D1791613

CHILTON'S

TRUCK and VAN SERVICE MANUAL

Publisher and Editor-in-Chief Kerry A. Freeman, S.A.E
Managing Editors Peter M. Conti, Jr. □ W. Calvin Settle, Jr., S.A.E
Assistant Managing Editor Nicholas L. D'Andrea
Senior Editors Debra Gaffney □ Michael L. Grady □ Richard J. Rivele, S.A.E.
Richard T. Smith □ Jim Taylor □ Ronald T. Webb
Project Managers Lawrence C. Braun, S.A.E. □ Michael M. Carroll □ Robert E. Doughten
Jacques Gordon □ Ben Greisler, S.A.E. □ Martin J. Gunther □ Jeffrey M. Hoffman □ James B. Steele
Service Editors Chris Armenti □ Thomas P. Browne III
Dean G. Callahan □ William C. Cottman □ Leonard Davis A.S.E. □ Joseph DeFrancesco, A.S.E.
Mike DiFurio □ Robert F. Dougherty, Jr. □ John J. Ferraro □ Sam Fiorani □ Andrew J. Folz □ Matthew Frederick
Edward J. Giacomucci, A.S.E. □ Al Gibbs □ Shawn Hibbert □ William Kessler □ Neil Leonard, A.S.E. □ Kevin Maher
Robert McAnally □ Raymond K. Moore □ Craig P. Nangle, A.S.E. □ Norman D. Norville □ Charles T. Ramsey
Roy Ripple, A.S.E. □ Don Schnell, A.S.E., S.A.E. □ Rich Schwartz
Larry E. Stiles □ Anthony Tortorici, A.S.E., S.A.E.

Director of Manufacturing Mike D'Imperio
Assistant Manager of Manufacturing Robin S. Norman
Production Manager Andrea Steiger
Assistant Production Manager Marsha Park Herman
Production Specialists Alan Bond □ Christine Davis □ Joel Greenberg
Daniel Harvey □ Kim Hayes □ Joseph McGinty □ Margaret Stoner

National Sales Manager Lawrence R. Rufo
National Administrator, Sales Mark Amentt
Eastern Regional Manager Howie Freeman
Western Regional Manager Larry W. Marshall
Mid West Regional Manager Bruce McCorkle
Special Accounts Manager Herbert Marshall
National Accounts Manager Kevin Mullen

OFFICERS
President, Chilton Enterprises David S. Loewith
Senior Vice President Ronald A. Hoxter

CHILTON PROFESSIONAL AUTOMOTIVE
ONE OF THE **DIVERSIFIED PUBLISHING COMPANIES,**
A PART OF **CAPITAL CITIES/ABC, INC.**
Manufactured in USA   ©1992 Chilton Book Company • Chilton Way, Radnor, Pa. 19089
ISBN 0-8019-8281-2   2345678901 3210987654   ISSN 0742-0331

SAFETY NOTICE

Proper service and repair procedures are vital to the safe, reliable operation of all motor vehicles, as well as the personal safety of those performing repairs. This manual outlines procedures for servicing and repairing vehicles using safe, effective methods. The procedures contain many NOTES, CAUTIONS and WARNINGS which should be followed along with standard safety procedures to eliminate the possibilty of personal injury or improper service which could damage the vehicle or compromise its safety.

It is important to note that the repair procedures and techniques, tools and parts for servicng motor vehicles, as well as the skill and experience of the individual performing the work vary widely. It is not possible to anticipate all of the conceivable ways or conditions under which vehicles may be serviced, or to provide cautions as to all of the possible hazards that may result. Standard and accepted safety precautions and equipment should be used when handling toxic or flammable fluids, and safety glasses or other protection should be used during cutting, grinding, chiseling, prying, or any other process that can cause material removal or projectiles.

Some procedures require the use of tools specially designed for a specific purpose. Before substituting another tool or procedure, you must be completely satisfied that neither your personal safety, nor the performance of the vehicle will be endangered

---

PART NUMBERS

Part numbers listed in this reference are not recomendations by Chilton for any product by brand name. They are references that can be used with interchange manuals and aftermarket supplier catalogs to locate each brand supplier's discrete part number.

Although information in this manual is based on industry sources and is complete as possible at the time of publication, the possibilty exists that some vehicle manufacturers made later changes which could not be included here. While striving for total accuracy, Chilton Book Company cannot assume responsibility for any errors, changes or omissions that may occur in the compilation of this data.

Pub 1796 67.90

SPECIFICATIONS

VEHICLE IDENTIFICATION CHART

It is important for servicing and ordering parts to be certain of the vehicle and engine identification. The VIN (vehicle identification number) is a 17 digit number visible through the windshield on the driver's side of the dash and contains the vehicle and engine identification codes. The tenth digit indicates model year and the eighth digit indicates engine code. It can be interpreted as follows:

Engine Code						Model Year	
Code	**Cu. In.**	**Liters**	**Cyl.**	**Fuel Sys.**	**Eng. Mfg.**	**Code**	**Year**
X	239	3.9	6	EFI	Chrysler	J	1988
Y	318	5.2	8	EFI	Chrysler	K	1989
W	360	5.9	8	4 BBL carb.	Chrysler	L	1990
Z	360	5.9	8	EFI	Chrysler	M	1991
5 ①	360	5.9	8	EFI	Chrysler	N	1992
8	360	5.9	6	Turbo Diesel	Cummins		

EFI—Electronic Fuel Injection
① Heavy Duty Chassis

ENGINE IDENTIFICATION

Year	Model	Engine Displacement cu. in. (liter)	Engine Series Identification (VIN)	No. of Cylinders	Engine Type
1988	B100 Van	239 (3.9)	X	6	OHV
	B100 Van	318 (5.2)	Y	8	OHV
	B150 Van	239 (3.9)	X	6	OHV
	B150 Van	318 (5.2)	Y	8	OHV
	B250 Van	239 (3.9)	X	6	OHV
	B250 Van	318 (5.2)	Y	8	OHV
	B250 Van	360 (5.9)	W	8	OHV
	B350 Van	318 (5.2)	Y	8	OHV
	B350 Van	360 (5.9)	W	8	OHV
	D100 Pick-Up	239 (3.9)	X	6	OHV
	D100 Pick-Up	318 (5.2)	Y	8	OHV
	D100 Pick-Up	360 (5.9)	W	8	OHV
	W100 Pick-Up	318 (5.2)	Y	8	OHV

ENGINE IDENTIFICATION

Year	Model	Engine Displacement cu. in. (liter)	Engine Series Identification (VIN)	No. of Cylinders	Engine Type
1988	W100 Pick-Up	360 (5.9)	W	8	OHV
	D150 Pick-Up	239 (3.9)	X	6	OHV
	D150 Pick-Up	318 (5.2)	Y	8	OHV
	D150 Pick-Up	360 (5.9)	W	8	OHV
	W150 Pick-Up	318 (5.2)	Y	8	OHV
	W150 Pick-Up	360 (5.9)	W	8	OHV
	AD150 Ramcharger	318 (5.2)	Y	8	OHV
	AD150 Ramcharger	360 (5.9)	W	8	OHV
	AW150 Ramcharger	318 (5.2)	Y	8	OHV
	AW150 Ramcharger	360 (5.9)	W	8	OHV
	D250 Pick-Up	239 (3.9)	X	6	OHV
	D250 Pick-Up	318 (5.2)	Y	8	OHV
	D250 Pick-Up	360 (5.9)	W	8	OHV
	W250 Pick-Up	318 (5.2)	Y	8	OHV
	W250 Pick-Up	360 (5.9)	W	8	OHV
	D350 Pick-Up	318 (5.2)	Y	8	OHV
	D350 Pick-Up	360 (5.9)	W	8	OHV
	W350 Pick-Up	318 (5.2)	Y	8	OHV
	W350 Pick-Up	360 (5.9)	W	8	OHV
1989	B100 Van	239 (3.9)	X	6	OHV
	B100 Van	318 (5.2)	Y	8	OHV
	B150 Van	360 (5.9)	W	8	OHV
	B150 Van	318 (5.2)	Y	8	OHV
	B250 Van	239 (3.9)	X	6	OHV
	B250 Van	318 (5.2)	Y	8	OHV
	B250 Van	360 (5.9)	W	8	OHV
	B350 Van	318 (5.2)	Y	8	OHV
	B350 Van	360 (5.9)	W	8	OHV
	D100 Pick-Up	239 (3.9)	X	6	OHV
	D100 Pick-Up	318 (5.2)	Y	8	OHV
	D100 Pick-Up	360 (5.9)	W	8	OHV
	W100 Pick-Up	318 (5.2)	Y	8	OHV
	W100 Pick-Up	360 (5.9)	W	8	OHV
	D150 Pick-Up	239 (3.9)	X	6	OHV
	D150 Pick-Up	318 (5.2)	Y	8	OHV
	D150 Pick-Up	360 (5.9)	W	8	OHV
	W150 Pick-Up	239 (3.9)	X	6	OHV
	W150 Pick-Up	318 (5.2)	Y	8	OHV
	W150 Pick-Up	360 (5.9)	W	8	OHV
	AD150 Ramcharger	318 (5.2)	Y	8	OHV
	AD150 Ramcharger	360 (5.9)	W	8	OHV
	AW150 Ramcharger	318 (5.2)	Y	8	OHV
	AW150 Ramcharger	360 (5.9)	W	8	OHV
	D250 Pick-Up	239 (3.9)	X	6	OHV

ENGINE IDENTIFICATION

Year	Model	Engine Displacement cu. in. (liter)	Engine Series Identification (VIN)	No. of Cylinders	Engine Type
1989	D250 Pick-Up	318 (5.2)	Y	8	OHV
	D250 Pick-Up	360 (5.9)	W	8	OHV
	D250 Pick-Up	360 (5.9)	8	6	OHV Turbo diesel
	W250 Pick-Up	318 (5.2)	Y	8	OHV
	W250 Pick-Up	360 (5.9)	W	8	OHV
	W250 Pick-Up	360 (5.9)	8	6	OHV Turbo diesel
	D350 Pick-Up	360 (5.9)	W	8	OHV
	D350 Pick-Up	360 (5.9)	8	6	OHV Turbo diesel
	W350 Pick-Up	360 (5.9)	W	8	OHV
	W350 Pick-Up	360 (5.9)	8	6	OHV Turbo diesel
1990	B150 Van	239 (3.9)	X	6	OHV
	B150 Van	318 (5.2)	Y	8	OHV
	B250 Van	239 (3.9)	X	6	OHV
	B250 Van	318 (5.2)	Y	8	OHV
	B250 Van	360 (5.9)	W	8	OHV
	B250 Van	360 (5.9)	5	8	OHV
	B350 Van	318 (5.2)	Y	8	OHV
	B350 Van	360 (5.9)	W	8	OHV
	B350 Van	360 (5.9)	5	8	OHV
	D150 Pick-Up	239 (3.9)	X	6	OHV
	D150 Pick-Up	318 (5.2)	Y	8	OHV
	D150 Pick-Up	360 (5.9)	Z	8	OHV
	W150 Pick-Up	239 (3.9)	X	6	OHV
	W150 Pick-Up	318 (5.2)	Y	8	OHV
	W150 Pick-Up	360 (5.9)	Z	8	OHV
	AD150 Ramcharger	318 (5.2)	Y	8	OHV
	AD150 Ramcharger	360 (5.9)	Z	8	OHV
	AD150 Ramcharger	360 (5.9)	5	8	OHV
	AW150 Ramcharger	318 (5.2)	Y	8	OHV
	AW150 Ramcharger	360 (5.9)	Z	8	OHV
	AW150 Ramcharger	360 (5.9)	5	8	OHV
	D250 Pick-Up	239 (3.9)	X	6	OHV
	D250 Pick-Up	318 (5.2)	Y	8	OHV
	D250 Pick-Up	360 (5.9)	Z	8	OHV
	D250 Pick-Up	360 (5.9)	5	8	OHV
	D250 Pick-Up	360 (5.9)	8	6	OHV Turbo diesel
	W250 Pick-Up	318 (5.2)	Y	8	OHV
	W250 Pick-Up	360 (5.9)	Z	8	OHV
	W250 Pick-Up	360 (5.9)	5	8	OHV
	W250 Pick-Up	360 (5.9)	8	6	OHV Turbo diesel
	D350 Pick-Up	360 (5.9)	Z	8	OHV
	D350 Pick-Up	360 (5.9)	5	8	OHV
	D350 Pick-Up	360 (5.9)	8	6	OHV Turbo diesel
	W350 Pick-Up	360 (5.9)	Z	8	OHV

ENGINE IDENTIFICATION

Year	Model	Engine Displacement cu. in. (liter)	Engine Series Identification (VIN)	No. of Cylinders	Engine Type
1990	W350 Pick-Up	360 (5.9)	5	8	OHV
	W350 Pick-Up	360 (5.9)	8	6	OHV Turbo diesel
1991–92	B150 Van	239 (3.9)	X	6	OHV
	B150 Van	318 (5.2)	Y	8	OHV
	B250 Van	239 (3.9)	X	6	OHV
	B250 Van	318 (5.2)	Y	8	OHV
	B250 Van	360 (5.9)	W	8	OHV
	B250 Van	360 (5.9)	5	8	OHV
	B350 Van	318 (5.2)	Y	8	OHV
	B350 Van	360 (5.9)	W	8	OHV
	B350 Van	360 (5.9)	5	8	OHV
	D150 Pick-Up	239 (3.9)	X	6	OHV
	D150 Pick-Up	318 (5.2)	Y	8	OHV
	D150 Pick-Up	360 (5.9)	Z	8	OHV
	W150 Pick-Up	239 (3.9)	X	6	OHV
	W150 Pick-Up	318 (5.2)	Y	8	OHV
	W150 Pick-Up	360 (5.9)	Z	8	OHV
	AD150 Ramcharger	318 (5.2)	Y	8	OHV
	AD150 Ramcharger	360 (5.9)	Z	8	OHV
	AD150 Ramcharger	360 (5.9)	5	8	OHV
	AW150 Ramcharger	318 (5.2)	Y	8	OHV
	AW150 Ramcharger	360 (5.9)	Z	8	OHV
	AW150 Ramcharger	360 (5.9)	5	8	OHV
	D250 Pick-Up	239 (3.9)	X	6	OHV
	D250 Pick-Up	318 (5.2)	Y	8	OHV
	D250 Pick-Up	360 (5.9)	Z	8	OHV
	D250 Pick-Up	360 (5.9)	5	8	OHV
	D250 Pick-Up	360 (5.9)	8	6	OHV Turbo diesel
	W250 Pick-Up	318 (5.2)	Y	8	OHV
	W250 Pick-Up	360 (5.9)	Z	8	OHV
	W250 Pick-Up	360 (5.9)	5	8	OHV
	W250 Pick-Up	360 (5.9)	8	6	OHV Turbo diesel
	D350 Pick-Up	360 (5.9)	Z	8	OHV
	D350 Pick-Up	360 (5.9)	5	8	OHV
	D350 Pick-Up	360 (5.9)	8	6	OHV Turbo diesel
	W350 Pick-Up	360 (5.9)	Z	8	OHV
	W350 Pick-Up	360 (5.9)	5	8	OHV
	W350 Pick-Up	360 (5.9)	8	6	OHV Turbo diesel

OHV—Overhead valves

GENERAL ENGINE SPECIFICATIONS

Year	VIN	No. Cylinder Displacement cu. in. (liter)	Fuel System Type	Net Horsepower @ rpm	Net Torque @ rpm (ft. lbs.)	Bore × Stroke (in.)	Compression Ratio	Oil Pressure @ rpm
1988	X	6-239 (3.9)	EFI	125 @ 4000	195 @ 2000	3.91 × 3.31	9.2:1	30–80 @ 3000
	Y	8-318 (5.2)	EFI	170 @ 4000	260 @ 2000	3.91 × 3.31	9.2:1	30–80 @ 3000
	W	8-360 (5.9)	4bbl	185 @ 4000	283 @ 1600	4.00 × 3.58	8.1:1	30–80 @ 3000
1989	W	8-360 (5.9)	4bbl	120 @ 3600	245 @ 1600	4.00 × 3.58	8.1:1	30–80 @ 3000
	X	6-239 (3.9)	EFI	125 @ 4000	195 @ 2000	3.91 × 3.31	9.0:1	30–80 @ 3000
	Y	8-318 (5.2)	EFI	170 @ 4000	260 @ 2000	3.91 × 3.31	9.2:1	30–80 @ 3000
	8	6-360 (5.9)	Turbo diesel	160 @ 2500	400 @ 1700	4.02 × 4.72	17.5:1	30–70 @ 2500
1990	W	8-360 (5.9)	EFI	190 @ 4000	292 @ 2400	4.00 × 3.58	8.1:1	30–80 @ 3000
	X	6-239 (3.9)	EFI	125 @ 4000	195 @ 2000	3.91 × 3.31	9.2:1	30–80 @ 3000
	Y	8-318 (5.2)	EFI	170 @ 4000	260 @ 2000	3.91 × 3.31	9.2:1	30–80 @ 3000
	Z	8-360 (5.9)	EFI	193 @ 4000	292 @ 2400	4.00 × 3.58	8.1:1	30–80 @ 3000
	5	8-360 (5.9)	EFI	193 @ 4000	292 @ 2400	4.00 × 3.58	8.1:1	30–80 @ 3000
	8	6-360 (5.9)	Turbo diesel	160 @ 2500	400 @ 1700	4.02 × 4.72	17.5:1	30–70 @ 2500
1991–92	W	8-360 (5.9)	EFI	190 @ 4000	292 @ 2400	4.00 × 3.58	8.1:1	30–80 @ 3000
	X	6-239 (3.9)	EFI	125 @ 4000	195 @ 2000	3.91 × 3.31	9.2:1	30–80 @ 3000
	Y	8-318 (5.2)	EFI	170 @ 4000	260 @ 2000	3.91 × 3.31	9.2:1	30–80 @ 3000
	Z	8-360 (5.9)	EFI	193 @ 4000	292 @ 2400	4.00 × 3.58	8.1:1	30–80 @ 3000
	5	8-360 (5.9)	EFI	193 @ 4000	292 @ 2400	4.00 × 3.58	8.1:1	30–80 @ 3000
	8	6-360 (5.9)	Turbo diesel	160 @ 2500	400 @ 1700	4.02 × 4.72	17.5:1	30–70 @ 2500

EFI—Electronic Fuel Injection

GASOLINE ENGINE TUNE-UP SPECIFICATIONS

Year	VIN	No. Cylinder Displacement cu. in. (liter)	Spark Plugs Type	Gap (in.)	Ignition Timing (deg.) MT	AT	Compression Pressure (psi) ①	Fuel Pump (psi)	Idle Speed (rpm) MT	AT	Valve Clearance In.	Ex.
1988	X	6-239 (3.9)	RN12YC	0.035	10B	10B	100	13.0–16.0	750	750	Hyd.	Hyd.
	Y	8-318 (5.2)	RN12YC	0.035	10B	10B	100	13.0–16.0	700	700	Hyd.	Hyd.
	W	8-360 (5.9)	RN12YC	0.035	13B	10B	100	5.0–7.0	750	750	Hyd.	Hyd.
1989	W	8-360 (5.9)	RN12YC	0.035	13B	10B	100	5.0–7.0	750	750	Hyd.	Hyd.
	X	6-239 (3.9)	RN12YC	0.035	10B	10B	100	13.0–16.0	750	750	Hyd.	Hyd.
	Y	8-318 (5.2)	RN12YC	0.035	10B	10B	100	13.0–16.0	700	700	Hyd.	Hyd.
1990	X	6-239 (3.9)	RN12YC	0.035	10B	10B	100	13.0–16.0	750	750	Hyd.	Hyd.
	Y	8-318 (5.2)	RN12YC	0.035	10B	10B	100	13.0–16.0	700	700	Hyd.	Hyd.
	W	8-360 (5.9)	RN12YC	0.035	10B	10B	100	13.0–16.0	750	750	Hyd.	Hyd.
	Z	8-360 (5.9)	RN12YC	0.035	10B	10B	100	13.0–16.0	700	700	Hyd.	Hyd.
	5	6-360 (5.9)	RN12YC	0.035	10B	10B	100	13.0–16.0	700	700	Hyd.	Hyd.
1991	X	6-239 (3.9)	RN12YC	0.035	10B	10B	100	13.0–16.0	750	750	Hyd.	Hyd.
	Y	8-318 (5.2)	RN12YC	0.035	10B	10B	100	13.0–16.0	700	700	Hyd.	Hyd.
	W	8-360 (5.9)	RN12YC	0.035	10B	10B	100	13.0–16.0	750	750	Hyd.	Hyd.
	Z	8-360 (5.9)	RN12YC	0.035	10B	10B	100	13.0–16.0	700	700	Hyd.	Hyd.
	5	6-360 (5.9)	RN12YC	0.035	10B	10B	100	13.0–16.0	700	700	Hyd.	Hyd.
1992		SEE UNDERHOOD SPECIFICATIONS STICKER										

Hyd.—Hydraulic
B—Before top dead center
① Minimum specification

DIESEL ENGINE TUNE-UP SPECIFICATIONS

Year	VIN	No. Cylinder Displacement cu. in. (liter)	Valve Clearance Intake (in.)	Valve Clearance Exhaust (in.)	Intake Valve Opens (deg.)	Injection Pump Setting (deg.)	Injection Nozzle Pressure (psi) New	Injection Nozzle Pressure (psi) Used	Idle Speed (rpm)	Cranking Compression Pressure (psi)
1989	8	6-360 (5.9)	0.010	0.020	NA	①	3550②	NA	③	NA
1990	8	6-360 (5.9)	0.010	0.020	NA	①	3550②	NA	③	NA
1991	8	6-360 (5.9)	0.010	0.020	NA	①	3550②	NA	③	NA
1992	SEE UNDERHOOD SPECIFICATIONS STICKER									

NA—Not available
① Align the alignment marks on the pump flange and gear housing.
② Injector operating or pop pressure
③ Automatic transmission, air conditioning ON—700
Manual transmission, air conditioning ON—750

FIRING ORDERS

NOTE: To avoid confusion, always replace spark plug wires one at a time.

5.2L and 5.9L Engines
Engine Firing Order: 1–8–4–3–6–5–7–2
Distributor Rotation: Clockwise

3.9L Engine
Engine Firing Order: 1–6–5–4–3–2
Distributor Rotation: Clockwise

Cummins 5.9L Turbodiesel Engine
Engine Firing Order: 1–5–3–6–2–4

CAPACITIES

Year	Model	VIN	No. Cylinder Displacement cu. in. (liter)	Engine Crankcase with Filter	Engine Crankcase without Filter	Transmission (pts.) 4-Spd	Transmission (pts.) 5-Spd	Transmission (pts.) Auto.	Drive Axle (pts.)	Fuel Tank (gal.)	Cooling System (qts.)
1988	B100 Van	X	6-239 (3.9)	4	4	7	4	①	②	④	14.6
	B100 Van	Y	8-318 (5.2)	5	4	7	4	①	②	④	16.5
	B150 Van	X	6-239 (3.9)	4	4	7	4	①	②	④	14.6
	B150 Van	Y	8-318 (5.2)	5	4	7	4	①	②	④	16.5
	B250 Van	X	6-239 (3.9)	4	4	7	4	①	②	④	14.6
	B250 Van	Y	8-318 (5.2)	5	4	7	4	①	②	④	16.5
	B250 Van	W	8-360 (5.9)	5	4	7	4	①	②	④	15⑧
	B350 Van	Y	8-318 (5.2)	5	4	7	—	①	②	④	16.5
	B350 Van	W	8-360 (5.9)	5	4	7	—	①	②	④	15⑧
	D100 Pick-Up	X	6-239 (3.9)	4	4	7	4	①	②	⑤	15.1
	D100 Pick-Up	Y	8-318 (5.2)	5	4	7	4	①	②	⑤	17
	D100 Pick-Up	W	8-360 (5.9)	5	4	7	4	①	②	30	15.5
	W100 Pick-Up	Y	8-318 (5.2)	5	4	7	—	①	② ③	⑤	17
	W100 Pick-Up	W	8-360 (5.9)	5	4	7	4	①	②	30	15.5
	D150 Pick-Up	X	6-239 (3.9)	4	4	7	4	①	②	⑤	15.1
	D150 Pick-Up	Y	8-318 (5.2)	5	4	7	4	①	②	⑤	17
	D150 Pick-Up	W	8-360 (5.9)	5	4	7	—	①	② ③	30	15.5
	W150 Pick-Up	Y	8-318 (5.2)	5	4	7	—	①	② ③	⑤	17
	W150 Pick-Up	W	8-360 (5.9)	5	4	7	—	①	②	34	15.5
	AD150 Ramcharger	Y	8-318 (5.2)	5	4	7	—	①	②	34	17
	AD150 Ramcharger	W	8-360 (5.9)	5	4	7	—	①	② ③	34	15.5
	AW150 Ramcharger	Y	8-318 (5.2)	5	4	7	—	①	② ③	34	17
	AW150 Ramcharger	W	8-360 (5.9)	5	4	7	—	①	②	30	15.5
	D250 Pick-Up	X	6-239 (3.9)	4	4	7	—	①	②	⑤	15.1
	D250 Pick-Up	Y	8-318 (5.2)	5	4	7	—	①	②	⑤	17
	D250 Pick-Up	W	8-360 (5.9)	5	4	7	—	①	②	30	15.5
	W250 Pick-Up	Y	8-318 (5.2)	5	4	7	—	①	② ③	⑤	17
	W250 Pick-Up	W	8-360 (5.9)	5	4	7	—	①	② ③	30	15.5
	D350 Pick-Up	Y	8-318 (5.2)	5	4	7	—	①	②	⑤	17
	D350 Pick-Up	W	8-360 (5.9)	6	5	7	—	①	②	30	15.5
	M350 Pick-Up	Y	8-318 (5.2)	5	4	7	—	①	② ③	⑤	17
	W350 Pick-Up	W	8-360 (5.9)	5	4	7	—	①	② ③	30	15.5
1989	B100 Van	X	6-239 (3.9)	4	4	—	4	① ⑥	②	④	14.6
	B100 Van	Y	8-318 (5.2)	5	4	—	4	① ⑥	②	④	16.5
	B150 Van	W	8-360 (5.9)	5	4	—	4	① ⑥	②	④	14.6
	B150 Van	Y	8-318 (5.2)	5	4	—	4	① ⑥	②	④	16.5
	B250 Van	X	6-239 (3.9)	4	4	—	4	① ⑥	②	④	14.6
	B250 Van	Y	8-318 (5.2)	5	4	—	4	① ⑥	②	④	16.5
	B250 Van	W	8-360 (5.9)	5	4	—	4	① ⑥	②	④	15⑧
	B350 Van	Y	8-318 (5.2)	5	4	—	—	① ⑥	②	④	16.5
	B350 Van	W	8-360 (5.9)	5	4	—	—	① ⑥	②	④	15⑧
	D100 Pick-Up	X	6-239 (3.9)	4	4	7	4	① ⑥	②	⑤	15.1
	D100 Pick-Up	Y	8-318 (5.2)	5	4	7	4	① ⑥	②	⑤	17

CHRYSLER CORPORATION
D/W SERIES (PICK-UP) • RAMCHARGER • B SERIES (VAN)

CAPACITIES

Year	Model	VIN	No. Cylinder Displacement cu. in. (liter)	Engine Crankcase with Filter	Engine Crankcase without Filter	Transmission (pts.) 4-Spd	Transmission (pts.) 5-Spd	Transmission (pts.) Auto.	Drive Axle (pts.)	Fuel Tank (gal.)	Cooling System (qts.)
1989	D100 Pick-Up	W	8-360 (5.9)	5	4	7	4	① ⑥	②	30	15.5
	W100 Pick-Up	Y	8-318 (5.2)	5	4	7	—	① ⑥	② ③	⑤	17
	W100 Pick-Up	W	8-360 (5.9)	5	4	7	—	① ⑥	② ③	30	15.5
	D150 Pick-Up	X	6-239 (3.9)	4	4	7	4	① ⑥	②	⑤	15.1
	D150 Pick-Up	Y	8-318 (5.2)	5	4	7	4	① ⑥	②	⑤	17
	D150 Pick-Up	W	8-360 (5.9)	5	4	7	4	① ⑥	②	30	15.5
	W150 Pick-Up	X	6-239 (3.9)	4	4	7	—	①	② ③	⑤	15.1
	W150 Pick-Up	Y	8-318 (5.2)	5	4	7	—	①	② ③	⑤	17
	W150 Pick-Up	W	8-360 (5.9)	5	4	7	—	①	② ③	30	15.5
	AD150 Ramcharger	Y	8-318 (5.2)	5	4	7	4	① ⑥	②	34	17
	AD150 Ramcharger	W	8-360 (5.9)	5	4	7	4	① ⑥	②	34	15.5
	AW150 Ramcharger	Y	8-318 (5.2)	5	4	7	—	①	② ③	34	17
	AW150 Ramcharger	W	8-360 (5.9)	5	4	7	—	①	② ③	34	15.5
	D250 Pick-Up	X	6-239 (3.9)	4	4	7	4	① ⑥	②	30	15.1
	D250 Pick-Up	Y	8-318 (5.2)	5	4	7	4	① ⑥	②	⑤	17
	D250 Pick-Up	W	8-360 (5.9)	5	4	7	4	① ⑥	②	30	15.5
	D250 Pick-Up	8	6-360 (5.9)	12	11	—	7	22	⑦	30	⑨
	W250 Pick-Up	Y	8-318 (5.2)	5	4	7	—	①	② ③	⑤	17
	W250 Pick-Up	W	8-360 (5.9)	5	4	7	—	①	② ③	30	15.5
	W250 Pick-Up	8	6-360 (5.9)	12	11	—	7	22	⑦	30	⑨
	D350 Pick-Up	W	8-360 (5.9)	5	4	7	4	①	②	30	15.5
	D350 Pick-Up	8	6-360 (5.9)	12	11	—	7	22	⑦	30	⑨
	W350 Pick-Up	W	8-360 (5.9)	5	4	7	—	①	② ③	30	15.5
	W350 Pick-Up	8	6-360 (5.9)	12	11	—	7	22	⑦	30	⑨
1990	B150 Van	X	6-239 (3.9)	4	4	7	4	① ⑥	②	④	14.6
	B150 Van	Y	8-318 (5.2)	5	4	7	4	① ⑥	②	④	16.5
	B250 Van	X	6-239 (3.9)	4	4	7	—	① ⑥	②	④	14.6
	B250 Van	Y	8-318 (5.2)	5	4	7	—	① ⑥	②	④	16.5
	B250 Van	W	8-360 (5.9)	5	4	7	—	① ⑥	②	④	15⑧
	B250 Van	5	8-360 (5.9)	5	4	7	—	① ⑥	②	④	15⑧
	B350 Van	Y	8-318 (5.2)	5	4	7	—	① ⑥	②	④	16.5
	B350 Van	W	8-360 (5.9)	5	4	7	—	① ⑥	②	④	15⑧
	B350 Van	5	8-360 (5.9)	5	4	7	—	① ⑥	②	④	15⑧
	D150 Pick-Up	X	6-239 (3.9)	4	4	7	4	①	②	⑤	15.1
	D150 Pick-Up	Y	8-318 (5.2)	5	4	7	4	①	②	⑤	17
	D150 Pick-Up	Z	8-360 (5.9)	5	4	7	4	①	②	30	15.5
	W150 Pick-Up	X	6-239 (3.9)	4	4	7	—	①	② ③	⑤	15.1
	W150 Pick-Up	Y	8-318 (5.2)	5	4	7	—	①	② ③	⑤	17
	W150 Pick-Up	Z	8-360 (5.9)	5	4	7	—	①	② ③	30	15.5
	AD150 Ramcharger	Y	8-318 (5.2)	5	4	7	—	①	②	34	17
	AD150 Ramcharger	Z	8-360 (5.9)	5	4	7	—	①	②	34	15.5
	AD150 Ramcharger	5	8-360 (5.9)	5	4	7	—	①	②	34	15.5
	AW150 Ramcharger	Y	8-318 (5.2)	5	4	7	—	①	② ③	34	16.5
	AW150 Ramcharger	Z	8-360 (5.9)	5	4	7	—	①	② ③	34	15

CAPACITIES

Year	Model	VIN	No. Cylinder Displacement cu. in. (liter)	Engine Crankcase with Filter	Engine Crankcase without Filter	Transmission (pts.) 4-Spd	Transmission (pts.) 5-Spd	Transmission (pts.) Auto.	Drive Axle (pts.)	Fuel Tank (gal.)	Cooling System (qts.)
1990	AW150 Ramcharger	5	8-360 (5.9)	5	4	7	—	①	②③	34	15
	D250 Pick-Up	X	6-239 (3.9)	4	4	7	4	①	②	⑤	15.1
	D250 Pick-Up	Y	8-318 (5.2)	5	4	7	4	①	②	⑤	17
	D250 Pick-Up	Z	8-360 (5.9)	5	4	7	4	①	②	30	15.5
	D250 Pick-Up	5	8-360 (5.9)	5	4	7	4	①	②	30	15.5
	D250 Pick-Up	8	6-360 (5.9)	12	11	—	7	22	⑦	30	⑨
	W250 Pick-Up	Y	8-318 (5.2)	5	4	7	4	①	②③	⑤	17
	W250 Pick-Up	Z	8-360 (5.9)	5	4	7	4	①	②③	30	15.5
	W250 Pick-Up	5	8-360 (5.9)	5	4	7	4	①	②③	30	15.5
	W250 Pick-Up	8	6-360 (5.9)	12	11	—	7	22	⑦	30	⑨
	D350 Pick-Up	Z	8-360 (5.9)	5	4	7	4	①	②	30	15.5
	D350 Pick-Up	5	8-360 (5.9)	5	4	7	4	①	②	30	15.5
	D350 Pick-Up	8	6-360 (5.9)	12	11	—	7	22	⑦	30	⑨
	W350 Pick-Up	Z	8-360 (5.9)	5	4	7	4	①	②③	30	15.5
	W350 Pick-Up	5	8-360 (5.9)	5	4	7	4	①	②③	30	15.5
	W350 Pick-Up	8	6-360 (5.9)	12	11	—	7	22	⑦	30	⑨
1991–92	B150 Van	X	6-239 (3.9)	4	4	7	4	①⑥	②	④	14.6
	B150 Van	Y	8-318 (5.2)	5	4	7	4	①⑥	②	④	16.5
	B250 Van	X	6-239 (3.9)	4	4	7	—	①⑥	②	④	14.6
	B250 Van	Y	8-318 (5.2)	5	4	7	—	①⑥	②	④	16.5
	B250 Van	W	8-360 (5.9)	5	4	7	—	①⑥	②	④	15⑧
	B250 Van	5	8-360 (5.9)	5	4	7	—	①⑥	②	④	15⑧
	B350 Van	Y	8-318 (5.2)	5	4	7	—	①⑥	②	④	16.5
	B350 Van	W	8-360 (5.9)	5	4	7	—	①⑥	②	④	15⑧
	B350 Van	5	8-360 (5.9)	5	4	7	—	①⑥	②	④	15⑧
	D150 Pick-Up	X	6-239 (3.9)	4	4	7	4	①	②	⑤	15.1
	D150 Pick-Up	Y	8-318 (5.2)	5	4	7	4	①	②	⑤	17
	D150 Pick-Up	Z	8-360 (5.9)	5	4	7	4	①	②	30	15.5
	W150 Pick-Up	X	6-239 (3.9)	4	4	7	—	①	②③	⑤	15.1
	W150 Pick-Up	Y	8-318 (5.2)	5	4	7	—	①	②③	⑤	17
	W150 Pick-Up	Z	8-360 (5.9)	5	4	7	—	①	②③	30	15.5
	AD150 Ramcharger	Y	8-318 (5.2)	5	4	7	—	①	②	34	17
	AD150 Ramcharger	Z	8-360 (5.9)	5	4	7	—	①	②	34	15.5
	AD150 Ramcharger	5	8-360 (5.9)	5	4	7	—	①	②	34	15.5
	AW150 Ramcharger	Y	8-318 (5.2)	5	4	7	—	①	②③	34	16.5
	AW150 Ramcharger	Z	8-360 (5.9)	5	4	7	—	①	②③	34	15
	AW150 Ramcharger	5	8-360 (5.9)	5	4	7	—	①	②③	34	15
	D250 Pick-Up	X	6-239 (3.9)	4	4	7	4	①	②	⑤	15.1
	D250 Pick-Up	Y	8-318 (5.2)	5	4	7	4	①	②	⑤	17
	D250 Pick-Up	Z	8-360 (5.9)	5	4	7	4	①	②	30	15.5
	D250 Pick-Up	5	8-360 (5.9)	5	4	7	4	①	②	30	15.5
	D250 Pick-Up	8	6-360 (5.9)	12	11	—	7	22	⑦	30	⑨
	W250 Pick-Up	Y	8-318 (5.2)	5	4	7	4	①	②③	⑤	17
	W250 Pick-Up	Z	8-360 (5.9)	5	4	7	4	①	②③	30	15.5

CAPACITIES

Year	Model	VIN	No. Cylinder Displacement cu. in. (liter)	Engine Crankcase with Filter	Engine Crankcase without Filter	Transmission (pts.) 4-Spd	Transmission (pts.) 5-Spd	Transmission (pts.) Auto.	Drive Axle (pts.)	Fuel Tank (gal.)	Cooling System (qts.)
1991–92	W250 Pick-Up	5	8-360 (5.9)	5	4	7	4	①	② ③	30	15.5
	W250 Pick-Up	8	6-360 (5.9)	12	11	—	7	22	⑦	30	⑨
	D350 Pick-Up	Z	8-360 (5.9)	5	4	7	4	①	②	30	15.5
	D350 Pick-Up	5	8-360 (5.9)	5	4	7	4	①	②	30	15.5
	D350 Pick-Up	8	6-360 (5.9)	12	11	—	7	22	⑦	30	⑨
	W350 Pick-Up	Z	8-360 (5.9)	5	4	7	4	①	② ③	30	15.5
	W350 Pick-Up	5	8-360 (5.9)	5	4	7	4	①	② ③	30	15.5
	W350 Pick-Up	8	6-360 (5.9)	12	11	—	7	22	⑦	30	⑨

① A-904T/A-999/A-998 Transmissions—
  17.1 pts.
  A-727 Transmission with lockup—16.7 pts.
  A-727 Transmission without lockup—17.1 pts.
② Chrysler 8⅜ in.—4.5 pts.
  Chrysler 9¼ in.—4.5 pts.
  Spicer or Dana 60—6.0 pts.
  Dana 70—7.0 pts.
③ Front axle except W250 and W350—5.6 pts.
  Front axle—W250 and W350—6.5 pts.

④ Standard—22 gals.
  Optional—35 gals.
⑤ Standard—22 gals.
  Optional—30 gals.
⑥ A500 Transmission—20.4 pts.
⑦ Rear axle—7.0 pts.
  Front axle—6.3 pts.
⑧ Add 1 qt. when equipped with rear heater
⑨ With manual transmission—15.5 qts.
  With automatic transmission—16.5 qts.

CAMSHAFT SPECIFICATIONS
All measurements given in inches.

Year	VIN	No. Cylinder Displacement cu. in. (liter)	Journal Diameter 1	Journal Diameter 2	Journal Diameter 3	Journal Diameter 4	Journal Diameter 5	Lobe Lift In.	Lobe Lift Ex.	Bearing Clearance	Camshaft End Play
1988	X	6-239 (3.9)	1.998–1.999	1.967–1.968	1.951–1.952	1.5605–1.5615	—	0.373	0.400	0.001–0.005	0.002–0.010
	Y	8-318 (5.2)	1.998–1.999	1.982–1.983	1.967–1.968	1.951–1.952	1.561–1.562	0.373	0.400	0.001–0.005	0.002–0.010
	W	8-360 (5.9)	1.998–1.999	1.982–1.983	1.967–1.968	1.951–1.952	1.561–1.562	0.410	0.410	0.001–0.005	0.002–0.010
1989	X	6-239 (3.9)	1.998–1.999	1.967–1.968	1.951–1.952	1.5605–1.5615	—	0.373	0.400	0.001–0.005	0.002–0.010
	Y	8-318 (5.2)	1.998–1.999	1.982–1.983	1.967–1.968	1.951–1.952	1.561–1.562	0.373	0.400	0.001–0.005	0.002–0.010
	W	8-360 (5.9)	1.998–1.999	1.982–1.983	1.967–1.968	1.951–1.952	1.561–1.562	0.410	0.410	0.001–0.005	0.002–0.010
	8	6-360 (5.9)	2.125 ①	2.125	2.125	2.125	—	1.852 ②	1.841 ②	0.001–0.005	0.006–0.010
1990	X	6-239 (3.9)	1.998–1.999	1.967–1.968	1.951–1.952	1.5605–1.5615	—	0.373	0.400	0.001–0.005	0.002–0.010
	Y	8-318 (5.2)	1.998–1.999	1.982–1.983	1.967–1.968	1.951–1.952	1.561–1.562	0.373	0.400	0.001–0.005	0.002–0.010
	Z	8-360 (5.9)	1.998–1.999	1.982–1.983	1.967–1.968	1.951–1.952	1.561–1.562	0.410	0.410	0.001–0.005	0.002–0.010
	5	8-360 (5.9)	1.998–1.999	1.982–1.983	1.967–1.968	1.951–1.952	1.561–1.562	0.410	0.410	0.001–0.005	0.002–0.010

CAMSHAFT SPECIFICATIONS
All measurements given in inches.

Year	VIN	No. Cylinder Displacement cu. in. (liter)	Journal Diameter					Lobe Lift		Bearing Clearance	Camshaft End Play
			1	2	3	4	5	In.	Ex.		
1990	8	6-360 (5.9)	2.125 ①	2.125	2.125	2.125	—	1.852 ②	1.841 ②	0.001–0.005	0.006–0.010
	W	8-360 (5.9)	1.998 1.999	1.982 1.983	1.967–1.968	1.951–1.952	1.561 1.562	0.410	0.410	0.001–0.005	0.002–0.010
1991–92	X	6-239 (3.9)	1.998–1.999	1.967–1.968	1.951–1.952	1.5605–1.5615	—	0.373	0.400	0.001–0.005	0.002–0.010
	Y	8-318 (5.2)	1.998–1.999	1.982–1.983	1.967–1.968	1.951–1.952	1.561 1.562	0.373	0.400	0.001–0.005	0.002–0.010
	Z	8-360 (5.9)	1.998–1.999	1.982–1.983	1.967–1.968	1.951–1.952	1.561 1.562	0.410	0.410	0.001–0.005	0.002–0.010
	5	8-360 (5.9)	1.998–1.999	1.982–1.983	1.967–1.968	1.951–1.952	1.561 1.562	0.410	0.410	0.001–0.005	0.002–0.010
	8	6-360 (5.9)	2.125 ①	2.125	2.125	2.125	—	1.852 ②	1.841 ②	0.001–0.005	0.006–0.010
	W	8-360 (5.9)	1.998 1.999	1.982 1.983	1.967–1.968	1.951–1.952	1.561 1.562	0.410	0.410	0.001–0.005	0.002–0.010

① Minimum wear limit
② Minimum diameter at peak of lobe

CRANKSHAFT AND CONNECTING ROD SPECIFICATIONS
All measurements are given in inches.

Year	VIN	No. Cylinder Displacement cu. in. (liter)	Crankshaft				Connecting Rod		
			Main Brg. Journal Dia.	Main Brg. Oil Clearance	Shaft End-play	Thrust on No.	Journal Diameter	Oil Clearance	Side Clearance
1988	X	6-239 (3.9)	2.4995–2.5005	①	0.002–0.010	2	2.124–2.125	0.0005–0.0022	0.006–0.014
	Y	8-318 (5.2)	2.4995–2.5005	①	0.002–0.010	3	2.124–2.125	0.0005–0.0022	0.006–0.014
	W	8-360 (5.9)	2.8095–2.8105	①	0.002–0.010	3	2.124–2.125	0.0005–0.0022	0.006–0.014
1989	X	6-239 (3.9)	2.4995–2.5005	①	0.002–0.010	2	2.124–2.125	0.0005–0.0022	0.006–0.014
	Y	8-318 (5.2)	2.4995–2.5005	①	0.002–0.010	3	2.124–2.125	0.0005–0.0022	0.006–0.014
	W	8-360 (5.9)	2.8095–2.8105	①	0.002–0.010	3	2.124–2.125	0.0005–0.0022	0.006–0.014
	8	6-360 (5.9)	3.2662 ②	0.0047 ③	0.005–0.012	6	2.715 ②	0.0035 ③	0.004–0.012

CRANKSHAFT AND CONNECTING ROD SPECIFICATIONS

All measurements are given in inches.

Year	VIN	No. Cylinder Displacement cu. in. (liter)	Crankshaft				Connecting Rod		
			Main Brg. Journal Dia.	Main Brg. Oil Clearance	Shaft End-play	Thrust on No.	Journal Diameter	Oil Clearance	Side Clearance
1990	X	6-239 (3.9)	2.4995–2.5005	①	0.002–0.010	2	2.124–2.125	0.0005–0.0022	0.006–0.014
	Y	8-318 (5.2)	2.4995–2.5005	①	0.002–0.010	3	2.124–2.125	0.0005–0.0022	0.006–0.014
	Z	8-360 (5.9)	2.8095–2.8105	①	0.002–0.010	3	2.124–2.125	0.0005–0.0022	0.006–0.014
	5	8-360 (5.9)	2.8095–2.8105	①	0.002–0.010	3	2.124–2.125	0.0005–0.0022	0.006–0.014
	8	6-360 (5.9)	3.2662 ②	0.0047 ③	0.005–0.012	6	2.715 ②	0.0035 ③	0.004–0.012
	W	8-360 (5.9)	2.8095–2.8105	①	0.002–0.010	3	2.124–2.125	0.0005–0.0022	0.006–0.014
1991–92	X	6-239 (3.9)	2.4995–2.5005	①	0.002–0.010	2	2.124–2.125	0.0005–0.0022	0.006–0.014
	Y	8-318 (5.2)	2.4995–2.5005	①	0.002–0.010	3	2.124–2.125	0.0005–0.0022	0.006–0.014
	Z	8-360 (5.9)	2.8095–2.8105	①	0.002–0.010	3	2.124–2.125	0.0005–0.0022	0.006–0.014
	5	8-360 (5.9)	2.8095–2.8105	①	0.002–0.010	3	2.124–2.125	0.0005–0.0022	0.006–0.014
	8	6-360 (5.9)	3.2662 ②	0.0047 ③	0.005–0.012	6	2.715 ②	0.0035 ③	0.004–0.012
	W	8-360 (5.9)	2.8095–2.8105	①	0.002–0.010	3	2.124–2.125	0.0005–0.0022	0.006–0.014

① No. 1—0.0005–0.0015 in.
Nos. 2–5—0.0005–0.0025 in.
② Minimum wear limit
③ Maximum clearance

VALVE SPECIFICATIONS

Year	VIN	No. Cylinder Displacement cu. in. (liter)	Seat Angle (deg.)	Face Angle (deg.)	Spring Test Pressure (lbs.)	Spring Installed Height (in.)	Stem-to-Guide Clearance (in.)		Stem Diameter (in.)	
							Intake	Exhaust	Intake	Exhaust
1988	X	6-239 (3.9)	45–45.5	44.5–45	②	③	0.001–0.017	0.002–0.017	0.372–0.373	0.371–0.372
	Y	8-318 (5.2)	45–45.5	44.5–45	②	③	0.001–0.017	0.002–0.017	0.372–0.373	0.371–0.372
	W	8-360 (5.9)	45–45.5	44.5–45	②	③	0.001–0.017	0.002–0.017	0.372–0.373	0.371–0.372

VALVE SPECIFICATIONS

Year	VIN	No. Cylinder Displacement cu. in. (liter)	Seat Angle (deg.)	Face Angle (deg.)	Spring Test Pressure (lbs.)	Spring Installed Height (in.)	Stem-to-Guide Clearance (in.)		Stem Diameter (in.)	
							Intake	Exhaust	Intake	Exhaust
1989	X	6-239 (3.9)	45–45.5	44.5–45	②	③	0.001–0.017	0.002–0.017	0.372–0.373	0.371–0.372
	Y	8-318 (5.2)	45–45.5	44.5–45	②	③	0.001–0.017	0.002–0.017	0.372–0.373	0.371–0.372
	W	8-360 (5.9)	45–45.5	44.5–45	②	③	0.001–0.017	0.002–0.017	0.372–0.373	0.371–0.372
	8	8-360 (5.9)	④	④	65⑤	2.19①	0.002–0.006	0.002–0.006	0.313–0.314	0.313–0.314
1990	X	6-239 (3.9)	45–45.5	44.5–45	②	③	0.001–0.017	0.002–0.017	0.372–0.373	0.371–0.372
	Y	8-318 (5.2)	45–45.5	44.5–45	②	③	0.001–0.017	0.002–0.017	0.372–0.373	0.371–0.372
	Z	8-360 (5.9)	45–45.5	44.5–45	②	③	0.001–0.017	0.002–0.017	0.372–0.373	0.371–0.372
	5	8-360 (5.9)	45–45.5	44.5–45	②	③	0.001–0.017	0.002–0.017	0.372–0.373	0.371–0.372
	8	6-360 (5.9)	④	④	65⑤	2.19①	0.002–0.006	0.002–0.006	0.313–0.314	0.313–0.314
	W	8-360 (5.9)	45–45.5	44.5–45	②	③	0.001–0.017	0.002–0.017	0.372–0.373	0.371–0.372
1991–92	X	6-239 (3.9)	45–45.5	44.5–45	②	③	0.001–0.017	0.002–0.017	0.372–0.373	0.371–0.372
	Y	8-318 (5.2)	45–45.5	44.5–45	②	③	0.001–0.017	0.002–0.017	0.372–0.373	0.371–0.372
	Z	8-360 (5.9)	45–45.5	44.5–45	②	③	0.001–0.017	0.002–0.017	0.372–0.373	0.371–0.372
	5	8-360 (5.9)	45–45.5	44.5–45	②	③	0.001–0.017	0.002–0.017	0.372–0.373	0.371–0.372
	8	6-360 (5.9)	④	④	65⑤	2.19①	0.002–0.006	0.002–0.006	0.313–0.314	0.313–0.314
	W	8-360 (5.9)	45–45.5	44.5–45	②	③	0.001–0.017	0.002–0.017	0.372–0.373	0.371–0.372

① Free standing length
② Intake—170–184 lbs.
Exhaust—318 CID (5.2L) and 239 CID (3.9L)—180–194 lbs.
Exhaust—360 CID (5.9L)—181–197 lbs.
③ Intake—1.625–1.688 in.
Exhaust—1.453–1.516 in.
④ Intake—30 degrees
Exhaust—45 degrees
⑤ Minimum acceptable load at 1.94 in.

PISTON AND RING SPECIFICATIONS

All measurements are given in inches.

Year	VIN	No. Cylinder Displacement cu. in. (liter)	Piston Clearance	Ring Gap			Ring Side Clearance		
				Top Compression	Bottom Compression	Oil Control	Top Compression	Bottom Compression	Oil Control
1988	X	6-239 (3.9)	0.0005–0.0015	0.010–0.020	0.010–0.020	0.015–0.055	0.0015–0.0030	0.0015–0.0030	0.0002–0.0050
	Y	8-318 (5.2)	0.0005–0.0015	0.010–0.020	0.010–0.020	0.015–0.055	0.0015–0.0030	0.0015–0.0030	0.0002–0.0050
	W	8-360 (5.9)	0.0005–0.0015	0.010–0.020	0.010–0.020	0.015–0.055	0.0015–0.0030	0.0015–0.0030	0.0002–0.0050
1989	X	6-239 (3.9)	0.0005–0.0015	0.010–0.020	0.010–0.020	0.015–0.055	0.0015–0.0030	0.0015–0.0030	0.0002–0.0050
	Y	8-318 (5.2)	0.0005–0.0015	0.010–0.020	0.010–0.020	0.015–0.055	0.0015–0.0030	0.0015–0.0030	0.0002–0.0050
	W	8-360 (5.9)	0.0005–0.0015	0.010–0.020	0.010–0.020	0.015–0.055	0.0015–0.0030	0.0015–0.0030	0.0002–0.0050
	8	8-360 (5.9)	NA	0.016–0.028	0.010–0.021	0.010–0.021	0.0030–0.0060	0.0030–0.0060	0.0020–0.0050
1990	X	6-239 (3.9)	0.0005–0.0015	0.010–0.020	0.010–0.020	0.015–0.055	0.0015–0.0030	0.0015–0.0030	0.0002–0.0050
	Y	8-318 (5.2)	0.0005–0.0015	0.010–0.020	0.010–0.020	0.015–0.055	0.0015–0.0030	0.0015–0.0030	0.0002–0.0050
	Z	8-360 (5.9)	0.0005–0.0015	0.010–0.020	0.010–0.020	0.015–0.055	0.0015–0.0030	0.0015–0.0030	0.0002–0.0050
	W	8-360 (5.9)	0.0005–0.0015	0.010–0.020	0.010–0.020	0.015–0.055	0.0015–0.0030	0.0015–0.0030	0.0002–0.0050
	5	8-360 (5.9)	0.0005–0.0015	0.010–0.020	0.010–0.020	0.015–0.055	0.0015–0.0030	0.0015–0.0030	0.0002–0.0050
	8	8-360 (5.9)	NA	0.016–0.028	0.010–0.021	0.010–0.021	0.0030–0.0060	0.0030–0.0060	0.0020–0.0050
1991–92	X	6-239 (3.9)	0.0005–0.0015	0.010–0.020	0.010–0.020	0.015–0.055	0.0015–0.0030	0.0015–0.0030	0.0002–0.0050
	Y	8-318 (5.2)	0.0005–0.0015	0.010–0.020	0.010–0.020	0.015–0.055	0.0015–0.0030	0.0015–0.0030	0.0002–0.0050
	Z	8-360 (5.9)	0.0005–0.0015	0.010–0.020	0.010–0.020	0.015–0.055	0.0015–0.0030	0.0015–0.0030	0.0002–0.0050
	W	8-360 (5.9)	0.0005–0.0015	0.010–0.020	0.010–0.020	0.015–0.055	0.0015–0.0030	0.0015–0.0030	0.0002–0.0050
	5	8-360 (5.9)	0.0005–0.0015	0.010–0.020	0.010–0.020	0.015–0.055	0.0015–0.0030	0.0015–0.0030	0.0002–0.0050
	8	8-360 (5.9)	NA	0.016–0.028	0.010–0.021	0.010–0.021	0.0030–0.0060	0.0030–0.0060	0.0020–0.0050

NA—Not available

TORQUE SPECIFICATIONS
All readings in ft. lbs.

Year	VIN	No. Cylinder Displacement cu. in. (liter)	Cylinder Head Bolts	Main Bearing Bolts	Rod Bearing Bolts	Crankshaft Pulley Bolts	Flywheel Bolts	Mainfold Intake	Mainfold Exhaust	Spark Plugs
1988	X	6-239 (3.9)	105	85	45	135③	55	45	④	30
	Y	8-318 (5.2)	105	85	45	100③	55	45	④	30
	W	8-360 (5.9)	105	85	45	100③	55	45	④	30
1989	X	6-239 (3.9)	105	85	45	135③	55	45	④	30
	Y	8-318 (5.2)	105	85	45	100③	55	40	④	30
	W	8-360 (5.9)	105	85	45	100③	55	40	④	30
	8	6-360 (5.9)	⑤	⑥	②	92③	101	①	32	NA
1990	X	6-239 (3.9)	105	85	45	135③	55	45	④	30
	Y	8-318 (5.2)	105	85	45	100③	55	40	④	30
	Z	8-360 (5.9)	105	85	45	100③	55	40	④	30
	W	8-360 (5.9)	105	85	45	100③	55	40	④	30
	5	8-360 (5.9)	105	85	45	100③	55	40	④	30
	8	6-360 (5.9)	⑤	⑥	②	92③	101	①	32	NA
1991-92	X	6-239 (3.9)	105	85	45	135③	55	45	④	30
	Y	8-318 (5.2)	105	85	45	100③	55	40	④	30
	Z	8-360 (5.9)	105	85	45	100③	55	40	④	30
	W	8-360 (5.9)	105	85	45	100③	55	40	④	30
	5	8-360 (5.9)	105	85	45	100③	55	40	④	30
	8	6-360 (5.9)	⑤	⑥	②	92③	101	①	32	NA

NA—Not available
① Intake manifold cover
② Stage 1—26
  Stage 2—51
  Stage 3—73

③ Vibration dampener bolt
④ Bolts—20 ft. lbs.
  Nuts—15 ft. lbs.

⑤ Stage 1—29
  Stage 2—62
  Stage 3—93
⑥ Stage 1—45
  Stage 2—88
  Stage 3—129

BRAKE SPECIFICATIONS
All measurements in inches unless noted.

Year	Model	Lug Nut Torque (ft. lbs.)	Master Cylinder Bore	Brake Disc Minimum Thickness	Brake Disc Maximum Runout	Standard Brake Drum Diameter	Minimum Lining Thickness Front	Minimum Lining Thickness Rear
1988	B100 Van	85–110	1.125	1.180	0.004	11	0.062	0.062
	B150 Van	85–110	1.125	1.180	0.004	11	0.062	0.062
	B250 Van	85–110	1.125	1.180	0.004	11	0.062	0.062
	B350 Van	①	1.125	②	0.004	12	0.062	0.062
	D100 Pick-Up	①	1.125	1.180	0.004	11	0.062	0.062
	W100 Pick-Up	①	1.125	1.180	0.004	11	0.062	0.062
	D150 Pick-Up	①	1.125	1.180	0.004	11	0.062	0.062
	W150 Pick-Up	①	1.125	1.180	0.004	11	0.062	0.062
	AD150 Ramcharger	①	1.125	1.180	0.004	11	0.062	0.062
	AW150 Ramcharger	①	1.125	1.180	0.004	11	0.062	0.062
	D250 Pick-Up	①	1.125	②	0.005	12	0.062	0.062
	W250 Pick-Up	①	1.125	1.125	0.005	12	0.062	0.062
	D350 Pick-Up	①	1.125	1.125	0.005	12	0.062	0.062
	W350 Pick-Up	①	1.125	1.125	0.005	12	0.062	0.062
1989	B100 Van	85–110	1.125	1.180	0.004	11	0.062	0.062
	B150 Van	85–110	1.125	1.180	0.004	11	0.062	0.062
	B250 Van	85–110	1.125	1.180	0.004	11	0.062	0.062
	B350 Van	①	1.125	②	0.004	12	0.062	0.062
	D100 Pick-Up	①	1.125	1.180	0.004	11	0.062	0.062
	W100 Pick-Up	①	1.125	1.180	0.004	11	0.062	0.062
	D150 Pick-Up	①	1.125	1.180	0.004	11	0.062	0.062
	W150 Pick-Up	①	1.125	1.180	0.004	11	0.062	0.062
	AD150 Ramcharger	①	1.125	1.180	0.004	11	0.062	0.062
	AW150 Ramcharger	①	1.125	1.180	0.004	11	0.062	0.062
	D250 Pick-Up	①	1.125	②	0.005	12	0.062	0.062
	W250 Pick-Up	①	1.125	1.125	0.005	12	0.062	0.062
	D350 Pick-Up	①	1.125	1.125	0.005	12	0.062	0.062
	W350 Pick-Up	①	1.125	1.125	0.005	12	0.062	0.062
1990	B150 Van	85–110	1.125	1.180	0.004	11	0.062	0.062
	B250 Van	85–110	1.125	1.180	0.004	11	0.062	0.062
	B350 Van	①	1.125	②	0.004	12	0.062	0.062
	D150 Pick-Up	①	1.125	1.180	0.004	11	0.062	0.062
	W150 Pick-Up	①	1.125	1.180	0.004	11	0.062	0.062
	AD150 Ramcharger	①	1.125	1.180	0.004	11	0.062	0.062
	AW150 Ramcharger	①	1.125	1.180	0.004	11	0.062	0.062
	D250 Pick-Up	①	1.125	②	0.005	12	0.062	0.062
	W250 Pick-Up	①	1.125	1.125	0.005	12	0.062	0.062
	D350 Pick-Up	①	1.125	1.125	0.005	12	0.062	0.062
	W350 Pick-Up	①	1.125	1.125	0.005	12	0.062	0.062

BRAKE SPECIFICATIONS

All measurements in inches unless noted.

Year	Model	Lug Nut Torque (ft. lbs.)	Master Cylinder Bore	Brake Disc Minimum Thickness	Brake Disc Maximum Runout	Standard Brake Drum Diameter	Minimum Lining Thickness Front	Minimum Lining Thickness Rear
1991–92	B150 Van	85–110	1.125	1.180	0.004	11	0.062	0.062
	B250 Van	85–110	1.125	1.180	0.004	11	0.062	0.062
	B350 Van	①	1.125	②	0.004	12	0.062	0.062
	D150 Pick-Up	①	1.125	1.180	0.004	11	0.062	0.062
	W150 Pick-Up	①	1.125	1.180	0.004	11	0.062	0.062
	AD150 Ramcharger	①	1.125	1.180	0.004	11	0.062	0.062
	AW150 Ramcharger	①	1.125	1.180	0.004	11	0.062	0.062
	D250 Pick-Up	①	1.125	②	0.005	12	0.062	0.062
	W250 Pick-Up	①	1.125	1.125	0.005	12	0.062	0.062
	D350 Pick-Up	①	1.125	1.125	0.005	12	0.062	0.062
	W350 Pick-Up	①	1.125	1.125	0.005	12	0.062	0.062

① 1/2 × 20 cone lug nut—105 ft. lbs.
5/8 × 18 cone lug nut—200 ft. lbs.
5/8 × 18 flanged lug nut—325 ft. lbs.
② With 3300 lb. or 3600 lb. front axle—1.180 in.
With 4000 lb. front axle—1.125 in.

WHEEL ALIGNMENT

Year	Model	Caster Range (deg.)	Caster Preferred Setting (deg.)	Camber Range (deg.)	Camber Preferred Setting (deg.)	Toe-in (in.)	Steering Axis Inclination (deg.)
1988	B100 Van	1.25P–3.75P	2.5P	0.6N–0.6P	0	0	NA
	B150 Van	1.25P–3.75P	2.5P	0.6N–0.6P	0	0	NA
	B250 Van	1.25P–3.75P	2.5P	0.6N–0.6P	0	0	NA
	B350 Van	1.25P–3.75P	2.5P	0.6N–0.6P	0	0	NA
	D100 Pick-Up	1N–2P	0.5P	0–1P	0.5P	0.25	NA
	M100 Pick-Up	0.5P–3.5P	2P	0.5P–1.5P	1P	0.20	8.5①
	D150 Pick-Up	1N–2P	0.5P	0–1P	0.5P	0.25	NA
	M150 Pick-Up	0.5P–3.5P	2P	0.5P–1.5P	1P	0.20	8.5①
	AD150 Ramcharger	1N–2P	0.5P	0–1P	0.5P	0.25	NA
	AW150 Ramcharger	0.5P–3.5P	2P	0.5P–1.5P	1P	0.20	8.5①
	D250 Pick-Up	1N–2P	0.5P	0–1P	0.5P	0.25	NA
	M250 Pick-Up	0.5P–3.5P	2P	0.5P–1.5P	1P	0.20	8.5①
	D350 Pick-Up	1N–2P	0.5P	0–1P	0.5P	0.25	NA
	M350 Pick-Up	0.5P–3.5P	2P	0.5P–1.5P	1P	0.20	8.5①

WHEEL ALIGNMENT

Year	Model	Caster Range (deg.)	Caster Preferred Setting (deg.)	Camber Range (deg.)	Camber Preferred Setting (deg.)	Toe-in (in.)	Steering Axis Inclination (deg.)
1989	B100 Van	1.25P–3.75P	2.5P	0.6N–0.6P	0	0	NA
	B150 Van	1.25P–3.75P	2.5P	0.6N–0.6P	0	0	NA
	B250 Van	1.25P–3.75P	2.5P	0.6N–0.6P	0	0	NA
	B350 Van	1.25P–3.75P	2.5P	0.6N–0.6P	0	0	NA
	D100 Pick-Up	1N–2P	0.5P	0–1P	0.5P	0.25	NA
	W100 Pick-Up	0.5P–3.5P	2P	0.5P–1.5P	1P	0.20	8.5①
	D150 Pick-Up	1N–2P	0.5P	0–1P	0.5P	0.25	NA
	W150 Pick-Up	0.5P–3.5P	2P	0.5P–1.5P	1P	0.20	8.5①
	AD150 Ramcharger	1N–2P	0.5P	0–1P	0.5P	0.25	NA
	AM150 Ramcharger	0.5P–3.5P	2P	0.5P–1.5P	1P	0.20	8.5①
	D250 Pick-Up	1N–2P	0.5P	0–1P	0.5P	0.25	NA
	W250 Pick-Up	0.5P–3.5P	2P	0.5P–1.5P	1P	0.20	8.5①
	D350 Pick-Up	1N–2P	0.5P	0–1P	0.5P	0.25	NA
	W350 Pick-Up	0.5P–3.5P	2P	0.5P–1.5P	1P	0.20	8.5①
1990	B150 Van	1.25P–3.75P	2.5P	0.6N–0.6P	0	0	NA
	B250 Van	1.25P–3.75P	2.5P	0.6N–0.6P	0	0	NA
	B350 Van	1.25P–3.75P	2.5P	0.6N–0.6P	0	0	NA
	D150 Pick-Up	1N–2P	0.5P	0–1P	0.5P	0.25	NA
	W150 Pick-Up	0.5P–3.5P	2P	0.5P–1.5P	1P	0.20	8.5①
	AD150 Ramcharger	1N–2P	0.5P	0–1P	0.5P	0.25	NA
	AW150 Ramcharger	0.5P–3.5P	2P	0.5P–1.5P	1P	0.20	8.5①
	D250 Pick-Up	1N–2P	0.5P	0–1P	0.5P	0.25	NA
	W250 Pick-Up	0.5P–3.5P	2P	0.5P–1.5P	1P	0.20	8.5①
	D350 Pick-Up	1N–2P	0.5P	0–1P	0.5P	0.25	NA
	W350 Pick-Up	0.5P–3.5P	2P	0.5P–1.5P	1P	0.20	8.5①
1991–92	B150 Van	1.25P–3.75P	2.5P	0.6N–0.6P	0	0	NA
	B250 Van	1.25P–3.75P	2.5P	0.6N–0.6P	0	0	NA
	B350 Van	1.25P–3.75P	2.5P	0.6N–0.6P	0	0	NA
	D150 Pick-Up	1N–2P	0.5P	0–1P	0.5P	0.25	NA
	W150 Pick-Up	0.5P–3.5P	2P	0.5P–1.5P	1P	0.20	8.5①
	AD150 Ramcharger	1N–2P	0.5P	0–1P	0.5P	0.25	NA
	AW150 Ramcharger	0.5P–3.5P	2P	0.5P–1.5P	1P	0.20	8.5①
	D250 Pick-Up	1N–2P	0.5P	0–1P	0.5P	0.25	NA
	W250 Pick-Up	0.5P–3.5P	2P	0.5P–1.5P	1P	0.20	8.5①
	D350 Pick-Up	1N–2P	0.5P	0–1P	0.5P	0.25	NA
	W350 Pick-Up	0.5P–3.5P	2P	0.5P–1.5P	1P	0.20	8.5①

NA—Not available
N—Negative
P—Positive
① King pin inclination

ENGINE ELECTRICAL

NOTE: Disconnecting the negative battery cable on some vehicles may interfere with the functions of the on board computer systems and may require the computer to undergo a relearning process, once the negative battery cable is reconnected.

Distributor

Removal and Installation

1. Disconnect the negative battery cable.
2. Disconnect the distributor pickup lead wires and vacuum hose, if equipped.
3. Unfasten the distributor cap retaining clips and lift off the distributor cap with all ignition wires still connected. Remove the coil wire if necessary.
4. Matchmark the rotor to the distributor housing.

NOTE: Do not crank the engine during this procedure. If the engine is cranked, the matchmark must be disregarded.

5. Remove the hold-down bolt and clamp.
6. Remove the distributor from the engine.

Installation

TIMING NOT DISTURBED

1. Install a new distributor housing O-ring.
2. Install the distributor in the engine so the rotor is aligned with the matchmark on the housing and the housing is aligned with the matchmark on the engine. Make sure the distributor is fully seated and the distributor shaft is fully engaged.
3. Install the hold-down clamp and snug the hold-down bolt.
4. Connect the distributor pickup lead wires.
5. Install the distributor cap and snap the retaining clips into place.
6. Connect the negative battery cable.
7. Adjust the ignition timing and tighten the hold-down bolt.

TIMING DISTURBED

1. Install a new distributor housing O-ring.
2. Position the engine so the No. 1 piston is at TDC of the compression stroke and the mark on the vibration damper is aligned with **0** on the timing indicator.
3. Install the distributor in the engine so the rotor is aligned with the position of the No. 1 ignition wire on the distributor cap and the housing is aligned with the matchmark on the engine. Make sure the distributor is fully seated and the distributor shaft is fully engaged.
4. Install the hold-down clamp and snug the hold-down bolt.
5. Connect the distributor pickup lead wires.
6. Install the distributor cap and snap the retaining clips into place.
7. Connect the negative battery cable.
8. Adjust the ignition timing and tighten the hold-down nut or bolt.

Ignition Timing

Adjustment

1. Start the engine, set the parking brake and run the engine until normal operating temperature is reached. Keep all lights and accessories **OFF**.
2. If a magnetic timing unit is available, insert the probe into the receptacle near the timing scale. The scale is located on the timing chain cover above and to the left of the vibration damper on Pick-Ups and below the damper on Vans.
3. If a magnetic timing unit is not available, connect a con-

ventional power timing light to the No. 1 cylinder spark plug wire.
4. Connect the red lead of a tachometer to the negative primary terminal of the coil and connect the black lead to a good ground.
5. If equipped with a carburetor, ground the carburetor switch with a jumper wire. Set the idle speed according to the Vehicle Emission Control Information (VECI) label. Disconnect and plug the distributor vacuum advance hose at the distributor or computer, if equipped.
6. If equipped with Electronic Fuel Injection (EFI), connect the Diagnostic Readout Box II (DRBII) and access the Basic Timing Mode. If the DRBII is not available, disconnect the coolant sensor located near the thermostat housing and confirm that the Check Engine light on the instrument panel is **ON**.
7. Aim the timing light at the timing scale or read the magnetic timing unit.
8. If the timing is advanced (higher than the specification on the VECI label), the distributor should be turned clockwise. If the timing is retarded, (lower than the specification on the VECI label), the distributor should be turned counterclockwise.
9. Loosen the distributor hold-down bolt just enough so the disributor can be rotated. Turn the distributor in the proper direction until the specified timing is reached. Tighten the hold-down bolt and recheck the timing and idle speed.
10. Turn the engine off. Remove the jumper wire, if used. Connect the vacuum hose or coolant sensor (make sure the Check Engine light does not come on when started). Disconnect the timing apparatus and tachometer.
11. If the coolant temperature sensor was disconnected, erase the created fault code using the Erase Fault Code mode on the DRBII. If the DRBII is not available, the code can be erased by disconnecting the battery, although it is not recommended.

NOTE: If the battery is disconnected, radio memory will be lost and other fault codes that may have been stored in the computer's memory will be erased. If the coolant sensor code is not erased at this point, it will disappear after 50–100 vehicle key on/off cycles providing there is no problem with that circuit.

Alternator

For further information, please refer to "Alternators" in the Unit Repair section.

Precautions

Several precautions must be observed when working with the alternator to avoid damaging the unit.
• If the battery is removed for any reason, make sure it is reconnected with the correct polarity. Reversing the battery connections may result in damage to the one-way rectifiers.
• When utilizing a booster battery as a starting aid, always connect the positive to positive terminals and the negative terminal from the booster battery to a good engine ground on the vehicle being started.
• Never use a fast charger as a booster to start vehicles.
• Disconnect the battery cables when charging the battery with a fast charger.
• Never attempt to polarize the alternator.
• Do not use test lights of more than 12 volts when checking diode continuity.
• Do not short across or ground any of the alternator terminals.
• The polarity of the battery, alternator and regulator must be matched and considered before making any electrical connections within the system.

• Never separate the alternator on an open circuit. Make sure all connections within the circuit are clean and tight.

• Disconnect the battery ground terminal when performing any service on electrical components.

• Disconnect the battery if arc welding is to be done on the vehicle.

Belt Tension Adjustment

NOTE: The belt tension is automatically adjusted by the tensioner on the 5.9L diesel engine. Periodic adjustment is not necessary.

1. Disconnect negative battery cable.
2. Loosen alternator pivot bolt slightly.
3. Loosen the adjuster strap nut or bolt just enough so the alternator can be moved.
4. If the alternator bracket is not equipped with an adjuster bolt, use a prybar and apply tension to the alternator until the belt(s) deflect about ¼–½ in. under a 10 lb. load. Torque the adjuster strap bolt to 200 inch lbs. (23 Nm). Torque the pivot bolt to 30 ft. lbs. (41 Nm).
5. If the bracket is equipped with an adjuster bolt, tighten it until the belts deflect about ½ in. under a 10 lb. load. Torque the adjuster strap nut to 200 inch lbs. (23 Nm). Torque the pivot bolt to 30 ft. lbs. (41 Nm).
6. Reconnect negative battery cable.

Removal and Installation

1. Disconnect the negative battery cable.
2. On the 5.9L diesel engine, use a ⅜ in. drive breaker bar to lift the belt tensioner and remove the belt. On all other engines, loosen the mounting bolts, move the alternator toward the engine and remove the drive belt(s).

NOTE: On some Vans, it may be easier to remove the alternator through the right front wheelwell since the fan shroud and possibly air conditioning and heater plumbing under the hood will prevent removal from in front of the vehicle. Lift the vehicle and safely support. Remove the right front wheel and gain access to the alternator on these applications.

3. Remove the mounting bolts, spacers and adjuster bolt. Remove the alternator from the brackets.
4. Remove the battery positive, field and ground terminals from the rear of the alternator. Remove the wire harness hold-down screw from the alternator.

To install:

5. Connect all wiring to the proper terminals on the rear of the alternator and install the wire harness hold-down screw.
6. Position the alternator in the mounting brackets.

Chrysler 60 and 78 amp alternator terminals

Chrysler 114 amp alternator terminals

Chrysler 90HS, 120HS and Nippondenso alternator terminals

7. Install the spacers, pivot bolt, adjuster strap bolt or nut and adjuster bolt.
8. On the 5.9L diesel engine, torque the upper bolt to 18 ft. lbs. (24 Nm), the lower bolt to 32 ft. lbs. (43 Nm) and install the belt. On all other engines, install the drive belt(s) and adjust to specification. Torque the adjuster strap nut or bolt to 200 inch lbs. (23 Nm). Torque the pivot bolt to 30 ft. lbs. (41 Nm).
9. Connect the negative battery cable.

Voltage Regulator

For further information, please refer to "Alternators" in the Unit Repair section.

Removal and Installation

NOTE: The voltage regulator is integrated into the circuitry of the Single Module Engine Controller (SMEC) or Single Board Engine Controller (SBEC) on vehicles with EFI and is not serviceable.

1. Disconnect the negative battery cable.
2. Unplug the connector from the voltage regulator.

3. Remove the retaining screws and remove the regulator from the vehicle.

4. The installation is the reversal of the removal procedure. Make sure the connector retainer is properly clipped in place.

Starter

For further information, please refer to "Starters" in the Unit Repair section.

Removal and Installation

1. Disconnect the negative battery cable.
2. Raise the vehicle and support safely.
3. Remove the heat shield from the starter.
4. Disconnect the solenoid lead wires from the starter.
5. Unbolt the starter, remove the exhaust bracket and automatic transmission oil cooler tube bracket, if equipped, and remove the starter from the vehicle.

To install:

6. Install the starter to the bell housing and install the upper mounting bolt loosely.
7. Install the automatic transmission oil cooler tube bracket and exhaust bracket, if equipped. Install the lower mounting nut or bolts. Torque the mounting nut and bolt evenly to 50 ft. lbs. (68 Nm) on all engines except the 5.9L diesel engine. On 5.9L diesel engine, torque the mounting bolts to 32 ft. lbs. (43 Nm).
8. Connect the solenoid lead wires.
9. Install the heat shield.
10. Connect the negative battery cable and check the starter for proper operation.

Intake Manifold Heater

Removal and Installation

5.9L DIESEL ENGINE

1. Disconnect the negative battery cable.
2. Remove the intercooler outlet duct from air inlet tube, if equipped.
3. Remove the 4 bolts that attach the air crossover to the intake manifold. Loosen the lower throttle control bracket mounting bolt and move the bracket away from the engine.

View of crossover tube and turbocharger—5.9L diesel engine

Rotating the throttle bracket away from the engine— 5.9L diesel engine

INTAKE MANIFOLD HEATER

Intake manifold heater and related parts—5.9L diesel engine

4. Loosen the hose clamps on the turbocharger end of the crossover tube and remove the tube and gasket. Cover the turbocharger opening with a clean shop towel.
5. Disconnect the electrical wiring from the intake manifold heater, remove the heater and remove the gasket.

To install:

6. Clean the gasket mounting surface and install a new gasket.
7. Install the intake manifold heater and connect the wiring.
8. Remove the towel from the turbocharger opening and install the air crossover tube and gasket. Tighten the hose clamps.
9. Rotate the throttle control bracket back into place. Torque all mounting bolts to 18 ft. lbs. (24 Nm).
10. Attach the throttle rod to the throttle lever. Reconnect negative battery cable.

Testing

1. Disconnect the negative battery cable.
2. Disconnect the wires from the intake manifold heater.
3. Using an ohmmeter, check the resistance from a good ground to each heater terminal.
4. If there is any resistance, or if the circuit is open, inspect the assembly for dirty or corroded connections.
5. If the resistance is 0 ohms, the heater is functioning properly.
6. If the circuit is open, the heater is defective.

CHASSIS ELECTRICAL

Heater Blower Motor

Removal and Installation

VAN

Without Air Conditioning

1. Disconnect the negative battery cable.
2. Remove the air intake duct and top half of the fan shroud, if necessary. Disconnect the blower connector.
3. Remove the 7 screws that fasten the back plate to the heater housing.
4. Remove the blower motor from the vehicle.
5. Remove the spring clip fastening the blower wheel to the blower shaft and pull off the wheel.
6. Remove the vent tube.
7. Remove the nuts fastening the blower motor to the back plate and remove the motor.

To install:

8. Check the seal for breaks or poor adhesion; repair as needed.
9. Install the blower motor to the back plate.
10. Install the vent tube.
11. Install the blower wheel to the shaft and secure the spring clip.
12. Install the assembly to the heater housing and install the 7 screws.
13. Install electrical connector.
14. Install the fan shroud and air duct if removed.
15. Connect the negative battery cable and check the blower motor for proper operation.

With Air Conditioning

1. Disconnect the negative battery cable.
2. Remove the air intake duct and top half of the fan shroud.
3. Disconnect the blower connector.
4. Remove the blower motor cooling tube.

5. Remove the retaining nuts and washers from the studs holding the blower.
6. Pull the air conditioning lines inboard and upward while removing the blower assembly from the vehicle. Remove the spring clip fastening the blower wheel to the blower shaft and pull off the wheel.

To install:

7. Install the blower wheel to the shaft and install the spring clip. Inspect the blower mounting plate seal and repair as needed. Apply rubber adhesive to the seal to aid in assembly.
8. Install the blower into the housing and install the washers and nuts.
9. Install the cooling tube.
10. Reconnect the electrical connector.
11. Install the fan shroud and air intake duct.
12. Connect the negative battery cable and check the blower motor for proper operation.

PICK-UP AND RAMCHARGER

1. Disconnect the negative battery cable.
2. Disconnect the blower connector.
3. Remove the blower motor cooling tube.
4. Remove the screws or retaining nuts retaining the blower plate to the housing.
5. Remove the assembly from the housing.
6. Remove the spring clip fastening the blower wheel to the blower shaft and pull off the wheel. Remove the blower from the plate.

To install:

7. Inspect the blower mounting plate seal and repair as necessary.
8. Install the blower to the plate. Install the blower wheel to the shaft and install the spring clip.
9. Install the blower into the housing and install the screws or washers and nuts.
10. Install the cooling tube.
11. Connect the connector.

Underhood location of the blower motor—Van with air conditioning

12. Connect the negative battery cable and check the blower motor for proper operation.

Windshield Wiper Motor

Removal and Installation

1. Disconnect the negative battery cable.
2. Disconnect the wires from the wiper motor.
3. Remove the mounting bolts.
4. Pull the motor out far enough to gain access to the crank arm to motor link retainer bushing.
5. Remove the crank arm from the drive link by prying the retainer bushing from the crank arm.
6. Remove the motor from the vehicle.
7. Hold the crank arm with a wrench while removing the crank nut to prevent from overloading the gears.
8. Remove the crank arm from the motor.

To install:

9. Index the slot correctly and position the crank arm on the motor shaft. Start the crank nut making sure the crank arm does not move from its slotted position.
10. Hold the crank arm with a wrench and torque the nut to 95 inch lbs. (11 Nm).
11. Lubricate the drive link retainer bushing and install the crank arm pin to the bushing by snapping them together.
12. Install the motor to the vehicle and torque the mounting bolts to 55 inch lbs. (6 Nm).
13. Connect the wires to the motor.
14. Connect the negative battery cable and check the wiper motor for proper operation.

Windshield Wiper Switch

Removal and Installation

NOTE: On 1991–92 vehicles, the windshield wiper switch is part of the combination switch.

1988–90
Except Tilt Wheel

1. Disconnect the negative battery cable.
2. Remove the lower steering column cover.
3. Remove the horn pad mounting screws from behind the steering wheel and remove the horn pad.
4. Remove the steering wheel nut, matchmark the steering wheel to the shaft and remove steering wheel.
5. Remove the plastic wiring channel from the underside of the steering column.

Typical steering column wiring harness

Typical windshield wiper motor and linkage—Van

Removing the wiper switch—standard column

12. Run the wiring through the opening and down the steering column, position the switch and install the hex-head screw. Make sure the dimmer switch rod is properly engaged.

13. Install the side lock housing cover.

14. Connect the wires and install the wiring channel.

15. Install the steering wheel torque the nut to 45 ft. lbs. (61 Nm).

16. Install the horn pad.

17. Connect the negative battery cable and check the wiper and washer, cruise control, turn signal switch and dimmer switch for proper operation.

18. Install the lower column cover.

Tilt Wheel

1. Disconnect the negative battery cable.

2. Remove the lower steering column cover. Remove the plastic wiring channel from the underside of the steering column.

3. Remove the horn pad mounting screws from behind the steering wheel and remove the horn pad.

4. Remove the steering wheel nut, matchmark the steering wheel to the shaft and remove the steering wheel.

5. Depress the lock plate with the proper depressing tool, remove the retaining ring from its groove and remove the tool, ring, lock plate, cancelling cam and spring.

6. Remove the switch stalk actuator screw and arm.

7. Remove the hazard switch knob.

8. Disconnect the turn signal switch, wiper switch, intermittent module and cruise control connectors, if equipped.

9. Remove the 3 screws and remove the turn signal switch. Tape the connector to the wires to aid in removal.

10. Remove the ignition key light.

11. Place the key in the **LOCK** position and remove the key. Insert a thin tool into the slot next to the switch mounting screw boss, depress the spring latch at the bottom of the slot releasing the lock. Remove the lock cylinder.

12. Remove the buzzer switch and wedge spring.

13. Remove the 3 housing cover screws and remove the housing cover.

14. Remove the wiper switch pivot pin with a punch and remove the switch.

Ignition key light removal

6. Disconnect the wiper switch connector, intermittent wipe module connector and cruise control connector, if equipped.

7. Remove the side lock housing cover.

8. Remove the slotted hex-head screw that attaches the wiper switch to the turn signal switch and remove the switch.

9. Remove the control knob from the end of the stalk. Pull the round nylon hider up the control stalk and remove the screws that attach the control stalk sleeve to the wiper switch.

10. Rotate the control stalk shaft to the full clockwise position and remove the shaft from the wiper switch by pulling it straight out.

To install:

11. Install the control shaft to the wiper switch, install the screws, the hider and the control knob.

Bearing housing, lock plate spring and lock plate location

15. Remove the control knob from the end of the stalk. Pull the round nylon hider up the control stalk and remove the revealed screws that attach the control stalk sleeve to the wiper switch.

16. Rotate the control stalk shaft to the full clockwise position and remove the shaft from the wiper switch by pulling it straight out.

To install:

17. Install the control shaft to the wiper switch, install the screws, the hider and the control knob.

18. Run the wiring through the opening and down the steering column, position the switch and install the wiper switch pivot pin.

19. Install the housing cover.

20. Install the buzzer switch and wedge spring.

21. Install the lock cylinder.

22. Install the ignition key light.

23. Install the turn signal switch, switch stalk actuator arm and hazard switch knob.

24. Install the spring, cancelling cam, lock plate and ring on the steering shaft. Depress the plate with the depressing tool and install the ring securely in the groove. Remove the tool slowly.

25. Connect the turn signal switch, wiper switch, intermittent module and cruise control connectors, if equipped. Install the channel.

26. Install the steering wheel torque the nut to 45 ft. lbs. (61 Nm).

27. Install the horn pad.

28. Connect the negative battery cable and check the wiper and washer, cruise control, turn signal switch and dimmer switch for proper operation.

29. Install the lower column cover.

Instrument Cluster

Removal and Installation

VAN

1. Disconnect the negative battery cable.

2. Open the glove box. Remove the screws that fasten the hood and bezel assembly. Pull the bezel off of the upper retaining clips.

3. Disconnect the gearshift pointer cable from the arm on the steering column, if equipped.

4. Remove the cluster screws. Pull the cluster out far enough to disconnect the speedometer cable by releasing the spring clip.

5. Remove all printed circuit board multiple connectors and the message center connector.

6. Remove the cluster assembly.

7. To remove the speedometer, remove the cluster lens, unplug the Emissions Maintenance Reminder (EMR) timer wires from the speedometer, if equipped, and remove the retaining screws.

To install:

8. Install the speedometer if removed and connect the EMR wiring, if equipped. Position the cluster to the panel and connect the speedometer cable, multiple connectors and message center connector.

9. Push the cluster in place and install the retaining screws.

10. Connect the gearshift pointer cable to the arm on the steering column, if equipped, and adjust if necessary.

11. Install the hood and bezel assembly and install the retaining screws.

12. Connect the negative battery cable.

PICK-UP AND RAMCHARGER

1. Disconnect the negative battery cable.

2. Remove the map light.

3. Remove 6 screws which attach the faceplate to the base panel. There is a screw below the heater-air conditioning control panel which is not visible from above.

4. If equipped with automatic transmission, place the shift lever in its lowest position.

5. Remove the faceplate by pulling the top edge rearward to clear the brow and pulling the bottom out, disengaging the attaching clips. If equipped with 4WD, disconnect the indicator wires.

6. Remove the upper and lower steering column covers. Disconnect the shift indicator actuator cable from the steering column, if equipped.

7. Loosen the heater and air conditioning control and pull it out enough to clear the cluster housing.

8. Remove the screws that retain the cluster and pull the cluster out far enough to disconnect the speedometer cable by releasing the spring clip.

9. Remove all printed circuit board multiple connectors.

10. Remove the cluster assembly.

11. To remove the speedometer, remove the cluster lens, unplug the EMR timer wires from the speedometer, if equipped, and remove the retaining screws.

To install:

12. Install the speedometer, if removed, and connect the EMR wiring, if equipped. Position the cluster to the panel and connect the speedometer cable and multiple connectors.

13. Push the cluster in place and install the retaining screws.

14. Install the heater air conditioning control screws.

15. Connect the shift indicator actuator cable and check for alignment.

16. Install the upper and lower steering column covers.

17. Connect the 4WD indicator, if equipped. Install the cluster faceplate and map light.

18. Connect the negative battery cable.

Headlight Switch

Removal and Installation

VAN

1. Disconnect the negative battery cable.

2. Remove the lower steering column cover.

3. Unscrew the hood release handle and lower.

4. Working under the instrument panel, depress the spring button on the headlight switch and pull the stem out.

5. Open the glove box. Remove the screws that fasten the dash bezel assembly. Pull the bezel off of the upper retaining clips.

Headlight switch removal—Van

6. Remove the switch bezel and remove the illumination bulb socket.

7. Remove the switch mounting nut from the panel, remove the switch and disconnect the wiring.

To install:

8. Connect the switch, install the switch to the panel and install the mounting nut.

9. Install the illumination bulb socket to the switch bezel and install the bezel.

10. Install the dash bezel and headlight switch stem.

11. Connect the negative battery cable and check the switch for proper operation.

12. Install the hood release handle and lower steering column cover.

PICK-UP AND RAMCHARGER

1. Disconnect the negative battery cable.

2. Remove the map light.

3. Remove 6 screws which attach the faceplate to the base panel. There is a screw below the heater-air conditioning control panel which is not visible from above.

4. If equipped with automatic transmission, place the shift lever in its lowest position.

5. Remove the faceplate by pulling the top edge rearward to clear the brow and pulling the bottom out, disengaging the attaching clips. If equipped with 4WD, disconnect the indicator wires.

6. Reach under the instrument panel, depress the spring button and remove the headlight switch knob.

7. Remove the wiper and power mirror switch knobs off their levers, if equipped.

8. Remove the bezel.

9. Remove the switch mounting nut from the panel, remove the switch and disconnect the wiring.

To install:

10. Connect the switch, install the switch to the panel and install the mounting nut.

11. Install the bezel.

12. Install the headlight stem and wiper and power mirror switch knobs, if removed.

13. Connect the 4WD indicator, if equipped. Install the cluster faceplate and map light.

14. Connect the negative battery cable and check the switch for proper operation.

Dimmer Switch

Removal and Installation

NOTE: On 1991–92 vehicles, the dimmer switch is part of the combination switch.

FLOOR MOUNTED

1. Disconnect the negative battery cable.

2. Raise the carpeting around the switch.

3. Unbolt the switch from the floor.

4. Unplug the switch and remove it from the vehicle.

5. The installation is the reversal of the removal procedure.

6. Connect the negative battery cable and check the switch for proper operation.

COLUMN MOUNTED

1. Disconnect the negative battery cable.

2. Remove the lower steering column cover.

3. Unplug the switch.

4. Holding the actuating rod against its upper seat, remove the bolts that attach the switch to the column and remove the switch.

5. The installation is the reversal of the removal procedure. Adjust the switch as required.

6. Connect the negative battery cable and check the switch for proper operation.

Column mounted dimmer switch location

Turn Signal Switch

Removal and Installation

NOTE: On 1991–92 vehicles, the turn signal switch is part of the combination switch.

1988–90 STANDARD COLUMN

1. Disconnect the negative battery cable.

2. Remove the lower steering column cover.

3. Remove the horn pad mounting screws from behind the steering wheel and remove the horn pad.

4. Remove the steering wheel nut, matchmark the steering wheel to the shaft and remove the steering wheel.

5. Remove the plastic wiring channel from the underside of the steering column and disconnect the turn signal switch connector.

6. Remove the hazard switch knob. Remove the slotted hex-head screw that attaches the wiper switch to the turn signal switch.

7. Remove the 3 screws and pull the turn signal switch out of the column.

To install:

8. Run the wiring through the opening and down the steering column, position the switch and install the hex-head screw. Make sure the dimmer switch rod is properly engaged.

9. Install the 3 screws and the hazard switch knob.

10. Connect the wires and install the wiring channel.

11. Install the steering wheel. Torque the nut to 45 ft. lbs. (61 Nm).

12. Install the horn pad.

13. Connect the negative battery cable and check the turn signal switch and dimmer switch for proper operation.

14. Install the lower column cover.

1988–90 TILT COLUMN

1. Disconnect the negative battery cable.

2. Remove the lower steering column cover. Remove the plastic wiring channel from the underside of the steering column.

3. Remove the horn pad mounting screws from behind the steering wheel and remove the horn pad.

4. Remove the steering wheel nut, matchmark the steering wheel to the shaft and remove the steering wheel.

5. Depress the lock plate with the proper depressing tool, remove the retaining ring from its groove and remove the tool, ring, lock plate, cancelling cam and spring.

6. Remove the stalk actuator screw and arm.

7. Remove the hazard switch knob.

8. Disconnect the turn signal switch connector.

9. Remove the 3 screws and remove the turn signal switch. Tape the connector to the wires to aid in removal.

To install:

10. Run the wiring through the opening and down the steering column, install the turn signal switch, switch stalk actuator arm and hazard switch knob.

11. Install the spring, cancelling cam, lock plate and ring on the steering shaft. Depress the plate with the depressing tool and install the ring securely in the groove. Remove the tool slowly.

12. Connect the turn signal switch connector and install the channel.

13. Install the steering wheel. Torque the nut to 45 ft. lbs. (61 Nm).

14. Install the horn pad.

15. Connect the negative battery cable and check the turn signal switch and dimmer switch for proper operation.

16. Install the lower column cover.

Combination Switch

Removal and Installation

1991–92 VEHICLES

1. Disconnect the negative battery cable.
2. Remove the tilt lever, if equipped.
3. Remove the steering column covers.
4. Remove the combination switch tamper-proof mounting screws and pull the switch away from the steering column.
5. Loosen the connector screw; the screw will remain in the connector.
6. Disconnect the connector from the switch.
7. The installation is the reverse of the removal procedure.
8. Connect the negative battery cable and check all functions of the combination switch for proper operation.

Ignition Lock

Removal and Installation

1988–90

Standard Column

1. Disconnect the negative battery cable.
2. Remove the horn pad mounting screws from behind the steering wheel and remove the horn pad.

3. Remove the steering wheel nut, matchmark the steering wheel to the shaft and remove the steering wheel.

4. Remove the hazard switch knob. Remove the slotted hex-head screw that attaches the wiper switch to the turn signal switch.

5. Remove the 3 screws and pull the turn signal switch out of the column as far as it will go. Unplug it below if necessary.

6. Remove the ignition switch key light.

7. Place the key in the **LOCK** position and remove the key.

8. Insert 2 small diameter tools into the release holes and push inward to release the spring loaded lock retainers while simultaneously pulling the key lock cylinder out of its bore.

To install:

9. Install the key cylinder.

10. Install the ignition switch key light.

11. Install the turn signal switch and hazard switch knob. Connect the wires if they were disconnected.

12. Install the steering wheel and torque the nut to 45 ft. lbs. (61 Nm).

13. Install the horn pad.

14. Connect the negative battery cable and check the lock cylinder for proper operation.

15. Install the lower column cover.

Tilt Column

1. Disconnect the negative battery cable.
2. Remove the horn pad mounting screws from behind the steering wheel and remove the horn pad.
3. Remove the steering wheel nut, matchmark the steering wheel to the shaft and remove the steering wheel.
4. Depress the lock plate with the proper depressing tool, remove the retaining ring from its groove and remove the tool, ring, lock plate, cancelling cam and spring.
5. Remove the stalk actuator screw and arm.
6. Remove the hazard switch knob.
7. Remove the 3 screws and pull the turn signal switch out of the column as far as it will go. Unplug it below if necessary.
8. Remove the ignition key light.
9. Place the key in the **LOCK** position and remove the key. Insert a thin tool into the slot next to the switch mounting screw boss, depress the spring latch at the bottom of the slot releasing the lock and remove the lock cylinder.

To install:

10. Install the lock cylinder.
11. Install the ignition key light.

Removing the key lock cylinder—standard column

Removing the key lock cylinder—tilt column

12. Install the turn signal switch, switch stalk actuator arm and hazard switch knob.

13. Install the spring, cancelling cam, lock plate and ring on the steering shaft. Depress the plate with the depressing tool and install the ring securely in the groove. Remove the tool slowly.

14. Connect the wires if disconnected.

15. Install the steering wheel and torque the nut to 45 ft. lbs. (61 Nm).

16. Install the horn pad.

17. Connect the negative battery cable and check the turn signal switch for proper operation.

18. Install the lower column cover, if removed.

Ignition Switch

Removal and Installation

1988–90 VEHICLES

1. Disconnect the negative battery cable.

2. Remove the lower steering column cover.

3. Remove the steering column retaining nuts and allow the steering wheel to rest on the driver's seat.

4. Remove the 2 screws that attach the ignition switch to the column.

5. Rotate the switch 90 degrees and pull up to disengage it from the ignition switch rod.

To install:

6. Engage the switch with the rod, rotate the switch 90 degrees and push down until fully engaged.

7. Install the mounting screws finger-tight.

8. Place the key in the **LOCK** position and remove the key. Adjust the switch by pushing up gently on the switch to take up all slack in the rod.

9. Tighten the mounting screws. Connect negative battery cable and check the switch for proper operation in all positions.

10. Install the steering column and cover.

Ignition Lock/Switch

Removal and Installation

1991–92 VEHICLES

1. Disconnect the negative battery cable.

2. Remove the tilt lever, if equipped.

3. Remove the upper and lower column covers.

4. Remove the 3 ignition switch tamper-proof Torx screws; APEX 440–TX20H or equivalent is required.

5. Pull the switch away from the column. Release the connector locks on the 2 wiring connectors and disconnect them from the switch.

6. Remove the key lock cylinder from the ignition switch by performing the following:

   a. Insert the key and turn the switch in the **LOCK** position. Using a small tool, depress the key cylinder retaining pin flush with the key cylinder surface.

   b. Rotate the key clockwise to the **OFF** position to unseat the key cylinder from the ignition switch assembly. The cylinder bezel should be about ⅛ in. above the ignition switch halo light ring. Do not attempt to remove the key cylinder at this point.

   c. With the key cylinder in the unseated position, rotate the key counterclockwise to the **LOCK** position and remove the key.

   d. Remove the key cylinder from the ignition switch.

To install:

7. Connect the wiring connectors.

8. Mount ignition switch to the column by performing the following:

   a. Position the shifter in **P** position. The park lock dowel pin on the ignition switch assembly must engage with the column park lock slider linkage.

   b. Verify that the ignition switch is in the **LOCK** position. The flag should be parallel to the ignition switch terminals. Apply a small amount of grease to the flag and pin.

   c. Position the park lock link to mid-travel.

   d. Align the locating pin hole and its pin and position the ignition switch against the lock housing face. Make sure the pin is inserted into the park lock link contour slot. Torque the retaining screws to 17 inch lbs.

9. With the key cylinder and ignition switch in the **LOCK** position, key not in cylinder, gently insert the key cylinder into the ignition switch until it bottoms.

10. Insert the key. Simultaneously push in on the cylinder and rotate the key to the **RUN** position. This action should fully seat the cylinder in the ignition switch.

11. Install the column covers and the tilt lever, if equipped.

12. Connect the negative battery cable and check the push-to-lock and park lock functions, halo lighting and all ignition switch positions for proper operation.

Stoplight Switch

Adjustment

1. Push the stoplight switch forward in the mounting bracket as far as it will go; the brake pedal should move forward slightly.

2. Pull back on the brake pedal bringing the striker toward the switch until the pedal will not go back any farther. This will cause the switch to ratchet backward into position and automatically adjust.

Removal and Installation

1. Disconnect the negative battery cable.

2. Remove the switch mounting bracket assembly from the brake pedal bracket.

3. Remove the switch from its bracket.

4. The installation is the reversal of the removal procedure.

5. Connect the negative battery cable and check the switch for proper operation.

Neutral Safety Switch

Removal and Installation

1. Disconnect negative battery cable.

2. Raise and safely support the vehicle. Position drain pan under switch.

3. Disconnect switch wiring harness.

4. Remove switch from case.

5. Verify that switch operating lever fingers are centered in the switch opening in the case when in **P** and **N**.

6. Install new seal on switch and install switch into case. Torque to 25 ft. lbs.

7. Test continuity of new switch. Connect wire harness and negative battery cable.

8. Add transmission fluid as required to correct level.

Fuses, Circuit Breakers and Relays

Location

The fuse block and relay bank is located to the left of the glove box on Vans and directly under the steering column on Pick-Ups and Ramchargers. Circuit breakers are also located on the fuse block. The auto shutdown relay, starter relay, A/C cutout relay and part throttle unlock relay are located in the engine compartment near the 50-way bulkhead connector

Computers

Location

The Single Module Engine Controller (SMEC) is located in engine compartment, mounted to the left or right fender depending to model. The Electronic Control Unit (ECU) is located on the righ side of the dash panel in engine compartment.

Flashers

Location

The turn signal flasher and the hazard flasher are located in the fuse block.

Cruise Control

For further information, please refer to Chilton's Chassis Electronics Service Manual.

Adjustment
DIESEL ENGINE

1. The clearance between the throttle stud and cable clevis should be as small as possible without moving the throttle. If gap is not correct, remove adjustment clip.
2. Push protective sleeve into housing to decrease gap or pull sleeve out of housing to increase gap. Install adjustment clip.

ENGINE COOLING

Radiator

Removal and Installation

1. Disconnect the negative battery cable.
2. Drain cooling system. Remove heater hoses from core and cap.
3. Remove the upper hose and coolant reserve tank hose from the radiator.
4. Remove the shroud from the radiator and position aside.
5. Remove the upper radiator mounting screws. On Van, the radiator will be removed from the bottom of the vehicle. Raise and safely support vehicle.
6. Remove the lower hose from the radiator.
7. Disconnect the automatic transmission cooler lines, if equipped, position aside and cap ends.
8. Remove the mounting screws and carefully lift or lower the radiator out of the engine compartment.

To install:

9. Lift or lower the radiator into position and install the mounting screws.
10. Connect the automatic transmission cooler lines, if removed.
11. Connect the lower hose.
12. Install the upper radiator mounting bolts and shroud.
13. Reconnect negative battery cable.
14. Connect the upper radiator hose and coolant reserve tank hose.
15. Fill the cooling system.
16. Run the vehicle until normal operating temperature is reached. Recheck coolant level and automatic transmission fluid level and add as required.

Heater Core

For further information, please refer to Chilton's Air Conditioning and Heating Manual.

Removal and Installation

VAN

Without Air Conditioning

1. Disconnect the negative battery cable.
2. Drain the cooling system. Disconnect and plug the heater hoses.
3. Disconnect the temperature control cable from the heater core cover and the blend door crank. Disconnect the vent cable.
4. Disconnect the blower motor power feed and ground wire connector.
5. Remove the screws retaining the heater assembly aside

cowl and the nuts fastening the heater assembly to the dash panel.
6. Remove the heater unit from the vehicle.
7. Remove the back plate and remove the screws holding the heater core cover to the heater housing. Lift the cover from the housing.
8. Remove the retaining screws from the heater core and remove the core from the heater housing.

To install:

9. Clean out the inside of the housing. Place the heater core into the housing and fasten.
10. Position the blend air door and right vent door in the housing and fasten the heater core cover to the housing.
11. Check the dash panel and side cowl seals for breaks or lack of adhesion and repair as needed.
12. Install the heater assembly to the vehicle.
13. Connect the blower motor power feed and ground wire connector.
14. Position temperature control cable on blend air door crank and attach cable to heater core cover. Connect and adjust vent cable.
15. Connect the heater hoses. Connect negative battery cable.
16. Refill the cooling system.
17. Run the vehicle until normal operating temperature is reached. Recheck coolant level and automatic transmission fluid level and add as required.

With Air Conditioning

1. Disconnect the negative battery cable. Discharge the air conditioning system.
2. Disconnect the freeze control connector from the wire harness at the H-valve.
3. Drain the cooling system. Place a layer of non-conductive waterproof material over the alternator to prevent coolant from spilling on it when disconnecting the heater hoses. Disconnect and cap the heater hoses.
4. Slowly disconnect the refrigerant plumbing from the H valve. Remove the 2 screws from the filter drier bracket and swing the plumbing out of the way. Cap open air conditioning lines to prevent contamination of the system.
5. Remove the temperature control cable from the cover.
6. Working from inside the vehicle, remove the glove box, spot cooler bezel and the appearance shield. Working through the glove box opening and under the instrument panel, remove the screws and nuts attaching the evaporator core housing to the dash panel.
7. Remove the 2 screws from the flange connection to the blower housing. Separate the evaporator core housing from the blower housing.
8. Carefully remove the evaporator core housing from the vehicle.

HEATER
CORE

EVAPORATOR
COIL

FREEZE
CONTROL
PROBE

Heater core removal—Van with air conditioning

9. Remove the cover from the housing. Remove 1 screw from strap on heater core tubes and pull core out of housing.
To install:
10. Clean the inside of the housing. Place the heater core into the housing and install the retaining strap and screw.
11. Install the housing cover.
12. Attach the blower housing to the evaporator housing.
13. Inspect all air seals and mating surfaces for possible breaks and leaks and repair as needed.
14. Through the glove box opening and under the dash, install the screws and nuts attaching evaporator housing assembly to dash panel.
15. Install the appearance shield, spot cooler bezel and glove box.
16. Attach the temperature control cable to the cover.
17. Position the plumbing and install the 2 screws onto the filter drier bracket.
18. Install a new gasket and connect the refrigerant plumbing to the H-valve.
19. Connect the heater hoses and remove the waterproof material from the alternator. Connect the freeze control wire harness.
20. Evacuate and recharge the air conditioning system.
21. Connect the negative battery cable. Refill the cooling system.
22. Run the vehicle until normal operating temperature is reached. Recheck coolant level and add as required. Check the operation of the entire climate control system.

PICK-UP AND RAMCHARGER

Without Air Conditioning

1. Disconnect the negative battery cable.
2. Drain the cooling system. Remove and plug the heater core hoses.
3. Remove the right side cowl trim panel, if equipped. Remove the glove box assembly. Remove the structural brace through the glovebox opening.
4. Remove the right half of the instrument panel lower reinforcement and disconnect the radio ground strap.
5. Disconnect the control cables from the heater housing and the blower motor wires on the engine side.
6. Remove the retaining screw between the package to cowl side sheet metal.
7. Remove the 6 heater housing retaining nuts on the engine

side of the heater assembly and remove the heater housing assembly.
8. Remove the heater housing cover retaining screws and the mode door crank. Separate the cover from the housing.
9. Carefully lift the heater core from the heater housing.
To install:
10. Clean the inside of the housing. Install the heater core into the housing.
11. Install the housing cover.
12. Inspect the dash panel seal for damage and repair as required.
13. Install the assembly to the dash panel and install the retaining nuts.
14. Install the cowl side retaining screws.
15. Connect the blower motor connector.
16. Connect the control cables.
17. Install the right lower instrument panel reinforcement, structural brace, glove box and cowl side trim panel, if equipped.
18. Connect the heater hoses.
19. Refill the radiator.
20. Connect the negative battery cable.
21. Run the vehicle until normal operating temperature is reached. Check coolant level and add as required.

With Air Conditioning

1. Disconnect the negative battery cable. Discharge the air condition system. Drain the cooling system. Disconnect and plug the heater hoses and the refrigerant lines.
2. Remove the condensation tube from the housing.
3. Move the transfer case and gear shift levers away from the instrument panel.
4. Remove the right side cowl trim panel, if equipped. Remove the glove box and swing it out from the bottom.
5. Remove the structural brace from the through hole in the glove box opening. Remove the ash tray.
6. Remove the right lower half of the dash reinforcement by removing the retaining screws holding it to the instrument panel and to the cowl side trim panel.
7. Disconnect the radio ground strap. Remove the center and floor air distribution ducts.
8. Disconnect the temperature control cable from the assembly and tape it out of the way.
9. Disconnect the vacuum lines from the extension on the control unit and unclip the vacuum lines from the defroster duct.
10. Remove the wiring connector from the resistor block. Remove the blower motor electrical connector from the engine side of the assembly.
11. Disconnect the vacuum lines on the engine side and make sure the grommet is free from the dash panel.
12. Remove the retaining nuts on the engine side. Remove the screw that retains the assembly to the cowl side of the sheetmetal.
13. Remove the assembly from the vehicle.
14. Remove the vacuum actuators, door crank levers, evaporator case cover retaining nuts and screws and the heater core retaining screws. Lift the cover off of the assembly and remove the heater core from its mounting.
To install:
15. Clean the inside of the housing. Install the heater core into the housing.
16. Install the housing cover, retaining screws and nuts, levers and actuators.
17. Inspect the dash panel seals for damage and repair as required.
18. Feed the vacuum lines through the hole in the dash panel, install the assembly to the dash panel and install all retaining nuts and screws.
19. Connect the resistor block and blower motor.
20. Connect the vacuum lines to the extension on the control unit and clip the vacuum lines to the defroster duct.

Evaporator heater assembly—Pick-Up and Ramcharger with air conditioning

21. Connect the temperature control cable to the assembly.
22. Connect the radio ground strap. Install the center and floor air distribution ducts.
23. Install the dash reinforcement, structural brace, glove box and right side cowl trim panel, if equipped. Install the ash tray.
24. Install the condensation tube.
25. Connect the heater hoses and vacuum lines.
26. Install a new gasket and connect the refrigerant lines.
27. Evacuate and recharge the air conditioning system. Refill the radiator and connect negative battery cable.
28. Run the vehicle until normal operating temperature is reached. Recheck coolant level and add as required. Check operation of the entire climate control system.

Water Pump

Removal and Installation

------------------------------ CAUTION ------------------------------

If the water pump is being replaced due to bearing or shaft damage, the mechanical cooling fan should be carefully inspected for fatigue cracks, loose blades or loose rivets resulting from excessive vibration. If the fan is damaged in any way, it could snap at any time, possibly causing serious personal injury or damage to the vehicle.

GASOLINE ENGINES

1. Disconnect the negative battery cable. Drain the coolant.
2. Remove the shroud from the radiator and slide it over the fan, if 1-piece.
3. Remove the radiator and lower hose.
4. Remove the fan blade, spacer or viscous drive unit, pully, bolts and shroud (if it was not removed in Step 2) together. Remove the air pump belt and power steering pump belt.

NOTE: Do not place the viscous fan in an upright position because the silicone fluid in the drive could drain into the bearing and contaminate its lubricant.

5. Loosen the alternator mounting bolts and remove the alternator/air conditioner belts.
6. Remove the alternator bracket. This bracket also supports the air conditioner compressor or idler pulley, which will remain supported by its rear mount.
7. Remove the air pump(s) and the air pump bracket.
8. Unbolt the power steering pump bracket with the pump still attached and position it out of the way.
9. Disconnect the heater and bypass hoses.
10. Remove the remaining pump retaining bolts and remove the pump from the engine.
To install:
11. Clean and dry the pump mating surfaces. Install a new bypass hose to the engine.

12. Install a new gasket and install the water pump to the engine.
13. Install any bolts that do not retain a bracket. Tighten the bypass hose clamps. Install the heater hose.
14. Install the water pump to compressor front mount bolts and bracket, if removed.
15. Install all remaining brackets and components that were removed during the removal procedure. Torque all water pump retaining bolts that do not go through adjusting slots to 30 ft. lbs. (41 Nm).
16. Install and adjust the alternator/air conditioner belts. Install the remaining belts.
17. Install the fan blade, spacer or viscous drive unit, pulley and bolts along with the shroud (if it is a 1-piece unit) together.
18. Install the radiator, lower hose and shroud.
19. Adjust all belts and torque the remaining water pump retaining bolts to 30 ft. lbs. (41 Nm).
20. Fill the radiator with coolant.
21. Connect the negative battery cable, run the vehicle until the thermostat opens, fill the radiator completely and check for leaks.
22. Once the vehicle has cooled, recheck the coolant level.

5.9L DIESEL ENGINE

1. Disconnect the negative battery cable.
2. Drain the coolant.
3. Use a ⅜ in. drive breaker bar to lift the belt tensioner and remove the belt.
4. Remove the 2 water pump retaining bolts and remove the pump from the engine.
5. Remove the O-ring from the pump groove.
To install:
6. Clean the O-ring groove and install a new O-ring.
7. Clean the pump mating surfaces and install the pump to the engine.
8. Torque the mounting bolts to 18 ft. lbs. (24 Nm). Fill the radiator with coolant.
9. Install the drive belt.
10. Connect the negative battery cable, run the vehicle until the thermostat opens, fill the radiator completely and check for leaks.
11. Once the vehicle has cooled, recheck the coolant level.

5.9L diesel engine water pump

Thermostat

Removal and Installation

EXCEPT 5.9L DIESEL ENGINE

1. Disconnect the negative battery cable. Drain the coolant down to thermostat level or below.
2. Remove the thermostat housing.
3. Remove the thermostat and discard the gasket.

4. Clean the housing mating surfaces and use a new gasket.

5. The installation is the reversal of the removal procedure.

6. Connect the negative battery cable, run the vehicle until the thermostat opens, fill the radiator completely and check for leaks.

7. Once the vehicle has cooled, recheck the coolant level.

5.9L DIESEL ENGINE

1. Disconnect the negative battery cable.

2. Drain the coolant.

3. Use a ⅜ in. drive breaker bar to lift the belt tensioner and remove the belt.

4. Disconnect the upper radiator hose from the thermostat housing.

5. Loosen the alternator mounting bolts and lower the alternator.

6. Unbolt the thermostat housing and remove the housing, engine lifting bracket and thermostat with seal.

To install:

7. Install the new thermostat to the housing, making sure the tang on the thermostat is aligned with the slot in the housing. This will ensure correct positioning of the jiggle pins in the housing. This is important because during cooling system filling. Air vents through the jiggle pin openings, through the upper hose and out the radiator fill neck.

8. Clean the pump mating surfaces.

9. Install the engine lifting bracket, new seal, thermostat and housing. Make sure the seal is installed with the beveled side facing out.

10. Torque the thermostat housing bolts to 18 ft. lbs. (24 Nm). Connect the upper hose to the housing.

11. Reinstall the alternator into position. Torque the upper bolt to 18 ft. lbs. (24 Nm) and the lower bolt to 32 ft. lbs. (43 Nm).

12. Install the drive belt.

5.9L diesel engine thermostat

Installing the thermostat in the housing—5.9L diesel engine

Proper positioning of the rubber seal—5.9L diesel engine

13. Connect the negative battery cable, run the vehicle until the thermostat opens, fill the radiator completely and check for leaks.

14. Once the vehicle has cooled, recheck the coolant level.

Cooling System Bleeding

Air trapped in the cooling system gathers under the radiator cap during engine operation. The next time the engine is operated thermal expansion of coolant will force trapped air past the radiator cap and into the coolant reserve tank where it is vented into the atmosphere. As the engine cools down coolant will be drawn from the reserve tank into the radiator to replace the vented air.

GASOLINE FUEL SYSTEM

Fuel System Service Precautions

Safety is the most important factor when performing not only fuel system maintenance but any type of maintenance. Failure to conduct maintenance and repairs in a safe manner may result in serious personal injury or death. Maintenance and testing of the vehicle's fuel system components can be accomplished safely and effectively by adhering to the following rules and guidelines.

• To avoid the possibility of fire and personal injury, always disconnect the negative battery cable unless the repair or test procedure requires that battery voltage be applied.

• Always relieve the fuel system pressure prior to disconnecting any fuel system component (injector, fuel rail, pressure regulator, etc.), fitting or fuel line connection. Exercise extreme caution whenever relieving fuel system pressure to avoid exposing skin, face and eyes to fuel spray. Please be advised that fuel under pressure may penetrate the skin or any part of the body that it contacts.

• Always place a shop towel or cloth around the fitting or connection prior to loosening to absorb any excess fuel due to spillage. Ensure that all fuel spillage (should it occur) is quickly removed from engine surfaces. Ensure that all fuel soaked cloths or towels are deposited into a suitable waste container.

• Always keep a dry chemical (Class B) fire extinguisher near the work area.

• Do not allow fuel spray or fuel vapors to come into contact with a spark or open flame.

• Always use a backup wrench when loosening and tightening fuel line connection fittings. This will prevent unnecessary stress and torsion to fuel line piping. Always follow the proper torque specifications.

• Always replace worn fuel fitting O-rings with new. Do not substitute fuel hose or equivalent where fuel pipe is installed.

Relieving Fuel System Pressure

1. Loosen the fuel filler cap to release fuel tank pressure.
2. Disconnect the injector wiring harness from the engine harness.
3. Connect a jumper wire to ground terminal 1 of the injector harness to engine ground.
4. Being careful not to allow contact between the jumper leads, connect a jumper wire to pin 2 next to the 1 that is grounded and touch the other end of the jumper to the positive battery post for no longer than 5 seconds. This will relieve fuel pressure.
5. Remove the jumper wires and connect the connector.

FUEL INJECTORS

FUEL INJECTORS WIRING CONNECTOR

Injector wiring connector location

TERMINAL #1

TERMINAL #2

Fuel Injector Harness Connectors

Fuel Tank

Removal and Installation

1. Disconnect negative battery cable.
2. Relieve the fuel pressure.
3. Raise the vehicle and support safely..
4. Using the proper equipment, drain the fuel tank.
5. Remove vent hoses from hose routing bracket attacked to the top of the frame rail. Disconnect the electrical connection.
6. Place a transmission jack or equivalent, under the center of the tank and apply slight pressure. Remove the tank straps.
7. Lower tank slightly to provide access to the fuel supply and return hoses, and disconnect hoses. Disconnect fuel vapor line from pressure relief/rollover valve.
8. Lower tank from vehicle.

To install:

9. Raise the tank into position and connect all electrical harnesses and vacuum hoses.
10. Install the tank straps and tighten the retaining nuts.
11. Install vent hoses, if not done, and check all connections.
12. Fill fuel tank, install fuel filler cap and reconnect negative battery cable.

Fuel Filter

Removal and Installation

CARBURETED ENGINE

1. Disconnect the negative battery cable.
2. Raise the vehicle and support safely.
3. Remove the fuel filter with hoses.

NOTE: Some vehicles may be equipped with a field package designed to combat driveability problems associated with fuel foaming. Affected vehicles have a special replaceable filter/reservoir mounted inboard on the right front frame rail. When the kit is installed, the conventional filter is discarded. Do not install a conventional filter or conventional clamps or hoses in place of the special replacement parts; they are not compatible with the electronic fuel pump installed with the kit.

4. Install the new filter, hoses and clamps.
5. If equipped with a Rochester Quadrajet carburetor, a second filter mounted in the carburetor can also be replaced. Remove the air cleaner assembly, disconnect the fuel line, remove the fuel inlet nut, gasket, filter and spring. The installation is the reversal of the removal procedure.
6. Connect the negative battery cable, start the engine and check for leaks.

FUEL INJECTED ENGINE

─────── **CAUTION** ───────

Do not use conventional fuel hoses or clamps when servicing this fuel system. They are not compatible with the injection system and could fail, causing personal injury or damage to the vehicle. Use only hoses and clamps specifically designed for fuel injection.

1. Relieve the fuel pressure.
2. Disconnect the negative battery cable.
3. Remove the filter retaining screw and remove the filter assembly from the mounting plate.
4. Loosen the outlet hose clamp on the filter and inlet hose clamp on the rear fuel tube.
5. Wrap a shop towel around the hoses to absorb fuel. Remove the hoses from the filter and fuel tube and discard the clamps and the filter.

To install:

6. Install the inlet hose on the fuel tube and tighten the new clamp to 10 inch lbs. (1 Nm).
7. Install the outlet hose on the filter outlet fitting and tighten the new clamp to 10 inch lbs. (1 Nm).

Fuel filter location—fuel injected engine

8. Position the filter assembly on the mounting plate and tighten the mounting screw to 75 inch lbs. (8 Nm).
9. Connect the negative battery cable, start the engine and check for leaks.

Mechanical Fuel Pump

Pressure Testing

1. Raise the vehicle and support safely.
2. Connect a pressure gauge (0–15 psi minimum range) to the fuel pump outlet fitting.
3. Crank the engine several times while observing the gauge.
4. The engines should develop 5.75–7.25 psi. If equipped with the field package noted above, fuel pressure should be 13–15 psi.

Removal and Installation

1. Disconnect the negative battery cable.
2. Raise the vehicle and support safely.
3. Disconnect the fuel lines from the pump and plug them.
4. Remove the fuel pump retaining bolts and remove the pump from the engine.
5. Clean and dry the mounting surfaces and bolt holes.
6. The installation is the reversal of the removal procedure.
7. Connect the negative battery cable, start the engine and check for leaks.

Electric Fuel Pump

Pressure Testing

1. Relieve the fuel pressure.
2. Disconnect the larger diameter fuel supply hose from the engine fuel line assembly.
3. Connect the fuel system pressure tester C–4799B or equivalent, between the fuel supply hose and the engine fuel line assembly.
4. With the key in the **RUN** position, put the DRB I or II in the activate auto shutdown relay mode; this will activate the fuel pump and pressurize the system.
5. The pressure specification is 13.5–15.5 psi. If the pressure is within specifications, reinstall the fuel hose.
6. If fuel pressure is below specifications, install the tester in the fuel supply line between the tank and the filter and repeat the test.
7. If the pressure is 5 psi higher than in Step 5, replace the fuel filter. If no change is observed, squeeze the return hose. If

pressure increases, replace the pressure regulator. If no change is observed, the problem is either a plugged in-tank sock filter or a defective pump.

8. If fuel pressure is above specifications, remove the fuel return line hose from the chassis line at the fuel tank and connect a 3 foot piece of fuel hose to the return line. Put the other end into a 2 gallon minimum capacity approved gasoline container. Repeat the test. If pressure is now correct, check the in-tank return hose for kinking. Replace the fuel pump assembly if the in-tank reservoir check valve or aspirator jet is obstructed.

9. If pressure is still above specifications, remove the fuel return hose from the throttle body. Connect a substitute hose to the throttle body return nipple and place the other end of the hose in a clean container. Repeat the test. If pressure is now correct, check for a restricted fuel return line. If no change is observed, replace the fuel pressure regulator.

Removal and Installation

The fuel pump module is installed in the top of the fuel tank. It contains the fuel pump, fuel pump reservoir, pressure relief/rollover valve, electrical connector for the sending unit, fuel filler vent, supply and return tube connections and the drain tube nipple.

1. Disconnect negative battery cable.
2. Relieve the fuel pressure.
3. Raise the vehicle and support safely.
4. Using the proper equipment, drain the fuel tank.
5. Remove vent hoses from hose routing bracket attacked to the top of the frame rail. Disconnect the electrical connection.
6. Place a transmission jack or equivalent, under the center of the tank and apply slight pressure. Remove the tank straps.
7. Lower tank slightly to provide access to the fuel supply and return hoses and disconnect hoses. Disconnect fuel vapor line from pressure relief/rollover valve. Lower tank from vehicle.
8. Remove the fuel pump module collar and module from tank. Mark position of sender wires and disconnect. Remove sender unit from module.
9. Replace module and pump assembly as a unit. Reinstall sender to module and reposition into tank. Install collar to original position.
10. Raise the tank into position and connect all harnesses and vacuum hoses. Install the tank straps and tighten the retaining nuts.
11. Connect fuel filler tube and vent hoses.
12. Fill fuel tank, install fuel filler cap and reconnect negative battery cable.

Carburetor

Removal and Installation

1. Disconnect the negative battery cable.
2. Remove the air cleaner assembly.
3. Remove and install the fuel tank cap to relieve any pressure in the tank.
4. Matchmark all vacuum hoses and electrical connectors and remove from the carburetor.
5. Disconnect the throttle, cruise control, choke and kickdown cables and linkages, if equipped.
6. Disconnect and plug the fuel inlet line.
7. Remove the mounting bolts and/or nuts and remove the carburetor from the intake manifold.
To install:
8. Clean the mounting surface of the manifold and install a new base gasket.
9. Install the mounting bolts and/or nuts and tighten them alternately to compress the base gasket evenly.
10. Connect the fuel line.
11. Connect the throttle, cruise control, choke and kickdown cables and linkages, if equipped.

12. Install all vacuum hoses and electrical connectors in their proper locations.

13. Install the air cleaner.

14. Connect the negative battery cable, start the engine and perform all necessary adjustments.

Idle Speed Adjustment

1. Start the engine and run until at normal operating temperature. Check and adjust the ignition timing. Turn the engine OFF.

2. Disconnect and plug the EGR hose. Disconnect the oxygen sensor, if equipped.

3. Disconnect and plug the $\frac{3}{16}$ in. hose at the canister.

4. Remove the PCV valve from the valve cover and allow it to draw underhood air.

5. Ground the carburetor switch with a jumper wire, if equipped.

6. Disconnect the vacuum hose from the computer, if equipped, and connect an auxiliary vacuum supply of 16 in. Hg.

7. Make sure all accessories are OFF. Install a tachometer and start the engine.

8. Allow the engine to run for 2 minutes to stabilize. Turn the idle speed screw until the correct idle speed according to the VECI label is reached.

9. Connect all wires and hoses that were previously disconnected. It is normal for the idle speed to vary after all hoses and wires are reconnected; do not readjust.

Idle Mixture Adjustment

1. Disconnect and plug the EGR hose. Disconnect the oxygen sensor, if equipped.

2. Disconnect and plug the $\frac{3}{16}$ in. hose at the canister.

3. Remove the PCV valve from the valve cover and allow it to draw underhood air.

4. Ground the carburetor switch with a jumper wire, if equipped.

5. Disconnect the vacuum hose from the computer, if equipped, and connect an auxiliary vacuum supply of 16 in. Hg.

6. Remove the concealment plug. Disconnect the vacuum supply hose to the tee and install a propane supply hose in its place.

7. Make sure all accessories are off. Install a tachometer and start the engine. Allow the engine to run for 2 minutes to stabilize.

8. Open the main propane valve. Slowly open the propane metering valve until the maximum engine rpm is reached. When too much propane is added, the engine will begin to stumble; at this point back OFF until the engine stabilizes.

9. Adjust the idle rpm to obtain the specified propane rpm. Fine tune the metering valve to obtain the highest rpm again. If there has been a change to the maximum rpm, readjust the idle screw to the specified propane rpm.

10. Turn the main propane valve off and allow the engine to run for 1 minute to stabilize.

11. Adjust the mixture screw to obtain the smoothest idle at the specified idle rpm.

12. Open the main propane valve. Fine tune the metering valve to obtain the highest rpm. If the maximum engine speed is more than 25 rpm different than the specified propane rpm, repeat the procedure.

13. Turn the propane valves off and remove the propane canister. Reinstall the vacuum supply hose to the tee.

14. Perform the idle speed adjustment procedure.

15. Connect all wires and hoses that were previously disconnected.

Service Adjustments.

For all carburetor service adjustment procedures and Specifications, please refer to "Carburetor Service" in the Unit Repair section.

Fuel Injection

For further information, please refer to Chilton's Electronic Engine Controls Manual.

Idle Speed Adjustment

1. Start the engine and allow it to reach normal operating temperature. If engine is already hot, run for 2 minutes.

2. Turn the engine OFF and allow 1 minute for the Idle Speed Control (ISC) actuator shaft to fully extend.

3. Disconnect the ISC actuator connector and the coolant temperature sensor.

4. Connect a tachometer to the engine and start the engine.

5. Adjust the extension screw on the actuator shaft until the rpm is within specifications.
   3.9L engine—2500–2600 rpm
   5.2L and 5.9L engines—2750–2850 rpm

6. Turn the engine OFF. Reconnect the ISC actuator connector and the coolant temperature sensor. Remove the tachometer.

Idle Mixture Adjustment

There is no idle mixture adjustment provided with this fuel injection system.

Adjusting the idle speed—fuel injected engine

Fuel Injector

Removal and Installation

1. Remove the air cleaner assembly.
2. Relieve the fuel pressure.
3. Disconnect the negative battery cable.

NOTE: There is a small spacer below the injector hold-down clamp. Take the proper precaution to prevent this spacer from falling into the throttle body.

4. Remove the injector hold-down Torx screw, the hold-down and the spacer.

5. Using a small flat-tipped tool, lift the caps off of the injector.

6. Using the same tool, gently pry the injector from its pod.

7. Remove the lower O-ring from the pod.

Injector hold-down and spacer—fuel injected engine

Removing the injector from its pod—fuel injected engine

To install:

8. Install the new lower O-ring on the injector.

9. Align the injector terminal housing with the locating socket in the injector cap.

10. Press the injector cap so the upper O-ring flange is flush with the lower surface of the cap.

11. Spray the inner surfaces of the injector pod with a carburetor parts cleaner to remove residual varnish and gasoline.

12. Lubricate the O-rings sparingly with unmedicated petroleum jelly.

13. Place the injector and cap into the injector pod and align the cap locating pin with the locating hole in the casting. The right side locating pin in 5mm in diameter and will not fit into the other hole.

14. Press firmly on the injector cap until it is flush with the casting surface.

15. Install the spacer and align the holes in the hold-down with the pins on the caps and install.

16. Push down on the caps, install the screw and torque to 35 inch lbs. (4 Nm).

Installing the injector to the cap—fuel injected engine

17. Connect the negative battery cable and check for leaks using the DRB I or II to activate the fuel pump.

18. Install the air cleaner.

DIESEL FUEL SYSTEM

Fuel System Service Precaution

Safety is the most important factor when performing not only fuel system maintenance but any type of maintenance. Failure to conduct maintenance and repairs in a safe manner may result in serious personal injury or death. Maintenance and testing of the vehicle's fuel system components can be accomplished safely and effectively by adhering to the following rules and guidelines.

• To avoid the possibility of fire and personal injury, always disconnect the negative battery cable unless the repair or test procedure requires that battery voltage be applied.

• Always relieve the fuel system pressure prior to disconnecting any fuel system component (injector, fuel rail, pressure regulator, etc.), fitting or fuel line connection. Exercise extreme caution whenever relieving fuel system pressure to avoid exposing skin, face and eyes to fuel spray. Please be advised that fuel under pressure may penetrate the skin or any part of the body that it contacts.

• Always place a shop towel or cloth around the fitting or connection prior to loosening to absorb any excess fuel due to spillage. Ensure that all fuel spillage (should it occur) is quickly removed from engine surfaces. Ensure that all fuel soaked cloths or towels are deposited into a suitable waste container.

• Always keep a dry chemical (Class B) fire extinguisher near the work area.

• Do not allow fuel spray or fuel vapors to come into contact with a spark or open flame.

• Always use a backup wrench when loosening and tightening fuel line connection fittings. This will prevent unnecessary stress and torsion to fuel line piping. Always follow the proper torque specifications.

• Always replace worn fuel fitting O-rings with new. Do not substitute fuel hose or equivalent where fuel pipe is installed.

Fuel Filter

Replacement

1. Disconnect the negative battery cable.
2. Disconnect the Water In Filter (WIF) sensor connector.
3. Remove the separator filter assembly from the filter head with a standard oil filter wrench.
4. Remove the square cut O-ring from the filter mounting bushing.
5. Drain the fuel/water separator filter and remove the assembly from the fuel filter.

To install:

6. Install a new O-ring to the WIF assembly and install to the new separator filter.
7. Install a new square cut O-ring to the mounting bushing.
8. Fill the fuel/water separator filter with clean diesel fuel.
9. Apply a light coat of oil to the sealing surface of the separator filter.
10. Install the assembly and tighten it ½ turn after the seal contacts the filter head.
11. Reconnect the WIF sensor connector.
12. Connect the negative battery cable, start the engine and check for leaks.

Draining Water From the System

Filtration and separation of water from the fuel is important for trouble free operation and long life of the fuel system. Regular maintenence, including draining moisture from the fuel/water separator filter is essential to keep water out of the fuel pump. To remove collected water place drain pan under drain tube on separator. Push up on the drain at the bottom filter separator.

Hold drain open until all water and contaminants have been removed and clean fuel exits the drain.

Diesel Injection Pump

Removal and Installation

NOTE: The Bosche VE lever is indexed to the shaft during pump calibration. Do not remove it from the pump during removal.

1. Disconnect the negative battery cable.
2. Remove the throttle linkage and bracket.
3. Disconnect the fuel drain manifold.
4. Remove the injection pump supply line.
5. Remove the high pressure lines.
6. Disconnect the electrical wire to the fuel shut off valve.
7. Remove the fuel air control tube.
8. Remove the pump support bracket.
9. Remove the oil fill tube bracket and adapter from the front gear cover.
10. Place a shop towel in the gear cover opening in a position that will prevent the nut and washer from falling into the gear housing. Remove the gear retaining nut and washer.
11. Install the turning tool into the flywheel housing opening on the exhaust side of the engine. Place a ½ in. drive universal joint in the turning tool and attach enough extensions to the joint to make it convenient to turn the tool.
12. Using a ratchet to turn the turning tool, turn the engine until the key way on the fuel pump shaft is pointing approximately in the 6 o'clock position.
13. Locate TDC for cylinder No. 1 by turning the engine slowly

1. Fuel from supply tank
2. Lift (fuel) pump
3. Low pressure supply line
4. Fuel/water separator filter
4a. Fuel heater
4b. Fuel/water drain valve
4c. Fuel/water separator filter
4d. WIF sensor
5. Thirmistor
6. Bleed screw
7. Robert Bosch low pressure supply line
8. Robert Bosch VE distributor type injection pump
9. Turbo boost control line
10. Control module
11. Fuel drain manifold (returns fuel to the tank)
12. High pressure lines
13. Robert Bosch 17mm, closed nozzle, hole type injector
14. KSB valve
15. Manual shut down switch
16. TDC timing pin

Fuel system components—5.9L diesel engine

Installing the turning tool—diesel fuel injection system

Locating TDC with the TDC pin—diesel fuel injection system

while pushing in on the TDC pin. Stop turning the engine as soon as the pin engages with the gear timing hole. Disengage the pin after locating TDC and remove the turning equipment.

14. Loosen the lockscrew, remove the special washer from the injection pump and wire it to the line above it so it will not get misplaced. Retighten the lockscrew to 22 ft. lbs. (30 Nm) to lock the driveshaft.

15. Using a puller, extract the pump drive gear from the driveshaft.

NOTE: Be careful not to drop the drive gear key into the front cover when removing or installing the pump. If it does drop in, it must be removed before proceeding.

16. Remove the 3 mounting nuts and remove the injection pump from the vehicle.

17. Remove the gasket and clean the mounting surface.

To install:

18. Install a new gasket.

NOTE: The shaft of a new or reconditioned pump is locked so the key aligns with the drive gear keyway with cylinder No. 1 at TDC.

19. Install the pump and finger-tighten the mounting nuts; the pump must be free to move in the slots.

Removing the special washer from the injection pump

20. Install the pump drive gear, washer and nut to the driveshaft. The pump will rotate slightly because of gear helix and clearance. This is acceptable providing the pump is free to move on the flange slots and the crankshaft does not move. Torque the nut to 11–15 ft. lbs. (15–20 Nm). This is not the final torque; do not overtighten.

21. If installing the original pump, rotate the pump to align the original timing marks and torque the mounting nuts to 18 ft. lbs. (24 Nm).

22. If installing a replacement pump, take up gear lash by rotating the pump counterclockwise toward the cylinder head and torque the mounting nuts to 18 ft. lbs. (24 Nm). Permanently mark the new injection pump flange to match the mark on the gear housing.

23. Loosen the lockscrew and install the special washer under the lockscrew. Torque to 19 ft. lbs. (13 Nm). Disengage the TDC pin.

24. Install the injection pump support bracket. finger-tighten the bolts initially, then torque them to 18 ft. lbs. (24 Nm) in the following sequence
   a. Bracket to block bolts.
   b. Bracket to injection pump bolts.
   c. Throttle support bracket bolts

25. Now perform the final torque of the pump drive gear retaining nut to 48 ft. lbs. (65 Nm).

26. Install the oil filler tube assembly and clamp. Torque the bolts to 32 ft. lbs. (43 Nm).

27. Install all fuel lines and the electrical connector to the fuel shut off valve. Tighten the high pressure lines to 18 ft. lbs. (24 Nm).

28. Install the fuel air control tube. Torque the banjo fitting bolt to 9 ft. lbs. (12 Nm).

29. Install the throttle bracket and linkage. When connecting the cable to the control lever, adjust the legnth so the lever has stop-to-stop movement.

30. Connect the negative battery cable.

CAUTION

Do not place any part of the hand near the base of the high pressure line. A fuel leak from a high pressure fuel line has sufficient pressure to penetrate the skin and cause serious bodily harm. Do not bleed the lines if the engine is hot. Fuel spilling onto a hot exhaust manifold creates the danger of fire.

31. To bleed air from the system, run or crank the engine and carefully loosen the high pressure fitting from each injector 1 at a time. Retighten the fitting after the air has expelled before going on to the next injector fitting. The operation is complete

when the engine runs smoothly. If the air cannot be removed, check the pump and supply line for suction leaks.

32. Adjust the idle speed, if necessary.

Idle Speed Adjustment

1. Start the engine and run until normal operating temperature is reached.

2. An optical tachometer must be used to read engine speed; a conventional tachometer connected to the coil is useless in this instance.

3. Turn the air conditioning **ON**, if equipped.

4. Turn the idle speed screw until the desired idle speed is obtained. The specification if equipped with automatic transmission is 700 rpm or if equipped with manual transmission is 750 rpm.

Injection Pump Timing

Adjustment

1. Install the turning tool into the flywheel housing opening on the exhaust side of the engine. Place a ½ in. drive universal joint in the turning tool and attach enough extensions to the joint to make it convenient to turn the tool.

2. Using a ratchet to turn the tool, turn the engine until the key way on the fuel pump shaft is pointing approximately in the 6 o'clock position.

3. Locate TDC for cylinder No. 1 by turning the engine slowly while pusing in on the TDC pin. Stop turning the engine as soon

Removing the plug from the pump—diesel fuel injection system

Installing the timing indicator-diesel fuel injection system

as the pin engages with the gear timing hole. Disengage the pin after locating TDC.

4. Remove the plug from the end of the pump.

5. Install the special timing indicator, allowing for adequate indicator pin travel. It may be necessary to disconnect 1 or more fuel lines to properly install the indicator.

NOTE: The indicator is marked in increments of 0.01mm. One revolution of the indicator needle is equal to 0.050mm.

6. Turn the engine counterclockwise until the indicator needle stops moving. Adjust the indicator face to read zero.

7. Rotate the engine back to TDC and count the number of revolutions of the indicator needle. The reading shown when the engine timing pin engages is the amount of plunger lift the pump has at that point.

8. Readjust the indicator face to read zero. Loosen the pump mounting nuts and rotate the pump clockwise toward the cylinder head until the indicator reads the correct value for plunger lift (the reading in Step 7). Torque the mounting nuts to 18 ft. lbs. (24 Nm).

9. Remove the engine turning equipment and timing indicator. Install the timing plug and torque to 7.5 ft. lbs. (10 Nm). Connect any fuel lines that were disconnected.

10. Road test the vehicle.

Fuel Injector

Removal and Installation

1. Disconnect the negative battery cable. Remove the throttle linkage and bracket, if necessary.

2. Disconnect the high pressure fuel supply line to the injector.

3. Disconnect the fuel drain manifold.

4. Clean the area around the injector.

5. Using a 24mm deepwell socket, remove the injector from the cylinder head.

To install:

6. Clean the injector bore with a bore brush.

7. Assemble the injector and 1 new copper sealing washer. Never use more than 1 copper washer.

8. Apply a thin coat of anti-sieze compound to the threads of the injector hold-down nut and between the top of the nut and the injector body.

9. Align the protrusion in the injector with the notch in the bore and install the injector. Torque the injector retainer nut to 44 ft. lbs. (60 Nm).

10. Push the O-ring into the groove at the top of the injector.

11. Using new sealing washers, assemble the fuel drain mani-

Installing the fuel injector—diesel fuel injection system

fold and high pressure lines. Torque the banjo fitting bolt to 6 ft. lbs. (8 Nm). Leave the high pressure line loose temporarily.

CAUTION

Do not place any part of the hand near the base of the high pressure line. A fuel leak from a high pressure fuel line has sufficient pressure to penetrate the skin and cause serious bodily harm. Do not bleed the lines if the engine is hot. Fuel spilling onto a hot exhaust manifold creates the danger of fire.

12. Reconnect negative battery cable. Install the throttle linkage and bracket, if removed.
13. To bleed air from the system, run or crank the engine and tighten the fitting after the air has expelled. If more than 1 injector was replaced, tighten each fitting after the air has expelled before going on to the next injector fitting. Torque the fittings to 18 ft. lbs. (24 Nm). The operation is complete when the engine runs smoothly. If the air cannot be removed, check the pump and supply line for suction leaks.

EMISSION CONTROLS

Emissions Warning Lamp

For further information, please refer to Chilton's Emission Controls Manual.

Resetting
1988 VEHICLES

1. Locate the EMR switch module. It is a red, green or tan plastic box located either on the lower portion of the steering column or to the left of the steering column on Vans and behind the right side of the glove box on Pick-Up and Ramcharger.

2. Reset the switch by inserting a small rod into a hole in the case of the module, which closes a switch and turns the light off.

1989–92 VEHICLES

1. Connect the DRBII to the diagnostic connector.
2. Turn the ignition switch to the **RUN** position and access the Emissions EMR Tests on the DRBII.
3. Select EMR Memory Check.
4. Select Reset EMR Light. This will reset the EMR timing in the computer and turn the light OFF.
5. Disconnect the DRBII.

GASOLINE ENGINE MECHANICAL

NOTE: Disconnecting the negative battery cable on some vehicles may interfere with the functions of the on board computer systems and may require the computer to undergo a relearning process, once the negative battery cable is reconnected.

Engine Assembly

Removal and Installation

1. Relieve the fuel pressure, if equipped with fuel injection. Disconnect the battery cables and remove battery from the vehicle.
2. Scribe hinge position on hood and remove the hood. Remove the oil dipstick and tube. Discharge the air conditioning.
3. Raise the vehicle and support safely. Drain the engine oil and coolant. Remove the lower radiator hose.
4. Remove the starter. Remove the engine to transmission struts, if equipped.
5. Remove the exhaust pipe from the exhaust manifold(s).
6. If equipped with manual transmission, remove the transmission.
7. If equipped with an automatic transmission, remove the inspection plate. Matchmark the flexplate to the converter, remove the torque converter bolts and push the torque converter backwards as far as it will go. Remove the lower bell housing bolts.
8. Remove the engine mount lower nuts.
9. Disconnect and plug the rubber fuel inlet and return hoses from the fuel lines at the right front of the vehicle. Lower the vehicle.
10. Remove the air cleaner assembly, disconnect all linkages and cables and remove the carburetor or throttle body. Stuff a clean shop towel into the intake manifold opening to prevent foreign objects from entering. Remove the left exhaust manifold and heat shield on Van.

11. Remove the discharge and suction lines from the air conditioning compressor. Cap the openings on the compressor to prevent foreign objects and moisture from entering the system.
12. On Van, remove the front bumper, grille and support brace. Remove the radiator, shroud, condenser and support as an assembly. On Pick-Up and Ramcharger, remove the radiator and shroud. Remove the fan and all related parts.
13. Unbolt the power steering pump brackets from the engine and position it aside.
14. Remove the alternator, air pump and all brackets. Disconnect the heater hoses.
15. Remove the distributor cap with all spark plug wires attached.
16. Disconnect all remaining electrical connectors, vacuum hoses and check for any other items preventing engine removal.
17. Attach an engine removal device to the intake manifold or cylinder head.
18. If equipped with an automatic transmission, support the transmission with a floor jack or equivalent. Remove the remaining bell housing bolts.
19. Remove the engine from the vehicle. Van may need to be raised slightly, depending on the size of the removal device.
To install:
20. Lower the engine into position and install the upper bell housing bolts. Remove the engine removal device. Install the left side exhaust manifold, if it was removed. Install the oil dipstick.
21. Raise the vehicle and support safely.
22. Install the engine mount nuts and the remaining bell housing bolts.
23. If equipped with a manual transmission, install the transmission and all related parts.
24. If equipped with an automatic transmission, align the torque converter and flexplate and install the bolts. Install the inspection plate, starter and the engine to transmission struts, if equipped.

25. Connect the rubber fuel inlet and return hoses to the fuel lines at the right front of the vehicle.

26. Install the exhaust pipe to the exhaust manifold(s). Install the air pump tube to the exhaust pipe, if equipped. Lower the vehicle.

27. Connect the heater hoses.

28. Install the alternator, air pump, power steering pump and all brackets.

29. Install the air conditioning compressor and connect the lines with new gaskets, if disconnected.

30. Install the throttle body or carburetor using a new base gasket and connect all linkages and cables. Connect all electrical connectors and vacuum hoses that were disconnected during the engine removal procedure.

31. Install the lower radiator hose. Install the fan and all related parts. Adjust all belt tensions.

32. On Van, install the radiator, shroud, condenser and support as an assembly. Install the support brace, grille and bumper. On Pick-Up and Ramcharger, install the radiator and shroud.

33. Install the distributor cap with all spark plug wires attached.

34. Install the air cleaner assembly.

35. Install the hood.

36. Fill the engine with the specified amount of oil and fill the radiator with coolant.

37. Connect the negative battery cable and set all adjustments to specification.

38. Evacuate and recharge the air conditioning system.

Engine Mounts

Removal and Installation

3.9L ENGINE

Rear Mount

1. Disconnect negative battery cable.

2. Raise and safely support vehicle. Remove skid plate, if equipped.

3. Install transmission jack into position and raise transmission slightly.

4. Remove rear mount through-bolt and nut.

5. Remove the flange nuts from the crossmember support bracket.

6. Raise rear of transmission and remove insulator flange nuts and remove mount. If necessary, remove attaching bolts holding transmission support bracket to transmission.

To install:

7. Install attaching bolts holding transmission support bracket to transmission.

8. Position insulator in transmission support bracket and install through-bolt.

9. With insulator installed in a level position tighten through bolt nut to 50 ft. lbs.

10. Position crossmember support bracket into insulator. Install flange nuts and tighten to 30 ft. lbs.

11. Using transmission jack, lower the insulator and crossmember support bracket onto the crossmember. Tighten flange nuts to 30 ft. lbs.

12. Remove transmission jack, install skid plate, if removed, lower vehicle and reconnect negative battery cable.

Front Mount

1. Disconnect negative battery cable. Remove skid plate, if equipped.

2. Position fan assembly to insure clearance for radiator and top hose when engine is moved. Install an engine support fixture.

3. Raise and safely support vehicle.

4. Remove nuts from front engine mounting brackets.

5. Raise engine with support fixture far enough to remove mounts, remove remaining bolts and mounts.

To install:

6. Install mounts to engine block.

7. Lower engine to original position and insert bolts through mounting brackets.

8. Install nuts and tighten to 75 ft. lbs. Install skid plate, if removed.

9. Lower vehicle and remove engine support fixture. Reconnect negative battery cable.

EXCEPT 3.9L ENGINE

Rear Mount

1. Disconnect negative battery cable.

2. Raise and safely support vehicle.

3. Install transmission jack into position and raise transmission slightly.

4. Remove rear mount through-bolt and nut.

5. Remove U-bracket from frame crossmember and remove insulator from U-bracket.

6. Remove rear engine mount from the bottom face of transmission extension housing.

To install:

7. Install rear mount to bottom of transmission. Torque bolts to 50 ft. lbs.

8. Install insulator to U-bracket. Tighten nuts to 30 ft. lbs.

9. Install through-bolt through the U-bracket/insulator assembly and the rear engine support. Tighten to 50 ft. lbs.

10. Attach U-bracket to crossmember tightening bolts to 30 ft. lbs. Remove transmission jack and lower vehicle. Connect negative battery cable.

Cylinder Head

Removal and Installation

1. Relieve the fuel pressure if equipped with fuel injection. Disconnect the negative battery cable from the battery and drain the cooling system.

2. Raise the vehicle and safely support. Disconnect the exhaust pipe from the manifolds.

3. Remove the alternator, if the right head is being removed, and the air pump and battery ground cable, if the left head is being removed.

4. Remove the air cleaner assembly. Unbolt the air conditioning compressor, if equipped, and lay it aside. Remove the distributor cap with all wires attached.

Cylinder head bolt torque sequence—3.9L engine

FRONT ⟶

⑦ ③ ① ⑤ ⑨

⑧ ④ ② ⑥ ⑩

Cylinder head bolt torque sequence—5.2L and 5.9L engines

5. Disconnect all wires, hoses, linkages and cables from the carburetor or throttle body. Disconnect the fuel line.

6. Disconnect the ignition coil, coolant temperature sending unit wire and all other connectors along the wiring harness connected to items on the intake manifold.

7. Disconnect the heater hose, upper radiator hose and the lower bypass hose clamp.

8. Remove the valve cover(s).

9. Remove the intake manifold assembly. Remove the exhaust manifold(s).

10. Remove the rocker arm and shaft assembly from the head(s). Do not disassemble unless service is required.

11. Remove the pushrods and identify them to ensure installation in their original locations.

12. Remove the head bolts and remove the cylinder head(s).

To install:

13. Clean and dry all gasket surfaces of the cylinder block and head. Inspect all surfaces with a straight-edge. If the flatness exceeds 0.0075 times the length of the span measured (in any direction), replace or machine the head gasket surface.

14. Using no sealer, install the new head gasket(s) to the block. Clean, dry and lightly oil all head bolts threads. Install the head(s) and install the head bolts.

15. Torque the head bolts in sequence to 50 ft. lbs. (68 Nm). Repeat the sequence retightening the bolts to a final torque of 105 ft. lbs. (143 Nm) and repeat the second step to ensure all bolts are accurately torqued.

16. Assemble the rocker shaft assembly, if it was serviced. Make sure all rocker arms with a **RH** stamp are installed to the right of those with an **LH**. Install the pushrods, rocker arms and shaft(s) with the notch on the end of the shaft pointing to the engine centerline and to the rear of the right bank or to the front of the left bank. Make sure the long stamped steel retainers are at the No. 2 and 4 positions. Torque the bolts evenly and gradually to 200 inch lbs. (23 Nm).

17. Clean and dry the intake manifold contact surfaces. Coat the intake manifold side gaskets lightly with sealer and install the gaskets to the heads. Cutouts at the front of the gaskets differentiate the right and left sides.

18. Apply a thin uniform coat of quick dry cement to the front and rear intake manifold gaskets and mounting surfaces on the block and apply a thin bead of sealer to each of 4 the corners. Install the front and rear gaskets engaging the hole in the block and the tangs from the head gaskets. Apply a second thin bead of sealer above the gaskets in the 4 corners.

19. Carefully lower the intake manifold into position engaging the bypass hose. Inspect the gaskets to make sure they have not become dislodged.

20. Install the intake manifold bolts and torque in sequence to 25 ft. lbs. (34 Nm). Repeat the sequence retightening the bolts to a final torque of 40 ft. lbs. (54 Nm). Repeat the second step to ensure all bolts are accurately torqued.

21. Install the exhaust manifold(s) and torque the bolts to 20 ft. lbs. (27 Nm). Torque the end nuts to 15 ft. lbs. (20 Nm).

22. Clean and dry the valve cover mating surfaces, bolts and bolt holes. Install the valve cover(s) each with a new gasket.

23. Connect the heater hose, upper radiator hose and the lower bypass hose clamp.

24. Connect the ignition coil, coolant temperature sending unit wire and all other connectors that were disconnected along the wiring harness.

25. Install the air conditioning compressor, if equipped. Install the distributor cap and all spark plug wires.

26. Install the alternator, battery ground and air pump, if removed.

27. Connect all wires, hoses, cables and the fuel line to the carburetor or throttle body. Install the air cleaner assembly.

28. Raise the vehicle and safely support. Connect the exhaust pipe to the manifolds.

29. Fill the cooling system.

30. Connect the negative battery cable and set all adjustments to specification.

Valve Lifters

Removal and Installation

1. Disconnect negative battery cable. Remove air cleaner.

2. Relieve the fuel pressure if equipped with fuel injection.

3. Remove the valve cover(s) and rocker arm assembly.

4. Remove the pushrods and identify them to ensure installation in their original locations.

5. Remove the intake manifold assembly, yoke retainer and aligning yokes.

6. Use an appropriate valve lifter removal tool to remove each lifter from its bore. If reinstalling the tappets, identify each upon removal to ensure installation in the original position.

7. If the tappet or bore in cylinder block is scored, scuffed or shows signs of sticking, ream the bore to the next oversize and replace with oversize tappet.

To install:

8. Lubricate the lifter(s) and bore(s) and install. Ensure that the oil feed hole in the side of the tappet body faces up.

9. Install aligning yokes with arrow toward camshaft. Install yoke retainer. Tighten bolts to 200 inch lbs. (23 Nm).

10. Install pushrods to their original positions. Install rocker arm and shaft assembly.

11. Install valve cover(s). Connect negative battery terminal and start vehicle. Check for oil leaks.

Service Tips

IMPROVED ROLLER TAPPET TO SILENCE LIFTER NOISE

Some vehicles equipped with the 3.9L, 5.2L and 5.9L engines, equipped with roller tappets, may experience excessive tappet noise. In order to solve this condition, a new design roller tappet is available. The new design tappet has an oil feed hole that was rotated 90 degrees to its original location. The location of the oil feed hole is identified by a paint mark on the tappet and when installed is to face up. In rotating the feed hole, more oil will be retained in the tappet resulting in reduced engine noise during start-up. In 1990 the new design roller tappet was entered into production.

Rocker Arms and Shaft

Removal and Installation

1. Disconnect the negative battery cable.
2. Remove the valve cover and gasket.
3. Note the positioning of the notch and remove the rocker arms and shaft assembly from the head.
4. Disassemble the assembly as required and replace all worn parts.

NOTE: If equipped with exhaust valve rotators, the exhaust rocker arm must have relief for clearance.

To install:

5. Make sure all rocker arms with an **RH** stamp are installed to the right of those with an **LH**. Install the assembly with the notch on the end of the shaft pointing to the engine centerline and to the rear of the right bank or to the front of the left bank. Make sure the long stamped steel retainers are at the No. 2 and 4 positions. Torque the bolts evenly starting from the center bolts and working outward to 200 inch lbs. (23 Nm). Allow 20 minutes bleed down time before starting the engine.
6. Clean and dry the valve cover mating surfaces, bolts and bolt holes. Install the valve cover with a new gasket. Torque the screws or nuts to 95 inch lbs. (11 Nm).
7. Connect the negative battery cable and check for leaks.

Intake Manifold

Removal and Installation

1. Relieve the fuel pressure if equipped with fuel injection. Disconnect the negative battery cable from the battery and drain the cooling system.
2. Remove the air pump and bracket. Removal of the bracket will allow for easier installation of the left front corner of the intake manifold.
3. Remove the air cleaner assembly. Remove the air conditioning compressor or unbolt it and lay it aside, if equipped. Remove the distributor cap with all wires attached.
4. Disconnect all wires, hoses, linkages and cables from the carburetor or throttle body. Disconnect the fuel line.
5. Disconnect the ignition coil, coolant temperature sending unit wire and all other connectors along the wiring harness connected to items on the intake manifold.
6. Disconnect the heater hose, upper radiator hose and the lower bypass hose clamp.
7. Remove the valve covers.
8. Unbolt the intake manifold from the heads and remove the intake manifold assembly. Disassemble the manifold as required and clean out the exhaust crossover passages.

To install:

9. Clean and dry the intake manifold contact surfaces. Coat the intake manifold side gaskets lightly with sealer and install the gaskets to the heads. Cutouts at the front of the gaskets differentiate the right and left sides.
10. Apply a thin uniform coat of quick dry cement to the front and rear intake manifold gaskets and mounting surfaces on the block and apply a thin bead of sealer to each of 4 the corners. Install the front and rear gaskets engaging the hole in the block and the tangs from the head gaskets. Apply a second thin bead of sealer above the gaskets in the 4 corners.
11. Carefully lower the intake manifold into position engaging the bypass hose. Inspect the gaskets to make sure they have not dislodged.
12. Install the intake manifold bolts with the aspirator tube, air pump bracket and kickdown linkage bracket in place. Torque the bolts in sequence to 25 ft. lbs. (34 Nm). Repeat the sequence retightening the bolts to a final torque of 40 ft. lbs. (54 Nm). Repeat this step to ensure bolts are accurately torqued.
13. Clean and dry the valve cover mating surfaces, bolts and

Identifying and assembling the rocker assembly— 5.2L and 5.9L engines—3.9L engine parts are similar

Intake manifold bolt torque sequence—3.9L engine

bolt holes. Install the valve covers with a new gasket. Torque the screws or nuts to 95 inch lbs. (11 Nm).
14. Connect the heater hose, upper radiator hose and the lower bypass hose clamp.
15. Connect the ignition coil, coolant temperature sending unit wire and all other connectors that were disconnected along the wiring harness.

Intake manifold bolt torque sequence—5.2L and 5.9L engine

Exhaust manifold installation—3.9L engine (right side shown)

16. Install the air conditioning compressor, if equipped. Install the distributor cap and all spark plug wires.
17. Install air pump.
18. Connect all wires, hoses, cables and the fuel line to the carburetor or throttle body. Install the air cleaner assembly.
19. Fill the cooling system.
20. Connect the negative battery cable and check for leaks.

Exhaust Manifold

Removal and Installation

1. Disconnect the negative battery cable. Remove the hot air tube and heat shield.
2. Raise the vehicle and support safely. Remove the exhaust pipe from the exhaust manifold. Lower the vehicle.
3. Take note of all conical washer locations and remove the bolts, nuts and washers attaching the manifold to the head.
4. Remove the manifold.

To install:

5. If either of the end studs came out with the nuts, install a new stud using sealer on the coarse threads.
6. Position the manifold on the end studs. Install conical washers and nuts on the studs.
7. Install the remaining bolts and washers in their proper locations. The inner bolts are not mounted with washers. Working outward from the center, torque the bolts to 20 ft. lbs. (27 Nm) and the nuts to 15 ft. lbs. (20 Nm).
8. Install the exhaust pipe to the manifold.
9. Connect the negative battery cable and check for exhaust leaks.

Timing Chain Front Cover

Removal and Installation

1. Disconnect the negative battery cable.
2. Drain the cooling system.
3. Remove the radiator, fan and all related parts. Remove the water pump from the engine.
4. Remove the crankshaft pulley.
5. Remove the vibration damper using the proper puller.
6. Disconnect the fuel lines from the fuel pump, if equipped with a mechanical pump.
7. Remove the 2 front bolts from the oil pan.
8. Unbolt the chain cover from the block and remove using

Exhaust manifold installation—5.2L and 5.9L engines

caution to avoid damaging the oil pan gasket. Remove the fuel pump from the cover, if equipped.

To install:

9. Clean and dry the mating surfaces of the cover and block. Apply a thin bead of sealer to the oil pan gasket.
10. Install a new cover gasket and install the cover. Torque bolts to 30 ft. lbs. (41 Nm).
11. Install the water pump with a new gasket.
12. Install the damper with tool C–3638 or equivalent. Install the bolt and washer and torque to specification. Apply a small amount of sealer to the bolts and install the crankshaft pulley.
13. Install the mechanical fuel pump using a new gasket, if equipped, and connect the fuel lines. Install the 2 oil pan bolts.
14. Install the radiator, fan and all related parts.
15. Fill the cooling system.
16. Connect the negative battery cable and check for leaks.

Front Cover Oil Seal

Replacement

1. Disconnect the negative battery cable.
2. Remove the belts from the crankshaft pulley.
3. Remove the fan and shroud from the vehicle.
4. Remove the crankshaft pulley.
5. Remove the vibration damper using the proper puller.
6. Using a seal remover pry outward behind the lip of the oil seal. Take care not to damage the crankshaft seal surface of the cover.

To install:

7. Install the new seal by installing the threaded shaft part of the special tool C–4251 into the threads of the crankshaft.

Installing the front cover oil seal—3.9L, 5.2L and 5.9L engines

Alignment of timing marks—3.9L, 5.2L and 5.9L gasoline engines

8. Place the seal into the opening with the spring toward the engine. Place the installing adapter C–4251–3 or equivalent, with the thrust bearing and nut on the shaft. Tighten the nut until the tool is flush with the timing chain cover. Remove the tool.

9. Install vibration damper using tool C–3638 or equivalent. Install the bolt and washer and torque to specification.

10. Apply a small amount of sealer to the bolts and install the crankshaft pulley.

11. Install the fan and shroud.

12. Connect the negative battery cable and check for leaks.

Timing Chain and Sprockets

Removal and Installation

1. If possible, crank the engine around so the No. 1 cylinder is at TDC on the compression stroke. Remove the distributor cap to confirm and line the timing mark on the damper pulley with **0** on the timing scale. This will aid in aligning timing marks when installing the timing gears. Disconnect the negative battery cable.

2. Drain the cooling system.

3. Remove the radiator, fan and all related parts. Remove the water pump from the engine.

4. Remove the crankshaft pulley.

5. Remove the vibration damper using the proper puller.

6. Disconnect the fuel lines from the fuel pump, if equipped.

7. Remove the 2 front bolts from the oil pan.

8. Unbolt the chain cover from the block and remove, using caution to avoid damaging the oil pan gasket. Remove the fuel pump from the cover, if equipped.

9. Remove the camshaft gear retaining bolt, cup washer and fuel pump eccentric, if equipped. Remove the timing chain and gears.

To install:

10. Place both camshaft and crankshaft gears on the bench with the timing marks on the exact imaginary center line through both gear bores as they are installed on the engine. Place the timing chain around both sprockets.

11. Turn the crankshaft and camshaft so the keys line up with the keyways in the gears when the timing marks are in proper position.

12. Slide both gears over their respective shafts and use a straight-edge to check timing mark alignment.

13. Install the fuel pump eccentric and cup washer, if equipped. Torque the camshaft gear retaining bolt to 35 ft. lbs. (47 Nm).

14. Clean and dry the mating surfaces of the timing chain cover and block. Apply a thin bead of sealer to the oil pan gasket.

15. Install a new cover gasket and install the cover. Torque the bolts to 30 ft. lbs. (41 Nm).

16. Install the water pump with a new gasket.

17. Install the vibration damper with tool C–3638 or equivalent. Install the bolt and washer and torque to specification. Apply a small amount of sealer to the bolts and install the crankshaft pulley.

18. Install the fuel pump using a new gasket, if equipped, and connect the fuel lines. Install the 2 oil pan bolts.

19. Install the radiator, fan and all related parts.

20. Fill the cooling system.

21. Connect the negative battery cable, set all adjustments to specifications and check for leaks.

Camshaft

Removal and Installation

1. If possible, crank the engine around so the No. 1 cylinder is at TDC on the compression stroke. Remove the distributor cap to confirm and line the timing mark on the damper pulley with **0** on the timing scale. This will aid in aligning timing marks when installing the timing gears. If equipped with fuel injection, relieve the fuel pressure. Disconnect the negative battery cable.

2. Drain the cooling system.

3. Remove the engine from the vehicle.

4. Remove the valve cover(s).

5. Remove the rocker shaft assembly(s). Identify and remove the pushrods.

6. Remove the intake manifold, identify and remove all lifters.

7. Remove the distributor. Lift out the oil pump and distributor driveshaft.

8. Remove the radiator, fan and all related parts.

9. Remove the fuel pump, if equipped. Remove the timing chain cover, timing chain and gears.

10. Note the location of the oil tab and remove the camshaft thrust plate.

11. Install a long bolt into the front of the camshaft to facilitate removal. Remove the camshaft, being careful not to damage any of the cam bearings with the cam lobes.

To install:

12. Install the camshaft to within 2 in. of its final installation position. Install the camshaft Gear Installer tool C–3509 with tongue in back of distributor drive gear. Bolt it in place with the distributor lock plate bolt. This will prevent the camshaft from being pushed in too far and knocking out the welch plug at the rear of the block. This tool should remain in place until the timing chain installation has been completed.

13. Install the camshaft thrust plate and chain oil tab with 3

bolts. Make sure the tang of the oil tab enters the lower right hole in the thrust plate. Torque the bolts to 210 inch lbs. (24 Nm). Make sure the top edge of the oil tab is flat against the thrust plate or it will not feed oil to the chain.

14. Place both camshaft and crankshaft gears on the bench with the timing marks on the exact imaginary center line through both gear bores as they are installed on the engine. Place the timing chain around both sprockets.

15. Turn the crankshaft and camshaft so the keys line up with the keyways in the gears when the timing marks are in proper position.

16. Slide both gears over their respective shafts and use a straight-edge to check timing mark alignment.

17. Install the fuel pump eccentric and cup washer, if equipped. Torque the camshaft gear retaining bolt to 35 ft. lbs. (47 Nm). Remove the camshaft blocking tool.

18. Measure camshaft endplay. Replace the thrust plate, if not within specifications.

19. Coat the oil pump and distributor driveshaft with oil. Install 3.9L engine shaft so when the gear spirals into place and drops into the oil pump, the slot in the top of the gear is pointing directly to the left front intake manifold bolt hole. Install 5.2L and 5.9L engine shaft in a similar manner, except position it so the slot is parallel with the center line of the camshaft.

20. If the camshaft was not replaced, lubricate and install the lifters in their original locations. If the camshaft was replaced, new lifters must be used.

21. Install the pushrods and rocker shaft assembly.

22. Install the intake manifold. Install the valve cover(s).

23. Install the distributor so the rotor points to the No. 1 spark plug wire position on the cap.

24. Install the timing chain cover and all related parts, fuel pump, if equipped, and radiator.

25. Install the engine into the vehicle.

26. When everything is bolted in place, change the engine oil and replace the oil filter.

NOTE: If the camshaft or lifters have been replaced, add 1 pint of Mopar crankcase conditioner or equivalent, when replenishing the oil to aid in break in. This mixture should be left in the engine for a minimum of 500 miles and drained at the next normal oil change.

27. Fill the radiator with coolant.

28. Connect the negative battery cable, set all adjustments to specifications and check for leaks.

Piston and Connecting Rod

Positioning

Installed distributor drive gear position—3.9L engine

Installed distributor drive gear position—5.2L and 5.9L gasoline engine

Piston ring and piston installation—5.2L and 5.9L gasoline engines—3.9L engine is similar

DIESEL ENGINE MECHANICAL

NOTE: Disconnecting the negative battery cable on some vehicles may interfere with the functions of the on board computer systems and may require the computer to undergo a relearning process, once the negative battery cable is reconnected.

Engine

Removal and Installation

CAUTION

This engine has a dry weight of 880 lbs. Make sure the engine removal equipment is rated adequately, or personal injury may result.

1. Scribe location of hood hinge bolts for proper alignment and remove the hood.
2. Disconnect the cables from the battery and from the engine. Remove the battery from the vehicle.
3. Drain the coolant.
4. Remove the radiator, shroud, belt, fan and all related parts.
5. Remove the air inlet tube from the turbocharger and the air intake housing. Remove the exhaust pipe from the turbocharger outlet flange. Remove the inlet duct from the turbocharger and inlet duct. Remove the outlet duct.
6. Remove the air conditioner compressor and set aside.
7. Disconnect and remove the alternator and all other electrical connections to the engine.
8. Disconnect the acclerator linkage, the speed control linkage and the throttle valve linkage.
9. Raise the vehicle and support safely. Remove the starter.
10. If equipped with automatic transmission, remove the torque converter bolts and remove the lower bell housing bolts. If equipped with manual transmission, remove the transmission.
11. Drain the oil from the engine.
12. Disconnect the transmission oil cooler lines from their brackets, if equipped.
13. Lower vehicle, disconnect and plug the fuel lines. Disconnect the power steering lines and vacuum pump lines.
14. Hoist the engine slightly using the lifting eyes and support the transmission if still installed.
15. Remove the motor mounts.
16. Remove the upper bell housing bolts.
17. Remove the engine from the vehicle.

To install:

18. Position the engine in the engine compartment and install the motor mounts. Torque the nuts and bolts to 57 ft. lbs. (77 Nm).
19. Install the bell housing bolts and torque converter bolts, if equipped. Install the manual transmission, if equipped.
20. Install the starter.
21. Connect the exhaust pipe.
22. Connect the transmission oil cooler lines to their brackets, if equipped.
23. Connect the fuel lines.
24. Connect the power steering lines.
25. Connect all engine driven accessories.
26. Connect the accelerator linkage.
27. Connect the throttle linkage to the control lever.
28. Mount the air conditioner compressor.
29. Connect the alternator and all other electrical connections to the engine.
30. Install the intake and exhaust pipes and air ducts to the turbocharger and intercooler.
31. Install the fan and all related parts, shroud and radiator.
32. Fill the enine with the proper amount of diesel engine oil.
33. Fill the radiator with coolant.
34. Install and connect the battery cables. Set all adjustments to specifications and check for leaks.

Engine Mounts

Removal and Installation
ENGINE REAR MOUNT

1. Disconnect negative battery cable.
2. Raise and safely support vehicle. Remove skid plate , if equipped.
3. Install transmission jack into position and raise transmission slightly.
4. Remove rear mount through-bolt and nut.
5. Remove the flange nuts from the crossmember support bracket.
6. Raise rear of transmission and remove insulator flange nuts and remove mount. If necessary, remove attaching bolts holding transmission support bracket to transmission.

To install:

7. Install attaching bolts holding transmission support bracket to transmission.
8. Position insulator in transmission support bracket and install through-bolt.
9. With insulator installed in a level position tighten through bolt nut to 50 ft. lbs.
10. Position crossmember support bracket into insulator. Install flange nuts and tighten to 30 ft. lbs.
11. Using transmission jack, lower the insulator and crossmember support bracket onto the crossmember. Tighten flange nuts to 30 ft. lbs.
12. Remove transmission jack, install skid plate if removed, lower vehicle and reconnect negative battery cable.

ENGINE FRONT MOUNT

1. Disconnect negative battery cable. Remove skid plate, if equipped.
2. Position fan assembly to insure clearance for radiator and top hose when engine is moved. Install an engine support fixture.
3. Raise and safely support vehicle.
4. Remove nuts from front engine mounting brackets.
5. Raise engine with support fixture far enough to remove mounts, remove remaining bolts and mounts.

To install:

6. Install mounts to engine block.
7. Lower engine to original position and insert bolts through mounting brackets.
8. Install nuts and tighten to 75 ft. lbs. Install skid plate, if removed.
9. Lower vehicle and remove engine support fixture. Reconnect negative battery cable.

Cylinder Head

NOTE: The cylinder head design was changed in mid–1991, and the new design is not interchanged with earlier models.

Removal and Installation

1. Disconnect the negative battery cable.
2. Drain the coolant.
3. Disconnect the radiator hose and heater hoses.
4. Remove the turbocharger and air crossover.
5. Remove the exhaust manifold.
6. Remove all fuel lines from the injection pump and remove injector nozzles. Remove the fuel filter.
7. Remove the valve covers.
8. Remove the rocker arms and pushrods.
9. Unbolt the cylinder head from the block. Remove the cylinder head.

Cylinder head bolt tightening sequence—5.9L diesel engine

10. Inspect the coolant passages. A large accumulation of rust or lime will require service to the block.

11. Inspect the surface of the head for flatness. The maximum variation is 0.0004 in. (0.010mm) within any 2 in. diameter area or 0.012 in. (0.30mm) overall end-to-end or side-to-side.

To install:

12. Thoroughly clean and dry the mating surfaces of the head and block. Position the new head gasket on the dowels.

13. Install the head onto the dowels on the block.

14. Lubricate the pushrod sockets and install the pushrods and rocker arms.

15. Clean, dry and lightly lubricate the head bolts. Install and torque in sequence first to 66 ft. lbs. (90 Nm) and then to 89 ft. lbs. (120 Nm). Tighten an additional 90 degrees. Tighten the 8 mm bolts to 18 ft. lbs. (24 Nm).

16. Install the rocker arm pedastal bolts. Torque to 18 ft. lbs. (24 Nm).

17. Adjust the valve clearance.

18. Install the valve covers with new gaskets. Torque the bolts to 18 ft. lbs. (24 Nm).

19. Install all fuel lines and the fuel filter.

20. Install the exhaust manifold.

21. Install the turbocharger and air crossover.

22. Connect the radiator hose and heater hoses.

23. Fill the radiator with coolant.

24. Connect the negative battery cable, set all adjustments to specifications and check for leaks.

Valve Lifters

Removal and Installation

1. Disconnect negative battery cable.

2. Remove the valve covers.

3. Drain the cooling system. Remove the rocker lever assemblies and push rods.

4. Remove the drive belts and fan hub assembly.

5. Remove the vibration damper.

6. Remove the gear housing cover. Remove the lift pump.

7. Insert the dowel tool through the push tube holes and into the top of each tappet. Pull the tappets up and wrap a rubber band around the top of the dowel rods. This will prevent the tappets from dropping into the engine.

8. Align the engine timing marks and remove the bolts in the thrust plate. Remove the camshaft, gear and thrust plate.

9. Insert a trough the full length of the cam bore. Make sure the trough is in the position to catch any falling tappets. Cum-

mins tappet changing tool 3822513 or equivalent, should be used for this procedure.

10. Remove the wooden dowel and catch the tappet in trough. Move the trough so the tappet falls over in the bottom of the trough. Mark each tappet for proper assembly, each tappet must be installed into their original location.

11. Carefully pull the trough and tappet from the cam bore. Repeat as needed to remove each tappet. Inspect the tappet socket, stem and face for excess wear, cracks and other damage. Minimum tappet stem diameter is 0.627 inch (15.925mm). If out of limits, replace tappet.

To install:

12. Install the trough into the cam bore. Feed the installation tool down the tappet bore and into the trough.

13. Feed the installation tool cord through the cam bores. Carefully pull the trough and installation tool out the front.

14. Lubricate the tappets with lubriplate 105 or equivalent.

15. Insert the installation tool into the tappet. Place the tappet and tool in the trough and slide the trough back into the cam bore.

16. Align the tappet below the proper bore and lift the tappet into the bore. After the tappet is in position, rotate the trough 180 degrees to hold tappet in position while the installation tool is removed. Install the dowel and rubber band to hold tappet in the bore and repeat process as required.

17. Lubricate camshaft lobes, journals and thrust washer and install camshaft into bore. Install lift pump, gear housing cover and vibration damper.

18. Install fan hub assembly and drive belts.

19. Install pushrods, rocker lever assemblies and valve covers.

20. Reconnect negative battery cable, refill coolant and oil as required. Start and check for leaks.

Valve Lash

Adjustment

1. Perform the adjustment when the engine is below 140°F (60°C).

2. Disconnect the negative battery cable.

3. Use the timing pin to locate TDC for cylinder No. 1. Disengage the pin.

4. Remove the valve covers.

5. With the engine is in this position, the first group of valves may be adjusted:

   No. 1 intake: 0.10 in. (0.254mm)
   No. 1 exhaust: 0.20 in. (0.508mm)
   No. 2 intake: 0.10 in. (0.254mm)
   No. 3 exhaust: 0.20 in. (0.508mm)
   No. 4 intake: 0.10 in. (0.254mm)
   No. 5 exhaust: 0.20 in. (0.508mm)

6. Mark the pulley and rotate the engine 360 degrees.

First group of valves to be adjusted—5.9L diesel engine

Second group of valves to be adjusted—5.9L diesel engine

7. With the engine is in this position, the second group of valves may be adjusted:

No. 2 exhaust: 0.20 in. (0.508mm)
No. 3 intake: 0.10 in. (0.254mm)
No. 4 exhaust: 0.20 in. (0.508mm)
No. 5 intake: 0.10 in. (0.254mm)
No. 6 intake: 0.10 in. (0.254mm)
No. 6 exhaust: 0.20 in. (0.508mm)

8. Torque all locknuts to 18 ft. lbs. (24 Nm).
9. Install the valve covers with new gaskets. Torque the bolts to 18 ft. lbs. (24 Nm).
10. Connect the negative battery cable.

Service Tips

ENGINE NOISE DUE TO BROKEN CONVERTER DRIVEPLATE

Some 1989 Pick-Ups equipped with automatic transmission and the Cummins diesel engine may experience excess engine noise. The noise will be located at the rear of the engine and sound like an engine knock or grinding type noise. The vehicle may also experience a no drive condition. A possible cause would be a cracked torque converter driveplate. The plate has been noted to crack around the plate-to-crankshaft bolts. The repair requires replacement of the torque converter driveplate, crankshaft bolt backing plate and the transmission torque converter. The driveplate bolts are to be torqued in a star pattern to 101 ft. lbs. (137 Nm).

Rocker Arm and Pedestal Assembly

Removal and Installation

1. Disconnect the negative battery cable. Remove the crossover tube.
2. Remove the valve covers.

3. Loosen the adjusting screw locknuts. Loosen the screws until they stop.
4. Remove the 8mm bolt and 12mm head bolt from the pedestal.
5. Remove the pedestal and rocker arm assembly. Remove the pushrods if necessary.
6. Remove the retaining ring and thrust washer.
7. Remove the rocker arm from the pedestal.

NOTE: Do not disassemble the rocker shaft and pedestal; they must be replaced as an assembly.

8. Remove the locknut and adjusting screw from the rocker arm.

To install:

9. Install the adjusting screw and locknut.
10. Lubricate the shaft with oil and install the rocker arm to the shaft. Install the thrust washer and snapring.
11. Install the pushrods to the engine, if removed.
12. Install the pedestal and rocker arm assembly to the head aligning the dowel in the pedestal with the dowel bore in the head. If the pushrod is holding the pedestal off the head, turn the engine until the pedestal will set on the head without interference.
13. Lubricate the threads of the bolt with oil. Install and torque first to 29 ft. lbs. (40 Nm), then to 62 ft. Lbs. (85 Nm) and finally to 93 ft. lbs. (126 Nm). If all of the pedestals were removed, follow the entire head bolt torque sequence including those head bolts that were not removed in this procedure.
14. Tighten the 8mm bolts to 18 ft. lbs. (24 Nm).
15. Adjust the valves.
16. Install the valve cover with a new gasket. Torque the bolts to 18 ft. lbs. (24 Nm).
17. Connect the negative battery cable.

Intake Manifold Cover

Removal and Installation

1. Disconnect negative battery cable.
2. Remove the intercooler outlet duct from air inlet tube, if equipped.
3. Remove the 4 bolts that attach the air crossover to the intake manifold. Loosen the lower throttle control bracket mounting bolt and move the bracket away from the engine.
4. Loosen the hose clamps on the turbocharger end of the crossover tube and remove the tube and gasket. Cover the turbocharger opening with a clean shop towel.

Removing the rocker arm and pedestal assembly—5.9L diesel engine

Removing or installing the rocker arm from the pedestal

Intake manifold cover and gasket—5.9L diesel engine

Proper rocker arm installation—5.9L diesel engine

Exhaust manifold bolt torque sequence—5.9L diesel engine

5. Disconnect the electrical wiring from the intake manifold heater, remove the heater and remove the gasket.

6. Disconnect the charge air temperature sensor, fuel heater ground wire and the air temperature switch from the intake manifold cover.

7. Remove the manifold intake cover and gasket. Clean all sealing surfaces.

To install:

8. Using a new gasket inatall intake manifold cover.

9. Connect the charge air temperature sensor, fuel heater ground wire and the air temperature switch to the intake manifold cover.

10. Some of the intake manifold bolt holes are drilled through and must be sealed. Apply liquid teflon sealant to the bolts. Install the intake manifold cover bolts and tighten to 18 ft. lbs. (24 Nm).

11. Clean the gasket mounting surface and install a new gasket between the intake manifold cover and the air intake heater.

12. Install the intake manifold heater and connect the wiring.

13. Remove the towel from the turbocharger opening and install the air crossover tube and gasket. Tighten the hose clamps.

14. Rotate the throttle control bracket back into place. Torque all mounting bolts to 18 ft. lbs. (24 Nm).

15. Attach the throttle rod to the throttle lever.

16. Connect the negative battery cable.

Exhaust Manifold

Removal and Installation

1. Disconnect negative battery cable.

2. Disconnect air intake and exhaust pipes.

3. Disconnect the turbocharger oil supply line and the oil drain tube from the turbocharger.

4. Disconnect the intercooler inlet duct from the turbocharger. Remove the turbocharger and gasket.

5. Remove the cab heater supply and return lines. Remove the exhaust manifold and gasket. Clean all sealing surfaces.

To install:

6. Install manifold and new gasket. Tighten bolts in sequence to 32 ft. lbs. (32 Nm).

7. Install turbocharger. Tighten the turbocharger mounting nuts to 24 ft. lbs. (32 Nm).

8. Position the intercooler inlet duct to the turbocharger. Tighten the clamp to 72 inch lbs. (8 Nm).

9. Position the air intake pipe and the exhaust pipe onto the turbocharger and tighten clamps to 72 inch lbs. (8 Nm).

10. Install oil drain tube and oil supply line to the turbocharger. Tighten the drain tube bolts to 18 ft. lbs. (24 Nm). Tighten the oil supply line fitting to 11 ft. lbs. (15 Nm).

11. Connect the cab heater supply and return lines. Tighten line nuts to 18 ft. lbs. (24 Nm).

12. Reconnect the negative battery cable, start the engine and check for exhaust leaks.

Turbocharger

Removal and Installation

1. Disconnect negative battery cable.

2. Disconnect air intake and exhaust pipes.

3. Disconnect the turbocharger oil supply line and the oil drain tube from the turbocharger.

4. Disconnect the intercooler inlet duct from the turbocharger. Remove the turbocharger and gasket.

To install:

5. Inspect the mounting surface for cracks and damage. In-

stall the turbocharger. Apply anti-sieze compound to the mounting studs and tighten the turbocharger mounting nuts to 24 ft. lbs. (32 Nm).

6. Position the intercooler inlet duct to the turbocharger. Tighten the clamp to 72 inch lbs. (8 Nm).

7. Position the air intake pipe and the exhaust pipe onto the turbocharger and tighten clamps to 72 inch lbs. (8 Nm).

8. New turbochargers must be prelubricated with fresh engine oil before operation. To do so, poor 2–3 oz. of oil into the supply fitting and rotate the turbine wheel to circulate the oil. Install oil drain tube and oil supply line to the turbocharger. Tighten the drain tube bolts to 18 ft. lbs. (24 Nm). Tighten the oil supply line fitting to 11 ft. lbs. (15 Nm).

9. Connect the cab heater supply and return lines. Tighten line nuts to 18 ft. lbs. (24 Nm).

10. Reconnect the negative battery cable, start the engine and check for leaks.

Timing Chain Front Cover

Removal and Installation

1. Disconnect the negative battery cable.
2. Remove the fan drive assembly and belt.
3. Remove the belt tensioner.
4. Remove the oil fill tube and adaptor.
5. Remove the crankshaft pulley.
6. Remove all bolts that attach the cover to the gear housing.
7. Gently pry the gear cover away from the housing and remove from the engine.

To install:

8. Clean the gasket sealing surfaces.
9. Lubricate the gear train with oil.
10. Thoroughly clean and dry the seal area of the crankshaft.
11. Install the front cover and a new gasket. Install the bolts finger-tight.
12. Using the alignment/installation tool, align the cover to the crankshaft.
13. Torque the cover bolts to 18 ft. lbs. (24 Nm). Remove the tool.
14. Install the oil fill tube and adaptor.
15. Install the crankshaft pulley but do not torque the bolts at this point.
16. Install the fan, belt tensioner and belt.
17. Torque the crankshaft pulley bolts to 92 ft. lbs. (125 Nm).
18. Connect the negative battery cable and check for leaks.

Front Cover Oil Seal

Replacement

1. Disconnect the negative battery cable.
2. Remove the drive belt.
3. Remove the crankshaft pulley.
4. Drill two ⅛ in. holes into the seal face, 180 degrees apart.
5. Using a slide hammer with a No. 10 sheet metal screw, pull the seal out alternating from side to side until the seal is out.
6. Thoroughly clean and dry the crankshaft.

To install:

7. Apply a bead of Loctite®277 to the outside diameter of the seal.
8. Install the pilot from the seal kit onto the crankshaft.
9. Install the seal onto the pilot and start it into the front cover seal bore. Remove the pilot.
10. Use the alignment/installation tool and a plastic hammer to fully install the seal.
11. Install the crankshaft pulley but do not torque the bolts at this point.
12. Install the drive belt.
13. Torque the crankshaft pulley bolts to 92 ft. lbs. (125 Nm).
14. Connect the negative battery cable and check for leaks.

ALIGNMENT/INSTALLATION TOOL

Aligning the cover with the crankshaft—5.9L diesel engine

Timing Sprockets

Removal and Installation

1. Disconnect the negative battery cable.
2. Remove the fan drive assembly and belt.
3. Remove the belt tensioner.
4. Remove the oil fill tube and adaptor.
5. Remove the crankshaft pulley.
6. Remove all bolts that attach the cover to the gear housing.
7. Gently pry the gear cover away from the housing and remove from the engine.
8. Using a puller, remove the camshaft gear from the camshaft. Remove the key and replace.
9. Remove the crankshaft gear using heavy duty puller. Remove and install new alignment pin leaving it protrude 0.063 inch above crankshaft surface.

To install:

10. Heat the camshaft gear and crankshaft gear to 250°F (121°C) for 45 minutes. Lubricate the gear mount surface with Lubriplate® 105. Install the gears with the timing marks facing away from the shafts and aligned.
11. Clean the gasket sealing surfaces.
12. Lubricate the gear train with oil.
13. Install the front cover and a new gasket. Install the bolts finger-tight.
14. Using the alignment/installation tool, align the cover to the crankshaft.
15. Torque the cover bolts to 18 ft. lbs. (24 Nm). Remove the tool.
16. Install the oil fill tube and adaptor.
17. Install the crankshaft pulley but do not torque the bolts at this point.
18. Install the fan, belt tensioner and belt.
19. Torque the crankshaft pulley bolts to 92 ft. lbs. (125 Nm).
20. Connect the negative battery cable and check for leaks.

Camshaft

Removal and Installation

1. Disconnect the negative battery cable.
2. Remove the valve covers.
3. Remove the rocker pedestal and arm assemblies.
4. Remove the pushrods.
5. Remove the drive belt.

Crankshaft gear and camshaft gear timing marks—5.9L diesel engine

Camshaft gear and injection pump gear timing marks—5.9L diesel engine

6. Drain the cooling system. Remove the fan assembly, radiator and all related parts.
7. Remove the crankshaft pulley.
8. Remove the front gear cover.
9. Remove the fuel pump.
10. Insert the special dowels into the pushrod holes and onto the top of each lifter. When properly installed, the dowels can be use to hold the tappets up securely. Wrap rubber bands around the top of the dowels to prevent them from dropping down.
11. Rotate the crankshaft to align the crankshaft to camshaft timing marks.
12. Remove the bolts from the thrust plate.
13. Remove the camshaft and thrust plate.
14. Press the gear from the camshaft and remove the key.

To install:

15. Install the key on the camshaft.
16. Heat the camshaft gear to 250°F (121°C) for 45 minutes. Lubricate the gear mount surface with Lubriplate® 105. Install the gear to the camshaft with the timing marks facing away from the shaft.
17. Lubricate the camshaft bores, lobes, journals and thrust washer with Lubriplate® 105.

NOTE: Do not push the camshaft in too far or it may dislodge the plug in the rear of the camshaft bore, possibly creating a leak.

18. Install the camshaft and thrust washer so the **E** timing mark on the injection pump gear aligns with the **C** timing mark on the camshaft gear and the timing mark on the crankshaft gear align with those on the camshaft gear.
19. Install the thrust washer bolts and torque to 18 ft. lbs. (24 Nm).
20. Check the endplay of the camshaft. The specification is 0.006–0.010 in. (0.152–0.254mm).

21. Check the backlash of the camshaft gear. The specification is 0.003–0.013 in. (0.080–0.330mm).
22. Install the tappets and pushrods.
23. Install the rocker pedestal and arm assemblies.
24. Install the front cover and crankshaft pulley.
25. Install the drive belt and fan assembly.
26. Install the fuel pump.
27. Adjust the valves.
28. Install the valve covers. Refill cooling system.
29. Connect the negative battery cable and check for leaks.

Piston and Connecting Rod

Positioning

The "FRONT" marking and the number on the rod should be oriented as shown—5.9L diesel engine

ENGINE LUBRICATION

Oil pan

Removal and Installation

1. Disconnect the negative battery cable.
2. Remove the engine oil dipstick and engine controller.
3. On Vans, remove the engine cover. Remove the air intake duct.
4. Raise the vehicle and support safely. Drain the engine oil.
5. Remove the transmission support braces.
6. Remove the starter and torque converter inspection cover, if equipped.
7. Remove the oxygen sensor and air injection tube, if equipped.
8. Lower the exhaust crossover pipe.

9. Remove the nut on right engine mount. Loosen nut on left mount. Remove the rear transmission insulator bolts.

10. Using the proper equipment, support the transmission.

11. Support the engine with a jackstand. Raise the engine and transmission as required to allow for pan removal.

12. Remove the oil pan bolts and remove the pan from the vehicle.

To install:

13. Using a new pan gasket set, apply a thin bead of sealer to the 4 corners where the rubber seals and cork gasket meet.

14. Thoroughly clean and dry all bolts and bolt holes. Install the pan and tighten the bolts to 75 inch lbs. (4 Nm), then retighten to 200 inch lbs. (23 Nm).

15. Lower the engine and transmission and install the engine mount nuts and transmission mount bolts.

16. Install the exhaust crossover pipe. Install the oxygen sensor and air injection tube, if equipped.

17. Install the torque converter inspection cover, if equipped. Install the starter and support braces. Lower the vehicle.

18. Install the dipstick, air intake duct and engine cover, if removed.

19. Fill the engine with the proper amount of oil.

20. Connect the negative battery cable and check for leaks.

Oil Pump

Removal and Installation

EXCEPT 5.9L DIESEL ENGINE

1. Disconnect the negative battery cable.
2. Remove the oil pan.
3. Remove the screen.
4. Unbolt the oil pump from the rear main bearing cap and remove it from the vehicle.

To install:

5. Prime the pump by pouring clean oil into the pump intake and turning the driveshaft until oil comes out the pressure port. Repeat a few times until no air bubbles are present. Install the oil pump with a rotating motion to ensure proper pump driveshaft engagement.

6. Hold the pump flush against the main cap and finger-tighten the attaching bolts.

7. Torque the bolts to 30 ft. lbs. (41 Nm).

8. Install the screen.

9. Install the oil pan with a new gasket.

10. Connect the negative battery cable and check the oil pressure.

5.9L DIESEL ENGINE

1. Disconnect the negative battery cable.
2. Remove the drive belt.
3. Remove the radiator.
4. Remove the fan assembly.
5. Remove the oil fill tube and adaptor.
6. Remove the crankshaft pulley and damper.
7. Remove the front cover.
8. Remove the 4 pump mounting bolts and remove the pump from the block.

To install:

9. Prime the pump by pouring clean oil into the pump intake and turning the driveshaft until oil comes out the pressure port. Repeat a few times until no air bubbles are present. Align the idler gear pin with the locating bore in the block and install the pump.

10. Tighten the mounting bolts in the proper sequence to 44 inch lbs. (5 Nm), then repeat the sequence torquing to 18 ft. lbs. (24 Nm).

NOTE: When the pump is correctly installed, the flange on the pump should not touch the block; the back plate on the pump seats against the bottom of the bore.

Oil pump attaching bolts tightening sequence—5.9L diesel engine

11. Measure the backlash of the idler to pump drive gears. The specification is 0.003–0.013 in. (0.08–0.33mm).

12. Measure the backlash of the idler to crankshaft gears. The specification is 0.003–0.013 in. (0.08–0.33mm).

13. Install the front cover, crankshaft damper and pulley.

14. Install the oil fill tube and adaptor.

15. Install the fan assembly, radiator and drive belt.

16. Connect the negative battery cable and check the oil pressure.

Checking

EXCEPT 5.9L DIESEL ENGINE

1. Disassemble the pump.

2. Replace the pump assembly, if the cover is scratched, grooved or warped more than 0.0015 in. (0.038mm).

3. The minimum thickness of the outer rotor is 0.825 in. (20.96mm). The minimum diameter of the outer rotor is 2.469 in. (62.70mm). The minimum thickness of the inner rotor is 0.825 in. (20.96mm). If any of the above measurements are not within specifications, replace the shaft and both rotors.

4. The maximum clearance between the outer rotor and the pump body is 0.014 in. (0.356mm). Replace the pump assembly, if not within specifications.

5. Install the inner rotor and place a straight-edge across the bolt holes. If a feeler gauge of 0.004 in. (0.101mm) or more fits, replace the pump assembly.

6. The maximum clearance between the rotors is 0.080 in. (0.254mm). Replace the shaft and both rotors if not within specifications.

7. Inspect the relief valve plunger for scoring. Small marks may be removed with 400-grit wet of dry sandpaper.

8. The relief valve spring should have a freelength of 1.95 in. (49.5mm). Replace the spring if it fails to meet specifications.

9. Assemble the pump using new parts where necessary.

5.9L DIESEL ENGINE

1. Inspect the drive and idle gears for damage of any type. The maximum backlash between the gears is 0.015 in. (0.38mm).

2. Remove the back plate.

3. The maximum tip clearance of the rotors is 0.007 in. (0.178mm).

4. Place a straight-edge across the rotors. The maximum clearance is 0.005 in. (0.127mm).

5. The maximum rotor to body clearance is 0.015 in. (0.381mm).

6. Remove the rotor and inspect all parts for visible damage.

7. Assemble the pump using new parts where necessary.

Exploded view of the oil pump—5.2L and 5.9L gasoline engines

Lower rear main seal—5.9L gasoline engine

Rear Main Bearing Oil Seal.

The 3.9L and 5.2L engines rear main seal is a 2 piece, fitted rope type seal. The 5.9L engine rear main seal is a split rubber type. In all cases, the upper half can be installed with the crankshaft in place. The 2 halves should always be replaced as a set.

Removal and Installation

3.9L AND 5.2L ENGINES

1. Raise the vehicle and support safely. Drain the engine oil. Remove the oil pan and oil pump.
2. Remove the rear main bearing cap.
3. Remove the lower seal from the cap.
4. To remove the upper rope seal, use oil seal remover and installer kit KD–492 or equivalent, following the instructions provided with the tool.

To install:

5. Wipe the crankshaft surface clean and coat it lightly with oil.
6. Use oil seal remover and installer kit KD–492 or equivalent, to install the upper rope seal. Trim the ends of the upper seal to eliminate frayed ends.
7. Install the lower rope seal in the main cap so both ends protrude. Use tool C–3511 to seat the seal in its groove. Cut of the portions of the seal that extend above the cap on both sides and install the end seals to the cap.
8. Install the main cap to the block and torque the bolts to 85 ft. lbs. (115 Nm).
9. Install the pan and fill the engine with the proper amount of oil.
10. Connect the negative battery cable and check for leaks.

5.9L GASOLINE ENGINE

1. Raise the vehicle and support safely. Drain the engine oil. Remove the oil pan and oil pump.
2. Remove the rear main bearing cap.
3. Remove the lower seal from the cap.
4. To remove the upper seal, press on one end of the seal with a small blunt tool, rotate the crankshaft slightly and pull out the other end of the seal.

To install:

5. Wipe the crankshaft surface clean and coat it lightly with oil.
6. When installing the upper seal, hold the seal (with the paint stripe to the rear) tightly against the crankshaft and rotate the crankshaft while sliding the seal into the groove. If any rubber has peeled off of the back of the new seal, do not use it; it will leak.
7. When installing the lower rubber seal, make sure the paint stripe is positioned to the rear and place a drop of sealer next to both ends of the seal.
8. Install the main cap to the block and torque the bolts to 85 ft. lbs. (115 Nm).
9. Install the oil pump and pan and fill the engine with the proper amount of oil.
10. Connect the negative battery cable and check for leaks.

5.9L DIESEL ENGINE

The rear crankshaft seal is mounted in a housing that is bolted to the rear of the block. A double lipped teflon seal is used.

1. Disconnect the negative battery cable.
2. Remove the transmssion.
3. Remove the clutch cover and plate, if equipped.
4. Remove the flywheel.
5. Drill two ⅛ in. holes 180 degrees apart into the seals. Be extremely careful not to drill against the crankshaft.
6. Using a No. 10 sheet metal screw and a slide hammer, remove the rear seal.

To install:

7. Thoroughly clean and dry the crankshaft surface. Do not oil the crankshaft or seal prior to installation or the seal will leak.
8. Install the seal pilot included in the replacement seal kit, on the crankshaft. Push the seal on the pilot and crankshaft. Remove the pilot.
9. If the new seal has a rubber outer diameter, lubricate it with soapy water. If the seal does not have a rubber outer diameter, use Loctite®277 or equivalent on the outer diameter.
10. Use the alignment tool to install the seal to the proper depth in the housing. Drive the seal in gradually and evenly until the alignment tool stops against the housing.
11. Install flywheel and clutch and cover, if equipped.
12. Install transmission and reconnect negative battery cable. Add oil to correct level, start vehicle and check for leaks.

TORQUE SPECIFICATIONS

Component	English	Metric
Camshaft sprocket bolt	50 ft. lbs.	68 Nm
Camshaft thrust plate	18 ft. lbs.	24 Nm
Clutch cover mounting to flywheel	17 ft. lbs.	23 Nm
Chain case cover bolts	35 ft. lbs.	47 Nm
Connecting rod nuts		
3.9L engine	45 ft. lbs.	61 Nm
5.2L engine	45 ft. lbs.	61 Nm
5.9L engine	45 ft. lbs.	61 Nm
5.9L diesel engine		
Step 1:	26 ft. lbs.	35 Nm
Step 2:	51 ft. lbs.	51 Nm
Step 3:	73 ft. lbs.	73 Nm
Crankshaft pulley (vibration damper) bolt		
3.9L engine	135 ft. lbs.	181 Nm
5.2L engine	100 ft. lbs.	136 Nm
5.9L engine	100 ft. lbs.	136 Nm
5.9L diesel engine	92 ft. lbs.	125 Nm
Cylinder Head bolt		
3.9L engine	105 ft. lbs.	143 Nm
5.2L engine	105 ft. lbs.	143 Nm
5.9L engine	105 ft. lbs.	143 Nm
5.9L diesel engine		
Step 1	29 ft. lbs.	40 Nm
Step 2,	62 ft. lbs.	82 Nm
Step 3,	93 ft. lbs.	126 Nm
Engine-to-transmission bolt	30 ft. lbs.	41 Nm
Exhaust Manifold bolts		
3.9L engine	20 ft. lbs.	27 Nm
5.2L engine	20 ft. lbs.	27 Nm
5.9L engine	20 ft. lbs.	27 Nm
5.9L diesel engine	32 ft. lbs.	44 Nm
Exhaust Manifold nut		
3.9L engine	15 ft. lbs.	20 Nm
5.2L engine	15 ft. lbs.	20 Nm
5.9L engine	15 ft. lbs.	20 Nm
5.9L diesel engine	32 ft. lbs.	44 Nm
Exhaust flange-to-manifold nuts	24 ft. lbs.	33 Nm
Fan blade attaching bolts	17 ft. lbs.	23 Nm
Flywheel/flex plate–to–crankshaft bolts		
3.9L engine	55 ft. lbs.	75 Nm
5.2L engine	55 ft. lbs.	75 Nm
5.9L engine	55 ft. lbs.	75 Nm
5.9L diesel engine	101 ft. lbs.	138 Nm
Flywheel-to-converter bolts	23 ft. lbs.	31 Nm
3.9L engine	23 ft. lbs.	31 Nm
5.2L engine	23 ft. lbs.	31 Nm
5.9L engine	23 ft. lbs.	31 Nm
5.9L diesel engine	35 ft. lbs.	47 Nm
Intake manifold bolts	45 ft. lbs.	61 Nm
Intake manifold cover bolts		
5.9L diesel engine	18 ft. lbs.	24 Nm
Main bearing cap bolts		
3.9L engine	85 ft. lbs.	115 Nm
5.2L engine	85 ft. lbs.	115 Nm
5.9L engine	85 ft. lbs.	115 Nm
5.9L diesel engine		
Step 1:	45 ft. lbs.	60 Nm
Step 2:	88 ft. lbs.	119 Nm
Step 3:	129 ft. lbs.	176 Nm

TORQUE SPECIFICATIONS

Component	English	Metric
Oil Pan–to–block	17 ft. lbs.	23 Nm
Oil pan drain plug		
3.9L engine	20 ft. lbs.	27 Nm
5.2L engine	20 ft. lbs.	27 Nm
5.9L engine	20 ft. lbs.	27 Nm
5.9L diesel engine	60 ft. lbs.	80 Nm
Oil pump attaching bolts		
3.9L engine	30 ft. lbs.	41 Nm
5.2L engine	30 ft. lbs.	41 Nm
5.9L engine	30 ft. lbs.	41 Nm
5.9L diesel engine	18 ft. lbs.	24 Nm
Oil pump cover bolt	8 ft. lbs.	11 Nm
Oil Pressure Sending Unit		
3.9L engine	5 ft. lbs.	7 Nm
5.2L engine	5 ft. lbs.	7 Nm
5.9L engine	5 ft. lbs.	7 Nm
5.9L diesel engine	12 ft. lbs.	16 Nm
Rocker shaft bracket/support bolt	17 ft. lbs.	23 Nm
Spark plug	30 ft. lbs.	41 Nm
Starter-to-block bolts		
3.9L engine	50 ft. lbs.	68 Nm
5.2L engine	50 ft. lbs.	68 Nm
5.9L engine	50 ft. lbs.	68 Nm
5.9L diesel engine	32 ft. lbs.	43 Nm
Thermostat housing		
3.9L engine	16 ft. lbs.	23 Nm
5.2L engine	16 ft. lbs.	23 Nm
5.9L engine	16 ft. lbs.	23 Nm
5.9L diesel engine	18 ft. lbs.	24 Nm
Valve cover nut/bolt		
3.9L engine	7 ft. lbs.	9 Nm
5.2L engine	7 ft. lbs.	9 Nm
5.9L engine	7 ft. lbs.	9 Nm
5.9L diesel engine	18 ft. lbs.	24 Nm
Water Pump to chain cover/housing bolt	30 ft. lbs.	41 Nm
Water Pump mounting bolt		
5.9L diesel engine	30 ft. lbs.	41 Nm

MANUAL TRANSMISSION

For further information, please refer to Chilton's Transmission Service Manual.

Transmission Assembly

Removal and Installation

1. Disconnect the negative battery cable.
2. Remove the shift lever. If equipped with the NP–435 4 speed, push the retainer (not the gearshift lever itself) down and rotate it counterclockwise slightly to release. If equipped with the NP–2500 5 speed, unbolt the shifter base assembly from the transmission. If equipped with the A–833 4 speed, label and disconnect the linkages to the shifter assembly and unbolt the shifter from its support. If equipped with the G–360 5 speed, remove snaping under lower boot on shift tower.
3. Raise the vehicle and support safely. Remove the skid plates, if equipped. Drain the transmission and transfer case.
4. Disconnect the distance sensor and the speedometer cable from the transmission or transfer case.
5. Matchmark and remove the driveshaft(s). Disconnect the PTO, if equipped.
6. If equipped with 4WD, disconnect all linkage, electrical connectors and vacuum lines from the transfer case. Using a jack, support the transfer case, unbolt the transfer case from the transmission and slide backward to remove from the vehicle.
7. Disconnect the reverse light switch connector and remove all wiring from any clips on the transmission case.

New Process 435 shifter components

New Process 2500 transmission

Getrag G-360 transmission coupled with the 5.9L diesel engine

8. Install an appropriate engine support fixture to hold the engine in place.

9. Support the transmission with a transmission jack.

10. Remove the transmission crossmember.

11. Remove the transmission to bell housing bolts.

12. Slide the transmission backwards until the input shaft clears the clutch disc. Remove the transmission from the vehicle.

To install:

13. Lubricate the pilot bushing and input shaft splines very lightly with high temperature lubricant.

14. Mount the transmission securely on a transmission jack and lift it in place until the input shaft is centered in the bell housing opening. Roll the transmission forward until the input shaft splines fully engage with the clutch disc.

15. Install the transmission to bell housing bolts. Torque the bolts to 50 ft. lbs. (68 Nm).

16. Install the transmission crossmember. Remove the transmission and engine support fixtures.

17. Install the transfer case and connect all linkage, electrical connectors and vacuum lines to the transfer case.

18. Connect the reverse light switch connector and clip all wiring to the transmission case.

19. Connect speedometer cable and distance sensor, if equipped.

20. Install the driveshaft(s) and connect the PTO, if equipped.

21. Fill the transmission and transfer case with the proper lubricant.

22. Install the shifter assembly and linkages.

23. Install the skid plates, if equipped.

24. Connect the negative battery cable and check the transmission for proper operation.

Linkage Adjustment

A–833 4 SPEED

1. Place the shifter in the neutral position.

2. Raise the vehicle and support safely.

3. Install the fabricated aligning tool to hold the levers in the neutral crossover position.

4. Disconnect the control rods from the levers in the shifter assembly. Make sure the levers are still in the neutral position.

5. Rotate the threaded ends of the shift control rods to adjust the rod length. Starting with the 1/2 rod, adjust it so the fabricated tool does not bind. Repeat with the 3/4 and the reverse rods.

6. Install the rods to their levers with the washers and clips.

7. Remove the alignment tool and check the shifting action for smoothness.

A-833 shifter and linkage

CLUTCH

Clutch Assembly

Removal and Installation

1. Disconnect the negative battery cable.
2. Raise the vehicle and support safely.
3. Remove the transmission and transfer case, if equipped.
4. Remove the clutch housing, release fork and bearing assembly, if equipped.
5. Remove the clutch cover bolts. If cover is to be reused, loosen cover bolts evenly a few threads at a time to avoid warping the cover.
6. Remove the clutch cover and disc.

To install:

7. Install the clutch cover and disc. Use a clutch aligning tool or spare input shaft to center the disc. Tighten all of the bolts finger-tight.
8. The cover bolts must be turned gradually, evenly and to the proper torque to avoid distorting the cover. Torque ⁵⁄₁₆ in. diameter bolts in the aforementioned manner to 17 ft. lbs. (23 Nm). Torque ⅜ in. diameter bolts similarly to 30 ft. lbs. (41 Nm).
9. Install the transmission and transfer case, if equipped.
10. Install the inspection cover.
11. Connect the negative battery cable and check the clutch for proper operation.

Pedal Height/Free-Play Adjustment

NOTE: Chrysler uses a hydraulic clutch release system on their full size Pick-Ups and Vans. There is no adjustment for free-play on vehicles with this system.

Clutch Master Cylinder and Slave Cylinder

The clutch master cylinder, remote reservoir, slave cylinder and connecting lines are all serviced as a complete assembly. The cylinders and connecting lines are sealed units. They are prefilled with fluid from the factory and cannot be disassembled or serviced separately.

Removal and Installation

1. Disconnect the negative battery cable.
2. Raise the vehicle and support safely. On diesel models, remove the slave cylinder shield from the clutch housing.
3. Remove the nuts attaching the slave cylinder to the bell housing.
4. Remove the slave cylinder and clip from the housing.
5. Lower the vehicle. On diesel models, disconnect the clutch pedal interlock switch wires.
6. Remove the locating clip from the clutch master cylinder mounting bracket.

Hydraulic clutch release components—Pick-Up and Ramcharger

7. Remove the retaining ring, flat washer and wave washer that attach the clutch master cylinder pushrod to the clutch pedal. Slide the pushrod off of the pedal pin. Inspect the bushing on the pedal pin and replace if it is excessively worn.

8. Verify that the cap on the clutch master cylinder reservoir is tight so fluid will not spill during removal.

9. Remove the screws attaching the reservoir and bracket, if equipped, to the dash panel and remove the reservoir.

10. Pull the clutch master cylinder rubber seal from the dash panel.

11. Rotate the clutch master cylinder counterclockwise 45 degrees to unlock it. Remove the cylinder from the dash panel.

12. Remove the clutch master cylinder, remote reservoir, slave cylinder and connecting lines from the vehicle.

To install:

13. Verify that the cap on the fluid reservoir is tight so fluid will not spill during installation.

14. Position the components in the replacement kit in their places on the vehicle.

15. Insert the master cylinder in the dash. Rotate clockwise 45 degrees to lock in place.

16. Lubricate the rubber seal with a lubricant to ease installation. Seat the seal around the cylinder in the dash.

17. Install the fluid reservoir and bracket, if equipped, to the dash panel.

18. Install the master cylinder pushrod to the clutch pedal pin. Secure the rod with the wave washer, flat washer and retaining ring. Install the locating clip. Do not remove the plastic shipping stop from the pushrod until the slave cylinder has been installed.

19. Raise the vehicle and support safely.

20. Insert the slave cylinder pushrod through the opening and make sure the cap on the end of the pushrod is securely engaged in the release lever before tightening the attaching nuts. Torque the nuts to 200 inch lbs. (23 Nm).

21. Install slave cylinder cover, if equipped. Lower the vehicle. Remove the plastic shipping stop from the master cylinder pushrod. Connect clutch pedal interlock switch wires.

22. Operate the clutch pedal a few times to verify proper operation of the system. The system will self-bleed any air in the system and vent through the reservoir.

23. Connect the negative battery cable and road test the vehicle.

AUTOMATIC TRANSMISSION

For further information, please refer to Chilton's Transmission Service Manual.

Transmission Assembly

Removal and Installation

1. Disconnect the negative battery cable.

2. Raise the vehicle and support safely. Drain the transmission and transfer case, if equipped.

3. Disconnect and lower or remove any exhaust parts as required.

4. Remove the skid plates, if equipped.

5. Matchmark and remove the driveshaft(s).

6. Disconnect the distance sensor, if equipped, and the speedometer cable.

7. If equipped with 4WD, disconnect all linkage, electrical connectors and vacuum lines from the transfer case. Support the transfer case, unbolt the transfer case from the transmission and slide it backwards to remove from the vehicle.

8. Remove the engine to transmission struts.

9. Remove the starter and the fluid cooler lines bracket.

10. Remove the torque converter inspection cover.

11. Matchmark the converter to the flexplate. Remove the torque converter bolts.

12. Disconnect the wires to the neutral safety switch and lockup solenoid, if equipped.

13. Disconnect the oil cooler lines from the transmission.

14. Disconnect the gearshift rod and torque shaft assembly from the transmission.

15. Disconnect the throttle rod from the lever.

16. Unbolt the oil filler tube brace and lift the oil filler tube out of its bore.

17. Install an appropriate engine support fixture to hold the engine in place when the transmission is out of the vehicle.

18. Raise the transmission slightly.

19. Remove the transmission crossmember.

20. Remove the oil filter, if necessary. Remove all bell housing bolts and remove the transmission from the vehicle.

To install:

21. Install the transmission securely on the transmission jack. Rotate the converter so it will align with the positioning of the flexplate.

22. Apply a coating of high temperature grease to the torque converter pilot hub.

23. Raise the transmission into place and push it forward until the dowels engage and the bell housing is flush with the block.

24. Install the bell housing bolts and torque to 30 ft. lbs. (41 Nm). Install the oil filler tube. Install the oil filter, if removed.

25. Install the transmission crossmember. Remove the engine support fixture and the transmission jack.

26. Install the torque converter bolts and torque as follows:

    a. On models with 9.5 inch, 3-lug converter, tighten bolts to 40 ft. lbs. (54 Nm).

    b. On models with 9.5 inch, 4-lug converter, tighten bolts to 55 ft. lbs. (74 Nm).

    c. On models with 10.75 inch, 4-lug converter, tighten bolts to 270 inch lbs. (31 Nm).

27. Connect the oil cooler lines.

28. Connect the throttle rod to the lever and adjust, if necessary.

29. Connect the gearshift rod and torque shaft assembly to the transmission and adjust if necessary.

30. Connect the wires to the neutral safety switch, and lockup solenoid, if equipped. Make sure all wires are routed correctly and clipped in place.

31. Install the torque converter inspection cover, starter and transmission struts.

32. Install the transfer case, if equipped.

33. Connect the distance sensor, if equipped.

34. Connect the the speedometer cable.

35. Install the driveshaft(s).

36. Install exhaust parts that were removed.

37. Fill the transfer case, if equipped. Lower the vehicle.

38. Connect the negative battery cable.

39. Fill the transmission with the proper amount of Dexron® II.

40. Road test the vehicle, check for leaks and recheck the fluid level.

Shift Linkage Adjustment

NOTE: Do not attempt to adjust the linkage if any of the parts are excessively worn. If any rods are removed from the plastic grommets, new grommets should be installed. Pry only where the grommet and rod attach, not on the rod itself. Use pliers to snap the rod into the new grommet.

1. Shift the transmission into **P**.
2. Raise the vehicle and support safely.
3. Loosen the shift rod adjusting swivel lock screw. Make sure the swivel turns freely on the rod.
4. Make sure the valve body is in the **PARK** position by moving lever all the way rearward.
5. Adjust the swivel position on the shift rod to obtain a free pin fit in the toque shaft lever. Tighten the lock screw.
6. If the vehicle starts in any gear other than **P** or **N**, or does not start in both **P** and **N**, then either the adjustment is wrong or another problem exists.

Throttle Linkage Adjustment

EXCEPT 5.9L DIESEL ENGINE

1. If the engine is carbureted, perform the adjustment with the engine at normal operating temperature and off of the fast idle cam.
2. If the engine is fuel injected, retract the ISC actuator by doing one of the following:

   a. If the DRBII is available, connect its connector to the diagnostic connector. Start the engine and place the DRBII in the "Throttle Body Minimum Air Flow Test" mode. Disconnect the electrical connector on the ISC actuator. Shut off the engine and disconnect the DRBII; the actuator is now fully retracted.

   b. If the DRBII is not available, 2 jumper wires may be used. With the engine OFF, disconnect the connector to the ISC actuator. Connect a pair of jumper wires to the battery. Connect the negative jumper to the top pin of the ISC actuator and the positive jumper to the other pin. Do not leave the jumpers connected for more than 5 seconds. Disconnect the jumpers and the ISC actuator is fully retracted.
3. Raise the vehicle and support safely.

4. Loosen the adjustable swivel lock screw on the throttle rod enough so the rod travels freely in the swivel.
5. Hold the throttle lever firmly forward against its internal stop and tighten the lock screw. Lower the vehicle.
6. Reconnect the ISC actuator, if equipped.
7. If equipped with fuel injection, turn the ignition key to the **RUN** position for at least 5 seconds but do not start the engine. Turn the key to the **OFF** position.
8. Start the engine and road test the vehicle.

Throttle Cable Adjustment

5.9L DIESEL ENGINE

1. Perform the adjustment with the engine at normal operating temperature.
2. While the throttle lever is seated against the low idle stop screw, the clearance between the actuation pin and the rear end of the slotted cable should be 0.180 inch (4.57 mm).
3. If it is not at specification, lift the locking pawl and slide the cable to the proper position to obtain the specified clearance.
4. Lock the pawl back into place and road test the vehicle.

Unlocking and locking the throttle cable pawl

TRANSFER CASE

Transfer Case Assembly

Removal and Installation

1. Disconnect the negative battery cable.
2. Raise the vehicle and support safely.
3. Remove the skid plates, if equipped. Drain the transfer case fluid.
4. Disconnect the distance sensor, if equipped, and disconnect the speedometer cable from the transfer case.
5. Matchmark and remove front and rear driveshafts.
6. Disconnect the PTO, if equipped.
7. Disconnect the linkage, electrical connectors and vacuum lines from the transfer case. Support the transfer case, unbolt the transfer case from the transmission and slide it backwards to remove it from the vehicle.

To install:

8. Apply silicone sealer to both sides of transfer case-to-transmission gasket and position on transmission.
9. Align and seat transfer case on transmission making sure gear splines are aligned with transmission output shaft. If nec-

essary, align splines by rotating transfer case rear output shaft yoke.
10. Install and tighten attaching nuts to 35 ft. lbs. (47 Nm).
11. Install rear crossmember. Remove transmission support.
12. Align and connect driveshafts.
13. Connect distance sensor wires. Reconnect transfer case shift lever to range lever tightening locknut to 90 inch lbs. (10 Nm).
14. Fill transfer case with lubricant. Install skid plate and lower vehicle.
15. Reconnect negative battery cable and check operation of transfer case.

Linkage Adjustment

NEW PROCESS 205

1. Shift the transfer case into neutral.
2. Move the shift rod boot upward for access.
3. Loosen the shift bracket bolts and move the bracket as far forward as possible. Tighten the bolts.
4. Check the smoothness of operation of the transfer case.

NEW PROCESS 208 AND 241

1. Move the transfer case shift lever boot aside for access to the shift lever and gate.
2. Move the shift lever into the **4H** position. Make sure the lever is against the **4H** gate.
3. Raise the vehicle and support safely.

4. Loosen the shift rod clamp screw until the shift rod is free to slide in the swivel.
5. Verify that the lever is in the **4H** position and correct location if moved out of position.
6. Tighten the clamp screw.
7. Check the smoothness of operation of the transfer case.

DRIVE AXLE

Rear Driveshaft

Removal and Installation
ONE-PIECE REAR DRIVEHSHAFT

1. Raise the vehicle and support safely.
2. Matchmark the driveshaft and the rear axle drive pinion gear shaft yoke.
3. Remove the rear U-joint attaching bolts and both strap clamps from the rear axle drive pinion gear shaft yoke.
4. Fluid may run from the rear of the extension housing or transfer case when the shaft is removed, so position a drain pan under the area.
5. Remove the driveshaft from the transmission or transfer case.
6. The installation is the reversal of the removal procedure. Torque ¼–28 clamp bolts to 14 ft. lbs. (19 Nm) and ⁵⁄₁₆–24 to 25 ft. lbs. (34 Nm).

TWO-PIECE REAR DRIVESHAFT

1. Raise the vehicle and support safely.
2. Matchmark the driveshaft and the rear axle drive pinion gear shaft yoke.
3. Remove the rear U-joint attaching bolts and both strap clamps from the rear axle drive pinion gear shaft yoke.
4. Detach the protective boot clamp from the front shaft splines, if equipped, and slide the rear shaft slip yoke from the front shaft at the center bearing. Remove the rear shaft from the vehicle.
5. Matchmark the yokes at the transmission or transfer case and remove the clamp retaining bolts and clamp straps.
6. Remove the center bearing retaining bolts and nuts and remove the front shaft with center bearing from the vehicle.
To install:
7. Lubricate shaft splines. Install front yoke of front shaft to transmission or transfer case and install retaining screws loosely. Loosely install retaining nuts and bolts in center support. As applicable, tighten ¼-inch clamp screws to 14 ft. lbs. (19 Nm). Torque ⁵⁄₁₆–clamp screw to 25 ft. lbs. (34 Nm).
8. Align master spline in shafts and slide together. Position boot over front splines, if equipped.
9. Align the reference marks, position rear U-Joint in axle yoke saddles and install straps and bolts. Torque ¼–28 clamp bolts to 14 ft. lbs. (19 Nm) and ⁵⁄₁₆–24 to 25 ft. lbs. (34 Nm).
10. Raise ans safely support the vehicle. Rotate the driveshaft via the engine to allow the center bearing to self-align. Torque the center bearing bolts and nuts to 50 ft. lbs. (68 Nm).

Front Driveshaft—4WD

Removal and Installation

1. Raise the vehicle and support safely.
2. Remove the skid plate, if equipped.
3. Matchmark the driveshaft and the front axle drive pinion gear shaft yoke.
4. Remove the joint to transfer case flange capscrews and lockwashers.

5. Remove the front U-joint attaching bolts and both strap clamps.
6. Remove the front driveshaft from the vehicle.
To install:
7. Install driveshaft and front U-joint attaching bolts and both strap clamps. Torque ¼–28 clamp bolts to 14 ft. lbs. (19 Nm) and ⁵⁄₁₆–24 to 25 ft. lbs. (34 Nm).
8. Install the joint to transfer case flange capscrews and lockwashers and torque to 25 ft. lbs. (34 Nm).
9. Install the skid plate and lower vehicle.

Rear Driveshaft Center Bearing

Removal and Installation

1. Remove the shafts and center bearing from the vehicle.

NOTE: Do not clamp the driveshaft tube in a vise. Clamp only the forged portion of the welded yoke in a vise. Do not overtighten the vise jaws.

2. Clamp the front shaft in a vise and remove the bearing support and rubber insulator from the center bearing.
3. Bend the slinger away from the center bearing to provide sufficient clearance for installing a puller.
4. Remove the bearing from the front shaft with a puller and remove the slinger. The replacement package contains the bearing, slinger and retainer.
To install:
5. Press the replacement slinger, bearing and retainer onto the front shaft until seated on shoulder.
6. Install the shafts and center support bearing on vehicle.

Single Cardan Universal Joint

Removal and Installation

1. Remove the driveshaft from the vehicle.

NOTE: Do not clamp the driveshaft tube in a vise. Clamp only the forged portion of the welded yoke or the slip yoke in a vise. Do not overtighten the vise jaws.

2. Clamp the yoke in a vise and remove the bearing cap retainers.
3. Place a socket which has an inside diameter larger than the outside diameter of the bearing cap, against the yoke around the perimeter of the first cap to be removed. Place a socket which is slightly smaller than the cap, on the cap opposite the cap to be removed. Then position the yoke in a vise.
4. Compress the jaws until the smaller socket has driven the other cap into the larger socket.
5. Release the jaws and remove the cap that is partially out of the yoke.
6. Repeat the procedure for the remaining cap(s).
To install:
7. Clean and remove any rust from the yoke bores and lubricate lightly with lithium based grease.
8. Position the spider cylinders in the yoke bores. Insert the

Single cardan universal joint components

U-joint removal and installation

seals into the yoke bores and against the spider cylinders. Tap the bearing caps into the yoke bores far enough to keep the spider in place.

9. Place the socket that is slightly smaller than the cap against the first cap and position the assembly in a vise.

10. Compress the jaws to force the bearing caps into the yoke bores far enough so the retainer grooves are visible.

11. Repeat the procedure for remaining caps.

12. Install the retaining clips.

13. Install the driveshaft assembly to the vehicle.

Double Cardan Joint—4WD

Removal and Installation

1. Remove the front driveshaft from the vehicle.

2. Matchmark the yokes before disassembling so they will be installed in their original locations to retain driveshaft balance.

3. To expedite removal, remove the bearing caps in the sequence indicated.

4. Support the driveshaft horizontally and aligned with the base plate of the press. Shear the bearing cap plastic retaining ring and position the first link yoke rear arm over a 1⅛ in. socket. Place spider press tool C–4365–1 or equivalent, on the bearing caps in the flange yoke arms. Force the bearing cap out of the yoke with a press.

5. If the bearing cap is not completely removed, insert a spacer between the spider and bearing cap and complete the removal.

6. Rotate the driveshaft 180 degrees and repeat the procedure.

7. Disengage the spider trunnions from the link yoke. Pull the flange yoke and the spider from the centering ball on the ball support tube yoke.

8. To remove the ball socket, separate the joint between the link yoke and the flange yoke by forcing the spider trunnion bushing from the link yoke. Pull the flange yoke and the spider with the ball socket from the centering ball as an assembly.

9. Pry the seal from the ball socket and remove the washers, spring and 3 ball seats.

10. Remove the centering ball from the ball socket using tool set C–4365 or equivalent.

To install:

11. Install the centering ball in the socket using special tool C–

Bearing cap removal sequence

LARGE WASHER   3 BALL SEATS
SEAL   SMALL WASHER
REPLACEABLE BALL
SPRING

Double cardan joint components

4365–3. Force the ball into the socket until it is seated firmly against the shoulder at the base of the socket.

12. To install the spider, insert one bearing cap partially into one of the yoke bores and then rotate the yoke 180 degrees. Insert the spider into the yoke bore and seat the spider trunnion in the bearing cap. Partially insert the opposite bearing cap in the remaining yoke bore.

13. Force the bearing caps inward while pivoting the spider back and forth to provide free movement of the trunnions in the bearing.

14. When the retainer grooves become visible, install the retainer.

15. Continue to force the caps inward until the opposite retainer can be installed in its groove.

16. Lubricate the centering ball and socket with the lubricant provided in the replacement kit.

17. Repeat the installation procedure with the remaining portion of the assembly.

Front Axle Shaft, Bearing and Seal

Removal and Installation

MODEL 44

Right Side Shaft

1. Raise the vehicle and support safely.
2. Remove the wheel and remove the brake caliper from the rotor. Do not allow the caliper to hang by the hose.
3. Remove the dust cap and driving hub snapring.
4. Remove the driving hub and retaining spring.
5. Remove the wheel bearing nut lock using tool C–4170–A or

equivalent. Remove the retaining washer and the wheel bearing adjusting nut.

6. Remove the rotor/hub with wheel bearings and retainer spring plate. Remove the grease seal and bearing from the rotor.

7. Remove the splash shield and spindle from the steering knuckle.

8. Remove the brake caliper adaptor from the knuckle.

9. Remove the axle shaft from the axle housing. Remove the seal and stone guard from the shaft.

To install:

10. Install the seal on the axle shaft stone shield with the lip facing toward the axle shaft splines.

11. Insert the axle assembly into the axle housing making sure not to damage the differential seal.

12. Install the brake caliper adaptor to the knuckle. Install the spindle and splash shield and torque the nuts to 30 ft. lbs. (41 Nm).

13. Lubricate and install the inner wheel bearing in the rotor and install a new seal.

14. Install the assembly to the spindle. Install the adjusting nut and tighten it with 50 ft. lbs. (68 Nm) of torque. Loosen the nut and tighten with 35 ft. lbs. (48 Nm) of torque. Loosen the adjusting nut about ⅜ turn. Position the retaining washer on the adjusting nut by rotating the nut so the alignment pin pressed into the nut will enter the nearest hole in the retaining washer. Install and tighten the nut lock with 50 ft. lbs. (68 Nm) of torque. The final bearing endplay should be 0.001–0.010 in.

15. Install the retaining spring, driving hub and retaining ring.

16. Apply sealant to the edge of the dust cap and install.

17. Install the brake components and wheel.

18. Road test the vehicle and check for leaks.

Left Side Shaft

1. Raise the vehicle and support safely.
2. Remove the wheel and remove the brake caliper from the rotor. Do not allow the caliper to hang by the hose.
3. Remove the dust cap and driving hub snapring.
4. Remove the driving hub and retaining spring.
5. Remove the wheel bearing nut lock using tool C–4170–A or equivalent. Remove the retaining washer and the wheel bearing adjusting nut.
6. Remove the rotor/hub with wheel bearings and retainer spring plate. Remove the grease seal and bearing from the rotor.
7. Remove the splash shield and spindle from the steering knuckle.
8. Remove the brake caliper adaptor from the knuckle.
9. Disconnect the vacuum hoses and electrical connector from the disconnect housing assembly.
10. Remove the disconnect housing assembly, cover and shield from the axle.
11. Remove the intermediate axle shaft from the axle tube.
12. Remove the shift collar from the disconnect housing.
13. Remove the inner axle shaft seal from the axle tube and remove from the housing. If equipped with a seal guard, discard it; the guard is not used with the replacement seal.
14. Remove the needle bearing from intermediate axle shaft with remover D–354–1. Remove the front differential cover.
15. Force the inner axle shaft toward the center of the vehicle and remove the C-lock from the recessed groove in the shaft.
16. Remove the inner axle shaft using tools D–354–4 and D–354–3 or equivalent.
17. Use tool D–354–1 and puller C–637 or equivalent, to remove the inner axle shaft bearing.

To install:

18. Use tool D–354–4 and C–637 or equivalent, to install the inner axle shaft bearing.

19. Install the inner axle shaft using D–354–4 and D–354–2 or equivalent. Slide the axle shaft into the side gear and install the C-lock in the groove.

20. Install the replacement seal using the replacing tools.

Model 44 left side front axle

21. Install the shift collar on the splined end of the inner axle shaft.

22. Install the needle bearing in the end of the intermediate shaft using installer D–328 and driver handle C–4171. Lubricate splined end of shaft with multi-purpose lubricant and install the intermediate axle shaft through the axle tube.

23. Install the disconnect housing assembly and gasket. Make sure the shift fork is properly guided into the shift collar groove. Install the shield.

24. Connect the vacuum hoses and electrical connector to the diaphram and switch on the disconnect housing assembly.

25. Install the brake caliper adaptor to the knuckle. Install the spindle and splash shield and torque the nts to 30 ft. lbs. (41 Nm).

26. Lubricate and install the inner wheel bearing in the rotor and install a new seal.

27. Install the assembly to the spindle. Install the adjusting nut and tighten it with 50 ft. lbs. (68 Nm) of torque. Loosen the nut and tighten with 35 ft. lbs. (48 Nm) of torque. Loosen the adjusting nut about ⅜ turn. Position the retaining washer on the adjusting nut by rotating the nut so the alignment pin pressed into the nut will enter the nearest hole in the retaining washer. Install and tighten the lock nut with 50 ft. lbs. (68 Nm) of torque. The final bearing endplay should be 0.001–0.010 in.

28. Install the retaining spring, driving hub and retaining ring.

29. Apply sealant to the edge of the dust cap and install.

30. Install the brake components and wheel.

31. Road test the vehicle and check for leaks.

DANA 60

1. Raise the vehicle and support safely.

2. Remove the wheel and remove the brake caliper and pads from the rotor. Do not allow the caliper to hang by the hose.

3. Turn the shift knob to the **ENGAGE** position.

4. Apply pressure to the face of the shift knob and remove the 3 retaining screws located nearest to the flange. Pull outward and remove the shift knob from the base.

5. Remove the snapring from the axle shaft.

6. Remove the capscrews and lockwashers from the base flange.

7. Remove the locking hub from the rotor/hub. Remove and discard the gasket.

8. Straighten the lock ring tangs and use tool DD–1241–JD or equivalent, to remove the outer locknut and the lock ring. Remove the inner locknut and the outer wheel bearing.

9. Remove the rotor/hub with the inner wheel bearing. Remove the grease seal and bearing from the rotor.

10. Remove the splash shield, caliper adaptor and spindle from the steering knuckle.

11. Slide the inner and outer axle shafts with the bronze spacer, seal and slinger from the axle shaft tube and the steering knuckle.

To install:

12. Position the bronze spacer on the axle shaft with the chamfer facing the U–joint. Slide the axle shaft into the steering knuckle and the axle shaft tube.

13. Install the spindle, the brake adaptor and the splash shield. Torque the nuts to 65 ft. lbs. (86 Nm). Position the inner pad on the adaptor.

14. Lubricate and install the inner wheel bearing in the rotor and install a new seal. Install the rotor to the spindle. Install the outer wheel bearing and inner locknut.

15. Install the locknut nut and tighten it with 50 ft. lbs. (68 Nm) of torque. Loosen the nut and tighten with 35 ft. lbs. (48 Nm) of torque. Loosen the adjusting nut about ⅜ turn. Install the lock ring and outer locknut. Install and tighten the locknut with 65 ft. lbs. (88 Nm) of torque. Bend one tang over each of the locknuts. The final bearing endplay should be 0.001–0.010 in.

16. Install a new gasket on the hub. Install the drive flange and torque the nuts to 35 ft. lbs. (48 Nm). Install the snapring.

17. Position the locking hub shift knob on its base. Align the splines by pushing inward on the shift knob and rotating it clockwise to lock it in place.

18. Install and tighten the 3 screws.

19. Install the brake components and wheel.

20. Road test the vehicle and check for leaks.

Rear Axle Shaft, Bearing and Seal

Removal and Installation

CHRYSLER 8⅜ IN. AND 9¼ IN.

1. Raise the vehicle and support safely.

2. Remove the wheel and brake drum.

3. Remove the differential housing cover.

4. Rotate the differential case as required to expose the lock screw and remove it. Remove the pinion mate gear shaft from the case.

5. Force the axle shaft toward the center of the vehicle and remove the axle shaft C–clip lock from the recessed groove in the axle shaft.

6. Remove the axle shaft from the axle housing.

7. Pry the axle shaft seal from the end of the axle tube using a prybar.

8. To remove the bearing from an 8⅜ in. rear, use removal

Removing the lock screw

Removing the C–clip lock

tool C–637 attached to a slide hammer. To remove the bearing from an 9¼ in. rear, use removal tool C–4828 attached to a slide hammer.

To install:

9. Clean the bearing bore in the axle tube.

10. Insert the new axle shaft bearing onto the pilot of tool C–4198 for 8⅜ in. rear or tool C–4826 for 9¼ in. rear. The bearing is fully installed when it is seated firmly against the shoulder in the axle tube.

11. Install the new seal to the axle tube.

12. Lubricat the bearing bore and seal lip with grease and insert the axle shaft into the axle tube engaging its splines with the differential side gear splines.

13. Install the C–clip lock in the groove at the end of the shaft. Force the shaft outward to seat the C–clip.

14. Insert the differential pinion gear mate shaft into the case and through the thrust washers and pinion gears. Align the hole in the shaft with the lock screw hole in the differential case and install the lock screw. Torque the screw to 14 ft. lbs. (19 Nm).

15. Thoroughly clean and dry the case cover, mating surface, bolts and bolt holes. Apply silicone sealer to the cover and install.

16. Install the drum and wheel.

17. Fill the differential with the proper lubricant.

18. Road test the vehicle and check for leaks.

MODEL 60, 60M AND 70

1. Raise the vehicle and support safely.

2. Remove the axle flange lock bolts or nuts.

3. Remove the axle shaft.

4. Remove the locknut and remove the special adjustment nut.

5. Remove the outer bearing, brake drum and inner bearing. Remove the inner seal from the drum.

To install:

6. Lubricate and install the inner bearing to the drum and install a new seal.

7. Install the drum to the axle housing. Install the outer bearing to the drum.

8. Tighten the adjustment nut with 130 ft. lbs. (175 Nm) while rotating the wheel.

9. Loosen the adjustment nut ⅓–turn to provide about–0.005–inch of bearing endplay. Install the locknut.

10. Install the axle with a new flange gasket.

11. Install the axle flange bolts and torque to 70 ft. lbs. (95 Nm).

Front Wheel Knuckle/Spindle and Bearings

Removal and Installation

MODEL 44–2WD VEHICLES

1. Disconnect negative battery cable.

2. Raise and safely support vehicle.

3. Remove brake caliper and rotor from spindle.

4. Remove brake splash shield and dust seal.

5. Remove the cotter pin and nut from tie rod ball stud.

6. Install puller C–3894A or equivalent, and loosen tie rod end ball stud from the steering knuckle arm.

7. Remove the shock absorber from vehicle.

8. Install spring compressor tool DD–1278 or equivalent, in the spring and snug nut by hand.

9. Remove cotter pins and lower and upper ball stud nuts at the steering knuckle.

10. Loosen upper and lower joint studs from the steering knuckle and remove ball studs. Slowly loosen tension on spring until spring is in a relaxed position.

11. Remove steering knuckle from vehicle. Remove the brake adapter and steering knuckle attaching bolts and separate knuckle from the steering arm.

To install:

12. Install brake adapter on steering knuckle and tighten to 100 ft. lbs. (136 Nm).

13. Install steering knuckle arm to steering knuckle bolts and torque to 215 ft. lbs. (291 Nm).

14. Mount the knuckle to the suspension arms and torque upper nut to 105 ft. lbs. (142 Nm). Torque lower nut as follows:

    a. If ¹¹⁄₁₆–16 bolt to 135 ft. lbs. (183 Nm). Install cotter pin.

    b. If ¾–16 bolt to 175 ft. lbs. (237 Nm). Install cotter pin.

15. Connect the tie rod end. Install nut and tighten to 45 ft. lbs. (61 Nm). Install cotter pin.

16. Install new dist seal on steering knuckle. Install splash shield.

17. Install shock absorber. Install rotor and brake caliper.

18. Install wheel and tire assembly and reconnect negative battery cable.

19. Road test vehicle for proper operation.

MODEL 44 AND 60–4WD VEHICLE

1. Raise and safely support vehicle.

2. Remove the wheel tire assembly.

3. Remove the cotter pin and retaining nut from the drag link.

4. Install puller C–4150 or equivalent, on the drag link ball stud and separate from knuckle arm.

5. Remove 3 steering knuckle arm to steering knuckle nuts

and washers. Remove the steering knuckle arm from the vehicle.

To install:

6. Position steering knuckle arm to steering knuckle. Install nuts and tighten to 90 ft. lbs. (122 Nm).

7. Connect drag link to steering knuckle arm and tighten nut to 60 ft. lbs. (81 Nm). Install new cotter pin. Lower vehicle.

Manual Locking Hubs

Removal and Installation

1. Raise the vehicle and support safely.
2. Remove the wheel and remove the brake caliper and pads from the rotor. Do not allow the caliper to hang by the hose.
3. Turn the shift knob to the **ENGAGE** position.
4. Apply pressure to the face of the shift knob and remove the 3 retaining screws located nearest to the flange. Pull outward and remove the shift knob from the base.
5. Remove the snapring from the axle shaft.
6. Remove the capscrews and lockwashers from the base flange.
7. Remove the locking hub from the rotor/hub. Remove and discard the gasket.

To install:

8. Install a new gasket on the hub. Install the drive flange and torque the nuts to 35 ft. lbs. (48 Nm). Install the snapring.
9. Position the locking hub shift knob on its base. Align the splines by pushing inward on the shift knob and rotating it clockwise to lock it in place.
10. Install and tighten the 3 screws.
11. Install the brake components and wheel.
12. Road test the vehicle and check for leaks.

Pinion Seal

Removal and Installation

1. Raise the vehicle and support safely.
2. Matchmark and remove the driveshaft.
3. Remove the rear wheel and brake drums to prevent any drag.
4. Using an inch lb. torque wrench, measure the pinion bearing preload. Read the torque while the handle of the wrench is moving through several complete revolutions.

5. Using the proper tools, hold the companion flange and remove the drive pinion nut and washer.
6. Remove the companion flange using tool C–452 or equivalent. Lower the rear of the vehicle to prevent fluid loss.
7. Using a seal remover tool, remove the seal from the carrier and clean the seal seat.

To install:

8. The outside diameter of the seal is precoated with a special sealer so no sealing compound is required for installation. The seal is properly installed when the flange contacts the housing flange face.
9. Install the companion flange and the washer with the convex side out.
10. For 8⅜ and 9¼ rears, tighten the pinion nut to 210 ft. lbs. (285 Nm) and check the pinion bearing preload. If the preload is less than the original preload measured, continue tightening the nut in very small increments until the proper preload is reached.
11. For 60, 60M and 70 rears, torque the pinion nut to 260 ft. lbs. (350 Nm).
12. Install the driveshaft, drums and rear wheels.
13. Refill the differential with the proper lubricant.
14. Road test the vehicle.

Differential Case

Removal and Installation

CHRYSLER 8⅜ IN. AND 9¼ IN.

1. Raise the vehicle and support safely.
2. Remove the wheels and the brake drums.
3. Remove the rear housing cover and drain the lubricant.
4. Remove the rear wheel anti-lock brake sensor, if equipped.
5. Remove both axle shafts.
6. Matchmark the bearing caps to the differential housing.
7. Remove the differential bearing threaded adjuster lock from each cap.
8. Loosen but do not remove the bearing caps.
9. Loosen the side adjusters using tool C-4164.
10. Remove the bearing caps, the threaded adjusters and the differential case.

To install:

11. Position the assembled differential case in the housing.

Dualmatic Locking Hub

12. Install the bearing caps in their original positions according to the matchmarks made during the disassembly.

13. Torque the upper bolts to 10 ft. lbs. (14 Nm) and finger-tighten the bottom bolts.

14. Tighten the side adjusters until the proper backlash specifications are reached with each adjuster tightened to 10 ft. lbs. (14 Nm).

15. Torque the bearing caps bolts to 70 ft. lbs. (95 Nm) for 8⅜ in. rears or 100 ft. lbs. (136 Nm) for 9¼ in. rears.

16. Install threaded adjuster locks. Tighten lock screw to 90 inch lbs. (10 Nm) torque. Check and adjust side clearance, if necessary.

17. Install both axle shafts.

18. Install the rear wheel anti-lock brake sensor, if equipped.

19. Install the housing cover and fill with the proper lubricant.

20. Install the drums and wheels.

21. Road test the vehicle.

MODEL 60, 60M AND 70

1. Raise the vehicle and support safely.

2. Remove both axle shafts. Remove the wheels and the brake drums.

3. Remove the housing cover and drain the lubricant.

4. Remove the rear wheel anti-lock brake sensor, if equipped.

5. Matchmark the bearing caps to the differential housing.

6. Remove the bearing caps.

7. Position a housing spreader on the housing with the dowels seated securely in the locating holes.

8. Spread the case no more than 0.015 in. (0.38mm).

9. Remove the differential case from the housing using a small prying tool, if necessary.

To install:

10. Spread the housing and install the assembled case.

11. Install the bearing caps in their original positions according to the matchmarks made during the disassembly.

12. Torque the cap bolts to 85 ft. lbs. (115 Nm).

13. Check and adjust all measurements to specifications.

14. Install the rear wheel anti-lock brake sensor, if equipped.

15. Install the housing cover and fill with the proper lubricant. Include hypoid gear lubricant if the differential is a TraC–Lok.

16. Install the brake drums and wheels.

17. Install both axle shafts.

18. Road test the vehicle.

Axle Housing

Removal and Installation

1. Disconnect the negative battery cable. Raise vehicle and support safely.

2. Remove the rear wheel anti-lock brake sensor, if equipped.

3. Remove the rear wheels.

4. Disconnect the brake hose at the T-fitting.

5. Disconnect the parking brake cables.

6. Matchmark and remove the driveshaft.

7. Support the weight of the assembly with the proper equipment. Disconnect the shock absorbers and remove the leaf spring nuts and U-bolts.

8. Remove the assembly from vehicle.

To install:

9. Position rear axle spring pads over spring center bolts and install U-bolts and nuts.

10. Connect the parking brake cables and rear shocks.

11. Reconnect the brake hoses. Align the reference marks and install driveshaft. Tighten the clamp bolts to 185 inch lbs. (22 Nm).

12. Install rear wheels and lower vehicle. Fill brake system, bleed and adjust brakes.

STEERING

Steering Wheel

Removal and Installation

1. Disconnect the negative battery cable.

2. Remove the horn pad.

3. Remove the steering wheel hold-down nut. Matchmark the steering wheel to the shaft.

4. Using a steering wheel puller, pull the steering wheel off the shaft.

To install:

5. Install steering wheel onto shaft and torque to 45 ft. lbs. (61 Nm).

6. Install horn pad and connect negative battery cable.

Steering Column

Removal and Installation

1. Disconnect the negative battery cable.

2. Remove the horn pad.

3. Remove the steering wheel hold-down nut. Matchmark the steering wheel to the shaft.

4. Using a steering wheel puller, pull the steering wheel off the shaft.

5. Matchmark column shaft to coupler and remove steering coupling screws.

6. Remove lower dash cover and fuse block cover.

7. If equipped with column shift, disconnect the link rod from shift lever. Position shift lever in **P** and remove indicator cable.

8. Remove tilt lever, if equipped.

9. Remove upper and lower shrouds. Remove the turn signal multi-function switch with 7 mm socket.

10. Remove wiring harness from column by removing retainer clips. Disconnect connectors at base of column.

11. Remove the lower dash panel and support bracket. Remove nuts from upper bracket and remove column.

To install:

12. Install column in vehicle and install mount brackets and fasteners loosely in place.

13. Align master splines on steering gear shaft and coupler. Engage the coupler with the shaft and install the roll pin. Tighten mounting nuts.

14. Fasten the wiring harness and multi-function switch to the steering column and connect wires to connectors at base of column.

15. Install the gear indicator cable. Install lower fixed shroud.

16. Install the lock housing shrouds and tilt lever, if equipped.

17. Install steering wheel to shaft and tighten to 45 ft. lbs. (61 Nm).

18. Install horn pad and connect negative battery cable.

19. Check operation of multi-function switch and any other related switches.

Manual Steering Gear

Removal and Installation

1. Disconnect the negative battery cable.
2. Remove the 2 bolts from the wormshaft to steering shaft coupler.
3. Raise the vehicle and support safely.
4. Matchmark and remove the pitman arm from the pitman shaft using tool C–4150 or equivalent.
5. Remove the steering gear mounting bolts and remove the gear from the vehicle.
6. The installation is the reversal of the removal procedure. Torque the pitman arm nut to 175 ft. lbs. (237 Nm).

Exploded view of the manual steering gear

Adjustment

WORMSHAFT PRELOAD TORQUE

1. Raise the vehicle and support safely.
2. Remove the pitman arm from the pitman shaft.
3. Remove the horn pad.
4. Loosen the sector shaft adjusting screw locknut and back off the adjusting screw about 1½ turns.
5. Turn the steering wheel to the right stop and then back ½ turn. Measure the torque required to turn the steering while back to the straight ahead position. The specification is 4–6 inch lbs.
6. If not within specifications, loosen the large adjustment cap locknut and turn the adjustment cap until the proper preload is reached. Turning the adjuster clockwise increases the preload torque.
7. Tighten the locknut and recheck the preload.
8. Tighten the sector shaft adjuster screw locknut.

SECTOR SHAFT

1. Perform the wormshaft preload procedure.
2. Center the steering wheel.
3. Loosen the sector shaft adjuster screw locknut and screw the adjuster screw all the way down. Tighten the locknut.
4. Rotate the steering wheel ¼ turn away from the overcenter position. Measure the torque required to rotate the wheel past the overcenter position. The specification is 14 inch lbs.
5. If not within specifications, adjust the screw accordingly and tighten the locknut.
6. Install the horn pad.
7. Install the pitman arm.

Power Steering Gear

Adjustment

1. If the vehicle wanders of the steering has too much play, the sector shaft can be adjusted.
2. Loosen the adjusting screw locknut and turn the screw all the down.
3. Back the screw off ¼–½ turn.
4. Tighten the locknut.
5. Road test the vehicle. If the steering wheel does not return easily after a turn, back the screw off until the wheel returns easily.

Removal and Installation

1. Place the wheels in the straight ahead position.
2. Remove the windshield washer solvent reservoir and the coolant overflow tank, if necessary.
3. Position a drain pan under the steering gear.
4. Disconnect the fluid hoses from the gear and plug them.
5. Disconnect the steering column shaft from the stub shaft.
6. Raise the vehicle and support safely. Matchmark and remove the pitman arm from the center link on 2WD vehicles. On 4WD vehicles, disconnect the drag link from the pitman arm. Remove the pitman arm from the pitman shaft.
7. Remove the retaining bolts and remove the steering gear from the vehicle.
To install:
8. For 2WD vehicles, position steering gear at frame rail and install bolts loosely. Align steering shaft and stub shaft and install bolts to 33 ft. lbs. (45 Nm) torque. Realign gear at frame and torque bolts to 100 ft. lbs. (136 Nm).

9. On 4WD vehicles, install steering gear to reinforcement and tighten screws to 100 ft. lbs. (136 Nm). Position steering gear at frame rail and install bolts loosely. Align steering shaft and stub shaft and install bolts to 33 ft. lbs. (45 Nm) torque. Realign gear at frame and torque bolts to 100 ft. lbs. (136 Nm).
10. Install pitman arm to steering shaft and torque nut to 175 ft. lbs. (237 Nm). Connect steering linkage to arm. Install replacement cotter pins.

Power Steering Pump

Removal and Installation

GASOLINE ENGINE

1. Disconnect the negative battery cable.
2. Position a drain pan under the power steering pump.
3. Disconnect the fluid hoses from the pump and plug them.
4. Remove the front bracket attaching bolts and remove the belt from the pulley.
5. Remove the rear pump to bracket nut and remove the pump.
6. Remove the bracket from the pump.
7. Remove the pulley from the pump with the proper puller. Install the pulley on the new pump using the special installation tools.
To install:
8. Position pump in rear bracket and install retaining bolts.
9. Install pump to engine and install retainer bolts. Attach fluid lines.
10. Tighten all mounting bolts. Add power steering fluid to reservoir. Install drive belt to correct tension.

DIESEL ENGINE

1. Disconnect the negative battery cable.
2. Position a drain pan under the power steering pump.
3. Disconnect and cap vacuum and steering pump hoses.
4. Disconnect oil pressure sender electrical connector and remove sender from block.
5. Disconnect and cap the oil feed from bottom of vacuum pump.
6. Remove lower vacuum/steering pump mounting bolts, gasket and pump from the engine.
7. Remove the steering pump to vacuum pump bracket attaching nuts and slide the steering pump from bracket.
To install:
8. Install body spacers to pump and install pump into bracket. The steering pump and spacer must mate completely with vacuum pump bracket.
9. Install new gasket to pump assembly using sealer to retain the gasket. Install pump assembly to engine.
10. Install oil pressure sending unit and electrical connector.
11. Install oil feed line and vacuum hoses to vacuum pump. Install fluid hoses to power steering pump.
12. Fill reservoir with power steering fluid. Connect negative battery cable, start engine and check for leaks.

Belt Adjustment

1. Loosen the bracket mounting bolts.
2. Using a ½ in. drive breaker bar in the square hole provided in the bracket, move the pump away from the engine. Do not pry against the fluid reservoir.
3. With the pump moved enough so the belt deflects about ¼–½ in. under a 10 lb. load, tighten the bolts.

System Bleeding

1. Fill the reservoir with power steering fluid.
2. Turn the wheels to the full left turn position and add fluid until the reservoir is full.
3. Start the engine and add fluid to bring the level to the correct level.
4. To purge the system of air, turn the steering wheel from side to side without contacting the stops.
5. Return the wheel to the straight ahead position and operate the engine for 2 minutes before road testing. This should bleed the system completely.

Tie Rod Ends

Removal and Installation

1. Raise the vehicle and support safely.
2. Remove the cotter pin and nut from the tie rod end.
3. Using a puller, remove the tie rod from the steering knuckle or center link.
4. Loosen the sleeve clamp nut and bolt and unscrew the tie rod end from the sleeve.
5. The installation is the reversal of the removal procedure. Torque the stud nuts to 45 ft. lbs. (61 Nm) and install a new cotter pin.
6. Perform a front end alignment as required to adjust toe-in.

Removing the tie rod end

BRAKES

For all brake system repair and service procedure not detailed below, please refer to "Brakes" in the Unit Repair section.

Master Cylinder

Removal and Installation

1. Disconnect the negative battery cable.
2. Disconnect and plug the brake lines from the master cylinder.
3. Remove the nuts attaching the master cylinder to the power booster.
4. Remove the master cylinder from the mounting studs.
To install:
5. Bench bleed the master cylinder.
6. Install to the studs and install the nuts.
7. Install the brake lines to the master cylinder loosely.
8. Slowly push brake pedal to the floor and hold in this position while tightening brake lines at master cylinder. Refill master cylinder and check for leaks and proper pedal resistance.

Proportioning/Combination Valve

Removal and Installation

1. Disconnect the negative battery cable.
2. Raise the vehicle and support safely.
3. Tag and disconnect the brake lines from the valve.
4. Disconnect the wires to the pressure switch.

5. Remove the combination valve from the frame bracket.
6. The installation is the reversal of the removal procedure.
7. Bleed the brakes in the following order:
   a. Rear Wheel Anti-Lock valve
   b. Right rear wheel cylinder
   c. Left rear wheel cylinder
   d. Right front caliper
   e. Left front caliper

Power Brake Booster

Removal and Installation

1. Disconnect the negative battery cable. Disconnect the vacuum hose(s) from the booster.
2. Remove the nuts attaching the master cylinder to the booster and move the master cylinder aside.
3. From inside of the vehicle, remove the clip that secures the booster pushrod to the brake pedal.
4. Remove the nuts that attach the booster to the dash panel and remove it from the vehicle.
5. Transfer the check valve to the new booster.
To install:
6. Position booster on dash panel and install retainer nuts.
7. Install booster pushrod on brake pedal and install new retainer clip.
8. Install brake master cylinder to booster and secure. Install vacuum hose to booster check valve.

Brake Caliper

Removal and Installation

1. Raise the vehicle and support safely. Remove the tire and wheel assembly.
2. Remove the caliper retaining clips and anti-rattle springs.
3. Lift the caliper off of the rotor. Remove the outer pad from the caliper.
4. Remove the brake hose retaining bolt from the caliper.

To install:

5. Install the brake hose to the caliper using new copper washers.
6. Adjust the ears of the outer pad to provide a tight fit in the caliper recesses.
7. Position the caliper over the rotor so the caliper engages the adaptor correctly.
8. Install the anti-rattle springs and retaining clips.
9. Fill the master cylinder and bleed the brake system.

Disc Brake Pads

Removal and Installation

1. Remove some of the fluid from the master cylinder. Raise the vehicle and support safely. Remove the tire and wheel assemblies.
2. Remove the caliper and remove the outer pad from the caliper.
3. Remove the inner pad from the adaptor.

To install:

4. Use a large C–clamp to compress the piston back into the caliper bore.
5. Adjust the ears of the outer pad to provide a tight fit in the caliper recesses.
6. Install the inner pad to the adaptor.
7. Position the caliper over the rotor so the caliper engages the adaptor correctly.
8. Install the anti-rattle springs and retaining bolt(s).
9. Install tire and wheel assembly. Refill the master cylinder. Pump brake pedal before moving the vehicle.

Brake Rotor

Removal and Installation

CHRYSLER DISC BRAKE

1. Raise the vehicle and support safely.
2. Remove the wheel.
3. Remove the caliper and disc brake pads. It is not necessary to remove the brake line from the caliper
4. Remove the dust cap.
5. Remove the cotter pin, locknut, wheel bearing nut and washer from the spindle.
6. Remove the outer wheel bearing.
7. Remove the rotor with the inner wheel bearing from the spindle. Remove the grease seal.

To install:

8. Lubricate and install the inner wheel bearing. Install a new grease seal.
9. Install the rotor to the spindle.
10. Lubricate and install the outer wheel bearing, washer and nut. When the bearing preload is properly set, install the nut lock and a new cotter pin.
11. Install the grease cap.
12. Install the brake pads and caliper.
13. Install the wheel. Pump brake pedal before moving vehicle.

BENDIX DISC BRAKE

1. Raise and safely support vehicle.
2. Remove wheel and tire assembly.

3. Remove support key retaining screw and support key. Remove caliper from adapter.
4. Remove hub cap. Remove drive flange snapring, flange nuts and lockwashers. Remove drive flange and gasket.
5. Straighten tang on lockring. Remove locknut, lockring, inner adjusting nut and bearing.
6. Remove hub and rotor from spindle.

To install:

7. Repack wheel bearings and install in hub. Install hub and rotor on spindle.
8. Install outer bearing and adjuster nut and tighten to 50 ft. lbs. (68 Nm). Back off adjusting nut and retorque to 40 ft. lbs. (54 Nm) while rotating wheel. Back off adjuster nut ⅜ turn. Install lockring and nut. Bearing endplay should be 0.001–0.010 in.
9. Bend 1 tang of lock-ring over locknut and 1 tang over adjusting nut.
10. Install hub with new gasket, drive flange, lockwashers and nuts. Tighten nuts to 35 ft. lbs.
11. Install flange snapring and hub cap. Install caliper, brake shoes and wheel assembly. Pump brake pedal before moving vehicle.

Brake Drums

Removal and Installation

EXCEPT DANA AXLE

1. Raise the vehicle and support safely.
2. Remove the wheel.
3. Remove the factory clips from the wheel studs, if equipped.
4. Remove the drum. If the drum is difficult to remove, remove the plug from the rear of the backing plate and push the self adjuster lever away from the star wheel. Rotate the star wheel to retract the shoes.
5. The installation is the reverse of the removal procedure.

DANA AXLE

1. Raise the vehicle and support safely.
2. Remove the axle shafts.
3. Remove the bearing adjuster nut and the outer bearing.
4. Remove the drum. If the drum is difficult to remove, remove the plug from the rear of the backing plate and push the self adjuster lever away from the star wheel. Rotate the star wheel to retract the shoes.
5. The installation is the reversal of the removal procedure.

Brake Shoes

Removal and Installation

11 INCH BRAKE DRUM

1. Raise the vehicle and support safely. Remove the wheels and drums. Remove the primary and secondary shoe return springs from the anchor pin.
2. Lift the adjuster lever and disconnect the actuator cable.
3. Remove the shoe retainers and springs.
4. Remove the shoes (held together by the lower spring) while separating the parking brake actuating lever from the shoe with a twisting motion.

To install:

5. Thoroughly clean and dry the backing plate. To prepare the backing plate, lubricate the bosses, anchor pin and parking brake actuating lever pivot surface lightly with lithium based grease.
6. Remove, clean and dry all parts still on the old shoes. Lubricate the star wheel shaft threads with anti-sieze lubricant and transfer all parts to their proper locations on the new shoes.
7. Spread the shoes apart, engage the parking brake lever and position them on the backing plate so the wheel cylinder pins engage and the anchor pins hold the shoes.

11 in. drum brakes

8. Install the parking brake strut and hold-down spring assemblies.

9. Install the anchor plate. Lubricate the sliding surface of the actuator cable plate lightly and install the cable.

10. Install the shoe return spring opposite the cable, then install the remaining spring.

11. Adjust the star wheel.

12. Remove any grease from the linings and install the drum.

13. Complete the brake adjustment with the wheels installed.

12 INCH BRAKE DRUM

1. Raise the vehicle and support safely. Remove the axles and drums.

2. Unhook the adjuster lever return spring from the lever.

3. Remove the lever and return spring from the lever pin.

4. Unhook the adjuster cable from the lever.

5. Remove the shoe to shoe upper spring.

6. Remove the shoe hold-down springs.

7. Disconnect the parking brake cable from the parking brake lever.

8. Remove both brake shoes, the lower spring and star wheel assembly.

To install:

9. Thoroughly clean and dry the backing plate. To prepare the backing plate, lubricate the bosses, anchor pin and parking brake actuating lever pivot surface lightly with lithium based grease.

10. Remove, clean and dry all parts still on the old shoes. Lubricate the star wheel shaft threads with anti-sieze lubricant

12 in. drum brakes

and transfer all parts to their proper locations on the new shoes. Install the assemblies to the backing plate.

11. Install the shoe hold-down springs and pins.
12. Connect the parking brake cable to the lever.
13. Install the upper spring.
14. Position the adjuster lever return spring on the pin. Install the adjuster lever and attach the cable.
15. Adjust the star wheel.
16. Remove any grease from the linings and install the drum.
17. Complete the brake adjustment with the wheels (but not the axles) installed.
18. Install the axles.

Wheel Cylinder

Removal and Installation

1. Raise the vehicle and support safely.
2. Remove the wheel, drum and brake shoes.
3. If equipped with a 12 in. drum, remove the anchor bolt and nut, washer, spring, parking brake lever, adjuster cable, cam plate and anchor spring bushing.
4. Remove the brake line from the wheel cylinder.
5. Remove the wheel cylinder bolts and remove the cylinder from the backing plate.

To install:

6. Install cylinder to backing plate and install bolts. Install brake line to cylinder.
7. If equipped with a 12 in. drum, install the anchor bolt and nut, washer, spring, parking brake lever, adjuster cable, cam plate and anchor spring bushing.
8. Install brake shoes, drum and wheel.
9. Bleed wheel cylinder and correct brake fluid level.

Parking Brake Cable

Adjustment

1. Release the parking brakes fully.
2. Raise the vehicle and support safely.
3. Adjust the rear brakes.
4. Loosen the nut on the front cable until there is slack in all the cables.
5. Rotate the rear wheels and tighten the cable adjusting nut until there is a slight drag at the wheels.
6. Continue to rotate the rear wheels and loosen the nut until all drag is eliminated.
7. Back off the nut an additional 2 turns.
8. Apply and release the parking brake several times. Upon the last release, verify that there is no drag at the rear wheels.
9. To check the operation, make sure the parking brake holds on an incline.

Removal and Installation

FRONT BRAKE CABLE

1. Raise the vehicle and support safely.
2. Remove the front cable adjusting nut.
3. Remove the clip securing the cable to the anchor bracket and slide the cable out of the bracket.
4. Remove the retainer attaching the cable to the pedal assembly frame. Disengage the cable from the pedal clevis.
5. Remove the cable grommet from the floor pan and remove the cable.
6. The installation is the reversal of the removal procedure.

REAR BRAKE CABLE

1. Release the parking brake fully.
2. Raise the vehicle and support safely.
3. Remove the adjusting nut from the front cable.
4. Remove the brake drums. Remove the shoes, if necessary.

Disconnect the cable from the lever and compress the cable retainer tabs and remove the cable from the backing plate.

5. Remove the cable from the equalizer and ratio lever.
6. The installation is the reversal of the removal procedure.

Brake System Bleeding

1. If master cylinder service has been performed, bleed master cylinder on bench before installing on vehicle.
2. Clean master cylinder reservoir cap to prevent contamination. Open cap and fill with brake fluid.
3. If pressure bleeding, follow instructions with bleeder for preparation and operation, and bleed the system in the following order:
   a. Master cylinder
   b. RWAL hydraulic valve
   c. Right rear wheel
   d. Left rear wheel
   e. Right front wheel
   f. Left front wheel
4. If manual bleeding, follow the above order of bleeding.
5. Open the bleeder valve and have a helper depress brake pedal to the floor. While pedal is held on the floor, tighten bleeder and repeat procedure until no air is expelled from the bleeder. Check the fluid level in the master cylinder and repeat at next site until complete system is free of air.
6. If brake light on dash remains on or the pedal feels spongy, there is air in system. Repeat procedure as required.

Anti-Lock Brake System Service

Precautions

Failure to observe the following precautions may result in system damage.

• Before performing electric arc welding on the vehicle, disconnect the Electronic Brake Control Module (EBCM) and the hydraulic modulator connectors.
• When performing painting work on the vehicle, do not expose the Electronic Brake Control Module (EBCM) to temperatures in excess of 185°F (85°C) for longer than 2 hrs. The system may be exposed to temperatures up to 200°F (95°C) for less than 15 min.
• Never disconnect or connect the Electronic Brake Control Module (EBCM) or hydraulic modulator connectors with the ignition switch ON.
• Never disassemble any component of the Anti-Lock Brake System (ABS) which is designated non-servicable; the component must be replaced as an assembly.
• When filling the master cylinder, always use brake fluid which meets DOT-3 specifications; petroleum-based fluid will destroy the rubber parts.

Electronic Control Module

Removal and Replacement

1. Disconnect negative battery cable.
2. The module is located by the blower motor resistor board and defroster duct. Remove the mounting screws, disconnect the harness connector and remove the module.
3. Installation is the reverse of the removal procedure.

Speed Sensor

Removal and Replacement

1. Raise and safely support vehicle.
2. Remove sensor mounting bolt on rear axle housing.
3. Remove sensor shield and sensor from housing. Disconnect sensor wire harness.
4. Installation is the reversal of the removal process.

Hydraulic Control Valve

Removal and Installation

1. Disconnect negative battery cable.
2. Raise and safely support vehicle.
3. Disconnect valve to sensor harness connector.
4. Disconnect brake lines connecting valve to rear brakes and to combination valve.
5. Remove valve attaching screws and remove valve.
To install:
6. Install brake lines into hydraulic valve and install valve to frame bracket.
7. Bleed hydraulic valve and brake system. Add brake fluid as required.

Exciter Ring

Removal and Installation

1. Raise and safely support vehicle.
2. Remove rear axle cover, drain fluid and remove ring gear.
3. Remove old exciter ring with a hammer and drift, wearing proper eye protection.
To install:
4. Heat replacement exciter ring with heat light or by immersing in a hot liquid not to exceed a temperature of 300 degrees Fahrenheit. Do not use a torch.
5. After heating, quickly position ring on differential case adjacent to the flange.
6. Install ring gear, cover and fluid to rear axle.

FRONT SUSPENSION

Shock Absorbers

Removal and Installation

1. Raise the vehicle and support safely.
2. On 2WD vehicles, remove the upper shock nut, washer and bushing. Remove the lower mounting bolts and remove the shock from the vehicle.
3. On 4WD vehicles, remove the upper mounting nut, lower mounting stud and retainers. Remove the shock from the vehicle.
4. The installation is the reversal of the removal procedure.

Coil Springs

Removal and Installation

1. Raise the vehicle and support safely.
2. Remove the shock absorber.
3. Remove the strut bar and disconnect the sway bar from the lower control arm, if equipped.
4. Install spring compressor tool DD–1278 or equivalent, to the coil spring and tighten the nut finger-tight, then back off nut ½ turn.
5. Remove the cotter pin and lower ball joint nut.
6. Release the lower ball joint taper using ball stud loosening tool C–3564–A or equivalent.
7. Remove the tool and remove the ball stud from the control arm. Release the compressor tool from the coil spring.
8. Pull the arm down and remove the spring with the rubber isolation pad from the vehicle.
To install:
9. Install the spring with the rubber isolators. Install the compressor tool and compress it enough so the lower ball joint can be inserted through the knuckle.
10. Torque $^{11}/_{16} - 16$ lower ball joint nuts to 135 ft. lbs. (183 Nm). Torque ¾ – 16 nuts to 175 ft. lbs. (237 Nm). Install a new cotter pin. Remove the spring compressor.
11. Install the strut bar and connect the sway bar from the lower control arm, if equipped.
12. Install the shock absorber.

Leaf Springs

Removal and Installation

1. Raise the vehicle and support safely.
2. Using the proper equipment, support the weight of the front axle.

3. Remove the nuts, washers and U-bolts attaching the springs to the axle housing. Remove the spring pad.
4. Remove the spring shackle bolts, shackle and spring front bolt.
5. Remove the spring from the vehicle.
6. The installation is the reverse of the removal procedure. Torque the U-bolt nuts to 110 ft. lbs. (149 Nm).

Upper Ball Joint

Inspection

To inspect the ball joints, unload the suspension. Upper ball joints on 2WD vehicles and any ball joint on 4WD vehicles should be replaced if any play exists at all.

Removal and Installation

2WD VEHICLES

1. Raise the vehicle and support safely.
2. Position a support at the outer end of the lower control arm and lower the vehicle so the support compresses the coil spring.
3. Remove the tire and wheel assembly.
4. Release the upper ball joint taper using ball stud loosening tool C–3564–A or equivalent.
5. Unthread the ball joint from the control arm with tool C–3561 or equivalent.
6. The installation is the reversal of the removal procedure. Torque the ball joint itself to 125 ft. lbs. (169 Nm).
7. Torque the upper ball stud nut to 135 ft. lbs. (183 Nm).

4WD VEHICLES

1. Raise the vehicle and support safely.
2. Remove the front axle shaft.
3. Disconnect the tie rod end from the steering knuckle. On the left side, disconnect the drag link ball stud from the steering knuckle.
4. On the left side, remove the nuts and washers from the steering knuckle arm and remove the arm and spring, if equipped, from the knuckle.
5. If equipped with a Model 44 front axle, remove the ball joint nuts and discard the lower nut. Use a brass drift and hammer to separate the steering knuckle from the axle tube yoke. Use tool C–4169 to remove the sleeve from the upper yoke arm.
6. Remove the snapring from the ball joint. Install the knuckle in a vise and use tools D–150–1, D–150–3 and C–4212–L or equivalent, to remove the ball joint from the knuckle.

Removing the upper ball joint from the knuckle

Removing or installing the upper socket pin

7. If equipped with a Dana 60 front axle, remove the bolts from the knuckle lower cap. Dislodge the cap from the steering knuckle and axle tube yoke. Remove the steering knuckle. Use tool D–192 or equivalent, to remove the upper socket pin from the axle tube upper arm bore. Remove the seal.

To install:

8. If equipped with a Model 44, use tools C–4212–L and C–4288 or equivalent, to force the upper ball joint into the steering knuckle. Install the snapring and install a new rubber boot. Thread the replacement sleeve into the upper yoke bore so 2 threads are exposed at the top of the yoke. Position the knuckle on the axle tube yoke and install a new lower ball stud nut. Torque to 80 ft. lbs. (108 Nm). Using the special socket, torque the sleeve to 40 ft. lbs. (54 Nm). Install the upper ball stud nut and torque to 100 ft. lbs. (136 Nm) and install a new cotter pin.

9. If equipped with a Dana 60 front axle, use tool D–192 or equivalent, to install the upper socket pin to the axle tube upper arm bore. Install a new seal. Torque to 500–600 ft. lbs. (668–813

Nm). Position the knuckle over the socket pin. Fill the lower socket cavity with grease. Install the lower cap and torque the bolts to 80 ft. lbs. (110 Nm).

10. On the left side, install the spring, if equipped, and the steering knuckle arm to the steering knuckle.

11. Connect the tie rod to the end of the steering knuckle. On the left side, connect the drag link ball stud to the steering knuckle.

12. Install the front axle shaft and all related components.

Lower Ball Joint

Inspection

To inspect the ball joints, unload the suspension. Lower ball joints on 2WD vehicles should be replaced if the have more than 0.020 in. play. Any ball joint on 4WD vehicles should be replaced if any play exists.

Removal and Installation

2WD VEHICLES

1. Raise the vehicle and support safely.
2. Remove the shock absorber.
3. Remove the strut bar and disconnect the sway bar from the lower control arm, if equipped.
4. Install spring compressor tool DD–1278 or equivalent, to the coil spring and tighten the nut finger-tight, then back off half a turn.
5. Remove the cotter pin and lower ball joint nut.
6. Release the lower ball joint taper using ball stud loosening tool C–3564–A or equivalent.
7. Remove the tool and remove the ball stud from the control arm. Release the compressor tool from the coil spring.
8. Pull the arm down and remove the spring with the rubber isolation pad from the vehicle. Remove the ball joint boot. Use tool C–4212 or a ball joint press, to remove the ball joint from the arm.

To install:

9. Use the remover tool to press the ball joint into the arm. Install a new rubber boot. Install the spring with the rubber isolators. Install the compressor tool and compress it enough so the lower ball joint can be inserted through the knuckle.

10. Torque $^{11}/_{16}$–16 lower ball joint nuts to 135 ft. lbs. (183 Nm). Torque $^{3}/_{4}$–16 nuts to 175 ft. lbs. (237 Nm). Install a new cotter pin. Remove the spring compressor.

11. Install the strut bar and connect the sway bar from the lower control arm, if equipped.

12. Install the shock absorber.

4WD VEHICLES

1. Raise the vehicle and support safely.
2. Remove the front axle shaft.
3. Disconnect the tie rod end from the steering knuckle. On the left side, disconnect the drag link ball stud from the steering knuckle.
4. On the left side, remove the nuts and washers from the steering knuckle arm and remove the arm and spring, if equipped, from the knuckle.
5. If equipped with a Model 44 front axle, remove the ball joint nuts and discard the lower nut. Use a brass drift and hammer to separate the steering knuckle from the axle tube yoke.
6. Remove the snapring from the ball joint. Install the knuckle in a vise and use tools D–150–1, D–150–3 and C–4212–L to remove the ball joint from the knuckle.
7. If equipped with a Dana 60 front axle, use tools C–4212–L, C–4366–1 and C–4366–2 to remove the lower ball joint.

To install:

8. If equipped with a Model 44, use tools C–4212–L and C–4288 or equivalent, to force the lower ball joint into the steering knuckle. Install the snapring and install a new rubber boot. Po-

sition the knuckle on the axle tube yoke and install a new lower ball stud nut. Torque to 80 ft. lbs. (108 Nm). Install the upper ball stud nut and torque to 100 ft. lbs. (136 Nm) and install a new cotter pin.

9. If equipped with a Dana 60 front axle, use tools C–4212–L, C–4366–3 and C–4366–4 to install the seal and lower bearing cup into the axle tube yoke lower bore. Reposition the tools and install the lower bearing and seal into the bore. Position the knuckle over the socket pin. Fill the lower socket cavity with grease. Install the lower cap and torque the bolts to 80 ft. lbs. (110 Nm).

10. On the left side, install the spring, if equipped, and the steering knuckle arm to the steering knuckle.

11. Connect the tie rod to the end of the steering knuckle. On the left side, connect the drag link ball stud to the steering knuckle.

12. Install the front axle shaft and all related components.

Upper Control Arm

Removal and Installation

1. Raise the vehicle and support safely.
2. Remove the shock absorber.
3. Remove the strut bar and disconnect the sway bar from the lower control arm, if equipped.
4. Install spring compressor tool DD–1278 or equivalent, to the coil spring and tighten the nut finger-tight, then back off nut ½ turn.
5. Remove the cotter pin and upper ball joint nut. Suspend the rotor assembly with a wire so there is not excessive pull on the brake hose.
6. Release the upper ball joint taper using ball stud loosening tool C–3564–A or equivalent.
7. Remove the tool and remove the ball stud from the control arm.
8. Remove the pivot bar retaining bolts on Vans or the cam bolt assemblies on Pick-Up and Ramcharger and remove the arm from the vehicle.

To install:

9. Install the arm to the frame rail bracket and install the retaining bolts.
10. Torque the ball joint nut to 135 ft. lbs. (183 Nm). Install a new cotter pin. Remove the spring compressor.
11. Install the strut bar and connect the sway bar to the lower control arm, if equipped.
12. Install the shock absorber.
13. Align the front end. When all settings are at specifications,

Upper control arm and related components— 2 wheel drive Pick-Up and Ramcharger

Upper control arm—Van

torque the pivot bar retaining bolts on Vans to 195 ft. lbs. (264 Nm). Torque the cam bolts to 70 ft. lbs. (95 Nm) on Pick-Up and Ramcharger.

Lower Control Arm

Removal and Installation

1. Raise the vehicle and support safely.
2. Remove the shock absorber.
3. Remove the strut bar and disconnect the sway bar from the lower control arm, if equipped.
4. Install spring compressor tool DD–1278 or equivalent, to the coil spring and tighten the nut finger-tight, then back off half a turn.
5. Remove the cotter pin and lower ball joint nut.
6. Release the lower ball joint taper using ball stud loosening tool C–3564–A or equivalent.
7. Remove the tool and remove the ball stud from the control arm. Release the compressor tool from the coil spring.
8. Pull the arm down and remove the spring with the rubber isolation pad from the vehicle. Remove the lower control arm pivot bolt from the crossmember and remove the arm from the vehicle.

To install:

9. Install the arm to the crossmember finger-tight. Install the spring with the rubber isolators. Install the compressor tool and compress it enough so the lower ball joint can be inserted through the knuckle.
10. Torque $\frac{11}{16}-16$ lower ball joint nuts to 135 ft. lbs. (183 Nm). Torque $\frac{3}{4}-16$ nuts to 175 ft. lbs. (237 Nm). Install a new cotter pin. Remove the spring compressor.
11. Install the strut bar and connect the sway bar from the lower control arm, if equipped.
12. Install the shock absorber.
13. Lower the vehicle completely. When the weight of the vehicle is off of the lifting apparatus, torque the lower arm pivot bolts to 175 ft. lbs. (237 Nm) on Vans or 225 ft. lbs. (305 Nm) on Pick-Up and Ramcharger.
14. Align the front end as required.

Sway Bar

Removal and Installation

1. Raise the vehicle and support safely.
2. Remove the front sway bar brackets and retainers.

3. Remove the sway bar connecting links to the control arm or front axle. Remove the sway bar from the vehicle.

4. The installation is the reversal of the removal procedure. Tighten the nuts just enough so the bushings compress to the same outer diameter as the washer adjacent to it.

Front Wheel Bearings

Removal and Installation

For 4WD models, please refer to "Drive Axle" in this manual.
1. Raise the vehicle and support safely.
2. Remove the tire and wheel assembly.
3. Remove the caliper and disc brake pads.
4. Remove the dust cap.
5. Remove the cotter pin, castelated locknut, wheel bearing nut and washer from the spindle.
6. Remove the outer wheel bearing.
7. Remove the rotor with the inner wheel bearing from the spindle. Remove the grease seal and inner wheel bearing.
8. If bearing replacement is required, remove bearing races with brass drift or puller. Install races with an appropriate installation tool.

To install:
9. Lubricate and install the inner wheel bearing. Install a new grease seal.
10. Install the rotor to the spindle.
11. Lubricate and install the outer wheel bearing, washer and nut. When the bearing preload is properly set, install the locknut and a new cotter pin.
12. Install the grease cap.
13. Install the brake pads and caliper.
14. Install the wheel.

Adjustment

1. Tighten the wheel bearing nut to 240–300 inch lbs. (27–34 Nm) while turning the rotor.
2. Loosen the wheel bearing adjusting nut completely.
3. Tighten the nut finger-tight.
4. Check the wheel bearing endplay. The specification is 0.0001–0.003 in.
5. Install the locknut and cotter pin.

REAR SUSPENSION

Shock Absorber

Removal and Installation

1. Raise the vehicle and support safely.
2. Remove the bolts that attach the shock to the frame or bracket.
3. Remove the shock from the vehicle.
4. The installation is the reversal of the removal procedure.

Leaf Springs

Removal and Installation

1. Raise the vehicle and support safely.
2. Using the proper equipment, support the weight of the axle.
3. Remove the nuts, washers and U-bolts attaching the springs to the axle housing. Remove the spacer.

Rear suspension components-150—models

Rear suspension with auxiliary springs—D and W—250 and 350—models

4. Remove the spring shackle bolts, shackle and spring front bolt.

5. Remove the springs and auxiliary spring, if equipped, from the vehicle.

To install:

6. Install spring on the axle tube so the spring center bolt is inserted into the locating hole in the axle tube spring pad.

7. Align front of spring at eye and install pivot bolt and nut. Install rear eye bolt and nut. Tighten mounting bolts on front and rear of spring until all separation between metal is removed.

8. Install U-bolts with new lockwashers and retaining nuts.

Align auxiliary spring with primary spring, if equipped. Lower vehicle.

Rear Wheel Bearings

For rear wheel bearing removal and installation procedures, refer to Drive Axle section.

Rear Axle Assembly

For rear axle removal and installation procedures, refer to Drive Axle section.

SPECIFICATIONS

VEHICLE IDENTIFICATION CHART

It is important for servicing and ordering parts to be certain of the vehicle and engine identification. The VIN (vehicle identification number) is a 17 digit number visible through the windshield on the driver's side of the dash and contains the vehicle and engine identification codes. The tenth digit indicates model year and the eighth digit indicates engine code. It can be interpreted as follows:

			Engine Code				Model Year	
Code	Cu. In.	Liters	Cyl.	Fuel Sys.	Eng. Mfg.	Code		Year
C	135	2.2	4	Carb	Chrys	J		1988
K	153	2.5	4	EFI	Chrys	K		1989
J	153	2.5	4	Turbo	Chrys	L		1990
3	181	3.0	6	EFI	Mitsubishi	M		1991
R	201	3.3	6	EFI	Chrys	N		1992
M	239	3.9	6	EFI	Chrys			
X	239	3.9	6	EFI	Chrys			
Y	318	5.2	8	EFI	Chrys			

EFI—Electronic Fuel Injection

ENGINE IDENTIFICATION

Year	Model	Engine Displacement cu. in. (liter)	Engine Series Identification (VIN)	No. of Cylinders	Engine Type
1988	Caravan	153 (2.5)	K	4	OHC
	Caravan	181 (3.0)	3	4	OHC
	Voyager	153 (2.5)	K	6	OHC
	Voyager	181 (3.0)	3	6	OHC
	Dakota	135 (2.2)	C	4	OHC
	Dakota	239 (3.9)	M	6	OHV
1989	Caravan	153 (2.5)	K	4	OHC
	Caravan	153 (2.5)	J	4	OHC
	Caravan	181 (3.0)	3	6	OHC
	Voyager	153 (2.5)	K	4	OHC
	Voyager	153 (2.5)	J	4	OHC
	Voyager	181 (3.0)	3	6	OHC
	Dakota	153 (2.5)	K	4	OHC
	Dakota	239 (3.9)	X	6	OHV

ENGINE IDENTIFICATION

Year	Model	Engine Displacement cu. in. (liter)	Engine Series Identification (VIN)	No. of Cylinders	Engine Type
1990	Caravan	153 (2.5)	K	4	OHC
	Caravan	153 (2.5)	J	4	OHC
	Caravan	181 (3.0)	3	6	OHC
	Caravan	201 (3.3)	R	6	OHV
	Voyager	153 (2.5)	K	4	OHC
	Voyager	153 (2.5)	J	4	OHC
	Voyager	181 (3.0)	3	6	OHC
	Voyager	201 (3.3)	R	6	OHV
	Town & Country	201 (3.3)	R	6	OHV
	Dakota	153 (2.5)	K	4	OHC
	Dakota	239 (3.9)	X	6	OHV
1991	Caravan	153 (2.5)	K	4	OHC
	Caravan	181 (3.0)	3	6	OHC
	Caravan	201 (3.3)	R	6	OHV
	Voyager	153 (2.5)	K	4	OHC
	Voyager	181 (3.0)	3	6	OHC
	Voyager	201 (3.3)	R	6	OHV
	Town & Country	201 (3.3)	R	6	OHV
	Dakota	153 (2.5)	K	4	OHC
	Dakota	239 (3.9)	X	6	OHV
	Dakota	318 (5.2)	Y	8	OHV
1992	Caravan	153 (2.5)	K	4	OHC
	Caravan	181 (3.0)	3	6	OHC
	Caravan	201 (3.3)	R	6	OHV
	Voyager	153 (2.5)	K	4	OHC
	Voyager	181 (3.0)	3	6	OHC
	Voyager	201 (3.3)	R	6	OHV
	Town & Country	201 (3.3)	R	6	OHV
	Dakota	153 (2.5)	K	4	OHC
	Dakota	239 (3.9)	X	6	OHV
	Dakota	318 (5.2)	Y	8	OHV

OHC—Overhead Cam
OHV—Overhead Valves

GENERAL ENGINE SPECIFICATIONS

Year	VIN	No. Cylinder Displacement cu. in. (liter)	Fuel System Type	Net Horsepower @ rpm	Net Torque @ rpm (ft. lbs.)	Bore × Stroke (in.)	Compression Ratio	Oil Pressure @ rpm
1988	C	4-135 (2.2)	2 bbl	96 @ 5200	140 @ 2800	3.44 × 3.62	9.5:1	50 @ 2000
	K	4-153 (2.5)	EFI	100 @ 4800	135 @ 2800	3.44 × 4.09	8.9:1	30–80 @ 3000
	3	6-181 (3.0)	EFI	142 @ 5000	173 @ 2800	3.59 × 2.99	8.9:1	30–80 @ 3000
	M	6-239 (3.9)	EFI	125 @ 4000	195 @ 2000	3.91 × 3.31	9.0:1	30–80 @ 3000
1989	K	4-153 (2.5)	EFI	100 @ 4800	135 @ 2800	3.44 × 4.09	8.9:1	30–80 @ 3000
	J	4-153 (2.5)	Turbo	150 @ 4800	180 @ 2000	3.44 × 4.09	7.8:1	30–80 @ 3000
	3	6-181 (3.0)	EFI	142 @ 5000	173 @ 2800	3.59 × 2.99	8.9:1	30–80 @ 3000
	X	6-239 (3.9)	EFI	125 @ 4000	195 @ 2000	3.91 × 3.31	9.0:1	30–80 @ 3000
1990	K	4-153 (2.5)	EFI	100 @ 4800	135 @ 2800	3.44 × 4.09	8.9:1	30–80 @ 3000
	J	4-153 (2.5)	Turbo	150 @ 4800	180 @ 2000	3.44 × 4.09	7.8:1	30–80 @ 3000
	3	6-181 (3.0)	EFI	142 @ 5000	173 @ 2800	3.59 × 2.99	8.9:1	30–80 @ 3000
	R	6-201 (3.3)	EFI	150 @ 4000	185 @ 3600	3.66 × 3.19	8.9:1	30–80 @ 3000
	X	6-239 (3.9)	EFI	125 @ 4000	195 @ 2000	3.91 × 3.31	9.0:1	30–80 @ 3000
1991	K	4-153 (2.5)	EFI	100 @ 4800	135 @ 2800	3.44 × 4.09	8.9:1	30–80 @ 3000
	3	6-181 (3.0)	EFI	142 @ 5000	173 @ 2800	3.59 × 2.99	8.9:1	30–80 @ 3000
	R	6-201 (3.3)	EFI	150 @ 4000	185 @ 3600	3.66 × 3.19	8.9:1	30–80 @ 3000
	X	6-239 (3.9)	EFI	125 @ 4000	195 @ 2000	3.91 × 3.31	9.0:1	30–80 @ 3000
	Y	8-318 (5.2)	EFI	230 @ 4800	280 @ 3200	3.91 × 3.31	9.0:1	30–80 @ 3000
1992	K	4-153 (2.5)	EFI	100 @ 4800	135 @ 2800	3.44 × 4.09	8.9:1	30–80 @ 3000
	3	6-181 (3.0)	EFI	142 @ 5000	173 @ 2800	3.59 × 2.99	8.9:1	30–80 @ 3000
	R	6-201 (3.3)	EFI	150 @ 4000	185 @ 3600	3.66 × 3.19	8.9:1	30–80 @ 3000
	X	6-239 (3.9)	EFI	125 @ 4000	195 @ 2000	3.91 × 3.31	9.0:1	30–80 @ 3000
	Y	8-318 (5.2)	EFI	230 @ 4800	280 @ 3200	3.91 × 3.31	9.0:1	30–80 @ 3000

EFI—Electronic Fuel Injection

GASOLINE ENGINE TUNE-UP SPECIFICATIONS

Year	VIN	No. Cylinder Displacement cu. in. (liter)	Spark Plugs Type	Spark Plugs Gap (in.)	Ignition Timing (deg.) MT	Ignition Timing (deg.) AT	Compression Pressure (psi) ①	Fuel Pump (psi)	Idle speed (rpm) MT	Idle speed (rpm) AT	Valve Clearance In.	Valve Clearance Ex.
1988	C	4-135 (2.2)	RN12YC	0.035	6B	—	100	4.5–6	850	—	Hyd.	Hyd.
	K	4-153 (2.5)	RN12YC	0.035	12B	12B	100	15	850	850	Hyd.	Hyd.
	3	6-181 (3.0)	RN11YC4	0.040	—	12B	178	48	—	700	Hyd.	Hyd.
	M	6-239 (3.9)	RN12YC	0.035	10B	10B	100	13–16	750	750	Hyd.	Hyd.
1989	K	4-153 (2.5)	RN12YC	0.035	12B	12B	100	15	850	850	Hyd.	Hyd.
	J	4-153 (2.5)	RN12Y C	0.035	12B	12B	100	55	950	900	Hyd.	Hyd.
	3	6-181 (3.0)	RN11YC4	0.040	—	12B	178	48	—	700	Hyd.	Hyd.
	X	6-239 (3.9)	RN12YC	0.035	10B	10B	100	13–16	750	750	Hyd.	Hyd.
1990	K	4-153 (2.5)	RN12YC	0.035	12B	12B	100	15	850	850	Hyd.	Hyd.
	J	4-153 (2.5)	RN12Y C	0.035	12B	12B	100	55	950	900	Hyd.	Hyd.
	3	6-181 (3.0)	RN11YC4	0.040	—	12B	178	48	—	700	Hyd.	Hyd.
	R	6-201 (3.3)	RN16YC5	0.050	—	16B	100	43–53	—	750	Hyd.	Hyd.
	X	6-239 (3.9)	RN12YC	0.035	10B	10B	100	13–16	750	750	Hyd.	Hyd.

GASOLINE ENGINE TUNE-UP SPECIFICATIONS

Year	VIN	No. Cylinder Displacement cu. in. (liter)	Spark Plugs Type	Gap (in.)	Ignition Timing (deg.) MT	Ignition Timing (deg.) AT	Compression Pressure (psi) ①	Fuel Pump (psi)	Idle speed (rpm) MT	Idle speed (rpm) AT	Valve Clearance In.	Valve Clearance Ex.
1991	K	4-153 (2.5)	RN12YC	0.035	12B	12B	100	15	850	850	Hyd.	Hyd.
	3	6-181 (3.0)	RN11YC4	0.040	—	12B	178	48	—	700	Hyd.	Hyd.
	R	6-201 (3.3)	RN16YC5	0.050	—	16B	100	43–53	—	750	Hyd.	Hyd.
	X	6-239 (3.9)	RN12YC	0.035	10B	10B	100	39	750	750	Hyd.	Hyd.
	Y	8-318 (5.2)	RN12YC	0.035	10B	10B	100	39	750	750	Hyd.	Hyd.
1992	K	4-153 (2.5)	RN12YC	0.035	12B	12B	100	15	850	850	Hyd.	Hyd.
	3	6-181 (3.0)	RN11YC4	0.040	—	12B	178	48	—	700	Hyd.	Hyd.
	R	6-201 (3.3)	RN16YC5	0.050	—	16B	100	43–53	—	750	Hyd.	Hyd.
	X	6-239 (3.9)	RN12YC	0.035	10B	10B	100	39	750	750	Hyd.	Hyd.
	Y	8-318 (5.2)	RN12YC	0.035	10B	10B	100	39	750	750	Hyd.	Hyd.

Hyd.—hydraulic
① Minimum specification

FIRING ORDERS
NOTE: To avoid confusion, always replace spark plug wires one at a time.

2.2L and 2.5L Engines
Engine Firing Order: 1–3–4–2
Distributor Rotation: Clockwise

3.3L Engine
Engine Firing Order: 1–2–3–4–5–6
Distributorless Ignition System

3.0L Engine (Mitsubishi)
Engine Firing Order: 1–2–3–4–5–6
Distributor Rotation: Counterclockwise

FIRING ORDERS

3.9L Engine
Engine Firing Order: 1–6–5–4–3–2
Distributor Rotation: Clockwise

FRONT OF ENGINE

CLOCKWISE ROTATION
1-8-4-3-6-5-7-2

5.2L Engine
Engine Firing Order: 1–8–4–3–6–5–7–2
Distributor Rotation: Clockwise

CAPACITIES

Year	Model	VIN	No. Cylinder Displacement cu. in (liter)	Engine Crankcase with Filter	Engine Crankcase without Filter	Transmission (pts.) 4-Spd	Transmission (pts.) 5-Spd	Transmission (pts.) Auto.	Drive Axle (pts.)	Fuel Tank (gal.)	Cooling System (qts.)
1988	Caravan	K	4-153 (2.5)	4	4	—	4.8	①	—	④	8.5
	Caravan	3	6-181 (3.0)	4	4	—	—	①	—	④	10.5
	Voyager	K	4-153 (2.5)	4	4	—	4.8	①	—	④	8.5
	Voyager	3	6-181 (3.0)	4	4	—	—	①	—	④	10.5
	Dakota	C	4-135 (2.2)	4	4	—	4.0	15.6	②	⑤	9.8
	Dakota	M	6-239 (3.9)	4	4	—	4.0	17.2	② ③	⑤	⑥
1989	Caravan	K	4-153 (2.5)	4	4	—	4.8	①	—	④	8.5
	Caravan	J	4-153 (2.5)	4	4	—	4.8	①	—	④	8.5
	Caravan	3	6-181 (3.0)	4	4	—	—	①	—	④	10.5
	Voyager	K	4-153 (2.5)	4	4	—	4.8	①	—	④	8.5
	Voyager	J	4-153 (2.5)	4	4	—	4.8	①	—	④	8.5
	Voyager	3	6-181 (3.0)	4	4	—	—	①	—	④	10.5
	Dakota	K	4-153 (2.5)	4	4	—	4.0	15.6	②	⑤	9.8
	Dakota	X	6-239 (3.9)	4	4	—	4.0	17.2	② ③	⑤	⑥
1990	Caravan	K	4-153 (2.5)	4.5	4	—	4.8	①	—	④	8.5
	Caravan	J	4-153 (2.5)	4.5	4	—	4.8	①	—	④	8.5
	Caravan	3	6-181 (3.0)	4.5	4	—	—	①	—	④	10.5
	Caravan	R	6-201 (3.3)	4.5	4	—	—	①	—	④	10.5
	Voyager	K	4-153 (2.5)	4.5	4	—	4.8	①	—	④	8.5
	Voyager	J	4-153 (2.5)	4.5	4	—	4.8	①	—	④	8.5
	Voyager	3	6-181 (3.0)	4.5	4	—	—	①	—	④	10.5
	Voyager	R	6-201 (3.3)	4.5	4	—	—	①	—	④	10.5
	Town & Country	R	6-201 (3.3)	4.5	4	—	—	18.2	—	④	10.5
	Dakota	K	4-153 (2.5)	4.5	4	—	4.0	—	②	⑤	9.8
	Dakota	X	6-239 (3.9)	4.5	4	—	4.0	20.4	② ③	⑤	⑥

CAPACITIES

Year	Model	VIN	No. Cylinder Displacement cu. in (liter)	Engine Crankcase with Filter	Engine Crankcase without Filter	Transmission (pts.) 4-Spd	Transmission (pts.) 5-Spd	Transmission (pts.) Auto.	Drive Axle (pts.)	Fuel Tank (gal.)	Cooling System (qts.)
1991	Caravan	K	4-153 (2.5)	4.5	4	—	4.8	①	—	④	8.5
	Caravan	R	6-201 (3.3)	4.5	4	—	—	①	—	④	10.5
	Caravan	3	6-181 (3.0)	4.5	4	—	—	①	—	④	10.5
	Voyager	K	4-153 (2.5)	4.5	4	—	4.8	①	—	④	8.5
	Voyager	R	6-201 (3.3)	4.5	4	—	—	①	—	④	10.5
	Voyager	3	6-181 (3.0)	4.5	4	—	—	①	—	④	10.5
	Dakota	K	4-153 (2.5)	4.5	4	—	4.0	15.6	②	⑤	9.8
	Dakota	X	6-239 (3.9)	4.5	4	—	4.0	17.2	② ③	⑤	⑥
	Dakota	Y	8-318 (5.2)	4.5	4	—	4.0	20.4	② ③	⑤	⑥
1992	Caravan	K	4-153 (2.5)	4.5	4	—	4.8	①	—	④	8.5
	Caravan	3	6-181 (3.0)	4.5	4	—	—	①	—	④	10.5
	Caravan	R	6-201 (3.3)	4.5	4	—	—	①	—	④	10.5
	Voyager	K	4-153 (2.5)	4.5	4	—	4.8	①	—	④	8.5
	Voyager	3	6-181 (3.0)	4.5	4	—	—	①	—	④	10.5
	Voyager	R	6-201 (3.3)	4.5	4	—	—	①	—	④	10.5
	Town & Country	R	6-201 (3.3)	4.5	4	—	—	18.2	—	④	10.5
	Dakota	K	4-153 (2.5)	4.5	4	—	4.0	—	②	⑤	9.8
	Dakota	X	6-239 (3.9)	4.5	4	—	4.0	—	② ③	⑤	⑥
	Dakota	Y	8-318 (5.2)	4.5	4	—	4.0	20.4	② ③	⑤	⑥

① A413/A470 automatic transaxles (except
fleet): 17.8 pts.
A413/A470 automatic transaxles (fleet):
18.4 pts.
A413/A670 automatic transaxles with lockup:
17.0 pts.
A604: 18.2 pts.
② 7¼ in.: 3.0 pts.
8¼ in.: 4.4 pts.
③ Front axle: 2.6 pts.
④ Standard: 15 gal.
Optional: 20 gal.
⑤ Standard: 15 gal.
Optional: 22 gal.
⑥ Standard radiator: 14 qts.
Heavy duty radiator: 14.3 qts.

CAMSHAFT SPECIFICATIONS
All measurements given in inches.

Year	VIN	No. Cylinder Displacement cu. in. (liter)	Journal Diameter 1	Journal Diameter 2	Journal Diameter 3	Journal Diameter 4	Journal Diameter 5	Lobe Lift In.	Lobe Lift Ex.	Bearing Clearance	Camshaft End Play
1988	C	4-135 (2.2)	1.375–1.376	1.375–1.376	1.375–1.376	1.375–1.376	1.375–1.376	NA	NA	—	0.005–0.020
	K	4-153 (2.5)	1.375–1.376	1.375–1.376	1.375–1.376	1.375–1.376	1.375–1.376	NA	NA	—	0.005–0.020
	3	6-181 (3.0)	NA	NA	NA	NA	NA	①	①	—	NA
	M	6-239 (3.9)	1.998–1.999	1.967–1.968	1.951–1.952	1.561–1.562	—	0.373	0.400	0.001–0.005	0.002–0.010

CAMSHAFT SPECIFICATIONS
All measurements given in inches.

Year	VIN	No. Cylinder Displacement cu. in. (liter)	Journal Diameter 1	2	3	4	5	Lobe Lift In.	Ex.	Bearing Clearance	Camshaft End Play
1989	K	4-153 (2.5)	1.375–1.376	1.375–1.376	1.375–1.376	1.375–1.376	1.375–1.376	NA	NA	—	0.005–0.020
	J	4-153 (2.5)	1.375–1.376	1.375–1.376	1.375–1.376	1.375–1.376	1.375–1.376	NA	NA	—	0.005–0.020
	3	6-181 (3.0)	NA	NA	NA	NA	NA	①	①	—	NA
	X	6-239 (3.9)	1.998–1.999	1.967–1.968	1.951–1.952	1.561–1.562	—	0.373	0.400	0.001–0.005	0.002–0.010
1990	K	4-153 (2.5)	1.375–1.376	1.375–1.376	1.375–1.376	1.375–1.376	1.375–1.376	NA	NA	—	0.005–0.020
	J	4-153 (2.5)	1.375–1.376	1.375–1.376	1.375–1.376	1.375–1.376	1.375–1.376	NA	NA	—	0.005–0.013
	3	6-181 (3.0)	NA	NA	NA	NA	NA	①	①	—	NA
	R	6-201 (3.3)	1.997–1.999	1.980–1.982	1.965–1.967	1.949–1.952	—	0.400	0.400	0.001–0.005	0.005–0.012
	X	6-239 (3.9)	1.998–1.999	1.967–1.968	1.951–1.952	1.561–1.562	—	0.373	0.400	0.001–0.005	0.002–0.010
1991	K	4-153 (2.5)	1.375–1.376	1.375–1.376	1.375–1.376	1.375–1.376	1.375–1.376	NA	NA	—	0.005–0.020
	3	6-181 (3.0)	NA	NA	NA	NA	NA	①	①	—	NA
	R	6-201 (3.3)	1.997–1.999	1.980–1.982	1.965–1.967	1.949–1.952	—	0.400	0.400	0.001–0.005	0.005–0.012
	X	6-239 (3.9)	1.998–1.999	1.967–1.968	1.951–1.952	1.561–1.562	—	0.373	0.400	0.001–0.005	0.002–0.010
	Y	8-318 (5.2)	1.998–1.999	1.982–1.983	1.967–1.968	1.951–1.952	1.5605–1.5615	0.373	0.400	0.001–0.003	0.002–0.010
1992	K	4-153 (2.5)	1.375–1.376	1.375–1.376	1.375–1.376	1.375–1.376	1.375–1.376	NA	NA	—	0.005–0.020
	3	6-181 (3.0)	NA	NA	NA	NA	NA	①	①	—	NA
	R	6-201 (3.3)	1.997–1.999	1.980–1.982	1.965–1.967	1.949–1.952	—	0.400	0.400	0.001–0.005	0.005–0.012
	X	6-239 (3.9)	1.998–1.999	1.967–1.968	1.951–1.952	1.561–1.562	—	0.373	0.400	0.001–0.005	0.002–0.010
	Y	8-318 (5.2)	1.998–1.999	1.982–1.983	1.967–1.968	1.951–1.952	1.5605–1.5615	0.373	0.400	0.001–0.003	0.002–0.010

NA—Not available
① Height of cam lobe: 1.604–1.624 in.

CRANKSHAFT AND CONNECTING ROD SPECIFICATIONS
All measurements are given in inches.

Year	VIN	No. Cylinder Displacement cu. in. (liter)	Crankshaft				Connecting Rod		
			Main Brg. Journal Dia.	Main Brg. Oil Clearance	Shaft End-play	Thrust on No.	Journal Diameter	Oil Clearance	Side Clearance
1988	C	4-135 (2.2)	2.362–2.363	0.0003–0.0031	0.002–0.007	3	1.968–1.969	0.0008–0.0034	0.005–0.013
	K	4-153 (2.5)	2.362–2.363	0.0003–0.0031	0.002–0.007	3	1.968–1.969	0.0008–0.0034	0.005–0.013
	3	6-181 (3.0)	2.361–2.363	0.0006–0.0020	0.002–0.010	3	1.968–1.969	0.0008–0.0028	0.004–0.010
	M	6-239 (3.9)	2.500–2.501	①	0.002–0.010	2	2.124–2.125	0.0005–0.0022	0.006–0.014
1989	K	4-153 (2.5)	2.362–2.363	0.0003–0.0031	0.002–0.007	3	1.968–1.969	0.0008–0.0034	0.005–0.013
	J	4-153 (2.5)	2.362–2.363	0.0004–0.0023	0.002–0.010	3	1.968–1.969	0.0008–0.0034	0.005–0.013
	3	6-181 (3.0)	2.361–2.363	0.0006–0.0020	0.002–0.010	3	1.968–1.969	0.0008–0.0028	0.004–0.010
	X	6-239 (3.9)	2.500–2.501	①	0.002–0.010	2	2.124–2.125	0.0005–0.0022	0.006–0.014
1990	K	4-153 (2.5)	2.362–2.363	0.0003–0.0031	0.002–0.007	3	1.968–1.969	0.0008–0.0034	0.005–0.013
	J	4-153 (2.5)	2.362–2.363	0.0004–0.0023	0.002–0.010	3	1.968–1.969	0.0008–0.0034	0.005–0.013
	3	6-181 (3.0)	2.361–2.363	0.0006–0.0020	0.002–0.010	3	1.968–1.969	0.0008–0.0028	0.004–0.010
	R	6-201 (3.3)	2.519	0.0007–0.0022	0.001–0.007	2	2.283	0.0008–0.0030	0.005–0.015
	X	6-239 (3.9)	2.500–2.501	①	0.002–0.010	2	2.124–2.125	0.0005–0.0022	0.006–0.014
1991	K	4-153 (2.5)	2.362–2.363	0.0003–0.0031	0.002–0.007	3	1.968–1.969	0.0008–0.0034	0.005–0.013
	3	6-181 (3.0)	2.361–2.363	0.0006–0.0020	0.002–0.010	3	1.968–1.969	0.0008–0.0028	0.004–0.010
	R	6-201 (3.3)	2.519	0.0007–0.0022	0.001–0.007	2	2.283	0.0008–0.0030	0.005–0.015
	X	6-239 (3.9)	2.500–2.501	①	0.002–0.010	2	2.124–2.125	0.0005–0.0022	0.006–0.014
	Y	8-318 (5.2)	2.4995–2.5005	①	0.002–0.007	3	2.124–2.125	0.0005–0.0022	0.006–0.014
1992	K	4-153 (2.5)	2.362–2.363	0.0003–0.0031	0.002–0.007	3	1.968–1.969	0.0008–0.0034	0.005–0.013
	3	6-181 (3.0)	2.361–2.363	0.0006–0.0020	0.002–0.010	3	1.968–1.969	0.0008–0.0028	0.004–0.010
	R	6-201 (3.3)	2.519	0.0007–0.0022	0.001–0.007	2	2.283	0.0008–0.0030	0.005–0.015
	X	6-239 (3.9)	2.500–2.501	①	0.002–0.010	2	2.124–2.125	0.0005–0.0022	0.006–0.014
	Y	8-318 (5.2)	2.4995–2.5005	①	0.002–0.007	3	2.124–2.125	0.0005–0.0022	0.006–0.014

① No. 1: 0.0005–0.0015 in.

VALVE SPECIFICATIONS
All measurements given in inches.

Year	VIN	No. Cylinder Displacement cu. in. (liter)	Seat Angle (deg.)	Face Angle (deg.)	Spring Test Pressure (lbs.)	Spring Installed Height (in.)	Stem-to-Guide Clearance (in.)		Stem Diameter (in.)	
							Intake	Exhaust	Intake	Exhaust
1988	C	4-135 (2.2)	45	45	95	1.65	0.001–0.003	0.0030–0.0047	0.3124	0.3103
	K	4-153 (2.5)	45	45	115	1.65	0.001–0.003	0.0030–0.0047	0.3124	0.3103
	3	6-181 (3.0)	44.5	45.5	73	1.59	0.001–0.002	0.002–0.003	0.313–0.314	0.312–0.313
	M	6-239 (3.9)	45	45	①	②	0.001–0.003	0.002–0.004	0.372–0.373	0.371–0.372
1989	K	4-153 (2.5)	45	45	115	1.65	0.001–0.003	0.0030–0.0047	0.3124	0.3103
	J	4-153 (2.5)	45	45	115	1.65	0.001–0.003	0.0030–0.0047	0.3124	0.3103
	3	6-181 (3.0)	44.5	45.5	73	1.59	0.001–0.002	0.002–0.003	0.313–0.314	0.312–0.313
	X	6-239 (3.9)	45	45	①	②	0.001–0.003	0.002–0.004	0.372–0.373	0.371–0.372
1990	K	4-153 (2.5)	45	45	115	1.65	0.001–0.003	0.0030–0.0047	0.3124	0.3103
	J	4-153 (2.5)	45	45	115	1.65	0.001–0.003	0.0030–0.0047	0.3124	0.3103
	3	6-181 (3.0)	44.5	45.5	73	1.59	0.001–0.002	0.002–0.003	0.313–0.314	0.312–0.313
	R	6-201 (3.3)	45	44.5	60	1.56	0.001–0.003	0.002–0.006	0.311–0.312	0.311–0.312
	X	6-239 (3.9)	45	45	①	②	0.001–0.003	0.002–0.004	0.372–0.373	0.371–0.372
1991	K	4-153 (2.5)	45	45	115	1.65	0.001–0.003	0.0030–0.0047	0.3124	0.3103
	3	6-181 (3.0)	44.5	45.5	73	1.59	0.001–0.002	0.002–0.003	0.313–0.314	0.312–0.313
	R	6-201 (3.3)	45	44.5	60	1.56	0.001–0.003	0.002–0.004	0.311–0.312	0.311–0.312
	X	6-239 (3.9)	45	45	①	②	0.001–0.003	0.002–0.004	0.372–0.373	0.371–0.372
	Y	8-318 (5.2)	45	45	①	②	0.001–0.003	0.002–0.004	0.3125	0.3215

VALVE SPECIFICATIONS
All measurements given in inches.

Year	VIN	No. Cylinder Displacement cu. in. (liter)	Seat Angle (deg.)	Face Angle (deg.)	Spring Test Pressure (lbs.)	Spring Installed Height (in.)	Stem-to-Guide Clearance (in.)		Stem Diameter (in.)	
							Intake	Exhaust	Intake	Exhaust
1992	K	4-153 (2.5)	45	45	115	1.65	0.001–0.003	0.0030–0.0047	0.3124	0.3103
	3	6-181 (3.0)	44.5	45.5	73	1.59	0.001–0.002	0.002–0.003	0.313–0.314	0.312–0.313
	R	6-201 (3.3)	45	44.5	60	1.56	0.001–0.003	0.002–0.006	0.311–0.312	0.311–0.312
	X	6-239 (3.9)	45	45	①	②	0.001–0.003	0.002–0.004	0.372–0.373	0.371–0.372
	Y	8-318 (5.2)	45	45	①	②	0.001–0.003	0.002–0.004	0.3125	0.3125

① Intake: 170–184 lbs.
Exhaust: 180–194 lbs.
② Intake: 1.625–1.688 in.
Exhaust: 1.453–1.516 in.

PISTON AND RING SPECIFICATIONS
All measurements are given in inches.

Year	VIN	No. Cylinder Displacement cu. in. (liter)	Piston Clearance	Ring Gap			Ring Side Clearance		
				Top Compression	Bottom Compression	Oil Control	Top Compression	Bottom Compression	Oil Control
1988	C	4-135 (2.2)	0.0005–0.0015	0.010–0.021	0.011–0.021	0.015–0.035	0.0015–0.0031	0.0015–0.0031	0.0002–0.0080
	K	4-153 (2.5)	0.0005–0.0015	0.010–0.021	0.011–0.021	0.015–0.035	0.0015–0.0031	0.0015–0.0031	0.0002–0.0080
	3	6-181 (3.0)	0.0008–0.0015	0.012–0.018	0.010–0.016	0.012–0.035	0.0020–0.0035	0.0008–0.0020	NA
	M	6-239 (3.9)	0.0005–0.0015	0.010–0.020	0.010–0.020	0.015–0.055	0.0015–0.0030	0.0015–0.0030	0.0002–0.0050
1989	K	4-153 (2.5)	0.0005–0.0015	0.010–0.021	0.011–0.021	0.015–0.035	0.0015–0.0031	0.0015–0.0031	0.0002–0.0080
	J	4-153 (2.5)	0.0006–0.0018	0.010–0.020	0.008–0.019	0.015–0.055	0.0016–0.0030	0.0016–0.0030	0.0002–0.0080
	3	6-181 (3.0)	0.0008–0.0015	0.012–0.018	0.010–0.016	0.012–0.035	0.0020–0.0035	0.0008–0.0020	NA
	X	6-239 (3.9)	0.0005–0.0015	0.010–0.020	0.010–0.020	0.015–0.055	0.0015–0.0030	0.0015–0.0030	0.0002–0.0050
1990	K	4-153 (2.5)	0.0005–0.0015	0.010–0.021	0.011–0.021	0.015–0.035	0.0015–0.0031	0.0015–0.0031	0.0002–0.0080
	J	4-153 (2.5)	0.0006–0.0018	0.010–0.020	0.008–0.019	0.015–0.055	0.0016–0.0030	0.0016–0.0030	0.0002–0.0080
	3	6-181 (3.0)	0.0008–0.0015	0.012–0.018	0.010–0.016	0.012–0.035	0.0020–0.0035	0.0008–0.0020	NA
	R	6-201 (3.3)	0.0009–0.0022	0.012–0.022	0.012–0.022	0.010–0.040	0.0012–0.0037	0.0012–0.0037	0.0005–0.0089
	X	6-239 (3.9)	0.0005–0.0015	0.010–0.020	0.010–0.020	0.015–0.055	0.0015–0.0030	0.0015–0.0030	0.0002–0.0050

PISTON AND RING SPECIFICATIONS
All measurements are given in inches.

| Year | VIN | No. Cylinder Displacement cu. in. (liter) | Piston Clearance | Ring Gap | | | Ring Side Clearance | | |
				Top Compression	Bottom Compression	Oil Control	Top Compression	Bottom Compression	Oil Control
1991	K	4-153 (2.5)	0.0005–0.0015	0.010–0.021	0.011–0.021	0.015–0.035	0.0015–0.0031	0.0015–0.0031	0.0002–0.0080
	3	6-181 (3.0)	0.0008–0.0015	0.012–0.018	0.010–0.016	0.012–0.035	0.0020–0.0035	0.0008–0.0020	NA
	R	6-201 (3.3)	0.0009–0.0022	0.012–0.022	0.012–0.022	0.010–0.040	0.0012–0.0037	0.0012–0.0037	0.0005–0.0089
	X	6-239 (3.9)	0.0005–0.0015	0.010–0.020	0.010–0.020	0.015–0.055	0.0015–0.0030	0.0015–0.0030	0.0002–0.0050
	Y	8-318 (5.2)	0.0005–0.0015	0.010–0.020	0.010–0.020	0.015–0.055	0.0015–0.0030	0.0015–0.0030	0.0002–0.0050
1992	K	4-153 (2.5)	0.0005–0.0015	0.010–0.021	0.011–0.021	0.015–0.035	0.0015–0.0031	0.0015–0.0031	0.0002–0.0080
	3	6-181 (3.0)	0.0008–0.0015	0.012–0.018	0.010–0.016	0.012–0.035	0.0020–0.0035	0.0008–0.0020	NA
	R	6-201 (3.3)	0.0009–0.0022	0.012–0.022	0.012–0.022	0.010–0.040	0.0012–0.0037	0.0012–0.0037	0.0005–0.0089
	X	6-239 (3.9)	0.0005–0.0015	0.010–0.020	0.010–0.020	0.015–0.055	0.0015–0.0030	0.0015–0.0030	0.0002–0.0050
	Y	8-318 (5.2)	0.0005–0.0015	0.010–0.020	0.010–0.020	0.015–0.055	0.0015–0.0030	0.0015–0.0030	0.0002–0.0050

NA—Not available

TORQUE SPECIFICATIONS
All readings in ft. lbs.

| Year | VIN | No. Cylinder Displacement cu. in. (liter) | Cylinder Head Bolts | Main Bearing Bolts | Rod Bearing Bolts | Crankshaft Pulley Bolts | Flywheel Bolts | Manifold | | Spark Plugs |
								Intake	Exhaust	
1988	C	4-135 (2.2)	①	30②	40②	50	70	17	17	26
	K	4-153 (2.5)	①	30②	40②	50	70	17	17	26
	3	6-181 (3.0)	80	60	38	110	70	17	17	20
	M	6-239 (3.9)	105	85	45	135	55	45	④	30
1989	K	4-153 (2.5)	①	30②	40②	50	70	17	17	26
	J	4-153 (2.5)	①	30②	40②	50	70	17	17	26
	3	6-181 (3.0)	80	60	38	110	70	17	17	20
	X	6-239 (3.9)	105	85	45	135	55	45	④	30
1990	K	4-153 (2.5)	①	30②	40②	50	70	17	17	26
	J	4-153 (2.5)	①	30②	40②	50	70	17	17	26
	3	6-181 (3.0)	80	60	38	110	70	17	17	20
	R	6-201 (3.3)	③	30②	40②	40	70	17	17	30
	X	6-239 (3.9)	105	85	45	135	55	45	④	30

TORQUE SPECIFICATIONS
All readings in ft. lbs.

Year	VIN	No. Cylinder Displacement cu. in. (liter)	Cylinder Head Bolts	Main Bearing Bolts	Rod Bearing Bolts	Crankshaft Pulley Bolts	Flywheel Bolts	Manifold Intake	Manifold Exhaust	Spark Plugs
1991	K	4-153 (2.5)	①	30②	40②	50	70	17	17	26
	3	6-181 (3.0)	80	60	38	110	70	17	17	20
	R	6-201 (3.3)	③	30②	40②	40	70	17	17	30
	X	6-239 (3.9)	105	85	45	135	55	45	④	30
	Y	8-318 (5.2)	105	85	45	135	55	45	④	30
1992	K	4-153 (2.5)	①	30②	40②	50	70	17	17	26
	3	6-181 (3.0)	80	60	38	110	70	17	17	20
	R	6-201 (3.3)	③	30②	40②	40	70	17	17	30
	X	6-239 (3.9)	105	85	45	135	55	45	④	30
	Y	8-318 (5.2)	105	85	45	135	55	45	④	30

① Sequence: 45, 65, 65 plus ¼ turn
② Plus ¼ turn
③ Sequence: 45, 65, 65 plus ¼ turn, torque the small bolt in the rear of the head to 25 ft. lbs. last.
④ Bolts: 20 ft. lbs.
 Nuts: 15 ft. lbs.

BRAKE SPECIFICATIONS
All measurements in inches unless noted

Year	Model	Lug Nut Torque (ft. lbs.)	Master Cylinder Bore	Brake Disc Minimum Thickness	Brake Disc Maximum Runout	Standard Brake Drum Diameter	Minimum Lining Thickness Front	Minimum Lining Thickness Rear
1988	Caravan	95	0.94	0.80	0.005	9	0.06	0.06
	Voyager	95	0.94	0.80	0.005	9	0.06	0.06
	Dakota	85	NA	0.81	0.004	9	0.06	0.06
1989	Caravan	95	0.94	0.80	0.005	9	0.06	0.06
	Voyager	95	0.94	0.80	0.005	9	0.06	0.06
	Dakota	85	NA	0.81	0.004	9	0.06	0.06
1990	Caravan	95	0.94	0.80	0.005	9	0.06	0.06
	Voyager	95	0.94	0.80	0.005	9	0.06	0.06
	Town & Country	95	0.94	0.80	0.005	9	0.06	0.06
	Dakota	85	NA	0.81	0.004	9	0.06	0.06
1991	Caravan	95	0.94	0.80	0.005	9	0.06	0.06
	Voyager	95	0.94	0.80	0.005	9	0.06	0.06
	Town & Country	95	0.94	0.80	0.005	9	0.06	0.06
	Dakota	85	NA	0.81	0.004	9	0.06	0.06
1992	Caravan	95	0.94	0.80	0.005	9	0.06	0.06
	Voyager	95	0.94	0.80	0.005	9	0.06	0.06
	Town & Country	95	0.94	0.80	0.005	9	0.06	0.06
	Dakota	85	NA	0.81	0.004	9	0.06	0.06

NA—Not available

WHEEL ALIGNMENT

Year	Model		Caster Range (deg.)	Caster Preferred Setting (deg.)	Camber Range (deg.)	Camber Preferred Setting (deg.)	Toe-in (in.)	Steering Axis Inclination (deg.)
1988	Caravan	front	①	②	0.25N–0.75P	0.30P	0.06	—
		rear	—	—	1.00N–0.50P	0.25N	0.00	—
	Voyager	front	①	②	0.25N–0.75P	0.30P	0.06	—
		rear	—	—	1.00N–0.50P	0.25N	0.00	—
	Dakota	—	0.50P–2.50P	1.50P	0–1P	0.50P	0.25	—
1989	Caravan	front	①	②	0.25N–0.75P	0.30P	0.06	—
		rear			1.00N–0.50P	0.25N	0.00	
	Voyager	front	①	②	0.25N–0.75P	0.30P	0.06	
		rear	—	—	1.00N–0.50P	0.25N	0.00	—
	Dakota	—	0.50P–2.50P	1.50P	0–1P	0.50P	0.25	—
1990	Caravan	front	①	②	0.25N–0.75P	0.30P	0.06	—
		rear	—	—	1.00N–0.50P	0.25N	0.00	—
	Voyager	front	①	②	0.25N–0.75P	0.30P	0.06	—
		rear	—	—	1.00N–0.50P	0.25N	0.00	—
	Town & Country	front	①	②	0.25N–0.75P	0.30P	0.06	—
		rear	—	—	1.00N–0.50P	0.25N	0.00	—
	Dakota	—	0.50P–2.50P	1.50P	0–1P	0.50P	0.25	—
1991	Caravan	front	①	②	0.25N–0.75P	0.30P	0.06	—
		rear	—	—	1.00N–0.50P	0.25N	0.00	—
	Voyager	front	①	②	0.25N–0.75P	0.30P	0.06	—
		rear	—	—	1.00N–0.50P	0.25N	0.00	—
	Town & Country	front	①	②	0.25N–0.75P	0.30P	0.06	—
		rear	—	—	1.00N–0.50P	0.25N	0.00	—
	Dakota	—	0.50P–2.50P	1.50P	0–1P	0.50P	0.25	—
1992	Caravan	front	①	②	0.25N–0.75P	0.30P	0.06	—
		rear	—	—	1.00N–0.50P	0.25N	0.00	—
	Voyager	front	①	②	0.25N–0.75P	0.30P	0.06	—
		rear	—	—	1.00N–0.50P	0.25N	0.00	—
	Town & Country	front	①	②	0.25N–0.75P	0.30P	0.06	—
		rear	—	—	1.00N–0.50P	0.25N	0.00	—
	Dakota	—	0.50P–2.50P	1.50P	0–1P	0.50P	0.25	—

N—Negative
P—Positive
① Not adjustable; maximum variation between sides should not exceed 1.5°
② Van: 0.40P   Wagon: 0.70P

ENGINE ELECTRICAL

NOTE: Disconnecting the negative battery cable on some vehicles may interfere with the functions of the on board computer systems and may require the computer to undergo a relearning process, once the negative battery cable is reconnected.

Distributor

Removal

EXCEPT 1992 3.9L AND 5.2L ENGINES

1. Disconnect the negative battery cable.
2. Disconnect the distributor pickup lead wires. Remove the splash shield, if equipped.
3. Unscrew the distributor cap hold-down screws and lift off the distributor cap with all ignition wires connected. Remove the coil wire, if necessary.
4. Matchmark the rotor to the distributor housing and the distributor housing to the engine.

NOTE: Do not crank the engine during this procedure. If the engine is cranked, the matchmark must be disregarded.

5. Remove the hold-down bolt and clamp.
6. Remove the distributor from the engine.

1992 3.9L AND 5.2L ENGINES

1. Disconnect negative battery cable.
2. Matchmark the original position of the distributor housing to the engine.
3. Unscrew the distributor cap hold-down screws and lift off the distributor cap with all ignition wires still connected. Remove the coil wire, if necessary.
4. Before distributor is removed the No. 1 piston must be at TDC of the compression stroke and the mark on the vibration damper must be aligned with **0** on the timing indicator.
5. Check to assure alignment of the distributor rotor to the alignment mark on the distributor switch plate. If mark is not aligned, reset engine position.
6. Disconnect distributor switch plate wiring harness and remove distributor rotor from shaft.
7. Remove the hold-down bolt and clamp.
8. Remove the distributor from the engine.

Distributor cap terminal routing—3.0L engine

Installation

TIMING NOT DISTURBED

1. Install a new distributor housing O-ring.
2. Install the distributor in the engine so the rotor is aligned with the matchmark on the housing and the housing is aligned with the matchmark on the engine. Make sure the distributor is fully seated and the distributor shaft is fully engaged. On 1992 3.9L and 5.2L engines, install distributor in engine so the matchmark on housing is aligned and the rotor is aligned with mark on the switch plate. Turn housing to align, if necessary.
3. Install the hold-down clamp and snug the hold-down bolt or install the nut.
4. Connect the distributor pickup lead wires. Install the splash shield, if equipped.
5. Install the distributor cap and tighten the retaining screws.
6. Connect the negative battery cable.
7. Adjust the ignition timing and tighten the hold-down bolt. On 1992 3.9L and 5.2L engines, base ignition timing can not be adjusted.

TIMING DISTURBED

1. Install a new distributor housing O-ring.
2. Position the engine so the No. 1 piston is at TDC of the compression stroke and the mark on the vibration damper is aligned with **0** on the timing indicator.
3. Install the distributor in the engine so the rotor is aligned with the position of the No. 1 ignition wire on the distributor cap and the housing is aligned with the matchmark on the engine. On 1992 3.9L and 5.2L engines, install the distributor in engine so the matchmark on housing is aligned and the rotor is aligned with the No.1 ignition wire. Turn the distributor housing as needed to align the rotor with the mark on the switch plate. Make sure the distributor is fully seated and the distributor shaft is fully engaged.

NOTE: There are distributor cap runners inside the cap on 3.0L engine. Make sure the rotor is pointing to where the No. 1 runner originates inside the cap and not where the No. 1 ignition wire plugs into the cap.

4. Install the hold-down clamp and snug the hold-down bolt or install the nut.
5. Connect the distributor pickup lead wires. Install the splash shield, if equipped.

Rotor alignment mark—1992 3.9L and 5.2L engines

6. Install the distributor cap and tighten the screws.

7. Connect the negative battery cable.

8. Adjust the ignition timing and tighten the hold-down nut or bolt. On 1992 3.9L and 5.2L engines, base ignition timing can not be adjusted.

Distributorless Ignition

Removal and Installation

IGNITION COIL

1. Disconnect the negative battery cable.
2. Remove the spark plug wires from the coil.
3. Disconnect the electrical connector.
4. Remove the coil fasteners.
5. Remove the coil from the ignition module.
6. The installation is the reverse of the removal procedure.

CRANKSHAFT POSITION SENSOR

1. Disconnect the negative battery cable.
2. Disconnect the sensor lead at the harness connector.
3. Remove the sensor retaining bolt.
4. Pull the sensor straight up out the transaxle housing.
5. If the sensor is being reinstalled, remove any remains of the old spacer completely and attach a new spacer to the sensor. If a new spacer is not used, the sensor will not function properly. New sensors are packaged with a new spacer.

To install:

6. Install the sensor to the tranaxle housing and push the sensor down until it contacts the drive plate.
7. Hold in this position and install the retaining bolt. Torque to 9 ft. lbs. (12 Nm).
8. Connect the sensor lead wire.

CAMSHAFT POSITION SENSOR

1. Disconnect the negative battery cable.
2. Disconnect the sensor lead at the harness connector.
3. Loosen the sensor retaining bolt sufficiently to allow the slotted mounting surface to slide past.
4. Pull the sensor straight up and out of the chain case cover. Resistance may be high due to the rubber O-ring.
5. If the sensor is being reinstalled, remove any remains of the old spacer completely and attach a new spacer to the sensor.

Crank position sensor location—3.3L engine

Cam position sensor location—3.3L engine

If a new spacer is not used, the sensor will not function properly. New sensors are packaged with a new spacer.

To install:

6. Inspect the O-ring for damage and replace if necessary.
7. Lubricate the O-ring with oil. Install the sensor to the chain case cover and push the sensor into its bore until contact is made with the cam timing gear.
8. Hold in this position and tighten the bolt to 9 ft. lbs. (12 Nm).
9. Connect the wire and position away from the accessory drive belt.

Ignition Timing

Adjustment

NOTE: The ignition timing on the distributorless 3.3L engine and 1992 3.9L and 5.2L engines cannot be checked or changed.

1. Start the engine, set the parking brake and run the engine until normal operating temperature is reached. Keep all lights and accessories **OFF**.
2. If a magnetic timing unit is available, insert the probe into

Ignition coil removal and installation—3.3L engine

the receptacle near the timing scale. The scale is located near the crankshaft pulley on 3.0L, 3.9L and 5.2L engines or on the bell housing on 2.2L and 2.5L engines.

3. If a magnetic timing unit is not available, connect a conventional power timing light to the No. 1 cylinder spark plug wire.

4. Connect the red lead of a tachometer to the negative primary terminal of the coil and connect the black lead to a good ground.

5. Disconnect and plug the distributor vacuum advance hose at the computer or distributor. If equipped with a carbureted 2.2L engine, disconnect the carburetor 6-way electrical connector and remove the violet wire from the connector and reconnect the connector. This disables the electronic spark advance. Set the idle speed according to the Vehicle Emission Control Information (VECI) label.

6. If equipped with Electronic Fuel Injection (EFI), disconnect the coolant sensor located near the thermostat housing. The Check Engine light on the instrument panel must be **ON**. On 1989–92 vehicles, connect the Diagnostic Readout Box II (DRB II) and access the Basic Timing Mode. If the DRB II is not available, disconnect the coolant sensor located near the thermostat housing. The Check Engine light on the instrument panel must be **ON**.

7. Aim the timing light at the timing scale or read the magnetic timing unit.

8. Loosen the distributor hold-down bolt just enough so the disributor can be rotated.

9. Turn the distributor in the proper direction until the specified timing according to the VECI label is reached. Tighten the hold-down bolt and recheck the timing and idle speed.

10. Turn the engine OFF. Remove the jumper wire, if used. Connect the vacuum hose(s) or coolant sensor (make sure the Check Engine light does not come on when restarted). Disconnect the timing apparatus and tachometer. Reinstal the violet wire into the carburetor connector, if removed.

11. If the coolant temperature sensor was disconnected, erase the created fault code using the Erase Fault Code mode on the DRB II. If the DRB II is not available, the code can be erased by disconnecting the battery, although it is not recommended.

NOTE: If the battery is disconnected, radio memory will be lost and other fault codes that may have been stored in the computer's memory will be erased. If the coolant sensor code is not erased at this point, it will disappear after 50–100 vehicle key on/off cycles providing there is no problem with that circuit.

Alternator

For further information, please refer to "Alternators" in the Unit Repair section.

Precautions

Several precautions must be observed when working with the alternator to avoid damaging the unit.

• If the battery is removed for any reason, make sure it is reconnected with the correct polarity. Reversing the battery connections may result in damage to the one-way rectifiers.

• When utilizing a booster battery as a starting aid, always connect the positive to positive terminals and the negative terminal from the booster battery to a good engine ground on the vehicle being started.

• Never use a fast charger as a booster to start vehicles.

• Disconnect the battery cables when charging the battery with a fast charger.

• Never attempt to polarize the alternator.

• Do not use test lights of more than 12 volts when checking diode continuity.

• Do not short across or ground any of the alternator terminals.

• The polarity of the battery, alternator and regulator must be matched and considered before making any electrical connections within the system.

• Never separate the alternator on an open circuit. Make sure all connections within the circuit are clean and tight.

• Disconnect the battery ground terminal when performing any service on electrical components.

• Disconnect the battery if arc welding is to be done on the vehicle.

Belt Tension Adjustment

NOTE: The belt tension is automatically adjusted by a dynamic tensioner on the 3.0L, 3.3L, 3.9L and 5.2L engines. Periodic adjustment is not necessary.

1. Loosen the pivot bolt slightly.

2. Raise the vehicle and support safely, if necessary. Remove the splash shield, if equipped. Loosen the adjuster slot nut or bolt just enough so the alternator can be moved.

3. Apply tension to the alternator until the belt(s) deflect about ¼–½ in. under a 10 lb. load. Torque the adjuster strap bolt to 17 ft. lbs. (23 Nm). Torque the pivot bolt to 30 ft. lbs. (41 Nm).

4. If the bracket is equipped with an adjuster bolt, first loosen the locknut, if equipped and tighten the bolt until the belt(s) deflect about ¼–½ in. under a 10 lb. load. Tighten the adjuster slot bolt and pivot bolt.

Removal and Installation

1. Disconnect the negative battery cable.

2. On some 2.2L and 2.5L engines, remove the air conditioning compressor and position it to the side. Remove the oil filter to allow the alternator to be removed from above, if possible.

3. On 3.0L, 3.3L, 3.9L and 5.2L engines, release the dynamic belt tensioner and remove the belt. On all other engines, loosen the mounting bolts, move the alternator toward the engine and remove the drive belt(s).

4. Remove the mounting bolts, spacers and adjuster bolt. Remove the alternator from the brackets. On 1992 3.9L and 5.2L engine the factory recommends removal of the idler pulley.

5. Remove the battery positive, field and ground terminals from the rear of the alternator. Remove the wire harness hold-down screw from the alternator, if equipped.

To install:

6. Connect all wiring to the proper terminals on the rear of the alternator and install the wire harness hold-down screw, if equipped.

7. Position the alternator in the mounting brackets.

8. Install the spacers, pivot bolt, adjuster slot bolt or nut and adjuster bolt, if equipped. Install the air conditioning compressor and oil filter, if removed.

9. Install idler pulley and bushing, if removed and tighten bolts to 30 ft. lbs. (41 Nm).

10. Install belt(s) and adjust the belt tension, if necessary.

11. Connect the negative battery cable.

Voltage Regulator

For further information, please refer to "Alternators" in the Unit Repair section.

Removal and Installation

NOTE: The voltage regulator is integrated into the circuitry of the Single Module Engine Controller (SMEC) or Single Board Engine Controller (SBEC) on vehicles equipped with EFI and is not serviceable.

1. Disconnect the negative battery cable.

2. Unplug the connector from the voltage regulator.

3. Remove the retaining screws and remove the regulator from the vehicle.

4. The installation is the reverse of the removal procedure. Make sure the connector retainer is properly clipped in place.

Starter

For further information, please refer to "Starters" in the Unit Repair section.

Removal and Installation

EXCEPT 1992 3.9L AND 5.2L ENGINES WITH 4WD

1. Disconnect the negative battery cable.
2. Some engines are equipped with bolts that attach starter to flywheel housing. Remove as required.
3. Raise the vehicle and support safely. Remove skid plate, if equipped.
4. Remove the rear mount from the starter. Remove the heat shield from the starter, if equipped.
5. Unbolt the starter, remove the exhaust bracket and automatic transmission oil cooler tube bracket, if equipped. To aid in removal slide starter forward to clear starter gear housing nose and allow starter to come down past the exhaust pipe.
6. Disconnect the solenoid lead wires from the starter and remove the starter from the vehicle.

To install:

7. Connect the solenoid lead wires and install the heat shield, if equipped.
8. Install the starter to bell housing attaching bolt, if equipped. Install the mounting bolt loosely. Install the automatic transmission oil cooler tube bracket and exhaust bracket, if equipped. Install the lower mounting nut. On 3.9L and 5.2L engines, torque starter upper mounting bolt to 50 ft. lbs. (68 Nm) and the stud nut to 20 ft. lbs. (27 Nm).
9. On all other engines, install mounting bolts to 40 ft. lbs. (54 Nm). Install the rear mount to the starter.
10. Connect the negative battery cable and check the starter for proper operation.

1992 3.9L AND 5.2L ENGINES WITH 4WD

1. Disconnect negative battery cable.

Removing or installing the starter—2.2L and 2.5L engines

2. Raise and safely support vehicle.
3. Remove skid plate, if equipped.
4. Remove lower retaining nut from stud through the front of the vehicle.
5. Lower vehicle and remove 15mm steering shaft coupler bolt.
6. Rotate coupler clip on shaft and slide the upper half of the shaft toward the rear of the vehicle.
7. Remove the upper starter mounting bolt. Move starter forward to clear the stud and lift starter upward to gain access to the cable connections.
8. Remove cable from terminal adapter and remove starter motor.

To install:

9. Install cable to starter adapter and install into position. Install upper mounting bolt to 50 ft. lbs. (68 Nm). Install lower retainer nut to 20 ft. lbs. (27 Nm).
10. Install steering shaft and tighten bolt to 35 ft. lbs. (47 Nm).
11. Install negative battery cable and skid plate. Check operation of starter motor.

CHASSIS ELECTRICAL

Air Bag

Disarming

To disarm the air bag, disconnect the negative battery. Allow system capacitor to discharge for 2 minutes before working on system. Failure to disarm the system may result in deployment of the air bag and possible personal injury.

Heater Blower Motor

Removal and Installation

WITHOUT AIR CONDITIONING

1988–90 Caravan, Voyager and Town & Country

1. Disconnect the negative battery cable.
2. Lower right side instrument panel trim cover and right cowl trim panel, as required. Disconnect the blower lead wire connector.
3. Remove the 2 screws at the top of the blower housing that secure it to the unit cover.

4. Remove the 5 screws from around the blower housing and separate the blower housing from the unit.
5. Remove the 3 screws that secure the blower assembly to the heater housing and remove the assembly from the unit. Remove the fan from the blower motor.
6. The installation is the reverse of the removal procedure.
7. Connect the negative battery cable and check the blower motor for proper operation.

Except—1988–90 Caravan, Voyager and Town & Country

1. Disconnect negative battery cable.
2. Remove the lower steering column cover, ash receiver and the intermittent wiper control module.
3. Remove the lower instrument panel module retaining screw to the right of the steering column at cluster bezel.
4. Remove the center distribution duct retaining screws and panel support screw at the bottom of the module.
5. Remove the courtesy light at the lower right corner of the module and the screw near the ash receiver. Disconnect the blower motor wire harness.

6. Open the glovebox and remove the screws along the top edge.

7. Move the module rearward and down far enough to unclip the wiring harness and antenna cable and disconnect the speaker wire (if equipped with monaural radio) and glovebox light wire. Remove the module from the vehicle.

8. Remove the 2 screws at the top of the blower housing that secure it to the unit cover.

9. Remove the 5 screws from around the blower housing and separate the blower housing from the unit.

10. Remove the 3 screws that secure the blower assembly to the heater housing and remove the assembly from the unit. Remove the fan from the blower motor.

To install:

11. Install blower motor assembly to the heater housing and install retainer screws.

12. Install 2 screws at top of blower housing that secure it to cover. Connect the blower motor wire harness.

13. Connect radio wiring harness, antenna cable, the speaker wire (if equipped with monaural radio) and glovebox light wire.

14. Install module in vehicle. Open the glovebox and install the retaining screws along the top edge.

15. Install the courtesy light at the lower right corner of the module and the screw near the ash receiver.

16. Install the center distribution duct retaining screws and panel support screw at the bottom of the module.

17. Install the lower instrument panel module retaining screw to the right of the steering column at cluster bezel.

18. Install the lower steering column cover, ash receiver and the intermittent wiper control module.

19. Reconnect negative battery cable.

WITH AIR CONDITIONING

1988–90 Caravan, Voyager and Town & Country

1. Disconnect the negative battery cable.

2. Lower right side instrument panel trim cover and right cowl trim panel, as required. Disconnect the blower lead wire connector.

3. Disconnect the 2 vacuum lines from the recirculating door actuator.

4. Remove the 2 screws at the top of the blower housing that secure it to the unit cover.

5. Remove the 5 screws from around the blower housing and separate the blower housing from the unit.

6. Remove the 3 screws that secure the blower assembly to the heater housing and remove the assembly from the unit. Remove the fan from the blower motor.

7. The installation is the reverse of the removal procedure.

8. Connect the negative battery cable and check the blower motor for proper operation.

Except–1988–90 Caravan, Voyager and Town & Country

1. Disconnect negative battery cable.

2. Remove the lower steering column cover, ash receiver and the intermittent wiper control module.

3. Remove the lower instrument panel module retaining screw to the right of the steering column at cluster bezel.

4. Remove the center distribution duct retaining screws and panel support screw at the bottom of the module.

5. Remove the courtesy light at the lower right corner of the module and the screw near the ash receiver.

6. Open the glovebox and remove the screws along the top edge.

7. Move the module rearward and down far enough to unclip the wiring harness and antenna cable and disconnect the speaker wire, if equipped with monaural radio, and glovebox light wire. Remove the module from the vehicle.

8. Disconnect 2 vacuum lines from the recirulating air door actuator and the blower motor wire harness. Remove the 2

screws at the top of the blower housing that secure it to the unit cover.

9. Remove the 5 screws from around the blower housing and separate the blower housing from the unit.

10. Remove the 3 screws that secure the blower assembly to the heater housing and remove the assembly from the unit. Remove the fan from the blower motor.

To install:

11. Install blower motor assembly to the heater housing and install retainer screws.

12. Install 2 screws at top of blower housing that secure it to cover.

13. Connect radio wiring harness, antenna cable, the speaker wire, if equipped with monaural radio, and glovebox light wire.

14. Reconnect the blower motor electrical harness and the vacuum lines to the recirculating air door actuator. Install module in vehicle. Open the glovebox and install the retaining screws along the top edge.

15. Install the courtesy light at the lower right corner of the module and the screw near the ash receiver.

16. Install the center distribution duct retaining screws and panel support screw at the bottom of the module.

17. Install the lower instrument panel module retaining screw to the right of the steering column at cluster bezel.

18. Install the lower steering column cover, ash receiver and the intermittent wiper control module.

19. Reconnect negative battery cable.

Windshield Wiper Motor

Removal and Installation

CARAVAN, VOYAGER AND TOWN & COUNTRY

1. Disconnect the negative battery cable.

2. Remove the wiper arms.

3. Open the hood and remove the cowl top plenum grille and the plastic screen.

4. Remove the wiper pivot retaining screws and push the pivots down into the plenum chamber.

5. Remove the nut from the wiper motor output shaft and remove the linkage assembly from the motor.

6. Disconnect the wiper motor harness, remove the mounting nuts and remove the motor from the vehicle.

To install:

7. Install wiper motor and mounting screws and nuts tightening to 60–70 inch lbs. (8 Nm) torque. Connect wiper harness connector.

8. Install the linkage assembly to the motor. Install the nut onto the wiper motor output shaft and tighten to 95 inch lbs. (10 Nm).

9. Install wiper pivot retaining screws and torque to 65 inch lbs. (8 Nm).

10. Install the plastic screen, the cowl top plenum grille and the wiper arms.

11. Reconnect the negative battery cable and check wiper operation.

DAKOTA

1. Disconnect the negative battery cable.

2. Disconnect the connector from the motor.

3. Remove 3 motor mounting nuts. Remove the wiper arms.

4. Remove the cowl panel mounting screws making sure to remove the screw in the center of the grille to the right of the right side pivot assembly.

5. Disengage the rear of the cowl grille from the windshield weather strip by pulling forward and remove cowel panel.

6. Pry up on clips in screen cover and remove.

7. Hold the drive crank with a wrench while remove the crank nut. Remove the drive crank.

8. Remove the motor from the vehicle.

To install:

9. Position motor on 3 studs on dash panel making certain rubber gasket and spacer between motor and dash panel are properly positioned.

10. Install 3 mounting nuts and torque to 65 inch lbs. (8 Nm).

11. Connect wiring harness. Align flats on the drive crank arm with flats on motor shaft and install tightening nut to 95 inch lbs. (11 Nm).

12. Connect negative battery cable and check wiper operation.

13. Install screen and hose in place and secure. Install cowl grille and wiper arms.

Liftgate Wiper Motor

Removal and Installation

CARAVAN, VOYAGER AND TOWN & COUNTRY

1. Disconnect the negative battery cable.

2. Remove the liftgate wiper using the special removal tool.

NOTE: Prying the arm off of the shaft with a prying device could damage the arm and possibly cause it to pop off of the shaft while in operation. This would cause poor rear vision for the driver and a dangerous situation for the driver behind. Do not bend or push the spring clip at the base of the arm to release the arm; it is self-releasing. Use only the indicated tool.

3. Open the liftgate and remove the inside trim panel.

4. Remove the motor mounting screws, disconnect the wiring harness and remove the motor from the liftgate.

5. The installation is the reverse of the removal procedure.

6. Connect the negative battery cable and check the rear wiper for proper operation.

Windshield Wiper Switch

Removal and Installation

NOTE: On 1991–92 vehicles, the windshield wiper switch is part of the combination switch.

1988–90 EXCEPT TILT WHEEL

1. Disconnect the negative battery cable.

2. Remove the lower steering column cover.

3. Remove the horn pad mounting screws from behind the steering wheel and remove the horn pad.

4. Remove the steering wheel nut, matchmark the steering wheel to the shaft and remove steering wheel.

5. Remove the plastic wiring channel from under the steering column.

Removing the wiper switch—except tilt wheel

6. Disconnect the wiper switch connector, intermittent wipe module connector and cruise control connector, if equipped.

7. Remove the side lock housing cover.

8. Remove the slotted hex-head screw that attaches the wiper switch to the turn signal switch and remove the switch.

9. Remove the control knob from the end of the stalk. Pull the round nylon hider up the control stalk and remove the screws that attach the control stalk sleeve to the wiper switch.

10. Rotate the control stalk shaft to the full clockwise position and remove the shaft from the wiper switch by pulling it straight out.

Removing the liftgate wiper arm

To install:

11. Install the control shaft to the wiper switch, install the screws, the hider and the control knob.

12. Run the wiring through the opening and down the steering column, position the switch and install the hex-head screw. Make sure the dimmer switch rod is properly engaged.

13. Install the side lock housing cover.

14. Connect the wires and install the wiring channel.

15. Install the steering wheel torque the nut to 45 ft. lbs. (61 Nm).

16. Install the horn pad.

17. Connect the negative battery cable and check the wiper and washer, cruise control, turn signal switch and dimmer switch for proper operation.

18. Install the lower column cover.

1988–90 TILT WHEEL

1. Disconnect the negative battery cable.

2. Remove the lower steering column cover. Remove the plastic wiring channel from the underside of the steering column.

3. Remove the horn pad mounting screws from behind the steering wheel and remove the horn pad.

4. Remove the steering wheel nut, matchmark the steering wheel to the shaft and remove the steering wheel.

5. Depress the lock plate with the proper depressing tool, remove the retaining ring from its groove and remove the tool, ring, lock plate, cancelling cam and spring.

6. Remove the switch stalk actuator screw and arm.

7. Remove the hazard switch knob.

8. Disconnect the turn signal switch, wiper switch, intermittent module and cruise control connectors, if equipped.

9. Remove the 3 screws and remove the turn signal switch. Tape the connector to the wires to aid in removal.

10. Remove the ignition key light.

11. Place the key in the **LOCK** position and remove the key. Insert a thin tool into the slot next to the switch mounting screw boss, depress the spring latch at the bottom of the slot releasing the lock. Remove the lock cylinder.

12. Remove the buzzer switch and wedge spring.

13. Remove the 3 housing cover screws and remove the housing cover.

14. Remove the wiper switch pivot pin with a punch and remove the switch.

15. Remove the control knob from the end of the stalk. Pull the round nylon hider up the control stalk and remove the revealed screws that attach the control stalk sleeve to the wiper switch.

16. Rotate the control stalk shaft to the full clockwise position and remove the shaft from the wiper switch by pulling it straight out.

To install:

17. Install the control shaft to the wiper switch, install the screws, the hider and the control knob.

18. Run the wiring through the opening and down the steering column, position the switch and install the wiper switch pivot pin.

19. Install the housing cover.

20. Install the buzzer switch and wedge spring.

21. Install the lock cylinder.

22. Install the ignition key light.

23. Install the turn signal switch, switch stalk actuator arm and hazard switch knob.

24. Install the spring, canceling cam, lock plate and ring on the steering shaft. Depress the plate with the depressing tool and install the ring securely in the groove. Remove the tool slowly.

25. Connect the turn signal switch, wiper switch, intermittent module and cruise control connectors, if equipped. Install the channel.

26. Install the steering wheel torque the nut to 45 ft. lbs. (61 Nm).

27. Install the horn pad.

28. Connect the negative battery cable and check the wiper and washer, cruise control, turn signal switch and dimmer switch for proper operation.

29. Install the lower column cover.

Instrument Cluster

Removal and Installation

1. Disconnect the negative battery cable.

2. Remove the warning indicator grill, if equipped.

3. If equipped with warning indicator module assembly, remove warning module mounting screws, disconnect wire harness and remove module.

4. Remove steering column cover. Apply parking brake and put gear selector into low.

5. Remove the instrument cluster bezel and disconnect wire connectors. Remove 4 cluster retaining screws.

6. If equipped with gear selector cable, disconnect cable from shift housing slot.

7. If equipped with indicator guide tube, remove 4 screws attaching mask to housing and rotate mask down and disconnect buttons. Remove 2 screws attaching gear indicator to cluster and remove indicator.

8. Disconnect speedometer cable, if equipped. Remove cluster from vehicle.

9. When only removing gauge(s) or the speedometer, remove the trip odometer reset knob, if equipped, remove the mask and lens assembly and remove the desired gauge from the cluster. Disconnect the speedometer cable, if removing the speedometer.

To install:

10. Postion the cluster and feed the gear indicator cable through slot in shift housing. If equipped with an indicator guide tube, install onto cluster.

11. Connect all wiring and install the speedometer cable to the speedometer, if equipped. Make sure it is securely clicked in place.

12. Install the cluster retaining screws. Install warning indicator module and grille, if equipped.

13. Install the cluster bezel and steering column cover.

14. Connect the negative battery cable. Check all gauges and the speedometer for proper operation. Make sure the gearshift indicator is properly aligned.

Headlight Switch

Removal and Installation

CARAVAN, VOYAGER AND TOWN & COUNTRY

1988–90

1. Disconnect the negative battery cable.

2. Remove the headlight and accessory switch trim bezel.

3. Remove the switch plate from the lower panel, pull the assembly out and disconnect the wiring.

4. Depress the spring button and remove the headlight switch knob and stem.

5. Remove the headlight switch retainer and remove the switch.

6. Attach headlight switch to headlight switch plate with retainer and secure.

7. Install headlight switch knob and stem. Reconnect wiring connectors to switch.

8. Install 4 screws attaching switch to lower panel. Install trim bezel.

9. Connect negative battery cable and check operation of switch.

1991–92

1. Disconnect negative battery cable.

2. Remove warning indicator grille by prying up with a flat blade tool.

Headlight and accessory switch removal and installation—Caravan, Voyager and Town & Country

Headlight switch assembly—Dakota

3. Remove 3 mounting screws from warning indicator module and remove module.
4. Remove steering column cover, apply parking brake and remove cluster bezel.
5. Disconnect switch wire connectors and remove switch by unsnapping from back side of cluster bezel.

To install:
6. Install switch to cluster bezel and reconnect electrical connector.
7. Install steering column cover. Install warning indicator module and grille.
8. Connect negative battery cable and check operation of switch.

DAKOTA
1. Disconnect the negative battery cable.
2. Remove the steering column cover and remove the instrument panel bezel. Two screws are hidden behind the steering column cover.
3. Remove the screws from the headlight switch bezel, pull the assembly out and disconnect the wiring.
4. Remove the nut retaining the bezel to the bracket. Depress the spring button on the right side of the switch and remove the headlight switch knob and stem.
5. Remove the spanner nut and remove the switch.
6. The installation is the reverse of the removal procedure.

Dimmer Switch

Removal and Installation

NOTE: On 1991–92 vehicles, the dimmer switch is part of the combination switch.

1. Disconnect the negative battery cable.
2. Remove the lower steering column cover.
3. Unplug the switch, located on the lower portion of the steering column.
4. Holding the actuating rod against its upper seat, remove the bolts that attach the switch to the column and remove the switch.
5. The installation is the reverse of the removal procedure. Adjust the switch as required.
6. Connect the negative battery cable and check the switch for proper operation.

Turn Signal Switch

NOTE: On 1991–92 vehicles, the turn signal switch is part of the combination switch.

Removal and Installation
1988–90 VEHICLES
Standard Column
1. Disconnect the negative battery cable.
2. Remove the lower steering column cover.
3. Remove the horn pad mounting screws from behind the steering wheel and remove the horn pad.
4. Remove the steering wheel nut, matchmark the steering wheel to the shaft and remove the steering wheel.
5. Remove the plastic wiring channel from the underside of the steering column and disconnect the turn signal switch connector.
6. Remove the hazard switch knob. Remove the slotted hex-head screw that attaches the wiper switch to the turn signal switch.
7. Remove the 3 screws and pull the turn signal switch out of the column.

To install:
8. Run the wiring through the opening and down the steering column, position the switch and install the hex-head screw. Make sure the dimmer switch rod is properly engaged.
9. Install the 3 screws and the hazard switch knob.
10. Connect the wires and install the wiring channel.
11. Install the steering wheel. Torque the nut to 45 ft. lbs. (61 Nm).
12. Install the horn pad.
13. Connect the negative battery cable and check the turn signal switch and dimmer switch for proper operation.
14. Install the lower column cover.

Tilt Column
1. Disconnect the negative battery cable.
2. Remove the lower steering column cover. Remove the plastic wiring channel from the underside of the steering column.
3. Remove the horn pad mounting screws from behind the steering wheel and remove the horn pad.
4. Remove the steering wheel nut, matchmark the steering wheel to the shaft and remove the steering wheel.
5. Depress the lock plate with the proper depressing tool, remove the retaining ring from its groove and remove the tool, ring, lock plate, canceling cam and spring.
6. Remove the stalk actuator screw and arm.
7. Remove the hazard switch knob.
8. Disconnect the turn signal switch connector.
9. Remove the 3 screws and remove the turn signal switch. Tape the connector to the wires to aid in removal.

To install:

10. Run the wiring through the opening and down the steering column, install the turn signal switch, switch stalk actuator arm and hazard switch knob.

11. Install the spring, canceling cam, lock plate and ring on the steering shaft. Depress the plate with the depressing tool and install the ring securely in the groove. Remove the tool slowly.

12. Connect the turn signal switch connector and install the channel.

13. Install the steering wheel. Torque the nut to 45 ft. lbs. (61 Nm).

14. Install the horn pad.

15. Connect the negative battery cable and check the turn signal switch and dimmer switch for proper operation.

16. Install the lower column cover.

Combination Switch

Removal and Installation

TURN SIGNAL/HEADLIGHT BEAM/WIPER CONTROL SWITCH

This switch contains circuitry for turn signals, headlight beam select, headlight optical horn, windshield wiper, pulse wipe, and windshield washer switching. On 1991 Caravan, Voyager and Town & Country the front and rear wiper and washer is controlled by a combination pod switch.

1. Disconnect the negative battery cable.

2. Remove the tilt lever, if equipped.

3. Remove the steering column covers.

4. Remove the combination switch tamper-proof mounting screws and pull the switch away from the steering column.

5. Loosen the connector screw; the screw will remain in the connector.

6. Disconnect the connector and remove the switch.

To install:

7. Install wiring connector to switch and tighten connector retaining screw to 17 inch lbs. (2 Nm).

8. Mount multi-function switch to column and tighten retaining screws 17 inch lbs. (2 Nm).

9. Install steering column covers and tilt lever if removed.

10. Connect negative battery cable and check operation of multi-function switch.

FRONT AND REAR WIPER/WASHER POD SWITCH

1. Disconnect negative battery cable.

2. Remove 8 screws mounting cluster bezel to the instrument panel.

3. Gently pull cluster bezel out to gain access to the switch mounting fingers. Release fingers and push switch through mounting hole for pod switch.

4. Remove electrical connectors for switch.

To install:

5. Position cluster bezel for assembly and pull wiring connectors through mounting hole for pod switch assembly.

6. Install wiring connector to switch and verify proper function of the front and rear wipe/wash system.

7. Install switch into bezel making sure fingers snap into position. Assemble cluster bezel into instrument panel and tighten retaining screws.

Ignition Lock

Removal and Installation

1988–90 VEHICLES

Standard Column

1. Disconnect the negative battery cable.

2. Remove the horn pad mounting screws from behind the steering wheel and remove the horn pad.

Removing the key lock cylinder—except tilt wheel

3. Remove the steering wheel nut, matchmark the steering wheel to the shaft and remove the steering wheel.

4. Remove the hazard switch knob. Remove the slotted hex-head screw that attaches the wiper switch to the turn signal switch.

5. Remove the 3 screws and pull the turn signal switch out of the column as far as it will go. Unplug it below if necessary.

6. Remove the ignition switch key light.

7. Place the key in the **LOCK** position and remove the key.

8. Insert 2 small diameter tools into the release holes and push inward to release the spring loaded lock retainers while simultaneously pulling the key lock cylinder out of its bore.

To install:

9. Install the key cylinder.

10. Install the ignition switch key light.

11. Install the turn signal switch and hazard switch knob. Connect the wires if disconnected.

12. Install the steering wheel and torque the nut to 45 ft. lbs. (61 Nm).

13. Install the horn pad.

14. Connect the negative battery cable and check the lock cylinder for proper operation.

15. Install the lower column cover.

Removing the key lock cylinder—tilt column

Tilt Column

1. Disconnect the negative battery cable.
2. Remove the horn pad mounting screws from behind the steering wheel and remove the horn pad.
3. Remove the steering wheel nut, matchmark the steering wheel to the shaft and remove the steering wheel.
4. Depress the lock plate with the proper depressing tool, remove the retaining ring from its groove and remove the tool, ring, lock plate, canceling cam and spring.
5. Remove the stalk actuator screw and arm.
6. Remove the hazard switch knob.
7. Remove the 3 screws and pull the turn signal switch out of the column as far as it will go. Unplug it below if necessary.
8. Remove the ignition key light
9. Place the key in the **LOCK** position and remove the key. Insert a thin tool into the slot next to the switch mounting screw boss, depress the spring latch at the bottom of the slot releasing the lock and remove the lock cylinder.

To install:

10. Install the lock cylinder.
11. Install the ignition key light.
12. Install the turn signal switch, switch stalk actuator arm and hazard switch knob.
13. Install the spring, canceling cam, lock plate and ring on the steering shaft. Depress the plate with the depressing tool and install the ring securely in the groove. Remove the tool slowly.
14. Connect the wires if disconnected.
15. Install the steering wheel and torque the nut to 45 ft. lbs. (61 Nm).
16. Install the horn pad.
17. Connect the negative battery cable and check the turn signal switch for proper operation.
18. Install the lower column cover, if removed.

Ignition Switch

Removal and Installation

1988–90 VEHICLES

1. Disconnect the negative battery cable.
2. Remove the lower steering column cover.
3. Remove the steering column retaining nuts and allow the steering wheel to rest on the driver's seat.
4. Remove the 2 screws that attach the ignition switch to the column.
5. Rotate the switch 90 degrees and pull up to disengage it from the ignition switch rod.

To install:

6. Engage the switch with the rod, rotate the switch 90 degrees and push down until fully engaged.
7. Install the mounting screws finger-tight.
8. Place the key in the **LOCK** position and remove the key. Adjust the switch by pushing up gently on the switch to take up all slack in the rod.
9. Tighten the mounting screws. Connect negative battery cable and check the switch for proper operation in all positions.
10. Install the steering column and cover.

Ignition Lock/Switch

Removal and Installation

1991–92 VEHICLES

1. Disconnect the negative battery cable.

NOTE: If equipped with an airbag, it is imperative that the steering wheel removal and installation procedure under Steering is followed.

2. Remove the tilt lever, if equipped.
3. Remove the upper and lower column covers.

4. Remove the 3 ignition switch tamper-proof Torx screws; APEX 440–TX20H or equivalent is required.
5. Pull the switch away from the column. Release the connector locks on the 2 wiring connectors and disconnect them from the switch.
6. Remove the key lock cylinder from the ignition switch by performing the following:
   a. Insert the key and turn the switch in the **LOCK** position. Using a small tool, depress the key cylinder retaining pin flush with the key cylinder surface.
   b. Rotate the key clockwise to the **OFF** position to unseat the key cylinder from the ignition switch assembly. The cylinder bezel should be about ⅛in. above the ignition switch halo light ring. Do not attempt to remove the key cylinder at this point.
   c. With the key cylinder in the unseated position, rotate the key counterclockwise to the **LOCK** position and remove the key.
   d. Remove the key cylinder from the ignition switch.

To install:

7. Connect the wiring connectors.
8. Mount ignition switch to the column by performing the following:
   a. Position the shifter in **PARK** position. The park lock dowel pin on the ignition switch assembly must engage with the column park lock slider linkage.
   b. Verify that the ignition switch is in the **LOCK** position. The flag should be parallel to the ignition switch terminals. Apply a small amount of grease to the flag and pin.
   c. Position the park lock link to mid-travel.
   d. Align the locating pin hole and its pin and position the ignition switch against the lock housing face. Make sure the pin is inserted into the park lock link contour slot. Torque the retaining screws to 17 inch lbs.
9. With the key cylinder and ignition switch in the **LOCK** position, key not in cylinder, gently insert the key cylinder into the ignition switch until it bottoms.
10. Insert the key. Simultaneously push in on the cylinder and rotate the key to the **RUN** position. This action should fully seat the cylinder in the ignition switch.
11. Install the column covers and the tilt lever, if equipped.
12. Connect the negative battery cable and check the push-to-lock and park lock functions, halo lighting and all ignition switch positions for proper operation.

Stoplight Switch

Adjustment

1. Push the stoplight switch forward in the mounting bracket as far as it will go; the brake pedal should move forward slightly.
2. Pull back on the brake pedal bringing the striker toward the switch until the pedal will not go back any farther. This will cause the switch to ratchet backward into position and automatically adjust.

Removal and Installation

1. Disconnect the negative battery cable.
2. Remove the switch mounting bracket assembly from the brake pedal bracket.
3. Remove the switch from its bracket.
4. The installation is the reverse of the removal procedure.
5. Connect the negative battery cable and check the switch for proper operation.

Neutral Safety Switch

Removal and Installation

1. Disconnect negative battery cable.

2. Raise and safely support the vehicle. Position drain pan under switch.

3. Disconnect switch wiring harness.

4. Remove switch from case.

5. Verify that switch operating lever fingers are centered in the switch opening in the case when in Park and Neutral.

6. Install new seal on switch and install switch into case. Torque to 25 ft. lbs.

7. Test continuity of new switch. Connect wire harness and negative battery cable.

8. Add transmission fluid as required to correct level.

Fuses, Circuit Breakers and Relays

Location

The fuse block and relay bank is located to the left of the steering column, covered by a removable access panel. Additional relays are located in the power distribution center which is mounted to the left fender wall.

Computers

Location

1988–89

Single Module Engine Controller (SMEC)—located in engine compartment, to the left of the battery.

1990–92

Single Board Engine Controller (SBEC)—located in the engine compartment, to the left of the battery.

1991–92

Rear Wheel Anti-Lock (RWAL) brake control module—located on the passenger side cowl panel under the instrument panel.

1992

The Bendix Anti-Lock—10 Brake Controller (CAB)—located under the battery tray.
The Air Bag Diagnostic Module (ASDM)—located under the center console of the instrument panel.

Body Controller—located inside the passenger compartment, behind the right side kick panel.

Flashers

Location

1988–91

The turn signal and hazard flashers are located in the fuse block to the left of the steering column.

1992

The electronic combination flasher module provides both turn signal and hazard flasher operation. The module plugs into the lower left corner of the relay bank to the left of the fuse block.

Cruise Control

For further information, please refer to Chilton's Chassis Electronics Service Manual.

Adjustment

2.5L ENGINE

1. The clearance between the throttle stud and cable clevis should be $\frac{1}{16}$ in.

2. To adjust the cable, remove the retaining clip or loosen the retaining clamp nut at the throttle bracket.

3. Pull all slack out of the cable using a $\frac{1}{16}$ in. diameter tool to account for proper clearance. Make sure the curb idle position of the throttle blade is not affected.

4. Reinstall the retaining clip or nut.

3.0L ENGINE

1. Grip the cable core and lightly push toward the servo.

2. While holding the position, mark the core wire next to the protective sleeve.

3. Pull the core wire away from the servo. There should be a 0.24 in. (6mm) gap between the mark on the core wire and the protective sleeve.

4. If the gap is not correct, remove the adjustment clip from the throttle bracket and move the sleeve to bring the gap into specification.

5. Reinstall the clip.

ENGINE COOLING

Radiator

Removal and Installation

1. Disconnect the negative battery cable. Unclip throttle cable at fan shroud, if equipped.

2. Open the radiator petcock and drain the antifreeze. Once the antifreeze has stopped draining, close the petcock.

3. Remove the upper hose and coolant reserve tank hose from the radiator.

4. Remove the fan shroud and electric cooling fan from radiator. On 5.2L and 3.9L engines, move fan shroud towards engine, it is not necessary to remove from the vehicle.

5. Disconnect the automatic transmission or transaxle cooler hoses, if equipped and plug them.

6. Remove upper mounting screws and lift radiator from lower supports.

To install:

7. Lower the radiator into position and install the mounting screws.

8. Connect the automatic transmission or transaxle cooler lines, if removed.

9. Connect the lower radiator hose.

10. Install the shroud or electric cooling fan, if removed.

11. Connect the upper hose and coolant reserve tank hose.

12. Fill the system with coolant.

13. Connect the negative battery cable. Run the vehicle until the thermostat opens, fill the radiator completely and check the coolant and transmission fluid levels and add as required.

14. Once the vehicle has cooled, recheck the coolant level.

Electric Cooling Fan

Testing

————— **CAUTION** —————

Make sure the key is in the OFF position when checking the electric cooling fan. If not, the fan could turn on at any time, causing serious personal injury.

Service Tips

ENGINE OVERHEATING

Some 1988–90 Caravan/Voyager "LE" models equipped with a soft fascia on the front bumper could experience an overheating condition due to inadequate air flow around the radiator and engine. This condition would occur under any of the following conditions:

  a. While pulling trailer and/or if vehicle is fully loaded.

  b. While vehicle is being operated on mountainous or hilly terrain.

  c. When the ambient temperature is 90°F or above.

If condition occurs check the cooling system for signs of a coolant leak. If no leaks are evident, then inadequate air flow may be the cause. To repair this condition it will be necessary to install a lower air dam onto the bottom of the front fascia. This will redirect air and lower engine temperatures to eliminate overheating conditions caused by inadequate air flow.

1. Unplug the fan connector.
2. Using a jumper wire, connect the female terminal of the fan connector to the negative battery terminal.
3. The fan should come on when the other wire is connected to the positive battery terminal.
4. If fan does not turn, the fan is defective and should be replaced.

Removal and Installation

1. Disconnect the negative battery cable.
2. Unplug the connector.
3. Remove the mounting screws.
4. Remove the fan assembly from the vehicle.
5. The installation is the reverse of the removal procedure.

Heater Core

For further information, please refer to Chilton's Air Conditioning and Heating Manual.

Removal and Installation

WITHOUT AIR CONDITIONING

Caravan, Voyager and Town & Country

1. Disconnect the negative battery cable. Drain the cooling system.
2. Remove the lower steering column cover and both side under panel silencers.
3. Remove the lower reinforcement under the steering column, right side cowl and sill trim. Remove the bolt holding the right side instrument panel to the right cowl.
4. Loosen the 2 brackets supporting the lower edge of the heater housing. Remove the instrument panel trim covering and reinforcement. Remove the retaining screws from the right side to the steering column.
5. Disconnect the vacuum line at the brake booster. Remove the accessory switch carrier and storage module.
6. Clamp off the heater hoses near the heater core and remove the hoses from the core tubes. Plug the hose ends and the core tubes to prevent spillage of coolant. Remove the heater assembly retaining nuts at the firewall.
7. Disconnect the blower motor wiring, resistor wiring and the temperature control cable. Disconnect the hanger strap from the package and rotate it out of the way.
8. Pull the right side of the instrument panel out as far as possible. Fold the carpeting and insulation back to provide a little more working room and to prevent spillage from staining the carpeting.
9. Pull the heater core assembly out from under instrument panel and remove it from the vehicle.
10. Remove vacuum harness and top cover from assembly. Remove nut and lever from the door shaft and remove the temperature door from the cover.
11. Remove the retaining screw from the heater core and remove the core from the housing assembly.

To install:

12. Clean out the inside of the housing. Wrap the heater core with foam tape and place it in position. Secure it with its retainer screw. Install temperature door and vacuum harness to heater unit.
13. Install the cover to the heater unit.
14. Install the assembly to the vehicle and install the nuts to the firewall. Fold the carpeting back into position.
15. Connect the hanger strap from the package and rotate it out of the way. Install the 2 brackets supporting the lower edge of the heater housing. Connect the blower motor wiring, resistor wiring and the temperature control cable.
16. Install the retaining screws from the right side to the steering column. Install the instrument panel trim covering and reinforcement.
17. Install the bolt holding the right side instrument panel to the right cowl. Install the lower reinforcement under the steering column, right side cowl and sill trim.
18. Install the heater hoses to the core tubes. Install the storage compartment and accessory switch carrier to original position.
19. Connect the vacuum line at the brake booster.
20. Fill the cooling system.
21. Connect the negative battery cable and check the heater for proper operation and leaks.

Dakota

1. Disconnect the negative battery cable. Drain the coolant.
2. Remove the steering column cover, intermittent wiper control, if equipped and the lower instrument panel module retaining screw to the right of the steering column.
3. Remove the center distribution duct retaining screws and panel support screw at the bottom of the module.
4. Remove the courtesy light at the lower right corner of the module and the screw near the ash tray.
5. Open the glovebox and remove the screws along the top edge.
6. Move the module out and down far enough to unclip the wiring harness and antenna cable and disconnect the speaker wire, if equipped with monaural radio, and glovebox light wire. Remove the module from the vehicle.
7. Remove the center air distribution duct.
8. Remove the antenna wire from retaining clip at the right end of the heater unit.
9. Disconnect the blower motor connector and remove the terminal insulator retainer from the heater unit.
10. Disconnect the demister hoses from the adaptor at the top of the heater unit.
11. Disconnect the vacuum feed line from the check valve.

12. Disconnect the temperature control cable flag retainer from the heater unit.

13. Remove the adjusting clip from the blend air door crank.

14. Disconnect the heater hoses from the core tubes and plug them.

15. Remove 4 heater unit attaching nuts from the rear engine compartment dash panel.

16. Remove the heater unit support attaching screw and rotate the brace out of the way.

17. Remove the heater unit from the vehicle.

18. To disassemble the housing assembly, vacuum diaphragm and retaining screws from the cover and remove the cover.

19. Remove the retaining screw from the heater core and remove the core from the housing assembly.

To install:

20. Remove the temperature control door from the unit and clean the unit out with solvent. Lubricate the lower pivot rod and its well and install. Wrap the heater core with foam tape and place it in position. Secure it with its screw.

21. Assemble the unit, making sure all vacuum tubing is properly routed.

22. Install the assembly to the vehicle and connect the vacuum harness. Install the nuts to the firewall. Install the support brace to the heater unit.

23. Connect the demister hoses to the adaptor at the top of the heater unit.

24. Connect the blower motor connector and install the thermal insulator retainer to the heater unit.

25. Connect the vacuum feed line to the check valve.

26. Connect the temperature control cable flag retainer to the heater unit and install the adjusting clip from the blend air door crank.

27. Install the center air distribution duct.

28. Install the antenna wire from retaining clip at the right end of the heater unit.

29. Install the instrument panel module and all related parts.

30. Connect the heater hoses to the core tubes.

31. Fill the cooling system.

32. Connect the negative battery cable and check the heater for proper operation and leakage.

WITH AIR CONDITIONING

Caravan, Voyager and Town & Country

1. Disconnect the negative battery cable. Properly discharge the air conditioning system. Drain the cooling system.

2. Remove the lower steering column cover. Remove the left and right under panel silencers.

3. Remove the lower reinforcement under the steering column, right side cowl and sill trim. Remove the bolt holding the right side instrument panel to the right cowl.

4. Loosen the 2 brackets supporting the lower edge of the heater housing. Remove the instrument panel trim covering and reinforcement. Remove the retaining screws from the right side to the steering column.

5. Disconnect the vacuum lines at the brake booster and water valve.

6. Clamp off the heater hoses near the heater core and remove the hoses from the core tubes. Plug the hose ends and the core tubes to prevent spillage of coolant.

7. Disconnect the H-valve connection at the valve and remove the H-valve. Remove the retaining nuts from the package mounting studs at the firewall.

8. Disconnect the blower motor wiring, resistor wiring and the temperature control cable. Disconnect the vacuum harness at the connection at the top of the heater unit.

9. Disconnect the hanger strap from the package and rotate it out of the way. Remove the rubber condensate drain tube located in the engine compartment.

10. Pull the right side of the instrument panel out as far as possible. Fold the carpeting and insulation back to provide a lit-tle more working room and to prevent spillage from staining the carpeting.

11. Remove the entire housing assembly from the dash panel and remove it from the vehicle.

12. To disassemble the housing assembly, remove the vacuum diaphragm, vacuum harness and retaining screws from the cover and remove the cover.

13. Remove the retaining screw from the heater core and remove the core from the housing assembly.

To install:

14. Remove the temperature control door from the unit and clean the unit out with solvent. Lubricate the lower pivot rod and its well and install. Wrap the heater core with foam tape and place it in position. Secure it with its screw.

15. Assemble the unit, making sure all vacuum tubing is properly routed.

16. Install the assembly to the vehicle and connect the vacuum harness. Install the nuts to the firewall and install the condensation tube. Fold the carpeting back into position.

17. Connect the hanger strap from the package and rotate it out of the way. Install the 2 brackets supporting the lower edge of the heater housing. Connect the blower motor wiring, resistor wiring and the temperature control cable.

18. Install the retaining screws from the right side to the steering column. Install the instrument panel trim covering and reinforcement.

19. Install the bolt holding the right side instrument panel to the right cowl. Install the lower reinforcement under the steering column, right side cowl and sill trim.

20. Connect the vacuum lines at the brake booster and water valve.

21. Connect the heater hoses to the core tubes.

22. Using new gaskets, install the H-valve and connect the hose connection at the valve.

23. Evacuate and recharge the air conditioning system.

24. Fill the cooling system.

25. Connect the negative battery cable and check the entire climate control system for proper operation and leakage.

Dakota

1. Disconnect the negative battery cable. Properly discharge the air conditioning system. Drain the coolant.

2. Remove the steering column cover, intermittent wiper control and the lower instrument panel module retaining screw to the right of the steering column.

3. Remove the center distribution duct retaining screws and panel support screw at the bottom of the module.

4. Remove the courtesy light at the lower right corner of the module and the screw near the ash tray.

5. Open the glovebox and remove the screws along the top edge.

6. Move the module out and down far enough to unclip the wiring harness and antenna cable and disconnect the speaker wire, if equipped with monaural radio, and glovebox light wire. Remove the module from the vehicle.

7. Remove the center air distribution duct.

8. Remove the antenna wire from retaining clip at the right end of the heater unit.

9. Disconnect the blower motor connector and remove the terminal insulator retainer from the heater unit.

10. Disconnect the demister hoses from the adaptor at the top of the heater unit.

11. Disconnect the vacuum harness connector from the air conditioning control hose and vacuum feed line from the check valve.

12. Disconnect the temperature control cable flag retainer from the heater unit and remove the adjusting clip from the blend air door crank.

13. Disconnect the heater hoses from the core tubes and plug them.

14. Remove the condensation drain tube.

15. Remove 4 heater-air conditioning unit attaching nuts from the rear engine compartment dash panel.

16. Remove the heater-air conditioning unit support attaching screw and rotate the brace out of the way.

17. Remove the heater-air conditioning unit from the vehicle.

18. To disassemble the housing assembly, vacuum diaphragm and retaining screws from the cover and remove the cover.

19. Remove the retaining screw from the heater core and remove the core from the housing assembly.

To install:

20. Remove the temperature control door from the unit and clean the unit out with solvent. Lubricate the lower pivot rod and its well and install. Wrap the heater core with foam tape and place it in position. Secure it with its screw.

21. Assemble the unit, making sure all vacuum tubing is properly routed.

22. Install the assembly to the vehicle and connect the vacuum harness. Install the nuts to the firewall and install the condensation tube. Install the support brace to the heater-air conditioning unit.

23. Connect the demister hoses to the adaptor at the top of the heater unit.

24. Connect the blower motor connector and install the thermal insulator retainer to the heater unit.

25. Connect the vacuum harness connector to the air conditioning control hose and vacuum feed line to the check valve.

26. Connect the temperature control cable flag retainer to the heater unit and install the adjusting clip from the blend air door crank.

27. Install the center air distribution duct.

28. Install the antenna wire from retaining clip at the right end of the heater unit.

29. Install the instrument panel module and all related parts.

30. Connect the heater hoses to the core tubes.

31. Using new gaskets, install the H-valve and connect the hose connection at the valve.

32. Evacuate and recharge the air conditioning system.

33. Fill the cooling system.

34. Connect the negative battery cable and check the entire climate control system for proper operation and leakage.

Water Pump

Removal and Installation

2.2L AND 2.5L ENGINES

1. Disconnect the negative battery cable.

2. Drain the cooling system. Remove the alternator and position aside.

3. If equipped with air conditioning, remove the compressor from the bracket and position it to the side.

4. Raise the vehicle and support safely, if necessary and remove the alternator and bracket. Remove the pulley from the water pump.

5. Disconnect the lower radiator hose and heater hose from the water pump.

6. Remove the water pump housing attaching screws and remove the assembly from the vehicle. Discard the O-ring.

7. Remove the water pump from the housing.

To install:

8. Using a new gasket or silicone sealer, install the water pump to the housing.

9. Install a new O-ring to the housing and install to the engine. Torque top 3 bolts to 21 ft. lbs. (30 Nm). Install lower screw and tighten to 50 ft. lbs. (68 Nm).

10. Install the water pump pulley and belt. Connect the radiator hose and heater hose to the water pump.

11. Install all items removed to gain access to the water pump and adjust the belts.

12. Remove the hex-head plug or vacuum switching valve on the top of the thermostat housing. Fill the radiator with coolant

Water pump—2.2L and 2.5L engines

until the coolant comes out the plug hole. Install the plug or valve and continue to fill the radiator.

13. Connect the negative battery cable, run the vehicle until the thermostat opens, fill the radiator completely and check for leaks.

14. Once cool, recheck the coolant level.

3.0L ENGINE

1. Disconnect the negative battery cable.

2. Drain the cooling system.

3. Remove the upper front outer timing cover. If the same timing belt will be reused, mark the direction of the timing belt's rotation, for installation in the same direction. Make sure the engine is positioned so No. 1 cylinder is at the TDC of it's compression stroke and the sprockets timing marks are aligned with the engine's timing mark indicators.

4. Loosen the timing belt tensioner bolt and remove the belt. Position the tensioner as far away from the center of the engine as possible and tighten the bolt. Remove the water pump

Water pump assembly—3.0L engine

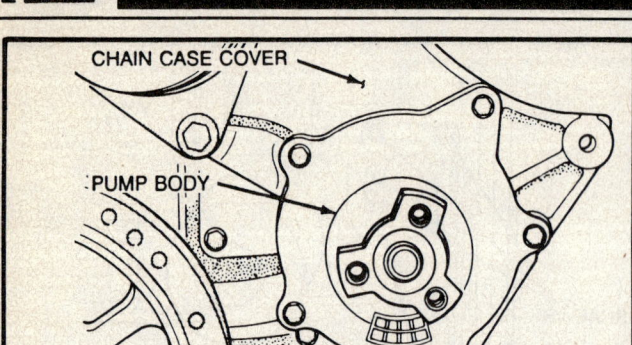

CHAIN CASE COVER

PUMP BODY

Water pump—3.3L engine

mounting bolts, separate the pump from the water inlet pipe and remove the pump from the engine.

To install:

5. Clean all gasket and O-ring surfaces on pump and install new O-ring on water inlet pipe. Dampen O-ring with water to ease in assembly. Install the pump with a new gasket to the engine. Torque the water pump mounting bolts to 20 ft. lbs. (27 Nm).

6. Position both camshafts so the marks line up with timing marks on the alternator bracket (rear bank) and inner timing cover (front bank). Rotate the crankshaft so the timing mark aligns with the mark on the oil pump.

7. Install the timing belt on the crankshaft sprocket and while keeping the belt tight on the tension side (right side), install the belt on the front camshaft sprocket.

8. Install the belt on the water pump pulley, rear camshaft sprocket and then the belt tensioner.

9. Rotate the front camshaft counterclockwise to tension the belt between the front camshaft and the crankshaft. If the timing marks came out of line, repeat the procedure.

10. Install the crankshaft sprocket flange.

11. Loosen the tensioner bolt and allow the spring to tension the belt.

12. Turn the crankshaft 2 full turns in the clockwise direction until the timing marks align again. Now that the belt is properly tensioned, torque the tensioner lock bolt to 21 ft. lbs. (29 Nm).

13. Refill the cooling system. This system uses a self-bleeding thermostat, so there is no need to bleed the system. Connect the negative battery cable and road test the vehicle.

3.3L ENGINE

1. Disconnect the negative battery cable.
2. Drain the cooling system.
3. Remove the serpentine belt.
4. Raise the vehicle and support safely. Remove the right front tire and wheel assembly and lower fender shield.
5. Remove the water pump pulley.
6. Remove the 5 mounting screws and remove the pump from the engine.
7. Discard the O-ring.

To install:

8. Using a new O-ring, install the pump to the engine. Torque the mounting bolts to 9 ft. lbs. (12 Nm).

9. Install the water pump pulley and torque screws to 21 ft. lbs. (30 Nm).

10. Install the fender shield and tire and wheel assembly. Lower the vehicle.

11. Install the serpentine belt.

12. Remove the engine temperature sending unit. Fill the radiator with coolant until the coolant comes out the sending unit hole. Install the sending unit and continue to fill the radiator.

13. Connect the negative battery cable, run the vehicle until the thermostat opens, fill the radiator completely and check for leaks.

14. Once cool, recheck the coolant level.

3.9L AND 5.2L ENGINES

1. Disconnect the negative battery cable. Drain the coolant.

2. Remove the shroud from the radiator and slide it over the fan. Unclip the throttle cable and coolant overflow bottle from the fan shroud.

3. Remove the upper radiator hose at the radiator.

4. Remove the fan blade, spacer or viscous drive unit, pulley, bolts and shroud together. Remove the air pump belt and power steering pump belt.

NOTE: Do not place the viscous fan in an upright position because the silicone fluid in the drive could drain into the bearing and contaminate its lubricant.

5. Remove the accessory drive belt(s).

6. Remove the air pump. Remove the air pump bracket and unbolt the power steering pump bracket with the pump still attached and position it out of the way.

7. Remove the water pump pulley from the pump.

8. Disconnect the heater hose, bypass hose and lower hose from the pump.

9. Remove the remaining water pump mounting bolts. Remove the pump from the engine.

To install:

10. Clean and dry the pump mating surfaces. Install a new bypass hose to the engine.

11. Install a new gasket and install the water pump to the engine.

12. Install any bolts that do not retain a bracket. Tighten the bypass hose clamps. Install the heater hose.

13. Install water pump pulley and tighten bolts to 20 ft. lbs. (27 Nm).

14. Install the water pump to compressor front mount bolts and bracket, if removed.

15. Install all remaining brackets and components that were removed during the removal procedure. Torque all water pump retaining bolts that do not go through adjusting slots to 30 ft. lbs. (41 Nm).

16. Install the fan blade, spacer or viscous drive unit, pulley and bolts along with the shroud.

17. Install and adjust the accessory drive belt(s) as required.

FLANGE IN GROOVE   AIR VENT VALVE   FLANGE IN GROOVE

THERMOSTAT

CASTING WALL

Thermostat with air vent valve—3.0L engine

18. Install the upper radiator hose and fan shroud. Reattach the throttle cable and overflow bottle to radiator shroud.

20. Fill the radiator with coolant. This cooling system is self-bleeding, so system bleeding is not required.

21. Connect the negative battery cable, run the vehicle until the thermostat opens, fill the radiator completely and check for leaks.

22. Once cool, recheck the coolant level.

Thermostat

Removal and Installation

EXCEPT 3.9L AND 5.2L ENGINES

1. Disconnect the negative battery cable. Drain the coolant down to thermostat level or below.

2. Remove the radiator hose from the thermostat and remove the thermostat housing.

3. Remove the thermostat and discard the gasket.

4. Clean the housing mating surfaces and use a new gasket.

To install:

5. Install the thermostat into the engine and install housing using new gasket. Install the upper radiator hose.

6. On 2.2L and 2.5L engines, remove the hex-head plug or vacuuum switching valve on the thermostat housing. Fill the radiator with coolant until the coolant comes out the plug hole. Install the plug or valve and continue to fill the radiator. On the 3.3L engine, remove the engine temperature sending unit. Fill the radiator with coolant until the coolant comes out the sending unit hole. Install the sending unit and continue to fill the radiator. All other engines are self-bleeding.

7. Connect the negative battery cable, run the vehicle until the thermostat opens, fill the radiator completely and check for leaks.

8. Once cool, recheck the coolant level.

3.9L AND 5.2L ENGINES

1. Disconnect the negative battery cable. Drain the coolant down to thermostat level or below.

2. Remove the thermostat housing.

3. Remove the thermostat and discard the gasket.

4. Clean the housing mating surfaces and use a new gasket.

5. The installation is the reversal of the removal procedure.

6. Connect the negative battery cable, run the vehicle until the thermostat opens, fill the radiator completely and check for leaks.

7. Once the vehicle has cooled, recheck the coolant level.

Cooling System Bleeding

The thermostat in the 3.0L engines is equipped with a small air vent valve that allows trapped air to bleed from the system during refilling. This valve negates the need for cooling system bleeding in those engines. The 3.9L and 5.2L engines cooling

Cooling system bleed plug—2.2L and 2.5L engines

Engine temperature sending unit—3.3L engine

system is also self-bleeding and does not require bleeding when refilling.

To bleed air from the 2.2L and 2.5L engines, remove the 8mm hex-head plug on the top of the thermostat housing (some engines have a vacuum switching valve at that location). On the 3.3L engine, remove the engine temperature sending unit. Fill the radiator with coolant until the coolant comes out the hole. Install the plug, valve or switch and continue to fill the radiator. This will vent all trapped air from the engine.

FUEL SYSTEM

Fuel System Service Precaution

Safety is the most important factor when performing not only fuel system maintenance but any type of maintenance. Failure to conduct maintenance and repairs in a safe manner may result in serious personal injury or death. Maintenance and testing of the vehicle's fuel system components can be accomplished safely and effectively by adhering to the following rules and guidelines.

• To avoid the possibility of fire and personal injury, always disconnect the negative battery cable unless the repair or test procedure requires that battery voltage be applied.

• Always relieve the fuel system pressure prior to disconnecting any fuel system component (injector, fuel rail, pressure regulator, etc.), fitting or fuel line connection. Exercise extreme caution whenever relieving fuel system pressure to avoid exposing skin, face and eyes to fuel spray. Please be advised that fuel under pressure may penetrate the skin or any part of the body that it contacts.

• Always place a shop towel or cloth around the fitting or connection prior to loosening to absorb any excess fuel due to spillage. Ensure that all fuel spillage (should it occur) is quickly removed from engine surfaces. Ensure that all fuel soaked cloths or towels are deposited into a suitable waste container.

• Always keep a dry chemical (Class B) fire extinguisher near the work area.

• Do not allow fuel spray or fuel vapors to come into contact with a spark or open flame.

• Always use a backup wrench when loosening and tightening fuel line connection fittings. This will prevent unnecessary stress and torsion to fuel line piping. Always follow the proper torque specifications.

• Always replace worn fuel fitting O-rings with new. Do not substitute fuel hose or equivalent where fuel pipe is installed.

Relieving Fuel System Pressure

EXCEPT 1992 3.9L AND 5.2L ENGINES

1. Loosen the fuel filler cap to release fuel tank pressure.

Fuel injector harness connector terminals—except 3.9L engine

Fuel injector harness connector location—2.5L non-turbocharged engine

Fuel injector harness connector location—2.5L turbocharged engine

Fuel injector harness connector location—3.0L engine

2. Locate the fuel injector harness connector.

3. Connect a jumper wire from terminal No. 1 of the appropriate connector to ground.

4. Being careful not to allow contact between the jumper leads, connect a jumper wire to terminal No. 2 of the connector and touch the other end of the jumper to the positive battery post for no longer than 5 seconds. This will relieve fuel pressure.

5. Remove the jumper wires and connect the connector.

1992 3.9L AND 5.2L ENGINES

1. Loosen the fuel filler cap to release fuel tank pressure.

2. Disconnect negative battery cable.

3. Remove the protective cap from pressure test port on the fuel rail. Do not allow fuel to spill onto the intake manifold or exhaust manifold. Place shop towels under and around the port to absorb any fuel when the pressure is released from the fuel rail.

4. Obtain the fuel pressure gauge/hose assembly from tool set

Fuel injector harness connector location—3.3L engine

Injector wiring harness connector—3.9L engine

5069 and remove the gauge from the hose. Place 1 end of the hose in an approved gasoline container.

5. Place a shop towel under the test port.
6. Screw the other end of the hose to the test pressure port. Install the protective cap after all pressure has been released.

Fuel Tank

Removal and Installation

1. Disconnect the negative battery cable.
2. Relieve the fuel pressure.
3. Raise the vehicle and support safely.

4. Using the proper equipment, drain the fuel tank.
5. On Van, remove the screws that fasten the filler tube to the inner and outer fender. On All Wheel Drive Van, remove the fasteners that hold the park brake cable support bracket in place.
6. Disconnect the electrical wiring and all hoses from the tank.
7. Place a transmission jack or equivalent, under the center of the tank and apply slight pressure.
8. Remove the nuts from the mounting straps and remove tank straps.
9. Lower the tank far enough to allow access to the fuel supply and return hoses, and disconnect hoses. Disconnect fuel vapor line from pressure relief/rollover valve.
10. Lower tank from vehicle.

To install:

11. Raise the tank into position and connect all electrical harnesses and vacuum hoses.
12. Install the tank straps and tighten the retaining nuts to 35–40 ft. lbs. (47–54 Nm).
13. Install vent hoses, if not done, and check all connections.
14. Fill fuel tank, install fuel filler cap and reconnect negative battery cable. Pressurize the fuel system and inspect for leaks.

Fuel Filter

Removal and Installation

CARBURETED ENGINE

1. Disconnect the negative battery cable.
2. Raise the vehicle and support safely, if necessary.
3. Remove the air cleaner assembly, if necessary. Remove the fuel filter and any hoses that are included with the new filter kit.

NOTE: Some vehicles may be equipped with a field package designed to combat driveability problems associated with fuel foaming. Affected vehicles have a special replaceable filter/reservoir mounted either on a plate on the carburetor or near the thermostat. When the kit is installed on a 2.2L engine, the conventional filter is discarded. Do not install a conventional filter or conventional clamps or hoses in place of the special replacement parts; they are not compatible with the electronic fuel pump installed with the kit.

4. Install the new filter, hoses and clamps.
5. Connect the negative battery cable, start the engine and check for leaks.

FUEL INJECTED ENGINE

——— **CAUTION** ———

Do not use conventional fuel filters, hoses or clamps when servicing this fuel system. They are not compatible with the injection system and could fail, causing personal injury or damage to the vehicle. Use only hoses and clamps specifically designed for fuel injection.

1. Relieve the fuel pressure.
2. Disconnect the negative battery cable. On All Wheel Drive Van, it will be necessary to remove the exhaust heat shield and the converter support bracket.
3. The filter is located on the frame rail towards the rear of the vehicle. Raise the vehicle and support safely. Remove the filter retaining screw and remove the filter assembly from the mounting plate.
4. Loosen the outlet hose clamp on the filter and inlet hose clamp on the rear fuel tube.
5. Wrap a shop towel around the hoses to absorb fuel. Remove the hoses from the filter and fuel tube and discard the clamps and the filter.

To install:

6. Install the inlet hose on the fuel tube and tighten the new clamp to 10 inch lbs.

7. Install the outlet hose on the filter outlet fitting and tighten the new clamp to 10 inch lbs.

8. Position the filter assembly on the mounting plate and tighten the mounting screw to 75 inch lbs. (8 Nm).

9. Connect the negative battery cable, start the engine and check for leaks.

Mechanical Fuel Pump

Pressure Testing

1. Raise the vehicle and support safely.

2. Connect a pressure gauge (0–15 psi minimum range) to the fuel pump outlet fitting.

3. Crank the engine several times while observing the gauge.

4. The 2.2L should develop 4.5–6.0 psi. If equipped with the field package noted above, fuel pressure should be 13–15 psi.

Removal and Installation

1. Disconnect the negative battery cable.

2. Raise the vehicle and support safely, if necessary. Remove the oil filter.

3. Disconnect the fuel lines from the pump and plug.

4. Remove the fuel pump retaining bolts or nuts and remove the pump from the engine.

5. Clean and dry the mounting surfaces and bolt holes. Install new gasket on mating surface.

6. The installation is the reverse of the removal procedure.

7. Connect the negative battery cable, start the engine and check for leaks.

Electric Fuel Pump

Pressure Testing

1. Relieve the fuel pressure.

2. Properly connect the fuel system pressure tester.

3. With the key in the **RUN** position, put the DRB I or II in the activate auto shutdown relay mode; this will activate the fuel pump and pressurize the system.

4. If the pressure is within specifications, remove pressure tester from the fuel system.

5. If fuel pressure is below specifications, install the tester in the fuel supply line between the tank and the filter and repeat the test.

6. If the pressure is 5 psi higher than in Step 5, replace the fuel filter. If no change is observed, squeeze the return hose. If pressure increases, replace the pressure regulator. If no change is observed, the problem is either a plugged in-tank sock filter or a defective pump.

7. If fuel pressure is above specifications, remove the fuel return line hose from the chassis line at the fuel tank and connect a 3 foot piece of fuel hose to the return line. Put the other end into a 2 gallon minimum capacity approved gasoline container. Repeat the test. If pressure is now correct, check the in-tank return hose for kinking. Replace the fuel pump assembly if the in-tank reservoir check valve or aspirator jet is obstructed.

8. If pressure is still above specifications, remove the fuel return hose from the throttle body. Connect hose to the throttle body return nipple and place the other end of the hose in a clean container. Repeat the test. If pressure is now correct, check for a restricted fuel return line. If no change is observed, replace the fuel pressure regulator.

Removal and Installation
CARAVAN, VOYAGER AND TOWN & COUNTRY
Front Wheel Drive

The fuel pump/level unit assembly is installed in the top of the fuel tank. It consists of the fuel pump, fuel pump reservoir, pressure relief/rollover valve, electrical connector for the send-

Removing the fuel pump from the tank – Caravan, Voyager and Town & Country

ing unit, fuel filler vent, supply and return tube connections and the drain tube nipple. The level unit can be serviced separately from the pump.

1. Relieve the fuel pressure.

2. Disconnect the negative battery cable.

3. Raise the vehicle and support safely.

4. Using the proper equipment, drain the fuel tank.

5. Remove the screws that hold the filler neck to the quarter panel.

6. Disconnect the wiring and hoses from the tank.

7. Place a transmission jack or equivalent, under the center of the tank and apply slight pressure. Remove the tank straps.

8. Lower the tank and remove the filler tube from the tank.

9. Disconnect the vapor separator rollover valve hose and remove the fuel tank from the vehicle.

10. To remove fuel pump/level unit, use a hammer and a brass drift and tap the lock ring counterclockwise to release the pump.

11. Remove the fuel pump from the tank.

12. To remove fuel inlet strainer from the pump/level unit, gently pry sock from the ferrule and pump body with broad bladed tool taking care not to damage the pump inlet. On 1990–92 pumps, gently bend locking tabs on pump reservoir body to clear locking tangs on the fuel pump strainer. Remove strainer. To install new strainer, lubricate strainer O-ring and insert strainer onto the inlet of the fuel pump reservoir body. Bend locking tabs into position.

To install:

13. Install a new O-ring to the pump.

14. Install the pump with the new inlet filter and locknut into the tank.

15. Install the lock ring with a hammer and brass punch turning the ring clockwise.

16. Install the fuel tank into the vehicle.

17. Connect the negative battery cable, start the engine and check for leaks.

All Wheel Drive

The fuel pump module is installed in the top of the fuel tank. It contains the fuel pump, fuel pump reservoir, pressure relief/rollover valve, electrical connector for the sending unit, fuel filler vent, supply and return tube connections and the drain tube nipple. The level unit can be serviced separately from the pump. The factory recommends that the locknut be replaced when the module is removed.

1. Relieve the fuel pressure.

2. Disconnect the negative battery cable.

3. Raise the vehicle and support safely.

4. Using the proper equipment, drain the fuel tank.

5. Remove the screws that hold the filler neck to the quarter panel.

6. Disconnect the wiring and hoses from the tank. Remove the support bracket for the parking brake cable and the bracket for the converter.

7. Place a transmission jack or equivalent, under the center of the tank and apply slight pressure. Remove the tank straps.

8. Lower the tank and remove the filler tube from the tank.

9. Disconnect the vapor separator rollover valve hose and remove the fuel tank from the vehicle.

10. Remove the fuel module from the tank. It will be necessary to hold down on module while removing the retainer clamp or nut. The module is spring loaded into the tank. Mark position of sender wires and disconnect. Remove sender unit from module. Replace module and pump assembly as a unit.

11. To remove the inlet strainer, gently bend locking tabs on pump reservoir to clear locking tangs on the fuel pump filter. Remove strainer. To install new strainer, lubricate strainer O-ring and insert strainer onto the inlet of the fuel pump reservoir body. Bend locking tabs into position.

To install:

12. Install a new O-ring to the pump module.

13. Install the module with the new inlet filter and locknut into the tank. Align the arrow on the edge of the module so it lies between the lines on the lip of the gas tank.

14. Tighten the retaining clamp or nut while holding down on the module.

15. Install the fuel tank into the vehicle.

16. Connect the negative battery cable, start the engine and check for leaks.

DAKOTA

The fuel pump module is installed in the top of the fuel tank. It contains the fuel pump, fuel pump reservoir, pressure relief/rollover valve, electrical connector for the sending unit, fuel filler vent, supply and return tube connections and the drain tube nipple. The level unit can be serviced separately from the pump. The factory recommends that the locknut be replaced when the module is removed.

1. Relieve the fuel pressure.

2. Disconnect the negative battery cable.

3. Raise the vehicle and support safely.

4. Using the proper equipment, drain the fuel tank.

5. Disconnect the vent hoses and filler hose from the tank and remove the hoses from the bracket attached to the top of the frame rail, if equipped.

6. Place a transmission jack or equivalent, under the center of the tank and apply slight pressure.

7. Remove the inboard retaining strap J-bolt nuts and remove the straps.

8. Lower the tank enough to reach in and disconnect the electrical connector and the remaining fuel tubes from the top of the module. Lower the tank from the vehicle.

9. Remove the fuel module from the tank. It will be necessary to hold down on module while removing the retainer clamp or nut. The module is spring loaded into the tank. Mark position of sender wires and disconnect. Remove sender unit from module. Replace module and pump assembly as a unit.

10. To remove the inlet strainer, gently bend locking tabs on pump reservoir to clear locking tangs on the fuel pump filter. Remove strainer. To install new strainer, lubricate strainer O-ring and insert strainer onto the inlet of the fuel pump reservoir body. Bend locking tabs into position.

To install:

11. Install a new O-ring to the pump module.

12. Install the module with the new inlet filter and locknut into the tank. Align the arrow on the edge of the module so it lies between the lines on the lip of the gas tank.

13. Tighten the retaining clamp or nut while holding down on the module.

14. Install the fuel tank into the vehicle.

15. Connect the negative battery cable, start the engine and check for leaks.

Carburetor

Removal and Installation

1. Disconnect the negative battery cable.

2. Remove the air cleaner assembly.

3. Remove and install the fuel tank cap to relieve any pressure in the tank.

4. Matchmark all vacuum hoses and electrical connectors and remove them from the carburetor.

5. Disconnect the throttle, cruise control, choke and kickdown cables and linkages, if equipped.

6. Disconnect and plug the fuel inlet line.

7. Remove the mounting bolts and/or nuts and remove the carburetor from the intake manifold.

To install:

8. Clean the mounting surface of the manifold and install a new base gasket.

9. Install the mounting bolts and/or nuts and tighten them alternately to compress the base gasket evenly.

10. Connect the fuel line.

11. Connect the throttle, cruise control, choke and kickdown cables and linkages, if equipped.

12. Install all vacuum hoses and electrical connectors in their proper locations.

13. Install the air cleaner.

14. Connect the negative battery cable, start the engine and perform all necessary adjustments.

Idle Speed Adjustment

2.2L ENGINE

1. Before checking or adjusting the idle speed, check ignition timing and adjust if necessary.

2. Disconnect and plug the vacuum connector at the coolant vacuum switch cold closed valve.

3. Unplug the connector at the radiator fan and install a jumper wire so the fan will run continuously.

4. Remove the PCV valve from the valve cover and allow it to draw under hood air.

5. Connect a tachometer to engine.

6. Ground the carburetor switch with a jumper wire.

7. Disconnect the oxygen system test connector located on left fender shield, if equipped.

8. Start and run the engine until normal operating temperature is reached.

9. If tachometer indicates idle speed is not at specifications, turn the idle speed screw until correct idle speed is obtained. The screw is located on top of the solenoid mounted on the back of the carburetor.

10. Reconnect the PCV valve, oxygen connector and vacuum connector.

11. Remove jumper wire and reconnect the radiator fan.

12. After Steps 9 and 10 are completed, the idle speed may change slightly. This is normal and engine speed should not be readjusted.

13. Make sure the solenoid kicker moves the throttle blade adequately so the idle does not change when the air conditioning is working.

3.9L ENGINE

1. Start the engine and run until at normal operating temperature. Check and adjust the ignition timing. Turn the engine **OFF**.

2. Disconnect and plug the EGR hose. Disconnect the oxygen sensor, if equipped.

3. Disconnect and plug the $\frac{3}{16}$ in. hose at the canister.

4. Remove the PCV hose from the valve cover and allow it to draw under hood air.

5. Ground the carburetor switch with a jumper wire, if equipped.

6. Disconnect the vacuum hose from the computer, if equipped and connect an auxiliary vacuum supply of 16 in. Hg.

7. Make sure all accessories are off. Install a tachometer and start the engine.

8. Allow the engine to run for 2 minutes to stabilize. Turn the idle speed screw until the correct idle speed according to the Vehicle Emission Control Information label is reached.

9. Connect all wires and hoses. It is normal for the idle speed to vary after all hoses and wires are reconnected; do not readjust.

Idle Mixture Adjustment

1. Disconnect and plug the EGR hose. Disconnect the oxygen sensor, if equipped.

2. Disconnect and plug the $\frac{3}{16}$ in. hose at the canister.

3. Remove the PCV hose from the valve cover and allow it to draw under hood air.

4. Ground the carburetor switch with a jumper wire, if equipped.

5. Disconnect the vacuum hose from the computer, if equipped, and connect an auxiliary vacuum supply of 16 in. Hg.

6. Remove the concealment plug. Disconnect the vacuum supply hose to the tee and install a propane supply hose in its place.

7. Make sure all accessories are OFF. Install a tachometer and start the engine. Allow the engine to run for 2 minutes to stabilize.

8. Open the main propane valve. Slowly open the propane metering valve until the maximum engine speed is reached. When too much propane is added, the engine will begin to stumble; at this point back off until the engine stabilizes.

9. Adjust the idle speed to obtain the specified propane rpm. Fine tune the metering valve to obtain the highest rpm again. If there has been a change to the maximum rpm, readjust the idle screw to the specified propane rpm.

10. Turn the main propane valve off and allow the engine to run for 1 minute to stabilize.

11. Adjust the mixture screw to obtain the smoothest idle at the specified idle rpm.

12. Open the main propane valve. Fine tune the metering valve to obtain the highest rpm. If the maximum engine speed is more that 25 rpm different than the specified propane rpm, repeat the procedure.

13. Turn the propane valves off and remove the propane canister. Reinstall the vacuum supply hose to the tee.

14. Perform the idle speed adjustment procedure.

15. Connect all wires and hoses.

Service Adjustments

For all carburetor service adjustment procedures and Specifications, please refer to "Carburetor Service" in the Unit Repair section.

Fuel Injection

For further information, please refer to Chilton's Electronic Engine Controls Manual.

Idle Speed Adjustment

SINGLE AND DUAL POINT INJECTION

1. Start the engine and allow it to reach normal operating temperature. If it is already hot, run it for 2 minutes.

2. Turn the engine OFF and allow 1 minute for the Idle Speed Control (ISC) actuator shaft to fully extend.

Adjusting the idle speed—Single and Dual Point Injection

3. Disconnect the ISC actuator connector and the coolant temperature sensor.

4. Connect a tachometer to the engine and start the engine.

5. Adjust the extension screw on the actuator shaft until the rpm is within specifications.

6. Turn the engine OFF. Reconnect the ISC actuator connector and the coolant temperature sensor. Remove the tachometer.

EXCEPT SINGLE AND DUAL POINT INJECTION

The idle speed is controlled by the automatic idle speed motor (AIS) which is controlled by the logic module. The logic module receives data from various sensors and switches in the system and adjusts the engine idle to a predetermined speed. Idle speed specifications can be found on the Vehicle Emission Control Information (VECI) label located in the engine compartment. If the idle speed is not within specifications and there are no problems with the system, the throttle body should be replaced.

Idle Mixture Adjustment

There is no idle mixture adjustment provided with any Chrysler fuel injection system.

Fuel Injector

Removal and Installation

SINGLE AND DUAL POINT INJECTION

2.5L and 3.9L Engines

1. Remove the air cleaner assembly.
2. Relieve the fuel pressure.
3. Disconnect the negative battery cable.

NOTE: On the 3.9L engine, there is a small spacer below the injector hold-down clamp. Take the proper precaution to prevent this spacer from falling into the throttle body.

4. Remove the injector hold-down Torx screw, the hold-down and the spacer, if equipped.

5. Using a small flat-tipped tool, lift the cap off of the injector.

6. Using the same tool, gently pry the injector from its pod.

7. Remove the lower O-ring from the pod.

Injector hold-down and spacer—Single and Dual Point Injection

Installing the injector to the cap—Single and Dual Point Injection

To install:

8. Install the new lower O-ring on the injector.

9. Align the injector terminal housing with the locating socket in the injector cap.

10. Press the injector into cap so the upper O-ring flange is flush with the lower surface of the cap.

11. Spray the inner surfaces of the injector pod with suitable carburetor parts cleaner to remove residual varnish and gasoline.

12. Lubricate the O-rings sparingly with unmedicated petroleum jelly.

13. Place the injector and cap into the injector pod and align the cap locating pin with the locating hole in the casting. On the 3.9L engine, the right side locating pin in 5mm in diameter and will not fit into the other hole. The left side pin is 4mm in diameter and will be loose in the other hole.

14. Press firmly on the injector cap until it is flush with the casting surface.

15. Install the spacer, if equipped and align the holes in the hold-down with the pins on the caps and install.

16. Push down on the caps, install the screw and torque to 35 inch lbs. (4 Nm).

17. Connect the negative battery cable and check for leaks using the DRB I or II to activate the fuel pump.

18. Install the air cleaner.

Fuel injector removal and installation—2.5L turbocharged engine

MULTI-PORT INJECTION

2.5L Turbocharged Engine

1. Relieve the fuel pressure.

2. Disconnect the negative battery cable.

3. Disconnect the injector wiring connector from the injector.

4. Unbolt the fuel rail from engine and remove. Position the fuel rail assembly so the fuel injectors are easily accessible.

5. Remove the injector clip from the fuel rail and injector. Pull the injector straight out of the fuel rail receiver cup.

6. Check the injector O-ring for damage. If the O-ring is damaged, replace it. If the injector is being reused, install a protective cap on the injector tip to prevent damage.

7. Repeat the procedure for the remaining injectors.

To Install:

8. Before installing an injector the rubber O-ring should be lubricated with a drop of clean engine oil to aid in installation.

9. Install injector top end into fuel rail receiver cup.

10. Install injector clip by sliding the open end into top slot of the injector and onto the receiver cup ridge.

11. Repeat the steps for the remaining injectors.

12. Install the fuel rail to the engine and secure.

13. Connect the negative battery cable and check for leaks using the DRB I or II to activate the fuel pump.

3.0L Engine

1. Relieve the fuel pressure.

2. Disconnect the negative battery cable.

3. Remove the air cleaner to throttle body hose.

4. Disconnect the throttle cable from the throttle body and disconnect the kickdown linkage. Remove the throttle cable bracket attaching bolts.

5. Disconnect the electrical connectors to the throttle body.

6. Matchmark and carefully remove the vacuum hoses from the throttle body.

7. Remove the PCV and brake booster hoses from the air intake plenum.

8. Remove the ignition coil from the intake plenum, if mounted there.

9. Remove the EGR tube flange from the intake plenum, if equipped.

10. Unplug the coolant temperature sensor and charge temperature sensor, if equipped.

Fuel rail assembly—3.0L engine

Fuel Rail Installed—3.3L Engine

11. Remove the vacuum connection from the air intake plenum vacuum connector.

12. Remove the fuel hoses from the fuel rail and plug them.

13. Remove the air intake plenum to intake manifold bolts and remove the plenum and gaskets. Cover the intake manifold openings.

14. Remove the vacuum hoses from the fuel rail.

15. Disconnect the fuel injector wiring harness.

16. Remove the fuel rail attaching bolts and remove the fuel rail from vehicle. Position the rail on the bench upside down so the injectors are easily accessible.

17. Remove the small connector retainer clip and unplug the injector. Remove the injector clip off the fuel rail and injector. Pull the injector straight out off the rail.

To install:

18. Lubricate the rubber O-ring with clean oil and install to the rail receiver cap. Install the injector clip to the **TOP** slot of the injector, plug in the connector and install the connector clip.

19. Install the fuel rail to the vehicle and plug in the injector harness. Connect the vacuum hoses to the fuel rail.

20. Install new intake plenum gaskets with the beaded sealer side up and install the intake plenum. Torque the attaching bolts and nuts to 115 inch lbs. (13 Nm).

21. Install the fuel hoses to the fuel rail.

22. Install or connect all items that were removed or disconnected from the intake plenum and throttle body.

23. Connect the negative battery cable and check for leaks using the DRB I or II to activate the fuel pump.

3.3L Engine

1. Relieve the fuel pressure.

2. Disconnect the negative battery cable.

3. Remove the air cleaner and hose assembly.

4. Disconnect the throttle cable. Remove the wiring harness from the throttle cable bracket and intake manifold water tube.

5. Remove the vacuum hose harness from the throttle body.

6. Remove the PCV and brake booster hoses from the air intake plenum.

7. Remove the EGR tube flange from the intake plenum, if equipped.

8. Unplug the charge temperature sensor and unplug all vacuum hoses from the intake plenum.

9. Remove the cylinder head to intake plenum strut.

10. Disconnect the MAP sensor and oxygen sensor connector. Remove the engine mounted ground strap.

11. Release the fuel hose quick disconnect fittings and remove the hoses from the fuel rail. Plug the hoses.

12. Remove the Direct Ignition System (DIS) coils and the alternator bracket to intake manifold bolt.

13. Remove the intake manifold bolts and rotate the manifold back over the rear valve cover. Cover the intake manifold.

14. Remove the vacuum harness from the pressure regulator.

15. Remove the fuel tube retainer bracket screw and fuel rail attaching bolts. Spread the retainer bracket to allow for clearance when removing the fuel tube.

16. Remove the fuel rail injector wiring clip from the alternator bracket.

17. Disconnect the cam sensor, coolant temperature sensor and engine temperature sensor.

18. Remove the fuel rail.

19. Position the rail on the bench so the injectors are easily accessible.

20. Remove the small connector retainer clip and unplug the injector. Remove the injector clip off the fuel rail and injector. Pull the injector straight out of the rail.

To install:

21. Lubricate the rubber O-ring with clean oil and install to the rail receiver cap. Install the injector clip to the slot in the injector, plug in the connector and install the connector clip.

22. Install the fuel rail.

23. Connect the cam sensor, coolant temperature sensor and engine temperature sensor.

24. Install the fuel rail injector wiring clip to the alternator bracket.

25. Install the fuel rail attaching bolts and fuel tube retainer bracket screw.

26. Install the vacuum harness to the pressure regulator.

27. Install the intake manifold with a new gasket. Install the bolts only finger-tight. Install the alternator bracket to intake manifold bolt and the cylinder head to intake manifold strut and bolts. Torque the intake manifold mounting bolts to 21 ft. lbs. (28 Nm) starting from the middle and working outward. Torque the bracket and strut bolts to 40 ft. lbs. (54 Nm).

28. Install or connect all items that were removed or disconnected from the intake manifold and throttle body.

29. Connect the fuel hoses to the rail. Push the fittings in until they click in place.

30. Install the air cleaner assembly.

31. Connect the negative battery cable and check for leaks using the DRB I or II to activate the fuel pump.

3.9L and 5.2L Engines

1. Disconnect negative battery cable.

Fuel rail assembly—1992 3.9L and 5.2L engines

2. Relieve the fuel pressure.
3. Remove the air cleaner. Remove the throttle body from intake manifold.
4. Disconnect the electrical connectors at fuel injectors.
5. Remove vacuum line at fuel pressure regulator.

6. On 3.9L engine, disconnect electrical connector at Charge Air Temperature sensor.
7. Remove canister purge solenoid and bracket assembly from intake manifold. Disconnect 2 fuel lines at the rear of the fuel rail and remove the remaining fuel rail mounting bolts.
8. Gently rock the left side fuel rail until the injectors start to clear the injector bores. Repeat the procedure on the right side fuel rail. Work both side fuel rails until the clearance is large enough to extract both fuel rails from the engine.
9. Remove the clips retaining the fuel injector to the fuel rail. Remove the injector from the fuel rail by pulling straight out from the rail.

To install:
10. Lubricate the rubber O-ring with clean oil and install to the rail receiver cap. Install the injector clip to the slot in the injector, plug in the connector and install the connector clip.
11. Install the fuel rail to the engine.
12. Push the right and left side fuel rail down alternately until the fuel injectors have bottomed on the injector shoulder. Install fuel rail mounting bolts.
13. Install purge solenoid to intake manifold. Connect the electrical connector to the Charge Air Temperature sensor.
14. Connect wire harness to fuel injectors. Install throttle body and new base gasket to intake manifold.
15. Install vacuum lines to fuel pressure regulator. Install 2 fuel lines to rear of the fuel rail.
16. Install the air cleaner and the negative battery cable. Start the engine and check for leaks.

EMISSION CONTROLS

For further information, please refer to Chilton's Emission Controls Manual.

Emission Warning Lamps

Resetting

1988 VEHICLES

1. Locate the EMR switch module. It is a plastic box located either on the lower portion of the steering column or to the left of the steering column.
2. Remove the 9 volt battery (under the small black panel) from the module. Some do not have the 9 volt battery.

3. Reset the switch by inserting a small rod into a hole in the case of the module, which closes a switch and turns the light off.
4. Install a new 9 volt battery, if equipped.

1989–92 VEHICLES

1. Connect the DRB II to the diagnostic connector.
2. Turn the ignition switch to the **RUN** position and access the Emissions EMR Tests on the DRB II.
3. Select EMR Memory Check.
4. Select Reset EMR Light. This will reset the EMR timing in the computer and turn the light off.
5. Disconnect the DRB II.

ENGINE MECHANICAL

NOTE: Disconnecting the negative battery cable on some vehicles may interfere with the functions of the on board computer systems and may require the computer to undergo a relearning process, once the negative battery cable is reconnected.

Engine Assembly

Removal and Installation

CARAVAN, VOYAGER AND TOWN & COUNTRY

2.2L and 2.5L Engines

1. If equipped with fuel injection, relieve the fuel pressure. Disconnect the negative battery cable and all engine ground straps.
2. Mark the hood hinge outline on the hood and remove the hood.

3. Drain the cooling system. Remove the radiator hoses, fan assembly, radiator shroud and radiator.
4. Remove the air cleaner, duct hoses and oil filter.
5. Unbolt the air conditioning compressor from its mount, if equipped, and position it to the side.
6. Remove the power steering pump mounting bolts and position the pump to the side, without disconnecting any fluid lines.
7. Label and disconnect all electrical connectors from the engine, alternator and carburetor or fuel injection system.
8. Disconnect the fuel line, heater hoses and accelerator linkage.
9. Disconnect the air pump lines and remove the pump, if equipped.
10. Remove the alternator.
11. Disconnect the shift linkage(s), clutch linkage, as required, and speedometer cable.
12. Raise the vehicle and support safely. Disconnect the ex-

haust pipe from the manifold. Remove the right inner fender shield.

13. If equipped with a manual transaxle, remove the transaxle.

14. If equipped with an automatic transaxle, perform the following procedures:

    a. Remove the lower cover from the transaxle case.

    b. Remove the exhaust pipe-to-exhaust manifold bolts. Separate the pipe from the manifold.

    c. Remove the starter and set it aside.

    d. Matchmark the flexplate to the torque converter, for installation purposes.

    e. Remove the torque converter bolts. Separate the converter from the flexplate. Remove the lower bell housing bolts.

15. Lower the vehicle and support the transaxle (if still in the vehicle) with a floor jack or equivalent. Attach an engine lifting device to the engine.

16. To lower the engine, separate the right side engine bracket from the yoke bracket. To raise the engine, remove the yoke/insulator long bolt.

NOTE: If removing the insulator-to-rail screws, first mark the position of the insulator on the side rail to insure proper alignment during reinstallation.

17. Remove the remaining bell housing bolts. Remove the front engine mount nut/bolt and the left insulator through bolt or the insulator bracket-to-transaxle bolts.

18. Lift the engine from the vehicle.

To install:

19. Lower the engine into the engine compartment. Loosely install all of the mounting bolts. With all bolts installed, torque the:

    Engine to mount bolts to 40 ft. lbs.

    Engine to transaxle bolts to 70 ft. lbs.

    Torque converter bolts to 40 ft. lbs.

20. Remove the engine hoist and transmission holding fixture.

21. Secure ground strap. Install right inner splash shield and starter assembly.

22. Connect the exhaust system to the engine manifold.

23. Reinstall the alternator, power steering pump and the air conditioner compressor.

24. Connect the fuel line, heater hoses and the accelerator cable. Reconnect all electrical connectors.

25. Install oil filter and refill the engine crankcase to the correct level.

26. Reinstall the radiator hoses, fan assembly, radiator shroud and radiator. Add coolant to the proper level.

27. Install the hood.

28. Start the engine and run until operating temperature is reached. Recheck all fluid levels and add as required.

3.0L and 3.3L Engines

1. If equipped with fuel injection, relieve the fuel pressure. Disconnect the negative battery cable.

2. Matchmark the hinge-to-hood position and remove the hood.

3. Drain the cooling system. Disconnect and label all engine electrical connections.

4. Remove the coolant hoses from the radiator and engine. Remove the radiator and cooling fan assembly.

5. Remove the air cleaner assembly. Disconnect the fuel lines from the engine. Disconnect the accelerator cable from the engine.

6. Raise the vehicle and support safely. Drain the engine oil.

7. Remove the air conditioning compressor mounting bolts, the drive belt(s) and position the compressor to the side. Disconnect the exhaust pipe from the exhaust manifold.

8. Remove the transaxle inspection cover, matchmark the converter to the flexplate and remove the torque converter bolts.

9. Remove the power steering pump mounting bolts and set the pump aside, upright, with the fluid lines attached.

10. Remove the lower bell housing bolts. Disconnect and label the starter motor wiring and remove the starter motor from the engine.

11. Lower the vehicle. Disconnect and label the vacuum hoses and engine ground straps.

12. Support the transaxle with a floor jack or equivalent. Attach an engine lifting device to the engine.

13. Remove the upper transaxle-to-engine bolts.

14. To separate the engine mounts from the insulators, mark the right insulator-to-right frame support and remove the mounting bolts. Remove the front engine mount through bolt. Remove the left insulator through bolt, from inside the wheel housing. Remove the insulator bracket-to-transaxle bolts.

15. Lift and remove the engine from the vehicle.

To install:

16. Lower the engine into the engine compartment. Align the engine mounts and install the bolts; do not tighten the bolts until all bolts have been installed. Install the upper transaxle-to-engine mounting bolts and torque to 75 ft. lbs.

17. Remove the engine lifting fixture from the engine.

18. Raise the vehicle and support safely.

19. Align the converter marks and install the torque converter bolts. Install the transaxle inspection cover.

20. Connect the exhaust pipe to the exhaust manifold. Install the starter motor and connect the wiring.

21. Install the power steering pump and air conditioning compressor. Adjust the drive belt tension, if necessary.

22. Lower the vehicle. Reconnect all vacuum hoses and electrical connections to the engine.

23. Connect the fuel lines and accelerator cable.

24. Install the radiator and fan assembly. Connect the fan motor wiring. Connect the radiator hoses and refill the cooling system.

25. Refill the engine with the proper oil to the correct level.

26. Connect the engine ground straps. Install the hood and connect the battery.

27. Start and run the engine until normal operating temperature is reached. Check for leaks and correct levels.

DAKOTA

2.5L Engine

1. If equipped with fuel injection, relieve the fuel pressure. Disconnect the negative battery cable and all engine ground straps.

2. Mark the hood hinge outline on the hood and remove the hood.

3. Drain the cooling system. Remove the radiator hoses, heater hoses, radiator shroud and radiator.

4. Remove the air cleaner, duct hoses and oil filter.

5. Unbolt the air conditioning compressor from its mount, if equipped, and position it to the side.

6. Remove the power steering pump mounting bolts and position the pump to the side, without disconnecting any fluid lines.

7. Label and disconnect all electrical connectors from the engine, alternator and carburetor or fuel injection system.

8. Disconnect the fuel line, heater hoses and accelerator linkage.

9. Disconnect the air pump lines and remove the pump, if equipped.

10. Remove the alternator. Remove the charcoal canister and the horn(s).

11. Disconnect the shift linkage(s), clutch linkage, as required, and speedometer cable.

12. Raise the vehicle and support safely. Disconnect the exhaust pipe from the manifold. Remove the right inner fender shield.

13. Remove the exhaust pipe-to-exhaust manifold bolts. Separate the pipe from the manifold. Remove the starter and set it aside.

14. Matchmark the flexplate to the torque converter, for installation purposes. Remove the torque converter bolts. Separate the converter from the flexplate.

15. Remove the lower bell housing bolts.

16. Lower the vehicle and support the transmission, if still in the vehicle, with a floor jack or equivalent. Attach an engine lifting device to the engine.

17. Remove the engine mount bolts.

18. Lift the engine from the vehicle.

To install:

19. Lower the engine into the engine compartment. Loosely install all of the mounting bolts. With all bolts installed, torque the:

Transmission to clutch housing bolts to 30 ft. lbs.
Engine front mount through bolts and nuts to 50 ft. lbs.
Torque converter bolts to 40 ft. lbs.

20. Remove the engine hoist and transmission holding fixture.

21. Secure ground strap. Install right inner splash shield and starter assembly.

22. Connect the exhaust system to the engine manifold.

23. Reinstall the alternator, power steering pump and the air conditioner compressor.

24. Connect the fuel line, heater hoses and the accelerator cable. Reconnect all electrical connectors.

25. Install throttle body with new gasket to intake manifold and torque mounting nuts to 50 ft. lbs. (68 Nm).

26. Install oil filter and refill the engine crankcase to the correct level.

27. Reinstall the radiator hoses, heater hoses, radiator shroud and radiator. Add coolant to fill to the proper level.

28. Install the hood.

29. Start the engine and run until operating temperature is reached. Recheck all fluid levels and add as required.

3.9L and 5.2L Engines

1. If equipped with fuel injection, relieve the fuel pressure. Disconnect the negative battery cable and all engine ground straps.

2. Mark the hood hinge outline on the hood and remove the hood.

3. Drain the cooling system. Remove the radiator hoses, heater hoses, radiator shroud and radiator.

4. Remove the air cleaner, duct hoses and oil filter. Remove the distributor cap with the wires installed.

5. Unbolt the air conditioning compressor from its mount, if equipped and position it to the side.

6. Remove the power steering pump mounting bolts and position the pump to the side, without disconnecting any fluid lines.

7. Label and disconnect all electrical connectors from the engine, alternator and carburetor or fuel injection system.

8. Disconnect the fuel line, heater hoses and accelerator linkage.

9. Disconnect the air pump lines and remove the pump, if equipped.

10. Remove the alternator. Remove the charcoal canister and the horn(s).

11. Disconnect the shift linkage(s), clutch linkage (as required) and speedometer cable.

12. Raise the vehicle and support safely. Disconnect the exhaust pipe from the manifold. Remove the right inner fender shield.

13. Remove the exhaust pipe-to-exhaust manifold bolts. Separate the pipe from the manifold. Remove the starter and set it aside.

14. Matchmark the flexplate to the torque converter, for installation purposes. Remove the torque converter bolts. Separate the converter from the flexplate.

15. Remove the lower bell housing bolts.

16. On manual transmission, support transmission with a stand and disconnect the clutch release mechanism. Remove the

Interconnected motor mounts—Dakota with 4WD

transmission to clutch housing bolts. Move the engine forward until the drive pinion clears the clutch disc.

17. Remove the engine mount bolts.

18. Install the engine lifting fixture. Do not lift the engine by the intake manifold.

19. If equipped with 2WD, remove the engine front mount nuts.

20. If equipped with 4WD, the engine and front driving axle are connected through insulators and support brackets. Support the axle and separate as follows:

a. On the left side, remove the 2 bolts attaching the bracket to the transmission bell housing and 2 bracket to pinion nose adaptor bolts. Separate the engine from the insulator by removing the upper nut washer assembly and through-bolt from the engine support bracket.

b. On the right side, remove the 2 bracket to axle bolts and 1 bracket to bellhouisng bolt. Separate the engine from the insulator by removing the upper nut washer assembly and the through-bolt from the engine support bracket.

21. Lower the vehicle and remove the engine.

To install:

22. Lower the engine into position and install the engine mount bolts. Install the upper bell housing bolts. Remove the engine removal device. Install the oil dipstick.

23. Raise the vehicle and support safely.

24. Install the engine mount and interconnect nuts and bolts. Install the remaining bell housing bolts.

25. If equipped with a manual transmission, install the transmission and all related parts.

26. If equipped with an automatic transmission, align the torque converter and flexplate and install the bolts. Install the inspection plate, starter and the engine to transmission struts, if equipped.

27. Connect the rubber fuel inlet and return hoses to the fuel lines at the front of the vehicle.

28. Install the exhaust pipe to the exhaust manifold(s). Install the lower radiator hose.

29. Lower the vehicle. Install the horn(s) and the charcoal canister.

30. Connect the heater hoses to the engine.

31. Make sure the negative battery cable is not connected to the battery. Connect the engine side of the negative cable to the engine. Install the alternator, air pump, power steering pump and all brackets.

32. Install the air conditioning compressor.

33. Install the throttle body, if equipped using a new base gasket and connect all linkages and cables. Connect all electrical connectors and vacuum hoses that were disconnected during the engine removal procedure.

34. Install accessory drive belts and adjust belt tensions as required.

35. Install the radiator and shroud.

36. Install the distributor cap with all spark plug wires attached.

37. Install the air cleaner assembly.

38. Install the hood.

39. Fill the engine with the specified amount of oil and fill the radiator with coolant.

40. Connect the negative battery cable and set all adjustments to specification.

Engine Mounts

Removal and Installation

FRONT MOUNT

2.2L and 2.5L Engines

1. Disconnect negative battery cable. Remove skid plate, if equipped.

2. Position fan assembly to insure clearance for radiator and top hose when engine is moved. Install an engine support fixture.

3. Raise and safely support vehicle.

4. Remove nuts from front engine mounting brackets.

5. Remove the insulator support to crossmember bracket bolts and nuts.

6. Raise engine with support fixture far enough to remove mounts, remove remaining bolts and mount.

To install:

7. Install mounts to engine block. Tighten the bolts to 40 ft. lbs. (54 Nm).

8. If removed, install the insulator support to crossmember bracket bolts and nut and tighten to 30 ft. lbs. (41 Nm).

9. Lower engine to original position and insert bolts through mounting brackets and tighten to 50 ft. lbs. (68 Nm).

10. Install skid plate, if removed.

11. Lower vehicle and remove engine support fixture. Reconnect negative battery cable.

3.0L and 3.3L Engines

1. Disconnect negative battery cable.

2. Support engine and transmission so it will not rotate. Remove the bolt from the insulator and the front crossmember mounting bracket.

3. Remove the front engine mount bracket to crossmember screws and nuts. Remove the insulator.

4. The installation is the reverse of the removal procedure.

3.9L and 5.2L Engines Without 4WD

1. Disconnect negative battery cable. Remove skid plate, if equipped.

2. Position fan assembly to insure clearance for radiator and top hose when engine is moved. Install an engine support fixture. Do not lift engine by the intake manifold.

3. Raise and safely support vehicle.

4. Remove bolts and washers holding insulator to the adapter and remove the insulator bolt.

5. Raise engine with the lifting fixture and remove insulator.

To install:

6. If adapter was removed, install to block and tighten bolts to 30 ft. lbs. (41 Nm).

7. If bracket was removed, install and tighten bolts to 30 ft. lbs. (41 Nm).

8. Position the insulator onto the adapter and install bolts and washers. Lower the engine.

9. Install insulator to bracket bolt and tighten nut to 50 ft. lbs. (68 Nm). Lower vehicle and remove support fixture.

3.9L And 5.2L Engines With 4WD

The front engine mount on the 4WD vehicle attaches directly to engine adapters and the axle housing. The engine and front axle must be supported during any serrvice procedures involving these insulators.

1. Disconnect negative battery cable. Remove skid plate, if equipped.

2. Position fan assembly to insure clearance for radiator and top hose when engine is moved. Install an engine support fixture. Do not lift engine by the intake manifold.

3. Raise and safely support vehicle.

4. Install front axle lifting fixture. Remove insulator thru bolt and nut. Remove the nut and washer attaching the engine mount bracket to the insulator bracket.

5. Raise engine slightly to clear insulator bracket stud. Remove bolts attaching the insulator to the axle housing.

6. Remove insulator to frame bolt and remove insulator.

To install:

7. Position insulator in frame and align attaching points. Install bolts and tighten nuts to 75 ft. lbs. (102 Nm).

8. Lower engine while guiding engine bracket onto insulator stud and install nut and bolt. Tighten stud nut to 30 ft. lbs. (41 Nm). Tighten bolt to 75 ft. lbs. (102 Nm).

9. Remove front axle lifting fixture, lower vehicle and remove the engine supporting fixture.

LEFT SIDE MOUNT

3.0L and 3.3L Engines

1. Disconnect negative battery cable.

2. Raise and safely support vehicle.

3. Remove the left front wheel and tire assembly.

4. Remove the inner splash shield. Support transmission and remove the insulator bolt from the mount.

5. Remove the transmission mount fasteners and remove the mount.

6. The installation is the reverse of the removal procedure.

RIGHT SIDE MOUNT

3.0L and 3.3L Engines

1. Remove the right engine mount insulator vertical fasteners from the frame rail.

2. Support the engine in a way that releases the load from the engine mounts.

3. Remove the bolt in the insulator assembly. Remove the insulator.

4. Installation is the reverse of the removal procedure.

Cylinder Head

Removal and Installation

2.2L AND 2.5L ENGINES

1. Relieve the fuel pressure if equipped with fuel injection. Disconnect the negative battery cable and unbolt it from the head. Drain the cooling system. Remove the dipstick bracket nut from the thermostat housing.

2. Remove the air cleaner assembly. Remove the upper radiator hose and disconnect the heater hoses.

3. Disconnect and label the vacuum lines, hoses and wiring connectors from the manifold(s), carburetor or throttle body and from the cylinder head. Remove the air pump, if equipped.

4. Disconnect all linkages and the fuel line from the carburetor or throttle body. Unbolt the cable bracket. Remove the ground strap attaching screw from the firewall.

5. If equipped with air conditioning, remove the upper compressor mounting bolts. The cylinder head can be remove with the compressor and bracket still mounted. Remove the upper part of the timing belt cover.

6. Raise the vehicle and support safely. Disconnect the converter from the exhaust manifold. Disconnect the water hose and oil drain from the turbocharger, if equipped.

Cylinder head bolt torque sequence—2.2L and 2.5L engines

7. Rotate the engine by hand, until the timing marks align (No. 1 piston at TDC). Lower the vehicle.

8. With the timing marks aligned, remove the camshaft sprocket. The camshaft sprocket can be suspended to keep the timing intact. Remove the spark plug wires from the spark plugs.

9. Remove the valve cover and curtain, if equipped. Remove the cylinder head bolts and washers, starting from the middle and working outward.

10. Remove the cylinder head from the engine.

NOTE: Before disassembling or repairing any part of the cylinder head assembly, identify factory installed oversized components. To do so, look for the tops of the bearing caps pained green and O/SJ stamped rearward of the oil gallery plug on the rear of the head. In addition, the barrel of the camshaft is painted green and O/SJ is stamped onto the rear end of the camshaft. Installing standard sized parts in an head equipped with oversized parts—or visa versa—will cause severe engine damage.

11. Clean the cylinder head gasket mating surfaces.

12. Using new gaskets and seals, install the head to the engine. Using new head bolts assembled with the old washers, torque the cylinder head bolts in sequence, to 45 ft. lbs. Repeating the sequence, torque the bolts to 65 ft. lbs. With the bolts at 65 ft. lbs., turn each bolt an additional ¼ turn.

NOTE: Head bolt diameter is 11mm. These bolts are identified with the No. 11 on the head of the bolt. The 10mm bolts used on previous vehicles will thread into an 11mm bolt hole but will permanently damage the cylinder block. Make sure the correct bolts are being used when replacing old head bolts.

13. Install the camshaft sprocket and timing belt.

14. Install valve cover using new side cover gaskets. Install all vacuum hoses, upper air conditioning compressor mounting bolts and throttle linkage.

15. Install all electrical wiring and oil fill tube retainer nut.

16. Raise vehicle and reinstall exhaust pipe to engine manifold. Install turbocharger lines, if equipped.

17. Adjust all engine fluid levels as required and reconnect negative battery cable. Start the engine and check for leaks.

3.0L ENGINE

1. Relieve the fuel pressure. Disconnect the negative battery cable. Drain the cooling system.

2. To remove the accessory drive belt, insert a ½ in. drive breaker bar into the square hole of the serpentine drive belt ten-

Service Tips

VALVE COVER GASKET LEAK

On some 1989 and early 1990 engines, the valve cover gasket may dislocate and allow engine oil to leak. Depending upon the size and location of the leak, a fire in the engine compartment may result. To prevent this condition, install the replacement parts package number C3940364, which consists of: a revised valve cover, 2 new valve cover end seals, 4 studs with washers and 5 screws with washers; use RTV sealant part number 4318025 or equivalent, to seal the parts. If no RTV sealant/or gasket tabs are extending up through the slots in the sealing surface on the long sides of the valve cover, the new cover has already been installed.

sioner and rotate it counterclockwise to reduce the belt tension. Remove the drive belt. Remove the alternator and power steering pump from the brackets and move them aside.

3. Remove the air conditioning compressor from its mount and support it aside. Remove the adjustable drive belt tensioner from the block.

4. Raise the vehicle and support safely. Remove the right front wheel assembly and the right inner splash shield.

4. Remove the crankshaft pulleys and the torsional damper.

5. Lower the vehicle. Using a floor jack and a block of wood positioned under the oil pan, raise the engine slightly. Remove the engine mount bracket from the timing cover end of the engine.

6. Remove the timing belt covers. If the same timing belt will be reused, mark the direction of the timing belt's rotation, for installation in the same direction. Make sure the engine is positioned so No. 1 cylinder is at the TDC of it's compression stroke and the sprockets timing marks are aligned with the engine's timing mark indicators.

7. Loosen the timing belt tensioner bolt and remove the belt.

NOTE: When removing the timing belt from the camshaft sprocket, make sure the belt does not slip off of the other camshaft sprocket. Support the belt so it can not slip off of the crankshaft sprocket and opposite side camshaft sprocket.

8. Hold camshaft sprocket with spanner wrench and remove bolt and washer. Remove camshaft sprocket. Remove valve cover(s) and install auto lash adjuster retainers tool MD998443 or equivalent, on the rocker arms.

9. If removing the right cylinder head, matchmark the distributor rotor to the distributor housing and the housing to distributor extension locations. Remove the distributor and the distributor extension.

10. Note position of rocker arms and bearing caps and loosen but do not remove the bolts from the camshaft bearing caps. Remove the rocker arm, rocker shafts and bearing caps as an assembly. Remove the camshafts from the cylinder head and inspect them for damage, if necessary.

11. Remove the intake manifold assembly.

12. Remove the exhaust manifold.

13. Remove the air cleaner assembly. Label and disconnect the spark plug wires and the vacuum hoses.

Cylinder head bolt torque sequence—3.0L engine

14. Remove the cylinder head bolts starting from the outside and working inward. Remove the cylinder head from the engine.

15. Clean the gasket mounting surfaces and check the heads for warpage; the maximum warpage allowed is 0.008 in. (0.20mm).

To install:

16. Install the new cylinder head gaskets over the dowels on the engine block.

17. Install the cylinder heads on the engine and torque the cylinder head bolts in sequence using 3 even steps, to 80 ft. lbs. (108 Nm).

18. Install the air cleaner assembly. Install spark plug wires and vacuum hoses.

19. Install exhaust and intake manifold to engine.

20. Install rocker arm assembly to cylinder head making sure to torque in the correct order. Install distributor drive and adaptor assembly.

21. Install the camshaft sprocket(s).

22. Install and align timing belt as follows:

a. Position both camshafts so the marks line up with timing marks on the alternator bracket (rear bank) and inner timing cover (front bank). Rotate the crankshaft so the timing mark aligns with the mark on the oil pump.

b. Install the timing belt on the crankshaft sprocket and while keeping the belt tight on the tension side (right side), install the belt on the front camshaft sprocket.

c. Install the belt on the water pump pulley, rear camshaft sprocket and then the belt tensioner.

d. Rotate the front camshaft counterclockwise to tension the belt between the front camshaft and the crankshaft. If the timing marks came out of line, repeat the procedure.

e. Install the crankshaft sprocket flange.

f. Loosen the tensioner bolt and allow the spring to tension the belt.

g. Turn the crankshaft 2 full turns in the clockwise direction until the timing marks align again. Now that the belt is properly tensioned, torque the tensioner lock bolt to 21 ft. lbs. (29 Nm).

23. Refill the cooling system. Connect the negative battery cable. Start the engine and check for leaks. Adjust the timing as required.

3.3L ENGINE

1. Relieve the fuel pressure. Disconnect the negative battery cable. Drain the cooling system.

2. Remove the intake manifold with throttle body.

3. Disconnect the coil wires, sending unit wire, heater hoses and bypass hose.

4. Remove the closed ventilation system, evaporation control system and cylinder hear cover.

5. Remove the exhaust manifold.

6. Remove the rocker arm and shaft assemblies. Remove the pushrods and identify them in ensure installation in their original positions.

7. Remove the head bolts and remove the cylinder head from the block.

To install:

8. Clean the gasket mounting surfaces and install a new head gasket to the block.

9. Install the head to the block. Before installing the head bolts, inspect them for stretching. Hold a straight edge up to the threads. If the threads are not all on line, the bolt is stretched and should be replaced.

10. Torque the bolts in sequence to 45 ft. lbs. (61 Nm). Repeat the sequence and torque the bolts to 65 ft. lbs. (88 Nm). With the bolts at 65 ft. lbs., turn each bolt an additional ¼ turn.

11. Torque the lone head bolt to 25 ft. lbs. (33 Nm) after the other 8 bolts have been properly torqued.

12. Install the pushrods, rocker arms and shafts and torque the bolts to 21 ft. lbs. (12 Nm).

13. Place a drop of silicone sealer onto each of the 4 manifold to cylinder head gasket corners.

─── **CAUTION** ───

The intake manifold gasket is composed of very thin and sharp metal. Handle this gasket with care or damage to the gasket or personal injury could result.

Checking the head bolt for stretching

Cylinder head bolt torque sequence—3.3L engine

14. Install the intake manifold gasket and torque the end retainers to 105 inch lbs. (12 Nm).

15. Install the intake manifold and torque the bolts in sequence to 10 inch lbs. Repeat the sequence increasing the torque to 17 ft. lbs. (23 Nm) and recheck each bolt for 17 ft. lbs. of torque. After the bolts are torqued, inspect the seals to ensure that they have not become dislodged.

16. Lubricate the injector O-rings with clean oil and position the fuel rail in place. Install the rail mounting bolts.

17. Install the valve cover with a new gasket. Install the exhaust manifold.

18. Install or connect all remaining items that were removed or disconnected during the removal procedure.

19. Refill the cooling system. Connect the negative battery cable. Start the engine and check for leaks.

3.9L ENGINE

1. Relieve the fuel pressure if equipped with fuel injection. Disconnect the negative battery cable and drain the cooling system.

2. Raise the vehicle and safely support. Disconnect the exhaust pipe from the manifolds.

3. Remove the alternator if the right head is being removed. Remove the air pump and battery ground cable if the left head is being removed.

4. Remove the air cleaner assembly. Unbolt the air conditioning compressor and lay it to the side, if equipped. Remove the distributor cap with all wires attached.

5. Disconnect all wires, hoses, linkages and cables from the carburetor or throttle body. Disconnect and plug the fuel line.

6. Disconnect the ignition coil and coolant temperature sending unit electrical connectors.

7. Disconnect the heater hose, upper radiator hose and the lower bypass hose clamp.

8. Remove the valve covers.

9. Remove the intake manifold assembly. Remove the exhaust manifolds.

10. Remove the rocker arm and shaft assembly from the heads. Do not disassemble unless service is required.

11. Remove the pushrods and identify them to ensure installation in their original locations.

12. Remove the head bolts and remove the cylinder head(s).

To install:

13. Clean and dry all gasket surfaces of the cylinder block and head. Inspect all surfaces with a straightedge. If the flatness exceeds 0.0075 times the length of the span measured, in any direction, replace or machine the head gasket surface.

Cylinder head bolt torque sequence—3.9 L engine

14. Using no sealer, install the new head gasket(s) to the block. Clean, dry and lightly oil all head bolts threads. Install the heads and install the bolts.

15. Torque the head bolts in sequence to 50 ft. lbs. (68 Nm). Repeat the sequence retightening the bolts to a final torque of 105 ft. lbs. (143 Nm) and repeat the second step to ensure all bolts are accurately torqued.

16. Assemble the rocker shaft assembly, if it was serviced. Make sure all rocker arms with an **RH** stamp are installed to the right of those with **LH**. Install the pushrods, rocker arms and shaft(s) with the notch on the end of the shaft pointing to the engine centerline and to the rear of the right bank or to the front of the left bank. Make sure the long stamped steel retainers are at the No. 2 and 4 positions. Torque the bolts evenly and gradually to 17 ft. lbs. (23 Nm).

17. Clean and dry the intake manifold contact surfaces. Coat the intake manifold side gaskets very lightly with sealer and install the gaskets to the heads. Cutouts at the front of the gaskets differentiate the right and left sides.

18. Apply a thin uniform coat of quick dry cement to the front and rear intake manifold gaskets and mounting surfaces on the block and apply a thin bead of sealer to each of 4 the corners. Install the front and rear gaskets engaging the hole in the block and the tangs from the head gaskets. Apply a second thin bead of sealer above the gaskets in the 4 corners.

19. Carefully lower the intake manifold into position engaging the bypass hose; after it is satisfactorily in place, inspect the gaskets to make sure they have not become dislodged.

20. Install the intake manifold bolts. On 1988–91 engine torque in sequence to 25 ft. lbs. (34 Nm). Repeat the sequence retightening the bolts to a final torque of 40 ft. lbs. (54 Nm) and repeat the second step to ensure all bolts are accurately torqued. On 1992 engine torque in steps to 6 ft. lbs. (8 Nm). Repeat torque procedure to 12 ft. lbs. (16 Nm). Repeat to assure all bolts are torqued to 12 ft. lbs. (16 Nm).

21. Install the exhaust manifold(s) and torque the bolts to 20 ft. lbs. (27 Nm). Torque the end nuts to 15 ft. lbs. (20 Nm).

22. Clean and dry the valve cover mating surfaces, bolts and bolt holes. Install the valve covers each with a new gasket.

23. Connect the heater hose, upper radiator hose and the lower bypass hose clamp.

24. Connect the ignition coil, coolant temperature sending unit wire and all other connectors that were disconnected along the wiring harness.

25. Install the air conditioning compressor, if equipped. Install the distributor cap and all spark plug wires.

26. Install the alternator, battery ground and air pump, if removed.

27. Connect all wires, hoses, cables and the fuel line to the carburetor or throttle body. Install the air cleaner assembly.

28. Raise the vehicle and safely support. Connect the exhaust pipe to the manifolds.

29. Fill the cooling system.

30. Connect the negative battery cable and set all adjustments to specification. Start vehicle and check for leaks.

5.2L ENGINE

1. Relieve the fuel pressure if equipped with fuel injection. Disconnect the negative battery cable from the battery and drain the cooling system.

2. Raise the vehicle and safely support. Disconnect the exhaust pipe from the manifolds.

3. Remove the alternator, if the right head is being removed, and the air pump and battery ground cable, if the left head is being removed.

4. Remove the air cleaner assembly. Unbolt the air conditioning compressor, if equipped, and lay it aside. Remove the distributor cap with all wires attached.

5. Disconnect all wires, hoses, linkages and cables from the carburetor or throttle body. Disconnect the fuel line.

6. Disconnect the ignition coil, coolant temperature sending

Cylinder head torque sequence—1992 5.2L engine

unit wire and all other connectors along the wiring harness connected to items on the intake manifold.

7. Disconnect the heater hose, upper radiator hose and the lower bypass hose clamp.

8. Remove the valve cover(s).

9. Remove the intake manifold assembly. Remove the exhaust manifold(s).

10. Remove the rocker arm and shaft assembly from the head(s). Do not disassemble unless service is required.

11. Remove the pushrods and identify them to ensure installation in their original locations.

12. Remove the head bolts and remove the cylinder head(s).

To install:

13. Clean and dry all gasket surfaces of the cylinder block and head. Inspect all surfaces with a straight-edge. If the flatness exceeds 0.0075 times the length of the span measured (in any direction), replace or machine the head gasket surface.

14. Using no sealer, install the new head gasket(s) to the block. Clean, dry and lightly oil all head bolts threads. Install the head(s) and install the head bolts.

15. Torque the head bolts in sequence to 50 ft. lbs. (68 Nm). Repeat the sequence retightening the bolts to a final torque of 105 ft. lbs. (143 Nm) and repeat the second step to ensure all bolts are accurately torqued.

16. Assemble the rocker shaft assembly, if it was serviced. Make sure all rocker arms with a **RH** stamp are installed to the right of those with an **LH**. Install the pushrods, rocker arms and shaft(s) with the notch on the end of the shaft pointing to the engine centerline and to the rear of the right bank or to the front of the left bank. Make sure the long stamped steel retainers are at the No. 2 and 4 positions. Torque the bolts evenly and gradually to 200 inch lbs. (23 Nm).

17. Clean and dry the intake manifold contact surfaces. Coat the intake manifold side gaskets lightly with sealer and install the gaskets to the heads. Cutouts at the front of the gaskets differentiate the right and left sides.

18. Apply a thin uniform coat of quick dry cement to the front and rear intake manifold gaskets and mounting surfaces on the block and apply a thin bead of sealer to each of 4 the corners. Install the front and rear gaskets engaging the hole in the block and the tangs from the head gaskets. Apply a second thin bead of sealer above the gaskets in the 4 corners.

19. Carefully lower the intake manifold into position engaging the bypass hose. Inspect the gaskets to make sure they have not become dislodged.

20. Install the intake bolts and torque to 6 ft. lbs. (8 Nm). Repeat torque procedure to 12 ft. lbs. (16 Nm). Repeat to assure all bolts are torqued to 12 ft. lbs. (16 Nm).

21. Install the exhaust manifold(s) and torque the bolts to 20 ft. lbs. (27 Nm). Torque the end nuts to 15 ft. lbs. (20 Nm).

22. Clean and dry the valve cover mating surfaces, bolts and bolt holes. Install the valve cover(s) each with a new gasket.

23. Connect the heater hose, upper radiator hose and the lower bypass hose clamp.

24. Connect the ignition coil, coolant temperature sending unit wire and all other connectors that were disconnected along the wiring harness.

25. Install the air conditioning compressor, if equipped. Install the distributor cap and all spark plug wires.

26. Install the alternator, battery ground and air pump, if removed.

27. Connect all wires, hoses, cables and the fuel line to the carburetor or throttle body. Install the air cleaner assembly.

28. Raise the vehicle and safely support. Connect the exhaust pipe to the manifolds.

29. Fill the cooling system.

30. Connect the negative battery cable and set all adjustments to specification.

Valve Lifters

Removal and Installation

2.2L AND 2.5L ENGINES

1. Disconnect the negative battery cable.

2. Remove the valve cover and curtain. If removing all lifters, remove the camshaft and rocker arms.

3. If only removing 1 lifter, rotate the crankshaft until the low point of the desired cam lobe is contacting the rocker arm.

4. Using the special valve spring compressor tool 4682 or equivalent, depress the valve spring without dislodging the keepers and slide the rocker arm out.

5. Remove the valve lifter(s) from the bore(s).

6. Lubricate the lifter(s) and their bore(s) with clean engine oil.

7. The installation is the reverse of the removal procedure.

8. Connect the negative battery cable and check the lifters for proper operation.

3.0L ENGINE

1. Disconnect the negative battery cable. Remove the air cleaner assembly.

2. Remove the valve cover.

3. Using the valve lifter retainer tools MD998443 or equivalent, install them on the rocker arms to keep the lifters from falling out.

4. On the right side cylinder head, remove the distributor extension.

5. Have a helper hold the rear end of the camshaft down. If the rear of the camshaft cannot be held down, the belt will dislodge and the valve timing will be lost. Loosen the camshaft cap bolts but do not remove them from the caps. Remove the caps, arms, shafts and bolts all as an assembly.

6. Remove the lifter(s) from the rocker arm(s).

7. Lubricate the lifter(s) and their bore(s) with clean engine oil.

8. The installation is the reverse of the removal procedure.

9. Connect the negative battery cable and check the lifters for proper operation.

3.3L ENGINE

1. Disconnect the negative battery cable. Relieve the fuel pressure.

2. Remove the cylinder head(s) to gain access to the valve lifter(s).

3. Remove the yoke retainer and aligning yoke(s).

4. Use an appropriate valve lifter removal tool to remove each lifter from its bore. If reinstalling the tappets, identify each upon removal to ensure installation in the original position.

To install:

5. Lubricate the lifter(s) and bore(s) and install.

6. Install aligning yoke(s).

7. Install the yoke retainer and torque the bolts to 105 inch lbs. (12 Nm).

8. Install the cylinder head(s) and all related components.

9. Connect the negative battery cable and check the lifters for proper operation.

3.9L AND 5.2L ENGINES

1. Disconnect negative battery cable. Remove air cleaner.

2. Relieve the fuel pressure if equipped with fuel injection.

3. Remove the valve cover(s) and rocker arm assembly.

4. Remove the pushrods and identify them to ensure installation in their original locations.

5. Remove the intake manifold assembly, yoke retainer and aligning yokes.

6. Use an appropriate valve lifter removal tool to remove each lifter from its bore. If reinstalling the tappets, identify each upon removal to ensure installation in the original position.

Identifying the rocker shafts—3.0L engine

7. If the tappet or bore in cylinder block is scored, scuffed or shows signs of sticking, ream the bore to the next oversize and replace with oversize tappet.

To install:

8. Lubricate the lifter(s) and bore(s) and install. Ensure that the oil feed hole in the side of the tappet body faces up.

9. Install aligning yokes with arrow toward camshaft. Install yoke retainer. Tighten bolts to 200 inch lbs. (23 Nm).

10. Install pushrods to their original positions. Install rocker arm and shaft assembly.

11. Install valve cover(s). Connect negative battery terminal and start vehicle. Check for oil leaks.

Rocker Arms and Shafts

Removal and Installation

2.2L AND 2.5L ENGINES

1. Disconnect the negative battery cable.

2. Remove the valve cover.

3. Rotate the crankshaft until the low point of the desired cam lobe is contacting the rocker arm.

4. Use the special valve spring compressor tool or equivalent, depress the valve spring (without dislodging the keepers) and slide the rocker arm out.

5. The installation is the reverse of the removal procedure.

3.0L ENGINE

1. Disconnect the negative battery cable. Remove the air cleaner assembly.

2. Remove the valve cover.

3. Using the auto lash adjuster retainer tools MD998443 or equivalent, install them on the rocker arms to keep the lash adjusters from falling out.

Rocker shafts/arms assembly—3.0L engine

Rocker shaft/arms assembly—3.3L engine

4. On the right side cylinder head, remove the distributor extension.

5. Have a helper hold the rear end of the camshaft down. If the rear of the camshaft cannot be held down, the belt will dislodge and the valve timing will be lost. Loosen the camshaft cap bolts but do not remove them from the caps. Remove the caps, arms, shafts and bolts all as an assembly.

6. Disassemble the unit keeping all parts in order and repair as required.

7. The installation is the reverse of the removal procedure. Apply a drop of sealant to the rear edge of the rear cap. Torque the cap bolts first to 85 inch lbs. (19 Nm), then to 180 inch lbs. (19 Nm) in the following order: No. 3 cap, No. 2 cap, No. 1 cap, No. 4 cap.

3.3L ENGINE

1. Disconnect the negative battery cable.
2. Remove the upper intake manifold assembly.
3. Remove the valve cover.
4. Remove the rocker shaft retaining bolts and retainers.
5. Remove the rocker shaft and arm assembly. Disassemble and repair as required.
6. The installation is the reverse of the removal procedure. Torque the retaining bolts gradually and evenly to 21 ft. lbs. (28 Nm).
7. Allow 20 minutes tappet bleed down time after rocker shaft installation before starting the engine.

3.9L AND 5.2L ENGINES

1988–91

1. Disconnect the negative battery cable.
2. Remove the valve cover and gasket.
3. Note the positioning of the oil notch and remove the rocker arms and shaft assembly from the head.
4. Disassemble the unit as required and replace all worn parts.

NOTE: On engines with exhaust valve rotators, the exhaust rocker arm must have relief for clearance.

To install:

5. Make sure all rocker arms with an **RH** stamped on them are installed to the right of those with an **LH**. Install the assembly with the notch on the end of the shaft pointing to the engine centerline and to the rear of the right bank or to the front of the left bank. Make sure the longer stamped steel retainers are at the No. 2 and 4 positions. Torque the bolts evenly and gradually to 21 ft. lbs. (28 Nm).
6. Install the valve cover.
7. Connect the negative battery cable and check for leaks.

Rocker shaft/arms assembly—1988-91 3.9L and 5.2L engines

1992

1. Disconnect the negative battery cable.
2. Remove the valve cover and gasket.

Rocker arm assembly—1992 5.2L engine

3. Remove the rocker arm bolts and pivots and place on bench in order of removal. Remove pushrod as required keeping in order of removal. Replace parts as required.

4. Installation is the reverse of the removal procedure. Torque rocker arm bolts to 21 ft. lbs. (28 Nm).

Intake Manifold

Removal and Installation

3.0L ENGINE

1. Relieve the fuel system pressure. Disconnect the negative battery cable.
2. Drain the cooling system.
3. Remove the throttle body to air cleaner hose.
4. Remove the throttle body and transaxle kickdown linkage.
5. Remove the AIS motor and TPS wiring connectors from the throttle body.
6. Remove and label the vacuum hose harness from the throttle body.
7. From the air intake plenum, remove the PCV and brake booster hoses and the EGR tube flange.
8. Disconnect and label the charge temperature sensor wiring at the intake manifold.
9. Remove the vacuum connections from the air intake plenum vacuum connector.
10. Remove the fuel hoses from the fuel rail.
11. Remove the air intake plenum mounting bolts and remove the plenum.
12. Remove the vacuum hoses from the fuel rail and pressure regulator.
13. Disconnect the fuel injector wiring harness from the engine wiring harness.
14. Remove the fuel pressure regulator mounting bolts and remove the regulator from the fuel rail.
15. Remove the fuel rail mounting bolts and remove the fuel rail from the intake manifold.
16. Separate the radiator hose from the thermostat housing and heater hoses from the heater pipe.
17. Remove the intake manifold mounting bolts and remove the manifold from the engine.
18. Clean the gasket mounting surfaces on the engine and intake manifold.

To install:

19. Using new gaskets, position the intake manifold on the engine and install the mounting nuts and washers.
20. Torque the mounting nuts gradually and evenly, in sequence, to 15 ft. lbs. (20 Nm).
21. Make sure the injector holes are clean. Lubricate the injector O-rings with a drop of clean engine oil and install the injector assembly onto the engine.
22. Install and torque the fuel rail mounting bolts to 10 ft. lbs. (14 Nm).
23. Install the fuel pressure regulator onto the fuel rail.

Intake manifold bolt torque sequence—3.0L engine

Air intake plenum bolt torque sequence—3.0L engine

24. Install the fuel supply and return tube and the vacuum crossover hold-down bolt.
25. Connect the fuel injection wiring harness to the engine wiring harness.
26. Connect the vacuum harness to the fuel pressure regulator and fuel rail assembly.
27. Remove the cover from the lower intake manifold and clean the mating surface.
28. Place the intake plenum gasket with the beaded sealant side up, on the intake manifold. Install the air intake plenum and torque the mounting bolts gradually and evenly, in sequence, to 10 ft. lbs. (14 Nm).
29. Connect or install all remaining items that were disconnected or removed during the removal procedure.
30. Refill the cooling system. Connect the negative battery cable and check for leaks using the DRB I or II to activate the fuel pump.

3.3L ENGINE

1. Disconnect the negative battery cable. Relieve the fuel pressure. Drain the cooling system.
2. Remove the air cleaner to throttle body hose assembly.
3. Disconnect the throttle cable and remove the wiring harness from the bracket.
4. Remove AIS motor and TPS wiring connectors from the throttle body.
5. Remove the vacuum hose harness from the throttle body.
6. Remove the PCV and brake booster hoses from the air intake plenum.
7. Disconnect the charge temperature sensor electrical con-

Intake manifold bolt torque sequence—3.3L engine

nector. Remove the vacuum harness connectors from the intake plenum.

8. Remove the cylinder head to the intake plenum strut.

9. Disconnect the MAP sensor and oxygen sensor connectors. Remove the engine mounted ground strap.

10. Remove the fuel hoses from the fuel rail and plug them.

11. Remove the DIS coils and the alternator bracket to intake manifold bolt.

12. Remove the upper intake manifold attaching bolts and remove the upper manifold.

13. Remove the vacuum harness connector from the fuel pressure regulator.

14. Remove the fuel tube retainer bracket screw and fuel rail attaching bolts. Spread the retainer bracket to allow for clearance when removing the fuel tube.

15. Remove the fuel rail injector wiring clip from the alternator bracket.

16. Disconnect the cam sensor, coolant temperature sensor and engine temperature sensor.

17. Remove the fuel rail.

18. Remove the upper radiator hose, bypass hose and rear intake manifold hose.

19. Remove the intake manifold bolts and remove the manifold from the engine.

20. Remove the intake manifold seal retaining screws and remove the manifold gasket.

21. Clean out clogged end water passages and fuel runners.

To install:

22. Clean and dry all gasket mating surfaces.

23. Place a drop of silicone sealer onto each of the 4 manifold to cylinder head gasket corners.

CAUTION

The intake manifold gasket is composed of very thin and sharp metal. Handle this gasket with care or damage to the gasket or personal injury could result.

---

24. Install the intake manifold gasket and torque the end retainers to 10 ft. lbs. (12 Nm).

25. Install the intake manifold and torque the bolts in sequence to 10 inch lbs. Repeat the sequence increasing the torque to 17 ft. lbs. (23 Nm) and recheck each bolt for 17 ft. lbs. torque. After the bolts are torqued, inspect the seals to ensure that they have not become dislodged.

26. Lubricat the injector O-rings with clean oil and position the fuel rail in place. Install the rail mounting bolts.

27. Connect the cam sensor, coolant temperature sensor and engine temperature sensor.

28. Install the fuel rail injector wiring clip to the alternator bracket.

29. Install the fuel rail attaching bolts and fuel tube retainer bracket screw.

30. Install the vacuum harness to the pressure regulator.

31. Install the upper intake manifold with a new gasket. Install the bolts only fingertight. Install the alternator bracket to intake manifold bolt and the cylinder head to intake manifold strut and bolts. Torque the intake manifold mounting bolts to 21 ft. lbs. (28 Nm) starting from the middle and working outward. Torque the bracket and strut bolts to 40 ft. lbs. (54 Nm).

32. Install or connect all items that were removed or disconnected from the intake manifold and throttle body.

33. Connect the fuel hoses to the rail. Push the fittings in until they click in place.

34. Install the air cleaner assembly.

35. Connect the negative battery cable and check for leaks using the DRB I or II to activate the fuel pump.

3.9L AND 5.2L ENGINES

1988–91

1. Relieve the fuel pressure if equipped with fuel injection. Disconnect the negative battery cable from the battery and drain the cooling system.

2. Remove the air pump and bracket. Removal of the bracket will allow for easier installation of the left front corner of the intake manifold.

3. Remove the air cleaner assembly. Unbolt the air conditioning compressor and lay it to the side, if equipped. Remove the distributor cap with all wires attached. Remove the alternator.

4. Disconnect all wires, hoses, linkages and cables from the carburetor or throttle body. Disconnect the fuel line.

5. Disconnect the ignition coil, coolant temperature sending unit wire and all other connectors along the wiring harness connected to items on the intake manifold.

6. Disconnect the heater hose, upper radiator hose and the lower bypass hose clamp.

7. Remove the valve covers.

8. Unbolt the intake manifold from the heads and remove the intake manifold assembly. Disassemble the manifold as required and clean out the exhaust crossover passages.

To install:

9. Clean and dry the intake manifold contact surfaces. Coat the intake manifold side gaskets very lightly with sealer and install the gaskets to the heads. Cutouts at the front of the gaskets differentiate the right and left sides.

Intake manifold bolt torque sequence—3.9L engine

10. Install the front and rear gaskets engaging the hole in the block and the tangs from the head gaskets. Apply a thin bead of sealer above the gaskets in the 4 corners.

11. Carefully lower the intake manifold into position engaging the bypass hose; after it is satisfactorily in place, inspect the gaskets to make sure they have not become dislodged.

12. Install the intake manifold bolts with the aspirator tube, air pump bracket and kickdown linkage bracket in place, if equipped. Torque the bolts in sequence to 25 ft. lbs. (34 Nm). Repeat the sequence retightening the bolts to a final torque of 40 ft. lbs. (54 Nm) and repeat the second step to ensure all bolts are accurately torqued.

13. Clean and dry the valve cover mating surfaces, bolts and bolt holes. Install the valve covers with a new gasket. Torque the screws or nuts to 95 inch lbs. (11 Nm).

14. Connect the heater hose, upper radiator hose and the lower bypass hose clamp.

15. Connect the ignition coil, coolant temperature sending unit wire and all other connectors that were disconnected along the wiring harness.

16. Install the air conditioning compressor, if equipped. Install the distributor cap and all spark plug wires.

17. Install air pump.

18. Connect all wires, hoses, cables and the fuel line to the carburetor or throttle body. Install the air cleaner assembly.

19. Fill the cooling system.

20. Connect the negative battery cable. Use the DRB II to activate the fuel pump on fuel injected vehicles. Check for leaks.

1992 3.9L ENGINE

1. Relieve the fuel pressure. Disconnect the negative battery cable from the battery and drain the cooling system.

2. Remove the alternator and fuel lines from the fuel rail.

3. Disconnect the accelerator linkage, speed control and transmission kickdown cables.

4. Remove the distributor cap and wires. Disconnect the coil wires, heat indicator sending unit, heater hoses and bypass hose.

5. Remove the closed crankcase ventilation and evaporation control systems.

6. Remove the intake manifold bolts and lift the intake from the engine. Remove and discard the flange side gaskets and the rear cross-over gaskets.

7. Clean and dry all mating surfaces and inspect for flatness.
To install:

8. Install 4 plastic locator dowels into the block and install the new flange gaskets into position. Ensure **MANIFOLD SIDE** is visible on each flange gasket. Apply silicone sealant to the 4 corner joints. Install the front and rear cross-over gaskets onto the dowels.

9. Carefully lower the intake manifold onto the engine block and cylinder heads. Check gasket alignment.

10. Tighten the intake mounting bolts following the torque sequence as follows:

  a. Tighten bolts 1 and 2 to 72 inch lbs. (8 Nm).

  b. Tighten bolts 3 thru 12 in sequence to 72 inch lbs. (8 Nm).

  c. Check that all bolts are tightened to 72 inch lbs. (8 Nm).

  d. Tighten bolts in sequence to 12 ft. lbs. (16 Nm).

  e. Check that all bolts are tightened to 12 ft. lbs. (16 Nm).

11. Install the closed crankcase ventilation and evaporation control systems.

12. Install the distributor cap and wires. Connect the coil wires, heat indicator sending unit, heater hoses and bypass hose.

13. Install the distributor cap and wires.

14. Connect the accelerator linkage, speed control and transmission kickdown cables.

15. Install alternator and drive belt. Adjust belt tension as required. Install fuel lines.

16. Install the air cleaner and refill the cooling system. Reconnect the negative battery cable and start engine. Check for leaks and allow engine to reach normal operating temperature. Recheck fluid levels and add as required.

1992 5.2L ENGINE

1. Relieve the fuel pressure. Disconnect the negative battery cable from the battery and drain the cooling system.

2. Remove the alternator and fuel lines.

3. Disconnect the accelerator linkage, speed control and transmission kickdown cables. Remove the return spring.

4. Remove the distributor cap and wires. Disconnect the coil wires, heat indicator sending unit, heater hoses and bypass hose.

5. Remove the closed crankcase ventilation and evaporation control systems.

6. Remove the intake manifold bolts and lift the intake from the engine. Remove and discard the flange side gaskets and the rear cross-over gaskets.

7. Clean and dry all mating surfaces and inspect for flatness.
To install:

8. Install 4 plastic locator dowels into the block and install the new flange gaskets into position. Ensure **MANIFOLD SIDE** is visible on each flange gasket. Apply silicone sealant to the 4 corner joints. Install the front and rear cross-over gaskets onto the dowels.

Intake manifold torque sequence—1992 3.9L engine

Intake manifold torque sequence—1992 5.2L engine

9. Carefully lower the intake manifold onto the engine block and cylinder heads. Check gasket alignment.

10. Tighten the intake following the torque sequence as follows:

    a. Tighten bolts 1 thru 4 in sequence to 72 inch lbs. (8 Nm).

    b. Tighten bolts 5 thru 12 in sequence to 72 inch lbs. (8 Nm).

    c. Check that all bolts are tightened to 72 inch lbs. (8 Nm).

    d. Tighten bolts in sequence to 12 ft. lbs. (16 Nm).

    e. Check that all bolts are tightened to 12 ft. lbs. (16 Nm).

11. Install the closed crankcase ventilation and evaporation control systems.

12. Install the distributor cap and wires. Connect the coil wires, heat indicator sending unit, heater hoses and bypass hose.

13. Install the distributor cap and wires.

14. Connect the accelerator linkage, speed control and transmission kickdown cables. Install the return spring.

15. Install alternator and drive belt. Adjust belt tension as required. Install fuel lines.

16. Install the air cleaner and refill the cooling system. Reconnect the negative battery cable and start engine. Check for leaks and allow engine to reach normal operating temperature. Recheck fluid levels and add as required.

Exhaust Manifold

Removal and Installation

3.0L ENGINE

1. Disconnect the negative battery cable. Raise and safely support the vehicle.

2. Disconnect the exhaust pipe from the rear exhaust manifold, at the articulated joint.

3. Disconnect the EGR tube from the rear manifold and the oxygen sensor wire.

4. Remove the crossover pipe to manifold bolts.

5. Remove the rear manifold to cylinder head nuts and the manifold.

6. Lower the vehicle and remove the heat shield from the manifold.

7. Remove the front manifold to cylinder head nuts and the manifold.

8. Clean the gasket mounting surfaces. Inspect the manifolds for cracks, flatness and/or damage.

To install:

9. When installing, the numbers 1–3–5 on the gaskets are used with the rear cylinders and 2–4–6 are on the gasket for the front cylinders. Torque the manifold to cylinder head nuts to 14 ft. lbs. (19 Nm).

10. Install the crossover pipe to the manifold.

11. Connect the EGR tube and oxygen sensor wire.

12. Connect the exhaust pipe to the rear exhaust manifold, at the articulated joint.

13. Connect the negative battery cable and check the manifolds for leaks.

3.3L ENGINE

1. Disconnect the negative battery cable.

2. If removing the rear manifold, raise the vehicle and support safely. Disconnect the exhaust pipe from the rear exhaust manifold at the articulated joint.

3. Separate the EGR tube from the rear manifold and disconnect the oxygen sensor wire.

4. Remove the alternator/power steering support strut.

5. Remove the bolts attaching the crossover pipe to the manifold.

6. Remove the bolts attaching the manifold to the head and remove the manifold.

7. If removing the front manifold, remove the heat shield,

Exhaust manifold bolt installation—3.9L engine

bolts attaching the crossover pipe to the manifold and the nuts attaching the manifold to the head.

8. Remove the manifold from the engine.

9. Install rear exhaust manifold and torque all exhaust manifold attaching bolts to 17 ft. lbs. (23 Nm).

10. Attach exhaust pipe to exhaust manifold and tighten bolts to 21 ft. lbs. (28 Nm).

11. Attach cross-over to exhaust manifold and tighten to 25 ft. lbs. (33 Nm). Connect the oxygen sensor electrical connector.

12. Install EGR tube and alternator and power steering strut.

13. Install front exhaust manifold and attach the cross-over pipe. Install front manifold heat shield.

14. Connect negative battery cable. Start the engine and check for exhaust leaks.

3.9L AND 5.2L ENGINES

1. Disconnect the negative battery cable. Remove the hot air tube and heat shield, if necessary.

2. Raise the vehicle and support safely. Remove the exhaust pipe from the exhaust manifolds. Lower the vehicle.

3. Take note of all conical washer locations and remove the bolts, nuts and washers attaching the manifold to the head.

4. Remove the manifold.

To install:

5. If either of the end studs came out with the nuts, install a new stud using sealer on the coarse threads.

6. Position the manifold on the end studs. Install conical washers and nuts on the studs.

7. Install the remaining bolts and washers in their proper locations. The inner bolts are not mounted with washers. Working outward from the center, torque the bolts to 20–25 ft. lbs. (27–34 Nm) and the nuts to 15 ft. lbs. (20 Nm).

8. Install the exhaust pipe to the manifolds.

9. Connect the negative battery cable and check for exhaust leaks.

Combination Manifold

Removal and Installation

2.2L AND 2.5L ENGINES

Without Turbocharger

NOTE: On some vehicles, some of the manifold attaching bolts are not accessible or too heavily sealed from the factory and cannot be removed on the vehicle. Head removal would be necessary in these situations.

1. Disconnect the negative battery cable.

2. Drain the cooling system.

3. Remove the air cleaner and disconnect all vacuum lines,

Combination manifold attaching nuts and bolts—2.2L and 2.5L non-turbocharged engine

electrical wiring and fuel lines from the carburetor or throttle body.

4. Disconnect the throttle linkage.

5. Loosen the power steering pump and remove the drive belt. On Dakota, remove the power steering and air pump support bracket.

6. Remove the power brake vacuum hose from the intake manifold.

7. On Canadian models, remove the coupling hose from the diverter valve to the exhaust manifold air injection tube assembly.

8. Remove the water hoses from the water crossover.

9. Raise and safely support the vehicle. Disconnect the exhaust pipe from the exhaust manifold.

10. On Caravan, Voyager and Town & Country, remove the power steering pump and set it aside.

11. Remove the intake manifold support bracket, if equipped.

12. Remove the EGR tube.

13. On Canadian models, remove the air injection tube bolts and the air injection tube assembly.

14. Remove the intake manifold bolts.

15. Lower the vehicle and remove the intake manifold.

16. Remove the exhaust manifold nuts.

17. Remove the exhaust manifold.

To install:

18. Install new combination intake and exhaust manifold gasket to engine. Coat lightly the manifold side with Mopar gasket sealer or equivalent. Install the exhaust manifold and torque the manifold to cylinder head nuts to 17 ft. lbs. (23 Nm).

19. Install the intake manifold. Raise vehicle and torque bolt, starting from the center and working outward, to 17 ft. lbs. (23 Nm).

20. Install the EGR tube with new gasket and tighten attaching bolts to 17 inch lbs. (23 Nm).

21. Install the exhaust pipe to manifold and tighten bolts to 20 ft. lbs. (27 Nm). Lower vehicle.

22. Connect the water hoses to the cross-over. Install diverter valve assembly and the air tube to the exhaust manifold.

23. Install the power steering and air pump support bracket. Install the power brake vacuum hose to the intake manifold.

24. Install the air cleaner and connect all vacuum hoses to the throttle body.

25. Fill the cooling system, connect the negative battery cable and start the engine. Check for exhaust leaks.

With Turbocharger

1. Disconnect the negative battery cable. Drain the cooling system. Raise and safely support the vehicle.

2. Disconnect the exhaust pipe at the articulated joint. Disconnect the oxygen sensor at the electrical connection.

3. Remove the turbocharger to engine support bracket.

4. Loosen the oil drain back tube connector hose clamps. Move the tube down on the engine block fitting.

5. Disconnect the turbocharger coolant inlet tube from the engine block and disconnect the tube support bracket.

6. Remove the air cleaner assembly, including the throttle body adaptor, hose and air cleaner box with support bracket.

7. Disconnect the accelerator linkage, throttle body electrical connector and vacuum hoses.

8. Relocate the fuel rail assembly. Remove the bracket to intake manifold screws and the bracket to heat shield clips. Lift and secure the fuel rail (with injectors, wiring harness and fuel lines intact) up and out of the way.

9. Disconnect the turbocharger oil feed line at the oil sending unit Tee fitting.

10. Disconnect the upper radiator hose from the thermostat housing.

11. Remove the cylinder head, manifolds and turbocharger as an assembly.

12. With the assembly on a workbench, loosen the upper turbocharger discharge hose end clamp.

NOTE: Do not disturb the center deswirler retaining clamp.

13. Remove the throttle body to intake manifold screws and throttle body assembly. Disconnect the turbocharger coolant return tube from the water box. Disconnect the retaining bracket on the cylinder head.

14. Remove the heat shield to intake manifold screws and the heat shield.

15. Remove the turbocharger to exhaust manifold nuts and the turbocharger assembly.

16. Remove the intake manifold bolts and the intake manifold.

17. Remove the exhaust manifold nuts and the exhaust manifold.

To install:

18. Place a new 2-sided Grafoil type intake/exhaust manifold gasket; do not use sealant.

19. Position the exhaust manifold on the cylinder head. Apply anti-seize compound to threads, install and torque the retaining nuts, starting at center and progressing outward in both directions, to 17 ft. lbs. (23 Nm). Repeat this procedure until all nuts are at 17 ft. lbs. (23 Nm).

20. Position the intake manifold on the cylinder head. Install and torque the retaining screws, starting at center and progressing outward in both directions, to 19 ft. lbs. (26 Nm). Repeat this procedure until all screws are at 19 ft. lbs. (26 Nm).

21. Connect the turbocharger outlet to the intake manifold inlet tube. Position the turbocharger on the exhaust manifold. Apply anti-seize compound to threads and torque the nuts to 30 ft. lbs. (41 Nm). Torque the connector tube clamps to 30 ft. lbs. (41 Nm).

22. Install the tube support bracket to the cylinder head.

23. Install the heat shield on the intake manifold. Torque the screws to 105 inch lbs. (12 Nm).

24. Install the throttle body air horn into the turbocharger inlet tube. Install and torque the throttle body to intake manifold screws to 21 ft. lbs. (28 Nm). Torque the tube clamp to 30 inch lbs.

25. Install the cylinder head/manifolds/turbocharger assembly on the engine.

26. Reconnect the turbocharger oil feed line to the oil sending unit Tee fitting and bearing housing, if disconnected. Torque the tube nuts to 10 ft. lbs. (14 Nm).

27. Install the air cleaner assembly. Connect the vacuum lines and accelerator cables.

28. Reposition the fuel rail. Install and torque the bracket screws to 21 ft. lbs. (28 Nm). Install the air shield to bracket clips.

29. Connect the turbocharger inlet coolant tube to the engine block. Torque the tube nut to 30 ft. lbs. (41 Nm). Install the tube support bracket.

30. Install the turbocharger housing to engine block support bracket and the screws hand tight. Torque the block screw 1st to 40 ft. lbs. (54 Nm). Torque the screw to the turbocharger housing to 20 ft. lbs. (27 Nm).

31. Reposition the drain back hose connector and tighten the hose clamps. Reconnect the exhaust pipe.

32. Connect the upper radiator hose to the thermostat housing.

33. Refill the cooling system.

34. Connect the negative battery cable and check the manifolds for leaks.

Turbocharger

Removal and Installation

NOTE: On some vehicles, some of the turbocharger to exhaust manifold nuts are not accessible enough to loosen and cannot be removed on the vehicle. Head removal would be necessary in these situations.

1. Disconnect the negative battery cable. Drain the cooling system.

2. Disconnect the EGR valve tube at the EGR valve.

3. Disconnect the turbocharger oil feed at the oil sending unit hex and the coolant tube at the water box. Disconnect the oil/coolant support bracket from the cylinder head.

4. Remove the right intermediate shaft, bearing support bracket and outer halfshaft assemblies.

5. Remove the turbocharger to engine block support bracket.

6. Disconnect the exhaust pipe at the articulated joint. Disconnect the oxygen sensor at the electrical connection.

7. Loosen the oil drain-back tube connector clamps and move the tube hose down on the nipple.

8. Disconnect the coolant tube nut at the block outlet (below steering pump bracket) and tube support bracket.

9. Remove the turbocharger to exhaust manifold nuts. Carefully routing the oil and coolant lines, move the assembly down and out of the vehicle.

To Install:

NOTE: Before installing the turbocharger assembly, be sure it is first charged with oil. Failure to do this may cause damage to the assembly.

10. Position the turbocharger on the exhaust manifold. Apply an anti-seize compound, Loctite® 771–64 or equivalent, to the threads and torque the retaining nuts to 40 ft. lbs. (54 Nm).

11. Connect the coolant tube to engine block fitting. Torque the tube nut to 30 ft. lbs. (41 Nm).

12. Position the oil drain-back hose and torque the clamps to 30 inch lbs.

13. Install and torque the:
    Turbocharger to engine support bracket block screw to 40 ft. lbs. (54 Nm).
    Turbocharger housing screw to 20 ft. lbs. (27 Nm).
    Articulated joint shoulder bolts to 21 ft. lbs. (28 Nm).

14. Install the right driveshaft assembly, the starter and the oil feed line at the sending unit hex. Torque the oil feed tube nut to 10 ft. lbs. (14 Nm) and the EGR tube to EGR valve nut to 60 ft. lbs. (81 Nm).

15. Refill the cooling system. Connect the negative battery cable and check the turbocharger for proper operation.

Timing Chain Front Cover

Removal and Installation

3.3L ENGINE

1. Disconnect the negative battery cable. Drain the cooling system.

2. Support engine and remove the right side motor mount.

3. Raise the vehicle and support safely. Drain the engine oil, remove the oil pan and oil pickup tube.

4. Remove the right wheel and tire assembly and the splash shield.

5. Remove the drive belt.

6. Unbolt the air conditioning compressor and position it to the side. Remove the compressor mounting bracket.

7. Remove the crankshaft pulley bolt and pulley.

8. Remove the idler pulley from the engine bracket and remove the bracket.

9. Remove the cam sensor from the timing chain cover.

10. Unbolt and remove the cover from the engine. Make sure the oil pump inner rotor does not fall out. Remove the 3 O-rings from the coolant passages and the oil pump outlet.

Timing chain cover—3.3L engine

Timing chain cover removed—3.3L engine

11. Thoroughly clean and dry the gasket mating surfaces. Install new O-rings to the block.

12. Remove the crankshaft oil seal from the cover. The seal must be removed from the cover when installing to ensure proper oil pump engagement.

To install:

13. Using a new gasket, install the chain case cover to the engine.

14. Make certain the oil pump is engaged onto the crankshaft before proceeding, or severe engine damage will result. Install the attaching bolts and torque to 20 ft. lbs. (27 Nm).

15. Install the crankshaft oil seal and pulley. Make sure the pulley bottoms out on the crankshaft seal diameter.

16. Install the engine bracket and torque the bolts to 40 ft. lbs. (54 Nm). Install the idler pulley to the engine bracket.

17. To install the cam sensor, first clean off the old spacer from the sensor face completely. Inspect the O-ring for damage and replace if necessary. A new spacer must be attached to the cam sensor prior to installation; if a new spacer is not used, engine performance will be adversely affected. Oil the O-ring lightly and push the sensor into its bore in the chain case cover until contact is made with the cam timing gear. Hold in this position and tighten the bolt to 9 ft. lbs. (12 Nm).

18. Install the air conditioning compressor and bracket.

19. Install the accessory drive belt.

20. Install the inner splash shield and the wheel and tire assembly.

21. Install the oil pump and pickup tube. Install the oil pan with a new gasket.

22. Install the motor mount.

23. Remove the engine temperature sensor and fill the cooling system until the level reaches the sensor hole. Install the sensor and continue to fill the radiator. Fill the engine with the proper amount of oil.

24. Connect the negative battery cable, start the engine and check for leaks.

3.9L AND 5.2L ENGINES

1. Disconnect the negative battery cable.
2. Drain the cooling system.
3. Remove the radiator, fan and all related parts. Remove the water pump.
4. Remove the crankshaft pulley.
5. Remove the vibration damper using the proper puller.
6. Disconnect the fuel lines from the fuel pump, if equipped.
7. Remove the 2 front bolts from the oil pan.
8. Unbolt the chain cover from the block and remove, using caution to avoid damaging the oil pan gasket. Remove the fuel pump from the cover, if equipped.

To install:

9. Clean and dry the mating surfaces of the cover and block. Apply a thin bead of sealer to the oil pan gasket.

10. Install a new cover gasket and install the cover. Do not tighten the mounting bolts at this time.

11. Lubricate seal lip with lubriplate or equivalent. Position damper hub slot in crankshaft, this will act as a pilot for crankshaft seal. Press damper on crankshaft. Torque the cover bolts to 30 ft. lbs. (41 Nm).

12. Install vibration damper bolt and washer and torque to 135 ft. lbs. (183 Nm). Install crankshaft pulley and the water pump with a new gasket.

13. Install the fuel pump using a new gasket, if equipped and connect the fuel lines. Install the 2 oil pan bolts.

14. Install the radiator, fan and all related parts.

15. Fill the cooling system.

16. Connect the negative battery cable and check for leaks.

Front Cover Oil Seal

Removal and Installation

3.3L ENGINE

1. Disconnect the negative battery cable.
2. Raise the vehicle and support safely. Remove the right front tire and wheel assembly and the inner splash shield.
3. Remove the drive belt.
4. Remove the crankshaft bolt and pulley.
5. Use tool C–4991 to remove the seal.

To install:

6. Clean out the bore. Place the seal with the spring toward the engine. Install the new seal using tool C–4992 until it is flush with the cover.

7. Install the crankshaft pulley and retainer bolt.

8. Install the accessory drive belt and adjust tension as desired.

9. Install the splash shield and the tire and wheel assembly.

10. Connect the negative battery cable and check for leaks.

3.9L ENGINE

1. Disconnect the negative battery cable.
2. Remove the belts from the crankshaft pulley.
3. Remove the fan and shroud from the vehicle.
4. Remove the crankshaft pulley.
5. Remove the vibration damper using the proper puller.
6. Using a flat bladed tool behind the lips of the oil seal, carefully pry outward. Take care not to damage the crankshaft seal surface of the cover.

To install:

7. Install the new seal by installing the threaded shaft part of the special tool C–4251 into the threads of the crankshaft.

8. Place the seal into the opening with the spring toward the engine. Place the installing adapter C–4251–3 with the thrust bearing and nut on the shaft. Tighten the nut until the tool is flush with the timing chain cover. Remove the tool.

9. Install the damper with tool C–3638, install the bolt and washer and torque to specification.

10. Apply a small amount of sealer to the bolts and install the crankshaft pulley.

11. Install the fan and shroud.

12. Connect the negative battery cable and check for leaks.

Timing Chain and Sprockets

Removal and Installation

3.3L ENGINE

1. If possible, position the engine so No. 1 piston is at TDC on the compression stroke. Disconnect the negative battery cable. Drain the coolant.

2. Remove the timing chain case cover and chain snubber.

3. Remove the camshaft gear attaching cup washer and bolt and remove the timing chain with the camshaft gear attached. Remove the crankshaft sprocket with suitable puller taking care not to damage the crankshaft surface.

To install:

4. Install the crankshaft sprocket onto the crankshaft making sure sprocket is seated into position. Rotate sprocket to position timing mark in the 12 o'clock position.

5. Place timing chain around camshaft sprocket and align timing mark in the 6 o'clock position. Place timing chain around the crankshaft sprocket and install camshaft sprocket in position.

6. Check alignment of gears with straight edge.

7. Install camshaft bolt and washer and tighten bolt to 35 ft. lbs. (47 Nm).

8. Check camshaft endplay. The specification with a new plate is 0.005–0.012 in. (0.0127–0.304mm) or 0.012 in.

Timing mark alignment—3.3L engine

Timing mark alignment—3.9L and 5.2L engines

(0.31mm) maximum with a used plate. Replace the thrust plate if not within specifications.

9. Install the timing chain snubber. For 1992 engine, these bolts are 20mm long and should **NOT** be used with previous year engines.

10. Thoroughly clean and dry the gasket mating surfaces.

11. Install new O-rings to the block.

12. Remove the crankshaft oil seal from the cover. The seal must be removed from the cover when installing to ensure proper oil pump engagement.

13. Using a new gasket, install the chain case cover to the engine.

14. Make certain the oil pump is engaged onto the crankshaft before proceeding or severe engine damage will result. Install the attaching bolts and torque to 20 ft. lbs. (27 Nm).

15. Install the crankshaft oil seal, crankshaft pulley and bolt. Make sure the pulley bottoms out on the crankshaft seal diameter.

16. Install engine bracket, idler pulley, air conditioning bracket and accessory belt(s).

17. To install the cam sensor, first clean off the old spacer from the sensor face. Inspect the O-ring for damage and replace if necessary. A new spacer must be attached to the cam sensor prior to installation; if a new spacer is not used, engine performance will be adversely affected. Oil the O-ring lightly and push the sensor into its bore in the chain case cover until contact is made with the cam timing gear. Hold in this position and tighten the bolt to 10 ft. lbs. (12 Nm).

18. Install the inner splash shield and tire and wheel assembly.

19. Install the oil pump pickup tube and oil pan. Install engine mount, lower vehicle and fill crankcase to proper level.

20. Refill the cooling system.

21. Connect the negative battery cable, road test the vehicle and check for leaks.

3.9L AND 5.2L ENGINES

1. If possible, crank the engine so No. 1 cylinder is at TDC on the compression stroke. Remove the distributor cap to confirm and line the timing mark on the damper pulley with **0** on the timing scale. This will aid in aligning timing marks when installing the timing gears. Disconnect the negative battery cable.

2. Drain the cooling system.

3. Remove the radiator, fan and all related parts. Remove the water pump.

4. Remove the crankshaft pulley.

5. Remove the vibration damper using the proper puller.

6. Disconnect the fuel lines from the fuel pump, if equipped.

7. Remove the 2 front bolts from the oil pan.

8. Unbolt the chain cover from the block and remove, using caution to avoid damaging the oil pan gasket. Remove the fuel pump from the cover, if equipped.

9. Remove the camshaft gear retaining bolt, cup washer and fuel pump eccentric, if equipped. Remove the timing chain and gears.

To install:

10. Place both camshaft and crankshaft gears on the bench with the timing marks on the exact imaginary center line through both gear bores as they are installed on the engine. Place the timing chain around both sprockets.

11. Turn the crankshaft and camshaft so the keys line up with the keyways in the gears when the timing marks are in proper position.

12. Slide both gears over their respective shafts and use a straightedge to check timing mark alignment.

13. Install the fuel pump eccentric and cup washer, if equipped. Torque the camshaft gear retaining bolt to 35 ft. lbs. (47 Nm).

14. Clean and dry the mating surfaces of the timing chain cover and block. Apply a thin bead of sealer to the oil pan gasket.

15. Install a new cover gasket and install the cover. Do not tighten the mounting bolts at this time.

16. Lubricate seal lip with lubriplate or equivalent. Position damper hub slot in crankshaft, this will act as a pilot for crankshaft seal. Press damper on crankshaft. Torque the cover bolts to to 30 ft. lbs. (41 Nm).

17. Install vibration damper bolt and washer and torque to 135 ft. lbs. (183 Nm). Install crankshaft pulley and the water pump with a new gasket.

18. Install the fuel pump using a new gasket, if equipped and connect the fuel lines. Install the 2 oil pan bolts.

19. Install the radiator, fan and all related parts.

20. Fill the cooling system.

21. Connect the negative battery cable and check for leaks.

Timing Belt Cover

Removal and Installation

2.2L AND 2.5L ENGINES

1. Disconnect the negative battery cable.

2. Remove the nuts that attach the upper cover to the valve cover. Remove the bolt that attaches the upper cover to the lower cover.

3. Remove the upper cover.

4. Raise the vehicle and support safely. Remove the right side splash shield.

5. Remove the crankshaft pulley, water pump pulley and the accessory belts.

6. Remove the lower cover attaching bolts. Remove the lower cover.

7. The installation is the reverse of the removal procedure.

3.0L ENGINE

1. Disconnect the negative battery cable.

2. If equipped with air conditioning, loosen the adjustment pulley locknut, turn the screw counterclockwise to reduce the drive belt tension and remove the belt.

3. To remove the serpentine drive belt, insert a ½ in. breaker bar in to the square hole of the tensioner pulley, rotate it counterclockwise to reduce the drive belt tension and remove the belt.

4. Remove the air conditioning compressor and the air compressor bracket if equipped, power steering pump and alternator from the mounts; support them aside. Remove power steering pump/alternator automatic belt tensioner bolt and the tensioner.

5. Raise and safely support the vehicle. Remove the right inner fender splash shield.

6. Remove the crankshaft pulley bolt and the pulley/damper assembly from the crankshaft.

7. Lower the vehicle and place a floor jack under the engine to support it.

8. Separate the front engine mount insulator from the bracket. Raise the engine slightly and remove the mount bracket.

9. Remove the timing belt cover bolts and the upper and lower covers from the engine.

10. Install upper and lower timing belt covers and install retaining screws.

11. Install the mount bracket and connect the engine mount insulator to the mount bracket.

12. Raise and safely support vehicle. Install crankshaft pulleys and damper. Install right inner splash shield and wheel and tire assembly.

13. Install the air conditioner bracket and compressor to the engine.

14. Install power steering pump, automatic belt tensioner and the accessory drive belt to the engine.

15. Connect the negative battery cable.

Adjusting the timing belt—2.2L and 2.5L engines

(SPECIAL TOOL / HORIZONTAL (WITHIN 15°))

Timing Belt and Tensioner

Adjustment

2.2L AND 2.5L ENGINES

1. Disconnect the negative battery cable.

2. Raise the vehicle and support safely. Remove the right front inner splash shield.

3. Remove the timing belt upper and lower covers.

4. Position camshaft so the timing marks are in the proper position and check crankshaft and intermediate shaft for proper alignment.

5. If properly aligned, turn the crankshaft ¼ turn counterclockwise. Install tensioning weight onto the hex of the tensioner and loosen the adjuster bolt. Slowly turn the crankshaft clockwise to remove any slack that might be in the timing belt. Secure tensioner adjuster nut. Rotate crankshaft clockwise for 2 engine revolutions and recheck engine timing marks.

6. If not properly aligned, inspect belt for wear and replaced as required. Adjust engine timing and belt tension.

7. Reinstall timing belt covers and install splash shield.

3.0L ENGINE

1. Loosen the bolt that holds the timing belt tensioner in place. The bolt is located to the left of the accessory belt tensioner mounting.

2. Allow the spring to pull the tensioner in automatically.

3. Tighten the tensioner locking bolt.

Removal and Installation

2.2L AND 2.5L ENGINES

1. If possible, position the engine so No. 1 piston is at TDC. Disconnect the negative battery cable.

2. Remove the timing belt covers. Remove the timing belt tensioner and allow the belt to hang free.

3. Place a floor jack under the engine and separate the right motor mount. Raise the engine from the mount slightly.

4. Remove the air conditioning compressor belt idler pulley, if equipped and remove the mounting stud. Unbolt the compressor/alternator bracket and position it to the side.

5. Remove the timing belt from the vehicle.

To install:

6. Remove spark plugs from the engine. Turn the crankshaft sprocket and intermediate shaft sprocket until the marks are in line. Use a straightedge from bolt to bolt to confirm alignment.

COVER (REFERENCE)   COVER TIMING HOLE PLUG

Alignment of the arrows on the camshaft sprocket with the camshaft bearing cap to cylinder head mounting line—2.2L and 2.5L engines

Alignment of the crankshaft sprocket and intermediate shaft sprocket—2.2L and 2.5L engines

CAMSHAFT SPROCKET
SMALL HOLE IN
VERTICAL CENTER LINE

PARTING LINE—CAMSHAFT
CAP TO CYLINDER HEAD

NUMBER ONE
CYLINDER-TDC

CRANKSHAFT
SPROCKET
"O" MARK

INTERMEDIATE SHAFT
SPROCKET NOTCH

Timing belt installation—2.2L and 2.5L engines

7. Install timing belt onto engine and lower engine into engine mount. Tighten retainer bolts and nut and remove the floor jack.

8. Turn the camshaft until the small hole in the sprocket is at the top and rows on the hub are in line with the camshaft cap to cylinder head mounting lines. Use a mirror to see the alignment so it is viewed straight on and not at an angle from above. Install belt over camshaft pulley. Turn the idler pulley counterclock-

wise slightly and install belt over the idler pulley. Hold belt in position and turn idler pulley clockwise until the slack is out of the belt. The timing mark should be in aligned with the crankshaft timing mark. If not, repeat this step until the mark on the pulley is aligned with crankshaft mark.

9. Repeat this step for the crankshaft pulley working back to the idler pulley. Do not rotate the belt far enough to disturb the camshaft pulley.

10. Install the weight on the hex of the tensioner and allow to hang freely. Rotate the crankshaft 2 engine revolutions clockwise and recheck engine timing. Tighten the adjuster nut while holding the tensioner in position.

NOTE: If the timing marks are in line but slack exists in the belt between either the camshaft and intermediate shaft sprockets or the intermediate and crankshaft sprockets, the timing will be incorrect when the belt is tensioned.

11. Install the air conditioning compressor/alternator bracket and the idler pulley.

12. Connect the negative battery cable and road test the vehicle.

3.0L ENGINE

1. If possible, position the engine so No. 1 cylinder is at TDC. Disconnect the negative battery cable. Remove the timing covers from the engine.

2. If the same timing belt will be reused, mark the direction of the timing belt's rotation, for installation in the same direction. Make sure the engine is positioned so the No. 1 cylinder is at the TDC of it's compression stroke and the sprockets timing marks are aligned with the engine's timing mark indicators.

3. Loosen the timing belt tensioner bolt and remove the belt. If not removing the tensioner, position it as far away from the center of the engine as possible and tighten the bolt.

4. If the tensioner is being removed, paint the outside of the spring to ensure that it is not installed backwards. Unbolt the tensioner and remove it along with the spring.

To install:

5. Install the tensioner, if removed and hook the upper end of the spring to the water pump pin and the lower end to the tensioner in exactly the same position as originally installed. If not already done, position both camshafts so the marks line up with those on the alternator bracket (rear bank) and inner timing cover (front bank). Rotate the crankshaft so the timing mark aligns with the mark on the oil pump.

6. Install the timing belt on the crankshaft sprocket and while keeping the belt tight on the tension side (right side), install the belt on the front camshaft sprocket.

7. Install the belt on the water pump pulley, then the rear camshaft sprocket and the tensioner.

8. Rotate the front camshaft counterclockwise to tension the belt between the front camshaft and the crankshaft. If the timing marks came out of line, repeat the procedure.

9. Install the crankshaft sprocket flange.

10. Loosen the tensioner bolt and allow the spring to tension the belt.

11. Turn the crankshaft 2 full turns in the clockwise direction only until the timing marks align again. Now that the belt is properly tensioned, torque the tensioner lockbolt to 21 ft. lbs. (29 Nm).

12. Install the timing belt covers and all related parts.

13. Connect the negative battery cable and road test the vehicle.

Timing Sprockets

Removal and Installation

2.2L AND 2.5L ENGINES

1. Disconnect the negative battery cable. Remove the timing belt.

Timing belt installation—3.0L engine

2. Remove the crankshaft sprocket bolt. Using the puller tool C–4685 or equivalent, and the button from tool L–4524 or equivalent, remove the crankshaft sprocket.

3. Using the tool C–4687 or equivalent, hold the camshaft and/or intermediate sprocket, remove the center bolt and the sprocket(s).

4. The installation is the reverse of the removal procedure. Torque the camshaft and intermediate sprocket bolts to 65 ft. lbs. (88 Nm) and the crankshaft sprocket bolt to 50 ft. lbs. (68 Nm).

3.0L ENGINE

1. Disconnect the negative battery cable.
2. Remove the timing belt.
3. To remove the camshaft sprocket, hold the sprocket with tool MB990775 or equivalent, and remove the retaining bolt and washer.
4. To remove the crankshaft sprocket, remove the bolt and remove the sprocket from the crankshaft.
5. The installation is the reverse of the removal procedure. Torque the camshaft sprocket bolt to 70 ft. lbs. (95 Nm) while holding the sprocket with the holding tool. Torque the crankshaft sprocket bolt. to 110 ft. lbs. (150 Nm).

Camshaft

Removal and Installation

2.2L AND 2.5L ENGINES

1. Disconnect the negative battery cable. Relieve the fuel pressure, if equipped with fuel injection.
2. Turn the crankshaft so the No. 1 piston is at the TDC of the compression stroke. Remove the upper timing belt cover. Remove the air pump pulley, if equipped.

3. Remove the camshaft sprocket bolt and the sprocket and suspend tightly so the belt does not lose tension. If it does, the belt timing will have to be reset.
4. Remove the valve cover.
5. If the rocker arms are being reused, mark them for installation identification and loosen the camshaft bearing bolts, evenly and gradually.
6. Using a soft mallet, tap the rear of the camshaft a few times to break the bearing caps loose.
7. Remove the bolts, bearing caps and the camshaft with both end seals.

NOTE: Before replacing the camshaft, identify factory installed oversized components. To do so, look for the tops of the bearing caps pained green and O/SJ stamped rearward of the oil gallery plug on the rear of the head. In addition, the barrel of the camshaft is painted green and "O/SJ" is stamped onto the rear end of the camshaft. Installing standard sized parts in an head equipped with oversized parts—or visa versa—will cause severe engine damage.

Also, take note of the color of the paint stripe on the rear camshaft seal. These stripes differentiate seal sizes. If a seal with a different color stripe is installed, a severe leak will develop if the seal is too small or the cap will not be able to be fully installed if the seal is too big.

8. Check the oil passages for blockages and the parts for wear and damage and replace parts, as required. Clean the gasket mounting surfaces.
To install:
9. Transfer the sprocket key to the new camshaft. New rocker arms and a new camshaft sprocket bolt are normally included with the camshaft package. Install the rocker arms and lubricated camshaft.

10. Install the bearing caps with No. 1 at the timing belt end and No. 5 at the transaxle end. The camshaft bearing caps are numbered and have arrows facing forward. Torque the camshaft bearing bolts evenly and gradually to 18 ft. lbs. (24 Nm).

11. Install a small amount of sealer into No. 1 and No. 5 camshaft cap and install seals into place. Check for proper alignment of seals.

12. Mount a dial indicator to the front of the engine and check the camshaft endplay. Play should not exceed 0.006 in.

13. Install the camshaft sprocket using the new bolt. Install the air pump pulley, if equipped.

14. Install the valve cover with a new gaskets.

15. Connect the negative battery cable and check for leaks.

3.0L ENGINE

1. Disconnect the negative battery cable. Remove the air cleaner assembly, timing belt covers and valve covers.

2. Install auto lash adjuster retainers MD998443 or equivalent on the rocker arms. Remove the timing belt from the camshaft sprocket.

3. If removing the right side (front) camshaft, remove the distributor extension.

4. Remove the camshaft bearing caps but do not remove the bolts from the caps.

5. Remove the rocker arms, rocker shafts and bearing caps, as an assembly.

6. Remove the camshaft from the cylinder head.

7. Inspect the bearing journals on the camshaft, cylinder head and bearing caps.

To install:

8. Lubricate the camshaft journals and camshaft with clean engine oil and install the camshaft in the cylinder head.

9. Install the rocker arm shaft assembly making sure the arrow on the bearing cap and the arrow mark on the cylinder head are in the same direction. The direction of the arrow marks on the front and rear assemblies are opposite to each other.

10. Torque the bearing cap bolts, in the following sequence: No. 3, No. 2, No. 1 and No. 4 to 85 inch lbs. (10 Nm).

11. Repeat the sequence increasing the torque to 175 inch lbs. (18 Nm).

12. Install the distributor extension, if it was removed.

13. Install the valve cover and all related parts.

3.3L ENGINE

1. Relieve the fuel pressure. Disconnect the negative battery cable.

2. Remove the engine from the vehicle. Remove the intake manifold, cylinder heads, timing chain cover and timing chain from the engine.

3. Remove the rocker arm and shaft assemblies.

4. Label and remove the pusrods and lifters.

5. Remove the camshaft thrust plate.

6. Install a long bolt into the front of the camshaft to facilitate its removal. Remove the camshaft being careful not to damage the cam bearings with the cam lobes.

To install:

7. Install the camshaft to within 2 in. of its final installation position.

8. Install the camshaft thrust plate and 2 bolts and torque to 105 inch. lbs. (12 Nm).

9. Place both camshaft and crankshaft gears on the bench with the timing marks on the exact imaginary center line through both gear bores as they are installed on the engine. Place the timing chain around both sprockets.

10. Turn the crankshaft and camshaft so the keys line up with the keyways in the gears when the timing marks are in proper position.

11. Slide both gears over their respective shafts and use a straightedge to check timing mark alignment.

12. Measure camshaft endplay. If not within specifications, replace the thrust plate.

13. If the camshaft was not replaced, lubricate and install the lifters in their original locations. If the camshaft was replaced, new lifters must be used.

14. Install the pushrods and rocker shaft assemblies.

15. Install the timing chain cover, cylinder heads and intake manifold.

16. Install the engine in the vehicle.

17. Change the engine oil and replace the oil filter.

NOTE: If the camshaft or lifters have been replaced, add 1 pint of Mopar crankcase conditioner or equivalent, when replenishing the oil to aid in break in. This mixture should be left in the engine for a minimum of 500 miles and drained at the next normal oil change.

18. Fill the radiator with coolant.

19. Connect the negative battery cable, set all adjustments to specifications and check for leaks.

3.9L AND 5.2L ENGINES

1. If possible, crank the engine around so No. 1 cylinder is at TDC on the compression stroke. Remove the distributor cap to confirm and line the timing mark on the damper pulley with **0** on the timing scale. This will aid in aligning timing marks when installing the timing gears.

2. If equipped with fuel injection, relieve the fuel pressure. Drain the cooling system.

3. Removal of the engine is required for this procedure.

4. After engine is removed, remove the valve covers and rocker shaft assemblies. Identify and remove the pushrods.

5. Remove the intake manifold. Identify and remove all lifters.

6. Remove the distributor.

7. Lift out the oil pump and distributor driveshaft.

8. Remove the fuel pump, if equipped. Remove the timing chain cover, timing chain and gears.

9. Note the location of the oil tab and remove the camshaft thrust plate.

10. Install a long bolt into the front of the camshaft to facilitate removal. Remove the camshaft, being careful not to damage any of the cam bearings with the cam lobes.

To install:

11. Install the camshaft to within 2 in. of its final installation position.

12. Install the camshaft blocking tool C–3509 and bolt it in place with the distributor hold-down bolt. This will prevent the camshaft from being pushed in too far and knocking out the welch plug at the rear of the block. This tool should remain in place until the timing chain installation has been completed.

13. Install the camshaft thrust plate and chain oil tab. Make

Installing the camshaft blocking tool—3.9L and 5.2L engines

Installed distributor drive gear position—3.9L engine

Position of installed distributor drive gear caps—5.2L engine

sure the tang of the oil tab enters the hole in the thrust plate at the lower right. Torque the bolts to 18 ft. lbs. (24 Nm). Make sure the top edge of the oil tab is flat against the thrust plate or it will not feed oil to the chain.

14. Place both camshaft and crankshaft gears on the bench with the timing marks on the exact imaginary center line through both gear bores as they are installed on the engine. Place the timing chain around both sprockets.

15. Turn the crankshaft and camshaft so the keys line up with the keyways in the gears when the timing marks are in proper position.

16. Slide both gears over their respective shafts and use a straightedge to check timing mark alignment.

17. Install the fuel pump eccentric, cup washer and retainer bolt. Remove the camshaft blocking tool, if it was installed.

18. Measure camshaft endplay, if applicable. Replace the thrust plate if not within specifications.

19. Coat the oil pump and distributor driveshaft with oil. On 3.9L engine, install the shaft so when the gear spirals into place and drops into the oil pump, the slot in the top of the gear is pointing directly to the left front intake manifold bolt hole. On 5.2L engine, install the shaft so when the gear spirals into place and drops into the oil pump, the slot in the top of the gear is

pointing in a direction parallel to the centerline of the crankshaft.

20. If the camshaft was not replaced, lubricate and install the lifters in their original locations. If the camshaft was replaced, new lifters must be used.

21. Install the pushrods and rocker shaft assemblies.

22. Install the intake manifold, if it was removed. Install the valve covers.

23. Install the distributor so the rotor points to the No. 1 spark plug wire position on the cap.

24. Install the timing chain cover and all related parts.

25. Install the fuel pump.

26. Install the engine.

27. Change the engine oil and replace the oil filter.

NOTE: If the camshaft or lifters have been replaced, add 1 pint of Mopar crankcase conditioner or equivalent, when replenishing the oil to aid in break in. This mixture should be left in the engine for a minimum of 500 miles and drained at the next normal oil change.

28. Fill the radiator with coolant.

29. Connect the negative battery cable, set all adjustments to specifications and check for leaks.

Intermediate/Balance Shaft

Removal and Installation

INTERMEDIATE SHAFT

2.2L and 2.5L Engines

1. Disconnect the negative battery cable.

2. Crank the engine around until the No. 1 piston is at TDC. Remove the timing belt covers to confirm that all timing marks are lined up.

3. Remove the fuel pump, if equipped. Remove the distributor. Looking down at the oil pump, the slot in the shaft must be parallel with the center line of the crankshaft. Remove the oil pan, dipstick tube and oil pump.

4. Remove the timing belt. Remove the intermediate sprocket using tool C–4685. Remove the seal retainer mounting bolts and remove the retainer from the block.

5. Remove the retainer and the intermediate shaft from the block.

6. If necessary, remove the front intermediate shaft bushing using tool C–4697–2 and the rear bushing using tool C–4686–2.
To install:

7. If replacement of the intermediate shaft bushings are required, install the front bushing using tool C–4697–1 until the tool is flush with the block. Install the rear bushing using tool C–4686–1 until the tool is flush with the block.

Alignment of balance shaft sprockets—2.5L engine

8. Lubricate the distributor drive gear and install the intermediate shaft into the block.

9. Install the intermediate shaft sprocket and the timing belt.

10. With the timing belt properly installed, install the oil pump so the slot is parallel to the center line of the crankshaft. Install the distributor so the rotor is aligned with the No. 1 spark plug wire tower on the cap.

11. Install the fuel pump, if equipped.

12. Connect the negative battery cable and road test the vehicle.

BALANCE SHAFT

2.5L Engine

1. Disconnect the negative battery cable. Raise the vehicle and support safely.

2. Remove the timing belt. Remove the oil pan, the oil pickup, the crankshaft belt sprocket and the front crankshaft oil seal retainer.

3. Remove the balance shafts chain cover, guide and tensioner. Remove the balance shaft gear and chain sprocket retaining screws and crankshaft chain sprocket torx screws. Remove chain and sprocket assembly.

4. Remove the gear cover retaining stud. Remove cover and balance shaft gears.

5. Remove the carrier rear cover and balance shafts.

To install:

6. Install balance shafts and rear carrier cover to the block. Install gears and set gear timing as follows:

    a. Turn balance shafts until both shaft keyways are parallel to the vertical centerline of the engine. (facing up)

    b. Install short hub drive gear on sprocket driven shaft.

    c. Install the long hub gear on gear drivenshaft.

    d. Check that the timing marks on the gears are facing each other and that the keyways are facing up.

7. Install the gear cover and tighten double ended stud/washer to 105 inch lbs. (12 Nm).

8. Install crankshaft sprocket and tighten head torx screw to 130 inch lbs. (13 Nm).

9. Rotate the crankshaft to position the No. 1 cylinder on the TDC of the compression stroke; the timing marks on the chain sprocket should align with the parting line on the left side of the No. 1 main bearing cap.

10. Position the balance shaft sprocket into the balance chain so the sprocket (yellow dot) timing mark mates with the yellow link on the chain.

11. Install the balance chain/sprocket assembly onto the crankshaft and the balance shaft. Torque the sprocket to shaft bolts to 21 ft. lbs. (28 Nm). If necessary to secure the crankshaft while tightening the bolts, place a block of wood between the crankcase and the crankshaft counterbalance.

Exploded view of the balance shafts and related parts—2.5L engine

Adjusting the balance shaft chain tensioner—2.5L engine

12. Loosely install the chain tensioners and place a shim (0.039 in. × 2.75 in.) between the chain and the tensioner. Apply firm pressure (to reduce the chain slack) to the tensioner shoe. Torque the tensioner to front gear cover bolts to 8.5 ft. lbs. (12 Nm). Remove the shim.

13. Install the chain cover and the rear cover to the carrier housing and torque the bolts to 8.5 ft. lbs. (12 Nm).

14. Replace the crankshaft retainer seal, apply silicone sealer to the mating surface and install the retainer.

15. Install the oil pickup and oil pan.

16. Install the crankshaft sprocket and the timing belt.

17. Connect the negative battery cable and road test the vehicle.

Piston and Connecting Rod

Positioning

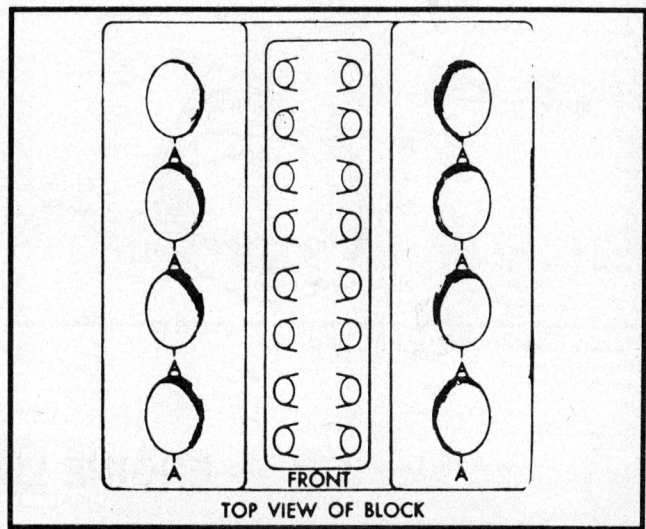

Piston positioning—3.9L and 5.2L engines

Timing the balance shaft sprocket with the crankshaft sprocket—2.5L engine

Piston positioning—3.3L engine

2-63

Piston positioning—3.0L engine

Piston positioning—2.2L and 2.5L engines

2.2L and 2.5L engines—piston differences

ENGINE LUBRICATION

Oil Pan

Removal and Installation

CARAVAN, VOYAGER AND TOWN & COUNTRY

2.2L and 2.5L Engines

1. Disconnect the negative battery cable. Remove the oil dipstick.
2. Raise the vehicle and support safely.
3. Drain the engine oil.
4. Remove the engine to transaxle struts, if equipped.
5. Remove the torque converter or clutch inspection cover, if equipped.
6. Remove the oil pan retaining screws and remove the oil pan and the side seals.

To install:

7. Thoroughly clean and dry all sealing surfaces, bolts and bolt holes.
8. Apply silicone sealer to the 4 end seal to block corners and install the end seals making sure the corners are not twisted.
9. Apply silicone to the 4 pan to block corners. Install a new pan gasket or apply silicone sealer to the sealing surface of the pan and install to the engine making sure not to dislodge the end seals.

10. Install the retaining screws and torque to 17 ft. lbs. (23 Nm).
11. Install the torque converter inspection cover and engine to transaxle struts, if equipped. Lower the vehicle.
12. Install the dipstick. Fill the engine with the proper amount of oil.
13. Connect the negative battery cable and check for leaks.

3.0L and 3.3L Engines

1. Disconnect the negative battery cable.
2. Raise the vehicle and support safely.
3. Remove the torque converter bolt access cover, if equipped.
4. Drain the engine oil.
5. Remove the oil pan retaining screws and remove the oil pan and gasket.

To install:

6. Thoroughly clean and dry all sealing surfaces, bolts and bolt holes.
7. Apply silicone sealer to the chain cover to block mating seam and the rear main seal retainer to block seam, if equipped.
8. Install a new pan gasket or apply silicone sealer to the sealing surface of the pan and install to the engine.
9. Install the retaining screws.
10. Install the torque converter bolt access cover, if equipped. Lower the vehicle.

11. Install the dipstick. Fill the engine with the proper amount of oil.

12. Connect the negative battery cable and check for leaks.

DAKOTA

2.2L and 2.5L Engines

1. Disconnect the negative battery cable. Remove the oil dipstick.

2. Disconnect the air pump relief valve upper hose. Raise the vehicle and support safely.

3. Remove the clutch housing to engine strut and clutch inspection cover.

4. Remove the lower radiator hose support bracket.

5. Slightly loosen the right motor mount through bolt just enough to relieve the tension.

6. Using the proper equipment, support the weight of the engine. Loosen the left motor mount through bolt enough to clear the bracket.

7. Raise the left side of the engine about 2 inches.

8. Remove the oil pan retaining screws and remove the oil pan and gasket.

To install:

9. Thoroughly clean and dry all sealing surfaces, bolts and bolt holes.

10. Apply silicone sealer to the 4 end seal to block corners and install the end seals making sure the corners are not twisted.

11. Apply silicone to the 4 pan to block corners. Install a new pan gasket or apply silicone sealer to the sealing surface of the pan and install to the engine making sure not to dislodge the end seals.

12. Install the pan retaining screws and torque to 17 ft. lbs. (23 Nm).

13. Lower the engine. Torque the motor mount through bolts to 50 ft. lbs. (68 Nm).

14. Install the clutch inspection cover and housing to engine strut. Install the lower radiator hose support bracket. Lower the vehicle.

15. Install the dipstick and air pump hose. Fill the engine with the proper amount of oil.

16. Connect the negative battery cable and check for leaks.

3.9L Engine With 2WD

1. Disconnect the negative battery cable. Remove the oil dipstick. Disengage the distributor cap and remove it away from the firewall.

2. Raise the vehicle and support safely. Drain the engine oil.

3. Remove the exhaust crossover.

4. Loosen the motor mount bolts. Using the proper equipment, raise the engine. When the engine is high enough, install replacement bolts (similar in size to the motor mount bolts), in the engine mount attaching points on the frame brackets. Lower the engine so the bottom of the motor mounts rest on the 2 replacement bolts. Remove the torque converter inspection cover, if equipped.

5. Remove the oil pan retaining screws and remove the oil pan and gaskets.

To install:

6. Thoroughly clean and dry all sealing surfaces, bolts and bolt holes.

7. Place a drop of silicone sealer to the timing chain cover to block mating seam.

8. Install the new gaskets to the engine and add a drop of silicone sealer to the corners where the rubber and cork meet. Install the rubber seals to the pan.

9. Install the pan to the engine and torque the retaining screws to 17 ft. lbs. (23 Nm). Install the torque converter inspection cover, if equipped.

10. Reinstall the engine to the mount and install the exhaust crossover. Lower the vehicle.

11. Install the distributor cap.

12. Install the dipstick. Fill the engine with the proper amount of oil.

13. Connect the negative battery cable and check for leaks.

3.9L Engine With 4WD

1. Disconnect the negative battery cable. Remove the oil dipstick.

2. Raise the vehicle and support safely.

3. Using the proper equipment, support the weight of the engine. Remove the front driving axle.

4. Remove the exhaust crossover and the lower transmission cover.

5. Remove the oil pan retaining screws and remove the oil pan and gaskets.

To install:

6. Thoroughly clean and dry all sealing surfaces, bolts and bolt holes.

7. Place a drop of silicone sealer to the timing chain cover to block mating seam.

8. Install the new gaskets to the engine and add a drop of silicone sealer to the corners where the rubber and cork meet. Install the rubber seals to the pan.

9. Install the pan to the engine and torque the retaining screws to 17 ft. lbs. (23 Nm). Install the lower transmission cover, if equipped.

10. Install the exhaust crossover.

11. Install the front driving axle. Lower the vehicle.

12. Install the dipstick. Fill the engine with the proper amount of oil.

13. Connect the negative battery cable and check for leaks.

5.2L Engine

1. Disconnect the negative battery cable. Remove the engine dipstick.

2. Raise the vehicle and support safely.

3. Drain the engine oil. Remove the exhaust crossover pipe.

4. Remove left engine to transmission strut.

5. Remove oil pan retaining bolts and remove oil pan.

To install:

6. Using a new pan gasket, add drop of sealer at corners of rubber and cork. Install pan and tighten bolts to 200 inch lbs. (23 Nm).

7. Install engine to strut and exhaust crossover. Lower vehicle.

8. Install oil dipstick. Connect negative battery cable, add engine oil, start engine and check for leaks.

Oil Pump

Removal and Installation

2.2L AND 2.5L ENGINES

1. Crank the engine around so No. 1 piston is at TDC. Disconnect the negative battery cable.

2. Matchmark the rotor to the block and remove the distributor to confirm that the slot in the oil pump shaft is parallel to the centerline of the crankshaft. Matchmark the slot to the distributor bore, if desired.

3. Remove the dipstick. Raise the vehicle and support safely. Drain the engine oil and remove the pan.

4. Remove the oil pickup.

5. Remove the 2 mounting bolts and remove the oil pump from the engine.

To install:

6. Prime the pump by pouring fresh oil into the pump intake and turning the driveshaft until oil comes out the pressure port. Repeat a few times until no air bubbles are present.

7. Apply sealer Loctite® 515 or equivalent, to the pump body to block machined surface interface. Lubricate the oil pump and distributor driveshaft.

8. Align the slot so it will be in the same position as when it

Aligning the slot in the oil pump shaft—2.2L and 2.5L engines

was removed. If it is not, the distributor will not be timed correctly. Install the pump fully and rotate back and forth to ensure proper positioning between the pump mounting surface and the machined surface of the block.

9. Install the mounting bolts fingertight and lower the vehicle to confirm proper slot positioning. If the slot is not properly positioned, raise the vehicle and move the gear as required. If the slot is correct, hold the pump firmly against the block and torque the mounting bolts to 17 ft. lbs. (23 Nm).

10. Clean out the oil pickup or replace as required. Replace the oil pickup O-ring and install the pickup to the pump.

11. Install the oil pan using new gaskets. Lower the vehicle.

12. Install the distributor.

13. Install the dipstick. Fill the engine with the proper amount of oil.

14. Connect the negative battery cable, check the timing and check the oil pressure.

3.0L ENGINE

1. Disconnect the negative battery cable. Remove the dipstick.

2. Raise the vehicle and support safely. Remove the timing

Exploded view of the oil pump—3.0L engine

Oil pump components—3.3L engine

Exploded view of the oil pump—3.9L engine

belt, drain the engine oil and remove the oil pan from the engine. Remove the oil pickup.

3. Remove the oil pump mounting bolts and remove the pump from the front of the engine. Note the different length bolts and their position in the pump for installation.

To install:

4. Clean the gasket mounting surfaces of the pump and engine block.

5. Prime the pump by pouring fresh oil into the pump and turning the rotors or, using petroleum jelly, pack the inside of the oil pump. Using a new gasket, install the oil pump on the engine and torque all bolts to 11 ft. lbs. (15 Nm).

6. Install the balancer and crankshaft sprocket to the end of the crankshaft.

7. Clean out the oil pickup or replace as required. Replace the oil pickup gasket ring and install the pickup to the pump.

8. Install the timing belt, oil pan and all related parts.

9. Install the dipstick. Fill the engine with the proper amount of oil.

10. Connect the negative battery cable, start the engine and check the oil pressure.

3.3L ENGINE

1. Disconnect the negative battery cable. Remove the dipstick.

2. Raise the vehicle and support safely. Drain the oil and remove the oil pan.

3. Remove the oil pickup.

4. Remove the chain case cover.

5. Disassemble the oil pump as required.

To install:

6. Assemble the pump. Torque the cover screws to 10 ft. lbs. (12 Nm).

7. Prime the oil pump by filling the rotor cavity with fresh oil and turning the rotors until oil comes out the pressure port. Repeat a few times until no air bubbles are present.

8. Install the chain case cover.

9. Clean out the oil pickup or replace as required. Replace the oil pickup O-ring and install the pickup to the pump.

10. Install the oil pan.

11. Install the dipstick. Fill the engine with the proper amount of oil.

12. Connect the negative battery cable, start the engine and check the oil pressure.

3.9L AND 5.2L ENGINES

1. Disconnect the negative battery cable.

2. Raise the vehicle and support safely. Drain the oil and remove the oil pan.

3. Remove the screen.

4. Unbolt the oil pump from the rear main bearing cap and remove it from the vehicle.

To install:

5. Prime the pump by pouring fresh oil into the pump intake and turning the driveshaft until oil comes out the pressure port. Repeat a few times until no air bubbles are present. Install the oil pump with a rotating motion to ensure proper pump driveshaft engagement.

6. Hold the pump flush against the main cap and finger-tighten the attaching bolts.

7. Torque the bolts to 30 ft. lbs. (41 Nm).

8. Install the screen.

9. Install the oil pan with a new gasket and lower vehicle.

10. Connect the negative battery cable and add oil to correct the level. Start the engine and check the oil pressure. Check for oil leaks.

Checking

2.2L AND 2.5L ENGINES

1. Remove the cover from the oil pump.

2. Check endplay of the inner rotor using a feeler gauge and a straight edge placed across the pump body. The specification is 0.001–0.004 in. (0.03–0.09mm).

3. Measure the clearance between the inner and outer rotors. The maximum clearance is 0.008 in. (0.20mm).

4. Measure the clearance between the outer rotor and the pump body. The maximum clearance is 0.014 in. (0.35mm).

5. The minimum thickness of the outer rotor is 0.944 in. (23.96mm). The minimum diameter of the outer rotor is 2.77 in. (62.70mm). The minimum thickness of the inner rotor is 0.943 in. (23.95mm).

6. Check the cover for warpage. The maximum allowable is 0.003 in. (0.076mm).

7. Check the pressure relief valve for damage. The spring's freelength specification is 1.95 in. (49.50mm).

8. Assemble the outer rotor with the larger chamfered edge in the pump body. Torque the cover screws to 10 ft. lbs. (12 Nm).

3.0L ENGINE

1. Remove the rear cover.

2. Remove the pump rotors and inspect the case for excessive wear.

3. Measure the diameter of the inner rotor hub that sits in the case. Measure the inside diameter of the inner rotor hub bore. Subtract the first measurement from the second; if the result is over 0.006 in. (0.15mm), replace the oil pump assembly.

4. Measure the clearance between the outer rotor and the case. The specification is 0.004–0.007 in. (0.10–0.18mm).

5. Check the side clearance of the rotors using a feeler gauge and a straightedge placed across the case. The specification is 0.0015–0.0035 in. (0.04–0.09mm).

6. Check the relief plunger and spring for damage and breakage. Replace as required.

7. Install the rear cover to the case.

3.3L ENGINE

1. Thoroughly clean and dry all parts. The mating surface of the chain case cover should be smooth. Replace the pump cover if it is scratched or grooved.

2. Lay a straightedge across the pump cover surface. If a 0.003 in. (0.076mm) feeler gauge can be inserted between the cover and straightedge, the cover should be replaced.

3. The minimum thickness of the outer rotor is 0.301 in. (7.63mm). The minimum diameter of the outer rotor is 3.14 in. (79.78mm). The minimum thickness of the inner rotor is 0.301 in. (7.64mm).

4. Install the outer rotor onto the chain case cover, press to one side and measure the clearance between the rotor and case. If the measurement exceeds 0.022 in. (56mm) and the rotor is good, replace the chain case cover.

5. Install the inner rotor to the chain case cover and measure the clearance between the rotors. If the clearance exceeds 0.008 in. (0.203mm), replace both rotors.

6. Place a straightedge over the chain case cover between bolt holes. If a 0.004 in. (0.102mm) thick feeler gauge can be inserted under the straightedge, replace the pump assembly.

7. Inspect the relief valve plunger for scoring and freedom of movement. Small marks may be removed with 400 grit wet or dry sandpaper.

8. The relief valve spring should have a freelength of 1.95 in.

9. Assemble the pump using new parts where necessary.

3.9L AND 5.2L ENGINES

1. Disassemble the pump.

2. Replace the pump assembly if the cover is scratched or grooved or if the cover is warped more than 0.0015 in. (0.038mm).

3. The minimum thickness of the outer rotor is 0.825 in. (20.96mm). The minimum diameter of the outer rotor is 2.469 in. (62.70mm). The minimum thickness of the inner rotor is 0.825 in. (20.96mm). If any of the above measurements are not within specifications, replace the shaft and both rotors.

4. The maximum clearance between the outer rotor and the pump body is 0.014 in. (0.356mm). Replace the pump assembly if not within specifications.

Service Tips

REAR ENGINE OIL LEAK

Some 1990 engines my exhibit an oil leak in the area of the rear crankshaft seal. The leak may be the result of 1 or more of the 4 untapped holes in the rear crankshaft flange being drilled too deep. If over-drilled, untapped holes are the problem, they must be sealed with plugs, part number(s) T3075032, coated with Stud N Bearing Mount number 04318032 and driven into position so they are slightly below the block's surface. Install new torque converter-to-driveplate bolts, part number(s) 06501193, and torque the bolts to 70 ft. lbs. (95 Nm).

5. Install the inner rotor and place a straightedge across the bolt holes. If a feeler gauge of 0.004 in. (0.101mm) or more fits, replace the pump assembly.

6. The maximum clearance between the rotors is 0.010 in. (0.254mm). Replace the shaft and both rotors if not within specifications.

7. Inspect the relief valve plunger for scoring. Small marks may be removed with 400 grit wet or dry sandpaper.

8. The relief valve spring should have a freelength of 1.9 in. Replace the spring if it fails to meet specifications.

9. Assemble the pump using new parts where necessary.

Rear Main Bearing Oil Seal

Removal and Installation

EXCEPT 3.9L AND 5.2L ENGINES

1. Disconnect the negative battery cable.

2. Remove the transmission or transaxle. Remove the flywheel or flexplate.

3. If there is any leakage coming from the rear seal retainer, drain the engine oil and remove the oil pan, if necessary. Remove the rear main oil seal retainer.

4. Remove the seal from the retainer.

To install:

5. Lightly coat the seal outer diameter with Loctite® Stud N' Bearing Mount or equivalent.

6. Install the seal to the retainer.

7. If removed, thoroughly clean and dry the retainer to block sealing surfaces. Install a new gasket or apply silicone sealer and install the retainer to the block. Install the pan, if removed.

8. Install the flywheel or flexplate and the transmission or transaxle.

9. Connect the negative battery cable and check for leaks.

3.9L AND 5.2L ENGINES

1. Raise the vehicle and support safely. Drain the engine oil. Remove the oil pan and oil pump.

2. Remove the rear main bearing cap.

3. Remove the lower seal from the cap.

4. To remove the upper rope seal, use oil seal remover and installer kit KD–492 or equivalent, following the instructions provided with the tool.

Service Tips

REAR ENGINE OIL LEAK

Some 1990–91 Town & Country Vans equipped with 3.3L engines may exhibit an oil leak at the rear of the engine. This condition may be the result of excessive engine thrust bearing wear. To verify this condition, check the crankshaft end-play for measurement which exceeds 0.015 inch. If the reading is above specification, replacement of the crankshaft, main bearings, rod bearings and rear seal retainer will be required to repair leak. If reading is below specification, the replacement of these parts are not required. Identify and repair oil leak as required.

To install:

5. Wipe the crankshaft surface clean and coat it lightly with oil.

6. Use oil seal remover and installer kit KD–492 or equivalent to install the upper rope seal. Trim the ends of the upper seal to eliminate frayed ends.

7. Install the lower rope seal in the main cap so both ends protrude. Use tool C–3511 to seat the seal in its groove. Cut of the portions of the seal that extend above the cap on both sides and install the end seals to the cap.

8. Install the main cap to the block and torque the bolts to 85 ft. lbs. (115 Nm).

9. Install the pan and fill the engine with the proper amount of oil.

10. Connect the negative battery cable, start engine and check for leaks.

TORQUE SPECIFICATIONS

Component	English	Metric
Camshaft sprocket bolt		
2.2L engine	65 ft. lbs.	88 Nm
2.5L engine	65 ft. lbs.	88 Nm
3.0L engine	70 ft. lbs.	95 Nm
3.3L engine	40 ft. lbs.	54 Nm
3.9L engine	50 ft. lbs.	68 Nm
5.2L engine	50 ft. lbs.	68 Nm
Camshaft thrust plate		
3.3L engine	9 ft. lbs.	12 Nm
3.9L engine	210 inch lbs.	24 Nm
5.2L engine	210 inch lbs.	24 Nm
Chain case cover bolts		
2.2L engine	9 ft. lbs.	12 Nm
2.5L engine	9 ft. lbs.	12 Nm
3.3L engine (8 x 1.25 thread size)	20 ft. lbs.	47 Nm
3.3L engine (10 x 1.5 thread size)	40 ft. lbs.	54 Nm
3.9L engine	30 ft. lbs.	41 Nm
5.2L engine	30 ft. lbs.	41 Nm

TORQUE SPECIFICATIONS

Component	English	Metric
Connecting rod cap bolts		
2.2L engine	40 ft. lbs. + ¼ turn	54 Nm + ¼ turn
2.5L engine	40 ft. lbs. + ¼ turn	54 Nm + ¼ turn
3.0L engine	38 ft. lbs.	52 Nm
3.3L engine	40 ft. lbs. + ¼ turn	54 Nm + ¼ turn
3.9L engine	45 ft. lbs.	61 Nm
5.2L engine	45 ft. lbs.	61 Nm
Crankshaft pulley (vibration damper) bolt		
2.2L engine	50 ft. lbs.	68 Nm
2.5L engine	50 ft. lbs.	68 Nm
3.0L engine	38 ft. lbs.	52 Nm
3.3L engine	40 ft. lbs.	54 Nm
3.9L engine	135 ft. lbs.	183 Nm
5.2L engine	135 ft. lbs.	183 Nm
Cylinder head bolt		
2.2L engine		
Step 1	45 ft. lbs.	62 Nm
Step 2	65 ft. lbs.	88 Nm
Step 3	65 ft. lbs.	88 Nm
Step 4	+ ¼ turn	+ ¼ turn
2.5L engine		
Step 1	45 ft. lbs.	62 Nm
Step 2	65 ft. lbs.	88 Nm
Step 3	65 ft. lbs.	88 Nm
Step 4	+ ¼ turn	+ ¼ turn
3.0L engine	80 ft. lbs.	108 Nm
3.3L engine (8 x 1.25 thread bolt)	25 ft. lbs.	33 Nm
3.3L engine (11 x 1.5 thread bolt)		
Step 1	45 ft. lbs.	62 Nm
Step 2	65 ft. lbs.	88 Nm
Step 3	65 ft. lbs.	88 Nm
Step 4	+ ¼ turn	+ ¼ turn
3.9L engine		
Step 1	50 ft. lbs.	68 Nm
Step 2,	105 ft. lbs.	143 Nm
5.2L engine		
Step 1	50 ft. lbs.	68 Nm
Step 2,	105 ft. lbs.	143 Nm
Exhaust flange nuts	21 ft. lbs.	28 Nm
Exhaust manifold bolts		
3.9L engine	25 ft. lbs.	34 Nm
5.2L engine	25 ft. lbs.	34 Nm
Exhaust manifold crossover bolts	25 ft. lbs.	33 Nm
Exhaust Manifold nut		
2.2L engine	17 ft. lbs.	23 Nm
2.5L engine	17 ft. lbs.	23 Nm
3.0L engine	17 ft. lbs.	23 Nm
3.3L engine	17 ft. lbs.	23 Nm
3.9L engine	25 ft. lbs.	34 Nm
5.2L engine	25 ft. lbs.	34 Nm
Exhaust manifold crossover nuts	25 ft. lbs.	33 Nm
Flywheel bolts		
2.2L engine	70 ft. lbs.	95 Nm
2.5L engine	70 ft. lbs.	95 Nm
3.0L engine	70 ft. lbs.	95 Nm
3.3L engine	70 ft. lbs.	95 Nm
3.9L engine	55 ft. lbs.	75 Nm
5.2L engine	55 ft. lbs.	75 Nm
Front crankshaft oil seal retainer bolts	105 inch lbs.	12 Nm

TORQUE SPECIFICATIONS

Component	English	Metric
Intake manifold bolts		
2.2L engine	17 ft. lbs.	23 Nm
2.5L engine	17 ft. lbs.	23 Nm
3.0L engine	17 ft. lbs.	23 Nm
3.3L engine	17 ft. lbs.	23 Nm
3.9L engine		
Step 1	72 inch lbs.	8 Nm
Step 2	12 ft. lbs.	16 Nm
5.2L engine		
Step 1	72 inch lbs.	8 Nm
Step 2	12 ft. lbs.	16 Nm
Intake manifold cover (plenum) bolts	21 ft. lbs.	28 Nm
Main bearing cap bolts		
2.2L engine	30 ft. lbs. + ¼ turn	41 Nm + ¼ turn
2.5L engine	30 ft. lbs. + ¼ turn	41 Nm + ¼ turn
3.3L engine	30 ft. lbs. + ¼ turn	41 Nm + ¼ turn
3.0L engine	60 ft. lbs.	80 Nm
3.9L engine	85 ft. lbs.	115 Nm
5.2L engine	85 ft. lbs.	115 Nm
Oil pan–to–block		
2.2L engine	17 ft. lbs.	23 Nm
2.5L engine	17 ft. lbs.	23 Nm
3.0L engine	5 ft. lbs.	6 Nm
3.9L engine	17 ft. lbs.	23 Nm
5.2L engine	17 ft. lbs.	23 Nm
Oil pan drain plug		
2.2L engine	20 ft. lbs.	27 Nm
2.5L engine	20 ft. lbs.	27 Nm
3.3L engine	20 ft. lbs.	27 Nm
3.0L engine	30 ft. lbs.	40 Nm
3.9L engine	25 ft. lbs.	34 Nm
5.2L engine	25 ft. lbs.	34 Nm
Oil pump attaching bolts		
2.2L engine	17 ft. lbs.	23 Nm
2.5L engine	17 ft. lbs.	23 Nm
3.0L engine	11 ft. lbs.	15 Nm
3.9L engine	30 ft. lbs.	41 Nm
5.2L engine	30 ft. lbs.	41 Nm
Oil pump cover bolt	9 ft. lbs.	12 Nm
Oil Pressure Sending Unit	5 ft. lbs.	7 Nm
Oil Pressure Sending Unit	5 ft. lbs.	7 Nm
Rocker shaft bracket/support bolt		
3.0L engine	15 ft. lbs.	20 Nm
3.3L engine	21 ft. lbs.	28 Nm
3.9L engine	21 ft. lbs.	28 Nm
5.2L engine	21 ft. lbs.	28 Nm
Rod bearing bolt		
2.2L engine		
Step 1	40 ft. lbs.	54 Nm
Step 2	+ ¼ turn	+ ¼ turn
2.5L engine		
Step 1	40 ft. lbs.	54 Nm
Step 2	+ ¼ turn	+ ¼ turn
3.0L engine	38 ft. lbs.	52 Nm
3.3L engine		
Step 1	40 ft. lbs.	54 Nm
Step 2	+ ¼ turn	+ ¼ turn
3.9L engine	45 ft. lbs.	61 Nm
5.2L engine	45 ft. lbs.	61 Nm

TORQUE SPECIFICATIONS

Component	English	Metric
Spark plug		
2.2L engine	20 ft. lbs	27 Nm
2.5L engine	20 ft. lbs	27 Nm
3.0L engine	20 ft. lbs	27 Nm
3.3L engine	20 ft. lbs	27 Nm
3.9L engine	30 ft. lbs.	41 Nm
5.2L engine	30 ft. lbs.	41 Nm
Starter-to-block bolts		
2.2L engine	40 ft. lbs.	55 Nm
2.5L engine	40 ft. lbs.	55 Nm
3.0L engine	50 ft. lbs.	68 Nm
3.3L engine	50 ft. lbs.	68 Nm
3.9L engine upper bolt	50 ft. lbs.	68 Nm
3.9L engine stud nut	20 ft. lbs.	27 Nm
5.2L engine upper bolt	50 ft. lbs.	68 Nm
5.2L engine stud nut	20 ft. lbs.	27 Nm
Sway bar end bracket bolt	50 ft. lbs.	70 Nm
Thermostat housing	16 ft. lbs.	23 Nm
Valve cover nut/bolt		
2.2L engine	9 ft. lbs.	12 Nm
2.5L engine	9 ft. lbs.	12 Nm
3.0L engine	7 ft. lbs.	10 Nm
3.3L engine	7 ft. lbs.	10 Nm
3.9L engine	7 ft. lbs.	9 Nm
5.2L engine	7 ft. lbs.	9 Nm
Water pump to chain cover/housing bolt	9 ft. lbs.	12 Nm
Water pump pulley bolts	22 ft. lbs.	30 Nm
Water pump mounting bolt		
2.2L engine (top bolts)	21 ft. lbs.	28 Nm
2.2L engine (lower bolts)	40 ft. lbs.	54 Nm
2.5L engine (top bolts)	21 ft. lbs.	28 Nm
2.5L engine (lower bolts)	40 ft. lbs.	54 Nm
3.0L engine	20 ft. lbs.	27 Nm
3.3L engine	9 ft. lbs.	12 Nm
3.9L engine	30 ft. lbs.	40 Nm
5.2L engine	30 ft. lbs.	40 Nm
Wheel stud lug nut	85–115 ft. lbs.	110–135 Nm

MANUAL TRANSMISSION

For further information, please refer to Chilton's Transmission Service Manual.

Transmission Assembly

Removal and Installation

2WD VEHICLE

1. Disconnect the negative battery cable.
2. Shift the transmission into Neutral and remove the upper shift lever. On 1992 models, do not remove the upper shift lever at this point.
3. Raise the vehicle and support safely. Remove the skid plate(s), if equipped. Drain the transmission lubricant.
4. Mark the location of the engine timing sensor, if equipped and remove sensor.
5. Matchmark and remove the driveshaft(s).
6. Disconnect the wires from the distance sensor, if equipped.

Then loosen the sensor coupling and remove the sensor from the speedometer adaptor.
7. Disconnect the reverse light switch and reposition harness.
8. Install engine support fixture C–3487–A or equivalent, to support the engine. Raise the engine slightly with the support fixture.
9. Disconnect the insulator from the extension housing.
10. Using the proper equipment, support the transmission and remove the crossmember.
11. Disconnect and remove the Y-pipe from the exhaust system.
12. On 1992 models remove the upper shift lever as follows:
    a. Lower transmission 3–4 in.
    b. Reach up and around transmission case unseat shift lever dust boot from the transmission shift tower. Move boot upward on on lever.
    c. Press shift lever retainer downward with your finger.
    d. Turn retainer counterclockwise to release retainer. Lift lever and retainer out of shift tower.

13. Remove the slave cylinder from the clutch housing. Remove the transmission to clutch housing bolts.

14. Slide the transmission rearward until the input shaft clears the clutch disc.

15. Pull the transmission completely away from the clutch housing and remove the transmission from the vehicle.

To install:

16. Lubricate the pilot bushing and input shaft splines very lightly with high temperature lubricant.

17. Mount the transmission on transmission jack and lift it in place until the input shaft is centered in the clutch housing opening. Roll the transmission forward until the input shaft splines fully engage with the clutch disc.

18. Install the transmission to clutch housing bolts. Torque the bolts to 28 ft. lbs. (38 Nm).

19. On 1992 models, lower transmission for access to the shift tower. Reach up and around the transmission and install the shift lever and retainer into the shift tower.

20. Press the retainer downward and turn clockwise to lock into position. Install the lever dust boot in place.

21. Install the transmission crossmember. Remove the transmission and engine support fixtures.

22. Connect the reverse light switch connector and clip all wiring to the transmission case.

23. Connect speedometer cable and distance sensor, if equipped.

24. Install the engine timing sensor in the position prior to removal.

25. Align U-joints and install the driveshaft(s).

26. Fill the transmission with the proper amount of 75W-90 or equivalent, API grade GL5 gear lubricant.

27. Apply silicone sealer to the perimeter of the shifter base and install the shifter assembly, if applicable.

28. Install the skid plate(s), if equipped.

29. Connect the negative battery cable and check the transmission for proper operation.

4WD VEHICLE

1. Disconnect the negative battery cable.

2. Shift the transmission into Neutral and remove the upper shift lever. On 1992 models, do not remove the upper shift lever at this point.

3. Raise the vehicle and support safely. Remove the skid plate(s), if equipped. Drain the transmission lubricant.

4. Mark the location of the engine timing sensor, if equipped and remove sensor.

5. Matchmark and remove the driveshaft(s).

6. Disconnect the wires from the distance sensor, if equipped. Then loosen the sensor coupling and remove the sensor from the speedometer adaptor.

7. Disconnect the vacuum switch hoses at transfer case. Disconnect the transfer case shift linkage at transfer case range lever. Remove the shift linkage bracket at the transfer case and position aside.

8. Remove shift motor vacuum tank and bracket from rear crossmember. Remove transfer case from transmission adapter housing.

9. Disconnect the reverse light switch and reposition harness.

10. Install engine support fixture C-3487-A or equivalent, to support the engine. Raise the engine slightly with the support fixture.

11. Using the proper equipment, support the transmission and remove the crossmember.

12. Disconnect and remove the Y-pipe from the exhaust system.

13. On 1992 models remove the upper shift lever as follows:
   a. Lower transmission 3-4 in.
   b. Reach up and around transmission case unseat shift lever dust boot from the transmission shift tower. Move boot upward on on lever.
   c. Press shift lever retainer downward with your finger.
   d. Turn retainer counterclockwise to release retainer. Lift lever and retainer out of shift tower.

14. Remove the slave cylinder from the clutch housing. Remove the transmission to clutch housing bolts.

15. On some models, it may be necessary to remove the oil filter and the front axle struts to gain removal clearance. Remove only if necessary. Slide the transmission rearward until the input shaft clears the clutch disc.

16. Pull the transmission completely away from the clutch housing and remove the transmission from the vehicle.

To install:

17. Lubricate the pilot bushing and input shaft splines very lightly with high temperature lubricant.

18. Mount the transmission on transmission jack and lift it in place until the input shaft is centered in the clutch housing opening. Roll the transmission forward until the input shaft splines fully engage with the clutch disc.

19. Install the transmission to clutch housing bolts. Torque the bolts to 28 ft. lbs. (38 Nm).

20. On 1992 models, lower transmission for access to the shift tower. Reach up and around the transmission and install the shift lever and retainer into the shift tower.

21. Press the retainer downward and turn clockwise to lock into position. Install the lever dust boot in place.

22. Install the transmission crossmember. Remove the transmission and engine support fixtures.

23. Connect the reverse light switch connector and clip all wiring to the transmission case.

24. Install slave cylinder in clutch housing. Install strut and fasteners, if removed.

25. Install transfer case and tighten bolts to 35 ft. lbs. (47 Nm). Install and connect the transfer case shift linkage.

26. Connect vacuum harness connector to switch at transfer case. Install vacuum tank and bracket on rear crossmember.

27. Connect speedometer cable and distance sensor, if equipped.

28. Install the engine timing sensor in the position prior to removal.

Manual transmission wiring harness routing—NP-2500 transfer case

29. Align U-joints and install the driveshaft(s).
30. Fill the transmission with the proper amount of 75W–90 or equivalent, API grade GL5 gear lubricant.
31. Apply silicone sealer to the perimeter of the shifter base and install the shifter assembly, if applicable.
32. Install the skid plate(s), if equipped.
33. Connect the negative battery cable and check the transmission for proper operation.

MANUAL TRANSAXLE

For further information, please refer to Chilton's Transmission Service Manual.

Transaxle Assembly

Removal and Installation

NOTE: If vehicle is going to be rolled while the transaxle is out of the vehicle, obtain 2 outer CV-joints to install to the hubs. If vehicle is rolled without the proper torque applied to the front wheel bearings, the bearings will be destroyed.

1. Disconnect the negative battery cable.
2. Remove the air cleaner assembly if it is preventing access to the upper bell housing bolts. Remove the upper bell housing bolts. Disconnect the reverse light switch and the ground wire.
3. Remove the starter attaching nut and bolt at the top of the bell housing.
4. Raise the vehicle and support safely. Remove the tire and wheel assemblies. Remove the axle end cotter pins, nut locks, spring washers and axle nuts.
5. Remove the ball joint retaining bolts and pry the control arm from the steering knuckle. Position a drain pan under the transaxle where the axles enter the differential or extension housing. Remove the axles from the transaxle or center bearing. Unbolt the center bearing and remove the intermediate axle from the transaxle, if equipped.
6. Remove the anti-rotation link from the crossmember. Disconnect the shifter cables from the transaxle and unbolt the cable bracket.
7. Remove the speedometer cable adaptor bolt and remove the adaptor from the transaxle.
8. Remove the rear mount from the starter, unbolt the starter and position it to the side.
9. Using the proper equipment, support the weight of the engine.
10. Remove the front motor mount and bracket.
11. Position a transaxle jack under the transaxle.
12. Remove the lower bell housing bolts.
13. Remove the left side splash shield. Remove the transaxle mount bolts.
14. Carefully separate the transaxle from the engine.
15. Slide the transaxle rearward until the input shaft clears the clutch disc.
16. Pull the transaxle completely away from the clutch housing and remove from the vehicle.
17. To prepare the vehicle for rolling, support the engine or reinstall the front motor mount to the engine. Then reinstall the ball joints to the steering knuckle and install the retaining bolt. Install the obtained outer CV-joints to the hubs, install the washers and torque the axle nuts to 180 ft. lbs. (244 Nm). The vehicle may now be safely rolled.
To install:
18. Lubricate the pilot bushing and input shaft splines very lightly with high temperature lubricant.

19. Mount the transaxle securely on jack and and install the left side mount bolts. Lift it in place until the input shaft is centered in the clutch housing opening. Roll the transaxle forward until the input shaft splines fully engage with the clutch disc.
20. Install the transaxle to clutch housing bolts.
21. Raise the transaxle up and install the front motor mount and bracket.
22. Remove the engine and transaxle support fixtures.
23. Install the starter to the transaxle and install the lower bolt finger-tight.
24. Install a new O-ring to the speedometer cable adaptor and install to the extension housing; make sure it snaps in place. Install the retaining bolt.
25. Install the shift cable bracket and snap the cable ends in place. Install the anti-rotation link.
26. Install the axles and center bearing, if equipped. Install the ball joints to the steering knuckles and install new cotter pins. Fill the transaxle with SAE 5W–30 engine oil. Install the splash shield and install the wheels. Lower the vehicle.
27. Install the upper bell housing bolts.
28. Install the starter attaching nut and bolt at the top of the bell housing. Raise the vehicle again and tighten the starter bolt from under the vehicle. Lower the vehicle.
29. Connect the reverse light switch and the ground wire.
30. Install the air cleaner assembly, if removed.
31. Connect the negative battery cable and check the transaxle for proper operation.

Cable Adjustment

1. Working over the left front fender, remove the lock pin from the transaxle selector shaft housing.
2. Reverse the lock pin (long end down) and insert it into the same threaded hole while pushing the selector shaft into the selector housing. A hole in the selector shaft will align with the lock pin, allowing the lock pin to be screwed into the housing. This operation locks the selector shaft in the neutral position between either 1st and 2nd gears or 3rd and 4th gears.
3. Remove the gearshift knob, the retaining nut and the pull-up ring from the gearshift lever.
4. If necessary, remove the shift lever boot and console to expose the gearshift linkage.
5. Fabricate 2 cable adjusting pins: $\frac{3}{16}$ in. diameter × 5 in. long with a $\frac{1}{2}$ in. 90 degrees bend at one end.
6. Place a pin in the hole provided at the right side and the other in the hole provided at the rear side of the shifting mechanism (make sure the alignment holes match). Torque the selector (right side) and the crossover (left side) adjusting bolts to 4–5 ft. lbs.
7. Remove the lock pin from the selector shaft housing and reinstall the lock pin (with the long end up) in the selector shaft housing. Torque the lock pin to 70 inch lbs. (8 Nm).
8. Check the first/reverse shifting and blockout into reverse.
9. Reinstall the console, boot, pull-up ring, retaining nut and knob.

CLUTCH

Clutch Assembly

Removal and Installation

CARAVAN AND VOYAGER

1. Disconnect the negative battery cable. Remove the transaxle.

2. Matchmark the clutch/pressure plate cover and flywheel. Insert a clutch plate alignment tool into the clutch disc hub.

3. Loosen the flywheel to pressure plate bolts gradually and evenly to avoid warpage.

4. Remove the pressure plate/clutch assembly from the flywheel.

5. Sand the flywheel or replace it, if scored, cracked or heat damaged.

To install:

6. Sparingly apply anti-sieze compound to the input shaft and clutch disc splines. Install a new release bearing.

7. Mount clutch assembly on flywheel taking care to align marks made before removal.

8. Install clutch alignment tool and apply pressure while tightening bolts to 21 ft. lbs. Make sure to step tighten bolts in a cross pattern to prevent any distortion of the clutch cover.

9. Install the transaxle and related parts that were removed.

10. Reconnect negative battery cable and check operation of the clutch.

DAKOTA

1. Disconnect the negative battery cable.
2. Raise the vehicle and support safely.
3. Remove the transmission and transfer case, if equipped.

4. Remove the clutch housing from the engine.
5. Remove the clutch cover bolts gradually in a cross pattern so the cover is not distorted.
6. Remove the clutch cover and disc.

To install:

7. Sparingly apply anti-sieze compound to the input shaft and clutch disc splines. Install a new release bearing.

8. Raise the clutch cover and disc into place and use a clutch aligning tool or spare input shaft to center the disc. Tighten all of the bolts finger-tight.

9. The cover bolts must be tightened gradually, evenly and to the proper torque to avoid distorting the cover. Torque $5/16$ in. diameter bolts to 17 ft. lbs. (23 Nm). Torque $3/8$ in. diameter bolts to 30 ft. lbs. (42 Nm).

10. Install the clutch housing, transmission and transfer case, if equipped.

11. Install the inspection cover, if removed.

12. Connect the negative battery cable and check the clutch for proper operation.

Pedal Free-play Adjustment

NOTE: The Caravan and Voyager are equipped with a self-adjusting cable operated mechanism and no adjustment is provided. The Dakota has been equipped with a hydraulic clutch release system. There is no adjustment for free-play on this system.

Clutch pedal, cable and related parts—1988–90 Caravan and Voyager

Clutch hydraulic linkage components — Dakota

Clutch Cable

Removal and Installation

1. Disconnect the negative battery cable.
2. Remove the clip from the cable mounting bracket on the shock tower and remove the cable from the bracket.
3. Remove the retainer from the clutch release lever on the transaxle.
4. Pry out the ball end of the cable from the position adjuster inside the pedal.
5. The installation is the reverse of the removal procedure. After installing, push the clutch pedal 2 or 3 times to allow the self-adjuster mechanism to function.

Clutch Master Cylinder and Slave Cylinder

The clutch master cylinder, remote reservoir, slave cylinder and connecting lines are all serviced as a complete assembly. The cylinders and connecting lines are sealed units. They are prefilled with fluid from the factory and cannot be disassembled or serviced separately.

Removal and Installation

1. Disconnect the negative battery cable.

2. Raise the vehicle and support safely.
3. Remove the nuts attaching the slave cylinder to the bell housing.
4. Remove the slave cylinder and clip from the housing.
5. Lower the vehicle.
6. Remove the locating clip from the clutch master cylinder mounting bracket.
7. Remove the retaining ring, flat washer and wave washer that attach the clutch master cylinder pushrod to the clutch pedal. Slide the pushrod off the pedal pin. Inspect the bushing on the pedal pin and replace, if excessively worn.
8. Verify that the cap on the clutch master cylinder reservoir is tight so fluid will not spill during removal.
9. Remove the screws attaching the reservoir and bracket to the dash panel and remove the reservoir.
10. Pull the clutch master cylinder rubber seal from the dash panel.
11. Rotate the clutch master cylinder 45 degrees to unlock it. Remove the cylinder from the dash panel.
12. Remove the clutch master cylinder, remote reservoir, slave cylinder and connecting lines from the vehicle.
To install:
13. Verify that the cap on the fluid reservoir is tight so fluid will not spill during installation.
14. Position the components in the replacement kit in their places on the vehicle.
15. Insert the master cylinder in the dash. Rotate it 45 degrees to lock it in place.

16. Lubricate the rubber seal with lubricant to ease installation. Seat the seal around the cylinder in the dash.

17. Install the fluid reservoir and bracket, if equipped, to the dash panel.

18. Install the master cylinder pushrod to the clutch pedal pin. Secure the rod with the wave washer, flat washer and retaining ring. Install the locating clip. Do not remove the plastic shipping stop from the pushrod until the slave cylinder has been installed.

19. Raise the vehicle and support safely.

20. Insert the slave cylinder pushrod through the opening and make sure the cap on the end of the pushrod is securely engaged in the release lever before tightening the attaching nuts. Torque the nuts to 17 ft. lbs. (23 Nm).

21. Lower the vehicle. Remove the plastic shipping stop from the master cylinder pushrod.

22. Operate the clutch pedal a few times to verify proper operation of the system.

23. Connect the negative battery cable and road test the vehicle.

AUTOMATIC TRANSMISSION

For further information, please refer to Chilton's Transmission Service Manual.

Transmission Assembly

Removal and Installation

2WD VEHICLE

1. Disconnect the negative battery cable.

2. Raise the vehicle and support safely. Drain the transmission and transfer case, if equipped.

3. Remove the exhaust crossover pipe from the exhaust system and reposition remaining exhaust pipes.

4. Remove the skid plates, if equipped. Remove the engine timing sensor marking original position for installation.

5. Matchmark and remove the driveshaft(s).

6. Disconnect the distance sensor, if equipped, and the speedometer cable.

7. Remove the engine to transmission struts.

8. Remove the starter and the fluid cooler lines bracket.

9. Remove the torque converter inspection cover.

10. Matchmark the converter to the flexplate. Remove the torque converter bolts.

11. Disconnect the wires to the neutral safety switch and lockup solenoid, if equipped.

12. Disconnect and plug the oil cooler lines from the transmission.

13. Disconnect the gearshift rod and torque shaft assembly from the transmission.

14. Disconnect the throttle rod from the lever.

15. Unbolt the oil filler tube brace and lift the oil filler tube out of its bore.

16. Install an appropriate engine support fixture to hold the engine in place when the transmission is out of the vehicle.

17. Raise the transmission slightly using transmission jack.

18. Remove the transmission crossmember.

19. Remove the oil filter, if necessary. Remove all bell housing bolts and remove the transmission from the vehicle.

To install:

20. Install the transmission securely on the transmission jack. Rotate the converter so it will align with the positioning of the flexplate.

21. Apply a coating of high temperature grease to the torque converter pilot hub.

22. Raise the transmission into place and push it forward until the dowels engage and the bell housing is flush with the block.

23. Install the oil filler tube. Install the bell housing bolts and torque to 30 ft. lbs. (41 Nm). Install the oil filter, if removed.

24. Install the transmission crossmember. Remove the engine support fixture and the transmission jack.

25. Install the torque converter bolts. If new bolts are being installed, it is essential that the correct length bolt be used.

26. Connect the oil cooler lines.

27. Connect the throttle rod to the lever and adjust, if necessary.

28. Connect the gearshift rod and torque shaft assembly to the transmission and adjust if necessary.

29. Connect the wires to the neutral safety switch and lockup solenoid, if equipped. Make sure all wires are routed correctly and clipped in place.

30. Install the torque converter inspection cover, starter and transmission struts.

31. Connect the distance sensor, if equipped.

32. Connect the the speedometer cable.

33. Install the driveshaft(s).

34. Install exhaust parts that were removed in order to remove the transmission.

35. Lower the vehicle. Connect the negative battery cable.

36. Fill the transmission with the proper amount of Dexron® II.

37. Road test the vehicle, check for leaks and recheck the fluid level.

4WD VEHICLE

1. Disconnect the negative battery cable.

2. Raise the vehicle and support safely. Drain the transmission and transfer case.

3. Remove the exhaust crossover pipe from the exhaust system and reposition remaining exhaust pipes.

4. Remove the skid plates, if equipped. Mark the location of the engine timing sensor and remove sensor.

5. Matchmark and remove the driveshafts.

6. Disconnect the vacuum switch hoses at transfer case. Disconnect the transfer case shift linkage at transfer case range lever. Remove the shift linkage bracket at the transfer case and position aside.

7. Remove shift motor vacuum tank and bracket from rear crossmember. Remove transfer case from transmission adapter housing.

8. Remove the starter and the fluid cooler lines bracket. Remove the engine to transmission struts.

9. Remove the torque converter inspection cover.

10. Matchmark the converter to the flexplate. Remove the torque converter bolts.

11. Disconnect the wires to the neutral safety switch and lockup solenoid, if equipped.

12. Disconnect and plug the oil cooler lines from the transmission.

13. Disconnect the gearshift rod and torque shaft assembly from the transmission.

14. Disconnect the throttle rod from the lever.

15. Unbolt the oil filler tube brace and lift the oil filler tube out of its bore.

16. Install an appropriate engine support fixture to hold the engine in place when the transmission is out of the vehicle.

17. Remove transmission fill tube. Raise the transmission slightly using transmission jack.

18. Remove the transmission crossmember.

19. Remove the oil filter, if necessary. Remove all bell housing bolts and remove the transmission from the vehicle.

To install:

20. Install the transmission securely on the transmission jack. Rotate the converter so it will align with the positioning of the flexplate.

21. Apply a coating of high temperature grease to the torque converter pilot hub.

22. Raise the transmission into place and push it forward until the dowels engage and the bell housing is flush with the block.

23. Install the oil filler tube. Install the bell housing bolts and torque to 30 ft. lbs. (41 Nm). Install the oil filter, if removed.

24. Install the transmission crossmember. Remove the engine support fixture and the transmission jack.

25. Install the torque converter bolts. If new bolts are being used, it is essential that the correct length be used.

26. Connect the oil cooler lines.

27. Install engine timing sensor to original position.

28. Connect the throttle rod to the lever and adjust, if necessary.

29. Connect the gearshift rod and torque shaft assembly to the transmission. Adjust if necessary.

30. Connect the wires to the neutral safety switch and lockup solenoid, if equipped. Make sure all wires are routed correctly and clipped in place.

31. Install the torque converter inspection cover, starter and transmission struts.

32. Install transfer case and tighten bolts to 35 ft. lbs. (47 Nm). Install and connect the transfer case shift linkage.

33. Connect vacuum harness connector to switch at transfer case. Install vacuum tank and bracket on rear crossmember.

34. Connect the distance sensor, if equipped.

35. Connect the speedometer cable.

36. Align and install the driveshafts.

37. Install exhaust parts that were removed in order to remove the transmission.

38. Fill the transfer case. Lower the vehicle.

39. Connect the negative battery cable.

40. Fill the transmission with the proper amount of Dexron® II.

41. Road test the vehicle, check for leaks and recheck the fluid level.

Shift Linkage Adjustment

NOTE: Do not attempt to adjust the linkage if any of the parts are excessively worn. If any rods are removed from the plastic grommets, new grommets should be installed. Pry only where the grommet and rod attach, not on the rod itself. Use pliers to snap the rod into the new grommet.

1. Shift the transmission into **P**.

2. Raise the vehicle and support safely.

3. Loosen the shift rod adjusting swivel lock screw. Make sure the swivel turns freely on the rod.

4. Make sure the valve body is in the **P** position by moving it all the way rearward.

5. Adjust the swivel position on the shift rod to obtain a free pin fit in the toque shaft lever. Tighten the lock screw.

6. If the vehicle starts in any gear other than **P** or **N** or does not start in both **P** and **N**, then either the adjustment is wrong or another problem exists.

Throttle Linkage Adjustment

1. If carbureted, perform the adjustment with the engine at normal operating temperature and off of the fast idle cam.

2. If fuel injected, retract the ISC actuator by doing one of the following:

a. If the DRB II is available, connect its connector to the diagnostic connector. Start the engine and place the DRB II in the "Throttle Body Minimum Air Flow Test" mode. Disconnect the electrical connector on the ISC actuator. Shut off the engine and disconnect the DRB II; the actuator is now fully retracted.

b. If the DRB II is not available, 2 jumper wires may be used. With the engine off, disconnect the connector to the ISC actuator. Connect a pair of jumper wires to the battery. Connect the negative jumper to the top pin of the ISC actuator and the positive jumper to the other pin. Do not leave the jumpers connected for more than 5 seconds. Disconnect the jumpers and the ISC actuator is fully retracted.

3. Raise the vehicle and support safely.

4. Loosen the adjustable swivel lock screw on the throttle rod enough so the rod travels freely in the swivel.

5. Hold the throttle lever firmly forward against its internal stop and tighten the lock screw. Lower the vehicle.

6. Reconnect the ISC actuator, if equipped.

7. If equipped with fuel injection, turn the ignition key to the **RUN** position for at least 5 seconds, but do not start the engine. Turn the key to the **OFF** position.

8. Start the engine and road test the vehicle.

AUTOMATIC TRANSAXLE

For further information, please refer to Chilton's Transmission Service Manual.

Transaxle Assembly

Removal and Installation

NOTE: If vehicle is going to be rolled while the transaxle is out of the vehicle, obtain 2 outer CV-joints to install to the hubs. If vehicle is rolled without the proper torque applied to the front wheel bearings, the bearings will be destroyed. If equipped with All Wheel Drive, the Power Transfer Unit (PTU) must be removed before removing the transaxle.

1. Disconnect the negative battery cable. If equipped with 3.0L or 3.3L engine, drain the coolant. Remove the dipstick.

2. Remove the air cleaner assembly if it is preventing access to the upper bell housing bolts. Remove the upper bell housing bolts and water tube, where applicable. Unplug all electrical connectors from the transaxle.

3. Install engine support fixture.

4. If equipped with a 2.2L or 2.5L engine, remove the starter attaching nut and bolt at the top of the bell housing.

5. Raise the vehicle and support safely. Remove the tire and wheel assemblies.

6. Remove the P.T.U. as follows:

a. Position a drainpan under the transaxle where the axles enter the differential, P.T.U. or extension housing. Support the P.T.U.

b. Remove the ball joint retaining bolts and pry the control arm from the steering knuckle. Unbolt the center bearing and remove the intermediate axle from the transaxle, if equipped. Remove the axles.

c. Remove the power steering hose bracket at front crossmember.

d. Remove front Bobble strut bolt at front crossmember.

e. Remove crossmember bridge bolts.

f. Remove the mounting bolts and remove unit from vehicle.

7. Drain the transaxle. Disconnect and plug the fluid cooler hoses. Disconnect the shifter and kickdown linkage from the transaxle, if equipped.

8. Remove the speedometer cable adaptor bolt and remove the adaptor from the transaxle.

9. Remove the starter. Remove the torque converter inspection cover, matchmark the torque converter to the flexplate and remove the torque converter bolts.

10. Disconnect the electrical connector at the PRNDL switch and the neutral safety switch.

11. Remove the front motor mount and bracket.

12. If equipped with Distributorless Ignition System (DIS), remove the crankshaft position sensor.

13. Position a transaxle jack under the transaxle.

14. Remove the lower bell housing bolts.

15. Remove the left side splash shield. Remove the transaxle mount bolts.

16. Carefully separate the transaxle from the engine.

17. Slide the transaxle rearward until the dowels disengage from the mating holes in the transaxle case.

18. Pull the transaxle away from the engine and remove from the vehicle.

19. To prepare the vehicle for rolling, support the engine with a support or reinstall the front motor mount to the engine. Then reinstall the ball joints to the steering knuckle and install the retaining bolt. Install the obtained outer CV-joints to the hubs, install the washers and torque the axle nuts to 180 ft. lbs. (244 Nm). The vehicle may now be safely rolled.

To install:

20. Install the transmission securely on the transmission jack. Rotate the converter so it will align with the positioning of the flexplate.

21. Apply a coating of high temperature grease to the torque converter pilot hub.

22. Raise the transaxle into place and push it forward until the dowels engage and the bell housing is flush with the block.

23. Install the transaxle to bell housing bolts.

24. Jack the transaxle up and install the left side mount bolts. Install the torque converter bolts and torque to 55 ft. lbs. (74 Nm).

25. Install the front motor mount and bracket. Remove the engine and transaxle support fixtures.

26. Install the starter to the transaxle. Install the bolt finger-tight if equipped with a 2.2L or 2.5L engine.

27. Install the crankshaft position sensor to the bell housing.

28. Install a new O-ring to the speedometer cable adaptor and install to the extension housing; make sure it snaps in place. Install the retaining bolt.

29. Install the P.T.U. to the transaxle and secure the mounting bolts. Install the crossmember supports.

30. Connect the shifter and kickdown linkage to the transaxle, if equipped.

31. Install the axles and center bearing, if equipped. Install the ball joints to the steering knuckles. Torque the axle nuts to 180 ft. lbs. (244 Nm) and install new cotter pins.

32. Install the splash shield and install the wheels. Lower the vehicle.

33. Install the dipstick. Install the upper bell housing bolts.

34. Install the water pipe, if removed.

35. If equipped with 2.2L or 2.5L engine, install the starter attaching nut and bolt at the top of the bell housing. Raise the vehicle again and tighten the starter bolt from under the vehicle.

36. Lower the vehicle. Connect all electrical wiring to the transaxle.

37. Install the air cleaner assembly, if it was removed. Fill the transaxle with the proper amount of Dexron® II.

38. Connect the negative battery cable and check the transaxle for proper operation.

Upshift and Kickdown Learning Procedure

A-604 ULTRADRIVE TRANSAXLE

In 1989, the A-604 4 speed, electronic transaxle was introduced; it is the first to use fully adaptive controls. The controls perform their functions based on real time feedback sensor information. Although, the transaxle is conventional in design, its functions are controlled by the ECM.

Since the A-604 is equipped with a learning function, each time the battery cable is disconnected, the ECM memory is lost. In operation, the transaxle must be shifted many times for the learned memory to be reinputed in the ECM; during this period, the vehicle will experience rough operation. The transaxle must be at normal operating temperature when learning occurs.

1. Maintain constant throttle opening during shifts. Do not move the accelerator pedal during upshifts.

2. Accelerate the vehicle with the throttle 1/8–1/2 open.

3. Make 15–20 1/2, 2/3 and 3/4 upshifts. Accelerating from a full stop to 50 mph each time at the aforementioned throttle opening is sufficient.

4. With the vehicle speed below 25 mph, make 5–8 wide open throttle kickdowns to 1st gear from either 2nd or 3rd gear. Allow at least 5 seconds of operation in 2nd or 3rd gear prior to each kickdown.

5. With the vehicle speed greater than 25 mph, make 5 part throttle to wide open throttle kickdowns to either 3rd or 2nd gear from 4th gear. Allow at least 5 seconds of operation in 4th gear, preferably at road load throttle prior to performing the kickdown.

Shift Linkage Adjustment

1. Place the shifter in the **P** detent.

2. Loosen the clamp bolt on the gearshift cable bracket.

3. Pull the shift lever all the way to the front detent position and tighten the lock screw.

4. Check for proper neutral safety switch operation.

Throttle Pressure Cable Adjustment

1. Run the engine until it reaches normal operating temperature.

2. Loosen the cable mounting bracket lock screw.

3. Position the bracket so both alignment tabs are touching the transaxle case surface and tighten the lock screws.

4. Release the cross lock on the cable assembly by pulling the cross lock up.

5. To ensure proper adjustment, the cable must be free to slide all the way toward the engine against its stop after the cross lock is released.

6. Move the transaxle throttle control lever fully clockwise and press the cross lock down until it snaps into position.

7. Road test the vehicle and check the shift points.

Throttle Pressure Rod Adjustment

1. Run the engine until it reaches normal operating temperature.

2. Loosen the adjustment swivel lock screw.

3. To ensure proper adjustment, the swivel must be free to slide along the flat end of the throttle rod. Disassembly, clean and lubricate as required.

4. Hold the transaxle throttle control lever firmly toward the engine and tighten the swivel screw.

5. Road test the vehicle and check the shift points.

TRANSFER CASE

Transfer Case Assembly

Removal and Installation
EXCEPT ALL WHEEL DRIVE

1. Disconnect the negative battery cable.
2. Raise the vehicle and support safely.
3. Remove the skid plates, if equipped. Drain the transfer case fluid.
4. Disconnect the distance sensor, if equipped and disconnect the speedometer cable from the transfer case.
5. Matchmark and remove the driveshafts.
6. Disconnect the PTO, if equipped.
7. Disconnect the linkage, electrical connectors and vacuum lines from the transfer case.
8. Remove the vacuum tank and bracket on rear crossmember.
9. Using a jack, support the transfer case and remove the crossmember.
10. Unbolt the transfer case from the transmission and slide it backwards to remove it from the vehicle.

To install:

11. Install transfer case and retaining bolts. Install and connect the transfer case shift linkage.
12. Connect vacuum harness connector to switch at transfer case. Install vacuum tank and bracket on rear crossmember.
13. Connect the distance sensor, if equipped.
14. Connect the the speedometer cable.
15. Align and install the driveshafts.

16. Fill transfer case with Dexron® II to the correct level.

ALL WHEEL DRIVE P.T.U.

1. Raise the vehicle and support safely. Remove the tire and wheel assemblies.
2. Position a drainpan under the transaxle where the axles enter the P.T.U. Support the P.T.U.
3.. Remove the ball joint retaining bolts and pry the control arm from the steering knuckle. Unbolt the center bearing and remove the intermediate axle from the transaxle, if equipped. Remove the axles.
4. Remove front Bobble strut bolt at front crossmember.
5. Remove the mounting bolts and remove unit from vehicle.
6. The installation is the reverse of the removal procedure.

Linkage Adjustment

1. Move the transfer case shift lever boot aside for access to the shift lever and gate.
2. Move the shift lever into the **4H** position. Make sure the lever is against the appropriate gate. Insert a ⅛ inch spacer between the shift lever and gate and secure the lever with tape.
3. Raise the vehicle and support safely.
4. Loosen the shift rod clamp screw until the shift rod is free to slide in the swivel.
5. Verify that the lever is in the **4H** position and move it, if it has moved out of position.
6. Tighten the clamp screw.
7. Check the smoothness of operation of the transfer case.

DRIVE AXLE

Halfshaft

Removal and Installation

1. Disconnect the negative battery cable.
2. Raise the vehicle and support safely.
3. Remove the tire and wheel assembly.
4. Remove the cotter pin from the end of the halfshaft. Remove the nut lock, spring washer, axle nut and washer.
5. Remove the ball joint retaining bolt and pry the control arm down to release the ball stud from the steering knuckle.
6. If removing the right side drive axle, it is necessary to remove the speedometer driven gear from the transaxle.
7. Position a drain pan under the transaxle where the halfshaft enters the differential or extension housing. Remove the halfshaft from the transaxle or center bearing. Unbolt the center bearing from the block and remove the intermediate shaft from the transaxle, if equipped.

To install:

8. Install the halfshaft or intermediate shaft to the transaxle, being careful not to damage the side seals. Make sure the inner joint clicks into pace inside the differential. Install the center bearing retaining bolts, if equipped. Install the outer shaft to the center bearing if equipped.
9. Pull the front strut out and insert the outer joint into the front hub.
10. Turn the ball joint stud, if necessary to position the bolt retaining indent to the inside of the vehicle. Install the ball joint stud into the steering knuckle. Install the retaining bolt and nut.
11. Install the axle nut washer and nut and torque the nut to 180 ft. lbs. (244 Nm). Install the spring washer, nut lock and a new cotter pin.

12. Install the speedometer driven gear into the transaxle and secure retaining bolt.
13. Install the tire and wheel assembly.

CV-Boot

Removal and Installation

NOTE: Use only clamps provided with the replacement package when servicing. Plastic wire ties and other straps will not clamp tightly enough and grease will sling out causing costly damage to the joint.

INNER JOINT
Except 4WD Vehicle

1. Raise the vehicle and support safely. Remove the halfshaft from the vehicle.
2. If cutting the boot away, mark and note the boot positioning on the shaft relative to the raised shoulders. Remove the boot clamps to gain access to the tripod retention system.
3. Separate the housing from the tripod according to the following:

NOTE: Always hold the rollers in place when removing the housing from the tripod or the needle bearing may fall out.

a. S.S.G.—Uses a wire ring tripod retainer which expands into a groove around the top of the housing. Use a tool to pry the wire ring, without damaging it, out of the groove and slide the tripod from the housing.

b. G.K.N.—Has retaining tabs integral with the housing cover. Hold the shaft on an angle while gently pulling on the

Driveshaft identification chart—axle boot identification

shaft until 1 of the tripod bearings is free of the retainer collar. Repeate until all rollers are free of the retainer collar.

4. Remove the snapring from the end of the shaft and remove the tripod.

5. If not already done, mark the boot positioning on the shaft, relative to the raised shoulders and remove the boot from the shaft.

6. Remove as much old grease as possible from the joint. Inspect all parts for wear or damage.

NOTE: Do not use petroleum-based solvents on the joints, shaft or boot to clean; it will ruin hidden rubber seals within the joint. Use only chlorine-based cleaner or hot soapy water to clean the joint, if necessary. Make sure the joint is completely dry before assembling.

To install:

7. If equipped, slide a new rubber washer seal over the stub shaft and down into the groove provided.

8. If the clamping device is not a staight strap, install it on the shaft first, then install the boot to the shaft in the proper position. Using the proper tool, C-4975 for crimping with plastic boot, C-4124 for crimping with rubber boot or C-4653 for clamping a strap, secure the clamp.

9. Install the tripod onto the shaft as follows:

   a. G.K.N—Slide the tripod on the shaft with the non-chamfered edge facing the tripod retainer ring groove.

   b. S.S.G.—Place the wire ring tripod retainer over the shaft, then slide on the tripod. The tripod may be installed either way; both ends are the same.

10. Install the new snapring into its groove on the shaft to lock the tripod in position.

11. Distribute the grease provided in the grease package as follows, or according to the instructions in the package:

   a. G.K.N—If equipped with 3 packets of grease, distribute

2 of the 3 packets into the boot and the remaining packet into the housing. Otherwise, distribute ½ of the packet of grease into the boot and the remaining amount into the housing.

   b. S.S.G.—Distribute ½ of the packet of grease into the boot and the remaining amount into the housing.

12. Position the spring in the housing spring pocket with the spring cup attached to the exposed end of the spring. Place a dab of grease on the concave surface of the spring cup.

13. Keeping the spring centered, install the housing to the tripod as follows:

   a. G.K.N—Slip the housing onto the tripod so the tripod assembly is resting on top of the plastic retainer collar. Hold shaft at an angle and push down on the shaft until the roller locks into the retainer collar. Insert each of the tripod rollers into the retainer collar 1 at a time. Check for proper retention ability.

   b. S.S.G.—Slip the housing onto the tripod and install the tripod wire retaining ring. Check for proper retention ability.

14. Position the larger end of the boot over the housing.

15. Using the proper tool, C-4975 for crimping with plastic boot, C-4124 for crimping with rubber boot or C-4653 for clamping a strap, secure the clamp.

16. Install the halfshaft to the vehicle. Fill the transaxle if fluid was lost when removing the halfshaft.

17. Road test the vehicle.

4WD Vehicle

1. Remove the cotter pin, nut lock and spring washer from the stub shaft.

2. Remove the halfshaft from the vehicle.

3. Raise and safely support the vehicle. Remove the skip plate, if equipped.

4. Remove the wheel and tire assembly.

5. Remove the bolts that attach the inner housing to the axle shaft flange.

6. Separate the joint housing from the hub. Remove the CV-driveshaft from the vehicle.

7. Remove the inner rubber boot retaining clamps and clamp protector. Pull the inner boot back onto the shaft.

8. Pull the tripod and shaft straight out from the inner CV-joint housing.

9. Move the snapring from the groove behind the tripod. Slide the tripod toward the conter of the shaft and remove the C-clip on the outer end of the shaft.

10. Remove the joint and the boot from the shaft.

11. Remove as much old grease as possible from the joint. Inspect all parts for wear or damage.

NOTE: Do not use petroleum-based solvents on the joints, shaft or boot to clean; it will ruin hidden rubber seals within the joint. Use only chlorine-based cleaner or hot soapy water to clean the joint, if necessary. Make sure the joint is completely dry before assembling.

To install:

12. If the clamping device is not a straight strap, install it on the shaft first, then install the boot to the shaft in the proper position. Using the proper tool, C–4975 for crimping with plastic boot, C–4124 for crimping with rubber boot or C–4653 for clamping a strap, secure the clamp.

13. Install the tripod onto the shaft making sure the chamfered end on the tripod is adjacent to the C-clip retaining ring groove. Install the C-clip onto the groove. Slide the tripod out against the clip and the snap ring in the inner groove.

14. Apply the lubricant supplied with the boot. Insert and seat the tripod in the housing and position the large end of the boot over the housing.

15. Install retainer clamps on the outer portion of the boot.

16. Insert the driveshaft stub into the hub. Attach the inner joint flange to the axle shaft flange and tighten bolts to 65 ft. lbs. (90 Nm).

17. Install the hub nut to the shaft and tighten to 190 ft. lbs. (258 Nm). Install the spring washer, nut lock and new cotter pin.

18. Install the wheel and tire assembly.

OUTER JOINT

Except 4WD Vehicle

1. Remove the halfshaft from the vehicle.

2. If cutting the boot away, mark and note the boot positioning on the shaft relative to the raised shoulders. Remove the boot clamps to gain access to the joint retention system.

3. Separate the housing from the tripod according to the following:

   a. G.K.N – Using a soft-jaw vise, support the halfshaft. Strike the joint assembly sharply with a soft-face hammer to dislodge the internal circlip and remove from the shaft.

   b. S.S.G. – Loosen the damper weight bolts and slide it and the boot toward the inner joint. Expand the snapring and slide the joint from the shaft. Reinstall the damper weight and torque the bolts to 21 ft. lbs. (28 Nm).

4. If damaged, remove the wear sleeve from the CV-joint machined ledge.

5. Remove the circlip from the groove.

6. If not already done, mark the boot positioning on the shaft, relative to the raised shoulders and remove the boot from the shaft.

7. Remove as much old grease as possible from the joint. Inspect all parts for wear or damage.

NOTE: Do not use petroleum-based solvents on the joints, shaft or boot to clean; it will ruin hidden rubber seals within the joint. Use only chlorine-based cleaner or hot soapy water to clean the joint, if necessary. Make sure the joint is completely dry before assembling.

To install:

8. If the clamping device is not a straight strap, install it on the shaft first, then install the boot to the shaft in the proper position. Using the proper tool, C–4975 for crimping with plastic boot, C–4124 for crimping with rubber boot or C–4653 for clamping a strap, secure the clamp.

9. Install a new circlip if provided in the replacement package. Fill the boot with the proper amount of grease according to the instructions provided with the package.

10. Position the outer joint on the shaft with hub nut installed, engage the splines and strike sharply with a soft-face hammer to install. Make sure the circlip did not become dislodged.

11. Position the larger end of the boot over the housing.

12. Using the proper tool, C–4975 for crimping with plastic boot, C–4124 for crimping with rubber boot or C–4653 for clamping a strap, secure the clamp.

13. Install the halfshaft to the vehicle. Fill the transaxle if fluid was lost when removing the halfshaft.

14. Road test the vehicle.

4WD Vehicle

1. Remove the halfshaft from the vehicle.

2. If cutting the boot away, mark and note the boot positioning on the shaft relative to the raised shoulders. Remove the boot clamps to gain access to the joint retention system.

3. To separate the housing from the tripod, expand the snapring and slide the joint from the shaft.

4. If damaged, remove the slinger from the CV-joint .

5. If not already done, mark the boot positioning on the shaft, relative to the raised shoulders and remove the boot from the shaft.

7. Remove as much old grease as possible from the joint. Inspect all parts for wear or damage.

NOTE: Do not use petroleum-based solvents on the joints, shaft or boot to clean; it will ruin hidden rubber seals within the joint. Use only chlorine-based cleaner or hot soapy water to clean the joint, if necessary. Make sure the joint is completely dry before assembling.

To install:

8. If the clamping device is not a straight strap, install it on the shaft first, then install the boot to the shaft in the proper position. Using the proper tool, C–4975 for crimping with plastic boot, C–4124 for crimping with rubber boot or C–4653 for clamping a strap, secure the clamp.

9. Fill the boot with the proper amount of grease according to the instructions provided with the package.

10. Align the outer CV-joint splines with the axle shaft splines and push joint onto axle until the snap ring seats in the groove. Ensure the snapring is properly seated in the housing.

11. Place the large end of the boot onto the housing and secure with clamp.

12. Install the axle into the vehicle.

Driveshaft and U-Joints

The driveshaft on the All Wheel Drive (AWD) model is a hollow shaft with a plunging tripod joint on the front of the shaft and a fixed tripod joint on the rear of the shaft. The shaft is serviced as an assembly only. The flange patterns are different at each end to insure proper installation.

Removal and Installation

EXCEPT ALL WHEEL DRIVE VEHICLE

1. Raise the vehicle and support safely.

2. Matchmark the driveshaft and the rear axle drive pinion gear shaft yoke. Unbolt the support collar from the frame, if equipped.

DIFFERENTIAL HOUSING

LEFT AXLE SHAFT

BEARING

SEAL

Left side axle shaft assembly

3. Remove the rear U-joint attaching bolts and both strap clamps from the rear axle drive pinion gear shaft yoke.

4. Fluid may run from the rear of the extension housing or transfer case when the shaft is removed, so position a drain pan under the area.

5. Remove the driveshaft from the transmission or transfer case.

6. The installation is the reverse of the removal procedure.

ALL WHEEL DRIVE VEHICLE

1. Place vehicle in neutral. Raise and safely secure the vehicle.

2. Remove the driveshaft rear mounting bolts.

3. Remove the driveshaft from the vehicle. Do not allow the driveshaft to hang freely while installing.

4. To install, reverse the removal procedure making sure mating surfaces are clean.

Front Axle Shaft, Seal and Bearing

Removal and Installation

LEFT SIDE SHAFT

1. Raise the vehicle and support safely.

2. Disconnect the left CV-driveshaft from the axle shaft flange.

3. Remove the differential housing cover. Rotate the differential case so the differential pinion mate gear shaft lock screw is accessible. Remove the lock screw and the pinion mate gear shaft from the differential case.

4. Force the left axle shaft toward the center of the vehicle and remove the shaft C-clip lock from the recessed groove in the axle shaft.

5. Remove the axle shaft from the differential housing. Inspect the axle shaft bearing contact surface for brinelling, spalling and pitting. If any of these conditions exist, replace the axle shaft and bearing.

6. Remove the axle shaft seal from the end of the housing bore with a prybar. Remove the axle shaft bearing only if it is being replaced; do not reinstall used bearings. Use removal tool C–4167 and slide hammer tool C–637 to remove the bearing.

To install:

7. Thoroughly clean and dry the bearing bore in the differential housing.

8. Insert the new bearing into the pilot of bearing installation tool C–4198 and attach to the handle. Insert the bearing to the housing until it is seated against the bore shoulder.

9. Install the new seal using tool C–4203 with the flat side of the tool facing the seal. When the installation tool contacts the housing flange face, the seal is installed to the correct depth.

10. Lubricate the bearing bore and seal lip, insert the axle

shaft into the housing and engage the splines. With the shaft in place, install the C-clip lock and push the shaft outward to seal the lock.

11. Install the mate shaft, align the hole in the shaft with the lock screw hole in the differential case and install the lock screw. Torque the lock screw to 8 ft. lbs. (11 Nm).

12. Thoroughly clean and dry the case cover, mating surface, bolts and bolt holes. Apply silicone sealer to the cover and install.

13. Connect the CV-driveshaft.

14. Level the vehicle and fill the differential with multi-purpose gear lubricant.

15. Road test the vehicle and check for leaks and correct front axle operation.

RIGHT SIDE AND INTERMEDIATE SHAFT

1. Raise the vehicle and support safely.

2. Remove the tire and wheel assembly.

3. Remove the cotter pin, nut lock and spring washer from the stub shaft. Remove the hub nut and washer.

4. Remove the bolts that attach the inner CV-joint to the axle shaft flange.

5. Separate the stub shaft splines from the hub bearing splines and remove the CV-joint shaft.

6. Remove the differential housing cover.

7. Disconnect the 4WD indicator light switch and the vacuum tube from the shift motor. Remove the shift motor, housing cover and gasket from the shift motor housing.

8. Remove the bearing seal/retainer attaching screws accessible via the holes in the axle shaft flange.

9. Remove the outer axle shaft from the differential housing.

10. Remove the snapring and the splined gear from the outer axle shaft. Separate the bearing and seal from the outer axle shaft.

11. Remove the shift collar from the shift motor housing.

12. Rotate the differential case so the differential pinion mate gear shaft lock screw is accessible. Remove the lock screw and the pinion mate gear shaft from the differential case.

13. Force the intermediate shaft toward the center of the vehicle and remove the shaft C-clip lock from the recessed groove in the axle shaft. Remove the intermediate shaft from the differential housing and tube.

To install:

14. Insert the axle shaft into the tube and housing and engage the splines. With the shaft in place, install the C-clip lock and push the shaft outward to seat the lock.

15. Install the mate shaft, align the hole in the shaft with the lock screw hole in the differential case and install the lock screw. Torque the lock screw to 8 ft. lbs. (11 Nm).

BOLT AND WASHER

REMOTE VENT

SHIFT MOTOR HOUSING

INDICATOR LAMP SWITCH

E-CLIP

SHIFT PADS

GASKET

SHIFT FORK

E-CLIP

VACUUM TUBE PORTS

GASKET

HOUSING COVER

ARMATURE

SHIFT MOTOR

Shift motor and related parts—Dakota with 4WD

Shift collar and related parts—Dakota with 4WD

Right side axle shaft assembly—Dakota with 4WD

16. Install the shift collar to the intermediate shaft.

17. Install a new seal to the seal retainer and install to the outer shaft. Press on the new bearing, install the splined gear and the snapring.

18. Insert the outer axle shaft into the shift motor housing. Torque the attaching screws to 17 ft. lbs. (23 Nm).

19. Install the shift motor housing cover and gasket. Ensure that the shift fork is correctly engaged in the collar groove. Install the cover bolts. Connect the vacuum tubes to the shift motor and the connector to the 4WD light switch.

20. Thoroughly clean and dry the case cover, mating surface, bolts and bolt holes. Apply silicone sealer to the cover and install.

21. Lubricate the contact surface area of the CV-driveshaft wear sleeve with grease and install the CV-driveshaft. Torque the hub nut to 190 ft. lbs. (258 Nm). Install the spring washer, nut lock and a new cotter pin.

22. Level the vehicle and fill the differential with multi-purpose gear lubricant.

23. Road test the vehicle and check for leaks and correct front axle operation.

Rear Axle Shaft, Bearing and Seal

Removal and Installation

1. Raise the vehicle and support safely.
2. Remove the wheel and brake drum.
3. Remove the differential housing cover.
4. Rotate the differential case so the differential pinion mate gear shaft lock screw is accessible. Remove the lock screw and the pinion mate gear shaft from the differential case.

5. Force the axle shaft toward the center of the vehicle and remove the axle shaft C-clip lock from the recessed groove in the axle shaft.

6. Remove the axle shaft from the axle housing.

7. Pry the axle shaft seal from the end of the axle tube using a pry bar.

8. To remove the bearing, use tool C–4167 attached to a slide hammer.

To install:

9. Clean the bearing bore in the axle tube.

10. Insert the new axle shaft bearing onto the pilot of tool C–4198. The bearing is fully installed when it is seated firmly against the shoulder in the axle tube.

11. Install the new seal to the axle tube.

12. Lubricate the bearing bore and seal lip with grease and insert the axle shaft into the axle tube engaging its splines with the differential side gear splines.

13. Install the C–clip lock in the groove at the end of the shaft. Force the shaft outward to seat the C–clip.

14. Insert the differential pinion gear mate shaft into the case and through the thrust washers and pinion gears. Align the hole in the shaft with the lock screw hole in the differential case and install the lock screw. Torque the screw to 8 ft. lbs. (11 Nm).

15. Thoroughly clean and dry the case cover, mating surface, bolts and bolt holes. Apply silicone sealer to the cover and install.

16. Install the drum and wheel.

17. Fill the differential with the proper lubricant.

18. Road test the vehicle and check for leaks.

Front Wheel Hub, Knuckle and Bearings

Removal and Installation

CARAVAN, VOYAGER AND TOWN & COUNTRY

1. Raise the vehicle and support safely.

2. Remove the tire and wheel assembly. Remove the brake caliper from the adaptor and remove the adaptor. Remove the brake disc.

3. Remove the halfshaft.

4. Disconnect the tie rod from the knuckle.

5. Remove the 2 strut clamp bolts and remove the knuckle from the vehicle.

6. Attach the hub removal tool C–4811 or equivalent, and the triangular adapter, to the 3 rear threaded holes of the steering knuckle housing with the thrust button inside the hub bore.

7. Tighten the bolt in the center of the tool, to press the hub from the steering knuckle. Remove the tools.

8. Remove the bolts and bearing retainer from the outside of the steering knuckle.

9. Carefully pry the bearing seal from the machined recess of the steering knuckle and clean the recess.

10. Insert the tool C–4811 or equivalent, through the hub bearing and install bearing removal adapter to the outside of the steering knuckle. Tighten the tool to press the hub bearing from the steering knuckle. Discard the bearing and the seal.

To install:

11. Use tool C–4811 or equivalent, and the bearing installation adapter to press in the hub bearing into the steering knuckle.

12. Install a new seal, the bearing retainer and the bolts to the steering knuckle.

13. Use the tool C–4811 or equivalent, and the hub installation adapter, to press the hub into the hub bearing.

14. Using the bearing installation tool C–4698 or equivalent, drive the new dust seal into the rear of the steering the hub and bearing from the knuckle as required.

15. Install the knuckle on the vehicle and insert lower ball joint nut into knuckle.

CAM BOLT NUT

ADAPTOR SCREW AND WASHER

WEAR SLEEVE

SEAL

BRAKE CALIPER

WASHER PLATE

BEARING

RETAINER

HUB

WASHER

COTTER PIN

GASKET

CLAMP BOLT

KNUCKLE

NUT LOCK

HUB NUT

WHEEL BOLT

LOWER CONTROL ARM

Front suspension components—Caravan, Voyager and Town & Country

16. Install the tie rod through the knuckle and install attaching nut. Tighten nut to 35 ft. lbs. (47 Nm). Install new cotter pin into tie rod end.

17. Install the stub axle into the hub assembly. Install the 2 strut clamp bolts in place.

18. Install the rotor, adaptor and brake caliper.

19. Install the washer and hub nut onto the stub shaft and tighten nut to 180 ft. lbs. (244 Nm). Install spring washer, nut lock and new cotter pin.

20. Install the front wheel and tire assembly. Lower vehicle and align. Before moving vehicle, make sure to pump brake pedal to seat caliper piston against rotor.

DAKOTA

2WD

1. Raise the vehicle and support safely.
2. Remove the tire and wheel assembly.
3. Remove the brake caliper and rotor from the steering knuckle.
4. Disconnect the tie rod end from the steering knuckle.
5. Disconnect both ball joints from the steering knuckle.
6. Remove the steering knuckle from the vehicle. Remove the splash shield and the steering arm from the knuckle.
7. The installation is the reverse of the removal procedure. Torque the steering arm to knuckle nuts to 217 ft. lbs. (294 Nm).

4WD

1. Raise the vehicle and support safely. Remove the tire and wheel assembly.
2. Remove the cotter pin, nut lock and spring washer from the end of the CV-driveshaft. Remove the hub nut and washer.
3. Remove the brake caliper and the rotor from the hub.

BEARING SEAL

BOLT

CALIPER ADAPTOR

STEERING ARM

STEERING KNUCKLE

HUB AND BEARING

Front wheel hub removal and installation—Dakota with 4WD

4. Remove the bolts that attach the wheel hub to the steering knuckle.
5. Remove the wheel hub from the steering knuckle and the stub shaft.
6. Disconnect the tie rod end from the knuckle.
7. Remove the tension from the torsion bar, if equipped. Remove the lower shock absorber attaching bolt.
8. Disconnect the stabilizer bar from the lower suspension arm, if equipped.
9. Disconnect both ball joints from the steering knuckle.

10. Remove the steering knuckle from the vehicle and remove the bearing seal from the knuckle.
To install:
11. Install the wheel hub on the steering knuckle and torque the retaining bolts to 110 ft. lbs. (149 Nm).
12. Fill the cavity between the seal lip and the knuckle with multi-purpose lubricant. Position the new seal in the bore at the inner side of the knuckle and seat it with tool C–4698.
13. Lubricate the contact surface area of the CV-driveshaft wear sleeve with grease and install the steering knuckle, engaging the splines of the CV-driveshaft with those in the wheel hub. Torque the upper ball stud nut to 105 ft. lbs. (142 Nm) and the lower nut to 120 ft. lbs. (163 Nm).
14. Install the torsion bar.
15. Install the stabilizer bar and shock bolt.
16. Install the tie rod to the steering knuckle and torque the nut to 40 ft. lbs. (54 Nm).
17. Torque the hub nut to 190 ft. lbs. (258 Nm). Install the spring washer, nut lock and a new cotter pin.
18. Install the tire and wheel assembly.
19. Set the front suspension height so the difference between the distance from the surface that the tires are on to the lower suspension arm inner pivot and the distance that the tires are on to the outer end of the arm is 1–1½ in.
20. Align the front end.
21. Road test the vehicle.

Pinion Seal

Removal and Installation

1. Raise the vehicle and support safely.
2. Matchmark and remove the driveshaft.
3. Remove the rear wheel and brake drums to prevent any drag.
4. Using an inch lb. torque wrench, measure the pinion bearing preload. Read the torque while the handle of the wrench is moving through several complete revolutions.
5. Using the proper tools, hold the companion flange and remove the drive pinion nut and washer.
6. Remove the companion flange. Lower the rear of the vehicle to prevent fluid loss.
7. Using a seal remover tool, remove the seal from the carrier and clean the seal seat.
To install:
8. The outside diameter of the seal is precoated with a special sealer so no sealing compound is required for installing. The seal is properly installed when the flange contacts the housing flange face.
9. Install the companion flange and the washer with the convex side out.
10. Tighten the pinion nut to 210 ft. lbs. (285 Nm) and check the pinion bearing preload. If the preload is less than the original preload measured, continue tightening the nut in very small increments until the proper preload is reached.
11. Install the driveshaft, drums and rear wheels.
12. Refill the differential with the proper lubricant.
13. Road test the vehicle and check for leaks.

Differential Carrier

Removal and Installation

CARAVAN, VOYAGER AND TOWN & COUNTRY

NOTE: The differential case can be removed from some vehicles with the transaxle installed. To do so, remove the halfshafts, remove the 2 K-frame mounting nuts and 2 bolts and lower the K-frame to provide enough room to pull the differential case out of its housing and over the lowered frame.

1. Disconnect negative battery cable.
2. Remove the axle shafts from the vehicle.
3. Remove the right side extension housing and the P.T.U., if equipped.
4. Remove the differential cover.
5. Remove the bolts and remove the right side differential bearing retainer using tool L–4435 or equivalent.
6. Remove the differential case from the transaxle.
To install:
7. Use new seals and gasket material when assembling. Install the differential case into the transaxle and install the right side differential bearing retainer. Torque bearing retainer bolts to 21 ft. lbs. (28 Nm).
8. Install the differential cover and fill with the proper lubricant.
9. Install the extension housing and P.T.U., if removed.
10. Install the axle shafts and connect negative battery cable.

DAKOTA

1. Raise the vehicle and support safely.
2. Remove the wheels. If removing the rear axle, remove the brake drums.
3. Remove the housing cover and drain the lubricant.
4. Remove the rear wheel anti-lock brake sensor, if equipped.
5. Remove both axle shafts.
6. Matchmark the bearing caps to the differential housing.
7. Remove the differential bearing threaded adjuster lock from each cap.
8. Loosen but do not remove the bearing caps.
9. Loosen the side adjusters using tool C–4164.
10. Remove the bearing caps, the threaded adjusters and the differential case.
To install:
11. Position the assembled differential case in the housing.
12. Install the bearing caps in their original positions according to the matchmarks made during the disassembly.
13. Torque the upper bolts to 10 ft. lbs. (14 Nm) and finger-tighten the bottom bolts.
14. Tighten the side adjusters until the proper side play specifications are reached.
15. Torque the bearing caps bolts to 45 ft. lbs. (61 Nm) for 7¼ in. rear or 100 ft. lbs. (136 Nm) for 8¼ in. rears.
16. Install both axle shafts.
17. Install the rear wheel anti-lock brake sensor, if equipped.
18. Install the housing cover and fill with the proper lubricant.
19. Install the drums if removed. Install the wheels.
20. Road test the vehicle.

Axle Housing

Removal and Installation

FRONT AXLE HOUSING

1. Disconnect the negative battery cable.
2. Raise vehicle and support safely. Remove skid plate, if equipped.
3. Remove the CV-driveshafts from the axle shaft flanges.
4. Remove the front propeller shaft from the transfer case.
5. Disconnect the vacuum hoses and wire connections from the shift motor.
6. Support the differential housing and remove the attaching bolts.
7. Remove the axle housing and the propeller shaft from the vehicle.
To install:
8. Install the axle housing and the propeller shaft into the vehicle. Install the attaching bolts.
9. Connect the vacuum hoses and wire connections to the shift motor.
10. Install the front propeller shaft from the transfer case.
11. Install the CV-driveshafts from the axle shaft flanges.

12. Install the skid plate and connect the negative battery cable.

REAR AXLE HOUSING

1. Disconnect the negative battery cable.
2. Raise vehicle and support safely. Remove skid plate, if equipped.
3. Remove the rear wheel anti-lock brake sensor, if equipped.
4. Remove the rear wheels.
5. Disconnect the rear brake hose at the T-fitting.
6. Remove the driveshafts from the vehicle.
7. Disconnect the parking brake cables and reposition.

8. Support the weight of the assembly with the proper equipment. Disconnect the shock absorbers and remove the leaf spring nuts and U-bolts.
9. Remove the assembly from vehicle.
10. Install the axle housing into the vehicle. Install the shock absorbers and the leaf spring nuts and U-bolts.
11. Connect the parking brake cables. Install the drive shafts.
12. Connect the rear brake hose at the T-fitting.
13. Install the rear wheel anti-lock brake sensor, if equipped. Install the rear wheels.
14. Install the skid plate, if equipped.
15. Connect the negative battery cable.

STEERING

Note: On 1992 models equipped with an Air bag, failure to disarm the system may result in deployment of the air bag and possible personal injury. To disarm the air bag, disconnect the negative battery. Allow system capacitor to discharge for 2 minutes before working on system.

Steering Wheel

Removal and Installation

1. Disconnect the negative battery cable. Disarm Air bag, if equipped.
2. Straighten the steering wheel so the front tires are pointing straight forward. Remove the horn pad and related parts.
3. Remove the steering wheel hold-down nut. Matchmark the steering wheel to the shaft.
4. Using a steering wheel puller, pull the steering wheel off of the shaft.
5. The installation is the reverse of the removal procedure.

Steering Column

Removal and Installation

1. Disconnect the negative battery cable.
2. Remove trim bezel, steering column cover and lower reinforcement, as required.
3. Disconnect all wiring connectors from below the instrument panel that lead up into the steering column.
4. Disconnect gear indicator cable and lock bar from column as required.
5. Remove the nuts that attach the steering column assembly to the instrument panel support.
6. Firmly grasp the steering wheel and pull the steering column out, separating the stub shaft from the steering gear coupling.
7. The installation is the reverse of the removal procedure.
8. Connect the negative battery cable and check the steering column and all related components for proper operation.

Manual Steering Gear

Removal and Installation
DAKOTA WITH 4WD

1. Disconnect the negative battery cable.
2. Raise the vehicle and support safely. Center the steering.
3. Disconnect the pitman arm from the center link.
4. Disconnect the steering gear to shaft coupling.
5. Remove the steering gear mount bolts and remove the gear from the vehicle.

6. Matchmark and remove the pitman arm from the sector shaft.
7. The installation is the reverse of the removal procedure. Torque the pitman arm nut to 175 ft. lbs. (237 Nm) and the mount bolts to 100 ft. lbs. (136 Nm).

Adjustment

1. If the vehicle wanders of the steering has too much play, the sector shaft can be adjusted.
2. Loosen the adjusting screw locknut and turn the screw all the down.
3. Back the screw off ¼–½ turn.
4. Tighten the locknut.
5. Road test the vehicle. If the steering wheel does not return easily after a turn, back the screw off until the wheel returns easily.

Manual Rack and Pinion

Removal and Installation
CARAVAN, VOYAGER AND TOWN & COUNTRY

1. Disconnect the negative battery cable.
2. Raise the vehicle and support safely. Remove the front wheel assemblies.
3. Remove the tie rod ends from the steering knuckles.
4. Remove the steering column from vehicle.
5. On All Wheel Drive models, remove the 2 bolts and nuts attaching the bridge to the front crossmember.
6. If equipped, remove the the the air diverter valve bracket, from the left side of the crossmember.
7. Remove the front suspension crossmember attaching bolts and nuts.
8. Lower the crossmember.
9. Remove the lower steering column coupler from the steering gear. Remove the steering coupler roll pin and separate coupler from steering gear shaft.
10. Remove the axle boot shield, if equipped.
11. Remove the steering gear bolts from the front suspension crossmember.
12. Remove the steering gear from the left side of the vehicle.
To install:
13. Install the steering gear from the left side of the vehicle. Install the steering gear bolts in the front suspension crossmember.
14. Install the lower steering column coupler to the steering gear. Install the steering coupler roll pin.
15. Install the lower crossmember and the attaching bolts. The right rear crossmember bolt is a pilot bolt that correctly locates the crossmember, tighten it first. Torque the crossmember bolts to 90 ft. lbs.

16. On All Wheel Drive models, install the 2 bolts and nuts attaching the bridge to the front crossmember.

17. Install the steering column. Install the tie rod ends from the steering knuckles.

18. Install the tire and wheel assemblies on the vehicle.

DAKOTA WITH 2WD

1. Disconnect the negative battery cable.
2. Remove the tie rod ends from the steering knuckle.
3. Remove the coupling pin.
4. Remove the bolts attaching the rack to the crossmember.
5. Remove the gear from the vehicle.
6. The installation is the reverse of the removal procedure. Torque the mounting bolts to 150 ft. lbs. (203 Nm).

Power Steering Gear

Removal and Installation
DAKOTA WITH 4WD

1. Disconnect the negative battery cable.
2. Raise the vehicle and support safely. Center the steering.
3. Disconnect the pitman arm from the center link.
4. Disconnect and plug the pressure and return hoses.
5. Disconnect the steering gear to shaft coupling.
6. Remove the steering gear mount bolts and remove the gear from the vehicle.
7. Matchmark and remove the pitman arm from the sector shaft.
8. The installation is the reverse of the removal procedure. Torque the pitman arm nut to 175 ft. lbs. (237 Nm) and the mount bolts to 100 ft. lbs. (136 Nm).
9. Refill the power steering pump.

Adjustment

1. If the vehicle wanders of the steering has too much play, the sector shaft can be adjusted.
2. Loosen the adjusting screw locknut and turn the screw all the down.
3. Back the screw off ¼–½ turn.
4. Tighten the locknut.
5. Road test the vehicle. If the steering wheel does not return easily after a turn, back the screw off until the wheel returns easily.

Power Rack and Pinion

Removal and Installation
CARAVAN, VOYAGER AND TOWN & COUNTRY

1. Disconnect the negative battery cable.
2. Raise the vehicle and support safely. Remove the front wheel assemblies.
3. Remove the tie rod ends from the steering knuckles.
4. Remove the steering column from vehicle.
5. On All Wheel Drive models, remove the 2 bolts and nuts attaching the bridge to the front crossmember.
6. If equipped, remove the the air diverter valve bracket, from the left side of the crossmember.
7. Disconnect and plug the oil lines from the rack.
8. Remove the front suspension crossmember attaching bolts and nuts. Lower the crossmember.
9. Remove the lower steering column coupler from the steering gear. Remove the steering coupler roll pin and separate coupler from steering gear shaft.
10. Remove the axle boot shield, if equipped.
11. Remove the steering gear bolts from the front suspension crossmember.
12. Remove the steering gear from the left side of the vehicle.

To install:

13. Install the steering gear from the left side of the vehicle. Install the steering gear bolts in the front suspension crossmember.

14. Install the lower steering column coupler to the steering gear. Install the steering coupler roll pin.

15. Install the lower crossmember and the attaching bolts. The right rear crossmember bolt is a pilot bolt that correctly locates the crossmember, tighten it first. Torque the crossmember bolts to 90 ft. lbs.

16. On All Wheel Drive models, install the 2 bolts and nuts attaching the bridge to the front crossmember.

17. Install the steering fluid lines. Refill the power steering pump.

18. Reinstall the steering column. Insert the tie rod ends into the steering knuckles.

19. Install the tire and wheel assemblies on the vehicle.

DAKOTA WITH 2WD

1. Disconnect the negative battery cable.
2. Remove the tie rod ends from the steering knuckle.
3. Disconnect and plug the power steering fluid lines.
4. Remove the coupling pin.
5. Remove the bolts attaching the rack to the crossmember.
6. Remove the gear from the vehicle.
7. The installation is the reverse of the removal procedure. Torque the mounting bolts to 150 ft. lbs. (203 Nm).

Power Steering Pump

Removal and Installation

1. Disconnect the negative battery cable.
2. Position a drainpan under the power steering pump.
3. Disconnect the fluid hoses from the pump and plug them.
4. Remove the front bracket attaching bolts and remove the belt from the pulley.
5. Remove the rear pump to bracket nut and remove the pump.
6. Remove the bracket from the pump.
7. Remove the pulley from the pump with the proper puller. Install the pulley on the new pump using the installation tools.
8. The installation is the reverse of the removal procedure.

Belt Adjustment

NOTE: The belt tension is automatically adjusted by a dynamic tensioner on the 3.0L and 3.3L engines and late 1991 3.9L and 5.2L engines. Adjustment is not possible.

1. Loosen the bracket mounting bolts.
2. Using a ½ in. drive breaker bar in the square hole provided in the bracket, move the pump away from the engine. Do not pry against the fluid reservoir.
3. With the pump moved enough so the belt deflects about ¼–½ in. under a 10 lb. load, tighten the bolts.

System Bleeding

1. Fill the reservoir with power steering fluid.
2. Turn the wheels to the full left turn position and add fluid until the reservoir is full.
3. Start the engine and add fluid to bring the level to the correct level.
4. To purge the system of air, turn the steering wheel from side to side without contacting the stops.
5. Return the wheel to the straight ahead position and operate the engine for 2 minutes before road testing. This should bleed the system completely.

Rack and pinion steering gear mounting—Caravan, Voyager and Town & Country

Rack and pinion steering gear mounting—2WD Dakota

Tie Rod Ends

Removal and Installation

1. Raise the vehicle and support safely.
2. Remove the cotter pin and nut from the tie rod end.
3. Using puller, remove the tie rod from the steering knuckle or center link, if equipped.

4. Loosen the sleeve clamp nut and bolt, if equipped and unscrew the tie rod end from the sleeve or inner tie rod.
5. The installation is the reverse of the removal procedure. Torque the stud nuts to 45 ft. lbs. (61 Nm) and install a new cotter pin.
6. Perform a front end alignment as required.

BRAKES

For all brake system repair and service procedure not detained below, please refer to "Brakes" in the Unit Repair section.

Master Cylinder

Removal and Installation

1. Disconnect the negative battery cable.
2. Disconnect and plug the brake lines from the master cylinder.
3. Remove the nuts attaching the master cylinder to the power booster.
4. Remove the master cylinder from the mounting studs.
5. Remove the fluid reservoir from the cylinder.
To install:
6. Bench bleed the master cylinder.
7. Install to the studs and install the nuts.
8. Install the brake lines to the master cylinder loosely.
9. While depressing the brake pedal slowly to floor tighten brake fluid lines to master cylinder. Fill brake fluid reservoir and pump brake pedal. If pedal feels spoongy or low, check adjustment of the rear brake shoes and bleed the brake system as required.

Combination Valve

Removal and Installation

1. Disconnect the negative battery cable.
2. Raise the vehicle and support safely.
3. Tag and disconnect the brake lines from the valve.
4. Disconnect the wires to the pressure switch.
5. Remove the combination valve from the frame bracket.

FROM MASTER CYLINDER

PRESSURE DIFFERENTIAL SWITCH AND CONNECTOR

TO REAR BRAKES

FROM MASTER CYLINDER

TO FRONT BRAKES

METERING VALVE STEM

COMBINATION VALVE

Combination switch—Dakota

6. The installation is the reverse of the removal procedure.
7. Bleed the brakes in the following order:
   a. Rear wheel anti-lock valve, if equipped
   b. Right rear wheel
   c. Left rear wheel
   d. Right front wheel
   e. Left front wheel

Height Sensing Proportioning Valve Assembly

Removal and Installation

CARAVAN, VOYAGER AND TOWN & COUNTRY

1. Disconnect the negative battery. Remove the rear stone shield.
2. Remove the actuator assembly.
3. Tag and disconnect the brake lines from the valve.
4. Remove the valve from the frame bracket.
5. The installation is the reverse of the removal procedure.

Adjustment

1. With the vehicle lifted so the rear suspension is hanging free, disconnect the shock absorbers.
2. Remove the rear tire and wheel assemblies and loosen both front spring hanger pivot bolts.
3. Make sure the actuator hook is properly seated on the valve lever. Loosen the adjustment nut on the actuator assembly.
4. Pull the actuator assembly toward the spring hanger until the valve lever bottoms on the valve body and hold the position.
5. Tighten the adjustment nut to 25 inch lbs. This will complete the adjustment.
6. Tighten the spring bolts, install the shocks and wheels and road test the vehicle.

Power Brake Booster

Removal and Installation

1. Disconnect the negative battery cable. Disconnect the vacuum hose(s) from the booster.
2. Remove the nuts attaching the master cylinder to the booster and move the master cylinder to the side.
3. From inside of the vehicle, remove the clip that secures the booster pushrod to the brake pedal.
4. Remove the nuts that attach the booster to the dash panel and remove it from the vehicle.
5. Transfer the check valve to the new booster.
6. The installation is the reverse of the removal procedure.

Brake Caliper

Removal and Installation

1. Raise the vehicle and support safely.

SNOW/STONE SHIELD

HEIGHT SENSING
PROPORTIONING
VALVE

ACTUATOR ASSEMBLY

ADJUSTMENT NUT

PLASTIC
RETAINER

ACTUATOR BRACKET
ASSEMBLY

Height sensing proportioning valve—Caravan, Voyager and Town & Country

2. Remove the tire and wheel assembly. Remove the hold-down spring on Dakota.
3. Remove the caliper mounting pin(s).
4. Lift the caliper off of the rotor. Remove the outer pad from the caliper.
5. Remove the brake hose retaining bolt from the caliper.
To install:
6. Install the brake hose to the caliper using new copper washers.
7. Position the caliper over the rotor so the caliper engages the adaptor correctly. Install the mounting pin(s). Install the hold-down spring, if equipped.
8. Fill the master cylinder and bleed the brakes.

Disc Brake Pads

Removal and Installation

1. Remove ½ of the brake fluid from the master cylinder resrevoir.
2. Raise the vehicle and support safely. Remove the tire and wheel assemblies.
3. Remove the hold-down spring on Dakota. Remove the caliper and remove the outer pad from the caliper.
4. Remove the inner pad from the adaptor.
To install:
5. Use a large C-clamp to compress the piston back into the caliper bore.
6. Install the inner pad to the adaptor.
7. Position the caliper over the rotor so the caliper engages the adaptor correctly and install the retainer pin(s).
8. Install the hold-down spring, if equipped.
9. Refill the master cylinder.

Brake Rotor

Removal and Installation

CARAVAN, VOYAGER AND TOWN & COUNTRY

1. Raise the vehicle and support safely. Remove the tire and wheel assembly.

2. Remove the caliper and brake pads.
3. Remove the factory installed clips, if equipped. It is not necessary to reinstall these clips.
4. Remove the rotor from the hub.
5. The installation is the reverse of the removal procedure.

DAKOTA

1. Raise the vehicle and support safely.
2. Remove the wheel and tire assembly.
3. Remove the caliper and disc brake pads.
4. Remove the dust cap.
5. Remove the cotter pin, nut lock, wheel bearing nut and washer from the spindle.
6. Remove the outer wheel bearing.
7. Remove the rotor and inner wheel bearing from the spindle. Remove the grease seal and inner wheel bearing from the back of the rotor.
To install:
8. Lubricate and install the inner wheel bearing into race in the rotor. Install a new grease seal.
9. Lubricate the spindle and install the rotor onto the spindle.
10. Lubricate and install the outer wheel bearing, washer and nut. When the bearing preload is properly set, install the nut lock and a new cotter pin.
11. Install the grease cap.
12. Install the brake pads and caliper.
13. Install the wheel and tire assembly.

Brake Drums

Removal and Installation

CARAVAN, VOYAGER AND TOWN & COUNTRY

1. Raise the vehicle and support safely.
2. Remove the wheel and tire assembly.
3. Remove the dust cap.
4. Remove the cotter pin and nut lock.
5. Remove the wheel bearing nut and washer from the spindle.
6. Remove the outer wheel bearing.

7. Remove the drum with the inner wheel bearing from the spindle. If the drum is difficult to remove, remove the plug from the rear of the backing plate and push the self adjuster lever away from the star wheel. Rotate the star wheel to retract the shoes. Remove the drum. Remove the grease seal from the drum.

To install:

8. Lubricate and install the inner wheel bearing in drum. Install a new grease seal.

9. Install the drum to the spindle.

10. Lubricate and install the outer wheel bearing, washer and nut. When the bearing preload is properly set, install the nut lock and a new cotter pin.

11. Install the grease cap.

12. Install the wheel and tire assembly. Adjust the rear brakes as required.

DAKOTA

1. Raise the vehicle and support safely.

2. Remove the wheel.

3. Remove the factory clips from the wheel studs, if equipped. It is not necessary to reinstall these clips.

4. Remove the drum. If the drum is difficult to remove, remove the plug from the rear of the backing plate and push the self adjuster lever away from the star wheel. Rotate the star wheel to retract the shoes and remove the drum.

5. The installation is the reverse of the removal procedure.

6. Adjust the rear brakes as required.

Brake Shoes

Removal and Installation

1. Raise the vehicle and support safely. Remove the wheel and tire assemblies and the brake drums.

2. Remove the primary and secondary shoe return springs from the anchor pin.

3. Lift the adjuster lever and disconnect the actuator cable.

4. Remove the shoe retainers and springs.

5. Remove the shoes (held together by the lower spring) while

BACKING PLATE
RETURN SPRING
ANCHOR PLATE
RETURN SPRING
CABLE GUIDE
PARKING BRAKE LEVER
PARKING BRAKE STRUT AND SPRING
ADJUSTER CABLE AND SPRING
PRIMARY SHOE
SHOE RETAINER, SPRING AND PIN
SHOE SPRING
SECONDARY SHOE
ADJUSTER SCREW ASSEMBLY
ADJUSTER LEVER
LEVER SPRING

Typical rear brake shoe assembly

separating the parking brake actuating lever from the shoe with a twisting motion.

To install:

6. Thoroughly clean and dry the backing plate. To prepare the backing plate, lubricate the bosses, anchor pin and parking brake actuating lever pivot surface lightly with lithium based grease.

7. Remove, clean and dry all parts still on the old shoes. Lubricate the star wheel shaft threads with anti-sieze lubricant and transfer all parts to their proper locations on the new shoes.

8. Spread the shoes apart, engage the parking brake lever and position them on the backing plate so the wheel cylinder pins engage and the anchor pins hold the shoes.

9. Install the parking brake strut and hold-down spring assemblies. Install the anchor plate. Lubricate the sliding surface of the actuator cable plate lightly and install the cable.

10. Install the shoe return spring opposite the cable, then install the remaining cable.

11. Adjust the star wheel.

12. Remove any grease from the linings and install the drum.

13. Complete the brake adjustment with the wheels installed.

Wheel Cylinder

Removal and Installation

1. Raise the vehicle and support safely.

2. Remove the wheel, drum and brake shoes.

3. Remove the brake line from the wheel cylinder.

4. Remove the wheel cylinder bolts and remove the cylinder from the backing plate.

To install:

5. Apply a very thin coating of silicone sealer to the cylinder mounting surface, install the cylinder to the backing plate and install the retaining bolts.

6. Connect the brake line to the wheel cylinder.

7. Install all brake parts that were removed.

8. Install the tire and wheel assembly.

9. Bleed the brake system.

Parking Brake Cable

Adjustment

1. Release the parking brakes fully.

2. Raise the vehicle and support safely.

3. Adjust the rear brakes.

4. Loosen the nut on the front cable until there is slack in all the cables.

5. Rotate the rear wheels and tighten the cable adjusting nut until there is a slight drag at the wheels.

6. Continue to rotate the rear wheels and loosen the nut until all drag is eliminated.

7. Back off the nut an additional 2 turns.

8. Apply and release the parking brake several times. Upon the least release, verify that there is no drag at the wheels.

9. To check the operation, make sure the parking brake holds on an incline.

Removal and Installation

FRONT PARKING BRAKE CABLE

1. Raise the vehicle and support safely. Remove the front cable adjusting nut.

2. Remove the clip securing the cable to the anchor bracket, if equipped and slide the cable out of the bracket.

3. Remove the retainer attaching the cable to the pedal assembly frame. Disengage the cable from the pedal clevis.

4. Remove the cable grommet from the floor pan and remove the cable.

5. The installation is the reverse of the removal procedure.

INTERMEDIATE BRAKE CABLE

1. Raise the vehicle and support safely.
2. Loosen the parking brake adjuster until cable is slack.
3. Disengage the adjuster hook from the frame rail.
4. Disengage the intermediate cable from the connectors and the right side cable guide.
5. Remove the cable.
6. The installation is the reverse of the removal procedure.

REAR PARKING BRAKE CABLE

1. Release the parking brake.
2. Raise the vehicle and support safely.
3. Remove the adjusting nut from the front cable.
4. Remove the brake drums and the shoes, if necessary. Disconnect the cable from the lever and compress the cable retainer tabs. Remove the cable from the backing plate.
5. Remove the cable from the guides connectors or equalizer and remove the retaining clips from the frame bracket.
6. The installation is the reverse of the removal procedure.

Brake System Bleeding

EXCEPT ANTI-LOCK BRAKES

NOTE: If using a pressure bleeder, follow the instructions furnished with the unit and choose the correct adaptor for the application. Do not substitute an adapter that "almost fits" as it will not work and could be dangerous.

Master Cylinder

If the master cylinder is off the vehicle it can be bench bled.

1. Connect 2 short pieces of brake line to the outlet fittings, bend them until the free end is below the fluid level in the master cylinder reservoirs.
2. Fill the reservoir with fresh brake fluid. Pump the piston slowly until no more air bubbles appear in the reservoirs.
3. Disconnect the 2 short lines, refill the master cylinder and securely install the cylinder caps.
4. If the master cylinder is on the vehicle, it can still be bled, using a flare nut wrench.
5. Open the brake lines slightly with the flare nut wrench while pressure is applied to the brake pedal by a helper inside the vehicle.
6. Be sure to tighten the line before the brake pedal is released.
7. Repeat the process with both lines until no air bubbles come out.

Calipers and Wheel Cylinders

1. Fill the master cylinder with fresh brake fluid. Check the level often during the procedure.
2. Starting with the right rear wheel, remove the protective cap from the bleeder, and place where it will not be lost. Clean the bleed screw.

CAUTION

When bleeding the brakes, keep face away from the brake area. Spewing fluid may cause facial and/or visual damage. Do not allow brake fluid to spill on the car's finish; it will remove the paint.

---

3. If the system is empty, the most efficient way to get fluid down to the wheel is to loosen the bleeder about ½–¾ turn, place a finger firmly over the bleeder and have a helper pump the brakes slowly until fluid comes out the bleeder. Once fluid is at the bleeder, close it before the pedal is released inside the vehicle.

NOTE: If the pedal is pumped rapidly, the fluid will churn and create small air bubbles, which are almost impossible to remove from the system. These air bubbles will eventually congregate and a spongy pedal will result.

4. Once fluid has been pumped to the caliper or wheel cylinder, open the bleed screw again, have the helper press the brake pedal to the floor, lock the bleeder and have the helper slowly release the pedal. Wait 15 seconds and repeat the procedure (including the 15 second wait) until no more air comes out of the bleeder upon application of the brake pedal. Remember to close the bleeder before the pedal is released inside the vehicle each time the bleeder is opened. If not, air will be induced into the system.
5. If a helper is not available, connect a small hose to the bleeder, place the end in a container of brake fluid and proceed to pump the pedal from inside the vehicle until no more air comes out the bleeder. The hose will prevent air from entering the system.
6. Repeat the procedure on remaining wheel cylinders in order:
    a. Left rear
    b. Right front
    c. Left front
7. Hydraulic brake systems must be totally flushed if the fluid becomes contaminated with water, dirt or other corrosive chemicals. To flush, bleed the entire system until all fluid has been replaced with new fluid.
8. Install the bleeder cap(s) on the bleeder to keep dirt out. Always road test the vehicle after brake work of any kind is done.

ANTI-LOCK BRAKES

Pressure Bleeding

The brake lines may be pressure bled, using a standard diaphragm type pressure bleeder. Only diaphragm type pressure bleeding equipment should be used to bleed the system.

1. The ignition should be turned **OFF** and remain **OFF** throughout this procedure.
2. Depressurize the hydraulic accumulator.

CAUTION

Failure to depressurize the hydraulic accumulator, prior to performing this operation may result in personal injury and/or damage to the painted surfaces.

---

3. Remove the electrical connector from fluid level sensor on the reservoir cap(s) and remove the reservoir cap(s).
4. Install the pressure bleeder adapter.
5. Attach the bleeding equipment to the bleeder adapter. Charge the pressure bleeder to approximately 20 psi (138 kPa).
6. Connect a transparent hose to the bleed screw. Submerge the free end of the hose in a clear glass container, which is partially filled with clean, fresh brake fluid.
7. With the pressure turned **ON**, open the bleed screw ½–¾ turn and allow fluid to flow into the container. Leave the bleed screw open until clear, bubble-free fluid slows from the hose. If the reservoir has been drained or the hydraulic assembly removed from the vehicle prior to the bleeding operation, slowly pump the brake pedal 1–2 times while the bleed screw is open and fluid is flowing. This will help purge air from the hydraulic assembly. Tighten the bleeder screw to 7.5 ft. lbs. (10 Nm).
8. Repeat Step 7 at all wheels. Wheels should be bled in the following order:
    a. Left rear
    b. Right rear
    c. Left front
    d. Right front
9. After bleeding all 4 wheels, remove the pressure bleeding equipment and bleeder adapter by closing the pressure bleeder valve and slowly unscrewing the bleeder adapter from the hydraulic assembly reservoir. Failure to release pressure in the reservoir will cause spillage of brake fluid and could result in injury or damage to painted surfaces.
10. Using a syringe or equivalent method, remove excess fluid from the reservoir to bring the fluid level to full level.

11. Install the reservoir cap and connect the fluid level sensor connector. Turn the ignition **ON** and allow the pump to charge the accumulator.

Manual Bleeding

1. Depressurize the hydraulic accumulator.

— CAUTION —

Failure to depressurize the hydraulic accumulator, prior to performing this operation may result in personal injury and/or damage to the painted surfaces.

2. Connect a transparent hose to the caliper bleed screw. Submerge the free end of the hose in a clear glass container, which is partially filled with clean, fresh brake fluid.

3. Slowly pump the brake pedal several times, using full strokes of the pedal and allowing approximately 5 seconds between pedal strokes. After 2 or 3 strokes, continue to hold pressure on the pedal, keeping it at the bottom of its travel.

4. With pressure on the pedal, open the bleed screw ½–¾ turn. Leave the bleed screw open until fluid no longer flows from the hose. Tighten the bleed screw and release the pedal.

5. Repeat this procedure until clear, bubble-free fluid flows from the hose.

6. Repeat all steps at each of the calipers. Calipers should be bled in the following order:
   a. Left rear
   b. Right rear
   c. Left front
   d. Right front

Anti-Lock Brake System Service

Precautions

Failure to observe the following precautions may result in system damage.

- Before performing electric arc welding on the vehicle, disconnect the Electronic Brake Control Module (EBCM) and the hydraulic modulator connectors.

- When performing painting work on the vehicle, do not expose the Electronic Brake Control Module (EBCM) to temperatures in excess of 185°F (85°C) for longer than 2 hrs. The system may be exposed to temperatures up to 200°F (95°C) for less than 15 min.

- Never disconnect or connect the Electronic Brake Control Module (EBCM) or hydraulic modulator connectors with the ignition switch ON.

- Never disassemble any component of the Anti-Lock Brake System (ABS) which is designated non-servicable; the component must be replaced as an assembly.

- When filling the master cylinder, always use brake fluid which meets DOT-3 specifications; petroleum-based fluid will destroy the rubber parts.

Depressurizing the Hydraulic Accumulator

1. With the ignition **OFF**, pump the brake pedal a minimum of 40 times, using approximately 50 lbs. (222 N) pedal force. A noticeable change in pedal feel will occur when the accumulator is discharged.

2. When a definite increase in pedal effort is felt, stroke the pedal a few additional times. This should remove all hydraulic pressure from the system.

Hydraulic Assembly

Removal and Installation

1. Disconnect the negative battery cable. Depressurize the hydraulic accumulator.

— CAUTION —

Failure to depressurize the hydraulic accumulator, prior to performing this operation may result in personal injury and/or damage to the painted surfaces.

2. Remove the fresh air intake ducts. Remove the washer fluid tank from the vehicle.

3. Disconnect all electrical connectors from the hydraulic unit and pump/motor.

4. Remove as much of the fluid as possible from the reservoir on the hydraulic assembly.

5. Remove the pressure hose fitting (banjo bolt) from the hydraulic assembly. Use care not to drop the 2 washers used to seal the pressure hose fitting to the hydraulic assembly inlet.

6. Disconnect the return hose from the reservoir nipple. Cap the spigot on the reservoir.

7. Disconnect all brake tubes from the hydraulic assembly.

8. Remove the driver's side sound insulation panel.

9. Disconnect the pushrod from the brake pedal by using a small, flat tool to release the retainer clip on the brake pedal pin. The center tang on the clip must be moved back enough to allow the lock tab to clear the pin. Disconnect the pushrod from the pedal pin.

10. Remove the 4 underdash hydraulic assembly mounting nuts.

11. Remove the hydraulic assembly.

To install:

12. Position the hydraulic assembly on the vehicle.

13. Install and torque the mounting nuts to 21 ft. lbs. (28 Nm).

14. Using Lubriplate® or equivalent, coat the bearing surface of the pedal pin.

15. Connect the pushrod to the pedal and install a new retainer clip.

16. Install the brake tubes. If the proportioning valves were removed from the hydraulic assembly, reinstall valves and tighten to 20 ft. lbs. (27 Nm).

17. Install the return hose to the nipple on the reservoir.

18. Install the pressure hose to the hydraulic assembly; be sure the 2 washers are in there proper position. Tighten the bango bolt to 13 ft. lbs. (18 Nm).

19. Fill the reservoir to the top of the screen.

20. Connect all electrical connectors to the hydraulic assembly.

21. Bleed the entire brake system.

22. Install the cross brace, if disturbed. Install the fresh air intake duct and the washer tank.

23. Connect the negative battery cable and check the assembly for proper operation.

Wheel Speed Sensors

Removal and Installation

FRONT SENSOR

1. Raise the vehicle and support safely. Remove the wheel and tire assembly.

2. Remove the screw from the clip that holds the sensor to the fender shield.

3. Carefully pull the sensor assembly grommet from the fender shield.

4. Unplug the connector from the harness. Remove the retaininer clip from the strut damper bracket.

5. Remove the sensor mounting screw.

6. Carefully remove the sensor.

To install:

7. Coat the sensor with high temperature multi-purpose anti-corrosion compound before installing into the steering knuckle. Install the screw and tighten to 60 inch lbs. (7 Nm).

8. Connect the sensor connector to the harness and install the sensor connector lock.

9. Install the sensor assembly grommet and attach the clip to the fender shield.

NOTE: Proper installation of the wheel speed sensor cables is critical to continued system operation. Be sure the cables are installed in retainers. Failure to install the cables in the retainers may result in contact with moving parts and/or over-extension of the cables, resulting in an open circuit.

10. Install the wheel.

REAR SENSOR

1. Raise the vehicle and support safely. Remove the wheel and tire assembly.
2. Carefully pull the sensor assembly grommet from the underbody and pull the harness through the hole.
3. Unplug the connector from the harness. Remove the retaininer clip from the strut damper bracket.
4. Remove the sensor spool grommet clip retaining screw from the body hose bracket, located in front of the inside of the trailing arm.
5. Remove the outboard sensor assembly retaining nut and sensor mounting screw.
6. Carefully remove the sensor.

To install:

7. Coat the sensor with high temperature multi-purpose anti-corrosion compound before installing into the steering knuckle. Install the screw and tighten to 60 inch lbs. (7 Nm). Install the retaining nut.
8. Install the sensor spool grommet clip retaining screw.
9. Feed the sensor connector wire through the grommet and connect to the harness.
10. Install the sensor assembly grommet.
11. Install the wheel.

Hydraulic Bladder Accumulator

Removal and Installation

1. Release pressure in the hydraulic accumulator. Disconnect the negative battery cable.

─── **CAUTION** ───

Failure to depressurize the hydraulic accumulator, prior to performing this operation may result in personal injury and/or damage to the painted surfaces.

2. Using oil filter band wrench C–4065, loosen bladder accumulator.
3. Remove the bladder accumulator and brake fluid shield from the hydraulic assembly.

To install:

4. Install the brake fluid shield onto the hydraulic accumulator and install the bladder accumulator onto the hydraulic assembly.
5. Torque bladder to 35 ft. lbs. (48 Nm) using band wrench. Make sure the O-ring on the bladder is fulley seated on the hydraulic assembly.
6. Turn the ignition switch to the run position to energize the pump/motor assembly and pressurize the system. Check for leaks in the system.
7. Depressurize the accumulator again and check the brake fluid level in the reservoir. Add as required to correct the level.

Controller Anti-Lock Brake Module

Removal and Installation

1. Turn the vehicle ignition to the **OFF** position.
2. Remove the speed control servo from vehicle.
3. Disconnect the wiring harness connector from the Controller Anti-Lock Brake (CAB) module. Remove the 3 mounting bolts on the fender and remove the CAB from the vehicle.

To install:

4. Install the CAB module to the fender and tighten the attaching bolts to 105 inch lbs. (12 Nm).
5. Install the electrical connector and tignten the retaining bolt to 40 inch lbs. (5 Nm).

FRONT SUSPENSION

Shock Absorbers

Removal and Installation

1. Remove the upper shock nut, washer and bushing.
2. Raise and safely support the vehicle.
3. Remove the lower mounting bolts and remove the shock from the vehicle.
4. The installation is the reverse of the removal procedure.

MacPherson Strut

Removal and Installation

1. Remove the 3 mounting nuts from the shock tower under the hood.
2. Raise the vehicle and support safely.
3. Remove the brake hose bracket screw from the strut.
4. Remove the strut to knuckle bolts, nuts and nut washer.
5. The installation is the reverse of the removal procedure. Torque the upper mounting nuts to 20 ft. lbs. (27 Nm).
6. Perform a front end alignment. Torque the strut to knuckle nuts to 75 ft. lbs. (100 Nm) plus ¼ turn.

Coil Spring

Removal and Installation

CARAVAN, VOYAGER AND TOWN & COUNTRY

1. Raise the vehicle and support safely. Remove the MacPherson strut from the vehicle.
2. Compress the coil spring using tool C–4838 or MacPherson spring compressor.
3. Remove the upper assembly retaining nut.
4. Remove the damper assembly and plastic strut tube, if equipped.

To install:

5. Install the compressed spring to the strut, making sure the spring end is seated in the recess.
6. Install the damper assembly to the strut rod.
7. Align the alignment notch or tab with the lower bracket.
8. Tighten the upper assembly retaining nut to 60 ft. lbs. (81 Nm). Make sure the spring and damper assembly are still aligned before releasing the compressor tool.
9. Release the compressor tool.
10. Install the strut to the vehicle.

MacPherson strut assembly

11. Perform a front end alignment.

DAKOTA WITH 2WD

1. Raise the vehicle and support safely.
2. Remove the shock absorber.
3. Disconnect the sway bar from the lower control arm, if equipped.
4. Install spring compressor tool DD–1278 or equivalent, to the coil spring and tighten the nut finger-tight, then back off half a turn.
5. Remove the cotter pin and lower ball joint nut.
6. Release the lower ball joint taper using ball stud loosening tool C–3564–A, or equivalent.
7. Remove the tool and remove the ball stud from the control arm. Release the compressor tool from the coil spring.
8. Pull the arm down and remove the spring with the rubber isolation pad from the vehicle.

To install:

9. Install the spring with the rubber isolator. Install the compressor tool and compress it enough so the lower ball joint can be inserted through the knuckle.
10. Torque the ball joint nut to 135 ft. lbs. (183 Nm). Install a new cotter pin. Remove the spring compressor.
11. Connect the sway bar to the lower control arm, if equipped.
12. Install the shock absorber.

Torsion Bar

Removal and Installation
DAKOTA WITH 4WD

NOTE: The left and right side torsion bars are not interchangeable. The bars are identified by the letter R or L stamped into one end of the bar. The bars do not have a front or rear, though and can be installed with either end facing foward.

1. Remove the upper control arm jounce bumper.
2. Raise the vehicle with the front suspension hanging free and support safely.
3. Release the load from the torsion bar by turning the adjustment bolt counterclockwise.

Installing and aligning the damper assembly—1988–92 Caravan, Voyager and Town & Country

Front Suspension—Dakota with 2WD

4. Remove the adjustment bolt from the swivel and then remove the torsion bar and the anchor together from the vehicle. Remove the torsion bar from the anchor.
5. Remove any dirt, rust or pebbles from the hex shaped socket in the anchor and lower control arm.
6. Inspect the anchor and bolt and replace them, if any damage or corrosion exists.

Torsion Bar assembly—Dakota with 4WD

To install:

7. Insert the torsion bar ends into the sockets.

8. Position the anchor and the bushing in the crossmember, insert the adjustment bolt and thread it into the swivel.

9. Turn the adjustment bolt clockwise to apply a load on the bar.

10. Lower the vehicle.

11. Set the front suspension height so the difference between the distance from the road surface to the lower control arm inner pivot and the distance from the road surface to the outer end of the arm is 1–1½ in.

12. Install the upper control arm jounce bumper.

Upper Ball Joint

Inspection

To inspect the ball joints, unload the suspension. Upper ball joints on 2WD vehicles or any ball joint on 4WD vehicles should be replaced if any play exists at all.

Removal and Installation

DAKOTA

2WD

1. Raise the vehicle and support safely.

2. Position a support at the outer end of the lower control arm and lower the vehicle so the support compresses the coil spring.

3. Remove the tire and wheel assembly.

4. Release the upper ball joint taper using ball stud loosening tool C–3564–A or equivalent.

5. Unthread the ball joint from the control arm with tool C–3561 or equivalent.

To install:

6. Thread new ball joint into control arm with tool C–3561. Tighten ball stud with 125 ft. lbs. (170 Nm) torque. Install new seal over stud.

7. Install steering knuckle on upper ball stud. Tighten upper nut to 105 ft. lbs. (142 Nm) torque. Install new cotter pin.

8. Install wheel and tire assembly.

4WD

1. Raise the vehicle and support safely.

2. Remove the CV-driveshaft from the vehicle.

3. Turn the torsion bar adjustment nut counterclockwise to relieve all tension from the torsion bar.

4. Remove the cotter pin from the upper ball stud.

5. Release the upper ball joint taper using ball stud loosening tool C–3564–A or equivalent. Remove the tool.

6. Remove the upper ball stud seal.

7. Force the ball joint from the arm using the ball stud removal and installation tool C–4212.

To install:

8. Install the new ball joint using the ball stud removal and installation tool C–4212.

9. Install the ball stud seal.

10. Insert the upper ball stud in the steering knuckle arm bore and install the nut. Torque the nut to 105 ft. lbs. (142 Nm) and install a new cotter pin.

11. Turn the torsion bar adjustment nut clockwise to apply a load on the bar.

12. Install the CV-driveshaft and all related parts.

13. Lower the vehicle.

14. Set the front suspension height so the difference between the distance from the surface that the tires are on to the lower control arm inner pivot and the distance that the tires are on to the outer end of the arm is 1–1½ in.

Lower Ball Joint

Inspection

To inspect the ball joints on Caravan, Voyager and Town & Country, grasp the grease fitting by hand with the vehicle on the ground. If the grease fitting can be moved at all by hand, the ball joint should be replaced.

To inspect the lower ball joints on Dakota, unload the suspension. Lower ball joints on 2WD vehicles should be replaced, if they have more than 0.020 in. play. Any ball joint on 4WD vehicles should be replaced if any play exists.

Removal and Installation

CARAVAN, VOYAGER AND TOWN & COUNTRY

1988–91

The ball joints are welded to the lower control arms. This necessitates replacement of the control arm assembly. Do not attempt to replace ball joints that are welded to the control arm; replacement control arms are equipped a new ball joint.

1992

1. Raise and safely support the vehicle. Remove tire and wheel assembly.

2. Remove brake rotor.

3. Remove the ball joint to steering knuckle clamp nut and bolt. Remove the lower ball joint stud from the steering knuckle.

4. Remove the seal from the joint. Install remover tool C–4699–2 over ball joint stud and against the joint upper housing.

5. Press the ball joint from the control arm.

To install:

6. Install ball joint onto the control arm and press into place using tool C–4699–2. Install seal on joint stud. Insert stud into steering knuckle and install knuckle clamp bolt and nut.

7. Install brake rotor, tire and wheel assembly.

DAKOTA

2WD

1. Raise the vehicle and support safely.

2. Remove the shock absorber.

3. Disconnect the sway bar from the lower control arm, if equipped.

4. Install spring compressor tool DD–1278 or equivalent, to the coil spring and tighten the nut finger-tight, then back off half a turn.

5. Remove the cotter pin and lower ball joint nut.

6. Release the lower ball joint taper using ball stud loosening tool C–3564–A or equivalent.

7. Remove the tool and remove the ball stud from the control arm. Release the compressor tool from the coil spring.

8. Pull the arm down and remove the spring with the rubber isolation pad from the vehicle. Remove the ball joint boot. Use tool C–4212, or an appropriate ball joint press to remove the ball joint from the arm.

Front Suspension—Dakota with 4WD

Upper control arm—Dakota with 2WD

To install:

9. Use the remover tool to press the ball joint into the arm. Install a new rubber boot. Install the spring with the rubber isolators. Install the compressor tool and compress it enough so the lower ball joint can be inserted through the knuckle.

10. Torque the lower ball joint nut to 130 ft. lbs. (176 Nm). Install a new cotter pin. Remove the spring compressor.

11. Connect the sway bar to the lower control arm, if equipped.

12. Install the shock absorber.

4WD

1. Raise the vehicle and support safely.

2. Remove the CV-driveshaft. Remove the brake rotor, if necessary.

3. Remove the torsion bar.

4. Remove the shock absorber lower attaching bolt.

5. Disconnect the stabilizer bar from the lower control arm.

6. Remove the cotter pin and the nut from the lower ball stud. Separate the lower ball stud from the steering knucle.

7. Pry the peened ball joint retainer sections upward from the lower control arm and remove the ball joint from the arm.

To install:

8. Install the new ball joint in the control arm. Peen the ball joint housing retainer over to secure the ball joint.

9. Install the grease seal.

10. Insert the ball stud into the steering knuckle bore. Torque the nut to 120 ft. lbs. (163 Nm) and install a new cotter pin.

11. Attach the stabilizer bar to the control arm and install the shock mount bolt.

12. Install the torsion bar and turn the adjustment bolt clockwise to apply a load to the bar.

13. Install the CV-driveshaft and all related parts.

14. Lower the vehicle.

15. Set the front suspension height so the difference between the distance from the surface that the tires are on to the lower control arm inner pivot and the distance that the tires are on to the outer end of the arm is 1–1½ in.

16. Perform a front end alignment.

Upper Control Arm

Removal and Installation

DAKOTA

2WD

1. Raise the vehicle and support safely.

2. Remove the shock absorber.

3. Disconnect the sway bar from the lower control arm, if equipped.

4. Install spring compressor tool DD–1278 or equivalent, to the coil spring and tighten the nut finger-tight, then back off half a turn.

5. Remove the cotter pin and upper ball joint nut. Suspend the rotor assembly with a wire so there is not excessive pull on the brake hose.

6. Release the upper ball joint taper using ball stud loosening tool C–3564–A or equivalent.

7. Remove the tool and remove the ball stud from the control arm.

8. Remove the pivot bar retaining bolts and remove the arm from the vehicle.

To install:

9. Install the arm to the frame rail bracket and install the retaining bolts.

10. Torque the ball joint nut to 135 ft. lbs. (183 Nm). Install a new cotter pin. Remove the spring compressor.

11. Connect the sway bar from the lower control arm, if equipped.

12. Install the shock absorber.

13. Align the front end. When all settings are at specifications, torque the pivot bar retaining bolts to 155 ft. lbs. (210 Nm).

4WD

1. Raise the vehicle and support safely.

2. Remove the CV-driveshaft from the vehicle.

3. Turn the torsion bar adjustment nut counterclockwise to

relieve all tension from the torsion bar. Remove the screws that attach the brake hose bracket to the upper arm. Remove the shock absorber.

4. Remove the cotter pin from the upper ball stud.

5. Release the upper ball joint taper using ball stud loosening tool C–3564–A or equivalent. Remove the tool. Remove the ball stud from the steering knuckle.

6. Remove the pivot bar retaining bolts.

7. Remove the arm from the vehicle.

To install:

8. Position the arm at the frame rail bracket.

9. Install the pivot arm nuts and bolts.

10. Insert the upper ball stud in the steering knuckle arm bore and install the nut. Torque the nut to 125 ft. lbs. (170 Nm) and install a new cotter pin. Install the shock absorber and attach the brake hose bracket.

11. Turn the torsion bar adjustment nut clockwise to apply a load on the bar.

12. Install the CV-driveshaft and all related parts.

13. Lower the vehicle.

14. Set the front suspension height so the difference between the distance from the surface that the tires are on to the lower control arm inner pivot and the distance that the tires are on to the outer end of the arm is 1–1½ in.

Lower Control Arm

Removal and Installation

CARAVAN, VOYAGER AND TOWN & COUNTRY

1. Raise the vehicle and support safely. Remove the tire and wheel assembly.

2. Remove the sway bar.

3. Remove the ball joint stud retaining bolt and nut.

4. Pry the lower control arm from the steering knuckle.

5. Remove the control arm to crossmember bolts, nuts bushings and retainers.

6. Remove the control arm from the vehicle.

7. Transfer all reusable parts to the new control arm and lubricate.

8. The installation is the reverse of the removal procedure. Torque the front pivot bolt to 120 ft. lbs. (163 Nm) and the rear mounting nut to 70 ft. lbs. (95 Nm).

9. Perform a front end alignment as required.

DAKOTA

2WD

1. Raise the vehicle and support safely.

2. Remove the shock absorber.

3. Disconnect the sway bar from the lower control arm, if equipped.

4. Install spring compressor tool DD–1278 or equivalent, to the coil spring and tighten the nut finger-tight, then back off half a turn.

5. Remove the cotter pin and lower ball joint nut.

6. Release the lower ball joint taper using ball stud loosening tool C–3564–A or equivalent.

7. Remove the tool and remove the ball stud from the control arm. Release the compressor tool from the coil spring.

8. Pull the arm down and remove the spring with the rubber isolation pad from the vehicle. Remove the lower control arm pivot bolts from the crossmember and remove the arm from the vehicle.

To install:

9. Install the arm to the crossmember finger-tight. Install the spring with the rubber isolators. Install the compressor tool and compress. Insert the lower ball joint through the knuckle.

10. Torque the lower ball joint nut to 135 ft. lbs. (183 Nm). Install a new cotter pin. Remove the spring compressor.

11. Connect the sway bar from the lower control arm, if equipped.

12. Install the shock absorber.

13. Lower the vehicle completely. When the weight of vehicle is off of the lifting apparatus, torque the front lower arm pivot bolt to 130 ft. lbs. (176 Nm) and the rear nut to 80 ft. lbs. (108 Nm).

14. Align the front end as required.

4WD

1. Raise the vehicle and support safely.

2. Remove the CV-driveshaft.

3. Remove the torsion bar.

4. Remove the shock absorber lower attaching bolt.

5. Disconnect the stabilizer bar from the lower control arm.

6. Remove the cotter pin and the nut from the lower ball stud. Separate the lower ball stud from the steering knuckle.

7. Remove the pivot bolts and remove the arm from the vehicle.

To install:

8. Install the new control arm to the vehicle.

9. Install the pivot bolts.

10. Insert the ball stud into the steering knuckle bore. Install the nut, torque to 120 ft. lbs. (163 Nm) and install a new cotter pin.

11. Attach the stabilizer bar to the control arm and install the shock mount bolt.

12. Install the torsion bar and turn the adjustment bolt clockwise to apply a load to the bar.

13. Install the CV-driveshaft and all related parts.

14. Lower the vehicle so the weight of vehicle is completely off of the lifting apparatus.

15. Torque the front pivot nut to 80 ft. lbs. (108 Nm) and the rear nut to 130 ft. lbs. (176 Nm).

16. Set the front suspension height so the difference between the distance from the surface that the tires are on to the lower control arm inner pivot and the distance that the tires are on to the outer end of the arm is 1–1½ in.

17. Perform a front end alignment.

Sway Bar

Removal and Installation

1. Raise the vehicle and support safely.

2. Remove the front sway bar brackets and retainers.

3. Remove the sway bar support brackets and bushings from the lower control arm. Remove the sway bar from the vehicle.

4. The installation is the reverse of the removal procedure.

Front Wheel Bearings

For FWD, AWD & 4WD model removal and installation procedures, refer to Drive Axle section.

Adjustment

1. Tighten the wheel bearing nut to 20–25 ft. lbs. (27–34 Nm) while turning the rotor.

2. Loosen the wheel bearing adjusting nut completely.

3. Tighten the nut finger-tight.

4. Check the wheel bearing endplay. The specification is 0.0001–0.003 in.

5. Install the nut lock and cotter pin.

Removal and Installation

1. Raise the vehicle and support safely.

2. Remove the tire and wheel assembly.

3. Remove the caliper and disc brake pads.

4. Remove the dust cap.

5. Remove the cotter pin, castelated nut lock, wheel bearing nut and washer from the spindle.

6. Remove the outer wheel bearing.

7. Remove the rotor with the inner wheel bearing from the spindle. Remove the grease seal.

To install:

8. Lubricate and install the inner wheel bearing. Install a new grease seal.

9. Install the rotor to the spindle.

10. Lubricate and install the outer wheel bearing, washer and nut. When the bearing preload is properly set, install the nut lock and a new cotter pin.

11. Install the grease cap.

12. Install the brake pads and caliper.

13. Install the wheel.

REAR SUSPENSION

Shock Absorber

Removal and Installation

1. Raise the vehicle and support safely.

2. Remove the bolts that attach the shock to the frame or bracket.

3. Remove the shock from the vehicle.

4. The installation is the reverse of the removal procedure.

Leaf Springs

Removal and Installation

CARAVAN, VOYAGER AND TOWN & COUNTRY

1. Raise the vehicle and support safely.

2. Disconnect the actuator valve for the height sensing proportional valve.

3. Using floor stands under the axle asembly, raise the rear axle assembly to relieve weight on the rear springs.

4. Disconnect the shock absorbers from the axle brackets.

5. Remove the U-bolt nuts and washers and remove the U-bolts.

6. Lower the rear axle assembly allowing the spring to hang free.

7. Remove the bolts from the front hanger.

8. Remove the rear spring shackle nuts and plate and remove the shackle from the spring.

9. Remove the front pivot bolt from the front spring hanger and remove the springs from the vehicle.

To install:

10. Assembly the shackle bushings and plate on the rear of the spring and ear spring hanger and start the shackle bolts.

11. Assembly the front spring hanger to the front of the spring eye and install the pivot bolt and nut. The pivot bolt must face inboard to prevent structural damage during installation.

12. Raise the front of the spring to the vehicle and install the 4 hanger bolts and torque to 45 ft. lbs. (61 Nm). Connect the actuator assembly for the height sensing proportioning valve.

13. Raise the axle assembly to the correct position with the axle centered under the spring center bolt.

14. Install the U-bolts, washers and nuts and torque the nuts to 60 ft. lbs. (81 Nm).

15. Install the shock absorbers.

16. Lower the vehicle so the full weight of vehicle is off of the lifting apparatus.

17. Torque the front pivot bolts to 105 ft. lbs. (142 Nm).

18. Torque the shackle nuts to 45 ft. lbs. (61 Nm).

19. Adjust the height sensing proportioning valve.

DAKOTA

1. Raise the vehicle and support safely.

2. Using the proper equipment, support the weight of the axle.

3. Remove the nuts, washers and U-bolts attaching the springs to the axle housing. Remove the spacer.

Rear suspension—Caravan, Voyager and Town & Country

4. Remove the spring shackle bolts, shackle and spring front bolt.

5. Remove the springs and auxiliary spring, if equipped, from the vehicle.

6. The installation is the reverse of the removal procedure.

Rear Wheel Bearings

Removal and Installation

CARAVAN, VOYAGER AND TOWN & COUNTRY

Except All Wheel Drive Vehicle

1. Raise the vehicle and support safely.
2. Remove the tire and wheel assembly.
3. Remove the dust cap.
4. Remove the cotter pin, nut lock and nut.
5. Remove the thrust washer and the outer wheel bearing.
6. Remove the drum with the inner wheel bearing and the grease seal.
7. Remove the grease seal and remove the inner bearing.

To install:

8. Lubricate the inner bearing and install to the drum.
9. Install a new grease seal.
10. Install the drum to the vehicle.
11. Lubricate and install the outer wheel bearing to the spindle.
12. Install the thrust washer.
13. Install and tighten the wheel bearng nut to 20–25 ft. lbs. (27–34 Nm) while rotating the drum.
14. Back off the adjusting nut ¼ turn then tighten it finger-tight.
15. Install the nut lock and a new cotter pin.

All Wheel Drive Vehicle

The rear wheel bearings and hub are serviced as an assembly.

1. Raise the vehicle and support safely.

2. Remove the tire and wheel assembly.

3. Remove the halfshaft flange retaining bolts. Compress inner halfshaft joint and pull downward to clear rear carrier assembly. Remove the halfshaft.

NOTE: The halfshaft acts as a bolt and secures the hub/bearing assembly. If vehicle is to be supported or moved on its wheels, install and torque a bolt through the hub. This will assure no damage is done to the bearing/hub assembly.

4. Remove the wheel bearing retainer bolts and remove hub/bearing assembly from the vehicle.

To install:

5. Install new hub/bearing assembly with new gasket onto the vehicle.
6. Install the retaining screws and tighten to 96 ft. lbs. (130 Nm).
7. Install halfshaft, washer and hub nut after cleaning foreign material from threads. Torque nut to 180 ft. lbs. (244 Nm).
8. Install spring washer, nut lock and new cotter pin. Install the tire and wheel assembly.

Rear Axle Assembly

Removal and Installation

CARAVAN, VOYAGER AND TOWN & COUNTRY

1. Raise the vehicle and support safely.
2. Disconnect the brake hose connection from the axle tube.
3. Unclip the brake tubes from the axle housing.
4. Support the axle tube with jack stands.
5. Unbolt the shock absorbers and the sway bar bushing retainers from the axle tube.
6. Unbolt the axle tube from the leaf springs.
7. Remove the axle from the vehicle.
8. The installation is the reverse of the removal procedure.

SPECIFICATIONS

VEHICLE IDENTIFICATION CHART

It is important for servicing and ordering parts to be certain of the vehicle and engine identification. The VIN (vehicle identification number) is a 17 digit number visible through the windshield on the driver's side of the dash and contains the vehicle and engine identification codes. The tenth digit indicates model year and the eighth digit indicates engine code. It can be interpreted as follows:

		Engine Code					Model Year	
Code	Cu. In.	Liters	Cyl.	Fuel Sys.	Eng. Mfg.		Code	Year
Y	300	4.9	6	EFI	Ford		J	1988
N	302	5.0	8	EFI	Ford		K	1989
H	351	5.8	8	EFI	Ford		L	1990
M	445	7.3	8	Diesel	Navistar		M	1991
G	460	7.5	8	EFI	Ford		N	1992

EFI—Electronic Fuel Injection

ENGINE IDENTIFICATION

Year	Model	Engine Displacement cu. in. (liter)	Engine Series Identification (VIN)	No. of Cylinders	Engine Type
1988	Bronco	300 (4.9)	Y	6	OHV
	Bronco	302 (5.0)	N	8	OHV
	Bronco	351 (5.8)	H	8	OHV
	E-150	300 (4.9)	Y	6	OHV
	E-150	302 (5.0)	N	8	OHV
	E-150	351 (5.8)	H	8	OHV
	E-250	300 (4.9)	Y	6	OHV
	E-250	302 (5.0)	N	8	OHV
	E-250	351 (5.8)	H	8	OHV
	E-250	445 (7.3)	M	8	Diesel
	E-250	460 (7.5)	G	8	OHV
	E-350	300 (4.9)	Y	6	OHV
	E-350	351 (5.8)	H	8	OHV
	E-350	445 (7.3)	M	8	Diesel
	E-350	460 (7.5)	G	8	OHV

Ford Motor Company
BRONCO • F SERIES (PICK-UP) • E SERIES (VAN)

ENGINE IDENTIFICATION

Year	Model	Engine Displacement cu. in. (liter)	Engine Series Identification (VIN)	No. of Cylinders	Engine Type
1988	F-150	300 (4.9)	Y	6	OHV
	F-150	302 (5.0)	N	8	OHV
	F-150	351 (5.8)	H	8	OHV
	F-250	300 (4.9)	Y	6	OHV
	F-250	302 (5.0)	N	8	OHV
	F-250	351 (5.8)	H	8	OHV
	F-250	445 (7.3)	M	8	Diesel
	F-250	460 (7.5)	G	8	OHV
	F-350	300 (4.9)	Y	6	OHV
	F-350	351 (5.8)	H	8	OHV
	F-350	445 (7.3)	M	8	Diesel
	F-350	460 (7.5)	G	8	OHV
	F-Super Duty	445 (7.3)	M	8	Diesel
	F-Super Duty	460 (7.5)	G	8	OHV
1989	Bronco	300 (4.9)	Y	6	OHV
	Bronco	302 (5.0)	N	8	OHV
	Bronco	351 (5.8)	H	8	OHV
	E-150	300 (4.9)	Y	6	OHV
	E-150	302 (5.0)	N	8	OHV
	E-150	351 (5.8)	H	8	OHV
	E-250	300 (4.9)	Y	6	OHV
	E-250	302 (5.0)	N	8	OHV
	E-250	351 (5.8)	H	8	OHV
	E-250	445 (7.3)	M	8	Diesel
	E-250	460 (7.5)	G	8	OHV
	E-350	300 (4.9)	Y	6	OHV
	E-350	351 (5.8)	H	8	OHV
	E-350	445 (7.3)	M	8	Diesel
	E-350	460 (7.5)	G	8	OHV
	F-150	300 (4.9)	Y	6	OHV
	F-150	302 (5.0)	N	8	OHV
	F-150	351 (5.8)	H	8	OHV
	F-250	300 (4.9)	Y	6	OHV
	F-250	302 (5.0)	N	8	OHV
	F-250	351 (5.8)	H	8	OHV
	F-250	445 (7.3)	M	8	Diesel
	F-250	460 (7.5)	G	8	OHV
	F-350	300 (4.9)	Y	6	OHV
	F-350	351 (5.8)	H	8	OHV
	F-350	445 (7.3)	M	8	Diesel
	F-350	460 (7.5)	G	8	OHV
	F-Super Duty	445 (7.3)	M	8	Diesel
	F-Super Duty	460 (7.5)	G	8	OHV

ENGINE IDENTIFICATION

Year	Model	Engine Displacement cu. in. (liter)	Engine Series Identification (VIN)	No. of Cylinders	Engine Type
1990	Bronco	300 (4.9)	Y	6	OHV
	Bronco	302 (5.0)	N	8	OHV
	Bronco	351 (5.8)	H	8	OHV
	E-150	300 (4.9)	Y	6	OHV
	E-150	302 (5.0)	N	8	OHV
	E-150	351 (5.8)	H	8	OHV
	E-250	300 (4.9)	Y	6	OHV
	E-250	302 (5.0)	N	8	OHV
	E-250	351 (5.8)	H	8	OHV
	E-250	445 (7.3)	M	8	Diesel
	E-250	460 (7.5)	G	8	OHV
	E-350	300 (4.9)	Y	6	OHV
	E-350	351 (5.8)	H	8	OHV
	E-350	445 (7.3)	M	8	Diesel
	E-350	460 (7.5)	G	8	OHV
	F-150	300 (4.9)	Y	6	OHV
	F-150	302 (5.0)	N	8	OHV
	F-150	351 (5.8)	H	8	OHV
	F-250	300 (4.9)	Y	6	OHV
	F-250	302 (5.0)	N	8	OHV
	F-250	351 (5.8)	H	8	OHV
	F-250	445 (7.3)	M	8	Diesel
	F-250	460 (7.5)	G	8	OHV
	F-350	300 (4.9)	Y	6	OHV
	F-350	351 (5.8)	H	8	OHV
	F-350	445 (7.3)	M	8	Diesel
	F-350	460 (7.5)	G	8	OHV
	F-Super Duty	445 (7.3)	M	8	Diesel
	F-Super Duty	460 (7.5)	G	8	OHV
1991–92	Bronco	300 (4.9)	Y	6	OHV
	Bronco	302 (5.0)	N	8	OHV
	Bronco	351 (5.8)	H	8	OHV
	E-150	300 (4.9)	Y	6	OHV
	E-150	302 (5.0)	N	8	OHV
	E-150	351 (5.8)	H	8	OHV
	E-250	300 (4.9)	Y	6	OHV
	E-250	302 (5.0)	N	8	OHV
	E-250	351 (5.8)	H	8	OHV
	E-250	445 (7.3)	M	8	Diesel
	E-250	460 (7.5)	G	8	OHV
	E-350	300 (4.9)	Y	6	OHV
	E-350	351 (5.8)	H	8	OHV
	E-350	445 (7.3)	M	8	Diesel

ENGINE IDENTIFICATION

Year	Model	Engine Displacement cu. in. (liter)	Engine Series Identification (VIN)	No. of Cylinders	Engine Type
1991–92	E-350	460 (7.5)	G	8	OHV
	F-150	300 (4.9)	Y	6	OHV
	F-150	302 (5.0)	N	8	OHV
	F-150	351 (5.8)	H	8	OHV
	F-250	300 (4.9)	Y	6	OHV
	F-250	302 (5.0)	N	8	OHV
	F-250	351 (5.8)	H	8	OHV
	F-250	445 (7.3)	M	8	Diesel
	F-250	460 (7.5)	G	8	OHV
	F-350	300 (4.9)	Y	6	OHV
	F-350	351 (5.8)	H	8	OHV
	F-350	445 (7.3)	M	8	Diesel
	F-350	460 (7.5)	G	8	OHV
	F-Super Duty	445 (7.3)	M	8	Diesel
	F-Super Duty	460 (7.5)	G	8	OHV

OHV—Overhead Valves

GENERAL ENGINE SPECIFICATIONS

Year	VIN	No. Cylinder Displacement cu. in. (liter)	Fuel System Type	Net Horsepower @ rpm	Net Torque @ rpm (ft. lbs.)	Bore × Stroke (in.)	Compression Ratio	Oil Pressure @ rpm
1988	Y	6-300 (4.9)	EFI	①	②	4.00 × 3.98	8.8:1	40–60 @ 2000
	N	8-302 (5.0)	EFI	185 @ 3800	270 @ 2400	4.00 × 3.00	9.0:1	40–60 @ 2000
	H	8-351 (5.8)	EFI	210 @ 3800	315 @ 2800③	4.00 × 3.50	8.8:1	40–65 @ 2000
	M	8-445 (7.3)	Diesel	180 @ 3300④	345 @ 1400⑤	4.11 × 4.18	21.5:1	40–70 @ 2000
	G	8-460 (7.5)	EFI	230 @ 3600	390 @ 2000	4.36 × 3.85	8.5:1	40–65 @ 2000
1989	Y	6-300 (4.9)	EFI	①	②	4.00 × 3.98	8.8:1	40–60 @ 2000
	N	8-302 (5.0)	EFI	185 @ 3800	270 @ 2400	4.00 × 3.00	9.0:1	40–60 @ 2000
	H	8-351 (5.8)	EFI	210 @ 3800	315 @ 2800③	4.00 × 3.50	8.8:1	40–65 @ 2000
	M	8-445 (7.3)	Diesel	180 @ 3300④	345 @ 1400⑤	4.11 × 4.18	21.5:1	40–70 @ 2000
	G	8-460 (7.5)	EFI	230 @ 3600	390 @ 2000	4.36 × 3.85	8.5:1	40–65 @ 2000
1990	Y	6-300 (4.9)	EFI	①	②	4.00 × 3.98	8.8:1	40–60 @ 2000
	N	8-302 (5.0)	EFI	185 @ 3800	270 @ 2400	4.00 × 3.00	9.0:1	40–60 @ 2000
	H	8-351 (5.8)	EFI	210 @ 3800	315 @ 2800③	4.00 × 3.50	8.8:1	40–65 @ 2000
	M	8-445 (7.3)	Diesel	180 @ 3300④	345 @ 1400⑤	4.11 × 4.18	21.5:1	40–70 @ 2000
	G	8-460 (7.5)	EFI	230 @ 3600	390 @ 2200	4.36 × 3.85	8.5:1	40–65 @ 2000
1991–92	Y	6-300 (4.9)	EFI	①	②	4.00 × 3.98	8.8:1	40–60 @ 2000
	N	8-302 (5.0)	EFI	185 @ 3800	270 @ 2400	4.00 × 3.00	9.0:1	40–60 @ 2000
	H	8-351 (5.8)	EFI	210 @ 3800	315 @ 2800③	4.00 × 3.50	8.8:1	40–65 @ 2000
	M	8-445 (7.3)	Diesel	180 @ 3300④	345 @ 1400⑤	4.11 × 4.18	21.5:1	40–70 @ 2000
	G	8-460 (7.5)	EFI	230 @ 3600	390 @ 2200	4.36 × 3.85	8.5:1	40–65 @ 2000

EFI—Electronic Fuel Injection
① Bronco, F150 and E150 with 2.73/3.08 axle ratio—145 @ 3400
All other vehicles—150 @ 3400
② Bronco, F150 and E150 with 2.73/3.08 axle ratio—265 @ 2000
All other vehicles—260 @ 2000
③ 310 @ 2800 on vehicles over 8500 lbs. GVWR.
④ 160 @ 3300 on high altitude applications
⑤ 305 @ 1400 on high altitude applications

GASOLINE ENGINE TUNE-UP SPECIFICATIONS

Year	VIN	No. Cylinder Displacement cu. in. (liter)	Spark Plugs Type	Spark Plugs Gap (in.)	Ignition Timing (deg.) MT	Ignition Timing (deg.) AT	Compression Pressure (psi)	Fuel Pump (psi)	Idle speed (rpm) MT	Idle speed (rpm) AT	Valve Clearance ① In.	Valve Clearance ① Ex.
1988	Y	6-300 (4.9)	BSF-44C	0.044	10B	10B	①	50–60③	②	②	Hyd.	Hyd.
	N	8-302 (5.0)	ASF-42C	0.044	10B	10B	①	35–45③	②	②	Hyd.	Hyd.
	H	8-351 (5.8)	ASF-32C	0.044	10B	10B	①	35–45③	②	②	Hyd.	Hyd.
	G	8-460 (7.5)	ASF-42C	0.044	10B	10B	①	35–45③	②	②	Hyd.	Hyd.
1989	Y	6-300 (4.9)	BSF-44C	0.044	10B	10B	①	50–60③	②	②	Hyd.	Hyd.
	N	8-302 (5.0)	ASF-42C	0.044	10B	10B	①	35–45③	②	②	Hyd.	Hyd.
	H	8-351 (5.8)	ASF-32C	0.044	10B	10B	①	35–45③	②	②	Hyd.	Hyd.
	G	8-460 (7.5)	ASF-42C	0.044	10B	10B	①	35–45③	②	②	Hyd.	Hyd.
1990	Y	6-300 (4.9)	BSF-44C	0.044	10B	10B	①	50–60③	②	②	Hyd.	Hyd.
	N	8-302 (5.0)	ASF-42C	0.044	10B	10B	①	35–45③	②	②	Hyd.	Hyd.
	H	8-351 (5.8)	ASF-32C	0.044	10B	10B	①	35–45③	②	②	Hyd.	Hyd.
	G	8-460 (7.5)	ASF-42C	0.044	10B	10B	①	35–45③	②	②	Hyd.	Hyd.
1991	Y	6-300 (4.9)	BSF-44C	0.044	10B	10B	①	50–60③	②	②	Hyd.	Hyd.
	N	8-302 (5.0)	ASF-42C	0.044	10B	10B	①	35–45③	②	②	Hyd.	Hyd.
	H	8-351 (5.8)	ASF-32C	0.044	10B	10B	①	35–45③	②	②	Hyd.	Hyd.
	G	8-460 (7.5)	ASF-44P	0.044	10B	10B	①	35–45③	②	②	Hyd.	Hyd.
1992		SEE UNDERHOOD SPECIFICATIONS STICKER										

Hyd.—Hydraulic
① The compression pressure in the lowest cylinder must be at least 75% of that in the highest cylinder
② See underhood emissions information label
③ High pressure pump

DIESEL ENGINE TUNE-UP SPECIFICATIONS

Year	VIN	No. Engine Displacement cu. in. (liter)	Valve Clearance Intake (in.)	Valve Clearance Exhaust (in.)	Intake Valve Opens (deg.)	Injection Pump Setting (deg.)	Injection Nozzle Pressure (psi) New	Injection Nozzle Pressure (psi) Used	Idle Speed (rpm)	Cranking Compression Pressure (psi)
1988	M	8-445 (7.3)	Hyd.	Hyd.	—	8.5B①	1875	1425	②	③
1989	M	8-445 (7.3)	Hyd.	Hyd.	—	8.5B①	1875	1425	②	③
1990	M	8-445 (7.3)	Hyd.	Hyd.	—	8.5B①	1875	1425	②	③
1991	M	8-445 (7.3)	Hyd.	Hyd.	—	8.5B①	1875	1425	②	③
1992		SEE UNDERHOOD SPECIFICATIONS STICKER								

Hyd.—Hydraulic
① @ 2000
② See underhood emission information label
③ The compression pressure in the lowest cylinder must be at least 75% of that in the highest cylinder. The minimum pressure is 195 psi, the maximum 440 psi.

FIRING ORDERS

NOTE: To avoid confusion, always replace spark plug wires one at a time.

4.9L Engine
Engine Firing Order: 1–5–3–6–2–4
Distributor Rotation: Clockwise

7.3L Diesel Engine
Engine Firing Order: 1–2–7–3–4–5–6–8

5.8L Engine
Engine Firing Order: 1–3–7–2–6–5–4–8
Distributor Rotation: Counterclockwise

5.0L and 7.5L Engines
Engine Firing Order: 1–5–4–2–6–3–7–8
Distributor Rotation: Counterclockwise

CAPACITIES

Year	Model	VIN	No. Cylinder Displacement cu. in (liter)	Engine Crankcase with Filter	Engine Crankcase without Filter	Transmission (pts.) 4-Spd	Transmission (pts.) 5-Spd	Transmission (pts.) Auto.	Drive Axle (pts.)	Fuel Tank (gal.)	Cooling System (qts.)
1988	Bronco	Y	6-300 (4.9)	6	5	7	①	②	③	32	⑥
	Bronco	N	8-302 (5.0)	6	5	7	①	②	③	32	⑦
	Bronco	H	8-351 (5.8)	6	5	7	①	②	③	32	⑧
	E-150	Y	6-300 (4.9)	6	5	7	①	②	③	④	⑩
	E-150	N	8-302 (5.0)	6	5	7	①	②	③	④	⑪
	E-150	H	8-351 (5.8)	6	5	7	①	②	③	④	⑫
	E-250	Y	6-300 (4.9)	6	5	7	①	②	③	④	⑩
	E-250	N	8-302 (5.0)	6	5	7	①	②	③	④	⑪
	E-250	H	8-351 (5.8)	6	5	7	①	②	③	④	⑫
	E-250	M	8-445 (7.3)	10	9	7	①	②	③	④	31
	E-250	G	8-460 (7.5)	6	5	7	①	②	③	④	28

CAPACITIES

Year	Model	VIN	No. Cylinder Displacement cu. in (liter)	Engine Crankcase with Filter	Engine Crankcase without Filter	Transmission (pts.) 4-Spd	Transmission (pts.) 5-Spd	Transmission (pts.) Auto.	Drive Axle (pts.)	Fuel Tank (gal.)	Cooling System (qts.)
1988	E-350	Y	6-300 (4.9)	6	5	7	①	②	③	④	⑩
	E-350	H	8-351 (5.8)	6	5	7	①	②	③	④	⑫
	E-350	M	8-445 (7.3)	10	9	7	①	②	③	④	31
	E-350	G	8-460 (7.5)	6	5	7	①	②	③	④	28
	F-150	Y	6-300 (4.9)	6	5	7	①	②	③	⑤	⑥
	F-150	N	8-302 (5.0)	6	5	7	①	②	③	⑤	⑦
	F-150	H	8-351 (5.8)	6	5	7	①	②	③	⑤	⑨
	F-250	Y	6-300 (4.9)	6	5	7	①	②	③	⑤	⑥
	F-250	N	8-302 (5.0)	6	5	7	①	②	③	⑤	⑦
	F-250	H	8-351 (5.8)	6	5	7	①	②	③	⑤	⑨
	F-250	M	8-445 (7.3)	10	9	7	①	②	③	⑤	29
	F-250	G	8-460 (7.5)	6	5	7	①	②	③	⑤	18
	F-350	Y	6-300 (4.9)	6	5	7	①	②	③	⑤	⑥
	F-350	H	8-351 (5.8)	6	5	7	①	②	③	⑤	⑨
	F-350	M	8-445 (7.3)	10	9	7	①	②	③	⑤	29
	F-350	G	8-460 (7.5)	6	5	7	①	②	③	⑤	18
1989	Bronco	Y	6-300 (4.9)	6	5	7	①	②	③	32	⑥
	Bronco	N	8-302 (5.0)	6	5	7	①	②	③	32	⑦
	Bronco	H	8-351 (5.8)	6	5	7	①	②	③	32	⑧
	E-150	Y	6-300 (4.9)	6	5	7	①	②	③	④	⑩
	E-150	N	8-302 (5.0)	6	5	7	①	②	③	④	⑪
	E-150	H	8-351 (5.8)	6	5	7	①	②	③	④	⑫
	E-250	Y	6-300 (4.9)	6	5	7	①	②	③	④	⑩
	E-250	N	8-302 (5.0)	6	5	7	①	②	③	④	⑪
	E-250	H	8-351 (5.8)	6	5	7	①	②	③	④	⑫
	E-250	M	8-445 (7.3)	10	9	7	①	②	③	④	31
	E-250	G	8-460 (7.5)	6	5	7	①	②	③	④	28
	E-350	Y	6-300 (4.9)	6	5	7	①	②	③	④	⑩
	E-350	H	8-351 (5.8)	6	5	7	①	②	③	④	⑫
	E-350	M	8-445 (7.3)	10	9	7	①	②	③	④	31
	E-350	G	8-460 (7.5)	6	5	7	①	②	③	④	28
	F-150	Y	6-300 (4.9)	6	5	7	①	②	③	⑤	⑥
	F-150	N	8-302 (5.0)	6	5	7	①	②	③	⑤	⑦
	F-150	H	8-351 (5.8)	6	5	7	①	②	③	⑤	⑨
	F-250	Y	6-300 (4.9)	6	5	7	①	②	③	⑤	⑥
	F-250	N	8-302 (5.0)	6	5	7	①	②	③	⑤	⑦
	F-250	H	8-351 (5.8)	6	5	7	①	②	③	⑤	⑨
	F-250	M	8-445 (7.3)	10	9	7	①	②	③	⑤	29
	F-250	G	8-460 (7.5)	6	5	7	①	②	③	⑤	18
	F-350	Y	6-300 (4.9)	6	5	7	①	②	③	⑤	⑥
	F-350	H	8-351 (5.8)	6	5	7	①	②	③	⑤	⑨
	F-350	M	8-445 (7.3)	10	9	7	①	②	③	⑤	29
	F-350	G	8-460 (7.5)	6	5	7	①	②	③	⑤	18

FORD MOTOR COMPANY
BRONCO • F SERIES (PICK-UP) • E SERIES (VAN)

CAPACITIES

Year	Model	VIN	No. Cylinder Displacement cu. in (liter)	Engine Crankcase with Filter	Engine Crankcase without Filter	Transmission (pts.) 4-Spd	Transmission (pts.) 5-Spd	Transmission (pts.) Auto.	Drive Axle (pts.)	Fuel Tank (gal.)	Cooling System (qts.)
1990	Bronco	Y	6-300 (4.9)	6	5	7	①	②	③	32	⑥
	Bronco	N	8-302 (5.0)	6	5	7	①	②	③	32	⑦
	Bronco	H	8-351 (5.8)	6	5	7	①	②	③	32	⑧
	E-150	Y	6-300 (4.9)	6	5	7	①	②	③	④	⑩
	E-150	N	8-302 (5.0)	6	5	7	①	②	③	④	⑪
	E-150	H	8-351 (5.8)	6	5	7	①	②	③	④	⑫
	E-250	Y	6-300 (4.9)	6	5	7	①	②	③	④	⑩
	E-250	N	8-302 (5.0)	6	5	7	①	②	③	④	⑪
	E-250	H	8-351 (5.8)	6	5	7	①	②	③	④	⑫
	E-250	M	8-445 (7.3)	10	9	7	①	②	③	④	31
	E-250	G	8-460 (7.5)	6	5	7	①	②	③	④	28
	E-350	Y	6-300 (4.9)	6	5	7	①	②	③	④	⑩
	E-350	H	8-351 (5.8)	6	5	7	①	②	③	④	⑫
	E-350	M	8-445 (7.3)	10	9	7	①	②	③	④	31
	E-350	G	8-460 (7.5)	6	5	7	①	②	③	④	28
	F-150	Y	6-300 (4.9)	6	5	7	①	②	③	⑬	⑥
	F-150	N	8-302 (5.0)	6	5	7	①	②	③	⑬	⑦
	F-150	H	8-351 (5.8)	6	5	7	①	②	③	⑬	⑨
	F-250	Y	6-300 (4.9)	6	5	7	①	②	③	⑬	⑥
	F-250	N	8-302 (5.0)	6	5	7	①	②	③	⑬	⑦
	F-250	H	8-351 (5.8)	6	5	7	①	②	③	⑬	⑨
	F-250	M	8-445 (7.3)	10	9	7	①	②	③	⑬	29
	F-250	G	8-460 (7.5)	6	5	7	①	②	③	⑬	18
	F-350	Y	6-300 (4.9)	6	5	7	①	②	③	⑬	⑥
	F-350	H	8-351 (5.8)	6	5	7	①	②	③	⑬	⑨
	F-350	M	8-445 (7.3)	10	9	7	①	②	③	⑬	29
	F-350	G	8-460 (7.5)	6	5	7	①	②	③	⑬	18
1991-92	Bronco	Y	6-300 (4.9)	6	5	7	①	②	③	32	⑥
	Bronco	N	8-302 (5.0)	6	5	7	①	②	③	32	⑦
	Bronco	H	8-351 (5.8)	6	5	7	①	②	③	32	⑧
	E-150	Y	6-300 (4.9)	6	5	7	①	②	③	④	⑩
	E-150	N	8-302 (5.0)	6	5	7	①	②	③	④	⑪
	E-150	H	8-351 (5.8)	6	5	7	①	②	③	④	⑫
	E-250	Y	6-300 (4.9)	6	5	7	①	②	③	④	⑩
	E-250	N	8-302 (5.0)	6	5	7	①	②	③	④	⑪
	E-250	H	8-351 (5.8)	6	5	7	①	②	③	④	⑫
	E-250	M	8-445 (7.3)	10	9	7	①	②	③	④	31
	E-250	G	8-460 (7.5)	6	5	7	①	②	③	④	28
	E-350	Y	6-300 (4.9)	6	5	7	①	②	③	④	⑩
	E-350	H	8-351 (5.8)	6	5	7	①	②	③	④	⑫
	E-350	M	8-445 (7.3)	10	9	7	①	②	③	④	31
	E-350	G	8-460 (7.5)	6	5	7	①	②	③	④	28
	F-150	Y	6-300 (4.9)	6	5	7	①	②	③	⑬	⑥
	F-150	N	8-302 (5.0)	6	5	7	①	②	③	⑬	⑦

CAPACITIES

Year	Model	VIN	No. Cylinder Displacement cu. in (liter)	Engine Crankcase with Filter	Engine Crankcase without Filter	Transmission (pts.) 4-Spd	Transmission (pts.) 5-Spd	Transmission (pts.) Auto.	Drive Axle (pts.)	Fuel Tank (gal.)	Cooling System (qts.)
	F-150	H	8-351 (5.8)	6	5	7	①	②	③	⑬	⑨
	F-250	Y	6-300 (4.9)	6	5	7	①	②	③	⑬	⑥
	F-250	N	8-302 (5.0)	6	5	7	①	②	③	⑬	⑦
	F-250	H	8-351 (5.8)	6	5	7	①	②	③	⑬	⑨
	F-250	M	8-445 (7.3)	10	9	7	①	②	③	⑬	29
	F-250	G	8-460 (7.5)	6	5	7	①	②	③	⑬	18
	F-350	Y	6-300 (4.9)	6	5	7	①	②	③	⑬	⑥
	F-350	H	8-351 (5.8)	6	5	7	①	②	③	⑬	⑨
	F-350	M	8-445 (7.3)	10	9	7	①	②	③	⑬	29
	F-350	G	8-460 (7.5)	6	5	7	①	②	③	⑬	18

① Mazda M50D transmission—7.6
  S5-42 ZF transmission—7.0
② C6 transmission with 2WD—23.5
  C6 transmission with 4WD—27
  AOD transmission—24.6
  E40D transmission with 2WD—31
  E40D transmission with 4WD—32
③ Front axle
  Dana 44—3.9
  Dana 50—4.1
  Dana 60—5.8
  Rear Axle
  Dana 60-3—6.3
  Dana 60-1v-1988–89—7.0, 1990–92—6.3
  Dana 61-1—5.8
  Dana 70-2v—6.6
  70HD—7.4
  Dana 80—8.5
  Ford 8.8 in.—5.5
  Ford 10.25 in.—6.5
④ 124 in. wheel base—18
  138 in., 158 in., and 176 in. wheelbase
  Rear mounted tank—22
  Front mounted tank—16

⑤ Rear mounted tank
  Diesel—18.2
  Gas—19.0
  Front mounted tank—
  116.8 in. and 138.8 in. wheelbase—16.5
  Except 116.8 and 138.8 in. wheelbase—19.0
  with E40D transmission—23
⑥ Standard cooling—13
  Manual transmission with air conditioning and/or super cool—14
  Automatic transmission with air conditioning or super cool—14
  Automatic transmission with air conditioning and super cool—15
⑦ Manual transmission with standard cool—13
  Automatic transmission with standard cool—14
  Manual or automatic transmission with air conditioning—14
  Super cool or super cool and air conditioning—15
⑧ Automatic transmission with standard cool or air conditioning—16
  Automatic transmission with super cool or super cool and air conditioning—17

⑨ Manual transmission with standard cool—15
  Automatic transmission with standard cool—16
  Manual and automatic transmission with air conditioning—16
  Manual and automatic transmission with super cool and air conditioning—17
⑩ Without air conditioning—15
  With air conditioning or super cool—18
⑪ Standard and air conditioning—17.5
  Super cool—18.5
⑫ Standard cooling—20
  Air conditioning or super cooling—21
⑬ Rear mounted tank
  F-250 4WD with 133 in. wheelbase
  F-350 except 155 in. wheelbase
  and 133 in. wheelbase with diesel engine—19
  All other F-series—18.2

CAMSHAFT SPECIFICATIONS

Year	VIN	No. Cylinder Displacement cu. in. (liter)	Journal Diameter 1	2	3	4	5	Lobe Lift In.	Lobe Lift Ex.	Bearing Clearance	Camshaft End Play
1988	Y	6-300 (4.9)	2.017–2.018	2.017–2.018	2.017–2.018	2.017–2.018	—	0.247–0.249	0.247–0.249	0.001–0.003	0.001–0.007
	N	8-302 (5.0)	2.0805–2.0815	2.0655–2.0665	2.0505–2.0515	2.0355–2.0365	2.0205–2.0215	0.2375	0.2474	0.001–0.003	0.001–0.007
	H	8-351 (5.8)	2.0805–2.0815	2.0655–2.0665	2.0505–2.0515	2.0355–2.0365	2.0205–2.0215	0.2600	0.2600	0.001–0.003	0.001–0.007
	M	8-445 (7.3)	2.099–2.100	2.099–2.100	2.099–2.100	2.099–2.100	2.099–2.100	NA	NA	0.0015–0.0035	0.002–0.009
	G	8-460 (7.5)	2.1238–2.1248	2.1238–2.1248	2.1238–2.1248	2.1238–2.1248	2.1238–2.1248	0.252	0.278	0.001–0.003	0.001–0.006

Ford Motor Company
BRONCO • F SERIES (PICK-UP) • E SERIES (VAN)

CAMSHAFT SPECIFICATIONS

Year	VIN	No. Cylinder Displacement cu. in. (liter)	Journal Diameter 1	2	3	4	5	Lobe Lift In.	Ex.	Bearing Clearance	Camshaft End Play
1989	Y	6-300 (4.9)	2.017–2.018	2.017–2.018	2.017–2.018	2.017–2.018	—	0.247–0.249	0.247–0.249	0.001–0.003	0.001–0.007
	N	8-302 (5.0)	2.0805–2.0815	2.0655–2.0665	2.0505–2.0515	2.0355–2.0365	2.0205–2.0215	0.2375	0.2474	0.001–0.003	0.001–0.007
	H	8-351 (5.8)	2.0805–2.0815	2.0655–2.0665	2.0505–2.0515	2.0355–2.0365	2.0205–2.0215	0.2600	0.2600	0.001–0.003	0.001–0.007
	M	8-445 (7.3)	2.099–2.100	2.099–2.100	2.099–2.100	2.099–2.100	2.099–2.100	NA	NA	0.0015–0.0035	0.002–0.009
	G	8-460 (7.5)	2.1238–2.1248	2.1238–2.1248	2.1238–2.1248	2.1238–2.1248	2.1238–2.1248	0.252	0.278	0.001–0.003	0.001–0.006
1990	Y	6-300 (4.9)	2.017–2.018	2.017–2.018	2.017–2.018	2.017–2.018	—	0.247–0.249	0.247–0.249	0.001–0.003	0.001–0.007
	N	8-302 (5.0)	2.0805–2.0815	2.0655–2.0665	2.0505–2.0515	2.0355–2.0365	2.0205–2.0215	0.2375	0.2474	0.001–0.003	0.001–0.007
	H	8-351 (5.8)	2.0805–2.0815	2.0655–2.0665	2.0505–2.0515	2.0355–2.0365	2.0205–2.0215	0.2600	0.2600	0.001–0.003	0.001–0.007
	M	8-445 (7.3)	2.099–2.100	2.099–2.100	2.099–2.100	2.099–2.100	2.099–2.100	NA	NA	0.0015–0.0035	0.002–0.009
	G	8-460 (7.5)	2.1238–2.1248	2.1238–2.1248	2.1238–2.1248	2.1238–2.1248	2.1238–2.1248	0.252	0.278	0.001–0.003	0.001–0.006
1991–92	Y	6-300 (4.9)	2.017–2.018	2.017–2.018	2.017–2.018	2.017–2.018	—	0.247–0.249	0.247–0.249	0.001–0.003	0.001–0.007
	N	8-302 (5.0)	2.0805–2.0815	2.0655–2.0665	2.0505–2.0515	2.0355–2.0365	2.0205–2.0215	0.2375	0.2474	0.001–0.003	0.001–0.007
	H	8-351 (5.8)	2.0805–2.0815	2.0655–2.0665	2.0505–2.0515	2.0355–2.0365	2.0205–2.0215	0.2780	0.2830	0.001–0.003	0.001–0.007
	M	8-445 (7.3)	2.099–2.100	2.099–2.100	2.099–2.100	2.099–2.100	2.099–2.100	NA	NA	0.0015–0.0035	0.002–0.009
	G	8-460 (7.5)	2.1238–2.1248	2.1238–2.1248	2.1238–2.1248	2.1238–2.1248	2.1238–2.1248	0.252	0.278	0.001–0.003	0.001–0.006

NA—Not available

CRANKSHAFT AND CONNECTING ROD SPECIFICATIONS

All measurements are given in inches.

Year	VIN	No. Cylinder Displacement cu. in. (liter)	Crankshaft Main. Brg. Journal Dia.	Main Brg. Oil Clearance	Shaft End-play	Thrust on No.	Connecting Rod Journal Diameter	Oil Clearance	Side Clearance
1988	Y	6-300 (4.9)	2.3982–2.3990	0.0010–0.0028	0.004–0.008	5	2.1228–2.1236	0.0007–0.0024	0.006–0.013
	N	8-302 (5.0)	2.2482–2.2490	0.0008–0.0026	0.004–0.008	3	2.1228–2.1236	0.0007–0.0024	0.010–0.020
	H	8-351 (5.8)	2.9994–3.0002	0.0008–0.0026	0.004–0.008	3	2.3103–2.3111	0.0008–0.0025	0.010–0.020
	M	8-445 (7.3)	3.1228–3.1236	0.0018–0.0046	0.0025–0.0085	3	2.4980–2.4990	0.0011–0.0036	0.012–0.024
	G	8-460 (7.5)	2.9994–3.0002	0.0008–0.0026	0.004–0.008	3	2.4992–2.5000	0.0008–0.0025	0.010–0.020

CRANKSHAFT AND CONNECTING ROD SPECIFICATIONS

All measurements are given in inches.

Year	VIN	No. Cylinder Displacement cu. in. (liter)	Crankshaft Main. Brg. Journal Dia.	Crankshaft Main Brg. Oil Clearance	Crankshaft Shaft End-play	Crankshaft Thrust on No.	Connecting Rod Journal Diameter	Connecting Rod Oil Clearance	Connecting Rod Side Clearance
1989	Y	6-300 (4.9)	2.3982–2.3990	0.0010–0.0028	0.004–0.008	5	2.1228–2.1236	0.0007–0.0024	0.006–0.013
	N	8-302 (5.0)	2.2482–2.2490	0.0008–0.0026	0.004–0.008	3	2.1228–2.1236	0.0007–0.0024	0.010–0.020
	H	8-351 (5.8)	2.9994–3.0002	0.0008–0.0026	0.004–0.008	3	2.3103–2.3111	0.0008–0.0025	0.010–0.020
	M	8-445 (7.3)	3.1228–3.1236	0.0018–0.0046	0.0025–0.0085	3	2.4980–2.4990	0.0011–0.0036	0.012–0.024
	G	8-460 (7.5)	2.9994–3.0002	0.0008–0.0026	0.004–0.008	3	2.4992–2.5000	0.0008–0.0025	0.010–0.020
1990	Y	6-300 (4.9)	2.3982–2.3990	0.0010–0.0028	0.004–0.008	5	2.1228–2.1236	0.0007–0.0024	0.006–0.013
	N	8-302 (5.0)	2.2482–2.2490	0.0008–0.0026	0.004–0.008	3	2.1228–2.1236	0.0007–0.0024	0.010–0.020
	H	8-351 (5.8)	2.9994–3.0002	0.0008–0.0026	0.004–0.008	3	2.3103–2.3111	0.0008–0.0025	0.010–0.020
	M	8-445 (7.3)	3.1228–3.1236	0.0018–0.0046	0.0025–0.0085	3	2.4980–2.4990	0.0011–0.0036	0.012–0.024
	G	8-460 (7.5)	2.9994–3.0002	0.0008–0.0026	0.004–0.008	3	2.4992–2.5000	0.0008–0.0025	0.010–0.020
1991–92	Y	6-300 (4.9)	2.3982–2.3990	0.0010–0.0028	0.004–0.008	5	2.1228–2.1236	0.0007–0.0024	0.006–0.013
	N	8-302 (5.0)	2.2482–2.2490	0.0008–0.0026	0.004–0.008	3	2.1228–2.1236	0.0007–0.0024	0.010–0.020
	H	8-351 (5.8)	2.9994–3.0002	0.0008–0.0026	0.004–0.008	3	2.3103–2.3111	0.0008–0.0025	0.010–0.020
	M	8-445 (7.3)	3.1228–3.1236	0.0018–0.0046	0.0025–0.0085	3	2.4980–2.4990	0.0011–0.0036	0.012–0.024
	G	8-460 (7.5)	2.9994–3.0002	0.0008–0.0026	0.004–0.008	3	2.4992–2.5000	0.0008–0.0025	0.010–0.020

VALVE SPECIFICATIONS

Year	VIN	No. Cylinder Displacement cu. in. (liter)	Seat Angle (deg.)	Face Angle (deg.)	Spring Test Pressure (lbs.)	Spring Installed Height (in.)	Stem-to-Guide Clearance (in.) Intake	Stem-to-Guide Clearance (in.) Exhaust	Stem Diameter (in.) Intake	Stem Diameter (in.) Exhaust
1988	Y	6-300 (4.9)	45	44	①	②	0.0010–0.0027	0.0010–0.0027	0.3416–0.3423	0.3416–0.3423
	N	8-302 (5.0)	45	44	③	④	0.0010–0.0027	0.0015–0.0032	0.3416–0.3423	0.3411–0.3418
	H	8-351 (5.8)	45	44	190–210 @ 1.20 in.	⑤	0.0010–0.0027	0.0015–0.0032	0.3416–0.3423	0.3411–0.3418
	M	8-445 (7.3)	⑥	⑥	80 @ 1.833 in.	⑦	0.0055	0.0055	0.37165–0.37235	0.37165–0.37235
	G	8-460 (7.5)	45	44	218–240 @ 1.33 in.	1.80–1.83	0.0010–0.0027	0.0010–0.0027	0.3415–0.3423	0.3415–0.3423

VALVE SPECIFICATIONS

Year	VIN	No. Cylinder Displacement cu. in. (liter)	Seat Angle (deg.)	Face Angle (deg.)	Spring Test Pressure (lbs.)	Spring Installed Height (in.)	Stem-to-Guide Clearance (in.)		Stem Diameter (in.)	
							Intake	Exhaust	Intake	Exhaust
1989	Y	6-300 (4.9)	45	44	①	②	0.0010–0.0027	0.0010–0.0027	0.3416–0.3423	0.3416–0.3423
	N	8-302 (5.0)	45	44	③	④	0.0010–0.0027	0.0015–0.0032	0.3416–0.3423	0.3411–0.3418
	H	8-351 (5.8)	45	44	190–210 @ 1.20 in.	⑤	0.0010–0.0027	0.0015–0.0032	0.3416–0.3423	0.3411–0.3418
	M	8-445 (7.3)	⑥	⑥	80 @ 1.833 in.	⑦	0.0055	0.0055	0.37165–0.37235	0.37165–0.37235
	G	8-460 (7.5)	45	44	218–240 @ 1.33 in.	1.80–1.83	0.0010–0.0027	0.0010–0.0027	0.3415–0.3423	0.3415–0.3423
1990	Y	6-300 (4.9)	45	44	①	②	0.0010–0.0027	0.0010–0.0027	0.3416–0.3423	0.3416–0.3423
	N	8-302 (5.0)	45	44	③	④	0.0010–0.0027	0.0015–0.0032	0.3416–0.3423	0.3411–0.3418
	H	8-351 (5.8)	45	44	190–210 @ 1.20 in.	⑤	0.0010–0.0027	0.0015–0.0032	0.3416–0.3423	0.3411–0.3418
	M	8-445 (7.3)	⑥	⑥	80 @ 1.833 in.	⑦	0.0055	0.0055	0.37165–0.37235	0.37165–0.37235
	G	8-460 (7.5)	45	44	218–240 @ 1.33 in.	1.80–1.83	0.0010–0.0027	0.0010–0.0027	0.3415–0.3423	0.3415–0.3423
1991–92	Y	6-300 (4.9)	45	44	①	②	0.0010–0.0027	0.0010–0.0027	0.3416–0.3423	0.3416–0.3423
	N	8-302 (5.0)	45	44	③	④	0.0010–0.0027	0.0015–0.0032	0.3416–0.3423	0.3411–0.3418
	H	8-351 (5.8)	45	44	190–210 @ 1.20 in.	⑤	0.0010–0.0027	0.0015–0.0032	0.3416–0.3423	0.3411–0.3418
	M	8-445 (7.3)	⑥	⑥	80 @ 1.833 in.	⑦	0.0055	0.0055	0.37165–0.37235	0.37165–0.37235
	G	8-460 (7.5)	45	44	218–240 @ 1.33 in.	1.80–1.83	0.0010–0.0027	0.0010–0.0027	0.3415–0.3423	0.3415–0.3423

① Intake 166–184 @ 1.240 in.
  Exhaust 166–184 @ 1.070 in.
② Intake 1.61–1.67
  Exhaust 1.44–1.50
③ Intake 196–212 @ 1.36 in.
  Exhaust 190–210 @ 1.20 in.
④ Intake 1.67–1.70
  Exhaust 1.58–1.61
⑤ Intake 1.77–1.80
  Exhaust 1.58–1.61
⑥ Intake 30°
  Exhaust 37.5°
⑦ Intake 1.767
  Exhaust 1.833

PISTON AND RING SPECIFICATIONS
All measurements are given in inches.

Year	VIN	No. Cylinder Displacement cu. in. (liter)	Piston Clearance	Ring Gap Top Compression	Ring Gap Bottom Compression	Ring Gap Oil Control	Ring Side Clearance Top Compression	Ring Side Clearance Bottom Compression	Ring Side Clearance Oil Control
1988	Y	6-300 (4.9)	0.0010–0.0018	0.0100–0.0200	0.0100–0.0200	0.0100–0.0350	0.0019–0.0036	0.0020–0.0040	SNUG
	N	8-302 (5.0)	0.0018–0.0026	0.0100–0.0200	0.0100–0.0200	0.0150–0.0350	0.0020–0.0040	0.0020–0.0040	SNUG
	H	8-351 (5.8)	0.0022–0.0030	0.0100–0.0200	0.0100–0.0200	0.0150–0.0350	0.0019–0.0036	0.0020–0.0040	SNUG
	M	8-445 (7.3)	①	0.0130–0.0450	0.0600–0.0850	NA	0.0020–0.0040	0.0020–0.0040	0.0010–0.0030
	G	8-460 (7.5)	0.0022–0.0030	0.0100–0.0200	0.0100–0.0200	0.0100–0.0350	0.0025–0.0045	0.0025–0.0045	SNUG
1989	Y	6-300 (4.9)	0.0010–0.0018	0.0100–0.0200	0.0100–0.0200	0.0150–0.0550	0.0019–0.0036	0.0020–0.0040	SNUG
	N	8-302 (5.0)	0.0013–0.0030	0.0100–0.0200	0.0100–0.0200	0.0150–0.0550	0.0013–0.0033	0.0020–0.0040	SNUG
	H	8-351 (5.8)	0.0018–0.0026	0.0100–0.0200	0.0100–0.0200	0.0150–0.0550	0.0013–0.0033	0.0020–0.0040	SNUG
	M	8-445 (7.3)	①	0.0130–0.0450	0.0600–0.0850	NA	0.0020–0.0040	0.0020–0.0040	0.0010–0.0030
	G	8-460 (7.5)	0.0022–0.0030	0.0100–0.0200	0.0100–0.0200	0.0100–0.0350	0.0025–0.0045	0.0025–0.0045	SNUG
1990	Y	6-300 (4.9)	0.0010–0.0018	0.0100–0.0200	0.0100–0.0200	0.0150–0.0550	0.0019–0.0036	0.0020–0.0040	SNUG
	N	8-302 (5.0)	0.0013–0.0030	0.0100–0.0200	0.0100–0.0200	0.0150–0.0550	0.0013–0.0033	0.0020–0.0040	SNUG
	H	8-351 (5.8)	0.0018–0.0026	0.0100–0.0200	0.0100–0.0200	0.0150–0.0550	0.0013–0.0033	0.0020–0.0040	SNUG
	M	8-445 (7.3)	①	0.0130–0.0450	0.0600–0.0850	NA	0.0020–0.0040	0.0020–0.0040	0.0010–0.0030
	G	8-460 (7.5)	0.0022–0.0030	0.0100–0.0200	0.0100–0.0200	0.0100–0.0350	0.0025–0.0045	0.0025–0.0045	SNUG
1991–92	Y	6-300 (4.9)	0.0010–0.0018	0.0100–0.0200	0.0100–0.0200	0.0150–0.0550	0.0019–0.0036	0.0020–0.0040	SNUG
	N	8-302 (5.0)	0.0013–0.0030	0.0100–0.0200	0.0100–0.0200	0.0150–0.0550	0.0013–0.0033	0.0020–0.0040	SNUG
	H	8-351 (5.8)	0.0018–0.0026	0.0100–0.0200	0.0100–0.0200	0.0150–0.0550	0.0013–0.0033	0.0020–0.0040	SNUG
	M	8-445 (7.3)	①	0.0130–0.0450	0.0600–0.0850	NA	0.0020–0.0040	0.0020–0.0040	0.0010–0.0030
	G	8-460 (7.5)	0.0022–0.0030	0.0100–0.0200	0.0100–0.0200	0.0100–0.0350	0.0025–0.0045	0.0025–0.0045	SNUG

NA—Not available
① Cylinder bores 1–6—0.0055–0.0085
Cylinder bores 7–8—0.0060–0.0085

FORD MOTOR COMPANY
BRONCO • F SERIES (PICK-UP) • E SERIES (VAN)

TORQUE SPECIFICATIONS
All readings in ft. lbs.

Year	VIN	No. Cylinder Displacement cu. in. (liter)	Cylinder Head Bolts	Main Bearing Bolts	Rod Bearing Bolts	Crankshaft Pulley Bolts	Flywheel Bolts	Manifold Intake	Manifold Exhaust	Spark Plugs
1988	Y	6-300 (4.9)	①	60–70	40–45	130–150	75–85	22–32	22–32	10–15
	N	8-302 (5.0)	②	60–70	19–24	70–90	75–85	23–25	18–24	10–15
	H	8-351 (5.8)	③	95–105	40–45	70–90	75–85	23–25	18–24	10–15
	M	8-445 (7.3)	④	⑤	⑥	90	47⑦	24	35	—
	G	8-460 (7.5)	⑧	95–105	40–45	70–90	75–85	⑨	22–30	5–10
1989	Y	6-300 (4.9)	①	60–70	40–45	130–150	75–85	22–32	22–32	10–15
	N	8-302 (5.0)	②	60–70	19–24	70–90	75–85	23–25	18–24	10–15
	H	8-351 (5.8)	③	95–105	40–45	70–90	75–85	23–25	18–24	10–15
	M	8-445 (7.3)	④	⑤	⑥	90	47⑦	24	35	—
	G	8-460 (7.5)	⑧	95–105	40–45	70–90	75–85	⑨	22–30	5–10
1990	Y	6-300 (4.9)	①	60–70	40–45	130–150	75–85	22–32	22–32	10–15
	N	8-302 (5.0)	②	60–70	19–24	70–90	75–85	23–25	18–24	10–15
	H	8-351 (5.8)	③	95–105	40–45	70–90	75–85	23–25	18–24	10–15
	M	8-445 (7.3)	④	⑤	⑥	90	47⑦	24	35	—
	G	8-460 (7.5)	⑧	95–105	40–45	70–90	75–85	⑨	22–30	5–10
1991-92	Y	6-300 (4.9)	①	60–70	40–45	130–150	75–85	22–32	22–32	10–15
	N	8-302 (5.0)	②	60–70	19–24	70–90	75–85	23–25	18–24	10–15
	H	8-351 (5.8)	③	95–105	40–45	70–90	75–85	23–25	18–24	10–15
	M	8-445 (7.3)	④	⑤	⑥	90	47⑦	24	35	—
	G	8-460 (7.5)	⑧	95–105	40–45	70–90	75–85	⑨	22–30	5–10

① Oil the bolt threads and tighten in 3 steps:
Step 1: 50–55
Step 2: 60–65
Step 3: 70–85

② Oil the bolt threads and tighten in 2 steps:
Step 1: 55–65
Step 2: 65–72

③ Oil the bolt threads and tighten in 3 steps:
Step 1: 85
Step 2: 95
Step 3: 105–112

④ Tighten in 4 steps:
Step 1: 65 ft. lbs. in numbered sequence
Step 2: 85 ft. lbs. in numbered sequence
Step 3: 100 ft. lbs. in line sequence
Step 4: 100 ft. lbs. in line sequence

⑤ Tighten in 2 steps:
Step 1: 75
Step 2: 95

⑥ Tighten in 2 steps:
Step 1: 38
Step 2: 51

⑦ Apply threadlocking compound prior to installation

⑧ Tighten in 3 steps:
Step 1: 80–90
Step 2: 100–110
Step 3: 130–140

⑨ Tighten in 3 steps:
Step 1: 8–12
Step 2: 12–22
Step 3: 22–35

BRAKE SPECIFICATIONS
All measurements in inches unless noted

Year	Model	Lug Nut Torque (ft. lbs.)	Master Cylinder Bore	Brake Disc Minimum Thickness	Brake Disc Maximum Runout	Standard Brake Drum Diameter	Minimum Lining Thickness Front	Minimum Lining Thickness Rear
1988	Bronco	100	NA	1.120	①	11.03	②	0.030
	E-150	100	NA	1.120	①	11.03	②	0.030
	E-250	140	NA	1.180	①	12.00	②	0.030
	E-350	140	NA	1.180	①	12.00	②	0.030
	F-150	100	NA	1.120	①	11.03	②	0.030
	F-250	140	NA	1.180	①	12.00	②	0.030
	F-350	140	NA	1.180	①	12.00	②	0.030

BRAKE SPECIFICATIONS
All measurements in inches unless noted

Year	Model	Lug Nut Torque (ft. lbs.)	Master Cylinder Bore	Brake Disc		Standard Brake Drum Diameter	Minimum Lining Thickness	
				Minimum Thickness	Maximum Runout		Front	Rear
1989	Bronco	100	NA	1.120	①	11.03	②	0.030
	E-150	100	NA	1.120	①	11.03	②	0.030
	E-250	140	NA	1.180	①	12.00	②	0.030
	E-350	140	NA	1.180	①	12.00	②	0.030
	F-150	100	NA	1.120	①	11.03	②	0.030
	F-250	140	NA	1.180	①	12.00	②	0.030
	F-350	140	NA	1.180	①	12.00	②	0.030
1990	Bronco	100	NA	1.120	①	11.03	②	0.030
	E-150	100	NA	1.120	①	11.03	②	0.030
	E-250	140	NA	1.180	①	12.00	②	0.030
	E-350	140	NA	1.180	①	12.00	②	0.030
	F-150	100	NA	1.120	①	11.03	②	0.030
	F-250	140	NA	1.180	①	12.00	②	0.030
	F-350	140	NA	1.180	①	12.00	②	0.030
1991-92	Bronco	100	NA	1.120	①	11.03	②	0.030
	E-150	100	NA	1.120	①	11.03	②	0.030
	E-250	140	NA	1.180	①	12.00	②	0.030
	E-350	140	NA	1.180	①	12.00	②	0.030
	F-150	100	NA	1.120	①	11.03	②	0.030
	F-250	140	NA	1.180	①	12.00	②	0.030
	F-350	140	NA	1.180	①	12.00	②	0.030

NA—Not available
① 2WD and 4WD with integral rotor—0.003
  2-piece rotor—0.005
② 0.060 in. above the bonding plate or 0.030 in. above the rivets.

WHEEL ALIGNMENT

Year	Model	Ride Height (in.)	Caster		Camber		Toe-in (in.)	Steering Axis Inclination (deg.)
			Range (deg.)	Preferred Setting (deg.)	Range (deg.)	Preferred Setting (deg.)		
1988	Bronco	3¼-3½	6P-8P	NA	1¾N-¼N	NA	1/32	NA
	Bronco	3½-3¾	5P-7P	NA	¾N-¾P	NA	1/32	NA
	Bronco	4-4¼	4P-6P	NA	¼P-1¾P	NA	1/32	NA
	Bronco	4¼-4½	3P-5P	NA	1¼P-2¾P	NA	1/32	NA
	E150	4-4½	7½P-9½P	NA	1¼N-¼P	NA	1/32	NA
	E150	4½-5	6¼P-8¼P	NA	⅛N-1¼P	NA	1/32	NA
	E150	5-5½	5P-7P	NA	⅞P-2¼P	NA	1/32	NA
	E150	5½-5¾	3¼P-5¼P	NA	1¾P-3¼P	NA	1/32	NA
	E250	3¾-4	7⅝P-9⅝P	NA	¾N-½P	NA	1/32	NA
	E250	4¼-4½	6¼P-8¼P	NA	¼P-1½P	NA	1/32	NA
	E250	4¾-5	5P-7P	NA	1¼P-2½P	NA	1/32	NA

WHEEL ALIGNMENT

Year	Model	Ride Height (in.)	Caster Range (deg.)	Caster Preferred Setting (deg.)	Camber Range (deg.)	Camber Preferred Setting (deg.)	Toe-in (in.)	Steering Axis Inclination (deg.)
1988	E250	5¼–5½	3¾P–5¾P	NA	2¼P–3½P	NA	¹/₃₂	NA
	E350	3¾–4	7⅝P–9⅝P	NA	¾N–½P	NA	¹/₃₂	NA
	E350	4¼–4½	6¼–8¼P	NA	¼P–1½P	NA	¹/₃₂	NA
	E350	4¾–5	5P–7P	NA	1¼P–2½P	NA	¹/₃₂	NA
	E350	5¼–5½	3¾P–5¾P	NA	2¼P–3½P	NA	¹/₃₂	NA
	F150 2WD	3¼–3½	5P–7P	NA	¾N–¾P	NA	¹/₃₂	NA
	F150 2WD	3½–4	4P–6P	NA	¼N–1¼P	NA	¹/₃₂	NA
	F150 2WD	4–4¼	3¼–5¼P	NA	½P–2P	NA	¹/₃₂	NA
	F150 2WD	4¼–4¾	2½P–4½P	NA	2P–3½P	NA	¹/₃₂	NA
	F150 2WD	4¾–5	1½P–3½P	NA	3P–4½P	NA	¹/₃₂	NA
	F150 4WD	3¼–3½	6P–8P	NA	1¾N–¼N	NA	¹/₃₂	NA
	F150 4WD	3½–3¾	5P–7P	NA	¾N–¾P	NA	¹/₃₂	NA
	F150 4WD	4–4¼	4P–6P	NA	¼P–1¾P	NA	¹/₃₂	NA
	F150 4WD	4¼–4½	3P–5P	NA	1¼P–2¾P	NA	¹/₃₂	NA
	F250 2WD	3¼–3½	5¾P–7¾P	NA	1N–½P	NA	³/₃₂	NA
	F250 2WD	3¾–4	4½P–6½P	NA	¼P–1¾P	NA	³/₃₂	NA
	F250 2WD	4¼–4½	3¼P–5¼P	NA	1½P–3P	NA	³/₃₂	NA
	F250 2WD	4¾–5	2¼P–4¼P	NA	2½P–4P	NA	³/₃₂	NA
	F250 2WD	5¼–5¾	1P–3P	NA	3¾P–5¼P	NA	³/₃₂	NA
	F250 4WD	5–5¼	3P–5P	NA	1¾N–¼N	NA	¹/₃₂	NA
	F250 4WD	5½–5¾	3⅛P–5⅛P	NA	¾N–¾P	NA	¹/₃₂	NA
	F250 4WD	6–6¼	3¼P–5¼P	NA	½P–2P	NA	¹/₃₂	NA
	F250 4WD	6¼–6½	3⅜P–5⅜P	NA	1½P–3P	NA	¹/₃₂	NA
	F250 4WD	6¾–7	3½P–5½P	NA	2½P–4P	NA	¹/₃₂	NA
	F350 2WD	3¼–3½	5¾P–7¾P	NA	1N–½P	NA	³/₃₂	NA
	F350 2WD	3¾–4	4½P–6½P	NA	¼P–1¾P	NA	³/₃₂	NA
	F350 2WD	4¼–4½	3¼P–5¼P	NA	1½P–3P	NA	³/₃₂	NA
	F350 2WD	4¾–5	2¼P–4¼P	NA	2½P–4P	NA	³/₃₂	NA
	F350 2WD	5¼–5¾	1P–3P	NA	3¾P–5¼P	NA	³/₃₂	NA
	F350 4WD①	4¾	NA	5P	NA	1½P	¹/₃₂	NA
	F350 4WD②	5–5¼	3P–5P	NA	1¾N–¼N	NA	¹/₃₂	NA
	F350 4WD②	5½–5¾	3⅛P–5⅛P	NA	¾N–¾P	NA	¹/₃₂	NA
	F350 4WD②	6–6¼	3¼P–5¼P	NA	½P–2P	NA	¹/₃₂	NA
	F350 4WD②	6¼–6½	3⅜P–5⅜P	NA	1½P–3P	NA	¹/₃₂	NA
	F350 4WD②	6¾–7	3½P–5½P	NA	2½P–4P	NA	¹/₃₂	NA
1989	Bronco	3¼–3½	5⅛P–7¾P	NA	1⅝N–1P	NA	¹/₃₂	NA
	Bronco	3½–3¾	4½P–7⅛P	NA	1N–1½P	NA	¹/₃₂	NA
	Bronco	4–4¼	3¼P–6½P	NA	0–2¾P	NA	¹/₃₂	NA
	Bronco	4¼–4½	2½P–5¼P	NA	¾P–3½P	NA	¹/₃₂	NA
	E150	3½–3¾	7P–9½P	NA	2N–½P	NA	¹/₃₂	NA
	E150	3¾–4	6½P–9P	NA	1½N–1P	NA	¹/₃₂	NA
	E150	4–4¼	6P–8½P	NA	1N–1½P	NA	¹/₃₂	NA
	E150	4¼–4½	5½P–8P	NA	½N–2P	NA	¹/₃₂	NA
	E150	4½–4¾	5P–7½P	NA	0–2½P	NA	¹/₃₂	NA

WHEEL ALIGNMENT

Year	Model	Ride Height (in.)	Caster Range (deg.)	Caster Preferred Setting (deg.)	Camber Range (deg.)	Camber Preferred Setting (deg.)	Toe-in (in.)	Steering Axis Inclination (deg.)
1989	E150	4¾–5	4½P–7P	NA	½P–3P	NA	1/32	NA
	E150	5–5¼	4P–6½P	NA	1P–3½P	NA	1/32	NA
	E150	5¼–5½	3½P–6P	NA	1½P–4P	NA	1/32	NA
	E250	3¾–4	6P–8½P	NA	1N–1½P	NA	1/32	NA
	E250	4–4¼	5½P–8P	NA	½N–2P	NA	1/32	NA
	E250	4¼–4½	5P–7½P	NA	0–2½P	NA	1/32	NA
	E250	4½–4¾	4½P–7P	NA	½P–3P	NA	1/32	NA
	E250	4¾–5	4P–6½P	NA	1P–3½P	NA	1/32	NA
	E250	5–5¼	3½P–6P	NA	1½P–4P	NA	1/32	NA
	E250	5¼–5½	3P–5½P	NA	2P–4½P	NA	1/32	NA
	E350	3¾–4	6P–8½P	NA	1N–1½P	NA	1/32	NA
	E350	4–4¼	5½P–8P	NA	½N–2P	NA	1/32	NA
	E350	4¼–4½	5P–7½P	NA	0–2½P	NA	1/32	NA
	E350	4½–4¾	4½P–7P	NA	½P–3P	NA	1/32	NA
	E350	4¾–5	4P–6½P	NA	1P–3½P	NA	1/32	NA
	E350	5–5¼	3½P–6P	NA	1½P–4P	NA	1/32	NA
	E350	5¼–5½	3P–5½P	NA	2P–4½P	NA	1/32	NA
	F150 2WD	3¾–4	5¾P–8¼P	NA	1⅝N–1P	NA	1/32	NA
	F150 2WD	4–4¼	4¾P–7¾P	NA	1N–1½P	NA	1/32	NA
	F150 2WD	4¼–4½	4P–6¾P	NA	½N–2P	NA	1/32	NA
	F150 2WD	4½–4¾	3½P–6P	NA	0–2¾P	NA	1/32	NA
	F150 2WD	4¾–5	2¾P–4½P	NA	¾P–3½P	NA	1/32	NA
	F150 4WD	3¼–3½	5⅛P–7¾P	NA	1⅝N–1P	NA	1/32	NA
	F150 4WD	3½–3¾	4½P–7⅛P	NA	1N–1½P	NA	1/32	NA
	F150 4WD	4–4¼	3¼P–6½P	NA	0–2¾P	NA	1/32	NA
	F150 4WD	4¼–4½	2½P–5¼P	NA	¾P–3½P	NA	1/32	NA
	F250 2WD	3¼–3¾	3⅞P–7¼P	NA	1¼N–1¾P	NA	3/32	NA
	F250 2WD	3¾–4¼	2¾P–5⅞P	NA	¼N–3P	NA	3/32	NA
	F250 2WD	4¼–4¾	1½P–4¾P	NA	1P–4P	NA	3/32	NA
	F250 2WD	4¾–5¼	½P–3½P	NA	2P–5P	NA	3/32	NA
	F250 4WD	5–5¼	3P–5P	NA	1¾N–¼N	NA	1/32	NA
	F250 4WD	5½–5¾	3⅛P–5⅛P	NA	¾N–¾P	NA	1/32	NA
	F250 4WD	6–6¼	3¼P–5¼P	NA	½P–2P	NA	1/32	NA
	F250 4WD	6¼–6½	3⅜P–5⅜P	NA	1½P–3P	NA	1/32	NA
	F250 4WD	6¾–7	3½P–5½P	NA	2½P–4P	NA	1/32	NA
	F350 2WD	3¼–3¾	3⅞P–7¼P	NA	1¼N–1¾P	NA	3/32	NA
	F350 2WD	3¾–4¼	2¾P–5⅞P	NA	¼N–3P	NA	3/32	NA
	F350 2WD	4¼–4¾	1½P–4¾P	NA	1P–4P	NA	3/32	NA
	F350 2WD	4¾–5¼	½P–3½P	NA	2P–5P	NA	3/32	NA
	F350 4WD ①	4¾	NA	5P	NA	1½P	1/32	NA
	F350 4WD ②	5–5¼	3P–5P	NA	1¾N–¼N	NA	1/32	NA
	F350 4WD ②	5½–5¾	3⅛P–5⅛P	NA	¾N–¾P	NA	1/32	NA
	F350 4WD ②	6–6¼	3¼P–5¼P	NA	½P–2P	NA	1/32	NA
	F350 4WD ②	6¼–6½	3⅜P–5⅜P	NA	1½P–3P	NA	1/32	NA

WHEEL ALIGNMENT

Year	Model	Ride Height (in.)	Caster Range (deg.)	Caster Preferred Setting (deg.)	Camber Range (deg.)	Camber Preferred Setting (deg.)	Toe-in (in.)	Steering Axis Inclination (deg.)
1989	F350 4WD②	6³⁄₄–7	3¹⁄₂P–5¹⁄₂P	NA	2¹⁄₂P–4P	NA	¹⁄₃₂	NA
1990	Bronco	3¹⁄₄–3¹⁄₂	5¹⁄₈P–7³⁄₄P	NA	1⁵⁄₈N–1P	NA	¹⁄₃₂	NA
	Bronco	3¹⁄₂–3³⁄₄	4¹⁄₂P–7¹⁄₈P	NA	1N–1¹⁄₂P	NA	¹⁄₃₂	NA
	Bronco	4–4¹⁄₄	3¹⁄₄P–6¹⁄₂P	NA	0–2³⁄₄P	NA	¹⁄₃₂	NA
	Bronco	4¹⁄₄–4¹⁄₂	2¹⁄₂P–5¹⁄₄P	NA	³⁄₄P–3¹⁄₂P	NA	¹⁄₃₂	NA
	E150	3¹⁄₂–3³⁄₄	7P–9¹⁄₂P	NA	2N–¹⁄₂P	NA	¹⁄₃₂	NA
	E150	3³⁄₄–4	6¹⁄₂P–9P	NA	1¹⁄₂N–1P	NA	¹⁄₃₂	NA
	E150	4–4¹⁄₄	6P–8¹⁄₂P	NA	1N–1¹⁄₂P	NA	¹⁄₃₂	NA
	E150	4¹⁄₄–4¹⁄₂	5¹⁄₂P–8P	NA	¹⁄₂N–2P	NA	¹⁄₃₂	NA
	E150	4¹⁄₂–4³⁄₄	5P–7¹⁄₂P	NA	0–2¹⁄₂P	NA	¹⁄₃₂	NA
	E150	4³⁄₄–5	4¹⁄₂P–7P	NA	¹⁄₂P–3P	NA	¹⁄₃₂	NA
	E150	5–5¹⁄₄	4P–6¹⁄₂P	NA	1P–3¹⁄₂P	NA	¹⁄₃₂	NA
	E150	5¹⁄₄–5¹⁄₂	3¹⁄₂P–6P	NA	1¹⁄₂P–4P	NA	¹⁄₃₂	NA
	E250	3³⁄₄–4	6P–8¹⁄₂P	NA	1N–1¹⁄₂P	NA	¹⁄₃₂	NA
	E250	4–4¹⁄₄	5¹⁄₂P–8P	NA	¹⁄₂N–2P	NA	¹⁄₃₂	NA
	E250	4¹⁄₄–4¹⁄₂	5P–7¹⁄₂P	NA	0–2¹⁄₂P	NA	¹⁄₃₂	NA
	E250	4¹⁄₂–4³⁄₄	4¹⁄₂P–7P	NA	¹⁄₂P–3P	NA	¹⁄₃₂	NA
	E250	4³⁄₄–5	4P–6¹⁄₂P	NA	1P–3¹⁄₂P	NA	¹⁄₃₂	NA
	E250	5–5¹⁄₄	3¹⁄₂P–6P	NA	1¹⁄₂P–4P	NA	¹⁄₃₂	NA
	E250	5¹⁄₄–5¹⁄₂	3P–5¹⁄₂P	NA	2P–4¹⁄₂P	NA	¹⁄₃₂	NA
	E350	3³⁄₄–4	6P–8¹⁄₂P	NA	1N–1¹⁄₂P	NA	¹⁄₃₂	NA
	E350	4–4¹⁄₄	5¹⁄₂P–8P	NA	¹⁄₂N–2P	NA	¹⁄₃₂	NA
	E350	4¹⁄₄–4¹⁄₂	5P–7¹⁄₂P	NA	0–2¹⁄₂P	NA	¹⁄₃₂	NA
	E350	4¹⁄₂–4³⁄₄	4¹⁄₂P–7P	NA	¹⁄₂P–3P	NA	¹⁄₃₂	NA
	E350	4³⁄₄–5	4P–6¹⁄₂P	NA	1P–3¹⁄₂P	NA	¹⁄₃₂	NA
	E350	5–5¹⁄₄	3¹⁄₂P–6P	NA	1¹⁄₂P–4P	NA	¹⁄₃₂	NA
	E350	5¹⁄₄–5¹⁄₂	3P–5¹⁄₂P	NA	2P–4¹⁄₂P	NA	¹⁄₃₂	NA
	F150 2WD	3³⁄₄–4	5³⁄₄P–8¹⁄₄P	NA	1⁵⁄₈N–1P	NA	¹⁄₃₂	NA
	F150 2WD	4–4¹⁄₄	4³⁄₄P–7³⁄₄P	NA	1N–1¹⁄₂P	NA	¹⁄₃₂	NA
	F150 2WD	4¹⁄₄–4¹⁄₂	4P–6³⁄₄P	NA	¹⁄₂N–2P	NA	¹⁄₃₂	NA
	F150 2WD	4¹⁄₂–4³⁄₄	3¹⁄₂P–6P	NA	0–2³⁄₄P	Setting	¹⁄₃₂	NA
	F150 2WD	4³⁄₄–5	2³⁄₄P–4¹⁄₂P	NA	³⁄₄P–3¹⁄₂P	NA	¹⁄₃₂	NA
	F150 4WD②	3¹⁄₄–3¹⁄₂	5¹⁄₈P–7³⁄₄P	NA	1⁵⁄₈N–1P	NA	¹⁄₃₂	NA
	F150 4WD	3¹⁄₂–3³⁄₄	4¹⁄₂P–7¹⁄₈P	NA	1N–1¹⁄₂P	NA	¹⁄₃₂	NA
	F150 4WD	4–4¹⁄₄	3¹⁄₄P–6¹⁄₂P	NA	0–2³⁄₄P	NA	¹⁄₃₂	NA
	F150 4WD	4¹⁄₄–4¹⁄₂	2¹⁄₂P–5¹⁄₄P	NA	³⁄₄P–3¹⁄₂P	NA	¹⁄₃₂	NA
	F250 2WD	3¹⁄₄–3³⁄₄	3⁷⁄₈P–7¹⁄₄P	NA	1¹⁄₄N–1³⁄₄P	NA	³⁄₃₂	NA
	F250 2WD	3³⁄₄–4¹⁄₄	2³⁄₄P–5⁷⁄₈P	NA	¹⁄₄N–3P	NA	³⁄₃₂	NA
	F250 2WD	4¹⁄₄–4³⁄₄	1¹⁄₂P–4³⁄₄P	NA	1P–4P	NA	³⁄₃₂	NA
	F250 2WD	4³⁄₄–5¹⁄₄	¹⁄₂P–3¹⁄₂P	NA	2P–5P	NA	³⁄₃₂	NA
	F250 4WD	5–5¹⁄₄	3P–5P	NA	1³⁄₄N–¹⁄₄N	NA	¹⁄₃₂	NA
	F250 4WD	5¹⁄₂–5³⁄₄	3¹⁄₈P–5¹⁄₈P	NA	³⁄₄N–³⁄₄P	NA	¹⁄₃₂	NA
	F250 4WD	6–6¹⁄₄	3¹⁄₄P–5¹⁄₄P	NA	¹⁄₂P–2P	NA	¹⁄₃₂	NA
	F250 4WD	6¹⁄₄–6¹⁄₂	3³⁄₈P–5³⁄₈P	NA	1¹⁄₂P–3P	NA	¹⁄₃₂	NA

WHEEL ALIGNMENT

Year	Model	Ride Height (in.)	Caster Range (deg.)	Caster Preferred Setting (deg.)	Camber Range (deg.)	Camber Preferred Setting (deg.)	Toe-in (in.)	Steering Axis Inclination (deg.)
1990	F250 4WD	6³/₄–7	3¹/₂P–5¹/₂P	NA	2¹/₂P–4P	NA	¹/₃₂	NA
	F350 2WD	3¹/₄–3³/₄	3⁷/₈P–7¹/₄P	NA	1¹/₄N–1³/₄P	NA	³/₃₂	NA
	F350 2WD	3³/₄–4¹/₄	2³/₄P–5⁷/₈P	NA	¹/₄N–3P	NA	³/₃₂	NA
	F350 2WD	4¹/₄–4³/₄	1¹/₂P–4³/₄P	NA	1P–4P	NA	³/₃₂	NA
	F350 2WD	4³/₄–5¹/₄	¹/₂P–3¹/₂P	NA	2P–5P	NA	³/₃₂	NA
	F350 4WD①	4³/₄	NA	5P	NA	1¹/₂P	¹/₃₂	NA
	F350 4WD②	5–5¹/₄	3P–5P	NA	1³/₄N–¹/₄N	NA	¹/₃₂	NA
	F350 4WD②	5¹/₂–5³/₄	3¹/₈P–5¹/₈P	NA	³/₄N–³/₄P	NA	¹/₃₂	NA
	F350 4WD②	6–6¹/₄	3¹/₄P–5¹/₄P	NA	¹/₂P–2P	NA	¹/₃₂	NA
	F350 4WD②	6¹/₄–6¹/₂	3³/₈P–5³/₈P	NA	1¹/₂P–3P	NA	¹/₃₂	NA
	F350 4WD②	6³/₄–7	3¹/₂P–5¹/₂P	NA	2¹/₂P–4P	NA	¹/₃₂	NA
1991–92	Bronco	3¹/₄–3¹/₂	5¹/₈P–7³/₄P	NA	1⁵/₈N–1P	NA	¹/₃₂	NA
	Bronco	3¹/₂–3³/₄	4¹/₂P–7¹/₈P	NA	1N–1¹/₂P	NA	¹/₃₂	NA
	Bronco	4–4¹/₄	3¹/₄P–6¹/₂P	NA	0–2³/₄P	NA	¹/₃₂	NA
	Bronco	4¹/₄–4¹/₂	2¹/₂P–5¹/₄P	NA	³/₄P–3¹/₂P	NA	¹/₃₂	NA
	E150	3¹/₂–3³/₄	7P–9¹/₂P	NA	2N–¹/₂P	NA	¹/₃₂	NA
	E150	3³/₄–4	6¹/₂P–9P	NA	1¹/₂N–1P	NA	¹/₃₂	NA
	E150	4–4¹/₄	6P–8¹/₂P	NA	1N–1¹/₂P	NA	¹/₃₂	NA
	E150	4¹/₄–4¹/₂	5¹/₂P–8P	NA	¹/₂N–2P	NA	¹/₃₂	NA
	E150	4¹/₂–4³/₄	5P–7¹/₂P	NA	0–2¹/₂P	NA	¹/₃₂	NA
	E150	4³/₄–5	4¹/₂P–7P	NA	¹/₂P–3P	NA	¹/₃₂	NA
	E150	5–5¹/₄	4P–6¹/₂P	NA	1P–3¹/₂P	NA	¹/₃₂	NA
	E150	5¹/₄–5¹/₂	3¹/₂P–6P	NA	1¹/₂P–4P	NA	¹/₃₂	NA
	E250	3³/₄–4	6P–8¹/₂P	NA	1N–1¹/₂P	NA	¹/₃₂	NA
	E250	4–4¹/₄	5¹/₂P–8P	NA	¹/₂N–2P	NA	¹/₃₂	NA
	E250	4¹/₄–4¹/₂	5P–7¹/₂P	NA	0–2¹/₂P	NA	¹/₃₂	NA
	E250	4¹/₂–4³/₄	4¹/₂P–7P	NA	¹/₂P–3P	NA	¹/₃₂	NA
	E250	4³/₄–5	4P–6¹/₂P	NA	1P–3¹/₂P	NA	¹/₃₂	NA
	E250	5–5¹/₄	3¹/₂P–6P	NA	1¹/₂P–4P	NA	¹/₃₂	NA
	E250	5¹/₄–5¹/₂	3P–5¹/₂P	NA	2P–4¹/₂P	NA	¹/₃₂	NA
	E350	3³/₄–4	6P–8¹/₂P	NA	1N–1¹/₂P	NA	¹/₃₂	NA
	E350	4–4¹/₄	5¹/₂P–8P	NA	¹/₂N–2P	NA	¹/₃₂	NA
	E350	4¹/₄–4¹/₂	5P–7¹/₂P	NA	0–2¹/₂P	NA	¹/₃₂	NA
	E350	4¹/₂–4³/₄	4¹/₂P–7P	NA	¹/₂P–3P	NA	¹/₃₂	NA
	E350	4³/₄–5	4P–6¹/₂P	NA	1P–3¹/₂P	NA	¹/₃₂	NA
	E350	5–5¹/₄	3¹/₂P–6P	NA	1¹/₂P–4P	NA	¹/₃₂	NA
	E350	5¹/₄–5¹/₂	3P–5¹/₂P	NA	2P–4¹/₂P	NA	¹/₃₂	NA
	F150 2WD	3³/₄–4	5³/₄P–8¹/₄P	NA	1⁵/₈N–1P	NA	¹/₃₂	NA
	F150 2WD	4–4¹/₄	4³/₄P–7³/₄P	NA	1N–1¹/₂P	NA	¹/₃₂	NA
	F150 2WD	4¹/₄–4¹/₂	4P–6³/₄P	NA	¹/₂N–2P	NA	¹/₃₂	NA
	F150 2WD	4¹/₂–4³/₄	3¹/₂P–6P	NA	0–2³/₄P	NA	¹/₃₂	NA
	F150 2WD	4³/₄–5	2³/₄P–4¹/₂P	NA	³/₄P–3¹/₂P	NA	¹/₃₂	NA
	F150 4WD	3¹/₄–3¹/₂	5¹/₈P–7³/₄P	NA	1⁵/₈N–1P	NA	¹/₃₂	NA
	F150 4WD	3¹/₂–3³/₄	4¹/₂P–7¹/₈P	NA	1N–1¹/₂P	NA	¹/₃₂	NA

WHEEL ALIGNMENT

Year	Model	Ride Height (in.)	Caster Range (deg.)	Caster Preferred Setting (deg.)	Camber Range (deg.)	Camber Preferred Setting (deg.)	Toe-in (in.)	Steering Axis Inclination (deg.)
1991-92	F150 4WD	4-4¼	3¼P-6½P	NA	0-2¾P	NA	¹⁄₃₂	NA
	F150 4WD	4¼-4½	2½P-5¼P	NA	¾P-3½P	NA	¹⁄₃₂	NA
	F250 2WD	3¼-3¾	3⅞P-7¼P	NA	1¼N-1¾P	NA	³⁄₃₂	NA
	F250 2WD	3¾-4¼	2¾P-5⅞P	NA	¼N-3P	NA	³⁄₃₂	NA
	F250 2WD	4¼-4¾	1½P-4¾P	NA	1P-4P	NA	³⁄₃₂	NA
	F250 2WD	4¾-5¼	½P-3½P	NA	2P-5P	NA	³⁄₃₂	NA
	F250 4WD	5-5¼	3P-5P	NA	1¾N-¼N	NA	¹⁄₃₂	NA
	F250 4WD	5½-5¾	3⅛P-5⅛P	NA	¾N-¾P	NA	¹⁄₃₂	NA
	F250 4WD	6-6¼	3¼P-5¼P	NA	½P-2P	NA	¹⁄₃₂	NA
	F250 4WD	6¼-6½	3⅜P-5⅜P	NA	1½P-3P	NA	¹⁄₃₂	NA
	F250 4WD	6¾-7	3½P-5½P	NA	2½P-4P	NA	¹⁄₃₂	NA
	F350 2WD	3¼-3¾	3⅞P-7¼P	NA	1¼N-1¾P	NA	³⁄₃₂	NA
	F350 2WD	3¾-4¼	2¾P-5⅞P	NA	¼N-3P	NA	³⁄₃₂	NA
	F350 2WD	4¼-4¾	1½P-4¾P	NA	1P-4P	NA	³⁄₃₂	NA
	F350 2WD	4¾-5¼	½P-3½P	NA	2P-5P	NA	³⁄₃₂	NA
	F350 4WD①	4¾	NA	5P	NA	1½P	¹⁄₃₂	NA
	F350 4WD②	5-5¼	3P-5P	NA	1¾N-¼N	NA	¹⁄₃₂	NA
	F350 4WD②	5½-5¾	3⅛P-5⅛P	NA	¾N-¾P	NA	¹⁄₃₂	NA
	F350 4WD②	6-6¼	3¼P-5¼P	NA	½P-2P	NA	¹⁄₃₂	NA
	F350 4WD②	6¼-6½	3⅜P-5⅜P	NA	1½P-3P	NA	¹⁄₃₂	NA
	F350 4WD②	6¾-7	3½P-5½P	NA	2½P-4P	NA	¹⁄₃₂	NA

NA—Not available
N—Negative
P—Positive
① With monobeam suspension
② Except monobeam suspension

ENGINE ELECTRICAL

NOTE: Disconnecting the negative battery cable on some vehicles may interfere with the functions of the on board computer systems and may require the computer to undergo a relearning process, once the negative battery cable is reconnected.

Distributor

Removal

1. Disconnect the negative battery cable.
2. Mark the position of the No. 1 cylinder wire tower on the distributor base. Remove the distributor cap and position the cap and ignition wires to the side.
3. Disconnect the wiring harness plug from the distributor connector. Disconnect and plug the vacuum hoses from the vacuum diaphragm assembly, if equipped.
4. Rotate the engine, in normal direction of rotation, until No. 1 piston is on Top Dead Center (TDC) of the compression stroke. The TDC mark on the crankshaft pulley and the pointer on the timing cover should align. The rotor tip should be pointing at the No. 1 spark plug wire position on the distributor cap.
5. Scribe a mark on the distributor body and the engine to in-dicate the position of the rotor tip and the position of the distributor in the engine.
6. Remove the hold-down bolt and clamp located at the base of the distributor. Remove the distributor from the engine. Pay attention to the direction the rotor tip points if it moves from the No. 1 position when the drive gear disengages. For reinstallation purposes, the rotor should be at this point to insure proper gear mesh and timing.
7. Avoid turning the engine, if possible, while the distributor is removed. If the engine is turned from TDC position, TDC timing marks will have to be reset before the distributor is installed.

Installation

NOTE: Before installing, visually inspect the distributor. The drive gear should be free of nicks, cracks and excessive wear. The distributor drive shaft should move freely, without binding. If equipped with an O-ring, it should fit tightly and be free of cuts.

TIMING NOT DISTURBED

1. Position the distributor in the engine with the rotor aligned to the marks made on the distributor or at the position

the rotor pointed when the distributor was removed. Engage the oil pump intermediate shaft and insert the distributor until fully seated on the engine. If the distributor does not fully seat, turn the engine slightly to fully engage the intermediate shaft.

2. After the distributor has been fully seated into the block, recheck the timing mark and rotor alignment. Install the hold-down clamp and bolt. Snug the mounting bolt so the distributor can be turned for ignition timing purposes.

3. Install the distributor cap and connect the distributor to the wiring harness.

4. Connect the negative battery cable. Check and, if necessary, set the ignition timing. Tighten the distributor hold-down clamp bolt to 17–25 ft. lbs. (23–34 Nm). Recheck the ignition timing after tightening the bolt.

5. If equipped, connect the vacuum diaphragm hoses.

TIMING DISTURBED

If the engine was cranked with the distributor removed, the following procedure will enable the proper setting of the timing.

1. Disconnect the No. 1 spark plug wire and remove the No. 1 spark plug.

2. Place a finger over the spark plug hole and crank the engine slowly until compression is felt.

3. Align the TDC mark on the crankshaft pulley with the pointer on the timing cover. This places the No. 1 cylinder at TDC on the compression stroke.

4. Turn the distributor shaft until the rotor points to the No. 1 spark plug tower on the cap.

5. Install the distributor into the engine, aligning the marks made on the block and the distributor housing. Install the distributor hold-down clamp and bolt. Snug the bolt so the distributor housing can be moved for timing purposes.

6. Install the No. 1 spark plug and connect the spark plug wire. Install the distributor cap and connect the distributor to the wiring harness.

7. Connect the negative battery cable and set the ignition timing. Tighten the distributor hold-down clamp bolt to 17–25 ft. lbs. (23–34 Nm). Recheck the ignition timing after tightening the bolt.

8. If equipped, connect the vacuum diaphragm hoses.

Ignition Timing

Adjustment

1. Locate the timing marks and pointer on the crankshaft pulley and the timing cover. Clean the marks so they will be visible with a timing light. Apply chalk or bright-colored paint, if necessary.

2. Place the transaxle in **P** or **N**. The air conditioning and heater controls should be in the **OFF** position.

3. On Non-EEC systems, disconnect the vacuum hoses from the distributor vacuum advance connection at the distributor and plug the hoses.

4. Connect a suitable inductive timing light and a tachometer according to the manufacturer's instructions.

5. On EEC-IV systems, disconnect the single wire in-line spout connector or remove the shorting bar from the double wire spout connector.

6. On Non-EEC systems, if equipped with a barometric pressure switch, disconnect it from the ignition module and place a jumper wire across the pins at the ignition module connector (yellow and black wires).

7. Start the engine and allow it to warm up to operating temperature.

NOTE: To set timing correctly, a remote starter should not be used. Use the ignition key only to start the vehicle. Disconnecting the start wire at the starter relay will cause the TFI module to revert to start mode timing after the vehicle is started. Reconnecting the start wire after the vehicle is running will not correct the timing.

8. With the engine at the timing rpm specified, check the initial timing by aiming the timing light at the timing marks and

Thick Film Integrated (TFI) ignition system with universal distributor

pointer. Refer to the underhood Vehicle Emission Information Label for specifications.

9. If the marks align, proceed to Step 10. If the marks do not align, shut off the engine and loosen the distributor hold-down clamp bolt. Start the engine, aim the timing light and turn the distributor until the timing marks align. Shut off the engine and tighten the distributor hold-down clamp bolt.

10. On EEC-IV systems, reconnect the single wire in-line spout connector or reinstall the shorting bar on the double wire spout connector. Check the timing advance to verify the distributor is advancing beyond the initial setting.

11. Remove the timing light and the tachometer.

12. On Non-EEC systems, unplug and reconnect the vacuum hoses. Remove the jumper wire from the ignition connector and reconnect, if applicable.

Alternator

For further information, please refer to "Alternators" in the Unit Repair section.

Precautions

Several precautions must be observed with alternator equipped vehicles to avoid damage to the unit.

• If the battery is removed for any reason, make sure it is reconnected with the correct polarity. Reversing the battery connections may result in damage to the one-way rectifiers.

• When utilizing a booster battery as a starting aid, always connect the positive to positive terminals and the negative terminal from the booster battery to a good engine ground on the vehicle being started.

• Never use a fast charger as a booster to start vehicles.

• Disconnect the battery cables when charging the battery with a fast charger.

• Never attempt to polarize the alternator.

• Do not use test lights of more than 12V when checking diode continuity.

• Do not short across or ground any of the alternator terminals.

• The polarity of the battery, alternator and regulator must be matched and considered before making any electrical connections within the system.

• Never separate the alternator on an open circuit. Make sure all connections within the circuit are clean and tight.

• Disconnect the battery ground terminal when performing any service on electrical components.

• Disconnect the battery if arc welding is to be done on the vehicle.

Belt Tension Adjustment

4.9L, 5.0L AND 5.8L ENGINES

Alternator belt tension is maintained by an automatic tensioner on these engines. Correct belt tension will be maintained if the correct length belt is on the engine. The tensioner is working properly if the belt length indicator mark on the tensioner is between the maximum and minimum marks.

7.3L AND 7.5L ENGINES

1. Position a suitable belt tension gauge midway on the longest accessible belt span.

2. Loosen the alternator adjustment and pivot bolts just enough to move the alternator.

3. Place a "C" clamp over the end of the adjusting arm and the adjusting bolt boss and tighten the belt to the correct tension. The correct tension is as follows:

7.3L engine with new belt—140–180 lbs.

7.3L engine with used belt (over 5 minutes engine operation)—95–115 lbs.

7.5L engine with new belt—160–200 lbs.

7.5L engine with used belt (over 5 minutes engine operation)—110–130 lbs.

Automatic belt tensioner—4.9L engine

Automatic belt tensioner—5.0L and 5.8L engines

Checking alternator belt tension

Diesel glow plug testing

4. Tighten the adjustment bolt to 30–40 ft. lbs. (40–55 Nm) and remove the "C" clamp.

5. Tighten the pivot bolt to 40–50 ft. lbs. (55–70 Nm). Check and readjust the belt tension, if necessary.

6. Start the engine and let it idle for 5 minutes.

7. Stop the engine and recheck the belt tension. If the tension is less than the used belt specification, then reset the belt tension to within the used belt tension limits.

8. If the belt will not hold tension, it must be replaced.

Removal and Installation

1. Disconnect the negative battery cable.
2. Disconnect the electrical connectors from the alternator.
3. Remove the alternator belt.
4. Remove the alternator mounting bolts and the alternator. Remove the alternator fan shield, if equipped.
5. Installation is the reverse of the removal procedure. Adjust the belt tension, if necessary.

Voltage Regulator

For further information, please refer to "Alternators" in the Unit Repair section.

Removal and Installation

NOTE: Always disconnect the connector plug from the regulator before removing the regulator mounting screws. Removing the connector from an ungrounded regulator with the ignition switch in RUN will destroy the regulator.

1. Disconnect the negative battery cable.
2. Disconnect the regulator from the wiring harness.
3. Remove the regulator mounting screws.
4. Installation is the reverse of the removal procedure.

Starter

For further information, please refer to "Starters" in the Unit Repair section.

Removal and Installation

1. Disconnect the negative battery cable.
2. Raise the vehicle and support it safely.
3. Disconnect the starter cable at the starter terminal.
4. Remove the starter mounting bolts and remove the starter.

To install:

5. Position the starter assembly to the flywheel housing and start the mounting bolts.

6. Snug all the bolts while holding the starter squarely against its mounting surface and fully inserted into the pilot hole. Tighten the bolts to 15–20 ft. lbs. (21–27 Nm).

7. Reconnect the starter cable at the starter terminal. Lower the vehicle. Connect the negative battery cable.

Diesel Glow Plugs

Removal and Installation

1. Disconnect the negative battery cable. Disconnect the glow plug electrical leads.

2. Remove the glow plugs by unscrewing them from the cylinder head.

3. Inspect the tips of the plugs for any evidence of distortion or missing tip ends and replace, as necessary.

4. Installation is the reverse of the removal procedure.

Testing

1. Turn the ignition switch OFF and disconnect the electrical connectors from the glow plugs.

2. Using a test light, check for continuity between the glow plug terminal and a power source with the glow plugs installed in the engine.

3. If there is no continuity, the glow plug must be replaced.

CHASSIS ELECTRICAL

Heater Blower Motor

Removal and Installation

1. Disconnect the negative battery cable.

2. If equipped, remove the emission module forward of the blower motor.

3. Disconnect the blower motor wiring connector.

4. Disconnect the blower motor cooling tube at the blower motor.

5. Remove the screws attaching the blower motor and wheel to the blower housing.

6. Holding the cooling tube aside, pull the blower motor and wheel from the heater blower assembly and remove it from the vehicle.

7. Remove the hub clamp and remove the blower wheel from the blower motor shaft.

To install:

8. Install the blower wheel onto the blower motor shaft. Install the hub clamp.

9. Holding the cooling tube aside, position the blower motor and wheel in the blower housing and install the attaching screws.

10. Connect the blower motor cooling tube and the wire harness connector.

11. If equipped, install the emission module forward of the blower motor.

12. Connect the negative battery cable and check the blower motor for proper operation.

Windshield Wiper Motor

Removal and Installation

1. Disconnect the negative battery cable.
2. On E series, remove the fuse panel and bracket assembly.
3. Remove both wiper arm and blade assemblies.
4. Disconnect the washer nozzle hose, if necessary and remove the cowl grille assembly.
5. Remove the wiper linkage clip from the motor output arm.
6. Disconnect the motor wiring connector.
7. Remove the 3 attaching screws and remove the motor.
8. Installation is the reverse of removal procedure. Always ensure the wiper motor is in the park position before installing. Torque the wiper motor retaining screws to 60–85 inch lbs. (6.7–9.5 Nm).

A/C EVAPORATOR LOWER HOUSING

A/C EVAPORATOR CASE TO DASH PANEL LOWER GASKET

A/C BLOWER MOTOR RESISTOR ASSY.

CLAMP

A/C BLOWER WHEEL

A/C BLOWER MOTOR ASSY.

BLOWER MOTOR ELECTRICAL CONNECTOR

A/C BLOWER HOUSING TO BLOWER MOTOR TUBE

Blower motor and wheel installation—E Series

SUCTION ACCUMULATOR DRIER

BLOWER MOTOR

BLOWER WHEEL

GASKET

SCREW

RETAINER

EVAPORATOR CASE (R.H.)

Blower motor and wheel installation—Bronco and F Series

Windshield Wiper Switch

Removal and Installation

BRONCO AND F SERIES

1. Disconnect the negative battery cable.
2. Remove the wiper switch knob, bezel nut and bezel.
3. Pull out the switch from under the instrument panel.
4. Disconnect the electrical connector from the switch and remove the switch.
5. Installation is the reverse of the removal procedure.

E SERIES

1. Disconnect the negative battery cable.
2. Remove the windshield wiper switch knob.
3. Remove the ignition switch bezel.
4. Remove the headlight switch knob and shaft by pulling the switch to the **ON** position. Then, depress the button on the top of the switch and pull the knob and shaft out.
5. Remove the 2 screws at the bottom of the finish panel, then pry the 2 upper retainers away from the instrument panel.
6. Disconnect the connector from the switch.
7. Remove the attaching screws and remove the switch.
8. Installation is the reverse of the removal procedure.

Instrument Cluster

Removal and Installation

BRONCO AND F SERIES

1. Disconnect the negative battery cable.
2. Remove the wiper/washer knob, using a hook tool to release each knob lock tab.
3. Remove the knob from the headlight switch. Remove the fog light switch knob, if equipped.
4. Remove the steering column shroud.

NOTE: If equipped with an automatic transmission, use care so as not to damage the transmission control selector indicator cable.

WIPER SWITCH ASSEMBLY

SCREW

SCREW

HEADLAMP SWITCH BUTTON

WIPER CONTROL KNOB

IGNITION SWITCH

HEADLAMP SWITCH

RETAINING CLIP

FINISH PANEL

BEZEL

LIGHT SWITCH KNOB

Windshield wiper switch installation—E Series

5. If equipped with an automatic transmission, remove the loop on the indicator cable assembly from the retainer pin. Remove the screw from the cable bracket and slide the bracket out of the slot in the tube.
6. Remove the cluster finish panel assembly.

Instrument cluster exploded view—E Series

7. Remove the 4 cluster attaching screws and disconnect the speedometer cable. Disconnect the wire connectors from the printed circuit and remove the cluster.

To install:

8. Position the cluster to the opening and connect the 2 connectors. Connect the speedometer cable and install the 4 cluster retaining screws.

9. If equipped with and automatic transmission, place the loop on the transmission indicator cable assembly over the retainer on the column.

10. Position the tab on the transmission indicator cable bracket into the slot on the column. Align the transmission indicator pointer and attach the screw. Adjust the transmission indicator as follows:

 a. With the engine off and the parking brake applied, place the transmission selector lever at the steering column in **D** or **OD** for automatic overdrive transmissions.

 b. Hold the lever against the **D** or **OD** stop using an approximate 8 lb. weight attached to the selector lever knob.

 c. Adjust the transmission indicator bracket to position the indicator in the rectangular adjustment band and attach the screw, taking care not to move the indicator.

 d. Change the transmission lever to **P** position and check the transmission indicator pointer. Shift the transmission lever to all shift positions and check the transmission indicator pointer position on each transmission shift position, verifying adjustment.

NOTE: The transmission indicator should only be adjusted using the adjustment window in the primary drive position and not adjusted in any other position.

11. Install the trim finish panel assembly and the column shroud.

12. Install the headlight switch knob. If equipped, install the fog light switch.

13. Install the wiper/washer control knobs.

14. Connect the negative battery cable. Check the operation of all gauges, lights, signals and transmission indicator pointer.

E SERIES

1. Disconnect the negative battery cable.

2. Remove the steering column shroud, if necessary.

3. If equipped with a tilt steering column, loosen the bolts which attach the column to the band support to provide sufficient clearance for cluster removal.

4. Remove the 7 cluster to panel retaining screws.

5. Position the cluster slightly away from the panel in order to disconnect the speedometer cable.

NOTE: If there is not sufficient access to disengage the speedometer cable from the speedometer, it may be necessary to remove the speedometer cable at the transmission and pull the cable through the cowl, to allow room to reach the speedometer quick disconnect.

6. Disconnect the harness connector plug from the printed circuit and remove the cluster assembly.

7. Installation is the reverse of the removal procedure. Before installation, apply an approximately $^3/_{16}$ in. diameter ball of silicone dielectric compound in the drive hole of the speedometer head.

Speedometer

Removal and Installation

1. Disconnect the negative battery cable. Remove the instrument cluster.

2. Remove the lens and mask from the cluster.

CABLE ASSEMBLY

SPEEDOMETER SHAFT

PRESS FLAT SURFACE AND PULL CABLE AWAY FROM SPEEDOMETER HEAD (PLACE INDEX FINGER ON METAL TUBE AND THUMB ON PLASTIC RING FLAT SURFACE)

Speedometer cable quick disconnect

3. Remove the 2 speedometer attaching screws and remove the speedometer.

4. Installation is the reverse of the removal procedure.

5. If a new speedometer is being installed, examine the square drive hole for sufficient lubrication. If lubrication is needed, apply a $^3/_{16}$ in. diamter dab of silicone grease in the drive hole.

Headlight Switch

Removal and Installation

BRONCO AND F SERIES

1. Disconnect the negative battery cable.

2. Remove the wiper/washer and headlight switch knobs using a hook tool to release each knob lock tab.

3. Remove the fog light switch knob, if equipped.

4. Remove the steering column shroud, if necessary and remove the cluster finish panel.

5. Unscrew the mounting nut and remove the switch from the instrument panel, then disconnect the wiring connector from the switch.

6. Installation is the reverse of the removal procedure.

E SERIES

1. Disconnect the negative battery cable.

2. Pull the headlight switch knob to the full **ON** position. Depress the shaft release button on the switch housing and pull the knob and shaft assembly out of the switch.

3. Unscrew the mounting nut. Remove the switch, then disconnect the wiring connector from the switch.

4. Installation is the reverse of the removal procedure. When installing the knob and shaft assembly, insert it all the way into the switch until a distinct click is heard. It may be necessary to rotate the shaft slightly until it engages the switch-contact carrier.

Dimmer Switch

Removal and Installation

1. Disconnect the negative battery cable.

2. Pull back the floor mat or carpet in the area of the switch. Remove the dimmer switch retaining screws.

3. Disconnect the electrical connection from the switch.

4. Installation is the reverse of the removal procedure.

Headlight switch—E Series

Turn Signal Switch

Removal and Installation

1. Disconnect the negative battery cable.
2. Remove the horn switch.
3. Remove the steering wheel.
4. Unscrew the turn signal switch lever from the steering column.
5. Remove the steering column shroud. On E Series, remove the steering column opening cover.
6. Disconnect the switch wiring connector plug by lifting up on the tabs and separating. Remove the screws that secure the switch to the column.
7. On Bronco and F Series equipped with a fixed column, remove the switch by lifting it out of the column and guiding the connector plug through the opening in the shift socket.
8. On E series equipped with a fixed column, proceed as follows:
    a. If equipped with an automatic transmission, remove the transmission indicator light assembly from the shift socket.
    b. Lift the switch and, if equipped, the transmission indicator light harness out of the column and guide the connector plug through the openings in the brake and clutch pedal support bracket and the shift socket.
    c. If the turn signal switch is to be replaced, the connector plug must be disassembled to remove the transmission indicator light and attaching harness. The transmission indicator light must be reused with the replacement switch.
9. Vehicles equipped with a tilt column require disassembly of the turn signal switch harness plug before removing the switch from the column, as the opening in the shift socket provided for the wiring harness is not large enough for the connector plug to pass through.

NOTE: On E Series, note the positions of each wire in the connector for reinstallation purposes. The color code sequence for this connector does not coincide with the color code of the wires in the harness connector plug.

10. On E series with automatic transmission, remove the transmission indicator light wire from the turn signal switch harness sheath prior to removal of the switch from the column.
11. Installation is the reverse of the removal procedure. Tighten the turn signal lever to 10–20 inch lbs. (1.2–2.2 Nm) and the steering wheel nut to 30–40 ft. lbs. (41–54 Nm).

Turn signal switch wire connector removal

Turn signal switch connector wire terminal removal— tilt wheel only

Ignition Lock

Removal and Installation

WITH KEY

1. Disconnect the negative battery cable.
2. If equipped with a fixed column, remove the steering wheel.
3. If equipped with an automatic transmission, place the shift lever in **P**.
4. Turn the lock cylinder with the ignition key to the **ON** position.
5. Place a ⅛ in. (3.17mm) diameter wire pin or small drift punch and depress the retaining pin while pulling out on the

IGNITION CYLINDER
IN "ON" POSITION

RETAINING
PIN

Lock retaining pin access slot—fixed column

lock cylinder to remove it from the column housing. The pin is located inside the column near the base of the lock cylinder on fixed column vehicles. On tilt column vehicles, the pin is located near the hazard warning button.

To install:

6. Lubricate the lock cylinder with grease.
7. Turn the lock cylinder to the **ON** position and depress the retaining pin, then insert the lock cylinder into its housing in the flange casting.
8. Make sure the cylinder is fully seated and aligned into the interlocking washer before turning the key to the **OFF** position. This will permit the cylinder retaining pin to extend into the cylinder casting housing hole.
9. Using the ignition key, rotate the lock cylinder to insure correct mechanical operation in all positions.
10. Install the steering wheel, if removed. Connect the negative battery cable.
11. Check for proper start in **P** or **N**. Make sure the vehicle cannot be started in **D** or **R**.

WITHOUT KEY

The following procedure applies to vehicles where the ignition lock is inoperative and the lock cylinder cannot be rotated due to a lost or broken ignition key and the key number not known or the lock cylinder cap is damaged and/or broken to the extent that the lock cylinder cannot be rotated.

Fixed Column

1. Disconnect the negative battery cable.
2. Remove the steering wheel and unscrew the turn signal lever.
3. Remove the steering column trim shrouds. Detach and lower the steering column assembly from the brake pedal support bracket.
4. Remove the ignition switch and key warning buzzer terminal and pin it in the **LOCK** position.
5. Remove the turn signal switch.
6. Remove the upper bearing snapring and the 2 T-bolt retaining nuts that secure the flange casting to the outer tube. Remove the entire flange casting assembly, the upper shaft bearing, the lock cylinder assembly, the ignition switch actuator and the actuator rod by pulling the assembly over the end of the steering column shaft.
7. If equipped with an automatic transmission, remove the lock actuator insert, the T-bolts and the transmission indicator insert. If equipped with a manual transmission, remove the key release lever assembly.

8. Replace the removed components with a new assembly consisting of the flange, lock cylinder assembly, steering column lock gear, steering column lock bearing, steering column upper bearing retainer and steering column lock actuator assembly.
9. If equipped with a manual transaxle, install the key release lever assembly. If equipped with an automatic transmission, install the transmission indicator insert. Install the T-bolts and lock actuator insert.

NOTE: Retain the ignition switch actuating rod from the removed casting assembly and use it with the new flange casting assembly.

To install:

10. Reassemble the parts listed in Step 8, install a new upper shaft bearing and set the actuator to drive gear—the last gear tooth aligns with the last tooth on the actuator when the actuator is fully rearward.
11. Install the turn signal switch and key warning buzzer.
12. Install the ignition switch and check and/or adjust for proper function.
13. Install the steering column assembly to the brake pedal support bracket.
14. Install the steering column trim shrouds, steering wheel and turn signal lever.
15. Using the ignition key, rotate the lock cylinder to insure correct mechanical operation in all positions.
16. Connect the negative battery cable. Check for proper start in **P** or **N**. Make sure the vehicle cannot be started in **D** or **R**.

Tilt Column

1. Disconnect the negative battery cable. Remove the steering column trim shrouds.
2. Tape the gap between the steering wheel hub and the cover casting. Cover the entire circumference of the casting.
3. Cover the adjacent seat and floor area with a suitable covering to protect the surrounding interior upholstery.
4. Pull out the hazard flasher switch and tape it down toward the floor to provide clearance for drilling out the lock cylinder retainer pin.
5. The tilt column lock cylinder retaining pin is located on the outside of the steering column cover casting near the hazard flasher button.
6. Tilt the steering column to the full up position and prepunch the lock cylinder retaining pin with a prick punch. Using a ⅛ in. (3.17mm) diameter drill with a right angle drive, drill out the retaining pin, going no deeper than ½ in. (12.7mm).

NOTE: When drilling out the retaining pin, be careful not to damage the cover cast housing or the hazard flasher switch.

7. Tilt the steering column to the full down position. Place a chisel at the base of the ignition lock cylinder cap and, using a hammer, strike the chisel with sharp blows to break the cap away from the lock cylinder.
8. Using a ⅜ in. (9.8mm) diameter drill, drill down the middle of the ignition lock key slot approximately 1¾ in. (45mm) until the lock cylinder breaks loose from the steering column cover casting. Remove the lock cylinder and the drill shavings from the base of the cover cast housing.
9. Remove the steering wheel.
10. Remove the turn signal lever, then remove the 2 attaching screws from the turn signal switch and 1 attaching screw from the key warning buzzer terminal. Lift the turn signal switch up and over the end of the steering shaft but do not disconnect it from the wiring harness.
11. Remove the 4 attaching screws from the cover casting and lift the casting over the end of the steering shaft allowing the turn signal switch to pass through the cover casting. Removal of the cover casting will expose the upper actuator. Remove the upper actuator.
12. Remove the drive gear, snapring and washer from the cov-

STEERING WHEEL TILTED TO THE FULL UP POSITION

RETAINING PIN ACCESS HOLE

⅛ IN. DIAMETER DRILL

APPLY FORCE IN THIS DIRECTION

CHISEL

LOCK CYLINDER CAP

PRNDD1

NOTE: DRILL DOWN THE MIDDLE OF THE LOCK CYLINDER REMAINING ON THE CENTER LINE FOR APPROXIMATELY 1¾ IN. (45MM) DEEP. REMOVE THE LOCK AND DRILL SHAVINGS.

NOTE REMOVAL OF CHROME CAP

⅜ IN. (9.8MM) DIAMETER DRILL

Ignition lock removal—tilt column without key

er casting along with the upper actuator. Thoroughly clean the components and inspect them for any damage resulting from the drilling operation. If any components show signs of damage, they must be replaced.

13. Clean the removed cover casting with compressed air to remove any drill shavings or foreign particles and carefully inspect it for damage. If the cover casting is damaged, it must be replaced.

To install:

14. Lubricate the tang of the lock cylinder with grease.

15. Attach the upper actuator to the lower actuator and lubricate the upper actuator. Reassemble the cover casting, upper actuator, turn signal switch and lever, lock drive gear, lock cylinder, steering wheel and the steering column trim shrouds.

16. Using the ignition key, rotate the lock cylinder to insure correct mechanical operation in all positions.

17. Connect the negative battery cable. Check for proper start in **P** or **N**. Make sure the vehicle cannot be started in **D** or **R**.

Ignition Switch

Removal and Installation

1. Disconnect the negative battery cable.

2. Remove the steering column shroud and lower the steering column.

3. Disconnect the switch wiring at the multiple plug.

4. Remove the 2 nuts that hold the switch to the steering column.

5. Lift the switch upward to disengage the actuator rod and remove the switch.

To install:

6. When installing the switch, both the locking mechanism at the top of the column and the switch itself must be in the **LOCK** position for correct adjustment.

7. To hold the mechanical parts of the column in the **LOCK** position, move the shift lever into **P**, if equipped with automatic

4. Remove the 2 switch retaining bolts, disconnect the electrical connectors and remove the switch.

To install:

5. Install the switch with the 2 retaining bolts.

6. With the transmission manual lever in **N**, check the location of the switch with the gauge pin. Using a No. 43 drill bit as a gauge pin, insert the gauge pin into the 3 gauge pin holes.

7. Tighten the switch attaching bolts to 55–75 inch lbs. (6.3–8.4 Nm) and remove the gauge pin.

8. Install the outer downshift lever and retaining nut and tighten the nut. Install the downshift linkage rod return spring between the lever and retaining clip on the low-reverse servo cover.

9. Connect the electrical connectors. The red connectors must be connected together and the blue connectors must be connected together.

10. Check the operation of the switch. The back-up lights should come on when the transmission is in **R**. The vehicle should start only with the transmission lever in **P** or **N**.

AUTOMATIC OVERDRIVE TRANSMISSION

1. Disconnect the negative battery cable. Raise and safely support the vehicle.

2. Disconnect the switch electrical connector by lifting straight up off the switch.

3. Using neutral switch socket tool T74P-77247-A, remove the switch and the O-ring.

To install:

4. Install a new O-ring seal on a new neutral safety switch. Lube the seal with transmission fluid.

5. Install the new switch and seal into the case, using the neutral switch socket tool. Tighten to 8–11 ft. lbs. (11–15 Nm).

6. Connect the electrical connector to the switch.

7. Lower the vehicle and connect the negative battery cable.

Fuses, Circuit Breakers and Relays

Location

FUSES

Fuses are located on the fuse panel. The fuse panel for the Bronco and F series vehicles is located on the firewall under the instrument panel left of the steering column. The fuse panel for the E series vehicles is located on the mounting bracket under the instrument panel left of the steering column.

NOTE: There is a 5 amp fuse, in-line, to protect the electric mirror circuit on Bronco and F Series, located on the harness near the fuse panel.

FUSE LINKS

A fuse link is a short length of special, Hypalon high temperature insulated wire, integral with the wiring harness. It is several wire gauges smaller than the circuit it protects. When heavy current flows, such as when a booster battery is connected incorrectly or when a short to ground occurs in the wiring harness, the fuse link burns out and protects the circuit.

The higher melting temperature and additional thickness of the Hypalon insulation will usually let the undersized internal fuse wire melt within the Hypalon casing with little damage to the high temperature insulation other than discoloration and/or bubbling of the insulation surface. In extreme cases of excessive circuit current, the insulation may separate after the fuse wire has disintegrated. However, the bare wire will rarely be exposed. If it is difficult to determine if the fuse link is burned open, perform a continuity test.

Bronco and F Series

12 Gauge Fuse Link—used to protect the alternator circuit on vehicles with 100 amp alternators; located at the starter relay.

14 Gauge Fuse Link—used to protect the auxiliary battery circuit; located near the right fender apron and dash panel.

14 Gauge Fuse Link—used to protect the alternator circuit on vehicles with 70 amp alternator; located at the starter relay.

14 Gauge Fuse Link—used to protect the ignition switch and fuse panel feed circuit on all Bronco and on F Series with ammeter; located near right fender apron and dash panel.

16 Gauge Fuse Link—used to protect the ignition switch and fuse panel feed circuit on F Series without ammeter; located near right fender apron and dash panel.

16 Gauge Fuse Link—used to protect the alternator circuit on vehicles with 40 or 60 amp alternators; located at the starter relay.

16 Gauge Fuse Link—(2) used to protect the trailer circuit; located at starter relay.

16 Gauge Fuse Link—used to protect the heated rear window circuit on Bronco; located on left fender apron.

16 Gauge Fuse Link—used to protect the headlight switch and fuse panel feed circuit; located near the right fender apron and dash panel.

18 Gauge Fuse Link—used to protect the trailer or auxiliary lights circuit; located on the left fender apron.

18 Gauge Fuse Link—used to protect the electronic engine controls circuit; located at the starter relay.

18 Gauge Fuse Link—used to protect the headlight switch and fuse panel feed circuit on F Super Duty vehicles; located at the starter relay.

20 Gauge Fuse Link—used to protect the ignition switch to engine feed circuit on F Super Duty vehicles; located at the starter relay.

E Series

14 Gauge Fuse Link—used to protect the glow plug right bank circuit; located at the starter relay.

14 Gauge Fuse Link—used to protect the glow plug left bank circuit; located at the starter relay.

16 Gauge Fuse Link—used to protect the ignition switch and fuse panel feed circuit; located near the air conditioning case.

18 Gauge Fuse Link—used to protect the headlight switch and fuse panel feed circuit; located near the air conditioning case.

18 Gauge Fuse Link—used to protect the auxiliary air conditioner/heater circuit; located on the left fender at the dash.

20 Gauge Fuse Link—used to protect the oxygen sensor circuit; located near the master cylinder.

20 Gauge Fuse Link—used to protect the ignition circuit; located near the master cylinder.

20 Gauge Fuse Link—used to protect the blower motor circuit; located on the right fender apron.

20 Gauge Fuse Link—used to protect the diesel engine fuel heater; located on the right fender at the dash.

CIRCUIT BREAKERS

Bronco and F Series

22 Amp Circuit Breaker—used to protect the headlight circuit; integral with light switch.

30 Amp Circuit Breaker—used to protect the power door locks, electric mirror and power tailgate circuits on 1988 vehicles; located on the fuse panel.

30 Amp Circuit Breaker—used to protect the power door locks and shift-on-the-fly circuits on 1989–92 vehicles; located on the fuse panel.

30 Amp Circuit Breaker—used to protect the power window circuit; located on the fuse panel.

E Series

7.5 Amp Circuit Breaker—used to protect the windshield wiper/washer circuit; located on the fuse panel.

20 Amp Circuit Breaker—used to protect the power door lock circuit; located on the fuse panel.

20 Amp Circuit Breaker—used to protect the power window circuit; located on the fuse panel.

RELAYS

Bronco and F Series

Charge Indicator Light Relay—located on the right fender apron, near the starter relay.

EEC Power Relay—located on the left side of engine compartment, on the relay assembly.

Fuel Pump Relay—located on the left side of engine compartment.

Horn Relay—located behind the right side of the instrument panel.

Starter Relay—located on the right fender apron.

Transmission Electronic Control Assembly Power Relay—located on the left side of the engine compartment.

E Series

Auxiliary Battery Relay—located on the left fender apron.

Auxiliary Blower Relay—located in the left rear corner of the engine compartment.

Blower Motor Relay—located in the right front corner of the engine compartment.

Door Lock/Unlock Control Relay—located behind the left side of the instrument panel, above the fuse panel.

EEC Power Relay—located on the right fender apron, near the battery.

Fuel Pump Relay—located on the right fender apron, near the battery.

Horn Relay—located behind the left side of the instrument panel, attached to the bottom of the steering column.

Starter Relay—located on the right front fender.

Transmission Electronic Control Assembly Power Relay—located on the right side of the firewall.

Trailer Exterior Lights Relay—located on the left rear of the vehicle, below the left tail light.

Computers

Location

The Electronic Engine Control (EEC) module is located on the left side of the firewall on Bronco and F Series and on the right side fender apron, under the blower motor on E Series.

Flashers

Location

The turn signal flasher is located on the front of the fuse panel. The hazard flasher is located on the rear of the fuse panel behind the turn signal flasher.

Cruise Control

Adjustment

ACTUATOR CABLE

1. Snap the molded cruise control actuator cable retainer over the accelerator cable end fitting attached to the throttle ball stud.
2. Remove the adjuster retainer clip, if installed, from the adjuster mounting tab.
3. Insert the cruise control actuator cable adjuster mounting tab in the slot provided in the accelerator cable support bracket.
4. Pull the cable through the adjuster until a slight tension is felt without opening the throttle plate or increasing idle rpm.
5. Insert the adjuster retainer clip slowly until engagement is felt and then push downward until it locks in position.

VACUUM DUMP VALVE

The vacuum dump valve releases the vacuum in the servo assembly whenever the brake pedal is depressed. It should be checked whenever brake application does not disconnect the cruise control.

1. Move the valve forward in the retaining clip with the valve plunger contacting the brake pedal adapter and the pedal in the released position until $\frac{1}{8}$ in. (3.2mm) or less of the plunger shows.
2. Make sure the brake pedal is against the stop in the release position after adjustment.

NOTE: If vacuum still does not release, replace the vacuum dump valve.

VIEW SHOWING CORRECTLY ADJUSTED DUMP VALVE

PAD ON BRAKE PEDAL

DUMP VALVE

$\frac{1}{8}$ INCH (3.2MM)

DUMP VALVE BLACK HOUSING MUST CLEAR WHITE PLASTIC PAD ON BRAKE PEDAL WITH BRAKE PEDAL PULLED TO REARMOST POSITION

Vacuum dump valve adjustment

ENGINE COOLING

Radiator

Removal and Installation

1. Disconnect the negative battery cable. Drain the cooling system by removing the cap and opening the drain cock located at the lower rear corner of the radiator.
2. Remove the overflow tube from the coolant recovery bottle and detach it from the radiator and shroud, if necessary.
3. Remove the radiator shroud retaining bolts, lift the shroud and drape it on the fan.
4. Disconnect the upper and lower radiator hoses from the radiator. If equipped, disconnect the heated water bypass hose from the radiator.
5. Disconnect the automatic transmission oil cooling lines from the radiator, if equipped.
6. Remove the radiator retaining bolts, tilt the radiator back to clear the radiator support and remove the radiator from the vehicle.

To install:

7. Position the radiator to the radiator support and install the attaching bolts. On F Series with diesel engine and E Series, tighten the bolts to 10–15 ft. lbs. (14–20 Nm). On Bronco and F

Series with gasoline engine, tighten the bolts to 8–11 ft. lbs. (11–14 Nm).

8. Connect the automatic transmission oil cooling lines, if equipped.

9. Connect the upper and lower radiator hoses and tighten the clamps. Attach the heated water bypass hose, if equipped.

10. Position the shroud to the radiator and install the retaining bolts. Tighten to 4–6 ft. lbs. (5.4–8.0 Nm).

11. Attach the overflow tube from the coolant recovery bottle to the radiator.

12. Make sure the radiator drain cock is closed. Fill the cooling system with a 50/50 mixture of water and anti-freeze.

13. Connect the negative battery cable, start the engine and operate for 15 minutes. Check for coolant leaks.

14. Check the coolant level and bring it up to within 1½ in. of the radiator filler neck. Install the radiator cap.

Heater Core

Removal and Installation

1. Disconnect the negative battery cable.
2. Drain the cooling system into a suitable container.
3. Disconnect the heater hoses from the heater core in the engine compartment.
4. On E Series, remove the 2 screws retaining the modesty panel to the underside of the instrument panel. Remove the modesty panel.
5. On Bronco and F Series, remove the glove compartment.
6. From inside the passenger compartment, remove the screws from the heater core cover and remove the cover. On Bronco and F Series, if necessary, disconnect the vacuum source but leave the vacuum harness attached to the cover.

7. On E Series, remove the screw and retaining bracket at the bottom of the heater core.
8. Remove the heater core and seal.

To install:

9. Position the heater core and seal into the heater case or plenum. On E Series, install the core retaining bracket and screw.

10. Position the heater core cover and install the attaching screws.

11. On E Series, install the modesty panel and the retaining screws. On Bronco and F Series, connect the vacuum harness to it's source connection and install the glove compartment.

12. Connect the heater hoses to the heater core.

13. Fill the cooling system to the proper level.

14. Connect the negative battery cable and check the system for proper operation and coolant leaks.

Water Pump

Removal and Installation

4.9L ENGINE

1. Disconnect the negative battery cable. Drain the cooling system.

2. Remove the alternator drive belt. If equipped with an air compressor, remove the compressor belt.

3. Remove the fan and the pulley.

4. Disconnect the heater hose, radiator lower hose and radiator supply line at the water pump.

5. Remove the water pump attaching bolts and the water pump.

Heater core removal—Bronco and F Series

HEATER CORE COVER

Heater core removal—E Series

To install:

6. Clean the gasket mating surfaces of the water pump and engine block.

7. If a new water pump is being installed, remove the fittings from the old pump and install them on the new pump.

8. Coat a new gasket on both sides with water-resistant sealer and install on the water pump. Position the water pump on the engine block.

9. Coat the threads of the mounting bolts with water-resistant sealer and install. Tighten the mounting bolts to 12–18 ft. lbs. (17–24 Nm).

10. Connect the hoses and install the pulley and fan.

11. Install the alternator belt. If equipped, install the compressor belt.

12. Connect the negative battery cable. Fill and bleed the cooling system. Operate the engine and check for leaks.

5.0L AND 5.8L ENGINES

1. Disconnect the negative battery cable and drain the cooling system. On E series, remove the air cleaner and intake duct assembly.

2. Remove the bolts securing the fan shroud to the radiator, if equipped and position the shroud over the fan. On E series, remove the radiator.

3. Disconnect the lower radiator hose, heater hose and bypass hose at the water pump. Remove the drive belts, fan, fan clutch and pulley. Remove the fan shroud, if equipped.

4. Remove the air conditioning compressor/power steering pump bracket and accessories to clear the stud bolt on the water pump housing.

5. Remove the bolts securing the water pump to the timing chain cover and remove the water pump.

To install:

6. Clean the gasket mating surfaces of the water pump and timing chain front cover.

7. Coat a new gasket on both sides with water-resistant sealer and position on the timing chain front cover. Install the pump with the attaching bolts and tighten to 12–18 ft. lbs. (17–24 Nm).

8. Connect the air conditioning compressor/power steering pump bracket and accessories to the cylinder head and water pump stud bolt.

9. Position the fan shroud over the water pump, if equipped. Install the pulley, fan clutch, fan and drive belts.

10. Install the radiator hose, heater hose and bypass hose. On E Series, install the radiator.

11. Install the fan shroud with the attaching bolts. Connect the negative battery cable.

12. Fill and bleed the cooling system. Operate the engine until normal operating temperature is reached. Check for leaks.

13. On E Series, install the air cleaner and intake duct assembly.

7.3L ENGINE

1. Disconnect the negative battery cable(s). Drain the cooling system and remove the fan shroud halves.

2. Remove the fan and clutch assembly using fan clutch pulley holder T83T-6312-A and fan clutch nut wrench T83T-6312-B or equivalent.

NOTE: The fan clutch nut has left hand thread. Remove by turning the nut clockwise.

3. Remove all drive belts and the water pump pulley.

4. Disconnect heater hose and remove the heater hose fitting from the water pump.

5. Remove the alternator adjusting arm and arm bracket.

6. Remove the air conditioning compressor and position the compressor out of the way. Remove the air conditioning compressor brackets.

Fan clutch assembly removal and installation—7.3L diesel engine

Water pump—7.3L diesel engine

7. Remove the power steering pump and bracket and position out of the way.

8. Remove water pump retaining bolts and remove the water pump from the engine.

To install:

9. Clean the gasket mating surfaces on the water pump and front cover. Clean the bolt threads.

10. Coat a new gasket on both sides with water-resistant sealer and install on the water pump. Position the pump on the front cover.

11. Coat the threads of the 2 top and 2 bottom water pump retaining bolts with water-resistant sealer and install along with the rest of the bolts. Tighten all bolts to 14 ft. lbs. (19 Nm).

12. Install the alternator adjusting arm bracket and the water pump pulley.

13. Coat the heater hose fitting with pipe sealant and install in the water pump. Connect the heater hose.

14. Install the power steering pump bracket, pump and drive belt. Install the air conditioning compressor bracket, compressor and drive belt.

15. Install the alternator adjusting arm and alternator drive belt.

16. Install the vacuum pump drive belt and adjust the tension on all accessory drive belts.

17. Install the fan and clutch assembly using the fan clutch pulley holder and the fan clutch nut wrench.

NOTE: The fan clutch nut has left hand thread. Tighten by turning the nut counterclockwise.

18. Install the radiator fan shroud halves. Fill and bleed the cooling system.

19. Connect the negative battery cables. Start the engine and bring to normal operating temperature. Check for leaks.

7.5L ENGINE

1. Disconnect the negative battery cable. Drain the cooling system and remove the fan shroud attaching bolts.

2. Remove the fan assembly attaching bolts and remove the shroud, fan and pulley.

3. Remove the power steering and air conditioning compressor, if equipped, drive belts.

4. If equipped with air conditioning, loosen the compressor attaching bolts and position the compressor aside. Remove the air conditioner and power steering pump bracket.

5. Loosen the alternator bolts and remove the alternator and air pump drive belt. Remove the air pump and bracket.

6. Disconnect the lower radiator hose, heater hose and bypass hose.

7. Remove the remaining water pump attaching bolts and remove the water pump from the cylinder front cover. Remove the separator plate from the water pump.

To install:

8. Clean the gasket mating surfaces on the water pump, cylinder front cover and separator plate.

9. Coat both sides of the new gaskets with water-resistant sealer. Install the gaskets, separator plate and water pump on the cylinder front cover with the attaching bolts. Tighten to 12–18 ft. lbs. (16–24 Nm).

10. Connect the bypass hose, heater hose and lower radiator hose.

11. Rotate the alternator and air pump bracket into position and install the attaching bolts. Install the air pump and alternator.

12. Install the air conditioning compressor bracket with the power steering pump in place. Install the compressor.

13. Install the pulley on the water pump and position the drive belts on their respective pulleys.

14. Lower the fan and shroud into position. Install the fan attaching bolts and tighten to 12–18 ft. lbs. (16–24 Nm).

15. Adjust the accessory drive belt tension. Fill and bleed the cooling system.

16. Connect the negative battery cable. Start the engine and bring to normal operating temperature. Check for leaks.

Thermostat

Removal and Installation

GASOLINE ENGINE

1. Disconnect the negative battery cable. Drain the radiator so the coolant level is below the thermostat.

2. If equipped with a V8 engine, disconnect the bypass hoses at the water pump and the intake manifold. Remove the bypass tube.

3. Remove the water outlet housing attaching bolts and pull the housing away from the engine to gain access to the thermostat. Remove the thermostat.

To install:

4. Clean the gasket mating surfaces on the water outlet and intake manifold or cylinder head.

5. Coat both sides of a new water outlet housing gasket with water-resistant sealer and position on the cylinder head or intake manifold.

Thermostat installation—4.9L engine

6. The water outlet housing on the 6 cylinder engine contains a locking recess into which the thermostat is turned and locked. Install the thermostat with the bridge section in the water outlet. Turn the thermostat clockwise to lock it in position on the flats cast into the water outlet.

7. If equipped with a V8 engine, install the thermostat in the intake manifold opening with the copper pellet or element toward the engine and the thermostat flange positioned in the recess.

8. Position the water outlet housing on the cylinder head or intake manifold. Install the attaching bolts and tighten to 12–15 ft. lbs. (17–20 Nm) on all except 7.5L engine. On 7.5L engine, tighten to 23–28 ft. lbs. (32–37 Nm).

9. If equipped with a V8 engine, install the bypass hose and tighten the clamps.

10. Fill and bleed the cooling system. Connect the negative battery cable, start the engine and bring to normal operating temperature. Check for leaks.

DIESEL ENGINE

1. Disconnect ground cables from both batteries.

2. Drain the radiator so the coolant level is below the thermostat.

3. Remove the alternator and vacuum pump drive belts.

4. Remove the alternator and the vacuum pump and bracket. Position out of the way.

5. Remove all but the lowest alternator/vacuum pump mounting casting bolt. Loosen the lowest bolt and pivot the alternator/vacuum pump casting outboard.

6. Remove the water outlet housing attaching bolts and pull the housing away from the engine to gain access to the thermostat. Remove the thermostat.

To install:

7. Clean the gasket mating surfaces on the water outlet housing and intake manifold.

8. Coat a new gasket with water-resistant sealer and position on the intake manifold opening.

9. Install the thermostat in the crankcase opening with the copper pellet or element toward the engine and the thermostat flange positioned in the recess.

10. Position the water outlet housing against the crankcase. Install the attaching bolts and tighten to 20 ft. lbs. (27 Nm).

11. Reposition the alternator/vacuum pump casting and install the attaching bolts.

12. Install the vacuum pump and bracket and the alternator. Install the drive belts.

13. Fill and bleed the cooling system. Connect the ground cables to both batteries.

Thermostat—7.3L diesel engine

14. Operate the engine until normal operating temperature is reached. Check the coolant level and check for leaks.

Cooling System Bleeding

When the entire cooling system is drained, the following procedure should be used to remove air from the cooling system and ensure a complete fill.

1. Close the radiator draincock and install the cylinder block drain plug, if removed.

2. Fill the cooling system with a 50/50 mixture of anti-freeze and water. Allow several minutes for trapped air to escape. When filling a cross flow radiator, allow time for the coolant to flow through the radiator tubes to the other end of the tank to ensure the radiator is full.

3. Disconnect the heater outlet hose at the water pump to bleed or release trapped air in the system. When the coolant begins to escape, connect the heater outlet hose.

4. Install the radiator cap to the pressure relief position by installing the cap to the fully installed position and then backing off to the 1st stop. This will allow any air to escape and will minimize spillage.

5. Slide the heater temperature and mode selection levers to the maximum heat position.

6. Start the engine and allow to operate at fast idle for approximately 3–4 minutes.

7. With the engine shut off, wrap the radiator cap with a

thick cloth, carefully remove the cap and add coolant to bring the coolant level up to 1½ in. below the cap seal.

8. Install the cap to the fully installed position. Then, back off to the 1st stop and operate the engine at fast idle until the thermostat opens and the upper radiator hose is warm. To check the coolant level, shut the engine off, wrap the cap with a thick cloth and cautiously remove the cap. Add additional coolant, if necessary. Install the cap to the fully installed position.

─────── **CAUTION** ───────

To avoid personal injury from scalding hot coolant or steam blowing out of the radiator, use extreme care when removing the cap from a hot radiator.

9. Fill the coolant recovery reservoir to the proper level with a 50/50 mix of anti-freeze and water.

GASOLINE FUEL SYSTEM

Fuel System Service Precautions

Safety is the most important factor when performing not only fuel system maintenance but any type of maintenance. Failure to conduct maintenance and repairs in a safe manner may result in serious personal injury or death. Maintenance and testing of the vehicle's fuel system components can be accomplished safely and effectively by adhering to the following rules and guidelines.

• To avoid the possibility of fire and personal injury, always disconnect the negative battery cable unless the repair or test procedure requires that battery voltage be applied.

• Always relieve the fuel system pressure prior to disconnecting any fuel system component (injector, fuel rail, pressure regulator, etc.), fitting or fuel line connection. Exercise extreme caution whenever relieving fuel system pressure to avoid exposing skin, face and eyes to fuel spray. Please be advised that fuel under pressure may penetrate the skin or any part of the body that it contacts.

• Always place a shop towel or cloth around the fitting or connection prior to loosening to absorb any excess fuel due to spillage. Ensure that all fuel spillage (should it occur) is quickly removed from engine surfaces. Ensure that all fuel soaked cloths or towels are deposited into a suitable waste container.

• Always keep a dry chemical (Class B) fire extinguisher near the work area.

• Do not allow fuel spray or fuel vapors to come into contact with a spark or open flame.

• Always use a backup wrench when loosening and tightening fuel line connection fittings. This will prevent unnecessary stress and torsion to fuel line piping. Always follow the proper torque specifications.

• Always replace worn fuel fitting O-rings with new. Do not substitute fuel hose or equivalent where fuel pipe is installed.

Relieving Fuel System Pressure

1. Locate and disconnect the electrical connection to either the fuel pump relay, the inertia switch or the in-line high pressure fuel pump.

2. Crank the engine for approximately 10 seconds. The engine may start and run for a short time. If so, crank the engine an additional 5 seconds after the engine stalls.

3. Connect the electrical connector that was disconnected in Step 1.

Fuel Line Couplings

Removal and Installation

There are 3 methods in use to connect the fuel lines and fuel system components, the hairpin clip push connect fitting, the duck bill clip push connect fitting and the spring lock coupling. Each requires a different procedure to disconnect and connect.

HAIRPIN CLIP PUSH CONNECT FITTING

1. Inspect the visible internal portion of the fitting for dirt accumulation. If more than a light coating of dust is present, clean the fitting before disassembly.

2. Some adhesion between the seals in the fitting and the tubing will occur with time. To separate, twist the fitting on the tube, then push and pull the fitting until it moves freely on the tube.

3. Remove the hairpin clip from the fitting by first bending and breaking the shipping tab. Next, spread the 2 clip legs by hand about ⅛ in. each to disengage the body and push the legs into the fitting. Lightly pull the triangular end of the clip and work it clear of the tube and fitting.

NOTE: Do not use hand tools to complete this operation.

4. Grasp the fitting and pull in an axial direction to remove the fitting from the tube. Be careful on 90 degree elbow connectors, as excessive side loading could break the connector body.

5. After disassembly, inspect and clean the tube end sealing surfaces. The tube end should be free of scratches and corrosion that could provide leak paths. Inspect the inside of the fitting for any internal parts such as O-rings and spacers that may have been dislodged from the fitting. Replace any damaged connector.

To install:

6. Install a new connector if damage was found. Insert a new clip into any 2 adjacent openings with the triangular portion pointing away from the fitting opening. Install the clip until the legs of the clip are locked on the outside of the body. Piloting with an index finger is necessary.

7. Before installing the fitting on the tube, wipe the tube end with a clean cloth. Inspect the inside of the fitting to make sure it is free of dirt and/or obstructions.

8. Apply a light coating of engine oil to the tube end. Align the fitting and tube axially and push the fitting onto the tube end. When the fitting is engaged, a definite click will be heard. Pull on the fitting to make sure it is fully engaged.

DUCK BILL CLIP PUSH CONNECT FITTING

1. Inspect the visible internal portion of the fitting for dirt accumulation. If more than a light coating of dust is present, clean the fitting before disassembly.

2. Some adhesion between the seals in the fitting and the tubing will occur with time. To separate, twist the fitting on the tube, then push and pull the fitting until it moves freely on the tube.

3. Align the slot on push connect disassembly tool T82L-9500–AH or equivalent, with either tab on the clip, 90 degrees from the slots on the side of the fitting and insert the tool. This disengages the duck bill retainer from the tube.

4. Holding the tool and the tube with 1 hand, pull the fitting away from the tube.

NOTE: Use hands only. Only moderate effort is required if the tube has been properly disengaged.

Typical push connect fittings

5. After disassembly, inspect and clean the tube end sealing surfaces. The tube end should be free of scratches and corrosion that could provide leak paths. Inspect the inside of the fitting for any internal parts such as O-rings and spacers that may have been dislodged from the fitting. Replace any damaged connector.

6. Some fuel tubes have a secondary bead which aligns with the outer surface of the clip. These beads can make tool insertion difficult. If there is extreme difficulty, use the following disassembly method:

   a. Using pliers with a jaw width of 0.2 in. (5mm) or less, align the jaws with the openings in the side of the fitting case and compress the portion of the retaining clip that engages the fitting case. This disengages the retaining clip from the case. Often 1 side of the clip will disengage before the other. The clip must be disengaged from both openings.

   b. Pull the fitting off the tube by hand only. Only moderate effort is required if the retaining clip has been properly disengaged.

   c. After disassembly, inspect and clean the tube end sealing surfaces. The tube end should be free of scratches and corrosion that could provide leak paths. Inspect the inside of the fitting for any internal parts such as O-rings and spacers that may have been dislodged from the fitting. Replace any damaged connector.

   d. The retaining clip will remain on the tube. Disengage the clip from the tube bead and remove.

To install:

7. Install a new connector if damage was found. Install the new replacement clip into the body by inserting 1 of the retaining clip serrated edges on the duck bill portion into 1 side of the window openings. Push on the other side until the clip snaps into place.

8. Before installing the fitting on the tube, wipe the tube end with a clean cloth. Inspect the inside of the fitting to make sure it is free of dirt and/or obstructions.

9. Apply a light coating of engine oil to the tube end. Align the fitting and tube axially and push the fitting onto the tube end. When the fitting is engaged, a definite click will be heard. Pull on the fitting to make sure it is fully engaged.

SPRING LOCK COUPLING

The spring lock coupling is a fuel line coupling held together by a garter spring inside a circular cage. When the coupling is connected together, the flared end of the female fitting slips behind the garter spring inside the cage of the male fitting. The garter spring and cage then prevent the flared end of the female fitting from pulling out of the cage. As an additional locking feature, most vehicles have a horseshoe shaped retaining clip that improves the retaining reliability of the spring lock coupling.

SPRING LOCK COUPLING CHART

FEMALE FITTING | O-RINGS | GARTER SPRING

MALE FITTINGS | CAGE

SPRING LOCK COUPLING DISCONNECTED

TO DISCONNECT COUPLING
CAUTION – DISCHARGE SYSTEM BEFORE DISCONNECTING COUPLING

TOOL

❶ BEFORE DISASSEMBLY, LOCATE WHITE INDICATOR RING WHICH MAY HAVE SLIPPED DOWN LENGTH OF FUEL LINE.

CAGE

WHITE INDICATOR RING (LOOSE)

❷ FIT TOOL TO COUPLING SO THAT TOOL CAN ENTER CAGE TO RELEASE THE GARTER SPRING.

TO CONNECT COUPLING

GARTER SPRING

❶ CHECK FOR MISSING OR DAMAGED GARTER SPRING – REMOVE DAMAGED SPRING WITH SMALL HOOKED WIRE – INSTALL NEW SPRING IF DAMAGED OR MISSING.

PUSH TOOL INTO CAGE

❸ PUSH THE TOOL INTO THE CAGE OPENING TO RELEASE THE FEMALE FITTING FROM THE GARTER SPRING.

B – INSTALL NEW O-RINGS

A – CLEAN FITTINGS

WHITE INDICATOR RING

C – LUBRICATE WITH CLEAN REFRIGERANT OIL

D. INSERT WHITE INDICATOR RING INTO CAGE ON MALE FITTING.
E. ASSEMBLE FITTING TOGETHER BY PUSHING WITH A SLIGHT TWISTING MOTION

❷

❹ PULL THE COUPLING MALE AND FEMALE FITTINGS APART.

WHITE INDICATOR RING (LOOSE)

GARTER SPRING

❸ AT REASSEMBLY, WHITE INDICATOR RING WILL POP FREE OF CAGE ON MALE FITTING WHEN JOINT IS FULL MADE. THIS INDICATES THAT GARTER SPRING INSIDE CAGE OF MALE FITTING IS PROPERLY SEATED OVER LIP OF FEMALE CONNECTOR.

❺ REMOVE THE TOOL FROM THE DISCONNECTED SPRING LOCK COUPLING.

Duck bill push connect fitting removal

Fuel Tank

Removal and Installation

BRONCO

1. Relieve the fuel system pressure and disconnect the negative battery cable.
2. Drain the fuel into a suitable container at the fuel hose between the fuel pump and the fuel tube.
3. Raise and safely support the vehicle.
4. Loosen the clamp on the fuel filler pipe and disconnect the hose from the pipe by pulling along the internal fuel tube from the tank filler neck.
5. Disconnect the fuel lines at the fuel gauge sending unit.
6. Support the tank and remove the lower support bracket bolts or skid plate bolts. Remove the support assembly or skid plate attaching nut at each tank mounting strap. Lower the support assemblies and lower the tank enough to gain access to the tank vent hose.
7. Disconnect the fuel sending unit electrical connector, fuel tank vent hose and fuel tank-to-vapor separator lines at the fuel tank.
8. Remove the fuel tank.

To install:

9. Position the forward edge of the tank and skid plate, if equipped, to the frame crossmember, support the tank and connect the vent hose and fuel sender electrical connector.
10. Position the tank, skid plate and straps and install the attaching parts. Apply threadlocking compound and tighten the bolts and nuts to 27–37 ft. lbs. (37–50 Nm).
11. Connect the fuel lines to the fuel sender.
12. Insert the internal fuel tube into the tank filler neck. Connect the filler pipe-to-tank hose and vent tube at the filler pipe and install the hose clamp. Tighten to 25–35 inch lbs. (3–4 Nm).
13. Lower the vehicle. Fill the tank and check all connections for leaks.
14. Connect the negative battery cable.

F SERIES

Midship Fuel Tank—Plastic

1. Relieve the fuel system pressure and disconnect the negative battery cable(s).
2. Drain the fuel into a suitable container by siphoning through the fuel hose at the fuel pump-to-fuel tube connection.
3. Remove the skid plate and heat shields.
4. Disconnect the fuel gauge sending unit wire at the fuel tank.
5. Loosen the fuel filler hose clamp at the tank and disconnect the fuel filler hose.
6. Disconnect the fuel tube push connect fittings at the fuel gauge sending unit.
7. Support the tank. Remove the bolts from the retaining straps and lower the tank to the floor.

To install:

8. Position the tank in the vehicle and secure the retaining straps to the frame with the attaching bolts hand-started.
9. Position and secure the fuel filler hose on the fuel tank filler neck. Tighten the hose clamp to 27–35 inch lbs. (3–4 Nm).
10. Clip the vapor valve hose to the frame rail. Connect the fuel tubes and electrical connector to the fuel gauge sender unit.
11. Tighten the strap attaching bolts to 12–18 ft. lbs. (16–24 Nm). Position the heat shield on the fuel tank retaining strap studs and tighten the attaching nuts to 6–8 ft. lbs. (8–11 Nm).
12. Position the skid plate in the vehicle and secure the skid plate and heat shield to the frame with the attaching bolts and nuts. Tighten to 6–8 ft. lbs. (8–11 Nm).
13. Fill the tank and check all connections for leaks. Connect the negative battery cable(s).

Midship Fuel Tank—Steel

1. Relieve the fuel system pressure and disconnect the negative battery cable.
2. Drain the fuel into a suitable container by siphoning through the fuel hose at the fuel pump-to-fuel tube connection.
3. Disconnect the fuel gauge sending unit wires at the fuel tank.
4. If equipped with dual tanks, disconnect the ground wire after draining both tanks. Loosen the clamp and disconnect the hose attached to the fuel tank by pulling along the rubber inner tube from the tank filler neck.
5. Disconnect the vapor line from the vapor emission control valve, if equipped.
6. Support the tank, remove the nuts and bolts from the retaining straps and lower the tank to the floor.

To install:

7. Raise the tank into place. Position the retaining straps around the fuel tank and attach the bolts and nuts. Tighten to 22–30 ft. lbs. (30–41 Nm).
8. Insert the rubber inner hose inside the filler neck and connect the hose to the tank. Tighten the clamps to 25–35 inch lbs. (3–4 Nm).
9. If equipped, connect the vapor lines to the emission control valve located in the top of the tank.
10. Fill the tank with fuel, connect the negative battery cable and start the engine. Check for leaks.

Aft-Of-Axle Fuel Tank

1. Relieve the fuel system pressure and disconnect the negative battery cable.
2. Raise and safely support the vehicle. Disconnect the fuel gauge sending unit wire at the fuel tank.
3. Siphon the fuel from the tank into a suitable container at the hose between the fuel pump and the fuel tube. If equipped with dual tanks, disconnect the ground wire after both tanks have been drained.
4. Disconnect the fuel line push connect fittings at the fuel gauge sending unit.
5. Loosen the clamp on the fuel filler pipe. Disconnect the filler pipe hose by pulling along the rubber inner tube from the tank filler neck.
6. If removing a metal tank, support the tank and remove the bolts attaching the tank supports to the frame. Carefully lower the tank and disconnect the vent tube(s) from the vapor emission control valve in the top of the tank. Finish removing the

filler pipe and filler pipe vent hose if not possible in Step 5. Remove the tank from under the vehicle.

7. If removing a plastic tank, support the tank and remove the bolts attaching the combination skid plate and tank support to the frame. Carefully lower the tank and disconnect the vent tube(s) from the vapor emission control valve in the top of the tank. Complete removing the filler pipe if not possible in Step 5. Remove the skid plate and tank from under the vehicle and disassemble the skid plate from the tank.

To install:

8. If installing a plastic tank, assemble the skid plate and support straps to the tank.

9. Raise the tank skid plate and support assembly and attach the vent hose(s) to the vapor emission control valve. Start the tank neck into the hose.

10. Position the tank assembly filler against the top straps of the frame. Install the attaching bolts and nuts using threadlocking compound. Tighten the attaching bolts and nuts to 27–37 ft. lbs. (37–50 Nm).

NOTE: The plastic tank attaching bolts and nuts do not use threadlocking compound. Tighten these bolts and nuts to 25–35 ft. lbs. (34–47 Nm).

11. Insert the rubber inner hose inside the tank filler neck and connect the filler pipe hose. Tighten the clamps to 25–35 inch lbs. (3–4 Nm).

12. Connect the sending unit electrical connector and the fuel lines. Install the drain plug, if equipped.

13. Lower the vehicle. Fill the tank and check all connections for leaks. Connect the negative battery cable.

E SERIES

Midship Tank

1. Relieve the fuel system pressure and disconnect the negative battery cable.

2. Drain the fuel into a suitable container by siphoning through the fuel line at the reservoir connection.

3. Raise and safely support the vehicle. Disconnect the fuel gauge sending unit wires at the fuel tank.

4. Support the tank in position. Disengage the mounting strap ends attached to the frame side rail. Remove the other end from the tank support by rotating the strap to disengage the T-shaped hook end.

5. Lower the tank enough to gain access to the vapor valve, fuel filler hose, fuel vent hose and fuel lines. Loosen the attaching clamps and push connectors and disconnect the lines. Disconnect the vapor valve hose from the carbon canister tube.

6. Lower the tank and remove it from under the vehicle.

To install:

7. Attach the T-shaped hook mounting strap ends in the tank supports. Raise the tank high enough and connect the vapor hose to the carbon canister line. Also connect the fuel filler hose, fuel vent hose and fuel lines. Tighten the clamps that attach the hoses to the mating tank parts to 25–35 inch lbs. (3–4 Nm).

8. Attach the mounting strap stud end to the frame side rail with the attaching nuts and tighten to 1¼–1½ in. (32–38mm) exposed thread length.

9. Connect the sending unit wire and lower the vehicle.

10. Fill the tank and check all connections for leaks. Connect the negative battery cable.

Aft Axle Body-Mounted Tank

1. Relieve the fuel system pressure and disconnect the negative battery cable.

2. Drain the fuel into a suitable container by siphoning through the fuel line at the reservoir connection.

3. Raise and safely support the vehicle. Disconnect the fuel gauge sending unit wires at the fuel tank.

4. Disconnect the fuel filler hose and vent hose at the tank neck.

5. Remove the fuel line hairpin clips if equipped with plastic connectors or use the plastic tool if equipped with steel connectors and disconnect the fuel lines from the fuel gauge sending unit.

6. Support the tank in position. Remove the nuts that attach the mounting straps to the T-bolts.

NOTE: The T-bolts are attached to the body brackets located at the rear of the tank. Disengage the straps from the T-bolts and the front body brackets. Lower the tank enough to gain access to the vapor valve.

7. Disconnect the carbon canister hose from the vapor control valve. Lower the fuel tank and remove it from under the vehicle.

To install:

8. Attach the front ends of the mounting straps to the front body brackets.

9. Raise the tank high enough to connect the carbon canister hose to the vapor valve and connect the hose.

10. Secure the strap ends to the T-bolts with the attaching nuts. Tighten the nuts so 1.65–1.85 in. (42–46mm) thread length is exposed.

11. Connect the fuel lnes to the sending unit. Connect the fuel filler hose and vent hose to the filler neck and vent neck at the tank. Tighten the hose clamps to 25–35 inch lbs. (3–4 Nm).

12. Connect the fuel gauge sending unit wires. Lower the vehicle.

13. Fill the tank and check all connections for leaks. Connect the negative battery cable.

Aft Axle Frame-Mounted Tank—Except 38 Gallon

1. Relieve the fuel system pressure and disconnect the negative battery cable.

2. Drain the fuel into a suitable container by siphoning through the fuel line at the reservoir connection.

3. Raise and safely support the vehicle. Disconnect the fuel gauge sending unit wires at the fuel tank.

4. Disconnect the fuel filler hose and vent hose from the tank. Remove the fuel line hairpin clips and disconnect the fuel lines from the fuel gauge sending unit.

5. Support the tank in position. Remove the nuts and bolts that attach the tank supports to the frame. Disengage the straps from the front tank support and the rear crossmember. Lower the tank enough to gain access to the vapor valve.

6. Disconnect the vapor hose from the vapor control valve. Lower the fuel tank and remove it from under the vehicle.

To install:

7. Attach the mounting straps to the rear crossmember. Raise the tank high enough to connect the vapor hose to the vapor valve and connect the hose.

8. Position the tank against the top straps and install the support and attaching bolts and nuts. Tighten the nuts to 30–42 ft. lbs. (41–56 Nm).

9. Connect the fuel hose(s) to the fuel gauge sending unit. Connect the fuel filler hose to the filler neck and vent hose to the vent neck at the tank. Tighten the hose clamps to 25–35 inch lbs. (3–4 Nm).

10. Connect the fuel gauge sending unit wires and lower the vehicle.

11. Fill the tank and check all connections for leaks. Connect the negative battery cable.

Aft Axle Frame-Mounted Tank—38 Gallon

1. Relieve the fuel system pressure and disconnect the negative battery cable.

2. Drain the fuel into a suitable container by siphoning through the fuel line at the reservoir connection.

3. Raise and safely support the vehicle.

4. Disconnect the fuel filler hose and vent hose at the fuel filler pipe assembly.

5. Disconnect the fuel supply and return lines at the front

fuel tank support; not at the fuel sender. Disconnect the vapor hose at the vapor tube.

6. Support the fuel tank in position and loosen the strap attachment nut at the rear that attaches the tank strap to the upper support. Disconnect the bolt that attaches the tank strap to the front crossmember and pivot the strap to the rear of the vehicle.

7. Lower the tank enough to gain access to the fuel gauge. Disconnect the fuel gauge sending unit wires at the fuel tank. If required, remove the front and rear attaching bolt and front heat shield.

8. Lower the fuel tank and remove it from under the vehicle.

To install:

9. Raise the fuel tank high enough to connect the vapor hose to the vapor tube and the fuel gauge sending unit wire.

10. Support the tank in position and tighten the strap attachment bolts at the front to 75–105 ft. lbs. (102–142 Nm). Tighten the rear nuts to 20–25 ft. lbs. (27–34 Nm). If required, attach the front and rear mounting bolts and reinstall the front heat shield.

11. Attach the fuel filler hose and vent hose at the pipe assembly and tighten the clamps to 20–25 ft. lbs. (34–47 Nm). Lower the vehicle.

12. Fill the tank and check all connections for leaks. Connect the negative battery cable.

Fuel Filter

Removal and Installation

NOTE: If the fuel filter is being serviced with the rear of the vehicle higher than the front, or if the tank is pressurized, fuel leakage or siphoning from the tank fuel lines could occur. To prevent this, keep the vehicle front end at or above the level of the rear of the vehicle. Also, relieve the tank pressure by loosening the fuel fill cap. The cap should be retightened after the pressure is relieved. If the vehicle is warm, change the fuel filter before the pressure rebuilds.

1. Relieve the fuel system pressure and disconnect the negative battery cable.

2. Raise and safely support the vehicle.

3. Loosen the screw clamp so the filter slides rearward easily.

4. Remove the push connect fittings at both ends of the filter. Install new retainer clips in each push connect fitting.

5. On E Series, remove the fuel filter from the metal bracket by rotating the fuel line and sliding the filter rearward. Be careful not to kink the fuel line.

6. On Bronco and F Series, gently pull the filter from the bracket, being careful not to kink the fuel line.

NOTE: Note the direction of the flow arrow prior to removal so the replacement filter may be installed in the same position.

To install:

7. On E Series, place the filter into the bracket with the flow arrow pointing toward the tab of the bracket. Slide the filter forward until it rests against the tab of the bracket.

8. On Bronco and F Series, position the filter and push to snap into the bracket.

9. On E Series, tighten the retaining screw of the screw clamp to 1.3–2.1 ft. lbs. (1.8–2.8 Nm).

10. Install the push connect fittings onto the filter ends.

11. Connect the negative battery cable. Turn the ignition switch from **OFF** to **RUN** position several times, without starting the engine. Check for fuel leaks.

12. Lower the vehicle.

Electric Fuel Pump

Pressure Testing
HIGH PRESSURE PUMP

1. Make sure there is an adequate fuel supply.
2. Relieve the fuel system pressure.
3. Turn the ignition key **OFF**.
4. Connect a suitable fuel pressure gauge to the schrader valve on the fuel rail.
5. Install a test lead to the **FP** terminal on the VIP test connector.
6. Turn the ignition key to the **RUN** position, then ground the test lead to run the fuel pump.
7. Observe the fuel pressure reading on the pressure gauge. The fuel pressure should be 35–45 psi on all except the 4.9L engine. On the 4.9L engine, the fuel pressure should be 50–60 psi.
8. Relieve the fuel system pressure and turn the ignition key **OFF**. Remove the fuel pressure gauge and the test lead.

LOW PRESSURE PUMP

It has been found that if the low pressure pump is running, it is almost certain that it is operating correctly. Flow testing of the pump is only necessary if there is good reason to suspect pump damage that would cause the pump to run but not pump.

1. Attach a test lead to the **FP** terminal on the VIP test connector. Make sure the lead is long enough to reach the work area under the vehicle.
2. Turn the ignition key to the **RUN** position.
3. Raise and safely support the vehicle. Bring the test lead to a convenient point for grounding.
4. Ground the test lead and listen at the fuel tank for low pressure pump operation. Use a stethoscope or other device to help hear the pump. The electrical connection to the high pressure pump may be disconnected to aid in hearing the low pressure pump run.
5. If the pump does not run, check the inertia switch, test connections, fuel pump relay and any other wiring problems that could prevent the pumps from running. Both pumps run from the same electrical circuit. If the high pressure pump runs, check the connections at the top of the fuel tank to pump for continuity and for voltage when the circuit is energized.
6. If the pump runs, remove the ground from the test lead and disconnect the pressure line from the pump at the reservoir inlet fitting.
7. Place the fuel line removed from the reservoir into a calibrated container of at least 1 qt. capacity. Ground the test lead and run the pump for 5 seconds. The fuel level should be at least 6 oz. (180ml).
8. If the fuel level is not at least 6 oz. (180ml), momentarily restrict the line to provide back pressure to prime the pump. If there is still no flow, check for blocked lines and replace the pump if no problem is found.

Removal and Installation

All E Series and 1988–89 Bronco and F Series are equipped with a low pressure fuel pump located inside the fuel tank and a high

FP LEAD
(SHORT END
OF CONNECTOR)

VIP test connector

pressure fuel pump mounted on the frame. Beginning in 1990, Bronco and F Series are only equipped with a high pressure fuel pump located in the fuel tank.

TANK MOUNTED PUMP

1. Relieve the fuel system pressure and disconnect the negative battery cable.
2. Raise and safely support the vehicle.
3. Remove the fuel tank.

4. Remove any dirt from the area around the sending unit/fuel pump assembly so it will not enter the tank.
5. Turn the locking ring counterclockwise and remove the locking ring, sending unit/fuel pump assembly and sealing gasket.

To install:

6. Clean the mounting surface on the fuel tank.
7. Place a new gasket in the groove of the fuel tank. Install the sending unit/fuel pump assembly into the tank so the tabs

Tank mounted fuel pump installation

Frame mounted fuel pump

are positioned into the tank slots. The gasket must remain in place during and after sending unit/fuel pump assembly installation.

8. Holding the sending unit/fuel pump assembly in place, install and rotate the locking ring clockwise. Metal locking rings should be rotated until the stop is against the retainer ring tab. Plastic locking rings should be tightened to 13–20 ft. lbs. (18–27 Nm) on 1988–89 vehicles or 40–55 ft. lbs. (54–75 Nm) on 1990–92 vehicles.

9. Install the fuel tank and lower the vehicle.

10. Fill the tank and check for leaks. Connect the negative battery cable.

FRAME MOUNTED PUMP

1. Relieve the fuel system pressure and disconnect the negative battery cable.

2. Raise and safely support the vehicle.

3. Disconnect and plug the inlet and outlet fuel lines. Disconnect the electrical connector at the pump.

4. Remove the pump from the mounting bracket.

6. Installation is the reverse of the removal procedure.

Fuel Injection

Idle Speed Adjustment

1988

1. Place the transmission in **P** or **N** and apply the parking brake.

2. Start the engine and bring to normal operating temperature. Make sure the air conditioner/heater and all accessories are **OFF**.

3. Check the ignition timing and adjust, if necessary.

4. Connect a tachometer according to the manufacturers instructions.

5. On all except 7.5L engine, check the curb idle speed. If it is not to the specification listed on the emission calibration decal, shut the engine **OFF**. Disconnect the negative battery terminal for 3 minutes and then reconnect it. Start the engine and let it idle for 5 minutes with the automatic transmission in **D**.

6. Check the curb idle speed. If it is not to specification, shut the engine **OFF**.

7. If equipped with a 7.5L engine, disconnect the air bypass solenoid.

8. Place the transmission in **N** or **P**. Run the 4.9L and 5.0L engines at 1800 rpm for 30 seconds, the 5.8L engine at 1800 rpm for 60 seconds or the 7.5L engine at 2500 rpm for 30 seconds.

9. If equipped with 5.8L engine, let the engine idle. If it stalls, turn the throttle stop screw 1 turn clockwise and repeat Steps 8 and 9.

10. Place the automatic transmission in **D** or the manual transmission in **N** on all except 7.5L engine. If equipped with 7.5L engine, place either transmission in **N**.

11. On the 4.9L engine, back out the throttle plate stop screw until the idle speed is 610 ± 40 rpm, if equipped with automatic transmission or 710 ± 40 rpm, if equipped with manual transmission, then back out the screw an additional ½ turn. The adjustment must be completed within 40 seconds; after that, the idle speed may change due to strategy parameter.

12. On the 5.0L engine, back out the throttle plate stop screw until the idle speed is 625 ± 25 rpm, if equipped with automatic transmission or 700 ± 25 rpm, if equipped with manual transmission, then back out the screw an additional ½ turn. The adjustment must be completed within 40 seconds; after that, the idle speed may change due to strategy parameter.

13. On the 5.8L engine, turn the throttle plate stop screw until the idle speed is 625 ± 25 rpm, if equipped with automatic transmission or 650 ± 25 rpm, if equipped with manual transmission.

14. On the 7.5L engine, turn the throttle plate stop screw until the idle speed is 650 rpm.

15. Reconnect the air bypass solenoid, if disconnected. Make sure the throttle is not stuck in the bore and the linkage is not preventing the throttle from closing.

Throttle body—4.9L, 5.0L and 5.8L engines

Throttle body—7.5L engine

1989–90

1. Place the transmission in **P** or **N** and apply the parking brake.
2. Start the engine and bring to normal operating temperature. Make sure the air conditioner/heater and all accessories are **OFF**.
3. Check the ignition timing and adjust, if necessary.
4. Connect a tachometer according to the manufacturers instructions.
5. On 5.8L and 7.5L engines, disconnect the negative battery cable for 3 minutes and then reconnect it.
6. Start the engine and let it stabilize for 2 minutes, then rev the engine and let it return to idle, lightly depress and release the accelerator and let the engine idle.
7. If the engine does not idle properly, shut the engine **OFF**.
8. With the engine off, install a 0.050 in. feeler gauge between the throttle plate stop screw and the throttle lever on all 4.9L engines and 5.0L engines with automatic transmission. Install a 0.030 in. feeler gauge between the throttle plate stop screw and the throttle lever on all 5.8L engines and on 5.0L engines with manual transmission.
9. Unplug the spout line and make sure the ignition timing is base ± 2 degrees BTDC on all except 7.5L engine.
10. Disconnect the air bypass solenoid.
11. Place the automatic transmission in **P** or the manual transmission in **N**. Let the engine idle for 2 minutes.
12. Turn the throttle plate stop screw until the idle speed is 650 ± 25 rpm on 4.9L engines with the following emission calibration decals: 7-52ER, 7-52JR, 7-52KR, 7-52MR, 7-52QR, 7-52RR, 7-52ZR and 7-72JR. Adjust the idle speed to 750 ± 25 rpm on all other 4.9L engines.
13. On the 5.0L engine, turn the throttle plate stop screw until the idle speed is 675 ± 50 rpm, if equipped with automatic transmission or 700 ± 50 rpm, if equipped with manual transmission.
14. On the 5.8L engine, turn the throttle plate stop screw until the idle speed is 780 ± 50 rpm, if equipped with the C6 automatic tranmsission or 730 ± 50 rpm, if equipped with electronic overdrive or manual transmissions.

NOTE: For Steps 12–14, if it is necessary to turn the throttle stop screw in, shut the engine off and make the estimated adjustment. Start the engine and repeat Steps 11–14.

15. On the 7.5L engine, turn the throttle plate stop screw until the idle speed is 650 ± 50 rpm, if equipped with automatic transmission or 650 ± 25 rpm, if equipped with manual transmission.
16. On the 4.9L and 5.0L engines, shut the engine off and disconnect the negative battery cable for 3 minutes.
17. On all except 7.5L engine, remove the feeler gauge from the throttle plate stop screw and throttle lever pad. Reconnect the spout line.
18. Reconnect the air bypass solenoid and verify the throttle is not stuck in the bore and the linkage is not preventing the throttle from closing.
19. Start the engine and stabilize for 2 minutes, then rev the engine and let it return to idle. Lightly depress and release the accelerator and let the engine idle.

NOTE: A condition may occur where the engine speed will oscillate. This can be caused by the throttle plates being open enough to allow purge flow. To verify this condition, disconnect the carbon canister purge line and plug it. If purge is present, the throttle plates must be closed until the purge flow induced idle oscillations stop.

20. If equipped with automatic overdrive transmission, check the TV pressure adjustment.

1991–92

Idle speed adjustment on 1991–92 engines requires the use of Super Star II tester 007–00028 or equivalent.

Idle Mixture Adjustment

The idle mixture is controlled by the electronic control unit and cannot be adjusted.

Fuel Injector

Removal and Installation

4.9L ENGINE

1. Relieve the fuel system pressure and disconnect the negative battery cable.
2. Disconnect the electrical connectors at the EGR valve position sensor, throttle position sensor and air bypass valve.
3. Disconnect the vacuum lines at the EGR valve, the evaporative lines to the throttle body and electronic purge, if equipped and the vacuum lines at the upper intake manifold vacuum tree. Tag the lines to aid in reinstallation.
4. Disconnect the PCV hose from the fitting located on the underside of the upper intake manifold.
5. Remove the throttle linkage shield and disconnect the throttle linkage and cruise control cables. Unbolt the accelerator cable from the bracket and position the cable away from the engine.
6. Disconnect the air inlet hoses from the throttle body.
7. Disconnect the EGR tube from the EGR valve and the rear exhaust manifold. Remove the tube from the engine.
8. Remove the thermactor tube assembly from the lower intake manifold by removing the 2 nuts retaining the tube. Remove the nut attaching the thermactor bypass valve bracket to the lower intake manifold.
9. On E Series, remove the nut attaching the transmission fill tube, then remove the tube bracket off the intake manifold stud.
10. Remove the studs and screws that retain the upper intake manifold.
11. Remove the screw and washer assembly attaching the upper intake manifold support bracket to the upper intake manifold.
12. Remove the upper intake manifold and throttle body assembly from the lower intake manifold.
13. Disconnect the electrical connectors from the fuel injectors.
14. Disconnect the fuel lines from the fuel supply manifold.
15. Remove the injector cooling manifold, if equipped. Disconnect the electrical connector from the fuel manifold temperature switch, if equipped.
16. Disconnect the vacuum line to the pressure regulator.
17. Remove the strap surrounding the fuel manifold, injector electrical harness and the main vacuum harness.
18. Remove the 3 fuel supply manifold retaining studs.
19. Carefully disengage the fuel supply manifold from the fuel injectors and remove the manifold.
20. Grasping the injector body, pull up while gently rocking the injector from side-to side. Remove and discard the injector O-rings.

To install:

21. Lubricate new O-rings with clean light grade oil and install 2 on each injector.

NOTE: Never use silicone grease as it will clog the injectors.

22. Install the injectors, using a light, twisting, pushing motion.
23. Install the fuel supply manifold, pushing down to make sure all the fuel injector O-rings are fully seated in the fuel supply manifold cups and intake manifold. Install the 3 retaining bolts or studs.

24. Install the injector cooling manifold, if equipped. Connect the electrical connector to the fuel manifold temperature switch.

25. Connect the fuel lines to the fuel supply manifold.

26. Before connecting the electrical connectors to the fuel injectors, connect the negative battery cable and turn the ignition switch **ON**. This will cause the fuel pump to run for 2–3 seconds and pressurize the system.

27. Check for fuel leaks where the fuel injector is installed into the fuel supply manifold.

28. Turn the ignition switch **OFF** and disconnect the negative battery cable.

29. Attach the vacuum line to the fuel pressure regulator.

30. Secure the main vacuum harness and the injector electrical harness to the fuel supply manifold with a strap positioned between the No. 5 and No. 6 intake manifold runners.

31. Connect the electrical connector to the electronic purge valve, if equipped.

32. Position a new upper intake gasket on the lower manifold, using the lower manifold dowels to position the gasket.

33. Position the upper intake manifold onto the lower intake manifold, using the dowels of the lower intake to locate the manifold holes. Install the studs and screws and hand-tighten.

34. Tighten the studs to 12–18 ft. lbs. (16.2–24.4 Nm).

35. Position the upper intake manifold support onto the boss of the upper intake, located under the throttle body. Install the retaining screw and tighten to 22–32 ft. lbs. (29.8–43.4 Nm).

36. Install the EGR tube between the EGR valve and the rear exhaust manifold. The tube is routed between the lower intake runners No. 4 and No. 5. Tighten both fittings to 25–35 ft. lbs. (33.8–47.5 Nm).

37. Connect the PCV hose to the fitting, located on the underside of the upper intake manifold.

38. Position the thermactor tube assembly onto the studs of the lower intake manifold and tighten the attachment nuts to 8–12 ft. lbs. (10.8–16.3 Nm).

39. On E Series, position the transmission fill tube onto the stud of the lower intake manifold. Tighten the attachment nut to 8–12 ft. lbs. (10.8–16.3 Nm).

40. Install the accelerator cable and throttle linkage shield onto the accelerator bracket of the throttle body.

41. Connect the air inlet hoses to the throttle body.

42. Connect the vacuum line to the EGR valve, the evaporative lines to the throttle body and the vacuum lines to the vacuum tree.

43. Connect the electrical connectors to the throttle position sensor, air bypass valve, EGR valve position sensor and, if equipped, the electronic purge valve.

44. Connect the negative battery cable, start the engine and let it idle for 2 minutes.

45. Turn the engine **OFF** and check for fuel leaks.

5.0L AND 5.8L ENGINES

1. Relieve the fuel system pressure and disconnect the negative battery cable.

2. Disconnect the electrical connectors at the air bypass valve, throttle position sensor and EGR position sensor.

3. Disconnect the throttle linkage at the throttle ball. Disconnect the automatic overdrive transmission linkage from the throttle body, if equipped. Remove the 2 bolts securing the throttle linkage bracket to the intake and position the bracket with the cables aside.

4. Disconnect the vacuum lines at the vacuum tree, EGR valve and fuel pressure regulator.

5. Disconnect the PCV hose from the fitting on the rear of the upper manifold.

6. Disconnect the canister purge line(s) from the fitting(s) on the throttle body.

7. Partially drain the cooling system and disconnect the water heater lines from the throttle body.

8. Disconnect the EGR tube from the EGR valve by removing the flange nut.

9. Remove the bolt from the upper intake support bracket to the upper manifold.

10. Remove the 6 upper intake manifold retaining bolts and remove the upper intake and throttle body assembly.

11. Disconnect the electrical connectors from the fuel injectors.

12. Disconnect the fuel lines from the fuel supply manifold.

13. Remove the 4 fuel supply manifold retaining bolts, carefully disengage the manifold from the fuel injectors and remove the manifold.

14. Grasping the injector body, pull up while gently rocking the injector from side-to-side. Remove and discard the injector O-rings.

To install:

15. Lubricate new O-rings with clean light grade oil and install 2 on each injector.

NOTE: Never use silicone grease at it will clog the injectors.

16. Install the injectors, using a light, twisting, pushing motion.

17. Install the fuel supply manifold, pushing down to make sure all the fuel injector O-rings are fully seated in the fuel supply manifold cups and intake manifold.

18. Install the 4 fuel supply manifold retaining bolts and tighten to 15–22 ft. lbs. (20–30 Nm).

19. Connect the fuel lines to the fuel supply manifold.

20. Before connecting the electrical connectors to the fuel injectors, connect the negative battery cable and turn the ignition switch **ON**. This will cause the fuel pump to run for 2–3 seconds and pressurize the system.

21. Check for fuel leaks where the fuel injector is installed into the fuel supply manifold.

22. Turn the ignition switch **OFF** and disconnect the negative battery cable.

23. Clean and inspect the mounting faces of the upper and lower intake manifolds.

24. Position a new gasket on the lower intake mounting face. The use of alignment studs may be helpful.

25. Install the upper intake manifold and throttle body assembly to the lower manifold making sure the gasket remains in place.

26. Install the 6 upper intake manifold retaining bolts and tighten to 12–18 ft. lbs. (16–24 Nm).

27. Install the upper intake support bracket to the upper manifold attaching bolt.

28. Install the EGR tube.

29. Connect the canister purge lines to the fittings on the throttle body.

30. Connect the water heater lines to the throttle body.

31. Connect the PCV hose to the rear of the upper manifold.

32. Connect the vacuum lines to the vacuum tree, EGR valve and fuel pressure regulator.

33. Position the throttle linkage bracket with the cables to the upper intake manifold. Install the 2 retaining bolts and tighten to 8–10 ft. lbs. (11–13 Nm). Connect the throttle cable and transmission cable to the throttle body.

34. Connect the electrical connectors to the air bypass valve, throttle position sensor and EGR position sensor.

35. Fill and bleed the cooling system.

36. Connect the negative battery cable, start the engine and let it idle for 2 minutes.

37. Turn the engine **OFF** and check for fuel and coolant leaks.

7.5L ENGINE

1. Relieve the fuel system pressure and disconnect the negative battery cable.

2. Disconnect the throttle linkage at the throttle ball and the automatic transmission linkage, if equipped, from the throttle body. Remove the bolts securing the bracket to the intake and position the bracket with the cable out of the way.

3. Remove the 2 canister purge lines from the fittings on the throttle body, if equipped.

4. Disconnect the electrical connectors at the air bypass valve, throttle position sensor and EGR position sensor.

5. Disconnect the vacuum lines to the MAP sensor and EGR valve.

6. Disconnect the EGR valve flange nut and the PCV hose at the rear of the upper manifold.

7. Disconnect and plug the water heater lines at the throttle body, if equipped.

8. Disconnect the bypass valve clean air supply hose, connected to the bypass port, if equipped.

9. Remove the 4 upper intake manifold retaining bolts and remove the upper intake manifold and throttle body assembly.

10. Disconnect the vacuum hose at the fuel pressure regulator.

11. Disconnect the electrical connectors at the injectors.

12. Disconnect the fuel lines from the fuel supply manifold.

13. Remove the 4 fuel supply manifold retaining bolts, carefully disengage the manifold from the fuel injectors and remove the manifold.

14. Grasping the injector body, pull up while gently rocking the injector from side-to-side. Remove and discard the injector O-rings.

15. Inspect the injector plastic pintle protection cap and washer for signs of deterioration. Replace the complete injector as required. If the plastic pintle protection cap is missing, look for it in the intake manifold.

NOTE: The plastic pintle protection cap is not available as a separate part.

To install:

16. Lubricate new O-rings with clean light grade oil and install 2 on each injector.

NOTE: Never use silicone grease at it will clog the injectors.

17. Install the injectors, using a light, twisting, pushing motion.

18. Install the fuel supply manifold, pushing down to make sure all the fuel injector O-rings are fully seated in the fuel supply manifold cups and intake manifold.

19. Install the 4 fuel supply manifold retaining bolts and tighten to 15–22 ft. lbs. (20–30 Nm).

20. Connect the fuel lines to the fuel supply manifold.

21. Before connecting the electrical connectors to the fuel injectors, connect the negative battery cable and turn the ignition switch **ON**. This will cause the fuel pump to run for 2–3 seconds and pressurize the system.

22. Check for fuel leaks where the fuel injector is installed into the fuel supply manifold.

23. Turn the ignition switch **OFF** and disconnect the negative battery cable.

24. Connect the electrical connectors to the fuel injectors.

25. Connect the vacuum hose to the fuel pressure regulator.

26. Clean and inspect the mounting faces of the upper and lower intake manifolds.

27. Position a new gasket on the lower intake mounting face. The use of alignment studs may be helpful.

1. Wiring harness
2. Fuel pressure regulator
3. Lower intake manifold
4. Fuel injector
5. Fuel supply manifold

Fuel Injector removal—7.5L engine

28. Install the upper intake manifold and throttle body assembly to the lower manifold making sure the gasket remains in place.

29. Install the 4 upper intake manifold retaining bolts and tighten to 12–18 ft. lbs. (16–24 Nm).

30. Install the EGR tube and connect the PCV hose to the rear of the upper manifold.

31. Connect the water heater lines to the throttle body, if equipped.

32. Connect the vacuum lines to the MAP sensor and EGR valve.

33. Position the throttle linkage bracket with the cable to the upper intake manifold. Install the 2 retaining bolts and tighten to 8–10 ft. lbs. (11–13 Nm). Connect the throttle cable and automatic transmission kickdown cable to the throttle body.

34. Connect the electrical connectors at the air bypass valve, throttle position sensor and EGR position sensor.

35. Connect the bypass valve clean air supply hose, if equipped.

36. Connect the negative battery cable, start the engine and let it idle for 2 minutes.

37. Turn the engine **OFF** and check for fuel leaks.

DIESEL FUEL SYSTEM

Fuel System Service Precautions

Safety is the most important factor when performing not only fuel system maintenance but any type of maintenance. Failure to conduct maintenance and repairs in a safe manner may result in serious personal injury or death. Maintenance and testing of the vehicle's fuel system components can be accomplished safely and effectively by adhering to the following rules and guidelines.

• To avoid the possibility of fire and personal injury, always disconnect the negative battery cable unless the repair or test procedure requires that battery voltage be applied.

• Always relieve the fuel system pressure prior to disconnecting any fuel system component (injector, fuel rail, pressure regulator, etc.), fitting or fuel line connection. Exercise extreme caution whenever relieving fuel system pressure to avoid exposing skin, face and eyes to fuel spray. Please be advised that fuel under pressure may penetrate the skin or any part of the body that it contacts.

• Always place a shop towel or cloth around the fitting or connection prior to loosening to absorb any excess fuel due to spillage. Ensure that all fuel spillage (should it occur) is quickly removed from engine surfaces. Ensure that all fuel soaked cloths or towels are deposited into a suitable waste container.

• Always keep a dry chemical (Class B) fire extinguisher near the work area.

• Do not allow fuel spray or fuel vapors to come into contact with a spark or open flame.

• Always use a backup wrench when loosening and tightening fuel line connection fittings. This will prevent unnecessary stress and torsion to fuel line piping. Always follow the proper torque specifications.

• Always replace worn fuel fitting O-rings with new. Do not substitute fuel hose or equivalent where fuel pipe is installed.

Fuel Filter

Replacement

1. Disconnect the battery ground cables from both batteries.

Fuel filter/water separator assembly—7.3L diesel engine

2. Place a container under the vehicle and drain the fuel from the fuel filter.
3. Remove the water drain tube from the bottom of the filter assembly.
4. Unscrew the water separator drain bowl and remove. Unscrew the filter element and discard.

To install:

5. Clean the gasket surfaces of the fuel filter adapter tp prevent contamination.
6. Lightly coat the filter sealing gaskets with clean diesel fuel.

NOTE: To avoid fuel contamination, do not add fuel directly to the new filter. Allow the engine to draw fuel through the filter.

7. Screw the new filter element onto the filter base until the seal contacts the flange. Tighten another 180–300 degree turn.
8. Screw on the water separator drain bowl. Tighten another 180–300 degree turn.
9. Install the water drain tube and clean any spilled fuel from the top of the engine.
10. Connect the negative battery cables. Run the engine and check for leaks.

Draining Water From The System

NOTE: Drain water from the water separator manual drain valve whenever the warning light comes on or every 5000 miles. The WATER IN FUEL light will glow when approximately 3.5 oz. of water accumulates in the separator.

1. Stop the vehicle and shut **OFF** the engine.
2. Place a container under the fuel filter/water separator drain tube to collect drain fluid.
3. Open the drain valve at the base of the water separator drain bowl. Allow the drain valve to remain open approximately 15 seconds or until clear, water-free diesel fuel flows from the drain tube.
4. Close the drain valve. Start the engine and make sure the WATER IN FUEL light is not on.

Diesel Injection Pump

Removal and Installation

NOTE: Before removing any fuel lines, clean the exterior with clean fuel oil or solvent to prevent entry of dirt into the engine when the fuel lines are removed.

1. Disconnect the negative battery cables from both batteries.
2. Remove the engine cover on E250 and E350.
3. Remove the adapter housing cover plate by removing the 2 retaining bolts.
4. Remove the bolts attaching the injection pump to the drive gear.
5. Disconnect the electrical connectors to the injection pump.
6. Remove the fast idle solenoid bracket assembly to provide access to the injection pump mounting nuts.
7. Disconnect the accelerator cable and cruise control cable from the throttle lever, if equipped.
8. Remove the air cleaner and install a suitable cover over the intake opening.
9. Remove the accelerator cable bracket, with the cables attached from the intake manifold and position aside.
10. On E series, disconnect the fuel inlet and return lines from the fuel filter and cap all lines.
11. On E series, remove the fuel filter bracket attaching bolts and remove the fuel filter and bracket as an assembly.
12. Remove the fuel return hose and clip from the 90 degree elbow at the governor cover. Cap the opening at the governor cover elbow.
13. Remove the fuel filter-to-injection pump fuel line and cap the fittings.

NOTE: It is not necessary to remove the injection lines from the injection pump to remove the injection pump. If the lines are to be removed, loosen the injection line fittings at the injection pump before removing it from engine.

14. Remove the fuel injection lines from the nozzles and cap the lines and nozzles to prevent entry of dirt into the system.

15. Remove the 3 nuts attaching the injection pump to the injection pump drive gear cover using injection pump mounting wrench T86T-9000-C or equivalent.

16. If the injection pump is to be replaced, loosen the injection line retaining clips and injection nozzle fuel lines and cap all fittings.

17. On F series, lift the injection pump, with the nozzle lines attached, up and out of the engine compartment. Do not carry the injection pump by the injection nozzle fuel lines.

18. On E series, remove the injection pump through the passenger compartment. Do not carry the injection pump by the injection nozzle fuel lines.

To install:

19. Install a new O-ring onto the drive gear end of the injection pump.

20. On F series, install injection pump by moving down and into position. On E series, install the injection pump from the passenger compartment.

21. Position the alignment dowel on the injection pump into the alignment hole on the drive gear. If necessary, rotate the pump driveshaft to align the drive slot.

22. Install the bolts attaching the injection pump to the drive gear and tighten to 25 ft. lbs. (34 Nm).

23. Install the nuts attaching the injection pump to the adapter. Align the scribe lines on the injection pump flange and injection pump adapter.

24. If the injection nozzle fuel lines were removed from the injection pump, install at this time.

25. Remove the protective caps from the nozzles and fuel lines. Install the fuel line nuts onto the nozzles and tighten to 22 ft. lbs. (30 Nm).

26. Connect the fuel inlet line from the filter and fuel return line to the injection pump.

27. Install the injection pump fitting adapter with a new O-ring.

28. Clean the old sealant from the injection pump elbow threads using clean solvent and dry thoroughly. Start the elbow into the injection pump adapter and then apply a light coating of pipe sealant.

29. Tighten the elbow in the injection pump adapter to a mini-

mum of 6 ft. lbs. (8 Nm). Then tighten further, if necessary, to align the elbow with the injection pump fuel inlet line, but do not exceed 360 degrees of rotation or 10 ft. lbs. (13 Nm).

30. Remove the caps and connect the fuel filter-to-injection pump fuel line.

31. On E Series, install the fuel filter and bracket as an assembly. Install the fuel filter inlet and return lines.

32. Install the accelerator cable bracket to the intake manifold. Remove the intake manifold cover and install the air cleaner.

33. Connect the accelerator and speed control cable, if equipped, to the throttle lever.

34. Install the fast idle solenoid bracket assembly. Reconnect the electrical connectors on the injection pump.

35. Clean the adapter housing cover plate sealing surfaces. Apply a ⅛ in. bead of sealant in the adapter housing grooves and install the adapter cover. Apply threadlocking compound to the retaining bolts and tighten to 14 ft. lbs. (19 Nm).

36. Connect the ground cables to both batteries. Start the engine and check for fuel leaks. If necessary, bleed the high pressure fuel lines of air by loosening the connector ½–1 turn and cranking the engine until bubble-free fuel flows from the connection.

Fuel return line location—7.3L diesel engine

Injection pump drive gear attaching bolt removal—7.3L diesel engine

Injection pump removal and installation—7.3L diesel engine

Injection pump cylinder numbering sequence—7.3L diesel engine

Idle speed adjusting screw location—7.3L diesel engine

— CAUTION —

Keep eyes and hands away from nozzle spray. Fuel spraying from the nozzle under high pressure can penetrate the skin and cause infection. Medical attention should be provided immediately in the event of skin penetration.

37. Check and adjust the injection pump timing.

Idle Speed Adjustment
CURB IDLE SPEED

1. Place the transmission in **N** or **P**.
2. Start the engine and bring to normal operating temperature.
3. Idle speed is measured with manual tranmission in **N** or automatic transmission in **D**.
4. Make sure the curb idle adjusting screw is against the stop. If not, correct the vehicle linkage.
5. Connect tachometer tool 055–00108 or equivalent, according to the manufacturers instructions.
6. Set the curb idle speed to the specification listed on the vehicle emission control information decal, using the idle speed adjusting screw.

7. Place the transmission in **N** or **P**. Rev the engine momentarily. Place the transmission in the specified gear and check the curb idle speed. Adjust again, if necessary.

FAST IDLE SPEED

1. Place the transmission in **N** or **P**.
2. Start the engine and bring to normal operating temperature.
3. Disconnect the fast idle solenoid from the wiring harness.
4. Apply battery voltage to the solenoid to activate it.
5. Rev the engine momentarily to set the solenoid to activate it.
6. Connect tachometer tool 055–00108 or equivalent, according to the manufacturers instructions.
7. Check the fast idle speed setting. The fast idle speed should be 825 ± 25 rpm. Adjust to specification by turning the solenoid plunger in or out.
8. Rev the engine momentarily and check the fast idle speed. Adjust as necessary.
9. Disconnect the battery voltage from the solenoid connector and connect to the wiring harness.

Diesel Injection Timing

Adjustment
STATIC TIMING

1. Remove the fast idle bracket and solenoid from the injection pump.
2. Break the torque, keeping the nuts snug, on 3 nuts attaching the injection pump to pump mounting adapter using tool T83T–9000–B or equivalent.
3. Install rotating tool T83T–9000–C or equivalent, on the front of the pump and rotate the injection pump to align the timing mark on the injection pump mounting flange with the timing mark on the pump mounting adapter, to with ± 0.030 in.
4. Remove the rotating tool and tighten the nuts.
5. Visually check the timing to verify the timing marks are aligned. Install the fast idle bracket and solenoid.

DYNAMIC TIMING

1. Bring the engine up to normal operating temperature. When checking or setting dynamic injection timing it is mandatory that the engine be stabilized at a normal operating temperature of 192–212°F (89–100°C). This temperature is needed to ensure proper fuel ignition in the precombustion chambers.
2. Stop the engine and install dynamic timing meter tool 078–00200 or equivalent, by placing the magnetic pickup in the timing pointer probe hole. Insert the pickup until it almost touches the vibration damper.
3. Attach the clamp from timing meter adapter tool 078–00201 or equivalent, to the line pressure sensor on the No. 1 injector nozzle (F series) or No. 4 injector nozzle (E series) and connect to the timing meter.
4. Connect the dynamic timing meter to the battery and dial in minus 20 degrees offset on the meter. Disconnect the cold start advance solenoid connector from the timing terminal.
5. With the transmission in **N** and the rear wheels raised off the ground, start the engine. Using throttle control tool D83T–9000–E or equivalent, set the engine speed to 2000 rpm with no accessory load. Observe the injection timing on the dynamic timing meter. The injection timing should be 8.5 degrees BTDC at 2000 rpm.
6. Apply battery voltage to the cold start advance solenoid terminal to activate it. Activating the cold start advance solenoid can result in engine speed increase. Adjust the throttle control to attain 2000 rpm, if necessary.
7. Check the timing at 2000 rpm. The timing should be advanced at least 1 degree before the timing obtained in Step 5. If the advance is less than 1 degree, replace the fuel injection pump top cover assembly.

Injection pump timing marks—7.3L diesel engine

Magnetic pickup—dynamic timing

Luminosity probe—dynamic timing

8. If the dynamic timing is not within ± 2 degrees of specification, adjustment of pump timing is necessary.

9. Turn the engine off. Note the timing mark alignment. Remove the fast idle bracket and solenoid from the injection pump. Break the torque (keeping nuts snug) on the nuts attaching the injection pump to the pump mounting adapter.

10. Install rotating tool T83T–9000–C or equivalent, on the front of the pump. Rotate clockwise (when viewed from front of engine) to retard or counterclockwise to advance the timing, by lightly tapping the tool with a rubber mallet. A 2 degree movement of dynamic timing is approximately 0.030 in. of timing mark movement.

11. Remove the rotating tool and tighten the nuts. Start the engine and recheck the timing. Repeat Steps 9, 10 and 11 as necessary, to set the timing to ± 1 degree of specification.

12. Turn the engine off. Remove the dynamic timing components. Install the fast idle bracket and solenoid.

Fuel Injector Nozzles

Removal and Installation

NOTE: Before removing the nozzle assemblies, clean the exterior of each nozzle assembly and the surrounding area with solvent to prevent entry of dirt into engine when nozzle assemblies are removed. Always cap all open fuel lines to prevent dirt from entering the system.

1. Disconnect the negative battery cable. Disconnect nozzle fuel inlet (high pressure) and fuel leak off tees from each nozzle assembly and position aside.

2. Remove fuel leak off lines as an assembly as follows:
   a. Remove the pump to fuel return tube hose at the fuel return elbow. Cap the elbow at the pump. Disconnect the hose from the leak-off tee to the fuel filter at the leak-off tee.
   b. Loosen the 2 fuel return tube retaining clamps, 1 at the intake manifold and 1 at the engine lifting eye. Remove the fuel return hose clamp at the CDR valve bracket.
   c. With the clamps removed, remove the return lines and tees as an assembly by lifting the tees off the nozzles.

3. Remove the injection nozzles by turning counterclockwise. Pull the nozzle assembly with the copper washer from the engine. Be careful not to strike the nozzle tip against any hard surface during removal. Note the position of the nozzles so they may be reinstalled in their original positions.

To install:

4. Thoroughly clean the nozzle bore in the cylinder head before reinserting the nozzle assembly. Pay particular attention to the seating surface, in order that no small particles of metal or carbon will cause the assembly to be cocked or permit blowby of combustion gases. Blow out the particles with compressed air.

5. Remove the protective cap and install a new copper gasket nozzle assembly with a small dab of multi-purpose grease. Apply anti-seize compound on the nozzle threads to aid installation and future removal.

6. Install the nozzle assembly into the cylinder head nozzle bore. Be careful that the nozzle tip does not strike against the recess wall. Tighten the nozzle assembly to 35 ft. lbs. (47 Nm).

7. Remove the protective caps from the nozzle assemblies and fuel lines. Install the leak-off tees and lines as an assembly by lowering onto the nozzles. Connect the clip and hose to the fuel return elbow at the pump. Install the line to retaining clamps.

NOTE: Install 2 new O-ring seals for each fuel return tee.

8. Connect the high pressure fuel lines. Start the engine. If necessary, bleed the fuel lines of air by loosening the connector ½–1 turn and cranking the engine until bubble-free fuel flows from the connection.

─── **CAUTION** ───

Keep eyes and hands away from nozzle spray. Fuel spraying from the nozzle under high pressure can penetrate the skin and cause infection. Medical attention should be provided immediately in the event of skin penetration.

9. Check for fuel leakage at the high-pressure connections.

Fuel line routing and installation

EMISSION CONTROLS

Emission Warning Lamps

For further information, please refer to Chilton's Emission Controls Manual.

Resetting

All vehicles are equipped with a "CHECK ENGINE" or "SER-VICE ENGINE SOON" warning light located on the instrument cluster. This light should come on briefly when the ignition key is turned **ON**, but should turn off when the engine starts. If the light does not come **ON** when the ignition key is turned **ON** or if it comes **ON** and stays **ON** when the engine is running, there is a malfunction in the electronic engine control system. After the malfunction has been remedied, using the proper procedures, the "CHECK ENGINE" or "SERVICE EN-GINE SOON" light will go out.

GASOLINE ENGINE MECHANICAL

Engine Assembly

Removal and Installation

4.9L ENGINE

Bronco and F Series

1. Disconnect the negative battery cable and relieve the fuel system pressure. Drain the cooling system and the crankcase.
2. Mark the position of the hood on the hinges and remove the hood. Remove the throttle body inlet tubes.
3. Disconnect the heater hose from the water pump and cool-ant outlet housing. Disconnect the flexible fuel line from the fuel supply manifold.
4. Remove the radiator and shroud. Remove the cooling fan, water pump pulley and fan drive belt.

NOTE: The fan clutch/water pump hub has a right-hand thread.

5. If equipped with air conditioning, discharge the refrigerant from the system and remove the compressor and the condenser. Cap all openings.

6. Disconnect the accelerator cable at the throttle body. Remove the throttle return spring.

7. Disconnect the power brake booster vacuum hose at the intake manifold. If equipped with automatic transmission, disconnect the transmission kickdown cable at the throttle body.

8. Disconnect the exhaust pipe from the exhaust manifold. Disconnect the body ground strap and the battery ground cable from the engine.

9. Tag and disconnect the Electronic Engine Control (EEC) harness from all sensors.

10. Tag and disconnect the engine wiring harness at the ignition coil, the coolant temperature sending unit and the oil pressure sending unit. Position the wiring harness aside.

11. Remove the alternator mounting bolts and position the alternator aside, leaving the wires attached.

12. Remove the power steering pump from the mounting brackets and move aside, leaving the lines attached. If equipped with an air compressor, bleed the air system and disconnect the 2 air pressure lines at the compressor.

13. Raise and safely support the vehicle.

14. Remove the starter and automatic transmission filler tube bracket, if equipped. Remove the rear engine plate upper right bolt.

15. If equipped with a manual transmission, remove the flywheel housing lower attaching bolts and disconnect the clutch return spring or clutch slave cylinder.

16. If equipped with an automatic transmission, remove the converter housing access cover assembly and remove the flywheel-to-converter attaching nuts. Secure the converter in the housing. Remove the transmission oil cooler lines from the retaining clip at the engine. Remove the lower converter housing-to-engine attaching bolts.

17. Remove the nut from each of the 2 front engine mounts.

18. Lower the vehicle and position a jack under the transmission to support it. Remove the remaining bell housing-to-engine attaching bolts.

19. Attach suitable engine lifting equipment. Raise the engine slightly and carefully pull it from the transmission. Lift the engine out of the vehicle.

To install:

20. Carefully lower the engine into the vehicle. Make sure the block dowels engage the holes in the bell housing.

21. If equipped with an automatic transmission, start the converter pilot into the crankshaft. Remove the retainer securing the converter in the housing.

22. If equipped with a manual transmission, start the transmission input shaft into the clutch disc. It may be necessary to adjust the position of the transmission in relation to the engine if the transmission input shaft will not enter the clutch disc. If the engine hangs up after the shaft enters, turn the crankshaft slowly, with the transmission in gear, until the shaft splines mesh with the clutch disc splines.

23. Install the bell housing upper attaching bolts and remove the jack supporting the transmission. Lower the engine until it rests on the engine mounts and remove the lifting equipment.

24. Install the engine mount attaching nuts and washers and tighten to 54–74 ft. lbs. (73–100 Nm). Install the automatic transmission oil cooler lines bracket.

25. Install the remaining bell housing bolts and connect the clutch return spring.

26. Install the starter and connect the starter cable. Attach the automatic transmission fluid filler tube bracket, if equipped.

27. If equipped, install the transmission oil cooler lines in the bracket at the cylinder block.

28. Install the exhaust pipe to the exhaust manifold with the lockwashers and nuts.

29. Connect the engine ground strap and the battery ground cable. Connect the EEC harness to all sensors.

30. Connect the accelerator linkage to the throttle body and install the retracting spring. If equipped, connect the kickdown cable to the throttle body.

31. Reconnect the power brake vacuum hose to the intake manifold.

32. Connect the coil primary wire, oil pressure and coolant temperature sending unit wires, flexible fuel line, heater hoses and the positive battery cable.

33. Install the alternator and power steering pump.

34. Install the water pump pulley, cooling fan and drive belt. Tighten the fan bolts to 12–18 ft. lbs. (16–24 Nm).

NOTE: The fan clutch/water pump hub has a right-hand thread.

35. Install the radiator and shroud. Connect the lower radiator hose to the water pump and the upper radiator hose to the coolant outlet housing. Connect the air compressor lines. If removed, install the air conditioning compressor and condenser.

36. If equipped with an automatic transmission, connect the oil cooler lines.

37. Install the hood, aligning the marks that were made during removal.

38. Fill the crankcase with the proper type and quantity of engine oil. Fill and bleed the cooling system.

39. Connect the negative battery cable, start the engine and operate at fast idle. Check for leaks.

40. If equipped with a manual transmission, check for correct clutch operation. If equipped with an automatic transmission, adjust the transmission control linkage and check the fluid level.

41. Install the throttle body intake tubes. If equipped, evacuate and charge the air conditioning system.

E Series

1. Disconnect the negative battery cable and relieve the fuel system pressure. Remove the engine cover, drain the coolant and the crankcase and remove the air cleaner.

2. Remove the front bumper, then remove the grille and lower gravel deflector as an assembly.

3. Disconnect the upper and lower radiator hoses at the radiator. Disconnect the transmission oil cooler lines at the radiator, if equipped. Remove the radiator and shroud.

4. Disconnect the heater hoses at the engine. Disconnect the alternator and move aside.

5. Remove the power steering pump and support from the engine and move aside. If equipped with air conditioning, discharge the system and remove the air conditioning compressor.

6. Disconnect and plug the fuel line at the fuel rail. Tag and disconnect the distributor and sender unit wires from the engine.

7. Tag and disconnect the Electronic Engine Control (EEC) harness from all sensors.

8. Disconnect the brake booster hose at the engine and disconnect the accelerator cable and remove the bracket.

9. Disconnect the automatic transmission kickdown cable at the throttle body, if equipped.

10. Remove the exhaust manifold heat deflector and unbolt the exhaust pipe from the manifold.

11. Disconnect both ends of the automatic transmission vacuum line from the intake manifold and from the junction.

12. Remove the upper engine-to-transmission bolts. If equipped, remove the automatic transmission dipstick tube support bolt at the intake manifold.

13. Raise and safely support the vehicle.

14. Remove the starter. Remove the flywheel inspection cover. Remove the automatic transmission torque converter retaining nuts, then remove the front engine support nuts. Remove the oil filter.

15. Remove the rest of the transmission-to-engine fasteners, then lower the vehicle.

16. Install suitable engine lifting equipment and remove the engine from the vehicle.

To install:

17. Position the engine in the vehicle and start the mounting bolts.

18. Remove the engine lifting equipment and connect the exhaust pipe to the exhaust manifold.

19. Connect the transmission dipstick tube, if equipped, to the intake manifold. Install the manifold heat shield.

20. Connect the automatic transmission kickdown cable, then install the upper transmission-to-engine bolts.

21. Connect the transmission vacuum line at the junction. Install the accelerator cable and bracket assembly.

22. Connect the distributor and sender unit wires. Connect the brake booster hose.

23. Unplug and connect the fuel line to the fuel rail. Connect the transmission vacuum line to the manifold.

24. Install the alternator and the power steering pump and support bracket. Install the air conditioning compressor, if equipped.

25. Install the accessory drive belt. Connect the heater hoses and install the radiator and shroud assembly.

26. Position the grille and lower gravel deflector. Connect the upper radiator hose, then install the grille and deflector bolts and screws.

27. Install the bumper, then raise and safely support the vehicle.

28. Install the converter nuts, then install the flywheel inspection cover bolts.

29. Install the starter and the oil filter. Install the front engine support nuts and the lower engine-to-transmission bolts. Tighten to 60–80 ft. lbs. (82–108 Nm).

30. Connect the lower radiator hose and the transmission cooler lines. Install the alternator splash shield, if equipped, and lower the vehicle.

31. Fill the crankcase with the proper type and quantity of engine oil. Fill and bleed the cooling system.

32. Connect the negative battery cable, start the engine and check for leaks. If equipped, evacuate and charge the air conditioning system.

33. Install the engine cover.

5.0L AND 5.8L ENGINES

Bronco and F Series

1. Disconnect the negative battery cable and relieve the fuel system pressure. Drain the cooling system and the crankcase.

2. Mark the position of the hood on the hinges and remove the hood.

3. Remove the air intake hoses, crankcase ventilation hose and carbon canister hose.

4. Disconnect the upper and lower radiator hoses and, if equipped, the automatic transmission oil cooler lines.

5. Disconnect and cap the power steering hoses. Disconnect the thermactor air pump hoses.

6. If equipped, discharge the air conditioning system and remove the condenser. Disconnect the air conditioning lines and the clutch wire at the compressor.

7. Remove the fan shroud and lay it over the fan. Remove the radiator and fan, shroud, pulley and belt.

8. Tag and disconnect the alternator wires. Remove the brackets for the air pump, alternator, power steering and compressor.

9. Disconnect the oil pressure sending unit lead from the sending unit. Disconnect and plug the flexible fuel line at the fuel tank line. Disconnect the evaporative emission hoses at the evaporative canister. Disconnect the chassis fuel line quick disconnects at the fuel rails.

10. Disconnect the accelerator cable at the throttle body. Disconnect the cruise control linkages, if equipped. Disconnect the automatic transmission kickdown rod and remove the return spring, if equipped.

11. Disconnect the power brake booster vacuum hose.

12. After disconnecting the accelerator and the TV cable from the throttle body, disconnect the throttle bracket from the upper intake manifold and swing out of the way with the cables still attached to the bracket.

13. Disconnect the heater hoses from the water pump and intake manifold or at the tee, if equipped. Disconnect the water temperature sending unit wire from the sending unit.

14. Remove the upper bell housing-to-engine attaching bolts.

15. Tag and disconnect the engine wire loom and position out of the way. Disconnect the ground strap from the cylinder block.

16. Raise and safely support the vehicle. Disconnect the starter cable from the starter. Remove the starter.

17. Disconnect the exhaust pipes and exhaust heat control valve, if equipped, from the exhaust manifolds.

18. Disconnect the engine mounts from the brackets on the frame.

19. If equipped with automatic transmission, remove the converter inspection plate and remove the torque converter-to-flywheel attaching bolts.

20. Remove the remaining bell housing-to-engine attaching bolts.

21. Lower the vehicle and support the transmission with a jack. Install suitable engine lifting equipment.

22. Raise the engine slightly and carefully pull it out from the transmission. Carefully lift the engine out of the engine compartment so the rear cover plate is not bent or other components damaged. Install the engine on a workstand.

To install:

23. Install suitable engine lifting equipment and remove the engine from the workstand. Lower the engine carefully into the engine compartment. Make sure the block dowels are through the rear cover plate, then engage the holes in the flywheel housing.

24. If equipped with a manual transmission, start the transmission input shaft into the clutch disc. It may be necessary to adjust the position of the transmission in relation to the engine if the transmission input shaft will not enter the clutch disc. If the engine hangs up after the shaft enters, turn the crankshaft slowly, with the transmission in gear, until the shaft splines mesh with the clutch disc splines.

25. Install the bell housing-to-engine upper bolts and the engine mount washers and attaching nuts. Remove the engine lifting equipment.

26. Raise and safely support the vehicle. Connect the exhaust pipes and the heat control valve, if equipped, to the manifolds.

27. Install the starter and the starter cable. Install the remaining bell housing-to-engine bolts.

28. If equipped with automatic transmission, install the converter-to-flywheel attaching bolts and install the converter inspection plate.

29. Remove the support from the transmission and lower the vehicle. Install the air conditioner and power steering bracket and components. Install the alternator/air pump bracket.

30. If equipped, connect the air conditioning compressor clutch lead wire. Connect the engine wire loom and the water temperature sending unit wire.

31. Connect the bellcrank/linkage bracket to the intake manifold. Connect the transmission shift rod or cable, if equipped and install the retracting spring. Connect the accelerator rod and cruise control linkage, if equipped.

32. Remove the plug from the fuel tank line and connect the fuel line and the oil pressure sending unit wire. Reconnect the evaporative emission hoses at the canister. Reconnect the chassis fuel lines to the fuel rail.

33. Install the pulley, clutch and fan and position the shroud over the fan. Install the accessory drive belt.

34. Position the alternator and install the mounting bolts. If equipped, connect the air conditioning lines to the compressor.

35. Install the radiator and connect the radiator hoses and transmission oil cooler lines, if equipped. Install the fan shroud.

36. If equipped, install the air conditioning condenser to the

radiator. Connect the heater hoses at the water pump and intake manifold.

37. Fill the crankcase with the proper type and quantity of engine oil. Fill and bleed the cooling system. Connect the power brake booster vacuum hose.

38. Connect the negative battery cable, start the engine and bring to normal operating temperature. Check for leaks. Purge the power steering system of any air.

39. Install the air cleaner and intake duct assembly including the crankcase ventilation hose and carbon canister hose. If equipped, evacuate and charge the air conditioning system.

40. Install the hood, aligning the marks that were made during removal.

E Series

1. Disconnect the negative battery cable and relieve the fuel system pressure. Drain the cooling system and the crankcase. Remove the engine cover.

2. Remove the grille assembly including the gravel deflector. Remove the air cleaner, air ducts and closure hose.

3. Remove the upper grille support bracket, hood lock support and condenser upper mounting brackets, if equipped.

4. If equipped, discharge the air conditioning system and remove the condenser. Disconnect the air conditioning lines at the compressor and remove the accelerator cable bracket. Disconnect the cruise control linkage, if equipped.

5. Disconnect the radiator hoses at the radiator. Disconnect the heater hoses from the engine and at the heater core and water valve. If equipped with automatic transmission, disconnect the oil cooler lines at the radiator.

6. Remove the fan shroud and fan assembly. Remove the radiator and the water pump pulley and drive belt.

7. Disconnect the alternator lead wires and the air conditioner compressor clutch wire. Disconnect the power steering, thermactor air pump, alternator and air conditioning compressor. Plug the hoses as necessary.

8. Remove the accessory brackets complete with the accessories. Remove the air cleaner assembly. Disconnect the fuel line from the fuel rail.

9. Disconnect the throttle linkage at the throttle body and remove the accelerator cable bracket from the engine. Disconnect the transmission shift rod, if equipped.

10. Raise and safely support the vehicle. Remove the oil filter.

11. Disconnect the exhaust pipes and exhaust heat control valve, if equipped, at the exhaust manifolds. Remove the 2 bolts retaining the transmission filler tube bracket to the right cylinder head.

12. Remove the engine mount attaching bolts and nuts. Remove the starter. If equipped with manual transmission, remove the housing-to-engine bolts.

13. If equipped with automatic transmission, remove the converter inspection cover bolts and remove the 4 nuts attaching the converter to the flexplate. Remove the 3 bolts retaining the adapter plate to the converter housing and remove the 4 converter housing-to-cylinder block lower bolts.

14. Remove the bolt retaining the ground cable to the cylinder block. Lower the vehicle and support the transmission with a floor jack.

15. Tag and disconnect the engine wire loom and position out of the way. Attach suitable engine lifting equipment and remove the remaining bell housing-to-engine bolts.

16. Carefully move the engine forward in the engine compartment so no components are damaged. Remove the engine from the vehicle and position on a workstand.

To install:

17. Install suitable engine lifting equipment and remove the engine from the workstand. Position the engine in the vehicle.

18. If equipped with automatic transmission, align the converter with the flexplate and the engine dowels with the converter housing.

19. If equipped with manual transmission, start the input

shaft into the clutch disc. It may be necessary to adjust the position of the transmission in relation to the engine if the input shaft will not enter the clutch disc. If the engine hangs up after the shaft enters, turn the crankshaft slowly, with the transmission in gear, until the shaft splines mesh with the clutch disc splines. Align the housing on the engine and install the housing-to-engine bolts. Tighten to 40–50 ft. lbs. (55–67 Nm).

20. If equipped with automatic transmission, install 2 converter housing-to-cylinder block bolts.

21. Remove the engine lifting equipment and remove the floor jack from under the transmission.

22. Install the brackets and accessories. If equipped, connect the air conditioning compressor clutch wire.

23. Position the accelerator cable mounting bracket and install 3 attaching bolts.

24. Position the engine wire harness in the retainers and connect at respective locations. Connect the vacuum lines at the center of the upper intake manifold and connect the power brake booster vacuum hose.

25. Connect the heater hoses and connect the air conditioning compressor, thermactor air pump, alternator and power steering pump.

26. Install the water pump pulley, clutch and fan to the water pump and position the shroud over the fan assembly.

27. Raise and safely support the vehicle. Install the bolt attaching the ground cable to the cylinder block. If equipped with automatic transmission, install the remaining converter housing-to-engine bolts.

28. If equipped with automatic transmission, install the 3 adapter plate-to-converter housing bolts. Install the 4 nuts retaining the converter to the flexplate and install the converter inspection cover.

29. Install the starter and connect the cable. Install the engine mount attaching bolts and nuts and tighten to 50–70 ft. lbs. (68–95 Nm).

30. Install the 2 bolts that retain the transmission filler tube bracket to the right cylinder head.

31. Connect the exhaust pipes and, if equipped, the heat control valve at the exhaust manifolds.

32. Connect the throttle and transmission linkage and cruise control linkage, if equipped, at the throttle body. Connect the alternator wires to the alternator and the fuel line to the fuel supply manifold.

33. Install the accessory drive belt. If equipped, connect the air conditioning lines to the compressor. Install the accelerator cable bracket to the dash.

34. Position the radiator to the radiator support and install the attaching bolts. Install the shroud.

35. Connect the transmission oil cooler lines, if equipped, and connect the radiator hoses at the radiator.

36. Install the air conditioning condenser to the radiator support, if equipped. Install the grille upper support bracket, hood lock support, condenser upper mounting brackets and the grille.

37. Fill the crankcase with the proper type and quantity of engine oil. Fill and bleed the cooling system. Install the air cleaner, air ducts and closure hose.

38. Connect the negative battery cable, start the engine and bring to normal operating temperature. Check for leaks.

39. Evacuate and charge the air conditioning system, if equipped. Install the engine cover.

7.5L ENGINE

F Series

1. Disconnect the battery cables and relieve the fuel system pressure. Drain the cooling system and the crankcase.

2. Mark the position of the hood on the hinges and remove the hood.

3. Disconnect the thermactor air pump inlet hose at the front of the air cleaner housing. Disconnect the air outlet tube assembly at the throttle body and upper intake manifold. Remove the

air cleaner assembly and air outlet tubes after disconnecting the air inlet tube at the air cleaner.

4. Remove the thermactor bypass valve hose connected to the air inlet tube and remove the air inlet tube.

5. Remove the air cleaner and intake duct assembly, including the crankcase ventilation hose and carbon canister hose.

6. Disconnect the radiator hoses at the radiator. If equipped with automatic transmission, disconnect the transmission oil cooler lines. If equipped with an engine oil cooler, disconnect the cooler lines at the oil filter adapter.

NOTE: Do not attempt to disconnect the engine oil cooler lines at the quick connect fittings behind or at the cooler, or damage to the fittings will occur.

7. If equipped, discharge the air conditioning system and remove the condenser. Disconnect the air conditioning lines at the compressor.

8. Remove the fan shroud and position it over the fan. Remove the radiator. Remove the fan shroud, fan clutch, belts and pulley.

9. Remove the alternator bolts and allow the alternator to swing down and out of the way.

10. Disconnect the throttle and transmission linkage at the throttle body and remove the accelerator cable bracket from the upper intake manifold. Remove the cruise control hardware, if equipped.

11. Disconnect the oil pressure sending unit wire from the sending unit. Disconnect the evaporative emission hoses at the evaporative canister.

12. Disconnect the fuel lines at the qick disconnect couplings. Tag and disconnect the vacuum lines at the intake manifold.

13. Disconnect the EGR tube at the left exhaust manifold and upper intake manifold. Plug the manifold opening.

14. Disconnect the power brake booster vacuum hose and disconnect the exhaust air supply bypass valve hose at the thermactor check valve. Disconnect the heater hoses from the water pump and intake manifold.

15. Remove the flywheel housing-to-engine upper bolts and disconnect the ground strap from the cylinder block. Remove the oil fill tube, dipstick and tube.

16. Raise and safely support the vehicle. Disconnect the starter cable and remove the starter.

17. Disconnect the exhaust pipes from the exhaust manifolds. Disconnect the engine mounts from the frame.

18. If equipped with automatic transmission, remove the converter inspection plate and remove the converter-to-flywheel attaching bolts. If equipped with manual transmission, remove the rear cover plate from the flywheel housing and remove the remaining flywheel housing-to-engine bolts.

19. If equipped, disconnect the air conditioner compressor clutch wire.

20. Lower the vehicle and support the transmission with a jack. Install suitable engine lifting equipment.

21. Raise the engine slightly and carefully pullit from the transmission. Carefully lift the engine out of the engine compartment so the rear cover plate is not bent or other components damaged. Install the engine on a workstand.

To install:

22. Attach the engine lifting equipment and remove the engine from the workstand. Lower the engine carefully into the engine compartment. Make sure the block dowels are through the rear cover plate, then engage the dowels with the holes in the flywheel housing.

23. If equipped with manual transmission, start the transmission input shaft into the clutch disc. It may be necessary to adjust the position of the transmission in relation to the engine if the input shaft will not enter the clutch disc. If the engine hangs up after the shaft enters, turn the crankshaft slowly, transmission in gear, until the shaft splines mesh with the clutch disc splines.

24. Install the flywheel housing upper bolts. Install the engine

mount-to-frame nuts and washers and tighten to 60–80 ft. lbs. (81–108 Nm). Remove the engine lifting equipment.

25. Raise and safely support the vehicle. Connect the exhaust pipes to the exhaust manifolds. Install the starter and the starter cable and install the remaining flywheel housing-to-engine bolts.

26. If equipped with automatic transmission, install the converter-to-flywheel attaching bolts and the inspection plate. On manual transmissions, install the rear cover plate. Remove the support from the transmission and lower the vehicle.

27. If equipped, connect the air conditioning compressor clutch wire. Connect the water temperature sending unit wire.

28. Connect the acclerator cable bracket to the intake manifold. Connect the transmission and throttle linkage to the throttle body and cruise control linkage, if equipped.

29. Connect the fuel lines and connect the evaporative emission hoses at the evaporative canister. Install the pulley, belt, spacer and fan. Position the shroud over the fan.

30. Position the alternator and install the bolts. Install the drive belt.

31. If equipped, connect the 2 air conditioning lines to the compressor.

32. Install the radiator and connect the radiator hoses. If equipped, connect the transmission oil cooler lines and engine oil cooler. Install the fan shroud.

33. If equipped, install the air conditioning condenser.

34. Connect the heater hose at the water pump. Fill and bleed the cooling system.

35. Fill the crankcase with the proper type and quantity of engine oil. Connect the power brake booster vacuum hose.

36. Connect the negative battery cable, start the engine and bring to normal operating temperature. Check for leaks.

37. Install the air outlet tubes to the throttle body and upper intake manifold including the crankcase ventilation hose and carbon canister hose.

38. Evacuate and charge the air conditioning system, if equipped. Install the hood, aligning the marks that were made during removal.

E Series

1. Remove the engine cover. Disconnect the negative battery cable and relieve the fuel system pressure. Drain the cooling system and the crankcase.

2. Remove the grille assembly including the gravel deflector.

3. Remove the 4 bolts that secure the air cleaner and bracket assembly at the body cowl and radiator support. Disconnect the thermactor air pump inlet hose at the front of the air cleaner housing.

4. Disconnect the air outlet tube assembly at the throttle body and upper intake manifold. Remove the air cleaner assembly and air outlet tubes, after disconnecting the air inlet tube at the air cleaner.

5. Remove the thermactor bypass valve hose connected to the air inlet tube and remove the air inlet tube. Remove the upper grille support bracket, hood lock support and condenser upper mounting brackets.

6. If equipped, discharge the air conditioning system and remove the condenser. Disconnect the air conditioning lines at the compressor.

7. Remove the accelerator cable bracket from the dash and disconnect the 2 heater hoses from the engine.

9. If equipped, disconnect the engine oil cooler lines at the oil filter adapter. Do not attempt to disconnect the lines at the quick disconnect fittings at the cooler, as the fittings or the cooler may become damaged.

10. Disconnect the radiator hoses at the radiator. Remove the fan shroud, fan and radiator. Pivot the alternator inward and disconnect the alternator wires.

11. Disconnect the throttle and transmission linkage at the throttle body and remove the accelerator cable bracket from the upper intake manifold. Remove the cruise control hardware, if equipped.

12. Disconnect the fuel lines at the quick disconnect couplings and vacuum lines to the intake manifold. Disconnect the EGR tube at the left exhaust manifold and upper intake manifold. Plug the manifold opening.

13. Raise and safely support the vehicle. Remove the oil filter.

14. Disconnect the exhaust pipes from the exhaust manifolds. Remove the 2 bolts retaining the transmission filler tube bracket to the right cylinder head.

15. Disconnect the exhaust air supply bypass valve hose at the check valve.

16. Remove the engine mount attaching bolts and nuts. Remove the starter and disconnect the cable.

17. Remove the converter inspection cover bolts and remove the 4 nuts attaching the converter to the flexplate. Remove the 3 bolts retaining the adapter plate to the converter housing.

18. Remove the 4 converter housing-to-cylinder block lower bolts. Remove the bolt attaching the ground cable to the cylinder block. Lower the vehicle.

19. Loosen the belt tensioner and remove the drive belt. Disconnect the air conditioning lines and compressor clutch wire, if equipped. Disconnect and plug the power steering pump lines. Remove the pump and bracket from the front of the engine.

20. Tag and disconnect any vacuum lines at the rear of the intake manifold. Disconnect the engine wire loom and position aside.

21. Place a jack under the transmission and attach suitable engine lifting equipment.

22. Remove the remaining bell housing-to-cylinder block bolts and remove the engine from the vehicle.

To install:

23. Position the engine in the vehicle, aligning the converter to the flexplate and the engine dowels to the transmission.

24. Install 2 bell housing-to-cylinder block upper bolts and remove the engine lifting equipment. Remove the floor jack from under the transmission.

25. If equipped, connect the air conditioning compressor clutch wire.

26. Position the accelerator cable mounting bracket and the cruise control servo to the intake manifold and install the attaching bolts.

27. Position the engine wire harness in the retainers and connect at the respective locations. Connect the vacuum lines at the rear of the intake manifold.

28. Connect the 2 heater hoses at the water outlet connector and at the water pump connector. Position the power steering bracket to the water pump and the left cylinder head and install the attaching bolts. Install the power steering pump to the bracket.

29. Position the power steering pump drive belt and install the automatic tensioner. If equipped, connect the 2 air conditioning lines to the compressor. Install the accelerator cable bracket to the dash.

30. Raise and safely support the vehicle. Install a new oil filter and install the bolt attaching the battery ground cable to the cylinder block.

31. Install the remaining bell housing-to-cylinder block bolts and install the adapter plate-to-converter housing bolts. Install the 4 nuts attaching the converter to the flexplate and install the converter inspection cover.

32. Install the starter motor and connect the cable. Install the engine mount attaching bolts and nuts and tighten to 50–70 ft. lbs. (68–94 Nm).

33. Install the 2 bolts attaching the transmission filler tube bracket to the right cylinder head. Connect the exhaust pipes at the exhaust manifolds.

34. Lower the vehicle. Connect the fuel lines and the vacuum lines. Connect the throttle and transmission linkage at the throttle body and connect the wires at the alternator.

35. Install the fan assembly to the water pump and position the shroud over the fan. Install the radiator, then install the shroud. Install the radiator hoses at the radiator.

36. Install the air conditioning condenser, if equipped. Connect the cruise control servo vacuum hose and secure the cable to the throttle body.

37. Install the grille upper support bracket, hood lock support and condenser upper mounting brackets. Install the grille assembly including gravel deflector.

38. Fill the crankcase with the proper type and quantity of engine oil. Fill and bleed the cooling system.

39. Connect the negative battery cable, start the engine and bring to normal operating temperature. Check for leaks.

40. Evacuate and charge the air conditioning system. Install the air cleaner assembly and the engine cover.

Engine Mounts

Removal and Installation

4.9L ENGINE

Bronco and F Series—Front Mounts

1. Remove the upper and lower nut and washer from the mount. If only 1 mount is being removed, loosen the nut and washer on the opposite mount.

2. Using a jack and a wood block placed under the oil pan, raise the engine just enough to allow clearance for removal of the mount.

3. Remove the mount and shield, if equipped. Remove the upper and lower brackets.

To install:

4. Install the lower bracket and tighten the bolts and nuts to 48–62 ft. lbs. (65–85 Nm). Install the upper bracket and tighten the bolts to 59–81 ft. lbs. (80–110 Nm).

5. Align the locator pin with the hole and position the mount on the lower bracket. Install the lower nut and washer finger-tight.

6. Position the shield on the right mount.

7. Lower the engine carefully to make sure the mount stud and pin engage the upper bracket mounting hole.

8. Install the nut and washer on the upper mount stud. Tighten the upper and lower stud nuts to 71–93 ft. lbs. (96–127 Nm).

9. If only 1 mount was removed, tighten the other mount at the brackets.

Bronco and F Series—Rear Mount

1. Remove the attaching bolts, nut and washers.

2. Raise the transmission slightly to provide clearance and remove the mount and mount retainer.

3. Installation is the reverse of the removal procedure. Tighten the mount-to-transmission bolts to 64–71 ft. lbs. (87–96 Nm) and the mount-to-crossmember nuts to 60–80 ft. lbs. (81–109 Nm).

E Series—Front Mounts

1. Raise and safely support the vehicle.

2. Remove the front mount-to-support bracket nuts and washers from both mounts.

3. Place a jack and a wood block under the engine oil pan. Raise the engine just enough to take the weight off the support brackets.

4. The support brackets are mounted to the frame crossmember with 4 bolts and locknuts. If these are to be removed, loosen the 4 locknuts on each support bracket and remove from the crossmember.

5. Remove the mount-to-cylinder block bolts and remove the mounts.

6. Installation is the reverse of the removal procedure. Tighten the mount-to-cylinder block bolts and the support bracket locknuts to 60–80 ft. lbs. (81–108 Nm). Tighten the mount-to-support bracket nuts to 57–74 ft. lbs. (67–100 Nm).

Front engine mount installation—Bronco and F Series with 4.9L engine

E Series—Rear Mount

1. Raise and safely support the vehicle. Place a transmission jack under the transmission and raise it slightly to take the weight off of the rear mount.
2. Remove the mount-to-crossmember and transmission extension housing locknuts and bolts. Remove the rear mount.
3. Installation is the reverse of the removal procedure. Tighten the mount locknuts to 50–70 ft. lbs. (68–94 Nm).

5.0L AND 5.8L ENGINES

Bronco and F Series—Front Mounts

1. Remove the bolts attaching the fan shroud to the radiator and position the shroud over the fan.
2. Remove the nut and washer attaching the mount to the chassis bracket.
3. Raise the engine. Remove the bolts and lockwashers attaching the mount to the cylinder block and remove the mount and the heat shield, if equipped.
4. Installation is the reverse of the removal procedure. Tighten the mount-to-engine bolts to 50–70 ft. lbs. (68–94 Nm) and the mount-to-chassis nut to 65–85 ft. lbs. (88–115 Nm).

Bronco and F Series—Rear Mount

1. Remove the mount-to-crossmember cttaching nuts.

2. Raise the transmission with a floor jack to provide clearance and remove the 2 bolts, insulator and spacers.
3. Installation is the reverse of the removal procedure. Tighten the mount-to-transmission bolts to 60–80 ft. lbs. (81–108 Nm) and the mount-to-crossmember nuts to 50–70 ft. lbs. (68–94 Nm).

E Series—Front Mounts

1. Disconnect the negative battery cable.
2. Remove the fan shroud bolts and the mount-to-frame nuts.
3. Position a jack and a wood block under the engine. Lift the engine and then remove the starter.
4. Remove the mount-to-engine bolts and alternator splash shield. Remove the mounts.
To install:
5. Clear the slots in the engine block of debris using a $^7/_{16}$-14 bottoming tap.
6. Install the mounts using new bolts and tighten to 50–70 ft. lbs. (68–96 Nm).
7. Install the starter, then lower the engine. Move the jack out of the way.
8. Install the mount-to-frame nuts and tighten to 50–70 ft. lbs. (68–95 Nm). Install the fan shroud and bolts.
9. Connect the negative battery cable.

E Series—Rear Mount

NOTE: On 138 in. wheelbase vehicles, first remove the fuel reservoir to eliminate any part damage due to removal of rear transmission support crossmember.

1. Raise and safely support the vehicle.
2. Remove the nuts securing the mount to the crossmember.
3. Raise the transmission with a jack so the mount clears the crossmember.
4. Remove the bolts securing the mount to the transmission and remove the mount.
5. Installation is the reverse of the removal procedure. Tighten the mount-to-transmission bolts and mount-to-crossmember nuts to 50–70 ft. lbs. (68–94 Nm).

7.5L ENGINE

Front Mount

1. Support the engine with a jack and a wood block placed under the oil pan.
2. Remove the locknuts from the bolts attaching the support bracket to the frame crossmember and frame side rail.
3. Remove the through bolt attaching the engine support bracket to the mount.
4. Raise the engine with the jack until the mount is clear of the cup-shaped engine bracket.
5. Remove the mount and frame bracket as an assembly.
6. Remove the nuts attaching the mount to the frame bracket.

To install:

7. Assemble the mount to the frame bracket and install the attaching nuts. The mount should be installed so the word **TOP** is visible on either side of the engine. Tighten the attaching nuts to 50–70 ft. lbs. (68–94 Nm).
8. Position the mount and frame bracket assembly to the engine mount bracket and the frame crossmember. Install the through bolt attaching the mount to the engine bracket. The through bolt for the right mount must be installed from the front of the engine and the through bolt for the left mount must be installed from the rear. Tighten the nut to 40–58 ft. lbs. (55–78 Nm) and install the cotter pin. Lower the engine.
9. Install the locknuts on the bolts attaching the frame bracket to the crossmember. Tighten the frame bracket attaching bolt locknuts to 35–50 ft. lbs. (48–67 Nm). Tighten the crossmember bolts and locknuts on the left support bracket to 72–105 ft. lbs. (98–142 Nm). Remove the jack and wood block.

Rear Mount

1. Remove the attaching bolts, nut and washer.
2. Raise the transmission slightly to provide clearance, then remove the mount.
3. Installation is the reverse of the removal procedure. Tighten the mount-to-transmission bolts to 44–59 ft. lbs. (60–80 Nm) on F Series or 50–70 ft. lbs. (68–94 Nm) on E Series. Tighten the mount-to-crossmember nuts to 50–70 ft. lbs. (68–94 Nm).

Cylinder Head

Removal and Installation

4.9L ENGINE

1. Relieve the fuel system pressure and disconnect the negative battery cable. Drain the cooling system and the crankcase.
2. Mark the position of the hood on the hinges and remove the hood. On E Series, remove the engine cover. Remove the throttle body inlet tubes.
3. If equipped, properly discharge the air conditioning system and remove the compressor and the condenser.
4. Disconnect the heater hose from the water pump and coolant outlet housing. Disconnect the fuel lines.
5. Remove the radiator, cooling fan, water pump pulley and fan drive belt.

6. Disconnect the accelerator cable at the throttle body and remove the cable retracting spring. If equipped with automatic transmission, disconnect the transmission kickdown cable at the throttle body. Disconnect the power brake booster vacuum line at the manifold.
7. Disconnect the exhaust pipe from the exhaust manifold. Disconnect the body ground strap and the battery ground cable at the engine.
8. Tag and disconnect the Electronic Engine Control (EEC) harness from all sensors. Tag and disconnect the engine wiring harness at the ignition coil, coolant temperature sending unit and oil pressure sending unit. Position the harness aside.
9. Remove the alternator mounting bolts and position the alternator aside, leaving the wires attached. Remove the air pump from the bracket, if equipped, and remove the alternator/air pump bracket from the engine.
10. Remove the power steering pump from the mounting brackets and position it aside, right side up, leaving the lines attached. If equipped with an air compressor, bleed the air system and disconnect the 2 air pressure lines at the compressor. Remove the power steering bracket.
11. Remove the coil bracket attaching bolts and position the coil aside.
12. Remove the rocker arm cover. Loosen the rocker arm bolts so the rocker arms can be rotated to 1 side. Remove the pushrods and identify them so they can be reinstalled in their original positions.
13. Tag and disconnect the spark plug wires at the spark plugs.
14. Remove the cylinder head bolts. Attach suitable lifting equipment and remove the cylinder head with the intake and exhaust manifolds. Do not pry between the head and block as the gasket surfaces may become damaged.
15. Separate the intake and exhaust manifolds from the cylinder head, if necessary.
16. Clean all gasket mating surfaces. Check the cylinder head gasket surface for flatness, using a feeler gauge and a straight edge. Warpage must not exceed 0.003 in. in any 6 in. or 0.006 in. overall. If machining is necessary, do not remove more than 0.010 in.

To install:

17. Position a new gasket over the dowel pins on the cylinder block. Attach suitable lifting equipment to the cylinder head and lower it into position on the cylinder block and dowel pins. Remove the lifting equipment.
18. Coat the threads of the cylinder head bolts with clean engine oil and install. Tighten the bolts, in sequence, in 3 steps, first to 50–55 ft. lbs. (67–75 Nm), then to 60–65 ft. lbs. (82–88 Nm) and finally to 70–85 ft. lbs. (94–115 Nm).
19. Apply multi-purpose grease to both ends of the pushrods and install them in their original positions. Apply multi-purpose grease to the valve stem tips.
20. Apply multi-purpose grease to the rocker arm fulcrum seat and the fulcrum seat socket in the rocker arm. Position the rocker arms and tighten the rocker arm bolt just enough to hold the pushrod in position. Check the valve clearance, then tighten the rocker arm bolts to 17–23 ft. lbs. (24–31 Nm).
21. Clean the rocker arm cover and position a new gasket on the cylinder head. Install the rocker arm cover retaining bolts and tighten to 70–105 inch lbs. (7.9–11.9 Nm), starting with the center bolts and working outward.
22. Connect the spark plug wires to the spark plugs. Connect the crankcase vent hose to the inlet tube in the intake manifold. Install the PCV valve in the rocker arm cover.
23. Connect the exhaust pipe to the exhaust manifold. Connect the engine ground strap and the battery ground cable. Connect the EEC harness to all sensors.
24. If equipped with automatic transmission, connect the kickdown cable to the throttle body. Connect the accelerator linkage to the throttle body and install the return spring.
25. Connect the power brake booster vacuum hose to the intake manifold. Connect the coil primary wire, oil pressure and

coolant temperature sending unit wires, fuel lines, heater hoses and positive battery cable.

26. Install the alternator and air pump on the mounting bracket and install the assembly on the engine. Install the power steering/air conditioning bracket on the engine and install the power steering pump and the air conditioning compressor, if equipped.

27. Install the water pump pulley, fan clutch, fan and drive belt. The fan clutch has right-hand thread. Tighten the fan bolts to 12–18 ft. lbs. (16.2–24.4 Nm).

28. Install the radiator and connect the radiator hoses. If removed connect the air compressor lines and/or the air conditioning condenser. If equipped, connect the transmission oil cooler lines.

29. Fill the crankcase with the proper type and quantity of engine oil. Fill and bleed the cooling system.

30. If removed, install the hood, aligning the marks that were made during removal.

31. Connect the negative battery cable, start the engine and bring to normal operating temperature. Check for leaks.

32. Install the throttle body intake tubes. On E Series, install the engine cover. If equipped, evacuate and charge the air conditioning system.

5.0L AND 5.8L ENGINES

1. Disconnect the negative battery cable and relieve the fuel system pressure. Drain the cooling system.

2. Remove the intake manifold and the rocker arm cover(s).

3. To remove the right cylinder head, remove the drive belt and then remove the alternator and air pump mounting bracket complete with accessories. Swing the alternator down and out of the way. If necessary, remove the ignition coil and air cleaner inlet duct from the left cylinder head.

4. To remove the left cylinder head, remove the air conditioning compressor/power steering bracket at the front of the cylinder and position the accessories aside. Remove the oil dipstick and tube and cruise control bracket, if equipped.

5. Raise and safely support the vehicle. Disconnect the exhaust pipe(s) from the manifold(s).

6. Loosen the rocker arm fulcrum bolts so the rocker arms can be rotated to the side. Remove the pushrods and identify them so they can be reinstalled in their original positions.

7. On E Series, remove the bolts holding the thermactor air supply manifold to the rear of the cylinder head and disconnect the hose at the air pump. Remove the hose, pump valve and air supply manifold as an assembly.

8. On Bronco and F Series, disconnect the thermactor air supply hoses at the check valves and plug the check valve.

9. Remove the cylinder head bolts and remove the cylinder head(s). Remove the exhaust manifold(s) from the cylinder head(s), if necessary.

10. Clean all gasket mating surfaces. Check the cylinder head gasket surface for flatness, using a feeler gauge and a straight edge. Warpage must not exceed 0.003 in. in any 6 in. or 0.006 in. overall. If machining is necessary, do not remove more than 0.010 in.

To install:

11. Position a new cylinder head gasket over the dowels on the cylinder block. Install the cylinder head on the block. Coat the threads of the cylinder head bolts with clean engine oil and install, finger-tight.

Cylinder head bolt torque sequence—4.9L engine

Cylinder head bolt torque sequence—5.0L, 5.8L and 7.5L engines

12. On the 5.0L engine, tighten the cylinder head bolts, in sequence, in 2 steps, first to 55–65 ft. lbs. (75–88 Nm) and then to 65–72 ft. lbs. (88–97 Nm).

13. On the 5.8L engine, tighten the cylinder head bolts, in sequence, in 3 steps, first to 85 ft. lbs. (115 Nm), then to 95 ft. lbs. (129 Nm) and finally to 105–112 ft. lbs. (143–151 Nm).

14. Apply multi-purpose grease to both ends of the pushrods and install them in their original positions. Apply multi-purpose grease to the valve stem tips.

15. Apply multi-purpose grease to the rocker arm fulcrum seat and the fulcrum seat socket in the rocker arm. Position the rocker arms and tighten the rocker arm bolt just enough to hold the pushrod in position. Check the valve clearance, then tighten the rocker arm bolts to 18–25 ft. lbs. (25–33 Nm).

16. Position new gasket(s) on the exhaust pipe(s), if required. Connect the exhaust pipe(s) to the exhaust manifold(s) and tighten the nuts to 25–38 ft. lbs. (34–52 Nm).

17. If the right cylinder head was removed, install the air pump/alternator bracket and accessories. Install the ignition coil and air cleaner inlet duct, if necessary. Install the drive belt.

18. If the left cylinder head was removed, install the power steering/air conditioning compressor bracket with accessories at the front of the cylinder head. Install the oil dipstick and tube and cruise control bracket, if equipped.

19. Clean the rocker arm cover(s) and install new gasket(s). Install the rocker arm cover(s) on the cylinder head(s) and install the retaining bolts. Tighten to 3–5 ft. lbs. (4–6 Nm).

20. Install the intake manifold.

21. Install the thermactor air supply manifold at the rear of the cylinder heads. Reconnect the air supply hose to the air pump, if removed. Unplug the check valve and connect the thermactor air supply hose.

22. Fill and bleed the cooling system. Connect the negative battery cable. Start the engine and bring to normal operating temperature. Check for leaks.

7.5L ENGINE

1. Disconnect the negative battery cable and relieve the fuel system pressure. Drain the cooling system.

2. Remove the intake manifold.

3. Raise and safely support the vehicle as necessary. Disconnect the exhaust pipe from the exhaust manifold.

4. Remove the accessory drive belts.

5. Remove the thermactor air pump and alternator. Remove the air pump bracket from the right cylinder head.

6. If equipped with air conditioning, shut off the compressor at the service valves and remove the valves and hoses from the compressor. Remove the nuts attaching the compressor support bracket to the water pump. Remove the bolts attaching the compressor to the upper mounting bracket and position the compressor aside. Remove the compressor/power steering pump mounting bracket.

7. If not equipped with air conditioning, remove the bolts attaching the power steering pump bracket to the left cylinder head and position the pump and bracket out of the way.

8. Disconnect the oil filler tube on E Series.

9. Remove the rocker arm covers. Remove the rocker arm fulcrum bolt, rocker arm, oil deflector, fulcrum and pushrod as-

semblies. Identify components so they can be reinstalled in their original positions.

10. Remove the cylinder head bolts and remove the cylinder heads and exhaust manifolds as assemblies. Remove the exhaust manifolds from the cylinder heads, if necessary.

NOTE: If necessary to loosen the cylinder head gasket seal, pry at the forward corners of the cylinder heads against the casting bosses provided on the cylinder block. Do not damage the machined surfaces of the head or block.

11. Clean all gasket mating surfaces. Check the cylinder head gasket surface for flatness, using a feeler gauge and a straight edge. Warpage must not exceed 0.003 in. in any 6 in. or 0.006 in. overall. If machining is necessary, do not remove more than 0.010 in.

To install:

12. If the exhaust manifold was removed, coat the cylinder head and manifold port areas with a film of graphite grease and install the manifold to the cylinder head.

13. Place 2 long head bolts in the 2 rear lower bolt holes of the left cylinder head. Place a long head bolt in the rear lower bolt hole of the right cylinder head. Use rubber bands to retain the bolts in position, above the head-to-block mating surface, until the cylinder heads are installed.

14. Position new head gaskets on the block over the dowels. Do not apply sealer to the head gasket surfaces. Place the cylinder heads on the block, guiding the exhaust manifold studs into the exhaust pipe connections.

15. Install the remaining head bolts, with the longer bolts in the lower row of bolt holes. Tighten the bolts, in sequence, in 3 steps, first to 80–90 ft. lbs. (108–122 Nm), then to 100–110 ft. lbs. (136–149 Nm) and finally to 130–140 ft. lbs. (177–189 Nm).

16. Apply multi-purpose grease to the pushrod ends and install them in their original positions. Apply multi-purpose grease to the valve stem tips. Lubricate and install the rocker arms, tightening the fulcrum bolts to 18–25 ft. lbs. (25–33 Nm). Perform a valve clearance check.

17. Tighten the exhaust pipe stud nuts to 25–38 ft. lbs. (34–52 Nm).

18. Install the intake manifold.

19. If equipped with air conditioning, install the compressor mounting bracket, with the power steering pump in place, to the left cylinder head and water pump. Attach the compressor to the mounting bracket and connect the service valves and hoses to the compressor.

20. If not equipped with air conditioning, attach the power steering pump and bracket to the left cylinder head and water pump.

21. On E Series, connect the oil filler tube.

22. Install the thermactor supply manifold to the exhaust manifold. Install the bolt attaching the alternator and air pump bracket to the right cylinder head. Install the air pump, alternator and the drive belt.

23. Install the air conditioning and power steering pump drive belt.

24. Fill and bleed the cooling system. Fill and bleed the power steering reservoir, as necessary.

25. Connect the negative battery cable, start the engine and bring to normal operating temperature. Check for leaks.

26. If equipped, evacuate and charge the air conditioning system.

Valve Lifters

Removal and Installation

EXCEPT 4.9L ENGINE

1. Disconnect the negative battery cable and relieve the fuel system pressure. Drain the cooling system.

2. Remove the intake manifold.

HYDRAULIC TAPPET PULLER

Valve lifter removal—5.0L, 5.8L and 7.5L engines

3. If necessary, disconnect the thermactor air supply hose at the air pump and place it aside.

4. Remove the rocker arm cover, then loosen the rocker arm bolts and rotate the rocker arms to the side.

5. Remove the pushrods and identify them so they can be reinstalled in their original positions.

6. Using lifter puller tool T70L–6500–A or equivalent, remove the lifters. If the lifters are to be reused, place them in a rack so they can be reinstalled in their original bores.

To install:

7. Clean the external surfaces and lubricate the lifters and lifter bores with clean engine oil. Install the lifters in their original positions. If new lifters are being installed, check each for a free fit in its bore.

8. Clean the pushrods in a suitable solvent and blow out the oil passages with compressed air. Check the pushrod ends for wear and/or damage. Check the pushrods for straightness by rolling them along a flat surface.

9. Apply multi-purpose grease to the pushrod ends and install them in their original positions. Apply multi-purpose grease to the valve stem tips.

10. Lubricate the rocker arms and fulcrum seats with multi-purpose grease and position the rocker arms over the pushrods. Tighten the rocker arm bolts to 18–25 ft. lbs. (25–33 Nm). Perform a valve clearance check.

11. Clean the rocker arm cover and cylinder head gasket surfaces. Install new gaskets and the rocker arm covers. Tighten the rocker arm cover bolts to 3–5 ft. lbs. (4–6 Nm) on 5.0L and 5.8L engines or 6–9 ft. lbs. (8–12 Nm) on 7.5L engine.

12. Install the intake manifold.

13. Fill and bleed the cooling system. Connect the negative battery cable, start the engine and bring to normal operating temperature. Check for leaks.

4.9L ENGINE

1. Disconnect the negative battery cable and relieve the fuel system pressure.

2. Disconnect the inlet air hose at the crankcase filter cap. Remove the throttle body inlet tubes.

3. Disconnect the accelerator cable at the throttle body and remove the return spring. Remove the accelerator cable bracket from the upper intake manifold and position the cable and bracket assembly aside.

4. Remove the fuel line from the fuel rail.

5. Remove the upper intake manifold and throttle body as follows:

a. Tag and disconnect the electrical connectors and vacuum lines at the upper intake manifold and the throttle body.

b. Disconnect the PCV hose from the fitting on the underside of the upper intake manifold.

c. Disconnect the EGR tube from the EGR valve and the rear exhaust manifold. Remove the tube from the engine.

d. Remove the thermactor tube from the lower intake manifold by removing the 2 nuts retaining the tube. Remove the nut attaching the thermactor bypass valve bracket to the lower intake manifold.

e. On E Series, remove the nut attaching the transmission fill tube. Then remove the tube bracket off the intake manifold stud.

f. Remove the 7 studs that retain the upper intake manifold. Remove the screw and washer attaching the upper intake manifold support bracket to the upper intake manifold.

g. Remove the upper intake manifold and throttle body.

6. Remove the coil bracket attaching bolt or "E" core assembly attaching nuts and position the coil aside.

7. Remove the rocker arm cover. Tag and disconnect the spark plug wires at the spark plugs. Disconnect the coil wire and remove the distributor cap and spark plug wire assembly.

8. Remove the pushrod cover. Loosen the rocker arm bolts and rotate the rocker arms to the side. Remove the pushrods and identify them so they can be reinstalled in their original positions.

9. Remove the lifters. If the lifters are to be reused, place them in a rack so they can be reinstalled in their original bores.

To install:

10. Clean all gasket mating surfaces. Clean the external surfaces of the lifters.

11. Apply multi-purpose grease to the camshaft lobes. Coat the lifters and the lifter bores with clean engine oil. Install the lifters in their original positions. If new lifters are being installed, check each for a free fit in its bore.

12. Clean the pushrods in a suitable solvent and blow out the oil passages with compressed air. Check the pushrod ends for wear and/or damage. Check the pushrods for straightness by rolling them atop a flat surface.

13. Apply multi-purpose grease to the pushrod ends and install them in their original positions. Apply multi-purpose grease to the valve stem tips.

14. Lubricate the rocker arms and fulcrum seats with multi-purpose grease and position the rocker arms over the pushrods. Tighten the rocker arm bolts to 17–23 ft. lbs. (24–31 Nm) and check the valve clearance.

15. Apply sealer to 1 side of a new pushrod cover gasket and install on the engine. Install the pushrod cover and tighten the screws to 25–35 inch lbs. (2.8–4.0 Nm).

16. Place a new gasket on the rocker arm cover and install on the cylinder head. Tighten the bolts to 70–105 inch lbs. (7.9–11.9 Nm). Install the PCV valve in the rocker arm cover.

17. Position the coil assembly on the cylinder head and install the attaching bolt or nuts. Install the distributor cap and spark plug wire assembly. Connect the spark plug wires at the spark plugs and the coil secondary high tension wire.

18. Install the upper intake manifold and throttle body assembly in the reverse order of removal. Tighten the attaching studs to 12–18 ft. lbs. (16.2–24.4 Nm) and the support screw to 22–32 ft. lbs. (29.8–43.4 Nm).

19. Install the accelerator cable bracket on the upper intake manifold and connect the cable to the throttle body.

20. Install the fuel line at the fuel rail. Install the throttle body inlet tubes. Connect the negative battery cable.

Valve Lash

Adjustment

Valve stem-to-valve rocker arm clearance should be within specification with the hydraulic lifter completely collapsed. Repeated machining operations, such as valve and/or valve seat refacing and cylinder head resurfacing or component replacement, will decrease the clearance to the point where if it is not compensated for, the hydraulic valve lifter will no longer function and the valve will be left open. For this reason, a 0.060 in. shorter or 0.060 in. longer pushrod is available to provide a means of compensating for dimensional changes in the valve train.

The positive stop rocker arm bolt eliminates the necessity to adjust the valve clearance. However, to obtain the proper valve clearance, all valve components must be in good condition and installed and tightened properly. Use the following service procedure to determine whether a shorter or longer pushrod is necessary.

4.9L ENGINE

1. Connect an auxiliary starter switch. Crank the engine with the ignition switch in the **OFF** position.

2. Make 2 marks on the crankshaft damper. Space the marks 120 degress apart so, with the timing mark, the damper is divided into 3 equal parts.

3. With No. 1 piston on TDC at the end of the compression stroke, tighten the rocker arm bolts of the No. 1 intake and exhaust valves to 17–23 ft. lbs. (24–31 Nm).

4. Using bleed down wrench T70P–6513–A or equivalent, slowly apply pressure to bleed down the lifter until the plunger is completely bottomed. Hold the lifter in this position and check the available clearance between the rocker arm and the valve stem tip with a feeler gauge. The clearance should be 0.125–0.175 in.

5. If the clearance is less than specified, install a shorter pushrod. If the clearance is greater than specified, install a longer pushrod.

6. Repeat this procedure for the rest of the valves, turning the crankshaft 1/3 turn at a time in the direction of rotation. Adjust the valves in the firing order sequence 1–5–3–6–2–4.

5.0L AND 5.8L ENGINES

1. Install an auxiliary starter switch. Crank the engine with the ignition switch **OFF** until No. 1 piston is on TDC after the compression stroke.

2. With the crankshaft in the positions designated in Steps 5a, 5b and 5c or Steps 6a, 6b and 6c, position the hydraulic lifter compressor tool T71P–6513–B or equivalent, on the rocker arm.

3. Slowly apply pressure to bleed down the hydraulic lifter until the plunger is completely bottomed. Hold the lifter in this position and check the available clearance between the rocker arm and the valve stem tip with a feeler gauge. The clearance should be 0.096–0.165 in. on 5.0L engine or 0.123–0.173 in. on 5.8L engine.

4. If the clearance is less than specified, install a shorter pushrod. If clearance is greater than specified, install a longer pushrod.

5. On 5.0L engine, clearance checking positions are as follows:

a. With the No. 1 piston on TDC at the end of the compression stroke, Position 1, check the following valves:

No. 1 intake

No. 1 exhaust

No. 7 intake

No. 5 exhaust

No. 8 intake

No. 4 exhaust

STEP 1 - SET NO. 1 PISTON ON T.D.C. AT END OF COMPRESSION STROKE ADJUST NO. 1 INTAKE AND EXHAUST

STEP 4 - CHECK NO. 6 INTAKE AND EXHAUST

STEP 2 - CHECK NO. 5 INTAKE AND EXHAUST

STEP 5 - CHECK NO. 2 INTAKE AND EXHAUST

STEP 3 - CHECK NO. 3 INTAKE AND EXHAUST

STEP 6 - CHECK NO. 4 INTAKE AND EXHAUST

Valve clearance adjustment positions—4.9L engine

WITH NO. 1 AT TDC AT THE END OF THE COMPRESSION STROKE MAKE A CHALK MARK AT POINTS 2 AND 3 APPROXIMATELY 90 DEGREES APART.

TIMING POINTER

POSITION 1—

NO. 1 AT TDC AT THE END OF THE COMPRESSION STROKE

POSITION 2—

ROTATE THE CRANKSHAFT 180 DEGREES (ONE HALF REVOLUTION) CLOCKWISE FROM POSITION 1

POSITION 3—

ROTATE THE CRANKSHAFT 270 DEGREES (THREE QUARTER REVOLUTION CLOCKWISE FROM POSITION 2

Valve clearance adjustment positions—5.0L and 5.8L engines

   b. Rotate the crankshaft to Position 2 and check the following valves:

   No. 5 intake

   No. 2 exhaust

   No. 4 intake

   No. 6 exhaust

   c. Rotate the crankshaft to Position 3 and check the following valves:

   No. 2 intake

   No. 7 exhaust

   No. 3 intake

   No. 3 exhaust

   No. 6 intake

   No. 8 exhaust

6. On 5.8L engine, clearance checking positions are as follows:

   a. With the No. 1 piston on TDC at the end of the compression stroke, Position 1, check the following valves:

   No. 1 intake

   No. 1 exhaust

   No. 4 intake

   No. 3 exhaust

   No. 8 intake

   No. 7 exhaust

   b. Rotate the crankshaft to Position 2 and check the following valves:

   No. 3 intake

   No. 2 exhaust

   No. 7 intake

   No. 6 exhaust

TAPPET BLEED DOWN WRENCH

Checking valve clearance

c. Rotate the crankshaft to Position 3 and check the following valves:

No. 2 intake
No. 4 exhaust
No. 5 intake
No. 5 exhaust
No. 6 intake
No. 8 exhaust

7.5L ENGINE

1. Install an auxiliary starter switch. Crank the engine with the ignition switch **OFF** until No. 1 piston is on TDC after the compression stroke.

2. With the crankshaft in the positions designated in Steps 5 and 6, position hydraulic lifter compressor tool T71P–6513–B or equivalent, on the rocker arm.

3. Slowly apply pressure to bleed down the hydraulic lifter until the plunger is completely bottomed. Hold the lifter in this position and check the available clearance between the rocker arm and the valve stem tip with a feeler gauge. The clearance should be 0.100–0.150 in.

4. If the clearance is less than specified, install a shorter pushrod. If clearance is greater than specified, install a longer pushrod.

5. With the No. 1 piston on TDC at the end of the compression stroke, Position 1, check the following valves:

No. 1 intake
No. 1 exhaust
No. 3 intake
No. 4 exhaust
No. 7 intake
No. 5 exhaust
No. 8 intake
No. 8 exhaust

6. Rotate the crankshaft 360 degrees to Position 2 and check the following valves:

No. 2 intake
No. 2 exhaust
No. 4 intake
No. 3 exhaust
No. 5 intake
No. 6 exhaust
No. 6 intake
No. 7 exhaust

Rocker Arms

Removal and Installation

4.9L ENGINE

1. Disconnect the negative battery cable and relieve the fuel system pressure. Disconnect the inlet air hose at the crankcase filter cap and remove the throttle body inlet tubes.

2. Disconnect the accelerator cable at the throttle body. Remove the cable retracting spring. Remove the accelerator cable bracket from the upper intake manifold and position the cable and bracket assembly aside.

3. Remove the fuel line from the fuel rail. Remove the upper intake and throttle body asembly as follows:

a. Tag and disconnect the electrical connectors and vacuum lines at the upper intake manifold and the throttle body.

b. Disconnect the PCV hose from the fitting on the underside of the upper intake manifold.

c. Disconnect the EGR tube from the EGR valve and the rear exhaust manifold. Remove the tube from the engine.

d. Remove the thermactor tube from the lower intake manifold by removing the 2 nuts retaining the tube. Remove the nut attaching the thermactor bypass valve bracket to the lower intake manifold.

e. On E Series, remove the nut attaching the transmission fill tube. Then remove the tube bracket off the intake manifold stud.

f. Remove the 7 studs that retain the upper intake manifold. Remove the screw and washer attaching the upper intake manifold support bracket to the upper intake manifold.

g. Remove the upper intake manifold and throttle body.

4. Remove the PCV valve from the rocker arm cover. Remove the crankcase filter. Remove the cover bolts and remove the rocker arm cover.

5. Remove the rocker arm bolt, fulcrum seat and rocker arm.

To install:

6. Clean all gasket mating surfaces. Check the rocker arm cover gasket sealing surface for damage and/or distortion. Repair or replace the cover, as necessary.

7. Apply multi-purpose grease to the top of the valve stems, the rocker arm fulcrum seat and the fulcrum seat socket in the rocker arm.

Valve clearance adjustment positions—7.5L engine

Rocker arm assembly

8. Install the rocker arm, fulcrum seat and rocker arm bolt. Tighten the rocker arm bolt to 17–23 ft. lbs. (24–31 Nm). Check the valve clearance.

9. Place a new gasket on the cylinder head, making sure the tabs of the gasket face down towards the head. Install the rocker arm cover, making sure the gasket seats evenly all around the head. Partially tighten the cover bolts, starting at the middle and working outwards, then tighten the bolts to 4–7 ft. lbs. (5–9 Nm) in the same way.

10. Install the PCV valve. Install the upper intake manifold and throttle body assembly in the reverse order of removal. Tighten the attaching studs to 12–18 ft. lbs. (16.2–24.4 Nm) and the support screw to 22–32 ft. lbs. (29.8–43.4 Nm).

11. Install the accelerator cable bracket on the upper intake manifold and connect the cable to the throttle body. Connect the fuel line.

12. Connect the inlet air hose to the crankcase filter cap and install the throttle body inlet tubes. Connect the negative battery cable.

5.0L AND 5.8L ENGINES

1. Disconnect the negative battery cable. Remove the air cleaner and intake duct assembly, including the closed crankcase ventilation hoses and tubes.

2. Remove the coil and the solenoid brackets.

3. For removal of the right side rocker arm cover, remove the lifting eye and the thermactor tube.

4. Remove the oil filler pipe hose from the left side rocker arm cover, if equipped.

5. Tag and disconnect the spark plug wires. Remove the wires and bracket assemblies from the rocker arm cover attaching stud and position aside.

6. Remove the vacuum harness and the electrical connectors to the vacuum solenoids mounted on the rocker arm covers, if equipped, and position aside.

7. Disconnect the evaporative system hoses from the canister or the chassis and position aside. Remove the thermactor air supply hose, if equipped.

8. Remove the rocker arm cover bolts and remove the rocker arm covers.

9. Remove the rocker arm bolt, fulcrum seat and rocker arm.

Rocker arm cover bolt torque sequence—5.0L and 5.8L engines

To install:

10. Clean all gasket mating surfaces. Check the rocker arm cover gasket sealing surface for damage and/or distortion. Repair or replace the cover, as necessary.

11. Apply multi-purpose grease to the top of the valve stems, the rocker arm fulcrum seat and the fulcrum seat socket in the rocker arm.

12. Install the fulcrum guide, rocker arm, fulcrum seat and bolt. Tighten to 18–25 ft. lbs. (25–32 Nm). Check the valve clearance.

13. Place new gaskets in the rocker arm covers, making sure the tabs of the gasket engage the notches in the cover. Position the covers on the cylinder heads, install the bolts and tighten, in sequence, to 3–5 ft. lbs. (4–6 Nm). Wait 2 minutes, then tighten the bolts again, in sequence, to the same specifications.

14. Retighten all intake manifold bolts to 23–25 ft. lbs. (32–33 Nm) in the proper sequence. Install the vacuum harness bracket and attaching nut and tighten to 12–18 ft. lbs. (17–24 Nm).

15. Reconnect the vacuum harnesses and electrical connectors to the vacuum solenoids on the rocker arm covers, if equipped.

16. Connect the spark plug wires and bracket assembly to the attaching stud on the rocker arm cover and connect the wires at the spark plugs.

17. Connect the thermactor air supply hose, if equipped. Connect the oil filler pipe hose to the left rocker arm, if equipped.

18. Install the closed crankcase ventilation hoses or tubes. Connect the negative battery cable.

7.5L ENGINE

1. Disconnect the negative battery cable(s). Remove the air cleaner and intake duct assembly.

2. Remove the thermactor exhaust air supply control valve and bracket assembly and the ignition coil mounting bracket.

3. Disconnect the MTA hose at the thermactor valve. Disconnect the thermactor air control valve to air pump hose and tube inlet assembly.

4. Tag and disconnect the spark plug wires from the spark plugs and position the wires aside.

5. For the right side rocker arm cover, remove the PCV valve and position the wiring and vacuum harnesses to gain access in order to remove the cover.

6. Remove the rocker arm covers. Remove the fulcrum bolt, oil deflector, fulcrum seat and rocker arm.

To install:

7. Clean the rocker arm covers and the cylinder head sealing surfaces.

8. Apply multi-purpose grease to the top of the valve stems and the rocker arm and fulcrum seats.

9. Position the No. 1 piston at TDC at the end of the compression stroke. Install the rocker arm, fulcrum seat, oil deflector and fulcrum bolt on the following valves: No. 1 intake, No. 1 exhaust, No. 3 intake, No. 8 exhaust, No. 7 intake, No. 5 exhaust, No. 8 intake and No. 4 exhaust.

10. Rotate the crankshaft 1 revolution clockwise and install the rocker arm, fulcrum seat, oil deflector and fulcrum bolt on the following valves: No. 2 intake, No. 2 exhaust, No. 4 intake, No. 3 exhaust, No. 5 intake, No. 6 exhaust, No. 6 intake and No. 7 exhaust.

11. Make sure the fulcrum seat base is inserted into its slot on the cylinder head before tightening the fulcrum bolts. Tighten the fulcrum bolts to 18–25 ft. lbs. (25–33 Nm). Check the valve clearance.

12. Position a new seal in the cover seal groove, making sure the seal tang is aligned with the notch in the cover.

13. Position the covers on the cylinder heads. Tighten the 4 rocker arm cover bolts to 9 ft. lbs. (12 Nm) working from right-to-left. Install the PCV valve in the right side cover.

14. Install the ignition coil mounting bracket and connect the spark plug wires to the spark plugs.

15. Connect the thermactor air control valve and bracket as-

sembly. Install the thermactor air supply tube and MTA hose at the thermactor valve.

16. Install the air cleaner and intake duct assembly. Connect the negative battery cable(s), start the engine and check for leaks.

Intake Manifold

Removal and Installation

5.0L AND 5.8L ENGINES

1. Disconnect the negative battery cable and relieve the fuel system pressure. Drain the cooling system. Remove the air intake duct assembly.

2. Tag and disconnect the electrical connectors at the air by-pass valve, throttle position sensor and EGR position sensor.

3. Disconnect the throttle linkage at the throttle ball and the transmission linkage from the throttle body. Remove the bolts that secure the bracket to the intake and position the bracket and cables out of the way.

4. Tag and disconnect the upper intake manifold vacuum fitting connections by removing all the vacuum lines at the vacuum tree, EGR valve and fuel pressure-regulator.

5. Disconnect the PCV system by disconnecting the hose from the fitting at the rear of the upper manifold.

6. Remove the canister purge lines from the fittings at the throttle body. Disconnect the water heater lines from the throttle body.

7. Disconnect the EGR tube from the EGR valve by removing the flange nut.

8. Remove the bolt from the upper intake support bracket to the upper manifold. Remove the upper manifold retaining bolts and remove the upper intake manifold and throttle body as an assembly.

9. Tag and disconnect the spark plug wires from the spark plugs. Disconnect the coil wire from the distributor cap and remove the cap and wires assembly.

10. Mark the position of the rotor and the distributor housing in relation to the engine, remove the distributor hold-down bolt and remove the distributor.

11. Tag and disconnect the electrical connections at the coolant temperature sensor, temperature sending unit, air charge temperature sensor, knock sensor, electrical vacuum regulator and thermactor solenoids.

12. Disconnect the injector wiring harness from the main harness assembly. Remove the oxygen sensor ground wire from the intake manifold stud.

NOTE: **The plated stud and ground wire must be reinstalled in the same position.**

13. Disconnect the fuel supply and return lines from the fuel supply manifold.

14. Remove the upper radiator hose from the thermostat housing. Remove the water bypass hose and remove the heater outlet hose at the intake manifold.

15. Remove the nut securing the coil bracket and move the bracket aside.

16. Remove the intake manifold mounting bolts and studs. Note the location of the bolts and studs for reinstallation. Remove the lower intake manifold assembly.

To install:

17. Clean all gasket mating surfaces.

18. Apply a $\frac{1}{16}$ in. bead of silicone sealer to the end seals–gaskets mating points. Install the end seals on the cylinder block and new gaskets on the cylinder heads. The gaskets must be interlocked with the seal tabs.

19. Install 2 locator pins into opposite corners and carefully lower the intake manifold assembly into position.

20. Install the intake manifold bolts and studs. Tighten all bolts and studs, in sequence, to 22–32 ft. lbs. (30–43 Nm). Wait 10 minutes and then tighten all bolts and studs again, in sequence, to specification.

21. Position the coil bracket and hold in place while tightening the nut. Install the coil and solenoid bracket to the intake manifold studs and exhaust manifold stud with the retaining nuts.

22. Connect the upper radiator hose and water bypass hose to

Lower intake manifold bolt torque sequence—5.0L and 5.8L engines

Lower intake manifold installation—5.0L and 5.8L engines

Upper intake manifold installation—5.0L and 5.8L engines

the thermostat housing. Connect the heater outlet hose to the intake manifold.

23. Connect the fuel supply and return lines to the fuel supply manifold. Connect the fuel line retaining clips.

24. Connect the electrical connectors to the coolant temperature sensor, engine temperature sending unit, air charge temperature sensor, knock sensor, electrical vacuum regulator and thermactor solenoids.

25. Install the distributor, aligning the rotor and distributor housing with the marks that were made during removal. Install the hold-down bolt and the cap and wires assembly. Connect the coil and spark plug wires.

26. Position a new gasket on the lower intake manifold mounting face. Using alignment studs may be helpful.

27. Install the upper intake and throttle body assembly on the lower manifold, making sure the gasket remains in place. Install the 6 upper intake manifold retaining bolts and tighten to 12–18 ft. lbs. (16–24 Nm).

28. Install the upper intake support bracket to the upper manifold attaching bolt. Install the EGR tube.

29. Connect the canister purge lines and the water heater lines to the throttle body. Connect the PCV hose to the rear of the upper manifold.

30. Connect the vacuum lines to the vacuum tree, EGR valve and fuel pressure regulator.

31. Install the throttle linkage bracket with the 2 retaining bolts. Connect the throttle cable and transmission cable to the throttle body.

32. Connect the electrical connectors at the air bypass valve, throttle position sensor and EGR position sensor.

33. Fill and bleed the cooling system. Connect the negative battery cable, start the engine and bring to normal operating temperature. Check for leaks.

34. Check the ignition timing and adjust, if necessary.

7.5L ENGINE

1. Disconnect the negative battery cable(s) and relieve the fuel system pressure. Drain the cooling system and remove the air cleaner and intake duct assembly.

2. Remove the thermactor system from the right side of the engine. Remove the ignition coil mounting bracket and remove the coil wire.

3. Disconnect and remove the external EGR tube.

4. Disconnect the upper radiator hose at the engine. Disconnect the heater hoses at the intake manifold and the water pump. Loosen the water pump bypass hose at the intake manifold.

5. Disconnect the PCV valve and hose at the right rocker arm cover. Tag and disconnect all of the vacuum lines at the rear of the intake manifold.

6. Tag and disconnect the wires at the spark plugs. Disconnect and remove the distributor cap and wires as an assembly.

7. Mark the position of the rotor and the distributor housing in relation to the engine, remove the hold-down bolt and remove the distributor.

8. Disconnect the accelerator linkage and transmission kickdown linkage at the throttle body. Remove the cruise control linkage bracket, if equipped, from the manifold and throttle body. Remove the bolts holding the accelerator linkage cable and position the linkage aside.

9. Disconnect the fuel line at the fuel supply manifold.

10. Disconnect the wiring harness from the main wiring harness. Remove lower intake manifold and wiring as an assembly.

11. Remove the intake manifold attaching bolts and lift the manifold and throttle body from the engine as an assembly. It may be necessary to pry the manifold away from the cylinder heads. Do not damage the gasket sealing surfaces.

To install:

12. Clean all gasket mating surfaces.

13. Apply a ⅛ in. bead of silicone sealer to the junction points of the cylinder heads and the cylinder block end rails.

14. Install the intake manifold gaskets and the front and rear manifold-to-cylinder block seals. Apply a $\frac{1}{16}$ in. bead of sealer for the full width of the seal.

15. Carefully lower the intake manifold into position over the 4 studs in the ends of the cylinder heads. When the intake manifold is in place, run a finger around the seal area to make sure the seals are in place. If the seals have shifted, remove the manifold and re-position the seals.

16. Install the attaching bolts, stud bolts and nuts and tighten as follows:

    a. Tighten bolts 1–12, in sequence, to 8–12 ft. lbs. (11–16 Nm). Tighten nuts 13–16, in sequence, to 8–12 ft. lbs. (11–16 Nm).

    b. Tighten bolts and nuts 1–16, in sequence, to 12–22 ft. lbs. (16–30 Nm).

    c. Tighten manifold bolts and nuts 1–16, in sequence, to 22–35 ft. lbs. (30–47 Nm).

17. Install the external EGR tube and thermactor exhaust air supply tubes.

18. Install the water pump bypass hose to the intake manifold fitting and heater hot water tube. Connect the radiator upper hose to the coolant outlet housing.

19. Install the distributor, aligning the rotor and the distributor housing with the marks that were made during removal. Install the hold-down bolt.

20. Connect the heater hoses at the intake manifold and water pump. Connect the PCV valve and hose to the right side rocker arm cover.

21. Connect the fuel lines to the fuel supply manifold and in-

Intake manifold bolt torque sequence—7.5L engine

stall the ignition coil mounting bracket. Connect all electrical connectors.

22. Position the accelerator linkage on the manifold and attach the accelerator linkage cable. Attach the cruise control linkage bracket to the intake manifold, if equipped. Connect the accelerator and kickdown linkage to the throttle body.

23. Connect the vacuum lines. Install the distributor cap and wires assembly. Connect the coil wire and the spark plug wires.

24. Fill and bleed the cooling system. Connect the negative battery cable(s), start the engine and bring to normal operating temperature. Check for leaks.

25. Check the ignition timing and adjust, if necessary.

26. While the engine is hot, tighten the manifold attaching nuts and bolts, in sequence, to 22–35 ft. lbs. (30–47 Nm).

27. Install the air cleaner and intake duct assembly.

Exhaust Manifold

Removal and Installation

5.0L AND 5.8L ENGINES

1. Disconnect the negative battery cable.

2. Remove the air cleaner and intake duct assembly, including the crankcase ventilation hose.

3. Remove the bolts attaching the air cleaner inlet duct, if equipped.

4. Raise and safely support the vehicle. Disconnect the muffler inlet pipes.

5. Lower the vehicle.

6. Remove the exhaust manifold heat shields, if equipped, attaching bolts and flat washers. On the left exhaust manifold, remove the oil dipstick tube assembly, cruise control bracket and exhaust heat control valve, if equipped. Then remove the exhaust manifold.

To install:

7. Clean the exhaust manifold and cylinder head mating surfaces. Clean the mounting flange spherical seat of the exhaust manifolds and muffler inlet pipes.

8. Position the exhaust manifolds on the cylinder heads and install the attaching bolts and flat washers. On the left exhaust manifold, install the oil dipstick tube and the cruise control bracket, if equipped. Working from the center to the ends, tighten the bolts to 18–24 ft. lbs. (25–33 Nm).

9. Raise and safely support the vehicle. Position new gaskets, if equipped, on the muffler inlet pipes. Position the muffler inlet pipes and exhaust heat control valve, if equipped, into the manifolds. Install and tighten the attaching nuts to 25–38 ft. lbs. (34–52 Nm).

10. Lower the vehicle. Install the air cleaner and intake duct assembly, including the crankcase ventilation hose.

7.5L ENGINE

1. Disconnect the negative battery cable.

2. If removing the right exhaust manifold, remove the spark plug heat shield.

3. Tag and disconnect the spark plug wires from the spark plugs.

4. Disconnect the thermactor air supply manifold, if equipped.

5. Disconnect the external EGR tube on the left exhaust manifold.

6. Raise and safely support the vehicle. Disconnect the muffler inlet pipes at the exhaust manifolds.

7. Lower the vehicle.

8. Remove the power steering pump support bracket. On E Series, remove the brace from the back of the power steering pump.

9. Remove the oil dipstick tube from the left exhaust manifold.

10. Remove the attaching bolts and remove the exhaust manifolds.

To install:

11. Clean the mating surfaces of the exhaust manifolds and cylinder heads. Clean the mounting flange of the manifolds and inlet pipes. Apply a light film of graphite grease to the exhaust manifolds.

12. Position the exhaust manifolds on the cylinder heads. Install the attaching bolts and washers, starting at the 4th bolt hole from the front of each manifold. Tighten the bolts to 22–30 ft. lbs. (30–41 Nm) working from the center of the manifold outwards.

13. Raise and safely support the vehicle. Position the inlet pipes to the manifolds and tighten the attaching nuts to 25–36 ft. lbs. (34–49 Nm).

14. Lower the vehicle. Install the power steering pump support bracket. Install the brace, if removed.

15. Connect the external EGR tube on the left exhaust manifold. Install the heat shield and spark plug wires.

16. Connect the negative battery cable. Start the engine and check for exhaust leaks.

Service Tips

LOOSE OR BREAKING EXHAUST MANIFOLD BOLTS OR STUDS

Exhaust manifold bolts or studs on the 7.5L engine, may break or loosen due to the type of alloy they are made of. Whenever the exhaust manifold bolts are replaced, use part number 390849–S101 only. Whenever the exhaust manifold studs are replaced, use part numbers 390850–S101 and 390851–S101 only. The bolts and studs are made of a special "A-286" stainless steel alloy.

Combination Manifold

Removal and Installation

4.9L ENGINE

1. Disconnect the negative battery cable and relieve the fuel system pressure. Disconnect the inlet air hose at the crankcase filter cap. Remove the throttle body inlet hoses.

2. Disconnect the accelerator cable at the throttle body. Remove the cable retracting spring. Remove the accelerator cable bracket and position the cable and bracket aside.

3. Disconnect the fuel line from the fuel supply manifold. Remove the upper intake manifold and throttle body assembly as follows:

   a. Tag and disconnect the electrical connectors and vacuum lines at the upper intake manifold and the throttle body.

   b. Disconnect the PCV hose from the fitting on the underside of the upper intake manifold.

   c. Disconnect the EGR tube from the EGR valve and the rear exhaust manifold. Remove the tube from the engine.

   d. Remove the thermactor tube from the lower intake manifold by removing the 2 nuts retaining the tube. Remove the nut attaching the thermactor bypass valve bracket to the lower intake manifold.

   e. On E Series, remove the nut attaching the transmission fill tube. Then remove the tube bracket off the intake manifold stud.

   f. Remove the 7 studs that retain the upper intake manifold. Remove the screw and washer attaching the upper intake manifold support bracket to the upper intake manifold.

   g. Remove the upper intake manifold and throttle body.

4. Tag and disconnect the vacuum lines. Raise and safely support the vehicle.

5. Disconnect the inlet pipe from the exhaust manifolds. Lower the vehicle.

6. Disconnect the power brake booster vacuum hose.

7. Remove the bolts attaching the manifolds to the cylinder head and lift the manifolds from the engine.

To install:

8. Clean the mating surfaces of the cylinder head and the manifolds.

9. If 1 of the manifolds is to be replaced, remove the tube fittings from the discarded manifolds and install them in the new manifolds, as required. Also install new studs in the new manifold.

10. Install a new intake manifold gasket.

NOTE: Combination intake/exhaust gasket is not to be used on a new exhaust manifold. Gasketing of the exhaust manifold is only recommended when the original exhaust manifold is reinstalled, in order to prevent leakage.

11. Coat the mating surfaces lightly with graphite grease. Place the manifold assemblies in position against the cylinder head, making sure the gasket has not become dislodged. Install the washers, bolts and nuts and tighten, in sequence, to 22–32 ft. lbs. (30–43 Nm).

12. Raise and safely support the vehicle. Connect the inlet pipe to the exhaust manifold and tighten the nuts to 25–36 ft. lbs. (34–49 Nm).

13. Lower the vehicle. Connect the crankcase vent hose to the intake manifold and position the hose clamp.

14. Install the upper intake manifold and throttle body assembly in the reverse order of removal. Tighten the attaching studs to 12–18 ft. lbs. (16.2–24.4 Nm) and the support screw to 22–32 ft. lbs. (29.8–43.4 Nm).

15. Connect the power brake booster vacuum hose and connect the vacuum lines. Connect the fuel line to the fuel supply manifold.

16. Install the accelerator cable bracket on the upper intake and connect the accelerator cable.

Combination manifold bolt torque sequence

17. Install the throttle body inlet hoses and connect the inlet air hose at the crankcase filter cap.

Cylinder Block Front Cover

Removal and Installation

4.9L ENGINE

1. Disconnect the negative battery cable and drain the cooling system. Remove the shroud and radiator.

3. Remove the drive belt, power steering bracket bolts and swing aside. Remove the fan and pulleys.

4. Remove the bolt and washer from the end of the crankshaft and remove the damper using a suitable puller.

5. Remove the front oil pan and front cover attaching bolts. Loosen the first 6 bolts on each side of the oil pan. Lightly push the pan down so it does not exert any upeard force on the front cover, which may affect front seal alignment.

NOTE: Keep foreign material from entering the crankcase during this procedure or the engine oil will have to be changed.

6. Remove the front cover and discard the gasket. Remove the front cover oil seal using seal remover tool T70P–6B070–B or equivalent.

To install:

7. Clean the front cover and block gasket surfaces. Clean any oil from the oil pan gasket as it will be used over. Install a new front cover oil seal using a suitable seal installer.

8. Coat the front cover gasket surfaces of the block and cover with oil-resistant sealer. Position a new front cover gasket on the block.

9. Apply silicone sealer to the block/pan junction and a small bead on the oil pan gasket sealing surface of the front cover. This provides an additional seal between the front cover and the used oil pan gasket.

NOTE: When applying silicone sealer, always use the specified bead size and join components within 15 minutes of application, before the sealer "sets-up".

10. Position the front cover over the end of the crankshaft and against the cylinder block. Start the cover and pan attaching screws. Slide front cover aligner tool T61P–6019–B or equivalent over the crank stub and into the seal bore of the cover. Tighten the oil pan bolts to 10–15 ft. lbs. (14–20 Nm) and the front cover bolts to 12–18 ft. lbs. (17–24 Nm).

NOTE: Tighten the front cover bolts first to obtain proper cover alignment.

11. Lubricate the crank stub, damper hub inside diameter and the seal rubbing surface with clean engine oil. Apply a ¼ in. bead of silicone to the inside of the keyway in the damper hub. Align the damper keyway with the crankshaft key and install the damper using damper replacer tool T52L–6306–AEE or equivalent.

12. Install the washer and damper retaining bolt and tighten to 130–150 ft. lbs. (177–203 Nm).

13. Install the pulleys, drive belt, fan, shroud, radiator and hoses.

14. Fill and bleed the cooling system. Change the engine oil, if necessary.

15. Connect the negative battery cable. Start the engine and bring to normal operating temperature. Check for leaks.

5.0L, 5.8L AND 7.5L ENGINES

1. Disconnect the negative battery cable and drain the cooling system. Discharge the air conditioning system on 7.5L engine vehicles, if equipped.

2. Remove the radiator on all except Bronco and F Series with 5.0L and 5.8L engines.

3. Remove the fan, accessory drive belt, pulleys and shroud. Disconnect the hoses from the water pump.

4. On 5.0L and 5.8L engines, remove the air conditioning compressor/power steering pump bracket and accessories.

5. On 7.5L engine, remove the alternator, air pump and air conditioning compressor, if equipped, and their respective brackets.

6. Remove the damper attaching bolt and washer. Remove the damper using a suitable puller.

7. Remove the oil pan-to-front cover attaching bolts. Use a thin-bladed knife to cut the oil pan gasket flush with the cylinder block face prior to separating the cover from the block. Remove the front cover and water pump as an assembly.

8. Remove the front cover oil seal using seal remover tool T70P–6B070–B or equivalent.

To install:

9. Clean the cylinder block, front cover and oil pan gasket surfaces. Clean the oil pan gasket surface where the oil pan and front cover fasten.

10. Install a new front cover oil seal, using a suitable seal installer.

11. Coat the gasket surface of the oil pan with sealer, then cut and position the required new gasket on the oil pan and apply sealer at the corners. Coat the block and cover gasket surfaces with sealer and position a new gasket on the block.

12. Position the front cover on the block and install front cover-to-seal alignment tool T61P–6019–B or equivalent. It may be necessary to force the cover downward to slightly compress the pan gasket. This can be done using a suitable tool at the front cover bolt hole locations.

13. Coat the threads of the attaching bolts with sealer and install. While pushing on the alignment tool, tighten the oil pan-to-cover bolts on 5.0L and 5.8L engines to 12–18 ft. lbs. (17–24 Nm) or to 7–9 ft. lbs. (10–12 Nm) on 7.5L engine. Tighten the cover-to-cylinder block bolts to 12–18 ft. lbs. (17–24 Nm).

14. Apply multi-purpose grease to the oil seal rubbing surface of the damper inner hub. Line up the damper keyway with the crankshaft key and install the damper using damper replacer tool T79T–6316–A or equivalent. Install the damper bolt and washer and tighten to 70–90 ft. lbs. (95–122 Nm).

15. Install the air conditioning compressor/power steering pump bracket and accessories on 5.0L and 5.8L engines. Install the alternator, air pump and air conditioning compressor and brackets on 7.5L engine.

16. Connect the hoses to the water pump. Install the pulleys, accessory drive belt, fan and shroud.

17. Install the radiator, if removed.

18. Fill and bleed the cooling system. Change the engine oil, if necessary.

19. Connect the negative battery cable, start the engine and bring to normal operating temperature. Check for leaks.

Front Cover Oil Seal

Removal and Installation

1. Disconnect the negative battery cable(s).
2. Remove the fan, shroud and accessory drive belt(s).
3. Remove the crankshaft pulley.
4. Remove the crankshaft damper retaining bolt and washer. Remove the damper using a puller.
5. Remove the front cover oil seal using seal replacer tool T70P–6B070–B or equivalent.

To install:

6. Coat a new front cover oil seal with clean engine oil and install, using seal replacer tool T70P–6B070–A or equivalent.

7. Apply clean engine oil to the oil seal rubbing surface of the damper inner hub. Line up the damper keyway with the crankshaft key and install the damper, using damper replacer tool T52L–6306–AEE or T79T–6316–A or equivalent.

Crankshaft damper removal

Crankshaft damper installation

8. Install the damper retaining bolt and washer. Tighten to 130–150 ft. lbs. (177–203 Nm) on 4.9L engine or 70–90 ft. lbs. (95–122 Nm) on 5.0L, 5.8L and 7.5L engines.

9. Install the crankshaft pulley, accessory drive belt(s), fan and shroud. Connect the negative battery cable(s).

Timing Chain and/or Timing Sprockets

Removal and Installation

4.9L ENGINE

1. Disconnect the negative battery cable and drain the cooling system and crankcase.

2. Remove the cylinder front cover assembly.

3. Crank the engine until the timing marks are aligned.

4. Install camshaft sprocket puller T82T–6256–A or equivalent, and remove the camshaft sprocket.

5. Install crankshaft damper remover T58P–6316–D or equivalent, and remove the crankshaft sprocket. Remove the key from the crankshaft.

To install:

6. Make sure the key spacer and camshaft thrust plate are properly installed. Align the camshaft sprocket keyway with the camshaft key and install the sprocket using camshaft sprocket replacing adapter tool T65L–6306–A or equivalent.

7. Install the key in the crankshaft keyway. Install the crankshaft sprocket using crankshaft damper replacer tool T52L–6306–AEE or equivalent. Make sure the timing marks are properly aligned. Install the oil slinger.

8. Install the cylinder front cover. Fill the crankcase with the proper type and quantity of engine oil. Fill and bleed the cooling system.

9. Connect the negative battery cable. Start the engine and bring to normal operating temperature. Check for leaks. Check the ignition timing and curb idle speed and adjust, if necessary.

5.0L, 5.8L AND 7.5L ENGINES

1. Disconnect the negative battery cable and drain the cooling system.

2. Remove the cylinder front cover assembly.

3. Rotate the crankshaft until the timing marks on the timing sprockets are aligned.

4. Remove the camshaft sprocket bolt, washer and eccentric, if equipped. Slide both sprockets and the timing chain forward and remove them as an assembly.

To install:

5. Install the sprockets and timing chain on the crankshaft and camshaft. Make sure the timing marks on the sprockets are positioned properly.

6. Install the eccentric, if equipped, the washer and camshaft retaining bolt. Tighten to 40–45 ft. lbs. (55–61 Nm).

7. Lubricate the timing chain and sprockets with heavy engine oil.

8. Install the cylinder front cover assembly.

Timing sprocket alignment—7.5L engine

Timing sprocket alignment—4.9L engine

Timing sprocket alignment—5.0L and 5.8L engines

9. Fill and bleed the cooling system. Connect the negative battery cable, start the engine and bring to normal operating temperature. Check for leaks.

10. Check the ignition timing and idle speed. Adjust, if necessary.

Camshaft

Removal and Installation

4.9L ENGINE

1. Disconnect the negative battery cable and drain the cooling system and crankcase.

2. Remove the shroud, radiator, lifters and cylinder front cover.

3. Disconnect the primary wire at the coil and remove the distributor.

4. Check the camshaft endplay using a dial indicator. The endplay should not exceed 0.009 in. Replace the thrust plate if the endplay is excessive.

5. Turn the crankshaft to align the timing marks on the timing sprockets.

6. Remove the camshaft thrust plate bolts. Remove the camshaft sprocket using sprocket puller T82T–6256–A or equivalent. Remove the key, thrust plate and spacer.

7. Remove the camshaft, being careful to avoid damaging the camshaft bearings.

To install:

8. Oil the camshaft bearing journals and apply multi-purpose grease to the lobes.

9. Assemble the key, spacer and thrust plate to the camshaft. Align the sprocket keyway with the key and install the sprocket on the camshaft using camshaft sprocket replacing adapter T65L–6306–A or equivalent.

10. Install the camshaft, sprocket and thrust plate as an assembly, making sure the timing marks are aligned. Be careful not to damage the camshaft bearings.

11. Tighten the thrust plate bolts to 9–12 ft. lbs. (13–16 Nm).

12. Turn the crankshaft until the timing marks are aligned. Do not turn the crankshaft again until the distributor is installed.

13. Install the cylinder front cover and damper, lifters, shroud and radiator.

14. Install the distributor, aligning the rotor with the No. 1 spark plug tower in the distributor cap.

15. Fill the crankcase with the proper type and quantity of engine oil. Fill and bleed the cooling system.

16. Connect the negative battery cable, start the engine and bring to normal operating temperature. Check for leaks.

17. Adjust the ignition timing.

5.0L, 5.8L AND 7.5L ENGINES

1. Disconnect the negative battery cable and relieve the fuel system pressure. Drain the cooling system.

2. If equipped, discharge the air conditioning system and remove the condenser.

3. Remove the radiator and fan shroud assembly. On all except F Series with 5.0L and 5.8L engines, remove the grille.

4. Remove the intake manifold and the rocker arm covers. Remove the lifters.

5. Remove the cylinder front cover and the timing chain and sprockets.

6. Remove the camshaft thrust plate and remove the camshaft, being careful not to damage the camshaft bearings.

To install:

7. Oil the camshaft journals and apply multi-purpose grease to the lobes. Carefully slide the camshaft through the bearings.

8. Lubricate the camshaft thrust plate with engine oil and install the with the groove toward the cylinder block. Tighten the thrust plate bolts to 9–12 ft. lbs. (13–16 Nm) on the 5.0L and 5.8L engines or 6–9 ft. lbs. (8–12 Nm) on 7.5L engine.

Camshaft assembly—4.9L engine

Typical camshaft assembly—5.0L, 5.8L and 7.5L engines

Service Tips

CAMSHAFT OR DISTRIBUTOR DRIVE GEAR FAILURE

A no start, hard start or rough idle and lack of power condition on the 7.5L engine, may be caused by a camshaft distributor drive gear that is out of specification. This can cause early camshaft or distributor gear failure at less than 10,000 miles.

Check the camshaft and distributor gear for signs of wear or failure. Replace both components if either gear is worn or has failed. Only use replacement camshaft part number C8SZ–6250–A. This camshaft has a green stripe located near the camshaft distributor gear.

When replacing the camshaft, remove the oil pan and the pump. Disassemble the pump and check for damage; replace if necessary. Install a new pickup tube, regardless of oil pump condition. Check the front of the cylinder block in the oil pan area and remove any metal shavings or other debris.

9. Check the camshaft endplay using a dial indicator. Endplay should not exceed 0.009 in. If endplay is excessive, replace the thrust plate.

10. Install the remaining components in the reverse order of their removal.

11. Fill and bleed the cooling system. Connect the negative battery cable, start the engine and bring to normal operating temperature. Check for leaks.

12. Check the ignition timing and idle speed; adjust if necessary. If equipped, evacuate and charge the air conditioning system.

Piston and Connecting Rod

Positioning

Piston and connecting rod assembly—4.9L engine

Piston and connecting rod assembly—7.5L engine

Piston and connecting rod assembly—5.0L and 5.8L engines

DIESEL ENGINE MECHANICAL

Engine Assembly

Removal and Installation

F SERIES

1. Disconnect battery ground cables from both batteries.
2. Scribe alignment marks at hood hinges and remove hood.
3. Drain cooling system.
4. Remove air cleaner and intake duct assembly. Position a suitable cover over the air intake opening.
5. Remove radiator fan shroud.
6. Remove fan and clutch assembly. The fan clutch nut has left-hand thread and must be removed by turning clockwise.
7. Disconnect radiator upper and lower hoses from radiator.
8. Disconnect and plug automatic transmission oil cooler lines at radiator, if equipped.
9. Remove radiator.
10. Loosen the air conditioning compressor, if equipped and remove drive belt.
11. Remove the air conditioning compressor from its mounting, if equipped and position it on radiator upper support.
12. Loosen power steering pump and remove drive belt. Remove power steering pump and position out of the way on left side of engine compartment.

13. Disconnect fuel supply line heater, if equipped, and alternator wires at alternator. Disconnect oil pressure sending unit wire at sending unit located at the back of the engine.

14. Disconnect accelerator cable from injection pump. Disconnect cruise control cable from injection pump, if equipped. Remove accelerator cable bracket with cables attached, from intake manifold and position out of the way.

15. Disconnect transmission kickdown rod from injection pump, if equipped. Disconnect main wiring harness connector from right side of engine. Disconnect engine ground strap from rear of engine. Disconnect fuel return hose from left rear of engine. Remove the vacuum supply hose from the vacuum pump, if equipped.

16. Remove upper transmission-to-engine attaching bolts.

17. Disconnect heater hoses from water pump and right cylinder head. Disconnect water temperature sender wire from sender on left front of engine block. Disconnect water temperature overheat light switch wire from switch on top front of left cylinder head. Position wires out of the way.

18. Raise and safely support the vehicle.

19. Disconnect both battery ground cables from lower front of engine.

20. Disconnect and cap fuel inlet line at fuel supply pump.

21. Disconnect starter cables at starter motor.

22. Disconnect muffler inlet pipe at exhaust manifolds.

23. Disconnect engine insulators from No. 1 crossmember. Remove flywheel inspection plate. Remove converter-to-flywheel attaching nuts, if equipped. Lower vehicle.

24. Support transmission with a floor jack. Remove lower transmission to engine attaching bolts.

25. Attach suitable engine lifting equipment. Raise engine high enough to clear number 1 crossmember and pull forward.

26. Rotate the front of the engine approximately 45 degrees to the left and lift it out of the engine compartment. Be careful not to damage the windshield wiper motor when lifting the engine from the vehicle.

To install:

NOTE: **If the engine to be installed has been overhauled or has been in storage, prime the entire engine lubricating system to fill the oil cooler, oil filter and cylinder block galleries with the proper type of oil. This will prevent piston and bearing scuffing.**

27. Lower the engine into the vehicle, being careful not to damage the windshield wiper motor.

28. Start transmission main shaft into clutch disc. It may be necessary to adjust position of transmission in relation to engine if main shaft binds or will not enter clutch disc. If engine hangs up after main shaft enters clutch disc, rotate crankshaft slowly with the transmission in gear, until mainshaft splines mesh with clutch disc splines. Align convertor to flywheel studs, if equipped.

29. Lower engine onto engine insulator brackets on the number 1 crossmember.

30. Install lower transmission to engine attaching bolts and tighten. Remove engine lifting equipment. Raise and safely support the vehicle.

31. Install converter to flywheel attaching nuts, if equipped. Install flywheel inspection plate.

32. Install engine insulator support to crossmember bracket attaching nuts and washers. Connect muffler inlet pipes to exhaust manifolds. Connect both battery ground cables to the lower front of the engine. Connect starter cables to starter. Install fuel pump inlet line onto fuel pump. Lower vehicle.

33. Connect water temperature sender wire to sender on left front of engine block. Connect wire to water temperature overheat light switch on top of left cylinder head. Install heater hoses onto right cylinder head and water pump and tighten clamps.

34. Connect engine ground strap at rear of engine. Connect fuel return hose at left rear of engine and vacuum supply hose to vacuum pump.. Connect transmission kickdown rod, if equipped.

35. Install accelerator cable bracket on intake manifold. Connect accelerator cable to injection pump. Connect cruise control cable, if equipped, to injection pump.

36. Connect oil pressure gauge sender wire to oil pressure sender.

37. Connect fuel supply line heater, if equipped, and alternator wires to alternator.

38. Install power steering pump and drive belt. Do not adjust belt at this time.

39. Install air conditioning compressor and drive belt. Adjust air conditioning compressor and power steering pump drive belts.

40. Install radiator. Connect automatic transmission oil cooler lines at radiator, if equipped. Connect upper and lower radiator hoses to radiator and tighten hose clamps. Fill and bleed the cooling system.

41. Install fan and clutch assembly. Turn nut counterclockwise to tighten.

42. Install radiator fan shroud.

43. Remove intake manifold cover and install air cleaner. Install intake duct assembly.

44. Install hood, aligning scribe marks drawn on hood at removal.

45. Connect battery ground cables at both batteries. Check the engine oil level and fill as required. Run engine and check for fuel, oil and coolant leaks.

E SERIES

1. Remove the engine cover.

2. Disconnect battery ground cables from both batteries.

3. Drain cooling system.

4. Remove the front bumper, grille assembly and gravel deflector.

5. Remove the cruise control servo bracket, if equipped, and position out of the way.

6. Mark the location and remove the hood latch and cable assembly from the grille upper support bracket. Remove the upper grille support.

7. Discharge the air conditioning system, if equipped. Disconnect the air conditioning lines from the condensor and remove the condensor.

8. Disconnect automatic transmission oil cooler lines at radiator, if equipped. Remove the transmission oil cooler and brackets.

9. Remove the radiator hoses at the engine and remove the shroud. Remove the radiator cooling fan. The fan clutch nut has left-hand thread and must be removed by turning clockwise.

10. Remove radiator attaching bolts and remove radiator.

11. Loosen and remove the vacuum pump and drive belt. Disconnect vacuum hose from the transmission shift modulator tube.

12. Loosen and remove the alternator adjusting arm, adjusting arm bracket and drive belt. Pivot the alternator inward toward the engine and disconnect the alternator wiring harness.

13. Disconnect the water temperature sender wire from the sender on the left front of the engine block and the water temperature overheat light switch wire from the switch on the top front of the left cylinder head. Position the wires aside.

14. Remove the 2 engine ground cables from the bottom front of the engine.

15. Remove the power steering pump and bracket from the engine. Disconnect and plug the power steering pump return line and position the power steering pump aside.

16. Remove air conditioning lines at the compressor. Remove the vacuum hose between the vacuum regulator valve and injection pump and position aside.

17. Disconnect and cap the fuel heater inlet line at the fuel filter filter and fuel pump. Remove the air cleaner assembly and inlet duct. Position a suitable cover over the air intake opening.

18. Disconnect and cap the fuel filter outlet line at the fuel filter ans injection pump. Cap the injection pump and fuel filter fittings. Remove the fuel filter return hose and remove the filter and bracket as an assembly.

19. Loosen the air conditioning compressor and rotate toward the engine. Remove and plug the fuel inlet hose at the fuel pump.

20. Remove the accelerator and cruise control cables from the injection pump and intake bracket and position aside. Remove the bracket. Remove the transmission kickdown rod.

21. Tag and disconnect the engine wiring harnesses from inside the vehicle and position aside. Disconnect the heater hose from the water pump and right cylinder head.

22. Remove the auxiliary heater and air conditioner hoses from the bracket at the left rear of the engine, if equipped. At the rear of the engine, disconnect the oil pressure sender wire from the sender and the fuel return line.

23. Remove the transmission dipstick tube attaching bolt and engine dipstick tube attaching nut. Remove the screw from the rocker arm cover bracket and remove the engine dipstick and tube.

24. Disconnect the ground cable from the cylinder block. Remove the top 4 transmission-to-engine attaching bolts.

25. Raise and safely support the vehicle. Remove the engine mount attaching nuts and disconnect the exhaust pipe at the manifolds.

26. Remove the converter inspection plate and the 4 converter-to-flywheel attaching nuts.

27. Disconnect the starter cable and position the fuel line on the No. 1 crossmember down and out of the way. Lower the vehicle.

28. Install suitable engine lifting equipment. Support the transmission and remove the remaining transmission-to-engine attaching bolts.

29. Separate the engine from the transmission, raise the engine high enough to clear the No. 1 crossmember, then pull the engine forward and out of the vehicle.

To install:

NOTE: If the engine to be installed has been overhauled or has been in storage, prime the entire engine lubricating system to fill the oil cooler, oil filter and cylinder block galleries with the proper type of oil. This will prevent piston and bearing scuffing.

30. Lower the engine into the vehicle and align the torque converter with the flywheel studs.

31. Position the transmission and install 2 lower transmission-to-engine attaching bolts.

32. Remove the engine lifting equipment and raise and safely support the vehicle.

33. Attach the starter cable. Install the 4 converter-to-flywheel nuts and the converter inspection plate.

34. Connect the exhaust pipe to the manifolds and install the engine mount attaching nuts.

35. Position the fuel line on the No. 1 crossmember and lower the vehicle. Install the top 4 transmission-to-engine attaching bolts.

36. Install the engine and transmission dipstick and tube assemblies. Connect the battery ground cable to the engine block.

37. At the left rear of the engine, connect the fuel return line and the auxiliary heater and air conditioner hoses, if equipped.

38. Install the transmission kickdown rod. Install the heater hoses on the right cylinder head and water pump.

39. Connect the engine wiring harness to the inside of the passenger compartment and the oil pressure sender wire to the sender at the rear of the engine.

40. Install the accelerator cable bracket to the intake manifold. Install the accelerator and cruise control cables to the bracket and the injection pump.

41. Remove the plug from the fuel inlet hose and install the hose to the fuel pump. Install the fuel filter and bracket.

42. Remove the caps from the fuel filter, outlet line and injection pump. Install the line between the fuel filter outlet and the injection pump. Connect the fuel filter return hose.

43. Remove the intake manifold cover and install the air cleaner and inlet duct assembly. Connect the fuel line between the fuel filter inlet and fuel pump.

44. Install the vacuum hose between the vacuum regulator valve and injection pump.

45. Connect the water temperature sender wire to the sender on the left front of the engine block and the water temperature overheat light switch wire to the switch on top of the left cylinder head.

46. If equipped, install the air conditioner drive belt and refrigerant lines to the compressor.

47. Remove the plug from the power steering pump return line and install the line. Install the power steering pump drive belt and bracket.

48. Connect the 2 engine ground cables to the bottom front of the engine. Connect the alternator wiring harness to the alternator and fuel line heater.

49. Loosely attach the alternator adjusting arm and adjusting bracket to the alternator and engine. Install the drive belt.

50. Loosely install the vacuum pump to the engine. Install the vacuum pump drive belt and connect the vacuum hose transmission modulator tube.

51. Adjust all accessory drive belts.

52. Install the radiator, cooling fan and shroud. The fan clutch nut has left-hand thread; tighten by turning counterclockwise.

53. Connect the radiator hoses and the transmission oil cooler lines.

54. If equipped, install the air conditioning condenser and connect the lines.

55. Install the upper grille support and install the hood latch and cable assembly to the grille upper support bracket. Install the cruise control servo bracket, if equipped.

56. Install the front bumper, grille assembly and gravel deflector.

57. Fill and bleed the cooling system. Check the engine oil level and fill as needed with the proper type of oil.

58. Connect the ground cables to both batteries. Start the engine and bring to normal operating temperature. Check for leaks.

59. Evacuate and charge the air conditioning system, if equipped. Install the engine cover.

Engine Mounts

Removal and Installation

FRONT MOUNTS

F Series

1. Disconnect both negative battery cables. Remove the fan shroud halves and raise and safely support the vehicle.

2. Remove the nuts attaching the mounts to the crossmember.

3. Disconnect the exhaust pipes at the manifolds.

4. Remove the bolts attaching the mounts to the engine block and lower the vehicle.

5. Attach suitable engine lifting equipment and raise the engine high enough for the mounts to clear the crossmember.

6. Remove the mount and bracket assemblies and remove the mount from the bracket.

To install:

7. Install the mount onto the mount bracket. Tighten the bolts to 60–80 ft. lbs. (81–108 Nm).

8. Install the mount and bracket assembly onto the engine block. Tighten the bolts to 75–95 ft. lbs. (102–129 Nm).

9. Lower the engine onto the crossmember and remove the engine lifting equipment. Raise and safely support the vehicle.

10. Install the mount-to-crossmember attaching nuts and washers. Tighten to 71–94 ft. lbs. (96–127 Nm).

11. Lower the vehicle and install the fan shroud. Connect both negative battery cables.

E Series

1. Disconnect both negative battery cables and remove the radiator fan shroud.

2. Loosen the vacuum pump and the alternator and remove the drive belts.

3. Disconnect the alternator wiring harness and remove the alternator adjusting bracket. Remove the alternator.

4. Remove the fuel filter/fuel heater/water separator inlet line from the fuel pump and fuel filter.

5. If equipped, discharge the air conditioning system, disconnect the refrigerant lines and remove the compressor and bracket.

6. Remove the engine cover. Remove the air cleaner and install a suitable cover over the air intake opening.

7. Remove and cap the fuel filter/fuel heater/water separator to injection pump fuel line. Cap the injection pump and fuel filter fittings.

8. Remove the fuel filter/fuel heater/water separator return line hose. Remove the fuel filter/fuel heater/water separator bracket bolts and remove the filter and bracket assembly.

9. Remove the kickdown rod from the injection pump. Raise and safely support the vehicle.

10. Disconnect the ground cables from the lower front of the engine and remove the nuts attaching the mounts to the No. 1 crossmember.

11. Disconnect and remove the transmission kickdown rod from the transmission. Lower the vehicle.

12. Attach suitable engine lifting equipment. Raise the engine until it contacts the body and remove the mount and bracket assemblies.

To install:

13. Install the mount to the bracket and tighten the bolts to 65–85 ft. lbs. (88–115 Nm).

14. Install the mount and bracket assembly onto the engine and tighten the bolts to 65–85 ft. lbs. (88–115 Nm).

15. Lower the engine and remove the lifting equipment. Raise and safely support the vehicle.

16. Install the mount to the No. 1 crossmember. Tighten the nuts to 54–74 ft. lbs. (73–100 Nm).

17. Install the transmission kickdown rod and connect to the transmission. Install the engine ground cables and lower the vehicle.

18. Install the fuel filter/fuel heater/water separator and bracket assembly. Uncap and install the fuel filter/fuel heater/water separator to injection pump fuel line. Install the fuel filter/fuel heater/water separator return hose.

19. Remove the intake opening cover and install the air cleaner.

20. If equipped, install the air conditioning compressor and bracket, connect the refrigerant lines and install the drive belt.

21. Install the fuel filter/fuel heater/water separator line.

22. Install the alternator, adjusting bracket and drive belt. Connect the alternator wiring.

23. Install the vacuum pump drive belt. Adjust all accessory drive belt tension.

24. Install the fan shroud. Connect both negative battery cables.

25. If equipped, evacuate and charge the air conditioning system. Install the engine cover.

REAR MOUNT

1. Remove the mount-to-support assembly bolt and locknut.

2. Remove the insulator-to-transmission housing bolts and lockwashers.

3. Raise the transmission with a jack and remove the mount and retainer.

4. Installation is the reverse of the removal procedure. Tighten the mount-to-transmission bolts and the mount-to-support bolts and nuts to 50–70 ft. lbs. (68–95 Nm).

Cylinder Head

Removal and Installation

1. Disconnect battery ground cables from both batteries.

2. Drain cooling system.

3. Remove the radiator fan shroud.

4. Remove the radiator cooling fan and clutch assembly. The fan clutch nut has left-hand thread and must be removed by turning clockwise.

5. Disconnect wiring from alternator and fuel filter/fuel heater/water separator.

6. Remove the alternator belt and alternator.

7. Remove the vacuum pump drive belt and vacuum pump.

8. Disconnect and cap all fuel lines. Remove alternator and vacuum pump mounting bracket. On F series, remove fuel filter with bracket as an assembly, for right side only.

9. Remove the heater hose from the cylinder head.

10. Remove the injection pump.

11. Remove the intake manifold and valley cover.

12. Raise and safely support the vehicle.

13. Disconnect the muffler inlet pipe from the exhaust manifolds.

14. For right side cylinder head, remove bolt holding the transmission dipstick tube to cylinder head.

15. Lower the vehicle. For right cylinder head, remove engine oil dipstick tube fasteners.

16. Remove the exhaust manifolds from the engine. For right cylinder head, remove the engine oil dipstick, dipstick tube and O-ring

17. Remove the rocker arm cover, rocker arm and pushrods.

18. Remove the injection nozzles and glow pugs.

19. Remove the cylinder head bolts. Attach suitable lifting equipment and lift the cylinder head from the engine.

NOTE: The prechambers may fall out of the cylinder head upon removal.

20. Clean and inspect the cylinder head gasket surface, prechambers and ports for cracks. Cracks in the prechambers are acceptable as long as they do not extend past the fire ring mark.

21. Check the cylinder head gasket surface for flatness using a straight edge and a feeler gauge. Remove the prechambers using a brass drift and hammer prior to checking, to avoid false readings. Warpage must not exceed 0.006 in. If warpage is excessive, the cylinder head must be replaced.

To install:

22. Apply a light coating of lubricant to the mounting edge of the prechambers and install into the cylinder head. Lightly tap with a plastic-tipped hammer, if necessary.

23. Clean the engine block head gasket surface. Position a new gasket on the engine block over the dowel pins. Install gasket with the words **THIS SIDE UP** facing installer.

24. Install the cylinder head, being careful to prevent the prechambers from falling into the cylinder bores. Do not slide the head across the gasket.

25. Lubricate the head bolt threads, bolt heads and washers with clean engine oil. Do not use anti-seize or grease. Install the head bolts and washers and tighten, as follows:

   a. Tighten bolts, in numbered sequence, to 65 ft. lbs. (88 Nm).

   b. Tighten bolts, in numbered sequence, to 85 ft. lbs. (115 Nm).

   c. Tighten bolts, in line sequence, to 100 ft. lbs. (136 Nm).

   d. Tighten bolts, in line sequence, to 100 ft. lbs. (136 Nm).

26. Install the pushrods, with the copper colored ends toward the rocker arms, making sure the pushrods are fully seated into the lifters.

27. Install the rocker arms, rocker arm covers, valley pan, intake manifold and injection pump.

28. Connect the heater hose to the cylinder head. Install the fuel filter/fuel heater/water separator, if removed.

29. Install the alternator and vacuum pump bracket. Remove the protective caps and install the fuel lines.

30. Loosely install the engine oil dipstick tube and O-ring, if removed. Raise and safely support the vehicle.

31. Install the exhaust manifold(s). Install the fasteners holding the engine oil dipstick tube in position.

32. If removed, install the bolt attaching the transmission oil dipstick to the cylinder head. Connect the exhaust pipe to the manifolds and lower the vehicle.

33. Install the vacuum pump, alternator and drive belts. Adjust the belts.

34. Connect the alternator and the fuel filter/fuel heater/water expansion wiring harnesses.

35. Remove the intake manifold cover and install the air clean-

INTAKE SIDE

LINE SEQUENCE START HERE STEPS NO. 3

15 11 7 3 2 6 10 14

16 17

8 1 9

12 4 5 13

EXHAUST SIDE

STEP 1. TIGHTEN BOLTS TO (65 FT-LB) IN NUMBERED SEQUENCE SHOWN ABOVE.

STEP 2. TIGHTEN BOLTS TO (85 FT-LB) IN NUMBERED SEQUENCE SHOWN ABOVE.

STEP 3. TIGHTEN BOLTS TO (100 FT-LB) IN LINE SEQUENCE SHOWN ABOVE.

STEP 4. REPEAT STEP NO. 3.

Cylinder head bolt torque sequence—7.3L diesel engine

GUIDE RETAINER

TAPPET

TAPPET GUIDE

Valve lifter removal—7.3L diesel engine

2. Remove the intake manifold, rocker arm covers, rocker arms and pushrods. Keep the rocker arms and pushrods in order so they may be reinstalled in their original positions.

3. Remove the Crankshaft Depression Regulator (CDR) tube and grommet from the valley pan.

4. Remove the bolts attaching the valley pan strap to the front of the engine block and remove the strap.

5. Remove the valley pan drain plug and remove the valley pan. Remove the lifter guide retainer.

6. Remove the lifter guides and the lifters. Keep them in order so they may be reinstalled in their original positions.

To install:

7. Clean all gasket mating surfaces.

8. Lubricate the lifters and bores with clean engine oil and install the lifters. If the old lifters are being reused, make sure they are installed in their original positions.

9. Install the lifter guides and the lifter guide retainer.

10. Install the pushrods in their original positions, with the copper colored ends toward the rocker arms. Install the rocker arms and rocker covers.

11. Install the valley pan and drain plug and install the CDR tube with a new grommet into the valley pan. Install a new O-ring and new back-up ring on the CDR valve.

12. Install the valley pan strap onto the front of the valley pan. Install the intake manifold.

13. Connect both negative battery cables. Run the engine and check for oil and fuel leaks.

14. If necessary, purge high-pressure fuel lines of air by loosening connector ½–1 turn and cranking engine until bubble-free fuel flows from the connection.

--- CAUTION ---

Keep eyes and hands away from nozzle spray. Fuel spraying from the nozzle under high-pressure can penetrate the skin and cause infection. Medical attention should be provided immediately in the event of skin penetration.

Service Tips

CYLINDER HEAD COOLANT LEAK

Coolant leaks on the 7.3L diesel engine, may be caused by a loose or improperly seated water passage steel seal ball in the cylinder head.

Remove the cylinder head from the vehicle. Using a suitable prying tool, remove the steel seal ball. Coat a new steel seal ball, part number E3TZ–6026–F, with sealer and drive the ball into the cylinder head using a hammer and punch. Reinstall the cylinder head.

The part number E3TZ–6026–F steel seal ball is 0.406 in. in diameter. Do not install a larger diameter ball, as this will cause the cylinder head to crack.

er. Install the fan and clutch assembly. The fan clutch nut has left-hand thread; tighten by turning counterclockwise.

36. Install the fan shroud. Fill and bleed the cooling system.

37. Connect both negative battery cables. Start the engine, bring to normal operating temperature and check for leaks.

38. If necessary, purge high-pressure fuel lines of air by loosening connector ½–1 turn and cranking engine until bubble-free fuel flows from the connection.

--- CAUTION ---

Keep eyes and hands away from nozzle spray. Fuel spraying from the nozzle under high-pressure can penetrate the skin and cause infection. Medical attention should be provided immediately in the event of skin penetration.

Valve Lifters

Removal and Installation

1. Disconnect both negative battery cables.

Valve Lash

Adjustment

1. Remove the rocker arm covers.

2. Rotate the crankshaft until the lifter to be checked is on the base circle of the camshaft.

3. Position bleed-down wrench T83T–6500–A or equivalent, over the rocker arm and push down, until the lifter is fully collapsed.

4. Check the gap between the valve tip and the rocker arm using a feeler gauge. The gap should not exceed 0.185 in.

5. Excessive clearance may be caused by loose rocker arm fulcrum bolts, or wear of the lifter roller, pushrod, rocker arm, rocker arm fulcrum or valve tip.

6. After checking is completed, reinstall the rocker arm covers.

Rocker Arms

Removal and Installation

1. Disconnect both negative battery cables.
2. On E series, remove the fan shroud and engine cover.
3. If removing the right side rocker arm cover on E Series, proceed as follows:

    a. Remove engine oil dipstick tube fasteners and remove dipstick, tube assembly and rocker arm cover bracket.

    b. Remove transmission filler tube fasteners and remove filler tube and dipstick.

    c. Raise and safely support the vehicle.

    d. Remove nuts attaching right engine mount to frame. Slightly raise right side of the engine until fuel filter header touches vehicle sheet metal. Install suitable wood block between insulator and frame. Lower engine on block.

    e. Lower the vehicle.

4. Remove the rocker arm cover retaining bolts and remove the covers. Remove the rocker arm post mounting bolts.

5. Remove the rocker arms, posts and pushrods in order and identify so they may be installed in their original positions.

To install:

6. Clean all gasket mating surfaces.

7. Install the pushrods in their original positions with the copper colored end of the pushrod toward the rocker arm, making sure they are fully seated in the lifter pushrod seats.

8. Install the rocker arms and posts in their original positions. Apply multi-purpose grease to the valve stem tips.

9. Turn the engine over by hand until the timing mark is at the 11 o'clock position as viewed from the front of the engine. Install all rocker arm post attaching bolts and tighten to 20 ft. lbs. (27 Nm).

10. Install new gaskets and install the rocker arm covers. Tighten the attaching bolts to 6 ft. lbs. (8 Nm).

11. If the right side rocker arm cover on E Series was removed, proceed as follows:

    a. Raise and safely support the vehicle. Raise engine, remove wood block and lower engine onto crossmember.

    b. Install engine mount attaching washers and nuts.

    c. Lower vehicle. Install transmission filler tube and transmission oil dipstick.

    d. Install engine oil dipstick tube and rocker arm cover bracket. Install engine oil dipstick.

12. Install radiator fan shroud halves, if removed. Connect both negative battery cables.

13. Run the engine and inspect for oil leaks.

Intake Manifold

Removal and Installation

1. Disconnect both negative battery cables.
2. On E series, remove the engine cover.
3. Remove the air cleaner and install a suitable cover over the air intake opening.
4. Remove the fuel inlet line and fuel return line from the fuel filter. Remove the fuel filter bracket attaching bolts and remove the fuel filter and bracket as an assembly.
5. Remove the injection pump.
6. On F series, remove the fuel return hoses from No. 7 and No. 8 (rear) nozzles and remove the return hose to the fuel tank.
7. Remove the glow plug harness and controller. Remove the engine wiring harness from the engine. Remove the engine harness ground cable from the back of the left cylinder head.

Rocker arm assembly—7.3L diesel engine

8. Remove the intake manifold retaining bolts and remove the intake manifold.

To install:

9. Clean the cylinder block and intake manifold gasket surfaces of any silicone sealer or oil. Apply a ⅛ in. bead of silicone sealer to each end of the cylinder block.

10. Install the intake manifold and tighten to specifications using the 2-step procedure.

11. Install the engine wiring harness on the engine. Connect the engine wiring harness ground wire to the rear of the left cylinder head.

12. Install the glow plug controller and harness.

13. On E series, install the fuel filter and bracket as as assembly and tighten the bolts to 24–39 ft. lbs. (33–52 Nm). Install the fuel filter return and inlet fuel lines.

14. Install the injection pump.

15. Connect the fuel tank return hose and No. 7 and No. 8 nozzle fuel return hoses.

16. Remove the intake manifold cover and install the air cleaner. Install the engine cover on E series.

17. Connect both negative battery cables. Run the engine and check for oil and fuel leaks.

18. If necessary, purge high-pressure fuel lines of air by loosening connector ½–1 turn and cranking engine until bubble-free fuel flows from the connection.

— CAUTION —

Keep eyes and hands away from nozzle spray. Fuel spraying from the nozzle under high-pressure can penetrate the skin and cause infection. Medical attention should be provided immediately in the event of skin penetration.

Intake manifold bolt torque sequence—7.3L diesel engine

Service Tips

OIL LEAK AT REAR CORNERS OF INTAKE MANIFOLD

Oil leaking from the rear corners of the intake manifold on the 7.3L diesel engine, on engines prior to serial number 438225, may be caused by the valley pan and gasket assembly.

Remove the intake manifold and valley pan. Clean all old sealant and gasket material from the intake manifold and cylinder block. Apply a ¼ in. bead of silicone sealant to the cylinder block rails and cylinder heads, overlapping the sealant ½ in. at each corner. Obtain valley pan and gasket assembly part number E8TZ-9439-A and coat the bottom of the gasket with Ford gasket eliminator part number E1FZ-19562-A. Install the valley pan, gasket, valley pan strap and bolts. Do not wipe off the excess sealant after valley pan installation, but allow it to seep at the cylinder block mating surfaces. Install the valley pan drain plug and tighten to 40 ft. lbs. (54 Nm), then install the intake manifold.

Exhaust Manifold

Removal and Installation

F SERIES

1. Disconnect both negative battery cables.
2. Raise and safely support the vehicle.
3. Disconnect the muffler inlet pipe from the exhaust manifolds.
4. If the right exhaust manifold is being removed, lower the vehicle. If the left exhaust manifold is being removed, leave the vehicle in the raised position.
5. Remove the exhaust manifold attaching bolts and the manifold.

To install:

6. Clean the mounting surfaces. Apply anti-seize compound on the exhaust manifold bolt threads and install the left manifold with a new gasket.
7. Tighten the bolts to specification, using the 2-step procedure.
8. Raise and safely support the vehicle. If the right manifold is being installed, repeat Steps 6 and 7.
9. Connect the muffler inlet pipe to the manifolds and tighten the nuts to 25–38 ft. lbs. (34–51 Nm). Lower the vehicle.
10. Connect the negative battery cables. Run the engine and check for exhaust leaks.

E SERIES

1. Remove the engine cover. Disconnect both negative battery cables.
2. For right side manifold removal only, remove the radiator fan shroud halves, engine oil dipstick and tube and transmission filler tube and dipstick.
3. Raise and safely support the vehicle.
4. For right side manifold removal only, remove the nuts attaching the engine mount to the frame. Slightly raise the right

side of the engine until the fuel filter header touches vehicle sheet metal. Install a wood block between the mount and frame. Lower the engine onto the block.
5. Remove the muffler inlet pipe from the exhaust manifolds. Lower the vehicle.
6. Remove the exhaust manifold retaining bolts and exhaust manifold.

To install:

7. Clean the mounting surfaces. Apply anti-seize compound to the manifold retaining bolts and install the manifold with a new gasket.
8. Tighten the bolts to specification using the 2-step procedure.
9. Raise and safely support the vehicle.
10. If the right manifold was installed, raise the engine, remove the wood block and lower the engine onto the crossmember. Install the engine mount attaching washers and nuts.
11. Install the muffler inlet pipe to the exhaust manifolds and tighten the nuts to 25–38 ft. lbs. (34–51 Nm). Lower the vehicle.
12. If the right manifold was installed, install the transmission filler tube and dipstick, the engine oil dipstick tube and dipstick and the radiator fan shroud halves.
13. Connect the negative battery cables. Run the engine and check for exhaust leaks. Install the engine cover.

Cylinder Block Front Cover

Removal and Installation

1. Disconnect both negative battery cables. Drain the cooling system.
2. Remove the air cleaner and install a suitable cover over the air intake opening.
3. Remove the fan shroud and fan and clutch assembly. Left-hand thread is used on the fan clutch nut; remove by turning the nut clockwise.
4. Remove the injection pump and injection pump adapter.
5. Remove the water pump.
6. Raise and safely support the vehicle.
7. Remove the crankshaft pulley and the damper attaching bolt. Remove the damper using a suitable puller.
8. Remove the ground cables at the front of the engine. Remove the bolts attaching the front cover to the engine block and oil pan.
9. Lower the vehicle. Remove the bolts attaching the engine front cover to the engine block and remove the front cover.

STEP 1. TIGHTEN BOLTS TO 35 FT-LB, IN NUMBERED SEQUENCE SHOWN ABOVE.

STEP 2. TIGHTEN BOLTS TO 35 FT-LB, IN LINE SEQUENCE SHOWN ABOVE.

Exhaust manifold bolt torque sequence—7.3L diesel engine

10. If the oil seal is to be replaced, support the front cover in a press and using drive handle tool T80T–4000–W or equivalent, and a 3¼ in. diameter spacer, drive the seal out of the cover.

To install:

11. Remove the old gasket material and clean all sealing surfaces.

12. Coat a new crankshaft oil seal with multi-purpose grease. Suuport the front cover and install the seal using seal replacer tool T83T–6700–A or equivalent, a suitable spacer and a press. When the tool is bottomed on the front cover surface, the seal is automatically installed at the proper depth.

13. Clean the outside surface of the front cover to remove any grease. Apply a ⅛ in. bead of silicone sealer around the outside diameter of the front seal and the edge of the front cover.

14. Install fabricated alignment dowels on the engine block and oil pan to align the front cover and gaskets.

15. Apply silicone sealer on the engine block and front cover sealing surfaces and install the gaskets on the engine block. Apply a ⅛ in. bead of silicone sealer to the rear corners of the oil pan and a ¼ in. bead of silicone sealer on the oil pan.

16. Install the front cover in position, on the oil pan dowels first, and install the attaching bolts. Remove the alignment dowels if required. Install and hand tighten the remaining front cover bolts.

17. Install the water pump gasket and water pump. Apply silicone sealer to the bolt threads and install the water pump attaching bolts. Remove the remaining alignment dowels.

18. Tighten the water pump bolts to 14 ft. lbs. (19 Nm). Tighten the front cover bolts. Install the injection pump adapter and injection pump.

19. Connect the heater hose to the water pump. Raise and safely support the vehicle.

20. Lubricate the damper seal nose with clean engine oil and install the crankshaft vibration damper, using damper replacer tool T83T–6316–B or equivalent. Add silicone sealer to the engine side of the retaining bolt washer to prevent oil leakage past the keyway. Install the vibration damper attaching bolt and tighten to 90 ft. lbs. (122 Nm).

21. Install the crankshaft pulley. Install both battery ground cables on the front of the engine and lower the vehicle.

22. Install the alternator adjusting arm bracket and water pump pulley.

23. Install the power steering pump bracket, power steering pump and drive belt.

24. Install the air conditioning compressor bracket, compressor and drive belt, if equipped.

25. Install the alternator adjusting arm, alternator and vacuum pump drive belts. Adjust all drive belts.

26. Install the fan and clutch assembly and the fan shroud halves.

Vibration damper removal—7.3L diesel engine

Cylinder block front cover installation—7.3L diesel engine

27. Remove the intake manifold cover, install the air cleaner and connect the negative battery cables.

28. Fill and bleed cooling system. Run the engine and inspect for coolant and oil leaks. If equipped, evacuate and charge the air conditioning system.

Front Cover Oil Seal

Removal and Installation

1. Disconnect both negative battery cables. Remove the radiator fan shroud.

2. Remove fan and clutch assembly. The fan clutch nut has left-hand thread; remove by turning clockwise.

3. Remove all drive belts. Raise and safely support the vehicle.

4. Remove the crankshaft pulley and the bolt attaching the damper to the crankshaft.

5. Install a suitable puller and remove the crankshaft vibration damper.

6. Pry out the front oil seal from the front cover using a small prybar. Use care to prevent damaging the front cover or crankshaft or breaking the oil pan seal by bending the front cover.

To install:

7. Coat a new seal with multi-purpose grease.

NOTE: It may be necessary to rotate the crankshaft to align the damper key with the seal installing tool.

8. On engines without 3 weldnuts on the front cover, place the seal into installation tool T83T–6700–A or equivalent, and install over the end of the crankshaft. Install damper replacer tool T83T–6316–B or equivalent, and tighten the nut against the washer and installation tool to force the seal into the front cover plate.

NOTE: Use care to prevent bending the front cover during oil seal installation and breaking the oil pan seal.

9. On engines with 3 weldnuts on the front cover, place the seal into installation tool T83T–6700–A or equivalent, install over the end of the crankshaft and attach the bridge to the weldnuts. Draw the seal into the front cover by rotating the center screw clockwise. The seal is automatically installed at the proper depth when the tool bottoms on the cover.

10. Clean the grease from the outside surfaces and apply a ⅛

in. bead of silicone sealer around the outside diameter of the front seal and the edge of the front cover.

11. Lubricate the damper seal nose with clean engine oil and install the crankshaft vibration damper using damper replacer tool T83T–6316–B or equivalent.

12. Apply silicone sealer to the engine side of the damper attaching bolt washer in the keyway area, to prevent oil leakage past the keyway. Install the bolt and tighten to 90 ft. lbs. (122 Nm).

13. Install the crankshaft pulley and lower the vehicle.

14. Install the drive belts and adjust the belt tension. Install the fan and clutch assembly. The fan clutch nut has left-hand thread; turn counterclockwise to tighten.

15. Install the fan shroud and connect the negative battery cables.

Crankshaft Drive Sprocket

Removal and Installation

1. Disconnect both negative battery cables. Remove the air filter and install a suitable cover on the intake manifold opening.

2. Drain the cooling system and remove the radiator fan shroud.

3. Remove the fan and clutch assembly. The fan clutch nut has left-hand thread; turn clockwise to remove.

4. Remove the alternator and vacuum pump belts.

5. Remove the air conditioning compressor and position out of the way. Remove the mounting bracket.

6. Remove the power steering pump and position out of the way. Remove the power steering pump bracket.

7. Remove the water pump pulley and water pump.

8. Remove the cylinder block front cover.

9. Install a suitable puller and remove the crankshaft sprocket.

To install:

10. Install the crankshaft sprocket using crankshaft sprocket replacer tool T83T–6316–B or equivalent, aligning the crankshaft drive sprocket timing mark with the camshaft drive sprocket timing mark.

NOTE: If necessary, the sprocket may be heated in an oven to 300–350°F (149–177°C) for ease of installation. Do not use a torch to heat the sprocket.

11. Clean all sealing surfaces. Install the cylinder block front cover.

12. Install the crankshaft vibration damper using damper replacer tool T83T–6316–B or equivalent. Apply silicone sealer to the engine side of the washer, in area of keyway only, to prevent

oil leakage past keyway. Install crankshaft vibration damper attaching bolt and tighten to 90 ft. lbs. (122 Nm).

13. Install the crankshaft pulley and water pump.

14. Install the injection pump adapter and injection pump.

15. Connect the heater hose to the water pump.

16. Install the power steering pump bracket, power steering pump and drive belt.

17. Install the air conditioning compressor bracket, compressor and drive belt, if equipped.

18. Install the alternator adjusting arm and the alternator and vacuum pump drive belts.

19. Adjust all drive belts. Check and set the injection pump timing.

20. Install the fan and clutch assembly and fan shroud halves. Fill and bleed the cooling system.

21. Remove the intake manifold cover. Install the air cleaner assembly and connect the negative cables to both batteries. Run the engine and inspect for oil and coolant leaks.

Injection Pump Drive Sprocket

Removal and Installation

1. Disconnect both negative battery cables. Remove the engine cover on E series.

2. Remove the air cleaner and install a suitable cover over the intake opening.

3. Remove the injection pump.

4. Remove the bolts attaching the injection pump drive sprocket cover to the engine block and remove the cover. Do not remove the drive sprocket yet.

5. Turn the engine over by hand to TDC on the compression stroke of No. 1 piston. Remove the glow plugs, to facilitate turning the engine over by hand.

6. To determine that No. 1 piston is at TDC on the compression stroke, position the injection pump drive sprocket dowel at the 4 o'clock position. The scribe line in the vibration damper should be at TDC.

NOTE: To aid aligning the timing marks, the pump drive sprocket and the camshaft sprocket are marked with "Y" timing marks. The crankshaft and camshaft sprockets are marked with "o" (dot) alignment marks. With the engine at TDC compression for No. 1 cylinder, the "Y" marks should be aligned.

7. Slide the injection pump sprocket back, but do not remove, to expose the top of the camshaft sprocket when looking down into the front cover. In addition to the "Y", the sprocket teeth adjacent to the "Y" on the camshaft sprocket are permanently dyed.

8. Remove the injection pump drive sprocket.

To install:

9. Clean all gasket and sealing surfaces.

NOTE: To determine that No. 1 piston is at TDC of compression stroke, position the injection pump drive sprocket dowel at the 4 o'clock position. The scribe line in the vibration damper should be at TDC.

10. With the drawn line on the drive sprocket at the 6 o'clock position, install the sprocket and align all drive sprocket timing marks. Use extreme care to avoid disturbing the injection pump drive gear, once it is in position.

11. Apply a 1/8 in. bead of silicone sealer along the bottom surface of the injection pump drive sprocket cover.

12. Install the injection pump drive sprocket cover and tighten the retaining bolts to 14 ft. lbs. (19 Nm). Apply sealing compound to the bolt threads before assembly. With the injection pump drive sprocket cover installed, the injection pump drive sprocket cannot jump timing.

13. Remove the intake manifold cover. Install the air cleaner and connect both negative battery cables.

Timing sprocket positioning—7.3L diesel engine

14. Run the engine and check for oil, fuel and coolant leaks.

15. If necessary, purge high-pressure fuel lines of air by loosening connector ½–1 turn and cranking engine until bubble-free fuel flows from the connection.

CAUTION

Keep eyes and hands away from nozzle spray. Fuel spraying from the nozzle under high-pressure can penetrate the skin and cause infection. Medical attention should be provided immediately in the event of skin penetration.

Camshaft Drive Sprocket

Removal and Installation

1. Disconnect both negative battery cables. Remove the air cleaner and install a suitable cover over the air intake opening.

2. Drain the cooling system.

3. Remove the alternator and vacuum pump drive belts.

4. Remove the air conditioning compressor mounting bolts and position the compressor out of the way. Remove the compressor mounting bracket.

5. Remove the power steering pump and position out of the way. Remove the power steering pump bracket.

6. Remove the water pump pulley and water pump.

7. Remove the cylinder block front cover. Remove the camshaft Allen screw and washer.

8. Install a suitable sprocket puller and remove the sprocket.

NOTE: At this point of the service procedure, the fuel pump cam and thrust flange spacer can be removed by first removing the the fuel pump, then by using a suitable puller to remove it from the camshaft.

To install:

9. Install a new thrust plate, if removed. Replace the fuel pump cam if damaged. If the fuel pump cam is replaced, replace the fuel pump.

10. Install the spacer and fuel pump cam against the camshaft thrust flange, using replacer tool T83T–6316–B or equivalent, if removed.

11. Install the camshaft drive sprocket against the fuel pump cam, aligning the timing mark with the mark on the crankshaft drive sprocket.

12. Install the camshaft Allen screw and tighten to 15 ft. lbs. (20 Nm).

13. Install the cylinder block front cover and water pump.

14. Install the injection pump sprocket and adapter. Install the injection pump.

Injection pump drive sprocket cover—7.3L diesel engine

Camshaft drive sprocket removal—7.3L diesel engine

15. Install the water pump pulley and power steering pump bracket. Install the power steering pump and drive belt.

16. Install the air conditioning compressor mounting bracket, compressor and drive belt. Install the alternator and vacuum pump drive belts. Adjust all drive belts.

17. Connect both negative battery cables. Remove the intake manifold cover and install the air cleaner.

18. Fill and bleed the cooling system. Run the engine and check for fuel, oil and coolant leaks.

19. If necessary, purge high-pressure fuel lines of air by loosening connector ½–1 turn and cranking engine until bubble-free fuel flows from the connection.

CAUTION

Keep eyes and hands away from nozzle spray. Fuel spraying from the nozzle under high-pressure can penetrate the skin and cause infection. Medical attention should be provided immediately in the event of skin penetration.

Camshaft

Removal and Installation

1. Remove the engine from the vehicle and position on an engine stand.

2. Remove the injection pump and adapter, intake manifold, lifters, cylinder block front cover and fuel supply pump.

3. Remove the camshaft drive sprocket, fuel supply pump cam, spacer and thrust plate from the camshaft.

4. Remove the camshaft. Use care to avoid damaging the camshaft bearings.

To install:

5. Coat the camshaft lobes with multi-purpose grease and lubricate the journals with engine oil. Carefully slide the camshaft through the bearings. Install the camshaft thrust plate.

6. Install the spacer and fuel pump cam against the camshaft thrust flange using installation tool T83T–6316–B or equivalent.

7. Install the camshaft drive sprocket against the fuel pump cam, aligning the timing mark with the timing mark on the crankshaft drive sprocket, using installation tool T83T–6316–B, or equivalent.

8. Install the camshaft allen screw and tighten to 15 ft. lbs. (20 Nm).

9. Install the fuel supply pump. Install a new crankshaft oil seal in the front cover and install the front cover.

10. Install the water pump and injection pump adapter.

11. Lubricate the valve lifters and their bores with clean en-

gine oil and install the lifters in their original positions. Install the lifter guides and lifter guide retainer.

12. Install the pushrods with the copper colored ends toward the rocker arms, making sure they are seated fully in the push-rod seats. Install the rocker arms and rocker arm covers.

13. Install the intake manifold and injection pump.

14. Install the engine into the vehicle and connect the negative battery cables. Fill and bleed the cooling system.

15. Run the engine and check for leaks. If necessary, purge high-pressure fuel lines of air by loosening connector ½–1 turn and cranking engine until bubble-free fuel flows from the connection.

—— CAUTION ——

Keep eyes and hands away from nozzle spray. Fuel spraying from the nozzle under high-pressure can penetrate the skin and cause infection. Medical attention should be provided immediately in the event of skin penetration.

16. Check the injection pump timing and road test the vehicle for proper operation.

Piston and Connecting Rod

Positioning

Piston orientation — 7.3L diesel engine

ENGINE LUBRICATION

Oil Pan

Removal and Installation

4.9L ENGINE

Bronco and F Series

1. Disconnect the negative battery cable. Drain the crankcase and the cooling system.

2. Remove the radiator. Remove the upper intake and throttle body assembly.

3. Raise and safely support the vehicle. Disconnect the starter cable and remove the starter.

4. Remove the engine front mount to support bracket nuts and washers. Use a transmission jack or equivalent, to raise the front of the engine, then install 1 in. thick wood blocks between the front mounts and support brackets. Lower the engine onto the blocks and remove the jack.

5. Remove the oil pan attaching bolts and lower the pan to the crossmember. Remove the 2 oil pump bolts and the 1 oil pump inlet tube nut, and drop the assembly in the oil pan. Remove the oil pan.

To install:

6. Clean all gasket mating surfaces and the oil pan.

7. Apply a pressure sensitive silicone based adhesive to the block rails and the front cover oil pan.

8. Apply a bead of silicone sealer to the parting lines between the front cover and block and to the rear bearing cap seal groove at the cylinder block junction. Immediately install the gasket to the block to facilitate pan installation.

9. Clean the inlet tube and screen assembly and place it in the oil pan.

10. Position the oil pan under the engine. Install the inlet tube and screen on the oil pump with a new gasket. Tighten the 2 screws to 10–15 ft. lbs. (14–20 Nm) and 1 nut to 22–32 ft. lbs. (30–43 Nm).

11. Raise the oil pan to the cylinder block and install the stiffener plates, if equipped, and attaching bolts. If not equipped with stiffener plates, tighten the bolts to 120–144 inch lbs. (14–16 Nm). If equipped with stiffener plates, tighten the bolts to 144–216 inch lbs. (16–24 Nm).

NOTE: Tighten the bolts in 2 steps. First, tighten all bolts except the 3 oil pan-to-front cover bolts installed through the curvature of the pan, then tighten those remaining 3 bolts.

12. Raise the engine with the jack and remove the wood blocks. Lower the engine until the mounts are positioned on the support brackets. Install the washers and nuts and tighten to 54–74 ft. lbs. (73–100 Nm).

13. Install the starter and connect the starter cable. Lower the vehicle.

14. Install the radiator. Install the upper intake and throttle body assembly.

15. Fill the crankcase with the proper type and quantity of oil. Fill and bleed the cooling system.

16. Connect the negative battery cable. Start the engine and check for leaks.

E Series

1. Disconnect the negative battery cable. Remove the engine cover. Remove the air cleaner and disconnect the air inlet tubes from the throttle body.

2. Drain the cooling system and crankcase. If equipped with air conditioning, discharge the system and remove the compressor.

3. Remove the EGR valve. If equipped, disconnect the thermactor check valve inlet hose and remove the check valve.

4. Remove the upper intake and throttle body assembly.

5. Remove the upper radiator hose. Unbolt the fan shroud and position it over the fan. If equipped with automatic transmission, disconnect the oil filler tube.

6. Disconnect the exhaust inlet pipe at the manifold. Raise and support the vehicle safely. Remove the starter.

7. Remove the front engine mount nuts. Remove the power steering return line clip which is located in front of the crossmember.

8. Disconnect the lower radiator hose and, if equipped, transmission oil cooler lines.

9. Raise the engine and place 3 in. wood blocks under the engine mounts. Remove the oil pan dipstick tube.

10. Remove the oil pan bolts and lower the oil pan. Remove the

pickup tube and screen from the oil pump and lay them in the pan. Remove the oil pan.

To install:

11. Clean all gasket mating surfaces and clean the oil pan.

12. Apply a pressure sensitive silicone based adhesive to the block rails and the front cover oil pan.

13. Apply a bead of silicone sealer to the parting lines between the front cover and block and to the rear bearing cap seal groove at the cylinder block junction. Immediately install the gasket to the block to facilitate pan installation.

14. Clean the inlet tube and screen assembly and place it in the oil pan.

15. Position the oil pan under the engine. Install the inlet tube and screen on the oil pump with a new gasket. Tighten the 2 screws to 10–15 ft. lbs. (14–20 Nm) and 1 nut to 22–32 ft. lbs. (30–43 Nm).

16. Raise the oil pan to the cylinder block and install the stiffener plates, if equipped, and attaching bolts. If not equipped with stiffener plates, tighten the bolts to 120–144 inch lbs. (14–16 Nm). If equipped with stiffener plates, tighten the bolts to 144–216 inch lbs. (16–24 Nm).

NOTE: Tighten the bolts in 2 steps. First, tighten all bolts except the 3 oil pan-to-front cover bolts installed through the curvature of the pan, then tighten those remaining 3 bolts.

17. Install the dipstick tube and lower the engine. Install the engine mount nuts.

18. Install the starter. Install the lower radiator hose and connect the transmission cooler lines, if equipped.

19. Install the power steering return line clip and position the line. Lower the vehicle.

20. Install the upper intake and throttle body. Install the EGR valve and connect the exhaust pipe. If equipped, install the thermactor check valve and connect the inlet hose.

21. Install the fan shroud and upper radiator hose. If equipped, install the air conditioning compressor.

22. Replace the oil filter and fill the crankcase with the proper type and quantity of oil. Fill and bleed the cooling system.

23. Connect the negative battery cable. Start the engine and check for leaks. If equipped, evacuate and charge the air conditioning system.

24. Install the air cleaner and air inlet tubes. Install the engine cover.

5.0L AND 5.8L ENGINES

Bronco and F Series

1. Disconnect the negative battery cable. Remove the oil dipstick, on pan entry vehicles only. Remove the bolts attaching the fan shroud to the radiator and position the shroud over the fan.

2. Remove the upper intake manifold.

3. Remove the nuts and lockwashers attaching the engine mounts to the chassis bracket.

4. Disconnect the oil cooler lines, if equipped with automatic transmission.

5. Raise and safely support the vehicle. Remove the exhaust system.

6. Raise the engine and place wood blocks under the engine mounts. Drain the crankcase.

7. Support the transmission with a jack stand and remove the transmission crossmember.

8. Remove the oil pan bolts and lower the oil pan onto the crossmember.

9. Remove the oil pump pick-up tube and screen and lower into the oil pan. Remove the oil pan.

To install:

10. Clean all gasket mating surfaces, the oil pan and the inlet tube and screen. Inspect the oil pan gasket sealing surfaces for damage and distortion due to overtightening. Repair as necessary.

11. Position a new oil pan gasket and seals on the cylinder block. Place the pickup tube and screen in the oil pan and position the pan on the crossmember.

12. Raise the pickup tube and screen into position. Attach the pickup tube to the pump with a new gasket and tighten the bolts to 12–18 ft. lbs. (16–24 Nm). Tighten the pickup tube nut to 22–32 ft. lbs. (30–43 Nm).

13. Raise the oil pan into position, install the attaching bolts and tighten to 9–11 ft. lbs. (13–14 Nm).

14. Install the transmission crossmember and remove the jackstand. Raise the engine and remove the wood blocks. Lower the engine, install the engine mount nuts and washers and tighten to 54–75 ft. lbs. (73–100 Nm).

15. Install the exhaust system and lower the vehicle.

16. If equipped, connect the transmission oil cooler lines. Install the fan shroud.

17. Install the upper intake manifold.

18. Fill the crankcase with the proper type and quantity of oil. Install the oil dipstick.

19. Connect the negative battery cable, start the engine and check for leaks.

E Series

1. Disconnect the battery and remove the engine cover. Remove the air cleaner and drain the cooling system.

2. If equipped with power steering, remove the pump and position it out of the way. If equipped, remove the air conditioning compressor retainers and clutch wire and position the compressor out of the way.

3. Disconnect the upper radiator hose. Remove the fan shroud bolts and oil filler tube. Remove the oil dipstick-to-exhaust manifold bolt. Raise and safely support the vehicle.

4. Remove the alternator splash shield. If equipped, disconnect the automatic transmission cooler lines at the radiator. Disconnect the lower radiator hose.

5. Disconnect and plug the fuel line at the fuel rail.

6. Remove the engine mount retaining nuts. Drain the crankcase and remove the dipstick tube.

7. Disconnect the muffler inlet pipe from the exhaust manifolds.

8. If equipped, remove the automatic transmission dipstick and tube. Disconnect the manual linkage at the transmission. Remove the center driveshaft support and remove the driveshaft from the transmission.

9. Place a transmission jack or equivalent, under the oil pan and insert a wood block between the pan and jack.

NOTE: The engine and transmission assembly will pivot around the rear engine mount. The engine assembly must be raised 4 inches, measured from the front motor mounts. The engine must remain centered in the engine compartment to obtain this much lift.

10. Raise the engine and transmission assembly. Insert wood blocks to support the engine in the uppermost position.

11. Remove the oil pan bolts and lower the oil pan. Remove the oil pump and the oil pickup tube and lay them in the oil pan on 5.0L engine. Remove the oil pan from the vehicle.

To install:

12. Clean all gasket mating surfaces, the oil pan and the inlet tube and screen. Inspect the oil pan gasket sealing surfaces for damage and distortion due to overtightening. Repair as necessary.

13. Position a new oil pan gasket and seals to the cylinder block. Position the pan with the pump to the engine and install the pump. Attach the pickup tube to the No. 3 main bearing cap stud. Install the oil pan and tighten the attaching bolts to 9–11 ft. lbs. (13–14 Nm). Install the dipstick tube.

14. Position the transmission jack, raise the engine and remove the wood blocks. Lower the engine and remove the jack. Install the engine mount attaching nuts and tighten to 50–70 ft. lbs. (68–95 Nm).

METAL-TO-METAL NOISE; CRANKSHAFT AND/OR THRUST BEARING FAILURE

Vehicles with 5.0L engine and Automatic Overdrive (AOD) transmission, may have an unusual metal-to-metal noise caused by an interference between the torque converter and the flywheel bolts. The interference can eventually cause the thrust bearing and the crankshaft to fail.

Install 6 new flywheel bolts, part number F1ZZ-6379-A. The bolts have reduced head height to provide additional clearance. When replacing a crankshaft due to thrust bearing failure, install a new crankshaft with a revised pilot hole, which will provide additional clearance for the torque converter.

15. Install the driveshaft and center driveshaft support. Connect the manual linkage at the transmission and install transmission filler tube.

16. Install the muffler inlet pipe and tighten the nuts to 25–38 ft. lbs. (34–52 Nm). Connect the lower radiator hose.

17. If equipped, connect the transmission cooler lines to the radiator. Connect the fuel line to the fuel rail and install the alternator splash shield. Lower the vehicle.

18. Install the fan shroud and connect the upper radiator hose. If equipped, install the power steering pump and bracket. Install the bolt attaching the dipstick tube to the exhaust manifold.

19. If equipped, install the air conditioning compressor. Install the accessory drive belt(s) and adjust the tension, if necessary.

20. Install the oil filler tube and the air cleaner. Fill the crankcase with the proper type and quantity of oil. Fill and bleed the cooling system.

21. Connect the negative battery cable, start the engine and check for leaks. Install the engine cover.

7.5L ENGINE

1. Remove the engine cover on E Series. Disconnect the battery and drain the cooling system.

2. Disconnect the air inlet tube and remove the air cleaner assembly. Disconnect the throttle and transmission linkage at the throttle body. Disconnect the power brake vacuum lines.

3. Disconnect the fuel lines at the fuel rail. Disconnect the air tubes at the throttle body.

4. Disconnect the radiator hoses. If equipped, disconnect the oil cooler lines. Remove the fan, shroud and radiator. If equipped, remove the power steering pump and position it aside.

5. Remove the front engine mount attaching bolts. Remove the engine oil dipstick tube from the exhaust manifold. Remove the oil filler tube and bracket.

6. If equipped, rotate the air conditioning lines, at the rear of the compressor, down to clear the dash. If necessary, discharge the system and remove the lines.

7. Remove the upper intake manifold and throttle body as an assembly.

8. Raise and support the vehicle safely. Drain the crankcase and remove the oil filter.

9. Remove the muffler inlet pipe assembly. Disconnect the manual and kickdown linkage from the transmission. Remove the driveshaft and coupling shaft assembly. Remove the transmission dipstick tube.

10. Remove the dipstick and tube from the oil pan. Place a transmission jack or equivalent, under the engine oil pan. Insert a wood block between the jack surface and the oil pan. Jack the engine upward, pivoting about the rear mount until the transmission contacts the floor. Block the engine in position at the engine mounts. The engine must remain centralized to obtain the maximum height. The engine must be raised 4 inches at the mounts to remove the oil pan.

11. Remove the oil pan bolts and lower the oil pan. Remove the oil pump and pick up tube attachments and drop them into the oil pan. Remove the oil pan rearward from the vehicle.

To install:

12. Clean all gasket mating surfaces, the oil pan and the oil pickup tube and screen. Prime the oil pump by filling the inlet opening with oil and rotate the pump shaft until oil emerges from the outlet opening.

13. Apply gasket sealer to the cylinder block surface. Position the gaskets and end seals or 1-piece gasket on the block and press lightly until the gasket(s) sticks to the surface.

NOTE: Vehicles built prior to March 30, 1989 use a 4-piece oil pan gasket set. Vehicles built after this date use a 1-piece oil pan gasket.

14. Position the oil pan with the oil pump and pickup tube assembly to the chassis. Install the oil pump assembly to the cylinder block and the pickup tube to the main cap. Tighten to 22–32 ft. lbs. (30–43 Nm).

15. Raise the oil pan into place on the cylinder block and install the attaching bolts. Tighten the ¼ in. bolts to 7–9 ft. lbs. (10–12 Nm) and the ⁵/₁₆ in. bolts to 8–11 ft. lbs. (11–15 Nm).

16. Place the jack under the engine and raise it enough to remove the blocks. Lower the engine and remove the jack.

17. Position the engine oil dipstick tube to the oil pan and exhaust manifold and install the attaching nut. Reposition the air conditioning lines, if equipped.

18. Install the engine mount bolts and connect the manual kickdown linkage at the tranmission. Install the driveshaft and coupling shaft.

19. Install the muffler inlet pipe and install a new oil filter. Lower the vehicle and install the engine oil filler tube and bracket. Attach the dipstick tube to the exhaust manifold.

20. Install the radiator. Connect the transmission oil cooler lines, if equipped.

21. Install the fan and shroud, then connect the radiator hoses.

22. Install the upper intake manifold and throttle body. Connect the throttle and transmission linkage at the throttle body. Connect the fuel lines at the fuel rail and connect the power brake vacuum line.

23. Install the power steering pump and drive belt. Adjust the belt tension, if necessary. Install the transmission filler tube to the right cylinder head.

24. Install the air cleaner assembly and fresh air tube. Fill the crankcase with the proper type and quantity of oil. Fill and bleed the cooling system.

25. Connect the negative battery cable, start the engine and check for leaks. If necessary, evacuate and charge the air conditioning system. On E Series, install the engine cover.

7.3L DIESEL ENGINE

1. Disconnect both negative battery cables.

2. Remove the engine oil dipstick and transmission dipstick, if equipped.

3. Remove the air cleaner and install a suitable cover over the intake opening.

4. Remove the fan and clutch assembly. The fan clutch nut has left-hand thread; turn clockwise to remove.

5. Drain the cooling system and remove the radiator hoses.

6. Disconnect the power steering return hose from the power steering pump. Plug the hose and the pump.

7. Disconnect the alternator and air conditioning compressor wiring harness and fuel line heater connector from the alternator. Position the harness away from the engine.

8. Raise and safely support the vehicle. Disconnect and plug the transmission oil cooler lines from the radiator, if equipped.

9. Disconnect and plug the fuel pump inlet fuel hose. Drain the crankcase and remove the oil filter.

10. Remove the transmission filler tube assembly. Remove the front pipe from the exhaust manifold and muffler. Remove the upper inlet pipe mounting stud from the right exhaust manifold.

11. Remove the nuts and washers attaching the engine mounts to the crossmember. If equipped with automatic transmission, remove the 2 bolts securing the shift linkage bell crank to the transmission. Lower the vehicle.

12. Using suitable engine lifting equipment, raise the engine until the transmission housing contacts the body.

13. Install wood blocks 2–2¾ in. thick between the engine mounts and crossmember. Lower the engine onto the blocks.

14. Raise and safely support the vehicle. Remove the flywheel inspection plate and position the fuel pump inlet line at the rear of the crossmember. Remove the transmission oil cooler lines, if equipped, and position out of the way.

15. Remove the oil pan attaching bolts. Remove the transmission mount retaining nuts and raise the transmission approximately 1 in. using a transmission jack.

16. On F Series, remove the oil pump and pickup tube from the engine and lay it in the oil pan. Remove the oil pan. The crankshaft may have to be turned to reposition counterweights to aid in removal of the oil pan.

17. On E Series, the oil pump and pickup tube can be removed at this time.

To install:

18. Clean the oil pan, engine block and front and rear covers of old gasket material. If removed, clean the mating surface of the oil pickup tube and install on the oil pump with a new gasket.

19. If removed, prime the oil pump with clean engine oil, rotating the pump drive gear to distribute oil within the pump body. The oil pump and pickup tube can be installed at this time, on E Series.

20. On F Series, place the oil pump and pickup tube in the oil pan and place the oil pan in position on the crossmember. Install the oil pump and pickup tube.

21. Apply a ⅛ in. bead of silicone sealer on the side rails of the engine block oil pan mating surface, and a ¼ in. bead of silicone sealer on the ends of the oil pan mating surface on the front and rear covers and in the mating corners.

22. Position the oil pan to the engine and install the attaching bolts.

23. Lower the transmission and install the transmission mount retaining nuts. Tighten to 70–94 ft. lbs. (96–128 Nm).

24. Install the flywheel inspection plate and lower the vehicle.

25. Raise the engine and remove the wood blocks. Lower the engine onto the crossmember and remove the engine lifting equipment. Raise and safely support the vehicle.

26. Install the automatic transmission filler tube with a new O-ring and install the retaining bolts. Install the nuts and washers attaching the engine mounts to the crossmember.

27. If equipped with automatic transmission, position the shift linkage bell crank to the transmission and tighten the bolts to 20–30 ft. lbs. (27–40 Nm).

28. Install the upper muffler inlet pipe mounting stud on the right exhaust manifold. Install the muffler inlet pipe.

29. Install the oil pan drain plug and new oil filter. Connect the fuel pump inlet hose to the fuel pump. Make sure the fuel line clip is installed in the crossmember.

30. Connect the transmission oil cooler lines, if equipped. Lower the vehicle.

31. Connect the alternator and air conditioning compressor wiring harness to the alternator and compressor. Connect the wiring harness to the top of the fuel filter/fuel heater/water separator.

32. Connect the power steering return hose to the power steering pump and connect the radiator hoses.

33. Install the fan and clutch assembly. The fan clutch nut has left-hand thread; tighten by turning counterclockwise.

34. Remove the intake manifold cover and install the air cleaner and intake tube. Install the engine oil and transmission oil dipsticks.

35. Fill the crankcase with the proper type and quantity of oil. Fill and bleed the cooling system.

36. Connect the negative battery cables. Run the engine and check for leaks. Check the power steering fluid and add, if necessary.

Oil Pump

Removal and Installation

1. Disconnect the negative battery cable(s). Raise and safely support the vehicle.

2. Remove the oil pan.

3. Remove the oil pump mounting bolts and pickup tube mounting nut and remove the oil pump and pickup tube.

To install:

4. Clean the pickup tube and screen assembly and install on the oil pump, using a new gasket.

5. Prime the pump by filling the inlet port with new engine oil. Rotate the pump shaft to distribute the oil within the pump body. If equipped, position the intermediate shaft into the oil pump.

6. Install the oil pump and pickup tube assembly. If equipped with an intermediate shaft, install the pump and shaft together.

NOTE: If equipped with an intermediate driveshaft, do not force the pump into position if it will not seat readily. The driveshaft hex may be misaligned with the distributor shaft. To align, rotate the intermediate driveshaft into a new position.

7. Install the oil pan and lower the vehicle.

Oil pump assembly—5.0L and 5.8L engines

8. Fill the crankcase with the proper type and quantity of engine oil. Connect the negative battery cable(s), start the engine and check for leaks.

Checking

1. Remove the pump and disassemble. Thoroughly clean all parts in solvent and dry with compressed air.

2. Check the inside of the pump housing and the inner and outer gears for damage or excessive wear. Check the mating surfaces of the pump cover for wear. Minor scuff marks are normal, but if the cover, gears or housing surfaces are excessively worn, scored or grooved, replace the entire pump.

3. Measure the inner to outer rotor tip clearance. With the rotor assembly removed from the pump and resting on a flat surface, the inner and outer rotor tip clearance must not exceed 0.012 in. (0.30mm) with a feeler gauge inserted ½ in. (13mm) minimum.

4. With the rotor assembly installed in the housing, place a straight edge over the rotor assembly and the housing. Measure the vertical clearance, the rotor endplay, between the straight edge and the inner rotor and outer race. Maximum clearance must not exceed 0.005 in. (0.13mm).

5. Inspect the relief valve spring for collapsed or worn condition. Check the spring tension. The tension should be 20.6–22.6 lbs. @ 2.49 in. for the 4.9L and 7.5L engines, 10.6–12.2 lbs. @

1.74 in. for the 5.0L engine or 18.2–20.2 lbs. @ 2.49 in. for the 5.8L engine. Check the relief valve piston and bore for scores and free operation.

6. If any part of the oil pump requires replacement, replace the complete pump assembly.

Rear Main Bearing Oil Seal

Removal and Installation

4.9L, 5.0L AND 5.8L ENGINES

1. Disconnect the negative battery cable. Raise and safely support the vehicle.

2. Remove the transmission. If equipped with manual transmission, remove the clutch assembly.

3. Remove the flywheel and the engine rear cover plate.

4. Using a sharp awl or equivalent, punch a hole into the seal metal surface between the lip and block. Screw in the threaded end of plug puller T77L-9533-B or equivalent, and remove the seal. Be careful to avoid scratching or damaging the oil seal surface.

5. When the seal has been removed, clean the mounting recess.

To install:

6. Coat the new seal and the crankshaft with a light film of engine oil. Do not use grease.

7. Start the seal into the recess with the seal lip facing forward and install it with rear oil seal replacer tool T65P-6701-A or equivalent. Keep the tool straight with the centerline of the crankshaft and install the seal until the tool contacts the cylinder block surface.

8. After removing the tool, inspect the seal to make sure it was not damaged during installation.

9. Install the engine rear cover plate. Position the flywheel on the crankshaft flange. Coat the threads of the flywheel bolts with an oil resistant sealing compound and install. Tighten to 75–85 ft. lbs. (102–115 Nm).

10. If equipped with manual transmission, install the clutch assembly. Install the transmission and starter and lower the vehicle.

11. Connect the negative battery cable, start the engine and check for leaks.

7.5L ENGINE

1. Disconnect the negative battery cable. Raise and safely support the vehicle.

Checking oil pump inner-to-outer rotor tip clearance

Checking oil pump rotor endplay

Installing 1 piece rear main bearing oil seal—4.9L, 5.0L and 5.8L engines

INSTALL SEAL WITH LIP TOWARDS FRONT OF ENGINE

FRONT | ENGINE

SEAL HALVES TO PROTRUDE BEYOND PARTING FACES THIS DISTANCE TO ALLOW FOR CAP TO BLOCK ALIGNMENT

REAR FACE OF REAR MAIN BEARING CAP AND CYLINDER BLOCK

VIEW LOOKING AT PARTING FACE OF SPLIT, LIP TYPE CRANKSHAFT SEAL

Installing 2 piece rear main bearing oil seal—7.5L engine

2. Remove the oil pan and oil pump. Loosen all main bearing cap bolts, lowering the crankshaft slightly, but not more than $\frac{1}{32}$ in.

3. Remove the rear main bearing cap and remove the seal half.

4. Remove the seal half from the block using a seal removal tool, or install a small metal screw in 1 end of the seal and pull on the screw to remove the seal. Be careful to prevent damaging the crankshaft seal surfaces.

To install:

5. Carefully clean the seal grooves in the block and cap with a brush and solvent. Dry the area thoroughly.

6. Dip the seal halves in clean engine oil.

7. Carefully install the upper seal half into the cylinder block, with the lip facing toward the front of the engine, until approximately $\frac{3}{8}$ in. protrudes below the parting surface. Make sure no rubber has been shaved from the outside diameter of the seal by the bottom edge of the groove.

8. Tighten all but the rear main bearing cap bolts to 95–105 ft. lbs. (129–142 Nm).

9. Install lower seal half in the rear main bearing cap with the lip facing toward the front of the engine. Allow the seal to protrude approximately $\frac{3}{8}$ in. above the parting surface to mate with the upper seal when the cap is installed.

10. Apply a $\frac{1}{16}$ in. bead of silicone sealer to the cylinder block, in the corner of the bearing cap recess next to the seal groove, and to the rear bearing cap, on the mating surface in line with the seal groove, leaving a $\frac{1}{8}$ in. gap between the sealer and the groove.

11. Install the rear main bearing cap and tighten the bolts to 95–105 ft. lbs. (129–142 Nm).

12. Install the oil pump and oil pan. Lower the vehicle.

13. Fill the crankcase with the proper type and quantity of oil. Connect the negative battery cable, start the engine and check for leaks.

7.3L DIESEL ENGINE

1. Disconnect the negative battery cables. Raise and safely support the vehicle.

2. Remove the transmission. If equipped with manual transmission, remove the clutch housing and clutch assembly.

3. Remove the flywheel mounting bolts and spacer and remove the flywheel. Remove the rear engine cover.

4. Support the rear cover in a suitable press. Using a $4\frac{1}{8}$ in. diameter spacer, remove the rear oil seal.

To install:

5. Clean the rear cover and engine block gasket surfaces. Remove old silicone sealer from the oil pan to rear cover sealing surface on the oil pan. Clean the sealing surfaces with suitable solvent and dry thoroughly.

6. Coat the rear engine cover seal bore inside diameter with gasket sealer. Support the rear engine cover in a suitable press and install the new seal, using seal replacer tool T83T–6701–A or equivalent.

NOTE: The seal must be installed from the engine block side of the rear cover flush with the seal bore inner surface.

7. Apply a $\frac{1}{8}$ in. bead of silicone sealer around the outside diameter of the rear seal and the edge of the rear cover.

8. Install rear crankshaft seal pilot tool T83T–6701–B or equivalent, onto the crankshaft.

9. Apply gasket sealer to the engine block and rear cover gasket surfaces. Install the rear cover gasket to the engine block.

10. Apply a $\frac{1}{4}$ in. bead of silicone sealer at the corners of the oil pan and on the oil pan sealing surface.

11. Push the rear cover into position on the engine block and install the attaching bolts. Remove the seal pilot.

12. Position the flywheel on the crankshaft flange. Coat the threads of the flywheel bolts with sealing compound and install the spacer, bolts and washers. Tighten to 47 ft. lbs. (64 Nm) in a criss-cross pattern.

13. Install the clutch assembly, if equipped. Install the transmission and lower the vehicle.

14. Connect the negative battery cables, start the engine and check for leaks.

Service Tips

REAR MAIN SEAL OIL LEAK

Oil leaking from the rear main seal on the 7.3L diesel engine, may be caused by a worn crankshaft flange surface. A sleeve and seal kit, part number E5TZ–6701–D, is available for repeat repairs.

If there is already a wear sleeve on the crank flange, remove it by striking it with a hammer and chisel. Be careful not to damage the crankshaft. Apply hydraulic sealant all the way around the crank flange and position the sleeve in the installation tool. Mount the sleeve and tool on the crank flange, making sure the sleeve is correctly aligned. Use a plastic hammer to drive the sleeve onto the crankshaft, until the tool bottoms against the crank flange face. Remove the tool and check to make sure the sleeve is flush with the rear face of the crank flange. Continue with the rear main seal installation.

TORQUE SPECIFICATIONS

Component	English	Metric
Camshaft sprocket bolt		
5.0L, 5.8L and 7.5L engines	40–45 ft. lbs.	55–61 Nm
7.3L diesel engine	15 ft. lbs.	20 Nm
Camshaft thrust plate-to-cylinder block bolts		
4.9L, 5.0L and 5.8L engines	9–12 ft. lbs.	13–16 Nm
7.5L engine	6–9 ft. lbs.	8–12 Nm
Combination manifold		
4.9L engine	22–32 ft. lbs.	30–43 Nm
Connecting rod nut		
4.9L, 5.8 and 7.5L engines	40–45 ft. lbs.	55–61 Nm
5.0L engine	19–24 ft. lbs.	26–32 Nm
7.3L diesel engine		
Step 1:	38 ft. lbs.	51 Nm
Step 2:	51 ft. lbs.	69 Nm
Crankshaft damper bolt		
4.9L engine	130–150 ft. lbs.	177–203 Nm
5.0L, 5.8L and 7.5L engines	70–90 ft. lbs.	95–122 Nm
7.3L diesel engine	90 ft. lbs.	122 Nm
Cylinder front cover		
4.9L, 5.0L, 5.8L and 7.5L engines	12–18 ft. lbs.	17–24 Nm
Cylinder head bolt		
4.9L engine*		
Step 1:	50–55 ft. lbs.	67–75 Nm
Step 2:	60–65 ft. lbs.	82–88 Nm
Step 3:	70–85 ft. lbs.	94–115 Nm
5.0L engine*		
Step 1:	55–65 ft. lbs.	75–88 Nm
Step 2:	65–72 ft. lbs.	88–97 Nm
5.8L engine*		
Step 1:	85 ft. lbs.	115 Nm
Step 2:	95 ft. lbs.	129 Nm
Step 3:	105–112 ft. lbs.	143–151 Nm
7.5L engine		
Step 1:	80–90 ft. lbs.	108–122 Nm
Step 2:	100–110 ft. lbs.	136–149 Nm
Step 3:	130–140 ft. lbs.	177–189 Nm
7.3L diesel engine**		
Step 1:	65 ft. lbs.	88 Nm
Step 2:	85 ft. lbs.	115 Nm
Step 3:	100 ft. lbs.	136 Nm
Step 4:	100 ft. lbs.	136 Nm

*NOTE: Oil the bolt threads
**NOTE: Refer to cylinder head removal and installation procedure in text for torque sequence

Component	English	Metric
EGR valve		
4.9L, 5.0L and 5.8L engines	12–18 ft. lbs.	17–24 Nm
7.5L engine	70–100 inch lbs.	8–11 Nm
Engine mounts		
4.9L engine		
Bronco and F Series		
Front mounts		
Lower bracket bolts and nuts	48–62 ft. lbs.	65–85 Nm
Upper bracket bolts	59–81 ft. lbs.	80–110 Nm
Upper and lower stud nuts	71–93 ft. lbs.	96–127 Nm
Rear mount		
Mount-to-transmission bolt	64–71 ft. lbs.	87–96 Nm
Mount-to-crossmember nuts	60–80 ft. lbs.	81–109 Nm

TORQUE SPECIFICATIONS

Component	English	Metric
Engine mounts		
E Series		
Front mounts		
Mount-to-cylinder block bolts	60–80 ft. lbs.	81–109 Nm
Support bracket locknuts	60–80 ft. lbs.	81–109 Nm
Mount-to-support bracket nuts	57–74 ft. lbs.	67–100 Nm
Rear mount		
Mount locknuts	50–70 ft. lbs.	68–95 Nm
5.0L and 5.8L engines		
Bronco and F Series		
Front mounts		
Mount-to-cylinder block bolts	50–70 ft. lbs.	68–95 Nm
Mount-to-chassis nut	65–85 ft. lbs.	88–115 Nm
Rear mount		
Mount-to-transmission bolts	60–80 ft. lbs.	81–108 Nm
Mount-to-crossmember nuts	50–70 ft. lbs.	68–95 Nm
E Series		
Front mounts		
Mount-to-cylinder block bolts	50–70 ft. lbs.	68–95 Nm
Mount-to-frame nuts	50–70 ft. lbs.	68–95 Nm
Rear mount		
Mount-to-transmission bolts	50–70 ft. lbs.	68–95 Nm
Mount-to-crossmember nuts	50–70 ft. lbs.	68–95 Nm
7.5L engine		
Front mount		
Mount-to-frame bracket nuts	50–70 ft. lbs.	68–95 Nm
Through bolt nut	40–58 ft. lbs.	55–78 Nm
Frame bracket bolt locknuts	35–50 ft. lbs.	48–67 Nm
Crossmember bolt locknuts	72–105 ft. lbs.	98–142 Nm
Rear mount		
Mount-to-transmission bolts	50 ft. lbs.	68 Nm
Mount-to-crossmember nuts	50–70 ft. lbs.	68–95 Nm
7.3L diesel engine		
Front mount		
F Series		
Mount-to-mount bracket bolts	60–80 ft. lbs.	81–108 Nm
Mount-to-cylinder block bolts	75–95 ft. lbs.	102–129 Nm
Mount-to-crossmember nuts	71–94 ft. lbs.	96–127 Nm
E Series		
Mount-to-bracket bolts	65–85 ft. lbs.	88–115 Nm
Mount-to-cylinder block	65–85 ft. lbs.	88–115 Nm
Mount-to-crossmember nuts	54–74 ft. lbs.	73–100 Nm
Rear mount		
Mount-to-transmission bolts	50–70 ft. lbs.	68–95 Nm
Mount-to-support bolts and nuts	50–70 ft. lbs.	68–95 Nm
Exhaust manifold		
5.0L and 5.8L engines	18–24 ft. lbs.	25–32 Nm
7.5L engine	22–30 ft. lbs.	30–41 Nm
7.3L diesel engine*	35 ft. lbs.	47 Nm.

*NOTE: Refer to removal and installation
procedure in text for torque sequence.

Component	English	Metric
Flywheel-to-crankshaft bolts		
4.9L, 5.0L, 5.8L and 7.5L engines	75–85 ft. lbs.	103–115 Nm
7.3L diesel engine*	47 ft. lbs.	64 Nm

*NOTE: Apply locking compound to the
threads prior to installation.

Component	English	Metric
Flywheel-to-torque converter nuts	20–30 ft. lbs.	28–40 Nm

TORQUE SPECIFICATIONS

Component	English	Metric
Intake manifold		
5.0L and 5.8L engines	23–25 ft. lbs.	32–33 Nm
7.5L engine		
Step 1:	8–12 ft. lbs.	11–16 Nm
Step 2:	12–22 ft. lbs.	16–30 Nm
Step 3:	22–35 ft. lbs.	30–47 Nm
7.3L diesel engine	24 ft. lbs.	33 Nm
Main bearing cap bolts		
4.9L and 5.0L engines	60–70 ft. lbs.	82–94 Nm
5.8L and 7.5L engines	95–105 ft. lbs.	129–142 Nm
7.3L diesel engine		
Step 1:	75 ft. lbs.	101 Nm
Step 2:	95 ft. lbs.	129 Nm
Oil pan bolts		
4.9L engine		
1988–89	120–144 inch lbs.	14–16 Nm
1990–92	144–216 inch lbs.	16–24 Nm
5.0L and 5.8L engines	9–11 ft. lbs.	13–14 Nm
7.5L engine		
¼ in. bolts	7–9 ft. lbs.	10–12 Nm
$^5/_{16}$ in. bolts	8–11 ft. lbs.	11–15 Nm
Oil pan drain plug		
4.9L, 5.0L, 5.8L and 7.5L engines	15–25 ft. lbs.	21–33 Nm
7.3L diesel engine	28 ft. lbs.	37 Nm
Oil pump-to-cylinder block		
4.9L engine	10–12 ft. lbs.	14–20 Nm
5.0L, 5.8L and 7.5L engines	22–32 ft. lbs.	30–43 Nm
Oil pickup tube-to-main bearing cap		
4.9L, 5.0L, 5.8L and 7.5L engines	22–32 ft. lbs.	30–43 Nm
Oil pickup tube-to-oil pump		
4.9L, 5.0L and 5.8L engines	10–15 ft. lbs.	14–20 Nm
7.5L engine	12–18 ft. lbs.	17–24 Nm
Rocker arm bolt		
4.9L engine	17–23 ft. lbs.	24–31 Nm
5.0L, 5.8L and 7.5L engines	18–25 ft. lbs.	25–32 Nm
7.3L diesel engine	20 ft. lbs.	27 Nm
Rocker arm cover bolts		
4.9L engine	4–7 ft. lbs.	5–9 Nm
5.0L and 5.8L engines	3–5 ft. lbs.	4–6 Nm
7.5L engine	9 ft. lbs.	12 Nm
7.3L diesel engine	6 ft. lbs.	8 Nm
Spark plugs		
4.9L, 5.0L and 5.8L engines	10–15 ft. lbs.	14–20 Nm
7.5L engine	5–10 ft. lbs.	7–13 Nm
Transmission-to-engine bolts	40–50 ft. lbs.	55–67 Nm
Water outlet housing		
4.9L, 5.0L and 5.8L engines	12–15 ft. lbs.	17–20 Nm
7.5L engine	23–28 ft. lbs.	32–37 Nm
7.3L diesel engine	20 ft. lbs.	27 Nm
Water pump		
4.9L, 5.0L, 5.8L and 7.5L engines	12–18 ft. lbs.	17–24 Nm
7.3L diesel engine	14 ft. lbs.	19 Nm

MANUAL TRANSMISSION

For further information, please refer to Chilton's Transmission Service Manual.

Transmission Assembly

Removal and Installation

BORG-WARNER T-18 FOUR SPEED

Bronco and F Series 4WD

1. Remove the 4 screws holding the floor mat. Remove the 11 screws holding the access cover to the floor pan. Place the shift lever in **R** and remove the cover.

2. Remove the insulator and the dust cover. Remove the transfer case shift lever, shift ball and boot as an assembly.

3. Remove the transmission shift lever, shift ball and boot as an assembly.

4. Raise and support the vehicle safely. Drain the transmission.

5. Disconnect the front and rear driveshafts from the transfer case and wire them out of the way.

6. Remove the the shift link and speedometer cable from the transfer case.

7. Position a transmission jack under the transfer case. Remove the 6 bolts holding the transfer case to the transmission and lower the transfer case from the vehicle.

8. Remove the 8 bolts that hold the rear support bracket to the transmission.

9. Position a transmission jack under the transmission and remove the rear support bracket and brace. Remove the 4 bolts that hold the transmission to the bell housing and remove the transmission.

To install:

10. Place the transmission on a transmission jack and install it in the vehicle. Install 2 guide pins in the bell housing top holes, to guide the transmission in place.

11. Install the 2 lower bolts, remove the guide pins and install the upper 2 bolts. Tighten to 35–50 ft. lbs. (47–67 Nm).

12. Place the rear support bracket in position and install the 8 retaining bolts. Install the 2 bolts at the rear mount bracket and remove the transmission jack.

13. Place the transfer case on the transmission jack and install the 6 retaining bolts and gasket. Position the transfer case on the transmission and tighten the bolts.

14. Install the transfer case shift link and the speedometer cable. Connect the front and rear driveshafts.

15. Fill the transmission and transfer case with the proper type and quantity of lubricant. Lower the vehicle.

16. Install the gasket and shift cover. Install the transfer case shift lever, shift ball and boot assembly and the transmission shift lever, shift ball and boot assembly.

17. Install the dust cover and insulator, the access cover-to-floor pan screws, and the floor mat screws.

F Series 2WD

1. Remove the floor mat, the body floor pan cover, the gearshift lever shift ball and boot as an assembly. and remove the transmission shift lever. Remove the isolator pad.

2. Raise and support the vehicle safely. Position a transmission jack under the transmission and disconnect the speedometer cable.

3. Disconnect the back-up light switch located at the rear of the gearshift housing cover.

4. Disconnect the driveshaft or coupling shaft and clutch actuator from the transmission and wire it to 1 side.

5. Disconnect the transmission mount and remove the transmission crossmember.

6. Remove the transmission attaching bolts.

7. Move the transmission to the rear until the input shaft clears the clutch housing and lower the transmission.

To install:

8. Place the transmission on a transmission jack, install guide studs in the clutch housing top holes, and raise the transmission until the input shaft splines are aligned with the clutch disc splines. The clutch release bearing and hub must be properly positioned in the release lever fork.

9. Slide the transmission forward on the guide studs until it is in position on the clutch housing. Install the top attaching bolts and tighten to 35–50 ft. lbs. (48–67 Nm). Remove the guide studs, install the 2 lower attaching bolts and tighten to 35–50 ft. lbs. (48–67 Nm).

10. Install the crossmember and transmission mount. Connect the speedometer cable and clutch actuator.

11. Install the bolts attaching the front U-joint of the coupling shaft to the transmission output shaft. Connect the back-up light switch and lower the vehicle.

12. Install the shift lever, boot and shift ball as an assembly and lubricate the spherical ball seat. Install the isolator pad, floor pan cover and floor mat.

13. Road test the vehicle for proper operation.

MAZDA M50D FIVE SPEED

2WD Vehicles

1. Shift the transmission into the **N** position. Disconnect the negative battery cable.

2. Remove the carpet or floor mat. Remove the shifter boot retainer screws and slide the boot up the shift lever shaft. Remove the shift lever retaining bolt and remove the shift lever.

3. Raise and support the vehicle safely. Disconnect the speedometer cable. Disconnect the back-up light switch located at the top left side of the transmission.

4. Remove the drain plug from the transmission and drain the transmission fluid into a suitable drain pan. Position a suitable transmission jack under the transmission.

5. Remove the driveshaft from the transmission. Disconnect the clutch slave cylinder hydraulic line.

6. Remove the transmission rear insulator and lower retainer. Remove the crossmember.

7. Remove the bolts that retain the transmission to the engine block. Move the transmission to the rear until the input shaft clears the clutch. Lower the transmission from the vehicle.

To install:

8. Place the transmission on a suitable transmission jack. Install guide studs into the engine block and raise the transmission up until the input shaft splines are aligned with the clutch disc splines.

9. Slide the transmission forward on the guide studs until the transmission is in position. Install the transmission retaining bolts and torque to 40–50 ft. lbs. (54–67 Nm). Remove the guide studs and install the remaining bolts. Tighten the 2 bolts for the lower plate to 9–12 ft. lbs. (12–16 Nm).

10. Install the crossmember. Position the mount and retainer between the transmission and crossmember. Install the bolts and tighten to 60–80 ft. lbs. (81–108 Nm). Install the nut retaining the mount and retainer to the crossmember. Tighten to 60–80 ft. lbs. (81–108 Nm) and remove the transmission jack.

11. Connect the speedometer cable and the clutch hydraulic line.

12. Connect the back-up light switch and install the driveshaft. Lower the vehicle.

13. Install the shift lever retaining bolt. Slide the shifter boot into position on the shifter shaft and install the boot retaining screws.

14. Install the carpet or floor mat. Connect the negative battery cable and road test for proper operation.

VEHICLE
IDENTIFICATION
NUMBER STAMPED
IN THIS AREA

FILL PLUG
(25-35 FT-LB)

IDENTIFICATION
TAG

BOLT
(35-50 FT-LB)

BACK-UP
LAMP SWITCH

**F-150 - F-350 (4x4) BRONCO
MAIN VIEW**

VEHICLE IDENTIFICATION
NUMBER STAMPED IN
THIS AREA

BACK-UP
LAMP SWITCH

IDENTIFICATION
TAG

BOLT
(35-50 FT-LB)

**F-150 - F-350 (4x2)
MAIN VIEW**

SPEEDOMETER GEAR AND CLIP USED ON
4x2 ONLY ASSEMBLE CLIP TO GEAR WITH
TABS ON BACK SIDE OF CLIP TOWARD
TEETH ON SPEEDOMETER GEAR

CLIP
17292

Borg-Warner T-18 manual transmission

4WD Vehicles

1. Shift the transmission into the **N** position. Disconnect the negative battery cable and remove the shift ball from the transfer case shift lever.

2. Remove the carpet or floor mat. Remove the shifter boot retainer screws and slide the boot up the shift lever shaft. Remove the shift lever retaining bolt and remove the shift lever.

3. Raise and support the vehicle safely. Remove the drain plugs and drain the transmission and transfer case.

4. Remove the front and rear driveshafts from the transfer case.

5. Disconnect the speedometer cable and the back-up light switch. If equipped, remove the skid pad from under the transfer case.

6. Support the transfer case, using a transmission jack. Remove the 6 bolts holding the transfer case to the transmission and carefully lower the transfer case from the vehicle, using care to ensure that the transfer case shift lever clears the opening in the floor pan.

7. Support the transmission with a transmission jack. Remove the transmission rear mount and lower retainer. Remove the crossmember.

8. Remove the bolts that retain the transmission to the engine block. Move the transmission to the rear until the input shaft clears the clutch. Lower the transmission from the vehicle.

To install:

9. Place the transmission on a transmission jack and install 2 guide studs in the transmission front case top holes. Raise the transmission up until the input shaft splines are aligned with the clutch disc splines.

10. Slide the transmission forward onto the guide studs until the transmission is in position. Install the 2 lower transmission retaining bolts and torque to 40–50 ft. lbs. (54–67 Nm). Remove the guide studs, install the upper bolts and tighten to 40–50 ft. lbs. (54–67 Nm).

11. Place the rear support bracket in position and install the retaining bolts. Install the crossmember. Position the mount between the transmission and crossmember. Remove the transmission jack.

12. Position the transfer case on the transmission jack. Position the transfer case onto the transmission, using care to guide the transfer case shift lever through the opening in the floor pan. Install the gasket and 6 retaining bolts.

13. Connect the speedometer cable and the back-up light switch.

14. Install the driveshafts.

15. Fill the transmission and transfer case with the proper type and quantity of lubricant. Lower the vehicle.

16. Install the shift lever retaining bolt. Slide the shifter boot into position on the shifter shaft and install the boot retaining screws.

17. Install the carpet or floor mat. Install the shift ball on the transfer case shift lever.

S5–42 ZF FIVE SPEED

2WD Vehicles

1. Shift the transmission into the **N** position. Disconnect the negative battery cable.

2. Remove the carpet or floor mat. Remove the boot and bezel assembly from the transmission opening cover. Remove the upper shift lever from the lower shift lever.

3. Raise and support the vehicle safely. Disconnect the speedometer cable. Disconnect the back-up light switch located at the top left side of the transmission.

4. Remove the drain plug from the transmission and drain the transmission fluid into a suitable drain pan. Position a suitable transmission jack under the transmission.

5. Disconnect the driveshaft and clutch linkage from the transmission and wire it to 1 side.

6. On F Super Duty, remove the transmission parking brake from the transmission.

7. Remove the transmission rear mount and lower retainer. Remove the crossmember.

8. Remove the bolts that retain the transmission to the engine block. Move the transmission to the rear until the input shaft clears the engine flywheel. Lower the transmission from the vehicle.

To install:

9. Place the transmission on a suitable transmission jack. Install guide studs in the front case and raise the transmission until the input shaft splines are aligned with the clutch disc splines. The clutch release bearing and hub must be properly positioned in the release lever fork.

10. Slide the transmission forward on the guide studs until the transmission is in position. Install the transmission retaining bolts and torque to 40–50 ft. lbs. (54–67 Nm). Remove the guide studs and install the 2 remaining bolts.

11. Install the crossmember. Position the mount and retainer between the transmission and crossmember. Install the bolts and tighten to 60–80 ft. lbs. (81–108 Nm). Install the nut retaining the mount and retainer to the crossmember. Tighten to 60–80 ft. lbs. (81–108 Nm) and remove the transmission jack.

12. Connect the speedometer cable, clutch linkage and back-up light switch.

13. On F Super Duty vehicles, install the transmission parking brake.

14. Connect the driveshaft. Fill the transmission with the proper type and quantity of lubricant and lower the vehicle.

15. Install the upper shift lever to the lower shift lever. Tighten the 2 retaining screws to 16–24 ft. lbs. (22–33 Nm). Install the boot and bezel assembly to the transmission opening cover.

16. Install the carpet or floor mat.

4WD Vehicles

1. Shift the transmission into the **N** position. Disconnect the negative battery cable.

2. Remove the carpet or floor mat. Remove the boot and bezel from the transmission opening cover. Remove the upper shift lever from the lower shift lever.

3. Raise and support the vehicle safely. Remove the drain plugs and drain the transmission and transfer case.

4. Disconnect the front and rear driveshafts from the transfer case and wire them out of the way.

5. Disconnect the speedometer cable and back-up light switch. If equipped, remove the skid pan from under the transfer case.

6. Support the transfer case using a transmission jack. Remove the 6 bolts holding the transfer case to the transmission and carefully lower the transfer case from the vehicle, using care to ensure that the transfer case shift lever clears the opening in the floor pan.

7. Support the transmission with the transmission jack. Remove the transmission rear mount and lower retainer. Remove the crossmember.

8. Remove the bolts that retain the transmission to the engine block. Move the transmission to the rear until the input shaft clears the engine flywheel housing. Lower the transmission from the vehicle.

To install:

9. Place the transmission on a transmission jack and install 2 guide studs in the transmission front case top holes. Raise the transmission up until the input shaft splines are aligned with the clutch disc splines.

10. Slide the transmission forward on the guide studs until the transmission is in position. Install the transmission retaining bolts and torque to 40–50 ft. lbs. (54–67 Nm). Remove the guide studs and install the remaining bolts.

11. Place the rear support bracket in position and install the

retaining bolts. Install the crossmember. Position the mount between the transmission and crossmember. Remove the transmission jack.

12. Position the transfer case on the transmission jack. Position the transfer case onto the transmission, using care to guide the transfer case shift lever through the opening in the floor pan. Install the gasket and 6 retaining bolts.

13. Connect the speedometer cable and the back-up light switch.

14. Install the front and rear driveshafts. Fill the transmission and transfer case with the proper type and quantity of lubricant. Lower the vehicle.

15. Install the upper shift lever to the lower shift lever and tighten the retaining bolts to 16–24 ft. lbs. (22–33 Nm). Install the boot and bezel assembly.

16. Install the carpet or floor mat. Install the shift ball on the upper shift lever and on the transfer case shift lever, if removed.

17. Road test the vehicle for proper shift operation.

ZF S5-42 TRANSMISSION – 4 x 4 AND F-SUPER DUTY VERSION

ZFS 5-42 TRANSMISSION – 4 x 2 VERSION

S5–42 ZF manual transmission

CLUTCH

Clutch Assembly

Removal and Installation

1. Disconnect the negative battery cable(s). Raise and safely support the vehicle.

2. Remove the clutch slave cylinder or the hydraulic line, as necessary.

3. Remove the dust cover and clutch release lever, if equipped.

4. Remove the transmission from the vehicle.

5. Mark the assembled position of the pressure plate to the flywheel, so they can be reinstalled in the same position.

6. Loosen the pressure plate attaching bolts evenly and remove the pressure plate and clutch disc.

7. Inspect the flywheel for wear, scoring and cracks. Machine or replace, as necessary. Inspect the clutch pilot bearing for wear and free movement. If replacement is necessary, remove using puller tool T58L–101–B or equivalent.

8. Inspect the clutch release bearing for wear and free movement; replace as necessary. If equipped with a concentric slave cylinder, remove the release bearing by twisting it until resistance is felt. Turning further will allow the preload spring to push the bearing assembly off the slave cylinder.

To install:

9. If the pilot bearing was removed, a new 1 must be installed. Install using replacer tool T74P–7137–A and clutch aligner tool T71P–7137–H or equivalent. Install the pilot bearing with the seal facing the transmission so the adapter is not cocked.

10. If the flywheel was removed, make sure the mating surfaces of the crank flange and flywheel are clean, and install the flywheel. Tighten the flywheel bolts to 75–85 ft. lbs. (102–115 Nm) on all except 7.3L diesel engine. On 7.3L diesel engine, apply locking compound to the bolts and tighten to 47 ft. lbs. (64 Nm).

11. Position the clutch disc on the flywheel so alignment tool D79T–7550–A or equivalent, can enter the pilot bearing and align the disc.

12. Install the pressure plate. If the original pressure plate is being reused, align the marks that were made during the removal procedure.

13. Install the pressure plate bolts and tighten in a gradual criss-cross pattern. The final torque should be 20–29 ft. lbs. (27–39 Nm) on all except 4.9L, 5.0L and 5.8L engines with 10 in. clutch and all 7.3L diesel and 7.5L engines, where the final torque should be 15–20 ft. lbs. (20–27 Nm).

14. Clean and lubricate the transmission bearing retainer. Clean and lubricate the bearing hub bore and install on the retainer. Clean and lubricate the release lever pivot stud, if equipped.

15. Install the transmission. If equipped, position the release lever in the bearing hub and align with the pivot stud. Push inward on the lever until it snaps into position. Install the dust boot, if equipped.

16. Install the slave cylinder, or attach the hydraulic line.

17. Connect the negative battery cable and bleed the hydraulic system, if necessary. Road test the vehicle for proper operation.

Pedal Height/Free Play Adjustment

The hydraulic clutch system provides automatic adjustment. No adjustment of clutch linkage or pedal position is required.

PILOT BEARING

CLUTCH DISC

BOLT
10" CLUTCH
(15-20 FT-LB)
11" CLUTCH
(20-29 FT-LB)

CLUTCH COVER

BOLT (15-20 FT-LB)

SLAVE CYLINDER ASSEMBLY

Clutch installation—Bronco, F Series and E Series with 4.9L, 5.0L and 5.8L engines

BOLT AND WASHER

PILOT BEARING

DISC ASSEMBLY

CLUTCH PRESSURE PLATE AND COVER ASSEMBLY

HUB AND BEARING ASSEMBLY

BOLT AND WASHER (40-50 FT-LB)

BOLT AND WASHER (40-50 FT-LB)

REAR ENGINE COVER PLATE

FLYWHEEL

LOCKWASHER

BOLT

CLUTCH RELEASE LEVER ASSEMBLY

BOLT AND WASHER

CLUTCH HOUSING DUST SHIELD

PART OF TRANSMISSION

CLUTCH HOUSING ASSEMBLY

CLUTCH LEVER RELEASE STUD

Clutch installation—Bronco and F Series with 4.9L and 5.0L engines and Warner transmission

Clutch installation—F Series with 7.3L diesel and 7.5L engines

Clutch Master Cylinder

Removal and Installation

NOTE: The master cylinder is removed with the hydraulic line attached.

1. Disconnect the negative battery cable.
2. From inside the vehicle, carefully pry the pushrod and retainer bushing from the cross-shaft lever pin. Disconnect the interlock switch connector plug.
3. If equipped with an external slave cylinder, remove the slave cylinder and use a $^3/_{32}$ in. diameter punch to drive out the pin that holds the tube in the slave cylinder. Disconnect and plug the tube.
4. If equipped with a concentric slave cylinder, disconnect the coupling at the transmission with coupling tool T88T–70522–A or equivalent, by sliding the white plastic sleeve toward the slave cylinder while applying a slight tug on the tube. Plug the tube.
5. Note the clutch tube routing to the slave cylinder, then remove the attaching hardware for the hydraulic tube retaining clips.
6. Remove the 2 nuts and support bracket retaining the clutch reservoir and master cylinder assembly to the firewall and remove the assembly. On Bronco and F Series, when the master cylinder studs are free of the dash panel, rotate the cylinder 105 degrees counterclockwise to permit the interlock switch to pass through the dash panel.
7. Installation is the reverse of the removal procedure. Press the pushrod with the retainer bushing onto the cross-shaft lever pin until the bushing tabs snap into position in the groove. The flanged side of the bushing must be towards the cross-shaft lever. Bleed the system.

Clutch Master Cylinder Pushrod Length Adjustment

To determine if the pushrod is adjusted properly, disconnect it and see if it will reassemble to the pin. When the pushrod is disconnected from the pin, the master cylinder piston is fully retracted and the clutch pedal blade is contacting the rubber bumper stop. If the pushrod and lever pin are not aligned, proceed as follows, only in the sequence given.

1. Tighten the clutch pedal attaching nut on the left side.
2. Reinstall the master cylinder pushrod to the cross-shaft lever pin.
3. Stroke the clutch pedal several times to reset the position of the shaft to the pedal slot. This Step is mandatory.
4. Remove the pushrod from the lever pin and check the alignment. If the pushrod and lever pin still do not align, replace the cross-shaft lever.

Clutch Slave Cylinder

Removal and Installation

EXTERNAL TYPE

NOTE: If the slave cylinder is disconnected with the hydraulic line attached, the master cylinder pushrod must be disconnected from the clutch pedal. If not disconnected, permanent damage to the slave cylinder will occur if the clutch pedal is depressed while the slave cylinder is disconnected.

1. Lift the 2 retaining tabs of the slave cylinder retaining bracket, using a small prybar. Disengage the tabs from the bell housing lugs and slide outward to remove.
2. Use a $^3/_{32}$ in. diameter punch to drive out the pin that holds the hydraulic tube in the slave cylinder. Disconnect and plug the tube.

To install:

3. Bleed the hydraulic system and connect the hydraulic tube. Install the retainer pin.
4. Push the slave cylinder pushrod into the cylinder. Engage the pushrod into the release lever and slide the slave cylinder into the bell housing lugs.

NOTE: A new slave cylinder contains a shipping strap that pre-positions the pushrod for installation and also provides a bearing insert. Following installation of the new slave cylinder, the first actuation of the clutch pedal will break the shipping strap and give normal system operation.

CONCENTRIC TYPE

1. Disconnect the negative battery cable.
2. Disconnect the hydraulic line coupling at the transmission with clutch coupling tool T88T–70522–A or equivalent, by sliding the white plastic sleeve toward the slave cylinder while applying a slight tug on the tube.
3. Remove the transmission from the vehicle.
4. To remove the clutch release bearing from the slave cylinder, twist the bearing until resistance is felt. Turning further will allow the preload spring to push the bearing assembly off the slave cylinder.
5. Remove the bolts retaining the slave cylinder to the transmission and remove the slave cylinder from the transmission input shaft.

To install:

6. Position the slave cylinder over the transmission input shaft with the bleed screw and coupling facing the left side of the transmission.
7. Install the slave cylinder attaching bolts and tighten to 15–20 ft. lbs. (20–27 Nm).
8. If removed, install the release bearing by pushing into place.
9. Install the transmission.
10. Insert the male coupling into the female coupling on the slave cylinder and check that the connection is secure.

Hydraulic Clutch System Bleeding

WITH EXTERNAL SLAVE CYLINDER

1. Clean the reservoir cap and slave cylinder in the area of the tube connection. Remove the slave cylinder from the transmission bell housing.
2. Using a $^3/_{32}$ in. diameter punch, drive out the pin that holds the tube. Remove the tube from the slave cylinder and place the tube into a container. Keep the fluid reservoir cap tight to minimize fluid loss.
3. Hold the slave cylinder so the connector port is at the highest point. Fill the cylinder with brake fluid through the connector port. It may be necessary to rock the cylinder around or gently push on the pushrod to expel all air. When all the air is expelled and no more bubbles come out of the port hole, reinstall the slave cylinder.

NOTE: Some fluid will be expelled from the connector port as the pushrod is compressed, attaching it to the transmission and lever.

4. Gravity fill the clutch master cylinder and tube as follows: Remove the reservoir cap and diaphragm. Fluid should flow out the open end of the tube into the container. Be sure to keep the reservoir full. When fluid is flowing out in a steady, uninterrupted flow and the fluid is level with the step in the reservoir, reinstall the cap and diaphragm. Install the end of the tube into the slave cylinder and replace the pin holding the tube in place.

WITH CONCENTRIC SLAVE CYLINDER

1. Clean dirt and grease from the reservoir cap. Remove the cap and diaphragm and fill reservior to the top with brake fluid.
2. Attach 1 end of a rubber tube to the slave cylinder bleed screw, located next to the inlet connection, and place the other end into a container.
3. Loosen the bleed screw, allowing fluid to move from the master cylinder down the tube to the slave cylinder. Be sure to

Clutch release bearing removal and installation— concentric slave cylinder

keep the reservoir full to make sure no additional air enters the system.

4. Bubbles should start to appear at the bleed screw outlet, indicating air is being expelled. When the slave cylinder is full, a steady flow of fluid will come from the slave outlet. Tighten the bleed screw. Be sure to maintain the fluid level at the step in the reservoir.

5. Depress the clutch pedal to the floor and hold for 2 seconds, then release the pedal as rapidly as possible. The pedal must be released completely, then pause for 2 seconds. Repeat 10 times.

6. Check the fluid level in the reservoir. The fluid should be level with the step when the diaphragm is removed.

7. Repeat Steps 5 and 6 five times. Replace the reservoir diaphragm and cap.

8. Have an assistant hold the clutch pedal to the floor. Crack open the bleed screw to allow any additional air to escape. Close the screw and release the pedal. Check the fluid level.

External slave cylinder bleeding

Concentric slave cylinder bleeding

AUTOMATIC TRANSMISSION

For further information, please refer to Chilton's Transmission Service Manual.

Transmission Assembly

Removal and Installation

FORD C6

Bronco and F Series

1. Disconnect the negative battery cable and disconnect the neutral switch wire at the plug connector. Raise and support the vehicle safely.

2. Place a drain pan under the transmission fluid pan. Starting at the rear of the pan and working toward the front, loosen the attaching bolts and allow the fluid to drain. Remove all the pan bolts except 2 at the front, to drain all of the fluid. After draining is completed, install 2 bolts at the rear of the pan to hold it in place.

3. Remove the converter access cover. Using a wrench on the crankshaft pulley, turn the engine over to gain access to and remove the converter-to-flywheel nuts. Place the drain pan under the converter and turn the crankshaft pulley to gain access to the converter drain plug. Remove the plug, drain the fluid and reinstall the plug.

4. On 2WD vehicles, remove the driveshaft.

5. Disconnect the speedometer cable from the extension housing.

6. Disconnect the throttle and manual linkage rods or cable controls from the levers at the transmission.

7. Disconnect the oil cooler lines from the transmission.

8. Remove the vacuum hose from the vacuum diaphragm unit. Remove the vacuum line from the retaining clip.

9. Disconnect the cable from the terminal on the starter motor. Remove the attaching bolts and remove the starter.

10. On 4WD vehicles, remove the transfer case.

11. Remove the 2 engine rear support and mount assembly attaching bolts.

12. Remove the 2 engine rear support and mount assembly-to-extension housing attaching bolts.

13. Remove the 6 bolts securing the No. 2 crossmember to the frame side rails.

14. Raise the transmission with a transmission jack and remove the crossmember.

15. Secure the transmission to the jack with the safety chain.

16. Remove the converter housing-to-engine attaching bolts.

17. Move the transmission away from the engine. Lower the transmission and remove it from under the vehicle.

To install:

18. Tighten the converter drain plug to 18–28 ft. lbs. (11–37 Nm). Position the converter on the transmission, making sure the converter drive flats are fully engaged in the pump gear.

19. With the converter properly installed, place the transmission on the jack. Secure the unit to the jack with the chain.

20. Rotate the converter so the studs and drain plug are in alignment with their holes in the flywheel.

21. Move the transmission forward into position, being careful not to damage the flywheel and the converter pilot.

NOTE: The converter must rest squarely against the flywheel. This indicates that the converter pilot is not binding in the engine crankshaft. Do not allow the converter drive flats to disengage from the pump gear.

22. Install the converter housing-to-engine bolts. On gasoline engines, tighten the retaining bolts to 40–50 ft. lbs. (55–67 Nm).

On diesel engines, tighten the retaining bolts to 50–65 ft. lbs. (67–87 Nm).

23. Remove the transmission jack safety chain from around the transmission.

24. Position the No. 2 crossmember to the frame side rails. Install the attaching bolts.

25. On 4WD vehicles, install the transfer case.

26. Position the engine rear support and mount assembly above the crossmember. Install the rear support and mount assembly-to-extension housing mounting bolts.

27. Lower the transmission and remove the jack.

28. Secure the engine rear support and mount assembly to the crossmember with the attaching bolts.

29. Connect the vacuum line to the vacuum diaphragm, making sure the metal line is secured in the retaining clip.

30. Connect the oil cooler lines to the transmission.

31. Connect the throttle and manual linkage rods or cable controls to their respective levers on the transmission.

32. Connect the speedometer cable to the extension housing.

33. Secure the starter in place with the attaching bolts. Connect the cable to the terminal on the starter.

34. Install a new O-ring on the lower end of the transmission filler tube and insert the tube in the case.

35. Secure the converter-to-flywheel attaching nuts and tighten to 20–30 ft. lbs. (28–40 Nm).

36. Install the converter housing access cover and secure it with the attaching bolts.

37. Connect the driveshaft.

38. Clean the gasket mating surfaces on the transmission pan and transmission. Install a new pan gasket and install the pan. Tighten the retaining bolts to 8–12 ft. lbs. (11–16 Nm).

39. Lower the vehicle. Fill the transmission to the correct level with the proper type of fluid. Adjust the shift linkage.

40. Connect the neutral switch wire to the plug connector and connect the negative battery cable.

41. Start the engine and check for leaks. Road test the vehicle and check for proper operation.

E Series

1. Disconnect the negative battery cable. Remove the engine cover from inside the vehicle.

2. Disconnect the neutral start switch wires at the plug connector.

3. If equipped with 8 cylinder engine, remove the flex hose from the air cleaner heat tube.

4. Remove the upper converter housing to engine attaching bolts. Remove the bolt securing the filler tube to the engine.

5. Raise the vehicle and support it safely.

6. Place a drain pan under the transmission fluid pan. Starting at the rear of the pan and working toward the front, loosen the attaching bolts and allow the fluid to drain. Remove all the pan bolts except 2 at the front, to drain all of the fluid. After draining is completed, install 2 bolts at the rear of the pan to hold it in place.

7. Remove the converter access cover. Using a wrench on the crankshaft pulley, turn the engine over to gain access to and remove the converter-to-flywheel nuts. Place the drain pan under the converter and turn the crankshaft pulley to gain access to the converter drain plug. Remove the plug, drain the fluid and reinstall the plug.

8. Disconnect the driveshaft and remove the fluid filler tube.

9. Disconnect the starter cable at the starter and remove the starter from the converter housing.

10. Position a suitable engine support bar to the frame and engine oil pan flanges.

11. Disconnect the cooler lines from the transmission. Disconnect the vacuum line from the diaphragm unit and remove the line from the retaining clip at the transmission.

12. Remove the speedometer driven gear from the extension housing.

13. Disconnect the manual and downshift linkage rods or cable controls from the control levers.

14. Position a transmission jack under the transmission. Install the safety chain to hold the transmission.

15. Remove the nuts securing the rear support and mount assembly to the crossmember. Remove the 6 bolts retaining the crossmember to the side rails and remove the 2 support gussets. Raise the transmission with the jack and remove the crossmember.

16. Remove the remaining converter housing-to-engine attaching bolts. Lower the jack and remove the converter and transmission assembly from under the vehicle.

To install:

17. Tighten the converter drain plug to 18–28 ft. lbs. (11–37 Nm). Position the converter on the transmission, making sure the converter drive flats are fully engaged in the pump gear.

18. With the converter properly installed, place the transmission on the jack. Secure the unit to the jack with the chain.

19. Rotate the converter so the studs and drain plug are in alignment with their holes in the flywheel.

20. Move the transmission forward into position, being careful not to damage the flywheel and the converter pilot.

NOTE: The converter must rest squarely against the flywheel. This indicates that the converter pilot is not binding in the engine crankshaft. Do not allow the converter drive flats to disengage from the pump gear.

21. Install the converter housing-to-engine bolts. On gasoline engines, tighten the retaining bolts to 40–50 ft. lbs. (55–67 Nm). On diesel engines, tighten the retaining bolts to 50–65 ft. lbs. (67–87 Nm).

22. Install the converter-to-flywheel attaching nuts and tighten to 20–30 ft. lbs. (28–40 Nm).

23. Install the crossmember. Install the rear support and mount assembly-to-crossmember attaching bolts and nuts.

24. Remove the safety chain and remove the jack from under the vehicle. Remove the engine support bar.

25. Install a new O-ring on the lower end of the transmission filler tube and insert the tube and dipstick in the case.

26. Connect the vacuum line to the vacuum diaphragm, making sure the line is secured in the retaining clip. Connect the oil cooler lines. Install the speedometer driven gear into the extension housing.

27. Connect the transmission linkage rods to the control levers. Be sure to use a new retaining ring and grommet. Attach the shift rod to the steering column shift lever. Align the flats of the adjusting stud with the flats of the rod slot and insert the stud through the rod. Assemble the adjusting stud nut and washer to a loose fit. Adjust the linkage.

28. Install the converter housing access cover and tighten the attaching bolts to 12–16 ft. lbs. (17–21 Nm).

29. Install the starter with the attaching bolts. Connect the starter cable.

30. Clean the gasket mating surfaces on the transmission pan and transmission. Install a new pan gasket and install the pan. Tighten the retaining bolts to 8–12 ft. lbs. (11–16 Nm).

31. Install the driveshaft and lower the vehicle.

32. If equipped with a V8 engine, install the flex hose to the air cleaner heat tube. Install the bolt that retains the filler tube to the cylinder block.

33. Connect the neutral start switch wires at the plug connector. Fill the transmission to the correct level with the proper type of fluid.

34. Connect the negative battery cable, start the engine and check for leaks. Adjust the throttle and manual linkage.

35. Install the engine compartment cover.

FORD AOD

1. Disconnect the negative battery cable. On E series, remove the engine cover. Raise the vehicle and support it safely.

2. Place the drain pan under the transmission fluid pan. Starting at the rear of the pan and working toward the front, loosen the attaching bolts and allow the fluid to drain. Finally

remove all of the pan attaching bolts except 2 at the front, to allow the fluid to further drain. With the fluid drained, install 2 bolts on the rear side of the pan to temporarily hold it in place.

3. Remove the converter drain plug access cover from the lower end of the converter housing.

4. Remove the converter-to-flywheel attaching nuts. Place a wrench on the crankshaft pulley attaching bolt to turn the converter to gain access to the nuts.

5. Place a drain pan under the converter to catch the fluid. With the wrench on the crankshaft pulley bolt, turn the converter to gain access to the converter drain plug and remove the plug. After the fluid has been drained, reinstall the plug.

6. Mark the rear driveshaft yoke and axle companion flange so they can be reinstalled in their original positions. Disconnect the driveshaft from the rear axle and slide the shaft rearward from the transmission. Install a seal installation tool or equivalent, in the extension housing to prevent fluid leakage.

7. Disconnect the cable from the terminal on the starter motor. Remove the attaching bolts and remove the starter motor. Disconnect the neutral start switch wires at the plug connector.

8. Remove the rear mount-to-crossmember attaching bolts and the 2 crossmember-to-frame attaching bolts.

9. Remove the 2 engine rear support-to-extension housing attaching bolts.

10. Disconnect the TV cable from the transmission TV lever. Disconnect the manual rod from the transmission manual lever at the transmission.

11. Remove the bolt securing the bellcrank bracket to the converter housing.

12. On 4WD vehicles, remove the transfer case from the vehicle.

13. Raise the transmission with a transmission jack, to provide clearance to remove the crossmember. Remove the rear mount from the crossmember and remove the crossmember from the side supports.

NOTE: 4WD vehicles have a deep well oil pan. Use a transmission jack that will allow clearance for the oil pan depth and still provide support for the transmission at the oil pan rail.

14. Lower the transmission to gain access to the oil cooler lines.

15. Disconnect each oil line from the fittings on the transmission.

16. Disconnect the speedometer cable from the extension housing.

17. Remove the bolt that secures the transmission fluid filler tube to the cylinder block. Lift the filler tube and the dipstick from the transmission.

18. Secure the transmission to the jack with the chain.

19. Remove the converter housing-to-cylinder block attaching bolts.

20. Carefully move the transmission and converter assembly away from the engine and, at the same time, lower the jack to clear the underside of the vehicle.

21. Remove the converter and mount the transmission in a holding fixture.

To install:

22. Tighten the converter drain plug to 8–28 ft. lbs. (11–38 Nm). Position the converter on the transmission, making sure the converter drive flats are fully engaged in the pump gear by rotating the converter.

23. Lube the pilot with chassis grease. With the converter properly installed, place the transmission on the jack. Secure the transmission to the jack with a chain.

24. Rotate the converter until the studs and drain plug are in alignment with the holes in the flywheel.

25. Move the converter and transmission assembly forward into position, using care not to damage the flywheel and the converter pilot. The converter must rest squarely against the flywheel. This indicates that the converter pilot is not binding in the engine crankshaft.

26. Install and tighten the converter housing-to-engine attaching bolts to 40–50 ft. lbs. (55–68 Nm).

NOTE: Before installing the torque converter-to-flywheel nuts, a check should be made to ensure the converter is properly seated. The converter should move freely with respect to the flywheel. Graps the stud; movement back and forth should result in a metallic clank noise if the converter is properly seated. If the converter will not move, the transmission must be removed and the converter repositioned so the impeller hub is properly engaged in the pump gear.

27. Remove the safety chain from around the transmission. Install a new O-ring on the transmission filler tube, lube the O-ring with transmission fluid, and install the tube in the transmission case. Install the tube retaining bolt.

28. Connect the speedometer cable to the extension housing and the oil cooler lines to the transmission case.

29. Secure the engine rear support to the extension housing and tighten the bolts to 60–80 ft. lbs. (82–108 Nm).

30. Position the crossmember on the side supports. Position the rear mount on the crossmember and install the attaching bolt and nut.

31. On 4WD vehicles, install the transfer case.

32. Lower the transmission and remove the jack. Secure the crossmember to the side supports.

33. Position the bellcrank to the converter housing and install the attaching bolt. Connect the TV cable to the transmission TV lever. Connect the manual linkage rod to the manual lever at the transmission.

34. Install the converter-to-flywheel nuts and tighten to 20–34 ft. lbs. (27–46 Nm). Install the converter housing access cover.

35. Install the starter and conect the starter cable. Connect the neutral start switch wires.

36. Lubricate the driveshaft yoke splines and install the driveshaft. Align the marks on the companion flange and rear yoke made during removal.

37. Clean the gasket mating surfaces on the transmission pan and transmission. Install a new pan gasket and install the pan. Tighten the retaining bolts to 6–10 ft. lbs. (8–14 Nm).

38. Adjust the shift linkage and throttle linkage. Lower the vehicle.

39. Fill the transmission to the correct level with the proper type of fluid. Connect the negative battery cable, start the engine and check for leaks. Road test and check for proper operation. Check the fluid level.

FORD E4OD

1. Disconnect the negative battery cable. Remove the transmission dipstick. On E series, remove the engine cover.

2. Place the transmission selector in **N** position. Raise and safely support the vehicle.

3. On 4WD vehicles, remove the front driveshaft. Remove the rear driveshaft. On F Super Duty vehicles, remove the transmission mounted parking brake.

4. Disconnect the shift linkage. On 4WD vehicles, remove the shift linkage from transfer case shift lever.

5. Remove the manual lever position sensor connector by squeezing the connector tabs and pulling on connector.

NOTE: Do not attempt to pry the tab with a prybar. Remove the heat shield from the transmission before attempting to remove the connector.

6. Remove the solenoid body connector heat shield.

7. Remove the solenoid body connector by pushing on the center tab and pulling on the wire harness.

8. On 4WD vehicles, remove the 4WD switch connector from the transfer case. Use care not to overextend the tabs.

9. Pry the wire harness locator from the extension housing wire bracket. On 4WD vehicles, remove the wire harness locators from the left side of the crossmember.

10. Remove the speedometer cable and the lower converter cover bolts.

11. Remove the rear engine cover plate bolts. Remove the starter.

12. Using a $^{15}/_{16}$ in. socket, rotate the crankshaft bolt to gain access to converter nuts. Remove the 4 converter mounting nuts and discard.

13. Place transmission stand fixture tool 014–00763 or equivalent, on a universal transmission jack and position under the transmission. Use a safety strap to secure the transmission to the transmission stand fixture.

14. Loosen the 2 rear transmission mounting pad nuts. Remove the retaining bolts and remove the crossmember from the transmission.

15. Remove the transmission cooler lines from the transmission case. Cap cooling lines and plug fittings at transmission.

16. Remove the 6 bell housing bolts. Back out the converter pilot from the flywheel and gently lower the transmission while checking for obstructions.

17. Install torque converter handles, T81P–8902–C or equivalent, on the converter with handles in the 6 and 12 o'clock positions.

18. Remove the transmission filler tube from the stub tube. On 4WD vehicles, remove the transfer case vent hose from the detent bracket and the transfer case from the transmission. On F Super Duty models, remove the transmission mounted parking brake.

To install:

19. Place the transmission onto transmission stand fixture tool 014–00763 or equivalent.

20. On 4WD vehicles, install the transfer case to the transmission. On F Super Duty vehicles, install the transmission mounted parking brake.

21. Install the torque converter using torque converter handles T81P–7902–C or the equivalent. Carry the converter with the handles in the 6 and 12 o'clock positions. Push and rotate the converter onto the pump until it bottoms out.

NOTE: Check the seating of the converter by placing a straightedge across the bell housing. There must be a gap between the converter pilot face and the straight edge.

22. Remove the converter handles. Check the condition of filler tube O-ring and replace if damaged or worn. Install the filler tube.

23. Rotate the converter studs to align with the flywheel mounting holes. Raise transmission into position while checking for any obstructions. Do not allow converter drive flats to disengage from pump gear. Use rubber converter drain plug cover to aid in the alignment of the converter studs.

NOTE: Use care not to damage the flywheel and converter pilot. The converter must rest squarely against the flywheel. This indicates that the converter pilot is not binding in the engine crankshaft.

24. Alternately snug up the bell housing bolts and final torque to 40–50 ft. lbs. (55–67 Nm).

25. Install the rubber converter drain plug cover and transmission cooling lines.

26. Install the crossmember and the transmission retaining bolts. Remove the safety strap and the transmission jack.

27. Rotate the crankshaft to gain access to converter studs. Install new stud nuts and torque to 20–30 ft. lbs. (28–40 Nm).

28. Install the starter, rear engine plate cover and lower dust cover.

29. Install the speedometer cable.

30. Completely seat the solenoid body connector into the solenoid valve body receptacle. An audible click sound indicates proper installation.

31. Install the solenoid body connector heat shield with offset bending inward.

Torque converter installation—E4OD automatic transmission

32. On 4WD vehicles, install wire harness locators into crossmember.

33. Install the wire harness locator into extension housing wire bracket.

34. On 4WD vehicles, install the 4WD switch connector and connect the transfer case shift linkage.

35. Install the manual lever position sensor connector. An audible click sound indicates proper installation.

36. Install the shift linkage. On 4WD vehicles, install the shift rod to transfer case shift lever.

37. Install the rear driveshaft and on 4WD vehicles, install the front driveshaft.

38. Lower the vehicle and connect the negative battery cable. Refill the transmission with the proper type and quantity of fluid. Start the engine and check the fluid level.

39. Road test vehicle for proper operation.

Shift Linkage Adjustment

1. With the engine stopped and the parking brake applied, place the selector lever at the steering column in the **D** position for C6 transmissions and in the **OD** position for AOD and E40D transmissions. Hold it against the stop by applying an 8 pound weight to the selector lever knob.

2. Loosen the shift rod adjusting nut at point "A".

3. Shift the manual lever at the transmission into the **D** or **OD** position, by moving the lever all the way rearward, then forward 2 detents.

4. With the selector lever and the manual lever in position, tighten the nut at point "A" to 12–18 ft. lbs. (17–24 Nm). Use care to prevent motion between the stud and rod.

5. Remove the 8 pound weight from the steering column selector lever knob.

6. Operate the shift lever in all positions to make sure the manual lever at the transmission is in full detent in all gear ranges. Re-adjust the linkage, if required.

7. On Bronco and F Series, check for correct operation of the automatic transmission selector indicator.

SHIFT ROD

SELECTOR LEVER

VIEW Z

PARTIAL VIEW SHOWING
TRANSMISSION GEAR SHIFT
ROD FOR 6.9L DIESEL

P R N D 2 1

VIEW Z

SHIFT ARM

STEERING COLUMN
ASSEMBLY

GEAR SHIFT ROD

BELLCRANK ASSEMBLY

VIEW Y

LEVER
CONTROL
ROD

MANUAL
LEVER

POINT "A"

GEAR SHIFT ROD

L1   SHIFT ARM

NUT AND WASHER

BELLCRANK
ASSEMBLY

BOLT

BOLT

NUT

L1

LEVER
CONTROL
ROD

LEVER

GASOLINE ENGINES
VIEW Y

Shift linkage adjustment—C6 transmission

Throttle Valve Control Cable Adjustment
AUTOMATIC OVERDRIVE TRANSMISSION
1988–89 4.9L Engine and All 5.0L Engines

1. Set the parking brake and put the selector in the **N** position. Remove the protective cover over the the cable linkage, if equipped.
2. Verify that the throttle lever is at the idle stop. If it is not, check for binding or interference in the throttle system. Do not attempt to adjust the idle stop.

3. Verify that the cable routing is free of sharp bends or pressure points and that the cable operates freely. Lubricate the TV lever ball stud. Check for damage to cable or rubber boot.
4. Unlock the locking tab at the throttle body end by prying up with a small prybar to free the cable.

CONTROL
CABLE

LOCKING TAB
(PRY OUT WITH
SCREWDRIVER
TO UNLOCK)

Unlocking TV cable locking tab—5.0L engine

BOOT OVER
RETURN SPRING

TRANSMISSION
CASE

TRANSMISSION
TV CONTROL LEVER

RETENSION
SPRING(S)

Installing retension springs—TV cable adjustment

5. A retention spring must be installed on the TV control lever at the transmission, to hold it in the idle position, as far to the rear as the lever will travel, with about 10 pounds of force. If a suitable single spring is not available, two V8 TV return springs may be used. Attach retention spring(s) to the transmission TV lever and hook the rear end of the spring to the transmission case.

6. With the TV cable locking tab unlocked and the retention spring in place, rotate the transmission outer TV lever 10–30 degrees and return slowly.

7. Push down on the locking tab until flush.

8. Remove the retension springs from the transmission TV lever.

Transmission Selector Indicator Adjustment

1. Remove the shroud.

2. With the engine stopped and the parking brake applied, place the transmission selector lever at the steering column in the **OD** position, or **D** position if equipped with C6 transmission. Hold the lever against the stop by applying an 8 lb. weight to the selector lever.

NOTE: This adjustment must be made in the OD or on C6 transmission, the D position.

3. Place the cable loop over the retainer pin on the shift socket casting. Place the cable bracket in the "T" slot in the column outer tube.

4. Adjust the cable bracket in the slot until the indicator flag totally fills the rectangular adjustment under the **OD** or on C6 transmission, the **D**.

5. Tighten the bracket screw to 20 inch lbs. (2.25 Nm) without disturbing the flag's position. Release the lever.

6. The indicator flag should totally fill the shift position letters or numerals in each shift position.

NOTE: After the shift lever indicator flag has been adjusted, the manual linkage must be checked.

TRANSFER CASE

Transfer Case Assembly

Removal and Installation
BORG WARNER MODEL 13–45

1. Raise the vehicle and support it safely.
2. Drain the fluid from the transfer case.
3. Disconnect the 4WD indicator switch wire connector at the transfer case.
4. Remove the skid plate from the frame, if equipped.
5. Disconnect the front driveshaft from the front output yoke.
6. Disconnect the rear driveshaft from the rear output shaft yoke.
7. Disconnect the speedometer driven gear from the transfer case rear bearing retainer.
8. Disconnect the shift rod between the transfer case shift lever and the control lever assembly.
9. Disconnect the vent hose from the transfer case.
10. Support the transfer case with a transmission jack.
11. Remove the bolts retaining the transfer case to the transmission adapter.
12. Slide the transfer case rearward off of the transmission output shaft and lower the transfer case from the vehicle. Remove the gasket between the transfer case and adapter.
To install:
13. Place a new gasket between the transfer case and the adapter.
14. Raise the transfer case with the transmission jack so the transmission output shaft aligns with the splined transfer case input shaft. Slide the transfer case forward onto the transmission output shaft and onto the dowel pin. Install the bolts retaining the transfer case to the adapter and tighten the bolts, in sequence, to 25–43 lbs. (34–58 Nm).
15. Remove the transmission jack from the transfer case.
16. Connect the rear driveshaft to the rear output shaft yoke. Tighten the nut to 8–15 ft. lbs. (11–20 Nm).
17. Connect the vent hose to the transfer case.
18. Attach the shift rod between the transfer case shift lever and the control lever assembly.
19. Connect the speedometer driven gear to the transfer case.
20. Connect the 4WD indicator switch wire connector at the transfer case.
21. Connect the front driveshaft to the front output yoke. Tighten the nut to 8–15 ft. lbs. (11–20 Nm).
22. Install the skid plate to the frame.
23. Install the drain plug and tighten to 6–14 ft. lbs. (9–18 Nm). Remove the filler plug and install 6.5 pints of the proper fluid. Install the filler plug and tighten to 15–25 ft. lbs. (21–33 Nm).
24. Lower the vehicle.

BORG WARNER MODEL 13–56
ELECTRONIC AND MANUAL SHIFT

1. Raise the vehicle and support it safely.
2. Remove the nuts, bolts and skid plate from the frame, if equipped.
3. Remove the plug and drain the fluid from the transfer case.
4. Remove the wire connector from the feed wire harness at the rear of the transfer case on the electronic shift transfer case. On manual shift transfer case, disconnect the 4WD indicator switch wire connector.
5. Disconnect the front driveshaft from the front output shaft yoke.
6. Disconnect the rear driveshaft from the transfer case rear output shaft yoke.
7. Disconnect the speedometer driven gear from the transfer case.
8. Disconnect the vent hose. On manual shift transfer case, disconnect the shift rod between the transfer case shift lever and the control lever assembly.

Transfer case-to-adapter bolt torque sequence—Borg Warner 13–45 transfer case

Transfer case installation—typical

Transfer case-to-adapter bolt torque sequence—Borg Warner 13–56 electronic and manual shift transfer cases

---
CAUTION

The catalytic converter is located beside the transfer case. Due to the extreme high temperatures generated by the converter, be careful when working around it, or personal injury may result.

---

9. Support the transfer case with a jack. Remove the bolts retaining the transfer case to the transmission and the extension housing.

10. Slide the transfer case rearward off the transmission output shaft and lower the transfer case from the vehicle. Remove the gasket from the transfer case and extension housing.

To install:

11. Clean the transmission and transfer case gasket surfaces and place a new gasket between the transfer case and extension housing.

12. Raise the transfer case with the transmission jack so the transmission output shaft aligns with the splined transfer case input shaft. Slide the transfer case forward onto the transmission output shaft and onto the dowel pin. Install the retaining bolts and tighten, in sequence, to 25–43 ft. lbs. (34–58 Nm).

13. Remove the transmission jack and connect the vent hose. Connect the speedometer cable.

14. Connect the rear driveshaft to the output shaft yoke. Tighten the bolts on the electronic shift transfer case and Bronco with manual shift transfer case, to 20–25 ft. lbs. (28–33 Nm). On F Series with manual shift transfer case, tighten the nut to 8–15 ft. lbs. (11–20 Nm).

15. If equipped with manual shift transfer case, attach the shift rod between the transfer case shift lever and the control lever assembly.

16. Connect the front driveshaft to the front output yoke. Tighten the nut to 8–15 ft. lbs. (11–20 Nm).

17. On electronic shift transfer case, connect the wire connectors on the rear of the transfer case, making sure the retaining tabs lock. On manual shift transfer case, connect the 4WD indicator switch wire connector at the transfer case.

18. Install the skid plate, if equipped.

19. Install the drain plug and tighten to 7–14 ft. lbs. (9–18 Nm). Remove the fill plug and install the proper type of fluid to the bottom of the fill hole plug. Install the fill plug and tighten to 14 ft. lbs. (18 Nm).

20. Lower the vehicle.

DRIVE AXLE

Driveshaft and U-Joints

Removal and Installation

ONE-PIECE DRIVESHAFT

1. Raise and safely support the vehicle.

2. To maintain driveline balance, if the yellow alignment marks are not visible, mark the relationship of the rear driveshaft yoke and the drive pinion flange of the axle, so they may be reinstalled in their original positions.

3. If equipped with a circular axle companion flange, proceed as follows:

a. Remove the bolts retaining the axle flange yoke to the companion flange and disconnect the driveshaft from the axle.

b. Lower the driveshaft and slide it rearward off the transmission output shaft.

c. Install a plug in the transmission extension housing to prevent fluid loss.

One-piece driveshaft

4. If equipped with a half round axle companion flange, proceed as follows:

a. Remove the nuts retaining the U-bolts to the axle companion flange.

b. Remove the U-bolts and disconnect the U-joint from the axle companion flange being careful not to drop the U-joint bearing cups.

c. Wrap tape around the U-joints to retain the bearing cups. Slide the driveshaft rearward off the transmission output shaft.

d. Install a plug in the transmission extension housing to prevent fluid loss.

NOTE: On 4WD vehicles equipped with a slip between the center driveshafts, disconnect the driveshaft at the transfer case during removal.

To install:

5. If the lugs on the half round axle companion flange are shaved or distorted so the bearings slide, replace the flange.

6. Lubricate the yoke spline and remove the plug from the extension housing. Install the yoke on the transmission output shaft, but do not allow the yoke assembly to bottom on the shaft with excessive force.

7. Install the driveshaft so the index marks or the yellow marks (if visible) on the yoke (light side) is in line with the yellow mark on the companion flange. This prevents vibration. If a vibration exists, the driveshaft should be disconnected from the axle, rotated 180 degrees, and reinstalled.

8. On half round axle companion flange, install the U-bolts and nuts attaching the U-joint to the companion flange. Tighten the U-bolt nuts to 8–15 ft. lbs. (11–20 Nm).

9. On circular axle companion flange, install the bolts retaining the axle flange yoke to the circular companion flange. Tighten to 70–95 ft. lbs. (95–129 Nm).

10. Lower the vehicle.

DRIVESHAFT/COUPLING SHAFT

1. Raise and safely support the vehicle.

2. Mark the relationship of the rear driveshaft yoke and the rear axle companion flange before removal, so they can be reinstalled in their original positions.

3. Disconnect the driveshaft from the rear axle companion flange and disconnect the driveshaft slip yoke from the coupling shaft yoke. Wrap tape type around the loose bearing caps to prevent the bearings from falling off the universal joint spiders.

4. Remove the 2 center bearing support-to-crossmember attaching bolts. Remove the coupling shaft and wrap tape around

the loose bearing caps. Install a plug in the transmission housing to prevent leakage.

5. Clean the male splines of the coupling shaft and driveshaft, removing hardened grease, dirt or rust, but do not remove the blue plastic coating. Inspect for worn or galled splines and remove any nicks, gouges or burrs from the driveshaft using a file or emery cloth.

6. Clean all dirt from the slip yoke internal splines and the slip yoke assembly. Inspect the splines for wear or twisting.

7. Clean all parts except the sealed center bearing and rubber insulator in solvent. Wipe the bearing and insulator clean with a cloth.

8. Inspect the slip yoke seal and replace, if necessary. Check the center support bearing for wear or rough action. Check the rubber insulator for hardening, cracking or deterioration. Replace if necessary.

To install:

9. Lubricate the coupling shaft slip yoke splines. Remove the plug from the transmission housing and install the front yoke of the coupling shaft assembly on the transmission ouput shaft. Do not allow the slip yoke assembly to bottom on the output shaft with excessive force.

10. Install the center bearing support bracket with the attaching bolts and spacers, if equipped.

11. Lubricate the splined stub shaft end of the coupling shaft assembly and the female splines of the slip yoke. Assemble the driveshaft slip yoke to the coupling shaft.

NOTE: If installing a new service driveshaft, align the factory made yellow paint mark at the rear of the driveshaft tube, with the factory made yellow paint mark on the outside diameter of the axle companion flange.

12. Connect the rear U-joint of the driveshaft to the rear axle companion flange and tighten the U-bolt nuts or strap bolts.

13. Using a hand grease gun, lubricate the driveshaft slip yoke at the grease fitting. Temporarily plug the vent hole in the welch plug at the slip yoke end while applying grease, to assure complete lubrication.

14. Lower the vehicle.

DOUBLE CARDAN U-JOINT DRIVESHAFT

1. Raise and safely support the vehicle.

2. If removing the rear driveshaft on Bronco, mark the driveshaft in relation to the transfer case and rear axle companion flange. Disconnect the double cardan U-joint from the transfer case flange and the single U-joint from the rear axle flange. Tape the loose bearing caps and remove the driveshaft.

Double Cardan U-joint assembly

3. If removing the front driveshaft on F 350, mark the driveshaft in relation to the transfer case and front axle companion flange. Disconnect the double cardan U-joint from the transfer case flange and the single U-joint from the front axle flange. Remove the driveshaft.

To install:

4. Align the index marks and position the single U-joint end of the driveshaft to the axle and install the U-bolts and nuts. Position the U-joint to the transfer case with the index marks aligned and install the bolts and lockwashers.

5. Tighten the bolts at the transfer case to 20–25 ft. lbs. (28–33 Nm) and the nuts at the axle to 8–15 ft. lbs. (11–20 Nm).

6. Lower the vehicle.

FRONT DRIVESHAFT

1. Raise and safely support the vehicle.

2. Mark the rear slip yoke in relation to the transfer case yoke for correct positioning during installation.

3. Remove the nuts and U-bolts, or bolts, that connect the rear slip yoke to the transfer case and the front yoke to the front axle.

4. Remove the driveshaft. Wrap tape around the loose bearing caps to prevent the bearings from falling out out of the U-joint spiders.

To install:

5. Install the driveshaft, aligning the marks on the slip yoke and transfer case.

6. Install the nuts and U-bolts that retain the slip yoke to the transfer case yoke. Tighten the nuts to 8–15 ft. lbs. (11–20 Nm). On F 350, tighten the bolts to 20–28 ft. lbs. (28–33 Nm).

7. Install the nuts and U-bolts that retain the front driveshaft yoke to the front drive axle yoke. Tighten the nuts to 8–15 ft. lbs. (11–20 Nm).

8. Lower the vehicle.

Front Axle Shaft, Bearing and Seal

Removal and Installation

DANA MODEL 60 MONOBEAM

1. Raise the vehicle and support it safely. Remove the front wheel and tire assembly.

2. Remove the disc brake caliper and wire it to the frame. Do not let the caliper hang by the brake hose.

3. Remove the 6 Allen head screws from the hub body and remove the cap. Remove the snapring that retains the axle shaft in the hub body.

4. Remove the lock ring seated in the groove of the hub and remove the body from the hub. If the body is difficult to remove, install 2 capscrews and pull the body assembly out of the hub.

5. Remove the outer locknut, lockwasher and the inner locknut from the spindle, using locknut wrench D85T–1197–A or equivalent. Remove the hub and rotor.

6. Remove the nuts retaining the spindle to the knuckle. Lightly tap the spindle with a rawhide hammer to remove it from the knuckle. Remove the splash shield and the caliper support from the knuckle.

7. Pull the axle shaft out of the steering knuckle. If required, remove the spacer from the axle shaft and the caged needle bearing from the spindle and remove the seal. Pull the bearing out of the spindle using collet D80L–100–T, actuator pin D80L–100–H and bridge assembly D80L–100–W or equivalents.

To install:

8. If removed, place a new caged needle bearing in the spindle bore. The writing on the bearing must face the rear of the spindle, toward the driving tool. Drive the bearing into the spindle with bearing replacer tool T80T–4000–R and driver handle tool T80T–4000–W or equivalents.

9. Pack the bearing with high temperature wheel bearing grease. Install the seal in the bore against the bearing. Pack the thrust face of the seal in the spindle bore and the V-seal on the axle shaft with high temperature wheel bearing grease.

10. Guide the axle shaft carefully through the knuckle and into the axle housing, making sure the axle shaft splines are engaged in the differential side gear splines.

11. Install the spacer on the axle shaft with the chamferred side inboard against the axle shaft. Install the splash shield and caliper support bracket on the steering knuckle.

12. Install the spindle on the steering knuckle and tighten the nuts to 50–60 ft. lbs. (68–81 Nm). Install the hub and rotor assembly on the spindle. Make sure the wheel bearings are adequately lubricated with high temperature wheel bearing grease.

13. Install the inner locknut on the spindle and seat the bearings by tightening the locknut to 50 ft. lbs. (68 Nm), with locknut wrench D85T–1197–A or equivalent.

14. Back off the inner locknut and retighten to 31–39 ft. lbs. (41–54 Nm) while rotating the hub and rotor. Back off the locknut 90 degrees.

15. Install the lockwasher so the key is positioned in the spindle groove. Tighten the inner locknut so the pin is aligned into the nearest hole in the lockwasher.

16. Install the outer locknut and tighten to 160–205 ft. lbs. (217–278 Nm), using locknut wrench D85T–1197–A or equivalent.

NOTE: The final wheel bearing end play should be 0–0.004 in. (0–0.15mm). The maximum allowable torque to rotate the hub is 20 inch lbs. (2.3 Nm).

17. Install the manual locking hub body assembly in the hub and rotor. Install the lock ring in the hub groove and the snapring on the end of the axle shaft.

18. Position the cap assembly with a new seal on the body. Install the 6 Allen-head screws and tighten to 35–45 inch lbs. (4–6 Nm).

19. Install the caliper and the front wheel and tire assembly. Lower the vehicle.

DANA MODELS 44 AND 50

1. Raise the vehicle and support it safely. Remove the front wheel and tire assembly.

2. Remove the disc brake caliper and wire it to the frame. Do not let the caliper hang by the brake hose.

3. Remove the hub locks, wheel bearings and locknuts.

4. Remove the hub and rotor assembly and the outer bearing from the spindle.

Dana model 60 Monobeam front drive axle assembly

5. Remove the nuts retaining the spindle to the steering knuckle. Tap the spindle with a nylon or rawhide hammer to jar the spindle from the knuckle. Remove the spash shield.

6. On the left side of the vehicle, remove the shaft and joint assembly by pulling the assembly out of the carrier.

7. On the right side of the vehicle, remove and discard the keystone clamp from the shaft and joint assembly and the stub shaft. Slide the rubber boot onto the stub shaft and pull the shaft and joint assembly from the splines of the stub shaft.

8. If the needle bearings are to be removed, place the spindle in a vise on the second step of the spindle. Wrap a shop towel around the spindle or use a brass-jawed vise to protect the spindle.

9. Remove the oil seal and needle bearing from the spindle with a slide hammer and bearing cup puller. Inspect the sealing surfaces of the spindle and the outer shaft of the axle shaft assembly for corrosion, pitts or wear. Replace as necessary.

To install:

10. Clean all dirt and grease from the spindle bearing bore. The bearing bores must be free from nicks and burrs.

11. Install a new needle bearing with the writing facing outward in the spindle bore, using bearing replacer tool T80T-4000–R or equivalent, on the Dana 50 or T80T–4000–S or equivalent, for the Dana 44 and driver handle tool T80T–4000–W or equivalent.

12. Install a new needle bearing seal with the seal lip directed away from the spindle. Pack the bearing and hub seal with high temperature wheel bearing grease. Install the seal with seal replacer tool T80T–4000–T and drive handle tool T80T–4000–W, or equivalents.

13. Remove and install the seal on top of the needle bearing. Apply a coating of grease to the leading ege of the seal lip. Place the thrust washer on the axle shaft.

14. Press a new slinger on the axle shaft using a suitable tool. Install the rubber V-seal on the slinger and axle shaft. The lip of the seal should face towards the spindle.

15. Install the plastic spacer on the axle shaft with the chamferred side inboard against the axle shaft. Pack the thrust face of the seal in the spindle bore and the V-seal on the axle shaft with grease.

16. On the right side of the vehicle, proceed as follows:

a. Install the rubber boot and the new keystone clamps on the stub shaft slip yoke.

b. Since the splines on the shaft are phased, there is only 1 way to assemble the right shaft and joint assembly through the knuckle and into the slip yoke.

c. Align the missing spline in the slip yoke barrel with the gapless male spline on the shaft and joint assembly.

d. Slide the right shaft and joint assembly through the knuckle and into the slip yoke making sure the splines are fully engaged.

e. Slide the boot over the assembly and crimp the keystone clamp using keystone clamp pliers T63P–9171–A or equivalent.

17. On the left side of the vehicle, slide the shaft and joint assembly through the knuckle and engage the splines on the shaft in the carrier.

18. Install the splash shield and spindle onto the steering knuckle with the attaching nuts. Tighten to 50–60 ft. lbs. (68–81 Nm).

19. Install the hub and rotor assembly and the outer wheel bearing. Make sure the grease seal lip totally encircles the spindle.

20. Install the wheel bearing, locknut, thrust bearing, snapring and locking hubs.

21. Install the caliper and the wheel and tire assembly. Lower the vehicle.

Rear Axle Shaft, Bearing and Seal

Removal and Installation
SEMI-FLOATING AXLE

1. Raise and safely support the vehicle. Remove the wheel and tire assembly and the brake drum.

2. Clean all dirt from the area of the carrier cover. Position a drain pan under the carrier housing and drain the rear axle lubricant by removing the housing cover.

3. Remove the differential pinion shaft lock bolt and differential pinion shaft.

NOTE: It is possible for Dana semi-float axles to be equipped with a lock bolt coated with either a locking compound treated thread or torque prevailing threads. The locking compound treated lock bolt has a $^5/_{32}$ in. hex socket head. The torque prevailing lock bolt has a 12-point drive head. The locking compound treated lock bolt must not be reused under any circumstances. The torque prevailing lock bolt may be reused up to 4 times, however, if there is any doubt concerning how many times it has been removed, replace the lock bolt.

4. Push the flanged end of the axle shaft toward the center of the vehicle and remove the C-clip from the button end of the shaft. If equipped, be careful not to damage the rubber O-ring in the axle shaft groove.

5. Remove the axle shaft from the housing, being careful not to damage the oil seal if it is to be reused.

6. Pry out the axle seal from the axle tube and discard. Use a suitable puller or slide hammer to remove the axle bearing from the tube.

**Spindle and Left Shaft and Joint
Installation—Typical**

**Right Hand Shaft and Joint Assembly
Installation—Typical**

Dana models 44 and 50 axle shaft and joint assemblies

To install:

7. Lubricate a new axle bearing with rear axle lubricant and install in the axle tube, using a suitable installer. Coat the lips of a new axle seal and install in the axle tube, using a seal installer. Be careful not to cock the bearing or seal in the tube during installation.

8. Slide the axle shaft into place in the axle housing far enough to install the C-clip. Be careful not to damage the oil seal.

9. Install the C-clip on the button end of the axle shaft and pull the shaft outward to lock the C-clip in the differential side gear.

NOTE: A rubber O-ring is used on all except Dana semi-float axles to hold the C-clip in position. Be sure the O-ring is in the groove at the button end of the axle shaft before installing the C-clip.

10. Install the differential pinion shaft through the case and pinions, aligning the hole in the shaft with the lock bolt hole. On Ford rear axle assemblies, apply thread-locking compound and install the lock bolt. Tighten to 15–30 ft. lbs. (20–40 Nm). On Dana rear axle assemblies, install the lock bolt and tighten to 20–25 ft. lbs. (27–34 Nm).

11. Clean the mating surface of the carrier and cover plate so they are free of any oil film or foreign material. Apply a $^1/_8$–$^3/_{16}$ in. bead of silicone sealer to the cover plate and install on the carrier with the attaching bolts. Tighten alternately and evenly to 30 ft. lbs. (41 Nm).

NOTE: Allow an hour cure time before filling the carrier with lubricant.

12. Fill the axle housing with the proper type and quantity of lubricant. Install the brake drum and the wheel and tire assembly.

13. Lower the vehicle.

FULL-FLOATING AXLE

Ford Full-Floating Axle

1. Set the parking brake and loosen the 8 axle shaft retaining bolts.

2. Raise and safely support the vehicle, keeping the axle parallel with the floor. Release the parking brake and back off the rear brake adjustment, if necessary.

3. Remove the wheel and tire assembly and remove the brake drum. If equipped, the push-on, sheet metal drum retainer nuts may be discarded.

4. Remove the axle shaft bolts and remove the axle shaft.

5. Remove the wheel bearing hub nuts using hub wrench T85T-4252-AH or equivalent, so the drive tangs of the tool engage the 4 slots in the hub nut.

NOTE: The left hub nut has left hand thread and must be removed by turning clockwise. Each hub nut is stamped RH for right hand thread or LH for left hand thread. Do not use power impact tools on hub nuts.

6. Install step plate adapter tool D80L-630-7 and puller tool D80L-1002-L or equivalents, and loosen the hub to the point of removal. Remove the puller tool and step plate and remove the hub assembly. Be careful not to drop the outer bearing.

7. Install the hub in a soft jawed vise and remove the hub seal using a small prybar. Remove the inner hub bearing and inspect both inner and outer bearings for wear. If bearing replacement is necessary, remove the bearing races from the hub with a brass drift.

To install:

8. Clean the hub and the bearings, if they are to be reused, in solvent and allow to dry.

9. If necessary, install new bearing races in the hub using a suitable installer. Pack the bearings with high temperature wheel bearing grease.

Removing the pinion shaft lock bolt—Dana rear axle

Installing the C-clip—Ford rear axles

10. Place the inner bearing in the hub and install a new oil seal, using a seal installer.

11. Clean the spindle thoroughly and then coat with axle lubricant. Push the hub and the outer bearing onto the spindle. Installing the hub this way causes the outer bearing to act as a pilot, making installation easier.

12. Install the hub nut on the spindle. Make sure the hub nut tab is located in the keyway prior to thread engagement. Turn the hub nut clockwise for right hand thread or counterclockwise for left hand thread.

13. Install hub wrench tool T85T-4252-AH or equivalent, on the spindle. Install a torque wrench and tighten the hub nut to 55–65 ft. lbs. (75–88 Nm), rotating the hub occasionally while tightening. The hub nut will ratchet as torque is applied.

14. For new bearings, ratchet back 5 teeth or notches on the hub nut. Five clicks must be heard during this operation to have performed it correctly.

15. For used bearings, ratchet back 8 teeth or notches on the

Rear axle shaft, bearing and hub assembly—Ford full-floating axle

hub nut. Eight clicks must be heard during this operation in order to have performed it correctly.

16. Inspect the axle shaft O-ring seal for cracks, nicks or wear and replace if necessary. Install the axle shaft.

17. Coat the threads of the axle shaft retaining bolts with thread-locking compound. Install the bolts and tighten until they seat. Do not final torque at this time.

18. Adjust the brakes so the brake diameter is 0.030 in. (0.762mm) less than the drum diameter and install the brake drum. Install the wheel and tire assembly.

19. Check the rear axle lubricant and fill, if necessary, to the bottom of the filler plug hole with the proper lubricant. Wipe off the particles from the magnetic filler plug and install. Tighten to 15–30 ft. lbs. (21–40 Nm).

20. Lower the vehicle and tighten the wheel lug nuts to 140 ft. lbs. (190 Nm). Tighten the axle shaft retaining bolts to 60–80 ft. lbs. (82–108 Nm).

Dana Full-Floating Axle

1. Set the parking brake and loosen the 8 axle shaft retaining bolts.

2. Raise and safely support the vehicle, keeping the axle parallel with the floor. Release the parking brake and back off the rear brake adjustment, if necessary.

3. Remove the wheel and tire assembly and remove the brake drum. If equipped, the push-on, sheet metal drum retainer nuts may be discarded.

4. Remove the axle shaft bolts and remove the axle shaft.

5. Remove the wheel bearing hub nuts using hub wrench T85T–4252–AH for E Series or T88T–4252–A for F Super Duty or equivalents, so the drive tangs of the tool engage the 4 slots in the hub nut.

NOTE: Do not use power impact tools on the hub nuts.

6. Remove the hub. Remove the hub seal using a small prybar. Remove the inner hub bearing and inspect both inner and outer bearings for wear. If bearing replacement is necessary, remove the bearing races from the hub with a brass drift.
To install:

7. Clean the hub and the bearings, if they are to be reused, in solvent and allow to dry.

8. If necessary, install new bearing races in the hub using a suitable installer. Check for proper seating by trying to insert a 0.0015 in. (0.038mm) feeler gauge between the races and the wheel hub in several places. The gauge should not enter under the race.

9. Pack the bearings with high temperature wheel bearing

grease. Place the inner bearing in the hub and install a new seal with a seal installer.

10. Thoroughly clean the spindle of the axle housing. Wrap the threads of the spindle with electrical tape and carefully slide the hub onto the spindle. Remove the tape.

11. Install the outer wheel bearing and start the hub nut, making sure the hub tab is properly located in the keyway prior to thread engagement.

12. Install locknut wrench tool T85T–4252 for E Series or T88T–4252–A for F Super Duty or equivalents, so the drive tangs of the tool engage the 4 slots of the nut.

13. Install a torque wrench to the tool and tighten to 65–75 ft. lbs. (88–102 Nm) while rotating the hub. If using tool T88T–4252–A or equivalent, apply inward pressure while tightening to separate the ratcheting components of the nut.

14. After torquing, back off 90 degrees, then retighten to 15–20 ft. lbs. (20–27 Nm).

15. Install the axle shaft with a new flange gasket, lock washers and axle shaft retaining bolts. Coat the threads of the bolts with thread adhesive and tighten the bolts until they seat. Do not torque at this time.

16. Install the brake drum and the wheel and tire assembly. Lower the vehicle and adjust the brakes.

17. Tighten the wheel lug nuts. Tighten the axle shaft retaining bolts to 41–55 ft. lbs. (55–75 Nm) on E Series or 70–85 ft. lbs. (95–115 Nm) on F Super Duty.

Front Wheel Knuckle

Removal and Installation

DANA MODEL 60 MONOBEAM

1. Raise and safely support the vehicle. Remove the axle shaft.

2. Alternately and evenly loosen the 4 bolts retaining the spindle cap to the knuckle; thereby relieving the spring compression. Remove the bolts.

3. Remove the spindle cap, compression spring and retainer. Remove and discard the gasket.

4. Remove the 4 bolts retaining the lower kingpin and retainer to the knuckle. Remove the lower kingpin and retainer from the knuckle.

5. Remove the tapered bushing from the top of the upper kingpin in the knuckle. Remove the knuckle from the axle yoke.
To install:

6. Install the knuckle on the axle yoke. Place the tapered bushing over the upper kingpin in the knuckle bore.

7. Place the lower kingpin and retainer assembly in the

knuckle and axle yoke. Install the 4 bolts and alternately and evenly tighten to 70–90 ft. lbs. (95–122 Nm).

8. Place the retainer and compression spring on the tapered bushing. Install a new gasket and the spindle cap on the knuckle. Install the 4 bolts and alternately and evenly tighten to 70–90 ft. lbs. (95–122 Nm).

9. Install the axle shaft. Lubricate the upper kingpin through the grease fitting and the lower through the flush type fitting.

10. Lower the vehicle.

DANA MODELS 44 AND 50

1. Raise and safely support the vehicle.

2. Remove the axle shafts and spindles. Disconnect the steering linkage.

3. Remove the cotter pin from the top ball joint stud. Loosen the nut on the top stud and the bottom nut inside the knuckle. Remove the top nut.

4. Sharply hit the top stud with a plastic or rawhide hammer, to free the knuckle from the axle arm. Remove and discard the bottom nut.

5. Mark the position of the camber adjuster and remove it by hand. If difficult to remove, use pitman arm puller T64P–3590–F or equivalent.

6. Place the knuckle in a vise and remove the snapring from the bottom ball joint socket, if equipped.

7. Using a suitable ball joint remover, press the lower ball joint from the knuckle. Always remove the lower ball joint first, then remove the upper ball joint.

To install:

8. Clean the steering knuckle bore and insert the lower ball joint as straight as possible. Press the ball joint into position using a suitable ball joint press. Repeat the procedure for the upper ball joint.

9. Install the knuckle to the axle arm arm. Install the camber adjuster, aligning the marks that were made during removal.

10. Install a new nut on the bottom socket finger tight. Install and tighten the nut on the top socket finger tight, then tighten the bottom nut to 80 ft. lbs. (109 Nm).

11. Tighten the top nut to 100 ft. lbs. (136 Nm), then advance the nut until the castellation aligns with the cotter pin hole. Install the cotter pin. Do not loosen the top nut to install the cotter pin.

12. Retighten the bottom nut to 90–110 ft. lbs. (123–150 Nm). Install the axle shaft and spindle assembly and lower the vehicle.

Manual Locking Hubs

Removal and Installation

1. Raise and support the vehicle safely.

2. Seperate the cap asembly from the body assembly by removing the 6 Allen head capscrews and remove the cap from the body.

3. Remove the snapring that retains the axle shaft in the hub body assembly.

4. Remove the lock ring seated in the groove of the wheel hub. Remove the body assembly from the hub. If the body is difficult to remove, install 2 capscrews and pull the body assembly out of the hub.

5. Installation is the reverse of the removal procedure. Tighten the Allen head retaining screws to 35–53 inch lbs. (4–6 Nm). Do not pack the cap assembly with grease, as excessive grease can cause excessive dialing effort.

Automatic Locking Hubs

Removal and Installation

1. Raise and support the vehicle safely.

2. Remove the capscrews from the body assembly. Remove the cover, being careful not to drop the spring, ball bearing, bearing race or retainer.

3. Remove the rubber seal.

4. Remove the seal bridge retainer from the retainer ring spacer.

5. Remove the retaining ring by closing the ends with needle nose pliers while pulling the hub lock assembly from the hub.

6. Installation is the reverse of the removal procedure. Tighten the retaining screws to 40–50 inch lbs. (4.5–5.6 Nm).

Pinion Seal

Removal and Installation

1. Raise and safely support the vehicle.

2. Mark the position of the driveshaft in relation to the pinion flange and remove the driveshaft.

3. On Ford 8.8 in. and 10.25 in. rear axles, proceed as follows:

   a. Remove the wheel and tire assemblies.

   b. Using and inch pound torque wrench on the pinion nut, record the torque required to rotate the pinion through several revolutions.

4. While holding the pinion flange with a suitable tool, remove the pinion nut. Remove the pinion flange. It may be necessary to use a puller to remove the flange.

5. Use a small prybar to remove the pinion seal.

To install:

6. Clean the pinion seal seat area. Coat the lips of a new seal with rear axle lubricant and install, using a seal installer.

7. Coat the inside of the pinion flange with a small amount of

Manual locking hub

Automatic locking hub

rear axle lubricant and install on the pinion. Install the pinion nut.

8. On Ford 8.8 in. and 10.25 in. rear axles, proceed as follows:

   a. Gradually tighten the pinion nut while holding the pinion flange with a suitable tool.

   b. Periodically check the torque required to rotate the pinion through several revolutions with the inch pound torque wrench.

   c. Tighten the pinion nut only to the point where the torque required to rotate the pinion through several revolutions is the same as was recorded during the removal procedure.

9. On all other axle assemblies, tighten the pinion nut to the following torque values:

Dana 60 and 61 rear axles—250–270 ft. lbs. (339–366 Nm).

Dana 80 rear axle—440–500 ft. lbs. (596–677 Nm).

Dana 60 Monobeam front axle—220–280 ft. lbs. (298–379 Nm).

Dana 44 and 50 front axles—200–220 ft. lbs. (271–298 Nm).

10. Install the driveshaft, aligning the marks that were made during removal.

11. Install the wheel and tire assemblies, if removed, and lower the vehicle.

Axle Housing

Removal and Installation

DANA MODEL 60 MONOBEAM FRONT AXLE

1. Raise and safely support the vehicle. Remove the front wheel and tire assemblies.

2. Remove the brake calipers and support with mechanics wire. Do not let the calipers hang by the brake hoses.

3. Disconnect the links from the stabilizer bar. If necessary, remove the stabilizer bar.

4. Remove the cotter pins and nuts securing the spindle connecting rod to the steering knuckles. Separate the connecting rods from the knuckles using pitman arm puller T64P-3590-F or equivalent, and wire the steering linkage to the springs.

5. Mark the position of the driveshaft on the pinion flange and remove the driveshaft. Disconnect the vent tube and plug the vent fitting at the axle housing.

6. On the right side of the vehicle, remove the nut and bolt and disconnect the tracking bar from the right spring cap.

7. Support the axle under the differential carrier with a suitable jack. Remove the retaining U-bolts and nuts and lower the axle from the vehicle.

To install:

8. Raise the axle into position with the jack. Make sure the retaining bolt head protruding from the leaf spring plate seats in the recessed portion of the axle spring mounting plate. Install the nuts, U-bolts and spring caps.

9. Connect the driveshaft to the pinion flange, aligning the marks that were made during removal.

10. On the right side of the vehicle, connect the tracking bar to the spring cap and tighten the nut and bolt to 163–203 ft. lbs. (221–275 Nm). Connect the vent tube.

11. Connect the spindle connecting rods to the steering knuckles. Install the nuts and tighten to 70–100 ft. lbs. (95–136 Nm). Install new cotter pins, advancing the nuts, if necessary, to align the castellations with the stud holes. Do not back off the nuts to line up the castellations and stud holes.

12. If removed, install the stabilizer bar. Connect the links to the stabilizer bar.

13. Install the brake calipers and the wheel and tire assemblies. Lower the vehicle.

DANA MODELS 44 AND 50 FRONT AXLES

With Coil Springs

1. Raise and safely support the vehicle. Remove the front wheel and tire assemblies.

2. Remove the brake calipers and support with mechanics wire. Do not let the calipers hang by the brake hoses.

3. Disconnect the steering linkage from the steering knuckles.

4. Position a jack under the axle arm assembly and remove the upper coil spring retainers. Lower the jack and remove the coil spring, spring cushion and lower spring seat.

NOTE: The axle arm must be supported with the jack throughout spring removal and installation and must not be permitted to hang by the brake hose. If necessary, remove the caliper and suspend it with mechanics wire. Do not let the caliper hang by the brake hose.

5. Disconnect the shock absorber at the radius arm and upper mounting bracket. Remove the stud and spring seat at radius arm and axle arm. Remove the bolt securing the upper attachment to axle arm radius arm to lower attachment axle arm.

6. Disconnect the vent tube at the differential housing and discard the hose clamps. Remove the vent fitting and install a ⅛ in. pipe plug.

NOTE: The vent tube may have been temporarily plugged to stop vent lube blowout while the axle vent was relocated during assembly. Check for lubricant leakage through the pinion seal, axle seals or support arm to housing to make sure the plastic plug has been removed. If the plug has not been removed, remove it from the end of the vent tube.

7. Remove the pivot bolt securing the right axle arm to the crossmember. Remove and discard the keystone clamps and remove the boot from the shaft. Remove the right drive axle and pull the axle shaft from the slip shaft.

8. Position a jack under the differential housing. Remove the bolt securing the left axle assembly to the crossmember and remove the left drive axle assembly.

To install:

9. Position the left drive axle at the radius arm. Secure the

drive axle to the crossmember with the pivot bolt. Tighten the bolt to 120–150 ft. lbs. (163–203 Nm).

10. Position the right axle assembly at the crossmember and radius arm. Align the axle shaft and install in the slip shaft. Install the boot on the shaft so the boot seats in the gooves. Position new keystone clamps over the grooves on the boot and crimp the clamp with keystone clamp pliers T63P-9171–A or equivalent. Secure the axle assembly to the crossmember with the pivot bolt and tighten to 120–150 ft. lbs. (163–203 Nm).

11. Install the vent fitting in the differential housing. Connect the vent tube to the vent fitting usinf new hose clamps.

12. Position the spring seat and install a new stud at the axle arm and upper radius arm. Install a new bolt at the axle assembly and lower radius arm. Tighten the bolts to 180–240 ft. lbs. (245–325 Nm).

13. Position the coil spring insulator and coil spring on the lower spring seat. Install the nut and tighten to 30–70 ft. lbs. (41–94 Nm). Position a jack under the axle assembly and raise the coil spring into position. Install the upper spring retainer and screw. Tighten to 13–18 ft. lbs. (18–24 Nm).

14. Lower the jack. Connect the shock absorbers to the upper and lower frame brackets.

15. Install the calipers and the wheel and tire assemblies. Connect the steering linkage.

16. Lower the vehicle and check the front end alignment.

With Leaf Springs

1. Raise and safely support the vehicle. Remove the wheel and tire assemblies.

2. Remove the brake calipers. Suspend the calipers with mechanics wire. Do not let the calipers hang by the brake hose.

3. Disconnect the steering linkage from the steering knuckles.

4. Position a jack under the right axle assembly. Remove the U-bolts securing the shock absorber mounting plate and leaf springs to the tube and yoke assembly.

5. Disconnect the vent tube at the differential housing. Remove the vent fitting and install a ⅛ in. pipe plug.

6. Remove the pivot bolt that secures the right axle assembly to the crossmember and remove the right axle assembly. Remove and discard the keystone clamps and remove the boot from the shaft. Pull the axle out of the slip shaft.

7. Position the jack under the left axle assembly. Remove the U-bolts securing the shock absorber mounting plate and leaf spring to the tube and yoke assembly.

8. Position a jack under the differential housing. Remove the pivot bolt securing the left axle assembly to the crossmember and remove the axle assembly.

To install:

9. Position the left axle assembly and install the pivot bolt that secures the axle to the crossmember. Secure the shock absorber mounting plate to the leaf spring and axle assembly with the 2 U-bolts. Tighten the bolts to 85–120 ft. lbs. (116–162 Nm).

10. Position the right axle assembly at the crossmember. Install the boot on the shaft so the boot seats in the grooves. Position new keystone clamps over the grooves on the boot and crimp the clamp with keystone clamp pliers T63P-9171–A or equivalent.

11. Align the axle shaft and install in the slip shaft. Install the pivot bolt that secures the axle assembly to the crossmember and tighten to 120–150 ft. lbs. (123–203 Nm).

12. Install the shock absorber mounting plate, leaf spring and axle assembly using 2 U-bolts. Tighten to 85–120 ft. lbs. (116–162 Nm).

13. Install the vent fitting to the differential housing and connect the vent tube to the vent using a new hose clamp.

14. Connect the steering linkage. Install the brake calipers and the wheel and tire assemblies.

15. Lower the vehicle. Check the front end alignment.

REAR AXLE

1. Raise and safely support the vehicle. Remove the wheel and tire assemblies and remove the brake drums.

2. Mark the position of the driveshaft on the pinion flange and remove the driveshaft.

3. Disconnect the parking brake cables from the brake shoes and backing plates. If equipped, disconnect the anti-lock brake sensor wiring.

4. Disconnect the flexible brake hose at the frame. Plug the hose and the line. Disconnect the axle vent hose.

5. Support the axle assembly with a suitable jack.

6. Disconnect the shock absorbers from the axle. Disconnect the stabilizer bar, if equipped.

7. Remove the nuts, U-bolts and spring seat caps and remove the axle assembly.

To install:

8. Raise the axle assembly into position and install the nuts, U-bolts and spring seat clamps. Connect the stabilizer bar, if equipped, and the shock absorbers. Remove the jack.

9. Connect the flexible brake hose and connect the parking brake cables at the backing plates and brake shoes. Connect the anti-lock brake sensor wiring, if equipped.

10. Install the driveshaft, aligning the marks that were made during removal. Connect the axle vent hose.

11. Install the brake drums and the wheel and tire assemblies. Check the rear axle lubricant level.

12. Lower the vehicle.

STEERING

Steering Wheel

Removal and Installation

1. Disconnect the negative battery cable.

2. Remove 1 screw from the underside of each steering wheel spoke and lift the steering wheel pad from the steering wheel.

3. Disconnect the horn switch wires by pulling the spade terminal from the blade connectors. If equipped with cruise control, squeeze or pinch the "J" clip ground wire terminal firmly and pull it out of the hole in the steering wheel. Do not pull the ground terminal out of the threaded hole without squeezing the terminal clip to relieve the spring retention of the terminal in the threaded hole.

4. Remove the horn switch and the steering wheel retaining nut. If the steering wheel and steering shaft do not have mating flats, mark the position of the wheel on the shaft so it can be reinstalled in the same position.

5. Using a suitable puller, remove the steering wheel from the steering shaft. Do not hammer on the steering wheel or use a knock-off type puller as either will damage the steering column.

To install:

6. Position the steering wheel on the column shaft, aligning the mating flats or the marks that were made during removal.

7. Install the retaining nut and tighten to 30–42 ft. lbs. (41–56 Nm).

8. Connect the horn and cruise control wires, if equipped.

9. Install the steering wheel pad. Tighten the screws to 7–11 inch lbs. (0.8–1.2 Nm).

10. Connect the negative battery cable and test the steering column for proper operation.

Steering Column

Removal and Installation

BRONCO AND F SERIES

1. Disconnect the negative battery cable and set the parking brake.

2. Remove the bolt and nut attaching the intermediate shaft to the steering column.

3. If equipped with automatic transmission, disconnect the shift linkage rod(s) from the column.

4. Remove the steering wheel. If equipped with tilt column, the steering wheel must be in the full up position when it is removed.

5. Remove the steering column floor opening cover plate screws.

6. Remove the shroud by loosening the screw at the bottom. If equipped with automatic transmission, place the selector lever in position **1**. Spread the shroud and withdraw it from the instrument panel opening while pulling up and away from the column.

7. Remove the instrument panel column opening cover. Remove the bolts attaching the column support bracket to the pedal support bracket.

8. Disconnect the turn signal-hazard warning and ignition switch wiring harnesses.

9. Remove the steering column from the vehicle and remove the steering column support bracket from the column.

To install:

10. Attach the steering column support bracket, making sure the turn signal-hazard warning wiring is on the outboard side of the column. Tighten the nuts to 13–38 ft. lbs. (18–51 Nm).

11. Start the floor opening cover clamp bolt and press the plate until the clamp flats touch the stops on the column outer tube.

12. Insert the column into the engine compartment through the floor opening. Connect the turn signal-warning hazard and ignition switch wiring harnesses.

13. Raise the column up to the pedal support bracket and hand start the 2 bolts. Fasten the floor opening cover plate to the floor and tighten to 6–10 ft. lbs. (8–14 Nm).

14. Tighten the 2 support bracket bolts to 19–27 ft. lbs. (26–37 Nm) and tighten the cover plate clamp bolt to 8–18 ft. lbs. (11–24 Nm).

15. Install and adjust the transmission indicator actuation cable, if equipped with automatic transmission. Install the instrument panel steering column opening cover.

16. Mount the shroud by selecting position **1**, if equipped with automatic transmission, and spreading the shroud around the steering column and through the opening in the instrument panel. Post on interior will index shroud when properly positioned.

17. Tighten the screw at the bottom of the shroud to 10–15 inch lbs. (1.1–1.7 Nm).

18. Attach the shift linkage rod to the column, if equipped with automatic transmission. Adjust the linkage, if required.

19. Fasten the intermediate shaft to the steering column and tighten to 35–50 ft. lbs. (46–68 Nm). Install the steering wheel and connect the negative battery cable.

E SERIES

1. Disconnect the negative battery cable and set the parking brake.

2. Remove the 2 nuts attaching the flexible coupling to the steering shaft flange.

3. If equipped with automatic transmission, disconnect the shift linkage rod(s) from the column.

4. Remove the steering wheel. If equipped with tilt column, the steering wheel must be in the full up position when it is removed.

5. Remove the steering column floor opening cover plate screws.

6. Remove the shroud by loosening the screw at the bottom. If equipped with automatic transmission, place the selector lever in position **1**. Spread the shroud and withdraw it from the instrument panel opening while pulling up and away from the column.

7. Remove the instrument panel column opening cover. Remove the bolts attaching the column support bracket to the pedal support bracket.

8. Disconnect the turn signal-hazard warning and ignition switch wiring harnesses.

9. Remove the steering column from the vehicle and remove the steering column support bracket from the column.

To install:

10. Attach the steering column support bracket and tighten the nuts to 13–38 ft. lbs. (18–51 Nm). Place the column in the vehicle.

11. Connect the turn signal-hazard warning and ignition switch wiring harnesses.

12. Insert the steering shaft flange through the floor opening so the flange engages the flexible coupling. Raise the column up to the pedal support bracket and loosely install the support bolts.

13. When the column has been removed, the flange will be fully telescoped into the column. Gently tap the flange down to engage the flexible coupling. Loosely install the flexible coupling flange nuts and floor plate fasteners.

14. Align the steering column and flexible coupling as follows:
   a. Make sure the coupling pin to flange cut-out clearance is 0.160 in. (4.06mm).
   b. Tighten the flange coupling nuts to 14–21 ft. lbs. (19–28 Nm).
   c. Tighten the steering column-to-support bracket bolts to 19–27 ft. lbs. (26–36 Nm).
   d. Tighten the steering column floor opening cover plate-to-dash panel bolts to 12–18 ft. lbs. (16–24 Nm).
   e. Tighten the steering column opening cover clamp bolt to 12–18 ft. lbs. (16–24 Nm).

15. Install the steering wheel. If equipped, attach the shift linkage rod and adjust the shift linkage, if necessary. Connect the negative battery cable.

Power Steering Gear

Adjustment

1. Make sure the wheels are in the straight ahead position. Remove the steering wheel pad. Disconnect the pitman arm from the sector shaft using a pitman arm puller.

2. Disconnect the fluid return line at the reservoir and cap the reservoir return tube. Place the end of the return line in a clean container and turn the steering wheel back and forth several times to empty the steering gear. Discard the fluid.

3. Turn the steering wheel to 45 degrees from the right stop.

4. Attach an inch pound torque wrench to the steering wheel nut and record the torque required to rotate the shaft slowly approximately ⅛ turn toward center from the 45 degree position.

5. Turn the steering gear back to center and record the torque required to rotate the shaft back and forth across the center position (± 90 degrees). If the vehicle has less than 5000 miles, the set torque measured rocking across center should be 14–18 inch lbs. (1.6–2.0 Nm) greater than that measured 45 degrees from the right stop. If the vehicle has more than 5000 miles, the set torque measured rocking across center should be 10–14 inch lbs. 1.13–1.6 Nm) greater than that measured 45 degrees from the right stop.

6. If reset is required, loosen the adjuster locknut and turn the sector shaft adjusting screw until the reading is the specified value greater than the torque at 45 degress from the stop. Hold the sector shaft screw in place and tighten the locknut.

7. Recheck the torque readings and install the pitman arm and steering wheel pad.

Power steering gear

Power steering gear installation—Bronco and F Series

Power steering gear installation—E Series

8. Connect the fluid return line to the reservoir and refill the system with fluid. Bleed the system. Adjust the belt tension, if necessary.

Removal and Installation

1. Make sure the wheels are in the straight ahead position. Disconnect the negative battery cable.
2. Disconnect the pressure and return lines from the steering gear. Plug the lines and the ports in the gear to prevent entry of dirt.
3. If equipped, remove the splash shield from the flex coupling. Disconnect the flex coupling at the steering gear.
4. Raise the vehicle and support it safely. Remove the pitman arm nut and washer. Remove the pitman arm using a pitman arm puller. Be careful not to damage the seals.
5. Support the steering gear and remove the attaching bolts. Work the steering gear free from the flex coupling and remove the gear from the vehicle.

To install:

6. If equipped, install the splash shield onto the steering gear lugs.
7. Slide the flex coupling into place on the steering shaft assembly. Turn the steering wheel so the spokes are in the horizontal position.
8. Slide the steering gear input shaft into the flex coupling and into place on the frame side rail. Install the flex coupling attaching bolt and tighten to 25–34 ft. lbs. (34–46 Nm) on Bronco and F Series or 20–35 ft. lbs. (28–47 Nm) on E Series. Install the gear to frame bolts and tighten to 54–66 ft. lbs. (74–89 Nm).
9. Make sure the wheels are in the straight ahead position, then install the pitman arm on the sector shaft. Install the pitman arm washer and nut and tighten to 170–230 ft. lbs. (230–310 Nm).
10. Connect and tighten the pressure and return lines to 20–30 ft. lbs. (27–40 Nm).
11. Snap the flex coupling shield over the hose fitting and the splash shield. Fill the system with fluid and connect the negative battery cable. Bleed the system and check for fluid leaks.

Power Steering Pump

Removal and Installation

1. Disconnect the negative battery cable.
2. Disconnect the fluid return hose at the reservoir and drain

the power steering fluid into a container. Remove the pressure hose from the pump.
3. If equipped with an automatic tensioner, use a wrench on the tensioner pulley bolt to lift the tensioner arm and remove the belt. Do not allow the tensioner to snap back.
4. If the drive belt is manually tensioned, loosen the pivot and adjustment bolts and remove the belt.

5. Remove the pulley from the pump, if necessary. Remove the attaching bolts and remove the pump.

To install:

6. Install the pump and tighten the attaching bolts. If the drive belt is manually tensioned, leave the pivot and adjusting bolts slightly snug.

7. Install the power steering pulley, if removed.

8. If equipped with an automatic tensioner, lift the tensioner arm using a wrench on the tensioner pulley bolt. Install the belt over the pulleys and slowly release the tensioner arm.

9. If the belt is manually tensioned, adjust the tension and tighten the pivot and adjusting bolts.

10. Connect the pressure and return hoses and the negative battery cable. Fill the reservoir with fluid and bleed the system. Check for leaks.

Belt Adjustment

EXCEPT 7.3L DIESEL ENGINE

All engines except the 7.3L diesel engine are equipped with an automatic tensioner to maintain power steering drive belt tension. Correct belt tension will be maintained if the correct length belt is on the engine. The tensioner is working properly if the belt length indicator mark on the tensioner is between the maximum and minimum marks.

7.3L DIESEL ENGINE

1. Position a belt tension gauge midway between the pulleys on the longest accessible belt span.

2. Insert a square drive ratchet wrench or breaker bar in the square hole in the power steering bracket and adjust the belt to 140–180 lbs. tension for a new belt or 95–115 lbs. tension for a used belt. Used belts have more than 5 minutes running time.

3. Maintain the belt tension and tighten the power steering pivot and adjustment bolts. Recheck the belt tension after tightening.

4. Remove the tension gauge and the ratchet or breaker bar.

System Bleeding

1. Fill the power steering fluid reservoir.

2. On all except 7.3L diesel engine, proceed as follows:

    a. Disconnect the coil wire.

    b. Crank the engine with the starter and continue adding fluid until the level remains constant. Do not prolong cranking as the battery may be drained and the starter damaged.

    c. Rotate the steering wheel approximately 30 degrees each side of center while continuing to crank the engine.

    d. Recheck the fluid level and fill, as required.

    e. Reconnect the coil wire.

3. On all vehicles, start the engine and allow it to run for several minutes.

4. Rotate the steering wheel from stop to stop.

5. Shut off the engine and recheck the fluid level. Add fluid, as required.

6. If air is still trapped in the system, proceed as follows:

    a. On Bronco and F Series, fabricate a purging tool. On E Series, it will be necessary to modify a pump reservoir cap.

    b. Make sure the reservoir fluid level is correct.

    c. On Bronco and F Series, insert the rubber stopper end of the fabricated purging tool. On E Series install the modified pump reservoir cap.

    d. Connect a suitable length of hose to the purging tool or modified cap. Connect the other end of the hose to an air conditioner vacuum pump or distributor machine. Do not use engine vacuum.

    e. Start the engine and let it idle for approximately 15 minutes. Turn the steering wheel 1 full cycle every 5 minutes but do not hit the stops. This will assist in removing trapped air.

    f. Stop the engine and disconnect the vacuum source. Remove the purging tool or modified cap.

    g. Check the fluid level and install the reservoir dipstick.

Power steering pump installation—Bronco and F Series

Fabricated purging tool dimensions—Bronco and F Series

Modified pump reservoir cap—E Series

Steering linkage—4WD Bronco and F 150

Tie Rod Ends

Removal and Installation

1. Raise and safely support the vehicle. Remove the cotter pin and nut from the tie rod end ball stud.
2. Using removal tool T64P–3590–F or equivalent, remove the tie rod ball stud from the spindle or drag link.
3. Loosen the nuts on the adjusting sleeve clamps and unscrew the tie rod end from the adjusting sleeve. Count and record the number of turns required to remove the tie rod end from the sleeve.

To install:

4. Install the tie rod end in the adjusting sleeve, screwing in the same number of turns as was recorded during removal.

5. Tighten the adjusting sleeve clamp nuts to 30–42 ft. lbs. (40–57 Nm).
6. Insert the tie rod end ball stud into the spindle or drag link tapered hole. Install the nut and tighten to 50–75 ft. lbs. (68–101 Nm).
7. Install a new cotter pin.

NOTE: It may be necessary to further tighten the tie rod end ball stud nut to align the castellation in the nut with the hole in the ball stud, in order to install the cotter pin. Never loosen the nut to align the castellation and hole.

8. Lower the vehicle and check the toe setting.

BRAKES

For all brake system repair and service procedure not detailed below, please refer to "Brakes" in the Unit repair section.

Master Cylinder

Removal and Installation

1. Disconnect the negative battery cable. Push the brake pedal down to expel vacuum from the brake booster system.
2. Disconnect the fluid level indicator switch connector from the master cylinder.
3. Disconnect and plug the hydraulic lines at the master cylinder. Plug the master cylinder ports.

4. Remove the brake booster to master cylinder retaining nuts and remove the master cylinder from the brake booster.

To install:

5. Before installing the master cylinder, check the distance from the outer end of the vacuum booster assembly pushrod to the front face of the vacuum brake booster assembly. The distance should be 0.980–0.995 in. (24.89–25.27mm). Turn the pushrod adjusting screw in or out, as required, to obtain the proper length.
6. Install the master cylinder with the attaching nuts. Tighten to 18–25 ft. lbs. (24–34 Nm). Connect the fluid level indicator switch.
7. Obtain 2 short lengths of brake line the same diameter as that used on the vehicle to connect to the master cylinder. Bend

Vacuum brake booster pushrod-to-booster face dimension

Height Sensing Brake Proportioning Valve

Removal and Installation

1. On 1988–89 vehicles, raise and safely support the vehicle so the rear suspension hangs in the fully extended position.
2. On 1990–91 vehicles, lift and safely support the frame so there is 6⅝ in. clearance between the bottom edge of the rubber jounce bumper and the top of the axle tube on both sides. This is the correct position for installing the pre-indexed height sensing valve.
3. Remove the linkage arm from the height sensing valve.
4. Remove the flow bolt holding the brake hose to valve.
5. Disconnect the brake line from the valve.
6. Remove the bolts securing the valve to the mounting bracket and remove the valve.
7. Installation is the reverse of the removal procedure. Tighten the valve mounting bracket bolts to 12–18 ft. lbs. (17–24 Nm) and the linkage arm nut to 8–10 ft. lbs. (11–14 Nm). Bleed the brake system.

Power Brake Booster

Removal and Installation

1. Disconnect the negative battery cable. Support the master cylinder from the underside with a prop.
2. Disconnect the vacuum hose from the booster check valve and remove the check valve.
3. Remove the wrap-around clip from the booster inboard stud, if equipped.
4. If necessary, remove the nuts retaining the clutch master cylinder and retainer to the booster. Remove and position the clutch master cylinder and retainer so fluid does not spill from the cylinder.
5. Remove the master cylinder-to-booster retaining nuts. Pull the master cylinder off the booster and leave it supported by the prop, out of the way enough to allow booster removal.
6. Working inside the cab, remove the cotter pin and slide the stoplight switch, spacers and bushing off the brake pedal arm. Remove the nuts retaining the booster and remove the booster.
To install:
7. Mount the booster assembly on the engine side of the dash

the lines, using a tubing bender, so when installed on the master cylinder ports, the other end of the lines will be submerged in the master cylinder reservoir.

8. Fill the master cylinder with brake fluid.
9. Have an assistant push the brake pedal down and slowly release. Repeat this procedure until no more air bubbles can be seen coming out of the brake lines submerged in the master cylinder reservoir.
10. Remove the fabricated brake lines and connect the vehicle brake lines to the master cylinder.
11. Have the assistant push the brake pedal to the floor. Crack open the front brake line fitting to expel the remaining air. Tighten the fitting, then let the brake pedal return. Repeat this procedure until all air is expelled.
12. Repeat Step 12 on the rear brake line fitting.
13. Final tighten the brake line fittings. Bleed the brake system, if necessary. Check the master cylinder fluid level and add, as required.

Height sensing brake proportioning valve—1988–89 E Series

panel by sliding the bracket mounting bolts and valve operating rod in through the holes in the dash panel.

NOTE: Make sure the booster pushrod is positioned on the correct side of the brake pedal to install onto the push pin prior to tightening the booster to the dash.

8. Working inside the cab, install the booster mounting nuts and tighten to 13–25 ft. lbs. (18–33 Nm) on Bronco and F Series or 10–18 ft. lbs. (13–25 Nm) on E Series.

9. Install the master cylinder and tighten the retaining nuts to 13–25 ft. lbs. (18–33 Nm) on Bronco and F Series or 10–18 ft. lbs. (13–25 Nm) on E Series.

10. Install the wrap-around clip on the booster inboard stud, if equipped.

11. If necessary, install the retainer and clutch master cylinder. Tighten the nuts to 10–18 ft. lbs. (13–25 Nm).

12. Install the booster check valve and connect the vacuum hose. Check the hose routing to make sure the hose is not crimped.

13. Working inside the cab, install the bushing and position the switch on the end of the pushrod, then install the switch and rod on the pedal pin along with the spacers and cotter pin.

14. Connect the negative battery cable, start the engine and check brake operation.

Correct caliper pin installation

Brake Caliper

Removal and Installation

1. Siphon part of the brake fluid out of the master cylinder to avoid overflow when the caliper piston is pressed into the cylinder bore.

2. Raise the vehicle and support it safely. Remove the front wheel and tire assembly.

3. Position an 8 in. C-clamp on the caliper and tighten the clamp to bottom the piston(s) in the caliper cylinder bore. Remove the clamp.

NOTE: Do not pry the piston(s) away from the rotor.

4. Clean excess dirt from the area around the pin tabs. Tap the upper caliper pin towards the inboard side until the pin tabs touch the spindle face.

5. Insert a small prybar into the slot provided behind the pin tabs on the inboard side of the pin.

6. Use needle nose pliers to compress the outboard end of the pin while prying at the same time with the prybar, until the tabs slip into the spindle groove.

7. Place 1 end of a $^{7}/_{16}$ in. diameter punch against the end of the caliper pin and drive the pin out of the caliper slide groove.

8. Repeat the procedure for the lower pin.

9. Disconnect the brake hose and remove the caliper from the vehicle. Plug the brake hose.

To install:

10. Install the caliper on the spindle, making sure the mounting surfaces are free of dirt and lubricate the caliper grooves with disc brake caliper slide grease.

11. Install the pin with the pin retention tabs positioned next to the spindle groove. Tap the pin on the outboard end with a hammer and continue tapping inward until the retention tabs on the sides of the pin contact the spindle face. Repeat the procedure for the lower pin.

NOTE: Do not allow the tabs of the caliper pin to be tapped too far into the spindle groove or it will be necessary to tap the other end of the caliper pin until the tabs snap into place. The tabs on each end of the caliper pin must be free to catch on the spindle flanks.

12. Connect the brake hose to the caliper and bleed the brake system.

13. Install the wheel and tire assembly and lower the vehicle.

Disc Brake Pads

Removal and Installation

1. Raise and safely support the vehicle. Remove the caliper assembly.

NOTE: If the caliper is not being serviced, it is not necessary to disconnect the brake hose from the caliper. Suspend the caliper aside with mechanics wire; do not let it hang from the brake hose.

2. If equipped with single piston caliper, remove the outer pad, then remove the anti-rattle clips and the inner pad.

3. If equipped with 2 piston caliper, remove the inner and outer pads and the anti-rattle spring.

To install:

4. If equipped with single piston caliper, proceed as follows:

a. Place a new anti-rattle clip on the lower end of the inner pad. Make sure the tabs on the clip are positioned properly and the clip is fully seated.

b. Position the inner pad and anti-rattle clip in the pad abutment with the anti-rattle clip tab against the pad abutment and the loop-type spring away from the rotor. Compress the anti-rattle clip and slide the upper end of the pad in position.

c. Install the outer pad. Crimp or bend the outer pad tabs to prevent the pads from rattling in the caliper.

5. If equipped with 2 piston caliper, install the inner and out-

Installing anti-rattle clip on inner pad—single piston caliper

er pads and the anti-rattle spring. There is a raised section at 1 end of each pad so installation can be made in 1 direction only.

6. Install the caliper. Bleed the brakes if the brake hose was disconnected.

7. Install the wheel and tire assembly and lower the vehicle.

8. Apply the brakes several times to seat the pads, prior to moving the vehicle. Check the master cylinder fluid level.

Brake Rotor

Removal and Installation

1. Raise and safely support the vehicle. Remove the wheel and tire assembly.

2. Remove the caliper assembly from the rotor and support it out of the way with mechanics wire. Do not let the caliper hang from the brake hose.

3. On 4WD vehicles, remove the locking hub assembly.

4. Remove the dust cap, cotter pin, locknut, washer and outer bearing and remove the rotor from the spindle.

5. Inspect the rotor for scoring, wear and runout; machine or replace as necessary.

6. Install in the reverse order of removal. Adjust the wheel bearings.

Brake Drum

Removal and Installation

1. Raise and safely support the vehicle. Remove the wheel and tire assembly.

2. Remove the spring retaining nuts, if equipped, and remove the brake drum.

NOTE: If the brake drum will not come off, insert a narrow prybar through the brake adjusting hole in the backing plate and disengage the adjusting lever from the adjusting screw. While holding the adjusting lever away from the adjusting screw, loosen the adjusting screw with a brake adjusting tool.

3. Inspect the brake drum surface for wear, scoring and runout. Machine or replace, as necessary.

4. Installation is the reverse of the removal procedure.

Brake Shoes

Removal and Installation

BRONCO, F 150 AND E 150

1. Raise and safely support the vehicle. Remove the wheel and tire assembly and the brake drum.

2. Pull backward on the adjusting lever cable to disengage the adjusting lever from the adjusting screw. Move the outboard side of the adjusting screw upward and back off the pivot nut as far as it will go.

3. Pull the adjusting lever, cable and automatic adjuster spring down and toward the rear to unhook the pivot hook from the large hole in the secondary shoe web. Do not pry the pivot hook from the hole.

4. Remove the automatic adjuster spring and adjusting lever.

5. Remove the secondary shoe-to-anchor spring using a suitable brake spring removal/installation tool. Using the tool, remove the primary shoe-to-anchor spring and unhook the cable anchor. Remove the anchor pin plate, if equipped.

6. Remove the cable guide from the secondary shoe.

7. Remove the shoe hold-down springs, shoes, adjusting screw, pivot nut and socket. Note the color and position of each hold-down spring so they can be reassembled in the same position.

8. Remove the parking brake link and spring. Disconnect the parking brake cable from the parking brake lever.

9. Remove the secondary brake shoe and disassemble the parking brake lever from the shoe by removing the retaining clip and spring washer.

To install:

10. Clean the backing plate ledge pads and sand lightly. Apply a light coating of high temperature lithium grease to the points where the brake shoes touch the backing plate. Lubricate the adjusting cable eye and the anchor pin area.

11. Install the parking brake lever on the secondary shoe and secure with the spring washer and retaining clip.

12. Position the brake shoes on the backing plate and install the hold-down spring pins, springs and cups. Install the parking brake link, spring and washer. Connect the parking brake cable to the parking brake lever.

13. Install the anchor pin plate, if equipped, and place the cable anchor over the anchor pin with the crimped side toward the backing plate.

14. Install the primary shoe-to-anchor spring using the brake spring removal/installation tool.

15. Install the cable guide on the secondary shoe with the flanged hole fitted into the hole in the secondary shoe. Thread the cable around the cable guide groove.

NOTE: Make sure the cable is positioned in the groove and not between the guide and shoe web.

16. Install the secondary shoe-to-anchor (long) spring.

NOTE: Make sure the cable end is not cocked or binding on the anchor pin when installed. All parts should be flat on the anchor pin.

17. Apply high temperature lithium grease to the threads and the socket end of the adjusting screw. Turn the adjusting screw into the adjusting pivot nut to the end of the threads and then loosen, ½ turn.

18. Place the adjusting socket on the screw and install the assembly between the shoe ends with the adjusting screw nearest the secondary shoe.

NOTE: Be sure to install the adjusting screw on the same side of the vehicle from which it came. To prevent incorrect installation, the socket end of each adjusting screw is stamped with R or L, to indicate installation on the right or left side of the vehicle. The adjusting pivot nuts have lines machined around the body of the nut, 2 lines indicating the right side nut and 1 line indicating the left side nut.

19. Hook the cable hook into the hole in the adjusting lever from the outboard plate side. The adjusting levers are also stamped with an **R** or **L** to indicate right or left side installation.

20. Place the hooked end of the adjuster spring in the large hole in the primary shoe web and connect the loop end of the spring to the adjuster lever hole.

21. Pull the adjuster lever, cable and automatic adjuster spring down toward the rear to engage the pivot hook in the large hole in the secondary shoe web.

22. After installation, check the action of the adjuster by pulling the section of the cable between the cable guide and the adjusting lever toward the secondary shoe web far enough to lift the lever past a tooth on the adjusting screw wheel. The lever should snap into position behind the next tooth and releasing the cable should cause the adjuster spring to return the lever to its original position. This return action will turn the adjusting screw 1 tooth.

23. If pulling the cable does not produce the action described in Step 22 or if lever action is sluggish instead of positive and sharp, check the position of the lever on the adjusting screw toothed wheel. With the brake in a vertical position, anchor at the top, the lever should contact the adjusting wheel 1 tooth above the center line of the adjusting screw. If the contact point is below the center line, the lever will not lock on the adjusting

screw wheel teeth and the screw will not turn as the lever is actuated by the cable.

24. To find the cause of the condition described in Step 23, proceed as follows:

a. Check the cable end fittings. The cable should completely fill or extend slightly beyond the crimped section of the fittings. If this does not happen, the cable assembly may be damaged and should be replaced.

b. Check the cable guide for damage. The cable groove should be parallel to the shoe web and the body of the guide should lie flat against the web. Replace the guide if it shows damage.

c. Check the pivot hook on the lever. The hook surfaces should be square with the body on the lever for proper pivoting. Repair the hook or replace the lever if the hook shows damage.

d. Be sure the adjusting screw socket is properly seated in the notch in the shoe web.

25. Adjust the brake shoes using either a brake adjustment gauge or manually with the drums installed.

26. If using a brake adjustment gauge, proceed as follows:

a. Measure the inside diameter of the brake drum with the gauge.

b. Reverse the tool and adjust the brake shoes until they touch the gauge. The gauge contact points on the shoes must be parallel to the vehicle with the center line through the center of the axle.

c. Install the drum and wheel and tire assembly. Lower the vehicle.

d. Apply the brakes sharply several times while driving the vehicle in reverse. Check brake operation by maling several stops while driving forward.

27. If manually adjusting the brakes, proceed as follows:

a. Install the brake drum and wheel and tire assembly.

b. Remove the cover from the adjusting hole at the bottom of the backing plate and turn the adjusting screw, using a suitable brake adjusting tool, to expand the brake shoes until they drag against the brake drum.

c. When the shoes are against the drum, insert a narrow prybar through the brake adjusting hole and disengage the adjusting lever from the adjusting screw. While holding the adjusting lever away from the adjusting screw, loosen the adjusting screw with the brake adjusting tool, until the drum rotates freely without drag.

d. Install the adjusting hole cover and lower the vehicle.

e. Apply the brakes. If the pedal travels more than halfway to the floor, there is too much clearance between the brake shoes and drums. Repeat the adjustment procedure.

F 250, F 350, E 250 AND E 350

1. Raise and safely support the vehicle. Remove the wheel and tire assembly and the brake drum.

2. Remove the parking brake lever assembly retaining nut from behind the backing plate and remove the parking brake lever assembly.

3. Remove the adjusting cable assembly from the anchor pin, cable guide and adjusting lever.

4. Remove the brake shoe retracting springs. Remove the hold-down spring from each shoe.

5. Remove the brake shoes and the adjusting screw assembly. Disassemble the adjusting screw assembly.

To install:

6. Clean the backing plate ledge pads and sand lightly. Apply a light coating of high temperature lithium grease to the points where the brake shoes touch the backing plate.

7. Apply high temperature lithium grease to the threads and socket end of the adjusting screw.

8. Install the upper retracting spring on the primary and secondary shoes and position the shoe assembly on the backing plate with the wheel cylinder pushrods in the shoe slots.

9. Install the brake shoe hold-down springs.

Rear brake shoe assembly—Bronco, F 150 and E 150

10. Install the brake shoe adjustment screw assembly with the slot in the head of the adjusting screw toward the primary shoe.

11. Install the lower retracting spring, adjusting lever spring, adjusting lever assembly and connect the adjusting cable to the adjusting lever. Position the cable in the cable guide and install the cable anchor fitting on the anchor pin.

NOTE: Be sure to install the adjusting screw on the same side of the vehicle from which it came. To prevent incorrect installation, the socket end of each adjusting screw is stamped with R or L, to indicate installation on the right or left side of the vehicle. The adjusting pivot nuts have lines machined around the body of the nut, 2 lines indicating the right side nut and 1 line indicating the left side nut.

12. Install the parking brake assembly in the anchor pin and washer and secure with the retaining nut behind the backing plate.

13. Adjust the brake shoes using either a brake adjustment gauge or manually with the drums installed.

14. If using a brake adjustment gauge, proceed as follows:

a. Measure the inside diameter of the brake drum with the gauge.

b. Reverse the tool and adjust the brake shoes until they touch the gauge. The gauge contact points on the shoes must be parallel to the vehicle with the center line through the center of the axle.

c. Install the drum and wheel and tire assembly. Lower the vehicle.

d. Apply the brakes sharply several times while driving the vehicle in reverse. Check brake operation by maling several stops while driving forward.

15. If manually adjusting the brakes, proceed as follows:

a. Install the brake drum and wheel and tire assembly.

b. Remove the cover from the adjusting hole at the bottom of the backing plate and turn the adjusting screw, using a suitable brake adjusting tool, to expand the brake shoes until they drag against the brake drum.

c. When the shoes are against the drum, insert a narrow prybar through the brake adjusting hole and disengage the adjusting lever from the adjusting screw. While holding the adjusting lever away from the adjusting screw, loosen the adjusting

Rear brake shoe assembly—F 250, F 350, E 250 and E 350

CABLE TENSION LIMITER ASSEMBLY

Parking brake cable tension limiter assembly

screw with the brake adjusting tool, until the drum rotates freely without drag.

d. Install the adjusting hole cover and lower the vehicle.

e. Apply the brakes. If the pedal travels more than halfway to the floor, there is too much clearance between the brake shoes and drums. Repeat the adjustment procedure.

Wheel Cylinder

Removal and Installation

1. Raise and safely support the vehicle. Remove the wheel and tire assembly, brake drum and brake shoes.

2. Remove the cylinder to shoe connecting pins.

3. Disconnect the brake line from the wheel cylinder.

4. Remove the wheel cylinder retaining bolts and remove the cylinder from the brake backing plate.

5. Installation is the reverse of the removal procedure. Adjust the brakes and bleed the system.

Parking Brake Cable

Adjustment

INITIAL ADJUSTMENT PROCEDURE

NOTE: Use this service adjustment procedure when a new tension limiter is installed.

1. Depress the parking brake pedal fully to the last detent position.

2. Grip the tension limiter housing to prevent it from spinning and tighten the equalizer nut 3 in. up the rod.

3. Check to make sure the cinch strap hook has slipped (less than 1½ in. remaining).

FIELD ADJUSTMENT PROCEDURE

NOTE: Use this service adjustment procedure to correct a slack system, if a new tension limiter is not installed.

1. Make sure the brake drums are cold for correct adjustment. Depress the parking brake pedal fully, all the way to the floor.

2. Grip the tension limiter housing to prevent it from spinning and tighten the equalizer nut 6 full turns past its original position on the threaded rod until the cinch strap hooks begin to slip.

3. Using cable tension gauge 021–00018 or equivalent, behind the equalizer either toward the right or left drum, measure the cable tension. It should be at least 350 lbs. with the parking brake pedal fully in the last detent position. If the tension is low, repeat Step 2.

4. Release the parking brake and check for rear wheel drag. There should be no brake drag.

NOTE: The tension limiter will reset the parking brake tension any time the system is disconnected, as long as the distance between the bracket and the cinch strap hook is reduced during adjustment. When the cinch strap contacts the bracket, the system tension will greatly increase and over tension may result. If all available adjustment travel has been used, the tension limiter must be replaced.

Removal and Installation

EQUALIZER TO CONTROL ASSEMBLY

1. Raise the vehicle and support it safely.

2. Back off the equalizer nut and remove the slug of front cable from the tension limiter.

3. Remove the parking brake cable from the cab mount on Bronco and F Series or crossmember on E Series and all retaining clips. Lower the vehicle.

4. Remove the forward ball end of the parking brake cable from the control assembly clevis.

5. Remove the cable from the control assembly by compressing the conduit end fitting prongs.

6. Using a cord attached to the control lever end of the cable, remove the cable from the vehicle.

To install:

7. Transfer the cord to the new cable. Position the cable in the vehicle, routing the cable through the dash panel. Remove the cord and secure the cable to the control.

8. Connect the forward ball end of the brake cable to the clevis of the control assembly. Raise and safely support the vehicle.

9. Route the cable through the cab mount on Bronco and F Series or through the crossmembers on E Series and secure in place with the retaining clips.

10. Connect the slug of the cable to the tension limiter connector. Adjust the parking brake cable at the equalizer using the initial adjustment or field adjustment procedure, as necessary.

11. Rotate both rear wheels to make sure the parking brake is not dragging.

EQUALIZER TO REAR WHEEL

1. Raise the vehicle and support it safely.

2. Remove the wheel and tire assembly, tension limiter and brake drum.

3. Remove the locknut on the threaded rod and disconnect the cable from the equalizer.

4. Compress the prongs that retain the cable housing to the frame bracket on Bronco and F Series or the crossmember on E Series, and pull the cable and housing out of the bracket or crossmember.

5. Working on the wheel side, compress the prongs on the cable retainer so they can pass through the hole in the brake backing plate. Draw the cable retainer out of the hole.

6. With the spring tension off of the parking brake lever, lift the cable out of the slot in the lever and remove the cable through the brake backing plate hole.

To install:

7. Pull the cable through the backing plate until the end is inserted over the parking brake lever slot. Pull the excess slack from the cable and insert the cable housing into the brake backing plate access hole until the retainer prongs expand.

8. Insert the front of the cable housing through the frame crossmember bracket until the prong expands. Insert the ball end of the cable into the key hole slots on the equalizer, rotate the equalizer 90 degrees and recouple the tension limiter threaded rod to the equalizer.

NOTE: On F 250, F 350, E 250 and E 350, check the clearance between the parking brake operating lever and the cam plate. The clearance should be 0.015 in. (0.38mm), when the brakes are fully released.

9. Install the brake drum and wheel and tire assembly. Adjust the brake shoes.

10. Adjust the parking brake tension using the initial adjustment or field adjustment procedure, as necessary.

11. Rotate both rear wheels to make sure the parking brake is not dragging.

Brake System Bleeding

1. Clean all dirt from the master cylinder filler cap.

2. If the master cylinder is known or suspected to have air in the bore, it must be bled before any of the wheel cylinders or calipers. To bleed the master cylinder, loosen the upper secondary left front outlet fitting approximately ¾ turn. Have an assistant depress the brake pedal slowly through it's full travel. Close the outlet fitting and let the pedal return slowly to the fully released position. Wait 5 seconds and then repeat the operation until all air bubbles disappear.

3. Repeat Step 2 with the right-hand front outlet fitting.

4. Continue to bleed the brake system by removing the rubber dust cap from the wheel cylinder bleeder fitting at the right-hand rear of the vehicle. Place a suitable box wrench on the bleeder fitting and attach a rubber drain tube to the fitting. The end of the tube should fit snugly around the bleeder fitting. Submerge the other end of the tube in a container partially filled with clean brake fluid and loosen the fitting ¾ turn.

5. Have an assistant push the brake pedal down slowly through it's full travel. Close the bleeder fitting and allow the pedal to slowly return to it's full release position. Wait 5 seconds and repeat the procedure until no bubbles appear at the submerged end of the bleeder tube. Secure the bleeder fitting and remove the bleeder tube. Install the rubber dust cap on the bleeder fitting.

6. Repeat the procedure in Steps 4 and 5 and bleed the rest of the system in the following sequence: left rear, right front and left front.

NOTE: If equipped with rear anti-lock brakes, bleed the Rear Anti-lock Brake System (RABS) valve in between the left rear wheel and the right front wheel in the sequence.

7. Refill the master cylinder reservoir after each wheel cylinder or caliper has been bled and install the master cylinder cover

and gasket. When brake bleeding is completed, the fluid level should be filled to the maximum level indicated on the reservoir.

8. Always make sure the disc brake pistons are returned to their normal positions by depressing the brake pedal several times until normal pedal travel is established. If the pedal feels spongy, repeat the bleeding procedure.

Anti-lock Brake System Service

Precautions
● Use caution when disassembling any hydraulic components as the system will contain residual pressure. Cover the area around the component to be removed with a shop cloth to catch any brake fluid spray. Do not allow brake fluid to come in contact with painted surfaces.

Rear Anti-lock Brake System (RABS) Module

Removal and Installation
BRONCO AND F SERIES

1. Disconnect the negative battery cable.

2. Disconnect the wiring harness from the RABS module by depressing the plastic tab on the connector and pulling the connector off.

RABS valve installation—Bronco and F Series

RABS module location—Bronco and F Series

3. Remove the 2 screws that retain the module to the dash panel and remove the module.

4. Installation is the reverse of the removal procedure. Check the system for proper operation.

E SERIES

1. Disconnect the negative battery cable.
2. Remove the parking brake actuator assembly.
3. Remove the 2 screws that hold the module to the cowl panel. Remove the module.
4. Disconnect the wiring harness from the RABS module by depressing the plastic tab on the connector and pulling the connector off.
5. Installation is the reverse of the removal procedure. Check the RABS and parking brake systems for proper operation.

RABS Valve

Removal and Installation

1. Disconnect the negative battery cable.
2. Disconnect and plug the 2 brake lines connected to the RABS valve.
3. Disconnect the wiring harness from the valve harness.
4. Remove the screws or nuts retaining the valve and remove the valve.

To install:

5. Position the RABS valve and install the retaining screws or nuts. Tighten the retaining nuts on Bronco and F Series to 12–17 ft. lbs. (17–23 Nm). Tighten the retaining screws on E Series to 19–24 ft. lbs. (26–32 Nm).
6. Connect the brake valve wiring harness connector.
7. Connect the brake lines to the valve and tighten as follows:
   a. ½–20 threaded fittings—10–17 ft. lbs. (14–23 Nm).
   b. $^{7}/_{16}$–24 threaded fittings—10–15 ft. lbs. (14–20 Nm).

NOTE: Do not overtighten the fittings.

8. Bleed the brake system. It is not necessary to energize the valve electrically to bleed the rear brakes.
9. Connect the negative battery cable.

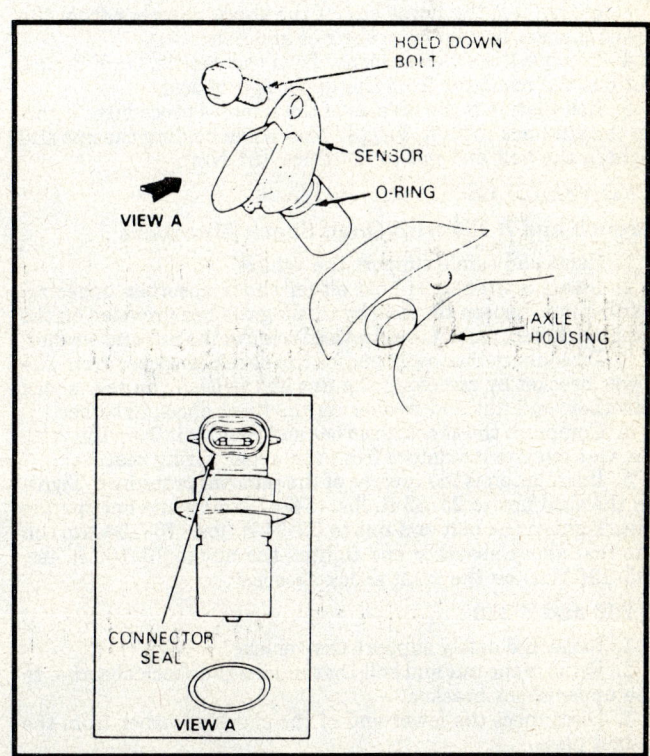

RABS sensor installation

RABS Sensor

Removal and Installation

1. Disconnect the negative battery cable.
2. Pull the wiring harness connector off.
3. Remove the sensor hold down bolt and remove the sensor from the axle housing.

To install:

4. Clean the axle mounting surface. Use care to prevent dirt from entering the axle housing.
5. Inspect and clean the magnetized sensor pole piece to ensure that it is free from loose metal particles which could cause erratic system operation. Inspect the sensor O-ring for damage and replace, if necessary.
6. Lightly lubricate the sensor O-ring with motor oil, align the sensor bolt hole and install. Do not apply force to the plastic sensor connector. The sensor flange should slide to the mounting surface. This will insure the air gap setting is between 0.005–0.045 in. (0.127–1.14mm).
7. Install the hold down bolt and tighten to 25–30 ft. lbs. (34–40 Nm).

8. Inspect the blue sensor connector seal and replace if missing or damaged. Push the connector on the sensor.
9. Connect the negative battery cable.

Excitor Ring

Inspection

1. Remove the RABS sensor.
2. View the excitor ring teeth through the sensor hole. Rotate the rear axle and check the excitor ring teeth for damage or breakage. Dented or broken teeth could cause the RABS system to function when not required.

Removal and Installation

To service the excitor ring, the differential case must be removed from the axle housing and the excitor ring pressed off the case.

NOTE: Upon removal, the excitor ring is to be discarded. It is not to be reused.

FRONT SUSPENSION

Shock Absorbers

Removal and Installation

2WD VEHICLES

1. Raise and safely support the vehicle.
2. Insert a wrench from the rear side of the spring upper seat to hold the shock absorber upper retaining nut. Loosen the stud by turning the hex provided on the exposed, lower, part of the stud and remove the nut and washer.
3. Disconnect the lower end of the shock absorber from the lower bracket by removing the nut and bolt.
4. Remove the shock absorber from the vehicle. On F Series, cut out the insulator from the upper spring seat.
5. Installation is the reverse of the removal procedure. Tighten the stud hex to 28 ft. lbs. (37 Nm) while holding the nut and tighten the bolt and nut to 60 ft. lbs. (81 Nm).

4WD VEHICLES

Bronco and F 150 with Quad Shock Absorbers

1. Raise and safely support the vehicle.
2. Insert a wrench to hold either shock absorber upper retaining nut. Loosen the stud by turning the hex provided on the exposed, lower, part of the stud and remove the nut and washer.
3. Disconnect the lower end of the shock absorber from the lower bracket by removing the nut and bolt on the rear shock absorber, and nut and washer on the front shock absorber.
4. Compress the shock absorber and remove it from the vehicle. Cut out the insulators from the upper spring seat.
5. Installation is the reverse of the removal procedure. Tighten the stud hex to 25–35 ft. lbs. (34–47 Nm) while holding the nut. Tighten the bolt and nut to 52–74 ft. lbs. (70–100 Nm) on the rear shock absorber and tighten the nut to 70–100 ft. lbs. (95–136 Nm) on the front shock absorber.

F 250 and F 350

1. Raise and safely support the vehicle.
2. Remove the nut and bolt that retains the shock absorber to the upper shock bracket.
3. Disconnect the lower end of the shock absorber from the U-bolt plate.
4. Compress the shock absorber and remove.

5. Reverse the removal procedure for installation. Tighten both nut and bolt assemblies to 52–74 ft. lbs. (70–100 Nm)

Coil Springs

Removal and Installation

2WD VEHICLES

1. Raise and safely support the vehicle. Position a jack under the front axle.

NOTE: The axle must be supported on the jack throughout spring removal and installation and must not be permitted to hang by the brake hose. If necessary, remove the brake caliper and suspend with mechanics wire. Do not let the caliper hang by the brake hose.

2. Disconnect the shock absorber from the lower bracket.
3. Remove the spring upper retainer attaching bolts or screws from the top of the spring upper seat and remove the retainer.
4. Remove the nut attaching the spring lower retainer to the lower seat and lower insulator and axle and remove the retainer. Slowly lower the axle and remove the spring.

To install:

5. Position the spring and slowly raise the front axle. Install the lower retainer over the stud, lower insulator, if equipped, and lower seat and install the attaching nut.
6. Install the upper retainer over the spring and against the spring upper seat and install the attaching screw.
7. Tighten the upper retainer attaching bolt to 13–18 ft. lbs. (18–24 Nm) on F Series or 20–30 ft. lbs. (28–40 Nm) on E Series. Tighten the lower retainer attaching nut to 70–100 ft. lbs. (95–135 Nm).
8. Connect the shock absorber and remove the jack from the axle. Lower the vehicle.

4WD VEHICLES

1. Raise and safely support the vehicle.
2. Remove the shock absorber-to-lower bracket attaching bolt and nut.
3. Remove the spring lower retainer attaching nut from the

Front suspension assembly—2WD F Series

inside of the coil spring. Remove the spring upper retainer attaching screw and remove the upper retainer.

4. Position a jack under the axle and lower it enough to relieve the tension from the spring.

NOTE: The axle must be supported on the jack throughout spring removal and installation and must not be permitted to hang by the brake hose. If necessary, remove the brake caliper and suspend with mechanics wire. Do not let the caliper hang by the brake hose.

5. Remove the spring lower retainer and remove the spring.
To install:
6. Position the spring and slowly raise the front axle. Make sure the spring is positioned correctly in the upper spring seats.

7. Install the lower retainer over the stud and lower seat and install the attaching nut. Tighten to 70–100 ft. lbs. (94–134 Nm).

8. Install the upper retainer over the spring and install the attaching screws. Tighten to 13–18 ft. lbs. (18–24 Nm).

9. Connect the shock absorber to the lower bracket and remove the jack from the axle. Lower the vehicle.

Leaf Springs

Removal and Installation

1. Raise the vehicle frame until the weight is off the front spring with the wheels still touching the floor. Support the axle.

2. Disconnect the lower end of the shock absorber from the U-bolt spacer. Remove the U-bolts, cap and the spacer.

3. If equipped with Dana Model 60 Monobeam axle, remove the 2 bolts that retain the tracking bar to the right spring cap and tracking bar mounting bracket.

4. Remove the nut from the hanger bolt retaining the spring at the rear. Drive out the hanger bolt.

5. Remove the nut connecting the front shackle and the spring eye. Drive out the shackle bolt and remove the spring.
To install:
6. Position the new spring on the spring seat. Install the shackle bolt through the shackle and spring and tighten to 120–150 ft. lbs. (163–203 Nm).

7. Position the rear of the spring to allow the rear hanger bolt to be installed. Install the nut and tighten to 120–150 ft. lbs. (163–203 Nm).

Front suspension assembly—F 350

8. Position the U-bolt spacer and place the U-bolts in position through the holes in the spring seat cap. Install, but do not tighten the U-bolt nuts. Make sure the spring center bolt is aligned with the indentation in the axle housing.

9. If equipped with a tracking bar, connect it to the crossmember mounting bracket and right spring seat cap.

10. Connect the lower end of the shock absorber to the U-bolt spacer. Lower the vehicle and tighten the U-bolt nuts to 85–120 ft. lbs. (115–163 Nm).

Upper Ball Joints

Inspection

NOTE: Always adjust the wheel bearings before any ball joint inspection procedure.

1. Raise the vehicle and place safety stands under the I-Beam axle beneath the spring.

2. Grasp the upper edge of the tire and move the wheel in and out. Observe the upper spindle arm and the upper part of the axle jaw.

3. A $\frac{1}{32}$ in. (0.794mm) or greater movement between the upper part of the axle jaw and the upper spindle arm indicates that the upper ball joint must be replaced.

Removal and Installation

2WD VEHICLES

1. Raise and safely support the vehicle. Remove the front wheel and tire assembly.

2. Remove the brake caliper and suspend with mechanics wire. Do not let the caliper hang by the brake hose.

3. Remove the dust cap, cotter pin, nut retainer, nut, washer and outer bearing and remove the rotor from the spindle. Remove the brake dust shield.

4. Remove the cotter pin and nut and disconnect the tie rod end from the spindle.

5. Remove the cotter pin and nut from the lower ball joint stud. Remove the nut from the axle clamp bolt and remove the bolt from the axle.

6. Remove the camber adjuster from the upper ball joint stud and axle beam. Strike the inside area of the axle with a hammer to pop the lower ball joint loose from the axle beam.

NOTE: Do not use a pickle fork to separate the ball joint from the axle as this will damage the seal and the ball joint socket.

7. Remove the spindle and ball joint assembly from the axle.

8. Install the spindle assembly in a vise. Remove the snapring from the lower ball joint and remove the ball joint from the spindle using C-frame tool T74P–3044–A1 and receiver cup tool D81T–3010–A or equivalents. Turn the forcing screw clockwise until the ball joint is removed from the spindle.

9. Assemble the C-frame and receiver cup tools to the upper ball joint and turn the forcing screw clockwise until the ball joint is removed from the spindle.

NOTE: Always remove the lower ball joint first. Do not heat the ball joint or the spindle to aid in removal.

To install:

10. Position the lower ball joint and assemble the C-frame and receiver cup tools with installation tool D81T–3010–A4 or equivalents on the spindle. Turn the forcing screw clockwise until the ball joint is seated.

NOTE: Always install the lower ball joint first. Do not heat the ball joint or the spindle to aid in installation.

11. Install the snapring onto the lower ball joint. To install the upper ball joint, repeat Step 10.

12. Remove the spindle assembly from the vise and install on the axle.

13. Install the nut on the lower ball joint stud and tighten to 95–110 ft. lbs. (129–149 Nm). Continue tightening until the castellated nut lines up with the hole in the stud. Install the cotter pin.

14. Install the camber adjuster in the upper spindle over the ball joint stud. Make sure the adjuster is aligned properly. Install the clamp bolt and nut into the axle boss and tighten the nut to 48–65 ft. lbs. (65–88 Nm).

15. Install the dust shield and the rotor. Install the outer wheel bearing, washer and nut. Adjust the wheel bearings and install the nut retainer, cotter pin and dust cap.

16. Install the brake caliper. Connect the tie rod end to the spindle and tighten the nut to 70–100 ft. lbs. (94–135 Nm). Install a new cotter pin.

17. Install the wheel and tire assembly and lower the vehicle. Check the front end alignment.

4WD VEHICLES

1. Raise and safely support the vehicle.

2. Remove the axle shafts and spindles. Disconnect the steering linkage.

3. Remove the cotter pin from the top ball joint stud. Loosen the nut on the top stud and the bottom nut inside the knuckle. Remove the top nut.

4. Sharply hit the top stud with a plastic or rawhide hammer, to free the knuckle from the axle arm. Remove and discard the bottom nut.

5. Mark the position of the camber adjuster and remove it by hand. If difficult to remove, use pitman arm puller T64P–3590–F or equivalent.

6. Place the knuckle in a vise and remove the snapring from the bottom ball joint socket, if equipped.

7. Using C-frame tool T74P–4635–C, plug tool T80T–3010–A4 and receiving cup tool T80T–3010–A2 or equivalents, turn the forcing screw clockwise until the bottom ball joint is removed from the steering knuckle.

NOTE: Always remove the lower ball joint first.

8. Repeat Step 7 to remove the upper ball joint.

To install:

9. Clean the steering knuckle bore and insert the lower ball joint as straight as possible. Assemble the C-frame tool with receiving cup tools T80T–3010–A3 and D81T–3010–A or equivalents to install the lower ball joint. Turn the forcing screw clockwise until the ball joint is firmly seated.

10. To install the upper ball joint, repeat Step 9, but use the C-frame tool with receiving cup tool T80T–3010–A3 and replacer tool T80T–3010–A1 or equivalents.

11. Install the knuckle to the axle arm arm. Install the camber adjuster, aligning the marks that were made during removal.

12. Install a new nut on the bottom socket finger tight. Install and tighten the nut on the top socket finger tight, then tighten the bottom nut to 80 ft. lbs. (109 Nm).

13. Tighten the top nut to 100 ft. lbs. (136 Nm), then advance the nut until the castellation aligns with the cotter pin hole. Install the cotter pin. Do not loosen the top nut to install the cotter pin.

14. Retighten the bottom nut to 90–110 ft. lbs. (123–150 Nm). Install the axle shaft and spindle assembly and lower the vehicle.

Lower Ball Joints

Inspection

NOTE: Always adjust the wheel bearings before any ball joint inspection procedure.

1. Raise the vehicle and place safety stands under the I-Beam axle beneath the spring.

2. Have an assistant grasp the lower edge of the tire and move

the wheel in and out. While the wheel is being moved, observe the lower spindle arm and the lower part of the axle jaw.

3. A $\frac{1}{32}$ in. (0.794) or greater movement between the lower part of the axle jaw and the lower spindle arm indicates that the lower ball joint must be replaced.

Removal and Installation

2WD VEHICLES

1. Raise and safely support the vehicle. Remove the front wheel and tire assembly.
2. Remove the brake caliper and suspend with mechanics wire. Do not let the caliper hang by the brake hose.
3. Remove the dust cap, cotter pin, nut retainer, nut, washer and outer bearing and remove the rotor from the spindle. Remove the brake dust shield.
4. Remove the cotter pin and nut and disconnect the tie rod end from the spindle.
5. Remove the cotter pin and nut from the lower ball joint stud. Remove the nut from the axle clamp bolt and remove the bolt from the axle.
6. Remove the camber adjuster from the upper ball joint stud and axle beam. Strike the inside area of the axle with a hammer to pop the lower ball joint loose from the axle beam.

NOTE: Do not use a pickle fork to separate the ball joint from the axle as this will damage the seal and the ball joint socket.

7. Remove the spindle and ball joint assembly from the axle.
8. Install the spindle assembly in a vise. Remove the snapring from the lower ball joint and remove the ball joint from the spindle using C-frame tool T74P–3044–A1 and receiver cup tool D81T–3010–A or equivalents. Turn the forcing screw clockwise until the ball joint is removed from the spindle.

NOTE: Do not heat the ball joint or the spindle to aid in removal.

To install:

9. Position the lower ball joint and sssemble the C-frame and receiver cup tools with installation cup tool D81T–3010–A4 or equivalents on the spindle. Turn the forcing screw clockwise until the ball joint is seated.

NOTE: Do not heat the ball joint or the spindle to aid in installation.

10. Install the snapring onto the lower ball joint.
11. Remove the spindle assembly from the vise and install on the axle.
12. Install the nut on the lower ball joint stud and tighten to 95–110 ft. lbs. (129–149 Nm). Continue tightening until the castellated nut lines up with the hole in the stud. Install the cotter pin.
13. Install the camber adjuster in the upper spindle over the ball joint stud. Make sure the adjuster is aligned properly. Install the clamp bolt and nut into the axle boss and tighten the nut to 48–65 ft. lbs. (65–88 Nm).
14. Install the dust shield and the rotor. Install the outer wheel bearing, washer and nut. Adjust the wheel bearings and install the nut retainer, cotter pin and dust cap.
15. Install the brake caliper. Connect the tie rod end to the spindle and tighten the nut to 70–100 ft. lbs. (94–135 Nm). Install a new cotter pin.
16. Install the wheel and tire assembly and lower the vehicle. Check the front end alignment.

4WD VEHICLES

1. Raise and safely support the vehicle.
2. Remove the axle shafts and spindles. Disconnect the steering linkage.
3. Remove the cotter pin from the top ball joint stud. Loosen

the nut on the top stud and the bottom nut inside the knuckle. Remove the top nut.
4. Sharply hit the top stud with a plastic or rawhide hammer, to free the knuckle from the axle arm. Remove and discard the bottom nut.
5. Mark the position of the camber adjuster and remove it by hand. If difficult to remove, use pitman arm puller T64P–3590–F or equivalent.
6. Place the knuckle in a vise and remove the snapring from the bottom ball joint socket, if equipped.
7. Using C-frame tool T74P–4635–C, plug tool T80T–3010–A4 and receiving cup tool T80T–3010–A2 or equivalents, turn the forcing screw clockwise until the bottom ball joint is removed from the steering knuckle.

To install:

8. Clean the steering knuckle bore and insert the lower ball joint as straight as possible. Assemble the C-frame tool with receiving cup tools T80T–3010–A3 and D81T–3010–A or equivalents, to install the lower ball joint. Turn the forcing screw clockwise until the ball joint is firmly seated.
9. Install the knuckle to the axle arm. Install the camber adjuster, aligning the marks that were made during removal.
10. Install a new nut on the bottom socket finger tight. Install and tighten the nut on the top socket finger tight, then tighten the bottom nut to 80 ft. lbs. (109 Nm).
11. Tighten the top nut to 100 ft. lbs. (136 Nm), then advance the nut until the castellation aligns with the cotter pin hole. Install the cotter pin. Do not loosen the top nut to install the cotter pin.
12. Retighten the bottom nut to 90–110 ft. lbs. (123–150 Nm). Install the axle shaft and spindle assembly and lower the vehicle.

Stabilizer Bar

Removal and Installation

2WD VEHICLES

F Series

1. Disconnect the left and right ends of the bar from the link assembly attached to the spring seat.
2. Disconnect the retainer bolts and remove the stabilizer bar.
3. Disconnect the link assemblies by looosening the right and left locknuts from their I-beam brackets.

To install:

4. Loosely assemble the entire stabilizer bar system with both link assemblies outboard of the stabilizer bar. Force the stabilizer bar rearward to connect the bar ends to the link assemblies.
5. Tighten the nuts and bolts retaining the link assemblies to the stabilizer bar and spring seat to 52–74 ft. lbs. (71–100 Nm).
6. Make sure the insulators are seated in the retainers and the stabilizer bar is centered in the assembly. Tighten the stabilizer bar-to-frame retainer nuts and bolts to 27–37 ft. lbs. (37–50 Nm).

E Series

1. Disconnect the left and right ends of the bar from the link assembly attached to the I-beam bracket.
2. Disconnect the retainer bolts and remove the stabilizer bar.
3. Disconnect the link assemblies by looosening the right and left locknuts from their I-beam brackets.

To install:

4. Connect the right and left stabilizer links to the I-beam brackets by sliding the bolt with the washer through the link, I-beam bracket hole and toward the inside of the side rail. Tighten the washer and locknut to 40–60 ft. lbs. (55–81 Nm).

NOTE: The link must be installed with the bend facing forward.

5. Connect the stabilizer bar to the frame side rails by placing the 2 retainers on the bottom of the side rails and tightening the 4 through bolts to 15–25 ft. lbs. (21–33 Nm).

6. Connect the stabilizer bar ends to the link assemblies. Tighten the retaining nuts to 18–28 ft. lbs. (25–37 Nm).

4WD VEHICLES

Bronco and F 150

1. Disconnect the stabilizer bar from the connecting links. Remove the nuts and bolts of the stabilizer bar retainer.

2. Remove the stabilizer bar retainer.

3. Remove the stabilizer bar and insulator. The stud does not have to be removed.

4. Installation is the reverse of the removal procedure. Tighten the retainer nuts to 27–37 ft. lbs. (37–50 Nm) and the link-to-stabilizer bolt and nut to 52–74 ft. lbs. (71–100 Nm).

F 250

1. Remove the bolts, washers and the nuts securing the links to the spring seat caps. If equipped with a Dana Model 60 Monobeam front axle, the links are secured to the mounting brackets.

2. Disconnect the links from the stabilizer bar and remove them.

3. Remove the retainers from the mounting bracket. Remove the stabilizer bar.

4. Installation is the reverse of the removal procedure. Tighten the nuts connecting the links to the spring seat caps to 52–74 ft. lbs. (70–100 Nm). Tighten the nuts connecting the links to the stabilizer bar to 15–25 ft. lbs. (21–33 Nm). Tighten the nuts and bolts connecting the retainers to the mounting bracket to 27–37 ft. lbs. (35–50 Nm).

F 350

1. Disconnect the left and right stabilizer bar ends from the link assembly.

2. Disconnect the retainer bolts and U-bolt and remove the stabilizer bar.

3. Disconnect the stabilizer links from the frame side rail mounting brackets.

To install:

4. Loosely assemble the entire stabilizer bar system with both link assemblies loosely attached to the frame mounting brackets and the stabilizer bar in position on the axle.

5. Make sure the stabilizer bar insulators are seated in the retainers and the stabilizer bar is centered between the leaf springs. Attach the stabilizer bar to the axle by assembling the retainers to the axle mounting brackets. Tighten the retaining bolts and U-bolt to 35–50 ft. lbs. (48–68 Nm).

6. Install the link assemblies to the frame mounting brackets and tighten the locknuts to 52–74 ft. lbs. (70–100 Nm).

7. Install the link assembly to the stabilizer bar and tighten the locknuts to 15–25 ft. lbs. (21–32 Nm).

King Pin and Bushings

Removal and Installation

2WD VEHICLES

1. Raise and support the vehicle safely. Remove the wheel and tire assembly.

2. Remove the brake caliper and suspend it with mechanics wire. Do not let the caliper hang from the brake hose.

3. Remove the rotor/hub and bearing assembly.

4. Disconnect the steering linkage from the spindle arm.

5. Remove the nut and lockwasher from the lock pin and remove the lock pin.

6. Remove the upper and lower king pin plugs, then drive the king pin out from the top of the axle. Remove the spindle and thrust bearing. Remove the king pin seal and thrust bearing.

7. Install the spindle in a vise. Remove and discard the seal from the bottom of the upper bushing bore of the upper spindle yoke.

8. Using suitable tools, drive the old bushings from the spindle bores.

To install:

9. Using a suitable driver, install a new top bushing. The bushing should be seated to a depth of 0.080 in. (2.03mm) minimum from the bottom of the upper spindle boss.

10. Using a suitable driver, install a new bottom spindle bushing. The bottom bushing should be seated to a depth of 0.130 in. (3.30mm) minimum from the top of the lower spindle boss.

11. Ream the new bushings to 0.001–0.003 in. (0.025–0.076mm) larger than the diameter of the new king pin. Clean all metal shavings from the bushings after reaming and coat the bushings with lubricant.

12. Make sure the king pin hole in the axle is free of nicks, burrs and dirt. Clean up the bore as necessary and lightly coat the surface with lithium grease.

13. Install a new king pin seal with the metal backing facing up towards the bushing into the spindle. Gently press the seal into position, being careful not to distort the casing.

14. Install a new thrust bearing with the lip flange facing down towards the lower bushing. Press until the bearing is firmly seated against the surface of the spindle.

15. Place the spindle in position on the axle with the thrust bearing.

16. Install the king pin with the **T** stamped on 1 end towards the top with the lock pin notch in the pin aligned with the lock pin hole in the axle. Insert the king pin through the bushings and axle from the top until the king pin notch is aligned with the lock pin hole.

17. Install a new lock pin with the threads pointing forward and the wedge groove facing the king pin notch. Firmly drive the lock pin into position and install the lock pin lockwasher and nut. Tighten the nut to 37–52 ft. lbs. (50–70 Nm). Install the king pin plugs at the top and bottom of the spindle and tighten to 35–50 ft. lbs. (48–67 Nm).

18. Lubricate the king pin and bushings with grease through both fittings until grease is visible seeping past the upper seal at the top and from the thrust bearing slip joint at the bottom. If grease does not appear, recheck the installation procedure.

19. Install the dust shield and the rotor/hub and bearing assembly. Adjust the wheel bearings.

20. Install the cailper assembly and connect the steering linkage to spindle. Install the wheel and tire assembly.

21. Lower the vehicle and check the front end alignment.

4WD VEHICLES

1. Raise and safely support the vehicle. Remove the axle shaft.

2. Alternately and evenly loosen the 4 bolts retaining the spindle cap to the knuckle; thereby relieving the spring compression. Remove the bolts.

3. Remove the spindle cap, compression spring and retainer. Remove and discard the gasket.

4. Remove the 4 bolts retaining the lower kingpin and retainer to the knuckle. Remove the lower kingpin and retainer from the knuckle.

5. Remove the tapered bushing from the top of the upper kingpin in the knuckle. Remove the knuckle from the axle yoke.

6. Remove the upper king pin from the axle yoke with a piece of 7/8 in. hex-shaped case hardened metal stock or with a suitable 7/8 in. ex socket. Discard the upper king pin and seal.

NOTE: The upper king pin is tightened to 500–600 ft. lbs. (678–813 Nm).

7. Press the lower king pin grease retainer, bearing cup, bearing and seal from the axle yoke lower bore with a 2-jaw puller

and suitable press plate. Discard the grease seal and retainer and lower bearing cup.

To install:

8. Coat the mating surface of a new lower king pin grease retainer with silicone sealer and install in the axle yoke bore so the concave portion of the retainer faces the upper king pin.

9. Using a suitable driver, drive a new bearing cup in the lower king pin bore until it bottoms against the grease retainer.

10. Pack the lower king pin bearing and the yoke bore with high-temperature wheel bearing grease. With a suitable driver, drive a new seal in the lower king pin bore.

11. Install a new seal, using installation tool T86T–3110–AH or equivalent. Install the upper king pin assembly in the yoke and tighten to 500–600 ft. lbs. (678–813 Nm).

12. Install the knuckle on the axle yoke. Place the tapered bushing over the upper kingpin in the knuckle bore.

13. Place the lower kingpin and retainer assembly in the knuckle and axle yoke. Install the 4 bolts and alternately and evenly tighten to 70–90 ft. lbs. (95–122 Nm).

14. Place the retainer and compression spring on the tapered bushing. Install a new gasket and the spindle cap on the knuckle. Install the 4 bolts and alternately and evenly tighten to 70–90 ft. lbs. (95–122 Nm).

15. Install the axle shaft. Lubricate the upper kingpin through the grease zerk and the lower through the flush type fitting.

16. Lower the vehicle.

Twin I-Beam Axle

Removal and Installation

1. Raise and safely support the vehicle. Remove the front wheel spindle, the front spring and the stabilizer bar, if equipped.

2. Remove the spring lower seat from the radius arm and then remove the bolt and nut that attaches the radius arm to the front axle.

3. Remove the axle to frame pivot bracket bolt and nut. Remove the axle assembly.

To install:

4. Position the axle to the frame pivot bracket and install the bolt and nut finger-tight.

5. Position the opposite end of the of the axle to the radius arm. Install the attaching bolt from underneath through the bracket, the radius arm and the axle.

6. Install the spring lower seat on the radius arm so the hole in the seat indexes over the arm-to-axle bolt and the pin on the spring seat engages the slot in the radius arm.

7. Install the front spring, wheel spindle and, if equipped, the stabilizer bar.

8. Lower the vehicle. With the weight on the suspension, tighten the axle-to-frame pivot bolt to 120–150 ft. lbs. (163–203 Nm).

Front Wheel Bearings

Adjustment

2WD VEHICLES

1. Raise the vehicle and support it safely.

2. Remove the wheel cover and the grease cap from the hub. Remove the cotter pin and the locknut.

3. Loosen the adjusting nut 3 turns. Try to obtain running clearance between the rotor and brake pads by rocking the wheel in and out or by tapping on the caliper housing.

NOTE: Do not pry on the caliper piston. If clearance cannot be obtained, remove the caliper and suspend it with mechanics wire. Do not let the caliper hang from the brake hose.

4. While rotating the wheel, tighten the adjusting nut to 17–25 ft. lbs. (23–34 Nm) to seat the bearings.

5. Back off the adjusting nut 120–180 degrees and install the retainer and new cotter pin without additional movement of the adjusting nut. Bearing endplay should be 0.00025–0.005 in. (0.006–0.127mm).

6. Check front wheel rotation. If the wheel rotates properly, reinstall the grease cap and wheel cover. If rotation is noisy or rough, remove and inspect the bearings.

7. Before driving the vehicle, pump the brake pedal several times to reseat the brake pads.

4WD VEHICLES

Bronco, F 150 and F 250 with Manual Locking Hubs

1. Raise the vehicle and support it safely.

2. Remove the hub lock assembly.

3. Using a torque wrench and spanner locknut wrench T86T–1197–A or equivalent, apply inward pressure to unlock the adjusting nut locking splines and turn the nut clockwise to tighten to 70 ft. lbs. (95 Nm) while rotating the wheel back and forth to seat the bearings.

4. Apply inward pressure to the locknut wrench to disengage the adjusting nut locking splines and back off the adjusting nut approximately 90 degress.

5. Retighten the adjusting nut to 15–20 ft. lbs. (20–27 Nm) and remove the tool and torque wrench. Check the final endplay of the hub and rotor on the spindle; it should be 0.00 in.

6. The torque required to rotate the hub and rotor assembly should not exceed 20 inch lbs. (2.3 Nm).

7. Install the hub lock assemblt and lower the vehicle.

Bronco and F 150 with Automatic Locking Hubs
F 250 and F 350 with Manual Locking Hubs

1. Raise and safely support the vehicle.

2. Remove the hub lock assembly.

3. Remove the outer locknut and lockwasher using spanner locknut wrench D85T–1197–A or equivalent.

4. Using the locknut wrench, tighten the inner locknut to 50 ft. lbs. (68 Nm) while rotating the hub back and forth, to seat the bearing.

5. Back off the inner locknut and retighten to 30–40 ft. lbs. (41–54 Nm).

6. Back off the locknut 90 degrees. Install the lockwasher so the key is positioned in the spindle groove. Tighten the inner locknut so the pin is aligned into the nearest lockwasher hole.

7. Install the outer locknut and tighten to 160–205 ft. lbs. (217–278 Nm). Check the final endplay of the spindle; it should be 0.000–0.004 in. (0.00–0.11mm).

8. The torque required to rotate the hub and rotor assembly should not exceed 20 inch lbs. (2.3 Nm).

9. Install the hub locks and lower the vehicle.

Removal and Installation

2WD VEHICLES

1. Raise and safely support the vehicle. Remove the front wheel and tire assembly.

2. Remove the brake caliper and suspend it with mechanics wire. Do not let the caliper hang from the brake hose.

3. Remove the grease cap, cotter pin, retainer adjusting nut and washer. Remove the outer bearing.

4. Pull the hub and rotor off the spindle. Remove and discard the grease seal.

5. Remove the inner bearing from the hub. Remove all traces of old lubricant from the bearings, hub and spindle with solvent and dry thoroughly.

6. Inspect the bearings and bearing races for scratches, pits, cracks or other wear. If the bearings or races are worn or damaged, remove the races using a brass drift.

To install:

7. If the inner or outer bearing races were removed, replace them in the hub with the proper tool. The races will be properly seated when they are fully bottomed.

8. Pack the inside of the hub with high temperature wheel bearing grease. Fill the hub until the grease is flush with the inside diameters of both bearing races.

9. Pack the bearings with wheel bearing grease, working as much lubricant as possible between the rollers and the cages.

10. Place the inner bearing in the inner race and install a new seal, using a seal installer.

11. Install the hub and rotor assembly on the spindle, being careful not to damage the seal. Install the outer bearing, washer and adjusting nut and adjust the wheel bearings.

12. Install the retainer, new cotter pin and grease cap. Install the caliper and the wheel and tire assembly.

13. Lower the vehicle. Before driving the vehicle, pump the brake pedal to reseat the brake pads.

REAR SUSPENSION

Shock Absorber

Removal and Installation

1. Raise the vehicle and support it safely.

2. Remove the shock absorber lower attaching nut and bolt and swing the lower end free of the mounting bracket on the axle housing.

3. Remove the nut and bolt or nut from the upper shock absorber mount.

To install:

4. Position the shock absorber to the upper mount and install the nut, bolt and washers.

5. Swing the lower end of the shock absorber into the mounting bracket on the axle housing. Install the mounting bolt, nut and washers. Tighten the nut and bolt to 52–74 ft. lbs. (70–100 Nm).

6. Install the upper nut or nut and bolt and tighten to 40–60 ft. lbs. (54–81 Nm) on Bronco and F Series or 25–35 ft. lbs. (33–47 Nm) on E Series.

7. Lower the vehicle.

Leaf Spring

Removal and Installation

BRONCO AND F SERIES

1. Raise and safely support the vehicle, so the weight is off the rear spring and the tires still touch the floor.

2. Remove the nuts from the spring U-bolts and drive the U-bolts from the U-bolt plate. If equipped, remove the auxiliary spring and spacer.

3. Remove the spring-to-bracket nut and bolt at the front of the spring.

4. Remove the shackle upper and lower nuts and bolts at the rear of the spring. Remove the spring and shackle assembly from the rear shackle bracket.

To install:

5. Position the spring in the shackle and install the upper shackle-to-spring bolt and nut with the bolt head facing outward.

6. Position the front end of the spring in the bracket and install the bolt and nut. Position the shackle in the rear bracket and install the bolt and nut.

7. Place the spring on top of the axle with the spring tie bolt centered in the hole provided in the seat. If equipped, install the auxiliary spring and spacer.

8. Install the spring U-bolts, U-bolt plate and nuts.

9. Lower the vehicle to the floor. Tighten the spring U-bolt nuts to 75–115 ft. lbs. (100–155 Nm) on Bronco, F 150 and F250 under 8500 lbs. or 150–210 ft. lbs. (200–280 Nm) on F 250 and F 350 over 8500 lbs. GVW.

10. Tighten the leaf spring-to-front bracket nut and bolt to 75–115 ft. lbs. (100–155 Nm) on 2WD F 150 or 150–177 ft. lbs. (200–240 Nm) on all other vehicles.

11. Tighten the leaf spring-to-rear shackle nut and bolt to 75–115 ft. lbs. (100–150 Nm) on all except 2WD F 250 and F 350, where the torque should be 150–210 ft. lbs. (200–280 Nm).

E 150

1. Raise and safely support the vehicle. Support the rear axle with a floor jack.

2. Disconnect the lower end of the shock absorber from the axle housing bracket. Remove the 2 U-bolts and plate.

3. Lower the axle and remove the upper and lower rear shackle bolts. Pull the rear shackle assembly from the bracket and spring.

4. Remove the nut and mounting bolt that secures the front end of the spring. Remove the spring assembly from the front shackle bracket.

To install:

5. Assemble the front eye of the spring to the front bracket with the front mounting bolt and nut but do not tighten at this time.

6. Mount the rear end of the spring with the upper bolt of the rear shackle assembly passing through the eye of the spring. Insert the lower bolt through the rear spring and shackle bracket.

7. Assemble the spring center bolt in the pilot hole in the axle and install the plate. Install the U-bolts through the plate but do not tighten the attaching nuts at this time.

8. Raise the axle with the jack until the shock absorbers can be connected to the axle housing brackets.

9. Tighten the leaf spring-to-front bracket nut and bolt to 150–204 ft. lbs. (204–276 Nm). Tighten the leaf spring-to-axle U-bolt nut to 74–107 ft. lbs. (101–145 Nm). Tighten the leaf spring-to-rear shackle nut and bolt to 74–107 ft. lbs. (101–145 Nm).

10. Lower the vehicle.

E 250 AND E 350

1. Raise and safely support the vehicle. Support the rear axle with a floor jack.

2. Disconnect the lower end of the shock absorber from the axle housing bracket. Remove the 2 U-bolts and plate.

3. Lower the axle and remove the spring front bolt from the hanger. Remove the 2 attaching bolts from the rear of the spring and remove the spring and shackle.

To install:

4. Assemble the upper end of the shackle to the spring with the attaching bolt. Connect the front of the spring to the front bracket with the attaching bolt.

5. Assemble the spring and shackle to the rear bracket with the attaching bolt. Place the U-bolt plate over the nut of the center bolt.

6. Raise the axle with a jack. Install the center bolt head through the pilot hole in the pad on the axle housing.

7. Install the spring U-bolts and attaching nuts and snug the nuts. Connect the shock absorber to the lower bracket.

8. Tighten the leaf spring-to-front bracket nut and bolt to 150–204 ft. lbs. (204–276 Nm). Tighten the leaf spring-to-axle U-bolt nut to 74–107 ft. lbs. (101–145 Nm) on light duty E 250 or 150–180 ft. lbs. (204–244 Nm) on heavy duty E 250 and E 350. Tighten the leaf spring-to-rear shackle nut and bolt to 74–107 ft. lbs. (101–145 Nm).

9. Lower the vehicle.

SPECIFICATIONS

VEHICLE IDENTIFICATION CHART

It is important for servicing and ordering parts to be certain of the vehicle and engine identification. The VIN (vehicle identification number) is a 17 digit number visible through the windshield on the driver's side of the dash and contains the vehicle and engine identification codes. The tenth digit indicates model year and the eighth digit indicates engine code. It can be interpreted as follows:

Engine Code						Model Year	
Code	Cu. In.	Liters	Cyl.	Fuel Sys.	Eng. Mfg.	Code	Year
C	122	2.0	4	Carb.	Ford	J	1988
A	140	2.3	4	EFI	Ford	K	1989
T	177	2.9	6	EFI	Ford	L	1990
U	183	3.0	6	EFI	Ford	M	1991
X	244	4.0	6	EFI	Ford	N	1992

EFI—Electronic Fuel Injection

ENGINE IDENTIFICATION

Year	Model	Engine Displacement cu. in. (liter)	Engine Series Identification (VIN)	No. of Cylinders	Engine Type
1988	Aerostar	183 (3.0)	U	6	OHV
	Bronco II	177 (2.9)	T	6	OHV
	Ranger	122 (2.0)	C	4	OHC
	Ranger	140 (2.3)	A	4	OHC
	Ranger	177 (2.9)	T	6	OHV
1989	Aerostar	183 (3.0)	U	6	OHV
	Bronco II	177 (2.9)	T	6	OHV
	Ranger	140 (2.3)	A	4	OHC
	Ranger	177 (2.9)	T	6	OHV
1990	Aerostar	183 (3.0)	U	6	OHV
	Aerostar	244 (4.0)	X	6	OHV
	Bronco II	177 (2.9)	T	6	OHV
	Ranger	140 (2.3)	A	4	OHC
	Ranger	177 (2.9)	T	6	OHV
	Ranger	244 (4.0)	X	6	OHV
1991–92	Aerostar	183 (3.0)	U	6	OHV
	Aerostar	244 (4.0)	X	6	OHV
	Explorer	244 (4.0)	X	6	OHV
	Ranger	140 (2.3)	A	4	OHC
	Ranger	177 (2.9)	T	6	OHV
	Ranger	183 (3.0)	U	6	OHV
	Ranger	244 (4.0)	X	6	OHV

OHV—Overhead Valve
OHC—Overhead Cam

GENERAL ENGINE SPECIFICATIONS

Year	VIN	No. Cylinder Displacement cu. in. (liter)	Fuel System Type	Net Horsepower @ rpm	Net Torque @ rpm (ft. lbs.)	Bore × Stroke (in.)	Compression Ratio	Oil Pressure @ rpm
1988	C	4-122 (2.0)	2 bbl	80 @ 4200	106 @ 2600	3.52 × 3.13	9.0:1	40–60 @ 2000
	A	4-140 (2.3)	EFI	90 @ 4000	134 @ 2000	3.78 × 3.13	9.5:1	40–60 @ 2000
	T	6-177 (2.9)	EFI	140 @ 4600	170 @ 2600	3.66 × 2.83	9.0:1	40–60 @ 2000
	U	6-183 (3.0)	EFI	145 @ 4800	165 @ 3600	3.50 × 3.14	9.3:1	40–60 @ 2500
1989	A	4-140 (2.3)	EFI	90 @ 4000	134 @ 2000	3.78 × 3.13	9.5:1	40–60 @ 2000
	T	6-177 (2.9)	EFI	140 @ 4600	170 @ 2600	3.66 × 2.83	9.0:1	40–60 @ 2000
	U	6-183 (3.0)	EFI	145 @ 4800	165 @ 3600	3.50 × 3.14	9.3:1	40–60 @ 2500
1990	A	4-140 (2.3)	EFI	100 @ 4600	133 @ 2600	3.78 × 3.13	9.2:1	40–60 @ 2000
	T	6-177 (2.9)	EFI	140 @ 4600	170 @ 2600	3.66 × 2.83	9.0:1	40–60 @ 2000
	U	6-183 (3.0)	EFI	145 @ 4800	165 @ 3600	3.50 × 3.14	9.3:1	40–60 @ 2500
	X	6-244 (4.0)	EFI	①	②	3.95 × 3.32	9.0:1	40–60 @ 2000
1991–92	A	4-140 (2.3)	EFI	100 @ 4600	133 @ 2600	3.78 × 3.13	9.2:1	40–60 @ 2000
	T	6-177 (2.9)	EFI	140 @ 4600	170 @ 2600	3.66 × 2.83	9.0:1	40–60 @ 2000
	U	6-183 (3.0)	EFI	145 @ 4800	165 @ 3600	3.50 × 3.14	9.3:1	40–60 @ 2500
	X	6-244 (4.0)	EFI	①	②	3.95 × 3.32	9.0:1	40–60 @ 2000

EFI—Electronic Fuel Injection
① 155 @ 4200—Explorer and Aerostar
  160 @ 4200—Ranger
② 215 @ 2400—Aerostar
  220 @ 2400—Explorer
  225 @ 2400—Ranger

ENGINE TUNE-UP SPECIFICATIONS

Year	VIN	No. Cylinder Displacement cu. in. (liter)	Spark Plugs Type	Gap (in.)	Ignition Timing (deg.) MT	AT	Compression Pressure (psi)	Fuel Pump (psi)	Idle Speed (rpm) MT	AT	Valve Clearance In.	Ex.
1988	C	4-122 (2.0)	AWSF-52C	0.044	6B	—	①	5–7	775–825	—	Hyd.	Hyd.
	A	4-140 (2.3)	AWSF-44C	0.044	10B	10B	①	35–45	②	645–795	Hyd.	Hyd.
	T	6-177 (2.9)	AWSF-42C	0.044	10B	10B	①	35–45	850	800	Hyd.	Hyd.
	U	6-183 (3.0)	AWSF-32P	0.044	10B	10B	①	35–45	②	②	Hyd.	Hyd.
1989	A	4-140 (2.3)	AWSF-32C	0.044	10B	10B	①	35–45	645–795	575–725	Hyd.	Hyd.
	T	6-177 (2.9)	AWSF-42C	0.044	10B	10B	①	35–45	850	800	Hyd.	Hyd.
	U	6-183 (3.0)	AWSF-32P	0.044	10B	10B	①	35–45	②	②	Hyd.	Hyd.
1990	A	4-140 (2.3)	AWSF-32C	0.044	10B	10B	①	35–45	645–795	575–725	Hyd.	Hyd.
	T	6-177 (2.9)	AWSF-42C	0.044	10B	10B	①	35–45	850	800	Hyd.	Hyd.
	U	6-183 (3.0)	AWSF-32P	0.044	10B	10B	①	35–45	②	②	Hyd.	Hyd.
	X	6-244 (4.0)	②	0.054	10B	10B	①	35–45	②	②	Hyd.	Hyd.
1991	A	4-140 (2.3)	AWSF-32C	0.044	10B	10B	①	35–45	②	575–725	Hyd.	Hyd.
	T	6-177 (2.9)	AWSF-42C	0.044	10B	10B	①	35–45	850	800	Hyd.	Hyd.
	U	6-183 (3.0)	AWSF-32P	0.044	10B	10B	①	35–45	②	②	Hyd.	Hyd.
	X	6-244 (4.0)	②	0.054	10B	10B	①	35–45	②	②	Hyd.	Hyd.
1992					SEE UNDERHOOD SPECIFICATION LABEL							

Hyd.—Hydraulic
① The compression pressure in the lowest cylinder must be at least 75% of that in the highest cylinder
② See Underhood Specification Label

FIRING ORDERS

NOTE: To avoid confusion, always replace spark plug wires one at a time.

1988 2.0L and 2.3L Engines
Engine Firing Order: 1–3–4–2
Distributor Rotation: Clockwise

FRONT OF CAR

1989–92 2.3L Engine
Engine Firing Order: 1–3–4–2
Distributorless Ignition System

2.9L and 3.0L Engines
Engine Firing Order: 1–4–2–5–3–6
Distributor Rotation: Clockwise

FRONT OF CAR

4.0L Engine
Engine Firing Order: 1–4–2–5–3–6
Distributorless Ignition System

CAPACITIES

Year	Model	VIN	No. Cylinder Displacement cu. in (liter)	Engine Crankcase with Filter	Engine Crankcase without Filter	Transmission (pts.) 4-Spd	Transmission (pts.) 5-Spd	Transmission (pts.) Auto.	Drive Axle (pts.)	Fuel Tank (gal.)	Cooling System (qts.)
1988	Aerostar	U	6-183 (3.0)	5.0	4.0	—	5.6	19	①	21	11.8
	Bronco II	T	6-177 (2.9)	5.0	4.0	—	②	③	④	23	⑤
	Ranger	C	4-122 (2.0)	5.0	4.0	—	②	—	④	⑥	6.5
	Ranger	A	4-140 (2.3)	5.0	4.0	—	②	19	④	⑥	⑦
	Ranger	T	6-177 (2.9)	5.0	4.0	—	②	③	④	⑥	⑤
1989	Aerostar	U	6-183 (3.0)	5.0	4.0	—	5.6	19.4	①	21	11.8
	Bronco II	T	6-177 (2.9)	5.0	4.0	—	②	⑧	④	23	⑤
	Ranger	A	4-140 (2.3)	5.0	4.0	—	②	19.4	⑨	⑩	⑦
	Ranger	T	6-177 (2.9)	5.0	4.0	—	②	⑧	⑨	⑩	⑤

CAPACITIES

Year	Model	VIN	No. Cylinder Displacement cu. in (liter)	Engine Crankcase with Filter	Engine Crankcase without Filter	Transmission (pts.) 4-Spd	Transmission (pts.) 5-Spd	Transmission (pts.) Auto.	Drive Axle (pts.)	Fuel Tank (gal.)	Cooling System (qts.)
1990	Aerostar	U	6-183 (3.0)	5.0	4.0	—	5.6	⑧	⑪	21	11.8
	Aerostar	X	6-244 (4.0)	5.0	4.0	—	5.6	⑧	⑪	21	⑫
	Bronco II	T	6-177 (2.9)	5.0	4.0	—	②	⑧	⑬	23	⑤
	Ranger	A	4-140 (2.3)	5.0	4.0	—	②	19.4	⑭	⑮	7.2
	Ranger	T	6-177 (2.9)	5.0	4.0	—	②	⑧	⑭	⑮	⑤
	Ranger	X	6-244 (4.0)	5.0	4.0	—	②	20.0	⑭	⑮	⑫
1991–92	Aerostar	U	6-183 (3.0)	5.0	4.0	—	5.6	⑧	⑪	21	11.8
	Aerostar	X	6-244 (4.0)	5.0	4.0	—	5.6	⑧	⑪	21	⑫
	Explorer	X	6-244 (4.0)	5.0	4.0	—	5.6	⑧	⑯	19.3	⑫
	Ranger	A	4-140 (2.3)	5.0	4.0	—	②	19.4	⑭	⑰	7.2
	Ranger	T	6-177 (2.9)	5.0	4.0	—	②	⑧	⑭	⑰	⑤
	Ranger	U	6-183 (3.0)	5.0	4.0	—	②	⑧	⑭	⑰	11.8
	Ranger	X	6-244 (4.0)	5.0	4.0	—	②	⑧	⑭	⑰	⑫

① Ford 7.5 in.—3.5
   Dana 30—2.5
② Mitsubishi 5 speed transmission—4.8
   Mazda M50D 5 speed transmission—5.6
③ 2WD—19
   4WD—20
④ Front axle—1.1
   Rear axle—5.5
⑤ Without air conditioning—7.2
   With air conditioning—7.8
⑥ Short wheel base vehicles—15.2
   Long wheel base vehicles—17.0
   Ranger supercab vehicles—14.5
   Auxiliary tank—13.0
⑦ Without air conditioning—6.5
   With air conditioning—7.2
⑧ 2WD—19.4
   4WD—20.0

⑨ Front axle—1.1
   Rear axle—5.0
⑩ Standard tank—17
   Optional tank—21
⑪ Front axle—2.2
   Rear axle
   Ford 7.5 in.—3.5
   Dana 35-1A—2.5
   Ford 8.8 in.—5.3
⑫ Standard cooling system,
   All transmissions and manual air
      conditioning—8.1
   Super cool with automatic transmission and
      air conditioning—8.5
⑬ Front axle:
   Dana 28—1.1
   Dana 35—3.5

   Rear axle—5.5
⑭ Front axle:
   Dana 28—1.1
   Dana 35—3.5
   Rear axle:
   Ford 7.5 in.—5.0
   Ford 8.8 in.—5.3
⑮ Short wheel base—17
   Long wheel base—17 or 21
   Ranger super cab—17 or 20
⑯ Front axle—3.5
   Rear axle—5.3
⑰ Standard tank except super cab—16.3
   Optional tank on long wheel base—19.6
   Super cab—19.6

CAMSHAFT SPECIFICATIONS
All measurements given in inches.

Year	VIN	No. Cylinder Displacement cu. in. (liter)	Journal Diameter 1	Journal Diameter 2	Journal Diameter 3	Journal Diameter 4	Journal Diameter 5	Lobe Lift In.	Lobe Lift Ex.	Bearing Clearance	Camshaft End Play
1988	C	4-122 (2.0)	1.7713–1.7720	1.7713–1.7720	1.7713–1.7720	1.7713–1.7720	—	0.2381	0.2381	0.0010–0.0030	0.0010–0.0070
	A	4-140 (2.3)	1.7713–1.7720	1.7713–1.7720	1.7713–1.7720	1.7713–1.7720	—	0.2381	0.2381	0.0010–0.0030	0.0010–0.0070
	T	6-177 (2.9)	1.7285–1.7293	1.7135–1.7143	1.6985–1.6992	1.6835–1.6842	—	NA	NA	0.0010–0.0026	0.0008–0.0040
	U	6-183 (3.0)	2.0074–2.0084	2.0074–2.0084	2.0074–2.0084	2.0074–2.0084	—	0.2600	0.2600	0.0010–0.0030	0.0070
1989	A	4-140 (2.3)	1.7713–1.7720	1.7713–1.7720	1.7713–1.7720	1.7713–1.7720	—	0.2381	0.2381	0.0010–0.0030	0.0010–0.0070
	T	6-177 (2.9)	1.7285–1.7293	1.7135–1.7143	1.6985–1.6992	1.6835–1.6842	—	NA	NA	0.0010–0.0026	0.0008–0.0040
	U	6-183 (3.0)	2.0074–2.0084	2.0074–2.0084	2.0074–2.0084	2.0074–2.0084	—	0.2600	0.2600	0.0010–0.0030	0.0070

CAMSHAFT SPECIFICATIONS

All measurements given in inches.

Year	VIN	No. Cylinder Displacement cu. in. (liter)	Journal Diameter					Lobe Lift		Bearing Clearance	Camshaft End Play
			1	2	3	4	5	In.	Ex.		
1990	A	4-140 (2.3)	1.7713–1.7720	1.7713–1.7720	1.7713–1.7720	1.7713–1.7720	—	0.2381	0.2381	0.0010–0.0030	0.0010–0.0070
	T	6-177 (2.9)	1.7285–1.7293	1.7135–1.7143	1.6985–1.6992	1.6835–1.6842	—	NA	NA	0.0010–0.0026	0.0008–0.0040
	U	6-183 (3.0)	2.0074–2.0084	2.0074–2.0084	2.0074–2.0084	2.0074–2.0084	—	0.2600	0.2600	0.0010–0.0030	0.0070
	X	6-244 (4.0)	1.9510–1.9520	1.9370–1.9380	1.9220–1.9230	1.9070–1.9080	—	NA	NA	0.0010–0.0026	0.0008–0.0040
1991–92	A	4-140 (2.3)	1.7713–1.7720	1.7713–1.7720	1.7713–1.7720	1.7713–1.7720	—	0.2381	0.2381	0.0010–0.0030	0.0010–0.0070
	T	6-177 (2.9)	1.7285–1.7293	1.7135–1.7143	1.6985–1.6992	1.6835–1.6842	—	NA	NA	0.0010–0.0026	0.0008–0.0040
	U	6-183 (3.0)	2.0074–2.0084	2.0074–2.0084	2.0074–2.0084	2.0074–2.0084	—	0.2600	0.2600	0.0010–0.0030	0.0070
	X	6-244 (4.0)	1.9510–1.9520	1.9370–1.9380	1.9220–1.9230	1.9070–1.9080	—	NA	NA	0.0010–0.0026	0.0008–0.0040

NA—Not available

CRANKSHAFT AND CONNECTING ROD SPECIFICATIONS

All measurements are given in inches.

Year	VIN	No. Cylinder Displacement cu. in. (liter)	Crankshaft				Connecting Rod		
			Main Brg. Journal Dia.	Main Brg. Oil Clearance	Shaft End-play	Thrust on No.	Journal Diameter	Oil Clearance	Side Clearance
1988	C	4-122 (2.0)	2.3982–2.3990	0.0008–0.0026	0.004–0.008	3	2.0462–2.0472	0.0008–0.0026	0.004–0.010
	A	4-140 (2.3)	2.3982–2.3990	0.0008–0.0026	0.004–0.008	3	2.0462–2.0472	0.0008–0.0026	0.004–0.010
	T	6-177 (2.9)	2.2433–2.2441	0.0005–0.0019	0.004–0.008	3	2.1252–2.1260	0.0005–0.0022	0.004–0.011
	U	6-183 (3.0)	2.5190–2.5198	0.0005–0.0023	0.004–0.008	3	2.1253–2.1261	0.0009–0.0027	0.006–0.014
1989	A	4-140 (2.3)	2.3982–2.3990	0.0008–0.0026	0.004–0.008	3	2.0462–2.0472	0.0008–0.0026	0.004–0.010
	T	6-177 (2.9)	2.2433–2.2441	0.0005–0.0019	0.004–0.008	3	2.1252–2.1260	0.0005–0.0022	0.004–0.011
	U	6-183 (3.0)	2.5190–2.5198	0.0005–0.0023	0.004–0.008	3	2.1253–2.1261	0.0009–0.0027	0.006–0.014
1990	A	4-140 (2.3)	2.3982–2.3990	0.0008–0.0026	0.004–0.008	3	2.0462–2.0472	0.0008–0.0026	0.004–0.010
	T	6-177 (2.9)	2.2433–2.2441	0.0005–0.0019	0.004–0.008	3	2.1252–2.1260	0.0005–0.0022	0.004–0.011
	U	6-183 (3.0)	2.5190–2.5198	0.0005–0.0023	0.004–0.008	3	2.1253–2.1261	0.0009–0.0027	0.006–0.014
	X	6-244 (4.0)	2.2433–2.2441	0.0005–0.0019	NA	3	2.1252–2.1260	0.0005–0.0022	NA

CRANKSHAFT AND CONNECTING ROD SPECIFICATIONS

All measurements are given in inches.

Year	VIN	No. Cylinder Displacement cu. in. (liter)	Crankshaft				Connecting Rod		
			Main Brg. Journal Dia.	Main Brg. Oil Clearance	Shaft End-play	Thrust on No.	Journal Diameter	Oil Clearance	Side Clearance
1991–92	A	4-140 (2.3)	2.2051–2.2059	0.0008–0.0026	0.004–0.008	3	2.0462–2.0472	0.0008–0.0026	0.004–0.010
	T	6-177 (2.9)	2.2433–2.2441	0.0005–0.0019	0.004–0.008	3	2.1252–2.1260	0.0005–0.0022	0.004–0.011
	U	6-183 (3.0)	2.5190–2.5198	0.0005–0.0023	0.004–0.008	3	2.1253–2.1261	0.0009–0.0027	0.006–0.014
	X	6-244 (4.0)	2.2433–2.2441	0.0005–0.0019	NA	3	2.1252–2.1260	0.0005–0.0022	NA

NA—Not available

VALVE SPECIFICATIONS

Year	VIN	No. Cylinder Displacement cu. in. (liter)	Seat Angle (deg.)	Face Angle (deg.)	Spring Test Pressure (lbs.)	Spring Installed Height (in.)	Stem-to-Guide Clearance (in.)		Stem Diameter (in.)	
							Intake	Exhaust	Intake	Exhaust
1988	C	4-122 (2.0)	45	44	128–142 @ 1.12 in.	1.49–1.55	0.0010–0.0027	0.0015–0.0032	0.3416–0.3423	0.3411–0.3418
	A	4-140 (2.3)	45	44	128–142 @ 1.12 in.	1.49–1.55	0.0010–0.0027	0.0015–0.0032	0.3416–0.3423	0.3411–0.3418
	T	6-177 (2.9)	45	44	138–149 @ 1.22 in.	1.58–1.61	0.0008–0.0025	0.0018–0.0035	0.3159–0.3167	0.3149–0.3156
	U	6-183 (3.0)	45	44	180 @ 1.16 in.	1.58	0.0010–0.0027	0.0015–0.0032	0.3126–0.3134	0.3121–0.3129
1989	A	4-140 (2.3)	45	44	128–142 @ 1.12 in.	1.49–1.55	0.0010–0.0027	0.0015–0.0032	0.3416–0.3423	0.3411–0.3418
	T	6-177 (2.9)	45	44	138–149 @ 1.22 in.	1.58–1.61	0.0008–0.0025	0.0018–0.0035	0.3159–0.3167	0.3149–0.3156
	U	6-183 (3.0)	45	44	180 @ 1.16 in.	1.58	0.0010–0.0027	0.0015–0.0032	0.3126–0.3134	0.3121–0.3129
1990	A	4-140 (2.3)	45	44	128–142 @ 1.12 in.	1.49–1.55	0.0010–0.0027	0.0015–0.0032	0.3416–0.3423	0.3411–0.3418
	T	6-177 (2.9)	45	44	138–149 @ 1.22 in.	1.58–1.61	0.0008–0.0025	0.0018–0.0035	0.3159–0.3167	0.3149–0.3156
	U	6-183 (3.0)	45	44	180 @ 1.16 in.	1.58	0.0010–0.0027	0.0015–0.0032	0.3126–0.3134	0.3121–0.3129
	X	6-244 (4.0)	45	44	138–1.49 @ 1.22 in.	1.58–1.61	0.0008–0.0025	0.0018–0.0035	0.3159–0.3167	0.3149–0.3156
1991–92	A	4-140 (2.3)	45	44	128–142 @ 1.12 in.	1.49–1.55	0.0010–0.0027	0.0015–0.0032	0.3416–0.3423	0.3411–0.3418
	T	6-177 (2.9)	45	44	138–149 @ 1.22 in.	1.58–1.61	0.0008–0.0025	0.0018–0.0035	0.3159–0.3167	0.3149–0.3156
	U	6-183 (3.0)	45	44	180 @ 1.16 in.	1.58	0.0010–0.0027	0.0015–0.0032	0.3126–0.3134	0.3121–0.3129
	X	6-244 (4.0)	45	44	138–149 @ 1.22 in.	1.58–1.61	0.0008–0.0025	0.0018–0.0035	0.3159–0.3167	0.3149–0.3156

PISTON AND RING SPECIFICATIONS

All measurements are given in inches.

Year	VIN	No. Cylinder Displacement cu. in. (liter)	Piston Clearance	Ring Gap			Ring Side Clearance		
				Top Compression	Bottom Compression	Oil Control	Top Compression	Bottom Compression	Oil Control
1988	C	4-122 (2.0)	0.0014–0.0022	0.0100–0.0200	0.0100–0.0200	0.0100–0.0490	0.0020–0.0040	0.0020–0.0040	Snug
	A	4-140 (2.3)	0.0014–0.0022	0.0100–0.0200	0.0100–0.0200	0.0100–0.0490	0.0020–0.0040	0.0020–0.0040	Snug
	T	6-177 (2.9)	0.0011–0.0019	0.0150–0.0230	0.0150–0.0230	0.0150–0.0550	0.0020–0.0033	0.0020–0.0033	Snug
	U	6-183 (3.0)	0.0012–0.0023	0.0100–0.0200	0.0100–0.0200	0.0100–0.0490	0.0016–0.0037	0.0016–0.0037	Snug
1989	A	4-140 (2.3)	0.0014–0.0022	0.0100–0.0200	0.0100–0.0200	0.0100–0.0490	0.0020–0.0040	0.0020–0.0040	Snug
	T	6-177 (2.9)	0.0011–0.0019	0.0150–0.0230	0.0150–0.0230	0.0150–0.0550	0.0020–0.0033	0.0020–0.0033	Snug
	U	6-183 (3.0)	0.0012–0.0023	0.0100–0.0200	0.0100–0.0200	0.0100–0.0490	0.0016–0.0037	0.0016–0.0037	Snug
1990	A	4-140 (2.3)	0.0014–0.0022	0.0100–0.0200	0.0100–0.0200	0.0100–0.0490	0.0020–0.0040	0.0020–0.0040	Snug
	T	6-177 (2.9)	0.0011–0.0019	0.0150–0.0230	0.0150–0.0230	0.0150–0.0550	0.0020–0.0033	0.0020–0.0033	Snug
	U	6-183 (3.0)	0.0012–0.0023	0.0100–0.0200	0.0100–0.0200	0.0100–0.0490	0.0016–0.0037	0.0016–0.0037	Snug
	X	6-244 (4.0)	0.0008–0.0019	0.0150–0.0230	0.0150–0.0230	0.0150–0.0550	0.0020–0.0033	0.0020–0.0033	Snug
1991–92	A	4-140 (2.3)	0.0024–0.0034	0.0100–0.0200	0.0100–0.0200	0.0150–0.0490	0.0016–0.0033	0.0016–0.0033	Snug
	T	6-177 (2.9)	0.0011–0.0019	0.0150–0.0230	0.0150–0.0230	0.0150–0.0550	0.0020–0.0033	0.0020–0.0033	Snug
	U	6-183 (3.0)	0.0012–0.0023	0.0100–0.0200	0.0100–0.0200	0.0100–0.0490	0.0016–0.0037	0.0016–0.0037	Snug
	X	6-244 (4.0)	0.0008–0.0019	0.0150–0.0230	0.0150–0.0230	0.0150–0.0550	0.0020–0.0033	0.0020–0.0033	Snug

TORQUE SPECIFICATIONS

All readings in ft. lbs.

Year	VIN	No. Cylinder Displacement cu. in. (liter)	Cylinder Head Bolts	Main Bearing Bolts	Rod Bearing Bolts	Crankshaft Pulley Bolts	Flywheel Bolts	Manifold		Spark Plugs
								Intake	Exhaust	
1988	C	4-122 (2.0)	①	②	③	103–133	59	④	⑤	10–15
	A	4-140 (2.3)	①	②	③	103–133	59	④	⑤	10–15
	T	6-177 (2.9)	⑥	65–75	19–24	85–96	47–52	⑦	20–30	10–15
	U	6-183 (3.0)	⑧	65–81	26	141–169	59	⑨	18	10–15
1989	A	4-140 (2.3)	①	②	③	103–133	59	④	⑤	10–15
	T	6-177 (2.9)	⑥	65–75	19–24	85–96	47–52	⑦	20–30	10–15
	U	6-183 (3.0)	⑧	60	26	107	59	⑨	19	10–15

TORQUE SPECIFICATIONS
All readings in ft. lbs.

Year	VIN	No. Cylinder Displacement cu. in. (liter)	Cylinder Head Bolts	Main Bearing Bolts	Rod Bearing Bolts	Crankshaft Pulley Bolts	Flywheel Bolts	Manifold Intake	Manifold Exhaust	Spark Plugs
1990	A	4-140 (2.3)	①	②	③	103–133	59	④	⑤	10–15
	T	6-177 (2.9)	⑥	65–75	19–24	85–96	47–52	⑦	20–30	10–15
	U	6-183 (3.0)	⑧	60	26	107	59	⑨	18	10–15
	X	6-244 (4.0)	⑪	66–77	19–24	⑫	59	⑦	19	10–15
1991–92	A	4-140 (2.3)	①	②	③	103–133	59	④	⑤	10–15
	T	6-177 (2.9)	⑥	65–75	19–24	85–96	47–52	⑦	20–30	10–15
	U	6-183 (3.0)	⑩	60	26	107	59	⑨	18	10–15
	X	6-244 (4.0)	⑪	66–77	19–24	⑫	59	⑦	19	10–15

① Tighten in 2 steps:
   Step 1: 50–60 ft. lbs.
   Step 2: 80–90 ft. lbs.
② Tighten in 2 steps:
   Step 1: 50–60 ft. lbs.
   Step 2: 75–85 ft. lbs.
③ Tighten in 2 steps:
   Step 1: 25–30 ft. lbs.
   Step 2: 30–36 ft. lbs.
④ Tighten in 2 steps:
   Step 1: 5–7 ft. lbs.
   Step 2: 15–22 ft. lbs.
⑤ Tighten in 2 steps:
   Step 1: 15–17 ft. lbs.
   Step 2: 20–30 ft. lbs.
⑥ Tighten in 4 steps:
   Step 1: 22 ft. lbs.
   Step 2: 51–55 ft. lbs.

   Step 3: Wait 5 minutes
   Step 4: Turn 90 degrees
⑦ Tighten in 4 steps:
   Step 1: 3–6 ft. lbs.
   Step 2: 6–11 ft. lbs.
   Step 3: 11–15 ft. lbs.
   Step 4: 15–18 ft. lbs.
⑧ Tighten in 2 steps:
   Step 1: 37 ft. lbs.
   Step 2: 68 ft. lbs.
⑨ Tighten in 2 steps:
   Step 1: 11 ft. lbs.
   Step 2: 19 ft. lbs.
⑩ Tighten in 4 steps:
   Step 1: 59 ft. lbs.
   Step 2: Back off 1 turn
   Step 3: 37 ft. lbs.
   Step 4: 68 ft. lbs.

⑪ Tighten in 7 steps:
   Step 1: Tighten cylinder head bolts
            to 44 ft. lbs.
   Step 2: Tighten intake manifold bolts
            to 3–6 ft. lbs.
   Step 3: Tighten cylinder head bolts
            to 59 ft. lbs.
   Step 4: Tighten intake manifold bolts
            to 6–11 ft. lbs.
   Step 5: Tighten cylinder head bolts
            another 85 degrees each
   Step 6: Tighten intake manifold bolts
            to 11–15 ft. lbs.
   Step 7: Tighten intake manifold bolts
            to 15–18 ft. lbs.
⑫ Tighten in 2 steps:
   Step 1: 30–37 ft. lbs.
   Step 2: Turn 90 degrees

BRAKE SPECIFICATIONS
All measurements in inches unless noted

Year	Model	Lug Nut Torque (ft. lbs.)	Master Cylinder Bore	Brake Disc Minimum Thickness	Brake Disc Maximum Runout	Standard Brake Drum Diameter	Minimum Lining Thickness Front	Minimum Lining Thickness Rear
1988	Aerostar	100	0.9375	0.81	0.003	①	0.12	0.030
	Bronco II	100	0.9375	0.81	0.003	②	0.12	0.030
	Ranger	100	0.9375	0.81	0.003	②	0.12	0.030
1989	Aerostar	100	0.9375	0.81	0.003	①	0.12	0.030
	Bronco II	100	0.9375	0.81	0.003	②	0.12	0.030
	Ranger	100	0.9375	0.81	0.003	②	0.12	0.030
1990	Aerostar	100	0.9375	0.81	0.003	①	0.12	0.030
	Bronco II	100	0.9375	0.81	0.003	②	0.12	0.030
	Ranger	100	0.9375	0.81	0.003	②	0.12	0.030
1991–92	Aerostar	100	0.9375	0.81	0.003	①	0.12	0.030
	Explorer	100	0.9375	0.81	0.003	②	0.12	0.030
	Ranger	100	0.9375	0.81	0.003	②	0.12	0.030

① Standard brakes—9.0
   Optional brakes—10.0
② Except 2WD Ranger Super Cab—9.0
   2WD Ranger Super Cab—10.0

WHEEL ALIGNMENT

Year	Model	Ride Height (in.)	Caster		Camber		Toe-in (in.)	Steering Axis Inclination (deg.)
			Range (deg.)	Preferred Setting (deg.)	Range (deg.)	Preferred Setting (deg.)		
1988	Aerostar	—	2¹/₂P–4¹/₂P	3¹/₂P	⁵/₁₆N–¹¹/₁₆P	³/₁₆P	¹/₃₂	NA
	Bronco II	2³/₄–3	5¹/₂P–8¹/₂P	NA	2N–¹/₂N	NA	¹/₃₂	NA
	Bronco II	3¹/₄–3¹/₂	4P–7P	NA	1N–¹/₂P	NA	¹/₃₂	NA
	Bronco II	3¹/₂–3³/₄	3P–6P	NA	0–1¹/₂P	NA	¹/₃₂	NA
	Bronco II	4–4¹/₄	2P–6P	NA	1P–2¹/₂P	NA	¹/₃₂	NA
	Bronco II	4¹/₄–4¹/₂	1P–4P	NA	2P–3¹/₂P	NA	¹/₃₂	NA
	Ranger 2WD ①	3¹/₄–3¹/₂	5¹/₄P–8¹/₄P	NA	2N–¹/₂N	NA	¹/₃₂	NA
	Ranger 2WD ①	3¹/₂–3³/₄	4¹/₂P–7¹/₂P	NA	1⁵/₈N–¹/₈N	NA	¹/₃₂	NA
	Ranger 2WD ①	3³/₄–4	3¹/₂P–6¹/₂P	NA	¹/₂N–1P	NA	¹/₃₂	NA
	Ranger 2WD ①	4–4¹/₄	3P–6P	NA	¹/₄P–1³/₄P	NA	¹/₃₂	NA
	Ranger 2WD ①	4¹/₂–4³/₄	1⁷/₈P–4⁷/₈P	NA	1¹/₄P–2³/₄P	NA	¹/₃₂	NA
	Ranger 2WD ②	3–3¹/₄	5¹/₄P–8¹/₄P	NA	2N–¹/₂N	NA	¹/₃₂	NA
	Ranger 2WD ②	3¹/₄–3¹/₂	4¹/₂P–7¹/₂P	NA	1⁵/₈N–¹/₈N	NA	¹/₃₂	NA
	Ranger 2WD ②	3¹/₂–3³/₄	3¹/₂P–6¹/₂P	NA	¹/₂N–1P	NA	¹/₃₂	NA
	Ranger 2WD ②	3³/₄–4	3P–6P	NA	¹/₄P–1³/₄P	NA	¹/₃₂	NA
	Ranger 2WD ②	4¹/₄–4¹/₂	1⁷/₈P–4⁷/₈P	NA	1¹/₄P–2³/₄P	NA	¹/₃₂	NA
	Ranger 4WD ③	2³/₄–3	5¹/₂P–8¹/₂P	NA	2N–¹/₂N	NA	¹/₃₂	NA
	Ranger 4WD ③	3¹/₄–3¹/₂	4P–7P	NA	1N–¹/₂N	NA	¹/₃₂	NA
	Ranger 4WD ③	3¹/₂–3³/₄	3P–6P	NA	0–1¹/₂P	NA	¹/₃₂	NA
	Ranger 4WD ③	4–4¹/₄	2P–5P	NA	1P–2¹/₂P	NA	¹/₃₂	NA
	Ranger 4WD ③	4¹/₄–4¹/₂	1P–4P	NA	2P–3¹/₂P	NA	¹/₃₂	NA
	Ranger 4WD ④	4¹/₄–4¹/₂	5¹/₂P–8¹/₂P	NA	2N–¹/₂N	NA	¹/₃₂	NA
	Ranger 4WD ④	4¹/₂–5	4P–7P	NA	1N–¹/₂P	NA	¹/₃₂	NA
	Ranger 4WD ④	5–5¹/₄	3P–6P	NA	0–1¹/₂P	NA	¹/₃₂	NA
	Ranger 4WD ④	5¹/₄–5³/₄	2P–5P	NA	1P–2¹/₂P	NA	¹/₃₂	NA
	Ranger 4WD ④	5³/₄–6	1P–4P	NA	2P–3¹/₂P	NA	¹/₃₂	NA
1989	Aerostar	—	2¹/₂P–4¹/₂P	3¹/₂P	⁵/₁₆N–¹¹/₁₆P	³/₁₆P	¹/₃₂	NA
	Bronco II	2³/₄–3	5¹/₄P–8P	NA	2N–¹/₂P	NA	0	NA
	Bronco II	3¹/₄–3¹/₂	4P–6¹/₂P	NA	⁷/₈N–1³/₄P	NA	0	NA
	Bronco II	3¹/₂–3³/₄	3¹/₄P–6P	NA	¹/₄N–2³/₈P	NA	0	NA
	Bronco II	3³/₄–4	2⁵/₈P–5¹/₄P	NA	³/₈P–2⁷/₈P	NA	0	NA
	Bronco II	4–4¹/₄	1⁷/₈P–4⁵/₈P	NA	⁷/₈P–3¹/₂P	NA	0	NA
	Bronco II	4¹/₄–4¹/₂	1¹/₈P–3⁷/₈P	NA	1¹/₂P–4¹/₄P	NA	0	NA
	Ranger 2WD	3¹/₄–3¹/₂	6¹/₈P–8³/₄P	NA	1¹/₂N–1P	NA	0	NA
	Ranger 2WD	3¹/₂–3³/₄	5¹/₂P–8¹/₈P	NA	1N–1³/₄P	NA	0	NA
	Ranger 2WD	3³/₄–4	4⁵/₈P–7¹/₂P	NA	¹/₄N–2³/₈P	NA	0	NA
	Ranger 2WD	4–4¹/₄	3³/₄P–6⁵/₈P	NA	³/₈P–3P	NA	0	NA
	Ranger 2WD	4¹/₄–4¹/₂	3¹/₄P–5³/₄P	NA	1P–4P	NA	0	NA
	Ranger 2WD	4¹/₂–4³/₄	2¹/₂P–5¹/₄P	NA	2P–4⁵/₈P	NA	0	NA
	Ranger 4WD ③	2³/₄–3	5¹/₄P–8P	NA	2N–¹/₂P	NA	0	NA
	Ranger 4WD ③	3¹/₄–3¹/₂	4P–6¹/₂P	NA	⁷/₈N–1³/₄P	NA	0	NA
	Ranger 4WD ③	3¹/₂–3³/₄	3¹/₄P–6P	NA	¹/₄N–2³/₈P	NA	0	NA

WHEEL ALIGNMENT

Year	Model	Ride Height (in.)	Caster Range (deg.)	Caster Preferred Setting (deg.)	Camber Range (deg.)	Camber Preferred Setting (deg.)	Toe-in (in.)	Steering Axis Inclination (deg.)
1989	Ranger 4WD③	3³⁄₄–4	2⁵⁄₈P–5¹⁄₄P	NA	³⁄₈P–2⁷⁄₈P	NA	0	NA
	Ranger 4WD③	4–4¹⁄₄	1⁷⁄₈P–4⁵⁄₈P	NA	⁷⁄₈P–3¹⁄₂P	NA	0	NA
	Ranger 4WD③	4¹⁄₄–4¹⁄₂	1¹⁄₈P–3⁷⁄₈P	NA	1¹⁄₂P–4¹⁄₄P	NA	0	NA
	Ranger 4WD④	4¹⁄₄–4¹⁄₂	5¹⁄₈P–8P	NA	2N–³⁄₈P	NA	0	NA
	Ranger 4WD④	4¹⁄₂–5	3³⁄₄P–7¹⁄₈P	NA	1⁵⁄₈N–1⁷⁄₈P	NA	0	NA
	Ranger 4WD④	5–5¹⁄₄	3¹⁄₈P–5³⁄₄P	NA	¹⁄₈N–2¹⁄₂P	NA	0	NA
	Ranger 4WD④	5¹⁄₄–5¹⁄₂	2¹⁄₂P–5¹⁄₈P	NA	¹⁄₂P–3¹⁄₂P	NA	0	NA
	Ranger 4WD④	5¹⁄₂–5³⁄₄	1³⁄₄P–4¹⁄₂P	NA	1¹⁄₄P–3⁵⁄₈P	NA	0	NA
	Ranger 4WD④	5³⁄₄–6	1P–3³⁄₄P	NA	1⁵⁄₈P–4¹⁄₄P	NA	0	NA
1990	Aerostar 2WD	—	2¹⁄₂P–4¹⁄₂P	3¹⁄₂P	³⁄₄N–³⁄₄P	0	¹⁄₃₂	NA
	Aerostar 4WD	—	2¹⁄₂P–4¹⁄₂P	3¹⁄₂P	³⁄₄N–³⁄₄P	0	¹⁄₃₂	NA
	Bronco II	2³⁄₄–3	5¹⁄₄P–8P	NA	2N–¹⁄₂P	NA	0	NA
	Bronco II	3¹⁄₄–3¹⁄₂	4P–6¹⁄₂P	NA	⁷⁄₈N–1³⁄₄P	NA	0	NA
	Bronco II	3¹⁄₂–3³⁄₄	3¹⁄₄P–6P	NA	¹⁄₄N–2³⁄₄P	NA	0	NA
	Bronco II	3³⁄₄–4	2⁵⁄₈P–5¹⁄₄P	NA	³⁄₈P–2⁷⁄₈P	NA	0	NA
	Bronco II	4–4¹⁄₄	1⁷⁄₈P–4⁵⁄₈P	NA	⁷⁄₈P–3¹⁄₂P	NA	0	NA
	Bronco II	4¹⁄₄–4¹⁄₂	1¹⁄₈P–3⁷⁄₈P	NA	1¹⁄₂P–4¹⁄₄P	NA	0	NA
	Ranger 2WD	3¹⁄₄–3¹⁄₂	6¹⁄₈P–8³⁄₄P	NA	1¹⁄₂N–1P	NA	0	NA
	Ranger 2WD	3¹⁄₂–3³⁄₄	5¹⁄₂P–8¹⁄₈P	NA	1N–1³⁄₄P	NA	0	NA
	Ranger 2WD	3³⁄₄–4	4⁵⁄₈P–7¹⁄₂P	NA	¹⁄₄N–2³⁄₈P	NA	0	NA
	Ranger 2WD	4–4¹⁄₄	3³⁄₄P–6⁵⁄₈P	NA	³⁄₈P–3P	NA	0	NA
	Ranger 2WD	4¹⁄₄–4¹⁄₂	3¹⁄₄P–5³⁄₄P	NA	1P–4P	NA	0	NA
	Ranger 2WD	4¹⁄₂–4³⁄₄	2¹⁄₂P–5¹⁄₄P	NA	2P–4⁵⁄₈P	NA	0	NA
	Ranger 4WD③	2³⁄₄–3	5¹⁄₄P–8P	NA	2N–¹⁄₂P	NA	0	NA
	Ranger 4WD③	3¹⁄₄–3¹⁄₂	4P–6¹⁄₂P	NA	⁷⁄₈N–1³⁄₄P	NA	0	NA
	Ranger 4WD③	3¹⁄₂–3³⁄₄	3¹⁄₄P–6P	NA	¹⁄₄N–2³⁄₈P	NA	0	NA
	Ranger 4WD③	3³⁄₄–4	2⁵⁄₈P–5¹⁄₄P	NA	³⁄₈P–2⁷⁄₈P	NA	0	NA
	Ranger 4WD③	4–4¹⁄₄	1⁷⁄₈P–4⁵⁄₈P	NA	⁷⁄₈P–3¹⁄₂P	NA	0	NA
	Ranger 4WD③	4¹⁄₄–4¹⁄₂	1¹⁄₈P–3⁷⁄₈P	NA	1¹⁄₂P–4¹⁄₄P	NA	0	NA
	Ranger 4WD④	4–4¹⁄₄	5¹⁄₈P–8P	NA	2P–³⁄₈P	NA	0	NA
	Ranger 4WD④	4¹⁄₂–5	3³⁄₄P–7¹⁄₈P	NA	1⁵⁄₈N–1⁷⁄₈P	NA	0	NA
	Ranger 4WD④	5–5¹⁄₄	3¹⁄₈P–5³⁄₄P	NA	¹⁄₈N–2¹⁄₂P	NA	0	NA
	Ranger 4WD④	5¹⁄₄–5¹⁄₂	2¹⁄₂P–5¹⁄₈P	NA	¹⁄₂P–3¹⁄₂P	NA	0	NA
	Ranger 4WD④	5¹⁄₂–5³⁄₄	1³⁄₄P–4¹⁄₂P	NA	1¹⁄₄P–3⁵⁄₈P	NA	0	NA
	Ranger 4WD④	5³⁄₄–6	1P–3³⁄₄P	NA	1⁵⁄₈P–4¹⁄₄P	NA	0	NA
1991–92	Aerostar 2WD	—	2¹⁄₂P–4¹⁄₂P	3¹⁄₂P	³⁄₄N–³⁄₄P	0	¹⁄₃₂	NA
	Aerostar 4WD	—	2¹⁄₂P–4¹⁄₂P	3¹⁄₂P	³⁄₄N–³⁄₄P	0	¹⁄₃₂	NA
	Explorer 2WD	1¹⁄₂–2	12P–14P	NA	5¹⁄₈N–3¹⁄₈N	NA	0	NA
	Explorer 2WD	2–2¹⁄₂	10P–12P	NA	3¹⁄₂N–1¹⁄₂N	NA	0	NA
	Explorer 2WD	2¹⁄₂–3	8P–10P	NA	2¹⁄₂N–¹⁄₂N	NA	0	NA
	Explorer 2WD	3–3¹⁄₂	6¹⁄₄P–8¹⁄₄P	NA	1¹⁄₂N–¹⁄₂P	NA	0	NA
	Explorer 2WD	3¹⁄₂–4	5¹⁄₄P–7¹⁄₄P	NA	¹⁄₂N–1¹⁄₂P	NA	0	NA

WHEEL ALIGNMENT

Year	Model	Ride Height (in.)	Caster Range (deg.)	Caster Preferred Setting (deg.)	Camber Range (deg.)	Camber Preferred Setting (deg.)	Toe-in (in.)	Steering Axis Inclination (deg.)
1991–92	Explorer 2WD	4–4½	3¾P–5¾P	NA	½N–2½P	NA	0	NA
	Explorer 2WD	4½–5	2¼P–4¼P	NA	1½P–3½P	NA	0	NA
	Explorer 4WD	1½–2	10P–12P	NA	5¾N–3¾N	NA	0	NA
	Explorer 4WD	2–2½	8P–10P	NA	4½N–2½N	NA	0	NA
	Explorer 4WD	2½–3	6P–8P	NA	3N–1N	NA	0	NA
	Explorer 4WD	3–3½	4½P–6½P	NA	1N–1P	NA	0	NA
	Explorer 4WD	3½–4	3¼P–5¼P	NA	½P–2½P	NA	0	NA
	Explorer 4WD	4–4½	2¾P–4¾P	NA	1¾P–3¾P	NA	0	NA
	Explorer 4WD	4½–5	½P–2½P	NA	3½P–5½P	NA	0	NA
	Ranger 2WD	3¼–3½	6⅛P–8¾P	NA	1½N–1P	NA	0	NA
	Ranger 2WD	3½–3¾	5½P–8⅛P	NA	1N–1¾P	NA	0	NA
	Ranger 2WD	3¾–4	4⅝P–7½P	NA	¼N–2⅜P	NA	0	NA
	Ranger 2WD	4–4¼	3¾P–6⅝P	NA	⅜P–3P	NA	0	NA
	Ranger 2WD	4¼–4½	3¼P–5¾P	NA	1P–4P	NA	0	NA
	Ranger 2WD	4½–4¾	2½P–5¼P	NA	2P–4⅝P	NA	0	NA
	Ranger 4WD	2–2½	9¾P–11¾P	NA	6¼N–4¼N	NA	0	NA
	Ranger 4WD	2½–3	8¾P–10¾P	NA	4¼N–2¼N	NA	0	NA
	Ranger 4WD	3–3½	7⅜P–9⅜P	NA	2N–0	NA	0	NA
	Ranger 4WD	3¾–4	5½P–7½P	NA	¼N–1¾P	NA	0	NA
	Ranger 4WD	4–4½	4P–6P	NA	1¼P–3¼P	NA	0	NA
	Ranger 4WD	4½–5	2½P–4½P	NA	2¾P–4¾P	NA	0	NA
	Ranger 4WD	5–5½	1¼P–3¼P	NA	4P–6P	NA	0	NA

NA—Not available
P—Positive
N—Negative
① With forged axle
② With stamped axle
③ Except STX
④ STX

ENGINE ELECTRICAL

NOTE: **Disconnecting the negative battery cable on some vehicles may interfere with the functions of the on board computer systems and may require the computer to undergo a relearning process, once the negative battery cable is reconnected.**

Distributor

Removal

1. Disconnect the negative battery cable. If equipped with the 2.0L engine, remove 1 alternator mounting bolt and the drive belt; swing the alternator to 1 side.

2. Remove the distributor cap and position aside. If it is necessary to remove the spark plug wires, tag each wire and mark it's position on the distributor cap.

3. Disconnect the electrical connector from the distributor. If equipped, disconnect and plug the vacuum advance hose.

4. Mark the position of the rotor in relation to the distributor housing and mark the position of the distributor housing in relation to the intake manifold or cylinder block.

5. Remove the distributor hold-down clamp and bolt and remove the distributor.

Installation

TIMING NOT DISTURBED

1. Install the distributor assembly, aligning the marks that were made during the removal procedure.

2. Install the distributor hold-down clamp and bolt and leave it snug.

3. Connect the electrical connector to the distributor.

4. Install the distributor cap. If the spark plug wires were removed, install them in their proper position, as marked during the removal procedure.

5. Connect the negative battery cable. Check the initial timing according to the proper procedure.

6. Adjust the timing, as necessary and tighten the distributor hold-down bolt. Connect the vacuum advance hose, if equipped.

TIMING DISTURBED

1. Disconnect the No. 1 spark plug wire and remove the No. 1 spark plug.

2. Place a finger over the spark plug hole and crank the engine slowly until compression is felt.

3. Align the TDC mark on the crankshaft pulley with the pointer on the timing cover. This places the No. 1 cylinder at TDC on the compression stroke.

4. Turn the distributor shaft until the rotor points to the No. 1 spark plug tower on the cap.

5. Install the distributor into the engine, aligning the marks made on the block or intake manifold and the distributor housing. Install the distributor hold-down clamp and bolt. Snug the bolt so the distributor housing can be moved for timing purposes.

6. Install the No. 1 spark plug and connect the spark plug wire. Install the distributor cap and connect the distributor electrical connector. If the spark plug wires were removed, install them in their proper position, as marked during the removal procedure.

7. Connect the negative battery cable and set the ignition timing. Tighten the distributor hold-down clamp bolt and recheck the ignition timing after tightening the bolt.

8. If equipped, connect the vacuum advance hose.

Distributorless Ignition

Removal and Installation

CRANKSHAFT SENSOR

2.3L Engine

1. Disconnect the negative battery cable.

2. Disconnect the crankshaft timing sensor assembly electrical connectors from the engine harness.

3. Remove the large electrical connector from the crankshaft timing sensor assembly by prying out the red retaining clip and removing the 4 wires.

4. Remove the crankshaft pulley assembly by removing the accessory drive belts and then the 4 bolts that retain it to the crankshaft pulley hub assembly.

5. Remove the timing belt outer cover.

6. Rotate the crankshaft so the keyway is at the 10 o'clock position. This will place the vane window of both inner and outer vane cups over the crankshaft timing sensor assembly.

NOTE: The vane cups are attached to the crankshaft pulley hub assembly.

7. Remove the 2 crankshaft timing sensor assembly retaining bolts and the plastic wire harness retainer which secures the crankshaft timing sensor harness to it's mounting bracket. Then remove the crankshaft timing sensor assembly, sliding the electrical wires out from behind the inner timing belt cover.

To install:

8. Remove the large electrical connector from the new crankshaft timing sensor assembly.

9. Position the crankshaft timing sensor assembly. First slide the electrical wires behind the inner timing belt cover. Then, hold the sensor assembly loosely in place with the retaining bolts, but do not tighten at this time.

10. Install the large electrical connector onto the crankshaft timing sensor assembly.

NOTE: Make sure the 4 wires to the large electrical connector are installed in the proper locations. The sensor will not function properly if the wires are installed in the wrong locations.

Positioning the crankshaft sensor—2.3L engine

11. Reconnect both of the crankshaft timing sensor electrical connectors to the engine harness.

12. Rotate the crankshaft so the outer vane on the crankshaft pulley hub assembly engages both sides of the crankshaft Hall effect sensor positioner tool T89P–6316–A or equivalent, and tighten the sensor assembly retaining bolts.

13. Rotate the crankshaft so the vane on the crankshaft pulley hub assembly is no longer engaged in the positioning tool. Remove the tool.

14. Install the new plastic wire harness retainer to secure the crankshaft timing sensor harness to it's mounting bracket. Trim off the excess.

15. Install the timing belt outer cover.

16. Install the crankshaft pulley assembly and tighten the 4 attaching bolts to 15–22 ft. lbs. (20–30 Nm). Install the accessory drive belts.

4.0L Engine

1. Disconnect the negative battery cable.

2. Disconnect the sensor electrical connector from the wiring harness.

3. Remove the crankshaft sensor mounting screws and remove the sensor.

4. Installation is the reverse of the removal procedure. Tighten the screws to 75–106 inch lbs. (8.5–12 Nm).

IGNITION MODULE

2.3L Engine

1. Disconnect the negative battery cable.

2. Disconnect the electrical connectors at the module.

3. Remove the module retaining screws and remove the module from the lower intake manifold.

To install:

4. Apply an even coating of silicone dielectric compound WA–10, D7AZ–19A331–A or equivalent, to the mounting surface of the module.

5. Install the module and the retaining screws. Tighten the screws to 22–31 inch lbs. (2.5–3.5 Nm).

6. Connect the electrical connectors to the module and connect the negative battery cable.

4.0L Engine

1. On Aerostar, disconnect the negative battery cable.

2. On Explorer and Ranger, disconnect the battery cables and remove the battery.

3. Disconnect the electrical connector at the module.

4. Remove the module retaining bolt and remove the module. On Ranger, slide the assembly up; on Aerostar slide toward the

front of the vehicle, to release the module from the tear-drop hole in the sheet metal.

5. Installation is the reverse of the removal procedure. Tighten the mounting bolt to 22–31 inch lbs. (2.5–3.5 Nm).

IGNITION COIL PACK

2.3L Engine

1. Disconnect the negative battery cable.
2. Squeeze the locking tabs of the coil wire retainer by hand and remove the spark plug wires with a twisting and pulling motion. Do not pull on the wire.
3. Disconnect the engine harness electrical connector from the ignition coil assembly.
4. Remove the ignition coil assembly by removing the 4 retaining screws.

NOTE: If equipped with power steering, it may be necessary to remove the intake coil and bracket as an assembly.

5. Installation is the reverse of the removal procedure.

4.0L Engine

1. Disconnect the negative battery cable.
2. Disconnect the electrical harness connector from the coil pack.
3. Remove the spark plug wires by squeezing the locking tabs to release the coil boot retainers.
4. Remove the coil pack retaining screws and remove the coil pack.
5. Installation is the reverse of the removal procedure. Tighten the screws to 40–62 inch lbs. (4.5–7.0 Nm).

Distributorless ignition system—2.3L engine

Ignition Timing

Adjustment

NOTE: Always refer to the Vehicle Emission Information Label to verify the timing adjustment procedure.

DISTRIBUTORLESS IGNITION SYSTEM

Base timing for distributorless engines is set from the factory at 10 degrees BTDC and is not adjustable.

DISTRIBUTOR IGNITION SYSTEM

1. Place automatic transmission in **P** or manual transmission in neutral. The air conditioning and heater controls should be in the **OFF** position.
2. On 2.0L engine, disconnect the distributor vacuum advance hose from the distributor and plug the hose.
3. Connect a suitable inductive timing light and a tachometer according to the manufacturer's instructions.
4. On all except 2.0L engine, disconnect the single wire in-line spout connector or remove the shorting bar from the double wire spout connector.
5. On 2.0L engine, if equipped with a barometric pressure switch, disconnect it from the ignition module and place a jumper wire across the pins at the ignition module connector (yellow and black wires).
6. Start the engine and bring to normal operating temperature.

NOTE: To set timing correctly, a remote starter should not be used. Use the ignition key only to start the vehicle. Disconnecting the start wire at the starter relay will cause the TFI module to revert to start mode timing after the vehicle is started. Reconnecting the start wire after the vehicle is running will not correct the timing.

7. With the engine at the timing rpm specified, check the initial timing by aiming the timing light at the timing marks and pointer. Refer to the underhood Vehicle Emission Information Label for specifications.
8. If the marks align, proceed to Step 9. If the marks do not align, shut off the engine and loosen the distributor hold-down clamp bolt. Start the engine, aim the timing light and turn the distributor until the timing marks align. Shut off the engine and tighten the distributor hold-down clamp bolt.
9. On all except 2.0L engine, reconnect the single wire in-line spout connector or reinstall the shorting bar on the double wire spout connector. Check the timing advance to verify the distributor is advancing beyond the initial setting.
10. Remove the timing light and tachometer.
11. On 2.0L engine, reconnect the vacuum advance hose at the distributor and, if equipped, remove the jumper wire and reconnect the barometric pressure switch.

Alternator

For further information, please refer to "Alternators" in the Unit Repair section.

Precautions

Several precautions must be observed with alternator equipped vehicles to avoid damage to the unit.

- If the battery is removed for any reason, make sure it is reconnected with the correct polarity. Reversing the battery connections may result in damage to the one-way rectifiers.
- When utilizing a booster battery as a starting aid, always connect the positive to positive terminals and the negative terminal from the booster battery to a good engine ground on the vehicle being started.
- Never use a fast charger as a booster to start vehicles.
- Disconnect the battery cables when charging the battery with a fast charger.
- Never attempt to polarize the alternator.
- Do not use test lights of more than 12V when checking diode continuity.
- Do not short across or ground any of the alternator terminals.
- The polarity of the battery, alternator and regulator must be matched and considered before making any electrical connections within the system.
- Never separate the alternator on an open circuit. Make sure all connections within the circuit are clean and tight.
- Disconnect the battery ground terminal when performing any service on electrical components.
- Disconnect the battery if arc welding is to be done on the vehicle.

Belt Tension Adjustment

NOTE: On 4.0L engine, belt tension is maintained by an automatic tensioner. No adjustment is necessary.

1. Disconnect the negative battery cable. Loosen the alternator adjustment and pivot bolts.
2. Position a suitable belt tension gauge on an accessible belt span mid-way between the 2 pulleys.
3. Position the alternator housing using a suitable tool to attain correct belt tension. Be careful not to damage the alternator housing.
4. The correct belt tension for a new belt should be 150–190 lbs. on all except 2.9L engine. New belt tension on 2.9L engine should be 120–160 lbs. The correct belt tension for a used belt should be 140–160 lbs., on all except 2.9L engine. Used belt tension on 2.9L engine should be 110–130 lbs.

NOTE: A used belt has more than 10 minutes of operation.

5. Tighten the adjustment bolt and release the pressure. Tighten the pivot bolt.
6. Check the belt tension and reset, if necessary.

Removal and Installation

1. Disconnect the negative battery cable.
2. Disconnect the electrical connectors from the alternator.
3. On all except 4.0L engine, loosen the alternator pivot bolt and remove the adjustment arm bolt. Remove the drive belt from the alternator pulley.
4. On 4.0L engine, loosen the drive belt tensioner and remove the drive belt from the alternator pulley.
5. Remove the pivot bolt or the mounting bolts and remove the alternator. Remove the alternator fan shield, if equipped.
6. Installation is the reverse of the removal procedure. Adjust the belt tension, if required.

Starter

For further information, please refer to "Starters" in the Unit Repair section.

Removal and Installation

1. Disconnect the negative battery cable.
2. Raise the vehicle and support it safely.
3. Disconnect the starter cable and, if equipped, the relay connector from the starter.
4. Remove the starter mounting bolts and remove the starter.
5. Installation is the reverse of the removal procedure. Tighten the mounting bolts to 15–20 ft. lbs. (20–27 Nm).

CHASSIS ELECTRICAL

Heater Blower Motor

Removal and Installation

WITHOUT AIR CONDITIONING

1. Disconnect the negative battery cable.
2. Remove the air cleaner or air inlet duct, as necessary.
3. On Aerostar, remove the 2 screws attaching the vacuum reservoir to the blower assembly and remove the reservoir.
4. Disconnect the wire harness connector from the blower motor by pushing down on the connector tabs and pulling the connector off of the motor.
5. Disconnect the blower motor cooling tube at the blower motor.
6. Remove the 3 screws attaching the blower motor and wheel to the heater blower assembly.
7. Holding the cooling tube aside, pull the blower motor and wheel from the heater blower assembly and remove it from the vehicle.
8. Remove the blower wheel push-nut or clamp from the motor shaft and pull the blower wheel from the motor shaft.

To install:

9. Install the blower wheel on the blower motor shaft.
10. Install the hub clamp or push-nut.
11. Holding the cooling tube aside, position the blower motor and wheel on the heater blower assembly and install the 3 attaching screws.
12. Connect the blower motor cooling tube and the wire harness connector.
13. On Aerostar, install the vacuum reservoir on the hoses with the 2 screws.
14. Install the air cleaner or air inlet duct, as necessary.
15. Connect the negative battery cable and check the system for proper operation.

WITH AIR CONDITIONING

1. Disconnect the negative battery cable.
2. In the engine compartment, disconnect the wire harness from the motor by pushing down on the tab while pulling the connection off at the motor.
3. Remove the air cleaner or air inlet duct, as necessary.
4. On Bronco II, Explorer and Ranger, remove the solenoid box cover retaining bolts and the solenoid box cover, if equipped.
5. Disconnect the blower motor cooling tube from the blower motor.
6. Remove the 3 blower motor mounting plate attaching screws and remove the motor and wheel assembly from the evaporator assembly blower motor housing.
7. Remove the blower motor hub clamp from the motor shaft and pull the blower wheel from the shaft.

To install:

8. Install the blower motor wheel on the blower motor shaft and install a new hub clamp.
9. Install a new motor mounting seal on the blower housing before installing the blower motor.
10. Position the blower motor and wheel assembly in the blower housing and install the 3 attaching screws.
11. Connect the blower motor cooling tube.
12. Connect the electrical wire harness hardshell connector to the blower motor by pushing into place.
13. On Bronco II, Explorer and Ranger, position the solenoid box cover, if equipped, into place and install the 3 retaining screws.
14. Install the air cleaner or air inlet duct, as necessary.
15. Connect the negative battery cable and check the blower motor in all speeds for proper operation.

Blower motor installation—Bronco II, Explorer and Ranger

Front wiper motor installation—Aerostar

Window Wiper Motor

Removal and Installation

FRONT

Aerostar

1. Turn the wiper switch **ON**. Turn the ignition switch to **RUN** until the wiper blades are in midpattern, then turn the ignition switch to **OFF** to keep the blades in this position.
2. Disconnect the negative battery cable, then disconnect the electrical connector from the wiper motor.
3. Remove both wiper arms and remove the cowl grille.
4. Remove the linkage retaining clip and disconnect the linkage from the motor crank arm.

5. Remove the motor retaining nuts while holding the motor to keep it from falling.

6. Installation is the reverse of the removal procedure.

Bronco II, Explorer and Ranger

1. Turn the wiper switch **ON**. Turn the ignition switch **ON** until the blades are straight up, then turn the ignition **OFF** to keep them there.

2. Disconnect the negative battery cable, then disconnect the electrical connector from the wiper motor.

3. Remove the right wiper arm and blade assembly. Remove the right pivot nut and allow the linkage to drop into the cowl.

4. Remove the linkage access cover, located on the right side of the dash panel, near the wiper motor.

5. Reach through the access cover opening and unsnap the wiper motor clip. Push the clip away from the linkage until it clears the nib on the crank pin, then push the clip off the linkage. Remove the linkage from the crank pin.

6. Remove the 3 attaching screws and remove the wiper motor.

To install:

7. Install the motor with the attaching screws. Tighten to 60–85 inch lbs. (6.8–9.6 Nm). Connect the motor electrical connector.

8. Install the clip completely onto the right linkage, making sure it is fully seated. Do not put the linkage on the motor crank pin and then try to install the clip.

9. Install the left and right linkage onto the wiper motor crank pin. Pull the linkage onto the crank pin until it snaps into place. The clip is properly installed if the nib is protruding through the center of the clip.

10. Install the right wiper pivot shaft and nut. Tighten the nut to 84–110 inch lbs. (9.5–12.5 Nm).

11. Connect the negative battery cable and turn the ignition **ON**. Turn the wiper switch **OFF** so the wiper motor will park, then turn the ignition **OFF**. Install the right linkage access cover.

12. Install the right wiper blade and arm assembly and test the system.

REAR

Aerostar

1. Disconnect the negative battery cable.

2. Remove the wiper arm.

3. Remove the motor shaft attaching nut and wedge block. Remove the liftgate trim panel.

4. Disconnect the electrical connector and remove the motor wiring pins from the inner panel. Remove the motor.

To install:

5. Position the motor so the motor shaft protrudes through the hole in the outer panel. Attach the motor to the liftgate panel with the bracket attaching screws but do not tighten at this time.

6. Install the rubber seal and wedge block over the shaft and install the pivot attaching nut. Tighten to 5.0–5.8 ft. lbs. (6.8–7.9 Nm). Tighten the motor bracket attaching screw to 5.5–6.3 ft. lbs. (7.5–8.5 Nm).

7. Attach the motor wiring to the liftgate inner panel by installing the wiring pushpins in the holes.

8. Install the articulating arm onto the drive pivot shaft.

9. Connect the negative battery cable and turn the ignition switch **ON**. Operate the wiper switch to cycle and park the wiper system in order to ensure the system linkage is in the **PARK** position before the wiper arm is installed.

10. Locate the blade in the proper position and install the arm onto the shaft with the slide latch in the unlocked position.

11. While applying a downward pressure on the arm head to ensure full seating, raise the other end of the arm sufficiently to allow the latch to slide under the pivot to the locked position. Use finger pressure only to slide the latch, then release the arm and blade against the rear window.

Bronco II and Explorer

1. Disconnect the negative battery cable.

2. Remove the wiper arm and blade assembly.

3. On Bronco II, remove the pivot shaft attaching nut washer and gasket.

4. Remove the liftgate inner trim panel.

5. On Bronco II, remove the motor bracket attaching screw and rectangular plate. On Explorer, remove the 3 motor bracket attaching screws and pull the motor and bracket assembly out of the rubber grommet.

6. Disconnect the electrical connector and disengage the wiring locator pins. Remove the motor.

To install:

7. On Bronco II, position the motor in the liftgate and loosely install the rectangular plate and attaching screw, but do not tighten at this time.

8. On Explorer, position the motor in the liftgate rubber grommet and install the attaching screws.

9. On Bronco II, install the gasket, washer and nut. Tighten the nut to 60–69 inch lbs. (6.8–7.9 Nm). Tighten the motor bracket attaching screw to 5–6 ft. lbs. (7.5–8.5 Nm).

10. Connect the electrical connector and install the wiring locator pins in the holes provided.

11. Install the wiper arm and blade assembly. Connect the negative battery cable and check wiper operation.

12. Install the liftgate inner trim panel.

Window Wiper Switch

Removal and Installation

FRONT

Aerostar

NOTE: The switch handle is an integral part of the switch and cannot be removed separately.

1. Disconnect the negative battery cable.

2. Remove the cluster finish panel retaining screws.

3. Remove the 3 left control pod retaining screws.

4. Remove the wiring connector from the switch.

5. Remove the 2 switch-to-control pod retaining screws and remove the switch.

6. Installation is the reverse of the removal procedure.

1988 Bronco II and Ranger

NOTE: The switch handle is an integral part of the switch and cannot be removed separately.

Front wiper switch location – 1988 Bronco II and Ranger

1. Disconnect the negative battery cable.
2. Remove the trim shrouds.
3. Disconnect the electrical connector.
4. Peel back the foam sight shield. Remove the 2 cross-recessed screws holding the switch and remove the switch.
5. Installation is the reverse of the removal procedure.

REAR

Aerostar

NOTE: The switch handle is an integral part of the switch and cannot be removed separately.

1. Disconnect the negative battery cable.
2. Remove the trim shrouds and the left switch pod.
3. Disconnect the electrical connector.
4. Remove the 2 cross-recessed screws holding the switch and remove the switch.
5. Installation is the reverse of the removal procedure.

1988 Bronco II

1. Disconnect the negative battery cable.
2. Remove the headlight switch knob.
3. Pull the finish panel away from the instrument panel and disconnect the electrical connector.
4. Remove the screw attaching the wiper switch to the finish panel and remove the wiper switch.
5. Installation is the reverse of the removal procedure.

Explorer and 1989–90 Bronco II

1. Disconnect the negative battery cable.
2. Remove the 2 ash tray retaining screws and remove the ash tray.
3. Remove the cluster trim panel, which is held on by clips.
4. Remove the snap-in switch mounting bezel containing the switches and disconnect the electrical connector.
5. Remove the switch from the mounting bezel by pushing on the switch from the connector side until the snap-in mounting clips release.
6. Installation is the reverse of the removal procedure.

Instrument Cluster

Removal and Installation

AEROSTAR

Conventional Cluster

1. Disconnect the negative battery cable.
2. Remove the 7 cluster housing-to-panel retaining screws and remove the cluster housing.
3. Remove the 4 instrument cluster-to-panel retaining screws.
4. Disconnect the 2 wiring harness connectors from the backplate.
5. Disconnect the speedometer cable and remove the cluster assembly.
6. Installation is the reverse of the removal procedure. Apply an approximately $3/16$ in. diameter ball of silicone dialectric compound in the drive hole of the speedometer head prior to installation.

Electronic Cluster

1. Disconnect the negative battery cable.
2. Remove the cluster binnacle.
3. Remove the 4 cluster mounting screws.
4. Pull the top of the cluster toward the steering wheel, then reach behind the cluster and unplug the 3 connectors.
5. Swing the bottom of the cluster out and remove.
6. Installation is the reverse of the removal procedure.

Rear wiper switch installation—Explorer and 1988 Bronco II

Speedometer cable quick disconnect

BRONCO II, EXPLORER AND RANGER

1988

1. Disconnect the negative battery cable(s).
2. Remove the 2 steering column shroud-to-panel retaining screws and remove the shroud.
3. Remove the 2 lower instrument trim panels and rotate the headlight switch trim cover to gain access to the cluster trim cover screws.

NOTE: Removal of the headlight switch knob is not required to gain access to the cluster trim cover attaching screws.

4. Remove the 8 retaining screws and remove the cluster trim cover from the instrument panel.
5. Remove the 4 cluster-to-panel retaining screws and pull the cluster away from the panel enough to gain access to the speedometer cable. Disconnect the speedometer cable, electrical connectors and bulb and socket assemblies and remove the instrument cluster.

NOTE: If there is not enough room to disengage the cable from the speedometer, it may be necessary to disconnect the cable at the transmission and pull the cable through the cowl, to allow room to reach the speedometer quick disconnect.

6. Installation is the reverse of the removal procedure. Apply an approximately $3/16$ in. diameter ball of silicone dialectric compound in the drive hole of the speedometer head prior to installation.

1989–92

1. Disconnect the negative battery cable.
2. Open the ash tray and remove the 2 screws attaching the ash tray and instrument cluster trim panel. Remove the ash tray.

Instrument cluster installation – Aerostar with conventional cluster

Instrument cluster installation – 1989–92 Bronco II, Explorer and Ranger

3. Unsnap the cluster trim panel by pulling rearward around the edge of the panel. Depress the hazard warning switch on the steering column and remove the cluster trim panel.

4. Remove the 4 screws securing the instrument cluster to the instrument panel.

5. If equipped with automatic transmission, remove the 2 screws attaching the shift position indicator to the cluster and slide the indicator down and out of the cluster. Leave the indicator connections undisturbed.

6. Pull the cluster assembly rearward to gain access to the speedometer cable. Disconnect the cable and the 2 wiring harness connectors and remove the cluster.

NOTE: If there is not enough room to disengage the cable from the speedometer, it may be necessary to disconnect the cable at the transmission and pull the cable through the cowl, to allow room to reach the speedometer quick disconnect.

7. Installation is the reverse of the removal procedure. Apply an approximately $^3/_{16}$ in. diameter ball of silicone dialectic compound in the drive hole of the speedometer head prior to installation.

Speedometer

Removal and Installation

1. Disconnect the negative battery cable. Remove the instrument cluster.
2. Remove the lens and mask from the cluster.
3. Remove the 2 speedometer attaching screws and remove the speedometer.
4. Installation is the reverse of the removal procedure.

Headlight Switch

Removal and Installation

AEROSTAR

1. Disconnect the negative battery cable.
2. Remove the 5 cluster finish panel assembly retaining screws and remove the cluster finish panel.
3. Remove the 3 left control pod assembly retaining screws.
4. Disconnect the electrical connector from the switch.
5. Remove the 2 switch-to-control pod retaining screws and remove the switch.
6. Installation is the reverse of the removal procedure.

BRONCO II, EXPLORER AND RANGER

1988

1. Disconnect the negative battery cable.
2. Pull the headlight switch knob to the full **ON** position. Depress the shaft release button and remove the knob and shaft assembly.
3. Remove the instrument panel finish panel.
4. Unscrew the mounting nut. Remove the switch, then remove the wiring connector from the switch.
5. Installation is the reverse of the removal procedure.

1989–92

1. Disconnect the negative battery cable.
2. Remove the ash tray and the 2 finish panel retaining screws.
3. Remove the finish panel, which snaps off.
4. Remove the rear wiper switch and rear defrost switch on Bronco II and Explorer, or the storage bin on Ranger.
5. Pull the headlight switch knob to the full **ON** position. Reach through the opening below the headlight switch, depress the shaft release button on the switch and remove the knob and shaft assembly.
6. Remove the headlight switch retaining bezel nut. Pull the switch downward and through the opening to disconnect the connector.
7. Installation is the reverse of the removal procedure.

Combination Switch

The combination switch incorporates the turn signal and dimmer switch functions on Aerostar and 1988 Bronco II and Ranger. On 1989–90 Bronco II, 1991–92 Explorer and 1989–92 Ranger, the combination switch incorporates the turn signal, dimmer and windshield wiper/washer switch functions.

Headlight switch—Bronco II, Explorer and Ranger

Combination switch assembly—Aerostar

Removal and Installation

AEROSTAR

1. Disconnect the negative battery cable.
2. Remove the steering wheel.
3. If equipped with tilt column, remove the upper extension shroud by squeezing it at the 6 and 12 o'clock positions and popping it free of the retaining plate at the 3 o'clock position.
4. Open the trim shroud by removing the 4 attaching screws. Swing the trim shroud down and remove the 2 screws attaching the shroud to the steering column assembly.
5. Remove the lock cylinder.
6. Remove the combination switch lever by grasping the lever and using a pulling and twisting motion, pull the lever straight out from the switch. Remove the shroud.

7. Peel back the foam sight shield from the switch. Remove the 2 self-tapping screws attaching the switch to the lock cylinder housing. Disengage the switch from the housing and disconnect the switch electrical connectors.

To install:

8. Connect the switch electrical connectors.

9. Install the switch with the self-tapping screws and tighten to 18–26 inch lbs. (2.0–2.9 Nm).

10. Stick the foam sight shield to the switch and install the trim shroud.

11. Install the lock cylinder. Install the tilt collar shroud, if equipped.

12. Install the lever into the switch by aligning the key on the lever with the keyway in the switch and pushing the lever into the switch to full engagement.

13. Install the steering wheel and connect the negative battery cable.

BRONCO II, EXPLORER AND RANGER

1988

1. Disconnect the negative battery cable.

2. Remove the 2 trim shroud halves by removing the 2 attaching screws.

3. If equipped with tilt column, remove the upper extension shroud by squeezing it at the 6 and 12 o'clock positions and popping it free of the retaining plate at the 3 o'clock position.

4. Remove the combination switch lever by grasping the lever and using a pulling and twisting motion, pull the lever straight out from the switch.

5. Peel back the foam sight shield from the switch. Remove the 2 self-tapping screws attaching the switch to the lock cylinder housing. Disengage the switch from the housing and disconnect the switch electrical connectors.

To install:

6. Connect the switch electrical connectors.

7. Install the switch with the self-tapping screws and tighten to 18–26 inch lbs. (2.0–2.9 Nm).

8. Stick the foam sight shield to the switch.

9. Install the lever into the switch by aligning the key on the lever with the keyway in the switch and pushing the lever into the switch to full engagement.

10. Install the steering column trim shrouds and connect the negative battery cable.

1989–92

1. Disconnect the negative battery cable.

Combination switch installation – 1989–92 Bronco II, Explorer and Ranger

2. Remove the steering column shroud.

3. Remove the 2 self-tapping screws that attach the combination switch to the steering column casting. Disengage the switch from the casting.

4. Disconnect the 3 electrical connectors, being careful not to damage the locking tabs. Do not damage the shift position indicator cable.

To install:

5. Connect the 3 switch electrical connectors. The wiring for the switch is to be routed under the shift position indicator cable.

6. Install the switch with the self-tapping screws. Tighten the screws to 18–27 inch lbs. (2–3 Nm).

7. If equipped with automatic transmission, make sure the shift position indicator adjustment is correct.

8. Install the shroud and connect the negative battery cable. Check the steering column for proper operation.

Ignition Lock

Removal and Installation

AEROSTAR AND 1988 BRONCO II AND RANGER

Functional Lock

NOTE: The following procedure should be used on vehicles with functional lock cylinders. Ignition keys are available for these vehicles or the ignition key numbers are known and the proper key can be made.

1. Disconnect the negative battery cable.

2. Remove the trim shroud and disconnect the electrical connector from the key warning switch.

3. Turn the lock cylinder to the **RUN** position.

4. Place a ⅛ in. diameter pin or small drift punch in the hole located at 4 o'clock and 1¼ in. from the outer edge of the lock cylinder housing. Depress the retaining pin and pull out the lock cylinder.

To install:

5. Before installing the lock cylinder, lubricate the cylinder cavity, including the drive gear, with a suitable lock lubricant.

6. Turn the lock cylinder to the **RUN** position, depress the retaining pin and insert it into the lock cylinder housing. Make sure the cylinder is fully seated and aligned into the inter-locking washer before turning the key to the **OFF** position. This will permit the cylinder retaining pin to extend into the hole in the lock cylinder housing.

7. Using the ignition key, rotate the lock cylinder to ensure correct mechanical operation in all positions. Connect the electrical connector to the key warning switch.

8. Connect the negative battery cable. Check for proper ignition functions and make sure the column is locked in the **LOCK** position.

9. Install the trim shrouds.

Non-Functional Lock

NOTE: The following procedure should be used on vehicles where the ignition lock is inoperative and the lock cylinder cannot be rotated due to a lost or broken ignition key, the key number is not known or the lock cylinder cap is damaged and/or broken.

1. Disconnect the negative battery cable.

2. Remove the steering wheel.

3. Remove the trim shrouds and disconnect the electrical connector from the key warning switch.

4. Using a ⅛ in. diameter drill bit, drill out the retaining pin, being careful not to drill deeper than ½ in.

5. Position a chisel at the base of the ignition lock cylinder cap and using a hammer, strike the chisel with sharp blows to break the cap away from the lock cylinder.

6. Using a ⅜ in. diameter drill bit, drill down the middle of

the ignition lock key slot approximately 1¾ in. until the lock cylinder breaks loose from the breakaway base of the lock cylinder. Remove the lock cylinder and drill shavings from the lock cylinder housing.

7. Remove the snapring, washer and ignition lock drive gear. Thoroughly clean all drill shavings and other foreign material from the casting.

8. Carefully inspect the lock cylinder housing for damage from the removal operation. If the housing is damaged, it must be replaced.

To install:

9. Install the ignition lock drive gear, washer and snapring.

10. Install the ignition lock cylinder.

11. Connect the key warning switch wire. Install the shroud with the 2 screws.

12. Install the steering wheel and connect the negative battery cable. Check for proper ignition and accessory functions and make sure the column locks in the **LOCK** position.

1989–92 BRONCO II, EXPLORER AND RANGER

Functional Lock

NOTE: The following procedure should be used on vehicles with functional lock cylinders. Ignition keys are available for these vehicles or the ignition key numbers are known and the proper key can be made.

1. Disconnect the negative battery cable.

2. Remove the steering wheel and shroud.

3. Using the ignition key, turn the lock cylinder to the **ON** position. If equipped with an automatic transmission, the selector lever must first be placed in **P**.

4. Push down on the lock cylinder retaining pin with a ⅛ in. diameter wire pin or small punch. Pull the lock cylinder from the column housing.

5. Disconnect the lock cylinder wiring plug from the horn brush wiring connector.

To install:

6. Lubricate the lock cylinder with grease.

7. Turn the lock cylinder to the **ON** position and depress the retaining pin.

8. Insert the lock cylinder into its housing in the flange casting, making sure the tab at the end of the cylinder aligns with the slot in the ignition drive gear.

9. Turn the key to the **OFF** position. This will allow the cylinder retaining pin to extend into the cylinder casting housing hole.

10. Using the ignition key, rotate the lock cylinder to ensure correct mechanical operation in all positions.

11. Connect the key warning wire plug and install the steering column lower shroud.

12. Install the steering column opening trim panel and connect the negative battery cable.

13. Check for proper start in **P** or **N**. Make sure the vehicle cannot be started in **D** and **R**.

Non-Functional Lock

NOTE: The following procedure should be used on vehicles where the ignition lock is inoperative and the lock cylinder cannot be rotated due to a lost or broken ignition key, the key number is not known or the lock cylinder cap is damaged and/or broken.

1. Disconnect the negative battery cable. If equipped with tilt wheel, tilt to the full up position.

2. Remove the steering wheel, tilt lever and steering column trim shrouds.

3. Punch the lock cylinder retaining pin with a prick punch, ⅛ in. maximum outside diameter. Using a ⅛ in. diameter drill, drill out the retaining pin going no deeper than ½ in. Be careful not to damage the cast housing.

4. Place a chisel at the base of the lock cylinder cap and, using a hammer, strike the chisel with sharp blows to break the cap away from the lock cylinder.

5. Using a ⅜ in. diameter drill bit, drill down the middle of the ignition lock key slot approximately 1¾ in. until the lock cylinder breaks loose from the steering column cover casting. Remove the lock cylinder and drill shavings from the base of the cover cast housing.

6. Remove the drive gear, bearing retainer and actuator from the casting. Toroughly clean and inspect all components. If any components or the casting are damaged, they must be replaced.

To install:

7. Lubricate the drive gear, bearing and retainer with grease and install. Lubricate the lock cylinder with grease.

8. Turn the lock cylinder to the **ON** position and depress the retaining pin. Insert the cylinder into its housing in the flange casting, making sure the tab at the end of the cylinder aligns with the slot in the ignition lock drive gear.

9. Turn the key to the **OFF** position. This will allow the cylinder retaining pin to extend into the cylinder casting housing hole.

10. Using the ignition key, rotate the lock cylinder to ensure correct mechanical operation in all positions.

11. Connect the key warning wire plug and install the steering column shrouds.

12. Install the steering wheel and connect the negative battery cable. Check for proper start in **P** or **N**. Make sure the vehicle cannot be started in **D** and **R**.

Ignition Switch

Removal and Installation

1. Rotate the lock cylinder to the **LOCK** position. Disconnect the negative battery cable.

2. Remove the steering wheel.

3. If equipped with tilt wheel, remove the upper extension housing shroud by squeezing it at the 6 and 12 o'clock positions and popping it free of the retaining plate at the 3 o'clock position.

4. On all except Aerostar, remove the trim shroud halves.

5. On Aerostar, proceed as follows:

   a. Remove the panel to the right of the steering column.

   b. Remove the trim shroud by removing the 4 screws at the bottom of the shroud. Swing the bottom panel of the shroud open and remove the 2 screws attaching the shroud to the retaining plate.

   c. Remove the lock cylinder.

   d. Remove the shroud by first raising the left side so the window for the combination switch lever is up past the lever receptacle, then pull up on the right side of the shroud until the lock cylinder embossment clears the lock cylinder housing.

   e. Work the shroud past the instrument panel.

6. Disconnect the switch electrical connector.

7. If equipped, remove the retaining nuts and disengage the ignition switch from the actuator pin.

8. If equipped with break-off head bolts, remove them using an ⅛ in. drill bit, then remove the bolts using an "easy-out" tool or equivalent. Disengage the ignition switch from the actuator pin.

NOTE: An alternate method of removing the break-off head bolts is to use a hammer and chisel to turn the bolts 1 revolution counterclockwise. Then, using a pair of adjustable pliers, grab the bolt head and continue to rotate the bolt until removed.

To install:

9. Rotate the ignition key to the **RUN** position and align the holes in the switch casting base with the holes in the lock cylinder housing.

10. Install the nuts or if equipped, new break-off head bolts. Tighten the break-off head bolts until the heads break off.

11. Connect the electrical connector to the ignition switch and install the steering column trim shrouds.

12. On Aerostar, install the lock cylinder.

13. Install the steering wheel. Connect the negative battery cable and check the ignition switch for proper operation.

Stoplight Switch

Removal and Installation

1. Disconnect the negative battery cable. Disconnect the electrical connector from the switch. The locking tab must be lifted before the connector can be removed.

2. Remove the hairpin clip and slide the switch, booster pushrod, nylon washer and bushing away from the pedal. Remove the washer, then the switch by sliding the switch up or down.

To install:

3. Position the switch so the U-shaped side is nearest the pedal and directly over/under the pin. Then slide the switch up/down installing the booster pushrod and bushing between the switch side plates.

4. Push the switch and pushrod assembly firmly toward the brake pedal arm. Install the outside plastic washer to the pin and install the hairpin clip. Do not substitute for this clip. Use only factory supplied hairpin clips.

5. Connect the electrical connector to the switch and connect the negative battery cable. Make sure the switch wire harness has sufficient length to travel with the switch during the full stroke of the brake pedal. Check the switch for proper operation.

Clutch Switch

Adjustment

1988 AEROSTAR

If the adjusting clip is out of position on the rod, remove both halves of the clip. Position the clip halves closer to the switch and snap the clips together on the rod. Depress the clutch pedal to the floor to adjust the switch.

Removal and Installation

EXCEPT 1988 AEROSTAR

1. Disconnect the negative battery cable. Disconnect the wiring harness from the switch.

2. Pull the orientation clip away from the switch to separate it from the pin on the switch.

3. Rotate the switch to expose the plastic retainer.

4. Push the tabs together to allow the retainer to slide rearward and separate from the switch.

5. Remove the switch from the pushrod.

6. Installation is the reverse of the removal procedure.

1988 AEROSTAR

1. Disconnect the negative battery cable.

2. Disconnect the electrical connector and remove the switch.

3. Installation is the reverse of the removal procedure. Depress the clutch pedal to the floor to set the position of the self-adjusting clips.

Neutral Safety Switch

Removal and Installation

1. Disconnect the negative battery cable.

2. Disconnect the electrical harness from the switch.

3. Remove the switch and O-ring using socket tool T74P-77247-A or equivalent.

Stoplight switch assembly

NOTE: The use of other tools could crush or puncture the walls of the switch.

4. Installation is the reverse of the removal procedure. Tighten the switch to 7–10 ft. lbs. (9.5–13.6 Nm).

5. Check the operation of the switch with the parking brake applied. The engine should start only with the transmission selector lever in **N** or **P**. The back-up lights should illuminate only with the selector lever in **R**.

Fuses

Location

Fuse Panel — located under the instrument panel, to the left of the steering column on all vehicles.

Power Distribution Box — located in the engine compartment, on the right inner fender on 1989–92 Bronco II, Explorer and Ranger. Contains only high current fuses.

Circuit Breakers

Location

AEROSTAR

Front Wiper/Washer Circuit — 6 amp circuit breaker located on the fuse panel.

Power Door Lock Circuit — 30 amp circuit breaker located on the fuse panel on 1988–89 vehicles.

Power Window Circuit — 20 amp circuit breaker located on the fuse panel.

Rear Cigar Lighter Circuit — 30 amp circuit breaker located on the fuse panel on 1988–89 vehicles.

BRONCO II, EXPLORER AND RANGER

Combination Switch Circuit — 20 amp circuit breaker located on the fuse panel on 1991–92 vehicles.

Cigar Lighter Circuit — 20 amp circuit breaker located on the fuse panel on 1989–92 vehicles.

Flash-to-Pass Circuit — 20 amp circuit breaker located on the fuse panel on 1989–92 vehicles.

Front Wiper/Washer Circuit — 6 amp circuit breaker located on the fuse panel.

Headlight Circuit — 22 amp circuit breaker, integral with the headlight switch.

Power Lumbar Support Circuit — 20 amp circuit breaker located on the fuse panel on 1989–92 vehicles.

Power Window Circuit — 20 amp circuit breaker located on the fuse panel on 1988–90 vehicles, 30 amp circuit breaker located on the fuse panel on 1991–92 vehicles.

Rear Wiper/Washer Circuit—4.5 amp circuit breaker located behind the instrument panel under the glove box on Bronco II and Explorer.

Relays

Location

AEROSTAR

Auxiliary Air Conditioner-Heater Power Relay—located at the multi-relay bracket on the left fender apron.

Courtesy Lamp Relay—located at the left rear corner of the cargo area on 1990 vehicles and in front of the left "D" pillar, above the grommet on 1991–92 vehicles.

Day/Night Illumination Relay—located behind the left side of the instrument panel.

Door Ajar Relay—located at the bottom of the right "B" pillar.

Door Locks Control Relay—located at the right cowl panel.

EEC Power Relay—located on the multi-relay bracket on the left fender apron.

Fuel Pump Relay—located on the multi-relay bracket on the left fender apron.

Horn Relay—located behind the left side of the instrument panel.

Low Oil Level Relay—located behind the left side of the instrument panel.

Starter Relay—located on the left fender apron, next to the battery.

Trailer Tow Relay Module—located behind the left wheelhouse.

Wide Open Throttle Cut-Out Relay—located at the multi-relay bracket on the left fender apron.

BRONCO II, EXPLORER AND RANGER

Air Conditioning Relay—located on the right fender apron.

Choke Relay—located near the test connector take off.

EEC Power Relay—located on the lower cowl, near the Electronic Control Assembly, on 1988 vehicles or on the right fender apron on 1989–92 vehicles.

Fuel Metering Relay—located at the cigar lighter takeoff.

Fuel Pump Relay—located on the right fender apron.

Horn Relay—located at the top of the steering column on 1988 vehicles or behind the instrument panel, to the right of the steering column on 1989–92 vehicles.

Lock/Unlock Relays—located on the left fender apron.

Low Oil Level Relay—located behind the lower right side of the instrument panel.

Starter Relay—located on the right fender apron.

Stop/Turn Signal Relay—located on left rear quarter panel on Explorer.

Tail Light Relay—located on left rear quarter panel on Explorer.

Trailer Lamps Relay—located on top of the left radiator support.

Wide Open Throttle Cut-Out Relay—located at the right fender apron.

Computers

Location

The engine Electronic Control Assembly (ECA) is located in the engine compartment, on the left side of the firewall on Aerostar or under the dash, at the right kick panel, on Bronco II, Explorer and Ranger.

Flashers

Location

Both the turn signal and hazard flashers are attached to the fuse panel.

Cruise Control

For further information, please refer to Chilton's Chassis Electronics Service Manual.

Adjustment

ACTUATOR CABLE

1. Remove the cable retaining clip.
2. Disengage the throttle positioner.
3. Set the engine at hot idle.
4. Pull on the actuator cable to take up any slack. Maintain a light tension on the cable.
5. While holding the cable, insert the cable retaining clip and snap securely.

VACUUM DUMP VALVE

1. Firmly hold the brake pedal in the up, released, position.
2. Push in the dump valve until the valve bottoms against the pad on the brake pedal.
3. The dump valve housing must clear the plastic pad on the brake pedal by 0.050–0.10 in. (1.27–2.54mm) with the brake pedal pulled to the rearmost position.

View showing correctly adjusted dump valve

ENGINE COOLING

Radiator

Removal and Installation

1. Disconnect the negative battery cable and remove the radiator cap.

——————— **CAUTION** ———————
Never remove the radiator cap while the engine is running or personal injury from scalding hot coolant or steam may result. If possible, wait until the engine has cooled to remove the radiator cap. If this is not possible, wrap a thick cloth around the radiator cap and turn it slowly to the first stop, to release the pressure in the cooling system. Step back while the pressure is released. After all pressure is released, remove the radiator cap completely.

2. Position a drain pan under the radiator and open the draincock to drain the radiator.

3. Disconnect the overflow hose from the radiator and the fan shroud, if necessary.

4. Remove the shroud or finger guard upper attaching screws. Lift the shroud out of the lower retaining clips and drape it on the fan.

5. Disconnect the radiator hoses from the radiator.

6. Disconnect and plug the automatic transmission oil cooling lines, if equipped.

7. Remove the radiator upper attaching screws, tilt the radiator back and lift directly upward, clear of the radiator support and cooling fan.

To install:

8. Make sure the radiator lower support rubber insulators are in place on the lower support.

9. Install the radiator, being careful to clear the fan. Make sure the mounting pins on the bottom of the radiator tanks are inserted into the holes in the lower support rubber insulators and the radiator is firmly seated on the insulators.

10. Install the radiator upper attaching screws. If equipped with automatic transmission, connect the transmission cooling lines.

11. Connect the radiator hoses to the radiator. Position the shroud in the retainer clips and install the attaching screws.

12. Connect the overflow hose and close the draincock. Connect the negative battery cable. Fill and bleed the cooling system.

Heater Core

For further information, please refer to Chilton's Air Conditioning and Heating Manual.

Removal and Installation

1. Disconnect the negative battery cable.
2. Drain the cooling system into a suitable container.
3. Disconnect the heater hoses from the heater core tubes. Use the snap-lock fitting disconnect procedure, if necessary.
4. In the passenger compartment, remove the screws attaching the heater core access cover to the plenum assembly. Remove the access cover.
5. Pull the heater core rearward and down, removing it from the plenum assembly.

To install:

6. Position the heater core and seal in the plenum assembly.
7. Install the heater core access cover to the plenum assembly and secure it with the screws.
8. Connect the heater hoses to the heater core tubes. Use the snap-lock fitting connection procedure.
9. Fill the cooling system to the proper level.
10. Connect the negative battery cable and check the system for proper operation and coolant leaks.

Water Pump

Removal and Installation

2.0L AND 2.3L ENGINES

1. Disconnect the negative battery cable and drain the cooling system.
2. Remove the bolts that retain the fan shroud and position the shroud back over the fan.
3. Remove the 4 bolts that retain the cooling fan, then remove the fan and shroud.
4. Remove the accessory drive belts.
5. Remove the water pump pulley and the vent hose to the canister.
6. Remove the heater hose at the water pump.
7. Remove the timing belt cover. Remove the lower radiator hose from the water pump.
8. Remove the water pump mounting bolts and the water pump. Clean all gasket mating surfaces.

Heater core installation—Explorer, 1990–92 Ranger and 1990 Bronco II

Fan and clutch assembly removal—2.9L and 4.0L engines

9. Installation is the reverse of the removal procedure. Coat the threads of the mounting bolts with sealer before installation and tighten to 14–21 ft. lbs. (20–30 Nm). Fill and bleed the cooling system.

2.9L AND 4.0L ENGINES

1. Disconnect the negative battery cable and drain the cooling system.
2. Remove the lower radiator hose and the heater return hose from the pump.
3. Remove the fan and clutch assembly using fan clutch pulley holder T83T-6312-A and fan clutch nut wrench T83T-6312-B or equivalents. The fan clutch nut has left hand thread; remove by turning clockwise.

SNAP-LOCK FITTING PROCEDURES

COMPLETE QUICK CONNECT
ASSEMBLY CONTAINS THE FOLLOWING:
2 - O-RINGS (SILICONE FLUID)
1 - SPACER
1 - COUPLING RETAINER
1 - HOUSING

SILICONE FLUID
ESF-M99B112-A

COUPLING
RETAINER
- 18D434 -

HEATER CORE TUBE

QUICK CONNECT COUPLING - DISCONNECTED

TO CONNECT COUPLING

ALWAYS USE NEW O-RINGS
WHEN RE-CONNECTING
TO HEATER CORE TUBES

NOTE:
LUBRICATE O-RINGS WITH
ESF-M99B112-A
SILICONE FLUID

INSPECT SPACER
FOR CRACKS OR DAMAGE —
REPLACE IF NECESSARY

INSPECT COUPLING RETAINER
FOR CRACKS OR DAMAGE —
REPLACE IF NECESSARY

(1)

CLEAN HEATER CORE
TUBE AND LUBRICATE
WITH SILICONE

(2) ASSEMBLE FITTINGS TOGETHER BY PUSHING TOGETHER —
LISTEN FOR COUPLING RETAINER TO SNAP IN PLACE.

HEATER HOSE
ASSEMBLY

TO HEATER
CORE

(3) TO ENSURE QUICK CONNECT ENGAGEMENT, LIGHTLY
PULL ON THE HEATER HOSE ASSEMBLY

TO DISCONNECT COUPLING

CAUTION — ENGINE SHOULD BE OFF BEFORE DISCONNECTING COUPLING

HEATER HOSE
DISCONNECT TOOL

EXTENSION HANDLE
T85T-18539-AH3

(1)

COUPLING RETAINER

HEATER HOSE
DISCONNECT TOOL

HEATER
CORE
TUBE

HEATER
HOSE
ASSEMBLY

PUSH HEATER HOSE ASSEMBLY TOWARDS HEATER CORE
TUBE TO ENSURE LOCKING TABS ARE FULLY EXPOSED, THEN
PUSH TOOL OVER COUPLING RETAINER WINDOWS TO
COMPRESS RETAINER LOCKING TABS — THEN PULL HOSE
ASSEMBLY AWAY FROM HEATER CORE TUBE.
REMOVE TOOL THEN CONTINUE PULLING HOSE ASSEMBLY
AWAY FROM HEATER CORE TUBE.

(2) NOTE: WHEN COMPRESSING WHITE COUPLING RETAINER,
THE TOOL MUST BE PERPENDICULAR AND ON THE HIGHEST
POINT OF THE COUPLING RETAINER AS SHOWN ABOVE.

SPREAD RETAINER APART
TO REMOVE FROM HEATER
CORE TUBE, AND REPLACE
WITH NEW RETAINER

WHEN THE QUICK CONNECT COUPLING IS DISCONNECTED — THE
WHITE COUPLING RETAINER WILL REMAIN ON THE HEATER CORE TUBE.
(3) INSTALL NEW COUPLING RETAINER, SPACER & NEW LUBRICATED
O-RINGS INTO QUICK CONNECT ASSEMBLY HOUSING BEFORE
RE-INSTALLING HEATER HOSE ASSEMBLY TO HEATER CORE TUBES.

4. Loosen the alternator mounting bolts and remove the belt. If equipped with air conditioning, remove the alternator and bracket.

5. Remove the water pump pulley.

6. Remove the water pump attaching bolts and remove the water pump. Note the length of the bolts when removing, so they can be reinstalled in the same positions.

7. Clean all gasket mating surfaces and install in the reverse order of removal. Tighten the water pump retaining bolts to 7–9 ft. lbs. (9–12 Nm) and the fan clutch nut to 30–100 ft. lbs. (40–135 Nm). Fill and bleed the cooling system.

3.0L ENGINE

1. Disconnect the negative battery cable and drain the cooling system.

2. Loosen the nut that attaches the fan clutch to the water pump shaft using a 22mm wrench. The nut has left-hand thread and must be turned clockwise to remove. Remove the fan and clutch assembly.

3. Loosen the 4 water pump pulley bolts, then remove the accessory drive belts. Remove the water pump pulley.

4. Remove the alternator adjusting arm and brace. Disconnect the heater hose and lower radiator hose from the pump.

5. Rotate the belt adjuster out of the way.

6. Remove the water pump attaching bolts, noting their positions for reinstallation and remove the water pump. Clean all gasket mating surfaces.

7. Installation is the reverse of the removal procedure. Apply sealer to the 8mm mounting bolt at the extreme passenger side, prior to installation. Tighten the 6mm mounting bolts to 7 ft. lbs. (10 Nm) and the 8mm mounting bolts to 19 ft. lbs. (25 Nm). Tighten the fan clutch nut to 30–100 ft. lbs. (40–135 Nm). Fill and bleed the cooling system.

Thermostat

Removal and Installation

1. Disconnect the negative battery cable and drain the cooling system.

2. Disconnect the upper radiator hose and, if equipped, the heater hose from the water outlet.

3. Remove the water outlet retaining bolts and remove the water outlet. Remove the thermostat from the water outlet.

To install:

4. Clean all gasket mating surfaces.

5. Apply gasket sealer to a new water outlet gasket and install on the cylinder head or intake manifold.

6. Install the thermostat in the water outlet with the bridge section toward the radiator hose. Turn the thermostat clockwise to lock it in position on the flats cast into the water outlet.

NOTE: If the water outlet is equipped with a heater outlet tube opening, check that the full width of the opening is visible within the thermostat port in the assembly. The correct port alignment is required to provide maximum coolant flow to the heater.

7. Install the water outlet with the mounting bolts. Tighten the bolts to 14–21 ft. lbs. (20–30 Nm) on 2.0L and 2.3L engines, 7–10 ft. lbs. (9–13 Nm) on 2.9L and 4.0L engines or 18 ft. lbs. (25 Nm) on the 3.0L engine.

8. Connect the radiator hose and, if equipped, the heater hose to the water outlet.

9. Connect the negative battery cable. Fill and bleed the cooling system.

Cooling System Bleeding

When the entire cooling system is drained, the following procedure should be used to remove air from the cooling system and ensure a complete fill.

1. Close the radiator draincock and install the cylinder block drain plug, if removed.

2. Fill the cooling system with a 50/50 mixture of anti-freeze and water. Allow several minutes for trapped air to escape. When filling a cross flow radiator, allow time for the coolant to flow through the radiator tubes to the other end of the tank to ensure the radiator is full.

3. Install the radiator cap to the pressure relief position by installing the cap to the fully installed position and then backing off to the 1st stop. This will allow any air to escape and will minimize spillage.

4. Slide the heater temperature and mode selection levers to the maximum heat position.

5. Start the engine and allow to operate at fast idle for approximately 3–4 minutes.

6. With the engine shut off, wrap the radiator cap with a thick cloth, carefully remove the cap and add coolant to bring the coolant level up to the filler neck seat.

7. Install the cap to the fully installed position. Then, back off to the 1st stop and operate the engine at fast idle until the thermostat opens and the upper radiator hose is warm. To check the coolant level, shut the engine off, wrap the cap with a thick cloth and cautiously remove the cap. Add additional coolant, if necessary. Install the cap to the fully installed position.

— CAUTION —

To avoid personal injury from scalding hot coolant or steam blowing out of the radiator, use extreme care when removing the cap from a hot radiator.

8. Fill the coolant recovery reservoir to the proper level with a 50/50 mix of anti-freeze and water.

FUEL SYSTEM

Fuel System Service Precautions

Safety is the most important factor when performing not only fuel system maintenance but any type of maintenance. Failure to conduct maintenance and repairs in a safe manner may result in serious personal injury or death. Maintenance and testing of the vehicle's fuel system components can be accomplished safely and effectively by adhering to the following rules and guidelines.

• To avoid the possibility of fire and personal injury, always disconnect the negative battery cable unless the repair or test procedure requires that battery voltage be applied.

• Always relieve the fuel system pressure prior to disconnecting any fuel system component (injector, fuel rail, pressure regulator, etc.), fitting or fuel line connection. Exercise extreme caution whenever relieving fuel system pressure to avoid exposing skin, face and eyes to fuel spray. Please be advised that fuel under pressure may penetrate the skin or any part of the body that it contacts.

• Always place a shop towel or cloth around the fitting or connection prior to loosening to absorb any excess fuel due to spillage. Ensure that all fuel spillage (should it occur) is quickly removed from engine surfaces. Ensure that all fuel soaked cloths or towels are deposited into a suitable waste container.

• Always keep a dry chemical (Class B) fire extinguisher near the work area.

• Do not allow fuel spray or fuel vapors to come into contact with a spark or open flame.

• Always use a backup wrench when loosening and tightening fuel line connection fittings. This will prevent unnecessary stress and torsion to fuel line piping. Always follow the proper torque specifications.

• Always replace worn fuel fitting O-rings with new. Do not substitute fuel hose or equivalent where fuel pipe is installed.

Relieving Fuel System Pressure

1. Disconnect the negative battery cable and remove the fuel filler cap.

2. Remove the cap from the pressure relief valve on the fuel supply manifold. Install pressure gauge T80L–9974–B or equivalent, to the pressure relief valve.

3. Direct the gauge drain hose into a suitable container and depress the pressure relief button.

4. Remove the gauge and replace the cap on the pressure relief valve.

NOTE: As an alternate method, disconnect the inertia switch and crank the engine for 15–20 seconds until the pressure is relieved.

Fuel Line Couplings

Removal and Installation

There are 3 methods in use to connect the fuel lines and fuel system components, the hairpin clip push connect fitting, the duck bill clip push connect fitting and the spring lock coupling. Each requires a different procedure to disconnect and connect.

HAIRPIN CLIP PUSH CONNECT FITTING

1. Inspect the visible internal portion of the fitting for dirt accumulation. If more than a light coating of dust is present, clean the fitting before disassembly.

2. Some adhesion between the seals in the fitting and the tubing will occur with time. To separate, twist the fitting on the tube, then push and pull the fitting until it moves freely on the tube.

3. Remove the hairpin clip from the fitting by first bending and breaking the shipping tab. Next, spread the 2 clip legs by hand about ⅛ in. each to disengage the body and push the legs into the fitting. Lightly pull the triangular end of the clip and work it clear of the tube and fitting.

NOTE: Do not use hand tools to complete this operation.

4. Grasp the fitting and pull in an axial direction to remove the fitting from the tube. Be careful on 90 degree elbow connectors, as excessive side loading could break the connector body.

5. After disassembly, inspect and clean the tube end sealing surfaces. The tube end should be free of scratches and corrosion that could provide leak paths. Inspect the inside of the fitting for any internal parts such as O-rings and spacers that may have been dislodged from the fitting. Replace any damaged connector.

To install:

6. Install a new connector if damage was found. Insert a new clip into any 2 adjacent openings with the triangular portion pointing away from the fitting opening. Install the clip until the legs of the clip are locked on the outside of the body. Piloting with an index finger is necessary.

7. Before installing the fitting on the tube, wipe the tube end with a clean cloth. Inspect the inside of the fitting to make sure it is free of dirt and/or obstructions.

8. Apply a light coating of engine oil to the tube end. Align the fitting and tube axially and push the fitting onto the tube end. When the fitting is engaged, a definite click will be heard. Pull on the fitting to make sure it is fully engaged.

FUEL PUMP SWITCH ASSEMBLY IN VEHICLE MUST HAVE RESET BUTTON ON TOP

INERTIA SWITCH

SCREW

HEATER

FLOOR (RH)

Typical inertia switch location

DUCK BILL CLIP PUSH CONNECT FITTING

1. Inspect the visible internal portion of the fitting for dirt accumulation. If more than a light coating of dust is present, clean the fitting before disassembly.

2. Some adhesion between the seals in the fitting and the tubing will occur with time. To separate, twist the fitting on the tube, then push and pull the fitting until it moves freely on the tube.

3. Align the slot on push connect disassembly tool T82L–9500–AH or equivalent, with either tab on the clip, 90 degrees from the slots on the side of the fitting and insert the tool. This disengages the duck bill retainer from the tube.

4. Holding the tool and the tube with 1 hand, pull the fitting away from the tube.

NOTE: Use hands only. Only moderate effort is required, if the tube has been properly disengaged.

5. After disassembly, inspect and clean the tube end sealing surfaces. The tube end should be free of scratches and corrosion that could provide leak paths. Inspect the inside of the fitting for any internal parts such as O-rings and spacers that may have been dislodged from the fitting. Replace any damaged connector.

6. Some fuel tubes have a secondary bead which aligns with the outer surface of the clip. These beads can make tool insertion difficult. If there is extreme difficulty, use the following disassembly method:

a. Using pliers with a jaw width of 0.2 in. (5mm) or less, align the jaws with the openings in the side of the fitting case and compress the portion of the retaining clip that engages the fitting case. This disengages the retaining clip from the case. Often 1 side of the clip will disengage before the other. The clip must be disengaged from both openings.

b. Pull the fitting off the tube by hand only. Only moderate effort is required, if the retaining clip has been properly disengaged.

c. After disassembly, inspect and clean the tube end sealing surfaces. The tube end should be free of scratches and corrosion that could provide leak paths. Inspect the inside of the fitting for any internal parts such as O-rings and spacers that may have been dislodged from the fitting. Replace any damaged connector.

d. The retaining clip will remain on the tube. Disengage the clip from the tube bead and remove.

To install:

7. Install a new connector if damage was found. Install the new replacement clip into the body by inserting 1 of the retaining clip serrated edges on the duck bill portion into 1 side of the window openings. Push on the other side until the clip snaps into place.

8. Before installing the fitting on the tube, wipe the tube end

with a clean cloth. Inspect the inside of the fitting to make sure it is free of dirt and/or obstructions.

9. Apply a light coating of engine oil to the tube end. Align the fitting and tube axially and push the fitting onto the tube end. When the fitting is engaged, a definite click will be heard. Pull on the fitting to make sure it is fully engaged.

SPRING LOCK COUPLING

The spring lock coupling is a fuel line coupling held together by a garter spring inside a circular cage. When the coupling is connected together, the flared end of the female fitting slips behind the garter spring inside the cage of the male fitting. The garter spring and cage then prevent the flared end of the female fitting from pulling out of the cage. As an additional locking feature, most vehicles have a horseshoe shaped retaining clip that improves the retaining reliability of the spring lock coupling.

Duck bill push connect fitting removal

HAIRPIN CLIP
O-RINGS
SHIPPING TAB
TUBE
SPACERS
BODY

TYPICAL 5/16 IN. PUSH CONNECT

HAIRPIN CLIP

TYPICAL 3/8 IN. PUSH CONNECT

O-RINGS
BODY
DUCK BILL CLIP
SPACERS
TUBE

TYPICAL 1/4 IN. PUSH CONNECT

Typical push connect fittings

SPRING LOCK COUPLING CHART

FEMALE FITTING — O-RINGS — GARTER SPRING — MALE FITTINGS — CAGE

SPRING LOCK COUPLING DISCONNECTED

TOOL — CAGE — WHITE INDICATOR RING (LOOSE)

❶ BEFORE DISASSEMBLY, LOCATE WHITE INDICATOR RING WHICH MAY HAVE SLIPPED DOWN LENGTH OF FUEL LINE.

❷ FIT TOOL TO COUPLING SO THAT TOOL CAN ENTER CAGE TO RELEASE THE GARTER SPRING.

TO CONNECT COUPLING

GARTER SPRING

❶ CHECK FOR MISSING OR DAMAGED GARTER SPRING - REMOVE DAMAGED SPRING WITH SMALL HOOKED WIRE - INSTALL NEW SPRING IF DAMAGED OR MISSING.

PUSH TOOL INTO CAGE

❸ PUSH THE TOOL INTO THE CAGE OPENING TO RELEASE THE FEMALE FITTING FROM THE GARTER SPRING

B - INSTALL NEW O-RINGS
A - CLEAN FITTINGS — WHITE INDICATOR RING
C - LUBRICATE WITH CLEAN REFRIGERANT OIL
D. INSERT WHITE INDICATOR RING INTO CAGE ON MALE FITTING
E. ASSEMBLE FITTING TOGETHER BY PUSHING WITH A SLIGHT TWISTING MOTION

❷

❹ PULL THE COUPLING MALE AND FEMALE FITTINGS APART.

WHITE INDICATOR RING (LOOSE) — GARTER SPRING

❸ AT REASSEMBLY, WHITE INDICATOR RING WILL POP FREE OF CAGE ON MALE FITTING WHEN JOINT IS FULL MADE. THIS INDICATES THAT GARTER SPRING INSIDE CAGE OF MALE FITTING IS PROPERLY SEATED OVER LIP OF FEMALE CONNECTOR.

❺ REMOVE THE TOOL FROM THE DISCONNECTED SPRING LOCK COUPLING.

Fuel Tank

Removal and Installation

AEROSTAR

1. Disconnect the negative battery cable and relieve the fuel system pressure.
2. Raise and safely support the vehicle.
3. Drain the fuel from the fuel tank.
4. Loosen the fuel fill pipe clamp and remove the heat shield.
5. Support the tank with a jack and remove the fuel tank straps.
6. Disconnect the fuel lines, vapor hose and electrical connector from the fuel tank.
7. Lower the tank from the vehicle.

To install:

8. Raise the tank into position and install the fuel tank straps.
9. Connect the fuel lines, vapor hose and electrical connector.
10. Install the heat shield and connect the fuel filler pipe.
11. Tighten the fuel tank strap retaining bolts to 35–45 ft. lbs. (47–61 Nm).
12. Remove the jack and lower the vehicle.
13. Fill the fuel tank and check for leaks. Connect the negative battery cable.

BRONCO II

1. Disconnect the negative battery cable and relieve the fuel system pressure.
2. Raise and safely support the vehicle.
3. Drain the fuel from the fuel tank. Remove the skid plate, if equipped.
4. Support the fuel tank with a jack and remove the fuel tank straps.
5. Disconnect the fill pipe and lower the tank enough to disconnect the fuel lines, vapor hoses and electrical connector.
6. Lower the tank from the vehicle.

To install:

7. Raise the fuel tank and connect the electrical connector vapor hoses and fuel lines.
8. Connect the fuel filler pipe and install the fuel tank straps. Install the skid plate, if equipped.
9. Remove the jack and lower the vehicle.
10. Fill the fuel tank and check for leaks. Connect the negative battery cable.

EXPLORER

1. Disconnect the negative battery cable and relieve the fuel system pressure.
2. Raise and safely support the vehicle.
3. Drain the fuel from the fuel tank.
4. Remove the shield, skid plate and fuel tank front strap.
5. Support the tank with a jack and remove the bolt from the fuel tank rear strap.
6. Disconnect the filler pipe and vent pipe and lower the tank. Disconnect the vapor hose, fuel lines and electrical connector.
7. Lower the tank from the vehicle.

To install:

8. Raise the fuel tank and connect the electrical connector, fuel lines and vapor hose.
9. Connect the filler pipe and vent pipe. Attach the rear fuel tank strap.
10. Install the shield, skid plate and front strap.
11. Remove the jack and lower the vehicle.
12. Fill the fuel tank and check for leaks. Connect the negative battery cable.

RANGER

1. Disconnect the negative battery cable and relieve the fuel system pressure.
2. Raise and safely support the vehicle.

3. Drain the fuel from the fuel tank.
4. Loosen the filler pipe clamp.
5. Remove the bolts securing the skid plate and shield assembly brackets to the frame, if equipped. Remove the skid plate and shield and the brackets as an assembly.
6. Remove the heat shield. Support the tank with a jack and remove the fuel tank straps.
7. Disconnect the fuel lines, vapor hose and electrical connector. Lower the fuel tank from the vehicle.

To install:

8. Raise the tank into position and attach the fuel tank straps.
9. Connect the electrical connector, vapor hose and fuel lines.
10. Connect the fuel filler pipe. Remove the jack.
11. Install the skid plate and heat shield and bracket assembly, if equipped. Install the heat shield and lower the vehicle.
12. Fill the fuel tank and check for leaks. Connect the negative battery cable.

Fuel Filter

Removal and Installation

EXCEPT 2.0L ENGINE

1. Disconnect the negative battery cable and relieve the fuel system pressure.
2. Raise and support the vehicle safely.
3. Disconnect the fuel lines from the fuel filter.
4. Remove the fuel filter from the bracket and the retainer, if equipped. Note the direction of the flow arrow so the replacement filter can be installed correctly.
5. Installation is the reverse of the removal procedure. Start the engine and check for leaks.

2.0L ENGINE

1. Disconnect the negative battery cable. Remove the air cleaner.
2. While holding the fuel filter with a backup wrench, disconnect the fuel line from the filter.
3. Unscrew the filter from the carburetor.

To install:

4. Apply a bead of teflon sealant to the external threads of a new filter. Thread the filter into the carburetor inlet port and tighten to 6.5–8.0 ft. lbs. (9.0–11.0 Nm).
5. Apply a small amount of engine oil to the fuel line nut and flare. Hand start the nut into the fuel filter inlet approximately 2 threads.
6. While holding the fuel filter with a backup wrench, tighten the fuel line nut to 15–18 ft. lbs. (20–24 Nm).
7. Connect the negative battery cable, start the engine and check for leaks. Install the air cleaner assembly.

Mechanical Fuel Pump

Pressure Testing

1. Remove the air cleaner. Disconnect the fuel line from the carburetor and attach a fuel pressure gauge to the line.
2. Start the engine and read the fuel pressure after 10 seconds. The fuel pressure should be 5–7 psi.

NOTE: The engine should be able to run for over 30 seconds on the fuel in the carburetor float bowl.

3. Shut off the engine and remove the pressure gauge. Connect the fuel line to the carburetor and install the air cleaner.

Removal and Installation

1. Disconnect the negative battery cable.
2. Loosen the mounting bolts approximately 2 turns. Apply hand force to loosen the pump if the gasket is stuck. Rotate the

engine until the fuel pump cam lobe is near its low position, in order to reduce the tension on the fuel pump.

3. Disconnect the fuel lines from the pump.

4. Remove the mounting bolts and the fuel pump. Clean all gasket mating surfaces.

5. Installation is the reverse of the removal procedure. Tighten the mounting bolts alternately and evenly to 14–21 ft. lbs. (19–29 Nm). Start the engine and check for leaks.

Electric Fuel Pump

All vehicles, except 1988 Bronco II and Ranger, are equipped with a single high-pressure pump located in the fuel tank. 1988 Bronco II and Ranger are equipped with 2 fuel pumps, a high-pressure pump mounted on the frame rail and a low-pressure pump located in the fuel tank.

Pressure Testing

HIGH PRESSURE PUMP

1. Make sure there is an adequate fuel supply.
2. Relieve the fuel system pressure.
3. Turn the ignition key **OFF**.
4. Connect a suitable fuel pressure gauge to the schrader valve on the fuel rail.
5. Install a test lead to the **FP** terminal on the VIP test connector.
6. Turn the ignition key to the **RUN** position, then ground the test lead to run the fuel pump.
7. Observe the fuel pressure reading on the pressure gauge. The fuel pressure should be 35–45 psi.
8. Relieve the fuel system pressure and turn the ignition key **OFF**. Remove the fuel pressure gauge and the test lead.

LOW PRESSURE PUMP

1. Relieve the fuel system pressure. Open the fuel line at the high pressure pump inlet.
2. Connect a hose to the line from the fuel tank. Position the other end of the hose in a calibrated container of at least 1 quart capacity.
3. Disconnect the high pressure fuel pump electrical connector from the wiring harness.
4. Install a test lead to the **FP** terminal on the VIP test connector.
5. Turn the ignition switch to the **RUN** position and ground the test lead to energize the pump for 10 seconds, then disconnect the test lead.

NOTE: It may be necessary to momentarily block the fuel hose to prime the low pressure pump. With the outlet open and under no back pressure on the outlet, this is normal.

6. If the fuel pump produces a minimum flow of 16 oz. of fuel in 10 seconds, the pump is operating correctly. If there is no flow from the pump, check the electrical circuit, check for inlet restriction and replace the pump if necessary.

7. If fuel pump noise comes from the low pressure pump, there may be a malfunction in the high pressure pump. To check this, compare the vibration of the inlet and outlet fuel lines at the high pressure pump. If there is a large difference between the lines in vibration level, replace the high pressure pump and recheck for noise.

Removal and Installation

TANK MOUNTED PUMP

NOTE: On Ranger, the fuel pump may be accessed by removing the pickup box from the chassis, instead of removing the fuel tank.

1. Disconnect the negative battery cable and relieve the fuel system pressure.

VIP test connector

Tank mounted electric fuel pump assembly

2. Raise and safely support the vehicle.
3. Remove the fuel tank.
4. Remove any dirt that has accumulated around the fuel pump attaching flange so it will not enter the fuel tank during removal and installation.
5. Turn the fuel pump locking ring counterclockwise using a suitable tool. Remove the locking ring.
6. Remove the fuel pump and discard the seal ring. Separate the fuel pump from the sending unit, if required.

To install:

7. Clean the fuel pump mounting flange and tank mounting surface and seal ring groove.
8. Apply a light coating of grease on a new seal ring and install it in the groove.
9. Install the fuel pump to the sending unit, if removed. Install the fuel pump assembly in the tank, making sure the locating keys are in the keyways and the seal ring is in place.
10. Hold the fuel pump assembly and the seal ring in place and install the locking ring. Rotate the ring clockwise using a suitable tool. Find the fuel tank part number on the front bottom of the tank and proceed as follows:

a. If equipped with part number E59A–9002–CAE tank, tighten the ring to 60–85 ft. lbs. (81–115 Nm), wait 5 minutes and retighten to the same specification. Use only the ring that was removed from the tank, do not replace with a ring from another tank.

b. If equipped with plastic retaining ring E99A–9A307–D, tighten to 40–55 ft. lbs. (54–74 Nm). Use the same ring that was removed from the tank. If a new tank is installed, use a new ring.

c. If equipped with part number E69A–9002–PA tank, tighten the locking ring once to 80–113 ft. lbs. (109–153 Nm).

d. On Ranger and Aerostar, tighten the polyethylene locking ring to 40–45 ft. lbs. (54–61 Nm).

11. Install the fuel tank in the vehicle.

12. Lower the vehicle and fill the fuel tank with at least 10 gallons of fuel. Connect the negative battery cable. Turn the ignition key to **RUN** for 3 seconds repeatedly, 5–10 times, to pressurize the system. Check for leaks.

13. Start the engine and check for leaks.

FRAME MOUNTED PUMP

1. Disconnect the negative battery cable and relieve the fuel system pressure.

2. Raise and support the vehicle safely.

3. Disconnect the fuel lines and electrical connector from the pump.

4. Remove the pump from the mounting bracket.

5. Installation is the reverse of the removal procedure. Start the engine and check for leaks.

Carburetor

Removal and Installation

1. Disconnect the negative battery cable. Remove the air cleaner, disconnecting the emission control hoses and air intake hose, as required.

2. Disconnect the fuel line and the accelerator linkage. Tag and disconnect the vacuum hoses and electrical connections.

3. Remove the retaining nuts and the carburetor. Cover the intake manifold opening with a cloth.

4. Installation is the reverse of the removal procedure. Tighten the carburetor retaining nuts to 13–14 ft. lbs. (17.7–19.0 Nm).

Idle Speed Adjustment

1. Apply the parking brake and place the transmission in **N**.

2. Bring the engine to normal operating temperature. Turn off all accessories.

Carburetor component locations—2.0L engine

3. Check the engine idle speed as specified on the vehicle emission information label. If the idle speed is correct, no adjustment is required. If not, proceed to Step 4.

4. Turn the ignition key to **OFF**.

5. Disconnect the Idle Speed Control (ISC) motor connector. Disconnect the vacuum hose at the fast idle cam breaker and plug. Connect insulated jumper clip leads from the battery terminals to the top 2 ISC motor terminals to retract the motor.

NOTE: If the motor extends instead of retracts, reverse the polarity across the motor terminals. Battery voltage must not be applied to the bottom terminals of the motor, the Idle Tracking Switch (ITS) terminals. Isolate the ITS terminals with electrical tape during this procedure.

6. Restart the engine and check the closed throttle rpm; it should be 700 rpm or less. If adjustment is required, remove the tamper proof cap and adjust the throttle stop adjusting screw.

7. Place the fast idle lever on the first step on the fast idle cam. Without touching the accelerator pedal, check/adjust the fast idle speed to specification with the fast idle adjusting screw.

8. Rev the engine momentarily, allowing it to return to closed throttle speed.

9. Reconnect the jumper leads the ISC motor terminals. If the motor retracts instead of extending, reverse polarity across the motor terminals. Disconnect the jumper leads after the motor has fully extended.

10. Check/adjust the ISC full stroke speed to 2000 ± 200 rpm using the full stroke speed adjusting screw.

11. Remove the electrical tape from the ITS terminals of the motor connector and reconnect the ISC motor to the engine wiring harness. Remove the plug from the fast idle cam breaker vacuum hose and reconnect.

12. Check the ISC function as follows:

  a. Turn off all accessories. The idle speed should adjust to that specified on the vehicle emission information label.

  b. Turn the ignition switch **OFF**.

  c. Disconnect the engine coolant temperature switch.

  d. Restart the engine. The idle speed should adjust to 1200 ± 75 rpm.

  e. Turn the ignition switch **OFF**, then reconnect the engine coolant temperature switch.

13. After adjustments are completed, reconnect all parts.

Idle Mixture Adjustment

Idle mixture adjustment requires propane enrichment tool T75L–9600–A or equivalent.

Service Adjustments

For all carburetor sevice adjustments procedures and specifications, please refer to "Carburetor Service" in the Unit Repair section.

Fuel Injection

For further information, please refer to Chilton's Electronic Engine Controls Manual.

Idle Speed Adjustment

1988–90

1. Apply the parking brake and place the transmission in **P** or **N**.

2. Start the engine and bring to normal operating temperature. Turn off the heater and all accessories.

3. Make sure the throttle lever is resting on the throttle plate stop screw and the ignition timing is set to specification.

4. Connect a tachometer according to the manufacturers instructions.

ISC MOTOR TERMINALS (CONNECT JUMPER WIRE)

ITS TERMINALS (COVER WITH TAPE)

ISC motor connectors

5. Shut the engine off and disconnect the negative battery cable for 5 minutes minimum, then reconnect it.

6. Start the engine and stabilize for 2 minutes, then rev the engine and let it return to idle. Lightly depress and release the accelerator and let the engine idle. If the engine does not idle properly, proceed to Step 7.

7. Disconnect the idle speed control-air bypass solenoid.

8. With the transmission in **N** or **P**, run the engine at 2500 rpm for 30 seconds.

9. On 1988 vehicles with 2.9L and 3.0L engines and 1989–90 vehicles with 3.0L engine, place the automatic transmission in **D**. On all other vehicles with automatic transmission, place the transmission in **P**.

10. Turn the throttle plate stop screw to adjust the idle speed to the following specifications:

  1988 2.3L engine – 625 ± 25 rpm.
  1989–90 2.3L engines – 575 ± 25 rpm.
  1988 2.9L engine – 700 rpm.
  1989–90 2.9L engines – 725 rpm.
  1988–90 3.0L engine with automatic transmission – 625 ± 25 rpm.
  1988–90 3.0L engine with manual transmission – 725 ± 25 rpm.
  1990 4.0L engine – 675 rpm.

11. On all except 2.3L engine, shut the engine off and repeat Steps 8, 9 and 10.

12. On all except 2.3L engine, shut the engine off and disconnect the battery for 3 minutes minimum.

13. With the engine off, reconnect the idle speed control-air bypass solenoid. Make sure the throttle is not stuck in the bore and the linkage not preventing the throttle from closing.

14. Start the engine and let it stabilize for 2 minutes, then rev the engine and let it return to idle. Lightly depress and release the accelerator and let the engine idle.

15. Vehicles with 3.0L engine and automatic transmission should now be idling at 700 ± 50 rpm. Vehicles with 3.0L engine and manual transmission should now be idling at 800 ± 50 rpm.

16. Remove all test equipment.

1991–92

Idle speed adjustment on 1991–92 engines requires the use of Super Star II tester 007-00028 or equivalent.

THROTTLE PLATE STOP SCREW

AIR BYPASS VALVE ASSEMBLY LOCATED AT THE INLET AIR FILTER

Throttle plate stop screw location – 2.3L engine

Throttle plate stop screw location—2.9L engine

Throttle plate stop screw location—3.0L engine

Idle Mixture Adjustment

The idle mixture is controlled by the electronic control unit and cannot be adjusted.

Fuel Injector

Removal and Installation

2.3L ENGINE

1. Disconnect the negative battery cable and relieve the fuel system pressure.
2. Disconnect the electrical connectors at the TPS, air bypass valve, injector wiring harness at the main engine harness and at the water temperature indicator sensor, ACT and ECT sensors and the ignition control assembly. Tag all lines prior to removal to aid reinstallation.
3. Remove the throttle linkage shield and disconnect the throttle linkage and cruise control. Unbolt the accelerator cable from the bracket and position out of the way.
4. Disconnect the vacuum lines at the upper intake manifold vacuum tree, EGR valve, fuel pressure regulator and canister purge line. Tag all lines prior to removal to aid reinstallation.
5. Disconnect the air intake hose and crankcase vent hose.
6. Disconnect the hose for the PCV system from the fitting on the underside of the upper intake manifold.
7. Disconnect the EGR tube from the EGR valve by removing the flange nut.
8. Remove the upper intake manifold retaining bolts and remove the upper intake manifold and throttle body assembly.
9. Disconnect the injector electrical connectors.

10. Disconnect the fuel lines from the fuel supply manifold.
11. Remove the 2 fuel supply manifold retaining bolts.
12. Carefully disengage the manifold and fuel injectors from the engine and remove the manifold and injectors.
13. Remove the injectors from the manifold by grasping the injector body and pulling while gently rocking the injector from side-to-side. Remove and discard the injector O-rings.

To install:

14. Lubricate new O-rings with clean light grade oil and install 2 on each injector.

NOTE: Never use silicone grease at it will clog the injectors.

15. Install the injectors, using a light, twisting, pushing motion.
16. Install the fuel supply manifold, pushing it down to make sure all the O-rings are seated in the fuel rail cups and intake manifold.
17. Install the manifold retaining bolts and tighten to 15–22 ft. lbs. (20–30 Nm) while holding the fuel manifold down.
18. Connect the fuel lines to the supply manifold.
19. After the fuel supply manifold has been installed and before the fuel injector wire connectors have been connected, connect the negative battery cable and turn the ignition **ON**. This will cause the fuel pump to run for 2–3 seconds and pressurize the fuel system.
20. Check for leaks where the fuel injector is installed into the fuel supply manifold.
21. Disconnect the negative battery cable.
22. Connect the fuel injector electrical connectors.
23. Make sure the gasket surfaces of the upper and lower intake manifolds are clean.
24. Place a new gasket on the lower intake manifold assembly and place the upper intake manifold and throttle body assembly in position.
25. Install the retaining bolts and tighten in sequence to 15–22 ft. lbs. (20–30 Nm).

NOTE: On 1989–92 vehicles, the 3 bolts with stud heads go in hole positions 2, 3 and 4.

26. Connect the EGR tube to the EGR valve and tighten to 18–28 ft. lbs. (25–30 Nm).
27. Connect the PCV system hose to the fitting on the underside of the upper intake manifold.
28. Connect all vacuum lines and electrical connectors according to the locations that were marked during the removal procedure.
29. Hold the accelerator cable bracket in position on the upper manifold and install the retaining bolts. Tighten to 10–15 ft. lbs. (13.5–20.5 Nm).
30. Install the accelerator cable to the bracket and connect the accelerator cable and cruise control. Install the throttle linkage shield.
31. Connect the air intake hose and crankcase vent hose.
32. Connect the negative battery cable. Start the engine and let it idle for 2 minutes.
33. Turn the engine **OFF** and check for fuel leaks.

2.9L ENGINE

1. Disconnect the negative battery cable and relieve the fuel system pressure.
2. Disconnect the electrical connectors at the air bypass valve, TPS, EGR sensor and ACT.
3. Remove the air inlet tube from the air cleaner to throttle body.
4. Remove the snow/ice shield to expose the throttle linkage. Disconnect the throttle cable from the ball stud.
5. Disconnect the upper intake manifold vacuum connectors; both the front and rear fittings including the EGR valve and the vacuum line to the fuel pressure regulator.
6. Disconnect the PCV closure tube from under the throttle

Upper intake manifold bolt torque sequence—1988 2.3L engine

FRONT OF ENGINE

Upper intake manifold bolt torque sequence—1989–92 2.3L engine

body and disconnect the PCV vacuum tube from under the manifold.

7. Remove the canister purge line from the fitting near the power steering pump.

8. Disconnect the EGR tube from the EGR valve by removing the flange nut.

9. Loosen the bolt that retains the air conditioning line at the upper rear of the upper manifold and disengage the retainer.

10. Remove the 6 upper intake manifold retaining bolts and remove the upper intake manifold and throttle body assembly.

11. Disconnect the fuel supply and return lines from the fuel supply manifold.

12. On 1990–92 vehicles, disconnect the fuel return line from the fuel pressure regulator as follows:

   a. Disengage the locking tabs on the connector retainer and separate the retainer halves.

   b. Inspect the visible internal portion of the fitting for dirt accumulation. Clean the fitting before disassembly.

   c. To disengage the fitting from the regulator, push the fitting toward the regulator, insert the fingers on fuel line coupling key T90P–9550–A or equivalent, into the slots in the coupling.

   d. Using the tool, pull the fitting from the regulator.

NOTE: If the fitting has been properly disengaged, the fitting should slide off the regulator with minimum effort.

13. Disconnect the electrical connectors from the fuel injectors.

14. Remove the 4 fuel supply manifold retaining bolts.

15. Carefully disengage the fuel supply manifold from the lower intake manifold. The fuel injectors are retained in the fuel supply manifold with clips.

16. Remove the retainer clips and inspect for corrosion and damage.

17. Remove the injector from the fuel supply manifold by grasping the injector body and pulling while gently rocking from side-to-side. Remove and discard the injector O-rings.

18. Inspect the injector plastic pintle protection cap and washer for signs of deterioration. Replace the complete injector as required. If the plastic pintle protection cap is missing, look for it in the intake manifold.

NOTE: The plastic pintle protection cap is not available as a separate part.

To install:

19. Lubricate new O-rings with clean light grade oil and install 2 on each injector.

NOTE: Never use silicone grease at it will clog the injectors.

20. Install the injectors, using a light, twisting, pushing motion.

Upper intake manifold assembly—2.9L engine

Fuel supply manifold assembly—2.9L engine

21. Install the fuel supply manifold, pushing down to make sure all the fuel injector O-rings are fully seated in the fuel supply manifold cups and intake manifold.

22. Install the 4 retaining bolts and tighten to 71–97 inch lbs. (8–11 Nm) while holding the fuel rail assembly down.

23. Connect the fuel supply and return lines to the fuel supply manifold. On 1990–92 vehicles, tighten the line nut to 15–18 ft. lbs. (20–24 Nm).

24. On 1990–92 vehicles, install the fuel return line to the fuel pressure regulator by pushing it onto the fuel pressure regulator line up to the shoulder on the regulator line.

NOTE: The connector should grip the regulator line securely.

25. Install the connector retainer and snap the 2 halves of the retainer together.

26. Install the fuel injector retaining clips to the injectors.

27. After the fuel supply manifold has been installed and before the fuel injector wire connectors have been connected, connect the negative battery cable and turn the ignition **ON**. This will cause the fuel pump to run for 2–3 seconds and pressurize the fuel system.

28. Check for leaks where the fuel injector is installed into the fuel supply manifold.

29. Disconnect the negative battery cable.

30. Connect the fuel injector electrical connectors.

31. Make sure the gasket surfaces of the upper and lower intake manifolds are clean.

32. Place a new gasket on the lower intake manifold assembly and place the upper intake manifold and throttle body assembly in position. The use of alignment studs may be helpful. Align the EGR tube in the valve.

33. Install the 6 upper intake manifold retaining bolts and tighten to 11–15 ft. lbs. (16–20 Nm).

34. Engage the air conditioner line retainer cup and tighten the bolt.

35. Tighten the EGR tube and flare fitting. Tighten the lower retainer nut at the exhaust manifold.

36. Connect the canister purge line, PCV vacuum hose and the PCV closure hose.

37. Connect the vacuum lines to the vacuum tree, EGR valve and fuel pressure regulator.

38. Connect the throttle cable to the throttle body and install the snow/ice shield.

39. Connect the electrical connectors at the air bypass valve, TPS and ACT sensor.

40. Install the air inlet tube from the throttle body to the air cleaner.

41. Connect the negative battery cable, start the engine and let it idle for 2 minutes.

42. Turn the engine **OFF** and check for fuel leaks.

3.0L ENGINE

1. Disconnect the negative battery cable and relieve the fuel system pressure.

2. Remove the air intake throttle body assembly as follows:

 a. Remove the engine air cleaner outlet tube between the air cleaner and throttle body.

 b. Remove the snow shield from the power steering pump bracket and accelerator cable bracket.

 c. Tag and disconnect the vacuum lines at the vacuum fittings on the intake manifold and PCV hose.

 d. Disconnect and remove the accelerator and cruise control cables from the accelerator mounting bracket and throttle lever.

 e. Remove the alternator support brace.

 f. Remove the throttle body-to-lower intake manifold retaining bolts and stud bolts. Remove the throttle body assembly.

3. Disconnect the fuel lines from the fuel supply manifold.

4. Disconnect the wiring harness from the injectors.

5. Disconnect the vacuum line from the fuel pressure regulator.

6. Remove the 4 fuel supply manifold retaining bolts.

7. Carefully disengage the fuel supply manifold from the fuel injectors by lifting and gently rocking the manifold.

8. Remove the injectors by lifting while gently rocking from side-to-side. Remove and discard the O-rings.

To install:

9. Lubricate new O-rings with clean light grade oil and install 2 on each injector.

NOTE: Never use silicone grease at it will clog the injectors.

10. Install the injectors in the fuel supply manifold, using a light, twisting, pushing motion.

11. Carefully install the fuel supply manifold and injectors into the lower intake manifold, 1 side at a time. Push the fuel supply manifold down to ensure that all injector O-rings are fully seated in the fuel supply manifold cups and intake manifold.

12. While holding the fuel supply manifold in place, install the 2 retaining bolts hand-tight and then tighten to 6–8 ft. lbs. (8–12 Nm).

13. Repeat Steps 11 and 12 for the other side of the fuel supply manifold.

14. Connect the fuel supply and return lines.

15. After the fuel supply manifold has been installed and before the fuel injector wire connectors have been connected, connect the negative battery cable and turn the ignition **ON**. This will cause the fuel pump to run for 2–3 seconds and pressurize the fuel system.

16. Check for leaks where the fuel injector is installed into the fuel supply manifold.

17. Disconnect the negative battery cable.

18. Connect the fuel injector electrical connectors.

19. Install the air intake throttle body in the reverse order of removal. Tighten the bolts, in sequence, to 19 ft. lbs. (25 Nm).

20. Connect the vacuum line to the fuel pressure regulator.

21. Connect the negative battery cable, start the engine and let it idle for 2 minutes.

22. Turn the engine **OFF** and check for fuel leaks.

4.0L ENGINE

1. Disconnect the negative battery cable and relieve the fuel system pressure.

2. Disconnect the electrical connectors at the air bypass valve, TPS and ACT sensor.

3. Remove the snow/ice shield to expose the throttle linkage. Remove the throttle cable bracket and disconnect the cable from the ball stud on the throttle body.

4. Remove the air inlet tube from the air cleaner to the throttle body.

5. Disconnect the PCV valve from the valve cover.

6. Disconnect the spark plug wires from the comb at the rear of the manifold.

7. Remove the canister purge line from the fitting in the throttle housing.

8. On Aerostar, remove the bolt retaining the engine oil dipstick tube.

9. Remove the bolt that retains the air conditioner line at the upper rear of the upper manifold.

10. Remove the 6 upper intake manifold retaining nuts and remove the upper intake and throttle body assembly.

11. Disconnect the fuel supply line fitting at the fuel manifold.

12. Disconnect the fuel return line from the fuel pressure regulator as follows:

 a. Disengage the locking tabs on the connector retainer and separate the retainer halves.

 b. Inspect the visible internal portion of the fitting for dirt accumulation. Clean the fitting before disassembly.

c. To disengage the fitting from the regulator, push the fitting toward the regulator, insert the fingers on fuel line coupling key T90P–9550–A or equivalent, into the slots in the coupling.

d. Using the tool, pull the fitting from the regulator.

NOTE: If the fitting has been properly disengaged, the fitting should slide off the regulator with minimum effort.

13. Disconnect the electrical connectors from the fuel injectors.

14. Remove the 6 bolts retaining the fuel supply manifold and remove the manifold.

15. Remove the injector retaining clips and remove the injectors from the manifold by grasping the injector body and pulling up while rocking the injector from side-to-side.

16. Remove and discard the injector O-rings.

17. Inspect the injector plastic pintle protection cap and washer for signs of deterioration. Replace the complete injector as required. If the plastic pintle protection cap is missing, look for it in the intake manifold.

NOTE: The plastic pintle protection cap is not available as a separate part.

To install:

18. Lubricate new O-rings with clean light grade oil and install 2 on each injector.

NOTE: Never use silicone grease at it will clog the injectors.

19. Install the injectors, using a light, twisting, pushing motion.

20. Install the fuel supply manifold, pushing down to make sure all the fuel injector O-rings are fully seated in the fuel supply manifold cups and intake manifold.

21. Install the 6 retaining bolts and tighten to 7–10 ft. lbs. (10–14 Nm). Install the retainer clips.

22. Install the fuel supply line and tighten the fitting to 15–18 ft. lbs. (20–24 Nm).

23. Install the fuel return line to the fuel pressure regulator by pushing it onto the fuel pressure regulator line up to the shoulder on the regulator line.

NOTE: The connector should grip the regulator line securely.

24. Install the connector retainer and snap the 2 halves of the retainer together.

25. Clean and inspect the mounting faces of the fuel manifold and upper intake manifold.

26. Position a new gasket on the mounting studs and install the upper intake manifold on the studs.

27. Install the 6 upper intake manifold retaining nuts and tighten to 15–18 ft. lbs. (20–25 Nm).

28. Connect the spark plug wires to the retainer comb at the rear of the intake manifold.

29. Attach the air conditioner line retainer and automatic transmission vacuum line retainer at the upper intake manifold.

30. Install the canister purge line on the throttle body fitting.

31. Connect the vacuum lines to the vacuum tree. Connect the electrical connectors at the air bypass valve, TPS and ACT sensor.

32. Install the PCV valve in the grommet at the rear of the right valve cover.

33. On Aerostar, attach the engine oil dipstick tube to the upper intake manifold.

34. Attach the throttle cable bracket to the upper intake manifold, then connect the throttle cable to the ball stud and install the snow/ice shield.

35. After the upper intake manifold has been installed and before the fuel injector wire connectors have been connected, connect the negative battery cable and turn the ignition switch **ON**. This will cause the fuel pump to run for 2–3 seconds and pressurize the system.

36. Check for fuel leaks where the fuel injector is installed into the fuel supply manifold.

37. Turn the ignition switch **OFF** and disconnect the negative battery cable.

38. Connect the injector wire connectors and the vacuum line to the regulator.

39. Install the air inlet tube from the throttle body to the air cleaner.

40. Connect the negative battery cable, start the engine and let it idle for 2 minutes.

41. Turn the engine **OFF** and check for fuel leaks.

EMISSION CONTROLS

For further information, please refer to Chilton's Emission Controls Manual.

Emission Warning Lamps

Resetting

EXCEPT 1988 2.0L AND 2.3L ENGINES

All vehicles are equipped with a "CHECK ENGINE" or "SERVICE ENGINE SOON" warning lamp located on the instrument cluster. This lamp should come on briefly when the ignition key is turned **ON**, but should turn off when the engine starts. If the lamp does not come ON when the ignition key is turned **ON** or if it comes ON and stays ON when the engine is running, there is a malfunction in the electronic engine control system. After the malfunction has been remedied, using the proper procedures, the "CHECK ENGINE" or "SERVICE ENGINE SOON" lamp will go out.

1988 2.0L ENGINE

The "CHECK ENGINE" lamp is used to indicate that maintenance of emission control devices is required. When the lamp stays on continuously, the required service should be performed. After the service is performed, the emission maintenance sensor, located above the right front corner of the glove box, must be reset as follows:

1. Turn the ignition switch to the **OFF** position.

2. Lightly push a small rod through the 0.2 in. diameter hole with the sticker labeled "RESET" and press down and hold.

3. While pressing the tool down, turn the ignition switch to the **RUN** position. The "CHECK ENGINE" lamp will then light and remain lit for as long as the rod is pressed down.

4. Hold the rod down for 5 seconds, then remove it. The lamp should go out within 2–5 seconds indicating a reset has occurred.

5. Turn the ignition switch to the **OFF** position then turn it to the **RUN** position. The "CHECK ENGINE" lamp will light for 2–5 seconds and will then go out. This verifies that a proper reset of the module has been accomplished.

NOTE: 1988 vehicles with 2.3L engines are not equipped with a "CHECK ENGINE" warning light.

ENGINE MECHANICAL

NOTE: Disconnecting the negative battery cable on some vehicles may interfere with the functions of the on board computer systems and may require the computer to undergo a relearning process, once the negative battery cable is reconnected.

Engine Assembly

Removal and Installation

2.0L AND 2.3L ENGINES

1. Disconnect the negative battery cable. On 2.3L engine, relieve the fuel system pressure.
2. Drain the cooling system. On 2.0L engine, remove the air cleaner and duct assembly. On 2.3L engine, disconnect the air cleaner tube at the throttle body. Disconnect the idle speed control hose and heat riser tube, if necessary.
3. Mark the location of the hinges on the hood and remove the hood.
4. Disconnect the radiator hoses and, if equipped, disconnect the transmission cooler lines. Remove the fan, fan shroud and radiator.
5. Remove the oil fill cap. Disconnect the engine wiring harness from the body wiring harness.
6. Disconnect the alternator wiring from the alternator, the starter cable from the starter and the accelerator cable from the carburetor or throttle body. If equipped, disconnect the transmission kickdown cable.
7. If equipped, remove the air conditioner compressor from the mounting bracket and position aside, leaving the refrigerant lines attached.
8. Disconnect the power brake vacuum hose. On 2.0L engine, disconnect the fuel line from the fuel pump. On 2.3L engine, disconnect the fuel lines from the fuel supply manifold.
9. Disconnect the heater hoses from the engine.
10. Remove the engine mount nuts. Raise and safely support the vehicle.
11. Drain the engine oil from the crankcase and remove the starter.
12. Disconnect the exhaust pipe at the exhaust manifold. If equipped with manual transmission, remove the dust cover. If equipped with automatic transmission, remove the converter inspection plate, then remove the converter-to-flywheel bolts.
13. Remove the lower flywheel housing or converter housing attaching bolts and lower the vehicle.
14. Support the transmission and flywheel housing or converter housing with a jack.
15. Remove the flywheel housing or converter housing upper attaching bolts.
16. Attach suitable engine lifting equipment. Carefully lift the engine out of the vehicle and install on a workstand.

To install:

17. Remove the engine from the workstand and carefully lower it into the engine compartment. If equipped with automatic transmission, start the converter pilot into the crankshaft.
18. If equipped with manual transmission, start the transmission input shaft into the clutch disc. It may be necessary to adjust the position of the transmission in relation to the engine if the input shaft will not enter the clutch disc. If the engine hangs up after the shaft enters, turn the crankshaft in the clockwise direction slowly, transmission in gear, until the shaft splines mesh with the clutch disc splines.
19. Install the flywheel or converter housing attaching bolts and remove the engine lifting equipment.
20. Remove the jack from under the vehicle and raise and safely support the vehicle.
21. If equipped with automatic transmission, install the converter-to-flywheel attaching bolts. Install the lower flywheel

housing or converter housing attaching bolts and install the dust plate or converter inspection cover.
22. Connect the exhaust pipe to the exhaust manifold. Install the starter and connect the starter cable.
23. Lower the vehicle and install the engine mount nuts. Tighten to 65–85 ft. lbs. (88–115 Nm).
24. Connect the heater hoses to the engine and the fuel lines to the fuel supply manifold or fuel pump. Connect the power brake vacuum hose.
25. Connect the wiring to the alternator and the accelerator cable to the carburetor or throttle body. If equipped, connect the transmission kickdown rod.
26. If equipped, install the air conditioning compressor in its mounting brackets.
27. Connect the engine wiring harness to the body wiring harness.
28. Install the fan, fan shroud and radiator. Connect the radiator hoses and, if equipped, the transmission cooler lines.
29. Install the hood, aligning the hinges with the marks that were made during removal.
30. On 2.0L engine, install the air cleaner assembly. On 2.3L engine, connect the air cleaner outlet tube at the throttle body. Connect the idle speed control hose and heat riser tube, if necessary.
31. Fill the crankcase with the proper type and quantity of engine oil. Install the oil cap.
32. Connect the negative battery cable. Fill and bleed the cooling system. Run the engine and check for leaks.

2.9L ENGINE

1. Disconnect the negative battery cable and relieve the fuel system pressure. Drain the cooling system.
2. Mark the position of the hood on the hinges and remove the hood. Remove the air cleaner intake hose.
3. Disconnect the radiator hoses and, if equipped with automatic transmission, disconnect the transmission cooler lines. Remove the fan shroud and radiator.
4. Remove the alternator and bracket and position the alternator aside. Disconnect the alternator ground wire from the engine block.
5. If equipped, remove the air conditioning compressor and power steering pump and position aside.
6. Disconnect the heater hoses at the intake manifold and water pump. Remove the ground wires from the cylinder block.
7. Disconnect the fuel lines from the fuel supply manifold. Disconnect the throttle cable shield and linkage at the throttle body and intake manifold.
8. Tag and disconnect all necessary vacuum lines and electrical connectors.
9. Raise and safely support the vehicle.
10. Disconnect the exhaust pipes from the exhaust manifolds. Disconnect the starter cable and remove the starter.
11. If equipped with manual transmission, remove the flywheel housing attaching bolts and remove the hydraulic clutch hose.
12. Remove the engine front mount-to-crossmember attaching nuts or through bolts.
13. If equipped with automatic transmission, remove the converter inspection cover and disconnect the converter from the flywheel.
14. Remove the cable. Remove the converter housing-to-engine bolts and the adapter plate-to-converter housing bolt.
15. Lower the vehicle and position a jack under the transmission. Install suitable engine lifting equipment.
16. Raise the engine slightly and carefully pull it from the transmission. Carefully lift the engine out of the engine compartment so the rear cover plate is not bent or components damaged. Install the engine on a workstand.

To install:

17. Remove the engine from the workstand and lower it carefully into the engine compartment. Make sure the exhaust manifolds are properly aligned with the exhaust pipes.

18. If equipped with manual transmission, start the transmission input shaft into the clutch disc. It may be necessary to adjust the position of the transmission in relation to the engine if the input shaft will not enter the clutch disc. If the engine hangs up after the shaft enters, turn the crankshaft in the clockwise direction slowly, transmission in gear, until the shaft splines mesh with the clutch disc splines.

19. Install the flywheel housing or converter housing upper bolts, making sure the dowels in the engine block engage the flywheel housing or converter housing. Tighten the bolts to 33–45 ft. lbs. (45–61 Nm).

20. Install the clutch hose and remove the jack from under the transmission. Remove the engine lifting equipment.

21. If equipped with automatic transmission, position the kickdown rod on the transmission and engine. Raise and safely support the vehicle.

22. If equipped with automatic transmission, position the transmission linkage bracket and install the remaining converter housing bolts. Install the adapter plate-to-converter housing bolt. Install the converter-to-flywheel nuts and the inspection cover. Connect the kickdown rod on the transmission.

23. If equipped with manual transmission, install the flywheel housing attaching bolts.

24. Install the starter and connect the cable. Connect the exhaust pipes at the exhaust manifolds.

25. Install the engine front mount-to-crossmember attaching nuts or through bolts. Lower the vehicle.

26. Connect all vacuum hoses and electrical connectors to the locations marked during removal.

27. Install the throttle linkage and connect the fuel lines. Connect the heater hoses at the water pump and engine block.

28. Install the alternator and bracket and connect the ground wire to the engine block. Install the drive belt and adjust the tension.

29. Install the air conditioning compressor and power steering pump, if equipped.

30. Install the radiator and fan shroud. Connect the radiator hoses and, if equipped, transmission cooler lines.

31. Connect the negative battery cable. Fill and bleed the cooling system. Run the engine and check for leaks.

32. If equipped, evacuate and charge the air conditioning system.

33. Install the intake hose. Install the hood, aligning the hinges with the marks that were made during removal.

3.0L ENGINE

Aerostar

1. Disconnect the negative battery cable and relieve the fuel system pressure. Drain the cooling system.

2. Disconnect the upper and lower radiator hoses.

3. Remove the air cleaner hose assembly. Removal should take place at the clamp retaining the hose to the air cleaner housing assembly.

4. Remove the engine fan retaining nut or bolts and remove the fan. Remove the fan shroud retaining screws and remove the shroud.

5. Disconnect the Barometric Manifold Absolute Pressure (BMAP) sensor electrical connector and vacuum line located on the dash panel.

6. Remove the shroud covering the throttle linkage and disconnect the linkage at the throttle body.

7. Loosen the idler arm and alternator jack screw retaining bolts and remove the accessory drive belts.

8. Disconnect the injector harness connector from the main harness. Disconnect the engine coolant temperature sensor, located near the thermostat housing and the engine coolant temperature sender.

9. Disconnect the canister purge solenoid hoses from both sides of the solenoid. If equipped with power steering, disconnect the pump pressure switch.

10. Mark the inlet and outlet heater hoses with chalk prior to removing them from the engine side of the ballast tube.

11. Remove the breather tubes from the air cleaner and rocker arm cover.

12. If equipped with automatic transmission, disconnect the transmission cooler lines from the radiator. Remove the radiator.

13. If equipped with air conditioning, remove the compressor retaining bolts and retain it to a sidemember with mechanics wire.

14. Disconnect the oil fill tube from the alternator bracket. If equipped with automatic transmission, disconnect the transmission fill tube from the manifold and gently pull out from the top of the vehicle.

15. Disconnect the electrical connectors from the alternator and the brake booster vacuum line from the booster. Remove the bolt retaining the steering gear at the top of the shaft.

16. From inside the vehicle, remove the engine cover. Tag and disconnect the electrical connectors for the radio frequency interference suppressor, distributor TFI module and oil pressure sender.

17. Disconnect the fuel lines from the fuel supply manifold.

18. If equipped with manual transmission, place the shift lever in **N** and remove the screws retaining the shift lever boot to the floor. Slide the boot up the shift lever. Remove the bolt retaining the shift lever assembly to the transmission and remove the lever assembly.

19. Raise and safely support the vehicle. Disconnect the oil level sensor connector from the oil pan.

20. Mark the driveshaft to flange position. From the rear of the vehicle, remove the 4 bolts retaining the driveshaft. Slide the driveshaft forward, pull down, then pull out to release. Set the driveshaft aside.

21. Remove the bolt retaining the speedometer cable bracket to the transmission. Pull the speedometer out of the rear of the transmission.

22. Remove the starter ground strap and remove the battery connection to the starter. Remove the starter bolts and remove the starter.

23. If equipped with manual transmission, disconnect the clutch hydraulic hose as follows:

    a. On 1988 vehicles, remove the lockpin retaining the hose to the slave cylinder in the clutch housing. Remove and plug the hose.

    b. On 1989–92 vehicles, disconnect the coupling at the transmission with tool T88T–70522–A or equivalent, by sliding the white plastic sleeve toward the slave cylinder while applying a slight tug on the tube.

24. If equipped with manual transmission, disconnect the backup lamp switch and neutral sensing switch wires from the transmission.

25. If equipped with automatic transmission, proceed as follows:

    a. Disconnect the electrical connectors for the neutral safety switch and 3–4 shift solenoid connectors. Disconnect the selector and kickdown cable from the transmission lever.

    b. Disconnect the vacuum hose from the transmission vacuum modulator.

    c. Remove the converter access cover and adapter plate bolts from the lower end of the converter housing.

    d. Remove the flywheel-to-converter attaching nuts. Place a 22mm socket and breaker bar on the crankshaft pulley bolt in order to turn the crankshaft and gain access to the flywheel-to-converter nuts.

    e. Disconnect the transmission cooler lines from the transmission.

26. Disconnect the oxygen sensor.

27. Position a jack under the transmission and a safety chain around the transmission. Slightly raise the transmission.

28. Remove the mount-to-crossmember attaching nuts. Remove the nuts and bolts attaching the crossmember to the 2 mounting brackets and remove the crossmember. If required, remove the bolts attaching the mount to the transmission and remove the mount.

29. Remove the converter housing-to-engine fasteners. Move the transmission to the rear so it disengages from the dowel pins and the converter disengages from the flywheel. Lower the transmission from the vehicle.

30. Disconnect and remove the exhaust pipe and catalytic converter. Remove both front wheel and tire assemblies.

31. Remove the engine block ground straps, 1 on the cylinder head just behind the power steering pump and the other just above where the exhaust manifold and exhaust pipe connect.

32. Remove the bar nuts and disconnect the stabilizer bar from the lower control arms. Discard the bar nuts.

33. Behind the spindles, disconnect and plug the brake lines at the bracket on the frame.

34. Position a jack under the lower control arm and raise the arm until tension is applied to the coil spring. Remove the bolt and nut retaining the spindle to the upper control arm ball joint. Slowly lower the jack to disconnect the spindle from the ball joint. Install safety chains around the lower control arm and spring seat.

35. Position drive train removal lift 109–00002 or equivalent, under the crossmember and engine assembly.

36. Slowly lower the vehicle until the crossmember rests on the removal lift. Place wood blocks under the front crossmember and rear of the engine block to keep the engine and crossmember assembly level. Install safety chains around the crossmember and lift.

37. With the engine and crossmember securely supported on the lift, remove the 3 nuts from the bolts that retain the engine crossmember assembly to the frame on each side of the vehicle.

38. Slowly lower the engine assembly out of the vehicle, making sure the air conditioning compressor and wiring harnesses do not interfere. When the assembly is clear, roll the lift out from under the vehicle.

39. Separate the engine from the crossmember and position on a workstand.

To install:

40. Remove the engine from the workstand. With the front crossmember securely positioned on drive train removal lift 109–00002 or equivalent, slowly lower the engine until the motor mount studs enter the crossmember holes. Install the retaining nuts and tighten to 71–94 ft. lbs. (96–127 Nm).

NOTE: Install wood blocks under the oil pan and crossmember.

41. Roll the removal lift under the vehicle. Align the lift, engine and crossmember assembly so the 3 mounting bolts on each side of the frame are in alignment with the holes in the crossmember.

42. Slowly lower the vehicle so the bolts are piloted in the crossmember holes. Raise the lift or lower the vehicle so the crossmember is against the frame. Install the nuts retaining the crossmember to the frame and tighten to 145–195 ft. lbs. (196–264 Nm). Raise the vehicle and remove the lift.

43. If equipped with automatic transmission, position the converter to the transmission making sure the converter hub is fully engaged in the pump gear. When the torque converter is fully installed, the distance between the converter pilot and the front of the converter housing should be $^7/_{16}$–$^9/_{16}$ in. Make sure the converter rotates freely and is not binding.

44. If equipped with manual transmission, install the transmission on a jack and lift into position. Make sure the transmission input shaft engages the pilot bearing in the flywheel and the flywheel housing holes are aligned with the engine block

dowel pins. Install the flywheel housing-to-engine block bolts and tighten to 28–38 ft. lbs. (38–51 Nm).

45. If equipped with automatic transmission, place the transmission on a jack and secure with safety chains. Rotate the converter so the drive studs are aligned with the flywheel holes. Lift the transmission into position and connect the transmission cooler lines to the case. Move the transmission forward into position, making sure the converter housing holes align with the engine block dowel pins. Install the converter housing-to-engine block bolts and tighten to 28–38 ft. lbs. (38–51 Nm).

46. Position the crossmember in the 2 mounting brackets and install the mounting nuts and bolts. Slowly lower the transmission so the mount studs are installed in the proper slots in the crossmember. Install the nuts and tighten to 71–94 ft. lbs. (97–127 Nm). Remove the safety chain and the jack.

47. Install the starter and tighten the mounting bolts to 15–20 ft. lbs. (21–27 Nm). Connect the starter cable.

48. If equipped with automatic transmission, connect the modulator vacuum hose. Position the selector cable in the case bracket and press the end of the cable on the ball stud on the lower portion of the selector lever. Install the retainer in the bracket.

49. If equipped with manual transmission, install the speedometer cable or connect the electronic speedometer wire. Connect the backup lamp and neutral sensor wires.

50. Remove the cap from the hydraulic clutch line. On 1988 vehicles, install the line and fitting in the slave cylinder and install the retaining clip. On 1989–92 vehicles, insert the male coupling into the female coupling on the slave cylinder and make sure the connection is secure.

51. Install the manual transmission shift lever to the shifter. Position the rubber shift boot on the floor and install the screws.

52. If equipped with automatic transmission, install the kickdown and selector cable. Adjust the cable. Connect the neutral safety switch, converter clutch solenoid and 3–4 shift solenoid connectors. Insert the speedometer driven gear into the transmission and retain with a clamp. Tighten the retaining screw to 20–25 inch lbs. (2.25–2.82).

53. Position a 22mm socket and breaker bar on the crankshaft pulley bolt. Rotate the pulley clockwise, as viewed from the front, to gain access to each torque converter studs. Install the nuts on the studs and tighten to 20–34 ft. lbs. (27–46 Nm).

54. Position the converter access cover and adapter plate on the converter housing. Install the bolts and tighten to 12–16 ft. lbs. (16–22 Nm).

55. Remove the safety chains from around the lower control arms and spring seat. Install a jack under the lower control arms. Slowly raise the control arm until the coil spring is under tension. Continue to raise the arm until the spindle is connected to the upper arm ball joint. Install a new nut and bolt and tighten to 27–37 ft. lbs. (37–50 Nm).

56. Connect the stabilizer bar to the lower control arms. Install new bar nuts and tighten to 12–18 ft. lbs. (16–24 Nm).

57. Connect the front brake lines to the caliper hoses at the frame brackets. Install the wheel and tire assemblies.

58. Install the driveshaft, aligning the marks that were made during removal.

59. Install new gaskets on the exhaust manifold and catalytic converter. Install the exhaust pipe and catalytic converter. Tighten the converter-to-muffler nuts and bolts to 18–26 ft. lbs. (25–35 Nm). Tighten the exhaust pipe-to-exhaust manifold nuts to 25–34 ft. lbs. (34–46 Nm).

60. Connect the oxygen sensor connector and install the engine ground straps. Connect the fuel lines and the low-oil level sensor.

61. If equipped with automatic transmission, connect the transmission oil cooler lines. Install the transmission oil fill tube and lower the vehicle.

62. From inside the vehicle, connect the radio frequency interference suppressor, TFI module connector and oil pressure

sender. Install the engine cover.

63. Connect the alternator electrical connectors and the brake booster vacuum hose. Connect the breather tube to the oil filler tube and attach the bolt retaining the steering gear to the top of the shaft.

64. If equipped, connect the power steering pressure switch. Connect the heater hoses to the ballast tube by matching the chalk lines to the specific inlet and outlet hoses.

65. Install the radiator. If equipped, connect the transmission oil cooler lines.

66. Connect the canister purge solenoid hoses from both sides of the solenoid. Connect the engine coolant temperature sensor, located near the thermostat housing and connect the engine coolant temperature sender.

67. If equipped with air conditioning, untie the compressor from the sidemember and position on the mounting bracket. Install the attaching bolts.

68. Install the alternator belt and tighten the idler arm. Place the injector harness behind the belt tension idler arm and tighten the idler arm.

69. Connect the throttle linkage to the ball stud located on the throttle body. Connect the shroud covering the throttle body.

70. Connect the BMAP sensor electrical connector and vacuum line located on the dash panel.

71. Install the fan and fan shroud. Connect the radiator hoses.

72. Connect the negative battery cable and install the air cleaner and duct assembly.

73. Bleed the brakes and the hydraulic clutch. Fill and bleed the cooling system. Check all fluid levels.

74. Run the engine and check for leaks and proper operation. Check the front end alignment.

Ranger

1. Disconnect the negative battery cable and relieve the fuel system pressure. Drain the cooling system.

2. Mark the position of the hood on the hinges and remove the hood. Remove the air cleaner intake hose.

3. Disconnect the radiator hoses at the radiator. Remove the fan shroud attaching bolts and position the shroud over the fan. Remove the radiator, then remove the shroud.

4. Remove the alternator and bracket and position the alternator aside. Disconnect the alternator ground wire from the cylinder block.

5. Remove the air conditioner compressor and power steering pump and position aside, if equipped.

6. Disconnect the heater hoses at the intake manifold and water pump. Remove the ground wires from the cylinder block.

7. Disconnect the fuel lines at the chassis to engine connections. Disconnect the throttle cable shield and linkage at the throttle body and intake manifold.

8. Tag and disconnect the vacuum connections at the rear fitting in the upper intake manifold.

9. Tag and disconnect the wires at the ignition coil. Disconnect the 3 body wiring connectors on top of the right rocker arm cover. Disconnect the oil pressure and engine coolant temperature sender connectors.

10. Disconnect the injector harness, air charge temperature sensor and throttle position sensor. Disconnect the oxygen sensor connector at the rear of the engine and disconnect the brake booster vacuum hose.

11. Remove the engine front mount-to-crossmember attaching nuts.

12. Raise and safely support the vehicle.

13. Remove 2 lower air conditioner compressor bracket-to-engine bolts. Disconnect the wiring from the low oil level sensor and oil pressure sending unit.

14. Remove the retaining bracket holding the transmission cooling lines to the right side of the engine block.

15. Disconnect the exhaust pipes at the manifolds. Disconnect the starter cable and remove the starter.

16. If equipped with manual transmission, disconnect the hydraulic clutch line and remove the flywheel housing-to-engine block bolts.

17. If equipped with automatic transmission, remove the converter inspection cover and disconnect the converter from the flywheel.

18. Disconnect the kickdown and shift cables at the transmission. Remove the converter housing-to-engine block bolts and adapter plate-to-converter housing bolt.

19. Lower the vehicle. Remove the 2 bolts from the air conditioner compressor and position aside.

20. Attach suitable engine lifting equipment and position a jack under the transmission.

21. Raise the engine slightly and carefully pull it from the transmission. Carefully lift the engine out of the engine compartment so the rear cover plate is not bent or components damaged. Install the engine on a workstand.

To install:

22. Remove the engine from the workstand and carefully lower it into the engine compartment. Make sure the exhaust manifolds are aligned with the exhaust pipes.

23. If equipped with manual transmission, start the transmission input shaft into the clutch disc. It may be necessary to adjust the position of the transmission in relation to the engine, if the input shaft will not enter the clutch disc. If the engine hangs up after the shaft enters, turn the crankshaft in the clockwise direction slowly, transmission in gear, until the shaft splines mesh with the clutch disc splines.

24. If equipped with automatic transmission, start the converter pilot into the crankshaft. Make sure the converter rotates freely and is not binding. When the converter is fully installed in the transmission, the distance between the converter pilot and the edge of the converter housing should be $^7/_{16}$–$^9/_{16}$ in.

25. Install the flywheel housing or converter housing upper bolts, making sure the engine block dowels engage the housing. If equipped, install the clutch hydraulic line.

26. Remove the jack from under the transmission and remove the engine lifting equipment. If equipped with automatic transmission, position the kickdown cable on the transmission and engine.

27. Raise and safely support the vehicle. If equipped with automatic transmission, position the transmission linkage bracket and install the remaining converter housing bolts.

28. Install the adapter plate-to-converter housing bolt. Install the converter-to-flywheel nuts and install the inspection cover. Connect the kickdown cable at the transmission.

29. If equipped with manual transmission, install the flywheel housing attaching bolts.

30. Install the starter and connect the cables. Connect the exhaust pipes at the manifolds.

31. Install the engine front mount nuts and washers or through bolts. Lower the vehicle.

32. Install the ground wires to the engine block. Connect the coil wires, the 3 body wiring connectors and the oxygen wiring connector. Connect the coolant temperature sending unit and oil pressure sending unit. Connect the brake booster vacuum hose.

33. Install the throttle linkage and connect the fuel lines. Connect the heater hoses at the water pump and cylinder block.

34. Install the alternator and bracket. Connect the alternator ground wire to the engine block. Install the drive belt and adjust the tension.

35. Install the air conditioning compressor and power steering pump, if equipped.

36. Position the fan shroud over the fan. Install the radiator and connect the radiator hoses. Install the fan shroud.

37. Connect the negative battery cable. Fill and bleed the cooling system.

38. Bleed the hydraulic clutch, if necessary. Evacuate and charge the air conditioning system, if necessary.

39. Run the engine and check for leaks and proper operation. Install the intake hose. Install the hood, aligning the marks that were made during removal.

4.0L ENGINE

Aerostar

1. Disconnect the negative battery cable and relieve the fuel system pressure.
2. Remove the front grille. Remove the air cleaner tube and the air cleaner assembly.
3. Discharge the refrigerant from the air conditioning system, if equipped. Disconnect and remove the air conditioner compressor.
4. Drain the engine oil. Drain disconnect and remove the power steering oil cooler.
5. Remove the front bumper cover. Drain, disconnect and remove the transmission oil cooler.
6. Drain the radiator and disconnect the radiator hoses. Disconnect the transmission oil cooler lines from the radiator.
7. Disconnect the fan shroud and position it over the fan. Remove the radiator and the shroud.
8. Remove the accessory drive belt and the right front air diverter flap. Remove the center hood latch support and remove the alternator.
9. If equipped, discharge the air conditioning system and remove the compressor.
10. Remove the engine oil fill tube. From inside the vehicle, remove the engine cover.
11. Remove the ice/snow shield. Remove the power steering hoses and remove the power steering pump and bracket.
12. Remove the transmission oil and engine oil dipsticks and tubes. Disconnect the exhaust system from the exhaust manifolds.
13. Disconnect and remove the starter. Working through the starter opening in the converter housing, remove the converter to flexplate bolts.
14. Remove the transmission oil cooler line bracket retaining bolt and remove the engine mount to frame bolts.
15. Remove the converter housing-to-engine bolts, except the upper bolts.
16. Remove the left motor mount from the engine, then remove the upper converter housing bolts.
17. Disconnect the transmission and transfer case electrical connectors. Disconnect the fuel lines at the fuel supply manifold.
18. Disconnect the throttle linkage and bracket and position aside. Disconnect the heater hoses.
19. Tag and disconnect the vacuum lines from the vapor canister, lower intake manifold and upper intake manifold vacuum tee.
20. Remove the spark plug wires from the coil assembly. Disconnect and remove the coil assembly with mounting bracket.
21. Disconnect the throttle position sensor electrical connector. Remove the throttle body from the upper intake manifold.
22. Tag and disconnect the engine wiring harness main connectors. Install suitable engine lifting equipment and remove the engine from the vehicle. Position the engine on a workstand.

To install:

23. Remove the engine from the workstand and position it in the vehicle. Remove the engine lifting equipment.
24. Connect the engine wiring harness main connectors. Install the throttle body on the upper intake manifold.
25. Install the ignition coil assembly and connect the spark plug wires and coil assembly wiring connector. Connect the electrical connector for the throttle position sensor.
26. Connect the heater hoses. Connect the vacuum lines to the vapor canister, lower intake manifold and upper intake manifold vacuum tee.
27. Connect the throttle linkage and bracket. Connect the fuel lines to the fuel supply manifold.

28. Install the left motor mount. Install the converter housing-to-engine bolts and connect the transmission and transfer case electrical connectors.
29. Install the engine mount-to-frame bolts and the transmission oil cooler line bracket retaining bolt.
30. Working through the starter opening in the converter housing, install the converter to flexplate bolts.
31. Install the starter and connect the starter wires. Connect the exhaust system to the exhaust manifolds.
32. Install the transmission oil and engine oil dipstick tubes and dipsticks.
33. Install the power steering pump and mounting bracket. Connect the power steering hoses.
34. Install the ice/snow shield and the engine oil fill tube. Install the engine cover.
35. Install and connect the air conditioner compressor, if equipped. Install and connect the alternator.
36. Install the center hood latch support and the right front air diverter flap. Install the accessory drive belt.
37. Install the radiator and fan shroud. Connect the transmission oil cooler lines and the radiator hoses.
38. Install the transmission oil cooler and the front bumper cover. Install and connect the power steering oil cooler.
39. Fill the engine with the proper type and quantity of engine oil.
40. Install and connect the air conditioner condenser, if equipped. Install the air cleaner assembly and air tube.
41. Install the front grille and connect the negative battery cable. Fill and bleed the cooling system.
42. If equipped, evacuate and charge the air conditioning system. Check all fluid levels.
43. Run the engine and check for leaks and for proper operation.

Explorer and Ranger

1. Disconnect the negative battery cable and relieve the fuel system pressure. Drain the cooling system.
2. Mark the position of the hood on the hinges and remove the hood. Remove the air cleaner intake hose.
3. Disconnect the radiator hoses at the radiator. Disconnect the fan shroud and position it over the fan. Remove the radiator, then the shroud.
4. Remove the alternator and bracket and position the alternator aside. Disconnect the alternator ground wire from the cylinder block.
5. Remove the air conditioning compressor and power steering pump and position aside, if equipped.
6. Disconnect the heater hoses at the intake manifold and water pump. Remove the ground wires from the cylinder block.
7. Disconnect the fuel lines from the fuel supply manifold. Disconnect the throttle cable shield and linkage at the throttle body and intake manifold.
8. Tag and disconnect the vacuum connections at the rear vacuum fitting in the upper intake manifold.
9. Disconnect the wiring from the ignition coil and oil pressure and engine coolant temperature senders. Disconnect the injector harness, air charge temperature sensor and throttle position sensor. Disconnect the brake booster vacuum hose.
10. Raise and safely support the vehicle. Disconnect the exhaust pipes at the manifolds. Disconnect the starter cable and remove the starter.
11. Remove the engine front mount-to-crossmember attaching nuts or through bolts.
12. Remove the converter inspection cover and disconnect the converter from the flywheel. Remove the cable.
13. Remove the converter housing-to-engine block bolts and the adapter plate-to-converter housing bolt. Lower the vehicle.
14. Position a jack under the transmission and install suitable engine lifting equipment.
15. Raise the engine slightly and carefully pull it from the transmission. Carefully lift the engine out of the engine com-

partment so the rear cover plate is not bent or components damaged. Install the engine on a workstand.

To install:

16. Remove the engine from the workstand and carefully lower it into the engine compartment. Make sure the exhaust manifolds are aligned with the exhaust pipes.

17. At the transmission, start the converter pilot into the crankshaft. Install the converter housing upper bolts, making sure the dowels in the cylinder block engage the flywheel housing. Tighten the bolts to 33–45 ft. lbs. (45–61 Nm).

18. Remove the jack from under the transmission and the engine lifting equipment.

19. Position the kickdown rod on the transmission and engine. Raise and safely support the vehicle.

20. Position the transmission linkage bracket and install the remaining converter housing bolts. Install the adapter plate-to-converter housing bolt. Install the converter-to-flywheel nuts and install the inspection cover. Connect the kickdown rod on the transmission.

21. Install the starter and connect the cable. Connect the exhaust pipes at the manifolds.

22. Install the engine front mount nuts and washers or through bolts. Lower the vehicle.

23. Install the ground wires to the engine block. Connect the ignition coil wiring, then connect the coolant temperature sending unit and oil pressure sending unit. Connect the brake booster vacuum hose.

24. Install the throttle linkage and connect the fuel lines at the fuel supply manifold.

25. Connect the ground cable at the engine block. Connect the heater hoses to the water pump and cylinder block.

26. Install the alternator and bracket. Connect the alternator ground wire to the engine block. Install the accessory drive belt.

27. Install the air conditioner compressor and power steering pump, if equipped.

28. Position the shroud over the fan. Install the radiator and connect the radiator upper and lower hoses. Install the fan shroud attaching bolts.

29. Connect the negative battery cable. Fill and bleed the cooling system.

30. Run the engine and check for leaks and proper operation. If equipped, evacuate and charge the air conditioning system.

31. Install the intake hose. Install the hood, aligning the marks that were made during removal.

Engine Mounts

Removal and Installation

FRONT MOUNTS

1. Remove the fan shroud attaching screws.

2. Support the engine using a wood block and a jack placed under the oil pan.

3. Remove the nuts and washers attaching the mounts to the engine bracket. Lift the engine enough to disengage the mount upper stud from the crossmember engine bracket.

4. Remove the bolt attaching the fuel pump shield to the left engine bracket, if necessary.

5. Remove the mount-to-crossmember attaching nut and washer assembly. Remove the engine mount.

To install:

6. Install the engine mount to the crossmember.

7. Install the bolt attaching the fuel pump shield to the left bracket, if necessary.

8. Lower the engine until the mount stud engages in the slot/hole of the engine bracket. Install the attaching nuts.

9. Remove the jack and wood block from the engine oil pan. Install the fan shroud attaching screws.

REAR MOUNT

1. Place a block of wood and a jack under the transmission.

2. Remove the 2 nuts attaching the mount to the crossmember. Raise the transmission enough to lift the mount from the crossmember.

3. Remove the bolts and nuts attaching the crossmember to the frame side rails and remove the crossmember.

4. If equipped, remove the fasteners attaching the exhaust hanger to the rear engine mount.

5. Remove the 2 bolts attaching the mount to the transmission and remove the mount and retainer assembly.

To install:

6. Position the mount and retainer assembly to the transmission and install the 2 attaching bolts.

7. If equipped, install the fasteners attaching the exhaust hanger to the mount.

8. Install the crossmember to the frame side rails with the attaching nuts and bolts.

9. Lower the transmission and install the mount crossmember attaching nuts. Remove the jack and wood block.

Cylinder Head

Removal and Installation

2.0L AND 2.3L ENGINES

1. Disconnect the negative battery cable. Drain the cooling system.

2. Remove the air cleaner assembly. Remove the heater hose retaining screw(s) to the rocker arm cover.

3. If equipped, disconnect the distributor cap and spark plug wires and remove the assembly.

4. Remove the spark plugs. If equipped with distributorless ignition, remove the spark plug wire harnesses.

5. Remove the engine and alternator wiring harnesses. Disconnect the oxygen sensor at the exhaust manifold.

6. Tag and disconnect the required vacuum hoses. Remove the dipstick tube and bracket.

7. Remove the rocker arm cover attaching bolts and remove the cover. Remove the intake manifold attaching bolts.

8. Loosen the alternator retaining bolts and remove the belt from the pulley. Remove the mounting bracket-to-head retaining bolts.

9. Remove the upper radiator hose. Remove the timing belt cover bolt(s) and remove the cover. If equipped with power steering, move the power steering pump bracket.

10. Loosen the timing belt idler retaining bolts. Position the idler in the unloaded position and tighten the retaining bolts. Remove the timing belt from the camshaft pulley and auxiliary pulley.

11. Remove the 4 nuts and/or stud bolts retaining the heat stove to the exhaust manifold. Remove the 8 exhaust manifold retaining bolts.

12. Remove the timing belt idler and 2 bracket bolts. Remove the timing belt idler spring stop from the cylinder head.

13. Remove the cylinder head retaining bolts and remove the cylinder head.

14. Clean all gasket mating surfaces. Check the cylinder head for flatness using a straight edge and a feeler gauge. The cylinder head must not be warped more than 0.003 in. in any 6 in. or more than 0.006 in. overall.

To install:

15. Position a new head gasket on the block. Properly position the camshaft in the cylinder head and install the cylinder head on the block.

16. Install the cylinder head bolts and tighten, in sequence, in 2 steps, first to 50–60 ft. lbs. (68–81 Nm) and then to 80–90 ft. lbs. (108–122 Nm).

17. Install a new intake manifold gasket and position the intake manifold to the cylinder head. Install the retaining bolts.

18. Install the timing belt idler spring stop to the cylinder head. Position the timing belt idler to the cylinder head and install the retaining bolts.

19. Install the 8 exhaust manifold retaining bolts and the 4 nuts and/or stud bolts retaining the heat stove to the exhaust manifold.

20. If equipped, align the distributor rotor with the No. 1 spark plug location in the distributor cap.

21. Align the cam gear with the pointer and the crank pulley with the pointer on the timing belt cover.

22. Position the timing belt to the pulleys. Loosen the idler retaining, rotate the engine and check the timing alignment.

23. Adjust the belt tensioner and tighten the retaining bolts. Install the timing belt cover and the retaining bolt(s).

24. Install the upper radiator hose. Position the alternator bracket to the cylinder head and install the retainers. Install the drive belt and adjust the belt tension.

25. Install a new rocker arm cover gasket on the rocker arm cover. Install the rocker arm cover on the cylinder head and install the retaining bolts.

26. Install the spark plugs. Install the spark plug wires and the distributor cap, if equipped.

27. Install the dipstick tube and bracket. Connect the vacuum hoses. Install the retaining heater hose screw(s) to the rocker arm cover.

28. Connect the negative battery cable. Fill and bleed the cooling system.

29. Start the engine and check for leaks. Install the air cleaner hose to the throttle body.

2.9L ENGINE

1. Disconnect the negative battery cable and relieve the fuel system pressure.

2. Drain the cooling system and remove the upper radiator hose.

3. Remove the intake tube from the throttle body and disconnect the throttle linkage and cover.

4. Tag the position of the spark plug wires and remove the distributor cap and wires as an assembly. Disconnect the distributor wiring harness.

5. Mark the position of the rotor in relation to the distributor housing and the position of the distributor housing in relation to the intake manifold. Remove the distributor hold-down bolt and clamp and remove the distributor.

6. Remove the rocker arm covers and rocker arm shafts.

7. Disconnect the fuel line from the fuel supply manifold. Remove the intake manifold.

8. Remove the pushrods, marking them so they can be reinstalled in their original positions.

9. Remove the exhaust manifolds.

10. Remove the cylinder head attaching bolts and remove the cylinder heads.

11. Clean all gasket mating surfaces. Check the cylinder head for flatness using a straight edge and a feeler gauge. The cylinder head must not be warped more than 0.003 in. in any 6 in. or more than 0.006 in. overall.

To install:

12. Position new cylinder head gaskets on the cylinder block.

NOTE: Gaskets are marked with the words "front" and "top" for correct positioning. Left and right cylinder head gaskets are not interchangeable.

13. Install fabricated alignment dowels in the cylinder block and install the cylinder heads.

14. Install new cylinder head bolts and remove the fabricated dowels. Tighten the bolts as follows:

    Step 1: Tighten in sequence to 22 ft. lbs. (30 Nm).
    Step 2: Tighten in sequence to 51–55 ft. lbs. (70–75 Nm).
    Step 3: Wait 5 minutes.
    Step 4: In sequence, turn all bolts 90 degrees.

15. Install the intake manifold.

16. Install the exhaust manifolds.

17. Apply engine oil to both ends of the pushrods and install them in their original positions.

Cylinder head installation—2.0L and 2.3L engines

Cylinder head bolt torque sequence—2.0L and 2.3L engines

Cylinder head bolt torque sequence—2.9L engine

18. Install the oil baffles and rocker arms.

19. Install the distributor, aligning the marks that were made during removal. Install the distributor hold-down bolt and clamp and connect the distributor wiring harness.

20. Adjust the valves and install the rocker arm covers.

21. Connect the fuel line to the fuel supply manifold.

22. Install the distributor cap and connect the spark plug wires.

23. Connect the negative battery cable. Fill and bleed the cooling system.

24. Run the engine and check for leaks. Check the ignition timing and idle speed and adjust, if necessary.

3.0L ENGINE

1. Disconnect the negative battery cable and relieve the fuel system pressure. Drain the cooling system.

2. Remove the air cleaner fresh air hose from the throttle body and air cleaner. If equipped, remove the engine oil filler adapter.

3. Disconnect the fuel lines. Tag and disconnect the necessary vacuum lines.

4. Disconnect the upper radiator hose and heater hose and position aside. On Ranger, disconnect the ignition coil electrical connector and remove the coil.

5. Remove the throttle body.

6. Remove the distributor cap. Mark the position of the rotor in relation to the distributor housing and the position of the distributor housing in relation to the intake manifold. Remove the distributor hold-down bolt and clamp and remove the distributor. Tag and disconnect the spark plug wires from the spark plugs and remove the distributor cap and wires assembly.

7. If removing the left cylinder head, proceed as follows:

   a. Remove the necessary accessory drive belt(s).

   b. On 1988 vehicles, remove the alternator adjusting arm.

   c. Remove the power steering pump and bracket, leaving the lines connected. Place the assembly aside in a position to prevent fluid leakage.

   d. On Aerostar, remove the ignition coil and bracket.

   e. Remove the engine oil dipstick tube.

   f. Remove the fuel line retaining bracket bolt from the front of the cylinder head, if equipped.

8. If removing the right cylinder head, proceed as follows:

   a. Remove the necessary accessory drive belt(s).

   b. Remove the accessory drive belt idler or tensioner.

   c. Remove the grounding strap throttle cable support bracket, if necessary.

   d. On 1989–92 vehicles, disconnect the alternator electrical harnesses and remove the alternator and bracket assembly.

9. Remove the spark plugs.

10. Disconnect the exhaust pipes and remove the exhaust manifolds.

11. Remove the rocker arm covers. Loosen the rocker arm fulcrum retaining bolts enough to allow the rocker arm to be lifted off the pushrod and rotated to 1 side.

NOTE: Regardless of which head is to be removed, the No. 3 cylinder intake valve pushrod must be removed to allow removal of the intake manifold.

12. Remove the pushrods, marking them so they can be reinstalled in their original positions.

13. Remove the intake manifold.

14. Remove the cylinder head attaching bolts and remove the cylinder heads.

15. Clean all gasket mating surfaces. Check the cylinder head for flatness using a straight edge and a feeler gauge. The cylinder head must not be warped more than 0.003 in. in any 6 in. or more than 0.006 in. overall.

To install:

16. Position new head gasket(s) on the cylinder block, using the dowels for alignment.

17. Install the cylinder head(s) on the block. Oil the threads of new cylinder head bolts and hand tighten.

18. On 1988–90 vehicles, tighten the cylinder head bolts, in sequence, in 2 steps, first to 37 ft. lbs. (50 Nm) and then to 68 ft. lbs. (92 Nm).

19. On 1991–92 vehicles, tighten the cylinder head bolts, in sequence, to 59 ft. lbs. (80 Nm). Back off all bolts a minimum of 1 full turn. Retighten the bolts, in sequence, in 2 steps, first to 37 ft. lbs. (50 Nm) and then to 68 ft. lbs. (92 Nm).

Cylinder head bolt torque sequence—3.0L engine

20. Install the intake manifold.

21. Install the distributor, aligning the marks that were made during removal. Install the hold-down bolt and clamp.

22. Dip each pushrod in heavy engine oil and install them in their original positions.

23. For each valve, rotate the crankshaft until the lifter rests on the base circle of the camshaft lobe, before tightening the rocker arm fulcrum attaching bolts. Position the rocker arms over the valves and pushrods, install the fulcrums and fulcrum bolts and tighten to 24 ft. lbs. (32 Nm).

NOTE: If the original valve train components are being installed, a valve clearance check is not required. If a component has been replaced, perform a valve clearance check.

24. Install the exhaust manifolds and the spark plugs.

25. Install the rocker arm covers. Install the dipstick tube.

26. Install the fuel injector harness to the injectors and in-board rocker arm cover studs. Connect the engine harness to the main harness.

27. Install the distributor cap and connect the spark plug wires to the spark plugs.

28. Install the throttle body. Install the ignition coil and bracket, if necessary and connect the electrical connector.

29. Install the fuel line retaining bracket to the front of the cylinder head, if equipped. Tighten the retaining bolts to 26 ft. lbs. (35 Nm).

30. Install the power steering pump and bracket, if removed. Install the alternator and bracket assembly, if removed and connect the electrical harness.

31. Install the accessory drive belt(s).

32. Connect the fuel lines to the fuel supply manifold. Connect the upper radiator and heater hoses.

33. Connect the vacuum lines. Install the engine oil filler adapter on Aerostar.

34. Change the engine oil and filter.

NOTE: Engine coolant is corrosive to all engine bearing material. Replacing engine oil after removal of a coolant carrying component helps prevent engine failure later.

35. Install the air cleaner fresh air hose to the throttle body and air cleaner. Connect the negative battery cable.

36. Fill and bleed the cooling system. Run the engine and check for leaks.

37. Check the ignition timing and idle speed and adjust, if necessary.

4.0L ENGINE

1. Disconnect the negative battery cable and relieve the fuel system pressure. Drain the cooling system.

2. Remove the upper and lower intake manifolds and rocker arm covers.

3. If the left cylinder head is being removed, proceed as follows:

    a. Remove the accessory drive belt.

    b. Discharge the refrigerant and remove the air conditioning compressor, if equipped.

    c. Remove the power steering pump and bracket and position aside.

    d. Remove the spark plugs.

4. If the right cylinder head is being removed, proceed as follows:

    a. Remove the accessory drive belt.

    b. Remove the alternator and alternator bracket.

    c. Remove the ignition coil and bracket assembly.

    d. Remove the spark plugs.

5. Disconnect the exhaust pipe and remove the exhaust manifold(s).

6. Remove the rocker arm shaft assembly. Remove the push-

Service Tips

COOLANT LEAKING AT CYLINDER HEAD

Coolant leaking at the cylinder head-to-engine block mating surface on the 3.0L engine, may be caused by broken cylinder head bolts. This can be corrected by installing new cylinder head bolts, part number E7DZ–6065–A and a new cylinder head gasket on the cylinder head that is leaking. If the cylinder head is not leaking, the bolts can be installed 1 at a time without head gasket replacement.

Cylinder head bolt torque sequence—4.0L engine

rods, marking them so they can be reinstalled in the same positions.

7. Remove and discard the cylinder head attaching bolts and remove the cylinder heads.

8. Clean all gasket mating surfaces. Check the cylinder head for flatness using a straight edge and a feeler gauge. The cylinder head must not be warped more than 0.003 in. in any 6 in. or more than 0.006 in. overall.

To install:

9. Position new cylinder head gasket(s) on the cylinder block. Install cylinder head locating dowels.

NOTE: The cylinder head(s) and intake manifold are torqued alternately and in sequence to insure correct fit and gasket crunch.

10. Install new cylinder head bolts and tighten, in sequence, to 44 ft. lbs. (60 Nm).

11. Apply silicone sealer to the block and cylinder head mating surfaces at the 4 corners of the lifter valley opening. Install the intake manifold gasket and again apply sealer in the same locations.

12. Position the lower intake manifold on the 2 guide studs and install the nuts and bolts hand tight. Tighten the lower intake manifold bolts, in sequence, to 3–6 ft. lbs. (4–8 Nm).

13. Tighten the cylinder head bolts, in sequence, to 59 ft. lbs. (80 Nm).

14. Tighten the intake manifold, in sequence, to 6–11 ft. lbs. (8–15 Nm).

15. Turn the cylinder head bolts 80–85 degrees tighter, in sequence.

16. Tighten the intake manifold, in sequence, to 11–15 ft. lbs. (15–21 Nm) and then to 15–18 ft. lbs. (21–25 Nm), in sequence.

17. Dip both ends of each pushrod in clean engine oil and install in their original locations. Install the rocker arm and shaft assemblies and tighten the rocker arm shaft support bolts evenly to 46–52 ft. lbs. (62–70 Nm).

18. Apply silicone sealer to the 4 locations at the joint where

the intake manifold and cylinder head meet. Install a new rocker arm cover gasket in each cover and install the rocker arm covers. Tighten the rocker arm cover bolts to 3–5 ft. lbs. (4–7 Nm), wait 2 minutes and then retighten to the same specification.

19. Install the upper intake manifold and tighten the nuts to 15–18 ft. lbs. (20–25 Nm).

20. Install the exhaust manifold(s) and connect the exhaust pipe.

21. Install the spark plugs and the ignition coil and bracket assembly.

22. Install the alternator and the accessory drive belt.

23. Install the power steering pump. Install the air conditioning compressor, if equipped.

24. Connect the negative battery cable. Fill and bleed the cooling system. Run the engine and check for leaks.

Valve Lifters

Removal and Installation

EXCEPT 2.0L AND 2.3L ENGINES

1. Disconnect the negative battery cable and relieve the fuel system pressure. Drain the cooling system.

2. Remove the intake manifold and rocker arm covers.

3. On 2.9L and 4.0L engines, loosen the rocker arm shaft support bolts 2 turns at a time until the rocker arm and shaft assembly can be removed.

4. On 3.0L engine, loosen the rocker arm fulcrum bolt enough so the rocker arm can be lifted from the pushrod and turned to 1 side.

5. Remove the pushrods, marking them so they can be reinstalled in their original positions.

6. On 2.9L engine, remove the cylinder heads.

7 Remove the lifters. Note the location of each lifter so it can be reinstalled in the same bore. If a lifter is stuck in the bore, use a suitable tool to rotate the lifter back and forth to loosen it from the gum and varnish that may have formed on the lifter.

NOTE: The 4.0L engine is equipped with roller lifters. Roller lifters have an alignment tab which fits into a locating groove in the lifter bore. Do not attempt to rotate a roller lifter in the bore.

To install:

8. Lubricate the lifters and bores with clean engine oil. Install each lifter in the same bore from which it was removed. On 4.0L engine, install the lifter with the alignment tab in the locating groove of the bore. If a new lifter is being installed, check for free fit in the bore.

9. On 2.9L engine, install the cylinder heads.

10. Check each pushrod for straightness and for damage, replace as necessary. Dip each pushrod end in clean engine oil and install in its original position.

11. On 2.9L and 4.0L engines, lubricate the rocker arm and shaft assembly and install. Draw the shaft support bolts down evenly, 2 turns at a time, until the shafts are fully down. Tighten the bolts to 43–50 ft. lbs. (59–67 Nm) on 2.9L engine or 46–52 ft. lbs. (62–70 Nm) on 4.0L engine.

12. On 3.0L engine, for each valve, rotate the crankshaft until the lifter rests on the base circle of the camshaft lobe, before tightening the rocker arm fulcrum attaching bolts. Position the rocker arms over the valves and pushrods, install the fulcrums and fulcrum bolts and tighten to 24 ft. lbs. (32 Nm).

13. Install the intake manifold and rocker arm covers.

14. Connect the negative battery cable. Fill and bleed the cooling system.

15. Run the engine and check for leaks.

2.0L AND 2.3L ENGINES

1. Disconnect the negative battery cable and remove the air cleaner or air intake duct. On 2.3L engine, remove the throttle body and EGR supply tube.

Valve lifter installation—4.0L engine

Cam follower removal—2.0L and 2.3L engines

2. Remove the rocker arm cover.

3. Rotate the crankshaft so the base circle of the cam is facing the applicable cam follower.

4. Using valve spring compressor lever tool T88T–6565–BH or equivalent, collapse the valve spring and slide the cam follower over the valve lifter and out.

5. Lift out the hydraulic valve lifter.

To install:

6. Rotate the crankshaft so the base circle of the cam is facing the applicable cam follower.

7. Coat the hydraulic lifter with clean engine oil and install it in the bore.

8. Collapse the valve spring using valve spring compressor lever T88T–6565–BH or equivalent. Position the cam follower over the valve lifter and the valve stem.

9. Clean the gasket surfaces of the rocker arm cover and cylinder head.

10. Coat the rocker arm cover and a new gasket with gasket adhesive and install the gasket to the cover.

11. Install the cover and tighten the retaining bolts to 5–8 ft. lbs. (7–11 Nm).

12. Install the throttle body and EGR supply tube, if necessary. Install the air cleaner or air intake duct.

13. Connect the negative battery cable.

Valve Lash

Adjustment

2.0L AND 2.3L ENGINES

1. Remove the rocker arm cover. Position the camshaft so the

base circle of the lobe is facing the cam follower of the valve to be checked.

2. Using tool valve spring compressor lever tool T88T–6565–BH or equivalent, slowly apply pressure to the cam follower until the valve lifter is completely collapsed. Hold the follower in this position and measure the clearance between the base circle of the cam and the follower. The allowable collapsed lifter gap is 0.035–0.055 in. at the camshaft.

3. If the clearance is excessive, remove the cam follower and inspect for damage.

4. If the cam follower is not excessively worn, measure the valve spring installed height to make sure the valve is not sticking. The installed height is 1.49–1.55 in.

5. If the valve spring installed height is correct, check the camshaft lobe lift. The lobe lift dimension is 0.2381 in.

6. If the cam follower, valve spring height and camshaft lobe lift are correct and the base circle-to-follower clearance is excessive, replace the valve lifter.

2.9L ENGINE

1. Remove the rocker arm cover assembly. On the cylinder to be adjusted, position the camshaft lobe so the lifters are on the base circle.

2. Loosen the adjusting screws until a distinct lash between the rocker arm pad and the valve tip end can be noticed. The plunger of the hydraulic lifter should now be fully extended under load of the internal spring.

3. Screw in the adjustment screws until the rocker arms slightly touch the valve stem.

4. To achieve the nominal working position of the plunger, turn in the adjusting screw 1½ turns, equivalent to 0.070 in.

3.0L ENGINE

1. Remove the rocker arm cover.

2. Rotate the crankshaft until the lifter is on the base circle of the cam on the valve to be checked.

3. Using a suitable tool, collapse the lifter fully and measure the clearance between the valve stem tip and rocker arm. The clearance should be 0.085–0.185 in. (2.15–4.69mm).

Rocker Arms/Shafts

Removal and Installation

2.0L AND 2.3L ENGINES

1. Disconnect the negative battery cable and remove the air cleaner or air intake duct. On 2.3L engine, remove the throttle body and EGR supply tube.

2. Remove the rocker arm cover.

3. Rotate the crankshaft so the base circle of the cam is facing the applicable cam follower.

4. Using valve spring compressor lever tool T88T–6565–BH or equivalent, collapse the valve spring and slide the cam follower over the valve lifter and out.

To install:

5. Rotate the crankshaft so the base circle of the cam is facing the applicable cam follower.

6. Collapse the valve spring using valve spring compressor lever T88T–6565–BH or equivalent. Position the cam follower over the valve lifter and the valve stem.

7. Clean the gasket surfaces of the rocker arm cover and cylinder head.

8. Coat the rocker arm cover and a new gasket with gasket adhesive and install the gasket to the cover.

9. Install the cover and tighten the retaining bolts to 5–8 ft. lbs. (7–11 Nm).

10. Install the throttle body and EGR supply tube, if necessary. Install the air cleaner or air intake duct.

11. Connect the negative battery cable.

Rocker arm shaft assembly installation—2.9L engine

2.9L ENGINE

1. Disconnect the negative battery cable and relieve the fuel system pressure.

2. Tag and disconnect the spark plug wires. If equipped, disconnect the transmission kickdown linkage.

3. Disconnect the fuel lines. If equipped with air conditioning, remove the dipstick tube and bracket and remove the left lifting eye.

4. Remove the PCV valve hose and breather. Remove the rocker arm cover attaching screws and load distribution washers. Note the position of the washers so they can be reinstalled in their original positions.

5. If equipped, remove the electrical connections from the right rocker arm cover.

6. Using a light plastic hammer, tap the rocker arm covers to break the seal. Remove the rocker arm covers.

7. Remove the rocker arm shaft stand attaching bolts by loosening them 2 turns at a time, in sequence. Lift off the rocker arm and shaft assembly and oil baffle.

To install:

8. Loosen the valve lash adjusting screws a few turns. Apply engine oil to the assembly to provide initial lubrication.

9. Install the oil baffle and rocker arm shaft assembly to the cylinder head. Guide the adjusting screws onto the pushrods.

10. Install the rocker arm stand attaching bolts, running them down 2 turns at a time, in sequence, until the shaft assembly is seated. Tighten the rocker arm stand attaching bolts to 43–50 ft. lbs. (59–67 Nm).

11. Adjust the valve lash.

12. Clean the gasket mating surfaces of the rocker arm covers and cylinder heads.

13. Install the rocker arm covers, using new gaskets. Install the attaching screws and load distribution washers, making sure the washers are installed in their original positions. Tighten to 3–5 ft. lbs. (4–7 Nm).

14. Connect the transmission kickdown linkage, if necessary. Connect the spark plug wires.

15. Connect the fuel lines and the negative battery cable. Start the engine and check for leaks.

3.0L ENGINE

1. Disconnect the negative battery cable. Remove the air cleaner fresh air hose, if necessary.

2. Tag and disconnect the spark plug wires from the spark plugs. Remove the spark plug wire/separator assembly from the rocker arm cover attaching bolt studs and position aside.

3. If the left rocker arm cover is being removed, proceed as follows:

    a. On 1988 vehicles, remove the oil fill cap and disconnect the closure system hose.

b. On 1989–92 vehicles, remove the throttle body assembly and the PCV valve.

c. On 1991–92 vehicles, remove the fuel injector harness stand-offs from the inboard rocker arm cover studs. Move the harness aside.

4. If the right rocker arm cover is being removed, proceed as follows:

a. On 1988 vehicles, remove the PCV valve and disconnect the heater hoses.

b. On 1989–92 Aerostar, remove the oil filler tube assembly and disconnect the closure hose from the oil fill adapter.

c. On Ranger, disconnect the engine harness connectors and remove the air cleaner closure hose from the oil fill adapter.

d. On 1991–92 vehicles, remove the fuel injector harness stand-offs from the inboard rocker arm cover studs. Move the harness aside.

5. Remove the rocker arm cover attaching bolts and studs, noting their locations. Remove the rocker arm cover.

6. Remove the rocker arm fulcrum bolt and remove the rocker arm and fulcrum.

To install:

7. Lubricate the valve stem tip, pushrod end, fulcrum and rocker arm fulcrum seat with clean engine oil.

8. For each valve, rotate the crankshaft until the lifter rests on the base circle of the camshaft lobe, before tightening the rocker arm fulcrum attaching bolts. Position the rocker arms over the valves and pushrods, install the fulcrums and fulcrum bolts and tighten to 24 ft. lbs. (32 Nm).

9. Clean the rocker arm cover and cylinder head gasket mating surfaces of all gasket material and/or old silicone sealer.

10. Apply a bead of silicone sealer at the cylinder head to intake manifold rail step and position the rocker arm cover on the cylinder head.

11. Install the bolts/studs in their original locations and tighten to 9 ft. lbs. (12 Nm).

12. Install the remaining components in the reverse order of their removal. Start the engine and check for leaks.

4.0L ENGINE

1. Disconnect the negative battery cable and relieve the fuel system pressure.

2. Tag and disconnect the spark plug wires. Disconnect the fuel lines.

3. If the left rocker arm cover is being removed, upper intake manifold removal may be required.

4. If the right rocker arm cover is being removed, proceed as follows:

a. Remove the ignition coil and bracket assembly and remove the PCV valve hose and breather.

b. On 1991–92 vehicles, remove the air inlet duct and the hose attached to the oil fill tube. Remove the accessory drive belt and remove the alternator.

c. On 1991–92 vehicles, drain the cooling system and remove the upper radiator hose. Remove the low pressure air conditioner hose bracket from the upper intake, if still installed and remove the vacuum hose from the air cleaner.

5. Remove the rocker arm cover attaching screws and load distribution washers. Note the position of the washers so they can be reinstalled in their original positions.

6. Using a light plastic hammer, tap the rocker arm covers to break the seal. Remove the covers.

7. Remove the rocker arm shaft stand attaching bolts by loosening the bolts 2 turns at a time, in sequence. Lift off the rocker arm and shaft assembly.

To install:

8. Apply engine oil to the valve train assembly to provide initial lubrication.

9. Install the rocker arm shaft assembly to the cylinder head, guiding the rocker arms onto the pushrods.

10. Install the rocker arm stand attaching bolts, running them

down 2 turns at a time, in sequence, until the shaft assembly is seated. Tighten the rocker arm stand attaching bolts to 46–52 ft. lbs. (62–70 Nm).

11. Clean all gasket material from the rocker arm cover and cylinder head.

12. Apply silicone sealer to the parting lines where the cylinder head and intake manifold seal. Install the rocker arm cover, using a new gasket.

13. Install the rocker arm cover attaching screws and load distribution washers, making sure the washers are in their original positions. Tighten to 3–5 ft. lbs. (4–7 Nm).

14. Install the remaining components in the reverse order of their removal. Start the engine and check for leaks.

Intake Manifold

Removal and Installation

2.0L ENGINE

1. Disconnect the negative battery cable and drain the cooling system. Remove the air cleaner.

2. Disconnect the accelerator cable. Tag and disconnect the necessary vacuum hoses. Remove the hot water hose from the manifold cover nipple fitting.

3. Remove the engine oil dipstick and disconnect the heat tube at the EGR valve. Disconnect the fuel line at the carburetor fuel filter.

4. Remove the dipstick retaining nut from the EGR valve.

5. Disconnect and remove the PCV at the engine and intake manifold.

6. Remove the distributor cap and position the cap and wires aside. Remove the plastic spark plug connector from the rocker arm cover.

7. Remove the intake manifold retaining bolts and remove the manifold from the vehicle.

To install:

8. Clean all gasket mating surfaces.

9. Position a new gasket and install the intake manifold. Install the attaching bolts and tighten, in sequence, in 2 steps, first to 5–7 ft. lbs. (7–9 Nm) and then to 15–22 ft. lbs. (19–29 Nm).

10. Install the distributor cap and the plastic spark plug connector.

11. Install the dipstick tube retaining nut and connect the fuel line.

12. Connect the PCV and connect the heat tube at the EGR valve.

13. Install the dipstick and connect the vacuum hoses. Connect the accelerator cable.

14. Install the hot water hose to the manifold nipple fitting and install the air cleaner.

15. Connect the negative battery cable. Fill and bleed the cooling system. Run the engine and check for leaks.

2.3L ENGINE

1. Disconnect the negative battery cable and relieve the fuel system pressure. Drain the cooling system.

Intake manifold bolt torque sequence—2.0L and 2.3L engines

2. Tag and disconnect the electrical connectors at the throttle position sensor, air charge temperature sensor, engine coolant temperature sensor and air bypass valve, if equipped. Disconnect the knock sensor connector, if equipped.

3. Disconnect the injector wiring harness at the main engine harness and at the water temperature indicator sensor. Disconnect the ignition control assembly connector, if equipped.

4. Tag and disconnect the vacuum lines at the upper intake manifold vacuum tree, EGR valve, fuel pressure regulator and canister purge line.

5. Remove the throttle linkage shield and disconnect the throttle linkage and cruise control. Disconnect the kickdown cable, if equipped. Unbolt the accelerator cable from the bracket and position the cable aside.

6. Disconnect the air intake hose and crankcase vent hose. Disconnect the air bypass hose, if equipped.

7. Disconnect the PCV system by disconnecting the hose from the fitting on the underside of the upper intake. Disconnect the water bypass line at the lower intake manifold.

8. Disconnect the EGR tube from the EGR valve. Remove the attaching bolts and remove the upper intake manifold and throttle body assembly.

9. Remove the engine oil dipstick tube bracket attaching bolt. Disconnect the fuel lines from the fuel supply manifold.

10. Disconnect the electrical connectors from the fuel injectors and position aside. Remove the fuel supply manifold attaching bolts and remove the fuel supply manifold.

11. Remove the attaching bolts and remove the lower intake manifold.

To install:

12. Clean all gasket mating surfaces. Clean and oil the manifold bolt threads.

13. Position a new gasket and install the lower intake manifold. Install the attaching bolts and tighten, in sequence, in 2 steps, first to 5–7 ft. lbs. (7–9 Nm) and then to 15–22 ft. lbs. (20–30 Nm).

14. Install the fuel supply manifold and injectors with the 2 attaching bolts. Tighten to 15–22 ft. lbs. (20–30 Nm). Connect the electrical connectors to the injectors.

15. Position a new gasket on the lower intake manifold and install the upper intake manifold. Install the attaching bolts and tighten, in sequence, to 15–22 ft. lbs. (20–30 Nm).

16. Install the engine oil dipstick tube and retaining bolt. Connect the fuel lines to the fuel supply manifold.

17. Connect the EGR tube to the EGR valve. Tighten to 18–28 ft. lbs. (25–30 Nm).

18. Connect the water bypass line and connect the PCV hose. Connect the vacuum lines to the locations marked during removal.

19. Hold the accelerator cable bracket in position on the upper manifold and install the attaching bolts. Tighten to 10–15 ft. lbs. (13.5–20.5 Nm).

20. Install the accelerator cable to the bracket. Connect the accelerator cable and cruise control. Install the throttle linkage shield.

21. Connect the electrical connectors to the locations marked during removal.

22. Connect the air intake hose and crankcase vent hose. Connect the air bypass hose, if equipped.

23. Connect the negative battery cable. Fill and bleed the cooling system. Run the engine and check for leaks.

2.9L ENGINE

1. Disconnect the negative battery cable and relieve the fuel system pressure. Drain the cooling system.

2. Remove air cleaner air intake duct from the throttle body.

3. Disconnect the throttle cable and bracket assembly.

4. Disconnect the EGR tube at the EGR valve, if equipped.

5. Tag and disconnect all vacuum hoses from the fittings on the upper intake manifold.

6. Disconnect the electrical connections at the throttle body,

Upper intake manifold retaining bolt torque sequence—1989–92 2.3L engine

Intake manifold assembly—1989–92 2.3L engine

Upper intake manifold retaining bolt torque sequence—1988 2.3L engine

intake manifold upper and lower, distributor and EGR pressure sensor, if equipped. Also disconnect the fuel injector sub harness from the main EEC harness.

7. Remove the upper intake manifold assembly.

8. Disconnect and remove the hose from the water outlet to radiator and heater supply. Disconnect the fuel lines from the fuel supply manifold.

9. Tag and disconnect the spark plug wires. Remove the distributor cap and wires as an assembly.

10. Mark the position of the distributor rotor in relation to the distributor housing and the housing in relation to the engine. Remove the distributor hold-down screw and clamp and lift out the distributor.

11. Remove the rocker arm covers.

12. Remove the intake manifold attaching bolts and nuts. Note the length of the manifold attaching bolts during removal so they can be installed in their original positions. Tap the manifold lightly with a plastic mallet to break the gasket seal. Remove the manifold.

13. Remove all old gasket material and sealing compound.

To install:

14. Apply sealing compound to the joining surfaces. Place the intake manifold gasket in position, making sure the tab on the right bank cylinder head gasket fits into the cutout of the manifold gasket.

15. Apply sealing compound to the attaching bolt bosses on the intake manifold and position the intake manifold. Install the attaching bolts/nuts and tighten, in sequence, in 4 steps, first to 3–6 ft. lbs. (4–8 Nm), 2nd to 6–11 ft. lbs. (8–15 Nm), 3rd to 11–15 ft. lbs. (15–21 Nm) and 4th to 15–18 ft. lbs. (21–25 Nm).

16. Install the distributor, aligning the marks that were made during removal. Install the distributor clamp and attaching bolt.

17. Replace the rocker arm cover gaskets and install the rocker arm covers.

18. Install the distributor cap and spark plug wires. Connect the distributor wiring harness.

19. Apply sealing compound at the joining surfaces of the upper and lower intake manifold. Install new upper intake manifold gaskets.

20. Install the upper intake manifold assembly and tighten the retaining bolts in sequence, center to end, in 2 steps, first to 7 ft. lbs. (10 Nm) and then to 15–18 ft. lbs. (21–25 Nm).

21. Connect all vacuum hoses to the fittings on the upper intake manifold.

22. Connect the electrical connectors at the throttle body, intake manifolds sub harness to EEC main harness and EGR pressure sensor, if equipped.

23. Install and adjust the throttle linkage bracket assembly and cover as required.

24. Connect the hoses from the water outlet to the radiator and the bypass hose from the thermostat housing rear cover to intake manifold.

25. Connect the fuel lines.

26. Connect the negative battery cable. Fill and bleed the cooling system.

27. Check the ignition timing and reset the engine idle speed to specification. Start the engine and check for coolant and oil leaks.

3.0L ENGINE

1. Disconnect the negative battery cable and relieve the fuel system pressure. Drain the cooling system.

2. Remove the air cleaner hoses to the throttle body and rocker arm cover. Disconnect the fuel lines from the fuel supply manifold.

3. Tag and disconnect the necessary vacuum lines.

4. Tag and disconnect the electrical connectors at the air charge temperature sensor, engine coolant temperature sensor, throttle position sensor, air bypass solenoid and coolant temperature sender.

Intake manifold bolt torque sequence—2.9L engine

Intake manifold bolt torque sequence—3.0L engine

5. Remove the snow shield from the power steering pump bracket and accelerator cable bracket.

6. Disconnect and remove the accelerator and cruise control cables from the accelerator mounting bracket and throttle lever.

7. Remove the alternator support brace.

8. Remove the throttle body-to-lower intake manifold retaining bolts and stud bolts and remove the throttle body assembly.

9. Disconnect the fuel injector harness stand-offs from the inboard rocker arm cover studs and each injector and remove from the engine.

10. Disconnect the upper radiator hose from the thermostat housing and disconnect the heater hoses.

11. Tag and disconnect the spark plug wires. Remove the distributor cap and wires as an assembly.

12. Mark the position of the distributor rotor in relation to the distributor housing and the housing in relation to the engine. Remove the distributor hold-down screw and clamp and lift out the distributor.

13. Remove the ignition coil from the rear of the left cylinder head, if required.

14. Remove the rocker arm covers. Loosen the No. 3 cylinder intake valve rocker arm fulcrum bolt and rotate the rocker arm away from the valve. Remove the pushrod.

15. Remove the intake manifold bolts. Break the gasket seal by wedging a large prybar between the manifold an the block using the lug on the water pump as a leverage point. Be careful to prevent damage to machines surfaces.

16. Remove the intake manifold.

To install:

17. Clean all gasket mating surfaces.

18. Apply silicone sealer to the intersection of the cylinder block and cylinder head at the 4 corners of the lifter valley opening.

19. Install the front and rear intake manifold seals and secure with the retaining features. Position the intake manifold gaskets on the cylinder heads and insert the locking tabs on the cylinder head gaskets.

20. Carefully lower the intake manifold into position being careful not to disturb the silicone sealer. Install the intake manifold bolts and tighten, in sequence, in 2 steps, first to 11 ft. lbs. (15 Nm) and then to 19 ft. lbs. (26 Nm).

21. Install the No. 3 cylinder intake valve pushrod. Apply oil to the pushrod and rocker arm fulcrum and position the rocker arm over the valve and pushrod. Rotate the crankshaft to place the lifter on the base circle of the cam, then tighten the fulcrum bolt to 24 ft. lbs. (32 Nm).

22. Install the rocker arm covers and the fuel injector electrical harness.

23. Install the throttle body using a new gasket. Tighten the throttle body attaching bolts, in sequence, to 19 ft. lbs. (25 Nm).

24. Install the alternator brace. Tighten the nuts to 12 ft. lbs. (16 Nm).

25. Connect the PCV valve hose. Connect the engine coolant temperature sensor, air charge temperature sensor, throttle position sensor, air bypass solenoid and coolant temperature sender connectors.

26. Install the distributor, aligning the marks that were made during removal. Install the distributor cap and connect the spark plug wires. Connect the distributor electrical connector.

27. Install the ignition coil, if removed.

28. Connect the heater hoses and the upper radiator hose. Connect the vacuum lines to the locations marked during removal.

29. Connect the fuel lines to the fuel supply manifold. Change the engine oil and filter.

NOTE: Engine coolant is corrosive to all engine bearing material. Changing the oil after removal of a coolant carrying component helps prevent engine failure.

30. Connect the negative battery cable. Fill and bleed the cooling system. Install the air cleaner hose.

31. Run the engine and check for leaks. Check the ignition timing, idle speed, throttle linkage and cruise control and adjust, if necessary.

4.0L ENGINE

1. Disconnect the negative battery cable and relieve the fuel system pressure.

2. Remove the air cleaner air intake duct from the throttle body.

3. Remove the snow/ice shield and disconnect the throttle cable and bracket assembly.

4. Tag and disconnect the vacuum hoses from the fittings on the upper intake manifold.

5. Tag and disconnect the electrical connectors at the throttle body, upper intake manifold, lower intake manifold and injectors.

6. Disconnect the fuel lines from the fuel supply manifold.

7. Remove the ignition coil and bracket assembly.

8. Remove the mounting nuts and remove the upper intake manifold.

Air intake throttle body bolt torque sequence—3.0L engine

9. Remove the rocker arm covers.

10. Remove the intake manifold attaching bolts and nuts. Tap the manifold lightly with a plastic mallet the break the gasket seal and remove the manifold.

To install:

11. Clean all gasket mating surfaces.

12. Apply silicone sealer to the block and cylinder head mating surfaces at the 4 corners of the lifter valley opening. Install the intake manifold gaskets and again apply sealer to the same locations.

13. Position the intake manifold on the 2 guide studs and install the nuts and bolts hand tight. Tighten the bolts, in sequence, in 4 steps, first to 3–6 ft. lbs. (4–8 Nm), then to 6–11 ft. lbs. (8–15 Nm), then to 11–15 ft. lbs. (15–21 Nm) and finally to 15–18 ft. lbs. (21–25 Nm).

14. Apply silicone sealer to the 4 locations where the intake manifold and the cylinder heads meet. Install the rocker arm covers with new gaskets and tighten evenly to 3–5 ft. lbs. (4–7 Nm). Wait 2 minutes and tighten the bolts again to the same specification.

Intake manifold bolt torque sequence—4.0L engine

15. Install the upper intake manifold and tighten the nuts to 15–18 ft. lbs. (20–25 Nm).

16. Install the ignition coil and bracket assembly. Connect the fuel lines to the fuel supply manifold.

17. Connect the electrical connectors at the throttle body, upper intake manifold, lower intake manifold and injectors.

18. Connect the vacuum hoses to the fittings on the upper intake manifold.

19. Install the throttle cable and bracket assembly and the snow/ice shield to the throttle body.

20. Connect the air cleaner air intake duct to the throttle body.

21. Connect the negative battery cable. Fill and bleed the cooling system. Run the engine and check for leaks.

Exhaust Manifold

Removal and Installation

2.0L AND 2.3L ENGINES

1. Disconnect the negative battery cable. Remove the air cleaner and duct assembly.

2. Remove the EGR tube at the exhaust manifold and loosen at the EGR valve.

3. Remove the check valve at the exhaust manifold and disconnect the hose at the end of the air bypass valve, if equipped.

4. Disconnect the oxygen sensor from the exhaust manifold, if equipped. Remove the sensor, if necessary.

5. Remove the screw attaching the heater hoses to the rocker arm cover. Disconnect the exhaust pipe from the exhaust manifold.

6. Remove the exhaust manifold mounting bolts and remove the manifold.

7. Installation is the reverse of the removal procedure. Tighten the exhaust manifold mounting bolts, in sequence, in 2 steps, first to 15–17 ft. lbs. (20–23 Nm) and then to 20–30 ft. lbs. (27–41 Nm).

2.9L ENGINE

1. Disconnect the negative battery cable.

2. Raise and safely support the vehicle, as necessary.

3. Disconnect the exhaust pipe from the exhaust manifold.

4. Disconnect the EGR tube at the manifold, if equipped.

5. Remove the manifold attaching bolts and remove the manifold.

6. Installation is the reverse of the removal procedure. Tighten the exhaust manifold bolts to 20–30 ft. lbs. (27–40 Nm).

3.0L ENGINE

1. Disconnect the negative battery cable.

2. Raise and safely support the vehicle, as necessary.

3. If removing the left exhaust manifold, remove the engine oil dipstick tube support bracket or retaining nut, as required. Rotate the tube out of the way or remove.

4. If removing the left exhaust manifold on 1988–90 vehicles, remove the power steering pump pressure and return hoses.

5. If removing the right exhaust manifold on 1988–89 vehicles, remove the heater hose support bracket and disconnect the heater hoses.

6. Remove the spark plugs. Disconnect the exhaust pipe from the manifold.

7. Remove the exhaust manifold attaching nuts and remove the manifold.

8. Installation is the reverse of the removal procedure. Tighten the manifold attaching bolts to 18 ft. lbs. (25 Nm).

4.0L ENGINE

1. Disconnect the negative battery cable.

2. Raise and safely support the vehicle, as necessary.

3. If removing the left manifold, remove the engine oil dip-

ＳｅｒｖｉｃｅＴｉｐｓ

EXHAUST SYSTEM NOISE

On all vehicles, a "buzz" or "rattle" noise from the exhaust system, may be caused by a loose heat shield at the muffler or catalytic converter. The noise is noticeable during normal driving or at engine idle. To correct this, install worm clamp(s), part number FOTZ–5A231–A to secure the heat shield to the muffler or catalytic converter. Tighten the clamps to no more than 60 inch lbs. (6.8 Nm) and trim the excess to approximately 1 in.

Exhaust manifold bolt torque sequence—2.0L and 2.3L engines

ＳｅｒｖｉｃｅＴｉｐｓ

CRACKED OR BROKEN EXHAUST MANIFOLD

The passenger's side exhaust manifold on the 3.0L engine in Aerostar, may become cracked or broken if the exhaust system or manifold is hit by a mis-adjusted vehicle hoist lifting arm. Use care when raising the vehicle, so there is no interference between the lift and the manifold or exhaust system. If the exhaust manifold is damaged, install a replacement, part number E69Z–9430–C.

stick tube support bracket. Remove the power steering pump pressure and return hoses, if necessary.

4. If removing the right manifold, remove the heater hose support bracket and disconnect the heater hoses.

5. Disconnect the exhaust pipe from the manifold.

6. Remove the manifold attaching bolts and remove the manifold.

7. Installation is the reverse of the removal procedure. Tighten the mounting bolts to 19 ft. lbs. (25 Nm).

Timing Chain Front Cover

Removal and Installation

2.9L AND 4.0L ENGINES

1. Disconnect the negative battery cable and drain the cooling system and crankcase.

2. Remove the oil pan and the radiator.

3. Remove the air conditioning compressor and power steering bracket, if equipped.

4. Remove the alternator and drive belt(s). Remove the fan.

5. Remove the water pump and heater and radiator hoses.

6. Remove the crankshaft pulley/damper assembly. On 4.0L engine, remove the crankshaft timing sensor.

7. Remove the front cover retaining bolts, noting their positions. If necessary, tap the cover lightly with a plastic hammer to break the gasket seal. Remove the front cover.

To install:

8. Clean all gasket mating surfaces. Apply sealer to the gasket surfaces on the cylinder block and the back side of the front cover plate. Install the guide sleeves.

9. Apply sealer to the front cover gasket surface and position a new gasket on the front cover.

10. Install the front cover with the retaining screws. Note the different bolt lengths on 4.0L engine. Tighten the bolts to 13–15 ft. lbs. (17–21 Nm).

11. On 4.0L engine, install the crankshaft timing sensor.

12. Install the crankshaft pulley/damper assembly. On 2.9L engine, tighten the attaching bolt to 85–96 ft. lbs. (115–130 Nm). On 4.0L engine, tighten the attaching bolt to 30–37 ft. lbs. (40–50 Nm), then tighten an additional 80–90 degrees.

13. Install the remaining components in the reverse order of their removal. Fill and bleed the cooling system. Run the engine and check for leaks.

3.0L ENGINE

Aerostar

1. Disconnect the negative battery cable. Remove the air cleaner fresh air hose.

2. Drain the cooling system and the crankcase. Remove the cooling fan.

3. Loosen the water pump hub bolts and remove the accessory drive belts. Remove the water pump pulley.

4. Remove the alternator adjusting arm and brace. Move the alternator aside.

5. Remove the air conditioning compressor mounting bolts, if equipped. Tie the compressor aside with mechanics wire and remove the bracket.

6. Remove the crankshaft pulley and damper. Remove the water pump, if required.

NOTE: The timing cover can be removed with the water pump installed by not removing the 6mm water pump attaching bolts.

7. Disconnect the lower radiator hose and heater hose.

8. Remove the oil pan assembly. Disconnect the oil level sensor, if equipped, before removal.

9. Remove the front cover attaching bolts and remove the front cover.

To install:

10. Clean all gasket mating surfaces. Use a seal removal tool to remove the front cover oil seal.

11. Install a new front cover oil seal, using a seal installer. Position a new front cover gasket on the engine block dowel pins.

12. Install the front cover with the attaching bolts. Apply sealer to the 3 attaching bolts on the passenger side of the cover, prior to installation. Tighten the 8mm bolts to 19 ft. lbs. (25 Nm) and the 6mm bolts to 7 ft. lbs. (10 Nm).

13. Install the oil pan. Install the water pump, if removed.

14. Install the crankshaft pulley and damper. Tighten the damper attaching bolt to 141–169 ft. lbs. (190–230 Nm) on 1988 vehicles or 107 ft. lbs. (145 Nm) on 1989–92 vehicles.

15. Install the lower radiator hose and heater hose. Install the air conditioning bracket, compressor and brace, if equipped.

16. Install the alternator assembly, bracket, oil fill tube support and throttle body brace.

17. Install the water pump pulley and accessory drive belts. Install the cooling fan and shroud.

18. Fill the crankcase with the proper type and quantity of engine oil. Connect the negative battery cable.

19. Fill and bleed the cooling system. Run the engine and check for leaks. Install the air cleaner fresh air hose.

Ranger

1. Disconnect the negative battery cable. Drain the cooling system and crankcase.

2. Remove the cooling fan and water pump pulley bolts. Remove the accessory drive belts and the water pump pulley.

3. Remove the alternator adjusting arm and the throttle body brace. Remove the heater air intake duct.

4. Remove the motor mount upper nuts. If equipped with automatic transmission and air conditioning, remove the air conditioning compressor upper bolts, then remove the front cover front nuts.

5. Remove the distributor assembly.

NOTE: Failure to remove the distributor assembly will result in a broken distributor.

6. Raise and safely support the vehicle. Remove the lower air conditioning compressor bolts and wire the compressor aside. Remove the compressor bracket.

7. Remove the crankshaft pulley and damper. Remove the oil pan. Disconnect the oil level sensor before pan removal.

8. Lower the vehicle and remove the lower radiator hose. Remove the water pump, if required.

NOTE: The timing cover can be removed with the water pump installed by not removing the 6mm water pump attaching bolts.

9. Remove the front cover attaching bolts and remove the front cover.

To install:

10. Clean all gasket mating surfaces. Use a seal removal tool to remove the front cover oil seal.

11. Install a new front cover oil seal, using a seal installer. Position a new front cover gasket on the engine block dowel pins.

12. Install the front cover with the attaching bolts. Apply sealer to the 3 attaching bolts on the passenger side of the cover, prior to installation. Tighten the 8mm bolts to 19 ft. lbs. (25 Nm) and the 6mm bolts to 7 ft. lbs. (10 Nm).

13. Raise and safely support the vehicle. Install the oil pan and connect the oil level sensor.

14. Install the water pump, if removed.

15. Install the crankshaft pulley and damper. Tighten the damper attaching bolt to 107 ft. lbs. (145 Nm).

16. Install the air conditioning compressor bracket, if equipped, position the compressor and install the lower bolts. Lower the vehicle.

17. Install the distributor. Install the front cover front nuts and the air conditioning compressor upper bolts, if equipped.

18. Install the motor mount upper nuts and the heater air intake duct. Install the alternator adjusting arm and brace.

19. Install the water pump pulley and accessory drive belts. Install the cooling fan and coolant hoses.

20. Fill the crankcase with the proper type and quantity of engine oil. Connect the negative battery cable.

21. Fill and bleed the cooling system. Run the engine and check for leaks. Check the ignition timing and adjust, if necessary.

Front Cover Oil Seal

Replacement

1. Disconnect the negative battery cable.

2. Drain the cooling system and remove the radiator, if necessary to provide access.

3. Remove the accessory drive belts and remove the crankshaft pulley and damper assembly.

4. Remove the seal from the front cover using a seal removal tool. Be careful not to damage the seal housing or crankshaft surfaces.

To install:

5. Coat a new oil seal with clean engine oil and install in the front cover, using a seal installer.

6. Install the crankshaft pulley and damper assembly. Tighten the damper attaching bolt to 85–96 ft. lbs. (115–130 Nm) on 2.9L engine, 141–169 ft. lbs. (190–230 Nm) on 1988 3.0L engine or 107 ft. lbs. (145 Nm) on 1989–92 3.0L engine. On 4.0L engine, tighten the attaching bolt to 30–37 ft. lbs. (40–50 Nm), then tighten an additional 80–90 degrees.

7. Install the accessory drive belts. Install the radiator, if removed.

8. Connect the negative battery cable. Fill and bleed the cooling system, if necessary.

Timing Chain and Sprockets

Removal and Installation

2.9L AND 3.0L ENGINES

1. Disconnect the negative battery cable and drain the cooling system.

2. Remove the timing chain front cover.

3. Rotate the crankshaft until No. 1 cylinder is at TDC and the crankshaft and camshaft sprocket timing marks are aligned.

4. Remove the camshaft sprocket retaining bolt and remove the sprocket and timing chain.

5. Remove the crankshaft sprocket.

To install:

6. Align the crankshaft sprocket with the key or dowel on the crankshaft and install the sprocket.

7. Make sure the sprocket timing marks are still in alignment.

8. Install the camshaft sprocket and timing chain. Install the camshaft sprocket retaining bolt and tighten to 19–28 ft. lbs. (26–38 Nm) on 2.9L engine or 46 ft. lbs. (63 Nm) on 3.0L engine.

NOTE: The camshaft retaining bolt on the 3.0L engine has a drilled oil passage for timing chain lubrication. If damaged, do not replace with a standard bolt. Clean the oil passage with solvent.

9. Install the timing chain front cover and the remaining components in the reverse order of their removal. Fill the crankcase with the proper type and quantity of engine oil. Fill and bleed the cooling system. Run the engine and check for leaks.

4.0L ENGINE

1. Disconnect the negative battery cable and drain the cooling system and crankcase.

Timing chain and sprocket alignment—3.0L engine

TIMING MARKS

Timing chain and sprocket alignment—4.0L engine

CAMSHAFT SPROCKET

CAMSHAFT TIMING MARK

TENSIONER

GUIDE RAIL

CRANKSHAFT TIMING MARK

CRANKSHAFT SPROCKET

CLIP

2. Remove the oil pan and radiator. Remove the accessory drive belt and crankshaft damper.

3. Remove the water pump and timing chain front cover.

4. Remove the camshaft sprocket retaining bolt and the crankshaft sprocket key. Remove the sprockets with the timing chain.

To install:

5. Install the timing chain guide to the cylinder block with the pin of the guide inserted into the oil hole in the block. Install the 2 retaining bolts and tighten to 7–9 ft. lbs. (10–12 Nm).

6. Position the camshaft and crankshaft so the sprocket timing marks will align.

7. Install the sprockets and timing chain together. Install the timing chain tensioner with the clip in place to lock the tensioner in the retracted position.

8. Install the crankshaft key and check the timing marks on the sprockets for correct alignment. Make sure the tensioner side of the timing chain is held inward and the guide side of the chain is straight and tight.

9. Install the camshaft sprocket retaining bolt and tighten to 44–50 ft. lbs. (60–68 Nm). Remove the clip from the tensioner assembly.

10. Install the timing chain front cover and the remaining components in the reverse order of their removal. Fill the crankcase with the proper type and quantity of engine oil. Fill and bleed the cooling system. Run the engine and check for leaks.

Timing Belt Front Cover

Removal and Installation

1. Disconnect the negative battery cable and drain the cooling system.
2. Loosen the thermactor pump bolts and remove the drive belt, if equipped.
3. Remove the fan blade and 4 water pump pulley bolts.
4. Loosen the alternator retaining bolts and remove the drive belt from the pulleys. Remove the upper radiator hose.
5. Remove the crankshaft pulley bolt and pulley. Remove the thermostat housing.
6. Loosen the power steering pump mounting bracket and position aside.
7. Remove the timing belt front cover retaining bolt(s). Release the cover interlocking tabs, if equipped. Remove the cover.

To install:

8. Install the front cover. If equipped, secure by snapping the interlocking tabs into place. Install the retaining bolt(s).
9. Install the power steering pump mounting bracket.
10. Install the thermostat housing and connect the upper radiator hose.
11. Install the crankshaft pulley and retaining bolt. Tighten to 103–133 ft. lbs. (140–180 Nm).
12. Position the alternator drive belt and adjust the belt tension. Install the water pump pulley and fan.
13. Position the thermactor pump drive belt, if equipped, and adjust the tension.
14. Connect the negative battery cable. Fill and bleed the cooling system. Run the engine and check for leaks.

Oil Seal Replacement

1. Disconnect the negative battery cable.
2. Remove the timing belt front cover, timing belt and sprockets.
3. Use seal removal tool T74P–6700–B or equivalent, to remove the crankshaft, camshaft or auxiliary shaft seals. Make sure the jaws of the tool are gripping the thin edge of the seal very tightly before operating the jack-screw portion of the tool.

To install:

4. Coat the new seal with engine oil and install, using seal installation tool T74P–6150–A or equivalent.
5. Install the timing sprockets, timing belt and timing belt front cover. Connect the negative battery cable.

Timing Belt and Tensioner

Removal and Installation

1. Disconnect the negative battery cable.
2. Remove the timing belt front cover.
3. Loosen the belt tensioner adjustment screw. Position belt tension adjusting tool T74P–6254–A or equivalent, on the tension spring rollpin and retract the belt tensioner. Tighten the adjustment screw to hold the tensioner in the retracted position.
4. On 1989–92 vehicles, remove the bolts holding the timing sensor in place and pull the sensor free of the dowel pin.
5. Remove the crankshaft pulley, hub and belt guide. Remove the timing belt.
6. If the timing belt tensioner is to be removed, remove the adjustment screw and the spring bolt and remove the tensioner.

To install:

7. If removed, install the timing belt tensioner. Install the spring bolt but do not tighten at this time. Position the tensioner in the fully retracted position and tighten the adjustment bolt.
8. Position the crankshaft sprocket to align with the TDC mark and the camshaft sprocket to align with the timing pointer. On 1988 vehicles, remove the distributor cap and set the dis-

Timing belt and sprockets alignment—2.0L and 2.3L engines

Timing belt, tensioner and sprockets installation—2.0L and 2.3L engines

tributor rotor to the No. 1 firing position by turning the auxiliary shaft.

9. Install the timing belt over the crankshaft sprocket and then counterclockwise over the auxiliary and camshaft sprockets. Align the belt fore and aft on the sprockets.
10. Loosen the tensioner adjustment bolt to allow the tensioner to move against the belt. If the spring does not have enough tension to move the roller against the belt and the belt hangs loose, it may be necessary to manually push the roller against the belt and tighten the bolt.

NOTE: The spring cannot be used to set belt tension. A wrench must be used on the tensioner assembly.

11. Remove a spark plug from each cylinder to make sure the engine does not jump time during Step 12.

12. Rotate the crankshaft 2 complete turns in the direction of normal rotation to remove the slack from the belt. Tighten the spring bolt to 28–40 ft. lbs. (38–54 Nm) and the adjustment bolt to 14–21 ft. lbs. (19–29 Nm).

13. Install the crankshaft belt guide.

14. On 1989–92 vehicles, proceed as follows:

   a. Install the timing sensor onto the dowel pin and tighten the 2 longer bolts.

   b. Rotate the crankshaft 45 degrees counterclockwise and install the crankshaft pulley and hub. Tighten the pulley bolt to 103–133 ft. lbs. (140–180 Nm).

   c. Rotate the crankshaft 90 degrees clockwise so the vane of the crankshaft pulley engages with timing sensor positioner tool T89P–6316–A or equivalent. Tighten the 2 shorter sensor bolts.

   d. Rotate the crankshaft 90 degrees counterclockwise and remove the sensor positioner tool.

   e. Rotate the crankshaft 90 degrees clockwise and measure the outer vane-to-sensor air gap. The air gap must be 0.018–0.039 in. (0.458–0.996mm).

15. Install the timing belt front cover and the remaining components in the reverse order of their removal.

Timing Sprockets

Removal and Installation

1. Disconnect the negative battery cable.
2. Remove timing belt front cover and timing belt.
3. Remove timing sprockets retaining bolt(s). Remove the timing sprocket with a suitable puller.
4. Installation is the reverse of the remove procedure. Tighten the camshaft sprocket bolt to 52–70 ft. lbs. (70–95 Nm). Tighten the auxiliary shaft sprocket bolt to 30–40 ft. lbs. (40–54 Nm).

Camshaft

Removal and Installation

EXCEPT 2.0L AND 2.3L ENGINES

1. Disconnect the negative battery cable and relieve the fuel system pressure. Drain the crankcase and the cooling system.

2. Remove the rocker arm covers, rocker arms or rocker arm shaft assemblies and pushrods. Note the position of each component so it can be reinstalled in the same place.

3. Remove the intake manifold.

4. Remove the lifters. Identify each lifter so it can be reinstalled in the original position.

5. Remove the front timing chain cover and the timing chain and gears.

6. Remove the thrust plate bolts and remove the thrust plate. Carefully remove the camshaft, being careful not to damage the journals, lobes or bearings.

To install:

7. Coat the camshaft lobes with grease and the journals with heavy engine oil. Carefully install the camshaft, being careful not to damage the journals, lobes or bearings.

8. Install the thrust plate and the thrust plate retaining bolts. Tighten the bolts to 13–16 ft. lbs. (17–21 Nm) on 2.9L engine, 7 ft. lbs. (10 Nm) on 3.0L engine or 7–10 ft. lbs. (10–13 Nm) on 4.0L engine.

9. Check the camshaft endplay using a dial indicator. The endplay should be 0.0008–0.004 in. on 2.9L and 4.0L engines or should not exceed 0.007 in. on 3.0L engine.

10. Install the remaining components in the reverse order of their removal. Fill the crankcase with the proper type and quantity of engine oil. Fill and bleed the cooling system. Run the engine and check for leaks.

Camshaft thrust plate positioning—2.9L engine

Camshaft installation—4.0L engine

2.0L AND 2.3L ENGINES

1. Disconnect the negative battery cable and drain the cooling system. Remove the air cleaner assembly.

2. Tag and disconnect the spark plug wires at the plugs and rocker arm cover and position aside. Tag and disconnect the necessary vacuum lines.

3. Remove the rocker arm cover. Remove the alternator mounting bracket-to-cylinder head mounting bolts and position aside.

4. Disconnect and remove the upper radiator hose. Remove the radiator shroud.

5. Remove the timing belt front cover. If equipped with power steering, remove the power steering pump bracket.

COVER ALIGNMENT PADS
3 PLACES
VIEW A

0.080–0.140 IN.
(2.0–3.5MM)

DOWEL

VIEW B

VIEW B

DOWEL

GEAR AND FUEL PUMP ECCENTRIC
MUST NOT BE ALLOWED TO TOUCH
BEARING SURFACES DURING
INSTALLATION

AUXILIARY SHAFT

RETAINING PLATE

SCREW AND
WASHER

PIN

BEARING

DIP SHAFT IN ENGINE OIL BEFORE
INSTALLING

CUT GASKET FOR SEPARATE REMOVAL
OR INSTALLATION OF COVERS.

SCREW AND
WASHER

AUXILIARY SHAFT
COVER

FRONT COVER ASSEMBLY

GUIDE PIN

VIEW A

FRONT COVER
ALIGNMENT TOOL

STUD BOLT

SCREW AND WASHER

GASKET

Auxiliary shaft installation—2.0L and 2.3L engines

Camshaft installation—2.0L and 2.3L engines

6. Remove the timing belt, camshaft followers and camshaft sprocket. Remove the camshaft seal using seal removal tool T74P-6700-B or equivalent.

7. Remove the 2 screws and the camshaft rear retainer.

8. Raise and support the vehicle safely. Remove the front motor mount bolts.

9. Position a jack under the engine and raise the engine carefully as far as it will go. Place blocks of wood between the engine mounts and chassis brackets and remove the jack.

10. Remove the camshaft, being careful to avoid damaging the journals, lobes and bearings.

To install:

11. Make sure the threaded plug is in the rear of the camshaft. If not, remove the threaded plug from the old camshaft and install. Tighten to 12–18 ft. lbs. (16–24 Nm).

12. Coat the camshaft lobes with grease and lubricate the journals with heavy engine oil. Carefully slide the camshaft through the bearings.

13. Install the camshaft rear retainer with the 2 screws. Tighten to 6–9 ft. lbs. (8–12 Nm).

14. Install a new camshaft seal using seal installation tool T74P-6150-A or equivalent.

15. Install the remaining components in the reverse order of their removal. Fill and bleed the cooling system. Run the engine and check for leaks.

Auxiliary Shaft

Removal and Installation

1. Disconnect the negative battery cable and drain the cooling system.

2. Remove the timing belt front cover.

3. Remove the timing belt and remove the auxiliary shaft sprocket.

4. Remove the auxiliary shaft cover bolts and the cover.

5. On 1988 vehicles, remove the distributor assembly.

6. Remove the auxiliary shaft retaining plate screws and remove the retaining plate.

7. Remove the auxiliary shaft, being careful not to damage the journals or bearings.

To install:

8. Coat the auxiliary shaft journals with heavy engine oil. Install the auxiliary shaft, being careful not to damage the journals or bearings.

9. Install the retaining plate. Tighten the retaining plate screws to 6–9 ft. lbs. (8–12 Nm).

10. Install the auxiliary shaft cover and tighten the screws to 6–9 ft. lbs. (8–12 Nm).

11. Install the remaining components in the reverse order of their removal. Fill and bleed the cooling system. Run the engine and check for leaks.

Piston and Connecting Rod

Positioning

Piston and connecting rod assembly—3.0L engine

Piston and connecting rod assembly—4.0L engine

Piston and Connecting Rod

Positioning

Piston and connecting rod assembly—2.0L and 2.3L engines

Piston and connecting rod assembly—2.9L engine

ENGINE LUBRICATION

Oil Pan

Removal and Installation

2.0L ENGINE

1. Disconnect the negative battery cable and remove the air cleaner assembly.

2. Remove the engine oil dipstick and remove the engine mount retaining nuts.

3. Remove the fan shroud. Raise and safely support the vehicle.

4. Disconnect the exhaust manifold tube to the inlet pipe bracket below the thermactor check valve. Drain the engine oil.

5. Disconnect the starter cable and remove the starter. Disconnect the right front lower shock absorber mount.

6. Position a jack under the engine. Raise the engine and position suitable wood blocks between the engine mounts and frame brackets. Remove the jack.

7. Remove the oil pan retaining bolts and lower the pan to the crossmember. Remove the oil pump drive and pickup tube assembly and remove the oil pan out the rear of the vehicle.

To install:

8. Clean all gasket mating surfaces and the oil pan.

9. Apply sealer to the oil pan surfaces and install the left and right gaskets to the oil pan. Apply sealer to the front and rear bearing caps and install the front and rear seals. Press the seal tabs firmly into the block.

10. Install 2 guide pins and position the oil pan under the block so it rests on the crossmember. Install the oil pump drive and pickup tube assembly and install the oil pan to the block.

11. Position the jack under the engine. Raise the engine, remove the wood blocks and lower the engine into position.

12. Install the right front lower shock absorber mount. Install the starter and connect the starter cable.

13. Install a new oil filter. Install the exhaust manifold tube to the inlet pipe bracket located below the thermactor check valve.

14. Remove the jack and lower the vehicle.

15. Install the fan shroud and the engine mount retainer nuts.

16. Install the engine oil dipstick and the air cleaner assembly.

17. Fill the crankcase with the proper type and quantity of engine oil. Connect the negative battery cable.

18. Run the engine and check for leaks.

2.3L ENGINE

1. Disconnect the negative battery cable and remove the air cleaner outlet tube at the throttle body.

2. Remove the engine oil dipstick and remove the engine mount retaining nuts.

3. Disconnect the oil cooler lines at the radiator, if equipped. Remove the fan shroud.

4. If equipped with automatic transmission, remove the radiator retaining bolts and position the radiator upward and wire to the hood.

5. Raise and safely support the vehicle. Drain the engine oil.

6. Disconnect the starter cable and remove the starter. Disconnect the exhaust manifold tube to the inlet pipe bracket at the thermactor check valve.

7. Disconnect the catalytic converter at the inlet pipe.

Service Tips

INCORRECT OIL DIPSTICK READING

On all engines, the markings on the engine oil level dipstick may not be read correctly or could possibly be misinterpreted. This could result in thinking that the engine has been overfilled with the specified amount of oil during oil and filter changes.

An engine filled with the proper amount of oil will appear to be overfilled. This occurs because the **FULL** mark on the dipstick represents the lowest level of oil that could occur when an engine is filled with the specified volume of oil. This variation is due to manufacturing tolerances and oil level checking conditions.

8. Remove the insulator and retainer assembly at the transmission. Remove the transmission mount retaining nuts to the crossmember.

9. If equipped with automatic transmission, remove the oil cooler lines from the retainer at the block and remove the front crossmember.

10. If equipped with manual transmission, disconnect the right front lower shock absorber mount.

11. Position a jack under the engine. Raise the engine and position suitable wood blocks between the engine mounts and frame brackets. Remove the jack.

12. If equipped with automatic transmission, position a jack under the transmission and raise slightly.

13. Remove the oil pan retaining bolts and lower the pan to the chassis. Remove the low oil level sensor assembly and the oil pump drive and pickup tube assembly.

14. If equipped with automatic transmission, remove the oil pan out the front of the vehicle. If equipped with manual transmission, remove the oil pan out from the rear.

To install:

15. Clean all gasket mating surfaces, the oil pan, oil pump exterior and pickup tube screen.

16. Install the low oil level sensor assembly and tighten to 20–30 ft. lbs. (27–41 Nm).

17. Press a new gasket into the oil pan groove. Retain the gasket in the oil pan by press fit only.

18. Position the oil pan on the crossmember. Install the oil pump drive and pickup tube assembly.

19. Apply sealer in 6 places on the engine and install the oil pan. Install the oil pan flange bolts tight enough to compress the gasket to the point that the 2 transmission holes are aligned with the 2 tapped holes in the oil pan, but loose enough to allow movement of the pan relative to the block.

20. Install the 2 oil pan-to-transmission bolts and tighten to 30–39 ft. lbs. (40–50 Nm) to align the oil pan with the transmission, then loosen the bolts ½ turn.

21. Tighten all oil pan flange bolts to 90–120 inch lbs. (10–13.5 Nm), then retighten the 2 oil pan-to-transmission bolts to 30–39 ft. lbs. (40–50 Nm).

22. Install a new oil filter. Position a jack under the engine and raise it enough to remove the wood blocks. Shift the engine/transmission backward to its original position.

23. Install the mount/bracket assembly to the crossmember and lower the engine. Install the front crossmember, if removed.

24. Raise the transmission with the jack and install the mount. Install the stabilizer brackets to the frame, if removed.

25. Connect the automatic transmission oil cooler line retainer clip to the engine, if equipped. Install the transmission mount retaining nuts.

26. Install a new gasket and connect the rear exhaust pipe just behind the catalytic converter.

27. Connect the low oil level sensor wire. Install the starter and connect the starter cable. Lower the vehicle.

28. Connect the vacuum tube to the clip at the front of the automatic transmission, if equipped.

29. Install the radiator and shroud. Connect the oil cooler lines, if equipped.

30. Connect the EGR valve and EGR tube. Install the engine mount retaining nuts.

31. Install the oil dipstick. Fill the crankcase with the proper type and quantity of engine oil.

32. Connect the negative battery cable, start the engine and check for leaks.

2.9L ENGINE

1. Disconnect negative battery cable and remove the air intake tube.

2. Remove the fan shroud and position over the fan.

Oil pan installation—2.3L engine

3. Remove the distributor cap and position forward of the dash panel. Remove the distributor and cover the bore opening.

4. Remove the nuts attaching the engine front mounts to the crossmember.

5. Raise and safely support the vehicle.

6. Drain the engine crankcase. If equipped with automatic transmission, remove the transmission fluid filler tube and plug the pan hole.

7. Remove the engine oil filter. Disconnect the muffler inlet pipe(s), except on 2WD Ranger vehicles.

8. Disconnect the oil cooler bracket and lower, if equipped. Remove the starter.

9. Position the transmission oil cooler lines aside, if equipped. Disconnect the front stabilizer bar and position forward, if equipped.

10. Position the jack under the engine. Raise the engine and install wooden blocks between the front engine mounts and No. 2 crossmember.

11. Lower the engine onto the blocks and remove the jack.

12. Remove the oil pan attaching bolts and lower the oil pan.

13. Remove the oil pump and pickup tube assembly, attached to the bearing cap. Lower into the oil pan, except on 2WD Ranger. Remove the oil pan.

To install:

14. Clean all gasket mating surfaces and the oil pan.

15. Apply sealer to the timing chain cover T-joint and a small amount to the groove in the rear main bearing.

16. Carefully lift the gasket over the 6 studs on the cylinder block, insert the ends into the grooves and align the gasket.

17. With the oil pump, oil pan baffle and pickup tube assembly positioned in the oil pan, install the oil pump and then the oil pan. Tighten the pan bolts in 2 steps. Start with bolt **A** and proceed in the direction of the arrows for the first step. Start with bolt **B** and proceed in the direction of the arrows for the second step. Final torque should be 4–6 ft. lbs. (5–8 Nm).

18. Position a jack under the engine and raise enough to remove the wooden blocks. Lower the engine and remove the jack.

19. Install the starter. Connect the muffler inlet pipes, if removed.

20. Connect the front stabilizer bar, if equipped. Position the transmission oil cooler lines and connect the cooler bracket, if equipped.

21. Install a new oil filter. If equipped with automatic transmission, unplug the oil pan and install the filler tube.

22. Lower the vehicle. Install the nuts attaching the engine front mounts to the crossmember.

23. Install the distributor assembly and cap. Install the fan shroud.

24. Fill the engine with the proper type and quantity of engine oil. Connect the negative battery cable.

25. Run the engine and check for leaks. Check the ignition timing and adjust, if necessary.

26. Install the air intake tube. Check the transmission fluid level.

Oil pan bolt tightening procedure—2.9L engine

Service Tips

OIL LEAK AT OIL FILTER

Oil leaking from around the oil filter on Aerostar with a 3.0L engine built from 6/1/89 to 12/31/89, may be caused by an oil filter that is improperly sealed to the engine mounting surface. This may be caused by an oil filter mounting insert that is too short. To correct this condition, install a new, longer oil filter mounting insert, part number E6DZ–6890–A. Tighten the insert so it bottoms on the threads; this will keep it from loosening when removing the oil filter. When installing the oil filter, make sure it turns at least 2½ turns after starting on the threads, before the seal contacts the mounting surface.

3.0L ENGINE

Aerostar

1. Disconnect the negative battery cable.

2. Remove the engine oil level dipstick. Raise the vehicle and support it safely.

3. If equipped with an oil level sensor, remove the retaining clip at the sensor. Disconnect the electrical connector from the sensor.

4. Drain the crankcase. Remove the starter and transmission inspection cover.

5. On 1988 vehicles, loosen the transmission bolts and slide the transmission ¼ in. rearward.

6. Remove the oil pan attaching bolts and remove the pan.

To install:

7. Clean all gasket mating surfaces and the oil pan.

8. Apply a ¹/₅ in. bead of silicone sealer to the junction of the rear main bearing cap and cylinder block and the junction of the front cover assembly and cylinder block.

9. Position the oil pan gasket to the oil pan and secure with sealer. Install the oil pan on the engine block with the attaching bolts and tighten to 9 ft. lbs. (12 Nm).

10. On 1988 vehicles, tighten the transmission bolts.

11. Install the starter and transmission inspection cover. Attach the low oil level sensor connector and install the retainer clip.

12. Lower the vehicle and install the engine oil level dipstick. Fill the crankcase with the proper type and quantity of engine oil.

13. Connect the negative battery cable, start the engine and check for leaks.

Ranger

1. Disconnect the negative battery cable. Remove the engine oil level dispstick.

2. Disconnect the fan shroud and drape it over the fan. Remove the motor mount nuts from the frame.

3. Mark the position of the distributor rotor in relation to the distributor housing and the position of the housing in relation to the engine. Remove the distributor.

4. Raise and safely support the vehicle. Remove the low oil level sensor retainer clip at the sensor. Disconnect the electrical connector from the sensor.

5. Drain the crankcase and remove the starter. Remove the transmission inspection cover.

6. Remove the right axle beam on 2WD vehicles.

NOTE: The brake caliper must be removed and wired out of the way.

7. Remove the oil pan bolts. Position a jack under the engine and raise it approximately 2 in. Remove the oil pan.

NOTE: The oil pan fits tightly between the transmission spacer plate and oil pump pickup tube. Use care when removing to avoid damaging the pickup tube.

To install:

8. Clean all gasket mating surfaces and the oil pan.

9. Apply a $\frac{1}{5}$ in. bead of silicone sealer to the junction of the rear main bearing cap and cylinder block and the junction of the front cover assembly and cylinder block.

10. Position the oil pan gasket to the oil pan and secure with sealer. Install the oil pan on the engine block with the attaching bolts and tighten to 9 ft. lbs. (12 Nm).

11. Install the low oil level sensor connector and the retainer clip. Lower the engine assembly.

12. Install the right axle beam, if removed.

13. Install the transmission inspection cover and the starter. Lower the vehicle.

14. Install the fan shroud and the motor mount nuts. Install the distributor, aligning the marks that were made during removal.

15. Install the engine oil level dipstick. Fill the crankcase with the proper type and quantity of engine oil.

16. Connect the negative battery cable, start the engine and check for leaks.

4.0L ENGINE

Aerostar

1. Disconnect the negative battery cable.

2. Raise and safely support the vehicle. Remove the starter.

3. On 4WD vehicles, proceed as follows:
   a. Remove the front wheel and tire assemblies.
   b. Remove the pivot bolts and nuts from both lower control arms, to allow the control arms to hang.
   c. Remove the control arm rear pivot crossmember.
   d. Remove the lower nuts from both motor mounts.
   e. Remove the front drive axle assembly.

4. Drain the crankcase and remove the oil filter. Disconnect the low oil level sensor from the engine oil pan.

5. Remove the 2 transmission-to-engine oil pan bolts. Remove the oil pan retaining bolts and nuts.

6. On 4WD vehicles, raise the engine approximately 1 in.

7. Remove the oil pan.

To install:

8. Clean all gasket mating surfaces and the oil pan.

9. Place a small amount of silicone sealer on the block at the corner where the oil pan, rear seal and block mate.

10. Install a new crankshaft rear main bearing cap wedge seal. The seal should fit snugly into the sides of the rear main bearing cap.

11. Position a new oil pan gasket into the groove in the oil pan and position the 2 oil pan spacers on the oil pan locating pads.

NOTE: If the same oil pan is being reused, the existing spacers may be used. If a new pan is being installed, the pan-to-transmission gap must be measured to find the needed spacer thickness. Failure to use the correct spacer can result in improper clearance between the oil pan and transmission, resulting in oil pan damage and/or an oil leak.

12. If a new oil pan is being installed, find the correct spacer thickness as follows:
   a. Position the oil pan on the engine without the spacers and install the retaining nuts on the 4 locating studs.
   b. Using a feeler gauge, measure the gap between the locating pads on the pan and the transmission converter housing.
   c. If the measured gap is 0.011–0.020 in. (0.27–0.51mm), a 0.010 in. (0.254mm) spacer is required. If the measured gap is 0.021–0.029 in. (0.52–0.76mm), a 0.020 in. (0.508mm) spacer is required. If the measured gap is 0.030–0.039 in. (0.77–1.00mm), a 0.030 in. (0.762mm) spacer is required.
   d. Remove the oil pan and position the correct spacers.

13. Install the oil pan with a new gasket on the engine and tighten the retaining bolts and nuts enough to compress the gasket so the transmission bolts align with the holes in the oil pan, but loose enough to allow the pan to move when the transmission bolts are installed.

14. Install the 2 transmission-to-oil pan bolts and tighten to 28–38 ft. lbs. (38–51 Nm) to align the oil pan with the transmission, then loosen the bolts ½ turn.

15. Tighten all the oil pan bolts and nuts evenly to 5–7 ft. lbs. (7–10 Nm), then retighten the 2 transmission-to-oil pan bolts to 28–38 ft. lbs. (38–51 Nm).

16. Connect the low oil level sensor. Install the drain plug and a new oil filter.

17. On 4WD vehicles, proceed as follows:
   a. Lower the engine and install the lower motor mount nuts.
   b. Install the front drive axle assembly.
   c. Install the control arm rear pivot crossmember.
   d. Reposition the lower control arms and install the pivot bolts and nuts.
   e. Install the front wheel and tire assemblies.

18. Install the starter. Lower the vehicle and fill the crankcase with the proper type and quantity of engine oil.

19. Connect the negative battery cable, start the engine and check for leaks.

Explorer and Ranger

1. Remove the engine assembly and install on a workstand with the oil pan facing up.

2. Remove the oil pan retaining bolts and remove the pan.

To install:

3. Clean all gasket mating surfaces and the oil pan.

4. Install a new crankshaft rear main bearing cap wedge seal. The seal should fit snugly into the sides of the rear main bearing cap.

5. Position a new oil pan gasket to the engine block and place the oil pan in position on the 4 locating studs. Tighten the retaining nuts and bolts evenly to 5–7 ft. lbs. (7–10 Nm).

6. Measure the gap between the surface of the rear face of the oil pan, at the spacer locations, and the rear face of the engine block as follows:
   a. With the oil pan installed on the engine, position a straight edge flat on the rear of the engine block so it extends over 1 of the oil pan/transmission bolt mounting pads.
   b. Using a feeler gauge, measure the gap between the mounting pad and the straight edge. Repeat the procedure for the other mounting pad.
   c. If the measured gap is 0.011–0.020 in. (0.27–0.51mm), a 0.010 in. (0.254mm) spacer is required. If the measured gap is 0.021–0.029 in. (0.52–0.76mm), a 0.020 in. (0.508mm) spacer is required. If the measured gap is 0.030–0.039 in. (0.77–1.00mm), a 0.030 in. (0.762mm) spacer is required.
   d. Install the selected spacers to the mounting pads on the rear of the oil pan before bolting the engine and transmission together.

Spacer thickness measurement procedure—Explorer and Ranger with 4.0L engine

NOTE: Failure to use the correct spacer can result in improper clearance between the oil pan and transmission, resulting in oil pan damage and/or an oil leak.

7. Remove the engine from the workstand and install in the vehicle.

Oil Pump

Removal and Installation

1. Disconnect the negative battery cable.
2. Remove the oil pan.
3. Remove the oil pump attaching bolts and, if equipped, remove the oil pump pickup tube retaining nut from the main bearing cap.
4. Remove the oil pump and oil pump driveshaft. Remove and clean the oil pump pickup tube and screen, as necessary.

To install:

5. Install the oil pump pickup tube and screen assembly, if removed.
6. Prime the oil pump by filling either the inlet or outlet port with clean engine oil. Rotate the pump shaft to distribute the oil within the pump body.
7. Insert the oil pump driveshaft into the opening in the block or main bearing cap. On 3.0L engine, assemble the shaft to the oil pump until the retainer clicks into place.
8. Install the oil pump, with a new gasket if equipped, and install the attaching bolts. Tighten the bolts to 14–21 ft. lbs. (19–29 Nm) on 2.0L and 2.3L engines, 6–10 ft. lbs. (9–13 Nm) on 2.9L engine, 35 ft. lbs. (48 Nm) on 3.0L engine or 13–15 ft. lbs. (17–21 Nm) on 4.0L engine.
9. On 2.0L and 2.3L engine, install the pickup tube retaining nut and tighten to 30–41 ft. lbs. (40–55 Nm).
10. Install the oil pan.
11. Fill the crankcase with the proper type and quantity of engine oil. Connect the negative battery cable, start the engine and check for leaks.

Checking

1. Remove the pump and disassemble. Thoroughly clean all parts in solvent and dry with compressed air.

Measuring the oil pump inner-to-outer rotor tip clearance

Measuring oil pump rotor endplay

2. Check the inside of the pump housing and the inner and outer gears for damage or excessive wear. Check the mating surfaces of the pump cover for wear. Minor scuff marks are normal, but if the cover, gears or housing surfaces are excessively worn, scored or grooved, replace the entire pump.
3. Measure the inner to outer rotor tip clearance. With the rotor assembly removed from the pump and resting on a flat surface, the inner and outer rotor tip clearance must not exceed 0.012 in. (0.30mm) with a feeler gauge inserted ½ in. (13mm) minimum.
4. With the rotor assembly installed in the housing, place a straight edge over the rotor assembly and the housing. Measure the vertical clearance, the rotor endplay, between the straight edge and the inner rotor and outer race. Maximum clearance must not exceed 0.005 in. (0.13mm).
5. Inspect the relief valve spring for collapsed or worn condition. Check the spring tension. The tension should be 12.6–14.5 lbs. at 1.20 in. on 2.0L and 2.3L engines, 13.6–14.7 lbs. at 1.39 in. on 2.9L engine and 4.0L engines or 9.1–10.1 lbs. at 1.11 in. on 3.0L engine.
6. If any part of the oil pump requires replacement, replace the complete pump assembly.

Rear Main Bearing Oil Seal

Removal and Installation

1. Disconnect the negative battery cable. Raise and safely support the vehicle.

2. Remove the transmission. If equipped with manual transmission, remove the clutch assembly.

3. Remove the flywheel and the engine rear cover plate.

4. Using a sharp awl or equivalent, punch a hole into the seal metal surface between the lip and block. Screw in the threaded end of plug puller T77L–9533–B or equivalent, and remove the seal. Be careful to avoid scratching or damaging the oil seal surface.

5. When the seal has been removed, clean the mounting recess.

To install:

6. Coat the new seal and the crankshaft with a light film of engine oil. Do not use grease.

7. Start the seal into the recess with the seal lip facing forward and install it with a suitable rear oil seal replacer tool. Keep the tool straight with the centerline of the crankshaft and install the seal until it is fully seated.

8. After removing the tool, inspect the seal to make sure it was not damaged during installation.

9. Install the engine rear cover plate. Position the flywheel on the crankshaft flange. Install the flywheel attaching bolts and tighten to 59 ft. lbs. (80 Nm) on all except 2.9L engine. Tighten the bolts on 2.9L engine to 47–52 ft. lbs. (64–70 Nm).

10. If equipped with manual transmission, install the clutch assembly. Install the transmission and starter and lower the vehicle.

11. Connect the negative battery cable, start the engine and check for leaks.

Rear main bearing oil seal installation—3.0L engine

REAR OIL SEAL

REAR MAIN
SEAL INSTALLER

Service Tips

REAR MAIN SEAL AND/OR ENGINE OIL DIPSTICK TUBE OIL LEAKS

Oil leaks at the rear main seal or engine oil dipstick tube on Aerostar with the 3.0L engine may be caused by excessive pressure in the engine crankcase. This may be caused by ice forming in the PCV closure hose in ambient temperatures of $-4°F$ ($-20°C$) and below. To correct this condition, install a filter and tee assembly in the crankcase ventilation closure hose.

Remove the hose and cut a 1⅛ in. piece from the hose. Make the cut 4 in. from the air cleaner end of the hose. Install part number FO9Z–6C652–A filter and tee assembly to both ends of the cut tube. Install the closure hose, filter and tee assembly with the filter in the vertical **DOWN** position.

Service Tips

REAR MAIN SEAL OIL LEAK DUE TO BROKEN MAIN BEARING CAP BOLTS

Oil leaking from the rear main seal on Aerostar with the 3.0L engine may be caused by broken rear main bearing cap bolts. A broken bolt will cause oil to leak through the bearing cap to the block mating surface, but not through the pan seal. To correct this condition, install new main bearing cap bolts, part number E9DZ–6345–D in the front and rear main bearing caps.

Before installation, check the top of each bolt hole in the front and rear main bearing caps for any ridges which may reduce bolt hole size. Use a file or stone to remove any ridges.

TORQUE SPECIFICATIONS

Component	English	Metric
Auxiliary shaft cover bolts	6–9 ft. lbs.	8–12 Nm
Auxiliary shaft retaining plate bolts	6–9 ft. lbs.	8–12 Nm
Auxiliary shaft sprocket bolt		
2.0L and 2.3L engines	30–40 ft. lbs.	40–54 Nm
Camshaft sprocket bolt		
2.0L and 2.3L engines	52–70 ft. lbs.	70–95 Nm
2.9L engine	19–28 ft. lbs.	26–38 Nm
3.0L engine	46 ft. lbs.	63 Nm
4.0L engine	44–50 ft. lbs.	60–68 Nm

TORQUE SPECIFICATIONS

Camshaft thrust plate bolts		
2.9L engine	13–16 ft. lbs.	17–21 Nm
3.0L engine	7 ft. lbs.	10 Nm
4.0L engine	7–10 ft. lbs.	10–13 Nm
Camshaft rear retainer bolts		
2.0L and 2.3L engines	6–9 ft. lbs.	8–12 Nm
Connecting rod nut		
2.0L and 2.3L engines		
Step 1:	25–30 ft. lbs.	34–41 Nm
Step 2:	30–36 ft. lbs.	41–49 Nm
2.9L and 4.0L engines	19–24 ft. lbs.	26–33 Nm
3.0L engine	26 ft. lbs.	35 Nm
Crankshaft damper bolt		
2.0L and 2.3L engines	103–133 ft. lbs.	140–180 Nm
2.9L engine	85–96 ft. lbs.	115–130 Nm
3.0L engine		
1988	141–169 ft. lbs.	190–230 Nm
1989–92	107 ft. lbs.	145 Nm
4.0L engine		
Step 1:	30–37 ft. lbs.	40–50 Nm
Step 2:	+ 90° turn	+ 90° turn
Cylinder head bolt		
2.0L and 2.3L engines		
Step 1:	50–60 ft. lbs.	68–81 Nm
Step 2:	80–90 ft. lbs.	108–122 Nm
2.9L engine		
Step 1:	22 ft. lbs.	30 Nm
Step 2:	51–55 ft. lbs.	70–75 Nm
Step 3:	Wait 5 minutes	Wait 5 minutes
Step 4:	+ 90° turn	+ 90° turn
3.0L engine		
1988–90		
Step 1:	37 ft. lbs.	50 Nm
Step 2:	68 ft. lbs.	92 Nm
1991–92		
Step 1:	59 ft. lbs.	80 Nm
Step 2:	Loosen 1 turn	Loosen 1 turn
Step 3:	37 ft. lbs.	50 Nm
Step 4:	68 ft. lbs.	92 Nm
4.0L engine*		
Step 1 (CYLINDER HEAD):	44 ft. lbs.	60 Nm
Step 2 (INTAKE MANIFOLD):	3–6 ft. lbs.	4–8 Nm
Step 3 (CYLINDER HEAD):	59 ft. lbs.	80 Nm
Step 4 (INTAKE MANIFOLD):	6–11 ft. lbs.	8–15 Nm
Step 5 (CYLINDER HEAD):	+ 85° turn	+ 85° turn
Step 6 (INTAKE MANIFOLD):	11–15 ft. lbs.	15–21 Nm
Step 7 (INTAKE MANIFOLD):	15–18 ft. lbs.	21–25 Nm

*NOTE: Refer to cylinder head removal
and installation procedure in text

Engine mounts		
2.0L and 2.3L engines		
Front mounts		
Mount-to-crossmember nuts	65–85 ft. lbs.	88–115 Nm
Mount-to-engine bracket nuts	65–85 ft. lbs.	88–115 Nm
Rear mount		
Mount-to-transmission bolts	60–80 ft. lbs.	82–108 Nm
Mount-to-crossmember nuts	65–80 ft. lbs.	88–109 Nm
2.9L engine		
Front mounts		
Mount-to-crossmember nuts	71–94 ft. lbs.	96–127 Nm
Mount-to-engine bracket nuts	71–85 ft. lbs.	96–115 Nm

TORQUE SPECIFICATIONS

Rear mount		
Mount-to-transmission bolts	60–80 ft. lbs.	82–108 Nm
Mount-to-crossmember nuts	65–85 ft. lbs.	88–115 Nm
3.0L engine		
Aerostar		
Front mounts		
Mount-to-crossmember nuts	71–94 ft. lbs.	96–127 Nm
Mount-to-engine bracket bolts	40–60 ft. lbs.	54–81 Nm
Rear mount		
Mount-to-transmission bolts	60–80 ft. lbs.	82–108 Nm
Mount-to-crossmember nuts	71–94 ft. lbs.	96–127 Nm
4.0L engine		
Aerostar		
Front mounts		
Mount-to-crossmember nuts	71–94 ft. lbs.	96–127 Nm
Mount-to-engine bracket bolts	40–60 ft. lbs.	54–81 Nm
Rear mount		
Mount-to-transmission bolts	60–80 ft. lbs.	82–108 Nm
Mount-to-crossmember nuts	71–94 ft. lbs.	96–127 Nm
Explorer		
Front mounts		
Mount-to-crossmember nuts	71–94 ft. lbs.	96–127 Nm
Mount-to-engine bracket nuts	65–85 ft. lbs.	88–115 Nm
Rear mount		
Mount-to-transmission bolts	60–80 ft. lbs.	82–108 Nm
Mount-to-crossmember nuts	65–85 ft. lbs.	88–115 Nm
Ranger		
Front mounts		
Mount-to-crossmember nuts	71–94 ft. lbs.	96–127 Nm
Mount-to-engine bracket nuts	65–85 ft. lbs.	88–115 Nm
Rear mount		
Mount-to-transmission bolts	60–80 ft. lbs.	82–108 Nm
Mount-to-crossmember nuts	65–85 ft. lbs.	88–115 Nm
Exhaust manifold		
2.0L and 2.3L engines		
Step 1:	15–17 ft. lbs.	20–23 Nm
Step 2:	20–30 ft. lbs.	27–41 Nm
2.9L engine	20–30 ft. lbs.	27–40 Nm
3.0L engine	18 ft. lbs.	25 Nm
4.0L engine	19 ft. lbs.	26 Nm
Flywheel-to-crankshaft bolts		
2.0L, 2.3L, 3.0L and 4.0L engines	59 ft. lbs.	80 Nm
2.9L engine	47–52 ft. lbs.	64–70 Nm
Flywheel-to-torque converter nuts	20–34 ft. lbs.	27–46 Nm
Intake manifold-to-cylinder head bolts		
2.0L and 2.3L engines		
Step 1:	5–7 ft. lbs.	7–9 Nm
Step 2:	15–22 ft. lbs.	20–30 Nm
2.9L and 4.0L engines		
Step 1:	3–6 ft. lbs.	4–8 Nm
Step 2:	6–11 ft. lbs.	8–15 Nm
Step 3:	11–15 ft. lbs.	15–21 Nm
Step 4:	15–18 ft. lbs.	21–25 Nm
3.0L engine		
Step 1:	11 ft. lbs.	15 Nm
Step 2:	19 ft. lbs.	26 Nm
Main bearing cap bolts		
2.0L and 2.3L engines		
Step 1:	50–60 ft. lbs.	68–81 Nm
Step 2:	75–85 ft. lbs.	102–115 Nm
2.9L engine	65–75 ft. lbs.	88–102 Nm

3.0L engine		
1988	65–81 ft. lbs.	88–110 Nm
1989–92	60 ft. lbs.	80 Nm
4.0L engine	66–77 ft. lbs.	90–104 Nm
Oil pan-to-block bolts/nuts		
2.0L and 2.3L engines	90–120 inch lbs.	10–13.5 Nm
2.9L engine	4–6 ft. lbs.	5–8 Nm
3.0L engine	9 ft. lbs.	12 Nm
4.0L engine	5–7 ft. lbs.	7–10 Nm
Oil pan-to-transmission bolts		
2.3L engine	30–39 ft. lbs.	40–50 Nm
4.0L engine	28–38 ft. lbs.	38–50 Nm
Oil pan drain plug		
2.0L, 2.3L, 2.9L and 4.0L engines	15–21 ft. lbs.	21–28 Nm
3.0L engine	10 ft. lbs.	14 Nm
Oil pump-to-cylinder block		
2.0L, 2.3L and 2.9L engines	14–21 ft. lbs.	19–28 Nm
3.0L engine	35 ft. lbs.	48 Nm
4.0L engine	13–15 ft. lbs.	17–21 Nm
Oil pickup tube-to-main bearing cap		
2.0L and 2.3L engines	30–41 ft. lbs.	40–55 Nm
Oil pickup tube-to-oil pump		
2.0L and 2.3L engines	15–22 ft. lbs.	19–29 Nm
2.9L and 4.0L engines	7–10 ft. lbs.	9–13 Nm
Rocker arm bolt		
3.0L engine	24 ft. lbs.	32 Nm
Rocker arm stand bolts		
2.9L engine	43–50 ft. lbs.	59–67 Nm
4.0L engine	46–52 ft. lbs.	62–70 Nm
Rocker arm cover bolts		
2.0L and 2.3L engines	5–8 ft. lbs.	7–11 Nm
2.9L and 4.0L engines	3–5 ft. lbs.	4–7 Nm
3.0L engine	9 ft. lbs.	12 Nm
Spark plugs	10–15 ft. lbs.	14–20 Nm
Starter-to-engine block bolts	15–20 ft. lbs.	20–27 Nm
Transmission-to-engine bolts	28–38 ft. lbs.	38–51 Nm
Timing belt cover bolts		
2.0L and 2.3L engines	6–9 ft. lbs.	8–12 Nm
Timing chain cover bolts		
2.9L and 4.0L engines	13–15 ft. lbs.	17–21 Nm
3.0L engine		
6mm bolts	7 ft. lbs.	10 Nm
8mm bolts	19 ft. lbs.	25 Nm
Upper-to-lower intake manifold bolts		
2.3L engine	15–22 ft. lbs.	20–30 Nm
2.9L engine		
Step 1:	7 ft. lbs.	10 Nm
Step 2:	15–18 ft. lbs.	21–25 Nm
3.0L engine	19 ft. lbs.	26 Nm
4.0L engine	15–18 ft. lbs.	20–25 Nm
Water outlet housing		
2.0L and 2.3L engines	14–21 ft. lbs.	20–30 Nm
2.9L and 4.0L engines	7–10 ft. lbs.	9–13 Nm
3.0L engine	18 ft. lbs.	25 Nm
Water pump		
2.0L and 2.3L engines	14–21 ft. lbs.	20–30 Nm
2.9L and 4.0L engines	7–9 ft. lbs.	9–12 Nm
3.0L engine		
6mm bolts	7 ft. lbs.	10 Nm
8mm bolts	19 ft. lbs.	25 Nm

MANUAL TRANSMISSION

For further information, please refer to Chilton's Transmission Service Manual.

Transmission Assembly

Removal and Installation

1. Disconnect the negative battery cable.
2. Place the gearshift lever in the **N** position.
3. Remove the shifter boot retainer screws and slide the boot up the shift lever shaft. Remove the shift lever attaching bolt(s) and remove the shift lever. Cover the opening in the transmission to prevent dirt from entering.
4. Raise and safely support the vehicle.
5. Mark the position of the driveshaft(s) on the flange(s) and remove the driveshaft(s). Plug the transmission or transfer case opening to prevent fluid leakage.
6. Disconnect the clutch hydraulic fluid line. Plug the line to prevent fluid leakage.
7. Disconnect the speedometer cable from the transmission or transfer case.
8. Disconnect the starter cable, backup lamp switch wire and neutral position switch wire.
9. Place a jack under the engine, with a wood block to protect the oil pan.
10. Remove the transfer case, if equipped.
11. Remove the starter. Place a transmission jack under the transmission.
12. Remove the bolts attaching the transmission and clutch housing to the engine. Remove the nuts and bolts attaching the transmission mount and damper to the crossmember.
13. Remove the nuts and/or bolts attaching the crossmember to the frame side rails and remove the crossmember.
14. Lower the engine jack. Work the clutch housing off the locating dowels and slide the clutch housing and transmission rearward until the input shaft clears the clutch disc. Remove the transmission.

15. Remove the clutch housing from the transmission, if necessary.

To install:

16. Make sure the machined mating surfaces and the locating dowels on the engine rear plate and the mating face of the clutch housing and locating dowel holes are free of burrs, dirt or paint. Install the clutch housing on the transmission, if removed.
17. Mount the transmission on a transmission jack and raise into position. Start the input shaft into the clutch disc, aligning the splines. Move the transmission forward until the clutch housing seats on the locating dowels.
18. Install the clutch housing-to-engine attaching bolts and tighten to 28–38 ft. lbs. (38–51 Nm). Remove the transmission jack.

FM146 manual transmission

4WD SAME AS 2WD EXCEPT AS SHOWN

M50D manual transmission

19. Install the starter.

20. Raise the engine and install the crossmember, insulator and damper with the attaching nuts and bolts. Install the nuts and bolts attaching the transmission mount to the crossmember.

21. Install the transfer case, if equipped.

22. Remove the plug(s) and install the driveshaft(s), aligning the marks on the flange(s) that were made during the removal procedure.

23. Connect the starter cable, backup lamp switch wire, shift indicator wire and neutral position switch wire, if equipped.

24. Connect the hydraulic clutch line and bleed the system.

25. Connect the speedometer cable.

26. Remove the fill plug and check the fluid level. Add if necessary.

27. Lower the vehicle and remove the cover from the transmission opening.

28. Install the gearshift lever with the attaching bolt(s). Install the shifter boot.

29. Connect the negative battery cable. Check the transmission for proper operation.

CLUTCH

Clutch Assembly

Removal and Installation

1. Disconnect the negative battery cable.

2. Disconnect the hydraulic clutch master cylinder from the clutch pedal.

3. Raise and safely support the vehicle. Remove the starter.

4. Use coupling disconnect tool T88T–70522–A or equivalent, to slide the white plastic sleeve toward the slave cylinder, then apply a slight tug on the tube to disconnect the hydraulic coupling. Plug the hose.

5. Remove the transmission.

6. Mark the position of the pressure plate on the flywheel so if the pressure plate is reused, it can be reinstalled in the same position.

7. Loosen the pressure plate attaching bolts evenly until the diaphragm spring is expanded. Remove the bolts, pressure plate and clutch disc.

8. Inspect the flywheel for wear, scoring and cracks. Machine or replace, as necessary. Inspect the clutch pilot bearing for wear and free movement. If replacement is necessary, remove using puller tool T58L–101–B or equivalent.

9. Inspect the clutch release bearing for wear and free movement; replace as necessary. Remove the release bearing by twisting it until resistance is felt. Turning further will allow the preload spring to push the bearing assembly off the slave cylinder.

To install:

10. If the pilot bearing was removed, a new 1 must be installed. Install using replacer tool T71P–7137–C and clutch driver tool T71P–7137–H or equivalent. Install the pilot bearing with the seal facing the transmission so the adapter is not cocked.

11. If the flywheel was removed, make sure the mating surfaces of the crank flange and flywheel are clean, and install the flywheel. Tighten the flywheel bolts to 59 ft. lbs. (80 Nm) on all except 2.9L engine. Tighten the bolts on 2.9L engine to 47–52 ft. lbs. (64–70 Nm).

12. Position the clutch disc on the flywheel so alignment tool T74P–7137–K or equivalent, can enter the pilot bearing and align the disc.

13. Install the pressure plate. If the original pressure plate is being reused, align the marks that were made during the removal procedure. Install the attaching bolts and tighten, in sequence, to 15–24 ft. lbs. (21–32 Nm), then remove the alignment tool.

14. Install the transmission. If equipped, reuse the aluminum washers under the attaching bolts to prevent galvanic corrosion.

15. Connect the hydraulic coupling by pushing the male coupling into the slave cylinder female coupling.

16. Lower the vehicle and connect the clutch master cylinder to the brake pedal. Bleed the clutch system, if necessary.

17. Connect the negative battery cable.

Clutch pressure plate bolt torque sequence

Pedal Height/Free Play Adjustment

The hydraulic clutch system provides automatic adjustment. No adjustment of clutch linkage or pedal position is required.

Clutch Master Cylinder

Removal and Installation

1. Disconnect the negative battery cable.

2. Disconnect the clutch master cylinder pushrod from the clutch pedal by prying the retainer bushing and pushrod off the pedal pin.

3. Remove the switch from the master cylinder assembly.

4. On Bronco II, Explorer and Ranger, remove the screw retaining the fluid reservoir to the cowl access cover. On Aerostar, slide the reservoir out of the relay bracket.

5. Use coupling disconnect tool T88T–70522–A or equivalent, to slide the white plastic sleeve toward the slave cylinder, then apply a slight tug on the tube to disconnect the hydraulic coupling.

6. Remove the retaining bolts and the clutch master cylinder.

To install:

7. Install the pushrod through the hole in the engine compartment. Make sure it is located on the correct side of the

clutch pedal. Install the master cylinder and tighten the bolts to 12 ft. lbs. (16 Nm).

8. Insert the coupling end into the slave cylinder and install the tube into the clips.

9. On Bronco II, Explorer and Ranger, install the fluid reservoir on the cowl access cover with the retaining screw. On Aerostar, slide the reservoir into the relay bracket.

10. Replace the retainer bushing in the clutch master cylinder pushrod if worn or damaged. Install the retainer and pushrod on the clutch pedal pin. Make sure the flange of the bushing is against the pedal blade. Install the switch.

11. Connect the negative battery cable and bleed the clutch hydraulic system, if necessary.

Clutch Slave Cylinder

Removal and Installation

NOTE: Before any vehicle service that requires slave cylinder removal, the clutch master cylinder pushrod must be disconnected from the clutch pedal. If not disconnected, permanent damage to the master cylinder will occur if the clutch pedal is depressed while the slave cylinder is disconnected.

1. Disconnect the negative battery cable.

2. Disconnect the coupling at the transmission using tool T88T–70522–A or equivalent, by sliding the white plastic sleeve toward the slave cylinder while applying a slight tug on the tube.

3. Raise and safely support the vehicle. Remove the transmission and clutch housing.

4. Remove the bolts retaining the slave cylinder to the transmission. Remove the slave cylinder from the transmission input shaft.

5. If necessary, remove the release bearing from the slave cylinder by twisting until resistance is felt, then turning further to allow the preload spring to push the bearing assembly off.

To install:

6. Push the release bearing into place, if removed.

7. Position the slave cylinder over the transmission input shaft with the bleed screw and coupling facing the left side of the transmission.

8. Install the slave cylinder attaching bolts and tighten to 13–19 ft. lbs. (18–26 Nm).

9. Install the transmission.

10. Insert the male coupling into the female coupling on the clutch slave cylinder and make sure the connection is secure.

11. Bleed the clutch hydraulic system, if necessary. Lower the vehicle and connect the negative battery cable.

Disconnecting the hydraulic tube from the slave cylinder

Slave cylinder installation

Clutch release bearing removal and installation

Hydraulic Clutch System Bleeding

NOTE: Under normal conditions, disconnecting the clutch coupling will not let air into the system. However, if there appears to be air in the system, indicated by a spongy pedal or insufficient bearing travel, the system must be bled.

1. Clean all dirt and grease from around the reservoir cap.
2. Remove the cap and fill the reservoir with heavy duty brake fluid.
3. Raise and safely support the vehicle, as necessary. Loosen the bleed screw, located in the slave cylinder body, next to the inlet connection.
4. Fluid will now begin to flow from the master cylinder, down the tube and into the slave cylinder.

NOTE: Keep the reservoir full at all times to make sure no additional air is drawn into the system.

5. Bubbles should begin to appear at the bleed screw outlet, indicating air is being expelled. When the slave cylinder is full, a steady stream of fluid will come from the slave cylinder outlet. Tighten the bleed screw.
6. Slowly depress the clutch pedal to the floor and hold. Loosen the bleed screw to allow air and excess fluid to be expelled. Retighten the bleed screw when fluid flow stops.
7. Depress and release the clutch pedal slowly, waiting 2 seconds between each cycle. Repeat 5 times.
8. Check the fluid level in the reservoir and add, if necessary. If evidence of air still exists, repeat Steps 6 and 7.

AUTOMATIC TRANSMISSION

For further information, please refer to Chilton's Transmission Service Manual.

Transmission Assembly

Removal and Installation

1. Disconnect the negative battery cable. Raise and safely support the vehicle.
2. Position a drain pan under the transmission fluid pan. On Explorer, pry the lower clips of the transmission heat shield back slightly to allow access to the pan bolts.
3. Starting at the rear of the transmission pan and working toward the front, loosen the attaching bolts and allow the fluid to drain. Remove all the bolts except the 2 at the front to allow the fluid to further drain. After all fluid has drained, reinstall 2 bolts at the rear of the pan to temporarily hold it in place.
4. Remove the converter access cover from the converter housing. On some applications, it may only be necessary to remove 1 bolt and swing the cover open.
5. Disconnect the starter cable and remove the starter.
6. Place a 22mm socket and breaker bar on the crankshaft pulley attaching bolt. Rotate the pulley clockwise, as viewed from the front, to gain access to each converter attaching nut. Remove the nuts.

NOTE: On 2.3L engine, the converter attaching nuts are accessed through the cover on the engine oil pan. On 2.9L and 4.0L engines, the converter attaching nuts are accessed through the starter mounting hole.

7. Mark the position of the driveshaft on the axle flange and remove the driveshaft. Plug the transmission to prevent fluid leakage.
8. Disconnect the speedometer cable from the transmission.
9. Disconnect the shift rod at the transmission manual lever. Remove the kickdown cable from the ball stud lever. Depress the tab on the cable downshift retainer and remove the cable from the bracket.
10. Disconnect the neutral safety switch wires and converter clutch solenoid connector. Disconnect the vacuum line from the vacuum modulator.
11. Position a transmission jack under the transmission and raise it slightly. Remove the engine rear support-to-crossmember bolts.
12. Remove the crossmember-to-frame side support attaching bolts and remove the crossmember insulator and support and damper.
13. Lower the jack under the transmission and allow the transmission to hang. On Bronco II, Explorer and Ranger, position a jack to the front of the engine and raise it to gain access to the 2 upper converter housing-to-engine attaching bolts.
14. Disconnect the oil cooler lines at the transmission. Plug the lines and transmission to prevent the entrance of dirt.
15. Remove the lower converter housing-to-engine attaching bolts and remove the transmission filler tube.
16. Secure the transmission to the jack with a safety chain. Remove the 2 upper converter housing-to-engine attaching bolts. Move the transmission to the rear so it disengages from the dowel pins and the converter is disengaged from the flywheel. Lower the transmission from the vehicle.

NOTE: If the transmission is to be removed for an extended period, support the engine with a safety stand and wood block.

To install:

17. Position the converter to the transmission making sure the converter hub is fully engaged in the pump gear. To make sure the converter is fully engaged, push and rotate the converter until 2 "bumps" are felt. Keep pushing and rotating until the distance between the converter pilot and the edge of the converter housing is $7/16$–$9/16$ in.
18. Place the transmission on a transmission jack and secure with a safety chain. Rotate the converter so the drive studs are in alignment with the holes in the flywheel.
19. Raise the transmission and move it forward into position, being careful not to damage the flywheel and converter pilot.

NOTE: When moving the transmission, do not let the front of the transmission tilt downward. This will cause the converter to move forward and disengage from the pump gear. The converter must rest squarely against the flywheel. This indicates that the converter pilot is not binding in the engine crankshaft.

20. Install 2 converter housing-to-engine attaching bolts at the engine dowel locations and tighten to 28–38 ft. lbs. (38–51 Nm). Install the remaining attaching bolts and tighten to the same specification.
21. Remove the safety chain from the transmission.
22. Insert the filler tube in the stub tube and secure it to the cylinder block with the attaching bolt. Tighten the bolt to 28–38 ft. lbs. (38–51 Nm). If the stub tube is loosened or dislodged, it should be replaced.
23. Install the oil cooler lines in the retaining clip at the cylinder block. Connect the lines to the transmission.
24. Remove the jack supporting the front of the engine.

25. Raise the transmission and position the crossmember, insulator and support and damper to the frame side supports. Install the attaching bolts and tighten to 20–30 ft. lbs. (27–41 Nm).

26. Lower the transmission and install the rear engine support-to-crossmember nut. Tighten the bolt to 60–80 ft. lbs. (82–108 Nm). Remove the transmission jack.

27. Install the vacuum hose on the vacuum modulator and attach the line to the clip. Connect the neutral safety switch plug and the converter clutch solenoid connector.

28. Install the flywheel-to-converter nuts and tighten to 20–34 ft. lbs. (27–46 Nm).

29. Install the converter access cover and adapter plate bolts and tighten to 12–16 ft. lbs. (16–22 Nm). On 2.3L engine, tighten the oil pan access cover bolts to 22–32 inch lbs. (2.5–3.6 Nm).

30. Install the starter and tighten the attaching bolts to 15–20 ft. lbs. (20–27 Nm). Connect the starter cable.

31. Connect the exhaust pipe to the exhaust manifold, if disconnected for removal.

32. Connect the shift rod to the manual lever and the downshift cable to the downshift lever. Connect the speedometer cable.

33. Install the driveshaft, aligning the marks on the axle flange. Adjust the manual and downshift linkage, as required.

34. Remove the bolts temporarily holding the transmission fluid pan and remove the pan. Discard the gasket and clean all old gasket material and dirt from the gasket mating surfaces.

35. Install the pan using a new gasket. Tighten the attaching bolts to 8–10 ft. lbs. (11–13.5 Nm).

36. Lower the vehicle and connect the negative battery cable. Fill the transmission with the proper type and quantity of fluid.

37. Run the vehicle and check for leaks and proper operation.

Shift Linkage Adjustment

AEROSTAR

1. Raise and safely support the vehicle, as necessary. Place the console shift lever in the **OD** position.

2. From below the vehicle, loosen the shift cable adjusting screw and remove the end fitting from the transmission manual control lever ball stud.

3. Position the manual control lever in the **OD** position by moving the lever all the way rearward, then moving it 3 detents forward. Hold the console shift lever against the rear **OD** stop.

4. Connect the cable end fitting to the manual control lever.

5. Tighten the adjustment screw to 45–60 inch lbs. (5–6 Nm).

6. Check the console shift lever in all detent positions with the engine running to ensure correct adjustment.

BRONCO II, EXPLORER AND RANGER

1988

1. Raise and safely support the vehicle, as necessary. Position

the selector control lever in the **D** position and loosen the trunnion bolt. Do not use the **OD** position.

NOTE: Make sure the shift lever detent pawl is held against the rearward Drive (D) detent stop during the linkage adjustment procedure.

2. Position the manual lever in the **D** position by moving the bell crank lever all the way rearward, then forward 4 detents.

3. With the floor shifter selector lever and manual lever in the **D** position, apply light forward pressure to the floor shifter lower arm while tightening the trunnion bolt to 13–23 ft. lbs. (18–31 Nm). Forward pressure on the floor shifter lower arm will ensure correct positioning within the **D** detent.

4. Check the selector lever in all detent positions with the engine running to ensure correct adjustment.

1989–92

1. Raise and safely support the vehicle, as necessary. From inside the vehicle, place the column shift selector lever in the **OD** position. Hang an 8 lb. weight on the selector lever.

2. From below the vehicle, pull down the lock tab on the shift cable and remove the fitting from the transmission manual control lever ball stud.

3. Position the transmission manual control lever in the **OD** position by moving the lever all the way rearward and then moving it 3 detents forward.

4. Connect the cable end fitting to the transmission manual control lever. Push up on the lock tab to lock the cable in the correctly adjusted position.

5. Remove the 8 lb. weight from the column shift selector.

6. After adjustment, check for **P** engagement. Check the column shift selector lever in all detent positions with the engine running to ensure correct adjustment.

Selector Indicator Adjustment

1989–92 BRONCO II, EXPLORER AND RANGER

1. Remove the steering column shroud.

2. With the engine stopped and the parking brake applied, place the transmission selector lever at the steering column in the **OD** position.

3. Secure a 3 lb. weight to the end of the transmission selector lever.

4. Loosen the selector indicator screw on the column casting. Move the selector indicator adjustment until the orange pointer is completely within the letter "D" inside the **OD** graphic.

5. Tighten the selector indicator screw on the column to 10–15 inch lbs. (1.1–1.7 Nm).

6. Install the steering column shroud.

TRANSFER CASE

Transfer Case Assembly

Removal and Installation

——— CAUTION ———

The catalytic converter is located beside the transfer case. Due to the extreme high temperatures generated by the converter, be careful when removing the transfer case or personal injury may result.

MECHANICAL SHIFT TYPE

1. Disconnect the negative battery cable. Raise and safely support the vehicle.

2. If equipped, remove the skid plate from the frame. Remove the damper from the transfer case, if equipped.

3. Place a drain pan under the transfer case, remove the drain plug and drain the fluid. Disconnect the 4WD indicator switch wire connector at the transfer case.

4. If equipped with Borg Warner model 13-50 transfer case, disconnect the front driveshaft from the axle input yoke and pull the driveshaft and front boot assembly out of the transfer case front output shaft.

5. If equipped with Borg Warner model 13-54 transfer case, disconnect the front driveshaft from the transfer case output shaft yoke and wire the driveshaft out of the way.

6. Disconnect the rear driveshaft from the transfer case output shaft flange and wire the driveshaft out of the way.

7. Disconnect the speedometer driven gear from the transfer case rear cover. Disconnect the vent hose from the control lever.

8. Disconnect the nut from the shift lever and remove the shift lever, if necessary.

9. Remove the large and small bolts retaining the shifter to the extension housing. Remove the lever assembly and bushing.

10. Support the transfer case with a transmission jack. Remove the 5 bolts retaining the transfer case to the transmission and extension housing.

11. Slide the transfer case rearward off the transmission output shaft and lower the transfer case from the vehicle. Remove the gasket from between the transfer case and extension housing.

To install:

12. Install a new gasket on the front mounting face of the transfer case assembly.

13. Raise the transfer case with the transmission jack so the transmission output shaft aligns with the transfer case input shaft. Slide the transfer case forward onto the transmission output shaft and onto the dowel pin. Install the 5 retaining bolts and tighten, in sequence, to 25–35 ft. lbs. (34–48 Nm).

14. Remove the transmission jack.

15. Install and adjust the shifter. Always tighten the large bolt retaining the shifter to the extension housing before tightening the small bolt.

16. Install the vent assembly so the white marking on the hose is in position in the notch in the shifter. The upper end of the vent hose should be ¾ in. above the top of the shifter and positioned just below the floor pan.

17. Connect the speedometer driven gear to the transfer case rear cover. Tighten the screw to 20–25 inch lbs. (2.3–2.8 Nm).

18. Connect the rear driveshaft to the transfer case output shaft flange. Tighten the bolts to 61–87 ft. lbs. (83–118 Nm).

19. If equipped with Borg Warner model 13–50 transfer case, clean the transfer case front output shaft female splines. Apply suitable lubricant to the splines and insert the front driveshaft male spline. Connect the front driveshaft to the axle input yoke and tighten the bolts to 12–16 ft. lbs. (16–22 Nm). Push the driveshaft boot to engage the external groove on the transfer case front output shaft.

20. If equipped with Borg Warner model 13–54 transfer case, connect the front driveshaft to the transfer case output shaft yoke. Tighten the bolts to 12–16 ft. lbs. (16–22 Nm).

21. Connect the 4WD indicator switch wire connector at the transfer case.

22. Install the drain plug and tighten to 14–22 ft. lbs. (19–30 Nm). Remove the fill plug and fill the transfer case with the proper type of fluid to the bottom of the fill hole. Install the fill plug and tighten to 14–22 ft. lbs. (19–30 Nm).

23. Install the damper to the transfer case, if equipped. Using new damper bolts, tighten to 25–35 ft. lbs. (34–48 Nm).

24. Install the skid plate, if equipped. Tighten the nuts and bolts to 15–20 ft. lbs. (20–27 Nm).

25. Lower the vehicle and connect the negative battery cable.

ELECTRONIC SHIFT TYPE

1. Disconnect the negative battery cable. Raise and safely support the vehicle.

2. If equipped, remove the nuts, bolts and skid plate from the frame. Remove the damper from the transfer case, if equipped.

3. Place a drain pan under the transfer case, remove the drain plug and drain the fluid.

4. Remove the wire connector from the feed wire harness at the rear of the transfer case. First squeeze the locking tabs, then pull the connectors apart.

NOTE: Do not pull directly on the wires or pull outwardly on the locking tabs.

Transfer case-to-extension housing bolt torque sequence

5. Remove the connector for the transfer case motor from the mounting bracket, if necessary.

6. If equipped with Borg Warner model 13–50 transfer case, disconnect the front driveshaft from the axle input yoke and pull the driveshaft and front boot assembly out of the transfer case front output shaft.

7. If equipped with Borg Warner model 13–54 transfer case, disconnect the front driveshaft from the transfer case ouput shaft yoke and wire the driveshaft out of the way.

8. Disconnect the rear driveshaft from the transfer case output shaft flange and wire the driveshaft out of the way.

9. Disconnect the speedometer driven gear from the transfer case rear cover. Disconnect the vent hose from the mounting bracket.

10. Support the transfer case with a transmission jack. Remove the 5 bolts retaining the transfer case to the transmission and extension housing.

11. Slide the transfer case rearward off the transmission output shaft and lower the transfer case from the vehicle. Remove the gasket from between the transfer case and extension housing.

To install:

12. Install a new gasket on the front mounting face of the transfer case assembly.

13. Raise the transfer case with the transmission jack so the transmission output shaft aligns with the transfer case input shaft. Slide the transfer case forward onto the transmission output shaft and onto the dowel pin. Install the 5 retaining bolts and tighten, in sequence, to 25–35 ft. lbs. (34–48 Nm).

14. Remove the transmission jack.

15. Install the vent hose so the white marking on the hose aligns with the notch in the mounting bracket.

16. Connect the speedometer driven gear to the transfer case rear cover. Tighten the screw to 20–25 inch lbs. (2.3–2.8 Nm).

17. Connect the rear driveshaft to the transfer case output shaft flange. Tighten the bolts to 61–87 ft. lbs. (83–118 Nm).

18. If equipped with Borg Warner model 13–50 transfer case, clean the transfer case front output shaft female splines. Apply suitable lubricant to the splines and insert the front driveshaft male spline. Connect the front driveshaft to the axle input yoke and tighten the bolts to 12–16 ft. lbs. (16–22 Nm). Push the driveshaft boot to engage the external groove on the transfer case front output shaft.

19. If equipped with Borg Warner model 13–54 transfer case, connect the front driveshaft to the transfer case output shaft yoke. Tighten the bolts to 12–16 ft. lbs. (16–22 Nm).

20. Attach the connector for the transfer case motor to the mounting bracket, if necessary.

21. Connect the wire connectors on the rear of the transfer case, making sure the retaining tabs lock.

22. Install the drain plug and tighten to 14–22 ft. lbs. (19–30 Nm). Remove the fill plug and fill the transfer case with the proper type of fluid to the bottom of the fill hole. Install the fill plug and tighten to 14–22 ft. lbs. (19–30 Nm).

23. Install the damper to the transfer case, if equipped. Using new damper bolts, tighten to 25–35 ft. lbs. (34–48 Nm).

24. Install the skid plate, if equipped. Tighten the nuts and bolts to 15–20 ft. lbs. (20–27 Nm).

25. Lower the vehicle and connect the negative battery cable.

Linkage Adjustment

MECHANICAL SHIFT TYPE

1. Raise the shift boot to expose the top surface of the cam plate.

2. Loosen the bolts "A" and "B" on the control lever assembly approximately 2 turns. Move the transfer case shift lever to the **4L** position.

3. Move the cam plate rearward until the bottom chamfered corner of the neutral lug just contacts the forward right edge of the shift lever, point "C".

4. Hold the cam plate in this position and tighten bolt "A" first to 70–90 ft. lbs. (94–122 Nm), then tighten bolt "B" to 31–42 ft. lbs. (43–56 Nm).

5. Move the transfer case in-cab shift lever to all shift positions to check the positive engagement. There should be clearance, not exceeding 0.13 in. (3.30mm), between the shift lever and cam plate in **2H** front **4H** rear and **4L** shift positions.

6. Install the shift boot assembly.

Transfer case linkage adjustment procedure

DRIVE AXLE

Halfshaft

Removal and Installation

4WD AEROSTAR

1. Raise and safely support the vehicle.
2. Remove the wheel and tire assembly and the hub retainer nut and washer. Discard the nut.
3. Mark the differential shaft flange in relation to the halfshaft so they can be reinstalled in their original position.
4. Remove the bolts and disconnect the halfshaft inboard flanges from the differential axle shaft flanges.
5. Support the end of the shaft by suspending it from an underbody component with mechanics wire. Do not allow the shaft to hang unsupported as damage to the outboard CV-joint may result.
6. Loosen the shock absorber on the lower control arm and move it to the side. Remove the rubber jounce bumper.
7. Separate the outboard CV-joint from the hub using front hub tools T81P-1104-C with T81P-1104-A and adapters T83P-1104-BH1 and T86P-1104-A1 or equivalents, and free the hub, bearing and knuckle assembly from the halfshaft by pushing in the CV-joint outer shaft until it is loose in the assembly.

NOTE: Never use a hammer to separate the outboard CV-joint stub shaft from the hub. Damage to the CV-joint threads and internal components may result.

8. Remove the halfshaft assembly from the vehicle. Once the halfshaft(s) have been removed, the vehicle must not be driven or rolled with the vehicle weight supported by the hub bearing.
To install:
9. Carefully align the splines of the outboard CV-joint stub shaft with the splines in the hub and push the shaft into the hub as far as possible.
10. Temporarily fasten the rotor to the hub with washers and 2 lug nuts. Insert a suitable steel rod into the rotor and rotate clockwise to contact the knuckle to prevent the rotor from turning during CV-joint installation.
11. Install the hub nut washer and a new hub retainer nut. Manually thread the nut onto the halfshaft as far as possible, then tighten to 170–210 ft. lbs. (230–283 Nm).
12. Install the inboard flange of the halfshaft to the differential output flange, aligning the marks that were made during removal. Install the flange bolts and tighten to 22–29 ft. lbs. (30–40 Nm).
13. Install the wheel and tire assembly and lower the vehicle.

CV-Boot

Removal and Installation

4WD AEROSTAR

1. Remove the halfshaft assembly from the vehicle.
2. Clamp the halfshaft in a vise equipped with jaw caps to prevent damage to machined surfaces. Do not allow the vise jaws to contact the boot or its clamp.
3. Remove the slip yoke boot clamps and separate the outboard shaft and joint assembly from the inboard slip yoke assembly. Remove and discard the slip yoke boot.
4. Cut the large boot clamp using suitable cutters and peel away from the boot. After removing the clamp, roll the boot back over the shaft and remove and discard the boot.
5. Clean all parts in suitable parts cleaning solvent.

NOTE: Do not submerge the slip yoke assembly U-joint in cleaning solvent.

6. Inspect the CV-joint and slip yoke assembly for excessive wear, pitting, rust and broken parts. If the CV-joint is no longer usable, the complete outer shaft assembly must be replaced.
To install:
7. Fill the CV-joint area around the balls with 2.8 oz. of suitable CV-joint grease. Then spread 1.4 oz. of grease evenly inside the large boot for a total combined fill of 4.2 oz.
8. Assemble the large outboard boot onto the outboard shaft and joint assembly, making sure the boot is seated in the boot grooves. Tighten the clamps using suitable crimping pliers, but do not overtighten, as it may damage the clamp and/or boot.
9. Assemble the small boot and clamps onto the outboard shaft and joint assembly, but do not crimp the clamps at this time.
10. Coat the spline end of the outboard shaft and joint assembly with lubricant and assemble into the inner slip yoke assembly.
11. Slip the boot into place, making sure the boot is seated in the boot grooves. Tighten the clamps using a suitable tool, but do not overtighten, as it may damage the clamp and/or boot.
12. Install the halfshaft in the vehicle.

Driveshaft and U-Joints

Removal and Installation

REAR DRIVESHAFT

1. Raise and safely support the vehicle.

Halfshaft assembly—4WD Aerostar

2. Mark the driveshaft in relation to the rear axle flange. If necessary, mark the relation of the driveshaft to the transfer case flange.

3. If equipped with a center bearing assembly, remove the retaining bolts and the spacers under the center bearing bracket, if installed.

4. Remove the attaching bolts and disconnect the driveshaft from the rear axle flange.

5. On 2WD vehicles, slide the driveshaft rearward until the slip yoke clears the transmission extension housing and remove the driveshaft. Plug the extension housing to prevent fluid leakage.

6. On 4WD vehicles, remove the bolts attaching the driveshaft to the transfer case flange and remove the driveshaft.

To install:

7. On 2WD vehicles, lubricate the splines of the slip yoke. Remove the plug from the extension housing and install the driveshaft assembly. Do not allow the slip yoke to bottom on the output shaft with excessive force.

8. On 4WD vehicles, install the driveshaft to the transfer case flange, aligning the marks that were made during removal. Install the attaching bolts and tighten to 61–87 ft. lbs. (83–118 Nm) if equipped with constant velocity U-joints or 12–16 ft. lbs. (17–22 Nm) if equipped with double cardan U-joints.

9. Connect the driveshaft to the rear axle flange, aligning the marks that were made during removal. Install the retaining bolts and tighten to 61–87 ft. lbs. (83–118 Nm) on 1988–89 vehicles or 70–95 ft. lbs. (95–129 Nm) on 1990–92 vehicles.

10. If equipped, install the center bearing attachment bolts and tighten to 27–37 ft. lbs. (37–50 Nm). Make sure the center bearing bracket is installed "square" to the vehicle. If spacers were installed under the center bearing bracket, make sure they are reinstalled.

11. Lower the vehicle.

FRONT DRIVESHAFT

1. Raise and safely support the vehicle.

2. Remove the bolts and straps or the flange bolts retaining the driveshaft to the transfer case. If necessary, remove the boot from the transfer case to gain access to the slip yoke.

3. Remove the bolts and straps retaining the front U-joint to the front axle and remove the front driveshaft.

To install:

4. If equipped, lubricate the slip yoke splines and the edge of the inner diameter of the rubber boot. Slide the driveshaft into the transfer case, making sure the wide-tooth splines are properly indexed. Reposition the boot and install the clamp.

5. If equipped, install the driveshaft to the transfer case flange and install the retaining bolts. Tighten to 12–16 ft. lbs. (17–22 Nm).

6. Install the driveshaft to the front axle flange with the straps and bolts. Tighten to 10–15 ft. lbs. (14–20 Nm).

7. Lower the vehicle.

Front Axle Shaft, Bearing And Seal

Removal and Installation

EXCEPT AEROSTAR

1. Raise and safely support the vehicle. Remove the front wheel and tire assemblies.

2. Remove the disc brake caliper and wire it to the frame. Do not let the caliper hang by the brake hose.

3. Remove the hub locks, wheel bearings and locknuts.

4. Remove the hub, rotor and outer wheel bearing.

5. Remove the grease seal from the rotor with a seal removal tool. Remove the inner wheel bearing.

6. If the wheel bearings are to be replaced, remove the inner and outer bearing races with a suitable puller or a hammer and brass drift.

7. Remove the nuts retaining the spindle to the steering knuckle. Tap the spindle with a plastic hammer to jar the spindle from the knuckle. Remove the splash shield.

8. On the left side of the vehicle, remove the shaft and joint assembly by pulling the assembly out of the carrier. On the right side of the carrier, remove and discard the clamp from the shaft and joint assembly and the stub shaft. Pull the shaft and joint assembly from the splines of the stub shaft.

9. If required, remove the oil seal and needle bearing from the spindle. If necessary, remove the slinger from the shaft by driving it off with a hammer.

To install:

10. If removed, install a new bearing and seal in the spindle and/or press on a new shaft slinger.

11. On the right side of the carrier, install the rubber boot and new keystone clamps on the stub shaft slip yoke. Slide the right shaft and joint assembly into the slip yoke making sure the splines are fully engaged. Slide the boot over the assembly and crimp the keystone clamp using suitable pliers.

NOTE: The Dana model 28 axle has phased splines; there is only 1 way to assemble the right shaft and joint assembly into the slip yoke. The Dana model 35 axle does not have a blind spline, therefore pay special attention to make sure the yoke ears are in phase (in line) during assembly.

12. On the left side of the carrier, slide the shaft and joint assembly through the knuckle and engage the splines on the shaft in the carrier.

13. Install the splash shield and spindle onto the steering knuckle. Install and tighten the spindle nuts to 45 ft. lbs. (61 Nm).

14. If removed, drive the bearing races into the rotor using a suitable driver. Pack the inner and outer wheel bearings and the lip of a new seal with high-temperature wheel bearing grease.

15. Position the inner wheel bearing in the race and install the seal using a seal installer. Install the rotor on the spindle and install the outer wheel bearing in the race.

16. Install the wheel bearing, locknut, thrust bearing, snapring and locking hubs.

17. Install the caliper and the wheel and tire assemblies. Lower the vehicle.

AEROSTAR

1. Remove the axle assembly from the sub-frame and the vehicle.

2. Remove the cover plate and drain the lubricant. Mount the axle assembly in a suitable fixture.

3. Rotate the shafts so the open side of the snapring is exposed. Remove the snaprings.

4. Remove the axle shafts. Remove and discard the oil seal and needle bearings.

To install:

5. Make sure the bearing bore is free from nicks and burrs. Install a new caged needle bearing on installation tool T83T–1244–A or equivalent, with the manufacturer name and part number facing outward towards the tool. Drive the needle bearing in until it is seated in the bore. The tool controls the installation depth of the seal and bearing.

6. Coat a new seal with lubricant and install using a seal installer.

7. Install the axle shafts into the carrier so the groove in the shaft is visible in the differential case.

8. Install the snapring in the axle shaft groove. Remove the axle assembly from the holding fixture.

9. Clean all old sealer from the carrier and cover surfaces. Apply a bead of RTV sealer ⅛–¼ in. wide. The bead should be continuous and should not pass through or outside the holes.

10. Install the cover and tighten the bolts to 20–25 ft. lbs. (27–34 Nm). Fill the carrier with the proper type and quantity of fluid.

11. Install the axle assembly in the vehicle.

Dana model 28 front drive axle assembly

Rear Axle Shaft, Bearing And Seal

Removal and Installation

FORD 7.5 IN. AND 8.8 IN. REAR AXLES

1. Raise and safely support the vehicle.
2. Remove the rear wheel and tire assemblies and the brake drums.
3. Clean all dirt from the carrier cover area. Position a drain pan under the carrier, remove the cover and drain the rear axle.

NOTE: Whenever a plastic rear axle cover is removed, it must be replaced with a new cover and bolts. Steel rear axle covers may be reused.

4. For all 8.8 in. axles and all 7.5 in. axles except 3.73: 1 and 4.10: 1 ratio axles, proceed as follows:
   a. Remove the differential pinion shaft lock bolt and pinion shaft.
   b. Push the flanged end of the axle shafts toward the center of the vehicle and remove the C-lock from the button end of the axle shaft.
   c. Remove the axle shaft from the housing.
   d. Reinstall the pinion shaft and lock bolt to ensure the pinion gears remain in place.
5. On 7.5 in. axles equipped with 3.73: 1 and 4.10: 1 axle ratios, proceed as follows:
   a. Remove the pinion shaft lock bolt.
   b. Push out the pinion shaft until the step on the shaft contacts the ring gear.
   c. Remove the C-lock from the axle shaft.
   d. Remove the axle shaft from the housing.
   e. Reinstall the pinion shaft and lock bolt to ensure the pinion gears remain in place.
6. Using bearing remover T85L–1225–AH or equivalent and a suitable slide hammer, remove the axle bearing and seal as a unit.

To install:
7. Lubricate a new bearing with rear axle lubricant and install in the housing bore using a suitable driver.
8. Apply grease to the lips of a new axle seal and install, using a seal installer.
9. Remove the pinion shaft lock bolt and pinion shaft. On 7.5 in. axles equipped with 3.73:1 and 4.10:1 axle ratios, push out the pinion shaft until the step contacts the ring gear.
10. Slide the axle shaft into the axle housing, being careful not to damage the seal or axle bearing. Start the splines into the side gear and push firmly until the button end of the axle shaft can be seen in the differential case.
11. Install the C-lock on the button end of the axle shaft, then pull the shaft outboard until the shaft splines engage and the C-lock seats in the counterbore of the differential side gear.

NOTE: On 8.8 in. axles, a rubber O-ring is used to hold the C-lock in position on the axle shaft. Make sure the O-ring is in the groove at the button end of the axle shaft before installing the C-lock.

12. Slide the pinion shaft through the case and pinion gears, aligning the hole in the shaft with the lock bolt hole. Install the lock bolt and tighten to 15–30 ft. lbs. (20–40 Nm).
13. Clean all old sealer from the carrier and cover surfaces. Apply a bead of RTV sealer ⅛–¼ in. wide. The bead should be continuous and should not pass through or outside the holes.
14. Install the cover and tighten the bolts to 15–20 ft. lbs. (21–27 Nm) if equipped with a plastic cover or 25–35 ft. lbs. (34–37 Nm) if equipped with a steel cover. Fill the carrier with the proper type and quantity of fluid.
15. Install the brake drums and the wheel and tire assemblies. Lower the vehicle.

Differential pinion shaft and pinion shaft lock bolt location—Ford 7.5 in. and 8.8 in. rear axles.

Axle shaft C-lock installation—Ford 7.5 in. and 8.8 in. rear axles.

DANA 30 AND 35–1A REAR AXLES

1. Raise and safely support the vehicle.
2. Remove the rear wheel and tire assemblies and the brake drums.
3. Working through the hole provided in the axle shaft flange, remove the nuts that secure the wheel bearing retainer plate. These are torque prevailing nuts and must not be reused.
4. Pull the axle shaft assembly out of the axle housing using puller adapter tool T66L–4234–A or equivalent, and a suitable slide hammer.
5. Remove the aaxle shaft carefully so as not to damage the outer seal. Remove the bearing race from the housing using a slide hammer type puller and bearing race puller tool T77F–1102–AA or equivalent. Remove the brake backing plate and wire it to the chassis.
6. Mount the axle shaft in a suitable fixture. Drill a ¼–½ in. hole in the outside diameter of the inner retainer ring to a depth approximately ⅜ in. the thickness of the retainer ring. Do not drill all the way through the retainer ring as this will damage the axle shaft.
7. After drilling the retainer ring, use a chisel positioned across the drilled hole and strike sharply to split the retainer ring.
8. Put the outer bearing race on the axle shaft assembly and place the axle shaft in tool T75L–1165–A, B, C or equivalent. Assemble the 2 halves of the remover collet and tighten the bolts.

9. Press the bearing and seal assembly off of the shaft. Never use heat as this would damage the axle shaft. Inspect the retainer plate for possible distortion and replace if damaged.

To install:

10. Install the outer retainer plate, if removed. Make sure it is not installed backwards.

11. Place a new lubricated seal and bearing on the axle shaft, making sure the race rib ring is facing the axle flange.

12. Press the tapered-bearing and seal assembly onto the axle shaft using tools T75L-1165-B, service plate and adapter tool T75L-1165-DA or equivalents. Apply enough pressure to seat the bearing against the axle shaft shoulder. Do not attempt to press on the bearing retainer at the same time.

13. Position a new bearing retainer on the shaft, then press it into position firmly against the bearing.

14. Apply lubricant to the outer diameter of the race and seal. Install the brake backing plate and attaching bolts.

15. Before sliding the shaft assembly into the axle housing, make sure the outer seal is fully mounted on the bearing.

16. Carefully slide the axle shaft into the housing, start the axle splines into the side gear and push the shaft in until the bearing bottoms in the housing.

17. Install the bearing retainer plate and nuts. Tighten the nuts to 25–35 ft. lbs. (34–47 Nm).

18. Install the brake drum and the wheel and tire assembly.

19. Add lubricant through the filler hole until the level reaches 3.8 ± ¼ in. below the bottom of the filler hole. The axle must be in the running position and the vehicle level.

20. Lower the vehicle.

Front Wheel Hub, Knuckle/Spindle and Bearings

Removal and Installation

EXCEPT AEROSTAR

1. Raise and safely support the vehicle. Remove the front wheel and tire assemblies.

2. Remove the disc brake caliper and wire it to the frame. Do not let the caliper hang by the brake hose.

3. Remove the hub locks, wheel bearings and locknuts.

4. Remove the hub, rotor and outer wheel bearing.

5. Remove the grease seal from the rotor with a seal removal tool. Remove the inner wheel bearing.

6. If the wheel bearings are to be replaced, remove the inner and outer bearing races with a suitable puller or a hammer and brass drift.

7. Remove the nuts retaining the spindle to the steering knuckle. Tap the spindle with a plastic hammer to jar the spindle from the knuckle. Remove the splash shield.

8. On the left side of the vehicle, remove the shaft and joint assembly by pulling the assembly out of the carrier. On the right side of the carrier, remove and discard the clamp from the shaft and joint assembly and the stub shaft. Pull the shaft and joint assembly from the splines of the stub shaft.

9. Place the spindle in a vise on the second step of the spindle. Wrap a shop towel around the spindle or use a brass-jawed vise to protect the spindle.

10. Remove the oil seal and needle bearing from the spindle with a slide hammer and seal remover TOOL–1175–AC or equivalent. If necessary, remove the slinger from the shaft by driving off with a hammer.

11. Remove the cotter pin from the tie rod nut and then remove the nut. Tap on the tie rod stud to free it from the steering arm.

12. Remove the upper ball joint snapring and remove the upper ball joint pinch bolt. Loosen the lower ball joint nut to the end of the stud.

13. Strike the inside of the knuckle near the upper and lower ball joints to break the knuckle loose from the ball joint studs.

14. Remove the camber adjuster sleeve. Note the position of the slot in the camber adjuster so it can be reinstalled in the same position during assembly.

15. Remove the lower ball joint nut. Place the knuckle in a vise and remove the snapring from the bottom ball joint socket, if equipped.

16. Assemble C-frame T74P-4635-C and ball joint remover T83T-3050-A or equivalents on the lower ball joint. Turn the forcing screw clockwise until the lower ball joint is removed from the steering knuckle.

17. Assemble the C-frame and ball joint remover on the upper ball joint and remove in the same manner.

NOTE: Always remove the lower ball joint first.

To install:

18. Clean the steering knuckle bore and insert the lower ball joint in the knuckle as straight as possible.

19. Assemble C-frame T74P-4635-C, ball joint installer T83T-3050-A and receiver cup T80T-3010-A3 or equivalents to install the lower ball joint. Turn the forcing screw clockwise until the lower ball joint is firmly seated. Install the snapring on the lower ball joint.

NOTE: The lower ball joint must always be installed first.

20. Assemble the C-frame, ball joint installer and receiver cup to install the upper ball joint. Turn the forcing screw clockwise until the ball joint is firmly seated.

21. Install the camber adjuster into the support arm, making sure the slot is in the original position.

NOTE: The torque sequence in Steps 22 and 23 must be followed exactly when securing the knuckle. Excessive knuckle turning effort may result in reduced steering returnability if this procedure is not followed.

22. Install a new nut on the bottom ball joint stud. Tighten the nut to 90 ft. lbs. (122 Nm) minimum, then tighten to align the next slot in the nut with the hole in the stud. Install a new cotter pin.

23. Install the snapring on the upper ball joint stud. Install the upper ball joint pinch bolt and tighten to 48–65 ft. lbs. (65–88 Nm).

NOTE: The camber adjuster will seat itself into the knuckle at a predetermined position during the tightening sequence. Do not attempt to adjust this position.

24. Clean all dirt and grease from the spindle bearing bore. The bearing bores must be free from nicks and burrs.

25. Place the bearing in the bore with the manufacturers identification facing outward. Drive the bearing into the bore using spindle bearing replacer T80T-4000-S and driver handle T80T-4000-W or equivalents.

26. Install the grease seal in the bearing bore with the lip side of the seal facing towards the tool. Drive the seal in the bore using the same tools as in Step 25. Coat the bearing seal lip with high-temperature lubricant.

27. If removed, press on a new shaft slinger.

28. On the right side of the carrier, install the rubber boot and new keystone clamps on the stub shaft slip yoke. Slide the right shaft and joint assembly into the slip yoke making sure the splines are fully engaged. Slide the boot over the assembly and crimp the keystone clamp using suitable pliers.

NOTE: The Dana model 28 axle has phased splines; there is only 1 way to assemble the right shaft and joint assembly into the slip yoke. The Dana model 35 axle does not have a blind spline, therefore pay special attention to make sure the yoke ears are in phase (in line) during assembly.

29. On the left side of the carrier, slide the shaft and joint as-

sembly through the knuckle and engage the splines on the shaft in the carrier.

30. Install the splash shield and spindle onto the steering knuckle. Install and tighten the spindle nuts to 45 ft. lbs. (61 Nm).

31. If removed, drive the bearing races into the rotor using a suitable driver. Pack the inner and outer wheel bearings and the lip of a new seal with high-temperature wheel bearing grease.

32. Position the inner wheel bearing in the race and install the seal using a seal installer. Install the rotor on the spindle and install the outer wheel bearing in the race.

33. Install the wheel bearing, locknut, thrust bearing, snapring and locking hubs.

34. Install the caliper and the wheel and tire assemblies. Lower the vehicle.

AEROSTAR

1. Place the front wheels in the straight ahead position. Raise and safely support the vehicle.

2. Raise and safely support the vehicle. Remove the wheel and tire assembly.

3. Remove the caliper and support it aside with mechanics wire. Do not let the caliper hang by the brake hose. Remove the brake rotor.

4. Remove the cotter pin and nut from the tie rod end stud. Disconnect the tie rod end from the steering knuckle.

5. Support the lower control arm. Remove the cotter pin and loosen the nut retaining the knuckle to the lower control arm ball joint. Disconnect the lower ball joint using tool T64P–3590–F or equivalent. Remove the tool and ball joint retaining nut.

6. With the vehicle body securely supported, pull down on the knuckle until the lower ball joint is disengaged from the steering knuckle.

7. Install hub remover T81P–1104–A with T81P–1104–C and hub knuckle adapters T83P–1104–BH1 and T88P–1104–A1 or equivalents, and free the hub, bearing and knuckle assembly from the halfshaft by pushing in the CV-joint outer shaft until it is loose in the assembly.

8. Remove the bolt and nut retaining the spindle to the upper control arm ball joint. While supporting the halfshaft, remove the knuckle by pulling the knuckle down and out of the upper ball joint and outward away from the halfshaft. Wire the halfshaft to the body to maintain it in a level position.

9. Remove the 3 bolts retaining the hub assembly to the steering knuckle and remove the hub assembly.

NOTE: The hub and bearing assembly is not serviceable. If the bearing requires replacement, it must be replaced as an assembly.

To install:

10. Install the hub assembly into the steering knuckle and tighten the 3 bolts.

11. Position the steering knuckle on the CV-joint outer shaft and into the lower ball joint. Make sure the splines of the CV-joint shaft are in proper mesh in the hub. Install the lower ball joint nut and tighten to 80–120 ft. lbs. (108–163 Nm). If required, continue turning the nut to the next castellation and install the cotter pin.

12. Temporarily install the rotor on the hub with washers and 2 lug nuts. Insert a steel rod into the rotor diameter and rotate clockwise to contact the knuckle.

13. Install the hub nut washer and a new hub nut. Rotate the nut clockwise to seat the CV-joint, but do not final torque at this time.

14. Position the upper control arm ball joint stud to the steering knuckle. Install the nut and bolt and tighten to 27–37 ft. lbs. (37–50 Nm).

15. Connect the tie rod end to the steering knuckle. Firmly seat the tie rod end stud into the tapered hole to prevent rotation while tightening. Install the nut and tighten to 52–74 ft.

Steering knuckle and hub assembly—4WD Aerostar

lbs. (70–100 Nm). If required, continue turning the nut to the next castellation and install the cotter pin.

16. Using a steel rod inserted into the rotor as in Step 12, tighten the hub nut to 170–210 ft. lbs. (230–285 Nm). Remove the wheel nuts and washers.

17. Install the dust shield, caliper, rotor and wheel and tire assembly. Lower the vehicle.

Manual Locking Hubs

Removal and Installation

1. Raise and support the vehicle safely.

2. Remove the lug nuts and remove the wheel and tire assembly.

3. Remove the retainer washers from the lug nut studs and remove the manual locking hub assembly. To remove the internal hub lock assembly from the outer body assembly, remove the outer lock ring seated in the hub body groove. The internal assembly, spring and clutch gear will now slide out of the hub body. Do not remove the screw from the plastic dial.

4. Rebuild the hub assembly in the reverse order of disassembly.

5. Adjust the wheel bearing if necessary. Install the manual locking hub assembly over the spindle and place the retainer washers on the lug nut studs.

6. Install the wheel and tire assembly and lower the vehicle.

Adjustment

1. Raise and safely support the vehicle. Remove the wheel and tire assembly.

2. Remove the retainer washers from the lug nut studs and remove the manual locking hub assembly from the spindle.

3. Remove the snapring from the end of the spindle shaft.

4. On Dana model 28 axles, remove the axle shaft spacer, needle thrust bearing and bearing spacer. On Dana model 35 axles, remove the axle shaft spacer.

5. Remove the outer wheel bearing locknut from the spindle using locknut wrench T86T–1197–A or equivalent. Make sure the tabs on the tool engage the slots in the locknut.

6. Remove the locknut washer from the spindle.

7. Loosen the inner wheel bearing locknut using locknut wrench T86T–1197–A or equivalent. Make sure the tabs on the tool engage the slots in the locknut and the slot in the tool is centered over the locknut pin.

8. Tighten the inner locknut to 35 ft. lbs. (47 Nm) to seat the bearings.

9. Spin the rotor and back off the inner locknut ¼ turn. Retighten the inner locknut to 16 inch lbs. (1.8 Nm). Install the

Manual locking hub assembly—Dana model 28 axle, model 35 similar

Automatic locking hub assembly—Dana model 28 axle, model 35 similar

lockwasher on the spindle. It may be necessary to tighten the inner locknut slightly so the pin on the locknut aligns with the closest hole in the lockwasher.

10. Install the outer wheel bearing locknut using locknut wrench T86T–1197–A or equivalent. Tighten the locknut to 150 ft. lbs. (203 Nm).

11. On Dana model 28 axles, install the bearing thrust spacer, needle thrust bearing and axle shaft spacer. On Dana model 35 axles, install the axle shaft spacer.

12. Clip the snapring onto the end of the spindle. Install the manual hub assembly over the spindle and install the retainer washers.

13. Install the wheel and tire assembly. Check the endplay of the wheel and tire assembly on the spindle. Final endplay should be 0–0.003 in. (0–0.08mm). The maximum torque to rotate the hub should be 25 inch lbs. (2.8 Nm).

14. Lower the vehicle.

Automatic Locking Hubs

Removal and Installation

1. Raise and support the vehicle safely. Remove the wheel lug nuts and remove the wheel and tire assembly.

2. Remove the retainer washers from the lug nut studs and remove the automatic locking hub assembly from the spindle.

3. Remove the snapring from the end of the spindle shaft.

4. On Dana model 28 axles, remove the axle shaft spacer, needle thrust bearing and the bearing spacer. On Dana model 35 axles, remove the axle shaft spacer.

5. Being careful not to damage the plastic moving cam, pull the cam assembly off the wheel bearing adjusting nut. On Dana model 28 axles, remove the thrust washer and needle thrust bearing from the adjusting nut. On Dana model 35 axles, remove the 2 plastic thrust spacers from the adjusting nut.

6. Using a magnet, remove the locking key. It may be necessary to rotate the adjusting nut slightly to relieve the pressure against the locking key, before the key can be removed.

NOTE: To prevent damage to the spindle threads, look into the spindle keyway under the adjusting nut and remove the separate locking key before removing the adjusting nut.

7. Loosen the wheel bearing adjusting nut from the spindle using a 2 ³⁄₈ in. hex socket tool.

8. While rotating the hub and rotor assembly, tighten the wheel bearing adjusting nut to 35 ft. lbs. (47 Nm) to seat the bearings. Spin the rotor and back off the nut ¼ turn.

9. Retighten the adjusting nut to 16 inch lbs. (1.8 Nm) using a torque wrench. Align the closest hole in the wheel bearing adjusting nut with the center of the spindle keyway slot. Advance the nut to the next lug if required. Install the separate locking key in the spindle keyway under the adjusting nut.

NOTE: Extreme care must be taken when aligning the spindle nut adjustment lug with the center of the spindle keyway slot to prevent damage to the separate locking key.

10. On Dana model 28 axles, install the locknut needle bearing and thrust washer in the reverse order of removal. On Dana model 35 axles, install the 2 thrust spacers. Push or press the cam assembly onto the locknut by lining up the key in the fixed cam with the spindle keyway.

NOTE: Extreme care must be taken when aligning the fixed cam key with the spindle keyway to prevent damage to the fixed cam.

11. On Dana model 28 axles, install the bearing thrust washer, needle thrust bearing and axle shaft spacer. On Dana model 35 axles, install the axle shaft spacer.
12. Clip the snapring onto the end of the spindle.
13. Install the automatic locking hub assembly over the spindle by lining up the 3 legs in the hub assembly with the 3 pockets in the cam assembly. Install the retainer washers.
14. Install the wheel and tire assembly. Check the endplay of the wheel and tire assembly on the spindle. Final endplay should be 0–0.003 in. (0–0.08mm). The maximum torque to rotate the hub should be 25 inch lbs. (2.8 Nm).
15. Lower the vehicle.

Pinion Seal

Removal and Installation

NOTE: This service procedure disturbs the pinion bearing preload and this preload must be carefully reset when assembling.

1. Raise the vehicle and support it safely.
2. Remove the wheels and the brake drums.
3. Mark the driveshaft and the axle companion flange so the driveshaft can be reinstalled in the same position. Remove the driveshaft.
4. Using an inch pound torque wrench on the pinion nut, record the torque required to maintain rotation of the pinion through several revolutions.
5. While holding the companion flange with a suitable tool, remove the pinion nut. Mark the companion flange in relation to the pinion shaft so the flange can be reinstalled in the same position.
6. Using a suitable puller, remove the rear axle companion flange. Use a small prybar to remove the seal from the carrier.
To install:
7. Make sure the splines of the pinion shaft are free of burrs.
8. Apply grease to the lips of the pinion seal and install, using a seal installer.
9. Check the seal surface of the companion flange for scratches, nicks or a groove. Replace the companion flange, as necessary. Apply a small amount of lubricant to the splines. Align the mark on the flange with the mark on the pinion shaft and install the companion flange.

NOTE: The companion flange must never be hammered on or installed with power tools.

10. Install a new nut on the pinion shaft. Hold the companion flange with a suitable tool while tightening the nut.
11. Tighten the pinion nut, rotating the pinion occasionally to ensure proper bearing seating. Take frequent pinion bearing torque preload readings until the original recorded preload reading is obtained or the following specification:
Ford 7.5 in. and 8.8 in. rear axles: 8–14 inch lbs.
Dana model 30 axle rear axles: 20–40 inch lbs.
Dana model 35-1A rear axles: 15–35 inch lbs.
Dana models 28 and Model 35 front axles: 15–25 inch lbs.
Dana model 28-2 front axles (4WD Aerostar): 15–35 inch lbs.

NOTE: Under no circumstances should the pinion nut be backed off to reduce preload. If reduced preload is required, a new collapsible pinion spacer and pinion nut must be installed.

12. Install the driveshaft and check the fluid level in the carrier. Lower the vehicle.

Axle Housing

Removal and Installation

FRONT AXLE

Aerostar

1. Raise and safely support the vehicle.
2. Mark the driveshaft and axle flanges so they can be reassembled in their original positions. Disconnect the driveshaft from the companion flange.
3. Remove the bolts that connect the inboard halfshaft flanges to the axle shafts. Wire the halfshafts to the body in a level position.
4. Remove the vent hose from the vent fitting on the axle tube and cap the fitting to prevent any fluid leakage.
5. Remove the snubber from the crossmember rear lateral support, located below the axle pinion.
6. Support the front axle with a jack. Remove the locknuts that connect the axle mounting brackets to the crossmember.
7. Lower the jack and remove the front axle assembly.
8. If necessary, remove the screws holding the mounting bracket to the axle housing and remove the bracket.
To install:
9. If removed, attach the axle mounting bracket to the axle housing, using thread locking compound on the 2 bolts. Tighten to 70–80 ft. lbs. (95–108 Nm).
10. Raise the axle into position. Insert the axle mounting bushing studs through the axle mounting bracket. Install the locknuts using thread locking compound and tighten to 65–85 ft. lbs. (88–115 Nm). Tighten in the following order: left front, right front, pinion, rear.

NOTE: When installing the axle assembly with new mounting bushings, each nut must be tightened to full torque in 1 step to avoid coring of the locking patch on the stud, before the nut is fully torqued.

11. Attach the vent hose to the vent fitting on the axle tube. Make sure the hose is not kinked.
12. Position the inboard halfshaft flanges to the axle shaft flanges, aligning the marks that were made during removal. Install the bolts and tighten to 22–29 ft. lbs. (30–40 Nm). Remove the wire that was supporting the halfshafts.
13. Position the front driveshaft flange to the front axle flange, aligning the marks that were made during removal. Install the bolts and tighten to 22–29 ft. lbs. (30–40 Nm).
14. Install the axle snubber on the crossmember just below the axle pinion. Tighten to 17–24 ft. lbs. (23–33 Nm).
15. Lower the vehicle.

Bronco II and Ranger

1. Raise the vehicle and support it safely under the radius arm brackets.
2. Mark the front axle yoke and the driveshaft so they can be reassembled in the same position. Disconnect the driveshaft from the front axle yoke.
3. Remove the front wheel and tire assemblies. Remove the disc brake calipers and support them on a frame rail. Do not let the calipers hang by the brake hoses.
4. Remove the cotter pin and nut retaining the steering linkage to the knuckle. Disconnect the linkage from the knuckle.
5. Position a jack under the axle arm and slightly compress the coil spring. Remove the nut that retains the lower part of the

spring to the axle arm. Slowly lower the jack and remove the coil spring, spacer, seat and stud.

6. Remove the nut and disconnect the shock absorber from the radius arm bracket. Remove the stud and bolts that connect the radius arm bracket and radius arm to the axle arm. Remove the bracket and radius arm.

7. Remove the pivot bolt that secures the right axle arm assembly to the crossmember.

8. Remove the clamps securing the axle shaft boot from the axle shaft slip yoke and axle shaft. Disconnect the outer axle shaft from the slip yoke assembly. Lower the jack and remove the right axle arm assembly.

9. Position another jack under the differential housing. Remove the bolt that connects the left axle arm to the crossmember. Lower the jacks and remove the left axle arm assembly.

To install:

10. Position a jack under the left support arm and raise the arm into position in the pivot bracket. Install the nut and bolt and tighten to 120–150 ft. lbs. (163–203 Nm). Do not remove the jack from under the differential housing at this time.

11. Place new clamps for the axle shaft boot on the axle shaft assembly. Position the right support arm on a jack and raise it so the right outer axle shaft slides onto the slip yoke and the support arm is in position in the right pivot bracket. Install the nut and bolt and tighten to 120–150 ft. lbs. (163–203 Nm). Do not remove the jack from the right support arm at this time.

NOTE: When installing the outer axle shaft into the inner slip yoke on Dana model 35 axles, the yoke ears must be in alignment with each other to assure proper phasing.

12. Position the radius arm and front bracket on the support arms. Install a new stud and nut on the top of the axle and radius arm assembly and tighten to 190–230 ft. lbs. (258–311 Nm). Install the bolts in the front of the bracket and tighten to 27–37 ft. lbs. (37–50 Nm).

13. Install the seat, spacer retainer and coil spring on the stud and nut. Raise the jack to compress the coil spring. Install the nut and tighten to 70–100 ft. lbs. (95–135 Nm).

14. Connect the shock absorber to the support arm assembly. Install the nut and tighten to 42–72 ft. lbs. (57–97 Nm).

15. Connect the tie rod ball joint to the knuckle. Install the nut and tighten to 50–75 ft. lbs. (68–101 Nm). Lower the jacks from the support arms.

16. Install the brake calipers and the wheel and tire assemblies.

17. Connect the driveshaft to the front axle yoke, aligning the marks that were made during removal. Install the U-bolts and tighten the nuts to 8–15 ft. lbs. (11–20 Nm).

18. Lower the vehicle.

Explorer

1. Raise and safely support the vehicle. Remove the front axle shaft and spindle assemblies.

2. Mark the front axle yoke and the driveshaft so they can be reassembled in the same position. Disconnect the driveshaft from the front axle yoke.

3. Remove the cotter pin and nut retaining the steering linkage to the knuckle. Disconnect the linkage from the knuckle.

4. Remove the left stabilizer bar link lower bolt and remove the link from the radius arm bracket.

5. Position a jack under the left axle arm and slightly compress the coil spring. Remove the shock absorber lower nut and disconnect the shock absorber from the radius arm bracket.

6. Remove the nut that retains the lower part of the spring to the axle arm. Slowly lower the jack and remove the coil spring, spacer, seat and stud.

7. Remove the stud and bolts that connect the radius arm bracket and radius arm to the axle arm. Remove the bracket and radius arm.

8. Position another jack under the differential housing. Re-

move the bolt that connects the left axle arm to the axle pivot bracket. Lower the jacks and remove the left axle arm assembly.

To install:

9. Position a jack under the left support arm and raise the arm into position in the pivot bracket. Install the nut and bolt and tighten to 120–150 ft. lbs. (163–203 Nm). Do not remove the jack from under the differential housing at this time.

10. Position the radius arm and front bracket on the left axle arm. Install a new stud and nut on the top of the axle and radius arm assembly and tighten to 190–230 ft. lbs. (258–311 Nm). Install the bolts in the front of the bracket and tighten to 27–37 ft. lbs. (37–50 Nm).

11. Install the seat, spacer retainer and coil spring on the stud and nut. Raise the jack to compress the coil spring. Install the nut and tighten to 70–100 ft. lbs. (95–135 Nm).

12. Connect the shock absorber to the radius arm. Install the nut and tighten to 42–72 ft. lbs. (57–97 Nm).

13. Connect the tie rod ball joint to the knuckle. Install the nut and tighten to 50–75 ft. lbs. (68–101 Nm). Install the stabilizer bar mounting bracket and tighten to 203–240 ft. lbs. (275–325 Nm).

14. Connect the front driveshaft to the front axle yoke, aligning the marks that were made during removal. Install the U-bolts and tighten the nuts to 8–15 ft. lbs. (11–20 Nm).

15. Install the spindle and axle shaft assemblies. Lower the vehicle.

REAR AXLE

Aerostar

1. Raise and safely support the vehicle.

2. Release the parking brake cable tension by pulling rearward on the front cable approximately 2 in. Clamp the cable behind the crossmember to release the tension on the rear parking brake cables.

3. Remove the parking brake cables from the equalizer. Compress the tabs on the retainers and pull the cables through the rear crossmember.

4. Mark the driveshaft to the rear axle so they can be reassembled in the same position. Remove the driveshaft. Remove the wheel and tire assemblies.

5. Disconnect the brake hose from the chassis brake line. Plug the line to prevent fluid loss.

6. Disconnect the shock absorbers from the lower control arm. Disconnect the axle vent tube from the clip on the frame.

7. Lower the axle until the springs are no longer under compression. Remove the spring retainers and the coil springs.

8. Raise the axle to the normal load position and disconnect the control arms at the axle.

9. Remove the bolt and nut retaining the upper control arm to the rear axle. Remove the upper control arm from the axle. Mark the position of the cam adjuster in the axle bushing.

10. Lower the axle from the vehicle.

To install:

11. Raise the axle into position.

12. Position the upper control arm over the cam adjuster and bushing. Make sure the marks scribed on the bushing and adjuster are still in alignment. Install the bolt, nut and retainer and tighten until snug. Do not final torque at this time.

13. Lower the axle to the spring unloaded position. Place the lower insulator on the control arm and the upper insulator on top of the spring. The white colored tapered coil must face upward. Install the spring in position on the control arm and axle.

14. Install the lower retainer and nut and tighten to 41–64 ft. lbs. (55–88 Nm). Install the upper retainer and bolt and tighten to 30–40 ft. lbs. (40–55 Nm).

15. Raise the axle to the normal load position and tighten the bolt and nut retaining the lower control arm to the axle to 100–129 ft. lbs. (133–176 Nm).

16. Connect the shock absorbers to the lower control arm. In-

UPPER CONTROL ARM

CAM ADJUSTER

SCRIBE MARK ON
CAM ADJUSTER AND
BUSHING

BUSHING

Rear axle housing removal—Aerostar

stall the shock bolt nut on the inside of the lower control arm bracket. Install the nut and tighten to 40–60 ft. lbs. (54–82 Nm).

17. Attach the brake hose to the frame and chassis brake line. Connect the axle vent hose, if equipped.

18. Install the wheel and tire assemblies. Install the driveshaft, aligning the marks that were made during removal.

19. Pull the parking brake cables and retainers through the clips on the vehicle underbody side rails and through the rear crossmember. Connect the brake cables to the equalizer. Unclamp the front parking brake cable to restore cable tension.

20. Bleed the brake system and lower the vehicle.

Bronco II and Ranger

1. Raise the vehicle and support it safely.

2. Remove the cover and drain the lubricant from the axle.

3. Remove the rear wheel and tire assemblies and remove the axle shafts.

4. Remove the 4 retaining nuts from each backing plate. Wire the backing plates to the underbody.

5. Disconnect the vent hose from the axle housing.

6. Remove the brake line from the clips that retain the line to the axle housing.

7. Remove the hydraulic brake T-fitting from the axle housing. Do not open the hydraulic brake system lines.

8. Mark the driveshaft and the axle companion flange so they can be reassembled in the same position. Remove the driveshaft.

9. Support the rear axle housing on a jack, then remove the spring clip U-bolt nuts. Remove the U-bolts and plates.

10. Disconnect the lower shock absorber studs or bolts from the mounting brackets on the axle housing. Lower the axle housing and remove it from under the vehicle.

To install:

11. Raise the axle housing into position so the spring clip U-bolt plates can be installed. Tighten the spring clip U-bolt nuts to 55–75 ft. lbs. (70–101 Nm).

12. Connect the lower shock absorber studs or bolts to the axle housing mounting bracket. Tighten the nut/bolt to 40–60 ft. lbs. (54–82 Nm).

13. Position the brake lines to the axle housing and secure with the retaining clips. Install the T-fitting.

14. Install the brake backing plates on the axle housing flanges. Tighten the nuts to 20–40 ft. lbs. (28–54 Nm).

15. Apply stud and bearing mount compound to the threads on the vent. Install the vent and vent tube.

16. Install the axle shafts, brake drums and wheel and tire assemblies.

17. Install the driveshaft, aligning the marks that were made during removal.

18. Clean all old sealer from the carrier and cover surfaces. Apply a bead of RTV sealer ⅛–¼ in. wide. The bead should be continuous and should not pass through or outside the holes.

19. Install the cover and tighten the bolts to 15–20 ft. lbs. (21–27 Nm) if equipped with a plastic cover or 25–35 ft. lbs. (34–37 Nm) if equipped with aa steel cover.

20. Add the proper type of rear axle lubricant until the level is $\frac{1}{4}$–$\frac{1}{9}$ in. below the bottom of the filler hole with the axle in running position.

21. Lower the vehicle.

Explorer

1. Raise the vehicle and support it safely.

2. Remove the cover and drain the lubricant from the axle.

3. Remove the rear wheel and tire assemblies and remove the rear anti-lock brake system sensor. Remove the axle shafts.

4. Remove the 4 retaining nuts from each backing plate. Wire the backing plates to the underbody.

5. Disconnect the vent hose from the axle housing. Remove the connector from the rear anti-lock sensor.

6. Remove the brake line from the clips that retain the line to the axle housing.

7. Remove the hydraulic brake junction block from the axle housing. Do not open the hydraulic brake system lines.

8. Mark the driveshaft and the axle companion flange so they can be reassembled in the same position. Remove the driveshaft.

9. Support the rear axle housing on a jack, then remove the axle housing U-bolt nuts. Remove the U-bolts and shock absorber plates. Leave the shock absorbers attached to the plates.

10. Remove the stabilizer bar attaaching bracket bolts from the axle housing and position the stabilizer bar assembly away from the axle housing.

11. Raise the axle housing off the springs with the jack and move to the right side of the vehicle. Lower the left side of the axle housing below the left spring enough to clear the spring.

12. Remove the axle housing from the vehicle by lowering the axle and moving to the left until the right axle tube clears the right spring.

To install:

13. Install the axle housing on the transmission jack. Guide the right side of the axle housing over the right spring. Lift the left side of the axle housing over the left spring and position the axle housing on the spring center bolts.

14. Install the stabilizer bar to the axle housing. Tighten the stabilizer bar bracket bolts to 30–42 ft. lbs. (40–57 Nm).

15. Install the axle housing U-bolts over the axle tube. Position the shock absorber plates under the springs and install the U-bolts through the holes. Install the nuts and tighten to 88–108 ft. lbs. (119–146 Nm).

16. Install the axle vent tube to the axle vent fitting and secure with a clamp. Connect the rear anti-lock sensor connector.

17. Install the brake backing plates on the axle housing flanges. Tighten the nuts to 20–40 ft. lbs. (28–54 Nm).

18. Position the brake lines to the axle housing and secure with the retaining clips. Position the brake junction block to the axle housing and install the retaining screw.

19. Install the axle shafts. Install the driveshaft, aligning the marks that were made during removal. Tighten the attaching bolts to 70–95 ft. lbs. (95–128 Nm).

20. Install the brake drums and the wheel and tire assemblies.

21. Clean all old sealer from the carrier surface. Apply a bead of RTV sealer ⅛–¼ in. wide. The bead should be continuous and should not pass through or outside the holes.

22. Install a new cover and tighten the bolts to 15–20 ft. lbs. (21–27 Nm) in a criss-cross pattern.

23. Add the proper type of lubricant through the filler hole until the lubricant level is ¼–⁹⁄₁₆ in. below the bottom of the filler hole with the axle in the running position.

24. Lower the vehicle.

STEERING

Steering Wheel

Removal and Installation

1. Disconnect the negative battery cable.

2. Remove the screws retaining the steering wheel pad to the steering wheel spokes. Pull the pad back and disconnect the horn switch/cruise control wires. Remove the steering wheel pad.

3. Remove the steering wheel attaching bolt and damper, if equipped.

4. Using a suitable puller, remove the steering wheel from the steering column shaft.

NOTE: Do not hammer on the steering wheel or steering shaft or use a knock-off type steering wheel puller, as either will damage the steering column.

To install:

5. Install the steering wheel on the steering column shaft, aligning the mark and flat on the steering wheel with the mark and flat on the steering shaft.

6. If equipped, install the damper and align the locators with the hole in the wheel hub.

7. Install the steering wheel attaching bolt and tighten to 23–33 ft. lbs. (31–45 Nm).

8. Connect the horn switch/cruise control wires and install the steering wheel pad. Install the pad retaining screws and tighten to 8–11.5 inch lbs. (0.9–1.3 Nm).

9. Connect the negative battery and check the steering column for proper operation.

Steering Column

Removal and Installation

AEROSTAR AND 1988 BRONCO II AND RANGER

1. Disconnect the negative battery cable.

2. Remove the bolt attaching the steering column shaft to the lower shaft assembly and disengage the shaft.

3. Remove the steering wheel.

4. Remove the steering column trim shrouds. If equipped with tilt column, remove the upper extension shroud by squeezing it at the 6 and 12 o'clock positions and popping it free of the retaining plate at the 3 o'clock position.

5. Remove the steering column cover directly under the column, on the instrument panel.

6. Disconnect the electrical connections to the steering column switches.

7. Loosen the 2 bolts retaining the steering column to the lower support bracket, but do not remove the bolts at this time.

8. Remove the 3 screws retaining the steering column toeplate/lower seal to the dash.

9. Remove the 2 bolts retaining the steering column to the lower support bracket.

10. Lower the steering column and pull it out from the vehicle.

To install:

11. Carefully insert the lower end of the steering column through the opening in the dash panel.

12. Align the lower support brackets and attach the bolts loosely, so the column hangs with clearance between the brackets.

13. Align the steering column toeplate 3 mounting holes to the dash weld nuts. Install the 3 bolts and tighten to 12 ft. lbs. (16 Nm).

14. Tighten the column support bolts to 17 ft. lbs. (23 Nm).

15. Connect the steering column switch electrical connectors.

16. Slide the lower steering shaft onto the steering column shaft and install the bolt and nut. On Aerostar, tighten to 30–42 ft. lbs. (41–57 Nm). On 1988 Bronco II and Ranger, tighten to 19–28 ft. lbs. (26–38 Nm).

17. Attach the trim shrouds that cover the steering column upper end. If equipped with tilt column, snap the upper extension shroud in place.

18. Install the steering wheel and the steering column cover on the instrument panel.

19. Connect the negative battery cable and check the steering column for proper operation.

1989–92 RANGER, 1989–90 BRONCO II AND 1991–92 EXPLORER

1. Disconnect the negative battery cable and apply the parking brake. Place automatic transmission in **N**.

2. Remove the bolt that holds the intermediate shaft to the steering column shaft. Using a prybar, compress the intermediate shaft until it is clear of the steering column shaft.

3. If equipped with automatic transmission, remove the nuts from the studs and remove the shift cable bracket from the steering column bracket. Disconnect the shift cable from the column lever.

4. Remove the steering wheel. If equipped with tilt column, make sure the steering wheel is in the full up position before removal.

5. If equipped with tilt column, remove the tilt lever and remove the column collar by pressing on the collar from the top and bottom while removing the collar.

6. Remove the retaining screws and remove the panel trim cover.

7. Remove the 2 screws from the bottom of the column shroud. Remove the bottom half of the shroud by pulling the shroud down and toward the rear of the vehicle. If equipped with automatic transmission, move the shift lever as required to ease shroud removal. Lift the top half of the shroud from the column.

8. If equipped with automatic transmission, disconnect the

STEERING COLUMN SHROUD

STEERING WHEEL ASSEMBLY

BOLT 23–33 FT. LBS. (30–46 NM)

BOLT AND WASHER 11–17 FT. LBS. (15–23 NM)

TURN SIGNAL HANDLE AND SHANK ASSEMBLY

NUT 30–42 FT. LBS. (41–57 NM)

TURN SIGNAL SWITCH COVER

UPPER BRACKET

SCREW 18–26 INCH LBS. (2.0–2.9 NM)

STEERING GEAR UPPER SHAFT ASSEMBLY

BOLT

LOWER BRACKET

STEERING COLUMN ASSEMBLY

BOLT AND WASHER 11–17 FT. LBS. (15–23 NM)

Steering column assembly—Aerostar

selector indicator cable by removing the screw from the column casting and the plastic plug at the end of the cable. To remove the plastic plug from the shift lever socket casting, push on the nose of the plug until the head clears the casting, then pull the plug from the casting.

9. Remove the plastic clip that holds the combination switch wiring to the steering column bracket. Remove the 2 screws from the combination switch and remove the switch from the column, leaving the wiring connectors attached to the switch. Position the switch and wiring aside.

10. Disconnect the key warning buzzer wire from the horn brush wire. Remove the screw that holds the horn brush connector to the column and remove the connector.

11. Remove the 5 screws that hold the toe plate to the dash panel and loosen the toe plate clamp bolt.

12. Support the column and remove the bolts that hold the breakaway bracket to the pedal support bracket. Pry apart the locking tabs and disconnect the ignition switch wiring harness.

13. Carefully remove the column from the vehicle.

To install:

14. Carefully position the column in the hole in the vehicle floor. Connect the ignition switch wiring harness to the column connector.

15. Install the bolts that hold the breakaway bracket to the pedal support bracket, but do not tighten at this time.

16. Tighten the bolts that hold the toe plate to the floor to 8 ft. lbs. (11 Nm), then tighten the breakaway bracket-to-pedal support bracket bolts to 19–27 ft. lbs. (25–36 Nm). Tighten the toe plate clamp to 6–13 ft. lbs. (8–18 Nm).

17. Install the horn brush connector to the column and tighten the retaining screw to 21–29 inch lbs. (2.3–3.3 Nm). Attach the key warning buzzer wire connector to the horn brush wire. Route the wiring to prevent contact with moving parts.

18. Position the combinaation switch on the column with the attaching screws. Tighten to 18–26 inch lbs. (2–3 Nm). Install the plastic clip that holds the switch wiring to the steering column breakaway bracket.

19. If equipped with automatic transmission, connect the selector indicator cable by pushing the plastic plug at the end of the cable into the shift lever socket casting. When installed, the nose of the plug should be facing the steering wheel and the head of the plug away from the wheel. Install the cable retaining screw in the column and adjust the cable. If the shift lever was removed, install it at this time.

20. Position the top half of the shroud on the column so the screw moldings on the shroud seat in the mounting bores in the column. Place the automatic transmission shift lever in the lowest position to aid assembly.

21. Install the bottom half of the shroud by sliding the guides in the shroud bottom half into the tabs in the shroud top half. Install the shroud retaining screws and tighten to 6–10 inch lbs. (0.7–1.1 Nm).

22. If equipped with tilt column, install the column collar by pressing on the collar from the top and bottom while installing the collar on the column. Install the tilt lever and tighten to 2.2–3.6 ft. lbs. (3–5 Nm).

23. If equipped, place the automatic transmission selector lever in **N**. Install the steering wheel and the lower trim cover panel.

24. If equipped with automatic transmission, install the nuts on the studs and install the shift cable bracket on the steering column bracket. Connect the shift cable to the column lever.

25. Connect the column shaft to the intermediate shaft U-joint and tighten the pinch bolt to 25–35 ft. lbs. (34–47 Nm). The intermediate shaft must be in collapsed state to align, both shafts have a flat side, and then pulled up the column shaft until the bolt holes align. Make sure the intermediate shaft does not contact the plastic retainer at the base of the column. If it does, pull the lower shaft of the column slightly out of the column.

26. Connect the negative battery cable and check the adjustment of the selector indicator cable. Pull the shift lever toward the steering wheel until the **OD** detent in the transmission is felt. Release the shift lever, it should be against the detent wall in the column.

27. Release the parking brake lever and test drive the vehicle.

Manual Steering Gear

Adjustment

PRELOAD AND MESHLOAD

Gear In Vehicle

1. Make sure that the steering column is properly aligned and that the intermediate shaft flex coupling is not distorted.
2. Raise and safely support the vehicle. Disconnect the Pitman arm at the ball stud.
3. Lubricate the wormshaft seal with a drop of power steering fluid.
4. Remove the horn pad assembly from the steering wheel and turn the wheel slowly to 1 stop.
5. Using an inch pound torque wrench on the steering wheel nut, measure the torque (preload) required to rotate the steering wheel at a constant speed for approximately 1½ turns.
6. If the preload is not within 2–6 inch lbs. the preload must be adjusted. The steering gear must be removed from the vehicle to adjust worm preload.
7. Rotate the steering wheel from stop to stop counting the number of turns then back halfway, placing the gear on center.
8. Place an inch pound torque wrench on the steering wheel nut. Observe the highest reading (meshload) by rotating the steering shaft back and forth 90 degrees either way across center. The meshload must be within 4–10 inch lbs. and at least 2 inch lbs. over the preload. Meshload can be adjusted in the vehicle.

Gear Removed From Vehicle

1. Tighten the sector cover bolts to 40 ft. lbs. to aid in meshload retention. Loosen the preload adjuster locknut and tighten the worm bearing adjuster nut until all endplay has been removed. Lubricate the wormshaft seal with a drop of power steering fluid.
2. Using an inch pound torque wrench and an $^{11}/_{16}$ in. 12-point socket, carefully turn the wormshaft all the way to the right. Measure the left turn torque (preload) required to rotate the wormshaft at a constant speed for approximately 1½ turns.
3. Tighten or loosen the adjuster nut as required until the correct preload of 5–6 inch lbs. is obtained. Tighten the adjuster locknut to 166–187 ft. lbs. (225–253 Nm).
4. Rotate the wormshaft from stop to stop, counting the total number of turns, then turn back halfway placing the gear on center.
5. Using the same torque wrench and socket, observe the highest reading (meshload) while the wormshaft is turned 90 degrees either way across center. If the reading is not within 9–11 inch lbs. and at least 4 inch lbs. over the preload, turn the sector shaft adjusting screw, as required.
6. Hold the sector shaft adjusting screw and tighten the locknut to 14–25 ft. lbs. (19–34 Nm).

Removal and Installation

1. Raise the vehicle and support it safely with the front wheels in the straight ahead position.
2. Disengage the flex coupling shield from the steering gear input shaft shield and slide it up the intermediate shaft.
3. Remove the bolt that retains the flex coupling to the steering gear.
4. Remove the nut and washer that secures the Pitman arm to the sector shaft.
5. Remove the Pitman arm using puller T64P–3590–F or equivalent.

NOTE: Do not hammer on the end of the sector shaft or the tool as this will damage the steering gear.

6. While supporting the steering gear, remove the bolts and washers that attach the gear to the side rail. Remove the gear.

Manual steering gear installation

To install:

7. Rotate the gear input shaft from stop-to-stop, counting the total number of turns, then turn back exactly half-way, placing the gear on center.
8. Slide the steering gear input shaft shield on the steering gear input shaft.
9. Position the flex coupling on the steering gear input shaft, making sure the flat on the gear input shaft is facing straight up and aligns with the flat on the flex coupling. Install the steering gear to the side rail with bolts and washers and tighten to 54–62 ft. lbs. (73–84 Nm).
10. Place the Pitman arm on the sector shaft and install the attaching washer and nut. Align the 2 blocked teeth on the Pitman arm with the 4 missing teeth on the steering gear sector shaft. Tighten the nut to 170–230 ft. lbs. (230–310 Nm).
11. Install the flex coupling to the steering gear input shaft with the attaching bolt and tighten to 25–35 ft. lbs. (34–47 Nm). Snap the flex coupling shield to the steering gear input shield.
12. Check the system to ensure equal turns from center to each lock position.

Power Steering Gear

Adjustment

1. Raise and safely support the vehicle. Disconnect the Pitman arm from the sector shaft using puller T64P–3590–F or equivalent.
2. Disconnect the fluid return line at the reservoir and cap the reservoir return line tube. Place the end of the return line in a clean container and turn the steering wheel from stop to stop several times to empty the steering gear. Discard the fluid.
3. Turn the steering wheel to 45 degrees from the right stop.
4. Attach an inch pound torque wrench to steering wheel nut and record the torque required to rotate the shaft slowly approximately ⅛ turn toward center from the 45 degree position.
5. Turn the steering gear back to center and record the torque required to rotate the shaft back and forth across the center position.
6. If the vehicle has less than 5000 miles, resetting is required if total meshload over center is not 12–24 inch lbs. If the vehicle has more than 5000 miles or the sector shaft has been replaced, resetting is required if meshload over center is less than 10 inch lbs. greater than the torque 45 degrees from the right stop.
7. The set torque specification is measured rocking across center to a value of 9–13 inch lbs. greater than that measured 45 degress from the right stop.
8. If reset is required, loosen the locknut and turn the sector

BOLT

STEERING GEAR SHAFT SHIELD

STEERING GEAR SHAFT SHIELD

STEERING GEAR INTERMEDIATE SHAFT ASSEMBLY

STEERING GEAR

WASHER

BOLT

WASHER

NUT

Power steering gear installation

shaft adjusting screw until the reading is the specified value greater than the torque at 45 degrees from the stop.

9. Tighten the adjusting screw locknut and recheck. Install the Pitman arm and steering wheel cover.

10. Connect the fluid return line to the reservoir and refill the system with fluid. Bleed the system.

Removal and Installation

1. Disconnect the pressure and return lines from the steering gear. Plug the lines and the ports in the gear to prevent entry of dirt.

2. Remove the upper and lower steering gear shaft U-joint shield from the flex coupling. Disconnect the flex coupling at the steering gear by removing the bolt.

3. Raise the vehicle and support it safely. Remove the Pitman arm attaching nut and washer. Remove the Pitman arm from the sector shaft using tool T64P-3590-F or equivalent. Be careful not to damage the seals.

4. Support the steering gear and remove the attaching bolts. Work the steering gear free from the flex coupling and remove the gear from the vehicle.

To install:

5. Install the lower U-joint shield onto the steering gear lugs. Slide the upper U-joint shield into place on the steering shaft assembly. Turn the steering wheel so the spokes are in the horizontal position.

6. Center the steering gear input shaft with the indexing flat facing down.

7. Slide the steering gear input shaft into the flex coupling and into place on the frame side rail. Install the attaching bolts and tighten to 50–62 ft. lbs. (68–84 Nm). Tighten the flex coupling bolt to 26–34 ft. lbs. (34–47 Nm).

8. Make sure the wheels are in the straight ahead position, then install the Pitman arm on the sector shaft. Install the attaching washer and nut and tighten to 170–228 ft. lbs. (230–310 Nm).

9. Connect and tighten the pressure and return lines to the steering gear to 20–30 ft. lbs. (27–40 Nm). Snap the upper and lower steering gear shaft U-joint shields together.

10. Fill and bleed the power steering system.

Power Rack and Pinion

Adjustment

Service adjustments are not required on the power rack and pinion gear.

Removal and Installation

EXCEPT 4WD AEROSTAR

1. Place the steering system in the on center position as follows:
   a. Start the engine.
   b. Rotate the steering wheel from lock-to-lock and record the number of steering wheel rotations.
   c. Divide the number of steering wheel rotations by 2 to give the required number of turns to place the system in the on center position.
   d. From the lock position, rotate the steering wheel the number of turns determined in Step c to place the gear in the on center position. Make sure the wheels are in the straight ahead position.
   e. Stop the engine.

2. Disconnect the negative battery cable and turn the ignition key to the **ON** position. Raise and safely support the vehicle.

3. Disconnect the pressure and return lines from the steering gear valve housing. Plug the lines and ports in the gear valve housing to prevent the entry of dirt.

4. Remove the bolt retaining the lower intermediate steering column shaft to the steering gear. Disconnect the shaft from the gear.

5. Remove the cotter pins and nuts from the tie rod ends. Separate the tie rod ends from the spindle arms.

Power rack and pinion steering gear

6. Support the steering gear and remove the 2 nuts, bolts and washers retaining the gear to the crossmember. Remove the gear from the vehicle.

To install:

7. Position the steering gear on the crossmember. Install the retaining nuts, bolts and washers and tighten to 80–105 ft. lbs. (108–142 Nm).

8. Connect the pressure and return lines to the gear valve housing ports. Tighten the fittings to 10–15 ft. lbs. (15–20 Nm) on 1988–89 vehicles or 20–25 ft. lbs. (27–34 Nm) on 1990–92 vehicles.

NOTE: The fitting design allows the hoses to swivel when properly tightened. Do not attempt to eliminate looseness by overtightening as this can damage the fittings.

9. With the steering gear, steering wheel and front wheels in the on center position, attach the tie rod ends to the spindle arms. Install the nuts and tighten to 52–73 ft. lbs. (70–100 Nm). If required, advance the nuts to the next castellation and install new cotter pins.

10. Connect the steering column lower intermediate shaft to the gear. Install the bolt and tighten to 30–42 ft. lbs. (41–56 Nm).

11. Lower the vehicle and turn the ignition key to the **OFF** position. Connect the negative battery cable.

12. Fill and bleed the steering system. Check the toe setting and adjust, if necessary.

4WD AEROSTAR

1. Place the steering system in the on center position as follows:

   a. Start the engine.

   b. Rotate the steering wheel from lock-to-lock and record the number of steering wheel rotations.

   c. Divide the number of steering wheel rotations by 2 to give the required number of turns to place the system in the on center position.

   d. From the lock position, rotate the steering wheel the number of turns determined in Step c to place the gear in the on center position. Make sure the wheels are in the straight ahead position.

   e. Stop the engine.

2. Disconnect the negative battery cable and turn the ignition key to the **ON** position. Raise and safely support the vehicle and remove the wheel and tire assemblies.

3. Disconnect the pressure and return lines from the steering gear valve housing. Plug the lines and ports in the gear valve housing to prevent the entry of dirt.

4. Remove the bolt retaining the lower intermediate steering column shaft to the steering gear. Disconnect the shaft from the gear. Retain any dust seals which may be present.

5. Remove the cotter pins and nuts from the tie rod ends. Separate the tie rod ends from the spindle arms.

6. Remove the nut and washer with the insulator retaining the shock absorbers to the front crossmember brackets. Remove the bolts retaining the shock absorbers to the bottom of the lower control arms and remove the shock absorbers.

NOTE: Be careful during shock absorber removal as the shock absorber may extend somewhat due to gas pressure.

7. Remove the front stabilizer bar.

8. Install a suitable spring compressor through each coil spring to secure the spring and prevent extension when the control arm pivot bolts are removed.

9. Remove the lower control arm pivot bolts. Reposition and secure the lower control arms away from the brackets. Be careful not to deform the control arm pivot brackets.

10. Remove the 5 nuts from the forward edge of the crossmember lower plate assembly. Remove the nut from the left rear and the bolts from the center and right rear positions at the rear of the assembly. Remove the crossmember lower plate.

Bolt and retainer flag positioning—4WD Aerostar

11. Support the steering gear and remove the 2 bolts, spacers and bushings retaining the steering gear. Remove the gear from the vehicle.

To install:

12. Position the steering gear on the crossmember with the attaching bolts and tighten to 61–82 ft. lbs. (83–111 Nm). The large end of the spacer is installed facing the steering rack.

13. Install the crossmember lower plate with the nuts and bolt in the proper locations.

14. Position the lower control arms within the brackets and install the pivot bolts. Properly position the retaining flags.

15. Tighten all lower control arm pivot bolt nuts to 100–140 ft. lbs. (136–190 Nm).

16. Install the coil springs and remove the spring compressors.

17. Install the shock absorbers through the lower control arms and install the insulators, nuts and washers. Tighten the nuts to 25–35 ft. lbs. (34–47 Nm). Install the lower shock absorber retaining bolts and tighten to 16–25 ft. lbs. (22–33 Nm).

18. Install the front stabilizer bar.

19. Connect the pressure and return lines to the gear valve housing ports. Tighten the fittings to 10–15 ft. lbs. (15–20 Nm).

NOTE: The fitting design allows the hoses to swivel when properly tightened. Do not attempt to eliminate looseness by overtightening as this can damage the fittings.

20. With the steering gear, steering wheel and front wheels in the on center position, attach the tie rod ends to the spindle arms. Install the nuts and tighten to 52–73 ft. lbs. (70–100 Nm). If required, advance the nuts to the next castellation and install new cotter pins.

21. Position the intermediate shaft and any dust seals over the steering rack input shaft spline and make sure no rotation from the on center position has occurred. Install the bolt and tighten to 30–42 ft. lbs. (41–56 Nm).

22. Install the wheel and tire assemblies. Lower the vehicle and turn the ignition key to the **OFF** position. Connect the negative battery cable.

23. Fill and bleed the steering system. Check the toe setting and adjust, if necessary.

Power Steering Pump

Removal and Installation

1. Remove the power steering fluid from the pump reservoir by disconnecting the fluid return hose at the reservoir and draining the fluid into a container.

2. Remove the pressure hose from the pump. If equipped, disconnect the power steering pump pressure switch.

3. If equipped with 2.0L, 2.3L and 3.0L engines, loosen the alternator or idler pulley assembly pivot and adjustment bolts to slacken belt tension. Remove the drive belt.

4. If equipped with 2.9L engine, loosen the adjustment nut and the slider bolts on the pump support to slacken belt tension. Remove the drive belt.

5. If equipped with 4.0L engine, slacken belt tension by lifting the tensioner pulley in a counterclockwise direction. Remove the drive belt from under the tensioner pulley and slowly lower the pulley to stop. Remove the drive belt.

6. Remove the engine oil dipstick tube, if necessary. Remove the power steering pump bracket support brace, if equipped.

7. Install steering pump pulley removal tool T69L–10300–B on the pulley. Hold the pump and rotate the tool nut counterclockwise to remove the pulley. Do not apply in and out pressure on the pump shaft as pressure will damage the internal thrust areas.

8. Remove the bolts attaching the pump to the bracket and remove the pump.

To install:

9. Install the pump on the bracket. Install and tighten the at-

taching bolts to 30–45 ft. lbs. (41–61 Nm). If equipped with 4.0L engine, tighten to 35–47 ft. lbs. (47–64 Nm), position the support on the bracket and install and tighten the mounting bolts to 35–47 ft. lbs. (47–64 Nm).

10. Install steering pump pulley replacement tool T65P–3A733–C and install the pulley. Remove the tool.

NOTE: Fore and aft location of the pulley on the pump shaft is critical for correct belt alignment. Make sure the pull-off groove on the pulley is facing front and flush with the end of the shaft ± 0.010 in. (0.254mm).

11. Install the drive belt.

12. If equipped with 4.0L engine, position and rotate the drive belt on the engine. While lifting the tensioner pulley in a counterclockwise direction, slide the belt under the tensioner pulley and lower the pulley to the belt.

13. If equipped with 2.0L, 2.3L or 3.0L engine, position the idler pulley or alternator to set the belt tension. Tighten the idler pulley or alternator pivot and adjustment bolts to 40 ft. lbs. (55 Nm) on the 2.0L and 2.3L engines or 35–47 ft. lbs. (47–64 Nm) on the 3.0L engine.

14. If equipped with the 2.9L engine, tighten the pump support adjustment nut to set the belt tension, then tighten the slider bolts to 35–47 ft. lbs. (47–64 Nm).

15. Install the power steering pump bracket support brace and/or engine dipstick tube, if removed.

16. Install the pressure hose to the pump fitting. Connect the return hose to the pump and tighten the clamp. If equipped, connect the power steering pump pressure switch.

17. Fill and bleed the power steering system. Check for leaks.

Belt Adjustment

EXCEPT 4.0L ENGINE

1. Loosen the accessory adjustment and pivot bolts.

2. Position a suitable belt tension gauge mid-way between the pulleys on the longest accessible belt span.

3. On 2.0L and 2.3L engines, move the alternator or idler pulley to apply tension to the belt. On 2.9L and 3.0L engines, move the power steering pump to apply tension to the belt.

4. On 2.0L, 2.3L and 3.0L engines, the tension should be 150–190 lbs. for a new belt or 140–160 lbs. for a used belt. On 2.9L engine, the tension should be 120–160 lbs. for a new belt or 110–130 lbs. for a used belt.

5. Tighten the adjustment bolt and release pressure, then tighten the pivot bolt.

6. Recheck the belt tension and adjust, if necessary.

Power steering pump installation – 3.0L engine

4.0L ENGINE

Belt tension is maintained by an automatic tensioner. No adjustment is necessary.

System Bleeding

1. Fill the power steering fluid reservoir.
2. Disconnect the coil wire.
3. Crank the engine with the starter and continue adding fluid until the level remains constant. Do not prolong cranking as the battery may be drained and the starter damaged.
4. Rotate the steering wheel approximately 30 degrees each side of center while continuing to crank the engine.
5. Recheck the fluid level and fill, as required.
6. Reconnect the coil wire.
7. Start the engine and allow it to run for several minutes.
8. Rotate the steering wheel from stop to stop.
9. Shut off the engine and recheck the fluid level. Add fluid, as required.
10. If air is still trapped in the system, proceed as follows:
    a. Fabricate a purging tool.
    b. Make sure the reservoir fluid level is correct.
    c. Insert the rubber stopper end of the fabricated purging tool tightly into the filler tube.
    d. Connect a suitable length of hose to the purging tool. Connect the other end of the hose to an air conditioner vacuum pump or distributor machine. Do not use engine vacuum.
    e. Start the engine and let it idle for approximately 15 minutes. Turn the steering wheel 1 full cycle every 5 minutes but do not hit the stops. This will assist in removing trapped air.
    f. Stop the engine and disconnect the vacuum source. Remove the purging tool.
    g. Check the fluid level and install the filler tube dipstick.

Tie Rod Ends

Removal and Installation

1. Place the front wheels in the straight ahead position. Raise and safely support the vehicle.
2. Remove the cotter pin and nut from the tie rod end ball stud. Discard the cotter pin.
3. Separate the tie rod end from the spindle or drag link using puller tool T64P-3590-F or equivalent.
4. On Aerostar, hold the tie rod with a wrench and loosen the tie rod jam nut. Mark the position of the tie rod end on the tie

Fabricated power steering system air purging tool

rod threads, grip the tie rod with suitable pliers and remove the tie rod end from the tie rod.
5. On Bronco II, Explorer and Ranger, loosen the bolts on the tie rod adjusting sleeve. Count the number of turns required to remove the tie rod from the tie rod adjusting sleeve and remove the tie rod.

To install:
6. On Aerostar, thread the replacement tie rod end onto the tie rod to the same location as the 1 that was removed. Hold the tie rod end with a wrench and tighten the jam nut to 35–50 ft. lbs. (48–68 Nm).
7. On Bronco II, Explorer and Ranger, install the tie rod into the adjusting sleeve the same number of turns required to remove it. With the adjusting sleeve clamps pointed down, tighten the adjusting sleeve nuts to 30–42 ft. lbs. (40–57 Nm).
8. Install the tie rod ball stud into the spindle or drag link. Install the nut and tighten to 50–75 ft. lbs. (70–100 Nm). Install a new cotter pin.

NOTE: If the cotter pin cannot be installed because the hole in the ball stud does not align with a castellation on the nut, continue to tighten the nut to align them. Never loosen the nut to align the hole and castellation.

9. Lower the vehicle. Check the toe-in setting and adjust, if necessary.

BRAKES

For all brake system repair and service procedure not detailed below, please refer to "Brakes" in the Unit repair section.

Master Cylinder

Removal and Installation

1. Disconnect the negative battery cable. If equipped, push the brake pedal down to expel vacuum from the brake booster system.
2. Disconnect the fluid level indicator switch connector from the master cylinder.
3. If equipped with non-power brakes, disconnect the wires from the stop light switch inside the cab below the instrument panel. Remove the lock pin and spacers securing the master cylinder pushrod to the brake pedal assembly. Remove the stop light switch from the pedal.
4. Disconnect and plug the hydraulic lines at the master cylinder. Plug the master cylinder ports.

5. Remove the master cylinder-to-booster or master cylinder-to-dash panel retaining nuts and remove the master cylinder.

NOTE: On 1990–92 Aerostar, use care when removing the cartridge master cylinder so as not to scratch the exposed primary piston.

To install:
6. If equipped with power brakes, before installing the master cylinder on all except 1990–92 Aerostar, check the distance from the outer end of the vacuum booster assembly pushrod to the front face of the vacuum brake booster assembly. The distance should be 0.980–0.995 in. (24.89–25.27mm). Turn the pushrod adjusting screw in or out, as required, to obtain the proper length.
7. On 1990–92 Aerostar, make sure the interface seal is located in the annular groove in the cartridge master cylinder body where the cartridge master cylinder seals with the booster. Do not assemble the cartridge master cylinder to the booster without this square section interface seal.

8. If equipped with non-power brakes and the dash spacer was removed, coat the spacer with sealer and install on the dash panel.

9. Install the master cylinder with the attaching nuts. On 1990–92 Aerostar, be careful not to scratch the exposed primary piston and make sure the primary piston socket engages the booster pushrod before tightening. Tighten the nuts to 20 ft. lbs. (27 Nm). Connect the fluid level indicator switch.

10. If equipped with non-power brakes, secure the pushrod to the brake pedal assembly with the pin or shoulder bolt. Make sure the bushings and spacers are installed properly. Install the lockpin and connect the wires to the stop light switch.

11. Connect the brake lines to the master cylinder and fill the master cylinder fluid reservoir. Wrap a shop cloth around the tubing below the fitting to be bled to absorb escaping brake fluid.

12. Have an assistant push the brake pedal to the floor. Crack open the brake line fitting to expel air trapped in the master cylinder. Tighten the fitting, then let the brake pedal return. Repeat this procedure until all air is expelled.

13. Repeat Step 12 on the remaining brake line fitting(s).

14. Final tighten the brake line fittings. Bleed the brake system, as required. Check the master cylinder fluid level.

Combination Valve

Removal and Installation

1. Disconnect and plug the brake lines at the valve.
2. Remove the valve attaching bolt and remove the valve.
3. Installation is the reverse of the removal procedure. Bleed the brake system.

Power Brake Booster

Removal and Installation

1. Disconnect the negative battery cable. Support the master cylinder from the underside with a prop.

2. Disconnect the vacuum hose from the booster check valve and remove the check valve.

3. Remove the master cylinder-to-booster retaining nuts. Pull the master cylinder off the booster and leave it supported by the prop, out of the way enough to allow booster removal.

4. Working inside the cab, remove the hairpin retainer and slide the stoplight switch, valve rod, spacers and bushing off the brake pedal arm. Remove the nuts retaining the booster and remove the booster.

To install:

5. Mount the booster assembly on the engine side of the dash panel by sliding the bracket mounting bolts and valve operating rod in through the holes in the dash panel.

6. Working inside the cab, install the booster mounting nuts and tighten to 13–25 ft. lbs. (18–33 Nm).

7. Before installing the master cylinder on all except 1990–92 Aerostar, check the distance from the outer end of the vacuum booster assembly pushrod to the front face of the vacuum brake booster assembly. The distance should be 0.980–0.995 in. (24.89–25.27mm). Turn the pushrod adjusting screw in or out, as required, to obtain the proper length.

8. Install the master cylinder and tighten the retaining nuts to 20 ft. lbs. (27 Nm). Remove the prop from under the master cylinder.

9. Install the booster check valve and connect the vacuum hose. Check the hose routing to make sure the hose is not crimped.

10. Working inside the cab, install the bushing and position the switch on the end of the valve rod, then install the switch and rod on the pedal arm along with the spacers and hairpin retainer.

Power brake booster dimensions

Master cylinder installation – 1990–92 Aerostar

NOTE: Use only the factory supplied hairpin retainer. Do not substitute other types of retainers.

11. Connect the negative battery cable, start the engine and check brake operation.

Brake Caliper

Removal and Installation

1. Siphon part of the brake fluid out of the master cylinder to avoid overflow when the caliper piston is pressed into the caliper bore.

2. Raise the vehicle and support it safely. Remove the wheel and tire assembly.

3. Position an 8 in. C-clamp on the caliper and tighten the clamp to move the caliper piston into the bore approximately ⅛ in. Avoid clamp contact with the outer shoe spring clip. Remove the clamp.

NOTE: Do not pry the piston away from the rotor.

4. Clean excess dirt from the pin tab area.

5. Using a ¼ in. drive socket, ⅜ in. deep and a light hammer, tap the upper caliper pin towards the outboard side until the pin tabs pass the spindle face.

6. Compress the inboard pin tab, if equipped, with pliers and, with a hammer, drive the pin out until the tab slips into the spindle groove.

7. Place 1 end of a ⁷/₁₆ in. diameter punch against the end of the caliper pin and tap the pin out of the caliper slide groove.

8. Repeat Steps 5, 6 and 7 to remove the lower pin.

9. Disconnect and plug the brake hose at the caliper. Remove the caliper from the rotor.

To install:

10. Make sure the caliper mounting surfaces are free of dirt. Lubricate the caliper grooves with disc brake caliper grease and install the caliper.

11. From the caliper outboard side, position the pin between the caliper and spindle grooves. The pin must be positioned so the tabs will be installed against the spindle outer face.

12. Tap the pin on the outboard end with a hammer until the retention tabs on the sides of the pin contact the spindle face.

13. Repeat Steps 11 and 12 for the lower pin.

NOTE: During installation, do not allow the tabs of the caliper pin to be tapped too far into the spindle groove. If this happens, it will be necessary to tap the other end of the caliper pin until the tabs snap in place. The tabs on each end of the pin must be free to catch on the spindle face.

14. Connect the brake hose to the caliper. Bleed the brake system.

15. Install the wheel and tire assembly and lower the vehicle. Check the brake fluid level and check the brakes for proper operation.

Disc Brake Pads

Removal and Installation

1. Siphon part of the brake fluid out of the master cylinder to avoid overflow when the caliper piston is pressed into the caliper bore.

2. Raise the vehicle and support it safely. Remove the wheel and tire assembly.

3. Remove the brake caliper, but do not disconnect the brake hose. Secure the caliper aside with mechanics wire.

NOTE: Do not let the caliper hang by the brake hose.

4. Compress the anti-rattle clip and remove the inner brake pad from the caliper.

5. Press each ear of the outer brake pad away from the caliper and slide the torque buttons out of the retention notches.

To install:

6. Bottom out the caliper piston in the caliper bore using an 8 in. C-clamp and a worn out inner brake pad or block of wood to push against the piston. Do not attempt to bottom out the piston with the outer brake pad installed.

7. Place a new anti-rattle clip on the lower end of the inner brake pad. Make sure the tabs on the clip are properly positioned and the clip is fully seated.

8. Position the inner brake pad and anti-rattle clip in the pad abutment with the ant-rattle clip tab against the pad abutment and the loop-type spring away from the rotor. Compress the anti-rattle clip and slide the upper end of the pad in position.

9. Install the outer pad, making sure the torque buttons on the pad are seated solidly in the matching holes in the caliper.

10. Install the caliper on the spindle.

11. Install the wheel and tire assembly and lower the vehicle. Apply the brakes several times before moving the vehicle to seat the pads.

SPINDLE FLANK

AFTER INSTALLATION INSPECT TO INSURE THAT PIN TABS ARE FREE TO CONTACT SPINDLE FLANKS ON EACH END OF PIN

Correct caliper pin installation

INNER BRAKE PAD

ANTI-RATTLE CLIP

VIEW A

SPRING CLIP

TORQUE BUTTON

OUTER BRAKE PAD

TORQUE BUTTONS

WARNING: OUTER SHOE TORQUE BUTTONS MUST BE SOLIDLY SEATED IN CALIPER HOLES OR TEMPORARY LOSS OF BRAKES MAY OCCUR

VIEW A

Correct brake pad installation

12. Check the brake fluid level. Check the brakes for proper operation.

Brake Rotor

Removal and Installation

1. Raise and safely support the vehicle. Remove the wheel and tire assembly.
2. Remove the caliper and support it aside with mechanics wire. Do not let the caliper hang by the brake hose.
3. On 2WD vehicles, remove the dust cap, cotter pin, nut, washer and outer bearing and remove the rotor from the spindle.
4. On 4WD Aerostar, remove the retainers and remove the brake rotor. On all other 4WD vehicles, remove the locking hub and remove the brake rotor.
5. Inspect the rotor for scoring, wear and runout; machine or replace as necessary.
6. Install in the reverse order of removal. Adjust the wheel bearings.

Brake Drum

Removal and Installation

1. Raise and safely support the vehicle. Remove the wheel and tire assembly.
2. Remove the spring retaining nuts, if equipped, and remove the brake drum.

NOTE: If the brake drum will not come off, insert a narrow prybar through the brake adjusting hole in the backing plate and disengage the adjusting lever from the adjusting screw. While holding the adjusting lever away from the adjusting screw, loosen the adjusting screw with a brake adjusting tool.

3. Inspect the brake drum surface for wear, scoring and runout. Machine or replace, as necessary.
4. Installation is the reverse of the removal procedure.

Brake Shoes

Removal and Installation

1. Raise and safely support the vehicle. Remove the wheel and tire assembly and the brake drum.
2. Pull backward on the adjusting lever cable to disengage the adjusting lever from the adjusting screw. Move the outboard side of the adjusting screw upward and back off the pivot nut as far as it will go.
3. Pull the adjusting lever, cable and automatic adjuster spring down and toward the rear to unhook the pivot hook from the large hole in the secondary shoe web. Do not pry the pivot hook from the hole.
4. Remove the automatic adjuster spring and adjusting lever.
5. Remove the secondary shoe-to-anchor spring using a suitable brake spring removal/installation tool. Using the tool, remove the primary shoe-to-anchor spring and unhook the cable anchor. Remove the anchor pin plate, if equipped.
6. Remove the cable guide from the secondary shoe.
7. Remove the shoe hold-down springs, shoes, adjusting screw, pivot nut and socket. Note the color and position of each hold-down spring so they can be reassembled in the same position.
8. Remove the parking brake link and spring. Disconnect the parking brake cable from the parking brake lever.
9. Remove the secondary brake shoe. On 9 in. rear brakes, remove the parking brake lever from the shoe. On 10 in. rear brakes, remove the retainer clip and spring washer and remove the parking brake lever.

To install:

10. Clean the backing plate ledge pads and sand lightly. Apply a light coating of high temperature lithium grease to the points where the brake shoes touch the backing plate. Lubricate the adjusting cable eye and the anchor pin area.
11. Install the parking brake lever on the secondary shoe. On 10 in. brakes, secure with the spring washer and retaining clip.
12. Position the brake shoes on the backing plate and install the hold-down spring pins, springs and cups. Install the parking brake link, spring and washer. Connect the parking brake cable to the parking brake lever.
13. Install the anchor pin plate, if equipped, and place the cable anchor over the anchor pin with the crimped side toward the backing plate.
14. Install the primary shoe-to-anchor spring using the brake spring removal/installation tool.
15. Install the cable guide on the secondary shoe with the flanged hole fitted into the hole in the secondary shoe. Thread the cable around the cable guide groove.

NOTE: Make sure the cable is positioned in the groove and not between the guide and shoe web.

16. Install the secondary shoe-to-anchor (long) spring.

NOTE: Make sure the cable end is not cocked or binding on the anchor pin when installed. All parts should be flat on the anchor pin.

17. Apply high temperature lithium grease to the threads and the socket end of the adjusting screw. Turn the adjusting screw into the adjusting pivot nut to the end of the threads and then loosen, ½ turn.
18. Place the adjusting socket on the screw and install the assembly between the shoe ends with the adjusting screw nearest the secondary shoe.

NOTE: Be sure to install the adjusting screw on the same side of the vehicle from which it came. To prevent incorrect installation, the socket end of each adjusting screw is stamped with R or L, to indicate installation on the right or left side of the vehicle. The adjusting pivot nuts have lines machined around the body of the nut, 2 lines indicating the right side nut and 1 line indicating the left side nut.

19. Hook the cable hook into the hole in the adjusting lever from the outboard plate side. The adjusting levers are also stamped with an **R** or **L** to indicate right or left side installation.
20. Place the hooked end of the adjuster spring in the large hole in the primary shoe web and connect the loop end of the spring to the adjuster lever.
21. Pull the adjuster lever, cable and automatic adjuster spring down toward the rear to engage the pivot hook in the large hole in the secondary shoe web.
22. After installation, check the action of the adjuster by pulling the section of the cable between the cable guide and the adjusting lever toward the secondary shoe web far enough to lift the lever past a tooth on the adjusting screw wheel. The lever should snap into position behind the next tooth and releasing the cable should cause the adjuster spring to return the lever to its original position. This return action will turn the adjusting screw 1 tooth.
23. If pulling the cable does not produce the action described in Step 22 or if lever action is sluggish instead of positive and sharp, check the position of the lever on the adjusting toothed wheel. With the brake in a vertical position, anchor at the top, the lever should contact the adjusting wheel 1 tooth above the center line of the adjusting screw. If the contact point is below the center line, the lever will not lock on the adjusting screw wheel teeth and the screw will not turn as the lever is actuated by the cable.

24. To find the cause of the condition described in Step 23, proceed as follows:

a. Check the cable and fittings. The cable should completely fill or extend slightly beyond the crimped section of the fittings. If this does not happen, the cable assembly may be damaged and should be replaced.

b. Check the cable guide for damage. The cable groove should be parallel to the shoe web and the body of the guide should lie flat against the web. Replace the guide if it shows damage.

c. Check the pivot hook on the lever. The hook surfaces should be square with the body on the lever for proper pivoting. Repair the hook or replace the lever if the hook shows damage.

d. Be sure the adjusting screw socket is properly seated in the notch in the shoe web.

25. Adjust the brake shoes using either a brake adjustment gauge or manually with the drums installed.

26. If using a brake adjustment gauge, proceed as follows:

a. Measure the inside diameter of the brake drum with the gauge.

b. Reverse the tool and adjust the brake shoes until they touch the gauge. The gauge contact points on the shoes must be parallel to the vehicle with the center line through the center of the axle.

c. Install the drum and wheel and tire assembly. Lower the vehicle.

d. Apply the brakes sharply several times while driving the vehicle in reverse. Check brake operation by making several stops while driving forward.

27. If manually adjusting the brakes, proceed as follows:

a. Install the brake drum and wheel and tire assembly.

b. Remove the cover from the adjusting hole at the bottom of the backing plate and turn the adjusting screw, using a suitable brake adjusting tool, to expand the brake shoes until they drag against the brake drum.

c. When the shoes are against the drum, insert a narrow prybar through the brake adjusting hole and disengage the adjusting lever from the adjusting screw. While holding the adjusting lever away from the adjusting screw, loosen the adjusting screw with the brake adjusting tool, until the drum rotates freely without drag.

d. Install the adjusting hole cover and lower the vehicle.

e. Apply the brakes. If the pedal travels more than halfway to the floor, there is too much clearance between the brake shoes and drums. Repeat the adjustment procedure.

Wheel Cylinder

Removal and Installation

1. Raise and safely support the vehicle. Remove the wheel and tire assembly, brake drum and brake shoes.
2. Remove the cylinder to shoe connecting pins.
3. Disconnect the brake line from the wheel cylinder.
4. Remove the wheel cylinder retaining bolts and remove the cylinder from the brake backing plate.
5. Installation is the reverse of the removal procedure. Adjust the brakes and bleed the system.

Parking Brake Cable

Adjustment

AEROSTAR

The parking brake system is self adjusting and requires no adjustment.

Rear brake shoe assembly

BRONCO II, EXPLORER AND RANGER

NOTE: Adjust the drum brakes before adjusting the parking brake. The brake drums must be cold for correct adjustment.

Initial Adjustment

Use this procedure when a new tension limiter is installed.

1. Apply the parking brake pedal to the fully engaged position.
2. Raise and safely support the vehicle, as necessary. Hold the threaded rod end of the right brake cable to keep it from spinning and thread the equalizer nut 2½ in. up the rod.
3. Check to make sure the cinch strap has slipped and there are less than 1⅜ in. remaining.
4. Release the parking brake and check for proper operation.

Field Adjustment

Use this procedure to correct a slack system if a new tension limiter is not installed.

1. Apply the parking brake pedal to the fully engaged position.
2. Raise and safely support the vehicle, as necessary. Grip the threaded rod to keep it from spinning and tighten the equalizer nut 6 full turns past its original position on the threaded rod.
3. Attach a suitable cable tension gauge in front of the equalizer assembly on the front cable and measure the cable tension. The cable tension should be 400–600 lbs. with the parking brake pedal in the last detent position. If tension is low, repeat Steps 2 and 3.
4. Release parking brake and check for rear wheel drag. There should be no brake drag.

Removal and Installation

FRONT CABLE

Aerostar

1. Place the parking brake control in the released position.

Release the parking brake cable tension as follows:

a. Remove the boot cover from the parking brake control assembly.

b. Insert a steel pin through the pawl lockout pin hole. The pin must be inserted from the inboard side of the control (larger hole) at a slightly upward and forward angle then moved downward and rearward to displace the self adjusting pawl to be inserted through the other hole. This locks out the self adjusting pawl.

c. Raise and safely support the vehicle with an assistant inside the vehicle. Pull rearward on the equalizer 1–2½ in. to rotate the self-adjuster reel backward.

d. Have the assistant insert a steel pin through the self-adjusting spring lock-out holes in the lever and control assembly. This locks the ratchet wheel in the cable released position.

NOTE: Do not remove the steel lock pin until the cables are connected to the equalizer. Pin removal releases the tension in the ratchet wheel causing the spring to unwind and release tension, requiring assembly removal to reset spring tension.

2. Raise and safely support the vehicle. Disconnect the rear parking brake cables from the equalizer. Remove the equalizer from the front cable.

3. Remove the bolts retaining the cover to the underbody reinforcement bracket and remove the cover. It may be necessary to loosen fuel tank straps and partially lower the fuel tank to gain access to the cover.

4. Remove the cable anchor pin from the pivot hole in the control assembly ratchet plate. Guide the front cable from the control assembly.

5. Insert a ½ in. box end 12-point distributor lock bolt wrench over the front fitting of the front cable. Push the wrench onto the cable retainer fitting in the crossmember. Compress the retainer fingers and push the retainer rearward through the hole.

6. Insert a ½ in. box end 12-point wrench over the rear fitting of the front cable. Push the wrench onto the cable retainer fitting in the crossmember. Compress the retainer fingers and push the retainer forward through the hole.

7. Pull the cable ends through the crossmembers and remove the cable:

To install:

8. Feed the front cable through the holes in both crossmembers. Push the retainers through the holes so the fingers expand over each hole.

9. Route the front cable around the control assembly pulley and insert the cable anchor pin in the pivot hole in the ratchet plate.

10. Slide the return spring over the rear end of the front cable. Connect the equalizer to the front and rear cables.

11. Remove the lock pins from the control assembly to apply cable tension. Position the cover on the reinforcement bracket. Install and tighten the bolts after visually checking to be sure the front cable is attached to the control.

12. Position the boot over the control. Install and tighten the screws.

13. Apply and release the control several times. Make sure the parking brakes are applied, and released and not dragging. Both pins must be removed for proper adjustment.

Bronco II, Explorer and Ranger

1. Raise and safely support the vehicle.

2. Back off the equalizer nut and remove slug of front cable on Bronco II and Ranger or intermediate cable on Explorer from the tension limiter.

3. On Bronco II and Ranger, remove the parking brake cable from the cable bracket. On Explorer, remove the intermediate cable from the bracket and disconnect the intermediate cable from the front cable.

Releasing parking brake cable tension—Aerostar

Front parking brake cable removal—Aerostar

4. Lower the vehicle. Remove the forward ball end of the parking brake cable from the control assembly clevis.

5. Remove the cable from the control assembly.

6. Using a cord attached to the control lever end of the cable, remove the cable from the vehicle pulling it up into the passenger compartment.

To install:

7. Transfer the cord to the new cable. Position the cable in the vehicle, routing the cable through the dash panel. Remove the cord and secure the cable to the control.

8. Connect the forward ball end of the brake cable to the clevis of the control assembly. Raise and safely support the vehicle.

9. Route the cable through the bracket. On Explorer, connect the front cable to the intermediate cable.

10. Connect the slug of the front or intermediate cable cable to the tension limiter connector. Adjust the parking brake cable at the equalizer using initial adjustment or field adjustment, as necessary.

11. Rotate both wheels to make sure the parking brakes are not dragging.

REAR CABLE

1. Release parking brake control.

2. On Aerostar, to release tension on the rear cables, pull rearward on the equalizer assembly about 1–2 in. and place a clamp on the front cable behind the crossmember.

3. Raise and safely support the vehicle. Remove the wheel and tire assembly and the brake drum.

4. On Bronco II, Explorer and Ranger, remove the locknut on the threaded rod at the equalizer. Disconnect the rear parking brake cable from the equalizer.

5. Compress the prongs that retain the cable housing to the frame bracket or crossmember and pull out the cable and housing.

6. Working on the wheel side of the backing plate, compress the prongs on the cable retainer so they can pass through the hole in the brake backing plate.

7. Lift the cable out of the slot in the parking brake lever, attached to the secondary brake shoe, and remove the cable through the brake backing plate hole.

To install:

8. Route the cable through the hole in the backing plate. Insert the cable anchor behind the slot in the parking brake lever. Make sure the cable is securely engaged in the parking brake lever so the cable return spring is holding the cable in the parking brake lever.

9. Push the retainer through the hole in the backing plate so the retainer prongs engage the backing plate.

10. Properly route the cable and insert the front of the cable through the frame bracket or crossmember until the prongs expand. Connect the rear cables to the equalizer.

11. On Bronco II, Explorer and Ranger, rotate the equalizer 90 degrees and recouple the threaded rod to the equalizer.

12. On Aerostar, remove the clamping device the reapply tension.

13. Install the brake drum and wheel and tire assembly. Adjust the rear brakes.

14. On Bronco II, Explorer and Ranger, adjust the parking brake tension using the initial adjustment or the field adjustment procedure, as necessary.

15. Apply and release the parking brake control several times. Rotate both wheels to make sure the parking brakes are applied and released and not dragging.

Brake System Bleeding

1. Clean all dirt from the master cylinder filler cap.

2. If the master cylinder is known or suspected to have air in the bore, it must be bled before any of the wheel cylinders or calipers. Proceed as follows:

a. Loosen the brake line fitting approximately ¾ turn. Wrap a shop cloth around the tubing below the fitting to absorb escaping brake fluid.

b. Have an assistant depress the brake pedal slowly through it's full travel to force air trapped in the master cylinder to escape at the fitting.

c. Tighten the fitting and let the pedal return slowly to the fully released position. Do not release the pedal until the fitting is tightened or air will re-enter the master cylinder.

d. Wait 5 seconds and then repeat the operation until all air bubbles disappear.

e. Repeat Steps a–d on the remaining master cylinder brake line fitting(s).

3. On Bronco II, Explorer and Ranger equipped with Rear Anti-lock Brakes (RABS), proceed as follows:

a. Place a box wrench on the bleeder fitting On the RABS valve. Attach a rubber drain hose to the bleeder fitting, making sure the end of the hose fits snugly around the bleeder fitting.

b. Submerge the other end of the hose in a container partially filled with clean brake fluid.

c. Loosen the bleeder fitting approximately ¾ turn. Have an assistant slowly press the brake pedal all the way down. Close the bleeder fitting and let the pedal return to the fully released position.

d. Repeat this procedure until no more air bubbles come from the submerged end of the tube. Close the fitting and remove the hose.

4. On 1990–92 Aerostar with cartridge master cylinder, proceed as follows:

a. Place a box wrench on the bleeder fitting located on the front of the cartridge master cylinder. Attach a rubber drain hose to the bleeder fitting, making sure the end of the hose fits snugly around the bleeder fitting.

b. Submerge the other end of the hose in a container partially filled with clean brake fluid.

c. Loosen the bleeder fitting approximately ¾ turn. Have an assistant slowly press the brake pedal all the way down. Close the bleeder fitting and let the pedal return to the fully released position.

d. Repeat this procedure until no more air bubbles come from the submerged end of the tube. Close the fitting and remove the hose.

5. Continue to bleed the brake system by removing the rubber dust cap from the wheel cylinder bleeder fitting at the right-hand rear of the vehicle. Place a box wrench on the bleeder fitting and attach a rubber drain hose to the fitting. The end of the tube should fit snugly around the bleeder fitting. Submerge the other end of the tube in a container partially filled with clean brake fluid and loosen the fitting ¾ turn.

6. Have an assistant push the brake pedal down slowly through it's full travel. Close the bleeder fitting and allow the pedal to slowly return to it's full release position. Wait 5 seconds and repeat the procedure until no bubbles appear at the submerged end of the bleeder tube. Secure the bleeder fitting and remove the bleeder hose. Install the rubber dust cap on the bleeder fitting.

7. Repeat the procedure in Steps 5 and 6 and bleed the rest of the system in the following sequence: left rear, right front and left front.

8. Refill the master cylinder reservoir after each wheel cylinder or caliper has been bled and install the master cylinder cover and gasket. When brake bleeding is completed, the fluid level should be filled to the maximum level indicated on the reservoir.

9. Always make sure the disc brake pistons are returned to their normal positions by depressing the brake pedal several times until normal pedal travel is established. If the pedal feels spongy, repeat the bleeding procedure.

Anti-lock Brake System Service

Precautions
• Use caution when disassembling any hydraulic components as the system will contain residual pressure. Cover the area around the component to be removed with a shop cloth to catch any brake fluid spray. Do not allow brake fluid to come in contact with painted surfaces.

Rear Anti-lock Brake System (RABS) Module

Removal and Installation

AEROSTAR

1. Disconnect the negative battery cable.
2. Disconnect the wiring harness from the RABS connector by depressing the plastic tab on the connector and pulling the connector off.
3. Remove the 2 nuts that retain the RABS module to the instrument panel anti-shake brace and remove the module.
4. Installation is the reverse of the removal procedure. Check the system for proper operation.

BRONCO II, EXPLORER AND RANGER

1. Disconnect the negative battery cable.
2. Disconnect the wiring harness from the RABS module by depressing the plastic tab on the connector and pulling the connector off.
3. Remove the 2 screws that retain the module to the dash panel and remove the module.
4. Installation is the reverse of the removal procedure. Check the system for proper operation.

RABS Valve

Removal and Installation

1. Disconnect the negative battery cable.
2. Disconnect and plug the 2 brake lines connected to the RABS valve.
3. Disconnect the wiring harness from the valve harness.
4. Remove the screw retaining the valve and remove the valve.

To install:

5. Position the RABS valve and install the retaining screw. Tighten the retaining screw on Bronco II, Explorer and Ranger to 11–14 ft. lbs. (15–20 Nm) or on Aerostar to 30–40 inch lbs. (3.3–4.5 Nm).
6. Connect the brake valve wiring harness connector.

VIEW X   MAIN VIEW

TUBE TO MASTER CYLINDER   SCREW

TUBE TO REAR BRAKES

FRONT OF VEHICLE

RABS VALVE

VIEW X

RABS valve location—Aerostar

RABS DIAGNOSTIC CONNECTOR

RABS MODULE

RABS module location—Bronco II, Explorer and Ranger

RABS valve location—Bronco II, Explorer and Ranger

7. Connect the brake lines to the valve and tighten as follows:
   a. ½–20 threaded fittings—10–17 ft. lbs. (14–23 Nm).
   b. ⁷/₁₆–24 threaded fittings—10–15 ft. lbs. (14–20 Nm).
   c. ³/₈–24 threaded fittings—10–15 ft. lbs. (14–20 Nm).

NOTE: Do not overtighten the fittings.

8. Bleed the brake system. It is not necessary to energize the valve electrically to bleed the rear brakes.
9. Connect the negative battery cable.

RABS Sensor

Removal and Installation

1. Disconnect the negative battery cable.
2. Pull the wiring harness connector off.
3. Remove the sensor hold-down bolt and remove the sensor from the axle housing.

To install:

4. Clean the axle mounting surface. Use care to prevent dirt from entering the axle housing.
5. Inspect and clean the magnetized sensor pole piece to ensure that it is free from loose metal particles which could cause erratic system operation. Inspect the sensor O-ring for damage and replace, if necessary.
6. Lightly lubricate the sensor O-ring with motor oil, align the sensor bolt hole and install. Do not apply force to the plastic sensor connector. The sensor flange should slide to the mounting surface. This will insure the air gap setting is between 0.005–0.045 in. (0.127–1.14mm).
7. Install the hold down bolt and tighten to 25–30 ft. lbs. (34–40 Nm).
8. Inspect the blue sensor connector seal and replace if missing or damaged. Push the connector on the sensor.
9. Connect the negative battery cable.

RABS sensor installation

Excitor Ring

Inspection

1. Remove the RABS sensor.
2. View the excitor ring teeth through the sensor hole. Rotate the rear axle and check the excitor ring teeth for damage or breakage. Dented or broken teeth could cause the RABS system to function when not required.

Removal and Installation

To service the excitor ring, the differential case must be removed from the axle housing and the excitor ring pressed off the case.

NOTE: Upon removal, the excitor ring is to be discarded. It is not to be reused.

FRONT SUSPENSION

Shock Absorbers

Removal and Installation

1. Raise and safely support the vehicle. Remove the nut and the washer that attaches the shock absorber to the spring seat or coil spring upper bracket.

2. On Bronco II, Explorer and Ranger, remove the nut or nut and bolt that retains the shock absorber to the radius arm.

3. On Aerostar, remove the 2 bolts that retain the shock absorber to the bottom of the lower control arm.

3. Slightly compress the shock absorber, as necessary and remove it from the vehicle.

4. Installation is the reverse of the removal procedure. Tighten the upper retaining nut to 25–35 ft. lbs. (34–38 Nm). Tighten the lower retaining bolts or nuts on Aerostar to 16–24 ft. lbs. (22–33 Nm). Tighten the lower retaining nut or nut and bolt on Bronco II, Explorer and Ranger to 42–53 ft. lbs. (57–72 Nm).

Coil Springs

Removal and Installation

AEROSTAR

1. Place the steering wheel and the steering system in the on center position.

2. Raise and safely support the vehicle. Remove the wheel and tire assembly.

3. Disconnect the stabilizer bar link bolt from the lower arm.

4. Remove the 2 nuts or bolts attaching the shock absorber to the lower arm. Remove the upper nut and washer and remove the shock absorber.

5. Using spring compressor tool D78P–5310–A or equivalent, install 1 plate with the pivot ball seat facing downward into the coils of the spring. Rotate the plate so it is flush with the upper surface of the lower arm.

6. Install the other plate with the pivot ball seat facing upward into the coils of the spring. Insert the upper ball nut through the coils of the spring, so the nut rests in the upper plate.

7. Insert the compression rod into the opening in the lower arm, through the upper and lower plate and upper ball nut. Insert the securing pin through the upper ball nut and the compression rod.

8. With the upper ball nut secured, turn the upper plate so it walks up the coil until it contacts the upper spring seat, then back off ½ turn.

9. Install the lower ball nut and thrust washer on the compression rod and screw on the forcing nut. Tighten the forcing nut until the spring is compressed enough so it is free in its seat.

10. Loosen the lower arm pivot bolts. Remove the cotter pin and loosen but do not remove the nut attaching the lower ball joint to the spindle. Using puller tool T64P–3590–F or equivalent, loosen the lower ball joint. Remove the puller tool. Support the lower control arm with a jack and remove the ball joint nut. Lower the control arm and remove the spring.

11. If a new spring is to be installed, mark the position of the plates on the spring with chalk. Compress a new spring for installation and measure the compressed length of the old spring.

12. Loosen the forcing nut to relieve spring tension and remove the tools from the spring.

To install:

13. Assemble the spring compressor and locate in the same positions indicated in Step 11.

14. Before compressing the spring, make sure the upper ball nut securing pin is inserted properly.

15. Compress the coil spring until the spring height reaches the dimension obtained in Step 11.

16. Position the coil spring in the lower control arm. To complete installation, reverse the removal procedure. Tighten the lower ball joint nut to 80–120 ft. lbs. (108–163 Nm).

BRONCO II, EXPLORER AND RANGER

1. Raise and safely support the vehicle. Place a jack under the axle.

FRONT OF VEHICLE

COIL SPRINGS

STEERING LINKAGE

CLAMPS

Front suspension–4WD Bronco II, Explorer and Ranger

FRONT OF VEHICLE

STEERING GEAR ASSEMBLY

UPPER A FRAME ARM

FRONT WHEEL SPINDLE ASSEMBLY

LOWER A FRAME ARM

TIE ROD END ASSEMBLY

JAM NUT

STABILIZER BAR LINK ASSEMBLY

TIE ROD

STABILIZER BAR

Front suspension—2WD Aerostar

AXLE PIVOT BRACKET

TWIN I-BEAM AXLES

FRONT OF VEHICLE

COIL SPRING

SHOCK ABSORBER

RADIUS ARM

SPINDLE

BALL JOINTS

TIE ROD END

ADJUSTING SLEEVE CLAMPS

STEERING LINKAGE

STABILIZER BAR

Front suspension—2WD Bronco II, Explorer and Ranger

2. Remove the nut or nut and bolt attaching the shock absorber to the radius arm.

3. Remove the nut securing the spring to the axle and remove the retainer.

4. Slowly lower the axle to relieve the spring tension. Remove the spring by rotating the upper coil out of the tabs in the upper spring seat.

To install:

5. Install the top of the spring in the upper seat, rotating into position.

6. Raise the axle until the spring is seated in the lower spring seat. Install the lower retainer and tighten the nut to 70–100 ft. lbs. (95–136 Nm).

7. Connect the shock absorber to the radius arm and lower the vehicle.

Upper Ball Joints

Inspection

NOTE: Always check and adjust the wheel bearings before ball joint inspection.

1. Raise and safely support the vehicle.

2. On Aerostar, place a jack under the lower control arm and raise to slightly compress the spring. On Bronco II, Explorer and Ranger, place a jack under the axle beneath the coil spring.

3. Grasp the upper edge of the tire and move the wheel in and out. A $1/32$ in. or greater movement between the upper spindle arm and the upper control arm or upper part of the axle jaw indicates that the upper ball joint must be replaced.

Removal and Installation

AEROSTAR

If upper ball joint replacement is necessary, the entire upper control arm must be replaced.

2WD BRONCO II, EXPLORER AND RANGER

1988

1. Raise and safely support the vehicle. Remove the wheel and tire assembly.

2. Remove the brake caliper and support it aside with mechanics wire. Do not let the caliper hang by the brake hose.

3. Remove the dust cap, cotter pin, nut retainer, washer and outer bearing and remove the brake rotor from the spindle. Remove the brake dust shield.

4. Disconnect the steering linkage from the spindle and spindle arm by removing the cotter pin and nut. Remove the tie rod end from the spindle arm.

5. Remove the nut from the upper ball joint stud. Remove the cotter pin from the lower ball joint stud and loosen but do not remove the lower ball joint nut to the end of the stud.

6. Strike the inside of the spindle near the upper and lower ball joints to break the spindle loose from the ball joint studs. Remove the lower ball joint nut and remove the spindle.

7. Remove the snapring from the upper ball joint. Assemble C-frame tool T74P-4635-C and receiving cup tool D81T-3010-A or equivalent and press the upper ball joint from the axle.

NOTE: Do not heat the ball joint or axle to aid in removal.

To install:

8. Assemble the C-frame tool along with receiver and installation cups D81T-3010-A5, D81T-3010-A1 and D81T-3010-A4 or equivalents and press in the upper ball joint.

NOTE: Do not heat the ball joint or axle to aid in installation.

9. Install the snapring onto the upper ball joint.

10. If removed, install the camber adjuster in the spindle up-per ball joint hole. Apply Loctite® 242 or equivalent, to the up-per and lower ball joint stud threads.

11. Place the spindle over the ball joints. Install the lower ball joint stud nut and partially tighten to 35 ft. lbs. (47 Nm).

12. Install the upper ball joint stud nut and tighten to 85–110 ft. lbs. (116–149 Nm). Finish tightening the lower ball joint stud nut to 104–146 ft. lbs. (141–197 Nm). Advance the nut to the next castellation and install the cotter pin.

13. Install the remaining components in the reverse order of their removal. Check and adjust the toe setting.

1989–92

1. Raise and safely support the vehicle. Remove the wheel and tire assembly.

2. Remove the brake caliper and support it aside with mechanics wire. Do not let the caliper hang by the brake hose.

3. Remove the dust cap, cotter pin, nut retainer, washer and outer bearing and remove the brake rotor from the spindle. Remove the brake dust shield.

4. Disconnect the steering linkage from the spindle and spindle arm by removing the cotter pin and nut. Remove the tie rod end from the spindle arm.

5. Remove the cotter pin and nut from the lower ball joint stud. Remove the axle clamp bolt from the axle.

6. Remove the camber adjuster from the upper ball joint stud and axle beam.

7. Strike the inside area of the axle to pop the lower ball joint loose from the axle beam. Remove the spindle and ball joint assembly from the axle.

NOTE: Do not use a pickle fork to separate the ball joint from the axle as this will damage the seal and ball joint socket.

To install:

8. Install the spindle assembly in a vise and remove the snapring from the lower ball joint. Remove the lower ball joint from the spindle using C-frame T74P-4635-C or equivalent and a suitable receiver cup to press the ball joint from the spindle.

NOTE: The lower ball joint must be removed first.

9. Repeat the procedure in Step 8 to remove the upper ball joint.

NOTE: Do not heat the ball joints or the spindle to aid in removal.

To install:

10. Assemble the C-frame and receiver cup and press in the upper ball joint.

11. Repeat the procedure in Step 10 to install the lower ball joint.

NOTE: Do not heat the ball joints or axle to aid in installation.

12. Install the snapring onto the ball joint.

13. Place the spindle and ball joints into the axle. Install the camber adjuster in the upper spindle over the ball joint stud making sure it is properly aligned.

14. Tighten the lower ball joint stud nut to 104–146 ft. lbs. (141–198 Nm). Continue tightening the castellated nut until it lines up with the hole in the stud, then install the cotter pin.

15. Install the clamp bolt into the axle boss and tighten to 48–65 ft. lbs. (65–88 Nm).

16. Install the remaining components in the reverse order of their removal.

4WD BRONCO II, EXPLORER AND RANGER

1. Raise and safely support the vehicle. Remove the front wheel and tire assemblies.

2. Remove the disc brake caliper and wire it to the frame. Do not let the caliper hang by the brake hose.

3. Remove the hub locks, wheel bearings and locknuts.

4. Remove the hub, rotor and outer wheel bearing.

5. Remove the nuts retaining the spindle to the steering knuckle. Tap the spindle with a plastic hammer to jar the spindle from the knuckle. Remove the splash shield.

6. On the left side of the vehicle, remove the shaft and joint assembly by pulling the assembly out of the carrier. On the right side of the carrier, remove and discard the clamp from the shaft and joint assembly and the stub shaft. Pull the shaft and joint assembly from the splines of the stub shaft.

7. Remove the cotter pin from the tie rod nut and then remove the nut. Tap on the tie rod stud to free it from the steering arm.

8. Remove the upper ball joint snapring and remove the upper ball joint pinch bolt. Loosen the lower ball joint nut to the end of the stud.

9. Strike the inside of the knuckle near the upper and lower ball joints to break the knuckle loose from the ball joint studs.

10. Remove the camber adjuster sleeve. Note the position of the slot in the camber adjuster so it can be reinstalled in the same position during assembly.

11. Remove the lower ball joint nut. Place the knuckle in a vise and remove the snapring from the bottom ball joint socket, if equipped.

12. Assemble C-frame T74P-4635-C and ball joint remover T83T-3050-A or equivalents on the lower ball joint. Turn the forcing screw clockwise until the lower ball joint is removed from the steering knuckle.

13. Assemble the C-frame and ball joint remover on the upper ball joint and remove in the same manner.

NOTE: Always remove the lower ball joint first.

To install:

14. Clean the steering knuckle bore and insert the lower ball joint in the knuckle as straight as possible.

15. Assemble C-frame T74P-4635-C, ball joint installer T83T-3050-A and receiver cup T80T-3010-A3 or equivalents to install the lower ball joint. Turn the forcing screw clockwise until the lower ball joint is firmly seated. Install the snapring on the lower ball joint.

NOTE: The lower ball joint must always be installed first.

16. Assemble the C-frame, ball joint installer and receiver cup to install the upper ball joint. Turn the forcing screw clockwise until the ball joint is firmly seated.

17. Install the camber adjuster into the support arm, making sure the slot is in the original position.

NOTE: The torque sequence in Steps 18 and 19 must be followed exactly when securing the knuckle. Excessive knuckle turning effort may result in reduced steering returnability if this procedure is not followed.

18. Install a new nut on the bottom ball joint stud. Tighten the nut to 90 ft. lbs. (122 Nm) minimum, then tighten to align the next slot in the nut with the hole in the stud. Install a new cotter pin.

19. Install the snapring on the upper ball joint stud. Install the upper ball joint pinch bolt and tighten to 48–65 ft. lbs. (65–88 Nm).

NOTE: The camber adjuster will seat itself into the knuckle at a predetermined position during the tightening sequence. Do not attempt to adjust this position.

20. On the right side of the carrier, install the rubber boot and new keystone clamps on the stub shaft slip yoke. Slide the right shaft and joint assembly into the slip yoke making sure the splines are fully engaged. Slide the boot over the assembly and crimp the keystone clamp using suitable pliers.

NOTE: The Dana model 28 axle has phased splines; there is only 1 way to assemble the right shaft and joint assembly into the slip yoke. The Dana model 35 axle does not have a blind spline, therefore pay special attention to make sure the yoke ears are in phase (in line) during assembly.

21. On the left side of the carrier, slide the shaft and joint assembly through the knuckle and engage the splines on the shaft in the carrier.

22. Install the splash shield and spindle onto the steering knuckle. Install and tighten the spindle nuts to 45 ft. lbs. (61 Nm).

23. Install the rotor on the spindle and install the outer wheel bearing in the race.

24. Install the wheel bearing, locknut, thrust bearing, snapring and locking hubs.

25. Install the caaliper and the wheel and tire assemblies. Lower the vehicle.

Lower Ball Joints

Inspection

NOTE: Always check and adjust the wheel bearings before ball joint inspection.

1. Raise and safely support the vehicle.

2. On Aerostar, place a jack under the lower control arm and raise to slightly compress the spring. On Bronco II, Explorer and Ranger, place a jack under the axle beneath the coil spring.

3. Grasp the lower edge of the tire and move the wheel in and out. A $1/32$ in. or greater movement between the lower control arm or lower axle and the spindle indicates that the lower ball joint must be replaced.

Removal and Installation

AEROSTAR

If lower ball joint replacement is necessary, the entire lower control arm must be replaced.

2WD BRONCO II, EXPLORER AND RANGER

1988

1. Raise and safely support the vehicle. Remove the wheel and tire assembly.

2. Remove the brake caliper and support it aside with mechanics wire. Do not let the caliper hang by the brake hose.

3. Remove the dust cap, cotter pin, nut retainer, washer and outer bearing and remove the brake rotor from the spindle. Remove the brake dust shield.

4. Disconnect the steering linkage from the spindle and spindle arm by removing the cotter pin and nut. Remove the tie rod end from the spindle arm.

5. Remove the nut from the upper ball joint stud. Remove the cotter pin from the lower ball joint stud and loosen but do not remove the lower ball joint nut to the end of the stud.

6. Strike the inside of the spindle near the upper and lower ball joints to break the spindle loose from the ball joint studs. Remove the lower ball joint nut and remove the spindle.

7. Remove the snapring from the upper ball joint. Assemble C-frame tool T74P-4635-C and receiving cup tool D81T-3010-A or equivalent and press the upper ball joint from the axle.

8. Repeat the procedure in Step 7 to remove the lower ball joint.

NOTE: Always remove the upper ball joint first. Do not heat the ball joint or axle to aid in removal.

To install:

9. Assemble the C-frame tool along with receiver and installation cups D81T-3010-A5, D81T-3010-A1 and D81T-3010-A4 or equivalents and press in the lower ball joint.

10. Repeat the procedure in Step 9 to install the upper ball joint.

NOTE: The lower ball joint must be installed first. Do not heat the ball joint or axle to aid in installation.

11. Install the snapring onto the ball joint.
12. If removed, install the camber adjuster in the spindle upper ball joint hole. Apply Loctite® 242 or equivalent, to the upper and lower ball joint stud threads.
13. Place the spindle over the ball joints. Install the lower ball joint stud nut and partially tighten to 35 ft. lbs. (47 Nm).
14. Install the upper ball joint stud nut and tighten to 85–110 ft. lbs. (116–149 Nm). Finish tightening the lower ball joint stud nut to 104–146 ft. lbs. (141–197 Nm). Advance the nut to the next castellation and install the cotter pin.
15. Install the remaining components in the reverse order of their removal. Check and adjust the toe setting.

1989–92

1. Raise and safely support the vehicle. Remove the wheel and tire assembly.
2. Remove the brake caliper and support it aside with mechanics wire. Do not let the caliper hang by the brake hose.
3. Remove the dust cap, cotter pin, nut retainer, washer and outer bearing and remove the brake rotor from the spindle. Remove the brake dust shield.
4. Disconnect the steering linkage from the spindle and spindle arm by removing the cotter pin and nut. Remove the tie rod end from the spindle arm.
5. Remove the cotter pin and nut from the lower ball joint stud. Remove the axle clamp bolt from the axle.
6. Remove the camber adjuster from the upper ball joint stud and axle beam.
7. Strike the inside area of the axle to pop the lower ball joint loose from the axle beam. Remove the spindle and ball joint assembly from the axle.

NOTE: Do not use a pickle fork to separate the ball joint from the axle as this will damage the seal and ball joint socket.

To install:

8. Install the spindle assembly in a vise and remove the snapring from the lower ball joint. Remove the lower ball joint from the spindle using C-frame T74P-4635-C or equivalent and a suitable receiver cup to press the ball joint from the spindle.

NOTE: Do not heat the ball joint or the spindle to aid in removal.

To install:

9. Assemble the C-frame and receiver cup and press in the lower ball joint.

NOTE: Do not heat the ball joint or axle to aid in installation.

10. Install the snapring onto the ball joint.
11. Place the spindle and ball joints into the axle. Install the camber adjuster in the upper spindle over the ball joint stud making sure it is properly aligned.
12. Tighten the lower ball joint stud nut to 104–146 ft. lbs. (141–198 Nm). Continue tightening the castellated nut until it lines up with the hole in the stud, then install the cotter pin.
13. Install the clamp bolt into the axle boss and tighten to 48–65 ft. lbs. (65–88 Nm).
14. Install the remaining components in the reverse order of their removal.

4WD BRONCO II, EXPLORER AND RANGER

1. Raise and safely support the vehicle. Remove the front wheel and tire assemblies.
2. Remove the disc brake caliper and wire it to the frame. Do not let the caliper hang by the brake hose.

3. Remove the hub locks, wheel bearings and locknuts.
4. Remove the hub, rotor and outer wheel bearing.
5. Remove the nuts retaining the spindle to the steering knuckle. Tap the spindle with a plastic hammer to jar the spindle from the knuckle. Remove the splash shield.
6. On the left side of the vehicle, remove the shaft and joint assembly by pulling the assembly out of the carrier. On the right side of the carrier, remove and discard the clamp from the shaft and joint assembly and the stub shaft. Pull the shaft and joint assembly from the splines of the stub shaft.
7. Remove the cotter pin from the tie rod nut and then remove the nut. Tap on the tie rod stud to free it from the steering arm.
8. Remove the upper ball joint snapring and remove the upper ball joint pinch bolt. Loosen the lower ball joint nut to the end of the stud.
9. Strike the inside of the knuckle near the upper and lower ball joints to break the knuckle loose from the ball joint studs.
10. Remove the camber adjuster sleeve. Note the position of the slot in the camber adjuster so it can be reinstalled in the same position during assembly.
11. Remove the lower ball joint nut. Place the knuckle in a vise and remove the snapring from the bottom ball joint socket, if equipped.
12. Assemble C-frame T74P-4635-C and ball joint remover T83T-3050-A or equivalents on the lower ball joint. Turn the forcing screw clockwise until the lower ball joint is removed from the steering knuckle.

To install:

13. Clean the steering knuckle bore and insert the lower ball joint in the knuckle as straight as possible.
14. Assemble C-frame T74P-4635-C, ball joint installer T83T-3050-A and receiver cup T80T-3010-A3 or equivalents to install the lower ball joint. Turn the forcing screw clockwise until the lower ball joint is firmly seated. Install the snapring on the lower ball joint.
15. Install the camber adjuster into the support arm, making sure the slot is in the original position.

NOTE: The torque sequence in Steps 16 and 17 must be followed exactly when securing the knuckle. Excessive knuckle turning effort may result in reduced steering returnability if this procedure is not followed.

16. Install a new nut on the bottom ball joint stud. Tighten the nut to 90 ft. lbs. (122 Nm) minimum, then tighten to align the next slot in the nut with the hole in the stud. Install a new cotter pin.
17. Install the snapring on the upper ball joint stud. Install the upper ball joint pinch bolt and tighten to 48–65 ft. lbs. (65–88 Nm).

NOTE: The camber adjuster will seat itself into the knuckle at a predetermined position during the tightening sequence. Do not attempt to adjust this position.

18. On the right side of the carrier, install the rubber boot and new keystone clamps on the stub shaft slip yoke. Slide the right shaft and joint assembly into the slip yoke making sure the splines are fully engaged. Slide the boot over the assembly and crimp the keystone clamp using suitable pliers.

NOTE: The Dana model 28 axle has phased splines; there is only 1 way to assemble the right shaft and joint assembly into the slip yoke. The Dana model 35 axle does not have a blind spline, therefore pay special attention to make sure the yoke ears are in phase (in line) during assembly.

19. On the left side of the carrier, slide the shaft and joint assembly through the knuckle and engage the splines on the shaft in the carrier.

20. Install the splash shield and spindle onto the steering knuckle. Install and tighten the spindle nuts to 45 ft. lbs. (61 Nm).

21. Install the rotor on the spindle and install the outer wheel bearing in the race.

22. Install the wheel bearing, locknut, thrust bearing, snapring and locking hubs.

23. Install the caaliper and the wheel and tire assemblies. Lower the vehicle.

Upper Control Arms

Removal and Installation

AEROSTAR

1. Place the steering wheel and the steering system in the on center position.

2. Raise the vehicle and support it safely under the body rails.

NOTE: Only remove and install 1 upper control arm at a time. Never service both sides at the same time.

3. Remove the spindle or steering knuckle, as required.

4. Remove the bolt retaining the bolt retainer plate and remove the plate.

5. Mark the position of the control arm mounting brackets on the flat plate.

6. Remove the bolt and washer retaining the front mounting bracket to the flat plate.

7. From under the rail, remove the 3 nuts from the bolts retaining the 2 upper control arm mounting brackets to the body rail.

8. Remove the 3 long bolts retaining the mounting brackets to the body rail by rotating the upper control arm out of position in order to remove the bolts.

9. Remove the upper control arm, upper ball joint and mounting bracket assembly and flat plate from the vehicle. If required, remove the damper assembly from the upper control arm.

To install:

10. If removed, install the damper assembly and tighten the retaining bolts to 22–29 ft. lbs. (30–39 Nm).

11. Place the flat plate for the mounting brackets in position on the body rail. Install the bolt and tighten to 10–14 ft. lbs. (14–18 Nm).

12. Place the mounting brackets and upper control arm assembly in position on the flat plate.

13. Install the 3 long bolts and washers retaining the mounting brackets to the body rail. Rotate or rock the upper control arm and mounting bracket assembly until the bolt heads rest against the mounting bracket and the studs extend through the body rail.

14. Move the mounting brackets into the position marked on the flat plate during removal.

15. Install and tighten the nuts retaining the mounting bracket bolts to the body rail to 145–195 ft. lbs. (196–264 Nm). Make sure the mounting brackets do not move from the marked position on the flat plate.

NOTE: The torque setting for the mounting bracket-to-body rail nuts and bolts is critical. They must be tightened to the specified torque.

16. Install and tighten the bolt retaining the front mounting bracket to the flat plate to 35–47 ft. lbs. (47–64 Nm).

17. Place the bolt retaining the plate in position on the mounting bracket and flat plate assembly. Install and tighten the bolt to 10–14 ft. lbs. (14–18 Nm).

18. Install the spindle or steering knuckle, as required.

19. Lower the vehicle and check the front end alignment.

Upper control arm installation—Aerostar

Lower Control Arms

Removal and Installation
AEROSTAR

1. Place the steering and the steering system in the on center position.
2. Raise the vehicle and support it safely under the frame.
3. Remove the coil spring.
4. Remove the bolts and nuts retaining the control arm to the No. 1 crossmember. Remove the lower control arm.
To install:
5. Position the control arm in the No. 1 crossmember and install the mounting bolts. Install the nuts and tighten until snug. Do not tighten to the specified torque at this time.
6. Install the coil spring.
7. With the vehicle in the normal ride position, tighten the lower control arm retaining nuts and bolts to 100–140 ft. lbs. (136–190 Nm).

Stabilizer Bar

Removal and Installation
AEROSTAR

1. Raise and safely support the vehicle. Remove the nuts retaining the stabilizer bar to the lower control arm link.
2. Remove the insulators and disconnect the bar from the links. If required, remove the nuts retaining the links to the lower control arm. Remove the insulators and remove the links.
3. Remove the bolts retaining the bar mounting bracket to the frame and remove the stabilizer bar. If required, remove the insulators from the stabilizer bar.
4. Installation is the reverse of the removal procedure. Tighten the mounting bracket bolts to 16–24 ft. lbs. (22–33 Nm). Tighten the link nuts to 9–12 ft. lbs. (12–16 Nm).

2WD BRONCO II AND EXPLORER

1. Raise and safely support the vehicle.
2. Remove the nut and washer and disconnect the stabilizer link assembly from the front I-beam axle.
3. Remove the mounting bolts and remove the stabilizer bar retainers from the stabilizer bar assembly. Remove the stabilizer bar.
4. Installation is the reverse of the removal procedure. Tighten the retainer bolts to 35–50 ft. lbs. (47–68 Nm). Tighten the stabilizer bar link nuts to 30–44 ft. lbs. (40–60 Nm).

2WD RANGER

1. Raise and safely support the vehicle.
2. On 1988–89 vehicles, remove the nuts and U-bolts retaining the lower shock bracket/stabilizer bar bushing to the radius arm.
3. On 1990–92 vehicles, remove the nuts and bolts retaining the stabilizer bar to the end links.
4. Remove the retainers and remove the stabilizer bar and bushings.
5. Installation is the reverse of the removal procedure. Tighten the retainer bolts to 35–50 ft. lbs. (47–68 Nm). On 1988–89 vehicles, tighten the U-bolt nuts to 48–68 ft. lbs. (66–92 Nm). On 1990–92 vehicles, tighten the end link nuts to 30–44 ft. lbs. (40–60 Nm).

4WD BRONCO II, EXPLORER AND RANGER

1. Raise and safely support the vehicle.
2. Remove the bolts and retainers from the center and right end of the stabilizer bar.
3. Remove the nut, bolt and washer retaining the stabilizer bar to the stabilizer link.
4. Remove the stabilizer bar and bushings.
5. Installation is the reverse of the removal procedure. Tight-

Lower control arm installation—Aerostar

en the retainer bolts to 35–50 ft. lbs. (48–68 Nm). Tighten the stabilizer bar link nut to 30–44 ft. lbs. (40–60 Nm).

I-Beam Axle

Removal and Installation

1. Raise and safely support the vehicle. Remove the front wheel spindle, the front spring and the stabilizer bar, if equipped.
2. Remove the spring lower seat from the radius arm and then remove the bolt and nut that attaches the stabilizer bar bracket, if equipped, and radius arm to the front axle.
3. Remove the axle-to-frame pivot bracket bolt and nut.
To install:
4. Position the axle to the frame pivot bracket and install the bolt and nut finger tight.
5. Position the opposite end of the of the axle to the radius arm, install the attaching bolt from underneath through the bracket, the radius arm and the axle. Install the nut and tighten to 191–220 ft. lbs. (258–298 Nm).
6. Install the spring lower seat on the radius arm so the hole in the seat indexes over the arm-to-axle bolt. Install the front spring.
7. Install the front wheel spindle and stabilizer bar, if equipped.
8. Lower the vehicle and with the weight on the suspension, tighten the axle-to-frame pivot bracket bolts to 120–150 ft. lbs. (163–203 Nm).

Front Wheel Bearings

Adjustment

1. Raise the vehicle and support it safely.
2. Remove the wheel cover and the grease cap from the hub. Remove the cotter pin and the retainer. Discard the cotter pin.
3. Loosen the adjusting nut 3 turns.
4. Obtain running clearance between the brake rotor and disc brake pads by rocking the entire wheel and tire assembly in and

out several times to push the caliper and brake pads away from the rotor.

NOTE: Do not pry on the caliper piston to obtain clearance.

5. While rotating the wheel, tighten the adjusting nut to 17–25 ft. lbs. (23–34 Nm) to seat the bearings.

6. Back off the adjusting nut ½ turn. Retighten the nut to 18–20 inch lbs. (2.0–2.3 Nm).

7. Install the retainer on the adjusting nut so the castellations line up with the hole in the spindle without moving the nut. Install a new cotter pin.

8. Check the front wheel rotation. If the wheel rotates properly, reinstall the grease cap and the wheel cover. If rotation is noisy or rough, remove, inspect and lubricate the bearings and bearing races.

9. Before driving the vehicle, pump the brake pedal several times to restore normal brake travel.

Removal and Installation

1. Raise and safely support the vehicle. Remove the wheel and tire assembly.

2. Remove the brake caliper and support it with mechanics wire. Do not let the caliper hang by the brake hose.

3. Remove the grease cap, cotter pin, retainer, adjusting nut and washer. Discard the cotter pin.

4. Remove the outer bearing and pull the hub and rotor off the spindle. Remove the grease seal using a seal removal tool. Discard the grease seal.

5. Remove the inner bearing from the hub. Remove all traces of old lubricant from the bearings, hub and spindle with solvent and dry thoroughly.

6. Inspect the bearings and bearing races for scratches, pits or cracks. If the bearings and/or races are worn or damaged, remove the races with a brass drift.

To install:

7. If the bearing races were removed, Install new races in the hub with suitable installation tools. Make sure the races are properly seated.

8. Using a bearing packer, pack the bearings with high-temperature wheel bearing grease. If a packer is not available, work as much grease as possible between the rollers and cages by hand.

9. Place a small amount of grease within the hub and grease the races. Install the inner bearing. Install a new wheel seal using a seal installer. Apply grease to the lips of the seal.

10. Install the hub and rotor assembly on the spindle. Install the outer bearing, washer and adjusting nut. Adjust the bearings.

11. Install the retainer, a new cotter pin and the grease cap.

12. Install the caliper and the wheel and tire assembly. Lower the vehicle.

13. Before driving the vehicle, pump the brake pedal several times to restore normal brake travel.

REAR SUSPENSION

Shock Absorber

Removal and Installation

1. Raise and safely support the vehicle.

2. Place a jack under the rear axle and raise slightly to take the load off the shock absorbers.

3. Remove the shock absorber lower attaching nut and bolt and swing the lower end free of the mounting bracket on the axle housing.

4. Remove the upper attaching bolt or nut(s) and remove the shock absorber.

5. Installation is the reverse of the removal procedure. Tighten the lower attaching nut and bolt to 41–53 ft. lbs. (55–72 Nm). On Aerostar, tighten the upper bolt to 41–63 ft. lbs. (55–85 Nm). On Bronco II and Ranger, tighten the upper attaching nut to 41–53 ft. lbs. (55–72 Nm). On Explorer, tighten the upper mounting nuts to 15–21 ft. lbs. (21–29 Nm).

Coil Springs

Removal and Installation

AEROSTAR

1. Raise and safely support the vehicle. Place safety stands or equivalent on the frame rear lift points.

2. Remove the nut and bolt retaining the shock absorber to the axle mount on the lower control arm. Disconnect the shock absorber from the axle bracket.

3. Lower the rear axle until the coil springs are no longer under compression.

4. Remove the nut retaining the lower retainer and spring to the control arm. Remove the bolt retaining the upper retainer and spring to the frame.

5. Remove the spring and retainers. Remove the upper and lower insulators.

To install:

6. Make sure the axle is in the spring unloaded position. Place the lower insulator on the control arm and the upper insulator on top of the spring.

7. Install the coil spring. The small diameter, white colored, tapered coils must face upward with the pigtail resting against the upper insulator rubber stop.

8. With the upper pigtail resting against the rubber stop, rotate the spring with the upper insulator until the lower pigtail points in the 3 o'clock position. Install the upper retainer and bolt and tighten to 30–40 ft. lbs. (40–55 Nm).

9. Install the lower retainer and nut and tighten to 41–65 ft. lbs. (55–88 Nm).

10. Raise the axle to the normal ride position and install the shock absorber. Lower the vehicle.

Leaf Springs

Removal and Installation

BRONCO II, EXPLORER AND RANGER

1. Raise the vehicle and safely support on the frame until the weight is off the rear spring, with the tires still touching the floor.

2. Remove the nuts from the spring U-bolts and drive the U-bolts from the U-bolt plate.

3. Remove the spring-to-bracket nut and bolt at the front of the spring.

4. Remove the shackle upper and lower nuts and bolts at the rear of the spring. Remove the spring and shackle assembly from the rear shackle bracket.

To install:

5. Position the spring in the shackle and install the upper shackle-to-spring bolt and nut with the bolt head facing outboard.

6. Position the front end of the spring in the bracket and in-

stall the bolt and nut. Position the shackle in the rear bracket and install the bolt and nut.

7. On Bronco II and Ranger, position the spring on top of the axle with the spring tie bolt centered in the hole provided in the seat. On Explorer, position the spring on the bottom of the axle with the spring tie bolt centered in the hole provided in the seat.

8. Install the spring U-bolts, U-bolt plate and nuts and lower the vehicle. On Bronco II and Ranger, tighten the spring U-bolt nuts to 65–75 ft. lbs. (88–102 Nm) and the front spring bolt and the rear shackle bolts and nuts to 75–115 ft. lbs. (100–155 Nm). On Explorer, tighten the spring U-bolt nuts to 88–108 ft. lbs. (119–146 Nm), the front spring bolt and nut to 64–91 ft. lbs. (87–123 Nm) and the rear shackle bolts and nuts to 75–115 ft. lbs. (100–155 Nm).

Rear Control Arms

Removal and Installation

AEROSTAR

Upper Arm

1. Raise the vehicle and support it safely. Place safety stands or equivalent on the frame rear lift points.

2. Remove the nut and bolt retaining the shock absorber to the lower axle bracket. Swing the lower end of the shock absorber free of the axle bracket.

3. Lower the rear axle assembly until the coil springs are no longer under compression.

4. Remove the bolt and nut retaining the upper control arm to the rear axle. Disconnect the upper control arm from the axle. Scribe a mark aligning the position of the cam adjuster in the axle bushing. The cam adjuster controls the rear axle pinion angle for driveline angularity.

5. Remove the bolt and nut retaining the upper control arm to the right frame bracket. Rotate the arm to disengage from the body bracket.

6. Remove the nut and washer retaining the upper control arm to the left frame bracket. Remove the outer insulator and spacer. Remove the control arm from the bracket. Remove the inner insulator from the control arm stud.

NOTE: If the left bracket attachments are loosened prior to disengaging the arm from the right bracket, the uncompressed left bushing will force the arm against the right bracket and make removal difficult.

To install:

7. Position the inner insulator on the control arm stud. Install the control arm so the stud extends through the left frame bracket. Install the spacer and outer insulator over the stud. Install nut and washer assembly and tighten until snug. Do not torque at this time.

8. Position the upper control arm in the right frame bracket. Install the bolt and nut and tighten until snug. Do not torque at this time.

9. Align the marks on the cam adjuster and axle bushing. Install the upper control arm to the axle housing. Install the nut

Rear upper control arm installation—Aerostar

Rear lower control arm installation—Aerostar

and bolt and tighten until snug. Do not torque at this time.

10. Raise the rear axle to the normal ride position and install the shock absorber. With the axle in the normal ride position, tighten the control arm-to-left frame bracket nut to 60–100 ft. lbs. (81–135 Nm), control arm-to-right frame bracket nut and bolt to 100–133 ft. lbs. (135–170 Nm) and control arm-to-axle housing to 100–145 ft. lbs. (135–197 Nm) on 1988–89 vehicles or 155–210 ft. lbs. (210–284 Nm) on 1990–92 vehicles.

11. Remove the safety stands and lower the vehicle.

Lower Arm

1. Raise and safely support the vehicle. Place safety stands under the frame rear lift points.

2. Remove the nut and bolt retaining the shock absorber to the lower axle bracket. Swing the lower end of the shock absorber free of the axle bracket.

3. Lower the rear axle until the coil springs are no longer under compression.

4. Remove the nut attaching the lower retainer and coil spring to the lower control arm. Remove the insulator from the arm.

5. Remove the bolt and nut retaining the lower control arm to the axle housing.

6. Remove the nut and bolt retaining the lower control arm to the frame bracket and remove the lower control arm.

To install:

7. Position the lower control arm in the bracket on the axle housing. Install the bolt so the head is inboard on the axle bracket. Install the nut but do not tighten at this time.

8. Install the insulator on the lower control arm. With the axle in the spring unloaded position, install the coil spring and lower retainer on the lower control arm.

9. Install the nut attaching the retainer and spring to the lower control arm. Tighten the nut to 41–65 ft. lbs. (55–88 Nm).

10. Raise the axle to the normal ride position. Tighten the lower control arm-to-axle housing nut and bolt and lower control arm-to-frame bracket nut and bolt to 95–130 ft. lbs. (129–177 Nm).

11. Install the shock absorber and lower the vehicle.

SPECIFICATIONS

VEHICLE IDENTIFICATION CHART

It is important for servicing and ordering parts to be certain of the vehicle and engine identification. The VIN (vehicle identification number) is a 17 digit number visible through the windshield on the driver's side of the dash and contains the vehicle and engine identification codes. The tenth digit indicates model year and the eighth digit indicates engine code. It can be interpreted as follows:

Engine Code						Model Year	
Code	Cu. In.	Liters	Cyl.	Fuel Sys.	Eng. Mfg.	Code	Year
Z	262	4.3	6	TBI	Chevrolet	J	1988
T	292	4.8	6	1bbl.	GM of Mexico	K	1989
H	305	5.0	8	4bbl.	Chevrolet	L	1990
M	350	5.7	8	4bbl.	Chevrolet	M	1991
K	350	5.7	8	TBI	Chevrolet	N	1992
C	379	6.2	8	Diesel	DDAD		
J	379	6.2	8	Diesel	DDAD		
F	400	6.5	8	Turbo Diesel	DDAD		
W	454	7.4	8	4bbl.	Chevrolet		
N	454	7.4	8	TBI	Chevrolet		

DDAD—Detroit Diesel Allison Division
TBI—Throttle Body Injection

ENGINE IDENTIFICATION

Year	Model	Engine Displacement cu. in. (liter)	Engine Series Identification (VIN)	No. of Cylinders	Engine Type
1988	C/K-Pick-Up	262 (4.3L)	Z	6	OHV
	C/K-Pick-Up	305 (5.0L)	H	8	OHV
	C/K-Pick-Up	350 (5.7L)	K	8	OHV
	C/K-Pick-Up	379 (6.2L)	C	8	OHV (Diesel)
	C/K-Pick-Up	379 (6.2L)	J	8	OHV (Diesel)
	C/K-Pick-Up	454 (7.4L)	N	8	OHV
	G Series—Van	262 (4.3L)	Z	6	OHV
	G Series—Van	305 (5.0L)	H	8	OHV
	G Series—Van	350 (5.7L)	K	8	OHV
	G Series—Van	350 (5.7L)	M	8	OHV

SECTION 5

GENERAL MOTORS CORPORATION
C/K SERIES (PICK-UP) • R/V SERIES (PICK-UP) • BLAZER/JIMMY • SUBURBAN • G SERIES (VAN)

ENGINE IDENTIFICATION

Year	Model	Engine Displacement cu. in. (liter)	Engine Series Identification (VIN)	No. of Cylinders	Engine Type
1988	G Series—Van	379 (6.2L)	C	8	OHV (Diesel)
	G Series—Van	379 (6.2L)	J	8	OHV (Diesel)
	G Series—Van	454 (7.4L)	N	8	OHV
	R/V Series—Pick-Up	292 (4.8L)	T	6	OHV
	R/V Series—Pick-Up	350 (5.7L)	K	8	OHV
	R/V Series—Pick-Up	350 (5.7L)	M	8	OHV
	R/V Series—Pick-Up	379 (6.2L)	C	8	OHV (Diesel)
	R/V Series—Pick-Up	379 (6.2L)	J	8	OHV (Diesel)
	R/V Series—Pick-Up	454 (7.4L)	N	8	OHV
	R/V Series—Pick-Up	454 (7.4L)	W	8	OHV
	R/V Series—Suburban	350 (5.7L)	K	8	OHV
	R/V Series—Suburban	379 (6.2L)	C	8	OHV (Diesel)
	R/V Series—Suburban	379 (6.2L)	J	8	OHV (Diesel)
	R/V Series—Suburban	454 (7.4L)	N	8	OHV
	V Series—Blazer/Jimmy	350 (5.7L)	K	8	OHV
	V Series—Blazer/Jimmy	379 (6.2L)	C	8	OHV (Diesel)
1989	C/K-Pick-Up	262 (4.3L)	Z	6	OHV
	C/K-Pick-Up	305 (5.0L)	H	8	OHV
	C/K-Pick-Up	350 (5.7L)	K	8	OHV
	C/K-Pick-Up	379 (6.2L)	C	8	OHV (Diesel)
	C/K-Pick-Up	379 (6.2L)	J	8	OHV (Diesel)
	C/K-Pick-Up	454 (7.4L)	N	8	OHV
	G Series—Van	262 (4.3L)	Z	6	OHV
	G Series—Van	305 (5.0L)	H	8	OHV
	G Series—Van	350 (5.7L)	K	8	OHV
	G Series—Van	379 (6.2L)	C	8	OHV (Diesel)
	G Series—Van	379 (6.2L)	J	8	OHV (Diesel)
	G Series—Van	454 (7.4L)	N	8	OHV
	R/V Series—Pick-Up	350 (5.7L)	K	8	OHV
	R/V Series—Pick-Up	379 (6.2L)	C	8	OHV (Diesel)
	R/V Series—Pick-Up	379 (6.2L)	J	8	OHV (Diesel)
	R/V Series—Pick-Up	454 (7.4L)	N	8	OHV
	R/V Series—Pick-Up	454 (7.4L)	W	8	OHV
	R/V Series—Suburban	350 (5.7L)	K	8	OHV
	R/V Series—Suburban	379 (6.2L)	C	8	OHV (Diesel)
	R/V Series—Suburban	379 (6.2L)	J	8	OHV (Diesel)
	R/V Series—Suburban	454 (7.4L)	N	8	OHV
	V Series—Blazer/Jimmy	350 (5.7L)	K	8	OHV
	V Series—Blazer/Jimmy	379 (6.2L)	C	8	OHV (Diesel)
1990	C/K-Pick-Up	262 (4.3L)	Z	6	OHV
	C/K-Pick-Up	305 (5.0L)	H	8	OHV
	C/K-Pick-Up	350 (5.7L)	K	8	OHV
	C/K-Pick-Up	379 (6.2L)	C	8	OHV (Diesel)
	C/K-Pick-Up	379 (6.2L)	J	8	OHV (Diesel)

ENGINE IDENTIFICATION

Year	Model	Engine Displacement cu. in. (liter)	Engine Series Identification (VIN)	No. of Cylinders	Engine Type
1990	C/K-Pick-Up	454 (7.4L)	N	8	OHV
	G Series—Van	262 (4.3L)	Z	6	OHV
	G Series—Van	305 (5.0L)	H	8	OHV
	G Series—Van	350 (5.7L)	K	8	OHV
	G Series—Van	379 (6.2L)	C	8	OHV (Diesel)
	G Series—Van	379 (6.2L)	J	8	OHV (Diesel)
	G Series—Van	454 (7.4L)	N	8	OHV
	R/V Series—Pick-Up	350 (5.7L)	K	8	OHV
	R/V Series—Pick-Up	379 (6.2L)	J	8	OHV (Diesel)
	R/V Series—Pick-Up	454 (7.4L)	N	8	OHV
	R/V Series—Suburban	350 (5.7L)	K	8	OHV
	R/V Series—Suburban	379 (6.2L)	C	8	OHV (Diesel)
	R/V Series—Suburban	379 (6.2L)	J	8	OHV (Diesel)
	R/V Series—Suburban	454 (7.4L)	N	8	OHV
	V Series—Blazer/Jimmy	350 (5.7L)	K	8	OHV
	V Series—Blazer/Jimmy	379 (6.2L)	C	8	OHV (Diesel)
1991	C/K-Pick-Up	262 (4.3L)	Z	6	OHV
	C/K-Pick-Up	305 (5.0L)	H	8	OHV
	C/K-Pick-Up	350 (5.7L)	K	8	OHV
	C/K-Pick-Up	379 (6.2L)	C	8	OHV (Diesel)
	C/K-Pick-Up	379 (6.2L)	J	8	OHV (Diesel)
	C/K-Pick-Up	454 (7.4L)	N	8	OHV
	G Series—Van	262 (4.3L)	Z	6	OHV
	G Series—Van	305 (5.0L)	H	8	OHV
	G Series—Van	350 (5.7L)	K	8	OHV
	G Series—Van	379 (6.2L)	C	8	OHV (Diesel)
	G Series—Van	379 (6.2L)	J	8	OHV (Diesel)
	G Series—Van	454 (7.4L)	N	8	OHV
	R/V Series—Pick-Up	350 (5.7L)	K	8	OHV
	R/V Series—Pick-Up	379 (6.2L)	J	8	OHV (Diesel)
	R/V Series—Pick-Up	454 (7.4L)	N	8	OHV
	R/V Series—Suburban	350 (5.7L)	K	8	OHV
	R/V Series—Suburban	379 (6.2L)	C	8	OHV (Diesel)
	R/V Series—Suburban	379 (6.2L)	J	8	OHV (Diesel)
	R/V Series—Suburban	454 (7.4L)	N	8	OHV
	V Series—Blazer/Jimmy	350 (5.7L)	K	8	OHV
	V Series—Blazer/Jimmy	379 (6.2L)	C	8	OHV (Diesel)
1992	C/K-Pick-Up	262 (4.3L)	Z	6	OHV
	C/K-Pick-Up	305 (5.0L)	H	8	OHV
	C/K-Pick-Up	350 (5.7L)	K	8	OHV
	C/K-Pick-Up	379 (6.2L)	C	8	OHV (Diesel)
	C/K-Pick-Up	379 (6.2L)	J	8	OHV (Diesel)
	C/K-Pick-Up	400 (6.5L)	F	8	OHV (Turbo Diesel)
	C/K-Pick-Up	454 (7.4L)	N	8	OHV

GENERAL MOTORS CORPORATION
C/K SERIES (PICK-UP) • R/V SERIES (PICK-UP) • BLAZER/JIMMY • SUBURBAN • G SERIES (VAN)

ENGINE IDENTIFICATION

Year	Model	Engine Displacement cu. in. (liter)	Engine Series Identification (VIN)	No. of Cylinders	Engine Type
1992	C/K Series—Suburban	350 (5.7L)	K	8	OHV
	C/K Series—Suburban	454 (7.4L)	N	8	OHV
	G Series—Van	262 (4.3L)	Z	6	OHV
	G Series—Van	305 (5.0L)	H	8	OHV
	G Series—Van	350 (5.7L)	K	8	OHV
	G Series—Van	379 (6.2L)	C	8	OHV (Diesel)
	G Series—Van	379 (6.2L)	J	8	OHV (Diesel)
	G Series—Van	454 (7.4L)	N	8	OHV
	K Series—Blazer/Yukon	350 (5.7L)	K	8	OHV

OHV—Overhead Valve

GENERAL ENGINE SPECIFICATIONS

Year	VIN	No. Cylinder Displacement cu. in. (liter)	Fuel System type	Net Horsepower @ rpm	Net Torque @ rpm (ft. lbs.)	Bore × Stroke (in.)	Compression Ratio	Oil Pressure @ rpm
1988	Z	8-262 (4.3)	EFI	145 @ 4000	230 @ 2400	4.00 × 3.48	9.3:1	35 @ 2000
	T	6-292 (4.8)	Carb.	115 @ 3400	215 @ 1600	3.88 × 4.12	8.0:1	50 @ 2000
	H	8-305 (5.0)	EFI	165 @ 4400	240 @ 2000	3.74 × 3.48	9.0:1	45 @ 2000
	K	8-350 (5.7)	EFI	—	—	4.00 × 3.48	8.5:1	45 @ 2000
	M	8-350 (5.7)	Carb.	185 @ 4000	285 @ 2400	4.00 × 3.48	8.3:1	45 @ 2000
	C	8-379 (6.2)	Diesel	130 @ 3600	240 @ 2000	3.98 × 3.80	21.0:1	35 @ 2000
	J	8-379 (6.2)	Diesel	135 @ 3600	240 @ 2000	3.98 × 3.80	21.0:1	35 @ 2000
	N	8-454 (7.4)	EFI	—	—	4.25 × 4.00	8.0:1	40 @ 2000
1989	Z	6-262 (4.3)	EFI	①	②	4.00 × 3.48	9.3:1	35 @ 2000
	H	8-305 (5.0)	EFI	170 @ 4000	270 @ 2400	3.74 × 3.48	9.3:1	30–55 @ 2000
	K	8-350 (5.7)	EFI	③	④	4.00 × 3.48	9.3:1	30–55 @ 2000
	C	8-379 (6.2)	Diesel	145 @ 3600	255 @ 1900	3.98 × 3.80	21.3:1	40–45 @ 2000
	J	8-379 (6.2)	Diesel	155 @ 3500	257–259 @ 2000	3.98 × 3.80	21.3:1	40–45 @ 2000
	N	8-454 (7.4)	EFI	230 @ 3600	385 @ 1600	4.25 × 4.00	7.9:1	40–60 @ 2000
	W	8-454 (7.4)	Carb.	230 @ 3800	370 @ 2800	4.25 × 4.00	7.9:1	40–60 @ 2000
1990	Z	6-262 (4.3)	EFI	①	②	4.00 × 3.48	9.3:1⑦	35 @ 2000
	H	8-305 (5.0)	EFI	170 @ 4000	270 @ 2400	3.74 × 3.48	9.3:1⑦	18⑨ @ 2000
	K	8-350 (5.7)	EFI	③	④	4.00 × 3.48	9.3:1⑦	18⑨ @ 2000
	C	8-379 (6.2)	Diesel	145 @ 3600	255 @ 1900	3.98 × 3.80	21.3:1	40–45 @ 2000
	J	8-379 (6.2)	Diesel	155 @ 3500	257–259 @ 2000	3.98 × 3.80	21.3:1	40–45 @ 2000
	N	8-454 (7.4)	EFI	230 @ 3600	385 @ 1600	4.25 × 4.00	7.9:1	40–60 @ 2000
1991	Z	6-262 (4.3)	EFI	①	②	4.00 × 3.48	9.3:1⑦	18⑨ @ 2000
	H	8-305 (5.0)	EFI	170 @ 4000	270 @ 2400	3.74 × 3.48	9.3:1	18⑨ @ 2000
	K	8-350 (5.7)	EFI	③	④	4.00 × 3.48	9.1:1⑧	18⑨ @ 2000
	C	8-379 (6.2)	Diesel	145 @ 3600	255 @ 1900	3.98 × 3.80	21.3:1	40–45 @ 2000
	J	8-379 (6.2)	Diesel	155 @ 3500	257–259 @ 2000	3.98 × 3.80	21.3:1	40–45 @ 2000
	N	8-454 (7.4)	EFI	230 @ 3600	385 @ 1600	4.25 × 4.00	7.9:1	40–60 @ 2000

GENERAL ENGINE SPECIFICATIONS

Year	VIN	No. Cylinder Displacement cu. in. (liter)	Fuel System type	Net Horsepower @ rpm	Net Torque @ rpm (ft. lbs.)	Bore × Stroke (in.)	Compression Ratio	Oil Pressure @ rpm
1992	Z	6-262 (4.3)	EFI	①	②	4.00 × 3.48	9.3:1	18⑨ @ 2000
	H	8-305 (5.0)	EFI	170 @ 4000	270 @ 2400	3.74 × 3.48	9.3:1⑦	18⑨ @ 2000
	K	8-350 (5.7)	EFI	③	④	4.00 × 3.48	9.1:1⑧	18⑨ @ 2000
	C	8-379 (6.2)	Diesel	145 @ 3600	255 @ 1900	3.98 × 3.80	21.3:1	40–45 @ 2000
	J	8-379 (6.2)	Diesel	155 @ 3500	257–259 @ 2000	3.98 × 3.80	21.3:1	40–45 @ 2000
	F	8-400 (6.5)	Turbo Diesel	⑤	⑥	4.05 × 3.80	21.0:1	40–45 @ 2000
	N	8-454 (7.4)	EFI	230 @ 3600	385 @ 1600	4.25 × 4.00	7.9:1	40–60 @ 2000

EFI—Electronic Fuel Injected
Carb.—Carbureted
① C/K Pick-Up—160 @ 4000
   C/K H.D. Pick-Up—155 @ 4000
   G Van—150 @ 4000
② C/K Pick-Up—235 @ 2400
   C/K H.D. Pick-Up—230 @ 2400
   G Van—230 @ 2400

③ Below 8500 GVWR—210 @ 4000
   Above 8500 GVWR—190 @ 4000
④ Below 8500 GVWR—300 @ 2800
   Above 8500 GVWR—300 @ 2400
⑤ Below 15,000 GVWR—190 @ 4000
   Above 15,000 GVWR—180 @ 3400
⑥ Below 8500 GVWR—380 @ 1700
   Above 8500 GVWR—360 @ 1700

⑦ Heavy duty—8.6:1
⑧ Heavy duty—8.3:1
⑨ Minimum psi.

GASOLINE ENGINE TUNE-UP SPECIFICATIONS

Year	VIN	No. Cylinder Displacement cu. in. (liter)	Spark Plugs Type	Spark Plugs Gap (in.)	Ignition Timing (deg.) MT	Ignition Timing (deg.) AT	Compression Pressure (psi)	Fuel Pump (psi)	Idle Speed (rpm) MT	Idle Speed (rpm) AT	Valve Clearance In.	Valve Clearance Ex.
1988	Z	6-262 (4.3)	CR43TS	0.040	0	0	④	9–13③	①	①	Hyd.	Hyd.
	T	6-292 (4.8)	R44T	0.035	8	8	④	5.0	700	700	Hyd.	Hyd.
	H	8-305 (5.0)	CR43TS	0.045	4	4	④	9–13③	700	700	Hyd.	Hyd.
	M	8-350 (5.7)	R44T	0.045	4	4	④	5.0③	700	700	Hyd.	Hyd.
	K	8-350 (5.7)	CR43TS	0.045	4	4	④	9–13③	700	700	Hyd.	Hyd.
	N	8-454 (7.4)	CR43TS	0.045	4	4	④	9–13③	700	700	Hyd.	Hyd.
	W	8-454 (7.4)	R44T	0.045	4	4	④	5.0	700	700	Hyd.	Hyd.
1989	Z	6-262 (4.3)	CR43TS	0.045	②	②	④	9–13③	②	②	Hyd.	Hyd.
	H	8-305 (5.0)	CR43TS	0.045	②	②	④	9–13③	②	②	Hyd.	Hyd.
	K	8-350 (5.7)	CR43TS	0.045	②	②	④	9–13③	②	②	Hyd.	Hyd.
	N	8-454 (7.4)	CR43TS	0.045	②	②	④	9–13③	②	②	Hyd.	Hyd.
	W	8-454 (7.4)	R44T	0.045	②	②	④	5.0③	②	②	Hyd.	Hyd.
1990	Z	6-262 (4.3)	CR43TS	0.045	②	②	④	9–13③	②	②	Hyd.	Hyd.
	H	8-305 (5.0)	CR43TS	0.045	②	②	④	9–13③	②	②	Hyd.	Hyd.
	K	8-350 (5.7)	CR43TS	0.045	②	②	④	9–13③	②	②	Hyd.	Hyd.
	N	8-454 (7.4)	CR43TS	0.045	②	②	④	9–13③	②	②	Hyd.	Hyd.
1991	Z	6-262 (4.3)	CR43TS	0.045	②	②	④	9–13③	②	②	Hyd.	Hyd.
	H	8-305 (5.0)	CR45TS	0.045	②	②	④	9–13③	②	②	Hyd.	Hyd.
	K	8-350 (5.7)	CR43TS	0.045	②	②	④	9–13③	②	②	Hyd.	Hyd.
	N	8-454 (7.4)	CR43TS	0.045	②	②	④	9–13③	②	②	Hyd.	Hyd.
1992	Z	6-262 (4.3)	CR43TS	0.045	②	②	④	9–13③	②	②	Hyd.	Hyd.
	H	8-305 (5.0)	CR43TS	0.045	②	②	④	9–13③	②	②	Hyd.	Hyd.
	K	8-350 (5.7)	CR43TS	0.045	②	②	④	9–13③	②	②	Hyd.	Hyd.

GENERAL MOTORS CORPORATION
C/K SERIES (PICK-UP) • R/V SERIES (PICK-UP) • BLAZER/JIMMY • SUBURBAN • G SERIES (VAN)

GASOLINE ENGINE TUNE-UP SPECIFICATIONS

Year	VIN	No. Cylinder Displacement cu. in. (liter)	Spark Plugs Type	Spark Plugs Gap (in.)	Ignition Timing (deg.) MT	Ignition Timing (deg.) AT	Compression Pressure (psi)	Fuel Pump (psi)	Idle Speed (rpm) MT	Idle Speed (rpm) AT	Valve Clearance In.	Valve Clearance Ex.
1992	N	8-454 (7.4)	CR43TS	0.045	②	②	④	9–13③	②	②	Hyd.	Hyd.

Hyd.—Hydraulic
① Controlled By ECM
② See Underhood Sticker
③ Fuel Injected

④ Minimum compression reading 100 psi
No cylinder should be more than 30% lower than that of the highest cylinder reading

DIESEL ENGINE TUNE-UP SPECIFICATIONS

Year	VIN	No. Engine Displacement cu. in. (liter)	Valve Clearance Intake (in.)	Valve Clearance Exhaust (in.)	Intake Valve Opens (deg.)	Injection Pump Setting (deg.)	Injection Nozzle Pressure (psi) New	Injection Nozzle Pressure (psi) Used	Idle Speed (rpm)	Cranking Compression Pressure (psi)
1988	C	8-379 (6.2)	Hyd.	Hyd.	—	—	—	—	②	380–400①
	J	8-379 (6.2)	Hyd.	Hyd.	—	—	—	—	②	380–400①
1989	C	8-379 (6.2)	Hyd.	Hyd.	—	—	—	—	②	380–400①
	J	8-379 (6.2)	Hyd.	Hyd.	—	—	—	—	②	380–400①
1990	C	8-379 (6.2)	Hyd.	Hyd.	—	—	—	—	②	380–400①
	J	8-379 (6.2)	Hyd.	Hyd.	—	—	—	—	②	380–400①
1991	C	8-379 (6.2)	Hyd.	Hyd.	—	—	—	—	②	380–400①
	J	8-379 (6.2)	Hyd.	Hyd.	—	—	—	—	②	380–400①
1992	C	8-379 (6.2)	Hyd.	Hyd.	—	—	—	—	②	380–400①
	F	8-400 (6.5)	Hyd.	Hyd.	—	—	—	—	②	380–400①
	J	8-379 (6.2)	Hyd.	Hyd.	—	—	—	—	②	380–400①

Hyd.—Hydraulic
① Minimum specified reading
All cylinders should be within 80% of highest cylinder reading
② Refer to emission control information label

FIRING ORDERS

NOTE: To avoid confusion, always replace spark plug wires one at a time.

4.8L Engine
Engine Firing Order: 1–5–3–6–2–4
Distributor Rotation: Clockwise

4.3L Engine
Engine Firing Order: 1–6–5–4–3–2
Distributor Rotation: Clockwise

5.0L, 5.7L and 7.4L Engines
Engine Firing Order: 1–8–4–3–6–5–7–2
Distributor Rotation: Clockwise

CAPACITIES

Year	Model	VIN	Engine cu. in./ (liters)	Engine with Filter	Crankcase without Filter	Transmission (pts.) 4-Spd	5-Spd	Auto.	Drive Axle (pts.)	Fuel Tank (gal.)	Cooling System (qts.)
1988	C/K—Pick-Up	Z	262 (4.3L)	5	4	①	3.6	②	③	26④	10.9
	C/K—Pick-Up	H	305 (5.0L)	5	4	①	3.6	②	③	26④	18
	C/K—Pick-Up	K	350 (5.7L)	5	4	①	3.6	②	③	26④	18
	C/K—Pick-Up	C	379 (6.2L)	7	7	①	3.6	②	③	26④	25
	C/K—Pick-Up	J	379 (6.2L)	7	7	①	3.6	②	③	26④	25
	C/K—Pick-Up	N	454 (7.4L)	6	5	①	3.6	②	③	26④	25
	G Series—Van	Z	262 (4.3L)	5	4	①	—	②	③	22⑤	11⑥
	G Series—Van	H	305 (5.0L)	5	4	①	—	②	③	22⑤	17⑥
	G Series—Van	K	350 (5.7L)	5	4	①	—	②	③	22⑤	17⑥
	G Series—Van	M	350 (5.7L)	5	4	①	—	②	③	22⑤	17⑥
	G Series—Van	C	379 (6.2L)	7	7	①	—	②	③	22⑤	24⑥
	G Series—Van	J	379 (6.2L)	7	7	①	—	②	③	22⑤	25.5⑥
	G Series—Van	N	454 (7.4L)	5	4	①	—	②	③	22⑤	17⑥
	R/V Series—Pick-Up	T	292 (4.8L)	5	4	①	—	②	⑦	20⑧	13.8
	R/V Series—Pick-Up	K	350 (5.7L)	5	4	①	—	②	⑦	20⑧	18
	R/V Series—Pick-Up	M	350 (5.7L)	5	4	①	—	②	⑦	20⑧	18
	R/V Series—Pick-Up	C	379 (6.2L)	7	7	①	—	②	⑦	20⑧	25
	R/V Series—Pick-Up	J	379 (6.2L)	7	7	①	—	②	⑦	20⑧	25
	R/V Series—Pick-Up	N	454 (7.4L)	6	5	①	—	②	⑦	20⑧	24.5
	R/V Series—Pick-Up	W	454 (7.4L)	6	5	①	—	②	⑦	20⑧	24.5
	R/V Series—Suburban	K	350 (5.7L)	5	4	—	—	②	⑦	25⑨	18
	R/V Series—Suburban	C	379 (6.2L)	7	7	—	—	②	⑦	27⑨	25
	R/V Series—Suburban	J	379 (6.2L)	7	7	—	—	②	⑦	27⑨	25
	R/V Series—Suburban	N	454 (7.4L)	6	5	—	—	②	⑦	27⑨	24.5
	V Series—Blazer/Jimmy	K	350 (5.7L)	5	4	①	—	②	⑦	25⑨	18
	V Series—Blazer/Jimmy	C	379 (6.2L)	7	7	①	—	②	⑦	27⑨	25
1989	C/K—Pick-Up	Z	262 (4.3L)	5	4	①	3.6	②	③	26④	10.9
	C/K—Pick-Up	H	305 (5.0L)	5	4	①	3.6	②	③	26④	18

GENERAL MOTORS CORPORATION
C/K SERIES (PICK-UP) • R/V SERIES (PICK-UP) • BLAZER/JIMMY • SUBURBAN • G SERIES (VAN)

CAPACITIES

Year	Model	VIN	Engine cu. in./ (liters)	Engine with Filter	Crankcase without Filter	Transmission (pts.)			Drive Axle (pts.)	Fuel Tank (gal.)	Cooling System (qts.)
						4-Spd	5-Spd	Auto.			
1989	C/K—Pick-Up	K	350 (5.7L)	5	4	[1]	3.6	[2]	[3]	26[4]	18
	C/K—Pick-Up	C	379 (6.2L)	7	7	[1]	3.6	[2]	[3]	26[4]	25
	C/K—Pick-Up	J	379 (6.2L)	7	7	[1]	3.6	[2]	[3]	26[4]	25
	C/K—Pick-Up	N	454 (7.4L)	6	5	[1]	3.6	[2]	[3]	26[4]	25
	G Series—Van	Z	262 (4.3L)	5	4	[1]	—	[2]	[3]	22[5]	11[6]
	G Series—Van	H	305 (5.0L)	5	4	[1]	—	[2]	[3]	22[5]	17[6]
	G Series—Van	K	350 (5.7L)	5	4	[1]	—	[2]	[3]	22[5]	17[6]
	G Series—Van	C	379 (6.2L)	7	7	[1]	—	[2]	[3]	22[5]	24[6]
	G Series—Van	J	379 (6.2L)	7	7	[1]	—	[2]	[3]	22[5]	25.5[6]
	G Series—Van	N	454 (7.4L)	6	5	[1]	—	[2]	[3]	22[5]	23[6]
	R/V Series—Pick-Up	K	350 (5.7L)	5	4	[1]	—	[2]	[3]	20	18.5[6]
	R/V Series—Pick-Up	C	379 (6.2L)	7	7	[1]	—	[2]	[3]	20	25[6]
	R/V Series—Pick-Up	J	379 (6.2L)	7	7	[1]	—	[2]	[3]	20	25[6]
	R/V Series—Pick-Up	N	454 (7.4L)	6	5	[1]	—	[2]	[3]	20	24[6]
	R/V Series—Pick-Up	W	454 (7.4L)	7[10]	6[10]	[1]	—	[2]	[3]	20	24[6]
	R/V Series—Suburban	K	350 (5.7L)	5	4	—	—	[2]	[3]	31[9]	18.5[6]
	R/V Series—Suburban	C	379 (6.2L)	7	7	—	—	[2]	[3]	32[9]	25[6]
	R/V Series—Suburban	J	379 (6.2L)	7	7	—	—	[2]	[3]	32[9]	25[6]
	R/V Series—Suburban	N	454 (7.4L)	6	5	—	—	[2]	[3]	31[9]	24[6]
	V Series—Blazer/Jimmy	K	350 (5.7L)	5	4	[1]	—	[2]	[3]	31	18.5[6]
	V Series—Blazer/Jimmy	C	379 (6.2L)	7	7	[1]	—	[2]	[3]	32	25[6]
1990	C/K—Pick-Up	Z	262 (4.3L)	5	4	[1]	3.6	[2]	[3]	[11]	10.9
	C/K—Pick-Up	H	305 (5.9L)	5	4	[1]	3.6	[2]	[3]	[11]	18
	C/K—Pick-Up	K	350 (5.7L)	5	4	[1]	3.6	[2]	[3]	[11]	18
	C/K—Pick-Up	C	379 (6.2L)	7	7	[1]	3.6	[2]	[3]	[11]	25
	C/K—Pick-Up	J	379 (6.2L)	7	7	[1]	3.6	[2]	[3]	[11]	25
	C/K—Pick-Up	N	454 (7.4L)	6	5	[1]	3.6	[2]	[3]	[11]	25
	G Series—Van	Z	262 (4.3L)	5	4	—	—	[2]	[3]	22[5]	10.9
	G Series—Van	H	305 (5.0L)	5	4	—	—	[2]	[3]	22[5]	18
	G Series—Van	K	350 (5.7L)	5	4	—	—	[2]	[3]	22[5]	18
	G Series—Van	C	379 (6.2L)	7	7	—	—	[2]	[3]	22[5]	25
	G Series—Van	J	379 (6.2L)	7	7	—	—	[2]	[3]	22[5]	25
	G Series—Van	N	454 (7.4L)	6	5	—	—	[2]	[3]	22[5]	25
	R/V Series—Pick-Up	K	350 (5.7L)	5	4	[1]	3.6	[2]	[3]	20	18
	R/V Series—Pick-Up	J	379 (6.2L)	7	7	[1]	3.6	[2]	[3]	20	25
	R/V Series—Pick-Up	N	454 (7.4L)	6	5	[1]	3.6	[2]	[3]	20	25
	R/V Series—Suburban	K	350 (5.7L)	5	4	[1]	—	[2]	[3]	31[9]	18
	R/V Series—Suburban	C	379 (6.2L)	7	7	—	—	[2]	[3]	32[9]	25
	R/V Series—Suburban	J	379 (6.2L)	7	7	—	—	[2]	[3]	32[9]	25
	R/V Series—Suburban	N	454 (7.4L)	6	5	—	—	[2]	[3]	31[9]	25
	V Series—Blazer/Jimmy	K	350 (5.7L)	5	4	[1]	3.6	[2]	[3]	31	18
	V Series—Blazer/Jimmy	C	379 (6.2L)	7	7	—	3.6	[2]	[3]	32	25
1991	C/K—Pick-Up	Z	262 (4.3L)	5	4	[1]	[12]	[2]	[3]	[11]	10.9
	C/K—Pick-Up	H	305 (5.0L)	5	4	[1]	[12]	[2]	[3]	[11]	18

CAPACITIES

Year	Model	VIN	Engine cu. in./(liters)	Engine with Filter	Crankcase without Filter	Transmission (pts.) 4-Spd	5-Spd	Auto.	Drive Axle (pts.)	Fuel Tank (gal.)	Cooling System (qts.)
1991	C/K—Pick-Up	K	350 (5.7L)	5	4	①	⑫	②	③	⑪	18
	C/K—Pick-Up	C	379 (6.2L)	7	7	①	⑫	②	③	⑪	25
	C/K—Pick-Up	J	379 (6.2L)	7	7	①	⑫	②	③	⑪	25
	C/K—Pick-Up	N	454 (7.4L)	7	6	①	⑫	②	③	⑪	25
	G Series—Van	Z	262 (4.3L)	5	4	—	—	②	③	22⑤	11⑥
	G Series—Van	H	305 (5.0L)	5	4	—	—	②	③	22⑤	17⑥
	G Series—Van	K	350 (5.7L)	5	4	—	—	②	③	22⑤	17⑥
	G Series—Van	C	379 (6.2L)	7	7	—	—	②	③	22⑤	24⑥
	G Series—Van	J	379 (6.2L)	7	7	—	—	②	③	22⑤	25.5⑥
	G Series—Van	N	454 (7.4L)	6	5	—	—	②	③	22⑤	23⑥
	R/V Series—Pick-Up	K	350 (5.7L)	5	4	8.4	3.6	②	③	20	18.5⑥
	R/V Series—Pick-Up	J	379 (6.2L)	7	7	8.4	3.6	②	③	20	25⑥
	R/V Series—Pick-Up	N	454 (7.4L)	7	6	8.4	3.6	②	③	20	24⑥
	R/V Series—Suburban	K	350 (5.7L)	5	4	8.4	3.6	②	③	37	18
	R/V Series—Suburban	C	379 (6.2L)	7	7	8.4	3.6	②	③	37	25
	R/V Series—Suburban	J	379 (6.2L)	7	7	8.4	3.6	②	③	37	25
	R/V Series—Suburban	N	454 (7.4L)	7	6	8.4	3.6	②	③	37	24
	V Series—Blazer/Jimmy	K	350 (5.7L)	5	4	8.4	3.6	②	③	31	18
	V Series—Blazer/Jimmy	C	379 (6.2L)	7	7	8.4	3.6	②	③	32	25
1992	C/K—Pick-Up	Z	262 (4.3L)	4.5	4	—	⑬	10	③	⑮	11
	C/K—Pick-Up	H	305 (5.0L)	5	4	—	⑬	10	③	⑮	18
	C/K—Pick-Up	K	350 (5.7L)	5⑭	4⑭	—	⑬	10	③	⑮	18⑯
	C/K—Pick-Up	C	379 (6.2L)	7	7	—	⑬	10	③	⑮	25
	C/K—Pick-Up	J	379 (6.2L)	7	7	—	⑬	10	③	⑮	25
	C/K—Pick-Up	F	400 (6.5L)	7	7	—	⑬	10	③	⑮	26.5
	C/K—Pick-Up	N	454 (7.4L)	7⑭	6⑭	—	⑬	10	③	⑮	25⑰
	C/K Series—Suburban	K	350 (5.7L)	5	4	—	—	10	③	34	18
	C/K Series—Suburban	N	454 (7.4L)	7	6	—	—	10	③	34	25
	G Series—Van	Z	262 (4.3L)	4.5	4	—	—	10	③	33⑱	11
	G Series—Van	H	305 (5.0L)	5	4	—	—	10	③	33⑱	18
	G Series—Van	K	350 (5.7L)	5	4	—	—	10	③	33⑱	18
	G Series—Van	C	379 (6.2L)	7	7	—	—	10	③	33⑱	25
	G Series—Van	J	379 (6.2L)	7	7	—	—	10	③	33⑱	25
	G Series—Van	N	454 (7.4L)	7	6	—	—	10	③	33⑱	25
	K Series—Blazer/Yukon	K	350 (5.7L)	5	4	—	⑬	10	③	⑮	18

① 85mm—3.6 pts.
117mm—8.4 pts.
② THM400 and 4L80—9.0 pts.
THM700R4 and 4L60—10.0 pts.
③ Front axle:
½ and ¾ ton—3.5 pts.
1 ton—4.4 pts.
Rear axle:
8½ in.—4.2 pts.
9½ and 10½ in.—6.5 pts.
9¾ in.—6.0 pts.
Transfer case:
½ and ¾ ton—2.8 pts.
1 tone—5.5 pts.

④ Deluxe tank (long bed)—34 gal.
⑤ Optional tank—33 gal.
⑥ Auxiliary heater— + 3.0 qts.
⑦ Front axle:
½ and ¾ ton—4.0 pts.
1 ton—6.0 pts.
Rear axle:
8½ in.—4.2 pts.
9½ and 10½ in.—6.5 pts.
9¾ in.—6.0 pts.
Transfer case:
½ and ¾ ton—10.4 pts.
1 ton—5.0 pts.
⑧ Dual tanks (gas eng.)
below 8600 GVWR—16 gal.

⑨ NK7 OPT.:
gas—31
diesel—32
NE2 OPT.:
gas—40
diesel—41
⑩ V Series—1 qt. less
⑪ Pick-up:
std. tank—25 gal.
opt. tank (long bed)—34 gal.
Chassis cab:
std. tank—22 or 34 gal.
opt. tank—30 gal.
⑫ 85mm—3.6 pts.
109mm—9.5 pts.

⑬ 85mm—4.4 pts.
Venture Gear 4500—8.0 pts.
⑭ CH3500 HD— + 1 qt.
⑮ Short bed—26 gal.
Long bed—34 gal.
4 Door—34 gal.
Chassis cab:
std. (side tank)—22 gal.
opt. (rear tank)—30 gal.
⑯ CH3500 HD—27 qts.
⑰ CH3500 HD—28.5 qts.
⑱ G series ½ TON:
122 in. wheel base—22 gal.

CAMSHAFT SPECIFICATIONS
All measurements given in inches.

Year	VIN	No. Cylinder Displacement cu. in. (liter)	Journal Diameter					Lobe Lift		Bearing Clearance	Camshaft End Play
			1	2	3	4	5	In.	Ex.		
1988	Z	6-262 (4.3)	1.8682–1.8692	1.8682–1.8692	1.8682–1.8692	1.8682–1.8692	—	0.357	0.390	—	0.004–0.012
	T	6-292 (4.8)	1.8677–1.8697	1.8677–1.8697	1.8677–1.8697	1.8677–1.8697	—	0.2315	0.2315	—	0.003–0.008
	H	8.305 (5.0)	1.8682–1.8692	1.8682–1.8692	1.8682–1.8692	1.8682–1.8692	1.8682–1.8692	0.2484	0.2667	—	0.004–0.012
	K	8-350 (5.7)	1.8682–1.8692	1.8682–1.8692	1.8682–1.8692	1.8682–1.8692	1.8682–1.8692	0.2600	0.2733	—	0.004–0.002
	M	8-350 (5.7)	1.8682–1.8692	1.8682–1.8692	1.8682–1.8692	1.8682–1.8692	1.8682–1.8692	0.2600	0.2733	—	0.004–0.002
	C	8-379 (6.2)	2.1642–2.1633	2.1642–2.1633	2.1642–2.1633	2.1642–2.1633	2.0067–2.0089	0.2808	0.2808	0.0010–0.0040	0.002–0.012
	J	8-379 (6.2)	2.1642–2.1633	2.1642–2.1633	2.1642–2.1633	2.1642–2.1633	2.0067–2.0089	0.2808	0.2808	0.0010–0.0040	0.002–0.012
	N	8-454 (7.4)	1.9482–1.9492	1.9482–1.9492	1.9482–1.9492	1.9482–1.9492	1.9482–1.9492	0.2343	0.2530	—	—
	W	8-454 (7.4)	1.9482–1.9492	1.9482–1.9492	1.9482–1.9492	1.9482–1.9492	1.9482–1.9492	0.2343	0.2530	—	—
1989	Z	6-262 (4.3)	1.8682–1.8692	1.8682–1.8692	1.8682–1.8692	1.8682–1.8692	—	0.357	0.390	—	0.004–0.012
	H	8.305 (5.0)	1.8682–1.8692	1.8682–1.8692	1.8682–1.8692	1.8682–1.8692	1.8682–1.8692	0.2484	0.2667	—	0.004–0.012
	K	8-350 (5.7)	1.8682–1.8692	1.8682–1.8692	1.8682–1.8692	1.8682–1.8692	1.8682–1.8692	0.2600	0.2733	—	0.004–0.012
	J	8-379 (6.2)	2.1642–2.1633	2.1642–2.1633	2.1642–2.1633	2.1642–2.1633	2.0067–2.0089	0.2808	0.2808	0.0010–0.0040	0.002–0.012
	C	8-379 (6.2)	2.1642–2.1633	2.1642–2.1633	2.1642–2.1633	2.1642–2.1633	2.0067–2.0089	0.2808	0.2808	0.0010–0.0040	0.002–0.012
	N	8-454 (7.4)	1.9482–1.9492	1.9482–1.9492	1.9482–1.9492	1.9482–1.9492	1.9482–1.9492	0.2343	0.2530	—	—
	W	8-454 (7.4)	1.9482–1.9492	1.9482–1.9492	1.9482–1.9492	1.9482–1.9492	1.9482–1.9492	0.2343	0.2530	—	—
1990	Z	6-262 (4.3)	1.8682–1.8692	1.8682–1.8692	1.8682–1.8692	1.8682–1.8692	—	0.357	0.390	—	0.004–0.012
	H	8.305 (5.0)	1.8682–1.8692	1.8682–1.8692	1.8682–1.8692	1.8682–1.8692	1.8682–1.8692	0.2484	0.2667	—	0.004–0.012
	K	8-350 (5.7)	1.8682–1.8692	1.8682–1.8692	1.8682–1.8692	1.8682–1.8692	1.8682–1.8692	0.2600	0.2733	—	0.004–0.012
	J	8-379 (6.2)	2.1642–2.1633	2.1642–2.1633	2.1642–2.1633	2.1642–2.1633	2.0067–2.0089	0.2808	0.2808	0.0010–0.0040	0.002–0.012
	C	8-379 (6.2)	2.1642–2.1633	2.1642–2.1633	2.1642–2.1633	2.1642–2.1633	2.0067–2.0089	0.2808	0.2808	0.0010–0.0040	0.002–0.012
	N	8-545 (7.4)	1.9482–1.9492	1.9482–1.9492	1.9482–1.9492	1.9482–1.9492	1.9482–1.9492	0.2343	0.2530	—	—
1991	Z	6-262 (4.3)	1.8682–1.8692	1.8682–1.8692	1.8682–1.8692	1.8682–1.8692	—	0.234	0.257	—	0.004–0.012
	H	8.305 (5.0)	1.8682–1.8692	1.8682–1.8692	1.8682–1.8692	1.8682–1.8692	1.8682–1.8692	0.2336	0.2565	—	0.004–0.012

CAMSHAFT SPECIFICATIONS

All measurements given in inches.

Year	VIN	No. Cylinder Displacement cu. in. (liter)	Journal Diameter 1	2	3	4	5	Lobe Lift In.	Ex.	Bearing Clearance	Camshaft End Play
1991	K	8-350 (5.7)	1.8682–1.8692	1.8682–1.8692	1.8682–1.8692	1.8682–1.8692	1.8682–1.8692	0.2565	0.2690	—	0.004–0.012
	C	8-379 (6.2)	2.1642–2.1633	2.1642–2.1633	2.1642–2.1633	2.1642–2.1633	2.0067–2.0089	0.2808	0.2808	0.0010–0.0040	0.002–0.012
	J	8-379 (6.2)	2.1642–2.1633	2.1642–2.1633	2.1642–2.1633	2.1642–2.1633	2.0067–2.0089	0.2808	0.2808	0.0010–0.0040	0.002–0.012
	N	8-545 (7.4)	1.9482–1.9492	1.9482–1.9492	1.9482–1.9492	1.9482–1.9492	1.9482–1.9492	0.2343	0.2530	—	—
1992	Z	6-262 (4.3)	1.8682–1.8692	1.8682–1.8692	1.8682–1.8692	1.8682–1.8692	—	0.357	0.390	—	0.004–0.012
	H	8.305 (5.0)	1.8682–1.8692	1.8682–1.8692	1.8682–1.8692	1.8682–1.8692	1.8682–1.8692	0.2484	0.2667	—	0.004–0.012
	K	8-350 (5.7)	1.8682–1.8692	1.8682–1.8692	1.8682–1.8692	1.8682–1.8692	1.8682–1.8692	0.2600	0.2733	—	0.004–0.012
	C	8-379 (6.2)	2.1642–2.1633	2.1642–2.1633	2.1642–2.1633	2.1642–2.1633	2.0067–2.0089	0.2808	0.2808	0.0010–0.0040	0.002–0.012
	J	8-379 (6.2)	2.1642–2.1633	2.1642–2.1633	2.1642–2.1633	2.1642–2.1633	2.0067–2.0089	0.2808	0.2808	0.0010–0.0040	0.002–0.012
	F	8-400 (6.5)	2.1644–2.1663	2.1644–2.1663	2.1644–2.1663	2.1644–2.1663	2.0068–2.0088	0.2808	0.2808	0.0010–0.0040	0.002–0.012
	N	8-545 (7.4)	1.9482–1.9492	1.9482–1.9492	1.9482–1.9492	1.9482–1.9492	1.9482–1.9492	0.2343	0.2530	—	—

CRANKSHAFT AND CONNECTING ROD SPECIFICATIONS

All measurements are given in inches.

Year	VIN	No. Cylinder Displacement cu. in. (liter)	Crankshaft Main Brg. Journal Dia.	Main Brg. Oil Clearance	Shaft End-play	Thrust on No.	Connecting Rod Journal Diameter	Oil Clearance	Side Clearance
1988	Z	6-262 (4.3)	①	②	0.0020–0.0060	4	2.2487–2.2497	0.0020–0.0030	0.0070–0.0150
	T	6-292 (4.8)	2.2979–2.2994	③	0.0020–0.0060	7	2.0990–2.1000	0.0010–0.0026	0.0060–0.0170
	H	8-305 (5.0)	①	④	0.0020–0.0060	5	2.0988–2.0998	0.0013–0.0035	0.0080–0.0140
	K	8-350 (5.7)	①	④	0.0020–0.0060	5	2.0988–2.0998	0.0013–0.0035	0.0080–0.0140
	M	8-350 (5.7)	①	④	0.0020–0.0060	5	2.0988–2.0998	0.0013–0.0035	0.0080–0.0140
	C	8-379 (6.2)	⑨	⑦	0.0020–0.0070	3	2.3480–2.3990	0.0017–0.0039	0.0070–0.0240
	J	8-379 (6.2)	⑨	⑦	0.0020–0.0070	3	2.3480–2.3990	0.0017–0.0039	0.0070–0.0240
	N	8-454 (7.4)	⑤	⑥	0.0060–0.0100	5	2.1990–2.2000	0.0009–0.0025	0.0130–0.0230

CRANKSHAFT AND CONNECTING ROD SPECIFICATIONS
All measurements are given in inches.

Year	VIN	No. Cylinder Displacement cu. in. (liter)	Crankshaft Main Brg. Journal Dia.	Crankshaft Main Brg. Oil Clearance	Crankshaft Shaft End-play	Crankshaft Thrust on No.	Connecting Rod Journal Diameter	Connecting Rod Oil Clearance	Connecting Rod Side Clearance
1988	W	8-434 (7.4)	⑤	⑥	0.0060–0.0100	5	2.1990–2.2000	0.0009–0.0025	0.0130–0.0230
1989	Z	6-262 (4.3)	①	⑧	0.0020–0.0060	4	2.2487–2.2497	0.0013–0.0035	0.0060–0.0140
	H	8-305 (5.0)	①	⑧	0.0020–0.0060	5	2.0988–2.0998	0.0013–0.0035	0.0060–0.0140
	K	8-350 (5.7)	①	⑧	0.0020–0.0060	5	2.0988–2.0998	0.0013–0.0035	0.0060–0.0140
	C	8-379 (6.2)	⑨	⑦	0.0040–0.0100	5	2.3981–2.3992	0.0018–0.0039	0.0060–0.0250
	J	8-379 (6.2)	⑨	⑦	0.0040–0.0100	5	2.3981–2.3992	0.0018–0.0039	0.0060–0.0250
	N	8-454 (7.4)	⑤	⑥	0.0060–0.0100	5	2.1990–2.2000	0.0009–0.0025	0.0130–0.0230
	W	8-454 (7.4)	⑤	⑥	0.0060–0.0100	5	2.1990–2.2000	0.0009–0.0025	0.0130–0.0230
1990	Z	6-262 (4.3)	①	⑧	0.0020–0.0060	4	2.2487–2.2497	0.0013–0.0035	0.0060–0.0140
	H	8-305 (5.0)	①	⑧	0.0020–0.0060	5	2.0988–2.0998	0.0013–0.0035	0.0060–0.0140
	K	8-350 (5.7)	①	⑧	0.0020–0.0060	5	2.0988–2.0998	0.0013–0.0035	0.0060–0.0140
	C	8-379 (6.2)	⑨	⑦	0.0040–0.0100	5	2.3981–2.3992	0.0018–0.0039	0.0060–0.0250
	J	8-379 (6.2)	⑨	⑦	0.0040–0.0100	5	2.3981–2.3992	0.0018–0.0039	0.0060–0.0250
	N	8-454 (7.4)	⑤	⑥	0.0060–0.0100	5	2.1990–2.2000	0.0009–0.0025	0.0130–0.0230
1991	Z	6-262 (4.3)	①	⑧	0.0020–0.0060	4	2.2487–2.2497	0.0013–0.0035	0.0060–0.0140
	H	8-305 (5.0)	①	⑧	0.0020–0.0060	5	2.0988–2.0998	0.0013–0.0035	0.0060–0.0140
	K	8-350 (5.7)	①	⑧	0.0020–0.0060	5	2.0988–2.0998	0.0013–0.0035	0.0060–0.0140
	C	8-379 (6.2)	⑨	⑦	0.0040–0.0100	5	2.3981–2.3992	0.0018–0.0039	0.0067–0.0248
	J	8-379 (6.2)	⑨	⑦	0.0040–0.0100	5	2.3981–2.3992	0.0018–0.0039	0.0067–0.0248
	N	8-454 (7.4)	⑤	⑥	0.0060–0.0100	5	2.1990–2.1996	0.0011–0.0029	0.0130–0.0230
1992	Z	6-262 (4.3)	①	⑧	0.0020–0.0060	4	2.2487–2.2497	0.0013–0.0035	0.0060–0.0140
	H	8-305 (5.0)	①	⑧	0.0020–0.0060	5	2.0988–2.0998	0.0013–0.0035	0.0060–0.0140
	K	8-350 (5.7)	①	⑧	0.0020–0.0060	5	2.0988–2.0998	0.0013–0.0035	0.0060–0.0140
	C	8-379 (6.2)	⑨	⑦	0.0040–0.0100	5	2.3981–2.3992	0.0018–0.0039	0.0067–0.0248

CRANKSHAFT AND CONNECTING ROD SPECIFICATIONS

All measurements are given in inches.

Year	VIN	No. Cylinder Displacement cu. in. (liter)	Crankshaft Main Brg. Journal Dia.	Crankshaft Main Brg. Oil Clearance	Crankshaft Shaft End-play	Crankshaft Thrust on No.	Connecting Rod Journal Diameter	Connecting Rod Oil Clearance	Connecting Rod Side Clearance
1992	J	8-379 (6.2)	⑨	⑦	0.0040–0.0100	5	2.3981–2.3992	0.0018–0.0039	0.0067–0.0248
	F	8-400 (6.5)	⑨	⑦	0.0040–0.0100	5	2.3981–2.3992	0.0018–0.0039	0.0060–0.0250
	N	8-454 (7.4)	⑤	⑥	0.0060–0.0100	5	2.1990–2.1996	0.0011–0.0029	0.0130–0.0230

① Front—2.4484–2.4493
  Inter.—2.4481–2.4490
  Rear—2.4479–2.4488
② Front—0.0010–0.0015
  Inter.—0.0010–0.0020
  Rear—0.0025–0.0030
③ 1–6—0.0010–0.0024
  7—0.0016–0.0035
④ 1—0.0008–0.0020
  2–4—0.0011–0.0023
  5—0.0017–0.0032

⑤ 1–4—2.7481–2.7490
  5—2.7476–2.7486
⑥ 1–4—0.0010–0.0030
  5—0.0024–0.0040
⑦ 1–4—0.0018–0.0033
  5—0.0022–0.0037
⑧ 1—0.0010–0.0015
  2–3—0.0010–0.0025
  4—0.0025–0.0035
⑨ 1–4—2.9495–2.9504
  5—2.9493–2.9502

VALVE SPECIFICATIONS

Year	VIN	No. Cylinder Displacement cu. in. (liter)	Seat Angle (deg.)	Face Angle (deg.)	Spring Test Pressure (lbs.)	Spring Installed Height (in.)	Stem-to-Guide Clearance (in.) Intake	Stem-to-Guide Clearance (in.) Exhaust	Stem Diameter (in.) Intake	Stem Diameter (in.) Exhaust
1988	Z	6-262 (4.3)	46	45	220 @ 1.25	1.70	0.0010–0.0027	0.0010–0.0027	0.3410–0.3417	0.3410–0.3417
	T	6-292 (4.8)	46	46	175 @ 1.26	1.66	0.0010–0.0027	0.0015–0.0032	0.3410–0.3417	0.3410–0.3417
	H	8-305 (5.0)	46	45	220 @ 1.25	1.70	0.0010–0.0027	0.0010–0.0027	0.3410–0.3417	0.3410–0.3417
	K	8-350 (5.7)	46	45	220 @ 1.25	1.70	0.0010–0.0027	0.0010–0.0027	0.3410–0.3417	0.3410–0.3417
	M	8-350 (5.7)	46	45	220 @ 1.25	1.70	0.0010–0.0027	0.0010–0.0027	0.3410–0.3417	0.3410–0.3417
	C	8-379 (6.2)	46	45	230 @ 1.38	1.81	0.0010–0.0027	0.0010–0.0027	0.3414	0.3414
	J	8-379 (6.2)	46	45	230 @ 1.38	1.81	0.0010–0.0027	0.0010–0.0027	0.3414	0.3414
	N	8-454 (7.4)	46	45	220 @ 1.40	1.80	0.0010–0.0027	0.0012–0.0027	0.3715–0.3722	0.3715–0.3722
	W	8-454 (7.4)	46	45	220 @ 1.40	1.80	0.0010–0.0027	0.0012–0.0027	0.3715–0.3722	0.3715–0.3722
1989	Z	6-262 (4.3)	46	45	220 @ 1.25	1.72	0.0010–0.0027	0.0010–0.0027	0.3414	0.3414
	H	8-305 (5.0)	46	45	200 @ 1.25	1.71	0.0010–0.0027	0.0010–0.0027	0.3414	0.3414
	K	8-350 (5.7)	46	45	200 @ 1.25	1.71	0.0010–0.0027	0.0010–0.0027	0.3414	0.3414

VALVE SPECIFICATIONS

Year	VIN	No. Cylinder Displacement cu. in. (liter)	Seat Angle (deg.)	Face Angle (deg.)	Spring Test Pressure (lbs.)	Spring Installed Height (in.)	Stem-to-Guide Clearance (in.) Intake	Stem-to-Guide Clearance (in.) Exhaust	Stem Diameter (in.) Intake	Stem Diameter (in.) Exhaust
1989	C	8-379 (6.2)	46	45	230 @ 1.39	1.81	0.0010–0.0027	0.0010–0.0027	0.3414	0.3414
	J	8-379 (6.2)	46	45	230 @ 1.39	1.81	0.0010–0.0027	0.0010–0.0027	0.3414	0.3414
	N	8-454 (7.4)	46	45	220 @ 1.40	1.80	0.0010–0.0027	0.0012–0.0027	0.3719	0.3719
	W	8-454 (7.4)	46	45	220 @ 1.40	1.80	0.0010–0.0027	0.0012–0.0027	0.3719	0.3719
1990	Z	6-262 (4.3)	46	45	220 @ 1.25	1.70	0.0010–0.0027	0.0010–0.0027	0.3414	0.3414
	H	8-305 (5.0)	46	45	200 @ 1.25	1.70	0.0010–0.0027	0.0010–0.0027	0.3414	0.3414
	K	8-350 (5.7)	46	45	200 @ 1.25	1.70	0.0010–0.0027	0.0010–0.0027	0.3414	0.3414
	C	8-379 (6.2)	46	45	230 @ 1.39	1.81	0.0010–0.0027	0.0010–0.0027	0.3414	0.3414
	J	8-379 (6.2)	46	45	230 @ 1.39	1.81	0.0010–0.0027	0.0010–0.0027	0.3414	0.3414
	N	8-454 (7.4)	46	45	220 @ 1.40	1.80	0.0010–0.0027	0.0012–0.0029	0.3719	0.3719
1991	Z	6-262 (4.3)	46	45	200 @ 1.25	1.70	0.0010–0.0027	0.0010–0.0027	NA	NA
	H	8-305 (5.0)	46	45	200 @ 1.25	1.70	0.0010–0.0027	0.0010–0.0027	NA	NA
	K	8-350 (5.7)	46	45	200 @ 1.25	1.70	0.0010–0.0027	0.0010–0.0027	NA	NA
	C	8-379 (6.2)	46	45	230 @ 1.39	1.81	0.0010–0.0027	0.0010–0.0027	NA	NA
	J	8-379 (6.2)	46	45	230 @ 1.39	1.81	0.0010–0.0027	0.0010–0.0027	NA	NA
	N	8-454 (7.4)	46	45	220 @ 1.40	1.80	0.0010–0.0027	0.0012–0.0029	NA	NA
1992	Z	6-262 (4.3)	46	45	200 @ 1.25	1.70	0.0010–0.0027	0.0010–0.0027	NA	NA
	H	8-305 (5.0)	46	45	200 @ 1.25	1.70	0.0010–0.0027	0.0010–0.0027	NA	NA
	K	8-350 (5.7)	46	45	200 @ 1.25	1.70	0.0010–0.0027	0.0010–0.0027	NA	NA
	C	8-379 (6.2)	46	45	230 @ 1.39	1.81	0.0010–0.0027	0.0010–0.0027	NA	NA
	J	8-379 (6.2)	46	45	230 @ 1.39	1.81	0.0010–0.0027	0.0010–0.0027	NA	NA
	F	8-400 (6.5)	46	45	230 @ 1.39	1.81	0.0010–0.0027	0.0010–0.0027	NA	NA
	N	8-454 (7.4)	46	45	220 @ 1.40	1.80	0.0010–0.0027	0.0012–0.0029	NA	NA

NA—Not available

PISTON AND RING SPECIFICATIONS

All measurements are given in inches.

Year	VIN	No. Cylinder Displacement cu. in. (liter)	Piston Clearance	Ring Gap			Ring Side Clearance		
				Top Compression	Bottom Compression	Oil Control	Top Compression	Bottom Compression	Oil Control
1988	Z	6-262 (4.3)	0.0007–0.0017	0.0100–0.0200	0.0100–0.0250	0.0150–0.0550	0.0012–0.0032	0.0012–0.0032	0.0020–0.0070
	T	6-292 (4.8)	0.0026–0.0036	0.0100–0.0200	0.0100–0.0200	0.0150–0.0550	0.0010–0.0027	0.0020–0.0040	0.0005–0.0055
	H	8-305 (5.0)	0.0007–0.0017	0.0100–0.0200	0.0100–0.0250	0.0150–0.0550	0.0012–0.0032	0.0012–0.0032	0.0020–0.0070
	K	8-350 (5.7)	0.0007–0.0017	0.0100–0.0200	0.0130–0.0250	0.0150–0.0550	0.0012–0.0032	0.0012–0.0032	0.0020–0.0070
	M	8-350 (5.7)	0.0007–0.0017	0.0100–0.0200	0.0130–0.0250	0.0150–0.0550	0.0012–0.0032	0.0012–0.0032	0.0020–0.0070
	C	8-379 (6.2)	①	0.0120–0.0220	0.0300–0.0400	0.0100–0.0210	0.0030–0.0071	0.0300–0.0400	0.0016–0.0038
	J	8-379 (6.2)	①	0.0120–0.0220	0.0300–0.0400	0.0100–0.0210	0.0030–0.0071	0.0300–0.0400	0.0016–0.0038
	N	8-454 (7.4)	0.0030–0.0040	0.0100–0.0200	0.0100–0.0200	0.0150–0.0550	0.0017–0.0032	0.0017–0.0032	0.0050–0.0065
	W	8-454 (7.4)	0.0030–0.0040	0.0100–0.0200	0.0100–0.0200	0.0150–0.0550	0.0017–0.0032	0.0017–0.0032	0.0050–0.0065
1989	Z	6-262 (4.3)	0.0007–0.0017	0.0100–0.0200	0.0100–0.0250	0.0150–0.0550	0.0012–0.0032	0.0012–0.0032	0.0020–0.0070
	H	8-305 (5.0)	0.0007–0.0017	0.0100–0.0200	0.0100–0.0250	0.0150–0.0550	0.0012–0.0032	0.0012–0.0032	0.0020–0.0070
	K	8-350 (5.7)	0.0007–0.0017	0.0100–0.0200	0.0130–0.0250	0.0150–0.0550	0.0012–0.0032	0.0012–0.0032	0.0020–0.0070
	M	8-350 (5.7)	0.0007–0.0017	0.0100–0.0200	0.0130–0.0250	0.0150–0.0550	0.0012–0.0032	0.0012–0.0032	0.0020–0.0070
	C	8-379 (6.2)	①	0.0120–0.0220	0.0300–0.0400	0.0100–0.0210	0.0030–0.0071	0.0300–0.0400	0.0016–0.0038
	J	8-379 (6.2)	①	0.0120–0.0220	0.0300–0.0400	0.0100–0.0210	0.0030–0.0071	0.0300–0.0400	0.0016–0.0038
	N	8-454 (7.4)	0.0030–0.0040	0.0100–0.0200	0.0100–0.0200	0.0150–0.0550	0.0017–0.0032	0.0017–0.0032	0.0050–0.0065
	W	8-454 (7.4)	0.0030–0.0040	0.0100–0.0200	0.0100–0.0200	0.0150–0.0550	0.0017–0.0032	0.0017–0.0032	0.0050–0.0065
1990	Z	6-262 (4.3)	0.0017–0.0017	0.0100–0.0250	0.0100–0.0250	0.0150–0.0550	0.0012–0.0032	0.0012–0.0032	0.0020–0.0070
	H	8-305 (5.0)	0.0007–0.0017	0.0100–0.0200	0.0100–0.0250	0.0150–0.0550	0.0012–0.0032	0.0012–0.0032	0.0020–0.0070
	K	8-350 (5.7)	0.0007–0.0017	0.0100–0.0200	0.0130–0.0250	0.0150–0.0550	0.0012–0.0032	0.0012–0.0032	0.0020–0.0070
	C	8-379 (6.2)	①	0.0120–0.0220	0.0300–0.0400	0.0100–0.0210	0.0030–0.0071	0.0300–0.0400	0.0016–0.0038
	J	8-379 (6.2)	①	0.0120–0.0220	0.0300–0.0400	0.0100–0.0210	0.0030–0.0071	0.0300–0.0400	0.0016–0.0038
	N	8-454 (7.4)	0.0030–0.0040	0.0100–0.0200	0.0100–0.0200	0.0150–0.0550	0.0017–0.0032	0.0017–0.0032	0.0050–0.0065

GENERAL MOTORS CORPORATION
C/K SERIES (PICK-UP) • R/V SERIES (PICK-UP) • BLAZER/JIMMY • SUBURBAN • G SERIES (VAN)

PISTON AND RING SPECIFICATIONS
All measurements are given in inches.

Year	VIN	No. Cylinder Displacement cu. in. (liter)	Piston Clearance	Ring Gap			Ring Side Clearance		
				Top Compression	Bottom Compression	Oil Control	Top Compression	Bottom Compression	Oil Control
1991	Z	6-262 (4.3)	0.0007–0.0017	0.0100–0.0200	0.0100–0.0250	0.0150–0.0550	0.0012–0.0032	0.0012–0.0032	0.0020–0.0070
	H	8-305 (5.0)	0.0007–0.0017	0.0100–0.0200	0.0100–0.0250	0.0150–0.0550	0.0012–0.0032	0.0012–0.0032	0.0020–0.0070
	K	8-350 (5.7)	0.0007–0.0017	0.0100–0.0200	0.0100–0.0250	0.0150–0.0550	0.0012–0.0032	0.0012–0.0032	0.0020–0.0070
	C	8-379 (6.2)	①	0.0120–0.0220	0.0295–0.0394	0.0100–0.0200	0.0030–0.0071	0.0300–0.0400	0.0016–0.0038
	J	8-379 (6.2)	①	0.0120–0.0220	0.0295–0.0394	0.0100–0.0200	0.0030–0.0071	0.0300–0.0400	0.0016–0.0038
	N	8-454 (7.4)	0.0030–0.0040	0.0100–0.0200	0.0160–0.0240	0.0100–0.0300	0.0012–0.0029	0.0012–0.0029	0.0050–0.0065
1992	Z	6-262 (4.3)	0.0007–0.0017	0.0100–0.0200	0.0100–0.0250	0.0150–0.0550	0.0012–0.0032	0.0012–0.0032	0.0020–0.0070
	H	8-305 (5.0)	0.0007–0.0021	0.0100–0.0200	0.0180–0.0260	0.0100–0.0300	0.0012–0.0032	0.0012–0.0032	0.0020–0.0070
	K	8-350 (5.7)	0.0007–0.0021	0.0100–0.0200	0.0180–0.0260	0.0100–0.0300	0.0012–0.0032	0.0012–0.0032	0.0020–0.0070
	C	8-379 (6.2)	①	0.0120–0.0220	0.0295–0.0394	0.0100–0.0200	0.0030–0.0071	0.0300–0.0400	0.0016–0.0038
	J	8-379 (6.2)	①	0.0120–0.0220	0.0295–0.0394	0.0100–0.0200	0.0030–0.0071	0.0300–0.0400	0.0016–0.0038
	F	8-400 (6.5)	①	0.0120–0.0220	0.0295–0.0394	0.0100–0.0236	0.0030–0.0071	0.0300–0.0400	0.0016–0.0038
	N	8-454 (7.4)	0.0030–0.0040	0.0100–0.0200	0.0160–0.0240	0.0100–0.0300	0.0012–0.0029	0.0012–0.0029	0.0050–0.0065

① Bohn Pistons
   1-6—0.0035–0.0045
   7-8—0.0040–0.0050

Zollner Pistons
   1-6—0.0044–0.0054
   7-8—0.0049–0.0059

TORQUE SPECIFICATIONS
All readings in ft. lbs.

Year	VIN	No. Cylinder Displacement cu. in. (liter)	Cylinder Head Bolts	Main Bearing Bolts	Rod Bearing Bolts	Crankshaft Pulley Bolts	Flywheel Bolts	Manifold		Spark Plugs
								Intake	Exhaust	
1988	Z	6-262 (4.3)	65	80	45	70	75	36	⑦	22
	T	6-292 (4.8)	95①	65	44	50	110	⑤	⑤	17–27
	H	8-305 (5.0)	65	④	45	70	60	35	⑦	17–27
	K	8-350 (5.7)	65	④	45	70	60	35	⑦	17–27
	M	8-350 (5.7)	65	④	45	70	60	35	⑦	17–27
	C	8-379 (6.2)	②	③	48	200	60	31	25	—
	J	8-379 (6.2)	②	③	48	200	60	31	25	—
	N	8-454 (7.4)	80	110	50	85	65	30	20	17–27
	W	8-454 (7.4)	80	110	50	85	65	30	20	17–27

TORQUE SPECIFICATIONS
All readings in ft. lbs.

Year	VIN	No. Cylinder Displacement cu. in. (liter)	Cylinder Head Bolts	Main Bearing Bolts	Rod Bearing Bolts	Crankshaft Pulley Bolts	Flywheel Bolts	Manifold		Spark Plugs
								Intake	Exhaust	
1989	Z	6-262 (4.3)	65	80	45	70	75	36	⑦	22
	H	8-305 (5.0)	65	④	45	70	60	35	⑦	17–27
	K	8-350 (5.7)	65	④	45	70	60	35	⑦	17–27
	M	8-350 (5.7)	65	④	45	70	60	35	⑦	17–27
	C	8-379 (6.2)	②	③	48	200	60	31	25	—
	J	8-379 (6.2)	②	③	48	200	60	31	25	—
	N	8-454 (7.4)	80	110	50	85	65	30	20	17–27
	W	8-454 (7.4)	80	110	50	85	65	30	20	17–27
1990	Z	6-262 (4.3)	65	80	45	70	75	36	⑦	22
	H	8-305 (5.0)	65	④	45	70	60	35	⑦	17–27
	K	8-350 (5.7)	65	④	45	70	60	35	⑦	17–27
	C	8-379 (6.2)	②	③	48	200	60	31	25	—
	J	8-379 (6.2)	②	③	48	200	60	31	25	—
	N	8-454 (7.4)	80	110	50	85	65	30	20	17–27
1991	Z	6-262 (4.3)	65	75	20⑥	75	75	36	⑦	22
	H	8-305 (5.0)	65	④	45	70	75	35	⑦	15
	K	8-350 (5.7)	65	④	45	70	60	35	⑦	15
	C	8-379 (6.2)	②	③	48	200	66	31	26	—
	J	8-379 (6.2)	②	③	48	200	66	31	26	—
	N	8-454 (7.4)	80	100	48	85	65	40	40	22
1992	Z	6-262 (4.3)	65	75	20⑥	70	75	36	⑦	22
	H	8-305 (5.0)	65	④	45	70	75	35	⑦	15
	K	8-350 (5.7)	65	④	45	70	60	35	⑦	15
	C	8-379 (6.2)	②	③	48	200	66	31	26	—
	J	8-379 (6.2)	②	③	48	200	66	31	26	—
	F	8-400 (6.5)	②	④	48	200	66	31	26	—
	N	8-454 (7.4)	80	100	48	85	65	40	40	22

① Left front bolt 85 ft. lbs.
② 1st step 20 ft. lbs.
  2nd step 50 ft. lbs.
  3rd step ¼ turn ft. lbs.
③ Inner bolts 110 ft. lbs.
  Outer bolts 100 ft. lbs.
④ All outer bolts on caps 2, 3, 4—70 ft. lbs.
  All other bolts 80 ft. lbs.
⑤ Intake manifold to exhaust manifold—44 ft. lbs.
  Manifold to cylinder head—38 ft. lbs.
⑥ Plus additional 60 degree turn
  Tubular stainless steel—26 ft. lbs.
⑦ Two center bolts—26 ft. lbs., all others—
  20 ft. lbs.

BRAKE SPECIFICATIONS
All measurements in inches unless noted.

Year	Model	Lug Nut Torque (ft. lbs.)	Master Cylinder Bore	Brake Disc Minimum Thickness	Brake Disc Maximum Runout	Standard Brake Drum Diameter	Minimum Lining Thickness Front	Minimum Lining Thickness Rear
1988	C10/1500 Pick-Up	90	—	0.979	0.004	10.00	③	③
	C20/2500 Pick-Up	90	—	0.979	0.004	11.15	③	③
	C20/2500 Pick-Up	90	—	1.230	0.004	13.00	③	③
	C30/3500 Pick-Up	90①	—	1.230	0.004	13.00	③	③
	K10/1500 Pick-Up	90	—	0.979	0.004	10.00	③	③
	K20/2500 Pick-Up	90	—	0.979	0.004	11.15	③	③
	K30/3500 Pick-Up	90①	—	1.230	0.004	13.00	③	③
	R20/2500 Pick-Up	120	—	1.230	0.004	13.00	③	③
	R30/3500 Pick-Up	120	—	1.230	0.004	13.00	③	③
	V30/3500 Pick-Up	120	—	1.230	0.004	13.00	③	③
	R10/1500 Suburban	100	—	0.979	0.004	11.15	③	③
	R20/2500 Suburban	120	—	1.230	0.004	13.00	③	③
	V10/1500 Suburban	100②	—	0.979	0.004	11.15	③	③
	V20/2500 Suburban	120	—	1.230	0.004	13.00	③	③
	V Blazer/Jimmy	100②	—	0.979	0.004	11.15	③	③
	G10/1500 Van	100	—	0.979	0.004	11.00	③	③
	G20/2500 Van	100	—	0.979	0.004	11.15	③	③
	G30/3500 Van	120	—	1.230	0.004	13.00	③	③
1989	C10/1500 Pick-Up	105	—	0.979	0.004	10.00	③	③
	C20/2500 Pick-Up	105	—	0.979	0.004	11.15	③	③
	C20/2500 Pick-Up	105	—	1.230	0.004	13.00	③	③
	C30/3500 Pick-Up	105①	—	1.230	0.004	13.00	③	③
	K10/1500 Pick-Up	105	—	0.979	0.004	10.00	③	③
	K20/2500 Pick-Up	105	—	0.979	0.004	11.15	③	③
	K30/3500 Pick-Up	105①	—	1.230	0.004	13.00	③	③
	R20/2500 Pick-Up	120	—	1.230	0.004	13.00	③	③
	R30/3500 Pick-Up	120	—	1.230	0.004	13.00	③	③
	V30/3500 Pick-Up	120	—	1.230	0.004	13.00	③	③
	R10/1500 Suburban	100	—	0.979	0.004	11.15	③	③
	R20/2500 Suburban	120	—	1.230	0.004	13.00	③	③
	V10/1500 Suburban	100②	—	0.979	0.004	11.15	③	③
	V20/2500 Suburban	120	—	1.230	0.004	13.00	③	③
	V Blazer/Jimmy	100②	—	0.979	0.004	11.15	③	③
	G10/1500 Van	100	—	0.979	0.004	11.00	③	③
	G20/2500 Van	100	—	0.979	0.004	11.15	③	③
	G30/3500 Van	120	—	1.230	0.004	13.00	③	③
1990	C10/1500 Pick-Up	105	—	0.979	0.004	10.00	③	③
	C20/2500 Pick-Up	105	—	0.979	0.004	11.15	③	③
	C20/2500 Pick-Up	105	—	1.230	0.004	13.00	③	③
	C30/3500 Pick-Up	105①	—	1.230	0.004	13.00	③	③
	K10/1500 Pick-Up	105	—	0.979	0.004	10.00	③	③
	K20/2500 Pick-Up	105	—	0.979	0.004	11.15	③	③
	K30/3500 Pick-Up	105①	—	1.230	0.004	13.00	③	③

BRAKE SPECIFICATIONS

All measurements in inches unless noted.

Year	Model	Lug Nut Torque (ft. lbs.)	Master Cylinder Bore	Brake Disc Minimum Thickness	Brake Disc Maximum Runout	Standard Brake Drum Diameter	Minimum Lining Thickness Front	Minimum Lining Thickness Rear
	R20/2500 Pick-Up	120	—	1.230	0.004	13.00	③	③
	R30/3500 Pick-Up	120	—	1.230	0.004	13.00	③	③
	V30/3500 Pick-Up	120	—	1.230	0.004	13.00	③	③
	R10/1500 Suburban	100	—	0.979	0.004	11.15	③	③
	R20/2500 Suburban	120	—	1.230	0.004	13.00	③	③
	V10/1500 Suburban	100②	—	0.979	0.004	11.15	③	③
	V20/2500 Suburban	120	—	1.230	0.004	13.00	③	③
	V Blazer/Jimmy	100②	—	0.979	0.004	11.15	③	③
	G10/1500 Van	100	—	0.979	0.004	11.00	③	③
	G20/2500 Van	100	—	0.979	0.004	11.15	③	③
	G30/3500 Van	120	—	1.230	0.004	13.00	③	③
1991	C10/1500 Pick-Up	105	—	0.979	0.004	10.00	③	③
	C10/1500 Pick-Up	105	—	1.230	0.004	10.00	③	③
	C20/2500 Pick-Up	105	—	0.979	0.004	11.15	③	③
	C20/2500 Pick-Up	105	—	1.230	0.004	13.00	③	③
	C30/3500 Pick-Up	105①	—	1.230	0.004	13.00	③	③
	K10/1500 Pick-Up	105	—	0.979	0.004	10.00	③	③
	K20/2500 Pick-Up	105	—	0.979	0.004	11.15	③	③
	K30/3500 Pick-Up	105①	—	1.230	0.004	13.00	③	③
	R20/2500 Pick-Up	120	—	1.230	0.004	13.00	③	③
	R30/3500 Pick-Up	120	—	1.230	0.004	13.00	③	③
	V30/3500 Pick-Up	120	—	1.230	0.004	13.00	③	③
	R10/1500 Suburban	100	—	0.979	0.004	11.15	③	③
	R20/2500 Suburban	120	—	1.230	0.004	13.00	③	③
	V10/1500 Suburban	100②	—	0.979	0.004	11.15	③	③
	V20/2500 Suburban	120	—	1.230	0.004	13.00	③	③
	V Blazer/Jimmy	100②	—	0.979	0.004	11.15	③	③
	G10/1500 Van	100	—	0.979	0.004	11.00	③	③
	G20/2500 Van	100	—	0.979	0.004	11.15	③	③
	G30/3500 Van	120	—	1.230	0.004	13.00	③	③
1992	C10/1500 Pick-Up	105	—	0.979	0.004	10.00	③	③
	C20/2500 Pick-Up	105	—	0.979	0.004	11.15	③	③
	C20/2500 Pick-Up	105	—	1.230	0.004	13.00	③	③
	C30/3500 Pick-Up	105①	—	1.230	0.004	13.00	③	③
	K10/1500 Pick-Up	105	—	0.979	0.004	10.00	③	③
	K20/2500 Pick-Up	105	—	0.979	0.004	11.15	③	③
	K30/3500 Pick-Up	105①	—	1.230	0.004	13.00	③	③
	C10/1500 Suburban	100	—	0.979	0.004	11.15	③	③
	C20/2500 Suburban	120	—	1.230	0.004	13.00	③	③
	K10/1500 Suburban	100②	—	0.979	0.004	11.15	③	③
	K20/2500 Suburban	120	—	1.230	0.004	13.00	③	③
	Blazer/Jimmy	100②	—	0.979	0.004	11.15	③	③
	G10/1500 Van	100	—	0.979	0.004	11.00	③	③

GENERAL MOTORS CORPORATION
C/K SERIES (PICK-UP) • R/V SERIES (PICK-UP) • BLAZER/JIMMY • SUBURBAN • G SERIES (VAN)

BRAKE SPECIFICATIONS
All measurements in inches unless noted.

Year	Model	Lug Nut Torque (ft. lbs.)	Master Cylinder Bore	Brake Disc Minimum Thickness	Brake Disc Maximum Runout	Standard Brake Drum Diameter	Minimum Lining Thickness Front	Minimum Lining Thickness Rear
1992	G20/2500 Van	100	—	0.979	0.004	11.15	③	③
	G30/3500 Van	120	—	1.230	0.004	13.00	③	③

NOTE: Minimum lining thickness is as recommended by the manufacturer. Because of variations in state inspection regulations, the minimum allowable thickness may be different than recommended by the manufacturer.
① Dual wheels—125 ft. lbs.
② Aluminum wheels—100 ft. lbs., Steel wheels—88 ft. lbs.
③ Within 1/32 inch of rivet head or shoe

WHEEL ALIGNMENT

Year	Model	Caster Range (deg.)	Caster Preferred Setting (deg.)	Camber Range (deg.)	Camber Preferred Setting (deg.)	Toe-in (in.)	Steering Axis Inclination (deg.)
1988	C10/1500 Pick-Up	2¾P–4¾P ①	3¾P	0–1P	½P	1/8	—
	K10/1500 Pick-Up	3P–5P ①	4P	13/32P–13/32P	29/32P	1/16	—
	C20/2500 Pick-Up	2¾P–4¾P ①	3¾P	0–1P	½P	1/8	—
	K20/2500 Pick-Up	3P–5P ①	4P	13/32P–1 13/32P	29/32P	1/16	—
	C30/3500 Pick-Up	2¾P–4¾P ①	3¾P	0–1P	½P	1/8	—
	K30/3500 Pick-Up	3P–5P ①	4P	¼P–1¼P	¾P	1/16	—
	R20/2500 Pick-Up	—	④	½N–1P	¼P	3/16	—
	R30/3500 Pick-Up	—	④	½N–1P	¼P	3/16	—
	U30/3500 Pick-Up	—	④	¾P–2P	1½P	1/8	—
	R10 Suburban	—	②	0–1 3/8P	11/16P	3/16	—
	V10 Suburban	—	③	¾P–2P	1½P	1/8	—
	R20 Suburban	—	④	½N–1P	¼P	3/16	—
	V20 Suburban	—	③	¾P–2P	1½P	1/8	—
	V Blazer/Jimmy	—	③	¾P–2P	1½P	1/8	—
	G10/1500 Van	—	⑤	¼N–1¼	½P	3/16	—
	G20/2500 Van	—	⑤	¼N–1¼	½P	3/16	—
	G30/3500 Van	—	⑤	½N–1P	¼P	3/16	—
1989	C1500 Pick-Up	2¾P–4¾P ①	3¾P	0–1P	½P	1/8	—
	K1500 Pick-Up	2P–4P ①	3P	5/32P–1 5/32P	21/32P	1/8	—
	C2500 Pick-Up	2¾P–4¾P ①	3¾P	0–1P	½P	1/8	—
	K2500 Pick-Up	2P–4P ①	3P	5/32P–1 5/32P	21/32P	1/8	—
	C3500 Pick-Up	2¾P–4¾P ①	3¾P	0–1P	½P	1/8	—
	K3500 Pick-Up	2P–4P ①	3P	¼P–1¼P	¾P	1/16	—
	R2500 Pick-Up	—	④	½N–1P	¼P	3/16	—
	R3500 Pick-Up	—	④	½N–1P	¼P	3/16	—
	V3500 Pick-Up	—	③	¾P–2P	1½P	1/8	—
	R1500 Suburban	—	②	0–1 3/8P	11/16P	3/16	—
	V1500 Pick-Up	—	③	¾P–2	1½P	1/8	—
	R2500 Suburban	—	④	½N–1P	¼P	3/16	—
	V2500 Suburban	—	③	¾P–2P	1½P	1/8	—

WHEEL ALIGNMENT

Year	Model	Caster Range (deg.)	Caster Preferred Setting (deg.)	Camber Range (deg.)	Camber Preferred Setting (deg.)	Toe-in (in.)	Steering Axis Inclination (deg.)
1989	V Blazer/Jimmy	—	③	$3/4$P–2P	$1^{1}/_{2}$P	$1/8$	—
	G10/1500 Van	—	⑤	$1/4$N–$1^{1}/_{4}$P	$1/2$P	$3/16$	—
	G20/2500 Van	—	⑤	$1/4$N–$1^{1}/_{4}$P	$1/2$P	$3/16$	—
	G30/3500 Van	—	⑤	$1/2$N–1P	$1/4$P	$3/16$	—
1990	C10/1500 Pick-Up	$2^{3}/_{4}$P–$4^{3}/_{4}$P ①	$3^{3}/_{4}$P	0–1P	$1/2$P	$1/8$	—
	K10/1500 Pick-Up	3P–5P ①	4P	$13/32$P–$13/32$P	$29/32$P	$1/16$	—
	C20/2500 Pick-Up	$2^{3}/_{4}$P–$4^{3}/_{4}$P ①	$3^{3}/_{4}$P	0–1P	$1/2$P	$1/8$	—
	K20/2500 Pick-Up	3P–5P ①	4P	$13/32$P–$1^{13}/_{32}$P	$29/32$P	$1/16$	—
	C30/3500 Pick-Up	$2^{3}/_{4}$P–$4^{3}/_{4}$P ①	$3^{3}/_{4}$P	0–1P	$1/2$P	$1/8$	—
	K30/3500 Pick-Up	3P–5P ①	4P	$1/4$P–$1^{1}/_{4}$P	$3/4$P	$1/16$	—
	R20/2500 Pick-Up	—	④	$1/2$N–1P	$1/4$P	$3/16$	—
	R30/3500 Pick-Up	—	④	$1/2$N–1P	$1/4$P	$3/16$	—
	U30/3500 Pick-Up	—	④	$3/4$P–2P	$1^{1}/_{2}$P	$1/8$	—
	R10 Suburban	—	②	0–$1^{3}/_{8}$P	$11/16$P	$3/16$	—
	V10 Suburban	—	③	$3/4$P–2P	$1^{1}/_{2}$P	$1/8$	—
	R20 Suburban	—	④	$1/2$N–1P	$1/4$P	$3/16$	—
	V20 Suburban	—	③	$3/4$P–2P	$1^{1}/_{2}$P	$1/8$	—
	V Blazer/Jimmy	—	③	$3/4$P–2P	$1^{1}/_{2}$P	$1/8$	—
	G10/1500 Van	—	⑤	$1/4$N–$1^{1}/_{4}$	$1/2$P	$3/16$	—
	G20/2500 Van	—	⑤	$1/4$N–$1^{1}/_{4}$	$1/2$P	$3/16$	—
	G30/3500 Van	—	⑤	$1/2$N–1P	$1/4$P	$3/16$	—
1991	C1500 Pick-Up	$2^{3}/_{4}$P–$4^{3}/_{4}$P ①	$3^{3}/_{4}$P	0–1P	$1/2$P	$1/8$	—
	K1500 Pick-Up	2P–4P ①	3P	$5/32$P–$1^{5}/_{32}$P	$21/32$P	$1/8$	—
	C2500 Pick-Up	$2^{3}/_{4}$P–$4^{3}/_{4}$P ①	$3^{3}/_{4}$P	0–1P	$1/2$P	$1/8$	—
	K2500 Pick-Up	2P–4P ①	3P	$5/32$P–$1^{5}/_{32}$P	$21/32$P	$1/8$	—
	C3500 Pick-Up	$2^{3}/_{4}$P–$4^{3}/_{4}$P ①	$3^{3}/_{4}$P	0–1P	$1/2$P	$1/8$	—
	K3500 Pick-Up	2P–4P ①	3P	$1/4$P–$1^{1}/_{4}$P	$3/4$P	$1/16$	—
	R2500 Pick-Up	—	④	$1/2$N–1P	$1/4$P	$3/16$	—
	R3500 Pick-Up	—	④	$1/2$N–1P	$1/4$P	$3/16$	—
	V3500 Pick-Up	—	③	$3/4$P–2P	$1^{1}/_{2}$P	$1/8$	—
	R1500 Suburban	—	②	0–$1^{3}/_{8}$P	$11/16$P	$3/16$	—
	V1500 Suburban	—	②	$3/4$P–2P	$1^{1}/_{2}$P	$1/8$	—
	R2500 Suburban	—	④	$1/2$N–1P	$1/4$P	$3/16$	—
	V2500 Suburban	—	③	$3/4$P–2P	$1^{1}/_{2}$P	$1/8$	—
	V Blazer/Jimmy	—	③	$3/4$P–2P	$1^{1}/_{2}$P	$1/8$	—
	G10/1500 Van	—	⑤	$1/4$N–$1^{1}/_{4}$P	$1/2$P	$3/16$	—
	G20/2500 Van	—	⑤	$1/4$N–$1^{1}/_{4}$P	$1/2$P	$3/16$	—
	G30/3500 Van	—	⑤	$1/2$N–1P	$1/4$P	$3/16$	—
1992	C1500 Pick-Up	$3^{3}/_{4}$P–$5^{3}/_{4}$P	$4^{1}/_{4}$P	$1/2$P–$1^{1}/_{2}$P	$3/4$P	$1/4$	—
	K1500 Pick-Up	1P–5P	3P	$5/8$N–$1^{5}/_{8}$P	$5/8$P	$1/4$	—
	C2500 Pick-Up	$3^{3}/_{4}$P–$5^{3}/_{4}$P	$4^{1}/_{4}$P	$1/2$P–$1^{1}/_{2}$P	$3/4$P	$1/4$	—
	K2500 Pick-Up	1P–5P	3P	0–1P	$1/2$P	$1/4$	—
	C3500 Pick-Up	$3^{3}/_{4}$P–$5^{3}/_{4}$P	$4^{1}/_{4}$P	$1/2$P–$1^{1}/_{2}$P	$3/4$P	$1/4$	—
	K3500 Pick-Up	1P–5P	3P	0–1P	$1/2$P	$1/4$	—

WHEEL ALIGNMENT

Year	Model	Caster Range (deg.)	Caster Preferred Setting (deg.)	Camber Range (deg.)	Camber Preferred Setting (deg.)	Toe-in (in.)	Steering Axis Inclination (deg.)
1992	C1500 Suburban	3¾P–5¾P	4¼P	½P–1½P	¾P	¼	—
	K1500 Suburban	1P–5P	3P	⅝N–1⅝P	⅝P	¼	—
	C2500 Suburban	3¾P–5¾P	4¼P	½P–1½P	¾P	¼	—
	K2500 Suburban	1P–5P	3P	½P–1½P	½P	¼	—
	K Blazer/Jimmy	—	③	¾P–2P	1½P	⅛	—
	G10/1500 Van	—	⑤	¼N–1¼P	½P	3/16	—
	G20/2500 Van	—	⑤	¼N–1¼P	½P	3/16	—
	G30/3500 Van	—	⑤	½N–1P	¼P	3/16	—

N—Negative
P—Positive

① Caster/camber adjustment kit must be installed to make adjustments
② If ride height is 2½, caster should be 3⅝P
If ride height is 3, caster should be 3⅛P
If ride height is 3½, caster should be 2⅝P
If ride height is 3¾, caster should be 2⅜P
If ride height is 4, caster should be 2⅛P

③ If ride height is 2½ to 4, caster should be 8P
④ If ride height is 2½, caster should be 1½P
If ride height is 3, caster should be 15/16P
If ride height is 3½, caster should be 5/16P
If ride height is 3¾, caster should be ⅛P
If ride height is 4, caster should be 0

⑤ If ride height is 1½, caster should be 3⅜P
If ride height is 2, caster should be 3P
If ride height is 2½, caster should be 2¹¹/₁₆P
If ride height is 3, caster should be 2⁵/₁₆P
If ride height is 3½, caster should be 2
If ride height is 3¾, caster should be 1¹³/₁₆P
If ride height is 4, caster should be 1¹¹/₁₆P

ENGINE ELECTRICAL

NOTE: Disconnecting the negative battery cable on some vehicles may interfere with the functions of the on board computer systems and may require the computer to undergo a relearning process, once the negative battery cable is reconnected.

Distributor

Removal

1. Disconnect the negative battery cable.
2. Remove all necessary components in order to gain access to the distributor assembly.
3. Disconnect the distributor electrical connectors. If equipped, disconnect the vacuum line. Mark and remove the spark plug wires.
4. Remove the distributor cap. Position the engine at TDC. Matchmark the rotor and the distributor body. Matchmark the distributor assembly and the engine block.
5. Remove the distributor retaining bolt. Carefully remove the distributor from the vehicle.

NOTE: As the distributor is removed from the engine, the rotor will turn counterclockwise. Observe and mark the start and finish rotation of the rotor. When reinstalling, position the rotor at the last mark and set the distributor into the engine. As the distributor drops into place, the rotor should turn to its original position, providing the engine crankshaft has not been rotated with the distributor out.

Installation

TIMING NOT DISTURBED

NOTE: To ensure correct ignition timing if the engine has not been disturbed, the distributor must be installed with the rotor in the same position as when removed.

1. Align the rotor to the last mark made and install the distributor in the engine.
2. The rotor should turn and end up at the first mark made. Ensure the distributor and oil pump rod are fully engaged.
3. Reconnect the distributor cap and wires.
4. Tighten the distributor hold-down bolt and set the timing.

TIMING DISTURBED

1. Remove the No. 1 spark plug. Place a finger over the spark plug hole and rotate the engine in the normal direction of rotation slowly, until compression is felt.
2. Align the timing mark on the crankshaft pulley to the **0** on the engine timing indicator by rotating the engine in the same direction slowly.
3. Position the rotor between No. 1 and No. 8 spark plug towers on the V8 engine or the No. 1 and No. 6 spark plug towers on the V6 engine.
4. Install the distributor, distributor cap, spark plug, wiring and connectors.
5. Check the engine timing and adjust, as required.

Ignition Timing

Connect the timing light per manufacturers instructions to the engine. Ensure the timing light is connected to the No. 1 spark plug wire. Connect the tachometer to the engine per manufacturers instructions. If equipped with a diesel engine, a special timing light and a digital tachometer must be used.

Adjustment

1. Locate the timing marks on the crankshaft pulley and the front of the timing case cover.
2. Clean off the timing marks.
3. Use chalk or white paint to color the mark on the scale that will indicate the correct timing, when aligned with the mark on the pulley or the pointer.

4. Attach a tachometer to the engine. Attach a timing light to the engine.

5. Disconnect and plug the vacuum lines to the distributor, if equipped. Loosen the distributor lock bolt slightly to permit the distributor to be turned.

6. Adjust the idle to the correct specification.

7. With the timing light aimed at the pulley and the marks on the engine, turn the distributor in the direction of rotor rotation to retard the spark or in the opposite direction of rotor rotation to advance the spark. Align the marks on the pulley and the engine with the flashes of the timing light.

Alternator

For further information, please refer to "Alternators" in the Unit Repair section.

Precautions

Several precautions must be observed with alternator equipped vehicles to avoid damage to the unit.

● If the battery is removed for any reason, make sure it is reconnected with the correct polarity. Reversing the battery connections may result in damage to the 1-way rectifiers.

● When utilizing a booster battery as a starting aid, always connect the positive to positive terminals and the negative terminal from the booster battery to a good engine ground on the vehicle being started.

● Never use a fast charger as a booster to start vehicles.

● Disconnect the battery cables when charging the battery with a fast charger.

● Never attempt to polarize the alternator.

● Do not use test lights of more than 12 volts when checking diode continuity.

● Do not short across or ground any of the alternator terminals.

● The polarity of the battery, alternator and regulator must be matched and considered before making any electrical connections within the system.

● Never separate the alternator on an open circuit. Make sure all connections within the circuit are clean and tight.

● Disconnect the battery ground terminal when performing any service on electrical components.

● Disconnect the battery if arc welding is to be done on the vehicle.

Removal and Installation

1. Disconnect the negative battery cable. Disconnect the electrical connectors at the alternator.

2. Remove the necessary components in order to gain access to the alternator assembly.

3. Remove the alternator belt. Remove the alternator retaining bolts. Remove the alternator from the vehicle.

4. Installation is the reverse of the removal procedure. Adjust the alternator belt to specification.

Belt Tension Adjustment

V-BELT

1. Place a belt tension gauge at the center of the greatest span of a warm not hot drive belt and measure the tension.

2. If the belt is below the specification, loosen the component mounting bracket and adjust to specification.

3. Run the engine at idle for 15 minutes to allow the belt to reseat itself in the pulleys.

4. Allow the drive belt to cool and re-measure the tension. Adjust as necessary to meet the following specifications:

    a. On the 4.3L, 5.0L, 5.7L, and 7.4L engines—old belt-90 lbs. (400 N) or new belt-135 lbs. (600 N).

    b. On the 4.8L engine—old belt-90 lbs. (400 N) or new belt-169 lbs. (750 N).

    c. On the 6.2L diesel engine—old belt-67 lbs. (300 N) or new belt-146 lbs. (650 N).

SERPENTINE BELTS

Serpentine belts use an automatic tensioner which is spring activated and can be turned to the left or the right to apply or release the pulley tension.

Starter

For further information, please refer to "Starters" in the Unit Repair section.

Removal and Installation

1. Disconnect the negative battery cable. As required, raise and support the vehicle safely.

2. Remove the flywheel cover. Remove the exhaust crossover pipe, as required.

3. Disconnect the electrical wiring harness and battery leads at the solenoid terminals.

4. Remove the starter mounting bolts and retaining nuts. Remove the starter assembly from the vehicle.

5. Installation is the reverse of the removal procedure. Install any shims that were removed with the starter and torque the bolts to specification.

Diesel Glow Plugs

Removal and Installation

1. Disconnect the negative battery cable.

2. Disconnect the electrical connection at the glow plug.

3. Using a suitable tool remove the glow plug.

4. Installation is the reverse of removal. Torque the glow plugs to 13 ft. lbs. (17 Nm).

Testing

INHIBIT SWITCH

Check the temperature controlled switch to make sure it is closed at low temperatures or open at temperatures above 125°F (52°C).

1. Remove the connector from the inhibit switch when the engine temperature is below 100°F (38°C).

2. Set the ohmmeter on a low range or use a self powered test light.

3. Test across the terminals. The switch should be closed (test light **ON** or a reading of less than 0.1 ohm on the meter).

Measuring flywheel to starter pinion clearance during starter installation

1. Glow plugs (6 volt)
2. Battery feed
3. 5/16-inch outer diameter studs
4. Glow plug controller
5. Glow plug feed
6. Glow plugs lamp
7. Glow plug inhibit temperature switch
8. Starter solenoid
9. Engine cranking sense input
10. Glow plug voltage sense input
11. Engine control
12. Ground
13. Engine control switch
14. Battery

Electronic glow plug system

1. Glow plug
2. Nozzle
3. Pre combustion chamber

Diesel engine glow plug location

◄FRT

Glow plug controller

4. Test terminals to ground with a test light or the ohmmeter on a high range. The light should be **OFF** or the meter show greater than 1.0 mega-ohm.

5. Replace the switch if it test open across the terminals or if either terminal is closed to the ground.

6. Disconnect the plug from the switch terminals when the engine is above 125°F.

7. Set the ohmmeter on the highest scale or use a self powered test light and test across the terminals. Test across each terminal to ground.

8. The switch should be open (test light **OFF** or high ohm reading of greater than 1 mega-ohm on the meter).

9. Replace the switch if it is closed. Use a socket wrench when installing the switch and torque to 17 ft. lbs. (21 Nm).

CONTROLLER

The glow plug controller provides glow plug operation after starting a cold engine.

1. With the engine cold 80°F (27°C), turn the engine control switch to the **RUN** position and let the glow plugs cycle.

2. After 2 minutes of letting the glow plugs cycle, crank the engine for 1 second; it is not important that the engine starts. Return the engine control switch to **RUN**. The glow plugs should cycle at least once after cranking.

3. If the plugs do not turn on, disconnect the controller connector and check terminal **B** with a grounded 12 volt test light. The light should be **OFF** with the engine control switch in **RUN**, and **ON** when the engine is cranked.

4. If the light does not operate as described, repair a short or open in the engine harness purple wire.

5. If the light works right but the afterstart glow plug feature does not, replace the controller.

CHASSIS ELECTRICAL

Heater Blower Motor

Removal and Installation
WITHOUT AIR CONDITIONING
Except G-Series

1. Disconnect the negative battery terminal.
2. Mark the position of the blower motor in relation to its case.
3. Remove the electrical connection at the motor.
4. Remove the blower attaching screws and remove the assembly.
5. The blower wheel can be removed from the motor shaft by removing the retaining nut.
6. Installation is the reverse of the removal procedure. Apply a bead of sealer to the mounting flange before installation.

G-Series

1. Disconnect the negative battery cable.
2. Remove the coolant overflow bottle.
3. Unplug the motor wiring.
4. Remove the attaching screws and lift out the blower motor.
5. Installation is the reverse of the removal procedure.

WITH AIR CONDITIONING
R/V-Series

1. Disconnect the negative battery terminal.
2. Remove the insulator attaching bolts and nuts. Remove the insulating shield from the case.
3. Mark the position of the blower motor in relation to its case.
4. Remove the electrical connection at the motor.
5. Disconnect the blower motor cooling tube.
6. Remove the blower attaching screws and remove the assembly.
7. The blower wheel can be removed from the motor shaft by removing the nut at the center.
8. Installation is the reverse of the removal procedure. Apply a bead of sealer to the mounting flange before installation.

C/K-Series

1. Disconnect the negative battery terminal.
2. Remove the electrical connection at the motor.
3. Remove the blower attaching screws and remove the assembly.
4. The blower wheel can be removed from the motor shaft by removing the nut at the center.
5. Installation is the reverse of removal. Apply a bead of sealer to the mounting flange before installation.

G-SERIES
1988–89

1. Disconnect the negative battery cable.
2. Remove the power antenna, if equipped.
3. Remove the coolant overflow bottle.
4. Unplug the motor wiring.

1. Blower motor
2. Screws
3. Gasket
4. Screw
5. Evaporator inlet line
6. Evaporator outlet line
7. Heater core tubes
8. Nut
9. Stud

Air conditioning blower motor installation—C/K Series

5. Remove the attaching screws and lift out the blower motor.
6. Installation is the reverse of removal.

1990–92

1. Disconnect the negative battery terminal.
2. Remove the coolant overflow bottle.
3. Unplug the motor wiring.
4. Remove the attaching screws and lift out the blower motor.
5. Installation is the reverse of removal.

Windshield Wiper Motor

Removal and Installation
R/V-SERIES

1. Make sure the wipers are in the parked position.
2. Disconnect the ground cable from the battery.
3. Disconnect the wiring harness at the wiper motor and the hoses from the washer pump.

1. Screw
2. Seal
3. Access hole
4. Drive rod retaining cap nuts
5. Drive rod
6. Crank arm pivot ball
7. Crank arm
8. Motor connector
9. Wiper motor harness
10. Park switch connector

Wiper motor mounting—R/V-Series

1. Screw
2. Wiper motor
3. Nut
4. Bracket
5. Transmission
6. Bolt

Wiper motor mounting—C/K-Series

4. Reach down through the access hole in the plenum and loosen the wiper drive rod attaching screws. Remove the drive rod from the wiper motor crank arm.

5. Remove the wiper motor attaching screws and the motor assembly and linkage.

6. To install, reverse the removal procedure.

NOTE: Lubricate the wiper motor crank arm pivot before reinstallation. Failure of the washers to operate or to shut off is often caused by grease or dirt on the electromagnetic contacts. Simply unplug the wire and pull off the plastic cover for access. Likewise, failure of the wipers to park is often caused by grease or dirt on the park switch contacts. The park switch is under the cover behind the pump.

C/K-SERIES

1. Disconnect the battery ground cable.
2. Pivot the wiper arm away from the windshield, move the latch to the open position and lift the wiper arm off of the driveshaft.
3. Remove the cowl vent grille.
4. Unplug the wiring from the motor.
5. Remove the drive link-to-crank arm screws and slide the links from the arm.
6. Remove the motor mounting bolts and lift the motor out.
7. Installation is the reverse of removal.

G-SERIES

1. Make sure the wipers are parked. The wiper arms should be in their normal **OFF** position.
2. Open the hood and disconnect the battery ground cable.
3. Remove the exposed cowl cover screws with the hood up.
4. Remove the wiper arms. This can be done by pulling the wiper arms away from the glass to release the clip underneath. The wiper arms are splined to the shafts and can be pulled off.
5. Remove the remaining screws securing the cowl panel and remove it.

1. Screw
2. Seal
3. Drive rod retaining cup nuts
4. Drive rod
5. Crank arm pivot ball
6. Crank arm
7. Motor connector
8. Wiper motor harness
9. Park switch connector

Wiper motor mounting—G-Series

6. Loosen the nuts holding the transmission linkage to the wiper motor crank arm.

7. Disconnect the power feed to the wiper arm at the connector next to the radio.

8. Remove the flex hose from the left defroster outlet to gain access to the wiper motor screws.

9. Remove the screw holding the left hand heater duct to the engine shroud and move the heater duct down and out.

10. Remove the windshield washer hoses from the pump.

11. Remove the 3 screws holding the wiper motor to the cowl and lift the wiper motor out from under the dash.

To install:

12. Position the wiper motor in the park position.

13. Position the wiper motor under the dash.

14. Install the 3 screws holding the wiper motor to the cowl.

15. Install the windshield washer hoses at the pump.

16. Install the screw holding the left hand heater duct to the engine.

17. Install the flex hose at the left defroster outlet.

18. Connect the power feed to the wiper arm at the connector next to the radio.

19. Tighten the nuts holding the transmission linkage to the wiper motor crank arm.

20. Install the cowl panel.

21. Install the wiper arms.

22. Install the cowl cover screws.

23. Connect the battery ground cable.

24. Be sure the wiper motor arm is in the parked position. The wiper arms should be in their normal **OFF** position.

Windshield Wiper Switch

Removal and Installation

1. Disconnect the negative battery cable. Remove the steering wheel. Remove the turn signal switch.

2. It may be necessary to loosen the 2 column mounting nuts and remove the 4 bracket to mast jacket screws, then separate the bracket from the mast jacket to allow the connector clip on

the ignition switch to be pulled out of the column assembly.

3. Disconnect the washer/wiper switch lower wire connector.

4. Remove the screws attaching the column housing to the mast jacket. Be sure to note the position of the dimmer switch actuator rod for reassembly in the same position. Remove the column housing and switch as an assembly.

NOTE: Some tilt columns have a removable plastic cover on the column housing. This provides access to the wiper switch without removing the entire column housing.

5. Turn the assembly upside down and use a drift to remove the pivot pin from the washer/wiper switch. Remove the switch.

6. Place the switch into position in the housing, then install the pivot pin.

7. Position the housing onto the mast jacket and attach by installing the screws. Install the dimmer switch actuator rod in the same position as noted earlier. Check switch operation.

8. Reconnect lower end of switch assembly.

9. Install remaining components in reverse order of removal. Be sure to attach column mounting bracket in original position.

Instrument Cluster

Removal and Installation

R/V-SERIES

1. Disconnect the battery ground cable.

2. Remove the headlight switch control knob.

3. Remove the radio control knobs, if required.

4. Remove the steering 4 column cover retaining screws.

5. Remove 8 screws and remove instrument bezel.

6. Reach under the dash, depress the speedometer cable tang, and remove the cable, if equipped.

7. Pull instrument cluster out just far enough to disconnect all lines and wires.

8. Remove the cluster.

9. Installation is the reverse of removal.

C/K-SERIES

1. Disconnect the battery ground cable.

2. Remove the radio control head.

3. Remove the heater control head.

4. Momentarily ground the cluster assembly by jumping from the metal retaining plate to a good ground.

5. On vehicles with automatic transmission, remove the cluster trim plate.

6. Remove the 4 cluster retaining screws.

7. Carefully pull the cluster towards you until you can reach the electrical connector. Unplug the connector. Avoid touching the connector pins.

8. Installation is the reverse of removal.

G-SERIES

1. Disconnect the battery ground cable.

2. Reach up behind the cluster, depress the speedometer cable retaining tang and pull out the cable, if equipped.

3. Remove the clock set stem knob, if equipped.

4. Remove the rear heater and fan controls knobs, if equipped.

5. Remove the interior light and headlight switch bezel.

6. Remove the instrument panel bezel screws and remove the bezel.

7. Remove the cluster bezel retaining screws and remove the bezel.

8. Pull the top of the cluster away from the panel and lift out the bottom of the cluster. Pull the cluster out just far enough to unplug the wiring and remove the speedometer cable.

9. Installation is the reverse of removal.

SECTION 5

GENERAL MOTORS CORPORATION
C/K SERIES (PICK-UP) • R/V SERIES (PICK-UP) • BLAZER/JIMMY • SUBURBAN • G SERIES (VAN)

1. Speedometer cable spring clip
2. Lamp bulb socket
3. Laminated circuit
4. Cluster case
5. Indicator lamp filter (turn signal)
6. Fuel gauge
7. Speedometer
8. Temperature gauge
9. Brake warning lamp filter
10. Ammeter
11. Oil pressure gauge
12. Transmission shift indicator
13. Instrument cluster lens
14. Instrument cluster bezel
15. Retainer

Exploded view of the cluster assembly—R/V-Series

1. Retainer
2. Retainer screw to cluster
3. Retainer screw to instrument panel
4. Lens cover
5. Lens cover screws
6. Speedometer
7. Oil pressure gauge
8. Temperature gauge
9. Fuel gauge
10. Voltage gauge
11. Speedometer retainer screw
12. Housing standoffs
13. Total and trip odometer
14. Housing
15. Circuit board
16. Cover
17. Cover screws

Exploded view of the cluster assembly—C/K-Series

1. Bolt (#8–32 x $^7/_{16}$ inch)
2. Speedometer mounting bushing
3. Nut
4. Flat washer
5. Laminated circuit
6. Screw (#8–18 x $^7/_{16}$ inch)
7. Fuel gauge
8. Engine oil pressure gage
9. Screw (#8–16 x $^7/_{16}$ inch)
10. Retainer
11. Speedometer
12. Gauge mask
13. Lens retainer
14. Lens
15. Bezel
16. Voltmeter
17. Lamp
18. Engine coolant temperature gauge
19. Fuel gauge
20. Instrument cluster with gauges
21. Instrument cluster without gauges

Exploded view of the cluster assembly—G-Series

Speedometer

Removal and Installation

R/V-SERIES

1. Disconnect the negative battery cable.
2. Remove the headlight switch knob assembly.
3. Remove the radio control knobs, if required.
4. Remove the clock adjuster stem.
5. Remove the instrument cluster bezel.
6. Remove the steering column cover.
7. Remove the instrument cluster lens.
8. Remove the transmission shift indicator.
9. Remove the cluster retainer.
10. Depress the spring clip and disconnect the speedometer cable.
11. Remove the cluster assembly and remove the speedometer assembly.
12. Installation is the reverse of removal.

C/K-SERIES

1. Disconnect the negative battery cable.
2. Remove the cluster.
3. Remove the speedometer mounting screws.
4. Carefully pull the speedometer from the circuit board. Avoid touching any of the circuit board pins.
5. Installation is the reverse of removal.

G-SERIES

1. Disconnect the negative battery cable.
2. Remove the cluster.
3. Remove the speedometer dial retaining screws.
4. Remove the 2 hex head screws and rubber grommets that hold the speedometer assembly to the cluster cover.
5. Disconnect the speedometer cable from the assembly and remove the speedometer.
6. Installation is the reverse of removal.

Headlight Switch

Removal and Installation

R/V-SERIES

1. Disconnect the negative battery cable.

2. Reaching up behind instrument cluster, depress shaft retaining button and remove switch knob and rod.
3. Remove instrument cluster bezel and trim panel screws.
4. Disconnect multiple wiring connectors at switch terminals.
5. Remove switch by rotating the switch locknut.
6. Installation is the reverse of removal.

C/K-SERIES

1. Disconnect the negative battery cable.
2. Remove the instrument cluster bezel.
3. Remove the headlight switch retaining screws.
4. Disconnect the wire connector and pull the switch away from the bezel.
5. Installation is the reverse of removal.

G-SERIES

1. Disconnect the negative battery cable.
2. Press the switch knob retaining pin and remove the knob.
3. Remove the left instrument panel trim plate.
4. Remove the retaining nut securing the switch.
5. Disconnect the electrical connector from the back of the switch.
6. Remove the switch from the instrument panel.
7. Reverse the procedure for installation.

1. Instrument panel cluster bezel
2. Headlamp switch
3. Screw

Headlight switch installation—C/K-Series

SECTION 5

GENERAL MOTORS CORPORATION
C/K SERIES (PICK-UP) • R/V SERIES (PICK-UP) • BLAZER/JIMMY • SUBURBAN • G SERIES (VAN)

Dimmer Switch

Removal and Installation

1. Disconnect the negative battery cable.
2. Remove the steering wheel.
3. Disconnect the switch wire connector.
4. Remove the screws attaching the dimmer switch to the column housing. Be sure to note the position of the dimmer switch actuator rod for reassembly in the same position. Remove the switch by prying up and away from the housing.
5. Installation is the reverse of the removal procedure. Check and adjust the switch as necessary.

Turn Signal Switch

Removal and Installation

1. Disconnect the negative battery cable.
2. Remove the steering wheel.
3. Using a steering wheel lock plate compressor, remove the snapring from the groove on the shaft.
4. Remove the lockplate, turn signal cam, the upper bearing preload spring and the thrust washer from the upper steering shaft.
5. Remove the steering column lower cover.
6. Remove the turn signal lever from the column.
7. If equipped with cruise control, disconnect the cruise control wire from the harness near the bottom of the column. Remove the harness protector from the cruise control wire. Remove the turn signal lever. Do not remove the wire from the column.
8. Disconnect the turn signal wiring and remove the wires from the plastic protector.
9. Remove the turn signal switch mounting screws.
10. Slide the switch connector out of the bracket on the steering column.
11. If the switch is to be replaced, cut the wires near the top of the switch and discard the switch. Before cutting the wires, verify that the wire color codes are the same. Tape the connector of the new switch to the old wires, and pull the new harness down through the steering column while removing the old switch.
12. If the original switch is to be reused, tape a piece of wire or string around the connector and pull the harness up through the column, while pulling the string up through the column to help with reinstallation later.
13. After freeing the switch wiring protector from its mounting, pull the turn signal switch straight up and remove the switch, switch harness, and the connector from the column.

To install:

14. Using the wire, string or switch wiring as previously described, pull the switch and wiring through the column and into position.
15. Position the switch connector onto the bracket on the column and reconnect the connector.
16. Install the turn signal switch mounting screws and turn signal lever.
17. Reconnect the cruise control wire connector, if equipped.
18. Install the steering column lower cover.
19. Install the lockplate, turn signal cam, the upper bearing preload spring and the thrust washer from the upper steering shaft.
20. Reinstall the lockplate and steering wheel.
21. Reconnect the negative battery cable.

Ignition Switch

Removal and Installation

1. Disconnect the negative battery cable. If equipped, remove the lower trim panel.

Removing the lock plate retaining ring

Turn signal switch location—typical

1. Retainer
2. Nut
3. Lock plate cover
4. Retainer
5. Lock plate
6. Cancelling cam
7. Bearing preload spring
8. Turn signal screws
9. Tap screw
10. Actuator cam
11. Turn signal switch
12. Turn signal housing screws
13. Washer
14. Tone alarm switch
15. Retainer clip
16. retainer screw
17. Ignition lock
18. Acuator sector
19. Housing assembly
20. Bearing
21. Bushing
22. Horn contact
23. Upper bearing retainer
24. Dimmer pivot and wiper switch
25. Shaft lock bolt
26. Switch rack preload spring
27. Actuator rack
28. Actuator pivot pin
29. Washer
30. Shift lever gate
31. Shift lever screw
32. Housing cover
33. Cover screw

Ignition switch shown in the LOCK position for removal

2. Remove the steering column retaining bolts. Lower the steering column assembly to gain access to the switch retaining screws. Extreme care is necessary to prevent damage to the collapsible column.

3. Make sure the switch is in the **LOCK** position. If the lock cylinder is out, pull the switch rod up to the stop, then go down 1 detent.

4. Remove the electrical connections from the switch. Remove the switch retaining screws. Remove the switch from the column.

5. Installation is the reverse of the removal procedure. Before installation, make sure the switch is in the **LOCK** position. Install the switch using the original screws. Use of screws that are too long could prevent the column from collapsing on impact.

Ignition Lock Cylinder

Removal and Installation

1. Disconnect the negative battery cable.
2. Remove the steering wheel.
3. Remove the turn signal switch. It is not necessary to completely remove the switch from the column. Pull the switch rearward far enough to slip it over the end of the shaft but do not pull the harness out of the column.
4. Turn the lock to **RUN**.
5. Remove the lock retaining screw and remove the lock cylinder.

NOTE: If the retaining screw is dropped on removal, it may fall into the column, requiring complete disassembly of the column to retrieve the screw.

To install:
6. Rotate the key to the stop while holding onto the cylinder.
7. Push the lock all the way in.
8. Install the screw. Tighten the screw to 40 inch lbs. for regular columns, 22 inch lbs. for adjustable columns.
9. Install the turn signal switch and the steering wheel.

Stoplight Switch

Removal and Installation

1. Disconnect the negative battery cable.
2. Disconnect the switch electrical connections. Remove the switch assembly from its mounting.
3. Installation is the reverse of the removal procedure. Adjust the switch, as required.

Adjustment

EXCEPT C/K-SERIES

1. Depress the brake pedal and press the switch in until it is firmly seated in its mounting.
2. Pull the brake pedal against the pedal stop until the switch does not make any noise.
3. Electrical contact should be made when the brake pedal is depressed from its fully released position.

C/K-SERIES

1. Depress the brake pedal fully.
2. Pull the lever on the brake switch back to its stop.
3. Pull the brake pedal back to its stop position.
4. Check for proper switch operation.

Fuses and Circuit Breakers

Location

FUSIBLE LINKS

In addition to circuit breakers and fuses, the wiring harness incorporates fusible links to protect the wiring. Links are used in place of a fuse in wiring circuits that are not normally fused, such as the ignition circuit. Fusible links are color coded red in the charging and load circuits to match the color of the circuits

Ignition lock cylinder removal and installation

Stoplight switch adjustment lever—C/K-Series

they protect. Each link is 4 gauges smaller than the cable it protects and the insulation is marked with the gauge size.

The engine compartment wiring harness has several fusible links. The same size wire with a special hypalon insulation must be used when replacing a fusible link. The links are located in the following areas:

1. A molded splice at the starter solenoid BAT terminal, a 14 gauge red wire.

2. A 16 gauge red fusible link at the junction block to protect the unfused wiring of 12 gauge or larger wire. This link stops at the bulkhead connector.

3. The alternator warning light and field circuitry is protected by a 20 gauge fusible link. The link is installed as a molded splice in the circuit at the junction block.

4. The ammeter circuit is protected by two 20 gauge fusible links installed as molded splices in the circuit at the junction block and battery to starter circuit.

CIRCUIT BREAKERS

A circuit breaker is an electrical switch which breaks the circuit in case of an overload. All models have a circuit breaker in the headlight switch to protect the headlight and parking light systems. An overload may cause the lights to flicker or flash ON and OFF, or in some cases, to remain OFF. Windshield wiper motors are protected by a circuit breaker at the motor.

FUSES

Fuses are located in the junction box below the instrument panel to the left of the steering column. Each fuse receptacle is marked as to the circuit it protects and the correct amperage of the fuse. Inline fuses are used on the underhood light and air conditioning.

FLASHERS

The turn signal flasher and the hazard/warning flasher plugs into the fuse block.

NOTE: A special heavy duty turn signal flasher is required to properly operate the turn signals when a trailer's lights are connected to the system.

Computers

Location

Electronic Control Module (ECM): located in the passenger compartment by the right side kick panel or behind the glove box on the R/V and C/K-Series vehicles or on the drivers side under the seat on the G-Series vans.

Wiper Delay Module:

R/V-Series: located on the steering column behind the lower cover.

C/K-Series: located on the wiper motor.

G-Series: located in the harness on the left side of the steering column.

Cruise Control Module:

R/V and G-Series: located on the back of instrument panel next to the steering column.

C/K-Series: located on the engine side of the cowl near the master cylinder.

Cruise Control

For further information, please refer to Chilton's Chassis Electronics Service Manual.

Servo Adjustment

R/V AND G-SERIES

1. Ensure ignition is **OFF** and the throttle valve fully closed before proceeding with adjustment.

2. If equipped with a gasoline engine, install the servo rod so the rod assembles over the stud per adjustment "B".

3. If equipped with a diesel engine, position the pin on the servo rod in the hole closest to the servo that allows for adjustment "C".

4. Install the servo rod retainer and verify system functions properly.

A. Unlocked Position

Unlocking cable for adjustment—C/K-Series

R/V TRUCK
B

B. 0.0394–0.197 in. (1.0–5.0mm)

1. Nut
2. Lever
3. Stud
4. Rod
5. Retainer
6. Servo
7. Bolt
8. Bracket
9. Tab

Cruise control servo mounting and adjustment—R/V and G-Series except Diesel engine

C. 0.0393 in. (1.0mm)
1. Lever
2. Rod
3. Retainer
4. Servo
5. Bolt
6. Bracket
7. Accelerator cable
8. Hose assembly

Cruise control servo mounting and adjustment—R/V and G-Series with Diesel engine

C/K-SERIES

1. Disconnect the engine end of the cruise control cable from the lever stud.
2. Pull lightly on the end of the cable.
3. If the cable does not pull out, the cable is adjusted properly. If the cable extends out, proceed as follows:
  a. Unlock the cable conduit lock mechanism.
  b. If equipped with a gasoline engine, move the cable until the throttle begins to open. Then move the cable in the opposite direction enough to close the throttle.
  c. If equipped with a diesel engine, move the cable until the injection pump lever moves off the idle stop screw. Then move the cable in the opposite direction far enough to return the lever to the idle stop screw.
  d. While holding the cable securely, push down on the cable conduit lock mechanism until it snaps into place.
  e. Verify the system functions properly.

ENGINE COOLING

Radiator

Removal and Installation

EXCEPT 6.2L DIESEL ENGINE

1. Disconnect the negative battery cable.
2. Drain the cooling system into a suitable container.
3. Disconnect the radiator upper and lower hoses and, if applicable, the transmission or engine oil cooler lines. Remove the coolant recovery hose.
4. Remove the radiator upper panel if equipped.
5. Remove the fan shroud attaching screws and clutch fan as required.
6. Remove the radiator from the vehicle.
7. Installation is the reverse of the removal procedure.

6.2L DIESEL ENGINE

1. Disconnect the negative battery cables.
2. Drain the cooling system.
3. Remove the air intake snorkel.
4. Remove the windshield washer bottle.
5. Remove the hood release cable.
6. Remove the upper fan shroud.
7. Disconnect the upper radiator hose.
8. Disconnect the transmission cooler lines.
9. Disconnect the low coolant sensor wire.
10. Disconnect the overflow hose.
11. Disconnect the engine oil cooler lines.
12. Disconnect the lower radiator hose.
13. On the G-Series, remove the brake master cylinder from the booster.
14. Unbolt and remove the radiator.

To install:

15. Install the radiator.
16. On G-Series Van, install the brake master cylinder on the booster.
17. Connect the lower radiator hose.
18. Connect the engine oil cooler lines.
19. Connect the overflow hose.
20. Connect the low coolant sensor wire.
21. Connect the transmission cooler lines.
22. Connect the upper radiator hose.
23. Install the upper fan shroud.
24. Install the hood release cable.
25. Install the windshield washer bottle.
26. Install the air intake snorkel.
27. Fill the radiator with the proper type and quantity of coolant and inspect the system for leaks.

Auxiliary Electric Cooling Fan

Removal and Installation

1. Disconnect the negative battery cable.
2. Remove the grille.
3. Unplug the fan harness connector.
4. Remove the fan-to-brace bolts and lift out the fan.
5. Installation is the reverse of removal. Torque the bolts to 53 inch lbs. (6 Nm).

Heater Core

Removal and Installation

R/V-SERIES

1. Disconnect the battery ground cable.
2. Disconnect the heater hoses at the core tubes and drain the engine coolant. Plug the core tubes to prevent spillage.
3. Remove the nuts securing the assembly from the engine firewall.
4. Remove the instrument panel.
5. Disconnect the air-defrost and temperature door cables.
6. Remove the floor outlet and remove the defroster duct-to-heater case screw.
7. Remove the heater case-to-instrument panel screws. Pull the assembly rearward to gain access to the wiring harness and disconnect the wires attached to the unit.
8. Remove the heater distributor from the vehicle.
9. Remove the heater core retaining straps and remove the core from the vehicle.
10. Installation is the reverse of removal. Be sure the core-to-case and case-to-dash panel sealer is intact. Fill the cooling system and check for leaks.

C/K-SERIES

1. Disconnect the negative battery cable.
2. Drain the cooling system into a suitable container.
3. Disconnect the heater hoses at the core tubes.
4. In the passenger compartment, remove the lower heater core cover-to-case screws.
5. Remove the bracket and screws securing the heater core to the case.
6. Remove the heater core.
7. Installation is the reverse of the removal procedure.

G-SERIES

1. Disconnect the negative battery cable.
2. Remove the coolant recovery bottle.
3. Place a pan under the vehicle and disconnect the heater intake and outlet hoses. Quickly remove and plug the hoses and support them in an upright position. Drain the coolant from the heater core into the pan.
4. Remove the heater distributor duct-to-case attaching screws and the duct-to-engine cover screw. Remove the duct.
5. Remove the engine housing cover.
6. Remove all the instrument panel attaching screws.
7. Carefully lower the steering column. Raise and support the right side of the instrument panel.
8. Remove the defroster duct-to-case attaching screws and the 2 screws attaching the distributor to the heater case.
9. Disconnect the temperature door cable. Carefully fold the cable back and out of the way.
10. Remove the 3 nuts from the engine compartment side of the heater case and the screw from the passenger compartment side.
11. Remove the heater case and core assembly.
12. Remove the core retaining straps and remove the core.

To install:

13. Install the core.
14. Install the core retaining straps.
15. Install the heater case and core assembly.
16. Install the 3 nuts on the engine compartment side of the distributor case and the screw on the passenger compartment side.
17. Connect the temperature door cable.
18. Install the defroster duct-to-case attaching screws and the 2 screws attaching the distributor to the heater case.
19. Install the steering column.
20. Install all the instrument panel attaching screws.
21. Install the engine cover.
22. Install the duct. Install the heater distributor duct-to-case attaching screws and the duct-to-engine cover screw.
23. Connect the heater intake and outlet hoses.
24. Fill the cooling system.
25. Install the coolant recovery bottle.
26. Connect the negative battery cable.

Water Pump

Removal and Installation

EXCEPT 6.2L DIESEL ENGINE

1. Disconnect the negative battery cable.
2. Drain the engine coolant into a suitable container.
3. Loosen the alternator and other accessories at their adjusting points, and remove the fan belts from the fan pulley.
4. Remove the fan shroud, fan clutch and pulley.
5. Remove all accessory brackets that will interfere with water pump removal.
6. Disconnect the lower radiator, bypass and the heater hoses from the water pump.
7. Remove the bolts, pump assembly and old gasket from the engine.

To install:

8. Ensure the gasket surfaces on the pump and engine are clean.
9. Install the pump assembly with a new gasket. On all except the 4.8L engine, tighten the bolts to 30 ft. lbs. (40 Nm). On the 4.8L engine, tighten the bolts to 15 ft. lbs. (20 Nm).
10. Connect the hose between the water pump inlet and the nipple on the pump.
11. Install any accessory brackets.
12. Install the fan and pulley.
13. Install and adjust the alternator and other accessories.
14. Install the fan belts from the fan pulley.
15. Fill the cooling system.
16. Connect the battery.

6.2L DIESEL ENGINE

1. Disconnect the negative battery cables.
2. Remove the fan and fan shroud.
3. Drain the engine coolant into a suitable container.
4. Remove the air conditioning hose bracket, as required.
5. Remove the oil filler tube, as required.

6. Remove the alternator pivot bolt and remove the alternator belt.

7. Remove the alternator upper and lower brackets.

8. Remove the power steering belt and pump assembly, secure it out of the way.

9. Remove the air conditioning belt, as required.

10. Disconnect the bypass hose and the lower radiator hose.

11. Remove the water pump bolts. Remove the water pump plate and gasket and water pump. If the pump gasket is to be replaced, remove the plate attaching bolts to the water pump and remove (and replace) the gasket.

To install:

12. When installing the pump, the flanges must be free of oil. Apply an anaerobic sealer GM part No. 1052357 or equivalent.

NOTE: The sealer must be wet to the touch when the bolts are torqued.

13. Attach the water pump and plate assembly. Torque the bolts to 30 ft. lbs. (41 Nm).

14. Connect the bypass hose and the lower radiator hose.

15. Install the air conditioning belt if equipped.

16. Install the power steering belt.

17. Install the alternator lower bracket.

18. Install the alternator pivot bolt.

19. Install the alternator belt.

20. Install the oil filler tube.

21. If equipped with air conditioning, install the air conditioning hose bracket nuts.

22. Fill the radiator with the proper type and quantity of antifreeze.

23. Install the fan and fan shroud.

24. Connect the batteries.

Thermostat

Removal and Installation

EXCEPT 6.2L DIESEL ENGINE

1. Disconnect the negative battery cable.

2. Drain the radiator until the level is below the thermostat level (below the level of the intake manifold).

3. Remove the thermostat housing from the engine. Remove the thermostat from inside the housing.

4. Install new thermostat in the reverse order of removal, making sure the thermostat is inserted correctly. Clean the gasket surfaces on the thermostat housing and the intake manifold. Use a new gasket when installing the elbow to the manifold. On the 4.8L engine, torque the thermostat housing bolts to 28 ft. lbs. or on all other engines to 20 ft. lbs. (27 Nm).

5. Refill the cooling system with the proper type and quantity of antifreeze.

6.2L DIESEL ENGINE

1. Disconnect the negative battery cables.

2. Remove the upper fan shroud.

3. Drain the cooling system to a point below the thermostat.

4. Remove the engine oil dipstick tube brace and the oil fill brace, as required.

5. Remove the upper radiator hose.

6. Remove the water outlet.

7. Remove the thermostat and gasket.

8. Installation is the reverse of removal. Use a new gasket coated with sealer. Torque the bolts to 35 ft. lbs. (47 Nm).

Cooling System Bleeding

1. Fill the cooling system to the lower edge of the radiator filler neck.

2. Start the engine and run with the radiator cap removed, until the upper radiator hose becomes hot and the thermostat is open.

3. With the engine idling, add coolant to the radiator until the level reaches the bottom of the filler neck.

4. Install the radiator cap and add coolant to the reservoir until the level reaches the **COLD** mark.

GASOLINE FUEL SYSTEM

Fuel System Service Precaution

When working with the fuel system certain precautions should be taken; always work in a well ventilated area, keep a dry chemical (Class B) fire extinguisher near the work area. Always disconnect the negative battery cable and do not make any repairs to the fuel system until all the necessary steps for repair have been reviewed.

Relieving Fuel System Pressure

The 220 TBI unit used on the V6 and V8 engines has a constant bleed in the pressure regulator to relieve pressure any time the engine is turned off, however a small amount of fuel may be released when the fuel line is disconnected. As a precaution, cover the fuel line with a cloth and dispose of the cloth properly. Also, loosen the fuel filler cap to relieve tank vapor pressure.

Fuel Tank

Removal and Installation

1. Disconnect the negative battery cable.

2. Properly drain the fuel tank into a suitable container.

3. Raise and support vehicle safely.

4. Safely support the fuel tank and remove the retaining straps.

5. Disconnect the fuel tank sending unit wire, ground straps and hoses.

6. With the help of an assistant, lower the tank and remove the assembly from the vehicle.

7. Installation is the reverse of the removal procedure.

Fuel Filter

Removal and Installation

CARBURETED ENGINE

Filter In Carburetor

1. Disconnect the negative battery cable.

2. Disconnect the fuel line connection at the intake fuel filter nut. Plug the opening to prevent loss of fuel.

3. Remove the intake fuel filter nut from the carburetor.

4. Remove the filter element and spring.

5. Check the element for restrictions by blowing air on the cone end. Air should pass freely.

6. Replace the element, as necessary.

7. Install the element spring, then the filter element in the

carburetor. Bronze filters should have the small section of the cone facing out.

8. Install a new gasket on the intake fuel nut. Install the nut in the carburetor body and tighten securely.

9. Install the fuel line and tighten the connection.

Inline Filter

Some vehicles may have an inline filter. This is a can shaped device located in the fuel line between the pump and the carburetor. It may be made of either plastic or metal. To replace the filter:

1. Disconnect the negative battery cable.

2. Place a cloth rags under the filter.

3. Use a pair of pliers to expand the clamp on one end of the filter, then slide the clamp down past the point to which the filter pipe extends in the rubber hose. Do the same with the other clamp.

4. Gently twist and pull the hoses free of the filter pipes. Remove and discard the old filter.

NOTE: Most replacement filters come with hoses and clamps that should be installed with a new filter.

5. Install the new filter in the correct flow direction, into the hoses, slide the clamps back into place, and check for leaks.

FUEL INJECTED ENGINE

1. Disconnect the negative battery cable.

2. Properly relieve the fuel system pressure.

3. Raise and support the vehicle safely.

4. Disconnect the fuel lines at the filter.

5. Remove the fuel filter from the retainer or mounting bolt.

6. To install, reverse the removal procedures ensuring the filter flow is in the correct direction. Start the engine and check for leaks.

NOTE: The filter has an arrow (fuel flow direction) on the side of the case, be sure to install it correctly in the system, the with arrow facing away from the fuel tank.

Mechanical Fuel Pump

Testing

Fuel pumps should always be tested on the vehicle. The larger line between the pump and tank is the suction side of the system and the smaller line, between the pump and carburetor, is the pressure side. A leak in the pressure side would be apparent because of dripping fuel. A leak in the suction side is usually only apparent because of a reduced volume of fuel delivered to the pressure side.

FLOW TEST

1. Verify there is a sufficient amount of fuel in the tank. Tighten any loose line connections and look for any kinks, restrictions and cracked hoses from the carburetor to the tank.

2. Disconnect the fuel line at the carburetor. Disconnect the distributor-to-coil primary wire. Place a container at the end of the fuel line and crank the engine. The fuel pump should supply a ½ pint in 15 seconds. If the fuel flow is insufficient, check for a restriction.

3. If there is no restriction, test the fuel pump for pressure and vacuum.

PRESSURE TEST

1. Disconnect the fuel line at the carburetor and install a low pressure gauge to the line.

2. If equipped with a vapor return system, squeeze off the return hose.

3. Run the engine at idle and note the reading on the gauge. Stop the engine and compare the reading to the specification. If the pump is operating properly, the pressure will be as specified

and will be constant at idle speed. If pressure varies sporadically or is too high or low, the pump should be replaced.

4. If the pressure is low, check for restrictions in the fuel tank sender unit filter, lines and hoses. If there are no restrictions, perform a vacuum test on the fuel pump inlet.

VACUUM TEST

1. Disconnect and plug the inlet hose at the fuel pump.

2. Connect a vacuum gauge to the pump inlet fitting.

3. Crank or run the engine until maximum vacuum is achieved.

4. If vacuum is less than 15 in. Hg, replace the pump.

5. If the reading is as specified, inspect the tank-to-pump lines and hoses for leaks, splits or kinks by disconnecting each section of line going back to the tank, connecting a vacuum gauge and retesting the pump.

Removal and Installation

1. Disconnect the negative battery cable.

2. Disconnect the fuel lines or hoses at the pump and plugging the pump inlet line.

3. Remove the 2 pump mounting bolts and lock washers; remove the pump and its gasket.

4. Install the fuel pump with a new gasket reversing the removal procedure. Apply chassis grease to hold the fuel pump pushrod up when installing the pump.

5. Connect the fuel lines and check for leaks.

Electric Fuel Pump

Testing

1. Ensure there is a sufficient quantity of fuel in the tank. Properly relieve the fuel system pressure.

2. Remove the air cleaner and plug the THERMAC vacuum port, as required.

3. Uncouple the fuel supply hose or line located in the engine compartment.

4. Install a fuel pressure gauge between the line. Tighten the line to ensure no leaks occur during testing.

5. Start the engine, check for leaks and observe the fuel pressure, it should be 9–13 psi.

6. Depressurize the fuel system, remove the testing tool, remove the plug from the THERMAC vacuum port, reconnect the fuel line, start the engine and check for fuel leaks.

Removal and Installation

1. With the engine turned off, properly relieve the fuel system pressure.

2. Disconnect the negative battery cable.

3. Raise and support the vehicle safely.

4. Drain the fuel tank and remove the assembly from the vehicle.

5. Using a suitable tool, turn the fuel lever sending unit and pump assembly locking ring (located on top of the fuel tank) counterclockwise, lift the assembly from the tank and remove the pump from the fuel lever sending device.

6. Pull the pump up into the attaching hose while pulling it outward away from the bottom support. Be careful not to damage the rubber insulator and strainer during removal. After the pump assembly is clear of the bottom support, pull it out of the rubber connector.

7. To install, reverse the removal procedures.

Carburetor

Removal and Installation

1. Disconnect the negative battery terminal. Remove the air cleaner assembly and gasket.

2. Disconnect the electrical connectors from the carburetor assembly.

3. Disconnect and tag the vacuum hoses at the carburetor.

4. Disconnect the accelerator linkage, downshift cable and cruise control linkage, if equipped.

5. Disconnect and plug the fuel line connection at the fuel inlet nut.

6. Remove the carburetor attaching bolts and the carburetor with the flange insulator.

7. Install the carburetor with a new flange gasket.

NOTE: It is good shop practice to fill the carburetor float bowl with fuel before installing the carburetor. This reduces strain on the starting motor and battery; and reduces the possibility of backfiring while attempting to start the engine. Operate the throttle several times and check the discharge from pump jets before installing the carburetor.

8. Install the carburetor attaching bolts and torque to specification. Torque the bolts in a criss-cross pattern.

9. Install the fuel line to the fuel inlet nut, cruise control cable, if equipped, downshift cable, accelerator linkage, vacuum hoses, electrical connectors to the choke and idle stop solenoid, air cleaner assembly with gasket and the negative battery terminal.

Idle Speed and Mixture Adjustment

In case of a major carburetor overhaul, throttle body replacement, or high idle CO (when indicated by an emissions inspection), the idle mixture may be adjusted. Adjusting the mixture by other than the following method may violate Federal and/or state laws. Idle mixture needle socket J–29030–B or equivalent is required for this adjustment.

1. Set the parking brake and block the drive wheels.

2. Remove the carburetor from the engine.

3. Drain the fuel from the carburetor into a container. Dispose of the fuel in an approved container.

4. Remove the idle mixture needle plugs as follows:

   a. Invert the carburetor and support it to avoid damaging external components.

   b. Make 2 parallel hacksaw cuts in the throttle body, between the locator points near one idle mixture needle plug. The distance between the cuts depends on the size of the punch to be used.

   c. Cut down to the plug but not more than ⅛ in. beyond the locator point.

   d. Place a flat punch at a point near the ends of the saw marks. Hold the punch at a 45 degree angle and drive it into the throttle body until the casting breaks away, exposing the steel plug.

   e. Use a center punch to break the plug apart, uncover idle mixture needle. Remove all loose pieces of plug.

   f. Repeat the previous steps for the other needle plug.

5. Use idle mixture needle socket J–29030–B or equivalent to lightly seat the idle mixture needles, then back them out 3 turns.

6. Reinstall the carburetor on the engine.

7. Place the transmission in **P** for automatic transmission or neutral for manual transmission.

8. Start the engine and bring it to a normal operating temperature, choke valve open and air conditioning off.

9. Connect a tachometer to the engine.

10. Check ignition timing, and adjust if necessary, by following the procedure described on the emission control information label located under the hood on the vehicle.

11. Use idle mixture needle socket J–29030–B or equivalent, to turn the mixture needles equally (⅛ turn at a time), in or out, to obtain the highest rpm (best idle).

12. Adjust the idle speed screw (throttle stop) to obtain the base idle speed specified on the underhood emission control information label.

13. Again try to readjust mixture needles to obtain the highest idle rpm. The adjustment is correct when the highest rpm (best idle) is reached with the minimum number of mixture needle turns from the seated position.

14. If necessary, readjust the idle speed screw (throttle stop) to obtain the specified base idle speed.

15. Check and if necessary, adjust the idle speed solenoid activated speed and fast idle speed. Refer to the underhood emission control information label.

16. Check the throttle kicker and adjust if necessary.

17. Turn **OFF** the engine, remove all test equipment and remove the block from the drive wheels.

Service Adjustments

For all carburetor service adjustment procedures and specifications, please refer to "Carburetor Service" in the Unit Repair section

Fuel Injection

Idle Speed Adjustment

This procedure should be performed only if parts of the throttle body have been replaced. The engine should be at normal operating temperature.

1. Remove the air cleaner, adapter and gaskets. Discard the gaskets. Plug any vacuum line ports, as necessary.

2. Leave the Idle Air Control (IAC) valve connected and ground the diagnostic terminal (ALDL connector).

3. Turn the ignition switch to the **ON** position; do not start the engine. Wait for at least 10 seconds; this allows the IAC valve pintle to extend fully and seat in the throttle body.

4. With the ignition switch still in the **ON** position, disconnect IAC electrical connector.

5. Remove the ground from the diagnostic terminal and start the engine. Let the engine reach normal operating temperature.

6. Apply the parking brake and block the drive wheels. Remove the plug from the idle stop screw by piercing it first with a suitable tool, then applying leverage to lift the plug out.

7. Connect a suitable tachometer to the engine.

8. Ensure the transmission is in the specified (N or D) position, the ECM in "Open or Closed" loop as specified.

9. Adjust the idle stop screw to obtain the specified RPM reading.

10. Turn the ignition **OFF** and reconnect the IAC valve con-

| 1 | IDLE STOP SCREW ASSEMBLY |
| 2 | IDLE STOP SCREW PLUG |

Removing idle stop screw plug for adjustment—TBI engines

Minimum Idle Air Rate—1988–89 Vehicles

MINIMUM IDLE AIR RATE

Engine	Transmission	Gear (D/N)	Engine Speed (RPM)	Open/Closed Loop*
2.5L	Man.	N	600 ± 50	CL
	Auto.	N	500 ± 50	CL
2.8L	Man.	N	700 ± 50	OL
4.3L	Man.	N	450 ± 50	CL
	Auto.	D	400 ± 50	CL
	Auto.(1)	N	475 ± 50	CL
5.0L	Man.	N	500 ± 25	OL
	Auto.	D	425 ± 25	OL
	Auto.(2)	D	425 ± 25	CL
5.7L (under 8500 GVW)	Man.	N	500 ± 25	OL
	Auto.	D	425 ± 25	OL
5.7L (over 8500 GVW)	Man.	N	550 ± 25	CL
	Auto.	D	450 ± 25	CL
7.4L	Man.	N	700 ± 25	OL
	Auto.	D	700 ± 25	OL

* Let engine idle until proper fuel control status (open/closed loop) is reached
(1) 4.3L ST series.
(2) 5.0L without AIR system.

Minimum Idle Air Rate—1990–92 Vehicles

MINIMUM IDLE SPEED

Engine	Transmission	Gear (D/N)	Engine Speed (RPM)**	Open/Closed Loop*
2.5L	Man.	N	600 ± 50	CL
	Auto.	N	500 ± 50	CL
2.8L	Man.	N	700 ± 50	OL
4.3L (under 8500 GVW)	Man.	N	400-525	CL
	Auto.	D	400 ± 50	CL
	Auto.(1)	D	475 ± 50	CL
4.3L (Over 8500 GVW)	Man.	N	400-525	CL
	Auto.	D	400 ± 50	CL
5.0L	Man.	N	500 ± 25	OL
	Auto.	D	425 ± 25	CL
5.7L (under 8500 GVW)	Man.	N	500 ± 25	OL
	Auto.	D	425 ± 25	CL
5.7L (over 8500 GVW)	Man.	N	550 ± 25	CL
	Auto.	D	450 ± 25	CL
7.4L	Man.	N	700 ± 25	OL
	Auto.	D	625 ± 25	OL

* Let engine idle until proper fuel control status (open/closed loop) is reached.
** If the engine has less than 500 miles or is checked at altitudes above 1500 feet, the idle rpm with a seated IAC valve should be lower than valves above.
(1) 4.3L High-Output ML Van Series

A DISTANCE OF PINTLE EXTENSION
B DIAMETER AND SHAPE OF PINTLE
C IAC VALVE GASKET

Typical IAC valve

Replacing the fuel meter cover on the TBI 220

nector. Unplug any plugged vacuum line ports and install the air cleaner, adapter and new gaskets.

11. Reset the IAC valve as follows:

NOTE: If installing a new IAC valve, measure and adjust the valve accordingly. If reinstalling a used IAC valve, do not push or pull on the pintle to adjust pintle length or damage to the IAC worm gear might occur. The valve is preset at the factory and will self adjust when the following procedure is performed.

a. Set a new IAC valve by measuring the distance between the tip of the pintle and the valve mounting surface.

b. If greater than 1.10 in. (28mm), use light finger pressure to slowly retract the pintle. The force required to retract a new valve will not damage the valve.

c. Install the valve and connect the wire connector.

d. Reset a used IAC valve pintle position by depressing the accelerator pedal slightly, start the engine and run for 5 seconds, turn the key **OFF** for 10 seconds, then restart the vehicle and check for proper idle operation.

Fuel Injector

Removal and Installation

NOTE: When removing the injectors, be careful not to damage the electrical connector pins (on top of the injector), the injector fuel filter and the nozzle. The fuel injector is serviced as a complete assembly only. The injector is an electrical component and should not be immersed in any kind of cleaner.

1. Disconnect the negative battery cable.

Removing the fuel injector on the TBI 220

2. Remove the air cleaner. Properly relieve the fuel system pressure.

3. Disconnect the injector electrical connector.

4. Remove the fuel meter cover and leave the cover gasket in place, if equipped with 2 injectors. Remove the retaining screw and injector retainer, if equipped with 1 injector.

5. Using a suitable tool or J–26868, carefully lift the injector until it is free from the fuel meter body.

6. Remove all O-rings and washers from the injector or housing.

7. Discard the fuel meter cover gasket.

8. To install, lubricate the O-rings with automatic transmission fluid and reverse the removal procedures.

DIESEL FUEL SYSTEM

Fuel Filter

Removal and Installation

1. Turn the ignition **OFF**. Remove the fuel tank cap to release any pressure or vacuum in the tank.

2. Drain the fuel from the fuel filter by opening both the air bleed and the water drain valve allowing the fuel to drain into a suitable container.

3. Unstrap both bail wires with a suitable tool and remove the filter.

To install:

4. Before installing the new filter, ensure that both filter mounting plate fittings are clear of dirt.

5. Snap the filter into place with the bail wires.

6. Close the water drain valve and open the air bleed valve. Connect a 1/8 in. (3mm) I.D. hose to the air bleed port and place the other end into a suitable container.

7. Disconnect the fuel injection pump shutdown solenoid wire.

8. Crank the engine for 10–15 seconds, then wait 1 minute

1. Water drain valve
2. Bail wires
3. Fuel meter element
4. Air bleed
5. Filter adapter
6. Air bleed port
7. Restriction switch
8. Fuel heater
9. Water sensor

Diesel engine fuel filter

Diesel shutdown solenoid location

for the starter motor to cool. Repeat until clear fuel is observed coming from the air bleed.

NOTE: If the engine is to be cranked or started with the air cleaner removed, care must be taken to prevent dirt from being pulled into the air inlet manifold which could result in engine damage.

9. Close the air bleed valve, reconnect the injection pump solenoid wire and replace the fuel tank cap.

10. Start the engine, allow it to idle for 5 minutes and check the fuel filter for leaks.

Draining Water From The System

Water is the worst enemy of the diesel fuel injection system. The injection pump, which is designed and constructed to extremely close tolerances, and the injectors can be easily damaged if

enough water is forced through them in the fuel. Engine performance will also be drastically affected and engine damage can occur.

Diesel fuel is much more susceptible than gasoline to water contamination. Diesel engine vehicles are equipped with an indicator light system located in the instrument panel if water (1–2½ gallons) is detected in the fuel tank. The light will come ON for 2–5 seconds each time the ignition is turned ON, assuring the driver the light is working. If there is water in the fuel, the light will come back ON after a 15–20 second off delay, and then remain ON.

PURGING THE FUEL TANK

The 6.2L diesel engines also use a water-in-fuel warning system. The fuel tank is equipped with a filter which screens out the water and lets it lay in the bottom of the tank below the fuel pick-up. When the water level reaches a point where it could be drawn into the system, a warning light flashes in the cab. A built-in siphoning system starting at the fuel tank and going to the rear spring hanger on some models, and at the midway point of the right frame rail on other models permits you to attach a hose at the shut-off and siphon out the water.

If it becomes necessary to drain water from the fuel tank, also check the primary fuel filter for water.

DRAINING THE FUEL TANK

NOTE: Disconnect the negative battery cable before beginning the draining operation.

If the vehicle is not equipped with a drain plug, use the following procedure to remove the fuel:

1. Using a 10 ft. (305cm) piece of ⅜ in. (9.525mm) hose cut a flap slit 18 in. (457mm) from one end.

2. Install a pipe nipple, of slightly larger diameter than the hose, into the opposite end of the hose.

3. Install the nipple end of the hose into the fuel tank with the natural curve of the hose pointing downward. Keep feeding the hose in until the nipple hits the bottom of the tank.

4. Place the other end of the hose in a suitable container and insert a air hose pointing it in the downward direction of the slit and inject air into the line.

NOTE: If the vehicle is to be stored, always drain the fuel from the complete fuel system including, fuel pump supply, fuel injection pump, fuel lines and tank.

Removal and Installation

1. Disconnect the negative battery cable.
2. Drain the tank.
3. Raise and support the vehicle safely.
4. Remove the clamp on the filler neck and the vent tube hose.
5. Remove the gauge hose which is attached to the frame.
6. While supporting the tank securely, remove the support straps.
7. Lower the tank until the gauge wiring can be removed.
8. Remove the tank.
9. Install the unit by reversing the removal procedure. Make certain the anti-squeak material is replaced during installation.

Diesel Injection Pump

Removal and Installation

1. Disconnect both battery negative cables.
2. Remove the intake manifold.
3. Remove the fuel injection lines.
4. Disconnect the accelerator cable at the injection pump and the detent cable, if equipped.
5. Tag and disconnect the necessary wires and hoses at the injection pump.

1. Injection pump gear
2. Alignment mark
3. Cam gear
4. Bolt
5. Nut
6. Gasket
7. Pump hub

Diesel injection pump installation

1. Driven gear
2. Pump hub

Diesel injection pump locating pin

6. Disconnect the fuel return line at the top of the injection pump.

7. Disconnect the fuel feed line at the injection pump.

8. Remove the air conditioning hose retainer bracket, if equipped.

9. Remove the oil fill tube, including the Crankcase Depression Regulator (CDR) valve vent hose assembly. Remove the grommet.

10. Scribe or paint a matchmark on the front cover and the injection pump flange.

11. Rotate the crankshaft and remove the injection pump drive gear bolts, accessing the bolts through the oil filler neck hole.

12. Remove the injection pump-to-front cover attaching nuts. Remove the pump and cap all open lines and nozzles.

To install:

13. Replace the pump gasket.

14. Align the locating pin on the pump hub with the slot in the injection pump driven gear. At the same time, align the timing marks.

15. Attach the injection pump to the front cover, aligning the timing marks before torquing the nuts to 30 ft. lbs. (40 Nm).

16. Install the drive gear to injection pump bolts, torquing the bolts to 20 ft. lbs. (25 Nm).

17. Install the grommet and oil fill tube.

18. Install the air conditioning bracket.

19. Connect the fuel feed line and torque to 20 ft. lbs. (25 Nm).

20. Connect the fuel return line to the pump.

21. Connect the accelerator and detent cables.

22. Connect all wires and hoses previously removed.

23. Connect the injector lines and install the intake manifold.

24. Connect the negative battery cables. Start the engine and check for leaks.

Idle Speed Adjustment

NOTE: A special tachometer suitable for diesel engines must be used. A gasoline engine type tachometer will not work with the diesel engine.

1. Set the parking brake and block the drive wheels.

2. Run the engine up to normal operating temperature. The air cleaner must be mounted and all accessories turned **OFF**.

3. Install the diesel tachometer as per the manufacturer's instructions.

4. Adjust the low idle speed screw on the fuel injection pump to manufacturer's specification per the emission control label.

NOTE: All idle speeds are to be set within 25 rpm of the specified values.

5. Adjust the fast idle speed as follows:

a. Remove the connector from the fast idle solenoid. Connect a jumper wire from the battery positive terminal to the solenoid terminal to energize the solenoid.

SOLENOID — FAST IDLE

SCREW
LOW IDLE

Diesel injection pump idle adjustment locations

Diesel injection timing alignment marks

Diesel injection nozzles

b. Open the throttle momentarily to ensure that the fast idle solenoid plunger is energized and fully extended.

c. Adjust the fast idle by turning the hex-head screw to manufacturers specification per the emission control label.

d. Remove the jumper wire and reinstall the connector to the fast idle solenoid.

6. Disconnect and remove the tachometer.

Injection Timing Adjustment

For the engine to be properly timed, the lines on the top of the injection pump adapter and the flange of the injection pump must be aligned.

1. The engine must be off for resetting the timing.

2. Loosen the 3 pump retaining nuts with tool J–26987, an injection pump intake manifold wrench or equivalent.

3. Align the mark on the injection pump with the marks on the front cover. Torque the nuts to 30 ft. lbs. (40 Nm). Use a ¾ in. open-end wrench on the boss at the front of the injection pump to aid in rotating the pump to align the marks.

Fuel Injector

Removal and Installation

1. Disconnect the negative cable on both batteries.

Diesel injection nozzle

2. Disconnect the fuel line clip, and remove the fuel return hose.

3. Remove the fuel injection line.

4. Using GM special tool J–29873, remove the injector. Always remove the injector by turning the 30mm hex portion of the injector. Cap the injector and fuel lines when disconnected, to prevent contamination.

5. Install the injector with new gasket and torque to 50 ft. lbs. (70 Nm). Connect the injection line and torque the nut to 20 ft. lbs. (25 Nm). Install the fuel return hose, fuel line clips and connect the batteries.

EMISSION CONTROLS

Emission Warning Lamps

For further information, please refer to Chilton's Emission Controls Manual.

Resetting

When the ECM sets a code, the **Service Engine Soon** light will come **ON** and a code will be stored in memory. If the problem is intermittent, the light will go out after 10 seconds when the fault goes away. However the code will stay in the memory for 50 starts or until the battery voltage to the ECM is removed. Removing battery voltage for 30 seconds will clear all stored codes. On 1988–90 vehicles, the ECM B fuse can also be used to clear codes on all vehicles, except the C/K-Series, which has a fuse link.

NOTE: To prevent damage to the ECM, the key must be OFF when disconnecting or connecting power to the ECM.

GASOLINE ENGINE MECHANICAL

NOTE: Disconnecting the negative battery cable on some vehicles may interfere with the functions of the on board computer systems and may require the computer to undergo a relearning process, once the negative battery cable is reconnected.

Engine Assembly

Removal and Installation

EXCEPT G-SERIES

1. Disconnect the negative battery cable.
2. Remove the hood.
3. Drain the cooling system.
4. Remove the air cleaner.
5. Remove the accessory drive belt, fan and water pump pulley.
6. Remove the radiator and shroud.
7. Disconnect the heater hoses at the engine.
8. Disconnect the accelerator, cruise control and detent linkage if used.
9. Disconnect the air conditioning compressor, if equipped, and lay aside.
10. Remove the power steering pump, if used, and lay aside.
11. Disconnect the engine wiring from the engine.
12. Release the fuel system pressure as required. Disconnect the fuel line.
13. Disconnect the vacuum lines from the intake manifold.
14. Raise the vehicle and support it safely.
15. Drain the engine oil.
16. Disconnect the exhaust pipes from the manifold.
17. Disconnect the strut rods at the engine mountings, if used.
18. Remove the flywheel or torque converter cover.
19. Disconnect the wiring along the oil pan rail.
20. Remove the starter.
21. Disconnect the wire for the fuel gauge.
22. On vehicles equipped with automatic transmission, remove the converter to flexplate bolts.
23. Lower the vehicle and suitably support the transmission. Attach a suitable lifting fixture to the engine.
24. Remove the bell housing to engine bolts.
25. Remove the rear engine mounting to frame bolts and the front through bolts and remove the engine.

To install:

26. Raise the vehicle and support it safely.
27. Lower the engine and install the engine mounting bolts. Torque the rear engine mounting to frame bolts or nuts, the front through bolts and the front nuts to specification.
28. Install the bell housing to engine bolts and torque to 35 ft. lbs. (44 Nm).
29. Install the converter to flex bolts and torque to specification.
30. Install the fuel gauge wiring and starter.
31. Install the flywheel or torque converter cover.
32. Connect the strut rods at the engine mountings, if used.
33. Install the exhaust pipes at the manifold.
34. Lower the vehicle.
35. Connect the vacuum lines to the intake manifold.
36. Install the fuel line.
37. Connect the engine wiring harness.
38. Install the power steering pump, if used.
39. Connect the air conditioning compressor, if used.
40. Connect the accelerator, cruise control and detent linkage.
41. Connect the heater hoses.
42. Install the radiator and shroud.
43. Install the accessory drive belts.
44. Install the hood.

45. Install the proper quantity and grade of coolant and engine oil.
46. Connect the negative battery cable.

G-SERIES

4.3L Engine

1. Disconnect the battery cables.
2. Remove the glove box, as required.
3. Drain the cooling system.
4. Remove the engine cover.
5. Remove the outside air duct.
6. Remove the power steering reservoir.
7. Remove the hood release cable, as required.
8. Remove the fan shroud and radiator assembly.
9. Remove the fan and pulley.
10. Remove the air cleaner.
11. Remove the cruise control servo, servo bracket and transducer, as required.
12. Tag and disconnect all vacuum hoses.
13. Disconnect the accelerator linkage and TVS cables.
14. Properly relieve the fuel system pressure and remove the TBI unit.
15. Remove the distributor cap with the wires attached.
16. Disconnect the heater hoses at the engine.
17. Remove the PCV valve, as required.
18. Properly discharge the air conditioning system and remove the air conditioning compressor and bracket.
19. Remove the alternator, as required.
20. Remove the upper half of the engine dipstick tube.
21. Remove the oil filler tube.
22. Remove the transmission dipstick tube and the accelerator cable at the tube.
23. Remove the fuel line at the fuel pump.
24. Remove the power steering pump.
25. Remove the headlight bezels and the grille.
26. Remove the upper radiator support.
27. Remove the lower fan shroud and filler panel.
28. Remove the hood latch support.
29. Remove the condenser. Cap all openings.
30. Raise and support the vehicle safely.
31. Drain the engine oil.
32. Disconnect the exhaust pipes at the manifolds.
33. Remove the strut rods at the torque converter or flywheel underpan.
34. Remove the torque converter or flywheel cover.
35. Remove the starter.
36. Remove the flexplate-to-torque converter bolts for automatic transmissions.
37. Remove the bell housing-to-engine bolts.
38. Remove the engine mounting through bolts.
39. Lower the vehicle and support the transmission using the proper equipment.
40. Attach an engine crane to the engine, pull the engine forward and upward and remove it from the vehicle.

To install:

41. Raise the engine into position.
42. Install the engine mount through bolts. Torque the bolts to specification.
43. Install the bell housing-to-engine bolts. Torque the bolts to specification.
44. Install the flexplate-to-torque converter bolts for automatic transmissions. Torque the bolts to specification.
45. Install the starter.
46. Install the torque converter or flywheel cover.

47. Install the strut rods at the torque converter or flywheel underpan.
48. Connect the exhaust pipes at the manifolds.
49. Install the fuel line at the fuel pump.
50. Install the condenser.
51. Install the hood latch support.
52. Install the lower fan shroud and filler panel.
53. Install the transmission dipstick tube and the accelerator cable at the tube.
54. Install the PCV valve.
55. Install the distributor cap.
56. Install the cruise control servo, servo bracket and transducer.
57. Install the oil filler pipe and the engine dipstick tube.
58. Install the thermostat housing.
59. Connect the heater hoses at the engine.
60. Connect the engine wiring harness from the firewall connection.
61. Install the air conditioning compressor, mounting bracket and alternator assembly.
62. Install the radiator and the shroud.
63. Install the radiator support bracket.
64. Install the TBI unit.
65. Connect the accelerator linkage and TVS cable.
66. Install the windshield wiper jar and bracket.
67. Install the air conditioning compressor.
68. Install the air conditioning vacuum reservoir.
69. Charge the air conditioning system, using the proper equipment.
70. If equipped with an automatic transmission, install the cooler lines at the radiator.
71. Install the power steering reservoir.
72. Install the hood release cable.
73. Connect the radiator hoses at the radiator.
74. Install the headlight bezels and the grille.
75. Install the air cleaner.
76. Install the outside air duct.
77. Install the engine cover.
78. Fill the cooling system with the proper type and quantity of antifreeze.
79. Fill the crankcase.
80. Connect the battery cables.
81. Install the glove box.

5.0L and 5.7L Engines

1. Disconnect the battery cables.
2. Drain the cooling system.
3. Remove the radiator coolant reservoir bottle.
4. Remove the upper radiator support.
5. Remove the grille and the lower grille valance.
6. Discharge the air conditioning system using the proper equipment.
7. Remove the air conditioning condenser from in front of the radiator.
8. If equipped with an automatic transmission, remove the fluid cooler lines from the radiator.
9. Disconnect the radiator hoses at the radiator.
10. Remove the radiator support bracket and remove the radiator and the shroud.
11. Remove the engine cover.
12. Remove the air cleaner.
13. Disconnect the accelerator linkage.
14. Disconnect all hoses and wires at the carburetor or TBI unit.
15. Relieve the fuel system pressure and remove the carburetor or TBI unit.
16. Disconnect the engine wiring harness from the firewall connection.
17. Tag and disconnect all vacuum lines.

18. Remove the power steering pump and lay the assembly aside.
19. Disconnect the heater hoses at the engine.
20. Remove the thermostat housing.
21. Remove the oil filler tube.
22. Remove the cruise control servo, servo bracket and transducer.
23. Raise and support the vehicle safely.
24. Drain the engine oil.
25. Disconnect the exhaust pipes at the manifolds.
26. Remove the driveshaft and plug the end of the transmission.
27. Disconnect the transmission shift linkage and the speedometer cable or speed sensor connector.
28. Disconnect the fuel and vapor return lines at the engine.
29. Remove the rear engine/transmission mount bolts.
30. Support the transmission and engine.
31. Remove the engine mount bracket-to-frame bolts.
32. Remove the engine mount through bolts.
33. Raise the engine slightly and remove the engine mounts.
34. Support the engine with a block of wood between the oil pan and the crossmember.
35. Lower the vehicle.
36. Install a suitable engine lifting device.
37. Remove the engine and transmission from the vehicle as an assembly.
38. Separate the engine and transmission as required.

To install:

39. Install the engine mount through bolts. Torque the bolts to specification.
40. Install the engine mount bracket-to-frame bolts. Torque the bolts to specification.
41. Remove the engine lifting device. Raise and support the vehicle safely.
42. Install the transmission mounting bolts. Torque the bolts to specification.
43. Connect the transmission shift linkage and the speedometer cable or speed sensor connector.
44. Install the driveshaft.
45. Install the condenser.
46. Install the hood latch support.
47. Install the lower fan shroud and filler panel.
48. Install the transmission dipstick tube and the accelerator cable at the tube.
49. Install the coolant hose at the intake manifold and the PCV valve.
50. Install the distributor cap and wires.
51. Install the cruise control servo, servo bracket and transducer.
52. Install the oil filler pipe and the engine dipstick tube.
53. Install the thermostat housing.
54. Connect the heater hoses at the engine.
55. Connect the engine wiring harness from the firewall connection.
56. Install the radiator and the shroud.
57. Install the radiator support bracket.
58. Install the carburetor or TBI unit.
59. Connect the accelerator linkage.
60. Install the windshield wiper jar and bracket.
61. Install the air conditioning compressor.
62. Connect the vacuum lines.
63. Charge the air conditioning system using the proper equipment.
64. If equipped with an automatic transmission, install the fluid cooler lines at the radiator.
65. Install the radiator coolant reservoir bottle.
66. Connect the radiator hoses at the radiator.

67. Install the upper radiator support the grille and the lower grille valance.
68. Install the air cleaner.
69. Install the air stove pipe.
70. Install the engine cover.
71. Fill the cooling system.
72. Connect the battery cables and inspect for leaks.

7.4L Engine

1. Disconnect the battery cables.
2. Drain the cooling system into a suitable container.
3. Remove the engine cover.
4. Remove the air cleaner and ducts.
5. Remove the cruise control servo, servo bracket and transducer, as required.
6. Remove the grille, lower grille valance, headlight bezels and all necessary sheetmetal to ease removal and installation of the engine and transmission assembly.
7. Remove the upper radiator support.
8. Discharge the air conditioning system using the proper equipment.
9. Remove the air conditioning condenser from in front of the radiator. Cap all lines.
10. Disconnect the radiator hoses at the radiator.
11. Disconnect the oil and transmission cooler lines.
12. Remove the radiator coolant reservoir bottle.
13. Remove the radiator support bracket and remove the radiator and the shroud.
14. Remove the power steering pump and position aside.
15. Remove the air conditioning compressor and brackets. Cap all open lines.
16. Disconnect the wiring, fuel lines and linkage at the TBI unit.
17. Properly relieve the fuel system pressure and remove the TBI unit.
18. Disconnect the ECS and MAP sensors with brackets. Disconnect the engine wiring harness from the firewall connection.
19. Disconnect the starter wires.
20. Disconnect the alternator wires.
21. Disconnect the temperature sensor wire.
22. Disconnect the oil pressure sender.
23. Disconnect the distributor and coil wiring.
24. Disconnect and plug the fuel supply and vapor lines.
25. Tag and disconnect all vacuum hoses.
26. Disconnect the heater hoses at the engine.
27. Remove the thermostat housing.
28. Remove the windshield wiper jar and bracket.
29. Remove the oil filler pipe and the engine dipstick tube.
30. Raise and support the vehicle safely.
31. Disconnect the exhaust pipes at the manifolds.
32. Remove the driveshaft and plug the end of the transmission.
33. Disconnect the transmission shift linkage and the speedometer cable.
34. Drain the engine oil.
35. Support the engine with a floor jack. Do not position the jack under the oil pan, crankshaft pulley or any sheetmetal!
36. Attach a suitable lifting device to the engine to relieve the weight.
37. Remove the transmission mount bolts and remove the crossmember.
38. Raise the engine slightly and remove the engine mounts. Support the engine with wood between the oil pan and the crossmember.
39. Lower the vehicle.
40. Raise the engine as necessary and maneuver the engine/transmission assembly from the vehicle.
41. Separate the engine and transmission as follows:
   a. Support the engine properly.

b. Remove the starter and converter housing underpan.
c. Remove the flywheel-to-converter attaching bolts.
d. Support the transmission on blocks.
e. Disconnect the detent cable.
f. Remove the transmission-to-engine mounting bolts.
g. Remove the blocks from the engine only and guide the engine away from the transmission.
42. Mount the engine on a work stand.

To install:

43. Install the automatic transmission as follows:
   a. Position the transmission and engine together.
   b. Install the transmission-to-engine mounting bolts. Torque the bolts to specification.
   c. Connect the throttle linkage detent cable, if equipped.
   d. Install the flywheel-to-converter attaching bolts. Torque the bolts to specification.
   e. Install the starter and converter shield.
44. Raise the engine/transmission and guide the assembly into position in the vehicle.
45. Raise the engine slightly and install the engine mounts. Torque the mount-to-block bolts to specification.
46. Install the engine mount through bolts. Torque the bolts to specification.
47. Install the engine mount bracket-to-frame bolts. Torque the front and the rear mount bolts to specification.
48. Install the transmission mounting bolts. Torque the nuts to specification.
49. Connect the transmission shift linkage and the speedometer cable.
50. Install the driveshaft.
51. Connect the exhaust pipes at the manifolds.
52. Install the oil filler pipe, engine and transmission dipstick tube.
53. Install the windshield wiper jar and bracket.
54. Install the thermostat housing.
55. Connect the heater hoses at the engine.
56. Connect all vacuum hoses.
57. Connect the fuel supply and vapor lines.
58. Connect the distributor and coil wiring.
59. Connect the oil pressure sender.
60. Connect the temperature sensor wire.
61. Connect the alternator wires.
62. Connect the starter wires.
63. Connect the engine wiring harness at the firewall connection.
64. Install the TBI unit.
65. Connect the wiring, fuel lines and linkage at the TBI unit.
66. Install the air conditioning compressor.
67. Install the power steering pump.
68. Install the radiator and the shroud.
69. Install the radiator support bracket.
70. Install the radiator coolant reservoir bottle.
71. Install the fluid cooler lines at the radiator.
72. Connect the radiator hoses at the radiator.
73. Install the air conditioning condenser.
74. Install the air conditioning vacuum reservoir.
75. Charge the air conditioning system using the proper equipment.
76. Install the upper radiator support.
77. Connect the radiator hoses at the radiator.
78. Install the grille and the lower grille valance.
79. Install the cruise control servo, servo bracket and transducer.
80. Fill the crankcase the proper type and quantity of oil.
81. Install the air cleaner.
82. Install the engine cover.
83. Fill the cooling system.
84. Connect the battery cables.

Engine Mounts

Removal and Installation

1. Disconnect the negative battery cable.
2. Raise and safely support the vehicle.
3. Support the engine with a suitable jack.

NOTE: Do not position the jack under the oil pan, any sheetmetal or the crankshaft pulley, otherwise damage may occur.

4. Remove the engine mount through-bolt.
5. Raise the engine to gain sufficient clearance for the mount to be removed, being careful not to crush the distributor against the firewall.
6. Remove the engine mount attaching bolts, nuts and washers.
7. Remove the mount assembly.
8. Installation is the reverse of the removal procedure.

Cylinder Head

Removal and Installation

4.3L ENGINE

1. Disconnect the negative battery cable.
2. Remove the engine cover, as required. Drain the cooling system into a suitable container.
3. Relieve the fuel system pressure and remove the intake manifold.
4. Remove the exhaust manifold.
5. Remove the air pipe at the rear of the head, if equipped.
6. Remove the air pump bolt and spacer at the right cylinder head, if equipped.
7. Remove the power steering pump and brackets from the cylinder head, and lay them aside (left cylinder head).
8. Remove the air conditioner compressor, accessory brackets and alternator and position aside, as required.
9. Remove the spark plugs wires, ground straps and engine wiring harness connectors.
10. Remove the fuel lines and brackets.
11. Remove the rocker arm covers, the rocker arms and pushrods.
12. Remove the cylinder head bolts.
13. Remove the cylinder head.

To install:

14. Clean all gasket mating surfaces, install a new gasket and reinstall the cylinder head.

NOTE: Apply sealer to both sides of steel gasket. If a composition gasket is used, do not use sealer.

15. Clean the bolts, apply sealer to the threads, and install the bolts hand tight.
16. Tighten the bolts in the proper sequence and torque specifications.
17. Install the rocker arms and pushrods.
18. Install the wiring harness and accessory brackets.
19. Install the spark plugs.
20. Install the rocker arm cover.
21. Install the air conditioner compressor.
22. Install the power steering pump and brackets.
23. Install the alternator mounting bolt at the cylinder head.
24. Install the air pipe at the rear of the head.
25. Install the exhaust manifold.
26. Install the intake manifold.
27. Install the engine cover.
28. Connect the negative battery cable.

4.8L ENGINE

1. Disconnect the negative battery cable. Drain cooling system. Remove air cleaner assembly.

Cylinder head bolt torque sequence—4.3L engine

Cylinder head bolt torque sequence—4.8L engine

Cylinder head bolt torque sequence—5.0L and 5.7L engines

2. Properly relieve the fuel pump pressure. Disconnect the fuel line at the carburetor. Disconnect the accelerator and transmission linkages. Disconnect all required electrical and vacuum lines.
3. Remove the combination manifold assembly retaining bolts. Remove the combination manifold from the engine.
4. Remove the valve cover. Remove the rocker arms and pushrods, placing them in order for reinstallation.
5. If equipped, disconnect the AIR injection hose at the check valve. Disconnect the upper radiator, heater and bypass hoses. Remove the battery ground strap.
6. Remove the cylinder head retaining bolts. Remove the cylinder head from the engine.

To install:

7. Install the gasket and cylinder head onto the block. Torque the cylinder head bolts to specification.
8. Connect the AIR injection hose at the check valve, if equipped. Connect the upper radiator, heater and bypass hoses.
9. Connect the battery ground strap. Install the combination manifold assembly and retaining bolts.
10. Install the rocker arms and pushrods, placing them in the same position from which they were removed. Install the valve cover and gasket.
11. Connect the fuel line at the carburetor. Connect the accelerator and transmission linkages. Connect all previously disconnected electrical and vacuum lines.
12. Connect the negative battery cable. Fill the cooling system with the proper type and quantity of antifreeze and inspect engine fo leaks. Install the air cleaner assembly.
13. Change oil and filter, as required.

5.0L AND 5.7L ENGINES

1. Disconnect the negative battery cable.
2. Properly relieve the fuel system pressure.
3. Drain the cooling system.
4. Remove the intake manifold.

5. Remove the exhaust manifolds and position out of the way.

6. Remove the air pump bolt and spacer.

7. If equipped with air conditioning, remove the compressor and the forward mounting bracket and lay the compressor aside. Do not disconnect any of the refrigerant lines.

8. Disconnect the wiring harness brackets, fuel lines and spark plug wires.

9. Remove the alternator, as required and position aside.

10. Remove the power steering pump, as required and position aside.

11. Remove the stud and nut securing the main accessory bracket to the cylinder head.

12. Remove the valve covers. Back off the rocker arm nuts and pivot the rocker arms out of the way and remove the pushrods. Mark the pushrods so they can be installed in their original positions.

13. Remove the cylinder head bolts and remove the heads.

To install:

14. Install the cylinder heads using new gaskets. Install the gaskets with the bead up. Coat a steel gasket on both sides with sealer. If a composition gasket is used, do not use sealer.

15. Clean the bolts, apply sealer to the threads, and install them hand tight.

16. Torque the head bolts to specification in the proper sequence.

17. Install the intake and exhaust manifolds.

18. Adjust the rocker arms and install the valve covers.

19. Install the exhaust manifolds.

20. Install the alternator, power steering pump and fuel lines.

21. Install the air pump and air conditioning compressor.

22. Connect all vacuum and electrical connectors. Install spark plugs and wires.

23. Fill the cooling system with the proper type and quantity of antifreeze.

24. Connect the negative battery cable.

7.4L ENGINE

1. Disconnect the negative battery cable.

2. Properly relieve the fuel system pressure.

3. Drain the cooling system into a suitable container.

4. Remove the intake manifold.

5. Remove the exhaust manifolds.

6. Remove the alternator and position aside.

7. Remove the power steering pump and position aside.

8. Remove the AIR pump and brackets, if equipped.

9. If equipped with air conditioning, remove the compressor and the forward mounting bracket and lay the compressor aside. Do not disconnect any of the refrigerant lines.

10. Remove the idler pulley and A/C compressor rear bracket on the vehicle, as required.

11. Remove the rocker arm covers.

12. Remove the spark plugs.

13. Remove the AIR pipes at the rear of the head, as required.

14. Disconnect the ground strap at the rear of the head.

15. Disconnect the sensor wire.

16. Back off the rocker arm nuts and pivot the rocker arms out

1.	Bolt
2.	Retainer
3.	Nuts
4.	Balls
5.	Rocker arms
6.	Pushrods
7.	Restrictor
8.	Hydrualic lifter

Cylinder head and components—4.3L engine

1.	Nut
2.	Ball
3.	Rocker arm
4.	Rocker arm stud
5.	Valve keepers
6.	Cap
7.	Rotator
8.	Spring with damper
9.	Exhaust valve
10.	Intake valve
11.	Pushrod guide
12.	Seal

Cylinder head bolt torque sequence—7.4L engine

Cylinder head and components—7.4L engine

1. Valve keeper
2. Cap
3. Shield
4. O-Ring seal
5. Seal
6. Damper
7. Spring
8. Intake valve
9. Rotator
10. Exhaust valve

Valves and components—4.3L, 5.0L and 5.7L engines

of the way so the pushrods can be removed. Identify the push-rods so they can be installed in their original positions.

17. Remove the cylinder head bolts and remove the head.

To install:

18. Thoroughly clean the mating surfaces of the head and block. Clean the bolt holes thoroughly.

19. Install the cylinder heads using new gaskets. Install the gaskets with the bead up.

NOTE: Coat a steel gasket on both sides with sealer. If a composition gasket is used, do not use sealer.

20. Clean the bolts, apply sealer to the threads, and install the bolts hand tight.

21. Torque the head bolts in sequence to the proper torque specifications.

22. Install the intake and exhaust manifolds.

23. Install the pushrods.

24. Install the rocker arms and adjust properly.

25. Connect the sensor wire.

26. Connect the ground strap at the rear of the head.

27. Install the AIR pipes at the rear of the head.

28. Install the spark plugs.

29. Install the rocker arm cover.

30. Install the air conditioning compressor and the forward mounting bracket.

31. Install the AIR pump.

32. Install the alternator.

Valve Lifters

Removal and Installation

EXCEPT 4.8L ENGINE

1. Disconnect the negative battery cable. Drain the cooling system into a suitable container. Properly relieve the fuel system pressure.

2. Remove the air cleaner assembly.

3. Remove the distributor assembly.

4. Remove the intake manifold, valve covers and pushrods.

5. Remove the retainer bolts and the valve lifter retainer, as required.

6. Remove the valve lifter restrictor plate, as required.

7. Remove the lifters and place them in the exact order of removal to ensure lifter is installed in original bore upon reinstallation.

To install:

8. Lubricate the lifter contact and/or roller points with a suitable engine oil supplement or Molylube®.

9. Install the used lifters in its original bore or new lifters in any bore.

10. Install the valve lifter restrictor plate, if equipped.

11. Install the retainer bolts and the valve lifter retainer, if equipped.

12. Install the intake manifold and pushrods. Adjust the valve lifters to specification; install the valve covers.

13. Install the distributor assembly.

14. Install the air cleaner assembly.

15. Connect the negative battery cable. Fill the cooling system with the proper type and quantity of antifreeze.

4.8L ENGINE

1. Disconnect the negative battery cable. Drain the cooling system into a suitable container. Properly relieve the fuel system pressure.

2. Remove the air cleaner assembly.

3. Remove the valve cover.

4. Remove the distributor assembly.

5. Remove the dipstick tube.

6. Remove the pushrod cover.

7. Remove the pushrods and remove the lifters placing them in the exact order of removal to ensure the lifter is installed in the original bore upon reinstallation.

To install:

8. Lubricate the lifter contact and/or roller points with a suitable engine oil supplement or Molylube®.

9. Install the used lifters in its original bore or new lifters in any bore.

10. Install the pushrods and pushrod cover.

11. Install the distributor assembly and dipstick tube.

12. Adjust the valve lifters to specification; install the valve cover.

13. Install the air cleaner assembly.

14. Connect the negative battery cable.

Valve Lash

Adjustment

All engines use hydraulic lifters, which require no periodic adjustment. In the event of cylinder head removal or any operation that requires disturbing the rocker arms, the rocker arms will have to be adjusted on all vehicles, except the 1991–92 7.4L engine, which use a positive stop bolt on the rocker arm instead of a stud and nut design.

EXCEPT 4.8L ENGINE

1. Remove the valve covers and gaskets.

2. Crank the engine until the mark on the damper aligns with the **TDC** or **0** mark on the timing tab and the engine is in No. 1 cylinder firing position. This can be determined by placing a finger on the No. 1 cylinder valves as the marks align. If the valves do not move, it is in the No. 1 firing position. If the valves move, it is in No. 6 firing position (No. 4 on the V6 engine) and the crankshaft should be rotated 1 more revolution to the No. 1 firing position.

3. With the engine in No. 1 firing position, the following valves can be adjusted:

V6 Engine
Exhaust—1, 5, 6
Intake—1, 2, 3

V8 Engine
Exhaust—1, 3, 4, 8
Intake—1, 2, 5, 7

4. To adjust the valves, proceed as follows:

a. Back off the adjusting nut until lash is felt at the pushrod.

b. Turn in the adjusting nut until all lash is removed and the pushrod is not capable of being rotated.

c. Turn the adjusting nut in an additional ¾–1 turn to center the lifter plunger.

5. Crank the engine 1 full revolution until the marks are again in alignment. This is No. 6 firing position (No. 4 on the V6 engine). The following valves can now be adjusted:

V6 Engine
Exhaust—2, 3, 4
Intake—4, 5, 6

V8 Engine
Exhaust—2, 5, 6, 7
Intake—3, 4, 6, 8

6. Repeat the adjustment procedure as directed in step 4.
7. Reinstall the valve covers using new gaskets.

4.8L ENGINE

1. Remove the valve covers and discard the gaskets.
2. Mark the distributor housing at the No. 1 and 6 plug wire positions.
3. Remove the distributor cap and set aside.
4. Turn the crankshaft until the rotor of the distributor points to the No. 1 cylinder position.
5. The following valves may be adjusted:

Exhaust—1, 3, 5
Intake—1, 2, 4

6. To adjust the valves, proceed as follows:
   a. Back off the adjusting nut until lash is felt at the pushrod.
   b. Turn in the adjusting nut until all lash is removed and the pushrod is not capable of being rotated.
   c. Turn the adjusting nut in an additional ¾–1 turn to center the lifter plunger.
7. Crank the engine until the distributor rotor points to the No. 6 cylinder position. The following valves can now be adjusted:

Exhaust—2, 4, 6
Intake—3, 5, 6

8. Repeat the adjustment procedure as directed in step 6.
9. Reinstall the valve covers using new gaskets.

Valve Arrangement

4.3L ENGINE

Left Side E–I–E–I–I–E
Right Side E–I–I–E–I–E

Adjusting hydraulic valves

4.8L ENGINE

E–I–E–E–I–I–E–E–I–I–E

5.0L AND 5.7L ENGINES

Left Side E–I–I–E–E–I–I–E
Right Side E–I–I–E–E–I–I–E

7.4L ENGINE

Left Side E–I–E–I–E–I–E–I
Right Side I–E–I–E–I–E–I–E

Rocker Arm

Removal and Installation

1. Disconnect the negative battery cable. On G-Series vehicle, remove the engine cover.
2. Remove all the necessary components in order to gain access to the engine valve covers. As required, properly relieve the fuel system pressure before disconnecting any fuel lines.
3. Remove the valve cover retaining bolts. Remove the valve cover from the engine.
4. Remove the rocker arm assemblies. Keep them in order for reinstallation.
5. Installation is the reverse of the removal procedure. Be sure to use new gaskets or RTV sealant, as necessary.

Intake Manifold

Removal and Installation

4.3L, 5.0L and 5.7L Engines

1. Disconnect the negative battery cable. Drain the cooling system.
2. Remove the air cleaner assembly.
3. Remove the thermostat housing and the bypass hose. It is not necessary to remove the top radiator hose from the thermostat housing.
4. Disconnect the heater hose at the rear of the manifold.
5. Disconnect all electrical connections and vacuum lines from the manifold. Remove the EGR valve if necessary.
6. Remove the power brake vacuum line from the vacuum booster to the manifold.
7. Remove the distributor.
8. Relieve the fuel system pressure and remove the fuel line at the TBI unit or carburetor.
9. Remove the accelerator linkage.
10. Remove the TBI unit or carburetor, as required.
11. Remove the intake manifold bolts. Remove the manifold and the gaskets.

Intake manifold installation—4.3L engine

5 GENERAL MOTORS CORPORATION
C/K SERIES (PICK-UP) • R/V SERIES (PICK-UP) • BLAZER/JIMMY • SUBURBAN • G SERIES (VAN)

SECTION

Intake manifold installation—5.0L and 5.7L engines

Intake manifold torque sequence—4.3L engine

Intake manifold torque sequence—5.0L and 5.7L engines

To install:

NOTE: Before installing the intake manifold, ensure the gasket surfaces are thoroughly clean.

12. Apply 3/16 in. (5mm) bead of sealant to the front and rear sealing surfaces of the engine block manifold. Extend the bead ½ in. (13mm) up each cylinder head to seal and retain the gaskets.

13. Install the manifold and the gaskets.

Intake manifold torque sequence—1988–90 7.4L engine

Intake manifold torque sequence—1990–92 7.4L engine

14. Install the intake manifold bolts and torque to the proper specification.
15. Install the TBI unit or carburetor assembly.
16. Install the accelerator linkage.
17. Install the fuel line.
18. Install the distributor.
19. Install the vacuum line between the vacuum booster and manifold.
20. Connect all electrical connections and vacuum lines at the manifold. Install the EGR valve if necessary.
21. Connect the heater hose at the rear of the manifold.
22. Install the thermostat housing and the bypass hose.
23. Install the air cleaner assembly.
24. Fill the cooling system with proper type and quantity of antifreeze.

7.4L Engine

1. Disconnect the negative battery cable.
2. Drain the cooling system.
3. Remove the air cleaner assembly.
4. Remove the upper radiator hose, thermostat housing and the bypass hose.
5. Disconnect the heater hose and pipe at the TBI unit, if equipped.
6. Tag and disconnect all electrical connections and vacuum lines from the manifold.
7. Disconnect the accelerator linkage.
8. Disconnect the cruise control cable.
9. Disconnect the TVS cable.

10. Properly relieve the fuel system pressure. Remove the fuel line at the TBI unit.

11. Remove the TBI unit.

12. Remove the distributor assembly.

13. Remove the cruise control transducer.

14. Disconnect and remove the ignition coil.

15. Remove the EGR solenoid and bracket.

16. Remove the MAP sensor and bracket.

17. Remove the air conditioning compressor rear bracket.

18. Remove the front alternator/AIR pump bracket.

19. Remove the intake manifold bolts.

20. Remove the manifold, gaskets and seals.

To install:

21. Install the manifold, gaskets and seals.

22. Install the intake manifold bolts. Torque the bolts to 30 ft. lbs. (40 Nm).

23. Install the front alternator/AIR pump bracket.

24. Install the air conditioning compressor rear bracket.

25. Install the MAP sensor and bracket.

26. Install the EGR solenoid and bracket.

27. Connect the ignition coil wires.

28. Install the cruise control transducer.

29. Install the distributor.

30. Install the TBI unit.

31. Install the fuel line at the TBI unit.

32. Connect the TVS cable.

33. Connect the cruise control cable.

34. Connect the accelerator linkage.

35. Connect all electrical connections and vacuum lines at the manifold.

36. Connect the heater hose and pipe.

37. Install the upper radiator hose, thermostat housing and the bypass hose.

38. Install the air cleaner assembly.

39. Fill the cooling system.

40. Connect the negative battery cable.

Exhaust Manifold

Removal and Installation

4.3L, 5.0L AND 5.7L ENGINES

1. Disconnect the negative battery cable. Remove the air cleaner.

2. Remove the hot air shroud, if equipped.

3. Loosen the alternator and remove the lower bracket, as required.

4. Remove the air conditioner compressor rear bracket and the diverter valve and bracket.

NOTE: On models with air conditioning, it may be necessary to remove the compressor, and tie it out of the way. Do not disconnect the compressor lines.

5. Disconnect the oxygen sensor wire, if equipped.

6. Remove the power steering pump rear bracket and the AIR hose at the check valve, as required.

7. Raise and support the vehicle safely.

8. Disconnect the crossover pipe from both manifolds.

9. Remove the manifold bolts and remove the manifold(s). Some models have lock tabs on the front and rear manifold bolts which must be removed before removing the bolts.

10. Installation is the reverse of removal. Torque the bolts to the proper specification and sequence.

7.4L Engine

1. Disconnect the negative battery cable.

2. Remove the heat stove pipe.

3. Remove the dipstick tube.

Service Tips

INTAKE MANIFOLD GASKET

The 1988–90 4.3L, 5.0L and 5.7L engines equipped with TBI have added a restrictor plate to the rear coolant passage of the gasket to prevent throttle plate icing. If the intake gasket is installed incorrectly the engine will overheat causing possible engine damage.

Ensure the gasket is installed with the restrictor to the rear of the engine.

The gasket may be checked without removing the manifold, the gasket has a metal locator tab that can be seen protruding from the end of the manifold/cylinder head. When installed correctly, on the 4.3L engine, the metal locator tab will at the rear of the engine or at the front of the engine, if equipped with the 5.0L or 5.7L engine.

Service Tips

TAILPIPE SMOKE ON STARTUP

The 1988–90 5.0L and 5.7L engines emitting white or bluish-white smoke from the tailpipe on initial start-up, may be caused by a loose joint between the intake manifold and cylinder head. If no unusual oil consumption is noted and the bolt torque is below 10 ft. lbs. or there are signs of threading in the manifold bolt holes, replace the manifold and gasket assembly.

1.	Heat shield	3.	Tab washer
2.	Washer	4.	Bolt/stud

Exhaust manifold installation–Typical

4. Disconnect the AIR hose at the check valve and AIR lines at the manifold, as required.

5. Remove the spark plugs and wires.

6. Raise and support the vehicle safely.

7. Disconnect the exhaust pipe at the manifold. Remove the heat shield, if equipped. Disconnect the oxygen sensor wire, as required.

8. Lower the vehicle and remove the manifold bolts and spark plug heat shields.

NOTE: It may be necessary to raise the engine slightly to gain sufficient clearance for removal of the manifold on G-Series vehicles.

9. Remove the manifold assemblies.
To install:

10. Clean the mating surfaces.

11. Clean the stud threads.

12. Install the manifold, spark plug heat shields and bolts. Tighten the bolts to 40 ft. lbs. (54 Nm). starting from the center bolts and working towards the outside.

13. Raise and safely support the vehicle. Connect the exhaust pipe, heat shields and oxygen sensor at the manifold.

14. Lower the vehicle. Install the spark plugs and wires.

15. Connect the AIR hose and lines.

16. Install the dipstick tube.

17. Install the heat stove pipe.

18. Connect the battery negative cable.

Combination Manifold

Removal and Installation

4.8L Engine

1. Disconnect the negative battery cable.

2. Remove the air cleaner.

3. Disconnect the throttle controls at the bellcrank.

4. Remove the carburetor, if necessary.

1. Bolt		6. Washer	
2. Clamp		7. Stud	
3. Nut		8. Gasket	
4. Exhaust manifold		9. Intake manifold	
5. Bolt		10. Nut	

Combination manifolds—4.8L engine

5. Disconnect the fuel and vacuum lines from the manifold.

6. Remove the AIR pump and bracket. Disconnect the PCV hose.

7. Raise and support the vehicle safely.

8. Disconnect the exhaust pipe at the manifold.

9. Lower the vehicle and remove the manifold heat stove.

10. Remove the clamps, bolts and washers and remove the combination manifold.

11. Separate the manifolds by removing the bolts and nuts.
To install:

12. Clean the mating surfaces.

13. Clean the stud threads.

14. Assemble the manifolds with a new gasket and leave the nuts finger-tight.

15. Install a new gasket over the manifold studs on the cylinder head and install the manifold assembly.

16. Install the bolts, clamps and nuts.

NOTE: Always tighten the manifold to cylinder head bolts and nuts to 38 ft. lbs. (52 Nm) before tightening the manifold center bolts and nuts to 44 ft. lbs. (60 Nm).

17. The remainder of the installation is reverse of the removal procedure.

Timing Chain Front Cover

Removal and Installation

EXCEPT 4.8L ENGINE

1. Disconnect the negative battery cable.

2. Drain the cooling system. Remove the fan shroud assembly.

3. Remove the belts, pulleys and water pump assembly.

4. Remove the crankshaft pulley and damper.

5. Remove the oil pan-to-front cover bolts.

6. Remove the screws holding the timing chain cover to the block, pull the cover forward enough to cut the front oil pan seal. Cut the seal flush with the block on both sides.

7. Pull off the cover and gaskets.

8. Use a suitable tool to pry the old seal out of the front face of the cover.
To install:

9. Using seal driver J–22102 or equivalent, install the new seal so the open end is toward the inside of the cover.

NOTE: Coat the lip of the new seal with oil prior to installation.

10. Install a new front pan seal, cutting the tabs off.

11. Coat a new cover gasket with adhesive sealer and position it on the block.

12. Apply a ⅛ in. bead of RTV gasket material to the front cover. Install the cover carefully onto the locating dowels.

13. Tighten the attaching screws to specification.

14. Tighten the cover-to-pan bolts to specification.

15. Install the torsional damper.

16. Install the water pump assembly.

17. Connect the battery cables.

18. Fill the cooling system with the proper type and quantity of antifreeze.

4.8L ENGINE

1. Disconnect the battery.

2. Drain the cooling system.

3. Remove the water pump.

4. Remove the crankshaft pulley and damper.

5. Remove the oil pan-to-front cover bolts.

6. Remove the screws holding the timing case cover to the block, pull the cover forward enough to cut the front oil pan seal. Cut the seal flush with the block on both sides.

7. Pull off the cover and gaskets.

Cut these portions off the front cover to pan seal—4.8L engine

8. Use a suitable tool to pry the old seal out of the front face of the cover.

To install:

9. Lubricate the new seal lip with engine oil and using a seal centering tool and installer J–23042 or equivalent, press the new seal into place. Leave the tool in position on the seal.

10. Install a new front pan seal, cutting the tabs off.

11. Coat a new cover gasket with adhesive sealer and position it on the block.

12. Apply a ⅛ in. bead of RTV gasket material to the front cover. Install the cover carefully in place with the centering tool still attached.

13. Tighten the timing gear cover to block bolts to 80 inch lbs. (9 Nm).

14. Tighten the cover-to-pan bolts to 45 inch lbs. (5 Nm).

15. Install the damper.

16. Install the water pump.

17. Connect the battery cables.

18. Fill the cooling system.

Front Cover Oil Seal

Replacement

1. Disconnect the negative battery cable.

2. Remove the fan shroud, belts, fan and pulleys.

3. Remove the accessory drive pulley.

4. Remove the torsional damper bolt, then the damper using tool J–23523–E.

5. Pry the front crankshaft seal using a suitable tool, being careful not to damage the cover.

NOTE: Ensure the seal contact area on the crankshaft is not scored or grooved, repair or replace as necessary.

To install:

6. Install the seal using an appropriate seal installation tool. Ensure the seal open end is facing inside the engine. Coat the seal with engine oil.

7. Install the torsional damper using tool J–23523–E, then install the bolt and washer; torque to specification.

8. Install the accessory drive pulley, fan, shroud and pulleys.

9. Connect the negative battery cable.

Timing Chain and Sprockets

Removal and Installation

4.3L, 5.0L, 5.7L AND 7.4L ENGINES

1. Disconnect the negative battery cable. Remove the fan shroud, water pump, the harmonic balancer and the timing chain front cover.

2. Crank the engine until the timing marks on both sprockets are nearest each other and in line between the shaft centers.

3. Remove the camshaft-to-gear attaching bolts. Remove the chain and the camshaft gear.

NOTE: A gear puller will be required to remove the crankshaft gear.

Service Tips

CAM GEAR MISORIENTATION

Some 1990 4.3L engines have been built with the crankshaft and camshaft gears misaligned, causing lack of performance and backfire. The problem may be identified by following a timing gear alignment checking procedure; once identified the timing cover will have to be removed and the chain and gears realigned.
The following VIN No.'s are applicable:
G Series: L7500878–L7501500
C/K Series:
    LZ501591–LZ504345 (Fort Wayne)
    LE500013–LE501336 (Pontiac East)

Service Tips

LEAK AT FRONT CRANKSHAFT SEAL OIL

Some 1990 4.3L engines may exhibit oil leaks coming from between the crankshaft seal and timing chain cover. This condition may be caused by a loose fit of the seal in the timing cover. To remedy the situation a new seal should be installed, first clean the timing cover and seal mating area with isopropyl alcohol; then inspect the timing cover hole for damage. Apply a bead of Loctite® 680 retaining compound around the outside diameter of the new seal and install the seal following the proper procedure. Do not use RTV or any other sealant in place of the Loctite® 680 compound.

To install:

4. Without disturbing the position of the engine, install the new crankshaft gear onto the shaft, and install the chain over the camshaft gear. Install the camshaft gear with the timing marks aligned. Position the camshaft locating dowel in the dowel hole of the cam sprocket.

5. Install the camshaft securing bolts and torque to specification.

6. After the gears are in place, turn the engine 2 full revolutions to make certain the timing marks are in correct alignment between the shaft centers.

Camshaft Timing Gear

Removal and Installation

4.8L ENGINE

The camshaft on this engines is gear driven, unlike the chain

A. Align Marks as Shown

Timing alignment marks—except 4.8L engine

1. Timing marks		4. Camshaft gear	
2. Camshaft		5. Thrust plate bolts	
3. Thrust plate		6. Crankshaft gear	

Camshaft and components installation and alignment—4.8L engine

Removing the camshaft thrust plate bolts—4.8L engine

driven V6 and V8 engines. The camshaft must be removed to replace the gear.

1. Disconnect the negative battery cable. Remove the camshaft and place the assembly in an arbor press.

NOTE: Support the camshaft gear not the thrust plate.

2. Press the gear off of the camshaft and remove the thrust plate and the spacer.

To install:

3. Support the camshaft at the front journal with tool J–22912–01 or equivalent, and mount the camshaft in a press.
4. Lubricate the thrust plate with engine oil.
5. Install the key if removed.
6. Install the spacer making sure the chamfer in the spacer faces toward the journal radius.
7. Install the thrust plate.
8. Install the camshaft gear on with the timing mark to the outside and press the gear on until it bottoms on the spacer.
9. Remove the camshaft from the press.

NOTE: The clearance between the camshaft and thrust plate should be 0.003–0.008 in.

Camshaft

Removal and Installation

4.3L ENGINE

1. Disconnect the negative battery cable and properly relieve the fuel system pressure.
2. Remove the rocker arm covers.
3. Remove the intake manifold, pushrods and hydraulic lifters.
4. Remove the outside air duct.
5. Remove the power steering reservoir out of the way.
6. Remove the upper fan shroud bolts.
7. Drain and remove the radiator.
8. Disconnect the hood release cable at the latch.
9. Remove the upper fan shroud.
10. Remove the water pump.
11. Remove the torsional damper.
12. Remove the front cover.
13. Align the timing marks and remove the camshaft sprocket bolts.
14. Remove the camshaft sprocket and timing chain. Loosen

the sprocket by tapping on the lower edge. Remove the camshaft thrust plate.
15. Remove the crankshaft sprocket, as required.
16. Remove the front grill and condenser assembly, as required.
17. Install two or three $\frac{5}{16}$–18 bolts 4–5 in. long into the camshaft threaded holes to handle the camshaft and carefully pull the camshaft from the block.
18. Inspect the shaft for signs of excessive wear or damage.

To install:

19. Liberally coat camshaft and bearings with heavy engine oil or engine assembly lubricant and insert the camshaft into the engine.
20. Install the condenser and grille assembly, if removed.
21. Align the timing marks on the camshaft and crankshaft gears.
22. Install the camshaft thrustplate, sprocket and chain. Tighten the bolts to specification.
23. Install the front cover assembly.
24. Install the torsional damper.
25. Install the water pump.
26. Install the fan shroud and radiator.
27. Connect the hood release cable at the latch.
28. Install the outside air duct.
29. Install the hydraulic lifters and pushrods.
30. Adjust the valves.
31. Install the rocker arm covers.
32. Install the intake manifold.
33. Refill the cooling system.
34. Connect the battery cable.

Camshaft removal and installation—4.3L, 5.0L, 5.7L and 7.4L engines

4.8L ENGINE

1. Disconnect the negative battery cable. Drain the cooling system into a suitable container. Remove the radiator, condenser and grille, as required.
2. Remove the fan and shroud assembly. Remove the air cleaner assembly.
3. Remove the fuel pump. Remove the crankshaft damper.
4. Remove the valve cover, pushrod cover and timing chain cover. Remove the distributor assembly.
5. Remove the hydraulic lifters and pushrods.
6. Align the timing marks on the camshaft and crankshaft gears.
7. Remove the thrust plate bolts.
8. Support and carefully remove the camshaft.
9. If either the camshaft or the camshaft gear is being renewed, the gear must be pressed off the camshaft. The replacement parts must be assembled in the same way. When placing the gear on the camshaft, press the gear onto the shaft until it bottoms against the gear spacer ring. The end clearance of the thrust plate should be 0.003–0.008 in.
10. Pre-lube the camshaft lobes with clean engine oil and then install the camshaft assembly in the engine. Be careful not to damage the bearings.
11. Turn the crankshaft and the camshaft gears so the timing marks align. Push the camshaft into position; install and torque the thrust plate bolts to 80 inch lbs. (9 Nm).
12. Check camshaft and crankshaft gear runout with a dial indicator. Camshaft gear runout should not exceed 0.004 in. (0.10mm) and crankshaft gear run-out should not be above 0.003 in. (0.08mm).
13. Using a dial indicator, check the backlash at several points between the camshaft and crankshaft gear teeth. Backlash should be 0.004–0.006 in. (0.10 0.10mm) with new gears or 0.008 in. (0.20mm) with used gears.
14. Install the timing gear cover.
15. Install the distributor assembly.
16. Install the fuel pump assembly.
17. Install the valve lifters and the pushrods.
18. Install the radiator, condenser and grille assembly.

5.0L AND 5.7L ENGINES

1. Disconnect the negative battery cable, Drain the cooling system and properly relieve the fuel system pressure.
2. On the G-Series, remove the engine cover.
3. Remove the air cleaner.
4. On the G-Series, remove the grille and center support.
5. Remove the air conditioning condenser and swing the condenser forward from its mounting, if equipped.
6. Remove the fan, the shroud and the radiator.
7. Remove the valve covers.
8. Remove the water pump assembly.
9. Align the timing marks and remove the torsional damper.
10. Remove the timing chain cover.
11. Disconnect the electrical and vacuum connections at the intake manifold.
12. Mark the distributor rotor-to-housing location. Remove the distributor assembly.
13. Remove the intake manifold, pushrods and hydraulic lifters.
14. Remove the fuel pump and pushrod, if equipped with a carburetor.
15. Remove the camshaft sprocket bolts, camshaft sprocket and timing chain. Tap the sprocket on its lower edge to loosen it.
16. Remove the crankshaft sprocket, as required.
17. As required, remove the front engine mount through bolts and raise the engine to gain sufficient clearance for camshaft removal.
18. Install two or three $5/16$–18 bolts 4–5 in. long into the camshaft threaded holes; carefully pull the camshaft from the block.
19. Inspect the shaft for signs of excessive wear or damage.

To install:

20. Liberally coat camshaft and bearing with heavy engine oil or engine assembly lubricant and insert the cam into the engine.
21. Lower the engine and install the engine mount through bolts.
22. Align the timing marks on the camshaft and crankshaft gears.
23. Install the camshaft sprocket and chain and tighten the bolts to specification.
24. Install the fuel pump and pushrod for carbureted engines.
25. Install the hydraulic lifters and pushrods and adjust the valves.
26. Install the distributor assembly.
27. Install the timing chain cover.
28. Install the torsional damper.
29. Install the water pump.
30. Install the valve covers.
31. Install the fan, the shroud and radiator.
32. Install the air conditioning condenser, if equipped.
33. On the G-Series, install the grille and center support.
34. Install the air cleaner.
35. On the G-Series, install the engine cover.
36. Connect the battery cable and fill the cooling system.

7.4L ENGINE

1. Disconnect the negative battery cable. Properly relieve the fuel system pressure.
2. Remove the engine cover, G-Series. Remove the air cleaner assembly.
3. Remove the grille and center support section, as required.
4. Properly discharge the air conditioning system. Remove the air conditioning compressor, condenser and auxiliary fan, if equipped.
5. Drain the cooling system.
6. Remove the fan, the shroud and radiator.
7. Remove the alternator belt, remove the alternator assembly, as required.
8. Remove the valve covers.
9. Disconnect the hoses from the water pump.
10. Remove the water pump.

SECTION 5

GENERAL MOTORS CORPORATION
C/K SERIES (PICK-UP) • R/V SERIES (PICK-UP) • BLAZER/JIMMY • SUBURBAN • G SERIES (VAN)

11. Align the timing marks at TDC. Remove the harmonic balancer and pulley.

12. Remove the engine front cover.

13. Mark the distributor rotor-to-housing location. Remove the distributor assembly.

14. Remove the intake manifold assembly.

15. Remove the lifters, pushrods, and rocker arms.

16. Rotate the camshaft so the timing marks align.

17. Remove the camshaft sprocket bolts. Remove the camshaft sprocket and timing.

18. Remove the engine mount through bolts. Raise and support the engine to aid in camshaft removal, as required.

19. Install two or three $5/16$-18 bolts in the holes in the front of the camshaft and carefully pull the camshaft from the block.

To install:

20. Liberally coat camshaft and bearing with heavy engine oil or engine assembly lubricant and insert the cam into the engine.

21. Align the timing marks on the camshaft sprocket and crankshaft gears.

22. Install the camshaft sprocket and chain and tighten the bolts to specification. Lower the engine and install the engine mount bolts.

23. Install the lifters and pushrods and adjust the valves.

24. Install the intake manifold.

25. Install the distributor using the locating marks made during removal.

26. Install the engine front cover.

27. Install the harmonic balancer and pulley.

28. Install the water pump.

29. Connect the hoses at the water pump.

30. Install the valve covers.

31. Install the alternator.

32. Install the fan shroud and radiator.

33. Fill the cooling system with the proper type and quantity of antifreeze.

34. Install the air conditioning condenser and compressor.

35. Install the grille and center support.

36. Install the air cleaner assembly.

37. Connect the battery.

Piston and Connecting Rod

Positioning

Correct relationship of the piston and rod—4.8L engine

Correct relationship of the piston and rod—7.4L engine

Correct relationship of the piston and rod—5.0L and 5.7L engines

Piston ring gap locations—4.3L, 5.0L and 5.7L engines

Piston ring gap locations—4.8L engine

Piston ring gap locations—7.4L engine

DIESEL ENGINE MECHANICAL

NOTE: Disconnecting the negative battery cable on some vehicles may interfere with the functions of the on board computer systems and may require the computer to undergo a relearning process.

Engine

Removal and Installation

6.2L ENGINE

Except G-Series

1. Remove the hood. Disconnect and remove the batteries from the vehicle.
2. Raise the vehicle and support it safely. Drain the engine oil.
3. Remove the flywheel cover. Disconnect the torque converter from the flexplate. Disconnect the exhaust pipes from the manifolds.
4. Remove the starter bolts and remove the starter. Remove the transmission bell housing to engine bolts, leaving 1 or more bolts loose to prevent separation.
5. Remove the engine mount through bolts. Disconnect the block heater, the wiring harness, transmission oil cooler lines and the front battery cable clamp at the oil pan.
6. Lower the vehicle. Properly relieve the fuel pump pressure. Disconnect and plug the fuel lines and the oil cooler lines at the engine block. Remove the lower fan shroud bolts.
7. Drain the engine coolant. Remove the air cleaner assembly. Disconnect the ground cable from the alternator bracket. Disconnect the alternator wires and clips.
8. Disconnect the TPS, EGR–EPR and the fuel cut-off at the injection pump. Remove the harness from the clips at the rocker covers and disconnect the glow plugs.
9. Disconnect the EGR–EPR solenoids, glow plugs, controller, temperature sender and move the harness aside. Disconnect the ground strap on the left or right side.
10. Remove the fan assembly. Remove the upper radiator hoses at the engine. Remove the fan shroud.
11. Remove the power steering pump and belt. Remove the reservoir and lay the pump and reservoir aside. If equipped with air conditioning, remove the compressor and position aside.
12. Disconnect the vacuum lines at the cruise servo and accelerator cable at the injection pump. Disconnect the heater hoses at the engine.
13. Disconnect the lower radiator hose, the oil cooler lines, the heater hose and the overflow hose at the radiator.
14. Remove the radiator assembly. Remove the detent cable.
15. Install an engine lifting device, remove the loose bolts in the bell housing. Properly support the transmission. Carefully remove the engine from the vehicle.

To install:

16. Lower the engine and install the engine mounting bolts. Torque the bolts and nuts to specification.
17. Install the bell housing to engine bolts and torque to 30 ft. lbs. (40 Nm).
18. Remove the engine lifting fixture and transmission jack.
19. Raise the vehicle and support it safely.
20. Install the converter to flex bolts and torque to specification.
21. Install the starter assembly.
22. Install the flywheel or torque converter cover.
23. Install the starter.
24. Install the exhaust pipes at the manifold.
25. Connect the wiring harness, transmission cooler lines and a battery cable clamp at the oil pan.
26. Connect the fuel return lines at the engine.
27. Connect the oil cooler lines at the engine.
28. Lower the vehicle.
29. Install the radiator.
30. Install the heater hose to the engine.
31. Connect the accelerator, cruise control and detent cables at the injection pump.
32. Connect the power steering pump and reservoir.
33. Install the fan and the upper fan shroud.
34. Install the ground strap.
35. Connect the wiring to the rocker cover including the glow plug wires.
36. Connect the EGR-EPR solenoids, glow plug controller and temperature solenoid harness.
37. Connect the alternator wires and clips.
38. Connect the wiring at the injector pump.
39. Install the air cleaner and air conditioning compressor.
40. Install the hood.
41. Connect the negative battery cable.

42. Install the proper quantity and type of coolant and engine oil.

G-Series

1. Disconnect the negative battery cables. Properly relieve the fuel system pressure.
2. Remove the upper radiator support.
3. Remove the grille.
4. Remove the bumper.
5. Remove the lower grille valance.
6. Remove the hood latch and the upper tie bar.
7. Drain the cooling system.
8. Remove the radiator coolant reservoir bottle.
9. Remove the radiator support bracket, if equipped.
10. Remove the radiator and the fan shroud.
11. Remove the engine cover.
12. Remove the air cleaner, resonator and bracket.
13. Properly discharge the air conditioning system.
14. Remove the air conditioning condenser and cap all openings.
15. Disconnect the air cleaner bracket at the valve cover.
16. Remove the crankcase ventilator bracket and move aside.
17. Remove the intake manifold assembly. Remove the injector pump.
18. Raise and support the vehicle safely.
19. Remove the power steering pump and position aside.
20. Disconnect the exhaust pipes at the manifolds.
21. Remove the flywheel cover and remove the torque converter-to-flywheel attaching bolts.
22. Remove the engine mount through bolts.
23. Disconnect the blocker heater wires.
24. Remove the starter assembly.
25. Disconnect the fuel line at the fuel pump (lift pump).
26. Lower the vehicle.
27. Remove the bell housing-to-engine bolts.
28. Remove the cruise control transducer, if equipped.
29. Remove the air conditioning compressor.
30. Remove the oil fill tube upper bracket.
31. Remove the wiring harness and connections from engine.
32. Unbolt the transmission dipstick tube and position aside.
33. Remove the heater hose at the engine.
34. Remove the alternator upper bracket.
35. Disconnect the glow plug temperature inhibit switch connector at the coolant crossover.
36. Remove the coolant crossover/thermostat assembly.
37. Connect a suitable engine lifting device to the center intake manifold bolt holes.
38. Support the transmission and remove the engine from the vehicle.

To install:

39. Install the engine into the vehicle. Raise and safely support the vehicle.
40. Install the engine mount through bolts and transmission bell housing bolts.
41. Install the flywheel-to-converter attaching bolts.
42. Install the starter and converter housing underpan.
43. Connect the blocker heater wires.
44. Connect the exhaust pipes to the manifold assembly.
45. Install the power steering pump. Lower the vehicle.
46. Install the coolant crossover/thermostat assembly.
47. Install the alternator upper bracket.
48. Install the heater hoses, transmission dipstick, air cleaner resonator and bracket assembly.
49. Install the wiring harness and connectors to the engine assembly.
50. Install the oil fill tube upper bracket.
51. Install the air conditioning compressor.
52. Install the injection pump and intake manifold.
53. Install the radiator, fan and lower shroud.
54. Install the air conditioning condenser.
55. Install the upper tie bar.

56. Install the fan lower shroud, coolant recovery bottle and battery cables.
57. Install the hood latch, lower valance, bumper, grille, and headlight bezels.
58. Fill the cooling system with the proper type and quantity of antifreeze. Check all fluid levels.
59. Evacuate and recharge the air conditioning system.
60. Install the engine cover. Inspect engine for leaks.

Engine Mounts

Removal and Installation

6.2L AND 6.5L ENGINE

1. Disconnect the negative battery cable.
2. Raise and safely support the vehicle.
3. Properly support the engine.

NOTE: Do not position the jack under the oil pan, any sheetmetal or the crankshaft pulley, otherwise damage may occur.

4. Remove the engine mount through-bolt.
5. Raise the engine to gain sufficient clearance for the mount to be removed.
6. Remove the engine mount attaching bolts, nuts and washers.
7. Remove the mount assembly.
8. Installation is the reverse of the removal procedure.

Cylinder Head

Removal and Installation

6.2L AND 6.5L ENGINE

Right Side

1. Disconnect the negative battery cable, relieve the fuel system pressure and drain the coolant system. Properly discharge the air conditioning system, if equipped.
2. Remove the intake manifold. Remove the fan upper shroud. Remove the compressor assembly, if equipped.
3. Raise and support the vehicle safely.
4. Remove the exhaust manifold. Lower the vehicle.
5. Remove the valve cover, rocker arm assemblies and pushrods. Mark all components so they may be returned to their original location.
6. Remove the air cleaner resonator and bracket.
7. Remove the transmission and oil dipstick tube; remove the oil fill tube from the coolant crossover pipe.
8. Remove the heater, radiator and bypass hoses.
9. Remove the alternator upper bracket and alternator.
10. Remove the fuel bleeder valve at the coolant crossover pipe.
11. Remove the fuel return crossover line clamp bolts from both cylinder heads.
12. Disconnect the wire connector from the sensor in the coolant crossover pipe.
13. Remove the coolant crossover pipe/thermostat assembly.
14. Remove the head bolts and the cylinder head.

To install:

15. Clean the mating surfaces of the head and block thoroughly.
16. Install a new head gasket on the engine block. Do not coat the gaskets with any sealer on either engine. The gaskets have a special coating that eliminates the need for sealer. Install the cylinder head onto the block.
17. Clean the head bolts thoroughly. Coat the threads of the head bolts with sealing compound GM part 1052080 or equivalent, before installation. Tighten the head bolts to 20 ft. lbs. (25 Nm). in the proper sequence, next tighten all bolts to 50 ft. lbs.

(65 Nm) in the proper sequence, and finally tighten all bolts an additional 90 degree (¼ turn).

18. Install the coolant crossover pipe and thermostat.
19. Install the fuel valve and alternator assembly.
20. Connect the bypass hose.
21. Connect the upper radiator hose.
22. Connect the heater hoses at the head.
23. Install the transmission and oil dipstick tube.
24. Install the air cleaner resonator and bracket.
25. Install the pushrods, hardened ends facing up.
26. Install the rocker arm assemblies.
27. Adjust the valves.
28. Install the valve cover. Install the alternator assembly.
29. Raise and support the vehicle safely.
30. Install the exhaust manifold. Lower the vehicle.
31. Install the upper fan shroud.
32. Install the intake manifold. Connect the negative battery cables.
33. Fill the cooling system with the proper type and quantity of antifreeze. Evacuate and recharge the air conditioning system.

Left Side

1. Disconnect the negative battery cables. Drain the cooling system into a suitable container. Properly discharge the air conditioning system.
2. Remove the intake manifold.
3. Remove the air conditioning compressor belt.
4. Remove the air conditioning compressor.
5. Remove the valve cover.
6. Remove the rocker arm assemblies. Mark the parts to ensure installation in their original location.
7. Remove the pushrods. Keep them in order.
8. Raise and support the vehicle safely.
9. Remove the exhaust manifold.
10. Remove the power steering pump and rear bracket, position the assembly aside. Lower the vehicle.
11. Remove the oil dipstick tube.
12. Disconnect the transmission detent cable.
13. Remove the glow plug controller and bracket.
14. Disconnect the wire connector from the sensor at the coolant crossover pipe.
15. Disconnect the oil fill tube, fuel bleeder valve and hoses from the coolant crossover pipe.
16. Disconnect the fuel crossover line from both cylinder heads.
17. Remove the air cleaner resonator and bracket.
18. Remove the alternator upper bracket.
19. Remove the coolant crossover pipe and thermostat.
20. Remove the head bolts.
21. Remove the cylinder head.

To install:

22. Clean the mating surfaces of the head and block thoroughly.
23. Install a new head gasket on the engine block. Do not coat the gaskets with any sealer on either engine. The gaskets have a

special coating that eliminates the need for sealer. Install the cylinder head onto the block.

24. Clean the head bolts thoroughly. Coat the threads of the head bolts with sealing compound GM part 1052080 or equivalent, before installation. Install the rear cylinder head bolt first. Tighten the head bolts to 20 ft. lbs. (25 Nm). in the proper sequence, next tighten all bolts to 50 ft. lbs. (65 Nm) in the proper sequence, and finally tighten all bolts an additional 90 degree (¼ turn).

25. Install the coolant crossover pipe and thermostat.
26. Install the fuel valve and alternator assembly.
27. Connect the bypass hose.
28. Connect the upper radiator hose.
29. Connect the heater hoses at the head.
30. Install the transmission and oil dipstick tube.
31. Install the air cleaner resonator and bracket.
32. Install the pushrods, hardened ends facing up.
33. Install the rocker arm assemblies.
34. Adjust the valves.
35. Install the valve cover. Install the air conditioner compressor and bracket assembly.
36. Raise and support the vehicle safely.
37. Install the exhaust manifold. Lower the vehicle.
38. Install the upper fan shroud.
39. Install the intake manifold. Connect the negative battery cables.
40. Fill the cooling system with the proper type and quantity of antifreeze. Evacuate and recharge the air conditioning system.

Valve Lifters

Removal and Installation

6.2L AND 6.5L ENGINE

1. Disconnect the negative battery cables.
2. Remove the valve covers, rocker arm shafts and pushrods. Position all components in the exact order which they were removed, so they may be reinstalled in their original bore.
3. Remove the cylinder head, as required.
4. Remove the valve lifter clamps and guide plates.
5. Remove the hydraulic lifters. Position the lifters in the exact order which they were removed, so they may be reinstalled in their original bore.

To install:

6. Coat the roller tips with GM part 1052365 or equivalent.

NOTE: All new lifters must be primed by working the plunger while submerged in kerosene or diesel fuel. Some engines will have 2 sizes of lifters being used, standard and oversized. The oversized lifter will be etched "10" on the side and the block will be stamped O.S. on the cast pad adjacent to the lifter bore.

7. Install the lifters in their original bores.
8. Install the guide plates and clamps. Torque the clamps bolts to 18 ft. lbs. (26 Nm).
9. Turn the engine 2 full turns and verify the lifters move freely in the guide plates. If the engine does not turn freely, 1 or more lifters are binding in the guide plate.
10. Install the cylinder head assembly.
11. Install the rocker arm shafts and pushrods assembly. Position all components in the exact order they were removed.
12. Install the valve covers.
13. Connect the negative battery cables.

Valve Lash

Adjustment

All engines use hydraulic lifters, which require no periodic adjustment.

Cylinder head bolt torque sequence—6.2L and 6.5L diesel engines

Rocker Arm and Shafts

Removal and Installation

1. Disconnect the negative battery cables. On the G-Series, remove the engine cover.

2. Remove all the necessary components in order to gain access to the engine valve covers. As required, properly relieve the fuel system pressure before disconnecting any fuel lines.

3. Remove the valve cover retaining bolts. Remove the valve cover from the engine.

4. Remove the rocker arm assemblies. Keep them in order for reinstallation.

5. Installation is the reverse of the removal procedure. Be sure to use new gaskets or RTV sealant, as necessary.

Intake Manifold

Removal and Installation

6.2L AND 6.5L ENGINE

1. Disconnect both negative battery cables.
2. Drain the cooling system and properly relieve the fuel system pressure.
3. Remove the engine cover, G-Series.
4. Remove the air cleaner assembly.
5. Remove the EPR/EGR valve bracket from the intake manifold.
6. Remove the CDR valve.
7. Remove the crankcase ventilator hose and EGR.
8. Remove the air conditioning rear bracket, if equipped.
9. Remove the fuel line bracket and ground strap.
10. Remove the fuel filter bracket at the intake manifold.
11. Remove the intake manifold bolts. The injection line clips are retained by these bolts.
12. Remove the intake manifold.

NOTE: If the engine is to be further serviced with the manifold removed, install protective covers over the intake ports.

To install:

13. Clean the manifold gasket surfaces on the cylinder heads and install new gaskets before installing the manifold.

NOTE: The gaskets have an opening for the EGR valve on light duty installations. An insert covers this opening on heavy duty installations.

14. Install the intake manifold.

1. Hydraulic lifter
2. Pushrod
3. Bolt
4. Rocker arm assembly
5. Clamp
6. Guide plate

Cylinder head and components—6.2L and 6.5L diesel engines

15. Install the intake manifold bolts and fuel injection line clips.
16. Install the fuel filter bracket at the intake manifold.
17. Install the fuel line bracket and ground strap.
18. Install the air conditioning rear bracket, if equipped.
19. Install the crankcase ventilator hose and EGR.
20. Install the CDR valve.
21. Install the EPR/EGR valve bracket from the intake manifold.
22. Install the air cleaner assembly.
23. Install the engine cover, G-Series.
24. Fill the cooling system with the proper type and quantity of antifreeze.
25. Connect both negative battery cables. Inspect for leaks.

Exhaust Manifold

Removal and Installation

6.2L AND 6.5L ENGINES

1. Disconnect the batteries.
2. Raise and support the vehicle safely.
3. Disconnect the exhaust pipe from the manifold flange and lower the vehicle.

LEFT SIDE   RIGHT SIDE

Intake manifold installation and torque sequence—6.2L and 6.5L diesel engines

4. Remove the engine cover and disconnect the glow plug wires.

5. Remove the air cleaner duct bracket.

6. Remove the glow plugs. Remove the turbocharger assembly, as required.

7. Remove the air conditioner compressor rear bracket, as required.

8. Remove the manifold bolts and remove the manifold.

9. Installation is the reverse of the removal procedure. Torque the manifold bolts to 26 ft. lbs. (35 Nm).

Timing Chain Front Cover

Removal and Installation

6.2L AND 6.5L ENGINES

1. Disconnect both negative battery cables. Drain the cooling system.

2. Remove the water pump and pulleys.

3. Rotate the crankshaft to align the marks on the torsional damper with the **0** mark on the timing tab.

4. Scribe a mark aligning the injection pump flange and the front cover, if not already marked.

5. Remove the crankshaft pulley and torsional damper.

6. Remove the front cover-to-oil pan bolts (4).

7. Remove the 2 fuel return line clips.

8. Remove the injection pump gear.

9. Remove the injection pump retaining nuts from the front cover.

10. Remove the baffle. Remove the remaining cover bolts and remove the front cover.

To install:

11. If the front cover oil seal is to be replaced, it can now be pried out of the cover with a suitable prying tool. Press the new seal into the cover evenly.

12. Clean both sealing surfaces until all traces of old sealer are gone. Apply a $\frac{3}{32}$ in. (2mm) bead of GM sealant 1052357 or equivalent to the sealing surface. Apply a $\frac{3}{16}$ in. (5mm) bead of RTV type sealer to the bottom portion of the front cover which attaches to the oil pan. Install the front cover.

13. Install the baffle.

14. Install the injection pump, making sure the scribe marks on the pump and front cover are aligned. Tighten the nuts to 31 ft. lbs. (42 Nm).

15. Install the injection pump driven gear, making sure the marks on the cam gear and pump are aligned. Torque the injection pump gear bolts to 17 ft. lbs. (23 Nm).

NOTE: Verify there is a minimum clearance of 0.040 in. (1.0mm) between the injection pump gear and baffle or noise may be result.

16. Install the fuel line clips, the front cover-to-oil bolts, and the torsional damper and crankshaft pulley. Torque the pan and the damper bolt to specification.

17. Install the water pump and pulley assembly.

18. Fill the cooling system with the proper type and quantity of antifreeze.

19. Connect the negative battery cables. Inspect engine for leaks.

Front Cover Oil Seal

Removal and Installation

NOTE: The oil seal can also be replaced with the front cover installed.

1. Disconnect both negative battery cables.

2. Remove the accessory drive belt.

3. Remove the crankshaft pulley and the torsional damper assembly.

1. Apply anarobic sealer
2. Minimum clearance 1.0 mm (0.040-inch)
3. Front cover
4. Baffle
5. Probe holder
6. Camshaft gear

Front cover and components—6.2L and 6.5L diesel engines

1. Torsional damper
2. Crankshaft pulley
3. Bolt
4. Bolt
5. Washer

Torsional damper and crankcase pulley installation—6.2L and 6.5L diesel engines

4. Pry the old seal out of the cover using a suitable tool. Use care not to damage the surface of the crankshaft. Install the new seal evenly into the cover.

5. The remaining installation is the reverse of the removal procedure.

Timing Chain

Removal and Installation

6.2L AND 6.5L ENGINES

1. Disconnect the negative battery cables. Remove the front cover assembly.

2. Remove the injection pump gear.

3. Align the camshaft timing gear marks and remove the bolt and washer attaching the camshaft gear.

4. Remove the camshaft sprocket with the timing chain. Remove the crankshaft sprocket.

1. Timing marks
2. Camshaft gear
3. Injection pump gear

Injection pump gear and timing marks—6.2L and 6.5L diesel engines

1. Timing marks
2. Camshaft gear
3. Camshaft sprocket
4. Crankshaft sprocket

Camshaft and sprockets—6.2L and 6.5L diesel engines

To install:

5. Install the cam sprocket, timing chain and crankshaft sprocket as a unit, aligning the timing marks on the sprockets.

6. Rotate the crankshaft to align the injection pump and camshaft gears. Install the injection pump gear.

7. Install the front cover. Connect the negative battery cables.

NOTE: The injection pump timing must be adjusted if a new chain, gears or sprockets were installed.

Camshaft

Removal and Installation

6.2L AND 6.5L ENGINES

R/V-Series

1. Disconnect the battery cables.
2. Drain the cooling system.
3. Remove the radiator shrouds and fan.
4. Remove the vacuum pump.

NOTE: Do not run the engine while the vacuum pump is removed. The oil pump is powered by the vacuum pump drive gear and thus the engine will not have any oil pressure.

5. Remove the power steering pump.
6. Remove the alternator.
7. Remove the air conditioning compressor leaving the refrigerant lines connected and position the compressor aside.
8. Remove the rocker arm covers.
9. Remove the rocker arm assemblies and pushrods. Mark the components so they can be reinstalled in their original position.

1. Inlet manifold
2. Centerline of engine
3. Rear face of case

Diesel engine vacuum pump positioning

10. Remove the hydraulic lifters keeping them in order so they can be returned to their original bore.
11. Remove the front cover.
12. Remove the injection pump.
13. Disconnect the air conditioning condenser mounting bolts and lift the condenser out of the way.
14. Remove the timing chain and camshaft sprocket.
15. Remove the engine mounting through bolts.
16. Raise the engine and support it safely.
17. Remove the camshaft thrust plate bolts and the thrust plate.
18. Carefully remove the camshaft from the block.
19. Remove the thrust plate spacer, if necessary.

To install:

20. Install the spacer with the ID chamfer toward the camshaft.

NOTE: It is recommended that the engine oil, oil filter and hydraulic lifters be replaced when installing a new camshaft.

21. Coat the camshaft lobes with Molykote® or equivalent.
22. Lubricate the camshaft journals with engine oil.
23. Insert the camshaft carefully into the block, install the thrust plate and bolts and torque to 17 ft. lbs. (23 Nm).
24. Lower the engine and install the engine mount through bolts.
25. Align the timing marks and install the timing chain and sprockets.
26. Install the air conditioner condenser, if equipped.
27. Install the injection pump.
28. Install the air conditioning condenser and front timing cover.
29. Install the hydraulic lifters in the same bore as they were removed.
30. Install the rocker arm assemblies and pushrods in their original locations.
31. Install the rocker arm covers.
32. Install the air conditioner compressor.
33. Install the alternator.
34. Install the power steering pump.
35. Install the vacuum pump and align the pump so the inlet tube faces the front of the engine at a 20 degree angle.
36. Install the fan, radiator and shrouds.
37. Connect the negative battery cables.
38. Fill the cooling system with the proper type and quantity of antifreeze.

C/K-Series

1. Disconnect the battery cables and relieve the fuel system pressure.
2. Drain the cooling system.
3. Remove the radiator, the shroud and fan assembly.
4. Remove the grille and parking light assembly.
5. Remove the hood latch and brace assembly.
6. Remove the oil pump drive.

7. Remove the power steering pump, alternator and air conditioner compressor and position aside.

8. Remove the rocker arm covers.

9. Remove the rocker arm assemblies and pushrods. Mark them so they can be returned to their original position.

10. Remove the hydraulic lifters and keep them in order so they can be returned to their original bore.

11. Remove the front cover.

12. Remove the timing chain and camshaft sprocket.

13. Remove the injector pump.

14. Raise the engine and support it safely.

15. Remove the front engine mounting through bolts.

16. Remove the air conditioner condenser mounting bolts and lift the condenser out.

17. Remove the thrust plate bolts and thrust plate.

18. arefully remove the camshaft from the block.

19. Remove the thrust plate spacer, if necessary.

To install:

20. Install the spacer with the ID chamfer toward the camshaft.

NOTE: It is recommended that the engine oil, oil filter and hydraulic lifters be replaced when installing a new camshaft.

21. Coat the camshaft lobes with Molykote® or equivalent.

22. Lubricate the camshaft journals with engine oil.

23. Insert the camshaft carefully into the block, install the thrust plate and bolts. Torque to 17 ft. lbs. (23 Nm).

24. Lower the engine and install the engine mount through bolts.

25. Align the timing marks and install the timing chain and sprockets.

26. Install the air conditioner condenser, if equipped.

27. Install the injector pump.

28. Install the front cover.

29. Install the hydraulic lifters in the same bore as they were removed.

30. Install the rocker arm assemblies and pushrods in their original locations.

31. Install the rocker arm covers.

32. Install the power steering pump, alternator and air conditioner compressor.

33. Install the oil pump drive.

34. Install the hood latch and brace.

35. Install the grille and parking light assembly.

36. Install the radiator, the shroud and fan assembly.

37. Fill the cooling system with the proper type and quantity of antifreeze.

38. Connect the negative battery cables.

G-Series

1. Disconnect the battery cables and relieve the fuel system pressure.

2. Remove the headlight bezels.

3. Remove the grille, bumper and lower valence panel.

4. Remove the hood latch.

5. Remove the coolant recovery bottle.

6. Remove the upper tie bar.

7. Remove the air conditioner compressor.

8. Drain the cooling system and remove the radiator and fan.

9. Remove the oil pump drive.

10. Remove the cylinder heads to gain clearance for lifter removal.

11. Remove the alternator lower bracket.

12. Remove the water pump.

13. Remove the torsional damper.

14. Remove the front cover.

15. Remove the injection pump.

16. Remove the rocker arm covers.

17. Remove the rocker arm assemblies and pushrods. Mark them so they can be returned to their original position.

18. Remove the hydraulic lifters and keep them in order so they can be returned to their original bore.

19. Remove the timing chain and camshaft sprocket.

20. Remove the thrust plate bolts and thrust plate.

21. Carefully remove the camshaft from the block.

22. Remove the thrust plate spacer, if necessary.

To install:

23. Install the spacer with the ID chamfer toward the camshaft.

NOTE: It is recommended that the engine oil, oil filter and hydraulic lifters be replaced when installing a new camshaft.

24. Coat the camshaft lobes with Molykote or equivalent.

25. Lubricate the camshaft journals with engine oil.

26. Insert the camshaft carefully into the block, install the thrust plate and bolts and torque to 17 ft. lbs.

27. Align the timing marks and install the timing chain and sprockets.

28. Install the hydraulic lifters in the same bore as they were removed.

29. Install the rocker arm assemblies and pushrods in their original locations.

30. Install the rocker arm covers.

31. Install the fuel pump.

32. Install the front cover.

33. Install the torsional damper and water pump.

34. Install the alternator lower bracket.

35. Install the cylinder heads.

36. Install the oil pump drive.

37. Install the radiator and fan.

38. Install the air conditioner compressor.

39. Install the upper tie bar.

40. Install the coolant recovery bottle.

41. Install the hood latch.

42. Install the grille, bumper and lower valence panel.

43. Install the headlight bezels.

44. Install the battery cables.

45. Fill the cooling system.

46. Evacuate and charge the air conditioner system.

Piston and Connecting Rod

Positioning

1. Oil control ring expander gap
2. Second compression ring gap
3. Centerline of piston pin
4. Oil control ring gap
5. Top compression ring gap

Piston ring gap locations—6.2L and 6.5L diesel engines

ENGINE LUBRICATION

Oil Pan

Removal and Installation

4.3L ENGINE

1. Disconnect the negative battery cable. Raise and support the vehicle safely. Drain the engine oil into a suitable container.
2. Remove the exhaust crossover pipe.
3. Remove the torque converter cover, if equipped with automatic transmission.
4. Remove the strut rods at the flywheel cover, if equipped.
5. Remove the strut rod at the front engine mounts, if equipped.
6. Remove the starter assembly.
7. Remove the oil pan bolts, nuts and reinforcements.
8. Remove the oil pan and gaskets.

To install:

9. Thoroughly clean all gasket surfaces and install a new gasket, using only a small amount of sealer at the front and rear corners of the oil pan.
10. Install the oil pan and new gaskets.
11. Install the oil pan bolts, nuts and reinforcements. Torque the pan bolts to specification.
12. Install the starter assembly.

13. Install the strut rod brackets at the front engine mounts.
14. Install the strut rods at the flywheel cover.
15. Install the torque converter cover, if equipped with automatic transmission.
16. Install the exhaust crossover pipe. Lower the vehicle.
17. Connect the negative battery cable.
18. Fill the engine with the proper quantity and type of oil.

4.8L ENGINE

1. Disconnect the negative battery cable. Raise the vehicle and support it safely. Drain the engine oil.
2. Remove the flywheel cover. Remove the starter assembly.
3. Remove the engine mount through bolts from the engine front mounts. Raise the engine enough to remove the oil pan.
4. Remove the oil pan retaining bolts. Remove the oil pan from the engine.
5. Installation is the reverse of the removal procedure. Use new gaskets or RTV sealant, as required. Torque the pan bolts to specification.

5.0L AND 5.7L ENGINES

1. Disconnect the negative battery cable. Raise the vehicle, support it safely, and drain the engine oil.
2. Remove the exhaust crossover pipe.
3. Remove the flywheel or torque converter cover.
4. Remove the strut rods at the front engine mountings, if used.
5. Remove the oil pan bolts, nuts and reinforcements.
6. Remove the oil pan and gaskets.

To install:

7. Thoroughly clean all gasket surfaces and install a new gasket, using a small amount of sealer at the front and rear corners of the oil pan.
8. Install the oil pan and new gaskets.
9. Install the oil pan bolts, nuts and reinforcements. Torque the pan bolts to specification.
10. Install the strut rods at the front engine mountings.
11. Install the torque converter or flywheel cover.
12. Install the exhaust crossover pipe.
13. Connect the negative battery cable.
14. Fill the crankcase with the proper type and quantity of oil.

Oil pan assembly—4.3L engine

1. Gasket
2. Reinforcement

Oil pan assembly—5.0L and 5.7L engines

6.2L AND 6.5L ENGINES

R/V-Series

1. Disconnect the battery cables.
2. Raise and support the vehicle safely.
3. Drain the engine oil and remove the filter.
4. Remove the flywheel cover and oil pan dipstick.
5. Remove the left engine mount through bolts. Remove the exhaust pipes at the manifold, as required. Raise the engine.
6. Remove the strut rods, as required. Remove the battery cables, cooler lines and clamps from the oil pan.
7. Remove the oil pan bolts and remove the oil pan. Remove the oil pan gaskets and seals.

To install:

8. Clean the old RTV sealant from the oil pan and block.
9. Apply a $\frac{3}{16}$ in. (5mm) bead of RTV sealant to the oil pan sealing surface, inboard of the bolt holes. The sealant must be wet to the touch when the oil pan is to be installed.
10. Install the oil pan rear seal.
11. Install the oil pan to the engine and install the retaining bolts. Torque the bolts to specification.
12. Lower the engine and install the oil pan dipstick.
13. Install the engine mount through bolt and nut.
14. Install the flywheel cover, strut rods.
15. Connect the battery cables, cooler lines and clamps to the oil pan and then lower the vehicle.
16. Refill with the proper grade and quantity of oil. Install the oil filter. Connect the negative battery cables.

C/K-Series

1. Disconnect the battery cables.
2. Raise the vehicle and support it safely.
3. Drain the engine oil. Remove the oil dipstick.
4. Remove the flywheel cover.
5. Disconnect the exhaust pipes from the manifolds.
6. Remove the front engine mount through bolts and raise the engine.
7. Remove the oil pan bolts and remove the oil pan.
8. Remove the oil pan rear seal.

To install:

9. Clean the old RTV sealant from the oil pan and block.
10. Apply a $\frac{3}{16}$ in. (5mm) bead of RTV sealant to the oil pan sealing surface, inboard of the bolt holes. The sealant must be wet to the touch when the oil pan is to be installed.
11. Install the oil pan rear seal.
12. Install the oil pan to the engine and install the retaining bolts. Torque all except the rear 2 bolts to 84 inch lbs. Torque the rear 2 bolts to 17 ft. lbs.
13. Lower the engine.
14. Install the engine mounting through bolt and nut.
15. Install the oil dipstick. Install the exhaust pipes to the manifolds.
16. Install the flywheel cover and lower the vehicle.
17. Refill with the proper grade and quantity of oil.
18. Install the battery cables.

G-Series

1. Disconnect the battery cables.
2. Remove the engine cover.
3. Remove the engine oil dipstick.
4. Remove the engine oil dipstick tube at the rocker cover.
5. Raise the vehicle and support it safely.
6. Remove the transmission flywheel cover.
7. Drain the engine oil.
8. Disconnect the oil cooler lines at the block.
9. Remove the starter. Remove the battery cables, transmission cooler lines and attaching clamps from the oil pan.
10. Remove the oil pan bolts and remove the oil pan and oil pan rear seal.

To install:

11 Apply a $\frac{3}{16}$ in. (5mm) bead of RTV sealant to the oil pan

sealing surface, inboard of the bolt holes. The sealant must be wet to the touch when the oil pan is to be installed.

12 Install the oil pan rear seal.
13 Install the oil pan to the engine and install the retaining bolts. Torque all bolts to specifications.
14 Install the starter. Install the transmission, battery cables and attaching clamps to the oil pan.
15. Install the engine oil cooler lines.
16. Install the transmission flywheel cover.
17. Lower the vehicle.
18. Install the engine oil dipstick tube at the rocker cover.
19. Install the engine oil dipstick.
20. Install the engine cover.
21. Refill with the proper grade and quantity of oil.
22. Install the battery cables.

7.4L ENGINE

NOTE: Removal of the transmission may be necessary on the G-Series vehicles.

1. Disconnect the negative battery cable.
2. Remove the fan shroud.
3. Remove the air cleaner.
4. Remove the distributor cap.
5. Raise and support the vehicle safely.
6. Drain the engine oil. Remove the starter assembly, if equipped with manual transmission.
7. Remove the torque converter or clutch housing cover.
8. Remove the oil filter.
9. Remove the oil pressure line from the side of the block.
10. Support the engine with a floor jack.
11. Remove the engine mount through bolts.
12. Raise the engine just enough to remove the pan.
13. Remove the oil pan bolts, the oil pan and discard the gaskets.

To install:

14. Clean all mating surfaces thoroughly.
15. Apply RTV gasket material to the front and rear corners of the gaskets.
16. Coat the gaskets with adhesive sealer and position them on the block.
17. Install the rear pan seal in the pan with the seal ends mating with the gaskets.
18. Install the front seal on the bottom of the front cover, pressing the locating tabs into the holes in the cover.
19. Install the oil pan.
20. Install the pan bolts, clips and reinforcements. Torque the pan bolts to specification.
21. Lower the engine onto the mounts.
22. Install the engine mount through-bolts.
23. Install the oil pressure line.
24. Install the oil filter. Install the starter assembly, if removed.
25. Install the torque converter or clutch housing cover.
26. Install the distributor cap.
27. Install the air cleaner.
28. Install the fan shroud.
29. Connect the battery.
30. Fill the crankcase with the proper type and quantity of oil.

Oil Pump

Removal and Installation

EXCEPT 4.8L ENGINE

1. Raise and support the vehicle safely and remove the oil pan.
2. Remove the bolt attaching the pump to the rear main bearing cap. Remove the pump and the extension shaft, which connects to the distributor/oil pump shaft.

To install:

3. If the pump has been disassembled and is being replaced or

for any reason oil has been removed, it must be primed. It can either be filled with oil before installing the cover plate and oil kept within the pump during handling or the entire pump cavity can be filled with petroleum jelly.

NOTE: If the pump is not primed, the engine could be damaged before it receives adequate lubrication when the engine is started.

4. Engage the extension shaft with the oil pump shaft. Align the slot on the top of the extension shaft with the drive tang on the lower end of the distributor/oil pump shaft, and then position the pump at the rear main bearing cap so the mounting bolt can be installed. No gasket is used. Install the bolt and torque to 65 ft. lbs. (90 Nm).

5. Install the oil pan.

4.8L ENGINE

1. Raise and support the vehicle safely.
2. Remove the oil pan.
3. Remove the oil pump tube bracket main bearing cap nut.
4. Remove the oil pump bolts and the oil pump.

To install:

5. Position the oil pump to the engine and align the slot in the oil pump shaft with the tang on the shaft. The oil pump should slide easily in place.

6. Install the oil pump bolts and tighten to 115 inch lbs. (13 Nm).

7. Install the oil pump pick-up tube to the main bearing cap nut and tighten to 25 ft. lbs. (34 Nm).

8. Install the oil pan.

Rear Main Bearing oil Seal

Removal and Installation

4.3L, 5.0L AND 5.7L ENGINES

1. Raise and support the vehicle safely.
2. Remove the transmission from the vehicle.
3. Remove the pressure plate/flywheel or flexplate assembly.
4. Insert a suitable tool into the notches provided in the seal retainer and pry the seal out.

NOTE: Care should be taken when removing the seal so as not to nick the crankshaft sealing surface.

5. Before installation lubricate the new seal with clean engine oil.

6. Install the seal on tool J–35621 or equivalent. Thread the tool into the rear of the crankshaft. Tighten the screws snugly.

Rear main seal removal notches—4.3L, 5.0L and 5.7L engines

Rear main seal installation—4.3L, 5.0L and 5.7L engines

This is to insure that the seal will be installed squarely over the crankshaft. Tighten the tool wing nut until it bottoms.

7. Remove the tool from the crankshaft.
8. Install the flywheel or flexplate and transmission assembly.

4.8L ENGINE

The rear main bearing oil seal, both halves, can be removed without removal of the crankshaft. Always replace the upper and lower halves together.

1. Raise and support the vehicle safely, drain the oil and remove the oil pan.
2. Remove the rear main bearing cap.
3. Remove the old oil seal from its groove in the retainer, prying from the bottom using a suitable tool.
4. Coat a new seal half completely with clean engine oil, and insert it into the bearing cap groove. Keep oil off of the parting line surface, as this surface is treated with glue. Gradually push the seal with a hammer handle until the seal is rolled into place.
5. To remove the upper half of the old seal, use a small hammer and a soft, blunt punch to tap one end of the oil seal out until it protrudes far enough to be removed with needle nosed pliers. Push the new seal into place with the lip toward the front of the engine.
6. Install the bearing cap and torque the bolts to a loose fit. With the cap fitted loosely, move the crankshaft first to the rear and then to the front with a rubber mallet. This will properly position the thrust bearing. Torque the bearing cap to a final torque of 65 ft. lbs. (90 Nm). Install the oil pan.

6.2L AND 6.5L ENGINES

2-Piece Seal

Engines are originally equipped with a 2-piece rope seal. This should be replaced with 2-piece lip seal, which is available as a service replacement.

1. Raise and support the vehicle safely. Drain the crankcase oil and remove the oil pan, pump and rear main bearing cap.
2. Using a suitable tool, remove the upper and lower rope seals.

To install:

3. Apply a light coat of oil to the seal lips where they contact the crankshaft. Roll 1 seal half into the block groove until a ½ in. (13mm) of one end is extending out of the block. Insert the other seal half into the opposite side of the seal groove in the block.

4. The ends of the seal halves should now be positioned at the 8 and 2 o'clock or 4 and 10 o'clock positions.

5. Lightly coat the seal groove in the main bearing with adhesive Loctite 414® or equivalent.

6. Apply a thin film of anaerobic sealant or equivalent, to the

Applying sealer to the block—4.8L and 7.4L engines

A. Oil relief slot   B. Apply anaerobic sealer

Applying sealer to the rear main bearing cap—6.2L and 6.5L diesel engines

INSTALLING THE UPPER SEAL HALF

13 mm (½-inch)

INSTALLING THE LOWER SEAL HALF

Rear main seal installation—6.2L and 6.5L diesel engines

main bearing cap as shown. Do not put sealant in the oil relief slot.
   7. Tap the bearing cap into place using a brass or leather mallet.
   8. Install the bearing cap bolts and torque to specification.
   9. Install the oil pump and oil pan.

1-Piece Seal

The 1-piece rear main seal may be serviced without removing the oil pan and rear main bearing cap.
   1. Raise and support the vehicle safely.
   2. Remove the transmission from the vehicle.
   3. Remove the pressure plate/flywheel or flexplate assembly.
   4. Insert a suitable tool into the notches provided in the seal retainer and pry the seal out.

NOTE: Care should be taken when removing the seal so as not to nick the crankshaft sealing surface.

To install:
   5. Before installation lubricate the new seal with clean engine oil.
   6. Install the seal with the spring cavity towards the crankshaft onto tool J–39084 or equivalent. Thread the tool into the rear of the crankshaft. Tighten the screws snugly. This is to insure that the seal will be installed squarely over the crankshaft. Tighten the tool wing nut until it bottoms.
   7. Remove the tool from the crankshaft.
   8. Install the flywheel or flexplate and transmission assembly.

7.4L ENGINE

2-Piece Seal

The rear main bearing oil seal, both halves, can be removed without removal of the crankshaft. Always replace the upper and lower halves together.
   1. Raise and support the vehicle safely, drain the oil and remove the oil pan.
   2. Remove the oil pump and the rear main bearing cap.
   3. Using a suitable tool, pry the oil seal from the rear main bearing cap.
   4. Using a small hammer and a brass pin punch, drive the top half of the oil seal from the rear main bearing.
   5. Using a non-abrasive cleaner, clean the rear main bearing cap and the crankshaft.
   6. Coat the new oil seal with engine oil; do not coat the ends of the seal.
   7. Position the new upper half seal into the main bearing cap groove and carefully roll the seal around the cap groove.

NOTE: Make sure the seal lip is positioned toward the front of the engine.

   8. Install the lower half onto the lower half of the rear main bearing cap.
   9. Apply sealant to the cap-to-case mating surfaces and install the lower rear main bearing half to the engine; keep the sealant off of the seal's mating line.
   10. Install the rear main bearing cap bolts and torque to 10 ft. lbs. (14 Nm). Using a lead hammer, tap the crankshaft forward and rearward, to line up the thrust surfaces. Torque the main bearing bolts to 110 ft. lbs. (150 Nm).
   11. Install the oil pan and pump assembly. Refill the crankcase with the proper type and quantity of engine oil.

TORQUE SPECIFICATIONS

Component	English	Metric
Bellhousing-to-transmission	74 ft. lbs.	100 Nm
Camshaft sprocket bolts		
4.3L, 5.0L and 5.7L engines	21 ft. lbs.	28 Nm
6.2L and 6.5L engines	74 ft. lbs.	100 Nm
7.4L engine	20 ft. lbs.	26 Nm
Connecting rod bearing cap bolts		
4.3L engine		
1988–90	45 ft. lbs.	60 Nm
1991–92		
Step 1:	20 ft. lbs.	27 Nm
Step 2:	+ 60° turn	+ 60° turn
4.8L engine	44 ft. lbs.	60 Nm
5.0L and 5.7L engines	45 ft. lbs.	60 Nm
6.2L, 6.5L and 7.4L engines	48 ft. lbs.	65 Nm
Crankshaft pulley bolt		
6.2L and 6.5L engine	30 ft. lbs.	40 Nm
Cylinder head nuts		
4.3L, 5.0L and 5.7L engines	65 ft. lbs.	90 Nm
4.8L engine		
Except left front bolt	95 ft. lbs.	130 Nm
Left front bolt	85 ft. lbs.	115 Nm
6.2L and 6.5L engines		
Step 1:	20 ft. lbs.	27 Nm
Step 2:	50 ft. lbs.	65 Nm
Step 3:	+ 45° turn	+ 45° turn
7.4L engine	80 ft. lbs.	110 Nm
Diesel injection nozzles	50 ft. lbs.	70 Nm
Diesel injection pump-to-front cover	40 ft. lbs.	30 Nm
Engine mount through bolts		
4.3L engine	44 ft. lbs.	59 Nm
4.8L engine	54 ft. lbs.	73 Nm
5.0L, 5.7L, 6.2L, 6.5L and 7.4L engines	70 ft. lbs.	95 Nm
Engine-to-transmission		
4L60 and 700R4 transmissions	35 ft. lbs.	47 Nm
3L80, 4L80 and 400/475 transmissions	33 ft. lbs.	44 Nm
Engine-to-bell housing		
1988–90	40 ft. lbs.	54 Nm
1991–92	29 ft. lbs.	39 Nm
Exhaust manifold		
4.3L, 5.0L and 5.7L engines		
Except 2 center bolts	26 ft. lbs.	36 Nm
2 center bolts	20 ft. lbs.	27 Nm
4.8L engine	44 ft. lbs.	60 Nm
6.2L and 6.5L engines	26 ft. lbs.	35 Nm
7.4L engine	40 ft. lbs.	54 Nm
Flywheel/flexplate-to-crankshaft bolts		
4.3L engine	75 ft. lbs.	100 Nm
4.8L engine	110 ft. lbs.	150 Nm
5.0L and 5.7L engines		
1988–89	65 ft. lbs.	90 Nm
1990–92	75 ft. lbs.	100 Nm
6.2L and 6.5L engines	66 ft. lbs.	90 Nm
7.4L engine	65 ft. lbs.	90 Nm
Intake manifold		
4.3L, 5.0L and 5.7L engines	35 ft. lbs.	48 Nm
4.8L engine	44 ft. lbs.	60 Nm
6.2L and 6.5L engines	31 ft. lbs.	42 Nm
7.4L engine		
1988–89	30 ft. lbs.	40 Nm
1990–92	40 ft. lbs.	54 Nm

TORQUE SPECIFICATIONS

Component	English	Metric
Main bearing cap bolts		
4.3L engine		
1988–90	80 ft. lbs.	109 Nm
1991–92	75 ft. lbs.	102 Nm
4.8L engine	65 ft. lbs.	88 Nm
5.0L and 5.7L engines		
Outer bolts on caps 2, 3, 4	70 ft. lbs.	95 Nm
All other cap bolts	80 ft. lbs.	109 Nm
6.2L and 6.5L engines		
Inner bolts	110 ft. lbs.	149 Nm
Outer bolts	100 ft. lbs.	136 Nm
7.4L engine		
1988–90	110 ft. lbs.	149 Nm
1991–92	100 ft. lbs.	135 Nm
Oil pump attaching bolt		
Except 4.8L engines	65 ft. lbs.	90 Nm
4.8L engine	115 inch lbs.	13 Nm
Pressure plate-to-flywheel bolts		
4.3L, 5.0L and 5.7L engines	22 ft. lbs.	30 Nm
6.2L and 6.5L engines	32 ft. lbs.	43 Nm
7.4L engine	24 ft. lbs.	33 Nm
Rocker arm bolts		
6.2L and 6.5L engines	40 ft. lbs.	54 Nm
7.4L engine (1991–92)	40 ft. lbs.	54 Nm
Spark plug		
4.3L and 7.4L engines	22 ft. lbs.	30 Nm
4.8L engine	15 ft. lbs.	20 Nm
5.0L and 5.7L engines		
1988–90	22 ft. lbs.	30 Nm
1991–92	15 ft. lbs.	20 Nm
Starter bolts		
Gas engine	35 ft. lbs.	47 Nm
Diesel engine		
Long bolt	35 ft. lbs.	47 Nm
Short bolt	24 ft. lbs.	32 Nm
Thermostat housing		
4.3L, 4.8L, 5.0L and 5.7L engines	21 ft. lbs.	28 Nm
6.2L and 6.5L engines	31 ft. lbs.	42 Nm
7.4L engine	27 ft. lbs.	37 Nm
Torque converter-to-flywheel bolts		
700R4 and 4L60 transmissions	50 ft. lbs.	65 Nm
400/475, 3L80 and 4L80 transmissions	33 ft. lbs.	45 Nm
Torsional damper		
4.3L engine	70 ft. lbs.	95 Nm
4.8L engine	50 ft. lbs.	70 Nm
5.0L and 5.7L engines	70 ft. lbs.	95 Nm
6.2L and 6.5L engines	200 ft. lbs.	270 Nm
7.4L engine	85 ft. lbs.	115 Nm
Transfer case-to-transmission	24 ft. lbs.	33 Nm
Turbocharger-to-exhaust manifold	37 ft. lbs.	50 Nm
Water Pump		
Gas engine	30 ft. lbs.	41 Nm
Diesel engine		
Long bolts and long studs	31 ft. lbs.	42 Nm
Short bolts and short studs	17 ft. lbs.	23 Nm

MANUAL TRANSMISSION

Transmission Assembly

For further information, please refer to Chilton's Transmission Service Manual.

Removal and Installation

R/V-SERIES

1. Raise and support the vehicle safely.
2. Drain the transmission.
3. Disconnect the speedometer cable/sensor and back-up light wire at transmission.
4. Remove the shifter boot. Remove the gearshift lever by pressing down firmly on the slotted collar plate with a pair of channel lock pliers and rotating counterclockwise. Plug the opening to keep out dirt.
5. Remove the transfer case, if equipped with 4 wheel drive.
6. Remove driveshaft after marking the position of the shaft to the flange.
7. Remove the exhaust and parking brake cables, as required. Position a transmission jack under the transmission to support it.
8. Remove the crossmember. Visually inspect to see if other equipment, brackets or lines, must be removed to permit removal of transmission.

NOTE: Mark position of crossmember when removing to prevent incorrect installation. The tapered surface should face the rear.

9. Remove the flywheel housing underpan.
10. Remove the top 2 transmission to housing bolts and insert 2 guide pins.

NOTE: The use of guide pins will not only support the transmission but will prevent damage to the clutch disc. Guide pins can be made by taking 2 bolts, the same as those just removed only longer, and cutting off the heads. Make a slot in the cut end of the bolt and use a suitable tool to install the special bolts. Be sure to support the clutch release bearing and support assembly during removal of the transmission. This will prevent the release from falling out of the flywheel housing.

11. Remove the 2 remaining bolts and slide transmission straight back from engine. Use care to keep the transmission drive gear straight in line with clutch disc hub.
12. Remove the transmission from the vehicle.

To install:

13. Place the transmission in high gear.
14. Coat the input shaft splines with high temperature grease.
15. Raise the transmission into position.
16. Install the guide pins in the top 2 bolt holes.
17. Roll the transmission forward and engage the clutch splines. Keep pushing the transmission forward until it mates with the engine.
18. Install the bolts, removing the guide pins. Torque the bolts to 75 ft. lbs.
19. Install the flywheel housing underpan.
20. Install the crossmember. Torque the crossmember-to-frame bolts to 55 ft. lbs.; the crossmember-to-transmission bolts to 40 ft. lbs.
21. Remove the transmission jack.
22. Install the driveshaft.
23. Install the gearshift lever.
24. Connect the speedometer cable/sensor and back-up light wire at transmission.
25. Fill the transmission with the proper quantity and type of oil.

NOTE: Do not force the transmission into the clutch disc hub. Do not let the transmission hang unsupported in the splined portion of the clutch disc.

C/K-SERIES

1. Disconnect the negative battery cable. Remove the shifter boot and lever.
2. Raise and support the vehicle safely. Drain the transmission.
3. Remove driveshaft after marking the position of the shaft to the axle flange.
4. Remove the exhaust pipes and parking brake cables.
5. Disconnect the wiring harness at the transmission.
6. Remove the transfer case, if equipped with 4 wheel drive.
7. Remove the clutch slave cylinder and support it out of the way.
8. On the 85mm (MG5) transmission, remove the flywheel housing-inspection cover.
9. Position a transmission jack or equivalent, under the transmission for support.
10. Remove the crossmember. Visually inspect to see if other equipment, brackets or lines, must be removed to permit removal of transmission.

NOTE: Mark position of crossmember when removing to prevent incorrect installation. The tapered surface should face the rear.

11. Remove the top 2 transmission to housing bolts and insert two guide pins.

NOTE: The use of guide pins will not only support the transmission but will prevent damage to the clutch disc. Guide pins can be made by taking 2 bolts, the same as those just removed only longer, and cutting off the heads. Make an adjustment slot. Be sure to support the clutch release bearing and support assembly during removal of the transmission. This will prevent the release from falling out of the flywheel housing.

12. Remove the remaining bolts and slide transmission straight back from engine. Use care to keep the transmission drive gear straight in line with clutch disc hub.
13. Remove the transmission from the vehicle.

To install:

14. Place the transmission in high gear. Coat the input shaft splines with high temperature grease.
15. Raise the transmission into position.
16. Install the guide pins in the top 2 bolt holes.
17. Roll the transmission forward and engage the clutch splines. Keep pushing the transmission forward until it mates with the engine.
18. Install the bolts, removing the guide pins. Torque the bolts to specification.
19. Install the transfer case, if equipped.
20. Install the crossmember. Torque the crossmember bolts to specification. Remove the transmission jack.
21. Install the slave cylinder.
22. Install the driveshaft.
23. Install the exhaust system.
24. Install the inspection cover on the 85mm transmission.
25. Install the gearshift lever.
26. Connect the wiring harness at the transmission.
27. Fill the transmission with the proper type and quantity of oil.

NOTE: Do not force the transmission into the clutch disc hub. Do not let the transmission hang unsupported in the splined portion of the clutch disc.

G-SERIES

1. Raise and support the vehicle safely.
2. Drain the transmission.
3. Disconnect the speedometer cable, back-up light and TCS switch.
4. Remove the shift controls from the transmission.
5. Disconnect the driveshaft and remove it from the vehicle.
6. Support the transmission using the proper equipment.
7. Remove the transfer case, if equipped with 4 wheel drive.
8. Inspect the transmission to be sure all necessary components have been removed or disconnected.
9. Mark the front of the crossmember to be sure it is installed correctly.
10. Remove the flywheel housing under pan and transmission mounting bolts.
11. Move the transmission slowly away from the engine, keeping the mainshaft in alignment with the clutch disc hub. Support the clutch release bearing to prevent it from falling out of the flywheel housing when the transmission is removed.
12. Remove the transmission from the vehicle.

To install:

13. Lightly coat the mainshaft with high temperature grease. Do not use much grease, since, under normal operation, the grease will be thrown onto the clutch, causing it to fail.
14. Raise the transmission into position under the vehicle.
15. Roll the unit forward, engaging the spline of the mainshaft with the splines in the clutch hub. Continue pushing forward until the transmission mates with the bell housing.
16. Install and tighten the transmission-to-bell housing bolts. Install the transfer case, if equipped.
17. Install the flywheel housing under pan.
18. Install the crossmember. Torque the bolts to 50 ft. lbs.
19. Inspect the transmission to be sure all necessary components have been installed or connected.
20. Connect the driveshaft.
21. Install the shift controls.
22. Connect the speedometer cable.
23. Connect the back-up light switch.
24. Connect the TCS switch.
25. Fill the transmission with the proper quantity and type of oil.
26. Road test the vehicle.

CLUTCH

Clutch Assembly

Removal and Installation

1. Raise and support the vehicle safely. Remove the transmission and place a support under the engine.
2. Remove the slave cylinder or clutch adjusting rod.
3. Remove the bell housing cover.
4. Remove the bell housing from the engine.
5. Remove the throwout spring and fork.
6. Remove the ball stud from the bell housing.
7. Install a pilot tool to support the clutch while removing the assembly.

NOTE: Before removing the clutch from the flywheel, matchmark the flywheel, clutch cover and one pressure plate lug, so these parts may be assembled in their same relative positions and retain the factory balance.

8. Loosen the clutch attaching bolts one turn at a time to prevent distortion of the clutch cover until the tension is released.
9. Remove the clutch pilot tool and the clutch from the vehicle.
10. Check the clutch assembly, flywheel and pilot bearing for signs of wear, scoring, overheating, etc. If the clutch plate, flywheel or pressure plate is oil-soaked, inspect the engine rear main seal and the transmission input shaft seal and correct leakage as required. Replace any damaged parts.

To install:

11. Assemble the pressure plate and disc assembly, as required.

NOTE: The manufacturer recommends that new pressure plate bolts and washers be used.

12. Turn the flywheel until the previously applied mark is at the bottom.

1. Lubrication fitting (R/V and C/K models only)
2. Clutch fork
3. Spring washer
4. Screw
5. Flywheel housing
6. Screw
7. Ball stud
8. Boot
9. Retainer
10. Release bearing
11. Cover assembly
12. Driveplate
13. Cover
14. Screw
15. Pilot bearing
16. Screw
17. Strap
18. Pressure plate

Exploded view of typical clutch assembly

13. Install the clutch disc, pressure plate and cover, using a suitable clutch aligning tool.

14. Turn the clutch until the matchmark on the clutch cover aligns with the mark on the flywheel.

15. Install the attaching bolts and tighten them a little at a time in a crossing pattern until the spring pressure is taken up.

16. Remove the aligning tool.

17. Coat the rounded end of the ball stud with high temperature wheel bearing grease.

18. Install the ball stud in the bell housing. Pack the ball stud from the lubrication fitting.

19. Pack the inside recess and the outside groove of the release bearing with high temperature wheel bearing grease and install the release bearing and fork.

20. Install the release bearing seat and spring.

21. Install the clutch housing. Torque the bolts to specification.

22. Install the cover.

23. Install the slave cylinder or clutch rod.

24. Install the transmission.

25. Bleed the hydraulic system or adjust the clutch as required.

Free Pedal Travel Adjustment

MECHANICAL CLUTCH

This adjustment is for the amount of clutch pedal free travel before the throwout bearing contacts the clutch release fingers. It is required periodically to compensate for clutch lining wear. Incorrect adjustment will cause gear grinding and clutch slippage or wear.

1. Raise and support the vehicle safely. Disconnect the clutch fork return spring at the fork on the clutch housing.

2. Loosen the outer locknut on the adjusting rod.

3. Move the clutch fork back until clutch spring pressure is felt.

4. Hold the clutch pedal against its bumper and turn the inner adjusting nut until it is 0.28 in. (7.1mm) from the cross lever.

5. Tighten the locknut against the cross lever.

6. Install the return spring.

7. Check the free travel at the pedal and readjust as necessary. It should be 1⅜ in. (34mm).

Clutch Master Cylinder

Removal and Installation

1. Disconnect the negative battery cable.

2. Remove the lower steering column covers.

3. Remove the lower left side air conditioning duct, if equipped.

4. Disconnect the pushrod from the clutch pedal.

5. Disconnect the reservoir hose, if equipped.

6. Disconnect and plug the secondary cylinder hydraulic line to the master cylinder.

7. Remove the master cylinder retaining nuts and remove the master cylinder.

8. To install, use a new gasket, reverse the removal procedure and bleed the clutch system.

Clutch Slave Cylinder

Removal and Installation

1. Disconnect the negative battery cable.

2. Raise the vehicle and support it safely.

3. Disconnect the hydraulic line from the secondary cylinder.

4. Disconnect the hydraulic line from the master cylinder.

5. Remove the nut retaining the hydraulic line and the speedometer cable to the cowl, then install the nut to hold the speedometer cable in place, as required.

6. Cover all hydraulic lines to prevent dirt and moisture from entering the system.

7. Installation is the reverse of removal. Bleed the clutch hydraulic system.

Bleeding The Hydraulic Clutch System

1. Fill the clutch master cylinder with the proper grade and type fluid. Raise and support the vehicle safely.

2. Remove the slave cylinder retaining bolts. Hold the cylinder about 45 degrees with the bleeder at the highest point.

3. Fully depress the clutch pedal and open the bleeder screw. Repeat until all air is expelled from the system.

4. Be sure the fluid level remains full in the clutch master cylinder throughout the bleeding procedure.

5. Test the clutch for proper operation.

1. Hydraulic line routing
2. Speedometer cable
3. Hydraulic line, secondary cylinder
4. Master cylinder
5. Nut
6. Nut
7. Bleeder Screw
8. Secondary cylinder

Typical secondary (slave) cylinder and hydraulic line

AUTOMATIC TRANSMISSION

For further information, please refer to Chilton's Transmission Service Manual.

Transmission Assembly

Removal and Installation

NOTE: It may be necessary to disconnect and remove the exhaust crossover pipe on 8 cylinder engines, and to disconnect the catalytic converter and remove its support bracket, if equipped.

2 WHEEL DRIVE

1. Disconnect the battery ground cable. Remove the air cleaner and disconnect the detent cable.
2. Raise and support the vehicle safely. Drain the transmission.
3. Matchmark the axle-to-driveshaft flanges and remove the driveshaft.
4. Disconnect the speedometer cable, downshift cable, vacuum modulator line, shift linkage, throttle linkage, fuel lines and fluid cooler lines at the transmission, as required. Remove the filler tube.
5. Support the transmission. Unbolt and remove the crossmember.
6. Remove the torque converter underpan, Matchmark the flywheel and converter, and remove the converter bolts.
7. Support the engine and lower the transmission slightly for access to the upper transmission to engine bolts.
8. Remove the transmission to engine bolts and pull the transmission back and out of the vehicle.

NOTE: Keep the front of the transmission up so the converter doesn't fall out.

9. Installation is the reverse of the removal procedure.

NOTE: Lubricate the internal yoke splines at the transmission end of the driveshaft with lithium base grease.

4 WHEEL DRIVE

1. Disconnect the battery ground cable and remove the transmission dipstick. Detach the downshift cable at the carburetor. Remove the transfer case shift lever knob and boot.
2. Raise and support the vehicle safely.
3. Remove the skid plate, if any. Remove the flywheel cover.
4. Matchmark the flywheel and torque converter, remove the bolts and secure the converter so it doesn't fall out of the transmission.
5. Detach the shift linkage, speedometer cable, vacuum modulator line, downshift cable, throttle linkage and cooler times at the transmission. Remove the filler tube.
6. Remove the exhaust crossover pipe to manifold bolts.
7. Unbolt the transfer case adapter from the crossmember. Support the transmission and transfer case. Remove the crossmember.

8. Move the exhaust system aside. Detach the driveshafts after matchmarking their flanges. Disconnect the parking brake cable.
9. Unbolt the transfer case from the frame bracket. Support the engine. Unbolt the transmission from the engine, pull the assembly back, and remove.
10. Reverse the procedure for installation.

Shift Linkage Adjustment

1. Raise and support the vehicle safely.
2. Loosen the shift lever bolt or nut at the transmission lever so the lever is free to move on the rod.
3. Set the column shift lever to the neutral gate notch. Do not use the indicator pointer as a reference to position the shift lever, as this will not be accurate.
4. Set the transmission lever in the neutral position by moving it clockwise to the park detent, then counterclockwise 2 detents to neutral.
5. Hold the rod tightly in the swivel and tighten the nut or bolt to 17 ft. lbs. (23 Nm).
6. Move the column shifter to **P** and check that the engine starts. Check the adjustment by moving the selector to each gear position.

Neutral Start Switch Adjustment

This switch prevents the engine from being started unless the transmission is in **N** or **P**. It is located on the steering column. This switch also activates the back-up lights.

NOTE: The manual transmission back-up light switch is on the rear of the transmission.

1. Move the switch housing all the way toward the low gear position.
2. Move the gear selector to the **P** position. The main housing and housing back should ratchet, providing proper switch adjustment.

Throttle Valve Cable Adjustment

The adjustment is made at the engine end of the cable with the engine off, by rotating the throttle lever by hand. Do not use the accelerator pedal to rotate the throttle lever.

1. Remove the air cleaner.
2. Depress and hold down the metal adjusting tab at the end of the cable.
3. Move the slider until it stops against the fitting.
4. Release the adjusting tab.
5. Rotate the throttle lever to the full extent of it travel.
6. The slider must move towards the lever when the lever is at full travel. Make sure the cable moves freely.

NOTE: The cable may appear to function properly with the engine cold. Recheck it with the engine hot.

7. Road test the vehicle.

TRANSFER CASE

Transfer Case Assembly

Removal and Installation

1. Disconnect the negative battery cable. Raise and support the vehicle safely.

2. Drain the fluid from the transfer case. Disconnect the speedometer cable, if equipped. Remove the skid plate, the crossmember and supports, as required.
3. Matchmark the transfer case front output shaft yoke and driveshaft for reassembly. Disconnect the driveshaft from the transfer case.

4. Matchmark the rear axle yoke and the driveshaft for reassembly. Remove the driveshaft. Disconnect the shift linkage and electrical connections from the transfer case.

5. Remove the parking cables, as required.

6. Properly support the transfer case assembly. Remove the transfer case retaining bolts.

7. Remove the transfer case from the vehicle.

8. Installation is the reverse of the removal procedure.

Linkage

Adjustment
MODEL 208 AND NP241

1. Position the transfer case lever in the 4H detent. Push the lower shift lever forward to the 4H stop.

2. Install the rod swivel in the shift lever hole. Hang a 0.200 in. (5.19mm) gauge rod behind the swivel.

3. Install the rear rod nut against the gauge with the shifter against the 4hi stop.

4. Remove the gauge tool. Push the rear of the swivel rearward against the nut.

5. Tighten the front rod nut against the swivel. Check for proper operation.

MODEL 205

1. Raise and support the vehicle safely. Remove the swivel from the transfer case shift lever.

2. Turn the swivel inward or outward to determine the correct shift detent.

3. Reinstall the swivel to the shift lever.

MODEL 1370

1. Position the transfer case lever in the 4H position.

2. Raise and support the vehicle safely.

3. Disconnect the linkage rod from the console shift lever.

4. Shift the transfer case into the 4H position (transfer shift lever in the forward detent).

5. Adjust the swivel to align with the hole in the console shift lever.

6. Lower the vehicle.

MANUAL TRANSMISSIONS

AUTOMATIC TRANSMISSIONS

1. Transmission
2. Gasket
3. Bolt
4. Spring washer
5. Seal
6. Adapter
7. Bolt
8. Mounting
9. Bolt

Typical transfer case installation

DRIVE AXLE

NOTE: The K-Series truck is the only vehicle using a halfshaft consisting of a CV-joint and boot; and is located only on the left front axle. The right side consists of an axle and tube assembly.

Halfshaft

Removal and Installation
K-SERIES
Left Side Only

1. Raise and support the vehicle safely.

2. Remove the wheel and tire assembly.

3. Remove the skid plate, as required.

4. Remove the drive axle hub nut and washer.

5. Remove the brake line support bracket from the upper control arm to allow extra travel of the control arm.

6. Remove the left outer tie rod attaching nut and cotter pin. Separate the tie rod from the steering knuckle using a suitable tie rod end splitter.

7. Position the tie rod aside and push steering linkage to the opposite side of the vehicle.

8. Remove the lower shock attaching nut and bolt; position the shock aside.

9. Remove the left stabilizer bar bracket and bushing at the frame. Remove the stabilizer bar bolt, spacer and bushings at the lower control arm.

10. Lower the vehicle, taking pressure off the upper control arm by placing a jack or jackstand below the lower control arm between the spring seat and the ball joint.

11. Remove the upper ball joint cotter pin and loosen (do not remove) the upper ball joint attaching nut. Using a suitable ball joint splitter, separate the ball joint stud from the steering knuckle. Remove the attaching nut.

NOTE: Cover the shock mounting bracket and lower ball joint stud with a towel to prevent the axle boot from tearing during removal and installation.

12. Separate the axle shaft from the hub and rotor using tool J–28733 or equivalent.

13. Remove the axle shaft inner flange bolts. Remove the shaft.

To install:

14. Lubricate the axle and hub splines with an approved high temperature wheel bearing grease. Position the shaft in the hub and install the inboard CV-joint-to-flange bolts.

15. Install the upper ball joint to steering knuckle and torque the stud nut to 61 ft. lbs. (83 Nm). Install a cotter pin through the upper ball joint stud and nut. Lubricate the ball joint as required.

16. Install the left stabilizer bar bracket and bushing at the frame. Install the stabilizer bar bolt, spacer and bushings at the lower control arm.

17. Position the lower shock in the mount bracket and install the attaching nut and bolt.

18. Connect the left tie rod end at the steering knuckle. Torque the nut to 35 ft. lbs. (47 Nm). Install a cotter pin through the tie rod stud and nut.

19. Connect the brake line bracket to the control arm, ensuring the line and/or hose is not twisted or kinked.

20. Install the skid plate, as required.

21. Install the axle hub washer and nut. Insert a drift through the rotor vanes to keep the axle from turning and torque the hub nut to 180 ft. lbs. (245 Nm) and the inboard CV-joint flange bolts to 60 ft. lbs. (80 Nm).

22. Remove the drift, install the wheel and tire assembly. Remove stands and lower the vehicle.

CV-Boot

Removal and Installation

OUTER

1. Raise and support the vehicle safely.
2. Remove the wheel and tire assembly.
3. Remove the skid plate, as required.
4. Remove the drive axle and place the assembly in a suitable holding fixture.
5. Remove the large (swage) ring using a chisel, being careful not to damage the housing surface.
6. Cut and remove the small clamp on the CV-boot.
7. Slide the boot back off of the joint housing. Clean excess grease from the joint area.
8. Spread the ears of the joint retaining clip and slide the joint off of the axle shaft.
9. Remove the boot from the axle shaft.

To install:

10. Place the small clamp on the small neck of the CV-boot. Do not crimp the clamp.
11. Slide the boot onto the axle shaft and into the groove on the axle shaft.
12. Crimp the small clamp using tool J–35910 or equivalent.
13. Disassemble the joint and thoroughly clean out old grease. Place a sufficient quantity of approved CV-joint grease inside the boot and in the joint.
14. Pinch the large CV-boot securing ring in an oval shape and slide the ring onto the boot large end.
15. Push the CV-joint onto the axle shaft until the retaining ring is seated in the groove on the axle shaft.
16. Slide the large diameter of the CV-boot with the ring in place over the outside of the CV-joint housing and locate the seal lip in the housing groove. Release any air trapped inside the boot using a thin flat blunt tool between the boot and housing.
17. Using a suitable ring installer tool, press the ring onto the housing until fully seated.

1. Hub assembly
2. Bolt
3. Drive axle
4. Washer
5. Nut

Drive axle removal and installation – C/K-Series

18. Install the halfshaft assembly, skid plate and the wheel and tire.
19. Lower the vehicle and road test.

INNER

1. Raise and support the vehicle safely.
2. Remove the wheel and tire assembly.
3. Remove the skid plate, as required.
4. Remove the drive axle and place the assembly in a suitable holding fixture.
5. Remove the large (swage) ring using a chisel, being careful not to damage the housing surface.
6. Cut and remove the small clamp on the CV-boot.
7. Slide the boot back off of the joint housing. Remove the joint and axle shaft from the joint housing.
8. Spread the ears of the joint retaining clip and slide the joint back on the axle shaft. Remove the forward retaining ring and slide the joint off of the shaft. Handle the joint with care to avoid disassembly.
9. Remove the rear retaining ring and remove the boot from the axle shaft.

To install:

10. Place the small clamp on the small neck of the CV-boot. Do not crimp the clamp.
11. Slide the boot onto the axle shaft and into the groove on the axle shaft.
12. Crimp the small clamp using tool J–35910 or equivalent. Install the forward joint retaining ring onto the axleshaft.
13. Thoroughly clean the old grease from the joint, boot and housing assembly. Place a sufficient quantity of approved CV-joint grease inside the boot.
14. Slide the joint assembly with the counterbore facing the axleshaft onto the shaft against the retaining ring.
15. Install the forward retaining ring in the groove on the axleshaft. Slide the joint towards the end of the shaft and move the inside retaining ring into the groove.
16. Pack the joint sufficient quantity of approved CV-joint

1. Tri-pot housing
2. Shaft retaining ring
3. Tri-pot joint spider
4. Needle retainer ring
5. Needle retainer
6. Tri-pot joint ball
7. Needle roller
8. Spacer ring
9. Swage ring
10. Tri-pot joint seal
11. Seal retaining clamp
12. Axle shaft
13. CV-joint seal
14. Race retaining ring
15. Ball
16. CV-joint inner race
17. CV-joint cage
18. CV-joint outer race
19. Sensor ring
20. Deflector Ring

Front drive axle components—K-Series

grease. Pinch the large CV-boot securing ring in an oval shape and slide the ring onto the boot large end.

17. Push the CV-joint onto the axle shaft.

18. Slide the large diameter of the CV-boot with the ring in place over the outside of the CV-joint housing and locate the seal lip in the housing groove. Release any air trapped inside the boot using a thin flat blunt tool between the boot and housing.

19. Using a suitable ring installer tool, press the ring onto the housing until fully seated.

20. Install the halfshaft assembly, skid plate and the wheel and tire.

21. Lower the vehicle and road test.

Driveshaft and U-Joints

Removal and Installation

1. Raise and support the vehicle safely.

SWAGE CLAMP SIZE CHART

TOOL NO.	DESCRIPTION	APPLICATION
J 36652-1	Split Plate Swage Clamp	K 10/20
J 36652-2	Split Plate Swage Clamp	K 30 (Outboard)
J 36652-3	Split Plate Swage Clamp	K 30 (Inboard)

MAKE SURE SWAGE RING AND SWAGE RING CLAMP ARE IN PROPER ALIGNMENT

9

HOUSING

SEAL

SWAGE RING CLAMP

J 36652

AXLE ASSEMBLY

9

VISE

SWAGE RING CLAMP

9. Swage Ring

Pressing axle boot in place—K-Series

2. Mark the relationship of the driveshaft to the front axle and transfer case flange.

3. Remove the skid plate, if equipped.

4. Remove the bolts, nuts, washers and U-bolts/retainers from the front axle flange-to-driveshaft.

5. Remove the slip yoke from the front axle.

NOTE: Do not let the u-joint caps fall off the yoke, tape the bearing caps in place to avoid loss of the bearing rollers.

6. Remove the bolts at the transfer case flange, slide the driveshaft forward and disengage the assembly from the transfer case.

7. Place the driveshaft into a holding fixture.

8. Remove the retaining rings.

9. Using 2 sockets, one with a diameter just smaller than the bearing cap; the other with an opening large enough to accept a bearing cap, press out the bearing caps in a vice.

10. Remove the trunnion from the slip yoke.

To install:

11. Place the trunnion in between the yoke ears of the driveshaft and begin installing both bearing caps by hand, finish the installation using a vice.

12. Use a socket with a smaller diameter than the bearing cap and press the bearing cap in past the retainer ring groove. Install the retaining ring.

13. Turn the driveshaft over and repeat the process.

14. Install the slip yoke over the trunnion and repeat the procedure for the remaining bearing caps.

15. Install the driveshaft, U-bolt/retainers, nuts and bolts, aligning the shaft with the previous made marks on the transfer case and front axle.

16. Lower the vehicle and roadtest.

Front Axle Shaft, Bearing and Seal

Removal and Installation

V-SERIES

1. Raise and support the vehicle safely.

2. Remove the wheel and tire assembly.

3. Remove the brake caliper and position the assembly aside.

4. Remove the locking hub assembly. Remove the hub and bearing assembly as follows:

a. Using either wheel bearing nut wrench (J–6893–D on ½ or ¾ ton vehicles or J–26878–A on 1 ton vehicles), remove the locknut, ring and adjusting nut.

b. Remove the hub and rotor assembly, bearing careful not to let the bearing fall out of the hub.

5. Remove the splash shield and brake bracket.

6. Remove the spindle from the steering knuckle.

7. Remove the axle shaft as follows.

To install:

8. Lube the spindle and spindle bearing with the recommended lubricant.

9. Install the spindle seal and spacer onto the axle shaft with the spacer's chamfer points facing toward the oil deflector.

10. Install the axle shaft into the housing.

11. Install the steering knuckle, brake caliper bracket and splash shield and secure with nuts and washers. Torque nuts to 65 ft. lbs. (88 Nm). Ensure the seal and oil deflector are in place on the steering knuckle.

12. Install the hub and rotor assembly as follows:

a. If replacing the bearing, drive the races out of the hub assembly.

b. Using a brass drift and hammer, drive the inner bearing and seal out of the hub.

1.	Axle shaft	16.	Seal
2.	Deflector	17.	Bolt
3.	Seal	18.	Lock
4.	Bearing	19.	Bolt
5.	Axle tube	20.	Pilot bearing
6.	Clip	21.	Inner output shaft
7.	Thrust washer	22.	Carrier case
8.	Connector	23.	Carrier bushing
9.	Snap ring	24.	Drain plug
10.	Sleeve	25.	Fill plug
11.	Front axle switch	26.	Washer
12.	Front axle solenoid	27.	Seal
13.	Bolt	28.	Snap ring
14.	Shift fork	29.	Deflector
15.	Spring	30.	Output shaft

Front axle components—K-Series

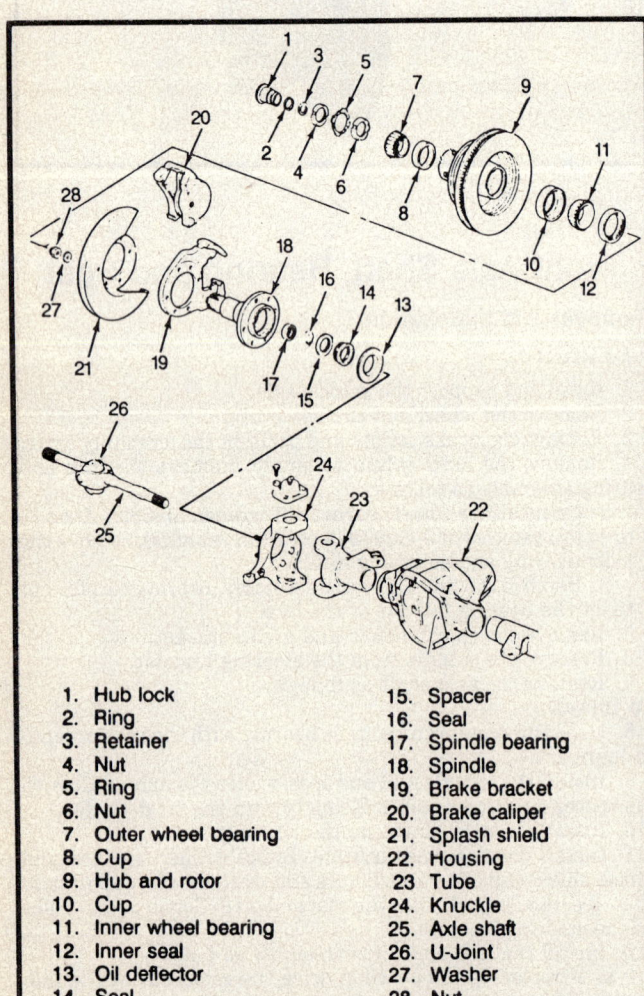

1.	Hub lock	15.	Spacer
2.	Ring	16.	Seal
3.	Retainer	17.	Spindle bearing
4.	Nut	18.	Spindle
5.	Ring	19.	Brake bracket
6.	Nut	20.	Brake caliper
7.	Outer wheel bearing	21.	Splash shield
8.	Cup	22.	Housing
9.	Hub and rotor	23.	Tube
10.	Cup	24.	Knuckle
11.	Inner wheel bearing	25.	Axle shaft
12.	Inner seal	26.	U-Joint
13.	Oil deflector	27.	Washer
14.	Seal	28.	Nut

Front driving axle components—except K-Series

c. Remove all grease from the bearings, hub and spindle assembly using a suitable solvent.

d. Inspect the bearings, races and spindle for heat stress, cracking or scores, repair or replace as necessary.

e. Using a bearing race installer, drive the new races into the hub assembly until fully seated.

f. Using an approved high-temperature wheel bearing grease pack the bearings, working the grease in between the rollers and apply a small quantity to the spindle and hub assembly.

g. Install the inner wheel bearing and a new seal into the hub.

h. Install the rotor/hub assembly onto the spindle.

i. Install the outer wheel bearing and push onto the spindle until fully seated against the race. Install the adjusting nut torque to 50 ft. lbs. (60 Nm) while spinning the rotor assembly.

j. Back off the adjusting nut and retorque the nut to 35 ft. lbs. (47 Nm) for automatic hubs or 50 ft. lbs. (60 Nm) for manual hubs.

k. Back off the adjusting nut a maximum of ⅜ of a turn for automatic hubs or just enough to free the bearing for manual hubs.

l. Install the ring and locknut, ensuring the tang on the inside diameter of the ring passes is aligned in the slot on the spindle.

m. The hole in the ring must align with the pin on the lock nut. Move the adjusting nut to align the pin.

n. Torque the locknut to 160 ft. lbs. (217 Nm).

13. Install the locking hub assembly.
14. Install the brake caliper assembly.
15. Install the wheel and tire assembly.
16. Lower the vehicle, check and add gear oil to the front axle as required. Road test the vehicle.

K-SERIES

1. Raise and support the vehicle safely.
2. Remove the right wheel.
3. Position a drain pan under the axle.
4. Remove the stabilizer bar.
5. Remove the skid plate.
6. Disconnect the right inner tie rod end at the relay rod.
7. Remove the left halfshaft-to-axle flange bolts, turn the

wheel to loosen the axle from the axle tube, push the axle towards the front of the truck and tie the axle out of the way.

8. Unplug the indicator switch and actuator electrical connectors.

9. Remove the drain plug and drain the fluid from the case.

10. Remove the right axle tube-to-frame bolts.

11. Remove the axle tube-to-carrier bolts.

12. Remove the axle tube/shaft assembly. Keep the open end up.

13. Disassemble the axle tube assembly as follows:

   a. Position the axle tube, open end up, in a vise by clamping on the mounting flange.

   b. Remove the snapring, sleeve, gear and thrust washer from the shaft end.

   c. Tap out the axle shaft with a soft mallet.

   d. Turn the axle tube over and pry out the deflector and seal.

   e. Using a slide hammer and bearing remover, remove the bearing.

   f. Clean all parts in a non-flammable solvent and inspect them for wear or damage. Clean off all old gasket material.

To install:

14. To install, perform the following procedures:

   a. Using a bearing driver, install the new outer bearing in the tube.

   b. Coat the lips of a new seal with wheel bearing grease and tap it into place in the tube.

   c. Install the deflector.

   d. Insert the axle shaft into the tube.

   e. Coat the thrust washer with grease to hold it in place and position it on the tube end. Make sure the tabs index the slots.

   f. Install the gear, sleeve, and snapring.

15. Position a new gasket, coated with sealer, on the carrier. Raise the tube assembly into position and install the tube-to-carrier bolts. Torque the bolts to 30 ft. lbs. (40 Nm).

16. Install the left halfshaft-to-flange bolts and torque to specification.

17. Install the axle tube-to-frame bolts. Torque the ½ and ¾ ton vehicle to 75 ft. lbs. (100 Nm) or the 1 ton vehicles to 106 ft. lbs. (145 Nm).

18. Connect the tie rod end to the relay rod.

19. Install the stabilizer bar.

20. Connect the actuator and indicator switch.

21. Install the drain plug. Tighten it to 24 ft. lbs. (33 Nm).

22. Fill the axle with the correct quantity and type of gear oil. Tighten the filler plug to 24 ft. lbs. (33 Nm).

23. Install the skid plate. Tighten the bolts to 25 ft. lbs.

Rear Axle Shaft, Bearing and Seal

Removal and Installation

SEMI FLOATING DIFFERENTIAL (8½ AND 9½ INCH)

1. Raise and support the vehicle safely. Remove the tire and wheel assembly. Remove the brake drums.

2. Remove the carrier cover retaining bolts. Remove the carrier cover.

3. If not equipped with a locking differential, remove the rear axle pinion shaft lock screw and the rear axle pinion shaft.

4. If equipped with a locking differential, remove the shaft lock screw and pull the pinion shaft partially out. Rotate the differential until the pinion shaft touches the top of the housing. Using a suitable tool, rotate the C-lock until aligned with the thrust block.

5. Push the flanged end of the axle shaft toward the center of the vehicle. Remove the C-lock clip from the button end of the shaft.

6. Remove the axle shaft from the housing. Be careful not to damage the oil seal.

7. When removing the axle shaft on vehicles equipped with

the 9½ in. ring gear, be sure the thrust washer in the differential case does not slide out.

8. Using a seal and bearing removal tool J-2619-01 and J-23689 for 8½ ring gear axle, insert the tool into the bore so the tool grasps behind the bearing. Slide the washer against the outside of the seal. Turn the nut finger-tight. Using a slide hammer remove the bearing and seal.

9. If equipped with the 9½ in. ring gear, use tool J-29712. Insert the tool into the axle tube so it grasps behind the bearing. Center the receiver on the axle tube and tighten the nut. Back off the nut and remove the bearing and seal from the tool.

To install:

10. Lubricate the space between where the bearing and the seal will seat with wheel bearing lubricant.

11. Using tool J-23690 for the 8½ ring gear or J-29709 for the 9½ ring gear axle, install the bearing into the housing until the tool bottoms against the tube.

12. Using tool J-21128 for the 8½ ring gear or J-29713 for the 9½ ring gear axle, install the seal until it is flush with the end of the axle tube.

13. Being careful not to damage the seal, insert the axle shaft into the housing allowing the splines to engage with the differential.

14. If not equipped with a locking differential, place the C-lock on the inside end of the axle shaft; then pull the axle shaft outward to seat the C-lock in the differential side gear. Install the pinion shaft and lock screw.

15. If equipped with a locking differential, install the pinion shaft partially into the differential; then rotate the differential until the shaft touches the top of the housing. Position the C-lock in the assembly as specified. Pull the axle shaft outward to seat the C-lock in the differential gear. Install the pinion shaft and lock screw.

16. Torque the lock screw to 25 ft. lbs. (34 Nm).

17. Install the carrier cover and gasket. Torque the bolts to 30 ft. lbs. (41 Nm)

18. Fill the axle assembly with the correct type of gear oil to the filler hole level.

19. Install the brake drum, wheel and tire assembly. Inspect the axle for leaks.

20. Lower the vehicle and road test.

FULL FLOATING DIFFERENTIAL (9¾ AND 10½ INCH)

1. Raise and support the vehicle safely. Remove the tire and wheel assembly.

2. Remove the bolts that retain the axle shaft flange to the wheel hub.

3. Tap the flange with a soft mallet and loosen the axle shaft.

4. Twist the shaft assembly and remove it from the axle tube.

5. Remove the hub assembly retaining ring, key, adjusting nut, and washer. Remove the hub and drum assembly.

6. Remove the oil seal from its mounting.

7. Using a hammer and a long brass drift pin, knock the inner bearing and cup from the hub assembly.

8. Using a snapring pliers, remove the retaining ring. Using tool J-24424 and J-8092, drive the outer bearing and cup from the hub assembly.

To install:

9. Thoroughly clean all parts with a non-flammable cleaner. Inspect all parts for wear, cracks, chips or other damage, replace as necessary.

10. Place the outer bearing cup into the hub, drive the cup in using tool J-8608 upside down on tool J-8092 beyond the retaining ring.

11. Place the retaining ring into the groove and drive the cup back onto the retaining ring using tool J-24426.

12. Install the inner bearing cup using tool J-24426 and J-8092 into place until it is seated against the hub shoulder.

13. Install the inner bearing and seal into the hub.

14. Install the hub and drum assembly, ensuring the bearings

**SAGINAW
8.50-IN.
10 BOLT
PATTERN**

**SAGINAW
9.50-IN.
14 BOLT
PATTERN**

**SAGINAW
10.50-IN.
14 BOLT
PATTERN
(COVER STYLE DIFFERENT)**

3 1/8"   12" APPROX.

**DANA MODEL
60 HD
9.75-IN.**

4"   12.8" APPROX.

**ROCKWELL MODEL
12.0-IN.**

**DANA MODEL
70 OU AND HD
10.50-IN.**

Rear axle identification

1. Drum
2. Bolt
3. Shaft
4. Lock
5. Seal
6. Bearing
7. Housing
8. Clip
9. Bolt
10. Carrier cover

Semi-floating rear axle assembly

1. Pinion shaft
2. Differential case
3. Housing

Pinion shaft pin removal and installation—Semi-floating rear axle

1. Pinion shaft
2. Thrust block
3. Side gear
4. C-Lock
5. Shaft

CORRECT

C-lock alignment for removal and installation—Semi-floating rear axle

A. Dana axles with disc brakes
B. Dana and saginaw axles with drum brakes

1. Outer locknut
2. Lock washer
3. Adjusting nut
4. Washer
5. Outer bearing
6. Retaining ring
7. Inner bearing
8. Oil seal
9. Drum
10. Hub
11. Stud
12. Gasket
13. Shaft
14. Axle shaft flange
15. Washer
16. Bolt
17. Retaining ring
18. Key
19. Adjusting nut
20. Outer bearing
21. Retaining ring
22. Inner bearing
23. Oil seal
24. Axle tube

Full floating axle and components

are positioned properly. Apply a light coat of high melting point EP bearing lubricant to the contact surfaces and the outside of the axle tube.

15. Install the washer with the tang inserted in the keyway.

16. Install the nut and torque to 50 ft. lbs. (68 Nm), while rotating the hub and drum assembly. If the adjusting nut is not aligned with the keyway, back the nut off not more than 1 slot of the lock or the axle spindle using tool J-2222-C.

17. Place a new gasket or apply RTV sealant over the axle shaft flange. Position the shaft in the housing so the shaft splines enter the differential side gear.

18. Align the axle shaft flange holes with the hub and install the attaching bolts. Torque the bolts to 15 ft. lbs. (156 Nm).

19. Install the wheel assembly. Check the differential fluid level and add as required. Lower the vehicle and roadtest.

Front Wheel Hub, Knuckle/Spindle and Bearings

Removal and Installation

R AND G-SERIES

1. Raise and support the vehicle safely.
2. Remove the wheels.
3. Dismount the caliper and suspend it out of the way without disconnecting the brake lines.
4. Remove the hub/rotor assembly as follows:
   a. Remove the dust cap, cotter pin, nut and washer.
   b. Pull the hub and rotor off the spindle and remove the outer bearing.
   c. Place the rotor upside down on a workbench and remove the inner bearing and seal.
5. Unbolt the splash shield and discard the old gasket.
6. Using a tie rod separator, disconnect the tie rod end from the knuckle.
7. Position a floor jack under the lower control arm, near the spring seat. Raise the jack to take up the weight of the suspension, compressing the spring. Safety-chain the coil spring to the lower arm.
8. Remove the upper and lower ball joint nuts.
9. Using tool J-23742 or equivalent, break loose the upper ball joint from the knuckle.
10. Raise the upper control arm to disconnect the upper ball joint.
11. Using the same procedure, break loose the lower ball joint.
12. Lift the knuckle off of the lower ball joint.
13. Inspect and clean the ball stud bores in the knuckle. Make sure there are no cracks or burrs. If the knuckle is damaged in any way, replace the assembly.
14. Check the spindle for wear, heat discoloration or damage. If at all damaged, replace the assembly.

To install:

15. Maneuver the knuckle onto both ball joints.
16. Install both nuts. On ½ ton series, torque the upper nut to 50 ft. lbs. (68 Nm) and the lower nut to 90 ft. lbs. (122 Nm). On ¾ and 1 ton series, torque both nuts to 90 ft. lbs. (122 Nm).
17. Install the cotter pins. Advance the nut to align the cotter pin hole.

NOTE: On the upper nut which was originally torque to 50 ft. lbs. (68 Nm), do not exceed 90 ft. lbs. (122 Nm) when aligning the hole. On nuts torqued originally to 90 ft. lbs. (122 Nm), don't exceed 130 ft. lbs. (175 Nm) to align the cotter pin hole.

18. Remove the floor jack.
19. Install a new gasket and the splash shield. Torque the bolts to 10 ft. lbs. (13.5 Nm).
20. Connect the tie rod end.
21. Install the hub/rotor assembly as follows:
   a. If replacing the bearings, drive the races out using a brass drift and hammer; place the drift behind the race in the notches in the hub.
   b. Clean all the bearings and hubs with a non-flammable solvent. Do not spin the bearings with compressed air to dry, otherwise damage may result.
   c. If reinstalling the original bearings, inspect both the race and bearing for cracks, heat stress or pitting; if either the bearing or race are damaged, replace both components.
   d. Using a suitable race installer, drive the inner and outer races into the hub until fully seated.
   e. Using an approved high temperature grease and bearing packer, fill the inner and outer wheel bearing with lubricant. Place a small amount inside the hub, in the dust cap and on the spindle.
   f. Place the inner bearing into the hub and flat block to install the seal so it is flush with the hub flange.

1. Steering knuckle
2. Shield
3. Seal
4. Inner wheel bearing
5. Wheel hub bolt
6. Outer race
7. Outer wheel bearing
8. Washer
9. Nut
10. Dust cap
11. Cotter pin
12. Wheel hub/rotor
13. Inner race
14. Bolt
15. Washer
16. Gasket

Hub and bearing assembly—R-Series

   g. Install the hub and rotor assembly onto the spindle, install the outer wheel bearing, washer and nut.
   h. Torque the nut to 12 ft. lbs. (16 Nm) while rotating the rotor assembly. Back off the nut until the "just loose" position. finger-tighten the nut until the cotter pin hole in the spindle lines up with the hole in the nut or cage. Do not back off the nut more than ½ of a flat.
   i. Install a new cotter pin.
   j. Rotor endplay should measure between 0.0012–0.0050 in. (0.03–0.13mm) when properly adjusted.
22. Install the caliper.
23. Install the wheels and check the front end alignment.

V-SERIES

Except 30/3500-Series

1. Raise and support the vehicle safely.
2. Remove the wheels.
3. Remove the caliper, hub and rotor assemblies.
4. Remove the spindle attaching nuts and plate. Remove the spindle assembly.
5. Disconnect the tie rod end from the knuckle.
6. Remove the knuckle-to-steering arm nuts and adapters.
7. Remove the steering arm from the knuckle.
8. Remove the cotter pins and nuts from the upper and lower ball joints.

NOTE: Do not remove the adjusting ring from the knuckle. If it is necessary to loosen the ring to remove the knuckle, don't loosen it more than 2 threads. The non-hardened threads in the yoke can be easily damaged by the hardened threads in the adjusting ring if caution is not used during knuckle removal.

9. Insert a ball joint separator between the lower ball joint and the yoke. Drive the prybar in to break the knuckle free.
10. Repeat the procedure at the upper ball joint.
11. Lift off the knuckle.

To install:

12. Position the knuckle on the yoke.

13. Start the ball joints into their sockets. Place the nuts onto the ball studs. The nut with the cotter pin slot is the upper nut. Tighten the lower nut to 30 ft. lbs. (40 Nm).

14. Using tool J–23447, tighten the adjusting ring to 50 ft. lbs. (70 Nm).

15. Tighten the upper ball joint nut to 100 ft. lbs. (135 Nm). Install a new cotter pin. Never loosen the nut to align the cotter pin hole, always tighten the nut.

16. Finish tightening the lower nut to 70 ft. lbs. (95 Nm).

17. Attach the steering arm to the knuckle using adapters and new nuts. Torque the nuts to 90 ft. lbs. (120 Nm).

18. Connect the tie rod end to the knuckle.

19. Install the spindle as follows:

   a. Mount the spindle in a holding fixture and remove the bearing seal and shaft bearing.

   b. Remove the spacer, seal and oil deflector from the shaft.

   c. Inspect all components for wear, heat stress and scoring. Replace as necessary.

   d. Lubricate the shaft bearing and spindle with a high melting point wheel bearing grease.

   e. Using tool J–8092 and J–23445–A, install the bearing and seal into the spindle.

   f. Install the oil seal onto the oil deflector with the deflector lip toward the spindle. Install the oil deflector and seal onto the axle shaft.

   g. Install the spacer onto the axle shaft with the chamfer pointing toward the oil deflector.

   h. Install the spindle onto the steering knuckle.

   i. Install the spindle plate. Install new nuts and washers. Torque the nuts to 65 ft. lbs. (88 Nm).

20. Install the hub/rotor assembly and wheel bearings. Adjust the bearings.

21. Install the locking hubs and caliper assembly.

22. Install the wheel and lower the vehicle.

30/3500-SERIES

1. Raise and support the vehicle safely.
2. Remove the wheel.
3. Remove the caliper assembly.
4. Remove the hub and rotor assembly.
5. Remove the spindle attaching nuts, washers plate and bracket. Remove the spindle assembly.
6. Remove the upper cap from the knuckle and/or steering arm from the knuckle, by loosening the bolts and/or nuts a little at a time in an alternating pattern. This will safely relieve spring pressure under the cap and/or arm. Once spring pressure

A. Chamfer toward the seal
B. Shaft yokes
C. Universal joint
1. Spindle
2. Spacer
3. Seal
4. Oil deflector

Front spindle assembly—V-Series

A. 0.10 in. (2.54mm) depth
1. Spindle
2. Bearing seal
3. Spacer
4. Seal
5. Oil deflector

Front spindle assembly—V-Series

is relieved, remove the bolts and/or nuts, washers and cap and/or steering arm.

7. Remove the gasket and compression spring.

8. Remove the bolts and washers and remove the lower bearing cap and the lower kingpin.

9. Remove the upper kingpin bushing by pulling it out through the knuckle.

10. Remove the knuckle from the axle yoke.

11. Remove the retainer from the knuckle.

12. Using a large breaker bar and adapter J-26871, remove the upper kingpin from the axle yoke by applying 500–600 ft. lbs. (677–813 Nm) of torque to the kingpin to break it free.

13. Using a hammer and blunt drift, drive out the retainer, race bearing and seal from the axle yoke all at once.

To install:

14. Using tool J-7817, install a new retainer and race in the axle yoke.

15. Fill the recessed area in the retainer and race with an approved high temperature wheel bearing lubricant.

16. Completely pack the upper yoke roller bearing with wheel bearing grease. A cone-type bearing packer is preferable but the bearing may be packed by hand.

17. Install the bearing and a new seal in the upper axle yoke, using a bearing driver such as J-22301. Don't distort the seal. It should protrude slightly above the yoke when fully seated.

18. Using adapter tool J-28871, install the upper kingpin. The kingpin must be torque to 550 ft. lbs. (745 Nm).

19. Position the knuckle in the yoke. Working through the knuckle, install a new felt seal over the kingpin and position the knuckle on the kingpin.

20. Install the bushing over the kingpin.

21. Install the compression spring, gasket, bearing cap and/or steering arm and bolts and/or nut and washer. Torque the bolts and/or nuts, in an alternating pattern, to 80 ft. lbs. (108 Nm).

22. Install the lower bearing cap and kingpin. Torque the bolts to 80 ft. lbs. (108 Nm) in an alternating pattern.

23. Thoroughly lube both kingpins through the grease fittings.

24. Install the spindle as follows:

   a. Mount the spindle in a holding fixture and remove the bearing seal and shaft bearing.

   b. Remove the spacer, seal and oil deflector from the shaft.

   c. Inspect all components for wear, heat stress and scoring. Replace as necessary.

   d. Lubricate the shaft bearing and spindle with a high melting point wheel bearing grease.

   e. Using tool J-8092 and J-21465-17, install the bearing and seal into the spindle.

   f. Install the oil seal onto the oil deflector with the deflector lip toward the spindle. Install the oil deflector and seal onto the axle shaft.

   g. Install the spacer onto the axle shaft with the chamfer pointing toward the oil deflector.

   h. Install the spindle onto the steering knuckle.

   i. Install the spindle bracket and plate. Install new nuts and washers. Torque the nuts to 65 ft. lbs. (88 Nm).

25. Install the hub and rotor assembly. Adjust the bearings.

26. Install the locking hubs and caliper assembly.

27. Install the wheel and tire assembly.

28. Lower the vehicle and check the front end alignment.

C-SERIES

1. Raise and support the vehicle safely. Let the control arms hang freely.

2. Remove the wheels.

3. Disconnect the tie rod end from the knuckle.

4. Dismount the caliper and suspend it out of the way without disconnecting the brake lines.

5. Remove the hub/rotor assembly as follows:

   a. Remove the dust cap, cotter pin, nut and washer.

   b. Pull the hub and rotor off the spindle and remove the outer bearing.

1. Cap
2. Cotter pin
3. Nut
4. Washer
5. Outer bearing
6. Outer cup
7. Bolt
8. Hub/disc
9. Inner cup
10. Inner bearing
11. Seal
12. Bolts
13. Caliper
14. Knuckle
15. Gasket
16. Shield

Hub and bearing assembly — C-Series

   c. Place the rotor upside down on a workbench and remove the inner bearing and seal.

6. Unbolt the splash shield from the knuckle and discard the old gasket.

7. If a new knuckle is being installed, remove the knuckle seal carefully, without damaging it.

8. Position a floor jack under the lower control arm, near the spring seat. Raise the jack to take up the weight of the suspension, compressing the spring. Safety chain the coil spring to the lower arm.

9. Remove the upper and lower ball joint nuts.

10. Using tool J-23742 or equivalent, break loose the upper ball joint from the knuckle.

11. Raise the upper control arm just enough to disconnect the ball joint.

12. Using tool J-23742 or equivalent, break loose the lower ball joint.

13. Lift the knuckle off of the lower ball joint.

14. Inspect and clean the ball stud bores in the knuckle. Make sure there are no cracks or burrs. If the knuckle is damaged in any way, replace it.

15. Check the spindle for wear, heat discoloration or damage. If at all damaged, replace it.

To install:

16. Maneuver the knuckle onto both ball joints.

17. Install both nuts. Torque the nuts to 84 ft. lbs. (115 Nm).

18. Install new cotter pins. Always advance the nut to align the cotter pin hole.

19. Install the knuckle seal.

20. Remove the floor jack.

21. Install a new gasket and the splash shield. Torque the bolts to 19 ft. lbs. (26 Nm).

22. Connect the tie rod end.

23. Install the hub/rotor assembly as follows:

   a. If replacing the bearings, drive the races out using a

brass drift and hammer; place the drift behind the race in the notches in the hub.

b. Clean all the bearings and hubs with a non-flammable solvent. Do not spin the bearings with compressed air to dry, otherwise damage may result.

c. If reinstalling the original bearings, inspect both the race and bearing for cracks, heat stress or pitting; if either the bearing or race are damaged, replace both components.

d. Using a suitable race installer, drive the inner and outer races into the hub until fully seated.

e. Using an approved high temperature grease and bearing packer, fill the inner and outer wheel bearing with lubricant. Place a small amount inside the hub, in the dust cap and on the spindle.

f. Place the inner bearing into the hub and flat block to install the seal so it is flush with the hub flange.

g. Install the hub and rotor assembly onto the spindle, install the outer wheel bearing, washer and nut.

h. Torque the nut to 12 ft. lbs. (16 Nm) while rotating the rotor assembly. Back off the nut until the "just loose" position. Finger-tighten the nut until the cotter pin hole in the spindle lines up with the hole in the nut or cage. Do not back off the nut more than ½ of a flat.

i. Install a new cotter pin.

j. Rotor endplay should measure between 0.0012–0.0050 in. (0.03–0.13mm) when properly adjusted.

24. Install the caliper assembly.
25. Install the wheels.
26. Lower the vehicle and check the front end alignment.

K-SERIES

1. Disconnect the negative battery cable.
2. Remove ⅔ of the brake fluid from the reservoir.
3. Raise and support the vehicle safely.
4. Remove the wheel, caliper and brake disc.
5. Remove the drive axle nut and washer.

6. Remove the tie rod nut and remove the tie rod end from the end of the washer.
7. Remove the hub and bearing assembly, using a puller.
8. Remove the drive axle.
9. Remove the splash shield bolts.
10. Remove the splash shield.
11. Support the lower control arm with a jack.
12. Remove the upper and lower ball joint nut and disconnect the upper and lower ball joint from the knuckle.
13. Remove the knuckle and the knuckle seal, as required.

To install:
14. Install the seal into the knuckle, using tool J–36605 or equivalent.
15. Install the knuckle to the upper and lower ball joints and tighten the nuts to 84 ft. lbs. (115 Nm). Tighten the nuts to align the new cotter pin, but do not tighten more than ⅙ turn. Bend the pin ends against the nut flats.
16. Install the splash shield and tighten the bolts to 19 ft. lbs. (26 Nm)
17. Install the drive axle.
18. Install the hub and bearing assembly. Align the threaded holes and tighten the bolts to 133 ft. lbs. (180 Nm).
19. Install the tie rod end to the knuckle, and tighten the tie rod nut to 35 ft. lbs. (48 Nm).
20. Install the washer and axle nut and torque to 173 ft. lbs. (245 Nm).
21. Install the brake disc and caliper.
22. Install the axle joint cover.
23. Install the wheel and tire assembly.
24. Lower the vehicle and check the front end alignment.

Manual Locking Hubs

The engagement and disengagement of the hub is a manual operation which must be performed at each hub assembly. The

Hub, knuckle and ball joints—C/K-Series

1. Internal snapring
2. Hub body
3. Inner drive gear
4. Spring
5. Clutch ring
6. Axle shaft snapring
7. Screw
8. Hub cap
9. Compression spring
10. Clutch cup
11. O-ring seal
12. Dial screw
13. Clutch nut
14. Seal
15. Lock ring

Manual hub components—R-Series

hubs should be placed completely into the **LOCK** or **FREE** position or damage will result.

Locking hubs should be run in the Lock position periodically for a few miles to assure proper differential lubrication.

NOTE: Do not place the transfer case in either 4-wheel mode unless the hubs are in the Lock position!

Removal and Installation

1. Raise and support the vehicle safely.
2. Remove the wheel and tire assembly.
3. Remove the cap retaining bolts and take off the cap, O-ring, and knob assembly.
4. Remove the lock ring from the axle shaft.
5. Remove the internal snapring from the hub.
6. Remove the body assembly. Install 2 screws into the hub body and use as leverage to withdraw the assembly.
7. Installation is the reverse of the removal procedure.

Automatic Locking Hubs

Removal and Installation

NOTE: The following procedure covers removal and installation only, for the hub assembly. The hub should be disassembled only if overhaul is necessary. In that event, an overhaul kit will be required. Follow the instructions in the overhaul kit to rebuild the hub.

1. Remove the screws and washers from the hub.
2. Remove the cap and spring.
3. Remove the bearing race, bearing and retainer.
4. Remove the keeper from the outer clutch housing.

1. Brake band retainer
2. Screw
3. O-ring seal
4. Cover
5. Seal
6. Spring
7. Inner race
8. Bearing
9. Ring
10. Retainer
11. Outer clutch housing
12. Keeper
13. Ring
14. Retainer plate
15. Retainer
16. Return spring
17. Retainer
18. Clutch gear
19. Sleeve
20. Stop ring
21. Conical spring
22. Cam follower
23. Outer cage
24. Inner cage
25. Ring
26. Brake band
27. Drag sleeve
28. Spacer
29. Retaining ring
30. Adjusting nut
31. Lock ring
32. Lock ring
33. Nut with pin
34. Ring

Automatic hub components—R-Series

5. Remove the large snapring to release the locking unit. The snapring is removed by squeezing the ears of the snapring with needle-nose pliers.

6. Remove the locking unit from the hub by threading 2 hub cap screws into the outer clutch housing and pulling out the assembly.

7. Installation is the reverse of the removal procedure.

Pinion Seal

Removal and Installation

1. Raise and support the vehicle safely. It would help to have the front end slightly higher than the rear to avoid fluid loss.

2. Mark and remove the driveshaft.

3. Release the parking brake.

4. Remove the rear wheels. Rotate the rear wheels by hand to make sure there is absolutely no brake drag. If there is brake drag, remove the drums.

5. Using an inch lb. torque wrench on the pinion nut, record the force needed to rotate the pinion.

6. Mark the pinion shaft, nut and flange. Count the number of exposed threads on the pinion shaft.

7. Install a holding tool on the pinion. A very large adjustable wrench will do or if 1 is not available, put the drums back on and set the parking brake as tightly as possible.

8. Remove the pinion nut.

9. Slide the flange off of the pinion. A puller may be necessary.

10. Center punch the oil seal to distort it and pry the seal out, being careful to avoid scratching the bore.

To install:

11. Pack the cavity between the lips of the seal with a lithium-based chassis lube.

12. Use a seal installer, as necessary, and position the seal in the bore and carefully drive it into place, leaving a space between the flange and oil seal of approximately ⅛ in.

13. Place the flange on the pinion and push it on as far as it will go.

14. Install the pinion washer and nut on the shaft and force the pinion into place by turning the nut.

NOTE: Never hammer the flange into place.

15. Tighten the nut, rotating the pinion occasionally until the exact number of threads previously noted appear and the scribed marks are aligned.

16. Measure the rotating torque of the pinion under the same

circumstances as before. Compare both readings. As necessary, tighten the pinion nut in very small increments until the torque necessary to rotate the pinion is 3 inch lbs. higher than the originally recorded torque.

17. Install the driveshaft and check rear fluid level.

18. Lower the vehicle and roadtest.

Front Axle Housing

Removal and Installation

V-SERIES

1. Raise and support the vehicle safely.

2. Matchmark and remove the driveshaft.

3. Disconnect the connecting rod from the steering arm.

4. Disconnect the brake caliper and position it out of the way, without disconnecting the brake line.

5. Disconnect the shock absorbers from the axle brackets.

6. Remove the front stabilizer bar.

7. Disconnect the axle vent tube clip at the differential housing.

8. Take up the weight of the axle assembly using a jack.

9. Remove the nuts, washers, U-bolts and plates from the axle and separate the axle from the springs. Remove the axle assembly from the vehicle.

To install:

10. Position the axle under the vehicle.

11. Install the plates, U-bolts, washers and nuts. Tighten the nuts to specification.

12. Remove the jack.

13. Connect the axle vent tube clip at the differential housing.

14. Install the front stabilizer bar.

15. Connect the shock absorbers at the axle brackets. Torque the bolts to specification.

16. Install the brake caliper assembly.

17. Connect the connecting rod at the steering arm.

18. Install the driveshaft and lower the vehicle.

K-SERIES

1. Raise and support the vehicle safely.

2. Remove the wheels.

3. Remove the skid plate.

4. Drain the carrier.

5. Matchmark and remove the front driveshaft.

6. Disconnect the right axle shaft at the tube flange.

7. Disconnect the left axle shaft at the carrier flange.

8. Wire both axle shafts out of the way.

1. Differential carrier
2. Bushing
3. Clamp
4. Screw
5. Screw
6. Washer
7. Screw
8. Washer
9. Nut
10. Nut
11. Connectors
12. Frame

Front differential carrier mounting – K-Series

9. Unplug the connectors at the indicator switch and actuator.

10. Disconnect the carrier vent hose.

11. Remove the axle tube-to-frame bolts, washers and nuts.

12. Remove the lower carrier mounting bolt.

13. Disconnect the right side inner tie rod end at the relay rod.

14. Depending on model, it may be necessary to remove the engine oil filter.

15. Support the carrier on a floor jack

16. Remove the upper carrier mounting bolt.

17. Lower the carrier assembly from the truck.

To install:

18. Raise the carrier into position.

19. Install the upper carrier mounting bolt, washers and nut. Then, install the lower carrier mounting bolt, washers and nut. Torque the bolts to 80 ft. lbs.

20. Remove the jack.

21. Install the oil filter.

22. Connect the tie rod end. Torque the nut to specification.

23. Install the axle tube-to-frame bolts, washers and nuts. Torque the nuts to specification.

24. Connect the vent hose.

25. Connect the wiring.

26. Connect the axle shafts at the flanges. Torque the bolts to specification.

27. Connect the driveshaft. Torque the bolts to specification.

28. Fill the carrier with SAE 85W-90 gear oil.

29. Install the wheels. Lower the vehicle.

30. Add any engine oil lost when the filter was removed.

Rear Axle Housing

Removal and Installation

ALL SERIES

1. Raise and support the vehicle safely.

2. For the 9¾ in. ring gear and the 10½ in. ring gear axles, place jackstands under the frame side rails for support.

3. Drain the lubricant from the axle housing and remove the driveshaft.

4. Remove the wheel, the brake drum or hub and the drum assembly.

5. Disconnect the parking brake cable from the lever and at the brake flange plate.

6. Disconnect the hydraulic brake lines from the connectors.

7. Disconnect the shock absorbers from the axle brackets.

8. Remove the vent hose from the axle vent fitting, if equipped.

9. Disconnect the height sensing and brake proportional valve linkage, if equipped.

10. Support the stabilizer shaft assembly with a hydraulic jack and remove, if equipped.

11. Remove the nuts and washers from the U-bolts.

12. Remove the U-bolts, spring plates and spacers from the axle assembly.

13. Lower the jack and remove the axle assembly.

To install:

14. Raise the axle assembly into position.

15. Install the U-bolts, spring plates and spacers.

16. Install the nuts and washers on the U-bolts. Torque the nuts to specification.

17. Install the stabilizer shaft.

18. Connect the height sensing and brake proportional valve linkage.

19. Install the vent hose at the axle vent fitting.

20. Connect the shock absorbers at the axle brackets. Torque the nuts to 80 ft. lbs.

21. Connect the hydraulic brake lines.

22. Connect the parking brake cable.

23. Install the wheels.

24. Install the driveshaft.

25. Fill the axle housing.

STEERING

Steering Wheel

Removal and Installation

1. Disconnect the battery ground cable.

2. Remove the horn button cap. On some models, it may be necessary to disconnect the horn wire.

3. Mark the steering wheel-to-steering shaft relationship.

4. Remove the snapring from the steering shaft.

5. Remove the nut and washer from the steering shaft.

6. Remove the steering wheel using a suitable puller.

7. Installation is the reverse of removal. The turn signal control assembly must be in the neutral position to prevent damaging the canceling cam and control assembly. Torque the nut to 30 ft. lbs. (40 Nm).

Manual Steering Gear

Removal and Installation

1. Set the front wheels in straight-ahead position by driving vehicle a short distance on a flat surface.

2. Raise and support the vehicle safely, as required.

4. Remove the steering shaft shield. Matchmark the relationship of the universal yoke to the wormshaft.

5. Remove the universal yoke pinch bolt.

6. Mark the relationship of the pitman arm to the pitman shaft.

7. Remove the pitman shaft nut and then remove the pitman arm from the pitman shaft, using puller J–6632 or J–29107.

8. Remove the steering gear to frame bolts and remove the gear assembly.

To install:

9. Ensure the steering gear is the centered position. Install the steering gear, guiding the steering gear shaft into the universal yoke.

10. Install the steering gear to frame bolts and torque to 100 ft. lbs. (135 Nm).

11. Install the yoke pinch bolt. Torque the pinch bolt to 22 ft. lbs. (30 Nm). Install the steering shaft shield.

12. Install the pitman arm onto the pitman shaft, lining up the marks made at removal. Install the pitman shaft nut torque to 185 ft. lbs. (250 Nm).

Adjustment

Before any steering gear adjustments are made, it is recommended that the front end of the vehicle be raised and supported safely and a thorough inspection be made for stiffness or lost motion in the steering gear, steering linkage and front suspension. Worn or damaged parts should be replaced, since a satisfactory adjustment of the steering gear cannot be obtained, if bent or badly worn parts exist.

It is also very important that the steering gear be properly aligned in the vehicle. Misalignment of the gear places a stress on the steering worm shaft, therefore a proper adjustment is impossible. To align the steering gear, loosen the steering gear-to-frame mounting bolts to permit the gear to align itself. Check the steering gear to frame mounting seat. If there is a gap at any of the mounting bolts, proper alignment may be obtained by placing shims where excessive gap appears. Tighten the steering gear-to-frame bolts. Alignment of the gear in the G-Series is very important and should be done carefully so a satisfactory, trouble-free gear adjustment may be obtained.

The steering gear is of the recirculating ball nut type. The ball nut, mounted on the worm gear, is driven by means of steel balls which circulate in helical grooves in both the worm and nut. Ball return guides attached to the nut serve to recirculate the 2 sets of balls in the grooves. As the steering wheel is turned to the right, the ball nut moves upward. When the wheel is turned to the left, the ball nut moves downward.

Before doing the adjustment procedures given below, ensure that the steering problem is not caused by faulty suspension components, bad front end alignment, etc. Then, proceed with the following adjustments.

Bearing Drag

1. Mark the pitman arm-to-shaft relationship. Remove the pitman arm from the shaft.
2. Disconnect the battery ground cable.
3. Loosen the wormshaft nut and back the adjuster off a ¼ turn. Remove the horn cap.
4. Turn the steering wheel gently to the left stop, then back ½ turn.
5. Position an inch-pound torque wrench on the steering wheel nut and rotate it through a 90 degree arc. Note the torque required to turn the shaft. Proper torque is 5–8 inch lbs. (0.6–1 Nm).

NOTE: Do not use a torque wrench with a maximum torque reading of over 50 inch lbs. (6 Nm).

6. If the torque is incorrect, tighten the adjuster plug until the proper torque reading is achieved.
7. Hold the plug and tighten the adjuster locknut to 85 ft. lbs. (115 Nm).

NOTE: If the gear feels lumpy after adjustment this is probably due to a previous out of adjustment condition and damage has been done to the bearings. The gear will need to be replaced or rebuilt to correct the condition.

Overcenter Preload

1. Turn the steering wheel lock-to-lock counting the total number of turns. Turn the wheel back ½ the total number of turns to the centered position.
2. Turn the lash (sector shaft) adjuster screw clockwise to remove all lash between the ball nut and sector teeth. Tighten the locknut to 22 ft. lbs. (30 Nm).
3. Using a torque wrench on the steering wheel nut, observe the highest reading while the gear is turned through the center position. It should be 16 inch lbs. (1.8 Nm) maximum torque.
4. If necessary repeat the adjustment procedure. Tighten the locknut to 22 ft. lbs. (30 Nm).

Power Steering Gear

Removal and Installation

R/V-SERIES

1. Set the front wheels in straight-ahead position by driving vehicle a short distance on a flat surface. Raise and support the vehicle safely as required.
2. Place a drain pan below the steering gear.
3. Disconnect the negative battery cable.
4. Disconnect the fluid lines. Cap the openings.

5. Mark the relationship of the pitman arm to the pitman shaft.
6. Remove the pitman shaft nut and then remove the pitman arm from the pitman shaft, using puller J–6632.
7. Remove the steering gear to frame bolts and remove the gear assembly.

To install:

8. Align the flat of the flexible coupling with the flat on the shaft. Push the coupling onto the shaft until the wormshaft bottoms against the end of the shaft.
9. Install the pinch bolt. Make sure the bolt passes through the shaft undercut. Tighten the pinch bolt to 75 ft. lbs. (102 Nm).
10. Place the steering gear into position, guiding the coupling bolts into the proper holes in the shaft flange.
11. Install the steering gear to frame bolts and torque to 66 ft. lbs. (90 Nm).
12. Install the coupling flange nuts and washers. Make sure the coupling alignment pins are centered in the flange slots. Tighten the nuts to 20 ft. lbs. (27 Nm). Maintain a coupling to flange dimension of 0.250–0.375 inches (6.4–9.5mm).
13. Install the pitman arm.
14. Install the hoses.

1. Mounting bolt	
2. Spring washer	
3. Pinch bolt	
4. Steering shaft	
5. Coupling nut	9. Adjusting screw
6. Spring washer	10. Side cover
7. Coupling flange	11. Side cover bolt
8. Coupling	12. Adjusting screw jam nut

Power steering gear installation—R-Series

1. Mounting bolt	7. Coupling
2. Pinch bolt	8. Spacer
3. Steering shaft	9. Adjusting screw
4. Coupling nut	10. Side cover
5. Spring washer	11. Side cover bolt
6. Coupling flange	12. Adjusting screw jam nut

Power steering gear installation—V-Series

1. Mounting bolt
2. Pinch bolt
3. Washer
4. Adjusting screw
5. Side cover
6. Side cover bolt
7. Adjusting screw jam nut

Power steering gear installation—G-Series

1. Steering gear
2. Jam nut
3. Adjuster screw
4. Lower intershaft clamp
5. Lower clamp bolt
6. Upper clamp bolt
7. Upper clamp
8. Retaining nut
9. Main shaft
10. Intershaft
11. Steering shaft
12. Feed
13. Return
14. Mounting bolt
15. Washer
16. Shield

Power steering gear installation—C/K-Series

1988–90 C/K-SERIES

1. Set the front wheels in straight-ahead position by driving

vehicle a short distance on a flat surface. Raise and support the vehicle safely, as required.
  2. Place a drain pan below the steering gear.
  3. Disconnect the negative battery cable.
  4. Disconnect the fluid lines. Cap the openings.
  5. Remove the shield, scribe alignment marks on the clamp and the steering shaft and remove the lower clamp bolt. Remove the clamp from the shaft.
  6. Remove the pitman shaft nut and then remove the pitman arm from the pitman shaft, using puller J–6632.
  7. Remove the steering gear to frame bolts and remove the gear assembly.
To install:
  8. Install the steering gear to the frame, the bolts and washers and tighten to 69 ft. lbs. (93 Nm).
  9. Install the pitman arm.
  10. Make sure the alignment marks line up and install the clamp and tighten the bolt to 30 ft. lbs. (41 Nm).
  11. Install the hoses and tighten the hose coupling to 33 ft. lbs. (45 Nm). Bleed the system.

G-SERIES

  1. Set the front wheels in straight-ahead position by driving vehicle a short distance on a flat surface. Raise and support the vehicle safely, as required.
  2. Place a drain pan below the steering gear.
  3. Disconnect the negative battery cable.
  4. Disconnect the fluid lines. Cap the openings.
  5. Matchmark the relationship of the universal yoke to the stubshaft.
  6. Remove the universal yoke pinch bolt.
  7. Mark the relationship of the pitman arm to the pitman shaft.
  8. Remove the pitman shaft nut and then remove the pitman arm from the pitman shaft, using puller J–6632.
  9. Remove the steering gear to frame bolts and remove the gear assembly.
To install:
  10. Ensure the gear is in the centered position. Install the steering gear, guiding the steering gear shaft into the universal yoke.
  11. Install the steering gear to frame bolts and torque to 66 ft. lbs. (90 Nm).
  12. Install the yoke pinch bolt. Torque the pinch bolt to 46 ft. lbs. (62 Nm).
  13. Install the pitman arm onto the pitman shaft, lining up the marks made at removal.
  14. Connect the fluid lines and refill the reservoir. Bleed the system.

Adjustments

For proper adjustment, remove the gear from the vehicle and drain all the fluid from the gear and place the gear in a holding fixture.

It is important that the adjustments be made in the order given.

Worm Bearing Preload

  1. Loosen the adjuster plug locknut.
  2. Turn the adjuster plug in clockwise until firmly bottomed. Then, tighten it to 20 ft. lbs. (27 Nm).
  3. Place an index mark on the gear housing in line with one of the holes in the adjuster plug.
  4. Measure counterclockwise from the mark about ¼ inch and make another mark on the housing.
  5. Rotate the adjuster plug counterclockwise until the hole is aligned with the second mark.
  6. Install the locknut. Hold the plug and tighten the locknut to 81 ft. lbs. (110 Nm).
  7. Place an inch pound torque wrench and 12-point deep

socket on the stub shaft and measure the stub shaft rotating torque, starting with the torque wrench handle in a vertical position to a point ¼ turn to either side. Note your reading. The proper torque should be 4–10 inch lbs. (0.45–1.13 Nm). If the reading is incorrect, either your adjustment was done incorrectly or there is gear damage.

Overcenter Preload

1. Loosen the locknut and turn the pitman shaft adjuster screw counterclockwise until it is all the way out. Then, turn it in ½ turn.
2. Rotate the stub shaft from stop to stop, counting the total number of turns, then turn the shaft ½ that number to center the gear.
3. Place the torque wrench in a vertical position on the stub shaft and measure the torque necessary to rotate the shaft to a point 45 degrees to either side of center. Record the highest reading.
   On gears with less than 400 miles, the reading should be 6–10 inch lbs. higher than the worm bearing preload torque previously recorded, but not to exceed 18 inch lbs. (2 Nm).
   On gears with more than 400 miles, the reading should be 4–5 inch lbs. higher, but not to exceed 14 inch lbs. (1.5 Nm).
4. If necessary, adjust the torque reading by turning the adjuster screw.
5. When the adjustment is made, hold the screw and tighten the locknut to 35 ft. lbs. (47 Nm).
6. Install the gear and bleed the system.

Power Steering Pump

Removal and Installation

1. Place a drain pan under the pump.
2. Disconnect the negative battery cable.
3. Disconnect and cap the hoses at the pump.

NOTE: If equipped with a remote reservoir, disconnect and cap the reservoir hose at the pump.

4. Loosen the pump adjusting bolts and nuts and remove the pump belt.
5. Remove the pulley from the pump as required using a suitable pulley remover/installer tool J–29785–A or equivalent, as required.
6. Remove the adjusting bolts, nuts and brackets and remove the pump assembly.
To install:
7. Connect the brackets to the pump.
8. Place the pulley on the end of the pump shaft and install tool J–25033–B or equivalent.

NOTE: On models with a remote reservoir fill the pump housing with as much fluid as possible before mounting.

9. Install the pump assembly and attaching parts loosely to the engine.
10. Install the hoses to the pump and fill the reservoir. Bleed the pump by turning the pulley backwards (counterclockwise as viewed from the front) until the air bubbles cease to appear.
11. Tighten all retaining bolts and nuts.
12. Install the pump belt over the pulley and adjust.
13. Fill and bleed the system.

System Bleeding

1. Fill the reservoir to the proper level and let the fluid remain undisturbed for at least 2 minutes.
2. Start the engine and run it for only about 2 seconds.
3. Add fluid as necessary.
4. Repeat Steps 1–3 until the level remains constant.
5. Raise the front of the vehicle so the front wheels are off the ground. Set the parking brake and block both rear wheels front and rear. Manual transmissions should be in neutral; automatic transmissions should be in **P**.
6. Start the engine and run it at approximately 1500 rpm.
7. Turn the wheels (off the ground) to the right and left, lightly contacting the stops.
8. Add fluid as necessary.
9. Lower the vehicle and turn the wheels right and left on the ground.
10. Check the level and refill as necessary.
11. If the fluid is extremely foamy, let the vehicle stand for a few minutes with the engine off and repeat the procedure. Check the belt tension and check for a bent or loose pulley. The pulley should not wobble with the engine running.
12. Check that no hoses are contacting any parts of the vehicle, particularly sheet metal.
13. Check the fluid level and refill as necessary.
14. Check for air in the fluid. Aerated fluid appears milky. If air is present, repeat the above operation. If it is obvious that the pump will not respond to bleeding after several attempts, a pressure test may be required.

Tie Rod Ends

Removal and Installation

C/K, R AND G-SERIES

NOTE: Before servicing, note the position of the tie rod adjuster tube and the direction from which the bolts are installed. Do not attempt to disengage the tie rod ball stud using a wedge type tool, because seal damage could result.

1. Raise and support the vehicle safely. As required, remove the tire and wheel assembly.
2. Remove the cotter pins and nuts. Using the proper removal tool J–6627A separate the outer tie rod from the steering knuckle.
3. Disconnect the inner tie rod from the relay rod using tool J–6627A. Remove the tie rod ends from the adjuster tubes, counting the number of turns to aid in installation.
To install:
4. Grease the threads and turn the new tie rod end in as many turns as were needed to remove it. This will give approximately correct toe-in. Tighten the clamp bolts to 14 ft. lbs.
5. Secure the tie rod ends to the relay rod and steering knuckle with a new nut. Tighten the nuts to 40 ft. lbs. (54 Nm) and install new cotter pins. Tighten the nut to align the cotter pin, do not loosen it.
6. Install the tire and wheel assembly.
7. Lower the vehicle and check the front end alignment.

V-SERIES

1. Raise and support the vehicle safely. As required, remove the tire and wheel assembly.
2. Remove the cotter pins and nuts from the rod assembly. Disconnect the shock absorber from the tie rod assembly.
3. Using the proper removal tool, J–6627A, separate the outer tie rods from the steering knuckle.

NOTE: Do not attempt to disengage the ball joint from the steering knuckle using a wedge type tool, because seal damage could result.

4. Disconnect the tie rod end bodies. Count the number of turns needed to remove the end bodies. Remove the tie rod ends from the adjuster tube.
5. Note the position of the adjuster tube and the direction from which the bolts are installed.
To install:
6. Install the tie rod ends the same number of turns as counted previously. Tighten the locknuts.

◀FRT

1. Idler arm
2. Relay rod
3. Tie rod assembly
4. Steering knuckle
5. Pitman arm
6. Steering gear
7. Idler arm frame support

Steering linkage—R-Series

1. Tie rod assembly (V30)
2. Tie rod assembly
3. Steering knuckle
4. Pitman arm
5. Shock absorber
6. Connecting rod assembly
7. Tie rod jam nut

Steering linkage—V-Series

1. Tie rod outer ball joint nut
2. Idler arm frame bolts
3. Steering gear
4. Frame
5. Pitman arm ball stud
6. Knuckle
7. Tie rod ball stud
8. Clamp
9. Clamp nut
10. Adjuster tube
11. Pitman arm nut
12. Tie rod inner ball joint nut
13. Idler arm frame nut
14. Relay rod
15. Idler arm ball joint
16. Idler arm ball joint nut
17. Idler arm mounting bracket
18. Tie rod inner ball joint

Steering linkage – C-Series

1. Tie rod outer ball joint nut
2. Idler arm frame bolts
3. Steering gear
4. Frame
5. Pitman arm ball stud
6. Knuckle
7. Tie rod ball stud
8. Clamp
9. Clamp nut
10. Adjuster tube
11. Pitman arm nut
12. Tie rod inner ball joint nut
13. Idler arm frame nut
14. Relay rod
15. Idler arm ball joint
16. Idler arm ball joint nut
17. Idler arm mounting bracket
18. Tie rod inner ball joint

Steering linkage – K-Series

7. Install the tie rod assembly in the knuckles and tighten the castellated nuts to 40 ft. lbs. (55 Nm). Always advance the nut to align the cotter pin hole. Never back it off.

8. Tighten the tie rod end jam nuts to 175 ft. lbs. (237 Nm).

9. Install the tire and wheel assembly. Lower the vehicle and adjust the front alignment, as required.

1. Idler arm
2. Relay rod
3. Tie rod assembly
4. Steering knuckle
5. Pitman arm
6. Steering gear
7. Shock absorber
8. Bracket
9. Idler arm frame support

Steering linkage—G-Series

BRAKE SYSTEM

For all brake system repair and service procedures not detailed below, please refer to "Brakes" in the Unit Repair section.

Master Cylinder

Removal and Installation

1. Disconnect the negative battery cable. Disconnect any electrical connections from the master cylinder, as required. Disconnect and plug the fluid lines.

2. If equipped with power brakes, remove the master cylinder to power booster retaining bolts. Remove the Rear Wheel Anti-Lock (RWAL) control module assembly, if equipped. Do not allow fluid to leak onto the module.

3. If equipped with manual brakes, remove the master cylinder pushrod from the brake pedal and remove the RWAL control module assembly.

4. Remove the master cylinder from the vehicle. If equipped with power brakes remove the vacuum booster pushrod.

5. Installation is the reverse of the removal procedure. Bench bleed the master cylinder prior to installation. If equipped with power brakes be sure to install the vacuum booster pushrod. Bleed the system, as required.

Proportioning Valve

Removal and Installation

EXCEPT C/K-SERIES

1. Disconnect the negative battery cable. Disconnect the hydraulic lines and plug to prevent dirt from entering the system.

2. Disconnect the warning switch harness.

3. Remove the retaining bolts and remove the valve.

4. Installation is the reverse of removal procedure. Bleed the brake system.

C/K-SERIES

1. Disconnect the negative battery cable. Disconnect the hy-

draulic lines and plug to prevent dirt from entering the system.

2. Disconnect the warning switch harness.

3. Remove the RWAL control module assembly from the bracket.

4. Remove the bolts holding the Isolation/Dump Valve to the bracket.

5. Remove the nuts that hold the master cylinder and bracket to the brake booster.

6. Remove the bracket and combination valve assembly.

7. Installation is the reverse of removal. Tighten the nuts that hold the master cylinder and bracket to the brake booster to 20 ft. lbs. (27 Nm) and the bolts holding the Isolation/Dump Valve to the bracket to 17 ft. lbs. (24 Nm).

8. Bleed the brake system.

Power Brake Boosters

Removal and Installation

VACUUM BOOSTER

1. Disconnect the negative battery cable. Apply the parking brakes.

2. Support the master cylinder and remove the master cylinder mounting nuts.

3. Disconnect the vacuum hose from the check valve.

4. Disconnect the booster pushrod.

5. Remove the booster mounting nuts from inside the vehicle and remove the booster.

6. Installation is the reverse of removal.

HYDRAULIC BOOSTER (HYDRA-BOOST)

1. Disconnect the negative battery cable. Apply the parking brakes.

2. Disconnect the hydraulic lines from the booster.

3. Support the master cylinder and remove the master cylinder mounting nuts.

4. Disconnect the booster pushrod.

5. Remove the booster mounting nuts from inside the vehicle and remove the booster.

6. Installation is the reverse of removal. Bleed the brake system, as follows:

a. To bleed the hydro-boost system, fill the power steering pump to the proper level. Allow the fluid to remain undisturbed for a few minutes.

b. Start the engine and add fluid until the level is constant with the engine running.

c. Raise and support the vehicle safely. Start the engine and turn the wheels from stop to stop, add fluid as required. Turn the engine **OFF** and lower the vehicle.

d. Start the engine and depress the brake pedal several times while rotating the steering wheel from stop to stop. Turn the engine off and pump the brake pedal 4 or 5 times.

e. If the power steering fluid is extremely foamy, allow the vehicle to sit for a short time and then perform the procedure again.

Brake Caliper

Removal and installation

NOTE: There are 2 caliper designs and they can be identified by the method used to secure the assembly to the spindle bracket. The Delco 3000/3100 caliper is secured by a bolt and sleeve combination. The Bendix caliper assembly is secured by a slider, spring and bolt.

1. Remove the cover on the master cylinder and siphon enough fluid out of the reservoirs to bring the level to ⅓ full. This step prevents spilling fluid when the piston is pushed back.

2. Raise and support the vehicle safely. Remove the front wheels and tires.

3. Position a C-clamp around the outside pad and caliper; tighten the C-clamp until the caliper piston bottoms in its bore.

4. Remove the brake hose from the caliper by removing the inlet fitting.

5. Remove the bolt and sleeve or bolt and slider assemblies which hold the caliper and then lift the caliper off the rotor.

6. Remove the inboard and outboard shoe.

To install:

7. Install the pads onto the caliper.

8. Position the caliper onto the knuckle/rotor assembly and secure the asseembly with the mounting bolts or sliders.

9. Reconnect the brake line to the caliper.

10. Pump the brake pedal and verify there is minimal brake pedal travel.

11. Check the brake fluid level. Install the tire and wheel assembly.

12. Lower the vehicle.

1. Inboard pad
2. Outboard pad
3. Bolt
4. Support key
5. Spring
6. Anti-rattle spring

Replacing the disc brake pads—Bendix type

Compressing the caliper piston

1. Bolt boot
2. Mounting bolt assembly
3. Bushing
4. Mounting bolt seal
5. Outboard shoe and lining
6. Wear sensor
7. Inboard shoe and lining
8. Boot
9. Piston
10. Piston seal
11. Bleeder valve
12. Caliper housing

Replacing the disc brake pads—Delco type

Disc Brake Pads

Removal and Installation

DELCO TYPE

1. Remove the cover on the master cylinder and siphon out ⅔ of the fluid. This step prevents spilling fluid when the piston is pushed back into the caliper bore.
2. Raise and support the vehicle safely.
3. Remove the wheels.
4. Compress the brake piston back into its bore using a C-clamp.
5. Remove the 2 bolts which hold the caliper and then lift the caliper off the disc.

NOTE: Do not let the caliper assembly hang by the brake hose.

6. Remove the inboard and outboard shoe.
7. Remove the pad support spring from the piston, if equipped.

To install:

8. Thoroughly inspect, clean and lubricate all caliper slide points, bolts and hardware.
9. Position the retainer spring on the inner pad and insert the assembly into the center cavity of the piston.
10. Push down on the inner pad until it lays flat against the caliper. It is important to push the piston all the way into the caliper if new linings are installed or the caliper will not fit over the rotor.
11. Position the outboard pad with the ears of the pad over the caliper ears and the tab at the bottom engaged in the caliper cutout.
12. With the 2 pads in position, place the caliper over the brake disc and align the holes in the caliper with those of the mounting bracket.

NOTE: Make certain the brake hose is not twisted or kinked.

13. Install the mounting bracket bolts through the sleeves in the inboard caliper ears and through the mounting bracket, making sure the ends of the bolts pass under the retaining ears on the inboard pad.
14. Tighten the mounting bolts to 35 ft. lbs. (48 Nm). After both calipers are mounted pump the brake pedal to seat the pad against the rotor. Use a pair of channel lock pliers to bend over the upper ears of the outer pad so it isn't loose.
15. Install the wheels and lower the vehicle.
16. Add fluid to the master cylinder reservoirs so they are ¼ in. (6.35mm) from the top.
17. Test the brake pedal by pumping it to obtain a hard pedal. Check the fluid level again and add fluid as necessary. Do not move the vehicle until a pedal is obtained.

BENDIX

1. Remove approximately ⅓ of the brake fluid from the master cylinder. Discard the used brake fluid.
2. Raise and support the vehicle safely and remove the wheel.
3. Push the piston back into its bore. This can be done by using a C-clamp.
4. Remove the bolt at the caliper slider. Use a brass drift pin to remove the slider and spring.
5. Rotate the caliper up and forward from the bottom and lift it off the caliper support.
6. Tie the caliper out of the way with a piece of wire. Be careful not to damage the brake line.

7. Remove the inner shoe from the caliper support. Discard the inner shoe clip.
8. Remove the outer shoe from the caliper.

To install:

9. Thoroughly clean, inspect and lubricate the caliper, slider and spring with silicone.
10. Install a new inboard shoe clip on the shoe.
11. Install the lower end of the inboard shoe into the groove provided in the support. Slide the upper end of the shoe into position. Be sure the clip remains in position.
12. Position the outboard shoe in the caliper with the ears at the top of the shoe over the caliper ears and the tab at the bottom of the shoe engaged in the caliper cutout. If assembly is difficult, a C-clamp may be used. Be careful not to damage the lining.
13. Position the caliper over the brake disc, top edge first. Rotate the caliper downward onto the support.
14. Place the spring over the caliper support key, install the assembly between the support and lower caliper groove. Tap into place until the key retaining screw can be installed.
15. Install the screw and torque to 15 ft. lbs. (20 Nm). The boss must fit fully into the circular cutout in the key.
16. Install the wheel and add brake fluid as necessary.

Brake Drums

Removal and Installation

SEMI-FLOATING AXLES

1. Raise and support the vehicle safely.
2. Mark the relationship of the wheel to the hub and remove the wheel.
3. Mark the relationship of the drum to the hub and pull the drum from the brake assembly. If the brake drums have been scored from worn linings, the brake adjuster must be backed off so the brake shoes will retract from the drum. The adjuster can be backed off by inserting a brake adjusting tool through the access hole provided. In some cases the access hole is provided in the brake drum. A metal cover plate is over the hole. This may be removed by using a hammer and chisel.
4. To install, reverse the removal procedure.

FULL FLOATING AXLES

To remove the drums from full floating rear axles, the axle shaft will have to be removed. Full floating rear axles can readily be identified by the bearing housing protruding through the center of the wheel.

1. Raise and support the vehicle safely.
2. Remove the wheel.
3. Remove the axle shaft.
4. Remove the retaining ring, key and adjusting nut.
5. Remove the hub and drum.

To install:

6. Install the hub and drum to the tube.
7. Install the adjusting nut and torque to specification.
8. Install the key and retaining ring.
9. Install the axle shaft and wheel.

Brake Shoes

Adjustment

1. Raise and support the vehicle safely.
2. Remove the lanced area in the backing plate.
3. Turn the adjusting screw until the wheel can just be turned by hand.

4. Back the adjuster screw off 33 notches. There should be no brake drag felt after the adjuster is backed off 15 notches.

5. Install an adjuster hole plug in the backing plate.

6. Repeat the procedure for both wheels.

Removal and Installation

LEADING/TRAILING BRAKES

NOTE: This brake system is used on the lower GVW rated vehicles.

1. Raise the vehicle and support it safely.
2. Remove the tire and wheel assembly.
3. Remove the brake drums.

NOTE: The brake pedal must not be depressed while the drums are removed.

4. Raise the lever arm of the actuator until the upper end is clear of the slot in the adjuster screw.

5. Slide the actuator off the adjuster pin. Disconnect the actuator spring from the shoe.

6. Remove the hold-down spring assemblies and pins.

7. Pull the bottom ends of the shoes apart and lift the lower return spring over the anchor plate. Allow the shoe ends to come together and remove the spring.

8. Remove the shoe assembly, along with the upper return spring and the adjusting screw assembly.

9. Remove the upper return spring and the adjusting screw assembly from the shoes.

10. Remove the retaining ring, pin, spring washer, and parking brake lever.

To install:

11. Clean adjuster wheel and the backing plates with a suitable cleaner. Lubricate the backing plate contact points, levers and adjuster with a suitable lubricant.

12. Assemble the parking lever, spring washer (concave side facing the brake lever), pin, and retaining ring onto the rearward shoe.

13. Install the adjuster pin in the forward shoe with the pin projecting 0.276 in. (7mm) from the side of the shoe web where the adjuster actuator is installed.

14. With the brake shoes laying on a flat surface (the shoe with the parking lever to the rear of the vehicle), install the upper return spring.

15. Install the adjuster screw assembly with the spring clip facing the backing plate.

16. Place the shoes in position on the backing plate. Do not place the lower shoe webs under the anchor plate.

17. Install the lower return spring, spread the bottom of the shoes and position the shoe against the backing plate.

18. Install the hold-down pins and spring assemblies.

19. Install the adjuster actuator over the end of the adjuster pin so the top leg engages the notch in the adjuster screw.

20. Install the actuator spring, being careful not to over-stretch it more than 3.27 in. (83mm).

21. Install the parking brake cable to the lever.

22. Adjust the parking brake if the shoes will not totally retract.

23. Install the drum, tire and wheel assembly. Adjust the rear brakes and lower the vehicle.

DUO-SERVO BRAKES

1. Raise the vehicle and support it safely.
2. Remove the tire and wheel assembly.
3. Remove the brake drums.

1. Actuator spring
2. Upper return spring
3. Adjuster actuator
4. Lower return spring
5. Hold-down spring assembly
6. Hold-down pin
7. Adjuster shoe and lining
8. Shoe and lining
9. Retaining ring
10. Pin
11. Spring washer
12. Park brake lever
13. Access hole plug
14. Inspection cover
15. Backing plate assembly
16. Adjuster pin
17. Adjusting screw assembly
18. Anchor plate
19. Wheel cylinder assembly

Left Side Shown —
Right Side Opposite

Exploded view of the rear drum brake assembly— Leading/Trailing type

1. Hold-down pins
2. Backing plate
3. Parking brake lever
4. Washer
5. Secondary shoe
6. Retaining ring
7. Shoe guide
8. Parking brake strut
9. Strut spring
10. Actuator lever
11. Actuator link
12. Return spring
13. Return spring
14. Hold down spring
15. Lever pivot
16. Lever return spring
17. Adjusting screw assembly
18. Adjusting screw spring
19. Primary shoe

Exploded view of the rear drum brake assembly — Duo-Servo type

NOTE: The brake pedal must not be depressed while the drums are removed.

4. Using a brake tool, remove the shoe return springs.
5. Remove the shoe guide.
6. Remove the hold-down springs and pins.
7. Remove the actuator lever and pivot.
8. Remove the lever return spring.
9. Remove the actuator link, parking brake strut, spring retaining ring.
10. Remove the parking brake lever and washer.
11. Remove the shoe assemblies.
12. Remove the adjuster screw and spring from the shoe assembly.

To install:

13. Use a brake cleaning fluid to remove dirt from the brake drum. Check the drums for scoring, cracks and for out-of-round; service the drums as necessary.
14. Check the wheel cylinders by carefully pulling the lower edges of the wheel cylinder boots away from the cylinders. If there is excessive leakage, the inside of the cylinder will drip fluid; repair or replace as necessary.
15. Check the flange plate, which is located around the axle, for leakage of differential lubricant.
16. Lightly lubricate the parking brake cable, parking brake lever where it enters the shoe and the backing plate-to-shoe contact points. Use high temperature, waterproof, grease or special brake lube.
17. Install the parking brake lever into the secondary shoe with the attaching bolt, spring washer, lockwasher, and nut. It is important that the lever move freely before the shoe is attached. Move the assembly and check for proper action.
18. Lubricate the adjusting screw and make sure it works freely.
19. Connect the adjuster screw and spring to the bottom portion of both shoes. Ensure the spring does not interfere with the adjuster rotation when installed. The primary (smaller shoe pad area) to the front and secondary shoe (larger shoe pad area) to the rear of the vehicle.
20. Install the shoe assembly. Ensuring the shoe webs are positioned correctly against the wheel cylinder.
21. Install the parking brake cable.
22. Secure the primary shoes with the holddown pin and spring.
23. Install the parking brake strut and the strut spring.

24. Install the actuator lever and pivot, securing the assembly with the holddown pin and spring. Install the actuator link and spring.
25. Install the return springs.
26. Check the operation of the self-adjusting mechanism by moving the actuating lever by hand.
27. Adjust the brakes and install the drum.
28. Adjust the parking brake.
29. Install the tire and wheel assembly.
30. Lower the vehicle.

Wheel Cylinders

Removal and Installation

1. Raise and support the vehicle safely.
2. Remove the wheel.
3. Back off the brake adjuster, if necessary, and remove the drum.
4. Disconnect and plug the brake line.
5. Remove the brake shoe upper return springs or remove the shoes, as necessary.
6. Remove the bolts securing the wheel cylinder to the backing plate.
7. Disengage the wheel cylinder pushrods from the brake shoes and remove the wheel cylinder.
8. Installation is the reverse of the removal procedure. Bleed the system.

Parking Brake Cable

Removal and Installation

Front Cable

1. Raise and support the vehicle safely.
2. Remove adjusting nut from equalizer.
3. Remove retainer clip from rear portion of front cable at frame and from lever arm.
4. Disconnect front brake cable from parking brake pedal or lever assemblies. Remove front brake cable. On some models, it may assist installation of the new cable if a heavy cord is tied to other end of cable in order to guide new cable through proper routing.
5. Installation is the reverse of the removal procedure.
6. Adjust the parking brake.

Center Cable

1. Raise and support the vehicle safely.
2. Remove adjusting nut from equalizer.
3. Unhook connector at each end and disengage hooks and guides.
4. Install new cable by reversing removal procedure.
5. Adjust parking brake.
6. Apply parking brake 3 times with heavy pressure and repeat adjustment.

Rear Cable

1. Raise and support the vehicle safely.
2. Remove rear wheel and brake drum.
3. Loosen adjusting nut at equalizer.
4. Disengage rear cable at connector.
5. Bend retainer fingers.
6. Disengage cable at brake shoe operating lever.
7. Install new cable by reversing removal procedure.
8. Adjust parking brake.

Adjustment

The rear brakes serve a dual purpose. They are used as service brakes and as parking brakes. To obtain proper adjustment of the parking brake, the service brakes must first be properly adjusted. Inspect the cables for binding or sticking.

R/V AND G-SERIES

Foot Pedal Type

1. Apply the parking brake 4 notches from the fully released position.
2. Raise and support the vehicle.
3. Loosen the jam nut at the equalizer.
4. Tighten or loosen the adjusting nut until a light drag is felt when the rear wheels are rotated forward.
5. Tighten the check nut.
6. Release the parking brake and rotate the rear wheels. No drag should be felt. If even a light drag is felt, readjust the parking brake.
7. Lower the vehicle.

NOTE: If a new parking brake cable is being installed, pre-stretch it by applying the parking brake hard about three times before making adjustments.

Lever Type

1. Raise and support the vehicle safely. Turn the adjusting knob on the parking brake lever counterclockwise until it stops.
2. Apply the parking brake. Loosen the equalizer nut.
3. Tighten the equalizer nut until light drag is felt while rotating the rear wheels in the forward motion.
4. Adjust the knob on the parking brake lever until a definite snap over center is felt.
5. Release the parking brake. Rotate the rear wheels in the forward motion. There should be no brake drag.

Driveshaft Type

1. Raise and support the vehicle safely. Remove the clevis pin connecting the pull rod and the relay lever.
2. Rotate the brake drum to align the access hole with the adjusting screw. If equipped with manual transmission the access hole is located at the bottom of the backing plate. If equipped with automatic transmission the access hole is located at the top of the shoe.
3. For first time adjustment it will be necessary to remove the driveshaft and the drum in order to remove the lanced area from the drum and clean out the metal shavings.
4. Adjust the screw until the drum cannot be rotated by hand. Back off the adjusting screw 10 notches, the drum should rotate freely.
5. Position the parking brake lever in the fully released position. Take up the slack in the cable to overcome spring tension.

6. Adjust the clevis of the pull rod to align with the hole in the relay lever. Install the clevis pin. Install a new cover in the drum access hole.

C/K-SERIES

1. Raise and support the vehicle safely. Matchmark the wheel to the axle flange. Remove the tire and wheel assembly.
2. Matchmark the drum to the axle flange. Remove the brake drum.
3. Using tool J–21177A or equivalent, measure and record the brake drum inside diameter.
4. Turn the adjuster nut and adjust the shoe and lining to a diameter 0.010–0.020 in. less than the measured inside diameter of the brake drum.
5. Be sure the stops on the parking brake levers are against the edge of the brake shoe web. If not, loosen the parking brake cable adjustment.
6. Tighten the parking brake cable at the adjuster nut until the lever stops begin to move off of the shoe webs. Loosen the adjustment nut until the lever stops move back, barely touching the shoe webs. The final clearance between the stops and either web should be 0.5mm.
7. Install the drums and wheels. Align the assemblies with the matchmarks made during removal.
8. Apply and release the service brake pedal 30–35 times using normal pedal force. Pause about one second between each pedal application.
9. Depress the parking brake six clicks. Check the rear wheels they should not rotate.
10. Release the parking brake lever. Check for free wheel rotation.

Brake System Bleeding

The brake system must be bled when any brake line is disconnected or there is air in the system.

NOTE: Never bleed a wheel cylinder when a drum is removed.

1. Clean the master cylinder of excess dirt and remove the cylinder cover and the diaphragm.
2. Fill the master cylinder to the proper level. Check the fluid level periodically during the bleeding process and replenish it, as necessary. Do not allow the master cylinder fall below ½ full.
3. If the master cylinder is suspected or known to have air in the bore, bleed it before any wheel cylinder or caliper as follows:
    a. Disconnect the forward brake line connection at the master cylinder.
    b. Allow brake fluid to fill the master cylinder bore until it begins to flow from the forward line connector port.
    c. Connect the forward brake line to the master cylinder and tighten.
    d. Have an assistant depress the brake pedal slowly, 1 at a time and hold while loosening the forward brake line connection at the master cylinder to purge the air from the bore. Tighten the connection and then have an assistant release the brake pedal slowly. Wait 15 seconds and repeat the sequence. Repeat the sequence, including the 15 second wait until all air is removed from the bore.
    e. After all air is removed at the forward connection, repeat the above procedure for the rear connection at the master cylinder.
4. Bleed the individual wheel cylinders or calipers only after all air is removed from the master cylinder.
    a. Attach the proper size box end wrench over the bleeder valve.
    b. Attach a length of vinyl hose to the bleeder screw of the brake to be bled. Insert the other end of the hose into a clear jar half full of clean brake fluid, so the end of the hose is beneath the level of fluid. The correct sequence for bleeding is to

work from the brake farthest from the master cylinder to the 1 closest; right rear, left rear, right front, left front.

5. Have an assistant depress and release the brake pedal 1 time and hold. Loosen the bleeder valve to purge the air from the cylinder. Tighten the bleeder screw and slowly release the pedal and wait 15 seconds. Repeat the sequence including the 15 second wait until all air is removed.

NOTE: Make sure an assistant presses the brake pedal to the floor slowly. Rapid pumping of the brake pedal pushes the master cylinder secondary piston down the bore in a way that makes it difficult to bleed the rear side of the system.

6. Repeat this procedure at each of the wheels. Remember to check the master cylinder level occasionally. Use only fresh fluid to refill the master cylinder, not the fluid bled from the system.

7. When the bleeding process is complete, refill the master cylinder, install its cover and diaphragm and discard the fluid bled from the brake system.

Anti-Lock Brake System Service

There are 3 different systems used, Four Wheel Anti-Lock (4WAL) which is used on 1992 C/K-Series vehicles, Zero Pressure Rear Wheel Anti-Lock (ZPRWAL) which is used only on the 1992 3500 HD-Series vehicle and Rear Wheel Anti-Lock (RWAL) which is used on all 1990-92 R/V and G-Series and C/K-Series except those equipped with 4WAL.

Precaution

Failure to observe the following precautions may result in system damage.
- Before performing electric arc welding on the vehicle, disconnect the electronic brake control unit .
- When performing painting work on the vehicle, do not expose the electronic brake control unit to temperatures in excess of 185°F (85°C) for longer than 2 hours. The system may be exposed to temperatures up to 200°F (95°C) for less than 15 minutes.
- Never disconnect or connect the electronic brake control unit connector with the ignition switch ON.
- Never disassemble any component of the Anti-Lock Brake System (ABS) which is designated non-serviceable; the component must be replaced as an assembly.
- When filling the master cylinder, always use Delco Supreme 11 brake fluid or equivalent, which meets DOT-3 specifications; petroleum base fluid will destroy the rubber parts. Do not allow fluid to be spilled on the Electronic Brake Control Unit.

Electronic Brake Control Module

Removal and Installation

EXCEPT 4WAL SYSTEM

1. Disconnect the negative battery cable.
2. Disconnect the electrical connectors from the module.

3. Remove the module from the master cylinder/proportioning valve bracket.
4. Installation is the reverse of the removal procedure.

4WAL SYSTEM

1. Disconnect the negative battery cable.
2. Disconnect the electrical connectors from the module.
3. Disconnect and plug the brake lines at the module.
4. Remove the bolts attaching the module to the fenderwell.
5. Remove the module and bracket assembly from the vehicle.
6. Remove the bracket from the module.
7. Installation is the reverse of the removal procedure.

Isolation/Dump Valve

Removal and Installation

RWAL AND ZPRWAL SYSTEMS

1. Disconnect the negative battery cable.
2. Disconnect and plug the brake line fittings at the isolation/dump valve located under the master cylinder.
3. Remove the master cylinder bracket bolts.
4. Disconnect the electronic brake control unit connector.
5. Remove the isolation/dump valve.
6. Installation is the reverse of the removal procedure.

Front Wheel Speed Sensor

Removal and Installation

4WAL SYSTEM

2 Wheel Drive

1. Disconnect the negative battery cable.
2. Raise and support the vehicle safely.
3. Remove the wheel and tire assembly.
4. Remove the brake caliper, hub and rotor assembly.
5. Remove the sensor wire from the clips on the upper control arm and disconnect the connector.
6. Remove the sensor and backing plate attaching bolts and remove the assembly.
7. Installation is the reverse of the removal procedure.

4 Wheel Drive

1. Disconnect the negative battery cable.
2. Raise and support the vehicle safely.
3. Remove the wheel and tire assembly.
4. Disconnect the sensor wire connector.
5. Remove the bolts securing the sensor and sensor wire.
6. Remove the sensor from the spindle.
7. Installation is the reverse of the removal procedure.

FRONT SUSPENSION

Shock Absorbers

Removal and Installation

R-SERIES AND G-SERIES

1. Raise and support the vehicle safely. Properly support the

lower control arm assembly, as required. Remove the tire and wheel assembly.

2. Remove the upper shock absorber retaining bolt. Remove the lower shock absorber retaining bolt. Vehicles equipped with quad shocks have a spacer between them.

3. Remove the shock absorber from the vehicle.

4. Installation is the reverse of the removal procedure. On the R-Series vehicle, torque the bolts to specification.

V-SERIES

1. Raise and support the vehicle safely.
2. Remove the nuts and eye bolts securing the upper and lower shock absorber eyes. Quad shocks have a spacer between the lower end bushings.
3. Remove the shock absorber(s) and inspect the rubber eye bushings for wear or the shock for leaks, replace the shock absorber assembly as necessary.
4. Installation is the reverse of removal. Make sure the spacer is installed at the bottom end on quad shocks. Torque the upper end nut to 65 ft. lbs. (88 Nm). On dual shocks, torque the lower end to 65 ft. lbs. (88 Nm). On quad shocks, torque the lower end to 89 ft. lbs. (120 Nm).

C-SERIES

1. Remove the upper shock absorber retaining bolt. Raise and support the vehicle safely.
2. Properly support the lower control arm, as required. Remove the lower shock absorber retaining bolt.
3. Remove the shock absorber from the vehicle.
4. Installation is the reverse of removal. Tighten the upper nut to 100 inch lbs. (11 Nm); tighten the lower mounting bolts to 20 ft. lbs. (27 Nm).

K-SERIES

1. Raise and support the vehicle safely.
2. Remove the upper end bolt, nut and washer.
3. Remove the lower end bolt, nut and washer.
4. Remove the shock absorber and inspect the rubber bushings for wear and the shock for leaks, replace the shock absorber assembly necessary.
5. Installation is the reverse of removal. Torque the both nuts to 66 ft. lbs. (90 Nm). Make sure the bolts are inserted in the proper direction. The bolt head on the upper end should be forward; the bottom end bolt head is rearward.

Coil Springs

Removal and Installation

R-SERIES AND G-SERIES

1. Raise and support the vehicle safely under the frame rails. The control arms should hang freely.
2. Remove the wheel.
3. Disconnect the shock absorber at the lower end and move it aside.
4. Disconnect the stabilizer bar from the lower control arm.
5. Support the lower control arm and install a spring compressor on the spring or chain the spring to the control arm as a safety precaution.

NOTE: On vehicles with an air cylinder inside the spring, remove the valve core from the cylinder and expel the air by compressing the cylinder with a prybar. With the cylinder compressed, replace the valve core so the cylinder will stay in the compressed position. Push the cylinder as far as possible towards the top of the spring.

6. Raise the jack to remove the tension from the lower control arm crossshaft and remove the 2 U-bolts securing the cross-shaft to the crossmember.

NOTE: The cross-shaft and lower control arm keeps the coil spring compressed. Use care when lowering the assembly.

7. Slowly release the jack and lower the control arm until the spring can be removed. Be sure all compression is relieved from the spring.

8. If the coil spring was chained, remove the chain and spring. If a compressor was used, remove the spring and slowly release the compressor.
9. Remove the air cylinder, if equipped.

To install:

10. Install the air cylinder so the protector plate is towards the upper control arm. The schrader valve should protrude through the hole in the lower control arm.
11. Install the chain and spring or compress the spring and install the assembly.
12. Slowly raise the jack and lower control arm. Line up the indexing hole in the shaft with the crossmember attaching studs.
13. Install the 2 U-bolts securing the cross-shaft to the crossmember. Torque the nuts to 85 ft. lbs. (115 Nm).
14. Remove the jack.
15. Connect the stabilizer bar to the lower control arm. Torque the nuts to 24 ft. lbs.
16. Connect the shock absorber at the lower end. Torque the bolt to specification.
17. If equipped with air cylinders, inflate the cylinder to 60 psi.
18. Install the wheel.
19. Lower the vehicle. Once the weight of the vehicle is on the wheels, reduce the air cylinder pressure to 50 psi.
20. Check the front end alignment.

C-SERIES

1. Raise and support the vehicle safely. Allow the control arms to hang free. Remove the tire and wheel assembly. Remove the shock absorber assembly, as required.
2. Install tool J–23028 under the lower control arm using a suitable jack. Install a safety chain around the spring and through the lower control arm.
3. Remove the stabilizer shaft from the lower control arm. Raise the jack and remove the tension on the lower control arm bolts.
4. Remove the lower control arm rear bolt, than remove the other retaining bolt.
5. Lower the jack and allow the lower control arm to hang free. Remove the spring assembly from the vehicle.

To install:

6. Install the chain and spring. If you used spring compressors, install the spring and compressors.
   a. Make sure the insulator is in place.
   b. Make sure the tape is at the lower end. New springs will have an identifying tape.
   c. Make sure the gripper notch on the top coil is in the frame bracket.
   d. Make sure 1 drain hole in the lower arm is covered by the bottom coil and the other is open.
7. Slowly raise the jack and lower control arm. Guide the control arm into place with a prybar.
8. Install the pivot shaft bolts, front one first. The bolts must be installed with the heads towards the front of the vehicle. Remove the safety chain or spring compressors.

NOTE: Do not torque the bolts yet. The bolts must be torque with the vehicle at its proper ride height.

9. Remove the jack.
10. Connect the stabilizer bar to the lower control arm. Torque the nuts to specification.
11. Install the shock absorber.
12. Install the wheel.
13. Lower the vehicle. Once the weight of the vehicle is on the wheels check the "Z" height as follows:
    a. Lift the front bumper about 1½ in. (38mm) and let it drop.
    b. Repeat this procedure 2 or 3 more times.
    c. Draw a line on the side of the lower control arm from the centerline of the control arm pivot shaft, dead level to the outer end of the control arm.

A. C-Series	7. Steering knuckle lower corner
B. K-Series	8. Nut
C. K-Series torsion bar	9. Torsion bar support assembly
D. C/K-Series rear suspension	10. Torsion bar adjustment arm
1. Lower ball joint	11. Bolt—1 turn equals 6mm height change
2. Lower control arm	12. Frame
3. Pivot bolt center line	13. Bottom surface of jounce bracket
4. "Z" Height C1, 2, 3—89–101mm K1, 2—151–163mm K3—139–151mm	14. "D" Height
5. Lower ball joint extrusion	15. Rear axle
6. Steering knuckle	16. Jounce bumper

Trim height adjustment—C/K-Series

d. Measure the distance between the lowest corner of the steering knuckle and the line on the control arm. Record the figure.

e. Push down about 38mm on the front bumper and let it return. Repeat the procedure 2 or 3 more times.

f. Re-measure the distance at the control arm.

g. Determine the average of the 2 measurements.

h. If the figure is correct, tighten the control arm pivot nuts to 121 ft. lbs. (165 Nm). Align the front end. If the figure is incorrect, replace the coil spring.

Leaf Spring

Removal and Installation

V-SERIES

1. Raise and support the vehicle and front axle safely so all tension is taken off of the front leaf springs.

2. Remove the shackle retaining bolts, nuts and spacers.

3. Remove the front spring-to-frame bracket bolt, washer and nut.

4. On the 10/1500 and 20/2500 both sides and the 30/3500 left side: remove the U-bolt nuts, washers, U-bolts, plate and spacers.

5. On the 30/3500 right side: remove the inboard spring plate bolts, U-bolt nuts, washers, U-bolt, plate and spacers.

6. To replace the bushing, place the spring in a press or vise and press out the bushing. Press in the new bushing. The new bushing should protrude evenly on both sides of the spring.

7. Installation is the reverse of removal. Coat all bushings with silicone grease prior to installation. Install all bolts and nuts finger-tight. When all fasteners are installed, torque the bolts. Torque the U-bolt nuts, including the inboard right side 30/3500 series bolts, in the crisscross pattern shown, to 150 ft. lbs. (213 Nm). Torque the shackle nuts to 50 ft. lbs. (68 Nm). Torque the front eye bolt nut to 90 ft. lbs. (122 Nm).

Torsion Bar

Removal and Installation

K-SERIES

1. Raise and support the vehicle safely.
2. Remove the wheels.
3. Support the lower control arm with a floor jack.
4. Matchmark the both torsion bar adjustment bolt positions.
5. Using tool J-36202, increase the tension on the adjusting arm.
6. Remove the adjustment bolt and retaining plate.
7. Move the tool aside.
8. Slide the torsion bars forward.
9. Remove the adjusting arms.
10. Remove the nuts and bolts from the torsion bar support crossmember and slide the support crossmember rearward.
11. Matchmark the position of the torsion bars and note the markings on the front end of each bar. They are not interchangeable. Remove the torsion bars.
12. Remove the support crossmember.
13. Remove the retainer, spacer and bushing from the support crossmember.

To install:
14. Assemble the retainer, spacer and bushing on the support.
15. Position the support assembly on the frame, out of the way.
16. Align the matchmarks and install the torsion bars, sliding them forward until they are supported.
17. Install the adjuster arms on the torsion bars.
18. Bolt the support crossmember into position. Torque the center nut to 18 ft. lbs. (24 Nm); the edge nuts to 46 ft. lbs. (62 Nm).
19. Install the adjuster retaining plate and bolt on each torsion bar.
20. Using tool J-36202, increase tension on both torsion bars.
21. Install the adjustment retainer plate and bolt on both torsion bars.
22. Set the adjustment bolt to the marked position.
23. Release the tension on the torsion bar until the load is take up by the adjustment bolt.
24. Remove the tool.
25. Install the wheels.
26. Check the front end alignment and "Z" height.

Ball Joints

Inspection

1. Raise the vehicle and position floor stands under the left and right lower control arm as near as possible to each lower ball joint. There should be sufficient space between the upper control arm bumper and frame after the lower control arm has been supported.
2. Position a dial indicator against the wheel rim.

3. Grasp the front wheel; push in on bottom of the tire while pulling out at the top. Read the gauge, then reverse the push-pull procedure. Horizontal deflection on the dial indicator should not exceed 1.125 in. (3.18mm).

4. If the indicator exceeds 1.125 in. (3.18mm) or if the ball stud, when disconnected from the knuckle assembly, can be twisted in its socket by hand, replace the ball joint.

Upper Ball Joints

Removal and Installation

R-SERIES AND G-SERIES

1. Raise and support the vehicle safely. Properly support the lower control arm.
2. Remove the wheel assembly. Remove the brake caliper and position it to the side.
3. Remove the cotter pin and the upper ball joint retaining bolt. Using the proper tool separate the upper joint from its mounting. Support the knuckle assembly so its weight will not damage the brake hose.
4. Remove the rivets from the ball joint assembly, using the proper tools. Remove the ball joint from the upper control arm.
To install:
5. Install the new ball joint into the control arm. Position the bleed vent in the rubber boot facing inward.
6. Secure the ball joint to the control arm using the new nuts and bolts.
7. Lower the upper arm ball joint stud into the steering knuckle.
8. Install the ball stud nut and torque to specification. Tighten the nut to align the cotter pin hole.
9. Install the brake caliper, if removed.
10. Install a new lube fitting and lubricate the new joint.
11. Install the tire and wheel.
12. Lower the vehicle.

V-SERIES

1. Raise and support the vehicle safely. Remove the tire and wheel assembly.
2. Remove the hub and rotor assembly. Remove the spindle.
3. Remove the steering knuckle assembly. If removing the left axle yoke ball joints, remove the steering arm. Position the steering knuckle assembly in a suitable vise.
4. The lower ball joint must be removed before service can be performed on the upper ball joint. first. Remove the snapring from the lower ball joint and press the ball joint from the knuckle assembly, using the proper tools.
5. Press the upper ball joint from the knuckle assembly, using the proper tools.
6. Installation is the reverse of the removal procedure. Check and adjust front alignment, as required.

C-SERIES

1. Raise and support the vehicle safely. Properly support the lower control arm, using the necessary equipment.
2. Remove the tire and wheel assembly. Remove the brake caliper and position it to the side.
3. Remove the cotter pin and the upper ball joint retaining bolt. Using the proper tool separate the upper joint from its mounting. Support the knuckle assembly so its weight will not damage the brake hose.
4. Remove the rivets from the ball joint assembly, using the proper tools. Remove the ball joint from the upper control arm.
To install:
5. Install the replacement ball joint in the control arm, using the bolts and nuts supplied. Torque the nuts to 18 ft. lbs. (24 Nm).

6. Position the ball stud in the knuckle. Make sure it is squarely seated. Torque the ball stud nut to 84 ft. lbs. (115 Nm).

7. Install a new cotter pin.

8. Install a new lube fitting and lubricate the new joint.

9. If removed, install the brake caliper.

10. Install the wheel and lower the vehicle. Check and align the front end.

K-SERIES

1. Raise and support the vehicle safely.

2. Remove the wheel.

3. Unbolt the brake hose bracket from the control arm.

4. Using a 1/8 in. drill bit, drill a pilot hole through each ball joint rivet.

5. Drill out the rivets with a 1/2 in. drill bit. Punch out any remaining rivet material.

6. Remove the cotter pin and nut from the ball stud.

7. Support the lower control arm with a floor jack.

8. Using a ball joint separator, separate the stud from the knuckle.

To install:

9. Position the new ball joint on the control arm.

NOTE: Service replacement ball joints come with nuts and bolts to replace the rivets.

10. Install the bolts and nuts. Tighten the nuts to 17 ft. lbs. (23 Nm) for 15 and 25-Series; 52 ft. lbs. (70 Nm) for 35-Series.

NOTE: The bolts are inserted from the bottom.

11. Start the ball stud into the knuckle. Make sure it is squarely seated. Install the ball stud nut and pull the ball stud into the knuckle with the nut. Torque the nut after the vehicle wheel are on the ground and the suspension is loaded.

12. Install the wheel.

13. Lower the vehicle. Once the weight of the vehicle is on the wheels tighten the nut to 84 ft. lbs. (115 Nm).

Lower Ball Joint

Removal and Installation

R-SERIES AND G-SERIES

1. Raise and support the vehicle safely. Properly support the lower control arm, using the necessary equipment.

2. Remove the tire and wheel assembly. As required, remove the brake caliper and position it to the side.

3. Remove the cotter pin and the lower ball joint retaining bolt. Using the proper tool separate the ball joint from its mounting. Support the knuckle assembly so its weight will not damage the brake hose.

4. Press the ball joint out of the lower control arm, using the proper tool.

To install:

5. Start the new ball joint into the control arm. Position the bleed vent in the rubber boot facing inward.

6. Press the ball joint into the control arm until fully seated.

7. Lower the upper arm and insert the lower ball joint stud into the steering knuckle.

8. Install the brake caliper, if removed.

9. Install the ball stud nut and torque to 90 ft. lbs. (122 Nm) plus the additional torque necessary to align the cotter pin hole. Do not exceed 130 ft. lbs. (175 Nm) or back the nut off to align the holes with the pin.

10. Install a new lube fitting and lubricate the new joint.

11. Install the tire and wheel.

12. Lower the vehicle.

C-SERIES

1. Raise and support the vehicle safely. Properly support the lower control arm, using the necessary equipment.

2. Remove the tire and wheel assembly. As required, remove the brake caliper and position it to the side.

3. Remove the cotter pin and the lower ball joint retaining nut. Using the proper tool separate the ball joint from its mounting. Support the knuckle assembly so its weight will not damage the brake hose.

4. Remove the rivets from the ball joint assembly, using the proper tools. Remove the ball joint from the control arm.

To install:

5. Secure the new ball joint to the control arm.

6. Position the ball joint into the knuckle. Install the nut and tighten it to 84 ft. lbs. (115 Nm).

7. Advance the nut to align the cotter pin hole and insert the new cotter pin.

8. Install the brake caliper, if removed.

9. Install a new lube fitting and lubricate the new joint.

10. Install the wheel.

11. Lower the vehicle.

12. Check the front end alignment.

K-SERIES

1. Raise and support the vehicle safely.

2. Remove the wheel.

3. Remove the splash shield from the knuckle.

4. Disconnect the inner tie rod end from the relay rod using a ball joint separator.

5. Remove the hub nut and washer. Insert a long drift or dowel through the vanes in the brake rotor to hold the rotor in place.

6. Remove the axle shaft inner flange bolts.

7. Using a puller, force the outer end of the axle shaft out of the hub. Remove the shaft.

8. Using a 1/8 in. drill bit, drill a pilot hole through each ball joint rivet.

9. Drill out the rivets with a 1/2 in. drill bit. Punch out any remaining rivet material.

10. Remove the cotter pin and nut from the ball stud.

11. Support the lower control arm with a floor jack.

12. Matchmark the both torsion bar adjustment bolt positions.

13. Using tool J-36202, increase the tension on the adjusting arm.

14. Remove the adjustment bolt and retaining plate.

15. Move the tool aside.

16. Slide the torsion bars forward.

17. Using a screw-type forcing tool, separate the ball joint from the knuckle.

To install:

18. Position the new ball joint on the control arm.

NOTE: Service replacement ball joints come with nuts and bolts to replace the rivets.

19. Install the bolts and nuts. Tighten the nuts to 45 ft. lbs.

NOTE: The bolts are inserted from the bottom.

20. Start the ball stud into the knuckle. Make sure it is squarely seated. Install the ball stud nut and pull the ball stud into the knuckle with the nut. Don't final-torque the nut yet.

21. Using tool J-36202, increase tension on both torsion bars.

22. Install the adjustment retainer plate and bolt on both torsion bars.

23. Set the adjustment bolt to the marked position.

24. Release the tension on the torsion bar until the load is take up by the adjustment bolt.

25. Remove the tool.

26. Position the shaft in the hub and install the washer and hub nut. Leave the drift in the rotor vanes and tighten the hub nut to 175 ft. lbs.

27. Install the flange bolts. Tighten them to 59 ft. lbs. Remove the drift.

28. Connect the inner tie rod end at the steering relay rod. Torque the nut to 35 ft. lbs.
29. Install the splash shield.
30. Install the wheel.
31. Lower the vehicle. Once the weight of the vehicle is on the wheels:

a. Lift the front bumper about 1-½ in. (38mm) and let it drop.

b. Repeat this procedure 2 or 3 more times.

c. Draw a line on the side of the lower control arm from the centerline of the control arm pivot shaft, dead level to the outer end of the control arm.

d. Measure the distance between the lowest corner of the steering knuckle and the line on the control arm. Record the figure.

e. Push down about 1½ in. (38mm) on the front bumper and let it return. Repeat the procedure 2 or 3 more times.

f. Re-measure the distance at the control arm.

g. Determine the average of the 2 measurements. The average distance should be as specified.

h. If the figure is correct, tighten the control arm pivot nuts to 94 ft. lbs. (128 Nm).

i. If the figure is not correct, tighten the pivot bolts to 94 ft. lbs. (128 Nm) and have the front end alignment corrected.

V-SERIES

1. Raise and support the vehicle safely.
2. Remove the wheels.
3. Remove the locking hubs.
4. Remove the spindle.
5. Disconnect the tie rod end from the knuckle.
6. Remove the knuckle-to-steering arm nuts and adapters.
7. Remove the steering arm from the knuckle.
8. Remove the cotter pins and nuts from the upper and lower ball joints.

NOTE: Do not remove the adjusting ring from the knuckle. If it is necessary to loosen the ring to remove the knuckle, don't loosen it more than 2 threads. The non-hardened threads in the yoke can be easily damaged by the hardened threads in the adjusting ring if caution is not used during knuckle removal.

9. Insert the wedge-shaped end of the heavy prybar or wedge-type ball joint tool, between the lower ball joint and the yoke. Drive the prybar in to break the knuckle free.
10. Repeat the procedure at the upper ball joint.
11. Lift off the knuckle.
12. Secure the knuckle in a vise.
13. Remove the snapring from the lower ball joint. Using tools J–9519–30, J–23454–1 and J–23454–4 or their equivalent screw-type forcing tool, force the lower ball joint from the knuckle.
14. Using tools J–9519–30, J–23454–3 and J–23454–4 or their equivalent screw-type forcing tool, force the upper ball joint from the knuckle.
To install:
15. Position the lower ball joint (the one without the cotter pin hole) squarely in the knuckle. Using tools J–9519–30, J–23454–2 and J–23454–3 or their equivalent screw-type forcing tool, force the lower ball joint into the knuckle until it is fully seated.
16. Install the snapring.
17. Position the upper ball joint (the one with the cotter pin hole) squarely in the knuckle. Using tools J–9519–30, J–23454–2 and J–23454–3 or their equivalent screw-type forcing tool, force the upper ball joint into the knuckle until it is fully seated.
18. Position the knuckle on the yoke.
19. Start the ball joints into their sockets. Place the nuts onto the ball studs. The nut with the cotter pin slot is the upper nut. Tighten the lower nut to 30 ft. lbs. (40 Nm), for now.
20. Using tool J–23447, tighten the adjusting ring to 50 ft. lbs. (68 Nm).

21. Tighten the upper nut to specification. Install a new cotter pin. Never loosen the nut to align the cotter pin hole; always tighten it.
22. Tighten the lower nut to specification.
23. Attach the steering arm to the knuckle using adapters and new nuts.
24. Connect the tie rod end to the knuckle.
25. Install the spindle.
26. Install the hub/rotor assembly and wheel bearings. Adjust the bearings.
27. Install the locking hubs.
28. Install the wheel.
29. Check the front end alignment.

Upper Control Arm

Removal and Installation

R-SERIES AND G-SERIES

1. Note and record the amount of shims. These shims must be installed in the same location as removed. Remove the nuts and the shims.
2. Raise and support the vehicle safely. Properly support the lower control arm, using the necessary equipment. The control arm must be supported so the spring and the control arm remain intact.
3. Remove the tire and wheel assembly. Remove the brake caliper assembly and position it to the side. Loosen the upper ball joint from the steering knuckle, using the proper tool. Support the hub assembly.
4. Remove the upper control arm retaining bolts. Remove the upper control arm from the vehicle.
To install:
5. Place the control arm in position and install the nuts. Before tightening the nuts, insert the caster and camber shims in the same order as when installed.
6. Install the nuts securing the control arm shaft studs to the crossmember bracket. Tighten the nuts to 70 ft. lbs. (95 Nm) for 10/1500 series; 105 ft. lbs. (142 Nm) for all other series.
7. Install the ball stud nut. Torque the nut to 50 ft. lbs. (68 Nm) for 10/1500 series; 90 ft. lbs. (122 Nm) for all other series.
8. Install the cotter pin. Never back off the nut to install the cotter pin. Always advance it.
9. Install the brake caliper. Remove the spring compressor.
10. Install the wheel.
11. Check the front end alignment.

C/K-SERIES

1. Raise and support the vehicle safely.
2. Support the lower control arm with a floor jack.
3. Remove the wheel.
4. Unbolt the brake hose bracket from the control arm.
5. Remove the air cleaner extension.
6. Remove the cotter pin from the upper control arm ball stud and loosen the stud nut until the bottom surface of the nut is slightly below the end of the stud.
7. Install a spring compressor on the coil spring for safety.
8. Using a screw-type forcing tool, break loose the ball joint from the knuckle.
9. Remove the nuts and bolts securing the control arm to the frame brackets.
10. The 35-Series bushings are replaceable. The 15/25-Series bushings are welded in place.
To install:
11. Place the control arm in position and install the shims, bolts and new nuts. Both bolt heads must be inboard of the control arm brackets. Tighten the nuts finger-tight for now.

NOTE: Do not torque the bolts yet. The bolts must be torque with the vehicle at its proper ride height.

12. Install the ball stud nut. Torque the nut to 84 ft. lbs. (115 Nm). Install the cotter pin. Never back off the nut to install the cotter pin.

13. Install the brake caliper.

14. Remove the spring compressor or safety chain.

15. Install the wheel.

16. Install the brake hose.

17. Install the air cleaner extension.

18. Install the battery ground cable.

19. Lower the vehicle. Once the weight of the vehicle is on the wheels:

a. Lift the front bumper about 38mm and let it drop.

b. Repeat this procedure 2 or 3 more times.

c. Draw a line on the side of the lower control arm from the centerline of the control arm pivot shaft, dead level to the outer end of the control arm.

d. Measure the distance between the lowest corner of the steering knuckle and the line on the control arm. Record the figure.

e. Push down about 38mm on the front bumper and let it return. Repeat the procedure 2 or 3 more times.

f. Re-measure the distance at the control arm.

g. Determine the average of the 2 measurements. The average distance should be as specified.

h. If the figure is correct, tighten the control arm pivot nuts to 139 ft. lbs. (190 Nm).

i. If the figure is not correct, adjust or repair the ride height.

Lower Control Arm

Removal and Installation

R-SERIES AND G-SERIES

1. Raise and support the vehicle safely. Properly support the lower control arm assembly. Remove the tire and wheel assembly. Remove the brake caliper and position it to the side.

2. Remove the control arm u-bolts and remove the coil spring. Remove the lower ball joint cotter pin and retaining nut. Using the proper tool, separate the lower ball joint from the steering knuckle.

3. Remove the lower control arm from the vehicle.

To install:

4. Install the lower control arm and spring assembly. Torque the U-bolts to 85 ft. lbs. (115 Nm).

5. Install the ball stud nut. Torque the nut to 90 ft. lbs. (122 Nm). Install the cotter pin. Never back off the nut to install the cotter pin.

6. Install the brake caliper.

C-SERIES

1. Raise and support the vehicle safely. Remove the tire and wheel assembly. Properly support the lower control arm assembly. Remove the lower control arm bolts and coil spring.

2. Remove the lower ball joint cotter pin and retaining nut. Using the proper tool, separate the lower ball joint from the steering knuckle.

3. Remove the lower control arm from the vehicle.

To install:

4. Slowly raise the jack and lower control arm with the coil spring. Guide the control arm into place with a prybar.

5. Install the pivot shaft bolts, front one first. The bolts must be installed with the heads towards the front of the vehicle. Remove the safety chain or spring compressors.

NOTE: Do not torque the bolts yet. The bolts must be torque with the vehicle at its proper ride height.

6. Remove the jack.

7. Connect the stabilizer bar to the lower control arm. Torque the nuts to specification.

8. Install the shock absorber.

9. Install the wheel.

10. Lower the vehicle. Once the weight of the vehicle is on the wheels proceed as follows:

a. Lift the front bumper about 1½ in. (38mm) and let it drop.

b. Repeat this procedure 2 or 3 more times.

c. Draw a line on the side of the lower control arm from the centerline of the control arm pivot shaft, dead level to the outer end of the control arm.

d. Measure the distance between the lowest corner of the steering knuckle and the line on the control arm. Record the figure.

e. Push down about 1½ in. (38mm) on the front bumper and let it return. Repeat the procedure 2 or 3 more times.

f. Re-measure the distance at the control arm.

g. Determine the average of the 2 measurements. The average distance should be 73.6mm ± 6mm.

h. If the figure is correct, tighten the control arm pivot nuts to specification.

i. If the figure is not correct, tighten the pivot bolts and check the front end alignment corrected.

K-SERIES

1. Raise and support the vehicle safely.

2. Remove the wheel.

3. Remove the splash shield from the knuckle.

4. Disconnect the stabilizer bar from the control arm.

5. Remove the shock absorber.

6. Disconnect the tie rod end from the relay rod.

7. Remove the hub nut and washer. Insert a long drift or dowel through the vanes in the brake rotor to hold the rotor in place.

8. Remove the axle shaft inner flange bolts.

9. Using a puller, force the outer end of the axle shaft out of the hub. Remove the shaft.

10. Support the lower control arm with a floor jack.

11. Matchmark the both torsion bar adjustment bolt positions.

12. Using tool J-36202, increase the tension on the adjusting arm.

13. Remove the adjustment bolt and retaining plate.

14. Move the tool aside.

15. Slide the torsion bars forward.

16. Remove the adjusting arm.

17. Remove the cotter pin from the lower ball stud and loosen the nut.

18. Loosen the lower ball stud in the steering knuckle using a ball joint stud removal tool. When the stud is loose, remove the nut from the stud. It may be necessary to remove the brake caliper and wire it to the frame to gain clearance.

19. Remove the control arm-to-frame bracket bolts, nuts and washers.

20. Remove the lower control arm and torsion bar as a unit.

21. Separate the control arm and torsion bar.

22. On 15 and 25-Series, the bushings are not replaceable. If they are damaged, the control arm will have to be replaced. On 35-Series, proceed as follows:

a. FRONT BUSHING: Unbend the crimps with a punch. Force out the bushings with tools J-36618-2, J-9519-23, J-36618-4 and J-36618-1.

b. REAR BUSHING: Force out the bushings with tools J-36618-5, J-9519-23, J-36618-3 and J-36618-2. There are no crimps.

To install:

23. On 35-Series, install a new front bushings, then a new rear bushing using the removal tools.

24. Assemble the control arm and torsion bar.

25. Raise the control arm assembly into position. Insert the front leg of the control arm into the crossmember first, then the rear leg into the frame bracket.

26. Install the bolts, front one first. The bolts must be installed with the front bolt head heads towards the front of the vehicle and the rear bolt head towards the rear of the vehicle!

NOTE: Do not torque the bolts yet. The bolts must be torque with the vehicle at its proper ride height.

27. Start the ball joint into the knuckle. Make sure it is squarely seated. Tighten the nut to 96 ft. lbs. and install a new cotter pin. Always advance the nut to align the cotter pin hole. Never back it off.

28. Install the adjuster arm.

29. Using tool J-36202, increase tension on both torsion bars.

30. Install the adjustment retainer plate and bolt on both torsion bars.

31. Set the adjustment bolt to the marked position.

32. Release the tension on the torsion bar until the load is take up by the adjustment bolt.

33. Remove the tool.

34. Position the shaft in the hub and install the washer and hub nut. Leave the drift in the rotor vanes and tighten the hub nut to specification.

35. Install the flange bolts. Tighten to specification. Remove the drift.

36. Connect the inner tie rod end at the steering relay rod. Torque the nut to specification.

37. Install the splash shield.

38. Connect the stabilizer bar to the lower control arm. Torque the nuts to specification.

39. Install the shock absorber.

40. Install the wheel.

41. Lower the vehicle. Once the weight of the vehicle is on the wheels proceed as follows:

   a. Lift the front bumper about 1½ in. (38mm) and let it drop.

   b. Repeat this procedure 2 or 3 more times.

   c. Draw a line on the side of the lower control arm from the centerline of the control arm pivot shaft, dead level to the outer end of the control arm.

   d. Measure the distance between the lowest corner of the steering knuckle and the line on the control arm. Record the figure.

   e. Push down about 1½ in. (38mm) on the front bumper and let it return. Repeat the procedure 2 or 3 more times.

   f. Re-measure the distance at the control arm.

   g. Determine the average of the 2 measurements. The average distance should be 73.6mm ± 6mm.

   h. If the figure is correct, tighten the control arm nuts to specification.

22. Washer	7. Washer
23. Nut	8. Reinforcement
24. Nut	9. Bracket
25. Retainer	10. Nut
26. Bushing	11. Rivet
27. Nut	12. Fitting
28. Upper control arm	13. Upper ball joint
29. Pivot shaft	14. Nut
30. Bumper	15. Cotter pin
31. Steering knuckle	16. Nut
32. Coil spring	17. Washer
33. Bumper	18. Shim pack
34. Cotter pin	19. Spacer
35. Nut	20. Shock absorber
36. Lower control arm	21. Bolt
37. Lower ball joint	1. Bolt
38. Nut	2. Washer
39. Washer	3. Nut
40. Bushing	4. Bolt
41. Washer	5. Washer
42. Bracket	6. Bolt
43. Bolt	54. Bolt
44. U-bolt	55. Washer
45. Rivet	56. Bracket
46. Bushing	57. Washer
47. Bracket	58. Nut
48. Washer	59. Stabilizer bar
49. Nut	60. Bolt
50. Pivot shaft	61. Washer
51. Rivet	62. Washer
52. Bracket	63. Nut
53. Bushing	64. Brace
	65. Bolt
	66. Washer
	67. Nut
	68. Seal
	69. Air cylinder

Front suspension assembly—R and G-Series

1. Bolt
2. Shackle
3. Bushing
4. nut
5. Washer
6. Bracket
7. Bumper
8. Rivet
9. Nut
10. Bracket
11. Bumper
12. Nut
13. Washer
14. hanger
15. Rivet
16. Spacer
17. Washer
18. Nut
19. Bolt
20. Shock absorber
21. Leaf spring
22. Nut
23. Washer
24. Plate
25. Bolt
26. Spacer
27. Bolt
28. Washer
29. Bolt
30. Stabilizer shaft
31. Nut
32. Washer
33. Bracket
34. Bushing
35. Rivet
36. Rivet
37. Bracket
38. Bolt
39. Nut
40. Washer
41. Hanger
42. Bolt
43. Reinforcement
44. Bracket
46. Spacer
47. Bracket
48. Bolt
A. K3500 Series — right side
B. Quad shock

Front suspension assembly — V-Series

i. If the figure is not correct, tighten the pivot bolts to specification and have the front end alignment corrected.

Sway Bar

Removal and Installation

R-SERIES AND G-SERIES

1. Raise and support the vehicle safely. As required, remove the tire and wheel assemblies.

2. Properly support the stabilizer bar assembly. Remove the stabilizer shaft bushing retaining bolts. Remove the stabilizer link bushing nuts and bolts.

3. Remove the stabilizer bar from the vehicle.

4. Installation is the reverse of removal. Note, the split in the bushing faces forward. Coat the bushings with silicone grease

prior to installation. Install all fasteners and torque to 24 ft. lbs. (33 Nm).

V-SERIES

1. Raise and support the vehicle safely.
2. Remove the wheels.
3. Remove the stabilizer bar-to-frame clamps.
4. Remove the stabilizer bar-to-spring plate bolts.
5. Remove the stabilizer bar and bushings.
6. Check the bushings for wear or splitting. Replace any damaged bushings.

7. Installation is the reverse of removal. The split in the bushing faces forward. Coat the bushings with silicone grease prior to installation. Torque the stabilizer bar-to-frame nuts to 52 ft. lbs. (70 Nm). Torque the stabilizer bar-to-spring plate bolts to 133 ft. lbs. (180 Nm).

C-SERIES

NOTE: The end link bushings, bolts and spacers are not interchangeable from left to right.

1. Raise and support the vehicle safely.
2. Remove the nuts from the end link bolts.
3. Remove the bolts, bushings and spacers.
4. Remove the bracket bolts and remove the stabilizer bar.
5. Inspect the bushings for wear or damage. Replace them as necessary.
6. Installation is the reverse of removal. Coat the bushings with silicone grease prior to assembly. The slit in the bushings faces the front of the vehicle. Torque the frame bracket bolts to 24 ft. lbs. (33 Nm); the end link nuts to 13 ft. lbs. (18 Nm).

K-SERIES

NOTE: The end link bushings, bolts and spacers are not interchangeable from left to right.

1. Raise and support the vehicle safely.
2. Remove the nuts, bolts, spacer and clamp from the stabilizer bar.
3. Remove the stabilizer bar and remove the insulator.
4. Inspect all parts for wear or damage and replace them as necessary.
5. Installation is the reverse of removal.
6. Unload the torsion bar tension using tool J–36202.
7. Coat the bushings with silicone grease prior to assembly. Torque the frame bracket bolts to 13 ft. lbs. (18 Nm); the end link nuts to 12 ft. lbs. (17 Nm).

Kingpins

Removal and Installation

1. Raise and support the vehicle safely.
2. Remove the tire and wheel assembly.
3. Remove the caliper, hub and rotor assembly.
4. Remove the backing plate and steering arm.
5. Remove the upper kingpin cap, gasket and brake hose bracket.
6. Remove the lower cap and gasket. Discard the gasket.
7. Remove the locking pin and nut from the axle.
8. Drive the kingpin out using a suitable drift punch. The spacer and bushings will also come out with the kingpin.
9. Remove the steering knuckle from the drive axle.
10. Remove the dust seal, shim and thrust bearing.

To install:

11. Install new bushings into the steering knuckle and ream the new bushings to 1.1804–1.1820 in. (29.982–30.022mm). Install the steering knuckle onto the axle.
12. Prelube the thrust bearing and install the bearing, shim, and dust seal.
13. Prelube the kingpin; install the kingpin and lock pin, inserting the spacers in the correct order. Torque the lock pin to 29 ft. lbs. (40 Nm).
14. Install the upper and lower gasket and kingpin caps. Install the upper brake hose bracket.
15. Install the steering arm and backing plate. Torque the bolts to 12 ft. lbs. (16 Nm) and the nuts to 230 ft. lbs. (312 Nm).
16. Install the hub, rotor and caliper assembly.
17. Install the tire and wheel assembly.
18. Lower the vehicle and check the front end alignment.

I-Beam Axle

Removal and Installation

1. Raise and support the vehicle safely. Properly support the front axle beam.
2. Remove the tire and wheel assembly.

1. Coil spring	12. Bushing
2. Lower control arm	13. Bushing
3. Upper control arm	14. Screw
4. Upper ball joint	15. Nut
5. Nut	16. Screw
6. Cotter pin	17. Nut
7. Lower ball joint	18. Nut
8. Nut	19. Washer
9. Screw	20. Bushing
10. Insulator	21. Nut
11. Bumper	22. Bracket
	23. Screw

Front suspension assembly — C-Series

1. Frame	7. Nut
2. Upper control arm	8. Bracket
3. Upper ball joint	9. Screw
4. Nut	10. Nut
5. Pin	11. Bushing
6. Bolt	12. Washer

Upper control arm installation — K-Series

3. Remove the steering arm, knuckle and spindle assembly.
4. Remove the shock absorber.
5. Remove the stabilizer link and bushings.
6. Remove the U-bolts from the axle.

7. Remove the U-bolt spacer and shock plate.
8. Remove the leaf spring, as required.
9. Remove the steering damper and remove the I-Beam axle.
10. Installation is the reverse of removal.

1. Spring hanger
2. Insulator
3. Clamp
4. Stabilizer shaft
5. Bolt
6. U-Bolt
7. Stabilizer link
8. Spacer
9. Spring hanger
10. Spring stop
11. Shock absorber
12. Front spring
13. Front axle
14. Spring spacer
15. Shim
16. Dust seal
17. Lock pin
18. Thrust bearing
19. Steering arm
20. Splash shield
21. Gasket
22. Cap
23. Cap
24. Gasket
25. Kingpin
26. Bushing
27. Spacer
28. Steering knuckle
29. Brake caliper
30. Anchor plate

Front I-Beam suspension—C3HD-Series

1. Nut
2. Shock absorber assembly
3. Nut
4. Lower control arm
5. Bolt
6. Frame
7. Bolt
8. Washer

Shock absorber installation—K-Series

1. Bumper location
2. Lower control arm
3. Ball joint
4. Bolt
5. Bumper
6. Washer
7. Bushing
8. Frame bracket
9. Nut
10. Bolt
11. Bushing
12. Nut
13. Nut
14. Crossmember

Lower control arm installation—K-Series

REAR SUSPENSION

Shock Absorbers

Removal and Installation

1. Raise and support the vehicle safely. Properly support the rear axle assembly.
2. Remove the upper and lower shock absorber bolts.
3. Remove the shock absorber from the vehicle.
4. Installation is the reverse of the removal procedure.

Leaf Spring

Removal and Installation

R/V-SERIES AND G-SERIES

1. Raise and support the vehicle safely. Properly support the rear axle assembly to relieve tension on the springs.
2. If equipped, remove the stabilizer bar. Loosen, but do not remove the spring to shackle nut and bolt.
3. Remove the nut and bolt securing the shackle to the rear hanger. Remove the nut and bolt securing the leaf spring to the front hanger.
4. Remove the leaf spring from the front hanger. Remove the nut and bolt securing the shackle to the leaf spring. Remove the shackle.

U-bolt tightening sequence—R/V and G-Series

SECTION 5

GENERAL MOTORS CORPORATION
C/K SERIES (PICK-UP) • R/V SERIES (PICK-UP) • BLAZER/JIMMY • SUBURBAN • G SERIES (VAN)

6. Rear shackle
7. Anchor plate
8. U-bolt
9. Shim
10. Leaf spring
11. Nut
12. Spring washer
13. Rear shock absorber
14. Bolt
15. Spring washer
16. Nut
17. Front hanger
18. Axle bumper
19. Bumper bracket
20. Washer
21. Nut
22. Bracket
23. Cushion
24. Rear hanger reinforcement
25. Leaf spring eye bushing
26. Bolt
27. Nut
28. Nut
29. Bolt
30. Spacer
31. Optional rear auxiliary spring
32. Bolt
33. Washer
34. Nut
35. Stabilizer bar anchor
36. Spacer
37. Spring clip

1. Bracket
2. Bolt
3. Washer
4. Rear hanger
5. Nut

Rear suspension assembly—R/V 30/3500-Series

1. Bracket
2. Bolt
3. Washer
4. Rear hanger
5. Nut
6. Rear shackle
7. Anchor plate
8. U-bolt
9. Shim
10. Leaf spring
11. Nut
12. Spring washer
13. Rear shock absorber
14. Bolt
15. Spring washer
16. Nut
17. Front hanger support
18. Front hanger
19. Axle bumper
20. Bumper bracket
21. Washer
22. Nut

Rear suspension assembly—R/V 10/1500, 20/2500 Series

1. Nut
2. Washer
3. Anchor plate
4. U-bolt
5. Spacer
6. Nut
7. Washer
8. Bolt
9. Nut
10. Washer
11. Bolt
12. Shackle
13. Rear bracket
14. Nut
15. Washer
16. Bolt
17. Front bracket
18. Spring assembly

Rear leaf spring and components—C/K-Series

1. Bracket
2. Bolt
3. Washer
4. Rear hanger
5. Nut
6. Rear shackle
7. Anchor plate
8. U-bolt
9. Shim
10. Leaf spring
11. Nut
12. Spring washer
13. Rear shock absorber
14. Bolt
15. Spring washer
16. Nut
17. Front hanger support
18. Front hanger
19. Axle bumper
20. Bumper bracket
21. Washer
22. Nut
23. Rear hanger reinforcement
24. Spacer
25. Bolt

Rear suspension assembly—G10/1500–G30/3500 Series

1. Bracket
2. Bolt
3. Washer
4. Nut
5. Rear shackle
6. Anchor plate
7. U-bolt
8. Shim
9. Nut
10. Nut
11. Spring washer
12. Rear shock absorber
13. Bolt
14. Spring washer
15. Nut
16. Front hanger support
17. Front hanger
18. Axle bumper
19. Bumper bracket
20. Washer
21. Nut
22. Rear hanger reinforcement
23. Leaf spring eye bushing
24. Bolt
25. Nut
26. Nut
27. Bolt
28. Spacer
29. Bolt
30. Spring clip

Rear suspension assembly—G30/3500-Series

U-bolt tightening sequence—C/K-Series

5. Remove the nuts and washers holding the spring to the frame. If equipped, remove the rear stabilizer anchor plate, spacers, shims and auxiliary spring.

6. Remove the U-bolts from the assembly. Remove the leaf spring from the vehicle.

7. Installation is the reverse of the removal procedure.

C/K-SERIES

1. Raise and support the vehicle safely. Properly support the rear axle assembly to relieve tension on the springs.

2. Remove the shock absorber. Remove the U-bolt nuts, washers, anchor plate and U-bolt.

3. Remove the shackle to frame bolt, washers and nut. Remove the spring assembly to front bracket nut, washers and bolt.

4. Remove the spring assembly from the vehicle. As required, separate the spring from the shackle.

5. Installation is the reverse of the removal procedure.

6. Tighten the U-bolt nuts in a diagonal sequence to specification. The spring height must be adjusted to obtain a measurement of 7.17 in. (182mm) between the top surface of the axle jounce pad and the bottom surface of the frame jounce pad.

SPECIFICATIONS

VEHICLE IDENTIFICATION CHART

It is important for servicing and ordering parts to be certain of the vehicle and engine identification. The VIN (vehicle identification number) is a 17 digit number visible through the windshield on the driver's side of the dash and contains the vehicle and engine identification codes. The tenth digit indicates model year and the eighth digit indicates engine code. It can be interpreted as follows:

Engine Code						Model Year	
Code	Cu. In.	Liters	Cyl.	Fuel Sys.	Eng. Mfg.	Code	Year
A	151	2.5	4	EFI	CPC	J	1988
E	151	2.5	4	EFI	CPC	K	1989
R	173	2.8	6	EFI	CPC	L	1990
D	189	3.1	6	EFI	CPC	M	1991
L	231	3.8	6	SFI	BOC	N	1992
B	262	4.3	6	EFI	CPC		
W	262	4.3	6	CPI	CPC		
Z	262	4.3	6	EFI	CPC		
Z①	262	4.3	6	MPFI	CPC		

EFI—Electronic Fuel Injection
CPI—Central Port Injection
MPFI—Multi-Port Fuel Injection
SFI—Sequential Fuel Injection
BOC—Buick/Oldsmobile/Cadillac
CPC—Chevrolet/Pontiac Canada
① Turbocharged LB4/ZR9 Engine

ENGINE IDENTIFICATION

Year	Model	Engine Displacement cu. in. (liter)	Engine Series Identification (VIN)	No. of Cylinders	Engine Type
1988	S10/15 Pick-Up 2WD	151 (2.5)	E	4	OHV
	S10/15 Pick-Up 2WD	173 (2.8)	R	6	OHV
	S10/15 Pick-Up 4WD	151 (2.5)	E	4	OHV
	S10/15 Pick-Up 4WD	173 (2.8)	R	6	OHV
	S10/15 Cab-Chassis	173 (2.8)	R	6	OHV
	S10/15 Blazer/Jimmy 2WD	151 (2.5)	E	4	OHV
	S10/15 Blazer/Jimmy 2WD	173 (2.8)	R	6	OHV
	S10/15 Blazer/Jimmy 4WD	173 (2.8)	R	6	OHV
	S10/15 Blazer/Jimmy 4WD	262 (4.3)	Z	6	OHV
	Astro/Safari	151 (2.5)	E	4	OHV
	Astro/Safari	262 (4.3)	Z	6	OHV

ENGINE IDENTIFICATION

Year	Model	Engine Displacement cu. in. (liter)	Engine Series Identification (VIN)	No. of Cylinders	Engine Type
1989	S10/15 Pick-Up 2WD	151 (2.5)	E	4	OHV
	S10/15 Pick-Up 2WD	173 (2.8)	R	6	OHV
	S10/15 Pick-Up 4WD	173 (2.8)	R	6	OHV
	S10/15 Pick-Up 4WD	262 (4.3)	Z	6	OHV
	S10/15 Blazer/Jimmy 2WD	151 (2.5)	E	4	OHV
	S10/15 Blazer/Jimmy 2WD	173 (2.8)	R	6	OHV
	S10/15 Blazer/Jimmy 2WD	262 (4.3)	Z	6	OHV
	S10/15 Blazer/Jimmy 4WD	173 (2.8)	R	6	OHV
	S10/15 Blazer/Jimmy 4WD	262 (4.3)	Z	6	OHV
	Astro/Safari	151 (2.5)	E	4	OHV
	Astro/Safari	262 (4.3)	Z	6	OHV
1990	S10/15 Pick-Up 2WD	151 (2.5)	E	4	OHV
	S10/15 Pick-Up 2WD	173 (2.8)	R	6	OHV
	S10/15 Pick-Up 2WD	262 (4.3)	Z	6	OHV
	S10/15 Pick-Up 4WD	262 (4.3)	Z	6	OHV
	S10/15 Blazer/Jimmy 2WD	262 (4.3)	Z	6	OHV
	S10/15 Blazer/Jimmy 4WD	262 (4.3)	Z	6	OHV
	Astro/Safari 2WD	151 (2.5)	E	4	OHV
	Astro/Safari 2WD	262 (4.3)	Z	6	OHV
	Astro/Safari 4WD	262 (4.3)	Z	6	OHV
	Lumina APV/Silhouette/Trans Sport	189 (3.1)	D	6	OHV
1991	S10/15 Pick-Up 2WD	151 (2.5)	A	4	OHV
	S10/15 Pick-Up 2WD	173 (2.8)	R	6	OHV
	S10/15 Pick-Up 2WD	262 (4.3)	Z	6	OHV
	S10/15 Pick-Up 4WD	262 (4.3)	Z	6	OHV
	Sonoma	151 (2.5)	A	4	OHV
	Sonoma	173 (2.8)	R	6	OHV
	Sonoma	262 (4.3)	Z	6	OHV
	Syclone ①	262 (4.3)	Z	6	OHV
	S10/15 Blazer/Jimmy 2WD	262 (4.3)	Z	6	OHV
	S10/15 Blazer/Jimmy 4WD	262 (4.3)	Z	6	OHV
	Bravada	262 (4.3)	Z	6	OHV
	Astro/Safari 2WD	262 (4.3)	B	6	OHV
	Astro/Safari 2WD	262 (4.3)	Z	6	OHV
	Astro/Safari 4WD	262 (4.3)	Z	6	OHV
	Lumina APV/Silhouette/Trans Sport	189 (3.1)	D	6	OHV
1992	S10/15 Pick-Up 2WD	151 (2.5)	A	4	OHV
	S10/15 Pick-Up 2WD	173 (2.8)	R	6	OHV
	S10/15 Pick-Up 2WD	262 (4.3)	Z	6	OHV
	S10/15 Pick-Up 4WD	262 (4.3)	Z	6	OHV
	Sonoma	151 (2.5)	A	4	OHV
	Sonoma	173 (2.8)	R	6	OHV
	Sonoma	262 (4.3)	W	6	OHV
	Sonoma	262 (4.3)	Z	6	OHV

ENGINE IDENTIFICATION

Year	Model	Engine Displacement cu. in. (liter)	Engine Series Identification (VIN)	No. of Cylinders	Engine Type
1992	Syclone ①	262 (4.3)	Z	6	OHV
	S10/15 Blazer/Jimmy 2WD	262 (4.3)	Z	6	OHV
	S10/15 Blazer/Jimmy 4WD	262 (4.3)	Z	6	OHV
	Bravada	262 (4.3)	W	6	OHV
	Bravada	262 (4.3)	Z	6	OHV
	Typhoon ①	262 (4.3)	Z	6	OHV
	Astro/Safari 2WD	262 (4.3)	W	6	OHV
	Astro/Safari 2WD	262 (4.3)	Z	6	OHV
	Astro/Safari 4WD	262 (4.3)	W	6	OHV
	Astro/Safari 4WD	262 (4.3)	Z	6	OHV
	Lumina APV/Silhouette/Trans Sport	189 (3.1)	D	6	OHV
	Lumina APV/Silhouette/Trans Sport	231 (3.8)	L	6	OHV

OHV—Overhead valves
① Turbocharged engine

GENERAL ENGINE SPECIFICATIONS

Year	VIN	Engine No. Cyl. cu. in. (liters)	Fuel System Type	SAE Net Horsepower @ rpm	SAE Net Torque @ rpm (ft. lbs.)	Bore × Stroke (in.)	Compression Ratio	Oil Pressure @ rpm
1988	E	4-151 (2.5)	EFI	92 @ 4400	130 @ 3200	4.00 × 3.00	8.3:1	41 @ 2000
	R	6-173 (2.8)	EFI	125 @ 4800	150 @ 2400	3.50 × 2.99	8.9:1	50 @ 2000
	Z	6-262 (4.3)	EFI	150 @ 4000	230 @ 2400	4.00 × 3.48	9.3:1	30 @ 2000
1989	E	4-151 (2.5)	EFI	92 @ 4400	130 @ 3200	4.00 × 3.00	8.3:1	41 @ 2000
	R	6-173 (2.8)	EFI	125 @ 4800	150 @ 2400	3.50 × 2.99	8.9:1	50 @ 2000
	Z	6-262 (4.3)	EFI	160 @ 4000	230 @ 2800	4.00 × 3.48	9.3:1	18 @ 2000
1990	E	4-151 (2.5)	EFI	105 @ 4800	135 @ 3200	4.00 × 3.00	8.3:1	41 @ 2000
	R	6-173 (2.8)	EFI	125 @ 4800	150 @ 2400	3.50 × 2.99	8.9:1	50 @ 2000
	D	6-189 (3.1)	EFI	120 @ 4400	175 @ 2200	3.50 × 3.30	8.9:1	15 @ 1100
	Z	6-262 (4.3)	EFI	160 @ 4000	230 @ 2800	4.00 × 3.48	9.3:1	18 @ 2000
1991	A	4-151 (2.5)	EFI	105 @ 4800	135 @ 3200	4.00 × 3.00	8.3:1	41 @ 2000
	R	6-173 (2.8)	EFI	125 @ 4800	150 @ 2400	3.50 × 2.99	8.9:1	50 @ 2000
	D	6-189 (3.1)	EFI	120 @ 4400	175 @ 2200	3.50 × 3.30	8.9:1	15 @ 1100
	B	6-262 (4.3)	EFI	170 @ 4600	225 @ 2200	4.00 × 3.48	9.3:1	18 @ 2000
	Z	6-262 (4.3)	EFI	160 @ 4000	230 @ 2800	4.00 × 3.48	9.3:1	18 @ 2000
	Z①	6-262 (4.3)	MPFI	280 @ 4200	350 @ 3600	4.00 × 3.48	8.35:1	18 @ 2000
1992	A	4-151 (2.5)	EFI	105 @ 4800	135 @ 3200	4.00 × 3.00	8.3:1	41 @ 2000
	R	6-173 (2.8)	EFI	125 @ 4800	150 @ 2400	3.50 × 2.99	8.9:1	50 @ 2000
	D	6-189 (3.1)	EFI	120 @ 4400	175 @ 2200	3.50 × 3.30	8.9:1	15 @ 1100
	L	6-231 (3.8)	SFI	165 @ 4300	220 @ 3200	3.80 × 3.40	8.5:1	60 @ 1850
	W	6-262 (4.3)	CPI	200 @ 4500	260 @ 3600	4.00 × 3.48	9.1:1	18 @ 2000
	Z	6-262 (4.3)	EFI	160 @ 4000	230 @ 2800	4.00 × 3.48	9.3:1	18 @ 2000
	Z①	6-262 (4.3)	MPFI	280 @ 4200	350 @ 3600	4.00 × 3.48	8.35:1	18 @ 2000

EFI—Electronic Fuel Injection
CPI—Central Port Injection
SFI—Sequential Fuel Injection
MPI—Multi-Port Fuel Injection
① Turbocharged engine

TUNE-UP SPECIFICATIONS CHART

Year	VIN	Engine No. Cyl. cu. in. (liters)	Spark Plugs Type	Spark Plugs Gap (in.)	Ignition Timing (deg.) MT	Ignition Timing (deg.) AT	Compression Pressure (psi)	Fuel Pump (psi)	Idle Speed (rpm) MT	Idle Speed (rpm) AT	Valve Clearance In.	Valve Clearance Ex.
1988	E	4-151 (2.5)	R43TS6	0.060	①	①	②	9–13	①	①	Hyd.	Hyd.
	R	6-173 (2.8)	R42TS	0.045	①	①	②	9–13	①	①	Hyd.	Hyd.
	Z	6-262 (4.3)	R43TS	0.045	①	①	②	9–13	①	①	Hyd.	Hyd.
1989	E	4-151 (2.5)	R43TS6	0.060	①	①	②	9–13	①	①	Hyd.	Hyd.
	R	6-173 (2.8)	R43TSK	0.045	①	①	②	9–13	①	①	Hyd.	Hyd.
	Z	6-262 (4.3)	CR43TS	0.045	①	①	②	9–13	①	①	Hyd.	Hyd.
1990	E	4-151 (2.5)	R43TS6	0.060	①	①	②	9–13	①	①	Hyd.	Hyd.
	R	6-173 (2.8)	R43TSK	0.045	①	①	②	9–13	①	①	Hyd.	Hyd.
	D	6-189 (3.1)	R43TS	0.045	①	①	②	9–13	①	①	Hyd.	Hyd.
	Z	6-262 (4.3)	CR43TS	0.035	①	①	②	9–13	①	①	Hyd.	Hyd.
1991	A	4-151 (2.5)	R43TS6	0.060	①	①	②	9–13	①	①	Hyd.	Hyd.
	R	6-173 (2.8)	R43TSK	0.045	①	①	②	9–13	①	①	Hyd.	Hyd.
	D	6-189 (3.1)	R43TS	0.045	①	①	②	9–13	①	①	Hyd.	Hyd.
	B	6-262 (4.3)	CR43TS	0.035	①	①	②	9–13	①	①	Hyd.	Hyd.
	Z	6-262 (4.3)	CR43TS	0.035	①	①	②	9–13	①	①	Hyd.	Hyd.
	Z④	6-262 (4.3)	CR42TS	0.045	①	①	②	35–38③	①	①	Hyd.	Hyd.
1992	A	4-151 (2.5)	R43TS6	0.060	①	①	②	9–13	①	①	Hyd.	Hyd.
	R	6-173 (2.8)	R43TSK	0.045	①	①	②	9–13	①	①	Hyd.	Hyd.
	D	6-189 (3.1)	R43TS	0.045	①	①	②	9–13	①	①	Hyd.	Hyd.
	L	6-231 (3.8)	R45LTS6	0.060	①	①	②	41–47③	①	①	Hyd.	Hyd.
	W	6-262 (4.3)	CR43TS	0.035	①	①	②	54–64③	①	①	Hyd.	Hyd.
	Z	6-262 (4.3)	CR43TS	0.035	①	①	②	9–13	①	①	Hyd.	Hyd.
	Z④	6-262 (4.3)	CR42TS	0.045	①	①	②	35–38③	①	①	Hyd.	Hyd.

Hyd.—Hydraulic
① See underhood emission sticker
② The lowest recorded reading should be within 70% of the highest reading
③ Key on; engine off
④ Turbocharged engine

FIRING ORDERS

NOTE: To avoid confusion, always replace spark plug wires one at a time.

2.5L Engine
Engine Firing Order: 1–3–4–2
Distributor Rotation: Clockwise

FIRING ORDER 1-2-3-4-5-6

2.8L Engine
Engine Firing Order: 1–2–3–4–5–6
Distributor Rotation: Clockwise

FIRING ORDERS

NOTE: To avoid confusion, always replace spark plug wires one at a time.

3.1L Engine
Engine Firing Order: 1–2–3–4–5–6
Distributor Rotation: Clockwise

CYLINDER NUMBERING

◀ FRT

4.3L Engine
Engine Firing Order: 1–6–5–4–3–2
Distributor Rotation: Clockwise

3.8L Engine
Engine Firing Order: 1–6–5–4–3–2
Distributorless Ignition System

CAPACITIES

Year	Model	VIN	Engine cu. in (liters)	Engine Crankcase with Filter	Engine Crankcase without Filter	Transmission (pts.) 4-Spd	Transmission (pts.) 5-Spd	Transmission (pts.) Auto.	Drive Axle (pts.)	Fuel Tank (gal.)	Cooling System (qts.)
1988	S10/15 Pick-Up	E	4-151 (2.5)	3.5	3.0	—	4.4	10	3.8④	13①	11.5
	S10/15 Pick-Up	R	6-173 (2.8)	4.5	4.0	—	4.4	10	3.8④	13①	10.5
	S10/15 Blazer/Jimmy	E	4-151 (2.5)	3.5	3.0	—	4.4	10	3.8④	13①	11.5
	S10/15 Blazer/Jimmy	R	6-173 (2.8)	4.5	4.0	—	4.4	10	3.8④	13①	10.5
	S10/15 Blazer/Jimmy	Z	6-262 (4.3)	5.0	4.0	—	4.4	10	3.8④	13①	13.5
	Astro/Safari	E	4-151 (2.5)	3.5	3.0	—	4.4	10	3.8	17②	10.0⑤
	Astro/Safari	Z	6-262 (4.3)	5.0	4.0	—	4.4	10	3.8	17②	13.5⑥
1989	S10/15 Pick-Up	E	4-151 (2.5)	3.5	3.0	—	4.4	10	3.8④	13①	11.5
	S10/15 Pick-Up	R	6-173 (2.8)	4.5	4.0	—	4.4	10	3.8④	13①	10.5
	S10/15 Pick-Up	Z	6-262 (4.3)	5.0	4.0	—	4.4	10	3.8④	13①	13.5
	S10/15 Blazer/Jimmy	E	4-151 (2.5)	3.5	3.0	—	4.4	10	3.8④	13①	11.5
	S10/15 Blazer/Jimmy	R	6-173 (2.8)	4.5	4.0	—	4.4	10	3.8④	13①	10.5
	S10/15 Blazer/Jimmy	Z	6-262 (4.3)	5.0	4.0	—	4.4	10	3.8④	13①	13.5
	Astro/Safari	E	4-151 (2.5)	3.5	3.0	—	4.4	10	3.8	17②	10.0⑤
	Astro/Safari	Z	6-262 (4.3)	5.0	4.0	—	2.2	10	3.8	17②	13.5⑥

GENERAL MOTORS CORPORATION
ASTRO • S/T PICK-UP/SYCLONE • S10 BLAZER/S15 JIMMY • BRAVADA/TYPHOON

CAPACITIES

Year	Model	VIN	Engine cu. in (liters)	Engine with Filter	Crankcase without Filter	Transmission (pts.) 4-Spd	5-Spd	Auto.	Drive Axle (pts.)	Fuel Tank (gal.)	Cooling System (qts.)
1990	S10/15 Pick-Up	E	4-151 (2.5)	3.5	3.0	—	4.4	10	3.8④	13①	11.5
	S10/15 Pick-Up	R	6-173 (2.8)	4.5	4.0	—	4.4	10	3.8④	13①	10.5
	S10/15 Pick-Up	Z	6-262 (4.3)	4.5	4.0	—	4.4	10	3.8④	13①	13.5
	S10/15 Blazer/Jimmy	Z	6-262 (4.3)	4.5	4.0	—	4.4	10	3.8④	13①	13.5
	Astro/Safari	Z	6-262 (4.3)	4.5	4.0	—	4.4	10	3.8④	27	16.5
	Lumina/Silhouette/Trans Sport	D	6-189 (3.1)	4.5	4.0	—	—	8	—	18	13.4
1991	S10/15 Pick-Up	A	4-151 (2.5)	3.5	3.0	—	4.4	③	3.5⑧	20⑦	11.5
	S10/15 Pick-Up	R	6-173 (2.8)	4.5	4.0	—	4.4	③	3.5⑧	20⑦	10.5
	S10/15 Pick-Up	Z	6-262 (4.3)	4.5	4.0	—	4.4	③	3.5⑧	20⑦	12.1
	Sonoma	A	4-151 (2.5)	3.5	3.0	—	4.4	③	3.5⑧	20⑦	11.5
	Sonoma	R	6-173 (2.8)	4.5	4.0	—	4.4	③	3.5⑧	20⑦	10.5
	Sonoma	Z	6-262 (4.3)	4.5	4.0	—	4.4	③	3.5⑧	20⑦	12.1
	Syclone	Z⑨	6-262 (4.3)	4.5	4.0	—	—	10.0	3.5⑧	20	12.1
	S10/15 Blazer/Jimmy	Z	6-262 (4.3)	4.5	4.0	—	4.4	③	3.5⑧	20⑦	12.1
	Bravada	Z	6-262 (4.3)	4.5	4.0	—	—	10.0	3.5⑧	20	11.9
	Astro/Safari	B	6-262 (4.3)	5	4.0	—	—	10.0	—	27	16.5
	Astro/Safari	Z	6-262 (4.3)	5	4.0	—	—	10.0	—	27	16.5
	Lumina/Silhouette/Trans Sport	D	6-189 (3.1)	4.0	4.0	—	—	8	—	18	13.4
1992	S10/15 Pick-Up	A	4-151 (2.5)	3.5	3.0	—	4.4	10.0	3.5⑧	20	11.5
	S10/15 Pick-Up	R	6-173 (2.8)	4.0	4.0	—	4.4	10.0	3.5⑧	20	10.5
	S10/15 Pick-Up	Z	6-262 (4.3)	4.0	4.0	—	4.4	10.0	3.5⑧	20	12.1
	Sonoma	A	4-151 (2.5)	3.5	3.0	—	4.4	③	3.5⑧	20⑦	11.5
	Sonoma	R	6-173 (2.8)	4.5	4.0	—	4.4	③	3.5⑧	20⑦	10.5
	Sonoma	W	6-262 (4.3)	4.5	4.0	—	—	10.0	3.5⑧	20	12.0
	Sonoma	Z	6-262 (4.3)	4.5	4.0	—	4.4	③	3.5⑧	20⑦	12.1
	Syclone	Z⑨	6-262 (4.3)	4.5	4.0	—	—	10.0	3.5⑧	20	12.1
	S10/15 Blazer/Jimmy	Z	6-262 (4.3)	4.0	4.0	—	4.4	10.0	3.5⑧	20	12.1
	Bravada	W	6-262 (4.3)	4.5	4.0	—	—	10.0	3.5⑧	20	12.0
	Bravada	Z	6-262 (4.3)	4.5	4.0	—	—	10.0	3.5⑧	20	12.0
	Typhoon	Z⑨	6-262 (4.3)	4.5	4.0	—	—	10.0	3.5⑧	20	12.1
	Astro/Safari	W	6-262 (4.3)	5	4.0	—	—	10.0	3.5⑧	27	16.5⑥
	Astro/Safari	Z	6-262 (4.3)	5	4.0	—	—	10.0	3.5⑧	27	16.5⑥
	Lumina/Silhouette/Trans Sport	D	6-189 (3.1)	4.0	4.0	—	—	8	—	20	⑩
	Lumina/Silhouette/Trans Sport	L	6-231 (3.8)	4.0	4.0	—	—	12	—	20	⑩

① 20 gallon tank optional
② 27 gallon tank optional
③ THM180C (3L30)—6 pts.
  THM700R4 (4L60)—10 pts.
④ Front axle—2.6 pts.
⑤ 13 qts. with rear heater
⑥ 16.5 qts. with rear heater
⑦ 2WD—13 gallon tank optional
⑧ Front and rear axle capacity
⑨ Turbocharged engine

⑩ Option (C40) with heater—o/s air, w/fan, elec. cont.:
  Copper-brass—11.4 qts.
  Aluminum—11.2 qts.
Option C40 and (C36) with rear heater:
  Copper-brass—13.0 qts.
  Aluminum—12.8 qts.
Option (C67) air conditioner—frt. elec. cont.:
  Copper-brass—11.7 qts.
  Aluminum—10.8 qts.
Option C67 and (C34) air conditioner/heater combination—rear:
  Copper-brass—13.3 qts.
  Aluminum—12.4 qts.

CAMSHAFT SPECIFICATIONS

| Year | VIN | Engine No. Cyl. cu. in. (liters) | Journal Diameter (in.) | | | | | Lobe Lift | | Bearing Clearance (in.) | Camshaft End Play (in.) |
			1	2	3	4	5	Intake	Exhaust		
1988	E	4-151 (2.5)	1.869	1.869	1.869	—	—	0.398	0.398	0.0007–0.0027	0.0015–0.0050
	R	6-173 (2.8)	1.867–1.869	1.867–1.869	1.867–1.869	1.867–1.869	—	0.262	0.273	0.0010–0.0040	—
	Z	6-262 (4.3)	1.868–1.869	1.868–1.869	1.868–1.869	1.868–1.869	—	0.357	0.390	—	0.0004–0.0012
1989	E	4-151 (2.5)	1.869	1.869	1.869	—	—	0.398	0.398	0.0007–0.0027	0.0015–0.0050
	R	6-173 (2.8)	1.867–1.869	1.867–1.869	1.867–1.869	1.867–1.869	—	0.262	0.273	0.0010–0.0040	—
	Z	6-262 (4.3)	1.868–1.869	1.868–1.869	1.868–1.869	1.868–1.869	—	0.357	0.390	—	0.0004–0.0012
1990	E	4-151 (2.5)	1.869	1.869	1.869	—	—	0.398	0.398	0.0007–0.0027	0.0015–0.0050
	R	6-173 (2.8)	1.867–1.869	1.867–1.869	1.867–1.869	1.867–1.869	—	0.262	0.273	0.0010–0.0040	—
	D	6-189 (3.1)	1.868–1.882	1.868–1.882	1.868–1.882	1.868–1.882	—	0.231	0.262	0.0010–0.0040	—
	Z	6-262 (4.3)	1.868–1.869	1.868–1.869	1.868–1.869	1.868–1.869	—	0.357	0.390	—	0.0004–0.0012
1991	E	4-151 (2.5)	1.869	1.869	1.869	—	—	0.398	0.398	0.0007–0.0027	0.0015–0.0050
	R	6-173 (2.8)	1.867–1.869	1.867–1.869	1.867–1.869	1.867–1.869	—	0.262	0.273	0.0010–0.0040	—
	D	6-189 (3.1)	1.868–1.882	1.868–1.882	1.868–1.882	1.868–1.882	—	0.231	0.262	0.0010–0.0040	—
	B	6-262 (4.3)	1.868–1.869	1.868–1.869	1.868–1.869	1.868–1.869	—	0.269	0.276	—	0.0004–0.0012
	Z	6-262 (4.3)	1.868–1.869	1.868–1.869	1.868–1.869	1.868–1.869	—	0.234	0.257	—	0.0004–0.0012
	Z①	6-262 (4.3)	1.868–1.869	1.868–1.869	1.868–1.869	1.868–1.869	—	0.357	0.390	—	0.0004–0.0012
1992	A	4-151 (2.5)	1.869	1.869	1.869	—	—	0.251	0.251	0.0007–0.0027	0.0015–0.0050
	R	6-173 (2.8)	1.867–1.869	1.867–1.869	1.867–1.869	1.867–1.869	—	0.262	0.273	0.0010–0.0040	—
	D	6-189 (3.1)	1.868–1.882	1.868–1.882	1.868–1.882	1.868–1.882	—	0.231	0.262	0.0010–0.0040	—
	L	6-231 (3.8)	1.785–1.786	1.785–1.786	1.785–1.786	1.785–1.786	—	0.250	0.255	0.0005–0.0035	—
	W	6-262 (4.3)	1.868–1.869	1.868–1.869	1.868–1.869	1.868–1.869	—	0.288	0.294	—	0.0001–0.0009
	Z	6-262 (4.3)	1.868–1.869	1.868–1.869	1.868–1.869	1.868–1.869	—	0.234	0.257	—	0.0004–0.0012
	Z①	6-262 (4.3)	1.868–1.869	1.868–1.869	1.868–1.869	1.868–1.869	—	0.357	0.390	—	0.0004–0.0012

① Turbocharged engine

CRANKSHAFT AND CONNECTING ROD SPECIFICATIONS

Year	VIN	Engine No. Cyl. cu. in. (liters)	Crankshaft Main Brg. Journal Dia.	Main Brg. Oil Clearance	Shaft End-play	Thrust on No.	Connecting Rod Journal Diameter	Oil Clearance	Side Clearance
1988	E	4-151 (2.5)	2.3000	0.0005–0.0022	0.0035–0.0085	5	2.0000	0.0005–0.0026	0.0020–0.0060
	R	6-173 (2.8)	①	0.0016–0.0032	0.0024–0.0083	3	④	0.0014–0.0037	0.0063–0.0252
	Z	6-262 (4.3)	②	③	0.0020–0.0060	4	2.2487–2.2497	0.0013–0.0035	0.0060–0.0140
1989	E	4-151 (2.5)	2.3000	0.0005–0.0022	0.0035–0.0085	5	2.0000	0.0005–0.0026	0.0020–0.0060
	R	6-173 (2.8)	①	0.0016–0.0032	0.0024–0.0083	3	④	0.0014–0.0037	0.0063–0.0252
	Z	6-262 (4.3)	②	③	0.0020–0.0060	4	2.2487–2.2497	0.0013–0.0035	0.0060–0.0140
1990	E	4-151 (2.5)	2.3000	0.0005–0.0022	0.0035–0.0085	5	2.0000	0.0005–0.0026	0.0020–0.0060
	R	6-173 (2.8)	①	0.0016–0.0032	0.0024–0.0083	3	④	0.0014–0.0037	0.0063–0.0252
	D	6-189 (3.1)	2.6473–2.6483	0.0012–0.0027	0.0024–0.0083	3	1.9983–1.9994	0.0011–0.0032	0.0140–0.0267
	Z	6-262 (4.3)	②	③	0.0020–0.0060	4	2.2487–2.2497	0.0013–0.0035	0.0060–0.0140
1991	A	4-151 (2.5)	2.3000	0.0005–0.0022	0.0035–0.0085	5	2.0000	0.0005–0.0026	0.0020–0.0060
	R	6-173 (2.8)	①	0.0016–0.0032	0.0024–0.0083	3	④	0.0014–0.0037	0.0063–0.0252
	D	6-189 (3.1)	2.6473–2.6483	0.0012–0.0027	0.0024–0.0083	3	1.9983–1.9994	0.0011–0.0032	0.0140–0.0267
	B	6-262 (4.3)	②	③	0.0020–0.0060	4	2.2487–2.2497	0.0013–0.0035	0.0060–0.0140
	Z	6-262 (4.3)	②	③	0.0020–0.0060	4	2.2487–2.2497	0.0013–0.0035	0.0060–0.0140
	Z⑥	6-262 (4.3)	②	③	0.0020–0.0060	4	2.2487–2.2497	0.0013–0.0035	0.0060–0.0140
1992	A	4-151 (2.5)	2.2984–2.2992	0.0005–0.0022	0.0050–0.0100	5	1.9963–2.0001	0.0005–0.0030	0.0020–0.0060
	R	6-173 (2.8)	①	0.0013–0.0027	0.0024–0.0083	3	④	0.0011–0.0033	0.0142–0.0236
	D	6-189 (3.1)	2.6473–2.6483	0.0012–0.0027	0.0024–0.0083	3	1.9983–1.9994	0.0011–0.0032	0.0140–0.0267
	L	6-231 (3.8)	2.4988–2.4998	0.0008–0.0022	0.0030–0.0110	2	2.2487–2.2499	0.0008–0.0022	0.0030–0.0150
	W	6-262 (4.3)	⑤	③	0.0020–0.0070	4	2.2487–2.2497	0.0013–0.0035	0.0060–0.0140
	Z	6-262 (4.3)	②	③	0.0020–0.0060	4	2.2487–2.2497	0.0013–0.0035	0.0060–0.0140
	Z⑥	6-262 (4.3)	②	③	0.0020–0.0060	4	2.2487–2.2497	0.0013–0.0035	0.0060–0.0140

① Journals with 3 dot: 2.6472–2.6475
Journals with 2 dot: 2.6475–2.6479
Journals with 1 dot: 2.6479–2.6482
② Journal #1: 2.4484–2.4493
Journals #2 & 3: 2.4481–2.4490
Journal #4: 2.4479–2.4488

③ Journal #1: 0.0008–0.0020
Journals #2 & 3: 0.0011–0.0023
Journal #4: 0.0017–0.0032
④ Journals with 2 dot: 1.9983–1.9989
Journals with 1 dot: 1.9989–1.9994

⑤ Journal #1: 2.4480–2.4495
Journals #2 & 3: 2.4485–2.4494
Journal #4: 2.4480–2.4489
⑥ Turbocharged engine

VALVE SPECIFICATIONS

Year	VIN	No. Cyl. cu. in. (liters)	Seat Angle (deg.)	Face Angle (deg.)	Spring Test Pressure (lbs.)	Spring Installed Height (in.)	Stem-to-Guide Clearance (in.)		Stem Diameter (in.)	
							Intake	Exhaust	Intake	Exhaust
1988	E	4-151 (2.5)	46	45	158–170 @ 1.040	1.440	0.0010–0.0025	0.0013–0.0030	0.3133–0.3138	0.3128–0.3135
	R	6-173 (2.8)	46	45	195 @ 1.181	1.574	0.0010–0.0027	0.0010–0.0027	—	—
	Z	6-262 (4.3)	46	45	194–206 @ 1.250	1.720	0.0010–0.0027	0.0010–0.0027	—	—
1989	E	4-151 (2.5)	46	45	158–170 @ 1.040	1.440	0.0010–0.0025	0.0013–0.0030	0.3133–0.3138	0.3128–0.3135
	R	6-173 (2.8)	46	45	195 @ 1.181	1.574	0.0010–0.0027	0.0010–0.0027	—	—
	Z	6-262 (4.3)	46	45	194–206 @ 1.250	1.720	0.0010–0.0027	0.0010–0.0027	—	—
1990	E	4-151 (2.5)	46	45	158–170 @ 1.040	1.440	0.0010–0.0025	0.0013–0.0030	0.3133–0.3138	0.3128–0.3135
	R	6-173 (2.8)	46	45	195 @ 1.181	1.574	0.0010–0.0027	0.0010–0.0027	—	—
	D	6-189 (3.1)	46	45	191 @ 1.187	1.574	0.0010–0.0027	0.0010–0.0027	—	—
	Z	6-262 (4.3)	46	45	194–206 @ 1.250	1.720	0.0010–0.0027	0.0010–0.0027	—	—
1991	A	4-151 (2.5)	46	45	158–170 @ 1.040	1.440	0.0010–0.0025	0.0013–0.0030	0.3133–0.3138	0.3128–0.3135
	R	6-173 (2.8)	46	45	195 @ 1.181	1.574	0.0010–0.0027	0.0010–0.0027	—	—
	D	6-189 (3.1)	46	45	191 @ 1.187	1.574	0.0010–0.0027	0.0010–0.0027	—	—
	B	6-262 (4.3)	46	45	194–206 @ 1.250	1.720	0.0010–0.0027	0.0010–0.0027	—	—
	Z	6-262 (4.3)	46	45	194–206 @ 1.250	1.720	0.0010–0.0027	0.0010–0.0027	—	—
	Z③	6-262 (4.3)	46	45	194–206 @ 1.250	1.720	0.0010–0.0027	0.0010–0.0027	—	—
1992	A	4-151 (2.5)	46	45	210–230 @ 1.239	1.679	0.0010–0.0025	①	0.3131–0.3138	②
	R	6-173 (2.8)	46	45	195 @ 1.181	1.574	0.0010–0.0027	0.0010–0.0027	—	—
	D	6-189 (3.1)	46	45	191 @ 1.187	1.574	0.0010–0.0027	0.0010–0.0027	—	—
	L	6-231 (3.8)	46	45	210 @ 1.315	1.690–1.720	0.0015–0.0035	0.0015–0.0032	—	②
	W	6-262 (4.3)	46	45	194–206 @ 1.250	1.690–1.710	0.0011–0.0027	0.0011–0.0027	—	—
	Z	6-262 (4.3)	46	45	194–206 @ 1.250	1.720	0.0010–0.0027	0.0010–0.0027	—	—
	Z③	6-262 (4.3)	46	45	194–206 @ 1.250	1.720	0.0010–0.0027	0.0010–0.0027	—	—

① Upper: 0.0013–0.0030
　Lower: 0.0024–0.0041
② Upper: 0.3129–0.3137
　Lower: 0.3118–0.3126
③ Turbocharged engine

PISTON AND RING SPECIFICATIONS

Year	VIN	Engine No. Cyl. cu. in. (liters)	Piston Clearance	Ring Gap Top Compression	Ring Gap Bottom Compression	Ring Gap Oil Control	Ring Side Clearance Top Compression	Ring Side Clearance Bottom Compression	Ring Side Clearance Oil Control
1988	E	4-151 (2.5)	0.0014–0.0022	0.0100–0.0200	0.0100–0.0200	0.0200–0.0600	0.0020–0.0030	0.0010–0.0030	0.0150–0.0550
	R	6-173 (2.8)	0.0007–0.0017	0.0098–0.0197	0.0098–0.0197	0.0200–0.0551	0.0012–0.0028	0.0016–0.0037	0.0078
	Z	6-262 (4.3)	0.0007–0.0017	0.0100–0.0200	0.0100–0.0250	0.0150–0.0550	0.0012–0.0032	0.0012–0.0032	0.0020–0.0070
1989	E	4-151 (2.5)	0.0014–0.0022	0.0100–0.0200	0.0100–0.0200	0.0200–0.0600	0.0020–0.0030	0.0010–0.0030	0.0150–0.0550
	R	6-173 (2.8)	0.0007–0.0017	0.0098–0.0197	0.0098–0.0197	0.0200–0.0551	0.0012–0.0028	0.0016–0.0037	0.0078
	Z	6-262 (4.3)	0.0007–0.0017	0.0100–0.0200	0.0100–0.0250	0.0150–0.0550	0.0012–0.0032	0.0012–0.0032	0.0020–0.0070
1990	E	4-151 (2.5)	0.0014–0.0022	0.0100–0.0200	0.0100–0.0200	0.0200–0.0600	0.0020–0.0030	0.0010–0.0030	0.0150–0.0550
	R	6-173 (2.8)	0.0007–0.0017	0.0098–0.0197	0.0098–0.0197	0.0200–0.0551	0.0012–0.0028	0.0016–0.0037	0.0078
	D	6-189 (3.1)	0.0009–0.0022	0.0100–0.0200	0.0200–0.0280	0.0100–0.0300	0.0020–0.0035	0.0020–0.0035	0.0080
	Z	6-262 (4.3)	0.0007–0.0017	0.0100–0.0200	0.0100–0.0250	0.0150–0.0550	0.0012–0.0032	0.0012–0.0032	0.0020–0.0070
1991	A	4-151 (2.5)	0.0014–0.0022	0.0100–0.0200	0.0100–0.0200	0.0200–0.0600	0.0020–0.0030	0.0010–0.0030	0.0150–0.0550
	R	6-173 (2.8)	0.0007–0.0017	0.0098–0.0197	0.0098–0.0197	0.0200–0.0551	0.0012–0.0028	0.0016–0.0037	0.0078
	D	6-189 (3.1)	0.0009–0.0022	0.0100–0.0200	0.0200–0.0280	0.0100–0.0300	0.0020–0.0035	0.0020–0.0035	0.0080
	B	6-262 (4.3)	0.0007–0.0017	0.0100–0.0200	0.0100–0.0250	0.0150–0.0550	0.0012–0.0032	0.0012–0.0032	0.0020–0.0070
	Z	6-262 (4.3)	0.0007–0.0017	0.0100–0.0200	0.0100–0.0250	0.0150–0.0550	0.0012–0.0032	0.0012–0.0032	0.0020–0.0070
	Z①	6-262 (4.3)	0.0015–0.0030	0.0100–0.0200	0.0100–0.0250	0.0150–0.0550	0.0012–0.0032	0.0012–0.0032	0.0020–0.0070
1992	A	4-151 (2.5)	0.0015–0.0035	0.0100–0.0150	0.0100–0.0200	0.0150–0.0550	0.0015–0.0030	0.0015–0.0032	0.0005–0.0070
	R	6-173 (2.8)	0.0007–0.0017	0.0098–0.0197	0.0098–0.0197	0.0106–0.0492	0.0012–0.0028	0.0016–0.0037	0.0078
	D	6-189 (3.1)	0.0009–0.0022	0.0100–0.0200	0.0200–0.0280	0.0100–0.0300	0.0020–0.0035	0.0020–0.0035	0.0080
	L	6-231 (3.8)	0.0004–0.0022	0.0100–0.0250	0.0100–0.0250	0.0150–0.0550	0.0013–0.0031	0.0013–0.0031	0.0011–0.0081
	W	6-262 (4.3)	0.0007–0.0017	0.0100–0.0200	0.0180–0.0260	0.0150–0.0550	0.0014–0.0032	0.0014–0.0032	0.0014–0.0032
	Z	6-262 (4.3)	0.0007–0.0017	0.0100–0.0200	0.0100–0.0250	0.0150–0.0550	0.0012–0.0032	0.0012–0.0032	0.0020–0.0070
	Z①	6-262 (4.3)	0.0015–0.0030	0.0100–0.0200	0.0100–0.0250	0.0150–0.0550	0.0012–0.0032	0.0012–0.0032	0.0020–0.0070

① Turbocharged engine

TORQUE SPECIFICATIONS

All readings in ft. lbs.

Year	VIN	No. Cylinder Displacement cu. in. (liter)	Cylinder Head Bolts	Main Bearing Bolts	Rod Bearing Bolts	Crankshaft Pulley Bolts	Flywheel Bolts	Manifold Intake	Manifold Exhaust	Spark Plugs
1988	E	4-151 (2.5)	③	70	32	160	55④	25	①	11
	R	6-173 (2.8)	⑤	70	39	70	52	23	25	22
	Z	6-262 (4.3)	65	75	45	70	75	35	②	22
1989	E	4-151 (2.5)	③	70	32	160	55④	30	①	11
	R	6-173 (2.8)	⑤	70	39	70	52	23	25	22
	Z	6-262 (4.3)	65	80	45	70	75	35	②	22
1990	E	4-151 (2.5)	③	65	32	160	55④	25	①	11
	R	6-173 (2.8)	⑤	70	39	70	52	23	25	22
	D	6-189 (3.1)	⑤	72	39	85	52	10	19	18
	Z	6-262 (4.3)	65	75	45	70	75	35	②	22
1991	A	4-151 (2.5)	③	70	32	160	55④	25	①	11
	R	6-173 (2.8)	⑤	70	39	70	52	15	25	11
	D	6-189 (3.1)	⑤	72	39	75	52	⑩	25	18
	B	6-262 (4.3)	65	75	⑥	70	75	⑪	②	11
	Z	6-262 (4.3)	65	75	⑥	70	75	⑫	②	11
1992	A	4-151 (2.5)	③	70	32	160	55④	25	①	11
	R	6-173 (2.8)	⑤	70	39	70	52	15	25	11
	D	6-189 (3.1)	⑤	72	39	75	52	⑩	25	18
	L	6-231 (3.8)	⑨	⑮	⑦	⑧	⑭	⑪	18	12
	W	6-262 (4.3)	65	75	⑥	70	75	⑬	②	11
	Z⑯	6-262 (4.3)	65	75	⑥	70	75	⑫	②	11

① Inner bolts: 36 ft. lbs.
  Outer bolts: 32 ft. lbs.
② Center Bolts: 26 ft. lbs.
  Outer bolts: 20 ft. lbs.
③ Step 1: 18 ft. lbs.
  Step 2: Except studs—26 ft. lbs.
  Studs—18 ft. lbs.
  Step 3: additional 90° turn
④ Manual transmission—65 ft. lbs.
⑤ Step 1: 40 ft. lbs.
  Step 2: additional 90° turn

⑥ Step 1: 20 ft. lbs.
  Step 2: additional 60° turn
⑦ Step 1: 20 ft. lbs.
  Step 2: additional 50° turn
⑧ Step 1: 110 ft. lbs.
  Step 2: additional 76° turn
⑨ Step 1: 35 ft. lbs.
  Step 2: additional 130° turn
  Step 3: (4 center bolts) additional 30° turn
⑩ Step 1: 13 ft. lbs.
  Step 2: 19 ft. lbs.

⑪ Lower—88 inch lbs.
  Upper—22 ft. lbs.
⑫ Except position No. 9—35 ft. lbs.
  Position No. 9—41 ft. lbs.
⑬ Lower—35 ft. lbs.
  Upper—124 inch lbs.
⑭ Step 1: 11 ft. lbs.
  Step 2: additional 50° turn
⑮ Step 1: 26 ft. lbs.
  Step 2: additional 45° turn
⑯ Including turbocharged engine

BRAKE SPECIFICATIONS

Year	Model	Lug Nut Torque (ft. lbs.)	Master Cylinder Bore	Brake Disc Minimum Thickness	Brake Disc Maximum Runout	Standard Brake Drum Diameter	Minimum Lining Thickness Front	Minimum Lining Thickness Rear
1988	S10/15 Pick-Up	①	—	0.965	0.004	9.500	0.030	0.030
	S10/15 Blazer/Jimmy	①	—	0.965	0.004	9.500	0.030	0.030
	Astro/Safari	90	—	0.965	0.004	9.500	0.030	0.030
1989	S10/15 Pick-Up	①	—	0.965	0.004	9.500	0.030	0.030
	S10/15 Blazer/Jimmy	①	—	0.965	0.004	9.500	0.030	0.030
	Astro/Safari	90	—	0.965	0.004	9.500	0.030	0.030

BRAKE SPECIFICATIONS

Year	Model	Lug Nut Torque (ft. lbs.)	Master Cylinder Bore	Brake Disc		Standard Brake Drum Diameter	Minimum Lining Thickness	
				Minimum Thickness	Maximum Runout		Front	Rear
1990	S10/15 Pick-Up	①	—	0.965	0.004	9.500	0.030	0.030
	S10/15 Blazer/Jimmy	①	—	0.965	0.004	9.500	0.030	0.030
	Astro/Safari	90	—	0.965	0.004	9.500	0.030	0.030
	Lumina	100	0.944	0.957	0.004	8.863	0.030	0.030
	Silhouette	100	0.944	0.957	0.004	8.863	0.030	0.030
	Trans Sport	100	0.944	0.957	0.004	8.863	0.030	0.030
1991	S10/15 Pick-Up	①	—	0.965	0.004	9.500	0.030	0.030
	Sonoma	②	—	0.965	0.004	9.500	0.030	0.030
	Syclone	100	—	0.965	0.004	9.500	0.030	0.030
	S10/15 Blazer/Jimmy	①	—	0.965	0.004	9.500	0.030	0.030
	Bravada	90	—	0.965	0.004	9.500	0.030	0.030
	Astro/Safari	90	—	0.965	0.004	9.500	0.030	0.030
	Lumina	100	0.944	0.957	0.004	8.863	0.030	0.030
	Silhouette	100	0.944	0.957	0.004	8.863	0.030	0.030
	Trans Sport	100	0.944	0.957	0.004	8.863	0.030	0.030
1992	S10/15 Pick-Up	90	—	0.965	0.004	9.500	0.030	0.030
	Sonoma	②	—	0.965	0.004	9.500	0.030	0.030
	Syclone	100	—	0.965	0.004	9.500	0.030	0.030
	S10/15 Blazer/Jimmy	90	—	0.965	0.004	9.500	0.030	0.030
	Bravada	90	—	0.965	0.004	9.500	0.030	0.030
	Typhoon	100	—	0.965	0.004	9.500	0.030	0.030
	Astro/Safari	90	—	0.965	0.004	9.500	0.030	0.030
	Lumina	100	0.944	0.957	0.004	8.863	0.030	0.030
	Silhouette	100	0.944	0.957	0.004	8.863	0.030	0.030
	Trans Sport	100	0.944	0.957	0.004	8.863	0.030	0.030

① Steel wheels—73 ft. lbs.
  Aluminum wheels—90 ft. lbs.
② 2 wheel drive—80 ft. lbs.
  4 wheel drive—100 ft. lbs.

WHEEL ALIGNMENT SPECIFICATIONS

Year	Model	Caster (deg.)		Camber (deg.)		Toe-In (in.)	Steering Axis Inclination (deg.)
		Range	Preferred Setting	Range	Preferred Setting		
1988	S10/15 Pick-Up	1P–3P	2P	0–1⅝P	¹³/₁₆P	⁵/₆₄P	NA
	S10/15 Blazer/Jimmy	1P–3P	2P	0–1⅝P	¹³/₁₆P	⁵/₆₄P	NA
	Astro/Safari 2WD	1¹/₁₆P–3¹¹/₁₆P	2¹¹/₁₆P	0–1¹⁹/₃₂P	¹³/₁₆P	⁵/₆₄P	NA
1989	S10/15 Pick-Up	1P–3P	2P	0–1⅝P	¹³/₁₆P	⁵/₆₄P	NA
	S10/15 Blazer/Jimmy	1P–3P	2P	0–1⅝P	¹³/₁₆P	⁵/₆₄P	NA
	Astro/Safari 2WD	1¹/₁₆P–3¹¹/₁₆P	2¹¹/₁₆P	0–1¹⁹/₃₂P	¹³/₁₆P	⁵/₆₄P	NA

WHEEL ALIGNMENT SPECIFICATIONS

Year	Model	Caster (deg.) Range	Caster (deg.) Preferred Setting	Camber (deg.) Range	Camber (deg.) Preferred Setting	Toe-In (in.)	Steering Axis Inclination (deg.)
1990	S10/15 Pick-Up	1P–3P	2P	0–1⅝P	¹³/₁₆P	⁵/₆₄P	NA
	S10/15 Blazer/Jimmy	1P–3P	2P	0–1⅝P	¹³/₁₆P	⁵/₆₄P	NA
	Astro/Safari 2WD	1¹/₁₆P–3¹¹/₁₆P	2¹¹/₁₆P	0–1¹⁹/₃₂P	¹³/₁₆P	³/₃₂P	NA
	Astro/Safari 4WD	2¹/₁₆P–4¹/₁₆P	3¹/₁₆P	0–1¾P	⅞P	³/₃₂P	NA
	Lumina	¹¹/₁₆P–2¹¹/₁₆P	1¹¹/₁₆P	½N–½P	0	0	NA
	Silhouette	¹¹/₁₆P–2¹¹/₁₆P	1¹¹/₁₆P	½N–½P	0	0	NA
	Trans Sport	¹¹/₁₆P–2¹¹/₁₆P	1¹¹/₁₆P	½N–½P	0	0	NA
1991	S10/15 Pick-Up	1P–3P	2P	0–1⅝P	¹³/₁₆P	⁵/₆₄P	NA
	Sonoma	1P–3P	2P	0–1⅝P	¹³/₁₆P	⁵/₆₄P	NA
	Syclone	2½P–4½P	3½P	¾N–1⁹/₁₆P	0	⁵/₆₄P	NA
	S10/15 Blazer/Jimmy	1P–3P	2P	0–1⅝P	¹³/₁₆P	⁵/₆₄P	NA
	Bravada	1P–3P	2P	0–1⅝P	¹³/₁₆P	⁵/₆₄P	NA
	Astro/Safari 2WD	1¹¹/₁₆P–3¹¹/₁₆P	2¹¹/₁₆P	0–1¹⁹/₃₂P	¹³/₁₆P	³/₃₂P	NA
	Astro/Safari 4WD	2¹/₁₆P–4¹/₁₆P	3¹/₁₆P	0–1¾P	⅞P	³/₃₂P	NA
	Lumina	¹¹/₁₆P–2¹¹/₁₆P	1¹¹/₁₆P	½N–½P	0	0	NA
	Silhouette	¹¹/₁₆P–2¹¹/₁₆P	1¹¹/₁₆P	½N–½P	0	0	NA
	Trans Sport	¹¹/₁₆P–2¹¹/₁₆P	1¹¹/₁₆P	½N–½P	0	0	NA
1992	S10/15 Pick-Up	1P–3P	2P	0–1⅝P	¹³/₁₆P	⁵/₆₄P	NA
	Sonoma	1P–3P	2P	0–1⅝P	¹³/₁₆P	⁵/₆₄P	NA
	Syclone	2½P–4½P	3½P	¾N–1⁹/₁₆P	0	⁵/₆₄P	NA
	S10/15 Blazer/Jimmy	1P–3P	2P	0–1⅝P	¹³/₁₆P	⁵/₆₄P	NA
	Bravada	1P–3P	2P	0–1⅝P	¹³/₁₆P	⁵/₆₄P	NA
	Typhoon	2½P–4½P	3½P	¾N–1⁹/₁₆P	0	⁵/₆₄P	NA
	Astro/Safari 2WD	1¹¹/₁₆P–3¹¹/₁₆P	2¹¹/₁₆P	0–1¹⁹/₃₂P	¹³/₁₆P	³/₃₂P	NA
	Astro/Safari 4WD	2¹/₁₆P–4¹/₁₆P	3¹/₁₆P	0–1¾P	⅞P	³/₃₂P	NA
	Lumina	¹¹/₁₆P–2¹¹/₁₆P	1¹¹/₁₆P	½N–½P	0	0	NA
	Silhouette	¹¹/₁₆P–2¹¹/₁₆P	1¹¹/₁₆P	½N–½P	0	0	NA
	Trans Sport	¹¹/₁₆P–2¹¹/₁₆P	1¹¹/₁₆P	½N–½P	0	0	NA

NA—Not available
N—Negative
P—Positive

ENGINE ELECTRICAL

NOTE: Disconnecting the negative battery cable on some vehicles may interfere with the functions of the on board computer systems and may require the computer to undergo a relearning process.

Distributor

Removal and Installation

1. Disconnect the negative battery cable.
2. Remove all necessary components in order to gain access to the distributor assembly.
3. Disconnect the distributor electrical connectors. Mark and remove the spark plug wires.

4. Remove the distributor cap. Position the engine at TDC. Match Mark the rotor and the distributor body. Matchmark the distributor assembly and the engine block.
5. Remove the distributor retaining bolt. Carefully remove the distributor from the vehicle.

NOTE: As the distributor is removed from the engine, the rotor will turn counterclockwise. Observe and mark the start and finish rotation of the rotor. When reinstalling, position the rotor at the last mark and set the distributor into the engine. As the distributor drops into place, the rotor should turn to its original position, providing the engine crankshaft had not been rotated with the distributor out.

Installation

TIMING NOT DISTURBED

NOTE: To ensure correct ignition timing if the engine has not been disturbed, the distributor must be installed with the rotor in the same position as when removed.

1. Align the rotor to the last mark made and install the distributor in the engine.
2. The rotor should turn and end up at the first mark made. Ensure the distributor and oil pump rod are fully engaged.
3. Reconnect the distributor cap and wires.
4. Tighten the distributor hold-down bolt and set the timing.

TIMING DISTURBED

1. Remove the No. 1 spark plug. Place a finger over the spark plug hole and rotate the engine in the normal direction of rotation slowly, until compression is felt.
2. Align the timing mark on the crankshaft pulley to the **0** on the engine timing indicator by rotating the engine in the same direction slowly.
3. Turn the distributor shaft of the rotor until it points to the No. 1 spark plug tower on the cap.
4. Install the distributor, distributor cap, spark plug, wiring and connectors.
5. Check the engine timing and adjust, as required.

Distributorless Ignition System

Removal and Installation

IGNITION COILS

NOTE: Any one of the 3 coils may be removed individually of the other 2 coils.

1. Disconnect the negative battery cable.
2. Remove the secondary ignition wires from the coil being removed.
3. Remove the coil mounting screws.
4. Remove the ignition coil assembly.
5. Installation is the reverse of the removal procedure.

IGNITION MODULE

1. Disconnect the negative battery cable.
2. Disconnect the wire connector from the module.
3. Remove the screws securing the module and coils to the mounting plate.
4. Separate the ignition coils from the module by pulling straight up on the coils.
5. Position the coils and wiring so the assembly will not be hanging from the wires.
6. Installation is the reverse of the removal procedure.

CRANKSHAFT SENSOR

1. Disconnect the negative battery cable.
2. Remove the serpentine belt from the crankshaft pulley.
3. Raise and support the vehicle safely.
4. Remove the right front tire and wheel assembly.
5. Remove the right inner fender access cover.
6. Using a 28mm socket, remove the harmonic balancer retaining bolt.
7. Using a harmonic balancer pulley removal tool, remove the balancer assembly. Remove the sensor shield.
8. Disconnect the sensor electrical connector. Remove the sensor and pedestal from the engine block.
9. Remove the sensor from the pedestal.

To install:
10. Loosely install the crankshaft sensor on the pedestal.
11. Position the sensor with the pedestal attached onto tool J–37089.
12. Position the assembly onto the crankshaft.

Install crankshaft sensor using tool J–37089—3.8L engine

13. Install the pedestal securing bolts and torque to 14–28 ft. lbs. (20–40 Nm).
14. Torque the pedestal pinch bolt to 36–40 inch lbs. (4–4.5 Nm).
15. Remove the tool. Install the crankshaft sensor shield.
16. Reconnect the wire connector.
17. Place tool J–37089 on the harmonic balancer; if any vane of the balancer touches the tool, replace the balancer assembly.
18. Position the balancer onto the crankshaft.
19. Apply sealer to the threads of the balancer bolt and torque the bolt to 110 ft. lbs. (150 Nm) plus turn the bolt an additional 76 degrees.
20. Install the fender shield, tire and wheel assembly.
21. Lower the vehicle.
22. Install the serpentine belt and connect the negative battery cable.

Ignition Timing

The 3.8L engine uses a Distributorless Ignition System (DIS) which is nonadjustable.

Adjustment

1. Locate and clean off the timing marks.
2. Use chalk or white paint to color the mark on the scale that will indicate the correct timing when aligned with the mark on the pulley or the pointer.
3. Attach a tachometer and timing light to the engine per manufacturers recommendation.
4. On some engines, it is necessary to disconnect the EST connector to set the timing. See the underhood emission control label.
5. Adjust the idle to the correct specification.
6. Loosen the distributor retaining bolt so the distributor can be turned with a little resistance.
7. With the timing light aimed at the timing marks, turn the distributor in the direction of rotor rotation to retard the timing, and in the opposite direction of rotor rotation to advance the timing. Set the timing marks to specification.
8. Turn the engine **OFF**, tighten the distributor holdown bolt and recheck the timing.

Alternator

For further information, please refer to "Alternators" in the Unit Repair section.

Precautions

Several precautions must be observed with alternator equipped vehicles to avoid damage to the unit.

• If the battery is removed for any reason, make sure it is reconnected with the correct polarity. Reversing the battery connections may result in damage to the 1-way rectifiers.

• When utilizing a booster battery as a starting aid, always connect the positive to positive terminals and the negative terminal from the booster battery to a good engine ground on the vehicle being started.

• Never use a fast charger as a booster to start vehicles.

• Disconnect the battery cables when charging the battery with a fast charger.

• Never attempt to polarize the alternator.

• Do not use test lamps of more than 12 volts when checking diode continuity.

• Do not short across or ground any of the alternator terminals.

• The polarity of the battery, alternator and regulator must be matched and considered before making any electrical connections within the system.

• Never separate the alternator on an open circuit. Make sure all connections within the circuit are clean and tight.

• Disconnect the battery ground terminal when performing any service on electrical components.

• Disconnect the battery if arc welding is to be done on the vehicle.

Removal and Installation

1. Disconnect the negative battery cable. Disconnect the electrical connectors at the alternator.

2. Remove the necessary components in order to gain access to the alternator assembly. On Astro and Safari, remove the upper radiator fan shroud.

3. Remove the alternator belt. If equipped, relieve the tension

Alternator mounting—2.5L engine

Alternator mounting—2.8L engine

Alternator mounting—3.1L engine

on the serpentine drive belt and remove the serpentine drive belt.

4. Remove the alternator retaining bolts and remove the alternator from the vehicle.

5. Installation is the reverse of the removal procedure. Adjust the alternator belt, as required.

Belt Tension Adjustment

SERPENTINE DRIVE BELT

The serpentine belt grooves must match the grooves in the pulleys. The tensioner is spring loaded. After removing the belt the tensioner will return the tension position.

1. Insert a ½ in. breaker bar into the tensioner pulley.

1. Bolt
2. Engine wiring harness bracket
3. Alternator
4. Crankshaft torsional damper
5. Coolant pump pulley

Alternator mounting—3.8L engine

Alternator mounting—4.3L engine

2. Rotate the tensioner to loosen the belt, then remove the belt.

3. Route the new belt over all the pulleys except the water pump.

4. Insert a ½ in. breaker bar into the tensioner pulley.

5. Rotate the tensioner pulley.

6. Install the belt over the water pump pulley.

7. Check the belt for correct V groove tracking.

Starter

For further information, please refer to "Starters" in the Unit Repair section.

Removal and Installation

PICK-UP, BLAZER, BRAVADA, JIMMY, SONOMA, SYCLONE AND TYPHOON

2WD Vehicle

1. Disconnect the negative battery cable.
2. Raise and support the vehicle safely.
3. Disconnect the solenoid wiring.
4. On the 2.5L engine, disconnect the end mounting bracket and wiring.
5. Remove the 2 bolts and washers; then remove the starter and the shim.
6. Installation is the reverse of removal. Install the shim and torque the mounting bolts to specification.

4WD Vehicle

1. Disconnect the negative battery cable.
2. Raise and support the vehicle safely.
3. Disconnect the solenoid wiring.
4. On the 2.5L engine, disconnect the end mounting bracket and wiring.
5. Remove the 4 bolts on the skid plate, if equipped and remove the skid plate.
6. Remove the bolts and 2 brackets holding the brake line to the crossmember.
7. Remove the 3 bolts on each side and remove the crossmember.
8. Remove the bracket holding the transmission cooler lines to the flywheel housing, brace rod to the flywheel housing, and the flywheel housing as necessary.

9. Remove the 2 bolts and washers and remove the starter and the shim.

10. Installation is the reverse of removal. Install the shim and torque the mounting bolts to specification.

ASTRO AND SAFARI

1. Disconnect the negative battery cable.
2. Raise and support the vehicle safely.
3. Disconnect the solenoid wiring.
4. Remove the 2 bolts and washers and remove the starter and the shim.
5. Installation is the reverse of removal. Install the shim, if used, and torque the mounting bolts to specification.

LUMINA APV, SILHOUETTE AND TRANS SPORT

3.1L Engine

1. Disconnect the negative battery cable.
2. Raise and support the vehicle safely.
3. Remove the air conditioning compressor brace.

4. Disconnect the oil pressure sensor electrical connector and remove the sensor.
5. Remove the solenoid cover and disconnect the solenoid wiring.
6. Remove the 2 bolts and washers and remove the starter and the shim.
7. Installation is the reverse of removal. Install the shim, if used, and torque the mounting bolts to specification.

3.8L Engine

1. Disconnect the negative battery cable.
2. Raise and support the vehicle safely.
3. Disconnect the solenoid wiring and position aside.
4. Remove the flywheel cover. Remove the starter bolts and shim.
5. Remove the starter assembly.
6. Installation is the reverse of removal. Install the shim, if used, and torque the mounting bolts to specification.

CHASSIS ELECTRICAL

Heater Blower Motor

Removal and Installation

PICK-UP, BLAZER, BRAVADA, JIMMY, SONOMA, SYCLONE AND TYPHOON

1. Disconnect the battery ground cable.
2. Disconnect the blower motor electrical connections.
3. Remove the blower motor attaching screws.
4. Remove the blower motor from the vehicle.
5. Installation is the reverse of the removal procedure.

ASTRO AND SAFARI

1. Disconnect the negative battery cable.
2. Remove the engine coolant bottle. Remove the 2 bolts from the windshield washer bottle and position the assembly aside.
3. Disconnect the electrical connections and cooling tube from the heater blower assembly. Remove the blower motor relay bracket, as required.
4. Remove the blower motor retaining screws and remove the motor from the vehicle.
5. Installation is the reverse of the removal procedure. Transfer the blower motor cage, as required.

LUMINA APV, SILHOUETTE AND TRANS SPORT

1. Disconnect the negative battery cable.
2. Remove the engine air cleaner.
3. Disconnect the left windshield wiper arm linkage.
4. Disconnect the blower motor electrical harness.
5. Remove the blower motor retaining screws and remove the blower motor assembly.
6. Installation is the reverse of removal.

Windshield Wiper Motor

Removal and Installation

PICK-UP, BLAZER, BRAVADA, JIMMY, SONOMA, SYCLONE AND TYPHOON

1. Disconnect the negative battery cable.
2. Remove the windshield wiper arms.
3. Remove the cowl vent grille and screen.
4. Mark the position of the wiper motor arm. Remove the wiper motor arm nut and remove the arm.
5. Disconnect the electrical wiring from the motor assembly.

6. Remove the motor retaining screws. Remove the windshield wiper motor while guiding it through the hole.
7. Installation is the reverse of the removal procedure. Install the arm in alignment with the previously made mark.

ASTRO AND SAFARI

1. Disconnect the negative battery cable.
2. Remove the cowl vent grille.
3. Disconnect the transmission link from the crank arm on the motor by prying it toward the rear of the vehicle.
4. Remove the motor mounting bolts and remove the motor.
5. Installation is the reverse of removal.

LUMINA APV, SILHOUETTE AND TRANS SPORT

1988–90

1. Run the wipers to the park position.
2. Disconnect the negative battery cable.
3. Disconnect the washer hoses.
4. Remove the nut from each wiper arm.
5. Lift each wiper arm and insert a suitable pin completely through the 2 holes located next to the pivot of the arm, then using tool J–22888 or equivalent, remove the arms from the driveshafts.
6. Remove the air cleaner.
7. Disconnect the wiring harness from the wiper motor.
8. Using a Torx® bit, remove the 2 wiper housing bolts.
9. Remove the 3 mounting nuts and washers and remove the module from the vehicle.
10. Loosen the 2 crank arm socket screws and lockwashers until the socket releases from the crank arm ball.

NOTE: Do not remove the crank arm from the motor.

11. Remove the 3 wiper motor retaining screws and remove the wiper motor from the frame.

To install:

12. Make sure the wiper motor is in the park position and secure the motor to the frame with the 3 screws.
13. Attach the crank arm socket to the crank arm ball and tighten the 2 screws.
14. Install the wiper module into the vehicle and secure with mounting screws.
15. Connect the wiring harness to the wiper motor.
16. Install the air cleaner assembly.
17. Install the wiper arms onto the shafts and secure with nuts.

Instrument cluster assembly—Pick-Up, Blazer, Bravada and Jimmy

Instrument cluster assembly—Astro and Safari

18. Remove pin near each arm pivot.

19. Measure from the tip of the blade to the bottom edge of the glass and ensure the left wiper blade measurement is 5.8 in. (147mm) and the right wiper blade measurement is 1.3 in. (33mm). Hold the blade and torque the nut to 41 ft. lbs. (55 Nm).

20. Reconnect the washer hose and battery negative cable.

1991–92

1. Disconnect the negative battery cable.

Instrument cluster assembly—Silhouette

2. Disconnect the wiper motor wiring harness connector.

3. Disconnect the transmission link from the crank arm on the motor by loosening the 2 crank arm screws.

4. Remove the motor mounting bolts and slide the motor out of its mounting.

5. Installation is the reverse of removal.

Windshield Wiper Switch

Removal and Installation

EXCEPT TRANS SPORT AND SILHOUETTE

The wiper switch is part of the multifunction switch on the column.

1. Disconnect the negative battery cable.
2. Remove the wiring protector cover under the column.
3. Disconnect the multifunction switch.
4. Disconnect the cruise control wire.
5. Remove the switch.
6. Installation is the reverse of removal.

Instrument cluster assembly—Trans Sport

TRANS SPORT AND SILHOUETTE

1. Disconnect the negative battery cable.
2. Grip the pod and carefully pull the wiper switch out to release the 2 spring retaining clips.
3. Disconnect the electrical connector and remove the switch.
4. Installation is the reverse of removal.

Instrument Cluster

Removal and Installation

PICK-UP, BLAZER, BRAVADA, JIMMY, SONOMA, SYCLONE AND TYPHOON

1. Disconnect the negative battery cable.
2. Remove the lamp switch trim plate screws and remove the trim plate.
3. Disconnect the lamp switch harness.
4. Remove the air conditioner and heater control assembly retaining screws and remove the control assembly.
5. Disconnect the air conditioner and heater control assembly harness.
6. Remove the filler panel screws and remove the filler panel.
7. Remove the instrument cluster housing nuts and remove the instrument cluster housing.
8. Remove the instrument cluster nuts. Disconnect the harness and remove the instrument cluster.
9. Installation is the reverse of the removal procedure.

ASTRO AND SAFARI

1. Disconnect the negative battery cable.
2. Remove the instrument panel cluster trim plate and screws.
3. Remove the instrument panel cluster and screws.
4. Disconnect the instrument panel cluster harness connectors and speedometer cable, as required.
5. Remove the instrument panel cluster.
6. Installation is the reverse of the removal procedure.

LUMINA APV

1. Disconnect the negative battery cable.
2. Remove the 4 screws securing the instrument panel pad to the instrument panel lower trim pad.
3. On Canadian models, if equipped, disconnect the daytime running lights sensor attached to the pad under the front left hand speaker grille.
4. Lift the instrument panel trim pad up and pull the pad rearward to disengage the pad from the 4 slots in the lower trim pad and remove the pad assembly.
5. Grip the pod and carefully pull the wiper switch out to release the 2 spring retaining clips.
6. Disconnect the electrical connector and remove the switch.
7. Remove the 2 cluster housing screws attaching the trim to the instrument panel lower trim pad.
8. Feed the instrument panel harness through the switch pod openings in the housing.
9. Lift the housing up while pulling rearward to release the 2 tabs on the pad from the slots in the housing and remove the cluster housing.
10. Remove the 4 bolts securing the cluster to the right and left hand retainers.
11. Disconnect the instrument panel harness connector and remove the cluster.

To install:

12. Connect the harness to the instrument cluster.
13. Lift the housing up and push the 2 tabs on the pad into the slots in the housing.
14. Install the 2 cluster housing screws attaching the trim to the instrument panel lower trim pad.
15. Connect the electrical connector and install the switch.
17. Install the instrument panel trim pad.
18. On Canadian models, if equipped, connect the daytime running lights sensor attached to the pad under the front left hand speaker grille.
19. Install the 4 screws securing the instrument panel pad to the instrument panel lower trim pad.
21. Connect the negative battery cable.

SILHOUETTE AND TRANS SPORT

1. Disconnect the negative battery cable.
2. Open the glove box door to access the 2 screws securing the lower instrument panel trim pad assembly to the instrument panel pad assembly.
3. Remove the 2 screws securing the instrument cluster trim panel to the instrument panel pad.
4. Remove the screw retaining the headlamp switch pod to the cluster trim panel and remove the headlamp switch pod. Disconnect the wiring harness to the pod.
5. Remove the screw retaining the windshield wiper switch pod to the cluster trim panel and remove the wiper switch pod. Disconnect the wiring harness to the pod.
6. Remove the 2 screws behind each switch pod securing the cluster trim panel to the left and right instrument cluster mounting brackets.
7. Remove the steering column opening filler.
8. Disconnect the **PRNDL** cable clip.
9. Disconnect the instrument panel harness connector to the instrument cluster.
10. Remove the 2 screws on each side from the left and right cluster retainer brackets and remove the instruments cluster.

To install:

11. Connect the instrument panel harness connector to the instrument cluster.
12. Install the instrument cluster and secure the cluster retainer brackets with 2 screws.
13. Connect the **PRNDL** cable clip.
14. Install the steering column opening filler.
15. Install the 2 screws behind each switch pod securing the cluster trim panel to the left and right instrument cluster mounting brackets.

16. Connect the wiring harness to the pod. Install the wiper switch pod.

17. Connect the wiring harness to the pod. Install the headlamp switch pod.

18. Install the 2 screws securing the instrument cluster trim panel to the instrument panel pad.

19. Install the 2 screws securing the lower instrument panel trim pad assembly to the instrument panel pad assembly, behind the glove box door.

20. Connect the negative battery cable.

Speedometer

The cable driven speedometers were replaced with electronic controlled units as of 1989 and the speedometer assembly is non-serviceable.

Removal and Installation

PICK-UP, BLAZER AND JIMMY

1. Remove the instrument cluster.
2. Remove the cluster case retaining screws.
3. Remove the speedometer to cluster case retaining screws.
4. Remove the cluster panel from the cluster case.
5. Remove the speedometer mounting screws and remove the speedometer.
6. Installation is the reverse of removal.

ASTRO AND SAFARI

1. Remove the instrument cluster.
2. Remove the speedometer head retaining screws and remove the speedometer head.
3. Installation is the reverse of removal.

Dimmer Switch

Removal and Installation

1. Disconnect the negative battery cable. If equipped, remove the lower trim panel.
2. Remove the steering column retaining bolts. Lower the steering column assembly to gain access to the switch retaining screws. Extreme care is necessary to prevent damage to the collapsible column.
3. Make sure the ignition switch is in the **LOCK** position.
4. Remove the electrical connections from the switch. Remove the switch retaining screws. Remove the switch from the column.

To install:

5. Attach the switch to the column with the screws finger-tight. To adjust the dimmer switch, depress the switch slightly to allow insertion of a ú/32 in. drill bit into the hole above the actuator rod. Force the switch upward to remove all lash, then tighten the screw.
7. Connect the switch wire harness.
8. Raise and secure the column the steering column. Install the lower trim plate, if removed.
9. Connect the negative battery cable.

Turn Signal Switch

Removal and Installation

1. Disconnect the negative battery cable.
2. Remove the steering wheel.
3. Remove the instrument panel trim cover. Remove the turn signal wire harness cover and disconnect the turn signal harness connector.

NOTE: To save time, attach a piece of wire or string to turn signal harness connector before pulling the har-

ness up through the column. Then attach the string or wire to the new switch to help guide the harness back down through the column upon installation.**

4. Insert a suitable tool in the slot in the lock plate cover and remove the cover.
5. Use lock plate compressing tool J–23653–A or equivalent, on the steering shaft and compress the lock plate. Pry the retaining ring off the shaft and remove the lock plate.

NOTE: If the column is being disassembled on a bench, the shaft could slide out of the end of the mast jacket when the snapring is removed.

6. Remove the turn signal canceling cam, upper bearing spring, thrust washer, multifunction lever screw and lever.
7. Press the hazard warning knob inward and then unscrew.
8. Remove the turn signal switch mounting screws. Pull the switch straight up, guiding the wiring harness and cover through the column housing.

To install:

9. Route the harness down through the column and secure the switch to the column.
10. Install the hazard warning knob and the screw.
11. Install the turn signal canceling cam, upper bearing spring, thrust washer, multifunction lever screw and lever.
12. Use lock plate compressing tool J–23653–A or equivalent on the steering shaft and compress the lock plate. Install the retaining ring onto the shaft
13. Install the lock plate cover and steering wheel.
14. Connect the turn signal harness connector. Install the turn signal wire harness cover and the instrument panel trim cover.
15. Connect the negative battery cable.

Combination Switch

Removal and Installation

1. Disconnect the negative battery cable.
2. Remove the wiring protector cover under the column.
3. Connect a piece of wire to the multifunction switch connector to help guide the wire down the column on installation.
4. Disconnect the cruise control wire connector.
5. Remove the mutlifunction lever by turning and pulling lever out.
6. Installation is the reverse of removal. Feed the cruise control wire into the column using the wire attached to the connector.

Ignition Lock Cylinder

Removal and Installation

1. Disconnect the negative battery cable.
2. Place the lock cylinder in the **RUN** position.
3. Remove the steering wheel.
4. Remove the turn signal switch. Pull the switch rearward far enough to slip it over the shaft. Do not pull the harness out of the column.
5. Remove the retaining screw and remove the lock cylinder.

To install:

6. Align the cylinder and key with the keyway in the housing, rotate clockwise and push all the way in.
7. Install the retaining screw.
8. Install the turn signal switch and steering wheel.
9. Connect the negative battery cable.

Ignition Switch

Removal and Installation

1. Disconnect the negative battery cable. If equipped, remove the lower trim panel.

2. Remove the steering column retaining bolts. Lower the steering column assembly to gain access to the switch retaining screws. Extreme care is necessary to prevent damage to the collapsible column.

3. Make sure the switch is in the **LOCK** position. If the lock cylinder is out, pull the switch rod up to the stop, then go down one detent.

4. Remove the electrical connections from the switches. Remove the switch retaining screws. Remove the switch from the column.

5. Installation is the reverse of the removal procedure. Before installation, make sure the ignition switch is in the **LOCK** position.

Stoplight Switch

Adjustment

1. Depress the brake pedal and press the switch in until it is firmly seated in its mount.
2. Pull the brake pedal back against the pedal stop.
3. Electrical contact should be made when the brake pedal is depressed from its fully released position.

Removal and Installation

1. Disconnect the negative battery cable. Remove the under dash trim panel.
2. Disconnect the switch electrical connections. Remove the switch assembly from its mount.
3. Installation is the reverse of the removal procedure. Adjust the switch, as required.

Clutch Switch

Adjustment

The clutch switch is automatic adjusting upon installation and initial pedal depression.

Removal and Installation

1. Disconnect the negative battery cable. Remove the under dash trim panel.
2. Disconnect the switch electrical connections.
3. Remove the switch retaining screw, if equipped and remove the switch from the clutch pedal.
To install:
4. Move the slider to the rear of the shaft.
5. Push the clutch pedal to the floor.
6. Move the slider down the shaft.
7. Release the clutch pedal.
8. Install the electrical connector.
9. Install the trim panel. Reconnect the negative battery cable.

Neutral Safety Switch

Adjustment

1. Move the switch all the way toward the **L** gear position.
2. Move the selector to the **P** position.
3. The main housing and housing back should ratchet, providing proper switch adjustment.

Removal and Installation

1. Disconnect the negative battery cable.
2. Place the gear selector in **N** position.
3. Remove the steering column lower trim cover and disconnect the switch wire connector.
4. Spread the tangs on the housing and remove the switch.

To install:
5. Align the actuator on the switch with the hole in the shift tube.
6. Position the rear portion of the switch (wire connector side) to fit into the cutout in the lower jacket.
7. Push down on the front of the switch to engage the 2 tangs.
8. Move the gear selector to the **N** position and the switch is adjusted. Reconnect the switch wire connector.
9. Install the lower trim cover and connect the negative battery cable.

Fuses, Circuit Breakers and Relays

Location

ASTRO, BLAZER, BRAVADA, JIMMY, PICK-UP, SAFARI, SONOMA, SYCLONE AND TYPHOON

Fuse Block—located at the far left side of the instrument panel.

Convenience Center—located at the far left side of the instrument panel.

Hazard Warning Relay—mounted on the convenience center.

Horn Relay—mounted on the convenience center.

Alarm Module or Buzzers—mounted on the convenience center.

Circuit Breakers—mounted on the convenience center.

A/C Low Fan Relay—mounted on the convenience center.

LUMINA APV, SILHOUETTE AND TRANS SPORT

Fuse Panel—located inside the glove compartment.

Convenience Center—mounted to a bracket behind the glove compartment. It can be reached by removing the right sound insulator panel. It contains the hazard warning flasher, horn relay and circuit breakers, which can be removed by pulling straight out. It also contains the chime module and A/C low fan relay. To remove the chime module first release the locking tab.

Computers

Location

ASTRO AND SAFARI

Electronic Control Module (ECM)—located in the passenger compartment behind the right side cowl panel.

Electronic Spark Control (ESC) Module (4.3L engine)—located at the right side of the engine above the valve cover.

Cruise Control Module (Electronic Cluster)—located on the left, near the brake booster.

Cruise Control Module (Standard Cluster)—located on the left side of the instrument panel on the rear of the dash.

BLAZER, BRAVADA, JIMMY, PICK-UP, SONOMA, SYCLONE AND TYPHOON

Electronic Control Module (ECM)—located in the passenger compartment behind the right side of instrument panel.

Electronic Spark Control (ESC) Module—located at the center of the firewall.

Cruise Control Module—located behind the instrument panel on the left side of the steering column.

LUMINA, SILHOUETTE AND TRANS SPORT

Electronic Control Module (ECM)—located below the right side of instrument panel, behind the convenience center.

Electronic Spark Control (ESC) Module—located behind the instrument panel, behind the convenience center.

Cruise Control Module—located behind the instrument panel on the left side.

Cruise Control

For further information, please refer to Chilton's Chassis Electronics Service Manual.

Servo Adjustment

1. Remove the cruise control cable from the servo.
2. Ensure ignition and fast idle cam are **OFF** and throttle is fully closed before adjusting servo.
3. Connect the cable to the servo. The rod should have 0.039–0.150 in. (1–4mm) of clearance at the stud.
4. Install the cable retainer and check for proper operation.

ENGINE COOLING

Radiator

Removal and Installation

ASTRO, BLAZER, BRAVADA, JIMMY, PICK-UP, SAFARI AND SONOMA

1. Disconnect the negative battery cable.
2. Drain the coolant from the radiator.
3. Remove the overflow hose.
4. Remove the upper fan shroud.
5. Disconnect the hoses.
6. Disconnect and plug the transmission fluid cooler lines, if equipped.
7. Disconnect and plug the engine oil cooler lines, if equipped.
8. Remove the radiator retaining bolts and remove the radiator.
9. Installation is the reverse of the removal procedure.

LUMINA APV, SILHOUETTE AND TRANS SPORT

1. Disconnect the negative battery cable.
2. Drain the coolant from the radiator.
3. Disconnect the engine forward strut bracket at the radiator, loosen the bolt at the other end and swing the strut rearward.
4. Disconnect the forward lamp harness from the fan frame and unplug the fan connector.
5. Remove the fan attaching bolts and remove the fan and frame assembly.
6. Scribe the latch location then remove the hood latch from the radiator support.
7. Disconnect the coolant hoses from the radiator and the coolant recovery tank hose from the radiator neck.
8. Disconnect and plug the transaxle oil cooler lines.
9. Remove the radiator to support attaching bolts and clamps and remove the radiator from the vehicle.
10. Installation is the reverse of removal.

SYCLONE AND TYPHOON

1. Disconnect the battery cables; remove the battery and tray assembly.
2. Remove the turbocharger inlet elbow.
3. Drain the cooling system into a suitable container.
4. Remove the heater and coolant reservoir hoses from the radiator.
5. Remove the upper fan shroud.
6. Remove the upper and lower radiator hoses from the radiator.
7. Disconnect and plug the transmission and oil cooler lines.
8. Remove the radiator assembly.
9. Installation is the reverse of the removal procedure.

Electric Cooling Fan

Removal and Installation
LUMINA APV, SILHOUETTE AND TRANS SPORT

1. Disconnect the negative battery cable.

2. Disconnect the engine forward strut bracket from the radiator frame and swing it rearward.
3. Disconnect the forward lamp harness from the fan frame.
4. Remove the fan attaching bolts.
5. Disconnect the fan wiring.
6. Remove the fan and frame assembly from the vehicle.
7. Installation is the reverse of the removal procedure.

Heater Core

For further information, please refer to Chilton's Air Conditioning and Heating Manual.

Removal and Installation
BLAZER, BRAVADA, JIMMY, PICK-UP, SONOMA, SYCLONE AND TYPHOON

1. Disconnect the negative battery cable.
2. Drain the cooling system.
3. Remove and plug the heater hoses at the heater core.

2.8L ENGINE

1. Coolant pump
2. Gasket
3. Nut
4. Bolts

2.5L ENGINE

Water pump assembly mounting—2.5L and 2.8L engines

1. Water pump
2. Gasket
3. 89 inch lbs. (10 Nm)
4. Locator— Must be vertical

Water pump assembly mounting—3.1L engine

1. Water pump
2. Engine front cover assembly
3. Gasket
4. 97 inch lbs. (11 Nm)
5. 29 ft. lbs. (39 Nm)

Water pump assembly mounting—3.8L engine

4. Remove the heater core cover attaching screws and remove the cover.
5. Remove the screw retainers at the end of the heater core.
6. Remove the core from under the dash assembly.
7. Installation is the reverse of the removal procedure.

ASTRO AND SAFARI

1. Disconnect the negative battery cable. Drain the engine coolant.
2. Remove the engine coolant bottle. Remove the bolts from the windshield washer bottle and position it aside. Remove and plug the heater hoses at the heater core.
3. Remove the instrument panel lower right filler panel. Remove the air distributor duct. Remove the engine cover as needed.
4. Remove the air duct. Remove vacuum lines and control cables as required.
5. Remove the heater core assembly retaining screws.
6. Remove the heater core cover plate. Remove the heater core.
7. Installation is the reverse of the removal procedure.

LUMINA APV, SILHOUETTE AND TRANS SPORT

1. Disconnect the negative battery cable.
2. Drain the cooling system.
3. Disconnect the heater hoses.
4. Remove the right side sound insulator from under the instrument panel.
5. Remove the glove box.
6. Disconnect the vacuum hoses and wiring from in front of the heater core cover.
7. Remove the heater core cover and remove the heater core.
8. Installation is the reverse of the removal procedure.

Water Pump

Removal and Installation

1. Disconnect the negative battery cable. Drain the coolant. Remove the fan shroud, as necessary. Remove the drive belts. Remove the fan shroud, fan and pulley assembly.
2. Remove the necessary components in order to gain access to the water pump retaining bolts.
3. Remove the water pump retaining bolts. Remove the water pump assembly from the engine.
4. Installation is the reverse of the removal procedure. Use a new gasket and torque all bolts to specification.

Thermostat

Removal and Installation

1. Disconnect the negative battery cable.
2. Drain the engine coolant.
3. Disconnect the upper radiator hose from the thermostat outlet.
4. Remove the thermostat housing bolts and remove the housing.
5. Remove the thermostat from the housing.

1. Water pump
2. Gasket
3. Bolt

Water pump assembly mounting—4.3L engine

6. Installation is the reverse of the removal procedure. Torque the housing bolts to specification.

7. Bleed the cooling system.

Cooling System Bleeding

1. To bleed the system, start with the system cool, the radiator cap off and the radiator filled to about an inch below the filler neck.

2. Start the engine and run it at slightly above normal idle speed. If air bubbles appear and the coolant level drops, fill the system with an antifreeze/water mixture to bring the level back to the proper level.

3. Run the engine until the thermostat opens and coolant flow is visible.

4. At this point, air is often expelled and the level may drop. Keep refilling the system until the level is near the top of the radiator and remains constant.

5. Fill the radiator to the filler neck. Replace the radiator filler cap and ensure the coolant reservoir is filled to the correct level.

FUEL SYSTEM

Fuel System Service Precaution

Relieving Fuel System Pressure

EXCEPT 3.8L AND 4.3L (MPI AND CPI) ENGINES

The Throttle Body Injection (TBI) system used on the 2.5L, 2.8L, 3.1L and 4.3L (VIN Z) engines have a built in bleed feature which requires no pressure relief before servicing. The Multi-Port Injection (MPI) and Central Port Injection (CPI) systems used with the 3.8L and 4.3L (VIN W) engines do require pressure relief before servicing system components.

3.8L AND 4.3L (MPI AND CPI) ENGINES

1. Place the transmission selector in the **P** position for automatic transmission or neutral for a manual transmission.

2. Set the parking brake and block the drive wheels.

3. Disconnect the negative battery cable.

4. Connect a fuel pressure gauge to the fuel line. Install a bleed hose into an approved container and slowly open the valve to relieve the system pressure.

5. Service the system as required.

Fuel Tank

Removal and Installation

EXCEPT LUMINA APV, SILHOUETTE AND TRANS SPORT

1. Disconnect the negative battery cable.

2. Properly relieve the fuel system pressure and, using an approved pump, drain the fuel from the tank into a suitable container.

3. Raise and support the vehicle safely.

4. Remove the fuel tank plastic shield.

5. Loosen the filler neck hose clamp at the tank and disconnect the filler neck.

6. Properly support the fuel tank and remove the tank brackets.

7. Lower the tank and remove the fuel/vapor hoses and electrical connections at the sender.

8. Remove the tank from the vehicle. Remove the fuel sender and seal ring using tool J–36608, as required.

To install:

9. Install the fuel sender and seal ring using tool J–36608, if removed.

10. With the aid of an assistant, raise the tank into position.

11. With the tank in position, connect the fuel/vapor hoses and electrical connections at the sender.

12. Install the fuel tank and brackets.

13. Connect the filler neck and tighten the filler neck hose clamp at the tank.

14. Install the fuel tank plastic shield.

15. Connect the negative battery cable.

16. Lower the vehicle. Refill the tank and inspect for leaks.

LUMINA APV, SILHOUETTE AND TRANS SPORT

1. Disconnect the negative battery cable.

2. Properly relieve the fuel system pressure and, using an approved pump, drain the fuel from the tank into a suitable container.

3. Raise and support the vehicle safely.

4. Remove the tail pipe, muffler and converter hangers.

5. Remove the exhaust heat shield attaching bolts. Support the exhaust and move the heat shield to gain access to the right side fuel tank retaining strap attaching bolts.

6. Remove the in-line fuel filter body clips.

7. Grasp both ends of 1 fuel line at both the inlet side of the in-line fuel filter and the return line connections and twist a ¼ turn in each direction to loosen any dirt in the quick connect fitting.

8. Squeeze the plastic tabs of the male ends of the connectors and pull the connections apart.

9. Loosen the filler neck hose clamp at the tank and disconnect the filler neck.

10. Lower the tank and remove the fuel vapor/vent hoses and electrical connections at the sender.

11. Properly support the fuel tank and remove the strap bolts and the fuel tank straps.

12. Remove the tank from the vehicle. Remove the fuel sender and seal ring using tool J–35731, as required.

To install:

13. Install the fuel sender and seal ring using tool J–35731, if removed.

14. With the aid of an assistant, raise the tank into position.

15. With the tank in position, connect the fuel vapor/vent hoses and electrical connections at the sender.

16. Secure the fuel tank with the brackets.

17. Connect the filler neck and tighten the filler neck hose clamp at the tank.

18. Apply oil to the fuel feed/return line quick connect fitting and push connectors together until a snap is heard. Pull on both lines and verify they are secure.

19. Secure the in-line fuel filter with new body clips.

20. Install the exhaust heat shield, the tail pipe, muffler and converter hangers.

21. Lower the vehicle an fill the tank.

22. Connect the negative battery cable.

23. Turn the ignition key **ON** for 2 seconds and then **OFF** for 10 seconds, repeat the procedure; then check the system for leaks.

Fuel Filter

Removal and Installation

2.5L ENGINE

1. Relieve the fuel system pressure.

2. Disconnect the negative battery cable.

1. Fuel return pipe
2. Clamp
3. Fuel return hose
4. In-line fuel filter
5. Clamp
6. Fuel feed hose
7. O-ring
8. Tighten nut to 20 ft. lbs. (26 Nm)

Fuel filter removal and installation—2.8L engine

1. Fuel feed pipe
2. In-line fuel filter
3. Left frame side member
4. Front fuel feed pipe

Fuel filter removal and installation—4.3L engine

MODEL 700 TBI

TBI INJECTOR

THROTTLE BODY PRESSURE REGULATOR

FUEL RETURN LINE

IN-LINE FUEL FILTER

FLEX HOSE

FUEL PRESSURE LINE

IN-TANK PUMP

FUEL CAP

FUEL PRESSURE GAGE TEST

FUEL TANK

PUMP INLET FILTER

MODEL 220 TBI

TBI UNIT INJECTORS

THROTTLE BODY PRESSURE REGULATOR

FUEL RETURN LINE

FLEX HOSE

FUEL PRESSURE LINE

FUEL CAP

IN-LINE FUEL FILTER

IN-TANK FUEL PUMP

FUEL PRESSURE GAGE TEST POINT

FUEL TANK

PUMP INLET FILTER

Fuel system pressure testing—2.5L, 2.8L and 4.3L (VIN Z) TBI engines

3. Remove the fuel line connections from the filter.

4. Remove the filter mounting clamp bolt and remove the filter.

5. Installation is the reverse of the removal procedure.

2.8L, 3.1L AND 3.8L ENGINES

1. Disconnect the negative battery cable.

2. Remove the fuel line connections from the filter. If equipped with quick connect fittings, use tool J–37088A to separate the lines.

3. Remove the filter mounting clamp bolt and remove the filter.

4. Installation is the reverse of the removal procedure.

4.3L ENGINE

The fuel filter is located along the frame rail of the vehicle.

1. Disconnect the negative battery cable.

2. Raise and safely support the vehicle.

3. Remove the fuel line connections from the filter.

4. Remove the filter mounting clamp bolt and remove the filter.

5. Installation is the reverse of the removal procedure.

Electric Fuel Pump

Pressure Testing

THROTTLE BODY INJECTION (TBI)

2.5L, 2.8L, 3.1L and 4.3L (VIN Z) Engines

1. Turn the engine **OFF** and relieve the fuel system pressure.

2. Disconnect the negative battery cable.

3. Disconnect the fuel supply line in the engine compartment. Install a suitable pressure gauge and T in the fuel line.

4. Connect the negative battery cable. Verify there is a sufficient quantity of fuel in the tank.

5. Start the engine and observe the pressure reading. The fuel pressure should be 9–13 psi.

6. If the fuel pressure reading is not as specified, inspect the fuel pump for proper operation, the lines and filter for kinks or clogging.

MULTI-PORT FUEL INJECTION

3.8L Engine

1. Turn the engine **OFF** and relieve the fuel system pressure.

2. Disconnect the negative battery cable.

3. Connect a suitable pressure gauge to the pressure regulator service fitting.

4. Reconnect the negative battery terminal and verify there is a sufficient quantity of fuel in the tank.

5. Turn the ignition switch **ON**, the fuel pump should run for 2 seconds and turn **OFF**; the pressure gauge reading should be approximately 41–47 psi.

6. Turn the ignition switch **OFF** and observe the pressure gauge, the reading should not leak down.

7. Start the vehicle and observe the gauge, the pressure should be 3–10 psi lower because of vacuum applied to the regulator.

8. If not as specified, inspect the pump, regulator, filter and lines for proper operation, kinks or clogging.

4.3L (VIN Z) Turbocharged Engine

1. Turn the engine **OFF** and relieve the fuel system pressure.

2. Disconnect the negative battery cable.

3. Connect a suitable pressure gauge to the pressure regulator service fitting.

4. Reconnect the negative battery terminal and verify there is a sufficient quantity of fuel in the tank.

5. Turn the ignition switch **ON**, the fuel pump should run for 2 seconds and turn **OFF**; the pressure gauge reading should be approximately 35–38 psi.

6. Turn the ignition switch **OFF** and observe the pressure gauge, the reading should not leak down.

7. Start the vehicle and observe the gauge, the pressure should be 25–30 psi because of vacuum applied to the regulator.

8. If not as specified, inspect the pump, regulator, filter and lines for proper operation, kinks or clogging.

CENTRAL PORT INJECTION (CPI)

4.3L (VIN W) Engine

1. Turn the engine **OFF** and relieve the fuel system pressure.

2. Disconnect the negative battery cable.

3. Connect a suitable pressure gauge to the pressure connection fitting.

4. Reconnect the negative battery terminal and verify there is a sufficient quantity of fuel in the tank.

5. Turn the ignition switch **ON**, the fuel pump should run for 2 seconds and turn **OFF**; the pressure gauge reading should be approximately 54–64 psi.

6. Turn the ignition switch **OFF** and observe the pressure gauge, the reading should not leak down.

7. Start the vehicle and observe the gauge, the pressure should be noticeably lower because of vacuum applied to the regulator.

8. If not as specified, inspect the pump, regulator, filter and lines for proper operation, kinks or clogging.

Fuel system pressure testing—3.1L engine

1. Pressure regulator
2. Fuel pressure gauge fitting
3. Quick connect fittings
4. Fuel return line
5. Inline filter
6. Fuel pressure line
7. To throttle body vacuum source

J 37287

Fuel system pressure testing—3.8L engine

BLEED HOSE

J 34730-1 FUEL PRESSURE GAGE ASSEMBLY

FUEL OUTLET

FUEL PRESSURE CONNECTION

FUEL RETURN LINE

FUEL CAP

FLEX HOSE

FUEL PRESSURE LINE

FUEL INLET

IN-LINE FUEL FILTER

FUEL TANK

IN-TANK FUEL PUMP

PUMP INLET FILTER

Fuel system pressure testing—4.3L (VIN W) CPI engine

Fuel system pressure testing—4.3L (VIN Z) Turbocharged engine

Removal and Installation

1. Properly relieve the fuel system pressure, as required.
2. Disconnect the negative battery cable.
3. Drain the fuel from the vehicle, into a suitable container.
4. Raise and safely support the vehicle.
5. Disconnect the fuel lines from the fuel tank. Disconnect the electrical leads from the fuel tank.
6. Disconnect the fuel filler neck from the tank.
7. Remove the tank mounting bolts and carefully lower the tank from the vehicle.
8. Remove the pump and pickup assembly retaining ring and remove the pump from the tank.
9. Installation is the reverse of the removal procedure.

Fuel Injection

For further information, please refer to Chilton's Electronic Engine Controls Manual.

Idle Speed Adjustment

2.5L ENGINE

The throttle stop screw that is used to adjust the idle speed of the vehicle, is preset at the factory. The throttle stop screw is then covered with a steel plug to prevent adjustment in the field. If it is necessary to gain access to the throttle stop screw, the following procedure will allow access to the throttle stop screw without removing the TBI unit from the manifold.

1. Using a small punch or equivalent, mark the center line of the throttle stop screw. Drill a ú/32 in. diameter hole through the casting of the hardened steel plug.
2. Using a ú/16 in. diameter punch or equivalent, punch out the steel plug.

3. With the transmission in **P** for automatic transmission or neutral for manual transmission equipped vehicles, the parking brake applied and the drive wheels blocked, remove the air cleaner and plug the thermac vacuum port, as required.
4. If equipped with automatic transmission, remove the transmission detent cable from the throttle control bracket in order to gain access to the minimum air adjustment screw.
5. Connect a tachometer to the engine and disconnect the idle air control motor connector.
6. Start the engine and let the engine reach normal operating temperature and the rpm to stabilize.
7. Install special tool J-33047 or equivalent, in the idle air passage of the throttle body. Be sure to seat the tool in the air passage until it is bottomed and no air leaks exist.
8. On the 2.5L engine, use a No. 20 Torx head bit or equivalent, turn the throttle stop screws until the minimum idle rpm is within specification.
9. If removed install the isolator. Install the transmission detent cable, as required.
10. Shut down the engine and remove the special tool or equivalent from the throttle body.
11. Reconnect the idle air control motor connector and seal the hole drilled through the throttle body housing with silicone sealant or equivalent.
12. Check the throttle position sensor voltage as required. Install the air cleaner and thermac vacuum line.

2.8L, 3.1L AND 4.3L (VIN Z) TBI ENGINES

1. Remove the air cleaner, adapter and gaskets. Discard the gaskets. Plug any vacuum line ports, as necessary.
2. Leave the Idle Air Control (IAC) valve connected and with the engine **OFF**, ground the diagnostic terminal (ALDL connector).
3. Turn the ignition switch to the **ON** position, do not start

the engine. Wait for at least 30 seconds; this allows the IAC valve pintle to extend and seat in the throttle body.

4. With the ignition switch still in the **ON** position, disconnect IAC electrical connector.

5. Remove the ground from the diagnostic terminal and start the engine. Let the engine reach normal operating temperature.

6. Apply the parking brake and block the drive wheels. Remove the plug from the idle stop screw by piercing it with a suitable tool and then applying leverage to the tool to lift the plug out.

7. With the engine in the proper shift selector range, adjust the idle stop screw to set the minimum idle to specification.

8. Turn the ignition **OFF** and reconnect the IAC valve connector. Unplug any plugged vacuum line ports and install the air cleaner, adapter and new gaskets.

Fuel Injector

Removal and Installation

2.5L ENGINE

1. Relieve the fuel system pressure. Disconnect the negative battery cable. Remove the air cleaner assembly.

2. Remove the fuel injector wire. Remove the fuel injector retainer clip screws. Remove the fuel injector retainer clip.

3. Using a suitable tool, gently pry the injector out.

4. Discard the upper and lower O-rings.

5. Installation is the reverse of the removal procedure. Lubricate both O-rings with light oil before installation.

2.8L, 3.1L AND 4.3L (VIN Z) TBI ENGINES

1. Relieve the fuel system pressure. Disconnect the negative battery cable. Remove the air cleaner assembly.

2. Remove the fuel injector wire. Remove the fuel meter cover assembly.

3. Using a suitable tool, gently pry the injector out.

4. Discard the upper and lower O-rings.

5. Installation is the reverse of the removal procedure. Lubricate both O-rings with light oil before installation.

NOTE: Be sure the replacement injectors have an identical part number. The 4.3L (VIN Z) uses 2 different injectors with 2 different flow rates. Injectors with part 5235134 (color coded orange and green) is located on the throttle lever side and part No. 5235342 (color coded pink and brown) located on the TPS side.

1. Fuel meter cover gasket
2. Removing fuel injector

Removing fuel injector—TBI

1. TBI model number
2. Throttle position sensor
3. Throttle lever
4. Injector P/N 5235134 (orange/green)
5. Injector P/N 5235342 (pink/brown)

Fuel injector location—4.3L (VIN Z) engine

3.8L AND 4.3L (VIN Z) MPI ENGINES

1. Relieve the fuel system pressure. Disconnect the negative battery cable. Remove the upper intake plenum, if equipped with turbocharger.

2. Remove the fuel supply and return lines from the fuel rail by squeezing the tabs and pulling the lines apart. Cap all open lines to prevent dirt and contaminants from entering.

3. Disconnect the vacuum line from the pressure regulator. Disconnect the fuel injector wire connectors.

4. Remove the fuel rail securing bolts and lift the rail up with equal force on both sides.

5. Remove the injector retaining clips and remove the injectors.

6. Installation is the reverse of the removal procedure.

4.3L (VIN W) CPI ENGINE

NOTE: The 4.3L (VIN W) engine is equipped with a non-repairable injector assembly which consists of the following: a fuel meter body, gasket seal, fuel pressure regulator, fuel injector and 6 poppet nozzles with fuel tubes. The assembly is housed in the lower manifold assembly.

1. Relieve the fuel system pressure. Disconnect the negative battery cable. Remove the upper intake plenum.

2. Disconnect the injector wire connector at the CPI unit.

3. Remove the fuel fitting clip and discard.

4. Remove the fuel inlet and return line.

5. Squeeze the poppet nozzle locking tabs together and lift the nozzles out of the casting.

6. Lift the CPI assembly out of the manifold.

To install:

7. Align the CPI assembly grommet with the casting grommet slot and push the assembly down until firmly seated in the bottom guide hole.

8. Push the poppet nozzles into the casting sockets.

— CAUTION —

Ensure the nozzles are firmly seated and locked in their casting sockets. An unlocked nozzle may work loose and create a fuel leak in the manifold.

9. Install new o-rings on the fuel inlet and return lines and coat them lightly with engine oil. Connect the inlet and return fuel lines to the CPI unit and install a new fuel fitting clip.

10. Pressurize the fuel system and verify no fuel leakage.

11. Install the upper intake manifold assembly.

12. Connect the negative battery cable.

13. Inspect for leaks.

1. IAC valve screw
2. IAC valve
3. IAC valve seal
4. MAP sensor seal
5. MAP sensor bolt
6. MAP sensor assembly
7. Intake manifold tuning valve bolt
8. Intake manifold tuning valve assembly
9. Intake manifold tuning valve o-ring
10. Power brake booster fitting
11. Upper intake manifold nut
12. CPI injector connector
13. CPI injector assembly
14. Fuel feed and return line clip
15. Fuel feed and return line o-ring
16. Upper intake manifold stud
17. Lower intake manifold fuel feed and return line seal
18. Fuel feed line
19. Fuel pressure connection fitting cap
20. Fuel pressure connection fitting
21. Fuel pressure connection seal
22. Fuel return line
23. Fuel line retainer bolt
24. Fuel line returner
25. Upper intake manifold locating pin
26. CPI injection wiring
27. CTS assembly
28. EGR valve bolt
29. EGR valve
30. EGR valve gasket
31. Lower intake manifold assembly
32. CPI injector assembly seal
33. Upper intake manifold gasket
34. TPS assembly screw
35. TPS assembly
36. Fuel vapor canister purge tube
37. Upper intake manifold assembly with throttle body

Fuel injector location—4.3L (VIN W) engine

EMISSION CONTROLS

For further information, please refer to Chilton's Emission Controls Manual.

Emission Warning Lamps

These vehicles are equipped with an "Service Engine Soon" light. This will illuminate when the key is turned to the **ON** position and when a malfunction in the computer command control system occurs. The light cannot be reset until the malfunction is corrected and the ECM memory is cleared of the fault. A light that turns **ON** and **OFF** during engine operation indicates an intermittent problem and a light that remains **ON** indicates a permanent component failure.

Resetting

1. Perform a diagnostic check of computer system codes.
2. Repair the failure.
3. Disconnect the negative battery cable for 15 seconds.
4. Reconnect the battery cable and check for failure codes.

ENGINE MECHANICAL

NOTE: Disconnecting the battery cable on some vehicles may interfere with the functions of the on board computer systems and may require the computer to undergo a relearning process.

Engine Assembly

Removal and Installation

BLAZER, BRAVADA, JIMMY, PICK-UP AND SONOMA

1. Disconnect the negative battery cable. Matchmark the hood hinges and remove the hood.
2. Drain the cooling system and disconnect the upper radiator hose at the radiator. Disconnect the coolant overflow hose.
3. Remove the upper fan shroud and disconnect the oil cooler lines.
4. Remove the radiator and the cooling fan. Disconnect the heater hoses.
5. Remove the air cleaner assembly and disconnect the vacuum hoses. Disconnect all necessary wires at the bulkhead and all of the main feed wires.
6. Disconnect the throttle cable and cruise control cable, if equipped. Remove the distributor cap.
7. Raise and safely support the vehicle. Disconnect the converter-to-exhaust pipe bolts. Remove the front drive shaft on 4WD vehicles.
8. Disconnect the exhaust pipes at the manifolds. Disconnect the strut rods at the bell housing. Remove the flywheel cover.
9. Remove the torque converter bolts on automatic transmission equipped vehicles. Remove the second crossmember on 4WD vehicles.
10. Remove the rear catalytic converter shield and disconnect the converter hanger at the exhaust pipe.
11. Remove the lower fan shroud and disconnect the fuel lines. Remove the 2 outer air dam bolts.
12. Remove the 2 left body mount bolts and, using a suitable jack, raise the body slightly. Remove the engine-to-transmission bolts.
13. Lower the body and remove the lower motor mount bolts. Lower the vehicle.
14. Remove the air conditioning compressor and power steering pump with their brackets from the engine. Do not disconnect the fluid or refrigerant lines.
15. Support the transmission with a suitable jack. Attach a suitable lifting device to the engine and remove the engine from the vehicle.

To install:

16. Carefully lower the engine into position in the vehicle.
17. Remove the transmission support. Raise and safely support the vehicle. Install the motor mount bolts, tighten to 52 ft. lbs. (70 Nm). Install the lower bell housing bolts. Tighten to 32 ft. lbs. (44 Nm).
18. Raise the body and install the upper bell housing bolts. Tighten to 32 ft. lbs. (44 Nm).
19. Lower the body and install the body mount bolts. Install the outer air dam bolts. Connect the fuel lines and install the lower fan shroud.
20. Connect the converter hanger at the exhaust pipe and install the shield at the converter. Install the torque converter bolts and install the flywheel cover.
21. Connect the strut rods at the bell housing. Connect the exhaust pipes to the manifolds. Connect the converter to the exhaust pipes.
22. Lower the vehicle. Install the air conditioning compressor and power steering pump. Install the distributor cap.
23. Connect the throttle cable and cruise control cable. Connect all electrical wires and vacuum hoses.
24. Install the air cleaner and connect the heater hoses. Install

the fan and radiator. Connect the oil cooler lines. Install the upper fan shroud.
25. Connect the overflow hose and the radiator hose. Fill the cooling system.
26. Install the hood. Connect the negative battery cable and run the engine. Bleed the cooling system.

ASTRO AND SAFARI

1. Disconnect the negative battery cable.
2. Drain the cooling system.
3. Raise and safely support the vehicle. Disconnect the exhaust pipes at the manifolds.
4. Disconnect the strut rods at the flywheel housing. Remove the flywheel cover. Remove the torque converter bolts. Drain the engine oil.
5. Remove the starter and oil filter. Disconnect the wires at the transmission. Disconnect the fuel lines.
6. Disconnect the oil cooler lines. Remove the lower fan shroud. Remove the motor mount bolts.
7. Lower the vehicle. Remove the headlight bezels and grille. Remove the radiator close out panel and the radiator support brace. Remove the lower tie bar.
8. Remove the hood latch mechanism. Remove the master cylinder and the upper fan shroud.
9. Remove the upper radiator core support and the radiator. If equipped, properly discharge the air conditioning system.
10. Remove the radiator filler panels. Remove the engine cover. Remove the air conditioning hose at the accumulator and remove the air conditioning compressor.
11. Remove the power steering pump. Disconnect the vacuum hoses at the intake manifold and the wiring at the bulkhead.
12. Remove the right kickpanel. Disconnect the harness at the ESC module and it through the bulkhead.
13. Remove the distributor cap. Remove the air conditioning accumulator, if equipped.
14. Disconnect the fuel lines. Remove the diverter valve. Remove the transmission dipstick tube.
15. Disconnect the heater hoses at the heater core. Remove the horn and remove the AIR system check valves. Remove the engine-to-transmission bolts.
16. Attach a suitable lifting device to the engine and remove the engine from the vehicle.

To install:

17. Install the engine into the vehicle. Install the bell housing bolts.
18. Install the AIR system check valves. Install the horn and connect the heater hoses, Install the transmission dipstick tube.
19. Install the diverter valve and connect the fuel lines. Install the accumulator and install the distributor cap.
20. Connect the harness to the ESC module. Install the right kick panel.
21. Connect the bulkhead wiring and the vacuum hoses. Install the power steering pump and the air conditioning compressor.
22. Connect the refrigerant line to the accumulator. Install the engine cover.
23. Install the radiator filler panel and the radiator. Install the radiator supports and the upper fan shroud.
24. Install the hood latch and the master cylinder. Install the lower tie bar. Install the lower radiator close out panel.
25. Install the grille and headlight bezels. Raise and safely support the vehicle.
26. Install the engine mount bolts and tighten to 75 ft. lbs. (100 Nm). Connect the oil cooler lines. Connect the fuel hoses and the wires at the transmission.
27. Install the oil filter and the starter. Install the torque converter bolts. Install the flywheel cover.
28. Install the strut rods at the flywheel housing. Connect the exhaust pipes. Lower the vehicle.

29. Connect the negative battery cable. Fill the cooling system and the crankcase. Charge the air conditioning system. Fill and bleed the brake system.

SYCLONE AND TYPHOON

1. Disconnect the negative battery cable. Matchmark the hood hinges and remove the hood.
2. Drain the coolant from the engine radiator and turbocharger air cooler. Remove the air cleaner and duct. Remove the turbocharger air inlet elbow.
3. Remove the upper fan shroud. Remove the serpentine belt and fan pulley.
4. Remove the battery tray and vacuum tank.
5. Raise and safely support the vehicle. Remove the front tire and wheel assemblies.
6. Remove the wheelhouse panels.
7. Disconnect the mufflers and tailpipe from the catalytic converter. Remove the catalytic converter support bolts.
8. Remove the turbocharger outlet pipe bracket and nuts. Move the outlet pipe and catalytic converter away from the turbocharger.
9. Disconnect the electrical connectors from the turbocharger air cooler radiator temperature sensor and hoses.
10. Remove the turbocharger air cooler radiator.
11. Remove the exhaust crossover pipe and lower the vehicle.
12. Remove the oil cooler lines, overflow hoses and upper and lower hoses from the radiator. Remove the radiator assembly.
13. Remove the oil lines at the filter adapter.
14. Remove the power steering pump hoses from the steering gear.
15. Remove the engine coolant reservoir. Remove the air conditioning compressor and position aside. Do not discharge or disconnect the compressor lines.
16. Remove the turbocharger air cooler clamps, ducts and hoses. Remove the air cooler from the supports.
17. Remove the throttle body assembly from the upper intake plenum and position aside.
18. Remove the upper intake manifold. Disconnect the fuel rail from the fuel lines.
19. Disconnect all necessary vacuum and electrical connections from the engine.
20. Raise and safely support the vehicle and transmission. Remove the front and rear driveshaft.
21. Remove the transmission crossmember and mount. Remove the torque converter cover and remove the bolts securing the converter to the flywheel.
22. Disconnect the shift linkage from the transmission.
23. Disconnect the fuel hoses from the pipes near the transfer case. Remove the fuel line bracket from the transfer case.
24. Disconnect and remove the fuel line clips, electrical clips and connectors from the transmission and transfer case.
25. Remove the transfer case from the vehicle.
26. Disconnect the T.V. cable and cooler lines from the transmission.
27. Remove the transmission from the vehicle.
28. Remove the fuel line clips, oil line clips and wiring harness clips from the cylinder head.
29. Remove the starter motor.
30. Remove the engine mount through bolts and lower the vehicle.
31. Attach a suitable lifting device to the engine and remove the engine from the vehicle, disconnecting any necessary connections.
To install:
32. Position all wires and hoses out of the way during engine installation.
33. Carefully lower the engine into position in the vehicle.
34. Install the engine mount through bolts and lower the vehicle.
35. Install the starter motor.

36. Connect the fuel line clips, oil line clips and wiring harness clips to the cylinder head.
37. Install the transmission assembly.
38. Connect the T.V. cable and cooler lines to the transmission.
39. Install the transfer case assembly.
40. Connect the fuel line clips, electrical clips and connectors to the transmission and transfer case.
41. Connect the fuel hoses to the pipes near the transfer case. Connect the fuel line bracket to the transfer case.
42. Connect the shift linkage to the transmission.
43. Install the transmission crossmember and mount. Install the bolts securing the converter to the flywheel and install the torque converter cover.
44. Install the front and rear driveshafts
45. Connect all vacuum and electrical connections previously removed from the engine.
46. Connect the fuel rail to the fuel lines. Install the upper intake manifold.
47. Install the throttle body assembly onto the upper intake plenum.
48. Install the air cooler. Install the turbocharger air cooler clamps, ducts and hoses.
49. Install the engine coolant reservoir. Install the air conditioning compressor.
50. Connect the power steering pump hoses to the steering gear and the engine oil lines at the filter adapter.
51. Install the radiator assembly. Connect the oil cooler lines, overflow hoses and upper and lower hoses to the radiator.
52. Raise and support the vehicle safely. Install the exhaust crossover pipe and lower the vehicle.
53. Install the turbocharger air cooler radiator.
54. Install and connect the electrical connectors to the turbocharger air cooler radiator temperature sensor and hoses.
55. Raise and support the vehicle safely. Connect the turbocharger outlet pipe bracket and nuts.
56. Connect the mufflers and tailpipe to the catalytic converter. Install the catalytic converter support bolts.
57. Install the wheelhouse panels.
58. Install the front tire and wheel assemblies. Lower the vehicle.
59. Install the serpentine belt and fan pulley. Install the battery tray and vacuum tank. Install the upper fan shroud.
60. Fill the cooling system with the proper type and quantity of antifreeze. Install the air cleaner and duct. Install the turbocharger air inlet elbow.
61. Connect the negative battery cable. Install the hood, aligning the marks previously.

LUMINA, APV, SILHOUETTE AND TRANS SPORT
3.1L Engine

1. Disconnect the negative battery cable.
2. Drain the cooling system. Disconnect the air flow tube from the air cleaner.
3. Disconnect the electrical connector from the ECM and push it through to the engine compartment. Disconnect the harness from the clips on the body and lay it across the engine.
4. Disconnect the engine harness at the bulkhead connector. Disconnect the throttle and TV cables.
5. Disconnect the fuel lines. Disconnect the transaxle shift linkage.
6. Disconnect the cooler lines at the radiator. Disconnect the radiator and heater hoses.
7. Remove the air conditioning compressor from the bracket and support it aside. Remove the upper engine support strut.
8. Raise and safely support the vehicle. Remove the front wheel and tire assemblies.
9. Remove the stabilizer bar. Disconnect the tie rod ends and the lower control arm ball joints.
10. Disconnect the halfhsafts and support them aside. Disconnect the steering shaft pinch bolt.

11. Remove the starter.

12. Disconnect the exhaust pipe at the manifold. Support the engine and sub-frame with a suitable jack.

13. Remove the sub-frame bolts and lower the engine/transaxle and subframe from the vehicle.

To install:

14. Raise the engine assembly into position and install the subframe bolts. Tighten to 35 ft. lbs.

15. Connect the exhaust pipe at the rear manifold. Install the starter.

16. Connect the steering shaft and install the pinch bolt. Connect the halfshafts to the transaxle.

17. Connect the lower control arm ball joints to the steering knuckles.

18. Install the stabilizer bar. Install the upper engine strut.

19. Install the wheel and tire assemblies. Lower the vehicle. Install the radiator and heater hoses.

20. Install the shift linkage. Connect the fuel lines and the throttle and TV cables.

21. Connect the harness to bulkhead connector. Connect the ECM harness to the ECM.

22. Connect the air cleaner hose and the radiator upper support.

23. Fill the cooling system. Install the air conditioning compressor.

24. Connect the negative battery cable.

3.8L Engine

1. Disconnect the negative battery cable. Properly relieve the fuel system pressure.

2. Remove the air cleaner and duct assembly. Remove the fuel lines from the fuel rail and the mounting bracket.

3. Disconnect the throttle cables from the throttle body and mounting bracket.

4. Drain the cooling system into a suitable container. Remove the radiator and heater hoses. Remove the engine cooling fan.

5. Remove the torque strut and brackets.

6. Disconnect the transaxle cooler lines and remove the radiator assembly.

7. Disconnect the relay center wiring.

8. Disconnect the fuel vapor canister hoses.

9. Disconnect the battery cables at the engine ground and starter assembly.

10. Disconnect the shift cables from the transaxle.

11. Disconnect and remove the ECM main harness and engine wiring.

12. Remove the serpentine belt. Remove the air conditioning compressor and position aside.

13. Disconnect the power steering line attachment at the lower right hand rail.

14. Raise and safely support the vehicle. Remove the front wheel and tire assemblies.

15. Remove the stabilizer shaft, tie rod ends and lower ball joints from the steering knuckle. Remove the drive axles from the transaxle.

16. Remove the intermediate steering shaft pinch bolt.

17. Remove the starter assembly and flywheel cover. Remove the torque converter bolts.

18. Remove the exhaust pipe at the rear manifold.

19. Safely support the engine, frame and transaxle assembly. Remove the frame bolts.

20. Lower the engine, frame and transaxle assembly.

21. Remove the transaxle to engine mount bracket.

22. Remove the exhaust crossover, the left and right exhaust manifolds.

23. Remove the engine to frame front mount.

24. Remove the left and right engine mounts to frame.

25. Remove the transaxle to engine bolts and separate the assembly.

To install:

26. Position the assembly together and install the transaxle to engine bolts.

27. Install the left and right engine mounts to frame.

28. Install the engine to frame front mount.

29. Install the exhaust crossover, the left and right exhaust manifolds.

30. Install the transaxle to engine mount bracket.

31. Raise the engine, frame and transaxle assembly into position.

32. Safely support the engine, frame and transaxle assembly and install the frame bolts.

33. Install the exhaust pipe at the rear manifold.

34. Install the starter assembly and the torque converter bolts. Install the flywheel cover.

35. Install the intermediate steering shaft pinch bolt.

36. Install the drive axles into the transaxle. Install the stabilizer shaft, tie rod ends and lower ball joints from the steering knuckle.

37. Lower the vehicle. Install the front wheel and tire assemblies.

38. Connect the power steering line attachment at the lower right hand rail.

39. Install the air conditioning compressor and position aside. Install the serpentine belt.

40. Reconnect the ECM main harness and engine wiring.

41. Connect the shift cables to the transaxle.

42. Connect the battery cables at the engine ground and starter assembly.

43. Connect the fuel vapor canister hoses.

44. Connect the relay center wiring.

45. Connect the transaxle cooler lines and remove the radiator assembly.

46. Install the torque strut and brackets.

47. Install the engine cooling fan. Install the radiator and heater hoses. Fill the cooling system with the proper type and quantity of antifreeze.

48. Connect the throttle cables to the throttle body and mounting bracket.

49. Install the air cleaner and duct assembly. Connect the fuel lines to the fuel rail and the mounting bracket.

50. Connect the negative battery cable.

Engine Mounts

NOTE: When lifting or raising the engine for any reason, do not support the assembly under the oil pan, any sheet metal or the crankshaft pulley.

Removal and Installation

2.5L ENGINE

1. Disconnect the negative battery cable.

2. Raise and support the vehicle safely. Support the engine with a suitable lifting fixture.

3. Remove the engine mount through bolt and nut.

4. Raise the engine enough to permit removal of the engine mounting.

5. Remove the mount assembly attaching bolts, nuts and washers. Remove the mount assembly.

6. Installation is the reverse of the removal procedure.

2.8L ENGINE

1. Disconnect the negative battery cable.

2. Raise and support the vehicle safely. Support the engine with a suitable lifting fixture.

3. Remove the fan shroud and right front wheel.

4. Remove the engine mount through bolt and nut.

5. Raise the engine enough to permit removal of the engine mounting and block in position.

6. Remove the tie rod at the drag link. Remove the stabilizer link from the control arm.

7. Remove the lower shock absorber bolts.

8. Remove the lower control arm pivot bolts and position control aside.

9. Remove the mount assembly attaching bolts, nuts and washers. Remove the mount assembly.

10. Installation is the reverse of the removal procedure.

3.1L AND 3.8L ENGINES

1. Disconnect the negative battery cable.

2. Raise and support the vehicle safely. Support the engine with a suitable lifting fixture.

3. Remove the engine mount nuts from below the engine frame mounting bracket.

4. Raise the engine enough to permit removal of the engine mounting and block in position.

5. Remove the mount assembly to engine bracket nuts and washers. Remove the mount assembly.

6. Installation is the reverse of the removal procedure.

4.3L ENGINE

Except Astro and Safari

1. Disconnect the negative battery cable.

2. Raise and support the vehicle safely. Support the engine with a suitable lifting fixture.

3. Remove the cab or body mounting bolts. Raise the body and block in position.

4. Remove the engine mount through bolts.

5. Raise the engine enough to permit removal of the engine mounting and block in position.

6. Remove the mount assembly to frame bolts. Remove the mount assembly.

7. Installation is the reverse of the removal procedure.

Astro and Safari

1. Disconnect the negative battery cable.

2. Raise and support the vehicle safely. Support the engine with a suitable lifting fixture.

3. Remove the engine mount through bolts.

4. Raise the engine enough to permit removal of the engine mounting and block in position.

5. Remove the mount assembly to frame bolts. Remove the mount assembly.

6. Installation is the reverse of the removal procedure.

Cylinder Head

Removal and Installation

2.5L ENGINE

1. Disconnect the negative battery cable. Drain the cooling system. On Astro and Safari vehicles, remove the engine cover. Remove the air cleaner assembly.

2. Remove the air conditioning compressor and position it aside. Remove the rocker arm cover. Remove the rocker arms and pushrods. Keep them in order for reinstallation.

3. Properly relieve the fuel system pressure. Disconnect the fuel line from the TBI unit. Disconnect all necessary electrical and vacuum lines.

4. Disconnect the accelerator cable, the cruise control cable and the TV cables. Remove the alternator and brackets.

5. Remove the water pump bypass hose. Disconnect the heater hoses at the intake manifold. Remove the upper radiator hose.

6. Disconnect the exhaust pipe from the exhaust manifold. Remove the fuel filter and filter brackets at the rear of the cylinder head assembly.

7. Remove the coil wire and spark plug wires. Disconnect the oxygen sensor electrical wire.

8. Remove the cylinder head retaining bolts. Remove the cylinder head along with the intake and exhaust manifold assembly.

To install:

9. Ensure the cylinder bolt threads in the block and threads on the bolts are cleaned, as dirt will affect bolt torque.

Cylinder head bolt torque sequence—2.5L engine

Cylinder head bolt torque sequence—2.8L and 3.1L engines

Cylinder head bolt torque sequence—4.3L engine

Cylinder head bolt torque sequence—3.8L engine

10. Coat the threads of the 2 cylinder head studs with sealing compound 1052080 or equivalent.

11. Position the new gasket over the dowel pins. Torque the cylinder head bolts gradually to 18 ft. lbs. (25 Nm) in the proper sequence. Then tighten all bolts except stud (position No. 9) to 26 ft. lbs. (35 Nm); tighten No. 9 to 18 ft. lbs. (25 Nm). Finally, tighten all bolts and studs an additional 90 degree turn.

12. Connect the coil wire and spark plug wires.

13. Connect the oxygen sensor electrical wire.

14. Connect the exhaust pipe to the exhaust manifold. Connect the fuel filter and filter brackets to the rear of the cylinder head assembly.

15. Install the water pump bypass hose. Connect the heater hoses to the intake manifold. Install the upper radiator hose.

16. Connect the accelerator cable, the cruise control cable and the TV cables. Install the alternator and brackets.

17. Connect the fuel line from the TBI unit. Connect all electrical and vacuum lines.

18. Install the air conditioning compressor and position it aside. Install the rocker arm cover. Install the rocker arms and pushrods in the same order they were removed.

19. Connect the negative battery cable. Fill the cooling system with the proper type and quantity of antifreeze. Install the air cleaner assembly. On Astro and Safari vehicles, install the engine cover.

2.8L AND 3.1L ENGINES

1. Disconnect the negative battery cable. Drain the radiator. Remove the intake manifold.

2. Remove the valve covers. Remove the rocker arms and pushrods. Keep them in order for reinstallation.

3. Raise and support the vehicle safely. Disconnect the exhaust manifolds from the exhaust pipes. On the left side disconnect the dipstick tube attachment. On the right side remove the alternator bracket. Lower the vehicle.

4. Remove the cylinder head retaining bolts. Remove the cylinder head from the engine along with the exhaust manifold.

To install:

5. Ensure that the cylinder bolt threads in the block and threads on the bolts are cleaned, as dirt will affect bolt torque.

6. Coat the threads of the cylinder head bolts with sealing compound 1052080 or equivalent.

7. Position the new gasket over the dowel pins with THIS SIDE UP showing.

8. Install the cylinder head onto the engine along with the exhaust manifold. Install the cylinder head retaining bolts. Torque the cylinder head bolts gradually in the proper sequence to 41 ft. lbs. (55 Nm). Then turn each bolt an additional 90 degrees.

9. Raise and support the vehicle safely. Connect the exhaust manifolds to the exhaust pipes. On the left side, connect the dipstick tube. On the right side, install the alternator bracket. Lower the vehicle.

10. Install the valve covers. Install the rocker arms and pushrods keeping them in the same order as removed.

11. Install the intake manifold assembly.

12. Connect the negative battery cable. Fill the cooling system with the proper type and quantity of antifreeze.

3.8L ENGINE

1. Disconnect the negative battery cable. Remove the engine cover. Drain the coolant into a suitable container.

2. Remove the intake and exhaust manifolds.

3. Remove the alternator bracket and 1 air conditioner bracket bolt. Remove the power steering pump.

4. Remove the valve covers. Remove the rocker arms, pushrods and guide plates. Keep them in order for reinstallation. Remove the coil and spark plug wires.

5. Remove the belt tensioner assembly. Remove the fuel pump heat shield.

6. Remove the cylinder head retaining bolts. Remove the cylinder head from the engine.

To install:

7. Ensure that the cylinder bolt threads in the block and threads on the bolts are cleaned, as dirt will affect bolt torque.

8. Coat the underside of the bolt heads with sealing compound 1052080 or equivalent. Coat the threads of the bolts with thread lock.

9. Position the new gasket with the arrow pointing to the front of the engine.

10. Install the cylinder head onto the engine. Install the cylinder head retaining bolts and torque as follows:

  a. Torque the cylinder head bolts gradually in the proper sequence to 35 ft. lbs. (47 Nm).

  b. Then turn each bolt an additional 130 degree turn in sequence.

  c. Finally turn the 4 center bolts an additional 30 degrees.

11. Install the rocker arms, pushrods and guide plates in the same position from which they were removed. Torque the rocker arm bolts to 28 ft. lbs. (38 Nm).

12. Install the intake manifold and valve covers.

13. Raise and support the vehicle safely. Connect the exhaust manifolds to the exhaust pipes. Lower the vehicle.

14. Install the alternator and bracket. Install the air conditioner bracket bolt.

15. Install the ignition coil and spark plug wires.

16. Install the belt tensioner and power steering pump assembly.

17. Install the fuel pump heat shield.

18. Connect the negative battery cable. Fill the cooling system with the proper type and quantity of antifreeze.

4.3L ENGINE

1. Disconnect the negative battery cable. Remove the engine cover, if equipped. Drain the engine and turbocharger air cooler radiator, if equipped. Remove the intake manifold. Remove the required electrical and vacuum connections.

2. Remove the valve covers. Remove the rocker arms and pushrods. Keep them in order for reinstallation. Remove the spark plugs.

3. Raise and support the vehicle safely. Remove the exhaust manifolds. On the left side, disconnect the dipstick tube attachment. Lower the vehicle.

4 Remove the alternator, power steering and brackets. Remove the air conditioner compressor and belt tensioner bracket and position aside.

5. Remove the cylinder head retaining bolts. Remove the cylinder head from the engine.

To install:

6. Ensure that the cylinder bolt threads in the block and threads on the bolts are cleaned, as dirt will affect bolt torque.

7. If a steel gasket is used, be sure to coat both sides with sealer. Coat the threads of the cylinder head bolts with sealing compound 1052080 or equivalent.

8. Position the new gasket over the dowel pins with the bead up. Torque the cylinder head bolts gradually in the proper sequence as follows:

  a. The first sequence to 25 ft. lbs. (34 Nm).

  b. The second sequence to 45 ft. lbs. (61 Nm).

  c. The final sequence to 65 ft. lbs. (90 Nm).

9. Install the cylinder head onto the engine. Install the cylinder head retaining bolts.

10. Install the alternator, power steering and brackets. Install the air conditioner compressor and belt tensioner bracket.

11. Raise and support the vehicle safely. Install the exhaust manifolds. On the left side, Connect the dipstick tube attachment. Lower the vehicle.

12. Install the rocker arms and pushrods in the same order as removed. Install the valve covers. Install the spark plugs and wires.

13. Install the intake manifold. Connect all electrical and vacuum connections.

Valve adjustment—2.8L and 4.3L (VIN Z) engines

14. Connect the negative battery cable. Install the engine cover. Fill the radiator with the proper type and quantity of antifreeze.

Valve Lash

Adjustment

2.8L AND 4.3L (VIN Z) ENGINES

1. On Astro and Safari, remove the engine cover. Remove the rocker covers.

2. Crank the engine until the mark on the damper aligns with the **0** mark on the timing tab and the engine is in the No. 1 firing position. This can be achieved by placing a finger on No. 1 intake valve as the damper approaches TDC; if the valve is closed, the engine is on the firing stroke. If the valve moves when the damper is approaching TDC the engine is on No. 4 firing position and will need to be turned 1 additional turn to reach No. 1 firing position.

3. With the engine in the No. 1 firing position, the following valves may be adjusted on the 2.8L engine:
    a. Exhaust—1, 2, 3
    b. Intake—1, 5, 6

4. With the engine in the No. 1 firing position, the following valves may be adjusted on the 4.3L (VIN Z) engine:
    a. Exhaust—1, 5, 6
    b. Intake—1, 2, 3

5. Back out the adjusting nut until the pushrod can be turned with finger pressure and lash is felt. Then turn in the nut until all lash is removed and the pushrod cannot be turned. When all lash has been removed, turn the adjusting nut in 1½ turn on the 2.8L engine or 1 full turn on the 4.3L (VIN Z) engine.

6. Crank the engine until the mark on the damper aligns with the **0** mark on the timing tab. This is the No. 4 firing position.

7. With the engine in the No. 4 timing position, the following valves can be adjusted on the 2.8L engine:
    a. Exhaust—4, 5, 6
    b. Intake—2, 3, 4

8. With the engine in the No. 4 timing position, the following valves can be adjusted on the 4.3L (VIN Z) engine:
    a. Exhaust—2, 3, 4
    b. Intake—4, 5, 6

9. Back out the adjusting nut until lash is felt at the pushrod then turn in the nut until all lash is removed. When all lash has been removed, turn the adjusting nut in 1½ turn on the 2.8L engine or 1 full turn on the 4.3L (VIN Z) engine.

10. After all valves are adjusted, install the valve covers.

Rocker Arms

Removal and Installation

1. Disconnect the negative battery cable. On Astro and Safari, remove the engine cover.

2. Remove all the necessary components in order to gain access to the engine valve covers. Properly relieve the fuel system pressure before disconnecting any fuel lines.

3. Remove the valve cover retaining bolts. Remove the valve cover from the engine.

4. Remove the rocker arm assemblies. Keep them in order for reinstallation.

5. Installation is the reverse of the removal procedure.

Intake Manifold

Removal and Installation

2.5L ENGINE

1. Disconnect the negative battery cable. Remove the air cleaner assembly.

2. Drain the cooling system. Disconnect the vacuum pipe hold-down at the exhaust and thermostat housing.

3. Disconnect the electrical and vacuum connections, as required.

4. Disconnect the accelerator, TV and cruise cable at the TBI unit.

5. Properly relieve the fuel pressure. Disconnect and plug the fuel lines at the intake manifold.

6. Disconnect the heater hoses at the intake manifold.

7. Remove the alternator bracket retaining bolts. Remove the alternator and position it aside. Remove the ignition coil wires.

8. Remove the intake manifold retaining bolts. Remove the intake manifold.

Intake manifold bolt torque sequence—2.8L engine

Intake manifold bolt torque sequence—3.1L engine

1. Intake manifold upper bolt
2. Intake manifold gasket
3. Intake manifold seal
4. Intake manifold lower
5. Intake manifold upper
6. Intake manifold lower bolt

Intake manifold assembly—3.8L engine

Intake manifold bolt torque sequence—3.8L engine

Lower intake manifold bolt torque sequence—4.3L (VIN W) engine

To install:

9. Install the manifold and gasket into position. Install the retaining bolts and tighten in sequence to the correct torque.

10. Install the alternator and bracket. Connect the heater hoses, vacuum and fuel lines.

11. Connect the accelerator, TV and cruise cable. Install the air cleaner assembly. Install the coil wires.

12. Connect the negative battery cable. Fill the cooling system with the proper type and quantity of antifreeze. Run the engine, check the idle speed and check for leaks.

2.8L AND 3.1L ENGINES

1. Disconnect the negative battery cable. Remove the air cleaner. Drain the cooling system. If equipped, remove the AIR pump and bracket.

2. Remove the distributor. Remove the heater and radiator hoses from the intake manifold. Remove the rocker arm covers.

3. Disconnect and label all vacuum hoses and electrical con-nections at the manifold. Remove the EFE pipe from the rear of the manifold. Remove the accelerator linkage. Disconnect and plug the fuel line.

4. As required, remove the TBI unit. Remove the intake manifold retaining bolts. Remove the intake manifold from the engine.

To install:

5. The gaskets are marked for right and left side installation. Do not interchange them. Clean the sealing surface of the engine block and apply a ú/16 in. bead of silicone sealer to each ridge.

Upper intake manifold bolt torque sequence—4.3L (VIN W) engine

Intake manifold removal—4.3L (VIN Z) turbocharged engine

6. Install the new gaskets onto the heads. The gaskets will have to be cut slightly to fit past the center pushrods. Do not cut any more material than necessary. Hold the gaskets in place by extending the ridge bead of sealer ¼ in. onto the gasket ends. Install the manifold and tighten the bolts in sequence to the correct torque.

INITIAL TIGHTENING SEQUENCE

FINAL TIGHTENING SEQUENCE

Intake manifold bolt torque sequence—4.3L (VIN Z) engine

7. When the intake manifold is installed the area between the ridges and the manifold should be completely sealed.

8. Install the intake manifold onto the engine. Install the intake manifold retaining bolts and torque in the proper sequence to specification. As required, install the TBI unit.

9. Connect all vacuum hoses and electrical connections at the manifold. Install the EFE pipe from the rear of the manifold. Install the accelerator linkage. Connect the fuel line.

10. Install the distributor. Install the heater and radiator hoses from the intake manifold. Install the rocker arm covers. Install the AIR pump and bracket.

11. Fill the cooling system with the proper type and quantity of antifreeze. Install the air cleaner.

12. Connect the negative battery cable.

3.8L ENGINE

1. Disconnect the negative battery cable. Drain the cooling system into a suitable container.

2. Remove the spark plug wires on the right side of the engine.

3. Remove the air intake duct. Properly relieve the fuel system pressure and remove the fuel rail.

4. Remove the exhaust heat shield.

5. Remove the cable bracket to cylinder head mounting bolt.

6. Remove the upper intake manifold bolts and upper manifold.

7. Remove the power steering pump support bracket.

Service Tips

INTAKE MANIFOLD GASKET

The 1988–90 4.3L engine, with TBI, has added a restrictor plate to the rear coolant passage of the gasket to prevent throttle plate icing. If the intake gasket is installed incorrectly, the engine will overheat causing possible engine damage.

Ensure the gasket is installed with the restrictor to the rear of the engine.

The gasket may be checked without removing the manifold, the gasket has a metal locator tab that can be seen protruding from the end of the manifold/cylinder head. When installed correctly, the metal locator tab will be at the rear of the engine.

Service Tips

ENGINE NOISE, ROUGH IDLE, LOW POWER

Vehicles experiencing engine rough idle, noise or reduced power after an intake manifold removal and installation may be missing a spacer. The 1988–89 2.5L engine uses a spacer on the intake manifold bolt which prevents the bolt from binding the pushrod on the No. 4 cylinder. If the spacer is missing, two ⅛ inch thick, ⅜ flat washers may be substituted; the pushrod should also be removed and inspected for damage. Retorque the bolt to 22–30 ft. lbs. (28–40 Nm).

8. Loosen the alternator and move aside to obtain clearance.
9. Remove the heater pipes and bypass hose.
10. Remove the lower intake manifold bolts and remove the assembly.

To install:

11. Thoroughly clean all manifold mating surfaces, bolts and bolt holes. Apply sealant to the ends of the manifold seals and coat the bolt threads with Loctite®. Install the lower intake manifold, gasket and bolts. Torque the lower manifold bolts in sequence, twice, to 88 inch lbs. (10 Nm).
12. Install the heater pipes and bypass hose.
13. Install the alternator.
14. Install the power steering pump support bracket.
15. Install the upper intake manifold and torque the bolts to 22 ft. lbs. (30 Nm).
16. Install the cable bracket to cylinder head mounting bolt.
17. Install the exhaust heat shield.
18. Install the air intake duct. Install the fuel rail.
19. Install the spark plug wires on the right side of the engine.
20. Connect the negative battery cable. Fill the cooling system with the proper type and quantity of antifreeze.

4.3L (VIN W) ENGINE

1. Disconnect the negative battery cable. Drain the cooling system into a suitable container.
2. Remove the plastic cover on the top of the intake manifold.
3. Remove the wiring harness, which includes disconnecting the TPS, IAC motor, MAP sensor and the intake manifold tuning valve.
4. Remove the throttle and TV linkage from the upper intake manifold.
5. Remove the ignition coil and PCV hose from the manifold.
6. Remove the vacuum hoses from the manifold.
7. Mark the installation location of all studs. Remove the upper manifold bolts and studs.
8. Remove the distributor and wiring.
9. Properly relieve the fuel system pressure. Remove the fuel supply and return line at the rear of the manifold.
10. Remove the upper radiator and heater hoses.
11. Remove the air conditioner compressor bracket at the intake manifold.
12. Disconnect the wiring harness, including the fuel injectors, EGR valve and coolant temperature sensor.
13. Remove the lower intake manifold bolts and manifold assembly.

To install:

14. Thoroughly clean all gasket mating surfaces, including

bolts. Apply GM sealer 1052080 or equivalent to the bolts. Apply a (5mm) bead of sealer to the front and rear sealing surfaces of the block, extending the bead ½ in. (13mm) up each cylinder head to seal and retain the gaskets.
15. Install the gaskets to the cylinder head with the port blocking plates facing the rear of the engine and the "THIS SIDE UP" stamping facing up.
16. Install the lower intake manifold and torque the bolts in sequence to 35 ft. lbs. (48 Nm).
17. Connect the wiring harness, including the fuel injectors, EGR valve and coolant temperature sensor.
18. Install the air conditioner compressor bracket at the intake manifold.
19. Install the upper radiator and heater hoses.
20. Connect the fuel supply and return line at the rear of the manifold.
21. Install the distributor and wiring.
22. Install the upper intake manifold and gaskets with the green sealing lines facing up. Install the manifold bolts and studs in there previously marked positions. Torque the bolts and studs in sequence to 124 inch lbs. (14 Nm).
23. Install the vacuum hoses at the manifold.
24. Install the ignition coil and PCV hose at the manifold.
25. Install the throttle and TV linkage onto the upper intake manifold.
26. Install the wiring harness, which includes connecting the TPS, IAC motor, MAP sensor and the intake manifold tuning valve.
27. Install the plastic cover on the top of the intake manifold.
28. Connect the negative battery cable. Fill the cooling system with the proper type and quantity of antifreeze.

4.3L (VIN Z) EXCEPT TURBOCHARGED ENGINE

Except Astro and Safari

1. Disconnect the negative battery cable. Remove the air cleaner and heat stove assembly. Drain the cooling system and remove the upper radiator hose.
2. Remove the 2 braces at the rear of the drive belt tensioner.
3. Remove the emission relays with brackets.
4. Remove the wiring harness from the clips and position aside.
5. Remove the ground cable from the manifold stud.
6. Remove the power brake vacuum pipe.
7. Remove the heater hose pipe at the manifold.
8. Properly relieve the fuel system pressure and disconnect the fuel lines at the manifold.
9. Remove the distributor cap, ignition wires and coil. Disconnect the ESC connector and remove the distributor.
10. Disconnect all necessary sensor wire connectors and vacuum lines at the manifold.
11. Disconnect the throttle, TV and cruise control cables at the throttle body.
12. Remove the intake manifold bolts and remove the assembly.

To install:

13. Thoroughly clean all gasket mating surfaces, including bolts. Apply GM sealer 1052080 or equivalent to the bolts.
14. Apply a (5mm) bead of sealer to the front and rear sealing surfaces of the block, extending the bead ½ in. (13mm) up each cylinder head to seal and retain the gaskets.
15. Install the gaskets to the cylinder head with the port blocking plates facing up and to the rear.
16. Install the intake manifold and torque the bolts in sequence to 35 ft. lbs. (48 Nm).
17. Connect the throttle, TV and cruise control cables at the throttle body.
18. Connect all necessary sensor wire connectors and vacuum lines at the manifold.
19. Install the distributor cap, ignition wires and coil. Connect the ESC connector and install the distributor.

20. Connect the fuel lines at the manifold.
21. Install the heater hose pipe at the manifold.
22. Install the power brake vacuum pipe.
23. Install the ground cable from the manifold stud.
24. Install the wiring harness onto the clips.
25. Install the emission relays with brackets onto the manifold.
26. Install the 2 braces at the rear of the drive belt tensioner.
27. Install the upper radiator hose and fill the cooling system with the proper type and quantity of antifreeze. Install the air cleaner and heat stove assembly.
28. Connect the negative battery cable.

Astro and Safari

1. Disconnect the negative battery cable. Remove the engine cover assembly. Remove the air cleaner assembly. Drain the cooling system.
2. Remove the distributor cap and ignition wires. Disconnect the ESC connector and remove the distributor.
3. Remove the cruise control transducer, if equipped.
4. Remove the detent, cruise and accelerator cables.
5. Remove the transmission and engine oil filler tubes at the alternator brace.
6. If equipped, remove the air conditioning compressor and idler pulley at the alternator brace. Remove the alternator brace.
7. Disconnect the fuel lines. Remove the necessary vacuum hoses and electrical wires.
8. Remove the AIR hoses and brackets, if equipped. Remove the upper radiator hose. Remove the heater hose at the manifold. As required, remove the TBI unit.
9. Remove the intake manifold retaining bolts. Remove the intake manifold from the engine.

To install:

10. The gaskets are marked for right and left side installation. Do not interchange them. Clean the sealing surface of the engine block and apply a ú/16 in. bead of silicone sealer to each ridge.
11. Install the new gaskets onto the heads. The gaskets will have to be cut slightly to fit past the center pushrods. Do not cut any more material than necessary. Hold the gaskets in place by extending the ridge bead of sealer 1/4 in. onto the gasket ends. Install the manifold and tighten the bolts in sequence to the correct torque.
12. When the intake manifold is installed the area between the ridges and the manifold should be completely sealed.
13. Install the intake manifold and torque the bolts in sequence to 35 ft. lbs. (47 Nm) except position No. 9 which is torqued to 41 ft. lbs. (56 Nm).
14. Install the AIR hoses and brackets, if equipped. Install the upper radiator hose. Install the heater hose at the manifold. Install the TBI unit.
15. Connect the fuel lines. Install the necessary vacuum hoses and electrical wires.
16. If equipped, install the air conditioning compressor and idler pulley at the alternator brace. Install the alternator brace.
17. Install the transmission and engine oil filler tubes at the alternator brace.
18. Install the detent, cruise and accelerator cables.
19. Install the cruise control transducer, if equipped.
20. Install the distributor, cap and ignition wires. Connect the ESC connector to the distributor.
21. Install the air cleaner assembly. Fill the cooling system with the proper type and quantity of antifreeze.
22. Connect the negative battery cable. Install the engine cover assembly.

4.3L (VIN Z) TURBOCHARGED ENGINE

1. Disconnect the negative battery cable. Remove the air cleaner wing bolt and position the assembly aside. Drain the en-

gine and turbocharger air cooler radiator antifreeze into a suitable container.
2. Remove the turbocharger air cooler, ducts, hoses and center support.
3. Disconnect all necessary vacuum and electrical connections from the upper and lower intake manifolds.
4. Remove the lower intake manifold left rear multi-use bracket.
5. Remove the throttle body, gasket and bracket from the upper intake manifold.
6. Remove the upper intake manifold bolts and remove the assembly.
7. Disconnect the heater hose and turbocharger coolant inlet pipe.
8. Disconnect the injector wire connectors and remove the fuel rail assembly.
9. Remove the air conditioner rear compressor bracket.
10. Disconnect the turbocharger coolant return line. Remove the upper radiator hose from the intake manifold.
11. Remove the distributor assembly.
12. Remove the lower intake manifold bolts and remove the assembly.

To install:

13. Thoroughly clean all gasket mating surfaces. Apply a 3/16 in. (5mm) bead of GM sealant No. 1052366 or equivalent to the front and rear of the cylinder block; extend the bead up each cylinder head 1/2 in. (13mm) to seal and retain the gaskets.
14. Lower the intake manifold onto the cylinder head and torque the bolts to 35 ft. lbs. (47 Nm).
15. Install the distributor assembly.
16. Connect the turbocharger coolant return line. Install the upper radiator hose at the intake manifold.
17. Install the air conditioner rear compressor bracket.
18. Install the fuel rail assembly and connect the injector wire connectors
19. Connect the heater hose and turbocharger coolant inlet pipe.
20. Install the upper intake manifold and bolts. Torque the bolts to 18 ft. lbs. (24 Nm) starting with the center bolts and working outward.
21. Install the throttle body, gasket and bracket at the upper intake manifold.
22. Install the lower intake manifold left rear multi-use bracket.
23. Connect all vacuum and electrical connections previously removed from the upper and lower intake manifolds.
24. Install the turbocharger air cooler, ducts, hoses and center support.
25. Connect the negative battery cable. Install the air cleaner and duct assembly.
26. Fill the cooling system with the proper type and quantity of antifreeze.

Exhaust Manifold

Removal and Installation

2.5L ENGINE

1. Disconnect the negative battery cable.
2. Remove the exhaust stove pipe at the manifold. Disconnect the oxygen sensor wire.
3. Raise and safely support the vehicle. Disconnect the exhaust pipe at the exhaust manifold.
4. Remove the air conditioning compressor and brackets, if equipped.
5. Remove the exhaust manifold retaining bolts. Remove the manifold from the engine.
6. Installation is the reverse of the removal procedure. Torque the manifold bolts to specification.

Exhaust manifold bolt torque sequence—2.5L engine

2.8L ENGINE

1. Disconnect the negative battery cable. Raise and support the vehicle safely.
2. Disconnect the exhaust pipe from the manifold. Remove the 4 rear manifold retaining bolts. Lower the vehicle.
3. Remove the air management hoses, pump and alternator brackets. Remove the heat stove tube.
4. If equipped, remove the power steering pump bracket.
5. Remove the remaining manifold attaching bolts. Remove the manifold from the engine.
6. Installation is the reverse of the removal procedure.

3.1L ENGINE

1. Disconnect the negative battery cable.
2. To remove the front exhaust manifold proceed as follows:
   a. Remove the serpentine belt and the air conditioning compressor.
   b. Remove the engine strut and bracket.
   c. Remove the crossover pipe.

Exhaust manifold mounting—2.8L engine

   d. Remove the exhaust manifold attaching bolts and remove the manifold.
3. To remove the rear exhaust manifold proceed as follows:
   a. Disconnect the oxygen sensor wire.
   b. Remove the crossover pipe.
   c. Raise and support the vehicle safely.
   d. Disconnect the exhaust pipe.
   e. Support the rear center of the frame.

A. Left Side
B. Right Side
1. Lock tab
2. Bolt
3. Bolt
4. Stud
5. Washer
6. Heat shield
7. Right exhaust manifold
8. Heat shield
9. Left exhaust manifold

Exhaust manifold mounting—4.3L engine

Exhaust manifold mounting—3.1L engine

1. Stud
2. Right (rear) exhaust manifold

Exhaust manifold mounting—3.8L engine

HEAT SHIELD
WASHER
TAB WASHER
BOLT/STUD

Exhaust manifold mounting—4.3L engine

f. Remove the rear frame mount bolts.

g. Lower the frame 8–10 in.

h. Remove the exhaust manifold bolts and remove the assembly.

4. Installation is the reverse of the removal procedure.

3.8L ENGINE

1. Disconnect the negative battery cable.

2. To remove the front exhaust manifold proceed as follows:

  a. Remove the crossover pipe.

  b. Remove the spark plug wires.

  c. Remove the exhaust manifold bolts and dipstick tube.

  d. Remove the exhaust manifold assembly.

3. To remove the rear exhaust manifold proceed as follows:

  a. Disconnect the oxygen sensor wire.

  b. Remove the spark plug wires.

  c. Remove the throttle cable bracket.

  d. Remove the crossover pipe heat shield and remove the crossover pipe.

  e. Remove the transaxle dipstick and tube assembly.

  f. Disconnect the oxygen sensor lead.

  g. Remove the plastic vacuum tank mounted on the cowl.

  h. Raise and support the vehicle safely.

  i. Remove the catalytic converter heat shield and hanger.

  j. Remove the front exhaust pipe to the manifold attaching nuts.

  k. Remove the front exhaust pipe from the manifold. Lower the vehicle.

  l. Remove the engine lift bracket and remove the manifold attaching nuts.

  m. Remove the exhaust manifold assembly.

4. Installation is the reverse of the removal procedure.

4.3L ENGINE

Non-Turbocharged Engine

1. Disconnect the negative battery cable. On Astro and Safari, remove the engine cover. Raise and support the vehicle safely.

2. Disconnect the exhaust pipes from the exhaust manifolds. Lower the vehicle.

3. To remove the right manifold, disconnect the heat stove pipe and the dipstick tube bracket.

4. To remove the left manifold, disconnect the oxygen sensor wire.

5. Disconnect the power steering bracket at the manifold, if equipped. Disconnect the alternator bracket at the manifold.

6. Remove the AIR hoses at the check valve, if equipped. Remove the exhaust manifold retaining bolts. Remove the manifold from the engine.

7. Installation is the reverse of the removal procedure.

Turbocharged Engine

1. Disconnect the negative battery cable.

2. Raise and support the vehicle safely.

3. Remove the left and right front wheel assembly and wheelhouse.

4. Lower the vehicle and remove the left exhaust manifold as follows:

  a. Remove the air cleaner and duct assembly.

  b. Remove the turbocharger air inlet elbow.

  c. Remove the upper fan shroud and loosen the fan nuts.

  d. Remove the serpentine drive belt, fan and pulley assembly.

  e. Remove the power steering pump pulley.

  f. Remove the rear alternator brace.

  g. Raise and support the vehicle safely.

  h. Place a drain pan under the power steering pump and remove the power steering pump inlet and outlet hose.

  i. Remove the oil filter lines bracket from the power steering pump.

  j. Remove the intermediate shaft.

  k. Remove the exhaust crossover pipe at the left manifold.

  l. Remove the power steering pump and rear brace as an assembly from the front bracket.

  m. Remove the spark plug wires and remove the spark plugs.

  n. Remove the exhaust manifold bolts, studs, washers, lock tabs and heat shields.

o. Remove the exhaust manifold and lower the vehicle.

5. Remove the right exhaust manifold as follows:

a. Drain the engine coolant into a suitable container.

b. Remove the battery tray with the vacuum tank.

c. Disconnect the turbocharger oil feed hose and coolant return pipe.

d. Disconnect the oxygen sensor wire.

e. Raise and safely support the vehicle.

f. Remove the muffler and tailpipe from the catalytic converter.

g. Remove the catalytic converter support bolts and lower the vehicle.

h. Disconnect the turbocharger solenoid electrical connector.

i. Loosen the turbocharger coolant feed line.

j. Remove the turbocharger outlet pipe nuts.

k. Raise and safely support the vehicle.

l. Remove the turbocharger outlet pipe support bolt. Move the catalytic converter and outlet pipe away from the turbocharger.

m. Disconnect the turbocharger oil return pipe from the turbocharger.

n. Remove the turbocharger mounting nuts.

o. Disconnect the turbocharger coolant feed pipe from the turbocharger and remove the assembly.

p. Remove the exhaust crossover pipe from the right exhaust manifold.

q. Remove the spark plug wires and remove the spark plugs.

r. Remove the turbocharger air cooler lower supports.

s. Remove the exhaust manifold bolts, studs, washers, lock tabs and heat shields.

t. Remove the exhaust manifold and lower the vehicle.

To install:

6. Install the exhaust manifold, bolts, studs, washers, lock tabs and heat shields. Torque the manifold bolts and studs to 33 ft. lbs. (45 Nm).

7. Install the spark plugs and wires.

8. Install the left exhaust assembly as follows:

a. Install the power steering pump and rear brace.

b. Install the exhaust crossover pipe at the left manifold and torque the bolts to 12 ft. lbs. (16 Nm).

c. Install the intermediate shaft.

d. Install the oil filter lines bracket to the power steering pump.

e. Install the power steering pump inlet and outlet hose.

f. Install the rear alternator brace.

g. Install the power steering pump pulley.

h. Install the serpentine drive belt, fan and pulley assembly.

i. Install the upper fan shroud.

j. Install the turbocharger air inlet elbow.

k. Install the air cleaner and duct assembly.

9. Install the right exhaust assembly as follows:

a. Install the turbocharger air cooler lower supports.

b. Install the exhaust crossover pipe at the right exhaust manifold.

c. Connect the turbocharger and coolant feed pipe assembly.

d. Install the turbocharger mounting nuts and torque to 33 ft. lbs. (45 Nm).

e. Connect the turbocharger oil return pipe at the turbocharger.

f. Install the turbocharger outlet pipe and nuts.

g. Install the turbocharger outlet pipe support bolt.

h. Connect the turbocharger solenoid electrical connector.

i. Install the catalytic converter support bolts.

j. Install the muffler and tailpipe at the catalytic converter and lower the vehicle.

k. Connect the oxygen sensor wire.

l. Connect the turbocharger oil feed hose and coolant return pipe.

m. Install the battery tray with the vacuum tank.

10. Raise and support the vehicle safely.

11. Install the left and right front wheel assembly and wheelhouse.

12. Connect the battery cables.

Turbocharger

Removal and Installation

1. Disconnect and remove the battery, tray and vacuum tank assembly.

2. Drain the antifreeze into a suitable container.

3. Remove the turbocharger air intake duct.

4. Remove the air intake duct.

5. Disconnect the solenoid wire connector at the turbocharger.

6. Raise and safely support the vehicle.

7. Remove the right wheel and tire assembly.

8. Remove the right wheelhouse panel.

9. Remove the turbocharger outlet pipe at the turbocharger. Lower the vehicle.

10. Remove the turbocharger coolant feed and return lines.

11. Remove the turbocharger oil feed and return lines.

12. Remove the turbocharger mounting bolts and remove the assembly.

To install:

13. Install the turbocharger, gasket and mounting bolts.

14. Install the turbocharger oil feed and return lines.

15. Install the turbocharger coolant feed and return lines.

16. Raise and safely support the vehicle. Install the turbocharger outlet pipe at the turbocharger.

17. Install the right wheelhouse panel.

18. Install the right wheel and tire assembly.

19. Lower the vehicle.

20. Connect the solenoid wire connector at the turbocharger.

21. Install the air intake duct.

22. Install the turbocharger air intake duct.

23. Fill the cooling system with the proper type and quantitiy of antifreeze.

24. Connect and Install the battery, tray and vacuum tank assembly.

25. Bleed the cooling system.

Timing Gear Front Cover

Removal and Installation

2.5L ENGINE

1. Disconnect the negative battery cable. Drain the cooling system.

2. Remove the power steering fluid reservoir from its mounting and support it aside.

3. Remove the upper fan shroud. Remove the accessory drive belt.

4. Disconnect the wiring from the alternator. Remove the alternator and its mounting brackets.

5. Using a suitable puller, remove the crankshaft pulley bolt and hub assembly. Disconnect the lower radiator hose at the water pump.

6. Remove the cover retaining bolts and remove the cover.

To install:

7. Lubricate the crankshaft seal with clean oil. Apply a 10mm bead of RTV sealer to oil pan lips. Apply a 6mm wide bead of RTV to the timing cover.

8. Install the cover in position on the engine. Tighten the retaining bolts to 90 inch lbs. (10 Nm).

9. Install the crankshaft pulley and hub. Connect the lower radiator hose to the water pump.

Front cover assembly—2.5L engine

10. Install the alternator and its mounting brackets. Install the accessory drive belt.
11. Install the fan shroud and the power steering reservoir.
12. Refill the cooling system and connect the negative battery cable.
13. Run the engine and check for leaks.

Timing Chain Front Cover

Removal and Installation

2.8L AND 4.3L ENGINES

1. Disconnect the negative battery cable.
2. Drain the cooling system. Remove the fan shroud assembly.
3. Remove the accessory drive belt and pulley.
4. Remove the water pump. Remove the power steering pump bracket.
5. Remove the crankshaft pulley and damper.
6. Disconnect the lower radiator hose. Remove the front cover retaining bolts.
7. Remove the front cover. Remove the old gasket material from the engine and the cover.

To install:

8. Install a new gasket in position. Install the front cover and tighten the retaining bolts to 18 ft. lbs. (24 Nm).
9. Install the water pump. Connect the lower radiator hose.
10. Install the crankshaft damper and pulley. Install the power steering mounting bracket.
11. Refill the cooling system to the correct level.
12. Connect the negative battery cable and bleed the cooling system.

3.1L ENGINE

1. Disconnect the negative battery cable.
2. Drain the cooling system.
3. Remove the accessory drive belt and tensioner.
4. Remove the power steering pump.
5. Raise and safely support the vehicle. Remove the inner splash shield.
6. Drain the engine oil. Remove the crankshaft pulley and damper. Remove the starter and support it aside.
7. Place a suitable jack under the engine-to-transaxle mount.
8. Remove the engine mount bolts and the engine mount. Raise the engine slightly.
9. Remove the lower front cover bolts and lower the oil pan. Remove the radiator hose at the water pump.

OIL LEAK AT FRONT CRANKSHAFT SEAL

Some 1990 4.3L engines may exhibit oil leaks coming from between the crankshaft seal and timing chain cover; this condition may be caused by a loose fit of the seal in the timing cover. To remedy the situation, a new seal should be installed, first clean the timing cover and seal mating area with isopropyl alcohol; then inspect the timing cover hole for damage. Apply a bead of Loctite® 680 retaining compound around the outside diameter of the new seal and install the seal following the proper procedure. Do not use RTV or any other sealant in place of the Loctite® 680 compound.

10. Remove the heater hose at the cooling system fill pipe. Remove the bypass and overflow hoses.
11. Remove the remaining front cover bolts and remove the front cover.

To install:

12. Clean all gasket mating surfaces. Install a new gasket in position on the engine block.
13. Apply sealer to the lower edges of the front cover. Install the front cover in position on the engine block. Tighten the upper bolts to 20 ft. lbs. (27 Nm).
14. Install the oil pan in position. Install the lower cover bolts and tighten to 28 ft. lbs. (38 Nm).
15. Install the engine mount to the engine and lower the engine into position.
16. Install the crankshaft damper and pulley. Install the flywheel cover and inner splash shield.
17. Install the starter. Connect the heater bypass hose an the slower radiator hose to the water pump. Lower the vehicle.
18. Install the power steering pump bracket. Install the accessory drive belt and tensioner.

1. Front cover
2. Gasket
3. Bolt
4. Bolt
5. Sealer

Front cover assembly—3.1L engine

1. Shield assembly
2. Crankshaft balancer
3. Attaching bolts

J 38197

Removing crankshaft pulley hub assembly—3.8L engine

1. Oil seal
2. Cover
3. Gasket
4. Bolt
5. Stud

Front cover assembly—3.8L engine

19. Refill the cooling system and the crankcase to the correct levels.
20. Connect the negative battery cable. Run the engine to normal operating temperature and check for leaks.

3.8L ENGINE

1. Disconnect the negative battery cable.
2. Drain the cooling system.
3. Remove the torque mount, accessory drive belt and tensioner.
4. Remove crankshaft damper using GM tool J–38197 or equivalent, while holding the flywheel in place using tool J–37096 or equivalent.
5. Remove the sensor shield.

6. Remove the oil pan to front cover bolts and the front cover attaching bolts.
7. Remove the front cover assembly.
8. Installation is the reverse of the removal procedure.

Front Cover Oil Seal

Replacement

The front cover seal can be replaced while the front cover is still on the vehicle. It is recommended by the manufacturer that the seal be replaced whenever the front cover is removed.

1. Disconnect the negative battery cable.
2. Remove the accessory drive belt.
3. Remove the crankshaft pulley and damper.
4. Using a suitable tool, pry the seal from the cover.
5. Lubricate the replacement seal with clean engine oil.
6. Using a suitable seal installer, position the seal on the crankshaft.
7. Install the crankshaft damper and pulley.
8. Install the accessory drive belt.
9. Connect the negative battery cable.

Timing Chain and Sprockets

Removal and Installation

2.8L ENGINE

1. Disconnect the negative battery cable. Drain the coolant.
2. Remove the front cover assembly.
3. Place the No. 1 piston at top dead center with the marks on the camshaft and crankshaft sprockets aligned (No. 4 cylinder firing).
4. Remove the bolts that hold the camshaft sprocket to the camshaft. This sprocket is a light press fit on the camshaft.
5. Remove the timing chain. Using a suitable puller, remove the crankshaft sprocket, as required.

To install:

6. Install the crankshaft sprocket using tool J–5590, ensuring the timing marks face outward.

#1 AT TDC

#4 AT TDC

Timing mark alignment—2.8L engine

7. Lubricate the thrust surface of the camshaft gear with Molykote® or equivalent. Install the chain onto camshaft sprocket.

8. Holding the sprocket vertically with the chain hanging down, align the marks on the camshaft and crankshaft sprockets and install the assembly onto the camshaft.

9. Install the camshaft to gear attaching bolts and torque to 17 ft. lbs. (23 Nm). After the sprockets are in place, turn the engine 2 full revolutions to make certain the timing marks are in correct alignment between the shaft centers.

10. Lubricate the chain with engine oil and install the front cover.

11. Connect the negative battery cable. Fill the cooling system with the proper type and quantity of antifreeze.

3.1L ENGINE

1. Disconnect the negative battery cable. Drain the coolant.

NOTE: ALIGN TIMING MARKS ON CAM & CRANK SPROCKETS USING ALIGNMENT MARKS ON DAMPER STAMPING OR CAST ALIGNMENT MARKS ON CYLINDER & CASE

1. Damper
2. Alignment marks
3. Timing chain
4. Crank sprocket
5. 21 ft. lbs. (28 Nm)
6. Camshaft sprocket

Timing mark alignment—3.1L engine

2. Remove the right front tire and wheel assembly.

3. Remove the front cover assembly. Ensure the marks on the crankshaft and camshaft gears are aligned using the marks on the damper stamping or cast alignment marks on cylinder and case.

4. Remove the bolts that hold the camshaft sprocket to the camshaft. This sprocket is a light press fit on the camshaft.

5. Remove the timing chain. Using a suitable puller, remove the crankshaft sprocket, as required.

To install:

6. Install the crankshaft sprocket.

7. Lubricate the camshaft thrust plate surface with Molykote® or equivalent. Install the chain onto camshaft sprocket.

8. Holding the sprocket vertically with the chain hanging down, align the marks on the camshaft and crankshaft sprockets and install the assembly onto the camshaft.

9. Install the camshaft to gear attaching bolts and torque to 18 ft. lbs. (24 Nm). After the sprockets are in place, turn the engine 2 full revolutions to make certain the timing marks are in correct alignment between the shaft centers.

10. Lubricate the chain with engine oil and install the front cover.

11. Connect the negative battery cable. Fill the cooling system with the proper type and quantity of antifreeze.

1. Key
2. Damper assembly
3. Crankshaft sprocket
4. Bolt
5. Timing chain
6. Camshaft sprocket
7. Camshaft gear

Exploded view of timing chain assembly—3.8L engine

ALIGN MARKS

ALIGN MARKS

BALANCE SHAFT TO CAMSHAFT

CAMSHAFT TO CRANKSHAFT

Timing mark alignment—3.8L engine

ALIGN TIMING MARKS AS SHOWN

Timing mark alignment—4.3L engine

3.8L ENGINE

1. Disconnect the negative battery cable. Drain the coolant.
2. Align the marks on the crankshaft damper and timing cover with the engine in the No. 1 firing position. Remove the front cover assembly.
3. Ensure the marks on the crankshaft and camshaft gears are aligned.
4. Remove the timing chain damper and camshaft sprocket.
5. Remove the timing chain. Using a suitable puller, remove the crankshaft sprocket, as required.

To install:

6. Install the crankshaft sprocket.
7. Install the chain onto camshaft sprocket.
8. Holding the sprocket vertically with the chain hanging down, align the marks on the camshaft and crankshaft sprockets and install the assembly onto the camshaft.
9. Install the camshaft to gear attaching bolt and torque to 74 ft. lbs. (100 Nm) and then an additional 105 degree turn. Install the damper and torque to 16 ft. lbs. (22 Nm).
10. After the sprockets are in place, turn the engine 2 full revolutions to make certain the timing marks are in correct alignment between the shaft centers.
11. Lubricate the chain with engine oil and install the front cover.
12. Connect the negative battery cable. Fill the cooling system with the proper type and quantity of antifreeze.

Service Tips

CAM GEAR MISORIENTATION

Some 1990 4.3L engines have been built with the crankshaft and camshaft gears misaligned, causing lack of performance and backfire. The problem may be identified by following a timing gear alignment checking procedure; once identified the timing cover will have to be removed and the chain and gears realigned.
The following VIN No.'s are applicable:
G Series: L7500878–L7501500
C/K Series:
    LZ501591–LZ504345 (Fort Wayne)
    LE500013–LE501336 (Pontiac East)

THRUST PLATE
CAMSHAFT GEAR
CAMSHAFT
BOLTS
CAMSHAFT GEAR
TIMING MARKS
CRANKSHAFT GEAR

Timing gear assembly and timing mark alignment— 2.5L engine

4.3L ENGINE

1. Disconnect the negative battery cable. Drain the coolant.
2. Align the marks on the crankshaft damper and timing cover with the engine in the No. 1 firing position. Remove the front cover assembly.
3. Ensure the marks on the crankshaft and camshaft gears are aligned.
4. Remove the bolts that hold the camshaft sprocket to the camshaft. Remove the timing chain.
5. Using a suitable puller, remove the crankshaft sprocket, as required.

To install:

6. Install the crankshaft sprocket using tool J–5590, ensuring the timing marks face outward.
7. Lubricate the thrust surface of the camshaft gear with Molykote® or equivalent. Install the chain onto the camshaft sprocket.
8. Holding the sprocket vertically with the chain hanging down, align the marks on the camshaft and crankshaft sprockets and install the assembly onto the camshaft.
9. Install the camshaft to gear attaching bolts and torque to specification. After the sprockets are in place, turn the engine 2 full revolutions to make certain the timing marks are in correct alignment between the shaft centers.
10. Lubricate the chain with engine oil and install the front cover.
11. Connect the negative battery cable. Fill the cooling system with the proper type and quantity of antifreeze.

Camshaft and Timing Gear

Removal and Installation

2.5L ENGINE

1. Disconnect the negative battery cable. Drain the cooling system. Remove the radiator.
2. Remove the engine side cover. Remove the air cleaner assembly. Remove the EGR valve.
3. Disconnect the power steering reservoir and position it aside. Remove the drive belts and pulleys. Remove the upper fan shroud. Remove the front cover.
4. Rotate the crankshaft until the timing marks are aligned at TDC. Remove the distributor assembly. Remove the oil pump drive shaft cover and drive shaft.

Service Tips

SERVICING TIMING GEARS

When servicing the camshaft and/or crankshaft gear on the 1988–90 2.5L engine, it is recommended the gears be replaced with a new gear kit part No. 10101790. The kit will provide improved wear resistance.

5. Remove the rocker cover. Remove the rockers and pushrods. Keep them in order for reinstallation. Remove the valve lifters. Keep them in order for reinstallation.

6. If equipped with air conditioning, it may be necessary to reposition the condenser in order to withdraw the camshaft from the engine. If the condenser must be removed, properly discharge the system before condenser removal.

7. Remove the headlight bezel and grille assembly.

8. Remove the camshaft thrust plate bolts. Carefully remove the camshaft from the vehicle. Press the gear off of the camshaft.

To install:

9. Lubricate the camshaft lobes with Molykote or equivalent before installation. Press the camshaft gear, spacer and thrust plate onto the camshaft. The camshaft to thrust plate clearance, measured with a feeler gauge should be approximately 0.0015–0.0050 in.

10. Install the camshaft into the block, use care not to damage the bearings. Align the timing marks on the camshaft gear and the crankshaft gear.

11. Install the thrust plate bolts and tighten to 90 inch lbs.

12. Install the front cover. Install the distributor and the oil pump shaft cover.

13. Install the lifters, pushrods, rocker arms and the engine side cover.

14. Install the remaining components in the reverse order of removal.

15. Refill the cooling system and connect the negative battery cable.

Camshaft

Removal and Installation

2.8L ENGINE

1. Disconnect the negative battery cable.
2. Drain the cooling system.
3. Remove the upper fan shroud.
4. Remove the radiator.
5. Remove the valve cover and the valve train components. Remove the intake manifold assembly and remove the lifters.
6. Remove the front cover assembly.
7. Remove the timing chain and sprocket.
8. Remove the camshaft from the block. Insert 3 bolts approximately 3 in. long into the camshaft gear bolt holes to supply leverage while removing the camshaft. Use care not to damage the bearings.

To install:

9. Lubricate the camshaft with Molykote or equivalent, before installation.

10. Install the camshaft into the cylinder block, use care not to damage the bearings.

11. Install the timing chain and sprocket. Make sure the timing marks align correctly.

12. Install the front cover assembly and hydraulic lifters.

13. Install the intake manifold assembly. Install the valve train components, adjust the valves and install the valve cover.

14. Install the radiator and the fan shroud.

15. Fill the cooling system to the correct level and connect the negative battery cable.

3.1L AND 3.8L ENGINES

1. Disconnect the negative battery cable.
2. Drain the cooling system.
3. Remove the engine from the vehicle and support it in a suitable holding fixture.
4. Remove the intake manifold. Remove the valve cover and the valve train components.
5. Remove the front cover assembly.
6. Remove the timing chain and sprocket. Remove the thrust plate, if equipped.
7. Remove the camshaft from the block. Insert 3 bolts approximately 3 in. long into the camshaft gear bolt holes to supply leverage while removing the camshaft. Use care not to damage the bearings.

To install:

8. Lubricate the camshaft with Molykote or equivalent, before installation.

9. Install the camshaft into the cylinder block, use care not to damage the bearings.

10. Install the thrust plate, if equipped. Install the timing chain and sprocket. Make sure the timing marks align correctly.

11. Install the front cover assembly.

12. Install the intake manifold assembly. Install the valve train components and the valve cover.

13. Install the engine into the vehicle.

14. Fill the cooling system to the correct level and connect the negative battery cable.

4.3L ENGINE

1. Disconnect the negative battery cable.
2. Drain the cooling system.
3. Remove the upper fan shroud, if required.
4. Remove the radiator.
5. Remove the valve cover and the valve train components. Remove the intake manifold assembly and remove the lifters.
6. Remove the front cover assembly.
7. Remove the timing chain and camshaft sprocket. Remove the balance shaft drive gear, if equipped. Remove the camshaft thrust plate.
8. Remove the camshaft from the block. Insert 3 bolts approximately 3 in. long into the camshaft gear bolt holes to supply leverage while removing the camshaft. Use care not to damage the bearings.

To install:

9. Lubricate the camshaft with Molykote or equivalent, before installation.

10. Install the camshaft into the cylinder block, use care not to damage the bearings. Install the thrust plate, if equipped. Install the balance shaft drive gear, if equipped.

11. Install the timing chain and sprocket. Make sure the timing marks align correctly.

12. Install the front cover assembly and hydraulic lifters.

13. Install the intake manifold assembly. Install the valve train components, adjust the valves and install the valve cover.

14. Install the radiator and the fan shroud.

15. Fill the cooling system to the correct level and connect the negative battery cable.

Balance Shaft

Removal and Installation

3.8L ENGINE

1. Disconnect the negative battery cable.
2. Remove the engine from the vehicle.
3. Remove the flywheel and intake manifold.
4. Remove the lifter guide retainer.
5. Remove the timing chain cover.
6. Remove the balance shaft drive gear bolt, the camshaft sprocket and timing chain.
7. Remove the balance shaft retainer bolts, retainer and gear.
8. Using tool J–6125–B, remove the balance shaft.
9. Remove the balance shaft rear plug. Using tool J–36995–5, remove the balance shaft rear bearing.

NOTE: The balance shaft and bearings are only to be serviced or replaced as a complete assembly.

To install:

10. Dip the bearings in clean engine oil before installation.
11. Using tool J–36995–5, install the balance shaft rear bearing with the rolled edge facing into the engine and the manufacturer's markings facing the flywheel side.
12. Dip the front balance shaft bearing into engine oil. Using tool J–36996, install the balance shaft into the block.
13. Temporarily install the balance shaft retainer and bolts. Install the balance shaft drive gear. Apply Loctite® to the bolt and torque to 14 ft. lbs. (20 Nm) plus turn the bolt an additional 35 degrees.
14. Install the balance shaft rear plug.
15. Measure the balance shaft end play. End play should be 0–0.008 in. (0–0.203mm).
16. Measure the balance shaft radial play at both the front and rear. The front radial play should be 0–0.0011 in. (0–0.028mm). The rear radial play should be 0.0005–0.0047 in. (0.0127–0.119mm).
17. Temporarily install the camshaft gear and align the timing

MEASURING END PLAY

MEASURING REAR RADIAL PLAY

MEASURING FRONT RADIAL PLAY

MEASURING GEAR LASH

Balance shaft clearance measuring—3.8L engine

marks point straight down. Remove the camshaft gear and align the balance shaft marks point straight down. Install the camshaft gear and align the marks by turning the balance shaft.

18. Ensure the No. 1 piston is at TDC and install the camshaft sprocket and timing chain.

19. Measure the gear lash at 4 places, every ¼ turn. The lash should be 0.002–0.005 in. (0.050–0.127mm).

20. Tighten the balance shaft front bearing retainer to 22 ft. lbs. (30 Nm).

21. Install the timing chain cover.

22. Install the lifter guide retainer.

23. Install the flywheel and intake manifold.

24. Install the engine into the vehicle.

25. Connect the negative battery cable.

1. Washer
2. Bolt
3. Balancer shaft gear
4. Nut
5. Pin
6. Bolt
7. Retainer
8. Plug
9. Bearing

J 6125–B

REMOVING SHAFT

J 36995–1

INSTALLING REAR BEARING

J 36995–5

J 36995

J 36996

J 21465–13

4   1

REMOVING REAR BEARING

INSTALLING SHAFT

Balance shaft service—3.8L engine

1. Camshaft sprocket bolt
2. Camshaft sprocket
3. Balance shaft driven gear bolt
4. Balance shaft driven gear
5. Balance shaft drive gear
6. Nut
7. Stud

Balance shaft drive gears—4.3L (VIN W) engine

1. Balance shaft retainer
2. Balance shaft
3. Screw
4. Bearing
5. Plug

Balance shaft assembly—4.3L (VIN W) engine

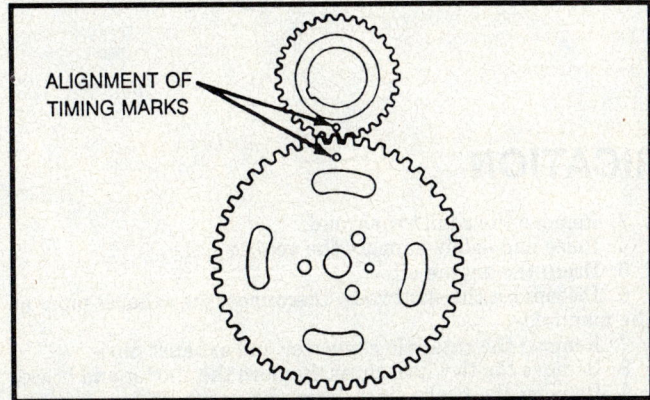

ALIGNMENT OF TIMING MARKS

Balance shaft alignment marks—4.3L (VIN W) engine

4.3L (VIN W) ENGINE

1. Disconnect the negative battery cable. Drain the cooling system into a suitable container. Properly relieve the fuel system pressure and discharge the air conditioning system.
2. Remove the air cleaner and air intake duct.
3. Remove the upper radiator shroud.
4. Remove the oil and transmission cooler lines at the radiator.
5. Remove the hoses from the radiator and remove the radiator.
6. Remove the air conditioner condenser and fan assembly.
7. Remove the serpentine belt.
8. Remove the brace at the coolant pump and remove the pump.
9. Remove the torsional damper.
10. Raise and support the vehicle safely.
11. Remove the flywheel cover. Drain the engine oil and loosen

6–53

the oil pan bolts; remove the 2 nuts and bolts at the front of the oil pan.

12. Remove the front timing cover bolts and cover.

NOTE: Use care when removing the front cover, as not to damage the oil pan gasket.

13. Remove the crankshaft front cover oil seal.
14. Remove the camshaft sprocket, timing chain and balance shaft drive gear.
15. Remove the balance shaft retainer.
16. Remove the intake manifold assembly.
17. Remove the hydraulic lifter retainer.
18. Remove the balance shaft from the bearing using a soft faced mallet.
19. Remove the rear bearing using tool J–38834 and J–26941.

NOTE: The balance shaft and bearings are only to be serviced or replaced as a complete assembly.

To install:

20. Dip the bearings in clean engine oil before installation.
21. Using tool J–38834, install the balance shaft rear bearing with the flat edge and the manufacturer's markings facing the front of engine.
22. Dip the front balance shaft bearing into engine oil. Using tool J–36996 and J–8092, install the balance shaft into the block.
23. Install the balance shaft retainer and torque the bolts to 120 inch lbs. (14 Nm).
24. Install the balance shaft drive gear. Apply Loctite® to the bolt and torque to 15 ft. lbs. (20 Nm) plus turn the bolt an additional 35 degrees.
25. Install the lifter retainer and turn the balance shaft to ensure proper clearance.
26. Install the balance shaft rear plug.
27. Turn the camshaft so the balance shaft drive gear timing marks are aligned.
28. Install the balance shaft drive gear retaining stud and torque to 12 ft. lbs. (16 Nm).
29. Install the intake manifold assembly.
30. Install the timing chain and gears with the timing marks dot-to-dot; this is the No. 4 cylinder firing position, so set the distributor rotor to the No. cylinder firing position when installing. Torque the camshaft bolts and nut to 21 ft. lbs. (28 Nm).
31. Install the distributor assembly.
32. Install the timing cover oil seal and install the cover.
33. Raise and support the vehicle safely.
34. Install the flywheel cover.
35. Tighten the oil pan bolts; install the 2 nuts and bolts at the front of the oil pan.
36. Install the torsional damper.
37. Install the brace at the coolant pump and install the pump.
38. Install the serpentine belt.
39. Install the air conditioner condenser and fan assembly.
40. Install the radiator and hoses.

41. Install the oil and transmission cooler lines at the radiator.
42. Install the upper radiator shroud.
43. Install the air cleaner and air intake duct.
44. Connect the negative battery cable. Fill the cooling system with proper type and quantity of antifreeze. Properly recharge the air conditioning system. Fill the engine with the correct quantity and grade of engine oil.

Piston and Connecting Rod

Positioning

The connecting rod bearing tang slots must be on the side opposite of the camshaft except the 3.8L engine.

a. Oil ring rail gaps
b. Second compression ring gap
c. Notch in piston
d. Oil ring spacer gap
e. Top compression ring gap

Piston and ring positioning

Piston installed position—3.8L engine

ENGINE LUBRICATION

Oil Pan

Removal and Installation

2.5L ENGINE

2WD Vehicle

1. Disconnect the negative battery cable.
2. Remove the power steering reservoir and position aside.

3. Remove the radiator shroud.
4. Raise and safely support the vehicle.
5. Drain the engine oil.
6. Disconnect the strut rods. Disconnect the exhaust pipes at the manifolds.
7. Remove the catalytic converter and exhaust pipe.
8. Remove the flywheel cover. Remove the starter and brace.
9. Remove the brake lines from the crossmember. Remove the front engine mounting bolts.

Oil pan assembly—V6 engine

10. Raise the engine slightly, with a suitable lifting device and insert wooden blocks to hold it.

11. Remove the oil pan retaining bolts and remove the oil pan.

To install:

12. Apply RTV sealant to the oil pan flange and block. Install the oil pan into position.

13. Install the oil pan bolts and tighten to 90 inch lbs. (10 Nm).

14. Remove the blocks and lower the engine. Install the engine mount bolts.

15. Connect the brake line at the crossmember. Install the starter and brace.

16. Install the flywheel cover. Install the catalytic converter and the exhaust pipe.

17. Install the strut rods. Lower the vehicle. Install the radiator shroud.

18. Install the power steering reservoir. Refill the crankcase with the correct level of oil.

19. Connect the negative battery cable.

4WD Vehicle

1. Disconnect the negative battery cable.

2. Remove the power steering pump from the fan shroud and remove the fan shroud.

3. Remove the crankcase dipstick. Raise and safely support the vehicle.

4. Drain the engine oil. Remove the brake line from the clips at the crossmember. Remove the crossmember.

5. Remove the transmission cooler lines at the flywheel cover bracket, if equipped.

6. Disconnect the exhaust pipe at the manifold. Remove the catalytic converter hanger.

7. Remove the flywheel cover. Remove the driveshaft splash shield.

8. Disconnect the idler arm assembly. Remove the steering gear retaining bolts and pull the gear and linkage forward.

9. Place a suitable support under the front differential housing and remove the differential support bracket bolts.

10. Move the differential assembly forward.

11. Remove the starter and brace.

12. Disconnect the front driveshaft at the pinion. Remove the engine mount through bolts.

13. Raise the engine slightly, using a suitable jack.

14. Remove the oil pan retaining bolts and remove the oil pan.

To install:

15. Clean all sealant from the block and the oil pan.

16. Apply a bead of RTV to the oil pan flange and to the sealing surfaces of the block.

17. Install the oil pan in position and install the retaining bolts. Tighten to 90 inch .lbs.

18. Lower the engine and install the engine mount through bolts. Connect the front driveshaft at the drive pinion.

19. Install the starter and brace. Pull the differential back into position and install the retaining bolts.

20. Install the steering gear and idler arm assembly mounting bolts.

21. Install the driveshaft shield and the flywheel cover.

22. Install the catalytic converter hanger and the connect the exhaust pipe at the manifold.

23. Reconnect the transmission cooler lines to the clips at the flywheel housing.

24. Install the crossmember and reposition the brake lines. Lower the vehicle.

25. Install the dipstick. Refill the crankcase with oil. Install the upper fan shroud.

26. Install the power steering fluid reservoir. Connect the negative battery cable.

2.8L ENGINE

1. Disconnect the negative battery cable.

2. Raise and safely support the vehicle.

3. Drain the engine oil and remove the filter.

4. Remove the engine assembly.

5. Remove the oil pan attaching bolts, nuts and reinforcements.

6. Remove the oil pan and gasket.

To install:

7. Install a new oil pan gasket, apply GM sealer 1052914 between the 2 rear oil pan bolts and install the oil pan. Tighten all oil pan bolts and nuts except the 2 rear bolts to 7 ft. lbs. (10 Nm) and torque the 2 rear oil pan bolts to 18 ft. lbs. (25 Nm).

8. Install the engine into the vehicle.

9. Install the oil filter and connect the negative battery cable.

3.1L ENGINE

1. Disconnect the negative battery cable. Remove the accessory drive belt.

2. Raise and safely support the vehicle.

3. Remove the crankshaft damper and pulley.

4. Drain the engine oil. Remove the flywheel shields.

5. Remove the starter. Support the engine with a suitable jack.

6. Remove the engine mounting bolts.

7. Raise the engine slightly.

8. Remove the oil pan bolts and the oil pan.

To install:

9. Install a new oil pan gasket and install the oil pan. Tighten M8 oil pan bolts to 19 ft. lbs. (25 Nm) and the M6 oil pan bolts to 7 ft. lbs. (10 Nm).

10. Lower the engine and install the engine mounting bolts.

11. Install the starter and flywheel shields.

12. Install the crankshaft damper and pulley.

13. Lower the vehicle and install the accessory drive belt.

14. Refill the crankcase and connect the negative battery cable.

3.8L ENGINE

1. Disconnect the negative battery cable. Remove the accessory drive belt.

2. Raise and safely support the vehicle.

3. Remove the crankshaft damper and pulley.

4. Drain the engine oil. Remove the flywheel shields.

5. Remove the starter. Support the engine with a suitable jack.

6. Remove the engine mounting bolts.

7. Raise the engine slightly.

8. Remove the oil pan bolts and the oil pan.

To install:

9. Install a new oil pan gasket and install the oil pan. Tighten the oil pan bolts to 124 inch lbs. (14 Nm).

10. Lower the engine and install the engine mounting bolts.

11. Install the starter and flywheel shields.

12. Install the crankshaft damper and pulley.

13. Lower the vehicle and install the accessory drive belt.

14. Refill the crankcase and connect the negative battery cable.

4.3L ENGINE

2WD Vehicle

1. Disconnect the negative battery cable.

2. Drain the oil and remove the engine from the vehicle.

3. Remove the oil pan bolts, nuts and reinforcements.

4. Remove the oil pan and gasket.

To install:

5. Install a new oil pan gasket, apply GM sealer 1052914 between the 2 front and rear oil pan bolts and install the oil pan. Tighten all oil pan bolts and nuts except the 4 front and rear nuts to 100 inch lbs. (11 Nm) and torque the 4 front and rear oil pan nuts to 17 ft. lbs. (23 Nm).

6. Install the engine into the vehicle.

7. Install the oil filter and connect the negative battery cable.

4WD Vehicle

1. Disconnect the negative battery cable.

2. Remove the crankcase dipstick. Raise and safely support the vehicle. Drain the engine oil.

3. Remove the drive belt splash shield.

4. Remove the axle shield and skid plate.

5. Remove the flywheel cover.

6. Remove the left and right engine mount through bolts. Raise the engine and block in position.

7. Remove the oil cooler lines and oil filter adapter.

8. Remove the pitman and idler arm.

9. Remove the front differential through bolts.

10. Remove the front propeller shaft and roll the differential forward.

11. Remove the starter and brace.

12. Remove the oil pan retaining bolts and remove the oil pan.

To install:

13. Clean all sealant from the block and the oil pan.

14. Apply a bead of RTV to the oil pan flange and to the sealing surfaces of the block. Install the oil pan gasket and seal.

15. Install the oil pan and the retaining bolts. Torque the bolts to 100 inch lbs. (11 Nm) and the nuts to 17 ft. lbs. (23 Nm).

16. Install the starter and brace.

17. Pull the differential back into position and install the retaining bolts.

18. Connect the front driveshaft at the drive pinion.

19. Lower the engine and install the engine mount through bolts.

20. Install the pitman and idler arm assembly.

21. Install the transfer case shield and the flywheel cover.

22. Install the front skid plate and axle shield.

23. Reconnect the oil cooler lines and oil filter adapter.

24. Install the drive belt splash shield. Lower the vehicle.

25. Install the dipstick. Refill the crankcase with oil.

26. Connect the negative battery cable.

Oil Pump

Removal and Installation

EXCEPT 3.8L ENGINE

1. Disconnect the negative battery cable.

2. Raise and safely support the vehicle.

3. Drain the engine oil. Remove the engine as required. Remove the oil pan.

Oil pump mounting—2.8L, 3.1L and 4.3L engines

4. Remove the oil pump retaining bolt and lower the pump from the block.

5. Remove the pump shaft.

6. Install the pump onto the block, ensure the pump shaft and driven shaft are properly aligned. No gasket is used.

7. Install the pump retaining bolt and torque to specification.

8. Install the oil pan. Install the engine, if removed.

9. Lower the vehicle. Refill the crankcase with oil.

10. Connect the negative battery cable. Disable the ignition system; crank engine for approximately 10 seconds to aid in priming the oil pump and reducing the risk of engine damage.

NOTE: If the oil pump does not build up oil pressure almost immediately, remove the pan and check for a loose oil pump to pick-up tube attachment. If necessary dismantle the pump and pack the pump cavity with petroleum jelly. Running the engine without measurable oil pressure will cause extensive damage.

3.8L ENGINE

1. Disconnect the negative battery cable.

2. Remove the front timing cover assembly.

3. Remove the oil pump cover attaching screws and remove the pump gears.

1. Pump outer gear
2. Pump inner gear
3. Oil pump cover
4. Screw
5. Front cover

Oil filter adapter and oil pressure valve—3.8L engine

1. Spring
2. Valve—Oil pressure
3. Gasket
4. Oil filter adapter
5. Oil cooler adapter
6. Connector
7. Oil filter
8. Stud
9. Oil drip shield

Oil pump gears and housing assembly—3.8L engine

4. Remove the oil filter drip shield.
5. Remove the oil filter.
6. Remove the 4 bolts securing the adapter to the front cover.
7. Remove the adapter, gasket, the oil pressure valve and spring.

To install:
8. Clean all part in solvent and remove the old gaskets.
9. Check all parts for scoring, cracks or excessive wear. Check pressure regulator spring for loss of tension and replace as necessary.
10. Install the oil filter adapter, a new gasket, the oil pressure valve and spring.
11. Install the 4 adapter to front cover screws and torque to 22 ft. lbs. (30 Nm).
12. Install the oil filter.
13. Install the oil filter drip shield.
14. Install the pump gears into the cover assembly and pack with petroleum jelly. Install the oil pump cover attaching screws and torque to 97 inch lbs. (11 Nm).
15. Install the front timing cover assembly.
16. Connect the negative battery cable.

NOTE: If the oil pump pick-up screen is thought to be possibly clogged or dirty the oil pan should be removed and the screen removed and cleaned with solvent.

Checking

1. Disconnect the negative battery cable.
2. Remove the oil pressure sending unit.
3. Connect a suitable oil pressure gauge in place of the sending unit.
4. Reconnect the negative battery cable.
5. Ensure oil level is within specification.
6. Start the engine and set to specified test RPM.

ALIGNMENT HOLE
DUST LIP
DOWEL PIN
SEAL
ATTACHING SCREWS
MANDRIL
COLLAR

One piece rear main seal tool and installation

7. Verify oil pressure reading meets specifications.
8. Remove the gauge and reinstall the sending unit.

Rear Main Oil Seal

Removal and Installation

1. Disconnect the negative battery cable.
2. Raise and safely support the vehicle.
3. Remove the engine and/or transmission from the vehicle, as required.
4. Remove the flywheel. Remove the clutch assembly, if equipped with manual transmission.
5. Remove the oil seal by prying it out with a suitable tool.
6. Coat the seal lips with oil and using a suitable tool, install the seal.
7. Install the flywheel and clutch assembly.
8. Install the transmission assembly.
9. Lower the vehicle. Connect the negative battery cable.

TORQUE SPECIFICATIONS

Component	English	Metric
Camshaft sprocket bolt		
2.8L engine	17 ft. lbs.	23 Nm
3.1L engine	18 ft. lbs.	24 Nm
3.8L engine		
Step 1:	74 ft. lbs.	100 Nm
Step 2:	+ 105° turn	+ 105° turn
4.3L engine	21 ft. lbs.	28 Nm
Connecting rod bearing cap bolts		
2.5L engine	32 ft. lbs.	45 Nm
2.8L engine	39 ft. lbs.	53 Nm
3.1L engine	39 ft. lbs.	53 Nm
3.8L engine		
Step 1:	20 ft. lbs.	27 Nm
Step 2:	+ 50° turn	+ 50° turn
4.3L engine		
Step 1:	20 ft. lbs.	27 Nm
Step 2:	+ 60° turn	+ 60° turn
Crankshaft damper bolt		
2.5L engine	160 ft. lbs.	220 Nm
2.8L engine	70 ft. lbs.	95 Nm
3.1L engine	75 ft. lbs.	102 Nm
3.8L engine		
Step 1:	110 ft. lbs.	150 Nm
Step 2:	+ 76° turn	+ 76° turn
4.3L engine	70 ft. lbs.	95 Nm
Crankshaft pulley bolt		
2.5L engine	25 ft. lbs.	34 Nm
Cylinder head bolt		
2.5L engine		
Step 1:	18 ft. lbs.	25 Nm
Step 2:		
Except position No. 9	27 ft. lbs.	35 Nm
Position No. 9	18 ft. lbs.	25 Nm
Step 3:	+ 90° turn	+ 90° turn
2.8L and 3.1L engines		
Step 1:	40 ft. lbs.	55 Nm
Step 2:	+ 90° turn	+ 90° turn
3.8L engine		
Step 1:	35 ft. lbs.	47 Nm
Step 2:	+ 130° turn	+ 130° turn
Step 3: 4 center bolts only	+ 30° turn	+ 30° turn
4.3L engine	65 ft. lbs.	90 Nm
EGR valve-to-intake plenum		
2.5L engine	18 ft. lbs.	25 Nm
2.8L and 3.1L engines	17 ft. lbs.	24 Nm
4.3L engine with TBI	15 ft. lbs.	20 Nm
Engine-to-transmission/transaxle	55 ft. lbs.	75 Nm
Exhaust manifold		
2.5L engine		
Center bolts (3)	36 ft. lbs.	50 Nm
Outer bolts (4)	32 ft. lbs.	43 Nm
2.8L and 3.1L engines	25 ft. lbs.	34 Nm
3.8L engine	18 ft. lbs.	52 Nm
4.3L engine		
Center bolts (2)	26 ft. lbs.	36 Nm
All others	20 ft. lbs.	27 Nm
Exhaust pipe-to-exhaust manifold nuts		
2.5L, 2.8 and 4.3L engines	15 ft. lbs.	20 Nm
3.1L and 3.8L engines	22 ft. lbs.	30 Nm

TORQUE SPECIFICATIONS

Component	English	Metric
Flywheel/flexplate-to-crankshaft bolts		
2.5L engine		
Automatic transmission/transaxle	55 ft. lbs.	75 Nm
Manual transmission/transaxle	65 ft. lbs.	90 Nm
2.8L and 3.1L engines	52 ft. lbs.	70 Nm
3.8L engine		
Step 1:	11 ft. lbs.	15 Nm
Step 2:	+ 50° turn	+ 50° turn
4.3L engine	75 ft. lbs.	100 Nm
Flywheel-to-converter bolts		
Except 3T40 transaxle	46 ft. lbs.	63 Nm
3T40 transaxle	35 ft. lbs.	47 Nm
Engine mount through bolt		
2.5L engine		
Nut	30 ft. lbs.	42 Nm
Bolt	50 ft. lbs.	65 Nm
2.8L engine		
Nut	53 ft. lbs.	72 Nm
Bolt	85 ft. lbs.	115 Nm
4.3L engine	52 ft. lbs.	70 Nm
Intake manifold		
2.5L engine	25 ft. lbs.	34 Nm
2.8L engine		
1988–90	23 ft. lbs.	31 Nm
1991–92	15 ft. lbs.	21 Nm
3.1L engine		
Step 1:	13 ft. lbs.	18 Nm
Step 2:	19 ft. lbs.	26 Nm
3.8L engine		
Lower	88 inch lbs.	10 Nm
Upper	22 ft. lbs.	30 Nm
4.3L (VIN W) engine		
Lower	35 ft. lbs.	48 Nm
Upper	124 inch lbs.	14 Nm
4.3L (VIN Z) engine		
Except position No. 9	35 ft. lbs.	47 Nm
Position No. 9	41 ft. lbs.	56 Nm
Main bearing cap bolts		
2.5L and 2.8L engine	70 ft. lbs.	95 Nm
3.1L engine	72 ft. lbs.	98 Nm
3.8L engine		
Step 1:	26 ft. lbs.	35 Nm
Step 2:	+ 45° turn	+ 45° turn
4.3L engine	75 ft. lbs.	110 Nm
Oil pan		
2.5L engine	96 inch lbs.	10 Nm
2.8L engine		
Except 2 rear bolts	96 inch lbs.	10 Nm
2 rear bolts	18 ft. lbs.	25 Nm
3.1L engine	15 ft. lbs.	20 Nm
3.8L engine	124 inch lbs.	14 Nm
4.3L engine		
Nuts	17 ft. lbs.	23 Nm
Bolts	97 inch lbs.	11 Nm
Oil pan drain plug		
Except 3.8L engine	18 ft. lbs.	25 Nm
3.8L engine	30 ft. lbs.	40 Nm
Oil pump attaching bolts		
2.5L engine	22 ft. lbs.	30 Nm
2.8L and 3.1L engines	30 ft. lbs.	41 Nm
4.3L engine	65 ft. lbs.	90 Nm

TORQUE SPECIFICATIONS

Component	English	Metric
Rocker arm bolt		
2.5L engine	22 ft. lbs.	30 Nm
3.8L engine	28 ft. lbs.	38 Nm
Rocker (valve) cover		
2.5L engine	48 inch lbs.	5 Nm
2.8L engine	72 inch lbs.	8 Nm
3.1L, 3.8L and 4.3L engines	89 inch lbs.	10 Nm
Spark plug		
2.5L engine	11 ft. lbs.	15 Nm
2.8L and 4.3L engines		
1988–90	22 ft. lbs.	30 Nm
1991–92	11 ft. lbs.	15 Nm
3.1L engine	18 ft. lbs.	24 Nm
3.8L engine	12 ft. lbs.	16 Nm
TBI fuel meter cover screws	27 inch lbs.	3 Nm
TBI-to-fuel meter body screws	35 inch lbs.	4 Nm
TBI fuel feed/return line	20 ft. lbs.	27 Nm
TBI mounting bolts/nuts	16 ft. lbs.	22 Nm
Timing cover		
2.5L engine	90 inch lbs.	10 Nm
2.8L engine		
10mm bolts (4)	37 ft. lbs.	50 Nm
8mm bolts (6)	22 ft. lbs.	30 Nm
3.8L engine	22 ft. lbs.	30 Nm
4.3L engine	124 inch lbs.	14 Nm
Water pump		
2.5L engine	17 ft. lbs.	23 Nm
2.8L engine	22 ft. lbs.	30 Nm
3.1L engine	89 inch lbs.	10 Nm
3.8L engine		
Water pump-to-block	29 ft. lbs.	39 Nm
Water pump-to-front cover	97 inch lbs.	11 Nm
4.3L engine	22 ft. lbs.	30 Nm

MANUAL TRANSMISSION

For further information, please refer to Chilton's Transmission Service Manual.

Transmission Assembly

Removal and Installation

1. Disconnect the negative battery cable.
2. Shift the transmission into neutral and remove the shift lever boot. Raise and support the vehicle safely. Drain the fluid.
3. Remove the shift lever assembly. Remove the parking brake cables for clearance.
4. Remove the driveshaft and skid plate. If equipped, drain and remove the transfer case.
5. Disconnect the speedometer cable at the transmission. Disconnect all electrical wires, as required.
6. Disconnect and remove exhaust components, as required. Remove the fuel lines, as required. Properly support the transmission assembly. Remove the clutch slave cylinder from its mounting.

7. Remove the transmission assembly retaining bolts. Remove the transmission crossmember retaining bolts. Remove the transmission mount retaining bolts. Remove the crossmember from the vehicle.
8. Properly support the clutch release bearing. Remove the engine-to-transmission bolts.
9. Properly support the engine assembly. Carefully remove the transmission assembly from the vehicle.

To install:

10. Put a thin layer of high temperature grease on the transmission main shaft. Shift the transmission into high gear (5th) before installing. Carefully install the transmission assembly onto the engine. Rotate the transmission clockwise onto the clutch hub splines.
11. Install the engine-to-transmission bolts and torque to specification.
12. Install the crossmember and retaining bolts.
13. Install the exhaust system. Install the fuel lines. Install the clutch slave cylinder.

10. Bolt
11. Drain Plug
12. Brace
13. Screw
14. Seal
15. Nut

1. Transmission
2. Spring washer
3. Screw
4. Filler plug
5. Rear extension seal
6. Retainer
7. Screw
8. Speed sensor connector
9. Vehicle speed sensor

Manual transmission assembly—Astro and Safari

1. Bolt
2. Transmission
3. Stud

FRT

New Venture Gear 5LM60 manual transmission assembly—S-10 Series

14. Connect the speedometer cable at the transmission. Connect all electrical wires, as required.

15. Install the driveshaft and skid plate. Install the transfer case and fill with the proper type and quantity of oil. Fill the transmission with the proper type and quantity of oil.

16. Install the parking brake cables.

17. Lower the vehicle.

18. Install the shift lever assembly. Connect the negative battery cable. Check for proper clutch operation.

1. Bolt
2. Flywheel housing
3. Transmission

Borg-Warner T-5 manual transmission assembly—S-10 Series

CLUTCH

Clutch Assembly

Removal and Installation

1. Disconnect the negative battery cable. Raise and support the vehicle safely. Remove the transmission assembly. As required, remove the flywheel cover.
2. Remove the slave cylinder retaining bolts. Remove the slave cylinder from its mounting.
3. Remove the bell housing retaining bolts. Remove the bell housing from the vehicle, as required.
4. Slide the clutch fork from the ball stud. Inspect the ball stud and replace as required.
5. Install the clutch removal tool and support the clutch assembly. Matchmark the clutch and pressure plate for reassembly.
6. Loosen the clutch plate retaining bolts slowly and evenly one at a time until all pressure is released from the pressure plate assembly.
7. Remove the clutch, pressure plate and removal tool from the vehicle. Check the flywheel for damage, repair or replace, as required.
8. Inspect the pilot bearing and replace as necessary.

To install:

9. Lubricate the pilot bearing with a few drops machine oil. Install the flywheel, if removed.
10. Using a clutch alignment tool, support the clutch assembly. Align the clutch and pressure plate matchmarks, made previously.
11. Install the clutch pressure plate and disc assembly.
12. Tighten the clutch plate retaining bolts slowly and evenly one at a time to avoid warping the assembly. Remove the alignment tool.
13. Lubricate the ball stud with high temperature grease and slide the clutch fork onto the ball stud. The fork must be installed so the fingers and tabs fit into the groove of the release bearing.
14. Inspect the release bearing for roughness or heat stress, replace if necessary. Apply high temperature grease to the inside and outside groove of the release bearing.
15. Install the bell housing and retaining bolts, as required.
16. Install the slave cylinder and retaining bolts.
17. Install the transmission assembly. As required, install the flywheel cover.
18. Connect the negative battery cable. Lower the vehicle safely. Bleed the hydraulic clutch system, as required.

Clutch Master Cylinder

Removal and Installation

1. Disconnect the negative battery cable. Remove the under

Clutch and pressure plate assembly

dash hush panel. Remove the lower steering column cover, as required. Remove the left side air conditioning duct work, as required.

2. Disconnect the pushrod from the clutch pedal. Disconnect the clutch master cylinder retaining nuts.

3. Disconnect and plug the reservoir hose at the clutch master cylinder assembly.

4. Disconnect and plug the fluid line to the slave cylinder at the clutch master cylinder assembly.

5. Remove the clutch master cylinder from the vehicle.

6. Installation is the reverse of the removal procedure. Bleed the hydraulic clutch system.

Clutch Slave Cylinder

Removal and Installation

1. Disconnect the negative battery cable.

2. Raise and support the vehicle safely. Disconnect and plug the fluid line at the slave cylinder.

3. Remove the slave cylinder retaining bolts. Remove the slave cylinder from the vehicle.

4. Installation is the reverse of the removal procedure. Bleed the system, as required.

Hydraulic Clutch System Bleeding

1. Fill the clutch master cylinder with the proper grade and type fluid. Raise and support the vehicle safely.

2. Remove the slave cylinder retaining bolts. Hold the cylinder at about a 45 degree angle with the bleeder at the highest point.

3. Fully depress the clutch pedal and open the bleeder screw. Close the bleeder screw after the pedal reaches the floor and repeat the procedure until all air is expelled from the system.

4. Ensure that the fluid level remains full in the clutch master cylinder throughout the bleeding procedure.

Clutch master cylinder mounting

Clutch slave cylinder mounting

AUTOMATIC TRANSMISSION

For further information, please refer to Chilton's Transmission Service Manual.

Transmission Assembly

Removal and Installation

EXCEPT TURBOCHARGED ENGINE

1. Disconnect the negative battery cable. Remove the air cleaner assembly. Disconnect the throttle valve cable and the throttle linkage.

2. Raise and support the vehicle safely.

3. Drain the transmission fluid. Disconnect the shift linkage. Properly relieve the fuel system pressure and remove the fuel lines.

4. Remove the driveshaft. If equipped with a transfer case, also remove the front driveshaft.

5. Disconnect and remove all required exhaust system components. Support the transmission using the proper equipment.

6. Remove the crossmember retaining bolts. Remove the transmission mount retaining bolts. Remove the crossmember from the vehicle and lower the transmission enough to gain access to other components.

7. Remove the transmission dipstick and tube. Disconnect the speedometer cable. If equipped, disconnect the vacuum modulator line.

8. Disconnect all electrical connections from the transmission assembly. Disconnect and plug the fluid cooler lines.

9. Remove the damper and support, as required. Remove the flywheel housing cover and torque converter to flywheel bolts. If equipped, remove the transfer case assembly.

10. Properly support the engine assembly. Remove the transmission to engine retaining bolts. Carefully remove the automatic transmission from the vehicle.

To install:

11. Install the transmission into position, making sure the converter is properly seated.

12. Install the engine-to-transmission and torque converter-to-flywheel bolts. Torque the bolts to specification.

13. Install the converter housing cover. Install the damper and support.

14. Connect all electrical leads to the transmission and connect the speedometer cable.

15. Install the dipstick tube. Install the crossmember and install the transmission mount retaining bolts. Reconnect the fuel lines.

16. Connect all exhaust system components. Install the front driveshaft on 4WD vehicles.

17. Connect the shift linkage and install the skid plate, if equipped. Lower the vehicle.

18. Connect the TV cable and throttle linkage.

19. Install the air cleaner assembly. Connect the negative battery cable.

20. Check the fluid level and operation of the transmission.

TURBOCHARGED ENGINE

1. Disconnect the negative battery cable. Raise and safely support the vehicle.

2. Remove the transfer case assembly.

3. Remove the converter cover. Remove the torque converter-to-flywheel bolts.

4. Remove the shift control cable.

5. Remove the clip retaining the fuel line and speed sensor harness. Position the fuel line and harness aside.

6. Disconnect the T.V. cable.

7. Remove the oil cooler lines at the transmission.

8. Remove the transmission vent hose.

9. Remove the transmission dipstick, filler tube and bracket.

10. Remove the transmission retaining bolts and remove the assembly.

To install:

11. Install the transmission assembly and torque the bolts to 35 ft. lbs. (47 Nm).

12. Install the transmission dipstick, filler tube and bracket.

13. Install the transmission vent hose.

14. Install the oil cooler lines at the transmission.

15. Connect the T.V. cable.

16. Install the clip retaining the fuel line and speed sensor harness.

17. Install the shift control cable.

18. Tighten the torque converter-to-flywheel bolts to specifications. Install the converter cover.

19. Install the transfer case assembly. Fill the transfer case, as required.

20. Connect the negative battery cable. Lower the vehicle. Add transmission fluid, as necessary.

Shift Linkage Adjustment

1. As required, raise and support the vehicle safely.

2. Loosen the linkage rod retaining nut. Note the position of

TV cable adjustment procedure

any washers, spacers and insulators. Position the transmission selector lever in the **N** position.

3. Do not use the indicator to determine the **N** position. Check the transmission shift lever bracket to determine that the transmission is in the **N** position.

4. Hold the selector rod and tighten the swivel to 17 ft. lbs. (23 Nm). Position the selector lever in the **P** detent.

5. Check the adjustment. The selector lever must go into all positions. The engine must only start in the **P** or **N** position. Align the selector indicator, as required.

TV Cable Adjustment

1. As required, remove the air cleaner assembly.

2. Depress and hold down the metal readjust tab at the engine end of the throttle valve cable.

3. Move the slider until it stops against the fitting. Release the readjustment tab.

4. Rotate the throttle lever to its full travel position. The slider must move toward the lever when the lever is rotated to its full travel position.

5. Check for proper operation. When the engine is cold, the cable may appear to be functioning properly, check the cable when the engine is hot.

6. Road test the vehicle.

AUTOMATIC TRANSAXLE

For further information, please refer to Chilton's Transmission Service Manual.

Transaxle Assembly

The automatic transaxle equipped in the Lumina APV, Silhouette and Trans Sport can only be removed as an assembly with the engine and transaxle/sub-frame.

Removal and Installation

1. Disconnect the negative battery cable.

2. Drain the cooling system. Disconnect the air flow tube from the air cleaner.

3. Disconnect the electrical connector from the ECM and push it through to the engine compartment. Disconnect the harness from the clips on the body and lay it across the engine.

4. Disconnect the engine harness at the bulkhead connector. Disconnect the throttle and TV cables.

5. Disconnect the fuel lines. Disconnect the transaxle shift linkage.

6. Disconnect the cooler lines at the radiator. Disconnect the radiator and heater hoses.

7. Remove the air conditioning compressor from the bracket and support it aside. Remove the upper engine support strut.

8. Raise and safely support the vehicle. Remove the front wheel and tire assemblies.

9. Remove the stabilizer bar. Disconnect the tie rod ends and the lower control arm ball joints.

10. Disconnect the halfhsafts and support them aside. Disconnect the steering shaft pinch bolt.

11. Remove the starter. Remove the torque converter bolts.

12. Disconnect the exhaust pipe at the manifold. Support the engine and sub-frame with a suitable jack.

13. Remove the sub-frame bolts and lower the engine/transaxle and subframe from the vehicle. Remove the engine-to-transmission bolts.

To install:

14. Position the engine and transmission together in the subframe assembly and torque the engine-to-transmission bolts to 55 ft. lbs. (75 Nm). Raise the engine assembly into position and install the subframe bolts. Tighten to 38 ft. lbs. (52 Nm).

15. Connect the exhaust pipe at the rear manifold. Install the starter.

16. Connect the steering shaft and install the pinch bolt. Connect the halfshafts to the transaxle. Install the torque converter-to-flywheel bolts and torque to 35 ft. lbs. (47 Nm).

17. Connect the lower control arm ball joints to the steering knuckles.

18. Install the stabilizer bar. Install the upper engine strut.

19. Install the wheel and tire assemblies. Lower the vehicle. Install the radiator and heater hoses.

20. Install the shift linkage. Connect the fuel lines and the throttle and TV cables.

21. Connect the harness to bulkhead connector. Connect the ECM harness to the ECM.

22. Connect the air cleaner hose and the radiator upper support.

23. Fill the cooling system. Install the air conditioning compressor.

24. Connect the negative battery cable.

TV Cable Adjustment

1. As required, remove the air cleaner assembly.

2. Depress and hold down the metal readjust tab at the engine end of the throttle valve cable.

3. Move the slider until it stops against the fitting. Release the readjustment tab.

4. Rotate the throttle lever to its full travel position. The slider must move toward the lever when the lever is rotated to its full travel position.

5. Check for proper operation. When the engine is cold, the cable may appear to be functioning properly, check the cable when the engine is hot.

6. Road test the vehicle.

Neutral Safety Switch Adjustment

1. Place the transaxle in the **N** position.

2. Loosen the switch attaching screws.

3. Insert a ⅛ in. gauge pin into the service adjustment hole.

4. Rotate the switch on the shifter assembly to align the service hole in the switch with the hole in the carrier. When the gauge pin drops into the service adjustment hole, tighten the bolts and nut.

5. Remove the gauge pin and check the operation of the switch.

6. The vehicle should only start in the **N** or **P** position.

TRANSFER CASE

Transfer Case Assembly

Removal and Installation

1. Disconnect the negative battery cable. Shift the transfer case into the **4HI** position, as required.

2. Raise and support the vehicle safely. If equipped, remove the skid plate. Drain the fluid from the transfer case.

3. Matchmark the transfer case front output shaft yoke and driveshaft for reassembly. Disconnect the driveshaft from the transfer case.

4. Matchmark the rear axle yoke and the driveshaft for reassembly. Remove the driveshaft.

5. Disconnect the speedometer cable, as required. Disconnect the vacuum harness and electrical connections at the transfer case. Remove the catalytic converter hanger bolts at the converter assembly.

6. Support the transmission and transfer case assembly. Remove the transmission mount retaining bolts. Lower the transmission and transfer case assembly to gain additional clearance.

7. Remove the transfer case retaining bolts.

8. As required, remove the shift lever bracket mounting bolts from the transfer case adapter in order to remove the upper left transfer case retaining bolt.

9. Separate the transfer case from its mounting and remove it from the vehicle.

To install:

10. Install a new gasket to the transmission. Install the transfer case into the vehicle.

11. Tighten the transfer case mounting bolts to specification.

12. Install the shift lever bracket bolts. Support the transmission, raise the transmission slightly.

13. Install the converter mounting bracket. Install the rear transmission mounting bolts.

14. Connect the transfer case linkage. Connect the speedometer cable.

15. Install the driveshafts. Install the skid plate if equipped.

16. Fill the transfer case to the correct level.

17. Lower the vehicle. Connect the negative battery cable.

Linkage Adjustment

1. Remove the console assembly. Raise the shifter boot aside.

2. Loosen the selector lever retaining bolt. Loosen the shifter pivot bolt. Shift the transfer case into the **4HI** position.

3. Install a Ñ/8 in. (8mm) gauge pin through the shifter and into the bracket. Install a service bolt at the transfer case shift lever. This will lock the transfer case in the **4HI** position.

4. Tighten the selector lever retaining bolt 25–35 ft. lbs. Tighten the shifter pivot bolt 88–103 ft. lbs.

5. Remove the service bolt. Remove the gauge pin. Install the console and shifter boot.

6. Check for proper operation.

DRIVE AXLE

Halfshaft

Removal and Installation

EXCEPT LUMINA APV, SILHOUETTE AND TRANS SPORT

1. Raise and support the vehicle safely. Remove the tire and wheel assemblies.

2. Remove the cotter pin, retainer, nut and washer. Remove the brake line support bracket.

3. Matchmark the axle tube-to-flange location. Loosen but do not remove the axle tube-to-flange bolts. Using the proper tools, remove the tie rods at the steering knuckles.

4. Remove the lower shock absorber retaining bolts and move the shock absorbers aside.

5. Separate the upper ball joint from the steering knuckle. Suspend the steering knuckle from the frame using a piece of wire.

6. As required, remove the skid plate. Remove the halfshaft to axle tube bolts.

7. Move the inner part of the halfshaft forward. Support it away from the frame. Using a suitable tool, remove the shaft from the hub and bearing assembly.

8. Remove the halfshaft from the vehicle.

To install:

9. Install the halfshaft into position. Push it into the hub.

Front drive axle assembly—4WD vehicles

10. Install the shaft retaining nut and washer. Tighten the halfshaft retaining nut to 160–200 ft. lbs. (220–270 Nm).

11. Install the cotter pin in the nut. Install the halfshaft-to-axle tube bolts and tighten to 60 ft. lbs. (80 Nm).

12. Install the lower shock absorber bolts. Connect the tie rods to the steering knuckle.

13. Install the skid plate, if equipped.

14. Install the wheel and tire assemblies. Lower the vehicle

LUMINA APV, SILHOUETTE AND TRANS SPORT

1. Raise and safely support the vehicle.

2. Remove the tire and wheel assemblies.

3. Remove the halfshaft retaining nut and washer.

4. Remove the brake caliper from the rotor and support it aside.

5. Remove the brake rotor from the hub.

6. Disconnect the stabilizer shaft from the control arm and disconnect the ball joint from the steering knuckle.

7. Using a suitable axle seal protector to guard against possible boot damage. Remove the halfshaft from the transaxle using a suitable tool.

8. Remove the halfshaft from the hub and bearing assembly.

To install:

9. Install the halfshaft into the hub and bearing assembly.

10. Connect the lower ball joint to the steering knuckle.

11. Connect the stabilizer shaft to the control arm. Install the rotor.

12. Install the brake caliper. Install a new halfshaft nut and tighten the nut to 185 ft. lbs. (250 Nm).

13. Seat the halfshaft into the transaxle, by pushing it in firmly. Check that the shaft is seated by pulling on it.

14. Install the wheel and tire assemblies.

15. Lower the vehicle.

CV-Boot and Joint

Removal and Installation

OUTER

1. Raise and safely support the vehicle.

2. Remove the tire and wheel assemblies.

3. Remove the halfshaft from the vehicle and place the assembly in a vice with soft jaws.

4. Cut the seal clamps and remove the boot. Slide the boot down away from the joint.

5. Clean the grease around the joint. Spread the snapring and remove the joint.

6. Discard the boot, if damaged.

7. Using a brass drift punch and hammer, tap on the joint cage until it moves enough to remove a ball, then remove the other balls in the same fashion.

8. Remove the cage and inner race by turning the assembly straight up 90 degrees to the center line of the outer housing. Maneuver the cage and inner race out of the outer race housing assembly. Then remove the inner race from the cage assembly.

To install:

9. Thoroughly clean all part in solvent. Apply grease to the ball grooves of the inner and outer race.

Separating outer joint from the axle shaft—FWD and 4WD vehicles

1. Outer race	
2. Cage	
3. Inner race	10. Snapring
4. Outboard boot	11. Spider assembly
5. Clamp	12. Spacer ring
6. Clamp	13. Axle shaft
7. Inboard boot	14. Clamp
8. Clamp	15. Snapring
9. Housing	16. Ball

Halfshaft assembly—FWD and 4WD vehicles

A. Land
B. Window
1. Outer Race
2. Cage

Positioning outer joint cage and race for removal and installation—FWD and 4WD vehicles

10. Install the inner race into the cage.
11. Install the cage assembly into the housing.
12. Tilt the cage up and install the ball into the assembly. Pack the assembly with grease.
13. Install the small boot clamp onto the axle shaft.
14. Install the axle boot onto the shaft and secure the small boot clamp using a suitable tool.
15. Install the joint assembly onto the axle shaft, the snapring will snap into place automatically. Pack the boot and outer joint with a sufficient quantity of grease.
16. Position the boot over the joint housing. Secure with the large clamp, using a suitable tool.
17. Reinstall the axle shaft assembly into the vehicle.
18. Install the tire and wheel assembly.
19. Lower the vehicle.

INNER

1. Raise and safely support the vehicle.
2. Remove the tire and wheel assemblies.
3. Remove the halfshaft from the vehicle and place the assembly in a vice with soft jaws.
4. Cut the seal clamps and remove the boot. Slide the joint housing off of the joint and shaft assembly.
5. Clean the grease around the joint. Spread the snapring and remove the joint.
6. Discard the boot, if damaged.

To install:

7. Thoroughly clean all part in solvent.
8. Install the small boot clamp onto the axle shaft.
9. Install the axle boot onto the shaft and secure the small boot clamp using a suitable tool.
10. Install the joint assembly with the snapring counterbore facing (out) the axle shaft housing, the snapring will snap into place automatically.

SHAFT RETAINING RING
SPIDER ASSEMBLY
SPACER RING
AXLE SHAFT

SLIDE SPACER RING AND SPIDER ASSEMBLY BACK ON SHAFT. REMOVE RETAINING RING AND SLIDE SPIDER ASSEMBLY OFF OF SHAFT.

Inner joint and snapring removal—FWD and 4WD vehicles

J-8059

A. Counterbore in spider assembly must face this end of axle

1. Snapring
2. Spider assembly
3. Spacer ring
4. Axle shaft

Inner joint installation—FWD and 4WD vehicles

11. Install the spacer ring onto the axle shaft, ensuring the ring is fully seated in the groove.
12. Position the axle housing onto the joint and shaft assembly. Pack the boot and joint with a sufficient quantity of grease.
13. Position the boot over the joint housing. Secure with the large clamp, using a suitable tool.
14. Reinstall the axle shaft assembly into the vehicle.
15. Install the tire and wheel assembly.
16. Lower the vehicle.

Driveshaft and U-Joints

Removal and Installation

FRONT 1 PIECE

Except Astro and Safari

1. Raise and support the vehicle safely.
2. If equipped, remove the skid plate.
3. Matchmark the rear yoke of the driveshaft to the transfer case. Matchmark the front of the driveshaft to the differential housing.
4. Remove the bolts and retainers from the rear of the driveshaft. Remove the driveshaft from the vehicle.
5. Installation is the reverse of the removal procedure. Tighten the bolts to 15 ft. lbs. (20 Nm).

Astro and Safari

1. Raise and support the vehicle safely.
2. Matchmark the rear of the driveshaft to the transfer case. Matchmark the front of the driveshaft to the differential housing.
3. Remove the bolts from the rear flange of the driveshaft. Remove the bolts from the front flange of the driveshaft. Lower the driveshaft and remove it from the vehicle.
4. Installation is the reverse of the removal procedure. Tighten the front flange bolts to 53 ft. lbs. (72 Nm) and the rear flange bolts to 92 ft. lbs. (125 Nm).

REAR 1 PIECE

1. Raise and support the vehicle safely.
2. If equipped, remove the skid plate.
3. Matchmark the front yoke of the driveshaft to the transmission. Matchmark the rear of the driveshaft to the differential housing.
4. Remove the bolts and retainers from the rear of the driveshaft. Remove the driveshaft from the vehicle.
5. Installation is the reverse of the removal procedure. Tighten the bolts to 15 ft. lbs. (20 Nm).

REAR 2 PIECE

1. Raise and support the vehicle safely.
2. As required, remove the skid plate.

3. Matchmark the front yoke of the driveshaft to the transmission. Matchmark the rear of the driveshaft to the differential housing.

4. Remove the center bearing bolts and washers. Remove the center bearing.

5. Remove the front driveshaft. Remove the rear driveshaft bolts and retainers. Remove the rear driveshaft.

6. Installation is the reverse of the removal procedure. When installing the center bearing, be sure to align it 90 degrees to the driveshaft center lines. Tighten the center bearing bolts to 25 ft. lbs. (34 Nm), and the driveshaft bolts to 15 ft. lbs. (20 Nm).

Rear Axle Shaft, Bearing and Seal

Removal and Installation

1. Raise and support the vehicle safely. Remove the tire, wheel and drum assemblies. Drain the lubricant.

2. Remove the carrier cover retaining bolts. Remove the carrier cover.

3. Remove the rear axle pinion shaft lock screw and the rear axle pinion shaft. Discard the lock screw.

4. Push the flanged end of the axle shaft toward the center of the vehicle. Remove the C-lock clip from the button end of the shaft.

5. Mark the axles left or right and remove the axle shaft from the housing. Be careful not to damage the oil seal.

6. Remove the rear wheel speed sensor, if equipped.

7. Remove the rear axle seal, using a suitable tool.

8. Remove the axle bearing from the housing using a suitable puller and slide hammer.

To install:

9. Install the axle bearing into the housing until the bearing bottoms against the housing shoulder, using a suitable tool.

10. Using a suitable tool, install the seal until flush with the axle housing.

11. Lubricate the seal with gear oil. Install the rear wheel speed sensor, if equipped.

12. Slide the axle into position and install the C-lock clip, use care not to damage the oil seal. Pull the axle out to secure the C-lock in place.

13. Install the pinion shaft through the case and pinion.

14. Install a new pinion shaft lock bolt, tighten it to 25 ft. lbs. (34 Nm).

15. Install the carrier cover, using a new gasket. Tighten the cover bolts to 20 ft. lbs. (27 Nm).

16. Fill the differential to within $^3/_8$ in. of the filler opening.

17. Install the brake drum. Install the wheel and tire assembly.

Front Wheel Hub, Knuckle and Bearing

Removal and Installation

EXCEPT LUMINA APV, SILHOUETTE AND TRANS SPORT

2WD Vehicle

1. Raise and safely support the vehicle.

2. Remove the wheel and tire assemblies.

3. Remove the brake caliper and remove the brake rotor. Use care not to drop the bearings from the rotor.

4. Remove the splash shield attaching bolts and remove the splash shield from the knuckle.

5. Remove the tie rod end from the knuckle. Remove the ball studs from the knuckle.

6. Remove the steering knuckle from the lower ball stud and the knuckle from the vehicle.

To install:

7. Install the upper and lower ball joint to the knuckle.

1. Cap
2. Cotter pin
3. Nut
4. Washer
5. Outer bearing
6. Outer cup
7. Bolt
8. Rotor
9. Inner cup
10. Inner bearing
11. Seal
12. Bolts
13. Caliper
14. Knuckle
15. Gasket
16. Shield

Front rotor, knuckle and bearing assembly – RWD vehicles

8. Attach the splash shield to the knuckle and tighten the bolts to 10 ft. lbs. (14 Nm).

9. Connect the tie rod end to the knuckle.

10. Install the rotor and bearings onto the spindle. Adjust the bearings.

11. Install the caliper. Install the wheel and tire assembly.

12. Lower the vehicle. Check the front end alignment.

4WD Vehicle

1. Raise and safely support the vehicle.

2. Remove the wheel and tire assembly.

3. Remove the brake caliper and support it aside.

4. Remove the brake rotor. Remove the halfshaft retaining nut.

5. Disconnect the tie rod end from the knuckle.

6. Remove the hub and bearing assembly mounting bolts and remove the assembly from the steering knuckle.

7. Remove the splash shield from the knuckle. Remove the ball joints from the knuckle.

8. Remove the knuckle from the ball joints and remove the spacer from the knuckle.

To install:

9. Install the spacer on the knuckle. Install the knuckle in position on the ball joints.

10. Install the ball joint nuts and cotter pins. Install the splash shield to the knuckle.

11. Install the hub and bearing assembly to the knuckle. Tighten the hub mounting bolts to 86 ft. lbs. (116 Nm). Install the halfshaft retaining nut.

12. Connect the tie rod to the knuckle. Install the brake rotor and the brake caliper.

13. Install the wheel and tire assembly. Lower the vehicle.

1. Hub and bearing
2. Steering knuckle
3. Shield
4. Washer
5. Hub nut
6. Seal
7. Retaining bolt
8. O-ring

Front hub and bearing assembly – Lumina APV, Silhouette and Trans Sport

B. Forward
1. Bushing
2. Bolt
3. Washer
4. Nut
5. Bolt
6. Nut
7. Carrier assembly

Front carrier assembly removal—4WD vehicle

14. Check the front end alignment.

LUMINA APV, SILHOUETTE AND TRANS SPORT

1. Raise and safely support the vehicle.
2. Remove the wheel and tire assembly.
3. Remove the brake caliper and support it aside.
4. Remove the brake rotor. Remove the halfshaft retaining nut.
5. Disconnect the tie rod end from the knuckle.
6. Remove the hub and bearing assembly mounting bolts and remove the assembly from the steering knuckle.
7. Matchmark the strut-to-knuckle positioning. Remove the strut mounting bolts from the knuckle. Remove the splash shield from the knuckle. Remove the ball joint from the knuckle.
8. Remove the knuckle from the ball joint and remove the knuckle from the vehicle.

To install:
9. Install the knuckle in position on the ball joint. Slide the knuckle onto the halfshaft.
10. Install the ball joint nut and cotter pin. Install the splash shield to the knuckle.
11. Install the hub and bearing assembly to the knuckle. Tighten the hub mounting bolts to 86 ft. lbs. (116 Nm). Install the halfshaft retaining nut.
12. Connect the tie rod to the knuckle. Install the brake rotor and the brake caliper.
13. Install the wheel and tire assembly. Lower the vehicle.
14. Check the front end alignment.

Pinion Seal

Removal and Installation

1. Raise and support the vehicle safely. Remove the tire,

wheel and drum assembly. Matchmark the driveshaft and the pinion flange.
2. Disconnect the driveshaft from the rear differential. Support the driveshaft aside.
3. Mark the position of the pinion flange, pinion shaft and nut. Using an inch lb. torque wrench, turn the pinion flange nut and record the amount of torque required to turn the pinion flange. Remove the pinion flange nut and washer.
4. Remove the pinion flange. Position a drain pan under the assembly to catch any excess lubricant.
5. Using the proper tool, remove the seal from its mounting.
6. Installation is the reverse of the removal procedure. Refill the differential to the correct level. Tighten the pinion flange nut until the torque required to turn the flange is 3–5 inch lbs. higher than the pre-disassembly reading.

Front Axle Housing

Removal and Installation

1. Unlock the steering column so the linkage is free to move. Disconnect the negative battery cable.
2. Raise and support the vehicle safely. Remove both front wheel and tire assemblies.
3. Insert a drift through the opening in the top of the brake caliper into the vanes of the brake rotor to keep the axle from turning. Remove the front driveshaft.
4. Remove the axle vent hose from the carrier fitting.
5. Disconnect the right and left halfshafts from the carrier by removing the retaining bolts.
6. Properly support the carrier assembly. Remove the carrier and axle tube to frame retaining bolts.
7. Remove the differential carrier assembly from the vehicle.
8. Installation is the reverse of the removal procedure.

Rear Axle Housing

Removal and Installation

EXCEPT ASTRO AND SAFARI

1. Raise and support the vehicle safely. Drain the axle assembly.
2. Remove the tire, wheel and drum assemblies. Properly support the rear axle assembly.
3. Disconnect the shock absorbers. Matchmark the driveshaft and the pinion flange. Remove the driveshaft and position aside.
4. Remove the brake line at the axle housing and backing plate. Disconnect the rear wheel antilock speed sensor connector at the junction block, if equipped.
5. Remove the U bolts and anchor plates.
6. Remove the vent hose from the axle housing.
7. Move the axle housing from above the spring.
8. Installation is the reverse of the removal procedure. Fill and bleed the brake system.

ASTRO AND SAFARI

1. Raise and support the vehicle safely. Remove the tire, wheel and drums assemblies. Properly support the rear axle assembly.
2. Disconnect the shock absorbers from the anchor plate. Matchmark the driveshaft and the pinion flange. Remove the driveshaft and position aside.
3. Disconnect the brake lines from the axle housing and backing plates. Disconnect the rear wheel anti-lock speed sensor connectors, if equipped.
4. Remove the stabilizer bar, if equipped. Remove the U bolts and anchor plates.
5. Lower the axle assembly and remove the lower spring shackle bolts.
6. Disconnect the vent hose from the axle housing. Remove the axle housing from the vehicle.
7. Installation is the reverse of the removal procedure. Fill and bleed the brake system.

STEERING

Steering Wheel

Removal and Installation

1. Disconnect the negative battery cable.
2. Remove the horn pad retaining screws. Remove the horn pad and disconnect the electrical lead.
3. Matchmark the steering wheel and the shaft.
4. Remove the steering wheel retaining clip and nut.
5. Remove the steering wheel, using a suitable puller.
6. Installation is the reverse of removal. Align the matchmarks made during removal and tighten the steering wheel retaining nut to 30 ft. lbs. (40 Nm).

Steering Column

Removal and Installation

EXCEPT LUMINA APV, SILHOUETTE AND TRANS SPORT

1. Disconnect the negative battery cable.
2. Remove the transmission shift linkage from the column.
3. Remove the column upper clamp bolt; mark the relationship of the joint to the steering shaft.
4. Remove the steering column support bracket under the dash.
5. Remove the column to floor seal.
6. Remove the steering wheel. Disconnect the wire harness connector under the dash.
7. Rotate the column so the shift levers clear the floor opening and remove the assembly.
8. Installation is the reverse of the removal procedure.

LUMINA APV, SILHOUETTE AND TRANS SPORT

1. Disconnect the negative battery cable.

STANDARD STEERING WHEEL

LEATHER WRAPPED WHEEL

Steering wheel removal

1. Steering column assembly
2. support bracket
3. Seal
4. Nut
5. Steering column bolts
6. Support bracket bolts

Steering column removal—except Lumina APV, Silhouette and Trans Sport

1. Support
2. Steering column
3. Bolt—21 ft. lbs. (29 Nm)
4. Nut—22 ft. lbs. (31 Nm)
5. Support
6. Bolt—12 ft. lbs. (16 Nm)
7. Steering column opening filler

VIEW A

VIEW B

VIEW C

Steering column removal—Lumina APV, Silhouette and Trans Sport

1. Seal—properly aligned when X is inside O
2. Intermediate shaft
3. Steering column
4. 35 ft. lbs. (48 Nm)

Intermediate steering shaft—Lumina APV, Silhouette and Trans Sport

1. Steering gear
2. Jam nut
3. Adjuster screw
4. Adapter
5. Lower clamp
6. Lower clamp bolt
7. Intermediate shaft
8. Upper clamp bolt
9. Clamp
10. Retaining nut
11. Mainshaft
12. Wormshaft
13. Adapter nut and washer
14. Washer
15. Mounting bolt
16. Shield

Steering gear mounting—Pick-Up, Blazer, Bravada, Jimmy, Astro and Safari

2. Remove the left instrument panel sound insulator and trim pad. Remove the steering column trim collar.
3. Remove the steering wheel, if column is to be disassembled.
4. Remove the column upper clamp bolt; mark the relationship of the joint to the steering shaft.
5. Remove the steering column support bracket under the dash. Remove the shift indicator cable.
6. Disconnect the wire harness connector under the dash.
7. Remove the shift cable at the actuator and housing holder.
8. Remove the column assembly.
9. Installation is the reverse of the removal procedure.

Manual Steering Gear

Removal and Installation

1. Disconnect the negative battery cable. Raise and support the vehicle safely. Position the wheels in the straight ahead position.
2. If equipped, remove the steering gear coupling shield. Remove the steering gear lower coupling bolt. On some vehicles it may be necessary to separate the coupling at the upper and lower flange bolts.
3. Matchmark the pitman arm to the steering gear. Remove the pitman arm retaining nut and washer. Using the proper tool, separate the pitman arm from the steering gear assembly.
4. Remove the steering gear retaining bolts. Separate steering gear from the intermediate shaft and remove the assembly from the vehicle.
To install:
5. Position the steering gear into in the vehicle.
6. Install the mounting bolts. Tighten the mounting bolts to 55 ft. lbs. (75 Nm).

7. Connect the steering gear and intermediate shaft, install the coupling flange bolts.
8. Connect the pitman arm to the steering gear in the previously marked position. Tighten the pitman arm retaining bolt to 185 ft. lbs. (250 Nm).
9. Install the coupling shield. Lower the vehicle
10. Connect the negative battery cable.

Adjustment

1. Raise and safely support the vehicle.
2. Remove the coupling shield. Remove the pitman arm nut and washer.
3. Matchmark the pitman arm to the pitman shaft.
4. Remove the pitman arm, using a suitable puller.
5. Loosen the adjuster nut on the steering gear, then back out the adjuster a ¼ turn.
6. Lower the vehicle, keeping it just above the ground.
7. Remove the horn pad. Center the steering wheel by turning the wheel all the way in one direction until stopped by the gear, then turn the wheel back 1½ turns to the center position.
8. Install an inch lb. torque wrench on the steering wheel nut. Use a torque wrench with no more than a 50 inch lbs. reading capability. Check the thrust bearing preload as follows:
   a. Turn the torque wrench and steering wheel through a 90 degree arc.
   b. Tighten the adjuster plug until the proper preload is achieved, 5–8 inch lbs. (0.6–1.0 Nm).
   c. Tighten the adjuster nut to 85 ft. lbs.
   d. Turn the steering wheel to check the adjustment. The gear should turn smooth and not lumpy, from lock to lock.
8. To check the overcenter preload:
   a. Turn the steering wheel from lock to lock counting the total number of turns.
   b. Turn the wheel back, to exactly the ½ way point.
   c. Turn the over center adjuster screw clockwise, to take out all of the lash between the ball nut and the pitman shaft sector teeth.
   d. Tighten the jam nut to 22 ft. lbs. (30 Nm).
   e. Check the torque at the steering wheel, taking the highest reading as the wheel is turned.
   f. If necessary, loosen the adjuster nut and tighten the adjuster plug to obtain 4–10 inch lbs. (0.5–1.2 Nm).
To install:
9. Install the pitman arm onto the pitman shaft, aligning the matchmarks made during disassembly.
10. Install the pitman arm washer and nut. Install the coupling shield.
11. Lower the vehicle completely and install the horn pad.
12. Connect the negative battery cable.

Power Steering Gear

Removal and Installation

1. Disconnect the negative battery cable. Position the wheels in the straight ahead position.
2. Disconnect and cap the fluid lines.
3. If equipped, remove the steering gear coupling shield. Matchmark and remove the steering gear to lower coupling and bolt. On some vehicles, it may be necessary to separate the coupling at the upper and lower flange bolts.
4. Raise and support the vehicle safely. Matchmark the pitman arm to the steering gear. Remove the pitman arm retaining nut and washer. Using the proper tool, separate the pitman arm from the steering gear assembly.
5. Remove the steering gear retaining bolts. Remove steering gear from the vehicle.
To install:
6. Install the steering gear in position in the vehicle.
7. Install the mounting bolts. Tighten the mounting bolts to 55 ft. lbs. (75 Nm).

8. Connect the steering gear coupling at the flange bolts.

9. Connect the pitman arm to the steering gear. Tighten the pitman arm retaining bolt to 185 ft. lbs. (250 Nm).

10. Connect the fluid lines. Install the coupling shield. Lower the vehicle.

11. Connect the negative battery cable. Fill and bleed the power steering system.

Adjustments

For proper adjustment, remove the gear from the vehicle and drain all the fluid from the gear and place the gear in a holding fixture.

It is important that the adjustments be made in the order given.

Worm Bearing Preload

1. Loosen the adjuster plug locknut.

2. Turn the adjuster plug in clockwise until firmly bottomed. Then, tighten it to 20 ft. lbs. (27 Nm).

3. Place an index mark on the gear housing in line with one of the holes in the adjuster plug.

4. Measure counterclockwise from the mark about ½ inch and place another mark on the housing.

5. Rotate the adjuster plug counterclockwise until the hole is aligned with the second mark.

6. Install the locknut. Hold the plug and tighten the locknut to 81 ft. lbs. (110 Nm).

7. Place an inch lb. torque wrench and 12-point deep socket on the steering gear stub shaft and measure the stub shaft rotating torque, starting with the torque wrench handle in a vertical position to a point ¼ turn to either side. Note your reading. The proper torque should be 4–10 inch lbs. (0.45–1.13 Nm). If the reading is incorrect, either the adjustment was done incorrectly or there is gear damage.

Overcenter Preload

1. Loosen the locknut and turn the pitman shaft adjuster screw counterclockwise until it is all the way out. Then, turn it in 1 turn.

2. Rotate the stub shaft from stop to stop, counting the total number of turns, then turn the shaft back ⅔ that number to center the gear. The stub shaft flat spot should face up.

3. Place the torque wrench in a vertical position on the stub shaft and measure the torque necessary to rotate the shaft to a point 45 degrees to either side of center. Record the highest reading.

4. Turn the adjuster in until the reading is 6–10 inch lbs. higher then the previous reading.

5. If necessary, adjust the torque reading by turning the adjuster screw.

6. When the adjustment is made, hold the screw and tighten the locknut to 20 ft. lbs. (27 Nm).

7. Install the gear and bleed the system.

Power Steering Rack and Pinion

Adjustment

RACK BEARING PRELOAD

1. Raise and support the vehicle safely. Ensure the steering wheel is centered.

2. Loosen the adjuster plug locknut and turn the adjuster plug clockwise until it bottoms in the housing; then back off 50–70 degrees.

3. Check the returnability of the steering wheel after the adjustment.

4. Tighten the locknut to 50 ft. lbs. (70 Nm), while holding the adjuster plug stationary.

5. Lower the vehicle.

Removal and Installation

1. Disconnect the negative battery cable.

2. Remove the air cleaner assembly.

3. Remove the dust boot from the steering gear.

4. Remove the intermediate shaft lower pinch bolt and disconnect the intermediate shaft from the lower stub shaft.

5. Remove the fluid line retaining clips at the pump and disconnect the lines.

6. Raise and safely support the vehicle.

7. Remove the wheel and tire assemblies. Disconnect the tie rod ends at the steering knuckle.

8. Remove the remaining brackets and clips at the crossmember. Support the body safely with the appropriate equipment, to allow lowering of the subframe.

9. Remove the rear subframe mounting bolts and carefully lower the rear of the subframe approximately 5 in. (128mm).

10. Remove the rack and pinion mounting bolts and remove the rack through the left wheel opening.

To install:

11. Install the rack and pinion through the left wheel opening.

12. Install the rack and pinion mounting nuts, tighten to 70 ft. lbs. (95 Nm).

13. Raise the subframe assembly and install the rear mounting bolts.

14. Remove any supports and install the brackets and clips to the crossmember.

15. Install the wheel and tire assemblies. Lower the vehicle.

16. Connect the fluid lines at the pump and tighten to 18 ft. lbs. (25 Nm).

17. Install the line retaining clips. Connect the intermediate shaft to the stub shaft.

18. Install the dust boot over the steering gear.

19. Install the air cleaner assembly and connect the negative battery cable.

20. Fill and bleed the steering system.

Power Steering Pump

Removal and Installation

EXCEPT TURBOCHARGED ENGINE

1. Disconnect the negative battery cable. Disconnect and cap the power steering pump hoses. Remove the accessory drive belt.

2. As required, remove the power steering pump pulley using a suitable puller tool or equivalent.

3. Remove the pump mounting bolts. Remove the pump from the vehicle.

4. Installation is the reverse of the removal procedure. Bleed the power steering system.

TURBOCHARGED ENGINE

1. Disconnect the negative battery cable.

2. Remove the air cleaner and duct assembly.

3. Remove the upper fan shroud.

4. Loosen the fan nuts and remove the serpentine belt.

5. Remove the fan and pulley assembly.

6. Remove the power steering pump pulley as follows:

   a. Install tool J–25034–B, ensure the pilot bolt bottoms in the pump shaft.

   b. Hold the pilot bolt with a suitable wrench.

   c. Turn the shaft locknut counterclockwise and remove the pulley.

7. Raise and safely support the vehicle.

8. Remove the left tire and wheel assembly.

9. Remove the left wheelhouse panel.

10. Remove the power steering hose bracket.

11. Place a drain pan below the pump and remove the power steering pressure and return lines, capping the lines to prevent dirt from entering.

12. Remove the bolts from the rear bracket at the alternator.

13. Lower the vehicle and remove the assembly.

14. Remove the bracket from the pump as necessary.

To install:

15. Install the bracket to the pump, if removed.

16. Install the pump assembly and torque the bolts to 37 ft. lbs. (50 Nm).

17. Install the bolts to the rear bracket at the alternator.

18. Install the power steering pressure and return lines.

19. Install the power steering hose bracket.

20. Raise and safely support the vehicle.

21. Install the left wheelhouse panel.

22. Install the left tire and wheel assembly. Lower the vehicle.

23. Install the power steering pump pulley as follows:

    a. Place the pulley on the shaft.

    b. Install tool J–25033–B, ensure the pilot bolt bottoms in the pump shaft.

    c. Hold the pilot bolt with a suitable wrench.

    d. Turn the shaft locknut clockwise and install the pulley.

24. Install the fan and pulley assembly.

25. Tighten the fan pulley nuts and install the serpentine belt.

26. Install the upper fan shroud.

27. Install the air cleaner and duct assembly.

28. Connect the negative battery cable. Fill and bleed the power steering system. Check system for leaks.

System Bleeding

1. Fill the fluid reservoir to the proper level.

2. Start the engine and let it run for at least 2 minutes. Turn the engine off.

3. Add fluid if necessary, then run the engine again. Repeat this until the fluid level remains constant.

4. Raise the front of the vehicle slightly, until the front wheels are just off the ground.

5. Start the engine and slowly turn the steering wheel from lock to lock, until the wheel contacts the stop.

6. Add fluid if necessary. Lower the vehicle to the ground.

7. Start the engine and again move the wheels side to side. Check the fluid level.

Tie Rod Ends

Removal and Installation

EXCEPT LUMINA APV, SILHOUETTE AND TRANS SPORT

1. Raise and support the vehicle safely. Remove the tire and wheel assemblies.

2. Remove the cotter pins and nuts. Using the proper removal tool, separate the outer tie rod from the steering knuckle.

3. Disconnect the inner tie rod from the relay rod using the proper tool. Remove the tie rod ends from the adjuster tubes.

4. Installation is the reverse of the removal procedure. Tighten the inner tie rod ball stud nut to 35 ft. lbs. (47 Nm). Tighten the outer tie rod ball stud to the steering knuckle to 35 ft. lbs. (47 Nm). The number of threads on both the inner and outer tie rod ends must be equal within 3 threads.

5. Adjust the front end alignment, as required.

LUMINA APV, SILHOUETTE AND TRANS SPORT

Outer

1. Raise and support the vehicle safely. Remove the tire and wheel assemblies.

2. Remove the cotter pins and nuts. Using the proper removal tool, separate the outer tie rod from the steering knuckle.

3. Disconnect the inner tie rod from the relay rod using the proper tool. Remove the tie rod ends from the adjuster tubes.

4. Installation is the reverse of the removal procedure. Tighten the inner tie rod ball stud nut to 35 ft. lbs. (47 Nm). Tighten the outer tie rod ball stud to the steering knuckle to 35 ft. lbs. (47 Nm). The number of threads on both the inner and outer tie rod ends must be equal within 3 threads.

5. Adjust the front end alignment, as required.

Inner

1. Disconnect the negative battery cable.

2. Raise and support the vehicle safely.

3. Remove the rack and pinion assembly.

4. Place the assembly in a holding fixture.

5. Remove the outer tie rod assembly. Remove the inner tie rod jam nut.

6. Remove the tie rod end boot clamps. Remove the boot.

7. Remove the shock dampner from the inner tie rod assembly.

8. Remove the tie rod from the rack. Place a wrench on the flat of the rack assembly and another wrench on the flats of the inner tie rod housing.

9. Installation is the reverse of the removal procedure.

BRAKES

For all brake system repair and service procedures not detailed below, please refer to "Brakes" in the Unit Repair section.

Master Cylinder

Removal and Installation

1. Disconnect the negative battery cable.

2. Disconnect the electrical connections from the master cylinder, as required. Disconnect and plug the fluid lines.

NOTE: On Lumina APV, Silhouette and Trans Sport, the master cylinder reservoir can be removed to ease master cylinder removal.

3. Remove the master cylinder to power booster retaining bolts. Remove the RWAL control module assembly, if equipped with anti-lock brakes.

4. Remove the master cylinder from the vehicle. Remove the vacuum booster pushrod.

To install:

5. Install the master cylinder in position on the booster. Connect the booster pushrod.

6. Install the master cylinder retaining bolts and tighten to 20 ft. lbs. (27 Nm).

7. Connect the fluid lines to the master cylinder. Connect the RWAL control unit, if equipped with anti-lock brakes, to the bracket.

8. Connect the negative battery cable. Refill the master cylinder and bleed the brake system.

Combination Valve

Removal and Installation

ASTRO, BLAZER, JIMMY, PICK-UP, SAFARI, SONOMA, SYCLONE AND TYPHOON

The combination valve is mounted on the master cylinder

1. Proportional valve cap assembly
2. O-Ring
3. Spring
4. Proportional valve piston
5. Proportional valve seal

MAKE SURE SEAL LIPS POINT UPWARD TOWARD CAP (2)

Proportioning valve replacement—Lumina APV, Silhouette and Trans Sport

bracket. On vehicles with anti-lock brakes, the combination valve is replaced with a dump/isolation valve. It is removed in the same manner.

1. Disconnect the negative battery cable.
2. Disconnect the brake lines from the combination valve.
3. Remove the mounting bolts and remove the valve from the bracket.
4. Installation is the reverse of the removal procedure. Bleed the brake system.

Proportioning Valve

Removal and Installation

LUMINA APV, SILHOUETTE AND TRANS SPORT

1. Disconnect the negative battery cable.
2. Remove the electrical connector from the master cylinder.
3. Drain and remove the master cylinder reservoir.
4. Remove the proportioning valve caps from the master cylinder.
5. Remove the O-rings, springs and the valve pistons. Use care not to scratch the valves in any way.
6. Remove the valve seals from the valve pistons.

To install:

7. Install new seals on the valve pistons. Lubricate the seals and the pistons with silicon grease.
8. Install the valve pistons and O-rings into the master cylinder.

9. Install the valve cap assemblies and tighten to 20 ft. lbs. (27 Nm).
10. Install the reservoir assembly. Connect the electrical leads.
11. Connect the negative battery cable. Bleed the brake system.

Power Brake Booster

Removal and Installation

1. Disconnect the negative battery cable. Do not disconnect the master cylinder fluid lines, unless there is a clearance problem. Remove the master cylinder and position aside.
2. Remove the vacuum booster pushrod. Disconnect the vacuum hose from the booster assembly.
3. From inside the vehicle, remove the mounting studs which secure the vacuum booster to the fire wall.
4. Pull the booster away from the cowl and remove it from the vehicle.
5. Installation is the reverse of the removal procedure. Be sure to properly install the vacuum booster pushrod. Bleed the system.

Brake Caliper

Removal and Installation

1. Remove $2/3$ of the brake fluid from the master cylinder reservoir.
2. Raise and support the vehicle safely. Remove the tire and wheel assembly.
3. Disconnect and plug the caliper fluid line. Remove the bolts retaining the caliper to the rotor. Remove the caliper from the rotor.

NOTE: If the caliper is being removed for brake pad replacement, the fluid line do not need to be disconnected.

4. Remove the disc brake pads from the caliper. Remove the disc brake pad retaining clips from inside the caliper.

To install:

5. Clean and lubricate the sleeves and bushings with silicon grease. Install the pads in the caliper.
6. Install the caliper in position over the rotor and install the

1. Bolt boot
2. Mounting bolt and sleeve
3. Bushing
5. Outboard shoe and lining
6. Wear sensor
7. Inboard shoe and lining
8. Boot
9. Piston
10. Piston seal
11. Bleeder valve
12. Caliper housing

Brake caliper—exploded view

mounting bolts. Tighten the mounting bolts to 38 ft. lbs. (51 Nm).

7. Connect the fluid lines to the caliper, if disconnected, and tighten to 33 ft. lbs. (45 Nm).

8. Install the wheel and tire assembly.

9. Lower the vehicle and refill the master cylinder to the correct level. Bleed the brake system if the fluid lines were disconnected from the caliper.

Disc Brake Pads

Removal and Installation

1. Remove $^2/_3$ of the brake fluid from the master cylinder.

2. Raise and safely support the vehicle.

3. Place a C-clamp around the outer pad and caliper; tighten the C-clamp until the piston is fully compressed in the caliper. Remove the brake caliper.

4. Remove the inboard pad and retaining spring from the caliper.

5. Remove the outboard pad from the caliper.

6. Remove the sleeves and bushings.

To install:

7. Clean and lubricate the sleeves and bushing with silicon lubricant and install them in the caliper.

8. Clip the retaining spring onto the inboard pad and install the pad in the caliper.

9. Install the outboard pad into the caliper.

10. Install the caliper in position over the rotor and install the mounting bolts. Bend the tabs, on the outboard brake pad, over the caliper.

11. Install the wheel and tire assemblies.

12. Lower the vehicle, refill the master cylinder and pump pedal to attain full brake pedal before road testing the vehicle.

Brake Rotor

Removal and Installation

EXCEPT LUMINA APV, SILHOUETTE AND TRANS SPORT

2WD Vehicle

1. Remove $^2/_3$ of the brake fluid from the master cylinder.

2. Raise and support the vehicle safely. Remove the tire and wheel assembly.

3. Remove the bolts retaining the caliper to the rotor. Remove the caliper from the rotor and position it aside. Do not allow the caliper to hang unsupported.

4. Remove the dust cap, cotter pin, spindle nut, washer and outer wheel bearings.

5. Remove the rotor from the vehicle. On Astro and Safari with 4 wheel anti-lock brakes, remove the wheel speed sensor from behind the rotor.

6. Installation is the reverse of the removal procedure. Adjust the wheel bearings, as required.

4WD Vehicle

1. Remove $^2/_3$ of the brake fluid from the master cylinder.

2. Raise and safely support the vehicle.

3. Remove the wheel and tire assemblies.

4. Remove the brake caliper from the rotor and support it aside. Do not disconnect the brake lines.

5. Remove the rotor from the hub.

To install:

6. Install the rotor on the hub. Install the brake caliper.

7. Install the wheel and tire assemblies.

8. Lower the vehicle and refill the master cylinder.

LUMINA APV, SILHOUETTE AND TRANS SPORT

1. Remove $^2/_3$ of the brake fluid from the master cylinder. Raise and safely support the vehicle.

2. Remove the wheel and tire assemblies.

3. Remove the brake caliper from the rotor and support it aside. Do not disconnect the brake lines.

4. Remove the rotor from the hub.

To install:

5. Install the rotor on the hub. Install the brake caliper.

6. Install the wheel and tire assemblies.

7. Lower the vehicle and refill the master cylinder.

Brake Drums

Removal and Installation

1. Raise and safely support the vehicle.

2. Remove the wheel and tire assembly.

3. Remove the brake drum from the vehicle. If the drum will not pull of the axle, use a rubber mallet and tap it around the edge.

4. Install the drum on the axle and install the wheel and tire assembly.

1. Hold-down pins
2. Backing plate
3. Parking brake lever
4. Secondary shoe
5. Shoe guide
6. Parking brake strut
7. Actuator lever
8. Actuator link
9. Return spring
10. Return spring
11. Hold-down springs
12. Lever pivot
13. Lever return spring
14. Strut spring
15. Adjusting screw assembly
16. Adjusting screw spring
17. Primary shoe

Drum brake assembly—Pick-Up, Blazer, Bravada, Jimmy, Astro and Safari

5. Lower the vehicle.

Brake Shoes

Removal and Installation

EXCEPT LUMINA APV, SILHOUETTE AND TRANS SPORT

1. Raise and safely support the vehicle.
2. Remove the wheel and tire assembly.
3. Remove the brake drum.
4. Remove the return springs from the brake shoes. Remove the shoe guide.
5. Remove the hold-down springs and pins. Remove the actuator lever and pivot.
6. Remove the lever return spring. Remove the actuator link.
7. Remove the parking brake strut and spring. Remove the parking brake lever.
8. Remove the brake shoes and the adjuster assembly.

To install:

9. Lubricate the contact points on the backing plate and the adjuster with lithium grease.
10. Install the parking brake lever, adjusting screw and spring assembly.
11. Install the shoe assembly onto the backing plate.
12. Install the parking brake lever, strut and strut spring.
13. Install the actuator lever and lever pivot. Install the actuator link.
14. Install the lever spring, the hold-down pins and springs.
15. Install the shoe guide. Install the return springs and install the brake drum in position.
16. Adjust the brakes as follows:
    a. Remove the knockout area in the backing plate, behind the adjuster assembly.
    b. Ensure the parking brake system is adjusted properly with no tension on the cables or parking brake lever. The tops of the shoes should be firmly seated against the upper spring retaining anchor, if not as specified, loosen the parking brake cables.
    c. Install the drum and turn the brake adjuster until the wheels can just be turned by hand.
    d. Then, back the adjuster off 24 notches. No brake drag should be felt after 12 notches.
    e. Install an adjusting hole plug in the backing plate to prevent dirt and moisture from entering.
    f. Readjust the parking brake cable as necessary.
17. Install the wheel and tire assemblies.

LUMINA APV, SILHOUETTE AND TRANS SPORT

1. Raise and safely support the vehicle.
2. Remove the wheel and tire assembly.
3. Remove the brake drum.
4. Remove the actuator spring from the brake shoes. Remove the retractor spring from the shoe web, being careful not to over stretch the spring.
5. Remove the adjuster shoe, adjuster actuator and adjusting screw assembly.
6. Do not remove the parking brake cable from the parking brake lever, unless the lever is being replaced. Remove the parking brake shoe.
7. Remove the retractor spring, as required.

To install:

8. Lubricate the contact points on the backing plate with lithium grease. Clean and lubricate the adjuster with lithium grease.
9. Install the retractor spring, if removed.
10. Install the parking brake shoe against the backing plate and snap the retractor spring into the slot on the brake shoe. Install the parking brake lever onto the parking brake shoe.

1. Adjuster socket
2. Adjuster screw
3. Pivot nut
4. Retractor spring
5. Adjuster shoe and lining
6. Wheel cylinder
7. Bleeder valve
8. Bolt
9. Access hole plug
10. Backing plate
11. Park brake shoe and lining
12. Park brake lever
13. Actuator spring
14. Adjuster actuator
15. Adjusting screw assembly

Drum brake assembly—Lumina APV, Silhouette and Trans Sport

11. Install the adjuster shoe and adjusting screw assembly. Install the retractor spring into the slot on the adjuster shoe web.

12. Lubricate and install the adjuster actuator onto the adjuster shoe. Install the actuator spring.

13. Ensure the parking brake system is adjusted properly with no tension on the cables or parking brake lever. The tops of the shoes should be firmly seated against the upper spring retaining anchor, if not as specified, loosen the parking brake cables.

14. Adjust the brakes using J–21177–A or equivalent. Turn the adjuster screw until the brake lining diameter is 0.050 in. (1.27mm) less than the inside diameter of the brake drum. Install the brake drum.

15. Install the wheel and tire assembly.

16. Lower the vehicle.

Wheel Cylinder

Removal and Installation

1. Raise and safely support the vehicle.
2. Remove the wheel and tire assemblies.
3. Remove the brake drum. Remove the brake shoes, as necessary.
4. Disconnect the brake fluid line from the wheel cylinder.
5. Remove the wheel cylinder retainer or bolt.
6. Remove the wheel cylinder from the backing plate.

To install:

7. Install the wheel cylinder in position on the backing plate.
8. Install the retainer or bolt. Connect the brake line to the wheel cylinder.
9. Install the brake linings and the brake drum.
10. Install the wheel and tire assembly. Lower the vehicle.
11. Bleed the brake system.

Parking Brake Cable

Adjustment

EXCEPT LUMINA APV, SILHOUETTE AND TRANS SPORT

1. Raise and support the vehicle safely. Loosen the equalizer nut. Some vehicles may require the removal of the cable guide on the equalizer.
2. Set the parking brake pedal 2 clicks for 2WD vehicles or 3 clicks for 4WD vehicles.
3. Tighten the equalizer nut until the rear wheels will not rotate without excessive force in the forward motion.
4. Back off the equalizer nut until there is light drag when the wheels are rotated in the forward motion.
5. If removed, install the cable guide. Release the parking brake.
6. Rotate the rear wheels in the forward motion. There should be no brake drag.

LUMINA APV, SILHOUETTE AND TRANS SPORT

1. Set the parking brake pedal 4 clicks.
2. Raise and support the vehicle safely. Remove the access plug in the backing plate.
3. Adjust the parking brake until an ⅛ in. drill can be inserted through the access hole into the space between the shoe web and park brake lever. Satisfactory adjustment will be obtained when an ⅛ in. drill bit will fit but a ¼ in. drill bit will not.
4. Release the parking brake and verify the rear wheels will rotate freely.
5. Replace the access plug and lower the vehicle. Check for proper operation of the parking brake.

Removal and Installation

REAR

1. Raise and support the vehicle safely. Remove the tire and wheel assembly. Remove the brake drum.

Parking brake cable routing—Pick-Up, Blazer, Jimmy, Astro and Safari

2. Loosen the equalizer and disconnect the cable at the center retainer.
3. Compress the plastic retainer fingers and remove the retainer from the frame bracket.
4. Remove the rear brake shoe assembly. Disconnect the parking brake cable. Remove the cable from the frame and from the brake backing plate.
5. Installation is the reverse of the removal procedure. Adjust the rear brakes, as required. Adjust the parking brake.

FRONT

1. Raise and support the vehicle safely. Loosen the adjuster nut and disconnect the front cable from the connector.
2. Compress the retainer fingers and loosen the assembly at the frame. Remove the supports.
3. Lower the vehicle. As required, remove dash trim panels to gain access to the parking brake pedal assembly.
4. Disconnect the cable from the parking brake pedal, compress the retainer fingers. Remove the cable from the vehicle.
5. Installation is the reverse of the removal procedure. Adjust the parking brake.

Brake System Bleeding

The brake system must be bled when any brake line is disconnected or there is air in the system.

NOTE: Never bleed a wheel cylinder when a drum is removed.

1. Clean the master cylinder of excess dirt and remove the cylinder cover and the diaphragm.
2. Fill the master cylinder to the proper level. Check the fluid level periodically during the bleeding process and replenish it, as necessary. Do not allow the master cylinder fall below ½ full.
3. If the master cylinder is suspected or known to have air in the bore, bleed it before any wheel cylinder or caliper as follows:

   a. Disconnect the forward brake line connection at the master cylinder.

   b. Allow brake fluid to fill the master cylinder bore until it begins to flow from the forward line connector port.

   c. Connect the forward brake line to the master cylinder and tighten.

   d. Have an assistant depress the brake pedal slowly, 1 depression at a time and hold while loosening the forward brake line connection at the master cylinder to purge the air from the bore. Tighten the connection and then have an assistant release the brake pedal slowly. Wait 15 seconds and repeat the sequence. Repeat the sequence, including the 15 second wait until all air is removed from the bore.

   e. After all air is removed at the forward connection, repeat the above procedure for the rear connection at the master cylinder.

4. Bleed the individual wheel cylinders or calipers only after all air is removed from the master cylinder.

   a. Attach the proper size box end wrench over the bleeder valve.

   b. Attach a length of vinyl hose to the bleeder screw of the brake to be bled. Insert the other end of the hose into a clear jar half full of clean brake fluid, so the end of the hose is under the level of fluid. The correct sequence for bleeding is to work from the brake farthest from the master cylinder to the 1 closest; right rear, left rear, right front, left front.

5. Have an assistant depress and release the brake pedal 1 time and hold. Loosen the bleeder valve to purge the air from the cylinder. Tighten the bleeder screw and slowly release the pedal and wait 15 seconds. Repeat the sequence including the 15 second wait until all air is removed.

NOTE: Make sure an assistant presses the brake pedal to the floor slowly. Rapid pumping of the brake pedal pushes the master cylinder secondary piston down the bore in a way that makes it difficult to bleed the rear side of the system.

6. Repeat this procedure at each of the wheels. Remember to check the master cylinder level occasionally. Use only fresh fluid to refill the master cylinder, not the fluid bled from the system.

7. When the bleeding process is complete, refill the master cylinder, install its cover and diaphragm and discard the fluid bled from the brake system.

Anti-Lock Brake System Service

There are 3 systems used, first, the Four Wheel Anti-Lock (4WAL) which is used on all 1990–92 vehicles, except the Lumina APV, Silhouette and Trans Sport. Second, the Rear Wheel Anti-Lock (RWAL) which is used only on the 1989–92 vehicles, except the Bravada, Lumina APV, Silhouette and Trans Sport and third, the Anti-Lock Brake System (ABS) which is used only on the Lumina APV, Silhouette and Trans Sport.

Precaution

Failure to observe the following precautions may result in system damage.

• Before performing electric arc welding on the vehicle, disconnect the Electronic Brake Control Unit.

• When performing painting work on the vehicle, do not expose the Electronic Brake Control Unit to temperatures in excess of 185°F (85°C) for longer than 2 hours. The system may be exposed to temperatures up to 200°F (95°C) for less than 15 minutes.

• Never disconnect or connect the Electronic Brake Control Unit connector with the ignition switch ON.

• Never disassemble any component of the Anti-Lock Brake System which is designated non-serviceable; the component must be replaced as an assembly.

• When filling the master cylinder, always use Delco Supreme 11 brake fluid or equivalent, which meets DOT-3 specifications; petroleum base fluid will destroy the rubber parts. Do not allow fluid to be spilled on the Electronic Brake Control Unit.

Control Module

Removal and Installation

RWAL SYSTEM

Electronic Control Unit (ECU)

1. Disconnect the negative battery cable.
2. Disconnect the electrical connectors from the module.
3. Remove the module from the master

cylinder/proportioning valve bracket.

4. Installation is the reverse of the removal procedure.

4WAL SYSTEM

Electro-Hydraulic Control Unit (EHCU)

1. Disconnect the negative battery cable.
2. Disconnect the electrical connectors from the module.
3. Disconnect and plug the brake lines at the module.
4. Remove the bolts attaching the module to the fenderwell.
5. Remove the module and bracket assembly from the vehicle.
6. Remove the bracket from the module.
7. Installation is the reverse of the removal procedure.

ANTILOCK BRAKE SYSTEM (ABS)

Electronic Brake Control Module (EBCU)

1. Disconnect the negative battery cable.
2. Remove the lower sound insulator under the steering column.
3. Remove the screws attaching the module to the dash panel.
4. Disconnect the electrical connectors from the module.
5. Remove the module from the vehicle.
6. Installation is the reverse of the removal procedure.

Isolation/Dump Valve

Removal and Installation

RWAL SYSTEM

1. Disconnect the negative battery cable.
2. Disconnect and plug the brake line fittings at the isolation/dump valve located under the master cylinder.
3. Remove the master cylinder bracket bolts.
4. Disconnect the Electronic Control Unit connector.
5. Remove the isolation/dump valve.
6. Installation is the reverse of the removal procedure.

Front Wheel Speed Sensor

Removal and Installation

4WAL SYSTEM

2 Wheel Drive

1. Disconnect the negative battery cable.
2. Raise and support the vehicle safely.
3. Remove the wheel and tire assembly.
4. Remove the brake caliper, hub and rotor assembly.
5. Remove the sensor wire from the clips on the upper control arm and disconnect the connector.
6. Remove the sensor and backing plate attaching bolts and remove the assembly.
7. Installation is the reverse of the removal procedure.

4 Wheel Drive

1. Disconnect the negative battery cable.
2. Raise and support the vehicle safely.
3. Remove the wheel and tire assembly.
4. Remove the hub and rotor assembly.
5. Disconnect the sensor wire connector.
6. Remove the bolts securing the sensor and sensor wire.
7. Remove the sensor from the spindle.
8. Installation is the reverse of the removal procedure.

ANTI-LOCK BRAKE SYSTEM (ABS)

1. Disconnect the negative battery cable.
2. Raise and support the vehicle safely.
3. Remove the wheel and tire assembly.
4. Remove the hub and rotor assembly.
5. Disconnect the sensor wire connector.
6. Remove the sensor from the hub assembly.

NOTE: The speed sensor cannot be removed from the hub assembly without damaging the sensor, therefore the sensor must be replaced. The sensor has 2 parts, which must be replaced as an assembly.

7. Installation is the reverse of the removal procedure.

Rear Wheel Speed Sensor

Removal and Installation

4WAL SYSTEM

1. Disconnect the negative battery cable.
2. Raise and support the vehicle safely.
3. Remove the wheel, tire and drum assembly.
4. Remove the primary (forward) brake shoe.

5. Disconnect the sensor wire connector and remove the sensor wire from the rear axle clips.
6. Remove the bolts securing the sensor and sensor wire.
7. Remove the sensor from the backing plate.
8. Installation is the reverse of the removal procedure.

ANTI-LOCK BRAKE SYSTEM (ABS)

1. Disconnect the negative battery cable.
2. Raise and support the vehicle safely.
3. Remove the wheel, tire and drum assembly.
4. Remove the bolts and nuts attaching the rear wheel bearing and speed sensor assembly.
5. Remove the wheel bearing and speed sensor assembly.
6. Disconnect the sensor wire connector.
7. Installation is the reverse of the removal procedure.

FRONT SUSPENSION

Shock Absorbers

Removal and Installation

1. Remove the top shock mounting nut and grommet.
2. Raise and safely support the vehicle.
3. Remove the wheel and tire assembly.
4. Remove the lower shock mounting bolts and remove the shock absorber.
5. Installation is the reverse of the removal procedure.

MacPherson Strut Assembly

All front wheel drive vehicles came equipped with a MacPherson strut front suspension.

Removal and Installation

LUMINA APV, SILHOUETTE AND TRANS SPORT

NOTE: Do not remove the top center nut from the strut assembly. This nut should only be removed when the strut assembly is out of the vehicle, mounted in a holding fixture and the coil spring is in a compressed position using the proper strut coil spring compressor.

1. Remove the 3 nuts that retain the top of the strut assembly.
2. Raise and safely support the vehicle.
3. Remove the wheel and tire assembly. Remove the brake line bracket from the strut mount.
4. Remove the lower strut mounting bolts.
5. Remove the strut assembly from the vehicle and place the strut in a suitable holding fixture.
6. Disassemble the strut as follows:
   a. With the strut coil spring in a compressed position approximately ½ its normal length, remove the nut from the top of the strut.
   b. Place tool J–34013–27 or equivalent guide rod on top of the damper shaft. Use the rod to guide the damper shaft straight down through the bearing cap while decompressing the spring.
   c. Remove the coil spring and other components.
7. Installation is the reverse of the removal procedure. Ensure the spring seat flat should face 10 degrees forward of the centerline of the strut assembly spindle.

1. Strut assembly
2. Nut
3. Knuckle and hub assembly
4. Lower control arm
5. Frame assembly
6. Bolt
7. Nut
8. Bracket
9. Mount washer
10. Shock tower

Strut assembly mounting—Lumina APV, Silhouette and Trans Sport

8. Tighten the strut lower bolts to 140 ft. lbs. (190 Nm) and the upper mounting nuts to 18 ft. lbs. (25 Nm).

Coil Springs

All 2 wheel rear drive vehicles came equipped with a coil spring front suspension.

MacPherson strut disassembly and assembly— Lumina APV, Silhouette and Trans Sport

Removal and Installation

ASTRO, BLAZER, BRAVADA, JIMMY, PICK-UP, SAFARI AND SONOMA

2WD Vehicle

1. Raise and support the vehicle safely. Remove the wheel and tire assembly. Remove the shock absorber lower retaining bolts.

2. Push the shock absorber through the control arm and into the spring.

3. With the vehicle supported so the control arms hang free, install tool J–23028 or equivalent, onto a suitable jack and into the lower control arm bushings. Remove the stabilizer bar from the control arm.

4. Remove the stabilizer to lower control arm attachment. Raise the jack and remove the tension on the lower control arm bolts.

5. Install a safety chain around the spring and through the lower control arm. Remove the lower control arm rear pivot bolt, than remove the other pivot bolt.

6. Lower the jack and allow the lower control arm to hang free. Remove the spring assembly from the vehicle.

7. Installation is the reverse of the removal procedure. When positioning the spring in the lower control arm, be sure the spring insulator is in the proper position before lifting the control arm in place.

Torsion Bars and Support

All 4 wheel drive vehicles came equipped with a torsion bar front suspension instead of coil spring.

Torsion bar spring mounting—4WD Pick-Up, Blazer, Bravada, Jimmy, Astro and Safari

Removal and Installation

ASTRO, BLAZER, JIMMY, PICK-UP, SAFARI, SONOMA, SYCLONE AND TYPHOON

1. Raise and safely support the vehicle. Remove the wheel and tire assemblies.
2. Remove the torsion bar adjusting bolt using tool J–36202 or equivalent. Count the number of tool turns required to remove the bolt.
3. Remove the torsion bar support retainer plate and insulator.
4. Remove the torsion bar by sliding it forward into the control arm and lowering it from the vehicle.
5. Remove the torsion bar support from the vehicle. Remove the adjusting arm and the adjusting arm bolt.

To install:

6. Install the adjusting arm to the support and loosely install the adjusting bolt.
7. Install the support to the frame and the insulator to the frame end.
8. Install the retainer to the support. Install the retainer mounting bolts and tighten to 26 ft. lbs. (35 Nm).
9. Tighten the center retainer bolt to 25 ft. lbs. (34 Nm).
10. Install the torsion bar to the lower control arm and raise and slide the torsion bar into the adjusting arm. The torsion bar should have 6mm clearance at the support.
11. Attach tool J–36202 to the support and tighten it against the adjusting arm the recorded number of turns.
12. Install the adjusting bolt and turn it in until it contacts the adjusting arm. Remove the tool.
13. Install the wheel and tire assemblies. Lower the vehicle.

Upper Ball Joint

Inspection

1. Raise and safely support the lower control arm.
2. Wipe the ball joint clean and check the seal for cuts or tears.
3. Check the wheel bearings for proper adjustment.
4. Position a dial indicator against the lowest outside point of the tire. Rock the wheel in and out.
5. Check the reading on the dial indicator. The reading should be no more than 0.125 inch (3.18mm).

Removal and Installation

1. Raise and support the vehicle safely. Properly support the lower control arm.

NOTE: The control arm must be supported so the spring and the control arm remain intact.

2. Remove the tire and wheel assembly. As required, remove the brake caliper and position it aside.
3. Remove the cotter pin and the upper ball joint retaining bolt. Using the proper tool separate the upper joint from its mounting. Support the knuckle assembly so its weight will not damage the brake hose.
4. Remove the rivets from the ball joint assembly, using a drill with an ⅛ in. and then ½ in. bit. Remove the ball joint from the upper control arm.
5. Installation is the reverse of the removal procedure. Tighten the replacement bolts to 17 ft. lbs. (23 Nm). Check and adjust the front end alignment, as required.

Lower Ball Joint

Inspection

EXCEPT LUMINA APV, SILHOUETTE AND TRANS SPORT

1. Raise and safely support the vehicle.

2. The ball joint wear is indicated by the position of the grease fitting on the bottom of the joint.
3. The round portion of the grease nipple must protrude from the bottom of the joint. If the nipple is flush with or inside of the joint, it must be replaced.

LUMINA APV, SILHOUETTE AND TRANS SPORT

1. Raise and safely support the lower control arm.
2. Wipe the ball joint clean and check the seal for cuts or tears.
3. Check the wheel bearings for proper adjustment.
4. Position a dial indicator against the lowest outside point of the tire. Rock the wheel in and out.
5. Check the reading on the dial indicator. The reading should be no more than 0.125 inch (3.18mm).

Removal and Installation

EXCEPT LUMINA APV, SILHOUETTE AND TRANS SPORT

1. Raise and support the vehicle safely. Properly support the lower control arm.

NOTE: The control arm must be supported so the spring and the control arm remain intact.

2. Remove the tire and wheel assembly. As required, remove the brake caliper and position it aside.
3. Remove the cotter pin and the lower ball joint retaining bolt. Using the proper tool separate the ball joint from its mounting. Support the knuckle assembly so its weight will not damage the brake hose.
4. Remove the rivets from the ball joint assembly, using a drill with a ⅛ in. bit. Remove the ball joint from the control arm.
5. Installation is the reverse of the removal procedure. Be sure to use the nuts and bolts that are supplied with the replacement ball joint assembly. Tighten the replacement bolts to 17 ft. lbs. (23 Nm). Check and adjust the front end alignment, as required.

LUMINA APV, SILHOUETTE AND TRANS SPORT

1. Raise and support the vehicle safely. Properly support the lower control arm.

NOTE: The control arm must be supported so the spring and the control arm remain intact.

2. Remove the tire and wheel assembly. As required, remove the brake caliper and position it aside.
3. Remove the pinch bolt from the lower ball joint. Using the proper tool separate the upper joint from the steering knuckle. Support the knuckle assembly so its weight will not damage the brake hose.
4. Remove the rivets from the ball joint assembly, using a drill with an ⅛ in. and then ½ in. bit.
5. Remove the stabilizer shaft bushing assembly nut.
6. Remove the ball joint from the lower control arm.
7. Installation is the reverse of the removal procedure. Tighten the ball joint pinch bolt to 33 ft. lbs. (45 Nm). Check and adjust the front end alignment, as required.

Upper Control Arms

Removal and Installation

1. Note and record the amount of shims used at the control arm retaining bolts. These shims must be installed in the same location as removed. Remove the nuts and the shims.
2. Raise and support the vehicle safely. Properly support the lower control arm. The control arm must be supported so the spring and the control arm remain intact.
3. Remove the wheel and tire assembly. Separate the upper ball joint from the steering knuckle, using the proper tool. Support the hub assembly.

Front suspension components—2WD Pick-Up, Blazer, Jimmy, Astro and Safari

4. Remove the upper control arm retaining bolts. Remove the upper control arm from the vehicle.

5. Installation is the reverse of the removal procedure. Tighten the upper control arm nuts to 65 ft. lbs. (88 Nm). Check and adjust the front end alignment, as required.

Lower Control Arms

Removal and Installation

EXCEPT LUMINA APV, SILHOUETTE AND TRANS SPORT

1. Raise and support the vehicle safely.
2. Remove the wheel and tire assemblies. Properly support the lower control arm assembly.
3. Remove the coil spring.
4. Remove the lower ball joint cotter pin and retaining nut.
5. Using the proper tool, separate the lower ball joint from the steering knuckle.
6. Remove the lower control arm from the vehicle.
7. Installation is the reverse of the removal procedure. Check and adjust front alignment, as required.

LUMINA APV, SILHOUETTE AND TRANS SPORT

1. Raise and safely support the vehicle so the suspension hangs freely.
2. Remove the wheel and tire assemblies.

3. Remove the stabilizer shaft-to-control arm mounting bolt. Remove the lower ball joint pinch bolt.
4. Separate the steering knuckle from the lower ball joint.
5. Remove the lower control arm mounting bolts and remove the control arm from the vehicle.

To install:

6. Install the control arm in position on the vehicle frame. Do not tighten the control arm bolts at this time.
7. Install the stabilizer shaft to the control arm, do not tighten the bolts at this time.
8. Connect the steering knuckle to the control arm using a new pinch bolt. Tighten to 33 ft. lbs. (45 Nm). Lower the vehicle so the weight is supported by the control arms.
9. Tighten the control arm bolts to 61 ft. lbs. (83 Nm). Tighten the stabilizer shaft bolts to 32 ft. lbs. (43 Nm).
10. Install the wheel and tire assemblies. Lower the vehicle completely.

Stabilizer Shaft

Removal and Installation

1. Raise and safely support the vehicle.
2. Remove the wheel and tire assembly.
3. Remove the left and right side stabilizer mounting bolts. Keep the sides separate for installation.
4. Remove the center stabilizer insulators and lower the stabilizer from the vehicle.

To install:

5. Install the stabilizer in position in the vehicle. Tighten the left and right mounting bolts to 24 ft. lbs. and the center bushing supports to 35 ft. lbs.
6. Install the wheel and tire assemblies and lower the vehicle.

Front Wheel Bearings

Adjustment

ASTRO, BLAZER, JIMMY, PICK-UP, SAFARI AND SONOMA

1. Raise and safely support the vehicle.
2. Remove the brake caliper and the dust cap from the wheel hub.
3. Remove the cotter pin from the castle nut.

Stabilizer bar mounting—Pick-Up, Blazer, Bravada, Jimmy, Astro and Safari

Front suspension components—Lumina APV, Silhouette and Trans Sport

4. Tighten the castle nut to 12 ft. lbs. (16 Nm) while turning the rotor forward.

5. Loosen the castle nut, then tighten it, by hand to a just loose position.

6. Back the nut off slightly, until the hole in the spindle aligns with a slot in the nut. Do not back the nut off more than ½ of a flat.

7. Install a new cotter pin. Measure the rotor end play at the castle nut, it should not exceed 0.0005 in. (0.13mm).

8. Install the bearing dust cover and install the wheel and tire assembly.

9. Lower the vehicle.

Removal and Installation

ASTRO, BLAZER, JIMMY, PICK-UP, SAFARI AND SONOMA

NOTE: All front and 4 wheel drive vehicles, refer to the drive axle section.

1. Raise and support the vehicle safely. Remove the tire and wheel assembly.

2. Remove the brake caliper and position it aside. Remove the dust cover, cotter pin, washer and spindle nut.

3. Remove the outer wheel bearing assembly. Remove the brake rotor. Remove the inner wheel bearing assembly.

4. Installation is the reverse of the removal procedure. When installing new bearings, be sure to install new bearing races inside the rotor.

5. Pack new bearings with the proper grade and type wheel bearing grease. Adjust the wheel bearings.

REAR SUSPENSION

Shock Absorbers

Removal and Installation

EXCEPT LUMINA APV, SILHOUETTE AND TRANS SPORT

1. Raise and support the vehicle safely.
2. Properly support the rear axle assembly.
3. Remove the upper shock absorber retaining bolt.
4. Remove the lower shock absorber bolt.
5. Remove the shock absorber from the vehicle.

To install:

6. Install the shock in position and install the mounting bolts.

7. Tighten the top mounting bolts to 17 ft. lbs. (23 Nm) and the lower mounting bolts to 47 ft. lbs. (64 Nm).

8. Lower the vehicle.

LUMINA APV, SILHOUETTE AND TRANS SPORT

1. Open the lift gate and open the trim cover.
2. Remove the upper shock mounting nut and grommet.
3. Raise and safely support the vehicle. Properly support the rear axle assembly.
4. If equipped with electronic level control suspension, remove the air line from the shock absorber. Allow the air to bleed off.
5. Remove the lower mounting bolt and remove the shock from the vehicle.

To install:

6. Install the shock in position and install the lower mounting bolt. Tighten to 44 ft. lbs. (59 Nm). Connect the air line to the shock, if equipped.

7. Lower the vehicle and install the upper shock retaining nut, tighten it to 16 ft. lbs. (22 Nm). Install the trim cover.

1. Bolt
2. Nut
3. Shock absorber
4. Washer
5. Nut

Typical shock absorber mounting

Coil Springs

Removal and Installation

LUMINA APV, SILHOUETTE AND TRANS SPORT

1. Raise and safely support the vehicle.
2. Safely support the rear axle assembly.
3. Remove the right and left brake line-to-axle attaching screws. Allow the brake lines to hang freely.
4. Disconnect the track bar-to-axle attaching bolt.
5. Disconnect the lower shock absorber mounting bolts.
6. Slowly lower the rear axle and remove the springs and insulators.
7. Installation is the reverse of the removal procedure.

Leaf Springs

Removal and Installation

ASTRO, BLAZER, JIMMY, PICK-UP, SAFARI, SONOMA, SYCLONE AND TYPHOON

1. Raise and support the vehicle safely. Properly support the rear axle assembly to relieve tension on the springs.

2. Remove the shock absorbers. Remove the U bolt nuts, washers, anchor plates and the U bolts.

3. Remove the shackle to frame bolt, washers and nut. Remove the spring assembly to front bracket nut, washers and bolt.

4. Remove the spring assembly from the vehicle. As required, separate the spring from the shackle.

5. Installation is the reverse of the removal procedure. Tighten the U bolts to 85 ft. lbs. (115 Nm) in 2 gradual steps. Tighten the front and rear shackle nuts to 92 ft. lbs. (125 Nm).

Rear Wheel Hub and Bearing Assembly

Removal and Installation

LUMINA APV, SILHOUETTE AND TRANS SPORT

1. Raise and safely support the vehicle.
2. Remove the wheel and tire assemblies.
3. Remove the brake drum.
4. Remove the hub and bearing assembly mounting bolts and remove it from the vehicle. Support the brake assembly with a wire.
5. Installation is the reverse of the removal procedure. Tighten the hub assembly mounting bolts to 45 ft. lbs. (60 Nm).

Track Bar

Removal and Installation

LUMINA APV, SILHOUETTE AND TRANS SPORT

1. Raise and safely support the vehicle.
2. Remove the track bar mounting bolts from the body and the axle.

Rear track bar mounting—Lumina APV, Silhouette and Trans Sport

Rear axle assembly mounting—Lumina APV, Silhouette and Trans Sport

3. Lower the track bar from the vehicle.

To install:

4. Install the track bar at the axle, loosely install the bolt.

5. Connect the other end of the track bar at the frame.

6. Tighten the bolt at the axle to 44 ft. lbs. (60 Nm) and the track bar-to-frame bolt to 35 ft. lbs. (47 Nm).

7. Lower the vehicle.

Rear Axle Assembly

Removal and Installation

LUMINA APV, SILHOUETTE AND TRANS SPORT

1. Raise and safely support the vehicle.

2. Properly support the rear axle assembly.

3. Remove the wheel and tire assemblies. Remove the brake drums.

4. Disconnect the parking brake cable from the brake system.

5. Disconnect the brake line brackets from the axle assembly.

6. Disconnect the shock absorbers from the axle.

7. Disconnect the track bar bolt at the rear axle.

8. Lower the rear axle slightly and remove the coil springs and insulator.

9. Remove the hub and bearing assemblies, support the backing plate and brake assemblies with wire from the vehicle.

NOTE: Do not allow the backing plates to hang by the brake lines.

10. Remove the control arm to frame bracket attaching bolts and lower the axle assembly from the vehicle.

To install:

11. Raise the axle assembly to the vehicle and install the control arm bolts. Torque control arm bracket bolts to 84 ft. lbs. (115 Nm). Torque the control arm to bracket pivot bolts to 28 ft. lbs. (38 Nm).

12. Install the backing plate, hub and bearing assembly. Use car not to kink the brake lines.

13. Install the brake line brackets to the axle assembly. Connect the parking brake cable to the brake assembly.

14. Position the coil springs and insulators on the axle and raise the axle.

15. Connect the shock absorber lower bolts to the axle.

16. Connect the track bar to the rear axle.

17. Install the brake drums. Install the wheel and tire assemblies.

18. Lower the vehicle.

SPECIFICATIONS

VEHICLE IDENTIFICATION CHART

It is important for servicing and ordering parts to be certain of the vehicle and engine identification. The VIN (vehicle identification number) is a 17 digit number visible through the windshield on the driver's side of the dash and contains the vehicle and engine identification codes. The tenth digit indicates model year and the fourth digit indicates engine code. It can be interpreted as follows:

Engine Code						Model Year	
Code	Cu. In.	Liters	Cyl.	Fuel Sys.	Eng. Mfg.	Code	Year
H	150	2.5	4	TBI	AMC	J	1988
M	243	4.0	6	MPI	Chrysler		
C	258	4.2	6	2bbl	AMC		
N	360	5.9	8	2bbl	AMC		

TBI—Throttle Body Injection
MPI—Multi-Port Fuel Injection

VEHICLE IDENTIFICATION CHART

It is important for servicing and ordering parts to be certain of the vehicle and engine identification. The VIN (vehicle identification number) is a 17 digit number visible through the windshield on the driver's side of the dash and contains the vehicle and engine identification codes. The tenth digit indicates model year and the eighth digit indicates engine code. It can be interpreted as follows:

Engine Code						Model Year	
Code	Cu. In.	Liters	Cyl.	Fuel Sys.	Eng. Mfg.	Code	Year
E	150	2.5	4	TBI	Chrysler	K	1989
L	243	4.0	6	MPI	Chrysler	L	1990
M	258	4.2	6	2bbl	Chrysler	M	1991
7	360	5.9	8	2bbl	Chrysler	N	1992
P	150	2.5	4	MPI	Chrysler		
S	243	4.0	6	MPI	Chrysler		

TBI—Throttle Body Injection
MPI—Multi-Port Fuel Injection

ENGINE IDENTIFICATION

Year	Model	Engine Displacement cu. in. (liter)	Engine Series Identification (VIN)	No. of Cylinders	Engine Type
1988	Comanche	150 (2.5)	H	4	OHV
	Comanche	243 (4.0)	M	6	OHV
	Wrangler	150 (2.5)	H	4	OHV
	Wrangler	258 (4.2)	C	6	OHV
	Cherokee	150 (2.5)	H	4	OHV
	Cherokee	243 (4.0)	M	6	OHV
	Wagoneer	243 (4.0)	M	6	OHV
	Grand Wagoneer	360 (5.9)	N	8	OHV
	J10 Pick-Up	258 (4.2)	C	6	OHV
	J10 Pick-Up	360 (5.9)	N	8	OHV
	J20 Pick-Up	360 (5.9)	N	8	OHV
1989	Comanche	150 (2.5)	E	4	OHV
	Comanche	243 (4.0)	L	6	OHV
	Wrangler	150 (2.5)	E	4	OHV
	Wrangler	258 (4.2)	M	6	OHV
	Cherokee	150 (2.5)	E	4	OHV
	Cherokee	243 (4.0)	L	6	OHV
	Wagoneer	243 (4.0)	L	6	OHV
	Grand Wagoneer	360 (5.9)	7	8	OHV
1990	Comanche	150 (2.5)	E	4	OHV
	Comanche	243 (4.0)	L	6	OHV
	Wrangler	150 (2.5)	E	4	OHV
	Wrangler	258 (4.2)	M	6	OHV
	Cherokee	150 (2.5)	E	4	OHV
	Cherokee	243 (4.0)	L	6	OHV
	Wagoneer	243 (4.0)	L	6	OHV
	Grand Wagoneer	360 (5.9)	7	8	OHV
1991-92	Comanche	150 (2.5)	P	4	OHV
	Comanche	243 (4.0)	S	6	OHV
	Wrangler	150 (2.5)	P	4	OHV
	Wrangler	243 (4.0)	S	6	OHV
	Cherokee	150 (2.5)	P	4	OHV
	Cherokee	243 (4.0)	S	4	OHV
	Grand Wagoneer	360 (5.9)	7	8	OHV

OHV—Overhead Valves

GENERAL ENGINE SPECIFICATIONS

Year	VIN	No. Cylinder Displacement cu. in. (liter)	Fuel System Type	Net Horsepower @ rpm	Net Torque @ rpm (ft. lbs.)	Bore × Stroke (in.)	Compression Ratio	Oil Pressure @ rpm
1988	H	4-150 (2.5)	TBI	83 @ 4200	116 @ 2600	3.876 × 3.188	9.2:1	40 @ 2000
	M	6-243 (4.0)	MPI	173 @ 4500	220 @ 2500	3.875 × 3.876	9.2:1	40 @ 2000
	C	6-258 (4.2)	2bbl	110 @ 3200	210 @ 1800	3.750 × 3.895	8.0:1	37 @ 2000
	N	8-360 (5.9)	2bbl	175 @ 4000	285 @ 2900	4.080 × 3.440	8.25:1	37 @ 2000

GENERAL ENGINE SPECIFICATIONS

Year	VIN	No. Cylinder Displacement cu. in. (liter)	Fuel System Type	Net Horsepower @ rpm	Net Torque @ rpm (ft. lbs.)	Bore × Stroke (in.)	Compression Ratio	Oil Pressure @ rpm
1989	E	4-150 (2.5)	TBI	121 @ 5250	141 @ 3250	3.876 × 3.188	9.2:1	37 @ 1600①
	L	6-243 (4.0)	MPI	177 @ 4500	224 @ 2500	3.880 × 3.440	9.2:1	37 @ 1600①
	M	6-258 (4.2)	2bbl	112 @ 3000	210 @ 2000	3.750 × 3.895	9.2:1	37 @ 1600①
	7	8-360 (5.9)	2bbl	144 @ 3200	280 @ 1500	4.080 × 3.440	8.25:1	37 @ 1600①
1990	E	4-150 (2.5)	TBI	121 @ 5250④	141 @ 3250⑦	3.876 × 3.188	9.2:1	37 @ 1600①
	L	6-243 (4.0)	MPI	177 @ 4500	224 @ 2500	3.880 × 3.440	9.2:1	37 @ 1600①
	M	6-258 (4.2)	2bbl	112 @ 3000	210 @ 2000	3.750 × 3.895	9.2:1	37 @ 1600①
	7	8-360 (5.9)	2bbl	144 @ 3200	280 @ 1500	4.080 × 3.440	8.25:1	37 @ 1600①
1991–92	P	4-150 (2.5)	MPI	123 @ 5250②	139 @ 3250⑤	3.88 × 3.19	9.1:1	37 @ 1600①
	S	6-243 (4.0)	MPI	180 @ 4750⑤	220 @ 4000⑥	3.88 × 3.41	8.8:1	37 @ 1600①
	7	8-360 (5.9)	2bbl	144 @ 3200	280 @ 1500	4.22 × 4.72	8.25:1	37 @ 1600①

TBI—Throttle Body Injection
MPI—Multi-Port Fuel Injection
① Above 1600 rpm, pressure can vary to a maximum of 75 psi.
② Cherokee and Comanche 130 @ 5250
③ Cherokee and Comanche 190 @ 4750
④ Wrangler 117 @ 5250
⑤ Cherokee and Comanche 149 @ 3250
⑥ Cherokee and Comanche 225 @ 4000
⑦ Wrangler 138 @ 3500

ENGINE TUNE-UP SPECIFICATIONS

Year	VIN	No. Cylinder Displacement cu. in. (liter)	Spark Plugs Type	Gap (in.)	Ignition Timing (deg.)② MT	AT	Compression Pressure (psi)	Fuel Pump (psi)	Idle Speed (rpm) MT	AT	Valve Clearance In.	Ex.
1988	H	4-150 (2.5)	RC12LYC	0.035	④	④	①	14–15	④	④	Hyd.	Hyd.
	M	6-243 (4.0)	RC9YC	0.035	④	④	①	31	④	④	Hyd.	Hyd.
	C	6-258 (4.2)	RFN14LY	0.035	9⑤	9⑤	①	4–5	700	600	Hyd.	Hyd.
	N	8-360 (5.9)	RN12Y	0.035	8	8	①	5–6.5	600	500	Hyd.	Hyd.
1989	E	4-150 (2.5)	RC12LYC	0.035	④	④	①	14–15	④	④	Hyd.	Hyd.
	L	6-243 (4.0)	RC9YC	0.035	④	④	①	31	④	④	Hyd.	Hyd.
	M	6-258 (4.2)	RFN14LY	0.035	9⑤	9⑤	①	4–5	700	600	Hyd.	Hyd.
	7	8-360 (5.9)	RN12Y	0.035	8	8	120–140①	5–6.5	600	500	Hyd.	Hyd.
1990	E	4-150 (2.5)	RC12LYC	0.035	④	④	①	14–15	④	④	Hyd.	Hyd.
	L	6-243 (4.0)	RC9YC	0.035	④	④	①	31	④	④	Hyd.	Hyd.
	M	6-258 (4.2)	RFN14LY	0.035	9⑤	9⑤	①	4–5	700	600	Hyd.	Hyd.
	7	8-360 (5.9)	RN12Y	0.035	8	8	120–140①	5–6.5	600	500	Hyd.	Hyd.
1991–92	P	4-150 (2.5)	RC12LYC	0.035	④	④	①	39–41	④	④	Hyd.	Hyd.
	S	6-243 (4.0)	RC12LYC	0.035	④	④	①	39–41	④	④	Hyd.	Hyd.
	7	8-360 (5.9)	RN12YC	0.035	8	8	120–140	5–6.5	600	600③	Hyd.	Hyd.

Hyd.—Hydraulic
① Check all cylinders. Difference between all cylinders should be no more than 25%.
② BTDC
③ 500 with solenoid de-energized
④ Not adjustable
⑤ At 1600 rpm: at high altitude—16 @ 1600 rpm

CAMSHAFT SPECIFICATIONS

Year	VIN	No. Cylinder Displacement cu. in. (liter)	Journal Diameter 1	2	3	4	5	Lobe Lift In.	Ex.	Bearing Clearance	Camshaft End Play
1988	H	4-150 (2.5)	2.0300–2.0290	2.0200–2.0190	2.0100–2.0009	2.0000–1.9990	—	0.2650	0.2650	0.0010–0.0030	0
	M	6-243 (4.0)	2.0300–2.0290	2.0200–2.0190	2.0100–2.0090	2.0000–1.9990	—	0.2530	0.2530	0.0010–0.0030	0
	C	6-258 (4.2)	2.0300–2.0290	2.0200–2.0190	2.0100–2.0090	2.0000–1.9990	—	0.2531	0.2531	0.0010–0.0030	0
	N	8-360 (5.9)	2.1195–2.1205	2.0895–2.0905	2.0595–2.0605	2.0295–2.0305	1.9995–2.0005	0.2660	0.2660	0.0010–0.0030	0
1989	E	4-150 (2.5)	2.0300–2.0290	2.0200–2.0190	2.0100–2.0009	2.0000–1.9990	—	0.2650	0.2650	0.0010–0.0030	0
	L	6-243 (4.0)	2.0300–2.0290	2.0200–2.0190	2.0100–2.0090	2.0000–1.9990	—	0.2530	0.2530	0.0010–0.0030	0
	M	6-258 (4.2)	2.0300–2.0290	2.0200–2.0190	2.0100–2.0090	2.0000–1.9990	—	0.2531	0.2531	0.0010–0.0030	0
	7	8-360 (5.9)	2.1195–2.1205	2.0895–2.0905	2.0595–2.0605	2.0295–2.0305	1.9995–2.0005	0.2660	0.2660	0.0010–0.0030	0
1990	E	4-150 (2.5)	2.0300–2.0290	2.0200–2.0190	2.0100–2.0009	2.0000–1.9990	—	0.2650	0.2650	0.0010–0.0030	0
	L	6-243 (4.0)	2.0300–2.0290	2.0200–2.0190	2.0100–2.0090	2.0000–1.9990	—	0.2530	0.2530	0.0010–0.0030	0
	M	6-258 (4.2)	2.0300–2.0290	2.0200–2.0190	2.0100–2.0090	2.0000–1.9990	—	0.2531	0.2531	0.0010–0.0030	0
	7	8-360 (5.9)	2.1195–2.1205	2.0895–2.0905	2.0595–2.0605	2.0295–2.0305	1.9995–2.0005	0.2660	0.2660	0.0010–0.0030	0
1991–92	P	4-150 (2.5)	2.0300–2.0290	2.0200–2.0190	2.0100–2.0009	2.0000–1.9990	—	0.2650	0.2650	0.0010–0.0030	0
	S	6-243 (4.0)	2.0300–2.0290	2.0200–2.0190	2.0100–2.0090	2.0000–1.9990	—	0.2530	0.2530	0.0010–0.0030	0
	7	8-360 (5.9)	2.1195–2.1205	2.0895–2.0905	2.0595–2.0605	2.0295–2.0305	1.9995–2.0005	0.2660	0.2660	0.0010–0.0030	0

FIRING ORDERS

NOTE: To avoid confusion, always replace spark plug wires one at a time.

2.5L Engine
Engine Firing Order: 1–3–4–2
Distributor Rotation: Clockwise

4.0L and 4.2L Engines
Engine Firing Order: 1–5–3–6–2–4
Distributor Rotation: Clockwise

FRONT ▷

CLOCKWISE ROTATION
1-8-4-3-6-5-7-2

5.9L Engine
Engine Firing Order: 1–8–4–3–6–5–7–2
Distributor Rotation: Clockwise

CAPACITIES

Year	Model	VIN	No. Cylinder Displacement cu. in. (liter)	Engine Crankcase with Filter	without Filter	Transmission (pts.) 4-Spd	5-Spd	Auto. ⑤	Drive Axle (pts.)	Fuel Tank (gal.)	Cooling System (qts.)
1988	Comanche	H	4-150 (2.5)	4	4	4.0①	4.9	17.0	2.5	13.5②	9.0
	Comanche	M	6-243 (4.0)	6	6	4.0①	4.9	17.0	2.5	13.5②	12.0
	Wrangler	H	4-150 (2.5)	4	4	4.0①	4.9	17.0	2.5	15②	7.8
	Wrangler	C	6-258 (4.2)	6	6	4.0①	4.9	17.0	2.5	15②	10.5
	Cherokee	H	4-150 (2.5)	4	4	4.0①	4.9	17.0	2.5	13.5②	9.0
	Cherokee	M	6-243 (4.0)	6	6	4.0①	4.9	17.0	2.5	13.5②	12.0
	Wagoneer	M	6-243 (4.0)	6	6	3.5	4.9	17.0	2.5	13.5②	12.0
	Grand Wagoneer	N	8-360 (5.9)	5	5	—	—	17.0	3.8	20	15.0
	J-10 Pick-Up	C	6-258 (4.2)	6	6	3.5	—	17.0	4.8	18	10.5
	J-10 Pick-Up	N	8-360 (5.9)	5	5	3.5	—	17.0	4.8	18	15.0
	J-20 Pick-Up	N	8-360 (5.9)	5	5	—	—	15.8	6	18	15.0
1989	Comanche	E	4-150 (2.5)	4	4	4.0①	4.9	17.0	2.5	18.5	9.0
	Comanche	L	6-243 (4.0)	6	6	4.0①	4.9	17.0	2.5	18.5	12.0
	Wrangler	E	4-150 (2.5)	4	4	4.0①	4.9	17.0	2.5	20.0	7.8
	Wrangler	M	6-258 (4.2)	6	6	4.0①	4.9	17.0	2.5	20.0	10.5
	Cherokee	E	4-150 (2.5)	4	4	4.0①	4.9	17.0	2.5	20.0	9.0
	Cherokee	L	6-243 (4.0)	6	6	4.0①	4.9	17.0	2.5	20.0	12.0
	Wagoneer	L	6-243 (4.0)	6	6	3.5	4.9	17.0	2.5	20.0	12.0
	Grand Wagoneer	7	8-360 (5.9)	5	5	—	—	17.0	3.8	20.0	15.0

CAPACITIES

Year	Model	VIN	No. Cylinder Displacement cu. in. (liter)	Engine Crankcase with Filter	Engine Crankcase without Filter	Transmission (pts.) 4-Spd	Transmission (pts.) 5-Spd	Transmission (pts.) Auto. ⑤	Drive Axle (pts.)	Fuel Tank (gal.)	Cooling System (qts.)
1990	Comanche	E	4-150 (2.5)	4	4	4.0①	4.9	17.0	2.5	18.0	9.0
	Comanche	L	6-243 (4.0)	6	6	4.0①	4.9	17.0	2.5	18.0	12.0
	Wrangler	E	4-150 (2.5)	4	4	4.0①	4.9	17.0	2.5	15②	7.8
	Wrangler	M	6-258 (4.2)	6	6	4.0①	4.9	17.0	2.5	15②	10.5
	Cherokee	E	4-150 (2.5)	4	4	4.0①	4.9	17.0	2.5	20.3	9.0
	Cherokee	L	6-243 (4.0)	6	6	4.0①	4.9	17.0	2.5	20.3	12.0
	Wagoneer	L	6-243 (4.0)	6	6	3.5	4.9	17.0	2.5	20.2	12.0
	Grand Wagoneer	7	8-360 (5.9)	5	5	—	—	17.0	3.8	20.2	15.0
1991–92	Comanche	P	4-150 (2.5)	4	4	7.0	7.4⑥	8.5	2.5③	18.5④	10.0
	Comanche	S	6-243 (4.0)	6	6	7.0	6.7	8.5	2.5③	18.5④	12.0
	Wrangler	P	4-150 (2.5)	4	4	—	7.4⑥	8.0	2.5③	15.0②	9.0
	Wrangler	S	6-243 (4.0)	6	6	—	6.7	8.0	2.5③	15.0②	12.0
	Cherokee	P	4-150 (2.5)	4	4	—	7.4⑥	8.5	2.5	20.2	10.0
	Cherokee	S	6-243 (4.0)	6	6	—	6.7	8.5	2.5	20.2	12.0
	Grand Wagoneer	7	8-360 (5.9)	5	5	—	—	8.5	3.8	20.3	15.5

① Aisin Warner—7.4 pts.
② Optional—20 gal.
③ Heavy Duty Axle—3.0 pts.
④ Long bed 23.5 gal.
⑤ Quantity will vary with fluid remaining in converter.
⑥ With 4WD—7.0 pts.

CRANKSHAFT AND CONNECTING ROD SPECIFICATIONS

All measurements are given in inches

Year	VIN	No. Cylinder Displacement cu. in. (liter)	Crankshaft Main Brg. Journal Dia.	Crankshaft Main Brg. Oil Clearance	Crankshaft Shaft End-play	Crankshaft Thrust on No.	Connecting Rod Journal Diameter	Connecting Rod Oil Clearance	Connecting Rod Side Clearance
1988	H	4-150 (2.5)	2.4996–2.5001	0.0010–0.0025	0.0015–0.0065	2	2.0934–2.0955	0.0010–0.0025	0.0100–0.0190
	M	6-243 (4.0)	2.4996–2.5001	0.0010–0.0025	0.0015–0.0065	3	2.0934–2.0955	0.0010–0.0030	0.0100–0.0190
	C	6-258 (4.2)	2.4996–2.5001	0.0010–0.0025	0.0015–0.0065	3	2.0934–2.0955	0.0010–0.0030	0.0100–0.0190
	N	8-360 (5.9)	2.7474–2.7489	0.0010–0.0020	0.0030–0.0080	3	2.0934–2.0955	0.0010–0.0030	0.0060–0.0180
1989	E	4-150 (2.5)	2.4996–2.5001	0.0010–0.0025	0.0015–0.0065	2	2.0934–2.0955	0.0010–0.0025	0.0100–0.0190
	L	6-243 (4.0)	2.4996–2.5001	0.0010–0.0025	0.0015–0.0065	3	2.0934–2.0955	0.0010–0.0030	0.0100–0.0190
	M	6-258 (4.2)	2.4996–2.5001	0.0010–0.0025	0.0015–0.0065	3	2.0934–2.0955	0.0010–0.0030	0.0100–0.0190
	7	8-360 (5.9)	2.7474–2.7489	0.0010–0.0020	0.0030–0.0080	3	2.0934–2.0955	0.0010–0.0030	0.0060–0.0180

CRANKSHAFT AND CONNECTING ROD SPECIFICATIONS

All measurements are given in inches

| Year | VIN | No. Cylinder Displacement cu. in. (liter) | Crankshaft | | | | Connecting Rod | | |
			Main Brg. Journal Dia.	Main Brg. Oil Clearance	Shaft End-play	Thrust on No.	Journal Diameter	Oil Clearance	Side Clearance
1990	E	4-150 (2.5)	2.4996–2.5001	0.0010–0.0025	0.0015–0.0065	2	2.0934–2.0955	0.0010–0.0025	0.0100–0.0190
	L	6-243 (4.0)	2.4996–2.5001	0.0010–0.0025	0.0015–0.0065	3	2.0934–2.0955	0.0010–0.0030	0.0100–0.0190
	M	6-258 (4.2)	2.4996–2.5001	0.0010–0.0025	0.0015–0.0065	3	2.0934–2.0955	0.0010–0.0025	0.0100–0.0190
	7	8-360 (5.9)	2.7474–② 2.7489	0.0010–① 0.0030	0.0030–0.0080	3	2.0934–2.0955	0.0010–0.0030	0.0060–0.0180
1991–92	P	4-150 (2.5)	2.4996–2.5001	0.0010–0.0025	0.0015–0.0065	2	2.0934–2.0955	0.0010–0.0025	0.0100–0.0190
	S	6-243 (4.0)	2.4996–2.5001	0.0010–0.0025	0.0015–0.0065	3	2.0934–2.0955	0.0010–0.0030	0.0100–0.0190
	7	8-360 (5.9)	2.7474–② 2.7489	0.0010–① 0.0030	0.0030–0.0080	3	2.0934–2.0955	0.0010–0.0030	0.0060–0.0180

① Rear Main: .002–.004
② Rear Main: 2.7464–2.7479

VALVE SPECIFICATIONS

| Year | VIN | No. Cylinder Displacement cu. in. (liter) | Seat Angle (deg.) | Face Angle (deg.) | Spring Test Pressure (lbs. @ in.) | Spring Installed Height (in.) | Stem-to-Guide Clearance (in.) | | Stem Diameter (in.) | |
							Intake	Exhaust	Intake	Exhaust
1988	H	4-150 (2.5)	45	45	200 @ 1.216	1.640	0.0010–0.0030	0.0010–0.0030	0.3110–0.3120	0.3110–0.3120
	M	6-243 (4.0)	44.5	45	210 @ 1.200	1.625	0.0010–0.0030	0.0010–0.0030	0.3120	0.3120
	C	6-258 (4.2)	①	②	195 @ 1.411	1.786	0.0010–0.0030	0.0010–0.0030	0.3715–0.3725	0.3715–0.3725
	N	8-360 (5.9)	①	②	200 @ 1.356	1.786	0.0010–0.0030	0.0010–0.0030	0.3715–0.3725	0.3715–0.3725
1989	E	4-150 (2.5)	45	45	200 @ 1.216	1.640	0.0010–0.0030	0.0010–0.0030	0.3110–0.3120	0.3110–0.3120
	L	6-243 (4.0)	44.5	45	210 @ 1.200	1.625	0.0010–0.0030	0.0010–0.0030	0.3120	0.3120
	M	6-258 (4.2)	①	②	195 @ 1.411	1.786	0.0010–0.0030	0.0010–0.0030	0.3715–0.3725	0.3715–0.3725
	7	8-360 (5.9)	①	②	200 @ 1.356	1.786	0.0010–0.0030	0.0010–0.0030	0.3715–0.3725	0.3715–0.3725
1990	E	4-150 (2.5)	44.5	44.5	200 @ 1.216	1.640	0.0010–0.0030	0.0010–0.0030	0.3110–0.3120	0.3110–0.3120
	L	6-243 (4.0)	44.5	45	210 @ 1.200	1.625	0.0010–0.0030	0.0010–0.0030	0.3120	0.3120
	M	6-258 (4.2)	①	②	195 @ 1.411	1.786	0.0010–0.0030	0.0010–0.0030	0.3715–0.3725	0.3715–0.3725
	7	8-360 (5.9)	①	②	200 @ 1.356	1.786	0.0010–0.0030	0.0010–0.0030	0.3715–0.3725	0.3715–0.3725

VALVE SPECIFICATIONS

Year	VIN	No. Cylinder Displacement cu. in. (liter)	Seat Angle (deg.)	Face Angle (deg.)	Spring Test Pressure (lbs. @ in.)	Spring Installed Height (in.)	Stem-to-Guide Clearance (in.) Intake	Exhaust	Stem Diameter (in.) Intake	Exhaust
1991–92	P	4-150 (2.5)	44.5	45	200 @ 1.216	1.640	0.0010–0.0030	0.0010–0.0030	0.3110–0.3120	0.3110–0.3120
	S	6-243 (4.0)	44.5	45	210 @ 1.200	1.625	0.0010–0.0030	0.0010–0.0030	0.3120	0.3120
	7	8-360 (5.9)	①	②	200 @ 1.356	1.786	0.0010–0.0030	0.0010–0.0030	0.3715–0.3725	0.3715–0.3725

① Intake: 30 degrees
  Exhaust: 44.5 degrees
② Intake: 29 degrees
  Exhaust: 44 degrees

PISTON AND RING SPECIFICATIONS

All measurements are given in inches

Year	VIN	No. Cylinder Displacement cu. in. (liter)	Piston Clearance	Ring Gap Top Compression	Bottom Compression	Oil Control	Ring Side Clearance Top Compression	Bottom Compression	Oil Control
1988	H	4-150 (2.5)	0.0013–0.0021	0.0100–0.0200	0.0100–0.0200	0.0150–0.0550	0.0010–0.0032	0.0010–0.0032	0.0010–0.0021
	M	6-243 (4.0)	0.0009–0.0017	0.0100–0.0200	0.0100–0.0200	0.0100–0.0250	0.0017–0.0032	0.0017–0.0032	0.0010–0.0080
	C	6-258 (4.2)	0.0009–0.0017	0.0100–0.0200	0.0100–0.0200	0.0100–0.0250	0.0015–0.0030	0.0015–0.0030	0.0010–0.0080
	N	8-360 (5.9)	0.0012–0.0020	0.0100–0.0200	0.0100–0.0200	0.0150–0.0450	0.0015–0.0035	0.0015–0.0035	0.0010–0.0070
1989	E	4-150 (2.5)	0.0013–0.0021	0.0100–0.0200	0.0100–0.0200	0.0150–0.0550	0.0010–0.0032	0.0010–0.0032	0.0010–0.0021
	L	6-243 (4.0)	0.0009–0.0017	0.0100–0.0200	0.0100–0.0200	0.0100–0.0250	0.0017–0.0032	0.0017–0.0032	0.0010–0.0080
	M	6-258 (4.2)	0.0009–0.0017	0.0100–0.0200	0.0100–0.0200	0.0100–0.0250	0.0015–0.0030	0.0015–0.0030	0.0010–0.0080
	7	8-360 (5.9)	0.0012–0.0020	0.0100–0.0200	0.0100–0.0200	0.0150–0.0450	0.0015–0.0035	0.0015–0.0035	0.0010–0.0070
1990	E	4-150 (2.5)	0.0013–0.0021	0.0100–0.0200	0.0100–0.0200	0.0150–0.0550	0.0010–0.0032	0.0010–0.0032	0.0010–0.0085
	L	6-243 (4.0)	0.0013–0.0021	0.0100–0.0200	0.0100–0.0200	0.0100–0.0250	0.0010–0.0032	0.0010–0.0032	0.0010–0.0095
	M	6-258 (4.2)	0.0009–0.0017	0.0100–0.0200	0.0100–0.0200	0.0100–0.0250	0.0017–0.0032	0.0012–0.0032	0.0010–0.0080
	7	8-360 (5.9)	0.0012–0.0020	0.0100–0.0200	0.0100–0.0200	0.0150–0.0450	0.0015–0.0035	0.0015–0.0035	0.0010–0.0070
1991–92	P	4-150 (2.5)	0.0013–0.0021	0.0100–0.0200	0.0100–0.0200	0.0150–0.0550	0.0010–0.0032	0.0010–0.0032	0.0010–0.0085
	S	6-243 (4.0)	0.0013–0.0021	0.0100–0.0200	0.0100–0.0200	0.0100–0.0250	0.0017–0.0032	0.0017–0.0032	0.0010–0.0095
	7	8-360 (5.9)	0.0012–0.0020	0.0100–0.0200	0.0100–0.0200	0.0150–0.0450	0.0015–0.0035	0.0015–0.0035	0.0000–0.0070

TORQUE SPECIFICATIONS
All readings in ft. lbs.

Year	VIN	No. Cylinder Displacement cu. in. (liter)	Cylinder Head Bolts	Main Bearing Bolts	Rod Bearing Bolts	Crankshaft Pulley Bolts	Flywheel Bolts	Manifold Intake	Manifold Exhaust	Spark Plugs
1988	H	4-150 (2.5)	①	80	33	75–85	40	⑦	30	28
	M	6-243 (4.0)	②	80	30–35	80	100–110	⑧	③	28
	C	6-258 (4.2)	85	75–85	30–35	75–85	100–110	20–25	③	28
	N	8-360 (5.9)	110	100	33	90	95	43	⑥	28
1989	E	4-150 (2.5)	①	80	33	75–85	40	⑦	30	28
	L	6-243 (4.0)	②	80	30–35	80	100–110	⑧	③	28
	M	6-258 (4.2)	85	75–85	30–35	75–85	100–110	20–25	③	28
	7	8-360 (5.9)	110	100	33	90	95	43	⑥	28
1990	E	4-150 (2.5)	①	80	33	75–85④	50⑤	⑦	30	27
	L	6-243 (4.0)	②	80	33	80④	100–110	⑧	③	27
	M	6-258 (4.2)	85	80	33	75–85④	100–110	23	③	28
	7	8-360 (5.9)	110	100	33	90④	95	43	⑥	27
1991–92	P	4-150 (2.5)	①	80	33	75–85④	50⑤	⑦	30	27
	S	6-243 (4.0)	②	80	33	80④	100–110	⑧	⑤	27
	7	8-360 (5.9)	110	100	33	90④	95	43	⑥	27

① Step 1—Tighten all bolts to 22 ft. lbs.
 Step 2—Tighten all bolts to 45 ft. lbs.
 Step 3—Tighten bolts 1–7 to 110 ft. lbs.
 Step 4—Tighten bolt 8 to 100 ft. lbs.
 Step 5—Tighten bolts 9–10 to 110 ft. lbs.
② Step 1—Tighten all bolts to 22 ft. lbs.
 Step 2—Tighten all bolts to 45 ft. lbs.

Step 3—Tighten bolts 1–10 & 12–14 to 110 ft. lbs.
Step 4—Tighten bolt 11 to 100 ft. lbs.
③ Middle nuts to 30 ft. lbs.
 Outside nuts to 23 ft. lbs.
④ Damper bolt (tighten pulley bolts to 20 ft. lbs.; 30 ft. lbs. on 5.9L engine)

⑤ Plus 60° rotation
⑥ Outer bolts to 15 ft. lbs.
 Inner bolts to 25 ft. lbs.
⑦ Bolts 1, 6 and 7 to 30 ft. lbs.
 Bolts 2–5 to 23 ft. lbs.
⑧ Bolts 1–5 and 8–11 to 23 ft. lbs.
 Bolts 6 and 7 to 17 ft. lbs.

BRAKE SPECIFICATIONS
All measurements in inches unless noted.

Year	Model	Lug Nut Torque (ft. lbs.)	Master Cylinder Bore	Brake Disc Minimum Thickness	Brake Disc Maximum Runout	Standard Brake Drum Diameter	Minimum Lining Thickness ② Front	Minimum Lining Thickness ② Rear
1988	Comanche	75	0.937	0.815	0.004	10.00	0.031	0.031
	Wrangler	75	0.937	0.815	0.004	10.00	0.031	0.031
	Cherokee	75	0.937	0.815	0.004	10.00	0.031	0.031
	Wagoneer	75	0.937	0.815	0.004	10.00	0.031	0.031
	Grand Wagoneer	75	1.125	1.215	0.005	11.00	0.031	0.031
	J10 Pick-Up	75	1.125	1.215	0.005	11.00	0.031	0.031
	J20 Pick-Up	75	1.125	1.215	0.005	12.00	0.031	0.031
1989	Comanche	75	0.937	0.815	0.004	10.00	0.031	0.031
	Wrangler	75	0.937	0.815	0.004	10.00	0.031	0.031
	Cherokee	75	0.937	0.815	0.004	10.00	0.031	0.031
	Wagoneer	75	0.937	0.815	0.004	10.00	0.031	0.031
	Grand Wagoneer	75	1.125	1.215	0.005	11.00	0.031	0.031
1990	Comanche	75	0.937	0.86④	0.005	9.5①	0.031	0.031
	Wrangler	75	0.937	0.94	0.005	9.5①	0.031	0.031
	Cherokee	75	0.937	0.86④	0.005	9.5①	0.031	0.031
	Wagoneer	75	0.937	0.86④	0.005	9.5①	0.031	0.031
	Grand Wagoneer	75	1.125	1.215	0.005	11.00	0.031	0.031

BRAKE SPECIFICATIONS

All measurements in inches unless noted.

Year	Model	Lug Nut Torque (ft. lbs.)	Master Cylinder Bore	Brake Disc		Standard Brake Drum Diameter	Minimum Lining Thickness ②	
				Minimum Thickness	Maximum Runout		Front	Rear
1991–92	Comanche	75	0.937	0.86③	0.005	9.0⑤	0.031	0.031
	Wrangler	75	0.937	0.86	0.005	9.0⑤	0.031	0.031
	Cherokee	75	0.937	0.86③	0.005	9.0⑤	0.031	0.031
	Grand Wagoneer	75	1.125	1.215	0.005	11.00	0.031	0.031

① 10.5 with heavy duty axle
② Bonded lining 0.062
③ 0.890 w/4WD
④ 0.94 w/4WD
⑤ 10.0 with heavy duty axle

WHEEL ALIGNMENT

Year	Model	Caster		Camber		Toe-in (in.)	Steering Axis Inclination (deg.)
		Range (deg.)	Preferred Setting (deg.)	Range (deg.)	Preferred Setting (deg.)		
1988	Comanche	7P–8P	7½P	½N–½P	0	1/16P	NA
	Wrangler	①	②	½N–½P	0	1/32P	NA
	Cherokee	7P–8P	7½P	½N–½P	0	1/16P	NA
	Wagoneer	7P–8P	7½P	½N–½P	0	1/16P	NA
	Grand Wagoneer	3P–5P	4P	½N–½P	0	3/64P–3/32P	8½
	J10 Pick-Up	3P–5P	4P	½N–½P	0	3/64P–3/32P	8½
	J20 Pick-Up	3P–5P	4P	½N–½P	0	3/64P–3/32P	8½
1989	Comanche	7P–8P	7½P	½N–½P	0	1/16P	NA
	Wrangler	①	②	½N–½P	0	1/32P	NA
	Cherokee	7P–8P	7½P	½N–½P	0	1/16P	NA
	Wagoneer	7P–8P	7½P	½N–½P	0	1/16P	NA
	Grand Wagoneer	3P–5P	4P	½N–½P	0	3/64P–3/32P	8½
1990	Comanche	5–9P	6P	¾N–½P	0	0	NA
	Wrangler	①	②	½N–½P	0	0	NA
	Cherokee	5–9P	6P	¾N–½P	0	0	NA
	Wagoneer	5–9P	6P	¾N–½P	0	0	NA
	Grand Wagoneer	4P–5P	4P	0–½P	0	0–5/32P	8½
1991–92	Comanche	5–9P	6P	¾N–½P	0	0	NA
	Wrangler	③	④	½N–½P	0	0	NA
	Cherokee	5–9P	6P	¾N–½P	0	0	NA
	Grand Wagoneer	3P–5P	4P	0–½P	0	0–3/16P	8½

NA—Not available
N—Negative
P—Positive
① With manual transmission   7½P–8½P
   With automatic transmission   6P–7P
② With manual transmission   8P
   With automatic transmission   6½P
③ With automatic transmission—5¼ to 7¼
   manual transmission—6½ to 9
④ With automatic transmission—8.0
   manual transmission—6.5

ENGINE ELECTRICAL

NOTE: Disconnecting the battery cable on some vehicles may interfere with the functions of the on board computer systems and may require the computer to undergo a relearning process, once the negative battery cable is disconnected.

Distributor

Removal

1. Disconnect the negative battery cable.
2. Label and remove the high tension wires from the distributor cap.
3. Remove the primary lead from the terminal post at the side of the distributor. Disconnect the vacuum line, if equipped.
4. Turn the engine, using a socket on the end of the crankshaft damper bolt, until the rotor is pointing to the No. 1 spark plug wire post and the timing mark on the damper aligns with the 0 on the timing scale; No. 1 cylinder is at TDC on the compression stroke.
5. Remove the distributor cap. Note the position of the rotor and distributor. Scribe a mark on the base of the distributor and the engine as an installation reference.
6. Remove the bolt for the distributor hold-down clamp.
7. Remove the distributor from the engine.

Installation

TIMING NOT DISTURBED

1. Using a new distributor gasket, install the distributor in the engine noting the scribe marks made during removal. It may be necessary to move the rotor slightly to engage the the oil pump shaft.

NOTE: When properly installed, the rotor should be aligned with the No. 1 spark plug wire terminal, the scribe marks should be aligned and the distributor should be fully seated on the engine block.

2. Install the distributor hold-down clamp. Leave the hold-down bolt loose enough so the distrubutor can be rotated with heavy hand pressure.
3. Connect the primary wire to the distributor side of the coil. Install the distributor cap.
4. Install the high tension wires. Ensure that the wires are routed correctly.
5. Start the engine and set the ignition timing. Tighten the distributor hold-down bolt to 17 ft. lbs. (23 Nm).

TIMING DISTURBED

1. Remove the No. 1 spark plug. Rotate the engine until the No. 1 piston is at TDC on the compression stroke.
2. Using a flat blade tool, rotate the oil pump gear so the slot in the oil pump shaft is in the correct position for distributor installation.

NOTE: On the 2.5L and 4.0L engines with non-adjustable timing, the position of the oil pump shaft is critical. The 2.5L engine should be at the 3 o'clock position. The 4.0L should be at the 11 o'clock position.

3. Using a new distributor gasket, install the distributor in the engine noting the scribe marks made during removal. It may be necessary to move the rotor slightly to engage the the oil pump shaft.

NOTE: When properly installed, the rotor should be aligned with the No. 1 spark plug wire terminal, the scribe marks should be aligned, and the distributor should be fully seated on the engine block.

4. Install the distributor hold-down clamp. Leave the hold-

Distributor rotor alignment for installation

down bolt loose enough so the distributor can be rotated with heavy hand pressure.

5. Connect the primary wire to the distributor side of the coil. Install the distributor cap.
6. Install the high tension wires. Ensure that the wires are routed correctly.
7. Start the engine and set the ignition timing. Tighten the distributor hold-down bolt to 17 ft. lbs. (23 Nm).

Ignition Timing

Adjustment

NOTE: The ignition timing for the 2.5L or 4.0L engine is controlled by the ECU and is not adjustable. However, the ignition timing may still be checked using the standard procedure.

4.2L AND 5.9L ENGINES

1. Locate the timing marks on the crankshaft pulley and the front of the timing case cover. Clean the marks so they are clearly visible.
2. Use chalk or white paint to color the mark on the scale that will indicate the correct timing, when aligned with the mark on the pulley or the pointer.
3. Attach a tachometer to the negative side of the coil and ground. Attach a timing light to the battery and connect the inductive probe to the No. 1 plug wire. Place the probe as close to the spark plug as possible.
4. Start the engine and allow it to reach operating temperature. Place the transmission in **P** and turn **OFF** all accessories.
5. On the 4.2L engine, disconnect and plug the vacuum switch located on the rocker arm cover. On both engines, disconnect and plug the vacuum lines to the distributor.
6. On the 4.2L engine, disconnect the knock sensor wire and ground it with a jumper wire to the engine block.
7. Loosen the distributor lock bolt just enough so the distributor can be turned with a little resistance.
8. Start the engine and check the idle, if necessary adjust it to the correct specification.
9. With the timing light aimed at the pulley and the marks on the engine, turn the distributor in the direction of rotor rotation

Timing mark location—5.9L engine

Serpentine drive belt routing—2.5L and 4.2L engines

Timing mark location—2.5L, 4.0L and 4.2L engines

Serpentine drive belt routing—4.0L engine

to retard the spark, and in the opposite direction of rotor rotation to advance the spark. Align the marks on the pulley and the engine with the flashes of the timing light.

10. Tighten the hold-down bolt and recheck the timing. Turn the engine **OFF**.

11. Remove the timing light and tachometer. Reconnect all vacuum lines and electrical connectors.

Alternator

For further information, please refer to "Alternators" in the Unit Repair section.

Belt Tension Adjustment

WITH V-BELTS

The belt tension should be checked using the gauge method.

The gauge should be placed in the section of belt being checked. The correct specification for a new V-belt is 120–160 ft. lbs. (533–711 Nm) and the correct tension for a used V-belt is 90–115 ft. lbs. (400–511 Nm).

To adjust the belt tension:

1. If equipped with the 2.5L or 4.0L engine, loosen the power steering pump mounting bolts. If equipped with the 5.9L or 4.2L engine, loosen the alternator mounting bolts.

2. Pry the alternator or power steering pump, away from the engine to tension the belt.

3. Tighten the mounting bolts to 20 ft. lbs. (27 Nm).

WITH SERPENTINE BELT

The belt tension should be checked using the gauge method. The gauge should be placed in the section of belt being checked. The correct specification for a new serpentine belt is 180–200 ft. lbs. (800–900 Nm) and the correct tension for a used serpentine belt is 140–160 ft. lbs. (623–712 Nm).

To adjust the belt tension:

1. If equipped with the 2.5L or 4.0L engine, loosen the power steering pump mounting bolts. If equipped with the 4.2L or 5.9L engines, loosen the alternator mounting bolts.

2. Tighten the adjusting bolt to increase the belt tension and loosen it to release the belt tension.

3. Tighten the mounting bolts to 20 ft. lbs. (27 Nm).

Removal and Installation

GRAND WAGONEER, PICK-UP AND WRANGLER

1. Disconnect the negative battery cable.
2. Loosen the pivot bolt and remove the accessory drive belt.
3. Remove the wire terminals attached to the rear of the alternator.
4. Loosen the bolt holding the adjusting bar and the pivot bolt at the opposite side of the alternator.
5. Remove the adjusting bar and pivot bolts and remove the alternator from the engine.
To install:
6. Attach the alternator to the mounting bracket and tighten the bolts finger-tight.
7. Install the accessory drive belt.
8. Adjust the belt tension to specification.
9. Tighten the mounting bolts and connect the electrical leads.
10. Connect the negative battery cable.

CHEROKEE, COMANCHE AND WAGONEER

1. Disconnect the negative battery cable.
2. Loosen the pivot bolt and remove the accessory drive belt.
3. Raise and safely support the vehicle.

4. Disconnect the electrical connector at the rear of the alternator.
5. Remove the alternator mounting bolts.
6. Remove the alternator from below the vehicle.
To install:
7. Attach the alternator to the mounting bracket and tighten the bolts to 28 ft. lbs. (38 Nm).
8. Connect the electrical leads and lower the vehicle.
9. Install the accessory drive belt.
10. Adjust the belt tension to specification.
11. Connect the negative battery cable.

Starter

For further information, please refer to "Starters" in the Unit Repair section.

Removal and Installation

1. Disconnect the negative battery cable.
2. Raise and safely support the vehicle.
3. Disconnect the electrical leads from the starter.
4. Remove the starter mounting bolts and remove the starter from the vehicle. On 1989–92 vehicles equipped with a 2.5L engine, it is necessary to remove the exhaust clamp and bracket, and the transmission brace rod before removing the starter.
To install:
5. Install the starter in position.
6. Tighten the mounting bolts to 18 ft. lbs. (24 Nm) for 2.5L engine or 33 ft. lbs. (45 Nm) except 2.5L engine.
7. Connect the electrical leads and lower the vehicle.

1. Bushing
2. Overrunning clutch housing
3. Snapring
4. Stop ring
5. Overrunning clutch
6. Clutch yoke
7. Yoke washer
8. Retainer
9. Solenoid
10. Planetary annulus gear
11. Planetary carrier and pinion shaft
12. Planetary gears
13. Armature shaft ball
14. Sealing ring
15. Armature frame and magnet assembly
16. Armature
17. Bearing
18. Washer
19. Carbon brushes
20. Brush holder
21. Armature frame bolts
22. End cover

Mitsubishi starter used on the 4.0L, 4.2L and 5.9L engines

1. Bushing
2. Screw
3. Shield
4. Solenoid switch
5. Retainer
6. Stop ring
7. Bushing
8. Overrunning clutch drive
9. Fork
10. Bearing pedestal
11. Sealing rubber
12. Planetary gear system
13. Armature
14. Stator frame
15. Brush holder
16. Gasket
17. Commutator end shield
18. Bushing
19. Sealing ring
20. Shim
21. Shim
22. Retaining washer
23. Closure cap
24. Hexagon screw
25. Screw

Bosch starter used on the 2.5L engine

CHASSIS ELECTRICAL

Heater Blower Motor

Removal and Installation

1. Disconnect the negative battery cable. Remove the coolant overflow bottle.
2. If equipped with anti-lock brakes, remove the anti-lock brake pump and bracket and position it aside.
3. Remove the brake hose retaining bracket screw.
4. Unplug the blower motor wiring connector.
5. Remove the blower motor mounting screws and lift out the motor.

To install:

6. Install the blower motor into position and connect the electrical leads.

7. Connect the brake hose retaining bracket.
8. Install the anti-lock brake pump and bracket.
9. Install the coolant bottle and connect the negative battery cable.

Windshield Wiper Motor

Removal and Installation

WRANGLER

1. Disconnect the negative battery cable. Remove the necessary hard or soft top components from the windshield frame.
2. Remove the left and right windshield hold-down knobs and fold the windshield forward.

3. Remove the left access hole cover. Disconnect the drive link from the left wiper pivot. Disconnect the wiper motor harness from the switch.

4. Grasp the motor and pull the drive arm out of the access hole. Pry the arm off the motor pivot. Do not remove the pivot attaching nut.

5. Remove the screws holding the intermittent wiper module bracket to the bottom of the instrument panel. Remove the motor.

To install:

6. Install and connect the wiring harness.

7. Install the screws holding the intermittent wiper module.

8. Turn the motor **ON** and check for proper operation.

9. Install the drive arm on the motor pivot. Install the motor and tighten the attaching bolts to 96 inch lbs. (11 Nm).

10. Connect the drive link at the left wiper pivot and install the harness clips. Install the windshield and hard or soft top assembly.

GRAND WAGONEER AND PICK-UP

1. Disconnect the negative battery cable.

2. Remove the screws attaching the motor adapter plate to the dash panel.

3. Separate the wiper wiring harness connector at the wiper motor.

4. Pull the motor and the linkage out of the opening to expose the drive link to crank stud retaining clip.

5. Raise the lock tab of the clip and slide the clip off the stud.

6. Remove the wiper motor from the vehicle.

To install:

7. Install the motor, position the wiper motor assembly and insert the crank stud into the drive link bushing.

8. Press the retaining clip onto the stud and slide into place in the stud groove. Check for a good fit.

9. Install the wiper motor attaching screws and tighten to 25 inch lbs. (3 Nm).

WAGONEER, CHEROKEE AND COMANCHE

1. Disconnect the negative battery cable.

2. Remove the wiper arm assemblies. Remove the cowl and trim panel.

3. Disconnect the washer hose. Remove the cowl mounting bracket attaching bolts and the pivot pin attaching screws.

4. Disconnect the wiring harness and remove the assembly. The motor is protected by a rubber case, care should be used as not to damage this protective coat.

To install:

5. Install the wiper motor assembly and connect the wiring harness. Take care not to damage the rubber case.

6. Install the pivot pin attaching screws. Install the cowl mounting bracket and washer hose.

7. Install the wiper arm assemblies and test for proper operation. Tighten the wiper motor attaching screws to 35–50 inch lbs. (47–67 Nm).

1. Tell tale display
2. Lens
3. Gauge
4. Coolant temperature gauge
5. Fuel gauge
6. Tachometer
7. Tachometer module
8. Speedometer
9. Engine oil pressure gauge
10. Voltmeter/diesel boost gauge
11. Mounting bezel
12. PC overlay

Instrument cluster assembly—Comanche, Cherokee and Wagoneer

Instrument Cluster

Removal and Installation

GRAND WAGONEER AND PICK-UP

1. Disconnect the negative battery. Remove the cluster retaining screws.
2. Disconnect the speedometer cable.
3. Disconnect the cluster terminal pin plug. Disconnect the four terminal connector.
4. Mark the electrical connectors and hoses, disconnect them and the blend door air cable.
5. Remove the heater control panel lights. Disconnect the heater temperature control wire from the lever. Remove the cluster.

To install:

6. Install the heater control panel lights. Install the heater temperature control wire on the lever and install the cluster.
7. Install the blend door hoses and all electrical connectors. Install the speedometer cable.
8. Install the cluster retaining screws and connect the negative battery cable.

WRANGLER, WAGONEER, CHEROKEE AND COMANCHE

1. Disconnect the negative battery cable.
2. Remove the instrument panel bezel screws and lift off the bezel. The bezel unsnaps.
3. Remove the cigarette lighter housing screws.
4. Remove the rocker switch housing screws.
5. Remove the cluster screws.
6. Disconnect the speedometer cable, pull the cluster out slowly and disconnect the electrical connectors at the cluster back. Remove the cluster.

To install:

7. Install the cluster after connecting all electrical connectors and the speedometer cable.
8. Install the cluster screws, rocker switch housing screws, cigarette lighter housing screws and install the instrument panel bezel.
9. Connect the negative battery cable.

Speedometer

Removal and Installation

1. Disconnect the negative battery cable.
2. Remove the instrument cluster.
3. Remove the 2 attaching screws from the rear of the cluster.
4. Remove the screw from the front of the speedometer and pull it from the cluster. Pull the speedometer out of the circuit board carefully.
5. Install the speedometer in the reverse order of the removal procedure.

Headlight Switch

Removal and Installation

PULLOUT TYPE SWITCH

1. Disconnect the negative battery cable.
2. Pull the light switch control knob out as far as it will go. As required, remove the instrument panel trim plate.
3. From under the dash depress the headlight switch shaft retainer button. Pull the shaft along with the knob from the headlight switch assembly.
4. Remove the headlight switch retaining nut. Disconnect the electrical connector from the switch.
5. Remove the headlight switch from the vehicle.

To install:

6. Install the headlight switch and connect the electrical connector. Install the shaft and knob.
7. Check the operation of the switch after connecting the negative battery cable.

ROCKER TYPE SWITCH

1. Disconnect the negative battery cable.
2. Remove the instrument cluster shroud.
3. Remove the 2 screws retaining the switch and remove the switch from the instrument panel.

To install:

4. Install the headlight switch and connect the electrical connectors. Install the retaining screws.
5. Install the instrument cluster shroud and connect the negative battery cable. Check the operation of the switch.

Dimmer Switch

Removal and Installation

1. Disconnect the negative battery cable.
2. On Cherokee, Comanche or Wagoneer, remove the lower instrument panel cover.
3. On Wrangler, remove the instrument housing screws. Slide the housing towards the steering wheel and apply upward pressure to the housing and downward pressure to the indicator to release the holding tabs. Remove the instrument housing.
4. On Wrangler or Grand Wagoneer, remove the evaporator housing panel attaching screws and the housing mounting bracket. Lower the evaporator.
5. Disconnect the dimmer switch electrical connector and tape the actuator rod in place.
6. Remove the dimmer switch.

To install:

7. Install the dimmer switch and actuator rod.
8. Install the evaporator housing, instrument panel and lower instrument panel, as required.
9. Connect the negative battery cable.

Combination Switch

Removal and Installation

1. Disconnect the negative battery cable.
2. Remove the steering wheel.
3. Remove the lockplate cover by compressing with tool C–4156 or equivalent, and release the steering shaft retaining snapring.
4. Remove the lockplate, canceling cam, upper bearing preload spring, and thrust washer from the steering column.
5. Remove the hazard warning switch knob. Press the knob inward and remove it from the column by turning counterclockwise.
6. If equipped with a column shift, remove the 2 retaining screws and the gear selector indicator cover.
7. If equipped with a column shift, remove the gear selector indicator light bracket retaining screw. Do not remove the light and bracket at this time.
8. Remove the tilt-release lever.
9. Remove the combination lever by pulling it out straight from the column. The wiper switch must be in the OFF position.
10. Disconnect the turn signal wiring harness located at the lower end of the steering column. Wrap it with tape to prevent it from becoming entangled.
11. Remove the plastic protector from the wire harness.
12. Remove the turn signal switch retaining screws and the dimmer switch actuator arm, then remove the switch. Guide the switch straight up out of the steering column.

To install:

13. Install the turn signal switch and wiring harness. Install the dimmer switch actuator arm and turn signal switch retain-

ing screws. Tighten turn signal and dimmer switch attaching screws to 35 inch lbs. Install the combination lever and tilt release lever.

14. If equipped with a column shift, install both retaining screws and the gear selector indicator cover.

15. If equipped with a column shift, install the gear selector indicator light bracket retaining screw. Do not remove the light and bracket at this time.

16. Install the hazard warning switch knob. Press the knob inward and install it from the column by turning clockwise.

17. Install the lockplate, canceling cam, upper bearing preload spring, and thrust washer from the steering column.

18. Install the lockplate cover and install the steering shaft retaining snapring.

19. Install the steering wheel. Tighten nut to 25 ft. lbs.

20. Connect the negative battery cable.

Ignition Lock

Removal and Installation

1. Disconnect the negative battery cable. Remove the combination switch.

2. Insert the key in the lock cylinder and turn it **ON**.

3. Remove the key warning buzzer switch and contacts as an assembly using needle-nosed pliers or a paper clip with a 90 degree bend.

4. With the ignition switch still ON, insert a thin tool into the slot adjacent to the switch attaching screw boss (right-hand slot). Depress the spring latch located at the bottom of the slot to release the lock cylinder.

NOTE: Some steering columns may have a retaining screw holding the lock cylinder in the column. Simply remove the retaining screw and remove the lock cylinder.

5. Remove the lock cylinder.

To install:

6. To install the lock cylinder, turn the key to the LOCK position. Insert the lock cylinder in to the housing far enough to contact the driveshaft. Force it inward and move the ignition switch actuator rod up and down to align the components. When the components align, the cylinder will move inward and the spring-loaded retainer will snap into place locking the lock cylinder in the housing.

NOTE: If the lock cylinder is retained by a screw, tighten the screw to 40 inch lbs.

7. Install the key warning buzzer switch.

8. Ignition switch installation for non-tilt columns:

   a. Move the ignition switch slider to the OFF unlocked position (move the slider all the way down, then back 2 clicks). The remote rod hole in the ignition switch slider should now be centered.

   b. Insert the remote rod in the ignition switch slider hole and install the ignition switch on the steering column. Tighten the attaching screws to 35 inch lbs.

9. Ignition switch installation for tilt columns: Insert the ignition key in the lock cylinder and turn the cylinder to the OFF UNLOCK position. Move the ignition switch downward to eliminate any slack and tighten the attaching screws to 35 inch lbs.

10. Install the combination switch. Connect the negative battery cable.

Ignition Switch

Removal and Installation

1. Place the ignition lock in the OFF–LOCK position.

2. Remove the 2 switch mounting screws.

3. Disconnect the switch from the rod.

4. Disconnect the wiring and remove the switch.

To install:

5. Ignition switch installation for non-tilt columns:

   a. Move the ignition switch slider to the OFF unlocked position (move the slider all the way down, then back 2 clicks). The remote rod hole in the ignition switch slider should now be centered.

   b. Insert the remote rod in the ignition switch slider hole and install the ignition switch on the steering column. Tighten the attaching screws to 35 inch lbs.

6. Ignition switch installation for tilt columns: Insert the ignition key in the lock cylinder and turn the cylinder to the OFF UNLOCK position. Move the ignition switch downward to eliminate any slack and tighten the attaching screws to 35 inch lbs.

Brakelight Switch

NOTE: The brakelight switch used on 1988–90 Cherokee, Wagoneer or Wrangler, is not adjustable.

Adjustment

1991–92 CHEROKEE AND WRANGLER

1. Check the adjustment of the switch. Move the brake pedal forward by hand and note the operation of the plunger. The plunger should be fully extended when the pedal free-play is taken up and the brake application begins. A clearance of ⅛ inch should exist between the plunger and the pedal.

2. If adjustment is necessary, grasp the brake pedal and pull it rearward as far as possible. The switch plunger barrel will ratchet rearward in the retaining clip to the correct position.

3. Verify brakelight switch operation and proper clearance between the plunger and brake pedal.

NOTE: Ensure that the brake pedal returns to a fully released position after adjustment. The Switch can interfere with full pedal return if too far forward. The result will be brake drag caused by partial brake application.

GRAND WAGONEER AND PICK-UP

1. Hold the brake pedal in the applied position.

2. Push the stoplight switch through the mounting bracket until it stops against the brake pedal bracket. Release the pedal to set the switch in the proper position.

3. Check the position of the switch. The switch plunger should be in the ON position and activate the brake lights after a brake pedal travel of ⅜–⅝ in. (9.5–15.5mm).

Removal and Installation

EXCEPT 1988–90 WRANGLER, CHEROKEE, COMANCHE AND WAGONEER

1. Remove the steering column cover and lower trim panel for access, if necessary. Disconnect switch wiring harness.

2. Thread switch out of retainer or rock switch up/down and pull it rearward.

3. Inspect switch retainer and replace if worn or damaged.

4. Insert replacement switch in retainer. Thread switch into place or rock up/down until switch plunger contacts brake pedal.

5. Connect wiring harness and perform adjustment procedure below.

1988–90 WRANGLER, CHEROKEE, COMANCHE AND WAGONEER

1. Disconnect the switch electrical connector.

2. Remove the pushrod bolt and remove the switch from the pushrod. Note the position of the switch bushings and spacers for installation referance.

3. Install the bushings and spacers in the new switch and position the switch on the pushrod.

4. Secure the pushrod to the pedal with the bolt and new lock

nuts. Tighten the inner nut to 25 ft. lbs. (34 Nm). Tighten the outer nut to 75 inch lbs. (8.5 Nm).

5. Connect the switch electrical connector and check for proper operation.

Fuses and Circuit Breakers

Location

The fuse panel is located under the instrument panel on the driver's side of the vehicle. In addition to fuses, the fuse panel also houses the hazard flasher, turn signal flasher and chime module.

Circuit breakers may be located at the fuse box or internal to the component. Circuit breaker protected components for specific models are as follows:

Wrangler—windshield wiper, keyless entry system, door locks, power seats and trailer package.

Cherokee and Comanche—power windows, windshield wiper and washer.

Grand Wagoneer—power windows, power mirrors, power seats, power locks and windshield wiper.

Typical fuse panel—Comanche, Cherokee and Wagoneer

Computers

Location

Cruise Control Module—located under the right side of the dash, under the left side of the dash below the fuse box or on the transmission tunnel.

Diagnostic Connector—located next to the battery or next to the relay block on the right fender.

Electronic Control Unit—located under the instrument panel between the steering column and the heater housing.

Ignition Control Module—2.5L engine, except Wrangler—located on the right shock tower.

Ignition Control Module—2.5L engine, Wrangler—located to the left of the battery on the firewall.

Ignition Control Module—4.0L engine—located on the ignition coil assembly.

Ignition Control Module—4.2L engine—located at the bottom of the radiator overflow bottle.

Ignition Control Module—5.9L engine—located on the left wheel well.

Maintenance Reminder Module—located under the dash near the steering column.

Wiper Delay Module—located under the left side of the instrument panel.

Relays

Location

A/C Blower Relay—located under the dash near the heater box.

A/C Compressor Relay—located on the right side inner fender well.

Antenna Relay—located behind the right side kick panel.

Anti-Lock Brake Relay—located at the front of the right inner fender well.

Anti-Lock Brake Pump Relay—located at the pump motor hearness on the right side of the engine compartment.

B + Latch Relay—located at the right inner fender well or at the battery.

Cooling Fan Relay—located at the left inner fender.

Defogger Relay—located to the right of the steering column or at the left kick panel.

ECU Starter Relay—located at the battery hold-down bracket in the relay block or at the rear of the right fender well.

Fan Control Relay—located at the right fender well.

Fog Light Relay—located behind the left headlight or at the left front fender.

Horn Relay—located near the fuse box.

Oxygen Sensor Heater Relay—located at the right inner fender well.

Power Door Lock Relay—located under the right side of the dash.

Radio Light Relay—located behind the glove box.

Towing Light Relay—located in the left rear quarter panel.

Cruise Control

For further information, please refer to Chilton's Chassis Electronics Service Manual.

Operational Check

Perform the following tests with the cruise control switch ON and vehicle speed faster than 35 mph. More comprehensive testing can be accomplished with an AM P-C-1R cruise control diagnostic tool.

1. Press the SET button at the end of the multi-function lever. Vehicle should maintain speed.

2. Hold SET button IN and remove foot from accelerator. Vehicle should coast to a slower speed.

3. Release SET button. Cruise control will engage and hold a slower speed, provided speed is above 35 mph.

4. Slide cruise switch to R/A and hold. Vehicle should accelerate.

5. Release cruise switch back to ON. Vehicle will hold the new faster speed, if SET button has been pressed.

6. Tap brake pedal. Vehicle will decelerate. If equipped with a manual transmission, perform same check with clutch pedal.

7. Slide cruise switch to R/A. Vehicle will accelerate to former set speed.

8. While cruising, accelerate, then remove foot from accelerator. Vehicle will coast back to set speed.

9. While cruise is engaged, tap SET button. Vehicle will increase 1 mph for each time SET button is tapped.

Adjustment

CENTERING ADJUSTMENT

Adjustment is made by turning the centering adjustment screw on the cruise control module. If the controlled speed is more than 2 mph above or below the set speed, turn the adjustment screw counterclockwise to decrease; clockwise to increase.

Check for proper centering adjustment by engaging the speed control on a level road after each adjustment.

SENSITIVITY ADJUSTMENT

The sensitivity adjustment is on the opposite side of the cruise control module. The sensitivity by turning the screw counterclockwise to decrease; clockwise to increase.

Changes in the sensitivity setting affect centering, so if sensitivity is changed, check the centering again and adjust as required.

LOW SPEED SWITCH (ENGAGEMENT) ADJUSTMENT

If the low speed setting is not between 27–33 mph, trun the low speed switch adjusting screw counterclockwise to lower (slow) the speed; clockwise to increase (raise) the speed. The low speed switch adjustment screw is located next to the centering adjustment screw.

ENGINE COOLING

Radiator

Removal and Installation

1. Disconnect the negative battery cable.
2. Remove the front grille mounting screws and grille, as necessary. Drain the cooling system.

NOTE: On some vehicles the drain cock is located on the right side of the radiator behind the park/turn signal light.

3. Remove the radiator upper and lower hoses. If equipped, remove the transmission cooler lines. Remove the fan shroud mounting bolts and pull the fan shroud back to the engine.
4. Remove the alignment dowel E-clip from the lower radiator mounting bracket.
5. Disconnect the overflow tube from the radiator. Remove all attaching bolts and screws that secure the radiator to the radiator support.
6. Remove the condensor to radiator mounting bolts and pull the radiator out of the vehicle.
7. Remove the radiator by lifting straight up. Take care not to damage the radiator fins.
8. Empty the remaining coolant in the radiator. Store the radiator in a safe place.
To install:
9. Slide the radiator into position behind the condensor, if equipped. Align the dowel pin with the bottom mounting bracket and install the E-clip.
10. Tighten the condenser-to-radiator bolts to 55 inch lbs. (6.2 Nm).
11. Install the grille. Install and tighten the radiator mounting bolts.
12. Connect the transmission cooler lines, if equipped. Install the fan shroud.
13. Connect the radiator hoses. Connect the negative battery cable.
14. Fill the cooling system to the correct level.

Electric Cooling Fan

Removal and Installation

1. Disconnect the negative battery cable.
2. Disconnect the electrical lead from the fan assembly.
3. Remove the fan mounting bolts and remove the fan assembly from the shroud and radiator.
4. Installation is the reverse of the removal procedure.

Testing

1. Remove the fan relay, mounted on the left inner fender panel.

2. Using a jumper wire, with an in-line 25 amp fuse, supply battery voltage to the the No. 4 terminal of the relay connector.
3. If the fan operates, the motor is good. If the motor does not operate, check the continuity between the No. 4 terminal and the body ground connections on the fender panel. If continuity exists, replace the fan motor. If there is no continuity, repair the open circuit and retest.

Heater Core

For further information, please refer to Chilton's Air Conditioning and Heating Manual.

Removal and Installation

CHEROKEE, COMANCHE AND WAGONEER

1. Disconnect the negative battery cable. Drain the coolant.
2. Disconnect the heater hoses at the core tubes.
3. If equipped with air conditioning, discharge the refrigerant.

— **CAUTION** —

Use extreme caution when discharging the refrigerant. Refrigerant R–12 will freeze anything it comes in contact with, including skin and eyes.

4. Disconnect the air conditioning hose from the expansion valve and cap all openings. Always use a backup wrench on the fitting.
5. Disconnect the blower motor wires and vent tube.
6. Remove the center console, if equipped.
7. Remove the lower half of the instrument panel.
8. Disconnect the wiring at the air conditioner relay, blower motor resistors and air conditioner thermostat. Disconnect the vacuum hoses at the vacuum motor.
9. Cut the plastic retaining strap that retains the evaporator housing to the heater core housing.
10. Disconnect and remove the heater control cable.
11. Remove the 3 clips at the rear blower housing flange and remove the retaining screws.
12. Remove the housing attaching nuts from the studs on the engine compartment side of the firewall.
13. Remove the evaporator drain tube.
14. Remove the right kick panel and the instrument panel support bolt.
15. Gently pull out on the right side of the dash and rotate the housing down and toward the rear to disengage the mounting studs from the firewall. Remove the housing.

Auxiliary cooling fan system circuit

Auxiliary cooling fan connector

16. Unbolt and remove the core from the housing.
To install:
17. Install the core in the housing.
18. Position the housing on the mounting studs on the firewall.
19. Install the right kick panel and the instrument panel support bolt.
20. Install the evaporator drain tube.
21. Install the housing attaching nuts from the studs on the engine compartment side of the firewall.
22. Install the 3 clips at the rear blower housing flange and install the retaining screws.
23. Connect the heater control cable.
24. Install a new plastic retaining strap that retains the evaporator housing to the heater core housing.
25. Connect the wiring at the air conditioner relay, blower motor resistors and air conditioner thermostat.
26. Connect the vacuum hoses at the vacuum motor.
27. Install the lower half of the instrument panel.
28. Install the center console, if equipped.
29. Connect the blower motor wires and vent tube.
30. Connect the air conditioning hose at the expansion valve. Always use a backup wrench.
31. Connect the heater hoses at the core tubes.
32. Fill the cooling system.
33. Evacuate, charge and leak test the refrigerant system.

EXCEPT CHEROKEE, WAGONEER AND COMANCHE

1. Disconnect the negative battery cable. Drain the coolant.
2. Disconnect the heater hoses at the core tubes.
3. If equipped with air conditioning, discharge the refrigerant.

Heater and defroster assembly—typical Cherokee and Wagoneer

4. Disconnect the vent door cables and the blower motor electrical connectors. Disconnect the defroster duct.

5. Remove the nuts attaching the heater housing studs to the engine compartment side of the dash.

6. Remove the heater housing assembly by tilting it downward, to disengage it from the defroster duct, and pulling it rearward and out from under the instrument panel.

7. Remove the heater housing cover and remove the heater core.

To install:

8. Install the heater core in the housing and install the cover.

9. Position the heater hosuing on the dash panel and install the seals on the heater core outlet and inlet tubes, and over the blower housing.

10. Install the attaching nuts and tighten alternately until 2 threads are visible on each nut. Then tighten nuts to 46 inch lbs. (5 Nm).

NOTE: Overtightening the housing nuts can cause the housing to destort, resulting in air leaks.

11. Connect the defroster duct to the housing and the blower motor to the electrical connection.

12. Connect the vent door control cables and heater hoses.

13. Fill and bleed the cooling system. Check the system for proper operation.

Water Pump

Removal and Installation

EXCEPT 5.9L ENGINE

NOTE: Some vehicles with air conditioning use a serpentine drive belt and have a reverse rotating water pump coupled with a viscous fan drive assembly. The components are identified by the words REVERSE stamped on the cover of the viscous drive and on the inner side of the fan. The word REV is also cast into the body of the water pump.

1. Disconnect the negative battery cable. Drain the cooling system.

2. Disconnect the hoses at the pump.

3. Remove the drive belts.

4. Remove the power steering pump bracket.

5. Remove the fan and shroud.

6. Unbolt and remove the pump.

To install:

7. Clean the mating surfaces thoroughly.

8. Using a new gasket, install the pump and torque the bolts to 13 ft. lbs.

9. Reconnect the hoses at the pump and install accessory drive belt.

10. Install the power steering pump bracket. Install the fan and shroud.

11. Adjust the belt tension and fill the cooling system to the correct level.

12. On 2.5L engine, remove the coolant temperature sensor in the intake manifold to permit air to escape from the block. Reinstall the sensor when the cooling system is filled. Connect the negative battery cable.

13. Operate the engine with the heater control valve in the **HEAT** position until the thermostat opens to purge air from the system. Check coolant level and fill as required.

5.9L ENGINE

1. Disconnect the negative battery cable. Drain the cooling system.

2. Disconnect the upper radiator hoses at the radiator.

3. Loosen the accessory drive belts. Separate the fan shroud from the radiator and remove the fan assembly from the water pump.

4. Remove the water pump pulley. Remove the fan shroud.

5. Remove the alternator front mounting bracket. If equipped with air conditioning, remove the compressor bolts and pivot the compressor aside. Do not disconnect the compressor lines.

6. If equipped with power steering remove the stud/nut retaining the bracket and pivot the power steering/air pump assembly forward.

7. Disconnect the heater hose and bypass hose at the water pump. Disconnect the lower radiator hose at the water pump.

8. Remove the water pump mounting bolts and remove the pump from the engine.

To install:

9. Clean the gasket mating surfaces.

10. Install the water pump and gasket in position. Tighten the water pump-to-timing case bolts to 48 inch lbs. (5 Nm) and the water pump-to-block bolts to 28 ft. lbs. (38 Nm).

11. Install the power steering pump, air pump and bracket assembly.

12. Connect the heater hose, bypass hose and lower radiator hose. Pivot the air conditioning compressor into position.

13. Install the alternator front mounting brackets. Position the shroud against the engine and install the fan assembly.

14. Install the shroud to the radiator and install the accessory drive belts.

15. Connect the upper radiator hose. Connect the negative battery cable.

16. Fill the cooling system to the correct level and bleed the system.

Thermostat

Removal and Installation

1. Disconnect the negative battery cable. Remove the necessary hoses from the thermostat housing. Remove the 2 attaching screws and lift the housing from the engine.

2. Remove the thermostat and the gasket.

3. Clean all gasket surfaces throughly. Place the thermostat in the housing with the spring inside the engine.

4. Install a new gasket with a small amount of sealing compound applied to both sides. Install the water outlet and tighten the attaching bolts to 30 ft. lbs.

5. Refill the cooling system.

Cooling System Bleeding

After working on the cooling system, even to replace the thermostat, it must be bled. Air trapped in the system will prevent proper filling and leave the radiator coolant level low, causing a risk of overheating.

1. To bleed the system, start with the system cool, the radiator cap off and the radiator filled to about an inch below the filler neck.

NOTE: On 2.5L engine, remove the coolant temperature sensor in the intake manifold to permit air to escape from the block. Reinstall the sensor when the cooling system is filled.

2. Start the engine and run it at slightly above normal idle speed with the heater control in the **HEAT** position. This will insure adequate circulation. If air bubbles appear and the coolant level drops, fill the system with an antifreeze/water mixture to bring the level back to the proper level.

3. Run the engine this way until the thermostat opens. When this happens, coolant will move abruptly across the top of the radiator and the temperature of the radiator will suddenly rise.

4. At this point, air is often expelled and the level may drop quite a bit. Keep refilling the system until the level is near the top of the radiator and remains constant.

5. If equipped with an overflow tank, fill the radiator to the filler neck. Replace the radiator filler cap.

FUEL SYSTEM

Fuel System Service Precaution

Safety is the most important factor when performing not only fuel system maintenance but any type of maintenance. Failure to conduct maintenance and repairs in a safe manner may result in serious personal injury or death. Maintenance and testing of the vehicle's fuel system components can be accomplished safely and effectively by adhering to the following rules and guidelines.

• To avoid the possibility of fire and personal injury, always disconnect the negative battery cable unless the repair or test procedure requires that battery voltage be applied.

• Always relieve the fuel system pressure prior to disconnecting any fuel system component (injector, fuel rail, pressure regulator, etc.), fitting or fuel line connection. Exercise extreme caution whenever relieving fuel system pressure to avoid exposing skin, face and eyes to fuel spray. Fuel under pressure may penetrate the skin or any part of the body that it contacts.

• Always place a shop towel or cloth around the fitting or connection prior to loosening to absorb any excess fuel due to spillage. Ensure that all fuel spillage (should it occur) is quickly removed from engine surfaces. Ensure that all fuel soaked cloths or towels are deposited into a suitable waste container.

• Always keep a dry chemical (Class B) fire extinguisher near the work area.

• Do not allow fuel spray or fuel vapors to come into contact with a spark or open flame.

• Always use a backup wrench when loosening and tightening fuel line connection fittings. This will prevent unnecessary stress and torsion to fuel line piping. Always follow the proper torque specifications.

• Always replace worn fuel fitting O-rings with new. Do not substitute fuel hose or equivalent where fuel pipe is installed.

Relieving Fuel System Pressure

Fuel injection systems operate under high pressure, this makes it necessary to first relieve the system of pressure before servicing. The pressurized fuel when released may ignite or cause personal injury. the following outlined steps may be used for most fuel systems:

1. Disconnect the negative battery cable.

2. Remove the fuel tank filler cap.

3. Remove the cap from the pressure test port on the fuel rail in the engine compartment.

NOTE: Don't allow fuel to spray or spill on the engine or exhaust manifold. Place heavy shop towels under the pressure port to absorb any escaping fuel.

4. Using a small punch, push the test port valve in to relieve the fuel system pressure.

5. Reinstall the test port cap.

Fuel Tank

Removal and Installation

1. Disconnect the negative battery cable. Relieve the fuel system pressure.

2. Remove the fuel filler cap and drain the fuel tank.

3. Raise and support the vehicle safely.

4. Disconnect the fuel fill hose and vent hose from the filler neck.

5. Disconnect the fuel pump/gauge electrical connectors.

6. Label and disconnect all other fuel and vent hoses attached to the fuel tank.

7. If equipped, remove the skid plate. Remove the fuel tank shield.

NOTE: On Wrangler and Grand Wagoneer, the fuel tank and skid plate are removed as a unit. Do not loosen the fuel tank strap nuts. Remove the assembly by loosening the skid plate/fuel tank assembly mounting nuts.

8. Place a floorjack under the fuel tank. Remove the strap nuts and pull the straps away from the tank.

9. Lower the tank from the vehicle.

To install:

10. Raise the fuel tank into position and connect all fuel filler and vent hoses.

11. Wrap the straps around the fuel tank and tighten the nuts to: 100 inch lbs. (11 Nm) for Cherokee and Wagoneer; 65 inch lbs. (7 Nm) for 2 outer straps and 43 inch lbs. (5 Nm) for center strap on Comanche.

12. On Wrangler and Grand Wagoneer, tighten the skid plate/fuel tank assembly mounting nuts to 65 inch lbs. (7 Nm).

13. Install the tank shield and skid plate, as required.

14. Connect the fuel supply and vent hoses. Connect the fuel pump/gauge electrical connectors.

15. Lower the vehicle, fill the fuel tank, connect the negative battery cable, run the vehicle and check for leaks.

Fuel Filter

Removal and Installation

CARBURETED ENGINE

The fuel filter is located in the carburetor, at the inlet line.

1. Disconnect the negative battery cable.

2. Remove the fuel inlet line from carburetor.

3. Remove the large nut from the inlet port, use care not to loose the spring behind the nut.

4. Remove and clean or replace the filter.

5. Installation is the reverse of the removal procedure.

FUEL INJECTED ENGINE

The fuel filter is located at the rear of the vehicle, on the drivers side frame rail.

1. Disconnect the battery ground cable.

2. Remove the fuel tank filler cap.

3. Relieve the fuel system pressure.

4. Raise and support the rear of the vehicle safely.

5. Remove the hoses and clamps from the filter.

6. Remove the filter strap bolt and remove the filter.

NOTE: The filter is marked for installation. IN goes towards the fuel tank; OUT towards the engine.

7. Place the new filter on the frame rail and tighten the strap bolt to 106 inch lbs.

8. Install and securely clamp the hoses.

Mechanical Fuel Pump

Pressure Testing

1. Disconnect the fuel inlet line at the carburetor.

2. Install a T-fitting on the open end of the fuel line and refit the line to the carburetor.

3. Plug a pressure gauge into the remaining opening of the T-fitting. The hose leading to the pressure gauge should not be any longer than 6 in. On pumps with a fuel return line, the line must be plugged.

4. Start the engine and allow it to idle. Fuel pressure readings should be 4–5 psi @ idle for the 4.2L engine or 6.00–7.50 psi @ idle for the 5.9L engine.

Removal and Installation

1. Disconnect the negative battery cable. Remove all the necessary components in order to gain access to the fuel pump. Disconnect the fuel lines.

2. Remove the attaching bolts that hold the fuel pump to the engine and lift the fuel pump off of the engine.

3. Before installing the fuel pump, make sure all of the mating surfaces are clean.

To install:

4. Cement a new gasket to the mating surface of the fuel pump.

5. Position the fuel pump on the cylinder block so the cam lever of the pump rests on the camshaft.

6. Secure the pump to the engine with the retaining bolts and lock washers. Tighten bolts to 13 ft. lbs. (18 Nm).

7. Connect the fuel lines to the fuel pump. Tighten fuel lines to 18 ft. lbs. (25 Nm).

Electric Fuel Pump

The fuel pump for fuel injected vehicles is located in the fuel tank attached to the fuel gauge sending unit.

Pressure Testing

THROTTLE BODY INJECTION

1. Remove the fuel pressure test port plug from the throttle body.

2. Install a pressure test fitting in the port.

3. Connect an 0–30 psi. gauge to the fitting.

4. Start the engine and allow it to idle.

5. The pressure gauge should read 14–15 psi. If the pressure is not in this range, adjust the pressure regulator to obtain the correct reading.

6. To adjust the pressure regulator, turn the screw at the bottom of the regulator in to increase the pressure and out to reduce the pressure.

MULTI-PORT FUEL INJECTION

1. Connect an 0–60 psi fuel pressure gauge to the test port pressure fitting on the fuel rail.

2. Remove the vacuum line from the fuel pressure regulator.

3. Start the engine and note the gauge reading.

4. The fuel pressure should be approximately 39 psi.

5. Reconnect the vacuum line to the pressure regulator, the fuel pressure should be approximately 31 psi.

6. If the fuel pressure is not approximately 8–10 psi higher with the vacuum line removed, check the line for kinks or pinches.

7. If the fuel pressure is below, momentarily pinch shut the hose section of the fuel line. If the pressure remains low, inspect the fuel supply system for blockage.

Removal and Installation

1. Disconnect the negative battery cable.

2. Remove the fuel tank filler cap.

3. Drain the fuel from the fuel tank.

4. Raise and safely support the rear of the vehicle.

5. Remove the fuel inlet and outlet hoses from the sending unit.

6. Remove the sending unit wires.

7. Using a brass punch and hammer, remove the sending unit retaining lock ring by tapping it counterclockwise.

8. Remove the sending unit, which incorporates the electric fuel pump, along with the O-ring seal from the fuel tank. Discard the O-ring.

9. Remove and discard the pump inlet filter.

Electric fuel pumps—fuel injected vehicles

TBI
FUEL
PUMP

MPI
FUEL
PUMP

10. Disconnect the fuel pump terminal wires.
11. Remove the pump outlet hose and clamp.
12. Remove the pump top mounting bracket nut and remove the pump.
To install:
13. Install a new inlet filter on the pump.
14. Assemble the pump and bracket. Connect the hose and wiring.
15. Install the unit and new O-ring in the tank. The rubber stopper on the end of the fuel return tube must be inserted into the cup in the fuel tank reservoir.
16. Install the lock ring. Carefully tap it into place until it seats against the stop on the tank.
17. Connect the hoses.
18. Connect the wiring.
19. Lower the vehicle, refill the fuel tank, run the engine and check for leaks.

Carburetor

The 4.2L engine is equipped with a model BBD 2-barrel feedback carburetor. The 5.9L engine is equipped with a model 2150 2-barrel caburetor.

Removal and Installation

1. Disconnect the negative battery cable. Remove the air cleaner assembly.
2. Remove the necessary components in order to gain access to the carburetor retaining bolts. Disconnect and plug the fuel line. Disconnect all electrical connectors, as required.
3. Disconnect the accelerator linkage. Disconnect the automatic transmission linkage, as required.
4. Remove the carburetor retaining bolts. Remove the carburetor from the vehicle.
To install:
5. Clean the gasket mating surfaces throughly.
6. If equipped, position the spacer and gasket. Tighten the bolts alternately in a criss-cross pattern to 7 ft. lbs. (9 Nm).
7. Install the carburetor and tighten the mounting nuts to 16 ft. lbs. (22 Nm).
8. Connect the fuel line, accelerator linkage and automatic

transmission linkage. Install any previously removed component.
9. Connect the negative battery cable, start the engine and adjust the idle speed.

Idle Speed Adjustment

4.2L ENGINE WITH BBD CARBURETOR AND CEC SYSTEM

1. Run the engine until normal operating temperature is reached. Connect a tachometer to the ignition coil negative terminal. The carburetor choke and intake manifold heater must be **OFF**. This occurs when the engine coolant heats to approximately 160°F.
2. Remove the vacuum hose to the solevac vacuum actuator unit. Plug the vacuum hose. Disconnect the holding solenoid wire connector.
3. Adjust the curb idle speed screw to specification.
4. Apply a direct source of vacuum to the vacuum actuator, using a hand vacuum pump or its equivalent. When the solevac throttle positioner is fully extended, turn the vacuum actuator adjustment screw on the throttler lever until the specified engine rpm is obtained. Disconnect the vacuum source from the vacuum actuator.
5. With a jumper wire, apply battery voltage to energize the holding solenoid. The holding wire connector can be installed and either the rear window defroster or the air conditioner, with the compressor clutch wire disconnected, can be turned on to energize the holding solenoid.
6. Hold the throttle open manually to allow the throttle positioner to fully extend. Without the vacuum actuator, the throttle must be opened manually to allow the solevac throttle positioner to fully extend.
7. If the holding solenoid idle speed is not within specifications, adjust the idle using the ¼ in. hex head adjustment screw on the end of the solevac unit. .
8. Disconnect the jumper wire from the solevac solenoid wire connector, if used. Connect the wire connector to the solevac unit, if not connected. Install the original vacuum hose to the vacuum actuator.
9. Remove the tachometer and if disconnected, connect the compressor clutch wire.

5.9L ENGINE WITH 2150 CARBURETOR

NOTE: If equipped with automatic transmission, lock the parking brake, block the wheels and place the selector lever in DRIVE before adjusting the idle speed.

1. Connect a tachometer to the ignition coil negative terminal.
2. Start the engine and allow it to reach normal operating temperature.
3. Turn the hex head adjustment screw on the solenoid carriage to obtain the correct engine speed.
4. Disconnect the solenoid wire connector and adjust the curb idle speed screw to specification.
5. Reconnect the solenoid wire connector and stop the engine.
6. If equipped with a dashpot, position the throttle at the curb idle position and depress the dashpot stem.
7. Measure the clearance between the stem and the throttle lever. A clearance of 0.032 in. should exist.
8. Adjust the clearance as required by loosening the locknut and turning the dashpot until the correct clearance is obtained. Tighten the dashpot locknut.

Idle Mixture Adjustment

4.2L ENGINE WITH BBD CARBURETOR AND CEC SYSTEM

The idle mixture adjustment should only be performed if the adjustment screws were removed during a carburetor overhaul procedure. When the carburetor is mounted to the engine, it must be removed to gain access to the dowel pin locations, whose removal must be accomplished before any adjustment of the mixture screws can be made.

1. Connect a tachometer to the engine. Run the engine until normal operating temperature is reached.

2. Set the parking brake firmly and chock the wheels. Position the gear selector in neutral for manual transmission or in **D** for automatic transmission. Adjust the idle speed.

3. Adjust the idle mixture screws clockwise (lean) until a loss of engine rpm is noted. Idle drop specification is 50 rpm for both automatic and manual transmission.

4. Turn the idle mixture screws counterclockwise (rich) until the highest engine rpm indication is obtained.

NOTE: Do not turn the screws any further than the point at which the highest engine rpm is first obtained. This is referred to as best lean mixture. The engine idle speed will increase above the curb idle speed by an amount that corresponds approximately to the idle drop specifications listed on the Emission Information Label.

5. Turn the mixture screws clockwise (lean) to obtain the specified drop in engine rpm. Turn both mixture screws in small, equal amounts until the specified idle drop is achieved.

6. If the final engine rpm differs ±30 rpm from the original curb idle rpm, adjust the curb idle speed to specifications and repeat the mixture adjustment procedure.

7. Install the dowel pins after completing the idle mixture adjustment. Use care not to disturb the mixture screw positions. It is necessary to remove the carburetor to gain access to the dowel pin locations. After the carburetor has been reinstalled, again check the idle speed specifications and correct as required.

5.9L ENGINE WITH 2150 CARBURETOR

NOTE: The idle mixture adjustment screws are concealed by tamper resistant caps. The idle mixture should be adjusted only if the mixture adjustment screws were removed or altered during major carburetor overhaul or tampering.

Carburetor mounting and connections

Carburetor adjustment screw locations

1. Connect a tachometer to the engine.

2. Start the engine and allow it to reach normal operating temperature.

3. Set the parking brake and chock the wheels. Position the automatic transmission in **D**.

4. Be sure choke is completely off and the idle speed is set to specifications.

5. Turn the idle mixture adjusting screws clockwise (leaner) until a perceptible loss of engine speed is noted on the tachometer.

6. Turn the idle mixture adjusting screws counterclockwise (richer) until the highest engine speed is obtained.

7. This position of the idle mixture adjusting screws is referred to as the lean best idle.

8. Turn both idle mixture adjusting screws clockwise in small, equal amounts until the specified idle speed drop is noted on the tachometer.

Service Adjustments

For all carburetor service adjustment procedures and specifications, please refer to "Carburetor Service" in the Unit Repair section.

Fuel Injection

Idle Speed and Mixture Adjustment

Idle speed and mixture adjustment are controlled by the ECU and are not adjustable.

For further information, please refer to Chilton's Electronic Engine Controls Manual.

Fuel Injector

Removal and Installation

THROTTLE BODY INJECTION

1. Disconnect the negative battery cable. Remove the air

Throttle body fuel injector components

cleaner and hose assembly. Relieve the fuel system pressure as necessary.

2. Remove the throttle body upper and lower covers.

3. Remove the fuel injector wire by compressing the tabs and pulling it upwards.

4. Remove the fuel injector retainer clip screws. Remove the fuel injector retainer clip.

NOTE: The injector has a small locating tab that fits into a slot in the bottom of the injector bore of the throttle body. Do not twist the injector during removal.

5. Using a small pair of pliers, gently grasp the center collar of the injector, between the electrical terminals, and carefully remove the injector using a lifting-rocking motion.

6. Discard the centering ring and the upper and lower O-rings. Never reuse these rings!

7. Installation is the reverse of the removal procedure. Lubricate both O-rings with light oil before installation. Align the tab on the injector with the slot in the throttle body.

MULTI-PORT FUEL INJECTION

1. Disconnect the negative battery cable. Relieve fuel system pressure.

2. Disconnect the fuel lines at the ends of the fuel rail assembly.

3. Mark and disconnect the injector wire harness connectors.

4. Remove the fuel rail retaining bolts.

5. Disconnect the vacuum line from the fuel pressure regulator.

6. Remove the fuel rail assembly from the engine.

NOTE: On models with automatic transmission, it may be necessary to remove the automatic transmission throttle pressure cable and bracket to remove the fuel rail assembly.

Fuel rail assembly location and mounting—4.0L engine

7. Remove the clips that retain the injectors to the fuel rail and remove the injectors. An O-ring kit is available which consists of 6 brown seals and 7 black seals. The brown seals fit on the injector tip area and seal the injector to the intake manifold. The black seals fit on the rail end of the injector to to seal the injector when it is installed into the fuel rail. The last black seal is for the fuel pressure regulator to seal the pressure regulator to the fuel rail. These seals cannot be interchanged.

8. Installation is the reverse of removal. Tighten the fuel rail mounting bolts to 20 ft. lbs. (27 Nm).

EMISSION CONTROLS

For further information, please refer to Chilton's Emission Controls Manual.

Emission Warning Lamps

The emission maintenance reminder light is connected to a timer, which will activate a light when PCV valve and oxygen sensor service is required. The interval for this light is 82,500 miles, at which time the timer module must be replaced as part of the emission service. There is no way to reset the light, except to replace the timer module.

The timer module is located under the instrument panel, above the parking brake assembly.

ENGINE MECHANICAL

NOTE: Disconnecting the battery cable on some vehicles may interfere with the functions of the on board computer systems and may require the computer to undergo a relearning process, once the negative battery cable is disconnected.

Engine

Removal and Installation

2.5L ENGINE

1. Disconnect the negative battery cable. As required, relieve the fuel system pressure.
2. Matchmark the hood and hinges, and remove the hood.
3. Remove the air cleaner. Drain the coolant and engine oil.
4. Remove the radiator hoses. Remove the fan shroud and transmission cooler lines.
5. Discharge the refrigerant. Remove the condenser and radiator.
6. Remove the fan and install a $5/16$ in. × $1/2$ in. bolt through the pulley and into the water pump flange to maintain pulley alignment.
7. Disconnect the heater hoses.
8. Disconnect and tag all wires, hoses, and cables connected to the engine.
9. Remove the service ports from the air conditioning compressor and cap the openings.
10. Drain the power steering reservoir. Remove the power steering hoses at the gear.
11. Remove the check valve from the power brake vacuum hose.
12. Raise and safely support the vehicle.
13. Remove the starter. Disconnect the exhaust pipe at the manifold.
14. Remove the converter access plate, if equipped with an automatic transmission.
15. If equipped with automatic transmission, matchmark the torque converter and flywheel. Remove the attaching bolts.
16. Remove the upper flywheel housing-to-engine bolts; loosen the lower ones.
17. Lower the vehicle. Connect an engine lift to the engine and remove the weight from the engine.
18. Remove the engine mount bolts. Raise the engine off the mounts.
19. Support the transmission with a floor jack.
20. Remove the remaining engine-to-flywheel housing bolts.
21. Move the engine forward to clear the transmission and lift it from the vehicle.

To install:

22. Lower the engine into the vehicle.

NOTE: Be sure to align the engine with the mounts.

23. On vehicles with a manual transmission, engage the transmission input shaft with the clutch splines. Align the flywheel housing bolt holes and install the lower engine-to-transmission bolts finger-tight.
24. On vehicles with an automatic transmission, align the torque converter housing and engine. Loosely install the 4 lower transmission-to-engine bolts.
25. Lower the engine onto the mounts. Remove the lifting device.
26. If equipped with an automatic transmission, install the torque converter-to-flywheel bolts. Torque the bolts to 40 ft. lbs.
27. Install the converter housing access plate.
28. Install the remaining engine-to-flywheel housing bolts. Torque the upper bolts to 27 ft. lbs.; the lower bolts to 43 ft. lbs.
29. Install the engine mount bolts. Torque the bolts to 48 ft. lbs.
30. Connect the exhaust pipe at the manifold. Torque the bolts to 23 ft. lbs.
31. Install the starter. Install the check valve on the power brake vacuum hose.
32. Install the power steering hoses at the gear. Fill the power steering reservoir.
33. Install the service ports on the air conditioning compressor.
34. Connect all wires, hoses, and cables to the engine.
35. Install the fan and pulley. Install the condenser and radiator.
36. Install the fan shroud and transmission cooler lines. Connect the radiator hoses.
37. Fill the cooling system and crankcase to the correct levels.
38. Install the air cleaner. Install the hood.
39. Connect the negative battery cable.
40. Evacuate, charge and leak test the refrigerant system.

4.0L ENGINE

1. Disconnect the battery cables. Matchmark the hood and hinges and remove the hood.
2. Raise and safely support the vehicle. Drain the engine oil. Drain the cooling system. Lower the vehicle. Relieve the fuel system pressure.
3. Remove the battery and remove the air cleaner.
4. Remove the upper and lower radiator hoses.
5. Disconnect and cap the automatic transmission cooler lines, if equipped.
6. Remove the fan shroud and remove the radiator. Remove the electric cooling fan.
7. Disconnect the vacuum harness connector at the intake manifold.
8. Disconnect the electric fan switch. On vehicles with air conditioning, discharge the system, remove the compressor service valves and cap the ports.
9. Remove the radiator or radiator/condenser assembly. Disconnect the accelerator linkage. Disconnect the heater hoses at the engine.
10. Disconnect the cruise control cable, if equipped. Disconnect and tag all wires, hoses, cables, vacuum lines, etc., connected to the engine or in the way of engine removal.
11. Disconnect the injection system wiring harness at the firewall.
12. Disconnect the quick-connect fuel lines at the fuel rail and return line by squeezing the 2 tabs against the tube. Pull the fuel tube and retainer from the quick-connect fiting.
13. Remove the power brake vacuum check valve from the booster.
14. Disconnect the power steering hoses from the steering gear, drain the pump reservoir, and cap all openings.
15. Raise and safely support the vehicle. Remove the starter and disconnect the exhaust pipe at the support bracket and the manifold.
16. Disconnect the engine speed sensor wiring (2 screws). Remove the exhaust pipe support bracket.
17. If equipped with an automatic transmission, remove the inspection cover. Matchmark the torque converter and flexplate. Turning the engine by hand, remove each torque converter-to-flexplate bolt.
18. Remove the upper flywheel housing-to-engine bolts and loosen the bottom bolts.
19. Remove the engine front support-to-frame nuts and lower the vehicle.
20. Take up the weight of the engine with a lifting device. Support the transmission with a jack.
21. Remove the lower engine-to-bell housing bolts. Raise the engine, while guiding it forward and out of the vehicle.

To install:

22. Lower the engine into the vehicle.

NOTE: Be very careful to avoid damaging the trigger wheel on the flywheel, if equipped with an automatic transmission.

23. If equipped with a manual transmission, insert the input shaft into the clutch splines, align the flywheel housing with the engine and install the lower bolts finger-tight.
24. If equipped with an automatic transmission, align the engine and converter housing and install the 4 lower bolts finger-tight.
25. Install the engine mount bolts finger-tight.
26. Remove the transmission support and the engine lifting device.
27. Install the remaining flywheel housing-to-engine bolts and tighten all bolts to 28 ft. lbs. Raise and safely support the vehicle.
28. If equipped with an automatic transmission, turn the engine by hand and install each torque converter-to-flexplate bolt. Torque the bolts to 40 ft. lbs. Install the access cover.
29. Remove the exhaust pipe support bracket and connect the exhaust pipe.
30. Connect the engine speed sensor wiring (2 screws). Install the starter.
31. Connect the power steering hoses at the gear and fill the pump reservoir.
32. Install the power brake vacuum check valve at the booster.
33. Connect the quick-connect fuel lines at the fuel rail and return line.
34. Connect the injection system wiring harness at the firewall. Connect all wires, hoses, cables, vacuum lines, etc. Connect the cruise control cable.
35. Connect the accelerator linkage. Install the radiator or radiator/condenser assembly. If equipped with air conditioning, install the compressor service valves.
36. Install the electric cooling fan and connect the electric fan switch.
37. Connect the vacuum harness connector at the intake manifold. Install the fan shroud.
38. Connect the automatic transmission cooler lines. Install the upper and lower radiator hoses. Install the air cleaner and the battery.
39. Refill the cooling system and the crankcase. Install the hood.
40. Evacuate, charge and leak test the refrigerant system.

4.2L ENGINE

1. Disconnect the negative battery cable. As required, relieve the fuel system pressure. Remove the air cleaner. Drain the cooling system and the engine oil.
2. Disconnect the upper and lower radiator hoses.
3. If equipped with an automatic transmission, disconnect the cooler lines from the radiator. Remove the radiator and the fan. If equipped with air onditioning, evacuate the system, remove the condenser and cap all openings immediately.
4. If equipped, remove the power steering pump and the drive belt, and place the unit aside. Do not remove the power steering hoses.
5. If equipped with air conditioning, remove the compressor. Disconnect all wires, lines, linkage and hoses that are connected to the engine. Remove the oil filter.
6. Remove both of the engine front support cushion-to-frame retaining nuts.
7. Disconnect the exhaust pipe at the support bracket and exhaust manifold.
8. Support the weight of the engine with a lifting device.
9. Remove the front support cushion and bracket assemblies from the engine.
10. Remove the transfer case shift lever boot and the transmission access cover.
11. If equipped with an automatic transmission, remove the upper bolts securing the transmission bell housing to the engine. If equipped with a manual transmission, remove the upper bolts that secure the clutch housing to the engine.
12. Remove the starter motor. If equipped with an automatic transmission:

    a. Remove the engine to transmission adapter plate inspection covers.

    b. Mark the assembled position of the converter and flexplate and remove the converter-to-flexplate retaining screws.

    c. Remove the remaining bolts securing the transmission bell housing to the engine.

13. If equipped with a manual transmission, remove the lower cover of the clutch housing and the remaining bolts that secure the clutch housing to the engine.
14. Support the transmission with a floor jack.
15. Attach a lifting device to the engine and using a hoist, lift the engine upward and forward at the same time, removing it from the vehicle.

To install:

16. Lower the engine into the vehicle and slide it rearward to engage the transmission.

17. If equipped with an automatic transmission, install the upper bolts securing the transmission bell housing to the engine. Torque to 27 ft. lbs. If equipped with a manual transmission, install the upper bolts that secure the clutch housing to the engine. Torque to 27 ft. lbs.

18. If equipped with a manual transmission, install the lower cover of the clutch housing and the remaining bolts that secure the clutch housing to the engine. Torque the clutch housing spacer-to-bolts to 12–15 ft. lbs. Torque the clutch housing lower bolts to 43 ft. lbs.

19. If equipped with an automatic transmission:

a. Install the remaining bolts securing the transmission bell housing to the engine. Torque the bell housing lower bolts to 43 ft. lbs.

b. Mark the assembled position of the converter and flexplate and install the converter-to-flexplate retaining screws. Torque the bolts to 20–25 ft. lbs.

c. Install the engine to transmission adapter plate inspection covers.

20. Install the starter motor. Torque the mounting bolts to 18 ft. lbs.

21. Install the transfer case shift lever boot and the transmission access cover.

22. Install the front support cushion and bracket assemblies from the engine.

23. Remove the lifting device.

24. Connect the exhaust pipe at the support bracket and exhaust manifold. Torque the nuts to 20 ft. lbs.

25. Install both of the engine front support cushion-to-frame retaining nuts. Torque to 35 ft. lbs.

26. Connect all wires, lines, linkage, and hoses that are connected to the engine. Install the oil filter.

27. If equipped, install the power steering pump and the drive belt.

28. Install the radiator and the fan, and the condenser. Evacuate, charge and leak test the refrigerant system.

29. If equipped with an automatic transmission, connect the cooler lines to the radiator.

30. Connect the upper and lower radiator hoses and fill the cooling system.

31. Install the air cleaner. Connect the negative battery cable.

5.9L ENGINE

1. Disconnect the negative battery cable. Remove the air cleaner.

2. Drain the cooling system.

3. Disconnect the upper and lower radiator hoses.

4. If equipped with an automatic transmission, disconnect the cooler lines from the radiator.

5. Remove the radiator and the fan. If equipped with air conditioning, evacuate the system, remove the condenser and cap all openings immediately.

6. If equipped, remove the power steering pump and the drive belt, place the unit aside. Do not remove the power steering hoses.

7. If equipped with air conditioning, remove the compressor.

8. Disconnect all wires, lines, linkage and hoses that are connected to the engine. Raise and safely support the vehicle.

9. Remove both of the engine front support cushion-to-frame retaining nuts.

10. Disconnect the exhaust pipes at the support bracket and exhaust manifold.

11. Support the weight of the engine with a lifting device.

12. Remove the front support cushion and bracket assemblies from the engine.

13. Remove the transfer case shift lever boot and the transmission access cover.

14. If equipped with an automatic transmission, remove the upper bolts securing the transmission bell housing to the engine. If equipped with a manual transmission, remove the upper bolts that secure the clutch housing to the engine.

15. Remove the starter motor.

16. If equipped with an automatic transmission:

a. Remove the engine to transmission adapter plate inspection covers.

b. Mark the assembled position of the converter and flexplate and remove the converter-to-flexplate retaining screws.

c. Remove the remaining bolts securing the transmission bell housing to the engine.

17. If equipped with a manual transmission, remove the lower cover of the clutch housing and the remaining bolts that secure the clutch housing to the engine. Lower the vehicle.

18. Support the transmission with a jack.

19. Attach a lifting device to the engine and lift the engine upward and forward at the same time, removing it from the vehicle.

To install:

20. Lower the engine into the vehicle and slide it rearward to engage the transmission.

21. If equipped with an automatic transmission, install the upper bolts securing the transmission bell housing to the engine. Torque them to 27 ft. lbs. If equipped with a manual transmission, install the upper bolts that secure the clutch housing to the engine. Torque them to 27 ft. lbs.

22. If equipped with a manual transmission, install the lower cover of the clutch housing and the remaining bolts that secure the clutch housing to the engine. Torque the clutch housing spacer-to-bolts to 12–15 ft. lbs. Torque the clutch housing lower bolts to 43 ft. lbs.

23. If equipped with an automatic transmission:

a. Install the remaining bolts securing the transmission bell housing to the engine. Torque the bell housing lower bolts to 43 ft. lbs.

b. Mark the assembled position of the converter and flexplate and install the converter-to-flexplate retaining screws. Torque the bolts to 20–25 ft. lbs.

c. Install the engine to transmission adapter plate inspection covers.

24. Install the starter motor. Torque the mounting bolts to 18 ft. lbs.

25. Install the transfer case shift lever boot and the transmission access cover.

26. Install the front support cushion and bracket assemblies from the engine.

27. Remove the lifting device.

28. Connect the exhaust pipes at the support bracket and exhaust manifold. Torque the nuts to 20 ft. lbs.

29. Install both of the engine front support cushion-to-frame retaining nuts. Torque them to 35 ft. lbs.

30. Connect all wires, lines, linkage, and hoses to the engine.

31. If equipped, install the power steering pump and the drive belt.

NOTE: If the vehicle has air conditioning, mount and connect the air conditioning compressor.

32. Install the radiator, fan and the condenser.

33. Evacuate, charge and leak test the refrigerant system.

34. If equipped with an automatic transmission, connect the cooler lines to the radiator.

35. Connect the upper and lower radiator hoses.

36. Fill the cooling system and connect the negative battery cable.

37. Install the air cleaner.

Service Tips

4.0L AND 4.2L ENGINES VIBRATION DURING ACCELERATION

On some vehicles equipped with the 4.0L and 4.2L engines, a metalic vibration may be noticed during heavy acceleration. The noise will intensify if the drive train is in the 4WD mode. The vibration may be caused by a defective left motor mount.

Engine Mounts

Removal and Installation

1. Disconnect the negative battery cable. Raise and support the vehicle safely.
2. Support the engine using a floor jack and a block of wood under the oil pan.
3. Remove the nut from the through-bolt but do not remove the through-bolt.
4. Remove the retaining bolts and nuts from the engine support cushions.
5. Remove the engine support cushions.

To install:

6. If the engine support bracket was removed, position the bracket and install the attaching bolts. Tighten the bolts to 45 ft. lbs. (61 Nm).
7. Install the engine support cushion and the through-bolt. Install the engine support cushion attaching bolts and tighten to 30–48 ft. lbs. (40–65 Nm). Tighten the through-bolt to 48 ft. lbs. (65 Nm).
8. Remove the engine support, lower the vehicle and connect the negative battery cable.

Cylinder Head

Removal and Installation

2.5L ENGINE

1. Disconnect the negative battery cable. As required, relieve the fuel system pressure.
2. Drain the cooling system.
3. Disconnect the hoses at the thermostat housing.
4. Remove the air cleaner.
5. Remove the rocker arm cover. The cover seal is RTV sealer. Break the seal with a clean putty knife or razor blade. Don't attempt to remove the cover until the seal is broken. To remove the cover, pry where indicated at the bolt holes.
6. Remove the rocker arms and the pushrods. Keep them in their original order for installation.
7. Remove the power steering pump bracket. Suspend the pump aside.
8. Remove the intake and exhaust manifolds.
9. Remove the air conditioning compressor drive belt, if equipped.
10. Loosen the alternator drive belt. Remove the compressor/alternator bracket mounting bolt and unbolt the compressor. Suspend it aside without disconnecting the refrigerant lines.

Service Tips

2.5L AND 4.0L ENGINES VALVE SPRINGS AND RETAINERS

Two types of valve springs and retainers are used in early 1988 vehicles equipped with the 2.5L and 4.0L engines. Type 1 is cone shaped and measures 2 inches (50.8mm) long. Type 2 is cylinder shaped and measures 1.82 inches (46.2mm) long.

The two types of valve springs and retainers are not interchangeable. Engines equipped with Type 2 valve springs and retainers will be stamped with an **S** after the engine build date code.

Cylinder head bolt torque sequence—2.5L engine

11. Remove the spark plugs. Disconnect the temperature sending unit wire.
12. Remove the cylinder head bolts in the reverse order of the installation torque sequence.
13. Lift the head off the engine and remove the head gasket.
14. Thoroughly clean the gasket mating surfaces. Remove all traces of old gasket material. Remove all carbon deposits from the combustion chambers. Lay a straight-edge across the head and check for flatness. Total deviation should not exceed 0.025mm.

To install:

15. Install the head gasket. Do not apply sealer as the cylinder head gaskets are of a composition type.
16. Fabricate 2 cylinder head alignment dowels from used head bolts. Using the longest bolts, trim the hex head off and cut slots into the top.

NOTE: Cylinder head bolts should be reused only once. Replace the head bolts which were previously used or are marked with paint. If head bolts are to be reused, mark each head bolt with paint for future reference. Head bolts should be installed using sealer.

17. Install the cylinder head and tighten the head bolts in the proper sequence to the followng torque specifications:

a. 1988—Using 3 steps, tighten all bolts (except bolt 8) to 85 ft. lbs. Tighten bolt 8 to 75 ft. lbs.

b. 1989–92—First, tighten all bolts to 22 ft. lbs. Next, tighten all bolts to 45 ft. lbs. Third, tighten all bolts, except bolt 7, to 110 ft. lbs. Last, tighten bolt 7 to 100 ft. lbs.

18. Connect the temperature sending unit wire. Install the spark plugs. Install the compressor/alternator bracket mounting bolt.

19. Install the accessory drive belt. Install the intake and exhaust manifolds. Install the power steering pump bracket.

20. Install the pushrods and rocker arms in their original positions.

21. Install the rocker arm cover. The cover gasket is RTV sealer. Thoroughly clean the mating surfaces of the head and rocker cover. Run a ⅛ in. bead of RTV sealer along the length of the sealing surface of the head. Position the cover on the head within 10 minutes of applying the sealer. Torque the cover bolts, in a criss-cross pattern, to 55 inch lbs.

22. Install the air cleaner. Connect the hoses at the thermostat housing.

23. Fill the cooling system. Connect the negative battery cable.

24. Run the engine to normal operating temperature and check for leaks.

4.0L AND 4.2L ENGINES

1. Disconnect the negative battery cable. Drain the cooling system and disconnect the hoses at the thermostat housing. As required, relieve the fuel system pressure.

2. Remove the cylinder head cover (valve cover), the gasket, the rocker arm assembly and the pushrods.

NOTE: The pushrods must be replaced in their original positions.

3. Remove the intake and exhaust manifold from the cylinder head.

4. Disconnect the spark plug wires and the spark plugs to avoid damaging them.

5. Disconnect the temperature sending unit wire, ignition coil and bracket assembly from the engine.

6. Unbolt and set aside the power steering pump and bracket. Do not disconnect the hoses.

7. Remove the intake and exhaust manifold assembly.

8. Remove the air conditioning compressor drive belt pulley.

9. Loosen the serpentine belt tension.

10. Remove the alternator.

11. Unbolt the air conditioning compressor and set it aside. Don't disconnect the refrigerant lines.

12. Remove the ignition coil.

13. Remove the cylinder head bolts, the cylinder head and gasket from the block.

Cylinder head bolt torque sequence—4.0L and 4.2L engines

NOTE: On 1990–92 vehicles, bolt No. 14 cannot be removed until the head is moved forward. Pull the bolt out as far as it will go and suspend in place by wrapping with tape.

14. Discard the gasket. Thoroughly clean the head and block mating surfaces. Check them for warpage with a straight-edge. Deviation should not exceed 0.002 in. in a 6 in. span.

To install:

15. Coat a new head gasket with sealer and place it on the block. Most replacement gaskets will have the word **TOP** stamped on them.

NOTE: Apply sealing compound only to the cylinder head gasket. Do not allow sealing compund to enter the cylinder bore.

16. Install the cylinder head and bolts. The threads of bolt No. 11 must be coated with Loctite® 592 sealant before installation. Tighten the bolts in 3 steps, using the correct sequence, to 22 ft. lbs. Then, torque them to 45 ft. lbs. When complete, check the torque at 45 ft. lbs. Then, torque all the bolts, except bolt 11, in sequence to 110 ft. lbs. Tighten bolt 11 to 100 ft. lbs.

NOTE: Cylinder head bolts should be reused only once. Replace the head bolts which were previously used or are marked with paint. If head bolts are to be reused, mark each head bolt with paint for future reference. Head bolts should be installed using sealer.

17. Install the ignition coil.

18. Install the air conditioning compressor. Install the alternator.

19. Adjust the serpentine belt tension.

20. Install the air conditioning compressor drive belt pulley.

21. Install the intake and exhaust manifold assembly.

22. Install the power steering pump and bracket.

23. Connect the temperature sending unit wire, ignition coil and bracket.

24. Connect the spark plug wires.

25. Install the pushrods, rocker arm assembly, gasket and cylinder head cover.

26. Connect the hoses at the thermostat housing.

27. Fill the cooling system. Connect the negative battery cable.

28. Run the engine to normal operating temperature and check for leaks.

5.9L ENGINE

1. Disconnect the negative battery cable. Drain the cooling system.

Cylinder head bolt torque sequence—5.9L engine

2. When removing the right cylinder head, it may be necessary to remove the heater core housing from the firewall.

3. Remove the valve cover(s) and gasket(s).

4. Remove the rocker arm assemblies and the pushrods.

NOTE: The valve train components must be replaced in their original positions.

5. Remove the spark plugs to avoid damaging them.

6. Remove the intake manifold with the carburetor still attached.

7. Remove the exhaust pipes at the flange of the exhaust manifold. When replacing the exhaust pipes it is advisable to install new gaskets at the flange.

8. Loosen the accessory drive belts.

9. Disconnect the alternator bracket, air conditioner compressor bracket and remove the negative battery cable from the right cylinder head. Disconnect the air pump and power steering bracket from the left cylinder head.

10. Disconnect the air pump and power steering pump brackets from the left cylinder head.

11. Remove the cylinder head bolts and lift the head(s) from the cylinder block.

12. Remove the cylinder head gasket from the head or the block.

13. Thoroughly clean the gasket mating surfaces. Remove all traces of old gasket material. Remove all carbon deposits from the combustion chambers. Lay a straight-edge across the head and check for flatness. Total deviation should not exceed 0.001 in. (0.025mm).

To install:

14. Do not apply sealant to the head or block. Coat both sides of the gasket with sealer. The gasket should be stamped **TOP** for installation. Place the gasket on the block.

15. Install the head on the block. Insert the bolts and tighten, in sequence, to 80 ft. lbs. Then retighten to 110 ft. lbs.

16. Connect the air pump and power steering pump brackets to the left cylinder head.

17. Connect the alternator bracket to the right cylinder head.

18. Adjust all the accessory drive belts.

19. Install the exhaust pipes at the flange of the exhaust manifold. When replacing the exhaust pipes it is advisable to install new gaskets at the flange.

20. Install the intake manifold with the carburetor still attached.

21. Install the spark plugs.

22. Install the rocker arm assemblies and the pushrods.

NOTE: The valve train components must be replaced in their original positions.

23. Install the valve cover(s) and gasket(s).

24. Install the heater core housing on the firewall, if removed.

25. Fill the cooling system and connect the negative battery cable.

26. Run the engine to normal operating temperature and check for leaks.

Valve Lifters

Removal and Installation

1. Disconnect the negative battery cable. Remove the rocker arm cover.

2. Remove the rocker arm assembly by alternately loosening the capscrews 1 turn at a time.

3. Remove the pushrods. Keep all components in the order they were removed.

4. On the 5.9L engine, remove the intake manifold. Remove the lifters using a hydraulic lifter removal tool.

5. On all other engines, remove the lifter through the pushrod opening in the cylinder head using a hydraulic lifter removal tool.

To install:

6. Dip each lifter in MOPAR engine oil supplement or equivalent, and install into lifter bore. Install the rocker arm assembly components in their original positions. Tighten the rocker arm bolts to 19 ft. lbs. (26 Nm).

7. On the 5.9L engine, install the intake manifold.

8. Pour remaining engine oil supplement into engine. The engine oil supplement must remain in the engine for at least 1000 miles but need not be drained until the next scheduled oil change.

9. Install the rocker arm covers and connect the negative battery cable.

Rocker Arms and Shafts

Removal and Installation

1. Disconnect the negative battery cable. As required, relieve the fuel system pressure. Remove the valve cover.

2. Remove the 2 capscrews at each bridge and pivot assembly.

3. Remove the bridges, pivots and rocker arms.

NOTE: The valve train components must be replaced in their original positions.

Typical rocker arm assembly

4. Installation is the reverse of the removal procedure. Torque the capscrews to 19 ft. lbs. Be sure to use new gaskets or RTV sealant as required.

Intake Manifold

Removal and Installation

2.5L ENGINE

NOTE: It may be necessary to remove the throttle body from the intake manifold before the manifold is removed.

1. Disconnect the negative battery cable. As required, relieve the fuel system pressure.
2. Remove the air cleaner (air inlet assembly). Remove the accessory drive belts.
3. Remove the power steering pump and hang aside. Remove the gas cap and relieve the fuel system pressure.
4. On MPI equipped vehicles, disconnect the fuel supply and return lines from the fuel rail. On TBI equipped vehicles, disconnect the black and grey fuel lines from the throttle body.
5. Disconnect the accelerator cable and cruise control connector.

NOTE: When disconnecting the cruise control connector at the throttle body, do not pry the connector of with pliers. Use finger pressure only.

6. Disconnect all electrical connectors and pull the wiring harness away from the manifold.
7. Disconnect the crankcase ventilation, MAP sensor, EGR valve, vacuum brake booster and the molded vacuum harness.
8. Remove bolts No. 2–5, slightly loosen bolt No. 1 and nuts No. 6 and 7.
9. Remove the intake manifold and gaskets. Drain the coolant from the manifold.
To install:
10. Clean the gasket mating surfaces throughly. Install the intake manifold and install the bolts finger-tight. On TBI equipped vehicles, install EGR on the intake manifold.
11. Tighten the bolts, in sequence, to the following torque: bolt No. 1 to 30 ft. lbs. (41 Nm); bolts 2–5 to 23 ft. lbs. (31 Nm); nuts 6 and 7 to 30 ft. lbs. (41 Nm).
12. Connect the fuel lines, vacuum hoses and electrical connectors.
13. Connect the crankcase ventilation, MAP sensor, EGR valve and vacuum brake booster.
14. Connect the accelerator cable and cruise control connector.
15. Install the air cleaner (air inlet assembly) and accessory drive belts.
16. Connect the negative battery cable. Start the engine and check for leaks.

5.9L ENGINE

1. Disconnect the negative battery cable. Drain the coolant from the radiator.
2. Remove the air cleaner assembly.
3. Disconnect the spark plug wires. Remove the spark plug wire brackets from the valve covers and the bypass valve bracket.
4. Disconnect the upper radiator hose and the bypass hose from the intake manifold. Disconnect the heater hose from the rear of the manifold.
5. Disconnect the ignition coil bracket and lay the coil aside.
6. Disconnect the TCS solenoid vacuum valve from the right side valve cover.
7. Disconnect all lines, hoses, linkages and wires from the carburetor and intake manifold and TCS components as required.
8. Disconnect the air delivery hoses at the air distribution manifolds.

Intake manifold bolt torque sequence — 2.5L engine

9. Disconnect the air pump diverter valve and lay the valve and the bracket assembly, including the hoses, forward of the engine.
10. Remove the intake manifold retaining bolts and remove the intake manifold. Remove and discard the side gaskets and the end seals.
To install:
11. Clean the mating surfaces of the intake manifold and the cylinder head before replacing the intake manifold. Use new gaskets and tighten the bolts to 43 ft. lbs. (58 Nm).

NOTE: There is no specified tighten sequence for this intake manifold. Start at the center bolts and work outward.

12. Connect the air pump diverter valve.
13. Connect the air delivery hoses at the air distribution manifolds.
14. Connect all lines, hoses, linkages and wires to the carburetor and intake manifold and TCS components as required.
15. Install the TCS solenoid vacuum valve to the right side valve cover.
16. Install the ignition coil bracket.
17. Connect the upper radiator hose and the bypass hose to the intake manifold. Connect the heater hose to the rear of the manifold.
18. Connect the spark plug wires. Install the spark plug wire brackets on the valve covers and the bypass valve bracket.
19. Install the air cleaner assembly.
20. Fill the cooling system. Connect the negative battery cable.

Exhaust Manifold

Removal and Installation

2.5L ENGINE

1. Disconnect the negative battery cable. Remove the intake manifold.
2. Disconnect the EGR tube.
3. Disconnect the exhaust pipe at the manifold.
4. Disconnect the oxygen sensor wire.
5. Support the manifold and remove the nuts from the studs.
To install:
6. Clean the intake manifold and cylinder head mating surfaces. Loosely attach the EGR tube to the exaust manifold. Transsfer the oxygen sensor, as required, and tighten the sensor to 35 ft. lbs.
7. Using a new intake manifold gasket, position the intake and exhaust manifolds on the cylinder head, and place spacers over the end studs to center the exhaust manifold. Install the end stud nuts and washer clamps but do not tighten.
8. Install washer clamp and bolt at position 1 and tighten to 30 ft. lbs. (41 Nm).

1988–90 2.5L ENGINE EXHAUST MANIFOLD LEAK

A new design exhaust manifold (part number 33002509) and gasket (part number 53020112) have been made available for engines experiencing exhaust leaks. Also, spacers (part number 33003332) and washer clamps (part number 33004255) are now used on all procedures requiring the removal of the exhaust manifold. The spacers and washers center the exhaust manifold during installation.

9. Install bolts and washers at positions 2–5 and tighten to 23 ft. lbs. (31 Nm).

10. Tighten end stud nuts (positions 6 and 7) to 23 ft. lbs. (31 Nm).

11. Install all components removed from the intake manifold.

12. Connect the exhaust pipe and tighten the bolts to 23 ft. lbs. (31 Nm).

5.9L ENGINE

1. Disconnect the negative battery cable. Disconnect the spark plug wires. Disconnect the air delivery hose at the distribution manifold.

2. Remove the air distribution manifold and the injection tubes. Disconnect the exhaust pipe at the manifold.

3. Remove the exhaust manifold retaining bolts along with the spark plug shields. Remove the exhaust manifold from the vehicle.

4. Installation is the reverse of the removal procedure. Using a new gasket, install the exhaust manifold and tighten the 2 center bolts to 25 ft. lbs. (34 Nm) and the 4 outer bolts to 15 ft. lbs. (20 Nm). Tighten the exhaust pipe nuts to 20 ft. lbs. (27 Nm).

Combination Manifold

Removal and Installation

4.0L ENGINE

NOTE: The intake and exhaust manifold are mounted externally on the left side of the engine and are attached to the cylinder head. They are removed as a unit.

1. Disconnect the negative battery cable.

2. Remove the air cleaner assembly, throttle cable, cruise control cable and transmission line pressure cable.

3. Disconnect all electrical connectors on the intake manifold.

4. Disconnect and remove the fuel supply and return lines from the fuel rail assembly. Remove the fuel rail and injectors.

5. Loosen the accessory drive belts and remove the power steering pump.

6. Disconnect the exhaust pipe from the manifold and discard the seal.

7. Remove the intake and exhaust manifold.

To install:

8. Clean the gasket mating surfaces throughly. Install a new gasket over the alignment dowels and position the exhaust manifold to the cylinder head. Install bolt No. 3 finger-tight.

9. Install the intake manifold and the remaining bolts and washers.

Exhaust manifold bolt torque sequence—2.5L engine

Location of spacers and washer clamps—2.5L engine

Intake manifold bolt torque sequence—4.0L engine

10. Tighten bolts, in sequence, to the following torque specifications: 31 ft. lbs. (23 Nm) for bolts No. 1–5; 17 ft. lbs. (23 Nm) for bolts No. 6 and 7; 23 ft. lbs. (31 Nm) for bolts No. 8–11.

11. Install the fuel rail and injectors.

12. Install the power steering pump and tension the accessory belt to specificaiton.

13. Using new O-rings, install the fuel supply and return lines. Connect all electrical connectors, vacuum connectors, throttle cable, cruise control cable and transmission lines pressure cable.

14. Install the air cleaner assembly. Using a new seal, connect the exhaust pipe to the manifold and tighten the bolt to 23 ft. lbs. (31 Nm).

15. Connect the negative battery cable, start the engine and check for leaks.

4.2L ENGINE

1. Disconnect the negative battery cable. Drain the coolant and disconnect the coolant hoses from the manifold.

2. Remove the air cleaner. Disconnect the fuel pipe, carburetor air horn vent hose, idle speed control vacuum hose and wire connector.

3. Disconnect the throttle cable, throttle valve linkage for automatic transmission, PCV valve, coolant temperature valve vacuum hoses, computerized emission control electrical connectors, EGR vacuum hose and electric heater wire connection, if equipped.

4. Remove the carburetor with the vacuum hoses still attached and set aside in the engine compartment.

5. Remove the accessory drive belts and power steering pump.

6. Disconnect the EGR valve tube, remove the intake manifold attaching bolts and remove the manifold. Discard the gasket.

7. Disconnect the exhaust downpipe from the manifold.

8. Disconnect the oxygen sensor electrical connector and remove the sensor from the manifold.

9. Remove the exhaust manifold nuts and remove the manifold.

To install:

10. Clean the gasket mating surfaces throughly. Using a new gasket, position the exhaust manifold over the end studs on the cylinder head. Install the nuts finger-tight.

11. Using an anti-sieze compound, install the oxygen sensor and tighten to 35 ft. lbs. (48 Nm). Connect the electrical connection.

12. Connect the exhaust pipe and tighten the nuts to 20 ft. lbs. (27 Nm).

13. Install the EGR valve tube to the exhaust manifold and tighten the nut finger-tight.

14. Install the intake manifold and the remaining attaching hardware.

15. Tighten nuts and bolts in sequence to 23 ft. lbs. (31 Nm).

16. Install the carburetor, linkage and hoses. Tighten the carburetor mounting nuts to 14 ft. lbs. (19 Nm). Connect the fuel pipe, air horn vent tube, idle speed control vacuum hose and choke heater wire.

17. Install the power steering pump and accessory drive belts. Tension the belts to specification.

18. Connect all other vacuum and electrical connections. Install the air cleaner, refill the cooling system, start the engine and check for leaks.

Timing Chain Front Cover and Seal

Removal and Installation

2.5L ENGINE

1. Disconnect the negative battery cable. Remove the vibration damper and pulley using a suitable puller.

2. Remove the fan and fan shroud. Remove the accessory drive belts and brackets attached to the timing cover.

3. Remove the air conditioner compressor and alternator bracket. Remove the oil pan-to-timing case cover bolts and the cover-to-cylinder block bolts.

4. Remove the timing case cover front seal and gasket from the engine.

5. Cut off the oil pan side gasket end tabs and oil pan front seal tabs flush with the front face of the cylinder block. Remove the gasket tabs.

6. Clean the timing case cover, oil pan and cylinder block gasket surfaces. Remove the crankshaft seal oil seal by prying it out with a suitable tool.

To install:

7. Install a new seal in the timing cover using tool 6139 or equivalent.

8. Apply sealer to both sides of the replacement cover gasket and position the gasket on the cylinder block. Cut the end tabs off the replacement oil pan dise gaskets corresponding to those cut off the original gsket. Attach the end tabs to the oil pan with sealer.

9. Coat the front cover seal end tab recesses generously with sealer and position the seal on the timng cover. Apply engine oil to the crankshaft seal and position the cover on the cylinder block.

10. Insert the timing case cover alignment tool 6139 in the crankshaft opening. Install the cover bolts and tighten the cover-to-cylinder block bolts to 62 inch lbs. (7 Nm); the oil pan-to-cover bolts to 11 ft. lbs. (13 Nm).

Intake manifold bolt torque sequence—4.2L engine

Timing case cover and components

Timing case cover alignment and seal installation

Timing case cover end tabs—4.0L and 4.2L engines

11. Remove the cover alignment tool and position a replacement oil seal on the tool with the seal lip facing outward. Apply a light coat of sealer to the seal and a light coat of oil to the crankshaft. Install the seal on the timing cover.

12. Install the vibration damper using a suitable installation tool. Do not hammer the damper into place as damage may result to the damper or engine.

13. Tighten the crankshaft vibration damper bolt to 80 ft. lbs. (108 Nm). Install the crankshaft pulley and tighten the bolts to 20 ft. lbs. (27 Nm).

14. Install the accessory drive belts and brackets attached to the timing cover. Install the fan and fan shroud.

15. Install the air conditioner compressor and alternator bracket. Connect the negative battery cable, start the engine and check for leaks.

4.0L AND 4.2L ENGINES

1. Disconnect the negative battery cable. Remove the drive belts, engine fan and hub assembly, the accessory pulley and vibration damper.

2. Unbolt the air conditioning compressor and bracket and set it aside. Don't disconnect the refrigerant lines.

3. Remove the oil pan to timing chain cover bolts and the bolts that attach the cover to the block.

4. Raise the timing chain cover just high enough to detach the retaining nibs of the oil pan neoprene seal from the bottom side of the cover. This must be done to prevent pulling the seal end tabs away from the tongues of the oil pan gaskets, which would cause a leak.

5. Remove the timing chain cover and gasket from the engine.

To install:

6. Use a razor blade to cut off the oil pan seal end tabs flush with the front face of the cylinder block and remove the seal. Clean the timing chain cover, oil pan and cylinder block surfaces.

7. Remove the crankshaft oil seal from the timing chain cover. Thoroughly clean the mating surfaces.

8. Apply RTV gasket material to both sides of the new gasket and position the gasket on the block.

9. Cut the end tabs off of the replacement oil pan side gaskets, corresponding to those cut off of the original gasket. Cement the end tabs to the oil pan.

10. Coat the front cover end tab recesses with a generous amount of RTV gasket sealant and position the seal on the timing case cover. Apply a coat of clean engine oil to the seal-to-pan contact surfaces.

11. Position the case cover on the block.

12. Place cover alignment tool in the crankshaft opening of the cover.

13. Install the cover-to-block bolts and the oil pan-to-cover bolts. Torque the cover-to-block bolts to 62 inch lbs.; the cover-to-pan bolts to 11 ft. lbs.

14. Remove the alignment tool and position the seal on the tool with the lip facing outward.

15. Apply a light coat of sealer on the outside diameter of the seal.

16. Lightly coat the crankshaft with clean engine oil.

17. Position the tool and seal over the end of the crankshaft and insert a screw tool into the seal installation tool.

18. Tighten the nut against the tool until it contacts the cover.

19. Remove the tools and apply a light coating of engine oil on the vibration damper hub contact surface of the seal.

20. Install the damper.

21. Install the remaining components in reverse order of removal.

5.9L ENGINE

1. Disconnect the negative battery cable.

2. Drain the cooling system and disconnect the radiator hoses and bypass hose.

3. Remove all of the drive belts and the fan and spacer assembly.

4. Remove the alternator and the front portion of the alternator bracket as an assembly.

5. Disconnect the heater hose.

6. Remove the power steering pump and/or the air pump and the mounting bracket as an assembly. Do not disconnect the power steering hoses.

7. Remove the distributor cap and note the position of the rotor. Remove the distributor.

8. Remove the fuel pump.

9. Remove the vibration damper and pulley.

10. Remove the front oil pan bolts and the bolts which secure the timing chain cover to the engine block.

NOTE: The timing gear cover retaining bolts vary in length and must be installed in the same locations from which they were removed.

11. Remove the cover by pulling forward until it is free of the locating dowel pins.

12. Clean the gasket surface of the cover and the engine block.

13. Pry out the original seal from inside the timing chain cover and clean the seal bore.

To install:

14. Drive the new seal into place from the inside with a block of wood until it contacts the outer flange of the cover.

15. Apply a light film of motor oil to the lips of the new seal.

16. Before reinstalling the timing gear cover, remove the lower locating dowel pin from the engine block. The pin is required for correct alignment of the cover and must either be reused or a replacement dowel pin installed after the cover is in position.

17. Cut both sides of the oil pan gasket flush with the engine block with a razor blade.

18. Trim a new gasket to correspond to the amount cut off at the oil pan.

19. Apply sealer to both sides of the new gasket and install the gasket on the timing case cover.

20. Install the new front oil pan seal.

21. Align the tongues of the new oil pan gasket pieces with the oil pan seal and cement them into place on the cover.

22. Apply a bead of sealer to the cutoff edges of the original oil pan gaskets.

23. Place the timing case cover into position and install the front oil pan bolts. Tighten the bolts slowly and evenly until the cover aligns with the upper locating dowel.

24. Install the lower dowel through the cover and drive it into the corresponding hole in the engine block.

25. Install the cover retaining bolts in the same locations from which they were removed. Tighten to 25 ft. lbs.

26. Assemble the remaining components in the reverse order of removal.

Front Cover Oil Seal

Replacement

1. Disconnect the negative battery cable.

2. Remove the drive belts, vibration damper and fan shroud.

3. Using a suitable tool, pry the oil seal from the front cover. Take care not to damage the front cover.

To install:

4. Position the replacement oil seal on a seal installation tool with the lip facing outward. Apply a light film of sealer to the outer rim of the seal and a light coat of oil to the crankshaft.

5. Install the seal in the cover. Apply a light coat of oil to the vibration damper bore and install the damper using a suitable installation tool. Tighten the damper bolt to 80 ft. lbs. (108 Nm) except for the 5.9L engine; 90 ft. lbs. (122 Nm) for the 5.9L engine.

6. Install the crankshaft pulley and tighten the bolts to 20 ft. lbs. (27 Nm).

7. Install the drive belts and fan shroud. Connect the negative battery cable.

8. Start the engine and check for leaks.

Timing Chain and Sprockets

Removal and Installation

2.5L ENGINE

1. Disconnect the negative battery cable. Remove the drive belts and fan shroud.

2. Unscrew the vibration damper bolts and washer.

3. Using a puller, remove the vibration damper.

4. Remove the timing case cover.

5. Rotate the crankshaft until the O timing mark on the crankshaft sprocket is closest to and on a center line with the timing mark on the camshaft sprocket.

6. Remove the oil slinger from the crankshaft.

7. Remove the camshaft retaining bolt and remove the sprockets and chain as an assembly. If the timing chain tensioner is to be replaced, the oil pan must be removed.

Timing mark alignment—2.5L engine

Timing mark alignment—4.0L and 4.2L engines

To install:

8. Turn the timing chain tensioner lever to the unlock (down) position. Pull the tensioner block toward the tensioner lever to compress the spring. Hold the block and turn the tensioner lever to the lock (up) position.

9. Install the sprockets and timing chain. Ensure the timing marks on the sprockets are properly aligned.

10. Install the camshaft sprocket retaining bolt and tighten to 80 ft. lbs. (108 Nm).

11. To verify correct alignment, turn the crankshaft to position the camshaft sprocket timing mark at the 1 o'clock position. This positions the crankshaft sprocket timing mark where the adjacent tooth meshes with the chain at the 3 o'clock position. Count the number of chain pins between the timing marks of both sprockets; there must be 20 pins.

12. Install the oil slinger, timing case cover and all other components removed in reverse order.

13. Connect the negative battery cable, start the engine, check the ignition timing and check for leaks.

4.0L AND 4.2L ENGINES

1. Disconnect the negative battery cable. Remove the drive belts, engine fan and hub assembly, accessory pulley, vibration damper and timing chain cover.

2. Remove the tension spring and thrust pin from the preload bolt. Remove the oil seal from the timing chain cover.

3. Remove the crankshaft sprocket retaining bolt and washer.

4. Rotate the crankshaft until the timing mark on the crankshaft sprocket is closest to and in a center line with the timing pointer of the camshaft sprocket.

5. Remove the crankshaft sprocket, camshaft sprocket and timing chain as an assembly. Disassemble the chain and sprockets.

To install:

6. Assemble the timing chain, crankshaft sprocket and camshaft sprocket with the timing marks aligned.

7. Install the assembly to the crankshaft and the camshaft. Double check the alignment by counting the number of links or pins with the sprockets positioned as illustrated. There must be 15 pins between the timing marks on both sprockets.

8. Install the camshaft sprocket retaining bolt and washer and tighten to 80 ft. lbs.

9. Install the timing chain cover and a new oil seal.

10. Install the vibration damper, accessory pulley, engine fan and hub assembly and drive belts. Tighten the belts to the proper tension.

5.9L ENGINE

1. Disconnect the negative battery cable. Remove the timing chain cover and gasket. Remove the crankshaft oil slinger.

2. Remove the camshaft sprocket retaining bolt and washer, distributor drive gear and fuel pump eccentric.

3. Rotate the crankshaft until the timing mark on the crankshaft sprocket is adjacent to and on a center line with, the timing mark on the camshaft sprocket.

4. Remove the crankshaft sprocket, camshaft sprocket and

Timing mark alignment—5.9L engine

timing chain as an assembly. Disassemble the chain and sprockets.

To install:

5. Assemble the timing chain, crankshaft sprocket and camshaft sprocket with the timing marks on both sprockets aligned. Install the assembly to the crankshaft and the camshaft.

6. Install the fuel pump eccentric. The fuel pump eccentric must be installed with the stamped word **REAR** facing the camshaft sprocket.

7. Install the distributor drive gear, washer and retaining bolt. Tighten the bolt to 25–35 ft. lbs.

8. Install the crankshaft oil slinger. Install the timing chain cover using a new gasket and oil seal.

Camshaft

Removal and Installation

2.5L ENGINE

1. Disconnect the negative battery cable. If equipped with air conditioning, properly discharge the system.

2. Drain the cooling system.

3. Remove the radiator and air conditioning condenser, if equipped.

4. Remove the fuel pump.

5. Matchmark the distributor and engine for installation. Note the rotor position by marking it on the distributor body. Unbolt and remove the distributor and wires.

6. Remove the rocker arm cover.

7. Remove the rocker arm assemblies.

8. Remove the pushrods.

NOTE: Keep all valve train components in order for installation.

9. Using tool J–21884 or equivalent, remove the hydraulic lifters.

10. Remove the timing case cover.

NOTE: If the camshaft sprocket appears to have been rubbing against the cover, check the oil pressure relief holes in the rear cam journal for debris.

11. Remove the timing chain and sprockets.

12. Slide the camshaft from the engine.

To install:

13. Inspect the camshaft for wear and damage. Lubricate all moving components with engine oil.

14. Install the camshaft taking care not to damage the cam bearings.

15. Install the timing chain and sprockets. Ensure that the timing marks are correctly positioned. Torque the camshaft sprocket bolt to 50 ft. lbs.

16. Install the timing case cover, hydraulic lifters, pushrods, rocker arm assemblies, cylinder head cover, distributor and ignition wires.

17. Properly position the distributor by positioning the No. 1 cylinder at TDC on the compression stroke. Insert the distributor into the shaft with the rotor pointed to the No. 1 firing position on the cap.

NOTE: Some adjustment of the distributor shaft may be necessary to engage the oil pump shaft to the distributor.

18. With the distributor fully engaged in its correct location, the rotor should be at the 6 o'clock position.

19. Install all other components in reverse order of removal.

20. Start the engine and allow it to reach operating temperature. Check the timing.

4.0L AND 4.2L ENGINES

1. Disconnect the negative battery cable. Drain the cooling

system and remove the radiator. As required, relieve the fuel system pressure.

2. Remove the condensor and receiver/drier as a charged unit.

3. Remove the valve cover and gasket, the rocker assemblies, pushrods, cylinder head and the lifters.

NOTE: The pushrods must be replaced in their original locations.

4. Remove the drive belts, cooling fan, fan hub assembly, vibration damper and the timing chain cover.

5. Remove the distributor assembly, including the spark plug wires.

6. Remove the cylinder head.

7. Remove the valve lifters. Keep them in order for installation.

8. Rotate the crankshaft until the timing mark of the crankshaft sprocket is adjacent to, and on a center line with, the timing mark of the camshaft sprocket.

9. Remove the crankshaft sprocket, camshaft sprocket and the timing chain as an assembly.

10. Remove the front bumper or grille as required and carefully slide out the camshaft.

To install:

11. Lubricate the camshaft with an engine oil supplement.

12. Slide the camshaft into the block carefully to avoid damage to the bearings.

13. Install the crankshaft sprocket, camshaft sprocket and the timing chain as an assembly.

14. Make sure the timing mark of the crankshaft sprocket is adjacent to and on a center line with, the timing mark of the camshaft sprocket. Torque the camshaft sprocket bolt to 80 ft. lbs.

15. Lubricate the tension spring, thrust pin and pin bore in the preload bolt. Install the assembly on thr preload bolt. Install the timing cover. Install the vibration damper.

16. Install the valve lifters, cylinder head, pushrods, rocker assemblies, valve cover and gasket.

17. Install the distributor assembly.

18. Install the condenser and receiver/drier as a charged unit.

19. Install the radiator and fill the cooling system.

20. Connect the negative battery cable. Start the engine and allow it to reach operating temperature. Check the ignition timing.

5.9L ENGINE

1. Disconnect the negative battery cable.

2. Drain the radiator and both banks of the block. Remove the lower hose at the radiator, the bypass hose at the pump, the thermostat housing and the radiator. If equipped with air conditioning, remove the condenser and receiver assembly as a charged unit.

3. Remove the distributor, all wires and the coil from the manifold.

4. Remove the intake manifold as an assembly.

5. Remove the valve covers, rocker arms and pushrods.

6. Remove the lifters.

NOTE: The valve train components must be replaced in their original locations.

7. Remove the cooling fan and hub assembly, fuel pump and heater hose at the water pump.

8. Remove the alternator and bracket as an assembly. Move it aside, do not disconnect the wiring.

9. Remove the crankshaft pulley and the damper. Remove the lower radiator hose at the water pump.

10. Remove the timing chain cover.

NOTE: Reinstall the vibration damper as a means of rotating the engine during servicing.

11. Rotate the engine until the timing marks are properly

aligned. Remove the distributor/oil pump drive gear, fuel pump eccentric, sprockets and the timing chain.

12. Remove the grille.

13. Remove the camshaft carefully by sliding it forward out of the engine.

To install:

14. Coat all parts with engine oil supplement.

15. Slide the camshaft, carefully, into the engine.

16. Install the grille.

17. Install the distributor/oil pump drive gear, fuel pump eccentric, sprockets and the timing chain. Tighten the camshaft bolt to 30 ft. lbs. (41 Nm). Install the timing chain cover.

18. Install the crankshaft pulley and the damper. Tighten the damper bolt to 90 ft. lbs. (122 Nm); the pulley bolts to 30 ft. lbs. (41 Nm).

19. Install the lower radiator hose at the water pump. Install the alternator and bracket as an assembly.

20. Install the cooling fan and hub assembly. Install the fuel pump.

21. Install the heater hose at the water pump. Install the lifters.

NOTE: The valve train components must be replaced in their original locations.

22. Install the valve covers, rocker arms and pushrods.

23. Install the intake manifold as an assembly.

24. Install the distributor, all wires and the coil on the manifold.

25. Install the radiator.

26. If equipped with air conditioning, install the condenser and receiver assembly.

27. Install the thermostat and housing. Install the bypass hose at the pump.

28. Install the lower hose at the radiator. Fill the cooling system.

29. Connect the negative battery cable.

30. Start the engine and allow to reach operating temperature. Check the ignition timing. Check for leaks.

Piston and Connecting Rod

Positioning

Position the arrow toward the front of the engine—all engines except 5.9L engine

Position the notches toward the front of the engine— 5.9L engine

ENGINE LUBRICATION

Service Tips

1988 4.2L ENGINE OIL FILTER CHANGE

In 1988 Jeep introduced a new style oil filter for the 4.2L engine. This oil filter has a 20 mm connector thread and an internal oil bypass system. The oil bypass system ensures continuous oil flow in the event the filter becomes clogged. This new style oil filter must be used on 4.2L engines.

Checking oil pump gear tooth to body clearance

Oil Pan

Removal and Installation

1. Disconnect the negative battery cable.
2. Raise and support the vehicle safely.
3. Drain the oil.
4. Disconnect the exhaust pipe at the manifold, as required.
5. Remove the starter.
6. Remove the bell housing access plate.
7. Raise the engine and remove the motor mount through-bolts. Continue raising the engine to gain clearance for oil pan removal.
8. Unbolt and remove the oil pan.

To install:

9. Clean the gasket surfaces thoroughly.
10. Install a replacement seal at the bottom of the timing case cover and at the rear bearing cap. When installing the front oil pan seal to the timing chain cover, apply a generous amount of Permatex® No. 2 to the end tabs. Cement the oil pan side of the gaskets to the mating surface on the bottom of the engine block. Coat the inside curved surface of the new oil pan rear seal with soap and apply a generous amount of Permatex® No. 2 to the gasket contacting surface of the seal end tabs.
11. Using new gaskets coated with sealer, install the pan and torque the ¼–20 bolts to 80 inch lbs.; the ⁵⁄₁₆–18 bolts to 11 ft. lbs. On some engines, RTV sealant may be used in place of a gasket.
12. Install the motor mount through-bolts, bell housing access cover, starter and exhaust pipe.
13. Lower the vehicle and fill the engine with oil. Start the engine and ensure that there is adequate oil pressure.

Oil Pump

Removal and Installation

EXCEPT 5.9L ENGINE

1. Disconnect the negative battery cable. Raise and safely support the vehicle.
2. Drain the engine oil and remove the oil pan.
3. Unbolt and remove the pump assembly from the block. Discard the gasket.
4. Using a new gasket, install the pump on the block. Torque the short bolt to 10 ft. lbs. and the long bolt to 17 ft. lbs.
5. Install the oil pan.
6. Connect the negative battery cable.

5.9L ENGINE

1. Disconnect the negative battery cable. Drain the engine oil.
2. Remove the retaining bolts and separate the oil pump cover, gasket and oil filter as an assembly from the timing case cover.
3. Remove the drive gear assembly and idler gear by sliding them out of the body.
4. Remove the oil pressure relief valve from the pump cover for cleaning by removing the retaining cap and spring.
5. Assemble the oil pressure relief valve and install the idler shaft, gear and drive assembly.

NOTE: To ensure self priming of the oil pump, fill the pump with petroleum jelly prior to the installation of the oil pump cover. Do not use grease of any type.

6. Install the pump cover and oil filter assembly with a replacement gasket. Tighten the retaining bolts to 55 inch lbs. (6 Nm).

Gear to Body Clearance Check

1. With both oil pump gears in the body, check the clearance by inserting a feeler gauge between a gear tooth and the pump body.
2. Rotate the gears to measure each tooth to body clearance.
3. The correct tooth to body clearance is:

    a. 2.5L, 4.0L and 4.2L engines—0.002–0.006 in. (0.051–0.152mm)

    b. 5.9L engine—0.009–0.0011 in. (0.229–0.279mm)

Rear Main Bearing Oil Seal

Removal and Installation

2.5L ENGINE

1. Remove the transmission.
2. Remove the flywheel.
3. Pry out the seal from around the crankshaft flange.
4. Coat the inner lip of the new seal with clean engine oil.
5. Carefully position the seal into place. Using a rear main seal installer, tool 6271 or equivalent, install the seal flush with the cylinder block.

NOTE: The felt lip must be located inside the flywheel mounting surface. If the lip is not positioned correctly the flywheel could tear the seal.

6. Using new bolts install the flywheel and tighten to 50 ft. lbs. (68 Nm).

4.0L, 4.2L AND 5.9L ENGINES

1. Remove the transmission.
2. Remove the flywheel or flexplate.
3. Remove the rear main bearing cap and push the upper seal out of the groove. Ensure that the crankshaft is not damaged.
4. Remove the lower seal from the rear main bearing cap. Wipe clean the cap and crankshaft seal surfaces.
5. Apply a thin coat of engine oil to the seal surfaces of the cap and crankshaft.

6. Coat the lip of each seal half with clean engine oil.
7. Position the upper seal half in the block. The lip of the seal faces the front of the engine.
8. Coat both side of the lower seal's end tabs with RTV silicone gasket material. Don't get any on the seal lip.
9. Coat the outer, curved surface of the lower seal with soap.
10. Seat the lower seal firmly in the bearing cap recess.
11. Coat both chamfered edges of the bearing cap with RTV silicone gasket material.

NOTE: Avoid getting and RTV material on the bearing cap-to-block mating surfaces. Doing so would change the bearing cleanace.

12. Install the bearing cap.
13. Torque all the main bearing caps to 80 ft. lbs. (108 Nm).

Rear main seal installation—2.5L engine

Removing the rear main seal 2.5L engine

Installing the rear main seal on the installation tool—2.5L engine

Two piece rear main seal installation

TORQUE SPECIFICATIONS

Component	English	Metric
Camshaft sprocket bolt		
All except 5.9L engine	80 ft. lbs.	108 Nm
5.9L engine	30 ft. lbs.	41 Nm
Carburetor-to-manifold bolts	22 ft. lbs.	16 Nm
Connecting rod bearing cap bolts	33 ft. lbs.	45 Nm
Crankshaft damper bolt		
All except 5.9L engine	80 ft. lbs.	108 Nm
5.9L engine	90 ft. lbs.	122 Nm

TORQUE SPECIFICATIONS

Component	English	Metric
Crankshaft pulley bolt		
All except 5.9L engine	20 ft. lbs.	27 Nm
5.9L engine	30 ft. lbs.	41 Nm
Cylinder Head bolt		
2.5L engine		
Step 1	22 ft. lbs.	29 Nm
Step 2	45 ft. lbs.	61 Nm
Step 3 bolts 1–7 and 9–10	110 ft. lbs.	149 Nm
Step 4 bolt 8	100 ft. lbs.	136 Nm
4.0L engine		
Step 1	22 ft. lbs.	29 Nm
Step 2	45 ft. lbs.	61 Nm
Step 3 bolts 1–10 and 12–14	110 ft. lbs.	149 Nm
Step 4 bolt 11	100 ft. lbs.	136 Nm
4.2L engine	85 ft. lbs.	115 Nm
5.9L engine		
Step 1	80 ft. lbs.	108 Nm
Step 2	110 ft. lbs.	149 Nm
EGR valve-to-intake plenum	20 ft. lbs.	27 Nm
Engine-to-transmission	28 ft. lbs.	38 Nm
Exhaust Manifold		
2.5L engine	30 ft. lbs.	41 Nm
4.0L and 4.2L engines		
Middle nuts	30 ft. lbs.	41 Nm
Outside nuts	23 ft. lbs.	31 Nm
5.9L engine		
Center bolts	25 ft. lbs.	34 Nm
Outer bolts	15 ft. lbs.	20 Nm
Exhaust pipe-to-exhaust manifold nuts		
2.5L and 4.0L engines	23 ft. lbs.	31 Nm
4.2L and 5.9L engines	20 ft. lbs.	27 Nm
Flywheel/flexplate-to-crankshaft bolts		
1988–89 2.5L engine	40 ft. lbs.	54 Nm
1990–92 2.5L engine		
Step 1	50 ft. lbs.	68 Nm
Step 2	+ 60°	+ 60°
4.0L and 4.2L engines	100–110 ft. lbs.	136–149 Nm
5.9L engine	95 ft. lbs.	129 Nm
Flywheel-to-converter bolts		
AW-4 transmission	40 ft. lbs.	54 Nm
727/999 transmission	22 ft. lbs.	30 Nm
Fuel pump-to-block (mechanical)	13 ft. lbs.	18 Nm
Front engine mount through bolt		
Except 5.9L engine	45 ft. lbs.	61 Nm
5.9L engine	33 ft. lbs.	45 Nm
Intake Manifold		
2.5L engine		
Bolts 1, 6 and 7	30 ft. lbs.	41 Nm
Bolts 2–5	23 ft. lbs.	31 Nm
4.0L engine		
Bolts 1–5 and 8–11	23 ft. lbs.	31 Nm
Bolts 6 and 7	17 ft. lbs.	23 Nm
4.2L engine	23 ft. lbs.	31 Nm
5.9L engine	43 ft. lbs.	58 Nm

TORQUE SPECIFICATIONS

Component	English	Metric
Main bearing cap bolts		
Except 5.9L engine		
Step 1	40 ft. lbs.	54 Nm
Step 2	70 ft. lbs.	95 Nm
Step 3	80 ft. lbs.	108 Nm
5.9L engine		
Step 1	30 ft. lbs.	41 Nm
Step 2	60 ft. lbs.	81 Nm
Step 3	90 ft. lbs.	122 Nm
Step 4	100 ft. lbs.	136 Nm
Oil Pan		
¼–20 bolts	84 inch lbs.	9 Nm
⁵⁄₁₆–18 bolts	132 inch lbs.	15 Nm
Oil pan drain plug		
Except 2.5L engine	30 ft. lbs.	41 Nm
2.5L engine	25 ft. lbs.	34 Nm
Oil pump attaching bolts		
Short bolts	10 ft. lbs.	17 Nm
Long bolts	17 ft. lbs.	23 Nm
Oil pump cover screws		
Except 5.9L engine	70 inch lbs.	8 Nm
5.9L engine	55 inch lbs.	6 Nm
Rocker arm pivot bolt	19 ft. lbs.	26 Nm
Rocker (Valve) Cover		
2.5L and 4.2L engines	70 inch lbs.	8 Nm
4.0L and 5.9L engines	55 inch lbs.	5 Nm
Spark plug		
1988–89	28 ft. lbs.	38 Nm
1990–92	27 ft. lbs.	37 Nm
Starter-to-block bolts		
Except 5.9L engine	33 ft. lbs.	45 Nm
5.9L engine	18 ft. lbs.	24 Nm
Thermostat housing	13 ft. lbs.	18 Nm
Throttle body mounting bolts	9 ft. lbs.	12 Nm
Timing cover		
Except 5.9L engine	62 inch lbs.	7 Nm
5.9L engine	25 ft. lbs.	34 Nm
Water Pump		
Except 5.9L engine	13 ft. lbs.	18 Nm
5.9L engine		
Water pump-to-timing cover	48 inch lbs.	5 Nm
Water pump-to-cylinder block	28 ft. lbs.	38 Nm
Water pump pulley	18 ft. lbs.	24 Nm

MANUAL TRANSMISSION

For further information, please refer to Chilton's Transmission Service Manual.

Transmission Assembly

Removal and Installation

2WD VEHICLES

1. Disconnect the negative battery cable. Raise the outer gearshift lever boot and remove the upper part of the console.

2. Remove the lower part of the console.
3. Remove the inner boot.
4. Remove the gearshift lever.
5. Raise and safely support the vehicle.
6. Drain the transmission oil.
7. Matchmark the driveshaft and yoke for installation alignment.
8. Unbolt and remove the driveshaft.
9. Position a jack under the transmission and take the weight off the transmission slightly.

10. Unbolt and remove the rear crossmember.
11. Disconnect the speedometer cable.
12. Disconnect the backup light switch.
13. Disconnect all linkage and hoses from the transmission.
14. Unbolt the transmission from the engine and lower the transmission while pulling it back.

To install:

15. Lightly grease the input shaft splines.
16. Raise the transmission into position.
17. Roll the transmission forward and engage the input shaft and clutch disc spline. Wiggle the output shaft yoke to get the splines to mesh. Once the splines mesh, push the trasmission forward all the way and align the bell housing-to-engine bolt holes. Install the attaching bolts and torque them to 28 ft. lbs.
18. Connect all linkage and hoses at the transmission.
19. Connect the backup light switch.
20. Connect the speedometer cable.
21. Install the rear crossmember. Torque the crossmember attaching bolt to 30 ft. lbs.; the transmission to crossmember bolts to 33 ft. lbs.
22. Remove the transmission jack.
23. Install the driveshaft. New strap bolts should be used whenever the driveshaft is disconnected. Torque the nuts to 14 ft. lbs.
24. Fill the transmission to the correct level with transmission oil.
25. Lower the vehicle.
26. Install the gearshift lever and install the inner boot. Install the lower part of the console. Install the upper part of the console.
27. Connect the negative battery cable.

4WD VEHICLES

1. Disconnnect the negative battery cable. Raise the outer gearshift lever boot and remove the upper part of the console.
2. Remove the lower part of the console.
3. Remove the inner boot.
4. Remove the gearshift lever.
5. Raise and safely support the vehicle.
6. Drain the transmission and transfer case.
7. Matchmark the rear driveshaft and yoke for installation alignment.
8. Unbolt and remove the rear driveshaft.

9. Position a jack under the transmission and take up the weight slightly.
10. Unbolt and remove the rear crossmember.
11. Disconnect the speedometer cable.
12. Disconnect the backup light switch.
13. Disconnect the transfer case vent hose at the case.
14. Disconnect all linkage and hoses from the transfer case and transmission.
15. Matchmark the front driveshaft and yoke.
16. Remove the front driveshaft.
17. Support the transmission to the jack.
18. Unbolt the transmission/transfer case assembly from the engine and lower the jack while pulling back.

To install:

19. If the transmission and transfer case were separated, torque the bolts to 26 ft. lbs.
20. Lightly grease the input shaft splines.
21. Raise the transmission into position.
22. Roll the transmission forward and engage the input shaft and clutch disc spline. Wiggle the output shaft yoke to get the splines to mesh. Once the splines mesh, push the trasmission forward all the way and align the bell housing-to-engine bolt holes. Install the attaching bolts and torque them to 28 ft. lbs.
23. Install the front driveshaft. New strap bolts should be used every time the driveshaft is disconnected. Torque the strap bolt nuts to 14 ft. lbs.; the flange-to-transfer case bolts to 35 ft. lbs.
24. Connect all linkage and hoses at the transfer case and transmission.
25. Connect the transfer case vent hose at the case.
26. Connect the backup light switch.
27. Connect the speedometer cable.
28. Install the rear crossmember. Torque the crossmember attaching bolts to 30 ft. lbs.; the transmission-to-crossmember bolts to 33 ft. lbs.
29. Remove the floor jack.
30. Install the rear driveshaft. Use new strap bolts. Torque the strap bolt nuts to 14 ft. lbs.; the flange-to-transfer case bolts to 35 ft. lbs.
31. Fill the transmission and transfer case.
32. Lower the vehicle.
33. Install the gearshift lever and the inner boot.
34. Install the lower part of the console and the upper part of the console.
35. Connect the negative battery cable.

CLUTCH

Clutch Assembly

Removal and Installation

1. Remove the transmission or transmission/transfer case assembly.
2. Matchmark the pressure plate and flywheel. Loosen the pressure plate bolts, a little at a time, in rotation, to avoid warpage.
3. Remove the pressure plate and clutch disc.
4. Remove the pilot bearing and check for excessive wear or damage.

To install:

5. Install the pilot bearing after lubricating with grease. Seat the bearing in the crankshaft with a clutch alignment tool.
6. Check the clutch disc runout by installing the disc on the transmission input shaft. Runout should not exceed 0.020 in. (0.5mm) when measured ¼ inch from the outer edge of the facing.

7. Install the clutch alignment tool in the pilot bearing. Install the clutch disc on the tool.
8. Install the pressure plate and tighten the bolts finger-tight. The pressure plate bolts must be tightened a little at a time, in rotation, to avoid warpage. Torque the pressure plate bolts to:

2.5L engine: 23 ft. lbs.

4.0L, 4.2L and 5.9L engines: 40 ft. lbs.

Clutch Master Cylinder

Removal and Installation

1. Disconnect the hydraulic line at the master cylinder. Cap the line.
2. Disconnect the pushrod at the clutch pedal.
3. Unbolt the master cylinder from the firewall.
4. Installation is the reverse of removal. Torque the mounting nuts to 19 ft. lbs. Refill and bleed the system.

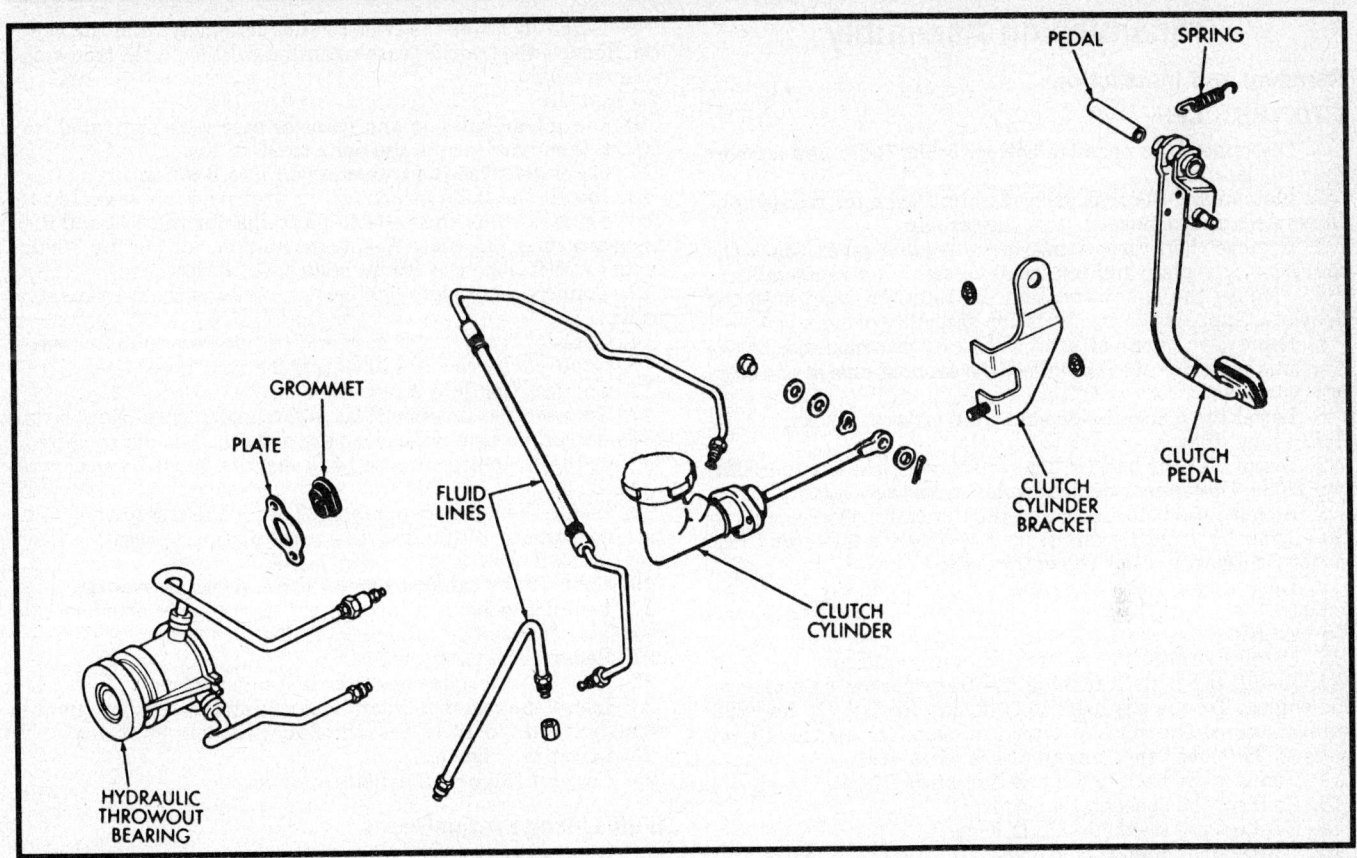

Hydraulic clutch system components — typical

Hydraulic Concentric Bearing

Removal and Installation

1. Disconnect the negative battery cable. Raise and support the vehicle safely.
2. Remove the transmission. Disconnect the clutch master cylinder fluid line.
3. Remove the insulator plate bolts and slide the plate off the bleed line. Remove the concentric bearing retaining nut.
4. Remove the concentric bearing from the transmission input shaft. If the bearing will be reused, secure the bearing and piston with rubber bands.

To install:

5. Inspect the bearing mounting pin and replace the front cover if the pin is damaged. Install the concentric bearing on the transmission input shaft.
6. Guide the bearing fluid and bleed lines through the openings in the clutch housing.
7. Position the bearing boss on the mounting pin and seat the bearing against the transmission. Install a new retaining nut and unhook the T-handle straps retaining the bearing.

8. Install the insulator and plate.
9. Install the transmission and transfer case and connect the clutch master cylinder fluid line.
10. Fill and bleed the clutch hydraulic system.

Hydraulic Clutch System Bleeding

1. Attach a hose to the clutch bleed screw and immerse the other end in a glass container filled with clutch fluid. Open the bleed screw.
2. Fill the clutch master cylinder reservoir until fluid is free of air bubbles. Close the bleed screw.
3. Check clutch pedal free-play. Press and release the clutch pedal several times and measure pedal free-play. If free-play exceeds ½ inch (13mm), continue the bleeding procedure.
4. Open the bleed screw and have an assistant press the clutch pedal to the floor. Tighten the bleed screw.
5. Continue until fluid entering glass jar is free of air bubbles. Do not allow the master cylinder reservoir to run out of fluid.
6. When clutch pedal free-play is within specification, top off the clutch master cylinder. Remove the bleed hose.

AUTOMATIC TRANSMISSION

The 727 transmission is used in the Grand Wagoneer; the 999 transmission is used in the Wrangler; the AW–4 is used in all other models.

For further information, please refer to Chilton's Transmission Service Manual.

Transmission Assembly

Removal and Installation

2WD VEHICLES

1. Disconnect the negative battery cable. Raise and support the vehicle safely.
2. Matchmark the rear driveshaft and yoke for reassembly. Disconnect and remove the rear driveshaft.
3. Remove the torque converter inspection cover. Mark the converter driveplate and converter assembly for reassembly.
4. Remove the bolts attaching the torque converter to the flexplate. Support the transmission assembly using a jack.
5. Remove the bolts attaching the rear crossmember to the transmission side rail. Disconnect the exhaust pipe at the catalytic converter.
6. Lower the transmission slightly in order to disconnect the fluid cooler lines.
7. Disconnect the backup light switch wire and the speedometer cable. Disconnect the transmission linkage.
8. Remove the bolts attaching the transmission assembly to the engine. Move the transmission assembly and the torque converter rearward to clear the crankshaft.
9. Carefully lower the transmission assembly from the vehicle.

To install:

10. Carefully raise the transmission into position.
11. Install the bolts attaching the transmission assembly to the engine. Torque the bolts to 30 ft. lbs. for the 727 and 999 transmissions. On the AW-4 transmission, torque the 10mm bolts to 25 ft. lbs.; the 12mm bolts to 42 ft. lbs.
12. Connect the backup light switch wire.
13. Connect the speedometer cable.
14. Connect the transmission linkage.
15. Connect the fluid cooler lines.
16. Install the rear crossmember. Torque the crossmember bolts to 30 ft. lbs.; the transmission-to-crossmember bolts to 33 ft. lbs.
17. Connect the exhaust pipe at the catalytic converter.
18. Install the bolts attaching the torque converter to the flexplate. Torque the bolts to 40 ft. lbs.
19. Remove the transmission jack.
20. Install the torque converter inspection cover.
21. Install the driveshaft. New strap bolts should be used every time the driveshaft is disconnected. Torque the nuts to 14 ft. lbs.
22. Lower the vehicle.
23. Connect the negative battery cable.

4WD VEHICLES

1. Disconnect the negative battery cable. Raise and support the vehicle safely.
2. Matchmark the rear driveshaft and yoke for reassembly. Disconnect and remove the rear driveshaft.
3. Remove the torque converter inspection cover. Mark the converter driveplate and converter assembly for reassembly.
4. Remove the bolts attaching the torque converter to the flexplate. Support the transmission assembly with a jack.
5. Remove the bolts attaching the rear crossmember to the transmission side rail. Disconnect the exhaust pipe at the catalytic converter.
6. Lower the transmission slightly in order to disconnect the fluid cooler lines. Matchmark the front driveshaft assembly for installation. Disconnect the driveshaft at the transfer case and secure the assembly aside.
7. Disconnect the backup light switch wire and the speedometer cable. Disconnect the transfer case and the transmission linkage. Disconnect the vacuum lines and the vent hose.
8. Remove the bolts attaching the transmission assembly to the engine. Move the transmission assembly and the torque converter rearward to clear the crankshaft.

9. Carefully lower the transmission assembly from the vehicle. Remove the transfer case retaining bolts from the transmission assembly.

To install:

10. If the transmission and transfer case were separated, re-attach them and torque the bolts to 26 ft. lbs.
11. Carefully raise the transmission into position.
12. Install the bolts attaching the transmission assembly to the engine. Torque the bolts to 30 ft. lbs. for the 727 and 999 transmissions. On the AW-4 transmission, torque the 10mm bolts to 25 ft. lbs.; the 12mm bolts to 42 ft. lbs.
13. Connect the backup light switch wire and the speedometer cable.
14. Connect the transfer case and the transmission linkage.
15. Connect the vacuum lines and the vent hose.
16. Connect the fluid cooler lines.
17. Connect the driveshaft at the transfer case. New strap bolts should be used whenever the driveshaft is disconnected. Torque the strap bolt nuts to 14 ft. lbs; the flange-to-case bolts to 35 ft. lbs.
18. Install the rear crossmember. Torque the crossmember attaching bolts to 30 ft. lbs.; the transmission-to-crossmember bolts to 33 ft. lbs.
19. Connect the exhaust pipe at the catalytic converter.
20. Install the bolts attaching the torque converter to the flexplate. Torque the bolts to 40 ft. lbs.
21. Remove the floor jack.
22. Install the torque converter inspection cover.
23. Install the rear driveshaft. Use new strap bolts. Torque strap bolt nuts to 14 ft. lbs.; the flange bolts to 35 ft. lbs.
24. Lower the vehicle.
25. Connect the negative battery cable.

Shift Linkage Adjustment

1. Raise and safely support the vehicle.
2. Loosen the shift rod trunnion jamnuts.
3. Remove the lockpin that retains the shift rod trunnion to the bell crank. Disengage the trunnion and shift rod at the bell crank.
4. Place the gear shift lever in the **P** position and lock the steering column.
5. Move the transmission lever rearward into the **P** detent. Be sure the lever is as far rearward as it will go.
6. Check the engagement of the park detent by trying to rotate the driveshaft with the rear wheels off of the ground. The shaft will not rotate if the park detent is engaged.
7. Adjust the trunnion until it will fit in the bell crank arm freely. Tighten the jamnuts. Install the lock pin.
8. Check engine starting in **P** and **N**, be sure it will not start in any other gear.

Throttle Cable Adjustment

AW-4 TRANSMISSION

1. Place the gear selector in **P** and turn the ignition switch to the **OFF** position.
2. Fully retract the cable plunger and press the cable button all the way down.
3. Rotate the throttle lever to wide open throttle position.
4. Hold the primary throttle lever in the wide open position and let the cable plunger extend. Release the lever when the plunger is fully extended. The cable is now adjusted.

999 TRANSMISSION

1. Place the gear selector in **P** and turn the ignition switch to the **OFF** position.
2. Press the cable release button all the way down and fully retract the cable plunger.

3. Rotate the throttle lever to wide open throttle position and the cable will ratchet to the correct adjustment point.

727 TRANSMISSION

1. Disconnect the throttle rod spring from the bellcrank.
2. Block the choke open and set the carburetor throttle off the fast idle cam.
3. If the carburetor has a throttle opoerated solenoid valve, turn the ignition switch **ON** position to energize the solenoid.

Then open the throttle halfway to allow the solenoid to lock and return the carburetor to the idle position.

4. Loosen the throttle rod retainer bolt.
5. Remove the spring clip from the nylon stop. Remove the stop from the lug and move the stop to the rear of the link.
6. Hold the bellcrank in place and push the end of the link to eliminate the lash. Tighten the link retaining bolt.
7. Install the nylon stop and spring clip. Connect the throttle rod spring.

TRANSFER CASE

Transfer Case Assembly

Removal and Installation

NEW PROCESS 207

1. Shift the case into **4H**.
2. Raise and safely support the vehicle.
3. Drain the transfer case.
4. Matchmark the rear driveshaft and remove it.
5. Disconnect the speedometer cable, vacuum hoses and vent hose from the case.
6. Support the transmission with a transmission jack.
7. Remove the crossmember.
8. Matchmark the front driveshaft and remove it.
9. Disconnect the shift lever linkage rod at the case.
10. Remove the shift lever bracket bolts.
11. Support the transfer case with a jack and remove the attaching bolts.
12. Pull the case out of the vehicle.

To install:

13. Raise the transfer case into position. Torque the attaching bolts to 26 ft. lbs.
14. Connect the shift lever linkage rod at the case.
15. Install the shift lever bracket bolts.
16. Install the front driveshaft. New strap bolts should be used. Torque the nuts to 14 ft. lbs. Torque the flange bolts to 35 ft. lbs.
17. Install the crossmember. Torque the bolts to 30 ft. lbs.
18. Remove the support jack.
19. Connect the speedometer cable, vacuum hoses and vent hose at the case.
20. Install the rear driveshaft. Use new strap bolts, torqued to 14 ft. lbs. Torque the flange bolts to 35 ft. lbs.
21. Fill the transfer case to the correct level.
22. Lower the vehicle.

NEW PROCESS 228

1. Raise and safely support the vehicle.
2. Drain the transfer case.
3. Disconnect the speedometer cable, vacuum hoses and vent hose from the case.
4. Disconnect the shift lever linkage rod at the case.
5. Support the transmission with a jack. Remove the rear crossmember.
6. Matchmark the rear driveshaft and remove it.
7. Matchmark the front driveshaft and remove it.
8. Remove the shift lever bracket bolts.
9. Support the transfer case with a jack and remove the attaching bolts.
10. Pull the case rearward out of the vehicle.

To install:

11. Position the transfer case in the vehicle. Torque the attaching bolts to 40 ft. lbs.
12. Install the shift lever bracket bolts.
13. Install the front and rear driveshafts. New strap bolts

should be used. Torque the strap bolt nuts to 14 ft. lbs.; the flange nuts to 35 ft. lbs.

14. Install the rear crossmember. Torque the bolts to 30 ft. lbs.
15. Connect the shift lever linkage rod at the case.
16. Connect the speedometer cable, vacuum hoses and vent hose from the case.
17. Fill the transfer case to the correct level.
18. Lower the vehicle.

NEW PROCESS 229

1. Raise and safely support the vehicle.
2. Drain the transfer case.
3. Disconnect the speedometer cable and vent hose. Disconnect the shift lever link at the operating lever.
4. Support the transmission with a jack.
5. Remove the rear crossmember.
6. Matchmark the driveshafts and remove them.
7. Disconnect the shift motor vacuum hoses.
8. Disconnect the shift linkage at the case.
9. Support the transfer case with a floor jack or transmission jack and remove the attaching bolts.
10. Pull the case rearward and remove it.
11. Clean the gasket mating surfaces and use new gasket material for installation.

To install:

12. Raise the transfer case into position. Make certain the case and transmission are mated without binding, before torquing the attaching bolts. Torque the bolts to 26 ft. lbs.
13. Connect the shift linkage at the case.
14. Connect the shift motor vacuum hoses.
15. Install the driveshafts. New strap bolts should be used. Torque the nuts to 14 ft. lbs.; torque the flange nuts to 35 ft. lbs.
16. Install the rear crossmember. Torque the bolts to 30 ft. lbs.
17. Remove the transmission support jack.
18. Connect the speedometer cable and vent hose.
19. Connect the shift lever link at the operating lever.
20. Fill the transfer case.
21. Lower the vehicle.

NEW PROCESS 231

1. Shift the transfer case into **N**.
2. Raise and support the vehicle safely.
3. Drain the lubricant.
4. Matchmark and remove the front and rear driveshafts.
5. Support the transmission with a jack.
6. Remove the rear crossmember.
7. Disconnect the speedometer cable.
8. Disconnect the linkage.
9. Disconnect the vent and vacuum hoses and the indicator wire.
10. Support the transfer case with a transmission jack.
11. Remove the transfer case-to-transmission bolts.
12. Pull the case rearward to disengage it and lower it from the truck.

To install:

13. Raise the transfer case into position. Make certain the case and transmission are mated without binding, before torquing the attaching bolts. Torque the bolts to 26 ft. lbs.
14. Connect the shift linkage at the case.
15. Connect the vacuum hoses.
16. Install the driveshafts. New strap bolts should be used. Torque the nuts to 14 ft. lbs.; torque the flange nuts to 35 ft. lbs.
17. Install the rear crossmember. Torque the bolts to 30 ft. lbs.
18. Remove the transmission floor jack.
19. Connect the speedometer cable and vent hose.
20. Connect the shift lever link at the operating lever.
21. Fill the transfer case to the correct level.
22. Lower the vehicle.

NEW PROCESS 242

1. Shift the transfer case into N.
2. Raise and safely support the vehicle.
3. Drain the lubricant.
4. Matchmark and remove the front and rear driveshafts.
5. Support the transmission with a jack.
6. Remove the rear crossmember.
7. Disconnect the speedometer cable.
8. Disconnect the linkage.
9. Disconnect the vent and vacuum hoses and the indicator wire.
10. Support the transfer case with a transmission jack.
11. Remove the transfer case-to-transmission bolts.
12. Pull the case rearward to disengage it and lower it from the vehicle.

To install:

13. Raise the transfer case into position. Make certain the case and transmission are mated without binding, before torquing the attaching bolts. Torque the bolts to 26 ft. lbs.
14. Connect the shift linkage at the case.
15. Connect the vacuum hoses.
16. Install the driveshafts. New strap bolts should be used. Torque the nuts to 14 ft. lbs.; torque the flange nuts to 35 ft. lbs.
17. Install the rear crossmember. Torque the bolts to 30 ft. lbs.
18. Remove the transmission floor jack.
19. Connect the speedometer cable and vent hose.
20. Connect the shift lever link at the operating lever.
21. Fill the transfer case.
22. Lower the vehicle.

Linkage Adjustment

1. Place the range selector in 2WD for the NP 207; HIGH for the NP 228/229 or 4 LOW for the NP 231/242.
2. Insert a ⅛ inch (3 mm) spacer between the shift lever gate and the lever. Hold the lever in this position.
3. Ensure that the transfer case lever is in the appropriate position.
4. Adjust the link, at the trunnion, to provide a free pin at the case outer lever.

Installing the shift lever adjusting spacer

Shift linkage adjusting trunnion

DRIVE AXLE

Driveshaft and U-Joints

Removal and Installation

FRONT

NOTE: These vehicles may come equipped with one of 2 different type front driveshafts. The first type has a conventional universal joint at the axle but a double offset joint at the transfer case. The second type has a conventional universal joint at the axle and a double cardan joint at the transfer case.

1. Place the transmission and transfer case in N.
2. Raise and safely support the vehicle.
3. Matchmark the shaft ends, axle and transfer case.
4. Remove the U-joint strap bolts at the front axle yoke.
5. Remove the double offset joint flange nuts at the transfer case.
6. Installation is the reverse of removal.

REAR

NOTE: Two different driveshafts are used on these ve-

hicles. With Command-Trac®, the driveshaft has welded yokes at each end. With Selec-Trac®, a welded yoke is used at the rear and a splined slip yoke is used at the front.

1. Place the transmission in **N**.
2. Raise and safely support the vehicle.
3. Matchmark the yokes and flanges.
4. On vehicles with Command-Trac®, the driveshaft may be removed by disconnecting it at the axle and sliding it from the front yoke, leaving the front yoke attached to the transfer case. If done this way, matchmark the driveshaft and front yoke before separation.
5. On vehicles with Selec-Trac®, disconnect the yokes from the axle and transfer case. Remove the driveshaft.
6. Installation is the reverse of removal. Torque the U-joint strap nuts to 19 ft. lbs.

NOTE: New U-joint straps should be used.

Front Axle Shaft, Bearing and Seal

Removal and Installation

EXCEPT GRAND WAGONEER

1. Raise and support the vehicle safely.
2. Remove the wheels, calipers and rotors.
3. Remove the cotter pin, locknut and axle hub nut.
4. Remove the hub-to-knuckle attaching bolts.
5. Remove the hub and splash shield from the steering knuckle.
6. Remove the axle shaft from the housing.
7. To remove the right shaft:
   a. Disconnect the vacuum harness from the shift motor.
   b. Remove the shift motor from the housing.
   c. Remove the axle shaft from the housing.

To install:

8. When installing the right axle shaft, ensure the shift collar is in position on the intermediate shaft and that the axle shaft is fully engaged in the intermediate shaft end.
9. Install the shift motor, making sure the fork engages with the collar. Tighten the bolts to 8 ft. lbs.
10. On the left side, install the axle shaft in the housing.
11. Partially fill the hub cavity of the knuckle with chassis lube and install the hub and splash shield.
12. Tighten the hub bolts to 75 ft. lbs.
13. Install the hub washer and nut. Torque the nut to 175 ft. lbs. Install the locknut. Install a new cotter pin.
14. Install the rotor, caliper and wheel.

GRAND WAGONEER

1. Raise and support the vehicle safely.
2. Remove the wheel, brake caliper and drive flange snapring.
3. Remove the inner and outer locknut and disc brake rotor/hub.
4. Remove the nuts and bolts attaching the spindle.
5. Remove the axle shaft, seal and bronze thrust washer.

To install:

6. Clean all components throughly. If damaged replace the bronze thrust washer.
7. Install the bronze thrust washer with the chamfered side inward. Install the replacement seal using a seal driver.
8. Pack wheel bearing grease around the inner face of the axle shaft and the seal. Install the axle shaft.
9. Position the spindle on the steering knuckle and install the retaining nuts. Tighten to 28 ft. lbs. (38 Nm).
10. Install the disc brake rotor and inner wheel bearing locknut. Tighten the locknut just enough to remove the endplay.
11. Install the wheel and tighten the lug nuts hand tight. Tighten the inner locknut to 50 ft. lbs. (68 Nm), then loosen 45–65 degrees. While turning the wheel tighten the locknut to seat the bearings. Install the washer and cotter pin.

12. Install teh outer locknut and tighten to 50 ft. lbs. (68 Nm). Remove the wheel.
13. Install the drive flange snapring, brake caliper and wheel. Tighten lug nuts to 75 ft. lbs. (102 Nm).

Rear Axle Shaft, Bearing and Seal

Removal and Installation

EXCEPT GRAND WAGONEER AND HEAVY DUTY AXLE

1. Raise and support the vehicle safely. Remove the wheel and brake drum.
2. Remove the rear differential cover and drain the lubricant.
3. Rotate the differential case and remove the lock screw and the pinion gear mate shaft.
4. Force the axle shaft toward the center of the vehicle and remove the C-clip. Remove the axle shaft.
5. Pry the axle shaft seal and bearing using tool 6310 or equivalent.

To install:

6. If the axle shaft seal and bearing were removed, install a new bearing and seal with tool C-4171 and 6437 or equivalent.
7. Install the axle shaft taking care not to damage the seal. Install the C-clip and force the axle shaft outward to seat the clip.
8. Insert the differentialpinion gear mate shaft and tighen the locking screw to 14 ft. lbs. (19 Nm).
9. Install the differential housing cover and tighten the attaching bolts to 35 ft. lbs. (47 Nm). Install the brake drum and wheel.
10. Fill the differential with lubricant and test drive. If equipped with Trac-Loc, drive the vehicle through 10–12 figure 8 turns to pump the lubricant through the clutch discs.

GRAND WAGONEER AND HEAVY DUTY AXLE

1. Raise and support the vehicle safely.
2. Remove the wheel and brake drum. Remove the nuts that attach the outer seal retainer to the axle tube. Discard the nuts.
3. Remove the axle shaft using tool J-25109-1 or equivalent.
4. Remove the axle shaft inner seal and discard.
5. Clamp the axle shaft in a vise. Center punch then drill a ¼ inch hole in the bearing retaining ring. Cut the retainig ring with a chisel and remove.
6. Use a bearing remover, tool 7650 or equivalent, and press the bearing off the shaft.
7. Remove the outer seal and replace the seal retainer, if damaged.

To install:

8. Clean all components throughly. Apply a light coat of wheel bearing grease to the bearing, seal and contact surfaces of the axle.
9. Install the inner seal with tool 8040 or equivalent. Install the retainer plate and outer seal on the shaft. Press the replacement bearing on the shaft with installer 7650 or equivalent.
10. Install the axle shaft into the rube and tighten the seal retainer nuts to 32 ft. lbs. (43 Nm).
11. Install the brake drum and wheel.

Steering Knuckle

Removal and Installation

EXCEPT GRAND WAGONEER

1. Raise and safely support the vehicle. Remove the wheel assembly.
2. Remove the brake caliper and anchor plate from the knuckle.
3. Remove the outer axle shaft.
4. Remove the knuckle-to-ball joint cotter pins and nuts.
5. Drive the knuckle out with a brass hammer.

Steering knuckle assembly—Grand Wagoneer

To install:

6. Install the axle shaft, brake caliper and the caliper anchor plate. Tighen the anchor plate bolts to 77 ft. lbs.

GRAND WAGONEER

1. Raise and support the vehicle safely.
2. Remove the axle shaft. Disconnect the tie rod end stud using a puller, if necessary.
3. Remove and discard the lower ball joint nut. Remove the cotter pin from the upper ball joint and loosen but do not remove the nut.
4. Unseat the upper and lower ball joints. Remove the upper ball joint. Remove the upper ball joint split ring the tool J-23447.

To install:

5. Install the upper ball joint spilt ring seat in the axle bore. The top of the seat should be flush with the top of the yoke.
6. Position the steering knuckle ball joints in the bores and install the lower ball joint nut finger-tight.
7. Using an appropriate installation kit, install the lower ball joint until it is firmly seated in the bore. Tighten the nut to 80 ft. lbs. (108 Nm).
8. Tighten the upper ball joint seat to 50 ft. lbs. (68 Nm). Install and tighten the upper ball joint nut to 100 ft. lbs. (136 Nm).
9. Connect the tie rod and tighten to 60 ft. lbs. (81 Nm). Install the axle shaft.

Pinion Seal

Removal and Installation

1. Raise and support the vehicle safely.
2. Matchmark and remove the driveshaft.
3. Rotate the pinion gear 3–4 times and measure the amount of torque necessary to rotate the pinion.

NOTE: Checking the pinion gear rotation torque is necessary to set the pinion gear preload after seal installation.

4. Matchmark the pinion yoke and remove the pinion gear nut and yoke.
5. Remove the pinion gear seal.

To install:

6. Lubricate and install the new pinion seal using a seal driver.
7. Align and install the yoke, washer and pinion nut. Tighten the pinion nut finger-tight.
8. Using a torque wrench, note the amount of torque necessary to rotate the pinion. The required pinion preload torque is equal to the measurement noted in the removal steps, plus 5 inch lbs.
9. Tighten the pinion nut in small increments and continue measureing preload torque until correct.
10. Align and install the driveshaft using new strap bolts. Tighten the bolts to 14 ft. lbs. (19 Nm).

GRAND WAGONEER

1. Raise and support the vehicle safely.
2. Matchamrk and remove the driveshaft.
3. Using a holding tool and socket wrench, remove the pinion yoke nut and washer. Discard the nut.
4. Using a puller, remove the yoke.
5. Punch the seal with a pin punch and pry it from the seal bore.

To install:

6. Drive the new seal into place using a seal driver.
7. Install the yoke, washer and a new nut. Torque the nut to 210 ft. lbs.
8. Check the amount of torque required to rotate the pinion gear, it should be 10–20 inch lbs.

NOTE: New strap bolts should be used whenever the driveshaft is disconnected.

9. Install the driveshaft. Torque the starp bolt nuts to 14 ft. lbs.

Differential Carrier

Removal and Installation

1. Raise the vehicle and support it safely. Drain the axle housing lubricant. Remove the axle housing cover.
2. Matchmark the driveshaft and remove. Remove the following components: wheels, disc brake rotors, hubs and bearings, shift motor, housing and axle shafts. If equipped with Command-Trac, remove the intermediate axle shaft retaining clup and disengage the shaft from the right side differential.
3. Mark the differential bearing caps for alignment during the assembly. Loosen the bearing cap bolts but do not remove. Disconnect the tie rod from the left steering knuckle and disconnect the track bar from the frame.
4. Install an axle housing spreader tool on the axle housing and secure with the hold-down clamps. Mount a dial indicator on the axle housing to measure the amount of spread. Zero the indicator dial.
5. Spread the axle housing no more than 0.015 in. for Grand Wagoneer and 0.020 in. for all others. Remove the differential bearing caps and the dial indicator from the housing. Using 2 prybars, remove the differential carrier from the axle housing.
6. Remove the spreader tool from the housing as soon as the differential carrier is removed to avoid the possibility of the axle housing taking a set.

To install:

7. Set the ring gear backlash and pinion depth as follows:
   a. Apply yellow ferrous oxide compound to both drive and coast sides of the ring gear teeth.
   b. Install the differential case in the housing. Tap the outer edges of the bearing cups with a mallet to seat them. Observe the installation regerence marks and install the bearing caps. Tighten bolts securely.
   c. Attach a dial indicator to the housing. Position the indicator plunger against the drive side of on ring gear tooth. Ensure that the plunger is at a right angle (90 degrees) to the tooth.
   d. Pry the ring gear toward the dial indicator and zero the indicator pointer while at this position. Pry the ring gear away from the drive pinion gear until the gear backlash indicated is 0.005–0.009 in.
   e. Temporarily insert shims between on differential housing bearing and the housing to maintain the established gear backlash during the remainder of the adjustment.
   f. Move the dial indicator aside and apply yellow ferrous oxide compound to the ring gear teeth. Rotate the ring gear on complete revolution in both directions to imprint the gear teeth contact patterns in the compound.
   g. Note the teeth patterns and refer to the Gear Teeth Contact Patterns chart. To increase backlash, subtract shims from the ring gear side of the case. To decrease backlash, add shims to the ring gear side of the case.
   h. Remove the differential and pinion gear and make any necessary adjustments to the shims. Reinstall the gears and repeat the gear contact pattern test until gear patterns are satisfactory.
8. Position the axle housing spreader tool on the axle housing and secure it in place with the hold-down clamps. Install a dial indicator and center the dial.
9. Spread the axle housing to a maximum of 0.020 in. Remove the dial indicator. Lubricate the differential side bearings and install the differential carrier in the axle housing. Tap the unit in place with a soft faced hammer. Remove the axle housing spreader tool.

Checking ring gear endplay

10. Install the bearing caps in their proper place and torque to 40 ft. lbs. on model 30 rear axle or to 80 ft. lbs. on all other models.
11. Install a dial indicator and recheck the ring gear backlash at 2 points. Correct as necessary. Complete the assembly in the reverse of the removal procedure.

Rear Axle Housing

Removal and Installation

1. Raise and support the vehicle safely. Remove the rear wheels.
2. Matchmark and remove the driveshaft. Disconnect the track bar, if equipped.
3. Disconnect the vent hose, parking brake cable and the shock absorbers.
4. Disconnect the brake hose at the junction. Do not disconnect the wheel cylinders.
5. Loosen the bolts that attach the spring front eyes to the frame. Remove the spring U-bolts and support the axle with a floorjack.
6. Raise the rear just enough to relieve the axle weight from the springs. Remove the bolts attaching the springs to the shackles and lower the rear.

To install:

7. Support the axle on the floorjack and raise into position. Install the spring shackle bolts but do not tighten them.

NOTE: The track bar and spring eye bushing bolts must be tightened with the vehicle at ride height.

8. Align the spring center bolts with the locating boles and lower the axle onto the springs. Install the U-bolts and brackets.
9. Tighten the U-bolts to 100 ft. lbs. (136 Nm) for the Grand Wagoneer or 90 ft. lbs. (122 Nm) for all others.
10. Connect the axle vent tube, parking brake cables and brake hose. Align and install the driveshaft. Tighten the bolts to 14 ft. lbs. (19 Nm).
11. Connect the track bar and shock absorbers. Bleed the brakes. Check the fluid level in the differential. Install the wheels and lower the vehicle.

Exploded view of the Dana 44 axle

Labels on the diagram:
- RING GEAR BOLTS
- DIFFERENTIAL CASE
- DIFFERENTIAL BEARING SHIMS
- DIFFERENTIAL BEARING
- BEARING CUP
- PINION GEAR
- PINION SHIMS
- AXLE HOUSING
- SLINGER
- PINION NUT
- WASHER
- YOKE
- DUST CAP
- SEAL
- PINION FRONT BEARING
- FRONT BEARING CUP
- BEARING
- OUTER SEAL
- RETAINER
- BEARING RETAINER RING
- INNER SEAL
- PRELOAD SHIMS
- REAR BEARING CUP
- PINION REAR BEARING
- PINION THRUST WASHERS
- SIDE GEAR
- PINION GEAR
- SIDE GEAR THRUST WASHERS
- RING GEAR
- COVER
- FILL PLUG
- PINION SHAFT
- LOCKPIN

Front Axle Housing

Removal and Installation

1. Raise and support the vehicle safely.
2. Remove the wheels, calipers and rotors.
3. Disconnect all vacuum hoses at the axle.
4. Matchmark and remove the driveshaft.
5. Disconnect the stabilizer bar, rod and center link, shock absorbers, steering damper, track bar and ABS brake sensors.
6. Support the front axle with a floorjack.
7. Disconnect the upper and lower control arms at the axle and lower the axle from the vehicle. Disconnect the spring bushing through bolts and U-bolts from the axle tube.
8. Lower the axle.

To install:

9. Raise and support the rear in position with a floor jack.
10. Install and tighten all suspension arm or spring shackle bolts. Tighten the bolts finger-tight.
11. Connect the stabilizer bar, rod and center link, shock absorbers, steering damper, track bar and ABS brake sensors. Lower the vehicle to normal ride height and tighten the suspension bolts as follows:

    Upper control arm-to-axle—55 ft. lbs.
    Lower control arm-to-axle—133 ft. lbs.
    Track bar-to-axle—74 ft. lbs.
    Steering damper-to-axle—55 ft. lbs.
    Shock absorber lower bolt—14 ft. lbs.
    Center link-to-knuckle—35 ft. lbs.
    Stabilizer bar-to-axle—70 ft. lbs.
    Stabilizer bar-to-connecting links—55 ft. lbs.
    U-joint strap nuts—14 ft. lbs.
    U-bolt retaining nuts—100 ft. lbs.

NOTE: Discard the U-joint straps. New replacement straps must be used whenever the straps are removed.

12. Align and install the driveshaft.
13. Connect all vacuum hoses at the axle.
14. Install the wheels, calipers and rotors.
15. Check the front wheel alignment.

Axle Shift Motor and Housing

Removal and Installation

1. Raise and safely support the vehicle.
2. Position a drain pan under the shift motor housing. Disconnect the vacuum harness from the shift motor.
3. Remove the housing attaching bolts and remove the housing, motor and shift fork unit as an assembly.
4. Mark the shift fork and housing for installtion reference.

Labels on the diagram:
- AXLE SHIFT MOTOR HOUSING
- AXLE SHIFT MOTOR

Axle shift motor and housing—location

Rotate the shift motor and remove the shift fork and motor retaining snaprings. Remove the shift motor.

5. Remove and discard the O-ring from the shift motor shaft.

To install:

6. Add 5 ounces of SAE 75W–90 axle oil to the axle through the shift motor opening. Install a replacement O-ring seal on the shift motor shaft.

7. Install the shift motor in the housing with the retaining snaprings and slide the shft fork onto the shaft with the reference mark aligned.

8. Engage the shift fork with the shift collar. Install and tighten the mounting bolts to 101 inch lbs. (11 Nm).

9. Connect the vacuum harness and lower the vehicle.

10. Check the operation of the shift mechanism.

STEERING

Steering Wheel

Removal and Installation

1. Disconnect the negative battery cable.
2. Set the front tires in a straight-ahead position.
3. Pull the horn button from the steering wheel. With sport wheel, remove the button, nut, washer, retainer and horn ring. It is necessary to remove the attaching screws from under the steering wheel spoke to remove the horn cover.
4. Remove the steering wheel nut and vibration damper.
5. Scribe a line mark on the steering wheel and steering shaft if there is not one already. Release the turn signal assembly from the steering post and install a puller.
6. Remove the steering wheel and spring.

To install:

7. To install, align the scribe marks on the steering shaft with the steering wheel and secure the steering wheel spring, steering wheel and horn button contact cup with the steering wheel nut. Tighten the nut to 25 ft. lbs. (34 Nm).
8. Install the horn button.
9. Connect the battery cable and test the horn.

Steering wheel components

Steering Column and Shaft

Removal and Installation

NOTE: When removed from the vehicle, a steering column must be handled very carefully. Otherwise, the plastic fasteners that maintain the rigidity of the energy-absorbing components could be damaged.

1. Disconnect the negative battery cable.
2. Matchmark the intermediate shaft and the steering shaft for assembly reference.
3. Disconnect the steering shaft from the intermediate shaft. If necessary, remove the lower part of the instrument panel.
4. Disconnect the automatic transmission shift indicator pointer cable from the shift housing and disconnect the column support bracket. Lower the steering wheel.
5. Disconnect the following wiring harnesses from the steering column: ignition switch, dimmer switch, turn signal, windshield wiper, cruise control and the park lock cable.
6. Disconnect the steering column toe plate from the instrument panel and remove the column.

To install:

7. Position the steering column in the vehicle paying close attention to the alignment marks. Connect the bracket to the steering column.
8. Connect all wiring harnesses and the park lock cable.
9. Connect the toe plate to the instrument panel and the shift indicator to the transmission.
10. Install the lower part of the insturment panel. Check the operation of the shift lever and indicator and adjust as necessary. Connect the negative battery cable.

Manual Steering Gear

Removal and Installation

1. Disconnect the steering shaft from the gear.
2. Raise and safely support the vehicle.
3. Disconnect the center link from the pitman arm.
4. Remove the front stabilizer bar.
5. Remove the pitman arm nut, matchmark the arm and shaft and remove the arm with a puller.
6. Unbolt and remove the gear.
7. Installation is the reverse of removal. The pitman arm nut must be securely staked. Observe the following torques:

    Steering gear-to-frame—65 ft. lbs.
    Pitman arm-to-shaft—185 ft. lbs.
    Stabilizer bar-to-frame—55 ft. lbs.
    Stabilizer bar-to-link—27 ft. lbs.
    Center link-to-pitman arm—55 ft. lbs.

Adjustment

1. Raise and safely support the vehicle.
2. Check the steering gear mounting bolt torque.

Exploded view of the manual steering gear

3. Matchmark the pitman arm and shaft and remove the pitman arm nut. Remove the arm with a puller.

4. Loosen the pitman adjusting screw locknut, then back off the adjusting screw 2–3 turns.

5. Remove the horn button and cover. Slowly turn the steering wheel in one direction as far as it will go, then back ½ turn.

6. Install a socket and torque wrench in the steering wheel nut. Measure the worm bearing preload by turning the wheel through a 90 degree arc (¼ turn) with the wrench. Preload should be 5–8 inch lbs.

7. If preload is not within specifications, turn the adjuster screw clockwise to increase or counterclockwise to decrease the preload.

8. When the desired preload is attained, tighten the adjuster locknut to 90 ft. lbs. and recheck the adjustment.

9. Rotate the steering wheel slowly from lock-to-lock, counting the number of turns. Turn the wheel back, ½ the number of turns to center the gear, then turn the wheel ½ turn off center.

10. Install the torque wrench and socket on the steering wheel nut. Measure the torque required to turn the gear through the center point of travel. The drag should equal the worm bearing preload torque plus 4–10 inch lbs. but not exceed a total of 18 inch lbs.

11. If adjustment is required, loosen the pitman shaft screw locknut and turn the adjusting screw to obtain the desired torque. Tighten the locknut to 25 ft. lbs. and recheck the overcenter drag.

12. Install all parts and check steering wheel alignment.

Power Steering Gear

Removal and Installation

1. Disconnect the steering shaft from the gear.
2. Raise and safely support the vehicle.
3. Disconnect the center link from the pitman arm.
4. Remove the front stabilizer bar.
5. Remove the pitman arm nut, matchmark the arm and shaft and remove the arm with a puller.
6. Disconnect and plug the power steering lines.
7. Unbolt and remove the gear.
8. Installation is the reverse of removal. The pitman arm nut must be securely staked. Observe the following torques:
   Steering gear-to-frame—65 ft. lbs.
   Pitman arm-to-shaft—185 ft. lbs.
   Stabilizer bar-to-frame—55 ft. lbs.
   Stabilizer bar-to-link—27 ft. lbs.
   Center link-to-pitman arm—55 ft. lbs.
9. Fill the power steering system to the correct level and bleed the system.

Worm Bearing Preload Adjustment

1. Remove the steering gear and place in on a clean workbench.
2. Remove the adjuster plug locknut. Seat the adjuster plug firmly by applying about 20 ft. lbs. of torque.
3. Place an index mark on the gear housing, opposite one of the adjuster plug holes.
4. Going counterclockwise, make another mark ³⁄₁₆–¼ in. from the first mark.

Wormshaft bearing preload adjustment

5. Turn the adjuster plug counterclockwise until the hole, which was aligned with the first mark, is now aligned with the second mark.

6. Install the adjuster plug locknut and torque it to 85 ft. lbs., making certain it does not move.

7. Turn the stub shaft clockwise to its stop, then turn it back ¼ turn.

8. Using an inch pound (inch lbs.) torque wrench with a 50 inch lbs. scale and a 12 point deep socket on the stub shaft, take a reading of effort when the beam of the torque wrench passes the vertical point while turning. Torque at this point must be 4–10 inch lbs. If the reading is not correct, the adjuster plug is either not set correctly or moved while tightening the locknut or there is internal damage in the gear.

Pitman Shaft Overcenter Drag Torque

1. Turn the pitman shaft adjuster screw counterclockwise until it is fully extended, then, turn it back ½ turn.

2. Rotate the stub shaft from stop to stop, counting the total number of full turns, then, turn it back ½ the number of full turns. This is the center point of its travel. When the gear is centered, the flat on the stub shaft should face upward and be parallel with the side cover. The master spline on the pitman shaft should be aligned with the adjuster screw.

3. Place an inch pound torque wrench with a 50 inch lbs. scale and a 12 point deep socket, on the stub shaft, with the torque wrench beam in the vertical position.

4. Rotate the torque wrench 45 degrees to each side of center and note the highest torque reading on or near the center point. Adjust the drag torque, by turning the adjusting screw clockwise, to the following values:

    a. New steering gears (used less than 400 miles), add 4–8 inch lbs. to the previously noted torque but don't exceed a total of 18 inch lbs.

    b. Used gears (used 400 miles or more), add 4–5 inch lbs. to the previously noted torque but don't exceed a total of 14 inch lbs.

5. When adjustment is complete, tighten the locknut to 20 ft. lbs.

6. Install the gear in the vehicle.

Power steering pump—exploded view

Power Steering Pump

Removal and Installation

SERPENTINE DRIVE BELT

NOTE: A belt tension gauge is needed to adjust the belt tension.

1. Disconnect the negative battery cable. Loosen the alternator adjustment and pivot bolts.

2. Insert the drive lug of a ½ in. drive ratchet into the adjustment hole in the alternator bracket and move the alternator to relieve tension on the belt.

3. Remove the drive belt.

4. Remove the air cleaner.

5. Disconnect the hoses at the pump and cap the hose ends.

6. Remove the front bracket-to-engine bolts.

7. Support the pump and remove the pump-to-rear bracket nuts.

8. Lift out the pump.

To install:

9. Install the pump in position and torque the pump-to-bracket nuts to 28 ft. lbs.; the bracket-to-engine bolts to 33 ft. lbs.

10. Install the drive belt. Using the ½ in. drive ratchet, move the alternator to put tension on the belt, tighten the alternator adjustment and pivot bolts and check the belt tension with a tension gauge at the mid-point of its longest straight run.

11. Belt tension should be 180–200 ft. lbs. for a new belt or 140–160 ft. lbs. for a used belt.

12. When the tension is achieved, tighten the alternator pivot bolt to 28 ft. lbs.; the adjustment bolt to 18 ft. lbs.

V-TYPE DRIVE BELT

1. Disconnect the negative battery cable. Loosen the power steering pump adjustment and pivot bolts.

2. Insert the drive lug of a ½ in. drive ratchet into the adjustment hole in the pump rear bracket and move the pump to relieve tension on the belt.

3. Remove the drive belt.

4. Remove the air cleaner.

5. Disconnect the hoses at the pump and cap the hose ends.

6. Remove the front bracket-to-engine bolts.

7. Support the pump and remove the pump-to-rear bracket nuts.

8. Lift out the pump.

9. Install the pump into position and torque the pump-to-

bracket nuts to 28 ft. lbs.; the bracket-to-engine bolts to 33 ft. lbs.

10. Install the drive belt. Using the ½ in. drive ratchet, move the pump to put tension on the belt, tighten the pump adjustment and pivot bolts and check the belt tension with a tension gauge at the mid-point of its longest straight run. Belt tension should be 120–160 ft. lbs. for a new belt or 90–115 ft. lbs. for a used belt.

11. When the tension is achieved, tighten the pump pivot nut to 21 ft. lbs.; the adjustment bolt to 21 ft. lbs.

System Bleeding

1. Raise the front of the vehicle and support safely.
2. With the wheels turned all the way to the left, add power steering fluid to the **COLD** mark on the fluid level indicator.
3. Start the engine and check the fluid level at fast idle. Add fluid, if necessary to bring the level up to the **COLD** mark.
4. Bleed air from the system by turning the wheels from side-to-side without hitting the stops. Keep the fluid level just above the internal pump casting or at the **COLD** mark.

5. Return the wheels to the center position and continue running the engine for 2–3 minutes.
6. Road test the vehicle to check steering function and re-check the fluid level with the system at its normal operating temperature. Fluid should be at the **HOT** mark.

Tie Rod Ends

Removal and Installation

1. Raise and safely support the vehicle.
2. Remove the cotter pins and retaining nuts at both ends of the tie rod.
3. Remove the tie rod ends from the steering arm and center link.
4. Count the number of visible threads on the tie rod and unscrew the tie rod ends.
5. Installation is the reverse of removal. Install the tie rod ends, leaving the same number of threads exposed. Torque the retaining nuts to 35 ft. lbs.

BRAKES

For all brake system repair and service procedures not detailed below, please refer to "Brakes" in the Unit Repair section.

Master Cylinder

Removal and Installation

1. Disconnect the negative battery cable. Disconnect and plug the brake lines.
2. Disconnect the wires from the stoplight switch.
3. Remove all attaching bolts and nuts and lift the assembly from the vehicle.
4. Prior to installation, fill the master cylinder and operate the pushrod until fluid squirts from the ports.
5. Installation is the reverse of removal. Torque the mounting nuts to 15–21 ft. lbs. Bleed the brake system.

Proportioning Valve

Removal and Installation
COMANCHE ONLY

1. Disconnect the linkage and spring.
2. Disconnect and cap the brake lines.
3. Unbolt and remove the valve.
4. Installation is the reverse of removal. Torque the valve bracket-to-frame bolts to 155 inch lbs.; the valve-to-bracket bolts to 118 inch lbs.

Adjustment

NOTE: **The vehicle must be unloaded and on a level surface for accurate valve adjustment. The valve bushing must also be replaced during adjustment. Failure to follow this procedure exactly can result in poor brake performance.**

1. Position the vehicle on a level surface with the bed unloaded. Remove the nut not attaching the lever to the valve shaft.
2. Pull the lever and retainer off the valve shaft. Remove and discard the old bushing. Clean the threads and splines on the valve shaft.

3. If the valve link was disconnected from the axle bracket, reconnect the link before continuing. Loosen the valve mounting bolts 2 full turns.
4. On 1990–92 models, turn the valve shaft until the shaft flat is between the 5:00 and 6:00 o'clock positions. On 1988–89 models, turn the valve shaft until the shaft flat is at the 4:00 o'clock position.
5. Install the valve adjusting gauge and position it on the mounting bolts and shaft. There should be no clearance between the gauge, shaft and bolts. The gauge must me seated on the shaft.
6. Install the retainer in the lever and insert a new bushing in the retainer and lever. Start the bushing and lever on the valve shaft. Finish pressing it on with a C-clamp.
7. Remove the adjustment gauge and tighten the lever nut to 100 inch lbs. Tighten the valve mounting bolts to 118 inch lbs.

Power Brake Booster

Removal and Installation

1. Loosen but do not remove the nuts attaching the master cylinder to booster.
2. Remove the instrument panel lower trim cover.
3. On Grand Wagoneer, remove the air conditioner duct and lower trim panel. Remove the cotter pin, washer and bushing attaching the booster pushrod pedal.
4. On all other models, remove the retaining clip attaching the booster pushrod to the brake pedal.
5. Remove the bolts and nuts attaching the booster to the dash panel and remove the vacuum hose.
6. Remove the master cylinder from the booster and carefully position it aside. Remove the booster.
To install:
7. Install the check valve and grommet in the booster. Position the booster on the vehicle and install the attaching nuts and bolts.
8. Attach the booster pushrod to the brake pedal. Tighten the booster mounting bolts and nuts to 22–30 ft. lbs. (30–41 Nm).
9. Connect the brake light electrical connector and reinstall the trim panels and air conditioner ducts.
10. Install the master cylinder on the booster and tighten the nuts to 15–25 ft. lbs. (21–34 Nm). Top off the master cylinder, connect the vacuum hose and check for proper operation of the system.

Brake Caliper

Removal and Installation

1. Drain ⅔ of the brake fluid from the front reservoir. Use the bleeder screw at the front outlet port to drain the fluid. If equipped with anti-lock brakes, relieve the system pressure.
2. Raise and safely support the vehicle.
3. Remove the wheels.
4. Place a C-clamp on the caliper so the solid end contacts the back of the caliper and the screw end contacts the metal part of the outboard brake pad.
5. Tighten the clamp until the caliper moves far enough to force the piston to the bottom of the piston bore. This will back the brake pads off of the rotor surface to facilitate the removal and installation of the caliper assembly.
6. Remove the C-clamp.

NOTE: Do not push down on the brake pedal or the piston and brake pads will return to their original positions up against the rotor.

7. Remove both of the allen head mounting bolts and lift the caliper off the rotor.

NOTE: If just the brake pads are being replaced, it is not necessary to remove the caliper assembly entirely from the vehicle. Do not remove the brake line. Rest the caliper on the front spring or other support. Do not allow the brake hose to support the weight of the caliper.

8. If the caliper is being removed, it is necessary to disconnect the brake fluid hose. Clean the brake fluid hose-to-caliper connection thoroughly. Remove the hose-to-caliper bolt. Cap or tape the open ends to keep dirt out. Discard the copper gaskets.
To install:
9. Install the caliper in the reverse order of removal. Torque the mounting bolts to 7–15 ft. lbs.

NOTE: If the brake fluid hose was disconnected, it will be necessary to bleed the hydraulic system.

10. Fill the master cylinder with fluid. Before driving the vehicle, pump the brakes several times to seat the pads.

Disc Brake Pads

Removal and Installation

1. Raise and safely support the vehicle.
2. Drain ⅔ of the brake fluid from the front reservoir. Use the bleeder screw at the front outlet port to drain the fluid. If equipped with anti-lock brakes, relieve the system pressure.
3. Raise and support the vehicle safely.
4. Remove the wheels.
5. Remove the brake caliper.
6. Hold the anti-rattle clip against the caliper anchor plate and remove the outboard brake pad.
7. Remove the inboard pad and its anti-rattle clip.
8. Clean all the mounting holes and bushing grooves in the caliper ears. Clean the mounting bolts. Replace the bolts if they are corroded or if the threads are damaged. Wipe the inside of the caliper clean, including the exterior of the dust boot. Inspect the dust boot for cuts or cracks and for proper seating in the piston bore. If evidence of fluid leakage is noted, the caliper should be rebuilt.

NOTE: Do not use abrasives on the bolts in order not to destroy their protective plating. Do not use compressed air to clean the inside of the caliper, as it may unseat the dust boot seal.

9. Install the inboard anti-rattle clip on the trailing end of the anchor plate. The split end of the clip must face away from the rotor.

10. Install the inboard pad in the caliper. The pad must lay flat against the piston.
11. Install the outboard pad in the caliper while holding the anti-rattle clip.
12. With the pads installed, position the caliper over the rotor. Line up the mounting holes in the caliper and the support bracket and insert the mounting bolts. Make sure the bolts pass under the retaining ears on the inboard shoes. Push the bolts through until they engage the holes of the outboard pad and caliper ears. Thread the bolts into the support bracket and tighten them to 30 ft. lbs.
13. Fill the master cylinder with brake fluid and pump the brake pedal to seat the pads. If equipped with ABS, turn the ignition **ON** and allow the pump to build pressure. After the pump has stopped running, pump the brakes.
14. Install the wheel assembly and lower the vehicle. Check the level of the brake fluid in the master cylinder and fill as necessary. Test the operation of the brakes before taking the vehicle onto the road.

Brake Rotor

Removal and Installation

2WD

1. Raise and safely support the vehicle.
2. Remove the wheels.
3. Remove the caliper without disconnecting the brake line. Suspend it aside.
4. Remove the grease cap, cotter pin, nut cap, nut and washer from the spindle.
5. Pull slowly on the hub and catch the outer bearing as it falls.
6. Remove the hub and rotor. The inner bearing and seal can be removed by prying out and discarding the inner seal.
To install:
7. Clean and repack the hub and bearings, install the inner bearing and a new seal.
8. Position the hub and rotor on the spindle and install the outer bearing.
9. Install the washer and nut.
10. While turning the rotor, torque the nut to 25 ft. lbs. to seat the bearings.
11. Back off the nut ½ turn and, while turning the rotor, torque the nut to 19 inch lbs.
12. Install the nut cap and a new cotter pin. Install the grease cap.
13. Install the caliper.
14. Install the wheels.

4WD

Except Grand Wagoneer

1. Loosen the lug nuts on the front wheels.
2. Raise and ssafely support the vehicle.
3. Remove the front wheels.
4. Remove the calipers but don't disconnect the brake lines. Suspend the calipers aside.
5. Remove the rotor.
6. Installation is the reverse of removal.

Grand Wagoneer

1. Raise and safely support the vehicle.
2. Remove the wheels.
3. Remove the caliper without disconnecting the brake line. Suspend it aside.
4. Remove the hub cap and snapring.
5. Remove the drive gear, pressure spring and spring cup.
6. Remove the outer nut, nut washer and inner nut.
7. Remove the rotor, grease seal and rear bearing. Remove the rotor shield, if necessary.

Rotor and bearing assemblies

To install:

8. Clean and repack the bearings with high temperature bearing grease. Also apply grease to the rotor hub cavity and spindle.

9. Install the rear bearing and new grease seal in the rotor. Install the rotor on the spindle.

10. Install the inner nut. Ensure that the locating peg on one side of the nut is facing outward.

11. Install the sheel but do not tighten the wheel nuts. Tighten the inner nut to 50 ft. lbs. (68 Nm). while rotating the wheel to seat the bearings. Continue rotating the wheel and back off the nut 45–65 degrees.

12. Install the nut washer and outer nut. Ensure the locating peg on the inner nut is seated in one of the washer holes before installing the outer nut.

13. Tighten the outer nut to a minimum of 50 ft. lbs. (68 Nm). Install the spring cup and pressure spring.

14. Install the drive gear then push the gear inward and install the snapring.

15. Remove the wheel, install the caliper, reinstall the wheel and lower the vehicle.

Brake Drums

Removal and Installation

1. Raise and safely support the vehicle.
2. Remove the wheel.
3. Remove the spring nuts from the lug bolts and remove the drum from the vehicle.

NOTE: It may be necessary to back off the brake adjusters to remove the drum.

4. When placing the drum on the hub, make sure the contacting surfaces are clean and flat.
5. Install the spring nuts on the lug bolts and install the wheel.

Rotor and bearing assembly— Grand Wagoneer and Pick-Up

Drum brake assembly—exploded view

Brake Shoes

Removal and Installation

1. Raise and safely support the vehicle.
2. Turn the adjustment starwheel so the brake shoes are retracted from the brake drum.
3. Remove the wheels and the drums to give access to the brake shoes.

4. Install wheel cylinder clamps to retain the wheel cylinder pistons in place and prevent leakage of brake fluid while replacing the shoes.
5. Remove the return springs with a brake spring remover tool.
6. Remove the adjuster cable, cable guide, adjuster lever and adjuster springs.
7. Remove the hold-down washers and springs and remove the brake shoes.

To install:

8. Clean the backing plate with a brush or cloth. Place a dab of Lubriplate® on each spot where the brake shoes rub on the backing plate.

9. Apply a thin coat of multi-purpose chassis lube to the mounting pads on the backing plate.

10. Transfer the parking brake actuating lever to the new secondary shoe.

NOTE: Always replace brake linings in axle sets. Never replace linings on one side or on a single wheel.

11. Position the brake shoes on the backing plate and install the hold-down springs. Engage the parking brake lever with the cable.

12. Install the parking brake actuating bar and spring between the parking brake lever and primary shoe.

13. Install the self-adjusting cable, cable guide and upper return springs.

14. Thoroughly clean the starwheel and lightly lubricate the threads with lithium based grease.

15. Install the starwheel.

16. Install the self-adjusting cam and lower spring.

17. Check the surface of the brake shoes for any grease.

18. Install the drum and reach through the adjusting opening in the backing plate with a brake adjusting tool. Turn the starwheel outward so the brakes lock the drum, then, holding the adjusting cam with a thin prybar, turn the starwheel back so the drum is free and no drag is felt.

19. Once the wheels are on and the vehicle is lowered, back it up several times, applying the brakes to actuate the self-adjusters.

Wheel Cylinders

Removal and Installation

1. Raise and safely support the vehicle. If equipped with anti-lock brakes, relieve the system pressure.

2. Remove the wheel and remove the brake drum.

3. Disconnect the brake line at the wheel cylinder.

4. Remove the brake shoes.

5. Remove the wheel cylinder attaching bolts and remove the wheel cylinder.

To install:

6. Position the wheel cylinder on the backing plate.

7. Connect the brake line to the cylinder fitting.

8. Install the wheel cylinder mounting bolts. On Wrangler, Comanche, Cherokee and Wagoneer, tighten the bolts to 90 inch lbs. (10 Nm); on the Grand Wagoneer and Pick-Up tighten bolts to 18 ft. lbs. (24 Nm).

9. Tighten the brake line fitting to 140 inch lbs. (16 Nm).

10. Install the brake shoes. Adjut the brake shoes.

11. Install the brake drum and wheel. Lower the vehicle.

12. Fill the brake system to the correct level and bleed the brakes.

Parking Brake Cable

Adjustment

CHEROKEE, COMANCHE AND WAGONEER

NOTE: This procedure requires the use of a special tool.

1. Ensure the rear brakes are properly adjusted. Place the parking brake lever in the fifth notch.

2. Raise and support the vehicle safely.

3. Place the adjustment tool J-34651 on the rear cable for Cherokee/Wagoneer or the front cable for Comanche. Using a torque wrench, apply a torque of 45–50 inch lbs.

Typical parking brake cable layout

4. Adjust the equalizer adjusting nut so that the gauge pointer is in the green band on the tool.

5. Apply and release the brake lever fully, 5 times and recheck the adjustment.

6. When adjustment is correct, stake the adjusting nut.

WRANGLER

1. Raise and support the vehicle safely.

2. Adjust the rear brakes. Fully apply the parking brakes.

3. Loosen the front cable locknut and tighten the front cable adjusting nut ½ inch. This will apply the necessary force to the front cable tensioner.

4. Hold the cable adjusting nut in position and tighten the cable locknut.

5. Release the parking brake pedal and verify that the rear wheels rotate freely without drag. Adjust as necessary.

GRAND WAGONEER AND PICK-UP

1. Raise and support the vehicle safely.

2. Apply and release the parking brake several times.

3. Loosen the equalizer locknuts and rotate the wheels. Tighten the nuts evenly until a light drag is felt at both rear wheels.

4. Loosen the adjusting nuts until the drag is eliminated and the wheels rotate freely.

5. Tighten the locknuts and verify correct operation.

Removal and Installation

REAR CABLE

1. Raise and support the vehicle safely. Fully release the parking brake.

2. Remove the rear wheel and brake drum. Disconnect the cable from the equalizer, as required.

3. Remove the secondary (rear) brake shoe and disengage the parking brake lever from the brakeshoe.

4. Compress the cable retainer with a hose clamp.

5. Remove the cable from the backing plate, then remove the cable mounting clips.

6. Disengage the cable from the equalizer and remove the cable.

7. Installation is the reverse of removal. Adjust the rear brakes. Adjust the parking brake cable.

FRONT CABLE

1. Raise and support the vehicle safely. Fully release the parking brake.

2. Remove the equalizer nuts and remove the front cable from the equalizer and cable bracket.

3. Lower the vehicle.

4. Move the carpet away from the pedal assembly. Then remove the pedal mounting bolts and move the pedal assembly away from the kick panel. Compress the cable retainer with a hose clamp and disconnect the front cable from the pedal.

5. Move the carper at the drivers side and rear of the cab to gain access to the cable floorpan clamps. Remove the clamps, unseat the cable grommet and remove the cable throught the floorpan.

6. Installation is the reverse of removal. Adjust the rear brakes. Adjust the parking brake cable.

Brake System Bleeding

Except Anti-Lock Brakes

When bleeding brakes, begin at the wheel most distant from the master cylinder first, the next most distant second and so on. During the bleeding operation, the master cylinder must be kept at least ¾ full of brake fluid.

NOTE: When bleeding the brakes, the metering section of the pressure differential valve must be held open. Loosen the front mounting bolt of the valve and insert Tool J–23709, J–26869 or equivalent, under the bolt. Push in on the metering valve stem to open it and re- tighten the bolt to hold the tool in place. When bleeding is finished, loosen the bolt, remove the tool and retighten the bolt.

To bleed the master cylinder: loosen one of the line fittings at the master cylinder. Have an assistant slowly depress the brake pedal and hold it at the floor. When the pedal reaches the floor, tighten the fitting. Repeat this procedure until just fluid emerges at the fitting. Repeat the entire bleeding procedure for the other brake line. Make sure that you have absorbant rags under the fittings to catch the fluid. Wear goggles to avoid any fluid spray from hitting your eyes.

To bleed the brakes: First carefully clean all dirt from around the master cylinder filler plug. Remove the filler plug and fill the master cylinder to the lower edge of the filler neck. Clean off the bleeder connections at all of the wheel cylinders or disc brake calipers. Attach the bleeder hose and fixture to the right rear wheel cylinder bleeder screw and place the end of the tube in a glass jar, submerged in brake fluid. Open the bleeder valve ½–¾ turn. Have an assistant depress the brake pedal and allow it to return slowly. Continue this pumping action to force any air out of the system. When bubbles cease to appear at the end of the bleeder hose, close the bleeder valve and remove the hose. Check the level of the brake fluid in the master cylinder and add fluid, if necessary.

After the bleeding operation at each caliper or wheel cylinder has been completed, fill the master cylinder reservoir and replace the filler plug.

NOTE: Never reuse brake fluid which has been removed from the lines through the bleeding process because it contains air bubbles and dirt.

Anti-lock brake system component layout

Anti-Lock Brake System Service

Precautions

-------------------- CAUTION --------------------

This brake system uses a hydraulic accumulator which, when fully charged, contains brake fluid at very high pressure. Before disconnecting any hydraulic lines, hoses or fittings be certain that the accumulator pressure is completely relieved. Failure to depressurize the accumulator may result in personal injury and/or vehicle damage.

- Certain components within the ABS system are not intended to be serviced or repaired individually. Only those components with removal and installation procedures should be serviced.
- Both the external accumulator and the smaller accumulator within the pump contain high pressure nitrogen charges to assist in pressurizing the system. The gas pressure is maintained even after fluid pressure in the system is reduced. Never puncture or attempt to disassemble either of these components.
- Do not use rubber hoses or other parts not specifically specified for the ABS system. When using repair kits, replace all parts included in the kit. Partial or incorrect repair may lead to functional problems and require the replacement of components.
- Lubricate rubber parts with clean, fresh brake fluid to ease assembly. Do not use lubricated shop air to clean parts; damage to rubber components may result.
- Use only DOT 3 brake fluid from an unopened container.
- If any hydraulic component or line is removed or replaced, it may be necessary to bleed the entire system.
- A clean repair area is essential. Always clean the reservoir and cap thoroughly before removing the cap. The slightest amount of dirt in the fluid may plug an orfice and impair the system function. Perform repairs after components have been thoroughly cleaned; use only denatured alcohol to clean components. Do not allow ABS components to come into contact with any substance containing mineral oil; this includes used shop rags.
- The anti-lock ECU is a microprocessor similar to other computer units in the vehicle. Insure that the ignition switch is **OFF** before removing or installing controller harnesses. Avoid static electricity discharge at or near the controller.

Relieving Anti-Lock System Pressure

-------------------- CAUTION --------------------

Depressurize the ABS accumulator and master cylinder assembly before performing any service operations. Failure to completely relieve the system could result in brake fluid under high pressure being sprayed on the technician and the vehicle. This can result in serious personal injury and vehicle damage.

1. Turn the ignition switch **OFF** and leave it **OFF** during repairs unless specifically directed otherwise.
2. Firmly apply and release the brake pedal a minimum of 45–50 times.
3. The pedal feel will become noticeably harder when the accumulator is completely discharged.
4. Do not turn the ignition switch **ON** after depressurizing the system unless service procedures specifically require it or all service operations have been performed.

NOTE: After the reserve pressure is depleted, the fluid level in the reservoir will rise above the MAX fill mark. This is normal; the reservoir will not overflow unless the system was overfilled to begin with.

5. Always wear safety goggles when disconnecting lines and fittings.

Speed Sensors

Removal and Installation

FRONT WHEEL

1. Elevate and safely support the vehicle. Turn the front wheel outward for easier access to the sensor.
2. Before disassembly, note sensor wire routing including location of all clips and retainers. The sensor wire must be routed correctly during reassembly to avoid damage from moving parts.
3. Carefully remove the wire ties holding the sensor wire to the brake lines and the steering knuckle.
4. If the sensor is coated with mud, slush, etc., clean the sensor and surrounding area. This will prevent damage to the sensor and tone wheel during removal.
5. Remove the sensor attaching screw and remove the sensor from the steering knuckle.
6. Loosen the grommet holding the sensor wire from the wheel arch panel.
7. In the engine compartment, disconnect the sensor wire connector from the ABS harness. Carefully remove the sensor and harness from the car.

To install:

8. The wheel sensors have a plastic spacing strip attached to the contact face. Inspect this spacer and note the condition. If the strip is securely attached and in good condition, no adjustment will be needed after installation. If the strip is damaged or not present, an air gap adjustment will be required.
9. Feed the sensor wire through the grommet hole in the wheelwell panel. Connect the sensor connector to the ABS harness and seat the rubber grommet in the panel.
10. Position the sensor on the steering knuckle and install the attaching bolt finger-tight.
11. If the spacer strip was intact and in good condition, lightly press the sensor against the tone wheel. Hold the sensor in this position and tighten the retaining bolt to 11 ft. lbs. (14 Nm).
12. If the spacer was missing or damaged, clean the contacts on the sensor with a clean shop towel. Remove the spacer strip completely if loose or torn. After the sensor is loosely held in position by the retaining bolt, use a brass feeler gauge to set the air gap from the sensor to the tone wheel. Correct air gap is 0.013–0.019 in. (0.33–0.48mm). Tighten the retaining bolt to 11 ft. lbs. (14 Nm) and recheck the air gap with the feeler gauge.

NOTE: Use of a brass or non-magnetic gauge is required. Do not use common steel feelers; the small magnets within the sensor may be damaged. Correct air gap is critical to the proper operation of the sensor.

13. Use new wire ties to secure the sensor wire to the brake lines and steering knuckle.

REAR WHEEL

1. Raise and fold forward the rear seat to gain access to the rear sensor connectors.
2. Disconnect the sensor connector from the ABS harness; push the sensor grommet and wiring through the floor pan.
3. Elevate and safely support the vehicle.
4. Remove the wheel and brake drum.
5. Carefully remove the wire ties holding the sensor wires to the brake lines and rear axle.
6. Loosen or unseat the backing plate grommet holding the sensor wire.
7. Remove the bolt holding the sensor to the bracket. Remove the sensor by pulling the wire through the grommet hole in the backing plate.

To install:

8. The wheel sensors have a plastic spacing strip attached to the contact face. Inspect this spacer and note the condition. If the strip is securely attached and in good condition, no adjust-

ment will be needed after installation. If the strip is damaged or not present, an air gap adjustment will be required.

9. Feed the sensor wire through the grommet hole in the backing plate and seat the grommet in the plate.

10. If the spacer strip was intact and in good condition, lightly press the sensor against the tone wheel. Hold the sensor in this position and tighten the retaining bolt to 11 ft. lbs. (14 Nm).

11. If the spacer was missing or damaged, clean the contacts on the sensor with a clean shop towel. Remove the spacer strip completely if loose or torn. After the sensor is loosely held in position by the retaining bolt, use a brass feeler gauge to set the air gap from the sensor to the tone wheel. Correct air gap is 0.030–0.036 in. (0.76–0.91mm). Tighten the retaining bolt to 11 ft. lbs. (14 Nm) and recheck the air gap with the feeler gauge.

NOTE: Use of a brass or non-magnetic gauge is required. Do not use common steel feelers; the small magnets within the sensor may be damaged. Correct air gap is critical to the proper operation of the sensor.

12. Route the sensor wire to the rear seat area and feed through the access hole. Seat the sensor wire grommets in the floorpan.

13. Use new wire ties to secure the sensor wiring to the brake lines and rear axle. Make certain that the wiring is clear of all moving and/or hot components.

14. Install the brake drum and wheel. Lower the vehicle to the ground.

15. Within the car, connect the sensor to the ABS harness. Reposition the seat and carpet.

Pump and Motor

Removal and Installation

1. Depressurize the brake system
2. Disconnect the negative battery cable.
3. Remove the strap holding the coolant reserve bottle and move the bottle aside. The hoses may be left attached; moving the bottle allows better access.
4. Remove the bolts holding the 2-piece mounting bracket to the firewall and inner fender panels.
5. Move or rotate the bracket with the pump assembly to one side for access to the wiring and hoses. Disconnect the pump motor wiring harness from the engine harness.
6. Slowly loosen the high pressure line at the pump and allow any residual high pressure to bleed off. Wear eye protection and wrap the joint in a clean shop towel to suppress any spray. Disconnect the line from the pump.
7. Place a container or catch pan under the return line to the pump. Loosen the hose clamp and remove the line. Do not reuse the brake fluid which drains from the line.
8. Remove the pump/motor and bracket as a complete assembly.
9. Remove the screw holding the relay to the bracket. Remove the screws holding the pump and motor to the bracket and remove the bracket.

To install:

10. Position the pump assembly onto the bracket and install the assembly attaching screws. Attach the pump/motor to the mounting bracket and attach the pump relay to the mounting bracket.
11. Connect the high-pressure and return lines to the pump.
12. Connect the electrical harness from the pump to the engine harness.
13. Place the bracket with the pump/motor and relay in place and install the retaining bolts.
14. Inspect the high-pressure and return lines; make certain they are not kinked or touching the engine.
15. Fill the master cylinder to the MAX level.
16. Connect the negative battery cable.
17. Turn the ignition switch **ON**; the pump should start run-

ning. Listen for a drop in pump rpm; this shows the pump is pressurizing the system. If there is no drop in pump rpm within 20 seconds, immediately shut the ignition **OFF** and check for hydraulic leaks.

NOTE: Severe pump damage will result if the pump runs without pressurizing the system for any length of time.

18. Add fluid to the reservoir as necessary. Do not overfill.
19. Reposition and secure the coolant reservoir.

Master Cylinder, Modulator and Accumulator

Removal and Installation

NOTE: The master cylinder, modulator and accumulator are serviced as an assembly only. Do not attempt to disassemble or repair these components.

1. Disconnect the negative battery cable.
2. Remove the screws holding the windshield washer fluid reservoir. Disconnect the hoses and wires and remove the reservoir.
3. Remove the air cleaner assembly.
4. Disconnect the ABS ECU wiring connectors at the pressure modulator.
5. Disconnect the wiring at the proportioning valve/differential switch.
6. Disconnect the brake line at the coupling on the underside of the proportioning valve.
7. Disconnect the high pressure line at the accumulator block and immediately cap the port to prevent entry of dirt.
8. Place a catch pan below the supply line at the reservoir. Disconnect the hose at the reservoir and discard the fluid drained from the line.
9. Remove the wires from the low pressure switch on the accumulator block, the modulator boost pressure switch and the fluid level switch.
10. Disconnect the front brake lines at the outboard side of the pressure modulator.
11. Inside the vehicle, disconnect the wiring to the brake pedal switch. It may be necessary to remove the instrument panel lower trim for access.
12. Remove the master cylinder pushrod bolt; disconnect the pushrod from the pedal. Immediately discard the nuts from the pushrod bolt—they are not reusable.
13. Remove the nuts from the brake mounting bracket studs.
14. Under the hood, carefully pull the hydraulic components and bracket forward until the studs clear the firewall. Lift the assembly up and out of the engine compartment.

To install:

15. Install the pad onto the new bracket and place the bracket with the brake components in place against the firewall. Make certain the studs are correctly seated in the holes.
16. Position the master cylinder/modulator/accumulator on the firewall and tighten the mounting nuts to 27 ft. lbs. (31 Nm).
17. Connect the wiring harness to the low pressure switch, the differential switch, the pressure modulator, the low fluid and boost pressure switches.
18. Inside the vehicle, install the nuts on the mounting studs and tighten them to 31 ft. lbs. (42 Nm).
19. Align the brake pedal, the brake light switch and the master cylinder pushrod. Install the pushrod bolt. The pushrod bolt must be correctly installed to avoid interference with the bracket. The bolt head must be on the left side of the brake pedal.
20. Use new nuts on the pushrod bolt. The inner locknut should be tightened to 25 ft. lbs. (34 Nm); the outer jam nut should be tightened to 75 inch lbs. (8.5 Nm).

21. Connect the wiring to the brake switch and replace the lower dashboard trim if removed.

22. In the engine compartment, connect the brake lines to the proportioning valve.

23. Connect the pressure and return lines to the accumulator.

24. Install the air cleaner assembly.

25. Connect hoses and wires to the windshield washer fluid reservoir and install it in position.

26. Inspect the high-pressure and return lines; make certain they are not kinked or touching the engine.

27. Fill the master cylinder to the MAX level.

28. Connect the negative battery cable.

29. Turn the ignition switch **ON**; the pump should start running. Listen for a drop in pump rpm; this shows the pump is pressurizing the system. If there is no drop in pump rpm within 20 seconds, immediately shut the ignition **OFF** and check for hydraulic leaks.

NOTE: Severe pump damage will result if the pump runs without pressurizing the system for any length of time.

30. Add fluid to the reservoir as necessary. Do not overfill.

31. Bleed the brake system.

Electronic Control Unit

Removal and Installation

1. Confirm that the ignition switch is **OFF**.
2. Fold the rear seat cushion forward for access to the ECU.
3. Remove the bracket holding the ECU from the floorpan, then remove the control unit from the bracket.
4. Carefully disconnect the wiring connectors from the ECU.

To install:

5. Connect the wiring harnesses to the replacement unit.
6. Mount the control unit on the bracket, then install the bracket to the floorpan. Make certain the bracket is in the correct position.
7. Reposition the rear seat cushion.

FRONT SUSPENSION

Shock Absorbers

Removal and Installation

NOTE: Before installing new shocks, they should be purged of air. To do this, hold the shock upright and fully extend it, then invert and compress it. Do this several times.

1. Raise and safely support the front of the vehicle.
2. Remove the locknuts and washers.
3. Pull the shock absorber eyes and rubber bushings from the mounting pins.
4. Install the shocks in the reverse order of the removal procedure. Torque the retaining nuts and bolts as follows:

Comanche, Cheerokee and Wagoneer: Lower—14 ft. lbs. Upper—8 ft. lbs.

Wrangler: Lower—45 ft. lbs. Upper—9 ft. lbs.

Grand Wagoneer and Pick-Up: Lower and Upper—45 ft. lbs.

Coil Springs

Removal and Installation

1. Raise and safely support the vehicle, allowing the front axle to hang.
2. Support the axle with a jack.
3. Remove the wheels.
4. On 4WD vehicles, matchmark and disconnect the front driveshaft from the axle.
5. Disconnect the lower control arm at the axle.
6. Disconnect the stabilizer bar links and the shock absorbers at the axle.
7. Disconnect the track bar at the sill bracket.
8. Disconnect the tie rod at the pitman arm.
9. Lower the axle until tension is removed from the spring, then loosen the spring retainer and remove the spring.

To install:

10. Position the replacement spring on the retainer, tighten the spring retainer bracket screw and lift the rear axle into position.
11. Connect the lower control arm to the axle. Tighten the control arm-to-axle bolt to 133 ft. lbs.

12. Remove the support jack. It is important that the front springs are supporting the weight of the vehicle when the track bar attaching bolts are tightened. Vehicle ride comfort could be adversely affected.

13. Connect the stabilizer bar links and the shock absorbers at the axle. tighten the shock absorber-to-axle bolt to 14 ft. lbs.; the stabilizer bar-to-axle bolt to 70 ft. lbs.

14. Connect the track bar at the sill bracket. Tighten the track bar-to-frame rail bolt to 35 ft. lbs.

15. Connect the tie rod at the pitman arm. Tighten the center link-to-pitman arm bolt to 35 ft. lbs.

NOTE: New strap bolts must be used each time the driveshaft is disconnected.

16. On 4WD vehicles, connect the front driveshaft. Tighten U-joint-to-axle bolt to 14 ft. lbs.

17. Install the wheels and lower the vehicle.

Leaf Springs

Removal and Installation

1. Raise the vehicle and support it safely.
2. Position a jack under the axle. Raise the axle to relieve the springs of the axle weight.
3. If equipped, disconnect the stabilizer bar. Remove the spring U-bolts and tie plates.
4. Remove the bolt attaching the spring front eye to the shackle. Remove the bolt attaching the spring rear eye to the shackle.
5. Remove the spring from its mounting.

To install:

6. Position the replacement spring front eye in the shackle. Loosely install the attaching bolt. Perform the same procedure for the rear spring eye.
7. Position and align the spring with the axle tube. Install spring bracket, U-bolts and nuts. Tighten the nuts to 100 ft. lbs. (136 Nm) for the Grand Wagoneer or 90 ft. lbs. (122 Nm) for the Wrangler.
8. Attach the stabilizer bar and tighten the attaching nut to 55 ft. lbs. (75 Nm).
9. Lower the vehicle and tighten the spring eye bolts to 100 fft. lbs. (136 Nm).

Upper and Lower Ball Joint

Removal and Installation

EXCEPT GRAND WAGONEER

1. Raise and safely support the vehicle. Remove the steering knuckle.
2. Position a ball joint removal tool J–34503–1 and 34503–3 or their equivalents, in a C-clamp and on the upper ball joint.
3. Tighten the clamp screw to remove the joint.
4. Use tools J–34503–5 and J–34503–12 or their equivalents, in a similar manner, to install the ball joint.
5. Install the knuckle. Tighten the ball joint nuts to 75 ft. lbs. (101 Nm).

GRAND WAGONEER

1. Raise and support the vehicle safely. Remove the steering knuckle.
2. Remove the ball joint retaining snaprings.
3. Clamp the steering knuckle in a vise and using tool J–25211 or equivalent, remove the ball joint.
4. Use the same tools in a similar manner to install the new ball joints.
5. Install the steering knuckle. Tighten the ball joint nuts to 80 ft. lbs. (108 Nm).

Upper Control Arm

Removal and Installation

1. Raise and safely support the vehicle, allowing the suspension to hang freely.
2. Remove the wheels.
3. Remove the control arm-to-axle bolt.
4. Remove the control arm-to-frame bolt and remove the arm.
5. Installation the upper control arm and tighten the bolts finger-tight.
6. Lower the vehicle and torque the control arm bolts to 55 fft. lbs. at the axle; 66 ft. lbs. at the frame.

Lower Control Arm

Removal and Installation

1. Raise and safely support the vehicle, allowing the suspension to hang freely.
2. Disconnect the lower control arm at the axle and rear bracket. Remove the arm.
3. Install the lower control arm and tighten the bolts finger-tight.
4. Lower the vehicle and tighten the bolts to 133 ft. lbs.

Front Stabilizer Bar

Removal and Installation

1. Raise and safely support the vehicle.
2. Remove the staibilizer bar-to-frame clamps and cushions.
3. Disconnect the stabilizer bar at the connecting links and remove the stabilizer bar. If necessary, disconnect the connecting links from the axle bracket.
4. Installation is the reverse of removal. Tighten the retaining bracket bolts to 55 ft. lbs. for the Grand Wagoneer, 27 ft. lbs. for the Cherokee, Comanche and Wagoneer or 45 ft. lbs. for the Wrangler.
5. Tighten the connecting rod link nuts to 35 ft. lbs. for the Grand Wagoneer, 55 ft. lbs. for the Cherokee, Comanche and Wagoneer or 30 ft. lbs. for the Wrangler.

Track Bar

Removal and Installation

1. Raise and safely support the vehicle.
2. Remove the cotter pin and nut securing the track bar to the frame bracket.
3. Remove the bolt and nut securing the track bar to the axle.
4. Install the track bar and tighten the nuts finger-tight.
5. Lower the vehicle and tighten the retaining nut at the axle shaft to 74 ft. lbs. (100 Nm). Tighten the retaining nut at the frome rail to 63 ft. lbs. (85 Nm) for Comanche, Cherokee and Wagoneer; 125 ft. lbs. (168 Nm) for Wrangler and Grand Wagoneer.

Front Wheel Bearings

Removal and Installation

2WD VEHICLES

1. Loosen the lug nuts on the front wheels.
2. Raise and safely support the vehicle.
3. Remove the front wheels.
4. Remove the calipers but don't disconnect the brake lines. Suspend the calipers aside.
5. Remove the dust cap, cotter pin, nut retainer, nut and thrust washer from the spindle.
6. Remove the rotor. Be ready to catch the outer bearing.
7. Carefully drive out the inner bearing and seal from the hub, using a wood block.
8. Inspect the bearing races for excessive wear, pitting or grooves. If they are cracked or grooved or if pitting and excess wear is present, drive them out with a drift or punch.
To install:
9. Check the bearing for excess wear, pitting or cracks or excess looseness.

NOTE: If it is necessary to replace either the bearing or the race, replace both. Never replace just a bearing or a race. These parts wear in a mating pattern. If just one is replaced, premature failure of the new part will result.

10. If the old parts are retained, thoroughly clean them in solvent and allow them to dry on a clean towel. Never spin dry them with compressed air.
11. Thoroughly clean the spindle.
12. Throughly clean the inside of the hub.
13. Pack the inside of the hub with EP wheel bearing grease. Add grease to the hub until it is flush with the inside diameter of the bearing cup.
14. Pack the bearing with the same grease.
15. If a new race is being installed, very carefully drive it into position until it bottoms all around, using a brass drift. Be careful to avoid scratching the surface.
16. Place the inner bearing in the race and install a new grease seal.
17. Position the hub and rotor on the spindle and install the outer bearing.
18. Install the washer and nut. Adjust the wheel bearing.
19. Install the nut cap and a new cotter pin. Install the grease cap.
20. Install the caliper and wheels. Lower the vehicle.

Adjustment

WRANGLER, CHEROKEE, COMANCHE AND WAGONEER

1. Raise and support the vehicle safely. Remove the tire and wheel. Remove the disc brake caliper as required. Remove the cotter pin, locknut and axle hub nut. Repack the bearings as necessary.

2. Loosen the axle hub nut and retighten to 21 ft. lbs. while spinning the rotor.

3. Loosen the hub nut ½ turn and tighten to 19 ft. lbs. while spinning the rotor.

4. Install the locknut and new cotter pins.

5. Install the caliper, if removed. Install the wheel. Lower the vehicle.

GRAND WAGONEER AND PICK-UP

1. Raise and support the vehicle safely.

2. If not equipped with front hubs, remove the wheel cover and hubcap. Remove the drive gear snapring. Remove the drive gear, pressure spring and spring cup.

3. If equipped with front hubs, Remove the socket head screws from the hub body and remove the body from the hub clutch assembly. Remove the large retaining ring from the hub. Remove the small retaining ring from the axle shaft. Remove the hub and clutch assembly. Remove the outer locknut and lock washer.

4. Seat the bearings by loosening and then tightening them to 50 ft. lbs. Back off the inner locknut about ⅙ of a turn while rotating the wheel.

5. Install the lock washer. Align one of the lock washer holes with the peg on the inner locknut and install the washer on the nut.

6. Install and torque the outer locknut to 50 ft. lbs. Recheck the bearing adjustment. Correct as required.

7. On vehicles without front hubs, The spring cup must be installed so the recessed side faces the bearing and the flat side faces the pressure spring. The pressure spring should contact the flat side of the cup only.

8. Install the spring cup and the pressure spring. Install the drive gear and the drive gear snapring.

9. If equipped with front hubs, Install the clutch assembly. Install the small retaining ring on the axle shaft. Install the large retaining ring on the hub.

10. Install the hub body on the hub clutch. Install the socket head screws in the hub and torque them to 30 inch lbs.

REAR SUSPENSION

Shock Absorbers

Removal and Installation

NOTE: Before installing new shocks, they should be purged of air. To do this, hold the shock upright and fully extend it, then invert and compress it. Do this several times.

1. Raise and safely support the front of the vehicle.

2. Remove the locknuts and washers.

3. Pull the shock absorber eyes and rubber bushings from the mounting pins.

4. Install the shocks in the reverse order of the removal procedure. Torque the retaining nuts and bolts as follows:

Comanche, Cheerokee and Wagoneer: Lower—44 ft. lbs. Upper—15 ft. lbs.

Wrangler: Lower and Upper—44 ft. lbs.

Grand Wagoneer and Pick-Up: Lower and Upper—45 ft. lbs.

Leaf Springs

Removal and Installation

1. Raise and safely support the vehicle, allowing the suspension to hang freely.

2. Take up the weight of the axle with a jack.

3. Disconnect the shock absorbers at the axle.

4. Remove the wheels.

5. Disconnect the stabilizer bar links at the spring plate.

6. Remove the U-bolts and spring plates.

7. Remove the rear spring-to-shackle bolt, then the front spring-to-shackle bolt.

8. Lower the axle and remove the spring.

9. Installation is the reverse of removal. Install all bolts finger tight and lower the rear axle until it is supported by the spring.

10. Tighten the spring U-bolts to 100 ft. lbs. on the Grand Wagoneer and Comanche; 122 ft. lbs. on the Wrangler or 52 ft. lbs. on the Cherokee and Wagoneer. Tigthen the spring eye bolts to 100 ft. lbs. on the Grand Wagoneer; 65 ft. lbs. on the Comanche, Cherokee and Wagoneer; 95–105 ft. lbs. on the Wrangler.

Rear Track Bar

Removal and Installation

1. Raise and safely support the vehicle.

2. Remove the cotter pin and nut securing the track bar to the frame bracket.

3. Remove the bolt and nut securing the track bar to the axle.

4. Install the track bar and tighten the nuts finger-tight.

5. Lower the vehicle and tighten the retaining nut at the axle shaft to 74 ft. lbs. (100 Nm). Tighten the retaining nut at the frome rail to 63 ft. lbs. (85 Nm) for Comanche, Cherokee and Wagoneer; 125 ft. lbs. (168 Nm) for Wrangler and Grand Wagoneer.

Rear Stabilizer Bar

Removal and Installation

1. Raise and safely support the vehicle.

2. Remove the staibilizer bar-to-frame clamps and cushions.

3. Disconnect the stabilizer bar at the connecting links and remove the stabilizer bar. If necessary, disconnect the connecting links from the axle bracket.

4. Installation is the reverse of removal. Tighten the retaining bracket bolts to 55 ft. lbs. for the Grand Wagoneer, 27 ft. lbs. for the Cherokee, Comanche and Wagoneer or 45 ft. lbs. for the Wrangler.

5. Tighten the connecting rod link nuts to 35 ft. lbs. for the Grand Wagoneer, 55 ft. lbs. for the Cherokee, Comanche and Wagoneer or 30 ft. lbs. for the Wrangler.

SPECIFICATIONS

ENGINE IDENTIFICATION

Year	Model	Engine Displacement cu. in. (cc/liter)	Engine Series Identification	No. of Cylinders	Engine Type
1988	Ram 50	122 (1997/2.0)	G63B	4	SOHC
	Ram 50	156 (2555/2.6)	G54B	4	SOHC
	Ram Raider	156 (2555/2.6)	G54B	4	SOHC
1989	Ram 50	122 (1997/2.0)	G63B	4	SOHC
	Ram 50	156 (2555/2.6)	G54B	4	SOHC
	Ram Raider	156 (2555/2.6)	G54B	4	SOHC
	Ram Raider	181 (2972/3.0)	6G72	6	DOHC
1990	Ram 50	143 (2350/2.4)	4G64	4	SOHC
	Ram 50	181 (2972/3.0)	6G72	6	DOHC
1991	Ram 50	143 (2350/2.4)	4G64	4	SOHC
	Ram 50	181 (2972/3.0)	6G72	6	DOHC
1992	Ram 50	143 (2350/2.4)	4G64	4	SOHC

SOHC—Single Overhead Cam
DOHC—Dual Overhead Cam

GENERAL ENGINE SPECIFICATIONS

Year	Model	Engine Displacement cu. in. (cc)	Fuel System Type	Net Horsepower @ rpm	Net Torque @ rpm (ft. lbs.)	Bore × Stroke (in.)	Compression Ratio	Oil Pressure @ rpm
1988	Ram 50	122 (1997)	2bbl	88 @ 5000	108 @ 3500	3.31 × 3.54	8.5:1	45–90 @ 3000
	Ram 50	156 (2555)	2bbl	109 @ 5000	142 @ 3500	3.59 × 3.86	8.7:1	45–90 @ 3000
	Ram Raider	156 (2555)	2bbl	109 @ 5000	142 @ 3500	3.59 × 3.86	8.7:1	45–90 @ 3000
1989	Ram 50	122 (1997)	2bbl	88 @ 5000	108 @ 3500	3.31 × 3.54	8.5:1	45–90 @ 3000
	Ram 50	156 (2555)	2bbl	109 @ 5000	142 @ 3500	3.59 × 3.86	8.7:1	45–90 @ 3000
	Ram Raider	156 (2555)	2bbl	88 @ 5000	108 @ 3500	3.31 × 3.54	8.7:1	45–90 @ 3000
	Ram Raider	181 (2972)	MPI	143 @ 5000	168 @ 2500	3.59 × 2.99	8.9:1	30–80 @ 3000
1990	Ram 50	143 (2350)	MPI	116 @ 5000	136 @ 3500	3.41 × 3.94	8.5:1	40–85 @ 3000
	Ram 50	181 (2972)	MPI	143 @ 5000	168 @ 2500	3.59 × 2.99	8.9:1	30–80 @ 3000
1991	Ram 50	143 (2350)	MPI	116 @ 5000	136 @ 3500	3.41 × 3.94	8.5:1	40–85 @ 3000
	Ram 50	181 (2972)	MPI	143 @ 5000	168 @ 2500	3.59 × 2.99	8.9:1	30–80 @ 3000
1992	Ram 50	143 (2350)	MPI	116 @ 5000	136 @ 3500	3.41 × 3.94	8.5:1	40–85 @ 3000

MPI—Multi-Port Fuel Injection
2bbl—2 barrel carb.

ENGINE TUNE-UP SPECIFICATIONS

Year	Model	Engine Displacement cu. in. (cc)	Spark Plugs Type	Spark Plugs Gap (in.)	Ignition Timing (deg.) MT	Ignition Timing (deg.) AT	Compression Pressure (psi)	Fuel Pump (psi)	Idle Speed (rpm) MT	Idle Speed (rpm) AT	Valve Clearance In.	Valve Clearance Ex.
1988	Ram 50	156 (2555)	RN9YC	0.039–0.043	7B	7B	170	3–4	800	800	Hyd. ③	Hyd. ③
	Ram 50	122 (1997)	RN9YC	0.039–0.043	8B	8B	170	3–4	750	750	Hyd.	Hyd.
	Ram Raider	156 (2555)	RN9YC	0.039–0.043	7B	7B	170	3–4	800	800	Hyd.	Hyd.

ENGINE TUNE-UP SPECIFICATIONS

Year	Model	Engine Displacement cu. in. (cc)	Spark Plugs Type	Gap (in.)	Ignition Timing (deg.) MT	AT	Compression Pressure (psi)	Fuel Pump (psi)	Idle Speed (rpm) MT	AT	Valve Clearance In.	Ex.
1989	Ram 50	156 (2555)	RN9YC	0.039–0.043	7B	7B	170	3–4	800	800	Hyd.	Hyd.
	Ram 50	122 (1997)	RN9YC	0.039–0.043	8B	8B	170	3–4	750	750	Hyd.	Hyd.
	Ram Raider	156 (2555)	RN9YC	0.039–0.043	7B	7B	170	3–4	800	800	Hyd. ③	Hyd. ③
	Ram Raider	181 (2972)	RN114C4	0.039–0.043	②	②	120	38	700	700	Hyd.	Hyd.
1990	Ram 50	143 (2350)	RN9YC	0.039–0.043	①	①	120	38	750	750	Hyd.	Hyd.
	Ram 50	181 (2972)	RN114C4	0.039–0.043	②	②	120	38	700	700	Hyd.	Hyd.
1991	Ram 50	143 (2350)	RN9YC	0.039–0.043	①	①	120	38	750	750	Hyd.	Hyd.
	Ram 50	181 (2972)	RN114C4	0.039–0.043	②	②	120	38	700	700	Hyd.	Hyd.
1992	Ram 50	143 (2350)	RN9YC	0.039–0.043	①	①	120	38	750	750	Hyd.	Hyd.

Hyd.—Hydraulic
① Basic timing: 5B
  Actual timing: 8B
② Basic timing: 5B
  Actual timing: 15B
③ Jet valve clearance (all engines): 0.010 in.
  (0.25 mm)

FIRING ORDERS

NOTE: To avoid confusion, always replace spark plug wires one at a time.

2.0L, 2.4L and 2.6L Engines
Engine Firing Order: 1–3–4–2
Distributor Rotation: Clockwise

3.0L Engine
Engine Firing Order: 1–2–3–4–5–6
Distributor Rotation: Counterclockwise

CAPACITIES

Year	Model	Engine Displacement cu. in. (cc)	Engine Crankcase (qts.) with Filter	without Filter	Transmission (pts.) 4-Spd	5-Spd	Auto.	Drive Axle (pts.)	Fuel Tank (gal.)	Cooling System (qts.)
1988	Ram 50	122 (1997)	4	3.5	—	5	14.4	3.2	⑨	8.3
	Ram 50	156 (2555)	①	②	—	5	⑩	⑧	⑨	8.3
	Ram Raider	156 (2555)	5	4.5	—	4.7	15.2	⑦	16	8.5
1989	Ram 50	122 (1997)	4	3.5	—	5	14.4	3.2	⑨	8.3
	Ram 50	156 (2555)	①	②	—	5	⑩	⑥	⑨	8.3
	Ram Raider	156 (2555)	5	4.5	—	5	—	⑤	16	8.5
	Ram Raider	181 (2972)	5	4.5	—	5	15.2	⑪	16	9.5
1990	Ram 50	143 (2350)	③	④	—	5	14.8	3.2	⑨	6.5
	Ram 50	181 (2972)	5.5	5	—	5	14.8	5.4	⑨	9
1991	Ram 50	143 (2350)	③	④	—	5	14.8	3.2	⑨	6.5
	Ram 50	181 (2972)	5.5	5	—	5	14.8	5.4	⑨	9
1992	Ram 50	143 (2350)	③	④	—	5	14.8	3.2	⑨	6.5

① 2WD: 4.5 qts.
   4WD: 5 qts.
② 2WD: 4 qts.
   4WD: 4.5 qts.
③ 2WD: 4.5 qts.
   4WD: 5.5 qts.
④ 2WD: 4 qts.
   4WD: 5 qts.

⑤ Front axle: 2.3 pts.
   Rear axle: 3.8 pts.
⑥ Front axle: 2.3 pts.
   Rear axle: 3.2 pts.
⑦ Front axle: 2.3 pts.
   Conventional rear axle: 2.3 pts.
   Limited-slip rear axle: 3.8 pts.
⑧ Front axle

Conventional rear axle: 2.7 pts.
Limited-slip rear axle: 3.2 pts.
⑨ 2WD standard body: 14 gals.
   2WD long body: 18 gals.
   4WD standard body: 16 gals.
   4WD long body: 20 gals.
⑩ 2WD: 14.4 pts.
   4WD: 15.2 pts.
⑪ Front axle:
   Rear axle:

CAMSHAFT SPECIFICATIONS

All measurements given in inches.

Year	Engine Displacement cu. in. (cc)	Journal Diameter 1	2	3	4	5	Lobe Lift ① In.	Ex.	Bearing Clearance	Camshaft End Play
1988	122 (1997)	1.34	1.34	1.34	1.34	1.34	1.66–1.68	1.66–1.68	0.002–0.004	0.004–0.016
	156 (2555)	1.34	1.34	1.34	1.34	1.34	1.65–1.67	1.65–1.67	0.001–0.002	0.004–0.016
1989	122 (1997)	1.34	1.34	1.34	1.34	1.34	1.66–1.68	1.66–1.68	0.002–0.004	0.004–0.016
	156 (2555)	1.34	1.34	1.34	1.34	1.34	1.65–1.67	1.65–1.67	0.001–0.002	0.004–0.016
	181 (2972)	1.34	1.34	1.34	1.34	—	1.60–1.62	1.60–1.62	0.002–0.004	NA
1990	143 (2350)	1.34	1.34	1.34	1.34	1.34	1.65–1.67	1.65–1.67	0.002–0.004	0.004–0.016
	181 (2972)	1.34	1.34	1.34	1.34	—	1.60–1.62	1.60–1.62	0.002–0.004	NA
1991	143 (2350)	1.34	1.34	1.34	1.34	1.34	1.65–1.67	1.65–1.67	0.002–0.004	0.004–0.016
	181 (2972)	1.34	1.34	1.34	1.34	—	1.60–1.62	1.60–1.62	0.002–0.004	NA
1992	143 (2350)	1.34	1.34	1.34	1.34	1.34	1.65–1.67	1.65–1.67	0.002–0.004	0.004–0.016

NA—Not available
① Diameter of cam lobe

CRANKSHAFT AND CONNECTING ROD SPECIFICATIONS

All measurements are given in inches.

| Year | Engine Displacement cu. in. (cc) | Crankshaft | | | | Connecting Rod | | |
		Main Brg. Journal Dia.	Main Brg. Oil Clearance	Shaft End-play	Thrust on No.	Journal Diameter	Oil Clearance	Side Clearance
1988	122 (1997)	2.24	0.001–0.004	0.002–0.016	3	NA	0.001–0.002	0.004–0.016
	156 (2555)	2.36	0.001–0.004	0.002–0.016	3	2.87	0.001–0.002	0.004–0.016
1989	122 (1997)	2.24	0.001–0.004	0.002–0.016	3	NA	0.001–0.002	0.004–0.016
	156 (2555)	2.36	0.001–0.004	0.002–0.016	3	2.87	0.001–0.002	0.004–0.016
	181 (2972)	2.36	0.001–0.004	0.002–0.012	3	1.97	0.001–0.004	0.004–0.016
1990	143 (2350)	2.24	0.001–0.004	0.002–0.016	3	NA	0.001–0.004	0.004–0.016
	181 (2972)	2.36	0.001–0.004	0.002–0.012	3	1.97	0.001–0.004	0.004–0.016
1991	143 (2350)	2.24	0.001–0.004	0.002–0.016	3	NA	0.001–0.004	0.004–0.016
	181 (2972)	2.36	0.001–0.004	0.002–0.012	3	1.97	0.001–0.004	0.004–0.016
1992	143 (2350)	2.24	0.001–0.004	0.002–0.016	3	NA	0.001–0.004	0.004–0.016

NA—Not available

VALVE SPECIFICATIONS

| Year | Engine Displacement cu. in (cc) | Seat Angle (deg.) | Face Angle (deg.) | Spring Test Pressure (lbs.) | Spring Installed Height (in.) | Stem-to-Guide Clearance (in.) | | Stem Diameter (in.) | |
						Intake	Exhaust	Intake	Exhaust
1988	122 (1997)	45	45–45.5	72	1.60	0.001–0.004	0.002–0.006	0.315	0.315
	156 (2555)	45	45–45.5	72	1.60	0.001–0.004	0.002–0.006	0.315	0.315
1989	122 (1997)	45	45–45.5	72	1.60	0.001–0.004	0.002–0.006	0.315	0.315
	156 (2555)	45	45–45.5	72	1.60	0.001–0.004	0.002–0.006	0.315	0.315
	181 (2972)	44–44.5	45–45.5	74	1.60	0.001–0.004	0.002–0.006	0.313	0.312
1990	143 (2350)	44–44.5	45–45.5	73	1.60	0.001–0.004	0.002–0.006	0.310	0.310
	181 (2972)	44–44.5	45–45.5	74	1.60	0.001–0.004	0.002–0.006	0.313	0.312
1991	143 (2350)	44–44.5	45–45.5	73	1.60	0.001–0.004	0.002–0.006	0.310	0.310
	181 (2972)	44–44.5	45–45.5	74	1.60	0.001–0.004	0.002–0.006	0.313	0.312
1992	143 (2350)	44–44.5	45–45.5	73	1.60	0.001–0.004	0.002–0.006	0.310	0.310

PISTON AND RING SPECIFICATIONS

All measurements are given in inches.

Year	Engine Displacement cu. in. (cc)	Piston Clearance	Ring Gap			Ring Side Clearance		
			Top Compression	Bottom Compression	Oil Control	Top Compression	Bottom Compression	Oil Control
1988	122 (1997)	0.0004–0.0012	0.010–0.031	0.008–0.031	0.008–0.039	0.001–0.004	0.001–0.004	NA
	156 (2555)	0.0008–0.0016	0.012–0.031	0.010–0.031	0.008–0.039	0.002–0.005	0.001–0.004	NA
1989	122 (1997)	0.0004–0.0012	0.010–0.031	0.008–0.031	0.008–0.039	0.001–0.004	0.001–0.004	NA
	156 (2555)	0.0008–0.0016	0.012–0.031	0.010–0.031	0.008–0.039	0.002–0.005	0.001–0.004	NA
	181 (2972)	0.0008–0.0016	0.012–0.031	0.010–0.031	0.008–0.039	0.001–0.004	0.001–0.004	NA
1990	143 (2350)	0.0008–0.0016	0.010–0.031	0.008–0.031	0.008–0.039	0.001–0.004	0.001–0.004	NA
	181 (2972)	0.0008–0.0016	0.012–0.031	0.010–0.031	0.008–0.039	0.001–0.004	0.001–0.004	NA
1991	143 (2350)	0.0008–0.0016	0.010–0.031	0.008–0.031	0.008–0.039	0.001–0.004	0.001–0.004	NA
	181 (2972)	0.0008–0.0016	0.012–0.031	0.010–0.031	0.008–0.039	0.001–0.004	0.001–0.004	NA
1992	143 (2350)	0.0008–0.0016	0.010–0.031	0.008–0.031	0.008–0.039	0.001–0.004	0.001–0.004	NA

NA—Not available

TORQUE SPECIFICATIONS

All readings in ft. lbs.

Year	Engine Displacement cu. in. (cc)	Cylinder Head Bolts	Main Bearing Bolts	Rod Bearing Bolts	Crankshaft Pulley Bolts	Flywheel Bolts	Manifold		Spark Plugs
							Intake	Exhaust	
1988	122 (1997)	70	38	38	20	95	13	13	18–20
	156 (2555)	70	58	37	87	95	13	13	18–20
1989	122 (1997)	70	38	38	20	95	13	13	18–20
	156 (2555)	70	58	37	87	95	13	13	18–20
	181 (2972)	70	60	38	130	55	13	13	18–20
1990	143 (2350)	70	38	37	20	95	13	13	18–20
	181 (2972)	70	60	38	130	55	13	13	18–20
1991	143 (2350)	70	38	37	20	95	13	13	18–20
	181 (2972)	70	60	38	130	55	13	13	18–20
1992	143 (2350)	70	38	37	20	95	13	13	18–20

BRAKE SPECIFICATIONS

All measurements in inches unless noted

Year	Model	Lug Nut Torque (ft. lbs.)	Master Cylinder Bore	Brake Disc		Standard Brake Drum Diameter	Minimum Lining Thickness	
				Minimum Thickness	Maximum Runout		Front	Rear
1988	Ram 50	87–101	①	0.80	0.006	10	0.06	0.06
	Ram Raider	72–87	0.94	0.80	0.006	10	0.06	0.06

BRAKE SPECIFICATIONS

All measurements in inches unless noted

Year	Model	Lug Nut Torque (ft. lbs.)	Master Cylinder Bore	Brake Disc Minimum Thickness	Brake Disc Maximum Runout	Standard Brake Drum Diameter	Minimum Lining Thickness Front	Minimum Lining Thickness Rear
1989	Ram 50	87–101	0.94	0.80	0.006	10	0.06	0.06
	Ram Raider	72–87	0.94	0.80	0.006	10	0.06	0.06
1990	Ram 50	87–101	0.94	0.80	0.006	10	0.06	0.06
1991	Ram 50	87–101	0.94	0.80	0.006	10	0.06	0.06
1992	Ram 50	87–101	0.94	0.80	0.006	10	0.06	0.06

① 2WD: 0.87 in.
   4WD: 0.94 in.

WHEEL ALIGNMENT

Year	Model	Caster Range (deg.)	Caster Preferred Setting (deg.)	Camber Range (deg.)	Camber Preferred Setting (deg.)	Toe-in (in.)	Steering Axis Inclination (deg.)
1988	2WD Ram 50	2P–4P	3P	¼P–1¼P	⅔P	0.10	NA
	4WD Ram 50	1P–3P	2P	½P–1½P	1P	0.10	NA
	Ram Raider	2½P–3½P	3P	½P–1½P	1P	0.20	8
1989	2WD Ram 50	1½P–3½P	2½P	¼P–1¼P	⅔P	0.20	NA
	4WD Ram 50	1P–3P	2P	½P–1½P	1P	0.20	NA
	Ram Raider	2P–4P	3P	½P–1½P	1P	0.20	8
1990	2WD Ram 50	1½P–3½P	2½P	¼P–1¼P	⅔P	0.20	NA
	4WD Ram 50	1P–3P	2P	½P–1½P	1P	0.20	NA
1991	2WD Ram 50	1½P–3½P	2½P	¼P–1¼P	⅔P	0.20	NA
	4WD Ram 50	1P–3P	2P	½P–1½P	1P	0.20	NA
1992	2WD Ram 50	1½P–3½P	2½P	¼P–1¼P	⅔P	0.20	NA
	4WD Ram 50	1P–3P	2P	½P–1½P	1P	0.20	NA

NA—Not available
P—Positive
N—Negative

ENGINE ELECTRICAL

NOTE: Disconnecting the negative battery cable on some vehicles may interfere with the functions of the on board computer systems and may require the computer to undergo a relearning process, once the negative battery cable is reconnected.

Distributor

Removal

1. Disconnect the negative battery cable.
2. Disconnect the distributor pickup lead wires and vacuum hose(s), if equipped.
3. Unfasten the distributor cap retaining clips or screws and lift off the distributor cap with all ignition wires connected. Remove the coil wire if necessary.
4. Matchmark the rotor to the distributor housing and the distributor housing to the engine.

NOTE: Do not crank the engine during this procedure. If the engine is cranked, the matchmark must be disregarded.

5. Remove the retaining nut and remove the distributor from the engine.

Installation

TIMING NOT DISTURBED

1. Install a new distributor housing O-ring.
2. Install the distributor in the engine so the rotor is aligned with the matchmark on the housing and the housing is aligned with the matchmark on the engine. Make sure the distributor is fully seated and the distributor shaft is fully engaged.
3. Install the retaining nut finger-tight only. Connect the vacuum hose(s), if removed.
4. Connect the distributor pickup electrical harness.

Distributor cap terminal routing viewed from the top of the cap—3.0L engine

5. Install the distributor cap and secure.
6. Connect the negative battery cable.
7. Check the ignition timing and adjust as required. Tighten the retaining nut.

TIMING DISTURBED

1. Install a new distributor housing O-ring.
2. Position the engine so No. 1 piston is on TDC of compression stroke and the timing mark on the vibration damper is aligned with **T** on the timing indicator.
3. Install the distributor so the rotor is aligned with the No. 1 ignition wire on the distributor cap. Take note that the distributor shaft is fully engaged and the housing is fully seated.

NOTE: There are distributor cap runners inside the cap on vehicles with 3.0L engine. Make sure the rotor is pointing to where the No. 1 runner originates inside the cap and not where the No. 1 ignition wire plugs into the cap.

4. Install the retaining nut finger-tight only. Connect the vacuum hose(s), if removed.
5. Connect the distributor electrical harness.
6. Install the distributor cap and secure.
7. Connect the negative battery cable.
8. Adjust the ignition timing and tighten the retaining nut.

Tachometer terminal—1988–89 Ram 50

Ignition Timing

Adjustment

CARBURETED ENGINE

1. Start the engine, set the parking brake and run the engine until normal operating temperature is reached. Keep all lights and accessories **OFF** and the transmission in neutral.
2. Connect a conventional power timing light to No. 1 cylinder spark plug wire.
3. Connect the red lead of a tachometer to the negative primary terminal of the coil and the black lead to an engine ground. Set the idle speed to specifications.
4. On 1988–89 vehicles, if working at an altitude of 3900 ft. (1200 meters) disconnect and plug the white-striped hose running to the sub-vacuum chamber on the bottom of the distributor; this step also applies to California engines equipped with dual-diaphragm distributor.
5. Aim the timing light at the timing scale.
6. Loosen the distributor retainer nut to allow for distributor rotation.
7. Turn the distributor in the proper direction until the specified timing is reached. Tighten the nut and recheck the ignition timing.
8. Turn the engine **OFF** and connect the vacuum hose. Start the engine and check the timing with the vacuum hose in place. This reading should equal to basic timing plus 5 degrees.

FUEL INJECTED ENGINE

1. Start the engine, set the parking brake and run the engine until normal operating temperature is reached. Keep all lights and accessories **OFF** and the transmission in neutral.
2. Without disconnecting the connector, insert a paper clip into the tachometer terminal. Connect the red lead of a tachom-

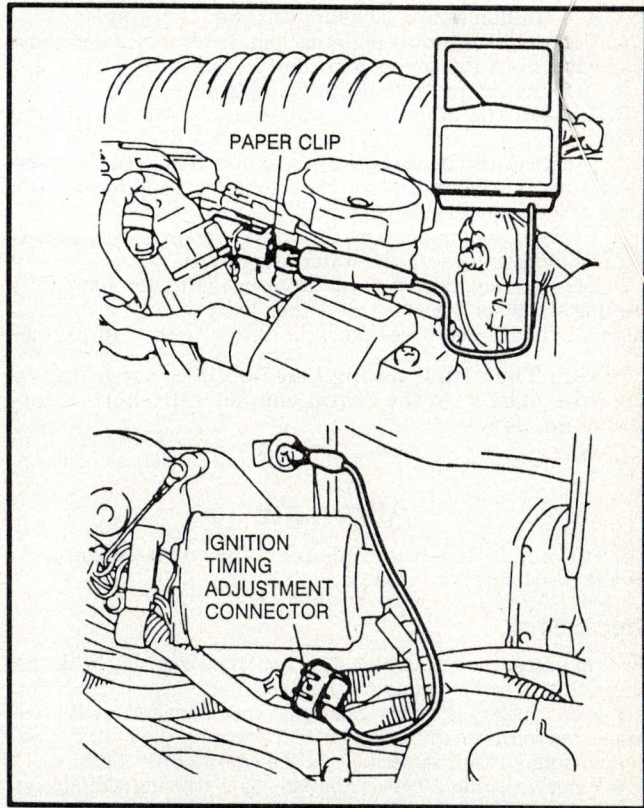

Tachometer terminal and ignition timing adjusting connector—Raider with 3.0L engine

2.4L ENGINE

3.0L ENGINE

Tachometer connector—1990–92 Ram 50

eter to the paper clip and connect the black lead to a ground. Set the idle speed to specifications.

3. Turn the engine **OFF**. Remove the water-proof cover from the ignition timing adjusting connector. Connect a jumper wire from the ignition timing adjusting terminal to ground.

4. Connect a conventional timing light to No. 1 cylinder spark plug wire. Start the engine and allow to idle.

5. Aim the timing light at the timing scale.

6. Loosen the distributor nut to allow for distributor rotation.

7. Turn the distributor in the proper direction until the specified timing is reached. Tighten the retainer nut and recheck the timing. Turn the engine **OFF**.

8. Remove the jumper wire from the ignition timing adjusting terminal and install the water-proof cover.

9. Start the engine and check the actual ignition timing. This reading should be 3 degrees more than basic timing for the 2.4L engine or 10 degrees more than basic timing for the 3.0L engine.

NOTE: The actual timing may fluctuate according to the control mode of the engine control unit; this is a normal condition.

10. Turn the engine **OFF** and remove all test equipment.

Alternator

For further information, please refer to "Alternators" in the Unit Repair section.

Precautions

Several precautions must be observed when working with the alternator to avoid damaging the unit.

• If the battery is removed for any reason, make sure it is reconnected with the correct polarity. Reversing the battery connections may result in damage to the one-way rectifiers.

• When utilizing a booster battery as a starting aid, always connect the positive to positive terminals and the negative terminal from the booster battery to a good engine ground on the vehicle being started.

• Never use a fast charger as a booster to start vehicles.

• Disconnect the battery cables when charging the battery with a fast charger.

• Never attempt to polarize the alternator.

• Do not use test lights of more than 12 volts when checking diode continuity.

• Do not short across or ground any of the alternator terminals.

• The polarity of the battery, alternator and regulator must be matched and considered before making any electrical connections within the system.

• Never separate the alternator on an open circuit. Make sure all connections within the circuit are clean and tight.

• Disconnect the battery ground terminal when performing any service on electrical components.

• Disconnect the battery if arc welding is to be done on the vehicle.

Belt Tension Adjustment

EXCEPT 3.0L ENGINE

1. Loosen the pivot bolt slightly.

2. Loosen the adjuster slot bolt or adjuster bolt locknut to allow for alternator movement. Raise and safely support the vehicle if necessary.

3. Apply tension to the alternator using adjuster bolt or prybar until the belt deflects ¼–½ in. under a 10 lb. load.

4. Torque the adjuster strap bolt or locknut to 10 ft. lbs. (15 Nm). and the pivot bolt to 16 ft. lbs. (23 Nm).

3.0L ENGINE

1. Loosen the tensioner pulley locknut.

2. Turn the adjusting bolt to displace tensioner pulley until the belt deflects ¼–½ in. under a 10 lb. load.

3. Tighten the locknut.

Removal and Installation

1. Disconnect the negative battery cable.

2. Remove the alternator cover, if equipped.

3. Remove the alternator drive belt.

4. Remove the alternator brace bolt(s), nut(s) and applicable spacers.

5. Remove the alternator from the mounting bracket, label and disconnect all wires from the rear of the unit.

To install:

6. Connect all wiring to their proper terminals on the rear of the alternator.

7. Position the alternator in the mounting bracket.

8. Install the alternator brace bolt(s), nut(s) and applicable spacers.

9. Install the alternator belt and adjust the tension as required.

10. Install the alternator cover, if equipped.

11. Connect the negative battery cable and check the alternator for proper operation.

Starter

For further information, please refer to "Starters" in the Unit Repair section.

Removal and Installation

1. Disconnect the negative battery cable.

2. Raise the vehicle and support safely.

3. Remove the starter cover, if equipped.

4. Label and disconnect the wiring to the starter motor.

5. Remove the starter mounting bolts.

6. Remove the starter motor from the vehicle.

7. The installation is the reverse of the removal procedure. Torque the mounting bolts to 20–25 ft. lbs. (27–34 Nm).

CHASSIS ELECTRICAL

Heater Blower Motor

Removal and Installation

WITHOUT AIR CONDITIONING

1. Disconnect the negative battery cable.
2. Remove the lap heater duct and the left side defroster duct.
3. On some vehicles, it will be necessary to remove the heater housing to extract the blower motor. Remove the housing as follows:

    a. Open the glove box lid and release the glove box stoppers. Remove the glove box from its hinge.

    b. Use a small prying device to remove the clip that holds the air selection control cable in place.

    c. Disconnect the air selection control cable from the end of the air selection damper lever.

    d. Remove the air distribution duct from the left side of the blower assembly.

    e. Disconnect the connector to the resistor block and remove the grounding screw.

    f. Remove the blower housing attaching bolts and remove the housing from the vehicle.

    g. Remove the resistor block and vent hose from the housing.

4. Remove the blower motor retaining screws and remove the motor assembly from the housing. Remove the fan from the motor.

To install:

5. Inspect the gasket on housing for cracking or breaks and repair as required.
6. Install the fan to the blower motor shaft. Install the blower motor assembly to the housing and install the retaining screws.
7. Install the heater housing as follows:

    a. Install the vent hose and resistor block.

    b. Install the assembled blower housing to the vehicle.

    c. Position the ground wire and install the grounding screw.

    d. Connect the resistor block connector.

    e. Install the air distribution duct to the blower housing.

    f. Move the air selection control lever to the recirculation position. Pull the air selection control damper lever up and connect the air selection control cable to the end of the air selection damper lever. Secure the cable with the retaining clip.

8. Install the lap heater duct, glove box and stopper.
9. Connect the negative battery cable and check the blower motor for proper operation.

WITH AIR CONDITIONING

1. Disconnect negative battery cable.
2. Remove the lap duct and the left side defroster duct.
3. If necessary remove the heater/air conditioner housing as follows:

    a. Open the glove box lid and release the glove box stoppers. Remove the glove box from its hinge.

    b. Use a small prying device to remove the clip that holds the air selection control cable in place.

    c. Disconnect the air selection control cable from the end of the air selection damper lever.

    d. Remove the air distribution duct from the left side of the blower assembly.

    e. Disconnect the connector to the resistor block and remove the grounding screw.

    f. Remove the blower housing attaching bolts and remove the housing from the vehicle.

    g. Remove the resistor block and vent hose from the housing.

4. Remove the blower motor retaining screws and remove the

1. Lap heater duct
2. Glove box
3. Air selection control cable
4. Duct
5. Blower assembly
6. Resistor
7. Vent hose
8. Blower motor
9. Gasket
10. Fan

Blower motor removal and installation

motor assembly from the housing. Remove the fan from the motor.

To install:

5. Inspect the gasket on housing for cracking or breaks and repair as required.
6. Install the fan to the blower motor shaft. Install the blower motor assembly to the housing and install the retaining screws.
7. Install the heater housing as follows:

    a. Install the vent hose and resistor block.

    b. Install the assembled blower housing to the vehicle.

    c. Position the ground wire and install the grounding screw.

    d. Connect the resistor block connector.

    e. Install the air distribution duct to the blower housing.

    f. Move the air selection control lever to the recirculation position. Pull the air selection control damper lever up and connect the air selection control cable to the end of the air selection damper lever. Secure the cable with the retaining clip.

8. Install the lap duct and the left side defroster duct.
9. Install the glove box and stopper.
10. Connect the negative battery cable and check the blower motor for proper operation.

Windshield Wiper Motor

Removal and Installation

FRONT WIPER

1. Disconnect the negative battery cable.
2. Disconnect the wiper motor electrical connector.
3. Remove the wiper motor retaining bolts and pull the motor out far enough to gain access to the wiper linkage.
4. Matchmark position of wiper linkage to aid installation. Pry the wiper linkage from the motor output shaft.
5. Remove the wiper motor from the vehicle.
6. The installation is the reverse of the removal procedure.

REAR WIPER

1. Disconnect the negative battery cable.
2. Tilt the wiper mount nut cover up and remove the wiper arm retaining nut. Remove the wiper arm from the shaft. Remove the wiper pivot nut and washer.
3. Remove the inside door handle cover. Remove rear door inside trim panel and waterproof film.
4. Disconnect the wiper motor wire connector.
5. Remove the wiper motor retaining bolts and remove the motor from the vehicle.

To install:

6. Install the wiper motor and torque retainers to 7 ft. lbs. (10 Nm).
7. Connect the wiper motor electrical harness.
8. Install waterproof film to rear door panel. Install rear door inside trim panel and handle cover.
9. Install the wiper pivot nut and washer to motor shaft. Install the wiper arm and retainer nut to the motor shaft and torque to 7 ft. lbs. (10 Nm).
10. Reconnect the negative battery cable and check operation of the rear wiper.

Windshield Wiper Switch

The front windshield wiper switch is part of the combination switch located on the steering column. The rear wiper switch is located on the instrument panel.

Removal and Installation

REAR WIPER SWITCH

1. Disconnect negative battery cable.
2. Insert a trim stick between the instrument panel and the switch housing. Pry switch out from the panel.
3. Disconnect electrical connector and service the wiper/washer switch, as required.

To install:

4. Connect the electrical connector and snap switch assembly into instrument panel.
5. Connect the negative battery cable and check operation of the wiper/washer assembly.

Instrument Cluster

Removal and Installation

1. Disconnect the negative battery cable.
2. On Ram 50, remove the hazard flasher switch and the matching cover on the other side of the column. Remove the screws under these covers.
3. If equipped with tilt steering, operate the tilt lever to bring the steering down.
4. Remove the hood attaching screws on the underside corners of the upper hood surface, if equipped.
5. Remove the hood from the instrument meter.
6. Remove the 4 cluster attaching screws and pull out cluster. Disconnect the speedometer cable from the back of the cluster by pushing the stopper of the plug on the speedometer cable side of the connection.
7. Disconnect the electrical connectors at the cluster and remove the cluster from the vehicle.
8. To remove the speedometer or gauges, remove the cover and glass. Remove the retaining screws and remove the speedometer or gauges as required.

To install:

9. Install the speedometer or gauges into the cluster and install the retaining screws. Install the glass and the cover.
10. Connect the electrical connectors and the speedometer to the cluster and install in vehicle. Install 4 retaining screws.
11. Install the instrument cluster hood and retaining screws.
12. Install the hazard flasher switch and the matching cover on the other side of the column, if equipped.
13. Connect the negative battery cable and check operation of all gauges.

Combination Switch

Removal and Installation

NOTE: The combination switch incorporates the windshield wiper/washer, headlight, dimmer and turn signal switch functions into a single switch assembly.

1. Disconnect negative battery cable.

Combination switch mounting

1. Column covers
2. Harness band
3. Ignition switch
4. Key reminder switch

Ignition switch and lock assembly

2. Remove the steering wheel pad. Matchmark and remove the steering wheel.
3. If equipped with tilt steering column, put the column in lowest position.
4. Remove the upper and lower column covers.
5. Remove the wiring harness band and disconnect the harness connectors.
6. Remove the combination switch mounting screws and remove the switch.
7. The installation is the reverse of the removal procedure. Torque the steering wheel nut to 30 ft. lbs. (41 Nm).

Ignition Lock/Switch

Removal and Installation

1. Disconnect the negative battery cable.
2. If equipped with tilt steering column, put the column in its lowest position.
3. Remove the upper and lower column covers.
4. Remove the wiring harness band and disconnect the ignition switch harness.
5. Remove the ignition switch to lock attaching screws, if equipped, and remove the switch from the lock.
6. Using a hacksaw blade, cut a groove into the head of the ignition switch break-off bolts and remove.
7. Remove the assembly from the steering column.
To install:
8. With the key inserted in the switch, install the switch and lock assembly to the steering column. Tighten the screws gradually making sure the key does not bind.
9. If using break-off bolts, tighten them until the heads break off.
10. Connect the switch harness and check the assembly for proper operation.
11. Install upper and lower column covers.

Stoplight Switch

Adjustment

1. Disconnect negative battery cable.
2. Loosen locknut on the brake light switch.
3. Turn the switch in the mounting bracket until the plunger does not contact the brake pedal.
4. Rotate the switch outward ½–1 revolution and secure the locknut. Reconnect the negative battery cable and check switch operation.

Removal and Installation

1. Disconnect the negative battery cable.
2. Unplug the connector to the switch.

0–0.04 IN.
(0–0.5MM)

Adjusting clutch switch—1992 Ram 50 with 2.4L engine

3. Remove the locknut and remove the switch from its mount bracket.
4. The installation is the reverse of the removal procedure.

Clutch Switch

Adjustment

1992 VEHICLE

1. Disconnect negative battery cable.
2. Loosen the locknut on the switch. Move the switch in the mounting bracket to adjust switch piston travel. Adjust the switch so distance from the bottom of the clutch pedal extension to the upper step of the switch, with the clutch depressed, measures 0–0.04 in. (0–0.5mm).
3. Reconnect the negative battery cable. Check operation of cruise control system making sure the cruise control is not operational when the pedal is depressed.

EXCEPT 1992 VEHICLE

1. Disconnect negative battery cable.
2. Loosen the locknut on the switch. Adjust the switch so the distance from the floorboard to the top of the pedal pad in a released position is 7½ in. for Raider or 6½ in. for Ram 50.
3. Reconnect the negative battery cable. Check operation of cruise control system making sure the cruise control is not operational when the pedal is depressed.

Removal and Installation

1992 VEHICLE

1. Disconnect negative battery cable.
2. Unplug the electrical connector from the clutch switch.
3. Remove the locknut from the top of the switch and pull the switch down from the mounting bracket.
4. The installation is the reverse of the removal procedure. Adjust switch after installed.

EXCEPT 1992 VEHICLE

1. Disconnect the negative battery cable.
2. Unplug the connector to the switch.
3. Remove the locknut and the switch from its mounting bracket.
4. The installation is the reverse of the removal procedure. Adjust clutch pedal travel after switch is installed.

Neutral Safety Switch

Removal and Installation

1. Disconnect negative battery cable.
2. Raise and safely support the vehicle.

Headlight circuit fuse location—Raider

Air conditioning fuse location—Raider

Electric door locks fuse location—1988–89 Raider

Electric door locks fuse location—1990–92 Raider

3. Remove the electrical connector from the switch. Place drain pan under the switch and remove the switch from the transmission.

4. Install switch with new seal into the transmission and tighten to 25 ft. lbs. (34 Nm).

5. Lower the vehicle and add transmission fluid to correct the level. Check operation of the switch.

Fuses, Circuit Breakers and Relays

Location

RAIDER

Main Fuse Block—located on the left side of the instrument panel, covered by a removable access panel. There are also several dedicated fuses located throughout the vehicle.

Main Fuse Link—located to the right side of the battery.

Sub Fuse Link—located in the engine compartment on the left fender by the device box.

Condenser Blower Motor Relay—located on the left front fender under the ignition coil.

Light Control Relay—located on the front corner of the left fender.

Auto Choke Relay—located in the engine compartment on the left fender by the device box.

Over Drive Control Relay—located on the right side kick panel in the passenger compartment.

Engine Control Relay—located on the right side of the instrument panel, mounted under a removable trim panel.

RAM 50

Fuse Block—located to the left of the steering column, covered by a removable access panel.

Main Fuse Link—located in the engine compartment between the battery and the fender.

Air Conditioning Relay—located behind the glove box.

Intermittent Wiper Relay—located inside of and is a function of the column combination switch.

Auto Choke Relay—located in the engine compartment on the left fender by the device box.

Over Drive Relay—located to the left of the fuse block.

Seat Belt Timer Relay—located to the left of the fuse block.

Engine Control Relay—located on the right side of the instrument panel behind a removable trim panel.

Computers

Location

Engine Control Unit (ECU)—located on the right side of the dash, under a removeable trim panel mounted to the kick-panel.

Automatic Free—Wheeling Hub Indicator Control Unit—located on the right side of the dash mounted to the kick panel.

Feed Back Carburetor Control Unit—located under the right side of the dash by the blower motor housing.

Auto—Cruise Control Unit—located to the left of the fuse block.

Flashers

Location

Turn Signal Flasher Unit—located in the central junction at the fuse block to the left of the steering column.

Hazard Warning Flasher Unit—located in the central junction at the fuse block to the left of the steering column.

Accelerator cable "A" adjustment—with cruise control

Accelerator cable "B" adjustment—with cruise control

Cruise Control

For further information, please refer to Chilton's Chassis Electronics Service Manual.

Adjustment

1. Run the vehicle until normal operating temperature is reached. Adjust the idle speed to match the emission sticker on the vehicle.
2. Turn the engine **OFF** and remove the actuator cover.

3. Loosen the locknuts on the accelerator cables and let the inner cables sag.
4. While keeping lever "P" and the stopper in contact with each other, turn the adjusting nut to lengthen the outer cable. Adjust until the lever "P" begins to operate. Turn the nut back ½ turn and secure the locknut. Accelerator cable "A" free-play should be 0-0.04 in. (0–1mm).
5. To adjust accelerator cable "B", alter the adjusting nuts on the carburator to meet the prefered free-play setting of 0–0.08 in. (0-2mm).
6. Install actuator cover and check operation of cruise control.

ENGINE COOLING

Radiator

Removal and Installation

1. Disconnect the negative battery cable. Remove the air duct, as required.
2. Drain the coolant from the radiator.
3. Remove the upper hose and coolant reserve tank hose from the radiator.
4. Remove the shroud assembly from the radiator.
5. Raise the vehicle and support safely.
6. Remove the lower hose from the radiator.
7. Disconnect and plug the automatic transmission cooler hoses, if equipped. Lower the vehicle.
8. Remove the mounting screws and carefully lift the radiator out of the engine compartment.
To install:
9. Lower the radiator into position and install the mounting screws.
10. Raise the vehicle and support safely. Connect the automatic transmission cooler hoses, if removed.
11. Connect the lower radiator hose. Lower the vehicle.
12. Install the shroud assembly.
13. Connect the upper hose and coolant reserve tank hose.
14. Fill the cooling system.
15. Connect the negative battery cable and run the vehicle until the thermostat opens. Fill the radiator completely and check the automatic transmission fluid level, if equipped.

16. Check for leaks. Once vehicle has cooled, recheck coolant level.
17. Reinstall the air duct, if removed.

Heater Core

For further information, please refer to Chilton's Air Conditioning and Heating Manual.

Removal and Installation
RAIDER

1. Disconnect the negative battery cable.
2. Set the temperature control to the extreme right position and drain the cooling system.
3. If equipped with 2.6L engine, remove the air cleaner assembly.
4. If equipped with 3.0L engine, remove the air intake plenum as follows:
   a. Relieve the fuel pressure.
   b. Remove the air intake hose from the throttle body.
   c. Disconnect all wires, hoses and linkages to the throttle body.
   d. Disconnect the EGR temperature sensor wire.
   e. Remove the ignition coil.
   f. Remove the engine oil filler neck bracket.
   g. Unbolt the EGR tube from the air intake plenum.

1. Lap heater duct
2. Lap heater duct
3. Hood release cable bracket
4. Left defroster grill
5. Right defroster grill
6. Glove box
7. Instrument cluster hood
8. Instrument cluster
9. Cover
10. Inclinometer pod
11. Center panel
12. Recirculation/fresh air selection cable
13. Mode selection cable
14. Water valve control cable
15. Center reinforcement
16. Horn pad
17. Steering wheel
18. Fuse box cover
19. Fuse box
20. Instrument panel
21. Heater case

Instrument panel assembly—Raider

h. Disconnect the PCV hose and vacuum hose cluster from the plenum.

i. Remove the plenum to engine brackets.

j. Unbolt the air intake plenum assembly from the intake manifold and remove.

k. Remove the gaskets and thoroughly clean and dry the mating surfaces of the intake plenum.

5. Remove the heater hose clamps and disconnect the heater hoses.

6. Remove the lap heater ducts and the hood release cable bracket.

7. Remove the side demister grills by carefully prying them from the instrument panel.

8. Remove the glove box and center console assembly. Remove the center reinforcement.

9. Remove the steering wheel.

10. Remove the instrument cluster.

11. Remove the oil pressure gauge, inclinometer and voltmeter pod cover and remove the gauge assembly.

12. Label and disconnect the recirculation/fresh air door control cable.

13. Label and disconnect the mode selection control cable.

14. Label and disconnect the water valve control cable.

15. Remove the fuse box retaining screw and position the fuse box aside.

16. Remove the instrument panel retaining nuts and bolts and carefully remove the instrument panel from the vehicle.

17. Remove the duct from the top of the heater case.

18. Remove the retaining nuts and bolts and remove the heater case from the vehicle.

19. Remove the water valve cover and carefully remove the water valve from the case.

20. Remove the foot/defroster selection link from the mode selection lever.

21. Move the lever up to a position which will not interfere with the removal of the heater core.

22. Remove the heater core from the heater case. If the mode lever is in the way, remove it.

To install:

23. Install the heater core to the heater case. Install the mode lever, if removed.

24. Install the foot/defroster selection link to the mode selection lever.

25. Install the water valve assembly and its cover to the case.

26. Install the assembled heater case to the vehicle and install the retaining nuts and bolts.

27. Install the duct to the top of the case.

28. Connect the heater hoses to the core tubes.

Instrument panel assembly—Ram 50

SPORTS MODEL

1. Hazard warning flasher switch
2. Screw cover
3. Instrument cluster hood
4. Instrument cluster
5. Fuse box cover
6. Fuse box
7. Glove box
8. Defroster duct
9. Air selection control cable
10. Mode selection control cable
11. Temperature control cable
12. Speaker grill
13. Parcel box or clock
14. Instrument panel attaching nut cover
15. Center cover
16. Shifter knob
17. Floor console
18. Instrunment panel
19. Heater case

29. Install the instrument panel and all related parts. Adjust the control cables if necessary.

30. If equipped with 3.0L engine, install the intake plenum as follows:

a. Using a new gasket, install the air intake plenum to the intake manifold. Torque the nuts and bolts to 12 ft. lbs. (16 Nm). Install the plenum to engine brackets.

b. Connect the PCV hose and vacuum hose cluster to the plenum.

c. Connect the EGR tube.

d. Install the engine oil filler neck bracket.

e. Install the ignition coil assembly.

f. Connect the EGR temperature sensor wire.

g. Connect all wires, hoses and linkages to the throttle body.

h. Install the air intake hose to the throttle body.

i. Connect the upper radiator hose to the thermostat housing.

j. Adjust accelerator cable.

31. If equipped with 2.6L engine, install the air cleaner assembly.

32. Fill the system with coolant.

33. Connect the negative battery cable, run the vehicle until the thermostat opens and fill the radiator completely.

34. Check for leaks. Once cooled, recheck the coolant level.

35. Check the entire climate control system and all gauges for proper operation.

RAM 50

1. Disconnect the negative battery cable. Position the heater controls in the extreme right position.

2. Drain the coolant. Disconnect the heater hoses from the core tubes.

3. Remove the hazard flasher switch and the matching cover on the other side of the column. Remove the instrument cluster.

4. Remove the fuse box cover and remove the fuse box retaining screws. Position the fuse box aside.

5. Remove the glove box assembly.

6. Remove the defroster ducts.

7. Label and disconnect the air, mode and temperature control cables from the heater case.

8. Remove the front speaker grilles.

9. Remove the parcel box or clock, as equipped.

10. Remove the nut cover from the top center of the instrument panel.

11. Remove the center cover.

12. Remove the shift knob and floor console assembly, if equipped.

13. Move the tilt steering column down as far as it will go.

14. Remove the instrument panel retaining nuts and bolts and carefully remove the instrument panel from the vehicle.

15. Remove the duct from the top center of the heater case.

16. Remove the defroster duct from the the left side of the case.

17. Remove the center reinforcement braces.

18. Remove the mounting nuts and remove the heater case from the vehicle.

19. Remove the hose cover, joint hose clamp and the plate from the case.

20. Remove the heater core from the case.

To install:

21. Install the heater core to the heater case.

22. Install the plate, joint hose clamp and hose cover.

23. Install the assembled heater case to the vehicle. Connect the heater hoses to the core tubes.

24. Install the center reinforcement braces.

25. Install the defroster and center ducts to the case.

26. Install the instrument panel and all related parts. Adjust the control cables if necessary.

27. Fill the system with coolant.

28. Connect the negative battery cable, run the vehicle until the thermostat opens and fill the radiator completely.

29. Check for leaks. Once cooled, recheck the coolant level.

30. Check the entire climate control system and all gauges for proper operation.

Water Pump

Removal and Installation

2.0L AND 2.4L ENGINES

1. Disconnect the negative battery cable.

2. Drain the cooling system.

3. Release the fuel pressure if equipped with fuel injection.

4. Remove the upper radiator shroud.

5. Remove all accessory belts. Remove the air conditioning compressor tensioner pulley, if equipped.

6. Remove the cooling fan assembly along with the water pump pulley.

7. Disconnect the radiator hose from the water pump.

8. Remove the crankshaft pulley(s).

9. Remove the timing belt covers. If the same timing belt will be reused, mark the direction of the timing belt's rotation, for installation in the same direction. Make sure the engine is positioned so the No. 1 cylinder is at the TDC of its compression stroke and the sprockets timing marks are aligned with the engine's timing mark indicators. Remove the timing belt.

10. The water pump bolts are different lengths, note their positions before removing. Remove the water pump mounting bolts and remove the pump from the block and the water pipe connection. Remove the O-ring from the water pipe connection.

To install:

11. Clean and dry the mating surfaces of the block and water pump. Install a new O-ring to the water pipe connection. Coat the new O-ring with water to aid in installation.

12. Install the water pump with a new gasket to the block and torque the bolts (except the alternator bracket bolt) to 10 ft. lbs. (13 Nm). Torque the aforementioned bolt to 17 ft. lbs. (23 Nm).

13. Install the timing belt(s) and covers.

14. Install the crankshaft pulley(s).

15. Connect the radiator hose to the water pump.

16. Install the water pump pulley and cooling fan assembly.

17. Install the air conditioning compressor tensioner pulley, if equipped, and install and adjust the accessory belts.

18. Install the upper radiator shroud.

19. Fill the system with coolant.

20. Connect the negative battery cable, run the vehicle until the thermostat opens and fill the radiator completely.

21. Check for leaks. Once cooled, recheck the coolant level.

2.6L ENGINE

1. Disconnect the negative battery cable.

2. Drain the cooling system.

3. Remove the upper radiator shroud, if equipped.

4. Remove all accessory belts.

5. Remove the cooling fan assembly along with the water pump pulley.

6. Disconnect the radiator hose and heater hose from the water pump.

7. The water pump bolts are different lengths, note their positions before removing. Remove the water pump retaining bolts and remove the water pump.

8. The installation is the reverse of the removal procedure. Torque the water pump and pulley bolts to 10 ft. lbs. (13 Nm).

3.0L ENGINE

1. Disconnect the negative battery cable.

2. Drain the cooling system. Remove the upper radiator hose, bypass hose and the upper radiator shroud.

3. If equipped with electric fuel pump, loosen the fuel filler

Water pump assembly—3.0L engine

cap to release fuel tank pressure and release the fuel pressure in the supply lines.

4. Remove the cooling fan assembly along with the water pump pulley. Remove all belts.

5. Remove the power steering pump from the bracket and remove the bracket.

6. Remove the tensioner pulley bracket, the air conditioning compressor and its bracket.

7. Remove the cooling fan bracket assembly. Remove the crankshaft pulley and flange.

8. Remove the timing belt covers. If the same timing belt will be reused, mark the direction of the timing belt's rotation, for installation in the same direction. Make sure the engine is positioned so the No. 1 cylinder is at the TDC of its compression stroke and the sprockets timing marks are aligned with the engine's timing mark indicators.

9. Loosen the timing belt tensioner bolt and remove the belt. Position the tensioner as far away from the center of the engine as possible and tighten the bolt. Remove the water pump mounting bolts, separate the pump from the water inlet pipe and remove the pump from the engine. Remove the water inlet fitting from the pump.

To install:

10. Clean and dry the mating surfaces of the block and water pump. Install a new O-ring to the water inlet pipe. Install the

pump and water inlet fitting with new gaskets to the engine and water pipe. Torque the water pump mounting bolts to 20 ft. lbs. (27 Nm).

11. If not already done, position both camshafts so the marks line up with those on the alternator bracket and inner timing cover. Rotate the crankshaft so the timing mark aligns with the mark on the oil pump.

12. Install the timing belt on the crankshaft sprocket and while keeping the belt tight on the tension side (right side), install the belt on the front camshaft sprocket.

13. Install the belt on the water pump pulley, then the rear camshaft sprocket and the tensioner.

14. Rotate the front camshaft counterclockwise to tension the belt between the front camshaft and the crankshaft. If the timing marks came out of line, repeat the procedure.

15. Install the crankshaft sprocket flange.

16. Loosen the tensioner bolt and allow the spring to tension the belt.

17. Turn the crankshaft 2 full turns in the clockwise direction only until the timing marks align again. Now that the belt is properly tensioned, torque the tensioner lock bolt to 21 ft. lbs. (29 Nm).

18. Install the timing belt covers and all related parts.

19. Fill the cooling system.

20. Connect the negative battery cable, run the vehicle until the thermostat opens and fill the radiator completely.

21. Check for leaks. Once cooled, recheck the coolant level.

Thermostat

Removal and Installation

1. Disconnect the negative battery cable. Drain the coolant down to thermostat level or below.

2. Disconnect the engine coolant temperature switch connector, if equipped.

3. Remove the thermostat housing.

4. Remove the thermostat and gasket from the housing.

5. Clean the housing mating surfaces and install a new gasket.

6. The installation is the reverse of the removal procedure.

Cooling System Bleeding

All engines are equipped with self-bleeding thermostats. Cooling system bleeding is not necessary in any vehicles when servicing the cooling system.

FUEL SYSTEM

Fuel System Service Precaution

Safety is the most important factor when performing not only fuel system maintenance but any type of maintenance. Failure to conduct maintenance and repairs in a safe manner may result in serious personal injury or death. Maintenance and testing of the vehicle's fuel system components can be accomplished safely and effectively by adhering to the following rules and guidelines.

• To avoid the possibility of fire and personal injury, always disconnect the negative battery cable unless the repair or test procedure requires that battery voltage be applied.

• Always relieve the fuel system pressure prior to disconnecting any fuel system component (injector, fuel rail, pressure regulator, etc.), fitting or fuel line connection. Exercise extreme caution whenever relieving fuel system pressure to avoid exposing skin, face and eyes to fuel spray. Please be advised that fuel

under pressure may penetrate the skin or any part of the body that it contacts.

• Always place a shop towel or cloth around the fitting or connection prior to loosening to absorb any excess fuel due to spillage. Ensure that all fuel spillage (should it occur) is quickly removed from engine surfaces. Ensure that all fuel soaked cloths or towels are deposited into a suitable waste container.

• Always keep a dry chemical (Class B) fire extinguisher near the work area.

• Do not allow fuel spray or fuel vapors to come into contact with a spark or open flame.

• Always use a backup wrench when loosening and tightening fuel line connection fittings. This will prevent unnecessary stress and torsion to fuel line piping. Always follow the proper torque specifications.

• Always replace worn fuel fitting O-rings with new. Do not substitute fuel hose or equivalent where fuel pipe is installed.

Fuel pump harness connector at the rear of the fuel tank—Raider

Fuel pump harness connector at the rear of the fuel tank—Ram 50

Relieving Fuel System Pressure

1. Disconnect the fuel pump harness connector.
2. Start the engine and allow the engine to run out of fuel.
3. Once the engine has stalled, turn the key to the **OFF** position and connect the electrical connector.
4. Disconnect the negative battery cable so pressure cannot build up until work has been completed.

Fuel Tank

Removal and Installation

1. If equipped with an electric fuel pump, release fuel pressure as follows:
   a. Disconnect the fuel pump harness connector.
   b. Start the engine and allow the engine to run out of fuel.
   c. Once engine has stalled, turn the key to the **OFF** position.
   d. Disconnect the negative battery cable so pressure cannot build up until work has been completed.
2. Raise the vehicle and support safely.
3. Using the proper equipment, drain the fuel tank.
4. Remove the side skirt panel, if equipped.
5. Disconnect the fuel gauge unit connector.
6. Disconnect the main hose connector.
7. Disconnect the return hose connector and the vapor hose connector.
8. Remove the filler hose connector and the breather hose connection.
9. Place a transmission jack or equivalent, under the center

of the tank and apply slight pressure. Remove the tank mounting nuts.
10. Lower the tank and disconnect any lines still conected.
11. Remove the tank from the vehicle.
To install:
12. Raise the tank into position and connect all harnesses and hoses.
13. Install the fuel tank mounting nuts and torque to 18–22 ft. lbs. (25–30 Nm).
14. Reconnect the fuel gauge unit connector.
15. Install the side skirt panel, if equipped.
16. Refill the fuel tank and start the engine. Check fuel system for leaks.

Fuel Filter

Removal and Installation
CARBURETED ENGINE

1. Disconnect the negative battery cable.
2. Raise the vehicle and support safely, if necessary.
3. Remove the air cleaner assembly, if necessary. Remove the fuel filter from its bracket. Inspect the hoses carefully.
4. Install the new filter, hoses and clamps if worn or cracked.
5. Connect the negative battery cable, start the engine and check for leaks.

FUEL INJECTED ENGINE

CAUTION

Do not use conventional fuel filters, hoses or clamps when servicing this fuel system. They are not compatible with the injection system and could fail, causing personal injury or damage to the vehicle. Use only replacement parts specifically designed for fuel injection.

---

1. Relieve the fuel pressure.
2. Disconnect the negative battery cable.
3. Raise the vehicle and support safely.
4. Remove the fuel filter protector plate, if equipped.
5. Disconnect the main and high pressure lines. Remove any other fuel hose that are damaged or worn.
6. Remove the filter mounting bolts and remove the filter from the vehicle.
To install:
7. Install new filter onto vehicle using new gaskets. Replace any hoses that are worn or damaged.
8. Install the protector plate, if equipped.
9. Connect the negative battery cable, check for leaks and road test the vehicle.

Mechanical Fuel Pump

Pressure Testing

1. Raise the vehicle and support safely.
2. Connect a pressure gauge to the fuel pump outlet fitting.
3. Crank the engine several times while observing the gauge.
4. The pump should develop 2.7–4.2 psi of pressure.

Removal and Installation

1. Disconnect the negative battery cable.
2. Disconnect the fuel lines from the pump and plug them.

NOTE: There is a fuel pump pushrod in the 2.0L engine. When removing or installing the pump, be careful not to drop the pushrod because it will drop down into the oil pan.

Also, it may be necessary to remove the rear thermostat housing bolt and/or the valve cover, on the 2.6L engine, to remove and install the pump.

Fuel pump activation terminal — Raider

Fuel pump activation terminal located behind the fuse box — Ram 50

Fuel pressure testing equipment. The hose is not used on Ram 50 with 2.4L engine

Fuel pressure gauge installation — 3.0L engine

Fuel pressure gauge installation — Ram 50 with 2.4L engine

3. Remove the fuel pump retaining bolts or nuts and remove the pump from the engine. Remove the pushrod, if equipped.

4. Clean and dry the mounting surfaces, bolts and bolt holes.

5. The installation is the reverse of the removal procedure. Use new gaskets and a new insulator.

6. Connect the negative battery cable, start the engine and check for leaks.

Electric Fuel Pump

Pressure Testing

1. Relieve the fuel pressure.

2. Disconnect the negative battery cable.

3. Cover the high pressure fuel hose hose with a clean shop towel to prevent fuel spray from residual pressure in the line. Disconnect the high pressure fuel hose at the delivery pipe.

4. Connect the proper fuel pressure gauge and accompanying special adaptor tools to the delivery pipe.

5. If not already done, place the key in the **OFF** position. Connect the negative battery cable.

6. Connect a jumper wire from the fuel pump activation terminal to the positive battery post. This will pressurize the system so the fuel pump installation assembly can be inspected for leaks. If a leak is found, repair it before proceeding.

7. Disconnect the jumper wire to stop the fuel pump.

8. Start the engine and allow to idle.

9. Measure the pressure during idling. The specification for all applications is 38 psi.

10. Disconnect and plug the vacuum hose from the fuel pressure regulator.

11. With the hose disconnected, the pressure should increase to 50 psi.

12. Race the engine a few times to make sure the fuel pressure does not deviate from specifications.

13. Press on the return hose while racing the engine to make sure there is pressure in the hose. Reconnect the vacuum hose.

14. Stop the engine and allow pressure to remain in the system. There should be no decrease in pressure for at least 2 minutes.

15. Release the fuel pressure.

16. Remove the fuel pressure measuring equipment.

17. Connect the high pressure fuel hose to the delivery pipe using new O-rings where necessary.

18. Connect the jumper wire from the fuel pump activation terminal to the positive battery post, inspect the system for leaks.

19. Road test the vehicle.

Removal and Installation

The electric fuel pump assembly is located in the fuel tank, ac-

Fuel tank assembly—Ram 50

1. Side skirt stay
2. Sending unit connector
3. Fuel pump connector
4. Main hose
5. Return hose
6. Vapor hose
7. Breather hose
8. Filler hose
9. Fuel tank protector (4WD)
10. Tank mounting nut
11. Fuel tank
12. Two-way overfill limiter valve
13. Fuel pump assembly
14. Gasket
15. Sending unit

cessible through an inspection plate on Raider. The fuel tank must be removed to service the fuel pump on Ram 50.

RAIDER

1. Relieve the fuel pressure.
2. Disconnect the negative battery cable.
3. Remove the pump and sending unit access panel.
4. Cover the high pressure fuel hose with a clean shop towel to prevent fuel spray from residual pressure in the line. Disconnect the fuel hose and pipe from the pump.
5. Remove the fuel pump mounting screws and remove the pump from the tank.
6. The installation is the reverse of the removal procedure.

RAM 50

1. Relieve the fuel pressure.
2. Disconnect the negative battery cable.
3. Raise the vehicle and support safely. Remove protective plates, if equipped.
4. Using the proper equipment, drain the fuel tank.
5. Remove the fuel tank from the vehicle.
6. Remove the overfill limiter.
7. Remove the pump retaining screws and remove the pump from the tank.

To install:

8. Clean the seal area of the tank. Install a new gasket.
9. Install the pump in the same position as originally installed.
10. Install the retaining screws and torque them to 15 inch lbs.
11. Install the fuel tank and all related parts.
12. Connect the negative battery cable. Connect the jumper wire from the fuel pump activation terminal to the positive battery post and inspect the system for leaks.
13. Road test the vehicle.

Carburetor

Removal and Installation

1. Disconnect the negative battery cable. The choke control element is water activated so it will be necessary to drain the cooling system.
2. Remove the air cleaner assembly.
3. Remove and install the fuel tank cap to relieve any pressure in the tank.
4. Matchmark all vacuum hoses and electrical connectors and remove them from the carburetor.
5. Disconnect the throttle, cruise control, choke, kickdown cables and linkages, as equipped.
6. Disconnect and plug the fuel inlet line.
7. Remove the mounting bolts and remove the carburetor from the intake manifold.

To install:

8. Thoroughly clean and dry the mounting surface of the manifold and install a new base gasket.
9. Install the mounting bolts and tighten them alternately to compress the base gasket evenly. Final torque should be 12 ft. lbs. (16 Nm).
10. Connect the fuel line.
11. Connect the throttle, cruise control, choke, kickdown cables and linkages as required.
12. Install all vacuum hoses and electrical connectors in their proper locations.
13. Install the air cleaner assembly.
14. Fill the cooling system.
15. Connect the negative battery cable, start the engine and perform all necessary adjustments.

Idle Speed Adjustment

1. Start the engine and allow it to reach normal operating temperature. Before checking or adjusting the idle speed, check ignition timing and adjust if necessary.
2. Turn all lights and accessories **OFF**. Connect a tachometer to the engine.
3. Open the throttle and run at 2500 rpm for 10 seconds. Allow the engine to idle for 2 minutes.
4. Check the idle speed. If the tachometer indicates rpm is not at specifications, turn the idle speed screw until the correct idle speed is obtained.

Carburetor adjusting screw locations

5. If equipped with air conditioning, engage compressor.

6. With the compressor running, set the idle to 900 rpm.

Idle Mixture Adjustment

1. Drill a 2mm pilot hole in the casting around the idle mixture screw. Drive out the concealment plug.

2. Run the engine until normal operating temperature is reached.

3. Check and adjust the idle speed and ignition timing.

4. Turn the engine **OFF.**

5. Disconnect the negative battery cable for 5 seconds, then reconnect.

6. Disconnect the oxygen sensor connector.

7. Open the throttle and run at 2500 rpm for 10 seconds. Allow the engine to idle for 2 minutes.

8. Using an emission tester, adjust the idle mixture screw until the CO at idle is below 0.30 percent and the idle is smooth.

9. Turn the engine **OFF.**

10. Connect the oxygen sensor connector.

11. Reinstall the concealment plug in the idle mixture screw hole.

Service Adjustments

For all carburetor service adjustment procedures and Specifications, please refer to "Carburetor Service" in the Unit Repair section.

Fuel Injection

For further information, please refer to Chilton's Electronic Engine Controls Manual.

Idle Speed Adjustment

The idle speed is automatically regulated by the idle speed control system which receives data from various sensors and switches in the system and adjusts the engine idle to a predetermined speed. Idle speed specifications can be found on the Vehicle Emission Control Information (VECI) label located in the engine compartment.

Idle Mixture Adjustment

There is no idle mixture adjustment provided with any Mitsubishi fuel injection system.

Fuel Injector

Removal and Installation

2.4L ENGINE

1. Relieve the fuel pressure.

2. Disconnect negative battery cable.

3. Drain the cooling system. Remove the air intake pipe.

4. Matchmark and remove all linkage and vacuum hoses from the throttle body.

5. Remove the throttle body from the intake manifold.

6. Cover the high pressure fuel hose with a clean shop towel to prevent fuel spray from residual pressure in the line. Disconnect the high pressure fuel hose from the fuel rail.

7. Remove the fuel return line and vacuum hose from the fuel pressure regulator.

8. Disconnect the electrical connectors from the injectors.

9. Remove the fuel rail retaining bolts.

10. Lift the rail with injectors attached up and away from the engine.

11. Remove the injector from the rail by pulling straight out away from rail. Remove the lower insulator.

To install:

12. Install a new grommet and O-rings onto the injector. Coat the O-rings lightly with gasoline.

13. Install the injector to the rail, making sure injector turns freely. If it does not turn, check for a damaged or misaligned O-ring and reinstall.

14. Replace the insulators in the intake manifold. Install the fuel rail with injectors onto the manifold. Make sure the rubber bushings are correctly seated in the installation holes.

15. Tighten fuel rail retaining bolts to 18 ft. lbs. (10 Nm).

16. Install the fuel return line and vacuum hose to the fuel pressure regulator.

17. Connect the electrical harness to the injectors.

18. Replace O-ring and connect the high pressure fuel line to delivery pipe.

19. Connect the boost hose to air plenum.

20. Install the throttle body using a new base gasket.

21. Refill the cooling system. Connect the negative battery cable.

22. Connect the jumper wire from the fuel pump activation terminal to the positive battery post and inspect the system for leaks.

3.0L ENGINE

1. Relieve the fuel pressure.

2. Disconnect negative battery cable.

3. Remove the air intake hose from the throttle body.

4. Disconnect all wires, hoses and linkages to the throttle body.

5. Disconnect the EGR temperature sensor wire.

6. Remove the ignition coil.

7. Remove the engine oil filler neck bracket.

8. Unbolt the EGR tube from the air intake plenum.

9. Disconnect the PCV hose and vacuum hose cluster from the plenum.

10. Remove the plenum to engine brackets.

11. Unbolt the air intake plenum assembly from the intake manifold and remove.

12. Cover the high pressure fuel hose with a clean shop towel to prevent fuel spray due to residual pressure in the line. Disconnect the high pressure fuel hose from the fuel rail.

13. Remove the fuel return line and vacuum hose from the fuel pressure regulator.

14. Remove electrical connectors from the injectors.

15. Remove the fuel rail retaining bolts.

16. Lift the rail with injectors attached up and away from the engine.

17. Remove the injectors from the fuel rail pulling straight out away from the rail. Remove the lower insulator.

1. Air intake hose
2. Breather hose
3. Wiring harness connector
4. Air intake pipe
5. Air hose
6. Accelerator cable
7. Kickdown cable
8. Water hose
9. Vacuum hose
10. Throttle body
11. Base plate
12. Fuel injector connector
13. High pressure fuel hose
14. Fuel return hose
15. Bolt
16. Fuel rail
17. Insulator
18. Injector
19. O-ring
20. Grommet
21. Insulator
22. Fuel pressure regulator
23. O-ring

Throttle body, fuel rail, injector and related parts – 2.4L engine

7. Harness connector
8. Fuel rail
9. Injector
10. O-ring
11. Grommet
12. Insulator
13. Insulator

1. Air intake plenum
2. High pressure fuel hose
3. Return hose
4. Vacuum hose
5. Fuel pressure regulator
6. O-ring

Fuel rail, injector and related parts – 3.0L engine

To install:

18. Install a new grommet and O-ring onto injector. Coat the O-ring lightly with gasoline to aid in assembly.

19. Install the injectors into the rail, making sure injector turns freely. If they do not, check for a misaligned O-ring and reinstall.

20. Replace the seats in the intake manifold. Install new rubber bushings onto mounting points of fuel rail. Install the assembled fuel rail with injectors onto the manifold.

21. Tighten the fuel rail bolts to 8 ft. lbs. (10 Nm).

22. Connect the electrical harness to the injectors.

23. Connect the fuel return hose and the vacuum hose to the pressure regulator.

24. Using a new O-ring coated lightly with gasoline, install the high pressure fuel line.

25. Install air intake plenum and all related parts.

26. Connect the negative battery cable.

27. Connect the jumper wire from the fuel pump activation terminal to the positive battery post inspect the system for leaks.

EMISSION CONTROLS

For further information, please refer to Chilton's Emission Controls Manual.

Emissions warning light reset switch—Raider

Emissions warning light reset switch—Ram 50

Emission Warning Lamps

Resetting

RAIDER

The reset switch is located on the back of the instrument cluster. Remove the instrument cluster to access the switch. To re-set the timer, simply flip the switch. The bulb may be removed after the 150,000 mile check is completed on Raider.

RAM 50

Remove the glass from the front of the instrument cluster to access the reset switch. To reset the timer, simply flip the switch. The bulb may be removed after the 120,000 mile check is completed.

ENGINE MECHANICAL

NOTE: Disconnecting the negative battery cable on some vehicles may interfere with the functions of the on board computer systems and may require the computer to undergo a relearning process, once the negative battery cable is reconnected.

Engine Assembly

Removal and Installation

EXCEPT VAN

1. Relieve the fuel pressure if equipped with fuel injection. Disconnect the negative battery cable from the battery and from the engine.

2. Matchmark and remove the hood. Remove the oil dipstick.

3. Raise the vehicle and support safely. Remove the engine under cover. Drain the engine oil and coolant.

4. Remove the starter. Remove the lower radiator hose.

5. Remove the exhaust pipe from the exhaust manifold(s).

6. If equipped with 4WD, remove transfer case from vehicle.

7. If equipped with a manual transmission, remove the transmission and all related parts.

8. If equipped with an automatic transmission and 2WD, remove the inspection plate, matchmark the flexplate to the converter, remove the torque converter bolts and move the torque converter back as far as it will go. Remove the lower bell housing bolts. Lower the vehicle.

9. If equipped with a carburetor, remove the air cleaner assembly. Remove all ductwork and air intake hoses. Disconnect all linkages and cables from the carburetor or throttle body.

10. Cover the fuel line connections with a clean shop rag and disconnect and plug the fuel lines.

11. If equipped with air conditioning, unbolt the air conditioning compressor from the engine and position aside. It is not necessary to remove the lines from the compressor.

12. Remove the radiator and shroud. Remove the fan and all related parts. Disconnet the heater hoses.

13. Unbolt the power steering pump from its brackets and position it to the side. Do not remove the hoses from the pump.

14. Remove the alternator. Remove the ignition coil and power transistor assembly, if equipped.

15. Label and disconnect all remaining electrical connectors, vacuum hoses and check for any other items preventing engine removal.

16. Attach an engine removal device to the engine support eyes on the engine.

17. If equipped with an automatic transmission, support the transmission with a floor jack or equivalent. Remove the remaining bell housing bolts.

18. Remove the engine mount nuts and remove the engine from the vehicle.

To install:

19. Lower the engine into position and install the engine mount nuts. Torque the nuts to 20 ft. lbs. (27 Nm). Install the upper bell housing bolts. Remove the engine removal device and the transmission support. Install the oil dipstick.

20. Raise the vehicle and support safely. Install the remaining bell housing bolts.

21. Install transfer case, if removed.

22. If equipped with a manual transmission, install the transmission and all related parts.

23. If equipped with an automatic transmission, align the torque converter and flexplate and install the bolts. Install the inspection plate and starter.

24. Install the exhaust pipe to the exhaust manifold(s) using new gaskets. Install the lower radiator hose. Lower the vehicle.

25. Connect the heater hoses.

26. Make sure the negative battery cable is not connected to the battery. Connect the engine side of the negative cable to the engine. Install the alternator, power steering pump and all brackets.

27. Install the air conditioning compressor.

28. Connect all linkages and cables to the carburetor or throttle body.

29. Install the ignition coil and power transistor assembly, if equipped. Connect all electrical connectors and vacuum hoses that were disconnected during the engine removal procedure.

30. Install the fan and all related parts. Adjust all belt tensions, as required.

31. Install the radiator, shroud and upper hose.

32. Install the air cleaner assembly, ducts and air intake hoses.

33. Fill the engine with the specified amount of oil and fill the radiator with coolant.

34. Connect the negative battery cable and connect the jumper wire from the fuel pump activation terminal, if equipped, to the positive battery post to inspect the system for leaks.

35. Check the automatic transmission fluid level, if equipped. Set all adjustments to specifications.

36. Install and align the hood.

Engine Mounts

Removal and Installation
FRONT MOUNT

1. Disconnect negative battery cable.

2. Install engine support fixture in place. Raise and safely support the vehicle.

3. Remove the engine front support insulator.

4. Remove the front insulator stopper.

5. Remove the heat protector.

6. Unbolt the rear crossmember or mount as required.

7. Raise engine with support fixture far enough to remove mounts, remove remaining bolts and mounts. Transfer insulator and stopper to new mount.

To install:

8. Install mounts to engine block. Install stopper and heat protector to the mount.

9. Lower engine to original position and insert bolts through mounting brackets. Tighten bolts to 22–29 ft. lbs. (30-40 Nm) and mount nut to 14–22 ft. lbs. (20–30 Nm).

10. Install heat protector to insulator. Tighten heat protector nut to 6–9 ft. lbs. (8-12 Nm).

11. Lower the vehicle and remove the engine support fixture. Reconnect the negative battery cable.

REAR MOUNT

1. Disconnect negative battery cable.

2. Install engine support fixture in place. Raise and safely support the vehicle.

3. Install transmission jack into position and raise transmission slightly.

4. Remove rear mount attaching bolts and crossmember attaching bolts. Remove crossmember from the vehicle and transfer mounting bracket, support insulator, and plate assembly to new mount.

5. Installation is the reverse of the removal procedure. Torque crossmember retaining bolts to 29–40 ft. lbs. (40–55 Nm). Torque the insulator to crossmember nuts to 14–18 ft. lbs. (20–25 Nm).

Cylinder Head

Removal and Installation
2.0L, 2.4L AND 2.6L ENGINES

1. Rotate the engine so No. 1 cylinder is at TDC. If equipped with fuel injection, relieve the fuel pressure.

2. Disconnect negative battery cable. Drain the cooling system.

3. Remove the upper radiator hose and disconnect the heater hoses. Remove the dipstick bracket bolt.

4. Remove the air cleaner assembly or air intake hose.

5. Disconnect all linkages and cables from the throttle body. Disconnect and plug the fuel lines to the carburetor or fuel rail. Remove the valve cover.

6. On the 2.0L and 2.4L engines, perform the following:

   a. Without disconnecting the lines, unbolt the power steering pump from its brackets and position it to the side, if equipped.

   b. Remove the timing belt upper cover.

   c. Align the timing mark, if not already aligned. Secure the timing belt to the sprocket with wire tie.

   d. Remove the camshaft bolt.

   e. Remove the sprocket from the camshaft and allow it to rest on the lower cover. If this is not possible, tie it to a fabricated device so the belt remains taut and the timing is not lost.

7. On the 2.6L engine, perform the following:

   a. Matchmark the distributor gear to its drive gear and remove the distributor.

   b. Remove the camshaft bolt and remove the distributor drive gear.

   c. Remove the camshaft gear (with the chain installed) from the camshaft and allow it to rest on the holder just below it. This will hold the valve timing. Do not crank the engine until the distributor has been reinstalled or the timing will be lost and timing components could be damaged.

8. Disconnect and label all vacuum lines, hoses and wiring connectors from the manifolds, carburetor or throttle body and cylinder head.

9. Raise the vehicle and support safely.

10. Remove the exhaust pipe from the exhaust manifold. Lower the vehicle.

11. On the 2.6L engine, remove the small head diameter end bolts from the head first.

12. Remove head bolts, starting from the outside and working inward. Remove the cylinder head from the engine.

Cylinder head bolt torque sequence—2.0L and 2.4L engines

Cylinder head bolt torque sequence—2.6L engine

Cylinder head bolt torque sequence—3.0L engine

13. Clean the cylinder head gasket mating surfaces.

To install:

14. On the 2.6L engine, apply a thin bead of sealant to the seam where the chain case and block meet. Install a new head gasket to the block and position the cylinder head assembly with all head bolts and washers. Torque the bolts in sequence to 30 ft. lbs. (41 Nm). Repeat the sequence increasing the torque to 50 ft. lbs. (68 Nm). Repeat the sequence a third time, increasing the torque to a final value of 69 ft. lbs. (94 Nm). On the 2.6L engine, tighten the small end bolts to 13 ft. lbs. (18 Nm) last.

15. Install the camshaft gear or sprocket. On the 2.6L engine, install the distributor drive gear, bolt and washer. Torque the bolt to 40 ft. lbs. (54 Nm). Install the distributor, aligning the matchmarks.

16. Install the timing belt cover, if equipped.

17. Install the power steering pump, if removed.

18. Connect the heater hoses.

19. Install the dipstick bracket bolt. Install the valve cover with a new gasket.

20. Connect and plug the fuel lines to the carburetor or fuel rail. Connect all linkages and cables to the throttle body.

21. Install the air cleaner assembly or air intake hose.

22. Connect the upper radiator hose.

23. Fill the radiator with coolant.

24. Connect the negative battery cable and connect the jumper wire from the fuel pump activation terminal to the positive battery post to inspect the system for leaks, if equipped.

25. Set all adjustments to specifications.

26. Install the seat underframe, if removed.

3.0L ENGINE

1. Relieve the fuel pressure. Disconnect the negative battery cable. Drain the cooling system. Disconnect the upper radiator hose.

2. Remove the drive belts, air conditioning compressor and power steering pump from the mounts and position them to the side.

3. Using a ½ in. drive breaker bar, insert it into the square hole of the serpentine drive belt tensioner, rotate it counterclockwise (to reduce the belt tension) and remove the belt.

4. Remove the alternator.

5. Remove the crankshaft pulley and the torsional damper.

6. To remove the timing belt, perform the following procedures:

a. Remove the covers. Rotate the crankshaft to position No. 1 cylinder on the TDC of its compression stroke; the crankshaft sprocket timing mark should align with the oil pan timing indicator and the camshaft sprockets timing marks (triangles) should align with the rear timing belt covers timing mark.

b. Mark the timing belt in the direction of rotation for reinstallation purposes.

c. Loosen the timing belt tensioner and remove the timing belt.

NOTE: When removing the timing belt from the camshaft sprocket, make sure the belt does not slip off of the other camshaft sprocket. Support the belt so it can not slip off of the crankshaft sprocket and opposite side camshaft sprocket.

7. Remove the air intake hose.

8. Label and disconnect the spark plug wires and vacuum hoses.

9. Remove the valve cover.

10. If removing the left cylinder head, matchmark the distributor rotor to the distributor housing and the housing to distributor extension locations. Remove the distributor and the distributor extension. Also, remove the EGR pipe.

11. Remove the air intake plenum and intake manifold assembly.

12. Remove the exhaust manifold.

13. Remove the cylinder head bolts starting from the outside and working inward.

14. Remove the cylinder head from the engine.

15. Clean the gasket mounting surfaces.

To install:

16. Install the new cylinder head gaskets over the dowels on the engine block.

17. Install the cylinder heads on the engine and torque the cyl-

inder head bolts in sequence using 3 even steps, to 70 ft. lbs. (95 Nm).

18. Install the intake and exhaust manifolds.
19. Install the EGR pipe with a new gasket, if removed.
20. Install the distributor and extension, if removed.
21. Install the timing belt and all related items. When installing the timing belt over the camshaft sprocket, use care not to allow the belt to slip off the opposite camshaft sprocket.
22. Make sure the timing belt is installed on the camshaft sprocket in the same position as when removed.
23. Install the alternator and power steering pump.
24. Install the air conditioning compressor and belts.
25. Connect the upper radiator hose.
26. Fill the radiator with coolant.
27. Connect the negative battery cable and connect the jumper wire from the fuel pump activation terminal to the positive battery post to inspect the system for leaks, if equipped.
28. Set all adjustments to specifications.

Valve Lifters

Removal and Installation

2.0L, 2.4L AND 2.6L ENGINES

1. Disconnect negative battery cable.
2. Remove the valve cover.
3. Have a helper hold the rear of the camshaft down during removal. Then install the rear cap loosely to hold the camshaft in position.
4. Loosen the camshaft cap bolts but do not remove them from the caps. Remove the caps, arms, shafts and bolts all as an assembly. Install tool MD998443-01 or equivalent, on the end of all rocker arms to assure the hydraulic lifters will not fall out of the rocker arms on removal of the assembly.

5. Disassemble the unit keeping all parts in the order of removal and repair as required.

NOTE: On the 2.0L and 2.4L engines, the rocker arms have identification marks on them. Arms with 1–3 on them should only be used on cylinders 1 or 3. Arms with 2–4 on them should only be used on cylinders 2 and 4. The arms on the 2.6L engine are not cylinder specific.

6. The installation is the reverse of the removal procedure. Make sure the arrows on the caps are all pointing to the front of the engine. Torque the cap bolts first to 85 inch lbs. (10 Nm), then to 175 inch lbs. (18 Nm) in the following order: No. 3 cap, No. 2 cap, No. 4 cap, Front cap and Rear cap.

3.0L ENGINE

1. Disconnect the negative battery cable. Remove the air cleaner assembly.
2. Remove the valve cover.
3. Using the auto lash adjuster retainer tools MD998443 or equivalent, install them on the rocker arms to keep the lash adjusters from falling out.
4. On the right side cylinder head, remove the distributor extension.
5. Have a helper hold the rear end of the camshaft down. If the rear of the camshaft cannot be held down, the belt will dislodge and the valve timing will be lost. Loosen the camshaft cap bolts but do not remove them from the caps. Remove the caps, arms, shafts and bolts all as an assembly.
6. Disassemble the unit keeping all parts in order and repair as required.
7. The installation is the reverse of the removal procedure. Apply a drop of sealant to the rear edge of the rear cap. Torque the cap bolts first to 85 inch lbs. (19 Nm), then to 180 inch lbs.

8. Spring
9. Cap No. 3
10. Intake rocker arm
11. Spring
12. Exhaust rocker arm
13. Cap No. 2
14. Exhaust rocker arm
15. Intake rocker arm
16. Spring
17. Wave washer
18. Right side shaft
19. Left side shaft
20. Front cap
21. Nut
22. Adjusting screw

1. Rear cap
2. Intake rocker arm
3. Spring
4. Exhaust rocker arm
5. Cap No. 4
6. Exhaust rocker arm
7. Intake rocker arm

Rocker arms/shafts assembly—2.0L and 2.4L engines. Note that 2.4L engine rocker arms are not equipped with jet valve extensions

Rocker arms/shafts assembly—2.6L engine

1. Rear cap
2. Exhaust rocker arm
3. Intake rocker arm
4. Spring
5. Cap No. 4
6. Exhaust rocker arm
7. Intake rocker arm
8. Spring
9. Cap No. 3
10. Exhaust rocker arm
11. Intake rocker arm
12. Spring
13. Cap No. 2
14. Exhaust rocker arm
15. Intake rocker arm
16. Wave washer
17. Right side shaft
18. Left side shaft
19. Front bearing cap
20. Nut
21. Adjusting screw

(19 Nm) in the following order: No. 3 cap, No. 2 cap, No. 1 cap and No. 4 cap.

Jet Valve Lash

Adjustment

2.0L AND 2.6L ENGINES

1. Run the engine until at normal operating temperature. Disconnect the negative battery cable and remove the valve cover.
2. In sequence, check that the head bolts are torqued to 75 ft. lbs. (103 Nm).
3. Position the piston at TDC on the compression stroke.
4. Loosen the jet valve adjuster locknut.
5. Adjust the valve clearance by turning the adjusting screw a little at a time while measuring the clearance with a feeler gauge.
6. The jet valve clearance specification on a hot engine is 0.010 in. (0.25mm).
7. Tighten the locknut securely while holding the adjustment screw stationary. Recheck the clearance after the locknut has been tightened.
8. Repeat the procedure for the remaining jet valves.
9. Install the valve cover with a new gasket.

Rocker Arms and Shafts

Removal and Installation

2.0L, 2.4L AND 2.6L ENGINES

1. Disconnect the negative battery cable.
2. Remove the valve cover.
3. Have a helper hold the rear of the camshaft down. Then install the rear cap loosely to hold the camshaft in position. If the rear of the camshaft cannot be held down, the belt will dislodge and the valve timing will be lost.
4. Loosen the camshaft cap bolts but do not remove them

from the caps. Remove the caps, arms, shafts and bolts all as an assembly. Install tool MD998443-01 or equivalent, on the end of all rocker arms to assure the hydraulic lifters will not fall out of the rocker arms on removal of the assembly.
5. Disassemble the unit keeping all parts in the order of removal and repair as required.

NOTE: On the 2.0L and 2.4L engines, the rocker arms have identification marks on them. Arms with 1–3 on them should only be used on cylinders 1 or 3. Arms with 2–4 on them should only be used on cylinders 2 and 4. The arms on the 2.6L engine are not cylinder specific.

6. The installation is the reverse of the removal procedure. Make sure the arrows on the caps are all pointing to the front of the engine. Torque the cap bolts first to 85 inch lbs. (10 Nm),

Service Tips

MATERIAL CHANGE AFFECTS INSTALLATION

In 1990, the composition of the water outlet fitting gasket has been changed from a joint-sheet composition to a rubber-coated metal design. Due to the new composition, the gasket now has a top and a bottom side. When installing the new gasket, install the side labeled "UP" facing the water outlet fitting or in the top side position. If using the old style gasket, either side may be installed on top.

Rocker arms/shafts assembly—3.0L engine

then to 175 inch lbs. (18 Nm) in the following order: No. 3 cap, No. 2 cap, No. 4 cap, Front cap and Rear cap.

3.0L ENGINE

1. Disconnect the negative battery cable. Remove the air cleaner assembly.
2. Remove the valve cover.
3. Using the auto lash adjuster retainer tools MD998443 or equivalent, install them on the rocker arms to keep the lash adjusters from falling out.
4. On the right side cylinder head, remove the distributor extension.
5. Have a helper hold the rear end of the camshaft down. If the rear of the camshaft cannot be held down, the belt will dislodge and the valve timing will be lost. Loosen the camshaft cap bolts but do not remove them from the caps. Remove the caps, arms, shafts and bolts all as an assembly.
6. Disassemble the unit keeping all parts in order and repair as required.
7. The installation is the reverse of the removal procedure. Apply a drop of sealant to the rear edge of the rear cap. Torque the cap bolts first to 85 inch lbs. (19 Nm), then to 180 inch lbs. (19 Nm) in the following order: No. 3 cap, No. 2 cap, No. 1 cap and No. 4 cap.

Intake Manifold

Removal and Installation

2.0L AND 2.6L ENGINES

1. Disconnect the negative battery cable.
2. Remove the air cleaner assembly. Remove the dipstick bracket bolt from the thermostat housing.
3. Drain the cooling system. Disconnect the heater hoses from the manifold.

4. Disconnect the upper radiator hose from the thermostat housing.
5. Remove and plug the fuel lines to the carburetor.
6. Remove the mounting bolts from the air conditioner compressor and position aside. It is not necessary to remove the lines from the air conditioner compressor. Remove the air conditioning compressor mounting bracket.
7. Disconnect and label the vacuum lines, hoses and wiring connectors from the manifold and carburetor.
8. Remove the starter motor cable clamp. Remove the thermo valve.
9. Disconnect all linkages from the carburetor.
10. Remove the manifold nuts and bolts, it may be necesary to remove the carburetor. Remove the intake manifold from the engine.

To install:

11. Install the intake manifold with new gasket in place. Install manifold bolts and nuts tightening to 12 ft. lbs. (17 Nm).
12. Install carburetor with new base gasket, if removed. Connect all linkages to the carburetor.
13. Install the starter motor cable clamp. Install the thermo valve.
14. Connect the vacuum lines, hoses and wiring connectors to the manifold and carburetor.
15. Install the air conditioner mounting bracket, compressor and mounting bolts.
16. Install the fuel lines to the carburetor.
17. Install the air cleaner assembly and the dipstick bracket bolt to the thermostat housing.
18. Reconnect the negative battery cable. Fill the cooling system. Start the engine and check for leaks.
19. Allow the engine to reach operating temperature and recheck cooling system for proper fluid level. Fill as required.

1. Air intake hose
2. Breater hose
3. Air intake pipe
4. Air hose
5. Accelerator and kickdown cables
6. Throttle body
7. Gasket
8. PCV hose
9. Brake booster vacuum hose
10. Vacuum hose cluster
11. Ignition coil wire
12. Ignition coil
13. Air intake plenum assembly
14. Gasket

Air intake plenum assembly—2.4L engine

1. High pressure fuel hose
2. Injector harness connector
3. Fuel rail
4. Insulator
5. Heater hose
6. Wiring harness connector
7. Coolant outlet fitting
8. Gasket
9. Thermostat
10. Distributor
11. Plenum bracket
12. Intake manifold bracket
13. Intake manifold
14. Gasket
15. Thermo switch (automatic transmission only)
16. Coolant temperature sensor
17. Coolant temperature sending unit
18. Coolant temperature switch (automatic transmission only)

Intake manifold assembly—2.4L engine

2.4L ENGINE

1. Relieve the fuel pressure.
2. Disconnect the negative battery cable.
3. Drain the engine coolant. Disconnect the upper radiator hose from the thermostat housing.
4. Remove the air intake hoses, breather hose and the air intake pipe.
5. Disconnect all wires, hoses and linkages to the throttle body.
6. Remove the ignition coil.
7. Disconnect the brake booster hose and vacuum hose cluster from the air intake plenum.
8. Unbolt the air intake plenum from the intake manifold and remove the plenum from the engine.
9. Cover the fuel line with a clean shop rag and disconnect the fuel lines from the fuel rail. Keep the line covered or plugged.
10. Remove the fuel rail assembly with injectors intact.
11. Disconnect the heater hose from the manifold.
12. Disconnect the wires to the engine coolant switches.
13. Matchmark the rotor to the housing and the housing to the cylinder head and remove the distributor.
14. Unbolt the intake manifold from the cylinder head and remove from the engine.
15. Clean and dry the mating surfaces of the manifold and cylinder head.

To install:

16. Using a new gasket, install the intake manifold to the head. Starting from the middle and working outward, torque the retaining nuts to 12 ft. lbs. (16 Nm).
17. Connect the wires to the engine coolant switches. Install the distributor with matchmarks aligned.
18. Install the fuel rail assembly to the manifold and connect the fuel line using a new O-ring.
19. Connect the heater hose to the manifold.

20. Install the air intake plenum with a new gasket. Torque the retaining bolts to 12 ft. lbs. (16 Nm).
21. Connect the vacuum hoses cluster, brake booster hose and all wires, hoses and linkages to the throttle body.
22. Install the ignition coil.
23. Install the air intake pipe and hoses.
24. Connect the upper radiator hose.
25. Fill the radiator with coolant.
26. Connect the negative battery cable and connect the jumper wire from the fuel pump activation terminal to the positive battery post to inspect the system for leaks.
27. Set all adjustments to specifications.

3.0L ENGINE

1. Relieve the fuel pressure.
2. Disconnect the negative battery cable.
3. Drain the engine coolant. Disconnect the upper radiator hose from the thermostat housing.
4. Remove the air intake hose from the throttle body.
5. Disconnect all wires, hoses and linkages to the throttle body.
6. Disconnect the EGR temperature sensor wire.
7. Remove the ignition coil.
8. Remove the engine oil filler neck bracket.
9. Unbolt the EGR tube from the air intake plenum.
10. Disconnect the PCV hose and vacuum hose cluster from the plenum.
11. Remove the plenum to engine brackets.
12. Unbolt the air intake plenum assembly from the intake manifold and remove.
13. Cover the fuel lines with a clean shop rag and disconnect the fuel lines from the fuel rail. Keep the lines covered.
14. Remove the fuel rail with injectors in place.
15. Disconnect the bypass hose and the upper radiator hose

1. Air intake hose
2. Throttle position sensor connector
3. Stepper motor connector
4. Accelerator cable adjusting bolt
5. Throttle control cable (automatic transmission only)
6. Accelerator cable
7. Coolant hoses
8. EGR temperature connector
9. Vacuum hose
10. Brake booster vacuum hose
11. Ignition coil wire
12. Ignition coil
13. Oil filler neck bracket
14. PCV hose
15. Vacuum hose cluster
16. EGR pipe attaching bolt
17. Gasket
18. Bracket bolt
19. Attaching bolt and nut
20. Air intake plenum and throttle body assembly
21. Gasket

Air intake plenum assembly—3.0L engine

1. High pressure fuel hose
2. Fuel return hose
3. Vacuum hose
4. Engine controller harness connector
5. Fuel rail
6. Vacuum hose and pipe
7. Upper radiator hose
8. Coolant bypass hose
9. Intake manifold
10. Gasket
11. Coolant outlet fitting
12. Gasket
13. Thermostat
14. Coolant temperature switch (automatic transmission only)
15. Coolant temperature sensor
16. Thermo switch
17. Coolant temperature sending unit
18. Thermo valve

Intake manifold assembly—3.0L engine

from the thermostat housing. Disconnect the wires to the coolant temperature switches.

16. Remove the intake manifold retaining nuts and remove the manifold from the cylinder heads.

17. Remove the gaskets and thoroughly clean and dry the mating surfaces of the manifold and heads.

To install:

18. Position the manifold over the studs and install the retaining nuts. Torque to 12 ft. lbs. (16 Nm), starting from the center and working outward.

19. Connect the hoses and connect the wires to the coolant switches.

20. Install the fuel rail assembly and connect the fuel hoses.

21. Using a new gasket, install the air intake plenum to the intake manifold. Torque the nuts and bolts to 12 ft. lbs. (16 Nm). Install the plenum to engine brackets.

22. Connect the PCV hose and vacuum hose cluster to the plenum.

23. Connect the EGR tube.

24. Install the engine oil filler neck bracket.

25. Install the ignition coil assembly.

26. Connect the EGR temperature sensor wire.

27. Connect all wires, hoses and linkages to the throttle body.

28. Install the air intake hose to the throttle body.

29. Connect the upper radiator hose to the thermostat housing.

30. Fill the radiator with coolant.

31. Connect the negative battery cable and connect the jumper wire from the fuel pump activation terminal to the positive battery post to inspect the system for leaks.

32. Set all adjustments to specifications.

Exhaust Manifold

Removal and Installation

2.0L, 2.4L AND 2.6L ENGINES

1. Disconnect the negative battery cable.
2. Remove the heat cowl from the exhaust manifold.
3. Remove the aspirator valve assembly, if equipped.

4. Raise the vehicle and support safely. Disconnect the exhaust pipe from the manifold. Lower the vehicle

5. Disconnect the oxygen sensor connector or ground cable, if equipped.

6. Remove the manifold mounting nuts and remove the manifold and gasket from the engine.

7. The installation is the reverse of the removal procedure. Torque the manifold mounting nuts to 13 ft. lbs. (18 Nm) starting from the middle and working outward.

8. Start the engine and check for exhaust leaks.

3.0L ENGINE

1. Disconnect the negative battery cable. Raise and safely support the vehicle.

2. Disconnect the exhaust pipe from the exhaust manifolds.

3. Remove the heat shield.

4. If removing the left manifold, remove EGR tube.

5. If removing the right manifold, remove alternator bracket.

6. Remove the manifold attaching nuts and remove manifold.

7. The installation is the reverse of the removal procedure. When installing, the numbers 1-3-5 on the gaskets are used with the right side cylinders and 2-4-6 are on the gasket for the left side cylinders. Torque the manifold nuts to 14 ft. lbs. (19 Nm).

8. Start the engine and check for exhaust leaks.

Timing Chain Front Cover

Removal and Installation

2.6L ENGINE

1. Disconnect the negative battery cable.

2. Drain the cooling system.

3. Remove the shroud, fan, belts and radiator as required.

4. Remove the power steering pump, alternator, air conditioning compressor and accompanying brackets, as required.

5. Remove the valve cover. Matchmark the distributor gear to its drive gear and remove the distributor.

6. Remove the 2 small front bolts from the cylinder head which screw into and seal the top of the timing cover.

7. Remove the crankshaft bolt and washer. Pull off the crankshaft pulley.

8. Raise the vehicle and support safely. Remove the engine undercover. Remove the bolts that attach the front of the oil pan to the chain case cover.

NOTE: As soon as the timing cover gasket seal is broken, antifreeze will run out from the water jacket extension in the cover. Place a large drain pan under the work area.

9. Remove the remaining timing cover retaining bolts. Position a drain pan under the timing cover and separate the cover from the block. Allow the coolant to drain from the block and remove the cover. If the oil pan gasket was damaged during this operation, remove the oil pan.

To install:

10. Clean and dry all sealing surfaces.

11. Replace the adjuster window gasket.

12. Pry the crankshaft oil seal out of the cover without scratching the seal bore. Install a new seal using a seal driver or installer.

13. Apply a thin coat of silicone sealer to the top of the timing chain cover to seal the head gasket extension. Install the cover to the block using new gaskets.

14. Install all cover bolts with the appropriate brackets in place. Torque the bolts to 10 ft. lbs. (13 Nm).

15. Install the crankshaft pulley. Thoroughly clean and dry the crankshaft pulley bolt and apply a very thin bead of Loctite® to the threads. Torque the bolt to 87 ft. lbs. (118 Nm).

16. Install the oil pan with a new gasket, if removed.

17. Clean and dry the 2 end bolts that attach the chain cover to the head. Install them and torque to 13 ft. lbs. (18 Nm).

18. Install the distributor aligning the matchmarks.

19. Install the valve cover with a new gasket.

20. Install the power steering pump, alternator, air conditioning compressor and any remaining brackets. Install the fan and adjust the belt tensions.

21. Install the radiator and shroud, if removed.

22. Refill the cooling system. Due to possible coolant contamination, replace the oil filter and change the engine oil.

23. Connect the negative battery cable, road test the vehicle and check for leaks.

Front Cover Oil Seal

Replacement

2.6L ENGINE

1. Disconnect the negative battery cable.

2. Remove the accessory drive belts.

3. Remove the crankshaft pulley.

4. Pry the crankshaft oil seal out of the cover without scratching the seal bore.

5. Install a new seal using a seal driver or installer.

6. Install the crankshaft pulley.

7. Clean and dry the crankshaft pulley bolt and apply a thin bead of Loctite® to the threads. Torque the bolt to 87 ft. lbs. (118 Nm).

8. Install the accessory drive belt and adjust the tension as required.

9. Reconnect the negative battery cable.

Timing Chain and Sprockets

Removal and Installation

2.6L ENGINE

1. If possible, position the engine so No. 1 piston is at TDC on the compression stroke. Disconnect the negative battery cable. Drain the coolant.

2. Remove the timing chain case cover.

3. Remove the 3 silent shaft chain guides. Label each bolt as it is removed. The bolts are of different lengths and styles and must be installed in the correct locations.

4. Remove the flange bolts from the right silent shaft and oil pump gears and carefully remove the chain with all 3 gears. Watch for the aligning keys on the oil pump shaft and right silent shaft. If the chain is removed individually, remove the gears afterward.

Camshaft position for chain installation — 2.6L engine

Timing chain, silent shaft chain and related parts— 2.6L engine

Timing chain installation—2.6L engine

NOTE: The 2 gears are identical, but the oil pump drive sprocket is installed with the concave side toward the engine while the right silent shaft sprocket has the concave side out.

Silent shaft chain installation—2.6L engine

5. The timing chain tensioner maintains constant spring pressure on the chain. To prevent it from popping out of the oil pump it must be fastened in place. Run a piece of wire around the plunger and the left side of the oil pump. Remove the remaining chain guides.

6. Remove the camshaft gear bolt and pry the distributor drive gear from the cam gear. Remove the cam gear from the camshaft and allow it to sit on the gear holder below it. Rotate the camshaft so the spring pin is at the 12 o'clock position.

7. Unbolt the holder and remove the chain with both gears. Remove the tensioner and spring from the oil pump.

8. Inspect all gears, guides and the chains themselves for wear and replace as required.

To install:

9. Assemble the new timing chain with the gears. Both the crankshaft sprocket and the camshaft sprocket have a small dot on their faces. Assemble the chain and sprockets so each dot aligns with the plated links on the chain. Both sets of marks and links must align.

10. Turn the crankshaft as required so the positions of the gears are correct.

11. Install the new tensioner and spring in the bore of the oil pump and hold it down with a piece of wire. Make sure the tensioner is equipped with black washer on the shaft. If the washer is missing, the chain will slap.

12. Install the crankshaft gear to the crankshaft. Install the cam gear holder while holding the gear in place. Allow the cam gear to rest on the holder.

13. Lift the cam gear onto the camshaft, install the distributor drive gear and install the bolt. Make certain sprocket engages the guide pin correctly. Tighten the bolt to 40 ft. lbs. (55 Nm).

14. Remove the wire holding the tensioner plunger and allow it to tension the chain. Install the right side guide.

15. Assemble the silent shaft gear, the oil pump gear and the silent shaft chain. Again, each sprocket is marked with a dot which must be aligned with the plated links on the chain. The sprocket for the silent shaft mounts with the concave side facing out (away from the engine block) and the sprocket for the oil pump mounts with the concave side facing the engine block.

16. Install the silent chain with gears onto the shafts. Turn the oil pump shaft and right silent shaft as required to keep the marks aligned.

17. Install the chain guides. Make sure the lock washer is installed between the tensioner guide pivot bolt and the timing chain guide under it. Torque all 10mm flanged bolts to 8 ft. lbs. (11 Nm). Adjust the upper guide so when the chain is pulled downward at the center, the clearance between the chain and the guide is 0.008–0.031 in. (0.20–0.80mm). Torque the tensioner guide locking bolt to 14 ft. lbs. (19 Nm).

18. Install the gear retaining bolts to the oil pump and right silent shaft. Torque the bolts to 25 ft. lbs. (34 Nm).

19. Install the timing chain case cover and all related parts.

20. Refill the cooling system and change the engine oil and filter.

21. Connect the negative battery cable, road test the vehicle and check for leaks.

Timing Belt Front Cover

Removal and Installation

2.0L AND 2.4L ENGINES

1. Disconnect the negative battery cable. Remove the spark plug wires from the tree on the upper cover.

2. Drain the cooling system. Remove the shroud, fan and accessory drive belts. Remove the radiator as required.

3. Remove the power steering pump, alternator, air conditioning compressor, tension pulley and accompanying brackets, as required.

4. Remove the upper front timing belt cover.

5. Remove the water pump pulley and the crankshaft pulley(s).

6. Remove the lower timing belt cover to engine screws and remove the cover.

7. The installation is the reverse of the removal procedure. Make sure the packing is positioned in the inner grooves of the covers properly when installing.

3.0L ENGINE

1. Disconnect the negative battery cable.

2. Drain the cooling system. Remove the drive belts.

3. Remove the upper radiator shroud.

4. Remove the fan and fan pulley.

5. Without disconnecting the lines, remove the power steering pump from its bracket and position it to the side. Remove the pump brackets.

6. Remove the belt tensioner pulley bracket.

7. Without releasing the refrigerant remove the air conditioning compressor from its bracket and position it to the side. Remove the bracket.

8. Remove the cooling fan bracket.

9. On some models it may be necessary to remove the pulley from the crankshaft to access the lower cover bolts.

10. Remove the timing belt cover bolts and the upper and lower covers from the engine.

To install:

11. Install the upper and lower covers to the engine and secure with the retaining screws. Make sure the packing is positioned in the inner grooves of the covers properly when installing.

12. Install the crankshaft pulley and bolts, if removed. Torque bolt to 110 ft. lbs. (150 Nm).

13. Install the air conditioning bracket and compressor to the engine. Install the belt tensioner.

14. Install the power steering pump into position. Install the fan pulley and fan.

15. Install the fan shroud to the radiator. Fill the cooling system, reconnect the negative battery cable and check for fluid leaks.

Timing Belt and Tensioner

Adjustment

2.0L AND 2.4L ENGINES

1. Disconnect the negative battery cable.

2. Remove the timing belt cover.

3. Adjust the silent shaft (inner) belt first. Loosen the pulley center bolt so the pulley may be moved.

4. Move the pulley up by hand so the center span of the long side of the belt deflects ¼ inch.

5. Hold the pulley tight so the pulley itself does not rotate when the bolt is tightened. Tighten the bolt to 15 ft. lbs. (20 Nm). If the pulley has moved, the belt will be too tight.

6. Check the timing (outer) belt tension.

7. To adjust the timing (outer) belt, first loosen the tensioner pulley bolts.

8. Allow the spring to take up any slack. Check that the the deflection of the longest span (between the camshaft and oil pump sprockets) is ½ inch. Do not overtighten the belt or it will howl.

9. First tighten the lower pulley bolts to 35 ft. lbs. (47 Nm) and then the upper bolt to the same value.

10. Install the covers and all related parts.

3.0L ENGINE

1. Loosen the bolt that holds the timing belt tensioner in place.

2. Allow the spring to pull the tensioner in automatically.

3. Tighten the tensioner locking bolt.

Silent shaft belt installation—2.0L and 2.4L engines

Removal and Installation

2.0L AND 2.4L ENGINES

1. If possible, crank the engine around so the No. 1 piston is at TDC.
2. Disconnect the negative battery cable. Remove the accessory drive belt(s).
3. Remove the timing belt covers. If the belt(s) are to be re-used, mark the direction of rotation on the belt.
4. Remove the timing (outer) belt tensioner and remove the belt. Unbolt the tensioner from the block and remove.
5. Remove the outer crankshaft sprocket and flange.
6. Remove the silent shaft (inner) belt tensioner and remove the inner belt. Unbolt the tensioner from the block and remove.

To install:

7. Align the timing mark of the silent shaft belt sprockets on the crankshaft and silent shaft with the marks on the front case. Wrap the silent shaft belt around the sprockets so there is not slack in the upper span of the belt and the timing marks are still in line.
8. Install the tensioner initially so the actual center of the pulley is above and to the left of the installation bolt.
9. Move the pulley up by hand so the center span of the long side of the belt deflects about ¼ inch.
10. Hold the pulley tightly so it does not rotate when the bolt is tightened. Tighten the bolt to 15 ft. lbs. (20 Nm). If the pulley has moved, the belt will be too tight.
11. Install the timing belt tensioner fully toward the water pump and temporarily tighten the bolts. Place the upper end of the spring against the water pump body. Align the timing marks of the cam, crankshaft and oil pump sprockets with the corresponding marks on the front case or head.

NOTE: If the following step is not followed exactly, there is a chance that the silent shaft alignment will be 180 degrees off. This will cause a noticeable vibration in the engine and the entire procedure will have to be repeated.

12. Before installing the timing belt, ensure that the left side silent shaft is in the correct position. It is possible to align the timing marks on the camshaft sprocket, crankshaft sprocket and the oil pump sprocket with the left balance shaft out of alignment. With the timing mark on the oil pump pulley aligned with the mark on the front case, check the alignment of the left balance shaft to assure correct shaft timing. To do so, remove the plug located on the left side of the block in the area of the starter. Insert a tool having a shaft diameter of 0.3 in. (8mm) into the hole. With the timing marks still aligned, the tool must be able to go in at least 2⅓ in. If it can only go in about 1 in. turn

the oil pump sprocket 1 complete revolution. Recheck the position of the balance shaft with the timing marks realigned. Leave the tool in place to hold the silent shaft while continuing.

13. Install the belt to the crankshaft sprocket, oil pump sprocket and the camshaft sprocket, in that order. While doing so, make sure there is no slack between the sprockets except where the tensioner will take it up when released.
14. Recheck the timing marks' alignment. If all are aligned, loosen the tensioner mounting bolt and allow the tensioner to apply tension to the belt.
15. Remove the tool that is holding the silent shaft in place and turn the crankshaft clockwise a distance equal to 2 teeth of the camshaft sprocket. This will allow the tensioner to automatically tension the belt the proper amount.

NOTE: Do not manually apply pressure to the tensioner. This will overtighten the belt and will cause a howling noise.

16. First tighten the lower mounting bolt and then tighten the upper spacer bolt.
17. To verify that belt tension is correct, check that the deflection of the longest span (between the camshaft and oil pump sprockets) is ½ inch.
18. Install the timing belt covers and all related parts.
19. Connect the negative battery cable and road test the vehicle.

3.0L ENGINE

1. If possible, position engine with No. 1 cylinder at TDC. Disconnect negative battery cable. Remove the timing covers from engine.
2. If the same timing belt will be reused, mark the direction of timing belt's rotation, for installation in the same direction.

Checking the left side silent shaft for positioning

Timing belt installation—2.0L and 2.4L engines

Timing belt installation—3.0L engine

Make sure engine is positioned so No. 1 cylinder is at the TDC of it's compression stroke and the sprockets timing marks are aligned with the engine's timing mark indicators.

3. Loosen the timing belt tensioner bolt and remove the belt. If not removing the tensioner, position it as far away from the center of the engine as possible and tighten the bolt.

4. If tensioner is being removed, mark outside of the spring to ensure that it is not installed backwards. Unbolt the tensioner and remove it along with the spring.

To install:

5. Install the tensioner, if removed, and hook the upper end of the spring to the water pump pin. Install the lower end of the spring to the tensioner in exactly the same position as originally installed. If not already done, position both camshafts so the timing marks line up with those on the alternator bracket (rear bank) and inner timing cover (front bank). Rotate the crankshaft so the timing mark aligns with the mark on the oil pump.

6. Install the timing belt on the crankshaft sprocket and while keeping the belt tight on the tension side (right side), install the belt on the front camshaft sprocket.

7. Install the belt on the water pump pulley, then the rear camshaft sprocket and the tensioner.

8. Rotate the front camshaft counterclockwise to tension the belt between the front camshaft and the crankshaft. If the timing marks came out of line, repeat the procedure.

9. Install the crankshaft sprocket flange.

10. Loosen the tensioner bolt and allow the spring to tension the belt.

11. Slowly turn the crankshaft 2 full turns in the clockwise direction until the timing marks align. Now that the belt is properly tensioned, torque the tensioner lock bolt to 21 ft. lbs. (29 Nm).

12. Install the timing belt covers and all related parts.

13. Connect the negative battery cable and road test the vehicle.

Timing Sprockets

Removal and Installation

1. Disconnect the negative battery cable.

2. Remove the timing belt(s).

3. To remove the camshaft sprocket, hold the sprocket with a holding tool and remove the retaining bolt and washer.

4. To remove the crankshaft sprocket, remove the bolt, if equipped, and remove the sprocket from the crankshaft.

5. To remove a silent shafts sprocket, remove the retaining bolt and pry the sprocket from its mounting shaft.

6. The installation is the reverse of the removal procedure. Torque the sprocket retaining bolt to specifications.

Camshaft

Removal and Installation

2.0L AND 2.4L ENGINES

1. Disconnect the negative battery cable. Remove the valve cover and the upper timing belt cover.

2. Matchmark the rotor to the distributor housing and remove the distributor.

3. Secure the belt to the sprocket and hold the sprocket up with a fabricated device to keep the belt taut. If timing is lost, it will have to be reset. Remove the camshaft sprocket from the camshaft.

4. Remove the camshaft cap bolts evenly and gradually. Install the auto lash adjuster retainers to the rocker arms.

5. Remove the caps, shafts, rocker arms and bolts together as an assembly.

6. Remove the camshaft with the front seal from the engine.

To install:

7. Install a new roll pin to the camshaft. Lubricate the cam-

shaft and install with the front seal in place. Install the camshaft so the hole in the sprocket will line up with the roll pin.

8. Install the caps, shafts and arms assembly. Tighten the camshaft bearing cap bolts in the following order to 85 inch lbs. (10 Nm): No. 3, No. 2, No. 4, front cap, rear cap. Repeat the sequence increasing the torque to 175 inch lbs. (19 Nm).

9. Install the sprocket to the camshaft, engaging the roll pin. Torque the bolt to 70 ft. lbs. (95 Nm). Install the distributor.

10. Install the valve cover and all related parts.

2.6L ENGINE

1. Disconnect the negative battery cable.
2. Remove the valve cover.
3. Remove the camshaft gear retaining bolt and matchmark the distributor gear to its drive gear.
4. Remove the distributor. Pry the distributor drive gear off of the cam gear.
5. Remove the cam gear from the camshaft and allow it to rest on the holder below it.
6. Remove the camshaft cap bolts evenly and gradually. Install the auto lash adjuster retaining tools to the rocker arms.
7. Remove the caps, shafts, rocker arms and bolts together as an assembly.
8. Remove the camshaft with rear seal from the engine.

To install:

9. Install a new roll pin to the camshaft. Lubricate the camshaft and install with the rear seal in place. Install the camshaft so the hole in the gear will line up with the roll pin.

10. Install the rocker caps, shafts and arms assembly. Tighten the camshaft bearing cap bolts in the following order to 85 inch lbs. (10 Nm): No. 3, No. 2, No. 4, front cap, rear cap. Repeat the sequence increasing the torque to 175 inch lbs. (19 Nm).

11. Install the gear to the camshaft engaging the roll pin. Install the distributor drive gear and install the bolt and washer. Torque the bolt to 40 ft. lbs. (54 Nm). Install the distributor.

12. Install the valve cover and all related parts.

3.0L ENGINE

1. Disconnect the negative battery cable. Remove the valve cover.
2. Remove the timing belt and remove the sprocket from the camshaft.
3. Install auto lash adjuster retainers MD998443 or equivalent on the rocker arms.
4. If removing the left side camshaft, remove the distributor and the distributor extension.
5. Remove the camshaft bearing caps but do not remove the bolts from the caps. Remove the rocker arms, rocker shafts and bearing caps, as an assembly.
6. Remove the camshaft from the cylinder head.
7. Inspect the bearing journals on the camshaft, cylinder head and bearing caps.

To install:

8. Lubricate the camshaft journals and camshaft with clean engine oil and install the camshaft in the cylinder head.
9. Align the camshaft bearing caps with the arrow mark (depending on cylinder numbers) and in numerical order. The arrow mark on the left rocker shaft bearing caps faces in same direction as the arrow marked on the left cylinder head which is away from the timing belt. The arrow on the right cylinder head and the right rocker bearing caps faces toward the timing belt.
10. Apply sealer at the ends of the bearing caps and install the assembly.
11. Torque the bearing cap bolts, in the following sequence: No. 3, No. 2, No. 1 and No. 4 to 85 inch lbs. (10 Nm).
12. Repeat the sequence increasing the torque to 175 inch lbs. (18 Nm).
13. Install the distributor, if removed.
14. Install the sprocket, timing belt and all related parts.
15. Install the valve cover.

Silent Shafts

Removal and Installation

2.0L AND 2.4L ENGINES

1. Disconnect the negative battery cable. Release fuel pressure if equipped with fuel injection.
2. Raise and safely support the vehicle. Drain the engine oil.
3. Remove the oil filter and the oil pan from the engine.
4. Remove the oil pressure electrical connector and the oil pressure switch.
5. Lower the vehicle. Remove the timing belt cover(s).
6. Remove the timing belts.
7. Remove the timing belt sprockets.
8. Remove the front case from the block.
9. Remove the oil pump components.
10. Remove the shafts from the block.

To install:

11. Coat the silent shafts with clean engine oil and install into the block.
12. Install the drive and driven gears into place so the timing marks are mated with each other. Coat gears with clean engine oil.
13. Attach the special tool to the end of the crankshaft and coat the outer surface with engine oil.
14. Install the front case assembly with a new front case gasket to the block. Install retaining bolts.
15. Install the oil filter bracket together with the oil filter bracket gasket and install retaining bolts with washers. Torque bolts to 15 ft. lbs. (22 Nm).
16. Install the timing belts, covers and related parts.
17. Connect the negative battery cable, add clean oil to correct level, start engine and check for leaks.

2.6L ENGINE

1. If possible, position the engine so No. 1 piston is at TDC on the compression stroke. Disconnect the negative battery cable. Drain the coolant.
2. Remove the timing chain case cover.
3. Remove the 3 silent shaft chain guides. Label each bolt as it is removed. The bolts are of different lengths and styles and must be installed in the correct locations.
4. Remove the flange bolts from the right silent shaft and oil pump gears and carefully remove the chain with all 3 gears. Watch for the aligning keys on the oil pump shaft and right silent shaft. If the chain is removed individually, remove the gears afterward.

NOTE: The 2 gears are identical, but the oil pump drive sprocket is installed with the concave side toward the engine while the right silent shaft sprocket has the concave side out.

5. The timing chain tensioner maintains constant spring pressure on the chain. To prevent it from popping out of the oil pump it must be fastened in place. Run a piece of wire around the plunger and the left side of the oil pump. Remove the remaining chain guides.
6. Remove the camshaft gear bolt and pry the distributor drive gear from the cam gear. Remove the cam gear from the camshaft and allow it to sit on the gear holder below it. Rotate the camshaft so the spring pin is at the 12 o'clock position.
7. Unbolt the holder and remove the chain with both gears. Remove the tensioner and spring from the oil pump.
8. Remove the retaining bolts from the oil pump and remove the oil pump. The right side silent shaft will come out with the pump. To remove the shaft from the pump, remove the retaining bolt on the pump and remove the shaft.

9. Remove the left silent shaft gear and spacer. To remove the thrust plate, remove the thrust plate retaining screws and install two $\frac{1}{32}$ in. screws into the threaded holes. Thread the screws in to aid in pulling the plate off.

10. Remove the silent shaft.

To install:

11. Coat the silent shaft(s) with oil and install left shaft into block. Install the right shaft attached to the oil pump into the block.

12. Install a new O-ring to the thrust plate. Install 2 fabricated guides into the threaded holes for mounting thrust plate. Slide the thrust plate over the guides. Remove the guides 1 at a time while installing retaining bolts tightening bolts to 25 ft. lbs. (34 Nm).

13. Install the oil pump gears to the pump body if removed, and align timing marks. Install the pump body in its original position before removal and add oil in the delivery port to prime pump.

14. Assemble the new timing chain with the gears. Both the crankshaft sprocket and the camshaft sprocket have a small dot on their faces. Assemble the chain and sprockets so each dot aligns with the plated links on the chain. Both sets of marks and links must align.

15. Install the new tensioner and spring in the bore of the oil pump and hold it down with a piece of wire. Make sure the tensioner is equipped with black washer on the shaft. If the washer is missing, the chain will slap.

16. Install the crankshaft gear to the crankshaft. Install the cam gear holder while holding the gear in place. Allow the cam gear to rest on the holder.

17. Lift the cam gear onto the camshaft, install the distributor drive gear and install the bolt. Make certain sprocket engages the guide pin correctly. Tighten the bolt to 40 ft. lbs. (55 Nm).

18. Remove the wire holding the tensioner plunger and allow it to tension the chain. Install the right side guide.

19. Assemble the silent shaft gear, the oil pump gear and the silent shaft chain. Again, each sprocket is marked with a dot which must be aligned with the plated links on the chain. The sprocket for the silent shaft mounts with the concave side facing out (away from the engine block) and the sprocket for the oil pump mounts with the concave side facing the engine block.

20. Install the silent chain with gears onto the shafts. Turn the oil pump shaft and right silent shaft as required to keep the marks aligned.

21. Install the chain guides. Make sure the lock washer is installed between the tensioner guide pivot bolt and the timing chain guide under it. Torque all 10mm flanged bolts to 8 ft. lbs. (11 Nm). Adjust the upper guide so when the chain is pulled downward at the center, the clearance between the chain and the guide is 0.008–0.031 in. (0.20–0.80mm). Torque the tensioner guide locking bolt to 14 ft. lbs. (19 Nm).

22. Install the gear retaining bolts to the oil pump and right silent shaft. Torque the bolts to 25 ft. lbs. (34 Nm).

23. Install the timing chain case cover and all related parts.

24. Refill the cooling system and change the engine oil and filter.

25. Connect the negative battery cable, road test the vehicle and check for leaks.

Piston and Connecting Rod

Positioning

Piston positioning—2.2L, 2.4L and 2.6L engines

Piston positioning—3.0L engine

ENGINE LUBRICATION

Oil Pan

Removal and Installation

1. Disconnect the negative battery cable.
2. Raise the vehicle and support safely.

3. Remove the skid plate(s), engine undercover, air guide plate and cross shaft plate as required.

4. Remove the front exhaust pipe and steering linkage components as required.

5. On some vehicles, unbolt the motor mounts and raise the engine safely using the proper equipment.

1. Drain plug
2. Gasket
3. Oil filter
4. Oil pressure sending unit
5. Oil pan
6. Oil screen
7. Gasket
8. Oil filter bracket
9. Gasket
10. Relief plug
11. Gasket
12. Relief spring
13. Relief plunger
14. Plug cap
15. O-ring
16. Driven gear bolt
17. Front case
18. Gasket
19. Oil seal
20. Oil seal
21. Oil seal
22. Oil pump cover
23. Driven gear
24. Drive gear
25. Left side silent shaft
26. Right side silent shaft
27. Front bearing
28. Right rear bearing
29. Left rear bearing

Engine lubrication components—2.0L and 2.4L engines

6. Drain the engine oil from the pan.

7. Disconnect the fluid level sensor wire, if equipped. Remove the attaching bolts and remove the pan.

8. The installation is the reverse of the removal procedure.

Oil Pump

Removal and Installation

2.0L AND 2.4L ENGINES

1. Disconnect the negative battery cable. Remove the timing belt covers, timing belts and sprockets.

2. Raise the vehicle and support safely. Drain the oil and remove the oil filter. Remove the oil pan and gasket. Remove the oil pump pickup and gasket.

3. Remove the oil pressure relief plunger plug and gasket. Remove the spring and plunger from the oil filter bracket.

4. Remove the 4 bracket mounting bolts and remove the oil filter mount and gasket.

5. Using special tool MD998162, remove the cap and gasket that covers the oil pump driven gear shaft. This is located on the right side of the front case at the front of the engine, just above the protruding drive gear shaft.

6. Using a long socket, remove the retaining bolt from the oil pump driven gear located behind the plug removed earlier.

7. Remove the front case mounting bolts and remove the case from the block.

8. Remove the case gasket from the block.

To install:

9. Prime the pump by pouring fresh oil into the pump intake and turning the driveshaft until oil comes out the pressure port. Repeat a few times until no air bubbles are present. Replace all seals on the case assembly.

10. Install a special seal guide to the crankshaft, MD998285 or equivalent so the smaller diameter faces outward. Coat the outer diameter of the seal with clean engine oil.

11. Install a new front case gasket and install the front case by carefully positioning the crankshaft seal over the seal guide and lining up all bolt holes. Install and tighten the bolts to 17 ft. lbs. (23 Nm).

Engine lubrication components—2.6L engine

12. Remove the plug from the left side of the block. Hold the left side silent shaft by inserting a tool in the plug hole and torque the driven gear bolt to 26 ft. lbs. (35 Nm). Using a new O-ring, install the plug cover.

13. Install the oil filter mounting bracket gasket. Install the mounting bracket and bolts tightening the oil filter mounting bracket bolts to 12 ft. lbs. (16 Nm).

14. Clean or replace the oil pickup screen and install with a new gasket.

15. Install the oil pan using a new gasket.
16. Install the timing sprockets, belts and covers.
17. Fill the engine with the proper amount of engine oil.
18. Connect the negative battery cable and check for proper oil pressure and leaks.

2.6L ENGINE

1. Disconnect the negative battery cable. Remove the dipstick.
2. Raise the vehicle and support safely. Drain the engine coolant and oil. Remove the oil pan and timing chain cover. Rotate the engine until all 3 silent chain gear marks are in a position to matchmark them to the corresponding chain link. Using different color paint, matchmark the chain to the gears. Remove the silent shaft chain. The lower guide bolts are also oil pump mounting bolts.
3. Remove the oil pump mounting bolts and remove the pump with the timing chain tensioner and the right side silent shaft.
4. Remove the silent shaft and its key from the oil pump.

To install:

5. Remove the gasket material from the block.
6. Prime the pump by pouring fresh oil into the pump intake and turning the driveshaft until oil comes out the pressure port. Repeat a few times until no air bubbles are present.
7. Install the silent shaft key to the oil pump and install the silent shaft to the pump.
8. Install the timing chain tensioner and spring into its bore it the pump housing. Make sure rubber washer is installed on the tensioner and is not damaged.
9. Install the new gasket to the oil pump. Install the pump to the block engaging the tensioner with the timing chain. Make sure the dowels are fully seated in their bores. Torque the mounting bolts to 13 ft. lbs. (18 Nm).
10. Install the silent shaft chain aligning the matchmarks.
11. Remove the oil pickup and clean or replace, as required. Reinstall with a new gasket.

1. Crankshaft sprocket
2. Oil pressure sending unit
3. Oil filter
4. Oil filter bracket
5. Gasket
6. Drain plug
7. Gasket
8. Oil pan
9. Oil screen
10. Gasket
11. Plug
12. Relief spring
13. Relief plunger
14. Front oil seal
15. Oil pump case
16. Gasket
17. Oil pump cover
18. Outer rotor
19. Inner rotor

Engine lubrication components—3.0L engine

12. Install the timing chain cover, oil pan and all related parts.
13. Install the dipstick. Fill the engine with the proper amount of oil.
14. Connect the negative battery cable and check the oil pressure.

3.0L ENGINE

1. Disconnect the negative battery cable. Remove the dipstick.
2. Raise the vehicle and support safely. Remove the timing belt, drain the engine oil and remove the oil pan from the engine. Remove the oil pickup.
3. Remove the oil pump mounting bolts and remove the pump from the front of the engine. Note the different length bolts and their position in the pump for installation.
To install:
4. Clean the gasket mounting surfaces of the pump and engine block.
5. Prime the pump by pouring fresh oil into the inlet and turning the rotors or by packing pump with petroleum jelly. Using a new gasket, install the oil pump on the engine and torque all bolts to 11 ft. lbs. (15 Nm).
6. Install the balancer and crankshaft sprockets.
7. Clean out the oil pickup or replace as required. Replace the oil pickup gasket ring and install the pickup to the pump.
8. Install the timing belt, oil pan and all related parts.
9. Install the dipstick. Fill the engine with the proper amount of oil.
10. Connect the negative battery cable and check the oil pressure.

Checking

2.0L AND 2.4L ENGINES

1. Remove the oil pump cover from the front case.
2. Check the case and gear cover for stepped wear from the gears.

Aligning the oil pump gear timing marks — 2.0L and 2.4L engines

Aligning the oil pump gear timing marks — 2.6L engine

3. Measure the drive gear tip clearance between the teeth and the case. The specification is 0.006–0.010 in. (0.16–0.25mm).
4. Check the driven gear tip clearance in the similar manner. The specification is 0.005–0.010 in. (0.13–0.25mm).
5. Place a straight-edge across the gears resting on the opposite sides of the case. If a 0.010 in. (0.25mm) feeler gauge can be inserted under the straight-edge, replace the assembly.
6. Check the relief plunger for freedom of movement and check the spring for deformation and rust.
7. If the gears were removed from the body, install them with the mating marks aligned. If not aligned properly, the silent shaft will be out of time.
8. Install the gear cover to the case using a new gasket. Torque the bolts to 12 ft. lbs. (16 Nm).

2.6L ENGINE

1. Remove the cover from the oil pump.
2. Measure the clearance between the gears and their bearings. The specification for both is 0.0008–0.0020 in. (0.02–0.05mm).
3. Check the clearance between the gears and the housing. The specification for both gears is 0.004–0.006 in. (0.11–0.15mm).
4. Check end-play of the gears using a feeler gauge and a straight-edge placed across the pump body. The specification for both is 0.002–0.004 in. (0.04–0.11mm).
5. Check the pressure relief valve for damage. The spring's freelength specification is 1.85 in. (47.00mm).
6. If the gears were removed from the body, install them with the markings aligned. If they are not aligned properly, the silent shaft will be out of time.
7. Torque the cover screws to 13 ft. lbs. (18 Nm).

3.0L ENGINE

1. Remove the rear cover.
2. Remove the pump rotors and inspect the case for excessive wear.
3. Measure the diameter of the inner rotor hub that sits in the case. Measure the inside diameter of the inner rotor hub bore. Subtract the first measurement from the second; if the result is over 0.006 in. (0.15mm), replace the oil pump assembly.
4. Measure the clearance between the outer rotor and the case. The specification is 0.004–0.007 in. (0.10–0.18mm).
5. Check the side clearance of the rotors using a feeler gauge and a straight-edge placed across the case. The specification is 0.0015–0.0035 in. (0.04–0.09mm).
6. Check the relief plunger and spring for damage and replace as required.
7. Install the rear pump cover to the case.

Rear Main Bearing Oil Seal

Removal and Installation

1. Disconnect the negative battery cable.
2. Support the weight of the engine using a jack stand with a block of wood to protect the oil pan. Remove the transmission from the vehicle.
3. If equipped with manual transmission, remove the clutch cover retainer bolts in a cross fashion gradually. Remove the clutch cover and disc. Remove the retaining bolt, flywheel and ball bearing from the engine.
4. If equipped with automatic transmission, remove the adapter plate, driveplate, crankshaft adapter and bushing.
5. Remove the rear engine plate and lower bell housing cover.
6. Remove the rear oil seal case and gasket from the back of the engine.
7. Remove the oil separator if remaining on the engine block.
To install:
8. Install the new oil seal into the seal case using seal installer.

9. Press the oil separator into the seal case making sure the separator oil hole is on the very bottom of the case. In the correct position, the hole is on the adjacent to the oil pan mounting surface.

10. Clean and dry the seal case to block sealing surfaces. Install seal case to the rear of the block using a new gasket.

11. Install the rear engine plate and the lower bell housing cover.

12. If equipped with automatic transmission, install the adapter plate, driveplate, crankshaft adapter and bushing.

13. If equipped with manual transmission, install the retaining bolt, flywheel and ball bearing to the engine.

14. Install the transmission into the vehicle. Lower the vehicle and remove the engine support. Connect the negative battery cable and check the oil level, adding as required.

TORQUE SPECIFICATIONS

Component	English	Metric
Air intake plenum-to-intake manifold	14 ft. lbs.	20 Nm
Camshaft sprocket bolt		
2.0L engine	43 ft. lbs.	60 Nm
2.4L engine	72 ft. lbs.	100 Nm
2.6L engine	43 ft. lbs.	60 Nm
3.0L engine	72 ft. lbs.	100 Nm
Camshaft bearing cap bolts		
2.0L engine		
8 x 25 bolt	19 ft. lbs.	27 Nm
8 x 65 bolt	15 ft. lbs.	21 Nm
2.4L engine		
8 x 25 bolt	19 ft. lbs.	27 Nm
8 x 65 bolt	15 ft. lbs.	21 Nm
2.6L engine	15 ft. lbs.	21 Nm
Connecting rod cap bolts		
2.0L engine	38 ft. lbs.	52 Nm
2.4L engine	38 ft. lbs.	52 Nm
2.6L engine	34 ft. lbs.	46 Nm
3.0L engine	38 ft. lbs.	52 Nm
Crankshaft main bearing bolt		
2.0L engine	38 ft. lbs.	52 Nm
2.4L engine	38 ft. lbs.	52 Nm
2.6L engine	58 ft. lbs.	79 Nm
3.0L engine	60 ft. lbs.	81 Nm
Crankshaft pulley (sprocket) bolt		
2.0L engine	80 ft. lbs.	110 Nm
2.4L engine	80 ft. lbs.	110 Nm
2.6L engine	87 ft. lbs.	118 Nm
3.0L engine	116 ft. lbs.	160 Nm
Cylinder head bolt (cold engine)	70 ft. lbs.	95 Nm
Exhaust flange nuts	29 ft. lbs.	40 Nm
Exhaust manifold		
Bolts	13 ft. lbs.	17 Nm
Nut	13 ft. lbs.	17 Nm
Flywheel bolts		
2.0L engine	95 ft. lbs.	129 Nm
2.4L engine	95 ft. lbs.	129 Nm
2.6L engine	95 ft. lbs.	129 Nm
3.0L engine	55 ft. lbs.	75 Nm
Intake manifold bolts	13 ft. lbs.	18 Nm
Oil pan-to-block		
2.0L engine	6 ft. lbs.	8 Nm
2.4L engine	6 ft. lbs.	8 Nm
2.6L engine	6 ft. lbs.	8 Nm
3.0L engine	5 ft. lbs.	7 Nm
Oil pan drain plug		
2.0L engine	26 ft. lbs.	35 Nm
2.4L engine	26 ft. lbs.	35 Nm
2.6L engine	26 ft. lbs.	35 Nm
3.0L engine	32 ft. lbs.	45 Nm

TORQUE SPECIFICATIONS

Component	English	Metric
Oil pump cover bolts		
2.0L engine	13 ft. lbs.	18 Nm
2.4L engine	13 ft. lbs.	18 Nm
2.6L engine	9 ft. lbs.	12 Nm
Oil pressure switch	6 ft. lbs.	8 Nm
Rocker cover bolt		
2.0L engine	5 ft. lbs.	7 Nm
2.4L engine	5 ft. lbs.	7 Nm
2.6L engine	5 ft. lbs.	7 Nm
3.0L engine	7 ft. lbs.	10 Nm
Spark plug	20 ft. lbs.	27 Nm
Starter-to-block bolts		
2.0L engine	23 ft. lbs.	32 Nm
2.4L engine	23 ft. lbs.	32 Nm
2.6L engine	25 ft. lbs.	34 Nm
3.0L engine	23 ft. lbs.	32 Nm
Thermostat housing	14 ft. lbs.	20 Nm
Throttle body-to-intake plenum	9 ft. lbs.	13 Nm
Water pump mounting bolt		
2.0L engine		
Bolt head 7T	20 ft. lbs.	27 Nm
Bolt head 4T	11 ft. lbs.	15 Nm
2.4L engine		
Bolt head mark 4T	11 ft. lbs.	15 Nm
Bolt head mark 7T	20 ft. lbs.	27 Nm
2.6L engine	11 ft. lbs.	15 Nm
3.0L engine		
Bolt head mark 4T	11 ft. lbs.	15 Nm
Bolt head mark 7T	20 ft. lbs.	27 Nm
Wheel stud lug nut	87–101 ft. lbs.	120–140 Nm

MANUAL TRANSMISSION

For further information, please refer to Chilton's Transmission Service Manual.

Transmission Assembly

Removal and Installation

1. Disconnect the negative battery cable.
2. Place the shifter(s) in the neutral position.
3. Unscrew the shift knob from the control lever. Remove the retainer screws from the dust cover retaining plate and slide plate and boot off of the lever.
4. Remove the retainer screws from the stopper plate and remove the lever assembly from the transmission. Cover the opening with a clean towel to prevent dirt from entering the transmission.
5. Raise the vehicle and support safely. Remove the skid plate, if equipped.
6. Drain the transmission fluid. If equipped with 4WD, drain the oil from the transfer case.
7. Matchmark and remove the driveshaft(s) from the vehicle.
8. Disconnect the speedometer cable from the transmission or transfer case.
9. Disconnect the clutch cable connection.
10. Disconnect the reverse light switch harness connector.
11. Remove the starter and the bell housing cover.
12. Support the weight of the engine using a jack stand with a block of wood to protect the oil pan.
13. Support the transmission with a transmission jack.
14. Remove the transfer case bracket, if equipped.
15. Remove the rear crossmember.
16. Remove the transmission to bell housing bolts.
17. Slide the transmission backwards until the input shaft clears the clutch disc. Remove the transmission from the vehicle.

To install:

18. Lubricate the pilot bushing and input shaft splines very lightly with high temperature lubricant.
19. Mount the transmission securely on a transmission jack and lift it in place until the input shaft is centered in the bell housing opening. Roll the transmission forward until the input shaft splines fully engage with the clutch disc.
20. Install the transmission to bell housing bolts. Torque the bolts to 35 ft. lbs. (47 Nm).
21. Lift the transmission using the transmission jack and install the rear crossmember into position. Install the transfer case bracket, if equipped. Torque the frame bolts to 50 ft. lbs. (68 Nm). Remove the transmission and engine support fixtures.
22. Install the starter and torque the mounting bolt to 20 ft. lbs. (27 Nm). Install the bell housing cover.
23. Connect the reverse light switch and clip all wiring to the transmission case.

24. Connect the speedometer cable.
25. Install the driveshaft(s) making sure to align matchmarks.
26. Connect the clutch cable, using a new cotter pin.
27. Fill the transmission and transfer case with the proper amount of SAE 80W or 75W/85W hypoid gear oil with an API classification of GL–4 or higher.
28. Install the skip plate, if equipped. Lower the vehicle.
29. Install the shift lever assembly, boot and console.

30. Connect the negative battery cable and check the transmission and transfer case for proper operation. Check operation of the reverse lights.

Linkage Adjustment

Since this transmission uses a direct engage shift mechanism, there are no provisions for adjustment.

CLUTCH

Clutch Assembly

Removal and Installation

1. Disconnect the negative battery cable.
2. Place the shifter(s) in the nuetral position.
3. Unscrew the shift knob from the control lever. Remove the retainer screws from the dust cover retaining plate and slide plate and boot off of the lever.
4. Remove the retainer screws from the stopper plate and remove the lever assembly from the transmission. Cover the opening with a clean towel to prevent dirt from entering the transmission.
5. Raise the vehicle and support safely. Remove the skid plate, if equipped.
6. Drain the transmission fluid. If equipped with 4WD, drain the oil from the transfer case.
7. Matchmark and remove the driveshaft(s) from the vehicle.
8. Disconnect the speedometer cable from the transmission or transfer case.
9. Disconnect the clutch cable connection.
10. Disconnect the reverse light switch harness connector.
11. Remove the starter and the bell housing cover.
12. Support the weight of the engine using a jack stand with a block of wood to protect the oil pan.
13. Support the transmission with a transmission jack.
14. Remove the transfer case bracket, if equipped.
15. Remove the rear crossmember.
16. Remove the transmission to bell housing bolts.
17. Slide the transmission backwards until the input shaft clears the clutch disc. Remove the transmission from the vehicle.
18. Remove the clutch cover retainer bolts in a cross fashion gradually. Remove the clutch cover and disc.

To install:
19. Raise the clutch cover and disc into place and use a clutch aligning tool or spare input shaft to center the disc. Apply Loctite® to the threads and tighten all of the bolts finger-tight.
20. Tighten cover bolts gradually, evenly and to the proper torque to avoid distorting the cover. Torque the bolts to 15 ft. lbs. (20 Nm).
21. Lubricate the pilot bushing and input shaft splines very lightly with high temperature lubricant.
22. Mount the transmission securely on a transmission jack and raise in place until the input shaft is centered in the bell housing opening. Roll the transmission forward until the input shaft splines fully engage with the clutch disc.
23. Install the transmission to bell housing bolts. Torque the bolts to 35 ft. lbs. (47 Nm).
24. Lift the transmission using the transmission jack and install the rear crossmember into position. Install the transfer case bracket, if equipped. Torque the frame bolts to 50 ft. lbs. (68 Nm). Remove the transmission and engine support fixtures.
25. Install the starter and torque the mounting bolt to 20 ft. lbs. (27 Nm). Install the bell housing cover.

26. Connect the reverse light switch and clip all wiring to the transmission case.
27. Connect the speedometer cable.
28. Install the driveshaft(s) making sure to align matchmarks.
29. Connect the clutch cable, using a new cotter pin.
30. Fill the transmission and transfer case with the proper amount of SAE 80W or 75W/85W hypoid gear oil with an API classification of GL–4 or higher.
31. Install the skip plate, if equipped. Lower the vehicle.
32. Install the shift lever assembly and boot.
33. Connect the negative battery cable and check the transmission and transfer case for proper operation. Check operation of the reverse lights.

Pedal Height/Free-Play Adjustment

1. Measure the distance from the face of the pedal pad to the floorboard. This distance should be about 6½–7 in.
2. If the pedal height is not correct, adjust the pedal stopper to contact the pedal at correct height.

Clutch Cable

Adjustment

1. Check the pedal's free-play. The specification is 1 inch.
2. Adjust the clutch cable by turning the star shaped adjusting wheel on the firewall. Turning the wheel counterclockwise will increase the amount of free-play in the pedal or vice-versa.

Removal and Installation

1. Disconnect the negative battery cable.
2. Turn the cable adjusting wheel counterclockwise to provide enough play to remove the cable end from the clutch lever inside the vehicle. Remove the cable from the lever.
3. Raise the vehicle and support safely.
4. Remove the cotter pin from the lever on the transmission.
5. Remove the clutch cable from the vehicle.
6. The installation is the reverse of the removal procedure. Make sure the insulator is positioning properly.

Clutch Master Cylinder

Removal and Installation

1. Disconnect the negative battery cable. Remove as much fluid as possible from the clutch master cylinder reservior.
2. Remove the cotter pin and remove the clevis pin from the clutch pedal.
3. Disconnect and plug the fluid line from the clutch master cylinder.
4. Remove the mounting nuts and remove the cylinder from the firewall.
5. Remove the reservoir from the cylinder.
6. The installation is the reverse of the removal procedure.
7. Bleed the clutch system.

Clutch Release Cylinder

Removal and Installation

1. Disconnect the negative battery cable.
2. Raise the vehicle and support safely.
3. Remove the eye-bolt and washer from the clutch hose at the release cylinder.
4. Remove the mounting bolts and remove the slave cylinder from the transmission case.
5. Replace the eye-bolt washer.
6. The installation is the reverse of the removal procedure.
7. Bleed the system.

Hydraulic Clutch System Bleeding

─── **CAUTION** ───

When bleeding, keep the facial area well away from the slave cylinder and protect all painted surfaces from fluid contact. Brake fluid will damage painted surfaces and could cause physical injury.

1. Fill the clutch master cylinder with fresh DOT 3 brake fluid.
2. Have a helper sit in the vehicle. Raise the vehicle and support safely.

3. Remove the bleeder screw cap.
4. If the system is empty, the most efficient way to get fluid down to the cylinder is to loosen the bleeder about ½–¾ turn, place a finger firmly over the bleeder and have the helper pump the brakes slowly until fluid pressure is felt at the bleeder. Once fluid is at the bleeder, close before the pedal is released.

NOTE: If the pedal is pump rapidly, the fluid will churn and create small air bubbles, which are difficult and time consuming to remove from the system. These air bubble will eventually congregate and will result in a spongy pedal.

5. Once fluid has been pumped to the slave cylinder, open the bleeder screw, have the helper depress the clutch pedal, lock the bleeder and have the helper release the pedal. Wait 15 seconds and repeat the procedure (including the 15 second wait) until no air bubbles flow from the bleeder. Remember to close the bleeder before the pedal is released. If the bleeder is left open when the pedal is released, air will be induced into the system.
6. If a helper is not available, connect a small hose to the bleeder, submerge the other end in a clean container of fresh brake fluid placed in a position that is visible from the driver's seat. Pump the pedal until no air comes out of the tube.

AUTOMATIC TRANSMISSION

For further information, please refer to Chilton's Transmission Service Manual.

Transmission Assembly

Removal and Installation

1. Disconnect the negative battery cable.
2. If equipped with 4WD, disconnect the 4WD indicator light switch connector and the ground cable at the transfer case. Remove the following components from the 4WD floor control console:
   a. Remove the shifter knob from the 4WD control.
   b. Remove the top trim panel around the outside of the boot, retaining screws and slide the boot(s) up and off of the shaft.
   c. Remove the center storage compartment and the rear cover plate. Remove the retaining screws the console from the vehicle.
3. Disconnect the pulse generator connector.
4. Raise and safely support the vehicle.
5. Remove the skid plate, if equipped. Drain the transmission and transfer case, as equipped.
6. Matchmark and remove the driveshaft(s).
7. Disconnect the speedometer cable from the transmission or transfer case.
8. Disconnect the shifter linkage or cable.
9. Unplug all transmission electrical connectors.
10. Remove the exhaust pipe from the vehicle. Remove the exhaust bracket from the transmission case.
11. Remove the filler neck and dipstick.
12. Remove the torque converter inspection plate. Matchmark the flexplate to the torque converter and remove the torque converter bolts.
13. Remove the starter assembly.
14. Disconnect and plug the oil cooler lines.
15. Using a transmission jack, support the transmission. Remove the retaining bolts at the crossmember.

16. Remove the rear crossmember.
17. Lower the transmission down slightly and unbolt the 4WD shifter from the transfer case, if equipped.
18. Remove the bell housing bolts and mounting brackets.
19. Pull the transmission assembly rearward to clear the aligning dowels and remove from the vehicle.

To install:
20. Install the transmission assembly to the engine using dowels as guides. Install the bell housing bolts and torque to 35 ft. lbs. (47 Nm).
21. Install the 4WD shifter, if equipped. Raise the assembly up into position and install the rear crossmember and mounting hardware. Torque the crossmember to frame bolts to 50 ft. lbs. (68 Nm).
22. Align the flexplate to torque converter. Apply Loctite® to the threads and install the torque converter bolts. Torque the bolts to 25 ft. lbs. (34 Nm). Install the inspection plate.
23. Install the filler tube with a new O-ring and the dipstick.
24. Install the exhaust and the support brackets.
25. Connect all switch connectors that were removed.
26. Connect the shifter linkage or cable and the throttle cable.
27. Align and install the driveshaft(s).
28. Install the ground wire and the 4WD indicator light switch connector to the transfer case, if equipped.
29. Fill the transfer case with hypoid gear oil with an API classification of GL–4 or higher.
30. Connect the throttle cable.
31. Install the skid plate, if equipped. Lower the vehicle.
32. Install the transfer case shifter boot and console, if equipped.
33. Fill the transmission with the proper amount of Dexron® II.
34. Connect the negative battery cable, start the engine and run through all gears. Add fluid until the transmission is properly filled.
35. Check the operation of the neutral safety switch and the reverse lights.
36. Road test the vehicle and check for leaks.

Throttle cable adjustment—carbureted engine

Throttle cable adjustment—fuel injected engine

Shift Linkage Adjustment

1. Position the shifter in the **N** detent.
2. Loosen the nut or bolt on the shifter linkage or cable.
3. Make sure the lever on the transmission is in the **N** detent and the needle in the indicator is also in the **N** position. Jiggle

Neutral safety switch adjustment

the selector rod to settle the assembly in position. If the rod is equipped with a notch, it should be at the 6 o'clock position.
4. Tighten the adjusting bolt or nut and check for proper assembly.
5. Check the operation of the neutral safely switch.
6. Liberally lubricate all pivoting points within the system.

Throttle Cable Adjustment

1. Depress the accelerator fully and make sure the throttle valve opens all the way. Adjust as required.
2. Measure the distance between the end of the rubber boot and the stopper on the cable at wide open throttle.
3. The specification for carbureted engines is 2.05–2.09 in. (52–52mm) or fuel injected engines is 0–0.04 in. (0–1mm).
4. Adjust the cable on carbureted engines by moving the bracket. Adjust the cable itself on fuel injected engines.
5. Road test the vehicle and check for proper shift points.

Neutral Safety Switch Adjustment

NOTE: Some vehicles are not equipped with an adjustable switch.

1. Adjust the shifter linkage.
2. Raise the vehicle and support safely. Place the shifter in the **N** detent. Loosen the mounting bolts.
3. Align the lever with the positioning boss.
4. Hold in position and tighten the bolts.
5. Check the switch and the reverse lights for proper operation.

TRANSFER CASE

Transfer Case Assembly

Removal and Installation

AUTOMATIC TRANSMISSION

1. Disconnect the negative battery cable.
2. Remove the transmission and transfer case assembly from the vehicle.
3. Remove the plug from the right side of the transfer case under the control housing.
4. Remove the select spring and plunger from the housing bore.
5. Remove the control lever housing assembly, cover and gasket.

6. Remove the transfer case to adapter attaching nuts. Pull transfer case from the adapter.

To install:

7. Install the transfer case to adapter and secure using retainer nuts. Torque nuts to 30 ft. lbs. (42 Nm).
8. Install the control lever housing assembly, cover and gasket.
9. Install the select spring and plunger into the housing and install plug in bore.
10. Install the transfer case and transmission into the vehicle, connect the negative battery cable and road test for proper operation.

1. Oil filler plug
2. Drain plug
3. Plug
4. Gasket
5. Selector spring
6. Selector plunger
7. Roll pin
8. Wire clamp
9. Wire clamp
10. Shift changer
11. Transfer case assembly
12. Gasket
13. Plug
14. Spring
15. Steel ball
16. Plug
17. Neutral return spring
18. Plunger
19. Plunger

Transfer case assembly

MANUAL TRANSMISSION

1. Disconnect the negative battery cable.
2. Remove the transmission and transfer case assembly from the vehicle.
3. Remove the plug from the right side of the transfer case under the control housing.
4. Remove the select spring and plunger from the housing bore.
5. Remove the spring pin that retains the shift changer to the control shaft using a pin punch.
6. Remove the transfer case to transmission attaching nuts and remove from the transmission.

To install:

7. Install the transfer case to transmission and tighten attaching nuts to 30 ft. lbs. (42 Nm).
8. Install the shift changer to the control shaft and install new roll pin.
9. Install select spring, plunger and plug into housing bore.
10. Install the transfer case and transmission into vehicle. Connect negative battery cable and road test for proper operation.

Linkage Adjustment

Since this transfer case uses a directly engaging shift mechanism, there are no provisions for adjustment.

DRIVE AXLE

Front Halfshaft

Removal and Installation

RIGHT HALFSHAFT

Outer

1. Place the free-wheeling hub in the free condition by placing the transfer lever in the **2H** position and moving in reverse for about 6 or 7 feet.

2. Disconnect negative battery cable.
3. Raise and safely support the vehicle. Remove the skid plate, if equipped.
4. Remove the tire and wheel assembly.
5. Remove the hub cover with the use of an oil filter wrench. Install a protective cloth between the wrench and the cover to avoid damage to the cover.
6. Remove the snapring from the inside of the hub. Remove the shim.

60 FT. LBS. (81 NM)

14

Left drive shaft

13   11

7   9   6   10   12

1   8

33 FT. LBS. (45 NM)

100 FT. LBS. 136 NM)   8

4   3   2

Right drive shaft

15

1. Under cover
2. Hub cover
3. Snapring
4. Shim
5. Caliper
6. Cotter pin
7. Tie rod end
8. Cotter pin
9. Lower ball joint
10. Cotter pin
11. Upper ball joint
12. Hub and knuckle assembly
13. Left side axle shaft
14. Circlip
15. Right side axle shaft

Front axle shafts and related parts

7. Remove the front brake caliper and brake pads from the vehicle. Do not allow the caliper to hang from the brake hose.

8. Separate the tie rod from the steering knuckle.

9. Separate the upper and lower ball joints from the steering knuckle.

10. Remove the front hub/knuckle assembly with the inner and outer bearings intact.

11. Remove the halfshaft to axle housing retaining nuts and remove the halfshaft from the vehicle.

To install:

12. Install the halfshaft and the retaining nuts and tighten to 43 ft. lbs. (60 Nm).

13. Install the front hub/knuckle and bearing assembly.

14. Install the upper ball joint to the knuckle and torque re-taining nut to 130 ft. lbs. (180 Nm). Install the lower ball joint to knuckle and torque retaining nut to 65 ft. lbs. (90 Nm). Install new cotter pins.

15. Install the tie rod end to the steering knuckle and torque to 33 ft. lbs. (45 Nm). Install new cotter pin.

16. Install the shim and snapring to the axle shaft. Install the front hub cover.

17. Install front brake caliper assembly.

18. Install the tire and wheel assembly. Install skid plate, if removed.

Inner

1. Disconnect negative battery cable.

2. Raise and safely support the vehicle.

3   2   5   4

1. Inner shaft
2. Bearing
3. Dust cover
4. Housing tube
5. Dust seal

Inner axle shaft and tube

3. Remove the skid plate, if equipped.
4. Remove the right outer halfshaft.
5. Remove the lower shock absorber mounting bolts.
6. Install slide hammer to inner shaft flange and pull from housing. Press the bearing from the axle, as required.

To install:

7. Press new bearing and seal on axle, as required. Install new circlip to inner halfshaft and install into housing. Drive the axle into position.
8. Install the lower shock absorber mounting bolts.
9. Install the right outer halfshaft and related parts.
10. Install the skid plate, if equipped.

LEFT HALFSHAFT

1. Place the free-wheeling hub in the free condition by placing the transfer lever in the **2H** position and moving in reverse for about 6 or 7 feet.
2. Disconnect negative battery cable.
3. Raise and safely support the vehicle. Remove the skid plate, if equipped.
4. Remove the tire and wheel assembly.
5. Remove the hub cover with the use of an oil filter wrench. Install a protective cloth between the wrench and the cover to avoid damage to the cover.
6. Remove the snapring from the inside of the hub. Remove the shim.
7. Remove the front brake caliper and brake pads from the vehicle. Do not allow the caliper to hang from the brake hose.
8. Separate the tie rod from the steering knuckle.
9. Separate the upper and lower ball joints from the steering knuckle.
10. Remove the front hub/knuckle assembly with the inner and outer bearings intact.
11. Pull the left halfshaft out from the differential carrier. Use care not to damage the oil seal with the splines of the shaft.

To install:

12. Replace circlip on the end of the shaft. Install the halfshaft into the front differential case and drive into position using a plastic hammer.
13. Install the front hub/knuckle and bearing assembly.
14. Install the upper ball joint to the knuckle and torque retaining nut to 130 ft. lbs. (180 Nm). Install the lower ball joint to knuckle and torque retaining nut to 65 ft. lbs. (90 Nm). Install new cotter pins.

15. Install the tie rod end to the steering knuckle and torque to 33 ft. lbs. (45 Nm). Install new cotter pin.
16. Install the shim and snapring to the axle shaft. Install the front hub cover.
17. Install front brake caliper assembly.
18. Install the tire and wheel assembly. Install skid plate, if removed.

CV-Boot

Removal and Installation

1. Disconnect negative battery cable.
2. Raise and safely support the vehicle.
3. Remove the skid plate, if equipped.
4. Remove the left halfshaft.
5. Remove the boot bands on the inner Double Offset Joint (DOJ). Remove the circlip.
6. Remove the DOJ outer race from the shaft.
7. Remove the dust cover from the DOJ outer race.
8. Remove the balls from the DOJ cage prying from the inside of the cage outward.
9. Rotate the cage while pushing toward the Birfield Joint (BJ). The cage will drop down to expose a snapring on the halfshaft. Remove the snapring.
10. Remove the DOJ cage and inner race from the halfshaft.
11. Wrap tape over the threads of the halfshaft. Remove the boot from the shaft.
12. Remove the dust cover from the BJ and the halfshaft.
13. Remove the boot bands. Remove the BJ boot from the DOJ end of the driveshaft.

NOTE: Do not disassemble the Birfield Joint (BJ).

To install:

14. Install the BJ boot and bands over the DOJ end of the driveshaft. Install the DOJ boot and bands onto the halfshaft. Apply ½ of supplied grease into the BJ boot and install the bands onto the boot.
15. Install the DOJ cage onto the halfshaft with the smaller diameter side of the cage facing the installed BJ boot. Install the snapring.
16. Apply remaining grease to the DOJ inner race, the DOJ cage and the balls. Insert the balls into the cage from the outside pushing in toward the shaft.

1. Boot band
2. Boot band
3. Circlip
4. DOJ outer race
5. Dust cover
6. Balls
7. DOJ cage
8. Snapring
9. DOJ inner race
10. DOJ boot
11. Dust cover
12. Boot protector band
13. Boot protector
14. Boot band
15. Boot band
16. BJ boot
17. Drive shaft and BJ
18. Circlip

Front halfshaft assembly—4WD Vehicle

17. Install the outer race over the DOJ cage assembly and install the retaining circlip.

18. Install the dust cover into place and install the boot bands.

19. Install the halfshaft into the vehicle.

20. Install the skid plate, if equipped.

Driveshaft and U-Joints

Removal and Installation

1. If equipped with 4WD, place the free-wheeling hub in the free condition by placing the transfer lever in the **2H** position and moving in reverse for about 6 or 7 feet.

2. Disconnect negative battery cable.

3. Raise and safely support the vehicle.

4. Remove the skid plate, if equipped.

5. Matchmark the flange yoke and the differential companion flange. Do not damage the oil seals when marking positions.

6. Drain the transfer case. Position a drain pan under the transmission tailshaft, as required. Fluid will leak from unit on removal of the driveshaft.

7. Remove the retaining bolts and nuts from the flange(s) and remove the shaft from the vehicle.

8. Remove the U-Joint from the driveshaft as follows:

   a. Make mating marks on the yokes of the universal joint that is to be disassembled.

   b. Remove the snaprings from the yoke. When disassembling, note the position of the snaprings so they may be reinstalled in the same positions.

   c. Remove the grease fitting from the journal.

   d. Remove the journal bearings from the propeller shaft yoke using tool MB990840–01.

   e. Remove the journal and the flange yoke or sleeve yoke from the shaft.

9. Inspect the propeller shaft yokes for wear, cracks or damage. Check the sleeve yoke and the flange yoke for wear, cracks or damage. Relpace as required.

To install:

10. Install the U-Joint on the driveshaft as follows:

   a. Install the sleeve yoke or flange yoke to the journal and the assembly to the driveshaft.

   b. Align the mating marks on the yokes and press the journal bearings to the yoke using tool MB990840–01.

   c. Install the snaprings in the position prior to removal. Install the grease fitting.

   d. Measure the clearance between the snaprings and the journal bearing. If the clearance is larger than 0.0024 in. (0.06mm), it will be necessary to replace the snapring.

11. With the mating marks aligned, install the driveshaft into the transfer case/transmission and the companion flange.

12. Clean the mounting nuts and bolts and install to the flange(s). Torque to 43 ft. lbs. (60 Nm).

13. Install the skid plate, if equipped.

Rear Axle Shaft, Bearing and Seal

Removal and Installation

1. Raise the vehicle and support safely.

2. Remove the rear tire and wheel assembly.

3. Remove the brake drum.

4. Disconnect the parking brake cable from the brake shoe and remove from the backing plate.

5. Disconnect and plug the brake line(s) at the wheel cylinder.

6. Remove the 4 nuts behind the backing plate.

7. Remove the backing plate, bearing case and the axle shaft as an assembly. If not possible by hand, use a slide hammer to remove the assembly.

1. Brake drum
2. Parking brake cable attaching bolt
3. Parking brake cable
4. Brake fluid lines
5. Nut
6. Rear axle shaft assembly
7. Shim
8. O-ring
9. Locknut
10. Lock washer
11. Washer
12. Axle shaft
13. Outer race
14. Seal
15. Bearing
16. Seal

Rear axle shaft assembly

8. Remove the O-ring and the bearing preload shims. Save the preload shims for reassembly.

9. Remove the oil seal from the axle tube with a hooked slide hammer.

10. To remove the axle shaft bearing, remove the notched locknut with tool MB990785–01 or a brass drift.

11. Remove the lock washer and flat washer.

12. Screw the locknut onto the axle shaft about 3 turns.

13. If tool MB990787–01 is not available, it will be necessary to fabricate a metal plate that fits over the axle shaft and butts the locknut. Drill 4 holes in the plate that align with the 4 bearing case studs and fit the plate. Refit 2 nuts and washers to the bearing case studs diagonally across from each other and tighten them evenly to release the bearing case and bearing.

14. Use a hammer and drift to remove the bearing outer race from the bearing case.

15. Remove the outer oil seal from the bearing case.

To install:

16. Apply grease to the outer surface on the bearing outer race and the lip of the outer oil seal. Drive into the bearing case.

17. Slide the bearing case and bearing over the rear axle shaft. Apply grease on the bearing rollers and install the inner race by pressing into place. Be careful not to damage the dust cover.

18. Pack the bearing with grease.

19. Install the washer, the crowned lock washer and the locknut in that order and torque the locknut to 130–159 ft. lbs. (176–220 Nm).

20. Bend the tab on the lock washer into the groove on the locknut. If the tab and the groove do not line up, tighten locknut slightly.

21. Lubricate and drive the new inner oil seal into place. Refit the assembly.

22. Install a new O-ring and the shims. Apply silicone rubber sealant to the face of the bearing case.

23. Install the entire assembly to the axle housing. Torque the retaining nuts to 40 ft. lbs. (54 Nm).

24. Check the axle shaft end-play. If not between 0.002–0.008 in. (0.05–0.20mm), proceed with the axle shaft end-play adjustment procedure.

25. Install all removed brake parts and bleed the system.

26. Install the tire and wheel assembly and road test the vehicle. Check for leaks.

End-play Adjustment Procedure

1. Begin with the left side rear axle assembly and insert a 0.04 in. (1mm) shim between the bearing case and the axle shaft housing. Torque the nuts to specification.

2. Install the right side axle assembly into the right side housing without its shim and O-ring. Torque the 4 nuts to about 50 inch. lbs.

3. Using a feeler gauge, measure the gap between the bearing case and the axle housing face.

4. Remove the axle shaft and select a shim or shims that is the equal to the sum of the clearance measured in Step 3 plus 0.002–0.008 in. (0.05–0.20mm) and install them on the housing. Install the O-ring and apply sealant.

5. Install the axle assembly and torque the nuts to 40 ft. lbs. (54 Nm).

6. Measure the end-play and complete the installation procedure.

Front Wheel Hub, Knuckle and Bearings

Removal and Installation

2WD VEHICLE

1. Raise the vehicle and support safely. Remove the tire and wheel assembly.

Measuring axle shaft end-play

2. Remove the brake caliper, pads and adaptor and position them out of the way.

3. Remove the grease cap.

4. Remove the cotter pin, castellated nut and washer. Remove the outer bearing.

5. Remove the front hub/rotor assembly from the steering knuckle. Remove the grease seal and inner bearing from the hub. Remove the splash shield.

6. Remove the nuts and bolts that attach the hub to the rotor and separate them. Clean out all of the old grease from the inside of the hub.

7. Remove the shock and stabilizer bar from the lower control arm, if equipped.

8. Support the lower control arm. Compress the coil spring with the special spring compressor, if equipped. Separate the ball joints and tie rod end from the knuckle.

9. Remove the steering knuckle.

To install:

10. Install the knuckle to the ball joint studs. Torque upper ball joint nuts to 65 ft. lbs. (90 Nm), and the lower joint nut to 130 ft. lbs. (180 Nm). Install new cotter pins. Remove the spring compressor, if used. Install the shock.

11. Connect the stabilizer bar to the lower control arm. Tighten the nut until the bushing is the same diameter as the washer.

12. Connect the tie rod end to the knuckle. Torque the nut to 30 ft. lbs. (41 Nm). Install a new cotter pin.

13. Assemble the rotor and front hub. Torque the nuts to 40 ft. lbs. (54 Nm).

14. Apply wheel bearing grease to the inside of the front hub.

15. Pack the inner bearing and install into hub.

16. Install a new oil seal into the hub so it is flush with the hub end face.

17. Install the assembly onto the steering knuckle, pack and install the outer bearing.

18. Install the washer and castellated nut. Spin the rotor and torque the nut to 22 ft. lbs. (30 Nm), loosen completely and re-tighten to 6 ft. lbs. (8 Nm) while turning the wheel.

19. Install a new cotter pin and install the grease cap.

20. Install the brake hardware and bleed the system, if opened.

21. Install the tire and wheel assembly and road test the vehicle.

Automatic Locking Hubs, Knuckle and Bearings

Removal and Installation

1. Place the free-wheeling hub in the free condition by placing the transfer lever in the **2H** position and moving in reverse for about 6 or 7 feet.

2. Disconnect negative battery cable.

1. Hub cover
2. Snapring
3. Shim
4. Caliper
5. Bolts
6. Automatic free-
   wheeling hub
   assembly
7. Lock washer
8. Locknut
9. Front hub and rotor

130–200 Nm→0 Nm→25 Nm
94–145 ft.lbs.→0 ft.lbs→18 ft.lbs.

Front hub and automatic hub assembly—4WD vehicles

1. Oil seal
2. Spacer
3. Needle bearing
4. Knuckle

Steering knuckle, needle bearing, spacer and seal—4WD vehicle

3. Raise and safely support the vehicle. Remove the skid plate, if equipped.

4. Remove the tire and wheel assembly.

5. Remove the hub cover with the use of an oil filter wrench. Install a protective cloth between the wrench and the cover to avoid damage to the cover.

6. Remove the snapring from the inside of the hub. Remove the shim.

7. Remove the front brake caliper and brake pads from the vehicle. Do not allow the caliper to hang from the brake hose.

8. Using hexagonal wrench, remove the automatic free wheeling hub assembly.

9. Remove the retaining screws from lock washer and remove lock washer.

10. Remove the outer bearing and front hub assembly from knuckle.

11. Remove the inner oil seal and inner bearing from the hub assembly.

12. To separate the hub from the brake disc, matchmark the brake disc to the front hub. Remove the retaining bolts and separate the hub from the disc.

13. Remove the dust cover from the spindle. Separate the tie rod from the steering knuckle.

14. Separate the upper and lower ball joints from the steering knuckle.

15. Remove the knuckle from the axle shaft.

16. Remove the knuckle oil seal and spacer. If damaged, drive out the needle bearing through the spindle end of the knuckle.
To install:

17. Use Chrysler tool C–4178 to press the new needle bearing into the knuckle. Lubricate the rollers and install the spacer with the chamfered side facing the center of the vehicle. Install a new seal until it is flush with the knuckle end face and lubricate the lip.

18. Install the knuckle to the ball joint studs. Torque lower ball joint nut to 130 ft. lbs. (180 Nm) and the upper nut to 65 ft. lbs. (90 Nm). Install new cotter pin through castellated nut.

19. Connect the tie rod end to the knuckle. Torque the nut to 30 ft. lbs. (41 Nm). Install a new cotter pin.

20. Clean out all of the old grease from inside the front hub.

21. Bolt the rotor and front hub together. Torque the nuts to 40 ft. lbs. (54 Nm). Install new races and apply wheel bearing grease to the inside of the front hub.

22. Pack the inner bearing and install to the race.

23. Install new oil seal into the front hub until it is flush with the front hub end face.

KEYWAY
KEY
BRAKE

Aligning the key in the automatic hub with the keyway in the spindle

24. Install the assembly onto the steering knuckle, pack and install the outer bearing with grease. Using special tool MB990954 or equivalent, which fits standard torque wrenches, torque the locknut to 95–145 ft. lbs. (130–200 Nm). Loosen the locknut completely, then retorque to 18 ft. lbs. (25 Nm). To complete the procedure, position the torque wrench at the 3 o'clock position and loosen the nut 30 degrees.

25. Install the lock washer. If the lock washer and locknut holes do not align, loosening the nut slightly.

26. Before installing the automatic hub assembly, measure the turning force of the front hub. If the measured value does not meet specifications of 2.5–11.5 inch lbs. and retorque the locknut. Also check the hub for an maximum end-play of 0.002 in. (0.05mm).

27. Apply even coating of sealant on the freewheeling hub body and front hub contact surface. Align the key of the brake and the keyway of the spindle and loosely install the automatic free wheeling hub assembly. The mounting surfaces of the automatic hub and the front hub must be perfectly flush before the mounting bolts are torqued.

28. Torque the automatic hub mounting bolts to 40 ft. lbs. (54 Nm).

29. Check the front hub turning resistance again. If the difference between the reading in Step 26 and this reading is more than 8.7 inch lbs., repair or replace the automatic hub, as required.

30. Install the shim and snapring. Rotate the axle shaft forward and backward and stop at a position midway between 2 heavy spots where there is a heavy feeling.

31. Set a dial indicator so the pin is resting on the end of the axle shaft. The end-play specification is 0.008–0.020 in. (0.2–0.5mm). If not within specifications, adjust by adding or removing shims.

32. Install the hub cover.

33. Install the brake hardware and install the wheel and tire assembly.

34. Road test the vehicle.

Pinion Seal

Removal and Installation

1. Raise the vehicle and support safely.

2. Matchmark and remove the driveshaft.

3. Check the turning torque of the pinion before proceeding. It should be 3.5–4.5 inch lbs. (0.4–0.5 Nm). This is the torque that must be reached during installation of the pinion nut.

4. Using a pinion flange holding tool, remove the pinion nut and washer.

5. Remove the companion flange from the drive pinion.

6. Pry the pinion seal out of the differential carrier.

7. Clean and inspect the sealing surface of the housing.

To install:

8. Using a seal driver, drive the new seal into the housing until the flange on the seal is flush with the carrier.

9. With the seal installed, the pinion bearing preload must be set.

10. Tighten the pinion nut, while holding the flange, until the turning torque is the same as before removal of the nut. The final pinion nut torque must be 137–181 ft. lbs. (190–250 Nm).

11. Align the matchmarks and install the drive shaft.

12. Check the level of the differential lubricant.

Differential Carrier

Removal and Installation

FRONT DIFFERENTIAL

1. Raise the vehicle and support safely. Remove the skid plate.

2. Remove both side outer and right side inner axle shafts.

3. Drain the front differential and remove the cover.

4. Remove the bearing cap retaining bolts, matchmark and remove the caps.

5. Pry the differential case out of the housing.

6. Label any loose parts as removed from the assembly.

To install:

7. Install the differential case to the housing.

8. Install the caps aligning the matchmarks made previously. Torque the retaining bolts evenly and gradually to 45 ft. lbs. (61 Nm).

9. Clean the sealing surfaces of the cover and the differential housing. Reseal the cover and install to the housing.

10. Install the axle shafts.

11. Level the vehicle and fill the differential with Hypoid gear

1. Brake drum
2. Parking brake cable attaching bolt
3. Parking brake cable
4. Brake fluid lines
5. Nut
6. Rear axle shaft
7. Driveshaft
8. Differential carrier

Differential carrier removal and installation

oil with an API classification of at least GL–5, until oil level reaches hole.

12. Install the skid plate and lower the vehicle.

13. Perform a road test and check the differential for leaks.

REAR DIFFERENTIAL

1. Raise the vehicle and support safely. Drain the rear differential.

2. Remove the rear tire and wheel assemblies and brake drums.

3. Remove the axle shafts.

4. Matchmark and remove the driveshaft.

5. Remove the differential carrier retaining nuts and remove the carrier from the axle housing.

6. The installation is the reverse of the removal procedure. Torque the carrier retaining nuts to 22 ft. lbs. (27 Nm).

Front Differential Housing

Removal and Installation

1. Raise the vehicle and support safely. Remove the skid plate and drain the differential.

2. Remove the hubs and knuckles from the vehicle.

3. Remove the outer and inner axle shafts.

4. Matchmark and remove the front driveshaft.

5. Support the differential housing with a jack.

6. Remove the differential mounting brackets.

7. Remove the front suspension crossmember.

8. Lower the differential housing and remove from the vehicle.

To install:

9. Mount the housing safely on jack and raise into position.

10. Lubricate the bushings and install the crossmember and housing brackets.

11. Torque all crossmember mounting nuts and bolt to 80 ft. lbs. (109 Nm) and the housing bracket mounting bolts to 65 ft. lbs. (88 Nm).

12. Replace the circlips and install the axle shafts.

13. Install the knuckle and hub assemblies.

14. Install the front driveshaft.

15. Level the vehicle and fill the differential with Hypoid gear oil with an API classification of at least GL–5, until oil level is up to the fill hole.

16. Install the under cover and lower the vehicle.

17. Perform a road test and check the differential for leaks.

Rear Axle Housing

Removal and Installation

EXCEPT RAIDER WITH COIL SPRINGS

1. Raise the vehicle and support safely. Drain the differential

2. Remove the tire and wheel assemblies. Remove the brake drums.

3. Remove the parking brake cable attaching bolts, disconnect the cables from the shoes and unclip them from the backing plates.

4. Disconnect the brake hose at the T-fitting.

5. Remove the load sensing proportioning valve spring support, if equipped.

6. Disconnect the breather hose, if equipped.

7. Matchmark and remove the driveshaft.

8. Place jack under the center of the differential housing and unbolt the shocks from their lower mounts.

9. Remove the U-bolts, shackle assemblies and remove the leaf springs.

10. Lower the axle and remove from vehicle.

1. Knuckle and axle shaft assembly
2. Inner shaft
3. Circlip
4. Front driveshaft
5. Locknut
6. Left side mounting bracket
7. Locknut
8. Bolt
9. Crossmember
10. Locknut

Front axle removal and installation

1. Brake drum
2. Parking brake cable attaching bolt
3. Parking brake cable
4. Brake hose
5. Breater hose
6. Driveshaft
7. Stabilizer bar mounting bolt
8. Trailing arm
9. Lateral rod
10. Shock absorber
11. Axle shaft
12. Coil spring
13. Stabilizer bar

4-door models

Rear axle assembly—Raider with coil springs

To install:

11. Raise the axle assembly into position and install the leaf springs. Make sure the shackle nuts are on the inside of the shackles. Tighten the shackle bolts to 43 ft. lbs. (60 Nm).
12. Install the U-bolt and bumper stops in position and tighten the new nuts to 87 ft. lbs. (120 Nm).
13. Install the lower shock mounting nuts tightening to 18 ft. lbs. (25 Nm).
14. Align and install the driveshaft.
15. Install the breather hose, if equipped.
16. Connect the brake hose.
17. Connect the parking brake cables and install the retaining bolts.
18. Install the load sensing spring support and spring, if equipped.
19. Level the vehicle and fill the differential using Hypoid gear oil with an API classification of at least GL–5, until level reaches the fill hole.

NOTE: If equipped with a limited slip differential, add the proper amount of limited slip friction modifier additive before filling the differential with gear oil.

20. Bleed the rear brakes. Install the brake drums and tire and wheel assemblies.
21. Lower the vehicle so full weight of the vehicle is on the ground. Unload any excess weight that may be weighing down the rear of the vehicle. Adjust the load sensing proportioning valve lever so the distance from the proportioning valve lever to the spring support is 7 in.
22. Road test the vehicle and check for leaks.

RAIDER WITH COIL SPRINGS

1. Raise the vehicle and support safely. Drain the differential.
2. Remove the tire and wheel assemblies. Remove the brake drums.
3. Remove the parking brake cable attaching bolts, disconnect the cables from the shoes and unclip from backing plates.
4. Disconnect the brake hose at the T-fitting.
5. Disconnect the breather hose.
6. Matchmark and remove the driveshaft.
7. Remove the rear stabilizer bar attaching bolts, links and bushings.
8. Place jack under the center of the differential housing and remove the rear trailing arm, if equipped.
9. Remove the lateral rod.
10. Unbolt the shocks from their lower mounts.
11. Lower the axle housing enough to remove the coil springs and the stabilizer bar.
12. Lower the axle assembly fully and remove from vehicle.

To install:
13. With the coil springs and stabilizer bar in place, raise the axle assembly into place and install the lower shock mounting bolts.
14. Install the lateral rod and tighten nuts loosely.

15. Assemble the trailing arm with its front mounting spacers, bushings and nuts. Make sure the washer's concave side faces away from the bushings. Install the trailing arm and torque the rear mount nuts to 90 ft. lbs. (122 Nm). If removed, tighten through bolt on lower control arm mounting bracket located on the rear axle housing to 159 ft. lbs. (220 Nm). Do not tighten the front mounting nuts yet.

16. Install the stabilizer bar and tighten the mounting nuts until the diameter of the bushing is the same as the diameter of the washers.

17. Install the driveshaft and breather hose.

18. Connect the parking brake cables and install the retaining bolts.

19. Level the vehicle and fill the differential with Hypoid gear oil with an API classification of at least GL–5, until it spills out the fill hole.

NOTE: If equipped with a limited slip differential, add the proper amount of limited slip friction modifier additive before filling the differential with gear oil.

20. Install the brake drums and tire and wheel assemblies. Bleed the rear brakes.

21. Lower vehicle so full weight of vehicle is on the ground. Torque the lateral rod mounting nuts to 90 ft. lbs. (122 Nm) and the front trailing arm mounting nuts to 100 ft. lbs. (150 Nm).

22. Road test the vehicle and check for leaks.

STEERING

Steering Wheel

Removal and Installation

1. Disconnect the negative battery cable.
2. Remove the center pad.
3. Remove the steering wheel jam nut. Matchmark the steering wheel to the shaft.
4. Using steering wheel puller, pull the steering wheel off of the shaft.
5. The installation is the reverse of the removal procedure. Tighten the jam nut to 33 ft. lbs. (45 Nm).

Steering Column and Shaft

Removal and Installation

1. Disconnect negative battery cable.
2. Remove the steering wheel from the vehicle.
3. Remove the upper and lower steering column covers.
4. Disconnect the electrical connectors at the base of the steering column.
5. Disconnect the key reminder switch and the ignition switch from the top at the steering column.
6. Remove the gear indicator cable connection at the top of the steering column, if equipped.
7. Remove the brake pedal return spring from the lower portion of the steering column, if equipped.
8. Remove the bolt in the steering shaft coupler above the steering gear.
9. Remove the column retainer bolts at the floor panel and under the instrument panel. Remove the steering column and shaft from the vehicle.
To install:
10. Install the steering column into the vehicle positioning the steering shaft over the bevel gear or steering gear shaft.
11. Install the under dash retaining bolts loosely.
12. Install the bolt at the lower steering coupler and torque to 25 ft. lbs. (35 Nm).
13. Tighten the bolts under the instrument panel to 14 ft. lbs. (20 Nm). Install the bolts in the column retainer at the floor panel tightening to 4 ft. lbs. (6 Nm).
14. Reconnect the electrical connectors at the base of the steering column.
15. Connect the gear indicator cable, if removed.
16. Install the upper and lower steering column covers.
17. Align and install the steering wheel tightening the jam nut to 36 ft. lbs. (50 Nm).
18. Install the horn pad. Reconnect the negative battery cable and check operation of all related electrical components.

Manual Steering Gear

Removal and Installation

1. Disconnect negative battery cable.
2. Remove the cotter pin and nut on the pitman arm. Separate the relay rod from the pitman arm.
3. Remove the bolt from the steering shaft to steering gear coupling.
4. Remove the steering gear mounting bolts and nuts, slide the gear from the steering shaft and remove the gear from the vehicle. Matchmark and remove the pitman arm, as required.
5. The installation is the reverse of the removal procedure. Torque the gear mounting nuts to 40 ft. lbs. (55 Nm). Torque the relay rod retainer nut to 33 ft. lbs. (45 Nm) and install new cotter pin.

Adjustment

1. Disconnect negative battery cable.
2. Remove the steering gear from the vehicle.
3. Turn the cross shaft 36 degrees. Position the mainshaft in the straight ahead position.
4. Using torque wrench, measure the starting torque of the mainshaft. The recommended value is 7.7–8.6 inch lbs. (0.9–1.0 Nm). If measured value is not within this value, Use tool MB990914 to screw adjusting cover to correct reading.

Power Steering Gear

Removal and Installation

1. Disconnect the negative battery cable. Raise the vehicle and support safely.
2. Fold back the dust boot which covers the steering shaft joint, if equipped. Remove the pinch bolt that holds the steering column shaft to the steering gear main shaft.
3. Remove the cotter pin, castellated nut the steering linkage from the pitman arm.
4. Disconnect and plug the fluid lines from the steering gear.
5. Remove the steering gear mounting nuts and remove the gear from the vehicle.
6. Matchmark and remove the pitman arm from the pitman shaft.
7. The installation is the reverse of the removal procedure. Torque the pitman arm nut to 100 ft. lbs. (136 Nm) and the gear mounting nuts to 28 ft. lbs. (38 Nm) on 2WD vehicles or 45 ft. lbs. (61 Nm) on 4WD vehicles.
8. Fill and bleed the system.

Adjustment

1. Attach special tool CT–1108 to the mainshaft and rotate

1. Pinch bolt
2. Pressure hose
3. Return hose
4. Cotter pin
5. Castellated nut
6. Steering linkage
7. Locknuts
8. Steering shaft
9. Power steering gear

Power steering gear and related parts—Raider and Ram 50

the pinion with an inch lb. torque wrench to measure the mainshaft starting torque.

2. The specification is 4–11 inch lbs (0.45–1.25 Nm).
3. If not within specifications, loosen the adjusting cover locknut and adjust by rotating the top cover until the proper starting torque is reached.
4. Tighten the valve housing locknut.

Power Steering Pump

Removal and Installation

1. Disconnect the negative battery cable.
2. Position a drain pan under the power steering pump.
3. Disconnect the fluid lines from the pump and plug them.
4. Remove the front bracket attaching bolts and remove the belt from the pulley.
5. Remove the pump from the vehicle.
6. The installation is the reverse of the removal procedure.
7. Adjust the belt tension, as required.
8. Fill and bleed the system.

Belt Adjustment

1. Loosen the pump mounting bolts. If equipped with tensioner pulley, loosen locknut on tensioner pulley only.
2. Using a prybar, move the pump away from the engine. If equipped with tensioner pulley, tighten the adjuster bolt to move the pulley.
3. Adjust the tension until the belt deflects about ¼–½ in. under a 10 lb. load, tighten the mounting bolts and adjuster bolts as required.

System Bleeding

1. Fill the reservoir with Dexron® II.
2. Raise the front end of the vehicle.
3. Disconnect the ignition coil wire.
4. Simultaneously crank the engine and turn the steering wheel from lock to lock. Repeat this several times.

NOTE: If the bleeding procedure is done with the engine running, high speed rotation of the pump will churn the fluid and create air bubbles filling the system with air. Bleed the system while cranking the engine only.

5. Lower the front end.
6. Connect one end of a tube to the breather plug on the steering box and place the other a container.
7. Start the engine and allow it to idle.
8. Loosen the breather plug and turn the steering wheel from lock to lock continuously until no more air bubbles appear in the fluid coming out the tube.

NOTE: Do not hold the steering wheel all the way against the stop for more than 5 seconds.

9. After the bleeding is done, tighten the breather plug and refill the reservoir.

Tie Rod Ends

Removal and Installation

1. Raise the vehicle and support safely.
2. Remove the cotter pin and nut from the tie rod end stud.
3. Using a puller, remove the tie rod from the steering knuckle or center link.
4. Loosen the sleeve clamp nut, if equipped, and unthread the tie rod end.
5. The installation is the reverse of the removal procedure. Torque the stud nuts to 33 ft. lbs. (45 Nm) and install a new cotter pin.
6. Lubricate the front end.
7. Align the front end.

BRAKES

For all brake system repair and service procedure not detained below, please refer to "Brakes" in the Unit Repair section.

Master Cylinder

Removal and Installation

1. Disconnect the negative battery cable. Disconnect the fluid level sensor connector.
2. Disconnect and plug the brake lines from the master cylinder.
3. Remove the nuts attaching the master cylinder to the power booster.
4. Remove the master cylinder from the mounting studs.
5. Remove the fluid reservoir from the cylinder.

To install:

6. Bench bleed the master cylinder.

Adjusting the load sensing proportioning valve

7. Install master cylinder on power booster studs and install the retaining nuts.

8. Install the brake lines loosely to the master cylinder.

9. Have a helper press down on the brake pedal, holding pedal to the floor. Tighten hydraulic lines at master cylinder. Release brake pedal.

10. Connect the fluid level sensor connector and refill reservoir as required.

Proportioning Valve

Removal and Installation
RAIDER

1. Disconnect the negative battery cable.

2. Raise the vehicle and support safely.

3. Identify and disconnect the brake lines from the proportioning valve.

4. Disconnect the wires to the valve, if any.

5. Remove the proportioning valve from the vehicle.

6. The installation is the reverse of the removal procedure.

7. Bleed the brakes in the following order:
   a. Right rear
   b. Left rear
   c. Right front
   d. Left front

Load Sensing Proportioning Valve

Removal and Installation
RAM 50

1. Disconnect the negative battery cable.

2. Raise the vehicle and support safely.

3. Identify and disconnect the brake lines from the valve.

4. Remove the mounting bolts and remove the valve leaving the spring hanging from the lever.

To install:

5. Install the valve to the vehicle engaging the spring.

6. Connect the brake lines.

7. Bleed the brakes in the following order:
   a. Right rear
   b. Load sensing proportioning valve
   c. Left rear
   d. Right front
   e. Left front

8. Lower the vehicle so the full weight of the vehicle is on the ground. Unload any excess weight that is weighing down the rear of the vehicle. Adjust the load sensing proportioning valve lever so the distance from the proportioning valve lever to the hole in the spring support is about 7 in.

Power Brake Booster

Removal and Installation

1. Disconnect the negative battery cable. Disconnect the vacuum hose from the booster.

2. Remove the nuts attaching the master cylinder to the booster and move the master cylinder to the side. Take care not to damage brake lines.

3. From inside of vehicle, remove the clevis pin that secures the booster pushrod to the brake pedal.

4. Remove the nuts that attach the booster to the dash panel and remove from the vehicle.

5. The installation is the reverse of the removal procedure.

Brake Caliper

Removal and Installation

1. Raise the vehicle and support safely.

2. Remove the tire and wheel assembly. Disconnect the brake line from the caliper.

3. Label and remove the 2 mounting bolts.

4. Lift the caliper off of the caliper support.

5. The installation is the reverse of the removal procedure. Make sure all anti-rattle and -squeal clips and pads are in place. Torque the guide pin bolt to 35 ft. lbs. (47 Nm) and the lock pin bolt to 30 ft. lbs. (41 Nm).

6. Bleed the brakes and road test the vehicle.

Disc Brake Pads

Removal and Installation

1. Remove ½ of the fluid from the master cylinder reservoir.

2. Raise the vehicle and support safely. Remove the tire and wheel assemblies.

3. Remove the calipers.

4. Remove the pads from the adaptor.

To install:

5. Use a large C-clamp to compress the piston into the caliper bore.

6. Install the pads to the adaptor with anti-rattle and anti-squeal clips in place.

7. Install the caliper and secure to the adapter.

8. Refill the master cylinder. Before moving the vehicle, pump brake pedal to seat brake pads against rotors.

9. Bleed the brakes if any brake lines were opened. Check the brake fluid.

Brake Rotor

Removal and Installation

1. Raise the vehicle and support safely.

2. Remove the tire and wheel assembly.

3. Remove the caliper and brake pads.

4. Remove the caliper adaptor.

5. If equipped with 4WD, remove the automatic hub, the shim, lock washer and locknut.

6. If equipped with 2WD, remove the dust cap, cotter pin, nut lock, nut, washer and outer bearing.

7. Remove the front hub and rotor assembly from the spindle.

8. To separate the hub from the rotor, remove the bolts and split the rotor from the hub.

To install:

9. Install the rotor to the hub and torque the attaching nuts and bolts to 40 ft. lbs. (54 Nm).

10. Install the hub and rotor assembly to the spindle and install the retaining nuts and bearings as removed. Adjust bearing preload.

1. Lock pin
2. Adaptor
3. Lock pin sleeve
4. Lock pin boot
5. Guide pin boot
6. Boot ring
7. Piston boot
8. Piston
9. Piston seal
10. Caliper
11. Guide pin
12. Guide pin sleeve
13. Outer anti-squeal plate
14. Brake pads
15. Inner anti-squeal plate
16. Pad and wear indicator
17. Anti-rattle clips

Front brakes—Raider and Ram 50

11. Install the caliper adaptor. Torque the bolts to 70 ft. lbs. (95 Nm).

12. Install the brake pads and caliper, making sure all anti-rattle and anti-squeal clips are in place.

13. Pump the brake pedal to seat the brake pads against the rotors. Bleed the brakes if any brake lines were opened. Check the brake fluid.

14. Install the tire and wheel assembly and road test the vehicle.

Brake Drums

Removal and Installation

1. Raise the vehicle and support safely.
2. Remove the tire and wheel assembly.
3. Remove the drum retaining screw with an impact driver if equipped.
4. Remove the drum. If difficult to remove the drum, remove the adjuster access cover in the backing plate and rotate the star wheel to loosen the adjustment on the rear brake shoes.
5. The installation is the reverse of the removal procedure.

Brake Shoes

Removal and Installation

1. Raise the vehicle and support safely.

2. Remove the tire and wheel assemblies and the brake drums.

3. Remove the upper return spring along with the adjuster.

4. Remove the adjuster spring.

5. Remove the lower retaining spring.

6. Remove the hold-down springs.

7. Remove the shoes, disengaging the parking brake lever.

To install:

8. Clean and dry the backing plate. Lubricate the bosses, anchor contacts and wheel cylinder piston grooves where the top of the shoe fits lightly with lithium based grease.

9. Lubricate the star wheel shaft threads with anti-sieze lubricant and transfer all parts to their proper locations on the new shoes. Make sure the longer end of the upper return spring is installed toward the shoe with the parking brake lever.

10. Spread the shoes apart, engage the parking brake lever and position them on the backing plate making sure the wheel cylinder pins engage the webs of the brake shoes.

11. Install the lower retaining spring and the hold-down springs.

12. Adjust the star wheel until the brake shoes are in contact with the brake drum when installed.

13. Remove any grease from the linings and install the brake drums.

14. Install the tire and wheel assemblies and complete the brake adjustment.

1. Brake drum
2. Upper return spring with adjuster
3. Adjuster spring
4. Lower retaining spring
5. Hold-down spring
6. Brake shoe
7. Brake shoe and parking brake lever
8. Hold-down pin

Rear brake shoes and hardware

Wheel Cylinder

Removal and Installation

1. Raise the vehicle and support safely.
2. Remove the wheel, drum and brake shoes.
3. Remove the hydraulic brake line from the wheel cylinder.
4. Remove the wheel cylinder mounting bolts and remove the cylinder from the backing plate.

To install:

5. Position the wheel cylinder on the backing plate and install the retaining bolts. Torque the bolts to 14 ft. lbs. (19 Nm).
6. Connect the brake line to the wheel cylinder.
7. Lubricate the backing plate and install the brake linings.
8. Install the brake drums, tire and wheel assemblies and adjust the brake linings.
9. Bleed the brakes system and refill the master cylinder reservoir.

Front Parking Brake Cable

Removal and Installation

FLOOR MOUNTED CONTROL

1. Raise the vehicle and support safely.
2. Remove the brake lever cover.
3. Remove the pin securing the cable to the equalizer and slide the cable out of the bracket.
4. Remove the pin or retainer attaching the cable to the handle assembly. Disengage the cable from the handle.
5. Remove the cable grommet from the floor pan and remove the cable from the vehicle.
6. The installation is the reverse of the removal procedure.

EXCEPT FLOOR MOUNTED CONTROL

1. Disconnect negative battery cable. Remove the front cable adjusting nut.
2. Disconnect the remove the parking brake switch from the control.
3. Remove the snapring located on the upper end of the cable.
4. Remove the pawl assembly from the ratchet. Push the parking brake pull rod in, disconnect the cable end from the control pull rod.

5. Remove the retainer clips and screws from the front cable.
6. Raise and safely support the vehicle.
7. Remove the pin securing the cable to the equalizer and disconnect the front cable from the rear brake cable equalizer lever. Remove the cable from the vehicle.

To install:

8. Instal the cable onto the rear brake cable actuator lever. Run cable under the vehicle and secure with retainers.
9. Lower the vehicle. Install cable into passenger compartment, install snapring to secure cable.
10. Attach the end of the cable into the parking brake control pull rod. Install paw and brake switch, adjust as required.
11. Adjust parking brake cables and connect the negative battery cable.

Rear Parking Brake Cable

Removal and Installation

1. Release the parking brakes fully.
2. Raise the vehicle and support safely.
3. Loosen the adjusting nut from the front cable.
4. Remove the brake drums. Remove the shoes, if necessary. Disconnect the cable from the lever.
5. Compress the cable retainer tabs to remove the cable from the backing plate.
6. Remove the cable from the equalizer and remove the retaining bolts from the frame.
7. The installation is the reverse of the removal procedure.

Adjustment

1. Release the parking brakes fully.
2. Raise the vehicle and support safely.
3. Adjust the rear brake linings.
4. Loosen the adjusting nut until there is slack in all the cables.
5. Rotate the rear wheels and tighten the cable adjusting nut until there is a slight drag at the wheels.
6. Continue to rotate the rear wheels and loosen the nut until all drag is eliminated.
7. Back off the nut an additional 2 turns.
8. Apply and release the parking brake several times. Upon

the last release, verify that there is no drag on the wheels. The pedal should depress 4–7 notches.

9. To check operation, make sure the parking brake holds on an incline.

Brake System Bleeding

—————— CAUTION ——————

If using a pressure bleeder, follow the instructions furnished with the unit and choose the correct adaptor for the application. Do not substitute an adapter that "almost fits" as it will not work and could be dangerous.

MASTER CYLINDER

If the master cylinder is off the vehicle it can be bench bled.

1. Connect short piece(s) of brake line to the outlet fitting(s), bend them until the free end is below the fluid level in the master cylinder reservoirs.

2. Fill the reservoir with fresh brake fluid. Pump the piston slowly until no more air bubbles appear in the reservoir(s).

3. Disconnect the lines, refill the master cylinder and securely install the cylinder cap.

4. If the master cylinder is on the vehicle, it can still be bled, using a flare nut wrench.

5. Open the brake line(s) slightly with the flare nut wrench while pressure is applied to the brake pedal by a helper inside the vehicle.

6. Be sure to tighten the line before the brake pedal is released.

7. Repeat the process with both lines until no air bubbles come out.

CALIPERS AND WHEEL CYLINDERS

1. Fill the master cylinder with fresh brake fluid. Check the level often during the procedure.

2. Starting with the right rear wheel, remove the protective cap from the bleeder and place where it will not be lost. Clean the bleed screw.

—————— CAUTION ——————

When bleeding the brakes, keep face away from the brake area. Spewing fluid may cause facial and/or visual damage. Do not allow brake fluid to spill on the car's finish; it will remove the paint.

3. If the system is empty, the most effecient way to get fluid down to the wheel is to loosen the bleeder about ½–¾ turn, place a finger firmly over the bleeder and have a helper pump the brakes slowly until fluid comes out the bleeder. Once fluid is at the bleeder, close it before the pedal is released inside the vehicle.

NOTE: If the pedal is pumped rapidly, the fluid will churn and create small air bubbles, which are almost impossible to remove from the system. These air bubbles will eventually congregate and a spongy pedal will result.

4. Once fluid has been pumped to the caliper or wheel cylinder, open the bleed screw again, have the helper press the brake pedal to the floor, lock the bleeder and have the helper slowly release the pedal. Wait 15 seconds and repeat the procedure (including the 15 second wait) until no more air comes out of the bleeder upon application of the brake pedal. Remember to close the bleeder before the pedal is released inside the vehicle each time the bleeder is opened. If not, air will be induced into the system.

5. If a helper is not available, connect a small hose to the bleeder, place the end in a container of brake fluid and proceed to pump the pedal from inside the vehicle until no more air comes out the bleeder. The hose will prevent air from entering the system.

6. Repeat the procedure on remaining wheel cylinders in order:
   a. Left rear
   b. Right front
   c. Left front

7. Hydraulic brake systems must be totally flushed if the fluid becomes contaminated with water, dirt or other corrosive chemicals. To flush, bleed the entire system until all fluid has been replaced with new fluid.

8. Install the bleeder cap(s) on the bleeder to keep dirt out. Always road test the vehicle after brake work of any kind is done.

FRONT SUSPENSION

Shock Absorbers

Removal and Installation

1. Raise and safely support the vehicle. Remove the upper shock nut, washer and bushing.

2. Raise the vehicle fully and support safely.

3. Remove the lower mounting bolt(s) and discard the shock.

4. The installation is the reverse of the removal procedure.

Coil Spring

Removal and Installation

1. Raise the vehicle and support safely.

2. Remove the shock absorber.

3. Disconnect the stabilizer bar from the lower control arm.

4. Install spring compressor tool MB990792 or equivalent, to the coil spring and to compress the spring.

5. Remove the cotter pin and lower ball joint nut.

6. Release the lower ball joint taper using Chrysler tool C–3564–A.

7. Remove the tool and the ball stud from the control arm. Release the compressor tool from the coil spring.

8. Pull the arm down and remove the spring with the rubber isolation pad from the vehicle.

To install:

9. Install the spring with the rubber isolator. Install the compressor tool and compress spring so the lower ball joint can be inserted through the knuckle.

10. Torque the lower ball joint nut to 100 ft. lbs. (136 Nm). Install a new cotter pin. Remove the spring compressor.

11. Connect the sway bar to the lower control arm, if equipped.

12. Install the shock absorber. Install the wheel and tire assembly.

Torsion Bar

Removal and Installation

1. Raise the vehicle and support safely. Remove skid plate, if equipped.

2. Support the lower control arm at a point away from the torsion bar mounting point to the arm.

Aligning the front of the torsion bar with the front anchor

Measure this distance when installing the torsion bar to the rear anchor

Measure this distance to initially set the riding height

Measure this distance to set the riding height

old bar is being reused. If a new bar has been installed, tighten the nut so the exposed length of the bolt threads is the specification:
    Raider left side—2.4 in.
    Raider right side—2.8 in.
    Ram 50 left side—3.9 in.
    Ram 50 right side—3.4 in.
10. Fill the dust covers with grease and fold them back into position.
11. Adjust the torsion to the correct riding height.

Adjusting the Torsion Bar

1. Lower the vehicle so its full weight is on the ground. If there is any excess weight in the vehicle, unload it.
2. To set the riding height, measure the distance from the rebound bumper to its stopper bracket on the frame. Adjust the torsion bar nut until that distance is within the specification:
    Raider—2.8 in.
    Ram 50—3.1 in.
3. If, after adjusting the riding height, the exposed portion of the adjusting bolt is protruding up or down far enough to interferes with any front suspension component or is hanging down too low, the bar must be removed and repositioned.
4. Road test the vehicle and remeasure the riding height. Readjust if necessary.

3. Fold the dust covers back and slide them away from the ends of the bar.
4. If the bars are to be reused, matchmark the torsion bar at both ends to the anchor and identify left from right.
5. Paint or measure the distance of the exposed threads of the rear mounting bolt down to the nut to aid in adjustment when installing. Remove the rear anchor arm mounting nut and bolt.
6. Remove the torsion bar from the front anchor arm.
To install:
7. If the bar is being reused, lubricate the ends and install the torsion bar aligning the matchmarks. If a new bar is being used, align the white stripe on the front splines with the mark on the anchor. There is a mark on the front of the torsion bar to differentiate between left and right. Do not install the bar with the mark facing the rear.
8. Install the torsion bar to the rear anchor so the length of the mounting bolt from the nut to the head of the bolt is the specified length with the rebound bumper in contact with the crossmember. The specifications are as follows:
    Raider left side—5.3–5.6 in.
    Raider right side—4.9–5.2 in.
    Ram 50 left side—5.5–5.9 in.
    Ram 50 right side—5.3–5.8 in.
9. To initially set the riding height, tighten the rear anchor mounting nut to the same point at which it was removed if the

Upper Ball Joint

Inspection

With the control arm removed, check the starting torque required to turn the ball stud. The specification for all vehicles is 7–30 inch lbs.

Removal and Installation

NOTE: The upper ball joint and upper control arm must be replaced as an assembly on Ram 50.

1. Raise the vehicle and support safely. Release the tension on the torsion bar and remove the upper control arm from the vehicle.
2. Remove the ring and boot from the ball joint. Remove the snapring.
3. Remove the ball joint from the control arm using special tool sets MB990800 and MB990799.

1. Shock absorber
   mounting nuts
2. Shock absorber
3. Cotter pin
4. Castellated nut
5. Rebound bumper
6. Alignment shims
7. Upper control arm

60 FT. LBS.
(81 NM)

Front suspension components—2WD Ram 50

To install:

4. Align the mating mark on the upper ball joint with the mark on the arm.

5. Press the ball joint in using the same tools that were used to remove the ball joint.

6. Install the snapring. If the snapring is loose, replace with a new one.

7. Fill the boot with grease and install the boot and ring.

8. Install the upper control arm.

9. Lubricate the ball joint with a grease gun.

10. Adjust the riding height, if equipped with a torsion bar and align the front end.

Lower Ball Joint

Inspection

With the control arm removed, check the up and down end-play of the ball stud. If it exceeds 0.02 in. (0.5mm), the ball joint should be replaced.

Removal and Installation

1. Raise the vehicle and support safely. Remove the lower control arm.

2. Remove the ball joint retaining nuts and bolts and remove the ball joint from the arm.

3. The installation is the reverse of the removal procedure. Torque the ball joint retaining nuts and bolts to 50 ft. lbs. (68 Nm) on 4WD vehicles or 28 ft. lbs. (38 Nm) on 2WD vehicles. Torque the ball stud nut to 100 ft. lbs. (136 Nm) and install a new cotter pin.

4. Lubricate the ball joint with a grease gun.

5. Adjust the riding height, if equipped with a torsion bar.

6. Align the front suspension.

Upper Control Arm

Removal and Installation

2WD RAM 50

1. Raise the vehicle and support safely. Remove the tire and wheel assembly.

1. Skid plate
2. Under cover
3. Torsion bar
4. Cotter pin
5. Lower ball joint
6. Stabilizer bar nut
7. Stabilizer bar
8. Shock absorber mounting bolts
9. Lower arm shaft
10. Front anchor arm
11. Lower control arm
12. Rebound bumper
13. Ball joint mounting nuts

100 FT. LBS. (136 NM)

110 FT. LBS. (149 NM)

80 FT. LBS. (109 NM)

Front suspension components—4WD Vehicle

2. Remove the shock absorber.

3. Install Chrysler tool DD–1278 or equivalent, to the coil spring and compress the spring.

4. Remove the cotter pin and upper ball joint nut.

5. Suspend the rotor assembly so there is not excessive pull on the brake hose.

6. Release the upper ball joint taper using Chrysler tool C–3564–A or equivalent.

7. Remove the tool and remove the ball stud from the knuckle.

8. Loosen the pivot bar retaining nuts and bolts, identify and remove the alignment shims, remove the nuts and bolts and remove the arm from the vehicle.

To install:

9. Install the arm to the frame rail bracket, install the shims in their original locations and install the retaining nuts and bolts. Torque the nuts initially to 40 ft. lbs. (54 Nm).

10. Torque the ball joint nut to 60 ft. lbs. (81 Nm). Install a new cotter pin. Remove the spring compressor.

11. Install the shock absorber.

12. Align the front end. When all settings are at specifications, torque the pivot bar retaining bolts to 80 ft. lbs. (109 Nm).

RAIDER AND 4WD RAM 50

1. Raise the vehicle and support safely. Remove the skid plate.

2. Remove the shock absorber.

3. Turn the torsion bar adjustment nut counterclockwise to relieve all tension from the torsion bar. Disconnect the brake hose from the brake line and remove the hose from the bracket.

4. Remove the cotter pin from the upper ball stud.

5. Release the upper ball joint taper using Chrysler tool C–3564–A or equivalent. Remove the tool. Remove the ball stud from the steering knuckle.

6. Loosen the pivot bar retaining nuts and bolts, identify and remove the alignment shims, remove the nuts and bolts.

7. Remove the control arm from the vehicle.

To install:

8. Position the arm at the frame rail bracket.

9. Install the shims in their original locations and install the

retaining nuts and bolts. Torque the nuts initially to 40 ft. lbs. (54 Nm).

10. Insert the upper ball stud in the steering knuckle arm bore and install the nut. Torque the nut to 60 ft. lbs. (81 Nm) and install a new cotter pin. Install the shock absorber and attach the brake hose.

11. Turn the torsion bar adjustment nut clockwise to apply a load on the bar.

12. Lower the vehicle.

13. Set the riding height. Align the front end. When all settings are at specifications, torque the pivot bar retaining bolts to 80 ft. lbs. (109 Nm).

Lower Control Arm

Removal and Installation

2WD RAM 50

1. Raise the vehicle and support safely.
2. Remove the shock absorber.
3. Disconnect the sway bar and strut bar from the lower control arm.
4. Install Chrysler spring compressor tool DD–1278 or equivalent, to the coil spring and compress the spring.
5. Remove the cotter pin and lower ball joint nut.
6. Release the lower ball joint taper using Chrysler tool C–3564–A or equivalent.
7. Remove the tool and remove the ball stud from the knuckle. Remove the spring compressor.
8. Pull the arm down and remove the spring with the rubber isolation pad from the vehicle. Remove the lower arm shaft mounting nuts and remove the arm from the vehicle.

To install:

9. Install the arm to the crossmember finger-tight. Install the spring with the rubber isolators. Install the compressor tool and compress spring so lower ball joint can be inserted through the knuckle.
10. Torque the lower ball joint slotted nut to 100 ft. lbs. (136 Nm). Install a new cotter pin. Remove the spring compressor.
11. Connect the sway bar and strut bar to the lower control arm.
12. Install the shock absorber.
13. Lower the vehicle completely. With the weight of the vehicle on suspension torque the lower control arm to crossmember mounting nut to 50 ft. lbs. (68 Nm).
14. Align the front suspension.

RAIDER AND 4WD RAM 50

1. Raise the vehicle and support safely.
2. Remove the skid plate.
3. Remove the torsion bar, anchors and lower arm shaft.
4. Remove the shock absorber lower attaching bolt.
5. Disconnect the stabilizer bar from the lower control arm.
6. Remove the cotter pin and the nut from the lower ball stud. Separate the lower ball stud from the steering knuckle using a puller.
7. Remove the pivot bolts and remove the arm from the vehicle.

To install:

8. Install the new control arm to the vehicle.
9. Install the pivot bolts, but do not torque.
10. Insert the ball stud into the steering knuckle bore. Install the slotted nut, torque to 100 ft. lbs. (136 Nm) and install a new cotter pin.
11. Attach the stabilizer bar to the control arm. Install the shock mount bolts.
12. Install the torsion bar and turn the adjustment bolt clockwise to apply a load to the bar.
13. Lower the vehicle so weight of the vehicle is on suspension.
14. Torque the pivot nuts to 110 ft. lbs. (149 Nm).
15. Set the riding height.
16. Align the front suspension.

Stabilizer Bar

Removal and Installation

1. Raise the vehicle and support safely.
2. Remove the front sway bar brackets and retainers.
3. Remove the sway bar support brackets and bushings from the lower control arm. Remove the sway bar from the vehicle.
4. The installation is the reverse of the removal procedure.

Front Wheel Bearings

For 4WD applications, please refer to "Drive Axles" in the Unit Repair section.

Adjustment

1. Tighten the wheel bearing nut to 22 ft. lbs. (30 Nm) while turning the rotor.
2. Loosen the wheel bearing adjusting nut completely.
3. Tighten the nut to 6 ft. lbs. (8 Nm).
4. Check the wheel bearing end-play. The specification is 0.001–0.003 in.
5. Install the nut lock and cotter pin.

Removal and Installation

1. Raise the vehicle and support safely.
2. Remove the tire and wheel assembly.
3. Remove the caliper, disc brake pads and adaptor.
4. Remove the dust cap.
5. Remove the cotter pin, castellated nut lock, wheel bearing nut and washer from the spindle.
6. Remove the outer wheel bearing.
7. Remove the hub and rotor assembly with the inner intact. Remove the grease seal and inner wheel bearing.

To install:

8. Lubricate and install the inner wheel bearing. Install a new grease seal.
9. Install the hub and rotor assembly to the spindle.
10. Lubricate and install the outer wheel bearing, washer and nut. When the bearing preload is properly set, install the nut lock and a new cotter pin.
11. Install the grease cap.
12. Install the brake pads and caliper.
13. Install the tire and wheel assembly.

REAR SUSPENSION

Shock Absorber

Removal and Installation

1. Raise the vehicle and support safely. If equipped with rear coil springs, support the rear axle using the proper equipment.
2. Remove the bolts that attach the shock to the frame or bracket.
3. Remove the shock from the vehicle.
4. The installation is the reverse of the removal procedure.

1. Coil spring
2. Axle bumper
3. Lower arm rear bushing
4. Lower control arm
5. Lower arm front bushing
6. Stabilizer bar
7. Shock absorber
8. Lateral arm bushing
9. Lateral arm

Coil spring rear suspension—Raider

Coil Springs

Removal and Installation

RAIDER WITH 3.0L ENGINE

1. Raise the vehicle and support safely. Remove the parking bake cable attaching bolt.
2. Using the proper equipment, support the weight of the axle.
3. Remove the bolt that attaches the lateral rod to the body.
4. Remove the lower shock mounting bolts.
5. Lower the axle and remove the coil springs with their seats.
6. The installation is the reverse of the removal procedure.

Leaf Springs

Removal and Installation

1. Raise the vehicle and support safely. Remove the parking bake cable attaching bolt.
2. Using the proper equipment, support the weight of the axle.
3. Remove the nuts, washers and U-bolts attaching the springs to the axle housing. Remove the seat and spacer.
4. Remove the spring shackle bolts, shackle and spring front bolt.
5. Remove the springs from the vehicle.
6. The installation is the reverse of the removal procedure. Make sure all shackle mounting nuts are on the inside of the springs. Torque the front spring mount nut to 116 ft. lbs. (160 Nm) and the rear shackle nuts to 43 ft. lbs. (60 Nm). Torque U-bolt nuts to 87 ft. lbs. (120 Nm).

SPECIFICATIONS

ENGINE IDENTIFICATION

Year	Model	Engine Displacement cu. in. (cc)	Engine Series Identification (VIN)	No. of Cylinders	Engine Type
1990	Rocky	97.0 (1589/1.6L)	—	4	SOHC
1991-92	Rocky	97.0 (1589/1.6L)	—	4	SOHC

SOHC—Single Overhead Cam

GENERAL ENGINE SPECIFICATIONS

Year	Model	Engine Displacement cu. in. (cc)	Fuel System Type	Net Horsepower @ rpm	Net Torque @ rpm (ft. lbs.)	Bore × Stroke (in.)	Compression Ratio	Oil Pressure @ rpm
1990	Rocky	97.0 (1589)	MPFI	94 @ 5700	94 @ 3200	2.99 × 3.45	9.5:1	35.6–71.0①
1991-92	Rocky	97.0 (1589)	MPFI	94 @ 5700	94 @ 3200	2.99 × 3.45	9.5:1	35.6–71.0①

MPFI—Multiport Fuel Injection
① @ 3000 rpm

GASOLINE ENGINE TUNE-UP SPECIFICATIONS

Year	Model	Engine Displacement cu. in. (cc)	Spark Plugs Type	Gap (in.)	Ignition Timing (deg.) MT	AT	Compression Pressure (psi)	Fuel Pump (psi)	Idle Speed (rpm) MT	AT	Valve Clearance In.	Ex.
1990	Rocky	97.0 (1589)	BKRGE-11	0.039–0.043	3	NA	149–199	36.3	850	NA	0.008–0.012	0.011–0.015
1991	Rocky	97.0 (1589)	BKRGE-11	0.039–0.043	3	NA	149–199	36.3	850	NA	0.008–0.012	0.011–0.015
1992	SEE UNDERHOOD STICKER											

NA—Not Available

FIRING ORDERS

NOTE: To avoid confusion, always replace spark plug wires one at a time.

1.6L Engine
Engine Firing Order: 1–3–4–2
Distributor Rotation: Counterclockwise

CAPACITIES

Year	Model	VIN	Engine Displacement cu. in. (cc)	Engine Crankcase with Filter	Engine Crankcase without Filter	Transmission (pts.) 4-Spd	Transmission (pts.) 5-Spd	Transmission (pts.) Auto.	Drive Axle (pts.)	Fuel Tank (gal.)	Cooling System (qts.)
1990	Rocky	NA	97.0 (1589)	3.5	3.3	NA	3.2	NA	①	15.9	6.1
1991-92	Rocky	NA	97.0 (1589)	3.5	3.3	NA	3.2	NA	①	15.9	6.1

NA—Not Available
① Front—1.7 pts.
  Rear—3.7 pts.

CAMSHAFT SPECIFICATIONS

All measurements are given in inches

Year	Engine Displacement cu. in. (cc)	Journal Diameter 1	2	3	4	5	Lobe Lift In.	Lobe Lift Ex.	Bearing Clearance	Camshaft End Play
1990	97.0 (1589)	NA	NA	NA	NA	NA	1.302–1.310	1.299–1.307	0.0014–① 0.0029	0.0067
1991-92	97.0 (1589)	NA	NA	NA	NA	NA	1.302–1.310	1.299–1.307	0.0014–① 0.0029	0.0067

NA—Not available
① 0.0067 limit

CRANKSHAFT AND CONNECTING ROD SPECIFICATIONS

All measurements are given in inches

Year	Engine Displacement cu. in. (cc)	Crankshaft Main Brg. Journal Dia.	Main Brg. Oil Clearance	Shaft End-play	Thrust on No.	Connecting Rod Journal Diameter	Oil Clearance	Side Clearance
1990	97.0 (1589)	1.9676–1.9685	0.0010–0.0016	0.006–0.018	3	0.858–0.860	0.0008–0.0017	NA
1991-92	97.0 (1589)	1.9676–1.9685	0.0010–0.0016	0.006–0.018	3	0.858–0.860	0.0008–0.0017	NA

NA—Not available

VALVE SPECIFICATIONS

Year	Engine Displacement cu. in. (cc)	Seat Angle (deg.)	Face Angle (deg.)	Spring Test Pressure (lbs.)	Spring Installed Height (in.)	Stem-to-Guide Clearance (in.) Intake	Exhaust	Stem Diameter (in.) Intake	Exhaust
1990	97 (1589)	45	45.5	58.2	1.5	0.0008–0.0024	0.0010–0.0025	NA	NA
1991-92	97 (1589)	45	45.5	58.2	1.5	0.0008–0.0024	0.0010–0.0025	NA	NA

NA—Not available

PISTON AND RING SPECIFICATIONS

All measurements are given in inches

| Year | Engine Displacement cu. in. (cc) | Piston Clearance | Ring Gap | | | Ring Side Clearance | | |
			Top Compression	Bottom Compression	Oil Control	Top Compression	Bottom Compression	Oil Control
1990	97.0 (1598)	0.0010–0.0018	0.0107–0.0165	0.0138–0.0196	0.008–0.028	0.0012–0.0027	0.0008–0.0023	—
1991–92	97.0 (1598)	0.0010–0.0018	0.0107–0.0165	0.0138–0.0196	0.008–0.028	0.0012–0.0027	0.0008–0.0023	—

TORQUE SPECIFICATIONS

All readings are given in ft. lbs.

| Year | Engine Displacement cu. in. (cc) | Cylinder Head Bolts | Main Bearing Bolts | Rod Bearing Bolts | Crankshaft Pulley Bolts | Flywheel Bolts | Manifold | | Spark Plugs |
							Intake	Exhaust	
1990	97.0 (1589)	43.4–49.2	32.5–39.8	25.4–32.5	65.1–72.0	57.9–72.3	10.8–15.9	21.7–32.5	10.8–15.9
1991–92	97.0 (1589)	43.4–49.2	32.5–39.8	25.4–32.5	65.1–72.0	57.9–72.3	10.8–15.9	21.7–32.5	10.8–15.9

BRAKE SPECIFICATIONS

All measurements are given in inches

| Year | Model | Lug Nut Torque (ft. lbs.) | Master Cylinder Bore | Brake Disc | | Standard Brake Drum Diameter | Minimum Lining Thickness | |
				Minimum Thickness	Maximum Runout		Front	Rear
1990	Rocky	65.1–87.0	0.875	0.49	0.45	10.00	0.06	0.04
1990–91	Rocky	65.1–87.0	0.875	0.49	0.45	10.00	0.06	0.04

WHEEL ALIGNMENT

| Year | Model | Caster | | Camber | | Toe-in (in.) | Steering Axis Inclination (deg.) |
		Range (deg.)	Preferred Setting (deg.)	Range (deg.)	Preferred Setting (deg.)		
1990	Rocky	1½P–2½P	2P	0–1P	1P	1/16N–1/16P	9
1991–92	Rocky	1½P–2½P	2P	0–1P	1P	1/16N–1/16P	9

N—Negative
P—Positive

ENGINE ELECTRICAL

NOTE: Disconnecting the negative battery cable on some vehicles may interfere with the functions of the on board computer systems and may require the computer to undergo a relearning process, once the negative battery cable is reconnected.

Distributor

Removal

1. Remove the negative battery terminal from the battery.
2. Disconnect vacuum hose and electrical connections.

NOTE: Do not bend or twist the spark plug wires to avoid internal damage. Grip the wire boot when removing or installing the wires.

3. Remove the distributor cap.
4. Mark the rotor position on the distributor housing and the distributor housing position on the engine.
5. Remove the distributor set bolt and remove the distributor.

Installation

TIMING NOT DISTURBED

1. Align the matchmarks on the distributor housing and on the engine to install properly and reverse the the removal procedure.
2. Set the timing to specification.

TIMING DISTURBED

1. Rotate the crankshaft in the clockwise position until the specified timing mark on the flywheel aligns with the timing matchmark on the engine.

Timing marks

Disconnection and plugging of vacuum hose at distributor

NOTE: After aligning the 2 marks, remove the cylinder head cover to visually confirm that the rocker arms are not riding on the camshaft cams at No. 1 cylinder. If the arms are found to be riding on the cams, turn the crankshaft 360 degrees to realign the 2 marks.

2. Position the rotor to the No. 1 cylinder position and install the distributor.
3. Re-attach the vacuum and electrical connections.
4. Adjust the ignition timing.

Ignition Timing

Adjustment

1. Start the engine and warm up to normal operating temperature. Prior to any adjustment, be sure all electrical accessories are **OFF**.
2. Check and/or adjust the idle speed.
3. Connect tachometer cable to negative terminal of the ignition coil.
4. Connect the timing light to the No. 1 cylinder spark plug wire.
5. Disconnect and plug the vacuum hose at the vacuum advance of the distributor.
6. With the engine running at the specified idle speed, direct the timing light to the crankshaft pulley. If the specified timing mark on the timing tab is aligned with the timing notch on the crankshaft pulley the ignition is properly timed.
7. If the timing is out of adjustment, loosen the distributor attaching bolt and adjust the distributor position to advance or retard the timing. Turn the distributor clockwise to advance the timing and counterclockwise to retard the timing.
8. After the adjustment, tighten the attaching bolt and recheck the timing.

Alternator

For further information, please refer to "Alternators" in the Unit Repair section.

Precautions

Several precautions must be observed with alternator equipped vehicles to avoid damage to the unit.
• If the battery is removed for any reason, make sure it is reconnected with the correct polarity. Reversing the battery connections may result in damage to the one-way rectifiers.
• When utilizing a booster battery as a starting aid, always connect the positive to positive terminals and the negative terminal from the booster battery to a good engine ground on the vehicle being started.
• Never use a fast charger as a booster to start vehicles.
• Disconnect the battery cables when charging the battery with a fast charger.
• Never attempt to polarize the alternator.
• Do not use test lights of more than 12 volts when checking diode continuity.
• Do not short across or ground any of the alternator terminals.
• The polarity of the battery, alternator and regulator must be matched and considered before making any electrical connections within the system.
• Never separate the alternator on an open circuit. Make sure all connections within the circuit are clean and tight.
• Disconnect the battery ground terminal when performing any service on electrical components.
• Disconnect the battery if arc welding is to be done on the vehicle.

Belt Tension Adjustment

1. Disconnect the negative battery cable.
2. Loosen the alternator bolt and pivot bolts.
3. Adjust the belt tension to 0.20–0.24 in. of deflection using a belt tension gauge placed half way between the top pulleys and the lower pulley.

Removal and Installation

1. Disconnect the negative battery cable.
2. Disconnect the wire coupler and lead wire from the alternator.
3. Remove the alternator mounting bolt and alternator belt adjusting bolt.
4. Remove alternator from the vehicle.
5. Installation is the reverse of the removal procedure. Adjust the drive belt tension.

Starter

For further information, please refer to "Starters" in the Unit Repair section.

Starter bolt location

Removal and Installation

1. Disconnect the negative battery cable.
2. Raise and support the vehicle safely.
3. Disconnect the lead wire and battery cable from the starter motor.
4. Support the starter and remove the mounting bolt.
5. Remove the starter.
6. Installation is the reverse of the removal procedure.

CHASSIS ELECTRICAL

Heater Blower Motor

Removal and Installation

1. Disconnect the negative battery cable.
2. Remove the glove compartment box.
3. Remove the instrument panel reinforcement.
4. Disconnect the electrical wire connector at the blower assembly.
5. Remove the 2 clamp bolts and remove the blower motor.
6. Installation is the reverse of the removal procedure.

Removal of Instrument cluster

Windshield Wiper Motor

Removal and Installation

1. Disconnect the negative battery cable.
2. Disconnect the electrical connector at the wiper motor.
3. Remove the 4 mounting bolts.
4. Disconnect the motor from the linkage. Remove the wiper motor.
5. Installation is the reverse of the removal procedure.

Instrument Cluster

Removal and Installation

1. Disconnect the negative battery cable.
2. Remove the lower instrument panel cover.
3. Loosen but do not remove the 2 upper steering column mounting bolts. Lower and support the steering column, if necessary.
4. Remove the instrument cluster cover by removing the 2 screws.
5. Remove the side cluster panel covers by removing the 4 screws.
6. Disconnect and tag the rear window defogger switch and the hazard warning switch.
7. Remove the 2 screws from the instrument cluster.
8. Disconnect the speedometer cable and the wire connector from the cluster.
9. Remove the instrument cluster.
10. Installation is the reverse of the removal procedure.

Combination Switch

The combination switch incorporates the turn signal, windshield wiper, dimmer and headlight switches.

Removal and Installation

1. Disconnect the negative battery cable.
2. Remove the horn pad assembly and disconnect horn wire.
3. Remove the steering wheel nut and remove the steering wheel.
4. Remove the upper and lower instrument finish panels.
5. Remove the upper and lower column cover screws and remove the covers.
6. Disconnect the wiring connector at the combination switch.
7. Remove the combination switch assembly screws.
8. Remove the combination switch from the steering column.
9. Installation is the reverse of the removal procedure.

Ignition Switch

Removal and Installation

1. Disconnect the negative battery cable.
2. Remove the steering wheel from the vehicle.
3. Remove the gauge cluster cover panel.
4. Remove the steering column upper and lower cover panels.
5. Disconnect wire connector at the ignition switch.
6. Remove the mounting bolts and remove the switch assembly.
7. Installation is the reverse of the removal procedure.

Ignition Lock

Removal and Installation

1. Disconnect the negative battery cable.
2. Remove the steering wheel from the vehicle.
3. Remove the gauge cluster cover panel.
4. Remove the steering column upper and lower cover panels.
5. Disconnect wire connector at the ignition switch.
6. Remove the mounting bolts and remove the switch assembly.
7. Set the key to **ACC** position.

8. Push in the lock button and draw out the ignition cylinder.
9. Installation is the reverse of the removal procedure.

Stoplight Switch

Removal and Installation

1. Disconnect the negative battery cable.
2. Push the brake pedal down and remove the stoplight locknut.
3. Disconnect the wire connector at the switch.
4. Remove the switch from the bracket.
5. Install the new switch on the bracket.
6. Adjust the switch so there is 0.02–0.04 in. clearance.
7. Replace the locknut and tighten to 7.5–10.5 ft. lbs.
8. Replace the negative battery cable.

Fuses and Relays

Location

FUSE BOX

The main fuse box is located under the dashboard on the drivers side.

RELAY BOX

The relay box under the hood is located next to the battery.

Computer

Location

The computer is located under the dash on the passenger's side.

Flashers

Location

The hazard warning and turn signal flashers are located under the dash on the driver's side.

ENGINE COOLING

Radiator

Removal and Installation

1. Disconnect the negative battery cable.
2. Drain the cooling system.
3. Remove the reserve tank and temporarily disconnect the power steering vane pump.
4. Remove upper and lower hoses from the radiator.
5. Remove the clamps for the clutch cable on the fan shroud.
6. Remove air cleaner and hose assembly.
7. Remove the 2 radiator shroud bolts and disconnect the lock section at the bottom of the shroud.
8. Remove the 4 radiator retaining bolts and remove the radiator.

To install:

9. Install the radiator mounting bolts and install the radiator.
10. Install fan shroud bolts.
11. Install air cleaner assembly and reinstall all hoses.
12. Install clutch cable clamps on fan shroud.
13. Install power steering vane pump.
14. Refill the cooling system.
15. Reconnect the negative battery cable.

Heater Core

For further information, please refer to Chilton's Air Conditioning and Heating Manual.

Removal and Installation

FRONT

1. Disconnect the negative battery cable. Drain the cooling system.
2. Remove the steering wheel and column covers.
3. Disconnect rear heater switch connector.
4. Remove duct below steering wheel and disconnect instrument panel wire connector.
5. Remove instrument panel cover and disconnect speedometer cable and wire connectors.
6. Remove speedometer cluster.
7. Remove the glove box door.
8. Disconnect the connectors for heater and air conditioner controls.
9. Disconnect heater control cables.
10. Remove defroster nozzles.
11. Remove dash panel hole covers and remove mounting screws.

Exploded view of water pump assembly

12. Remove the dashboard assembly from vehicle.
13. Remove defroster ductwork assembly.
14. Remove center dash support.
15. Remove blower motor assembly.
16. Remove the 4 heater attaching screws and pull out heater case.
17. Disconnect the heater hoses from the heater core tubes and remove assembly.
To install:
18. Install the heater core hoses and install the heater case.
19. Install the blower motor assembly.
20. Install the instrument panel supports and the defroster ductwork.
21. Install the instrument panel and all related parts.
22. Connect the heater control cables and electrical connectors.
23. Install the glove box door assembly.
24. Fill the cooling system with coolant.
25. Connect the negative battery cable, run the engine until the thermostat opens and fill the radiator completely.
26. Check for leaks. Once the engine has cooled, recheck the coolant level.
27. Check the electrical system for proper operation.

REAR

1. Disconnect the negative battery terminal.
2. Remove the passenger side front seat by removing the 4 bolts.
3. Disconnect the 2 heater hoses from the rear heater assembly and plug the hoses.
4. Disconnect the electrical connector and remove the heater assembly by removing the 2 nuts and the 2 bolts.
To install:
5. Install the heater assembly and replace the 2 nuts and 2 bolts.
6. Connect the electrical connector and the 2 water hoses.
7. Install the front seat and connect the negative battery terminal.

Water Pump

Removal and Installation

1. Disconnect the negative battery terminal.
2. Drain the cooling system.

3. Remove the air cleaner and air cleaner hose assembly.
4. Remove the radiator reserve tank.
5. If equipped, loosen the power steering tension and remove the belt. If equipped, loosen the air conditioning belt tension and remove the belt.
6. Remove the fan shroud.
7. Remove the 4 water pump attaching nuts and remove the fan and fluid coupling.
8. Remove the crankshaft pulley attaching bolts and remove the pulley.
9. Remove the timing belt cover mounting bolts and remove the cover.
10. Loosen the timing belt tensioner bolt and remove the timing belt.
11. Remove the 4 water pump mounting bolts and remove the water pump assembly.
12. Clean and inspect the gasket mounting surface of the engine before installation.
To install:
13. Using a new gasket, install the new water pump on the engine. Torque the mounting bolts to 10.8–15.9 ft. lbs.
14. Align the marks on the timing belt and the camshaft sprocket. Install the timing belt in the same position on the camshaft sprocket as when removed.
15. Adjust the timing belt to be free of any slack.
16. Install the timing belt cover, crankshaft pulley and the fan.
17. Replace fan shroud and belts. Adjust the belt tension.
18. Refill the cooling system with the proper coolant and replace the negative battery cable.

Thermostat removal and installation

Thermostat

Removal and Installation

1. Disconnect the negative battery cable.
2. Drain the cooling system.
3. If equipped, remove power steering pump assembly.
4. Remove the radiator hose from the water inlet.
5. Remove the water inlet and remove the thermostat.

To install:

6. Install the new thermostat with the new spring facing towards the engine.
7. Replace the water inlet and torque the bolts to 4.4–6.5 ft. lbs.
8. Replace the power steering pump, if equipped.
9. Refill the cooling system with the proper coolant and replace the negative battery cable.

FUEL SYSTEM

Fuel System Service Precaution

When working with the fuel system, certain precautions should be taken; always work in a well ventilated area, keep a dry chemical (Class B) fire extinguisher near the work area. Always disconnect the negative battery cable and do not make any repairs to the fuel system until all the necessary steps for repair have been reviewed.

Relieving Fuel System Pressure

1. Disconnect the negative battery terminal.
2. Remove the fuel filler cap from the fuel filler neck to release the fuel vapor pressure in the fuel tank.
3. Place an appropriate container under the fuel filter.
4. Cover the plug bolt on the fuel filter inlet union bolt with a rag and loosen the plug bolt slowly to release the fuel pressure gradually.
5. When the pressure has been released, tighten the plug bolt so the fuel does not leak.
6. Reconnect the negative battery cable.

Fuel Tank

Removal and Installation

1. Disconnect the negative battery cable.
2. Raise and support the vehicle safely.
3. Remove the fuel tank cover mounting screws and remove the cover.
4. Disconnect all fuel inlet, outlet and vent lines.
5. Disconnect fuel gauge wire connector.
6. Remove fuel tank mounting screws and lower tank.
7. Installation is the reverse of the removal procedure.

Fuel Filter

Removal and Installation

1. Disconnect the negative battery cable.

2. Remove the fuel filler cap to release the fuel vapor pressure in the tank.
3. Release the fuel pressure.
4. Disconnect the inlet and outlet hoses from the fuel filter.
5. Remove the fuel filter from the firewall.
6. Installation is the reverse of the removal procedure.

Electric Fuel Pump

Pressure Testing

1. Remove the fuel filler cap to release fuel vapor pressure in the fuel tank. Reinstall the cap.
2. Release the fuel presssure in the fuel feed line.
3. Remove the union bolt on the fuel filter and connect the proper fuel pressure gauge at the bolt.

NOTE: If the pressure in the fuel tank is not released prior to system service, the fuel in the fuel tank may be forced out through the fuel hoses during disconnection.

4. Measure the fuel pressure under each of the following conditions.
   a. With the ignition switch turned **ON** the fuel pressure should read: 33–40 psi.
   b. Within 3 minutes after the fuel pump has been turned **OFF**, the fuel pressure should read: 25.6 psi.
5. Release the fuel pressure and remove the fuel pressure gauge.
6. Install union bolt in fuel filter. Use a new gasket.
7. Start the engine and check for leaks.

Removal and Installation

1. Disconnect the negative battery terminal.
2. Release the pressure from the fuel system by removing the fuel cap.

NOTE: Place a rag or container under the connectors, because fuel will flow out.

3. At the frame mounting of the fuel pump, disconnect the front fuel line.
4. Disconnect the electrical coupler at the fuel pump.

Fuel tank removal procedure

Checking fuel pump pressure

5. Remove the fuel pump bracket from the frame by removing the 3 attaching bolts.

6. Remove the bracket from the pump by removing the 3 attaching bolts.

7. Remove the pump by disconnecting the rear fuel hose.

To install:

8. Connect the fuel hose to the rear of the fuel pump.

9. Install the fuel pump to the bracket and tighten the 3 attaching bolts.

10. Install the bracket to the frame and tighten the bolts to 11 ft. lbs.

11. Connect the front fuel line to the pump and connect the electrical coupler.

12. Connect the negative battery cable, run the engine and check for leaks.

Fuel Injection

For further information, please refer to Chilton's Electronic Engine Controls Manual.

Idle Speed Adjustment

1. With the transmission in neutral and the parking brake applied, warm engine to normal operating temperature.

2. Connect a tachometer to the engine and use a jumper wire to connect the brown test terminal to the black ground terminal.

3. Remove idle adjusting screw cap from the throttle body and race the engine to 2000 rpm for 2–3 times.

4. Adjust idle adjusting screw to specified rpm idle speed. Idle speed should be 800–850 rpm.

Fuel Injector

Removal and Installation

1. Relieve the fuel system pressure. Disconnect the negative battery cable.

2. Remove hoses from air chamber, unbolt chamber, unlock 2 clamps and remove air chamber.

3. Disconnect the electrical connectors at each injector.

4. Remove the fuel hose at the delivery pipe side.

Installing jumper wire at test terminal

Adjusting idle speed

5. Remove the fuel return hose from the pressure regulator.

6. Remove the vacuum hose from the vacuum pipe and remove the delivery pipe attaching nuts.

7. Remove delivery pipe and remove injectors from insulator.

To install:

8. Install the delivery pipe and injectors with new O-rings and tighten the attaching bolts to 15 ft. lbs.

9. Connect the fuel hoses and vaccum hoses.

10. Connect the fuel injector wiring connectors.

11. Connect the negative battery cable.

EMISSION CONTROLS

Emission Warning Lamp

The 0_2S light automatically comes on at 80,000 miles.

Resetting

After replacing the oxygen sensor, the bulb in the 0_2S warning light must be removed and then reinstalled to reset the warning system. The instrument cluster must be removed to reset the light.

For further information, please refer to Chilton's Emission Controls Manual.

ENGINE MECHANICAL

NOTE: Disconnecting the negative battery cable on some vehicles may interfere with the functions of the on board computer systems and may require the computer to undergo a relearning process, once the negative battery cable is reconnected.

Engine Assembly

Removal and Installation

1. Disconnect the negative and positive cables at the battery and remove the battery.

2. Remove the hood from the vehicle and drain the cooling system, transmission oil and engine oil.

3. Remove the radiator reservoir tank, fan shroud and cooling fan.

4. Properly discharge the air conditioning system and remove the air conditioning condenser, if equipped.

5. Remove the air cleaner assembly and hose.

6. Remove the air conditioner compressor.

7. Disconnect and tag the charcoal canister hoses at the surge tank side.

8. Remove the radiator grille.

9. Remove the radiator.

10. Disconnect the exhaust pipe from the manifold.

11. Remove the fuel tank filler cap to relieve the pressure. Reinstall the cap.

12. Relieve the fuel pressure in the fuel feed line. Disconnect and tag the fuel hose at the top of the fuel filter.

13. Remove the idle-up VSV and pressure sensor VSV from the firewall.

14. Disconnect the coil wire from coil and disconnect the wiring plug at the distributor.

15. Disconnect the accelerator cable.

16. Remove the positive wire clamp from the body and the battery ground cable from the body.

17. Disconnect the heater hoses from the heater core outlet pipes.

18. Disconnect the cowl wire and alternator wire.

19. Disconnect the engine wire and fuse block connector.

20. Disconnect the wire clamp at the cylinder block on the driver's side.

21. Remove the wire for the ECU by disconnecting the wire at the ECU under the passenger side cowl and pull the wire out through the engine compartment.

22. Support the transmission, using an appropriate stand or jack and remove the transmission attaching bolts.

23. Support the engine from the top using a hoist or equivalent means.

24. Remove the engine mount attaching bolts on both sides.

NOTE: Before lifting the engine, check to ensure all the hoses, wires and cables are disconnected from the engine.

25. Remove the engine assembly from the chassis and transmission by sliding towards the front side and carefully hoist the engine.

To install:

26. Install the engine into the engine compartment and connect to the transmission.

27. Install the engine mount attaching bolts. Tighten to 32 ft. lbs.

28. Remove the lifting device.

29. Install the nuts and bolts fastening the cylinder block and transmission. Tighten to 50 ft. lbs.

30. Install the exhaust pipe to the exhaust manifold and muffler.

31. Reinstall engine wire to ECU.

32. Connect cowl wire and alternator wire.

33. Connect engine wire and fuse block connectors.

34. Install wire clamp at fuse block.

35. Reconnect the oxygen sensor.

36. Connect the heater hoses at the inlet and outlet fittings.

37. Reconnect the accelerator cable and distributor wiring harness.

38. Reconnect the coil wire to the ignition coil.

39. Reattach the pressure sensor VSV and idle-up VSV to the firewall.

40. Connect the fuel hose to the fuel filter.

41. Install the fuel return hose to the pressure regulator pipe.

42. Install the hose between the charcoal cannister and the throttle body.

43. Install the radiator, cooling fan, fan shroud and radiator reservoir tank.

44. Install the air cleaner assembly and outlet hose. Refill the engine oil, the transmission oil and the coolant to the proper level.

45. Install the air conditioning condenser and properly recharge the air conditioning system, if equipped.

46. Install the hood and install the battery.

47. Adjust the accelerator and the clutch.

48. Before starting the engine, check to see if all the parts disassembled are secure.

49. Start the engine and check the timing. Check for any oil leaks.

Engine mounts

Removal and Installation

1. Disconnect the negative battery cable.

2. Raise and support the vehicle safely.

3. Support the engine.

4. Remove the mounting bolts and nuts and remove the mounts.

To install:

5. Installation is the reverse of the removal procedure. Torque the engine mounting bolts and nuts to 31 ft. lbs.

Cylinder Head

Removal and Installation

1. Disconnect the battery and remove. Drain the cooling system and the engine oil.

2. Remove the engine hood.

3. Remove the air intake chamber.

4. Remove the radiator reserve tank.

5. If equipped, loosen the power steering tension and remove the belt. If equipped, loosen the air conditioning belt tension and remove the belt.

6. Remove the fan shroud.

7. Remove the 4 water pump attaching nuts and remove the fan and fluid coupling.

8. Remove the crankshaft pulley attaching bolts and remove the pulley.

9. Remove the timing belt cover mounting bolts and remove the cover.

10. Loosen the timing belt tensioner bolt and remove the timing belt.

11. Remove the power steering pump and temporarily place pump in battery area.

12. Disconnect spark plug wires and remove spark plugs.

13. Disconnect vacuum hoses at the surge tank.

14. Disconnect the distributor wire connectors and remove the distributor.

15. Disconnect and remove the engine wire harness.

16. Disconnect the 4 fuel injector connectors.

Cylinder head bolt tightening sequence

17. Remove the top radiator hose.

18. Remove the fuel tank filler cap to relieve the pressure. Re-install the cap.

19. Release the fuel pressure in the fuel feed line.

20. Disconnect the fuel feed and return hoses.

21. Remove the water hose from the upper side throttle body.

22. Disconnect the surge tank from the surge tank stay.

23. Remove the exhaust manifold cover and the dipstick support.

24. Disconnect the exhaust pipe from the exhaust manifold.

25. Remove the cylinder head cover attaching bolts and remove the cylinder head cover.

26. Remove the cylinder head mounting bolts and remove the cylinder head with the manifolds from the engine using a chain type hoist.

27. Remove any oil and water in the cylinder bores and on top of the pistons.

28. Clean and inspect the sealing surfaces of the cylinder head and the engine block.

To install:

29. Install the cylinder head with manifolds using a new gasket.

30. Install the cylinder head mounting bolts and tighten to 43.4–49.2 ft. lbs.

31. Connect the exhaust pipe to the manifold with a new gasket and tighten to 25.3–36.2 ft. lbs.

32. Install the exhaust manifold cover and the oil dipstick support.

33. Secure the lower surge tank stay.

34. Connect the water hoses to the throttle body.

35. Connect the fuel return hose and the top hose to the fuel filter.

36. Install the timing belt, making sure the arrow on the belt is pointing in the correct direction.

37. Adjust the valve lash.

38. Install the cylinder head cover and install the oxygen sensor wire.

39. Install the timing belt cover.

40. Install the crankshaft pulley.

41. Install the fluid coupling with the fan and install the radiator and fan shroud.

42. Install the alternator belt and adjust.

43. Install engine wire harness and connect at the fuel injectors.

44. Connect wires at throttle position sensor, intake air temperature sensor, water temperature sensors and air conditioning sensors.

45. Replace the O-ring on the distributor and install the distributor.

46. Replace distributor cap and install spark plug wires and spark plugs.

47. Install the power steering pump and belt, if equipped.

48. Install the vacuum hoses at the surge tank.

49. Install air cleaner and sub assembly.

50. Install the radiator reserve tank.

51. Install the air chamber.

52. Connect the accelerator cable to the throttle body.

53. Refill the cooling system with the proper coolant and install the battery.

54. Check for any water and oil leaks when finished.

Valve Lash

Adjustment

NOTE: The valves are adjusted with the engine HOT. A hot engine condition is where the cooling water temperature is 167–185°F and the oil temperature should be above 149°F.

1. Remove the air chamber and the cylinder head cover.

Valve lash adjustment procedure

2. Rotate the crankshaft pulley until the No. 1 piston is at TDC of the compression stroke.

NOTE: To make sure the piston is on the correct stroke, remove the spark plug and place a finger over the hole. Feel for air being forced out of the spark plug hole. Both valves on No. 1 cylinder will be closed. Stop turning the crankshaft when the TDC timing mark on the crankshaft pulley is directly aligned with the timing mark pointer.

3. With the No. 1 piston at TDC of the compression stroke, adjust the clearances of the following valves:

Intake No. 1 and 2: 0.008–0.012 in.
Exhaust No. 1 and 3: 0.011–0.015 in.

4. Adjust the clearance by loosening the locknut and turning the adjusting screw. Retightening the locknut when the proper thickness feeler gauge passes between the camshaft or valve stem and has a slight drag when the clearance is corrected.

5. Rotate the crankshaft 1 complete revolution (360 degrees) to position the No. 4 piston at TDC of its compression stroke and adjust the clearances of the following valves:

Intake No. 3 and 4: 0.008–0.012 in.
Exhaust No. 2 and 4: 0.011–0.015 in.

6. After adjustment, use a new gasket, sealant and install the rocker arm cover.

Rocker Arms/Shafts

Removal and Installation

1. Disconnect the negative battery cable. Drain the cooling system.

2. Remove the front grille.

3. Remove the radiator cooling fan and fan shroud. Properly discharge the air conditioning system and remove the air conditioning flexible suction hose, if equipped.

4. Remove the radiator .

5. Remove the water pump drive belt and the water pump pulley.

6. Remove the timing belt outside cover, timing belt and the tensioner.

7. Disconnect the air intake case and remove the cylinder head cover.

8. Insert the proper size rod into the hole in the camshaft to lock the camshaft, loosen the pulley nut and remove the pulley.

9. Loosen all the valve lash adjusting screw locknuts and turn the adjusting screws out all the way.

10. Remove the rocker arm shaft screws.

11. Remove the intake and exhaust rocker arm shafts, rocker arms and springs.

12. Keep all the valve train parts in the order that they were removed.

To install:

13. Apply engine oil to the rocker arms, springs and shafts. In-

stall the shafts in the correct direction, into the cylinder head by placing the rocker arms and springs on the shafts as they are installed. With the rocker arms, springs and shafts installed, torque the rocker shaft mounting screws to 7.0–8.5 ft. lbs.

14. Install the timing belt pulley and inside cover by locking the camshaft with the proper size rod.

15. Install the camshaft pulley and tighten the camshaft pulley bolt to 10.9–15.9 ft. lbs.

16. The remainder of the installation is the reverse of the removal procedure.

Intake Manifold

Removal and Installation

1. Disconnect the battery terminals and remove the battery.
2. Disconnect the windshield washer hoses and remove the hood.
3. Remove the air intake chamber.
4. Remove the power steering pump, if equipped.
5. Tag and remove the spark plug wires.
6. Relieve the fuel pressure and disconnect the fuel lines at the fuel filter and at the return line.
7. Tag and remove the vaccum hoses at the surge tank side.
8. Disconnect the engine wire harness at the intake manifold.
9. Disconnect the 4 fuel injector connectors.
10. Remove the surge tank stay No. 3.
11. Remove the 8 bolts and 4 nuts and remove the intake manifold.

To install:
12. Install the intake manifold with a new manifold gasket and tighten the bolts and nuts to 15 ft. lbs.
13. Replace the surge tank stay No. 3 and connect the 4 fuel injector connectors.
14. Connect the engine wire harness and the vaccum hoses.
15. Connect the fuel lines at the fuel filter and at the return line.
16. Install the spark plug wires and the power steering pump.
17. Install the air intake chamber and install the hood.
18. Install the battery and connect both terminals.

Exhaust Manifold

Removal and Installation

1. Disconnect the negative battery terminal.
2. Drain the cooling system and remove the upper radiator hose assembly.
3. Remove the exhaust manifold cover by removing the 5 attaching bolts.
4. Disconnect the exhaust pipe from the exhaust manifold by removing the 3 attaching nuts.
5. Remove the 6 bolts and 2 nuts attaching the exhaust manifold to the head and remove the exhaust manifold.

To install:
6. Replace the exhaust manifold gasket and install the exhaust manifold and tighten the bolts and nuts to 30 ft. lbs.
7. Connect the exhaust pipe to the manifold and tighten the nuts to 34 ft. lbs.
8. Install the exhaust manifold cover and tighten the attaching bolts.
9. Replace the upper radiator hose and refill the cooling system.
10. Connect the negative battery terminal.

Timing Belt Front Cover

Removal and Installation

1. Disconnect the negative battery terminal.
2. Remove the air cleaner assembly and drain the cooling system.

3. Loosen and remove the power steering and air conditioning belts.
4. Remove the radiator fan shroud and radiator reserve tank.
5. Remove the fan and fluid coupling assembly.
6. Remove the crankshaft pulley.
7. Remove the timing belt cover.

To install:
8. Clean and inspect all mounting surfaces.
9. Install the timing belt cover and tighten the mounting bolts.
10. Install the crankshaft pulley and tighten to 14.4–21.6 ft. lbs.
11. Install the fan and fluid coupling.
12. Install fan shroud and radiator reserve tank.
13. Install power steering and air conditioning belts.
14. Replace air cleaner assembly and refill the cooling system with the proper coolant.
15. Connect the negative battery cable.

Oil Seal Replacement

1. Disconnect the negative battery cable.
2. Remove the the timing belt and the crankshaft sprocket.
3. Insert a suitable tool between the crankshaft and the oil seal and pull the seal outwards to remove it.

NOTE: Use care when removing or installing the oil seal, not to damage the crankshaft or the oil pump sealing surfaces.

4. Clean and inspect the surfaces of the crankshaft and the oil pump assembly.
5. Install the crankshaft sleeve, using the proper tool, onto the crankshaft.
6. Install the new seal over the crankshaft and into the oil pump, making sure the oil seal lip is not up-turned.
7. Install the crankshaft sprocket and the timing belt. Check the timing.
8. Connect the negative battery cable.

Timing Belt and Tensioner

Adjustment

1. Disconnect the negative battery cable.
2. Drain the cooling system.
3. Remove the air cleaner and air cleaner hose assembly.
4. Remove the radiator reserve tank.
5. If equipped, loosen the power steering tension and remove the belt. If equipped, loosen the air conditioning belt tension and remove the belt.
6. Remove the fan shroud and disconnect the engine wire connector at the relay box.
7. Remove the 4 water pump attaching nuts and remove the fan and fluid coupling.
8. Remove the crankshaft pulley attaching bolts and remove the pulley.
9. Remove the timing belt cover mounting bolts and remove the cover.
10. Align the "F" mark on the camshaft with the indicator at the top of the cylinder head cover. Align the drilled mark on the crankshaft pulley with the bottom indicator.
11. Remove any slack from the drive side of the timing belt and tighten the tensioner bolt to 21.7–32.5 ft. lbs.
12. To allow the belt to be free of any slack, turn the crankshaft clockwise 2 full rotations.
13. Install the timing cover and tighten the bolts to 1.4–2.9 ft. lbs.
14. Install the crankshaft pulley.
15. Install the fluid coupling with the fan and the fan shroud.
16. Install the V-ribbed belt and the power steering belt, if equipped.

1. Indicator
2. "F" mark
3. Drilled mark
4. Spring tensioner
5. Drilled mark
6. Indicator

Exploded view of the timing belt assembly

17. Install the coolant reserve tank.
18. Install the air cleaner assembly and the air intake chamber.
19. Fill the radiator with coolant and connect the negative battery cable.

Removal and Installation

1. Disconnect the negative battery terminal.
2. Drain the cooling system.
3. Remove the air cleaner and air cleaner hose assembly.
4. Remove the radiator reserve tank.
5. If equipped, loosen the power steering tension and remove the belt. If equipped, loosen the air conditioning belt tension and remove the belt.
6. Remove the fan shroud.
7. Remove the 4 water pump attaching nuts and remove the fan and fluid coupling.
8. Remove the crankshaft pulley attaching bolts and remove the pulley.
9. Remove the timing belt cover mounting bolts and remove the cover.
10. Loosen the timing belt tensioner bolt and remove the timing belt.

To install:

11. Align the "F" mark on the camshaft timing belt pulley with the indicator on the cylinder head cover.
12. Align the drilled mark of the crankshaft timing belt pulley with the lower indicator.
13. Align the timing belt mating marks with the drilled marks on the crankshaft and camshaft pulley and slide the belt onto the pulleys making sure that the arrow on the belt is pointing in the correct direction.
14. Loosen the attaching bolt of the timing belt tensioner and remove any slack on the drive side of the belt.
15. To assure that the belt is free of all slack, turn the crankshaft clockwise 2 full rotations.
16. Replace the timing cover and tighten the bolts to 1.4–2.9 ft. lbs.
17. Install the crankshaft pulley.

18. Install the fluid coupling with the fan and the fan shroud.
19. Install the V-ribbed belt and the power steering belt, if equipped.
20. Install the coolant reserve tank.
21. Install the air cleaner assembly and the air intake chamber.
22. Connect the negative battery cable.

Timing Sprockets

Removal and Installation

1. Disconnect the negative battery terminal.
2. Drain the cooling system.
3. Remove the air cleaner and air cleaner hose assembly.
4. Remove the radiator reserve tank.
5. If equipped, loosen the power steering tension and remove the belt. If equipped, loosen the air conditioning belt tension and remove the belt.
6. Remove the fan shroud.
7. Remove the 4 water pump attaching nuts and remove the fan and fluid coupling.
8. Remove the crankshaft pulley attaching bolts and remove the pulley.
9. Remove the timing belt cover mounting bolts and remove the cover.
10. Loosen the timing belt tensioner bolt and remove the timing belt.
11. Place the gear shift lever in the **5TH** gear position to prevent the crankshaft from being rotated and remove the pulley bolt.
12. Remove the camshaft timing belt pulley by inserting a proper size rod into the hole in the camshaft to lock the camshaft.
13. Remove the pulley mounting bolts and remove the pulley.

To install:

14. Install the camshaft pulley and the pulley mounting bolts.
15. Insert a rod into the hole in the camshaft to lock the camshaft and tighten the camshaft mounting bolts to 10.8–15.9 ft. lbs.
16. Install the crankshaft timing belt pulley on the crankshaft by aligning the pulley key groove.
17. Install the setting bolt and align the pulley with the drilled mark on the pulley and the lower indicator.
18. Tighten the crankshaft timing belt pulley belt to 65.1–72.0 ft. lbs.
19. Align the camshaft and crankshaft timing marks, install the timing belt, making sure the arrow on the belt is pointing in the correct direction and tighten the timing belt tensioner.
20. Install the timing cover and tighten the bolts to 1.4–2.9 ft. lbs.
21. Install the crankshaft pulley.
22. Install the fluid coupling with the fan and the fan shroud.
23. Install the V-ribbed belt and the power steering belt, if equipped.
24. Install the coolant reserve tank.
25. Install the air cleaner assembly and the air intake chamber.
26. Connect the negative battery cable.

Camshaft

Removal and Installation

1. Disconnect the negative battery cable. Drain the cooling system.
2. Remove the front grille.
3. Remove the radiator cooling fan and fan shroud. Properly discharge the air conditioning system and remove the air conditioning flexible suction hose, if equipped.
4. Remove the radiator .

5. Remove the water pump drive belt and the water pump pulley.

6. Remove the timing belt outside cover and the timing belt.

7. Disconnect the air intake case and remove the cylinder head cover.

8. Insert the proper size rod into the hole in the camshaft to lock the camshaft, loosen the pulley nut and remove the pulley.

9. Loosen all the valve lash adjusting screw locknuts and turn the adjusting screws out all the way.

10. Remove the rocker arm shaft screws.

11. Remove the intake and exhaust rocker arm shafts, rocker arms and springs.

12. Remove the camshaft bearing caps and remove the camshaft.

To install:

13. Lubricate the lobes and journals of the camshaft and the oil seal on the cylinder head with engine oil.

14. Install the camshaft to the cylinder head and replace the bearing caps.

15. Install the valve rocker shaft and tighten the bolts to the specified torque; M10 bolts to 25 ft. lbs. and M8 bolts to 11 ft. lbs.

16. Install the camshaft pulley and tighten the pulley to 13 ft. lbs.

17. Install the timing belt and timing belt cover.

18. Install the water pump pulley and belt and install the radiator.

19. Install the grille and refill the cooling system.

20. Adjust the valves and replace the valve cover with the gasket.

Piston and Connecting Rod

Positioning

1. Top ring
2. Second ring
3. Oil ring
4. Piston
5. Connecting rod
6. Connecting rod bearing cap
7. Connecting rod bearing
8. Piston pin

Exploded view of the piston and rod assembly

ENGINE LUBRICATION

Oil Pan

Removal and Installation

1. Raise and safely support the vehicle.

2. Drain the engine oil.

3. Remove the attaching bolts and nuts and remove the pan.

4. Clean and inspect the sealing surfaces of the oil pan and the engine block.

5. Using new gaskets install the oil pan and tighten the oil pan bolts and nuts to 5.1–8.7 ft. lbs.

6. Install the oil drain plug and tighten to 14.5–21.7 ft. lbs.

7. Lower the vehicle.

8. Refill the engine with oil. Run the engine and check for leaks.

Oil pan removal procedure

Oil Pump

Removal and Installation

1. Disconnect the negative battery cable.

2. Remove the radiator cooling fan, fan shroud, water pump pulley and water pump drive belt.

3. Remove the timing belt outside cover, timing belt and timing belt tensioner.

4. Disconnect the alternator and remove the bracket, if necessary.

5. If equipped, properly discharge the air conditioning system and remove the air compressor and bracket.

6. Disconnect the crankshaft timing belt pulley and the timing belt guide.

NOTE: To lock the crankshaft, engage a special tool (gear stopper) with the flywheel ring gear. With the crankshaft locked, remove the crankshaft timing belt pulley bolt.

7. Raise and safely support the vehicle. Drain the engine oil.

8. Remove the oil pan mounting bolts and remove the oil pan. Disconnect the oil pump strainer.

9. Remove the oil pump mounting bolts and remove the oil pump.

10. Clean and inspect the sealing surfaces of the oil pump and the engine block.

To install:

11. Using a new gasket, install the oil pump to the engine.

12. Install the No. 1 and No. 2 mounting bolts and tighten to 7.0–8.5 ft. lbs.

NOTE: To prevent the oil seal lip from being damaged when installing the oil pump to the crankshaft, use a proper seal guide tool when installing. After installing the oil pump, check to be sure the oil lip is not up-turned, then remove the special tool. The edge of the oil pump gasket might bulge out. If it does, cut off bulge with knife.

13. With the crankshaft locked, install the crankshaft timing belt guide and the timing belt pulley.

14. If equipped, install the air conditioning bracket and the air conditioning compressor, then properly recharge the air conditioning system.

15. Replace the alternator and the alternator bracket, if necessary.

16. Reinstall the timing belt tensioner, timing belt and timing belt outside cover.

17. Replace the water pump drive belt, water pump pulley, radiator cooling fan and fan shroud.

18. Refill the engine with engine oil and connect the negative battery cable.

19. Run the engine and check for any leaks.

Checking

With the oil pump removed from the engine, certain clearances must be checked on the oil pump, if it is being reused.

1. The radial clearance is the clearance between the oil pump outer rotor and the oil pump case. The maximum clearance is 0.0122 in.

2. The side clearance is measured with a straight-edge across the mounting surface of the oil pump. The measurement is taken between the oil pump gears and the straight-edge. The maximum clearance is 0.0094 in.

Rear Main Bearing Oil Seal

Removal and Installation

1. Raise and safely support the vehicle.

2. Support the engine and remove the transmission from the vehicle.

3. Disconnect the clutch and flywheel.

4. Using a suitable tool, remove the seal by pulling it outwards. Use care not to damage the sealing surface of the crankshaft.

5. Clean and inspect the sealing surfaces of the crankshaft and seal housing.

6. Using a seal driver, install the new seal into the seal housing with the lip of the seal facing the engine.

7. Install the flywheel and clutch.

8. Install the transmission in the vehicle.

9. Lower the vehicle and check all the fluids. Run the engine and check for any leaks.

TORQUE SPECIFICATIONS

Component	English	Metric
Camshaft timing belt pulley	10.8–15.9 ft. lbs.	14.8–21.6 Nm
Connecting rod bearing cap bolts	25.3–32.5 ft. lbs.	34.3–44.1 Nm
Crankshaft flywheel bolt	57.9–72.3 ft. lbs.	78.5–98.0 Nm
Crankshaft pulley bolt	65.1–72.0 ft. lbs.	88.3–98.0 Nm
Cylinder head bolt Step 1: Step 2:	22 ft. lbs. 45 ft. lbs.	29 Nm 61 Nm
O$_2$ sensor-to-exhaust manifold	21.7–28.9 ft. lbs.	29.4–39.2 Nm
Engine-to-transmission	36.2–50.6 ft. lbs.	49.0–68.6 Nm
Exhaust manifold	21.7–32.5 ft. lbs.	29.4–44.1 Nm
Exhaust pipe-to-exhaust manifold nuts	25.3–36.2 ft. lbs.	34.2–49.0 Nm
Flywheel/flexplate-to-crankshaft bolts	57.9–72.3 ft. lbs.	78.5–98.0 Nm
Flywheel-to-clutch cover bolts	10.8–15.9 ft. lbs.	14.7–21.6 Nm
Fuel pump-to-frame	7.2–11.6 ft. lbs.	9.8–15.7 Nm
Front engine mount bolt	21.7–32.5 ft. lbs.	29.4–44.1 Nm
Intake manifold	10.8–15.9 ft. lbs.	14.7–21.6 Nm
Main bearing cap bolts	32.5–39.8 ft. lbs.	44.1–53.9 Nm
Oil pan	5.1–8.7 ft. lbs.	6.9–11.8 Nm
Oil pan drain plug	14.5–21.7 ft. lbs.	19.6–21.4 Nm
Oil pump attaching bolts	18.1–25.3 ft. lbs.	24.5–34.3 Nm
Oil pump cover screws	5.8–9.4 ft. lbs.	7.8–12.7 Nm
Rocker shaft bolt M10 bolt M8 bolt	21.0–26.8 ft. lbs. 9.4–12.3 ft. lbs.	28.4–36.3 Nm 12.8–16.7 Nm
Rocker (valve) cover	2.2–3.6 ft. lbs.	3.0–4.9 Nm
Spark plug	10.8–15.9 ft. lbs.	14.7–21.6 Nm
Starter-to-transmission bolts	36.2–50.6 ft. lbs.	49.0–68.6 Nm
Thermostat housing	4.3–6.5 ft. lbs.	5.9–8.8 Nm

TORQUE SPECIFICATIONS

Surge tank-to-throttle body	10.8–15.9ft. lbs.	14.7–21.6 Nm
Surge tank-to-intake air temp. sensor	21.7–28.9ft. lbs.	29.4–39.2 Nm
Timing cover	1.4–2.9 ft. lbs.	2.0–3.9 Nm
Water pump	10.8–15.9 ft. lbs.	14.7–21.6 Nm
Water pump pulley-to-fluid coupling	7.2–13.0 ft. lbs.	9.8–17.7 Nm

MANUAL TRANSMISSION

For further information, please refer to Chilton's Transmission Service Manual.

Transmission Assembly

Removal and Installation

1. Disconnect the negative battery cable.
2. Remove the shift lever boots.
3. Remove the snapring and remove the gear shift lever.
4. Remove the transfer case lever shifter attaching bolts and remove the transfer case shift lever.
5. Remove the C-clip at the clutch cable adjuster at the firewall.
6. Disconnect the transmission breather hose at the connector.
7. Remove the connector bolt under the starter.
8. Raise and safely support the vehicle.
9. Remove the transmission under cover bolts and remove the cover.
10. Drain the transmission and the transfer of all fluid.
11. Disconnect the clutch cable at the clutch housing side.
12. Disconnect the electrical connector at the back-up light switch and at the transmission position detect switch.
13. Disconnect the speedometer cable at the transmission case.
14. Disconnect the flange bolts from the front driveshaft and remove the driveshaft.
15. Disconnect the flange bolts from the rear driveshaft and remove the driveshaft.
16. Separate the catalytic converter by removing the 2 mounting bolts.
17. Remove the exhaust pipe mounting brackets and remove the exhaust pipe.
18. Remove the 2 crossmember attaching bolts and remove the starter.
19. Remove the transmission connecting bolts and leave them inserted.
20. Position a transmission jack under the transmission.
21. Remove the crossmember attaching bolts and remove the transmission attaching bolts completely.
22. Move the transmission and transfer case rearwards and lower the transmission away from the engine.
To install:
23. Raise the transmission and transfer case on the transmission jack and place under the vehicle.
24. Install the crossmember and the attaching bolts.
25. Install the transmission attaching bolts and install the exhaust pipe and mounting bolts.

Transmission to crossmember mounting bolts

Transmission to engine mounting bolts

26. Install the transmission to crossmember mounting bolts.
27. Secure the catalytic converter and install both driveshafts.
28. Connect the speedometer cable, the back-up light switch and the transmission position detect switch.
29. Connect the clutch release cable.
30. Fill the transmission and the transfer case with the proper fluids.
31. Replace the starter bolts and the clutch cable C-clip at the firewall.
32. Connect the transmission breather hose.
33. Install the transmission shift lever and the transfer case lever and replace the 2 shift boots.
34. Connect the negative battery cable. Run the engine and check for any leaks.

CLUTCH

Clutch Assembly

Removal and Installation

1. Disconnect the negative battery cable.
2. Raise and safely support the vehicle.
3. Support the engine and remove the transmission from the vehicle.
4. Support the pressure plate and remove the 6 pressure plate to flywheel mounting bolts.
5. Remove the pressure plate and the clutch disc from the flywheel.
6. Inspect the condition of the flywheel, pressure plate and clutch disc and replace as necessary.
7. Remove the flywheel mounting bolts and remove the flywheel.

To install:

8. Install the flywheel and replace the mounting bolts, tighten to 41–47 ft. lbs.
9. Inspect the condition of the clutch release bearing and the input shaft bearing and replace, if necessary.
10. Align the clutch disc to the flywheel using a clutch disc alignment tool.
11. Install the pressure plate and evenly tighten the pressure plate bolts to 10.8–15.9 ft. lbs.

NOTE: Before assembling, make sure the clutch disc and the pressure plate are clean and dry.

12. With the engine supported, install the transmission in the vehicle.
13. Lower the vehicle. Connect the negative battery cable.
14. Check and adjust the clutch pedal height. Check the clutch operation when finished.

Clutch removal procedure

Clutch Cable

Removal and Installation

1. Disconnect the negative battery cable.
2. Remove clip at top cable holder and disconnect cable.
3. Disconnect cable at release fork and remove cable assembly.
4. Install the cable after applying grease to both cable end hooks.
5. The remainder of the installation is the reverse of the removal procedure.

Clutch pedal height adjustment

Clutch cable free travel adjustment

TRANSFER CASE

Transfer Case Assembly

Removal and Installation

1. Disconnect the negative battery cable.
2. Raise and safely support the vehicle.
3. Support the transmission and transfer case using a transmission jack.
4. Disconnect the speedometer cable from the transfer case.
5. Remove the transmission and transfer case from the vehicle.

6. Remove the 8 transmission-to-transfer case mounting bolts and separate the transfer case from the transmission.

To install:

7. Install the transmission to transfer case mounting bolts.
8. While supporting the transmission with a transmission jack, align and slide the transmission into the engine.
9. Install the crossmember and the attaching bolts.
10. Install the transmission attaching bolts and install the exhaust pipe and mounting bolts.
11. Install the transmission to crossmember mounting bolts.
12. Secure the catalytic converter and install both driveshafts.

13. Connect the speedometer cable, the back-up light switch and the transmission position detect switch.

14. Connect the clutch release cable.

15. Fill the transmission and the transfer case with the proper fluids.

16. Install the starter bolts and the clutch cable C-clip at the firewall.

17. Connect the transmission breather hose.

18. Install the transmission shift lever and the transfer case lever and replace the 2 shift boots.

19. Connect the negative battery cable. Run the engine and check for any leaks.

DRIVE AXLE

Halfshaft

Removal and Installation

1. Raise and safely support the vehicle. Drain the front differential oil.

2. Remove the front wheels.

3. Remove the stabilizer bar and the torsion spring.

4. Remove the brake caliper and support it.

5. Remove the front axle hub and disconnect the tie rod end from the steering knuckle.

6. Remove the 4 attaching nuts at the upper and lower ball joints and remove the steering knuckle.

7. Pull out the driveshaft by prying away from the differential assembly.

To install:

8. Install the inboard joint into the front differential.

9. Fill the front differential with oil.

10. Install the steering knuckle and attaching nuts at upper and lower ball joints. Tighten the upper ball joint nuts to 26 ft. lbs. and the lower ball joint nuts to 55 ft. lbs.

11. Install the front axle hub and brake caliper assembly.

12. Install the stabilizer bar and the torsion spring.

13. Install the front wheels and lower the vehicle.

Driveshaft and U-Joints

Removal and Installation

FRONT

1. Raise and safely support the vehicle.

2. Matchmark the driveshafts to the yokes on the transfer case and the differential.

3. Drain the transfer case oil.

4. Support the driveshaft and remove the attaching bolts.

5. Remove the driveshaft from the vehicle.

To install:

6. Install the driveshaft, by aligning the matchmarks to the vehicle.

7. Tighten the mounting bolts to 43.4–57.9 ft. lbs.

8. Refill the transfer case and lower the vehicle.

Removing the halfshaft assembly

REAR

1. Raise and safely support the vehicle.

2. Matchmark the driveshafts to the yokes on the transfer case and the differential.

3. Support the driveshaft and remove the attaching bolts.

4. Remove the driveshaft from the vehicle.

To install:

5. Install the driveshaft, by aligning the matchmarks to the vehicle.

6. Tighten the mounting bolts to 43.4–57.9 ft. lbs and lower the vehicle.

Rear Axle Shaft, Bearing and Seal

Removal and Installation

1. Raise and safely support the vehicle. Drain the rear differential assembly.

2. Make sure the rear brake is released.

3. Remove the rear wheels and remove the rear brake drums from the vehicle.

4. Disconnect the parking brake cables from the levers. Remove the parking brake lever stop plates.

5. Disconnect and plug the brake lines to the wheel cylinders.

6. Remove the backing plate mounting bolts.

7. Remove the rear axles with the backing plates attached using a slide hammer type puller.

8. Using a suitable tool, remove the axle seal from the housing.

9. If the axle, axle bearing or backing plate is being replaced, support the axle in a vise with additional support under the shaft next to the bearing.

— **CAUTION** —

Eye protection must be worn during the 3 steps. Failure to do so could cause injury.

10. With the axle shaft supported properly, grind the top and bottom of the axle bearing retainer to remove it without damaging the axle shaft.

11. Using a chisel, finish removing the retainer from the axle shaft.

Removing the steering knuckle assembly

1. Front axle inboard joint sub assembly
2. Retainer ring
3. Snapring
4. Inboard joint birfield assembly
5. Spacer
6. Ball bearing
7. Boot band
8. Front axle joint boot
9. Boot band
10. Driveshaft sub assembly
11. Boot band
12. Front axle joint boot
13. Boot band
14. Ball bearing
15. Spacer
16. Outboard joint birfield assembly
17. Snapring
18. Front axle outboard joint sub assembly

Exploded view of driveshaft assembly

12. Using a press or suitable bearing puller, remove the axle shaft bearing from the axle shaft.
13. Remove the backing plate from the axle shaft.

To install:

14. Using a seal driver, install the new seal with the lip facing the housing to the same depth as the old seal.
15. Install the backing plate on the axle shaft and using a press, install the bearing and the retainer on the axle shaft.
16. Install the axle shaft in the housing.
17. Install the backing plate mounting bolts and connect the brake lines to the wheel cylinders.
18. Install the parking brake lever plates and connect the brake cables to the parking brake lever.
19. Install the rear brake drums and install the rear wheels.
20. Adjust the brakes and bleed the brake system.
21. Refill the rear differential and safely lower the vehicle.

Front Wheel Hub, Knuckle/Spindle and Bearings

Removal and Installation

1. Raise and safely support the vehicle. Remove the front wheels.
2. Remove the hub cover attaching bolts.
3. Remove the brakes and suspend the caliper assembly.
4. Remove the hub cap and remove the driveshaft snapring.
5. Remove the locknut and with a slide hammer remove the complete hub assembly.
6. Remove the oil seal and remove the roller bearings.

To install:

7. Replace the roller bearings and pack with lithium grease.
8. Install the front axle hub to the steering knuckle.

9. Insert the outer bearing, replace the locknut and tighten to 100 ft. lbs.
10. Install the hub cover, tightening the attaching bolts to 50 ft. lbs. and replace the snapring.
11. Install brake assembly and replace the wheels.
12. Lower the vehicle.

Manual Locking Hubs

Removal and Installation

1. Disconnect the negative battery cable, raise and support the vehicle safely and remove the front wheels.
2. Turn the free-wheel cover handle to the FREE setting.
3. Remove the 5 free-wheel cover attaching bolts and remove the cover from the hub body.
4. Remove the snapring from the driveshaft.
5. Mark the hub body and hub with alignment marks for reassembly.
6. Remove the 5 hub body attaching bolts and remove the hub body assembly.

To install:

7. Install the hub body, aligning the mating marks and torque the hub body attaching bolts to 43.4–50.6 ft. lbs.
8. Install the snapring.
9. Install the flywheel cover and torque the bolts to 5.8–8.7 ft. lbs.
10. Install the front wheels, lower the vehicle and connect the negative battery cable.

Automatic Locking Hubs

Removal and Installation

1. Disconnect the negative battery cable and raise and support the vehicle safely.

2. Remove the front wheels and remove the hub cover and gasket.

3. Remove the center attaching nut and the washer.

4. Mark the hub body and brake rotor for proper alignment upon reassembly.

5. Remove the hub body and the center snapring.

6. Remove the hub body brake shoe by prying outward.

7. Remove the Torx screws around the hub center and remove the hub assembly.

To install:

8. Install the Torx screws around the hub center and install the hub and brake rotor assembly.

9. Torque the hub body attaching bolts to 43.4–50.6 ft. lbs.

10. Install the hub body brake shoe assembly.

11. Install the hub center snapring and the hub body.

12. Install the center attaching nut and washer.

13. Install the hub cover and gasket and replace the front wheels.

14. Connect the negative battery cable and lower the vehicle.

Pinion Seal

Removal and Installation

FRONT

1. Raise and safely support the vehicle.

2. Matchmark and remove the front driveshaft.

3. Bend back the tab on the locknut of the drive pinion.

4. Using a pinion flange holding tool, remove the pinion nut and the washer.

5. Remove the pinion flange from the differential carrier and pry out the pinion seal.

To install:

6. Clean and inspect the sealing surface of the carrier.

7. Using a seal driver, install the new seal into the carrier until the flange of the seal is flush with the carrier.

NOTE: Tightening the flange nut will preload the pinion bearings. Exceeding the preload specifications will compress the collapsible spacer to far and require the spacer to be replaced.

8. Install the pinion flange and using the pinion flange holding tool, replace the pinion nut and washer. Tighten the pinion nut to 145 ft. lbs. and bend the nut into the opening to lock into place.

9. Align the matchmarks and install the driveshaft and tighten to 57 ft. lbs.

10. Check the level of the differential fluid when finished.

REAR

1. Raise and safely support the vehicle.

2. Matchmark and remove the rear driveshaft.

3. Bend the tab out on the locknut to allow for removal.

4. Using a pinion flange holding tool, remove the pinion nut and the washer.

5. Remove the pinion flange from the differential carrier and pry out the pinion seal.

To install:

6. Clean and inspect the sealing surface of the carrier.

7. Using a seal driver, install the new seal into the carrier until the flange of the seal is flush with the carrier.

NOTE: Tightening the flange nut will preload the pinion bearings. Exceeding the preload specifications will compress the collapsible spacer to far and require the spacer to be replaced.

8. Install the pinion flange and using the pinion flange holding tool, replace the pinion nut and washer. Tighten the pinion nut to 160 ft. lbs. and bend the nut into the opening to lock into place.

9. Align the matchmarks, install the driveshaft and tighten to 57 ft. lbs.

10. Check the level of the differential fluid when finished.

Differential Carrier

Removal and Installation

1. Raise and safely support the vehicle. Drain the oil from the rear differential.

2. Remove the left and right axle shafts.

3. Disconnect the driveshaft.

4. Support the differential carrier with a jack.

5. Remove the differential carrier assembly by removing the 10 bolts.

6. Lower the differential assembly from the rear housing.

To install:

7. Clean and inspect the sealing surfaces of the carrier and the housing.

8. Using a liquid sealant on the carrier, install the carrier in the housing and tighten the nuts to 39.8–57.9 ft. lbs.

9. Connect the rear driveshaft and replace the left and rear axles.

10. Refill the rear differential to the proper level with SAE 75W–90W API GL5 Hypoid Gear Oil.

11. Lower the vehicle.

Rear Axle Housing

Removal and Installation

1. Raise and safely support the vehicle. Drain the rear differential assembly.

2. Make sure the parking brake is in the released position.

3. Remove the rear wheels and remove the rear brake drums from the vehicle.

4. Disconnect the parking brake cables from the levers. Remove the parking brake lever stop plates.

5. Disconnect and plug the brake lines to the wheel cylinders.

6. Remove the backing plate mounting bolts and remove the axle shafts with the backing plates attached.

7. Remove the brake line from the flexible hose and remove the E-clip.

8. Disconnect the brake clamps and remove the brake lines from the rear housing.

9. Disconnect the driveshaft and remove from the transmission.

10. Disconnect the mounting bolts to the rear suspension arm and remove the housing to leaf spring U-bolts and nuts.

11. Remove shock absorber lower mount bolt.

12. Slide the housing to one side while tilting the opposite side under the leaf spring and remove the housing from the vehicle.

To install:

13. Install the housing-to-leaf spring U-bolt mounting bolts and nuts. Torque the housing U-bolts to 80 ft. lbs.

14. Install the shock absorber lower mount nut and locknut and tighten to 21 ft. lbs.

15. Connect the driveshaft and tighten the bolts to 57 ft. lbs.

16. Connect the rear brake clamps and brake lines.

17. Replace the rear axle housing gasket and install the axle shaft into the housing and tighten the bolts to 39 ft. lbs.

18. Install the wheel cylinders and connect the brake lines.

19. Install the rear brakes and connect the parking brake cables.

20. Install the rear brake drums, refill the differential and bleed the brake system.

21. Install the rear wheels and lower the vehicle.

STEERING

Steering Wheel

Removal and Installation

1. Disconnect the negative battery cable.
2. Remove the horn pad attaching screw and remove the horn pad.
3. Disconnect the horn wiring connector.
4. Remove the steering wheel attaching nut and pull the steering wheel off of the shaft.

To install:

5. Install the steering wheel onto the shaft and tighten the steering wheel attaching nut to 21.7–36.2 ft. lbs.
6. Connect the horn wiring connector and install the horn pad and horn pad attaching screw.
7. Connect the negative battery cable.

Manual Steering Gear

Removal and Installation

1. Disconnect the negative battery cable.
2. Remove the air cleaner, air hose assembly and the clutch cable clamp bolts and hose bands.
3. Remove the intermediate shaft connecting bolts and disconnect the shaft.
4. Disconnect the pitman arm from the relay rod.
5. Remove the pitman arm attaching nut to the steering gear housing.
6. Remove the attaching nuts and bolts and remove the steering gear housing from the vehicle.

To install:

7. Install the steering gear housing and install the attaching nuts and bolts and tighten to 25 ft. lbs.
8. Attach the pitman arm to the steering gear housing and to the relay rod.
9. Install the intermediate shaft and install the connecting bolts and tighten to 25 ft. lbs.
10. Install the air cleaner, air hose assembly and the clutch cable clamp bolts and hose bands.
11. Connect the negative battery cable.

Steering wheel removal procedure

Power Steering Gear

Removal and Installation

1. Disconnect the negative battery cable.
2. Remove the air cleaner, air hose assembly and the clutch cable clamp bolts and hose bands.
3. Remove the intermediate shaft connecting bolts and disconnect the shaft.
4. Drain power steering fluid and disconnect the power steering line clamps.
5. Disconnect the pitman arm from the relay rod.
6. Remove the pitman arm attaching nut to the steering gear housing.
7. Remove the attaching nuts and bolts and remove the steering gear housing from the vehicle.

To install:

8. Install the steering gear housing and install the attaching nuts and bolts and tighten to 25 ft. lbs.
9. Attach the pitman arm to the steering gear housing and to the relay rod.
10. Connect the power steering line clamps and refill the power steering reservoir.
11. Install the intermediate shaft and install the connecting bolts and tighten to 25 ft. lbs.
12. Install the air cleaner, air hose assembly and the clutch cable clamp bolts and hose bands.
13. Connect the negative battery cable.

Power Steering Pump

Removal and Installation

NOTE: Before disconnecting the power steering pressure and return line at the pump assembly, make sure any dirt or grease is removed.

1. Disconnect the negative battery cable. Drain the power steering fluid.
2. Remove the radiator reserve tank.
3. Loosen the power steering pump adjusting and mounting bolts.
4. Remove the power steering belt.
5. Disconnect the power steering pressure and return hose and plug.
6. Disconnect the air hoses at the air control valve.
7. Remove the pressure feed tube clamp and remove the tube support bracket.
8. Remove the power steering pump mounting and adjusting bolts.
9. Remove the power steering pump.

Power steering pump bolts

To install:

10. Install the power steering pump and replace the pump mounting bolts. Do not tighten.
11. Replace the power steering pressure and return hoses.
12. Install the power steering belt and tighten the power steering pump mounting bolts to 21 ft. lbs.
13. Replace the pressure feed tube clamp and bracket.
14. Replace the coolant reservoir tank to the radiator and connect the negative battery cable. Refill the power steering pump.
15. Run the engine and operate the power steering. Recheck the fluid level and for any leaks.

Belt Adjustment

1. Adjust the drive belt tension by tightening the adjusting bolt.
2. Tighten the locknut on the adjustment bolt to 11 ft. lbs.

System Bleeding

1. Raise and support the vehicle safely.
2. Fill the power steering reservoir to the specified level.
3. Run the engine for 3–5 minutes, stop it and add fluid, if necessary to reach specified level.
4. With the engine stopped, turn the steering wheel to the left and to the right as far as it turns. Repeat a few times and refill the reservoir.
5. With the engine running at idle speed, bleed air from the system by loosening the bleeder valve at the gear assembly.
6. Repeat the stop to stop turn of the steering wheel until all the foam is gone.
7. Tighten the bleed valve securely. Recheck the fluid level in the reservoir.

Tie Rod Ends

Removal and Installation

1. Raise and safely support the vehicle and remove the wheels.
2. Remove the tie rod end from the steering knuckle, using a suitable tie rod end remover tool.
3. Mark the tie rod end locknut position on the tie rod thread.
4. Loosen the locknut and remove the tie rod end from the tie rod.
5. Install the tie rod end locknut and the tie rod end to the tie rod. Align the locknut with the mark on the tie rod thread and tighten the locknut to 88 ft. lbs.
6. Connect the tie rod end to the steering knuckle. Tighten the locknut to 88 ft. lbs.

BRAKES

For all brake system repair and service procedures not detailed below, please refer to "Brakes" in the Unit Repair section.

Master Cylinder

Removal and Installation

1. Disconnect the negative battery cable.
2. Drain the brake fluid at the wheel cylinders.
3. Disconnect the brake fluid level sensor connector.
4. Disconnect the hydraulic brake lines from the master cylinder.
5. Remove the brake master cylinder attaching bolts and remove the master cylinder.

To install:

6. Install the new master cylinder to the brake booster and tighten the mounting bolts to 7.52–11.3 ft. lbs.
7. Connect the hydraulic lines to the master cylinder and tighten the lines to 9.4–13.0 ft. lbs.
8. Install the brake fluid level sensor connector and refill the reservoir with the specified brake fluid.
9. Bleed the air from the brake hydraulic system and check the brake pedal play.

Removing the master cylinder assembly

Combination Valve

Removal and Installation

1. Drain the brake fluid from the front and rear bleeder valves.
2. Disconnect the brake lines from the combination valve.
3. Remove the attaching bolts and remove the combination valve.

To install:

4. Install the combination valve and tighten the attaching bolts to 9.4–13.0 ft. lbs.
5. Connect the brake lines to the combination valves.
6. Fill the brake reservoir to the proper level and bleed the brake hydraulic system.

Power Brake Booster

Removal and Installation

1. Disconnect the negative battery cable.
2. Drain the brake fluid from the brake system.
3. Remove the master cylinder.
4. Disconnect the brake booster hose at the brake booster.
5. Remove the cotter pin and clevis pin from the top of the brake pedal.
6. Remove the brake booster attaching nuts and remove the brake booster assembly.

To install:

7. Install the brake booster assembly and tighten the brake booster attaching nuts to 7.2–11.6 ft. lbs.
8. Connect the clevis pin and cotter pin to brake pedal.
9. Install the brake booster hose and the master cylinder.
10. Connect the negative battery cable, refill the brake reservoir and bleed the brake hydraulic system.

Brake Caliper

Removal and Installation

1. Disconnect the negative battery cable. Raise and safely support the vehicle.

1. Bolt
2. Boot
3. Bolt
4. Bleeder plug
5. Caliper body
6. Cylinder slide bushing
7. Dust boot/bushing
8. Brake piston
9. Piston seal
10. Set ring
11. Cylinder boot

Exploded view of front brake caliper

2. Remove the wheels. Disconnect and plug the brake line.
3. Remove the caliper mounting bolts and remove the caliper from the vehicle.

To install:
4. Install the caliper and tighten the mounting bolts to 23.1–30.3 ft. lbs.
5. Connect the hydraulic brake line, using 2 new washers. Install the front wheels.
6. Lower the vehicle. Connect the negative battery cable.
7. Fill the brake reservoir and bleed the hydraulic brake system.

Disc Brake Pads

Removal and Installation

1. Disconnect the negative battery cable. Raise and safely support the vehicle.
2. Remove the wheels.
3. Disconnect the brake caliper.

NOTE: Do not allow the caliper hang from the brake hose. Support it by the mounting bracket.

4. Remove the disc pads from the caliper. Disconnect the anti rattle springs and anti-squeal shims.

1. Anti-squeal shim
2. Brake pad guide plate
3. Brake pad guide plate
4. Anti-squeal shim

Exploded view of front brake pad assembly

To install:
5. Connect the anti rattle springs and anti squeal shims and install the brake pads on to caliper assembly.
6. Connect the brake caliper and install the front wheels.
7. Lower the vehicle. Connect the negative battery cable.

Brake Rotor

Removal and Installation

1. Disconnect the negative battery cable.
2. Raise and safely support the vehicle. Remove the wheel assembly.
3. Remove the brake caliper mounting bracket, with the caliper and the brake line attached, move it out of the way and support it.

NOTE: Do not allow the caliper hang from the brake hose. Support it by the mounting bracket.

4. Remove the front axle hub and rotor assembly by removing the locknut assembly.

To install:
5. Install the new brake rotor on the hub and tighten the locknut.
6. Install the caliper mounting bracket and caliper assembly.
7. Install the front wheels and lug nuts.
8. Lower the vehicle and connect the negative battery cable.

Brake Drums

Removal and Installation

1. Disconnect the negative battery cable. Raise and safely support the vehicle.
2. Make sure the parking brake is released.
3. Remove the lug nuts and the wheels.
4. Remove the brake drum.

To install:
5. Install the brake drums and wheels and tighten the lug nuts to 65.1–87.0 ft. lbs.

Brake Shoes

Removal and Installation

1. Disconnect the negative battery cable. Raise and safely support the vehicle.

1. Shoe hold-down pin
2. Hole plug
3. Brake backing plate
4. Bleeder plug
5. Rear wheel brake cylinder assembly
6. Rear wheel cylinder cap kit
7. Compression spring
8. Rear brake shoe
9. Shoe hold-down spring
10. Tension spring
11. Tension spring
12. Tension spring #2
13. Parking brake shoe lever
14. Rear brake shoe
15. Parking brake lever pin
16. Bolt
17. Automatic adjusting lever
18. Tension spring
19. Parking brake shoe strut

Exploded view of the rear brake assembly

2. Remove the rear wheels and the brake drums.

3. Remove the brake shoe tension springs and the hold-down springs.

4. Disconnect the parking brake cable from the parking brake shoe lever and remove the brake shoes.

To install:

5. Install the brake cable and install the brake shoes.

6. Install the brake shoe tension springs and hold-down springs.

7. Install the rear brake drums and rear wheels.

Wheel Cylinder

Removal and Installation

1. Disconnect the negative battery cable. Raise and safely support the vehicle.

2. Remove the rear wheels and brake drums.

3. Remove the rear brake shoes and disconnect the brake line from the rear of the wheel cylinder. Plug the brake line.

4. Remove the 2 rear wheel cylinder mounting bolts. Remove the rear wheel cylinder.

To install:

5. Install the wheel cylinder and tighten the mounting bolts to 8 ft. lbs.

6. Connect the brake line to the wheel cylinder and install the rear brake shoes.

7. Install the rear brake drums and the rear wheels.

8. Lower the vehicle. Connect the negative battery cable.

9. Bleed the brake system and check for any leaks when finished.

Parking Brake Cable

Removal and Installation

1. Raise and safely support the vehicle. Remove the rear wheels and brake drums.

2. Disconnect the parking brake cable at the equalizer and remove the brake cable clamps and bolts.

3. Remove the rear brake shoes and disconnect the parking brake cable from the parking brake shoe lever.

4. Remove the cable from the brake backing plate by squeezing the parking brake cable stop ring.

To install:

5. Install the brake cable at the backing plate and at the parking brake lever.

6. Install the rear brake shoes and brake drums.

7. Install the brake cable clamps and bolts and connect the brake cable at the equalizer.

Adjustment

1. Adjust the parking brake lever by loosening or tightening the self locking nut at the park brake lever.

2. The proper adjustment is when the park brake lever is within 4–6 notches, when the lever is pulled up at 66 lbs.

3. Check the rear drum for dragging after adjustment.

FRONT SUSPENSION

Shock absorbers

Removal and Installation

1. Raise and safely support the vehicle.
2. Support the axle assembly and remove the upper shock absorber mounting nut.
3. Remove the lower shock absorber mounting nut and remove the shock absorber.

To install:

4. Install the shock absorber and connect the upper and lower mounting bolts and nuts.
5. Torque the upper mounting nut to 22 ft. lbs. and the lower nut to 50 ft. lbs. and lower the vehicle.

Torsion Bars

Removal and Installation

1. Raise and safely support the vehicle.
2. Remove the rubber boot and mark both ends of the spring for installation purposes.
3. Measure and record the length of the protruding portion of the anchor bolt and loosen the nuts on the anchor arm until the spring reaction force is eliminated.
4. Remove the torque arm attaching bolt.
5. Remove the anchor arm bolt and stopper from the frame and remove the torsion bar spring.

To install:

6. Install the torsion bar spring and anchor arm bolt assembly.
7. Install the torque arm attaching bolt.
8. Install the torque arm, making sure the alignment marks match.
9. Adjust the anchor bolt so that the protruding dimension of the bolt is the same as it was prior to removal.

Upper Ball Joints

Inspection

1. Inspect for the smoothness of the rotation.
2. Check the ball stud for damage.
3. Inspect the dust shield for damage.

Removal and Installation

1. Raise and safely support the vehicle.
2. Remove the stabilizer bar and the torsion spring.
3. Remove the front brakes and front hub assembly.
4. Disconnect steering knuckle from the tie rod end.
5. Remove attaching bolts at the upper ball joint.
6. Remove the cotter pin and nut and remove the ball joint.

To install:

7. Install the ball joint and tighten the bolts to 65 ft. lbs.
8. Replace attaching bolts and connect steering knuckle to tie rod end.
9. Replace front brakes, hub assembly and torsion spring.

Lower Ball Joints

Inspection

1. Inspect for the smoothness of the rotation.
2. Check the ball stud for damage.
3. Inspect the dust shield for damage.

Removal and Installation

1. Raise and safely support the vehicle.
2. Remove the stabilizer bar and the torsion spring.
3. Remove the front brakes and front hub assembly.
4. Disconnect steering knuckle from the tie rod end.
5. Remove attaching bolts at the lower ball joint.
6. Remove the cotter pin and nut and remove the ball joint.

To install:

7. Install the ball joint and tighten the bolts to 65 ft. lbs.
8. Replace attaching bolts and connect steering knuckle to tie rod end.
9. Replace front brakes, hub assembly and torsion spring.

Lower Control Arms

Removal and Installation

1. Raise and safely support the vehicle.
2. Remove the stabilizer bar and the torsion spring.
3. Remove the front brakes and front hub assembly.
4. Remove the steering knuckle.
5. Remove the driveshaft and remove the lower shock absorber attaching bolts.

Exploded view of torsion bar assembly

6. Remove the lower arm attaching bolts and remove the lower arm assembly.

To install:

7. Install the control arm to the chassis and tighten the attaching bolts to 94 ft. lbs.

8. Attach the lower shock absorber bolts and install the driveshaft.

9. Install the steering knuckle.

10. Install the front hub and front brake assembly.

11. Install the stabilizer bar and the torsion spring.

Sway Bar

Removal and Installation

1. Disconnect the negative battery cable. Raise and safely support the vehicle.

2. Disconnect the stabilizer bar pivot bolts.

3. Remove the stabilizer bar mount bushing bracket bolts and nuts.

4. Remove the stabilizer bar.

To install:

5. Install the new stabilizer bar, using new bushings.

6. Replace the bracket, bolts and nuts.

7. Torque the stabilizer bar to lower control arm attaching bolts to 13 ft. lbs. and the stabilizer bracket cover attaching bolt to 21 ft. lbs.

8. Connect the negative battery cable.

REAR SUSPENSION

Shock Absorbers

Removal and Installation

1. Raise and safely support the vehicle. Support the rear axle housing.

2. Remove the upper and lower shock absorber mounting bolts.

3. Remove the rear shock absorber.

4. Install the the rear shock absorber.

5. Replace the mounting bolts and tighten to 21 ft. lbs.

Leaf Springs

Removal and Installation

1. Raise and safely support the vehicle. Remove the rear wheels.

2. Safely, support the rear axle housing separately.

3. Disconnect the rear shock absorbers at the lower mounting.

NOTE: Do not let the rear axle housing hang on the rear brake hoses or lines.

4. Remove the rear axle housing U-bolts nuts and bolts.

5. Raise the axle housing and remove the shackle plate.

6. Support the leaf spring and disconnect the front and the rear leaf spring mounting bolts.

7. Remove the rear leaf spring.

To install:

8. Connect the front section of the rear spring and install the attaching bolt and nut.

9. Connect the shackle pin to the frame and connect the leaf spring to the shackle pin.

10. Install the bracket to the shackle pin temporarily tighten the nuts.

11. Attach the bolt to the leaf spring at the rear axle housing.

12. Replace the U-bolts and U-bolt seat, tighten the nuts to 80 ft. lbs.

13. Connect the shock absorbers at the lower mounting and lower the vehicle.

14. Tighten the front spring mounting bolt and nut to 100 ft. lbs. and the rear spring shackle attaching nuts to 65 ft. lbs.

15. Tighten the rear shock absorber attaching nut to 22 ft. lbs. and install the locknut and tighten to 22 ft. lbs.

16. Replace the rear spring bumper and tighten the attaching bolts.

1. Rear spring shackle
2. Bushing
3. Bushing
4. Washer
5. Nut
6. Rear spring shackle
7. Washer
8. Nut
9. Bushing
10. Rear spring assembly
11. Bolt
12. Rear spring bumper
13. "U" bolt
14. Washer
15. Nut
16. Spring "U" bolt seat
17. Bushing
18. Nut
19. Bolt

Rear suspension assembly

SPECIFICATIONS

VEHICLE IDENTIFICATION CHART

It is important for servicing and ordering parts to be certain of the vehicle and engine identification. The VIN (vehicle identification number) is a 17 digit number visible through the windshield on the driver's side of the dash and contains the vehicle and engine identification codes. The tenth digit indicates model year and the eighth digit indicates engine code. It can be interpreted as follows:

Engine Code						Model Year	
Code	Cu. In.	Liters	Cyl.	Fuel Sys.	Eng. Mfg.	Code	Year
U	97.0	1.6	4	EFI	Suzuki	L	1990
						M	1991
						N	1992

EFI—Electronic Fuel Injection

ENGINE IDENTIFICATION

Year	Model	Engine Displacement cu. in. (cc/liter)	Engine Series Identification	No. of Cylinders	Engine Type
1990	Tracker	97.0 (1590/1.6)	U	4	SOHC
1991	Tracker	97.0 (1590/1.6)	U	4	SOHC
1992	Tracker	97.0 (1590/1.6)	U	4	SOHC

SOHC—Single Overhead Cam

GENERAL ENGINE SPECIFICATIONS

Year	Model	Engine Displacement cu. in. (cc)	Fuel System Type	Net Horsepower @ rpm	Net Torque @ rpm (ft. lbs.)	Bore × Stroke (in.)	Compression Ratio	Oil Pressure @ rpm
1990	Tracker	97.0 (1590)	EFI	80 @ 5400	94 @ 3000	2.95 × 3.54	8.9:1	51.2–62.6①
1991	Tracker	97.0 (1590)	EFI	80 @ 5400	94 @ 3000	2.95 × 3.54	8.9:1	51.2–62.6①
1992	Tracker	97.0 (1590)	EFI	80 @ 5400	94 @ 3000	2.95 × 3.54	8.9:1	51.2–62.6①

EFI—Electronic Fuel Injection
① @ 3000 rpm

ENGINE TUNE-UP SPECIFICATIONS

Year	Model	Engine Displacement cu. in. (cc)	Spark Plugs		Ignition Timing (deg.)		Com-pression Pressure (psi)	Fuel Pump (psi)	Idle Speed (rpm)		Valve Clearance	
			Type	Gap (in.)	MT	AT			MT	AT	In.	Ex.
1990	Tracker	97.0 (1590)	BPR5ES	0.028–0.031	8B	8B	170–199	34.1–39.8	800	800	①	②
1991	Tracker	97.0 (1590)	BPR5ES	0.028–0.031	8B	8B	170–199	34.1–39.8	800	800	①	②
1992	Tracker	97.0 (1590)	BPR5ES	0.028–0.031	8B	8B	170–199	34.1–39.8	800	800	①	②

① Intake
 Cold—0.0051–0.0067 in.
 Hot—0.009–0.011 in.
② Exhaust
 Cold—0.0063–0.0079 in.
 Hot—0.0102–0.0118 in.

FIRING ORDERS

NOTE: To avoid confusion, always replace spark plug wires one at a time.

FRONT →

1.6L Engine
Engine Firing Order: 1–3–4–2
Distributor Rotation: Clockwise

CAPACITIES

Year	Model	Engine Displacement cu. in. (cc)	Engine Crankcase		Transmission (pts.)			Drive Axle (pts.)	Fuel Tank (gal.)	Cooling System (qts.)
			with Filter	without Filter	4-Spd	5-Spd	Auto.			
1990	Tracker	97.0 (1590)	4.5	4.3	NA	3.2	10.8	②	11.1	①
1991	Tracker	97.0 (1590)	4.5	4.3	NA	3.2	6.0	②	11.1	①
1992	Tracker	97.0 (1590)	4.5	4.3	NA	3.2	6.0	②	11.1	①

NA—Not available
① Manual transmission—5.6 qts.
 Automatic transmission—5.5. qts.
② Front—2.1 pts.
 Rear—4.6 pts.

CAMSHAFT SPECIFICATIONS

All measurements are given in inches.

Year	Engine Displacement cu. in. (cc)	Journal Diameter					Lobe Lift		Bearing Clearance	Camshaft End Play
		1	2	3	4	5	In.	Ex.		
1990	97.0 (1590)	1.7372–1.7381	1.7451–1.7460	1.7530–1.7539	1.7609–1.7618	1.7687–1.7697	1.4763–1.4724	1.4763–1.4724	0.0020–0.0036 ①	0.0039
1991	97.0 (1590)	1.7372–1.7381	1.7451–1.7460	1.7530–1.7539	1.7609–1.7618	1.7687–1.7697	1.4763–1.4724	1.4763–1.4724	0.0020–0.0036 ①	0.0039
1992	97.0 (1590)	1.7372–1.7381	1.7451–1.7460	1.7530–1.7539	1.7609–1.7618	1.7687–1.7697	1.4763–1.4724	1.4763–1.4724	0.0020–0.0036 ①	0.0039

① 0.0059 limit

CRANKSHAFT AND CONNECTING ROD SPECIFICATIONS

All measurements are given in inches.

Year	Displacement cu. in. (cc)	Crankshaft				Connecting Rod		
		Main Brg. Journal Dia.	Main Brg. Oil Clearance	Shaft End-play	Thrust on No.	Journal Diameter	Oil Clearance	Side Clearance
1990	97.0 (1590)	①	0.0012–0.0023	0.0100–0.0149	3	1.7316–1.7323	0.0008–0.0031	0.0039–0.0137
1991	97.0 (1590)	①	0.0012–0.0023	0.0100–0.0149	3	1.7316–1.7323	0.0008–0.0031	0.0039–0.0137
1992	97.0 (1590)	①	0.0012–0.0023	0.0100–0.0149	3	1.7316–1.7323	0.0008–0.0031	0.0039–0.0137

① Bearing cap stamped
No. 1—2.0470–2.0472
No. 2—2.0468–2.0470
No. 3—2.0465–2.0468

VALVE SPECIFICATIONS

Year	Engine Displacement cu. in. (cc)	Seat Angle (deg.)	Face Angle (deg.)	Spring Test Pressure (lbs.)	Spring Installed Height (in.)	Stem-to-Guide Clearance (in.)		Stem Diameter (in.)	
						Intake	Exhaust	Intake	Exhaust
1990	97 (1590)	45	45	54.7–64.3 @ 1.63 in.	1.9074	0.0008–0.0019 ①	0.0014–0.0025 ②	0.2742–0.2748	0.2737–0.2742
1991	97 (1590)	45	45	54.7–64.3 @ 1.63 in.	1.9074	0.0008–0.0019 ①	0.0014–0.0025 ②	0.2742–0.2748	0.2737–0.2742
1992	97 (1590)	45	45	54.7–64.3 @ 1.63 in.	1.9074	0.0008–0.0019 ①	0.0014–0.0025 ②	0.2742–0.2748	0.2737–0.2742

① Maximum clearance—0.0027 in.
② Maximum clearance—0.0035 in.

PISTON AND RING SPECIFICATIONS

All measurements are given in inches.

Year	Engine Displacement cu. in. (cc)	Piston Clearance	Ring Gap			Ring Side Clearance		
			Top Compression	Bottom Compression	Oil Control	Top Compression	Bottom Compression	Oil Control
1990	97.0 (1590)	0.0008–0.0015	0.0079–0.0129	0.0079–0.0137	0.0079–0.0275	0.0012–0.0027	0.0008–0.0023	NA
1991	97.0 (1590)	0.0008–0.0015	0.0079–0.0129	0.0079–0.0137	0.0079–0.0275	0.0012–0.0027	0.0008–0.0023	NA
1992	97.0 (1590)	0.0008–0.0015	0.0079–0.0129	0.0079–0.0137	0.0079–0.0275	0.0012–0.0027	0.0008–0.0023	NA

NA—Not available

TORQUE SPECIFICATIONS

All readings are given in ft. lbs.

Year	Engine Displacement cu. in. (cc)	Cylinder Head Bolts	Main Bearing Bolts	Rod Bearing Bolts	Crankshaft Pulley Bolts	Flywheel Bolts	Manifold Intake	Manifold Exhaust	Spark Plugs
1990	97.0 (1590)	51–54	36–41	24–26	7–9	54–57	13–20	13–20	14–21
1991	97.0 (1590)	51–54	36–41	24–26	7–9	54–57	13–20	13–20	14–21
1992	97.0 (1590)	51–54	36–41	24–26	7–9	54–57	13–20	13–20	14–21

BRAKE SPECIFICATIONS

All measurements are given in inches.

Year	Model	Lug Nut Torque (ft. lbs.)	Master Cylinder Bore	Brake Disc Minimum Thickness	Brake Disc Maximum Runout	Standard Brake Drum Diameter	Minimum Lining Thickness Front	Minimum Lining Thickness Rear
1990	Tracker	36–57	NA	0.394	0.334	8.66	0.236 ①	0.120 ②
1991	Tracker	58–78	NA	0.394	0.315	8.66	0.315 ①	0.120 ②
1992	Tracker	58–78	NA	0.394	0.315	8.66	0.315 ①	0.120 ②

NA—Not available
① Lining plus pad rim
② Lining plus shoe rim

WHEEL ALIGNMENT

Year	Model	Caster Range (deg.)	Caster Preferred Setting (deg.)	Camber Range (deg.)	Camber Preferred Setting (deg.)	Toe-in (in.)	Steering Axis Inclination (deg.)
1990	Tracker	½P–2½P	1½P	½N–1½P	½P	5/16–¼	NA
1991	Tracker	½P–2½P	1½P	½N–1½P	½P	5/16–¼	NA
1992	Tracker	½P–2½P	1½P	½N–1½P	½P	5/16–¼	NA

NA—Not available
N—Negative
P—Positive

ENGINE ELECTRICAL

NOTE: Disconnecting the battery cable on some vehicles may interfere with the functions of the on board computer systems and may require the computer to undergo a relearning process, once the negative battery cable is disconnected.

Distributor

Removal

1. Disconnect the negative battery terminal from the battery.
2. Disconnect vacuum hose and electrical connections.

NOTE: Do not bend or twist the spark plug wires to avoid internal damage. Grip the the wire boot when removing or installing the wires.

3. Remove the distributor cap.
4. Mark the rotor position on the distributor housing and the distributor housing position on the engine.

5. Remove the distributor flange bolt and remove the distributor.

NOTE: Do not crank the engine with the distributor removed.

Installation

TIMING NOT DISTURBED

1. Install the distributor and align the marks on the distributor housing and on the engine.
2. Tighten the flange bolt to 11 ft. lbs. and install the distributor cap.
3. Connect the electrical connections and the vacuum hoses.
4. Connect the negative battery cable and set the timing to specification.

TIMING DISTURBED

1. Rotate the crankshaft in a clockwise position until the

specified timing mark on the flywheel aligns with the timing matchmark on the engine.

NOTE: After aligning the 2 marks, remove the cylinder head cover to visually check so the rocker arms are not riding on the camshaft cams at No. 1 cylinder. If the arms are found to be riding on the cams, turn the crankshaft 360 degrees to realign the 2 marks.

2. Position the rotor to the No. 1 cylinder position and install the distributor tightening the flange bolt to 11 ft. lbs.
3. Connect the vacuum and electrical connections.
4. Connect the negative battery cable and set the timing to specification.

Ignition Timing

Adjustment

1. Start the engine and warm to normal operating temperature. Prior to any adjustment, be sure all the electrical accessories are OFF .
2. After warming, make sure the idle speed is 800 rpm.
3. Remove cap from monitor coupler next to battery and connect terminals **C** and **D** with a jumper wire. Connect the timing light to the No. 1 cylinder spark plug wire.
4. With the engine running at the specified idle speed, direct the timing light to the crankshaft pulley. If the specified timing mark on the timing tab is aligned with the timing notch on the crankshaft pulley the ignition is properly timed.
5. If the timing is out of adjustment, loosen the distributor flange bolt and turn the distributor housing to advance or retard the timing. Turn the distributor counterclockwise to advance the timing and clockwise to retard the timing.
6. After the adjustment, tighten the flange bolt and recheck the timing.

Alternator

For further information, please refer to "Alternators" in the Unit Repair section.

Belt Tension Adjustment

1. Disconnect the negative battery cable.
2. Loosen the alternator bolt and pivot bolts.
3. Adjust the belt tension to 0.24 – 0.32 in. of deflection using a belt tension guage.

Removal and Installation

1. Disconnect the negative battery cable.

Timing mark location—Tracker

2. Disconnect the wire coupler and white lead wire from the alternator.
3. Remove the charcoal cannister mounting bracket, if necessary.
4. Remove the alternator mounting bolt and alternator drive belt adjusting bolt.
5. Remove the alternator from the vehicle.
To install:
6. Install the alternator and tighten the mounting bolt and drive belt adjusting bolt. Adjust the drive belt tension.
7. Install the shroud under the radiator and connect the wire coupler to the alternator.
8. Connect the negative battery cable.

Starter

For further information, please refer to "Starters" in the Unit Repair section.

Removal and Installation

1. Disconnect the negative battery cable.
2. Raise and support the vehicle safely.
3. Disconnect the lead wire and battery cable from the starter motor.
4. Support the starter and remove the 2 mounting bolts.
5. Remove the starter.
To install:
6. Install the starter and tighten the 2 mounting bolts to 22 ft. lbs.
7. Connect the lead wire to the starter.
8. Lower the vehicle and connect the negative battery cable.

CHASSIS ELECTRICAL

Heater Blower Motor

Removal and Installation

1. Disconnect the negative battery cable.
2. Remove the glove box assembly.
3. Disconnect the blower motor and resistor wire connectors.
4. Disconnect the fresh air control cable from the blower motor case.
5. Loosen but do not remove the blower housing fastener bolts.
6. Remove the 3 blower motor mounting screws.
7. Remove the blower motor.
To install:
8. Install the blower motor and secure with the 3 screws.

Heater blower motor mounting screws

9. Tighten the blower housing fastener bolts.

10. Connect the fresh air control cable to the blower motor case.

11. Connect the electrical connectors and install the glove box assembly.

12. Connect the negative battery cable.

Windshield Wiper Motor

Removal and Installation

1. Disconnect the negative battery cable.
2. Remove the right and left cowl grilles.
3. Remove the wiper linkage to wiper mounting nut.
4. Disconnect the wire connector from the wiper motor.
5. Remove the 4 wiper motor mounting bolts and remove the wiper motor.

To install:

6. Install the wiper motor and install the 4 mounting bolts.
7. Connect the electrical connector and connect the wiper linkage.
8. Install the cowl grilles and connect the negative battery cable.

Instrument Cluster

Removal and Installation

1. Disconnect the negative battery cable.
2. Remove the 4 screws from the front shroud.
3. Remove the front shroud.
4. Remove the 4 cluster mounting screws and slide the cluster outwards.
5. Disconnect the lead wires and speedometer cable from the speedometer.
6. Remove the instrument cluster assembly.

To install:

7. Install the lead wires and speedometer cable.
8. Install the 4 cluster screws and tighten.
9. Install the front shroud and install the 2 upper and 2 lower screws.
10. Connect the negative battery cable.

Radio

Removal and Installation

1. Disconnect the negative battery cable.
2. Remove the ashtray and the ashtray guide assembly.
3. Remove the 1 bolt that secures radio to the bracket.
4. Disconnect the electrical connections and antenna lead from the radio.
5. Remove the radio from the vehicle.

To install:

6. Install the radio and connect the antenna wire and electrical connector.
7. Install the 1 bolt between the radio and the bracket assembly.
8. Install the ashtray and guide assembly and connect the negative battery cable.

Combination Switch

The combination switch incorporates the turn signal, windshield wiper, dimmer and headlight switches into one switch.

Removal and Installation

1. Disconnect the negative battery cable.
2. Remove the horn button and the steering wheel retaining nut and remove the steering wheel.

3. Remove the upper and lower column cover screws and remove the covers.
4. Disconnect the lead wires from the combination switch at the connector.
5. Remove the combination switch assembly screws.
6. Remove the combination switch from the steering column.

To install:

7. Install the combination switch assembly and install the screws.
8. Connect the electrical connector.
9. Install the upper and lower column covers.
10. Install the steering wheel and tighten the shaft nut to 24 ft. lbs.
11. Install the horn button and connect the negative battery cable.

Ignition Switch

Removal and Installation

1. Disconnect the negative battery cable.
2. Remove the steering wheel from the vehicle.
3. Disconnect the wire connector at the ignition switch.
4. With the ignition switch in the **OFF** position, remove the mounting bolts and remove the switch.

To install:

5. Install the ignition switch and replace the mounting bolts.
6. Connect the electrical connector to the ignition switch.
7. Install the steering wheel and tighten the shaft nut to 24 ft. lbs.
8. Install the horn button and connect the negative battery cable.

Ignition Lock

1. Disconnect the negative battery cable.
2. Remove the steering wheel.
3. Disconnect the lead wires to the ignition and combination switches.
4. Disconnect the steering joint by removing the joint bolt.
5. Remove the steering column fastening bolts.
6. Remove the steering column assembly.
7. Using a center punch, loosen and remove the steering lock mounting bolts.
8. Turn the key to **ACC** or **ON** position and remove the steering lock assembly from the steering column.

To install:

9. To install the switch, position the oblong hole of the steering shaft in the center of the hole in the steering column.
10. Turn the ignition key to the **ACC** or **ON** position and install the steering lock assembly onto the column.
11. Turn the ignition key to the **LOCK** position and remove it.
12. Align the hub on the lock with oblong hole of the steering shaft.
13. Rotate the shaft to assure that the steering shaft is locked.
14. Tighten the 2 new steering lock mounting bolts.
15. Turn the ignition key to the **ACC** or **ON** position and check to be sure the steering shaft rotates smoothly. Also check the lock mechanism.
16. Install the steering column assembly by attaching the steering joint and joint bolt.
17. Install the steering column fastening bolts.
18. Reconnect the lead wires to the ignition and combination switches.
19. Replace the steering wheel and negative battery cable.

Stoplight Switch

Removal and Installation

1. Disconnect the negative battery cable. Remove the under dash trim panel, if equipped.

2. Push the brake pedal down and remove the stoplight switch locknut.

3. Disconnect the wire connector at the switch.

4. Remove the switch from the bracket.

To install:

5. Install the new switch on the bracket.

6. Adjust the switch so there is 0.02–0.04 in. clearance between the switch and the brake pedal.

7. Replace the locknut and tighten to 7.5–10.5 ft. lbs.

8. Replace the negative battery cable.

Clutch Switch

Removal and Installation

1. Disconnect the negative battery cable. Remove the under dash trim panel, if equipped.

2. Disconnect the clutch/start switch connector beside the clutch pedal bracket.

3. Remove the locknut and clutch/start switch.

To install:

4. Install the clutch/start switch and tighten the locknut.

5. Connect the electrical connector, connect the negative battery cable and install the under dash trim panel.

Fuses and Relays

Location

The fuse box and turn signal relay are located under the driver side of the dashboard.

Computer

Location

The Electronic Control Module (ECM) computer is located under the dash on the driver side of the vehicle.

Cruise control adjustment

Cruise Control

For further information, please refer to Chilton's Chassis Electronics Service Manual.

Adjustment

1. Remove the top cover from the actuator assembly.

2. Loosen the lock nuts on the cable.

3. Adjust the cable so the play range is between 0.04–0.08 in. when the actuator lever is fully closed.

4. Tighten the lock nut to 4 ft. lbs. and replace the top cover.

Flashers

Location

The flashers are located under the driver side of the dashboard.

ENGINE COOLING

Radiator

Removal and Installation

1. Disconnect the negative battery cable.

2. Drain the cooling system.

3. Disconnect and plug the transmission cooler lines, if equipped.

4. Loosen the water pump drive belt tension.

5. Remove the cooling fan and radiator shroud.

6. Disconnect the water hoses to the radiator.

7. Remove the radiator retaining bolts and remove the radiator.

To install:

8. Replace the radiator mounting bolts and install the radiator.

9. Reconnect the water hoses to the radiator.

10. Install the cooling fan and radiator shroud.

11. Tighten the water pump drive belt to the proper tension.

12. Reconnect the transmission cooler lines, if necessary to the radiator.

13. Refill the cooling system.

14. Reconnect the negative battery cable.

Heater Core

For further information, please refer to Chilton's Air Conditioning and Heating Manual.

Removal and Installation

1. Disconnect the negative battery cable. Drain the cooling system.

2. Disconnect the 2 heater hoses from the heater case.

3. Remove the steering wheel. Disconnect the lead wires from the ignition and combination switches.

4. Disconnect the wiring harness and remove the instrument panel.

5. Disconnect all the wiring connections and cables from the heater controls.

6. Disconnect the defroster duct and speedometer cable retaining bracket from the heater case.

7. Remove the heater assembly and remove the heater core.

To install:

8. Install the heater core and install the heater assembly.

9. Reconnect the defroster duct and speedometer cable retaining bracket to the heater case.

10. Reconnect the wiring connections and cables to the heater controls.

11. Reconnect the wiring harness and install the instrument panel.

12. Connect the lead wires to the ignition and combination switches.

13. Connect the heater hoses to the heater core.

14. Refill the cooling system with the proper coolant and replace the negative battery cable.

Water Pump

Removal and Installation

1. Disconnect the negative battery cable.
2. Drain the cooling system.
3. Loosen the drive belt tension and remove the drive belt. If equipped, loosen the air conditioning belt tension and remove the air conditioning belt.
4. Remove the radiator fan shroud mounting bolts and radiator fan mounting bolts. Remove the radiator shroud, fan and water pump pulley from the vehicle.
5. Remove the crankshaft pulley bolts and remove the crankshaft pulley.

NOTE: The crankshaft pulley bolt can be removed without removing the center crankshaft bolt.

6. Remove the timing belt cover mounting bolts and remove the cover.
7. Loosen the timing belt tensioner adjusting bolt and pivot nut. Hold the tensioner to loosen the timing belt and remove the belt from the camshaft pulley.
8. Remove the timing belt tensioner mounting bolts and remove the tensioner plate and spring.
9. Remove the water pump mounting bolts and remove the water pump assembly.
10. Remove the dipstick tube and the alternator bracket from the vehicle.

To install:

11. Clean and inspect the surface of the engine before installation.
12. Using a new gasket, install the new water pump on the engine. Torque the mounting bolts to 7.5–9.0 ft. lbs.
13. Install the dipstick tube and the alternator bracket to the vehicle.
14. Install the rubber seals between the water pump to cylinder head and water pump to oil pump.

15. Install the timing belt tensioner plate, tensioner and spring.
16. Align the marks on the timing belt and the camshaft sprocket. Install the timing belt in the same position on the camshaft sprocket as when removed.
17. Adjust the timing belt to be free of any slack. Torque the tensioner bolts to 7.5–9.0 ft. lbs.
18. Install the crankshaft and water pump pulleys. Torque the crankshaft and water pulley bolts to 7.5–9.0 ft. lbs.
19. Install the timing belt cover, cooling fan/clutch, shroud and drive belt. Adjust the belt tension.
20. As required, adjust the intake and exhaust valve lash.
21. Refill the cooling system with the proper coolant and replace the negative battery cable.

Thermostat

Removal and Installation

1. Disconnect the negative battery cable.
2. Drain the cooling system.
3. Disconnect the thermostat cap from the intake manifold and remove the thermostat.

To install:

4. Clean and inspect the surfaces of the housing and the engine.
5. Install the new thermostat with the spring facing towards the engine.
6. Install a new gasket and the thermostat cap to the intake manifold.
7. Refill the cooling system with the proper coolant and replace the negative battery cable.

Cooling System Bleeding

In the top portion of the thermostat, an air bleed valve is provided. This valve is for venting air, if any, that is accumulated in the system.

FUEL SYSTEM

Fuel System Service Precaution

When working with the fuel system, certain precautions should be taken; always work in a well ventilated area, keep a dry chemical (Class B) fire extinguisher near the work area. Always disconnect the negative battery cable and do not make any repairs to the fuel system until all the necessary steps for repair have been reviewed.

Relieving Fuel System Pressure

The fuel pressure must be relieved before performing any service on the fuel system.
1. Disconnect the negative battery cable.
2. Remove the fuel filler cap from the fuel filler neck to release the fuel vapor pressure in the fuel tank. Reinstall the fuel cap.
3. Raise and support the vehicle safely.
4. Place an appropriate container under the fuel filter.
5. Cover the plug bolt on the fuel filter inlet union bolt with a rag and loosen the plug bolt slowly to release the fuel pressure gradually.
6. When the pressure has been released, tighten the plug bolt to 7.5 ft. lbs. so the fuel does not leak.

7. Lower the vehicle.
8. Reconnect the negative battery cable.

Fuel Filter

Removal and Installation

1. Disconnect the negative battery cable.
2. Remove the fuel filler cap to release the fuel vapor pressure in the fuel tank. After releasing pressure, reinstall filler cap.
3. Raise and support the vehicle safely.
4. Release the fuel pressure.
5. Disconnect the inlet and outlet hoses from the fuel filter.
6. Remove the fuel filter from the chassis frame.

To install:

7. Install the new fuel filter to the frame and connect the inlet and outlet hoses.
8. Lower the vehicle and connect the negative battery terminal.

Electric Fuel Pump

Pressure Testing

1. Remove the fuel filler cap to release the fuel vapor pressure in the fuel tank. Reinstall the cap.

2. Raise and support the vehicle safely.

3. Release the fuel pressure in the fuel feed line.

4. Remove the plug bolt on the fuel filter union bolt and connect the proper fuel pressure gauge to the fuel filter inlet union bolt.

NOTE: If the pressure in the fuel tank is not released prior to system service, the fuel in the fuel tank may be forced out through the fuel hoses during disconnection.

5. Start the engine and warm to the proper operating temperature.

6. Measure the fuel pressure under each of the following conditions.

a. At a specified idle speed or with the fuel pump operating and the engine stopped the fuel pressure should read: 34.1–39.8 psi.

b. Within 1 minute after the fuel pump has stopped the fuel pressure should read: 21.3 psi.

7. Release the fuel pressure and remove the fuel pressure gauge.

8. Install the plug bolt to the fuel filter inlet bolt. Use a new gasket.

9. Start the engine and check for leaks.

10. Lower the vehicle.

Removal and Installation

NOTE: The fuel pump is located in the fuel tank. The fuel pump and the fuel gauge sending unit are located on the upper part of the fuel tank.

1. Disconnect the negative battery cable.

2. Remove the rear bumper assembly.

3. Disconnect the fuel gauge sending unit and fuel pump electrical connectors from the fuel tank.

4. Relieve the fuel system pressure.

5. Disconnect the fuel tank filler hose cover, filler hose and fuel tank inlet valve (breather hose).

6. Disconnect the inlet pipe from the fuel filter and remove the fuel vapor and return hoses.

7. If necessary, drain the fuel from the tank using a hand operating pump.

8. Disconnect the fuel tank protector and remove the fuel tank and cover from the vehicle.

9. Remove the fuel pump from the fuel tank.

To install:

10. Install the fuel pump to the fuel tank using a new gasket.

11. Install the fuel tank and cover to the vehicle and connect the fuel tank protector.

12. Replace the fuel vapor and return hoses and connect the inlet pipe to the fuel filter.

13. Reconnect the fuel tank inlet valve (breather hose), filler hose and fuel tank filler hose cover.

14. Connect the fuel pump and fuel gauge sending sending unit electrical connectors to the fuel tank.

15. Replace the bumper assembly and reconnect the negative battery cable.

16. If necessary, refill the fuel tank with any fuel that had been drained.

17. Start the engine and check for leaks when finished.

Fuel Injection

For further information, please refer to Chilton's Electronic Engine Controls Manual.

Idle Speed Adjustment

NOTE: Before starting the engine, place the gear shift lever in neutral for manual transmission or P for automatic transmission. Set the parking brake and block the drive wheels.

Checking fuel pump pressure

IDLE ADJUSTING SCREW

Idle adjustment

1. Warm the engine to the normal operating temperature.

2. Race the engine until the engine speed exceeds 1500 rpm and than let it slow down to idle speed.

3. Check and see if the idle speed is within 750–850 rpm.

Fuel Injector

Removal and Installation

1. Disconnect the negative battery cable.

2. Release the fuel pressure in the fuel feed line.

3. Remove the the air intake case from the throttle body.

4. Remove the fuel feed pipe clamp from the intake manifold and disconnect the fuel feed pipe from the throttle body.

5. Remove the injector cover.

6. Disconnect the injector coupler, release its wire harness from the clamp and remove its grommet from the throttle body.

7. Place a cloth over the injector and a hand on top of it. Using an air gun, blow low pressure compressed air into the fuel inlet port of the throttle body, and the injector can be removed.

NOTE: Be precise about the pressure of the compressed air. Using excessively high pressure may force the injector to jump out and may cause damage, not only to the injector itself but also to other parts.

To install:

8. Apply thin coating of gasoline to O-rings and then install the fuel injector to the throttle body.

9. Connect fuel injector wire connector and install injector cover.

10. Connect fuel feed pipe to throttle body.

11. Connect the negative battery cable and turn the ignition **ON** for 3 seconds and then **OFF** until fuel pressure is felt at the return hose.

12. Install air intake case assembly.

13. Secure all wires and check for any leaks in the system.

EMISSION CONTROLS

For further information, please refer to Chilton's Emission Controls Manual.

Emission Warning Lamps

The CHECK ENGINE light automatically comes on at 50,000, 80,000 and 100,000 miles.

Resetting

The lamp reset switch is located on the left side of the dashboard, mounted on the steering column support. The lamp can be reset by moving the switch upwards and then downwards. If the switch remains on after being reset, check the system.

Resetting the check engine light

ENGINE MECHANICAL

NOTE: Disconnecting the battery cable on some vehicles may interfere with the functions of the on board computer systems and may require the computer to undergo a relearning process, once the negative battery cable is disconnected.

Engine

Removal and Installation

1. Disconnect the negative and positive cables at the battery.
2. Remove the hood from the vehicle and drain the cooling system.
3. Remove the radiator reservoir tank, fan shroud, cooling fan and radiator.
4. Properly discharge the air conditioning system and remove the air conditioning condenser, if equipped.
5. Remove the air cleaner outlet hose.
6. Disconnect the accelerator and the automatic transmission kickdown cable from the throttle body, if equipped.
7. Disconnect and tag the throttle opener VSV and EGR VSV wires at the coupler.
8. Disconnect and tag the water temperature, oil pressure, air temperature and ground cable wires at the intake manifold.
9. Disconnect and tag the injector, throttle position sensor and idle speed control solenoid valve wires at their couplers, if equipped.
10. Disconnect the PTC heater wires at the coupler for automatic transmission vehicle, if equipped.
11. Disconnect and tag the wires at the starter and alternator.
12. Disconnect and tag the oxygen sensor and distributor wires at their couplers. Remove the coil wire.
13. Remove the starter motor and disconnect the ground wires from the distributor assembly.
14. Remove the fuel tank filler cap to relieve the pressure. Reinstall the cap.
15. Relieve the fuel pressure in the fuel feed line. Disconnect and tag the fuel feed and return hoses.
16. Remove the gear shift lever mounting bolts and remove the shifter.

17. Disconnect the canister purge hose and remove the pressure sensor hose from the fuel filter, if equipped.
18. Disconnect the brake booster hose from the intake manifold.
19. Remove the vacuum hose for the automatic transmission from the intake manifold, if equipped.
20. Disconnect the heater hoses from the heater core outlet pipe and the intake manifold.
21. Raise and safely support the vehicle.
22. Drain the engine oil and remove the exhaust pipe from the exhaust manifold and muffler.
23. Disconnect the clutch cable, if equipped with manual transmission.
24. Drain the automatic transmission fluid, if equipped.
25. Disconnect the clutch (torque converter) housing lower plate.
26. Remove the lock drive plate, using the special tool, if equipped with automatic transmission.
27. Lower the vehicle.
28. Remove the nuts and bolts fastening the cylinder block and transmission.
29. Support the transmission, using a stand or jack.
30. Support the engine from the top using a chain type hoist or equivalent means.
31. Remove the engine mounts with the chassis side mounting brackets.

NOTE: Before lifting the engine, check to ensure all the hoses, wires and cables are disconnected from the engine.

32. Remove the engine assembly from the chassis and transmission by sliding towards the front side and carefully hoist the engine.

To install:
33. Install the engine into the engine compartment and connect to the transmission.
34. Replace the engine mounts with the chassis side mounting brackets. Tighten to 41 ft. lbs.
35. Remove the lifting device.

36. Install the nuts and bolts fastening the cylinder block and transmission.

37. Raise and safely support the vehicle.

38. Replace the lock driveplate, if equipped.

39. Connect the clutch (torque converter) housing lower plate.

40. Connect the automatic transmission lines, if equipped.

41. Reconnect the clutch cable to the bracket, if equipped with manual transmission.

42. Replace the exhaust pipe to the exhaust manifold and muffler.

43. Lower the vehicle.

44. Reconnect the heater hoses to the heater core outlet pipe and the intake manifold.

45. Install the vacuum hose for the automatic transmission to the intake manifold, if equipped.

46. Replace the brake booster hose to the intake manifold.

47. Replace the pressure sensor hose to the fuel filter and connect the canister purge hose, if equipped.

48. Replace the fuel return and feed hoses.

49. Install the starter motor and connect the ground wire to the distributor.

50. Replace the coil wire and connect the oxygen sensor and distributor wires to their couplers.

51. Reconnect the wires at the alternator and starter motor.

52. Replace the PTC heater wires at the coupler, if equipped with automatic transmission.

53. Install the idle speed control solenoid valve, throttle position sensor and injector wires at their couplers, if equipped.

54. Connect the ground cable, air temperature, oil pressure and water temperature wires to the intake manifold.

55. Reconnect the throttle opener VSR and EGR VSR wires to their couplers, if equipped.

56. Connect the accelerator cable and the automatic transmission kickdown cable, if equipped, to the throttle body.

57. Replace the air cleaner outlet hose. Refill the engine oil and the transmission oil to the proper level.

58. Replace the air conditioning condenser and properly recharge the air conditioning system, if equipped.

59. Replace the radiator, cooling fan, fan shroud and radiator reservoir tank.

60. Replace the hood and refill the cooling system with the proper coolant.

61. Reconnect the positive and negative battery cables.

62. Adjust the accelerator, clutch and the automatic transmission kickdown cable, if equipped.

63. Before starting the engine, check to see if all the parts disassembled are back in place securely.

64. Start the engine and check the timing. Check for any oil leaks.

Cylinder Head

Removal and Installation

1. Disconnect the negative battery cable. Drain the cooling system.

2. Disconnect the air intake case.

3. Disconnect the brake booster hose from the intake manifold and the air valve water hose from the throttle body.

4. Disconnect the accelerator and the automatic transmission kickdown cable, if equipped, from the throttle body.

5. Disconnect and tag the throttle opener VSV and EGR VSV wires at the coupler.

6. Disconnect and tag the water temperature, oil pressure, air temperature sensor and ground cable wires at the intake manifold.

7. Disconnect and tag the injector, throttle position sensor and idle speed control solenoid valve wires at their couplers, if equipped.

8. Disconnect the PTC heater wires at the coupler, if equipped with automatic transmission.

CAMSHAFT PULLEY SIDE

DISTRIBUTOR SIDE

Cylinder head and bolt tightening sequence

9. Disconnect and tag the oxygen sensor and distributor wires at their couplers. Remove the coil wire.

10. Disconnect the ground wires from the distributor assembly.

11. Remove the fuel tank filler cap to relieve the pressure. Reinstall the cap.

12. Release the fuel pressure in the fuel feed line.

13. Disconnect the fuel feed and return hoses.

14. Disconnect the canister purge hose and remove the pressure sensor hose from the fuel filter, if equipped.

15. Disconnect the vacuum hose for the automatic transmission from the intake manifold, if equipped.

16. Disconnect the radiator cooling fan, fan shroud, water pump drive belt and water pump pulley.

17. Disconnect the crankshaft pulley, timing belt cover and the timing belt.

18. Raise and safely support the vehicle.

19. Disconnect the exhaust pipe from the exhaust manifold and lower the vehicle.

20. Disconnect the air conditioning compressor adjusting arm, if equipped.

21. Remove the cylinder head cover mounting bolts and remove the cylinder head cover.

22. Loosen all the valve adjusting screw locknuts, turn the adjusting screws back all the way to allow all the valves to close.

23. Remove the intake manifold with the carburetor attached, from the cylinder head.

24. Remove the distributor and distributor housing from the cylinder head.

25. Remove the cylinder head mounting bolts and remove the cylinder head from the engine.

26. Remove any oil and water in the cylinder bores and on top of the pistons.

27. Clean and inspect the sealing surfaces of the cylinder head and the engine block.

To install:

28. Install the cylinder head using a new gasket.

29. Replace the cylinder head mounting bolts, in sequence, and tighten to 46–54 ft. lbs.

30. Install the distributor and distributor housing to the cylinder head.

31. Replace the intake manifold with the carburetor attached, to the cylinder head.

32. Tighten all the valve adjusting screw nuts.

33. Adjust the valve lash.

34. Replace the cylinder head cover and connect the air conditioning compressor adjusting arm, if equipped.

35. Raise and safely support the vehicle.

36. Connect the exhaust pipe to the exhaust manifold and safely lower the vehicle.

37. Reconnect the timing belt, timing belt cover and crankshaft pulley.

38. Replace the water pump pulley, water pump drive belt, fan shroud and the radiator cooling fan.

39. Replace the vacuum hose for the automatic transmission to the intake manifold, if equipped.

40. Replace the pressure sensor hose to the fuel filter and connect the canister purge hose, if equipped.

41. Replace the fuel return and feed hoses.

42. Connect the ground wires to the distributor assembly.

43. Replace the coil wire. Connect the oxygen sensor and distributor wires to their couplers.

44. Connect the PTC wires to the coupler.

45. Connect the idle speed control valve, throttle position sensor and injector wires to their couplers, if equipped.

46. Reconnect the ground cable, air temperature, oil pressure and water temperature sensor wires to the intake manifold.

47. Replace the throttle opener VSV and EGR VSV wires to their couplers.

48. Connect the accelerator and the automatic transmission kickdown cables, if equipped, to the throttle body.

49. Replace the air valve water hose to the throttle body and connect the brake booster hose to intake manifold.

50. Reconnect the air intake case.

51. Refill the cooling system with the proper coolant and connect the negative battery.

52. Check for any water and oil leaks when finished.

Valve Lash

Adjustment

Valve lash can be adjusted with the engine hot or cold. Specifications are provided for both adjustments.

1. Remove the air intake case.

2. Remove the cylinder head cover assembly.

3. Turn the crankshaft clockwise so the **V** mark on the crankshaft pulley is aligned with the **0** mark on the timing belt cover.

4. Remove the distributor cap and confirm that the rotor is facing the No. 1 firing position. If the rotor is out of place, turn the crankshaft 360 degrees.

5. With the engine in this position, check the valve lash at valves 1, 2, 5 and 7. Clearance should be: Intake 0.0051–0.0067 in. (0.13–0.17mm) COLD or 0.009–0.011 in. (0.23–0.27mm) HOT. Exhaust 0.0063–0.0075 in. (0.15–0.19mm) COLD or 0.0102–0.0114 in. (0.25–0.29mm.) HOT.

NOTE: The valves are adjusted by loosening the locknut on the valve adjuster and turning the adjusting screw to obtain the proper clearance. Once the proper clearance is obtained, the locknut must be torqued to 11–13 ft. lbs. while holding the adjusting screw. Check the clearance after the locknut is torqued.

6. Rotate the crankshaft 360 degrees and check the valve lash at valves 3, 4, 6 and 8.

7. After adjusting and checking all the valves, install the cylinder head cover, distributor cover and intake hose.

Rocker Arms/Shafts

Removal and Installation

NOTE: The rocker arm shafts are not identical and must be kept in the proper order for installation. If the shafts get mixed up before installation, the intake rocker shaft has a 14mm stepped end and the exhaust rocker shaft has a 13mm stepped end. The stepped end of the intake rocker shaft faces the front of the engine and the stepped end of the exhaust rocker shaft faces the rear of the engine.

1. Disconnect the negative battery cable. Drain the cooling system.

2. Remove the front grille.

Valve lash adjustment

Locking the camshaft in position

3. Remove the radiator cooling fan and fan shroud. Properly discharge the air conditioning system and remove the air conditioning flexible suction hose, if equipped.

4. Remove the radiator.

5. Remove the water pump drive belt and the water pump pulley.

6. Remove the timing belt outside cover, timing belt and the tensioner.

7. Disconnect the air intake case and remove the cylinder head cover.

8. Remove the camshaft timing belt pulley and timing belt inside cover. Insert the proper size rod into the hole in the camshaft to lock the camshaft and loosen the pulley nut.

9. Loosen all the valve lash adjusting screw locknuts and turn the adjusting screws out all the way.

10. Remove the rocker arm shaft screws.

11. Remove the intake and exhaust rocker arm shafts, rocker arms and springs.

12. Keep all the valve train parts in the order that they were removed.

To install:

13. Apply engine oil to the rocker arms, springs and shafts. Install the shafts in the correct direction, into the cylinder head by placing the rocker arms and springs on the shafts as they are installed. With the rocker arms, springs and shafts installed, torque the rocker shaft mounting screws to 7.0–8.5 ft. lbs.

14. Install the timing belt pulley and inside cover by locking the camshaft with the proper size rod.

15. With the camshaft locked, tighten the camshaft pulley bolt to 41–46 ft. lbs.

16. The remainder of the installation is the reverse of the removal procedure.

Intake Manifold

Removal and Installation

1. Disconnect the negative battery cable. Drain the cooling system.
2. Remove the air intake case from the manifold.
3. Disconnect the accelerator cable and the automatic transmission kickdown cable, if equipped.
4. Disconnect the injector, throttle position sensor and idle speed control solenoid valve wires at their couplers, if equipped.
5. Disconnect the vacuum hoses from the throttle body and throttle opener. Remove the water hose from the air valve, if equipped.
6. Remove the fuel filler cap to release the fuel pressure in the fuel tank. Reinstall the cap.
7. Release the fuel pressure in the fuel line.
8. Disconnect the fuel line from the throttle body or carburetor and intake manifold.
9. Remove the fuel return hose.
10. Disconnect the throttle body from the intake manifold and remove the PCV hose from the cylinder head cover.
11. Disconnect the pressure sensor hose from the fuel filter, if equipped, and remove the brake booster hose from the intake manifold.
12. Disconnect the vacuum hose for the automatic transmission from the intake manifold, if equipped.
13. Remove the VSV (for throttle opener) hose from the intake manifold.
14. Disconnect the water hose from the thermostat cap. Remove the heater inlet and water bypass hose from the intake manifold.
15. Disconnect the hoses at the EGR valve and remove the ground wire from the intake manifold.
16. Disconnect the wire couplers from the air temperature sensor, water temperature sensor, water temperature gauge and PTC heater, if equipped with automatic transmission.
17. Disconnect the wire harnesses from their clamps.
18. Remove the intake manifold mounting bolts and remove the intake manifold from the cylinder head.
19. Remove the PCV valve, EGR valve, fuel filter, thermostat from the intake manifold.
20. Clean and inspect the sealing surfaces of the intake manifold and the cylinder head.

To install:
21. Install the thermostat, fuel filter, EGR valve and PCV valve to the intake manifold.
22. Using a new gasket, install the intake manifold and tighten the mounting bolts to 13–20 ft. lbs.
23. Reconnect the wiring harnesses to their clamps and fasten the wire couplers to the air temperature sensor, water temperature sensor, water temperature gauge and PTC heater, if equipped with automatic transmission.
24. Reconnect the ground wire to the intake manifold and replace the hoses at the EGR valve.
25. Install the water heater inlet and bypass hose to the intake manifold. Replace the water hose to the thermostat cap.
26. Replace the VSV (for throttle opener) hose to the intake manifold.
27. Connect the automatic transmission vacuum hose to the intake manifold, if equipped.
28. Replace the brake booster hose to the intake manifold and connect the pressure sensor to the fuel filter, if equipped.
29. Reconnect the fuel line to the throttle body to the intake manifold.
30. Replace the water hose to the air valve. Connect the vacuum hoses to the throttle body and throttle opener, if equipped.
31. Reconnect the injector, throttle position sensor and idle speed control wires to their couplers, if equipped.
32. Connect the accelerator cable and the automatic transmission kickdown cable, if equipped, to the throttle body.
33. Install the air intake case to the manifold.
34. Refill the cooling system with the proper coolant. Connect the negative battery cable.
35. Check for vacuum, water and oil leaks when finished.

Exhaust Manifold

Removal and Installation

1. Disconnect the negative cable.
2. Raise and safely support the vehicle.
3. Disconnect the exhaust pipe from the exhaust manifold and lower the vehicle.
4. Disconnect the oxygen sensor lead wire at the coupler and remove the air intake case bracket.
5. Disconnect the exhaust manifold upper and lower covers or heat shields from the exhaust manifold.
6. Remove the exhaust manifold mounting bolts and remove the exhaust manifold from the cylinder head.

To install:
7. Clean and inspect the sealing surfaces of the exhaust manifold and the cylinder head.
8. Using new gaskets, install the exhaust manifold to the cylinder head and tighten the mounting bolts to 13–20 ft. lbs.
9. The remainder of the installation is the reverse of the removal procedure.
10. Check for exhaust leaks when finished.

Timing Belt Front Cover

Removal and Installation

1. Disconnect the negative battery cable.
2. Remove the radiator cooling fan and fan shroud.
3. If equipped, disconnect the air conditioning compressor drive belt, properly discharge the air conditioning system and remove the air conditioning compressor flexible suction hose.
4. Loosen the alternator mounting bolts and remove the water pump drive belt and pulley.
5. Remove the crankshaft mounting bolts and remove the crankshaft pulley.

NOTE: The crankshaft drive belt pulley can be removed without loosening the center crankshaft bolt.

6. Disconnect the timing belt cover mounting bolts and remove the timing belt cover.

To install:
7. Clean and inspect all mounting surfaces.
8. Install the timing belt cover and tighten the bolts to 7.0–9.0 ft. lbs.
9. Install the crankshaft pulley. Replace the 5 mounting bolts and tighten to 7.0–9.0 ft. lbs.
10. Install the water pump drive belt pulley and replace the drive belt .
11. Adjust the belt tension and tighten the alternator mounting bolts.
12. Install the air conditioning flexible suction hose and replace the air conditioning compressor drive belt. Adjust the belt tension and properly recharge the air conditioning system, if equipped.
13. Replace the radiator cooling fan and fan shroud.
14. Connect the negative battery cable.

Oil Seal Replacement

1. Disconnect the negative battery cable.
2. Remove the the timing belt and the crankshaft sprocket.
3. Insert a suitable tool between the crankshaft and the oil seal and pull the seal outwards to remove it.

NOTE: Use care when removing or installing the oil seal, not to damage the crankshaft or the oil pump sealing surfaces.

4. Clean and inspect the surfaces of the crankshaft and the oil pump assembly.

5. Install the crankshaft sleeve, using the proper tool, onto the crankshaft.

6. Install the new seal over the crankshaft and into the oil pump, making sure the oil seal lip is not upturned.

7. Install the crankshaft sprocket and the timing belt. Check the timing.

8. Connect the negative battery cable.

Timing Belt and Tensioner

Adjustment

1. Disconnect the negative battery cable.
2. Remove the radiator cooling fan and fan shroud.
3. If equipped, disconnect the air conditioning compressor drive belt, properly discharge the air conditioning system and remove the air conditioning compressor flexible suction hose.
4. Loosen the alternator mounting bolts and remove the water pump drive belt and pulley.
5. Remove the crankshaft mounting bolts and disconnect the crankshaft pulley.

NOTE: The crankshaft drive belt pulley can be removed without loosening the center crankshaft bolt.

6. Disconnect the timing belt cover mounting bolts and remove the timing belt cover. Loosen but do not remove the tensioner bolt.

7. Disconnect the air intake case from the intake manifold.

8. Remove the cylinder head cover and loosen all the valve adjusting screws to permit free rotation of the camshaft.

9. Turn the camshaft pulley clockwise and align the timing marks.

10. Turn the crankshaft clockwise, using a 17mm wrench to crank the timing belt pulley bolt.

11. Align the punch mark on the timing belt pulley with the arrow mark on the oil pump.

12. With the 4 marks aligned, remove any slack from the drive side of the belt. Tighten the tensioner bolt to 17.5–21.5 ft. lbs.

13. To allow the belt to be free of any slack, turn the crankshaft clockwise 2 full rotations. Confirm that the 4 marks are aligned.

14. Replace the timing cover and tighten the bolts to 7.0–8.5 ft. lbs.

15. Adjust the valve lash and install the cylinder head cover, using a new gasket.

16. Connect the air intake case to the throttle body.

17. Install the crankshaft pulley and replace the 5 mounting bolts. Tighten to 7.0–8.5 ft. lbs.

18. Replace the water pump pulley, water pump drive belt and tighten the alternator mounting bolts.

19. Install the air conditioning compressor flexible suction hose and the air compressor belt. Properly recharge the air conditioning system, if equipped.

20. Replace the radiator cooling fan and fan shroud.

21. Connect the negative battery cable.

22. Properly recharge the air conditioning system, if equipped. Run the engine and check for any leaks.

Removal and Installation

1. Disconnect the negative battery cable.
2. Remove the radiator cooling fan and fan shroud.
3. If equipped, disconnect the air conditioning compressor drive belt, properly discharge the air conditioning system and remove the air conditioning compressor flexible suction hose.

Exploded view of the timing belt and the tensioner assembly

Timing marks on the camshaft pulley

4. Loosen the alternator mounting bolts and remove the water pump drive belt and pulley.

5. Remove the crankshaft mounting bolts and disconnect the crankshaft pulley.

NOTE: The crankshaft drive belt pulley can be removed without loosening the center crankshaft bolt.

6. Disconnect the timing belt cover mounting bolts and remove the timing belt cover. Loosen but do not remove the tensioner bolt.

7. Disconnect the air intake case from the intake manifold.

8. Loosen the timing belt tensioner adjusting bolt and pivot nut. Hold pressure on the tensioner to loosen the timing belt and remove the timing belt from the camshaft and crankshaft pulleys.

9. Remove the timing belt tensioner, tensioner plate and tensioner spring.

To install:

10. Install the timing belt tensioner, plate and spring. Hand tighten the tensioner bolt and stud only at this time.

11. Remove the cylinder head cover and loosen all the valve adjusting screws to permit free rotation of the camshaft.

12. Turn the camshaft pulley clockwise and align the timing marks.

13. Turn the crankshaft clockwise, using a 17mm wrench to crank the timing belt pulley bolt.

14. Align the punch mark on the timing belt pulley with the arrow mark on the oil pump

15. With the 4 marks aligned, remove any slack from the drive side of the belt. Tighten the tensioner bolt to 17.5–21.5 ft. lbs.

16. To allow the belt to be free of any slack, turn the crankshaft clockwise 2 full rotations. Confirm that the 4 marks are aligned.

17. Install the timing cover and tighten the bolts to 7.0–8.5 ft. lbs.

18. Adjust the valve lash and install the cylinder head cover, using a new gasket.

19. Connect the air intake case to the intake manifold.

20. Install the crankshaft pulley and replace the mounting bolts. Tighten to 7.0–8.5 ft. lbs.

21. Replace the water pump pulley, water pump drive belt and tighten the alternator mounting bolts.

22. If equipped, install the air conditioning compressor flexible suction hose and replace the air conditioning compressor belt.

23. Replace the radiator cooling fan and fan shroud.

24. Connect the negative battery cable.

25. If equipped, properly recharge the air conditioning system. Run the engine and check for any leaks.

Timing Sprockets

Removal and Installation

1. Disconnect the negative battery cable.

2. Remove the radiator cooling fan/clutch and fan shroud.

3. If equipped, disconnect the air conditioning compressor drive belt, properly discharge the air conditioning system and remove the air conditioning compressor flexible suction hose.

4. Loosen the alternator mounting bolts and remove the water pump drive belt and pulley.

5. Remove the crankshaft mounting bolts and disconnect the crankshaft pulley.

NOTE: The crankshaft drive belt pulley can be removed without loosening the center crankshaft bolt.

6. Disconnect the timing belt cover mounting bolts and remove the timing belt cover. Loosen but do not remove the tensioner bolt.

7. Disconnect the air intake case from the throttle body.

8. Remove the cylinder head cover and loosen all the valve adjusting screws to permit rotation of the camshaft.

9. Remove the camshaft timing belt pulley by inserting a proper size rod into the hole in the camshaft to lock the camshaft.

10. Remove the camshaft sprocket mounting bolt, sprocket and sprocket pin.

To install:

11. Install the camshaft sprocket pin in the sprocket and replace the sprocket and the bolt on the camshaft.

12. With the camshaft locked, tighten the sprocket bolt to 41–46 ft. lbs.

13. Remove the crankshaft sprocket by using a gear stopper to hold the flywheel for manual transmission or driveplate for automatic transmission vehicles. Remove the crankshaft timing belt pulley bolt, sprocket and key.

14. With the crankshaft locked, install the crankshaft timing

ARROW MARK

PUNCH MARK

CRANKSHAFT TIMING BELT PULLEY

Timing marks on the crankshaft pulley

belt sprocket and key. Replace the crankshaft pulley bolt and tighten to 47–54 ft. lbs.

15. Align the camshaft and crankshaft timing marks, install the timing belt and tighten the timing belt tensioner.

16. Adjust the valve lash and replace the cylinder head cover.

17. Reconnect the air intake hose to the throttle body.

18. If equipped, install the air conditioning compressor flexible suction hose and replace the air conditioning compressor belt.

19. Install the water pump pulley and replace the water pump drive belt.

20. Replace the radiator cooling fan and fan shroud.

21. Install the water pump pulley and replace the water pump drive belt.

22. Connect the negative battery cable.

23. If equipped, properly recharge the air conditioning system. Run the engine and check for any leaks.

Camshaft

Removal and Installation

1. Disconnect the negative battery cable. Drain the cooling system.

2. Disconnect the air intake case.

3. Disconnect the brake booster hose from the intake manifold and the air valve water hose from the throttle body.

4. Disconnect the accelerator and the automatic transmission kickdown cable, if equipped, from the throttle body.

5. Disconnect and tag the throttle opener VSV and EGR VSV wires at the coupler.

6. Disconnect and tag the water temperature, oil pressure, air temperature sensor and ground cable wires at the intake manifold.

7. Disconnect and tag the injector, throttle position sensor and idle speed control solenoid valve wires at their couplers, if equipped.

8. Disconnect the PTC heater wires at the coupler, if equipped with automatic transmission.

9. Disconnect and tag the oxygen sensor and distributor wires at their couplers. Remove the coil wire.

10. Disconnect the ground wires from the distributor assembly.

11. Remove the fuel tank filler cap to relieve the pressure. Reinstall the cap.

12. Release the fuel pressure in the fuel feed line.

13. Disconnect the fuel injector connections and fuel hoses.

14. Disconnect the canister purge hose and remove the pressure sensor hose from the fuel filter, if equipped.

15. Remove the vacuum hose for the automatic transmission from the intake manifold, if equipped.

16. Disconnect the radiator cooling fan, fan shroud, water pump drive belt and water pump pulley.

17. Disconnect the crankshaft pulley, timing belt cover and the timing belt.

18. Raise and safely support the vehicle.
19. Disconnect the exhaust pipe from the exhaust manifold and lower the vehicle.
20. Disconnect the air conditioner compressor adjusting arm, if equipped.
21. Remove the cylinder head cover mounting bolts and remove the cylinder head cover.
22. Loosen all the valve adjusting screw locknuts, turn the adjusting screws back all the way to allow all the valves to close.
23. Remove the intake manifold from the cylinder head.
24. Remove the distributor and distributor housing from the cylinder head.
25. Remove the cylinder head mounting bolts and remove the cylinder head from the engine.
26. Remove any oil and water in the cylinder bores and on top of the pistons.
27. Clean and inspect the sealing surfaces of the cylinder head and the engine block.
28. Disconnect the timing belt gear from the camshaft and remove the rocker arms, springs and rocker arm shafts.
29. Keep all the valve train parts in the order that they were removed.
30. Remove the camshaft from the rear of the cylinder head.

To install:
31. To install, lubricate the lobes and journals of the camshaft and the oil seal on the cylinder head with engine oil.
32. Install the camshaft to the cylinder head from the transmission side.
33. Install the cylinder head using a new gasket.
34. Install the cylinder head mounting bolts and tighten to 46–54 ft. lbs.
35. Install the distributor and distributor housing to the cylinder head.
36. Install the intake manifold to the cylinder head.
37. Tighten all the valve adjusting screw nuts.
38. Adjust the valve lash.
39. Install the cylinder head cover and connect the air conditioning compressor adjusting arm, if equipped.
40. Raise and safely support the vehicle.
41. Connect the exhaust pipe to the exhaust manifold and safely lower the vehicle.
42. Reconnect the timing belt, timing belt cover and crankshaft pulley.
43. Install the water pump pulley, water pump drive belt, fan shroud and the radiator cooling fan.
44. Install the vacuum hose for the automatic transmission to the intake manifold, if equipped.
45. Install the pressure sensor hose to the fuel filter and connect the canister purge hose, if equipped.
46. Install the fuel return and feed hoses.
47. Connect the ground wires to the distributor assembly.
48. Install the coil wire. Connect the oxygen sensor and distributor wires to their couplers.
49. Connect the PTC wires to the coupler.
50. Connect the idle speed control valve, throttle position sensor and injector wires to their couplers, if equipped.
51. Reconnect the ground cable, air temperature, oil pressure and water temperature sensor wires to the intake manifold.
52. Install the throttle opener VSV and EGR VSV wires to their couplers.
53. Connect the accelerator and the automatic transmission kickdown cables, if equipped, to the throttle body.
54. Install the air valve water hose to the throttle body and connect the brake booster hose to intake manifold.
55. Reconnect the air intake case.
56. Refill the cooling system with the proper coolant and connect the negative battery.
57. Check for any water and oil leaks when finished.

Camshaft removal

Piston and Connecting Rod

Positioning

Piston arrow marks to the cylinder head

1. Top ring	6. Connecting rod bearing cap
2. Second ring	7. Connecting rod bearing
3. Oil ring	8. Piston pin
4. Piston	
5. Connecting rod	

Exploded view of the piston and rod assembly

ENGINE LUBRICATION

Oil Pan

Removal and Installation

1. Raise and safely support the vehicle.
2. Drain and remove the front differential assembly from the chassis.
3. Drain the engine oil.
4. Remove the clutch housing lower plate or the torque converter housing lower plate.
5. Remove the oil pan mounting bolts and remove the pan.

To install:

6. Clean and inspect the sealing surfaces on the oil pan and the engine block.
7. Using new gaskets, install the oil pan and tighten the oil pan bolts to 7.0–8.5 ft. lbs.

NOTE: Tightening should begin at the center moving outward on both sides.

8. Install the oil drain plug and tighten to 22.0–28.5 ft. lbs.
9. Replace the clutch housing lower plate or the torque converter.
10. Install the front differential assembly to the chassis and fill with differential oil.
11. Lower the vehicle.
12. Refill the engine with engine oil. Run the engine and check for leaks.

Oil Pump

Removal and Installation

1. Disconnect the negative battery cable.
2. Remove the radiator cooling fan, fan shroud, water pump pulley and water pump drive belt.
3. Remove the timing belt outside cover, timing belt and timing belt tensioner.
4. Disconnect the alternator and remove the bracket, if neccesary.
5. If equipped, properly discharge the air conditioning system and remove the air compressor and bracket.
6. Disconnect the crankshaft timing belt pulley and the timing belt guide.

NOTE: To lock the crankshaft, engage a special tool (gear stopper) with the flywheel ring gear for manual transmission or driveplate ring gear for automatic transmission vehicles. With the crankshaft locked, remove the crankshaft timing belt pulley bolt.

7. Raise and safely support the vehicle. Drain the engine oil.
8. Remove the clutch (torque converter) housing lower plate.
9. Remove the oil pan mounting bolts and remove the oil pan. Disconnect the oil pump strainer.
10. Remove the oil pump mounting bolts and remove the oil pump.

To install:

11. Clean and inspect the sealing surfaces of the oil pump and the engine block.
12. Using a new gasket, install the oil pump to the engine.
13. Install the No. 1 and No. 2 mounting bolts and tighten to 7.0–8.5 ft. lbs.

NOTE: To prevent the oil seal lip from being damaged when installing the oil pump to the crankshaft, use a proper seal guide tool when installing. After installing the oil pump, check to be sure the oil lip is not upturned, then remove the special tool. The edge of the oil pump gasket might bulge out. If it does, cut off bulge with knife.

Oil pump installation—bolt location

14. With the crankshaft locked, install the crankshaft timing belt guide and the timing belt pulley.
15. Replace the clutch (torque converter) housing lower plate.
16. If equipped, replace the air conditioning bracket, the air conditioning compressor and properly rechargew the air conditioning system.
17. Replace the alternator and the alternator bracket, if necessary.
18. Reinstall the timing belt tensioner, timing belt and timing belt outside cover.
19. Replace the water pump drive belt, water pump pulley, radiator cooling fan and fan shroud.
20. Refill the engine with engine oil and connect the negative battery cable.
21. Run the engine and check for any leaks.

Checking

With the oil pump removed from the engine, certain clearances must be checked on the oil pump, if it is being reused.

1. The radial clearance is the clearance between the oil pump outer rotor and the oil pump case. The maximum clearance is 0.0122 in.
2. The side clearance is measured with a straight-edge across the mounting surface of the oil pump. The measurement is taken between the oil pump gears and the straight-edge. The maximum clearance is 0.0059 in.

Rear Main Bearing Oil Seal

Removal and Installation

1. Raise and safely support the vehicle.
2. Support the engine and remove the transmission from the vehicle.
3. Disconnect the clutch and flywheel for manual transmission vehicles or the driveplate for automatic transmission vehicles.
4. Using a suitable tool, remove the seal by pulling it outwards. Use care not to damage the sealing surface of the crankshaft.

To install:

5. Clean and inspect the sealing surfaces of the crankshaft and seal housing.
6. Using a seal driver, install the new seal into the seal housing with the lip of the seal facing the engine.
7. Install the flywheel and clutch for manual transmission vehicles or the driveplate for automatic transmission vehicles.
8. Install the transmission in the vehicle.
9. Lower the vehicle and check all the fluids. Run the engine and check for any leaks.

TORQUE SPECIFICATIONS

Component	English	Metric
Camshaft sprocket bolt	45 ft. lbs.	62 Nm
Carburetor-to-manifold bolts	17 ft. lbs.	25 Nm
Connecting rod bearing cap bolts	25 ft. lbs.	35 Nm
Crankshaft pulley bolt	9 ft. lbs.	13 Nm
Cylinder head bolt		
Step 1:	21 ft. lbs.	30 Nm
Step 2:	33 ft. lbs.	45 Nm
Step 3:	48 ft. lbs.	65 Nm
Engine-to-transmission	18 ft. lbs.	25 Nm
Exhaust manifold	19 ft. lbs.	26 Nm
Exhaust pipe-to-exhaust manifold nuts	43 ft. lbs.	60 Nm
Flywheel/flexplate-to-crankshaft bolts	55 ft. lbs.	78 Nm
Flywheel-to-converter bolts	38 ft. lbs.	53 Nm
Front engine mount through bolt	36 ft. lbs.	50 Nm
Intake manifold	20 ft. lbs.	28 Nm
Main bearing cap bolts	25 ft. lbs.	34 Nm
Oil pan	8.5 ft. lbs.	12 Nm
Oil pan drain plug	28.5 ft. lbs.	40 Nm
Oil pump attaching bolts	8.5 ft. lbs.	12 Nm
Oil pump cover screws	8.5 ft. lbs.	12 Nm
Rocker arm pivot bolt	8.5 ft. lbs.	12 Nm
Rocker (valve) cover	8.5 ft. lbs.	12 Nm
Spark plug	21.5 ft. lbs.	30 Nm
Starter-to-block bolts	20 ft. lbs.	28 Nm
Thermostat housing	20 ft. lbs.	27 Nm
Timing belt cover	8.5 ft. lbs.	12 Nm
Water pump	9 ft. lbs.	13 Nm
Water pump pulley	36 ft. lbs.	50 Nm

MANUAL TRANSMISSION

For further information, please refer to Chilton's Transmission Service Manual.

Transmission Assembly

Removal and Installation

1. Disconnect the negative battery cable.
2. Remove the console cover, remove the 4 gear shift boot mounting bolts and slide the boot upwards on the gear shifter.
3. Remove the boot clamp and remove the second boot from the shift lever case.
4. Push the gear shift lever control case down with fingers, turn it counterclockwise and remove the shift control lever.
5. Remove the transfer case shift control lever the same way.
6. Disconnect the breather hose and clamp at the rear of the cylinder head.
7. Remove the clamp at the rear of the intake manifold to free up the wiring harness. Disconnect the harness coupler.
8. Raise and safely support the vehicle. Drain the oil from the transmission and the transfer case.
9. Disconnect the starter lead wires and mounting bolts and remove the starter.
10. Remove the fuel line clamp on the transmission. Disconnect the bolts fastening the engine to the transmission.
11. Disconnect the flange bolts from the front driveshaft and remove and mark the shaft.
12. Disconnect the flange bolts from the rear driveshaft and remove and mark the shaft.
13. Disconnect the clutch cable and remove the clutch housing lower plate.
14. Disconnect the center exhaust pipe and remove the nuts from the joint with the engine.
15. Disconnect the speedometer cable from the transfer case.
16. Position a transmission jack and remove the engine rear mounting member from the vehicle. Move the transmission and transfer case rearwards and lower.
17. Disconnect the wiring harness and breather hose at the transmission.
18. Separate the gear shift lever case and transfer case from the transmission. Remove the transmission from the vehicle.

To install:

19. Install the gear shift lever case and transfer case to the transmission.
20. Install the transmission wiring harness and breather hose.

21. Raise the transmission and transfer case on the transmission jack and place under the vehicle.

22. Install the engine rear mounting member and tighten the bolts.

23. Connect the speedometer cable to the transfer case and joint with the engine.

24. Remove the transmission jack and replace the center exhaust pipe.

25. Replace the clutch housing lower plate and connect the clutch cable.

26. Install the front and rear driveshaft and replace the flange bolts and tighten to 37 ft. lbs.

27. Connect the bolts attaching the engine to the transmission and tighten to 37 ft. lbs. and replace the fuel line clamp on the transmission.

28. Install the starter and replace the mounting bolts and the lead wires to the starter.

29. Lower the vehicle. Refill the transmission and transfer case with the recommended gear oil.

30. Connect the wiring coupler and replace the clamp holding the wiring harness at the rear of the intake manifold.

31. Replace the breather hose and clamp at the rear of the cylinder head.

32. Install the transfer case and the gear shift control levers. Replace the gear shift lever boots and the console cover.

33. Connect the negative battery cable. Run the engine and check for any leaks.

CLUTCH

Clutch Assembly

Removal and Installation

1. Disconnect the negative battery cable.
2. Raise and safely support the vehicle.
3. Support the engine and remove the transmission from the vehicle.
4. Support the pressure plate and remove the 6 pressure plate to flywheel mounting bolts.
5. Remove the pressure plate and the clutch disc from the flywheel.
6. Inspect the condition of the flywheel, pressure plate and clutch disc and replace as necessary.
7. Remove the flywheel mounting bolts and remove the flywheel if necessary.

To install:

8. Install the new flywheel and replace the mounting bolts, tighten to 41–47 ft. lbs.
9. Inspect the condition of the clutch release bearing and the input shaft bearing and replace if necessary.
10. Align the clutch disc to the flywheel using a clutch disc alignment tool.
11. Install the pressure plate and evenly tighten the pressure plate bolts to 13–20 ft. lbs.

NOTE: Before assembling, make sure the clutch disc and the pressure plate are clean and dry.

12. With the engine supported, install the transmission in the vehicle.
13. Lower the vehicle. Connect the negative battery cable.

1. Flywheel
2. Cover bolt
3. Release shaft seal
4. Release shaft bushing
5. Clutch release shaft
6. Release return spring
7. Clutch release bearing
8. Clutch cover
9. Clutch disc
10. Input shaft bearing

Exploded view of the clutch assembly

14. Check and adjust the clutch pedal height. Check the clutch operation when finished.

Pedal Height/Free-play Adjustment

The only adjustment possible is the clutch pedal free-play. The free play is adjusted by moving the joint nut on the release bearing arm. Clutch linkage free-play should be between 0.6–1.1 in.

Clutch Cable

Removal and Installation

1. Disconnect the negative battery cable.
2. Raise and safely support the vehicle.
3. Disconnect the cable adjusting nuts on the clutch release and remove the adjusting nuts on the cable support bracket.
4. Disconnect the clutch cable from the 3 cable clamps.
5. Remove the clutch cable support bolts. Lower the vehicle.

Clutch pedal height adjustment

Clutch cable free travel adjustment

6. Disconnect the cable hook at the clutch pedal shaft arm and remove the clutch cable.

To install:

7. Install the cable after first applying grease to the cable end hook and the joint pin.
8. Connect the cable to the 3 cable clamps and install the clutch cable support bolts.
9. Lower the vehicle and connect the negative battery cable.

Adjustment

Adjust the clutch pedal height by adjusting the bolt located on the pedal bracket so the clutch pedal exceeds the height of the brake pedal by 0.2 in. (5mm). Tighten the locknut.

AUTOMATIC TRANSMISSION

For further information, please refer to Chilton's Transmission Service Manual.

Transmission Assembly

Removal and Installation

1. Disconnect the negative battery cable.
2. Disconnect the transmission shift control lever and remove the transfer case shift control lever knob.
3. Disconnect the breather hose from the clamp at the rear of the cylinder head.
4. Disconnect the wiring harness clamp at the rear end of the intake manifold to free up the harness.
5. Disconnect the wiring harness coupler and remove the detent cable at the throttle body, if equipped.
6. Remove the vacuum modulator hose at the intake manifold.
7. Raise and safely support the vehicle.
8. Disconnect the starter lead wires and mounting bolts, remove the starter motor.
9. Drain the oil from the transmission and transfer case.
10. Disconnect the flange bolts from the front driveshaft, remove and mark the shaft.
11. Disconnect the flange bolts from the rear driveshaft, remove and mark the shaft.
12. Disconnect the select cable from the transmission and the speedometer cable from the transfer cases.

13. Remove the torque converter housing lower plate and disconnect and plug the oil cooler lines.
14. Disconnect the transfer case skid plate and remove the kickdown cable from the transmission.
15. Remove the exhaust bracket at the catalytic converter and at the transmission. Disconnect the center exhaust pipe, if necessary.
16. Remove the transmission to engine retaining bolts and nuts.
17. Support the transmission using a transmission jack or equivalent. Disconnect the transmission crossmember mounting bolts and remove the crossmember.
18. Disconnect the lead wires and breather hose at the transmission and lower the transmission with the transfer case from the vehicle. Remove the torque converter to flywheel bolts.
19. Disconnect the transmission-to-transfer case bolts and separate the transmission from the transfer case.

To install:

20. Connect the transfer case to the transmission and tighten the bolts to 20 ft. lbs. Replace the torque converter to flywheel bolts.
21. Raise the transmission, connect the lead wires and breather to the transmission.
22. Replace the transmission to engine retaining bolts and tighten to 62 ft. lbs.
23. Install the transmission cross member and tighten the bolts to 62 ft. lbs.
24. Connect the exhaust bracket to the catalytic converter and the transmission.
25. Reconnect the center exhaust pipe, if necessary.

26. Connect the transfer case skid plate and replace the kickdown cable to the transmission.

27. Replace the torque converter housing lower plate and connect the transmission cooler lines.

28. Reconnect the select cable to the transmission and the speedometer cable to the transfer case.

29. Replace the front and rear driveshafts and tighten the flange bolts to 37 ft. lbs.

30. Install the starter and connect the lead wires to the starter.

31. Lower the vehicle and connect the vacuum modulator hose to the intake manifold.

32. Connect the wiring coupler at the rear of the intake manifold and replace the wiring harness clamp in the proper position.

33. Connect the breather hose to the clamp at the rear of the cylinder head.

34. Install the transmission shift control lever and replace the transfer case shift control lever knob.

35. Connect the negative battery cable and refill the transmission. Run the engine and check for leaks.

Shift Linkage Adjustment

1. Adjust the shift cable assembly by moving the shift selector to the **N** position and placing a pin in the selector to hold that position.

2. Put the manual select lever in **L** position and set the cable to the cable bracket with the E-clip.

3. Adjust the manual select lever back to the **N** position and tighten the cable end locknut to 5 ft. lbs.

NOTE: When the manual selector is moved to the N position, there should be a little clearance between the lever and the adjusting nut.

Throttle linkage Adjustment

Adjust the cable by loosening the cable locknut and adjust the cable to specifications. The cable endplay should be 0.12–0.20 in. when the throttle valve is in the idle position.

Detent Cable Adjustment

1. Make sure accelerator play is within specifications.

2. Loosen the kickdown cable nut and adjusting nut.

3. With the accelerator pedal fully depressed and the cable pulled towards the firewall, adjust the locknut-to-bracket clearance to 0.039 in. by turning the locknut.

Adjusting the shift cable assembly

Accelerator cable adjustment

NOTE: When adjusting the clearance make sure the adjusting nut does not rub against the bracket.

4. Release the accelerator pedal and adjust the locknut-to-bracket clearance by tightening the adjusting nut. Tighten the locknut securely.

TRANSFER CASE

Transfer Case Assembly

Removal and Installation

1. Disconnect the negative battery cable.

2. Raise and safely support the vehicle.

3. Support the transmission and transfer case using a transmission jack.

4. Disconnect the speedometer cable from the transfer case.

5. Remove the transmission and transfer case from the vehicle.

6. Remove the 10 transmission-to-transfer case mounting bolts and separate the transfer case from the transmission.

To install:

7. Install the 10 transmission-to-transfer case mounting bolts and tighten the bolts to 20 ft. lbs.

8. Install the transmission and transfer case into the vehicle and tighten the mounting bolts to 37 ft. lbs.

9. Connect the speedometer cable to the transfer case.

10. Lower the vehicle and connect the negative battery cable.

DRIVE AXLE

Halfshaft

Removal and Installation

1. Raise and safely support the vehicle. Drain the transmission.
2. Remove the front wheels and disconnect the locking hubs.
3. Disconnect the halfshaft snaprings and remove the stabilizer bar links.
4. Disconnect the tie rod ends and remove the brake caliper and brake disc. Support the brake caliper.
5. Disconnect the wheel hub and remove the steering knuckle.
6. Disconnect the differential side joint snapring and remove the right side halfshaft by prying the joint away from the differential assembly.
7. Disconnect the left side halfshaft bolts and remove the halfshaft from the left inner axle flange.

To install:

8. Install the left side halfshaft and the halfshaft bolts and tighten to 37 ft. lbs.
9. Install the right side halfshaft and install the snapring.
10. Install the steering knuckle and wheel hub assembly.
11. Install the brake caliper and connect the tie rod ends.
12. Install the left side driveshaft snapring and connect the stabilizer bar links.
13. Install the front wheels and lower the vehicle.
14. Refill the transmission with the proper fluid.

Driveshaft and U-Joints

Removal and Installation

1. Raise and safely support the vehicle.

2. Matchmark the driveshafts to the yokes on the transfer case and the differential.
3. Drain the transfer case oil when servicing the front driveshaft shaft.
4. Support the driveshaft and remove the attaching bolts.
5. Remove the driveshaft from the vehicle.

To install:

6. Install the driveshaft, by aligning the matchmarks to the vehicle.
7. Tighten the mounting bolts to 37 ft. lbs.
8. Refill the transfer case and lower the vehicle.

Rear Axle Shaft, Bearing and Seal

Removal and Installation

1. Raise and safely support the vehicle.
2. Remove the rear wheels and remove the rear brake drums from the vehicle.
3. Drain the gear oil from the rear axle housing.
4. Remove the rear wheel bearing retainer nuts from the rear axle housing.
5. Using a suitable tool, remove the axle shaft from the housing.

NOTE: Do not remove the backing plate with the axle. This may cause damage to the inner seal.

6. If the axle, axle bearing or backing plate is being replaced, support the axle in a vise with additional support under the shaft next to the bearing.

—————————————— CAUTION ——————————————
Eye protection must be worn during the 3 steps. Failure to do so could cause injury.
—————————————————————————————————————

Exploded view of the halfshaft assembly

7. With the axle shaft supported properly, grind the top and bottom of the axle bearing retainer to remove it without damaging the axle shaft.

8. Using a chisel, finish removing the retainer from the axle shaft.

9. Using a press or suitable bearing puller, remove the axle shaft bearing from the axle shaft.

10. Using a suitable tool, remove the seal from the axle housing.

To install:

11. Using a seal driver, install the new seal with the lip facing the housing to the same depth as the old seal.

12. Install the new bearing and the retainer on the axle shaft using a suitable press.

13. Install the axle shaft into the rear axle housing and replace the rear wheel bearing retaining nuts, tighten to 17 ft. lbs.

14. Replace the rear brake drums and replace the rear tires on the vehicle.

15. Refill the rear axle housing with the proper gear oil and safely lower the vehicle.

Front Wheel Hub, Knuckle and Bearings

Removal and Installation

1. Disconnect the negative battery cable. Raise and safely support the vehicle.

2. Remove the wheels and disconnect the locking hub assembly.

3. Remove the caliper mounting bracket and position the caliper out of the way. Support the caliper.

4. Disconnect the front wheel bearing lock plate and washer and remove the wheel hub complete with bearings and seals.

5. Remove the oil seal and race from the wheel hub.

6. Clean and inspect the hub and bearing seats. Install the new bearing, race and grease seal in the same position.

7. Support the suspension with a jack and remove the dust cover.

8. Disconnect the spindle by tapping with a hammer.

9. Remove the strut bracket bolts from the steering knuckle.

10. Disconnect the tie rod end from the knuckle and the knuckle from the control arm.

11. Remove the dust seal and the spindle from the knuckle.

To install:

12. Install the new seal and the spindle to the knuckle.

13. Connect the knuckle to the ball joint and tighten the nut to 40 ft. lbs.

14. Connect the knuckle to the strut damper and tighten the bolts to 66 ft. lbs.

15. Install the tie rod end to the knuckle and tighten the nut 30 ft. lbs.

16. Install the spindle and replace the dust cover and remove the jack from under the suspension.

17. Install the wheel hub assembly and connect the locking hub.

18. Install the wheels and lower the vehicle.

19. Connect the negative battery cable.

Manual Locking Hubs

Removal and Installation

1. Disconnect the negative battery cable and remove the locking hub cover.

2. Raise and support the vehicle safely.

3. Remove the locking hub body assembly.

NOTE: The manual locking hubs must not be packed with grease.

Wheel hub "LOCK" position

Wheel hub "FREE" position

To install:

4. Install a new O-ring to the locking hub assembly.

5. Install the locking hub body assembly to the wheel hub flange and tighten the hub body bolts to 18 ft. lbs.

6. Install a new gasket in the manual locking hub cover.

7. Replace the locking hub cover and connect the negative battery cable.

8. Lower the vehicle.

NOTE: The O mark on the hub knob must be in the FREE position. Tighten the locking hub cover bolts to 106 inch lbs.

Automatic Locking Hubs

Removal and Installation

1. Disconnect the negative battery cable and remove the automatic locking hub cover.

2. Disconnect the automatic hub body assembly.

To install:

3. Install a new O-ring to the automatic locking hub body assembly.

4. Connect the automatic locking hub body assembly to the wheel hub flange. Tighten the hub body assembly bolts to 18 ft. lbs.

5. Install a new gasket in the automatic locking hub cover and replace the hub cover.

6. Connect the negative battery cable.

Pinion Seal

Removal and Installation

1. Raise and safely support the vehicle.

2. Matchmark and remove the driveshaft.

3. Check the turning torque of the pinion before proceeding.

4. Using a pinion flange holding tool, remove the pinion nut and the washer.

5. Remove the pinion flange from the differential carrier and pry out the pinion seal.

To install:

6. Clean and inspect the sealing surface of the carrier.

7. Using a seal driver, install the new seal into the carrier until the flange of the seal is flush with the carrier.

NOTE: Tightening the flange nut will preload the pinion bearings. Exceeding the preload specifications will compress the collapsible spacer to far and require the spacer to be replaced.

8. Install the pinion flange and using the pinion flange holding tool, replace the pinion nut and washer. Tighten the pinion nut to the same torque as before.

9. Align the matchmarks and install the driveshaft.

10. Check the level of the differential fluid when finished.

Differential Carrier

Removal and Installation

1. Raise and safely support the vehicle and disconnect the negative battery cable. Drain the oil from the rear differential.

2. Remove the left and right axle shafts.

3. Disconnect the driveshaft.

4. Remove the 4 mounting bolts to the upper rear suspension arm.

5. Support the differential carrier with a proper jack.

6. Remove the differential case nuts and lower the differential assembly from the rear housing.

To install:

7. Clean and inspect the sealing surfaces of the carrier and the housing.

8. Using a liquid sealant on the carrier, install the carrier in the housing and tighten the nuts to 13–20 ft. lbs.

9. Replace the 4 mounting bolts to the upper rear suspension arm and tighten to 41 ft. lbs.

10. Connect the rear driveshaft and replace the left and rear axles.

11. Refill the rear differential to the proper level with SAE 75W–90W API GL5 Hypoid Gear Oil.

12. Lower the vehicle and connect the negative battery cable.

Front Axle Housing

Removal and Installation

1. Raise and safely support the vehicle. Remove the front wheels.

2. Drain the oil from the front differential.

3. Remove caliper assembly from brake disc and support caliper assembly.

4. Remove the tie rod end from the steering knuckle using a tie rod end remover.

5. Remove the 8 oil seal cover bolts and separate the felt pad, seal and retainer.

6. Remove the 4 kingpin bolts from the top and bottom and remove the kingpins from the knuckle.

7. Remove axle shafts from housing by pulling outward gradually.

8. Remove the bolts between the flange yoke and companion flange and disconnect the front drive shaft.

9. Remove the 8 U-joint nuts and remove the housing assembly.

To install:

10. Install the housing and torque the housing U-bolt nuts to 43 ft. lbs.

11. Connect the front drive shaft and install the bolts.

12. Install the front axle shafts and install the kingpins. Apply Loctite® to the kingpin bolts.

13. Install oil seal, felt pad and retainer and tighten the 8 cover bolts.

14. Install the tie rod end to the steering knuckle.

15. Install the front caliper to the disc and install the front wheels.

16. Refill the differential with the proper lubricant and bleed the brake system when finished.

Rear Axle Housing

Removal and Installation

1. Raise and safely support the vehicle. Drain the rear differential assembly.

2. Make sure the parking brake is in the released position.

3. Remove the rear wheels and remove the rear brake drums from the vehicle.

4. Disconnect the parking brake cables from the levers. Remove the parking brake lever stop plates.

5. Disconnect and plug the brake lines to the wheel cylinders.

6. Remove the rear wheel bearing retainer nuts and remove the axle shafts from the vehicle. Do not remove the axle shafts with the backing plates attached.

7. Remove the rear axle carrier assembly.

8. Disconnect the brake line from the flexible hose and remove the E-clip. Remove the brake lines from the rear housing.

9. Remove the breather hose from the axle housing and disconnect the rear driveshaft.

10. Support the rear axle housing with a jack.

11. Remove the ball joint bracket from the differential carrier and remove the carrier assembly.

12. Loosen the rear mount nut of the trailing rod. Do not remove it.

13. Disconnect the shock absorber lower mount bolt.

14. Lower the jack to relieve the tension of the coil springs and remove the rear mount bolt of the trailing rod.

15. Remove the rear axle housing.

To install:

16. Place the rear axle housing on a jack and install the trailing rod rear mounting bolts. Mount the nuts but do not tighten.

17. Install the coil spring on the spring seat and raise the axle housing.

18. Replace the shock absorber lower mounting bolts. Do not tighten.

19. Install the differential carrier assembly and replace the rear upper ball joint bracket onto the carrier assembly and tighten to 37 ft. lbs.

20. Install the rear driveshaft and remove the jack from under the axle housing.

21. Replace the breather hose and brake lines to axle housing. Tighten them securely.

22. Connect the flexible brake hose to the bracket on the axle housing and secure with the E-clip.

23. Tighten the trailing rod nuts and the shock absorber nuts to 66 ft. lbs.
24. Install the brake line to the flexible hose and replace the axle shafts.
25. Install the brake lines to the wheel cylinders and replace the brake drums.
26. Install the wheels and refill the rear differential assembly.
27. Bleed the brake system and lower the vehicle.

STEERING

Steering Wheel

Removal and Installation

1. Disconnect the negative battery cable.
2. Disconnect the horn button and remove the steering wheel shaft nut.
3. Make matchmarks on the steering wheel and the shaft to use as a guide during reinstallation.
4. Remove the steering wheel, using a suitable steering wheel puller.

To install:

5. Install the steering wheel onto the shaft, aligning the matchmarks.
6. Install and tighten the shaft nut to 24 ft. lbs.
7. Install the horn button and connect the negative battery cable.

Manual Steering Gear

Removal and Installation

1. As required, raise and support the vehicle safely. Disconnect the steering lower shaft mounting bolts.
2. Disconnect the center link end from the pitman arm.
3. Remove the 3 steering gear box mounting bolts.
4. Disconnect the steering lower shaft joint and remove the steering gear.

To install:

5. Install the steering gear box by connecting to the lower shaft joint.

NOTE: Align the flat part of the steering gear worm shaft with the bolt hole of the lower shaft joint.

6. Replace the steering gear box mounting bolts and tighten to 50–72 ft. lbs.
7. Attach the center link to the pitman arm and tighten the nut to 22–50 ft. lbs.
8. Connect the lower shaft mounting bolts and tighten to 14–22 ft. lbs.

Adjustment

1. Check the worm shaft to make sure it is free from thrust play.
2. Place the pitman arm in a position that is nearly parallel with the worm shaft.
3. With the pitman arm in this position, the front wheels are in a straight forward position.
4. Measure the worm shaft starting torque from it's straight foward position. The torque should be 0.4–0.7 ft. lbs.
5. Adjust the worm shaft adjusting bolt to specifications.

Power Steering Gear

Removal and Installation

1. Disconnect the negative battery cable.
2. Remove the coolant reservoir tank from the radiator.
3. Disconnect the steering column lower shaft from the gear box.
4. Raise and safely support the vehicle.

ADJUSTING BOLT

Adjusting the steering gear assembly

5. Remove the center link nut and lock washer and disconnect the center link from the pitman arm, using a piman arm puller.
6. Lower the vehicle. Remove the pressure hose from the power steering gear assembly and plug.
7. Disconnect the return hose and plug. Remove the 3 power steering gear mounting bolts.
8. Remove the power steering gear. Disconnect the pitman arm from the gear assembly, note the alignment marks.

To install:

9. Align the matchmarks on the pitman arm and the power steering gear sector shaft. Install the pitman arm to the gear assembly and tighten the nut to 95 ft. lbs.
10. Install the power steering gear assembly on the vehicle and tighten the mounting bolts to 72 ft. lbs.
11. Connect the power steering pressure and return hoses.
12. Raise and safely support the vehicle.
13. Install the center link to the pitman arm and tighten the nut to 40 ft. lbs. Lower the vehicle.
14. Connect the steering column lower shaft to the gear assembly and tighten the bolts to 29 ft. lbs.
15. Install the coolant reservoir tank to the radiator. Refill the power steering pump.
16. Connect the negative battery cable. Run the engine and operate the power steering. Recheck the fluid level and for any leaks.

Adjustment

1. Check the worm shaft to make sure it is free from thrust play.
2. Place the pitman arm in a position that is nearly parallel with the worm shaft.
3. With the pitman arm in this position, the front wheels are in a straight forward state.

4. Measure the worm shaft starting torque from it's straight forward state. The torque should be 0.4–0.7 ft. lbs.

5. Adjust the worm shaft adjusting bolt to specifications.

Power steering Pump

Removal and Installation

NOTE: Before disconnecting the power steering pressure and return line at the pump assembly, make sure any dirt or grease is removed.

1. Disconnect the negative battery cable. Remove the coolant reservoir tank from the radiator.

2. Loosen the air conditioning compressor adjusting and pivot bolts, if equipped.

3. Loosen the power steering pump adjusting and mounting bolts, if not equipped with air conditioning.

4. Remove the power steering belt.

5. Disconnect the power steering pressure and return hose and plug.

6. Disconnect the power steering pressure switch lead wire at the switch terminal.

7. Remove the engine oil filter.

8. Remove the power steering pump mounting and adjusting bolts.

9. Remove the power steering pump.

To install:

10. Install the power steering pump and replace the pump mounting bolts. Do not tighten.

11. Install the power steering pump pressure switch lead wire to the switch terminal.

12. Replace the power steering pressure and return hoses.

13. Install the power steering belt and tighten the power steering pump mounting bolts to 21 ft. lbs.

14. Tighten the air conditioning mounting bolts to 21 ft. lbs., if equipped.

15. Replace the coolant reservoir tank to the radiator and connect the negative battery cable. Refill the power steering pump.

16. Replace the oil filter and fill the crankcase to the proper level.

17. Run the engine and operate the power steering. Recheck the fluid level and for any leaks.

Belt Adjustment

1. To adjust the power steering belt tension, loosen the adjusting bolt of the air conditioning compressor, if equipped, or that of the power steering pump for vehicles without air conditioning.

2. Adjust the belt tension to 0.24–0.35 in. deflection, using the proper belt tension gauge.

3. Tighten the proper adjusting and mounting bolts to the specified torque.

System Bleeding

1. Raise and support the vehicle safely.

2. Fill the power steering reservoir to the specified level.

3. Run the engine for 3 to 5 minutes, stop it and add fluid if necessary to reach specified level.

4. With the engine stopped, turn the steering wheel to the left and to the right as far as it turns. Repeat a few times and refill the reservoir.

5. With the engine running at idle speed, bleed air from the system by loosening the bleeder valve at the gear assembly.

6. Repeat the stop to stop turn of the steering wheel until all the foam is gone.

7. Tighten the bleed valve securely. Recheck the fluid level in the reservoir.

NOTE: When air bleeding is not complete, it is indicated by a foaming fluid on the level indicator or a humming noise from the power steering pump.

Tie Rod Ends

Removal and Installation

1. Raise and safely support the vehicle and remove the wheels.

2. Remove the tie rod end from the steering knuckle, using a suitable tie rod end remover tool.

3. Mark the tie rod end locknut position on the tie rod thread.

4. Loosen the locknut and remove the tie rod end from the tie rod.

To install:

5. Install the tie rod end locknut and the tie rod end to the tie rod. Align the locknut with the mark on the tie rod thread and tighten the locknut to 48 ft. lbs.

6. Connect the tie rod end to the steering knuckle. Tighten the castle nut until the holes of the split pin are aligned but only within the specified torque 33 ft. lbs.

BRAKES

For all brake system repair and service procedures not detailed below, please refer to "Brakes" in the Unit Repair section.

Master Cylinder

Removal and Installation

1. Disconnect the negative battery cable. Remove the air cleaner case.

2. Disconnect the reservoir lead wire.

3. Clean the outside of the reservoir and remove the fluid from the reservoir.

4. Disconnect and plug the brake fluid lines at the master cylinder.

5. Remove the master cylinder to booster mounting bolts and remove the master cylinder.

To install:

6. Install the new master cylinder and tighten the mounting bolts to 12 ft. lbs.

7. Install the hydraulic brake lines to the master cylinder and tighten and tighten the flare nuts to 13 ft. lbs.

8. Replace the reservoir lead wire, if equipped.

9. Fill the reservoir with the specified brake fluid. Replace the air cleaner case.

10. Bleed the air from the brake hydraulic system and check the brake pedal play.

Proportioning Valve

Removal and Installation

1. Raise and safely support the vehicle.

2. Disconnect and plug the hydraulic brake lines from the proportioning valve assembly.

3. Remove the proportioning valve from the vehicle body.

NOTE: The proportioning valve should be removed with the spring attached.

To install:

4. Install the proportioning valve to the vehicle body and tighten the mounting bolts to 20 ft. lbs.

5. Connect the hydraulic brake lines to the proportioning valve and tighten the flare nuts to 13 ft. lbs.

6. Fill the brake reservoir to the proper level and bleed the brake hydraulic system. Lower the vehicle.

NOTE: Bleed the air from the proportioning valve bleeder valve.

Power Brake Booster

Removal and Installation

1. Disconnect the negative battery cable. Remove the air cleaner case.

2. Remove the fluid from the brake reservoir and remove the master cylinder.

3. Disconnect the vacuum hose from the booster. Remove the pushrod clevis pin and cotter pin from the brake pedal arm.

4. Disconnect the brake booster mounting nuts and remove the brake booster from the vehicle.

5. Disconnect the pedal attachment from the booster.

To install:

6. Connect the pedal attachment to the booster and install the booster to the vehicle. Tighten the mounting nuts to 7.5–11.5 ft. lbs.

7. Install the pushrod clevis pin and cotter pin to the brake pedal arm.

8. Connect the vacuum hose to the booster and install the master cylinder to the booster.

9. Replace the air cleaner case and connect the negative battery cable.

10. Fill the brake reservoir and bleed the brake hydraulic system.

Brake Caliper

Removal and Installation

1. Disconnect the negative battery cable. Raise and safely support the vehicle.

2. Remove the wheels. Disconnect and plug the brake line.

3. Remove the caliper mounting bolts and remove the caliper from the vehicle.

To install:

4. Install the caliper on the vehicle. Tighten the mounting bolts to 65 ft. lbs.

5. Connect the hydraulic brake line, using 2 new washers. Replace the front wheels.

6. Lower the vehicle. Connect the negative battery cable.

7. Fill the brake reservoir and bleed the hydraulic brake system.

Disc Brake Pads

Removal and Installation

1. Disconnect the negative battery cable. Raise and safely support the vehicle.

2. Remove the wheels.

3. Disconnect the brake caliper.

NOTE: Do not allow the caliper hang from the brake hose. Support it by the mounting bracket.

1. Brake caliper carrier
2. Disc brake outer pad
3. Disc brake inner pad
4. Brake pad spring
5. Cylinder boot
6. Disc brake piston
7. Piston seal
8. Disc brake caliper
9. Caliper pin
10. Caliper mounting bolt
11. Bleeder plug
12. Bleeder plug cap

Exploded view of the front disc brake assembly

1. Brake backing plate
2. Hold-down pin
3. Wheel bearing retainer nut
4. Wheel cylinder assembly
5. Parking brake rod
6. Shoe hold-down spring
7. Brake shoes
8. Shoe return spring
9. Shoe return upper spring

Exploded view of the rear brake drum assembly

4. Remove the disc pads from the caliper. Disconnect the anti-rattle springs.
To install:
5. Connect the anti rattle springs and install the brake pads on to caliper assembly.
6. Connect the brake caliper and install the front wheels.
7. Lower the vehicle. Connect the negative battery cable.

Brake Rotor

Removal and Installation

1. Disconnect the negative battery cable.
2. Raise and safely support the vehicle. Remove the wheel assembly.
3. Remove the brake caliper mounting bracket, with the caliper and the brake line attached, move it out of the way and support it.

NOTE: Do not allow the caliper hang from the brake hose. Support it by the mounting bracket.

4. Install 2 bolts into the threaded holes in the brake rotor and tighten them evenly. This will remove the rotor from the hub assembly.
To install:
5. Install the new brake rotor on the hub and install the caliper assembly.
6. Install the front wheels and tighten to 65 ft. lbs.
7. Lower the vehicle and connect the negative battery cable.

Brake Drums

Removal and Installation

1. Disconnect the negative battery cable. Raise and safely support the vehicle.
2. Make sure the parking brake is released.
3. Remove the wheels and the rear drum nuts from the vehicle.
4. Remove the brake drum, using a slide hammer puller.
To install:
5. Install the brake drum, tighten the brake drum nuts to 58 ft. lbs.
6. Install the rear wheels and lower the vehicle. Connect the negative battery cable.

Brake Shoes

Removal and Installation

1. Disconnect the negative battery cable. Raise and safely support the vehicle.
2. Remove the rear wheels from the vehicle. Remove the rear brake drums.
3. Remove the brake shoe holddown springs.
4. Disconnect the parking brake cable from the parking brake shoe lever and remove the brake shoes.

To install:
5. Install the brake shoes and install the parking brake lever and cable to the assembly.
6. Install the brake shoe hold-down springs and install the rear brake drums.
7. Install the rear wheels, lower the vehicle and connect the negative battery terminal.

Wheel Cylinder

Removal and Installation

1. Disconnect the negative battery cable. Raise and safely support the vehicle.
2. Remove the rear wheels and brake drums from the vehicle.
3. Remove the rear brake shoes and disconnect the brake line from the rear of the wheel cylinder. Plug the brake line.
4. Remove the 2 rear wheel cylinder mounting bolts. Remove the rear wheel cylinder.
To install:
5. Install the wheel cylinder and tighten the mounting bolts to 6.0–8.5 ft. lbs.
6. Connect the brake line to the wheel cylinder and install the rear brake shoes.
7. Replace the rear brake drums and the rear wheels.
8. Lower the vehicle. Connect the negative battery cable.
9. Bleed the brake system and check for any leaks when finished.

Parking Brake Cable

Removal and Installation

1. Disconnect the parking brake cable from the parking lever.
2. Raise and safely support the vehicle. Remove the rear wheels and brake drums from the vehicle.
3. Remove the rear brake shoes and disconnect the parking brake cable from the parking brake shoe lever.
4. Remove the cable from the brake backing plate by squeezing the parking brake cable stop ring.
To install:
5. Install the cable to the backing plate and to the brake shoe lever.
6. Install the brake shoes and install the rear brake drums.
7. Install the rear wheels and connect the cable to the parking brake lever.

Adjustment

1. Adjust the parking brake lever by loosening or tightening the self locking nut at the park brake lever.
2. The proper adjustment is when the parking brake lever is within 7–9 notches, when the lever is pulled up at 44 lbs.
3. Ckeck the rear drum for dragging after adjustment.

FRONT SUSPENSION

MacPherson Strut

Removal and Installation

1. Disconnect the negative battery cable.
2. Raise and safely support the vehicle. Allow the front suspension to hang free.
3. Remove the front wheel. Disconnect the E-clip mounting

the brake hose and remove the brake hose from the strut bracket.
4. Remove the strut bracket to steering knuckle bolts.
5. Lower the vehicle. Remove the strut support nuts, while holding the strut by hand. Remove the strut assembly.
To install:
6. Install the strut assembly and tighten the strut support nuts to 18 ft. lbs.

7. Raise and safely support the vehicle.

8. Install the strut bracket to steering knuckle bolts and tighten to 66 ft. lbs.

9. Connect the brake hose to the strut bracket using the E-clip.

10. Replace the front wheels and lower the vehicle.

11. Connect the negative battery cable.

Coil Springs

Removal and Installation

1. Disconnect the negative battery cable.

2. Raise and safely support the vehicle. Allow the front suspension to hang free.

3. Remove the front wheel and the locking hub assembly.

4. Remove the front axle circlip and washer.

5. Remove the brake caliper mounting bracket, with the caliper and the brake line attached, move it out of the way and support it.

6. Remove the brake disc and disconnect the stabilizer link from the control arm.

7. Disconnect the tie rod end and support the lower control arm using a jack.

8. Disconnect the strut bracket and remove the ball joint castle nut.

9. Remove the steering knuckle and the wheel hub assembly while lowering the jack.

10. Remove the coil spring from the vehicle.

To install:

11. Install the coil spring to the vehicle and install the wheel hub and steering knuckle while raising the jack.

12. Connect the strut bracket and install the ball joint castle nut.

13. Connect the tie rod end and connect the stabilizer link to the control arm.

14. Install the brake disc and connect the caliper assembly.

15. Install the front axle circlip and washer and install the locking hub assembly.

16. Install the front wheels, lower the vehicle and connect the negative battery cable.

Lower Ball Joints

Inspection

1. Inspect for the smoothness of the rotation.

2. Check the ball stud for damage.

3. Inspect the dust shield for damage.

Removal and Installation

1. Disconnect the negative battery cable. Remove the coil spring from the vehicle.

2. Remove the control arm mounting bolts.

3. Remove the control arm.

4. Disconnect the ball joint from the control arm and remove the ball joint.

To install:

5. Install the ball joint to the control arm and tighten the bolts to 63 ft. lbs.

6. Install the control arm to the chassis and tighten the bolts to 74 ft. lbs.

7. Install the coil spring and connect the negative battery cable.

Lower Control Arms

Removal and Installation

1. Disconnect the negative battery cable. Remove the coil spring from the vehicle.

2. Remove the control arm mounting bolts.

3. Remove the control arm.

To install:

4. Install the control arm to the chassis and tighten the bolts to 74 ft. lbs.

5. Install the coil spring and connect the negative battery cable.

Stabilizer Bar

Removal and Installation

1. Disconnect the negative battery cable. Raise and safely support the vehicle.

2. Disconnect the left and the right stabilizer ball joints from the front control arms.

3. Remove the stabilizer bar mount bushing bracket bolts and nuts.

4. Remove the stabilizer bar.

5. Remove the stabilizer links.

To install:

6. Install the new stabilizer bar, using new bushings.

7. Torque the stabilizer link nuts to 21 ft. lbs. and the stabilizer bar bracket bolts and nuts to 37 ft. lbs.

8. Lower the vehicle and connect the negative battery cable.

REAR SUSPENSION

Shock Absorbers

Removal and Installation

1. Raise and safely support the vehicle. Support the rear axle housing.

2. Remove the upper and lower shock absorber mounting bolts.

3. Remove the rear shock absorber.

To install:

4. Install the the rear shock absorber.

5. Replace the upper mounting bolts and tighten to 21 ft. lbs. Replace the lower mounting bolts and tighten to 63 ft. lbs.

Coil Springs

Removal and Installation

1. Raise and safely support the vehicle. Remove the rear wheels.

2. Support the rear axle housing , using a floor jack.

3. Remove the shock absorber lower mounting bolt.

4. Lower the rear axle housing so the coil spring can be removed.

5. Remove the coil spring from the vehicle.

To install:

6. Install the coil spring to the spring seat and raise the axle housing.

7. Install the lower shock absorber mounting bolt but do not tighten.

8. Connect the parking brake cable hangers and install the rear wheels.

9. Lower the vehicle and tighten the lower shock absorber nuts to 64 ft. lbs.

SPECIFICATIONS

ENGINE IDENTIFICATION

Year	Model	Engine Displacement cu. in. (cc/liter)	Engine Series Identification	No. of Cylinders	Engine Type
1988	Pick-Up	138 (2254/2.3)	4ZD1	4	OHC
	Pick-Up	156 (2559/2.6)	4ZE1	4	OHC
	Trooper II	156 (2559/2.6)	4ZE1	4	OHC
1989	Amigo	138 (2254/2.3)	4ZD1	4	OHC
	Amigo	156 (2559/2.6)	4ZE1	4	OHC
	Pick-Up	138 (2254/2.3)	4ZD1	4	OHC
	Pick-Up	156 (2559/2.6)	4ZE1	4	OHC
	Trooper/Trooper II	156 (2559/2.6)	4ZE1	4	OHC
	Trooper/Trooper II	173 (2828/2.8)	CPC	6	OHV
1990	Amigo	138 (2254/2.3)	4ZD1	4	OHC
	Amigo	156 (2559/2.6)	4ZE1	4	OHC
	Pick-Up	138 (2254/2.3)	4ZD1	4	OHC
	Pick-Up	156 (2559/2.6)	4ZE1	4	OHC
	Trooper/Trooper II	156 (2559/2.6)	4ZE1	4	OHC
	Trooper/Trooper II	173 (2828/2.8)	CPC	6	OHV
1991-92	Amigo	138 (2254/2.3)	4ZD1	4	OHC
	Amigo	156 (2559/2.6)	4ZE1	4	OHC
	Amigo	191 (3137/3.1)	CPC	6	OHV
	Pick-Up	138 (2254/2.3)	4ZD1	4	OHC
	Pick-Up	156 (2559/2.6)	4ZE1	4	OHC
	Pick-Up	191 (3137/3.1)	CPC	6	OHV
	Rodeo	156 (2559/2.6)	4ZE1	4	OHC
	Rodeo	191 (3137/3.1)	CPC	6	OHV
	Trooper/Trooper II	156 (2559/2.6)	4ZE1	4	OHC
	Trooper/Trooper II	173 (2828/2.8)	CPC	6	OHV

OHC—Overhead Cam
OHV—Overhead Valves

GENERAL ENGINE SPECIFICATIONS

Year	Model	Engine Displacement cu. in. (cc)	Fuel System Type	Net Horsepower @ rpm	Net Torque @ rpm (ft. lbs.)	Bore × Stroke (in.)	Compression Ratio	Oil Pressure @ rpm
1988	Pick-Up	138 (2254)	2 bbl	96 @ 4600	123 @ 2600	3.52 × 3.54	8.3:1	57 @ 3000
	Pick-Up	156 (2559)	MPFI	120 @ 4600	146 @ 2600	3.65 × 3.74	8.3:1	57–71 @ 4000
	Trooper II	156 (2559)	MPFI	120 @ 4600	146 @ 2600	3.65 × 3.74	8.3:1	57–71 @ 4000
1989	Amigo	138 (2254)	2 bbl	96 @ 4600	123 @ 2600	3.52 × 3.54	8.3:1	57 @ 3000
	Amigo	156 (2559)	MPFI	120 @ 4600	146 @ 2600	3.65 × 3.74	8.3:1	57–71 @ 4000
	Pick-Up	138 (2254)	2 bbl	96 @ 4600	123 @ 2600	3.52 × 3.54	8.3:1	57 @ 3000
	Pick-Up	156 (2559)	MPFI	120 @ 4600	146 @ 2600	3.65 × 3.74	8.3:1	57–71 @ 4000
	Trooper/Trooper II	156 (2559)	MPFI	120 @ 4600	146 @ 2600	3.65 × 3.74	8.3:1	57–71 @ 4000
	Trooper/Trooper II	173 (2828)	TBI	NA	NA	3.50 × 2.99	8.9:1	30–55 @ 2000

GENERAL ENGINE SPECIFICATIONS

Year	Model	Engine Displacement cu. in. (cc)	Fuel System Type	Net Horsepower @ rpm	Net Torque @ rpm (ft. lbs.)	Bore × Stroke (in.)	Compression Ratio	Oil Pressure @ rpm
1990	Amigo	138 (2254)	2 bbl	96 @ 4600	123 @ 2600	3.52 × 3.54	8.3:1	57 @ 3000
	Amigo	156 (2559)	MPFI	120 @ 4600	146 @ 2600	3.65 × 3.74	8.3:1	57–71 @ 4000
	Pick-Up	138 (2254)	2 bbl	96 @ 4600	123 @ 2600	3.52 × 3.54	8.3:1	57 @ 3000
	Pick-Up	156 (2559)	MPFI	120 @ 4600	146 @ 2600	3.65 × 3.74	8.3:1	57–71 @ 4000
	Trooper/Trooper II	156 (2559)	MPFI	120 @ 4600	146 @ 2600	3.65 × 3.74	8.3:1	57–71 @ 4000
	Trooper/Trooper II	173 (2828)	TBI	NA	NA	3.50 × 2.99	8.9:1	30–55 @ 2000
1991–92	Amigo	138 (2254)	2 bbl	96 @ 4600	123 @ 2600	3.52 × 3.54	8.3:1	57 @ 3000
	Amigo	156 (2559)	MPFI	120 @ 4600	146 @ 2600	3.65 × 3.74	8.3:1	57–71 @ 4000
	Amigo	191 (3137)	TBI	120 @ 4200	175 @ 2200	3.50 × 3.40	8.5:1	30–55 @ 2000
	Pick-Up	138 (2254)	2 bbl	96 @ 4600	123 @ 2600	3.52 × 3.54	8.3:1	57 @ 3000
	Pick-Up	156 (2559)	MPFI	120 @ 4600	146 @ 2600	3.65 × 3.74	8.3:1	57–71 @ 4000
	Pick-Up	191 (3137)	TBI	120 @ 4200	175 @ 2200	3.50 × 3.40	8.5:1	30–55 @ 2000
	Trooper/Trooper II	156 (2559)	MPFI	120 @ 4600	146 @ 2600	3.65 × 3.74	8.3:1	57–71 @ 4000
	Trooper/Trooper II	173 (2828)	TBI	125 @ 4800	150 @ 2400	3.50 × 2.99	8.9:1	30–55 @ 2000
	Rodeo	156 (2559)	MPFI	120 @ 4600	146 @ 2600	3.65 × 3.74	8.3:1	57–71 @ 4000
	Rodeo	191 (3137)	TBI	120 @ 4200	175 @ 2200	3.50 × 3.40	8.5:1	30–55 @ 2000

NA—Not available
MPFI—Multi Port Fuel Injection
TBI—Throttle Body Injection

ENGINE TUNE-UP SPECIFICATIONS

Year	Model	Engine Displacement cu. in. (cc)	Spark Plugs Type	Spark Plugs Gap (in.)	Ignition Timing (deg.) MT	Ignition Timing (deg.) AT	Compression Pressure (psi)	Fuel Pump (psi)	Idle Speed (rpm) MT	Idle Speed (rpm) AT	Valve Clearance ① In.	Valve Clearance ① Ex.
1988	Pick-Up	138 (2254)	R42XLS	0.040	6B	6B	—	3.5	900	900	0.006	0.010
	Pick-Up	156 (2559)	R42XLS	0.040	12B	12B	—	43	900	900	0.008	0.008
	Trooper II	156 (2559)	R42XLS	0.040	12B	12B	—	43	900	900	0.008	0.008
1989	Amigo	138 (2254)	R42XLS	0.040	6B	6B	—	3.5	900	900	0.006	0.010
	Amigo	156 (2559)	R42XLS	0.040	12B	12B	—	43	900	900	0.008	0.008
	Pick-Up	138 (2254)	R42XLS	0.040	6B	6B	—	3.5	900	900	0.006	0.010
	Pick-Up	156 (2559)	R43XLS	0.040	12B	12B	—	43	900	900	0.008	0.008
	Trooper/Trooper II	156 (2559)	R43XLS	0.040	12B	12B	—	43	900	900	0.008	0.008
	Trooper/Trooper II	173 (2828)	R43TSK	0.045	10B	10B	—	9–13	800	800	②	②
1990	Amigo	138 (2254)	R42XLS	0.040	6B	6B	—	3.5	900	900	0.006	0.010
	Amigo	156 (2559)	R42XLS	0.040	12B	12B	—	43	900	900	0.008	0.008
	Pick-Up	138 (2254)	R42XLS	0.040	6B	6B	—	3.5	900	900	0.006	0.010
	Pick-Up	156 (2559)	R43XLS	0.040	12B	12B	—	43	900	900	0.008	0.008
	Rodeo	156 (2559)	R42XLS	0.040	12B	12B	—	43	900	900	0.008	0.008
	Trooper/Trooper II	156 (2559)	R43XLS	0.040	12B	12B	—	43	900	900	0.008	0.008
	Trooper/Trooper II	173 (2828)	R43TSK	0.045	10B	10B	—	9–13	800	800	②	②

ENGINE TUNE-UP SPECIFICATIONS

Year	Model	Engine Displacement cu. in. (cc)	Spark Plugs Type	Gap (in.)	Ignition Timing (deg.) MT	AT	Com-pression Pressure (psi)	Fuel Pump (psi)	Idle Speed (rpm) MT	AT	Valve Clearance ① In.	Ex.
1991	Amigo	138 (2254)	R42XLS	0.040	6B	6B	—	3.5	900	900	0.006	0.010
	Amigo	156 (2559)	R42XLS	0.040	12B	12B	—	43	900	900	0.008	0.008
	Amigo	191 (3137)	R43TSK	0.045	10B	10B	—	9–13	800	800	②	②
	Pick-Up	138 (2254)	R42XLS	0.040	6B	6B	—	3.5	900	900	0.006	0.010
	Pick-Up	156 (2559)	R43XLS	0.040	12B	12B	—	43	900	900	0.008	0.008
	Pick-Up	191 (3137)	R43TSK	0.045	10B	10B	—	9–13	800	800	②	②
	Rodeo	156 (2559)	R42XLS	0.040	12B	12B	—	43	900	900	0.008	0.008
	Rodeo	191 (3137)	R43TSK	0.045	10B	10B	—	9–13	800	800	②	②
	Trooper/Trooper II	156 (2559)	R43XLS	0.040	12B	12B	—	43	900	900	0.008	0.008
	Trooper/Trooper II	173 (2828)	R43TSK	0.045	10B	10B	—	9–13	800	800	②	②
1992					SEE UNDERHOOD SPECIFICATIONS							

B—Before Top Dead Center
① Cold
② Zero lash, plus 1½ turns

FIRING ORDERS

NOTE: To avoid confusion, always replace spark plug wires one at a time.

2.3L and 2.6L Engines
Engine Firing Order: 1–3–4–2
Distributor Rotation: Counterclockwise

2.8L and 3.1L Engines
Engine Firing Order: 1–2–3–4–5–6
Distributor Rotation: Clockwise

CAPACITIES

Year	Model	Engine Displacement cu. in. (cc)	Engine Crankcase with Filter	without Filter	Transmission (pts.) 4-Spd	5-Spd	Auto.	Drive Axle (pts.)	Fuel Tank (gal.)	Cooling System (qts.)
1988	Pick-Up	138 (2254)	4.2	3.8	—	3.2	13.8	3.2④	②	9.5
	Pick-Up	156 (2559)	5.2	4.8	—	6.2①	13.8	3.8④	4	9.5
	Trooper II	156 (2559)	4.4	4.0	—	6.2①	24.0③	3.8④	21.9	8.5

CAPACITIES

Year	Model	Engine Displacement cu. in. (cc)	Engine Crankcase with Filter	Engine Crankcase without Filter	Transmission (pts.) 4-Spd	Transmission (pts.) 5-Spd	Transmission (pts.) Auto.	Drive Axle (pts.)	Fuel Tank (gal.)	Cooling System (qts.)
1989	Amigo	138 (2254)	4.2	3.8	—	3.2	13.8	3.2④	②	9.5
	Amigo	156 (2559)	5.2	4.8	—	6.2①	13.8	3.8④	②	9.5
	Pick-Up	138 (2254)	4.2	3.8	—	3.2	13.8	3.2④	②	9.5
	Pick-Up	156 (2559)	5.2	4.8	—	6.2①	13.8	3.8④	②	9.5
	Trooper/Trooper II	156 (2559)	5.2	4.8	—	6.2①	24.0③	3.8④	21.9	8.5
	Trooper/Trooper II	173 (2828)	4.5	4.0	—	6.2①	18.6	3.8④	21.9	10.6
1990	Amigo	138 (2254)	4.2	3.8	—	3.2	13.8	3.2④	②	9.5
	Amigo	156 (2559)	5.2	4.8	—	6.2①	13.8	3.8④	②	9.5
	Pick-Up	138 (2254)	4.2	3.8	—	3.2	13.8	3.2④	②	9.5
	Pick-Up	156 (2559)	5.2	4.8	—	6.2①	13.8	3.8④	②	9.5
	Trooper/Trooper II	156 (2559)	5.2	4.8	—	6.2①	24.0③	3.8④	21.9	8.5
	Trooper/Trooper II	173 (2828)	4.5	4.0	—	6.2①	18.6	3.8④	21.9	10.6
1991–92	Amigo	138 (2254)	4.2	3.8	—	3.2	13.8	3.2④	②	9.5
	Amigo	156 (2559)	5.2	4.8	—	6.2①	13.8	3.8④	②	9.5
	Amigo	191 (3137)	4.5	4.0	—	6.2①	—	3.8④	21.9	11.4
	Pick-Up	138 (2254)	4.2	3.8	—	3.2	13.8	3.2④	②	9.5
	Pick-Up	156 (2559)	5.2	4.8	—	6.2①	13.8	3.8④	②	9.5
	Pick-Up	191 (3137)	4.5	4.0	—	6.2①	—	3.8④	21.9	11.4
	Rodeo	156 (2559)	5.8	5.4	—	6.2①	19.0	4.0④	21.9	9.5
	Rodeo	191 (3137)	4.5	4.0	—	4.8①	19.0	4.0④	21.9	11.4
	Trooper/Trooper II	156 (2559)	5.2	4.8	—	6.2①	24.0③	3.8④	21.9	8.5
	Trooper/Trooper II	173 (2828)	4.5	4.0	—	6.2①	18.6	3.8④	21.9	10.6

① Transfer case—3.0 pts.
② Short wheel base—14.0 gal.
　Long wheel base—19.8 gal.
③ Transfer case—2.4 pts.
④ Front axle—3.2 pts.

CAMSHAFT SPECIFICATIONS

Year	Engine Displacement cu. in. (cc)	Journal Diameter 1	2	3	4	5	Lobe Lift In.	Lobe Lift Ex.	Bearing Clearance	Camshaft End Play
1988	138 (2254)	1.3390	1.3390	1.3390	1.3390	1.3390	NA	NA	0.0026–0.0043	0.008①
	156 (2559)	1.3390	1.3390	1.3390	1.3390	1.3390	NA	NA	0.0026–0.0043	0.008①
1989	138 (2254)	1.3390	1.3390	1.3390	1.3390	1.3390	NA	NA	0.0026–0.0043	0.008①
	156 (2559)	1.3390	1.3390	1.3390	1.3390	1.3390	NA	NA	0.0026–0.0043	0.008①
	173 (2828)	1.8678–1.8815	1.8678–1.8815	1.8678–1.8815	1.8678–1.8815	—	0.262	0.273	0.0010–0.0040	NA

CAMSHAFT SPECIFICATIONS

Year	Engine Displacement cu. in. (cc)	Journal Diameter					Lobe Lift		Bearing Clearance	Camshaft End Play
		1	2	3	4	5	In.	Ex.		
1990	138 (2254)	1.3390	1.3390	1.3390	1.3390	1.3390	1.451	1.451	0.0033– 0.0051	0.0002– 0.0059
	156 (2559)	1.3390	1.3390	1.3390	1.3390	1.3390	NA	NA	0.0026– 0.0043	0.0080 ①
	173 (2828)	1.8670– 1.8810	1.8670– 1.8810	1.8670– 1.8810	1.8670– 1.8810	—	0.262	0.273	0.0010– 0.0040	NA
1991–92	138 (2254)	1.3390	1.3390	1.3390	1.3390	1.3390	1.451	1.451	0.0033– 0.0051	0.0002– 0.0059
	156 (2559)	1.3390	1.3390	1.3390	1.3390	1.3390	NA	NA	0.0026– 0.0043	0.0080 ①
	173 (2828)	1.8670– 1.8810	1.8670– 1.8810	1.8670– 1.8810	1.8670– 1.8810	—	0.262	0.273	0.0010– 0.0040	NA
	191 (3137)	1.8670– 1.8810	1.8670– 1.8810	1.8670– 1.8810	1.8670– 1.8810	—	0.230	0.267	0.0010– 0.0040	NA

NA—Not available
① Limit

CRANKSHAFT AND CONNECTING ROD SPECIFICATIONS

Year	Engine Displacement cu. in. (cc)	Crankshaft				Connecting Rod		
		Main Brg. Journal Dia.	Main Brg. Oil Clearance	Shaft End-play	Thrust on No.	Journal Diameter	Oil Clearance	Side Clearance
1988	138 (2254)	2.2032– 2.2038	0.0006– 0.0026	0.0024– 0.0099	3	1.9276– 1.9282	0.0004– 0.0026	0.0078– 0.0130
	156 (2559)	2.2032– 2.2038	0.0009– 0.0020	0.0024– 0.0099	3	1.9276– 1.9282	0.0008– 0.0020	0.0078– 0.0130
1989	138 (2254)	2.2032– 2.2038	0.0006– 0.0026	0.0024– 0.0099	3	1.9276– 1.9282	0.0004– 0.0026	0.0078– 0.0130
	156 (2559)	2.2032– 2.2038	0.0009– 0.0020	0.0024– 0.0099	3	1.9276– 1.9282	0.0008– 0.0020	0.0078– 0.0130
	173 (2828)	2.6473– 2.6483	0.0016– 0.0033	0.0020– 0.0080	3	1.9983– 1.9993	0.0013– 0.0026	0.0060– 0.0170
1990	138 (2254)	2.2032– 2.2038	0.0006– 0.0026	0.0024– 0.0099	3	1.9276– 1.9282	0.0012– 0.0024	0.0078– 0.0130
	156 (2559)	2.2032– 2.2038	0.0009– 0.0020	0.0024– 0.0099	3	1.9276– 1.9282	0.0008– 0.0020	0.0078– 0.0130
	173 (2828)	2.6473– 2.6483	0.0016– 0.0033	0.0020– 0.0080	3	1.9983– 1.9993	0.0013– 0.0026	0.0060– 0.0170
1991–92	138 (2254)	2.2032– 2.2038	0.0006– 0.0026	0.0024– 0.0099	3	1.9276– 1.9282	0.0012– 0.0024	0.0078– 0.0130
	156 (2559)	2.2032– 2.2038	0.0009– 0.0020	0.0024– 0.0099	3	1.9276– 1.9282	0.0008– 0.0020	0.0078– 0.0130
	173 (2828)	2.6473– 2.6483	0.0016– 0.0033	0.0020– 0.0080	3	1.9983– 1.9993	0.0013– 0.0026	0.0060– 0.0170
	191 (3137)	2.6473– 2.6483	0.0016– 0.0033	0.0020– 0.0080	3	1.9983– 1.9993	0.0011– 0.0032	0.0014– 0.0267

VALVE SPECIFICATIONS

Year	Engine Displacement cu. in. (cc)	Seat Angle (deg.)	Face Angle (deg.)	Spring Test Pressure (lbs.)	Spring Installed Height (in.)	Stem-to-Guide Clearance (in.) Intake	Exhaust	Stem Diameter (in.) Intake	Exhaust
1988	138 (2254)	45	45	56	1.62	0.0009–0.0022	0.0015–0.0031	0.3150	0.3150
	156 (2559)	45	45	56	1.62	0.0009–0.0022	0.0015–0.0031	0.3150	0.3150
1989	138 (2254)	45	45	56	1.62	0.0009–0.0022	0.0015–0.0031	0.3150	0.3150
	156 (2559)	45	45	56	1.62	0.0009–0.0022	0.0015–0.0031	0.3150	0.3150
	173 (2828)	46	45	215	1.72	0.0010–0.0027	0.0010–0.0027	0.3410–0.3420	0.3410–0.3420
1990	138 (2254)	45	45	56 @ 1.61	1.62	0.0009–0.0022	0.0015–0.0031	0.3150	0.3150
	156 (2559)	45	45	56 @ 1.61	1.62	0.0009–0.0022	0.0015–0.0031	0.3150	0.3150
	173 (2828)	46	45	175 @ 1.26	1.72	0.0010–0.0027	0.0010–0.0027	0.3410–0.3420	0.3410–0.3420
1991–92	138 (2254)	45	45	56 @ 1.61	1.62	0.0009–0.0022	0.0015–0.0031	0.3150	0.3150
	156 (2559)	45	45	56 @ 1.61	1.62	0.0009–0.0022	0.0015–0.0031	0.3150	0.3150
	173 (2828)	46	45	175 @ 1.26	1.72	0.0010–0.0027	0.0010–0.0027	0.3410–0.3420	0.3410–0.3420
	191 (3137)	46	46	191 @ 1.18	1.57	0.0010–0.0027	0.0010–0.0027	0.3410–0.3420	0.3410–0.3420

PISTON AND RING SPECIFICATIONS

Year	Engine Displacement cu. in. (cc)	Piston Clearance	Ring Gap Top Compression	Bottom Compression	Oil Control	Ring Side Clearance Top Compression	Bottom Compression	Oil Control
1988	138 (2254)	0.0008–0.0016	0.0120–0.0180	0.0100–0.0160	0.008–0.028	0.0010–0.0024	0.0010–0.0024	—
	156 (2559)	0.0010–0.0018	0.0120–0.0180	0.0240–0.0280	0.008–0.028	0.0010–0.0024	0.0008–0.0022	—
1989	138 (2254)	0.0008–0.0016	0.0120–0.0180	0.0240–0.0280	0.008–0.028	0.0010–0.0024	0.0010–0.0024	—
	156 (2559)	0.0010–0.0018	0.0120–0.0180	0.0240–0.0280	0.008–0.028	0.0010–0.0024	0.0010–0.0024	—
	173 (2828)	0.0007–0.0017	0.0098–0.0196	0.0098–0.0196	0.0020–0.0550	0.0011–0.0027	0.0015–0.0037	0.0078 MAX
1990	138 (2254)	0.0008–0.0016	0.0120–0.0180	0.0240–0.0280	0.008–0.028	0.0010–0.0024	0.0010–0.0024	—
	156 (2559)	0.0010–0.0018	0.0120–0.0180	0.0240–0.0280	0.008–0.028	0.0010–0.0024	0.0010–0.0024	—
	173 (2828)	0.0007–0.0017	0.0098–0.0196	0.0098–0.0196	0.0020–0.0550	0.0011–0.0027	0.0015–0.0037	0.0078 MAX

PISTON AND RING SPECIFICATIONS

Year	Engine Displacement cu. in. (cc)	Piston Clearance	Ring Gap Top Compression	Ring Gap Bottom Compression	Ring Gap Oil Control	Ring Side Clearance Top Compression	Ring Side Clearance Bottom Compression	Ring Side Clearance Oil Control
1991–92	138 (2254)	0.0008–0.0016	0.0120–0.0180	0.0240–0.0280	0.008–0.028	0.0010–0.0024	0.0010–0.0024	—
	156 (2559)	0.0010–0.0018	0.0120–0.0180	0.0240–0.0280	0.008–0.028	0.0010–0.0024	0.0010–0.0024	—
	173 (2828)	0.0007–0.0017	0.0098–0.0196	0.0098–0.0196	0.0020–0.0550	0.0011–0.0027	0.0015–0.0037	0.0078 MAX
	191 (3137)	0.0009–0.0022	0.0100–0.0200	0.0200–0.0280	0.0100–0.0300	0.0020–0.0035	0.0020–0.0035	0.0080 MAX

TORQUE SPECIFICATIONS

Year	Engine Displacement cu. in. (cc)	Cylinder Head Bolts	Main Bearing Bolts	Rod Bearing Bolts	Crankshaft Pulley Bolts	Flywheel Bolts	Manifold Intake	Manifold Exhaust	Spark Plugs
1988	138 (2254)	①	65–80	42–45	79–102	40–47	14–18	14–18	10–17
	156 (2559)	①	65–80	42–45	79–102	40–47	14–18	14–18	10–17
1989	138 (2254)	①	65–80	42–45	79–102	40–47	14–18	14–18	10–17
	156 (2559)	①	65–80	42–45	79–102	40–47	14–18	14–18	10–17
	173 (2828)	②	70	39	70	52	23	25	22
1990	138 (2254)	①	65–80	42–45	76–98	40–47	14–18	14–18	10–17
	156 (2559)	①	65–80	42–45	79–102	40–47	14–18	14–18	10–17
	173 (2828)	②	70	39	70	52	23	25	22
1991–92	138 (2254)	①	65–80	42–45	76–98	40–47	14–18	14–18	10–17
	156 (2559)	①	65–80	42–45	79–102	40–47	14–18	14–18	10–17
	173 (2828)	②	70	39	70	52	23	25	22
	191 (3137)	②	72	39	85	52	19	19	25

① 1st pass—58
  2nd pass—72
② 1st step—41 ft. lbs.
  2nd step: Turn an additional 90 degrees
  (¼ turn)

BRAKE SPECIFICATIONS

Year	Model	Lug Nut Torque (ft. lbs.)	Master Cylinder Bore	Brake Disc Minimum Thickness	Brake Disc Maximum Runout	Standard Brake Drum Diameter	Minimum Lining Thickness Front	Minimum Lining Thickness Rear
1988	Pick-up	①	②	③	0.005	10.0	0.039	0.039
	Trooper II	①	1.000	③	0.005	—	0.039	0.039
1989	Amigo	①	②	③	0.005	10.0	0.039	0.039
	Pick-Up	①	②	③	0.005	10.0	0.039	0.039
	Trooper/Trooper II	①	1.000	③	0.005	—	0.039	0.039
1990	Amigo	①	②	③	0.005	10.0	0.039	0.039
	Pick-Up	①	②	③	0.005	10.0	0.039	0.039
	Trooper/Trooper II	①	1.000	③	0.005	—	0.039	0.039

BRAKE SPECIFICATIONS

Year	Model	Lug Nut Torque (ft. lbs.)	Master Cylinder Bore	Brake Disc		Standard Brake Drum Diameter	Minimum Lining Thickness	
				Minimum Thickness	Maximum Runout		Front	Rear
1991–92	Amigo	①	②	③	0.005	10.0	0.039	0.039
	Pick-Up	①	②	③	0.005	10.0	0.039	0.039
	Rodeo	①	1.000	0.811	0.005	10.0	0.039	0.039
	Trooper/ Trooper II	①	1.000	③	0.005	—	0.039	0.039

① Aluminum wheel: 80–94
  Steel wheel: 58–87
② 0.938 in.—2.3L engine
  1.000 in.—2.6L engine or 3.1L engine
③ Front: 0.811
  Rear: 0.417

WHEEL ALIGNMENT

Year	Model	Caster		Camber		Toe-in (in.)	Steering Axis Inclination (deg.)
		Range (deg.)	Preferred Setting (deg.)	Range (deg.)	Preferred Setting (deg.)		
1988	Pick-Up 2WD	1P–2P	1½P	½N–1½P	½P	0.08	10
	Pick-Up 4WD	1¼P–2¼P	1¾P	½N–1½P	½P	0.08	10
	Trooper II	2P–3P	2½P	0–1P	½P	0.08	10
1989	Amigo 2WD	1¾P–3¼P	2½P	0–1P	½P	0.08	10
	Amigo 4WD	1¾P–3¼P	2½P	0–1P	½P	0.08	10
	Pick-Up 2WD	1P–2P	1½P	½N–1½P	½P	0.08	10
	Pick-Up 4WD	1¼P–2¼P	1¾P	½N–1½P	½P	0.08	10
	Trooper/Trooper II	2P–3P	2½P	0–1P	½P	0.08	10
1990	Amigo	1¾P–3¼P	2½P	½N–1½P	½P	0.08	10
	Pick-Up 2WD①	⅞P–2⅜P	1⅝P	½N–1½P	½P	0.08	10
	Pick-Up 2WD②	1P–2¾P	1⅞P	½N–1½P	½P	0.08	10
	Pick-Up 4WD①	1 3/16P–2 11/16P	1 15/16P	½N–1½P	½P	0.08	10
	Pick-Up 4WD②	1 7/16P–2 15/16P	2 3/16P	½N–1½P	½P	0.08	10
	Trooper/Trooper II	2P–3P	2½P	0–1P	½P	0.08	10
1991–92	Amigo	1¾P–3¼P	2½P	½N–1½P	½P	0.08	10
	Pick-Up 2WD①	⅞P–2⅜P	1⅝P	½N–1½P	½P	0.08	10
	Pick-Up 2WD②	1P–2¾P	1⅞P	½N–1½P	½P	0.08	10
	Pick-Up 4WD①	1 3/16P–2 11/16P	1 15/16P	½N–1½P	½P	0.08	10
	Pick-Up 4WD②	1 7/16P–2 15/16P	2 3/16P	½N–1½P	½P	0.08	10
	Rodeo	1 9/16P–3 1/16P	2⅓P	½N–1½P	½P	0.08	10
	Trooper/Trooper II	2P–3P	2½P	0–1P	½P	0.08	10

N—Negative
P—Positive
① Short wheel base
② Long wheel base

ENGINE ELECTRICAL

NOTE: Disconnecting the negative battery cable on some vehicles may interfere with the functions of the on board computer systems and may require the computer to undergo a relearning process, once the negative battery cable is reconnected.

Distributor

Removal

2.3L AND 2.6L ENGINES

1. Disconnect the battery ground cable and the distributor wiring connector.
2. Turn the engine to TDC of cylinder No. 4. Remove the distributor cap and mark the position of the rotor to the distributor body and the distributor body to the engine block. This allows for easier installation.
3. Remove the distributor hold-down bolt and remove the distributor.

2.8L AND 3.1L ENGINES

1. Disconnect the negative battery cable.
2. Disconnect and label the spark plug wires at the distributor cap.
3. Remove the distributor cap from the distributor. Disconnect and label the distributor wiring.
4. Using a piece of chalk, matchmark the rotor to the distributor housing and the housing to the engine.
5. Remove the distributor hold-down nut, the clamp and lift the distributor from the engine.

NOTE: When removing the distributor, it may be necessary to rotate the distributor shaft slightly to disengage it from the drive gear.

Installation

TIMING NOT DISTURBED

1. Lower the distributor into the engine and align the rotor and distributor housing to the matchmarks.
2. Check and/or adjust the ignition timing when finished.

TIMING DISTURBED

2.8L and 3.1L Engines

1. Remove the No. 1 spark plug.
2. Rotate the crankshaft in the normal direction of rotation until compression is felt at the spark plug hole.
3. Continue rotating the engine in the same direction while observing the timing marks at the indicator line up when No. 1 cylinder is at TDC.
4. Install the distributor and align the rotor with the No. 1 lug on the distributor cap.
5. Check and/or adjust the ignition timing when finished.

2.3L and 2.6L Engines

1. Remove the valve cover. Turn the engine so cylinder No. 4 is on TDC of the compression stroke and the camshaft pulley setting mark is aligned with the setting mark on the front plate.
2. Lubricate the distributor O-ring with engine oil. Align the distributor setting mark with the distributor shaft setting mark.
3. Install the distributor on the cylinder head aligning the mark on the cylinder head with the mark on the distributor shaft.
4. Install the distributor hold-down bolt and valve cover. Install the distributor cap and the distributor wiring. Connect the negative battery terminal and time the engine. Torque the hold-down bolt to 14 ft. lbs. (19 Nm).

Ignition Timing

Adjustment

NOTE: The following procedures are basic outlines for timing the ignition system. As emission controls change and are updated, the timing procedures will change. Check the underhood emissions sticker for updated timing instructions and follow them exactly.

2.3L AND 2.6L ENGINES

NOTE: Set the air gap in the distributor before timing the engine.

The timing marks are located near the front crankshaft pulley and consist of a pointer with graduations attached to the engine block and a mark on the crankshaft pulley.
1. Check and correct the air gap in the distributor.
2. Locate and clean the timing marks on the crankshaft pulley and the front of the engine.
3. Using an inductive pick-up timing light, connect it to the No. 1 spark plug wire. Attach a timing light to the ignition coil.
4. If the distributor is equipped with a vacuum advance, disconnect and plug the vacuum line.
5. Make sure all wires from the timing light and tachometer are clear of the fan and belts. Start the engine.
6. Adjust the idle to the correct rpm.
7. Aim the timing light at the timing marks. Adjust the distributor until the timing marks are aligned.
8. Tighten the distributor mounting bolt and check the timing again.
9. Turn the engine **OFF** and remove the timing light and tachometer. Connect the distributor vacuum line.

2.8L AND 3.1L ENGINES

1. Set the parking brake and block the drive wheels.
2. Operate the engine to normal operating temperatures and turn the air conditioning **OFF**, if equipped.
3. Verify that the Check Engine light is not turned **ON**.
4. Place the Electronic Spark Timing (EST) into the bypass mode by disconnect the timing connector.

NOTE: The EST is a single wire connector, located under the center console in the passenger compartment. Do not disconnect the 4-wire connector from the distributor.

5. Using an inductive pick-up timing light, connect it to the No. 1 spark plug wire.
6. Check and/or adjust the engine speed to 800 rpm.
7. Loosen the distributor hold-down bolt and turn the distributor until the timing mark, on the crankshaft pulley, is aligned with the 10 degree BTDC timing mark on the timing cover.

TIMING MARK   CRANKSHAFT PULLEY

View of the ignition timing marks

Adjusting the air gap—2.3L engine

8. Tighten the distributor hold-down bolt.
9. Reconnect the timing connector and clear the ECM trouble code(s).

Air Gap Setting

The air gap setting in the distributor should be checked and adjusted before the ignition timing is adjusted.

Adjustment

1. Remove the distributor cap, O-ring and rotor.
2. Use a feeler gauge to measure the air gap at the pick-up coil projection. The gap should be 0.008–0.016 in. for 3.1L engine or 0.012–0.020 in. for 2.3L and 2.6L engines; adjust it, if necessary.
3. Loosen the screws and move the signal generator until the gap is correct. Tighten the screws and recheck the gap.

NOTE: The electrical parts in this system are not repairable. If found to be defective, they must be replaced.

Alternator

For further information, please refer to "Alternators" in the Unit Repair section.

Belt Tension Adjustment

2.3L AND 2.6L ENGINES

1. Loosen the alternator pivot bolt.
2. Rotate the alternator to produce a belt deflection of 0.40 in. (10mm).
3. Tighten the alternator pivot bolt.

2.8L AND 3.1L ENGINES

The 2.8L and 3.1L engines uses a single serpentine belt to drive all engine accessories. The belt tension is maintained by a spring loaded tensioner. The belt tensioner has the ability to control the belt tension over a broad range of belt lengths as the belt ages and stretches.

Removal and Installation

2.3L AND 2.6L ENGINES

1. Disconnect the negative battery cable. If equipped with an air pump, it may be necessary to remove it.
2. Disconnect and label the alternator wiring.
3. Remove the alternator pivot bolt on the lower part of the alternator. Remove the drive belt from the pulley.
4. Remove the alternator mounting bolt(s) and the alternator from the engine.
To install:
5. Install the alternator.
6. Adjust the belt tension and tighten the alternator mounting bolts.
7. Reconnect the alternator's wiring connectors. Connect the negative battery cable.

2.8L AND 3.1L ENGINES

1. Disconnect the negative battery cable.
2. Remove the terminal plug and the battery lead from the rear of the alternator.
3. Remove the drive belt.
4. Remove the bracket bolt from the rear of the alternator.
5. Remove the mounting bolts from the front of the alternator and the alternator from the vehicle.
To install:
6. Install the alternator and the mounting bolts.
7. Install the drive belt.
8. Torque the lower mounting bolt to 26 ft. lbs. (35 Nm), the upper mounting bolt to 18 ft. lbs. (25 Nm) and the air pump bracket bolt to 18 ft. lbs. (25 Nm).
9. Connect the terminal connector and the battery lead to the rear of the alternator. Reconnect the negative battery cable.

Starter

For further information, please refer to "Starters" in the Unit Repair section.

Removal and Installation

1. Disconnect the negative battery cable. Remove the skid plate if necessary.
2. On 4 cylinder engines, it may be necessary to disconnect and remove the EGR pipe.
3. Disconnect and label the starter wiring at the starter.
4. Remove the starter-to-engine bolts and the shims. Remove the starter from the vehicle.
To install:
5. Install the starter and shims to the engine and replace the bolts. Torque the bolts to 30 ft. lbs. (40 Nm).
6. Connect the electrical leads to the starter.
7. If the EGR pipe was removed, install it. Replace the skid plate, if removed.
8. Connect the negative battery cable.

CHASSIS ELECTRICAL

Heater Blower Motor

The heater blower motor is located under the right side of the dash.

Removal and Installation

1. Disconnect the negative battery cable.

2. Disconnect and label the blower motor electrical leads.
3. Remove the blower-to-heater unit screws and lower the blower motor assembly.
To install:
4. Install the heater blower motor, into the heater unit and install the screws.
5. Connect the electrical connectors to the heater blower motor.
6. Connect the negative battery cable.

Windshield Wiper Motor

Removal and Installation

FRONT

1. Disconnect the negative battery cable.
2. Disconnect the electrical connector from the wiper motor.
3. Remove the wiper motor bracket-to-chassis bolts.
4. Disconnect the wiper motor from the wiper linkage at the ball joint.

To install:

5. Connect the wiper motor to the wiper linkage at the ball joint.
6. Install the wiper motor-to-chassis bolts.
7. Connect the electrical connector to the wiper motor.
8. Connect the negative battery cable.

REAR

1. Disconnect the negative battery cable.
2. Remove the back door panel to expose the wiper motor and disconnect the motor wiring.
3. Remove the cover from the wiper arm retaining nut and remove the nut. Pull off the arm and remove the motor shaft mounting hardware.
4. Remove the motor from the door cavity.
5. Installation is reverse of removal.

1. Solenoid valve
2. Diaphragm assembly
3. Door spring and lever
4. Blower motor assembly
5. Thermo sensor assembly
6. Seal
7. Attaching parts
8. Left side case
9. Right side case
10. Blower motor housing
11. Blower motor fan

Exploded view of the heater blower motor

1. Wiper arm assembly
2. Link pivot nut
3. Center cover
4. Left cover
5. Wiring connector
6. Wiper motor assembly with link assembly
7. Link joint
8. Tank assembly

Exploded view of the wiper motor and linkage assembly

Windshield Wiper Switch

Removal and Installation

EXCEPT PICK-UP AND AMIGO

The windshield wiper switch is a part of the combination switch located on the steering column.

PICK-UP AND AMIGO

The windshield wiper switch is a part of the switch cluster located on the left side of the instrument cluster.

1. Disconnect the negative battery cable.
2. Remove the instrument cluster-to-dash screws.
3. Pull the instrument cluster forward and disconnect the electrical connector from the switch cluster.
4. From the rear of the instrument cluster, loosen the switch cluster-to-instrument cluster bolts.
5. Separate the windshield wiper switch from the switch cluster.

To install:

6. Install the windshield wiper switch to the switch cluster.
7. Tighten the switch cluster-to-instrument cluster bolts.
8. Connect the electrical connector to the switch cluster.
9. Install the instrument cluster.
10. Connect the negative battery cable.

Instrument Cluster

Removal and Installation

TROOPER/TROOPER II

1. Disconnect the negative battery cable.
2. Remove the steering wheel.
3. Remove the knob from the light switch.
4. Remove the cover-to-instrument panel screws and the cover.
5. Remove the instrument panel-to-dash screws and pull the panel forward.
6. Disconnect the electrical connectors and the speedometer cable from the rear of the instrument panel.
7. Remove the instrument panel from the vehicle.

To install:

8. Connect the speedometer cable and the electrical connectors to the rear of the instrument cluster.
9. Install the instrument cluster to the dash.
10. Install the cover to the instrument cluster.
11. Install the knob to the light switch.
12. Install the steering wheel.
13. Connect the negative battery cable.

PICK-UP, AMIGO AND RODEO

Tilt Steering Wheel

1. Disconnect the negative battery cable.
2. Move the steering wheel to the fully down position.
3. Remove the instrument cluster-to-dash screws and pull the instrument cluster forward.
4. Disconnect the electrical connectors and the speedometer cable from the instrument cluster.

To install:

5. Connect the speedometer cable and electrical connectors to the instrument cluster.
6. Install the instrument cluster to the dash.
7. Connect the negative battery cable.

Except Tilt Steering Wheel

1. Disconnect the negative battery cable.
2. Remove the steering wheel and the steering wheel cowl.
3. Remove the instrument cluster-to-dash screws and pull the instrument cluster forward.

Removing the instrument cluster—Trooper/Trooper II shown—Pick-Up similar

4. Disconnect the electrical connectors and the speedometer cable from the instrument cluster.

To install:

5. Connect the speedometer cable and electrical connectors to the instrument cluster.
6. Install the instrument cluster to the dash.
7. Install the steering column cowl and the steering wheel.
8. Connect the negative battery cable.

Auxiliary Gauge Panel

Removal and Installation

TROOPER/TROOPER II

1. Disconnect the negative battery cable.
2. Remove the 2 screws holding the auxiliary gauge panel face plate and remove the face plate.
3. Remove the screws holding the gauges and pull the gauges forward.
4. Disconnect the wiring to the gauges and remove the gauge.
5. Installation is the reverse of removal.

Speedometer

Removal and Installation

EXCEPT TROOPER/TROOPER II

1. Disconnect the negative battery terminal.
2. Remove the instrument cluster. Remove the instrument cluster glass.
3. Pull the indicator needles off the shafts of the speedometer and tachometer.
4. Remove the speedometer fastening screws and remove the speedometer.
5. Installation is the reverse of removal. Be sure to align the instrument indicator needles when pressing them onto their shafts.

TROOPER/TROOPER II

1. Disconnect the negative battery cable.
2. Remove the instrument cluster.
3. Remove the speedometer holding screws from the instrument cluster and remove the speedometer.

Exploded view of the speedometer—Trooper/Trooper II

To install:
4. Install the speedometer to the instrument cluster.
5. Install the instrument cluster.
6. Connect the negative battery cable.

Radio

Removal and Installation

TROOPER/TROOPER II

1. Disconnect the negative battery cable.
2. Remove the knobs, the nuts and washers.
3. Remove the face plate from the radio.
4. Remove the radio shroud screws and the shroud.
5. Disconnect the harness connector and the feeder cable.
6. Remove the radio-to-bracket screws and the radio.

To install:
7. Install the radio and the radio-to-bracket screws.
8. Connect the feeder cable and the harness connector.
9. Install the radio shroud and screws.
10. Install the radio faceplate.
11. Install the washers, nuts and knobs.
12. Connect the negative battery cable.

PICK-UP, RODEO AND AMIGO

1. Disconnect the negative battery cable.
2. Remove the radio console-to-dash screws and the console.
3. Disconnect the harness connector and the feeder cable, if equipped.
4. Remove the radio bracket-to-radio screws.
5. Remove the radio.

To install:
6. Install the radio and the radio bracket-to-radio screws.
7. Connect the harness connector and the feeder cable, if equipped.
8. Install the console and the radio console-to-dash screws.
9. Connect the negative battery cable.

Headlight Switch

Removal and Installation

TROOPER/TROOPER II

The headlight switch is located on the lower left side of the dash.
1. Disconnect the negative battery cable.
2. Remove the headlight switch knob.
3. Disconnect and label the headlight switch wiring under the dashboard.

4. Remove the headlight switch locknut and the switch from the dash.

To install:
5. Install the switch to the dash and secure with the locknut.
6. Connect the electrical connector to the headlight switch.
7. Install the headlight switch knob.
8. Connect the negative battery cable.

PICK-UP, RODEO AND AMIGO

The push button headlight switch, is a part of the switch cluster located on the left side of the dash.
1. Disconnect the negative battery cable.
2. Remove the instrument cluster-to-dash screws.
3. Pull the instrument cluster forward and disconnect the electrical connector from the switch cluster.
4. From the rear of the instrument cluster, loosen the switch cluster-to-instrument cluster bolts.
5. Separate the headlight switch from the switch cluster.

To install:
6. Install the headlight switch to the switch cluster.
7. Tighten the switch cluster-to-instrument cluster bolts.
8. Connect the electrical connector to the switch cluster.
9. Install the instrument cluster.
10. Connect the negative battery cable.

Combination Switch

Removal and Installation

1. Disconnect the negative battery cable.
2. From the rear of the steering wheel, remove the horn pad screw and lift the horn pad upward to remove it.
3. Disconnect the electrical connector from the horn pad.
4. Remove the steering wheel-to-steering column nut.
5. Matchmark the steering wheel to the steering shaft for reinstallation purposes.

NOTE: Never apply a blow to the steering wheel shaft with a hammer or other impact tool, to remove the steering wheel, for the steering shaft may become damaged.

6. Using a steering wheel puller, press the steering wheel from the steering column.
7. Remove the contact ring.
8. Remove the steering column covers.
9. Disconnect the electrical connector from the combination switch.
10. Remove the combination switch-to-steering column screws and the switch.

To install:
11. Install the combination switch to the steering column and secure it with screws.
12. Connect the combination switch electrical connector.
13. Install the steering column covers.
14. Install the contact ring.
15. Align the steering wheel-to-steering column matchmarks and torque the nut to 22–29 ft. lbs. (30–40 Nm).
16. Connect the electrical connector to the horn pad.
17. Install the horn pad and the horn pad screw.
18. Connect the negative battery cable.

Ignition Lock/Switch

Removal and Installation

1. Disconnect the negative battery cable.
2. From the rear of the steering wheel, remove the horn pad screw and lift the horn pad upward to remove it.
3. Remove the steering wheel-to-steering column nut.
4. Matchmark the steering wheel to the steering shaft for ease of installation purposes.

1. Horn shroud
2. Nut
3. Steering wheel
4. Steering cowl
5. Combination switch
6. Snapring
7. Bushing
8. Steering lock and bearing
9. Steering assembly

Exploded view of the steering column—Amigo and Pick-Up 1988–90—others are similar

NOTE: Never apply a blow to the steering wheel shaft with a hammer or other impact tool, to remove the steering wheel, for the steering shaft may become damaged.

5. Using the proper steering wheel puller, remove the steering wheel from the steering column.
6. Remove the horn contact ring.
7. Remove the steering column covers.
8. Disconnect the electrical connector from the combination switch.
9. Remove the combination switch-to-steering column screws and the switch.
10. On the Rodeo, Amigo and Pick-Up, remove the ignition lock/switch-to-steering column snapring and bushing.
11. Disconnect the electrical connector from the ignition lock/switch assembly.
12. On the Rodeo, Amigo and Pick-Up, remove the ignition lock/switch-to-steering column bolts and the lock/switch assembly. On the Trooper/Trooper II, remove the lock/switch pinch bolts and remove the lock/switch unit.

To install:

13. Install the ignition lock/switch-to-steering column bolts, the bushing and the snapring on the Rodeo, Amigo and Pick-Up. Install the lock/switch pinch bolts on the Trooper/Trooper II.
14. Install the combination switch to the steering column and tighten the screws.
15. Connect the combination switch electrical connector.
16. Install the steering column covers.
17. Install the contact ring.
18. Align the steering wheel-to-steering column matchmarks and torque the nut to 22–29 ft. lbs. (30–40 Nm) on the Trooper/Trooper II or 26 ft. lbs. (35 Nm) on the Rodeo, Pick-Up and Amigo.
19. Install the horn pad and the horn pad screw.
20. Connect the negative battery cable.

Stoplight Switch

Adjustment

1. Loosen the locknut on the stoplight switch.
2. Rotate the body off the switch to adjust the gap between the switch plunger and the brake pedal.
3. The gap should be 0.020–0.040 in. (0.5–1.0mm).
4. Once the gap has been set, hold the body of the stoplight switch to prevent it from rotating and tighten the locknut.

Removal and Installation

1. Disconnect the negative battery cable.
2. Locate the stoplight switch on the brake pedal support.
3. Disconnect the electrical connector from the stoplight switch.
4. Remove the locknut and the stoplight switch.

To install:

5. Install the switch on the support and adjust the switch so there is 0.020–0.040 in. (0.5–1.0mm) clearance between the switch and the brake pedal.
6. Hold the body of the stoplight switch to prevent it from turning and tighten the locknut.
7. Connect the wiring to the switch and the negative battery cable.
8. Check the operation of the switch.

Ignition Enable Clutch Switch

Adjustment

No adjustment is possible on the ignition enable clutch switch

Removal and Installation

1. Disconnect the negative battery cable. Remove the electrical leads at the clutch switch.
2. Remove the fastening screws on the switch body and remove the switch from the linkage.
3. Install the switch and tighten the mounting screws.
4. Connect the negative battery cable and check the operation of the switch.

Neutral Safety Switch

Adjustment

1. Adjustment of the neutral safety switch should be done when the engine will start in any transmission range other than **N** or **P**.
2. Loosen the hold-down bolt for the neutral safety switch on the transmission housing. Set the shifter to the **N** range.
3. Turn the switch so the groove and the neutral basic line are aligned.
4. Tighten the hold-down bolt 9 ft. lbs. (13 Nm).

View of the neutral start switch

5. While holding the brake pedal and with the wheels chocked, check that the engine will not start in any other range than **N** or **P**.

Removal and Installation

1. Disconnect the negative battery cable.
2. Disconnect the electrical connector to the neutral safety switch.
3. Disconnect the linkage and remove the hold-down bolt.
4. Remove the switch from the transmission body.
5. Installation is in reverse order. Adjust the switch for proper operation.

Fuses and Circuit Breakers

Location

The main fuse box is located at the lower left side of the instrument panel on vehicles other than the Trooper/Trooper II. On the Trooper/Trooper II, the fuse box is located on the left side valance panel inside the engine compartment.

On the Amigo, Rodeo and the Pick-Up the fuse/relay box is located at the right side of the engine compartment incorporating the fuseable links within it.

Fusible links are in a box located beside the battery on the Trooper/Trooper II.

Computers

Locations

AMIGO, PICK-UP AND RODEO

The ECM is located below the left side of the dash at the kick panel.

The rear wheel anti-lock controller is located under the right, front seat on Pick-Up and Rodeo. On Amigo, it is located behind the right side of the dash above the kick panel.

TROOPER/TROOPER II

The ECM is located on the center of the floor below the console.

The electronic spark control module is located on the right side of the engine compartment on the inner fender panel.

The electronic transmission controller is located behind the left side of the instrument panel, near the kick panel.

Flashers

Locations

The flasher unit of the Amigo, Rodeo and Pick-Up is located behind the left side of the dash above the kick panel.

The hazard relay on the Trooper/Trooper II is located below the left side of the instrument panel on the brake pedal support.

Cruise Control

For further information, please refer to Chilton's Chassis Electronics Service Manual.

Adjustment

ACTUATOR CABLE

1. The engine should be at normal idle speed when performing this adjustment.
2. Loosen the 2 nuts at the actuator end of the cruise control actuator cable.
3. Pull the outer cable towards the accelerator pedal and make sure there is no play in the inner cable.
4. Turn the nut on the accelerator side of the actuator so it contacts the bracket and tighten the nut on the other side of the bracket to lock the cable adjustment.

BRAKE AND CLUTCH SWITCHES

1. Loosen the locknut on the appropriate switch.
2. Rotate the body of the switch so the plunger is fully compressed and the body of the switch makes contact with the pedal arm.

3. On the brake switch back off the switch ½ turn. Back off the clutch switch 1 full turn for the Rodeo or ½ turn except for the Rodeo.
4. Tighten the locknut and check the operation of the switch.

ENGINE COOLING

Radiator

Removal and Installation

1. Disconnect the negative battery cable.
2. Drain the cooling system.
3. Remove the upper, lower and reservoir hoses from the radiator. Remove the air intake duct assembly, if necessary for Rodeo.
4. Remove the fan shroud-to-radiator bolts and the shroud. If equipped with a 2 piece shroud, unclip and remove the lower shroud section first, then unbolt and remove the main upper section.
5. Remove the automatic transmission cooling lines, if equipped.
6. Remove the radiator-to-chassis bolts and the radiator.

To install:

7. Install the radiator and the radiator-to-chassis bolts.
8. Install the automatic transmission cooling lines, if equipped.
9. Install the fan shroud and the shroud-to-radiator bolts.
10. Reconnect the radiator hoses. Replace the air intake duct.

11. Refill the cooling system.
12. Connect the negative battery cable.

Heater Core

For further information, please refer to Chilton's Air Conditioning and Heating Manual.

Removal and Installation

RODEO, AMIGO AND PICK-UP

1. Disconnect the negative battery cable. Drain the coolant into a clean container for reuse or dispose of the coolant in a safe and enviromentally sound way. If equipped with air conditioning, discharge the system using an appropriate refrigerant recycling unit.
2. Disconnect the heater hoses at the inlet of the heater unit. Plug the hoses and inlets to prevent excess coolant from dripping into the passenger compartment.
3. Remove the instrument panel:
   a. Remove the steering wheel and its cowling.

1. Heater hoses
2. Instrument panel assembly
3. Resistor connector
4. Duct (without air conditioning)
4a. Evaporator assembly (with air conditioning)
5. Instrument panel brace
6. Heater assembly

Heater unit parts removal order—Amigo, Rodeo and Pick-Up

A/T model only

1. Steering wheel and cowl assembly
2. Grill and bezel
2a. Driving pattern indicator panel (with air conditioning)
3. Gauge hood
4. Gauge cluster assembly
5. Gauge panel
6. Hood release handle
7. Steering lower cover
8. Fuse box
9. Side trim
10. ECM box
11. Front console
12. Lower reinforcement
13. Speaker grill
14. Glove box
15. Knob
16. Bezel
17. Control lever assembly
18. Illumination controller
19. Instrument panel

Instrument panel parts removal order—Amigo, Rodeo and Pick-Up

b. Remove the vent by inserting an appropriate prybar and carefully prying on the unit.

c. Remove the instrument panel nuts under the vents.

d. If equipped with an automatic transmission, remove the driving pattern indicator panel.

e. Remove the screws holding the gauge hood and remove.

f. Pull out the gauge cluster and remove the clips from the gauge hood.

g. Disconnect the wiring connector blocks from the back of the cluster and remove the speedometer connection. Remove the gauge cluster.

h. Remove the hood release handle by removing the screws on the underside of the handle.

i. Remove the steering column lower cover, the use box, the side trim, ECM box, the front console and the lower reinforcement.

j. Remove the screws holding the speaker grill and remove the speaker.

k. Remove the glove box hinge pins. Remove the heater control knobs and remove the bezel.

l. Remove the control lever assembly after disconnecting the control cables from the heater and blower units.

m. Remove the illumination controller from the instrument panel.

n. Remove the instrument panel nuts and bolts. Disconnect the instrument harness at the ECM location.

o. Remove the instrument panel from the vehicle. Take appropriate measures to prevent damage to the panel.

4. Disconnect the resistor connection.

5. Remove the duct or air conditioning evaporator unit as equipped. If removing the evaporator assembly, cap the refrigerant lines to prevent moisture and foriegn objects from contaminating the system.

6. Remove the instrument panel reinforcement.

7. Remove the heater unit after unclipping the harness and removing the nuts.

1. Refrigerant lines connection
2. Vacuum hose
3. Evaporator relay connection
4. Evaporator nuts
5. Evaporator unit assembly
5a. Duct—without air conditioner
6. Heater hose
7. Heater hose
8. Duct
9. Heater unit relay connectors
10. Heater unit nuts
11. Heater unit assembly
12. Blower unit connectors and vacuum hose
13. Blower unit nuts
14. Blower unit assembly

Heater unit parts removal order—Trooper/Trooper II

8. Remove the case section with the control levers.
9. Split the heater core case and remove the heater core.

To install:

10. Install the heater core in the heater core case and reassemble the heater unit.
11. Install the heater unit in the vehicle and replace the harness holding clip.
12. Install the instrument panel reinforcement and the duct or air conditioning evaporator unit as equipped. Connect the resistor wiring connection.
13. Install the instrument panel. Installation is the reverse of removal.
14. Connect the heater hoses and refill the cooling system. Recharge the air conditioning system, if equipped.
15. Connect the negative battery terminal.

TROOPER/TROOPER II

1. Disconnect the negative battery cable. Drain the coolant into a clean container for reuse or dispose of the coolant in a safe and enviromentally sound way. If equipped with air conditioning, discharge the system using an appropriate refrigerant recycling unit.
2. Disconnect the heater hoses at the inlet of the heater unit. Plug the hoses and inlets to prevent excess coolant from dripping into the passenger compartment.
3. Remove the instrument panel:
   a. Remove the gauge cluster.
   b. Remove the screws on the underside of the gauge hood and remove the gauge assembly.
   c. Remove the glove compartment and radio.
   d. Remove the side vents by turning the vents and prying out.
   e. Remove the 10 bolts holding the instrument panel. The

bolt heads are covered by a clip–on cover. Pry the covers off to expose the bolt heads.
   f. Remove the instrument panel taking care not to damage it or the interior of the vehicle.
4. Disconnect the refrigerant lines to the evaporator unit, if equipped.
5. Remove the vacuum line and the evaporator relay connection.
6. Remove the evaporator unit nuts and remove the evaporator unit, if equipped. If not air conditioner equipped, remove the duct.
7. Disconnect the air ducts from the unit.
8. Disconnect the heater unit relay connector.
9. Remove the heater unit nuts and remove the heater unit from the vehicle.
10. Remove the defroster door spring, rod and lever.
11. Remove the battery relay and air conditioning resistor.
12. Remove the plate and seal and the water valve rod.
13. Remove the core assembly.

To install:

14. Install the core assembly in the heater unit.
15. Reassemble the heater unit and install the unit in the vehicle.
16. Connect the electrical connector to the unit and install the ducts.
17. Install the evaporator unit and connect the refrigerant lines, vacuum and electric connections.
18. Install the instrument panel in reverse order of removal.
19. Connect the heater hoses and refill the cooling system. Recharge the air conditioning system, if equipped.
20. Connect the negative battery terminal.

1. Gauge panel
2. Gauge hood
3. Gauge assembly
4. Glove compartment
5. Radio
6. Vents
7. Bolts(10)
8. Instrument panel

Instrument panel parts removal order—Trooper/ Trooper II

Water Pump

Removal and Installation

2.3L AND 2.6L ENGINES

1. Disconnect the negative battery terminal. Drain the coolant from the system. Collect the coolant in a clean pan for reuse or dispose of the old coolant in an enviromentally safe and legally compliant way.

2. Disconnect the radiator hoses and remove the air duct assembly.

3. Unclip the lower fan shroud from the upper portion of the fan shroud and remove.

4. Remove the 4 bolts holding the upper fan shroud and remove the shroud from the engine compartment

5. Remove the 4 nuts holding the fan, fan clutch and pulley. Remove the assembly.

6. Remove the power steering drive belt, if equipped. Loosen the bolts at the pump bracket to remove tension from the belt.

7. Loosen the air pump adjustment and remove the drive belt. Loosen the idler for the air conditioning compressor drive belt and remove the belt.

8. Remove the 2 idler pulley bolts and remove the idler.

9. Loosen and remove the alternator drive belt.

*10. Remove the 4 bolts holding the water pump pulley to the water pump hub. Remove the pulley.

11. Remove the 2 bolts holding the starter. Disconnect the starter electrical leads. Remove the starter.

12. Hold the crankshaft stationary with a flywheel lock or equivalent, and loosen the crank pulley bolt. Remove the crank pulley.

13. Remove the the upper and lower timing covers.

14. Remove the 4 bolts and 1 nut holding the water pump and remove the water pump.

To install:

15. Installation is the reverse of removal. Torque the water pump bolts to 14 ft. lbs. (19 Nm). Torque the water pump nut to 20 ft. lbs. (25 Nm).

16. Torque the lower and upper timing cover bolts to 4 ft. lbs. (6 Nm). Torque the crank pulley to 90 ft. lbs. (122 Nm).

17. Torque the power steering pump bracket bolts to 32 ft. lbs. (43 Nm). Torque the fan and fan clutch nuts to 20 ft. lbs. (25 Nm).

18. Refill the cooling system and run the engine. Check for leaks.

2.8L AND 3.1L ENGINES

1. Disconnect the negative battery terminal. Drain the coolant from the system. Collect the coolant in a clean pan for reuse or dispose of the old coolant in an enviromentally safe and legally compliant way.

2. Remove the serpentine drive belt.

1. Radiator hose
2. Air duct assembly
3. Lower fan shroud
4. Upper fan shroud
5. Fan and fan clutch
6. Power steering pump drive belt
7. Air pump drive belt
8. Air conditioner compressor idler pulley
9. Air conditioner compressor drive belt
10. Alternator drive belt
11. Water pump pulley
12. Starter motor
13. Crank pulley
14. Timing belt upper cover
15. Timing belt lower cover
16. Water pump

Water pump removal—2.3L and 2.6L engines

1. Serpentine drive belt
2. Radiator upper hose
3. Air conditioner line bracket
4. Lower fan shroud
5. Upper fan shroud
6. Fan and fan clutch assembly
7. Water pump pulley
8. Air conditioner compressor and bracket
9. Power steering pump with bracket
10. Water pump bolts
11. Water pump

Water pump removal—2.8L and 3.1L engines

3. Remove the upper radiator hose. Remove the air conditioner line bracket from the radiator bracket.

4. Unclip the lower fan shroud from the upper portion of the fan shroud and remove.

5. Remove the 4 bolts holding the upper fan shroud and remove the shroud from the engine compartment

6. Remove the 4 nuts holding the fan, fan clutch and pulley. Remove the assembly.

7. Remove the water pump pulley and the air conditioner compressor along with its bracket.

8. Remove the power steering pump and its bracket.

9. Remove the water pump bolts and remove the water pump.

To install:

10. Installation is the reverse of removal.

11. Coat the water pump bolts with sealant and torque the water pump bolts to 22 ft. lbs. (30 Nm).

12. Torque the power steering pump bolts to 37 ft. lbs. (50 Nm).

13. Torque the air conditioning compressor bolts to 78 ft. lbs. (58 Nm).

14. Torque the fan and fan clutch bolts to 17 ft. lbs. (23 Nm).

15. Refill the cooling system and check the system for leaks.

Thermostat

Removal and Installation

The thermostat is located, under the thermostat housing, on top of the intake manifold at the front of the engine.

1. Disconnect the negative battery cable.

2. Drain the cooling system. Disconnect the upper radiator hose from the thermostat housing.

3. Remove the air cleaner assembly.

4. Remove the thermostat housing from the intake manifold.

5. Remove the gasket and the thermostat.

To install:

6. Install the thermostat, with the spring facing the engine.

7. Using a new gasket, install the thermostat housing.

8. Connect the radiator hose to the thermostat housing and refill the cooling system.

9. Install the air cleaner.

10. Connect the negative battery cable.

11. Operate the engine until normal operating temperatures are reached and check the thermostat operation.

Cooling System Bleeding

2.6L ENGINE

1. Check that the jiggle valve is located at the top of the thermostat.

2. Remove the thermal valve from the thermostat housing. Remove the radiator cap.

3. Set the heater on the highest setting. Fill the cooling system until coolant begins to flow from the thermal valve opening.

4. Apply Loctite® 262 or equivalent, to the thermal valve threads. Install the valve on the housing until the it stops. Using a wrench on the metal portion of the valve, tighten 1 full turn.

5. Continue to turn the thermal valve until the ports on the valve are parallel with the centerline of the thermostat housing mounting bolts.

6. Run the engine until it reaches operating temperature. When bubbles stop forming at the neck of the radiator, install the radiator cap.

7. Shut off engine and check the level of coolant in the reservoir tank.

FUEL SYSTEM

Fuel System Service Precautions

Disconnect the negative battery cable. Keep a Class B dry chemical fire extinguisher available. Always relieve the fuel pressure before disconnecting a fuel line. Wrap a shop cloth around the fuel line when disconnecting a fuel line. Always use new O-rings. Do not replace the fuel pipes with fuel hoses. Always use a backup wrench when opening or closing a fuel line.

Relieving Fuel System Pressure

CARBURETED ENGINE

1. Release the fuel vapor pressure in the fuel tank by removing the fuel tank cap and reinstalling it.

2. Cover the fuel line with an absorbent shop cloth and loosen the connection slowly to release the fuel pressure gradually.

FUEL INJECTED ENGINES

1. Allow the engine to cool. Then, remove the fuel pump fuse from the fuse block.

2. Crank the engine, it will start and run until the fuel supply remaining in the fuel lines is exhausted. When the engine stops, engage the starter again for 3.0 seconds to assure dissipation of any remaining pressure.

3. With the ignition **OFF**, replace the fuel pump fuse.

Fuel Filter

On the Rodeo, Amigo and Pick-Up, the fuel filer is located directly in front of the fuel tank. On the Trooper/Trooper II, the fuel filter is located along the inner side of the right frame rail, near the rear of the vehicle.

Removal and Installation

1. Properly relieve the fuel system pressure.

2. Raise and safely support the vehicle.

3. Remove the fuel hose clamps and the fuel hoses from each side of the filter.

4. Cap the open fuel lines to prevent spillage and the entry of contaminants into the fuel system.

5. Remove the mounting bolt and the filter.

To install:

6. Using a new filter, install it to the vehicle; be sure its directional arrow matches the fuel flow.

7. Install the fuel hoses and fuel hose clamps to the filter.

8. Start the engine and check for leaks at the filter.

Mechanical Fuel Pump

Removal and Installation

2.3L ENGINE

The fuel pump is located at the right side of the engine, directly under the intake manifold.

1. Relieve the fuel pressure.

2. Disconnect the negative battery cable.

3. Remove the air cleaner assembly.

4. Remove the intake manifold assembly.

5. Disconnect and plug the fuel lines at the fuel pump.

6. Remove the fuel pump-to-engine bolts and the pump assembly.

To install:

7. Remove the cylinder head cover.

8. Rotate the engine to position the No. 4 cylinder at TDC.

9. Lift the fuel pump pushrod toward the camshaft and hold it in the raised position.

10. Using a new gasket, install the fuel pump on the engine; torque the bolts to 15–25 ft. lbs. (20–4 Nm).

11. Connect the fuel hoses to the fuel pump.

12. Using a new gasket, install the intake manifold.

13. Install the air cleaner assembly.

14. Connect the negative battery cable.

15. Start the engine and check for fuel leaks.

Electric Fuel Pump

Pressure Testing

2.6L, 2.8L AND 3.1L ENGINES

1. Relieve the fuel pressure.

2. Disconnect the fuel line near the engine and install fuel pressure gauge T-connector in the line.

3. Connect the fuel pressure gauge to the T-connector.

4. Start the engine and check the fuel pressure; it should be 43 psi for 2.6L and 3.1L engines or 9–13 psi for 2.8L engine.

5. After checking, turn the engine **OFF**.

6. Relieve the fuel pressure.

7. Remove the pressure gauge from the fuel line and reconnect the fuel line.

8. Start the engine and check for leaks.

Removal and Installation

The electric fuel pump is located in the fuel tank.

2.6L, 2.8L AND 3.1L ENGINES

1. Relieve the fuel pressure.

2. Disconnect the negative battery cable.

3. Raise and safely support the vehicle.

4. Drain the fuel from the fuel tank.

5. Disconnect the electrical connectors and the fuel lines from the fuel tank.

6. Remove the fuel tank-to-vehicle supports and lower the tank from the vehicle.

7. Remove the fuel sending unit cover-to-fuel tank screws and lift the assembly from the tank.

8. Remove the fuel pump from the fuel sending unit.

To install:

9. Install the fuel pump to the fuel sending unit.

10. Using a new gasket, install the fuel sending unit to the fuel tank and tighten the screws.

11. Raise the fuel tank into the vehicle and install the tank-to-chassis connectors.

12. Connect the electrical connectors and the fuel lines to the fuel sending unit.

13. Lower the vehicle.

14. Refill the fuel tank.

15. Connect the negative battery cable.

16. Start the engine and check for fuel leaks.

Carburetor

Removal and Installation

1. Disconnect the negative battery cable.

2. Remove the air cleaner wing nut and disconnect the rubber hoses from the clips on the air cleaner cover.

3. Remove the bracket bolts, if equipped, at the air cleaner and remove the air cleaner cover and filter element.

4. Disconnect the hot air hose (to the hot air duct), the air hose to the air pump at the air cleaner and the vacuum hose at the joint nipple side of the intake manifold.

5. Loosen the bolt clamping the air cleaner to the carburetor. Separate the air cleaner body from the carburetor but do not remove it completely.

6. Disconnect the PCV hose (to the camshaft cover), the rubber hoses to the check and relief valve. Remove the air cleaner body.

7. Disconnect the vacuum hoses from the EGR valve.

8. Disconnect the choke control wire.

9. Disconnect the lead from the throttle solenoid.

10. Disconnect the throttle linkage return spring.

11. Disconnect the accelerator linkage.

12. Disconnect the fuel line at the carburetor.

13. Remove the carburetor-to-manifold nuts and the carburetor.

To install:

14. Using a new gasket, install the carburetor to the intake manifold.

15. Connect the fuel line and the accelerator linkage to the carburetor.

16. Connect the throttle linkage return spring, the throttle solenoid lead, the choke control wire and the vacuum hoses to the EGR and the PCV.

17. Install the air cleaner and any necessary hoses.

18. Start the engine and check for fuel leaks.

Idle Speed Adjustment

1. Firmly set the parking brake and block the drive wheels.

2. Place the transmission in **N**.

3. Operate the engine until it reaches normal operating temperatures. Be sure the choke is fully open and the air cleaner is installed. If equipped, turn the air conditioning **OFF**.

4. Disconnect and plug the distributor vacuum, the canister purge and EGR vacuum lines. Shut off the vacuum to the idle compensator by bending the rubber hose.

5. Turn the throttle adjusting screw to the required idle speed.

6. If equipped with air conditioning, turn air conditioning control to **MAX COLD** and the blower on **HIGH**.

7. Open throttle to approximately 1/3 opening and allow it to close.

NOTE: The speed-up solenoid should reach full travel.

8. Adjust the speed-up solenoid screw to 850–950 rpm.

View of the idle and throttle adjusting screws—carbureted models

Idle Mixture Adjustment

1. Firmly set the parking brake and block the drive wheels.

2. Place the transmission in **N**.

3. Remove the carburetor assembly.

4. Using a drill, drill a hole through the sealing plug covering the idle mixture screw and pry the plug from the carburetor.

5. Reinstall the carburetor.

6. Operate the engine until it reaches normal operating temperatures. Be sure the choke is fully open and the air cleaner is installed. If equipped, turn the air conditioning **OFF**.

7. Disconnect and plug the distributor vacuum, the canister purge and EGR vacuum lines. Shut off the vacuum to the idle compensator by bending the rubber hose.

8. Connect a dwell meter (4 cyl. scale) or duty meter to the duty monitor lead.

9. Turn the idle mixture screw all the way in and back out 1½ turns.

10. Turn the throttle adjusting screw until the engine speed is 900 rpm.

11. Adjust the idle mixture screw to achieve an average dwell of 36 degrees or duty of 40 percent.

NOTE: The dwell or duty reading specified is the average of the most constant variation.

12. Reset the throttle adjusting screw until the engine speed is 850–950 rpm.

13. Reinstall a mixture adjustment plug.

Service Adjustments

For all carburetor service adjustment procedures and Specifications, please refer to "Carburetor Service" in the Unit Repair section.

Fuel Injection

Idle Speed Adjustment

2.6L ENGINE

For further information, please refer to Chilton's Electronic Engine Controls Manual.

Location of the vacuum switching valve (VSV) electrical connector—2.6L engine

View of the throttle body adjusting screw to alter the idle speed—2.6L engine

1. Firmly set the parking brake and block the drive wheels.
2. Place the transmission in **N**.
3. Set the engine tachometer.
4. Make sure the throttle valve is fully closed.
5. If equipped with air conditioning, turn **OFF** the air conditioning.
6. Place the manual transmission in neutral or the automatic transmission in **P**.
7. Disconnect the electrical connector from the Vacuum Switching Valve (VSV) on the pressure regulator; the idle speed should 850–950 rpm.
8. If the idle speed is not correct, turn the adjusting screw **A** on the throttle body.

2.8L AND 3.1L ENGINES

The idle speed is controlled by the ECM and no adjustment is necessary or possible.

Idle Mixture Adjustment

No idle mixture adjustment is necessary or possible.

Fuel Injector

Removal and Installation

2.6L ENGINE

The engine is equipped 4 fuel injectors, with 1 located at each cylinder.

1. Relieve the fuel pressure.
2. Disconnect the negative battery cable.
3. Label and disconnect the electrical connectors from the fuel injectors.
4. Disconnect the fuel rail from the fuel system.
5. Remove the fuel rail from the intake manifold; pull the fuel rail with the injectors connected from the intake manifold.
6. Separate the fuel injectors from the fuel rail.

To install:

7. Replace the fuel injector O-rings.
8. Install the fuel injectors to the fuel rail.
9. Lubricate the fuel injector O-rings with automatic transmission fluid and press them, with the fuel rail, into the intake manifold.
10. Install the fuel rail-to-intake manifold bolts.
11. Connect the fuel rail to the fuel system.
12. Connect the electrical connectors to the fuel injectors.
13. Connect the negative battery cable.
14. Turn the ignition switch **ON** and check for fuel leaks at the fuel rail.

1. Fuel meter cover gasket
2. Removing fuel injector

Removing the fuel injectors from the throttle body— 2.8L and 3.1L engines

2.8L AND 3.1L ENGINES

The engine is equipped with 2 fuel injectors, both are located in the throttle body.

1. Relieve the fuel pressure.
2. Disconnect the negative battery cable.
3. Remove the air cleaner.
4. At the injector electrical connectors, squeeze the 2 tabs together and pull them straight upward.
5. Remove the fuel meter cover and leave the cover gasket in place.
6. Using a small prybar, carefully pry the injectors upward until they are free of the throttle body.
7. Remove the small O-ring from the nozzle end of the injector. Carefully rotate the injector's fuel filter back-and-forth to remove it from the base of the injector.
8. Discard the fuel meter cover gasket.
9. Remove the large O-ring and backup washer from the top of the counterbore of the fuel meter body injector cavity.

To install:

10. Lubricate the O-rings with automatic transmission fluid and push them into the fuel injector cavities.
11. Install the new fuel meter cover gasket and cover.
12. Install the electrical connectors to the injectors.
13. Install the air cleaner and connect the negative battery cable.

EMISSION CONTROLS

For further information, please refer to Chilton's Emission Controls Manual.

Emission Warning Lamps

Resetting

Once the problem in the system is corrected, the trouble codes must be cleared from the ECM memory. The Check Engine light can be reset by disconnecting the negative battery cable or the ECM fuse at the fuse box for at least 10 seconds and then reconnecting the cable.

ENGINE MECHANICAL

NOTE: Disconnecting the negative battery cable on some vehicles may interfere with the functions of the on board computer systems and may require the computer to undergo a relearning process, once the negative battery cable is reconnected.

Engine

Removal and Installation

2WD VEHICLES

1. Relieve the fuel pressure. Disconnect both battery cables, the negative cable first. Remove the battery.
2. Matchmark the hood-to-hinges and remove the hood.
3. Remove the undercover, if equipped. Open the drain plugs on the radiator and the cylinder and drain the cooling system.
4. Remove the air cleaner for 2.3L, 2.8L and 3.1L engines or air cleaner duct and hose for 2.6L engine. Using a clean shop cloth, cover the air cleaner port to prevent dirt from entering the engine.
5. Label and disconnect the necessary hoses, electrical connectors, control cables and control rods from the engine.
6. Label and disconnect the following items:
    a. Air switch valve hose.
    b. Oxygen sensor wire.
    c. Vacuum switch valve hose.
    d. Thermal vacuum switching valve hose.
    e. Pressure regulator vacuum hose.
    f. Canister hose.
    g. ECM harness.
    h. Fuel hose(s).
7. Remove the clutch return spring, if equipped, the clutch control cable, if equipped, the backup light switch connector and the speedometer cable from the transmission.
8. Remove the radiator grille from the deflector panel.
9. Disconnect the upper and lower radiator hoses and the reservoir tank hose.
10. Remove the fan shroud, fan blade assembly and the radiator.
11. If equipped with air conditioning, remove the compressor from the engine and move it aside; do not disconnect the pressure hoses.
12. Remove the gear shift lever by performing the following procedures:
    a. Place the gear shift lever in **N**.
    b. Remove the front console from the floor panel.
    c. Pull the shift lever boot and grommet upward.
    d. Remove the shift lever cover bolts and the shift lever.
13. Raise and safely support the vehicle. Remove the front wheels.
14. Drain the oil from the engine and the transmission fluid.
15. If equipped with an automatic transmission, perform the following procedures:
    a. Remove the oil level gauge and the tube.
    b. Disconnect the shift select control link rod from the select lever.
    c. Disconnect the downshift cable from the transmission.
    d. Disconnect and plug the fluid coolant lines from the transmission.
16. If equipped with a 1-piece driveshaft, remove the driveshaft flange-to-pinion nuts, lower the driveshaft and pull it from the transmission.
17. If equipped with a 2-piece driveshaft, perform the following procedures:
    a. Remove the rear driveshaft flange-to-pinion nuts.
    b. Remove the rear driveshaft flange-to-front driveshaft flange bolts and the rear driveshaft.
    c. Remove the center bearing-to-chassis bolts, move the front driveshaft rearward and from the transmission.
18. Remove the starter-to-engine bolts and the starter.
19. Remove the exhaust pipe-to-exhaust manifold nuts, the exhaust pipe bracket-to-transmission bolts, the front exhaust pipe-to-2nd exhaust pipe bolts and the front exhaust pipe from the vehicle.

20. Attach an engine hanger to the rear of the exhaust manifold.

21. Using an engine hoist, connect it to the engine hangers and support the engine.

22. If equipped with a manual transmission, perform the following procedures:

    a. Using a transmission jack, place it under the transmission; do not support it.

    b. Remove the rear mount-to-transmission nuts.

    c. Remove the rear mount-to-crossmember nuts/bolts and the mount.

NOTE: Further removal of the transmission may require an assistant.

    d. Remove the clutch cover and the transmission-to-engine bolts.

    e. Move the transmission rearward into the crossmember and floor pan area; the transmission may rest on the crossmember.

    f. Lower the front of the transmission toward the jack.

    g. Firmly, grasp the transmission the rear cover while the assistant raises the jack toward the transmission.

    h. Carefully lower the transmission onto the jack and center it.

    i. Lower the jack and move the transmission rearward.

23. If equipped with an automatic transmission, perform the following procedures:

NOTE: Removal of the transmission will require an assistant.

    a. Remove the torque converter-to-flexplate bolts through the starter hole.

    b. Using a transmission jack, place it under the transmission; do not support it.

    c. Remove the rear mount-to-transmission nuts.

    d. Remove the rear mount-to-crossmember nuts/bolts and the mount.

    e. Remove the transmission-to-engine bolts.

    f. Move the transmission rearward into the crossmember and floor pan area; the transmission may rest on the crossmember.

    g. Lower the front of the transmission toward the jack.

    h. Firmly, grasp the transmission the rear cover while the assistant raises the jack toward the transmission.

    i. Carefully, lower the transmission onto the jack and center it.

    j. Lower the jack and move the transmission rearward.

24. Remove the engine-to-mount nuts/bolts.

25. Using the hoist, slowly, lift the engine; be sure to hold the front of the engine higher than the rear.

26. Place the engine on a workstand.

To install:

27. Using the hoist, slowly, lower the engine into the vehicle; be sure to hold the front of the engine higher than the rear.

28. Install the engine-to-mount nuts/bolts.

29. If equipped with an automatic transmission, perform the following procedures:

NOTE: Installation of the transmission will require an assistant.

    a. Raise the transmission into position.

    b. Raise the rear of the transmission and move it into position on the crossmember.

    c. Move the transmission forward and engage it with the engine.

    d. Install the engine-to-transmission bolts.

    e. Install the mount and the rear mount-to-crossmember nuts/bolts.

    f. Install the rear mount-to-transmission nuts.

    g. Install the torque converter-to-flexplate bolts through the starter hole.

30. If equipped with a manual transmission, perform the following procedures:

NOTE: Installation of the transmission may require an assistant.

    a. Raise the transmission into position.

    b. Raise the rear of the transmission and move it into position on the crossmember.

    c. Move the transmission forward and engage it with the engine.

    d. Install the engine-to-transmission bolts.

    e. Install the mount and the rear mount-to-crossmember nuts/bolts.

    f. Install the rear mount-to-transmission nuts.

31. Remove the engine hoist and the engine hanger from the rear of the exhaust manifold.

32. Install the front exhaust pipe, exhaust pipe-to-exhaust manifold nuts, the exhaust pipe bracket-to-transmission bolts, the front exhaust pipe-to-2nd exhaust pipe bolts.

33. Install the starter and the starter-to-engine bolts.

34. If equipped with a 2-piece driveshaft, perform the following procedures:

    a. Install the front driveshaft into the transmission and the center bearing-to-chassis bolts.

    b. Install the rear driveshaft and the rear driveshaft flange-to-front driveshaft flange bolts.

    c. Install the rear driveshaft flange-to-pinion nuts.

35. If equipped with a 1-piece driveshaft, install the driveshaft into the transmission and the driveshaft flange-to-pinion nuts.

36. If equipped with an automatic transmission, perform the following procedures:

    a. Connect the fluid coolant lines to the transmission.

    b. Connect the downshift cable to the transmission.

    c. Connect the shift select control link rod to the select lever.

    d. Install the oil level gauge and the tube.

37. Install the front wheels and lower the vehicle.

38. Install the gear shift lever by performing the following procedures:

    a. Install the shift lever and the shift lever cover bolts.

    b. Push the grommet and shift lever boot downward.

    c. Install the front console to the floor panel.

39. If equipped with air conditioning, install the compressor to the engine.

40. Install the radiator, the fan blade assembly and the fan shroud.

41. Connect the upper and lower radiator hoses and the reservoir tank hose.

42. Install the radiator grille to the deflector panel.

43. Install the clutch return spring, if equipped, the clutch control cable, if equipped, the backup light switch connector and the speedometer cable to the transmission.

44. Connect the following items:

    a. Air switch valve hose.

    b. Oxygen sensor wire.

    c. Vacuum switch valve hose.

    d. Thermal vacuum switching valve hose.

    e. Pressure regulator vacuum hose.

    f. Canister hose.

    g. ECM harness.

    h. Fuel hose(s).

45. Connect the necessary hoses, electrical connectors, control cables and control rods to the engine.

46. Install the air cleaner for 2.3L engine or air cleaner duct and hose for 2.6L engine.

47. Refill the engine, the transmission and the cooling system. Install the undercover, if equipped.

48. Install the hood.

49. Install the battery and connect both battery cables, the positive cable first.

50. Adjust the belt tension. Start the engine, check for leaks.

51. Check and/or adjust the idle speed and ignition timing.

4WD VEHICLES

1. Relieve the fuel pressure. Disconnect both battery cables, the negative cable first. Remove the battery.

2. Matchmark the hood-to-hinges and remove the hood.

3. Remove the undercover, if equipped. Open the drain plugs on the radiator and the cylinder and drain the cooling system.

4. Remove the air cleaner for 2.3L, 2.8L and 3.1L engines or air cleaner duct and hose for 2.6L engine. Using a clean shop cloth, cover the air cleaner port to prevent dirt from entering the engine.

5. Label and disconnect the necessary hoses, electrical connectors, control cables and control rods from the engine.

6. Label and disconnect the following items:
  a. Air switch valve hose.
  b. Oxygen sensor wire.
  c. Vacuum switch valve hose.
  d. Thermal vacuum switching valve hose.
  e. Pressure regulator vacuum hose.
  f. Canister hose.
  g. ECM harness.
  h. Fuel hose(s).

7. Remove the clutch return spring, if equipped, the clutch control cable, if equipped, the backup light switch connector and the speedometer cable from the transmission.

8. Remove the radiator grille from the deflector panel.

9. Disconnect the upper and lower radiator hoses and the reservoir tank hose.

10. Remove the fan shroud, fan blade assembly and the radiator.

11. If equipped with air conditioning, remove the compressor from the engine and move it aside; do not disconnect the pressure hoses.

12. If equipped with a 2.8L or 3.1L engine, perform the following procedures:
  a. Remove the power steering pump-to-engine brackets and move the pump aside.
  b. Remove the spark plug wire from the No. 1 spark plug.
  c. Remove the distributor cap with the No. 1 spark plug wire.
  d. Remove the ignition coil.

13. Remove the gear shift lever by performing the following procedures:
  a. Place the gear shift lever in **N**.
  b. Remove the front console from the floor panel.
  c. Pull the shift lever boot and grommet upward.
  d. Remove the shift lever cover bolts and the shift lever.

14. Remove the transfer shift lever by performing the following procedures:
  a. Place the transfer shift lever in **H** for 2.3L or 2.6L engine or **2H** for 2.8L or 3.1L engine.
  b. Pull the shift lever boot and dust cover upward.
  c. Remove the shift lever retaining bolts.
  d. Pull the shift lever from the transfer case.

15. Raise and safely support the vehicle. Remove the front wheels. Drain the oil from the engine.

16. Drain the transmission and transfer case fluid.

17. If equipped with an automatic transmission, perform the following procedures:
  a. Remove the oil level gauge and the tube.
  b. Disconnect the shift select control link rod from the select lever.
  c. Disconnect the downshift cable from the transmission.
  d. Disconnect and plug the fluid coolant lines from the transmission.

18. If equipped with a 1-piece driveshaft, remove the driveshaft flange-to-pinion nuts, lower the driveshaft and pull it from the transmission.

19. If equipped with a 2-piece driveshaft, perform the following procedures:
  a. Remove the rear driveshaft flange-to-pinion nuts.
  b. Remove the rear driveshaft flange-to-front driveshaft flange bolts and the rear driveshaft.
  c. Remove the center bearing-to-chassis bolts, move the front driveshaft rearward and from the transmission.

20. Remove the front driveshaft's splined yoke flange-to-transfer case bolts and separate the front driveshaft from the transfer case; do not allow the splined flange to fall away from the driveshaft.

21. Remove the starter-to-engine bolts and the starter.

22. If equipped with a clutch slave cylinder, remove it from the transmission and move it aside.

23. Remove the exhaust pipe-to-exhaust manifold nuts, the exhaust pipe bracket-to-transmission bolts, the front exhaust pipe-to-2nd exhaust pipe bolts and the front exhaust pipe from the vehicle.

24. Attach an engine hanger to the rear of the exhaust manifold.

25. Using an engine hoist, connect it to the engine hangers and support the engine.

26. If equipped with a 2.8L engine, remove the catalytic converter and the parking brake cable bracket.

27. Remove the transmission/transfer case assembly by performing the following procedures:
  a. Using a transmission jack, place it under the transmission and support the assembly.
  b. Remove the rear mount-to-transmission nuts.
  c. Remove the rear mount-to-side mount member nuts/bolts and the mount.
  d. Remove the transmission-to-engine bolts.
  e. Move the transmission assembly rearward.
  f. Carefully lower the transmission.

28. Remove the engine-to-mount nuts/bolts.

29. Using the hoist, slowly, lift the engine; be sure to hold the front of the engine higher than the rear.

30. Place the engine on a work stand.

To install:

31. Using the hoist, slowly, lower the engine into the vehicle; be sure to hold the front of the engine higher than the rear.

32. Install the engine-to-mount nuts/bolts.

33. Install the transmission/transfer assembly by performing the following procedures:
  a. Raise the transmission into position.
  b. Move the transmission forward and engage it with the engine.
  c. Install the engine-to-transmission bolts.
  d. Install the rear mount and the rear mount-to-side mount member nuts/bolts.
  e. Install the rear mount-to-transmission nuts.
  f. Remove the transmission jack.

34. If equipped with a 2.8L or 3.1L engine, install the catalytic converter and the parking brake cable bracket.

35. Remove the engine hoist and the engine hanger from the rear of the exhaust manifold.

36. Install the front exhaust pipe, exhaust pipe-to-exhaust manifold nuts, the exhaust pipe bracket-to-transmission bolts, the front exhaust pipe-to-2nd exhaust pipe bolts.

37. If equipped with a clutch slave cylinder, install it onto the transmission.

38. Install the starter and the starter-to-engine bolts.

39. Install the front driveshaft's splinded yoke flange-to-transfer case bolts.

40. If equipped with a 2-piece driveshaft, perform the following procedures:
  a. Install the front driveshaft into the transmission and the center bearing-to-chassis bolts.
  b. Install the rear driveshaft and the rear driveshaft flange-to-front driveshaft flange bolts.
  c. Install the rear driveshaft flange-to-pinion nuts.

41. If equipped with a 1-piece driveshaft, install the driveshaft into the transmission and the driveshaft flange-to-pinion nuts.

42. If equipped with an automatic transmission, perform the following procedures:

    a. Connect the fluid coolant lines to the transmission.

    b. Connect the downshift cable to the transmission.

    c. Connect the shift select control link rod to the select lever.

    d. Install the oil level gauge and the tube.

43. Install the front wheels and lower the vehicle.

44. Install the transfer shift lever by performing the following procedures:

    a. Position the shift lever into the transfer case.

    b. Install the shift lever retaining bolts.

    c. Push the dust cover and the shift lever boot downward.

45. Install the gear shift lever by performing the following procedures:

    a. Install the shift lever and the shift lever cover bolts.

    b. Push the grommet and shift lever boot downward.

    c. Install the front console to the floor panel.

46. If equipped with a 2.8L or 3.1L engine, perform the following procedures:

    a. Install the ignition coil.

    b. Install the distributor cap with the No. 1 spark plug wire.

    c. Install the spark plug wire from the No. 1 spark plug and reconnect the wires to the distributor cap.

    d. Install the power steering pump-to-engine brackets.

47. If equipped with air conditioning, install the compressor to the engine.

48. Install the radiator, the fan blade assembly and the fan shroud.

49. Connect the upper and lower radiator hoses and the reservoir tank hose.

50. Install the radiator grille to the deflector panel.

51. Install the clutch return spring, if equipped, the clutch control cable, if equipped, the backup light switch connector and the speedometer cable to the transmission.

52. Connect the following items:

    a. Air switch valve hose.

    b. Oxygen sensor wire.

    c. Vacuum switch valve hose.

    d. Thermal vacuum switching valve hose.

    e. Pressure regulator vacuum hose.

    f. Canister hose.

    g. ECM harness.

    h. Fuel hose(s).

53. Connect the necessary hoses, electrical connectors, control cables and control rods to the engine.

54. Install the air cleaner for 2.3L, 2.8L and 3.1L engines or air cleaner duct and hose for 2.6L engine.

55. Refill the engine, the transmission, the transfer case and the cooling system. Install the undercover, if equipped.

56. Install the hood.

57. Install the battery and connect both battery cables, the positive cable first.

58. Adjust the belt tension. Start the engine, check for leaks.

59. Check and/or adjust the idle speed and ignition timing.

Engine Mounts

Removal and Installation

1. Disconnect the negative battery cable. Using a hoist, lift up on the engine hoisting tabs to remove weight from the engine mounts.

2. Loosen the engine mount hardware and remove the mounts from the engine and crossmember.

3. Install the mount and replace the hardware. Torque the bolts and nuts to 38 ft. lbs. (52 Nm).

4. Lower the engine and connect the negative battery cable.

Cylinder Head

Removal and Installation

2.3L AND 2.6L ENGINES

1. Relieve the fuel pressure. Disconnect the negative battery cable. Drain the cooling system.

2. Remove the drive belts from the power steering pump, the air pump, the air conditioning compressor, if equipped, and the cooling fan.

3. Rotate the engine to position the No. 1 cylinder on TDC.

4. Remove the distributor cap, high tension cables and the distributor.

5. Remove the exhaust manifold-to-exhaust pipe bolts.

6. Label and disconnect the electrical connectors and vacuum hoses which may be in the way.

7. On the 2.3L engine, remove the carburetor.

8. Remove the coolant hoses. It is not necessary to remove the radiator and the cooling fan assembly.

9. Remove the crankshaft pulley bolt and the pulley.

10. Remove the upper and lower timing belt covers, the tension spring and the timing belt.

11. Remove the camshaft pulley bolt, the pulley and the camshaft boss.

12. Remove the timing belt guide plate and the cylinder head front plate.

13. Remove the rocker arm cover and gasket.

14. Remove the cylinder head-to-engine bolts, the cylinder head and gasket.

15. Clean the gasket mounting surfaces.

To install:

16. Using a new gasket, install the cylinder head and torque the bolts, in sequence to 57 ft. lbs. in the 1st step and to 65–79 ft. lbs. in the final step.

17. Install the camshaft pulley.

18. Using a new gasket, install the rocker arm cover.

19. Align the camshaft pulley mark with the mark on the front plate. Make sure the keyway on the crankshaft if facing upward, aimed at the pointer on the engine block.

20. Install the timing belt in the following order: crankshaft pulley, the oil pump pulley, the camshaft and the tensioner.

21. Install the timing belt covers, using a new gasket.

22. Install the crankshaft pulley.

23. Install the cooling fan assembly, the radiator and the coolant hoses.

24. On the 2.3L engine, install the carburetor.

25. Connect the electrical connectors and vacuum hoses.

26. Install the exhaust manifold-to-exhaust pipe bolts.

27. Install the distributor, the distributor cap and the high tension cables.

28. Install the drive belts to the power steering pump, the air pump, the air conditioning compressor, if equipped, and the cooling fan.

View of the cylinder head bolt torquing sequence— 2.3L and 2.6L engines

29. Disconnect the negative battery cable. Refill the cooling system.

30. Start the engine and check for leaks.

2.8L AND 3.1L ENGINES

Left Side

1. Relieve the fuel pressure. Disconnect the negative battery cable. Drain the cooling system.

2. Remove the intake manifold.

3. Raise and safely support the vehicle.

4. Disconnect the exhaust pipe from the exhaust manifold and remove the exhaust manifold-to-cylinder head bolts.

5. Remove the dipstick tube from the engine.

6. Lower the vehicle.

7. Loosen the rocker arm nuts, turn the rocker arms and remove the pushrods; keep the pushrods in the same order as removed.

8. Remove the cylinder head bolts in stages and in the reverse order of torquing.

9. Remove the cylinder head; do not pry on the head to loosen it.

10. Clean the gasket mounting surfaces.

To install:

11. Position a new cylinder head gasket over the dowel pins with the words **This Side Up** facing upwards. Carefully, guide the cylinder head into place.

12. Install the pushrods; make sure the lower ends are in the lifter heads. Torque the rocker arm nuts to 14–20 ft. lbs. (20–27 Nm).

13. Install the intake manifold.

14. Install the dipstick tube to the engine.

15. Install the exhaust manifold-to-cylinder head bolts and the exhaust pipe-to-exhaust manifold nuts.

16. Refill the cooling system. Start the engine and check for leaks.

Right Side

1. Relieve the fuel pressure. Disconnect the negative battery cable. Drain the cooling system.

2. Remove the intake manifold.

3. If equipped, remove the cruise control servo bracket, the air management valve and hose.

4. Raise and safely support the vehicle.

5. Disconnect the exhaust pipe from the exhaust manifold and remove the exhaust manifold-to-cylinder head bolts.

6. Remove the exhaust pipe at crossover, the crossover and the heat shield, if equipped.

7. Lower the vehicle.

8. Label and disconnect the electrical wiring and vacuum hoses that may interfere with the removal of the right cylinder head.

9. Loosen the rocker arm nuts, turn the rocker arms and remove the pushrods; keep the pushrods in the same order as removed.

10. Remove the cylinder head bolts in stages and in the reverse order of torquing.

11. Remove the cylinder head; do not pry on the head to loosen it.

12. Clean the gasket mounting surfaces.

To install:

13. Position a new cylinder head gasket over the dowel pins with the words **This Side Up** facing upwards. Carefully, guide the cylinder head into place.

14. Install the pushrods; make sure the lower ends are in the lifter heads. Torque the rocker arm nuts to 14–20 ft. lbs. (20–27 Nm).

15. Install the intake manifold.

16. Install the exhaust pipe at crossover, the crossover and the heat shield, if equipped.

17. Install the exhaust manifold-to-cylinder head bolts and the exhaust pipe-to-exhaust manifold nuts.

19. Connect the electrical wiring and vacuum hoses to the right cylinder head.

20. If equipped, install the cruise control servo bracket, the air management valve and hose.

21. Refill the cooling system. Start the engine and check for leaks.

Valve Lifters

Removal and Installation

2.8L AND 3.1L ENGINES

1. Disconnect the negative battery cable.

2. Remove the rocker arm covers.

3. Remove the rocker arm nut, the pivot balls, the rocker arm and the pushrods. Keep all components separated so they may be reinstalled in the same location.

4. Remove the lifter from their bores using a hydraulic valve lifter J-929901 or equivalent.

NOTE: The intake and exhaust pushrods are of different lengths.

To install:

5. Lubricate the lifters with Molycote or equivalent, and install in the bores. Install the pushrods in their original location; be sure the lower ends are seated in the lifter.

6. Coat the bearing surfaces of the rocker arms and pivot balls with Molykote or equivalent.

7. Install the rocker arm nuts and torque them to 14–20 ft. lbs. (20–27 Nm).

8. Adjust the valve lash.

Valve Lash

Adjustment

2.3L AND 2.6L ENGINES

NOTE: The valves are adjusted with the engine COLD. It is best to allow an engine to sit overnight before beginning a valve adjustment. While all valve adjustments must be made as accurately as possible, it is better to have the valve adjustment slightly loose rather than slightly tight. A burned valve may result from overly tight valve adjustments.

1. Remove the rocker arm cover and discard the gasket.

2. Make sure both the cylinder head and camshaft retaining bolts are tightened to the proper torque.

3. Rotate the crankshaft pulley until the No. 1 piston is at TDC of the compression stroke.

View of the cylinder head bolt torquing sequence—
2.8L and 3.1L engines

Adjusting the valves—2.3L and 2.6L engines

NOTE: To make sure the piston is on the correct stroke, remove the spark plug and place a finger over the hole. Feel for air being forced out of the spark plug hole. Both valves on No. 1 cylinder will be closed. Stop turning the crankshaft when the TDC timing mark on the crankshaft pulley is directly aligned with the timing mark pointer.

4. With the No. 1 piston at TDC of the compression stroke, adjust the clearances of the following valves:
    Intake: 1 and 2
    Exhaust: 1 and 3
5. Adjust the clearance by loosening the locknut and turning the adjusting screw. Retightening the locknut when the proper thickness feeler gauge passes between the camshaft or valve stem and has a slight drag when the clearance is corrected.
6. Rotate the crankshaft 1 complete revolution (360 degrees) to position the No. 4 piston at TDC of its compression stroke and adjust the clearances of the following valves:
    Intake: 3 and 4
    Exhaust: 2 and 4
7. After adjustment, use a new gasket, sealant and install the rocker arm cover.

2.8L AND 3.1L ENGINES

1. Remove the valve covers.
2. Rotate the crankshaft until the No. 1 cylinder is on the TDC of its compression stroke.

NOTE: When the notch on the damper pulley is aligned with the 0 timing mark and the rocker arms of the No. 1 cylinder do not move, the engine is at the TDC of the compression stroke of the No. 1 cylinder.

3. With the engine at TDC of the No. 1 cylinder, adjust the following valves:
    Exhaust: 1, 2 and 3
    Intake: 1, 5 and 6
4. Back out the adjusting nut until lash is felt.
5. Tighten the adjusting nut until the lash is removed, then, turn the nut 1½ additional turns to center the lifter plunger.
6. Rotate the engine 1 complete revolution and reposition the notch on the damper pulley with the **0** mark on the timing tab; this is the No. 4 cylinder firing position.
7. With the engine at TDC of the No. 4 cylinder, adjust the following valves:
    Exhaust: 4, 5 and 6
    Intake: 2, 3 and 4
8. Back out the adjusting nut until lash is felt.
9. Tighten the adjusting nut until the lash is removed, plus, turn the nut 1½ additional turns to center the lifter plunger.
10. Using a new gasket and sealant, install the rocker arm covers.

Adjusting the valves—2.8L and 3.1L engines

Rocker Arms/Shafts

Removal and Installation

2.3L AND 2.6L ENGINES

1. Disconnect the negative battery cable. Remove the rocker cover. Remove the accessory drive belts and the engine cooling fan and water pump pulley. Remove the starter and crankshaft pulley. Remove the timing covers and timing belt.
2. Loosen the rocker arm shaft bracket nuts a little at a time, in sequence, starting with the outer nuts.
3. Remove the nuts from the rocker arm shaft brackets. Remove shaft assembly.
4. To disassemble the rockers and shafts; remove the spring from the rocker arm shaft, the rocker brackets and arms. Keep parts in order for reassembly.
5. Before installing apply a generous amount of clean engine oil to the rocker arm shaft, rocker arms and valve stems.
To install:
6. Install the longer shaft on the exhaust valve side and the shorter shaft on the intake side so the aligning marks on the shafts are turned on the front side of the engine.
7. Assemble the rocker arm shaft brackets and rocker arms to the shafts so the cylinder number, on the upper face of the brackets, points toward the front of the engine.
8. Align the mark on the No. 1 rocker arm shaft bracket with the mark on the intake and exhaust valve side rocker arm shaft.
9. Make certain the amount of projection of the rocker arm shaft beyond the face of the No. 1 rocker arm shaft bracket, is longer on the exhaust side shaft than on the intake shaft when the rocker arm shaft stud holes are aligned with the rocker arm shaft bracket stud holes.
10. Place the rocker arm shaft springs in position between the shaft bracket and rocker arm.
11. Check that the punch mark on the rocker arm shaft is facing upward, then, install the rocker arm shaft bracket assembly onto the cylinder head studs. Align the mark on the camshaft with the mark on the No. 1 rocker arm shaft bracket.
12. Torque the rocker arm shaft brackets-to-cylinder head nuts to 16 ft. lbs. and bolts to 6 ft. lbs.

NOTE: Hold the rocker arm springs while torquing the nuts to prevent damage to the spring. Start with the center nut and work outward.

1. Bracket
2. Rocker arm shaft
3. Rocker arm
4. Rocker arm spring
5. Rocker arm bracket nut

Exploded view of the rocker arm/shaft assembly—
2.3L and 2.6L engines

View of the rocker arm/shaft assembly torquing
sequence—2.3L and 2.6L engines

Exploded view of the cylinder head/rocker arm
assembly—2.8L and 3.1L engines

13. Adjust the valves and install the camshaft cover, with a new gasket and sealer. Install the timing covers, accessories and drive belts. Check the ignition timing.

2.8L AND 3.1L ENGINES

1. Disconnect the negative battery cable.
2. Remove the rocker arm covers.
3. Remove the rocker arm nut, the pivot balls, the rocker arm and the pushrods. Keep all components separated so they may be reinstalled in the same location.

NOTE: The intake and exhaust pushrods are of different lengths.

To install:

4. Install the pushrods in their original location; be sure the lower ends are seated in the lifter.
5. Coat the bearing surfaces of the rocker arms and pivot balls with Molykote or equivalent.
6. Install the rocker arm nuts and torque them to 14–20 ft. lbs. (20–27 Nm).
7. Adjust the valve lash.

Intake Manifold

Removal and Installation

2.3L ENGINE

1. Relieve the fuel pressure. Disconnect the negative battery cable and remove the air cleaner assembly.
2. Remove the EGR pipe clamp bolt at the rear of the cylinder head.
3. Raise and support the vehicle safely. Remove the EGR pipe from the intake and exhaust manifolds.
4. Remove the EGR valve and bracket assembly from the intake manifold.
5. Lower the vehicle and drain the cooling system.
6. Remove the upper coolant hoses from the manifold.
7. Disconnect the accelerator linkage, vacuum lines, electrical wiring and fuel line from the intake manifold.
8. Remove the intake manifold mounting nuts and remove the manifold from the cylinder head.
9. Remove the lower heater hose while holding the manifold away from the engine. Remove the manifold from the vehicle.

To install:

10. Connect the lower heater hose to the manifold. Using a new gasket, install the intake manifold.
11. Connect the accelerator linkage, vacuum lines, electrical wiring and fuel line to the intake manifold.
12. Connect the upper coolant hose to the intake manifold.
13. Install the EGR valve and bracket assembly to the intake manifold.
14. Install the EGR pipe to the intake and exhaust manifolds. Lower the vehicle.
15. Install the EGR pipe clamp bolt to the rear of the cylinder head.

Exploded view of the intake manifold—2.3L engine

RR

16. Install the air cleaner and connect the negative battery cable.

2.6L ENGINE

1. Relieve the fuel pressure. Disconnect the negative battery cable and remove the air duct.

2. Drain the cooling system. Remove the upper coolant hoses from the manifold.

3. Remove the air regulator rubber hose from the intake plenum.

4. Remove the EGR valve and bracket assembly from the intake manifold.

5. Disconnect the accelerator linkage, vacuum lines, electrical wiring and fuel line from the throttle body.

6. Remove the throttle body-to-plenum nuts and the throttle body.

7. Remove the plenum-to-intake manifold bolts and the plenum. Remove the fuel injector rail with the fuel injectors.

8. Remove the intake manifold-to-cylinder head nuts and the manifold from the cylinder head.

1. Intake manifold
2. Fuel injector with pipe
3. Thermostat
4. Water outlet pipe gasket
5. Water outlet pipe
6. Thermal valve
7. Air regulator
8. Coolant temperature sensor
9. Water temperature unit
10. Thermal vacuum valve
11. Plenum gasket
12. Plenum
13. Bolt
14. TBI gasket
15. TBI unit
16. EGR valve
17. Throttle valve switch
18. Pressure regulator
19. Power switch

Exploded view of the intake manifold assembly—2.6L engine

1. Intake manifold
2. Gaskets
3. Studs
4. Bolt/screw studs
5. Bolt/screw assembly
6. Bolt/screw assembly
7. Nut/washer assembly
8. Sealant
9. Cylinder head assembly

INLET MANIFOLD BOLT/SCREW
AND NUT TIGHTENING SEQUENCE
VIEW A

Exploded view of the intake manifold assembly—2.8L and 3.1L engines

To install:

9. Using a new gasket, install the intake manifold to the cylinder head. Install the fuel injector rail with the injectors.

10. Using a new gasket, install the plenum to the intake manifold.

11. Using a new gasket, install the throttle body to the plenum.

12. Connect the accelerator linkage, vacuum lines, electrical wiring and fuel line.

13. Install the EGR valve and bracket assembly to the intake manifold.

14. Install the air regulator rubber hose to the intake plenum.

15. Install the upper coolant hoses to the manifold.

16. Install the air duct. Connect the negative battery cable. Refill the cooling system.

2.8L AND 3.1L ENGINES

1. Relieve the fuel pressure. Disconnect the negative battery cable.

2. Remove the air cleaner. Drain the cooling system.

3. Label and disconnect the wires and hoses from the TBI unit and the intake manifold.

4. Disconnect and plug the fuel lines from the TBI unit.

5. Disconnect the accelerator cables from the TBI unit.

6. Disconnect the ignition wires from the spark plugs and the wires from the coil.

7. Remove the distributor cap with the wires.

8. Mark the location of the rotor to the distributor housing and the distributor housing to the intake manifold.

9. Remove the distributor hold-down clamp and the distributor.

10. Label and disconnect the EGR vacuum line and the emission hoses.

11. Remove the pipe brackets from the rocker arm covers.

12. Remove the rocker arm covers.

13. Remove the upper radiator hose and the heater hose.

14. Disconnect the electrical connectors from the coolant sensors.

15. Remove the intake manifold nuts/bolts, the manifold and gaskets.

16. Clean the gasket mounting surfaces.

To install:

17. Using RTV sealant, apply an 1/8 in. bead to the front and rear of the block; make sure no water or oil is present.

18. Using new gaskets, marked right and left side, apply a 1/4 in. bead of sealant to hold them in place and install them onto the cylinder heads; the gaskets may have to be cut to be installed around the pushrods.

19. Install the intake manifold and torque the nuts/bolts, in sequence, to 19 ft. lbs. (26 Nm) and retorque using the same sequence.

NOTE: Make sure the areas between the case ridges and the intake manifold are completely sealed.

20. Install the heater hose and the radiator to the manifold.

21. Using new gaskets, install the rocker arm covers.

22. Connect the electrical connectors to the coolant sensors.

23. Install the pipe brackets.

24. Align the matchmarks and install the distributor and the distributor cap.

25. Connect the fuel lines and the accelerator cables to the TBI unit.

26. Connect all the wires and vacuum hoses.

27. Install the air cleaner. Connect the negative battery cable. Refill the cooling system.

Exploded view of the exhaust manifold—2.6L engine

Exhaust Manifold

Removal and Installation

2.3L AND 2.6L ENGINES

1. Disconnect the negative battery cable and remove the air duct.
2. Remove the hoses from the air pump.
3. Remove the air pump bolts, remove the drive belt and the air pump.
4. Remove the EGR pipe clamp bolt at the rear of the cylinder head.
5. Raise and safely support the vehicle. Remove the EGR pipe from the intake and exhaust manifolds. If necessary, remove the dipstick and tube.
6. Disconnect the exhaust pipe from the exhaust manifold. Disconnect the electrical connector from the oxygen sensor.
7. Remove the manifold shield.
8. Remove the manifold-to-cylinder head nuts and the manifold from the engine.

To install:

9. Using a new gasket, install the exhaust manifold and torque the nuts to 33 ft. lbs. (44 Nm).
10. Install the heat shield. If the dipstick was removed, install the tube and the dipstick.
11. Connect the exhaust pipe to the exhaust manifold. Torque the nuts to 49 ft. lbs. (67 Nm). Connect the electrical connector to the oxygen sensor.
12. Install the EGR pipe to the intake and exhaust manifolds and lower the vehicle. Torque to 33 ft. lbs. (44 Nm).
13. Install the EGR pipe clamp bolt to the rear of the cylinder head.
14. Install the air duct. Connect the negative battery cable.

2.8L AND 3.1L ENGINES

1. Disconnect the negative battery cable.
2. Raise and safely support the vehicle.
3. Remove the exhaust pipe from the manifold.
4. Lower the vehicle and remove the rear manifold bolts.
5. On the right side, remove the diverter valve, the heat shield, the AIR pump bracket and alternator bracket.
6. On the left side, remove the heat stove tube and the power steering bracket.
7. Remove the exhaust manifold-to-cylinder head bolts and the manifold.
8. Clean the gasket mounting surfaces.

To install:

9. Using a new gasket, install the exhaust manifold-to-cylinder head bolts and torque the bolts to 25 ft. lbs. (34 Nm).
10. On the left side, install the power steering bracket and heat stove tube.
11. On the right side, install the AIR pump bracket, the alternator bracket, the diverter valve and the heat shield.

Exploded view of the exhaust manifolds—2.8L and 3.1L engines

12. Raise and safely support the vehicle.
13. Install the exhaust pipe-to-manifold bolts.
14. Lower the vehicle and connect the negative battery cable.

Timing Chain Front Cover

Removal and Installation

2.8L AND 3.1L ENGINES

1. Disconnect the negative battery cable.
2. Drain the cooling system. Remove the lower radiator hose from the front cover. Raise and support the vehicle.
3. Remove the stone guard and radiator undercover from beneath the vehicle. Remove the serpentine belt and suspension crossmember.
4. Remove the starter and the flywheel cover. Loosen the oil pan nuts and bolts but do not remove them. Remove the power steering bracket, if equipped.
5. Remove the upper radiator hose and the air conditioner pipe bracket. Remove the fan shrouds. Remove the fan and clutch assembly. Remove the water pump pulley.

6. Remove the damper and pulley bolts. Remove the damper with tool J–24420B or equivalent. Remove the front cover-to-engine bolts and the cover and discard the gasket.

7. Clean the gasket mounting surfaces.

NOTE: When the front cover is removed, replace the oil seal.

To install:

8. Installation is the reverse of removal. Using a new gasket and sealant, install the front cover. torque the bolts to 20 ft. lbs. (27 Nm).

9. Install the water pump and the lower radiator hose.

10. Install the crankshaft pulley and damper. Torque the damper bolts to 70 ft. lbs. (95 Nm).

11. Install the power steering pump bracket, if equipped.

12. Install the drive belt(s).

13. Connect the negative battery cable and refill the cooling system.

Front Cover Oil Seal

Replacement

2.8L AND 3.1L ENGINES

1. Disconnect the negative battery cable.

2. Remove the serpentine belt, starter, flywheel cover and damper bolt. Lock the flywheel in place and remove the crankshaft pulley and damper.

3. Using a small prybar, pry the oil seal from the front cover; be careful not to damage the sealing surface or the crankshaft.

4. Using an oil seal installation tool, lubricate the new seal with engine oil and drive it into the front cover; be careful not to cut the seal lip.

5. Install the crankshaft pulley and damper. Install the starter and flywheel cover.

6. Connect the negative battery cable.

Timing Chain and Sprockets

Removal and Installation

2.8L AND 3.1L ENGINES

1. Disconnect the negative battery cable.

2. Rotate the crankshaft to position the No. 1 cylinder at the TDC of its compression stroke.

3. Remove the front cover.

4. Inspect the sprocket for chipped teeth and wear.

5. Inspect the timing chain for wear; if the chain can be pulled out more than 0.374 in. (9.5mm) from the damper, replace the chain.

6. Remove camshaft sprocket-to-camshaft bolts, the sprocket and the timing chain; if necessary, use a mallet to tap the sprocket from the camshaft.

7. Using a puller tool, press the crankshaft sprocket from the crankshaft.

To install:

8. Using an installation tool and a hammer, drive the crankshaft sprocket onto the crankshaft; make sure the timing mark faces outward.

9. Using Molykote or equivalent, lubricate the camshaft sprocket thrust surface and install the timing chain onto the sprocket.

10. While holding the camshaft sprocket and chain vertically, align the marks on the camshaft and crankshaft sprockets.

11. Align the camshaft dowel with the camshaft sprocket hole. Install the camshaft sprocket and torque the bolts to 17 ft. lbs. (23 Nm).

12. Lubricate the timing chain with engine oil.

13. Install the front cover and crankshaft pulley.

14. Connect the negative battery cable.

15. Start the engine, then, check and/or adjust the timing.

A. No. 1 cylinder at TDC
B. No. 4 cylinder at TDC
30. Bolt

View of the timing chain alignment marks—2.8L and 3.1L engines

Service Tips

SERPENTINE BELT SQUEAKING

Trooper II vehicles equipped with a V6 engine and air conditioning may have a squeaking noise originating from the serpentine belt. This is caused by a misalignment of the air conditioning compressor pulley and the idler pulley.

To eliminate the noise the compressor should be shimmed out 1/32 in. (0.16mm) using part 2-90126–000–0 spacer shim. Disconnect the negative battery cable and loosen the serpentine belt. Loosen the mounting bolts for the compressor bracket and loosen the 12mm fasteners at the support bracket at the rear of the compressor. Slip the shim between the compressor bracket and the cylinder head. Make sure the shim is positioned so the tab does not contact the intake manifold.

Torque the compressor bracket bolts to 30–44 ft. lbs. (40–60 Nm) and the 12mm fasteners to 50–55 ft. lbs. (67–74 Nm). Install the belt and connect the battery cable. Test drive the vehicle to check that the noise has been eliminated. Repeat the procedure and add another shim if the noise has not been eradicated.

Timing Belt Front Cover

Removal and Installation

2.3L AND 2.6L ENGINES

1. Disconnect the negative battery cable.
2. Remove all accessory drive belts and the cooling fan assembly.
3. Remove the crankshaft pulley bolt and pulley.
4. Remove the upper timing belt cover.
5. Remove the lower timing belt cover.
6. To install, reverse the removal procedures.

Oil Seal Replacement

2.3L AND 2.6L ENGINES

1. Disconnect the negative battery cable. Remove the crankshaft pulley.
2. Remove the upper and lower timing belt covers.
3. Rotate the crankshaft to align the camshaft sprocket with the mark on the rear timing cover and the crankshaft sprocket keyway with the mark on the oil seal retainer cover.

NOTE: **With the timing marks aligned, the engine is positioned on the TDC of the No. 4 cylinder's compression stroke.**

4. Loosen the timing belt tensioner and relax the tension and remove the timing belt from the crankshaft sprocket.
5. Remove the crankshaft sprocket bolt, the sprocket, the key and deflector shield.
6. Using a small prybar, pry the oil seal from the oil seal retainer.

To install:

7. Using a new oil seal, lubricate it with engine oil and tap it into the retainer with an oil seal installation tool.
8. Install the deflector, the key, the crankshaft sprocket and bolt.
9. With the crankshaft sprocket aligned with the timing mark, install the timing belt.
10. Apply the tensioner pulley spring pressure to the timing belt.
11. Rotate the crankshaft 2 complete revolutions in the opposite direction of rotation and realign the timing marks.
12. Loosen the tensioner pulley bolt to allow the spring to adjust the correct tension. Torque the tensioner pulley bolt to 14 ft. lbs. (19 Nm).
13. Install the timing covers and the crankshaft pulley.
14. To complete the installation, reverse the removal procedures.

Timing Belt and Tensioner

Adjustment

2.3L AND 2.6L ENGINES

1. Disconnect the negative battery cable. Remove the crankshaft pulley.
2. Remove the upper and lower timing belt covers.
3. Loosen the timing belt tensioner and relax the belt tension.
4. Apply the tensioner pulley spring pressure to the timing belt.
5. Rotate the crankshaft 2 complete revolutions in the opposite direction of rotation and realign the timing marks.
6. Loosen the tensioner pulley bolt to allow the spring to ad-

1. Crankshaft pulley bolt
2. Timing belt cover
3. Timing belt
4. Tensioner pulley and spring
5. Crankshaft timing sprocket
6. Camshaft timing sprocket
7. Camshaft boss
8. Oil pump and pulley
9. Water pump
10. Rear timing belt covers

Exploded view of the timing belt assembly — 2.3L and 2.6L engines

View of the crankshaft sprocket alignment mark—2.3L and 2.6L engines

View of the camshaft sprocket alignment mark—2.3L and 2.6L engines

just the correct tension. Torque the tensioner pulley bolt to 14 ft. lbs. (19 Nm).

7. Install the timing covers and the crankshaft pulley.

8. To complete the installation, reverse the removal procedures.

Removal and Installation

2.3L AND 2.6L ENGINES

1. Disconnect the negative battery cable. Remove the crankshaft pulley.

2. Remove the upper and lower timing belt covers.

3. Rotate the crankshaft to align the camshaft sprocket with the mark on the rear timing cover and the crankshaft sprocket keyway with the mark on the oil seal retainer cover.

NOTE: With the timing marks aligned, the engine is positioned on the TDC of the No. 4 cylinder's compression stroke.

4. Loosen the timing belt tensioner and relax the tension and remove the timing belt from the crankshaft sprocket.

To install:

5. With the crankshaft and the camshaft sprockets aligned with the timing marks, install the timing belt. Install the timing belt using the following sequence: the crankshaft sprocket, the oil pump sprocket and the camshaft sprocket.

6. Apply the tensioner pulley spring pressure to the timing belt.

7. Rotate the crankshaft 2 complete revolutions in the opposite direction of rotation and realign the timing marks.

8. Loosen the tensioner pulley bolt to allow the spring to adjust the correct tension. Torque the tensioner pulley bolt to 14 ft. lbs.

9. Install the timing covers and the crankshaft pulley.

10. To complete the installation, reverse the removal procedures.

Timing Sprockets

Removal and Installation

2.3L AND 2.6L ENGINES

Camshaft Sprocket

1. Disconnect the negative battery cable.

2. Remove the timing belt.

3. Remove the camshaft sprocket-to-camshaft bolt and the sprocket.

NOTE: It may be necessary to use a mallet to tap the sprocket from the camshaft.

4. Remove and replace the camshaft oil seal.

To install:

5. Align the camshaft sprocket-to-rear plate timing marks. With the crankshaft sprocket aligned with the timing mark, install the timing belt.

6. Apply the tensioner pulley spring pressure to the timing belt.

7. Rotate the crankshaft 2 complete revolutions in the opposite direction of rotation and realign the timing marks.

8. Loosen the tensioner pulley bolt to allow the spring to adjust the correct tension. Torque the tensioner pulley bolt to 14 ft. lbs.

9. Install the timing covers and the crankshaft pulley.

10. To complete the installation, reverse the removal procedures.

Crankshaft Sprocket

1. Disconnect the negative battery cable.

2. Remove the timing belt.

3. Using a puller, press the sprocket from the crankshaft.

4. Remove and replace the crankshaft oil seal.

To install:

5. Align the crankshaft sprocket-to-oil seal retainer plate timing marks.

6. With the camshaft sprocket aligned with its timing mark, install the timing belt.

7. Apply the tensioner pulley spring pressure to the timing belt.

8. Rotate the crankshaft 2 complete revolutions in the opposite direction of rotation and realign the timing marks.

9. Loosen the tensioner pulley bolt to allow the spring to adjust the correct tension. Torque the tensioner pulley bolt to 14 ft. lbs.

10. Install the timing covers and the crankshaft pulley.

11. To complete the installation, reverse the removal procedures.

Camshaft

Removal and Installation

2.3L AND 2.6L ENGINES

1. Disconnect the negative battery cable.

2. Rotate the crankshaft to position the No. 4 cylinder on the TDC of its compression stroke.

3. Remove the distributor cap and move it aside. Matchmark the rotor to the distributor housing and the distributor housing to the engine. Remove the distributor.

4. Remove the rocker arm cover, the timing belt cover and the timing belt.

5. Remove the rocker arm assembly-to-cylinder head bolts, the rocker arm assembly and the camshaft. If necessary, remove the camshaft sprocket-to-camshaft bolt and the sprocket.

To install:

6. Lubricate the camshaft with engine oil and position it onto the cylinder head.

7. Install the rocker arm assembly and torque the bolts to bolts to 6 ft. lbs. (8 Nm) and the nuts to 16 ft. lbs. (22 Nm).

8. Align the timing marks and install the timing belt.

9. Using a new gasket, install the rocker arm cover.

10. Install the timing belt cover.

11. Align the matchmarks and install the distributor to the cylinder head.

12. To complete the installation, reverse the removal procedures.

13. Rotate the engine manually 2 times to check that there is no piston-to-valve interference. With the timing marks aligned, start the engine, then, check and/or adjust the engine timing.

2.8L AND 3.1L ENGINES

1. Relieve the fuel pressure. Disconnect the negative battery cable.

2. Drain the cooling system.

3. Remove the upper fan shroud and the radiator.

4. Disconnect the fuel line(s), the accelerator linkage, the vacuum hoses and electrical connectors from the throttle body unit.

5. Remove the rocker arm covers.

6. Loosen the valves, rotate them 90 degrees and remove the pushrods; be sure to keep them aligned so they may be installed in their original positions.

7. Remove the intake manifold. Using a hydraulic lifter removal tool, pull the valve lifters from the engine.

8. Remove the damper, front cover, timing chain and sprocket.

9. Using 3 long bolts, thread them into the camshaft holes. Grasp the bolts and carefully, pull the camshaft from the front of the engine.

NOTE: All the camshaft bearing journals are the same diameter; exercise care in removing the camshaft so the bearings do not become damaged.

10. Lubricate the camshaft with engine oil and install it into the engine.

11. Using a hydraulic lifter installation tool, install the hydraulic lifters into the engine.

12. Using new gaskets and sealant, install the intake manifold.

13. Install the pushrods and the rocker arms.

14. Install the camshaft sprocket, the timing chain and the front cover; be sure the timing marks are aligned.

15. Adjust the valves.

16. Using new gaskets, install the rocker arm covers.

17. To complete the installation, reverse the removal procedures. Refill the cooling system.

18. Start the engine and allow it to reach normal operating temperatures. Check and/or adjust the timing.

Piston and Connecting Rod

Positioning

Positioning of the piston and compression rings—2.3L and 2.6L engines

Positioning of the piston and compression rings—2.8L and 3.1L engines

ENGINE LUBRICATION

Oil Pan

Removal and Installation

2.3L AND 2.6L ENGINES

2WD Vehicles

1. Disconnect the negative battery cable.

2. Raise and safely support the vehicle.

3. Drain the engine oil. Remove the dipstick and the dipstick tube.

4. Remove the front splash shield, if equipped.

5. Remove the flywheel cover.

6. Disconnect the engine mount nuts and bolts. Raise the engine off the mounts to provide clearance for pan removal.

7. Remove the oil pan bolts and remove the oil pan.

8. Clean the gasket mounting surfaces.

9. Using a new gasket and sealant, install the oil pan. Torque the oil pan-to-engine bolts to 13 ft. lbs. (18 Nm).

10. To complete the installation, reverse the removal procedure. Torque the engine mount bolts to 41 ft. lbs. (55 Nm). Refill the crankcase.

4WD Vehicles—Upper Oil Pan

1. Disconnect the negative battery cable.

2. Raise and safely support the vehicle.

3. Drain the engine oil. Remove the dipstick and the dipstick tube.

4. Remove the front splash shield, if equipped.

5. Remove the flywheel cover.

6. Disconnect the engine mount nuts and bolts. Raise the engine off the mounts to provide clearance for pan removal.

7. Remove the oil pan bolts and remove the oil pan.

8. Clean the gasket mounting surfaces.

9. Using a new gasket and sealant, install the oil pan. Torque the oil pan-to-engine bolts to 13 ft. lbs. (18 Nm).

10. To complete the installation, reverse the removal procedure. Torque the engine mount bolts to 41 ft. lbs. (55 Nm). Refill the crankcase.

4WD Vehicles—Lower Oil Pan

1. Raise and safely support the vehicle.
2. Drain the crankcase.
3. Remove the lower oil pan-to-upper oil pan bolts and the lower pan.
4. Clean the gasket mounting surfaces.
5. Using a new gasket and sealant, install the lower oil pan and torque the bolts to 47–94 inch lbs.
6. Refill the crankcase.

2.8L AND 3.1L ENGINES

1. Disconnect the negative battery cable.
2. Remove the dipstick. Raise and safely support the vehicle. Drain the crankcase.
3. Remove the front skid plate and the crossmember.
4. Remove the exhaust pipe-to-catalytic converter bolts, the exhaust pipe-to-manifold bolts and the Y-exhaust pipe.
5. Remove the front driveshaft from the front differential.
6. Remove the braces from the flywheel cover.
7. Disconnect the electrical connectors from the starter. Remove the starter-to-engine bolts and the starter.
8. Remove the flywheel inspection cover.
9. Matchmark the pitman arm-to-pitman shaft for reassembly. Remove the pitman arm-to-pitman arm shaft nut and separate the pitman arm from the pitman shaft.
10. Remove the idler arm-to-shaft nut and separate the idler arm from the shaft.
11. Remove the rubber hose from the front axle vent and support the axle housing assembly.
12. Remove both bolts from the left axle housing isolator and the right axle housing isolator, then, lower the front axle housing assembly.
13. Remove the oil pan-to-engine bolts, the oil pan and discard the gasket.
14. Clean the gasket mounting surfaces.

To install:

15. Using a new gasket and sealant, install the oil pan. Torque both rear pan-to-engine bolts to 18 ft. lbs. (25 Nm) and the other bolts/nuts/studs to 7 ft. lbs. (10 Nm).
16. To complete the installation, reverse the removal procedures. Torque the following fasteners:

    Pitman arm-to-pitman shaft nut—159 ft. lbs. (215 Nm)
    Idler arm-to-shaft nut—86 ft. lbs. (117 Nm)
    Front drive axle shaft bolts—46 ft. lbs. (62 Nm)

17. Refill the crankcase. Connect the negative battery cable.
18. Start the engine and check for leaks.

Use sealant at the indicated points when installing the pan gasket—2.3L engine

Exploded view of the oil pan used with 4WD—2.3L and 2.6L engines—1988–90

A. Apply sealant here
35. Bolts
36. Bolts
37. Reinforcements
38. Nuts

Exploded view of the oil pan assembly—2.8L and 3.1L engines

Oil Pump

Removal and Installation

2.3L AND 2.6L ENGINES

The oil pump is attached to the front, lower right side of the engine and is driven by the timing belt.

1. Remove the upper and lower timing belt covers.
2. Remove the timing belt from the crankshaft and oil pump sprockets.
3. Remove the oil pump sprocket-to-oil pump nut and the sprocket from the oil pump.
4. Using a 6mm Allen wrench, remove the oil pump-to-engine bolts and the oil pump.

To install:

5. Using petroleum jelly, pack the oil pump.
6. Using a new O-ring, install the oil pump and torque the bolts to 10–17 ft. lbs. (13–23 Nm).
7. Install the sprocket to the oil pump and torque the nut to 48–62 ft. lbs.
8. Align the timing marks on the camshaft and crankshaft sprockets and install the timing belt.
9. To complete the installation, reverse the removal procedures.

2.8L AND 3.1L ENGINES

The oil pump is attached to the cylinder block and is located in the oil pan.

1. Disconnect the negative battery cable. Raise and safely support the vehicle.
2. Drain the crankcase. Remove the oil pan.
3. Remove the oil pump-to-engine bolts and the oil pump.

To install:

4. Align the oil pump shaft with the hexagon socket and install the pump. Torque the oil pump-to-engine bolts to 30 ft. lbs. (41 Nm).
5. Install the oil pan.
6. To complete the installation, reverse the removal procedures.
7. Connect the negative battery cable. Start the engine and check for leaks.

Checking

2.3L AND 2.6L ENGINES

1. Visually inspect the oil pump for wear, damage or other abnormal conditions.
2. Insert the oil pump vane into the cylinder block.
3. Place a straight-edge across the oil pump opening and a feeler gauge between the straight-edge and the vane; the clearance between the vane-to-cylinder block surface should be 0.002–0.004 in. (0.04–0.09mm), if not, replace the vane.
4. Using a feeler gauge, measure the side clearance between the cylinder block and the vane; it should be 0.009–0.0014 in. (0.24–0.36mm), if not, replace the vane.
5. Position the vane onto the rotor shaft.
6. Using a feeler gauge, measure the clearance between the rotor and the vane; it should be 0.005–0.006 in. (0.13–0.15mm), if not, replace the rotor and/or vane.

2.8L AND 3.1L ENGINES

1. Visually inspect the oil pump for wear, damage or other abnormal conditions.
2. Check that the regulator valve moves freely. Soak in solvent to free the piston, if stuck.
3. Lay a straight-edge across the body of the pump and the faces of the gears and measure the side lash with a feeler gauge between the straight-edge and the pump. The side lash should be 0.002–0.005 in. (0.05–0.13mm).

View of the oil pump—2.3L and 2.6L engines

Exploded view of the oil pump assembly—2.8L and 3.1L engines

A. Front
40. Bolt
41. Oil pump
42. Shaft

4. Check the gear lash between the body and the gear with a feeler gauge. The lash should be 0.009–0.105 in. (0.23–0.38mm).
5. Check the gear lash between the gears with a feeler gauge. The lash should be 0.003–0.004 in. (0.08–0.10mm).
6. Replace the pump if any of the measurements are out of specification.

Rear Main Bearing Oil Seal

Removal and Installation

1. Disconnect the negative battery cable. Raise and safely support the vehicle.
2. If equipped with an automatic transmission, remove the transmission. If equipped with a manual transmission, remove the transmission and clutch assembly.
3. Remove the starter without disconnecting the wires and secure it aside.
4. Remove the flywheel-to-crankshaft bolts and the flywheel.
5. Using a small prybar, carefully remove the oil seal work the tool around the diameter of the seal until the seal begins to lift out. Use care not to damage the seat and area around the seal.
6. Using a new oil seal, lubricate the seal lips with clean engine oil.
7. Using an oil seal installation tool, install the new oil seal.
8. To complete the installation, reverse the removal procedures.

TORQUE SPECIFICATIONS

Component	English	Metric
Camshaft sprocket bolt		
2.8L and 3.1L engines	17 ft. lbs.	23 Nm
2.3L and 2.6L engines	43 ft. lbs.	59 Nm
Connecting rod bearing cap bolts		
2.8L and 3.1L engines	39 ft. lbs.	53 Nm
2.3L and 2.6L engines	42–45 ft. lbs.	58–62 Nm
Crankshaft sprocket bolt		
2.3L and 2.6L engines	56 ft. lbs.	76 Nm
Crankshaft pulley bolt		
2.3L and 2.6L engines—1988–89	79–102 ft. lbs.	109–143 Nm
2.3L engine—1990–92	76–98 ft. lbs.	105–135 Nm
2.6L engine—1990–92	79–102 ft. lbs.	109–143 Nm
2.8L engine	70 ft. lbs.	94 Nm
3.1L engine	85 ft. lbs.	114 Nm
Cylinder Head bolt		
2.3L and 2.6L engines:		
Step 1:	58 ft. lbs.	78 Nm
Step 2:	72 ft. lbs.	97 Nm
2.8L and 3.1L engines:		
Step 1:	41 ft. lbs.	55 Nm
Step 2:	+90° turn	+90° turn
EGR valve-to-intake manifold		
2.8L and 3.1L engines	16 ft. lbs.	22 Nm
2.3L and 2.6L engines	6 ft. lbs.	8 Nm
Engine-to-transmission		
Manual transmission	27 ft. lbs.	37 Nm
Automatic transmission	47 ft. lbs.	65 Nm
Exhaust Manifold		
2.3L and 2.6L engines	14–18 ft. lbs.	19–25 Nm
2.8L engine	25 ft. lbs.	36 Nm
3.1L engine	19 ft. lbs.	26 Nm
Exhaust pipe-to-exhaust manifold nuts	49 ft. lbs.	67 Nm
Flywheel/flexplate-to-crankshaft bolts		
2.8L and 3.1L engines	52 ft. lbs.	70 Nm
2.3L and 2.6L engines	40–47 ft. lbs.	55–63 Nm
Flexplate-to-converter bolts	21 ft. lbs.	30 Nm
Intake Manifold		
2.3L and 2.6L engines	14–18 ft. lbs.	19–25 Nm
2.8L engine	23 ft. lbs.	34 Nm
3.1L engine	19 ft. lbs.	26 Nm
Main bearing cap bolts		
2.3L and 2.6L engines	65–80 ft. lbs.	87–107 Nm
2.8L engine	70 ft. lbs.	94 Nm
3.1L engine	72 ft. lbs.	96 Nm
Oil Pan		
2.3L and 2.6L engines	4 ft. lbs.	5 Nm
2.8L and 3.1L engines		
Rear bolts:	18 ft. lbs.	25 Nm
Others:	7 ft. lbs.	10 Nm
Oil pan drain plug	58 ft. lbs.	73 Nm
Oil pump attaching bolts		
2.3L and 2.6L engines	10–17 ft. lbs.	13–23 Nm
2.8L and 3.1L engines	30 ft. lbs.	41 Nm
Rocker (Valve) Cover		
2.3L and 2.6L engines	7 ft. lbs.	10 Nm
2.8L and 3.1L engines	6 ft. lbs.	8 Nm

TORQUE SPECIFICATIONS

Component	English	Metric
Spark plug		
2.3L and 2.6L engines	10–17 ft. lbs.	13–23 Nm
2.8L engine	22 ft. lbs.	30 Nm
3.1L engine	25 ft. lbs.	34 Nm
Starter-to-block bolts		
2.3L and 2.6L engines	63 ft. lbs.	86 Nm
2.8L and 3.1L engines	30 ft. lbs.	40 Nm
Thermostat housing		
2.3L and 2.6L engines	14 ft. lbs.	19 Nm
2.8L and 3.1L engines	21 ft. lbs.	28 Nm
Timing cover		
2.3L and 2.6L engines	4 ft. lbs.	6 Nm
2.8L and 3.1L engines	20 ft. lbs.	27 Nm
Throttle body-to-intake manifold		
TBI	18 ft. lbs.	25 Nm
MPI	14 ft. lbs.	19 Nm
Water Pump		
2.3L and 2.6L engines	14 ft. lbs.	19 Nm
2.8L and 3.1L engines	22 ft. lbs.	33 Nm
Water pump pulley		
2.3L and 2.6L engines	6 ft. lbs.	8 Nm
2.8L and 3.1L engines	17 ft. lbs.	23 Nm

MANUAL TRANSMISSION

For further information, please refer to Chilton's Transmission Service Manual.

Transmission Assembly

Removal and Installation

2WD VEHICLES

1. Disconnect the negative battery cable.
2. Remove the undercover, if equipped.
3. Remove the air cleaner for 2.3L, 2.8L and 3.1L engines or air cleaner duct and hose for 2.6L engine. Using a clean shop cloth, cover the air cleaner port to prevent dirt from entering the engine.
4. Label and disconnect the necessary hoses and electrical connectors.
5. Remove the clutch return spring, the clutch control cable, the backup light switch connector and the speedometer cable from the transmission.
6. Remove the gear shift lever by performing the following procedures:
   a. Place the gear shift lever in **N**.
   b. Remove the front console from the floor panel.
   c. Pull the shift lever boot and grommet upward.
   d. Remove the shift lever cover bolts and the shift lever.
7. Raise and safely support the vehicle. Remove the front wheels.
8. Drain the transmission fluid.
9. If equipped with a 1-piece driveshaft, remove the driveshaft flange-to-pinion nuts, lower the driveshaft and pull it from the transmission.
10. If equipped with a 2-piece driveshaft, perform the following procedures:
   a. Remove the rear driveshaft flange-to-pinion nuts.

   b. Remove the rear driveshaft flange-to-front driveshaft flange bolts and the rear driveshaft.
   c. Remove the center bearing-to-chassis bolts, move the front driveshaft rearward and from the transmission.
11. Remove the starter-to-engine bolts and the starter.
12. Remove the exhaust pipe-to-exhaust manifold nuts, the exhaust pipe bracket-to-transmission bolts, the front exhaust pipe-to-2nd exhaust pipe bolts and the front exhaust pipe from the vehicle.
13. Attach an engine hanger to the rear of the exhaust manifold.
14. Using an engine hoist, connect it to the engine hangers and support the engine.
15. Using a transmission jack, place it under the transmission; do not support it.
16. Remove the rear mount-to-transmission nuts.
17. Remove the rear mount-to-crossmember nuts/bolts and the mount.

NOTE: Further removal of the transmission may require an assistant.

18. Remove the clutch cover and the transmission-to-engine bolts.
19. Move the transmission rearward into the crossmember and floor pan area; the transmission may rest on the crossmember.
20. Lower the front of the transmission toward the jack.
21. Firmly, grasp the transmission the rear cover while the assistant raises the jack toward the transmission.
22. Carefully, lower the transmission onto the jack and center it.
23. Lower the jack and move the transmission rearward.

To install:

   NOTE: Installation of the transmission may require an assistant.

24. Raise the transmission into position.

25. Raise the rear of the transmission and move it into position on the crossmember.

26. Move the transmission forward and engage it with the engine.

27. Install the engine-to-transmission bolts.

28. Install the mount and the rear mount-to-crossmember nuts/bolts.

29. Install the rear mount-to-transmission nuts.

30. Remove the engine hoist and the engine hanger from the rear of the exhaust manifold.

31. Install the front exhaust pipe, exhaust pipe-to-exhaust manifold nuts, the exhaust pipe bracket-to-transmission bolts, the front exhaust pipe-to-2nd exhaust pipe bolts.

32. Install the starter and the starter-to-engine bolts.

33. If equipped with a 2-piece driveshaft, perform the following procedures:

   a. Install the front driveshaft into the transmission and the center bearing-to-chassis bolts.

   b. Install the rear driveshaft and the rear driveshaft flange-to-front driveshaft flange bolts.

   c. Install the rear driveshaft flange-to-pinion nuts.

34. If equipped with a 1-piece driveshaft, install the driveshaft into the transmission and the driveshaft flange-to-pinion nuts.

35. Install the front wheels and lower the vehicle.

36. Install the gear shift lever by performing the following procedures:

   a. Install the shift lever and the shift lever cover bolts.

   b. Push the grommet and shift lever boot downward.

   c. Install the front console to the floor panel.

37. Install the clutch return spring, the clutch control cable, the backup light switch connector and the speedometer cable to the transmission.

38. Connect the necessary hoses and electrical connectors.

39. Install the air cleaner for 2.3L, 2.8L and 3.1L engines or air cleaner duct and hose for 2.6L engine.

40. Refill the transmission. Install the undercover, if equipped.

41. Connect the negative battery cable.

4WD VEHICLES

1. Disconnect the negative battery cable.

2. Remove the undercover, if equipped.

3. Remove the air cleaner for 2.3L, 2.8L and 3.1L engines or air cleaner duct and hose for 2.6L engine. Using a clean shop cloth, cover the air cleaner port to prevent dirt from entering the engine.

4. Label and disconnect the necessary hoses and electrical connectors.

5. Remove the clutch return spring, the clutch control cable, the backup light switch connector and the speedometer cable from the transmission.

6. Remove the gear shift lever by performing the following procedures:

   a. Place the gear shift lever in **N**.

   b. Remove the front console from the floor panel.

   c. Pull the shift lever boot and grommet upward.

   d. Remove the shift lever cover bolts and the shift lever.

7. Remove the transfer shift lever by performing the following procedures:

   a. Place the transfer shift lever in **H** for 2.3L and 2.6L engines or **2H** for 2.8L and 3.1L engines.

   b. Pull the shift lever boot and dust cover upward.

   c. Remove the shift lever retaining bolts.

   d. Pull the shift lever from the transfer case.

8. Raise and safely support the vehicle. Remove the front wheels.

9. Drain the transmission and transfer case fluid.

10. If equipped with a 1-piece driveshaft, remove the driveshaft flange-to-pinion nuts, lower the driveshaft and pull it from the transmission.

11. If equipped with a 2-piece driveshaft, perform the following procedures:

   a. Remove the rear driveshaft flange-to-pinion nuts.

   b. Remove the rear driveshaft flange-to-front driveshaft flange bolts and the rear driveshaft.

   c. Remove the center bearing-to-chassis bolts, move the front driveshaft rearward and from the transmission.

12. Remove the front driveshaft's splined yoke flange-to-transfer case bolts and separate the front driveshaft from the transfer case; do not allow the splined flange to fall away from the driveshaft.

13. Remove the starter-to-engine bolts and the starter.

14. If equipped with a clutch slave cylinder, remove it from the transmission and move it aside.

15. Remove the exhaust pipe-to-exhaust manifold nuts, the exhaust pipe bracket-to-transmission bolts, the front exhaust pipe-to-2nd exhaust pipe bolts and the front exhaust pipe from the vehicle.

16. Attach an engine hanger to the rear of the exhaust manifold.

17. Using an engine hoist, connect it to the engine hangers and support the engine.

18. If equipped with a 2.8L or 3.1L engine, remove the catalytic converter and the parking brake cable bracket.

19. Using a transmission jack, place it under the transmission and support the assembly.

20. Remove the rear mount-to-transmission nuts.

21. Remove the rear mount-to-side mount member nuts/bolts and the mount.

22. Remove the transmission-to-engine bolts.

23. Move the transmission assembly rearward.

24. Carefully lower the transmission.

To install:

25. Raise the transmission into position.

26. Move the transmission forward and engage it with the engine.

27. Install the engine-to-transmission bolts.

28. Install the rear mount and the rear mount-to-side mount member nuts/bolts.

29. Install the rear mount-to-transmission nuts.

30. Remove the transmission jack.

31. If equipped with a 2.8L or 3.1L engine, install the catalytic converter and the parking brake cable bracket.

32. Remove the engine hoist and the engine hanger from the rear of the exhaust manifold.

33. Install the front exhaust pipe, exhaust pipe-to-exhaust manifold nuts, the exhaust pipe bracket-to-transmission bolts, the front exhaust pipe-to-2nd exhaust pipe bolts.

34. If equipped with a clutch slave cylinder, install it onto the transmission.

35. Install the starter and the starter-to-engine bolts.

36. Install the front driveshaft's splined yoke flange-to-transfer case bolts.

37. If equipped with a 2-piece driveshaft, perform the following procedures:

   a. Install the front driveshaft into the transmission and the center bearing-to-chassis bolts.

   b. Install the rear driveshaft and the rear driveshaft flange-to-front driveshaft flange bolts.

   c. Install the rear driveshaft flange-to-pinion nuts.

38. If equipped with a 1-piece driveshaft, install the driveshaft into the transmission and the driveshaft flange-to-pinion nuts.

39. Install the front wheels and lower the vehicle.

40. Install the transfer shift lever by performing the following procedures:

   a. Position the shift lever into the transfer case.

b. Install the shift lever retaining bolts.

c. Push the dust cover and the shift lever boot downward.

41. Install the gear shift lever by performing the following procedures:

a. Install the shift lever and the shift lever cover bolts.

b. Push the grommet and shift lever boot downward.

c. Install the front console to the floor panel.

42. Install the clutch return spring, the clutch control cable, the backup light switch connector and the speedometer cable to the transmission.

43. Connect the necessary hoses and electrical connectors.

44. Install the air cleaner for 2.3L, 2.8L and 3.1L engines or air cleaner duct and hose for 2.6L engine.

45. Refill the transmission and the transfer case. Install the undercover, if equipped.

46. Install the negative battery cable.

Linkage Adjustment

No adjustments are possible on the transmission or transfer case linkage.

CLUTCH

Clutch Assembly

Removal and Installation

1. Raise and support the vehicle safely.

2. On 2WD vehicles, remove the transmission. On 4WD models, remove the transmission and transfer case as an assembly.

3. Matchmark the clutch assembly to the flywheel so the clutch assembly can be reassembled in the same position. Lock the flywheel in place to prevent it from turning.

4. Loosen the pressure plate-to-flywheel bolts, 1 turn at a time in an alternating sequence, until the spring tension is relieved to avoid distorting or bending the pressure plate.

5. Using a clutch alignment tool, support the pressure plate and cover assembly and remove the bolts and clutch assembly.

To install:

6. Apply a thin coat of grease to the pressure plate fingers, diaphragm spring, clutch cover grooves and the drive bosses on the pressure plate.

7. Apply a thin coat of lubricant to the splines in the clutch disc.

8. Using a clutch alignment tool, assemble the clutch disc and pressure plate onto the flywheel.

9. Align the matchmarks and install the pressure plate-to-flywheel bolts and torque the bolts to 12–14 ft. lbs. (16–19 Nm) using a star pattern tightening sequence. Remove the aligning tool.

10. On 2WD vehicles, install the transmission. On 4WD models, install the transmission and transfer case as an assembly.

1. Bolt
2. Pressure plate assembly
3. Clutch disc
4. Spring
5. Shift collar with bearing
6. Clutch shift fork assembly
7. Flywheel bolt
8. Flywheel washer
9. Flywheel assembly
10. Crankshaft ball bearing

Exploded view of the clutch assembly

11. To complete the installation, reverse the removal procedures. Adjust the clutch cable linkage, if equipped.

Pedal Height Adjustment

The clutch pedal height is the distance from the center of the clutch pedal pad to the firewall.

1. Locate the clutch switch (with cruise control) or clutch pedal stop bolt (without cruise control) at the top of the clutch pedal under the dash.

2. Loosen the clutch switch or stop bolt as equipped. Loosen the clutch master cylinder pushrod yoke nut.

3. Adjust the clutch master cylinder pushrod to obtain a clutch pedal height of 6.7–7.1 in. (171–181mm) for Rodeo with 2.6L engine, 7.6–8.0 in. (192–202mm) for Rodeo with 3.1L en-

gine or 9.15–9.55 in. (232–242mm) for Trooper/Trooper II, Pick-Up and Amigo.

4. After adjusting the pedal height, tighten the pushrod yoke nut. Screw in the clutch switch until the plunger is fully depressed and then unscrew 1 full turn and tighten the locknut. Tighten the pedal stop bolt so it just touches the pedal and tighten the locknut.

Clutch Cable

Removal and Installation

1. Loosen the clutch cable lock and adjusting nuts. Remove the clutch cable clip in the engine compartment.

2. Raise and safely support the vehicle. Remove the spring from the shift fork end.

3. Disconnect the cable end from the shift fork and pull the cable assembly through the bracket.

4. Lower the vehicle enough to disengage the hooked part of the clutch pedal from the cable eye. Pull the cable assembly towards the engine compartment and remove the cable from the vehicle.

5. To install, reverse the removal procedures. Adjust the cable when finished.

Adjustment

1. Pull the outer cable, located under the hood, forward as far as possible and secure it.

2. Turn the adjusting nut inward it touches the damper rubber washer, located at the firewall.

3. Depress and release the clutch pedal 3 times.

4. Tighten the adjusting nut again.

FLOOR PANEL

Measuring the clutch pedal height

1. Clutch cable lock and adjusting nuts
2. Clutch cable clip
3. Return spring from shift fork end
4. Assist spring
5. Clutch damper
6. Clutch control cable
7. Clutch pedal

Exploded view of the clutch cable assembly

VEHICLE FRONT
⟵

0.2 IN. (5MM)

View of the clutch cable adjustment

5. Pull the outer cable forward again and fully tighten the adjusting nut.

6. Loosen the nut to provide a ⅛ in. clearance between the adjusting nut and the damper washer.

7. Release the outer cable and tighten the locknut to secure the adjusting nut.

Clutch Master Cylinder

The clutch master cylinder is located on the firewall inside the engine compartment.

Removal and Installation

1. Disconnect the negative battery cable. Remove the hydraulic line from the clutch master cylinder.

2. Disconnect the master cylinder pushrod from the clutch pedal.

3. Remove the master cylinder-to-firewall nuts and remove the master cylinder.

4. To install, reverse the removal procedures. Torque the master cylinder-to-firewall nuts to 8–15 ft. lbs. (12–20 Nm).

5. On master cylinders that use a banjo fitting, use new washers and torque the hydraulic line-to-master cylinder bolt to 22–29 ft. lbs. (30–39 Nm).

6. On master cylinders that use a flare fitting, torque the flare nut to 14.5 ft. lbs. (20 Nm).

7. Bleed the hydraulic clutch system.

Clutch Slave Cylinder

The clutch slave cylinder is attached to the bell housing.

Removal and Installation

1. Disconnect the negative battery cable. Remove the hydraulic line from the clutch slave cylinder.

2. Remove the slave cylinder-to-bell housing bolts and remove the slave cylinder.

3. To install, reverse the removal procedures.

4. On cylinders with flare fittings, torque the hydraulic line-to-slave cylinder fitting to 11–17 ft. lbs. (16–25 Nm).

5. On cylinders with banjo fittings, use new washers and torque the hydraulic line-to-slave cylinder fitting to 25 ft. lbs. (35 Nm).

6. Bleed the hydraulic clutch system.

1. Pin
2. Jaw joint pin
3. Pedal assembly
4. Oil line
5. Master cylinder
   assembly
6. Oil line
7. Slave cylinder assembly

Exploded view of the hydraulic system

Clutch Damper Cylinder

Removal and Installation

6 CYLINDER VEHICLES

1. Locate the clutch hydraulic damper in the clutch hydraulic line to the slave cylinder.
2. Disconnect the hydraulic fitting from the damper body.
3. Unbolt the damper from the mounting position bracket.
4. Remove the damper and cap the hydraulic lines to prevent dirt and moisture from contaminating the system.
5. Installation is the reverse of removal. Bleed the hydraulic system.

Bleeding the Hydraulic Clutch System

1. Firmly, set the parking brake.

2. Check the reservoir fluid level and refill, if necessary.
3. Bleed the damper cylinder first, if equipped, then the slave cylinder. The bleeding procedure, as outlined in steps 4 through 9, is the same for both the slave cylinder and the damper cylinder.
4. Using a vinyl tube, connect it to the bleeder screw and submerge the other end in a transparent container of brake fluid.
5. Have an assistant pump the clutch pedal several times and hold it.
6. Loosen the bleeder screw and allow the air bubble fluid to flow into the container, then, tighten the bleeder screw.
7. Release the clutch pedal.
8. Repeat this operation until the fluid is clear of air bubbles.
9. Refill the reservoir. Remove the vinyl tube and replace the rubber cap on the bleeder screw.

AUTOMATIC TRANSMISSION

For further information, please refer to Chilton's Transmission Service Manual.

Transmission Assembly

Removal and Installation

2WD VEHICLES

1. Disconnect the negative battery cable. Raise and safely support the vehicle.
2. Remove the undercover, if equipped.
3. Drain the transmission fluid from the oil pan.
4. Remove the throttle cable at the engine end. Remove the transmission dipstick.
5. Unbolt the starter and place it aside in a safe location. Support the starter so it does not strain the electrical connections.
6. If equipped with a 1-piece driveshaft, remove the driveshaft flange-to-pinion nuts, lower the driveshaft and pull it from the transmission.
7. If equipped with a 2-piece driveshaft, perform the following procedures:
    a. Remove the rear driveshaft flange-to-pinion nuts.
    b. Remove the rear driveshaft flange-to-front driveshaft flange bolts and the rear driveshaft.
    c. Remove the center bearing-to-chassis bolts, move the front driveshaft rearward and from the transmission.
8. Disconnect the shift lever at the shifter end.
9. Disconnect the speedometer cable.
10. Disconnect the oil cooler lines and place the cooler bypass line close to the transmission case to prevent damage during transmission removal.
11. Remove the torque converter-to-flexplate bolts through the starter hole.
12. Using a transmission jack, place it under the transmission and raise it slightly.
13. Remove the rear mount-to-transmission nuts.
14. Remove the rear mount-to-crossmember nuts/bolts and the mount.
15. Remove the transmission-to-engine bolts.
16. Move the transmission back and lower the transmission out of the vehicle.

To install:

NOTE: Installation of the transmission will require an assistant.

17. Raise the transmission into position.
18. Raise the rear of the transmission and move it into position on the crossmember.

19. Move the transmission forward and engage it with the engine.
20. Install the engine-to-transmission bolts and torque to 47 ft. lbs. (64 Nm).
21. Install the mount and the rear mount-to-crossmember nuts/bolts.
22. Install the rear mount-to-transmission nuts.
23. Install the torque converter-to-flexplate bolts through the starter hole and torque to 22 ft. lbs. (30 Nm).
24. Connect the oil cooler lines, speedometer cable and shift linkage.
25. If equipped with a 2-piece driveshaft, perform the following procedures:
    a. Install the front driveshaft into the transmission and the center bearing-to-chassis bolts.
    b. Install the rear driveshaft and the rear driveshaft flange-to-front driveshaft flange bolts.
    c. Install the rear driveshaft flange-to-pinion nuts.
26. If equipped with a 1-piece driveshaft, install the driveshaft into the transmission and the driveshaft flange-to-pinion nuts.
27. Install the starter.
28. Connect the downshift cable to the transmission.
29. Install the oil level dipstick and the tube.
30. Refill the transmission. Install the undercover, if equipped.
31. Connect the negative battery cable.
32. Start the engine, check for leaks.

4WD VEHICLES

Trooper/Trooper II

1. Disconnect the negative battery cable. Raise and safely support the vehicle.
2. Remove the undercover, if equipped.
3. Drain the transmission fluid from the oil pan.
4. Remove the throttle cable at the engine end. Remove the transmission dipstick.
5. Unbolt the starter and place it aside in a safe location. Support the starter so it does not strain the electrical connections.
6. Remove the front driveshaft.
7. To remove the 1-piece rear driveshaft, remove the driveshaft flange-to-pinion nuts and driveshaft-to-output flange bolts, lower the driveshaft.
8. Disconnect the shift lever at the shifter end.
9. Disconnect the speedometer cable.
10. Disconnect the oil cooler lines and place the cooler bypass line close to the transmission case to prevent damage during transmission removal.

11. Remove the torque converter-to-flexplate bolts through the starter hole.

12. Using a transmission jack, place it under the transmission and raise it slightly.

13. Remove the rear mount-to-transmission nuts.

14. Remove the rear mount-to-crossmember nuts/bolts and the mount.

15. Remove the transmission-to-engine bolts.

16. Move the transmission back and lower the transmission out of the vehicle.

To install:

NOTE: **Installation of the transmission will require an assistant.**

17. Raise the transmission into position.

18. Raise the rear of the transmission and move it into position on the crossmember.

19. Move the transmission forward and engage it with the engine.

20. Install the engine-to-transmission bolts and torque to 47 ft. lbs. (64 Nm).

21. Install the mount and the rear mount-to-crossmember nuts/bolts.

22. Install the rear mount-to-transmission nuts.

23. Install the torque converter-to-flexplate bolts through the starter hole and torque to 22 ft. lbs. (30 Nm).

24. Connect the oil cooler lines, speedometer cable and shift linkage.

25. Install the front driveshaft.

26. Install the rear driveshaft.

27. Install the starter.

28. Connect the downshift cable to the transmission.

29. Install the oil level dipstick and the tube.

30. Refill the transmission. Install the undercover, if equipped.

31. Connect the negative battery cable.

32. Start the engine, check for leaks.

Rodeo

1. Disconnect both battery cables.

2. Remove the center console housing. Remove the transfer case control lever.

3. Disconnect the transmission shifter control linkage.

4. Remove the undercover to expose the transmission housing.

5. Remove the rear driveshaft and the front driveshaft.

6. Disconnect the parking brake cable from the relay link.

7. Disconnect the speedometer cable from the transmission housing.

8. Remove the left side exhaust pipe.

9. Remove the transmission oil cooler lines.

10. Remove the starter motor and place off to the side.

11. Remove the mode switch from the side of the transmission.

12. Remove the breather hose, dipstick, flywheel cover and the torque converter bolts.

13. Remove the rear crossmember and the exhaust Y-assembly.

14. Number the transmission mounting bolts as they are removed and note the position from which they came. The bolts are of different lengths and this will ease reassembly.

15. Using a transmission jack, remove the transmission assembly.

To install:

16. Install the transmission assembly and replace the mounting bolts into their original locations. Torque the bolts to 55 ft. lbs. (75 Nm).

17. Install the dipstick, exhaust pipe Y-assembly and crossmember.

18. Install the torque converter bolts and torque to 40 ft. lbs. (54 Nm).

19. Install the flywheel cover and torque the M6 bolts to 6 ft. lbs. (8 Nm) and the M10 bolts to 25 ft. lbs. (34 Nm).

20. Install the breather hose.

21. Install the mode selector switch. Place the lever in the **N** position and install the switch on the transmission body. Align the slots on the support and back. Insert a 0.09 in. (2.34mm) pin into the ports and torque the mounting bolts to 104 inch lbs. (12 Nm). Remove the pin before moving the lever.

22. Install the starter motor and torque the mounting bolts to 30 ft. lbs. (40 Nm).

23. Install the oil cooler lines and torque the fittings to 33 ft. lbs. (44 Nm).

24. Install the left front exhaust pipe, the speedometer cable, the parking brake cable and the driveshafts.

Adjusting the automatic transmission shift linkage

THROTTLE
ADJUSTING SCREW

Location the throttle adjusting screw—1988 engine

0.032–0.059 IN. (0.8–1.5MM)   BOOT

INNER CABLE STOPPER

WHEN THROTTLE VALVE IS FULLY
CLOSED

View of the throttle cable adjustment—1988 engine

25. Install the undercover, the shift linkage, the transfer control linkage and the center console.

26. Connect the battery cables and refill the transmission. Check for proper operation.

Shift Linkage Adjustment

1. Loosen the shift linkage adjusting nut.
2. Push the shift lever fully rearward.
3. Return the shift lever 2 notches to the **N** position.
4. While holding the selector lever lightly toward the **R** range side, tighten the shift linkage nut.

Throttle Linkage Adjustment

1. Depress the accelerator pedal all the way and check that the throttle valve opens fully.

NOTE: If the valve does not open fully, adjust the accelerator link.

2. Fully depress the accelerator.
3. Loosen the adjustment nuts.
4. Adjust the cable housing so the distance between the end of the boot and stopper on the cable is the 0.03–0.06 in. (0.8–1.5mm).
5. Tighten the adjusting nuts.
6. Recheck the adjustment.

THROTTLE VALVE FULLY OPENED

Stroke 32.9$^{+1}_{0}$

0.8 — 1.5

View of the throttle cable adjustment — 1988–90 gasoline engine

TRANSFER CASE

Transfer Case Assembly

Removal and Installation

The transfer case is an integral part of the transmission housing. Although the 2 cases can be separated, the transfer case should be removed with the transmission. The transfer case linkage is not adjustable.

DRIVE AXLE

Driveshaft and U-Joints

Removal and Installation

2WD DRIVESHAFT

1. Raise and support the vehicle safely.
2. Matchmark the driveshaft to the yokes.
3. Remove the driveshaft flange retaining bolts and remove the driveshaft.
4. To install, reverse the removal procedures. Torque the bolts 46 ft. lbs. (63 Nm).

4WD DRIVESHAFT

Rear

1. Raise and safely support the vehicle.
2. Matchmark the driveshaft flange-to-differential pinion flange.
3. If equipped with a 1-piece driveshaft, remove the driveshaft flange-to-pinion nuts, lower the driveshaft and pull it from the transmission.
4. If equipped with a 2-piece driveshaft, perform the following procedures:
    a. Remove the rear driveshaft flange-to-pinion nuts.
    b. Remove the rear driveshaft flange-to-front driveshaft flange bolts and the rear driveshaft.

    c. Remove the center bearing-to-chassis bolts, move the front driveshaft rearward and from the transmission.

To install:

5. If equipped with a 2-piece driveshaft, perform the following procedures:
    a. Install the front driveshaft into the transmission and the center bearing-to-chassis bolts.
    b. Install the rear driveshaft and the rear driveshaft flange-to-front driveshaft flange bolts.
    c. Install the rear driveshaft flange-to-pinion nuts.
6. If equipped with a 1-piece driveshaft, install the driveshaft into the transmission and the driveshaft flange-to-pinion nuts.
7. To complete the installation, reverse the removal procedures. Torque the retaining bolts to 46 ft. lbs. (63 Nm).

Front

1. Raise and safely support the vehicle.
2. Matchmark the driveshaft flange-to-transfer case flange and the driveshaft-to-differential pinion flange.
3. Remove the front driveshaft's splined yoke flange-to-transfer case bolts and separate the front driveshaft from the transfer case; do not allow the splined flange to fall away from the driveshaft.
4. Remove the driveshaft flange-to-differential pinion flange bolts and separate the driveshaft from the front differential.

1. Differential side bolt
2. Flange bolt
3. 2nd propeller shaft assembly
4. Center bearing bracket bolt
5. 1st propeller shaft assembly

Exploded view of the rear driveshaft assembly

SPLINED YOKE   FRONT PROPELLER SHAFT

TRANSFER SIDE   SETTING MARK

View of the front driveshaft—4WD

5. To install, align the matchmarks and reverse the removal procedures. Torque the retaining bolts to 46 ft. lbs. (63 Nm).

U-JOINTS

1. Raise and support the vehicle safely. Remove the driveshaft.

2. If the front yoke is to be disassembled, matchmark the driveshaft and sliding splined yoke so driveline balance is preserved upon reassembly. Remove the snaprings that retain the bearing caps.

3. Select 2 press components, with 1 small enough to pass through the yoke holes for the bearing caps and the other large enough to receive the bearing cap.

4. Use a vise or a press and position the small and large press components on either side of the U-joint. Press in on the smaller press component so it presses the opposite bearing cap out of the yoke and into the larger press component. If the cap does not come all the way out, grasp it with a pair of pliers and work it out.

5. Reverse the position of the press components so the smaller press component presses on the cross. Press the other bearing cap out of the yoke.

6. Repeat the procedure on the other bearings.

7. To install, grease the bearing caps and needles thoroughly if they are not pregreased. Start a new bearing cap into a side of the yoke. Position the cross in the yoke.

NOTE: Some U-joints have a grease fitting that must be installed in the joint before assembly. When installing the fitting, make sure once the driveshaft is installed in the vehicle that the fitting is accessible to be greased at a later date.

8. Select 2 press components small enough to pass through the yoke holes. Put the press components against the cross and the cap and press the bearing cap ¼ in. below the surface of the yoke. If there is a sudden increase in the force needed to press the cap into place or if the cross starts to bind, the bearings are cocked. They must be removed and restarted in the yoke. Failure to do so will cause premature bearing failure.

9. Install a new snapring.

10. Start the new bearing into the opposite side. Place a press component on it and press in until the opposite bearing contacts the snapring.

11. Install a new snapring.

12. Install the other bearings in the same manner.

13. Check the joint for free movement. If binding exists, smack the yoke ears with a brass or plastic faced hammer to seat the bearing needles. If binding still exists, disassemble the joint and check to see if the needles are in place. Do not strike the bearings unless the shaft is supported firmly. Do not install the driveshaft until free movement exists at all joints.

1. Assembly of hub and disc, back plate, knuckle, knuckle arm and lower end
2. Propeller shaft
3. Nut and bolt
4. Washer
5. Front drive axle assembly
6. Washer

Exploded view of the front axle assembly—4WD

Front Axle Shaft, Bearing and Seal

Removal and Installation

AXLE SHAFT

1. Raise and safely support the vehicle.
2. Disconnect the front driveshaft from the differential.
3. Remove the wheels and skid plate.
4. Loosen the torsion bar completely with the height control adjusting bolts.
5. Remove the strut bars.
6. Disconnect the stabilizer bars from the lower control arms.
7. Remove the caliper assemblies and wire them to the frame; do not disconnect the brake lines.
8. Remove the ball joints from the tie rods.
9. Disconnect the upper control arms from the frame; make sure to note the number and positions of the shims.
10. Remove the steering link ends from the lower control arms.

11. Disconnect the shock absorbers from the lower control arms.
12. Disconnect the lower control arms from the frame.
13. Remove the locking hub.
14. Remove the rotors and upper links.
15. Remove the pitman arm and idler arm along with the steering linkage assembly.
16. Support the differential housing and lower it clear of the vehicle. Take care to avoid damaging the Birfield joints.
17. Drain the differential case and remove the 4 bolts attaching the axle mounting bracket to the case.
18. Pull the shaft assemblies from the case on both sides.
19. To install, reverse the removal procedures. Torque the axle mounting nuts to 112 ft. lbs. (152 Nm).
20. Check the level of the axle lubricant and bleed the brake system when finished.

AXLE SHAFT SEAL

1. Raise and safely support the vehicle. Remove the wheel assembly.

2. Remove the axle from the housing.

3. Remove the seal from the housing.

4. Clean and inspect the sealing surfaces of the housing and axle.

5. Using a seal installer tool, drive the new seal into the housing with the lip of the seal facing the housing.

6. Lightly coat the lip of the seal with oil and install the axle in the housing.

7. To complete the installation, reverse the removal procedures.

8. Check the level of the axle lubricant when finished.

AXLE SHAFT BEARINGS

1. Raise and safely support the vehicle.

2. Remove the axle shaft from the housing.

3. Support the axle shaft and remove the bearing retainer locknut and washer.

4. Remove the retainer, bearing and seal from the axle shaft.

5. To install, reverse the removal procedures.

6. Always replace the seal and lock washer when removing the axle shaft from the housing. Torque the bearing retainer nut to 188–195 ft. lbs.

WHEEL BEARINGS

1. Place the transfer case in **2H**. Raise and safely support the vehicle.

2. Remove the free wheeling hub cover assembly. Remove the brake caliper and hang aside.

3. Using wrench J-36827 or equivalent, remove the hub nut.

4. Remove the hub and disk assembly.

5. Remove the outer roller bearing assembly from the hub with a finger.

6. Using a brass or wood drift, drive out the inner bearing assembly along with the oil seal. Replace the seal.

7. Wash all parts in a non-flammable solvent.

8. Check all parts for cracks or wear. Thoroughly lubricate all bearing parts with a high-temperature wheel bearing grease. Remove any excess. Apply about 2 ounces of the grease to the hub.

To install:

9. Lightly coat the spindle with the same grease.

10. Place the inner bearing into the hub race and install a new seal and retaining ring.

11. Carefully install the hub on the spindle and install the outer bearing.

12. Install the spindle nut.

13. While rotating the hub, tighten the hub so the wheel can just be turned by hand.

14. Turn the hub 2–3 turns and back off the nut just enough so it can be loosened with the fingers.

15. Finger-tighten the nut so all play is taken up at the bearing.

16. Attach a pull scale to a lug nut and check the amount of pull needed to start the wheel turning. Initial pull should be 2.6–4.0 lbs. When performing this test, make sure the brake pads are not touching the rotor. If the rotating torque is not correct, tighten the spindle nut until it is.

17. Install the lockwasher so the bolt holes align. If the bolt holes do not align, reverse the position of the lock washer. The bolt head should be able to sink below the surface of the washer when tightened.

18. Clean the hub flange surface and areas surrounding the spindle and with the transfer case lever in the **2H** position, install the inner cam with the gear teeth facing out.

19. Lower the vehicle and install tools J-36835-2 and J-36836 or equivalent, on the axle shaft until it comes in contact with the lock washer.

20. Measure the gap between the tool and the snapring tool and select shims to reduce the gap to 0.00–0.10mm. Remove the tool.

21. Apply grease to the hub splines and lubrication grooves.

Install the drive clutch assembly. The cut portion of the drive clutch must be aligned with the concave part of the inner cam. Match the teeth of the cam to the inner cam by turning the axle shaft.

22. Install the snapring and previously selected shims, gasket and cover. Apply Loctite® 515 or equivalent, and torque the cover bolts to 43 ft. lbs. (59 Nm).

Rear Axle Shaft, Bearing and Seal

Removal and Installation

AXLE SHAFT

1. Raise and safely support the vehicle.

2. Remove the rear wheel assembly and brake drum. If equipped with rear disk brakes, remove the caliper and hang aside. Remove the brake rotor.

3. Remove the 4 axle retainer bolts.

4. Using a slide hammer on the axle, pull the axle out of the housing.

5. To install, reverse the removal procedures.

6. If equipped with drum brakes, torque the axle retention bolts to 55 ft. lbs. (75 Nm). If equipped with disk brakes, torque the axle retention bolts to 75 ft. lbs. (103 Nm).

AXLE SHAFT SEAL

1. Raise and safely support the vehicle.

2. Remove the axle shaft from the housing.

3. Support the axle shaft and remove the bearing retainer locknut.

4. Remove the retainer, bearing and seal from the axle shaft.

5. Using a seal driver tool, remove the seal and install the new seal in the retainer.

6. To install, reverse the removal procedures.

7. Torque the bearing retainer nut to 188–195 ft. lbs. (250–260 Nm).

8. Check the level of the axle lubricant when finished.

1. Differential carrier and case assembly	16. Wheel stud
2. Mounting bolt	17. Brake drum
3. Gasket	18. Wheel nut
4. Drain plug	19. Drum-to-flange screw
5. Filler plug	
6. Vent	
7. Through bolt	
8. Oil seal	
9. Shims	
10. Locknut	
11. Lockwasher	
12. Axle shaft bearing	
13. Bearing holder	
14. Grease seal	
15. Axle shaft	

Exploded view of the rear axle assembly

1. Bolt
2. Brake caliper
3. Hub cap
4. Split pin
5. Nut retainer
6. Hub nut
7. Lock washer
8. Outer bearing
9. Hub and disc assembly
10. Oil seal
11. Inner bearing and outer race
12. Bolt
13. Wheel pin

Exploded view of the front wheel assembly—2WD Pick-Up

1. Bolt
2. Brake caliper
3. Bolt
4. Cover
5. Lock washer
6. Hub nut
7. Hub and disc assembly
8. Outer bearing
9. Oil seal
10. Inner bearing
11. Bolt
12. Wheel pin

Exploded view of the front wheel assembly—2WD Amigo

Front Wheel Hub, Knuckle and Bearings

Removal and Installation

1. Raise and safely support the vehicle. Remove the wheel assembly.
2. Remove the brake caliper and support it on a wire. Remove the rotor and dust shield.
3. If equipped with 4WD, remove the axle shaft from the hub.
4. Remove the tie rod end-to-steering knuckle nut and separate the tie rod from the steering knuckle.
5. Support the lower control arm and separate the steering knuckle from the lower ball joint.
6. Separate the steering knuckle from the upper ball joint.
7. Remove the steering knuckle from the vehicle.
8. To install, reverse the removal procedures.
9. Torque the upper ball joint nut to 75 ft. lbs. (100 Nm), the lower ball joint nut to 95 ft. lbs. (127 Nm) and the steering linkage ball nut to 75 ft. lbs. (100 Nm).

Manual Locking Hubs

Removal and Installation

1. Place the transfer case in the **2H** position. Raise and safely the vehicle.
2. Set the hubs in the **FREE** position.
3. Remove the hub cover bolts and the hub cover.
4. While pushing the follower toward the knob, turn the clutch assembly clockwise and then remove the clutch assembly from the knob.
5. Remove the snapring and the knob from the cover. Do not loose the detent ball.
6. Remove the ball and spring from the knob.
7. Remove the X-ring from the knob by pressing it off.

1. Bolt
2. Housing assembly
3. Snapring and shims
4. Body assembly
5. Lock washer
6. Hub nut
7. Hub and disc assembly
8. Outer bearing
9. Oil seal
10. Inner bearing
11. Clutch assembly
12. Snapring
13. Knob
14. Compression spring
15. Follower
16. Retaining spring
17. Detent ball and spring
18. X-ring
19. Snapring
20. Inner assembly
21. Snapring
22. Ring
23. Spacer

Exploded view of the manual locking hub assembly— 4WD

NOTE: Do not use a sharp instrument to remove this ring because it may scratch the ring.

8. Remove the compression spring, retaining spring and the follower from the clutch assembly.

9. Remove the retaining spring from the clutch assembly by turning it counterclockwise.

10. Remove the snapring and the inner assembly from the body.

11. Separate the ring, inner and spacer by removing the snapring.

12. To install, reverse the removal procedures. Apply grease to the X-ring, the inner cover and the outside circumference of the knob.

Automatic Locking Hubs

Removal and Installation

1. Move the transfer case shift lever into **2H** and move the vehicle forward and rearward about 3 ft.

2. Remove the hub cap-to-housing bolts and the cap.

3. Loosen the wheel nuts

4. Raise and safely support the vehicle. Remove the front wheel(s).

5. Remove the brake caliper-to-steering knuckle bolts and support the caliper on a wire; do not disconnect the brake hose.

6. Using snapring pliers, remove the snapring and shims.

7. Remove the drive clutch assembly, the inner cam and lockwasher.

8. Using a hub nut wrench, loosen the hub nut.

9. Pull the hub from the spindle.

10. If necessary, use a brass drift and a hammer to drive the wheel bearings from the hub.

11. If removing the disc from the hub, scribe matchmarks, remove the disc-to-hub bolts and separate the disc from the hub.
To install:

12. To install, reverse the removal procedures.

13. When installing the hub nut, perform the following procedures:

    a. Torque the hub nut to 22 ft. lbs. and loosen the nut.

    b. Using a spring gauge, connect it to the stud bolt at 90 degrees.

    c. Retorque the hub nut until the spring gauge measures a bearing preload of 4.4–5.5 lbs. for new bearing and oil seal or 2.6–4.0 lbs. for used bearing and new oil seal.

14. Adjust the snapring clearance by performing the following procedures:

Using a feeler gauge to measure the shim clearance on the automatic locking hub assembly — 4WD

1. Bolt
2. Hub cap
3. Housing assembly
4. Snapring and shims
5. Drive clutch assembly
6. Inner cam
7. Lock washer
8. Hub nut
9. Hub and disc assembly
10. Outer bearing and outer race
11. Oil seal
12. Inner bearing and outer race
13. Bolt
14. Wheel pin

Exploded view of the automatic locking hub assembly — 4WD

a. Install the special adjusting tool onto the hub until it comes in contact with the lock washer.

b. Using a feeler gauge, measure the clearance **t** between the hub and the snapring groove on the axle shaft.

c. If the clearance is larger than the snapring groove, install shims on the shaft so clearance **t** is 0–0.039 in. (0–0.1mm).

15. To complete the installation, reverse the removal procedures. Apply Loctite® to the hub cap bolts and torque the hub cap-to-hub assembly bolts to 43 ft. lbs. (60 Nm).

Pinion Seal

Removal and Installation

1. Raise and safely support the vehicle. If necessary, remove the skid plate.

2. Matchmark and remove the front driveshaft.

3. Check the turning torque of the pinion before proceeding. This is the torque that must be reached during installation of the pinion nut.

NOTE: The amount of turning torque required to move the pinion gear should be 20–30 ft. lbs. of torque.

4. Using a pinion flange holding tool, remove the pinion nut and washer.

5. Remove the pinion flange from the pinion gear.

6. Pry the pinion seal out of the differential carrier.

7. Clean and inspect the sealing surface of the carrier.

To install:

8. Using a seal driver tool, drive the new seal into the carrier until the flange on the seal is flush with the carrier.

9. With the seal installed, the pinion bearing preload must be set.

10. Tighten the pinion nut while holding the flange, until the turning torque is the same as before removal of the nut.

11. Align the matchmarks and install the driveshaft.

12. Check the level of the differential lubricant when finished.

Differential Carrier

Removal and Installation

FRONT DRIVE AXLE

1. Raise and safely support the vehicle.

2. Drain the differential oil.

3. Matchmark and remove the front driveshaft.

4. Remove the axle shafts from the differential.

5. Remove the differential carrier mounting bolts and remove the carrier.

To install:

6. To install, reverse the removal procedures. Use a new gasket when installing. Torque the bolts to 19 ft. lbs. (26 Nm).

7. Fill the differential to the correct level when finished.

REAR DRIVE AXLE

1. Raise and safely support the vehicle.

2. Drain the differential oil.

3. Matchmark and remove the rear driveshaft. Remove the drum or caliper and rotor assemblies.

4. Remove the axle retainer bolts and remove the axle shafts from the axle housing.

5. Remove the differential carrier mounting bolts and the carrier.

To install:

6. To install, reverse the removal procedures. Use a new gasket when installing. Torque the differential mounting bolts to 47 ft. lbs. (64 Nm). Torque the bearing retainer bolts to 75 ft. lbs. (103 Nm) on disk brake models or 54 ft. lbs. (74 Nm) on drum brake models.

7. Fill the differential to the correct level when finished.

Axle Housing

Removal and Installation

FRONT HOUSING

1. Raise and safely support the vehicle.

2. Matchmark and disconnect the front driveshaft from the differential.

3. Remove the wheels and skid plate.

4. Loosen the torsion bar completely with the height control adjusting bolts.

5. Remove the strut bars.

6. Disconnect the stabilizer bars from the lower control arms.

7. Remove the caliper assemblies and suspend them on a wire; do not disconnect the brake lines.

8. Remove the tie rod ends from the steering knuckles.

9. Disconnect the upper control arms from the frame; note the number and positions of the shims.

10. Remove the steering link ends from the lower control arms.

11. Disconnect the shock absorbers from the lower control arms.

12. Disconnect the lower control arms from the frame.

13. Remove the locking hub.

14. Remove the rotors and upper links.

15. Remove the pitman arm and idler arm along with the steering linkage assembly.

16. Support the differential housing and lower it clear of the vehicle. Take care to avoid damaging the Birfield joints.

17. To install, reverse the removal procedures. Check the level of the axle lubricant when finished.

REAR HOUSING

1. Raise and safely support the vehicle. Remove the rear wheels.

2. Disconnect the shock absorbers from the spring plates.

3. Disconnect and plug the brake lines on the rear axle housing.

4. Disconnect the parking brake cables from the rear axle housing.

5. Support the rear axle housing and remove the housing to leaf spring U-bolts.

6. Remove the rear axle housing from the vehicle.

To install:

7. To install, reverse the removal procedures.

8. Torque the housing U-bolts to 36–43 ft. lbs. and the shock absorber bolts to 27–30 ft. lbs.

9. Bleed the brake system and check the level of the axle lubricant when finished.

STEERING

Steering Wheel

Removal and Installation

1. Disconnect the negative battery cable.

2. From the rear of the steering wheel, remove the horn pad screw. Pry the horn pad upward from the steering wheel.

3. Remove the steering wheel-to-steering column nut.

4. Matchmark the steering wheel-to-steering shaft.

1. Horn shroud
2. Nut
3. Steering wheel
4. Steering cowl
5. Combination switch
6. Snapring
7. Bushing
8. Steering lock and
   bearing
9. Steering column
   assembly

Exploded view of the steering column assembly — 1988–90

5. Using a steering wheel puller, press the steering wheel from the steering shaft.

6. To install, align the matchmarks and reverse the removal procedures. Torque the steering wheel nut to 22–29 ft. lbs. (30–39 Nm).

Steering Column

Removal and Installation

1. Disconnect the negative battery cable.

2. Mark the shaft and steering wheel hub and remove the steering wheel and the column cowling. Remove the instrument cluster on the Amigo, Pick-Up and Rodeo to remove the column cowling.

3. Disconnect the electrical connections to the combination switch and the ignition switch.

4. Mark the steering shaft and universal joint and remove the bolt from the steering shaft-to-steering box universal joint. Re-

move the bolts from the steering column bracket at the firewall. Remove the bolts from the steering bracket under the dash panel.

5. Remove the steering column from the vehicle.

To install:

6. Install the steering column in the vehicle and match the marks on the steering shaft and the universal joint. Connect the electrical connections to the combination switch and the ignition switch.

7. Insert the bolts into the steering bracket under the dash. Torque the bolts to 11–14 ft. lbs. (1.5–2.0 Nm).

8. Insert the bolts into the firewall bracket and torque to 10–17 ft. lbs. (1.4–2.4 Nm).

9. Install the universal joint bolt and torque to 14–22 ft. lbs. (2.0–3.0 Nm).

10. Install the steering wheel, matching the marks made during removal. Torque the nut to 22–29 ft. lbs. (3.0–4.0 Nm). Install the cowling and the instrument panel. Connect the battery.

Manual Steering Gear

Removal and Installation

1. Disconnect the negative battery cable. Raise and safely support the vehicle. Remove the skid plate, if equipped.
2. Remove pitman arm nut and washer. Matchmark the pitman arm-to-pitman shaft.
3. Using a puller tool, press the pitman arm from the pitman shaft.
4. Remove the steering gear-to-steering shaft clamp bolt.
5. Remove the steering gear-to-frame bolts and the steering gear from vehicle.

To install:

6. Place the steering gear in position and install and tighten the mounting bolts.
7. Install the steering gear-to-steering shaft clamp bolt and torque to 29–40 ft. lbs. (40–49 Nm).
8. Torque the steering column mounting bolts to 13 ft. lbs.
9. Install the pitman arm-to-pitman shaft and torque the nut to 145–174 ft. lbs. (196–236 Nm).
10. Install the skid plate, if equipped.
11. Lower the vehicle.

Adjustment

1. Position the front wheel in the straight ahead position.
2. Loosen the locknut on the adjusting screw of the steering unit.
3. Turn the adjusting screw clockwise to decrease the free-play or counterclockwise to increase it.
4. With the steering wheel free-play set at 0.4–1.2 in. (10–30mm), torque the locknut to 15–22 ft. lbs. (20–29 Nm).

Power Steering Gear

Removal and Installation

1. Raise and safely support the vehicle. Remove the skip plate, if equipped.
2. Remove pitman arm nut and washer. Matchmark the pitman arm-to-pitman shaft.
3. Using a puller tool, press the the pitman arm from the pitman shaft.
4. Disconnect and plug the power steering lines at the steering gear.
5. Remove the steering gear-to-steering shaft clamp bolt.
6. Remove the steering gear-to-frame bolts and the steering gear from vehicle.

To install:

7. Place the steering gear in position and install and tighten the mounting bolts. Connect the power steering lines to the steering gear.
8. Install steering gear-to-steering shaft bolts and torque to 29–40 ft. lbs. (40–49 Nm).
9. Torque steering column mounting bolts to 13 ft. lbs.
10. Install the pitman arm to the pitman shaft. Install washer and torque nut to 145–174 ft. lbs. (196–236 Nm).
11. Install the skid plate, if equipped.
12. Lower the vehicle. Refill and bleed the power steering system.

Adjustment

1. Position the front wheel in the straight ahead position.
2. Loosen the locknut on the adjusting screw of the steering unit.
3. Turn the adjusting screw clockwise to decrease the free-play or counterclockwise to increase it.
4. With the steering wheel free-play set at 0.4 in. (10mm), torque the locknut to 26–35 ft. lbs. (37–47 Nm).

Power Steering Pump

Removal and Installation

1. Disconnect the negative battery cable.
2. Disconnect and plug the inlet and outlet fluid lines from the power steering pump.
3. Remove the drive belt from the pump.
4. Remove the pump-to-bracket bolts and the pump from the brackets.
5. To install, reverse the removal procedures.
6. Connect the negative battery cable. Refill and bleed the power steering system.

Belt Adjustment

1. Loosen the power steering pump adjusting bolts.
2. Using finger pressure, between the idler pulley and the power steering pump pulley, check the belt deflection; it should be 0.4 in. (10mm).
3. With the power steering pump adjusted to the correct belt deflection, tighten the pump bolts.

System Bleeding

1. Fill the power steering reservoir to the proper level when cold.
2. Start and operate the engine until it reaches normal operating temperatures.
3. Turn the engine **OFF** and check the fluid level. If necessary, fill the reservoir to the proper level.
4. Run the engine and turn the steering wheel from lock-to-lock, in both directions, 3–4 times; do not hold the steering wheel at the lock position for more than 5 seconds or temperature rise will result.
5. Return the steering wheel to center, turn the engine **OFF** and allow the fluid to sit for 5 minutes before adding any more.
6. If necessary, repeat the bleeding procedure until the air bubbles are removed from the system.
7. Fill the system to the proper level when finished.

Tie Rod Ends

Removal and Installation

1. Raise and safely support the vehicle.
2. Matchmark the tie rod ends to the tie rod shaft for reinstallation purposes.
3. Remove the cotter pin and nut from the tie rod end and loosen the clamping bolts on the sleeve.
4. Using a tie rod end puller, separate the tie rod from the steering knuckle.
5. Unscrew the tie rod while counting the number of turns required to remove it.
6. Check the tie rod end for damage and replace it, if necessary.

To install:

7. Install the tie rod end in the sleeve the same number of turns as when removing it.
8. Install the tie rod end in the steering knuckle. Install the nut and new cotter pin.
9. Check the toe in when finished.

Intermediate Rod and Tie Rods

Removal and Installation

1. Raise and safely support the vehicle.
2. Remove cotter pin from the ball studs connecting tie rods-to-intermediate rod and the steering damper. Remove the cas-

1. Nut
2. Bolt
3. Steering damper
4. Nut
5. Pitman arm nut
6. Relay lever nut
7. Intermediate rod

Exploded view of the steering linkage assembly

tellated nuts. Using a ball joint separator tool, separate the parts.

3. Remove the nut and lockwasher on ball stud connecting the intermediate rod to idler arm. Using a ball joint separator tool, separate the intermediate rod from the idler arm.

4. Remove the intermediate rod with tie rods.

5. If the tie rod is replaced, disconnect the intermediate rod from tie rod.

To install:

6. Make sure the threads on the ball studs and nuts are clean and smooth.

7. Install the intermediate rod-to-idler arm and torque the nut to 50 ft. lbs. (67 Nm).

8. Raise the end of the rod and install it on the pitman arm. Torque the nut to 44 ft. lbs. (59 Nm). Tighten the nut just enough to insert cotter pin and install new cotter pin.

9. Install intermediate rod to steering damper end. Torque nut to 87 ft. lbs. (117 Nm), then, advance nut just enough to insert cotter pin and install new cotter pin.

10. Install the tie rods to adapter, torque nut to 44 ft. lbs. (59 Nm), then, advance nut just enough to insert cotter pin and install new cotter pin and lubricate tie rod ball studs.

BRAKES

For all brake system repair and service procedures not detailed below, please refer to "Brakes" in the Unit Repair section.

Master Cylinder

Removal and Installation

1. Disconnect the negative battery cable. Firmly, set the parking brake and block the wheels.
2. Draw off the brake fluid from the reservoir with a clean syringe. Disconnect and plug the brake lines from the master cylinder.

NOTE: Be careful not to spill any brake fluid on any painted surface. Brake fluid acts exactly like paint remover.

3. Remove the master cylinder-to-power brake unit nuts.
4. Remove the master cylinder from the booster.
5. Bleed the master cylinder before installing.
6. Install the master cylinder onto the booster.
7. Connect the fluid lines, refill the master cylinder with the proper brake fluid and bleed the brake system. Torque the flare fittings to 6.5–11 ft. lbs. (8.8–15 Nm). Torque the master cylinder-to-booster nuts to 7–1 ft. lbs. (10–16 Nm).

Bleeding

1. Set the parking brake and perform the bleeding operation with the engine running to prevent damage to the pushrod seal. Route the exhaust outside if working in an enclosed area. Carefully clean all dirt from around the master cylinder filler cap.
2. If a bleeder tank is used, follow the manufacturer's instructions.
3. Remove the filler cap and fill the master cylinder to the lower edge of the filler neck.
4. Clean off the bleeder connections at all of the wheel cylinders or disc brake calipers. Attach the bleeder hose and fixture to the right rear wheel cylinder bleeder screw and place the end of the tube in a glass jar, submerged in brake fluid.
5. Have an assistant pump the pedal several times and hold it down. Open the bleeder valve ½–¾ of a turn. Close the valve before the pressure is completely released. Repeat this procedure until bubbles cease to appear at the end of the bleeder hose.
6. Check the level of the brake fluid in the master cylinder and add fluid, if necessary. Repeat this procedure at the left rear wheel, then right front wheel and finishing at the left front. It is a good opportunity while the bleeding equipment is available to bleed the clutch hydraulic system using the same procedure.
7. After the bleeding operation at each caliper or wheel cylinder has been completed, refill the master cylinder reservoir, retract the filler cap diaphragm and replace the filler cap.

NOTE: Never reuse brake fluid which has been removed from the lines through the bleeding process because it contains moisture and dirt.

Proportioning Valve

The proportioning valve is located directly under the master cylinder.

Removal and Installation

1. Disconnect the negative battery cable. Firmly, set the parking brake and block the wheels.
2. Disconnect the electrical connector from the proportioning valve.
3. Disconnect and plug the fluid lines from the proportioning valve.

4. Remove the proportioning valve-to-chassis bolts and the valve.
5. To install, reverse the removal procedures.
6. Bleed the brake system.

Power Brake Booster

Removal and Installation

1. Disconnect the negative battery cable. Firmly, set the parking brake and block the wheels.
2. Disconnect the vacuum hose to the vacuum booster.
3. Disconnect and plug the brake fluid lines at the master cylinder. Place rags under the master cylinder to catch any leaking fluid.

NOTE: Be careful not to spill any brake fluid on any painted surface. Brake fluid will damage painted surfaces.

4. Inside the vehicle, remove the snapring from the clevis pin and separate the clevis pin from the brake pedal.
5. Remove the vacuum booster mounting nuts at the firewall and lift out the power unit and master cylinder/reservoir as an assembly.

To install:

6. Check the distance from the flange face of the vacuum booster to the end of the pushrod before installation of the master cylinder. The distance should be 0.709–0.717 in. (18.0–18.2mm). If the measurement deviates from the specified range, make an adjustment with the locknut at the end of the pushrod.

0.717 IN.
(18.2MM)

SCREW BOLT

LOCKNUT

View of the power booster pushrod adjustment

7. Apply sealer to the dashboard fitting face plate and mount the booster assembly and torque the mounting nuts to 16–23 ft. lbs. (22–32 Nm).
8. Connect the brake pedal clevis, brake lines and the vacuum hose. Torque the brake lines to 6.5–11 ft. lbs. (10–15 Nm).
9. Bleed the brake system.

Brake Caliper

Removal and Installation

1. Raise and safely support the vehicle. Remove the wheel assembly.
2. Disconnect and plug the brake fluid line from the caliper. On rear calipers disconnect parking brake cables.
3. Remove the brake caliper mounting bolts and the caliper from the mount.
4. Remove the brake pads and clips from the caliper. Inspect the brake pads for wear; replace them, if necessary.

3. Lock bolt
4. Bolt and washer
5. Caliper assembly
6. Pads and clips
7. Support bracket

★: REPAIR KIT

Exploded view of the rear disc brake assembly

OUTER SIDE

1. Brake flexible hose
2. Lock bolt
3. Pad assembly with shim
4. Pad clip
5. Caliper assembly
6. Support bracket
7. Front hub and disc assembly

★: REPAIR KIT

Exploded view of the front disc brake assembly

To install:

5. Fill the brake caliper with brake fluid and connect the fluid line to the caliper using new washers. Torque the brake line banjo fitting to 22–29 ft. lbs. (30–40 Nm). Install the brake pads and clips onto the caliper.

6. Install the caliper on the mounting bracket. Torque the caliper-to-mounting bracket bolts to 20–27 ft. lbs. (28–38 Nm) for front calipers or 12–17 ft. lbs. (16–24 Nm) for rear calipers.

7. Bleed the brake system. Install the wheel assembly and lower the vehicle.

Disc Brake Pads

Removal and Installation

FRONT

1. Raise and safely support the vehicle. Remove the wheel assembly.

2. Remove the brake caliper mounting bolts and remove the caliper without disconnecting the brake fluid line. Support the caliper so it does not hang on the brake line.

3. Remove the brake pads and retaining clips from the caliper.

4. Use a C-clamp and press the brake caliper piston into the caliper until it bottoms out.

To install:

5. Install the new brake pads and clips in the caliper and install the caliper in the mounting bracket.

6. Install the wheel assembly. Check the brake fluid level.

7. Pump the brake pedal until pressure is felt before moving the vehicle.

REAR

1. Raise and safely support the vehicle. Remove the wheel assembly.

2. Remove the brake caliper mounting bolts and remove the caliper without disconnecting the brake fluid line. Support the caliper so it does not hang on the brake line.

3. Remove the brake pads and retaining clips from the caliper.

4. Using tool J-37617 or equivalent, rotate the piston clockwise while retracting the piston into the bore. Align the notches of the piston face so the centerline of the notches is perpendicular to the centerline of the mounting bosses.

To install:

5. Install the new brake pads and clips in the caliper and install the caliper in the mounting bracket.

6. Install the wheel assembly. Check the brake fluid level.

7. Pump the brake pedal until pressure is felt before moving the vehicle.

Brake Rotor

Removal and Installation

FRONT

2WD Vehicle

1. Raise and safely support the vehicle. Remove the wheel assembly.

2. Remove the brake caliper without disconnecting the fluid line. Support the caliper aside.

3. Remove the brake caliper mounting bracket.

4. Remove the dust cover, cotter pin and locknut from the rotor.

5. Place a hand over the outer wheel bearing in the rotor and remove the rotor from the spindle.

6. Remove the rotor-to-hub bolts and pull off the rotor.

To install:

7. Install the rotor on the hub and torque the bolts to 75 ft. lbs. (105 Nm).

8. Torque the hub nut to 22 ft. lbs. (29 Nm) and loosen the nut. Using a spring gauge, connect it to the stud bolt at 90 degrees. Retorque the hub nut until the spring gauge measures a bearing preload of 1.8–2.2 lbs.

9. Install the caliper mounting bracket and torque the bolts to 103–126 ft. lbs. (142–174 Nm).

10. Install the caliper and torque the mounting bolts to 20–27 ft. lbs. (28–38 Nm).

11. Install the wheel and lower the vehicle.

4WD Vehicle

1. Place the transfer case in **2H**. Raise and safely support the vehicle.

2. Remove the free wheeling hub cover assembly. Remove the brake caliper and hang aside.

3. Using wrench J-36827 or equivalent, remove the hub nut.

4. Remove the hub and disk assembly. Unbolt the rotor from the hub.

5. Remove the outer roller bearing assembly from the hub with a finger.

6. Using a brass or wood drift, drive out the inner bearing assembly along with the oil seal. Replace the seal.

7. Wash all parts in a non-flammable solvent.

8. Check all parts for cracks or wear. Thoroughly lubricate all bearing parts with a high-temperature wheel bearing grease. Remove any excess. Apply about 2 ounces of the grease to the hub.

To install:

9. Bolt the rotor to the hub and torque the bolts to 75 ft. lbs. (105 Nm).

10. Lightly coat the spindle with the same grease. Place the inner bearing into the hub race and install a new seal and retaining ring.

11. Carefully install the hub on the spindle and install the outer bearing.

12. Install the spindle nut.

13. While rotating the hub, tighten the hub so the wheel can just be turned by hand.

14. Turn the hub 2–3 turns and back off the nut just enough so it can be loosened with the fingers.

15. Finger-tighten the nut so all play is taken up at the bearing.

16. Attach a pull scale to a lug nut and check the amount of pull needed to start the wheel turning. Initial pull should be 2.6–4.0 lbs. When performing this test, make sure the brake pads are not touching the rotor. If the rotating torque is not correct, tighten the spindle nut until it is.

17. Install the lockwasher so the bolt holes lineup. If the bolt holes do not line up, reverse the position of the lock washer. The bolt head should be able to sink below the surface of the washer when tightened down.

18. Clean the hub flange surface and areas surrounding the spindle and with the transfer case lever in the **2H** position, install the inner cam with the gear teeth facing out.

19. Lower the vehicle and install tools J-36835-2 and J-36836 or equivalent, on the axle shaft until it comes in contact with the lock washer.

20. Measure the gap between the tool and the snapring tool and select shims to reduce the gap to 0.00–0.10mm. Remove the tool.

21. Apply grease to the hub splines and lubrication grooves. Install the drive clutch assembly. The cut portion of the drive clutch must be aligned with the concave part of the inner cam. Match the teeth of the cam to the inner cam by turning the axle shaft.

22. Install the snapring and previously selected shims, gasket and cover. Apply Loctite® 515 or equivalent, and torque the cover bolts to 43 ft. lbs. (59 Nm).

23. Install the caliper mounting bracket and torque the bolts to 103–126 ft. lbs. (142–174 Nm).

24. Install the caliper and torque the mounting bolts to 20–27 ft. lbs. (28–38 Nm).

25. Mount the wheel assembly and lower the vehicle. Pump the brakes before moving the vehicle.

REAR

1. Raise and safely support the vehicle. Remove the wheel assembly.

2. Remove the brake caliper without disconnecting the fluid line. Support the caliper aside.

3. Remove the brake caliper from the mounting bracket. Remove the brake caliper mounting bracket.

4. Remove the rotor from the axle shaft.

5. To install, reverse the removal procedures. Torque the mounting bracket bolts to 69–84 ft. lbs. (95–116 Nm). Torque the caliper mounting bolt to 12–17 ft. lbs. (16–24 Nm).

Brake Drums

Removal and Installation

1. Raise and safely support the vehicle.

2. Remove the wheel and the brake drum.

3. To install, reverse the removal procedures.

Brake Shoes

Removal and Installation

1. Raise and safely support the vehicle. Remove the tire and wheel assembly.

2. Remove the brake drum.

3. Remove the return springs, the hold-down springs and lift the brake shoe assembly from the backing plate.

4. Disconnect the parking brake cable from the adjuster.

5. To install, reverse the removal procedures.

1. Brake line
2. Holding spring and cups
3. Lower return spring
4. Upper return spring (shoe-to-adjust lever)
5. Upper return spring (shoe-to-shoe)
6. Primary shoe assembly
7. Shoe assembly with lever
8. Retainer with pin
9. Wave washer
10. Automatic adjuster lever
11. Secondary shoe assembly
12. Adjuster assembly
13. Wheel cylinder assembly
14. Wheel cylinder boot
15. Piston assembly
16. Piston cup
17. Piston return spring
18. Wheel cylinder bleeder

Exploded view of the rear brake drum/shoe assembly

1. Nut
2. Equalizer bracket
3. Split pin with plain washer
4. Pin with curved washer
5. Front lower cable
6. Split pin with plain washer
7. Pin with curved washer
8. Intermediate cable
9. Clip
10. Fixing bracket clip
11. Rear cable assembly
12. 2nd relay lever assembly with return spring
13. 1st relay lever assembly

Exploded view of the parking brake cable assembly

Wheel Cylinder

Removal and Installation

1. Raise and safely support the vehicle. Remove the wheel assembly, brake drums and shoes.
2. Disconnect and plug the brake line at the wheel cylinder.
3. Remove the wheel cylinder-to-backing plate bolts and the cylinder.
4. Cap the openings of the brake line and the wheel cylinder.
5. To install, reverse the removal procedures. Bleed the brake system.

Parking Brake Cable

Removal and Installation

1. Raise and safely support the vehicle.
2. Loosen the cable adjusting nut and remove the lever return spring. Remove the adjusting nut.
3. Remove the cotter pin from the retaining pin on the 2nd lever assembly and remove the front cable.
4. Remove the 2 cotter pins from the retaining pins on the intermediate cable and remove the cable.
5. Remove the retaining clips from the rear fixing brackets and lower the rear brake cables.
6. Remove the rear wheel assemblies and brake drums. Remove the rear brake shoes and disconnect the rear brake cables from the lever in the rear brake shoes.
7. To install, reverse the removal procedures. Adjust the cables when finished.

Adjustment

NOTE: Adjustment of the parking brake is necessary every time the rear brake cables are disconnected or after overhauling the rear brake assembly.

1. Fully, release the parking brake lever and check the cable for free movement.
2. Firmly, grab the 2nd relay lever rod. Rotate the adjusting nut until all the slack is removed from the cable. Tighten the adjusting nut.
3. Apply the parking brake to the fully set position 3–4 times.
4. If the parking brake is properly adjusted, the traveling range should be between 12–14 notches. If the travel is incorrect, readjust to specifications.

Load Sensing Proportioning Valve

Adjusting

1. Connect a continuity meter between the mounting bracket and the linkage arm. The arm is insulated so be sure to cut through to the metal arm when attaching the lead.
2. Place weight into the vehicle bed to end up with a 1257 lbs. (570 kg) rear axle weight. Have an assistant sit in the drivers seat.
3. Loosen the locknut on the side of the valve body. Raise the valve body and allow to drop slowly. At the point where continuity is achieved, tighten the locknut. Torque the nut to 12 ft. lbs. (17 Nm).
4. If continuity is broken while tightening the nut, loosen the nut and lower the valve body slightly. Tighten the nut.

Rear Wheel anti-Lock brake component locations— Amigo and Pick-Up—Rodeo similar

Rear wheel anti-Lock brake system schematic

5. Check the adjustment by pressing down slightly on the linkage near to the valve. If continuity is broken then the adjustment is acceptable.

Removal and Installation

1. Disconnect the fluid lines to the valve body.
2. Disconnect the linkage at the axle housing.
3. Remove the mounting bolts at the bracket and remove the valve.
4. Mount the valve, attach the linkage and lines. Bleed the system.

Rear Wheel Anti-Lock Brake Valve

Removal and Installation

1. Disconnect the negative battery cable. Locate the valve body on the right side frame rail.
2. Disconnect the wiring harness connector from the valve body lead.
3. Disconnect the brake lines at the valve body. Cap the lines to prevent the ingress of dirt and moisture.
4. Remove the bolts holding the valve to the frame rail bracket and remove the valve.

5. Installation is the reverse of removal. Torque the brake line fittings to 11 ft. lbs. (15 Nm).

Speed Sensor

Removal and Installation

1. Disconnect the negative battery terminal. Locate the speed sensor on the top of the rear axle housing.
2. Disconnect the wiring harness lead from the sensor.
3. Remove the speed sensor bolt and remove the speed sensor.

4. Installation is the reverse of removal. Torque the bolt to 17 ft. lbs. (23 Nm).

Rear Wheel Anti-Lock Brake System ECM

Removal and Installation

1. Disconnect the negative battery terminal. Remove the 4 bolts holding the passenger seat assembly and remove the seat.
2. Disconnect the wiring harness from the ECM.
3. Unbolt the ECM from the floor and remove with the bracket.
4. Installation is the reverse of removal.

FRONT SUSPENSION

Shock Absorbers

Removal and Installation

1. Raise and support the vehicle safely.

2. Hold the upper stem of the shock absorber from turning and remove the upper stem retaining nut, retainer and rubber grommet. On some vehicles, it may be necessary to remove the bumpstops to gain access to the mounting bolts.
3. Remove the bolt retaining the lower shock absorber pivot

1. Adjust bolt, seat, lock plate and bolt
2. Height control arm
3. Torsion bar
4. Nut and washer
5. Rubber bushing and washer
6. Bolt and washer
7. Strut bar
8. Rubber bushing, washer and tube
9. Bolt
10. Bracket
11. Nut
12. Rubber bushing and washer
13. Rubber bushing and washer
14. Bracket
15. Bolt and nut
16. Rubber bushing and washer
17. Stabilizer bar
18. Nut
19. Rubber bushing and washer
20. Bolt, nut and washer
21. Shock absorber
22. Rubber bushing and washer
23. Lower link bumper
24. Upper link bumper

Exploded view of the front suspension—2WD

to the lower control arm and remove the shock absorber from the vehicle.

To install:

4. Install the shock absorber by first installing the lower retainer and rubber grommet over the upper stem and then, installing the shock fully extended up through the upper control arm so the upper stem passes through the mounting hole in the frame bracket.

5. Install the upper rubber grommet, retainer and attaching nut over the shock absorber upper stem.

6. Hold the upper stem of the shock absorber from turning and tighten the retaining nut. Torque to 15 ft. lbs. (20 Nm).

7. Install the retainers attaching the shock absorber lower pivot to the lower control arm and tighten them. Torque the mounting bolt to 60 ft. lbs. (84 Nm).

8. Install the bumpstops if removed. Lower the vehicle.

Torsion Bars

Removal and Installation

1. Raise and safely support the vehicle.

2. Mark the location of the height adjustment bolt and remove from the height control arm.

3. Mark the location and remove the height control arm from the torsion bar and the third crossmember.

4. Mark the location and withdraw the torsion bar from the lower control arm.

To install:

5. To install, apply a generous amount of grease to the serrated ends of the torsion bar.

6. Hold the rubber bumpers in contact with the lower control arm. Raise the vehicle up under the lower control arm to accomplish this.

7. Insert the front end of the torsion bar into the control arm.

8. Install the height control arm in position so it's end is reaching the adjusting bolt. Be sure to lubricate the part of the height control arm that fits into the chassis with grease.

9. Install a new cotter pin in the control arm.

10. Turn the adjusting bolt to the location marked before removal.

11. Lower the vehicle and check the vehicle height.

3AW
1. Adjusting bolt and seat
2. Height control arm
3. Torsion bar
4. Rubber seat
5. Bolt
6. Rubber bushing and bracket
7. Bolt, nut and washer
8. Rubber bushing and washer
9. Stabilizer bar
10. Nut
11. Rubber bushing and washer
12. Bolt, nut and washer
13. Shock absorber
14. Rubber bushing and washer
15. Lower link bumper

Exploded view of the front suspension—4WD

Upper Ball Joints

Inspection

Grasp the top of the front wheel and pull it in and out several times to check for excessive movement of the ball joint; if no movement exist, the joint is in good shape.

Removal and Installation

1. Raise and safely support the vehicle. Remove the wheel and tire assembly.
2. Mark the position of the torsion bar adjuster and remove the tension from the torsion bar.
3. Remove the upper ball joint-to-steering knuckle nut.
4. Using a ball joint separator tool, separate the upper ball joint from the steering knuckle.
5. Remove the upper ball joint-to-upper control arm bolts and the ball joint.
6. To install, reverse the removal procedures. Torque the upper ball joint-to-upper control arm bolts to 21–25 ft. lbs. (29–35 Nm) and the upper ball joint-to-steering knuckle nut to 72–87 ft. lbs. (96–117 Nm) for 2WD or to 65–80 ft. lbs. (88–108 Nm) for 4WD.
7. Adjust the tension on the torsion bar to its original position and lower the vehicle.

Lower Ball Joints

Inspection

1. Raise and safely support the front of the vehicle.
2. Using a large prybar, place it under the front wheel and try to pry the wheel upwards.
3. If excessive upward movement or clunking is noticed, the ball joint is damaged and requires replacement.

Removal and Installation

1. Raise and safely support the vehicle.
2. Remove the wheel and tire assembly.
3. Mark the position of the torsion bar adjuster and release the torsion bar tension.
4. Remove the cotter pin and castellated nut which retains the ball joint to the steering knuckle.
5. Remove the lower ball joint-to-lower control arm and strut rod.
6. Remove the ball joint.

To install:

7. Install the lower ball joint by mounting the joint to the lower control arm and torque the bolts to 45–56 ft. lbs. (61–76 Nm) for 2WD or to 68–83 ft. lbs. (93–113 Nm) for 4WD.
8. Install the ball joint stud into the steering knuckle and install the castellated nut and torque it to 101–116 ft. lbs. (137–

1. Nut and cotter pin
2. Nut and cotter pin
3. Nut and cotter pin
4. Steering link end
5. Knuckle
6. Upper end
7. Bolt and washer
8. Nut assembly
9. Upper link assembly
10. Nut and plate
11. Bushing
12. Fulcrum pin
13. Lower end
14. Bolt, nut and washer
15. Lower link assembly
16. Bushing

Exploded view of the steering knuckle and control arm assembly—2WD

157 Nm) for 2WD or to 87–111 ft. lbs. (117–137 Nm) for 4WD and just enough additional torque to align the cotter pin hole with a castellation on the nut. Install a new cotter pin.

9. Lubricate the lower ball joint through the grease fitting.
10. Adjust the torsion bar tension to its original position.
11. Install the wheel assembly and lower the vehicle.

Upper Control Arms

Removal and Installation

NOTE: The upper control arm and ball joint are replaced as an assembly.

1. Raise and safely support the vehicle.
2. Remove the wheel and tire assembly. Mark the position of the torsion bar adjuster and release the torsion bar tension.
3. Remove the cotter pin nut fastening the upper control arm and upper ball joint assembly and disconnect the upper control arm from the steering knuckle.

NOTE: Do not allow the steering knuckle to hang by the flexible brake line. Wire the steering knuckle up to the frame temporarily.

4. Remove the bolts from the upper pivot shaft and remove the upper control arm from the bracket. Be sure to note the position and number of shims used for adjusting the camber and caster angles when removing the upper control arm. The shims must be replaced in their original position.
5. To remove the pivot shaft and bushings from the upper control arm assembly, remove the bushing nuts from the pivot shaft by loosening them alternately, then remove the pivot shaft.

To install:

6. To install the upper control arm and ball joint assembly, first install the pivot shaft boots to the pivot shaft.
7. Fill the internal part of the bushings with grease and screw the bushings into the pivot shaft. Be sure to screw the right side and the left side bushings alternately into the pivot shafts carefully avoiding getting grease on the outer face of the bushings. Tighten the nuts to 250 ft. lbs. (333 Nm).

1. Front bushing
2. Rear bushing
3. Lower link assembly
4. Torsion bar arm
5. Bolt
6. Nut and washer
7. Bolt
8. Nut and washer
9. Lower end
10. Fulcrum pin
11. Bushing
12. Plate
13. Nut
14. Upper link assembly
15. Caster shims
16. Camber shims
17. Bolt and plate
18. Nut assembly
19. Upper end
20. Needle bearing
21. Washer
22. Oil seal
23. Knuckle assembly
24. Nut and cotter pin
25. Nut and cotter pin
26. Back plate

Exploded view of the steering knuckle and control arm assembly—4WD

NOTE: Be sure the control arm and bushings are centered properly and the control arm rotates with resistance but not binding on the pivot shaft when tightened to the proper torque.

8. Install the grease fittings and lubricate the parts with grease through the grease fittings.

9. Install the ball joint stud through the steering knuckle. Install the castellated nut and tighten it to 75 ft. lbs. and just enough additional torque to install the cotter pin. Use a new cotter pin.

10. Mount the upper control arm to the chassis frame and install the shims in their original positions between the pivot shaft and bracket. Tighten the pivot shaft attaching nuts to 55 ft. lbs.

NOTE: Tighten the thinner shim pack's nut first for improved shaft-to-frame clamping force and torque retention.

11. Install the dust cover. Adjust the torsion bar to its original position.

12. Install the wheel assembly and lower the vehicle.

Lower Control Arms

Removal and Installation

1. Raise and safely support the vehicle.

2. Remove the wheel and tire assembly. Mark the position of the torsion bar adjuster and release the torsion bar tension.

3. Remove the strut bar by removing the frame side bracket and the double nuts, washer and the rubber bushing from the front side of the strut bar. Remove the strut bar-to-lower control arm bolts and remove the bar.

4. Disconnect the stabilizer bar from the lower control arm.

5. Remove the torsion bar.

6. Disconnect the shock absorber from the lower control arm.

7. Remove the lower ball joint from the lower control arm joint.

8. Remove the retaining nut and drive out the bolt holding the lower control arm to the chassis with a soft metal drift. Remove the lower control arm from the vehicle.

To install:

9. To install the lower control arm, install the lower ball joint to the lower control arm. Tighten the retaining nuts to 45 ft. lbs.

10. Mount the lower control arm to the frame. Drive the bolt into position carefully. Use care not to damage the serrated portions. Tighten the nut on the end of the pivot bolt to 135 ft. lbs.

11. Install the stabilizer bar to the lower control arm.

12. Place the washers and bushings on the strut rod and install it through the frame bracket. Install the second set of washers and bushings on the strut rod together with the lockwashers and nut. Leave the nut loose temporarily.

13. Install the strut rod to the lower control arm and tighten the bolts to 45 ft. lbs.

14. Assemble the lower ball joint to the steering knuckle. Adjust the torsion bar to the original position.

15. Install the wheel assembly and lower the vehicle.

16. Tighten the 1st strut bar-to-chassis frame attaching nut to 175 ft. lbs. and the 2nd locknut to 55 ft. lbs. with the vehicle on the ground.

Stabilizer Bar

Removal and Installation

1. Raise and safely support vehicle.

2. Remove the endlink nuts and remove the endlinks

3. Unbolt the frame bushing brackets and remove the stabilizer bar.

4. Installation is the reverse of removal. Torque the bracket bolts to 20 ft. lbs. (28 Nm) and the endlink nuts to 10 ft. lbs. (14 Nm).

Front Wheel Bearings—2WD

Removal and Installation

1. Raise and safely support the vehicle. Remove the wheel assembly. Remove the hub assembly.

2. Remove the outer roller bearing assembly from the hub. Pry out the inner bearing lip seal and remove the inner bearing assembly.

3. Wash all parts in a cleaning solvent and allow to air dry.

4. Check the bearings for pitting or scoring. Also check for smooth rotation and lack of noise.

To install:

5. Thoroughly lubricate the bearings with new wheel bearing lubricant.

6. Apply a light coat of lubricant to the spindle and inside surface of the hub.

7. Place the inner bearing in the race of the hub and install a new grease seal.

8. Install the hub assembly on the spindle.

9. Install the outer wheel bearing, washer and adjust nut.

10. Adjust the wheel bearings.

11. Install the dust cap on the hub.

12. Install the brake caliper and support assembly.

13. Install the wheel assembly.

Adjustment

1. With the wheel raised, remove the hub cap and dust cap and then remove the cotter pin and nut retainer from the end of the spindle.

2. While rotating the wheel, tighten the spindle nut to 22 ft. lbs. (29 Nm).

3. Turn the hub 2–3 turns and loosen the nut just enough so it can be turned by hand.

4. Turn the nut all the way hand tight and check to be sure the hub has no free-play.

5. Measure the starting torque by pulling a wheel hub stud with a pull scale. Tighten the spindle nut so the pull scale reads 1.1–2.6 lbs. when the hub begins to rotate.

NOTE: Make sure the brake pads are not in contact with the drum when measuring rotating torque.

6. Install the nut retainer, new cotter pin, dust cap and hub cap.

REAR SUSPENSION

Shock Absorbers

Removal and Installation

1. Raise and safely support the vehicle.

2. Remove the shock absorber-to-lower mount nut, washers and bushings.

3. Remove the shock absorber-to-chassis nut, washers and bushings.

4. Remove the shock absorber.

5. To install, reverse the removal procedures. Torque the mounting nuts to 30 ft. lbs. (40 Nm.)

Leaf Springs

Removal and Installation

1. Raise and safely support the vehicle so the leaf springs are hanging freely. Remove the wheel assemblies.

2. Remove the rear shock absorbers.

3. Remove the parking brake cable clips.

4. Remove the nuts from the U-bolts holding the springs to the axle housing.

5. Support the rear axle housing to remove the weight of the axle housing from the springs.

6. Remove the front and rear shackle pin nuts.

7. Drive out the rear shackle pin by using a hammer and drift. Lower the rear end of the leaf spring assembly to the floor.

8. Drive out the front shackle pin and remove the leaf spring assembly rearward.

9. Remove the shackle pin from the rear spring bracket and remove the shackle.

10. Check the leaf springs for cracks, wear and broken leaves. Replace any leaves found to be cracked, broken, fatigued or seriously worn.

11. Check the shackles for bending and the pins for wear.

12. Check the U-bolts for distortion or other damage.

To install:

13. Mount the shackle to the bracket.

14. Align the front end of the leaf spring assembly with the front bracket and install the shackle pin.

15. Align the rear end of the leaf spring assembly with the shackle and install the shackle pin.

16. Loosely install the shackle pin nuts and install the U-bolts.

17. Install the shock absorbers.

18. Clip the parking brake cable to the bracket.

19. Tighten the front shackle pin nut to 112 ft. lbs. (152 Nm).

20. Tighten the rear shackle pin nuts to 72 ft. lbs. (98 Nm). Tighten the U-bolt nuts to 48 ft. lbs. (67 Nm).

21. Install the wheels. Remove the axle housing support and lower the vehicle so the weight is on the leaf springs.

1. Rubber bumper
2. Bushing
3. Leaf spring assembly
4. Spring pin, bolt and washer
5. Nut and washer
6. Rubber bushing
7. Rubber bushing
8. Shackle
9. Shackle plate
10. Nut and washer
11. Nut and washer
12. Lower clamp
13. U-bolt and nut
14. Shock absorber
15. Nut and washer
16. Nut and washer

Exploded view of the rear suspension assembly

SPECIFICATIONS

ENGINE IDENTIFICATION

Year	Model	Engine Displacement cu. in. (cc/liter)	Engine Series Identification	No. of Cylinders	Engine Type
1988	B2200	133 (2184/2.2)	F2	4	OHC
	B2600	156 (2555/2.6)	G54B	4	OHC
1989	B2200	133 (2184/2.2)	F2	4	OHC
	B2600	159 (2606/2.6)	G6	4	OHC
	MPV	159 (2606/2.6)	G6	4	OHC
	MPV	180 (2954/3.0)	JE	6	OHC
1990	B2200	133 (2184/2.2)	F2	4	OHC
	B2600i	159 (2606/2.6)	G6	4	OHC
	MPV	159 (2606/2.6)	G6	4	OHC
	MPV	180 (2954/3.0)	JE	6	OHC
1991	B2200	133 (2184/2.2)	F2	4	OHC
	B2600i	159 (2606/2.6)	G6	4	OHC
	MPV	159 (2606/2.6)	G6	4	OHC
	MPV	180 (2954/3.0)	JE	6	OHC
	Navajo	245 (4016/4.0)	X	6	OHV
1992	B2200	133 (2184/2.2)	F2	4	OHC
	B2600i	159 (2606/2.6)	G6	4	OHC
	MPV	159 (2606/2.6)	G6	4	OHC
	MPV	180 (2954/3.0)	JE	6	OHC
	Navajo	245 (4016/4.0)	X	6	OHV

OHC—Overhead cam   OHV—Overhead valve

GENERAL ENGINE SPECIFICATIONS

Year	Model	Engine Displacement cu. in. (L)	Fuel System Type	Net Horsepower @ rpm	Net Torque @ rpm (ft. lbs.)	Bore × Stroke (in.)	Compression Ratio	Oil Pressure @ rpm
1988	B2200	133 (2.2)	2bbl	85 @ 4500	118 @ 2500	3.395 × 3.700	8.6:1	43–57 @ 3000
	B2600	156 (2.6)	2bbl	105 @ 5000	139 @ 2500	3.586 × 3.858	8.7:1	78 @ 3000
1989	B2200	133 (2.2)	2bbl	85 @ 4500	118 @ 2500	3.395 × 3.700	8.6:1	43–57 @ 3000
	B2600i	159 (2.6)	MPI	121 @ 4600	149 @ 3500	3.622 × 3.858	8.4:1	44–58 @ 3000
	MPV	159 (2.6)	MPI	121 @ 4600	149 @ 3500	3.622 × 3.858	8.4:1	44–58 @ 3000
	MPV	180 (3.0)	MPI	150 @ 5000	165 @ 4000	3.540 × 3.050	8.5:1	53–75 @ 3000
1990	B2200	133 (2.2)	2bbl	85 @ 4500	118 @ 2500	3.395 × 3.700	8.6:1	43–57 @ 3000
	B2200	133 (2.2)	MPI	91 @ 4500	118 @ 2000	3.395 × 3.700	8.6:1	43–57 @ 3000
	B2600i	159 (2.6)	MPI	121 @ 4600	149 @ 3500	3.622 × 3.858	8.4:1	44–58 @ 3000
	MPV	159 (2.6)	MPI	121 @ 4600	149 @ 3500	3.622 × 3.858	8.4:1	44–58 @ 3000
	MPV	180 (3.0)	MPI	150 @ 5000	165 @ 4000	3.540 × 3.050	8.5:1	53–75 @ 3000
1991	B2200	133 (2.2)	2bbl	85 @ 4500	118 @ 2500	3.395 × 3.700	8.6:1	43–57 @ 3000
	B2200	133 (2.2)	MPI	91 @ 4500	118 @ 2000	3.395 × 3.700	8.6:1	43–57 @ 3000
	B2600i	159 (2.6)	MPI	121 @ 4600	149 @ 3500	3.622 × 3.858	8.4:1	44–58 @ 3000
	MPV	159 (2.6)	MPI	121 @ 4600	149 @ 3500	3.622 × 3.858	8.4:1	44–58 @ 3000
	MPV	180 (3.0)	MPI	150 @ 5000	165 @ 4000	3.540 × 3.050	8.5:1	53–75 @ 3000
	Navajo	245 (4.0)	MPI	155 @ 4200	220 @ 2400	3.950 × 3.320	9.0:1	40–60 @ 2000

GENERAL ENGINE SPECIFICATIONS

Year	Model	Engine Displacement cu. in. (L)	Fuel System Type	Net Horsepower @ rpm	Net Torque @ rpm (ft. lbs.)	Bore × Stroke (in.)	Com-pression Ratio	Oil Pressure @ rpm
1992	B2200	133 (2.2)	2bbl	85 @ 4500	118 @ 2500	3.395 × 3.700	8.6:1	43–57 @ 3000
	B2200	133 (2.2)	MPI	91 @ 4500	118 @ 2000	3.395 × 3.700	8.6:1	43–57 @ 3000
	B2600i	159 (2.6)	MPI	121 @ 4600	149 @ 3500	3.622 × 3.858	8.4:1	44–58 @ 3000
	MPV	159 (2.6)	MPI	121 @ 4600	149 @ 3500	3.622 × 3.858	8.4:1	44–58 @ 3000
	MPV	180 (3.0)	MPI	150 @ 5000	165 @ 4000	3.540 × 3.050	8.5:1	53–75 @ 3000
	Navajo	245 (4.0)	MPI	155 @ 4200	220 @ 2400	3.950 × 3.320	9.0:1	40–60 @ 2000

MPI—Multi Port Injection

GASOLINE ENGINE TUNE-UP SPECIFICATIONS

Year	Model	Engine Displacement cu. in. (L)	Spark Plugs Type	Gap (in.)	Ignition Timing (deg.) MT	AT	Com-pression Pressure (psi)	Fuel Pump (psi)	Idle Speed (rpm) MT	AT	Valve Clearance In.	Ex.
1988	B2200	133 (2.2)	BPR5ES	0.030	6B	6B	173	①	825	825	Hyd.	Hyd.
	B2600	156 (2.6)	BUR6EA-11	0.041	7B	7B	171	2.8–3.6	825	825	Hyd.	Hyd.
1989	B2200	133 (2.2)	BPR5ES	0.030	6B②	6B②	173	①	825	825	Hyd.	Hyd.
	B2600i	159 (2.6)	ZFR5A-11	0.041	5B②	5B②	185	64–85	750②	750②	Hyd.	Hyd.
	MPV	159 (2.6)	ZFR5A-11	0.041	5B②	5B②	185	64–85	750②	770②	Hyd.	Hyd.
	MPV	180 (3.0)	ZFR5A-11	0.041	11B②	11B②	164	64–85	800②	800②	Hyd.	Hyd.
1990	B2200	133 (2.2)	③	④	6B②	6B②	173	①	⑤②	⑥②	Hyd.	Hyd.
	B2600i	159 (2.6)	ZFR5F-11	0.041	5B②	5B②	185	64–85	750②	770②	Hyd.	Hyd.
	MPV	159 (2.6)	ZFR5F-11	0.041	5B②	5B②	185	64–85	750②	770②	Hyd.	Hyd.
	MPV	180 (3.0)	ZFR5F-11	0.041	11B②	11B②	164	64–85	800②	800②	Hyd.	Hyd.
1991	B2200	133 (2.2)	③	④	6B②	6B②	173	①	⑤②	⑥②	Hyd.	Hyd.
	B2600i	159 (2.6)	ZFR5F-11	0.041	5B②	5B②	185	64–85	750②	770②	Hyd.	Hyd.
	MPV	159 (2.6)	ZFR5F-11	0.041	5B②	5B②	185	64–85	750②	770②	Hyd.	Hyd.
	MPV	180 (3.0)	ZFR5F-11	0.041	11B②	11B②	164	64–85	800②	800②	Hyd.	Hyd.
	Navajo	245 (4.0)	⑦	0.054	10B	10B	⑧	35–45	⑦	⑦	Hyd.	Hyd.
1992	B2200	133 (2.2)	③	④	6B②	6B②	173	①	⑤②	⑥②	Hyd.	Hyd.
	B2600i	159 (2.6)	ZFR5F-11	0.041	5B②	5B②	185	64–85	750②	770②	Hyd.	Hyd.
	MPV	159 (2.6)	ZFR5F-11	0.041	5B②	5B②	185	64–85	750②	770②	Hyd.	Hyd.
	MPV	180 (3.0)	ZFR5F-11	0.041	11B②	11B②	164	64–85	800②	800②	Hyd.	Hyd.
	Navajo	245 (4.0)	⑦	0.054	10B	10B	⑧	35–45	⑦	⑦	Hyd.	Hyd.

Hyd.—Hydraulic
① Carbureted engine
  Manual transmission—mechanical pump:
  3.7–4.7 psi
  Automatic transmission—electric pump:
  2.8–3.6 psi
  Fuel injected engine: 64–85 psi
② With test connector grounded
③ Carbureted engine BPR5ES
  Fuel injected engine BPR5ES-11
④ Carbureted engine 0.030 in.
  Fuel injected engine 0.041 in.
⑤ Carbureted engine 800 rpm
  Fuel injected engine 750 rpm
⑥ Carbureted engine 800 rpm
  Fuel injected engine 770 rpm
⑦ See underhood emissions information label
⑧ The compression pressure in the lowest
  cylinder must be at least 75% of that in the
  highest cylinder

FIRING ORDERS

NOTE: To avoid confusion, always replace the spark plug wires one at a time.

2.2L Engine
Engine Firing Order: 1–3–4–2
Distributor Rotation: Clockwise

2.6L (2555cc) and 2.6L (2606cc) Engines
Firing Order: 1–3–4–2
Distributor Rotation: Clockwise

4.0L Engine
Engine Firing Order: 1–4–2–5–3–6
Distributorless Ignition System

3.0L Engine
Engine Firing Order: 1–2–3–4–5–6
Distributor Rotation: Clockwise

CAPACITIES

Year	Model	Engine Displacement cu. in. (L)	Engine Crankcase with Filter	Engine Crankcase without Filter	Transmission (pts.) 4-Spd	Transmission (pts.) 5-Spd	Transmission (pts.) Auto.	Drive Axle (pts.)	Fuel Tank (gal.)	Cooling System (pts.)
1988	B2200	133 (2.2)	4.4	4.1	3.6	4.2	15.8	2.6	①	②
	B2600	156 (2.6)	③	④	—	⑤	15.8	⑥	①	⑦
1989	B2200	133 (2.2)	4.3	4.1	3.6	4.2	15.8	2.6	①	⑦
	B2600i	159 (2.6)	5.0	4.8	—	6.8	15.8	⑧	14.8	14.4
	MPV	159 (2.6)	5.0	4.8	—	5.2	18.2	3.2	15.9	⑨
	MPV	180 (3.0)	5.0	4.8	—	5.2	18.2	3.2	19.6	⑩
1990	B2200	133 (2.2)	4.3	4.1	3.6	4.2	15.8	2.6	①	⑦
	B2600i	159 (2.6)	5.0	4.8	—	⑪	⑫	⑧	14.8	14.4
	MPV	159 (2.6)	5.0	4.8	—	5.2	⑫	⑬	15.9	⑨
	MPV	180 (3.0)	5.0	4.8	—	5.2	⑫	⑬	19.6	⑩
1991	B2200	133 (2.2)	4.3	4.1	3.6	4.2	15.8	2.6	①	②
	B2600i	159 (2.6)	5.0	4.8	—	⑪	⑫	⑧	14.8	②
	MPV	159 (2.6)	5.0	4.8	—	⑭	⑫	⑬	15.9	⑨
	MPV	180 (3.0)	5.0	4.8	—	⑭	⑫	⑬	19.6	⑩
	Navajo	245 (4.0)	5.0	4.0	—	5.6	⑮	⑯	19.3	⑰

CAPACITIES

Year	Model	Engine Displacement cu. in. (L)	Engine Crankcase with Filter	Engine Crankcase without Filter	Transmission (pts.) 4-Spd	Transmission (pts.) 5-Spd	Transmission (pts.) Auto.	Drive Axle (pts.)	Fuel Tank (gal.)	Cooling System (pts.)
1992	B2200	133 (2.2)	4.3	4.1	—	4.2	15.8	2.6	①	②
	B2600i	159 (2.6)	5.0	4.8	—	⑪	⑫	⑧	14.8	②
	MPV	159 (2.6)	5.0	4.8	—	6.0	⑫	⑬	15.9	⑨
	MPV	180 (3.0)	5.0	4.8	—	6.0	⑫	⑬	19.6	⑩
	Navajo	245 (4.0)	5.0	4.0	—	5.6	⑮	⑯	19.3	⑰

① Short bed, cab plus—14.8 gal.
   Long bed—17.4 gal.
② With heater—15.8 pts.
   Without heater—14.6 pts.
③ 2WD—4.4 qts.
   4WD—5.2 qts.
④ 2WD—4.0 qts.
   4WD—4.8 qts.
⑤ 2WD—6.0 qts.
   4WD—6.8 qts.
⑥ 2WD—2.8 pts.
   4WD
     Front—2.6 pts.
     Rear—3.6 pts.

⑦ With heater—15.8 pts.
   Without heater—14.8 pts.
⑧ Front axle—3.2 pts.
   Rear axle—3.6 pts.
⑨ With manual transmission—14.4 pts.
   With automatic transmission—15.2 pts.
⑩ With manual transmission—20.2 pts.
   With automatic transmission—20.6 pts.
⑪ 2WD—6.0 pts.
   4WD—6.8 pts.
⑫ Hydraulically controlled—15.8 pts.
   Electronically controlled—18.2 pts.
⑬ Front axle—3.6 pts.
   Rear axle—3.2 pts.

⑭ 2WD—5.2 pts.
   4WD—6.0 pts.
⑮ 2WD—19.4 pts.
   4WD—20.9 pts.
⑯ Front axle—3.5 pts.
   Rear axle—5.3 pts.
⑰ Standard cooling system, all transmissions and manual air conditioning—16.2 pts.
   Super cooling with automatic transmission and air conditioning—17.0 pts.

CAMSHAFT SPECIFICATIONS

All measurements given in inches.

Year	Engine Displacement cu. in. (L)	Journal Diameter 1	Journal Diameter 2	Journal Diameter 3	Journal Diameter 4	Journal Diameter 5	Lobe Lift In.	Lobe Lift Ex.	Bearing Clearance	Camshaft End Play
1988	133 (2.2)	1.2575–1.2584	1.2563–1.2573	1.2563–1.2573	1.2563–1.2573	1.2575–1.2584	1.4970–1.4990	1.4970–1.4990	①	0.0030–0.0060
	156 (2.6)	1.3360–1.3366	1.3360–1.3366	1.3360–1.3366	1.3360–1.3366	1.3360–1.3366	1.6690	1.6690	0.002–0.004	0.0008–0.0070
1989	133 (2.2)	1.2575–1.2584	1.2563–1.2573	1.2563–1.2573	1.2563–1.2573	1.2575–1.2584	1.4984	1.4984	①	0.0031–0.0063
	159 (2.6)	1.1787–1.1797	1.1776–1.1785	1.1776–1.1785	1.1776–1.1785	1.1787–1.1797	1.6423	1.6344	①	0.0008–0.0059
	180 (3.0)	1.9268–1.9274	1.9258–1.9266	1.9258–1.9266	1.9268–1.9274	—	1.6163	1.6257	②	0.0020–0.0071
1990	133 (2.2)	1.2575–1.2584	1.2563–1.2573	1.2563–1.2573	1.2563–1.2573	1.2575–1.2584	1.4984	1.4984	①	0.0031–0.0063
	159 (2.6)	1.1787–1.1797	1.1776–1.1785	1.1776–1.1785	1.1776–1.1785	1.1787–1.1797	1.6423	1.6531	①	0.0008–0.0059
	180 (3.0)	1.9268–1.9274	1.9258–1.9266	1.9258–1.9266	1.9268–1.9274	—	1.6163	1.6257	②	0.0020–0.0071
1991	133 (2.2)	1.2575–1.2584	1.2563–1.2573	1.2563–1.2573	1.2563–1.2573	1.2575–1.2584	1.4984	1.4984	①	0.0031–0.0063
	159 (2.6)	1.1788–1.1797	1.1776–1.1786	1.1776–1.1786	1.1776–1.1786	1.1788–1.1797	1.6423	1.6531	①	0.0008–0.0059
	180 (3.0)	1.9268–1.9274	1.9258–1.9266	1.9258–1.9266	1.9268–1.9274	—	1.6163	1.6257	②	0.0020–0.0071
	245 (4.0)	1.9510–1.9520	1.9370–1.9380	1.9220–1.9230	1.9070–1.9080	—	NA	NA	0.0010–0.0026	0.0008–0.0040

CAMSHAFT SPECIFICATIONS

All measurements given in inches.

Year	Engine Displacement cu. in. (L)	Journal Diameter					Lobe Lift		Bearing Clearance	Camshaft End Play
		1	2	3	4	5	In.	Ex.		
1992	133 (2.2)	1.2575–1.2584	1.2563–1.2573	1.2563–1.2573	1.2563–1.2573	1.2575–1.2584	1.4984	1.4984	①	0.0031–0.0063
	159 (2.6)	1.1788–1.1797	1.1776–1.1786	1.1776–1.1786	1.1776–1.1786	1.1788–1.1797	1.6423	1.6531	①	0.0008–0.0059
	180 (3.0)	1.9261–1.9267	1.9258–1.9266	1.9258–1.9266	1.9268–1.9274	—	1.6163	1.6257	②	0.0020–0.0071
	245 (4.0)	1.9510–1.9520	1.9370–1.9380	1.9220–1.9230	1.9070–1.9080	—	NA	NA	0.0010–0.0026	0.0008–0.0040

NA—Not available
① No. 1 and No. 5: 0.0014–0.0033 in.
   No. 2, 3 and 4: 0.0026–0.0045 in.
② No. 1 and No. 4: 0.0024–0.0035 in.
   No. 2 and No. 3: 0.0031–0.0045 in.
③ No. 1 and No. 4: 0.0031–0.0044 in.
   No. 2 and No. 3: 0.0031–0.0047 in.

CRANKSHAFT AND CONNECTING ROD SPECIFICATIONS

Year	Engine Displacement cu. in. (L)	Crankshaft				Connecting Rod		
		Main Brg. Journal Dia.	Main Brg. Oil Clearance	Shaft End-play	Thrust on No.	Journal Diameter	Oil Clearance	Side Clearance
1988	133 (2.2)	2.3597–2.3605	0.0012–0.0019	0.0031–0.0071	3	2.0055–2.0061	0.0011–0.0026	0.0040–0.0100
	156 (2.6)	2.3614–2.3622	0.0008–0.0020	0.0020–0.0071	3	2.0855–2.0866	0.0008–0.0024	0.0040–0.0100
1989	133 (2.2)	2.3597–2.3604	①	0.0031–0.0071	3	2.0055–2.0061	0.0011–0.0026	0.0043–0.0103
	159 (2.6)	2.3597–2.3604	0.0010–0.0017	0.0031–0.0071	4	2.0055–2.0061	0.0011–0.0026	0.0043–0.0103
	180 (3.0)	2.4385–2.4392	0.0010–0.0015	0.0031–0.0111	4	2.0842–2.0848	0.0009–0.0025	0.0070–0.0130
1990	133 (2.2)	2.3597–2.3604	①	0.0031–0.0071	3	2.0055–2.0061	0.0011–0.0026	0.0043–0.0103
	159 (2.6)	2.3597–2.3604	0.0010–0.0017	0.0031–0.0071	4	2.0055–2.0061	0.0011–0.0026	0.0043–0.0103
	180 (3.0)	2.4385–2.4392	0.0010–0.0015	0.0031–0.0111	4	2.0842–2.0848	0.0009–0.0025	0.0070–0.0130
1991	133 (2.2)	2.3597–2.3604	①	0.0031–0.0071	3	2.0055–2.0061	0.0011–0.0026	0.0043–0.0103
	159 (2.6)	2.3597–2.3604	0.0010–0.0017	0.0031–0.0071	4	2.0055–2.0061	0.0011–0.0026	0.0043–0.0103
	180 (3.0)	2.4385–2.4392	0.0010–0.0015	0.0031–0.0111	4	2.0842–2.0848	0.0009–0.0025	0.0070–0.0130
	245 (4.0)	2.2433–2.2441	0.0005–0.0019	NA	3	2.1252–2.1260	0.0005–0.0022	NA
1992	133 (2.2)	2.3597–2.3604	①	0.0031–0.0071	3	2.0055–2.0061	0.0011–0.0026	0.0043–0.0103
	159 (2.6)	2.3597–2.3604	0.0010–0.0017	0.0031–0.0071	4	2.0055–2.0061	0.0011–0.0026	0.0043–0.0103
	180 (3.0)	2.4385–2.4392	0.0010–0.0015	0.0031–0.0111	4	2.0842–2.0848	0.0009–0.0025	0.0070–0.0130
	245 (4.0)	2.2433–2.2441	0.0005–0.0019	NA	3	2.1252–2.1260	0.0005–0.0022	NA

NA—Not available
① No. 1, 2, 4 and 5: 0.001–0.0017 in.
   No. 3: 0.0012–0.0019 in.

VALVE SPECIFICATIONS

Year	Displacement cu. in. (L)	Seat Angle (deg.)	Face Angle (deg.)	Spring Test Pressure (lbs.)	Spring Installed Height (in.)	Stem-to-Guide Clearance (in.)		Stem Diameter (in.)	
						Intake	Exhaust	Intake	Exhaust
1988	133 (2.2)	45	45	NA	NA	0.0010–0.0024	0.0012–0.0026	0.3161–0.3167	0.3159–0.3165
	156 (2.6)	45	45	NA	NA	0.0010–0.0023	0.0020–0.0035	0.3130–0.3140	0.3120–0.3130
1989	133 (2.2)	45	45	①	NA	0.0010–0.0024	0.0012–0.0026	0.3161–0.3167	0.3159–0.3165
	159 (2.6)	45	45	43.8–49.7 @ 1.693 in.	NA	0.0010–0.0024	0.0012–0.0026	0.2744–0.2750	0.2742–0.2748
	180 (3.0)	45	45	②	NA	0.0010–0.0024	0.0012–0.0026	0.2744–0.2750	0.3159–0.3165
1990	133 (2.2)	45	45	①	NA	0.0010–0.0024	0.0012–0.0026	0.3161–0.3167	0.3159–0.3165
	159 (2.6)	45	45	43.8–49.7 @ 1.693 in.	NA	0.0010–0.0024	0.0012–0.0026	0.2744–0.2750	0.2742–0.2748
	180 (3.0)	45	45	③	NA	0.0010–0.0024	0.0012–0.0026	0.2744–0.2750	0.3159–0.3165
1991	133 (2.2)	45	45	①	NA	0.0010–0.0024	0.0012–0.0026	0.3161–0.3167	0.3159–0.3165
	159 (2.6)	45	45	43.8–49.7 @ 1.693 in.	NA	0.0010–0.0024	0.0012–0.0026	0.2744–0.2750	0.2742–0.2748
	180 (3.0)	45	45	③	NA	0.0010–0.0024	0.0012–0.0026	0.2744–0.2750	0.3159–0.3165
	245 (4.0)	45	44	138–149 @ 1.22 in.	1.58–1.61	0.0008–0.0025	0.0018–0.0035	0.3159–0.3167	0.3149–0.3156
1992	133 (2.2)	45	45	①	NA	0.0010–0.0024	0.0012–0.0026	0.3161–0.3167	0.3159–0.3165
	159 (2.6)	45	45	43.8–49.7 @ 1.693 in.	NA	0.0010–0.0024	0.0012–0.0026	0.2744–0.2750	0.2742–0.2748
	180 (3.0)	45	45	②	NA	0.0010–0.0024	0.0012–0.0026	0.2744–0.2750	0.3159–0.3165
	245 (4.0)	45	44	138–149 @ 1.22 in.	1.58–1.61	0.0008–0.0025	0.0018–0.0035	0.3159–0.3167	0.3149–0.3156

NA—Not available
① Outer spring—94.6 @ 1.22 in.
  Inner spring—66.0 @ 1.04 in.
② Intake
  Outer—29.3–33.2 @ 1.732 in.
  Inner—19.6–22.2 @ 1.555 in.

Exhaust
  Outer—51.9–58.7 @ 1.772 in.
  Inner—33.2–37.4 @ 1.594 in.
③ Intake
  Outer—31–33 @ 1.969 in.
  Inner—21–22 @ 1.555 in.

Exhaust
  Outer—51.9–58.7 @ 1.386 in.
  Inner—27.5–37.4 @ 1.496 in.

PISTON AND RING SPECIFICATIONS

Year	Displacement cu. in. (L)	Piston Clearance	Ring Gap			Ring Side Clearance		
			Top Compression	Bottom Compression	Oil Control	Top Compression	Bottom Compression	Oil Control
1988	133 (2.2)	0.0014–0.0030	0.008–0.014	0.006–0.012	0.012–0.035	0.0012–0.0028	0.0012–0.0028	Snug
	156 (2.6)	0.0008–0.0160	0.012–0.018	0.010–0.016	0.012–0.024	0.0020–0.0035	0.0008–0.0024	Snug

PISTON AND RING SPECIFICATIONS

Year	Displacement cu. in. (L)	Piston Clearance	Ring Gap			Ring Side Clearance		
			Top Compression	Bottom Compression	Oil Control	Top Compression	Bottom Compression	Oil Control
1989	133 (2.2)	0.0014–0.0030	0.008–0.014	0.006–0.012	0.008–0.028	0.0012–0.0028	0.0012–0.0028	Snug
	159 (2.6)	0.0023–0.0029	0.008–0.014	0.010–0.016	0.008–0.028	0.0012–0.0028	0.0012–0.0028	Snug
	180 (3.0)	0.0019–0.0026	0.008–0.014	0.006–0.012	0.008–0.028	0.0012–0.0028	0.0012–0.0028	Snug
1990	133 (2.2)	0.0014–0.0030	0.008–0.014	0.006–0.012	0.008–0.028	0.0012–0.0028	0.0012–0.0028	Snug
	159 (2.6)	0.0023–0.0029	0.008–0.014	0.010–0.016	0.008–0.028	0.0012–0.0028	0.0012–0.0028	Snug
	180 (3.0)	0.0019–0.0026	0.008–0.014	0.006–0.012	0.008–0.028	0.0012–0.0028	0.0012–0.0028	Snug
1991	133 (2.2)	0.0014–0.0030	0.008–0.014	0.006–0.012	0.008–0.028	0.0012–0.0028	0.0012–0.0028	Snug
	159 (2.6)	0.0023–0.0029	0.008–0.014	0.010–0.016	0.008–0.028	0.0012–0.0028	0.0012–0.0028	Snug
	180 (3.0)	0.0019–0.0026	0.008–0.014	0.006–0.012	0.008–0.028	0.0012–0.0028	0.0012–0.0028	Snug
	245 (4.0)	0.0008–0.0019	0.015–0.023	0.015–0.023	0.015–0.055	0.0020–0.0033	0.0020–0.0033	Snug
1992	133 (2.2)	0.0017–0.0024	0.008–0.014	0.006–0.012	0.008–0.028	0.0012–0.0028	0.0012–0.0028	Snug
	159 (2.6)	0.0023–0.0029	0.008–0.014	0.010–0.016	0.008–0.028	0.0012–0.0028	0.0012–0.0028	Snug
	180 (3.0)	0.0009–0.0022	0.008–0.014	0.006–0.012	0.008–0.028	0.0012–0.0028	0.0012–0.0028	Snug
	245 (4.0)	0.0008–0.0019	0.015–0.023	0.015–0.023	0.015–0.055	0.0020–0.0033	0.0020–0.0033	Snug

TORQUE SPECIFICATIONS

Year	No. Cylinder Displacement cu. in. (L)	Cylinder Head Bolts	Main Bearing Bolts	Rod Bearing Bolts	Crankshaft Pulley Bolts	Flywheel Bolts	Manifold		Spark Plugs
							Intake	Exhaust	
1988	133 (2.2)	59–64	61–65	48–51	9–13	71–76	14–19	19	11–15
	156 (2.6)	①	54–61	33–35	80–94	94–101	11–14	19	11–15
1989	133 (2.2)	59–64	61–65	48–51	9–13	71–76	14–19	19	11–15
	159 (2.6)	59–64	61–65	48–51	130–145	67–72	14–19	19	11–15
	180 (3.0)	②	③	④	116–123	76–81	14–19	19	11–15
1990	133 (2.2)	59–64	61–65	48–51	9–13	71–76	14–19	19	11–15
	159 (2.6)	59–64	61–65	48–51	130–145	67–72	14–19	19	11–15
	180 (3.0)	②	③	④	116–123	76–81	14–19	19	11–15
1991	133 (2.2)	59–64	61–65	48–51	9–13	71–76	14–19	19	11–15
	159 (2.6)	59–64	61–65	48–51	130–145	67–72	14–19	19	11–15
	180 (3.0)	②	③	④	116–123	76–81	14–19	19	11–15
	245 (4.0)	⑤	66–77	19–24	⑥	59	⑦	19	11–15

TORQUE SPECIFICATIONS

Year	No. Cylinder Displacement cu. in. (L)	Cylinder Head Bolts	Main Bearing Bolts	Rod Bearing Bolts	Crankshaft Pulley Bolts	Flywheel Bolts	Manifold Intake	Manifold Exhaust	Spark Plugs
1992	133 (2.2)	59–64	61–65	48–51	9–13	71–76	14–19	19	11–15
	159 (2.6)	59–64	61–65	48–51	130–145	67–72	14–19	19	11–15
	180 (3.0)	②	③	④	116–123	76–81	14–19	19	11–15
	245 (4.0)	⑤	66–77	19–24	⑥	59	⑦	19	11–15

① Bolts 1-10: 65–72 ft. lbs.
  Bolts 11-12: 11–16 ft. lbs.
② Tighten in 3 steps
  Step 1: 14 ft. lbs.
  Step 2: +90° turn
  Step 3: +90° turn
③ Tighten in 3 steps
  Step 1: 14 ft. lbs.
  Step 2: +90° turn
  Step 3: +45° turn
④ Tighten in 2 steps
  Step 1: 22 ft. lbs.
  Step 2: +90° turn

⑤ Tighten in 7 steps
  Step 1: Tighten cyl. head bolts to 44 ft. lbs.
  Step 2: Tighten intake man. bolts to 3–6 ft. lbs.
  Step 3: Tighten cyl. head bolts to 59 ft. lbs.
  Step 4: Tighten intake man. bolts to 6–11 ft. lbs.
  Step 5: Tighten cyl. head bolts to +85° ft. lbs.
  Step 6: Tighten intake man. bolts to 11–15 ft. lbs.

Step 7: Tighten intake man. bolts to 15–18 ft. lbs.
⑥ Tighten in 2 steps
  Step 1: 30–37 ft. lbs.
  Step 1: +90° turn
⑦ Tighten in 4 steps
  Step 1: 3–6 ft. lbs.
  Step 2: 6–11 ft. lbs.
  Step 3: 11–15 ft. lbs.
  Step 4: 15–18 ft. lbs.

BRAKE SPECIFICATIONS

All measurements in inches unless noted

Year	Model	Lug Nut Torque (ft. lbs.)	Master Cylinder Bore	Brake Disc Minimum Thickness	Brake Disc Maximum Runout	Standard Brake Drum Diameter	Minimum Lining Thickness Front	Minimum Lining Thickness Rear
1988	B2200	①	0.875	0.71	0.006	10.24	0.118	0.04
	B2600	①	0.875	0.79	0.006	10.24	0.118	0.04
1989	B2200	①	0.875	0.71	0.006	10.24	0.118	0.04
	B2600i	①	0.875	0.79	0.006	10.24	0.118	0.04
	MPV	65–87	0.940	0.87	0.004	10.24	0.080	0.04
1990	B2200	①	0.875	0.71	0.006	10.24	0.118	0.04
	B2600i	①	0.875	②	0.006	10.24	0.118	0.04
	MPV	65–87	0.940	0.87	0.004	10.24	0.080	0.04
1991	B2200	①	0.875	0.71	0.006	10.24	0.118	0.04
	B2600i	①	0.875	②	0.006	10.24	0.118	0.04
	MPV	65–87	0.940	③	0.004	10.24	0.080	0.04
	Navajo	100	0.937	0.81	0.003	10.00	0.120	0.03
1992	B2200	①	0.875	0.71	0.006	10.24	0.118	0.04
	B2600i	①	0.875	②	0.006	10.24	0.118	0.04
	MPV	65–87	0.940	③	0.004	10.24	0.080	0.04
	Navajo	100	0.937	0.81	0.003	10.00	0.120	0.03

① Design wheels 65–87 ft. lbs.
  Styled wheels 87–108 ft. lbs.
② 2WD—0.71 in.
  4WD—0.79 in.
③ 2WD—1.10 in.
  4WD—1.02 in.

WHEEL ALIGNMENT

Year	Model	Caster Range (deg.)	Caster Preferred Setting (deg.)	Camber Range (deg.)	Camber Preferred Setting (deg.)	Toe-in (in.)	Steering Axis Inclination (deg.)
1988	B2200	①	②	7/16P–1 1/4P	3/4P	1/8	8 1/4
	B2600	1 1/4P–2 3/4P	2P	11/16P–1 1/2P	1P	1/8	10 5/16

WHEEL ALIGNMENT

Year	Model	Caster Range (deg.)	Caster Preferred Setting (deg.)	Camber Range (deg.)	Camber Preferred Setting (deg.)	Toe-in (in.)	Steering Axis Inclination (deg.)
1989	B2200	①	②	7/16P–1¼P	¾P	⅛	8¼
	B2600i	1¼P–2¾P	2P	11/16P–1½P	1P	⅛	10 5/16
	MPV	4 11/16P–6 3/16P	5 7/16P	⅜N–1⅛P	⅜P	5/32	12 15/16
1990	B2200	①	②	7/16P–1¼P	¾P	⅛	8¼
	B2600i	①	②	③	④	⅛	⑤
	MPV	⑥	⑦	⑧	⑨	5/32	⑩
1991	B2200	①	②	7/16P–1¼P	¾P	⅛	8¼
	B2600i	①	②	③	④	⅛	⑤
	MPV	⑥	⑦	⑧	⑨	5/32	⑩
	Navajo	2½P–6P	NA	¾N–1¼P	NA	0	NA
1992	B2200	①	②	7/16P–1¼P	¾P	⅛	8¼
	B2600i	①	②	③	④	⅛	⑤
	MPV	⑥	⑦	⑧	⑨	5/32	⑩
	Navajo	2½P–6P	NA	¾N–1¼P	NA	0	NA

N—Negative
P—Positive
NA—Not available
① 2WD
   With manual steering 1/16P–1 9/16P
   With power steering 1 1/16P–2 9/16P
  4WD   1¼P–2¾P
② 2WD
   With manual steering 13/16P
   With power steering 1 13/16P
  4WD   2P

③ 2WD 7/16P–1¼P
   4WD 11/16P–1½P
④ 2WD ¾P
   4WD 1P
⑤ 2WD 8¼°
   4WD 10 5/16°
⑥ 2WD 4 11/16P–6 3/16P
   4WD 4¾P–6¼P
⑦ 2WD 5 7/16P
   4WD 5½P

⑧ 2WD ⅜N–1⅛P
   4WD 5/16N–1 1/16P
⑨ 2WD ⅜P
   4WD 3/16P
⑩ 2WD 12 15/16°
   4WD 11 13/16°

ENGINE ELECTRICAL

NOTE: **Disconnecting the negative battery cable on some vehicles may interfere with the functions of the on board computer systems and may require the computer to undergo a relearning process, once the negative battery cable is reconnected.**

Distributor

Removal

1. Disconnect the negative battery cable.
2. Remove the distributor cap from the distributor, leaving the spark plug wires attached. If spark plug wire removal is necessary to remove the distributor cap, tag the wires prior to removal so they can be reinstalled in the correct position.
3. Disconnect the electrical connectors and vacuum hose(s), if equipped, from the distributor.
4. Mark the position of the rotor in relation to the distributor housing and the position of the distributor housing on the cylinder head.
5. Remove the distributor hold-down bolt(s) and remove the distributor.
6. Check the distributor O-ring for cuts or other damage and replace, if necessary.

Installation

TIMING NOT DISTURBED

1. Lubricate the distributor O-ring with clean engine oil.
2. Install the distributor with the hold-down bolt(s), aligning the marks that were made during removal. Tighten the hold-down bolt(s) to 14–19 ft. lbs. (19–25 Nm).
3. Connect the electrical connectors and vacuum hose(s), if equipped.
4. Install the distributor cap on the distributor. Connect the spark plug wires, if removed.
5. Connect the negative battery cable. Start the engine and check the ignition timing.

TIMING DISTURBED

1. Disconnect the spark plug wire from the No. 1 cylinder spark plug and remove the spark plug. Place a finger over the spark plug hole.
2. Turn the crankshaft in the normal direction of rotation until compression is felt at the spark plug hole.
3. Align the mark on the crankshaft pulley with the TDC mark on the timing belt cover.
4. Lubricate the distributor O-ring with clean engine oil.

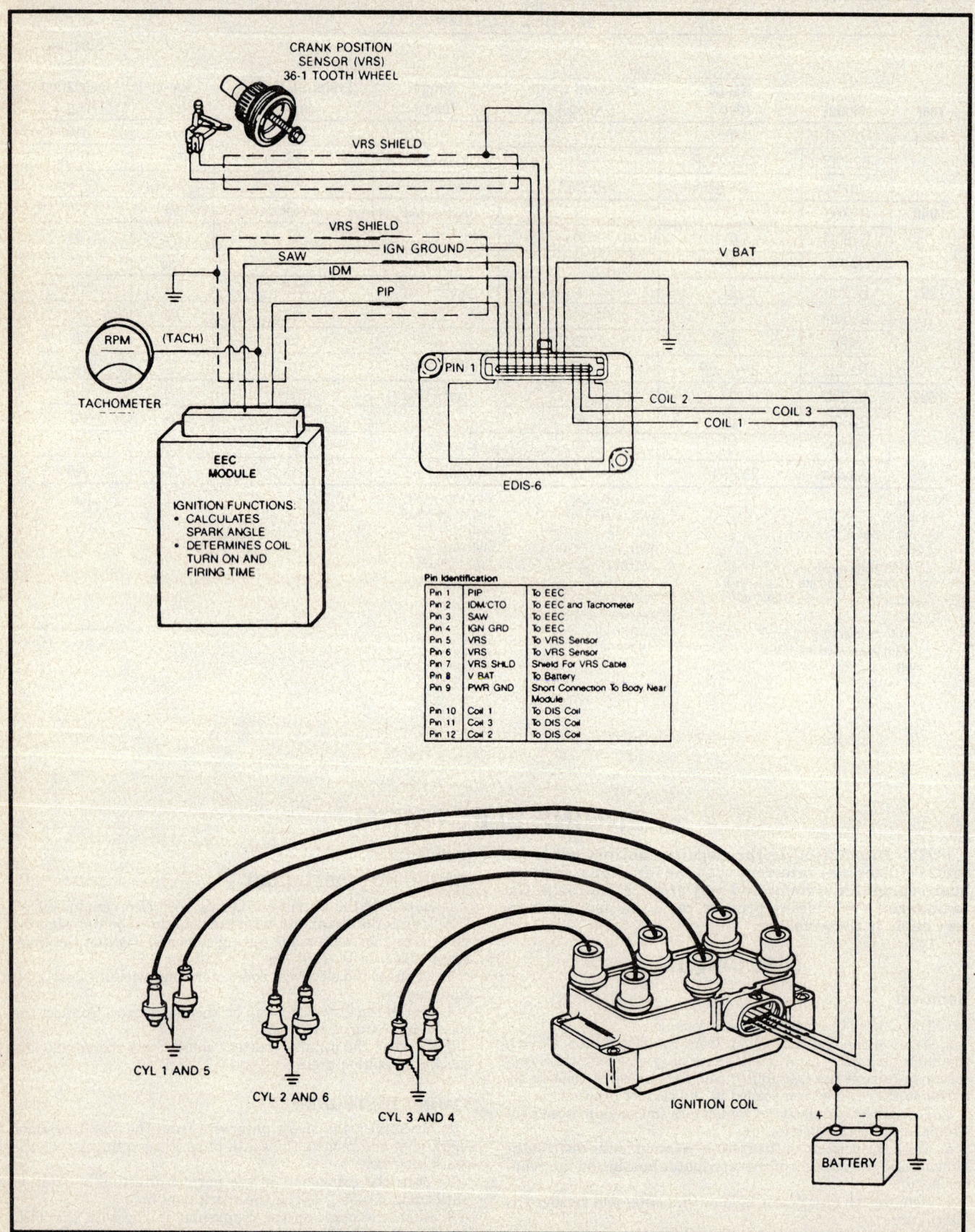

CRANK POSITION
SENSOR (VRS)
36-1 TOOTH WHEEL

VRS SHIELD

VRS SHIELD

SAW

IGN GROUND

IDM

PIP

V BAT

RPM

(TACH)

TACHOMETER

PIN 1

COIL 2

COIL 3

COIL 1

EDIS-6

EEC
MODULE

IGNITION FUNCTIONS:
• CALCULATES
  SPARK ANGLE
• DETERMINES COIL
  TURN ON AND
  FIRING TIME

Pin Identification

Pin 1	PIP	To EEC
Pin 2	IDM/CTO	To EEC and Tachometer
Pin 3	SAW	To EEC
Pin 4	IGN GRD	To EEC
Pin 5	VRS	To VRS Sensor
Pin 6	VRS	To VRS Sensor
Pin 7	VRS SHLD	Shield For VRS Cable
Pin 8	V BAT	To Battery
Pin 9	PWR GND	Short Connection To Body Near Module
Pin 10	Coil 1	To DIS Coil
Pin 11	Coil 3	To DIS Coil
Pin 12	Coil 2	To DIS Coil

CYL 1 AND 5

CYL 2 AND 6

CYL 3 AND 4

IGNITION COIL

BATTERY

Distributorless ignition system—4.0L engine

5. Turn the distributor shaft until the rotor points to the No. 1 spark plug tower on the distributor cap and install the distributor. Install the distributor hold-down bolt(s) and align the distributor housing with the mark made on the cylinder head during removal. Snug the bolt(s).

6. Connect the electrical connectors and vacuum hose(s), if equipped.

7. Install the distributor cap on the distributor. Connect the spark plug wires, if removed.

8. Install the spark plug in the No. 1 cylinder and connect the spark plug wire.

9. Connect the negative battery cable. Start the engine and adjust the ignition timing. Tighten the distributor hold-down bolt(s) to 14–19 ft. lbs. (19–25 Nm) after the timing has been set.

Distributorless Ignition

Removal and Installation

CRANKSHAFT SENSOR

1. Disconnect the negative battery cable.

2. Disconnect the sensor electrical connector from the wiring harness.

3. Remove the crankshaft sensor mounting screws and remove the sensor.

4. Installation is the reverse of the removal procedure. Tighten the screws to 75–106 inch lbs. (8.5–12 Nm).

IGNITION MODULE

1. Disconnect the battery cables and remove the battery.

2. Disconnect the electrical connector at the module.

3. Remove the module retaining bolt and remove the module.

4. Installation is the reverse of the removal procedure. Tighten the mounting bolt to 22–31 inch lbs. (2.5–3.5 Nm).

IGNITION COIL PACK

1. Disconnect the negative battery cable.

2. Disconnect the electrical harness connector from the coil pack.

3. Remove the spark plug wires by squeezing the locking tabs to release the coil boot retainers.

4. Remove the coil pack retaining screws and remove the coil pack.

5. Installation is the reverse of the removal procedure. Tighten the screws to 40–62 inch lbs. (4.5–7.0 Nm).

Ignition Timing

Adjustment

EXCEPT 4.0L ENGINE

1. Before starting the engine, clean and mark the timing marks on the timing belt cover and crankshaft pulley.

2. Connect a timing light and tachometer according to the manufacturers instructions.

3. Start the engine and bring to normal operating temperature. Turn all electric loads **OFF**.

4. On fuel injected vehicles, connect a jumper wire between the green 1-pin test connector and ground.

5. Check the idle speed and adjust, if necessary, to the specification on the underhood emission information label.

6. Aim the timing light and verify that the timing marks on the crankshaft pulley and timing belt cover are aligned. If the marks are aligned, proceed to Step 8.

7. If the marks are not aligned, loosen the distributor hold-down bolts and turn the distributor housing to adjust the timing. Tighten the hold-down bolts to 14–19 ft. lbs. (19–25 Nm) and recheck the timing.

8. Shut off the engine. Remove the jumper wire and all test equipment.

Timing mark location—2.2L and 1989–92 2.6L engines

Timing mark location—3.0L engine

4.0L ENGINE

Timing on the 4.0L engine is preset from the factory at 10 degrees BTDC and is not adjustable.

Alternator

For further information, please refer to "Alternators" in the Unit Repair section.

Precautions

Several precautions must be observed with alternator equipped vehicles to avoid damage to the unit.

• If the battery is removed for any reason, make sure it is reconnected with the correct polarity. Reversing the battery connections may result in damage to the one-way rectifiers.

• When utilizing a booster battery as a starting aid, always connect the positive to positive terminals and the negative terminal from the booster battery to a good engine ground on the vehicle being started.

• Never use a fast charger as a booster to start vehicles.

• Disconnect the battery cables when charging the battery with a fast charger.

• Never attempt to polarize the alternator.

• Do not use test lights of more than 12V when checking diode continuity.

• Do not short across or ground any of the alternator terminals.

• The polarity of the battery, alternator and regulator must be matched and considered before making any electrical connections within the system.

• Never separate the alternator on an open circuit. Make sure all connections within the circuit are clean and tight.

• Disconnect the battery ground terminal when performing any service on electrical components.

• Disconnect the battery if arc welding is to be done on the vehicle.

Belt Tension Adjustment

EXCEPT 4.0L ENGINE

1. Disconnect the negative battery cable.
2. Check the belt tension by applying approximately 22 lbs. pressure mid-way between the pulleys and measuring the belt deflection. Belt deflection specifications are as follows:

2.2L and 1988 2.6L engines—New belt: 0.28–0.31 in., Used belt: 0.31–0.35 in.

1989–92 2.6L engine—New belt: 0.39–0.47 in., Used belt: 0.43–0.51 in.

3.0L engine—New belt: 0.35–0.39 in., Used belt: 0.39–0.47 in.

3. If belt tension is incorrect, loosen the alternator pivot and adjusting bolts. Position the alternator housing using a suitable tool to attain correct belt tension. Be careful not to damage the alternator housing.
4. When correct belt tension is achieved, tighten the alternator adjusting bolt to 14–19 ft. lbs. (19–25 Nm) on all except 2.2L engine. On 2.2L engine, tighten the adjusting bolt to 23–34 ft. lbs. (31–46 Nm).
5. Tighten the alternator pivot bolt to 27–38 ft. lbs. (37–52 Nm).
6. Connect the negative battery cable.

4.0L ENGINE

Belt tension is maintained by an automatic tensioner; no adjustment is necessary.

Removal and Installation

1. Disconnect the negative battery cable.
2. Disconnect the electrical connectors at the alternator. Remove the wiring connector bracket on 4.0L engine.
3. On the 3.0L engine, loosen the power steering pump drive belt adjusting locknut and remove the drive belt. Remove the power steering pump pulley.
4. On all except 4.0L engine, loosen the alternator adjusting and pivot bolts and remove the drive belt. On 4.0L engine, loosen the drive belt tensioner and remove the drive belt.
5. Remove the alternator bolts and remove the alternator.
6. Installation is the reverse of the removal procedure. Tight-en the alternator mounting bolts on 4.0L engine to 22–30 ft. lbs. (30–40 Nm). Adjust the belt tension on all except 4.0L engine.
7. Tighten the power steering pump pulley nut to 29–43 ft. lbs. (39–59 Nm).

Starter

For further information, please refer to "Starters" in the Unit Repair section.

Removal and Installation

EXCEPT 4WD MPV

1. Disconnect the negative battery cable. Raise and safely support the vehicle.
2. Disconnect the electrical connectors from the starter.
3. Remove the starter mounting bolts and remove the starter.
4. Installation is the reverse of the removal procedure. Tight-en the starter mounting bolts to 24–33 ft. lbs. (32–46 Nm) on 1988 vehicles, 27–38 ft. lbs. (37–52 Nm) on 1989–92 vehicles except 4.0L engine or 15–20 ft. lbs. (21–27 Nm) on 4.0L engine.

4WD MPV

1. Disconnect the negative battery cable.
2. Remove the alternator.
3. Raise and safely support the vehicle. Remove the splash shields.
4. Remove the power steering pump mounting bolts and position the pump aside, without disconnecting the power steering hoses.
5. Remove the automatic transmission cooler line brackets.
6. Mark the position of the driveshaft on the axle flange and remove the front driveshaft.
7. Remove the wiring harness bracket and the automatic transmission cooler line bracket that is next to the starter.
8. Disconnect the electrical connectors from the starter.
9. Remove the fuel and brake line shield.
10. Remove the starter mounting bolts and remove the starter.
11. Installation is the reverse of the removal procedure. Tight-en the starter mounting bolts to 27–38 ft. lbs. (37–52 Nm).

CHASSIS ELECTRICAL

Heater Blower Motor

Removal and Installation

EXCEPT NAVAJO

1. Disconnect the negative battery cable.
2. On B Series Pick-Up, remove the ECU. On MPV, remove the passenger side lower panel and undercover.
3. Disconnect the electrical connector from the blower motor.
4. Remove the attaching screws and remove the blower motor.
5. Installation is the reverse of the removal procedure.

NAVAJO

1. Disconnect the negative battery cable.
2. Remove the air cleaner.
3. Disconnect the wire harness connector from the blower motor by pushing down on the tab while pulling the connector off at the motor.
4. If equipped with air conditioning, remove the 3 solenoid box cover retaining bolts and the solenoid box cover.
5. Disconnect the blower motor cooling tube at the blower motor.
6. Remove the 3 attaching screws and remove the blower motor.
7. If necessary, remove the blower wheel hub push-nut and remove the blower wheel.
8. Installation is the reverse of the removal procedure.

Window Wiper Motor

Removal and Installation

FRONT

B Series Pick-Up

1. Disconnect the negative battery cable. Remove the wiper arm/blade assembly.
2. Remove the rubber seal from the leading edge of the cowl grille.
3. Remove the attaching screws and remove the cowl grille.
4. Remove the access hole covers.

Blower motor assembly exploded view—MPV

Blower motor assembly exploded view—Navajo

5. Remove the bolts attaching the wiper shaft drives.

6. Matchmark the position of the wiper linkage in relation to the face of the wiper motor. Disconnect the wiper linkage from the wiper motor.

7. Disconnect the electrical connector from the wiper motor.

8. Remove the mounting bolts and the wiper motor.

To install:

9. Position the wiper motor and install the mounting bolts. Tighten to 61–87 inch lbs. (6.9–9.8 Nm).

10. Connect the electrical connector.

11. Attach the wiper linkage to the motor, aligning the mark that was made during removal.

12. Install the bolts attaching the wiper shaft drives and tighten to 61–87 inch lbs. (6.9–9.8 Nm).

13. Install the access hole covers, cowl grille and seal.

14. Install the wiper arm/blade assemblies. Adjust the arm height to 0.8 in. (20mm) from the lower windshield moulding and tighten the arm retaining nuts to 7.2–10 ft. lbs. (9.8–14 Nm).

15. Connect the negative battery cable and check wiper operation.

MPV

1. Disconnect the negative battery cable.

2. Disconnect the electrical connector from the wiper motor.

3. Disconnect the wiper linkage from the motor crank arm. If necessary to remove the crank arm from the motor, matchmark the arm to the bracket prior to removal.

4. Remove the mounting bolts and remove the wiper motor.

To install:

5. Position the wiper motor and install the mounting bolts. Tighten to 61–87 inch lbs. (6.9–9.8 Nm).

6. If removed, install the motor crank arm, aligning the marks that were made during removal.

7. Connect the wiper linkage to the motor crank arm. Connect the electrical connector.

8. Make sure when in the park position, the wiper blades are 0.98–1.38 in. (25–35mm) from the lower windshield moulding.

Navajo

1. Turn the wiper switch **ON**. Turn the ignition switch **ON** until the blades are straight up, then turn the ignition **OFF** to keep them there.

2. Disconnect the negative battery cable, then disconnect the electrical connector from the wiper motor.

3. Remove the right wiper arm and blade assembly. Remove the right pivot nut and allow the linkage to drop into the cowl.

4. Remove the linkage access cover, located on the right side of the dash panel, near the wiper motor.

5. Reach through the access cover opening and unsnap the wiper motor clip. Push the clip away from the linkage until it clears the nib on the crank pin, then push the clip off the linkage. Remove the linkage from the crank pin.

6. Remove the 3 attaching screws and remove the wiper motor.

To install:

7. Install the motor with the attaching screws. Tighten to 60–85 inch lbs. (6.8–9.6 Nm). Connect the motor electrical connector.

8. Install the clip completely onto the right linkage, making sure it is fully seated. Do not put the linkage on the motor crank pin and then try to install the clip.

9. Install the left and right linkage onto the wiper motor crank pin. Pull the linkage onto the crank pin until it snaps into place. The clip is properly installed if the nib is protruding through the center of the clip.

10. Install the right wiper pivot shaft and nut. Tighten the nut to 84–110 inch lbs. (9.5–12.5 Nm).

11. Connect the negative battery cable and turn the ignition **ON**. Turn the wiper switch **OFF** so the wiper motor will park, then turn the ignition **OFF**. Install the right linkage access cover.

12. Install the right wiper blade and arm assembly and test the system.

REAR

MPV

1. Disconnect the negative battery cable.

2. Remove the wiper arm cover, retaining nut and the wiper arm/blade assembly.

3. Remove the seal cap and outer bushing.

4. Remove the liftgate trim panel and screen.

5. Disconnect the electrical connector, remove the mounting bolts and remove the wiper motor.

To install:

6. Position the wiper motor and install the attaching bolts. Tighten to 61–87 inch lbs. (6.9–9.8 Nm).

7. Connect the electrical connector.

8. Install the screen and liftgate trim panel.

9. Install the seal cap and outer bushing.

10. Connect the negative battery cable. Set the motor shaft to the park position by turning the rear wiper switch from **ON** to **OFF**.

11. Install the wiper arm/blade assembly so the blade is 0.98–

1.38 in. (25–35mm) from the lower window moulding.

12. Install the arm retaining nut and tighten to 52–87 inch lbs. (5.9–9.8 Nm). Install the wiper arm cover.

Navajo

1. Disconnect the negative battery cable.
2. Remove the wiper arm and blade assembly.
3. Remove the liftgate inner trim panel.
4. Rmove the 3 motor bracket attaching screws and pull the motor and bracket assembly out of the rubber grommet.
5. Disconnect the electrical connector and disengage the wiring locator pins. Remove the motor.

To install:

6. Position the motor in the liftgate rubber grommet and install the attaching screws.
7. Connect the electrical connector and install the wiring locator pins in the holes provided.
8. Install the wiper arm and blade assembly. Connect the negative battery cable and check wiper operation.
9. Install the liftgate inner trim panel.

Window Wiper Switch

Removal and Installation

FRONT

The function of the front wipers is controlled by the combination switch.

REAR

MPV

1. Disconnect the negative battery cable.
2. Remove the front cluster panel.
3. Remove the attaching screws from the left cluster switch, disconnect the electrical connectors and remove the rear wiper switch.
4. Installation is the reverse of the removal procedure.

Navajo

1. Disconnect the negative battery cable.
2. Remove the 2 ash tray retaining screws and remove the ash tray.
3. Remove the cluster trim panel, which is held on by clips.
4. Remove the snap-in switch mounting bezel containing the switches and disconnect the electrical connector.
5. Remove the switch from the mounting bezel by pushing on the switch from the connector side until the snap-in mounting clips release.
6. Installation is the reverse of the removal procedure.

Instrument Cluster

Removal and Installation

B SERIES PICK-UP

1. Disconnect the negative battery cable.
2. Remove the screws and the instrument cluster hood.
3. Remove the instrument cluster attaching screws.
4. Pull the cluster rearward enough to gain access to the rear of the cluster. Disconnect the electrical connectors and speedometer cable.
5. Remove the instrument cluster.
6. Installation is the reverse of the removal procedure.

MPV

1. Disconnect the negative battery cable.
2. Remove the screws attaching the front cluster assembly. Disconnect the electrical connectors from the cluster assembly switches and remove the cluster assembly.
3. Remove the instrument cluster attaching screws.
4. Pull the cluster rearward enough to gain access to the rear

of the cluster. Disconnect the electrical connectors and speedometer cable.

5. If equipped with automatic transmission, remove the lock pin from the shift position indicator wire end.
6. Remove the instrument cluster.
7. Installation is the reverse of the removal procedure. If equipped with automatic transmission, adjust the shift position indicator as follows:

   a. Using moderate force, pull the shift position indicator wire end out fully to set the indicator position. Only pull the wire until the indicator is felt to bottom. Do not use excessive force.

   b. Using a small prybar, properly align the spring hook. Pull the indicator wire until it just stops. Be careful not to move the position indicator after aligning.

   c. Install a suitable adjusting pin in the position indicator wire end.

   d. Install the instrument cluster.

   e. Make sure the transmission selector lever is in **P**.

   f. Mount the shift position indicator wire housing to the outer bracket using the clip. Hook the position indicator wire to the selector.

   g. Turn the ignition switch to **ACC**. Move the selector lever from **P** to **L** to **P**.

   h. Remove the adjusting pin and install the lock pin.

NAVAJO

1. Disconnect the negative battery cable.
2. Open the ash tray and remove the 2 screws attaching the ash tray and instrument cluster trim panel. Remove the ash tray.
3. Unsnap the cluster trim panel by pulling rearward around the edge of the panel. Depress the hazard warning switch on the steering column and remove the cluster trim panel.
4. Remove the 4 screws securing the instrument cluster to the instrument panel.

Shift position indicator adjustment—MPV

INSTRUMENT CLUSTER

CLUSTER ASSEMBLY

SPEEDOMETER
CABLE

LOCK PIN (A/T)

Instrument cluster removal—MPV

A/T POSITION INDICATOR

MILEAGE
SENSOR

SPEED
SENSOR

SPEEDOMETER

WATER TEMPERATURE
GAUGE

TACHOMETER

FUEL GAUGE

Instrument cluster exploded view—MPV

Radio removal tool — Navajo

5. If equipped with automatic transmission, remove the 2 screws attaching the shift position indicator to the cluster and slide the indicator down and out of the cluster. Leave the indicator connections undisturbed.

6. Pull the cluster assembly rearward to gain access to the speedometer cable. Disconnect the cable and the 2 wiring harness connectors and remove the cluster.

NOTE: If there is not enough room to disengage the cable from the speedometer, it may be necessary to disconnect the cable at the transmission and pull the cable through the cowl, to allow room to reach the speedometer quick disconnect.

7. Installation is the reverse of the removal procedure. Apply an approximately $^3/_{16}$ in. diameter ball of silicone dialectric compound in the drive hole of the speedometer head prior to installation.

Speedometer

Removal and Installation

1. Disconnect the negative battery cable. Remove the instrument cluster.
2. Remove the trip meter and/or clock adjusting knob(s), if necessary.
3. Separate the lens and mask assembly from the cluster.
4. Remove the mounting screws and remove the speedometer.
5. Installation is the reverse of the removal procedure.

Headlight Switch

Removal and Installation
NAVAJO

1. Disconnect the negative battery cable.
2. Remove the ash tray and the 2 finish panel retaining screws.
3. Remove the finish panel, which snaps off.
4. Remove the rear wiper switch and rear defrost switch.
5. Pull the headlight switch knob to the full **ON** position. Reach through the opening below the headlight switch, depress the shaft release button on the switch and remove the knob and shaft assembly.
6. Remove the headlight switch retaining bezel nut. Pull the

Headlight switch installation — Navajo

switch downward and through the opening to disconnect the connector.

7. Installation is the reverse of the removal procedure.

Combination Switch

Removal and Installation
EXCEPT NAVAJO

1. Disconnect the negative battery cable.
2. Remove the steering wheel.
3. Remove the upper and lower column shroud halves.
4. Disconnect the electrical connectors to the switch.
5. Remove the attaching screw(s), release the lock, if required and remove the switch.
6. Installation is the reverse of the removal procedure.

RELEASE LOCK

Combination switch removal — MPV, B Series Pick-Up similar

NAVAJO

1. Disconnect the negative battery cable.
2. Remove the steering column shroud.
3. Remove the 2 self-tapping screws that attach the combination switch to the steering column casting. Disengage the switch from the casting.
4. Disconnect the 3 electrical connectors, being careful not to damage the locking tabs. Do not damage the shift position indicator cable.

To install:

5. Connect the 3 switch electrical connectors. The wiring for the switch is to be routed under the shift position indicator cable.
6. Install the switch with the self-tapping screws. Tighten the screws to 18–27 inch lbs. (2–3 Nm).
7. If equipped with automatic transmission, make sure the shift position indicator adjustment is correct.
8. Install the shroud and connect the negative battery cable. Check the steering column for proper operation.

Ignition Lock

Removal and Installation

EXCEPT NAVAJO

1. Disconnect the negative battery cable.
2. Remove the combination switch.
3. Use a chisel to make a groove in the head of each lock retaining bolt, then remove the bolts using a suitable tool.
4. Remove the lock assembly.
5. Installation is the reverse of the removal procedure. Install new lock retaining bolts and tighten them until the heads break off.

NAVAJO

Functional Lock

NOTE: **The following procedure should be used on vehicles with functional lock cylinders. Ignition keys are available for these vehicles or the ignition key numbers are known and the proper key can be made.**

1. Disconnect the negative battery cable.

2. Remove the steering wheel and shroud.
3. Using the ignition key, turn the lock cylinder to the **ON** position. If equipped with an automatic transmission, the selector lever must first be placed in **P**.
4. Push down on the lock cylinder retaining pin with a ⅛ in. diameter wire pin or small punch. Pull the lock cylinder from the column housing.
5. Disconnect the lock cylinder wiring plug from the horn brush wiring connector.

To install:

6. Lubricate the lock cylinder with grease.
7. Turn the lock cylinder to the **ON** position and depress the retaining pin.
8. Insert the lock cylinder into its housing in the flange casting, making sure the tab at the end of the cylinder aligns with the slot in the ignition drive gear.
9. Turn the key to the **OFF** position. This will allow the cylinder retaining pin to extend into the cylinder casting housing hole.
10. Using the ignition key, rotate the lock cylinder to ensure correct mechanical operation in all positions.
11. Connect the key warning wire plug and install the steering column lower shroud.
12. Install the steering column opening trim panel and connect the negative battery cable.
13. Check for proper start in **P** or **N**. Make sure the vehicle cannot be started in **D** and **R**.

Non-Functional Lock

NOTE: **The following procedure should be used on vehicles where the ignition lock is inoperative and the lock cylinder cannot be rotated due to a lost or broken ignition key, the key number is not known or the lock cylinder cap is damaged and/or broken.**

1. Disconnect the negative battery cable. If equipped with tilt wheel, tilt to the full up position.
2. Remove the steering wheel, tilt lever and steering column trim shrouds.
3. Punch the lock cylinder retaining pin with a prick punch, ⅛ in. maximum outside diameter. Using a ⅛ in. diameter drill, drill out the retaining pin going no deeper than ½ in. Be careful not to damage the cast housing.

4. Place a chisel at the base of the lock cylinder cap and, using a hammer, strike the chisel with sharp blows to break the cap away from the lock cylinder.

5. Using a ⅜ in. diameter drill bit, drill down the middle of the ignition lock key slot approximately 1¾ in. until the lock cylinder breaks loose from the steering column cover casting. Remove the lock cylinder and drill shavings from the base of the cover cast housing.

6. Remove the drive gear, bearing retainer and actuator from the casting. Thoroughly clean and inspect all components. If any components or the casting are damaged, they must be replaced.

To install:

7. Lubricate the drive gear, bearing and retainer with grease and install. Lubricate the lock cylinder with grease.

8. Turn the lock cylinder to the **ON** position and depress the retaining pin. Insert the cylinder into its housing in the flange casting, making sure the tab at the end of the cylinder aligns with the slot in the ignition lock drive gear.

9. Turn the key to the **OFF** position. This will allow the cylinder retaining pin to extend into the cylinder casting housing hole.

10. Using the ignition key, rotate the lock cylinder to ensure correct mechanical operation in all positions.

11. Connect the key warning wire plug and install the steering column shrouds.

12. Install the steering wheel and connect the negative battery cable. Check for proper start in **P** or **N**. Make sure the vehicle cannot be started in **D** and **R**.

Ignition Switch

Removal and Installation
EXCEPT NAVAJO

1. Disconnect the negative battery cable.
2. Remove the steering column covers.
3. Disconnect the electrical connectors from the switch.
4. Remove the attaching screw and remove the switch.
5. Installation is the reverse of the removal procedure.

NAVAJO

1. Rotate the lock cylinder to the **LOCK** position. Disconnect the negative battery cable.
2. Remove the steering wheel.
3. If equipped with tilt wheel, remove the upper extension housing shroud by squeezing it at the 6 and 12 o'clock positions and popping it free of the retaining plate at the 3 o'clock position.
4. Remove the trim shroud halves.
5. Disconnect the switch electrical connector.
6. Remove the retaining nuts and disengage the ignition switch from the actuator rod.
7. Installation is the reverse of the removal procedure.

Stoplight Switch

Adjustment
EXCEPT NAVAJO

1. Disconnect the negative battery cable.
2. Disconnect the electrical connector from the switch.
3. Loosen the switch locknut and turn the switch until it does not contact the pedal.
4. Loosen the booster pushrod locknut and turn the rod to adjust the pedal height to 7.09–7.28 in. (180–185mm) on B Series Pick-Up or 7.52–7.91 in. (191–201mm) on MPV.
5. Depress the brake pedal a few times to eliminate the vacuum in the system. Gently depress the pedal and check the free-play. Turn the booster pushrod to adjust the free-play to 0.16–0.28 in. (4–7mm).

Pedal height measurement location for stoplight switch and clutch switch adjustment

6. Tighten the booster pushrod locknut.
7. Turn the stoplight switch until it contacts the pedal, then turn an additional ½ turn. Tighten the switch locknut.
8. Connect the electrical connector and the negative battery cable.

NAVAJO

The stoplight switch is not adjustable.

Removal and Installation
EXCEPT NAVAJO

1. Disconnect the negative battery cable.
2. Disconnect the electrical connector from the switch.
3. Loosen the switch locknut and remove the switch.
4. Installation is the reverse of the removal procedure. Adjust the switch.

NAVAJO

1. Disconnect the negative battery cable. Disconnect the electrical connector from the switch. The locking tab must be lifted before the connector can be removed.
2. Remove the hairpin clip and slide the switch, booster pushrod, nylon washer and bushing away from the pedal. Remove the washer, then the switch by sliding the switch up or down.

To install:

3. Position the switch so the U-shaped side is nearest the pedal and directly over/under the pin. Then slide the switch up/down installing the booster pushrod and bushing between the switch side plates.
4. Push the switch and pushrod assembly firmly toward the brake pedal arm. Install the outside plastic washer to the pin and install the hairpin clip. Do not substitute for this clip. Use only factory supplied hairpin clips.
5. Connect the electrical connector to the switch and connect the negative battery cable. Make sure the switch wire harness has sufficient length to travel with the switch during the full stroke of the brake pedal. Check the switch for proper operation.

Clutch Switch

Adjustment

EXCEPT NAVAJO

1. Disconnect the negative battery cable.
2. Disconnect the electrical connector from the switch.
3. Loosen the switch locknut and turn the switch until the clutch pedal height is 7.13–7.52 in. (181–191mm) on B2200, 7.52–7.91 in. (191–201mm) on B2600 or 8.19–8.58 in. (208–218mm) on MPV.
4. Tighten the locknut.
5. Connect the electrical connector and the negative battery cable.

NAVAJO

The clutch switch is not adjustable.

Removal and Installation

EXCEPT NAVAJO

1. Disconnect the negative battery cable.
2. Disconnect the electrical connector from the switch.
3. Loosen the switch locknut and remove the switch.
4. Installation is the reverse of the removal procedure. Adjust the switch.

NAVAJO

1. Disconnect the negative battery cable. Disconnect the wiring harness from the switch.
2. Pull the orientation clip away from the switch to separate it from the pin on the switch.
3. Rotate the switch to expose the plastic retainer.
4. Push the tabs together to allow the retainer to slide rearward and separate from the switch.
5. Remove the switch from the pushrod.
6. Installation is the reverse of the removal procedure.

Neutral Safety Switch

Adjustment

EXCEPT NAVAJO

Hydraulically-Controlled Transmission

1. Raise and safely support the vehicle.
2. Move the manual shaft to the **N** position.
3. Loosen the switch mounting bolts.
4. Remove the screw on the switch body and move the switch so the screw hole is aligned with the small hole inside the switch. Check the alignment by inserting an approximately 0.079 in. (2mm) diameter pin through the holes.
5. Tighten the mounting bolts to 43–61 inch lbs. (4.9–6.9 Nm) and remove the alignment pin.
6. Install the screw in the switch body and check for proper operation. The starter should operate only when the transmission is in the **P** or **N** range.

Electronically-Controlled Transmission

1. Raise and safely support the vehicle.
2. Move the manual shaft to the **N** position.
3. Loosen the switch mounting bolts.
4. Align the holes of the switch and the manual shaft lever and insert an approximately 0.157 in. (4mm) diameter pin through the holes.
5. Tighten the mounting bolts to 22–35 inch lbs. (2.5–3.9 Nm) and remove the pin.
6. Check the switch for proper operation. The starter should operate only when the transmission is in the **P** or **N** range.

NAVAJO

The neutral safety switch is not adjustable.

Removal and Installation

EXCEPT NAVAJO

1. Disconnect the negative battery cable. Raise and safely support the vehicle.
2. Disconnect the manual shaft lever from the transmission.
3. Remove the mounting bolts and the switch.
4. Installation is the reverse of the removal procedure. Adjust the switch.

NAVAJO

1. Disconnect the negative battery cable.
2. Disconnect the electrical harness from the switch.
3. Remove the switch and O-ring using socket tool T74P–77247–A or equivalent.

NOTE: The use of other tools could crush or puncture the walls of the switch.

4. Installation is the reverse of the removal procedure. Tighten the switch to 7–10 ft. lbs. (9.5–13.6 Nm).
5. Check the operation of the switch with the parking brake applied. The engine should start only with the transmission selector lever in **N** or **P**. The back-up lights should illuminate only with the selector lever in **R**.

Fuses and Circuit Breakers

Location

B SERIES PICK-UP

The fuse box is located under the instrument panel, to the left of the steering column. There is also a small fuse box under the hood, on the right inner fender, that contains the main vehicle fuses.

MPV

The main fuse block is located on the right side of the engine compartment. There is also a fuse box located above the left kick panel.

NAVAJO

The fuse panel is located under the instrument panel to the left of the steering column. There is also a power distribution box located in the engine compartment on the right inner fender, next to the starter relay, which contains mostly high-current fuses.

NOTE: All circuit breakers on Navajo are located in the fuse panel except for a 4.5 amp circuit breaker for the rear wiper/washer and a 22 amp circuit breaker for the high beams which is integral with the headlight switch.

Relays

Location

B SERIES PICK-UP

Circuit Open Relay—located on the left kick panel.
Daytime Running Lights (DRL) Relay—located on the firewall in the engine compartment on Canadian vehicles.
EGI Main Relay—located at the right front of the engine compartment.
Fuel Cut Relay—located under the left side of the dash.
Horn Relay—located on the right inner fender in the engine compartment.

MPV

Air Conditioning Relay—located on the right inner fender in the engine compartment.
ALL Relay—located on the left inner fender in the engine compartment on 1990–92 vehicles.

Blower Motor Relay—located on the left inner fender in the engine compartment.

Change Motor Relay No. 1—located on the firewall in the engine compartment on 1990–92 vehicles.

Change Motor Relay No. 2—located on the firewall in the engine compartment on 1990–92 vehicles.

Circuit Opening Relay—located in the front of the engine compartment.

Condenser Fan Relay—located on the right inner fender in the engine compartment.

Daytime Running Light (DRL) Relay—located on the left inner fender in the engine compartment on 1990–92 vehicles.

EGI Main Relay—located on the left inner fender in the engine compartment.

Horn Relay—located on the left inner fender in the engine compartment.

Kickdown Relay—located on the left inner fender in the engine compartment.

Rear Blower Motor Relay—located on the rear blower unit.

Rear Cooler Relay No. 1—located on the rear cooling unit.

Rear Cooler Relay No. 2—located on the rear cooling unit.

Rear Cooler Relay No. 3—located on the rear cooling unit.

Rear Wheel Anti-Lock Brake Relay—located on the left inner fender in the engine compartment.

NAVAJO

Air Conditioning Cutoff Relay—located under the power distribution box at the right fender apron.

Fuel Pump Relay—located under the power distribution box at the right fender apron.

Stop/Turn Signal Relays—located on the left rear quarter panel.

Low Oil Level Relay—located on right side of dash panel.

Starter Relay—located on the fender apron in the right front of the engine compartment.

Tail light Relay—located at the left rear quarter panel.

Computers

Location

The Engine Control Unit (ECU) is located at the right kick panel on B Series Pick-Ups and Navajo or under the center of the dash on MPV.

Flashers

Location

The turn signal/hazard flasher unit is located under the left side of the dash on B Series Pick-Up or behind the driver's side kick panel on MPV. On Navajo, both the turn signal and hazard flashers are attached to the fuse panel.

Cruise Control

For further information, please refer to Chilton's Chassis Electronics Service Manual.

(B2200)

(B2600i)

Actuator cable free-play adjustment—B Series Pick-Up

Adjustment

ACTUATOR CABLE

Except Navajo

1. Remove the clamp.
2. Adjust the nut so the actuator cable free-play is 0.04–0.12 in. (1–3mm) when the cable is pressed lightly.
3. Reinstall the clamp.

Navajo

1. Remove the cable retaining clip.
2. Disengage the throttle positioner.
3. Set the engine at hot idle.
4. Pull on the actuator cable to take up any slack. Maintain a light tension on the cable.
5. While holding the cable, insert the cable retaining clip and snap securely.

VACUUM DUMP VALVE

Navajo

1. Firmly hold the brake pedal in the up, released, position.
2. Push in the dump valve until the valve bottoms against the pad on the brake pedal.

CLUTCH AND STOPLIGHT SWITCHES

Except Navajo

When replacing these switches, be sure to adjust the pedal height to the proper specification.

ENGINE COOLING

Radiator

Removal and Installation
EXCEPT NAVAJO

1. Disconnect the negative battery cable and remove the radiator cap.

------ **CAUTION** ------

Never remove the radiator cap while the engine is running or personal injury from scalding hot coolant or steam may result. If possible, wait until the engine has cooled to remove the radiator cap. If this is not possible, wrap a thick cloth around the radiator cap and turn it slowly to the first stop, to release the pressure in the cooling system. Step back while the pressure is released. After all pressure is released, remove the radiator cap completely.

2. Position a drain pan under the radiator and open the draincock to drain the radiator.
3. On MPV, remove the fresh air duct.
4. Disconnect the upper and lower radiator hoses and the coolant reservoir hose.
5. If equipped with automatic transmission, disconnect and plug the oil cooler lines at the radiator.
6. Remove the cooling fan retaining nuts and the fan.
7. Remove the fan shroud attaching bolts and remove the shroud. Disconnect the thermoswitch electrical connector, if necessary.
8. Remove the radiator attaching bolts and remove the radiator.

To install:

9. Position the radiator and install the attaching bolts. Tighten to 16–22 ft. lbs. (22–30 Nm).
10. Install the fan shroud with the attaching bolts and tighten to 69–95 inch lbs. (7.8–11.0 Nm). Connect the thermoswitch electrical connector, if necessary.
11. Install the cooling fan with the retaining nuts and tighten to 69–95 inch lbs. (7.8–11.0 Nm).
12. If equipped with automatic transmission, unplug and connect the oil cooler lines at the radiator.
13. Connect the coolant reservoir hose and the upper and lower radiator hoses.
14. On MPV, install the fresh air duct.
15. Close the draincock and connect the negative battery cable. Fill and bleed the cooling system.
16. Run the engine and check for leaks.

NAVAJO

1. Disconnect the negative battery cable and remove the radiator cap.

------ **CAUTION** ------

Never remove the radiator cap while the engine is running or personal injury from scalding hot coolant or steam may result. If possible, wait until the engine has cooled to remove the radiator cap. If this is not possible, wrap a thick cloth around the radiator cap and turn it slowly to the first stop, to release the pressure in the cooling system. Step back while the pressure is released. After all pressure is released, remove the radiator cap completely.

2. Position a drain pan under the radiator and open the draincock to drain the radiator.
3. Disconnect the overflow hose from the radiator and the fan shroud, if necessary.
4. Remove the shroud or fan guard upper attaching screws. Lift the shroud out of the lower retaining clips and drape it on the fan.
5. Disconnect the radiator hoses from the radiator.

6. Disconnect and plug the automatic transmission oil cooling lines, if equipped.
7. Remove the radiator upper attaching screws, tilt the radiator back and lift directly upward, clear of the radiator support and cooling fan.

To install:

8. Make sure the radiator lower support rubber insulators are in place on the lower support.
9. Install the radiator, being careful to clear the fan. Make sure the mounting pins on the bottom of the radiator tanks are inserted into the holes in the lower support rubber insulators and the radiator is firmly seated on the insulators.
10. Install the radiator upper attaching screws. If equipped with automatic transmission, connect the transmission cooling lines.
11. Connect the radiator hoses to the radiator. Position the shroud in the retainer clips and install the attaching screws.
12. Connect the overflow hose and close the draincock. Connect the negative battery cable. Fill and bleed the cooling system.

Heater Core

For further information, please refer to Chilton's Air Conditioning and Heating Manual.

Removal and Installation
B SERIES PICK-UP

1. Disconnect the negative battery cable. Drain the cooling system.
2. Disconnect the heater hoses from the heater unit and remove the grommet.
3. Remove the instrument panel as follows:
   a. Remove the steering wheel.
   b. Remove the upper and lower column covers and the combination switch.
   c. Remove the instrument cluster hood and the instrument cluster.
   d. Remove the left side panel from the instrument panel.
   e. Remove the hole cover from the upper right corner of the instrument panel center panel to expose a center panel attaching screw. Remove the center panel.
   f. Remove the glove compartment lid and the glove compartment.
   g. Remove the shifter knob and boot, then remove the console box.
   h. Remove the radio.
   i. Remove the instrument panel retaining bolt covers from the top and sides of the instrument panel.
   j. Remove the instrument panel retaining bolts and remove the instrument panel.
4. Disconnect the cables from the heater unit, remove the nuts and bolts and remove the heater unit.
5. Disassemble the heater unit and remove the heater core.

To install:

6. Install the heater core and assemble the heater unit.
7. Install the heater unit and tighten the retaining nuts and bolts to 69–95 inch lbs. (7.8–11.0 Nm). Connect the control cables.
8. Install the instrument panel in the reverse order of removal.
9. Install the grommet and connect the heater hoses.
10. Connect the negative battery cable. Fill and bleed the cooling system.
11. Run the engine and check heater operation. Check for leaks.

Heater unit disassembled view—B Series Pick-Up

MPV

1. Disconnect the negative battery cable. Drain the cooling system.

2. Remove the instrument panel as follows:

   a. Disconnect the hood release knob from the instrument panel.

   b. Remove the steering wheel.

   c. Remove the upper and lower column covers.

   d. Disconnect the electrical connectors from the combination switch. Loosen the screw, release the lock and remove the switch.

   e. Remove the front cluster assembly and the instrument cluster.

   f. Remove the covers from the left and right side of the instrument panel.

   g. If equipped, remove the undercover from the lower right side of the instrument panel.

   h. Remove the right and left lower panels.

   i. Remove the duct from the driver's side under the steering column.

   j. Remove the ashtray and radio trim panel.

   k. Remove the radio housing and the radio.

   l. Remove the knobs and the switch panel assembly.

   m. Remove the temperature and blower controls and the airflow mode control.

   n. Remove the bolt covers, 3 bolts and the upper garnish.

   o. Remove the retaining bolts and remove the instrument panel.

3. Disconnect the heater hoses from the heater core.

4. Remove the nuts and the instrument panel stay.

5. Remove the nuts and the heater unit case. Use caution to prevent spilling coolant from the heater core.

6. Disassemble the heater unit and remove the heater core.

To install:

7. Install the heater core and assemble the heater unit.

8. Install the heater unit case with the attaching nuts.

9. Install the instrument panel stay with the attaching nuts.

10. Connect the heater hoses to the heater core.

11. Install the instrument panel in the reverse order of removal. When attaching the airflow mode control wire, proceed as follows:

    a. Set the control knob to the far left position.

    b. Set the mode control link to the extreme stop position, then install the wire loop on the link.

    c. Clamp the wire into position with the clip.

    d. Move the mode lever to be sure the wire is attached. Make sure it can move the full stroke between DEF and VENT.

12. When attaching the Rec-Fresh control wire, proceed as follows:

    a. Set the control knob to the far right position.

    b. Set the air-mix control link to the extreme stop position, then install the wire loop on the link.

    c. Clamp the wire into position with the clip.

    d. Move the Rec-Fresh lever to be sure the wire is attached. Make sure it can move the full stroke between REC and FRESH.

13. When attaching the temperature control wire, proceed as follows:

    a. Set the control knob to the full clockwise position.

    b. Set the temperature control link to the extreme stop position, then install the wire loop on the link.

    c. Clamp the wire into position with the clip.

    d. Move the temperature control lever to be sure the wire is attached. Make sure it can move the full stroke between HOT and COLD.

14. Connect the negative battery cable. Fill and bleed the cooling system.

15. Run the engine and check heater operation. Check for leaks.

NAVAJO

1. Disconnect the negative battery cable.

2. Drain the cooling system into a suitable container.

3. Disconnect the heater hoses from the heater core tubes. Use the snap-lock fitting disconnect procedure, if necessary.

4. In the passenger compartment, remove the screws attaching the heater core access cover to the plenum assembly. Remove the access cover.

5. Pull the heater core rearward and down, removing it from the plenum assembly.

To install:

6. Position the heater core and seal in the plenum assembly.

7. Install the heater core access cover to the plenum assembly and secure it with the screws.

HEATER PLENUM CHAMBER

HEATER CORE

HEATER CORE COVER

SCREW

Heater core installation—Navajo

8. Connect the heater hoses to the heater core tubes. Use the snap-lock fitting connection procedure.
9. Fill the cooling system to the proper level.
10. Connect the negative battery cable and check the system for proper operation and coolant leaks.

Water Pump

Removal and Installation

2.2L ENGINE

1. Disconnect the negative battery cable. Drain the cooling system.
2. Remove the cooling fan and the fan shroud.
3. Remove the water pump drive belt and the water pump pulley.
4. Remove the timing belt front covers and the timing belt and tensioner. Remove the timing belt idler pulley.
5. Remove the coolant inlet pipe, if necessary.
6. Remove the mounting bolts and the water pump.

To install:
7. Clean all gasket mating surfaces.
8. Install a new water pump gasket and the water pump. Tighten the water pump mounting bolts to 14–19 ft. lbs. (19–25 Nm).
9. Install a new gasket and the coolant inlet pipe, if removed.
10. Install the timing belt idler pulley, timing belt and timing belt front cover.
11. Install the water pump pulley and drive belt. Install the cooling fan and shroud.
12. Adjust the drive belt tension. Connect the negative battery cable.
13. Fill and bleed the cooling system. Run the engine and check for leaks.

2.6L ENGINES

1. Disconnect the negative battery cable. Drain the cooling system.
2. Remove the cooling fan and the fan shroud.

Water pump installation—2.2L engine

3. Remove the water pump drive belt and the water pump pulley.

4. On 1988 vehicles, disconnect the water bypass hose.

5. Remove the mounting bolts/nuts and the water pump.

To install:

6. Clean all gasket mating surfaces.

7. Install a new gasket and the water pump. Tighten the mounting bolts/nuts to 14–19 ft. lbs. (19–25 Nm).

8. Connect the water bypass hose, if necessary.

9. Install the water pump pulley and the drive belt. Install the cooling fan and shroud.

10. Adjust the drive belt tension. Connect the negative battery cable.

11. Fill and bleed the cooling system. Run the engine and check for leaks.

3.0L ENGINE

1. Disconnect the negative battery cable. Drain the cooling system.

2. Remove the fresh air duct.

3. Remove the cooling fan and the fan shroud. Loosen the drive belt and remove the water pump pulley.

4. Remove the timing belt front covers and the timing belt.

5. Remove the water pump mounting bolts/nuts and the water pump.

To install:

6. Clean all gasket mating surfaces.

7. Install a new gasket and the water pump. Tighten the mounting bolts/nuts to 14–19 ft. lbs. (19–25 Nm).

8. Install the timing belt and the timing belt front covers.

9. Install the water pump pulley and drive belt. Install the cooling fan and shroud.

10. Adjust the drive belt tension. Install the fresh air duct.

11. Connect the negative battery cable. Fill and bleed the cooling system.

12. Run the engine and check for leaks.

4.0L ENGINE

1. Disconnect the negative battery cable and drain the cooling system.

2. Remove the lower radiator hose and the heater return hose from the pump.

Water pump installation—3.0L engine

3. Remove the fan and clutch assembly using fan clutch pulley holder 49 UN01 007 and fan clutch nut wrench 49 UN01 008 or equivalents. The fan clutch nut has left hand thread; remove by turning clockwise.

4. Loosen the alternator mounting bolts and remove the belt. If equipped with air conditioning, remove the alternator and bracket.

5. Remove the water pump pulley.

6. Remove the water pump attaching bolts and remove the water pump. Note the length of the bolts when removing, so they can be reinstalled in the same positions.

7. Clean all gasket mating surfaces and install in the reverse order of removal. Tighten the water pump retaining bolts to 7–9 ft. lbs. (9–12 Nm) and the fan clutch nut to 30–100 ft. lbs. (40–135 Nm). Fill and bleed the cooling system.

Fan clutch-to-water pump installation—4.0L engine

Thermostat installation—2.2L engine

Thermostat installation—3.0L engine

Thermostat

Removal and Installation

EXCEPT 4.0L ENGINE

1. Disconnect the negative battery cable. Drain the cooling system.

2. On 2.2L and 2.6L engines, disconnect the upper radiator hose from the water outlet. On 3.0L engine, disconnect the lower radiator hose from the water outlet.

3. Remove the water outlet and the thermostat.

To install:

4. Clean all gasket mating surfaces. On 3.0L engine, make sure the thermostat O-ring is not damaged.

5. Install the thermostat. If equipped, the jiggle pin should be on the side facing the water outlet.

6. On 2.2L and 2.6L engines, install a new gasket with the seal print facing the cylinder head.

7. Install the water outlet. On 3.0L engine, face the mark on the water outlet to the front of the engine.

8. Install the water outlet retaining bolts/nuts and tighten to 14–19 ft. lbs. (19–25 Nm).

9. Connect the radiator hose and the negative battery cable.

10. Fill and bleed the cooling system. Run the engine and check for leaks.

4.0L ENGINE

1. Disconnect the negative battery cable and drain the cooling system.

2. Disconnect the coolant hose from the water outlet.

3. Remove the water outlet retaining bolts and remove the water outlet. Remove the thermostat from the water outlet.

To install:

4. Clean all gasket mating surfaces.

5. Apply gasket sealer to a new water outlet gasket and install on the engine.

6. Install the thermostat in the water outlet with the bridge section toward the coolant hose. Turn the thermostat clockwise to lock it in position on the flats cast into the water outlet.

NOTE: Make sure the thermostat is aligned so the full width of the heater outlet tube opening is visible within the thermostat port in the assembly. The correct port alignment is required to provide maximum coolant flow to the heater.

7. Install the water outlet with the mounting bolts. Tighten the bolts to 7–10 ft. lbs. (9–13 Nm).

8. Connect the coolant hose.

9. Connect the negative battery cable. Fill and bleed the cooling system.

Cooling System Bleeding

EXCEPT NAVAJO

Use the following steps to remove air from the system and ensure a complete fill.

1. Close the radiator draincock and install the cylinder block drain plug, if removed.

2. Slowly pour a 50/50 mixture of water and antifreeze into the radiator up to the coolant filler port.

3. Fill the coolant reservoir with the same mixture up to the FULL level.

4. Install the radiator cap securely and start the engine.

5. Run the engine at idle speed until it reaches normal operating temperature.

NOTE: If the temperature increases beyond normal, there is excessive air in the system. Stop the engine, allow it to cool and repeat Steps 2–4.

6. Run the engine up to 2200–2800 rpm for 5 seconds and return to idle. Repeat several times.

7. Stop the engine and wait until the system has cooled down. Remove the radiator cap and check the coolant level. If the coolant level has dropped, repeat the procedure from Step 2.

NAVAJO

Use the following steps to remove air from the system and ensure a complete fill.

1. Close the radiator draincock and install the cylinder block drain plug, if removed.

2. Fill the cooling system with a 50/50 mixture of water and antifreeze. Allow several minutes for trapped air to escape and for coolant mixture to flow through the radiator.

3. Install the radiator cap to the fully installed position, then back off to the first stop.

4. Slide the heater temperature and mode selection levers to maximum heat position.

5. Start the engine and operate at approximately 2000 rpm for 3–4 minutes.

6. Shut the engine off. Wrap the radiator cap with a thick cloth and carefully remove the cap.

7. Add coolant mixture to bring the coolant level up to the filler neck seat.

— CAUTION —

Use cation when adding coolant to the radiator to avoid hot coolant or steam blowing out from the radiator and possibly causing personal injury.

8. Install the radiator cap to the fully installed position, then back off to the first stop.

9. Run the engine at fast idle until the upper radiator hose is warm, indicating the thermostat is open.

10. Shut the engine off. Wrap the radiator cap with a thick cloth and carefully remove the cap. Add coolant, if necessary and reinstall the cap to the fully installed position.

11. Remove the coolant reservoir cap and add 1.1 qts. of coolant mixture to the reservoir. Install the cap.

FUEL SYSTEM

Fuel System Service Precautions

Safety is the most important factor when performing not only fuel system maintenance but any type of maintenance. Failure to conduct maintenance and repairs in a safe manner may result in serious personal injury or death. Maintenance and testing of the vehicle's fuel system components can be accomplished safely and effectively by adhering to the following rules and guidelines.

• To avoid the possibility of fire and personal injury, always disconnect the negative battery cable unless the repair or test procedure requires that battery voltage be applied.

• Always relieve the fuel system pressure prior to disconnecting any fuel system component (injector, fuel rail, pressure regulator, etc.), fitting or fuel line connection. Exercise extreme caution whenever relieving fuel system pressure to avoid exposing skin, face and eyes to fuel spray. Please be advised that fuel under pressure may penetrate the skin or any part of the body that it contacts.

• Always place a shop towel or cloth around the fitting or connection prior to loosening to absorb any excess fuel due to spillage. Ensure that all fuel spillage (should it occur) is quickly removed from engine surfaces. Ensure that all fuel soaked cloths or towels are deposited into a suitable waste container.

• Always keep a dry chemical (Class B) fire extinguisher near the work area.

• Do not allow fuel spray or fuel vapors to come into contact with a spark or open flame.

• Always use a backup wrench when loosening and tightening fuel line connection fittings. This will prevent unnecessary stress and torsion to fuel line piping. Always follow the proper torque specifications.

• Always replace worn fuel fitting O-rings with new. Do not substitute fuel hose or equivalent where fuel pipe is installed.

Relieving Fuel System Pressure

Fuel lines on fuel injected vehicles will remain pressurized after the engine is shut off. This residual pressure must be relieved before any fuel lines or components are disconnected.

EXCEPT NAVAJO

1. Start the engine.

2. Disconnect the circuit opening relay connector, airflow meter connector or fuel pump connector.

3. After the engine stalls, turn **OFF** the ignition switch.

4. Reconnect the electrical connector.

NOTE: After releasing fuel system pressure, the system must be primed before starting the engine to avoid excessive cranking. To prime the system, connect the terminals of the yellow 2-pin test connector with a jumper wire and turn the ignition switch ON for approximately 10 seconds. Check for fuel leaks, then turn the ignition switch OFF and remove the jumper wire.

NAVAJO

1. Disconnect the negative battery cable and remove the fuel filler cap.

2. Remove the cap from the pressure relief valve on the fuel supply manifold. Install pressure gauge 49 UN01 010 or equivalent, to the pressure relief valve.

3. Direct the gauge drain hose into a suitable container and depress the pressure relief button.

4. Remove the gauge and replace the cap on the pressure relief valve.

NOTE: As an alternate method, disconnect the inertia switch and crank the engine for 15–20 seconds until the pressure is relieved.

Fuel Line Couplings

Removal and Installation

NAVAJO

There are 2 methods in use to connect the fuel lines and fuel system components on Navajo, the hairpin clip push connect fitting and the spring lock coupling. Each requires a different procedure to disconnect and connect.

Hairpin Clip Push Connect Fitting

1. Inspect the visible internal portion of the fitting for dirt accumulation. If more than a light coating of dust is present, clean the fitting before disassembly.

SPRING LOCK COUPLING CONNECT AND DISCONNECT PROCEDURE

FEMALE FITTING

O-RINGS SUPPLIED IN KIT

GARTER SPRING

MALE FITTINGS

CAGE

SPRING LOCK COUPLING DISCONNECTED

TO DISCONNECT COUPLING
CAUTION — DISCHARGE SYSTEM BEFORE DISCONNECTING COUPLING

TOOL

CAGE

❶ FIT TOOL TO COUPLING SO THAT TOOL CAN ENTER CAGE TO RELEASE THE GARTER SPRING.

TO CONNECT COUPLING

GARTER SPRING

REPLACEMENT GARTER SPRINGS
3/8 INCH
1/2 INCH
ALSO AVAILABLE IN KIT

● CHECK FOR MISSING OR DAMAGED GARTER SPRING — REMOVE DAMAGED SPRING WITH SMALL HOOKED WIRE — INSTALL NEW SPRING IF DAMAGED OR MISSING.

PUSH TOOL INTO CAGE

❷ PUSH THE TOOL INTO THE CAGE OPENING TO RELEASE THE FEMALE FITTING FROM THE GARTER SPRING.

A — CLEAN FITTINGS

B - INSTALL NEW O-RINGS — USE ONLY SPECIFIED O-RINGS — SUPPLIED IN KIT

C — LUBRICATE WITH CLEAN REFRIGERANT OIL

D — ASSEMBLE FITTING TOGETHER BY PUSHING WITH A SLIGHT TWISTING MOTION.

❸ PULL THE COUPLING MALE AND FEMALE FITTINGS APART.

GARTER SPRING

● VISUALLY CHECK TO BE SURE GARTER SPRING IS OVER FLARED END OF FEMALE FITTING, AND PULL ON FITTING TO ENSURE FULL ENGAGEMENT.

❹ REMOVE THE TOOL FROM THE DISCONNECTED SPRING LOCK COUPLING.

"HAIRPIN" CLIP

SHIPPING TAB

O-RINGS

STEEL OR NYLON TUBE

SPACERS

BODY

Hairpin clip push connect fitting—Navajo

2. Some adhesion between the seals in the fitting and the tubing will occur with time. To separate, twist the fitting on the tube, then push and pull the fitting until it moves freely on the tube.

3. Remove the hairpin clip from the fitting by first bending and breaking the shipping tab. Next, spread the 2 clip legs by hand about ⅛ in. each to disengage the body and push the legs into the fitting. Lightly pull the triangular end of the clip and work it clear of the tube and fitting.

NOTE: Do not use hand tools to complete this operation.

4. Grasp the fitting and pull in an axial direction to remove the fitting from the tube. Be careful on 90 degree elbow connectors, as excessive side loading could break the connector body.

5. After disassembly, inspect and clean the tube end sealing surfaces. The tube end should be free of scratches and corrosion that could provide leak paths. Inspect the inside of the fitting for any internal parts such as O-rings and spacers that may have been dislodged from the fitting. Replace any damaged connector.

To install:

6. Install a new connector if damage was found. Insert a new clip into any 2 adjacent openings with the triangular portion pointing away from the fitting opening. Install the clip until the legs of the clip are locked on the outside of the body. Piloting with an index finger is necessary.

7. Before installing the fitting on the tube, wipe the tube end with a clean cloth. Inspect the inside of the fitting to make sure it is free of dirt and/or obstructions.

8. Apply a light coating of engine oil to the tube end. Align the fitting and tube axially and push the fitting onto the tube end. When the fitting is engaged, a definite click will be heard. Pull on the fitting to make sure it is fully engaged.

Spring Lock Coupling

The spring lock coupling is a fuel line coupling held together by a garter spring inside a circular cage. When the coupling is connected together, the flared end of the female fitting slips behind the garter spring inside the cage of the male fitting. The garter spring and cage then prevent the flared end of the female fitting from pulling out of the cage. As an additional locking feature, most couplings have a horseshoe shaped retaining clip that improves the retaining reliability of the spring lock coupling.

Fuel Tank

Removal and Installation

B SERIES PICK-UP

1. Relieve the fuel system pressure and disconnect the negative battery cable.
2. Remove the fuel filler cap. Raise and safely support the vehicle.
3. Position a suitable container under the fuel tank. Remove the drain plug and drain the tank.
4. Disconnect the electrical connector from the sending unit or sending unit/fuel pump assembly.
5. Disconnect the fuel filler hose, evaporative hoses, breather hose and fuel lines.
6. Position a jack under the fuel tank and remove the tank attaching nuts. Lower the tank from the vehicle.

To install:

7. Raise the tank into position and install the attaching nuts. Remove the jack.
8. Connect the fuel lines and evaporative hoses, making sure they are pushed onto the fuel tank fittings at least 1 in. (25mm). Connect the breather hose.
9. Connect the fuel filler hose, making sure the hose is pushed onto the fuel tank pipe and filler pipe at least 1.4 in. (35mm).
10. Connect the electrical connector to the sending unit or sending unit/fuel pump assembly.
11. Install the drain plug and lower the vehicle.
12. Fill the fuel tank and install the filler cap. Check for leaks.
13. Start the engine and check for leaks.

MPV

1. Relieve the fuel system pressure and disconnect the negative battery cable.
2. Remove the fuel filler cap. Raise and safely support the vehicle.
3. Position a suitable container under the fuel tank. Remove the drain plug and drain the tank.
4. Disconnect the fuel pump electrical connector.
5. Disconnect the fuel lines, evaporative hoses, breather hose and fuel filler hose.
6. Support the tank with a jack. Remove the retaining bolts and the fuel tank straps.
7. Lower the fuel tank from the vehicle.

To install:

8. Raise the fuel tank into position and install the straps and retaining bolts. Tighten to 32–44 ft. lbs. (43–61 Nm). Remove the jack.
9. Connect the fuel lines and evaporative hoses, making sure they are pushed onto the fuel tank fittings at least 1 in. (25mm). Connect the breather hose.
10. Connect the fuel filler hose, making sure the hose is pushed onto the fuel tank pipe and filler pipe at least 1.4 in. (35mm).
11. Connect the fuel pump electrical connector.
12. Install the drain plug and lower the vehicle.
13. Fill the fuel tank and install the filler cap. Check for leaks.
14. Start the engine and check for leaks.

NAVAJO

1. Disconnect the negative battery cable and relieve the fuel system pressure.
2. Raise and safely support the vehicle.
3. Drain the fuel from the fuel tank.
4. Remove the shield, skid plate and fuel tank front strap.
5. Support the tank with a jack and remove the bolt from the fuel tank rear strap.
6. Disconnect the filler pipe and vent pipe and lower the tank. Disconnect the vapor hose, fuel lines and electrical connector.
7. Lower the tank from the vehicle.

To install:

8. Raise the fuel tank and connect the electrical connector, fuel lines and vapor hose.

9. Connect the filler pipe and vent pipe. Attach the rear fuel tank strap.

10. Install the shield, skid plate and front strap.

11. Remove the jack and lower the vehicle.

12. Fill the fuel tank and check for leaks. Connect the negative battery cable.

Fuel Filter

Removal and Installation

B SERIES PICK-UP

The fuel filter is located in the engine compartment on all except

Fuel filter location – B Series Pick-Up with fuel injection

Fuel filter location – MPV

Fuel filter location – Navajo

1988 B2600 and all B2200 with automatic transmission. On 1988 B2600 and all B2200 with automatic transmission, the fuel filter is located under the rear of the vehicle, near the fuel tank.

1. Relieve the fuel system pressure. Disconnect the negative battery cable.

2. Raise and safely support the vehicle, if necessary.

3. Disconnect the fuel lines from the fuel filter.

4. Remove the fuel filter or, if equipped, remove the fuel filter and bracket assembly.

5. Installation is the reverse of the removal procedure. Make sure the flow arrow on the fuel filter is facing in the proper direction of fuel flow.

MPV

The fuel filter is located in the engine compartment, next to the pulsation damper.

1. Relieve the fuel system pressure. Disconnect the negative battery cable.

2. Disconnect the fuel lines from the filter.

3. Remove the filter bracket bolts and remove the filter and bracket assembly.

4. Remove the fuel filter from the mounting bracket, if necessary.

5. Installation is the reverse of the removal procedure. Make sure the flow arrow on the fuel filter is facing in the proper direction of fuel flow.

NAVAJO

The fuel filter is located on the underside of the vehicle, attached to the frame rail.

1. Disconnect the negative battery cable and relieve the fuel system pressure.

2. Raise and support the vehicle safely.

3. Disconnect the fuel lines from the fuel filter.

4. Remove the fuel filter from the bracket. Note the direction of the flow arrow so the replacement filter can be installed correctly.

5. Installation is the reverse of the removal procedure. Start the engine and check for leaks.

Mechanical Fuel Pump

Pressure Testing

1. Disconnect the negative battery cable.

2. Disconnect the fuel line from the carburetor.

3. Connect a fuel pressure gauge to the fuel line.

4. Disconnect the fuel return hose from the fuel pump and plug the fuel pump return outlet.

5. Connect the negative battery cable and start the engine.

6. Check the fuel pressure while the engine is idling. The fuel pressure should be 3.7–4.7 psi.

7. Replace the pump if the pressure is not as specified.

1. Outlet hose
2. Inlet hose
3. Return hose
4. Fuel pump
5. Gasket
6. Insulator
7. Gasket

Mechanical fuel pump installation

8. Shut off the engine and disconnect the negative battery cable. Remove the fuel pressure gauge and reconnect the fuel lines.

9. Connect the negative battery cable.

Removal and Installation

1. Disconnect the negative battery cable.

2. Disconnect and plug the inlet, outlet and return hoses at the fuel pump.

3. Remove the fuel pump mounting bolts and remove the fuel pump, insulator and gaskets.

To install:

4. Clean all gasket mating surfaces.

5. Install new gaskets and the insulator and fuel pump. Install the mounting bolts and tighten to 14–19 ft. lbs. (19–25 Nm).

6. Unplug and connect the fuel lines.

7. Connect the negative battery cable, start the engine and check for leaks.

Electric Fuel Pump

Pressure Testing

EXCEPT NAVAJO

Carbureted Engines

1. Turn the ignition switch **OFF** and disconnect the negative battery cable.

2. Disconnect the main fuel hose and connect a pressure gauge to it.

3. Connect the negative battery cable. Connect a jumper wire between the **B** and **D** terminals of the fuel pump control unit.

4. Turn the ignition switch **ON** and check the fuel pressure. It should be 2.8–3.6 psi.

5. If the fuel pressure is not as specified, replace the fuel pump.

6. Turn the ignition switch **OFF** and disconnect the negative battery cable.

7. Remove the fuel pressure gauge and reconnect the main fuel hose. Remove the jumper wire from the fuel pump control unit.

8. Connect the negative battery cable.

Fuel Injected Engines

1. Relieve the fuel system pressure and disconnect the negative battery cable.

2. Disconnect the fuel line from the fuel filter outlet. Connect a fuel pressure gauge to the fuel filter outlet.

3. Connect the negative battery cable. Connect the terminals of the yellow 2-pin test connector with a jumper wire.

4. Turn the ignition switch **ON** to operate the fuel pump and check the fuel pressure. It should be 64–85 psi.

5. If the fuel pressure is not as specified, replace the fuel pump.

6. Turn the ignition switch **OFF** and disconnect the negative battery cable. Remove the jumper wire from the test connector.

7. Remove the fuel pressure gauge and reconnect the fuel line to the fuel filter outlet.

8. Connect the negative battery cable.

NAVAJO

1. Make sure there is an adequate fuel supply.

2. Relieve the fuel system pressure.

3. Turn the ignition key **OFF**.

4. Connect a suitable fuel pressure gauge to the schrader valve on the fuel rail.

5. Install a test lead to the **FP** terminal on the VIP test connector.

6. Turn the ignition key to the **RUN** position, then ground the test lead to run the fuel pump.

7. Observe the fuel pressure reading on the pressure gauge. The fuel pressure should be 35–45 psi.

8. Relieve the fuel system pressure and turn the ignition key **OFF**. Remove the fuel pressure gauge and the test lead.

Test connector location—B Series Pick-Up

Test connector location—MPV

Connecting the jumper wire to the fuel pump control unit

FP terminal location on VIP connector—Navajo

Removal and Installation

NOTE: The fuel pump is located inside the fuel tank, attached to the tank sending unit assembly.

B SERIES PICK-UP

1. Relieve the fuel system pressure and disconnect the negative battery cable.
2. Remove the fuel tank.
3. Remove any dirt that has accumulated around the sending unit/fuel pump assembly so it will not enter the fuel tank during removal and installation.
4. Remove the attaching screws and remove the sending unit/fuel pump assembly.
5. If necessary, disconnect the electrical connectors and the fuel hose and remove the pump from the sending unit assembly.
6. Installation is the reverse of the removal procedure. Be sure to install a new seal rubber gasket.

MPV

1. Relieve the fuel system pressure and disconnect the negative battery cable.
2. Remove the rear seat and lift up the rear floormat. Remove the fuel pump cover.
3. Disconnect the sending unit/fuel pump assembly electrical connector and the fuel lines.
4. Remove any dirt that has accumulated around the sending unit/fuel pump assembly so it will not enter the fuel tank during removal and installation.
5. Remove the attaching screws and remove the sending unit/fuel pump assembly.
6. If necessary, disconnect the electrical connectors and the fuel hose and remove the pump from the sending unit assembly.
7. Installation is the reverse of the removal procedure. Be sure to install a new seal rubber gasket.

NAVAJO

1. Disconnect the negative battery cable and relieve the fuel system pressure.
2. Raise and safely support the vehicle.
3. Remove the fuel tank.
4. Remove any dirt that has accumulated around the fuel pump attaching flange so it will not enter the fuel tank during removal and installation.
5. Turn the fuel pump locking ring counterclockwise using a suitable tool. Remove the locking ring.
6. Remove the fuel pump and discard the seal ring. Separate the fuel pump from the sending unit, if required.
To install:
7. Clean the fuel pump mounting flange and tank mounting surface and seal ring groove.
8. Apply a light coating of Molybdenum grease on a new seal ring and install it in the groove.
9. Install the fuel pump to the sending unit, if removed. Install the fuel pump assembly in the tank, making sure the locating keys are in the keyways and the seal ring is in place.
10. Hold the fuel pump assembly and the seal ring in place and install the locking ring. Rotate the ring clockwise using a suitable tool. Tighten the locking ring to 40–45 ft. lbs. (54–61 Nm).
11. Install the fuel tank in the vehicle.
12. Lower the vehicle and fill the fuel tank with at least 10 gallons of fuel. Connect the negative battery cable. Turn the ignition key to **RUN** for 3 seconds repeatedly, 5–10 times, to pressurize the system. Check for leaks.
13. Start the engine and check for leaks.

Carburetor

Removal and Installation

1. Disconnect the negative battery cable.
2. Remove the air cleaner assembly.
3. Disconnect the accelerator cable and, if equipped, the cruise control cable.
4. Tag and disconnect the vacuum hoses and electrical connectors.
5. Disconnect the fuel lines.
6. Remove the attaching nuts and remove the carburetor.
7. Installation is the reverse of the removal procedure. Be sure to use a new gasket. Tighten the carburetor attaching nuts in a criss-cross pattern.

Idle Speed Adjustment

Make sure the ignition timing, spark plugs, and carburetor float level are all in normal operating condition. Turn off all lights and other unnecessary electrical loads.

1. Connect a tachometer to the engine.
2. Start the engine and allow it to reach normal operating temperature. Make sure the choke valve has fully opened.
3. Check the idle speed. If necessary, adjust it to specification by turning the throttle adjusting screw. The idle speed should be 800–850 rpm with manual transmission in neutral or automatic transmission in **P**.

Idle Mixture Adjustment

2.2L ENGINE

1. Start the engine and allow it to reach normal operating temperature. Let the engine run at idle.
2. Connect a dwellmeter (90 degrees, 4 cylinder) to the air/fuel check connector (Br/Y).
3. Check the idle mixture at the specified idle speed. The idle mixture should be 20–70 degrees. If the idle mixture is not as specified, adjust as follows:
   a. Remove the carburetor and knock out the spring pin. Reinstall the carburetor.
   b. Install the air cleaner and make sure the idle compensator is closed. Make sure all vacuum hoses are properly connected.
   c. Connect a tachometer to the engine.
   d. Warm the engine and run it at idle. Make sure the idle speed is correct.
   e. Reconnect the dwellmeter to the air/fuel check connector.
   f. Adjust the idle mixture to 27–45 degrees by turning the mixture adjust screw.
   g. Tap in the spring pin.

1988 2.6L ENGINE

1. Start the engine and allow it to reach normal operating temperature. Let the engine run at idle.
2. Connect a dwellmeter (90 degrees, 4 cylinder) to the jet mixture solenoid valve connector (YG) wire. The check connector is located near the No. 3 ACV and reed valve case assembly.
3. Check the idle mixture at the specified idle speed. The idle mixture should be 27–45 degrees. If the idle mixture is not as specified, check the oxygen sensor, feedback control unit and the wiring between the sensor and control unit.
4. If the oxygen sensor, feedback control unit and wiring are okay, adjust the idle mixture as follows:
   a. Remove the carburetor and mount it in a vise with the mixture adjust screws facing up. Protect the gasket surface from the vise jaws.
   b. Drill a 0.079 in. (2mm) pilot hole in the casting toward the mixture adjust screw, then redrill the hole to 0.118 in. (3mm).
   c. Insert a blunt punch into the hole and drive out the antitamper plug. Reinstall the carburetor.
   d. Connect a tachometer to the engine. Start the engine and allow it to reach normal operating temperature. Let the engine run at idle. Make sure the idle speed is correct.
   e. Reconnect the dwell meter to the jet mixture solenoid

THROTTLE ADJUST SCREW

AIR/FUEL CHECK CONNECTOR

SPRING PIN

MIXTURE ADJUST SCREW

Idle speed and and idle mixture adjustment—2.2L engine

valve connector. Adjust the idle mixture to 36 ± 9 degrees by turning the mixture adjust screw.

    f. Press in a new anti-tamper plug.

Service Adjustments

For all carburetor service adjustment procedures and specifications, please refer to "Carburetor Service" in the Unit Repair section.

Fuel Injection

For further information, please refer to Chilton's Electronic Engine Controls Manual.

Idle Speed Adjustment

EXCEPT NAVAJO

1. Place manual transmission in neutral or automatic transmission in **P**.
2. Make sure all accessories are **OFF**.
3. Connect a tachometer and timing light to the engine.
4. Warm the engine to normal operating temperature.
5. Check the ignition timing and adjust, if necessary.
6. Ground the green 1-pin test connector to the body with a jumper wire.

7. Check the idle speed. Specifications are as follows:
    2.2L and 2.6L engines—Manual transmission: 730–770 rpm. Automatic transmission: 750–790 rpm.
    3.0L engine—Manual and automatic transmission: 780–820 rpm.

8. If the idle speed is not within specification, adjust by turning the air adjusting screw.
9. After adjustment, disconnect the jumper wire from the test connector. Recheck the ignition timing.

NAVAJO

1. Place manual transmission in neutral or automatic transmission in **P**. Apply the parking brake.
2. Make sure the heater and accessories are **OFF**.
3. Start the engine and bring to normal operating temperature. Make sure the throttle lever is resting on the throttle plate stop screw.
4. Check the ignition timing and adjust, if necessary.
5. Shut off the engine and disconnect the negative battery cable for 5 minutes minimum. Reconnect the negative battery cable.
6. Start the engine and let it stabilize for 2 minutes. Rev the engine and let it return to idle, lightly depress and release the accelerator and let the engine idle.
7. If the engine does not idle properly, shut off the engine and disconnect the idle speed control-air bypass solenoid.
8. Run the engine at 2500 rpm for 30 seconds, then let it idle for 2 minutes.
9. Check/adjust the idle rpm to 675 rpm by turning the throttle plate stop screw.

Test connector locations

Air adjusting screw locations

NOTE: If the screw must be turned in, shut the engine off and make the estimated adjustment, then start the engine and repeat Steps 8 and 9.

10. Shut the engine off and repeat Steps 8 and 9.

11. Shut the engine off and disconnect the negative battery cable for 5 minutes minimum.

12. With the engine off, reconnect the idle speed control-air bypass solenoid. Make sure the throttle is not stuck in the bore and the linkage is not preventing the throttle from closing.

13. Start the engine and let it stabilize for 2 minutes. Rev the engine and let it return to idle, lightly depress and release the accelerator and let the engine idle.

NOTE: A condition may occur where the engine rpm will oscillate. This can be caused by the throttle plates being open enough to allow purge flow. To make sure of this condition, disconnect the carbon canister purge line and plug it. If purge is present, the throttle plates must be closed until the purge flow induced idle oscillations stop.

Idle Mixture Adjustment

The idle mixture is controlled by the Electronic Control Unit (ECU) and is not adjustable.

Fuel Injector

Removal and Installation

2.2L AND 2.6L ENGINES

1. Relieve the fuel system pressure and disconnect the negative battery cable. Drain the cooling system.

2. Disconnect the intake air hose and the ventilation hose.

3. Remove the air pipe and resonance chamber on 2.6L engine.

4. Disconnect the accelerator cable from the throttle lever.

5. Disconnect the water hoses.

6. Tag and disconnect the electrical connectors from the idle speed control valve, throttle sensor and idle switch.

7. Remove the attaching nuts and the throttle body.

8. Remove the upper intake manifold brackets.

9. Tag and disconnect the vacuum hoses and PCV hose. Tag and disconnect the intake air thermosensor connector and ground wire.

Fuel supply manifold installation—2.2L and 2.6L engines

10. Remove the injector harness bracket. Remove the nuts and bolts and the upper intake manifold.

11. Disconnect the vacuum hose and fuel lines from the fuel supply manifold.

12. Remove the fuel supply manifold with the pressure regulator.

13. Disconnect the electrical connector(s) from the injector(s). Remove the grommet(s), injector(s) and insulator(s).

To install:

14. Clean all gasket mating surfaces.

15. Apply a small amount of clean engine oil to new O-ring(s) and install on the injector(s). Install the injector(s) and insulator(s) and connect the electrical connector(s).

16. Install the fuel supply manifold and tighten the attaching bolts to 14–19 ft. lbs. (19–25 Nm).

17. Connect the fuel lines and vacuum hose.

18. Position a new gasket on the lower intake manifold and install the upper intake manifold. Tighten the attaching nuts and bolts to 14–19 ft. lbs. (19–25 Nm).

19. Install the injector harness bracket.

20. Connect the ground wire and the intake air thermosensor connector. Connect the PCV hose and the vacuum hoses.

21. Install the upper intake manifold brackets and tighten the bolts to 14–19 ft. lbs. (19–25 Nm).

22. Position a new gasket and install the throttle body. Tighten the attaching nuts to 14–19 ft. lbs. (19–25 Nm).

23. Connect the electrical connectors to the idle speed control valve, throttle sensor and idle switch.

24. Connect the water hoses. Connect the accelerator cable to the throttle lever.

25. Install the air pipe and resonance chamber, if equipped.

26. Connect the ventilation hose and intake air hose.

27. Connect the negative battery cable. Fill and bleed the cooling system.

28. Run the engine and check for leaks.

3.0L ENGINE

1. Relieve the fuel system pressure and disconnect the negative battery cable. Drain the cooling system.

2. Tag and disconnect all necessary vacuum, air and water hoses. Remove the airflow meter-to-throttle body intake air tube.

3. Disconnect the accelerator cable and the throttle sensor connector.

4. Remove the throttle body attaching nuts and the throttle body.

5. Remove the bypass air control valve and remove the throttle body-to-upper intake manifold intake air pipe.

6. Remove the extension manifolds. Remove the upper intake manifold along with the shutter valve actuator.

7. Disconnect the fuel lines and remove the fuel supply manifold. Disconnect the electrical connector(s) from the injector(s). Remove the injector(s) and insulator(s).

Upper intake manifold, throttle body and related components—3.0L engine

To install:

8. Clean all gasket mating surfaces.

9. Apply a small amount of clean engine oil to new O-ring(s) and install on the injector(s). Install the injector(s) and insulator(s).

10. Install the fuel supply manifold and tighten the attaching nuts to 14–19 ft. lbs. (19–25 Nm).

11. Connect the fuel lines to the fuel supply manifold. Before installing the remaining components, check for fuel leaks as follows:

a. Connect the negative battery cable.

b. Connect the terminals of the fuel pump test connector with a jumper wire and turn the ignition switch **ON** to run the fuel pump and pressurize the system.

c. Check for fuel leaks and correct as necessary.

d. Turn the ignition switch **OFF**, remove the jumper wire and disconnect the negative battery cable.

12. Connect the electrical connectors to the fuel injectors.

13. Install a new O-ring on the lower intake manifold, then install the upper intake manifold and extension manifolds. Tighten the attaching nuts to 14–19 ft. lbs. (19–25 Nm).

14. Position a new gasket and install the intake air pipe. Tighten the attaching nuts/bolt to 14–19 ft. lbs. (19–25 Nm).

15. Position a new gasket and install the throttle body. Tighten the attaching nuts/bolt to 14–19 ft. lbs. (19–25 Nm).

16. Connect the accelerator cable and the throttle sensor connector.

17. Connect the intake air tube between the airflow meter and the throttle body. Connect all vacuum, air and water hoses.

18. Connect the negative battery cable. Fill and bleed the cooling system.

19. Run the engine and check for leaks.

4.0L ENGINE

1. Disconnect the negative battery cable and relieve the fuel system pressure.

2. Disconnect the electrical connectors at the air bypass valve, TPS and ACT sensor.

3. Remove the snow/ice shield to expose the throttle linkage. Remove the throttle cable bracket and disconnect the cable from the ball stud on the throttle body.

4. Remove the air inlet tube from the air cleaner to the throttle body.

5. Disconnect the PCV valve from the valve cover.

6. Disconnect the spark plug wires from the comb at the rear of the manifold.

7. Remove the canister purge line from the fitting in the throttle housing.

8. Remove the bolt that retains the air conditioner line at the upper rear of the upper manifold.

9. Remove the 6 upper intake manifold retaining nuts and remove the upper intake manifold and throttle body assembly.

10. Disconnect the fuel supply line fitting at the fuel manifold.

11. Disconnect the fuel return line from the fuel pressure regulator as follows:

a. Disengage the locking tabs on the connector retainer and separate the retainer halves.

b. Inspect the visible internal portion of the fitting for dirt accumulation. Clean the fitting before disassembly.

c. To disengage the fitting from the regulator, push the fitting toward the regulator, insert the fingers on fuel line coupling key 49 UN01 006 or equivalent, into the slots in the coupling.

d. Using the tool, pull the fitting from the regulator.

NOTE: If the fitting has been properly disengaged, the fitting should slide off the regulator with minimum effort.

12. Disconnect the electrical connectors from the fuel injectors.

13. Remove the 6 bolts retaining the fuel supply manifold and remove the manifold.

14. Remove the injector retaining clips and remove the injectors from the manifold by grasping the injector body and pulling up while rocking the injector from side-to-side.

15. Remove and discard the injector O-rings.

16. Inspect the injector plastic pintle protection cap and washer for signs of deterioration. Replace the complete injector as required. If the plastic pintle protection cap is missing, look for it in the intake manifold.

NOTE: The plastic pintle protection cap is not available as a separate part.

To install:

17. Lubricate new O-rings with clean light grade oil and install 2 on each injector.

NOTE: Never use silicone grease at it will clog the injectors.

18. Install the injectors, using a light, twisting, pushing motion.

19. Install the fuel supply manifold, pushing down to make sure all the fuel injector O-rings are fully seated in the fuel supply manifold cups and intake manifold.

20. Install the 6 retaining bolts and tighten to 7–10 ft. lbs. (10–14 Nm). Install the retainer clips.

21. Install the fuel supply line and tighten the fitting to 15–18 ft. lbs. (20–24 Nm).

22. Install the fuel return line to the fuel pressure regulator by pushing it onto the fuel pressure regulator line up to the shoulder on the regulator line.

NOTE: The connector should grip the regulator line securely.

23. Install the connector retainer and snap the 2 halves of the retainer together.

24. Clean and inspect the mounting faces of the fuel manifold and upper intake manifold.

25. Position a new gasket on the mounting studs and install the upper intake manifold on the studs.

26. Install the 6 upper intake manifold retaining nuts and tighten to 15–18 ft. lbs. (20–25 Nm).

27. Connect the spark plug wires to the retainer comb at the rear of the intake manifold.

28. Attach the air conditioner line retainer and automatic transmission vacuum line retainer at the upper intake manifold.

29. Install the canister purge line on the throttle body fitting.

30. Connect the vacuum lines to the vacuum tree. Connect the electrical connectors at the air bypass valve, TPS and ACT sensor.

31. Install the PCV valve in the grommet at the rear of the right valve cover.

32. Attach the throttle cable bracket to the upper intake manifold, then connect the throttle cable to the ball stud and install the snow/ice shield.

33. After the upper intake manifold has been installed and before the fuel injector wire connectors have been connected, connect the negative battery cable and turn the ignition switch **ON**. This will cause the fuel pump to run for 2–3 seconds and pressurize the system.

34. Check for fuel leaks where the fuel injector is installed into the fuel supply manifold.

35. Turn the ignition switch **OFF** and disconnect the negative battery cable.

36. Connect the injector wire connectors and the vacuum line to the regulator.

37. Install the air inlet tube from the throttle body to the air cleaner.

38. Connect the negative battery cable, start the engine and let it idle for 2 minutes.

39. Turn the engine **OFF** and check for fuel leaks.

EMISSION CONTROLS

For further information, please refer to Chilton's Emission Controls Manual.

Emission Warning Lamps

Resetting

B SERIES PICK-UP

On Federal and Canadian vehicles, the Malfunction Indicator Light (MIL) will come on at 60,000 and 80,000 mile intervals to indicate the need for scheduled maintenance of the emission control system.

On California vehicles, the MIL will come on any time an engine management input device malfunctions, indicating that service is necessary.

After the required service or maintenance has been performed, the MIL can be reset by changing the connector connections.

MPV

Federal and Canadian vehicles are equipped with a mileage sensor which is linked to the odometer. At every 80,000 miles, the mileage sensor will cause the Malfunction Indicator Light (MIL) to illuminate, indicating that the oxygen sensor must be replaced.

After replacing the oxygen sensor, remove the instrument

Resetting the MIL—B Series Pick-Up

Mileage sensor assembly — MPV

MIL reset screw location at rear of instrument cluster — MPV

cluster and reset the MIL by reversing the position of the MIL set screw.

NAVAJO

All vehicles are equipped with a "CHECK ENGINE" or warn-ing light located on the instrument cluster. This light should come on briefly when the ignition key is turned **ON**, but should turn off when the engine starts. If the light does not come ON when the ignition key is turned **ON** or if it comes ON and stays ON when the engine is running, there is a malfunction in the electronic engine control system. After the malfunction has been remedied, using the proper procedures, the "CHECK ENGINE" light will go out.

ENGINE MECHANICAL

NOTE: Disconnecting the negative battery cable on some vehicles may interfere with the functions of the on board computer systems and may require the computer to undergo a relearning process, once the negative battery cable is reconnected.

Engine Assembly

Removal and Installation

B SERIES PICK-UP

1. Relieve the fuel system pressure, disconnect the battery cables and remove the battery.
2. Raise and safely support the vehicle. Drain the engine oil and coolant. Remove the splash shields, as necessary.
3. Remove the starter and the transmission.
4. Disconnect the exhaust system from the exhaust manifold. Lower the vehicle.
5. Remove the air cleaner assembly, if carburetor equipped. Disconnect the accelerator cable.
6. Remove the cooling fan and the radiator shroud. Disconnect the radiator hoses and transmission oil cooler lines, if equipped and remove the radiator.
7. Disconnect the fuel lines, heater hoses and brake vacuum hose.
8. Tag and disconnect the necessary electrical connectors and vacuum hoses.
9. If carburetor equipped, disconnect the secondary air pipe assembly. On 1989-92 2.6L engine, remove the resonance chamber.
10. Remove the accessory drive belt(s). If equipped, remove the power steering pump pulley and the power steering pump. Position the pump aside, leaving the hoses connected.
11. If equipped, remove the air conditioning compressor and position aside, leaving the hoses attached.
12. Remove the gusset plates, if equipped. Remove the transmission oil cooler line retainers, if equipped.
13. Attach suitable engine lifting equipment to the engine. Remove the engine mount nuts and remove the engine from the vehicle.
14. Install the engine on a workstand.

To install:

15. Remove the engine from the workstand and position in the vehicle. Install the engine mount nuts and tighten to 30-36 ft. lbs. (40-49 Nm).
16. Install the gusset plates, if equipped. Attach the transmission oil cooler line retainers, if equipped.
17. Install the air conditioning compressor, if equipped. Tighten the mounting bolts to 29-40 ft. lbs. (39-54 Nm).
18. Install the power steering pump, if equipped. Tighten the mounting bolts to 23-34 ft. lbs. (31-46 Nm). Install the power steering pump pulley and tighten the nut to 36-43 ft. lbs. (49-59 Nm).
19. Install the secondary air pipe, if equipped. Install the resonance chamber, if equipped.
20. Connect all vacuum lines and electrical connectors. Connect the brake vacuum hose, heater hoses and fuel lines.
21. Install the accessory drive belt(s) and cooling fan. Install the fan shroud, radiator and radiator hoses.
22. Adjust the accessory drive belt tension.
23. Connect the accelerator cable. Install the air cleaner assembly on carbureted engine.

24. Raise and safely support the vehicle. Connect the exhaust pipe to the exhaust manifold and tighten the attaching nuts to 30–36 ft. lbs. (40–49 Nm).

25. Install the starter and the transmission assembly. Install the splash shields and lower the vehicle.

26. Fill the crankcase with the proper type and quantity of engine oil. Install the battery and connect the battery cables.

27. Fill and bleed the cooling system. Run the engine and check for leaks and proper operation.

MPV

1. Relieve the fuel system pressure, disconnect the battery cables and remove the battery.

2. Raise and safely support the vehicle. Drain the engine oil and coolant. Remove the splash shield.

3. Remove the starter and the transmission.

4. Disconnect the exhaust pipes from the exhaust manifolds and lower the vehicle.

5. Remove the fresh air duct and the radiator hoses. Disconnect the transmission oil cooler lines from the radiator, if equipped.

6. Remove the radiator, fan shroud and cooling fan. Remove the accessory drive belts.

7. Tag and disconnect the necessary electrical connectors and vacuum lines. Disconnect the brake vacuum hose, heater hoses and fuel lines.

8. On 2.6L engine, disconnect the accelerator cable and remove the resonance chamber and air cleaner. On 3.0L engine, disconnect the accelerator cable and remove the air cleaner and airflow meter.

9. Remove the shroud upper panel and the air conditioning pipe bracket. On 3.0L engine, remove the protector cover from the front of the engine.

10. If equipped, remove the power steering pump and position aside, leaving the hoses attached. It is necessary to remove the power steering pulley prior to removing the pump.

11. If equipped, remove the air conditioning compressor and position aside, leaving the hoses attached.

12. Remove the lower grille and radiator grille. Remove the shroud upper plate and the additional condenser fan, if equipped.

13. Attach suitable engine lifting equipment to the engine. Remove the engine mount nuts and remove the engine from the vehicle.

14. Install the engine on a workstand.

To install:

15. Remove the engine from the workstand. Lower the engine into the vehicle, being careful not to damage the piping.

NOTE: Lean the air conditioning condenser forward to ease engine installation.

16. Install the engine mount nuts and tighten to 25–36 ft. lbs. (34–49 Nm). Install the additional condenser fan, if equipped.

17. Apply a bead of sealer to each side of the front support, then install the shroud upper plate. Tighten the mounting bolts to 61–87 inch lbs. (6.9–9.8 Nm).

18. Install the radiator grille and lower grille.

19. Install the air conditioning compressor, if equipped. Tighten the mounting bolts to 13–20 ft. lbs. (18–26 Nm). Install the air conditioner pipe bracket and tighten the mounting nuts to 61–87 inch lbs. (6.9–9.8 Nm).

20. Install the power steering pump, if equipped. Tighten the mounting bolts to 23–34 ft. lbs. (31–46 Nm). Install the pump pulley and tighten the nut to 29–43 ft. lbs. (39–59 Nm).

21. Install the shroud upper panel and tighten the bolts to 69–95 inch lbs. (7.8–11.0 Nm).

22. Connect the accelerator cable. On 2.6L engine, install the resonance chamber and air filter. On 3.0L engine, install the air cleaner and airflow meter.

23. Connect all electrical connectors and vacuum hoses.

24. Connect the brake vacuum hose, heater hoses and fuel lines.

25. Install the accessory drive belts and the cooling fan. Install the fan shroud and the radiator. Adjust the drive belt tension.

26. Install the radiator hoses and fresh air duct. If equipped, connect the transmission oil cooler lines.

27. Raise and safely support the vehicle. Connect the exhaust pipes to the exhaust manifolds. Tighten the nuts to 25–36 ft. lbs. (34–49 Nm).

28. Install the starter and transmission assembly. Install the splash shield and lower the vehicle.

29. Install the battery and connect the negative battery cables. Fill the crankcase with the proper type and quantity of engine oil.

30. Fill and bleed the cooling system. Run the engine and check for leaks and proper operation.

NAVAJO

1. Disconnect the negative battery cable and relieve the fuel system pressure. Drain the cooling system.

2. Mark the position of the hood on the hinges and remove the hood. Remove the air cleaner intake hose.

3. Disconnect the radiator hoses at the radiator. Disconnect the fan shroud and position it over the fan. Remove the radiator, then the shroud.

4. Remove the alternator and bracket and position the alternator aside. Disconnect the alternator ground wire from the cylinder block.

5. Remove the air conditioning compressor and power steering pump and position aside, if equipped.

6. Disconnect the heater hoses at the intake manifold and water pump. Remove the ground wires from the cylinder block.

7. Disconnect the fuel lines from the fuel supply manifold. Disconnect the throttle cable shield and linkage at the throttle body and intake manifold.

8. Tag and disconnect the vacuum connections at the rear vacuum fitting in the upper intake manifold.

9. Disconnect the wiring from the ignition coil and oil pressure and engine coolant temperature senders. Disconnect the injector harness, air charge temperature sensor and throttle position sensor. Disconnect the brake booster vacuum hose.

10. Raise and safely support the vehicle. Disconnect the exhaust pipes at the manifolds. Disconnect the starter cable and remove the starter.

11. Remove the engine front mount-to-crossmember attaching nuts or through bolts.

12. Remove the converter inspection cover and disconnect the converter from the flywheel. Remove the cable.

13. Remove the converter housing-to-engine block bolts and the adapter plate-to-converter housing bolt. Lower the vehicle.

14. Position a jack under the transmission and install suitable engine lifting equipment.

15. Raise the engine slightly and carefully pull it from the transmission. Carefully lift the engine out of the engine compartment so the rear cover plate is not bent or components damaged. Install the engine on a workstand.

To install:

16. Remove the engine from the workstand and carefully lower it into the engine compartment. Make sure the exhaust manifolds are aligned with the exhaust pipes.

17. At the transmission, start the converter pilot into the crankshaft. Install the converter housing upper bolts, making sure the dowels in the cylinder block engage the flywheel housing. Tighten the bolts to 33–45 ft. lbs. (45–61 Nm).

18. Remove the jack from under the transmission and the engine lifting equipment.

19. Position the kickdown rod on the transmission and engine. Raise and safely support the vehicle.

20. Position the transmission linkage bracket and install the remaining converter housing bolts. Install the adapter plate-to-converter housing bolt. Install the converter-to-flywheel nuts

and install the inspection cover. Connect the kickdown rod on the transmission.

21. Install the starter and connect the cable. Connect the exhaust pipes at the manifolds.

22. Install the engine front mount nuts and washers or through bolts. Lower the vehicle.

23. Install the ground wires to the engine block. Connect the ignition coil wiring, then connect the coolant temperature sending unit and oil pressure sending unit. Connect the brake booster vacuum hose.

24. Install the throttle linkage and connect the fuel lines at the fuel supply manifold.

25. Connect the ground cable at the engine block. Connect the heater hoses to the water pump and cylinder block.

26. Install the alternator and bracket. Connect the alternator ground wire to the engine block. Install the accessory drive belt.

27. Install the air conditioner compressor and power steering pump, if equipped.

28. Position the shroud over the fan. Install the radiator and connect the radiator upper and lower hoses. Install the fan shroud attaching bolts.

29. Connect the negative battery cable. Fill and bleed the cooling system.

30. Run the engine and check for leaks and proper operation. If equipped, evacuate and charge the air conditioning system.

31. Install the intake hose. Install the hood, aligning the marks that were made during removal.

Engine Mounts

Removal and Installation

FRONT MOUNTS

1. Remove the fan shroud attaching bolts.
2. Support the engine using a wood block and a jack under the oil pan.
3. Remove the engine mount bracket nut(s). Raise the engine with the jack just enough to remove the mount.
4. Remove the attaching nuts/bolts and remove the mount.
5. Installation is the reverse of the removal procedure.

REAR MOUNTS

1. Raise and safely support the vehicle.
2. Support the transmission with a jack.
3. Remove the mount-to-crossmember nuts/bolts and the mount-to-transmission bolts.
4. Raise the transmission just enough to remove the mount.
5. Installation is the reverse of the removal procedure.

Cylinder Head

Removal and Installation

2.2L ENGINE

1. Relieve the fuel system pressure and disconnect the negative battery cable.
2. Remove the splash shield and drain the cooling system.
3. If carburetor equipped, remove the air cleaner assembly. If fuel injected, remove the air intake hose.
4. Disconnect the accelerator cable.
5. Remove the cooling fan and fan shroud.
6. Disconnect the fuel lines. If equipped with carburetor and manual transmission, remove the fuel pump.
7. Disconnect the heater hoses and brake vacuum hose. Tag and disconnect the necessary electrical connectors and vacuum hoses.
8. Tag and disconnect the spark plug wires and remove the spark plugs. Remove the distributor.
9. If carburetor equipped, disconnect the secondary air pipe assembly.

Cylinder head bolt removal sequence—2.2L engine

Cylinder head bolt torque sequence—2.2L engine

10. Disconnect the upper radiator and water bypass hoses.
11. Remove the intake and exhaust manifolds.
12. Remove the timing belt front cover and the timing belt tensioner and timing belt.
13. Remove the rocker arm cover.
14. Loosen the cylinder head bolts in 2–3 steps in the proper sequence. Remove the bolts and remove the cylinder head.
15. Clean all gasket mating surfaces. Measure the cylinder head for distortion in 6 directions using a straight-edge. The maximum allowable distortion is 0.006 in. (0.15mm).
16. If distortion is excessive, resurface or replace the cylinder head. If resurfacing, do not remove more than 0.008 in. (0.20mm). The cylinder head height should be 3.620–3.624 in. (91.95–92.05mm).

NOTE: If resurfacing the cylinder, it will be necessary to remove the rocker arm/shaft assemblies.

To install:

17. Position a new head gasket on the cylinder block and install the cylinder head. Apply oil to the threads and seat faces of the cylinder head bolts and install.
18. Tighten the cylinder head bolts in 2–3 steps in the proper sequence. The final torque specification is 59–64 ft. lbs. (80–86 Nm).
19. Apply silicone sealer to each side of the front and rear camshaft bearing caps where the cap meets the cylinder head. Install the rocker arm cover and tighten the bolts to 26–35 inch lbs. (2.9–3.9 Nm).

20. Install the timing belt and tensioner. install the timing belt front cover.

21. Install the intake and exhaust manifolds.

22. Install the upper radiator and water bypass hoses. If carburetor equipped, install the secondary air pipe.

23. Install the distributor. Install the spark plugs and connect the spark plug wires.

24. Connect all vacuum hoses and electrical connectors. Connect the heater hoses and the brake vacuum hose.

25. If equipped, install the fuel pump. Connect the fuel lines.

26. Install the cooling fan and shroud.

27. Connect the accelerator cable. Install the air cleaner or air intake hose.

28. Install the splash shield. Connect the negative battery cable.

29. Fill and bleed the cooling system. Run the engine and check for leaks.

30. Check and adjust the ignition timing.

2.6L ENGINE

1988

1. Relieve the fuel system pressure and disconnect the negative battery cable. Drain the cooling system.

2. Remove the air cleaner assembly.

3. Remove the bracket from the exhaust side of the cylinder head and remove the exhaust manifold.

4. Remove the water bypass pipe. Disconnect all necessary vacuum hoses and electrical connectors. Disconnect the fuel lines.

5. Remove the carburetor and intake manifold. Remove the distributor.

6. Remove the rocker arm cover. Remove the rocker arm and shaft assembly, leaving the bolts in place in the shaft to keep the assembly together. Install hydraulic lash adjuster holder tools 49 U012 001 or equivalent to keep the adjusters from falling.

7. Hold the crankshaft pulley bolt with a wrench to keep it from turning, then remove the camshaft sprocket bolt. Remove the camshaft. With the camshaft sprocket and timing chain meshed together, place the sprocket on the sprocket holder.

NOTE: Do not rotate the engine with the camshaft removed. Once the cylinder head is removed, do not allow the sprocket to fall from the sprocket holder.

8. Remove the cylinder head-to-timing chain case bolts.

9. Loosen the cylinder head bolts in 2–3 steps in the proper sequence. Remove the bolts and remove the cylinder head.

10. Clean all gasket mating surfaces. Measure the cylinder head for distortion in 6 directions using a straight-edge. The maximum allowable distortion is 0.008 in. (0.20mm).

11. If distortion is excessive, resurface or replace the cylinder head. If resurfacing, do not remove more than 0.008 in. (0.20mm). The cylinder head height should be 3.539–3.547 in. (89.9–90.1mm).

To install:

12. Apply a thin coat of sealer to the cylinder block and timing chain cover contact surfaces, install a new head gasket and the cylinder head. Do not apply sealer to the cylinder head gasket.

13. Apply oil to the threads and seat faces of the cylinder head bolts and install. With the engine cold, tighten the cylinder head bolts, in sequence in 2–3 steps. Final torque on bolts 1–10 should be 65–72 ft. lbs. (88–98 Nm) and on bolts 11 and 12, 11–16 ft. lbs. (15–22 Nm).

14. Apply engine oil to the camshaft journals and install the camshaft, aligning the dowel pin with the camshaft sprocket. Install the distributor drive gear and the lock bolt. Tighten the lock bolt by hand only at this time.

15. Coat the circular packing with sealant and install in the rear of the cylinder head. Install the rocker arms/shafts assembly and tighten the mounting bolts, in sequence, to 14–15 ft. lbs. (19–20 Nm) except for the No. 5 bearing cap rear bolt, which should be tightened to 15–20 ft. lbs. (20–26 Nm).

Cylinder head bolt removal sequence—1988 2.6L engine

Cylinder head bolt torque sequence—1988 2.6L engine

16. Tighten the distributor drive gear/camshaft sprocket lock bolt to 36–43 ft. lbs. (49–58 Nm).

17. Remove the hydraulic lash adjuster holders. Adjust the jet valve clearance.

18. Install the half-circle packing in the front of the cylinder head and apply sealer across the top of the packing and on both sides of the packing on the cylinder head. Install the rocker arm cover and tighten the bolts to 43–61 inch lbs. (5.0–6.8 Nm).

19. Install the remaining components in the reverse order of removal. Fill and bleed the cooling system. Run the engine and check for leaks. Check and adjust the ignition timing.

1989–92

1. Relieve the fuel system pressure and disconnect the negative battery cable. Drain the cooling system.

2. Disconnect the accelerator cable and remove the air intake pipe and resonance chamber.

3. Remove the air conditioning drive belt and idler.

4. Tag and disconnect the spark plug wires. Remove the spark plugs.

5. Remove the upper radiator and oil cooler water hoses. Disconnect the brake vacuum hose, canister hose and fuel line.

6. Tag and disconnect the oxygen sensor connector and emission harness connectors. Remove the solenoid valves.

7. Remove the rocker arm cover. Turn the crankshaft pulley until the timing mark on the camshaft sprocket is 90 degrees to the right. The mark should be parallel to the top of the cylinder head surface. Make sure the yellow crankshaft pulley timing mark is aligned with the indicator pin.

8. Mark the position of the distributor rotor in relation to the distributor housing and the distributor housing in relation to the cylinder head. Remove the distributor.

NOTE: Do not rotate the engine after distributor removal.

9. Hold the crankshaft pulley with a suitable tool and remove

the distributor drive gear/camshaft pulley retaining bolt and the drive gear.

10. Remove the service cover on the timing chain cover. Push the chain adjuster sleeve in toward the left and insert a 0.08 in. (2mm) diameter by 1.77 in. (45mm) long pin into the lever hole to hold it. Be careful that the pin does not fall.

11. Secure the camshaft sprocket and chain with a wire to hold the chain in place on the sprocket. Do not allow the sprocket and chain to fall down into the engine and cause the chain to become disengaged from the crankshaft sprocket.

12. Loosen the cylinder head bolts in 2–3 steps in the proper sequence. Remove the bolts and remove the cylinder head.

13. If necessary, remove the intake and exhaust manifolds from the cylinder head.

14. Clean all gasket mating surfaces. Measure the cylinder head for distortion in 6 directions using a straight-edge. The maximum allowable distortion is 0.006 in. (0.15mm).

15. If distortion is excessive, resurface or replace the cylinder head. If resurfacing, do not remove more than 0.008 in. (0.20mm). The cylinder head height should be 3.541–3.545 in. (89.95–90.05mm).

NOTE: It will be necessary to remove the rocker arm/ shaft assembly if resurfacing is necessary.

To install:

16. If removed, install the intake and exhaust manifolds.

17. Apply silicone sealer to the cylinder block head gasket surface at the mating junction of the cylinder block and the timing chain cover.

18. Position a new head gasket and install the cylinder head. Apply clean engine oil to the head bolt threads and seat faces and install the bolts.

19. Tighten the cylinder head bolts, in sequence, in 2–3 steps. The final torque specification is 59–64 ft. lbs. (80–86 Nm). Tighten the 2 cylinder head-to-timing chain cover bolts to 12–17 ft. lbs. (16–23 Nm).

20. Install the camshaft sprocket onto the camshaft dowel pin, then remove the wire securing the camshaft sprocket and chain.

21. Remove the retaining pin from the chain adjuster and install the service cover with a new gasket. Tighten the mounting bolts to 69–95 inch lbs. (7.8–11.0 Nm) and the mounting nuts to 61–87 inch lbs. (6.9–9.8 Nm).

22. Install the distributor drive gear with a new washer and lock bolt. Position a shop cloth to protect the cylinder head and place a small prybar between the cylinder head and the small tab on the camshaft between the lobes, to hold the camshaft in place. Tighten the lock bolt to 36–45 ft. lbs. (49–61 Nm).

23. Apply sealer to the cylinder head and install the half circle seals.

24. Make sure the timing mark on the camshaft sprocket is still positioned 90 degrees to the right and the yellow crankshaft pulley timing mark is aligned with the indicator pin.

25. Apply clean engine oil to a new O-ring and install on the distributor. Apply clean engine oil to the distributor driven gear and install the distributor, aligning the marks that were made during removal.

26. Apply clean engine oil to the valves, rocker arms and timing chain.

27. Coat a new rocker arm cover gasket with sealer and install on the rocker arm cover.

28. Apply silicone sealer to the front and rear half circle seals and install the rocker arm cover. Tighten the attaching bolts to 52–78 inch lbs. (5.9–8.8 Nm).

29. Install the solenoid valves. Connect all electrical connectors and vacuum hoses.

30. Connect the fuel line, brake vacuum hose, upper radiator hose and oil cooler water hose.

31. Install the spark plugs and the spark plug wires.

32. Install the air conditioner drive belt and idler, if equipped. Install the air intake pipe and resonance chamber and connect the accelerator cable.

Retaining the chain adjuster—1989–92 2.6L engine

Cylinder head bolt removal sequence—1989–92 2.6L engine

Cylinder head bolt torque sequence—1989–92 2.6L engine

33. Connect the negative battery cable. Fill and bleed the cooling system.

34. Run the engine and check for leaks. Check and adjust the ignition timing.

3.0L ENGINE

1. Relieve the fuel system pressure and disconnect the negative battery cable. Drain the cooling system.

2. Remove the air intake hose and disconnect the accelerator cable.

3. Turn the crankshaft to align the timing marks on the tim-

ing belt sprockets. Mark the direction of rotation on the belt and remove the timing belt.

4. Disconnect the brake vacuum hose and the fuel line. Tag and disconnect all necessary electrical connectors and vacuum hoses.

5. Mark the position of the distributor rotor in relation to the distributor housing and the distributor housing in relation to the cylinder head. Remove the distributor.

6. Remove the extension manifolds. Loosen the intake manifold bolts, in sequence, in 2–3 steps and remove the bolts and intake manifold.

7. Remove the rocker arm cover. Remove the center exhaust pipe insulator and center exhaust pipe.

8. Remove the exhaust manifold insulator and exhaust manifold. Remove the seal plate.

9. Loosen the cylinder head bolts, in sequence, in 2–3 steps and remove the bolts and cylinder head.

10. Clean all gasket mating surfaces. Measure the cylinder head for distortion in 6 directions using a straight-edge. The maximum allowable distortion is 0.004 in. (0.10mm).

11. If distortion is excessive, resurface or replace the cylinder head. If resurfacing, do not remove more than 0.006 in. (0.15mm). The cylinder head height should be 4.931–4.935 in. (125.25–125.35mm).

NOTE: It will be necessary to remove the rocker arm/shaft assembly if resurfacing is necessary.

To install:

12. Check the oil control plug projection from the cylinder block. It should be 0.209–0.224 in. (5.3–5.7mm).

13. Apply clean engine oil to a new O-ring and install on the oil control plug. Install a new cylinder head gasket, making sure the **L** mark, for left bank or **R** mark, for right bank, is facing upward.

14. Install the cylinder head, being careful not to damage the oil control plug O-ring.

15. Measure the length of the cylinder head bolts prior to installation and replace if not within specification. The intake side bolts should be 4.25 in. (108mm) and should not exceed 4.29 in. (109mm). The exhaust side bolts should be 5.43 in. (138mm) and should not exceed 5.47 in. (139mm).

16. Apply clean engine oil to the threads and the seat face of the cylinder head bolts and install. Tighten the bolts as follows:

    Step 1: Tighten each bolt, in sequence, to 14 ft. lbs. (20 Nm).

    Step 2: Tighten each bolt, in sequence, an additional 90 degree turn.

    Step 3: Repeat Step 2.

17. Install the seal plate, exhaust manifold and exhaust manifold insulator.

18. Install the center exhaust pipe and exhaust pipe insulator.

19. Coat a new rocker arm cover gasket with silicone sealant and install onto the rocker arm cover. Install the rocker arm cover with new seal washers and tighten the bolts to 30–39 inch lbs. (3.4–4.4 Nm).

20. Connect the injector harness and position a new intake manifold gasket. Install the intake manifold and tighten the bolts, in sequence in 2–3 steps. The final torque specification is 14–19 ft. lbs. (19–25 Nm).

21. Apply clean engine oil to new O-rings and install the extension manifolds with new gaskets. Tighten to 14–19 ft. lbs. (19–25 Nm).

22. Install the distributor, aligning the marks that were made during removal.

23. Connect all electrical connectors and vacuum hoses. Connect the fuel line and brake vacuum hose.

24. Install the timing belt.

25. Connect the accelerator cable and install the air intake hose.

26. Connect the negative battery cable. Fill and bleed the cooling system.

Cylinder head bolt removal sequence—3.0L engine

Cylinder head bolt torque sequence—3.0L engine

27. Run the engine and check for leaks. Check and adjust the ignition timing.

4.0L ENGINE

1. Disconnect the negative battery cable and relieve the fuel system pressure. Drain the cooling system.

2. Remove the upper and lower intake manifolds and rocker arm covers.

3. If the left cylinder head is being removed, proceed as follows:

    a. Remove the accessory drive belt.

    b. Discharge the refrigerant and remove the air conditioning compressor, if equipped.

    c. Remove the power steering pump and bracket and position aside.

    d. Remove the spark plugs.

4. If the right cylinder head is being removed, proceed as follows:

    a. Remove the accessory drive belt.

    b. Remove the alternator and alternator bracket.

    c. Remove the ignition coil and bracket assembly.

    d. Remove the spark plugs.

5. Disconnect the exhaust pipe and remove the exhaust manifold(s).

6. Remove the rocker arm shaft assembly. Remove the pushrods, marking them so they can be reinstalled in the same positions.

7. Remove and discard the cylinder head attaching bolts and remove the cylinder heads.

Cylinder head bolt torque sequence — 4.0L engine

8. Clean all gasket mating surfaces. Check the cylinder head for flatness using a straight-edge and a feeler gauge. The cylinder head must not be warped more than 0.003 in. in any 6 in. or more than 0.006 in. overall.

To install:

9. Position new cylinder head gasket(s) on the cylinder block. Install cylinder head locating dowels.

NOTE: The cylinder head(s) and intake manifold are torqued alternately and in sequence to insure correct fit and gasket crunch.

10. Install new cylinder head bolts and tighten, in sequence, to 44 ft. lbs. (60 Nm).

11. Apply silicone sealer to the block and cylinder head mating surfaces at the 4 corners of the lifter valley opening. Install the intake manifold gasket and again apply sealer in the same locations.

12. Position the lower intake manifold on the 2 guide studs and install the nuts and bolts hand tight. Tighten the lower intake manifold bolts, in sequence, to 3–6 ft. lbs. (4–8 Nm).

13. Tighten the cylinder head bolts, in sequence, to 59 ft. lbs. (80 Nm).

14. Tighten the intake manifold, in sequence, to 6–11 ft. lbs. (8–15 Nm).

15. Turn the cylinder head bolts 80–85 degrees tighter, in sequence.

16. Tighten the intake manifold, in sequence, to 11–15 ft. lbs. (15–21 Nm) and then to 15–18 ft. lbs. (21–25 Nm), in sequence.

17. Dip both ends of each pushrod in clean engine oil and install in their original locations. Install the rocker arm and shaft assemblies and tighten the rocker arm shaft support bolts evenly to 46–52 ft. lbs. (62–70 Nm).

18. Apply silicone sealer to the 4 locations at the joint where the intake manifold and cylinder head meet. Install a new rocker arm cover gasket in each cover and install the rocker arm covers. Tighten the rocker arm cover bolts to 3–5 ft. lbs. (4–7 Nm), wait 2 minutes and then retighten to the same specification.

19. Install the upper intake manifold and tighten the nuts to 15–18 ft. lbs. (20–25 Nm).

20. Install the exhaust manifold(s) and connect the exhaust pipe.

21. Install the spark plugs and the ignition coil and bracket assembly.

22. Install the alternator and the accessory drive belt.

23. Install the power steering pump. Install the air conditioning compressor, if equipped.

24. Connect the negative battery cable. Fill and bleed the cooling system. Run the engine and check for leaks.

Valve Lifters

Removal and Installation

EXCEPT 4.0L ENGINE

All engines except 4.0L are equipped with hydraulic lash adjusters located in the rocker arms. The hydraulic lash adjusters can be removed by hand or with suitable pliers after the rocker arm/shaft assembly is removed.

Valve lifters — 4.0L engine

4.0L ENGINE

1. Disconnect the negative battery cable and relieve the fuel system pressure. Drain the cooling system.

2. Remove the intake manifold and rocker arm covers.

3. Loosen the rocker arm shaft support bolts 2 turns at a time until the rocker arm and shaft assembly can be removed.

4. Remove the pushrods, marking them so they can be reinstalled in their original positions.

5. Remove the lifters. Note the location of each lifter so it can be reinstalled in the same bore. The roller lifters have an alignment tab which fits into a locating groove in the lifter bore. Do not attempt to rotate a roller lifter in the bore in an effort to remove it.

To install:

6. Lubricate the lifters and bores with clean engine oil. Install each lifter in the same bore from which it was removed. Install the lifter with the alignment tab in the locating groove of the bore. If a new lifter is being installed, check for free fit in the bore.

7. Check each pushrod for straightness and for damage, replace as necessary. Dip each pushrod end in clean engine oil and install in its original position.

8. Lubricate the rocker arm and shaft assembly and install. Draw the shaft support bolts down evenly, 2 turns at a time, until the shafts are fully down. Tighten the bolts to 46–52 ft. lbs. (62–70 Nm).

9. Install the intake manifold and rocker arm covers.

10. Connect the negative battery cable. Fill and bleed the cooling system.

11. Run the engine and check for leaks.

Valve Lash

Adjustment

NOTE: All engines are quipped with hydraulic adjusters which require no adjustment. The only adjustment necessary is on the jet valves, located beside the intake valves on 1988 2.6L engine.

1988 2.6L ENGINE

1. Start the engine and bring to normal operating temperature.

Adjusting jet valve clearance—1988 2.6L engine

Rocker arm/shaft assembly mounting bolts removal sequence—2.2L engine

Rocker arm/shaft assembly mounting bolts torque sequence—2.2L engine

2. Shut the engine off and disconnect the negative battery cable.

3. Remove the air cleaner and the rocker arm cover.

4. Bring the piston in the cylinder of the jet valve to be adjusted to TDC on the compression stroke.

5. Check the jet valve lash using a feeler gauge placed between the adjusting screw and the jet valve stem tip. The clearance should be 0.010 in. (0.25mm).

6. If the clearance is incorrect, loosen the locknut and turn the adjusting screw until proper clearance is obtained, then tighten the locknut.

7. Install the rocker arm cover and air cleaner. Connect the negative battery cable.

Rocker Arms/Shafts

Removal and Installation

2.2L ENGINE

1. Disconnect the negative battery cable.

2. Remove the air cleaner assembly or air intake hose, as required.

3. Remove the rocker arm cover.

4. Loosen the rocker arm/shaft assembly mounting bolts in 2–3 steps in the proper sequence. Remove the rocker arm/shaft assembly together with the bolts.

5. If necessary, disassemble the rocker arm/shaft assembly, noting the position of each component to ease reassembly.

6. Check for wear or damage to the contact surfaces of the shafts and rocker arms; replace as necessary.

7. Measure the rocker arm inner diameter, it should be 0.6300–0.6310 in. (16.000–16.027mm). Measure the rocker arm shaft diameter, it should be 0.6286–0.6293 in. (15.966–15.984mm).

8. Subtract the shaft diameter from the rocker arm diameter to get the oil clearance. The oil clearance should be 0.0006–0.0024 in. (0.016–0.061mm) and should not exceed 0.004 in. (0.10mm). Replace parts, as necessary, if the oil clearance is not within specification.

To install:

9. Apply clean engine oil to the rocker arm shafts and rocker arms and assemble the rocker arm/shaft assembly in the reverse order of disassembly. Make sure the rocker arm shaft oil holes in the center camshaft cap face each other.

NOTE: Use the mounting bolts for alignment.

10. Apply silicone sealant to the cylinder head on the front and rear camshaft cap mounting surface. Apply clean engine oil to the camshaft journals and valve stem tips.

11. Install the rocker arm/shaft assembly and tighten the bolts, in sequence, in 2–3 steps to a maximum torque of 13–20 ft. lbs. (18–26 Nm).

12. Apply silicone sealant to each side of the front and rear camshaft cap and the cylinder head in the area where the caps meet the cylinder head.

13. Install the rocker arm cover and tighten the mounting bolts to 26–35 inch lbs. (2.9–3.9 Nm).

Service Tips

ROCKER ARM NOISE

Noise coming from the rocker arms on 2.2L engine may be caused by insufficient oil supply to the hydraulic lash adjuster. Replacement rocker arms are available that have the oil passage to the hydraulic lash adjuster enlarged from 0.031 in. to 0.078 in. The hydraulic lash adjuster itself is not faulty and the original hydraulic lash adjuster can be installed in the replacement rocker arm. Be careful not to damage the hydraulic lash adjuster O-ring during installation.

The replacement rocker arms, without hydraulic lash adjusters, are available as part number F240 12 131B for rocker arm 1 and 3 and part number F240 12 151B for rocker arm 2 and 4. The replacement rocker arms, with hydraulic lash adjusters, are available as part number F240 12 130B for rocker arm 1 and 3 and part number F240 12 150B for rocker arm 2 and 4.

14. Install the air cleaner assembly or air intake tube. Connect the negative battery cable, start the engine and check for leaks and proper operation.

2.6L ENGINE

1988

1. Disconnect the negative battery cable.
2. Remove the air cleaner assembly.
3. Remove the rocker arm cover.
4. Install hydraulic lash adjuster holder tool 49 U012 001 or equivalent, over the ends of each rocker arm to keep the hydraulic lash adjuster from falling out when the rocker arm/shaft assembly is removed.
5. Loosen the rocker arm/shaft assembly mounting bolts and remove the assembly. Leave the mounting bolts in place in the shaft to keep the assembly together, if there will be no further disassembly.
6. If necessary, disassemble the rocker arm/shaft assembly, noting the position of each component to ease reassembly.
7. Check for wear or damage to the contact surfaces of the shafts and rocker arms; replace as necessary.
8. Measure the rocker arm inner diameter, it should be 0.7445–0.7452 in. (18.910–18.928mm). Measure the rocker arm shaft diameter, it should be 0.7435–0.7440 in. (18.885–18.898mm).
9. Subtract the shaft diameter from the rocker arm diameter to get the oil clearance. The oil clearance should be 0.0005–0.0017 in. (0.012–0.043mm) and should not exceed 0.004 in. (0.10mm). Replace parts, as necessary, if the oil clearance is not within specification.

To install:

10. Apply clean engine oil to the rocker arm shafts and rocker arms and assemble the rocker arm/shaft assembly in the reverse order of disassembly. Be sure to align the mating mark on the front of the shaft with the mating mark on the front camshaft cap.
11. Apply clean engine oil to the camshaft journals and valve stem tips.
12. Install the rocker arm/shaft assembly and tighten the mounting bolts, in sequence, in 2–3 steps to a maximum torque of 14–15 ft. lbs. (19–20 Nm).
13. Remove the hydraulic lash adjuster holder tools. Adjust the jet valve lash.
14. Install the rocker arm cover and tighten to 43–61 inch lbs. (5–7 Nm). Install the air cleaner assembly.
15. Connect the negative battery cable, start the engine and bring to normal operating temperature. Check for leaks and proper operation. With the engine warm, readjust the jet valve clearance.

1989–92

1. Disconnect the negative battery cable.
2. Remove the air intake hose.
3. Remove the rocker arm cover.
4. Loosen the rocker arm/shaft assembly mounting bolts in 2–3 steps in the proper sequence. Remove the rocker arm/shaft assembly together with the bolts.

Rocker arm/shaft assembly mounting bolts torque sequence—1988 2.6L engine.

Rocker arm/shaft assembly mounting bolts removal sequence—1989–92 2.6L engine

Rocker arm/shaft assembly mounting bolts torque sequence—1989–92 2.6L engine.

5. If necessary, disassemble the rocker arm/shaft assembly, noting the position of each component to ease reassembly.
6. Check for wear or damage to the contact surfaces of the shafts and rocker arms; replace as necessary.
7. Measure the rocker arm inner diameter, it should be 0.8268–0.8281 in. (21.000–21.033mm). Measure the rocker arm shaft diameter, it should be 0.8252–0.8260 in. (20.959–20.980mm).
8. Subtract the shaft diameter from the rocker arm diameter to get the oil clearance. The oil clearance should be 0.0008–0.0029 in. (0.020–0.074mm) and should not exceed 0.004 in. (0.10mm). Replace parts, as necessary, if the oil clearance is not within specification.

To install:

9. Apply clean engine oil to the rocker arm shafts and rocker arms and assemble the rocker arm/shaft assembly in the reverse order of disassembly, noting the following:
   a. The intake side shaft has twice as many oil holes as the exhaust side shaft.
   b. The No. 4 camshaft cap has an oil hole from the cylinder head; make sure it is installed correctly.
10. Apply clean engine oil to the camshaft journals and valve stem tips.
11. Install the rocker arm/shaft assembly and tighten the mounting bolts, in sequence, in 2–3 steps to a maximum torque of 14–19 ft. lbs. (19–25 Nm).
12. Coat a new gasket with silicone sealer and install on the rocker arm cover. Apply sealer to the cylinder head in the area of the half circle seals and install the rocker arm cover. Install the mounting bolts and tighten to 52–78 inch lbs. (5.9–8.8 Nm).
13. Install the air intake hose. Connect the negative battery cable, start the engine and check for leaks and proper operation.

3.0L ENGINE

1. Disconnect the negative battery cable.

2. If removing the driver's side rocker arm/shaft assembly, proceed as follows:

    a. Remove the air inlet tube.

    b. Disconnect the necessary electrical connectors and vacuum hoses from the throttle body and intake air pipe.

    c. Disconnect the throttle cable.

    d. Remove the throttle body and intake air pipe.

3. Remove the rocker arm cover.

4. Loosen the rocker arm/shaft assembly mounting bolts in sequence, in 2–3 steps. Remove the assembly with the bolts.

5. If necessary, disassemble the rocker arm/shaft assembly, noting the position of each component to ease reassembly.

6. Check for wear or damage to the contact surfaces of the shafts and rocker arms; replace as necessary.

7. Measure the rocker arm inner diameter, it should be 0.7480–0.7493 in. (19.000–19.033mm). Measure the rocker arm shaft diameter, it should be 0.7464–0.7472 in. (18.959–18.980mm).

8. Subtract the shaft diameter from the rocker arm diameter to get the oil clearance. The oil clearance should be 0.0008–0.0029 in. (0.020–0.074mm) and should not exceed 0.004 in. (0.10mm). Replace parts, as necessary, if the oil clearance is not within specification.

To install:

9. Apply clean engine oil to the rocker arm shafts and rocker arms and assemble the rocker arm/shaft assembly in the reverse order of disassembly, noting the following. The intake side shaft has twice as many oil holes as the exhaust side shaft.

10. Apply clean engine oil to the camshaft journals and valve stem tips.

11. Install the rocker arm/shaft assembly and tighten the mounting bolts, in sequence, in 2–3 steps to a maximum torque of 14–19 ft. lbs. (19–25 Nm).

NOTE: Be careful that the rocker arm shaft spring does not get caught between the shaft and mounting boss during installation.

12. Coat a new gasket with silicone sealant and install on the rocker arm cover. Install the rocker arm cover with new seal washers and tighten the bolts to 30–39 inch lbs. (3.4–4.4 Nm).

13. Install the intake air pipe, throttle body and air intake tube, if removed. Connect the throttle cable and the necessary electrical connectors and vacuum hoses.

14. Connect the negative battery cable, start the engine and check for leaks and proper operation.

4.0L ENGINE

1. Disconnect the negative battery cable. Remove the intake shield and air intake tube.

2. If removing the right rocker arm/shaft assembly, proceed as follows:

    a. Remove the alternator and the coil pack.

    b. Remove the retaining bolt from the air conditioning pipe over the upper intake manifold.

    c. Remove the spark plug wires from the clips on the valve cover.

    d. Remove the 2 wiring harnesses from the right rocker arm cover.

    e. Disconnect the vacuum hose at the coupling over the rocker arm cover.

    f. Remove the engine wiring harness clip from the rocker arm cover-to-intake manifold stud. Do not pull on the harness but rather lift up on the clip.

    g. Remove the right rocker arm cover bolts, reinforcement plate and the cover.

3. If removing the right rocker arm/shaft assembly, proceed as follows:

    a. Remove the bolt from the air conditioning pipe over the upper intake manifold, if not already done.

    b. Disconnect the air conditioning compressor clutch con-

Rocker arm/shaft assembly mounting bolts removal sequence—3.0L engine

Rocker arm/shaft assembly mounting bolts torque sequence—3.0L engine.

nector and remove the wiring harness from the back of the compressor.

    c. Remove the air conditioning compressor bolts, pull up the tube that goes around the back of the engine and reposition the compressor and tube aside.

    d. Tag and disconnect the power brake vacuum hose and other hoses from the vacuum tee on the plenum.

    e. Remove the PCV hose and valve. Remove the wiring harness from the valve cover and position aside.

    f. Tag and disconnect the spark plug wires from the spark plugs and clips on the rocker arm cover.

    g. Remove the engine wiring harness clip from the rocker arm cover-to-intake manifold stud. Do not pull on the harness but rather lift up on the clip.

    h. Remove the retaining bolt from the fuel hose clip to the front of the engine to allow the fuel hoses to be moved enough to gain access to the upper front rocker arm cover bolt.

    i. Remove the bolts, reinforcement plates and left rocker arm cover.

4. Remove the rocker arm shafts by loosening the support bolts 2 turns at a time until the shaft can be removed.

5. If necessary, disassemble the rocker arm/shaft assembly by removing the spring washer and pin from each end of the shaft and sliding the rocker arms, springs and rocker arm shaft supports off the shaft. Note the position of each component to ease reassembly.

6. Inspect all components for wear and replace, as necessary.

To install:

7. Coat the rocker arms and shafts with clean engine oil and reassemble. The oil holes in the shaft must point down when the shaft is installed. This position can be recognized by a notch on the front face of the shaft.

8. Lubricate the pushrod ends and valve stem tips.

9. Install the rocker arm/shaft assembly and draw the shaft support bolts down evenly, 2 turns at a time, until the rocker

arm/shaft assembly is fully down. Tighten the shaft support bolts to 46–52 ft. lbs. (62–70 Nm).

10. Clean all gasket mating surfaces.

11. Apply silicone sealant to the intake manifold-to-cylinder head parting seam and an ⅛ in. ball of sealer to the rocker arm cover bolt holes on the exhaust side.

12. Install a new gasket on the rocker arm cover and install the cover, reinforcing plates and bolts. Tighten the bolts to 53–70 inch lbs. (6–8 Nm) working in a criss-cross pattern and starting at the center bolts.

13. Install the remaining components in the reverse order of their removal. Connect the negative battery cable, start the engine and check for leaks and proper operation.

Intake Manifold

Removal and Installation

2.2L AND 2.6L ENGINES

Carbureted Engine

1. Relieve the fuel system pressure and disconnect the negative battery cable. Drain the cooling system.

2. Remove the air cleaner assembly.

3. Disconnect the accelerator cable. Tag and disconnect the necessary electrical connectors and vacuum hoses.

4. Disconnect the coolant hoses and fuel line.

5. Remove the intake manifold mounting nuts and remove the intake manifold.

To install:

6. Clean all gasket mating surfaces.

7. Position a new intake manifold gasket on the cylinder head and install the intake manifold.

8. Install the intake manifold mounting nuts and tighten, in 2–3 steps, to 14–19 ft. lbs. (19–25 Nm) on 2.2L engine or 11–14 ft. lbs. (15–19 Nm) on 2.6L engine. Tighten the nuts at the center of the manifold 1st and work towards the ends.

9. Connect the fuel line and the coolant hoses.

10. Connect the electrical connectors and vacuum hoses. Connect the accelerator cable.

11. Install the air cleaner assembly and connect the negative battery cable.

12. Fill and bleed the cooling system. Run the engine and check for leaks.

Fuel Injected Engine

1. Relieve the fuel system pressure and disconnect the negative battery cable. Drain the cooling system.

2. Disconnect the air intake tube and ventilation hose. Remove the air pipe and resonance chamber on 2.6L engine.

3. Disconnect the accelerator cable and coolant hoses. Tag and disconnect the electrical connectors to the solenoid valve, throttle sensor and idle switch.

4. Remove the throttle body.

5. Remove the upper intake manifold brackets.

6. Tag and disconnect the vacuum hoses and PCV hose. Tag and disconnect the intake air thermosensor connector and ground wire.

7. Remove the injector harness bracket and remove the upper intake manifold.

8. Tag and disconnect the vacuum hoses from the lower intake manifold. Disconnect the fuel lines.

9. Remove the fuel supply manifold and the injectors. Remove the injector harness and bracket.

10. Remove the pulsation damper and the intake manifold bracket. Remove the attaching nuts and remove the lower intake manifold.

To install:

11. Clean all gasket mating surfaces.

12. Position a new intake manifold-to-cylinder head gasket and install the lower intake manifold. Tighten the nuts to 14–19 ft. lbs. (19–25 Nm).

13. Install the intake manifold bracket and pulsation damper. Install the injector harness and bracket. Tighten the pulsation damper and injector harness bracket bolts to 69–95 inch lbs. (7.8–11.0 Nm).

14. Install the injectors and the fuel supply manifold. Tighten the fuel supply manifold attaching bolts and tighten to 14–19 ft. lbs. (19–25 Nm).

15. Connect the fuel lines. Connect the vacuum hoses to the lower intake manifold.

16. Position a new gasket and install the upper intake manifold. Tighten the attaching bolts/nuts to 14–19 ft. lbs. (19–25 Nm).

17. Install the injector harness bracket. Connect the ground wire and air thermosensor electrical connector. Connect the PCV hose and the vacuum hoses to the upper intake manifold.

18. Install the upper intake manifold brackets.

19. Position a new gasket and install the throttle body. Tighten the mounting nuts to 14–19 ft. lbs. (19–25 Nm).

20. Connect the electrical connectors at the idle switch, throttle sensor and solenoid valve.

21. Connect the coolant hoses and the accelerator cable. On 2.6L engine, install the air pipe and resonance chamber.

22. Connect the ventilation hose and air intake hose. Connect the negative battery cable.

23. Fill and bleed the cooling system. Run the engine and check for leaks and proper operation.

3.0L ENGINE

1. Relieve the fuel system pressure and disconnect the negative battery cable. Drain the cooling system.

2. Remove the air intake tube from the throttle body. Disconnect the accelerator cable.

3. Disconnect the throttle sensor connector and the coolant hoses. Remove the throttle body.

4. Tag and disconnect the vacuum hoses. Remove the bypass air control valve and the intake air pipe.

Intake manifold mounting nuts removal sequence—3.0L engine

Intake manifold mounting nuts torque sequence—3.0L engine

5. Remove the extension manifolds. Remove the upper intake plenum with the shutter valve actuator.

6. Remove the fuel supply manifold and the injectors. Disconnect the coolant hoses.

7. Loosen the lower intake manifold nuts, in sequence, in 2 steps and remove the lower intake manifold.

To install:

8. Clean all gasket mating surfaces.

9. Position new lower intake manifold-to-cylinder head gaskets and install the lower intake manifold.

10. Install the intake manifold washers with the white paint mark upward. Install the nuts and tighten, in sequence, in 2 steps to a maximum torque of 14–19 ft. lbs. (19–25 Nm).

11. Install the injectors and the fuel supply manifold. Tighten the attaching bolts to 14–19 ft. lbs. (19–25 Nm).

12. Connect the coolant hoses.

13. Install a new O-ring on the lower intake manifold and install the upper intake plenum. Apply clean engine oil to new O-rings and install on the extension manifolds. Position new gaskets and install the extension manifolds. Tighten the attaching nuts to 14–19 ft. lbs. (19–25 Nm).

14. Position a new gasket and install the intake air pipe. Install the bypass air control valve. Tighten the attaching bolts/nuts to 14–19 ft. lbs. (19–25 Nm).

15. Position a new gasket and install the throttle body. Tighten the attaching nuts to 14–19 ft. lbs. (19–25 Nm).

16. Connect the coolant and vacuum hoses. Connect the throttle sensor connector and accelerator cable.

17. Adjust the accelerator cable deflection to 0.039–0.118 in. (1–3mm).

18. Connect the air intake tube and the negative battery cable.

19. Fill and bleed the cooling system. Run the engine and check for leaks and proper operation.

4.0L ENGINE

1. Disconnect the negative battery cable and relieve the fuel system pressure.

2. Remove the air cleaner air intake duct from the throttle body.

3. Remove the snow/ice shield and disconnect the throttle cable and bracket assembly.

4. Tag and disconnect the vacuum hoses from the fittings on the upper intake manifold.

5. Tag and disconnect the electrical connectors at the throttle body, upper intake manifold, lower intake manifold and injectors.

6. Disconnect the fuel lines from the fuel supply manifold.

7. Remove the ignition coil and bracket assembly.

8. Remove the mounting nuts and remove the upper intake manifold.

9. Remove the rocker arm covers.

10. Remove the intake manifold attaching bolts and nuts. Tap the manifold lightly with a plastic mallet to break the gasket seal and remove the manifold.

To install:

11. Clean all gasket mating surfaces.

12. Apply silicone sealer to the block and cylinder head mating surfaces at the 4 corners of the lifter valley opening. Install the intake manifold gaskets and again apply sealer to the same locations.

13. Position the intake manifold on the 2 guide studs and install the nuts and bolts hand tight. Tighten the bolts, in sequence, in 4 steps, first to 3–6 ft. lbs. (4–8 Nm), then to 6–11 ft. lbs. (8–15 Nm), then to 11–15 ft. lbs. (15–21 Nm) and finally to 15–18 ft. lbs. (21–25 Nm).

14. Apply silicone sealer to the 4 locations where the intake manifold and the cylinder heads meet. Install the rocker arm covers with new gaskets and tighten evenly to 3–5 ft. lbs. (4–7 Nm). Wait 2 minutes and tighten the bolts again to the same specification.

Intake manifold bolts/nuts torque sequence—4.0L engine

15. Install the upper intake manifold and tighten the nuts to 15–18 ft. lbs. (20–25 Nm).

16. Install the ignition coil and bracket assembly. Connect the fuel lines to the fuel supply manifold.

17. Connect the electrical connectors at the throttle body, upper intake manifold, lower intake manifold and injectors.

18. Connect the vacuum hoses to the fittings on the upper intake manifold.

19. Install the throttle cable and bracket assembly and the snow/ice shield to the throttle body.

20. Connect the air cleaner air intake duct to the throttle body.

21. Connect the negative battery cable. Fill and bleed the cooling system. Run the engine and check for leaks.

Exhaust Manifold

Removal and Installation

1. Disconnect the negative battery cable. Raise and safely support the vehicle.

2. Disconnect the exhaust pipe from the exhaust manifold. If necessary, disconnect the electrical connector from the oxygen sensor.

3. Lower the vehicle.

4. Remove the exhaust manifold insulator, if equipped.

5. If necessary, remove the engine oil dipstick and the dipstick tube. On 4.0L engine, if necessary, remove the power steering pump pressure and return hoses.

6. On 3.0L engine, disconnect or remove the exhaust manifold crossover.

7. If removing the right manifold on 4.0L engine, remove the heater hose support bracket and disconnect the heater hoses.

Service Tips

EXHAUST SYSTEM NOISE

Noise coming from under the body on 1988 B2600 4WD vehicles may be caused by a broken exhaust hanger bolt. A stronger replacement assembly consisting of a front exhaust pipe and the hanger bolt, washer and nut is available to correct the problem. The replacement front exhaust pipe is available as part number AM09 40 500C. The replacement bolt is part number 9978 40 880. The replacement washer is part number 1845 40 357 and the nut is part number 9946 08 000.

8. Remove the exhaust manifold attaching bolts/nuts and remove the exhaust manifold.

9. Installation is the reverse of the removal procedure. Tighten the exhaust manifold attaching bolts/nuts to 19 ft. lbs. (25 Nm).

Timing Chain Front Cover

Removal and Installation

2.6L ENGINES

1. Relieve the fuel system pressure and disconnect the negative battery cable. Drain the cooling system.

2. Remove the air cleaner assembly or disconnect the air intake tube.

3. Remove the cylinder head.

4. Remove the cooling fan and fan shroud. Remove the accessory drive belts.

5. Remove the alternator mounting bolts and remove the alternator and bracket.

6. Remove the power steering pump mounting bolts and position the pump and bracket aside.

7. Remove the air conditioning compressor mounting bolts and position the compressor and bracket aside.

8. Remove the water pump and disconnect the bypass pipe, if equipped.

9. Raise and safely support the vehicle. Remove the splash shield, if equipped and drain the engine oil.

10. Remove the oil pan and lower the vehicle.

11. Remove the retaining bolt and the crankshaft pulley.

12. Remove the attaching bolts and remove the timing chain cover.

To install:

13. Clean all gasket mating surfaces.

14. Coat new timing chain cover gaskets with sealer and install on the cylinder block. Install the timing chain cover and tighten the mounting bolts to 104–122 inch lbs. (12–14 Nm) on 1988 vehicles or 14–19 ft. lbs. (19–25 Nm) on 1989–92 vehicles.

15. Install the crankshaft pulley. Tighten the retaining bolt to 80–94 ft. lbs. (108–128 Nm) on 1988 vehicles or 130–145 ft. lbs. (177–196 Nm) on 1989–92 vehicles.

16. Raise and safely support the vehicle. Install the oil pan and the splash shield, if equipped.

17. Lower the vehicle and install the water pump. If equipped, apply vegetable oil to a new O-ring and install the coolant bypass pipe. Tighten the attaching bolt to 27–38 ft. lbs. (37–52 Nm).

18. Install the air conditioning compressor, if equipped, power steering pump and alternator. Install the accessory drive belts.

19. Install the cooling fan and fan shroud. Adjust the drive belt tension.

20. Install the cylinder head.

21. Fill the crankcase with the proper type and quantity of engine oil.

22. Connect the negative battery cable. Fill and bleed the cooling system.

23. Run the engine and check for leaks and proper operation.

4.0L ENGINE

1. Disconnect the negative battery cable and drain the cooling system and crankcase.

2. Remove the oil pan and the radiator.

3. Remove the air conditioning compressor and power steering bracket, if equipped.

4. Remove the alternator and drive belt(s). Remove the fan.

GASKET, REPLACE

GASKET, REPLACE

TIMING CHAIN COVER

WATER PUMP

WATER PUMP PULLEY

CRANKSHAFT PULLEY

Timing chain cover installation—1989–92 2.6L engine

5. Remove the water pump and heater and radiator hoses.

6. Remove the crankshaft pulley/damper assembly and the crankshaft timing sensor.

7. Remove the front cover retaining bolts, noting their positions. If necessary, tap the cover lightly with a plastic hammer to break the gasket seal. Remove the front cover.

To install:

8. Clean all gasket mating surfaces. Apply sealer to the gasket surfaces on the cylinder block and the back side of the front cover plate. Install the guide sleeves.

9. Apply sealer to the front cover gasket surface and position a new gasket on the front cover.

10. Install the front cover with the retaining screws. Note the different bolt lengths. Tighten the bolts to 13–15 ft. lbs. (17–21 Nm).

11. Install the crankshaft timing sensor.

12. Install the crankshaft pulley/damper assembly. Tighten the attaching bolt to 30–37 ft. lbs. (40–50 Nm), then tighten an additional 80–90 degrees.

13. Install the remaining components in the reverse order of their removal. Fill and bleed the cooling system. Run the engine and check for leaks.

Front Cover Oil Seal

Replacement

1. Disconnect the negative battery cable and drain the cooling system.

2. Remove the cooling fan and fan shroud.

3. Disconnect the upper and lower radiator hoses and remove the radiator, if necessary to provide access.

4. Remove the accessory drive belt(s).

5. Remove the crankshaft pulley.

6. Pry the seal from the front cover, using a suitable prybar. Be careful not to damage the seal housing.

7. Clean the pulley and seal area. Inspect the crankshaft pulley surface for grooving or other damage. Repair or replace, as necessary.

To install:

8. Install a new seal into the cover using a seal installer. The seal must be flush with the edge of the timing chain cover.

9. Apply clean engine oil to the seal lip and the crankshaft pulley. Install the crankshaft pulley and tighten the retaining bolt to 80–94 ft. lbs. (108–128 Nm) on 1988 2.6L engine, 130–145 ft. lbs. (177–196 Nm) on 1989–92 2.6L engine or 30–37 ft. lbs. (40–50 Nm), then tighten an additional 80–90 degrees on 4.0L engine.

10. Install the accessory drive belt(s). Install the radiator, if removed.

11. Install the cooling fan and fan shroud. Adjust the drive belt tension.

12. Connect the negative battery cable, start the engine and check for leaks.

Timing Chain and Sprockets

Removal and Installation

1988 2.6L ENGINE

Conventional Method

1. Relieve the fuel system pressure and disconnect the negative battery cable. Drain the cooling system and engine oil.

2. Remove the cylinder head, oil pan and timing chain cover.

3. Loosen the balancer shaft sprocket bolts, then remove the balancer shaft chain guides. Remove the balancer shaft sprockets and chain assembly.

4. Push in and hold the chain tensioner head, then remove the timing chain and sprockets. If necessary, remove the timing chain guides.

5. Inspect the chain, sprockets and guides for damage and/or wear. Replace, as necessary.

To install:

6. Install the timing chain guides and tighten to 7.2–8.7 ft. lbs. (10–12 Nm).

7. Align the plated links of the timing chain with the timing marks on the sprockets as the chain and sprockets are assembled.

8. Hold the chain tensioner head in, then slide the crankshaft sprocket onto the crankshaft and place the camshaft sprocket on the sprocket holder.

9. Install the balancer shaft drive sprocket on the crankshaft. Assemble the balancer shaft sprockets to the balancer shaft chain, making sure the timing marks on the sprockets are aligned with the polished links on the chain.

NOTE: Be careful not to confuse the right and left sprockets as they are installed in opposite directions.

10. While holding the assembled sprockets and chain, align the timing mark on the crankshaft sprocket with the chain and install the balancer shaft sprockets. Temporarily tighten the bolts by hand.

11. Temporarily install chain guides A, B and C. Set chain guide C to the fully downward position and tighten chain guides A and C to 43–69 inch lbs. (4.9–7.8 Nm).

12. Tighten the balancer shaft sprocket bolt to 43–50 ft. lbs. (59–68 Nm) and the oil pump sprocket bolt to 22–29 ft. lbs. (29–39 Nm).

13. Rotate both balancer shaft sprockets slightly to position

Timing chain and sprocket alignment—1988 2.6L engine

Balancer chain and sprockets alignment—1988 2.6L engine

the chain slack at the center between the left balancer shaft sprocket and the oil pump sprocket.

14. Adjust the position of chain guide B so when the chain is pulled away from the guide with the fingertips, the clearance between chain guide B and the chain links is 0.008–0.031 in. (0.2–0.8mm), then tighten the bolts. Tighten the upper bolt to 69–78 inch lbs. (8–9 Nm) and the lower bolt to 11–15 ft. lbs. (15–21 Nm).

15. Install the remaining components in the reverse order of removal.

16. Fill the crankcase with the proper type and quantity of engine oil. Fill and bleed the cooling system. Run the engine and check for leaks and proper operation.

17. Check the idle speed and ignition timing and adjust, if necessary.

Alternate Method

The following procedure can be used to replace the timing chain without removing the cylinder head or timing chain cover.

1. Disconnect the negative battery cable and remove the air cleaner.

2. Remove the spark plugs and the rocker arm cover.

3. Turn the crankshaft until the polished link is at the top of the camshaft sprocket.

NOTE: Stuff rags between the camshaft sprocket and cylinder head to prevent objects from falling into the engine.

4. Remove the polished link by using chain link remover tool 49 4120 110 or equivalent.

To install:

5. Connect the new timing chain to the used chain as follows:
   a. Pass the joint link through the end of the used chain and the end of the new chain.
   b. Attach the polished link and secure it with the clip.

6. Insert suitable wooden wedges between the timing chain and the cylinder head to ensure the chain stays in contact with the sprocket.

7. Turn the crankshaft slowly to engage the new timing chain onto the camshaft sprocket. When the new chain is completely engaged, remove the old chain.

8. Connect the new timing chain as follows:
   a. Insert the intermediate link plate in the center of the chain.
   b. Align the holes and pass the joint link through them.
   c. Attach the polished link and secure with the clip. The open part of the clip must face the passenger's side of the vehicle.

9. Install the rocker arm cover and spark plugs. Install the air cleaner and connect the negative battery cable.

10. Run the engine and check for proper operation. Check the idle speed and the ignition timing.

1989–92 2.6L ENGINE

1. Relieve the fuel system pressure and disconnect the negative battery cable. Drain the cooling system and engine oil.

2. Remove the cylinder head, oil pan and timing chain cover.

3. Before replacing any further components, check the following:
   a. Check the timing chain tension; if the adjuster sleeve protrudes 13 notches or more, replace the timing chain.
   b. Push the chain lever towards the driver's side of the vehicle. If there is excessive movement, there will be a chain adjuster malfunction or worn chain lever, chain guide, camshaft sprocket or crankshaft sprocket. Inspect and replace as necessary.
   c. Push the chain adjuster sleeve towards the passenger's side of the vehicle. If it moves back, the chain adjuster ratchet will be faulty and the chain adjuster must be replaced.

4. Remove the crankshaft spacer.

5. Loosen the idler sprocket lock bolt, then remove the balancer shaft chain guides.

6. Remove the idler sprocket assembly, crankshaft balancer chain sprocket and balancer chain.

7. Remove the timing chain adjuster.

8. Remove the camshaft sprocket, timing chain and crankshaft sprocket. Remove the key from the crankshaft.

9. Remove the timing chain lever and chain guide.

10. Inspect all components for damage and/or wear and replace as necessary.

To install:

11. Install the chain guide and tighten the mounting bolts to 61–78 inch lbs. (6.9–8.8 Nm).

12. Install the chain lever and check that it moves smoothly from right to left. Tighten the mounting bolt to 69–95 inch lbs. (7.8–11.0 Nm).

13. Push the chain adjuster sleeve in toward the left and insert a 1.77 in. (45mm) long by 0.08 in. (2mm) diameter pin into the lever hole to hold it in position. Install the chain adjuster and tighten the mounting bolts to 69–95 inch lbs. (7.8–11.0 Nm).

14. Install the key into the crankshaft keyway. Install the crankshaft sprocket.

15. Install the timing chain on the crankshaft sprocket, aligning the 2 white links with the crankshaft sprocket timing mark.

16. Install the camshaft sprocket so the timing mark on the sprocket aligns with the single white link of the timing chain. Secure the timing chain to the sprocket with wire and temporarily rest it between the chain lever and guide.

17. Install the crankshaft balancer sprocket.

18. Set the balancer chain on the idler sprocket assembly so the timing mark on the idler sprocket assembly and the brown link of the balancer chain align.

19. Install the balancer chain so the 5 alignment marks on the chain, sprocket and block align and attach the idler sprocket assembly to the cylinder block. Loosely tighten the idler sprocket assembly lock bolt.

20. Install the right and left lower balancer chain guides and tighten the mounting bolts to 69–95 inch lbs. (7.8–11.0 Nm).

21. Install the upper chain guide and loosely tighten the mounting and adjusting bolts.

22. Tighten the idler sprocket assembly lock bolt to 27–38 ft. lbs. (37–52 Nm) and install the spacer.

23. On 1989 B Series Pick-Up and all MPV, adjust the balancer chain tension as follows:
   a. Loosen the upper chain guide adjusting bolt.
   b. Push on the chain guide just above the adjusting slot with a force of approximately 11 lbs., then pull back the guide 0.14 ± 0.012 in. (3.5 ± 0.3mm) and tighten the bolt to 69–95 inch lbs. (7.8–11.0 Nm). Tighten the guide pivot bolt to the same specification.
   c. The chain slack at the notch in the guide should be 0.12 in. (3mm) when the guide is properly adjusted.

24. On 1990–91 B Series Pick-Up with manual transmission, adjust the balancer chain tension as follows:
   a. Tighten the upper chain guide pivot bolt to 69–95 inch lbs. (7.8–11.0 Nm).
   b. Loosen the upper chain guide adjusting bolt.
   c. Push on the chain guide just above the adjusting slot with a force of approximately 11 lbs., then pull back the guide 0.24 ± 0.012 in. (6.0 ± 0.3mm) and tighten the bolt to 69–95 inch lbs. (7.8–11.0 Nm).
   d. The chain slack at the notch in the guide should be 0.23 in. (5.8mm) when the guide is properly adjusted.

25. On all 1992 and 1990–91 B Series Pick-Up with automatic transmission, adjust the balancer chain tension as follows:
   a. Fabricate a piece of wood, 0.118–0.138 in. (3.0–3.5mm) thick and 0.335–0.374 in. (8.5–9.5mm) wide.
   b. Insert the piece of wood in the notch in the upper chain guide.
   c. Push on the chain guide just above the adjusting slot

Timing chain and sprockets alignment—1989–92 2.6L engine

Timing chain and sprockets alignment—4.0L engine

Balancer chain and sprockets alignment—1989–92 2.6L engine

with a force of 2.9–3.7 lbs. and tighten the adjusting and pivot bolts to 69–95 inch lbs. (7.8–11.0 Nm).

d. Remove the wood from between the chain and chain guide, making sure no wood shavings are left.

e. Measure the chain slack. It should be 0.039–0.059 in. (1.0–1.5mm) at the notch in the guide.

NOTE: If the upper chain guide bottoms on the adjusting bolt during the adjustment procedure, the balancer chain must be replaced.

26. Install the remaining components in the reverse order of removal.

NOTE: Be sure to remove the pin from the timing chain adjuster before installing the service cover.

27. Fill the crankcase with the proper type and quantity of oil. Fill and bleed the cooling system.
28. Run the engine and check for leaks and proper operation. Check the idle speed and ignition timing.

4.0L ENGINE

1. Disconnect the negative battery cable and drain the cooling system and crankcase.

2. Remove the oil pan and radiator. Remove the accessory drive belt and crankshaft damper.
3. Remove the water pump and timing chain front cover.
4. Remove the camshaft sprocket retaining bolt and the crankshaft sprocket key.
5. Push the timing chain tensioner into the retracted position and install the retaining clip.
6. Remove the crankshaft and camshaft sprockets with the timing chain. Remove the tensioner and guide, as required.
To install:
7. Install the timing chain guide to the cylinder block with the pin of the guide inserted into the oil hole in the block. Install the 2 retaining bolts and tighten to 7–9 ft. lbs. (10–12 Nm).
8. Position the camshaft and crankshaft so the sprocket timing marks will align.
9. Install the sprockets and timing chain together. Install the timing chain tensioner with the clip in place to lock the tensioner in the retracted position.
10. Install the crankshaft key and check the timing marks on the sprockets for correct alignment. Make sure the tensioner side of the timing chain is held inward and the guide side of the chain is straight and tight.
11. Install the camshaft sprocket retaining bolt and tighten to 44–50 ft. lbs. (60–68 Nm). Remove the clip from the tensioner assembly.
12. Install the timing chain front cover and the remaining components in the reverse order of their removal. Fill the crankcase with the proper type and quantity of engine oil. Fill and bleed the cooling system. Run the engine and check for leaks.

Timing Belt Front Cover

Removal and Installation

2.2L ENGINE

1. Disconnect the negative battery cable and drain the cooling system.
2. Remove the cooling fan and fan shroud.
3. Remove the accessory drive belt(s) and the cooling fan pulley and bracket.
4. If carburetor equipped, remove the secondary air pipe assembly.
5. Remove the retaining bolts and the crankshaft pulley.

1. Cooling fan
2. Fan shroud
3. Alternator drive belt
4. Cooling fan pulley
5. Cooling fan bracket
6. Secondary air pipe
   (Carburetor)
7. Crankshaft pulley
8. Timing belt upper
   cover
9. Timing belt lower
   cover
10. Timing belt tensioner
    and spring
11. Timing belt

Timing belt covers and timing belt installation—2.2L engine

6. Remove the upper and lower timing belt covers.

7. Installation is the reverse of the removal procedure. Install the timing belt covers with new gaskets. Tighten the bolts to 61–87 inch lbs. (6.9–9.8 Nm).

8. Tighten the crankshaft pulley retaining bolts to 9–13 ft. lbs. (12–17 Nm). Fill and bleed the cooling system.

3.0L ENGINE

1. Disconnect the negative battery cable and drain the cooling system.

2. Tag and disconnect the spark plug wires from the spark plugs. Remove the spark plugs.

3. Remove the fresh air duct, cooling fan and fan shroud.

4. Remove the accessory drive belt(s) and the air conditioning compressor idler pulley.

5. Remove the retaining bolt and remove the crankshaft pulley.

6. Remove the coolant bypass hose and upper radiator hose.

7. Remove the timing belt covers and gaskets.

8. Installation is the reverse of the removal procedure. Install the timing belt covers with new gaskets. Tighten the 6mm bolts to 69–95 inch lbs. (7.8–11.0 Nm) and the 10mm bolt to 27–38 ft. lbs. (37–52 Nm).

9. Tighten the crankshaft pulley bolt to 116–123 ft. lbs. (157–167 Nm).

Oil Seal Replacement

2.2L ENGINE

Crankshaft Seal

1. Disconnect the negative battery cable and drain the engine oil.

2. Remove the timing belt cover and timing belt.

3. Remove the crankshaft sprocket retaining bolt and the crankshaft sprocket.

4. Remove the oil seal using a small prybar. Be careful not to damage the seal housing.

To install:

5. Apply clean engine oil to the lip of a new seal and fit the seal into the oil pump body.

Timing belt covers and timing belt installation—3.0L engine

6. Tap the seal in place using a seal installer until the seal is flush with the edge of the pump body.

7. Install the crankshaft sprocket and tighten the retaining bolt to 116–123 ft. lbs. (157–167 Nm).

8. Install the timing belt and timing belt cover. Connect the negative battery cable.

9. Fill the engine with the proper type and quantity of engine oil. Run the engine and check for leaks.

Camshaft Seal

1. Disconnect the negative battery cable and drain the cooling system.

2. Remove the timing belt cover and the timing belt.

3. Remove the camshaft sprocket retaining bolt and remove the sprocket.

4. Disconnect the upper radiator hose and remove the distributor.

5. Remove the front housing.

6. Pry or press the oil seal from the front housing.

To install:

7. Clean all gasket mating surfaces.

8. Apply engine oil to the front housing and a new oil seal. Press the seal into the front housing.

9. Apply engine oil to the seal lip and install the front housing with a new gasket. Tighten the mounting bolts to 14–19 ft. lbs. (19–25 Nm).

10. Connect the upper radiator hose and install the distributor.

11. Install the camshaft sprocket and tighten the retaining bolt to 35–48 ft. lbs. (47–65 Nm).

12. Install the timing belt and the timing belt cover. Connect the negative battery cable.

13. Fill and bleed the cooling system. Run the engine and check for leaks. Check the ignition timing.

3.0L ENGINE

Crankshaft Seal

1. Disconnect the negative battery cable. Drain the engine oil and the cooling system.

2. Remove the timing belt cover and timing belt. Remove the crankshaft sprocket.

3. Remove the thermostat assembly.

4. Remove the oil pan and oil pump pickup.

5. Remove the oil pump.

6. Remove the oil seal from the pump using a suitable driver. Be careful not to damage the seal housing.

To install:

7. Coat the lip of a new seal and the seal housing with clean engine oil. Install the seal using a seal installer.

8. Install the oil pump, pickup and oil pan.

9. Install the thermostat assembly.

10. Install the crankshaft sprocket, timing belt and timing belt covers.

11. Fill the crankcase with the proper type and quantity of engine oil. Connect the negative battery cable.

12. Fill and bleed the cooling system. Run the engine and check for leaks.

Camshaft Seal

1. Disconnect the negative battery cable.

2. Remove the timing belt cover and timing belt.

3. Remove the camshaft sprocket retaining bolt and remove the camshaft sprocket.

4. Remove the seal plate and the camshaft seal.

To install:

5. Lubricate the oil seal lip with clean engine oil and install in the cylinder head, using a seal installer.

6. Install the seal plate and tighten the bolts to 69–95 inch lbs. (7.8–11.0 Nm).

7. Install the camshaft sprocket and tighten the retaining bolt to 52–59 ft. lbs. (71–80 Nm).

8. Install the timing belt and timing belt cover. Connect the negative battery cable, start the engine and check for leaks.

Timing Belt and Tensioner

Removal and Installation

2.2L ENGINE

1. Disconnect the negative battery cable and drain the cooling system.

Timing belt sprocket matching marks—2.2L engine

Timing belt deflection checking point—2.2L engine

2. Remove the timing belt cover.

3. Turn the crankshaft to align the mark of the camshaft sprocket with the front housing matching mark.

4. Remove the tensioner and spring. Mark the timing belt direction of rotation if it is to be reused.

5. Remove the timing belt.

To install:

6. Make sure the mark on the crankshaft sprocket is aligned with the matching mark on the oil pump body.

7. Make sure the mark on the camshaft sprocket is aligned with the matching mark on the front housing.

8. Install the timing belt tensioner and spring. Temporarily secure it with the spring fully extended.

9. Install the timing belt so there is no looseness at the water pump pulley and idler pulley side. If the timing belt is being reused, it must be installed in the same direction of rotation.

10. Remove the spark plugs to make engine rotation easier.

11. Turn the crankshaft twice clockwise in the direction of rotation. Make sure the matching marks are correctly aligned; if not repeat the installation procedure.

12. Loosen the tensioner lock bolt and apply tension to the belt. Tighten the tensioner lock bolt to 27–38 ft. lbs. (37–52 Nm).

13. Turn the crankshaft twice clockwise in the direction of rotation and align the matching marks. Check the timing belt deflection. The deflection should be 0.31–0.35 in. (8–9mm) on a new belt or 0.35–0.39 in. (9–10mm) on a used belt. Do not apply tension other than that of the tensioner spring.

14. If the deflection is not correct, repeat Steps 11–13.

15. Install the remaining components in the reverse order of removal. Fill and bleed the cooling system.

16. Run the engine and check for leaks and proper operation. Check the idle speed and the ignition timing.

3.0L ENGINE

1. Disconnect the negative battery cable and drain the cooling system.

2. Remove the timing belt cover.

3. Remove the upper idler pulley.

4. Turn the crankshaft to align the matching marks on the sprockets. If the timing belt is to be reused, make an arrow on the belt to indicate rotation direction.

5. Remove the timing belt and automatic tensioner.

To install:

6. Set a plane washer at the bottom of the tensioner body to prevent damage to the body plug. Press in the tensioner rod slowly, using a press or a vise.

NOTE: Do not press the tensioner rod more than 2200 lbs.

7. Insert a pin to hold the tensioner rod in the body. Install the automatic tensioner and tighten the mounting bolts to 14–19 ft. lbs. (19–25 Nm).

8. Install the crankshaft pulley lock bolt and loosely tighten. Check the alignment of the matching marks on the sprockets.

9. With the upper idler pulley removed, install the timing belt, making sure there is no slack between the crankshaft and camshaft sprockets. If the timing belt is being reused, it must be installed in the same direction of rotation.

Timing belt sprocket matching marks—3.0L engine

Timing belt deflection checking point—3.0L engine

10. Install the upper idler pulley and tighten the attaching bolt to 27–38 ft. lbs. (37–52 Nm).

11. Turn the crankshaft twice in the direction of rotation and align the matching marks. If the marks do not align, repeat Steps 8–11.

12. Remove the pin from the automatic tensioner. Turn the crankshaft twice and align the matching marks. Make sure the marks are aligned.

13. Check the timing belt deflection. The deflection should be 0.20–0.28 in. (5–7mm). Do not apply tension other than that of the automatic tensioner.

14. If the deflection is not correct, repeat Steps 10–13.

15. Remove the crankshaft pulley lock bolt.

16. Install the remaining components in the reverse order of removal. Fill and bleed the cooling system.

17. Run the engine and check for leaks and proper operation. Check the idle speed and the ignition timing.

Timing Sprockets

Removal and Installation

1. Disconnect the negative battery cable.
2. Remove the timing belt cover and the timing belt.
3. Remove the sprocket retaining bolt and remove the sprocket.
4. Installation is the reverse of the removal procedure. Tighten the camshaft sprocket bolt to 35–48 ft. lbs. (47–65 Nm) on 2.2L engine or 52–59 ft. lbs. (71–80 Nm) on 3.0L engine. Tighten the crankshaft sprocket bolt to 116–123 ft. lbs. (157–167 Nm) on 2.2L engine.

Camshaft

Removal and Installation

2.2L ENGINE

1. Disconnect the negative battery cable and drain the cooling system. Remove the air cleaner assembly or air intake tube.

2. Remove the timing belt cover and the timing belt. Remove the camshaft sprocket.

3. Remove the rocker arm cover and rocker arm/shaft assembly.

4. Disconnect the upper radiator hose from the thermostat housing.

5. Remove the distributor.

6. Remove the front housing.

7. Remove the seal cap from the rear of the cylinder head and remove the camshaft.

8. Check the camshaft for wear and/or damage and replace, as necessary.

To install:

9. Clean all gasket mating surfaces.

10. Apply clean engine oil to the camshaft journals, lobes and bearings. Install the camshaft with the dowel pin facing straight up.

11. Apply silicone sealer to the cylinder head on the front and rear camshaft bearing cap mating surface. Install the rocker arm/shaft assembly and tighten the bolts in sequence, in 2–3 steps to 13–20 ft. lbs. (18–26 Nm).

12. Install a new camshaft seal in the front housing. Apply clean engine oil to the seal lip and install the housing using a new gasket. Tighten the bolts to 14–19 ft. lbs.

13. Apply silicone sealer to the cylinder head and both sides of the front and rear camshaft bearing caps where the caps meet the cylinder head. Install the rocker arm cover and tighten the bolts to 26–35 inch lbs. (2.9–3.9 Nm).

14. Install the camshaft sprocket and tighten the retaining bolt to 35–48 ft. lbs. (47–65 Nm).

15. Install the timing belt and timing belt cover.

16. Install the distributor.

17. Connect the upper radiator hose.

18. Install the remaining components in the reverse order of removal. Fill and bleed the cooling system.

19. Run the engine and check for leaks and proper operation. Check the idle speed and the ignition timing.

2.6L ENGINES

1. Disconnect the negative battery cable.
2. Remove the air cleaner assembly or air intake tube.
3. Remove the rocker arm cover.
4. Remove the distributor.
5. Remove the rocker arm/shaft assembly. On 1988 vehicles, install hydraulic lash adjuster holder tools 49 U012 001 or equivalent, over the ends of the rocker arms prior to removal.

6. On 1989–92 vehicles, remove the service cover on the timing chain cover. Push the chain adjuster sleeve toward the left and insert a 1.77 in. (45mm) long by 0.08 in. (2mm) diameter pin into the lever hole to hold it.

7. Remove the bolt and the distributor drive gear. Remove the camshaft sprocket from the camshaft and rest it on the sprocket support on 1988 vehicles or hold it in position with mechanics wire on 1989–92 vehicles.

NOTE: Do not allow the timing chain to become disconnected from the camshaft sprocket or engine timing will be disturbed.

8. Remove the camshaft. Inspect the camshaft for wear or damage and replace, if necessary.

To install:

9. Apply clean engine oil to the camshaft journals, lobes and bearings. Install the camshaft, aligning the dowel with the camshaft sprocket.

10. If equipped, coat the circular packing with sealant and install in the end of the cylinder head.

11. Install the rocker arm/shaft assembly and tighten the bolts, in sequence, in 2–3 steps to 14–15 ft. lbs. (19–20 Nm) on 1988 vehicles or 14–19 ft. lbs. (19–25 Nm) on 1989–92 vehicles. Remove the hydraulic lash adjuster holder tools on 1988 vehicles.

12. Install the camshaft sprocket to the camshaft. Install the distributor drive gear and lock bolt. Tighten the lock bolt to 36–43 ft. lbs. (49–58 Nm).

13. On 1989–92 vehicles, remove the chain adjuster sleeve retaining pin and install the service cover with a new gasket. Tighten the bolts to 69–95 inch lbs. (7.8–11.0 Nm) and the nuts to 61–87 inch lbs. (6.9–9.8 Nm).

14. On 1988 vehicles, adjust the jet valve clearance.

15. Apply sealant to the half circle seal(s) and install in the cylinder head. Apply sealer to the tops of the seals and to the cylinder head in the seal area.

16. Coat a new gasket with sealant and install the rocker arm cover. Tighten the bolts to 43–61 inch lbs. (5–7 Nm) on 1988 vehicles or 52–78 inch lbs. (5.9–8.8 Nm) on 1989–92 vehicles.

17. Install the distributor.

18. Install the air cleaner assembly or air intake tube. Connect the negative battery cable.

19. Run the engine and check for leaks and proper operation. Check the idle speed and ignition timing. On 1988 vehicles, readjust the jet valves when the engine is warm.

3.0L ENGINE

1. Disconnect the negative battery cable and drain the cooling system.

2. Remove the timing belt covers and timing belt.

3. Remove the rocker arm cover.

4. If removing the driver's side camshaft, remove the distributor and the distributor spacer.

5. Remove the bolt and the camshaft sprocket.

6. Remove the seal plate. Pry out the camshaft seal, being careful not to damage the seal housing.

7. Remove the rocker arm/shaft assembly.

8. Remove the thrust plate bolts and remove the thrust plate. Slide the camshaft out of the cylinder head. If removing the driver's side camshaft, remove the distributor drive gear.

NOTE: Components such as the radiator, radiator support and air conditioning condenser may have to be removed to allow camshaft removal. It may be necessary to remove the cylinder head to remove the camshaft.

9. Inspect the camshaft for wear and/or damage and replace if necessary.

To install:

10. If installing the driver's side camshaft, remove all old sealer from the distributor drive gear and apply sealer to the gear face, then seat the gear fully on the camshaft.

11. Apply clean engine oil to the camshaft journals, lobes and bearings. Install the camshaft and the thrust plate. Tighten the thrust plate to 69–95 inch lbs. (7.8–11.0 Nm).

12. Apply clean engine oil to a new camshaft seal lip and press the seal into the cylinder head, using a seal installer.

13. Install the rocker arm/shaft assembly and tighten the bolts, in sequence, in 2–3 steps to 14–19 ft. lbs. (19–25 Nm). Make sure the rocker arm shaft spring does not get caught between the shaft and mounting boss during installation.

14. Install the seal plates and tighten the bolts to 69–95 inch lbs. (7.8–11.0 Nm).

15. Install the camshaft sprocket and tighten the bolt to 52–59 ft. lbs. (71–80 Nm).

16. If installing the driver's side camshaft, apply clean engine oil to a new O-ring and install on the distributor spacer. Install the spacer and tighten the nuts to 69–95 inch lbs. (7.8–11.0 Nm).

17. Coat a new gasket with silicone sealant and install on the rocker arm cover. Install the cover and tighten the bolts to 30–39 inch lbs. (3.4–4.4 Nm).

18. Install the timing belt and timing belt covers.

19. Install the distributor.

20. Connect the negative battery cable. Fill and bleed the cooling system.

21. Run the engine and check for leaks and proper operation. Check the idle speed and ignition timing.

4.0L ENGINE

1. Disconnect the negative battery cable and relieve the fuel system pressure. Drain the crankcase and the cooling system.

2. Remove the rocker arm covers, rocker arm shaft assemblies and pushrods. Note the position of each component so it can be reinstalled in the same place.

3. Remove the intake manifold.

4. Remove the lifters. Identify each lifter so it can be reinstalled in the original position.

5. Remove the front timing chain cover and the timing chain and sprockets.

6. Remove the thrust plate bolts and remove the thrust plate. Carefully remove the camshaft, being careful not to damage the journals, lobes or bearings.

To install:

7. Coat the camshaft lobes with grease and the journals with heavy engine oil. Carefully install the camshaft, being careful not to damage the journals, lobes or bearings.

8. Install the thrust plate and the thrust plate retaining bolts. Tighten the bolts to 7–10 ft. lbs. (10–13 Nm).

9. Check the camshaft endplay using a dial indicator. The endplay should be 0.0008–0.004 in.

10. Install the remaining components in the reverse order of their removal. Fill the crankcase with the proper type and quantity of engine oil. Fill and bleed the cooling system. Run the engine and check for leaks.

Balancer Shafts

Removal and Installation

2.6L ENGINE

1988

1. Relieve the fuel system pressure and disconnect the negative battery cable. Drain the cooling system and the engine oil.

2. Remove the cylinder head, oil pan and timing chain cover.

3. Remove the balancer shaft chain and timing chain.

4. Remove the bolts, then push in and hold the chain tensioner head and remove the oil pump and passenger's side balancer shaft assembly.

5. Install 8mm bolts into the threaded holes of the flange and turn the bolts equally to remove the thrust plate. Remove the driver's side balancer shaft.

6. Inspect the balancer shaft for wear and/or damage. Make sure the oil passages are not clogged.

To install:

7. Install the timing chain guides, if removed. Install the timing chain on the sprockets, slide the crankshaft sprocket onto the crankshaft and place the camshaft sprocket on the sprocket holder.

8. Apply clean engine oil to the journals of the driver's side balancer shaft and install the shaft in the cylinder block, being careful not to damage the bearings.

NOTE: The driver's side and passenger's side balancer shafts are different and not interchangeable.

9. Install a new O-ring into the groove of the thrust plate and apply clean engine oil around the O-ring.

10. Install two 6mm × 50mm guides into the threaded holes for mounting the thrust plate.

NOTE: The guides must be used to install the thrust plate because damage to the O-ring may result if the plate is not properly aligned.

11. Remove the guides and install the thrust plate mounting bolts. Tighten to 87–95 inch lbs. (10–11 Nm).

12. Install the oil pump gears in the oil pump body, if removed and align the timing mark.

NOTE: The timing marks must be aligned correctly or the balancer shaft will be out of phase and engine vibration will result.

13. Install the oil pump cover on the body and tighten the screw. After installing the pump cover, put approximately 10cc of clean engine oil in the delivery port.

14. Install the balancer shaft into the oil pump driven gear and tighten to 43–50 ft. lbs. (59–68 Nm).

15. Apply clean engine oil to the journals of the balancer shaft and install the shaft, oil pump and adjuster assembly into the block. Push in the chain adjuster head and hold it during installation. Be careful not to damage the bearings.

16. Tighten the oil pump mounting bolts to 69–78 inch lbs. (8–9 Nm).

17. Install the balancer shaft drive sprocket on the crankshaft. Assemble the balancer shaft sprockets to the balancer shaft chain, making sure the timing marks on the sprockets are aligned with the polished links on the chain.

NOTE: Be careful not to confuse the right and left sprockets as they are installed in opposite directions.

18. While holding the assembled sprockets and chain, align the timing mark on the crankshaft sprocket with the chain and install the balancer shaft sprockets. Temporarily tighten the bolts by hand.

19. Temporarily install chain guides A, B and C. Set chain guide C to the fully downward position and tighten chain guides

A and C to 43–69 inch lbs. (4.9–7.8 Nm).

20. Tighten the balancer shaft sprocket bolt to 43–50 ft. lbs. (59–68 Nm) and the oil pump sprocket bolt to 22–29 ft. lbs. (29–39 Nm).

21. Rotate both balancer shaft sprockets slightly to position the chain slack at the center between the left balancer shaft sprocket and the oil pump sprocket.

22. Adjust the position of chain guide B so when the chain is pulled away from the guide with the fingertips, the clearance between chain guide B and the chain links is 0.008–0.031 in. (0.2–0.8mm), then tighten the bolts. Tighten the upper bolt to 69–78 inch lbs. (8–9 Nm) and the lower bolt to 11–15 ft. lbs. (15–21 Nm).

23. Install the remaining components in the reverse order of removal.

24. Fill the crankcase with the proper type and quantity of engine oil. Fill and bleed the cooling system. Run the engine and check for leaks and proper operation.

25. Check the idle speed and ignition timing and adjust, if necessary.

1989–92

1. Relieve the fuel system pressure and disconnect the negative battery cable. Drain the engine engine oil and the cooling system.

2. Remove the cylinder head, oil pan and timing chain cover.

3. Remove the balancer shaft chain.

4. Remove the thrust plate lock bolts and remove the balancer shaft(s). Be careful not to damage the balancer shaft journals and bushing during removal.

5. Check the balancer shaft(s) and bushings for wear and/or damage and replace as necessary.

To install:

6. Apply clean engine oil to the balancer shaft journals and install in the cylinder block, being careful not to damage the bushings and journals.

7. Loosely tighten the thrust plate lock bolts and make sure the balancer shaft(s) rotate smoothly. Tighten the lock bolts to 69–95 inch lbs. (7.8–11.0 Nm).

8. Install the crankshaft balancer sprocket.

9. Set the balancer chain on the idler sprocket assembly so the timing mark on the idler sprocket assembly and the brown link of the balancer chain align.

10. Install the balancer chain so the 5 alignment marks on the chain, sprocket and block align and attach the idler sprocket assembly to the cylinder block. Loosely tighten the idler sprocket assembly lock bolt.

11. Install the right and left lower balancer chain guides and tighten the mounting bolts to 69–95 inch lbs. (7.8–11.0 Nm).

12. Install the upper chain guide and loosely tighten the mounting and adjusting bolts.

13. Tighten the idler sprocket assembly lock bolt to 27–38 ft. lbs. (37–52 Nm) and install the spacer.

14. On 1989 B Series Pick-Up and all MPV, adjust the balancer chain tension as follows:

a. Loosen the upper chain guide adjusting bolt.

b. Push on the chain guide just above the adjusting slot with a force of approximately 11 lbs., then pull back the guide 0.14 ± 0.012 in. (3.5 ± 0.3mm) and tighten the bolt to 69–95 inch lbs. (7.8–11.0 Nm). Tighten the guide pivot bolt to the same specification.

c. The chain slack at the notch in the guide should be 0.12 in. (3mm) when the guide is properly adjusted.

15. On 1990–91 B Series Pick-Up with manual transmission, adjust the balancer chain tension as follows:

a. Tighten the upper chain guide pivot bolt to 69–95 inch lbs. (7.8–11.0 Nm).

b. Loosen the upper chain guide adjusting bolt.

c. Push on the chain guide just above the adjusting slot with a force of approximately 11 lbs., then pull back the guide

0.24 ± 0.012 in. (6.0 ± 0.3mm) and tighten the bolt to 69–95 inch lbs. (7.8–11.0 Nm).

d. The chain slack at the notch in the guide should be 0.23 in. (5.8mm) when the guide is properly adjusted.

16. On all 1992 and 1990–91 B Series Pick-Up with automatic transmission, adjust the balancer chain tension as follows:

a. Fabricate a piece of wood, 0.118–0.138 in. (3.0–3.5mm) thick and 0.335–0.374 in. (8.5–9.5mm) wide.

b. Insert the piece of wood in the notch in the upper chain guide.

c. Push on the chain guide just above the adjusting slot with a force of 2.9–3.7 lbs. and tighten the adjusting and pivot bolts to 69–95 inch lbs. (7.8–11.0 Nm).

d. Remove the wood from between the chain and chain guide, making sure no wood shavings are left.

e. Measure the chain slack. It should be 0.039–0.059 in. (1.0–1.5mm) at the notch in the guide.

NOTE: If the upper chain guide bottoms on the adjusting bolt during the adjustment procedure, the balancer chain must be replaced.

17. Install the remaining components in the reverse order of removal.

NOTE: Be sure to remove the pin from the timing chain adjuster before installing the service cover.

18. Fill the crankcase with the proper type and quantity of oil. Fill and bleed the cooling system.

19. Run the engine and check for leaks and proper operation. Check the idle speed and ignition timing.

Piston and Connecting Rod

Positioning

Install the piston with the L mark (left bank) and the R mark (right bank) facing the front of the engine — 3.0L engine

Piston and connecting rod positioning — 4.0L engine

Install the piston so the mark points toward the front of the engine—1988 2.6L engine

Install the piston with the F mark facing the front of the engine—2.2L and 1989–92 2.6L engine

ENGINE LUBRICATION

Oil Pan

Removal and Installation

B SERIES PICK-UP

1. Disconnect the negative battery cable.
2. Raise and support the vehicle safely.
3. Remove the necessary splash shields.
4. Position a drain pan under the oil pan. Remove the drain plug and drain the engine oil.
5. On 1988 2.6L engine, remove the rear subframe.
6. If equipped with 4WD, remove the front differential.
7. Remove the necessary steering linkage.
8. Remove the gusset plates and the clutch housing cover, if equipped.
9. Remove the oil pan mounting bolts and remove the oil pan. If necessary, insert a scraper or other suitable tool between the oil pan and block to separate them. Be careful not to bend the pan.

To install:

10. Clean all gasket mating surfaces and the oil pan.
11. Apply sealant to the cylinder block and install a new gasket.
12. Install the oil pan with the attaching bolts. Tighten the bolts to 61–104 inch lbs. (6.9–12.0 Nm) on 2.2L engine, 52–61 inch lbs. (6–7 Nm) on 1988 2.6L engine or 69–95 inch lbs. (7.8–11.0 Nm) on 1989–92 2.6L engine.

NOTE: Apply Loctite® to the bolt threads on 1989–92 2.6L engine before installation.

13. Install the remaining components in the reverse order of removal. Lower the vehicle and connect the negative battery cable.
14. Fill the crankcase with the proper type and quantity of engine oil. Run the engine and check for leaks.

MPV

2.6L Engine

1. Disconnect the negative battery cable. Remove the fan shroud.
2. Install engine support tool 49 G017 5A0 or equivalent. Remove the engine mount nuts and lift the engine slightly to gain removal clearance.
3. Raise and safely support the vehicle. Support the transmission with a transmission jack and remove the transmission lower mount.
4. Remove the splash shield.
5. Position a drain pan under the oil pan. Remove the drain plug and drain the engine oil.
6. Remove the gusset plates and stabilizer bar brackets.
7. Remove the oil pan mounting bolts and remove the oil pan. If necessary, insert a scraper or other suitable tool between the oil pan and block to separate them. Be careful not to bend the pan.

To install:

8. Clean all gasket mating surfaces and the oil pan.
9. Apply sealant to the cylinder block and install a new gasket.
10. Install the oil pan with the attaching bolts. Tighten the bolts to 69–95 inch lbs. (7.8–11.0 Nm). Apply Loctite® to the bolt threads before installation.
11. Install the remaining components in the reverse order of removal. Lower the vehicle and remove the engine support tool. Install the engine mount nuts.
12. Connect the negative battery cable. Fill the crankcase with the proper type and quantity of engine oil. Run the engine and check for leaks.

3.0L Engine—2WD

1. Disconnect the negative battery cable.
2. Raise and safely support the vehicle.
3. Remove the splash shield.
4. Position a drain pan under the oil pan. Remove the drain plug and drain the engine oil.
5. Remove the gusset plates.
6. Remove the oil pan mounting bolts and remove the oil pan. If necessary, insert a scraper or other suitable tool between the oil pan and block to separate them. Be careful not to bend the pan.

To install:

7. Clean all gasket mating surfaces and the oil pan.
8. Apply sealant to the cylinder block and install a new gasket.
9. Install the oil pan with the attaching bolts. Tighten to 61–87 inch lbs. (6.9–9.8 Nm).
10. Install the remaining components in the reverse order of removal. Lower the vehicle and connect the negative battery cable.
11. Fill the crankcase with the proper type and quantity of engine oil. Run the engine and check for leaks.

3.0L Engine—4WD

1. Disconnect the negative battery cable. Remove the fresh air duct and fan shroud.

2. Install engine support tool 49 G017 5A0 or equivalent. Remove the engine mount nuts and lift the engine slightly to gain removal clearance.

3. Raise and safely support the vehicle. Support the transmission with a transmission jack and remove the transmission lower mount.

4. Remove the splash shields.

5. Position a drain pan under the oil pan. Remove the drain plug and drain the engine oil.

6. If equipped with automatic transmission, disconnect and reposition the oil cooler hose and tube.

7. Remove the stabilizer bar.

8. Remove the oil pan mounting bolts and remove the oil pan. If necessary, insert a scraper or other suitable tool between the oil pan and block to separate them. Be careful not to bend the pan.

To install:

9. Clean all gasket mating surfaces and the oil pan.

10. Apply sealant to the cylinder block and install a new gasket.

11. Install the oil pan with the attaching bolts. Tighten to 61–87 inch lbs. (6.9–9.8 Nm).

12. Install the remaining components in the reverse order of removal. Lower the vehicle and remove the engine support tool. Install the engine mount nuts.

13. Connect the negative battery cable. Fill the crankcase with the proper type and quantity of engine oil. Run the engine and check for leaks.

NAVAJO

1. Remove the engine assembly and install on a workstand with the oil pan facing up.

2. Remove the oil pan retaining bolts and remove the pan.

To install:

3. Clean all gasket mating surfaces and the oil pan.

4. Install a new crankshaft rear main bearing cap wedge seal. The seal should fit snugly into the sides of the rear main bearing cap.

5. Position a new oil pan gasket to the engine block and place the oil pan in position on the 4 locating studs. Tighten the retaining nuts and bolts evenly to 5–7 ft. lbs. (7–10 Nm).

6. Measure the gap between the surface of the rear face of the oil pan, at the spacer locations, and the rear face of the engine block as follows:

   a. With the oil pan installed on the engine, position a straight-edge flat on the rear of the engine block so it extends over 1 of the oil pan/transmission bolt mounting pads.

   b. Using a feeler gauge, measure the gap between the mounting pad and the straight-edge. Repeat the procedure for the other mounting pad.

   c. If the measured gap is 0.011–0.020 in. (0.27–0.51mm), a 0.010 in. (0.254mm) spacer is required. If the measured gap is 0.021–0.029 in. (0.52–0.76mm), a 0.020 in. (0.508mm) spacer is required. If the measured gap is 0.030–0.039 in. (0.77–1.00mm), a 0.030 in. (0.762mm) spacer is required.

   d. Install the selected spacers to the mounting pads on the rear of the oil pan before bolting the engine and transmission together.

NOTE: Failure to use the correct spacer can result in improper clearance between the oil pan and transmission, resulting in oil pan damage and/or an oil leak.

7. Remove the engine from the workstand and install in the vehicle.

Measuring oil pan-to-transmission gap—Navajo

Oil Pump

Removal and Installation

2.2L AND 1989–92 2.6L ENGINES

1. Disconnect the negative battery cable and drain the cooling system.

2. Raise and safely support the vehicle. Remove the splash shield and drain the engine oil.

3. Remove the oil pan, stiffener and oil pump pickup.

4. Lower the vehicle.

5. On 2.2L engine, remove the timing belt cover, timing belt and crankshaft sprocket. Remove the oil pump mounting bolts and remove the oil pump.

6. On 2.6L engine, remove the cylinder head and the timing chain cover. The oil pump is part of the timing chain cover.

7. If necessary, disassemble the oil pump and check for wear and/or damage. Replace parts as necessary.

8. Pry out the crankshaft oil seal, being careful not to damage the seal housing.

To install:

9. Clean all gasket material.

Oil pump mounting bolt identification—2.2L engine

Oil pump exploded view—1989–92 2.6L engine

Labels in diagram:
OIL SEAL, REPLACE
TIMING CHAIN COVER
WASHER, REPLACE
FACE THE DIMPLE TOWARD THE PUMP COVER WHEN ASSEMBLING
PRESSURE RELIEF VALVE
38—61 (3.8—6.2, 28—45)
INNER ROTOR
OUTER ROTOR
WATER INLET PIPE GASKET
GASKET, REPLACE
PUMP COVER

10. Apply clean engine oil to the lip of a new seal and press the seal into the pump, using a seal installer.

11. On 2.2L engine, proceed as follows:

   a. Apply a continuous bead of silicone sealant to the contact surface of the oil pump. Do not allow sealant to get into the oil hole.

   b. Lubricate a new O-ring and install into the pump body.

   c. Install the oil pump and tighten the **A** bolts to 14–19 ft. lbs. (19–25 Nm) and the **B** bolts to 27–38 ft. lbs. (37–52 Nm).

   d. Install the crankshaft sprocket, timing belt and timing belt cover.

12. On 2.6L engine, install the timing chain cover and cylinder head.

13. Raise and safely support the vehicle.

14. Install the stiffener. Install a new gasket and the oil pump pickup. Tighten the bolts to 69–95 inch lbs. (7.8–11.0 Nm).

15. Install the oil pan and the splash shield.

16. Lower the vehicle and connect the negative battery cable. Fill the engine with the proper type and quantity of engine oil.

17. Run the engine and check for leaks and proper operation.

1988 2.6L ENGINE

1. Relieve the fuel system pressure and disconnect the negative battery cable. Drain the cooling system.

2. Raise and safely support the vehicle. Remove the splash shield and drain engine oil. Remove the oil pan.

3. Lower the vehicle.

4. Remove the cylinder head and timing chain cover.

5. Remove the left and right balancer shaft sprocket bolts and the oil pump drive sprocket bolt.

6. Remove the balancer shaft chain guides.

7. Remove the oil pump and balancer shaft sprockets and chain.

8. Remove the oil pump assembly.

Service Tips

LEAKING OIL PRESSURE SWITCH

Engine oil leakage in the area of the oil pressure switch on 1988 B2200 may be caused by a switch that has failed due to heat. A replacement switch is available that has a diaphragm with increased heat resistance. The replacement switch is part number E5D3 18 501.

TIMING BELT SPROCKET

OIL PUMP

STIFFENER

OIL PUMP PICK-UP

OIL PAN

Oil pan and pump removal—2.2L engine

9. If necessary, disassemble the pump and remove the chain tensioner oil pump cover and gears. Inspect all components for wear and/or damage and replace, if necessary.
To install:
10. Clean all gasket mating surfaces.
11. Assemble the oil pump gears, aligning the matching marks and install in the pump with the pump cover.
12. Before installing the pump, put approximately 10cc of clean engine oil in the delivery port.
13. Install the pump with a new gasket and tighten the bolts to 69–78 inch lbs. (8–9 Nm).
14. Install the balancer shaft drive sprocket on the crankshaft. Assemble the balancer shaft sprockets to the balancer shaft chain, making sure the timing marks on the sprockets are aligned with the polished links on the chain.

NOTE: Be careful not to confuse the right and left sprockets as they are installed in opposite directions.

15. While holding the assembled sprockets and chain, align the timing mark on the crankshaft sprocket with the chain and install the balancer shaft sprockets. Temporarily tighten the bolts by hand.
16. Temporarily install chain guides A, B and C. Set chain guide C to the fully downward position and tighten chain guides A and C to 43–69 inch lbs. (4.9–7.8 Nm).
17. Tighten the balancer shaft sprocket bolt to 43–50 ft. lbs. (59–68 Nm) and the oil pump sprocket bolt to 22–29 ft. lbs. (29–39 Nm).
18. Rotate both balancer shaft sprockets slightly to position the chain slack at the center between the left balancer shaft sprocket and the oil pump sprocket.
19. Adjust the position of chain guide B so when the chain is pulled away from the guide with the fingertips, the clearance between chain guide B and the chain links is 0.008–0.031 in. (0.2–

0.8mm), then tighten the bolts. Tighten the upper bolt to 69–78 inch lbs. (8–9 Nm) and the lower bolt to 11–15 ft. lbs. (15–21 Nm).
20. Install the remaining components in the reverse order of removal.
21. Fill the crankcase with the proper type and quantity of engine oil. Fill and bleed the cooling system. Run the engine and check for leaks and proper operation.
22. Check the idle speed and ignition timing and adjust, if necessary.

3.0L ENGINE

1. Disconnect the negative battery cable and drain the cooling system.
2. Raise and safely support the vehicle. Remove the splash shield and drain the engine oil. Remove the oil pan and oil pump pickup.
3. Lower the vehicle.
4. Remove the timing belt cover, timing belt and crankshaft sprocket.
5. Remove the thermostat assembly.
6. Remove the attaching bolts and remove the oil pump. Disassemble the pump, if necessary and inspect all components for wear and/or damage. Replace components, as necessary.
7. Pry out the crankshaft seal from the pump, being careful not to damage the seal housing.
To install:
8. Clean all gasket mating surfaces.
9. Apply clean engine oil to a new crankshaft seal and install in the pump, using a seal installer.
10. Install a new gasket and the oil pump. Tighten the mounting bolts to 14–19 ft. lbs. (19–25 Nm).
11. Install a new gasket and the thermostat housing. Tighten the mounting bolts to 14–19 ft. lbs. (19–25 Nm).

1. Air cleaner
2. Cooling fan
3. Drive belt
4. Water pump pulley
5. Radiator hose
6. Water bypass hose
7. Water pump and gasket
8. Crankshaft pulley
9. Alternator strap
10. Alternator
11. Cylinder head cover
12. Chain cover bolts
13. Timing chain cover and gaskets
14. Left balance shaft sprocket bolts
15. Oil pump drive sprocket bolt
16. Right balance shaft sprocket bolt
17. Chain guide A
18. Chain guide B
19. Chain guide C
20. Oil pump and balance shaft sprocket and chain
21. Oil pump assembly
22. Chain tensioner
23. Gasket
24. Oil pump cover
25. Drive gear
26. Driven gear

Exploded view of the oil pump assembly and related components—1988 2.6L engine

12. Install the crankshaft sprocket, timing belt and timing belt cover.

13. Raise and safely support the vehicle.

14. Lubricate and install a new O-ring and the oil pump pickup. Tighten the mounting bolts to 69–95 inch lbs. (7.8–11.0 Nm).

15. Install the oil pan and the splash shield. Lower the vehicle.

16. Fill the crankcase with the proper type and quantity of engine oil. Connect the negative battery cable.

17. Fill and bleed the cooling system. Run the engine and check for leaks and proper operation.

4.0L ENGINE

1. Remove the engine assembly.

2. Remove the oil pan.

3. Remove the oil pump attaching bolts and withdraw the oil pump driveshaft.

To install:

4. Prime the oil pump by filling either the inlet or outlet port with clean engine oil. Rotate the pump shaft to distribute the oil within the pump body.

5. Insert the oil pump driveshaft into the block with the pointed end facing inward. The pointed end is closest to the pressed-on flange. Position the pump with a new gasket and install the attaching bolts. Tighten to 13–15 ft. lbs. (17–21 Nm).

6. Clean and install the oil pump pickup with a new gasket. Tighten the bolts to 7–10 ft. lbs. (9–13 Nm).

7. Install the oil pan and install the engine assembly.

8. Fill the crankcase with the proper type and quantity of engine oil. Run the engine and check for leaks.

Checking
EXCEPT 4.0L ENGINE
1. Remove the pump and disassemble. Clean all parts in solvent and allow to dry.
2. Check for a distorted or damaged oil pump body or cover.
3. Check the relief valve plunger for wear or damage. Check for a weak or broken plunger spring. The spring free length should be 1.827 in. (46.4mm).
4. Check the rotor side clearance as follows: Lay a straightedge across the pump body and, using a feeler gauge, measure between the gear faces and the straight-edge. If the clearance exceeds 0.0039 in. (0.10mm) on 2.2L and 1989–92 2.6L engines or 0.0051 in. (0.13mm) on 3.0L engine, replace the pump.
5. Check the rotor tooth tip clearance as follows: Insert a feeler gauge between the gears at the gear tip. If the clearance exceeds 0.0071 in. (0.18mm) on 2.2L and 1989–92 2.6L engines or 0.0094 in. (0.24mm) on 3.0L engine, replace the gears or pump.
6. Check the outer rotor-to-pump body clearance as follows: Insert a feeler gauge between the outer gear and the pump body. If the clearance exceeds 0.0078 in. (0.20mm) on 2.2L and 1989–92 2.6L engine or 0.0091 in. (0.23mm) on 3.0L engine, replace the pump.
7. Apply clean engine oil to the pump components and reassemble. Apply oil to the lip of a new seal and install in the pump, using a seal installer.

4.0L ENGINE
1. Remove the pump and disassemble. Thoroughly clean all parts in solvent and dry with compressed air.
2. Check the inside of the pump housing and the inner and outer gears for damage or excessive wear. Check the mating surfaces of the pump cover for wear. Minor scuff marks are normal, but if the cover, gears or housing surfaces are excessively worn, scored or grooved, replace the entire pump.
3. Measure the inner to outer rotor tip clearance. With the rotor assembly removed from the pump and resting on a flat surface, the inner and outer rotor tip clearance must not exceed 0.012 in. (0.30mm) with a feeler gauge inserted ½ in. (13mm) minimum.
4. With the rotor assembly installed in the housing, place a straight-edge over the rotor assembly and the housing. Measure the vertical clearance, the rotor endplay, between the straight-edge and the inner rotor and outer race. Maximum clearance must not exceed 0.005 in. (0.13mm).
5. Inspect the relief valve spring for collapsed or worn condition. Check the spring tension. The tension should be 13.6–14.7 lbs. at 1.39 in.
6. If any part of the oil pump requires replacement, replace the complete pump assembly.

Oil pump checking—4.0L engine

Rear Main Oil Seal

Removal and Installation
EXCEPT 4.0L ENGINE
1. Disconnect the negative battery cable. Raise and safely support the vehicle.
2. Drain the engine oil.
3. Remove the transmission. If equipped with manual transmission, remove the clutch assembly.

SIDE CLEARANCE   TOOTH TIP CLEARANCE   OUTER ROTOR-TO-PUMP BODY CLEARANCE

Oil pump checking—2.2L engine; 1989–92 2.6L and 3.0L engines similar

4. Remove the flywheel.

5. Using a small prybar and a rag, remove the oil seal, being careful not to damage the crankshaft or seal housing.

6. When the seal has been removed, clean the mounting recess.

To install:

7. Coat the new seal and the crankshaft with a light film of clean engine oil.

8. Start the seal into the recess with the seal lip facing forward and install it with a suitable rear oil seal replacer tool. Install the seal until it is flush with the edge of the rear cover.

9. Position the flywheel on the crankshaft flange. Install the flywheel attaching bolts and tighten to 71–76 ft. lbs. (96–103 Nm) on 2.2L engine, 94–101 ft. lbs. (128–137 Nm) on 1988 2.6L engine, 67–72 ft. lbs. (91–98 Nm) on 1989–92 2.6L engine or 76–81 ft. lbs. (103–110 Nm) on 3.0L engine.

10. If equipped with manual transmission, install the clutch assembly. Install the transmission and lower the vehicle.

11. Fill the crankcase with the proper type and quantity of engine oil. Connect the negative battery cable, start the engine and check for leaks.

4.0L ENGINE

1. Disconnect the negative battery cable. Raise and safely support the vehicle.

2. Remove the transmission. If equipped with manual transmission, remove the clutch assembly.

3. Remove the flywheel.

4. Using a sharp awl or equivalent, punch 2 holes into the seal on opposite sides of the crankshaft and just above the bearing cap-to-cylinder block split line. Install a sheet metal screw in each hole.

5. Using 2 small prybars, pry against both screws and remove the seal. It may be necessary to place small blocks of wood against the cylinder block to provide a fulcrum point for the prybars. Be careful not to damage the crankshaft oil seal surface or seal housing.

6. When the seal has been removed, clean the mounting recess and the oil seal contact surface on the crankshaft.

To install:

7. Coat the new seal and the crankshaft with a light film of engine oil.

8. Start the seal into the recess with the seal lip facing forward and install it with a suitable rear oil seal replacer tool. Keep the tool straight with the centerline of the crankshaft and install the seal until it is fully seated.

9. After removing the tool, inspect the seal to make sure it was not damaged during installation.

10. Position the flywheel on the crankshaft flange. Install the flywheel attaching bolts and tighten to 59 ft. lbs. (80 Nm).

11. If equipped with manual transmission, install the clutch assembly. Install the transmission and lower the vehicle.

12. Connect the negative battery cable, start the engine and check for leaks.

TORQUE SPECIFICATIONS

Component	English	Metric
Balancer shaft sprocket bolts		
2.6L engine		
1988	43–50 ft. lbs.	59–68 Nm
1989–92	27–38 ft. lbs.	37–52 Nm
Balancer shaft thrust plate bolts		
2.6L engine		
1988	87–95 inch lbs.	10–11 Nm
1989–92	69–95 inch lbs.	7.8–11.0 Nm
Camshaft sprocket bolt		
2.2L engine	35–48 ft. lbs.	47–65 Nm
2.6L engine	36–43 ft. lbs.	49–58 Nm
3.0L engine	52–59 ft. lbs.	71–80 Nm
4.0L engine	44–50 ft. lbs.	60–68 Nm
Camshaft thrust plate bolts		
4.0L engine	7–10 ft. lbs.	10–13 Nm
Camshaft rear retainer bolts		
3.0L engine	69–95 inch lbs.	7.8–11.0 Nm
Connecting rod nut		
2.2L and 1989–92 2.6L engines	48–51 ft. lbs.	65–69 Nm
1988 2.6L engine	33–35 ft. lbs.	45–47 Nm
3.0L engine		
Step 1:	22 ft. lbs.	29 Nm
Step 2:	+ 90° turn	+ 90° turn
4.0L engine	19–24 ft. lbs.	26–33 Nm
Crankshaft damper bolt		
2.2L engine	9–13 ft. lbs.	12–17 Nm
2.6L engine		
1988	80–94 ft. lbs.	108–128 Nm
1989–92	130–145 ft. lbs.	177–196 Nm
3.0L engine	116–123 ft. lbs.	157–167 Nm
4.0L engine		
Step 1:	30–37 ft. lbs.	40–50 Nm
Step 2:	+ 90° turn	+ 90° turn

TORQUE SPECIFICATIONS

Component	English	Metric
Crankshaft sprocket bolt		
2.2L engine	116–123 ft. lbs.	157–167 Nm
Cylinder head bolt		
2.2L engine*	59–64 ft. lbs.	80–86 Nm
2.6L engine*		
1988		
Bolts 1–10	65–72 ft. lbs.	88–98 Nm
Bolts 11–12	11–16 ft. lbs.	15–22 Nm
1989–92	59–64 ft. lbs.	80–86 Nm
3.0L engine*		
Step 1:	14 ft. lbs.	20 Nm
Step 2:	+ 90° turn	+ 90° turn
Step 3:	+ 90° turn	+ 90° turn
4.0L engine*		
Step 1 (CYLINDER HEAD):	44 ft. lbs.	60 Nm
Step 2 (INTAKE MANIFOLD):	3–6 ft. lbs.	4–8 Nm
Step 3 (CYLINDER HEAD):	59 ft. lbs.	80 Nm
Step 4 (INTAKE MANIFOLD):	6–11 ft. lbs.	8–15 Nm
Step 5 (CYLINDER HEAD):	+ 85° turn	+ 85° turn
Step 6 (INTAKE MANIFOLD):	11–15 ft. lbs.	15–21 Nm
Step 7 (INTAKE MANIFOLD):	15–18 ft. lbs.	21–25 Nm

*NOTE: Refer to cylinder head removal and installation procedure in text

Component	English	Metric
Engine mounts		
2.2L engine		
Front mounts		
Mount-to-crossmember nut	30–41 ft. lbs.	40–55 Nm
Mount-to-engine bolts	27–46 ft. lbs.	37–63 Nm
Rear mount		
Manual transmission		
Mount-to-crossmember bolts	23–34 ft. lbs.	31–46 Nm
Mount-to-transmission bolts	12–17 ft. lbs.	16–23 Nm
Automatic transmission		
Mount-to-crossmember bolts	23–34 ft. lbs.	31–46 Nm
Mount-to-transmission bolts	7.2–17.0 ft. lbs.	9.8–23.0 Nm
2.6L engine		
Front mounts		
Mount-to-crossmember nut		
B Series Pick-Up	30–41 ft. lbs.	40–55 Nm
MPV	25–36 ft. lbs.	34–49 Nm
Mount-to-engine bolts		
1988	36–43 ft. lbs.	49–59 Nm
1989–92	32–45 ft. lbs.	43–61 Nm
Rear mount		
Manual transmission		
Mount-to-crossmember nuts	23–34 ft. lbs.	31–46 Nm
Mount-to-transmission bolts		
B Series Pick-Up	23–34 ft. lbs.	31–46 Nm
MPV	32–45 ft. lbs.	43–61 Nm
Automatic transmission		
2WD		
Mount-to-crossmember bolts		
B Series Pick-Up	23–34 ft. lbs.	31–46 Nm
MPV	32–45 ft. lbs.	43–61 Nm
Mount-to-transmission bolts		
B Series Pick-Up	7.2–17.0 ft. lbs.	9.8–23.0 Nm
MPV	14–21 ft. lbs.	20–28 Nm
4WD		
Mount-to-crossmember nuts	23–34 ft. lbs.	31–46 Nm
Mount-to-transmission bolts	23–34 ft. lbs.	31–46 Nm
3.0L engine		

TORQUE SPECIFICATIONS

Component	English	Metric
Front mounts		
Mount-to-crossmember nuts	25–36 ft. lbs.	34–49 Nm
Mount-to-engine bolts	29–42 ft. lbs.	39–57 Nm
Rear mount		
Manual transmission		
Mount-to-crossmember nuts	23–34 ft. lbs.	31–46 Nm
Mount-to-transmission bolts	32–45 ft. lbs.	43–61 Nm
Automatic transmission		
Mount-to-crossmember bolts		
2WD	32–45 ft. lbs.	43–61 Nm
Mount-to-crossmember nuts		
4WD	23–34 ft. lbs.	31–46 Nm
Mount-to-transmission bolts	32–45 ft. lbs.	43–61 Nm
4.0L engine		
Front mounts		
Mount-to-crossmember nuts	71–94 ft. lbs.	96–127 Nm
Mount-to-engine bracket nuts	65–85 ft. lbs.	88–115 Nm
Rear mount		
Mount-to-transmission bolts	60–80 ft. lbs.	82–108 Nm
Mount-to-crossmember nuts	65–85 ft. lbs.	88–115 Nm
Exhaust manifold	19 ft. lbs.	26 Nm
Flywheel-to-crankshaft bolts		
2.2L engine	71–76 ft. lbs.	96–103 Nm
2.6L engine		
1988	94–101 ft. lbs.	128–137 Nm
1989–92	67–72 ft. lbs.	91–98 Nm
3.0L engine	76–81 ft. lbs.	103–110 Nm
4.0L engine	59 ft. lbs.	80 Nm
Flywheel-to-torque converter bolts/nuts		
B Series Pick-Up		
2WD	25–36 ft. lbs.	34–49 Nm
4WD	27–40 ft. lbs.	36–54 Nm
MPV	27–40 ft. lbs.	36–54 Nm
Navajo	20–34 ft. lbs.	27–46 Nm
Intake manifold-to-cylinder head bolts		
2.2L engine	14–19 ft. lbs.	19–25 Nm
2.6L engine		
Carbureted engine	11–14 ft. lbs.	15–19 Nm
Fuel injected engine	14–19 ft. lbs.	19–25 Nm
3.0L engine	14–19 ft. lbs.	19–25 Nm
4.0L engine		
Step 1:	3–6 ft. lbs.	4–8 Nm
Step 2:	6–11 ft. lbs.	8–15 Nm
Step 3:	11–15 ft. lbs.	15–21 Nm
Step 4:	15–18 ft. lbs.	21–25 Nm
Main bearing cap bolts		
2.2L engine	61–65 ft. lbs.	82–88 Nm
2.6L engine		
1988	54–61 ft. lbs.	74–83 Nm
1989–92	61–65 ft. lbs.	82–88 Nm
3.0L engine		
Step 1:	14 ft. lbs.	20 Nm
Step 2:	+ 90° turn	+ 90° turn
Step 3:	+ 45° turn	+ 45° turn
4.0L engine	66–77 ft. lbs.	90–104 Nm
Oil pan-to-block bolts/nuts		
2.2L engine	61–104 inch lbs.	6.9–12.0 Nm
2.6L engine		
1988	52–61 inch lbs.	6–7 Nm
1989–92	69–95 inch lbs.	7.8–11.0 Nm
3.0L engine	61–87 inch lbs.	6.9–9.8 Nm
4.0L engine	5–7 ft. lbs.	7–10 Nm

TORQUE SPECIFICATIONS

Component	English	Metric
Oil pan-to-transmission bolts		
4.0L engine	28–38 ft. lbs.	38–50 Nm
Oil pan drain plug		
Except 4.0L engine	22–30 ft. lbs.	29–41 Nm
4.0L engine	15–21 ft. lbs.	21–28 Nm
Oil pump-to-cylinder block		
2.2L engine*		
Bolt A	14–19 ft. lbs.	19–25 Nm
Bolt B	27–38 ft. lbs.	37–52 Nm
2.6L engine		
1988	69–78 inch lbs.	8–9 Nm
1989–92	14–19 ft. lbs.	19–25 Nm
3.0L engine	14–19 ft. lbs.	19–25 Nm
4.0L engine	13–15 ft. lbs.	17–21 Nm
Oil pickup tube-to-oil pump		
2.2L engine	69–104 inch lbs.	7.8–12.0 Nm
2.6L engine		
1988	11–16 ft. lbs.	15–22 Nm
1989–92	69–95 inch lbs.	7.8–11.0 Nm
3.0L engine	69–95 inch lbs.	7.8–11.0 Nm
4.0L engine	7–10 ft. lbs.	9–13 Nm
Rocker arm shaft bolts		
2.2L engine	13–20 ft. lbs.	18–26 Nm
2.6L engine		
1988	14–15 ft. lbs.	19–20 Nm
1989–92	14–19 ft. lbs.	19–25 Nm
3.0L engine	14–19 ft. lbs.	19–25 Nm
4.0L engine	46–52 ft. lbs.	62–70 Nm
Rocker arm cover bolts		
2.2L engine	26–35 inch lbs.	2.9–3.9 Nm
2.6L engine		
1988	43–61 inch lbs.	5–7 Nm
1989–92	52–78 inch lbs.	5.9–8.8 Nm
3.0L engine	30–39 inch lbs.	3.4–4.4 Nm
4.0L engine	3–5 ft. lbs.	4–7 Nm
Spark plugs	11–15 ft. lbs.	15–20 Nm
Starter-to-engine block bolts		
1988 vehicles	24–33 ft. lbs.	32–46 Nm
1989–92 vehicles		
Except 4.0L engine	27–38 ft. lbs.	37–72 Nm
4.0L engine	15–20 ft. lbs.	21–27 Nm
Transmission-to-engine bolts		
Manual transmission		
B Series Pick-Up	51–65 ft. lbs.	69–88 Nm
MPV		
2.6L engine	51–65 ft. lbs.	69–88 Nm
3.0L engine	27–38 ft. lbs.	37–52 Nm
Navajo	28–38 ft. lbs.	38–52 Nm
Automatic transmission		
Except MPV	28–38 ft. lbs.	38–52 Nm
MPV*		
Small diameter bolts	27–38 ft. lbs.	37–52 Nm
Large diameter bolts	51–65 ft. lbs.	69–88 Nm
*NOTE: Refer to automatic transmission removal and installation procedure in text		
Timing belt cover bolts		
2.2L engine	61–87 inch lbs.	6.9–9.8 Nm
3.0L engine		
6mm bolts	69–95 inch lbs.	7.8–11.0 Nm
10mm bolts	27–38 ft. lbs.	37–52 Nm

TORQUE SPECIFICATIONS

Component	English	Metric
Timing chain cover bolts		
2.6L engine		
1988	104–122 inch lbs.	12–14 Nm
1989–92	14–19 ft. lbs.	19–25 Nm
4.0L engines	13–15 ft. lbs.	17–21 Nm
Upper-to-lower intake manifold bolts		
Except 4.0L engine	14–19 ft. lbs.	19–25 Nm
4.0L engine	15–18 ft. lbs.	20–25 Nm
Water outlet housing		
Except 4.0L engine	14–19 ft. lbs.	19–25 Nm
4.0L engine	7–10 ft. lbs.	9–13 Nm
Water pump		
Except 4.0L engine	14–19 ft. lbs.	19–25 Nm
4.0L engine	7–9 ft. lbs.	9–12 Nm

MANUAL TRANSMISSION

For further information, please refer to Chilton's Transmission Service Manual.

Transmission Assembly

Removal and Installation

B2200

1. Disconnect the negative battery cable.
2. Remove the gearshift knob and shift console attaching screws. Remove the console.
3. Remove the shift lever to extension housing attaching bolts and remove the shift lever.
4. Raise and support the vehicle safely.
5. Drain the transmission oil.
6. Matchmark and remove the driveshaft.
7. Disconnect the speedometer cable from the transmission.
8. Remove the starter motor.
9. Disconnect and the back-up light switch wiring at the transmission.
10. Disconnect the parking brake return spring and parking brake cables.
11. Disconnect the clutch slave cylinder from the transmission.
12. Remove the transmission-to-engine gusset plate.
13. Disconnect the exhaust pipe at the transmission and manifold.
14. Support the transmission and engine separately with jacks.
15. Remove the transmission crossmember.
16. Lower the transmission to gain access to the top bolts and remove the transmission-to-engine bolts.
17. Pull the transmission straight back, away from the engine and remove transmission from the vehicle.

To install:

18. Raise the transmission into position. Install the transmission-to-engine bolts and tighten to 51–65 ft. lbs. (69–88 Nm).
19. Install the transmission crossmember and tighten the crossmember-to-chassis bolts to 23–34 ft. lbs. (31–46 Nm).
20. Lower the transmission onto the crossmember and remove the jacks. Install the crossmember-to-mount bolts to 12–17 ft. lbs. (16–23 Nm).
21. Connect the exhaust pipe to the manifold and transmission bracket. Tighten the exhaust pipe-to-manifold nuts to 30–

41 ft. lbs. (40–55 Nm) and the exhaust pipe-to-transmission bracket bolt to 13–20 ft. lbs. (18–26 Nm).
22. Install the gusset plate and tighten the bolts to 27–38 ft. lbs. (37–52 Nm).
23. Install the clutch slave cylinder and tighten the bolts to 12–17 ft. lbs. (16–23 Nm).
24. Install the parking brake cables and the return spring.
25. Connect the back-up light switch wiring connector and connect the speedometer cable.
26. Install the driveshaft, aligning the marks that were made during removal.
27. Install the starter. Fill the transmission with the proper type and quantity of engine oil.
28. Lower the vehicle. Install the shift lever and tighten the attaching bolts to 69–95 inch lbs. (7.8–11.0 Nm).
29. Install the console and the shift knob.
30. Connect the negative battery cable. Check the transmission for leaks and proper operation.

B2600

NOTE: On 4WD vehicles, the transmission and transfer case are removed as a unit.

1. Disconnect the negative battery cable.
2. Remove the knobs from the transfer case, if equipped and transmission shifters.
3. Remove the console box, if equipped.
4. Remove the insulator plate and shifter boot.
5. Remove the attaching bolts and the shift lever(s).
6. Raise and support the vehicle safely. Drain the tranfer case, if equipped and transmission oil.
7. Remove the transmission and transfer case, if equipped, splash shields. Remove the starter.
8. Disconnect and remove the front exhaust pipe.
9. Matchmark and remove the driveshaft(s).
10. Disconnect the speedometer cable, 4WD switch, if equipped and backup light switch wires from the transmission or transmission/transfer case.
11. Remove the slave cylinder without disconnecting the fluid line. Support the slave cylinder aside.
12. Remove the transmission gusset plates and clutch housing cover. Support the transmission and engine with jacks.
13. Raise the transmission or transmission/transfer case and remove the crossmember.
14. Remove the transmission or transmission/transfer case.

To install:

15. Raise the transmission or transmission/transfer case assembly into position. Install the transmission-to-engine bolts and tighten to 51–65 ft. lbs. (69–88 Nm).

16. Install the crossmember and tighten the crossmember-to-chassis bolts to 23–34 ft. lbs. (31–46 Nm).

17. Lower the transmission or transmission/transfer case assembly and remove the jacks. Install the crossmember-to-transmission mount nuts and tighten to 23–34 ft. lbs. (31–46 Nm).

18. Install the gusset plates and clutch housing cover. Install the slave cylinder.

19. Connect the backup light and, if equipped, 4WD switch electrical connectors and the speedometer cable.

20. Install the driveshaft(s), aligning the marks that were made during removal.

21. Install the front exhaust pipe and the starter. Install the splash shields.

22. Fill the transmission and, if equipped, transfer case with the proper type and quantity of fluid. Lower the vehicle.

23. Install the shift lever(s) and tighten the mounting bolts to 25–37 ft. lbs. (34–50 Nm).

24. Install the shifter boot and insulator plate. Tighten the mounting bolts to 25–37 ft. lbs. (34–50 Nm).

25. Install the console box and the shifter knob(s).

26. Connect the negative battery cable. Check the transmission for leaks and proper operation.

MPV

NOTE: On 4WD vehicles, the transmission and transfer case are removed as a unit.

1. Disconnect the negative battery cable.

2. Remove the shift lever knob and boot.

3. Shift the transmission into N and unbolt and remove the shift lever.

4. Raise and safely support the vehicle.

5. Drain the transmission and, if equipped, transfer case fluid.

6. Disconnect the speedometer cable and, if equipped, the Hi-Lo shift cable.

7. Disconnect the electrical connectors at the transmission.

8. Matchmark and remove the driveshaft(s). Stuff a rag in the double offset joint to prevent damage to the boot from the driveshaft.

9. On the 2.6L engine, unbolt the support bracket from the transmission, if equipped.

10. Remove the starter.

11. Remove the clutch slave cylinder and hydraulic line bracket. It is not necessary to disconnect the hydraulic line. Remove the bellhousing inspection plate.

12. Remove the front exhaust pipe and heat shield.

13. Remove the gusset plates and support the transmission and engine with jacks.

14. Remove the transmission-to-crossmember bolts. Remove the crossmember.

15. Remove the transmission-to-engine bolts.

16. Pull the transmission straight back on the jack until the mainshaft clears the clutch. Lower the transmission and pull it out from under the vehicle.

To install:

17. Raise the transmission into position.

18. Push the transmission straight forward on the jack until the mainshaft enters the clutch and the transmission engages the locating dowels on the engine.

19. Install the transmission-to-engine bolts and tighten to 27–38 ft. lbs. (37–52 Nm) on 3.0L engine or 51–65 ft. lbs. (69–88 Nm) on 2.6L engine.

20. Install the starter. Install the crossmember and tighten the crossmember-to-chassis bolts to 32–45 ft. lbs. (43–61 Nm).

21. Lower the transmission and remove the jacks. Install the transmission-to-crossmember bolts and tighten the nuts to 23–34 ft. lbs. (31–46 Nm) or bolts/nuts to 32–45 ft. lbs. (43–61 Nm).

22. Install the front exhaust pipe and heat shield.

23. Install the transmission gusset plates. Install the clutch release cylinder and bracket.

24. Connect the speedometer cable and, if equipped, Hi-Lo shift cable. Connect the electrical wiring.

25. Install the driveshaft(s), aligning the marks that were made during removal. Install the bellhousing inspection plate.

26. Fill the transmission and, if equipped, transfer case with the proper type and quantity of fluid. Lower the vehicle.

27. Install the shift lever.

28. Install the shifter knob and boot.

29. Connect the negative battery cable. Check the transmission for leaks and proper operation.

NAVAJO

1. Disconnect the negative battery cable.

2. Place the gearshift lever in the N position.

3. Remove the shifter boot retainer screws and slide the boot up the shift lever shaft. Remove the shift lever attaching bolt(s) and remove the shift lever. Cover the opening in the transmission to prevent dirt from entering.

4. Raise and safely support the vehicle. Drain the transmission fluid.

5. Mark the position of the driveshaft(s) on the flange(s) and remove the driveshaft(s). Plug the transmission or transfer case opening to prevent fluid leakage.

6. Disconnect the clutch hydraulic fluid line. Plug the line to prevent fluid leakage.

7. Disconnect the speedometer cable from the transmission or transfer case.

8. Disconnect the starter and backup lamp switch wires.

9. Place a jack under the engine, with a wood block to protect the oil pan.

10. Remove the transfer case, if equipped.

11. Remove the starter. Place a transmission jack under the transmission.

12. Remove the bolts attaching the transmission and clutch housing to the engine. Remove the nuts and bolts attaching the transmission mount and damper to the crossmember.

13. Remove the nuts and/or bolts attaching the crossmember to the frame side rails and remove the crossmember.

14. Lower the engine jack. Work the clutch housing off the locating dowels and slide the clutch housing and transmission rearward until the input shaft clears the clutch disc. Remove the transmission.

15. Remove the clutch housing from the transmission, if necessary.

To install:

16. Make sure the machined mating surfaces and the locating dowels on the engine rear plate and the mating face of the clutch housing and locating dowel holes are free of burrs, dirt or paint. Install the clutch housing on the transmission, if removed.

17. Mount the transmission on a transmission jack and raise into position. Start the input shaft into the clutch disc, aligning the splines. Move the transmission forward until the clutch housing seats on the locating dowels.

18. Install the clutch housing-to-engine attaching bolts and tighten to 28–38 ft. lbs. (38–51 Nm). Remove the transmission jack.

19. Install the starter.

20. Raise the engine and install the crossmember, insulator and damper with the attaching nuts and bolts. Install the nuts and bolts attaching the transmission mount to the crossmember.

21. Install the transfer case, if equipped.

22. Remove the plug(s) and install the driveshaft(s), aligning the marks on the flange(s) that were made during the removal procedure.

23. Connect the starter cable and backup lamp switch wires.

24. Connect the hydraulic clutch line and bleed the system.
25. Connect the speedometer cable.
26. Fill the transmission with the proper type and quantity of fluid.
27. Lower the vehicle and remove the cover from the transmission opening.
28. Install the gearshift lever with the attaching bolt(s). Install the shifter boot.
29. Connect the negative battery cable. Check the transmission for leaks and proper operation.

CLUTCH

Clutch Assembly

Removal and Installation

1. Disconnect the negative battery cable.
2. On Navajo, disconnect the hydraulic clutch master cylinder from the clutch pedal.
3. Raise and safely support the vehicle. Remove the starter.
4. On all except Navajo, remove the slave cylinder, leaving the hydraulic line conected. On Navajo, use coupling disconnect tool T88T–70522–A or equivalent, to slide the white plastic sleeve toward the slave cylinder, then apply a slight tug on the tube to disconnect the hydraulic coupling. Plug the hose.
5. Remove the transmission.
6. Mark the position of the pressure plate on the flywheel so if the pressure plate is reused, it can be reinstalled in the same position.
7. Loosen the pressure plate attaching bolts evenly until the diaphragm spring is expanded. Remove the bolts, pressure plate and clutch disc.
8. Inspect the flywheel for wear, scoring and cracks. Machine or replace, as necessary. Inspect the clutch pilot bearing for wear and free movement. If replacement is necessary, remove using puller tool T58L–101–B or equivalent.
9. Inspect the clutch release bearing for wear and free movement; replace as necessary. On Navajo, remove the release bearing by twisting it until resistance is felt, then turning further will allow the preload spring to push the bearing assembly off the slave cylinder.

To install:

10. If the pilot bearing was removed, a new 1 must be installed. Install using a suitable driver. On Navajo, install the pilot bearing with the seal facing the transmission so the adapter is not cocked.
11. If the flywheel was removed, make sure the mating surfaces of the crank flange and flywheel are clean, and install the flywheel. Tighten the flywheel bolts to 71–76 ft. lbs. (96–103 Nm) on 2.2L engine, 94–101 ft. lbs. (128–137 Nm) on 1988 2.6L engine, 67–72 ft. lbs. (91–98 Nm) on 1989–92 2.6L engine, 76–81 ft. lbs. (103–110 Nm) on 3.0L engine or 59 ft. lbs. (80 Nm) on 4.0L engine.
12. Position the clutch disc on the flywheel so a suitable alignment tool can enter the pilot bearing and align the disc.
13. Install the pressure plate. If the original pressure plate is being reused, align the marks that were made during the removal procedure. Install the attaching bolts and tighten, in sequence, to 13–20 ft. lbs. (18–26 Nm) on all except 4.0L engine where the torque is 15–24 ft. lbs. (21–32 Nm), then remove the alignment tool.
14. On all except Navajo, lightly lubricate the release bearing fork pivot and release bearing contact surfaces with high temperature grease. Install the fork and the release bearing.
15. On Navajo, lubricate the release bearing bore and bearing carrier with high temperature grease and install over the transmission input shaft and onto the slave cylinder.
16. Install the transmission. If equipped, reuse the aluminum washers under the attaching bolts to prevent galvanic corrosion.
17. On all except Navajo, install the slave cylinder to the transmission. On Navajo, connect the hydraulic coupling by pushing the male coupling into the slave cylinder female coupling.
18. Lower the vehicle. On Navajo, connect the clutch master cylinder to the brake pedal and bleed the clutch system, if necessary.
19. Connect the negative battery cable.

Clutch pressure plate bolt torque sequence—except 4.0L engine

Clutch pressure plate bol torque sequence—4.0L engine

Pedal Height/Free-Play Adjustment

EXCEPT NAVAJO

1. Measure the distance from the top of the clutch pedal pad to the carpet. The distance should be as follows:
   B2200: 7.13–7.52 in. (181–191mm)
   B2600: 7.52–7.91 in. (191–201mm)
   MPV: 8.19–8.58 in. (208–218mm)
2. If the distance is not within specification, loosen the clutch

A. Locknut
B. Clutch switch
C. Locknut
D. Actuator rod

Clutch pedal height/free-play measurement points — except Navajo

switch locknut and turn the switch until the distance is correct. Tighten the lock nut.

3. Check the free-play by pressing the pedal by hand until clutch resistance is felt. The free-play should be 0.02–0.12 in. (0.6–3.0mm).

4. If the free-play is not within specification, loosen the locknut on the actuator rod and turn the actuator rod unitl the free-play is correct.

5. Check that the disengagement height from the upper surface of the pedal height to the carpet is correct when the pedal is fuuly depressed. The disengagement height should be as follows:

    B2200: 2.60 in. (66mm)
    B2600: 2.80 in. (71mm)
    MPV: 1.38 in. (35mm)

6. Tighten the actuator rod locknut to 8.7–12.0 ft. lbs. (12–17 Nm).

7. Recheck the pedal height.

NAVAJO

The hydraulic clutch system provides automatic adjustment. No adjustment of clutch linkage or pedal position is required.

Clutch Master Cylinder

Removal and Installation

EXCEPT NAVAJO

1. Disconnect the negative battery cable. Disconnect and plug the fluid outlet line at the fitting on the master cylinder.

2. Working inside the vehicle, remove the nuts mounting the master cylinder to the firewall.

3. On MPV, remove the fluid reservoir mounting bolts.

4. On B Series Pick-Up, remove the master cylinder from the firewall. On MPV, remove the master cylinder and the remote fluid reservoir as an assembly.

To install:

5. Start the pedal pushrod into the master cylinder and position the master cylinder on the firewall.

6. Working inside the vehicle, install the mounting nuts and tighten to 12–17 ft. lbs. (16–23 Nm) on B Series Pick-Up or 14–19 ft. lbs. (19–25 Nm) on MPV.

7. On MPV, install the remote fluid reservoir mounting bolts and tighten to 69–95 inch lbs. (7.8–11.0 Nm).

8. Connect the fluid outlet line to the master cylinder fitting.

9. Bleed the hydraulic clutch system.

10. Check the clutch pedal height/free-play and adjust if necessary.

NAVAJO

1. Disconnect the negative battery cable.

2. Disconnect the clutch master cylinder pushrod from the clutch pedal by prying the retainer bushing and pushrod off the pedal pin.

3. Remove the switch from the master cylinder assembly.

4. Remove the screw retaining the fluid reservoir to the cowl access cover.

5. Use coupling disconnect tool T88T–70522–A or equivalent, to slide the white plastic sleeve toward the slave cylinder, then apply a slight tug on the tube to disconnect the hydraulic coupling.

6. Remove the retaining bolts and the clutch master cylinder.

To install:

7. Install the pushrod through the hole in the engine compartment. Make sure it is located on the correct side of the clutch pedal. Install the master cylinder and tighten the bolts to 12 ft. lbs. (16 Nm).

8. Insert the coupling end into the slave cylinder and install the tube into the clips.

9. Install the fluid reservoir on the cowl access cover with the retaining screw.

10. Replace the retainer bushing in the clutch master cylinder pushrod if worn or damaged. Install the retainer and pushrod on the clutch pedal pin. Make sure the flange of the bushing is against the pedal blade. Install the switch.

11. Connect the negative battery cable and bleed the clutch hydraulic system, if necessary.

Clutch Slave Cylinder

Removal and Installation

EXCEPT NAVAJO

1. Disconnect the negative battery cable. Raise and support the vehicle safely.

2. Disconnect the flexible hose from the slave cylinder or hydraulic tube. Plug the hose.

3. Pull off the hose retaining clip, if equipped. Remove the tube from the slave cylinder on MPV.

4. Remove the slave cylinder attaching bolts and the slave cylinder.

5. Installation is the reverse of the removal procedure.

6. Tighten the slave cylinder mounting bolts to 12–17 ft. lbs. (16–23 Nm) on B Series Pick-Up or 14–19 ft. lbs. (19–25 Nm) on MPV.

7. Bleed the clutch hydraulic system.

NAVAJO

NOTE: Before any vehicle service that requires slave cylinder removal, the clutch master cylinder pushrod must be disconnected from the clutch pedal. If not disconnected, permanent damage to the master cylinder will occur if the clutch pedal is depressed while the slave cylinder is disconnected.

TRANSMISSION CLUTCH HOUSING

TRANSMISSION INPUT SHAFT

HYDRAULIC BLEED SCREW

HYDRAULIC CLUTCH LINE COUPLING

FRONT OF VEHICLE

CONCENTRIC SLAVE CYLINDER

BOLT

Slave cylinder installation—Navajo

1. Disconnect the negative battery cable.
2. Disconnect the coupling at the transmission using tool T88T–70522–A or equivalent, by sliding the white plastic sleeve toward the slave cylinder while applying a slight tug on the tube.
3. Raise and safely support the vehicle. Remove the transmission and clutch housing.
4. Remove the bolts retaining the slave cylinder to the transmission. Remove the slave cylinder from the transmission input shaft.
5. If necessary, remove the release bearing from the slave cylinder by twisting until resistance is felt, then turning further to allow the preload spring to push the bearing assembly off.
To install:
6. Push the release bearing into place, if removed.

7. Position the slave cylinder over the transmission input shaft with the bleed screw and coupling facing the left side of the transmission.
8. Install the slave cylinder attaching bolts and tighten to 13–19 ft. lbs. (18–26 Nm).
9. Install the transmission.
10. Insert the male coupling into the female coupling on the clutch slave cylinder and make sure the connection is secure.
11. Bleed the clutch hydraulic system, if necessary. Lower the vehicle and connect the negative battery cable.

Hydraulic Clutch System Bleeding

NOTE: On Navajo, under normal conditions, disconnecting the clutch coupling will not let air into the system. However, if there appears to be air in the system, indicated by a spongy pedal or insufficient bearing travel, the system must be bled.

1. Clean all dirt and grease from around the reservoir cap.
2. Remove the cap and fill the reservoir with heavy duty brake fluid.
3. Raise and safely support the vehicle, as necessary. Loosen the bleed screw, located in the slave cylinder body, next to the inlet connection.
4. Fluid should now begin to flow from the master cylinder, down the tube and into the slave cylinder.

NOTE: Keep the reservoir full at all times to make sure no additional air is drawn into the system.

5. Bubbles should begin to appear at the bleed screw outlet, indicating air is being expelled. When the slave cylinder is full, a steady stream of fluid will come from the slave cylinder outlet. Tighten the bleed screw.
6. Slowly depress the clutch pedal to the floor and hold. Loosen the bleed screw to allow air and excess fluid to be expelled. Retighten the bleed screw when fluid flow stops.
7. Depress and release the clutch pedal slowly, waiting 2 seconds between each cycle. Repeat 5 times.
8. Check the fluid level in the reservoir and add, if necessary. If evidence of air still exists, repeat Steps 6 and 7.

AUTOMATIC TRANSMISSION

For further information, please refer to Chilton's Transmission Service Manual.

Transmission Assembly

Removal and Installation

B SERIES PICK-UP

2WD

1. Disconnect the negative battery cable. Raise and safely support the vehicle.
2. Drain the transmission fluid.
3. Mark the position of the driveshaft on the axle flange and remove the driveshaft.
4. Disconnect the speedometer cable, vacuum hose and shift lever. Remove the vacuum line bracket from the transmission.
5. Remove the gusset plates and bellhousing cover.
6. Remove the torque converter attaching bolts from the flywheel.
7. Support the transmission and engine with jacks.
8. Remove the transmission mount and mount bracket.

9. Tag and disconnect the electrical connectors from the neutral safety switch, kickdown solenoid and overdrive cancel solenoid.
10. Remove the transmission fluid dipstick and tube.
11. Disconnect and plug the transmission fluid lines.
12. Remove the transmission.
To install:
13. Raise the transmission into position. Install the transmission-to-engine bolts and tighten to 27–38 ft. lbs. (37–52 Nm).
14. Unplug and connect the transmission fluid lines. Tighten the banjo bolts to 17–26 ft. lbs. (24–35 Nm).
15. Install the transmission fluid dipstick and tube.
16. Connect the electrical connectors.
17. Install the transmission mount and tighten the bolts to 7.2–17 ft. lbs. (9.8–23 Nm). Install the mount bracket to the crossmember and tighten the bolts to 23–34 ft. lbs. (31–46 Nm). Install the mount-to-mount bracket bolts to 23–34 ft. lbs. (31–46 Nm).
18. Remove the support jacks.
19. Install the torque converter attaching bolts and tighten to 25–36 ft. lbs. (34–49 Nm).
20. Install the gusset plates and bellhousing cover. Tighten the gusset plate bolts to 27–38 ft. lbs. (37–52 Nm).

21. Connect the shift lever, vacuum hose and speedometer cable. Attach the vacuum line bracket.

22. Install the driveshaft and lower the vehicle.

23. Connect the negative battery cable. Fill the transmission with the proper type and quantity of fluid.

24. Check the transmission for leaks and proper operation.

4WD

1. Disconnect the negative battery cable.

2. Remove the shifter knob and the console box.

3. Remove the insulator plate and boot. Remove the 4WD shift lever.

4. Raise and safely support the vehicle. Remove the splash shields and drain the transmission fluid.

5. Disconnect and remove the front exhaust pipe.

6. Mark the position of the driveshaft on the flanges and remove the driveshafts.

7. Disconnect the speedometer cable and the 4WD indicator switch connector, if equipped.

8. Disconnect the shift cable and vacuum hose, if equipped.

9. Remove the gusset plate, if equipped.

10. On 1990–92 vehicles, loosen the front differential mounting bolts and remove the No. 2 crossmember.

11. Remove the torque converter attaching bolts.

12. Support the transmission and engine with jacks. Remove the transmission-to-engine bolts.

13. Disconnect and plug the transmission fluid lines at the transmission. Remove the bracket from the transmission.

14. Remove the rear transmission crossmember.

15. Tag and disconnect the electrical connectors at the transmission.

16. Remove the transmission dipstick and tube.

17. Lower the transmission from the vehicle.

To install:

18. Raise the transmission into position and install the transmission-to-engine bolts. Tighten to 27–38 ft. lbs. (37–52 Nm).

19. Install the dipstick and tube.

20. Connect the electrical connectors.

21. Install the rear transmission crossmember and tighten the transmission-to-chassis bolts to 23–34 ft. lbs. (31–46 Nm).

22. Lower the transmission to the crossmember and install the mount-to-crossmember nuts. Tighten to 23–34 ft. lbs. (31–46 Nm). Remove the jacks.

23. Connect the transmission fluid lines to the transmission and tighten the banjo bolts to 17–26 ft. lbs. (24–35 Nm). Attach the fluid line bracket.

24. Install the torque converter attaching bolts and tighten to 27–40 ft. lbs. (36–54 Nm). Install the bellhousing cover.

25. Install the No. 2 crossmember.

26. Install the gusset plates, if equipped.

27. Connect the shifter cable and the bracket, if equipped. Connect the speedometer cable.

28. Install the driveshafts, aligning the marks that were made during removal.

29. Install the front exhaust pipe and the splash shields. Lower the vehicle.

30. Install the 4WD shift lever and the insulator plate and boot.

31. Install the console box and the shifter knob.

32. Connect the negative battery cable. Fill the transmission with the proper type and quantity of fluid.

33. Check the transmission for leaks and proper operation.

MPV

1. Disconnect the negative battery cable. Raise and safely support the vehicle.

2. Drain the transmission fluid.

3. Disconnect the speedometer cable. Tag and disconnect the necessary electrical connectors.

4. Disconnect and remove the front exhaust pipe and heat shield.

5. Mark the position of the driveshaft on the flanges and remove the driveshaft(s).

6. Disconnect and remove the shift linkage from the transmission.

7. Remove the dipstick and tube.

8. Remove the bellhousing cover and then remove the torque converter bolts.

9. Remove the starter and bracket, if equipped.

10. Remove the exhaust pipe bracket and the gusset plates.

11. Support the engine and transmission with jacks. Remove the transmission crossmember.

12. Disconnect and plug the transmission fluid lines at the transmission. Disconnect the vacuum line, if equipped.

13. Remove the transmission-to-engine bolts and lower the transmission from the vehicle.

To install:

14. Raise the transmission into position. Install the transmission-to-engine bolts. Tighten all bolts to 27–38 ft. lbs. (37–52 Nm) except the 4 larger diameter bolts on the hydraulically controlled transmission which are tightened to 51–65 ft. lbs. (69–88 Nm).

15. Install the transmission crossmember and tighten the crossmember-to-chassis bolts to 32–45 ft. lbs. (43–61 Nm). Tighten the mount-to-crossmember nuts to 23–34 ft. lbs. (31–46 Nm) or bolts/nuts to 32–45 ft. lbs. (43–61 Nm). Remove the jacks.

16. Connect the transmission fluid lines and tighten the banjo bolts to 17–26 ft. lbs. (24–35 Nm). Connect the vacuum line, if equipped.

17. Install the exhaust pipe bracket and gusset plates. Tighten the gusset plate bolts to 27–38 ft. lbs. (37–52 Nm).

18. Install the starter and the bracket, if equipped.

19. Install the torque converter bolts and tighten to 27–40 ft. lbs. (36–54 Nm). Install the bellhousing cover.

20. Install the dipstick and tube. Connect the shift linkage.

21. Install the driveshaft(s), aligning the marks that were made during removal.

22. Install the front exhaust pipe and heat shield.

23. Connect the electrical connectors and speedometer cable. Lower the vehicle.

24. Connect the negative battery cable. Fill the transmission with the proper type and quantity of fluid.

25. Check the transmission for leaks and proper operation.

NAVAJO

1. Disconnect the negative battery cable. Raise and safely support the vehicle.

2. Position a drain pan under the transmission fluid pan. Pry the lower clips of the transmission heat shield back slightly to allow access to the pan bolts.

3. Starting at the rear of the transmission pan and working toward the front, loosen the attaching bolts and allow the fluid to drain. Remove all the bolts except the 2 at the front to allow the fluid to further drain. After all fluid has drained, reinstall 2 bolts at the rear of the pan to temporarily hold it in place.

4. Disconnect the starter cable and remove the starter.

5. Place a 22mm socket and breaker bar on the crankshaft pulley attaching bolt. Rotate the pulley clockwise, as viewed from the front, to gain access to each converter attaching nut. Remove the nuts through the starter mounting hole.

6. Mark the position of the driveshaft on the axle flange and remove the driveshaft. Plug the transmission to prevent fluid leakage.

7. Disconnect the speedometer cable from the transmission.

8. Disconnect the shift cable at the transmission manual lever. Remove the kickdown cable from the ball stud lever. Depress the tab on the cable downshift retainer and remove the cable from the bracket.

9. Disconnect the neutral safety switch wires and converter clutch solenoid connector. Disconnect the vacuum line from the vacuum modulator.

10. Position a transmission jack under the transmission and raise it slightly. Remove the engine rear support-to-crossmember bolts.

11. Remove the crossmember-to-frame side support attaching bolts and remove the crossmember insulator and support and damper.

12. Lower the jack under the transmission and allow the transmission to hang. Position a jack to the front of the engine and raise it to gain access to the 2 upper converter housing-to-engine attaching bolts.

13. Disconnect the oil cooler lines at the transmission. Plug the lines and transmission to prevent the entrance of dirt.

14. Remove the lower converter housing-to-engine attaching bolts and remove the transmission filler tube.

15. Secure the transmission to the jack with a safety chain. Remove the 2 upper converter housing-to-engine attaching bolts. Move the transmission to the rear so it disengages from the dowel pins and the converter is disengaged from the flywheel. Lower the transmission from the vehicle.

NOTE: If the transmission is to be removed for an extended period, support the engine with a safety stand and wood block.

To install:

16. Position the converter to the transmission making sure the converter hub is fully engaged in the pump gear. To make sure the converter is fully engaged, push and rotate the converter until 2 "bumps" are felt. Keep pushing and rotating until the distance between the converter pilot and the edge of the converter housing is $^7/_{16}$–$^9/_{16}$ in.

17. Place the transmission on a transmission jack and secure with a safety chain. Rotate the converter so the drive studs are in alignment with the holes in the flywheel.

18. Raise the transmission and move it forward into position, being careful not to damage the flywheel and converter pilot.

NOTE: When moving the transmission, do not let the front of the transmission tilt downward. This will cause the converter to move forward and disengage from the pump gear. The converter must rest squarely against the flywheel. This indicates that the converter pilot is not binding in the engine crankshaft.

19. Install 2 converter housing-to-engine attaching bolts at the engine dowel locations and tighten to 28–38 ft. lbs. (38–51 Nm). Install the remaining attaching bolts and tighten to the same specification.

20. Remove the safety chain from the transmission.

21. Insert the filler tube in the stub tube and secure it to the cylinder block with the attaching bolt. Tighten the bolt to 28–38 ft. lbs. (38–51 Nm). If the stub tube is loosened or dislodged, it should be replaced.

22. Install the oil cooler lines in the retaining clip at the cylinder block. Connect the lines to the transmission.

23. Remove the jack supporting the front of the engine.

24. Raise the transmission and position the crossmember, insulator and support and damper to the frame side supports. Install the attaching bolts and nuts and tighten to 65–85 ft. lbs. (88–115 Nm).

25. Lower the transmission and install the rear engine support-to-crossmember nuts. Tighten the nuts to 65–85 ft. lbs. (88–115 Nm). Remove the transmission jack.

26. Install the vacuum hose on the vacuum modulator and attach the line to the clip. Connect the neutral safety switch plug and the converter clutch solenoid connector.

27. Install the flywheel-to-converter nuts and tighten to 20–34 ft. lbs. (27–46 Nm).

28. Install the starter and tighten the attaching bolts to 15–20 ft. lbs. (20–27 Nm). Connect the starter cable.

29. Connect the exhaust pipe to the exhaust manifold, if disconnected for removal.

30. Connect the shift cable to the manual lever and the downshift cable to the downshift lever. Connect the speedometer cable.

31. Install the driveshaft, aligning the marks on the axle flange. Adjust the manual and downshift linkage, as required.

32. Remove the bolts temporarily holding the transmission fluid pan and remove the pan. Discard the gasket and clean all old gasket material and dirt from the gasket mating surfaces.

33. Install the pan using a new gasket. Tighten the attaching bolts to 8–10 ft. lbs. (11–13.5 Nm).

34. Lower the vehicle and connect the negative battery cable. Fill the transmission with the proper type and quantity of fluid.

35. Run the vehicle and check for leaks and proper operation.

Shift Linkage Adjustment

B SERIES PICK-UP

1988 Three Speed Transmission

1. Move the gearshift lever to the **P** range.
2. Loosen locknuts A, B and C.
3. Be sure to shift the transmission to the **P** range by moving the select lever of the transmission.
4. Push and hold the gearshift lever forward with a force of approximately 22 lbs.
5. Tighten locknut A, locknut B, then locknut C.

1988 Four Speed Transmission

1. Move the gearshift lever to the **P** range.
2. Loosen locknuts A and B.
3. Be sure to shift the transmission to the **P** range by moving the select lever of the transmission.
4. Using a feeler gauge, adjust locknut A until there is 0.039 in. (1mm) between the adjust lever and the locknut.
5. Remove the feeler gauge and tighten locknut B to 69–95 inch lbs. (7.8–11.0 Nm).
6. Move the gearshift lever to the **N**, **D** and **P** ranges and make sure there is clearance between the select lever bracket and the guide pin.
7. If there is no clearance, readjust the lever by adjusting locknuts A and B.

1989–92 Hydraulically Controlled Transmission

1. Move the gearshift lever to the **P** range.
2. Loosen locknuts A and B so they are both at least 0.039 in. (1mm) away from the adjustment lever.
3. Shift the transmission to the **P** range by moving the manual shaft of the transmission.
4. With the link at 90 degrees to the lever, adjust the clearance using a feeler gauge to 0.039 in. (1mm) between the adjustment lever and locknut A.

Shift linkage adjustment—1988 B Series Pick-Up with 3-speed transmission

Shift linkage adjustment—1988 B Series Pick-Up with 4-speed transmission

5. Remove the feeler gauge and tighten locknut B to 69–95 inch lbs. (8–11 Nm).

6. Measure the clearance between the guide plate and the guide pin in the **P** range. There should be 0.039 in. (1mm) clearance in front of the pin and 0.020 in. (0.5mm) clearance behind the pin.

7. Move the gearshift lever to the **N** and **D** ranges and check that the clearance between the guide plate and guide pin is the same in both ranges. If not, readjust locknuts A and B.

1989–92 Electronically Controlled Transmission

1. Disconnect the negative battery cable to deactivate the shift-lock.

2. Remove the selector knob and console.

3. Loosen locknuts A and B and lock bolt C.

4. Shift the transmission manual shaft to the **P** range.

5. Push and hold the selector lever forward with a force of approximately 22 lbs., then tighten lock bolt C to 67–95 inch lbs. (8–11 Nm).

6. Turn locknut A by hand until it just touches the spacer, then tighten locknut B to 67–95 inch lbs. (8–11 Nm).

7. Check the lever so the clearance between the guide plate and the guide pin in the **P** range with the pushrod lightly depressed is as specified.

8. Move the selector lever to the **N** and **D** ranges and make sure there is the same clearance between the guide plate and guide pin. If not, readjust the lever.

9. Install the console. Clean and apply locking compound to the selector knob screw threads and tighten the screws to 13–26 inch lbs. (1.5–2.9 Nm).

10. Connect the negative battery cable.

MPV

1. Move the selector lever to the **P** range.

2. Remove the column covers.

3. Pull the selector lever rearward, toward the driver and insert a 0.197 in. (5mm) outer diameter pin into the gearshift rod assembly.

4. Remove the air intake tube.

5. Loosen the shift lever and the top lever mounting bolts.

6. Shift the transmission manual shaft to the **P** range position.

7. Adjust the clearance between the lower bracket and the shift lever bushing by sliding the shift lever assembly until there is no clearance.

8. Tighten the shift lever mounting bolts to 12–17 ft. lbs. (16–23 Nm).

9. Make sure the detent ball is positioned in the center of the **P** range detent. If not, loosen bolts A and turn the bracket to adjust the position, then retighten bolts A to 61–87 inch lbs. (6.9–9.8 Nm).

10. Adjust the clearance between the lower bracket and the shift lever bushing by turning the top lever until there is no clearance. Tighten the top lever mounting bolt A then retighten bolt B to 12–17 ft. lbs. (16–23 Nm).

11. Remove the pin from the gear shift rod assembly and install the column covers. Check selector lever operation.

NAVAJO

1. Raise and safely support the vehicle, as necessary. From

Shift linkage adjustment—1989–92 B Series Pick-Up with hydraulically controlled transmission

Shift linkage adjustment—1989–92 B Series Pick-Up with electronically controlled transmission

Shift linkage adjustment — MPV

inside the vehicle, place the column shift selector lever in the **OD** position. Hang an 8 lb. weight on the selector lever.

2. From below the vehicle, pull down the lock tab on the shift cable and remove the fitting from the transmission manual control lever ball stud.

3. Position the transmission manual control lever in the **OD** position by moving the lever all the way rearward and then moving it 3 detents forward.

4. Connect the cable end fitting to the transmission manual control lever. Push up on the lock tab to lock the cable in the correctly adjusted position.

5. Remove the 8 lb. weight from the column shift selector.

6. After adjustment, check for **P** engagement. Check the column shift selector lever in all detent positions with the engine running to ensure correct adjustment.

Kickdown Switch Adjustment

EXCEPT NAVAJO

1. Disconnect the negative battery cable.

2. Disconnect the switch connector, located above the accelerator pedal.

3. Loosen the locknut and back the switch out fully.

4. Depress the accelerator pedal fully and hold it.

5. With the accelerator pedal fully down, turn the kickdown switch clockwise until it turns **ON** (clicking sound heard), then turn the switch ¼ turn further clockwise.

6. Tighten the locknut to 10–13 ft. lbs. (14–18 Nm) and release the accelerator pedal.

7. Reconnect the connector and the negative battery cable.

8. Depress the accelerator pedal fully and verify that the kickdown switch clicks at the fully depressed position.

Selector Indicator Adjustment

NAVAJO

1. Remove the steering column shroud.

2. With the engine stopped and the parking brake applied, place the transmission selector lever at the steering column in the **OD** position.

3. Secure a 3 lb. weight to the end of the transmission selector lever.

4. On 1991 vehicles, proceed as follows:

  a. Loosen the selector indicator screw on the column casting. Move the selector indicator adjustment until the orange pointer is completely within the letter "D" inside the **OD** graphic.

  b. Tighten the selector indicator screw on the column to 10–15 inch lbs. (1.1–1.7 Nm).

5. On 1992 vehicles, rotate the thumb wheel until the orange pointer is completely within the letter "D" inside the **OD** graphic.

6. Install the steering column shroud.

TRANSFER CASE

Transfer Case Assembly

Removal and Installation

B SERIES PICK-UP

1. Disconnect the negative battery cable. Raise and safely support the vehicle.

2. Remove the transmission assembly from the vehicle.

3. Place the transmission in a vertical position, converter housing down.

4. Remove the control cover assembly, roll pin and control lever end from the transfer case.

5. Remove the extension housing-to-transfer case attaching bolts.

6. Lift the transfer case off vertically to prevent damaging the control rod.

To install:

7. Install the input sleeve, if removed.

8. Coat the contacting surfaces of the transfer case and extension housing with sealant.

9. Install the transfer case to the extension housing. Apply sealant to the bolt threads and tighten to 27–35 ft. lbs. (36–47 Nm).

10. Install the control lever end and secure with a new roll pin.

11. Coat the contacting surfaces of the control cover assembly and transfer case with sealant and install the control cover assembly on the transfer case.

12. Apply sealant to the bolt threads and tighten to 16–22 ft. lbs. (22–30 Nm).

13. Install the transmission assembly and lower the vehicle. Connect the negative battery cable.

14. Check the transfer case for leaks and proper operation.

MPV

1. Disconnect the negative battery cable. Raise and safely support the vehicle. Drain the transfer case.

2. Mark the position of the driveshafts on the flanges and remove the driveshafts. Push a rag into the double-offset joint to hold the rear driveshaft straight to prevent damaging the boot.

3. Support the transmission with a jack and remove the transmission lower mount. Remove the upper mount.

4. Remove the front exhaust pipe and heat insulator.

5. Disconnect the speedometer and transfer case shift cable. Tag and disconnect the electrical connectors.

6. Support the transfer case with a jack and remove the transfer case attaching bolts. Remove the transfer case.

To install:

7. Apply silicone sealant to the transfer case flange.

8. Support the transfer case with a jack and install the transfer case. Apply sealant to the bolt threads and tighten to 27–40 ft. lbs. (36–54 Nm).

9. Connect the electrical connectors, transfer case shift cable and speedometer cable. Adjust the transfer case shift cable.

10. Install the exhaust pipe and heat insulator.

11. Install the upper transmission mount.

12. Install the lower transmission mount. Loosely install the center washers and nuts and tighten the outer bolts to 32–45 ft. lbs. (43–61 Nm), then tighten the center nuts to 23–34 ft. lbs. (31–46 Nm).

13. Remove the support jacks.

14. Install the driveshafts, aligning the marks that were made during removal. Remove the rag from the double-offset joint and check the boot for damage.

15. Fill the transfer case with the proper type and quantity of fluid.

16. Lower the vehicle and connect the negative battery cable. Check the transfer case for leaks and proper operation.

NAVAJO

Mechanical Shift Type

1. Disconnect the negative battery cable. Raise and safely support the vehicle.

2. If equipped, remove the skid plate from the frame. Remove the damper from the transfer case, if equipped.

3. Place a drain pan under the transfer case, remove the drain plug and drain the fluid. Disconnect the 4WD indicator switch wire connector at the transfer case.

4. Disconnect the front driveshaft from the transfer case output shaft yoke and wire the driveshaft out of the way.

5. Disconnect the rear driveshaft from the transfer case output shaft flange and wire the driveshaft out of the way.

6. Disconnect the speedometer driven gear from the transfer case rear cover. Disconnect the vent hose from the control lever.

7. Disconnect the nut from the shift lever and remove the shift lever.

8. Remove the large and small bolts retaining the shifter to the extension housing. Remove the lever assembly and bushing.

9. Support the transfer case with a transmission jack. Remove the 5 bolts retaining the transfer case to the transmission and extension housing.

10. Slide the transfer case rearward off the transmission output shaft and lower the transfer case from the vehicle. Remove the gasket from between the transfer case and extension housing.

To install:

11. Install a new gasket on the front mounting face of the transfer case assembly.

12. Raise the transfer case with the transmission jack so the transmission output shaft aligns with the transfer case input shaft. Slide the transfer case forward onto the transmission output shaft and onto the dowel pin. Install the 5 retaining bolts and tighten, in sequence, to 25–43 ft. lbs. (34–58 Nm).

13. Remove the transmission jack.

14. Install and adjust the shifter. Always tighten the large bolt retaining the shifter to the extension housing before tightening the small bolt.

15. Install the vent assembly so the white marking on the hose is in position in the notch in the shifter. The upper end of the vent hose should be ¾ in. above the top of the shifter and positioned just below the floor pan.

16. Connect the speedometer driven gear to the transfer case rear cover. Tighten the screw to 20–25 inch lbs. (2.3–2.8 Nm).

17. Connect the rear driveshaft to the transfer case output shaft flange. Tighten the bolts to 61–87 ft. lbs. (83–118 Nm).

18. Connect the front driveshaft to the transfer case output shaft yoke. Tighten the bolts to 12–16 ft. lbs. (16–22 Nm).

19. Connect the 4WD indicator switch wire connector at the transfer case.

20. Install the drain plug and tighten to 14–22 ft. lbs. (19–30 Nm). Remove the fill plug and fill the transfer case with the proper type of fluid to the bottom of the fill hole. Install the fill plug and tighten to 14–22 ft. lbs. (19–30 Nm).

21. Install the damper to the transfer case, if equipped. Using new damper bolts, tighten to 25–35 ft. lbs. (34–48 Nm).

22. Install the skid plate, if equipped. Tighten the nuts and bolts to 15–20 ft. lbs. (20–27 Nm).

23. Lower the vehicle and connect the negative battery cable.

Electronic Shift Type

1. Disconnect the negative battery cable. Raise and safely support the vehicle.

2. If equipped, remove the nuts, bolts and skid plate from the frame. Remove the damper from the transfer case, if equipped.

3. Place a drain pan under the transfer case, remove the drain plug and drain the fluid.

4. Remove the wire connector from the feed wire harness at the rear of the transfer case. First squeeze the locking tabs, then pull the connectors apart.

NOTE: Do not pull directly on the wires or pull outwardly on the locking tabs.

5. Remove the connector for the transfer case motor from the mounting bracket.

6. Disconnect the front driveshaft from the transfer case ouput shaft yoke and wire the driveshaft out of the way.

7. Disconnect the rear driveshaft from the transfer case output shaft flange and wire the driveshaft out of the way.

8. Disconnect the speedometer driven gear from the transfer case rear cover. Disconnect the vent hose from the mounting bracket.

9. Support the transfer case with a transmission jack. Remove the 5 bolts retaining the transfer case to the transmission and extension housing.

10. Slide the transfer case rearward off the transmission output shaft and lower the transfer case from the vehicle. Remove the gasket from between the transfer case and extension housing.

To install:

11. Install a new gasket on the front mounting face of the transfer case assembly.

12. Raise the transfer case with the transmission jack so the transmission output shaft aligns with the transfer case input shaft. Slide the transfer case forward onto the transmission output shaft and onto the dowel pin. Install the 5 retaining bolts and tighten, in sequence, to 25–43 ft. lbs. (34–58 Nm).

13. Remove the transmission jack.

14. Install the vent hose so the white marking on the hose aligns with the notch in the mounting bracket.

15. Connect the speedometer driven gear to the transfer case rear cover. Tighten the screw to 20–25 inch lbs. (2.3–2.8 Nm).

16. Connect the rear driveshaft to the transfer case output shaft flange. Tighten the bolts to 61–87 ft. lbs. (83–118 Nm).

17. Connect the front driveshaft to the transfer case output shaft yoke. Tighten the bolts to 12–16 ft. lbs. (16–22 Nm).

18. Attach the connector for the transfer case motor to the mounting bracket.

19. Connect the wire connectors on the rear of the transfer case, making sure the retaining tabs lock.

20. Install the drain plug and tighten to 14–22 ft. lbs. (19–30 Nm). Remove the fill plug and fill the transfer case with the proper type of fluid to the bottom of the fill hole. Install the fill plug and tighten to 14–22 ft. lbs. (19–30 Nm).

21. Install the damper to the transfer case, if equipped. Using new damper bolts, tighten to 25–35 ft. lbs. (34–48 Nm).

22. Install the skid plate, if equipped. Tighten the nuts and bolts to 15–20 ft. lbs. (20–27 Nm).

23. Lower the vehicle and connect the negative battery cable.

Linkage Adjustment

MPV

NOTE: Make sure the Hi-Low lever and transfer case are in Low mode while adjusting the Hi-Low lever.

1. Shift the Hi-Low lever to the **4LO** position.
2. Remove the column covers.
3. Pull the column lever rearward, toward the driver and insert a 0.197 in. (5mm) outside diameter pin into the shift rod assembly.
4. Raise and safely support the vehicle.
5. Mark the position of the front driveshaft on the flanges and remove the front driveshaft.
6. Loosen the locknuts of the transfer case side.

Ø 5.0mm (0.197 in) O.D. PIN

Transfer case linkage adjustment—MPV

7. Remove the air intake tube.
8. Loosen the shift lever mounting bolts and adjust the clearance between the lower bracket and the shift lever bushing by sliding the shift lever assembly until there is no clearance.

Transfer case linkage adjustment—Navajo with mechanical shift transfer case

9. Tighten the shift lever mounting bolts to 12–17 ft. lbs. (16–23 Nm).

10. Install the air intake tube.

11. While pushing the outer cable toward the transfer case, turn locknut B until it touches Z surface. Tighten locknut A to 18–29 ft. lbs. (25–39 Nm) and locknut C to 25–37 ft. lbs. (34–50 Nm).

12. Install the front driveshaft, aligning the marks that were made during removal.

13. Remove the pin from the shift rod assembly and install the column covers. Check the Hi-Low lever operation.

NAVAJO

Mechanical Shift Type

1. Raise the shift boot to expose the top surface of the cam plate.

2. Loosen the bolts "A" and "B" on the control lever assembly approximately 1 turn. Move the transfer case shift lever to the **4L** position.

3. Rotate the cam plate clockwise around bolt "A" until the bottom chamfered corner of the neutral lug just contacts the forward right edge of the shift lever, point "C".

4. Hold the cam plate in this position and tighten bolt "A" first to 70–90 ft. lbs. (94–122 Nm), then tighten bolt "B" to 31–42 ft. lbs. (43–56 Nm).

5. Move the transfer case in-cab shift lever to all shift positions to check the positive engagement. There should be clearance, not exceeding 0.13 in. (3.30mm), between the shift lever and cam plate in **2H** front **4H** rear and **4L** shift positions.

6. Install the shift boot assembly.

DRIVE AXLE

Halfshaft

Removal and Installation

B SERIES PICK-UP

1. Raise and safely support the vehicle. Remove the wheel and tire assembly.

2. Remove the drive flange hub.

3. Remove the caliper, mounting support and knuckle arm. Support the caliper aside with rope or mechanics wire; do not let the caliper hang by the brake hose.

4. Disconnect the stabilizer bar and the tie rod end.

5. Remove the lower mountof the shock absorber.

6. Remove the snapring and spacer.

7. Support the lower control arm with a jack.

8. Disconnect the upper and lower ball joints and the knuckle.

9. Lower the lower control arm and remove the knuckle assembly.

10. Remove the splash shield.

11. Using a suitable prybar, pry out the halfshaft from the differential and remove the halfshaft from the vehicle. Be careful not to damage the dust cover or oil seal.

To install:

12. Install a new clip on the halfshaft. Coat the differential seal with clean transmission fluid.

13. Install the halfshaft in the differential, being careful not to damage the seal. After installation, attempt to pull the halfshaft outward to make sure it does not come out.

14. Install the knuckle and hub to the halfshaft and ball joints. Install the spacer and a new snapring.

15. Install the lower mount of the shock absorber and loosely tighten the bolt.

16. Connect the stabilizer bar and tie rod end.

17. Install the caliper assembly, knuckle arm and wheel and tire assembly. Apply sealant to the drive flange and install it.

18. Install the splash shield and lower the vehicle.

19. Tighten the lower shock absorber mount to 41–59 ft. lbs. (55–80 Nm).

20. Check the front end alignment.

MPV

1. Raise and safely support the vehicle. Remove the wheel and tire assembly.

2. Remove and discard the halfshaft locknut.

3. Disconnect the tie rod end from the knuckle.

4. Remove the caliper and brake rotor from the knuckle. Support the caliper aside with rope or mechanics wire; do not let it hang by the brake hose.

5. Remove the nut and bolts and remove the lower ball joint. Remove the bolts and nuts and remove the knuckle/hub assembly from the strut.

NOTE: If the halfshaft is stuck to the hub, install a used locknut so it is flush with the end of the shaft, then tap the nut with a soft mallet.

6. Remove the splash shield.

7. Using a suitable prybar, pry out the halfshaft from the differential and remove the halfshaft from the vehicle. Be careful not to damage the dust cover or oil seal.

To install:

8. Install a new clip on the halfshaft. Coat the differential seal with clean transmission fluid.

9. Install the halfshaft in the differential, being careful not to damage the seal. After installation, attempt to pull the halfshaft outward to make sure it does not come out.

10. Install the knuckle/hub assembly to the strut and tighten the nuts to 69–86 ft. lbs. (93–117 Nm).

11. Install the lower ball joint. Tighten the bolts to 75–101 ft. lbs. (102–137 Nm) and the nut to 115–137 ft. lbs. (157–187 Nm). Install a new cotter pin.

12. Install the brake rotor and caliper.

13. Connect the tie rod end to the knuckle.

14. Install a new locknut and tighten to 174–231 ft. lbs. (235–314 Nm). After tightening, stake the locknut using a blunt chisel.

15. Install the splash shield. Install the wheel and tire assembly and lower the vehicle.

16. Check the front end alignment.

CV-Boot

Removal and Installation

NOTE: Do not attempt to disassemble the outer CV-joint. If outer CV-boot replacement is necessary, the inner CV-joint and boot must first be removed.

INNER BOOT

1. Remove the halfshaft from the vehicle and mount it in a vise with protective jaw caps.

2. Pry up the boot band locking clips with a small prybar and remove the bands with pliers.

3. Slide the boot back on the shaft to expose the inner CV-joint.

4. Mark the CV-joint housing and cage for proper reassembly and remove the retaining clip with a small prybar. Remove the housing.

5. Mark the shaft, cage, balls and inner ring for reassembly and remove the snapring. Turn the cage about 30 degrees, remove the balls and remove the cage from the inner ring.

6. Remove the inner ring from the shaft with a press or drive it off with a hammer and brass drift.

7. Wrap the shaft splines with tape and remove the inner boot.

To install:

8. Wrap the shaft splines with tape and slide a new boot onto the shaft. Remove the tape.

NOTE: The inner and outer CV-boots are different and cannot be interchanged.

9. Install the inner ring on the shaft, aligning the marks that were made during removal.

10. Install the cage with the big end facing the snapring groove. Install the cage on the inner ring, aligning the marks made during removal and turn it 30 degrees. Install the balls into their proper positions and install a new snapring into the groove.

11. Fill the CV-joint housing with the proper quantity and type of CV-joint grease and apply the grease thoroughly to the cage, inner ring and ball assembly.

12. Align the marks and install the CV-joint housing on the shaft and install a new retaining clip.

13. Apply about 120 grams of CV-joint grease to the inside of the inner boot and slide the boot over the CV-joint. Carefully lift up the small end of the boot to release any trapped air.

14. Set the halfshaft to the required length before installing the boot bands. On B Series Pick-Up, the right side halfshaft length should be 24.49 in. (622mm) and the left side should be 21.81 in. (554mm). On MPV, the right side halfshaft length should be 22.30 in. (566.5mm) and the left side should be 19.63 in. (498.5mm).

15. Install the new CV-joint boot bands. Fold the band back by pulling the end with pliers, then lock the end of the band by bending the locking clips.

NOTE: The bands should always be mounted in the direction opposite the forward revolving direction of the halfshaft.

16. Remove the halfshaft from the vise and install it in the vehicle.

OUTER BOOT

1. Remove the halfshaft from the vehicle and mount it in a vise with protective jaw caps.

2. Remove the inner CV-boot.

3. Remove the dust cover, if equipped, using a hammer and a drift.

4. Pry up the boot band locking clips with a small prybar and remove the bands with pliers.

5. Slide the outer CV-boot off of the shaft.

To install:

6. Wrap the shaft splines with tape and slide a new boot onto the shaft. Remove the tape.

NOTE: The inner and outer CV-boots are different and cannot be interchanged.

7. Apply about 120 grams of CV-joint grease to the inside of the outer boot and slide the boot over the CV-joint. Carefully lift up the small end of the boot to release any trapped air.

8. Install new CV-joint boot bands. Fold the band back by pulling the end with pliers, then lock the end of the band by bending the locking clips.

RIGHT DRIVESHAFT

LEFT DRIVESHAFT

1. Dust cover
2. Boot protector
3. CV-joint housing
4. Clip
5. Snapring
6. Balls, inner ring and cage
7. Boot band
8. Boot
9. Clip
10. CV-joint

Halfshaft assembly exploded view – B Series Pick-Up

NOTE: **The bands should always be mounted in the direction opposite the forward revolving direction of the halfshaft.**

9. Press on a new dust cover, if equipped.
10. Install the inner CV-joint boot.
11. Install the halfshaft in the vehicle.

Driveshaft and U-Joints

Removal and Installation

1. Raise and safely support the vehicle.
2. Mark the position of the driveshaft flange on the transmission or transfer case flange and/or axle flange so the driveshaft can be reinstalled in the same position.
3. Remove the bolts/nuts, bolt/strap assemblies or U-bolt/nut assemblies attaching the driveshaft to the transmission or transfer case flange and/or axle flange.
4. If equipped with a center bearing support, remove the support attaching nuts.
5. If equipped with a double-offset joint, push a rag into the joint to hold the driveshaft straight and prevent damaging the boot.
6. Remove the driveshaft assembly. If equipped with a splined yoke, pull the driveshaft out until the yoke clears the extension housing or transfer case, then install a suitable plug to prevent fluid leakage.
7. Inspect the universal joints for binding, excessive looseness or other damage. If equipped, inspect the splined yoke for wear or other damage.
To install:
8. If equipped with a splined yoke, lubricate the splines with Molybdenum grease and remove the plug from the extension housing or transfer case. During installation, do not allow the yoke to bottom on the output shaft with excessive force.
9. Raise the driveshaft into position. Install the yoke on the output shaft or align the flange marks that were made during removal, as required.
10. Install the bolts/nuts, bolt/strap assemblies or U-bolt/nut assemblies attaching the driveshaft to the transmission or transfer case flange and/or axle flange. Tighten the bolts/nuts, if equipped, to 36–43 ft. lbs. (49–59 Nm) on all except Navajo. On Navajo, tighten the axle flange bolts to 70–95 ft. lbs. (95–129 Nm) and the transfer case bolts to 12–16 ft. lbs. (17–22 Nm).
11. On Navajo, if equipped with bolt/strap assemblies, tighten the bolts to 10–15 ft. lbs. (14–20 Nm). If equipped with U-bolt/nut assemblies, tighten the nuts to 8–15 ft. lbs. (11–20 Nm).
12. If equipped with a center bearing support, install and tighten the nuts or bolts to 27–39 ft. lbs. (36–53 Nm).
13. Lower the vehicle and road test for proper operation.

Front Axle Shaft, Bearing And Seal

Removal and Installation

NAVAJO

1. Raise and safely support the vehicle. Remove the front wheel and tire assemblies.
2. Remove the disc brake caliper and wire it to the frame. Do not let the caliper hang by the brake hose.
3. Remove the hub locks, wheel bearings and locknuts.
4. Remove the hub, rotor and outer wheel bearing.
5. Remove the grease seal from the rotor with a seal removal tool. Remove the inner wheel bearing.
6. If the wheel bearings are to be replaced, remove the inner and outer bearing races with a suitable puller or a hammer and brass drift.
7. Remove the nuts retaining the spindle to the steering knuckle. Tap the spindle with a plastic hammer to jar the spindle from the knuckle. Remove the splash shield.

8. On the left side of the vehicle, remove the shaft and joint assembly by pulling the assembly out of the carrier. On the right side of the carrier, remove and discard the clamp from the shaft and joint assembly and the stub shaft. Pull the shaft and joint assembly from the splines of the stub shaft.
9. If required, remove the oil seal and needle bearing from the spindle. If necessary, remove the slinger from the shaft by driving it off with a hammer.
To install:
10. If removed, install a new bearing and seal in the spindle and/or press on a new shaft slinger.
11. On the right side of the carrier, install the rubber boot and new keystone clamps on the stub shaft slip yoke. Slide the right shaft and joint assembly into the slip yoke making sure the splines are fully engaged. Slide the boot over the assembly and crimp the keystone clamp using suitable pliers.

NOTE: **Make sure the yoke ears are in phase (in line) during assembly.**

12. On the left side of the carrier, slide the shaft and joint assembly through the knuckle and engage the splines on the shaft in the carrier.
13. Install the splash shield and spindle onto the steering knuckle. Install and tighten the spindle nuts to 45 ft. lbs. (61 Nm).
14. If removed, drive the bearing races into the rotor using a suitable driver. Pack the inner and outer wheel bearings and the lip of a new seal with high-temperature wheel bearing grease.
15. Position the inner wheel bearing in the race and install the seal using a seal installer. Install the rotor on the spindle and install the outer wheel bearing in the race.
16. Install the wheel bearing, locknut, thrust bearing, snapring and locking hubs.
17. Install the caliper and the wheel and tire assemblies. Lower the vehicle.

Rear Axle Shaft, Bearing and Seal

Removal and Installation

B SERIES PICK-UP

1. Raise and safely support the vehicle. Remove the wheel and tire assembly.
2. Remove the brake drum and the brake shoes.
3. Disconnect the parking brake cable from the brake backing plate. Disconnect and plug the brake line at the wheel cylinder.
4. Remove the axle shaft/backing plate assembly from the axle housing, then pry out the axle seal. On 4WD vehicles, remove the O-ring from the axle housing.
5. Install the axle shaft in a vise, attached at the axle flange. Remove the lockwasher and the bearing locknut.

NOTE: **Left side axles have left-hand thread; remove by turning clockwise.**

6. Reposition the axle shaft in the vise so the jaws grip the shaft. Use protective jaw caps on the vise to protect the axle shaft.
7. Use a suitable puller to remove the bearing and bearing housing.
8. Remove the bearing and seal from the hub, then remove the outer bearing race using a suitable drift.
9. Clean all components and inspect for wear and/or damage. Replace as necessary. If bearing replacement is necessary, the bearing races must also be replaced.
To install:
10. Press in a new seal and inner race, using suitable drivers. Liberally apply high temperature wheel bearing grease to the area of the race and seal.
11. Using a suitable seal installer, tap a new seal into the axle housing until it is flush with the end of the housing. Coat the seal lip with grease.

12. Install the spacer on the axle shaft and position the axle shaft and backing plate in a press. Using suitable press tools, press the wheel bearing onto the axle shaft.

NOTE: The standard press-fit force should be 30,379–44,121 lbs. If the force is too high or too low, replace the bearing collar or shaft.

13. Position the axle shaft in a vise, attached at the axle flange. Install the bearing locknut and a new lockwasher. Tighten the locknut to 145–217 ft. lbs. (196–294 Nm). Align the lockwasher craws to the locknut notches and crimp the lockwasher.

14. Install a new O-ring in the axle housing, if removed. Install the axle shaft assembly, being careful not to damage the axle seal. Adjust the wheel bearing play as follows:

   a. There can only be 1 axle shaft installed in the housing during the adjustment procedure. If only 1 shaft was removed, remove the other shaft at this time. If both shafts were removed, leave the other shaft out of the axle housing for now.

   b. Attach a dial indicator to the backing plate and place the indicator foot on the end of the axle shaft.

   c. Check the axle shaft endplay; it should be 0.026–0.037 in. (0.65–0.95mm).

   d. If the bearing play is not within specification, remove the axle and install shims which are available from Mazda.

   e. If both axle shafts were removed, at this time, remove the axle shaft that has been adjusted and install and adjust the bearing play of the other shaft.

15. Install the backing plate mounting nuts and tighten to 72–87 ft. lbs. (98–118 Nm).

16. Connect the brake line and the parking brake cable.

17. Install the brake shoes and the brake drum.

18. Install the wheel and tire assembly. Bleed the brakes and lower the vehicle.

MPV

1. Raise and safely support the vehicle. Remove the wheel and tire assembly.

2. Remove the brake drum and the brake shoes.

3. Disconnect the parking brake cable from the brake backing plate. Disconnect and plug the brake line at the wheel cylinder.

4. Remove the axle shaft/backing plate assembly using a slide hammer. Remove the axle seal using a prybar.

5. Remove and discard the retaining ring from the axle shaft.

6. Using a suitable grinder, grind a section of the bearing collar until only approximately 0.0197 in. (0.5mm) remains. Be careful not to damage the axle shaft.

7. Cut the bearing collar with a chisel at the ground section and remove the bearing collar.

8. Use a suitable bearing puller to remove the bearing from the shaft. Remove the seal.

To install:

9. Apply grease to the lip of a new seal and install on the backing plate.

10. Install a new bearing over the axle shaft. Make sure there is no oil or grease on the new collar or axle shaft, then install the collar on the axle shaft.

11. Position the axle shaft/backing plate assembly in a press and press the bearing and collar onto the axle shaft.

NOTE: If the press-fit force of the collar is 5952 lbs. (2.7 tons) or less, replace the collar or the axle shaft.

12. Apply grease to the lip of a new axle seal and install the seal into the axle housing, using a suitable seal installer.

13. Install the axle shaft/backing plate assembly in the axle housing, being careful not to damage the axle seal. Install the backing plate nuts and tighten to 72–87 ft. lbs. (98–118 Nm).

14. Connect the brake line and the parking brake cable.

15. Install the brake shoes and the brake drum.

16. Install the wheel and tire assembly. Bleed the brakes and lower the vehicle.

NAVAJO

1. Raise and safely support the vehicle.

2. Remove the rear wheel and tire assemblies and the brake drums.

3. Clean all dirt from the carrier cover area. Position a drain pan under the carrier, remove the cover and drain the rear axle.

4. Remove the differential pinion shaft lock bolt and pinion shaft.

5. Push the flanged end of the axle shafts toward the center of the vehicle and remove the C-lock from the button end of the axle shaft. Be careful not to lose or damage the rubber O-ring which is in the axle shaft groove under the C-lock.

6. Remove the axle shaft from the housing.

7. Reinstall the pinion shaft and lock bolt to ensure the pinion gears remain in place.

8. Using bearing remover 49 UN01 033 or equivalent and a suitable slide hammer, remove the axle bearing and seal as a unit.

To install:

9. Lubricate a new bearing with rear axle lubricant and install in the housing bore using a suitable driver.

10. Apply grease to the lips of a new axle seal and install, using a seal installer.

11. Remove the pinion shaft lock bolt and pinion shaft.

12. Slide the axle shaft into the axle housing, being careful not to damage the seal or axle bearing. Start the splines into the side gear and push until the button end of the axle shaft can be seen in the differential case.

13. Install the C-lock on the button end of the axle shaft, then pull the shaft outboard until the shaft splines engage and the C-lock seats in the counterbore of the differential side gear. Make sure the O-ring is in the groove at the button end of the axle shaft before installing the C-lock.

14. Slide the pinion shaft through the case and pinion gears, aligning the hole in the shaft with the lock bolt hole. Apply stud and bearing mount compound and install the lock bolt. Tighten to 15–30 ft. lbs. (20–40 Nm).

15. Clean all old sealer from the carrier surface. Apply a bead of RTV sealer ⅛–¼ in. wide. The bead should be continuous and should not pass through or outside the holes.

16. Install a new cover and new bolts. Tighten the bolts to 15–20 ft. lbs. (21–27 Nm). Fill the carrier with the proper type and quantity of fluid.

17. Install the brake drums and the wheel and tire assemblies. Lower the vehicle.

Front Wheel Hub, Knuckle/Spindle and Bearings

Removal and Installation

B SERIES PICK-UP

1. Raise and safely support the vehicle. Remove the wheel and tire assembly.

2. Remove the drive flange.

3. Remove the brake caliper. Support the caliper aside with rope or mechanics wire; do not let the caliper hang by the brake hose.

4. Remove the snapring and spacer. Remove the set bolts and bearing set plate.

5. Remove the bearing locknut using a suitable removal tool. Remove the hub and rotor without letting the washer and bearing fall.

6. Remove the dust cover.

7. Disconnect the tie rod end from the knuckle. Disconnect the stabilizer bar and the lower shock mount.

8. Support the lower control arm with a jack. Remove the lower ball joint nut and separate the knuckle from the lower arm using a suitable tool.

9. Remove the upper ball joint nut and separate the knuckle from the lower arm using a suitable tool.

10. Lower the lower control arm and remove the knuckle.

11. Inspect the knuckle, hub and bearings for wear and or damage. Replace components, as necessary.

12. Remove the oil seal and the bearing inner race from the knuckle. Using a suitable drift, remove the bearing outer race by tapping lightly with a hammer.

13. Using a slide hammer, remove the needle bearing from the knuckle.

14. Mark the position of the disc brake rotor on the hub, then remove the bolts and disassemble the rotor and hub.

15. Remove the oil seal and the bearing inner race from the hub. Using a suitable drift, remove the bearing outer race by tapping lightly with a hammer.

To install:

16. Press a new needle bearing into the knuckle using a suitable driver.

17. After installing the inner bearing into the knuckle, press in a new oil seal. Apply wheel bearing grease to the oil seal lip.

18. Press fit the outer side bearing outer race, then the inner side bearing outer race, into the hub using suitable drivers. Press in a new oil seal until it is flush with the hub end surface. Apply wheel bearing grease to the seal lip.

19. Align the matching marks of the hub and brake rotor and tighten the mounting bolts to 40–51 ft. lbs. (54–69 Nm).

20. Liberally apply high temperature wheel bearing grease to the inside of the hub. Install the outer bearing race and washer in the hub.

21. Insert the halfshaft into the knuckle and install the nut for the lower ball joint. Tighten the nut by hand.

22. Raise the lower control arm with the jack until the upper ball joint is connected to the knuckle. Install the nut and tighten by hand.

23. Tighten the upper ball joint nut to 22–38 ft. lbs. (29–51

Nm) and the lower ball joint nut to 87–116 ft. lbs. (118–157 Nm). Install new cotter pins.

24. Connect the tie rod end to the knuckle, tighten the nut to 23–43 ft. lbs. (44–59 Nm) and install a new cotter pin.

25. Install the dust cover to the knuckle and tighten to 14–19 ft. lbs. (19–26 Nm).

26. After loosely installing the lower shock absorber mount, install the stabilizer bar.

27. Install the hub and rotor assembly, then adjust the bearing preload as follows:

a. Tighten the locknut, then turn the hub and rotor 2–3 times to seat the bearing.

b. Loosen the locknut so they can be turned by hand.

c. Attach a suitable pull scale to a wheel lug bolt and measure the frictional forces. The preload is the frictional force plus 1.3–2.6 lbs.

d. Tighten the locknut until the preload is as specified.

e. Install the bearing set plate using 2 bolts. Tighten the bolts to 43–61 inch lbs. (5–7 Nm).

f. Coat the spacer with grease and install it. Install a new snapring.

28. Install the caliper, wheel and tire assembly and drive flange. Lower the vehicle.

29. Tighten the lower shock mount to 41–59 ft. lbs. (55–80 Nm) with the vehicle unloaded.

30. Check the front end alignment.

MPV

1. Raise and safely support the vehicle. Remove the wheel and tire assembly.

2. Remove and discard the locknut from the end of the halfshaft.

3. Remove the brake caliper and disc brake rotor. Support the caliper aside with rope or mechanics wire; do not let the caliper hang by the brake hose.

1. Freewheel hub bolts
2. Snapring
3. Spacer
4. Bearing set plate
5. Locknut
6. Bearing
7. Hub assembly
8. Bearing
9. Oil seal
10. Rotor
11. Dust cover
12. Knuckle
13. Needle bearing
14. Halfshaft

Front hub, knuckle and bearing assembly—4WD B Series Pick-Up

4. Remove the cotter pin and nut and, using a suitable tool, disconnect the tie rod end from the knuckle.

5. Remove the cotter pin and loosen the lower ball joint nut. Separate the lower arm from the knuckle using a suitable tool.

6. Remove the knuckle-to-strut bolts and nuts and remove the knuckle/hub assembly from the vehicle.

7. Pry out the inner oil seal from the knuckle.

8. Position the knuckle/hub assembly in a press and, using a suitable driver, press the hub from the knuckle.

NOTE: If the inner bearing race remains on the hub, position the hub in a vise, secured by the flange. Move the race away from the hub using a hammer and chisel, then position the hub in a press and press the race off of the hub.

9. Pry out the outer oil seal from the knuckle.

10. Remove the retaining ring and position the knuckle in a press. Using a suitable driver, press the wheel bearing from the knuckle.

11. If necessary, mark the position of the dust shield on the knuckle and remove the dust shield, using a hammer and chisel. Do not reuse the dust cover, if removed.

To install:

12. If the dust cover was removed, mark the new cover in the same place as the old was marked during removal. Align the cover and knuckle marks and press the cover onto the knuckle.

13. Press a new wheel bearing into the knuckle, using a suitable driver. Install the retaining ring and a new outer seal. Apply grease to the seal lip.

14. Press the hub into the knuckle, using a suitable driver. Install a new inner seal and lubricate the seal lip with grease.

15. Install the knuckle/hub assembly onto the strut, install the bolts and nuts and tighten to 69–86 ft. lbs. (93–117 Nm).

16. Install the lower ball joint into the knuckle and tighten the nut to 115–137 ft. lbs. (157–187 Nm). Install a new cotter pin.

17. Connect the tie rod to the knuckle and install the nut.

Tighten to 43–58 ft. lbs. (59–78 Nm) and install a new cotter pin.

18. Install the brake rotor and caliper.

19. Install a new locknut on the end of the halfshaft and tighten to 174–231 ft. lbs. (235–314 Nm). After tightening, stake the nut with a blunt chisel.

20. Install the wheel and tire assembly and lower the vehicle. Check the front end alignment.

NAVAJO

1. Raise and safely support the vehicle. Remove the front wheel and tire assemblies.

2. Remove the disc brake caliper and wire it to the frame. Do not let the caliper hang by the brake hose.

3. Remove the hub locks, wheel bearings and locknuts.

4. Remove the hub, rotor and outer wheel bearing.

5. Remove the grease seal from the rotor with a seal removal tool. Remove the inner wheel bearing.

6. If the wheel bearings are to be replaced, remove the inner and outer bearing races with a suitable puller or a hammer and brass drift.

7. Remove the nuts retaining the spindle to the steering knuckle. Tap the spindle with a plastic hammer to jar the spindle from the knuckle. Remove the splash shield.

8. On the left side of the vehicle, remove the shaft and joint assembly by pulling the assembly out of the carrier. On the right side of the carrier, remove and discard the clamp from the shaft and joint assembly and the stub shaft. Pull the shaft and joint assembly from the splines of the stub shaft.

9. Place the spindle in a vise on the second step of the spindle. Wrap a shop towel around the spindle or use a brass-jawed vise to protect the spindle.

10. Remove the oil seal and needle bearing from the spindle with a slide hammer and seal remover TOOL-1175-AC or equivalent. If necessary, remove the slinger from the shaft by driving off with a hammer.

Front wheel hub, knuckle and bearing assembly – 4WD MPV

11. Remove the cotter pin from the tie rod nut and then remove the nut. Tap on the tie rod stud to free it from the steering arm.

12. Remove the upper ball joint snapring and remove the upper ball joint pinch bolt. Loosen the lower ball joint nut to the end of the stud.

13. Strike the inside of the knuckle near the upper and lower ball joints to break the knuckle loose from the ball joint studs.

14. Remove the camber adjuster sleeve. Note the position of the slot in the camber adjuster so it can be reinstalled in the same position during assembly.

15. Remove the lower ball joint nut. Place the knuckle in a vise and remove the snapring from the bottom ball joint socket, if equipped.

16. Assemble C-frame T74P–4635–C and ball joint remover T83T–3050–A or equivalents on the lower ball joint. Turn the forcing screw clockwise until the lower ball joint is removed from the steering knuckle.

17. Assemble the C-frame and ball joint remover on the upper ball joint and remove in the same manner.

NOTE: Always remove the lower ball joint first.

To install:

18. Clean the steering knuckle bore and insert the lower ball joint in the knuckle as straight as possible.

19. Assemble C-frame T74P–4635–C, ball joint installer T83T–3050–A and receiver cup T80T–3010–A3 or equivalents to install the lower ball joint. Turn the forcing screw clockwise until the lower ball joint is firmly seated. Install the snapring on the lower ball joint.

NOTE: The lower ball joint must always be installed first.

Front axle shaft, hub, knuckle and bearing assembly—Navajo

20. Assemble the C-frame, ball joint installer and receiver cup to install the upper ball joint. Turn the forcing screw clockwise until the ball joint is firmly seated.

21. Install the camber adjuster into the support arm, making sure the slot is in the original position.

NOTE: The torque sequence in Steps 22 and 23 must be followed exactly when securing the knuckle. Excessive knuckle turning effort may result in reduced steering returnability if this procedure is not followed.

22. Install a new nut on the bottom ball joint stud. Tighten the nut to 90 ft. lbs. (122 Nm) minimum, then tighten to align the next slot in the nut with the hole in the stud. Install a new cotter pin.

23. Install the snapring on the upper ball joint stud. Install the upper ball joint pinch bolt and tighten to 48–65 ft. lbs. (65–88 Nm).

NOTE: The camber adjuster will seat itself into the knuckle at a predetermined position during the tightening sequence. Do not attempt to adjust this position.

24. Clean all dirt and grease from the spindle bearing bore. The bearing bores must be free from nicks and burrs.

25. Place the bearing in the bore with the manufacturers identification facing outward. Drive the bearing into the bore using spindle bearing replacer T80T–4000–S and driver handle T80T–4000–W or equivalents.

26. Install the grease seal in the bearing bore with the lip side of the seal facing towards the tool. Drive the seal in the bore using the same tools as in Step 25. Coat the bearing seal lip with high-temperature lubricant.

27. If removed, press on a new shaft slinger.

28. On the right side of the carrier, install the rubber boot and new keystone clamps on the stub shaft slip yoke. Slide the right shaft and joint assembly into the slip yoke making sure the splines are fully engaged. Slide the boot over the assembly and crimp the keystone clamp using suitable pliers.

NOTE: The Dana model 35 axle does not have a blind spline, therefore pay special attention to make sure the yoke ears are in phase (in line) during assembly.

29. On the left side of the carrier, slide the shaft and joint assembly through the knuckle and engage the splines on the shaft in the carrier.

30. Install the splash shield and spindle onto the steering knuckle. Install and tighten the spindle nuts to 45 ft. lbs. (61 Nm).

31. If removed, drive the bearing races into the rotor using a suitable driver. Pack the inner and outer wheel bearings and the lip of a new seal with high-temperature wheel bearing grease.

32. Position the inner wheel bearing in the race and install the seal using a seal installer. Install the rotor on the spindle and install the outer wheel bearing in the race.

33. Install the wheel bearing, locknut, thrust bearing, snapring and locking hubs.

34. Install the caliper and the wheel and tire assemblies. Lower the vehicle.

Manual Locking Hubs

Removal and Installation

1988 B SERIES PICK-UP

1. Raise and safely support the vehicle. Remove the wheel and tire assembly.
2. Set the locking hub in the **FREE** position.
3. Remove the locking hub mounting bolts and remove the locking hub.
4. With the hub removed, install 2 bolts and nuts opposite each other to hold the hub together.

5. Check for smooth turning of the control handle.
6. Check for smooth rotation of the inner hub with the control lever in the **FREE** position.
7. Check for no rotation of the inner hub with the control lever in the **LOCK** position.

To install:
8. Coat the surface of the hub with sealant.
9. Place the control lever in the **FREE** position.
10. Install the hub on the vehicle and tighten the bolts to 22–25 ft. lbs. (29–34 Nm).
11. Install the wheel and tire assembly and check the operation of the hub. Lower the vehicle.

NAVAJO

1. Raise and support the vehicle safely.
2. Remove the lug nuts and remove the wheel and tire assembly.
3. Remove the retainer washers from the lug nut studs and remove the manual locking hub assembly. To remove the internal hub lock assembly from the outer body assembly, remove the outer lock ring seated in the hub body groove. The internal assembly, spring and clutch gear will now slide out of the hub body. Do not remove the screw from the plastic dial.
4. Rebuild the hub assembly in the reverse order of disassembly.
5. Adjust the wheel bearing if necessary. Install the manual locking hub assembly over the spindle and place the retainer washers on the lug nut studs.
6. Install the wheel and tire assembly and lower the vehicle.

Adjustment

NAVAJO

1. Raise and safely support the vehicle. Remove the wheel and tire assembly.
2. Remove the retainer washers from the lug nut studs and remove the manual locking hub assembly from the spindle.
3. Remove the snapring from the end of the spindle shaft.
4. Remove the axle shaft spacer.
5. Remove the outer wheel bearing locknut from the spindle using locknut wrench 49 UN01 042 or equivalent. Make sure the tabs on the tool engage the slots in the locknut.
6. Remove the locknut washer from the spindle.
7. Loosen the inner wheel bearing locknut using the locknut wrench. Make sure the tabs on the tool engage the slots in the locknut and the slot in the tool is centered over the locknut pin.
8. Tighten the inner locknut to 35 ft. lbs. (47 Nm) to seat the bearings.
9. Spin the rotor and back off the inner locknut ¼ turn. Retighten the inner locknut to 16 inch lbs. (1.8 Nm). Install the lockwasher on the spindle. It may be necessary to tighten the inner locknut slightly so the pin on the locknut aligns with the closest hole in the lockwasher.
10. Install the outer wheel bearing locknut using the locknut wrench. Tighten the locknut to 150 ft. lbs. (203 Nm).
11. Install the axle shaft spacer.
12. Clip the snapring onto the end of the spindle. Install the manual hub assembly over the spindle and install the retainer washers.
13. Install the wheel and tire assembly. Check the endplay of the wheel and tire assembly on the spindle. Final endplay should be 0–0.003 in. (0–0.08mm). The maximum torque to rotate the hub should be 25 inch lbs. (2.8 Nm).
14. Lower the vehicle.

Automatic Locking Hubs

Removal and Installation

NAVAJO

1. Raise and support the vehicle safely. Remove the wheel lug nuts and remove the wheel and tire assembly.

Manual locking hub assembly—Navajo

2. Remove the retainer washers from the lug nut studs and remove the automatic locking hub assembly from the spindle.

3. Remove the snapring from the end of the spindle shaft.

4. Remove the axle shaft spacer.

5. Being careful not to damage the plastic moving cam or thrust spacers, pull the cam assembly off the wheel bearing adjusting nut. Remove the 2 plastic thrust spacers from the adjusting nut.

6. Using a magnet, remove the locking key. It may be necessary to rotate the adjusting nut slightly to relieve the pressure against the locking key, before the key can be removed.

NOTE: To prevent damage to the spindle threads, look into the spindle keyway under the adjusting nut and remove the separate locking key before removing the adjusting nut.

7. Loosen the wheel bearing adjusting nut from the spindle using a $2\frac{3}{8}$ in. hex socket tool.

8. While rotating the hub and rotor assembly, tighten the wheel bearing adjusting nut to 35 ft. lbs. (47 Nm) to seat the bearings. Spin the rotor and back off the nut $\frac{1}{4}$ turn.

9. Retighten the adjusting nut to 16 inch lbs. (1.8 Nm) using a torque wrench. Align the closest hole in the wheel bearing adjusting nut with the center of the spindle keyway slot. Advance the nut to the next lug if required. Install the separate locking key in the spindle keyway under the adjusting nut.

NOTE: Extreme care must be taken when aligning the spindle nut adjustment lug with the center of the spindle keyway slot to prevent damage to the separate locking key.

10. Install the 2 thrust spacers. Push or press the cam assembly onto the locknut by lining up the key in the fixed cam with the spindle keyway.

NOTE: Extreme care must be taken when aligning the fixed cam key with the spindle keyway to prevent damage to the fixed cam.

11. Install the axle shaft spacer.

12. Clip the snapring onto the end of the spindle.

13. Install the automatic locking hub assembly over the spindle by lining up the 3 legs in the hub assembly with the 3 pockets in the cam assembly. Install the retainer washers.

14. Install the wheel and tire assembly. Check the endplay of the wheel and tire assembly on the spindle. Final endplay should be 0–0.003 in. (0–0.08mm). The maximum torque to rotate the hub should be 25 inch lbs. (2.8 Nm).

15. Lower the vehicle.

Freewheel Mechanism

Removal and Installation

NOTE: The Remote Freewheel Mechanism on 1989–92 4WD B Series Pick-Up and the Automatic Freewheel Mechanism on 1990–92 4WD MPV are used in place of automatic locking hubs.

1. Disconnect the negative battery cable. Raise and safely support the vehicle. Remove the left front wheel and tire assembly.

2. Drain the fluid from the front differential.

Automatic locking hub assembly—Navajo

17–20 FT. LBS. (23–26 NM)

REPLACE

27–40 FT. LBS. (36–54 NM)

27–40 FT. LBS. (36–54 NM)

1. Halfshaft
2. Vacuum hose
3. Electrical connector
4. Snap pin
5. Joint shaft assembly
6. Control box assembly
7. Gear sleeve
8. Output shaft

Remote Freewheel Mechanism Installation—4WD B Series Pick-Up; MPV similar

3. Remove the left side halfshaft assembly.

4. Tag and disconnect the vacuum hoses and electrical connector from the control box assembly.

5. Remove and discard the snap pin at the control box assembly.

6. Remove the attaching bolts and remove the joint shaft assembly.

7. Remove the attaching bolts and remove the control box assembly.

8. Remove the gear sleeve from the side of the differential, if necessary.

9. If necessary, remove the output shaft from the differential using a slide hammer.

To install:

10. If removed, install a new clip on the end of the output shaft and install in the differential. Install the gear sleeve, if removed.

11. Install the control box and tighten the attaching bolts to 17–20 ft. lbs. (23–26 Nm).

12. Install the joint shaft assembly and tighten the attaching bolts to 27–40 ft. lbs. (36–54 Nm). On MPV, install the attaching nut and tighten to 49–72 ft. lbs. (67–97 Nm).

13. Install a new snap pin at the control box assembly.

14. Connect the electrical connector and vacuum hoses at the control box assembly.

15. Install the left side halfshaft assembly.

16. Fill the differential with the proper type and quantity of fluid.

17. Install the wheel and tire assembly and lower the vehicle.

Pinion Seal

Removal and Installation

NOTE: This service procedure disturbs the pinion bearing preload and this preload must be carefully reset when assembling.

1. Raise the vehicle and support it safely.

2. Remove the wheels and the brake drums.

3. Mark the driveshaft and the axle companion flange so the driveshaft can be reinstalled in the same position. Remove the driveshaft.

4. Using an inch pound torque wrench on the pinion nut, record the torque required to maintain rotation of the pinion through several revolutions.

5. While holding the companion flange with a suitable tool, remove the pinion nut. Mark the companion flange in relation to the pinion shaft so the flange can be reinstalled in the same position.

6. Using a suitable puller, remove the rear axle companion flange. Use a small prybar to remove the seal from the carrier.

To install:

7. Make sure the splines of the pinion shaft are free of burrs.

8. Apply grease to the lips of the pinion seal and install, using a seal installer.

9. Check the seal surface of the companion flange for scratches, nicks or a groove. Replace the companion flange, as necessary. Apply a small amount of lubricant to the splines. Align the mark on the flange with the mark on the pinion shaft and install the companion flange.

NOTE: The companion flange must never be hammered on or installed with power tools.

10. Install a new nut on the pinion shaft. Hold the companion flange with a suitable tool while tightening the nut.

11. Tighten the pinion nut, rotating the pinion occasionally to ensure proper bearing seating. Take frequent pinion bearing torque preload readings until the original recorded preload reading is obtained.

NOTE: Under no circumstances should the pinion nut be backed off to reduce preload. If reduced preload is re-

quired, a new collapsible pinion spacer and pinion nut must be installed.

12. Install the driveshaft and check the fluid level in the carrier. Lower the vehicle.

Differential Carrier

Removal and Installation

FRONT

B Series Pick-Up

NOTE: On 1989–92 vehicles, the differential is removed as a unit with the freewheel mechanism. After removal, the differential can then be separated from the freewheel mechanism, if necessary.

1. Raise and safely support the vehicle. Remove the wheel and tire assemblies.
2. Remove the splash shield and drain the differential fluid.
3. Remove the halfshafts.
4. Mark the position of the driveshaft on the axle flange and remove the driveshaft.
5. On 1989–92 vehicles, tag and disconnect the vacuum hoses and electrical connector from the freewheel mechanism control box.
6. Support the differential with a jack.
7. Remove the crossmember bolts adjacent to the lower control arm. Lower the differential/crossmembers assembly from the vehicle.
8. Remove the crossmembers from the differential, if necessary. On 1989–92 vehicles, remove the freewheel mechanism from the differential, if necessary.
To install:
9. If removed, install the freewheel mechanism.
10. If removed, install the differential to the crossmembers.
11. Raise the differential/crossmembers assembly into position. Install the crossmember mounting bolts and tighten to 69–85 ft. lbs. (93–116 Nm). Remove the jack.
12. Install the remaining components in the reverse order of their removal. Fill the differential with the proper type and quantity of fluid.

MPV

NOTE: The differential is removed as a unit with the freewheel mechanism. After removal, the differential can then be separated from the freewheel mechanism, if necessary.

1. Raise and safely support the vehicle. Remove the wheel and tire assemblies.
2. Remove the splash shield and drain the differential fluid.
3. Remove the halfshafts.
4. Mark the position of the driveshaft on the axle flange and remove the driveshaft.
5. Tag and disconnect the vacuum hoses and electrical connector from the freewheel mechanism control box.
6. Support the differential with a jack.
7. Remove the bolts/nuts attaching the differential/freewheel mechanism assembly in 3 places and lower the assembly from the vehicle.
8. If necessary, separate the freewheel mechanism from the differential.
To install:
9. If removed, install the freewheel mechanism.
10. Raise the differential/freewheel mechanism assembly into position and install the attaching bolts/nuts. Tighten to 49–72 ft. lbs. (67–97 Nm). Remove the jack.
11. Install the remaining components in the reverse order of their removal. Fill the differential with the proper type and quantity of fluid.

REAR

1. Raise and safely support the vehicle. Remove the wheel and tire assemblies.
2. Drain the fluid from the differential.
3. Remove the axle shafts.
4. Mark the position of the driveshaft on the axle flange and remove the driveshaft.
5. Disconnect the rear wheel anti-lock brake sensor, if equipped.
6. Remove the differential attaching nuts/bolts and remove the differential.
To install:
7. Clean all old sealant from the axle housing and differential mating surfaces.
8. Apply sealant to the stud threads and the differential and axle housing surfaces.
9. Install the differential to the axle housing. Tighten the attaching nuts/bolts to 17–20 ft. lbs. (23–26 Nm)
10. Install the remaining components in the reverse order of removal. Fill the differential with the proper type and quantity of fluid.

Axle Housing

Removal and Installation

FRONT

Navajo

1. Raise and safely support the vehicle. Remove the front axle shaft and spindle assemblies.
2. Mark the front axle yoke and the driveshaft so they can be reassembled in the same position. Disconnect the driveshaft from the front axle yoke.
3. Remove the cotter pin and nut retaining the steering linkage to the knuckle. Disconnect the linkage from the knuckle.
4. Remove the left stabilizer bar link lower bolt and remove the link from the radius arm bracket.
5. Position a jack under the left axle arm and slightly compress the coil spring. Remove the shock absorber lower nut and disconnect the shock absorber from the radius arm bracket.
6. Remove the nut that retains the lower part of the spring to the axle arm. Slowly lower the jack and remove the coil spring, spacer, seat and stud.
7. Remove the stud and bolts that connect the radius arm bracket and radius arm to the axle arm. Remove the bracket and radius arm.
8. Position another jack under the differential housing. Remove the bolt that connects the left axle arm to the axle pivot bracket. Lower the jacks and remove the left axle arm assembly.
To install:
9. Position a jack under the left support arm and raise the arm into position in the pivot bracket. Install the nut and bolt and tighten to 120–150 ft. lbs. (163–203 Nm). Do not remove the jack from under the differential housing at this time.
10. Position the radius arm and front bracket on the left axle arm. Install a new stud and nut on the top of the axle and radius arm assembly and tighten to 190–230 ft. lbs. (258–311 Nm). Install the bolts in the front of the bracket and tighten to 27–37 ft. lbs. (37–50 Nm).
11. Install the seat, spacer retainer and coil spring on the stud and nut. Raise the jack to compress the coil spring. Install the nut and tighten to 70–100 ft. lbs. (95–135 Nm).
12. Connect the shock absorber to the radius arm. Install the nut and tighten to 42–72 ft. lbs. (57–97 Nm).
13. Connect the tie rod ball joint to the knuckle. Install the nut and tighten to 50–75 ft. lbs. (68–101 Nm). Install the stabilizer bar mounting bracket and tighten to 203–240 ft. lbs. (275–325 Nm).
14. Connect the front driveshaft to the front axle yoke, align-

ing the marks that were made during removal. Install the U-bolts and tighten the nuts to 8–15 ft. lbs. (11–20 Nm).

15. Install the spindle and axle shaft assemblies. Lower the vehicle.

REAR

2WD B Series Pick-Up

1. Raise and safely support the vehicle. Remove the rear wheel and tire assemblies.
2. Remove the brake drums and brake shoes. Disconnect the parking brake cables from the backing plate.
3. Mark the position of the driveshaft on the axle flange and remove the driveshaft.
4. Disconnect and plug the flexible brake hose at the axle housing or chassis.
5. Disconnect the rear wheel anti-lock brake sensor, if equipped.
6. Support the axle housing with a jack.
7. Disconnect the shock absorbers at the spring clamp.
8. Remove the nuts from the U-bolts and remove the U-bolts and spring clamp.
9. While supporting the axle housing with the jack, move the axle housing to 1 side of the vehicle until the axle flange clears the leaf spring.
10. Tilt the axle housing downward and move it to the other side of the vehicle while lowering the jack. Lower the axle housing completely when the other axle flange clears the leaf spring.
To install:
11. Raise the axle housing to just below the leaf springs.
12. Move the axle housing to 1 side of the vehicle until the axle flange will clear the leaf spring, then tilt the axle housing upward and raise it until 1 side of the axle housing is over the leaf spring.
13. Move the axle housing to the opposite side of the vehicle and raise it until the other side of the housing is above the leaf spring. Move the housing into position on the leaf springs.
14. Install the spring clamps, U-bolts and nuts. Tighten the nuts to 47–58 ft. lbs. (64–78 Nm).
15. Connect the shock absorbers to the spring clamp and tighten the nuts to 47–58 ft. lbs. (64–78 Nm). Remove the jack.
16. Install the remaining components in the reverse order of removal. Bleed the brake system.

4WD B Series Pick-Up

1. Raise and safely support the vehicle. Remove the rear wheel and tire assemblies.
2. Remove the brake drums and brake shoes. Disconnect the parking brake cables from the backing plate.
3. Mark the position of the driveshaft on the axle flange and remove the driveshaft.
4. Disconnect and plug the flexible brake hose at the axle housing or chassis.
5. Disconnect the rear wheel anti-lock brake sensor, if equipped.
6. Support the axle housing with a jack.
7. Disconnect the shock absorbers at the axle housing.
8. Remove the nuts from the U-bolts and remove the U-bolts and spring clamp.
9. Lower the axle housing from the vehicle.
To install:
10. Raise the axle housing into position.
11. Install the U-bolts and spring clamps and tighten to 88–101 ft. lbs. (120–137 Nm).
12. Connect the shock absorbers at the axle housing and tighten the nuts and bolts to 47–58 ft. lbs. (64–78 Nm). Remove the jack.
13. Install the remaining components in the reverse order of removal. Bleed the brake system.

MPV

1. Raise and safely support the vehicle. Remove the rear wheel and tire assemblies.
2. Remove the brake drums and brake shoes. Disconnect the parking brake cables from the backing plate.
3. Mark the position of the driveshaft on the axle flange and remove the driveshaft.
4. Disconnect and plug the flexible brake hose at the axle housing or chassis.
5. Disconnect the rear wheel anti-lock brake sensor, if equipped.
6. Remove the rear stabilizer bar, if equipped.
7. Support the axle housing with a jack.
8. Disconnect the shock absorbers at the axle housing.
9. If equipped, remove the nut and disconnect the height sensor link from the axle housing.
10. Remove the lateral rod.
11. Slowly lower the axle housing until the coil spring tension is relieved. Remove the coil springs.
12. Remove the upper and lower control arms from the axle housing and lower the housing from the vehicle.
To install:
13. Raise the axle housing into position.
14. Connect the upper and lower control arms to the axle housing and snug the attaching bolts and nuts.
15. Install the coil springs. Install the lateral rod and snug the attaching bolts. Connect the height sensor link, if equipped.
16. Connect the shock absorbers to the axle housing and snug the attaching bolts and nuts. Remove the jack from the axle housing.
17. Install the stabilizer bar and snug the attaching bolts.
18. Connect the rear wheel anti-lock brake sensor, if equipped. Connect the height sensor link to the axle housing, if equipped.
19. Connect the brake hose to the brake line.
20. Install the driveshaft, aligning the marks that were made during the removal procedure.
21. Connect the parking brake cables to the backing plates. Install the brake shoes and the brake drums.
22. Install the wheel and tire assemblies and lower the vehicle.
23. With the vehicle in the normal ride height position, tighten the following to specification:
   Control arm nuts and bolts: 108–127 ft. lbs. (146–167 Nm).
   Lateral arm nuts: 108–127 ft. lbs. (146–167 Nm)
   Shock absorber nuts and bolts: 56–76 ft. lbs. (76–103 Nm)
   Stabilizer bar bushing mount bolts: 23–38 ft. lbs. (34–51 Nm)

Navajo

1. Raise the vehicle and support it safely.
2. Remove the cover and drain the lubricant from the axle.
3. Remove the rear wheel and tire assemblies and remove the rear anti-lock brake system sensor. Remove the axle shafts.
4. Remove the 4 retaining nuts from each backing plate. Wire the backing plates to the underbody.
5. Disconnect the vent hose from the axle housing. Remove the connector from the rear anti-lock sensor.
6. Remove the brake line from the clips that retain the line to the axle housing.
7. Remove the hydraulic brake junction block from the axle housing. Do not open the hydraulic brake system lines.
8. Mark the driveshaft and the axle companion flange so they can be reassembled in the same position. Remove the driveshaft.
9. Support the rear axle housing on a jack, then remove the axle housing U-bolt nuts. Remove the U-bolts and shock absorber plates. Leave the shock absorbers attached to the plates.
10. Remove the stabilizer bar attaching bracket bolts from the axle housing and position the stabilizer bar assembly away from the axle housing.
11. Raise the axle housing off the springs with the jack and move to the right side of the vehicle. Lower the left side of the axle housing below the left spring enough to clear the spring.

12. Remove the axle housing from the vehicle by lowering the axle and moving to the left until the right axle tube clears the right spring.

To install:

13. Install the axle housing on the transmission jack. Guide the right side of the axle housing over the right spring. Lift the left side of the axle housing over the left spring and position the axle housing on the spring center bolts.

14. Install the stabilizer bar to the axle housing. Tighten the stabilizer bar bracket bolts to 30–42 ft. lbs. (40–57 Nm).

15. Install the axle housing U-bolts over the axle tube. Position the shock absorber plates under the springs and install the U-bolts through the holes. Install the nuts and tighten to 88–108 ft. lbs. (119–146 Nm).

16. Install the axle vent tube to the axle vent fitting and secure with a clamp. Connect the rear anti-lock sensor connector.

17. Install the brake backing plates on the axle housing flanges. Tighten the nuts to 20–40 ft. lbs. (28–54 Nm).

18. Position the brake lines to the axle housing and secure with the retaining clips. Position the brake junction block to the axle housing and install the retaining screw.

19. Install the axle shafts. Install the driveshaft, aligning the marks that were made during removal. Tighten the attaching bolts to 70–95 ft. lbs. (95–128 Nm).

20. Install the brake drums and the wheel and tire assemblies.

21. Clean all old sealer from the carrier surface. Apply a bead of RTV sealer ⅛–¼ in. wide. The bead should be continuous and should not pass through or outside the holes.

22. Install a new cover and tighten the bolts to 15–20 ft. lbs. (21–27 Nm) in a criss-cross pattern.

23. Add the proper type of lubricant through the filler hole until the lubricant level is $1/4$–$9/16$ in. below the bottom of the filler hole with the axle in the running position.

24. Lower the vehicle.

STEERING

Steering Wheel

Removal and Installation

1. Disconnect the negative battery cable.

2. Remove the steering wheel pad from the steering wheel. Pull the pad back and disconnect the horn switch and, if equipped, cruise control wires. Remove the steering wheel pad.

3. Remove the steering wheel attaching bolt or nut. Check to see if the steering wheel and steering shaft have alignment marks or flats. If there are no steering wheel-to-steering column shaft alignment marks or flats, matchmark the steering wheel and column shaft so they can be reassembled in the same position.

4. Using a suitable puller, remove the steering wheel from the steering column shaft.

NOTE: Do not hammer on the steering wheel or steering shaft or use a knock-off type steering wheel puller, as either will damage the steering column.

To install:

5. Install the steering wheel on the steering column shaft, aligning the marks or flats on the steering wheel with the marks or flats on the steering shaft.

6. On all except Navajo, install the steering wheel attaching nut and tighten to 29–36 ft. lbs. (39–49 Nm). On Navajo, install the steering wheel attaching bolt and tighten to 23–33 ft. lbs. (31–45 Nm).

7. Connect the horn switch and, if equipped, cruise control wires and install the steering wheel pad.

8. Connect the negative battery and check the steering column for proper operation.

Steering Column

Removal and Installation

EXCEPT NAVAJO

1. Disconnect the negative battery cable. Place the front wheels in the straight-ahead position.

2. Remove the steering wheel.

3. Remove the steering column covers and remove the combination switch.

4. Remove the necessary dash panels from under the steering column.

5. Disconnect the automatic transmission interlock cable, if equipped. Tag and disconnect the necessary electrical connectors.

6. Disconnect the steering column from the steering linkage by removing the bolt at the intermediate shaft universal joint. Mark the position of the intermediate shaft on the column shaft before disconnecting so they can be reassembled in the same position.

7. Remove the nuts attaching the column at the firewall.

8. Support the steering column and remove the bolts attaching the column to the underside of the dash. Remove the steering column.

9. Installation is the reverse of the removal procedure. Tighten the bolts attaching the steering column to the underside of the dash to 12–17 ft. lbs. (16–23 Nm). Tighten the nuts attaching the column at the firewall to 14–19 ft. lbs. (19–26 Nm) on B Series Pick-Up or 12–17 ft. lbs. (16–23 Nm) on MPV.

10. Align the marks that were made on the intermediate shaft and steering column shaft during removal. Tighten the intermediate shaft universal joint bolt to 13–18 ft. lbs. (18–25 Nm).

NAVAJO

1. Disconnect the negative battery cable and apply the parking brake. Place automatic transmission in **N**.

2. Remove the bolt that holds the intermediate shaft to the steering column shaft. Using a prybar, compress the intermediate shaft until it is clear of the steering column shaft.

3. If equipped with automatic transmission, remove the nuts from the studs and remove the shift cable bracket from the steering column bracket. Disconnect the shift cable from the column lever.

4. Remove the steering wheel. If equipped with tilt column, make sure the steering wheel is in the full up position before removal.

5. If equipped with tilt column, remove the tilt lever and remove the column collar by pressing on the collar from the top and bottom while removing the collar.

6. Remove the retaining screws and remove the panel trim cover.

7. Remove the 2 screws from the bottom of the column shroud. Remove the bottom half of the shroud by pulling the shroud down and toward the rear of the vehicle. If equipped with automatic transmission, move the shift lever as required to ease shroud removal. Lift the top half of the shroud from the column.

8. If equipped with automatic transmission, disconnect the selector indicator cable by removing the screw from the column

casting and the plastic plug at the end of the cable. To remove the plastic plug from the shift lever socket casting, push on the nose of the plug until the head clears the casting, then pull the plug from the casting.

9. Remove the plastic clip that holds the combination switch wiring to the steering column bracket. Remove the 2 screws from the combination switch and remove the switch from the column, leaving the wiring connectors attached to the switch. Position the switch and wiring aside.

10. Disconnect the key warning buzzer wire from the horn brush wire. Remove the screw that holds the horn brush connector to the column and remove the connector.

11. Remove the 5 screws that hold the toe plate to the dash panel and loosen the toe plate clamp bolt.

12. Support the column and remove the bolts that hold the breakaway bracket to the pedal support bracket. Pry apart the locking tabs and disconnect the ignition switch wiring harness.

13. Carefully remove the column from the vehicle.

To install:

14. Carefully position the column in the hole in the vehicle floor. Connect the ignition switch wiring harness to the column connector.

15. Install the bolts that hold the breakaway bracket to the pedal support bracket, but do not tighten at this time.

16. Tighten the bolts that hold the toe plate to the floor to 8 ft. lbs. (11 Nm), then tighten the breakaway bracket-to-pedal support bracket bolts to 19–27 ft. lbs. (25–36 Nm). Tighten the toe plate clamp to 6–13 ft. lbs. (8–18 Nm).

17. Install the horn brush connector to the column and tighten the retaining screw to 21–29 inch lbs. (2.3–3.3 Nm). Attach the key warning buzzer wire connector to the horn brush wire. Route the wiring to prevent contact with moving parts.

18. Position the combination switch on the column with the attaching screws. Tighten to 18–26 inch lbs. (2–3 Nm). Install the plastic clip that holds the switch wiring to the steering column breakaway bracket.

19. If equipped with automatic transmission, connect the selector indicator cable by pushing the plastic plug at the end of the cable into the shift lever socket casting. When installed, the nose of the plug should be facing the steering wheel and the head of the plug away from the wheel. Install the cable retaining screw in the column and adjust the cable. If the shift lever was removed, install it at this time.

20. Position the top half of the shroud on the column so the screw moldings on the shroud seat in the mounting bores in the column. Place the automatic transmission shift lever in the lowest position to aid assembly.

21. Install the bottom half of the shroud by sliding the guides in the shroud bottom half into the tabs in the shroud top half. Install the shroud retaining screws and tighten to 6–10 inch lbs. (0.7–1.1 Nm).

22. If equipped with tilt column, install the column collar by pressing on the collar from the top and bottom while installing the collar on the column. Install the tilt lever and tighten to 2.2–3.6 ft. lbs. (3–5 Nm).

23. If equipped, place the automatic transmission selector lever in **N**. Install the steering wheel and the lower trim cover panel.

24. If equipped with automatic transmission, install the nuts on the studs and install the shift cable bracket on the steering column bracket. Connect the shift cable to the column lever.

25. Connect the column shaft to the intermediate shaft U-joint and tighten the pinch bolt to 25–35 ft. lbs. (34–47 Nm). The intermediate shaft must be in collapsed state to align, both shafts have a flat side, and then pulled up the column shaft until the bolt holes align. Make sure the intermediate shaft does not contact the plastic retainer at the base of the column. If it does, pull the lower shaft of the column slightly out of the column.

26. Connect the negative battery cable and check the adjustment of the selector indicator cable. Pull the shift lever toward the steering wheel until the **OD** detent in the transmission is felt. Release the shift lever, it should be against the detent wall in the column.

27. Release the parking brake lever and test drive the vehicle.

Manual Steering Gear

Adjustment

B SERIES PICK-UP

1. Remove the steering gear and mount the assembly in a vise.

2. Set the toe of a dial indicator at the end of the Pitman arm.

3. Loosen the locknut and turn the adjusting screw until there is no backlash.

NOTE: Adjust the backlash with the steering gear in the center position. Otherwise, the backlash becomes excessively small and the gears may become damaged.

4. Reinstall the steering gear in the vehicle.

Removal and Installation

B SERIES PICK-UP

1. Position the front wheels in the straight-ahead position. Raise and safely support the vehicle.

2. Remove the pinch bolt securing the worm shaft to the intermediate shaft coupling.

3. Remove the cotter pin and nut from the Pitman arm stud. Use separator tool 49 0118 850C or equivalent, to separate the Pitman arm from the center link.

4. Support the steering gear and remove the steering gear attaching bolts/nuts. Remove the steering gear from the vehicle.

5. Installation is the reverse of the removal procedure. Tighten the steering gear-to-chassis bolts/nuts to 46–69 ft. lbs. (63–93 Nm). Tighten the Pitman arm stud nut to 33–43 ft. lbs. (44–59 Nm) and install a new cotter pin. Tighten the worm shaft-to-intermediate shaft coupling pinch bolt to 22–38 ft. lbs. (30–38 Nm).

Power Steering Gear

Adjustment

B SERIES PICK-UP

1. Remove the power steering gear from the vehicle and install in a suitable holding fixture.

2. Position the worm shaft in the center position.

3. Install tool 49 0180 510B or equivalent, on the end of the worm shaft and attach a pull scale to the end of the tool.

4. Set the sector shaft adjusting screw so the preload with the worm shaft in the center position is 1.3–2.0 lbs.

NOTE: The preload at the center position must be 0.4–0.9 lbs. higher than the preload when the worm shaft is turned 360 degrees to the left and right.

Manual steering gear adjustment—B Series Pick-Up

Power steering gear adjustment—B Series Pick-Up

5. If the specified preload is not obtained, disassemble the steering gear and check for dirt and foreign material and that the oil seal is correctly installed. Reassemble the steering gear and adjust the preload.

6. After adjustment, tighten the sector shaft adjusting screw locknut to 25–35 ft. lbs. (34–47 Nm).

7. Reinstall the steering gear in the vehicle.

NAVAJO

1. Raise and safely support the vehicle. Disconnect the Pit-man arm from the sector shaft using puller T64P–3590–F or equivalent.

2. Disconnect the fluid return line at the reservoir and cap the reservoir return line tube. Place the end of the return line in a clean container and turn the steering wheel from stop to stop several times to empty the steering gear. Discard the fluid.

3. Turn the steering wheel to 45 degrees from the right stop.

4. Attach an inch pound torque wrench to steering wheel nut and record the torque required to rotate the shaft slowly approximately 1/8 turn toward center from the 45 degree position.

5. Turn the steering gear back to center and record the torque required to rotate the shaft back and forth across the center position.

6. If the vehicle has less than 5000 miles, resetting is required if total mesh-load over center is not 12–24 inch lbs. If the vehicle has more than 5000 miles or the sector shaft has been replaced, resetting is required if mesh-load over center is less than 10 inch lbs. greater than the torque 45 degrees from the right stop.

7. The set torque specification is measured rocking across center to a value of 9–13 inch lbs. greater than that measured 45 degress from the right stop.

8. If reset is required, loosen the locknut and turn the sector shaft adjusting screw until the reading is the specified value greater than the torque at 45 degrees from the stop.

9. Tighten the adjusting screw locknut and recheck. Install the Pitman arm and steering wheel cover.

10. Connect the fluid return line to the reservoir and refill the system with fluid. Bleed the system.

Removal and Installation

B SERIES PICK-UP

1. Position the front wheels in the straight-ahead position. Raise and safely support the vehicle.

2. Remove the pinch bolt securing the worm shaft to the intermediate shaft coupling.

1. Nut and cotter pin
2. Outer tie rod end
3. Tie rod end nuts
4. Inner tie rod end
5. Center link
6. Idler arm
7. Bushing
8. Bolt, washers and nut
9. Idler arm bracket
10. Pressure pipe
11. Return pipe
12. Bolt
13. Bolt and washer
14. Bolt, washers and nut
15. Steering gear and pitman arm

Power steering gear and linkage exploded view—B Series Pick-Up

3. Disconnect and plug the power steering fluid lines at the steering gear.

4. Remove the cotter pin and nut from the Pitman arm stud. Use separator tool 49 0118 850C or equivalent, to separate the Pitman arm from the center link.

5. Support the steering gear and remove the steering gear attaching bolts/nuts. Remove the steering gear from the vehicle.

To install:

6. Install the steering gear and tighten the steering gear-to-chassis bolts/nuts to 46–69 ft. lbs. (63–93 Nm).

7. Connect the Pitman arm and tighten the Pitman arm stud nut to 33–43 ft. lbs. (44–59 Nm). Install a new cotter pin.

8. Connect the worm shaft-to-intermediate shaft coupling and tighten the worm shaft-to-intermediate shaft coupling pinch bolt to 22–38 ft. lbs. (30–38 Nm).

9. Connect the power steering fluid lines. Tighten the pressure line nut to 17–26 ft. lbs. (24–35 Nm) and the return line nut to 23–35 ft. lbs. (31–47 Nm).

10. Lower the vehicle. Fill and bleed the power steering system.

NAVAJO

1. Disconnect the pressure and return lines from the steering gear. Plug the lines and the ports in the gear to prevent entry of dirt.

2. Remove the upper and lower steering gear shaft U-joint shield from the flex coupling. Disconnect the flex coupling at the steering gear by removing the bolt.

3. Raise the vehicle and support it safely. Remove the Pitman arm attaching nut and washer. Remove the Pitman arm from the sector shaft using tool T64P-3590-F or equivalent. Be careful not to damage the seals.

4. Support the steering gear and remove the attaching bolts. Work the steering gear free from the flex coupling and remove the gear from the vehicle.

To install:

5. Install the lower U-joint shield onto the steering gear lugs. Slide the upper U-joint shield into place on the steering shaft assembly. Turn the steering wheel so the spokes are in the horizontal position.

6. Center the steering gear input shaft with the indexing flat facing down.

7. Slide the steering gear input shaft into the flex coupling and into place on the frame side rail. Install the attaching bolts and tighten to 50–62 ft. lbs. (68–84 Nm). Tighten the flex coupling bolt to 26–34 ft. lbs. (34–47 Nm).

8. Make sure the wheels are in the straight-ahead position, then install the Pitman arm on the sector shaft. Install the attaching washer and nut and tighten to 170–228 ft. lbs. (230–310 Nm).

9. Connect and tighten the pressure and return lines to the steering gear to 20–30 ft. lbs. (27–40 Nm). Snap the upper and lower steering gear shaft U-joint shields together.

10. Fill and bleed the power steering system.

Power Rack and Pinion

Removal and Installation

MPV

2WD

1. Place the front wheels in the straight-ahead position. Raise and safely support the vehicle.

2. Remove the wheel and tire assemblies. Remove the splash shield.

3. Remove the cotter pins and nuts from both tie rod end studs. Use separator tool 49 0727 575 or equivalent, to separate the tie rod ends from the knuckles.

4. Remove the pinch bolt from the intermediate shaft-to-pinion shaft coupling.

Change counter assembly location—MPV

5. Disconnect and plug the pressure line from the rack and pinion assembly. Loosen the clamp and disconnect the return line from the rack and pinion assembly. Plug the line.

6. If equipped with automatic transmission, remove the change counter assembly to remove the protector plate mounting bolt indicated by the arrow.

7. Remove the steering bracket mounting bolts and remove the rack and pinion assembly and brackets.

8. If necessary, remove the brackets.

To install:

9. If removed, install the brackets and tighten the mounting bolts, in sequence, to 54–69 ft. lbs. (74–93 Nm).

10. Install the rack and pinion assembly and brackets in the vehicle. Tighten the bracket-to-chassis bolts to 46–69 ft. lbs. (63–93 Nm).

11. If equipped with automatic transmission, install the change counter assembly.

12. Connect the return line and tighten the clamp. Connect the pressure line and tighten the nut to 23–35 ft. lbs. (31–47 Nm).

13. Install the pinch bolt in the intermediate shaft-to-pinion shaft coupling and tighten to 13–20 ft. lbs. (18–26 Nm).

14. Position the tie rod end studs in the knuckles and install the nuts. Tighten the nuts to 43–58 ft. lbs. (59–78 Nm) and install new cotter pins.

15. Install the splash shield and the wheel and tire assemblies. Lower the vehicle and bleed the power steering system.

4WD

1. Place the front wheels in the straight-ahead position. Raise and safely support the vehicle.

2. Remove the wheel and tire assemblies. Remove the splash shield.

3. Remove the cotter pins and nuts from both tie rod end studs. Use separator tool 49 0727 575 or equivalent, to separate the tie rod ends from the knuckles.

Power rack and pinion bracket mounting bolt torque sequence—2WD MPV

1. Cotter pin
2. Nut
3. Tie rod end and steering knuckle
4. Fixing bolt
5. Pressure pipe
6. Return hose
7. Steering bracket mounting bolts
8. Steering gear and linkage bracket assembly
9. Mounting bracket bolts
10. Mounting bracket and rubbers
11. Steering gear and linkage
12. Steering brackets

Power rack and pinion removal—2WD MPV

4. Disconnect and plug the pressure and return hoses at the pressure and return lines.

5. Remove the pressure and return lines from the rack and pinion assembly.

6. Remove the pinch bolt from the intermediate shaft-to-pinion shaft coupling.

7. Working inside the vehicle, remove the lower panel and column cover from under the steering column. Remove the steering column mounting bolts and nuts and pull the column and intermediate shaft rearward to separate the intermediate shaft from the pinion shaft.

8. Mark the position of the front driveshaft on the axle flange and remove the front driveshaft.

9. Remove the rack and pinion assembly mounting bracket bolts and the front differential/joint shaft assembly mounting bolts.

10. Slide the differential/joint shaft assembly rearward. Slide the rack and pinion assembly rearward and turn it 90 degrees, then remove it from the left side of the vehicle.

To install:

11. Install the rack and pinion assembly from the left side of

the vehicle, turn it 90 degrees and move it forward into position. Install the mounting bolts and tighten, in sequence, to 54–69 ft. lbs. (74–93 Nm).

12. Move the differential/joint shaft assembly forward, install the mounting bolts and tighten to 49–72 ft. lbs. (67–97 Nm).

13. Install the driveshaft, aligning the marks made during removal.

14. Working inside the vehicle, move the steering column and intermediate shaft forward to engage the intermediate shaft with the pinion shaft. Install and tighten the steering column nuts and bolts to 12–17 ft. lbs. (16–23 Nm). Install the lower panel and column cover.

15. Install the pinch bolt in the intermediate shaft-to-pinion shaft coupling and tighten to 13–20 ft. lbs. (18–26 Nm).

16. Install the pressure and return lines on the rack and pinion assembly. Connect the pressure and return hoses to the lines.

17. Position the tie rod end studs in the knuckles and install the nuts. Tighten the nuts to 43–58 ft. lbs. (59–78 Nm) and install new cotter pins.

18. Install the splash shield and the wheel and tire assemblies. Lower the vehicle and bleed the power steering system.

Power Steering Pump

Removal and Installation

EXCEPT NAVAJO

1. Disconnect the negative battery cable.

2. Loosen the adjusting nut and pivot bolt or loosen the idler pulley locknut and turn the adjusting bolt, as required, to loosen the drive belt. Remove the drive belt from the pulley.

3. Hold the power steering pulley with holder tool 49 W023 585A or equivalent, and remove the pulley locknut. Remove the pulley.

4. Disconnect and plug the power steering pressure and return hoses at the pump.

Power rack and pinion bracket mounting bolt torque sequence—4WD MPV

1. Oil pump belt
2. Locknut
3. Oil pump pulley
4. Pressure switch coupler
5. Pressure pipe
6. Return hose
7. Oil pump assembly

30 mm (1.18 in)

CLIP POSITION

Power steering pump installation—3.0L engine

5. If equipped, disconnect the fluid pressure switch electrical connector.

6. Remove the mounting bolts/nuts and remove the power steering pump.

To install:

7. Install the power steering pump and tighten the mounting bolts/nuts to 23–34 ft. lbs. (31–46 Nm).

8. If equipped, connect the fluid pressure switch electrical connector.

9. Connect the pressure and return hoses at the pump. Tighten the line nut to 23–35 ft. lbs. (31–47 Nm) or tighten the clamp, as required.

10. Install the power steering pulley on the pump. Hold the pulley with the holder tool and tighten the nut to 36–43 ft. lbs. (49–59 Nm).

11. Install the drive belt and adjust the tension. Fill and bleed the power steering system. Check for leaks

NAVAJO

1. Remove the power steering fluid from the pump reservoir by disconnecting the fluid return hose at the reservoir and draining the fluid into a container.

2. Remove the pressure hose from the pump.

3. Slacken belt tension by lifting the tensioner pulley in a counterclockwise direction. Remove the drive belt from under the tensioner pulley and slowly lower the pulley to stop. Remove the drive belt.

4. Install steering pump pulley removal tool 49 UN01 005 or equivalent, on the pulley. Hold the pump and rotate the tool nut counterclockwise to remove the pulley. Do not apply in and out pressure on the pump shaft as pressure will damage the internal thrust areas.

5. Remove the support and the bolts attaching the pump to the bracket and remove the pump.

To install:

6. Install the pump on the bracket and tighten the bolts to 30–40 ft. lbs. (40–55 Nm).

7. Install steering pump pulley replacement tool 49 UN01 006 or equivalent and press the pulley on the pump shaft.

NOTE: Fore and aft location of the pulley on the pump shaft is critical for correct belt alignment. Make sure the pull-off groove on the pulley is facing front and flush with the end of the shaft ± 0.010 in. (0.254mm).

8. Position and rotate the drive belt on the engine. While lifting the tensioner pulley in a counterclockwise direction, slide the belt under the tensioner pulley and lower the pulley to the belt.

9. Install the pressure hose to the pump fitting. Connect the return hose to the pump and tighten the clamp.

10. Fill and bleed the power steering system. Check for leaks.

Belt Adjustment

EXCEPT 4.0L ENGINE

1. On all except 1988 4WD B Series Pick-Up, adjust the belt tension by loosening the idler pulley locknut and turning the adjusting bolt until belt tension is as specified.

2. On 1988 4WD B Series Pick-Up, adjust the belt tension by loosening the adjusting nut and pivot bolt and moving the power steering pump until belt tension is as specified.

3. To obtain the correct belt tension, measure the belt deflection at the center of the belt span between the idler pulley and power steering pump pulley. Deflection specifications are as follows:

1988 2.2L Engine—New belt: 0.31–0.39 in. (8–10mm), Used belt: 0.43–0.51 in. (11–13mm)

1989–92 2.2L Engine—New belt: 0.28–0.31 in. (7–8mm), Used belt: 0.31–0.35 in. (8–9mm)

1988 2.6L Engine—New belt: 0.31–0.39 in. (8–10mm), Used belt: 0.43–0.51 in. (11–13mm)

1989–92 2.6L Engine—New belt: 0.26–0.28 in. (6.6–7.2mm), Used belt: 0.28–0.31 in. (7.2–8.0mm)

3.0L Engine—New belt: 0.28–0.30 in. (7.0–7.5mm), Used belt: 0.30–0.32 in. (7.5–8.2mm)

4. After correct belt tension is obtained, tighten the idler pulley locknut or the adjusting nut and pivot bolt, as required.

4.0L ENGINE

Belt tension is maintained by an automatic tensioner. No adjustment is necessary.

System Bleeding

EXCEPT NAVAJO

1. Raise and safely support the vehicle.
2. Check the fluid level and add, if necessary.
3. Turn the steering wheel fully left and right several times with the engine not running.
4. Recheck the fluid level and add, if necessary.
5. Repeat Steps 3 and 4 until the fluid level stabilizes. Lower the vehicle.
6. Start the engine and let it run at idle. Turn the steering wheel fully left and right several times. If noise is heard in the oil line, air is still present.
7. Put the wheels in the straight-ahead position and turn the engine **OFF**. The fluid level in the pump should not increase; if it does, air is still present. Repeat Step 6.
8. Recheck the fluid level and check for leaks.

NOTE: If air is still present in the system, raise the fluid temperature to 122–176°F (50–80°C) by turning the steering wheel right and left, stop the engine and repeat Step 6 for 5–10 minutes. Air can be completely bled in this manner.

NAVAJO

1. Fill the power steering fluid reservoir.
2. Disconnect the distributorless ignition module connector.
3. Crank the engine with the starter and continue adding fluid until the level remains constant. Do not prolong cranking as the battery may be drained and the starter damaged.
4. Rotate the steering wheel approximately 30 degrees each side of center while continuing to crank the engine.
5. Recheck the fluid level and fill, as required.
6. Reconnect the distributorless ignition module connector.
7. Start the engine and allow it to run for several minutes.
8. Rotate the steering wheel from stop to stop.
9. Shut off the engine and recheck the fluid level. Add fluid, as required.
10. If air is still trapped in the system, proceed as follows:
    a. Fabricate a purging tool.
    b. Make sure the reservoir fluid level is correct.
    c. Insert the rubber stopper end of the fabricated purging tool tightly into the filler tube.
    d. Connect a suitable length of hose to the purging tool. Connect the other end of the hose to an air conditioner vacuum pump or distributor machine. Do not use engine vacuum.
    e. Start the engine and let it idle for approximately 15 minutes. Turn the steering wheel 1 full cycle every 5 minutes but do not hit the stops. This will assist in removing trapped air.
    f. Stop the engine and disconnect the vacuum source. Remove the purging tool.
    g. Check the fluid level and install the filler tube dipstick.

Fabricated purging tool dimensions – Navajo

Tie Rod Ends

Removal and Installation

1. Place the front wheels in the straight-ahead position. Raise and safely support the vehicle.
2. Remove the cotter pin and nut from the tie rod end ball stud. Discard the cotter pin.
3. Separate the tie rod end from the knuckle or center link using separator tool 49 0118 850C or equivalent.
4. On all except Navajo, mark the position of the locknut and tie rod end on the tie rod threads. Grip the tie rod with suitable pliers, loosen the locknut and remove the tie rod end from the tie rod.
5. On Navajo, loosen the bolts on the tie rod adjusting sleeve. Count the number of turns required to remove the tie rod from the tie rod adjusting sleeve and remove the tie rod.

To install:

6. On all except Navajo, thread the replacement tie rod end onto the tie rod to the same location as the 1 that was removed. Hold the tie rod end with a wrench and tighten the locknut to 51–58 ft. lbs. (69–78 Nm).
7. On Navajo, install the tie rod into the adjusting sleeve the same number of turns required to remove it. With the adjusting sleeve clamps pointed down, tighten the adjusting sleeve nuts to 30–42 ft. lbs. (40–57 Nm).
8. Install the tie rod ball stud into the knuckle or center link. Install the nut and tighten to 33–43 ft. lbs. (44–59 Nm) on B Series Pick-Up, 43–58 ft. lbs. (59–78 Nm) on MPV or 50–75 ft. lbs. (70–100 Nm) on Navajo. Install a new cotter pin.

NOTE: If the cotter pin cannot be installed because the hole in the ball stud does not align with a castellation on the nut, continue to tighten the nut to align them. Never loosen the nut to align the hole and castellation.

9. Lower the vehicle. Check the toe-in setting and adjust, if necessary.

BRAKES

For all brake system repair and service procedures not covered below, please refer to "Brakes" in the Unit Repair section.

Master Cylinder

Removal and Installation

1. Disconnect the negative battery cable. Disconnect the fluid level sensor connector, if equipped.

2. Disconnect and plug the brake lines at the master cylinder.
3. Remove the attaching nuts from the power brake booster studs and remove the master cylinder.

To install:

4. On all except Navajo, adjust the power brake booster pushrod clearance as follows:
    a. Install clearance adjusting tool 49 F043 001 or equiva-

Master cylinder bench bleeding

Adjusting the load sensing G-valve—1988–89 4WD B Series Pick-Up and 1989 MPV

lent on the rear of the master cylinder. Turn the adjusting bolt until it bottoms in the pushrod hole in the piston.

b. Apply 19.7 in. Hg vacuum to the power brake booster with a vacuum pump.

c. Invert the clearance adjusting tool and place it on the power brake booster. Turn the pushrod locknut until there is no clearance between the tool and the pushrod.

5. On Navajo, measure the distance between the outer end of the booster pushrod and the front face of the booster assembly; the distance should be 0.995 in. Turn the pushrod adjusting screw in or out until the distance is as specified.

6. If a new or dry master cylinder is being installed, bench bleed the master cylinder as follows:

a. Support the master cylinder in a suitable holding fixture. Fill the reservoir with the proper type of brake fluid.

b. Install plugs in the brake outlet ports.

c. Loosen an outlet port plug and depress the master cylinder piston slowly to force air out of the master cylinder. Tighten the plug while the piston is depressed or air will enter the master cylinder.

d. Repeat the procedure until there is no more air at the outlet port.

e. Repeat the procedures in Steps c and d at the other outlet ports.

7. Install the master cylinder over the booster studs. Install the attaching nuts and tighten to 7.2–12.0 ft. lbs. (9.8–16.0 Nm) on all except Navajo. On Navajo, tighten the nuts to 20 ft. lbs. (27 Nm).

8. Remove the outlet port plugs and connect the brake lines to the master cylinder.

9. Connect the fluid level sensor connector, if equipped.

10. Bleed the brake system.

Proportioning/Bypass Valve

Removal and Installation

EXCEPT NAVAJO

1. Disconnect the negative battery cable. Disconnect the pressure differential switch connector, if equipped.

2. Disconnect and plug the brake lines at the valve.

3. Remove the attaching bolt(s) and the valve.

4. Installation is the reverse of the removal procedure.

5. Bleed the brake system.

Load Sensing Proportioning Valve

Removal and Installation

1989 MPV

1. Raise and support the vehicle safely.

2. Remove the nut attaching the bracket to the axle housing.

3. Disconnect and plug the brake lines at the valve.

4. Remove the valve attaching bolts and remove the valve.

5. Installation is the reverse of the removal procedure. Install the valve first, then the axle bracket.

6. When installing the axle bracket, position it so the length of the spring, measured between the 2 collars, is 5.93 in. (150.5mm), with no extra load in the vehicle.

7. Bleed the brake system.

Load Sensing G-Valve

Removal and Installation

1988–89 4WD B SERIES PICK-UP AND 1989 MPV

1. Raise and support the vehicle safely.

2. Disconnect and plug the brake lines.

3. Remove the valve mounting bolts and remove the valve.

4. Installation is the reverse of the removal procedure. Bleed the brake system.

5. Adjust the inclination angle of the valve as follows:

a. Place the vehicle on level ground.

b. Make sure there is no cargo in the vehicle.

c. Fill the tires to the recommended inflation pressure.

d. Attach angle gauge 49 U043 003 or equivalent, to the valve and check the inclination angle. The angle should be 7.5 degrees ± 1 degree on B Series Pick-Up or 8.5 degrees ± 1 degree on MPV.

e. If the inclination angle is not correct, loosen the valve mounting bolts and tilt the valve until the angle is as specified.

f. Tighten the bolts to 16–22 ft. lbs. (22–30 Nm) on B Series Pick-Up or 14–19 ft. lbs. (19–25 Nm) on MPV.

Power Brake Booster

Removal and Installation

EXCEPT NAVAJO

1. Disconnect the negative battery cable.

2. On MPV with 3.0L engine, remove the wiper arms, wiper motor and wiper linkage.

3. Remove the master cylinder.

4. Disconnect the vacuum hose at the booster.

5. Working inside the vehicle, remove the cotter pin and clevis pin from the booster pushrod. Remove the booster attaching nuts.

6. Remove the power brake booster and gasket.

7. Installation is the reverse of the removal procedure. Apply gasket sealant to the booster gasket and grease to the clevis pin prior to installation. Tighten the booster attaching nuts to 12–17 ft. lbs. (16–23 Nm) on B Series Pick-Up or 14–19 ft. lbs. (19–25 Nm) on MPV.

8. Bleed the brake system.

NAVAJO

1. Disconnect the negative battery cable. Support the master cylinder from the underside with a prop.

2. Disconnect the vacuum hose from the booster check valve and remove the check valve.

3. Remove the master cylinder-to-booster retaining nuts. Pull the master cylinder off the booster and leave it supported by the prop, out of the way enough to allow booster removal.

4. Working inside the cab, remove the hairpin retainer and slide the stoplight switch, valve rod, spacers and bushing off the brake pedal arm. Remove the nuts retaining the booster and remove the booster.

To install:

5. Mount the booster assembly on the engine side of the dash panel by sliding the bracket mounting bolts and valve operating rod in through the holes in the dash panel.

6. Working inside the cab, install the booster mounting nuts and tighten to 13–25 ft. lbs. (18–33 Nm).

7. Before installing the master cylinder, check the distance from the outer end of the vacuum booster assembly pushrod to the front face of the vacuum brake booster assembly. The distance should be 0.995 in. Turn the pushrod adjusting screw in or out, as required, to obtain the proper length.

8. Install the master cylinder and tighten the retaining nuts to 20 ft. lbs. (27 Nm). Remove the prop from under the master cylinder.

9. Install the booster check valve and connect the vacuum hose. Check the hose routing to make sure the hose is not crimped.

10. Working inside the cab, install the bushing and position the switch on the end of the valve rod, then install the switch and rod on the pedal arm along with the spacers and hairpin retainer.

NOTE: Use only the factory supplied hairpin retainer. Do not substitute other types of retainers.

11. Connect the negative battery cable, start the engine and check brake operation.

Brake Caliper

Removal and Installation

EXCEPT NAVAJO

1. Raise and safely support the vehicle. Remove the wheel and tire assembly.

2. Remove the banjo bolt and disconnect the brake hose from the caliper. Plug the hose to prevent fluid leakage.

3. On B Series Pick-Up, remove the caliper mounting bolt and pivot the caliper about the mounting pin and off of the brake rotor. Remove the caliper from the pin.

4. On MPV, remove the caliper mounting bolts and remove the caliper.

5. Installation is the reverse of the removal procedure. Lubricate the caliper mounting bolts or bolt and pin prior to installation.

6. Tighten the caliper mounting bolt(s) to 23–30 ft. lbs. (31–41 Nm) on B Series Pick-Up or 61–69 ft. lbs. (83–93 Nm) on MPV. Bleed the brake system.

NAVAJO

1. Siphon part of the brake fluid out of the master cylinder to avoid overflow when the caliper piston is pressed into the caliper bore.

2. Raise the vehicle and support it safely. Remove the wheel and tire assembly.

3. Position an 8 in. C-clamp on the caliper and tighten the clamp to move the caliper piston into the bore approximately ⅛ in. Avoid clamp contact with the outer shoe spring clip. Remove the clamp.

NOTE: Do not pry the piston away from the rotor.

4. Clean excess dirt from the pin tab area.

1. Brake pipe
2. Clip
3. Brake hose
4. Lockbolt
5. Brake caliper assembly
6. Disc pad
7. Shim
8. Guide plate
9. Bolt
10. Mounting support
11. Disc plate

Disc brake assembly – MPV

5. Using a ¼ in. drive socket, ⅜ in. deep and a light hammer, tap the upper caliper pin towards the outboard side until the pin tabs pass the spindle face.

6. Place 1 end of a $^7/_{16}$ in. diameter punch against the end of the caliper pin and tap the pin out of the caliper slide groove.

7. Repeat Steps 5 and 6 to remove the lower pin.

8. Disconnect and plug the brake hose at the caliper. Remove the caliper from the rotor.

To install:

9. Make sure the caliper mounting surfaces are free of dirt. Lubricate the caliper grooves with disc brake caliper grease and install the caliper.

10. From the caliper outboard side, position the pin between the caliper and spindle grooves. The pin must be positioned so the tabs will be installed against the spindle outer face.

11. Tap the pin on the outboard end with a hammer until the retention tabs on the sides of the pin contact the spindle face.

12. Repeat Steps 10 and 11 for the lower pin.

NOTE: During installation, do not allow the tabs of the caliper pin to be tapped too far into the spindle groove. If this happens, it will be necessary to tap the other end of the caliper pin until the tabs snap in place. The tabs on each end of the pin must be free to catch on the spindle face.

13. Connect the brake hose to the caliper. Bleed the brake system.

14. Install the wheel and tire assembly and lower the vehicle. Check the brake fluid level and check the brakes for proper operation.

Disc Brake Pads

Removal and Installation

EXCEPT NAVAJO

1. Siphon part of the brake fluid out of the master cylinder to avoid overflow when the caliper piston is pressed into the caliper bore.

2. Raise the vehicle and support it safely. Remove the wheel and tire assembly.

3. Remove the brake caliper, but do not disconnect the brake hose. Secure the caliper aside with mechanics wire.

NOTE: Do not let the caliper hang by the brake hose.

4. Remove the disc brake pads, shims and guide plates from the mounting support, noting the position of the shims and guide plates for reassembly.

To install:

5. Using a C-clamp or similar tool, bottom out the caliper piston in the caliper bore.

6. Install the new disc pads along with the shims and guide plates in the mounting support. Make sure the shims and guide plates are installed in their original positions.

7. Install the brake caliper.

8. Install the wheel and tire assembly and lower the vehicle. Apply the brakes several times before moving the vehicle to seat the pads.

9. Check the brake fluid level. Check the brakes for proper operation.

NAVAJO

1. Siphon part of the brake fluid out of the master cylinder to avoid overflow when the caliper piston is pressed into the caliper bore.

2. Raise the vehicle and support it safely. Remove the wheel and tire assembly.

3. Remove the brake caliper, but do not disconnect the brake hose. Secure the caliper aside with mechanics wire.

NOTE: Do not let the caliper hang by the brake hose.

4. Compress the anti-rattle clip and remove the inner brake pad from the caliper.

5. Press each ear of the outer brake pad away from the caliper and slide the torque buttons out of the retention notches.

To install:

6. Bottom out the caliper piston in the caliper bore using an 8 in. C-clamp and a worn out inner brake pad or block of wood to push against the piston. Do not attempt to bottom out the piston with the outer brake pad installed.

7. Place a new anti-rattle clip on the lower end of the inner brake pad. Make sure the tabs on the clip are properly positioned and the clip is fully seated.

8. Position the inner brake pad and anti-rattle clip in the pad abutment with the ant-rattle clip tab against the pad abutment and the loop-type spring away from the rotor. Compress the anti-rattle clip and slide the upper end of the pad in position.

9. Install the outer pad, making sure the torque buttons on the pad are seated solidly in the matching holes in the caliper.

10. Install the caliper on the spindle.

Correct disc brake pad installation—Navajo

11. Install the wheel and tire assembly and lower the vehicle. Apply the brakes several times before moving the vehicle to seat the pads.

12. Check the brake fluid level. Check the brakes for proper operation.

Brake Rotor

Removal and Installation

1. Raise and safely support the vehicle. Remove the wheel and tire assembly.

2. Remove the caliper and support it aside with mechanics wire; do not let the caliper hang by the brake hose. On all except Navajo, remove the disc brake pads and mounting support.

3. On 2WD B Series Pick-Up and Navajo, remove the dust cap, cotter pin, nut, washer and outer bearing and remove the rotor from the spindle.

4. On 4WD B Series Pick-Up, remove the locking hub or drive flange, snapring and spacer, set bolts and bearing set plate. Remove the bearing locknut using a suitable puller and remove the hub and rotor assembly, being careful not to let the washer and bearing fall.

5. On 4WD Navajo, remove the locking hub and remove the brake rotor.

6. On MPV, remove the attaching screw and remove the rotor.

7. Inspect the rotor for scoring, wear and runout; machine or replace as necessary.

8. If rotor replacement is necessary on B Series Pick-Up, remove the attaching bolts and separate the rotor from the hub.

9. Install in the reverse order of removal. On B Series Pick-Up, tighten the rotor-to-hub bolts to 40–51 ft. lbs. (54–69 Nm). Adjust the wheel bearings.

Brake Drums

Removal and Installation

1. Make sure the parking brake is released.

2. Raise and safely support the vehicle. Remove the wheel and tire assembly.

3. On all except Navajo, remove the retaining screw, if equipped, and remove the brake drum.

4. On Navajo, remove the spring retaining nuts, if equipped, and remove the brake drum.

NOTE: If the brake drum will not come off, insert a narrow prybar through the appropriate hole in the backing plate and disengage the adjusting lever from the adjusting screw. While holding the adjusting lever away from the adjusting screw, insert a brake adjusting tool through the backing plate hole adjacent to the star wheel of the adjusting screw and loosen the adjusting screw.

5. Inspect the brake drum surface for wear, scoring and runout. Machine or replace, as necessary.

6. Installation is the reverse of the removal procedure.

Brake Shoes

Removal and Installation

2WD B SERIES PICK-UP

1. Raise and safely support the vehicle. Remove the wheel and tire assembly and the brake drum.

2. Remove the upper and lower return springs from the brake shoes.

3. Compress the forward brake shoe spring and remove the forward brake shoe, spring and pin.

4. Remove the adjuster screw, pawl lever return spring and pawl lever.

5. Compress the rearward brake shoe spring and remove the rearward brake shoe, spring and pin.

6. Pull back the spring on the parking brake cable and disengage the brake shoe parking brake lever from the cable.

7. Remove the clip and pin and the parking brake lever from the brake shoe, if necessary.

To install:

8. Lubricate the adjusting screw threads, backing plate shoe sliding surfaces and wheel cylinder and anchor sliding points with a small amount of grease.

9. If removed, install the parking brake lever to the rearward brake shoe with the pin and clip. Make sure the clip is secure.

10. Pull back the spring on the parking brake cable and connect the cable end to the parking brake lever.

11. Install the brake shoes to the backing plate and secure with the pins and shoe springs.

12. Turn the adjusting screw all the way in and install the adjusting screw, pawl lever return spring and pawl lever.

13. Install the upper and lower return springs.

14. Install the brake drum.

15. Adjust the brake shoes as follows:

a. Remove the 2 adjusting hole plugs from the back of the backing plate.

b. Place a suitable brake adjusting tool against the star wheel of the adjust screw through the hole adjacent to the star wheel and turn the star wheel toward the arrow direction marked on the backing plate until the wheel is locked.

c. Insert a suitable drift through the other adjusting hole and push the pawl lever of the self-adjuster away from the star wheel, then back off the star wheel about 6–7 notches with the brake adjusting tool, so the drum rotates freely without drag.

d. Repeat the adjustment to the other wheel. The adjustment must be the same on both rear wheels.

e. Check the parking brake adjustment and install the backing plate plugs.

16. Install the wheel and tire assembly and lower the vehicle.

MPV AND 4WD B SERIES PICK-UP

1. Raise and safely support the vehicle. Remove the wheel and tire assembly and the brake drum.

2. Remove the upper return springs from the spring anchor and the primary and secondary shoes. Remove the adjuster lever link spring.

3. Remove the primary shoe holding spring assembly and disengage the primary shoe from the lower shoe spring. Remove the primary shoe and the holding spring pin.

NOTE: The primary shoe holding spring is yellow and the secondary shoe holding spring is white. The springs cannot be interchanged.

4. Remove the parking brake lever strut, lower shoe spring and adjuster screw assembly.

5. Remove the secondary shoe holding spring assembly and remove the secondary shoe, adjust lever and parking brake lever assembly and the holding spring pin.

6. Pull back the spring on the parking brake cable and disengage the brake shoe parking brake lever from the cable.

7. Remove the clip and the parking brake lever from the brake shoe, if necessary.

To install:

8. Lubricate the adjusting screw threads, backing plate shoe sliding surfaces and spring anchor sliding points with a small amount of grease.

9. If removed, install the parking brake lever to the secondary shoe with the clip. Make sure the clip is secure.

10. Pull back the spring on the parking brake cable and connect the cable end to the parking brake lever.

11. Install the secondary shoe with the adjust lever to the

1. Brake drum
2. Parking brake cable
3. Hold spring and sleeve
4. Adjust lever
5. Link
6. Pull-off spring
7. Shoe spring
8. Return spring
9. Return spring
10. Adjuster
11. Primary brake shoe
12. Secondary brake shoe
13. Strut
14. Wheel cylinder assembly

WHITE

YELLOW

Drum brake assembly—MPV and 4WD B Series Pick-Up

backing plate and secure with the pin and holding spring assembly.

12. Install the primary shoe to the backing plate and secure with the pin and holding spring assembly.

13. Install the lower shoe spring to the primary and secondary shoes.

14. Turn the adjuster screw assembly all the way in. Pry the shoes apart slightly and install the adjuster screw assembly between the shoes. Make sure the star wheel is toward the secondary shoe and is in contact with the adjust lever.

15. Install the parking brake lever strut.

16. Install the adjuster lever link spring between the adjust lever and the spring anchor.

17. Install the primary and secondary shoe upper return springs between the shoes and the spring anchor.

18. Install the brake drum.

19. Adjust the brake shoes as follows:

a. Remove the 2 adjusting hole plugs from the back of the backing plate.

b. Place a suitable brake adjusting tool against the star wheel of the adjust screw through the hole adjacent to the star wheel and turn the star wheel toward the arrow direction marked on the backing plate until the wheel is locked.

c. Insert a suitable drift through the other adjusting hole and push the pawl lever of the self-adjuster away from the star wheel, then back off the star wheel about 8–10 notches on B Series Pick-Up or 13–15 notches on MPV with the brake adjusting tool, so the drum rotates freely without drag.

d. Repeat the adjustment to the other wheel. The adjustment must be the same on both rear wheels.

e. Check the parking brake adjustment and install the backing plate plugs.

20. Install the wheel and tire assembly and lower the vehicle.

NAVAJO

1. Raise and safely support the vehicle. Remove the wheel and tire assembly and the brake drum.

2. Pull backward on the adjusting lever cable to disengage the adjusting lever from the adjusting screw. Move the outboard side of the adjusting screw upward and back off the pivot nut as far as it will go.

3. Pull the adjusting lever, cable and automatic adjuster spring down and toward the rear to unhook the pivot hook from the large hole in the secondary shoe web. Do not pry the pivot hook from the hole.

4. Remove the automatic adjuster spring and adjusting lever.

5. Remove the secondary shoe-to-anchor spring using a suitable brake spring removal/installation tool. Using the tool, remove the primary shoe-to-anchor spring and unhook the cable anchor. Remove the anchor pin plate, if equipped.

6. Remove the cable guide from the secondary shoe.

7. Remove the shoe hold-down springs, shoes, adjusting screw, pivot nut and socket. Note the color and position of each hold-down spring so they can be reassembled in the same position.

8. Remove the parking brake link and spring. Disconnect the parking brake cable from the parking brake lever.

9. Remove the secondary brake shoe. Remove the retainer clip and spring washer and remove the parking brake lever.

To install:

10. Clean the backing plate ledge pads and sand lightly. Apply a light coating of high temperature lithium grease to the points where the brake shoes touch the backing plate.

11. Install the parking brake lever on the secondary shoe and secure with the spring washer and retaining clip.

12. Position the brake shoes on the backing plate and install the hold-down spring pins, springs and cups. Install the parking brake link, spring and washer. Connect the parking brake cable to the parking brake lever.

13. Install the anchor pin plate, if equipped, and place the cable anchor over the anchor pin with the crimped side toward the backing plate.

14. Install the primary shoe-to-anchor spring using the brake spring removal/installation tool.

15. Install the cable guide on the secondary shoe with the flanged hole fitted into the hole in the secondary shoe. Thread the cable around the cable guide groove.

NOTE: **Make sure the cable is positioned in the groove and not between the guide and shoe web.**

16. Install the secondary shoe-to-anchor (long) spring.

NOTE: **Make sure the cable end is not cocked or binding on the anchor pin when installed. All parts should be flat on the anchor pin.**

17. Apply high temperature lithium grease to the threads and the socket end of the adjusting screw. Turn the adjusting screw into the adjusting pivot nut to the end of the threads and then loosen, ½ turn.

18. Place the adjusting socket on the screw and install the assembly between the shoe ends with the adjusting screw nearest the secondary shoe.

NOTE: **Be sure to install the adjusting screw on the same side of the vehicle from which it came. To prevent incorrect installation, the socket end of each adjusting screw is stamped with R or L, to indicate installation on the right or left side of the vehicle. The adjusting pivot nuts have lines machined around the body of the nut, 2 lines indicating the right side nut and 1 line indicating the left side nut.**

19. Hook the cable hook into the hole in the adjusting lever from the outboard plate side. The adjusting levers are also stamped with an **R** or **L** to indicate right or left side installation.

20. Place the hooked end of the adjuster spring in the large hole in the primary shoe web and connect the loop end of the spring to the adjuster lever hole.

21. Pull the adjuster lever, cable and automatic adjuster spring down toward the rear to engage the pivot hook in the large hole in the secondary shoe web.

22. After installation, check the action of the adjuster by pulling the section of the cable between the cable guide and the adjusting lever toward the secondary shoe web far enough to lift the lever past a tooth on the adjusting screw wheel. The lever should snap into position behind the next tooth and releasing the cable should cause the adjuster spring to return the lever to its original position. This return action will turn the adjusting screw 1 tooth.

23. If pulling the cable does not produce the action described in Step 22 or if lever action is sluggish instead of positive and sharp, check the position of the lever on the adjusting screw toothed wheel. With the brake in a vertical position, anchor at the top, the lever should contact the adjusting wheel 1 tooth above the center line of the adjusting screw. If the contact point is below the center line, the lever will not lock on the adjusting screw wheel teeth and the screw will not turn as the lever is actuated by the cable.

24. To find the cause of the condition described in Step 23, proceed as follows:

a. Check the cable and fittings. The cable should completely fill or extend slightly beyond the crimped section of the fittings. If this does not happen, the cable assembly may be damaged and should be replaced.

b. Check the cable guide for damage. The cable groove should be parallel to the shoe web and the body of the guide should lie flat against the web. Replace the guide if it shows damage.

c. Check the pivot hook on the lever. The hook surfaces should be square with the body on the lever for proper pivoting. Repair the hook or replace the lever if the hook shows damage.

d. Be sure the adjusting screw socket is properly seated in the notch in the shoe web.

25. Adjust the brake shoes using either a brake adjustment gauge or manually with the drums installed.

26. If using a brake adjustment gauge, proceed as follows:

a. Measure the inside diameter of the brake drum with the gauge.

Rear brake shoe assembly — Navajo

b. Reverse the tool and adjust the brake shoes until they touch the gauge. The gauge contact points on the shoes must be parallel to the vehicle with the center line through the center of the axle.

c. Install the drum and wheel and tire assembly. Lower the vehicle.

d. Apply the brakes sharply several times while driving the vehicle in reverse. Check brake operation by making several stops while driving forward.

27. If manually adjusting the brakes, proceed as follows:

a. Install the brake drum and wheel and tire assembly.

b. Remove the cover from the adjusting hole at the bottom of the backing plate and turn the adjusting screw, using a suitable brake adjusting tool, to expand the brake shoes until they drag against the brake drum.

c. When the shoes are against the drum, insert a narrow prybar through the brake adjusting hole and disengage the adjusting lever from the adjusting screw. While holding the adjusting lever away from the adjusting screw, loosen the adjusting screw with the brake adjusting tool, until the drum rotates freely without drag.

d. Install the adjusting hole cover and lower the vehicle.

e. Apply the brakes. If the pedal travels more than halfway to the floor, there is too much clearance between the brake shoes and drums. Repeat the adjustment procedure.

Wheel Cylinder

Removal and Installation

1. Raise and safely support the vehicle. Remove the wheel and tire assembly, brake drum and brake shoes.

2. Disconnect and plug the brake line at the wheel cylinder.

3. Remove the wheel cylinder retaining bolts and remove the cylinder from the brake backing plate.

4. Installation is the reverse of the removal procedure. Adjust the brakes and bleed the system.

Parking Brake Cable

Adjustment

EXCEPT NAVAJO

1. Make sure the rear brake shoes are properly adjusted.

2. Start the engine and depress the brake pedal several times while the vehicle is moving in reverse.

3. Stop the engine.

4. On MPV, remove the screw and remove the parking brake lever cover. Remove the adjusting nut clip.

5. On B Series Pick-Up, loosen the locknut at the end of the front cable, near the parking brake lever.

6. Turn the adjusting nut until the parking brake is fully applied when the lever is pulled 7–12 notches on B Series Pick-Up or 5–7 notches on MPV.

7. Tighten the locknut on B Series Pick-Up.

8. Install the adjusting nut clip and the parking brake lever cover on MPV.

NAVAJO

NOTE: Adjust the drum brakes before adjusting the parking brake. The brake drums must be cold for correct adjustment.

Initial Adjustment

Use this procedure when a new tension limiter is installed.

1. Apply the parking brake pedal to the fully engaged position.

2. Raise and safely support the vehicle, as necessary. Hold the threaded rod end of the right brake cable to keep it from spinning and thread the equalizer nut 2½ in. up the rod.

3. Check to make sure the cinch strap has slipped and there are less than 1⅜ in. remaining.

4. Release the parking brake and check for proper operation.

Field Adjustment

Use this procedure to correct a slack system if a new tension limiter is not installed.

1. Apply the parking brake pedal to the fully engaged position.

2. Raise and safely support the vehicle, as necessary. Grip the threaded rod to keep it from spinning and tighten the equalizer nut 6 full turns past its original position on the threaded rod.

3. Attach a suitable cable tension gauge in front of the equalizer assembly on the front cable and measure the cable tension. The cable tension should be 400–600 lbs. with the parking brake pedal in the last detent position. If tension is low, repeat Steps 2 and 3.

4. Release parking brake and check for rear wheel drag. There should be no brake drag.

Removal and Installation

FRONT

Except Navajo

1. Make sure the parking brake is fully released.

2. Remove the parking brake lever adjusting nut from the forward end of the front cable.

3. Remove the seat(s) and roll back the front floormat, as required. On MPV, remove the cable cover.

4. Raise and safely support the vehicle, as necessary.

5. Disengage the rear cables from the equalizer and remove the spring. Disconnect the front cable from the equalizer.

6. Remove the bolts from the cable retaining straps and remove the cable.

7. Installation is the reverse of the removal procedure. Adjust the parking brake.

Navajo

1. Raise and safely support the vehicle.

2. Back off the equalizer nut and remove the cable end of the intermediate cable from the tension limiter.

3. Remove the intermediate cable from the bracket and disconnect the intermediate cable from the front cable.

4. Lower the vehicle. Remove the forward ball end of the parking brake cable from the control assembly clevis.

5. Remove the cable from the control assembly.

6. Using a cord attached to the control lever end of the cable, remove the cable from the vehicle pulling it up into the passenger compartment.

To install:

7. Transfer the cord to the new cable. Position the cable in the vehicle, routing the cable through the dash panel. Remove the cord and secure the cable to the control.

8. Connect the forward ball end of the brake cable to the clevis of the control assembly. Raise and safely support the vehicle.

9. Route the cable through the bracket. Connect the front cable to the intermediate cable.

10. Connect the slug of the front or intermediate cable cable to the tension limiter connector. Adjust the parking brake cable at the equalizer using initial adjustment or field adjustment, as necessary.

11. Rotate both wheels to make sure the parking brakes are not dragging.

REAR

Except Navajo

1. Make sure the parking brake is fully released.

2. Loosen the parking brake lever adjusting nut.

3. Remove the seat(s) and roll back the front floormat, as required. On MPV, remove the cable cover.

4. Raise and safely support the vehicle.

5. Disconnect the rear cable from the equalizer.

6. Remove the rear wheel and tire assembly, brake drum and brake shoes.

7. Disconnect the cable from the backing plate.

8. Remove the bolts from the cable retaining straps and disconnect the spring from the cable. Remove the cable.

9. Installation is the reverse of the removal procedure. Adjust the parking brake.

Navajo

1. Release the parking brake control.

2. Raise and safely support the vehicle. Remove the wheel and tire assembly, brake drum and brake shoes.

3. Remove the locknut on the threaded rod at the equalizer. Disconnect the rear parking brake cable from the equalizer.

4. Compress the prongs that retain the cable housing to the frame bracket or crossmember and pull out the cable and housing.

5. Working on the wheel side of the backing plate, compress the prongs on the cable retainer so they can pass through the hole in the brake backing plate.

6. Lift the cable out of the slot in the parking brake lever, attached to the secondary brake shoe, and remove the cable through the brake backing plate hole.

To install:

7. Route the cable through the hole in the backing plate. Insert the cable anchor behind the slot in the parking brake lever. Make sure the cable is securely engaged in the parking brake lever so the cable return spring is holding the cable in the parking brake lever.

8. Push the retainer through the hole in the backing plate so the retainer prongs engage the backing plate.

9. Properly route the cable and insert the front of the cable through the frame bracket or crossmember until the prongs expand. Connect the rear cables to the equalizer.

10. Rotate the equalizer 90 degrees and recouple the threaded rod to the equalizer.

11. Install the brake shoes, brake drum and wheel and tire assembly. Adjust the rear brakes.

12. Adjust the parking brake tension using the initial adjustment or the field adjustment procedure, as necessary.

13. Apply and release the parking brake control several times. Rotate both wheels to make sure the parking brakes are applied and released and not dragging.

Brake System Bleeding

1. Clean all dirt from the master cylinder filler cap.

2. If the master cylinder is known or suspected to have air in the bore, it must be bled before any of the wheel cylinders or calipers. Proceed as follows:

    a. Loosen the brake line fitting approximately ¾ turn. Wrap a shop cloth around the tubing below the fitting to absorb escaping brake fluid.

    b. Have an assistant depress the brake pedal slowly through it's full travel to force air trapped in the master cylinder to escape at the fitting.

    c. Tighten the fitting and let the pedal return slowly to the fully released position. Do not release the pedal until the fitting is tightened or air will reenter the master cylinder.

    d. Wait 5 seconds and then repeat the operation until all air bubbles disappear.

    e. Repeat Steps a–d on the remaining master cylinder brake line fitting(s).

3. Continue to bleed the brake system by removing the rubber dust cap from the wheel cylinder bleeder fitting at the right-hand rear of the vehicle. Place a box wrench on the bleeder fitting and attach a rubber drain hose to the fitting. The end of the tube should fit snugly around the bleeder fitting. Submerge the other end of the tube in a container partially filled with clean brake fluid and loosen the fitting ¾ turn.

4. Have an assistant push the brake pedal down slowly through it's full travel. Close the bleeder fitting and allow the pedal to slowly return to it's full release position. Wait 5 seconds and repeat the procedure until no bubbles appear at the submerged end of the bleeder tube. Secure the bleeder fitting and remove the bleeder hose. Install the rubber dust cap on the bleeder fitting.

5. Repeat the procedure in Steps 3 and 4 and bleed the rest of the system in the following sequence: left rear, right front and left front.

NOTE: If equipped with anti-lock brakes, the electro-hydraulic valve must also be bled. It is not necessary to energize the valve to bleed it.

6. Refill the master cylinder reservoir after each wheel cylinder or caliper has been bled and install the master cylinder cover and gasket. When brake bleeding is completed, the fluid level should be filled to the maximum level indicated on the reservoir.

7. Always make sure the disc brake pistons are returned to their normal positions by depressing the brake pedal several times until normal pedal travel is established. If the pedal feels spongy, repeat the bleeding procedure.

Anti-lock Brake System Service

Precautions

● Use caution when disassembling any hydraulic components as the system will contain residual pressure.

● Cover the area around the component to be removed with a shop cloth to catch any brake fluid spray.

● Do not allow brake fluid to come in contact with painted surfaces.

Electronic Control Unit

Removal and Installation

1. Disconnect the negative battery cable.

CONTROL UNIT

Rear anti-lock brake system electronic control unit location – MPV

REAR ANTI-LOCK BRAKE SYSTEM DIAGNOSTIC CONNECTOR

ELECTRONIC CONTROL UNIT

Rear anti-lock brake system electronic control unit location – Navajo

2. On B Series Pick-Up, remove the driver's seat. On MPV, remove the inside trim panel from the left rear of the vehicle. The control unit is located under the dash on Navajo.

3. Disconnect the electrical connector from the control unit.

4. Remove the attaching screws and remove the control unit.

5. Installation is the reverse of the removal procedure. Check the system for proper operation.

Electro-Hydraulic Valve

Removal and Installation

1. Disconnect the negative battery cable.

2. Disconnect and plug the 2 brake lines connected to the valve.

3. Disconnect the wiring harness from the valve harness.

4. Remove the screw(s) retaining the valve and remove the valve.

5. Installation is the reverse of the removal procedure. Tighten the valve retaining screw(s) to 14–19 ft. lbs. (19–25 Nm) on all except Navajo where the torque is 11–14 ft. lbs. (15–20 Nm). Bleed the brake system.

Speed Sensor

Removal and Installation

EXCEPT NAVAJO

1. Disconnect the negative battery cable.

2. Pull the wiring harness connector off.

3. Remove the sensor hold-down bolt and remove the sensor from the axle housing.

To install:

4. Clean the axle mounting surface. Use care to prevent dirt from entering the axle housing.

5. Inspect the sensor O-ring for damage and replace, if necessary.

6. Check the sensor-to-sensor rotor clearance as follows:

   a. Measure the distance between the sensor attaching surface and the sensor rotor teeth.

   b. Measure the distance between the sensor attaching surface and the sensor pole piece.

   c. Subtract the distance recorded in Step b from the distance recorded in Step a.

   d. The clearance should be 0.020–0.039 in. (0.5–1.0mm) on B2200 or 0.020–0.047 in. (0.5–1.2mm) on B2600 and MPV.

7. If the clearance is less than specified, increase it using adjusting shim P049 27 155 or equivalent, during sensor installation. If the clearance is more than specified, replace the speed sensor.

8. Lubricate the speed sensor with clean engine oil and install the speed sensor. Tighten the attaching bolt to 12–17 ft. lbs. (16–23 Nm).

NAVAJO

1. Disconnect the negative battery cable.

2. Pull the wiring harness connector off.

3. Remove the sensor hold-down bolt and remove the sensor from the axle housing.

To install:

4. Clean the axle mounting surface. Use care to prevent dirt from entering the axle housing.

5. Inspect and clean the magnetized sensor pole piece to ensure that it is free from loose metal particles which could cause erratic system operation. Inspect the sensor O-ring for damage and replace, if necessary.

6. Lightly lubricate the sensor O-ring with motor oil, align the sensor bolt hole and install. Do not apply force to the plastic sensor connector. The sensor flange should slide to the mounting surface. This will insure the air gap setting is between 0.005–0.045 in. (0.127–1.14mm).

7. Install the hold-down bolt and tighten to 25–30 ft. lbs. (34–40 Nm).

8. Inspect the blue sensor connector seal and replace if missing or damaged. Push the connector on the sensor.

9. Connect the negative battery cable.

Sensor Rotor

Inspection

1. Remove the speed sensor.

2. View the sensor rotor teeth through the sensor hole. Rotate the rear axle and check the sensor rotor teeth for damage or breakage. Dented or broken teeth could cause the rear anti-lock brake system to function when not required.

Removal and Installation

To service the sensor rotor, the differential case must be removed from the axle housing and the sensor rotor pressed off the case.

NOTE: Upon removal, the sensor rotor is to be discarded. It is not to be reused.

FRONT SUSPENSION

Shock Absorbers

Removal and Installation

B SERIES PICK-UP

1. Raise and safely support the vehicle. Remove the wheel and tire assembly.

2. Remove the upper shock absorber nuts, retainer and bushing.

3. Remove the lower shock absorber-to-lower control arm mounting bolt, nut and washer.

4. Slightly compress the shock absorber and remove it from the vehicle. Remove the remaining retainers and bushing from the upper shock absorber stud.

To install:

5. Install the shock absorber and install the mounting bolts, nuts, washers and bushings. Do not tighten at this time.

6. Install the wheel and tire assembly and lower the vehicle.

7. With the vehicle unladen, tighten the upper shock absorber mounting nuts until the stud protrudes 0.28 in. (7mm) above the upper nut. Tighten the lower mounting bolt and nut to 41–59 ft. lbs. (55–80 Nm).

8. Check the front end alignment.

NAVAJO

1. Raise and safely support the vehicle. Remove the wheel and tire assembly.

2. Remove the shock absorber upper attaching nut, washer and bushing from the upper spring seat.

3. Remove the shock absorber lower mounting nut and washer from the radius arm stud.

4. Slide the shock absorber off the stud. Slightly compress the shock absorber and remove it from the vehicle.

5. Installation is the reverse of the removal procedure. Tight-

1. Shock absorber
2. Stabilizer
3. Torsion bar
4. Anchor arm
5. Anchor bolt
6. Tension rod
7. Upper arm
8. Lower arm

Front suspension assembly—2WD B Series Pick-Up

1. Shock absorber
2. Stabilizer
3. Torsion bar
4. Anchor arm
5. Anchor bolt
6. Upper arm
7. Lower arm

Front suspension assembly—4WD B Series Pick-Up

en the lower mounting nut to 39–53 ft. lbs. (53–72 Nm) and the upper mounting nut to 25–35 ft. lbs. (34–48 Nm).

MacPherson Strut

Removal and Installation

MPV

1. Raise and safely support the vehicle. Remove the wheel and tire assembly.
2. Support the lower control arm with a jack.
3. Remove the clip attaching the brake hose to the strut and disconnect the hose from the strut.
4. Remove the strut-to-knuckle attaching bolts and nuts.
5. Working in the engine compartment, remove the 4 attaching nuts from the strut tower and remove the strut assembly from the vehicle.
6. Remove the rubber cap from the upper mounting block. Loosen the upper attaching nut, but do not remove it.

7. Install a suitable spring compressor and compress the coil spring.
8. Remove the upper attaching nut and slowly relieve the tension on the coil spring, using the spring compressor. When the spring is no longer under tension, remove the spring compressor.
9. Remove the upper mounting block, upper spring seat, spring seat, coil spring, bump stopper and ring rubber from the strut.

To install:

10. Secure the strut in a vise equipped with protective jaw covers, so the strut will not be damaged.
11. Apply a suitable rubber grease to the ring rubber and install it on the bump stopper. Install the bump stopper on the strut.
12. Attach the spring compressor to the coil spring and compress the spring.
13. Install the compressed spring on the strut and install the spring seat.

14. Install the upper spring seat. The flat of the strut rod must fit correctly into the upper spring seat.

15. Install the upper mounting block. Install and loosely tighten the upper attaching nut.

16. Remove the spring compressor. Make sure the spring is properly seated in the upper and lower spring seats.

17. Secure the upper spring seat in a vise and tighten the upper attaching nut to 47–59 ft. lbs. (64–80 Nm). Install the rubber cap on the upper mounting block.

18. Install the strut assembly in the strut tower, making sure the white mark on the upper mounting block is in the front-inside direction. Install the attaching nuts and tighten to 22–27 ft. lbs. (29–36 Nm).

19. Install the strut to the knuckle and tighten the attaching bolts and nuts to 69–86 ft. lbs. (93–117 Nm).

20. Position the brake hose on the strut and install the clip. Remove the jack from under the lower control arm.

21. Install the wheel and tire assembly and lower the vehicle. Check the front end alignment.

Strut upper mounting block positioning—MPV

1. Nut
2. Upper mounting block
3. Upper spring seat
4. Spring seat
5. Coil spring
6. Bump stopper
7. Ring rubber
8. Strut

MacPherson strut assembly exploded view—MPV

Coil Springs

Removal and Installation

NAVAJO

1. Raise and safely support the vehicle. Place a jack under the axle.

2. Remove the nut attaching the shock absorber to the radius arm and slide the shock absorber off of the stud.

3. Remove the nut securing the spring to the axle and remove the retainer.

4. Slowly lower the axle to relieve the spring tension. Remove the spring by rotating the upper coil out of the tabs in the upper spring seat.

To install:

5. Install the top of the spring in the upper seat, rotating into position.

6. Raise the axle until the spring is seated in the lower spring seat. Install the lower retainer and tighten the nut to 70–100 ft. lbs. (95–136 Nm).

7. Connect the shock absorber to the radius arm and lower the vehicle.

Torsion Bar

Removal and Installation

B SERIES PICK-UP

1. Raise and safely support the vehicle. Remove the wheel and tire assembly.

2. Support the lower control arm with a jack.

3. Remove the cotter pin and nut from the lower ball joint stud. Separate the ball joint from the knuckle using tool 49 0727 575 or equivalent.

4. Remove the bolt, washer and nut attaching the shock absorber to the lower control arm.

5. Mark the position of the anchor bolt and swivel for reference during reassembly and remove the anchor bolt and swivel.

6. Mark the position of the torsion bar on the anchor arm and remove the anchor arm.

7. Mark the position of the torsion bar on the torque plate and remove the torsion bar. If removing the torsion bar from both sides of the vehicle, mark their positions as the torsion bars are not interchangeable.

8. Remove the attaching bolts and remove the torque plate.

9. Check the torsion bar for bending or for looseness between the serrations of the torsion bar and anchor arm and/or torque plate, replace as necessary.

To install:

10. Install the torque plate and tighten the attaching bolts to 55–69 ft. lbs. (75–93 Nm).

11. Coat the serrations of the torsion bar with grease and install in the torque plate, aligning the marks made during the removal procedure. If both torsion bars were removed, make sure the correct torsion bar is being installed.

12. Coat the serrations on the other end of the torsion bar with grease and install the anchor arm onto the torsion bar, aligning the marks made during the removal procedure.

13. Install the anchor bolt and swivel. Tighten the anchor bolt until the marks made during removal are aligned.

14. Connect the shock absorber to the lower control arm and loosely tighten the nut and bolt. Connect the lower ball joint to the knuckle; install the nut and tighten to 87–116 ft. lbs. (118–157 Nm). Install a new cotter pin.

15. Install the wheel and tire assembly and lower the vehicle. With the vehicle unladen, tighten the shock absorber-to-lower control arm bolt and nut to 41–59 ft. lbs. (55–80 Nm).

16. Check vehicle ride height as follows:

  a. Check the front and rear tire pressures and bring to specification.

b. Measure the distance from the center of each front wheel to the fender brim. The difference must not be greater than 0.39 in. (10mm).

c. If the difference is not as specified, turn the necessary torsion spring anchor bolt to adjust.

17. Check the front end alignment.

Upper Ball Joints

Inspection

B SERIES PICK-UP

1. Raise and safely support the vehicle. Remove the wheel and tire assembly.
2. Support the lower control arm with a jack.
3. Remove the clip attaching the brake hose to the upper control arm and disconnect the hose from the arm.
4. Remove the cotter pin and nut from the upper ball joint stud. Using tool 49 0727 575 or equivalent, separate the upper ball joint from the knuckle.
5. Install tool 49 0180 510B or equivalent to the ball joint stud and attach a suitable pull scale to the stud.
6. After rocking the ball joint stud back and forth 3–4 times, measure the pull scale reading while the ball joint stud is rotating. The pull scale reading should be 4.4–7.7 lbs.
7. If the pull scale reading is not as specified, replace the upper ball joint.

NAVAJO

NOTE: Always check and adjust the wheel bearings before ball joint inspection.

1. Raise and safely support the vehicle.
2. Place a jack under the axle beneath the coil spring.
3. Grasp the upper edge of the tire and move the wheel in and out. A $^1/_{32}$ in. or greater movement between the upper spindle arm and the upper control arm or upper part of the axle jaw indicates that the upper ball joint must be replaced.

Removal and Installation

B SERIES PICK-UP

1. Raise and safely support the vehicle. Remove the wheel and tire assembly.
2. Support the lower control arm with a jack.
3. Remove the clip attaching the brake hose to the upper control arm and disconnect the hose from the arm.
4. Remove the cotter pin and nut from the upper ball joint stud. Using tool 49 0727 575 or equivalent, separate the upper ball joint from the knuckle.
5. Remove the upper ball joint-to-upper control arm attaching bolts and remove the upper ball joint.
6. Installation is the reverse of the removal procedure. Tighten the upper ball joint-to-upper control arm attaching bolts to 18–25 ft. lbs. (25–33 Nm) and the upper ball joint stud nut to 22–38 ft. lbs. (29–51 Nm). Install a new cotter pin.
7. Check the front end alignment.

NAVAJO

2WD

1. Raise and safely support the vehicle. Remove the wheel and tire assembly.
2. Remove the brake caliper and support it aside with mechanics wire. Do not let the caliper hang by the brake hose.
3. Remove the dust cap, cotter pin, nut retainer, washer and outer bearing and remove the brake rotor from the spindle. Remove the brake dust shield.
4. Disconnect the steering linkage from the spindle and spindle arm by removing the cotter pin and nut. Remove the tie rod end from the spindle arm.

5. Remove the cotter pin and nut from the lower ball joint stud. Remove the axle clamp bolt from the axle.
6. Remove the camber adjuster from the upper ball joint stud and axle beam.
7. Strike the inside area of the axle to pop the lower ball joint loose from the axle beam. Remove the spindle and ball joint assembly from the axle.

NOTE: Do not use a pickle fork to separate the ball joint from the axle as this will damage the seal and ball joint socket.

To install:

8. Install the spindle assembly in a vise and remove the snapring from the lower ball joint. Remove the lower ball joint from the spindle using C-frame T74P-4635-C or equivalent and a suitable receiver cup to press the ball joint from the spindle.

NOTE: The lower ball joint must be removed first.

9. Repeat the procedure in Step 8 to remove the upper ball joint.

NOTE: Do not heat the ball joints or the spindle to aid in removal.

To install:

10. Assemble the C-frame and receiver cup and press in the upper ball joint.
11. Repeat the procedure in Step 10 to install the lower ball joint.

NOTE: Do not heat the ball joints or axle to aid in installation.

12. Install the snapring onto the ball joint.
13. Place the spindle and ball joints into the axle. Install the camber adjuster in the upper spindle over the ball joint stud making sure it is properly aligned.
14. Tighten the lower ball joint stud nut to 104–146 ft. lbs. (141–198 Nm). Continue tightening the castellated nut until it lines up with the hole in the stud, then install the cotter pin.
15. Install the clamp bolt into the axle boss and tighten to 48–65 ft. lbs. (65–88 Nm).
16. Install the remaining components in the reverse order of their removal.

4WD

1. Raise and safely support the vehicle. Remove the front wheel and tire assemblies.
2. Remove the disc brake caliper and wire it to the frame. Do not let the caliper hang by the brake hose.
3. Remove the hub locks, wheel bearings and locknuts.
4. Remove the hub, rotor and outer wheel bearing.
5. Remove the nuts retaining the spindle to the steering knuckle. Tap the spindle with a plastic hammer to jar the spindle from the knuckle. Remove the splash shield.
6. On the left side of the vehicle, remove the shaft and joint assembly by pulling the assembly out of the carrier. On the right side of the carrier, remove and discard the clamp from the shaft and joint assembly and the stub shaft. Pull the shaft and joint assembly from the splines of the stub shaft.
7. Remove the cotter pin from the tie rod nut and then remove the nut. Tap on the tie rod stud to free it from the steering arm.
8. Remove the upper ball joint snapring and remove the upper ball joint pinch bolt. Loosen the lower ball joint nut to the end of the stud.
9. Strike the inside of the knuckle near the upper and lower ball joints to break the knuckle loose from the ball joint studs.
10. Remove the camber adjuster sleeve. Note the position of the slot in the camber adjuster so it can be reinstalled in the same position during assembly.
11. Remove the lower ball joint nut. Place the knuckle in a vise

and remove the snapring from the bottom ball joint socket, if equipped.

12. Assemble C-frame T74P-4635-C and ball joint remover T83T-3050-A or equivalents on the lower ball joint. Turn the forcing screw clockwise until the lower ball joint is removed from the steering knuckle.

13. Assemble the C-frame and ball joint remover on the upper ball joint and remove in the same manner.

NOTE: Always remove the lower ball joint first.

To install:

14. Clean the steering knuckle bore and insert the lower ball joint in the knuckle as straight as possible.

15. Assemble C-frame T74P-4635-C, ball joint installer T83T-3050-A and receiver cup T80T-3010-A3 or equivalents to install the lower ball joint. Turn the forcing screw clockwise until the lower ball joint is firmly seated. Install the snapring on the lower ball joint.

NOTE: The lower ball joint must always be installed first.

16. Assemble the C-frame, ball joint installer and receiver cup to install the upper ball joint. Turn the forcing screw clockwise until the ball joint is firmly seated.

17. Install the camber adjuster into the support arm, making sure the slot is in the original position.

NOTE: The torque sequence in Steps 18 and 19 must be followed exactly when securing the knuckle. Excessive knuckle turning effort may result in reduced steering returnability if this procedure is not followed.

18. Install a new nut on the bottom ball joint stud. Tighten the nut to 90 ft. lbs. (122 Nm) minimum, then tighten to align the next slot in the nut with the hole in the stud. Install a new cotter pin.

19. Install the snapring on the upper ball joint stud. Install the upper ball joint pinch bolt and tighten to 48-65 ft. lbs. (65-88 Nm).

NOTE: The camber adjuster will seat itself into the knuckle at a predetermined position during the tightening sequence. Do not attempt to adjust this position.

20. On the right side of the carrier, install the rubber boot and new keystone clamps on the stub shaft slip yoke. Slide the right shaft and joint assembly into the slip yoke making sure the splines are fully engaged. Slide the boot over the assembly and crimp the keystone clamp using suitable pliers.

NOTE: The Dana model 35 axle does not have a blind spline, therefore pay special attention to make sure the yoke ears are in phase (in line) during assembly.

21. On the left side of the carrier, slide the shaft and joint assembly through the knuckle and engage the splines on the shaft in the carrier.

22. Install the splash shield and spindle onto the steering knuckle. Install and tighten the spindle nuts to 45 ft. lbs. (61 Nm).

23. Install the rotor on the spindle and install the outer wheel bearing in the race.

24. Install the wheel bearing, locknut, thrust bearing, snapring and locking hubs.

25. Install the caliper and the wheel and tire assemblies. Lower the vehicle.

Lower Ball Joints

Inspection

B SERIES PICK-UP AND 4WD MPV

1. Raise and safely support the vehicle. Remove the wheel and tire assembly.

2. On B Series Pick-Up, support the lower control arm with a jack.

3. On 4WD MPV, disconnect the stabilizer bar from the lower control arm.

4. Remove the cotter pin and nut from the lower ball joint stud. Separate the ball joint from the knuckle using tool 49 0727 575 or equivalent.

5. Install tool 49 0180 510B or equivalent to the ball joint stud and attach a suitable pull scale to the stud.

6. After rocking the ball joint stud back and forth 3-4 times, measure the pull scale reading while the ball joint stud is rotating. The pull scale reading should be 4.4-7.7 lbs.

7. If the pull scale reading is not as specified, replace the lower ball joint.

2WD MPV

1. Raise and safely support the vehicle. Remove the wheel and tire assembly.

2. Remove the brake caliper and support it aside with mechanics wire; do not let it hang by the brake hose.

3. Remove the nuts, bolts, spacer, washers and bushings and remove the compression rod from the lower control arm and chassis and disconnect the stabilizer bar from the lower control arm.

NOTE: The left-hand compression rod nut has left-hand thread.

4. Remove the cotter pin and nut and, using tool 49 0118 850C or equivalent, separate the tie rod end from the knuckle.

5. Remove the bolts and nuts and disconnect the strut from the knuckle.

6. Remove the cotter pin and nut from the lower ball joint stud. Using tool 49 0727 575 or equivalent, separate the lower ball joint from the knuckle.

7. Install tool 49 0180 510B or equivalent to the ball joint stud and attach a suitable pull scale to the stud.

8. After rocking the ball joint stud back and forth 3-4 times, measure the pull scale reading while the ball joint stud is rotating. The pull scale reading should be 39.6 lbs. or less. The rotation torque should be 156.2 inch lbs. (18 Nm) or less.

9. If the pull scale reading or rotation torque is not as specified, replace the entire lower control arm.

NAVAJO

NOTE: Always check and adjust the wheel bearings before ball joint inspection.

1. Raise and safely support the vehicle.

2. Place a jack under the axle beneath the coil spring.

3. Grasp the lower edge of the tire and move the wheel in and out. A $1/32$ in. or greater movement between the lower control arm or lower axle and the spindle indicates that the lower ball joint must be replaced.

Removal and Installation

B SERIES PICK-UP

1. Raise and safely support the vehicle. Remove the wheel and tire assembly.

2. Support the lower control arm with a jack.

3. On 2WD vehicles, remove the bolts attaching the tension rod to the lower control arm.

4. Remove the cotter pin and nut from the lower ball joint stud. Separate the ball joint from the knuckle using tool 49 0727 575 or equivalent.

5. Remove the bolts/nuts attaching the lower ball joint to the lower control arm and remove the lower ball joint.

6. Installation is the reverse of the removal procedure. Tighten the lower ball joint-to-lower control arm bolts/nuts to 32-40 ft. lbs. (43-54 Nm) on 2WD vehicles or 41-50 ft. lbs. (55-68 Nm) on 4WD vehicles. Tighten the lower ball joint stud nut to 87-116 ft. lbs. (118-157 Nm) and install a new cotter pin.

7. Check the front end alignment.

MPV

2WD

If the lower ball joint needs replacement, the entire lower control arm must be replaced.

4WD

1. Raise and safely support the vehicle. Remove the wheel and tire assembly.
2. Disconnect the stabilizer bar from the lower control arm.
3. Remove the cotter pin and nut from the lower ball joint stud. Separate the ball joint from the knuckle using tool 49 0727 575 or equivalent.
4. Remove the lower ball joint-to-lower control arm bolts and remove the lower ball joint.
5. Installation is the reverse of the removal procedure. Tighten the lower ball joint-to-lower control arm bolts to 75–101 ft. lbs. (102–137 Nm). Tighten the lower ball joint stud nut to 115–137 ft. lbs. (157–186 Nm) and install a new cotter pin.

NAVAJO

2WD

1. Raise and safely support the vehicle. Remove the wheel and tire assembly.
2. Remove the brake caliper and support it aside with mechanics wire. Do not let the caliper hang by the brake hose.
3. Remove the dust cap, cotter pin, nut retainer, washer and outer bearing and remove the brake rotor from the spindle. Remove the brake dust shield.
4. Disconnect the steering linkage from the spindle and spindle arm by removing the cotter pin and nut. Remove the tie rod end from the spindle arm.
5. Remove the cotter pin and nut from the lower ball joint stud. Remove the axle clamp bolt from the axle.
6. Remove the camber adjuster from the upper ball joint stud and axle beam.
7. Strike the inside area of the axle to pop the lower ball joint loose from the axle beam. Remove the spindle and ball joint assembly from the axle.

NOTE: Do not use a pickle fork to separate the ball joint from the axle as this will damage the seal and ball joint socket.

To install:

8. Install the spindle assembly in a vise and remove the snapring from the lower ball joint. Remove the lower ball joint from the spindle using C-frame T74P-4635-C or equivalent and a suitable receiver cup to press the ball joint from the spindle.

NOTE: Do not heat the ball joint or the spindle to aid in removal.

To install:

9. Assemble the C-frame and receiver cup and press in the lower ball joint.

NOTE: Do not heat the ball joint or axle to aid in installation.

10. Install the snapring onto the ball joint.
11. Place the spindle and ball joints into the axle. Install the camber adjuster in the upper spindle over the ball joint stud making sure it is properly aligned.
12. Tighten the lower ball joint stud nut to 104–146 ft. lbs. (141–198 Nm). Continue tightening the castellated nut until it lines up with the hole in the stud, then install the cotter pin.
13. Install the clamp bolt into the axle boss and tighten to 48–65 ft. lbs. (65–88 Nm).
14. Install the remaining components in the reverse order of their removal.

4WD

1. Raise and safely support the vehicle. Remove the front wheel and tire assemblies.
2. Remove the disc brake caliper and wire it to the frame. Do not let the caliper hang by the brake hose.
3. Remove the hub locks, wheel bearings and locknuts.
4. Remove the hub, rotor and outer wheel bearing.
5. Remove the nuts retaining the spindle to the steering knuckle. Tap the spindle with a plastic hammer to jar the spindle from the knuckle. Remove the splash shield.
6. On the left side of the vehicle, remove the shaft and joint assembly by pulling the assembly out of the carrier. On the right side of the carrier, remove and discard the clamp from the shaft and joint assembly and the stub shaft. Pull the shaft and joint assembly from the splines of the stub shaft.
7. Remove the cotter pin from the tie rod nut and then remove the nut. Tap on the tie rod stud to free it from the steering arm.
8. Remove the upper ball joint snapring and remove the upper ball joint pinch bolt. Loosen the lower ball joint nut to the end of the stud.
9. Strike the inside of the knuckle near the upper and lower ball joints to break the knuckle loose from the ball joint studs.
10. Remove the camber adjuster sleeve. Note the position of the slot in the camber adjuster so it can be reinstalled in the same position during assembly.
11. Remove the lower ball joint nut. Place the knuckle in a vise and remove the snapring from the bottom ball joint socket, if equipped.
12. Assemble C-frame T74P-4635-C and ball joint remover T83T-3050-A or equivalents on the lower ball joint. Turn the forcing screw clockwise until the lower ball joint is removed from the steering knuckle.

To install:

13. Clean the steering knuckle bore and insert the lower ball joint in the knuckle as straight as possible.
14. Assemble C-frame T74P-4635-C, ball joint installer T83T-3050-A and receiver cup T80T-3010-A3 or equivalents to install the lower ball joint. Turn the forcing screw clockwise until the lower ball joint is firmly seated. Install the snapring on the lower ball joint.
15. Install the camber adjuster into the support arm, making sure the slot is in the original position.

NOTE: The torque sequence in Steps 16 and 17 must be followed exactly when securing the knuckle. Excessive knuckle turning effort may result in reduced steering returnability if this procedure is not followed.

16. Install a new nut on the bottom ball joint stud. Tighten the nut to 90 ft. lbs. (122 Nm) minimum, then tighten to align the next slot in the nut with the hole in the stud. Install a new cotter pin.
17. Install the snapring on the upper ball joint stud. Install the upper ball joint pinch bolt and tighten to 48–65 ft. lbs. (65–88 Nm).

NOTE: The camber adjuster will seat itself into the knuckle at a predetermined position during the tightening sequence. Do not attempt to adjust this position.

18. On the right side of the carrier, install the rubber boot and new keystone clamps on the stub shaft slip yoke. Slide the right shaft and joint assembly into the slip yoke making sure the splines are fully engaged. Slide the boot over the assembly and crimp the keystone clamp using suitable pliers.

NOTE: The Dana model 35 axle does not have a blind spline, therefore pay special attention to make sure the yoke ears are in phase (in line) during assembly.

19. On the left side of the carrier, slide the shaft and joint as-

sembly through the knuckle and engage the splines on the shaft in the carrier.

20. Install the splash shield and spindle onto the steering knuckle. Install and tighten the spindle nuts to 45 ft. lbs. (61 Nm).

21. Install the rotor on the spindle and install the outer wheel bearing in the race.

22. Install the wheel bearing, locknut, thrust bearing, snapring and locking hubs.

23. Install the caliper and the wheel and tire assemblies. Lower the vehicle.

Upper Control Arms

Removal and Installation

B SERIES PICK-UP

1. Raise and safely support the vehicle. Remove the wheel and tire assembly.

2. Support the lower control arm with a jack.

3. Remove the clip attaching the brake hose to the upper control arm and disconnect the hose from the arm.

4. Remove the cotter pin and nut from the upper ball joint stud. Using tool 49 0727 575 or equivalent, separate the upper ball joint from the knuckle.

5. Remove the bolts and washers retaining the upper control arm shaft to the chassis and remove the upper control arm. Note the position of the alignment shims so they can be reassembled in their original positions.

6. Installation is the reverse of the removal procedure. Tighten the upper control arm shaft-to-chassis bolts to 54–69 ft. lbs. (74–93 Nm) on 2WD vehicles or 69–85 ft. lbs. (93–117 Nm) on 4WD vehicles. Tighten the upper ball joint stud nut to 22–38 ft. lbs. (29–51 Nm) and install a new cotter pin.

Lower Control Arms

Removal and Installation

B SERIES PICK-UP

1. Raise and safely support the vehicle. Remove the wheel and tire assembly.

2. Support the lower control arm with a jack.

3. Remove the cotter pin and nut from the lower ball joint stud. Separate the ball joint from the knuckle using tool 49 0727 575 or equivalent.

4. Remove the bolt, washer and nut attaching the shock absorber to the lower control arm.

5. Remove the torsion bar, anchor arm and torque plate assembly.

6. Remove the bolt(s) and nut(s) attaching the lower control arm to the frame.

7. On 2WD vehicles, remove the bolts attaching the tension rod to the lower control arm.

8. Remove the bolts, bushings, retainers, spacer and nuts connecting the stabilizer bar to the lower control arm.

9. Remove the lower control arm from the vehicle. Remove the lower ball joint, if necessary.

To install:

10. Position the lower control to the frame and install the attaching bolt(s) and nut(s), but do not tighten at this time.

11. Install the torsion bar, anchor arm and torque plate assembly.

12. On 2WD vehicles, install the tension rod bolt and tighten to 69–86 ft. lbs. (93–117 Nm).

13. Attach the stabilizer bar to the control arm with the bolts, bushings, retainers, spacer and nuts. Tighten the nuts so 0.73 in. (18.5mm) of thread is exposed at the end of the bolt.

14. Install the shock absorber to the lower control arm and loosely tighten the mounting bolt and nut.

15. Install the wheel and tire assembly and lower the vehicle.

16. With the vehicle unladen, tighten the lower control arm-to-frame bolt and nut on 2WD vehicles and the front side lower control arm-to-frame bolt and nut on 4WD vehicles to 87–116 ft. lbs. (118–157 Nm). Tighten the rear side lower control arm-to-frame bolt and nut on 4WD vehicles to 116–145 ft. lbs. (157–196 Nm).

17. With the vehicle unladen, tighten the shock absorber-to-lower control arm bolt and nut to 41–59 ft. lbs. (55–80 Nm).

18. Check vehicle ride height as follows:

   a. Check the front and rear tire pressures and bring to specification.

   b. Measure the distance from the center of each front wheel to the fender brim. The difference must not be greater than 0.39 in. (10mm).

   c. If the difference is not as specified, turn the necessary torsion spring anchor bolt to adjust.

19. Check the front end alignment.

MPV
2WD

1. Raise and safely support the vehicle. Remove the wheel and tire assembly.

2. Remove the brake caliper and support it aside with mechanics wire; do not let it hang by the brake hose.

3. Remove the nuts, bolts, spacer, washers and bushings and remove the compression rod from the lower control arm and chassis and disconnect the stabilizer bar from the lower control arm.

4. Remove the cotter pin and nut and, using tool 49 0118 850C or equivalent, separate the tie rod end from the knuckle.

5. Remove the bolts and nuts and disconnect the strut from the knuckle.

6. Remove the cotter pin and nut from the lower ball joint stud. Using tool 49 0727 575 or equivalent, separate the lower ball joint from the knuckle.

7. Remove the mounting bolt and nut and remove the lower control arm from the vehicle.

To install:

8. Position the lower control arm to the chassis and install the bolt and nut, but do not tighten at this time.

9. Install the knuckle to the lower control arm. Tighten the lower ball joint stud nut to 87–116 ft. lbs. (118–157 Nm) and install a new cotter pin.

10. Connect the strut to the knuckle and tighten the attaching bolts and nuts to 69–86 ft. lbs. (93–117 Nm).

11. Connect the tie rod end to the knuckle. Tighten the tie rod end stud nut to 43–58 ft. lbs. (59–78 Nm) and install a new cotter pin.

12. Install the compression rod to the lower control arm and chassis. Tighten the compression rod-to-lower control arm mounting bolts to 76–93 ft. lbs. (103–126 Nm) and the compression rod bushing-to-chassis bolts to 61–76 ft. lbs. (83–103 Nm). Install the compression rod nut but do not tighten at this time.

NOTE: The left-hand compression rod nut has left-hand thread.

13. Connect the stabilizer bar to the control arm with the bolt, washers, bushings, spacer and nuts. Tighten the nuts so 0.24 in. (6mm) of thread is exposed at the end of the bolt.

14. Install the caliper and the wheel and tire assembly. Lower the vehicle.

15. With the vehicle unladen, tighten the lower control arm-to-chassis bolt and nut to 94–108 ft. lbs. (146–172 Nm). Tighten the compression rod nut to 108–127 ft. lbs. (146–172 Nm).

16. Check the front end alignment.

4WD

1. Raise and safely support the vehicle. Remove the wheel and tire assembly.

2. Remove the bolt, retainers, bushings, spacer and nuts and disconnect the stabilizer bar from the lower control arm.

3. Remove the cotter pin and nut from the lower ball joint stud. Separate the ball joint from the knuckle using tool 49 0727 575 or equivalent.

4. Remove the lower control arm-to-chassis nuts and bolts and remove the lower control arm.

To install:

5. Position the lower control arm to the chassis and install the bolts and nuts. Do not tighten at this time.

6. Connect the lower ball joint to the knuckle and tighten the ball joint stud nut to 115–137 ft. lbs. (157–186 Nm). Install a new cotter pin.

7. Install the bolt, retainers, bushings, spacer and nuts and connect the stabilizer bar to the lower control arm. Tighten the nuts so 0.24 in. (6mm) of thread is exposed at the end of the bolt.

8. Install the wheel and tire assembly and lower the vehicle. With the vehicle unladen, tighten the lower control arm-to-chassis nuts and bolts to 101–127 ft. lbs. (137–172 Nm).

9. Check the front end alignment.

Stabilizer Bar

Removal and Installation

EXCEPT NAVAJO

1. Raise and safely support the vehicle. Remove the wheel and tire assembly.

2. On MPV, remove the splash shield.

3. Remove the bolt, retainers, bushings, spacer and nuts connecting the stabilizer bar end to the lower control arm.

4. Remove the stabilizer bar bushing bracket bolts and remove the stabilizer bar.

To install:

5. Install the stabilizer bar to the vehicle and loosely tighten the bushing bracket bolts.

6. Install the bolt, retainers, bushings, spacer and nuts connecting the stabilizer bar end to the lower control arm. Tighten the nuts so 0.73 in. (18.5mm) of thread is exposed at the end of the bolt on B Series Pick-Up or 0.24 in. (6mm) of thread is exposed at the end of the bolt on MPV.

7. Install the wheel and tire assembly and lower the vehicle.

8. With the vehicle unladen, tighten the stabilizer bar bushing bracket bolts to 16–20 ft. lbs. (22–26 Nm) on B Series pickup, 37–45 ft. lbs. (50–61 Nm) on 2WD MPV or 14–19 ft. lbs. (19–26 Nm) on 4WD MPV.

9. Check the front end alignment.

NAVAJO

2WD

1. Raise and safely support the vehicle.

2. Remove the nut and washer and disconnect the stabilizer link assembly from the front I-beam axle.

3. Remove the mounting bolts and remove the stabilizer bar retainers from the stabilizer bar assembly. Remove the stabilizer bar.

4. Installation is the reverse of the removal procedure. Tighten the retainer bolts to 35–50 ft. lbs. (47–68 Nm). Tighten the stabilizer bar link nuts to 30–44 ft. lbs. (40–60 Nm).

4WD

1. Raise and safely support the vehicle.

2. Remove the bolts and retainers from the center and right end of the stabilizer bar.

3. Remove the nut, bolt and washer retaining the stabilizer bar to the stabilizer link.

4. Remove the stabilizer bar and bushings.

5. Installation is the reverse of the removal procedure. Tighten the retainer bolts to 35–50 ft. lbs. (48–68 Nm). Tighten the stabilizer bar link nut to 30–44 ft. lbs. (40–60 Nm).

I-Beam Axle

Removal and Installation

2WD NAVAJO

1. Raise and safely support the vehicle. Remove the front wheel spindle, the front spring and the stabilizer bar, if equipped.

2. Remove the spring lower seat from the radius arm and then remove the bolt and nut that attaches the stabilizer bar bracket, if equipped, and radius arm to the front axle.

3. Remove the axle-to-frame pivot bracket bolt and nut.

To install:

4. Position the axle to the frame pivot bracket and install the bolt and nut finger tight.

5. Position the opposite end of the of the axle to the radius arm, install the attaching bolt from underneath through the bracket, the radius arm and the axle. Install the nut and tighten to 191–220 ft. lbs. (258–298 Nm).

6. Install the spring lower seat on the radius arm so the hole in the seat indexes over the arm-to-axle bolt. Install the front spring.

7. Install the front wheel spindle and stabilizer bar, if equipped.

8. Lower the vehicle and with the weight on the suspension, tighten the axle-to-frame pivot bracket bolts to 120–150 ft. lbs. (163–203 Nm).

Front Wheel Bearings

Adjustment

2WD VEHICLES

B Series Pick-Up

1. Raise and safely support the vehicle. Remove the wheel and tire assembly.

2. Remove the brake caliper and suspend it aside with rope or mechanics wire; do not let the caliper hang by the brake hose.

3. Remove the dust cap and cotter pin.

4. Tighten the locknut to 14–22 ft. lbs. (20–29 Nm) and turn the hub and rotor 2–3 times to seat the bearings.

5. Loosen the locknut until it can be turned by hand.

6. Attach a suitable pull scale to a wheel lug bolt and measure the frictional force.

7. Tighten the locknut until the pull scale reading, the initial turning torque, reaches the frictional force plus 1.3–2.4 lbs. Insert the retainer and secure with a new cotter pin.

8. Install the dust cap and the caliper. Install the wheel and tire assembly and lower the vehicle.

9. Before driving the vehicle, pump the brake pedal several times to restore normal brake travel.

Navajo

1. Raise the vehicle and support it safely.

2. Remove the wheel cover and the grease cap from the hub. Remove the cotter pin and the retainer. Discard the cotter pin.

3. Loosen the adjusting nut 3 turns.

4. Obtain running clearance between the brake rotor and disc brake pads by rocking the entire wheel and tire assembly in and out several times to push the caliper and brake pads away from the rotor.

NOTE: Do not pry on the caliper piston to obtain clearance.

5. While rotating the wheel, tighten the adjusting nut to 17–25 ft. lbs. (23–34 Nm) to seat the bearings.

6. Back off the adjusting nut ½ turn. Retighten the nut to 18–20 inch lbs. (2.0–2.3 Nm).

7. Install the retainer on the adjusting nut so the

castellations line up with the hole in the spindle without moving the nut. Install a new cotter pin.

8. Check the front wheel rotation. If the wheel rotates properly, reinstall the grease cap and the wheel cover. If rotation is noisy or rough, remove, inspect and lubricate the bearings and bearing races.

9. Before driving the vehicle, pump the brake pedal several times to restore normal brake travel.

Removal and Installation

2WD VEHICLES

1. Raise and safely support the vehicle. Remove the wheel and tire assembly.

2. Remove the brake caliper and support it with mechanics wire. Do not let the caliper hang by the brake hose.

3. Remove the grease cap, cotter pin, retainer, adjusting nut and washer. Discard the cotter pin.

4. Remove the outer bearing and pull the hub and rotor off the spindle. Remove the grease seal using a seal removal tool. Discard the grease seal.

5. Remove the inner bearing from the hub. Remove all traces of old lubricant from the bearings, hub and spindle with solvent and dry thoroughly.

6. Inspect the bearings and bearing races for scratches, pits or cracks. If the bearings and/or races are worn or damaged, remove the races with a brass drift.

To install:

7. If the bearing races were removed, install new races in the hub with suitable installation tools. Make sure the races are properly seated.

8. Using a bearing packer, pack the bearings with high-temperature wheel bearing grease. If a packer is not available, work as much grease as possible between the rollers and cages by hand.

9. Place a small amount of grease within the hub and grease the races. Install the inner bearing. Install a new wheel seal using a seal installer. Apply grease to the lips of the seal.

10. Install the hub and rotor assembly on the spindle. Install the outer bearing, washer and adjusting nut. Adjust the bearings.

11. Install the retainer, a new cotter pin and the grease cap.

12. Install the caliper and the wheel and tire assembly. Lower the vehicle.

13. Before driving the vehicle, pump the brake pedal several times to restore normal brake travel.

REAR SUSPENSION

Shock Absorber

Removal and Installation

1. Raise and safely support the vehicle.

2. Place a jack under the rear axle and raise slightly to take the load off the shock absorbers.

3. On MPV equipped with automatic load leveling, disconnect the air line from the shock absorber.

4. Remove the shock absorber lower attaching nut or nut and bolt and swing the lower end free of the mounting bracket or stud on the axle housing or spring plate.

5. Remove the upper attaching bolt and/or nut(s) and remove the shock absorber.

6. Installation is the reverse of the removal procedure. Tighten the lower attaching nut or nut and bolt to 47–58 ft. lbs. (64–78 Nm) on B Series Pick-Up, 56–76 ft. lbs. (76–103 Nm) on MPV or 41–53 ft. lbs. (55–72 Nm) on Navajo.

7. Tighten the upper attaching bolt and/or nut(s) to 47–58 ft. lbs. (64–78 Nm) on B Series Pick-Up, 56–76 ft. lbs. (76–103 Nm) on MPV or 15–21 ft. lbs. (21–29 Nm) on Navajo.

Coil Springs

Removal and Installation

MPV

1. Raise and safely support the vehicle. Remove the splash shield.

2. Remove the stabilizer bar.

3. Remove the nut and disconnect the height sensor from the rear axle.

4. Remove the bolt attaching the parking brake cable bracket.

5. Support the rear axle housing with a jack. Raise the jack slightly to take the load off the shock absorbers.

6. Remove the attaching bolts and nuts and disconnect the shock absorbers from the lower axle housing.

7. Slowly lower the axle housing until the spring tension is relieved. Remove the coil springs.

8. Remove the spring seats and bump stopper, if equipped.

To install:

9. Install the upper and lower spring seats and the bump stopper, if removed.

10. Install the coil springs, making sure the larger diameter coil is toward the axle housing.

11. Raise the axle housing enough to connect the shock absorbers. Install the attaching bolts and nuts and tighten to 56–76 ft. lbs. (76–103 Nm). Remove the jack.

12. Install the bolt attaching the parking brake cable bracket and the nut attaching the height sensor.

13. Install the stabilizer bar. Tighten the link bolt nut until 0.28 in. (7mm) of thread is exposed at the top of the link bolt. Do not tighten the stabilizer bar bushing bracket bolts at this time.

14. Lower the vehicle. With the vehicle unladen, tighten the stabilizer bar bushing bracket bolts to 23–38 ft. lbs. (34–51 Nm).

15. Install the splash shield.

Leaf Springs

Removal and Installation

B SERIES PICK-UP

2WD

1. Raise and safely support the vehicle. Remove the wheel and tire assembly.

2. Support the rear axle housing with a jack. Raise the jack slightly to take the load off the shock absorber.

3. Remove the nut and washers and slide the shock absorber off of the spring clamp stud. Lower the jack just enough to relieve the spring tension.

4. Remove the nuts and washers and remove the U-bolts, spring clamp and rubber stopper.

5. Support the leaf spring and remove the attaching bolts and the spring pin at the front of the leaf spring.

6. Remove the nuts and washers and remove the shackle pin and shackle plate at the rear of the leaf spring.

7. Remove the leaf spring and bushings.

8. Installation is the reverse of the removal procedure. Tighten the shackle pin nuts to 43–58 ft. lbs. (59–78 Nm). Tighten the

spring pin attaching bolts to 12–17 ft. lbs. (16–23 Nm) and the spring pin nut to 58–72 ft. lbs. (78–98 Nm).

9. Tighten the U-bolt nuts to 47–58 ft. lbs. (64–78 Nm) and the lower shock absorber mounting nut to 47–58 ft. lbs. (64–78 Nm).

4WD

1. Raise and safely support the vehicle. Remove the wheel and tire assembly.

2. Support the rear axle housing with a jack. Raise the jack slightly to take the load off the shock absorber.

3. Remove the nut and bolt and disconnect the shock absorber from the axle housing. Lower the jack just enough to relieve the spring tension.

4. Remove the nuts and washers and remove the U-bolts, spring clamp and rubber stopper.

5. Remove the attaching bolts and the spring pin at the front of the leaf spring.

6. Remove the nuts and washers and remove the shackle pin and shackle plate at the rear of the leaf spring.

7. Lower the axle enough to allow clearance for the leaf spring to be removed. Remove the leaf spring and bushings.

8. Installation is the reverse of the removal procedure. Tighten the shackle pin nuts to 43–58 ft. lbs. (59–78 Nm). Tighten the spring pin attaching bolts to 12–17 ft. lbs. (16–23 Nm) and the spring pin nut to 58–72 ft. lbs. (78–98 Nm).

9. Tighten the U-bolt nuts to 88–101 ft. lbs. (120–137 Nm) and the lower shock absorber mounting bolt and nut to 47–58 ft. lbs. (64–78 Nm).

NAVAJO

1. Raise the vehicle and safely support on the frame until the weight is off the rear spring, with the tires still touching the floor.

2. Remove the nuts from the spring U-bolts and drive the U-bolts from the U-bolt plate.

3. Remove the spring-to-bracket nut and bolt at the front of the spring.

4. Remove the shackle upper and lower nuts and bolts at the rear of the spring. Remove the spring and shackle assembly from the rear shackle bracket.

To install:

5. Position the spring in the shackle and install the upper shackle-to-spring bolt and nut with the bolt head facing outboard.

6. Position the front end of the spring in the bracket and install the bolt and nut. Position the shackle in the rear bracket and install the bolt and nut.

7. Position the spring on the bottom of the axle with the spring tie bolt centered in the hole provided in the seat.

8. Install the spring U-bolts, U-bolt plate and nuts and lower the vehicle. Tighten the spring U-bolt nuts to 88–108 ft. lbs. (119–146 Nm), the front spring bolt and nut to 64–91 ft. lbs. (87–123 Nm) and the rear shackle bolts and nuts to 75–115 ft. lbs. (100–155 Nm).

Rear Control Arms

Removal and Installation

MPV

Lateral Rod

1. Raise and safely support the vehicle.

2. Support the axle housing with a jack.

3. Remove the lateral rod-to-chassis stud bolt and nut and the lateral rod-to-axle housing nut.

4. Remove the lateral rod.

5. Installation is the reverse of the removal procedure. Make sure the lateral rod is installed with the identification mark toward the body.

6. Tighten the lateral rod-to-axle housing nut to 108–127 ft. lbs. (146–167 Nm). Tighten the lateral rod-to-chassis stud bolt and nuts to 94–127 ft. lbs. (128–167 Nm).

Lateral rod positioning—MPV

Rear control arm installation—MPV

Upper Control Arms

1. Raise and safely support the vehicle.
2. Support the axle housing with a jack.
3. Remove the upper control arm-to-chassis bolt and nut and the upper control arm-to-axle housing bolt and nut.
4. Remove the upper control arm.
5. Installation is the reverse of the removal procedure. Tighten the upper control arm attaching bolts and nuts to 94–127 ft. lbs. (128–167 Nm).

Lower Control Arms

1. Raise and safely support the vehicle.
2. Support the axle housing with a jack.
3. Remove the lower control arm-to-chassis bolt and nut and the lower control arm-to-axle housing bolt and nut.
4. Remove the lower control arm.
5. Installation is the reverse of the removal procedure. Tighten the upper control arm attaching bolts and nuts to 101–127 ft. lbs. (137–167 Nm).

SPECIFICATIONS

ENGINE IDENTIFICATION

Year	Model	Engine Displacement cu. in. (cc/liter)	Engine Series Identification	No. of Cylinders	Engine Type
1988	Montero	156 (2555/2.6)	G54B	4	SOHC
	Pick-Up	122 (1997/2.0)	G63B	4	SOHC
	Pick-Up	156 (2555/2.6)	G54B	4	SOHC
	Van	143 (2350/2.4)	G64B	4	SOHC
1989	Montero	156 (2555/2.6)	G54B	4	SOHC
	Montero	181 (2972/3.0)	6G72	6	DOHC
	Pick-Up	122 (1997/2.0)	G63B	4	SOHC
	Pick-Up	156 (2555/2.6)	G54B	4	SOHC
	Van	143 (2350/2.4)	4G64	4	SOHC
1990	Montero	181 (2972/3.0)	6G72	6	DOHC
	Pick-Up	143 (2350/2.4)	4G64	4	SOHC
	Pick-Up	181 (2972/3.0)	6G72	6	DOHC
	Van	143 (2350/2.4)	4G64	4	SOHC
1991–92	Montero	181 (2972/3.0)	6G72	6	DOHC
	Pick-Up	143 (2350/2.4)	4G64	4	SOHC
	Pick-Up	181 (2972/3.0)	6G72	6	DOHC

SOHC—Single overhead cam
DOHC—Dual overhead cam

GENERAL ENGINE SPECIFICATIONS

Year	Model	Engine Displacement cu. in. (cc)	Fuel System Type	Net Horsepower @ rpm	Net Torque @ rpm (ft. lbs.)	Bore × Stroke (in.)	Compression Ratio	Oil Pressure @ rpm
1988	Montero	156 (2555)	2bbl	109 @ 5000	142 @ 3500	3.59 × 3.86	8.7:1	45–90 @ 3000
	Pick-Up	122 (1997)	2bbl	88 @ 5000	108 @ 3500	3.31 × 3.54	8.5:1	45–90 @ 3000
	Pick-Up	156 (2555)	2bbl	109 @ 5000	142 @ 3500	3.59 × 3.86	8.7:1	45–90 @ 3000
	Van	143 (2350)	MPI	107 @ 5000	132 @ 3500	3.41 × 3.94	8.5:1	40–85 @ 3000
1989	Montero	156 (2555)	2bbl	109 @ 5000	142 @ 3500	3.59 × 3.86	8.7:1	45–90 @ 3000
	Montero	181 (2972)	MPI	143 @ 5000	168 @ 2500	3.59 × 2.99	8.9:1	30–80 @ 3000
	Pick-Up	122 (1997)	2bbl	88 @ 5000	108 @ 3500	3.31 × 3.54	8.5:1	45–90 @ 3000
	Pick-Up	156 (2555)	2bbl	109 @ 5000	142 @ 3500	3.59 × 3.86	8.7:1	45–90 @ 3000
	Van	143 (2350)	MPI	107 @ 5000	132 @ 3500	3.41 × 3.94	8.5:1	40–85 @ 3000
1990	Montero	181 (2972)	MPI	143 @ 5000	168 @ 2500	3.59 × 2.99	8.9:1	30–80 @ 3000
	Pick-Up	143 (2350)	MPI	116 @ 5000	132 @ 3500	3.41 × 3.94	8.5:1	40–85 @ 3000
	Pick-Up	181 (2972)	MPI	143 @ 5000	168 @ 2500	3.59 × 2.99	8.9:1	30–80 @ 3000
	Van	143 (2350)	MPI	107 @ 5000	132 @ 3500	3.41 × 3.94	8.5:1	40–85 @ 3000
1991–92	Montero	181 (2972)	MPI	143 @ 5000	168 @ 2500	3.59 × 2.99	8.9:1	30–80 @ 3000
	Pick-Up	143 (2350)	MPI	116 @ 5000	132 @ 3500	3.41 × 3.94	8.5:1	40–85 @ 3000
	Pick-Up	181 (2972)	MPI	143 @ 5000	168 @ 2500	3.59 × 2.99	8.9:1	30–80 @ 3000

MPI—Multi-port injection
2bbl—2 barrel carb.

ENGINE TUNE-UP SPECIFICATIONS

Year	Model	Engine Displacement cu. in. (cc)	Spark Plugs Type	Gap (in.)	Ignition Timing (deg.) MT	AT	Compression Pressure (psi)	Fuel Pump (psi)	Idle Speed (rpm) MT	AT	Valve Clearance ③ In.	Ex.
1988	Montero	156 (2555)	RN9YC	0.039–0.043	7B	7B	170	3–4	800	800	Hyd.	Hyd.
	Pick-Up	122 (1997)	RN9YC	0.039–0.043	8B	8B	170	3–4	750	750	Hyd.	Hyd.
	Pick-Up	156 (2555)	RN9YC	0.039–0.043	7B	7B	170	3–4	800	800	Hyd.	Hyd.
	Van	143 (2350)	RN9YC	0.039–0.043	—	①	120	28	—	750	Hyd.	Hyd.
1989	Montero	156 (2555)	RN9YC	0.039–0.043	7B	7B	170	3–4	800	800	Hyd.	Hyd.
	Montero	181 (2972)	RN114C4	0.039–0.043	②	②	120	38	700	700	Hyd.	Hyd.
	Pick-Up	122 (1997)	RN9YC	0.039–0.043	8B	8B	170	3–4	750	750	Hyd.	Hyd.
	Pick-Up	156 (2555)	RN9YC	0.039–0.043	7B	7B	170	3–4	800	800	Hyd.	Hyd.
	Van	143 (2350)	RN9YC	0.039–0.043	—	①	120	38	—	750	Hyd.	Hyd.
1990	Montero	181 (2972)	RN114C4	0.039–0.043	②	②	120	38	700	700	Hyd.	Hyd.
	Pick-Up	143 (2350)	RN9YC	0.039–0.043	①	①	120	38	750	750	Hyd.	Hyd.
	Pick-Up	181 (2972)	RN114C4	0.039–0.043	②	②	120	38	700	700	Hyd.	Hyd.
	Van	143 (2350)	RN9YC	0.039–0.043	—	①	120	38	—	750	Hyd.	Hyd.
1991	Montero	181 (2972)	RN114C4	0.039–0.043	②	②	120	38	700	700	Hyd.	Hyd.
	Pick-Up	143 (2350)	RN9YC	0.039–0.043	①	①	120	38	750	750	Hyd.	Hyd.
	Pick-Up	181 (2972)	RN114C4	0.039–0.043	②	②	120	38	700	700	Hyd.	Hyd.
1992	SEE UNDERHOOD SPECIFICATIONS STICKER											

Hyd.—Hydraulic
① Basic timing: 5B
   Actual timing: 8B
② Basic timing: 5B
   Actual timing: 15B
③ Jet valve clearance (all engines): 0.010 in.
   (0.25 mm)

FIRING ORDERS

NOTE: To avoid confusion, always replace spark plug wires one at a time.

2.0L, 2.4L and 2.6L Engines
Engine Firing Order: 1–3–4–2
Distributor Rotation: Clockwise

3.0L Engine
Engine Firing Order: 1–2–3–4–5–6
Distributor Rotation: Counterclockwise

CAPACITIES

Year	Model	Engine Displacement cu. in. (cc)	Engine Crankcase (qts.) with Filter	without Filter	Transmission (pts.) 4-Spd	5-Spd	Auto.	Drive Axle (pts.)	Fuel Tank (gal.)	Cooling System (qts.)
1988	Montero	156 (2555)	5	4.5	—	4.7	15.2	⑦	16	8.5
	Pick-Up	122 (1997)	4	3.5	—	5	14.4	3.2	⑨	8.3
	Pick-Up	156 (2555)	①	②	—	5	⑪	⑧	⑨	8.3
	Van	143 (2350)	4	3.5	—	—	14.4	3.2	14	8.5⑩
1989	Montero	156 (2555)	5	4.5	—	5	—	⑤	16	8.5
	Montero	181 (2972)	5	4.5	—	5	15.2	⑫	⑬	9.5
	Pick-Up	122 (1997)	4	3.5	—	5	14.4	3.2	⑨	8.3
	Pick-Up	156 (2555)	①	②	—	5	⑪	⑥	⑨	8.3
	Van	143 (2350)	4	3.5	—	—	14.4	3.2	14	8.5⑩
1990	Montero	181 (2972)	5.5	5	—	5	15.2	⑫	⑬	9.5
	Pick-Up	143 (2350)	③	④	—	5	14.8	3.2	⑨	6.5
	Pick-Up	181 (2972)	5.5	5	—	5	14.8	5.4	⑨	9
	Van	143 (2350)	4	3.5	—	—	14.4	3.2	14	8.5⑩
1991–92	Montero	181 (2972)	5.5	5	—	5	15.2	⑫	⑬	9.5
	Pick-Up	143 (2350)	③	④	—	5	14.8	3.2	⑨	6.5
	Pick-Up	181 (2972)	5.5	5	—	5	14.8	5.4	⑨	9

① 2WD: 4.5 qts.
4WD: 5 qts.
② 2WD: 4 qts.
4WD: 4.5 qts.
③ 2WD: 4.5 qts.
4WD: 5.5 qts.
④ 2WD: 4 qts.
4WD: 5 qts.

⑤ Front axle: 2.3 pts.
Rear axle: 3.8 pts.
⑥ Front axle: 2.3 pts.
Rear axle: 3.2 pts.
⑦ Front axle: 2.3 pts.
Conventional rear axle: 2.3 pts.
Limited-slip rear axle: 3.8 pts.

⑧ Front axle: 2.3 pts.
Conventional rear axle: 2.7 pts.
Limited-slip rear axle: 3.2 pts.
⑨ 2WD standard body: 14 gals.
2WD long body: 18 gals.
4WD standard body: 16 gals.
4WD long body: 20 gals.
⑩ Add ½ qt. with rear heater

⑪ 2WD: 14.4 pts.
4WD: 15.2 pts.

⑫ Front axle: 2.3 pts.
Rear axle: 2.6L engine—3.8 pts.
3.0L engine—5.2 pts.
⑬ 2 door: 20 gal.
4 door: 24 gal.

CAMSHAFT SPECIFICATIONS

All measurements given in inches.

Year	Engine Displacement cu. in. (cc)	Journal Diameter 1	2	3	4	5	Lobe Lift ① In.	Ex.	Bearing Clearance	Camshaft End Play
1988	122 (1997)	1.34	1.34	1.34	1.34	1.34	1.66–1.68	1.66–1.68	0.002–0.004	0.004–0.016
	143 (2350)	1.34	1.34	1.34	1.34	1.34	1.65–1.67	1.65–1.67	0.002–0.004	0.004–0.016
	156 (2555)	1.34	1.34	1.34	1.34	1.34	1.65–1.67	1.65–1.67	0.001–0.002	0.004–0.016
1989	122 (1997)	1.34	1.34	1.34	1.34	1.34	1.66–1.68	1.66–1.68	0.002–0.004	0.004–0.016
	143 (2350)	1.34	1.34	1.34	1.34	1.34	1.65–1.67	1.65–1.67	0.002–0.004	0.004–0.016
	156 (2555)	1.34	1.34	1.34	1.34	1.34	1.65–1.67	1.65–1.67	0.001–0.002	0.004–0.016
	181 (2972)	1.34	1.34	1.34	1.34	—	1.60–1.62	1.60–1.62	0.002–0.004	NA
1990	143 (2350)	1.34	1.34	1.34	1.34	1.34	1.65–1.67	1.65–1.67	0.002–0.004	0.004–0.016
	181 (2972)	1.34	1.34	1.34	1.34	—	1.60–1.62	1.60–1.62	0.002–0.004	NA
1991–92	143 (2350)	1.34	1.34	1.34	1.34	1.34	1.65–1.67	1.65–1.67	0.002–0.004	0.004–0.016
	181 (2972)	1.34	1.34	1.34	1.34	—	1.60–1.62	1.60–1.62	0.002–0.004	NA

NA—Not available

① Diameter of cam lobe

CRANKSHAFT AND CONNECTING ROD SPECIFICATIONS

All measurements are given in inches.

Year	Engine Displacement cu. in. (cc)	Crankshaft Main Brg. Journal Dia.	Main Brg. Oil Clearance	Shaft End-play	Thrust on No.	Connecting Rod Journal Diameter	Oil Clearance	Side Clearance
1988	122 (1997)	2.24	0.001–0.004	0.002–0.016	3	NA	0.001–0.002	0.004–0.016
	143 (2350)	2.24	0.001–0.004	0.002–0.016	3	NA	0.001–0.004	0.004–0.016
	156 (2555)	2.36	0.001–0.004	0.002–0.016	3	2.87	0.001–0.002	0.004–0.016
1989	122 (1997)	2.24	0.001–0.004	0.002–0.016	3	NA	0.001–0.002	0.004–0.016
	143 (2350)	2.24	0.001–0.004	0.002–0.016	3	NA	0.001–0.004	0.004–0.016
	156 (2555)	2.36	0.001–0.004	0.002–0.016	3	2.87	0.001–0.002	0.004–0.016
	181 (2972)	2.36	0.001–0.004	0.002–0.012	3	1.97	0.001–0.004	0.004–0.016
1990	143 (2350)	2.24	0.001–0.004	0.002–0.016	3	NA	0.001–0.004	0.004–0.016
	181 (2972)	2.36	0.001–0.004	0.002–0.012	3	1.97	0.001–0.004	0.004–0.016

CRANKSHAFT AND CONNECTING ROD SPECIFICATIONS

All measurements are given in inches.

| Year | Engine Displacement cu. in. (cc) | Crankshaft | | | | Connecting Rod | | |
		Main Brg. Journal Dia.	Main Brg. Oil Clearance	Shaft End-play	Thrust on No.	Journal Diameter	Oil Clearance	Side Clearance
1991–92	143 (2350)	2.24	0.001–0.004	0.002–0.016	3	NA	0.001–0.004	0.004–0.016
	181 (2972)	2.36	0.001–0.004	0.002–0.012	3	1.97	0.001–0.004	0.004–0.016

NA—Not available

VALVE SPECIFICATIONS

| Year | Engine Displacement cu. in (cc) | Seat Angle (deg.) | Face Angle (deg.) | Spring Test Pressure (lbs.) | Spring Installed Height (in.) | Stem-to-Guide Clearance (in.) | | Stem Diameter (in.) | |
						Intake	Exhaust	Intake	Exhaust
1988	122 (1997)	45	45–45.5	72	1.60	0.001–0.004	0.002–0.006	0.315	0.315
	143 (2350)	44–44.5	45–45.5	73	1.60	0.001–0.004	0.002–0.006	0.310	0.310
	156 (2555)	45	45–45.5	72	1.60	0.001–0.004	0.002–0.006	0.315	0.315
1989	122 (1997)	45	45–45.5	72	1.60	0.001–0.004	0.002–0.006	0.315	0.315
	143 (2350)	44–44.5	45–45.5	73	1.60	0.001–0.004	0.002–0.006	0.310	0.310
	156 (2555)	45	45–45.5	72	1.60	0.001–0.004	0.002–0.006	0.315	0.315
	181 (2972)	44–44.5	45–45.5	74	1.60	0.001–0.004	0.002–0.006	0.313	0.312
1990	143 (2350)	44–44.5	45–45.5	73	1.60	0.001–0.004	0.002–0.006	0.310	0.310
	181 (2972)	44–44.5	45–45.5	74	1.60	0.001–0.004	0.002–0.006	0.313	0.312
1991–92	143 (2350)	44–44.5	45–45.5	73	1.60	0.001–0.004	0.002–0.006	0.310	0.310
	181 (2972)	44–44.5	45–45.5	74	1.60	0.001–0.004	0.002–0.006	0.313	0.312

PISTON AND RING SPECIFICATIONS

All measurements are given in inches.

| Year | Engine Displacement cu. in. (cc) | Piston Clearance | Ring Gap | | | Ring Side Clearance | | |
			Top Compression	Bottom Compression	Oil Control	Top Compression	Bottom Compression	Oil Control
1988	122 (1997)	0.0004–0.0012	0.010–0.031	0.008–0.031	0.008–0.039	0.001–0.004	0.001–0.004	NA
	143 (2350)	0.0008–0.0016	0.010–0.031	0.008–0.031	0.008–0.039	0.001–0.004	0.001–0.004	NA
	156 (2555)	0.0008–0.0016	0.012–0.031	0.010–0.031	0.008–0.039	0.002–0.005	0.001–0.004	NA

PISTON AND RING SPECIFICATIONS

All measurements are given in inches.

Year	Engine Displacement cu. in. (cc)	Piston Clearance	Ring Gap			Ring Side Clearance		
			Top Compression	Bottom Compression	Oil Control	Top Compression	Bottom Compression	Oil Control
1989	122 (1997)	0.0004–0.0012	0.010–0.031	0.008–0.031	0.008–0.039	0.001–0.004	0.001–0.004	NA
	143 (2350)	0.0008–0.0016	0.010–0.031	0.008–0.031	0.008–0.039	0.001–0.004	0.001–0.004	NA
	156 (2555)	0.0008–0.0016	0.012–0.031	0.010–0.031	0.008–0.039	0.002–0.005	0.001–0.004	NA
	181 (2972)	0.0008–0.0016	0.012–0.031	0.010–0.031	0.008–0.039	0.001–0.004	0.001–0.004	NA
1990	143 (2350)	0.0008–0.0016	0.010–0.031	0.008–0.031	0.008–0.039	0.001–0.004	0.001–0.004	NA
	181 (2972)	0.0008–0.0016	0.012–0.031	0.010–0.031	0.008–0.039	0.001–0.004	0.001–0.004	NA
1991–92	143 (2350)	0.0008–0.0016	0.010–0.031	0.008–0.031	0.008–0.039	0.001–0.004	0.001–0.004	NA
	181 (2972)	0.0008–0.0016	0.012–0.031	0.010–0.031	0.008–0.039	0.001–0.004	0.001–0.004	NA

NA—Not available

TORQUE SPECIFICATIONS

All readings in ft. lbs.

Year	Engine Displacement cu. in. (cc)	Cylinder Head Bolts	Main Bearing Bolts	Rod Bearing Bolts	Crankshaft Pulley Bolts	Flywheel Bolts	Manifold		Spark Plugs
							Intake	Exhaust	
1988	122 (1997)	70	38	38	20	95	13	13	18–20
	143 (2350)	70	38	38	20	95	13	13	18–20
	156 (2555)	70	58	34	87	95	13	13	18–20
1989	122 (1997)	70	38	38	20	95	13	13	18–20
	143 (2350)	70	38	38	20	95	13	13	18–20
	156 (2555)	70	58	34	87	95	13	13	18–20
	181 (2972)	70	60	38	110	55	13	13	18–20
1990	143 (2350)	70	38	34	20	95	13	13	18–20
	181 (2972)	70	60	38	110	55	13	13	18–20
1991–92	143 (2350)	70	38	34	20	95	13	13	18–20
	181 (2972)	70	60	38	110	55	13	13	18–20

BRAKE SPECIFICATIONS

All measurements in inches unless noted

Year	Model	Lug Nut Torque (ft. lbs.)	Master Cylinder Bore	Brake Disc		Standard Brake Drum Diameter	Minimum Lining Thickness	
				Minimum Thickness	Maximum Runout		Front	Rear
1988	Montero	72–87	0.94	0.80	0.006	10	0.06	0.06
	Pick-Up	87–101	①	0.80	0.006	10	0.06	0.06
	Van	87–101	0.94	0.80	0.006	10	0.06	0.06

BRAKE SPECIFICATIONS
All measurements in inches unless noted

Year	Model	Lug Nut Torque (ft. lbs.)	Master Cylinder Bore	Brake Disc		Standard Brake Drum Diameter	Minimum Lining Thickness	
				Minimum Thickness	Maximum Runout		Front	Rear
1989	Montero	72–87	0.94	0.80	0.006	10	0.06	0.06
	Pick-Up	87–101	0.94	0.80	0.006	10	0.06	0.06
	Van	87–101	0.94	0.80	0.006	10	0.06	0.06
1990	Montero	72–87	0.94	0.80	0.006	10	0.06	0.06
	Pick-Up	87–101	0.94	0.80	0.006	10	0.06	0.06
	Van	87–101	0.94	0.80	0.006	10	0.06	0.06
1991–92	Montero	72–87	0.94	0.80	0.006	10	0.06	0.06
	Pick-Up	87–101	0.94	0.80	0.006	10	0.06	0.06

① 2WD: 0.87 in.
4WD: 0.94 in.

WHEEL ALIGNMENT

Year	Model	Caster		Camber		Toe-in (in.)	Steering Axis Inclination (deg.)
		Range (deg.)	Preferred Setting (deg.)	Range (deg.)	Preferred Setting (deg.)		
1988	Montero	2½P–3½P	3P	½P–1½P	1P	0.20	8
	2WD Pick-Up	2P–4P	3P	¼P–1¼P	⅔P	0.10	NA
	4WD Pick-Up	1P–3P	2P	½P–1½P	1P	0.10	NA
	Van	2½P–3½P	3P	0–1P	½P	0.12	NA
1989	Montero	2P–4P	3P	½P–1½P	1P	0.20	8
	2WD Pick-Up	1½P–3½P	2½P	¼P–1¼P	⅔P	0.20	NA
	4WD Pick-Up	1P–3P	2P	½P–1½P	1P	0.20	NA
	Van	2½P–3½P	3P	0–1P	½P	0.08	NA
1990	Montero	2P–4P	3P	½P–1½P	1P	0.20	8
	2WD Pick-Up	1½P–3½P	2½P	¼P–1¼P	⅔P	0.20	NA
	4WD Pick-Up	1P–3P	2P	½P–1½P	1P	0.20	NA
	Van	2P–4P	3P	¼N–1¼P	½P	0.08	NA
1991–92	Montero	2P–4P	3P	½P–1½P	1P	0.20	8
	2WD Pick-Up	1½P–3½P	2½P	¼P–1¼P	⅔P	0.20	NA
	4WD Pick-Up	1P–3P	2P	½P–1½P	1P	0.20	NA

NA—Not available
P—Positive
N—Negative

ENGINE ELECTRICAL

NOTE: Disconnecting the negative battery cable on some vehicles may interfere with the functions of the on board computer systems and may require the computer to undergo a relearning process, once the negative battery cable is reconnected.

Distributor

Removal

1. Disconnect the negative battery cable.

2. On Vans gain access to distributor as follows:
   a. Remove the battery cover.
   b. Disconnect the negative battery cable.
   c. Release the 2 catches and flip the passenger seat up.
   d. Remove the driver's seat.
   e. Remove the parking brake lever cover.
   f. Remove the parking brake lever and fuel filler release lever retaining screws and remove the levers from the lower seat frame.
   g. Remove the lower seat frame retaining screws and remove the frame from the vehicle.

3. Disconnect the distributor pickup lead wires and vacuum hose(s), if equipped.

4. Unfasten the distributor cap retaining clips or screws and lift off the distributor cap with all ignition wires connected. Remove the coil wire if necessary.

5. Matchmark the rotor to the distributor housing and the distributor housing to the engine.

NOTE: **Do not crank the engine during this procedure. If the engine is cranked, the matchmark must be disregarded.**

6. Remove the retaining nut and remove the distributor from the engine.

Installation

TIMING NOT DISTURBED

1. Install a new distributor housing O-ring.

2. Install the distributor in the engine so the rotor is aligned with the matchmark on the housing and the housing is aligned with the matchmark on the engine. Make sure the distributor is fully seated and that the distributor shaft is fully engaged.

3. Install the retaining nut finger-tight only. Connect the vacuum hose(s), if removed.

4. Connect the distributor pickup electrical harness.

5. Install the distributor cap and secure.

6. Connect the negative battery cable.

7. Check the ignition timing and adjust as required. Tighten the retaining nut.

TIMING DISTURBED

1. Install a new distributor housing O-ring.

2. Position the engine so No. 1 piston is on TDC of compression stroke and the timing mark on the vibration damper is aligned with **0** on the timing indicator.

3. Install the distributor so the rotor is aligned with the No. 1 ignition wire on the distributor cap. Take note that the distributor shaft is fully engaged and the housing is fully seated.

NOTE: **There are distributor cap runners inside the cap on vehicles with 3.0L engine. Make sure the rotor is pointing to where the No. 1 runner originates inside the cap and not where the No. 1 ignition wire plugs into the cap.**

Distributor cap terminal routing viewed from the top of the cap—3.0L engine

4. Install the retaining nut finger-tight only. Connect the vacuum hose(s), if removed.

5. Connect the distributor electrical harness.

6. Install the distributor cap and secure.

7. Connect the negative battery cable.

8. Adjust the ignition timing and tighten the retaining nut.

Ignition Timing

Adjustment

CARBURETED ENGINE

1. Start the engine, set the parking brake and run the engine until normal operating temperature is reached. Keep all lights and accessories **OFF** and the transmission in neutral.

2. Connect a conventional power timing light to No. 1 cylinder spark plug wire.

3. Connect the red lead of a tachometer to the negative primary terminal of the coil and the black lead to an engine ground. Set the idle speed to specifications.

Tachometer terminal—1988–89 Pick-Up

4. On 1988–89 vehicles, if working at an altitude of 3900 ft. (1200 meters) disconnect and plug the white-striped hose running to the sub-vacuum chamber on the bottom of the distributor; this step also applies to California engines equipped with dual-diaphragm distributor.

5. Aim the timing light at the timing scale.

6. Loosen the distributor retainer nut to allow for disributor rotation.

7. Turn the distributor in the proper direction until the specified timing is reached. Tighten the nut and recheck the ignition timing.

8. Turn the engine **OFF** and connect the vacuum hose. Start the engine and check the timing with the vacuum hose in place. This reading should equal to basic timing plus 5 degrees.

FUEL INJECTED ENGINE

1. Start the engine, set the parking brake and run the engine until normal operating temperature is reached. Keep all lights and accessories **OFF** and the transmission in neutral.

2. Without disconnecting the connector, insert a paper clip into the tachometer terminal. Connect the red lead of a tachometer to the paper clip and connect the black lead to a ground. Set the idle speed to specifications.

3. Turn the engine **OFF**. Remove the water-proof cover from the ignition timing adjusting connector. Connect a jumper wire from the ignition timing adjusting terminal to ground.

4. Connect a conventional timing light to No. 1 cylinder spark plug wire. Start the engine and allow to idle.

5. Aim the timing light at the timing scale.

6. Loosen the distributor nut to allow for distributor rotation.

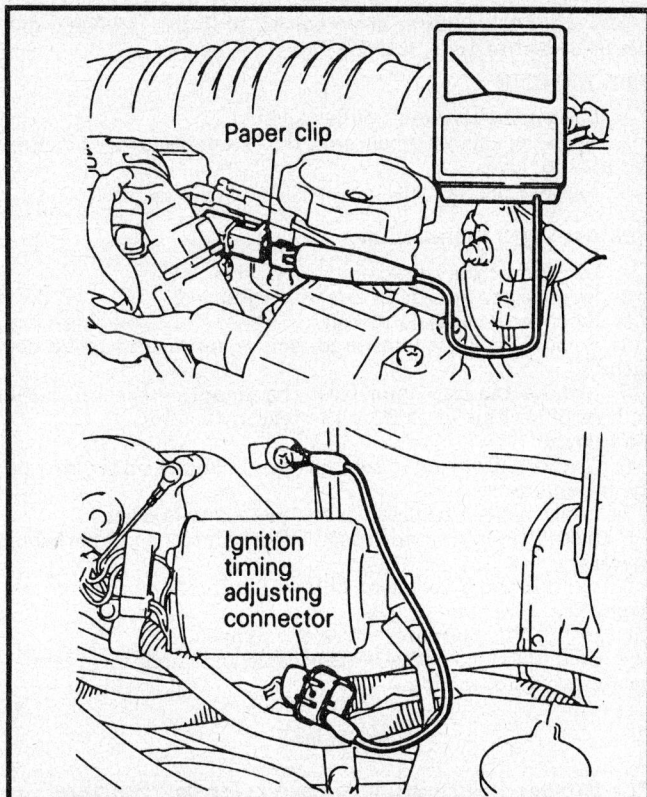

Tachometer terminal and ignition timing adjusting connector—Montero with 3.0L engine

Tachometer connector—1990–92 Pick-Up

Tachometer connector—Van

Ignition timing adjustment connector—1988–89 Van

Ignition timing adjustment connector—1990 Van

7. Turn the distributor in the proper direction until the specified timing is reached. Tighten the retainer nut and recheck the timing. Turn the engine **OFF** .

8. Remove the jumper wire from the ignition timing adjusting terminal and install the water-proof cover.

9. Start the engine and check the actual ignition timing. This reading should be 3 degrees more than basic timing for the 2.4L engine or 10 degrees more than basic timing for the 3.0L engine.

NOTE: The actual timing may fluctuate according to the control mode of the engine control unit; this is a normal condition.

10. Turn the engine **OFF** and remove all test equipment.

Alternator

For further information, please refer to "Alternators" in the Unit Repair section.

Precautions

Several precautions must be observed when working with the alternator to avoid damaging the unit.
- If the battery is removed for any reason, make sure it is reconnected with the correct polarity. Reversing the battery connections may result in damage to the one-way rectifiers.
- When utilizing a booster battery as a starting aid, always connect the positive to positive terminals and the negative terminal from the booster battery to a good engine ground on the vehicle being started.
- Never use a fast charger as a booster to start vehicles.
- Disconnect the battery cables when charging the battery with a fast charger.
- Never attempt to polarize the alternator.
- Do not use test lights of more than 12 volts when checking diode continuity.
- Do not short across or ground any of the alternator terminals.
- The polarity of the battery, alternator and regulator must be matched and considered before making any electrical connections within the system.
- Never separate the alternator on an open circuit. Make sure all connections within the circuit are clean and tight.
- Disconnect the battery ground terminal when performing any service on electrical components.
- Disconnect the battery if arc welding is to be done on the vehicle.

Belt Tension Adjustment

EXCEPT 3.0L ENGINE

1. Loosen the pivot bolt slightly.
2. Loosen the adjuster slot bolt so the alternator can be moved. Raise and safely support the vehicle if necessary.
3. On Montero, use a prybar and apply tension to the alternator until the belt deflects ¼–½ in. under a 10 lb. load.
4. Except Montero, loosen the brace bolt and increase the tension by tightening the adjustment bolt. The belt should deflect ¼–½ in. under a 10 lb. load.

5. Torque the adjuster strap bolt to 10 ft. lbs. (15 Nm). and the pivot bolt to 16 ft. lbs. (23 Nm).

3.0L ENGINE

1. Loosen the tensioner pulley locknut.
2. Turn the adjusting bolt until the belt deflects ¼–½ in. under a 10 lb. load.
3. Tighten the locknut.

Removal and Installation

1. Disconnect the negative battery cable.
2. Remove the alternator cover, if equipped.
3. Remove the alternator belt.
4. Remove the alternator brace bolt(s), nut(s) and applicable spacers.
5. Remove the alternator from the mounting bracket, label and disconnect all wires from the rear of the unit.
To install:
6. Connect all wiring to their proper terminals on the rear of the alternator.
7. Position the alternator in the mounting bracket.
8. Install the alternator brace bolt(s), nut(s) and applicable spacers.
9. Install the alternator belt and adjust the tension as required.
10. Install the alternator cover, if equipped.
11. Connect the negative battery cable and check the alternator for proper operation.

Starter

For further information, please refer to "Starters" in the Unit Repair section.

Removal and Installation

1. Disconnect the negative battery cable.
2. Raise the vehicle and support safely.
3. Remove the starter cover, if equipped.
4. Label and disconnect the wiring to the starter motor.
5. Remove the starter mounting bolts.
6. Remove the starter motor from the vehicle.
7. The installation is the reverse of the removal procedure. Torque the mounting bolts to 20–25 ft. lbs. (27–34 Nm).

CHASSIS ELECTRICAL

Heater Blower Motor

Removal and Installation

WITHOUT AIR CONDITIONING

1. Disconnect the negative battery cable.
2. Remove the lap heater duct and the left side defroster duct.
3. On Vans, it will be necessary to remove the heater housing to extract the blower motor. Remove the housing as follows:
   a. Open the glove box lid and release the glove box stoppers. Remove the glove box from its hinge.
   b. Use a small prying device to remove the clip that holds the air selection control cable in place.
   c. Disconnect the air selection control cable from the end of the air selection damper lever.
   d. Remove the air distribution duct from the left side of the blower assembly.
   e. Disconnect the connector to the resistor block and remove the grounding screw.

   f. Remove the blower housing attaching bolts and remove the housing from the vehicle.
   g. Remove the resistor block and vent hose from the housing.
4. Remove the blower motor retaining screws and remove the motor assembly from the housing. Remove the fan from the motor.
To install:
5. Inspect the gasket on housing for cracking or breaks and repair as required.
6. Install the fan to the blower motor shaft. Install the blower motor assembly to the housing and install the retaining screws.
7. Install the heater housing as follows:
   a. Install the vent hose and resistor block.
   b. Install the assembled blower housing to the vehicle.
   c. Position the ground wire and install the grounding screw.
   d. Connect the resistor block connector.
   e. Install the air distribution duct to the blower housing.

1. Lap heater duct
2. Glove box
3. Air selection control cable
4. Duct
5. Blower assembly
6. Resistor
7. Vent hose
8. Blower motor
9. Gasket
10. Fan

Blower motor removal and installation—except Van

Front heater blower motor removal and installation—Van

f. Move the air selection control lever to the recirculation position. Pull the air selection control damper lever up and connect the air selection control cable to the end of the air selection damper lever. Secure the cable with the retaining clip.
8. Install the lap heater duct, glove box and stopper.
9. Connect the negative battery cable and check the blower motor for proper operation.

WITH AIR CONDITIONING

Front Unit

1. Disconnect negative battery cable.
2. Remove the lap duct and the left side defroster duct.
3. If necessary remove the heater/air conditioner housing as follows:

a. Open the glove box lid and release the glove box stoppers. Remove the glove box from its hinge.
b. Use a small prying device to remove the clip that holds the air selection control cable in place.
c. Disconnect the air selection control cable from the end of the air selection damper lever.
d. Remove the air distribution duct from the left side of the blower assembly.
e. Disconnect the connector to the resistor block and remove the grounding screw.
f. Remove the blower housing attaching bolts and remove the housing from the vehicle.
g. Remove the resistor block and vent hose from the housing.
4. Remove the blower motor retaining screws and remove the motor assembly from the housing. Remove the fan from the motor.

To install:

5. Inspect the gasket on housing for cracking or breaks and repair as required.
6. Install the fan to the blower motor shaft. Install the blower motor assembly to the housing and install the retaining screws.
7. Install the heater housing as follows:
a. Install the vent hose and resistor block.
b. Install the assembled blower housing to the vehicle.
c. Position the ground wire and install the grounding screw.
d. Connect the resistor block connector.
e. Install the air distribution duct to the blower housing.
f. Move the air selection control lever to the recirculation position. Pull the air selection control damper lever up and connect the air selection control cable to the end of the air selection damper lever. Secure the cable with the retaining clip.
8. Install the lap duct and the left side defroster duct.
9. Install the glove box and stopper.
10. Connect the negative battery cable and check the blower motor for proper operation.

Rear Unit

1. Disconnect the negative battery cable.
2. Disconnect the blower motor connector.
3. Remove the blower motor cover.
4. Remove the vent hose.
5. Remove the blower motor retaining screws and remove the motor assembly from the housing. Remove the fan from the motor.
6. The installation is the reverse of the removal procedure.

Front Windshield Wiper Motor

Removal and Installation

EXCEPT VAN

1. Disconnect the negative battery cable.
2. Disconnect the wiper motor electrical connector.
3. Remove the wiper motor retaining bolts and pull the motor out far enough to gain access to the wiper linkage.
4. Matchmark position of wiper linkage to aid installation. Pry the wiper linkage from the motor output shaft.
5. Remove the wiper motor from the vehicle.
6. The installation is the reverse of the removal procedure.

VAN

1. Disconnect the negative battery cable.
2. Remove the steering wheel and column covers.
3. If equipped with a tilt column, move column to lowest position. If not equipped with a tilt column, remove the combination switch.
4. Remove the brake fluid level inspection cover on the left side of the instrument panel.

1. Wiper arm assembly
2. Wiper blade
3. Wiper arm
4. Instrument panel
5. Wiper motor assembly
6. Cap
7. Wiper pivot nut
8. Washer
9. Wiper linkage

Front wiper system—Van

5. Remove the lap heater ducts. Remove the switch panel and the instrument cluster assembly.
6. Remove the brake fluid reservoir mounting screws. Do not allow fluid to spill out onto any painted surface; brake fluid will damage a painted surface.
7. Remove the heater control knobs and the center trim panel.
8. Remove the heater control mounting screws and push the control panel towards the instrument panel.
9. Disconnect the electrical harnesses below the center of the instrument panel.
10. Remove the radio.
11. Remove the mounting screws across the bottom of the instrument panel.
12. Remove the bolt covers from the top of the instrument panel and remove the bolts.
13. Remove the defroster duct from the heater unit.
14. Carefully remove the instrument panel from the vehicle.
15. Disconnect the wiper motor electrical connector.
16. Remove the wiper motor retaining bolts and pull the motor out far enough to gain access to the wiper linkage.
17. Matchmark and pry the wiper linkage from the motor output shaft.
18. Remove the wiper motor from the vehicle.
To install:
19. Position wiper motor on vehicle and connect the linkage.
20. Install motor retaining bolts and connect the electrical harness. Make sure the motor works properly in all modes before installing the remaining parts. Disconnect the battery before proceeding.
21. Install the instrument panel and all related parts. Adjust control cables if necessary.
22. Install the combination switch, if removed. Install the steering wheel and column covers.
23. Connect the negative battery cable.
24. Check the entire climate control system and all gauges for proper operation.

Rear Wiper Motor

Removal and Installation

1. Disconnect the negative battery cable.

2. Tilt the wiper mount nut cover up and remove the nut. Remove the wiper arm from the shaft. Remove the wiper pivot nut and washer, if equipped.
3. Remove rear door inside trim panel and waterproof film.
4. Disconnect the wiper motor wire connector.
5. Remove the wiper motor retaining bolts and remove the motor from the vehicle.
6. The installation is the reverse of the removal procedure.

Windshield Wiper Switch

The front windshield wiper switch is part of the combination switch located on the steering column. The rear wiper switch is located on the instrument panel.

Removal and Installation
REAR WIPER SWITCH

1. Disconnect negative battery cable.
2. Insert a trim stick between the instrument panel and the switch housing. Pry switch out from the panel.
3. Disconnect electrical connector and service the wiper/washer switch, as required.
To install:
4. Connect the electrical connector and snap switch assembly into instrument panel.
5. Connect the negative battery cable and check operation of the wiper/washer assembly.

Instrument Cluster

Removal and Installation

1. Disconnect the negative battery cable.
2. On Pick-Up, remove the hazard flasher switch and the matching cover on the other side of the column.

INSTRUMENT
CLUSTER HOOD

INSTRUMENT
CLUSTER

WIRING
HARNESS

SPEEDOMETER
CABLE

Instrument cluster mounting

3. If equipped with tilt steering, operate the tilt lever to bring the steering down. Remove the hood attaching screws and remove the hood.

4. Remove the 4 cluster attaching screws and pull out cluster. Disconnect the speedometer cable from the back of the cluster by pushing the stopper of the plug on the speedometer cable side of the connection.

5. Disconnect the electrical connectors at the cluster and remove the cluster from the vehicle.

6. To remove the speedometer, remove the cover and glass. Remove the retaining screws and remove the speedometer or gauges as required.

To install:

7. Install the speedometer or gauges into the cluster and install the retaining screws. Install the cover and the glass.

8. Connect the electrical connectors and the speedometer to the cluster and install in vehicle. Install 4 retaining screws.

9. Install the instrument cluster hood and retaining screws.

10. Install the hazard flasher switch and the matching cover on the other side of the column.

11. Connect the negative battery cable.

Combination Switch

Removal and Installation

NOTE: The combination switch incorporates the windshield, headlight, dimmer and turn signal switches into a single switch assembly.

1. Disconnect negative battery cable.

2. Remove the steering wheel pad. Matchmark and remove the steering wheel.

3. If equipped with tilt steering column, put the column in lowest position.

4. Remove the upper and lower column covers.

5. Remove the wiring harness band and disconnect the harness connectors.

6. Remove the combination switch mounting screws and remove the switch.

7. The installation is the reverse of the removal procedure. Torque the steering wheel nut to 30 ft. lbs. (41 Nm).

Ignition Lock/Switch

Removal and Installation

1. Disconnect the negative battery cable.

2. If equipped with tilt steering column, put the column in its lowest position.

3. Remove the upper and lower column covers.

4. Remove the wiring harness band and disconnect the ignition switch harness.

5. Remove the ignition switch retaining screw, if equipped and remove the switch from the lock.

1. Column covers
2. Harness band
3. Ignition switch
4. Key reminder switch

Ignition switch and lock assembly

Combination switch mounting

6. Using a hacksaw blade, cut a groove into the head of the ignition switch break-off bolts and remove.

7. Remove the assembly from the steering column.

To install:

8. With the key inserted in the switch, install the switch and lock assembly to the steering column. Tighten the screws gradually making sure the key does not bind.

9. If using break-off bolts, tighten them until the heads break off.

10. Connect the switch harness and check the assembly for proper operation.

11. Install upper and lower column covers.

Stoplight Switch

Adjustment

1. Disconnect negative battery cable.

2. Loosen locknut on the brake light switch.

3. Turn the switch in the mounting bracket until the plunger does not contact the brake pedal.

4. Rotate the switch outward ½–1 revolution and secure the locknut. Reconnect the negative battery cable and check switch operation.

Removal and Installation

1. Disconnect the negative battery cable.

2. Unplug the connector to the switch.

3. Remove the locknut and remove the switch from its mount bracket.

4. The installation is the reverse of the removal procedure.

Clutch Switch

Adjustment

1. Disconnect negative battery cable.

2. Loosen the locknut on the switch. Adjust the switch so the distance from the floorboard to the top of the pedal pad in a released position is 7½ in. for Montero or 6½ in. for Pick-Up .

3. Reconnect the negative battery cable. Check operation of cruise control system making sure the cruise control is not operational when the pedal is depressed.

Removal and Installation

1. Disconnect the negative battery cable.

2. Unplug the connector to the switch.

3. Remove the locknut and the switch from its mounting bracket.

4. The installation is the reverse of the removal procedure.

Nuetral Safety Switch

Removal and Installation

1. Disconnect negative battery cable.

2. Raise and safely support the vehicle.

3. Remove the electrical connector from the switch. Place drain pan under the switch and remove the switch from the transmission.

3. Install switch with new seal into the transmission and tighten to 25 ft. lbs. (34 Nm).

4. Lower the vehicle and add transmission fluid to correct the level. Check operation of the switch.

Fuses, Circuit Breakers and Relays

Location

MONTERO

Main Fuse Block/Relay Box—located on the left side of the

instrument panel, covered by a removable access panel. There are also several dedicated fuses located throughout the vehicle.

Air Conditioning Compressor Power Relay—located in the engine compartment on the left fender.

Engine Control Relay—located on the right side of the instrument panel, mounted under a removable trim panel.

PICK-UP AND VAN

Fuse Block/Relay Box—located to the left of the steering column, covered by a removable access panel or mounted to the left kick-panel.

Air Conditioning Compressor Power Relay—located in the engine compartment on the left fender.

Engine Control Relay—located on the right side of the instrument panel behind a removable trim panel.

Headlight circuit fuse location—Montero

Air conditioning fuse location—Montero

Electric door locks fuse location—1988–89 Montero

Electric door locks fuse location—1990–92 Montero

Sunroof fuse location—1989–92 Montero

Dual air conditioning fuse location—1989–92 Montero

Computers

Location

Engine Control Unit (ECU)—located on the right side of the dash, under a removeable trim panel mounted to the kick-panel.

Auto-Cruise Control Unit—located on the left side of the steering column, under the instrument panel.

Automatic Transmission Control Unit—located on the right side of the instrument panel.

Flashers

Location

Turn Signal Flasher Unit—located in the central junction at the fuse block to the left of the steering column.

Hazard Warning Flasher Unit—located in the central junction at the fuse block to the left of the steering column.

Cruise Control

For further information, please refer to Chilton's Chassis Electronics Service Manual.

Adjustment

1. Run the vehicle until normal operating temperature is reached. Adjust the idle speed to match the emission sticker on the vehicle.
2. Turn the engine **OFF** and remove the actuator cover.
3. Loosen the locknuts on the accelerator cables and let the inner cables sag.
4. While keeping lever "P" and the stopper in contact with each other, turn the adjusting nut to lengthen the outer cable. Adjust until the lever "P" begins to operate. Turn the nut back ½ turn and secure the locknut. Accelerator cable "A" free-play should be 0–0.04 in. (0–1mm).
5. To adjust accelerator cable "B", alter the adjusting nuts on the carburator to meet the prefered free-play setting of 0–0.08 in. (0–2mm).
6. Install actuator cover and check operation of cruise control.

Accelerator cable "A" adjustment—with cruise control

Accelerator cable "B" adjustment—with cruise control

ENGINE COOLING

Radiator

Removal and Installation

EXCEPT VAN

1. Disconnect the negative battery cable.
2. Drain the coolant from the radiator.
3. Remove the upper hose and coolant reserve tank hose from the radiator.
4. Remove the shroud assembly from the radiator.
5. Raise the vehicle and support safely.
6. Remove the lower hose from the radiator.
7. Disconnect and plug the automatic transmission cooler hoses, if equipped. Lower the vehicle.
8. Remove the mounting screws and carefully lift the radiator out of the engine compartment.

To install:

9. Lower the radiator into position and install the mounting screws.
10. Raise the vehicle and support safely. Connect the automatic transmission cooler hoses, if removed.
11. Connect the lower radiator hose. Lower the vehicle.
12. Install the shroud assembly.
13. Connect the upper hose and coolant reserve tank hose.
14. Fill the cooling system.
15. Connect the negative battery cable and run the vehicle until the thermostat opens. Fill the radiator completely and check the automatic transmission fluid level, if equipped.
16. Check for leaks. Once vehicle has cooled, recheck coolant level.

VAN

1. Remove the battery cover and disconnect the negative battery cable.
2. Release the 2 catches and flip the passenger seat up.
3. Remove the driver's seat.
4. Remove the parking brake lever cover.
5. Remove the parking brake lever and fuel filler fuel release lever retaining screws and remove the levers from the seat under frame.
6. Remove the seat underframe retaining screws and remove the seat underframe from the vehicle.
7. Raise the vehicle and support safely. Drain the radiator.
8. Disconnect and plug the automatic transmission cooler hoses.
9. Remove the lower radiator mounting screws. Lower the vehicle.
10. Remove the upper hose and coolant reserve tank hose from the radiator.
11. Remove the shroud assembly from the radiator.
12. Remove the lower hose from the radiator.
13. Remove the upper mounting screws and carefully lift the radiator out of the engine compartment.

To install:

14. Lower the radiator into position and install the mounting screws.
15. Raise the vehicle and support safely. Connect the automatic transmission cooler hoses. Lower the vehicle.
16. Connect the lower hose.
17. Install the shroud assembly.
18. Connect the upper hose and coolant reserve tank hose.
19. Fill the cooling system.
20. Connect the negative battery cable and run the vehicle until the thermostat opens. Fill the cooling system completely.
21. Check the automatic transmission fluid level and add as required.
22. Check for leaks. Once cooled, recheck the coolant level.
23. Install the seat underframe and all related parts.

Electric Cooling Fan

An electric condenser cooling fan is used on the Montero. The condenser on Pick-Up and Van are cooled by the belt-driven fan.

Testing

1. Disconnect negative battery cable.

─────────── **CAUTION** ───────────

Make sure the key is in the OFF position when checking the electric cooling fan. If not the fan could turn on at any time, causing serious personal injury.

────────────────────────────────────

2. Disconnect the electrical connector from the condenser fan.
3. Connect the green-with-black-tracer wire to 12 volt supply and ground the black wire.
4. Make sure the fan runs smoothly, without abnormal noise or vibration.
5. Connect the negative battery cable.

Removal and Installation

1. Disconnect negative battery cable.
2. Open the hood and remove the grille. It is fastened with 3 screws along the top and 3 nuts along the bottom.
3. Disconnect the electrical connector from the fan.
4. Remove the mounting screws and the fan through the grille opening.
5. The installation is the reverse of the removal procedure.
6. Connect the negative battery cable and check the fan for proper operation.

Heater Core

For further information, please refer to Chilton's Air Conditioning and Heating Manual.

Removal and Installation

MONTERO

1. Disconnect the negative battery cable.
2. Set the temperature control to the extreme right position and drain the cooling system.
3. Remove the air filter assembly. Remove the heater hose clamps and disconnect the heater hoses.
4. Remove the lap heater ducts and the hood release cable bracket.
5. Remove the side demister grills by carefully prying them from the instrument panel.
6. Remove the glove box and center console assembly. Remove the center reinforcement.
7. Remove the steering wheel.
8. Remove the instrument cluster.
9. Remove the oil pressure gauge, inclinometer and voltmeter pod cover and remove the gauge assembly.
10. Label and disconnect the recirculation/fresh air door control cable.
11. Label and disconnect the mode selection control cable.
12. Label and disconnect the water valve control cable.
13. Remove the fuse box retaining screw and position the fuse box aside.
14. Remove the instrument panel retaining nuts and bolts and carefully remove the instrument panel from the vehicle.
15. Remove the air cleaner or air intake plenum, as required.
16. Remove the duct from the top of the heater case.
17. Remove the retaining nuts and bolts and remove the heater case from the vehicle.

1. Lap heater duct
2. Lap heater duct
3. Hood release cable bracket
4. Left defroster grill
5. Right defroster grill
6. Glove box
7. Instrument cluster hood
8. Instrument cluster
9. Cover
10. Inclinometer pod
11. Center panel
12. Recirculation/fresh air selection cable
13. Mode selection cable
14. Water valve control cable
15. Center reinforcement
16. Horn pad
17. Steering wheel
18. Fuse box cover
19. Fuse box
20. Instrument panel
21. Heater case

Instrument panel assembly—Montero

18. Remove the water valve cover and carefully remove the water valve from the case.

19. Remove the foot/defroster selection link from the mode selection lever.

20. Move the lever up to a position which will not interfere with the removal of the heater core.

21. Remove the heater core from the heater case. If the mode lever is in the way, remove it.

To install:

22. Install the heater core to the heater case. Install the mode lever, if removed.

23. Install the foot/defroster selection link to the mode selection lever.

24. Install the water valve assembly and its cover to the case.

25. Install the assembled heater case to the vehicle and install the retaining nuts and bolts.

26. Install the duct to the top of the case.

27. Connect the heater hoses to the core tubes and install the air cleaner or intake plenum.

28. Install the instrument panel and all related parts. Adjust the control cables if necessary.

29. Fill the system with coolant.

30. Connect the negative battery cable, run the vehicle until the thermostat opens and fill the radiator completely.

31. Check for leaks. Once cooled, recheck the coolant level.

32. Check the entire climate control system and all gauges for proper operation.

PICK-UP

1. Disconnect the negative battery cable. Position the heater controls in the extreme right position.

2. Drain the coolant. Disconnect the heater hoses from the core tubes.

3. Remove the hazard flasher switch and the matching cover on the other side of the column. Remove the instrument cluster.

4. Remove the fuse box cover and remove the fuse box retaining screws. Position the fuse box aside.

5. Remove the glove box assembly.

Sports model

1. Hazard warning flasher switch
2. Screw cover
3. Instrument cluster hood
4. Instrument cluster
5. Fuse box cover
6. Fuse box
7. Glove box
8. Defroster duct
9. Air selection control cable
10. Mode selection control cable
11. Temperature control cable
12. Speaker grill
13. Parcel box or clock
14. Instrument panel attaching nut cover
15. Center cover
16. Shifter knob
17. Floor console
18. Instrument panel
19. Heater case

Instrument panel assembly—Pick-Up

6. Remove the defroster ducts.

7. Label and disconnect the air, mode and temperature control cables from the heater case.

8. Remove the front speaker grilles.

9. Remove the parcel box or clock, as equipped.

10. Remove the nut cover from the top center of the instrument panel.

11. Remove the center cover.

12. Remove the shift knob and floor console assembly, if equipped.

13. Move the tilt steering column down as far as it will go.

14. Remove the instrument panel retaining nuts and bolts and carefully remove the instrument panel from the vehicle.

15. Remove the duct from the top center of the heater case.

16. Remove the defroster duct from the the left side of the case.

17. Remove the center reinforcement braces.

18. Remove the mounting nuts and remove the heater case from the vehicle.

19. Remove the hose cover, joint hose clamp and the plate from the case.

20. Remove the heater core from the case.

To install:

21. Install the heater core to the heater case.

22. Install the plate, joint hose clamp and hose cover.

23. Install the assembled heater case to the vehicle. Connect the heater hoses to the core tubes.

24. Install the center reinforcement braces.

25. Install the defroster and center ducts to the case.

26. Install the instrument panel and all related parts. Adjust the control cables if necessary.

27. Fill the system with coolant.

28. Connect the negative battery cable, run the vehicle until the thermostat opens and fill the radiator completely.

29. Check for leaks. Once cooled, recheck the coolant level.

30. Check the entire climate control system and all gauges for proper operation.

VAN

Front Heater Core

1. Disconnect the negative battery cable.

2. Drain the coolant.

3. Remove the steering wheel and column covers. If equipped with a tilt column, lower it to its lowest position. If not equipped with a tilt column, remove the combination switch.

4. Remove the brake fluid level inspection cover on the left side of the instrument panel.

5. Remove the lap heater ducts. Remove the switch panel and remove the instrument cluster assembly.

6. Remove the brake fluid reservoir mounting screws. Do not allow fluid to spill out onto any painted surface; brake fluid will ruin the paint.

7. Remove the heater control knobs and remove the center panel.

8. Remove the heater control mounting screws and push the control panel into the instrument panel.

1. Brake fluid level inspection cover
2. Switch panel
3. Instrument cluster hood
4. Instrument panel wiring harness
5. Speedometer cable
6. Instrument cluster
7. Brake fluid reservoir bracket mounting nut
8. Heater control knob
9. Center panel
10. Heater control mounting screws
11. Instrument panel wiring harnesses
12. Antenna cable
13. Radio bracket mounting screws
14. Instrument panel attaching screws
15. Screw covers
16. Instrument panel mounting bolts
17. Instrument panel

Instrument panel assembly—Van

1. Heater hose
2. Heater hose
3. Heater hose
4. Heater hose
5. Water pipe
6. Lap heater duct
7. Defroster duct
8. Instrument panel
9. Frame assembly
10. Heater control assembly
11. Air duct
12. Air flow box
13. Front heater unit
14. Joint duct

Front heater case and related parts—Van

9. Disconnect the harnesses below the center of the instrument panel.
10. Remove the radio.
11. Remove the mounting screws across the bottom of the instrument panel.
12. Remove the bolt covers across the top of the instrument panel and remove the bolts.
13. Remove the defroster duct from the heater unit.
14. Remove the instrument panel from the vehicle.
15. Remove the instrument panel frame and the control panel from the vehicle.
16. Raise the vehicle and support safely. Disconnect the heater hoses from the heater core tubes.
17. Label and disconnect all cables from the heater case. Remove the heater case mounting bolts. Tilt the case away from the bracket and remove it from the vehicle.
18. Disassemble the heater case and remove the heater core.

To install:
19. Install the heater core to the heater case.

20. Install the assembled case to the vehicle, making sure the floor pan seal is seated properly.
21. Connect the heater hoses to the core tubes. Make sure the hoses are not twisted and that the clamps are not touching other parts.
22. Install the instrument panel frame and position the heater control panel.
23. Install the instrument panel and all related parts. Adjust the control cables if necessary.
24. Install the combination switch, if removed. Install the steering wheel and column covers.
25. Fill the system with coolant.
26. Connect the negative battery cable, run the vehicle until the thermostat opens and fill the radiator completely.
27. Check for leaks. Once cooled, recheck the coolant level.
28. Check the entire climate control system and all gauges for proper operation.

Rear Heater Core

1. Disconnect negative battery cable.

1. Blower motor connector
2. Blower motor cover
3. Blower motor
4. Fan
5. Resistor
6. Water valve damper lever
7. Mode selection damper lever

8. Mode selection damper lever
9. Heater core

Rear heater assembly—Van

2. Drain the coolant.
3. Disconnect the heater hoses from the core tubes.
4. Remove the air duct assembly from the heater case.
5. Remove the blower motor cover and remove the blower motor.
6. Remove the upper half of the case.
7. Remove the heater core from the case.

To install:

8. Install heater core into case.
9. Install upper portion of case making sure the duct seals do not get dislodged.
10. Install the blower motor and cover to the case.
11. Install the air duct assembly to the heater case.
12. Install the heater hoses to the core tubes.
13. Fill the system with coolant.
14. Connect the negative battery cable, run the vehicle until the thermostat opens and fill the radiator completely.
15. Check for leaks. Once the vehicle has cooled, recheck the coolant level.
16. Check the rear heater system proper operation.

Water Pump

Removal and Installation

2.0L AND 2.4L ENGINES

1. Disconnect the negative battery cable.

2. Drain the cooling system. On Van, remove the seat underframe.
3. Release the fuel pressure if equipped with fuel injection.
4. Remove the upper radiator shroud.
5. Remove all accessory belts. Remove the air conditioning compressor tensioner pulley, if equipped.
6. Remove the cooling fan assembly along with the water pump pulley.
7. Disconnect the radiator hose from the water pump.
8. Remove the crankshaft pulley(s).
9. Remove the timing belt covers. If the same timing belt will be reused, mark the direction of the timing belt's rotation, for installation in the same direction. Make sure the engine is positioned so the No. 1 cylinder is at the TDC of its compression stroke and the sprockets timing marks are aligned with the engine's timing mark indicators. Remove the timing belt.
10. The water pump bolts are different lengths, note their positions before removing. Remove the water pump mounting bolts and remove the pump from the block and the water pipe connection. Remove the O-ring from the water pipe connection.

To install:

11. Clean and dry the mating surfaces of the block and water pump. Install a new O-ring to the water pipe connection. Coat the new O-ring with water to aid in installation.
12. Install the water pump with a new gasket to the block and torque the bolts (except the alternator bracket bolt) to 10 ft. lbs. (13 Nm). Torque the aforementioned bolt to 17 ft. lbs. (23 Nm).
13. Install the timing belt(s) and covers.
14. Install the crankshaft pulley(s).
15. Connect the radiator hose to the water pump.
16. Install the water pump pulley and cooling fan assembly.
17. Install the air conditioning compressor tensioner pulley, if equipped, and install and adjust the accessory belts.
18. Install the upper radiator shroud.
19. Fill the system with coolant.
20. Connect the negative battery cable, run the vehicle until the thermostat opens and fill the radiator completely.
21. Check for leaks. Once cooled, recheck the coolant level.
22. Install the seat underframe and all related parts, if removed.

2.6L ENGINE

1. Disconnect the negative battery cable.
2. Drain the cooling system.
3. Remove the upper radiator shroud, if equipped.
4. Remove all accessory belts.
5. Remove the cooling fan assembly along with the water pump pulley.
6. Disconnect the radiator hose and heater hose from the water pump.
7. The water pump bolts are different lengths, note their positions before removing. Remove the water pump retaining bolts and remove the water pump from the timing chain cover.
8. The installation is the reverse of the removal procedure. Torque the water pump and pulley bolts to 10 ft. lbs. (13 Nm).

3.0L ENGINE

1. Disconnect the negative battery cable.
2. Drain the cooling system. Remove the upper radiator hose and the upper radiator shroud.
3. If equipped with electric fuel pump, loosen the fuel filler cap to release fuel tank pressure and release the fuel pressure in the supply lines.
4. Remove the cooling fan assembly along with the water pump pulley. Remove all belts.
5. Remove the power steering pump from the bracket and remove the bracket.
6. Remove the tensioner pulley bracket, the air conditioning compressor and its bracket.
7. Remove the cooling fan bracket assembly. Remove the crankshaft pulley and flange.

Water pump assembly—3.0L engine

8. Remove the timing belt covers. If the same timing belt will be reused, mark the direction of the timing belt's rotation, for installation in the same direction. Make sure the engine is positioned so the No. 1 cylinder is at the TDC of its compression stroke and the sprockets timing marks are aligned with the engine's timing mark indicators.

9. Loosen the timing belt tensioner bolt and remove the belt. Position the tensioner as far away from the center of the engine as possible and tighten the bolt. Remove the water pump mounting bolts, separate the pump from the water inlet pipe and remove the pump from the engine. Remove the water inlet fitting from the pump.

To install:

10. Clean and dry the mating surfaces of the block and water pump. Install a new O-ring to the water inlet pipe. Install the pump and water inlet fitting with new gaskets to the engine and water pipe. Torque the water pump mounting bolts to 20 ft. lbs. (27 Nm).

11. If not already done, position both camshafts so the marks line up with those on the alternator bracket and inner timing cover. Rotate the crankshaft so the timing mark aligns with the mark on the oil pump.

12. Install the timing belt on the crankshaft sprocket and while keeping the belt tight on the tension side (right side), install the belt on the front camshaft sprocket.

13. Install the belt on the water pump pulley, then the rear camshaft sprocket and the tensioner.

14. Rotate the front camshaft counterclockwise to tension the belt between the front camshaft and the crankshaft. If the timing marks came out of line, repeat the procedure.

15. Install the crankshaft sprocket flange.

16. Loosen the tensioner bolt and allow the spring to tension the belt.

17. Turn the crankshaft 2 full turns in the clockwise direction only until the timing marks align again. Now that the belt is properly tensioned, torque the tensioner lock bolt to 21 ft. lbs. (29 Nm).

18. Install the timing belt covers and all related parts.

19. Fill the cooling system.

20. Connect the negative battery cable, run the vehicle until the thermostat opens and fill the radiator completely.

21. Check for leaks. Once cooled, recheck the coolant level.

Thermostat

Removal and Installation

1. Disconnect the negative battery cable. Drain the coolant down to thermostat level or below.

2. Disconnect the engine coolant temperature switch connector, if equipped.

3. Remove the thermostat housing.

4. Remove the thermostat and gasket from the housing.

5. Clean the housing mating surfaces and install a new gasket.

6. The installation is the reverse of the removal procedure.

Service Tips

MATERIAL CHANGE AFFECTS INSTALLATION

As of 1990, the composition of the water outlet fitting gasket has been changed from a joint-sheet composition to a rubber-coated metal design. Due to the new composition, the gasket now has a top and a bottom side. When installing the new gasket, install the side labeled "UP" facing the water outlet fitting or in the top side position. If using the old style gasket, either side may be installed on top.

Cooling System Bleeding

All engines are equipped with self-bleeding thermostats. Cooling system bleeding is not necessary in any vehicles when servicing the cooling system.

FUEL SYSTEM

Fuel System Service Precaution

Safety is the most important factor when performing not only fuel system maintenance but any type of maintenance. Failure to conduct maintenance and repairs in a safe manner may result in serious personal injury or death. Maintenance and testing of the vehicle's fuel system components can be accomplished safely and effectively by adhering to the following rules and guidelines.

● To avoid the possibility of fire and personal injury, always disconnect the negative battery cable unless the repair or test procedure requires that battery voltage be applied.

● Always relieve the fuel system pressure prior to disconnecting any fuel system component (injector, fuel rail, pressure regulator, etc.), fitting or fuel line connection. Exercise extreme caution whenever relieving fuel system pressure to avoid exposing skin, face and eyes to fuel spray. Please be advised that fuel under pressure may penetrate the skin or any part of the body that it contacts.

Fuel pump harness connector at the rear of the fuel tank—Montero

Fuel pump harness connector at the rear of the fuel tank—Pick-Up

Fuel pump harness connector at the left of the transmission extension housing—Van

• Always place a shop towel or cloth around the fitting or connection prior to loosening to absorb any excess fuel due to spillage. Ensure that all fuel spillage (should it occur) is quickly removed from engine surfaces. Ensure that all fuel soaked cloths or towels are deposited into a suitable waste container.

• Always keep a dry chemical (Class B) fire extinguisher near the work area.

• Do not allow fuel spray or fuel vapors to come into contact with a spark or open flame.

• Always use a backup wrench when loosening and tightening fuel line connection fittings. This will prevent unnecessary

stress and torsion to fuel line piping. Always follow the proper torque specifications.

• Always replace worn fuel fitting O-rings with new. Do not substitute fuel hose or equivalent where fuel pipe is installed.

Reliveing Fuel System Pressure

1. Disconnect the fuel pump harness connector.
2. Start the engine and allow the engine to run out of fuel.
3. Once the engine has stalled, turn the key to the **OFF** position and connect the electrical connector.
4. Disconnect the negative battery cable pressure cannot build up until work has been completed.

Fuel Tank

Removal and Installation

1. If equipped with an electric fuel pump, release fuel pressure as follows:
   a. Disconnect the fuel pump harness connector.
   b. Start the engine and allow the engine to run out of fuel.
   c. Once engine has stalled, turn the key to the **OFF** position.
   d. Disconnect the negative battery cable so pressure cannot build up until work has been completed.
2. Raise the vehicle and support safely.
3. Using the proper equipment, drain the fuel tank.
4. Remove the side skirt panel, if equipped.
5. Disconnect the fuel gauge unit connector.
6. Disconnect the main hose connector.
7. Disconnect the return hose connector and the vapor hose connector.
8. Remove the filler hose connector and the breather hose connection.
9. Place a transmission jack or equivalent, under the center of the tank and apply slight pressure. Remove the tank mounting nuts.
10. Lower the tank and remove disconnect any lines still conected.
11. Remove the tank from the vehicle.
To install:
12. Raise the tank into position and connect all harnesses and hoses.
13. Install the fuel tank mounting nuts and torque to 18–22 ft. lbs. (25–30 Nm).
14. Reconnect the fuel gauge unit connector.
15. Install the side skirt panel, if equipped.
16. Refill the fuel tank and start the engine. Check fuel system for leaks.

Fuel Filter

Removal and Installation

CARBURETED ENGINE

1. Disconnect the negative battery cable.
2. Raise the vehicle and support safely, if necessary.
3. Remove the air cleaner assembly, if necessary. Remove the fuel filter from its bracket. Inspect the hoses carefully.
4. Install the new filter, hoses and clamps if worn or cracked.
5. Connect the negative battery cable, start the engine and check for leaks.

FUEL INJECTED ENGINE

─────── **CAUTION** ───────

Do not use conventional fuel filters, hoses or clamps when servicing this fuel system. They are not compatible with the injection system and could fail, causing personal injury or damage to the vehicle. Use only replacement parts specifically designed for fuel injection.

1. Relieve the fuel pressure.

2. Disconnect the negative battery cable.
3. Raise the vehicle and support safely.
4. Remove the fuel filter protector plate, if equipped.
5. Disconnect the main and high pressure lines. Remove any other fuel hose that are damaged or worn.
6. Remove the filter mounting bolts and remove the filter from the vehicle.

To install:

7. Install new filter onto vehicle using new gaskets. Replace any hoses that are worn or damaged.
8. Install the protector plate, if equipped.
9. Connect the negative battery cable, check for leaks and road test the vehicle.

Mechanical Fuel Pump

Pressure Testing

1. Raise the vehicle and support safely.
2. Connect a pressure gauge to the fuel pump outlet fitting.
3. Crank the engine several times while observing the gauge.
4. The pump should develop 3–4 psi of pressure.

Removal and Installation

1. Disconnect the negative battery cable.
2. Disconnect the fuel lines from the pump and plug them.

NOTE: There is a fuel pump pushrod in the 2.0L engine. When removing or installing the pump, be careful not to drop the pushrod because it will drop down into the oil pan.

Also, it may be necessary to remove the rear thermostat housing bolt and/or the valve cover, on the 2.6L engine, to remove and install the pump.

3. Remove the fuel pump retaining bolts or nuts and remove the pump from the engine. Remove the pushrod, if equipped.
4. Clean and dry the mounting surfaces, bolts and bolt holes.
5. The installation is the reverse of the removal procedure. Use new gaskets and a new insulator.
6. Connect the negative battery cable, start the engine and check for leaks.

Electric Fuel Pump

Pressure Testing

1. Relieve the fuel pressure.
2. Disconnect the negative battery cable.
3. Cover the high pressure fuel hose hose with a clean shop towel to prevent fuel spray from residual pressure in the line. Disconnect the high pressure fuel hose at the delivery pipe.
4. Connect the proper fuel pressure gauge and accompanying special adaptor tools to the delivery pipe.
5. If not already done, place the key in the **OFF** position. Connect the negative battery cable.
6. Connect a jumper wire from the fuel pump activation terminal to the positive battery post. This will pressurize the system so the fuel pump installation assembly can be inspected for leaks. If a leak is found, repair it before proceeding.
7. Disconnect the jumper wire to stop the fuel pump.
8. Start the engine and allow it to idle.
9. Measure the pressure during idling. The specification for all applications is 38 psi.
10. Disconnect and plug the vacuum hose from the fuel pressure regulator.
11. With the hose disconnected, the pressure should increase to 50 psi.
12. Race the engine a few times to make sure the fuel pressure does not deviate from specifications.
13. Press on the return hose while racing the engine to make sure there is pressure in the hose. Reconnect the vacuum hose.

Fuel pump activation terminal—Montero

Fuel pump activation terminal located behind the fuse box—Pick-Up

Fuel pump activation terminal—Van

14. Stop the engine and allow pressure to remain in the system. There should be no decrease in pressure for at least 2 minutes.
15. Release the fuel pressure.
16. Remove the fuel pressure measuring equipment.
17. Connect the high pressure fuel hose to the delivery pipe using new O-rings where necessary.
18. Connect the jumper wire from the fuel pump activation terminal to the positive battery post, inspect the system for leaks.
19. Road test the vehicle.

Removal and Installation
MONTERO

1. Relieve the fuel pressure.
2. Disconnect the negative battery cable.

Fuel pressure testing equipment—except Van. The hose is not used on Pick-Up with 2.4L engine

Fuel pressure gauge installation—Pick-Up with 2.4L engine

Fuel pressure gauge installation—3.0L engine

Fuel pressure gauge installation—Van

1. Side skirt stay
2. Sending unit connector
3. Fuel pump connector
4. Main hose
5. Return hose
6. Vapor hose
7. Breather hose
8. Filler hose
9. Fuel tank protector (4WD)
10. Tank mounting nut
11. Fuel tank
12. Two-way overfill limiter valve
13. Fuel pump assembly
14. Gasket
15. Sending unit

Fuel tank assembly—Pick-Up

1. Fuel pump connector
2. Filler cap
3. Drain plug
4. Filler hose
5. Leveling hose
6. Main hose
7. Return hose
8. Vapor hose
9. Sending unit connector
10. Fuel tank
11. Two-way valve
12. Fuel pump assembly
13. Gasket
14. Sending unit

Fuel tank assembly—Van

3. Remove the pump and sending unit access panel.
4. Cover the high pressure fuel hose with a clean shop towel to prevent fuel spray from residual pressure in the line. Disconnect the fuel hose and pipe from the pump.
5. Remove the fuel pump mounting screws and remove the pump from the tank.
6. The installation is the reverse of the removal procedure.

PICK-UP AND VAN

1. Relieve the fuel pressure.
2. Disconnect the negative battery cable.
3. Raise the vehicle and support safely. Remove protective plates, if equipped.
4. Using the proper equipment, drain the fuel tank.
5. Remove the fuel tank from the vehicle.
6. Remove the pump retaining screws and remove the pump from the tank.
To install:
7. Clean the seal area of the tank. Install a new gasket.
8. Install the pump in the same position as originally installed.
9. Install the retaining screws and torque them to 15 inch lbs.
10. Install the fuel tank and all related parts.
11. Connect the negative battery cable. Connect the jumper wire from the fuel pump activation terminal to the positive battery post and inspect the system for leaks.
12. Road test the vehicle.

Carburetor

Removal and Installation

1. Disconnect the negative battery cable. The choke control

element is water activated so it will be necessary to drain the cooling system.
2. Remove the air cleaner assembly.
3. Remove and install the fuel tank cap to relieve any pressure in the tank.
4. Matchmark all vacuum hoses and electrical connectors and remove them from the carburetor.
5. Disconnect the throttle, cruise control, choke, kickdown cables and linkages, as equipped.
6. Disconnect and plug the fuel inlet line.
7. Remove the mounting bolts and remove the carburetor from the intake manifold.
To install:
8. Thoroughly clean and dry the mounting surface of the manifold and install a new base gasket.
9. Install the mounting bolts and tighten them alternately to compress the base gasket evenly. Final torque should be 12 ft. lbs. (16 Nm).
10. Connect the fuel line.
11. Connect the throttle, cruise control, choke, kickdown cables and linkages as required.
12. Install all vacuum hoses and electrical connectors in their proper locations.
13. Install the air cleaner assembly.
14. Fill the cooling system.
15. Connect the negative battery cable, start the engine and perform all necessary adjustments.

Idle Speed Adjustment

1. Start the engine and allow it to reach normal operating temperature. Before checking or adjusting the idle speed, check ignition timing and adjust if necessary.

IDLE SPEED SCREW

IDLE-UP SCREW

Carburetor adjusting screw locations

2. Turn all lights and accessories **OFF**. Connect a tachometer to the engine.

3. Open the throttle and run at 2500 rpm for 10 seconds. Allow the engine to idle for 2 minutes.

4. Check the idle speed. If the tachometer indicates rpm is not at specifications, turn the idle speed screw until the correct idle speed is obtained.

5. If equipped with air conditioning, engage compressor.

6. With the compressor running, set the idle to 900 rpm.

Idle Mixture Adjustment

1. Drill a 2mm pilot hole in the casting around the idle mixture screw. Drive out the concealment plug.

2. Run the engine until normal operating temperature is reached.

3. Check and adjust the idle speed and ignition timing.

4. Turn the engine **OFF.**

5. Disconnect the negative battery cable for 5 seconds, then reconnect.

6. Disconnect the oxygen sensor connector.

7. Open the throttle and run at 2500 rpm for 10 seconds. Allow the engine to idle for 2 minutes.

8. Using an emission tester, adjust the idle mixture screw until the CO at idle is below 0.30 percent and the idle is smooth.

9. Turn the engine **OFF.**

10. Connect the oxygen sensor connector.

11. Reinstall the concealment plug in the idle mixture screw hole.

Service Adjustments

For all carburetor service adjustment procedures and Specifications, please refer to "Carburetor Service" in the Unit Repair section.

Fuel Injection

For further information, please refer to Chilton's Electronic Engine Controls Manual.

Idle Speed Adjustment

The idle speed is automatically regulated by the idle speed control system which receives data from various sensors and switches in the system and adjusts the engine idle to a predetermined speed. Idle speed specifications can be found on the Vehicle Emission Control Information (VECI) label located in the engine compartment.

Idle Mixture Adjustment

There is no idle mixture adjustment provided with any Mitsubishi fuel injection system.

Fuel Injector

Removal and Installation

2.4L ENGINE

1. Relieve the fuel pressure.

2. Disconnect negative battery cable. Remove the front seat underframe as required.

3. Drain the cooling system.

4. Matchmark and remove all linkage and vacuum hoses from the throttle body and remove the throttle body from the intake manifold.

5. Remove the boost hose from opposite end of air plenum.

6. Cover the high pressure fuel hose with a clean shop towel to prevent fuel spray from residual pressure in the line. Disconnect the high pressure fuel hose from the fuel rail.

7. Remove the fuel return line and vacuum hose from the fuel pressure regulator.

8. Disconnect the electrical connectors from the injectors.

9. Remove the fuel rail retaining bolts.

10. Lift the rail with injectors attached up and away from the engine.

11. Remove the injector from the rail by pulling straight out away from rail. Remove the lower insulator.

To install:

12. Install a new grommet and O-rings onto the injector. Coat the O-rings lightly with gasoline.

13. Install the injector to the rail, making sure injector turns freely. If it does not turn, check for a damaged or misaligned O-ring and reinstall.

14. Replace the insulators in the intake manifold. Install the fuel rail with injectors onto the manifold. Make sure the rubber bushings are correctly seated in the installation holes.

15. Tighten fuel rail retaining bolts to 18 ft. lbs. (10 Nm).

16. Install the fuel return line and vacuum hose to the fuel pressure regulator.

17. Connect the electrical harness to the injectors.

18. Replace O-ring and connect the high pressure fuel line to delivery pipe.

19. Connect the boost hose to air plenum.

20. Install the throttle body using a new base gasket.

21. Refill the cooling system. Connect the negative battery cable.

22. Connect the jumper wire from the fuel pump activation terminal to the positive battery post and inspect the system for leaks.

3.0L ENGINE

1. Relieve the fuel pressure.

2. Disconnect negative battery cable.

3. Remove the air intake hose from the throttle body.

4. Disconnect all wires, hoses and linkages to the throttle body.

5. Disconnect the EGR temperature sensor wire.

6. Remove the ignition coil.

7. Remove the engine oil filler neck bracket.

8. Unbolt the EGR tube from the air intake plenum.

9. Disconnect the PCV hose and vacuum hose cluster from the plenum.

10. Remove the plenum to engine brackets.

11. Unbolt the air intake plenum assembly from the intake manifold and remove.

12. Cover the high pressure fuel hose with a clean shop towel to prevent fuel spray due to residual pressure in the line. Disconnect the high pressure fuel hose from the fuel rail.

1. Air intake hose
2. Breather hose
3. Wiring harness connector
4. Air intake pipe
5. Air hose
6. Accelerator cable
7. Kickdown cable
8. Water hose
9. Vacuum hose
10. Throttle body
11. Base plate
12. Fuel injector connector
13. High pressure fuel hose
14. Fuel return hose
15. Bolt
16. Fuel rail
17. Insulator
18. Injector
19. O-ring
20. Grommet
21. Insulator
22. Fuel pressure regulator
23. O-ring

Throttle body, fuel rail, injector and related parts— 2.4L engine

13. Remove the fuel return line and vacuum hose from the fuel pressure regulator.

14. Remove electrical connectors from the injectors.

15. Remove the fuel rail retaining bolts.

16. Lift the rail with injectors attached up and away from the engine.

17. Remove the injectors from the fuel rail pulling straight out away from the rail. Remove the lower insulator.

To install:

18. Install a new grommet and O-ring onto injector. Coat the O-ring lightly with gasoline to aid in assembly.

19. Install the injectors into the rail, making sure injector turns freely. If they do not, check for a misaligned O-ring and reinstall.

20. Replace the seats in the intake manifold. Install new rubber bushings onto mounting points of fuel rail. Install the assembled fuel rail with injectors onto the manifold.

21. Tighten the fuel rail bolts to 8 ft. lbs. (10 Nm).

22. Connect the electrical harness to the injectors.

23. Connect the fuel return hose and the vacuum hose to the pressure regulator.

24. Using a new O-ring coated lightly with gasoline, install the high pressure fuel line.

25. Install air intake plenum and all related parts.

26. Connect the negative battery cable.

27. Connect the jumper wire from the fuel pump activation terminal to the positive battery post inspect the system for leaks.

1. Air intake plenum
2. High pressure fuel hose
3. Return hose
4. Vacuum hose
5. Fuel pressure regulator
6. O-ring
7. Harness connector
8. Fuel rail
9. Injector
10. O-ring
11. Grommet
12. Insulator
13. Insulator

Fuel rail, injector and related parts—3.0L engine

EMISSION CONTROLS

For further information, please refer to Chilton's Emission Controls Manual.

Emission Warning Lamps

Resetting

EXCEPT PICK-UP

The reset switch is located on the back of the instrument cluster. Remove the instrument cluster to access the switch. To reset the timer, simply flip the switch. The bulb may be removed after the 150,000 mile check is completed on Montero.

PICK-UP

Remove the glass in from of the instrument cluster to access the reset switch. To reset the timer, simply flip the switch. The bulb may be removed after the 120,000 mile check is completed.

Emissions warning light reset switch—Montero

Emissions warning light reset switch — Van

Emissions warning light reset switch — Pick-Up

ENGINE MECHANICAL

NOTE: Disconnecting the negative battery cable on some vehicles may interfere with the functions of the on board computer systems and may require the computer to undergo a relearning process, once the negative battery cable is reconnected.

Engine

Removal and Installation

EXCEPT VAN

1. Relieve the fuel pressure if equipped with fuel injection. Disconnect the negative battery cable from the battery and from the engine.
2. Matchmark and remove the hood. Remove the oil dipstick.
3. Raise the vehicle and support safely. Remove the engine under cover. Drain the engine oil and coolant.
4. Remove the starter. Remove the lower radiator hose.
5. Remove the exhaust pipe from the exhaust manifold(s).
6. If equipped with a manual transmission, remove the transmission and all related parts.
7. If equipped with an automatic transmission, remove the inspection plate, matchmark the flexplate to the converter, remove the torque converter bolts and push the torque converter backwards as far as it will go. Remove the lower bell housing bolts. Lower the vehicle.
8. If equipped with a carburetor, remove the air cleaner assembly. Remove all ductwork and air intake hoses. Disconnect all linkages and cables from the carburetor or throttle body.
9. Cover the fuel line connections with a clean shop rag and disconnect and plug the fuel lines.
10. If equipped with air conditioning, unbolt the air conditioning compressor from the engine and position aside. It is not necessary to remove the lines from the compressor.
11. Remove the radiator and shroud. Remove the fan and all related parts. Disconnet the heater hoses.
12. Unbolt the power steering pump from its brackets and position it to the side. Do not remove the hoses from the pump.
13. Remove the alternator. Remove the ignition coil and power transistor assembly, if equipped.

14. Label and disconnect all remaining electrical connectors, vacuum hoses and check for any other items preventing engine removal.
15. Attach an engine removal device to the engine support eyes on the engine.
16. If equipped with an automatic transmission, support the transmission with a floor jack or equivalent. Remove the remaining bell housing bolts.
17. Remove the engine mount nuts and remove the engine from the vehicle.

To install:
18. Lower the engine into position and install the engine mount nuts. Torque the nuts to 20 ft. lbs. (27 Nm). Install the upper bell housing bolts. Remove the engine removal device. Install the oil dipstick.
19. Raise the vehicle and support safely.
20. Install the remaining bell housing bolts.
21. If equipped with a manual transmission, install the transmission and all related parts.
22. If equipped with an automatic transmission, align the torque converter and flexplate and install the bolts. Install the inspection plate and starter.
23. Install the exhaust pipe to the exhaust manifold(s) using new gaskets. Install the lower radiator hose. Lower the vehicle.
24. Connect the heater hoses.
25. Make sure the negative battery cable is not connected to the battery. Connect the engine side of the negative cable to the engine. Install the alternator, power steering pump and all brackets.
26. Install the air conditioning compressor.
27. Connect all linkages and cables to the carburetor or throttle body.
28. Install the ignition coil and power transistor assembly, if equipped. Connect all electrical connectors and vacuum hoses that were disconnected during the engine removal procedure.
29. Install the fan and all related parts. Adjust all belt tensions, as required.
30. Install the radiator, shroud and upper hose.
31. Install the air cleaner assembly, ducts and air intake hoses.

1. Throttle position sensor connector
2. Ignition coil connector
3. Power transistor connector
4. EGR temperature sensor connector
5. Coolant temperature sending unit connector
6. Coolant temperature sensor connector
7. Thermo switch connector (automatic transmission only)
8. Oxygen sensor connector
9. Alternator connector
10. Oil pressure sending unit connector
11. Coolant temperature switch connector (automatic transmission only)
12. Ground cable
13. Emission control vacuum hose
14. Brake booster vacuum hose
15. Ground cable
16. I.S.C. connector
17. Motor position sensor connector
18. Engine controller wiring harness
19. Heat shield
20. Engine mount bolt

Identifying electrical connectors—Pick-Up with 2.4L engine

32. Fill the engine with the specified amount of oil and fill the radiator with coolant.
33. Connect the negative battery cable and connect the jumper wire from the fuel pump activation terminal, if equipped, to the positive battery post to inspect the system for leaks.
34. Check the automatic transmission fluid level, if equipped. Set all adjustments to specifications.
35. Install and align the hood.

VAN

─────── **CAUTION** ───────

The engine is removed from the bottom of the Van. Before attempting to remove the engine, obtain the special OTC support fixture or equivalent, specifically designed for this operation. Do not attempt to remove the engine using a conventional transmission jack. Serious personal injury or damage to the engine or transmission may result if improper equipment is used. Transmission jacks are not rated at the proper weight capacity for engine removal.

─────────────────────────

1. Remove the seat underframe.
2. Relieve the fuel pressure.
3. Disconnect the negative battery cable.
4. Drain the antifreeze. Remove the upper radiator hose.
5. Remove the radiator shroud, cooling fan and all drive belts.
6. Unbolt the power steering pump from its brackets and position aside.
7. If equipped with air conditioning, unbolt the air conditioning compressor from the engine and position aside. Do not disconnect the lines from the air compressor.

8. Unbolt the battery ground cable from the block.
9. Remove the air intake hose from the throttle body.
10. Disconnect all linkages and cables from the throttle body.
11. Remove the alternator. Label and disconnect all remaining electrical connectors and vacuum hoses from the engine.
12. Raise the vehicle and support safely.
13. Matchmark the nut to the threads and remove both strut bars. Remove the driveshaft.
14. Remove the starter.
15. Disconnect the speedometer cable from the transmission. Disconnect the transmission harness connector.
16. Disconnect the transmission ground cable.
17. Remove the header pipe.
18. Disconnect the oil pressure sending unit wire.
19. Disconnect the transmission cooler lines.
20. Cover the fuel line connections with a clean shop rag. Disconnect and plug the fuel lines.
21. Disconnect the transmission gear selector cable.
22. Disconnect and plug the heater hoses.
23. Support the engine safely.
24. Suport the transmission if not removed from the vehicle. Remove the rear engine mount installation bolt.
25. Remove the engine to crossmember installation bolts and nuts.
26. Remove the engine and transmission from the vehicle.
To install:
27. Install the engine and transmission assembly into vehicle. Install the engine to crossmember bolts and torque the nuts to 65 ft. lbs. (88 Nm).

1. Alternator connector
2. Ignition coil and power transistor assembly
3. I.S.C. connector
4. Throttle position sensor connector
5. Coolant temperature switch connector (automatic transmission only)
6. Coolant temperature sensor connector
7. Thermo switch connector (automatic transmission only)
8. Coolant temperature sending unit connector
9. Emission control vacuum hose
10. Ground cable
11. Brake booster vacuum hose
12. Engine controller wiring harness
13. Ground cable
14. EGR temperature sensor connector
15. Oil pressure sending unit connector
16. Oil pressure sending unit connector
17. Ground cable
18. Heat shield

Identifying electrical connectors—3.0L engine

1. Fan shroud
2. Power steering pump
3. Fan
4. Lower radiator hose
5. Upper radiator hose
6. Engine controller wiring harness
7. Oxygen sensor connector
8. Accelerator cable
9. Kickdown cable
10. Vacuum hose cluster
11. Brake booster vacuum hose
12. Air conditioning compressor belt
13. Compressor
14. Ground cable

Identifying electrical connectors—Van

1. Fuel return hose
2. High pressure fuel hose
3. Heater hoses
4. Shifter cable
5. Driveshaft
6. Rear engine mount bolt
7. Engine mount to crossmember bolt

Engine mounting components—Van

28. Install the rear engine mount installation bolt and a new nut and torque the nut to 65 ft. lbs. (88 Nm).
29. Connect the heater hoses and secure the hose clamps.
30. Connect the transmission gear selector cable, speedometer cable, harness connector, ground cable and cooler lines.
31. Install the driveshaft and torque the nuts to 40 ft. lbs. (54 Nm).
32. Install the starter.
33. Connect the fuel lines.
34. Connect the oil pressure sending unit wire.
35. Install the header pipe using a new gasket.
36. Install the strut bars and tighten the nuts until the matchmarks are aligned. Lower the vehicle.
37. Install the alternator.
38. Connect all electrical connectors and vacuum hoses that are accessible from above the engine.
39. Connect all linkages and cables to the throttle body.
40. Make sure the ground cable is not touching the battery post and connect the ground cable to the block.
41. Install the power steering pump and air conditioning compressor.
42. Install the accessory drive belts, cooling fan and radiator shroud.
43. Install the air intake hose to the throttle body.
44. Fill the engine with the specified amount of oil and fill the radiator with coolant.
45. Connect the negative battery cable and connect the jumper wire from the fuel pump activation terminal to the positive battery post to inspect the system for leaks.
46. Check the automatic transmission fluid level. Set all adjustments to specifications.
47. Install the seat underframe.

Engine Mounts

Removal and Installation

FRONT MOUNT

1. Disconnect negative battery cable.

2. Install engine support fixture in place. Raise and safely support the vehicle.
3. Remove the engine front support insulator.
4. Remove the front insulator stopper.
5. Remove the heat protector.
6. Unbolt the rear crossmember or mount as required.
7. Raise engine with support fixture far enough to remove mounts, remove remaining bolts and mounts. Transfer insulator and stopper to new mount.

To install:
8. Install mounts to engine block. Install stopper and heat protector to the mount.
9. Lower engine to original position and insert bolts through mounting brackets. Tighten bolts to 22–29 ft. lbs. (30–40 Nm) and mount nut to 14–22 ft. lbs. (20–30 Nm).
10. Install heat protector to insulator. Tighten heat protector nut to 6–9 ft. lbs. (8–12 Nm).
11. Lower the vehicle and remove the engine support fixture. Reconnect the negative battery cable.

REAR MOUNT

1. Disconnect negative battery cable.
2. Install engine support fixture in place. Raise and safely support the vehicle.
3. Install transmission jack into position and raise transmission slightly.
4. Remove rear mount attaching bolts and crossmember attaching bolts. Remove crossmember from the vehicle and transfer mounting bracket, support insulatorprybar plate assembly to new mount.
5. Installation is the reverse of the removal procedure. Torque crossmember retaining bolts to 29–40 ft. lbs. (40–55 Nm). Torque the insulator to crossmember nuts to 14–18 ft. lbs. (20–25 Nm).

Cylinder Head

Removal and Installation

2.0L, 2.4L AND 2.6L ENGINES

1. On Van, remove the seat underframe. Rotate the engine so

No. 1 cylinder is at TDC. If equipped with fuel injection, relieve the fuel pressure.

2. Disconnect negative battery cable. Drain the cooling system.

3. Remove the upper radiator hose and disconnect the heater hoses. Remove the dipstick bracket bolt.

4. Remove the air cleaner assembly or air intake hose.

5. Disconnect all linkages and cables from the throttle body. Disconnect and plug the fuel lines to the carburetor or fuel rail. Remove the valve cover.

6. On the 2.0L and 2.4L engines, perform the following:

   a. Without disconnecting the lines, unbolt the power steering pump from its brackets and position it to the side, if equipped.

   b. Remove the timing belt upper cover.

   c. Align the timing mark, if not already aligned. Secure the timing belt to the sprocket with wire tie.

   d. Remove the camshaft bolt.

   e. Remove the sprocket from the camshaft and allow it to rest on the lower cover. If this is not possible, tie it to a fabricated device so the belt remains taut and the timing is not lost.

7. On the 2.6L engine, perform the following:

   a. Matchmark the distributor gear to its drive gear and remove the distributor.

   b. Remove the camshaft bolt and remove the distributor drive gear.

   c. Remove the camshaft gear (with the chain installed) from the camshaft and allow it to rest on the holder just below it. This will hold the valve timing. Do not crank the engine until the distributor has been reinstalled or the timing will be lost and timing components could be damaged.

8. Disconnect and label all vacuum lines, hoses and wiring connectors from the manifolds, carburetor or throttle body and cylinder head.

9. Raise the vehicle and support safely.

10. Remove the exhaust pipe from the exhaust manifold. Lower the vehicle.

11. On the 2.6L engine, remove the small end bolts from the head first. Remove head bolts, starting from the outside and working inward.

12. Remove the cylinder head from the engine.

13. Clean the cylinder head gasket mating surfaces.

To install:

14. On the 2.6L engine, apply a thin bead of sealant to the seam where the chain case and block meet. Install a new head gasket to the block and position the cylinder head assembly with all head bolts and washers. Torque the bolts in sequence to 30 ft. lbs. (41 Nm). Repeat the sequence increasing the torque to 50 ft. lbs. (68 Nm). Repeat the sequence a third time, increasing the torque to a final value of 69 ft. lbs. (94 Nm). On the 2.6L engine, tighten the small end bolts to 13 ft. lbs. (18 Nm) last.

15. Install the camshaft gear or sprocket. On the 2.6L engine, install the distributor drive gear, bolt and washer. Torque the bolt to 40 ft. lbs. (54 Nm). Install the distributor, aligning the matchmarks.

16. Install the timing belt cover, if equipped.

17. Install the power steering pump, if removed.

18. Connect the heater hoses.

19. Install the dipstick bracket bolt. Install the valve cover with a new gasket.

20. Connect and plug the fuel lines to the carburetor or fuel rail. Connect all linkages and cables to the throttle body.

21. Install the air cleaner assembly or air intake hose.

22. Connect the upper radiator hose.

23. Fill the radiator with coolant.

24. Connect the negative battery cable and connect the jumper wire from the fuel pump activation terminal to the positive battery post to inspect the system for leaks, if equipped.

25. Set all adjustments to specifications.

26. Install the seat underframe, if removed.

Cylinder head bolt torque sequence—2.0L and 2.4L engines

Cylinder head bolt torque sequence—2.6L engine

3.0L ENGINE

1. Relieve the fuel pressure. Disconnect the negative battery cable. Drain the cooling system. Disconnect the upper radiator hose.

2. Remove the drive belts, air conditioning compressor and power steering pump from the mounts and position them to the side.

3. Using a ½ in. drive breaker bar, insert it into the square hole of the serpentine drive belt tensioner, rotate it counterclockwise (to reduce the belt tension) and remove the belt.

4. Remove the alternator.

5. Remove the crankshaft pulley and the torsional damper.

6. To remove the timing belt, perform the following procedures:

   a. Remove the covers. Rotate the crankshaft to position No. 1 cylinder on the TDC of its compression stroke; the crankshaft sprocket timing mark should align with the oil pan timing indicator and the camshaft sprockets timing marks (triangles) should align with the rear timing belt covers timing marks.

   b. Mark the timing belt in the direction of rotation for reinstallation purposes.

   c. Loosen the timing belt tensioner and remove the timing belt.

NOTE: When removing the timing belt from the camshaft sprocket, make sure the belt does not slip off of the other camshaft sprocket. Support the belt so it can not slip off of the crankshaft sprocket and opposite side camshaft sprocket.

7. Remove the air intake hose.

8. Label and disconnect the spark plug wires and vacuum hoses.

10MM ALLEN HEX

CYLINDER HEAD BOLT AND WASHER

TIMING BELT END

Cylinder head bolt torque sequence—3.0L engine

9. Remove the valve cover.

10. If removing the left cylinder head, matchmark the distributor rotor to the distributor housing and the housing to distributor extension locations. Remove the distributor and the distributor extension. Also, remove the EGR pipe.

11. Remove the air intake plenum and intake manifold assembly.

12. Remove the exhaust manifold.

13. Remove the cylinder head bolts starting from the outside and working inward.

14. Remove the cylinder head from the engine.

15. Clean the gasket mounting surfaces.

To install:

16. Install the new cylinder head gaskets over the dowels on the engine block.

17. Install the cylinder heads on the engine and torque the cylinder head bolts in sequence using 3 even steps, to 70 ft. lbs. (95 Nm).

18. Install the intake and exhaust manifolds.

19. Install the EGR pipe with a new gasket, if removed.

20. Install the distributor and extension, if removed.

21. Install the timing belt and all related items. When installing the timing belt over the camshaft sprocket, use care not to allow the belt to slip off the opposite camshaft sprocket.

22. Make sure the timing belt is installed on the camshaft sprocket in the same position as when removed.

23. Install the alternator and power steering pump.

24. Install the air conditioning compressor and belts.

25. Connect the upper radiator hose.

26. Fill the radiator with coolant.

27. Connect the negative battery cable and connect the jumper wire from the fuel pump activation terminal to the positive battery post to inspect the system for leaks, if equipped.

28. Set all adjustments to specifications.

Valve Lifters

Removal and Installation

2.0L, 2.4L AND 2.6L ENGINES

1. Disconnect negative battery cable.

2. Remove the valve cover.

3. Have a helper hold the rear of the camshaft down during

removal. Then install the rear cap loosely to hold the camshaft in position.

4. Loosen the camshaft cap bolts but do not remove them from the caps. Remove the caps, arms, shafts and bolts all as an assembly. Install tool MD998443-01 or equivalent, on the end of all rocker arms to assure the hydraulic lifters will not fall out of the rocker arms on removal of the assembly.

5. Disassemble the unit keeping all parts in the order of removal and repair as required.

NOTE: On the 2.0L and 2.4L engines, the rocker arms have identification marks on them. Arms with 1–3 on them should only be used on cylinders 1 or 3. Arms with 2–4 on them should only be used on cylinders 2 and 4. The arms on the 2.6L engine are not cylinder specific.

6. The installation is the reverse of the removal procedure. Make sure the arrows on the caps are all pointing to the front of the engine. Torque the cap bolts first to 85 inch lbs. (10 Nm), then to 175 inch lbs. (18 Nm) in the following order: No. 3 cap, No. 2 cap, No. 4 cap, Front cap and Rear cap.

3.0L ENGINE

1. Disconnect the negative battery cable. Remove the air cleaner assembly.

2. Remove the valve cover.

3. Using the auto lash adjuster retainer tools MD998443 or equivalent, install them on the rocker arms to keep the lash adjusters from falling out.

4. On the right side cylinder head, remove the distributor extension.

5. Have a helper hold the rear end of the camshaft down. If the rear of the camshaft cannot be held down, the belt will dislodge and the valve timing will be lost. Loosen the camshaft cap bolts but do not remove them from the caps. Remove the caps, arms, shafts and bolts all as an assembly.

6. Disassemble the unit keeping all parts in order and repair as required.

7. The installation is the reverse of the removal procedure. Apply a drop of sealant to the rear edge of the rear cap. Torque the cap bolts first to 85 inch lbs. (19 Nm), then to 180 inch lbs. (19 Nm) in the following order: No. 3 cap, No. 2 cap, No. 1 cap and No. 4 cap.

Valve Lash

Adjustment

2.0L AND 2.6L ENGINES

1. Run the engine until at normal operating temperature. Disconnect the negative battery cable and remove the valve cover.

2. In sequence, check that the head bolts are torqued to 75 ft. lbs. (103 Nm).

3. Position the piston at TDC on the compression stroke.

4. Loosen the jet valve adjuster locknut.

5. Adjust the valve clearance by turning the adjusting screw a little at a time while measuring the clearance with a feeler gauge.

6. The jet valve clearance specification on a hot engine is 0.010 in. (0.25mm).

7. Tighten the locknut securely while holding the adjustment screw stationary. Recheck the clearance after the locknut has been tightened.

8. Repeat the procedure for the remaining jet valves.

9. Install the valve cover with a new gasket.

Rocker Arms and Shafts

Removal and Installation

2.0L, 2.4L AND 2.6L ENGINES

1. Disconnect the negative battery cable.

1. Rear cap
2. Intake rocker arm
3. Spring
4. Exhaust rocker arm
5. Cap No. 4
6. Exhaust rocker arm
7. Intake rocker arm
8. Spring
9. Cap No. 3
10. Intake rocker arm
11. Spring
12. Exhaust rocker arm
13. Cap No. 2
14. Exhaust rocker arm
15. Intake rocker arm
16. Spring
17. Wave washer
18. Right side shaft
19. Left side shaft
20. Front cap
21. Nut
22. Adjusting screw

Rocker arms/shafts assembly—2.0L and 2.4L engines. Note that 2.4L rocker arms are not equipped with jet valve extensions

1. Rear cap
2. Exhaust rocker arm
3. Intake rocker arm
4. Spring
5. Cap No. 4
6. Exhaust rocker arm
7. Intake rocker arm
8. Spring
9. Cap No. 3
10. Exhaust rocker arm
11. Intake rocker arm
12. Spring
13. Cap No. 2
14. Exhaust rocker arm
15. Intake rocker arm
16. Wave washer
17. Right side shaft
18. Left side shaft
19. Front bearing cap
20. Nut
21. Adjusting screw

Rocker arms/shafts assembly—2.6L engine

2. Remove the valve cover.

3. Have a helper hold the rear of the camshaft down. Then install the rear cap loosely to hold the camshaft in position. If the rear of the camshaft cannot be held down, the belt will dislodge and the valve timing will be lost.

4. Loosen the camshaft cap bolts but do not remove them from the caps. Remove the caps, arms, shafts and bolts all as an assembly. Install tool MD998443-01 or equivalent, on the end of all rocker arms to assure the hydraulic lifters will not fall out of the rocker arms on removal of the assembly.

5. Disassemble the unit keeping all parts in the order of removal and repair as required.

NOTE: On the 2.0L and 2.4L engines, the rocker arms have identification marks on them. Arms with 1–3 on them should only be used on cylinders 1 or 3. Arms with 2–4 on them should only be used on cylinders 2 and 4. The arms on the 2.6L engine are not cylinder specific.

Identifying rocker shafts – 3.0L engine

Service Tips

TICKING NOISE FROM VALVE TRAIN

Some 1990 Monteros equipped with 3.0L engines may emit a ticking noise from the valve train. This condition may be experienced at idle when the engine is cold or at normal operating temperature. The condition may be experienced on a continuous or intermittent basis. It appears that a small casting burr located on the side face of the rocker arm may be the cause of the noise. The burr will not allow full contact of the rocker arm with the side bearing surface of the bearing cap. To repair a ticking noise due to this condition, first isolate the noise to the right or left engine bank. Remove the rocker arm assembly and disassemble as required. Clean and inspect the rocker arm face wear pattern for complete contact. If complete contact is not evident, using a hard, smooth oil stone remove the burr in the rocker arm side face nearest the valve. Reassemble the rocker arm assembly as required and install onto the cylinder head.

Rocker arms/shafts assembly – 3.0L engine

6. The installation is the reverse of the removal procedure. Make sure the arrows on the caps are all pointing to the front of the engine. Torque the cap bolts first to 85 inch lbs. (10 Nm), then to 175 inch lbs. (18 Nm) in the following order: No. 3 cap, No. 2 cap, No. 4 cap, Front cap and Rear cap.

3.0L ENGINE

1. Disconnect the negative battery cable. Remove the air cleaner assembly.

2. Remove the valve cover.

3. Using the auto lash adjuster retainer tools MD998443 or equivalent, install them on the rocker arms to keep the lash adjusters from falling out.

4. On the right side cylinder head, remove the distributor extension.

5. Have a helper hold the rear end of the camshaft down. If the rear of the camshaft cannot be held down, the belt will dislodge and the valve timing will be lost. Loosen the camshaft cap bolts but do not remove them from the caps. Remove the caps, arms, shafts and bolts all as an assembly.

6. Disassemble the unit keeping all parts in order and repair as required.

7. The installation is the reverse of the removal procedure. Apply a drop of sealant to the rear edge of the rear cap. Torque the cap bolts first to 85 inch lbs. (19 Nm), then to 180 inch lbs. (19 Nm) in the following order: No. 3 cap, No. 2 cap, No. 1 cap and No. 4 cap.

Intake Manifold

Removal and Installation

2.0L AND 2.6L ENGINES

1. Disconnect the negative battery cable.

2. Remove the air cleaner assembly. Remove the dipstick bracket bolt from the thermostat housing.

3. Drain the cooling system. Disconnect the heater hoses from the manifold.

4. Disconnect the upper radiator hose from the thermostat housing.

5. Remove and plug the fuel lines to the carburetor.

6. Remove the mounting bolts from the air conditioner compressor and position aside. It is not necessary to remove the lines from the air conditioner compressor. Remove the air conditioning compressor mounting bracket.

7. Disconnect and label the vacuum lines, hoses and wiring connectors from the manifold and carburetor.

8. Remove the starter motor cable clamp. Remove the thermo valve.

9. Disconnect all linkages from the carburetor.

10. Remove the manifold nuts and bolts and remove the manifold from the engine.

To install:

11. Install the intake manifold with new gasket in place. Install manifold bolts and nuts tightening to 12 ft. lbs. (17 Nm).

1. Air intake hose
2. Breater hose
3. Air intake pipe
4. Air hose
5. Accelerator and kickdown cables
6. Throttle body
7. Gasket
8. PCV hose
9. Brake booster vacuum hose
10. Vacuum hose cluster
11. Ignition coil wire
12. Ignition coil
13. Air intake plenum assembly
14. Gasket

Air intake plenum assembly—2.4L engine

12. Connect all linkages to the carburetor.

13. Install the starter motor cable clamp. Install the thermo valve.

14. Connect the vacuum lines, hoses and wiring connectors to the manifold and carburetor.

15. Install the air conditioner mounting bracket, compressor and mounting bolts.

16. Install the fuel lines to the carburetor.

17. Install the air cleaner assembly and the dipstick bracket bolt to the thermostat housing.

18. Reconnect the negative battery cable. Fill the cooling system. Start the engine and check for leaks.

19. Allow the engine to reach operating temperature and re-check cooling system for proper fluid level. Fill as required.

2.4L ENGINE

1. Relieve the fuel pressure.

2. Disconnect the negative battery cable.

3. Drain the engine coolant. Disconnect the upper radiator hose from the thermostat housing.

4. Remove the air intake hoses and the air intake pipe.

5. Disconnect all wires, hoses and linkages to the throttle body.

6. Remove the ignition coil.

7. Disconnect the brake booster hose and vacuum hose cluster from the air intake plenum.

8. Unbolt the air intake plenum from the intake manifold and remove the plenum from the engine.

9. Cover the fuel line with a clean shop rag and disconnect the fuel lines from the fuel rail. Keep the line covered or plugged.

10. Remove the fuel rail assembly with injectors.

11. Disconnect the heater hose from the manifold.

12. Disconnect the wires to the engine coolant switches.

13. Matchmark the rotor to the housing and the housing to the cylinder head and remove the distributor.

14. Unbolt the intake manifold from the cylinder head and remove from the engine.

15. Clean and dry the mating surfaces of the manifold and cylinder head.

To install:

16. Using a new gasket, install the intake manifold to the head. Starting from the middle and working outward, torque the retaining nuts to 12 ft. lbs. (16 Nm).

17. Connect the wires to the engine coolant switches. Install the distributor with matchmarks aligned.

18. Install the fuel rail assembly to the manifold and connect the fuel line using a new O-ring.

19. Connect the heater hose to the manifold.

20. Install the air intake plenum with a new gasket. Torque the retaining bolts to 12 ft. lbs. (16 Nm).

21. Connect the vacuum hoses cluster, brake booster hose and all wires, hoses and linkages to the throttle body.

22. Install the ignition coil.

23. Install the air intake pipe and hoses.

24. Connect the upper radiator hose.

25. Fill the radiator with coolant.

26. Connect the negative battery cable and connect the jumper wire from the fuel pump activation terminal to the positive battery post to inspect the system for leaks.

27. Set all adjustments to specifications.

3.0L ENGINE

1. Relieve the fuel pressure.

2. Disconnect the negative battery cable.

3. Drain the engine coolant. Disconnect the upper radiator hose from the thermostat housing.

4. Remove the air intake hose from the throttle body.

1. High pressure fuel hose
2. Injector harness connector
3. Fuel rail
4. Insulator
5. Heater hose
6. Wiring harness connector
7. Coolant outlet fitting
8. Gasket
9. Thermostat
10. Distributor
11. Plenum bracket
12. Intake manifold bracket
13. Intake manifold
14. Gasket
15. Thermo switch (automatic transmission only)
16. Coolant temperature sensor
17. Coolant temperature sending unit
18. Coolant temperature switch (automatic transmission only)

Intake manifold assembly—2.4L engine

1. Air intake hose
2. Throttle position sensor connector
3. Stepper motor connector
4. Accelerator cable adjusting bolt
5. Throttle control cable (automatic transmission only)
6. Accelerator cable
7. Coolant hoses
8. EGR temperature connector
9. Vacuum hose
10. Brake booster vacuum hose
11. Ignition coil wire
12. Ignition coil
13. Oil filler neck bracket
14. PCV hose
15. Vacuum hose cluster
16. EGR pipe attaching bolt
17. Gasket
18. Bracket bolt
19. Attaching bolt and nut
20. Air intake plenum and throttle body assembly
21. Gasket

Air intake plenum assembly—3.0L engine

5. Disconnect all wires, hoses and linkages to the throttle body.

6. Disconnect the EGR temperature sensor wire.

7. Remove the ignition coil.

8. Remove the engine oil filler neck bracket.

9. Unbolt the EGR tube from the air intake plenum.

10. Disconnect the PCV hose and vacuum hose cluster from the plenum.

11. Remove the plenum to engine brackets.

12. Unbolt the air intake plenum assembly from the intake manifold and remove.

13. Cover the fuel lines with a clean shop rag and disconnect the fuel lines from the fuel rail. Keep the lines covered.

14. Remove the fuel rail with injectors in place.

15. Disconnect the bypass hose and the upper radiator hose from the thermostat housing. Disconnect the wires to the coolant temperature switches.

16. Remove the intake manifold retaining nuts and remove the manifold from the cylinder heads.

17. Remove the gaskets and thoroughly clean and dry the mating surfaces of the manifold and heads.

To install:

18. Position the manifold over the studs and install the retaining nuts. Torque to 12 ft. lbs. (16 Nm), starting from the center and working outward.

19. Connect the hoses and connect the wires to the coolant switches.

20. Install the fuel rail assembly and connect the fuel hoses.

21. Using a new gasket, install the air intake plenum to the intake manifold. Torque the nuts and bolts to 12 ft. lbs. (16 Nm). Install the plenum to engine brackets.

22. Connect the PCV hose and vacuum hose cluster to the plenum.

23. Connect the EGR tube.

24. Install the engine oil filler neck bracket.

25. Install the ignition coil assembly.

26. Connect the EGR temperature sensor wire.

27. Connect all wires, hoses and linkages to the throttle body.

28. Install the air intake hose to the throttle body.

29. Connect the upper radiator hose to the thermostat housing.

30. Fill the radiator with coolant.

31. Connect the negative battery cable and connect the jumper wire from the fuel pump activation terminal to the positive battery post to inspect the system for leaks.

32. Set all adjustments to specifications.

Exhaust Manifold

Removal and Installation

2.0L, 2.4L AND 2.6L ENGINES

1. Disconnect the negative battery cable.

2. Remove the heat cowl from the exhaust manifold.

3. Remove the aspirator valve assembly, if equipped.

4. Raise the vehicle and support safely. Disconnect the exhaust pipe from the manifold. Lower the vehicle

5. Disconnect the oxygen sensor connector or ground cable, if equipped.

6. Remove the manifold mounting nuts and remove the manifold and gasket from the engine.

7. The installation is the reverse of the removal procedure. Torque the manifold mounting nuts to 13 ft. lbs. (18 Nm) starting from the middle and working outward.

8. Start the engine and check for exhaust leaks.

1. High pressure fuel hose
2. Fuel return hose
3. Vacuum hose
4. Engine controller harness connector
5. Fuel rail
6. Vacuum hose and pipe
7. Upper radiator hose
8. Coolant bypass hose
9. Intake manifold
10. Gasket
11. Coolant outlet fitting
12. Gasket
13. Thermostat
14. Coolant temperature switch (automatic transmission only)
15. Coolant temperature sensor
16. Thermo switch
17. Coolant temperature sending unit
18. Thermo valve

Intake manifold assembly—3.0L engine

3.0L ENGINE

1. Disconnect the negative battery cable. Raise and safely support the vehicle.
2. Disconnect the exhaust pipe from the exhaust manifolds.
3. Remove the heat shield.
4. If removing the left manifold, remove the EGR tube.
5. If removing the right manifold, remove the alternator bracket.
6. Remove the manifold attaching nuts and remove the manifold.
7. The installation is the reverse of the removal procedure. When installing, the numbers 1–3–5 on the gaskets are used with the right side cylinders and 2–4–6 are on the gasket for the left side cylinders. Torque the manifold nuts to 14 ft. lbs. (19 Nm).
8. Start the engine and check for exhaust leaks.

Timing Chain Front Cover

Removal and Installation

2.6L ENGINE

1. Disconnect the negative battery cable.
2. Drain the cooling system.
3. Remove the shroud, fan, belts and radiator as required.
4. Remove the power steering pump, alternator, air conditioning compressor and accompanying brackets, as required.
5. Remove the valve cover. Matchmark the distributor gear to its drive gear and remove the distributor.
6. Remove the 2 small front bolts from the cylinder head which screw into and seal the top of the timing cover.
7. Remove the crankshaft bolt and washer. Pull off the crankshaft pulley.
8. Raise the vehicle and support safely. Remove the engine

undercover. Remove the bolts that attach the front of the oil pan to the chain case cover.

NOTE: As soon as the timing cover gasket seal is broken, antifreeze will run out from the water jacket extension in the cover. Place a large drain pan under the work area.

9. Remove the remaining timing cover retaining bolts. Position a drain pan under the timing cover and separate the cover from the block. Allow the coolant to drain from the block and remove the cover. If the oil pan gasket was damaged during this operation, remove the oil pan.

To install:

10. Clean and dry all sealing surfaces.

11. Replace the adjuster window gasket.

12. Pry the crankshaft oil seal out of the cover without scratching the seal bore. Install a new seal using a seal driver or installer.

13. Apply a thin coat of silicone sealer to the top of the timing chain cover to seal the head gasket extension. Install the cover to the block using new gaskets.

14. Install all cover bolts with the appropriate brackets in place. Torque the bolts to 10 ft. lbs. (13 Nm).

15. Install the crankshaft pulley. Thoroughly clean and dry the crankshaft pulley bolt and apply a very thin bead of Loctite® to the threads. Torque the bolt to 87 ft. lbs. (118 Nm).

16. Install the oil pan with a new gasket, if removed.

17. Clean and dry the 2 end bolts that attach the chain cover to the head. Install them and torque to 13 ft. lbs. (18 Nm).

18. Install the distributor aligning the matchmarks.

19. Install the valve cover with a new gasket.

20. Install the power steering pump, alternator, air conditioning compressor and any remaining brackets. Install the fan and adjust the belt tensions.

21. Install the radiator and shroud, if removed.

22. Refill the cooling system and fill the engine with oil.

23. Connect the negative battery cable, road test the vehicle and check for leaks.

Front Cover Oil Seal

Replacement

2.6L ENGINE

1. Disconnect the negative battery cable.

2. Remove the accessory drive belts.

3. Remove the crankshaft pulley.

4. Pry the crankshaft oil seal out of the cover without scratching the seal bore.

5. Install a new seal using a seal driver or installer.

6. Install the crankshaft pulley.

7. Clean and dry the crankshaft pulley bolt and apply a thin bead of Loctite® to the threads. Torque the bolt to 87 ft. lbs. (118 Nm).

8. Install the accessory drive belt and adjust the tension as required.

9. Reconnect the negative battery cable.

Timing Chain and Sprockets

Removal and Installation

2.6L ENGINE

1. If possible, position the engine so No. 1 piston is at TDC on the compression stroke. Disconnect the negative battery cable. Drain the coolant.

2. Remove the timing chain case cover.

3. Remove the 3 silent shaft chain guides. Label each bolt as

Timing chain, silent shaft chain and related parts – 2.6L engine

it is removed. The bolts are of different lengths and styles and must be installed in the correct locations.

4. Remove the flange bolts from the right silent shaft and oil pump gears and carefully remove the chain with all 3 gears. Watch for the aligning keys on the oil pump shaft and right silent shaft. If the chain is removed individually, remove the gears afterward.

NOTE: The 2 gears are identical, but the oil pump drive sprocket is installed with the concave side toward the engine while the right silent shaft sprocket has the concave side out.

5. The timing chain tensioner maintains constant spring pressure on the chain. To prevent it from popping out of the oil

pump it must be fastened in place. Run a piece of wire around the plunger and the left side of the oil pump. Remove the remaining chain guides.

6. Remove the camshaft gear bolt and pry the distributor drive gear from the cam gear. Remove the cam gear from the camshaft and allow it to sit on the gear holder below it. Rotate the camshaft so the spring pin is at the 12 o'clock position.

7. Unbolt the holder and remove the chain with both gears. Remove the tensioner and spring from the oil pump.

8. Inspect all gears, guides and the chains themselves for wear and replace as required.
To install:
9. Assemble the new timing chain with the gears. Both the crankshaft sprocket and the camshaft sprocket have a small dot on their faces. Assemble the chain and sprockets so each dot aligns with the plated links on the chain. Both sets of marks and links must align.

10. Turn the crankshaft as required so the positions of the gears are correct.

11. Install the new tensioner and spring in the bore of the oil pump and hold it down with a piece of wire. Make sure the tensioner is equipped with black washer on the shaft. If the washer is missing, the chain will slap.

12. Install the crankshaft gear to the crankshaft. Install the cam gear holder while holding the gear in place. Allow the cam gear to rest on the holder.

13. Lift the cam gear onto the camshaft, install the distributor drive gear and install the bolt. Make certain sprocket engages the guide pin correctly. Tighten the bolt to 40 ft. lbs. (55 Nm).

14. Remove the wire holding the tensioner plunger and allow it to tension the chain. Install the right side guide.

15. Assemble the silent shaft gear, the oil pump gear and the silent shaft chain. Again, each sprocket is marked with a dot which must be aligned with the plated links on the chain. The sprocket for the silent shaft mounts with the concave side facing

Camshaft position for chain installation—2.6L engine

Timing chain installation—2.6L engine

Silent shaft chain installation—2.6L engine

out (away from the engine block) and the sprocket for the oil pump mounts with the concave side facing the engine block.

16. Install the silent chain with gears onto the shafts. Turn the oil pump shaft and right silent shaft as required to keep the marks aligned.

17. Install the chain guides. Make sure the lock washer is installed between the tensioner guide pivot bolt and the timing chain guide under it. Torque all 10mm flanged bolts to 8 ft. lbs. (11 Nm). Adjust the upper guide so when the chain is pulled downward at the center, the clearance between the chain and the guide is 0.008–0.031 in. (0.20–0.80mm). Torque the tensioner guide locking bolt to 14 ft. lbs. (19 Nm).

18. Install the gear retaining bolts to the oil pump and right silent shaft. Torque the bolts to 25 ft. lbs. (34 Nm).

19. Install the timing chain case cover and all related parts.

20. Refill the cooling system and change the engine oil and filter.

21. Connect the negative battery cable, road test the vehicle and check for leaks.

Timing Belt Front Cover

Removal and Installation

2.0L AND 2.4L ENGINES

1. Disconnect the negative battery cable. Remove the spark plug wires from the tree on the upper cover.

2. Drain the cooling system. Remove the shroud, fan, belts and radiator as required.

3. Remove the power steering pump, alternator, air conditioning compressor, tension pulley and accompanying brackets, as required.

4. Remove the upper front timing belt cover.

5. Remove the water pump pulley and the crankshaft pulley(s).

6. Remove the lower timing belt cover to engine screws and remove the cover.

7. The installation is the reverse of the removal procedure. Make sure the packing is positioned in the inner grooves of the covers properly when installing.

3.0L ENGINE

1. Disconnect the negative battery cable.

2. Drain the cooling system. Remove the drive belts.

3. Remove the upper radiator shroud.

4. Remove the fan and fan pulley.

5. Without disconnecting the lines, remove the power steering pump from its bracket and position it to the side. Remove the pump brackets.

6. Remove the belt tensioner pulley bracket.

7. Without releasing the refrigerant remove the air conditioning compressor from its bracket and position it to the side. Remove the bracket.

8. Remove the cooling fan bracket.

9. Remove the crankshaft pulley bolt and the pulley from the crankshaft.

10. Remove the timing belt cover bolts and the upper and lower covers from the engine.

To install:

11. Install the upper and lower covers to the engine and secure with the retaining screws. Make sure the packing is positioned in the inner grooves of the covers properly when installing.

12. Install the crankshaft pulley and bolts. Torque bolt to 110 ft. lbs. (150 Nm).

13. Install the air conditioning bracket and compressor to the engine. Install the belt tensioner.

14. Install the power steering pump into position. Install the fan pulley and fan.

15. Install the fan shroud to the radiator. Fill the cooling system, reconnect the negative battery cable and check for fluid leaks.

Timing Belt and Tensioner

Adjustment

2.0L AND 2.4L ENGINES

1. Disconnect the negative battery cable.

2. Remove the timing belt cover.

3. Adjust the silent shaft (inner) belt first. Loosen the pulley center bolt so the pulley may be moved.

4. Move the pulley up by hand so the center span of the long side of the belt deflects ¼ inch.

5. Hold the pulley tight so the pulley itself does not rotate when the bolt is tightened. Tighten the bolt to 15 ft. lbs. (20 Nm). If the pulley has moved, the belt will be too tight.

6. Check the timing (outer) belt tension.

7. To adjust the timing (outer) belt, first loosen the tensioner pulley bolts.

8. Allow the spring to take up any slack. Check that the the deflection of the longest span (between the camshaft and oil pump sprockets) is ½ inch. Do not overtighten the belt or it will howl.

9. First tighten the lower pulley bolts to 35 ft. lbs. (47 Nm) and then the upper bolt to the same value.

10. Install the covers and all related parts.

3.0L ENGINE

1. Loosen the bolt that holds the timing belt tensioner in place.

2. Allow the spring to pull the tensioner in automatically.

3. Tighten the tensioner locking bolt.

Removal and Installation

2.0L AND 2.4L ENGINES

1. If possible, crank the engine around so the No. 1 piston is at TDC.

2. Disconnect the negative battery cable.

3. Remove the timing belt covers. If the belt(s) are to be reused, mark the direction of rotation on the belt.

4. Remove the timing (outer) belt tensioner and remove the belt. Unbolt the tensioner from the block and remove.

5. Remove the outer crankshaft sprocket and flange.

6. Remove the silent shaft (inner) belt tensioner and remove the inner belt. Unbolt the tensioner from the block and remove.

To install:

7. Align the timing mark of the silent shaft belt sprockets on the crankshaft and silent shaft with the marks on the front case. Wrap the silent shaft belt around the sprockets so there is not slack in the upper span of the belt and the timing marks are still in line.

Silent shaft belt installation—2.0L and 2.4L engines

8. Install the tensioner initially so the actual center of the pulley is above and to the left of the installation bolt.

9. Move the pulley up by hand so the center span of the long side of the belt deflects about ¼ inch.

10. Hold the pulley tightly so it does not rotate when the bolt is tightened. Tighten the bolt to 15 ft. lbs. (20 Nm). If the pulley has moved, the belt will be too tight.

11. Install the timing belt tensioner fully toward the water pump and temporarily tighten the bolts. Place the upper end of the spring against the water pump body. Align the timing marks of the cam, crankshaft and oil pump sprockets with the corresponding marks on the front case or head.

NOTE: If the following step is not followed exactly, there is a chance that the silent shaft alignment will be 180 degrees off. This will cause a noticeable vibration in the engine and the entire procedure will have to be repeated.

12. Before installing the timing belt, ensure that the left side silent shaft is in the correct position. To do so, remove the plug from the left side of the block and insert a suitable tool. With the timing marks still aligned, the tool must be able to go in at least

Checking the left side silent shaft for proper positioning

Timing belt installation—2.0L and 2.4L engines

2⅓ in. If it can only go in about 1 in. turn the oil pump sprocket 1 complete revolution, recheck and realign the timing marks. Leave the tool in place to hold the silent shaft while continuing.

13. Install the belt to the crankshaft sprocket, oil pump sprocket and the camshaft sprocket, in that order. While doing so, make sure there is no slack between the sprockets except where the tensioner will take it up when released.

14. Recheck the timing marks' alignment. If all are aligned, loosen the tensioner mounting bolt and allow the tensioner to apply tension to the belt.

15. Remove the tool that is holding the silent shaft in place and turn the crankshaft clockwise a distance equal to 2 teeth of the camshaft sprocket. This will allow the tensioner to automatically tension the belt the proper amount.

NOTE: Do not manually apply pressure to the tensioner. This will overtighten the belt and will cause a howling noise.

16. First tighten the lower mounting bolt and then tighten the upper spacer bolt.

17. To verify that belt tension is correct, check that the deflection of the longest span (between the camshaft and oil pump sprockets) is ½ inch.

18. Install the timing belt covers and all related parts.

19. Connect the negative battery cable and road test the vehicle.

3.0L ENGINE

1. If possible, position engine with No. 1 cylinder at TDC. Disconnect negative battery cable. Remove the timing covers from engine.

2. If the same timing belt will be reused, mark the direction of timing belt's rotation, for installation in the same direction. Make sure engine is positioned so No. 1 cylinder is at the TDC of it's compression stroke and the sprockets timing marks are aligned with the engine's timing mark indicators.

3. Loosen the timing belt tensioner bolt and remove the belt. If not removing the tensioner, position it as far away from the center of the engine as possible and tighten the bolt.

4. If tensioner is being removed, mark outside of the spring to ensure that it is not installed backwards. Unbolt the tensioner and remove it along with the spring.

To install:

5. Install the tensioner, if removed, and hook the upper end of the spring to the water pump pin. Install the lower end of the spring to the tensioner in exactly the same position as originally installed. If not already done, position both camshafts so the timing marks line up with those on the alternator bracket (rear bank) and inner timing cover (front bank). Rotate the crankshaft so the timing mark aligns with the mark on the oil pump.

6. Install the timing belt on the crankshaft sprocket and while keeping the belt tight on the tension side (right side), install the belt on the front camshaft sprocket.

7. Install the belt on the water pump pulley, then the rear camshaft sprocket and the tensioner.

8. Rotate the front camshaft counterclockwise to tension the belt between the front camshaft and the crankshaft. If the timing marks came out of line, repeat the procedure.

9. Install the crankshaft sprocket flange.

10. Loosen the tensioner bolt and allow the spring to tension the belt.

11. Turn the crankshaft 2 full turns in the clockwise direction until the timing marks align. Now that the belt is properly tensioned, torque the tensioner lock bolt to 21 ft. lbs. (29 Nm).

12. Install the timing belt covers and all related parts.

13. Connect the negative battery cable and road test the vehicle.

Timing belt installation—3.0L engine

Timing Sprockets

Removal and Installation

1. Disconnect the negative battery cable.
2. Remove the timing belt(s).
3. To remove the camshaft sprocket, hold the sprocket with a holding tool and remove the retaining bolt and washer.
4. To remove the crankshaft sprocket, remove the bolt, if equipped, and remove the sprocket from the crankshaft.
5. To remove a silent shafts sprocket, remove the retaining bolt and pry the sprocket from its mounting shaft.
6. The installation is the reverse of the removal procedure. Torque the sprocket retaining bolt to specifications.

Camshaft

Removal and Installation

2.0L AND 2.4L ENGINES

1. Disconnect the negative battery cable. Remove the valve cover and the upper timing belt cover.
2. Matchmark the rotor to the distributor housing and remove the distributor.
3. Secure the belt to the sprocket and hold the sprocket up with a fabricated device to keep the belt taut. If timing is lost, it will have to be reset. Remove the camshaft sprocket from the camshaft.
4. Remove the camshaft cap bolts evenly and gradually. Install the auto lash adjuster retainers to the rocker arms.
5. Remove the caps, shafts, rocker arms and bolts together as an assembly.
6. Remove the camshaft with the front seal from the engine.

To install:

7. Install a new roll pin to the camshaft. Lubricate the camshaft and install with the front seal in place. Install the camshaft so the hole in the sprocket will line up with the roll pin.
8. Install the caps, shafts and arms assembly. Tighten the camshaft bearing cap bolts in the following order to 85 inch lbs. (10 Nm): No. 3, No. 2, No. 4, front cap, rear cap. Repeat the sequence increasing the torque to 175 inch lbs. (19 Nm).
9. Install the sprocket to the camshaft, engaging the roll pin. Torque the bolt to 70 ft. lbs. (95 Nm). Install the distributor.
10. Install the valve cover and all related parts.

2.6L ENGINE

1. Disconnect the negative battery cable.
2. Remove the valve cover.
3. Remove the camshaft gear retaining bolt and matchmark the distributor gear to its drive gear.
4. Remove the distributor. Pry the distributor drive gear off of the cam gear.
5. Remove the cam gear from the camshaft and allow it to rest on the holder below it.
6. Remove the camshaft cap bolts evenly and gradually. Install the auto lash adjuster retaining tools to the rocker arms.
7. Remove the caps, shafts, rocker arms and bolts together as an assembly.
8. Remove the camshaft with rear seal from the engine.

To install:

9. Install a new roll pin to the camshaft. Lubricate the camshaft and install with the rear seal in place. Install the camshaft so the hole in the gear will line up with the roll pin.
10. Install the rocker caps, shafts and arms assembly. Tighten the camshaft bearing cap bolts in the following order to 85 inch lbs. (10 Nm): No. 3, No. 2, No. 4, front cap, rear cap. Repeat the sequence increasing the torque to 175 inch lbs. (19 Nm).

11. Install the gear to the camshaft engaging the roll pin. Install the distributor drive gear and install the bolt and washer. Torque the bolt to 40 ft. lbs. (54 Nm). Install the distributor.

12. Install the valve cover and all related parts.

3.0L ENGINE

1. Disconnect the negative battery cable. Remove the valve cover.

2. Remove the timing belt and remove the sprocket from the camshaft.

3. Install auto lash adjuster retainers MD998443 or equivalent on the rocker arms.

4. If removing the left side camshaft, remove the distributor and the distributor extension.

5. Remove the camshaft bearing caps but do not remove the bolts from the caps. Remove the rocker arms, rocker shafts and bearing caps, as an assembly.

6. Remove the camshaft from the cylinder head.

7. Inspect the bearing journals on the camshaft, cylinder head and bearing caps.

To install:

8. Lubricate the camshaft journals and camshaft with clean engine oil and install the camshaft in the cylinder head.

9. Align the camshaft bearing caps with the arrow mark (depending on cylinder numbers) and in numerical order.

10. Apply sealer at the ends of the bearing caps and install the assembly.

11. Torque the bearing cap bolts, in the following sequence: No. 3, No. 2, No. 1 and No. 4 to 85 inch lbs. (10 Nm).

12. Repeat the sequence increasing the torque to 175 inch lbs. (18 Nm).

13. Install the distributor, if removed.

14. Install the sprocket, timing belt and all related parts.

15. Install the valve cover.

Silent Shafts

Removal and Installation

2.0L AND 2.4L ENGINES

1. Disconnect the negative battery cable.
2. Remove the timing belts.
3. Remove the timing belt sprockets.
4. Remove the front case.
5. Remove the oil pump components.
6. Remove the shafts from the block.

To install:

7. Coat the silent shafts with clean engine oil and install into the block.

8. Install the drive and driven gears into place so the timing marks are mated with each other. Coat gears with clean engine oil.

9. Attach the special tool to the end of the crankshaft and coat the outer surface with engine oil.

10. Install the front case assembly with a new front case gasket to the block. Install retaining bolts loosely.

11. Install the oil filter bracket together with the oil filter bracket gasket and install retaining bolts with washers. Torque bolts to 15 ft. lbs. (22 Nm).

12. Install the timing belts, covers and related parts.

13. Connect the negative battery cable, start engine and check for leaks.

2.6L ENGINE

1. Disconnect the negative battery cable.

2. Matchmark the silent chain to the gears and remove the chain.

3. Remove the oil pump. The right side silent shaft will come out with the pump. To remove the shaft from the pump, remove the retaining bolt on the pump and remove the shaft.

4. Remove the left silent shaft gear and spacer. Remove the

thrust plate retaining screws and remove the thrust plate by installing two $\frac{1}{32}$ in. screws into the threaded holes and pulling the plate out.

5. Remove the silent shaft.

To install:

6. Coat the silent shaft(s) with oil and install into block. Install the right shaft attached to the oil pump.

7. Install a new O-ring to the thrust plate. Install 2 fabricated guides into the threaded holes for mounting thrust plate. Slide the thrust plate over the guides. Remove the guides 1 at a time and install retaining bolts tightening bolts to 25 ft. lbs. (34 Nm).

8. Install the oil pump gears to the pump body if removed, and align timing marks. Install the pump body in its original position before removal and add oil in the delivery port to prime pump.

9. Install the silent shafts chain and related parts.

10. Connect the negative battery cable and road test the vehicle.

Piston and Connecting Rod

Positioning

Piston positioning—2.2L, 2.4L and 2.6L engines

Piston positioning—3.0L engine

ENGINE LUBRICATION

Oil Pan

Removal and Installation

1. Disconnect the negative battery cable.
2. Raise the vehicle and support safely.
3. Remove the skid plate(s), engine undercover, air guide plate and cross shaft plate as required.
4. Remove the front exhaust pipe and steering linkage components as required.
5. On some vehicles, unbolt the motor mounts and raise the engine safely using the proper equipment.
6. Drain the engine oil from the pan.
7. Disconnect the fluid level sensor wire, if equipped. Remove the attaching bolts and remove the pan.
8. The installation is the reverse of the removal procedure.

Oil Pump

Removal and Installation

2.0L AND 2.4L ENGINES

1. Disconnect the negative battery cable. Remove the timing belt covers, timing belts and sprockets.
2. Raise the vehicle and support safely. Drain the oil and remove the oil filter. Remove the oil pan and gasket. Remove the oil pump pickup and gasket.

3. Remove the oil pressure relief plunger plug and gasket. Remove the spring and plunger from the oil filter bracket.
4. Remove the 4 bracket mounting bolts and remove the oil filter mount and gasket.
5. Using special tool MD998162, remove the cap and gasket that covers the oil pump driven gear shaft. This is located on the right side of the front case at the front of the engine, just above the protruding drive gear shaft.
6. Using a long socket, remove the retaining bolt from the oil pump driven gear located behind the plug removed earlier.
7. Remove the front case mounting bolts and remove the case from the block.
8. Remove the case gasket from the block.

To install:

9. Prime the pump by pouring fresh oil into the pump intake and turning the driveshaft until oil comes out the pressure port. Repeat a few times until no air bubbles are present. Replace all seals on the case assembly.
10. Install a special seal guide to the crankshaft MD998285 or equivalent so the smaller diameter faces outward. Coat the outer diameter of the seal with clean engine oil.
11. Install a new front case gasket and install the front case by carefully positioning the crankshaft seal over the seal guide and lining up all bolt holes. Install and tighten the bolts to 17 ft. lbs. (23 Nm).
12. Remove the plug from the left side of the block. Hold the left side silent shaft by inserting a tool in the plug hole and

1. Drain plug	12. Relief spring	24. Drive gear
2. Gasket	13. Relief plunger	25. Left side silent shaft
3. Oil filter	14. Plug cap	26. Right side silent shaft
4. Oil pressure sending unit	15. O-ring	27. Front bearing
5. Oil pan	16. Driven gear bolt	28. Right rear bearing
6. Oil screen	17. Front case	29. Left rear bearing
7. Gasket	18. Gasket	
8. Oil filter bracket	19. Oil seal	
9. Gasket	20. Oil seal	
10. Relief plug	21. Oil seal	
11. Gasket	22. Oil pump cover	
	23. Driven gear	

Engine lubrication components—2.0L and 2.4L engines

torque the driven gear bolt to 26 ft. lbs. (35 Nm). Using a new O-ring, install the plug cover.

13. Install the oil filter mounting bracket gasket. Install the mounting bracket and bolts tightening the oil filter mounting bracket bolts to 12 ft. lbs. (16 Nm).

14. Clean or replace the oil pickup screen and install with a new gasket.

15. Install the oil pan using a new gasket.

16. Install the timing sprockets, belts and covers.

17. Fill the engine with the proper amount of engine oil.

18. Connect the negative battery cable and check for proper oil pressure and leaks.

2.6L ENGINE

1. Disconnect the negative battery cable. Remove the dipstick.

2. Raise the vehicle and support safely. Drain the engine coolant and oil. Remove the oil pan and timing chain cover. Rotate the engine until all 3 silent chain gear marks are in a position to matchmark them to the corresponding chain link. Using different color paint, matchmark the chain to the gears. Remove the silent shaft chain. The lower guide bolts are also oil pump mounting bolts.

3. Remove the oil pump mounting bolts and remove the pump with the timing chain tensioner and the right side silent shaft.

4. Remove the silent shaft and its key from the oil pump.

To install:

5. Remove the gasket material from the block.

6. Prime the pump by pouring fresh oil into the pump intake and turning the driveshaft until oil comes out the pressure port. Repeat a few times until no air bubbles are present.

7. Install the silent shaft key to the oil pump and install the silent shaft to the pump.

8. Install the timing chain tensioner and spring into its bore it the pump housing. Make sure rubber washer is installed on the tensioner and is not damaged.

9. Install the new gasket to the oil pump. Install the pump to the block engaging the tensioner with the timing chain. Make sure the dowels are fully seated in their bores. Torque the mounting bolts to 13 ft. lbs. (18 Nm).

10. Install the silent shaft chain aligning the matchmarks.

11. Remove the oil pickup and clean or replace, as required. Reinstall with a new gasket.

12. Install the timing chain cover, oil pan and all related parts.

13. Install the dipstick. Fill the engine with the proper amount of oil.

14. Connect the negative battery cable and check the oil pressure.

3.0L ENGINE

1. Disconnect the negative battery cable. Remove the dipstick.

2. Raise the vehicle and support safely. Remove the timing belt, drain the engine oil and remove the oil pan from the engine. Remove the oil pickup.

3. Remove the oil pump mounting bolts and remove the pump from the front of the engine. Note the different length bolts and their position in the pump for installation.

To install:

4. Clean the gasket mounting surfaces of the pump and engine block.

5. Prime the pump by pouring fresh oil into the inlet and turning the rotors or by packing pump with petroleum jelly. Using a new gasket, install the oil pump on the engine and torque all bolts to 11 ft. lbs. (15 Nm).

6. Install the balancer and crankshaft sprockets.

7. Clean out the oil pickup or replace as required. Replace the oil pickup gasket ring and install the pickup to the pump.

Engine lubrication components—2.6L engine

1. Crankshaft sprocket
2. Oil pressure sending unit
3. Oil filter
4. Oil filter bracket
5. Gasket
6. Drain plug
7. Gasket
8. Oil pan
9. Oil screen
10. Gasket
11. Plug
12. Relief spring
13. Relief plunger
14. Front oil seal
15. Oil pump case
16. Gasket
17. Oil pump cover
18. Outer rotor
19. Inner rotor

Engine lubrication components—3.0L engine

8. Install the timing belt, oil pan and all related parts.

9. Install the dipstick. Fill the engine with the proper amount of oil.

10. Connect the negative battery cable and check the oil pressure.

Checking

2.0L AND 2.4L ENGINES

1. Remove the oil pump cover from the front case.

2. Check the case and gear cover for stepped wear from the gears.

3. Measure the drive gear tip clearance between the teeth and the case. The specification is 0.006–0.010 in. (0.16–0.25mm).

4. Check the driven gear tip clearance in the similar manner. The specification is 0.005–0.010 in. (0.13–0.25mm).

5. Place a straight-edge across the gears resting on the opposite sides of the case. If a 0.010 in. (0.25mm) feeler gauge can be inserted under the straight-edge, replace the assembly.

6. Check the relief plunger for freedom of movement and check the spring for deformation and rust.

7. If the gears were removed from the body, install them with the mating marks aligned. If not aligned properly, the silent shaft will be out of time.

8. Install the gear cover to the case using a new gasket. Torque the bolts to 12 ft. lbs. (16 Nm).

2.6L ENGINE

1. Remove the cover from the oil pump.

2. Measure the clearance between the gears and their bearings. The specification for both is 0.0008–0.0020 in. (0.02–0.05mm).

3. Check the clearance between the gears and the housing.

Aligning the oil pump gear timing marks—2.0L and 2.4L engines

Aligning the oil pump gear timing marks—2.6L engine

The specification for both gears is 0.004–0.006 in. (0.11–0.15mm).

4. Check endplay of the gears using a feeler gauge and a straight-edge placed across the pump body. The specification for both is 0.002–0.004 in. (0.04–0.11mm).

5. Check the pressure relief valve for damage. The spring's freelength specification is 1.85 in. (47.00mm).

6. If the gears were removed from the body, install them with the markings aligned. If they are not aligned properly, the silent shaft will be out of time.

7. Torque the cover screws to 13 ft. lbs. (18 Nm).

3.0L ENGINE

1. Remove the rear cover.

2. Remove the pump rotors and inspect the case for excessive wear.

3. Measure the diameter of the inner rotor hub that sits in the case. Measure the inside diameter of the inner rotor hub bore. Subtract the first measurement from the second; if the result is over 0.006 in. (0.15mm), replace the oil pump assembly.

4. Measure the clearance between the outer rotor and the case. The specification is 0.004–0.007 in. (0.10–0.18mm).

5. Check the side clearance of the rotors using a feeler gauge and a straight-edge placed across the case. The specification is 0.0015–0.0035 in. (0.04–0.09mm).

6. Check the relief plunger and spring for damage and replace as required.

7. Install the rear pump cover to the case.

Rear Main Bearing Oil Seal

Removal and Installation

1. Disconnect the negative battery cable.

2. Support the weight of the engine using a jack stand with a block of wood to protect the oil pan. Remove the transmission from the vehicle.

3. If equipped with manual transmission, remove the clutch cover retainer bolts in a cross fashion gradually. Remove the clutch cover and disc. Remove the retaining bolt, flywheel and ball bearing from the engine.

4. If equipped with automatic transmission, remove the adapter plate, driveplate, crankshaft adapter and bushing.

5. Remove the rear engine plate and lower bell housing cover.

6. Remove the rear oil seal case and gasket from the back of the engine.

7. Remove the oil separator if remaining on the engine block.

To install:

8. Install the new oil seal into the seal case using seal installer.

9. Press the oil separator into the seal case making sure the separator oil hole is on the very bottom of the case. In the correct position, the hole is on the adjacent to the oil pan mounting surface.

10. Clean and dry the seal case to block sealing surfaces. Install seal case to the rear of the block using a new gasket.

11. Install the rear engine plate and the lower bell housing cover.

12. If equipped with automatic transmission, install the adapter plate, driveplate, crankshaft adapter and bushing.

13. If equipped with manual transmission, install the retaining bolt, flywheel and ball bearing to the engine.

14. Install the transmission into the vehicle. Lower the vehicle and remove the engine support. Connect the negative battery cable and check the oil level, adding as required.

TORQUE SPECIFICATIONS

Component	English	Metric
Air intake plenum-to-intake manifold	14 ft. lbs.	20 Nm
Camshaft sprocket bolt		
2.0L engine	43 ft. lbs.	60 Nm
2.4 engine	72 ft. lbs.	100 Nm
2.6L engine	43 ft. lbs.	60 Nm
3.0L engine	72 ft. lbs.	100 Nm
Camshaft bearing cap bolts		
2.0L engine (8 x 25 bolt)	19 ft. lbs.	27 Nm
2.0L engine (8 x 65 bolt)	15 ft. lbs.	21 Nm
2.4L engine (8 x 25 bolt)	19 ft. lbs.	27 Nm
2.4L engine (8 x 65 bolt)	15 ft. lbs.	21 Nm
2.6L engine	15 ft. lbs.	21 Nm
Connecting rod cap bolts		
2.0L engine	38 ft. lbs.	52 Nm
2.4L engine	38 ft. lbs.	52 Nm
2.6L engine	34 ft. lbs.	46 Nm
3.0L engine	38 ft. lbs.	52 Nm
Crankshaft main bearing bolt		
2.0L engine	38 ft. lbs.	52 Nm
2.4L engine	38 ft. lbs.	52 Nm
2.6L engine	58 ft. lbs.	79 Nm
3.0L engine	60 ft. lbs.	81 Nm
Crankshaft pulley (sprocket) bolt		
2.0L engine	80 ft. lbs.	110 Nm
2.4L engine	80 ft. lbs.	110 Nm
2.6L engine	87 ft. lbs.	118 Nm
3.0L engine	130 ft. lbs.	180 Nm
Cylinder head bolt (cold engine)	70 ft. lbs.	95 Nm

TORQUE SPECIFICATIONS

Component	English	Metric
Exhaust flange nuts	29 ft. lbs.	40 Nm
Exhaust manifold bolts	13 ft. lbs.	17 Nm
Exhaust manifold nut	13 ft. lbs.	17 Nm
Flywheel bolts		
2.0L engine	95 ft. lbs.	129 Nm
2.4L engine	95 ft. lbs.	129 Nm
2.6L engine	95 ft. lbs.	129 Nm
3.0L engine	55 ft. lbs.	75 Nm
Intake manifold bolts	13 ft. lbs.	18 Nm
Oil pan-to-block		
2.0L engine	6 ft. lbs.	8 Nm
2.4L engine	6 ft. lbs.	8 Nm
2.6L engine	6 ft. lbs.	8 Nm
3.0L engine	5 ft. lbs.	7 Nm
Oil pan drain plug		
2.0L engine	26 ft. lbs.	35 Nm
2.4L engine	26 ft. lbs.	35 Nm
2.6L engine	26 ft. lbs.	35 Nm
3.0L engine	32 ft. lbs.	45 Nm
Oil pump cover bolts		
2.0L engine	13 ft. lbs.	18 Nm
2.4L engine	13 ft. lbs.	18 Nm
2.6L engine	9 ft. lbs.	12 Nm
Oil pressure switch	6 ft. lbs.	8 Nm
Rocker cover bolt		
2.0L engine	5 ft. lbs.	7 Nm
2.4L engine	5 ft. lbs.	7 Nm
2.6L engine	5 ft. lbs.	7 Nm
3.0L engine	7 ft. lbs.	10 Nm
Spark plug	20 ft. lbs.	27 Nm
Starter-to-block bolts		
2.0L engine	23 ft. lbs.	32 Nm
2.4L engine	23 ft. lbs.	32 Nm
2.6L engine	25 ft. lbs.	34 Nm
3.0L engine	23 ft. lbs.	32 Nm
Thermostat housing	14 ft. lbs.	20 Nm
Throttle body-to-intake plenum	9 ft. lbs.	13 Nm
Water pump mounting bolt		
2.0L engine (bolt head 7T)	20 ft. lbs.	27 Nm
2.0L engine (bolt head 4T)	11 ft. lbs.	15 Nm
2.4L engine (bolt head mark 4T)	11 ft. lbs.	15 Nm
2.4L engine (bolt head mark 7T)	20 ft. lbs.	27 Nm
2.6L engine	11 ft. lbs.	15 Nm
3.0L engine (bolt head mark 4T)	11 ft. lbs.	15 Nm
3.0L engine (bolt head mark 7T)	20 ft. lbs.	27 Nm
Wheel stud lug nut	87–101 ft. lbs.	120–140 Nm

MANUAL TRANSMISSION

For further information, please refer to Chilton's Transmission Service Manual.

Transmission Assembly

Removal and Installation

1. Disconnect the negative battery cable.

2. Place the shifter(s) in the nuetral position.

3. Unscrew the shift knob from the control lever. Remove the retainer screws from the dust cover retaining plate and slide plate and boot off of the lever.

4. Remove the retainer screws from the stopper plate and remove the lever assembly from the transmission. Cover the opening with a clean towel to prevent dirt from entering the transmission.

5. Raise the vehicle and support safely. Remove the skid plate, if equipped.

6. Drain the transmission fluid. If equipped with 4WD, drain the oil from the transfer case.

7. Matchmark and remove the driveshaft(s) from the vehicle.

8. Disconnect the speedometer cable from the transmission or transfer case.

9. Disconnect the clutch cable connection.

10. Disconnect the reverse light switch harness connector.

11. Remove the starter and the bell housing cover.

12. Support the weight of the engine using a jack stand with a block of wood to protect the oil pan.

13. Support the transmission with a transmission jack.

14. Remove the transfer case bracket, if equipped.

15. Remove the rear crossmember.

16. Remove the transmission to bell housing bolts.

17. Slide the transmission backwards until the input shaft clears the clutch disc. Remove the transmission from the vehicle.

To install:

18. Lubricate the pilot bushing and input shaft splines very lightly with high temperature lubricant.

19. Mount the transmission securely on a transmission jack and lift it in place until the input shaft is centered in the bell housing opening. Roll the transmission forward until the input shaft splines fully engage with the clutch disc.

20. Install the transmission to bell housing bolts. Torque the bolts to 35 ft. lbs. (47 Nm).

21. Lift the transmission using the transmission jack and install the rear crossmember into position. Install the transfer case bracket, if equipped. Torque the frame bolts to 50 ft. lbs. (68 Nm). Remove the transmission and engine support fixtures.

22. Install the starter and torque the mounting bolt to 20 ft. lbs. (27 Nm). Install the bell housing cover.

23. Connect the reverse light switch and clip all wiring to the transmission case.

24. Connect the speedometer cable.

25. Install the driveshaft(s) making sure to align matchmarks.

26. Connect the clutch cable, using a new cotter pin.

27. Fill the transmission and transfer case with the proper amount of SAE 80W or 75W/85W hypoid gear oil with an API classification of GL-4 or higher.

28. Install the skip plate, if equipped. Lower the vehicle.

29. Install the shift lever assembly, boot and console.

30. Connect the negative battery cable and check the transmission and transfer case for proper operation. Check operation of the reverse lights.

Linkage Adjustment

Since this transmission uses a direct engage shift mechanism, there are no provisions for adjustment.

CLUTCH

Clutch Assembly

Removal and Installation

1. Disconnect the negative battery cable.

2. Place the shifter(s) in the nuetral position.

3. Unscrew the shift knob from the control lever. Remove the retainer screws from the dust cover retaining plate and slide plate and boot off of the lever.

4. Remove the retainer screws from the stopper plate and remove the lever assembly from the transmission. Cover the opening with a clean towel to prevent dirt from entering the transmission.

5. Raise the vehicle and support safely. Remove the skid plate, if equipped.

6. Drain the transmission fluid. If equipped with 4WD, drain the oil from the transfer case.

7. Matchmark and remove the driveshaft(s) from the vehicle.

8. Disconnect the speedometer cable from the transmission or transfer case.

9. Disconnect the clutch cable connection.

10. Disconnect the reverse light switch harness connector.

11. Remove the starter and the bell housing cover.

12. Support the weight of the engine using a jack stand with a block of wood to protect the oil pan.

13. Support the transmission with a transmission jack.

14. Remove the transfer case bracket, if equipped.

15. Remove the rear crossmember.

16. Remove the transmission to bell housing bolts.

17. Slide the transmission backwards until the input shaft clears the clutch disc. Remove the transmission from the vehicle.

18. Remove the clutch cover retainer bolts in a cross fashion gradually. Remove the clutch cover and disc.

To install:

19. Raise the clutch cover and disc into place and use a clutch aligning tool or spare input shaft to center the disc. Apply Loctite® to the threads and tighten all of the bolts finger tight.

20. Tighten cover bolts gradually, evenly and to the proper torque to avoid distorting the cover. Torque the bolts to 15 ft. lbs. (20 Nm).

21. Lubricate the pilot bushing and input shaft splines very lightly with high temperature lubricant.

22. Mount the transmission securely on a transmission jack and raise in place until the input shaft is centered in the bell housing opening. Roll the transmission forward until the input shaft splines fully engage with the clutch disc.

23. Install the transmission to bell housing bolts. Torque the bolts to 35 ft. lbs. (47 Nm).

24. Lift the transmission using the transmission jack and install the rear crossmember into position. Install the transfer case bracket, if equipped. Torque the frame bolts to 50 ft. lbs. (68 Nm). Remove the transmission and engine support fixtures.

25. Install the starter and torque the mounting bolt to 20 ft. lbs. (27 Nm). Install the bell housing cover.

26. Connect the reverse light switch and clip all wiring to the transmission case.

27. Connect the speedometer cable.

28. Install the driveshaft(s) making sure to align matchmarks.

29. Connect the clutch cable, using a new cotter pin.

30. Fill the transmission and transfer case with the proper amount of SAE 80W or 75W/85W hypoid gear oil with an API classification of GL-4 or higher.

31. Install the skip plate, if equipped. Lower the vehicle.

32. Install the shift lever assembly and boot.

33. Connect the negative battery cable and check the transmission and transfer case for proper operation. Check operation of the reverse lights.

Pedal Height/Free-Play Adjustment

1. Measure the distance from the face of the pedal pad to the floorboard. This distance should be about 6½-7 in.

2. If the pedal height is not correct, adjust the pedal stopper to contact the pedal at correct height.

Clutch Cable

Adjustment

1. Check the pedal's free-play. The specification is 1 inch.
2. Adjust the clutch cable by turning the star shaped adjusting wheel on the firewall. Turning the wheel counterclockwise will increase the amount of free-play in the pedal or vice-versa.

Removal and Installation

1. Disconnect the negative battery cable.
2. Turn the cable adjusting wheel counterclockwise to provide enough play to remove the cable end from the clutch lever inside the vehicle. Remove the cable from the lever.
3. Raise the vehicle and support safely.
4. Remove the cotter pin from the lever on the transmission.
5. Remove the clutch cable from the vehicle.
6. The installation is the reverse of the removal procedure. Make sure the insulator is positioning properly.

Clutch Master Cylinder

Removal and Installation

1. Disconnect the negative battery cable. Remove as much fluid as possible from the clutch master cylinder reservoir.
2. Remove the cotter pin and remove the clevis pin from the clutch pedal.
3. Disconnect and plug the fluid line from the clutch master cylinder.
4. Remove the mounting nuts and remove the cylinder from the firewall.
5. Remove the reservoir from the cylinder.
6. The installation is the reverse of the removal procedure.
7. Bleed the system.

Clutch Slave Cylinder

Removal and Installation

1. Disconnect the negative battery cable.
2. Raise the vehicle and support safely.

3. Remove the eye-bolt and washer from the slave cylinder.
4. Remove the mounting bolts and remove the slave cylinder from the transmission case.
5. Replace the eye-bolt washer.
6. The installation is the reverse of the removal procedure.
7. Bleed the system.

Hydraulic Clutch System Bleeding

CAUTION

When bleeding, keep the facial area well away from the slave cylinder and protect all painted surfaces from fluid contact. Brake fluid will damage painted surfaces and could cause physical injury.

1. Fill the clutch master cylinder with fresh DOT 3 brake fluid.
2. Have a helper sit in the vehicle. Raise the vehicle and support safely.
3. Remove the bleeder screw cap.
4. If the system is empty, the most efficient way to get fluid down to the cylinder is to loosen the bleeder about ½–¾ turn, place a finger firmly over the bleeder and have the helper pump the brakes slowly until fluid pressure is felt at the bleeder. Once fluid is at the bleeder, close before the pedal is released.

NOTE: If the pedal is pump rapidly, the fluid will churn and create small air bubbles, which are difficult and time consuming to remove from the system. These air bubble will eventually congregate and will result in a spongy pedal.

5. Once fluid has been pumped to the slave cylinder, open the bleeder screw, have the helper depress the clutch pedal, lock the bleeder and have the helper release the pedal. Wait 15 seconds and repeat the procedure (including the 15 second wait) until no air bubbles flow from the bleeder. Remember to close the bleeder before the pedal is released. If the bleeder is left open when the pedal is released, air will be induced into the system.
6. If a helper is not available, connect a small hose to the bleeder, submerge the other end in a clean container of fresh brake fluid placed in a position that is visible from the driver's seat. Pump the pedal until no air comes out of the tube.

AUTOMATIC TRANSMISSION

For further information, please refer to Chilton's Transmission Service Manual.

Transmission Assembly

Removal and Installation

1. Disconnect the negative battery cable.
2. If equipped with 4WD, disconnect the 4WD indicator light switch connector and the ground cable at the transfer case.
3. Disconnect the pulse generator connector.
4. Raise and safely support the vehicle.
5. Remove the skid plate, if equipped. Drain the transmission and transfer case, as equipped.
6. Matchmark and remove the driveshaft(s).
7. Disconnect the speedometer cable from the transmission or transfer case.
8. Disconnect the shifter linkage or cable.
9. Unplug all transmission electrical connectors.
10. Remove the exhaust pipe from the vehicle. Remove the exhaust bracket from the transmission case.
11. Remove the filler neck and dipstick.

12. Remove the torque converter inspection plate. Matchmark the flexplate to the torque converter and remove the torque converter bolts.
13. Remove the starter assembly.
14. Disconnect and plug the oil cooler lines.
15. Using a transmission jack, support the transmission. Remove the retaining bolts at the crossmember.
16. Remove the crossmember on all vehicles except Van.
17. Lower the transmission down slightly and unbolt the 4WD shifter from the transfer case, if equipped.
18. Remove the bell housing bolts and mounting brackets.
19. Pull the transmission assembly rearward to clear the aligning dowels and remove from the vehicle.
To install:
20. Install the transmission assembly to the engine using dowels as guides. Install the bell housing bolts and torque to 35 ft. lbs. (47 Nm).
21. Install the 4WD shifter, if equipped. Raise the assembly up into position and install the rear crossmember and mounting hardware. Torque the crossmember to frame bolts to 50 ft. lbs. (68 Nm). Torque the through bolt and nut on Van to 60 ft. lbs. (81 Nm).

22. Align the flexplate to torque converter. Apply Loctite® to the threads and install the torque converter bolts. Torque the bolts to 25 ft. lbs. (34 Nm). Install the inspection plate.

23. Install the filler tube with a new O-ring and the dipstick.

24. Install the exhaust and the support brackets.

25. Connect all switch connectors that were removed.

26. Connect the shifter linkage or cable and the throttle cable.

27. Align and install the driveshaft(s).

28. Install the ground wire and the 4WD indicator light switch connector to the transfer case, if equipped.

29. Fill the transfer case with hypoid gear oil with an API classification of GL–4 or higher.

30. Connect the throttle cable.

31. Install the skid plate, if equipped. Lower the vehicle.

32. Install the transfer shifter boot, if equipped.

33. Fill the transmission with the proper amount of Dexron® II.

34. Connect the negative battery cable, start the engine and run through all gears. Add fluid until the transmission is properly filled.

35. Check the operation of the neutral safety switch and the reverse lights.

36. Road test the vehicle and check for leaks.

Shift Linkage Adjustment

1. On the Van, remove the floor console. Position the shifter in the **N** detent.

2. Loosen the nut or bolt on the shifter linkage or cable.

3. Make sure the lever on the transmission is in the **N** detent and the needle in the indicator is also in the **N** position. Jiggle the selector rod to settle the assembly in position. If the rod is equipped with a notch, it should be at the 6 o'clock position.

4. Tighten the adjusting bolt or nut and check for proper assembly.

5. Check the operation of the neutral safely switch.

6. Liberally lubricate all pivoting points within the system.

Throttle Cable Adjustment

1. Depress the accelerator fully and make sure the throttle valve opens all the way. Adjust as required.

2. Measure the distance between the end of the rubber boot and the stopper on the cable at wide open throttle.

3. The specification for carbureted engines is 2.05–2.09 in. (52–52mm) or fuel injected engines is 0–0.04 in. (0–1mm).

4. Adjust the cable on carbureted engines by moving the bracket. Adjust the cable itself on fuel injected engines.

5. Road test the vehicle and check for proper shift points.

Neutral Safety Switch Adjustment

NOTE: Some vehicles are not equipped with an adjustable switch.

1. Adjust the shifter linkage.

2. Raise the vehicle and support safely. Place the shifter in the **N** detent. Loosen the mounting bolts.

3. Align the lever with the positioning boss.

4. Hold in position and tighten the bolts.

5. Check the switch and the reverse lights for proper operation.

Throttle cable adjustment—carbureted engine

Throttle cable adjustment—fuel injected engine

Neutral safety switch adjustment

TRANSFER CASE

Transfer Case Assembly

Removal and Installation

AUTOMATIC TRANSMISSION

1. Disconnect the negative battery cable.
2. Remove the transmission and transfer case assembly from the vehicle.
3. Remove the plug from the right side of the transfer case under the control housing.
4. Remove the select spring and plunger from the housing bore.
5. Remove the control lever housing assembly, cover and gasket.
6. Remove the transfer case to adapter attaching nuts. Pull transfer case from the adapter.

To install:

7. Install the transfer case to adapter and secure using retainer nuts. Torque nuts to 30 ft. lbs. (42 Nm).
8. Install the control lever housing assembly, cover and gasket.
9. Install the select spring and plunger into the housing and install plug in bore.
10. Install the transfer case and transmission into the vehicle, connect the negative battery cable and road test for proper operation.

MANUAL TRANSMISSION

1. Disconnect the negative battery cable.
2. Remove the transmission and transfer case assembly from the vehicle.
3. Remove the plug from the right side of the transfer case under the control housing.
4. Remove the select spring and plunger from the housing bore.
5. Remove the spring pin that retains the shift changer to the control shaft using a pin punch.
6. Remove the transfer case to transmission attaching nuts and remove from the transmission.

To install:

7. Install the transfer case to transmission and tighten attaching nuts to 30 ft. lbs. (42 Nm).
8. Install the shift changer to the control shaft and install new roll pin.
9. Install select spring, plunger and plug into housing bore.
10. Install the transfer case and transmission into vehicle. Connect negative battery cable and road test for proper operation.

Linkage Adjustment

Since this transfer case uses a directly engaging shift mechanism, there are no provisions for adjustment.

1. Oil filler plug
2. Drain plug
3. Plug
4. Gasket
5. Selector spring
6. Selector plunger
7. Roll pin
8. Wire clamp
9. Wire clamp
10. Shift changer
11. Transfer case assembly
12. Gasket
13. Plug
14. Spring
15. Steel ball
16. Plug
17. Neutral return spring
18. Plunger
19. Plunger

Transfer case assembly

DRIVE AXLE

Front Halfshaft

Removal and Installation

RIGHT HALFSHAFT

Outer

1. Place the free-wheeling hub in the free condition by placing the transfer lever in the **2H** position and moving in reverse for about 6 or 7 feet.
2. Disconnect negative battery cable.
3. Raise and safely support the vehicle. Remove the skid plate, if equipped.
4. Remove the tire and wheel assembly.
5. Remove the hub cover with the use of an oil filter wrench. Install a protective cloth between the wrench and the cover to avoid damage to the cover.
6. Remove the snapring from the inside of the hub. Remove the shim.
7. Remove the front brake caliper and brake pads from the vehicle. Do not allow the caliper to hang from the brake hose.
8. Separate the tie rod from the steering knuckle.
9. Separate the upper and lower ball joints from the steering knuckle.

10. Remove the front hub/knuckle assembly with the inner and outer bearings intact.
11. Remove the halfshaft to axle housing retaining nuts and remove the halfshaft from the vehicle.

To install:

12. Install the halfshaft and the retaining nuts and tighten to 43 ft. lbs. (60 Nm).
13. Install the front hub/knuckle and bearing assembly.
14. Install the upper ball joint to the knuckle and torque retaining nut to 130 ft. lbs. (180 Nm). Install the lower ball joint to knuckle and torque retaining nut to 65 ft. lbs. (90 Nm). Install new cotter pins.
15. Install the tie rod end to the steering knuckle and torque to 33 ft. lbs. (45 Nm). Install new cotter pin.
16. Install the shim and snapring to the axle shaft. Install the front hub cover.
17. Install front brake caliper assembly.
18. Install the tire and wheel assembly. Install skid plate, if removed.

Inner

1. Disconnect negative battery cable.
2. Raise and safely support the vehicle.

Front axle shafts and related parts

60 FT. LBS. (81 NM)

14
Left drive shaft
13
11
7 9
6
33 FT. LBS. (45 NM)
10
100 FT. LBS. 136 NM)
8
12
4 3 2
1
Right drive shaft
15

1. Under cover	9. Lower ball joint	
2. Hub cover	10. Cotter pin	
3. Snapring	11. Upper ball joint	
4. Shim	12. Hub and knuckle assembly	
5. Caliper	13. Left side axle shaft	
6. Cotter pin	14. Circlip	
7. Tie rod end	15. Right side axle shaft	
8. Cotter pin		

1. Inner shaft
2. Bearing
3. Dust cover
4. Housing tube
5. Dust seal

Inner axle shaft and tube

3. Remove the skid plate, if equipped.
4. Remove the right outer halfshaft.
5. Remove the lower shock absorber mounting bolts.
6. Install slide hammer to inner shaft flange and pull from housing. Press the bearing from the axle, as required.

To install:
7. Press new bearing and seal on axle, as required. Install new circlip to inner halfshaft and install into housing. Drive the axle into position.
8. Install the lower shock absorber mounting bolts.
9. Install the right outer halfshaft.
10. Install the skid plate, if equipped.

LEFT HALFSHAFT

1. Place the free-wheeling hub in the free condition by placing the transfer lever in the **2H** position and moving in reverse for about 6 or 7 feet.
2. Disconnect negative battery cable.
3. Raise and safely support the vehicle. Remove the skid plate, if equipped.
4. Remove the tire and wheel assembly.
5. Remove the hub cover with the use of an oil filter wrench. Install a protective cloth between the wrench and the cover to avoid damage to the cover.
6. Remove the snapring from the inside of the hub. Remove the shim.

7. Remove the front brake caliper and brake pads from the vehicle. Do not allow the caliper to hang from the brake hose.
8. Separate the tie rod from the steering knuckle.
9. Separate the upper and lower ball joints from the steering knuckle.
10. Remove the front hub/knuckle assembly with the inner and outer bearings intact.
11. Pull the left halfshaft out from the differential carrier. Use care not to damage the oil seal with the splines of the shaft.

To install:
12. Replace circlip on the end of the shaft. Install the halfshaft into the front differential case and drive into position using a plastic hammer.
13. Install the front hub/knuckle and bearing assembly.
14. Install the upper ball joint to the knuckle and torque retaining nut to 130 ft. lbs. (180 Nm). Install the lower ball joint to knuckle and torque retaining nut to 65 ft. lbs. (90 Nm). Install new cotter pins.
15. Install the tie rod end to the steering knuckle and torque to 33 ft. lbs. (45 Nm). Install new cotter pin.
16. Install the shim and snapring to the axle shaft. Install the front hub cover.
17. Install front brake caliper assembly.
18. Install the tire and wheel assembly. Install skid plate, if removed.

1. Boot band
2. Boot band
3. Circlip
4. DOJ outer race
5. Dust cover
6. Balls
7. DOJ cage
8. Snapring
9. DOJ inner race
10. DOJ boot
11. Dust cover
12. Boot protector band
13. Boot protector
14. Boot band
15. Boot band
16. BJ boot
17. Drive shaft and BJ
18. Circlip

Front halfshaft assembly—4WD Vehicle

CV-Boot

Removal and Installation

1. Disconnect negative battery cable.
2. Raise and safely support the vehicle.
3. Remove the skid plate, if equipped.
4. Remove the left halfshaft.
5. Remove the boot bands on the inner Double Offset Joint (DOJ). Remove the circlip.
6. Remove the DOJ outer race from the shaft.
7. Remove the dust cover from the DOJ outer race.
8. Remove the balls from the DOJ cage prying from the inside of the cage outward.
9. Rotate the cage while pushing toward the Birfield Joint (BJ). The cage will drop down to expose a snapring on the halfshaft. Remove the snapring.
10. Remove the DOJ cage and inner race from the halfshaft.
11. Wrap tape over the threads of the halfshaft. Remove the boot from the shaft.
12. Remove the dust cover from the BJ and the halfshaft.
13. Remove the boot bands. Remove the BJ boot from the DOJ end of the driveshaft.

NOTE: Do not disassemble the Birfield Joint (BJ).

To install:

14. Install the BJ boot and bands over the DOJ end of the driveshaft. Install the DOJ boot and bands onto the halfshaft. Apply ½ of supplied grease into the BJ boot and install the bands onto the boot.
15. Install the DOJ cage onto the halfshaft with the smaller diameter side of the cage facing the installed BJ boot. Install the snapring.
16. Apply remaining grease to the DOJ inner race, the DOJ cage and the balls. Insert the balls into the cage from the outside pushing in toward the shaft.
17. Install the outer race over the DOJ cage assembly and install the retaining circlip.
18. Install the dust cover into place and install the boot bands.
19. Install the halfshaft into the vehicle.
20. Install the skid plate, if equipped.

Driveshaft and U-Joints

Removal and Installation

1. If equipped with 4WD, place the free-wheeling hub in the free condition by placing the transfer lever in the **2H** position and moving in reverse for about 6 or 7 feet.
2. Disconnect negative battery cable.
3. Raise and safely support the vehicle.
4. Remove the skid plate, if equipped.
5. Matchmark the flange yoke and the differential companion flange. Do not damage the oil seals when marking positions.
6. Drain the transfer case. Position a drain pan under the transmission tailshaft, as required. Fluid will leak from unit on removal of the driveshaft.
7. Remove the retaining bolts and nuts from the flange(s) and remove the shaft from the vehicle.
8. Remove the U-Joint from the driveshaft as follows:
   a. Make mating marks on the yokes of the universal joint that is to be disassembled.
   b. Remove the snaprings from the yoke. When disassembling, note the position of the snaprings so they may be reinstalled in the same positions.
   c. Remove the grease fitting from the journal.
   d. Remove the journal bearings from the propeller shaft yoke using tool MB990840–01.
   e. Remove the journal and the flange yoke or sleeve yoke from the shaft.
9. Inspect the propeller shaft yokes for wear, cracks or dam-age. Check the sleeve yoke and the flange yoke for wear, cracks or damage. Relpace as required.

To install:

10. Install the U-Joint on the driveshaft as follows:
    a. Install the sleeve yoke or flange yoke to the journal and the assembly to the driveshaft.
    b. Align the mating marks on the yokes and press the journal bearings to the yoke using tool MB990840–01.
    c. Install the snaprings in the position prior to removal. Install the grease fitting.
    d. Measure the clearance between the snaprings and the journal bearing. If the clearance is larger than 0.0024 in. (0.06mm), it will be necessary to replace the snapring.
11. With the mating marks aligned, install the driveshaft into the transfer case/transmission and the companion flange.
12. Clean the mounting nuts and bolts and install to the flange(s). Torque to 43 ft. lbs. (60 Nm).
13. Install the skid plate, if equipped.

Rear Axle Shaft, Bearing and Seal

Removal and Installation

1. Raise the vehicle and support safely.
2. Remove the rear tire and wheel assembly.
3. Remove the brake drum.
4. Disconnect the parking brake cable from the brake shoe and remove from the backing plate.
5. Disconnect and plug the brake line(s) at the wheel cylinder.
6. Remove the 4 nuts behind the backing plate.
7. Remove the backing plate, bearing case and the axle shaft as an assembly. If not possible by hand, use a slide hammer to remove the assembly.
8. Remove the O-ring and the bearing preload shims. Save the preload shims for reassembly.
9. Remove the oil seal from the axle tube with a hooked slide hammer.
10. To remove the axle shaft bearing, remove the notched locknut with tool MB990785–01 or a brass drift.
11. Remove the lock washer and flat washer.
12. Screw the locknut onto the axle shaft about 3 turns.
13. If tool MB990787–01 is not available, it will be necessary to fabricate a metal plate that fits over the axle shaft and butts the locknut. Drill 4 holes in the plate that align with the 4 bearing case studs and fit the plate. Refit 2 nuts and washers to the bearing case studs diagonally across from each other and tighten them evenly to release the bearing case and bearing.
14. Use a hammer and drift to remove the bearing outer race from the bearing case.
15. Remove the outer oil seal from the bearing case.

To install:

16. Apply grease to the outer surface on the bearing outer race and the lip of the outer oil seal. Drive into the bearing case.
17. Slide the bearing case and bearing over the rear axle shaft. Apply grease on the bearing rollers and install the inner race by pressing into place. Be careful not to damage the dust cover.
18. Pack the bearing with grease.
19. Install the washer, the crowned lock washer and the locknut in that order and torque the locknut to 130–159 ft. lbs. (176–220 Nm).
20. Bend the tab on the lock washer into the groove on the locknut. If the tab and the groove do not line up, tighten locknut slightly.
21. Lubricate and drive the new inner oil seal into place. Refit the assembly.
22. Install a new O-ring and the shims. Apply silicone rubber sealant to the face of the bearing case.
23. Install the entire assembly to the axle housing. Torque the retaining nuts to 40 ft. lbs. (54 Nm).
24. Check the axle shaft endplay. If not between 0.002–0.008

1. Brake drum
2. Parking brake cable attaching bolt
3. Parking brake cable
4. Brake fluid lines
5. Nut
6. Rear axle shaft assembly
7. Shim
8. O-ring
9. Locknut
10. Lock washer
11. Washer
12. Axle shaft
13. Outer race
14. Seal
15. Bearing
16. Seal

Rear axle shaft assembly

Measuring axle shaft endplay

in. (0.05–0.20mm), proceed with the axle shaft endplay adjustment procedure.

25. Install all removed brake parts and bleed the system.

26. Install the tire and wheel assembly and road test the vehicle. Check for leaks.

Endplay Adjustment Procedure

1. Begin with the left side rear axle assembly and insert a 0.04 in. (1mm) shim between the bearing case and the axle shaft housing. Torque the nuts to specification.

2. Install the right side axle assembly into the right side housing without its shim and O-ring. Torque the 4 nuts to about 50 inch. lbs.

3. Using a feeler gauge, measure the gap between the bearing case and the axle housing face.

4. Remove the axle shaft and select a shim or shims that is the equal to the sum of the clearance measured in Step 3 plus 0.002–0.008 in. (0.05–0.20mm) and install them on the housing. Install the O-ring and apply sealant.

5. Install the axle assembly and torque the nuts to 40 ft. lbs. (54 Nm).

6. Measure the endplay and complete the installation procedure.

Front Wheel Hub, Knuckle and Bearings

Removal and Installation

2WD VEHICLE

1. Raise the vehicle and support safely. Remove the tire and wheel assembly.

2. Remove the brake caliper, pads and adaptor and position them out of the way.

3. Remove the grease cap.

4. Remove the cotter pin, castellated nut and washer. Remove the outer bearing.

5. Remove the front hub/rotor assembly from the steering knuckle. Remove the grease seal and inner bearing from the hub. Remove the splash shield.

6. Remove the nuts and bolts that attach the hub to the rotor and separate them. Clean out all of the old grease from the inside of the hub.

7. Remove the shock and stabilizer bar from the lower control arm, if equipped.

8. Support the lower control arm. Compress the coil spring with the special spring compressor, if equipped. Separate the ball joints and tie rod end from the knuckle.

9. Remove the steering knuckle.

To install:

10. Install the knuckle to the ball joint studs. Torque all ball joint nuts, except the upper nut on Pick-Up to 100 ft. lbs. (136 Nm). Torque the nut on Pick-Up to 60 ft. lbs. (82 Nm). Install new cotter pins. Remove the spring compressor, if used. Install the shock.

11. Connect the stabilizer bar to the lower control arm. Tighten the nut until the bushing is the same diameter as the washer.

12. Connect the tie rod end to the knuckle. Torque the nut to 30 ft. lbs. (41 Nm). Install a new cotter pin.

13. Assemble the rotor and front hub. Torque the nuts to 40 ft. lbs. (54 Nm).

14. Apply wheel bearing grease to the inside of the front hub.

15. Pack the inner bearing and install into hub.

16. Install a new oil seal into the hub so it is flush with the hub end face.

17. Install the assembly onto the steering knuckle, pack and install the outer bearing.

18. Install the washer and castellated nut. Spin the rotor and torque the nut to 22 ft. lbs. (30 Nm), loosen completely and re-tighten to 6 ft. lbs. (8 Nm) while turning the wheel.

19. Install a new cotter pin and install the grease cap.

20. Install the brake hardware and bleed the system, if opened.

21. Install the tire and wheel assembly and road test the vehicle.

Automatic Locking Hubs, Knuckle and Bearings

Removal and Installation

1. Place the free-wheeling hub in the free condition by placing the transfer lever in the **2H** position and moving in reverse for about 6 or 7 feet.

2. Disconnect negative battery cable.

3. Raise and safely support the vehicle. Remove the skid plate, if equipped.

4. Remove the tire and wheel assembly.

5. Remove the hub cover with the use of an oil filter wrench. Install a protective cloth between the wrench and the cover to avoid damage to the cover.

6. Remove the snapring from the inside of the hub. Remove the shim.

7. Remove the front brake caliper and brake pads from the vehicle. Do not allow the caliper to hang from the brake hose.

8. Using hexagonal wrench, remove the automatic free wheeling hub assembly.

9. Remove the retaining screws from lock washer and remove lock washer.

10. Remove the outer bearing and front hub assembly from knuckle.

11. Remove the inner oil seal and inner bearing from the hub assembly.

12. To separate the hub from the brake disc, matchmark the brake disc to the front hub. Remove the retaining bolts and separate the hub from the disc.

13. Remove the dust cover from the spindle. Separate the tie rod from the steering knuckle.

14. Separate the upper and lower ball joints from the steering knuckle.

15. Remove the knuckle from the axle shaft.

16. Remove the knuckle oil seal and spacer. If damaged, drive out the needle bearing through the spindle end of the knuckle.

To install:

17. Use Mitsubishi tool MB990985 to press the new needle bearing into the knuckle. Lubricate the rollers and install the spacer with the chamfered side facing the center of the vehicle. Install a new seal until it is flush with the knuckle end face and lubricate the lip.

18. Install the knuckle to the ball joint studs. Torque all ball joint nuts except the upper nut on Pick-Up to 100 ft. lbs. (136 Nm). Torque the nut on Pick-Up to 60 ft. lbs. (82 Nm). Install new cotter pins.

19. Connect the tie rod end to the knuckle. Torque the nut to 30 ft. lbs. (41 Nm). Install a new cotter pin.

20. Clean out all of the old grease from inside the front hub.

21. Bolt the rotor and front hub together. Torque the nuts to 40 ft. lbs. (54 Nm). Install new races and apply wheel bearing grease to the inside of the front hub.

22. Pack the inner bearing and install to the race.

23. Install new oil seal into the front hub until it is flush with the front hub end face.

1. Hub cover
2. Snapring
3. Shim
4. Caliper
5. Bolts
6. Automatic free-wheeling hub assembly
7. Lock washer
8. Locknut
9. Front hub and rotor

130–200 Nm→0 Nm→25 Nm
94–145 ft.lbs.→0 ft.lbs→18 ft.lbs.

Front hub and automatic hub assembly—4WD vehicles

1. Oil seal
2. Spacer
3. Needle bearing
4. Knuckle

Steering knuckle, needle bearing, spacer and seal—4WD vehicle

24. Install the assembly onto the steering knuckle, pack and install the outer bearing with grease. Using special tool MB990954 or equivalent, which fits standard torque wrenches, torque the locknut to 95–145 ft. lbs. (130–200 Nm). Loosen the locknut completely, then retorque to 18 ft. lbs. (25 Nm). To complete the procedure, position the torque wrench at the 3 o'clock position and loosen the nut 30 degrees.

25. Install the lock washer. If the lock washer and locknut holes do not align, loosening the nut slightly.

26. Before installing the automatic hub assembly, measure the turning force of the front hub. If the measured value does not meet specifications of 2.5–11.5 inch lbs. and retorque the locknut. Also check the hub for an maximum endplay of 0.002 in. (0.05mm).

Keyway
Key
Brake

Aligning the key in the automatic hub with the keyway in the spindle

27. Apply even coating of sealant on the freewheeling hub body and front hub contact surface. Align the key of the brake and the keyway of the spindle and loosely install the automatic free wheeling hub assembly. The mounting surfaces of the automatic hub and the front hub must be perfectly flush before the mounting bolts are torqued.

28. Torque the automatic hub mounting bolts to 40 ft. lbs. (54 Nm).

29. Check the front hub turning resistance again. If the difference between the reading in Step 26 and this reading is more than 8.7 inch lbs., repair or replace the automatic hub, as required.

30. Install the shim and snapring. Rotate the axle shaft forward and backward and stop at a position midway between 2 heavy spots where there is a heavy feeling.

31. Set a dial indicator so the pin is resting on the end of the axle shaft. The endplay specification is 0.008–0.020 in. (0.2–0.5mm). If not within specifications, adjust by adding or removing shims.

32. Install the hub cover.

33. Install the brake hardware and install the wheel and tire assembly.

34. Road test the vehicle.

Pinion Seal

Removal and Installation

1. Raise the vehicle and support safely.
2. Matchmark and remove the driveshaft.
3. Check the turning torque of the pinion before proceeding. It should be 3.5–4.5 inch lbs. (0.4–0.5 Nm). This is the torque that must be reached during installation of the pinion nut.
4. Using a pinion flange holding tool, remove the pinion nut and washer.
5. Remove the companion flange from the drive pinion.
6. Pry the pinion seal out of the differential carrier.
7. Clean and inspect the sealing surface of the housing.

To install:

8. Using a seal driver, drive the new seal into the housing until the flange on the seal is flush with the carrier.
9. With the seal installed, the pinion bearing preload must be set.
10. Tighten the pinion nut, while holding the flange, until the turning torque is the same as before removal of the nut. The final pinion nut torque must be 137–181 ft. lbs. (190–250 Nm).
11. Align the matchmarks and install the drive shaft.
12. Check the level of the differential lubricant.

Differential Carrier

Removal and Installation

FRONT DIFFERENTIAL

1. Raise the vehicle and support safely. Remove the skid plate.
2. Remove both side outer and right side inner axle shafts.
3. Drain the front differential and remove the cover.
4. Remove the bearing cap retaining bolts, matchmark and remove the caps.
5. Pry the differential case out of the housing.
6. Label any loose parts as removed from the assembly.

To install:

7. Install the differential case to the housing.
8. Install the caps aligning the matchmarks made previously. Torque the retaining bolts evenly and gradually to 45 ft. lbs. (61 Nm).
9. Clean the sealing surfaces of the cover and the differential housing. Reseal the cover and install to the housing.
10. Install the axle shafts.
11. Level the vehicle and fill the differential with Hypoid gear oil with an API classification of at least GL–5, until oil level reaches hole.
12. Install the skid plate and lower the vehicle.
13. Perform a road test and check the differential for leaks.

REAR DIFFERENTIAL

1. Raise the vehicle and support safely. Drain the rear differential.
2. Remove the rear tire and wheel assemblies and brake drums.
3. Remove the axle shafts.
4. Matchmark and remove the driveshaft.
5. Remove the differential carrier retaining nuts and remove the carrier from the axle housing.
6. The installation is the reverse of the removal procedure. Torque the carrier retaining nuts to 22 ft. lbs. (27 Nm).

Differential carrier removal and installation

1. Brake drum
2. Parking brake cable attaching bolt
3. Parking brake cable
4. Brake fluid lines
5. Nut
6. Rear axle shaft
7. Driveshaft
8. Differential carrier

1. Knuckle and axle shaft assembly
2. Inner shaft
3. Circlip
4. Front driveshaft
5. Locknut
6. Left side mounting bracket
7. Locknut
8. Bolt
9. Crossmember
10. Locknut

Front axle removal and installation

Front Differential Housing

Removal and Installation

1. Raise the vehicle and support safely. Remove the skid plate and drain the differential.
2. Remove the hubs and knuckles from the vehicle.
3. Remove the outer and inner axle shafts.
4. Matchmark and remove the front driveshaft.
5. Support the differential housing with a jack.
6. Remove the differential mounting brackets.
7. Remove the front suspension crossmember.
8. Lower the differential housing and remove from vehicle.

To install:

9. Mount the housing safely on jack and raise into position.
10. Lubricate the bushings and install the crossmember and housing brackets.
11. Torque all crossmember mounting nuts and bolt to 80 ft. lbs. (109 Nm) and the housing bracket mounting bolts to 65 ft. lbs. (88 Nm).
12. Replace the circlips and install the axle shafts.
13. Install the knuckle and hub assemblies.
14. Install the front driveshaft.
15. Level the vehicle and fill the differential with Hypoid gear oil with an API classification of at least GL–5, until oil level is up to the fill hole.
16. Install the under cover and lower the vehicle.
17. Perform a road test and check the differential for leaks.

Rear Axle Housing

Removal and Installation

EXCEPT MONTERO WITH COIL SPRINGS

1. Raise the vehicle and support safely. Drain the differential
2. Remove the tire and wheel assemblies. Remove the brake drums.
3. Remove the parking brake cable attaching bolts, disconnect the cables from the shoes and unclip them from the backing plates.
4. Disconnect the brake hose at the T-fitting.
5. Remove the load sensing proportioning valve spring support, if equipped.
6. Disconnect the breather hose, if equipped.
7. Matchmark and remove the driveshaft.
8. Place jack under the center of the differential housing and unbolt the shocks from their lower mounts.
9. Remove the U-bolts, shackle assemblies and remove the leaf springs.
10. Lower the axle and remove from vehicle.

To install:

11. Raise the axle assembly into position and install the leaf springs. Make sure the shackle nuts are on the inside of the shackles.
12. Install the lower shock mounting bolts.
13. Matchmark and install the driveshaft.
14. Install the breather hose, if equipped.

1. Brake drum
2. Parking brake cable attaching bolt
3. Parking brake cable
4. Brake hose
5. Breater hose
6. Driveshaft
7. Stabilizer bar mounting bolt
8. Trailing arm
9. Lateral rod
10. Shock absorber
11. Axle shaft
12. Coil spring
13. Stabilizer bar

4-door models

Rear axle assembly—Montero with coil springs

15. Connect the brake hose.

16. Connect the parking brake cables and install the retaining bolts.

17. Install the load sensing spring support and spring, if equipped.

18. Level the vehicle and fill the differential using Hypoid gear oil with an API classification of at least GL-5, until level reaches the fill hole.

NOTE: If equipped with a limited slip differential, add the proper amount of limited slip friction modifier additive before filling the differential with gear oil.

19. Bleed the rear brakes. Install the brake drums and tire and wheel assemblies.

20. Lower the vehicle so full weight of the vehicle is on the ground. Unload any excess weight that may be weighing down the rear of the vehicle. Adjust the load sensing proportioning valve lever so the distance from the proportioning valve lever to the spring support is 7 in.

21. Road test the vehicle and check for leaks.

MONTERO WITH COIL SPRINGS

1. Raise the vehicle and support safely. Drain the differential.

2. Remove the tire and wheel assemblies. Remove the brake drums.

3. Remove the parking brake cable attaching bolts, disconnect the cables from the shoes and unclip from backing plates.

4. Disconnect the brake hose at the T-fitting.

5. Disconnect the breather hose.

6. Matchmark and remove the driveshaft.

7. Remove the rear stabilizer bar attaching bolts, links and bushings.

8. Place jack under the center of the differential housing and remove the rear trailing arm, if equipped.

9. Remove the lateral rod.

10. Unbolt the shocks from their lower mounts.

11. Lower the axle housing enough to remove the coil springs and the stabilizer bar.

12. Lower the axle assembly fully and remove from vehicle.

To install:

13. With the coil springs and stabilizer bar in place, raise the axle assembly into place and install the lower shock mounting bolts.

14. Install the lateral rod and tighten nuts loosely.

15. Assemble the trailing arm with its front mounting spacers, bushings and nuts. Make sure the washer's concave side faces away from the bushings. Install the trailing arm and torque the rear mount nuts to 90 ft. lbs. (122 Nm). Do not tighten the front mounting nuts yet.

16. Install the stabilizer bar and tighten the mounting nuts until the diameter of the bushing is the same as the diameter of the washers.

17. Install the driveshaft and breather hose.

18. Connect the parking brake cables and install the retaining bolts.

19. Level the vehicle and fill the differential with Hypoid gear oil with an API classification of at least GL-5, until it spills out the fill hole.

NOTE: If equipped with a limited slip differential, add the proper amount of limited slip friction modifier additive before filling the differential with gear oil.

20. Bleed the rear brakes. Install the brake drums and tire and wheel assemblies.

21. Lower vehicle so full weight of vehicle is on the ground. Torque the lateral rod mounting nuts to 90 ft. lbs. (122 Nm) and the front trailing arm mounting nuts to 100 ft. lbs. (150 Nm).

22. Road test the vehicle and check for leaks.

STEERING

Steering Wheel

Removal and Installation

1. Disconnect the negative battery cable.

2. Remove the center pad.

3. Remove the steering wheel jam nut. Matchmark the steering wheel to the shaft.

4. Using steering wheel puller, pull the steering wheel off of the shaft.

5. The installation is the reverse of the removal procedure.

Steering Column and Shaft

Removal and Installation

1. Disconnect negative battery cable.

2. Remove the steering wheel from the vehicle.

3. Remove the upper and lower steering column covers.

4. Disconnect the electrical connectors at the base of the steering column.

5. Remove the gear indicator cable connection at the top of the steering column, if equipped.

6. Remove the brake pedal return spring from the lower portion of the steering column, if equipped.

7. Remove the bolt in the steering shaft coupler above the steering gear. On Van, remove the bolt located on the top of the steering shaft to bevel gear assembly coupling.

8. Remove the column retainer bolts at the floor panel and under the instrument panel. Remove the steering column and shaft from the vehicle.

To install:

9. Install the steering column into the vehicle positioning the steering shaft over the bevel gear or steering gear shaft.

10. Install the under dash retaining bolts loosely.

11. Install the bolt at the lower steering coupler and torque to 25 ft. lbs. (35 Nm).

12. Tighten the bolts under the instrument panel to 14 ft. lbs. (20 Nm). Install the bolts in the column retainer at the floor panel tightening to 4 ft. lbs. (6 Nm).

13. Reconnect the electrical connectors at the base of the steering column.

14. Connect the gear indicator cable, if removed.

15. Install the upper and lower steering column covers.

16. Align and install the steering wheel tightening the jam nut to 36 ft. lbs. (50 Nm).

17. Install the horn pad. Reconnect the negative battery cable and check operation of all related electrical components.

Manual Steering Gear

Removal and Installation

1. Disconnect negative battery cable.

2. Remove the cotter pin and nut on the pitman arm. Separate the relay rod from the pitman arm.

3. Remove the bolt from the steering shaft to steering gear coupling.

4. Remove the steering gear mounting bolts and nuts, slide the gear from the steering shaft and remove the gear from the vehicle. Matchmark and remove the pitman arm, as required.

5. The installation is the reverse of the removal procedure. Torque the gear mounting nuts to 40 ft. lbs. (55 Nm). Torque the relay rod retainer nut to 33 ft. lbs. (45 Nm) and install new cotter pin.

Adjustment

1. Disconnect negative battery cable.
2. Remove the steering gear from the vehicle.
3. Turn the cross shaft 36 degrees. Position the mainshaft in the straight ahead position.
4. Using torque wrench, measure the starting torque of the mainshaft. The recommended value is 7.7–8.6 inch lbs. (0.9–1.0 Nm). If measured value is not within this value, Use tool MB990914 to screw adjusting cover to correct reading.

Manual Rack and Pinion

Removal and Installation

1. Disconnect the negative battery cable.
2. Raise the vehicle and support safely. Remove the under cover.
3. Remove the front tire and wheel assemblies.
4. Remove the cotter pins, castellated nuts and tie rod ends from the steering knuckles.
5. Disconnect the intermediate shaft from the steering gear yoke.
6. Remove the gear housing clamps and remove the gear from the vehicle. Transfer the mounting insulators to the new gear.
7. The installation is the reverse of the removal procedure. Torque the steering gear mounting bolt to 60 ft. lbs. (81 Nm).
8. Align the front end.

Adjustment

With the rack removed from the vehicle, total pinion torque can be checked and adjusted. Remove the boots before attempting to adjust, they will create an additional drag.

1. Attach special tool MB990228–01 to the pinion shaft and rotate the pinion with an inch lb. torque wrench. Turn the pinion 180 degrees to the right and left to measure.
2. The specification is 5–10 inch lbs.
3. If not within specifications, loosen the large locknut below the shaft and tighten the adjust cover until the proper turning torque is reached.
4. If the proper torque is not obtained after tightening the adjust cover 60 degrees, disassemble the unit and replace worn parts.

Power Steering Gear

Removal and Installation

1. Disconnect the negative battery cable. Raise the vehicle and support safely.
2. Fold back the dust boot which covers the steering shaft joint, if equipped. Remove the pinch bolt that holds the steering column shaft to the steering gear main shaft.
3. Remove the cotter pin, castellated nut the steering linkage from the pitman arm.
4. Disconnect and plug the fluid lines from the steering gear.
5. Remove the steering gear mounting nuts and remove the gear from the vehicle.
6. Matchmark and remove the pitman arm from the pitman shaft.
7. The installation is the reverse of the removal procedure. Torque the pitman arm nut to 100 ft. lbs. (136 Nm) and the gear mounting nuts to 28 ft. lbs. (38 Nm) on 2WD vehicles or 45 ft. lbs. (61 Nm) on 4WD vehicles.
8. Fill and bleed the system.

1. Pinch bolt
2. Pressure hose
3. Return hose
4. Cotter pin
5. Castellated nut
6. Steering linkage
7. Locknuts
8. Steering shaft
9. Power steering gear

Power steering gear and related parts—Montero and Pick-Up

Adjustment

1. Attach special tool MB990228–01 to the mainshaft and rotate the pinion with an inch lb. torque wrench to measure the starting torque.
2. The specification is 4–11 inch lbs.
3. If not within specifications, loosen the adjusting screw locknut and adjust the locknut until the proper starting torque is reached.
4. Tighten the adjusting bolt locknut.

Power Rack and Pinion Steering Gear

Removal and Installation

1. Disconnect the negative battery cable.
2. Raise the vehicle and support safely. Remove the under cover.
3. Remove the front tire and wheel assemblies.
4. Remove the cotter pins, castellated nuts and tie rod ends from the steering knuckles.
5. Disconnect the intermediate shaft from the steering gear yoke.
6. Disconnect and plug the fluid lines from the fittings on the rack.
7. Remove the gear housing clamps and remove the gear from the vehicle.
To install:
8. Transfer the mounting insulators to the new gear and replace the O-rings on the the fluid lines.
9. Install the gear and the gear housing clamps in place and torque the steering gear mounting bolts to 60 ft. lbs. (81 Nm).
10. Connect the fluid lines to the fittings on the rack. Connect the intermediate shaft to the steering gear yoke.

Power steering components — Van

11. Install the tie rod ends of the rack to the steering knuckles. Install the castellated nuts on tie rod end studs and install new cotter pins.

12. Install the tire and wheel assemblies.

13. Install the under cover, if equipped.

14. Lower the vehicle. Fill and bleed the power steering system.

15. Align the front end.

Adjustment

With the rack removed from the vehicle, total pinion torque can be checked and adjusted. Remove the boots before attempting to adjust, they will create an additional drag.

1. Attach special tool MB990228–01 to the pinion shaft and rotate the pinion with an inch lb. torque wrench. Turn the pinion 180 degrees to the right and left to measure.

2. The specification is 6–12 inch lbs.

3. If not within specifications, loosen the large locknut below the shaft and tighten the adjust cover until the proper turning torque is reached.

4. If the proper torque is not obtained after tightening the adjust cover 60 degrees, disassemble the unit and replace worn parts.

Bevel Gear and Intermediate Shaft

Removal and Installation

VAN

1. Disconnect the negative battery cable. Raise the vehicle and support safely.

2. Remove the pinch bolt that holds the steering column shaft to the bevel gear input shaft.

3. Remove the pinch bolt and remove the intermediate shaft from the bevel gear output shaft.

4. Remove the mounting bolts and remove the bevel gear from the vehicle.

5. Disconnect the intermediate shaft from the steering gear yoke and remove the shaft. Inspect the rubber coupling for damage.

6. The installation is the reverse of the removal procedure. Torque the bevel gear mounting bolt to 35 ft. lbs. (47 Nm).

Power Steering Pump

Removal and Installation

1. Disconnect the negative battery cable.

2. Position a drain pan under the power steering pump.

3. Disconnect the fluid lines from the pump and plug them.

4. Remove the front bracket attaching bolts and remove the belt from the pulley.

5. Remove the pump from the vehicle.

6. The installation is the reverse of the removal procedure.

7. Adjust the belt tension, as required.

8. Fill and bleed the system.

Belt Adjustment

EXCEPT 3.0L ENGINE

1. Loosen the pump mounting bolts.

2. Using a pry bar, move the pump away from the engine.

3. Adjust the tension until the belt deflects about ¼–½ in. under a 10 lb. load, tighten the mounting bolts.

3.0L ENGINE

1. Loosen the tensioner pulley locknut.

2. Tighten the adjuster bolt until the belt deflects about ¼–½ in. under a 10 lb. load
3. Tighten the tensioner lock bolt.

System Bleeding

EXCEPT VAN

1. Fill the reservoir with Dexron® II.
2. Raise the front end of the vehicle.
3. Disconnect the ignition coil wire.
4. Simultaneously crank the engine and turn the steering wheel from lock to lock. Repeat this several times.

NOTE: If the bleeding procedure is done with the engine running, high speed rotation of the pump will churn the fluid and create air bubbles filling the system with air. Bleed the system while cranking the engine only.

5. Lower the front end.
6. Connect one end of a tube to the breather plug on the steering box and place the other a container.
7. Start the engine and allow it to idle.
8. Loosen the breather plug and turn the steering wheel from lock to lock continuously until no more air bubbles appear in the fluid coming out the tube.

NOTE: Do not hold the steering wheel all the way against the stop for more than 5 seconds.

9. After the bleeding is done, tighten the breather plug and refill the reservoir.

VAN

1. Fill the reservoir with Dexron® II. Disconnect the ignition coil wire.

2. Simultaneously crank the engine and turn the steering wheel from steering stop to stop. Repeat this several times.

NOTE: If the bleeding procedure is done with the engine running, high speed rotation of the pump will churn the fluid and create air bubbles filling the system with air. Bleed the system while cranking the engine only.

3. Start the engine and allow it to idle.
4. Turn the steering wheel from lock to lock until no more bubbles are visible in the fluid reservoir.
5. Confirm that the fluid is not milky and that there is very little change in the fluid level when the steering wheel is turned.
6. If the fluid level rises when the engine is turned off, there is still air present in the system.

Tie Rod Ends

Removal and Installation

1. Raise the vehicle and support safely.
2. Remove the cotter pin and nut from the tie rod end stud.
3. Using a puller, remove the tie rod from the steering knuckle or center link.
4. Loosen the sleeve clamp nut, if equipped, and unthread the tie rod end.
5. The installation is the reverse of the removal procedure. Torque the stud nuts to 33 ft. lbs. (45 Nm) and install a new cotter pin.
6. Lubricate the front end.
7. Align the front end.

BRAKES

For all brake system repair and service procedure not detained below, please refer to "Brakes" in the Unit Repair section.

Master Cylinder

Removal and Installation

EXCEPT VAN

1. Disconnect the negative battery cable. Disconnect the fluid level sensor connector.
2. Disconnect and plug the brake lines from the master cylinder.
3. Remove the nuts attaching the master cylinder to the power booster.
4. Remove the master cylinder from the mounting studs.
5. Remove the fluid reservior from the cylinder.
To install:
6. Bench bleed the master cylinder.
7. Install master cylinder on power booster studs and install the retaining nuts.
8. Install the brake lines loosely to the master cylinder.
9. Have a helper press down on the brake pedal, holding pedal to the floor. Tighten hydraulic lines at master cylinder.
10. Connect the fluid level sensor connector and refill reservoir as required.

VAN

1. Disconnect the negative battery cable.
2. Remove the instrument cluster.

3. Disconnect and plug the fluid hoses that run from the reservoir to the actual cylinder. Make sure fluid is not leaking past the plugs.
4. Disconnect and plug the brake lines from the master cylinder.
5. Remove the nuts attaching the master cylinder to the power booster.
6. Remove the master cylinder from the mounting studs.
To install:
7. Bench bleed the master cylinder.
8. Install master cylinder to the mounting studs and install the retainer nuts.
9. Install the brake lines to the master cylinder.
10. Connect the fluid hoses to the cylinder.
11. Install the instrument cluster.
12. Bleed the brakes, if necessary.
13. Check the operation of all brake warning indicators on the instrument cluster.

Proportioning Valve

Removal and Installation

MONTERO

1. Disconnect the negative battery cable.
2. Raise the vehicle and support safely.
3. Identify and disconnect the brake lines from the proportioning valve.
4. Disconnect the wires to the valve, if any.
5. Remove the proportioning valve from the vehicle.

6. The installation is the reverse of the removal procedure.
7. Bleed the brakes in the following order:
   a. Right rear
   b. Left rear
   c. Right front
   d. Left front

Load Sensing Proportioning Valve

Removal and Installation

PICK-UP AND VAN

1. Disconnect the negative battery cable.
2. Raise the vehicle and support safely.
3. Identify and disconnect the brake lines from the valve.
4. Remove the mounting bolts and remove the valve leaving the spring hanging from the lever.

To install:

5. Install the valve to the vehicle engaging the spring.
6. Connect the brake lines.
7. Bleed the brakes in the following order:
   a. Right rear
   b. Load sensing proportioning valve
   c. Left rear
   d. Right front
   e. Left front

8. Lower the vehicle so the full weight of the vehicle is on the ground. Unload any excess weight that is weighing down the rear of the vehicle. Adjust the load sensing proportioning valve lever so the distance from the proportioning valve lever to the spring support is about 7 in.

Adjusting the load sensing proportioning valve

Power Brake Booster

Removal and Installation

EXCEPT VAN

1. Disconnect the negative battery cable. Disconnect the vacuum hose from the booster.
2. Remove the nuts attaching the master cylinder to the booster and move the master cylinder to the side.
3. From inside of the vehicle, remove the clevis pin that secures the booster pushrod to the brake pedal.
4. Remove the nuts that attach the booster to the dash panel and remove from the vehicle.
5. The installation is the reverse of the removal procedure.

VAN

1. Disconnect the negative battery cable.
2. Remove the driver's lap heater duct.
3. Remove the upper and lower column covers.
4. Disconnect the column electrical connectors.
5. Remove the steering column from the vehicle.

POWER BRAKE
BOOSTER

CLEVIS
PIN

PEDAL ASSEMBLY

Brake pedal assembly with booster attached—Van

6. Raise the vehicle and support safely. Remove the pinch bolt that retains the column shaft to the bevel gear input shaft. Lower the vehicle.
7. Remove the master cylinder.
8. Disconnect the stoplight switch connector.
9. Disconnect the vacuum hose from the booster.
10. Remove the entire brake pedal assembly with bracket and booster attached.
11. Remove the clevis pin that secures the booster pushrod to the brake pedal.
12. Remove the nuts that attach the booster to the brake pedal bracket.

To install:

13. Install the booster to the bracket and attach the pushrod to the brake pedal. Install the clevis pin and new cotter pin.
14. Install the assembly to the vehicle. Connect the vacuum hose.
15. Install the master cylinder and connect the stop light switch electrical connector.
16. Install the column and the lower steering linkage pinch bolt.
17. Install the upper and lower column covers and the lap duct.
18. Bleed the brakes, as required.

Brake Caliper

Removal and Installation

VAN

1. Raise the vehicle and support safely.
2. Remove the tire and wheel assembly.
3. Remove the brake hose from the brake tube and the caliper.
4. Remove the caliper mounting bolts and remove the caliper from the adapter.

To install:

5. Install the adapter onto the steering knuckle.
6. Install the caliper with brake pads in place, to the adapter.
7. Install the brake line to the caliper.

1. Lock pin
2. Adaptor
3. Lock pin sleeve
4. Lock pin boot
5. Guide pin boot
6. Boot ring
7. Piston boot
8. Piston
9. Piston seal
10. Caliper
11. Guide pin
12. Guide pin sleeve
13. Outer anti-squeal plate
14. Brake pads
15. Inner anti-squeal plate
16. Pad and wear indicator
17. Anti-rattle clips

Front brakes—Montero and Pick-Up

8. Make sure all anti-rattle and anti-squeal clips and pads are in place.
9. Bleed the brakes system.
10. Install the tire and wheel assembly.
11. Road test the vehicle.

EXCEPT VAN

1. Raise the vehicle and support safely.
2. Remove the tire and wheel assembly. Disconnect the brake line from the caliper.
3. Label and remove the 2 mounting bolts.
4. Lift the caliper off of the adaptor.
5. The installation is the reverse of the removal procedure. Make sure all anti-rattle and -squeal clips and pads are in place. Torque the guide pin bolt to 35 ft. lbs. (47 Nm) and the lock pin bolt to 30 ft. lbs. (41 Nm).
6. Bleed the brakes and road test the vehicle.

Disc Brake Pads

Removal and Installation

1. Remove ½ of the fluid from the master cylinder reservoir.
2. Raise the vehicle and support safely. Remove the tire and wheel assemblies.
3. Remove the calipers.
4. Remove the pads from the adaptor.

To install:
5. Use a large C-clamp to compress the piston into the caliper bore.
6. Install the pads to the adaptor with anti-rattle and anti-squeal clips in place.
7. Install the caliper and secure to the adapter.
8. Refill the master cylinder.
9. Bleed the brakes if any brake lines were opened.

Brake Rotor

Removal and Installation

1. Raise the vehicle and support safely.
2. Remove the tire and wheel assembly.
3. Remove the caliper and brake pads.
4. Remove the caliper adaptor.
5. If equipped with 4WD, remove the automatic hub, the shim, lock washer and locknut.
6. If equipped with 2WD, remove the dust cap, cotter pin, nut lock, nut, washer and outer bearing.
7. Remove the front hub and rotor assembly from the spindle.
8. To separate the hub from the rotor, remove the bolts and split the rotor from the hub.

To install:
9. Install the rotor to the hub and torque the attaching nuts and bolts to 40 ft. lbs. (54 Nm).

10. Install the hub and rotor assembly to the spindle and install the retaining nuts and bearings as removed. Adjust bearing preload.

11. Install the caliper adaptor. Torque the bolts to 70 ft. lbs. (95 Nm).

12. Install the brake pads and caliper, making sure all anti-rattle and anti-squeal clips are in place.

13. Bleed the brakes if any brake line was opened.

14. Install the tire and wheel assembly and road test the vehicle.

Brake Drums

Removal and Installation

1. Raise the vehicle and support safely.
2. Remove the tire and wheel assembly.
3. Remove the drum retaining screw with an impact driver if equipped.
4. Remove the drum. If difficult to remove the drum, remove the adjuster access cover in the backing plate and rotate the star wheel to loosen the adjustment on the rear brake shoes.
5. The installation is the reverse of the removal procedure.

Brake Shoes

Removal and Installation

1. Raise the vehicle and support safely.
2. Remove the tire and wheel assemblies and the brake drums.
3. Remove the upper return spring along with the adjuster.
4. Remove the adjuster spring.
5. Remove the lower retaining spring.
6. Remove the hold-down springs.
7. Remove the shoes, disengaging the parking brake lever.
To install:
8. Clean and dry the backing plate. Lubricate the bosses, anchor contacts and wheel cylinder piston grooves where the top of the shoe fits lightly with lithium based grease.
9. Lubricate the star wheel shaft threads with anti-sieze lubricant and transfer all parts to their proper locations on the

new shoes. Make sure the longer end of the upper return spring is installed toward the shoe with the parking brake lever.

10. Spread the shoes apart, engage the parking brake lever and position them on the backing plate making sure the wheel cylinder pins engage the webs of the brake shoes.

11. Install the lower retaining spring and the hold-down springs.

12. Adjust the star wheel until the brake shoes are in contact with the brake drum when installed.

13. Remove any grease from the linings and install the brake drums.

14. Install the tire and wheel assemblies and complete the brake adjustment.

Wheel Cylinder

Removal and Installation

1. Raise the vehicle and support safely.
2. Remove the wheel, drum and brake shoes.
3. Remove the hydraulic brake line from the wheel cylinder.
4. Remove the wheel cylinder mounting bolts and remove the cylinder from the backing plate.
To install:
5. Position the wheel cylinder on the backing plate and install the retaining bolts. Torque the bolts to 14 ft. lbs. (19 Nm).
6. Connect the brake line to the wheel cylinder.
7. Lubricate the backing plate and install the brake linings.
8. Install the brake drums, tire and wheel assemblies and adjust the brake linings.
9. Bleed the brakes system and refill the master cylinder reservoir.

Front Parking Brake Cable

Removal and Installation
VAN

1. Remove the parking brake cover from the inside of the passenger compartment.
2. Remove the adjuster from the front cable.
3. Remove the spring retainer clip from the cable housing.

1. Brake drum
2. Upper return spring with adjuster
3. Adjuster spring
4. Lower retaining spring
5. Hold-down spring
6. Brake shoe
7. Brake shoe and parking brake lever
8. Hold-down pin

Rear brake shoes and hardware

4. Raise and safely support the vehicle.

5. Remove the retainer bolts from the cable housing. Remove the cable retainer from the equalizer and remove the front cable.

6. The installation is the reverse of the removal procedure.

EXCEPT VAN

1. Raise the vehicle and support safely. Remove the front cable adjusting nut.

2. Remove the brake lever cover, if floor mounted.

3. Remove the pin securing the cable to the equalizer and slide the cable out of the bracket.

4. Remove the pin or retainer attaching the cable to the handle assembly. Disengage the cable from the handle.

5. Remove the cable grommet from the floor pan and remove the cable from the vehicle.

6. The installation is the reverse of the removal procedure.

Rear Parking Brake Cable

Removal and Installation

1. Release the parking brakes fully.

2. Raise the vehicle and support safely.

3. Loosen the adjusting nut from the front cable.

4. Remove the brake drums. Remove the shoes, if necessary. Disconnect the cable from the lever.

5. Compress the cable retainer tabs to remove the cable from the backing plate.

6. Remove the cable from the equalizer and remove the retaining bolts from the frame.

7. The installation is the reverse of the removal procedure.

Adjustment

1. Release the parking brakes fully.

2. Raise the vehicle and support safely.

3. Adjust the rear brake linings.

4. Loosen the adjusting nut until there is slack in all the cables.

5. Rotate the rear wheels and tighten the cable adjusting nut until there is a slight drag at the wheels.

6. Continue to rotate the rear wheels and loosen the nut until all drag is eliminated.

7. Back off the nut an additional 2 turns.

8. Apply and release the parking brake several times. Upon the last release, verify that there is no drag on the wheels. The pedal should depress 4–7 notches.

9. To check operation, make sure the parking brake holds on an incline.

Brake System Bleeding

——— CAUTION ———

If using a pressure bleeder, follow the instructions furnished with the unit and choose the correct adaptor for the application. Do not substitute an adapter that "almost fits" as it will not work and could be dangerous.

MASTER CYLINDER

If the master cylinder is off the vehicle it can be bench bled.

1. Connect short piece(s) of brake line to the outlet fitting(s), bend them until the free end is below the fluid level in the master cylinder reservoirs.

2. Fill the reservoir with fresh brake fluid. Pump the piston slowly until no more air bubbles appear in the reservoir(s).

3. Disconnect the lines, refill the master cylinder and securely install the cylinder cap.

4. If the master cylinder is on the vehicle, it can still be bled, using a flare nut wrench.

5. Open the brake line(s) slightly with the flare nut wrench while pressure is applied to the brake pedal by a helper inside the vehicle.

6. Be sure to tighten the line before the brake pedal is released.

7. Repeat the process with both lines until no air bubbles come out.

CALIPERS AND WHEEL CYLINDERS

1. Fill the master cylinder with fresh brake fluid. Check the level often during the procedure.

2. Starting with the right rear wheel, remove the protective cap from the bleeder and place where it will not be lost. Clean the bleed screw.

——— CAUTION ———

When bleeding the brakes, keep face away from the brake area. Spewing fluid may cause facial and/or visual damage. Do not allow brake fluid to spill on the car's finish; it will remove the paint.

3. If the system is empty, the most effecient way to get fluid down to the wheel is to loosen the bleeder about ½–¾ turn, place a finger firmly over the bleeder and have a helper pump the brakes slowly until fluid comes out the bleeder. Once fluid is at the bleeder, close it before the pedal is released inside the vehicle.

NOTE: If the pedal is pumped rapidly, the fluid will churn and create small air bubbles, which are almost impossible to remove from the system. These air bubbles will eventually congregate and a spongy pedal will result.

4. Once fluid has been pumped to the caliper or wheel cylinder, open the bleed screw again, have the helper press the brake pedal to the floor, lock the bleeder and have the helper slowly release the pedal. Wait 15 seconds and repeat the procedure (including the 15 second wait) until no more air comes out of the bleeder upon application of the brake pedal. Remember to close the bleeder before the pedal is released inside the vehicle each time the bleeder is opened. If not, air will be induced into the system.

5. If a helper is not available, connect a small hose to the bleeder, place the end in a container of brake fluid and proceed to pump the pedal from inside the vehicle until no more air comes out the bleeder. The hose will prevent air from entering the system.

6. Repeat the procedure on remaining wheel cylinders in order:
   a. Left rear
   b. Right front
   c. Left front

7. Hydraulic brake systems must be totally flushed if the fluid becomes contaminated with water, dirt or other corrosive chemicals. To flush, bleed the entire system until all fluid has been replaced with new fluid.

8. Install the bleeder cap(s) on the bleeder to keep dirt out. Always road test the vehicle after brake work of any kind is done.

FRONT SUSPENSION

Shock Absorbers

Removal and Installation

1. Raise and safely support the vehicle. Remove the upper shock nut, washer and bushing.
2. Raise the vehicle fully and support safely.
3. Remove the lower mounting bolt(s) and discard the shock.
4. The installation is the reverse of the removal procedure.

Coil Spring

Removal and Installation

1. Raise the vehicle and support safely.
2. Remove the shock absorber.
3. Disconnect the stabilizer bar from the lower control arm.
4. Install spring compressor tool MB990792 or equivalent, to the coil spring and to compress the spring.
5. Remove the cotter pin and lower ball joint nut.
6. Release the lower ball joint taper using Mitsubishi tool MB990809–01.
7. Remove the tool and the ball stud from the control arm. Release the compressor tool from the coil spring.
8. Pull the arm down and remove the spring with the rubber isolation pad from the vehicle.

To install:

9. Install the spring with the rubber isolator. Install the compressor tool and compress spring so the lower ball joint can be inserted through the knuckle.
10. Torque the lower ball joint nut to 100 ft. lbs. (136 Nm). Install a new cotter pin. Remove the spring compressor.
11. Connect the sway bar to the lower control arm, if equipped.
12. Install the shock absorber.

Torsion Bar

Removal and Installation

4WD VEHICLE

1. Raise the vehicle and support safely. Remove skid plate, if equipped.
2. Support the lower control arm at a point away from the torsion bar mounting point to the arm.
3. Fold the dust covers back and slide them away from the ends of the bar.
4. If the bars are to be reused, matchmark the torsion bar at both ends to the anchor and identify left from right.
5. Paint or measure the distance of the exposed threads of the rear mounting bolt down to the nut to aid in adjustment when installing. Remove the rear anchor arm mounting nut and bolt.
6. Remove the torsion bar from the front anchor arm.

To install:

7. If the bar is being reused, lubricate the ends and install the torsion bar aligning the matchmarks. If a new bar is being used, align the white stripe on the front splines with the mark on the anchor. There is a mark on the front of the torsion bar to differentiate between left and right. Do not install the bar with the mark facing the rear.
8. Install the torsion bar to the rear anchor so the length of the mounting bolt from the nut to the head of the bolt is the specified length with the rebound bumper in contact with the crossmember. The specifications are as follows:

    Montero left side—5.3–5.6 in.
    Montero right side—4.9–5.2 in.
    Pick-Up left side—5.5–5.8 in.
    Pick-Up right side—5.3–5.6 in.

9. To initially set the riding height, tighten the rear anchor

Aligning the front of the torsion bar with the front anchor—Except Van

Measure this distance when installing the torsion bar to the rear anchor—Except Van

Measure this distance to initially set the riding height—Except Van

mounting nut to the same point at which it was removed if the old bar is being reused. If a new bar has been installed, tighten the nut so the exposed length of the bolt threads is the specification:

    Montero left side—2.4 in.
    Montero right side—2.8 in.
    Pick-Up left side—3.9 in.
    Pick-Up right side—3.4 in.

10. Fill the dust covers with grease and fold them back into position.
11. Adjust the torsion to the correct riding height.

VAN

1. Raise the vehicle and support safely. Remove the skid plate, if equipped.

2. Support the lower control arm at a point away from where the torsion bar attaches to the arm.

3. Fold the dust covers back and slide them away from the ends of the bar.

4. If the bars are to be reused, matchmark the torsion bar at both ends to the anchor and identify left from right.

5. Paint or measure the distance of the exposed threads of the rear mounting bolt up to the nut to aid in adjustment when installing. Remove the rear anchor arm mounting nut and bolt.

6. Remove the torsion bar from the front anchor arm.

To install:

7. If the bar is being reused, lubricate the ends and install the torsion bar aligning the matchmarks. If a new bar is being used, align the white stripe on the front splines with the mark on the anchor. There is a mark on the rear of the torsion bar to differentiate between left and right. Do not install the bar with the mark facing the front.

Measure this distance when installing the torsion bar to the anchor—Van

Measure this distance to initially set the riding height—Van

8. Install the torsion bar to the rear anchor so the length of the mounting bolt from nut to head is 1.4 inch. Reposition the bar as required.

9. To initially set the riding height, tighten the rear anchor mounting nut to the same point prior to removal, if the old bar is being reused. If a new bar has been installed, tighten the nut so the exposed length of the bolt threads is 2.5 in.

10. Fill the dust covers with grease and fold them back into position.

11. Adjust the torsion bar to the correct riding height.

Adjusting the Torsion Bar

1. Lower the vehicle so its full weight is on the ground. If there is any excess weight in the vehicle, unload it.

Measure this distance to set the riding height—Except Van

UPPER ARM

UPPER ARM REBOUND STOPPER

Measure this distance to set the riding height—Van

2. To set the riding height, measure the distance from the rebound bumper to its stopper bracket on the frame. Adjust the torsion bar nut until that distance is within the specification:

    Montero—2.8 in.
    Pick-Up—3.1 in.
    Van—2.0 in.

3. If, after adjusting the riding height, the exposed portion of the adjusting bolt is protruding up or down far enough to interferes with any front suspension component or is hanging down too low, the bar must be removed and repositioned.

4. Road test the vehicle and remeasure the riding height. Readjust if necessary.

Upper Ball Joint

Inspection

With the control arm removed, check the starting torque required to turn the ball stud. The specification for all vehicles is 7–30 inch lbs.

Removal and Installation

EXCEPT VAN

NOTE: The upper ball joint and upper control arm must be replaced as an assembly on Pick-Up.

1. Raise the vehicle and support safely. Release the tension on the torsion bar and remove the upper control arm from the vehicle.

2. Remove the ring and boot from the ball joint. Remove the snapring.

3. Remove the ball joint from the control arm using tool sets MB990800 and MB990799.

To install:

4. Align the mating mark on the upper ball joint with the mark on the arm.

5. Press the ball joint in using the same tools that were used to remove the ball joint.

6. Install the snapring. If the snapring is loose, install a new one.

7. Fill the boot with grease and install the boot and ring.

8. Install the upper control arm.

9. Lubricate the ball joint with a grease gun.

10. Adjust the riding height, if equipped with a torsion bar and align the front end.

VAN

1. Raise the vehicle and support safely. Release the torque on the torsion bar and remove the upper control arm.

2. Remove the ball joint retaining bolts and remove the ball joint from the arm.

3. The installation is the reverse of the removal procedure. Torque the ball joint retaining bolts to 40 ft. lbs. (54 Nm) and the ball stud nut to 100 ft. lbs. (136 Nm). Install a new cotter pin.

4. Lubricate the ball joint with a grease gun.

5. Adjust the riding height, if equipped with a torsion bar and align the front end.

Lower Ball Joint

Inspection

EXCEPT VAN

With the control arm removed, check the up and down endplay of the ball stud. If it exceeds 0.02 in. (0.5mm), the ball joint should be replaced.

VAN

With the control arm removed, check the starting torque required to turn the ball stud. The specification is 9–30 inch lbs.

Removal and Installation

NOTE: The lower ball joint and lower control arm must be replaced as an assembly on the Van.

1. Raise the vehicle and support safely. Remove the lower control arm.

2. Remove the ball joint retaining nuts and bolts and remove the ball joint from the arm.

3. The installation is the reverse of the removal procedure. Torque the ball joint retaining nuts and bolts to 50 ft. lbs. (68 Nm) on 4WD vehicles or 28 ft. lbs. (38 Nm) on 2WD vehicles. Torque the ball stud nut to 100 ft. lbs. (136 Nm) and install a new cotter pin.

4. Lubricate the ball joint with a grease gun.

5. Adjust the riding height, if equipped with a torsion bar.

6. Align the front suspension.

Upper Control Arm

Removal and Installation

2WD PICK-UP

1. Raise the vehicle and support safely. Remove the tire and wheel assembly.

2. Remove the shock absorber.

3. Install Mitsubishi spring compressor tool MB990792 or equivalent, to the coil spring and compress the spring.

4. Remove the cotter pin and upper ball joint nut.

5. Suspend the rotor assembly so there is not excessive pull on the brake hose.

6. Release the upper ball joint taper using Mitsubishi tool MB990809–01 or equivalent.

7. Remove the tool and remove the ball stud from the knuckle.

8. Loosen the pivot bar retaining nuts and bolts, identify and remove the alignment shims, remove the nuts and bolts and remove the arm from the vehicle.

To install:

9. Install the arm to the frame rail bracket, install the shims in their original locations and install the retaining nuts and bolts. Torque the nuts initially to 40 ft. lbs. (54 Nm).

10. Torque the ball joint nut to 60 ft. lbs. (81 Nm). Install a new cotter pin. Remove the spring compressor.

11. Install the shock absorber.

12. Align the front end. When all settings are at specifications, torque the pivot bar retaining bolts to 80 ft. lbs. (109 Nm).

MONTERO AND 4WD PICK-UP

1. Raise the vehicle and support safely. Remove the skid plate.

2. Remove the shock absorber.

3. Turn the torsion bar adjustment nut counterclockwise to relieve all tension from the torsion bar. Disconnect the brake hose from the brake line and remove the hose from the bracket.

4. Remove the cotter pin from the upper ball stud.

5. Release the upper ball joint taper using Mitsubishi tool MB990809–01 or equivalent. Remove the tool. Remove the ball stud from the steering knuckle.

6. Loosen the pivot bar retaining nuts and bolts, identify and remove the alignment shims, remove the nuts and bolts.

7. Remove the control arm from the vehicle.

To install:

8. Position the arm at the frame rail bracket.

9. Install the shims in their original locations and install the retaining nuts and bolts. Torque the nuts initially to 40 ft. lbs. (54 Nm).

10. Insert the upper ball stud in the steering knuckle arm bore and install the nut. Torque the nut to 60 ft. lbs. (81 Nm) and install a new cotter pin. Install the shock absorber and attach the brake hose.

11. Turn the torsion bar adjustment nut clockwise to apply a load on the bar.

12. Lower the vehicle.

13. Set the riding height and align the front end.

VAN

1. Raise the vehicle and support safely.

2. Remove the rubber splash shield. Remove the shock absorber.

3. Turn the torsion bar adjustment nut counterclockwise to relieve all tension from the torsion bar. Remove the nuts and bolts that attach the front torsion bar anchor to the upper control arm.

4. Suspend the rotor assembly with a wire so there is not excessive pull on the brake hose. Remove the cotter pin from the upper ball stud.

5. Release the upper ball joint taper using Mitsubishi tool MB990809–01 or equivalent. Remove the tool. Remove the ball stud from the steering knuckle.

6. Remove the pivot bar retaining nuts and bolts.

7. Remove the arm from the vehicle.

To install:

8. Position the arm at the frame rail bracket.

9. Install the retaining nuts and bolts. Torque the nuts to 100 ft. lbs. (136 Nm).

10. Insert the upper ball stud in the steering knuckle arm bore and install the nut. Torque the nut to 100 ft. lbs. (136 Nm) and install a new cotter pin. Install the shock absorber.

11. Turn the torsion bar adjustment nut clockwise to apply a load on the bar.

12. Lower the vehicle.

13. Set the riding height and align the front end.

1. Shock absorber mounting nuts
2. Shock absorber
3. Cotter pin
4. Castellated nut
5. Rebound bumper
6. Alignment shims
7. Upper control arm

60 FT. LBS. (81 NM)

Front suspension components—2WD Pick-Up

Lower Control Arm

Removal and Installation

2WD PICK-UP

1. Raise the vehicle and support safely.
2. Remove the shock absorber.
3. Disconnect the sway bar and strut bar from the lower control arm.
4. Install Mitsubishi spring compressor tool MB990792 or equivalent, to the coil spring and compress the spring.
5. Remove the cotter pin and lower ball joint nut.
6. Release the lower ball joint taper using Mitsubishi tool MB990809-01 or equivalent.
7. Remove the tool and remove the ball stud from the knuckle. Remove the spring compressor.
8. Pull the arm down and remove the spring with the rubber isolation pad from the vehicle. Remove the lower arm shaft mounting nuts and remove the arm from the vehicle.

To install:

9. Install the arm to the crossmember finger tight. Install the spring with the rubber isolators. Install the compressor tool and compress spring so lower ball joint can be inserted through the knuckle.
10. Torque the lower ball joint nut to 100 ft. lbs. (136 Nm). Install a new cotter pin. Remove the spring compressor.
11. Connect the sway bar and strut bar to the lower control arm.
12. Install the shock absorber.
13. Lower the vehicle completely. With the weight of the vehicle on suspension torque the lower control arm to crossmember mounting nut to 50 ft. lbs. (68 Nm).
14. Align the front suspension.

MONTERO AND 4WD PICK-UP

1. Raise the vehicle and support safely.
2. Remove the skid plate.
3. Remove the torsion bar, anchors and lower arm shaft.

1. Skid plate
2. Under cover
3. Torsion bar
4. Cotter pin
5. Lower ball joint
6. Stabilizer bar nut
7. Stabilizer bar
8. Shock absorber mounting bolts
9. Lower arm shaft
10. Front anchor arm
11. Lower control arm
12. Rebound bumper
13. Ball joint mounting nuts

100 FT. LBS. (136 NM)

110 FT. LBS. (149 NM)

80 FT. LBS. (109 NM)

Front suspension components—4WD Vehicle

4. Remove the shock absorber lower attaching bolt.
5. Disconnect the stabilizer bar from the lower control arm.
6. Remove the cotter pin and the nut from the lower ball stud. Separate the lower ball stud from the steering knuckle using a puller.
7. Remove the pivot bolts and remove the arm from the vehicle.
To install:
8. Install the new control arm to the vehicle.
9. Install the pivot bolts, but do not torque.
10. Insert the ball stud into the steering knuckle bore. Install the nut, torque to 100 ft. lbs. (136 Nm) and install a new cotter pin.
11. Attach the stabilizer bar to the control arm. Install the shock mount bolts.
12. Install the torsion bar and turn the adjustment bolt clockwise to apply a load to the bar.
13. Lower the vehicle so weight of the vehicle is on suspension.
14. Torque the pivot nuts to 110 ft. lbs. (149 Nm).

15. Set the riding height.
16. Align the front suspension.

VAN
1. Raise the vehicle and support safely.
2. Remove the under cover.
3. Remove the shock absorber.
4. Disconnect the strut bar and stabilizer bar from the lower control arm.
5. Remove the cotter pin and the nut from the lower ball stud. Separate the lower ball stud from the steering knuckle using a puller.
6. Matchmark the head of the cam bolt to the alignment reference plate and remove the bolt, washer and nut.
7. Remove the arm from the vehicle.
To install:
8. Install the arm to the crossmember and install the bolt aligning the matchmarks. Torque the nut to about 40 ft. lbs. (54 Nm).

9. Insert the ball stud into the steering knuckle bore. Install the nut, torque to 100 ft. lbs. (136 Nm) and install a new cotter pin.

10. Install the strut bar and stabilizer bar to the control arm.

11. Install the shock absorber.

12. Align the front end. When all setting are at specifications, torque the lower arm pivot bolt nut to 94 ft. lbs. (130 Nm).

Stabilizer Bar

Removal and Installation

1. Raise the vehicle and support safely.
2. Remove the front sway bar brackets and retainers.
3. Remove the sway bar support brackets and bushings from the lower control arm. Remove the sway bar from the vehicle.
4. The installation is the reverse of the removal procedure.

Front Wheel Bearings

Adjustment

1. Tighten the wheel bearing nut to 22 ft. lbs. (30 Nm) while turning the rotor.
2. Loosen the wheel bearing adjusting nut completely.
3. Tighten the nut to 6 ft. lbs. (8 Nm).
4. Check the wheel bearing endplay. The specification is 0.001–0.003 in.
5. Install the nut lock and cotter pin.

Removal and Installation

1. Raise the vehicle and support safely.
2. Remove the tire and wheel assembly.
3. Remove the caliper, disc brake pads and adaptor.
4. Remove the dust cap.
5. Remove the cotter pin, castellated nut lock, wheel bearing nut and washer from the spindle.
6. Remove the outer wheel bearing.
7. Remove the hub and rotor assembly with the inner intact. Remove the grease seal and inner wheel bearing.

1. Shock absorber
2. Nut
3. Nut
4. Cotter pin
5. Lower ball joint
6. Control arm shaft with alignment cam
7. Lower control arm
8. Rebound bumper

100 FT. LBS. (136 NM)

90 FT.LBS. (122 NM)

Front suspension components—Van

To install:

8. Lubricate and install the inner wheel bearing. Install a new grease seal.
9. Install the hub and rotor assembly to the spindle.
10. Lubricate and install the outer wheel bearing, washer and nut. When the bearing preload is properly set, install the nut lock and a new cotter pin.
11. Install the grease cap.
12. Install the brake pads and caliper.
13. Install the tire and wheel assembly.

REAR SUSPENSION

Shock Absorber

Removal and Installation

1. Raise the vehicle and support safely. If equipped with rear coil springs, support the rear axle using the proper equipment.
2. Remove the bolts that attach the shock to the frame or bracket.
3. Remove the shock from the vehicle.
4. The installation is the reverse of the removal procedure.

Coil Springs

Removal and Installation

MONTERO WITH 3.0L ENGINE

1. Raise the vehicle and support safely. Remove the parking bake cable attaching bolt.
2. Using the proper equipment, support the weight of the axle.
3. Remove the bolt that attaches the lateral rod to the body.
4. Remove the lower shock mounting bolts.

5. Lower the axle and remove the coil springs with their seats.
6. The installation is the reverse of the removal procedure.

Leaf Springs

Removal and Installation

1. Raise the vehicle and support safely. Remove the parking bake cable attaching bolt.
2. Using the proper equipment, support the weight of the axle.
3. Remove the nuts, washers and U-bolts attaching the springs to the axle housing. Remove the seat and spacer.
4. Remove the spring shackle bolts, shackle and spring front bolt.
5. Remove the springs from the vehicle.
6. The installation is the reverse of the removal procedure. Make sure all shackle mounting nuts are on the inside of the springs. Torque the front spring mount nut to 116 ft. lbs. (160 Nm) and the rear shackle nuts to 43 ft. lbs. (60 Nm). Torque U-bolt nuts to 87 ft. lbs. (120 Nm).

SPECIFICATIONS

ENGINE IDENTIFICATION

Year	Model	Engine Displacement cu. in. (cc/liter)	Engine Series Identification (VIN)	No. of Cylinders	Engine Type
1988	Van	146 (2389/2.4)	Z24i	4	OHC
	Pick-Up 2WD	146 (2389/2.4)	Z24i	4	OHC
	Pick-Up 2WD	181 (2960/3.0)	VG30i	6	DOHC
	Pick-Up 4WD	146 (2389/2.4)	Z24i	4	OHC
	Pick-Up 4WD	181 (2960/3.0)	VG30i	6	DOHC
	Pathfinder	146 (2389/2.4)	Z24i	4	OHC
	Pathfinder	181 (2960/3.0)	VG30i	6	DOHC
1989	Pick-Up 2WD	146 (2389/2.4)	Z24i	4	OHC
	Pick-Up 2WD	181 (2960/3.0)	VG30i	6	DOHC
	Pick-Up 4WD	146 (2389/2.4)	Z24i	4	OHC
	Pick-Up 4WD	181 (2960/3.0)	VG 30i	6	DOHC
	Pathfinder 2WD	181 (2960/3.0)	VG30i	6	DOHC
	Pathfinder 4WD	146 (2389/2.4)	Z24i	4	OHC
	Pathfinder 4WD	181 (2960/3.0)	VG30i	6	DOHC
1990	Axxess 2WD	146 (2389/2.4)	KA24E	4	OHC
	Axxess 4WD	146 (2389/2.4)	KA24E	4	OHC
	Pick-Up 2WD	146 (2389/2.4)	KA24E	4	OHC
	Pick-Up 2WD	181 (2960/3.0)	VG30E	6	DOHC
	Pick-Up 4WD	146 (2389/2.4)	KA24E	4	OHC
	Pick-Up 4WD	181 (2960/3.0)	VG30E	6	DOHC
	Pathfinder	181 (2960/3.0)	VG30E	6	DOHC
1991–92	Pick-Up 2WD	146 (2389/2.4)	KA24E	4	OHC
	Pick-Up 2WD	181 (2960/3.0)	VG30E	6	DOHC
	Pick-Up 4WD	146 (2389/2.4)	KA24E	4	OHC
	Pick-Up 4WD	181 (2960/3.0)	VG30E	6	DOHC
	Pathfinder	181 (2960/3.0)	VG30E	6	DOHC

OHC—Overhead cam
DOHC—Dual overhead cam

GENERAL ENGINE SPECIFICATIONS

Year	Model	Engine Displacement cu. in. (cc)	Fuel System Type	Net Horsepower @ rpm	Net Torque @ rpm (ft. lbs.)	Bore × Stroke (in.)	Compression Ratio	Oil Pressure @ rpm
1988	Van	146 (2389)	EFI	103 @ 4800	134 @ 2800	3.50 × 3.78	8.3:1	55 @ 3000
	Pick-Up	146 (2389)	EFI	103 @ 4800	134 @ 2800	3.50 × 3.78	8.3:1	55 @ 3000
	Pick-Up	181 (2960)	EFI	152 @ 5200	162 @ 3600	3.43 × 3.27	9.0:1	60 @ 3200
	Pathfinder	146 (2389)	EFI	103 @ 4800	134 @ 2800	3.50 × 3.78	8.3:1	55 @ 3000
	Pathfinder	181 (2960)	EFI	152 @ 5200	162 @ 3600	3.43 × 3.27	9.0:1	60 @ 3200

GENERAL ENGINE SPECIFICATIONS

Year	Model	Engine Displacement cu. in. (cc)	Fuel System Type	Net Horsepower @ rpm	Net Torque @ rpm (ft. lbs.)	Bore × Stroke (in.)	Compression Ratio	Oil Pressure @ rpm
1989	Pick-Up	146 (2389)	EFI	103 @ 4800	134 @ 2800	3.50 × 3.78	8.3:1	55 @ 3000
	Pick-Up	181 (2960)	EFI	152 @ 5200	162 @ 3600	3.43 × 3.27	9.0:1	60 @ 3200
	Pathfinder	146 (2389)	EFI	103 @ 4800	134 @ 2800	3.50 × 3.78	8.3:1	55 @ 3000
	Pathfinder	181 (2960)	EFI	152 @ 5200	162 @ 3600	3.43 × 3.27	9.0:1	60 @ 3200
1990	Axxess	146 (2389)	MFI	138 @ 5600	148 @ 4400	3.50 × 3.78	8.6:1	65 @ 3000
	Pick-Up	146 (2389)	MFI	138 @ 5600	148 @ 4400	3.50 × 3.78	8.6:1	65 @ 3000
	Pick-Up	181 (2960)	MFI	153 @ 4800	180 @ 4000	3.43 × 3.27	9.0:1	60 @ 3200
	Pathfinder	146 (2389)	MFI	138 @ 5600	148 @ 4400	3.50 × 3.78	8.6:1	65 @ 3000
	Pathfinder	181 (2960)	MFI	153 @ 4800	180 @ 4000	3.43 × 3.27	9.0:1	60 @ 3200
1991–92	Pick-Up	146 (2389)	MFI	138 @ 5600	148 @ 4400	3.50 × 3.78	8.6:1	65 @ 3000
	Pick-Up	181 (2960)	MFI	153 @ 4800	180 @ 4000	3.43 × 3.27	9.0:1	60 @ 3200
	Pathfinder	146 (2389)	MFI	138 @ 5600	148 @ 4400	3.50 × 3.78	8.6:1	65 @ 3000
	Pathfinder	181 (2960)	MFI	153 @ 4800	180 @ 4000	3.43 × 3.27	9.0:1	60 @ 3200

EFI—Electronic fuel injection
MFI—Multi fuel injection

ENGINE TUNE-UP SPECIFICATIONS

Year	Model	Engine Displacement cu. in. (cc)	Spark Plugs Type	Gap (in.)	Ignition Timing (deg.) MT	AT	Compression Pressure (psi)	Fuel Pump (psi)	Idle Speed (rpm) MT	AT	Valve Clearance In.	Ex.
1988	Van	146 (2389)	BPR5ES①	0.033	10	10	173	36	800	750②	0.008	0.009
	Pick-Up	146 (2389)	BPR5ES①	0.033	10	10	173	36	800	750②	0.008	0.009
	Pick-Up	181 (2960)	BCPR5ES-11	0.041	12	12	173	36	800	750②	Hyd.	Hyd.
	Pathfinder	146 (2389)	BPR5ES①	0.033	10	10	173	36	800	750②	0.008	0.009
	Pathfinder	181 (2960)	BCPR5ES-11	0.041	12	12	173	36	800	750②	Hyd.	Hyd.
1989	Pick-Up	146 (2389)	BPR5ES①	0.033	10	10	173	36	800	750②	0.008	0.009
	Pick-Up	181 (2960)	BCPR5ES-11	0.041	12	12	173	36	800	750②	Hyd.	Hyd.
	Pathfinder	146 (2389)	BPR5ES①	0.033	10	10	173	36	800	750②	0.008	0.009
	Pathfinder	181 (2960)	BCPR5ES-11	0.041	12	12	173	36	800	750②	Hyd.	Hyd.
1990	Axxess	146 (2389)	ZFR5E-11	0.033	15	15	175	33	650	750③	Hyd.	Hyd.
	Pick-Up	146 (2389)	ZFR5E-11	0.041	15	15	192	33	800	750③	Hyd.	Hyd.
	Pick-Up	181 (2960)	BKR6EY	0.033	15	15	173	33	750	750②	Hyd.	Hyd.
	Pathfinder	146 (2389)	ZFR5E-11	0.041	15	15	192	33	800	750③	Hyd.	Hyd.
	Pathfinder	181 (2960)	BKR6EY	0.033	15	15	173	33	750	750②	Hyd.	Hyd.
1991–92	Pick-Up	146 (2389)	ZFR5E-11	0.041	15	15	192	33	800	750③	Hyd.	Hyd.
	Pick-Up	181 (2960)	BKR6EY	0.033	15	15	173	33	750	750②	Hyd.	Hyd.
	Pathfinder	146 (2389)	ZFR5E-11	0.041	15	15	192	33	800	750③	Hyd.	Hyd.
	Pathfinder	181 (2960)	BKR6EY	0.033	15	15	173	33	750	750②	Hyd.	Hyd.

Hyd.—Hydraulic
① Intake and exhaust sides
② Transmission in drive
③ Transmission in neutral

FIRING ORDER

NOTE: To avoid confusion, always replace spark plug wires one at a time.

2.4L (Z24i) Engine
Engine Firing Order: 1–3–4–2
Distributor Rotation: Counterclockwise

3.0L (VG30i and VG30E) Engines
Engine Firing Order: 1–2–3–4–5–6
Distributor Rotation: Counterclockwise

2.4L (KA24E) Engine
Engine Firing Order: 1–3–4–2
Distributor Rotation: Counterclockwise

CAPACITIES

Year	Model	Engine Displacement cu. in. (cc)	Engine Crankcase with Filter	Engine Crankcase without Filter	Transmission (pts.) 4-Spd	Transmission (pts.) 5-Spd	Transmission (pts.) Auto.	Drive Axle (pts.)	Fuel Tank (gal.)	Cooling System (qts.)
1988	Van	146 (2389)	4.4	3.9	—	4.25	14.8	2.8	17.1	9.6
	Pick-Up	146 (2389)	⑥	⑦	3.6	③	14.8	⑤	15.9	9.0
	Pick-Up	181 (2960)	①	②	—	④	14.8	⑤	21.1	10.5
	Pathfinder	146 (2389)	⑥	⑦	3.6	③	14.8	⑤	15.9	9.0
	Pathfinder	181 (2960)	①	②	—	④	14.8	⑤	21.1	10.5
1989	Pick-Up	146 (2389)	⑥	⑦	3.6	③	14.8	⑤	15.9	9.0
	Pick-Up	181 (2960)	①	②	—	④	14.8	⑤	21.1	10.5
	Pathfinder	146 (2389)	⑥	⑦	3.6	③	14.8	⑤	15.9	9.0
	Pathfinder	181 (2960)	①	②	—	④	14.8	⑤	21.1	10.5

CAPACITIES

Year	Model	Engine Displacement cu. in. (cc)	Engine Crankcase with Filter	Engine Crankcase without Filter	Transmission (pts.) 4-Spd	Transmission (pts.) 5-Spd	Transmission (pts.) Auto.	Drive Axle (pts.)	Fuel Tank (gal.)	Cooling System (qts.)
1990	Axxess	146 (2389)	3.8	3.4	—	10.0	15.8	2.1	—	8.0
	Pick-Up	146 (2389)	⑩	⑪	—	③	16.8	⑤	15.9	⑨
	Pick-Up	181 (2960)	①	②	—	④	16.8 ⑫	⑤	21.1	⑧
	Pathfinder	146 (2389)	⑩	⑪	—	③	16.8	⑤	15.9	⑨
	Pathfinder	181 (2960)	①	②	—	④	16.8 ⑫	⑤	21.1	⑧
1991–92	Pick-Up	146 (2389)	⑩	⑪	—	③	16.8	⑤	15.9	⑨
	Pick-Up	181 (2960)	①	②	—	④	16.8 ⑫	⑤	21.1	⑧
	Pathfinder	146 (2389)	⑩	⑪	—	③	16.8	⑤	15.9	⑨
	Pathfinder	181 (2960)	①	②	—	④	16.8 ⑫	⑤	21.1	⑧

① 2WD—4.25
   4WD—3.6
② 2WD—3.9
   4WD—3.1
③ 2WD—4.3
   4WD—8.5
④ 2WD—5.1
   4WD—7.6
⑤ 4WD front—4 cylinder engine—R180A—2.8
   4WD front—V6 engine—R200A—3.1
   4WD rear—4 cylinder engine—C200—2.8
   2WD—4 cylinder engine—H190A—3.1
   2WD or 4WD rear—V6 engine—H233B—5.9

⑥ 2WD—4.0
   4WD—4.5
⑦ 2WD—3.5
   4WD—4.0
⑧ 2WD—11.4
   4WD—12.4
⑨ 2WD—8.6
   4WD—9.5
⑩ 2WD—4.1
   4WD—3.5
⑪ 2WD—3.8
   4WD—3.1

CAMSHAFT SPECIFICATIONS
All measurements given in inches.

Year	Engine Displacement cu. in. (cc)	Journal Diameter 1	Journal Diameter 2	Journal Diameter 3	Journal Diameter 4	Journal Diameter 5	Lobe Lift In.	Lobe Lift Ex.	Bearing Clearance	Camshaft End Play
1988	146 (2389)	1.2961–1.2968	1.2961–1.2968	1.2961–1.2968	1.2961–1.2968	1.2961–1.2968	NA	NA	0.0024–0.0041	0.008
	181 (2960)	1.8866–1.8874–	1.8472–1.8480	1.8472–1.8480	1.8472–1.8480	1.6701–1.6709	NA	NA	0.0018–0.0035	0.0012–0.0024
1989	146 (2389)	1.2961–1.2968	1.2961–1.2968	1.2961–1.2968	1.2961–1.2968	1.2961–1.2968	NA	NA	0.0024–0.0041	0.008
	181 (2960)	1.8866–1.8874–	1.8472–1.8480	1.8472–1.8480	1.8472–1.8480	1.6701–1.6709	NA	NA	0.0018–0.0035	0.0012–0.0024
1990	146 (2389)	1.2967–1.2974	1.2967–1.2974	1.2967–1.2974	1.2967–1.2974	1.2967–1.2974	NA	NA	0.0018–0.0035	0.0028–0.0059
	181 (2960)	1.8866–1.8874–	1.8472–1.8480	1.8472–1.8480	1.8472–1.8480	1.6701–1.6709	NA	NA	0.0024–0.0041	0.0012–0.0024
1991–92	146 (2389)	1.2967–1.2974	1.2967–1.2974	1.2967–1.2974	1.2967–1.2974	1.2967–1.2974	NA	NA	0.0018–0.0035	0.0028–0.0059
	181 (2960)	1.8866–1.8874–	1.8472–1.8480	1.8472–1.8480	1.8472–1.8480	1.6701–1.6709	NA	NA	0.0024–0.0041	0.0012–0.0024

NA—Not available

CRANKSHAFT AND CONNECTING ROD SPECIFICATIONS

All measurements are given in inches.

Year	Engine Displacement cu. in. (cc)	Crankshaft				Connecting Rod		
		Main Brg. Journal Dia.	Main Brg. Oil Clearance	Shaft End-play	Thrust on No.	Journal Diameter	Oil Clearance	Side Clearance
1988	146 (2389)	2.3599–2.3604	①	0.0020–0.0071	3	1.9670–1.9675	0.0005–0.0021	0.008–0.012
	181 (2960)	2.4790–2.4793	0.0011–0.0022	0.0020–0.0067	4	1.9670–1.9675	0.0006–0.0021	0.008–0.014
1989	146 (2389)	2.3599–2.3604	①	0.0020–0.0071	3	1.9670–1.9675	0.0006–0.0019	0.008–0.012
	181 (2960)	2.4790–2.4793	0.0011–0.0022	0.0020–0.0067	4	1.9670–1.9675	0.0006–0.0021	0.008–0.014
1990	146 (2389)	2.5057–2.5060	0.0008–0.0019	0.0020–0.0071	3	2.3603–2.3612	0.0004–0.0014	0.008–0.016
	181 (2960)	2.4790–2.4793	0.0011–0.0022	0.0020–0.0067	4	1.9667–1.9675	0.0006–0.0021	0.008–0.014
1991–92	146 (2389)	2.5057–2.5060	0.0008–0.0019	0.0020–0.0071	3	2.3603–2.3612	0.0004–0.0014	0.008–0.016
	181 (2960)	2.4790–2.4793	0.0011–0.0022	0.0020–0.0067	4	1.9667–1.9675	0.0006–0.0021	0.008–0.014

① No. 1 and 5—0.0008–0.0024
No. 2, 3 and 4—0.0008–0.0030

VALVE SPECIFICATIONS

Year	Engine Displacement cu. in. (cc)	Seat Angle (deg.)	Face Angle (deg.)	Spring Test Pressure (lbs.)	Spring Installed Height (in.)	Stem-to-Guide Clearance (in.)		Stem Diameter (in.)	
						Intake	Exhaust	Intake	Exhaust
1988	146 (2389)	45	45.5	②	①	0.0008–0.0021	0.0016–0.0029	0.3136–0.3142	0.3128–0.3134
	181 (2960)	45	45.5	③	④	0.0008–0.0021	0.0016–0.0029	0.3136–0.3142	0.3128–0.3134
1989	146 (2389)	45	45.5	②	①	0.0008–0.0021	0.0016–0.0029	0.3136–0.3142	0.3128–0.3134
	181 (2960)	45	45.5	③	④	0.0008–0.0021	0.0016–0.0029	0.2742–0.2748	0.3128–0.3134
1990	146 (2389)	45	45.5	⑤	⑥	0.0008–0.0021	0.0016–0.0029	0.2742–0.2748	0.3128–0.3134
	181 (2960)	45	45.5	③	④	0.0008–0.0021	0.0012–0.0021	0.2742–0.2748	0.3136–0.3138
1991–92	146 (2389)	45	45.5	⑤	⑥	0.0008–0.0021	0.0016–0.0029	0.2742–0.2748	0.3128–0.3134
	181 (2960)	45	45.5	③	④	0.0008–0.0021	0.0012–0.0021	0.2742–0.2748	0.3136–0.3138

① Outer—1.58 in.
　Inner—1.34 in.
② Outer—51 lbs.
　Inner—24 lbs.
③ Outer—118 lbs.
　Inner—57 lbs.
④ Outer—1.18 in.
　Inner—0.98 in.

⑤ Outer intake—136 lbs.
　Outer exhaust—144 lbs.
　Inner intake—64 lbs.
　Inner exhaust—74 lbs.
⑥ Outer intake—1.48 in.
　Outer exhaust—1.34 in.
　Inner intake—1.28 in.
　Inner exhaust—1.15 in.

PISTON AND RING SPECIFICATIONS

All measurements are given in inches.

Year	No. Cylinder Displacement cu. in. (liter)	Piston Clearance	Ring Gap			Ring Side Clearance		
			Top Compression	Bottom Compression	Oil Control	Top Compression	Bottom Compression	Oil Control
1988	146 (2389)	0.0010–0.0018	0.011–0.015	0.010–0.014	0.008–0.023	0.0016–0.0029	0.0012–0.0025	NA
	181 (2960)	0.0010–0.0018	0.008–0.017	0.007–0.017	0.008–0.029	0.0016–0.0029	0.0012–0.0025	0.0006–0.0075
1989	146 (2389)	0.0010–0.0018	0.011–0.015	0.010–0.014	0.008–0.023	0.0016–0.0029	0.0012–0.0025	NA
	181 (2960)	0.0010–0.0018	0.008–0.017	0.007–0.017	0.008–0.029	0.0016–0.0029	0.0012–0.0025	0.0006–0.0075
1990	146 (2389)	0.0008–0.0016	0.012–0.020	0.017–0.027	0.008–0.027	0.0016–0.0031	0.0012–0.0028	0.0026–0.0053
	181 (2960)	0.0010–0.0018	0.008–0.017	0.007–0.017	0.008–0.029	0.0016–0.0029	0.0012–0.0025	NA
1991–92	146 (2389)	0.0008–0.0016	0.012–0.020	0.017–0.027	0.008–0.027	0.0016–0.0031	0.0012–0.0028	0.0026–0.0053
	181 (2960)	0.0010–0.0018	0.008–0.017	0.007–0.017	0.008–0.029	0.0016–0.0029	0.0012–0.0025	NA

NA—Not available

TORQUE SPECIFICATIONS

All readings in ft. lbs.

Year	Engine Displacement cu. in. (cc)	Cynlinder Head Bolts	Main Bearing Bolts	Rod Bearing Bolts	Crankshaft Pulley Bolts	Flywheel Bolts	Manifold		Spark Plugs
							Intake	Exhaust	
1988	146 (2389)	61	38	33	102	③	14	15	18
	181 (2960)	47	74	33	62	80	①	15	18
1989	146 (2389)	61	38	33	102	③	14	15	18
	181 (2960)	47	74	33	62	80	①	15	18
1990	146 (2389)	61	38	②	116	③	14	15	18
	181 (2960)	47	74	②	98	80	①	15	18
1991–92	146 (2389)	61	38	②	116	③	14	15	18
	181 (2960)	47	74	②	98	80	①	15	18

① Bolt—12–14
  Nut—17–20
② 10–12 ft. lbs., plus, 60–65 degrees
③ Manual—112
  Automatic—76

BRAKE SPECIFICATIONS

All measurements in inches unless noted

Year	Model	Lug Nut Torque (ft. lbs.)	Master Cylinder Bore	Brake Disc Minimum Thickness	Brake Disc Maximum Runout	Standard Brake Drum Diameter	Minimum Lining Thickness Front	Minimum Lining Thickness Rear
1988	Van	78	1.000	0.945	0.0028	10.24	0.079	0.059
	Pick-Up	98	①	③ ④	0.0028	②	0.079	0.059
	Pathfinder	98	①	③ ④	0.0028	②	0.079	0.059
1989	Pick-Up	98	①	③ ④	0.0028	⑤	0.079	0.059
	Pathfinder	98	①	③ ④	0.0028	⑤	0.079	0.059
1990	Axxess	78	0.938	0.787	0.0028	⑥	0.079	0.059
	Pick-Up	98	0.938	③ ④	0.0028	⑦	0.079	0.059
	Pathfinder	98	0.938	③ ④	0.0028	10.24	0.079	0.059
1991–92	Pick-Up	98	0.938	③ ④	0.0028	⑦	0.079	0.059
	Pathfinder	98	0.938	③ ④	0.0028	10.24	0.079	0.059

① 2WD light duty—LT26B: 0.938 and 1.000 in.
  Except 2WD light duty—LT26B: 0.938 in.
② 2WD light duty—LT26B: 10.24 in.
  2WD light duty—LT26B: 8.66 in.
③ 2WD with 4 cylinder—CL28VA: 0.787 in.
  Except 2WD with 4 cylinder—CL28VD: 0.945 in.
④ Sports package—AD14VB—0.630 in.

⑤ 2WD with 4 cylinder—LT26B—10.24 in.
  2WD/4WD heavy duty—DS25B and DS25C—10.00 in.
  Sports package—AD14VB—11.26 in.
  Sports package—DS19HB—7.48 in.
⑥ 2WD—5 passenger: 9.00 in.
  4WD and 2WD—7 passenger: 10.24 in.
⑦ Except 4WD Pick-Up—LT26B: 10.24 in.
  4WD Pick-Up—LT30A: 11.61 in.

WHEEL ALIGNMENT

Year	Model	Caster Range (deg.)	Caster Preferred Setting (deg.)	Chamber Range (deg.)	Chamber Preferred Setting (deg.)	Toe-in (in.)	Steering Axis Inclination (deg.)
1988	Van	¾P–2¼P	1½P	½N–1P	¼P	0.04	9–10
	Pick-Up 2WD	⅙N–⅚P	⅓P	1/12N–1¹¹/12P	¹¹/24P	0.12	9
	Pick-Up 4WD	5/16P–1⅚P	¹¹/12P	⅙P–1⅙P	⅔P	0.16	8
	Pathfinder 2WD	⅙N–⅚P	⅓P	1/12N–1¹¹/12P	¹¹/24P	0.12	9
	Pathfinder 4WD	⅚P–1⅚P	¹¹/12P	⅙P–1⅙P	⅔P	0.16	8
1989	Pick-Up 2WD	⅙N–⅚P	⅓P	1/12N–1¹¹/12P	¹¹/24P	0.12	9
	Pick-Up 4WD	⅚P–1⅚P	¹¹/12P	⅙P–1⅙P	⅔P	0.16	8
	Pathfinder	⅚P–1⅚P	¹¹/12P	⅙P–1⅙P	⅔P	0.16	8
1990	Axxess 2WD	¼N–1¼P	½P	⅓N–1P	⅓P	0.08	14
	Axxess 4WD	1/12N–1⁵/12P	⅔P	7/12N–1¹¹/12P	⅙P	0.08	14
	Pick-Up 2WD	⅙N–⅚P	⅓P	1/12N–1¹¹/12P	¹¹/24P	0.16	9
	Pick-Up 4WD	⅚P–1⅚P	¹¹/12P	⅙P–1⅙P	⅔P	0.16	8
	Pathfinder	⅚P–1⅚P	¹¹/12P	⅙P–1⅙P	⅔P	0.16	8
1991–92	Pick-Up 2WD	⅙N–⅚P	⅓P	1/12N–1¹¹/12P	¹¹/24P	0.16	9
	Pick-Up 4WD	⅚P–1⅚P	¹¹/12P	⅙P–1⅙P	⅔P	0.16	8
	Pathfinder	⅚P–1⅚P	¹¹/12P	⅙P–1⅙P	⅔P	0.16	8

N—Negative
P—Positive

ENGINE ELECTRICAL

NOTE: Disconnecting the negative battery cable on some vehicles may interfere with the functions of the on board computer systems and may require the computer to undergo a relearning process when the battery cable is reconnected. This usually requires only a few minutes of driving.

Distributor

Removal

1. Disconnect the negative battery cable.
2. Remove the distributor cap without disconnecting the spark plug wires. Unplug the distributor connector.
3. Rotate the crankshaft to TDC of No. 1 cylinder, if possible. Mark the position of the rotor to the distributor body and to the engine.
4. Remove the hold-down bolt and lift the distributor out of the engine.

Installation

TIMING NOT DISTURBED

1. If necessary, install a new O-ring on the distributor body. Lightly oil the O-ring and make sure the distributor mounting boss is clean.
2. If the crankshaft was not rotated with the distributor removed, align the rotor with the mark on the distributor body and insert the distributor into place. Some distributors have alignment marks on the shaft and housing. Align the shaft mark with the protruding mark on the housing.
3. The rotor may turn as the distributor is pushed in; remove it and turn the rotor back or forward 1 tooth and try again. When installing the distributor, it is important to make sure the rotor points to the mark made on the engine.
4. Check and adjust ignition timing as required.

TIMING DISTURBED

1. If the crankshaft was turned or if no alignment marks were made when the distributor was removed, make sure the engine is at TDC of No. 1 cylinder.
   a. Remove the spark plug from No. 1 cylinder.
   b. Rotate the crankshaft while holding a thumb over the spark plug hole to determine that the is coming up on the compression stroke.
   c. Align the red TDC mark on the crankshaft pulley with the pointer on the cover.
2. Check the O-ring on the distributor body and replace as necessary. Lightly lubricate the O-ring and make sure the mounting boss is clean.
3. Align the marks on the distributor shaft and body and in-

Some distributors have alignment marks on the shaft and body—3.0L engine shown

DISTRIBUTOR DRIVE GEAR
MARK ON SHAFT
PROTRUDING MARK ON HOUSING
INDENTED MARK ON HOUSING

CAP
CARBON POINT
ROTOR HEAD
METAL SUPPORT
HARNESS ASSEMBLY

Distributor for Z24i engine has 2 carbon points contacting the rotor head

Exploded view of the distributor—3.0L engine

stall the distributor. The rotor may turn as the distributor is pushed in; remove it and turn the rotor back or forward 1 tooth and try again. When installing the distributor, it is important to make sure the rotor points to the mark made on the engine.

4. Check and adjust ignition timing as required.

Ignition Timing

Adjustment

The ignition timing is controlled by the ECU, but a basic setting is required if the distributor has been removed. Always check and adjust ignition timing and idle speed together.

1. Locate the timing marks on the crankshaft pulley and the front of the engine. The timing marks are in 5 degree increments and the TDC mark is always painted red.

2. Connect a tachometer and a timing light to the engine, according to the manufacturer's instructions. Make sure the wires do not interfere with the fan.

3. Make sure all lights and accessories are switched **OFF** and run the engine to warm it to normal operating temperature.

4. With the transmission out of gear, run the engine at 2000

rpm for about 2 minutes, then check idle speed and ignition timing. If timing and idle speed are different from specification, look for another engine problem such as a vacuum leak or bad electrical connection. If no other obvious problem is found, a full diagnostic test should be run.

5. Check idle speed; on engines with throttle body fuel injection, ignition timing is not adjustable.

   a. On all 1988–89 models, idle speed should be 800 rpm with manual transmission, 750 rpm in **D** with automatic transmission.

   b. On 1990–92 models with automatic transmission, idle speed should be 750 rpm in **N**.

6. To adjust timing on 3.0L engines with multi-point fuel injection:

   a. If timing is not correct, disconnect the wiring for the air control valve at the back of the intake manifold. Idle speed should be 700 rpm. The adjusting screw is on the same body assembly as the air control valve.

   b. Reconnect the wiring, idle speed should be about 750 rpm. Do not change it with the wiring connected.

   c. Check and adjust timing as required to 12 degrees BTDC on 1988–89 models or 15 degrees BTDC on 1990–92 models. Adjust by rotating the distributor. Idle speed should remain at about 750 rpm.

7. To adjust timing on the 2.4L engine with multi-point fuel injection:

   a. Check idle speed at about 800 rpm. If not correct, disconnect the throttle sensor wiring and adjust the speed to less than 800 rpm.

   b. Check and adjust ignition timing to 15 degrees BTDC on Axxess or 10 degrees BTDC on Pick-Up, Pathfinder and Van.

8. Run the engine at 2000 rpm for about 2 minutes and check idle speed and timing again. If idle speed or timing are not correct, other problems exist with the engine control system and a full diagnostic test must be run.

Alternator

For further information, please refer to "Alternators" in the Unit Repair section.

Belt Tension Adjustment

Belt tension can be checked with a gauge made for the purpose. If a tension gauge is not available, belt deflection can be measured in inches. Press on the belt with 22 lbs. (10 kg) of force at a point halfway between the alternator and water pump pulleys. Deflection should be 0.200–0.310 in. (5–8mm) on the 3.0L engine or 0.310–0.470 in. (8–12mm) on the 2.4L engine.

1. Loosen the alternator's pivot bolt and the tension adjuster lock bolt.

2. Turn the adjuster bolt as required until the tension is correct.

3. Tighten the bolts and recheck the tension. If new belts have been installed, run the engine for a few minutes, then check tension again. The ideal adjustment is toward the looser end of the specification, belts adjusted too tight will cause bearing failure.

Removal and Installation

1. Disconnect the negative battery cable.

2. Label and disconnect the wiring from the alternator.

3. Loosen the drive belt tension and remove the belt from the pulley.

4. Remove the alternator-to-bracket bolts and the alternator from the vehicle.

5. To install, reverse the removal procedures. Adjust the drive belt tension and torque the lower bracket bolt to 35 ft. lbs. (47 Nm), the adjuster lock bolt to 10 ft. lbs. (13 Nm).

6. Connect all wiring before connecting the battery cable. Terminal **E** is always alternator ground.

Voltage Regulator

The voltage regulator on all models is an internal part of the alternator and cannot be removed separately. The regulator can be replaced when rebuilding the alternator.

Starter

For further information, please refer to "Starters" in the Unit Repair section.

Removal and Installation

1. If necessary, raise and safely support the vehicle.
2. Disconnect the negative battery cable.
3. Disconnect the electrical connectors from the starter, taking note of the positions for reinstallation purposes.
4. Remove the starter-to-engine bolts and the starter from the vehicle.
5. To install, reverse the removal procedures. Torque the starter mounting bolts to 29–36 ft. lbs. (39–49 Nm).

CHASSIS ELECTRICAL

Heater Blower Motor

Removal and Installation
VAN
Front Unit

1. Disconnect the negative battery cable.
2. Remove the package tray or glove box.
3. Disconnect the electrical connector from the blower motor.
4. Remove the blower motor-to-housing screws and the blower motor.
5. To install, reverse the removal procedures.

Rear Unit

1. Disconnect the negative battery cable.
2. Remove the rear heater unit cover panel.
3. Disconnect the electrical connector from the blower motor.
4. Remove the blower motor-to-housing screws and the blower motor.
5. To install, reverse the removal procedures.

EXCEPT VAN

The blower motor is accessible from under the right side of the instrument panel.
1. Disconnect the negative battery cable.
2. Disconnect the electrical connector from the blower motor.
3. Remove the blower motor-to-heater unit screws and the blower motor from the unit. It may be necessary to remove the glove box or package tray.
4. To install, reverse the removal procedures.

Windshield Wiper Motor

Removal and Installation
FRONT WIPER

1. Disconnect the negative battery cable.
2. Remove the wiper blades and arms as an assembly from the pivots. The arms are retained to the pivots by nuts; remove the nuts and pull the arms straight off.
3. Remove the cowl top grille screws (from the front edge) and pull the grille forward to disengage the rear tabs.
4. Remove the wiper motor arm-to-connecting rod stop ring.
5. From under the instrument panel, disconnect the electrical connector from the wiper motor harness.
6. Remove the wiper motor-to-cowl screws and the wiper motor from the vehicle.
To install:
7. Install the motor and secure the bolts. Install the cowl grille.
8. Before installing the wiper arms, be sure the motor is in the PARK position. To do this, connect the battery and wiper motor wiring and turn the ignition switch **ON**. Turn the wiper switch **ON** and cycle the motor 3–4 times, then turn the wiper switch **OFF**. The motor should stop in the correct PARK position.
9. When installing the arms, the blades should be the correct distance above the lower windshield molding:
   Pick-Up and Pathfinder – 0.98 in. (25mm)
   Axxess – 1.62 in. (40mm)
   Van – 1.12 in. (55mm) on the driver's side or 0.20 in. (5mm) on the passenger's side

REAR WIPER

1. Disconnect the negative battery cable.
2. From the rear door, remove the wiper blade/arm as an assembly from the pivot. The arm is retained to the pivots by a nut; remove the nut and pull the arm straight off.
3. From inside the rear door, remove wiper motor cover plate.
4. Remove the wiper motor arm-to-connecting rod stop ring.
5. Disconnect the wiring and remove the screws to remove the motor from the door.
6. Installation is the reverse of removal. Before installing the wiper arm, be sure the motor is in the PARK position. To do this, connect the battery and wiper motor wiring and turn the ignition switch **ON**. Turn the wiper switch **ON** and cycle the motor 3–4 times, then turn the wiper switch **OFF**. The motor should stop in the correct PARK position.

Windshield Wiper Switch

The windshield wiper switch is a part of the combination switch located on the steering column. The switch can be removed without removing the steering wheel.

Removal and Installation

1. Disconnect the negative battery cable.
2. Remove the steering column covers.
3. Disconnect the windshield wiper switch electrical connector.
4. Remove the windshield wiper switch-to-combination switch screws and the windshield wiper switch from the steering column.
5. To install, reverse the removal procedures.

Instrument Cluster

Removal and Installation

1. Disconnect the negative battery cable.
2. Remove the instrument cluster bezel screws and the bezel. Except on the Van, the bezel is also secured with clips; pull the bezel straight out after removing the screws.
3. Remove the instrument cluster-to-dash screws and pull the cluster assembly out far enough to disconnect the wiring and speedometer cable.
4. Installation is the reverse of removal.

Headlight and Turn Signal Switch

The headlight, turn signal and dimmer switches make up the combination switch located on the steering column.

Removal and Installation

1. Disconnect the negative battery cable.
2. Remove the steering column covers.
3. Disconnect the switch electrical connector.
4. Remove the switch-to-combination switch screws and remove the switch from the steering column.
5. To install, reverse the removal procedures.

Combination Switch

The combination switch includes switches for headlights and dimmer, windshield washer and wiper, turn signal, horn contacts and cruise control, if equipped. The steering wheel must be removed to remove the combination switch as an assembly. The 2 switch stalks can be removed separately as described above.

Removal and Installation

1. Disconnect the negative battery cable. Remove the steering column covers.
2. Remove the horn pad and the steering wheel nut. Use a puller to remove the steering wheel.
3. Disconnect the wiring harness from the clip which retains it to the lower instrument panel.
4. Disconnect the electrical connectors from the combination switch.
5. Loosen the combination switch-to-steering column screw and remove the switch assembly.
6. To install, align the hole in the steering column with the protrusion on the switch base and reverse the removal procedures.

HAZARD SWITCH

WIPER AND WASHER SWITCH

SWITCH BASE

LIGHTING SWITCH AND A.S.C.D. SET SWITCH

Combination switch assembly—the steering wheel must be remove to remove the base

Ignition Lock/Switch

Removal and Installation

1. Disconnect the negative battery cable.
2. From the upper steering column, remove the shell cover screws and the covers.
3. Disconnect the electrical connector from the rear of the ignition switch.
4. Drill out the 2 self shear screws from the ignition lock holder.
5. Remove the screws and the ignition switch.
6. To install, reverse the removal procedures. Torque the shear-type screws until the heads shear.

Stoplight Switch

The stoplight switch is attached to a bracket at the top of the brake pedal.

Removal and Installation

1. Disconnect the negative battery cable.
2. From under the dash, disconnect the electrical connector from the stoplight switch.
3. Loosen and remove the locknut from the stoplight switch.
4. Unscrew the stoplight switch from the brake pedal bracket.
5. To install, reverse the removal procedures. Adjust the switch, torque the stoplight switch locknut to 11 ft. lbs. (15 Nm) and adjust the pedal height and free-play.

Adjustment

1. Start the engine and press the brake pedal by hand until pushrod resistance is felt.
2. Use a feeler gauge to measure stoplight switch-to-brake pedal gap: it should be 0.012–0.039 in. (0.3–1.0mm).
3. If necessary, disconnect the electrical connector from the stoplight switch, loosen the switch locknut and adjust the gap. Torque the lock nut to 11 ft. lbs. (15 Nm).

Clutch Cruise Control Switch

If equipped with cruise control, the clutch switch is attached to a bracket mounted to the upper portion of the clutch pedal bracket. This switch replaces the stopper bolt and is used to set pedal height.

Removal and Installation

1. Disconnect the negative battery cable.
2. Disconnect the electrical connector from the clutch switch.
3. Loosen the locknut and unscrew the switch from the bracket.
4. To install, screw the clutch switch into the bracket until the correct pedal height is established and torque the locknut to 11 ft. lbs. (15 Nm).

Pick-Up and Pathfinder
2.4L engine—9.29–9.69 in. (236–246mm)
3.0L engine—8.94–9.33 in. (227–237mm)
Van—6.97–7.25 in. (177–184mm)
Axxess—6.97–7.25 in. (177–184mm)

PEDAL BRACKET

PUSHROD

PEDAL STOPPER BOLT OR CRUISE CONTROL SWITCH

LOCKNUT

INTERLOCK SWITCH

LOCKNUT

LOCKNUT

CLUTCH SWITCH OR ASCD SWITCH

A

FLOOR BOARD

MELT SHEET

DASH INSULATOR

Pad

90°

H

CARPETING

Clutch pedal switch adjustment; vehicles with cruise control use the switch to set pedal height

NOTE: The pedal height is the distance from the floor board to the pedal pad with the carpet removed.

Clutch Interlock Switch

The clutch interlock switch is attached to a bracket mounted to the cowl.

Removal and Installation

1. Disconnect the negative battery cable.
2. Disconnect the electrical connector from the clutch interlock switch.
3. Loosen the locknut and unscrew the switch from the bracket.
4. To install, use a feeler gauge and screw the clutch interlock switch into the bracket.
5. Fully depress the clutch pedal and adjust the gap between the clutch pedal stopper bracket and the threaded end of the clutch interlock switch. The gap should be 0.012–0.039 in. (0.3–1.0mm) on Pick-Up, Pathfinder and Axxess or 0.059–0.138 in. (1.5–3.5mm) on Van.
6. Torque the locknut to 11 ft. lbs. (15 Nm), reconnect the wiring and make sure the started operates only when the clutch pedal is fully depressed.

Fuses, Circuit Breakers and Relays

Location

AXXESS

The main fuse block is under the dashboard to the left of the steering column. Some of the relays are on the fuse block, the rest are on the secondary panel under the hood near the battery. All relays are color coded according to internal circuitry and should be replaced with relays of the same color.

VAN

The main fuse block is under the dashboard to the left of the steering column. The battery is under a panel in the floor behind the driver's seat. The turn signal flasher and all of the relays are in the right side dashboard behind the glove compartment.

PICK-UP AND PATHFINDER

The main fuse block is behind a panel to the right or the steering column. The turn signal flasher is to the left of the brake pedal. A series relays in mounted under the hood on the right fender. All relays are color coded according to internal circuitry and should be replaced with relays of the same color.

Computers

Location

AXXESS

The main engine ECU is under the dashboard immediately in front of the shift lever. The cruise control ECU is behind the driver's side kick panel and the power window amplifier is in the driver's door.

VAN

Most of the electronic control units are in the right side dashboard behind the glove compartment. The main engine ECU is behind the wall panel directly above the battery.

PICK-UP AND PATHFINDER

The main engine ECU is under the passenger's seat along with the automatic transmission control unit. The power window amplifier is behind the passenger's side kick panel. The door lock timer and cruise control ECU are under the driver's seat.

Turn Signal Flasher

Location

AXXESS

The turn signal flasher is next to the brake pedal.

VAN

The turn signal flasher is in the right side dashboard behind the glove compartment.

PICK-UP AND PATHFINDER

The turn signal flasher is to the left of the brake pedal.

ENGINE COOLING

Radiator

Removal and Installation

AXXESS

1. Disconnect the negative battery cable and the wiring for the electric fans.
2. Remove the fan shroud bolts and remove the shroud and fans as an assembly.
3. Raise and safely support the vehicle and drain the cooling system.
4. Disconnect the hoses from the radiator. If equipped with an automatic transaxle, disconnect the plug the oil cooler lines.
5. Remove the upper radiator-to-chassis bolts and lift the radiator from the vehicle.
6. Installation is the reverse of removal. Make sure the lower radiator mounting rubbers are in place before installing radiator.

7. If equipped with an automatic transmission, check and/or refill the transmission.

EXCEPT AXXESS

1. Disconnect the negative battery cable.
2. Drain the engine cooling system and disconnect the radiator hoses. If equipped with an automatic transmission, disconnect and plug the transmission oil cooler lines at the radiator.
3. On Pick-Up and Pathfinder, there is a lower section that can be removed from the fan shroud. Remove this section, unbolt the 2 upper radiator brackets and lift the radiator and shroud out together.
4. On Van, if the shroud will not clear the fan, unbolt the shroud and move it back away from the radiator. Remove the bolts and lift the radiator out.
5. Installation is the reverse of removal. Make sure the lower radiator mounting rubbers are in place before installing radiator.
6. If equipped with an automatic transmission, check and/or refill the transmission.

Electric Cooling Fan

Removal and Installation

AXXESS

1. Disconnect the negative battery cable and the wiring for the electric fans.
2. Remove the fan shroud bolts and remove the shroud and fans as an assembly.
3. Remove the nut in the center of the fan blade and pull the blade off the motor.
4. Remove the bolts to remove the motors from the shroud.
5. Installation is the reverse of removal.

Testing

The cooling fans are controlled by the ECU; testing must be performed on the vehicle.

1. Start the engine and turn the air conditioner and blower fan **ON**. Both fans should operate at low speed.
2. If the air conditioner compressor operates but both fans do not operate, check for power to the fan relays under the hood. These relays are operated by the main ECU.

3. To check high speed operation, stop the engine, disconnect the engine coolant temperature sensor, in the cylinder head near the oil filler cap, and start the engine. Both fans should run at high speed.
4. If either fan does not operate under any condition, stop the engine and unplug the connectors at the fans. Use jumper wires to provide 12 volts directly to the motors: the black wire and the yellow/black wire are both ground wires.

Heater Core

For further information, please refer to Chilton's Air Conditioning and Heating Manual.

Removal and Installation

PICK-UP, PATHFINDER AND VAN

1. The dashboard must be removed. Disconnect the negative battery cable. On vehicles with theft protected radios, obtain the security code.
2. Set the temperature control to full hot and drain the cooling system.
3. Disconnect the heater hoses at the engine compartment.

Pick-Up and Pathfinder dashboard assembly must be removed to remove the heater core

4. Remove the ash tray and remove the screws holding the center console face cover. Remove the cover, heater controls, radio and center vent.

5. Disconnect the control cables and wiring as needed to remove the dashboard.

6. Disconnect the ducts and remove the heater unit. Remove the clips or screws and split the case to remove the heater core. Note how the air flow control doors fit into the case.

To install:

7. Install the heater core and assemble the case halves. Use a new gasket and make sure the air flow doors work properly.

8. Install the heater unit and use a new gasket to seal it to the cooling unit or blower fan housing. Connect the ducts.

9. Install the instrument panel.

10. Install the heater control assembly, center vent and radio.

11. Adjust the heater controls and air flow doors as required.

12. Connect the heater hoses, fill the cooling system and start the engine to test the system.

AXXESS

1. The heater unit can be removed without removing the dashboard. Disconnect the negative battery cable. On vehicles with theft protected radios, obtain the security code.

2. Set the temperature control to full hot and drain the cooling system.

3. Disconnect the heater hoses at the engine compartment.

4. Remove the glove compartment, ash tray assembly and the radio.

5. Disconnect the heater control cables and wiring as required and remove the control assembly.

Water valve and air mix door control rod adjustment-Pick-Up, Pathfinder and Van.

Water valve and air mix door control rod adjustment-Axxess

6. Disconnect the ducting and remove the heater unit. Split the case to remove the heater core. Note the placement of the air flow control doors.

To install:

7. Install the heater core and assemble the case halves. Use a new gasket and make sure the air flow doors work properly.

8. Install the heater unit and use a new gasket to seal it to the cooling unit or blower fan housing. Connect the ducts.

9. Install the heater control assembly and radio.

10. Adjust the heater control cables and rods.

11. Connect the heater hoses, re-fill the cooling system and start the engine to test the system.

Water Pump

Removal and Installation

AXXESS

1. Disconnect the negative battery cable and drain the cooling system. Don't forget the block drain.

2. Remove the upper radiator hose to provide working room and loosen the alternator to remove the drive belt from the pulleys.

3. Disconnect the hoses and remove the bolts to remove the water pump and thermostat housing assembly from the block.

4. Remove the pulley bolts to remove the pulley from the pump. Remove the bolts to remove the pump from the housing.

To install:

5. Make sure all gasket surfaces are clean and use a new gasket or silicone sealer when installing the pump to the housing.

6. Install the housing to the block with a new gasket or silicone sealer.

7. Connect the hoses, install the belts and fill the cooling system to check for leaks.

VAN, PICK-UP AND PATHFINDER WITH 2.4L ENGINE

1. Disconnect the negative battery cable and drain the cooling system. Don't forget the block drain.

2. Remove the upper radiator hose to provide working room and loosen the alternator to remove the drive belt from the pulleys.

3. On Pick-Up and Pathfinder, remove the lower section of the fan shroud and remove the screws to lift the shroud from the engine. Hold the pulley and remove the nuts to remove the fan and pulley from the water pump.

4. On Van, remove the shroud screws and push the shroud back away from the radiator. Remove the fan pulley nuts and lift the fan and shroud out together.

5. Remove the bolts and remove the water pump from the engine.

To install:

6. Make sure all gasket surfaces are clean and use a new gasket or silicone sealer when installing the pump to the engine. Torque the 6mm bolts to 7 ft. lbs. (10 Nm) and the 8mm bolts to 12 ft. lbs. (16 Nm).

7. On Van, lower the shroud and fan into place and push the shroud back against the engine.

8. Install the fan clutch, fan and pulley and torque the nuts or bolts to 7 ft. lbs. (10 Nm).

9. Install the fan shroud and drive belts and fill the cooling system to check for leaks.

PICK-UP AND PATHFINDER WITH 3.0L ENGINE

1. The timing belt cover must be removed. Disconnect the negative battery cable and drain the cooling system. Don't forget the block drain.

2. Remove the radiator hoses and, on automatic transmission, disconnect and plug the fluid cooling lines.

3. Remove the lower section of the fan shroud and remove the

Water pump and thermostat assembly on Axxess

Water pump replacement on 2.4L engine in Pick-Up, Pathfinder and Van

The timing belt cover must be removed to remove the water pump on 3.0L engine—on 4WD, the pump is part of the rear belt cover

screws to lift the shroud from the engine. Remove the bracket bolts and lift the radiator out of the vehicle.

4. Remove all the accessory drive belts.
5. Hold the pulley and remove the nuts to remove the fan and pulley from the water pump.
6. Remove the timing belt covers.
7. Remove the bolts to remove the water pump from the engine.

To install:

8. Make sure all gasket surfaces are clean and use a new gasket or silicone sealer when installing the pump to the engine. Torque the bolts to 15 ft. lbs. (21 Nm).
9. Install the timing belt covers. On 4WD models, make sure the sealing surfaces are clean and carefully install the rubber seal when installing the cover. The timing belt must be properly protected from dirt and oil.
10. Install the pulley, fan clutch and the fan.
11. Install the accessory drive belts and adjust the tension.
12. Install the radiator and fan shroud and connect the cooling system hoses.
13. Fill the system and check for leaks.

Thermostat

The factory-installed thermostat opening temperature is 180°F

(USA) or 190°F (Canada). On the Z24i engine, the thermostat is located on the right front-side of the intake manifold; on the KA24E engine used with the Axxess, the thermostat is mounted in the water pump housing, attached to the left side of the engine; on the all other engines, the thermostat is located above the water pump.

Removal and Installation

1. Disconnect the negative battery cable.
2. Drain the engine coolant to a level below the thermostat housing.
3. Disconnect the coolant hose from the thermostat water outlet.
4. Remove the water outlet-to-thermostat housing bolts, gasket and thermostat.

NOTE:The thermostat spring must face the inside of the engine.

5. Clean the gasket mounting surfaces.

NOTE: If the thermostat is equipped with an air bleed or jiggle valve, be sure to position it in the upward direction.

6. To install, use a new gasket or sealant and reverse the removal procedures. Torque the thermostat housing bolts to 6 ft. lbs. (8 Nm) on the 1990–92 2.4L engine or 15 ft. lbs. (21 Nm) on all except 1990–92 2.4L engine.

Cooling System Bleeding

1. Set the heater temperature control to **HOT** and open the air relief plug. Pour coolant into the radiator until it comes out the relief plug, then close the plug.
2. Fill the reservoir and run the engine to warm it to operating temperature.
3. When the engine is cool again, check the coolant level in the reservoir.

Air relief plug location on Pick-Up, Pathfinder and Van with 2.4L engine.

Air relief plug on 3.0L engine

Air relief plug on Axxess

FUEL SYSTEM

Fuel System Service Precautions

- Keep a Class B dry chemical fire extinguisher available.
- Always relieve the fuel system pressure before disconnecting any fitting.
- Make sure the work area is well ventilated to minimize the possibility of explosion.
- Turn off any source of ignition, such as a heater or welding equipment before beginning work on a fuel system.
- Always use new O-rings or gaskets and do not replace the metal fuel pipes with hose.
- Always us a back-up wrench when opening or closing a fuel line. Wrap a rag around the fitting to catch any fuel spilled.
- Deposit of fuel soaked rags or clothing in a proper safety container.

Relieving Fuel System Pressure

1. Locate the fuel pump fuse or relay and remove it.
2. Start the engine and allow it to run.
3. After the engine stalls, crank it 2–3 times to make sure the pressure is released.
4. Turn the ignition switch **OFF** and replace the fuse. There may still be some pressure in the system, make sure to take proper precautions when loosening any fittings.

Fuel Filter

Removal and Installation

AXXESS

The fuel filter is located under the driver's side and attached to the chassis; it is concealed by a cover plate.
1. Relieve the fuel pressure.
2. Raise and safely support the vehicle.
3. Remove the fuel filter cover plate.
4. Loosen the hose clamps and remove the filter.
5. Installation is the reverse of removal. Be sure to use a high pressure type filter and that the flow direction arrow on the filter points to the front of the vehicle.

EXCEPT AXXESS

On Pick-Up and Pathfinder, the fuel filter is located in the right side of the engine compartment, near the power steering fluid reservoir. On Van, the filter is next to the cruise control vacuum actuator.
1. Release the fuel pressure.
2. Loosen the hose clamps at the fuel inlet and outlet lines and slide each line off the filter nipples.
3. Remove the fuel filter.
4. Installation is the reverse of removal. Be sure to use a high

pressure type filter and that the flow direction arrow on the filter points to the engine.

Electric Fuel Pump

The fuel pump is located in the fuel tank which must be removed to remove the fuel pump.

System Pressure Test

1. Relieve the fuel system pressure.
2. Disconnect the fuel filter outlet hose and install a 0–60 psi gauge on a Tee fitting. Connect the fuel hose to the other leg of the Tee.
3. Start the engine, check for leaks and note the system pressure on the gauge. At idle, the pressure should be more than 33 psi.
4. Disconnect the vacuum hose from the pressure regulator. The pressure should increase to about 43 psi.
5. If the pressure is not correct, check for a system leak or a faulty injector or pressure regulator before removing the pump.

Pump Delivery Test

1. Relieve the fuel system pressure and disconnect the outlet hose from the filter.
2. Connect a length of hose that has an inside diameter of ¼ in. (6mm). The diameter of the hose is important for accurate measurements.
3. Raise the end of the hose above the level of the pump. Turn the ignition switch **ON** and catch the gasoline in a graduated container. Pump output should be 1400cc in a minute or less.

Removal and Installation

1. Relieve the fuel system pressure. Disconnect the negative battery cable.
2. Siphon the fuel from the fuel tank or, if fuel tank is equipped with a drain plug, remove the plug and drain the fuel into a proper fuel container.
3. Raise and safely support the vehicle.
4. Disconnect the fuel lines and the electrical connector from the fuel pump assembly. For 4WD models, remove the fuel tank protector from the bottom of the fuel tank.
5. Remove the fuel tank filler tube-to-vehicle bolts or nuts and the outer plate.
6. Remove the fuel tank-to-chassis bolts and lower the tank from the vehicle.
7. Remove the fuel pump assembly-to-tank screws and lift the assembly from the tank.
8. To install, use a new fuel pump assembly-to-tank O-ring and reverse the removal procedures. Torque the fuel pump assembly-to-tank screws to 24 inch lbs. (3 Nm) and the fuel tank protectors-to-chassis bolts to 26 ft. lbs. (35 Nm).

Fuel Injection

For further information, please refer to Chilton's Electronic Engine Controls Manual.

Idle Speed Adjustment

NOTE: Idle speed and ignition timing must be checked together.

1. Visually inspect the air cleaner for clogging, the hoses/ducts for leaks, the EGR valve operation, the electrical connectors, the gaskets, the throttle valve and throttle sensor operation and the AIV hose.
2. Start the engine and allow it to reach normal operating temperature.
3. Operate the engine under no-load for 2 minutes at about

Idle speed adjustment on engines with multi-point fuel injection is on the Idle Air Adjusting unit—3.0L engine shown

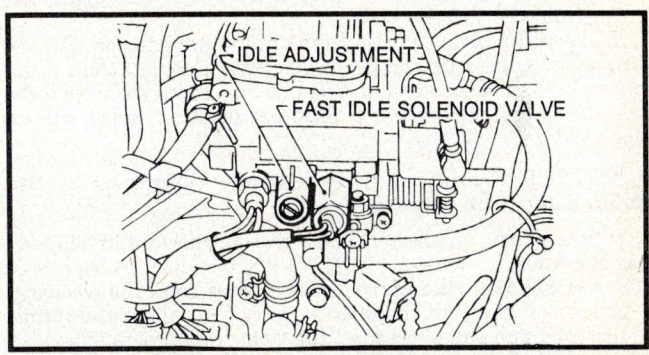

Idle speed adjustment on engines with throttle body fuel injection is on the throttle body

2000 rpm. Make sure all accessories and lights are **OFF**. Race the engine 2–3 times, then let it at idle speed for 1 minute.
4. To adjust idle speed on engines with throttle body fuel injection, turn the large adjusting screw that is next to the fast idle solenoid valve on the throttle body. Do not turn the throttle stop screw.
5. To adjust idle speed on the 3.0L engine with multi-point fuel injection:
   a. Disconnect the wiring for the Auxiliary Air Control (AAC) valve at the back of the intake manifold. Idle speed should drop to about 700 rpm. The adjusting screw is on the same body assembly as the AAC.
   b. Reconnect the wiring, idle speed should be about 750 rpm. Do not change it with the wiring connected. If idle speed is not correct, look for another problem in the engine control system.
   c. Check and adjust timing as required to 15 degrees BTDC by rotating the distributor. Idle speed should remain at about 750 rpm.
6. To adjust timing on the 2.4L engine with multi-point fuel injection:
   a. Check idle speed at about 800 rpm. If it is not correct, disconnect the throttle sensor wiring and adjust the speed to less than 800 rpm. The adjustment is on the throttle body Idle Air Adjusting (IAA) unit that has small engine coolant hoses connected to it.
   b. Check and adjust ignition timing to 15 degrees BTDC.
7. Run the engine at 2000 rpm for about 2 minutes and check idle speed and timing again. If idle speed or timing are not correct, other problems exist with the engine control system and a full diagnostic test must be run.

Fuel Injector

Removal and Installation

1988–89

The injectors are in the throttle body, 1 for the 2.4L engine or 2 for the 3.0L engine. The throttle body assembly must be removed and the injectors pushed out from the bottom.

1. Relieve the fuel system pressure.
2. Drain about 1⅛ qt. (1L) of coolant from the engine.
3. From the throttle body, remove or disconnect the following items:
   a. Air cleaner
   b. Label and disconnect all wiring
   c. Accelerator cable
   d. Fuel and coolant hoses
4. Remove the throttle body-to-intake manifold nuts and the throttle body.
5. Remove the rubber seal and the injector harness grommet from the throttle body.
6. Remove the injector cover-to-injector body screws and the cover from the throttle body.
7. Turn the throttle valve to the fully open position. Place a soft hollow tube, with and inside diameter of not less than ¼ in., on the bottom of the fuel injectors and tap the injectors from the throttle body. Do not use a solid rod or the injector will be damaged.

NOTE: If the injector tip becomes deformed by the tube, it must be replaced.

8. If replacing an injector with a new one, perform the following operation:
   a. Disconnect the faulty injector wires from the electrical connector, then cut the injector wires from the metal terminals and pull the injector wiring from the harness tube.
   b. Install the new wiring into the harness tube and connect new terminals to the injector wires.
   c. Install the terminals into the electrical harness connector.

NOTE: Be sure to install a new electrical harness grommet every time a new injector is installed.

To install:

9. To install, use new O-rings and push the injectors into the throttle body until the O-rings are fully seated. Invert the throttle body and look to make sure the injector tips are properly seated.
10. Using silicone sealant, apply it to the injector harness grommet. An airtight seal is essential to ensure a stable idling condition.
11. Apply a thread locking compound to the injector cover screw threads and install the injector cover. Torque the injector cover screws in a criss-cross pattern to 2.5 ft. lbs. (3 Nm). Do not over tighten or the O-rings will be damaged.
12. Using silicone sealant, coat the top of the throttle body and install the air cleaner rubber seal.

NOTE: Do not install the air cleaner until the air cleaner seal (silicone sealant) has hardened.

13. Install the throttle body and torque the throttle body-to-intake manifold nuts to 13 ft. lbs. (18 Nm).
14. To complete the installation, connect the wiring, hoses and cables and refill the cooling system.
15. Start the engine, check for leaks and check and adjust idle speed as required. Stop the engine and check to make sure the injector is fully closed; check for dripping fuel on the throttle valve.

1990–92

2.4L Engine

The engine is equipped 4 fuel injectors, with one located at each cylinder.

1. Relieve the fuel pressure.
2. Label and disconnect the electrical connectors from the fuel injectors.
3. Disconnect the fuel hoses from the rail.

The injectors are pushed out of the throttle body from below the throttle plates

When replacing throttle body injectors, feed the wires through the tube and attach the terminal

4. Remove the fuel rail with injectors attached from the intake manifold.
5. Separate the fuel injectors from the fuel rail.

To install:

6. Replace the fuel injector O-rings.
7. Install the fuel injectors to the fuel rail.
8. Lubricate the fuel injector O-rings with automatic transmission fluid and press them, with the fuel rail, into the intake manifold.
9. Install the fuel rail-to-intake manifold bolts.
10. Connect the fuel hoses to the rail.

11. Connect the electrical connectors to the fuel injectors.
12. Turn the ignition switch **ON** and check for fuel leaks at the fuel rail.

3.0L Engine

The engine is equipped 6 fuel injectors, with one located at each cylinder.

1. Relieve the fuel pressure.
2. Remove the air cleaner from the throttle body.
3. Label and disconnect the vacuum hoses, electrical connectors and throttle cable from the throttle body/upper intake manifold assembly.
4. Remove the upper intake manifold.
5. Disconnect the electrical connectors from the fuel injectors.
6. Disconnect the supply and return hoses from the fuel rail.
7. The injectors can be removed separately or as an assembly with the rail. Do not use the old O-rings or insulators when installing the injectors.

To install:

8. Replace the fuel injector O-rings.
9. Lubricate the fuel injector O-rings with automatic transmission fluid and press them into the fuel rail assembly.
10. Connect the electrical connectors to the fuel injectors.
11. Using a new gasket, install the upper intake manifold and torque the bolts to 16 ft. lbs. (22 Nm).
12. Connect the electrical connectors, the vacuum lines and the accelerator cable.
13. Install the air cleaner to the throttle body.
14. Turn the ignition switch **ON** and check for fuel leaks at the fuel rail.

EMISSION CONTROLS

For further information, please refer to Chilton's Emission Controls Manual.

Emission Warning Lamp

The check engine light is located on the instrument panel of California vehicles only and indicates an emission performance malfunction.

Resetting

1. Turn the ignition switch **ON**.
2. If the check engine light turns **ON**, perform the self-diagnosis procedures to determine the malfunction.
3. Turn the ignition switch **OFF**.
4. Locate and repair the malfunction.

NOTE: When the malfunction is repaired and the fault code memory cleared, the check engine light will stay OFF.

ENGINE MECHANICAL

NOTE: Disconnecting the negative battery cable on some vehicles may interfere with the functions of the on board computer systems and may require the computer to undergo a relearning process when the battery cable is reconnected. This usually requires only a few minutes of driving.

Engine

Removal and Installation

PICK-UP AND PATHFINDER

On 1990–92 vehicles equipped with the 3.0L engine, the transmission must be removed before removing the engine. If equipped with the 2.4L engine, the engine and transmission are

removed together. On vehicles with 4WD, the front torsion bar must be removed to remove the transfer case.

1. Relieve the fuel system pressure.
2. Disconnect the battery cables and remove the battery.
3. Using a scribing tool, mark the location of the hood hinges on the body and remove the hood.
4. Drain the engine oil and the cooling system, including the block drains. Dispose of old fluids properly.
5. Remove the air cleaner. Wrap a shop rag around the fuel filter outlet and disconnect the hose.
6. Raise and safely support the vehicle. If equipped, remove the splash pan from under the engine.
7. To remove the radiator:
   a. Remove the upper and lower radiator hoses.
   b. If equipped with an automatic transmission, disconnect

and plug the transmission oil cooler lines from the radiator.

c. Remove the lower radiator shroud.

d. Remove the bracket bolts and lift the radiator and shroud out together.

8. If equipped with air conditioning, loosen the belt tension and remove the belt. Disconnect the wiring, remove the compressor and secure it out of the way. Do not disconnect the pressure hoses.

9. If equipped with power steering, remove the drive belt and the power steering pump and secure it out of the way. Do not disconnect the pressure hoses.

10. Label and disconnect all wiring and vacuum hoses.

11. Disconnect the heater hoses from the engine and disconnect the throttle cable.

12. Remove the starter.

13. Matchmark the driveshaft flange at the rear pinion flange and remove the driveshaft. Plug the extension housing opening to prevent the oil from draining out.

14. If equipped with 4WD, matchmark both front driveshaft flanges so the shaft can be installed in the same position. Remove the driveshaft.

15. Disconnect the exhaust pipe from the manifold(s) and from the catalytic converter and remove the pipe.

16. Disconnect the speedometer cable and the wiring from the transmission.

17. If equipped an automatic transmission:

a. Disconnect the selector lever and throttle cables from the transmission.

b. Remove the dipstick tube and disconnect the cooler lines.

c. Remove the torque converter housing dust cover. Matchmark the converter with the driveplate for reassembly; these are balanced together at the factory. Remove the torque converter-to-driveplate (flywheel) bolts. Use a wrench on the crankshaft pulley bolt to rotate the crankshaft to expose the hidden torque converter bolts.

18. On vehicles with a manual transmission:

a. Remove the shifter knob and boot and remove the snapring to lift the shift lever out of the transmission. Stuff a rag in the opening to keep dirt out of the transmission.

b. Without disconnecting the hydraulic hose, remove the clutch slave cylinder from the transmission and secure it aside.

19. If equipped with 4WD:

a. Working under the vehicle, measure and note the length of the threads on the torsion bar adjustment. At the front of the bar, pull the boot back and matchmark the bar to the mounting plate. The spline on the bar must be re-installed in the same position on the plate.

b. Remove the locknut and adjustment nut from both torsion bars. Remove the 3 nuts at the mounting plate and remove the bars. Mark the bars left and right side for proper installation.

c. Remove the transfer case shift lever assembly from the transfer case.

d. If necessary, the transfer case can be removed at this point so the jack will be available to remove the transmission.

e. If equipped with a 3.0L engine, remove the gusset securing the engine to the transmission.

20. Using a chain hoist, attach it to the engine and lift the engine slightly to take the weight off the mounts. Using an appropriate transmission jack, properly support the transmission and remove the transmission mount and crossmember.

21. Remove the transmission-to-engine bolts and move the transmission back away from the engine. On automatic transmissions, secure the torque converter so it does not fall out. Lower the transmission from the vehicle.

NOTE: When removing the engine mounts, do not loosen the 4 mount cover nuts. The mount is fluid filled and will not function properly if the fluid leaks out.

Removing the transfer case shift lever on 4WD Pick-Up and Pathfinder

Do not remove these engine mount nuts—Pick-Up and Pathfinder

Measure thread length before removing torsion bar on 4WD Pick-Up and Pathfinder

22. Check to make sure all wires and hoses have been disconnected. Remove the front engine mount bolts and carefully lift the engine out.

To install:

23. Carefully guide the engine into place and start the mount bolts. Tighten the bolts temporarily.

24. On manual transmission:

a. Lightly grease the input shaft splines. On 4WD, apply a silicone sealant to the engine block or rear plate to seal the engine to the transmission.

b. Fit the transmission into place and start all the engine-to-transmission bolts. Make sure the input shaft fits properly into the clutch disc and pilot bearing.

c. Torque the 2.36 in. (60mm) and 2.56 in. (65mm) engine-to-transmission bolts to 36 ft. lbs. (49 Nm).

d. Torque the remaining bolts to 18 ft. lbs. (25 Nm) on the

2.4L cylinder engine, 29 ft. lbs. (39 Nm) on the 3.0L engine.

25. On automatic transmission:

a. Use a dial indicator to check the driveplate runout while turning the crankshaft. Maximum allowable runout is 0.020 in. (0.5mm); if beyond specifications, replace the driveplate.

b. Measure and adjust how far the torque converter is recessed into the transmission housing. The distance between the front mounting surface of the transmission and the torque converter–to–driveplate bolt boss should be at least 1.024 in. (26mm).

c. Install the transmission and torque transmission–to–engine bolts to 36 ft. lbs. (49 Nm). Torque to transmission–to–engine gusset bolts to 29 ft. lbs. (39 Nm).

26. Install the crossmember and torque the crossmember-to-chassis bolts to 38 ft. lbs. (52 Nm) on 2WD or 31 ft. lbs. (42 Nm) on 4WD.

27. Install the rear transmission mount bolts, loosen the engine mount bolts, then torque all the mount bolts to 31 ft. lbs. (42 Nm), starting at the rear.

28. On automatic transmission, align the matchmarks on the driveplate and torque converter, install the bolts and torque to 36 ft. lbs. (49 Nm). Turn the crankshaft after tightening the bolts to make sure there is no binding at the driveplate.

29. If the torsion bars were removed, install them in their original location. Make sure the splines are in their original position and set the adjustment to its original position.

30. If the transfer case was removed, apply silicone sealant to seal the case to the transmission. Install the transfer case and torque the bolts to 30 ft. lbs. (41 Nm). Install the shift lever.

31. When installing the driveshafts, be sure to align the matchmarks. Torque the bolts on the front driveshaft (4WD) to 33 ft. lbs. (44 Nm). On single piece rear driveshafts, torque the bolts to 65 ft. lbs. (88 Nm). On 2 piece driveshafts, torque the bolts to 33 ft. lbs. (44 Nm). Torque the center bearing bracket bolts to 16 ft. lbs. (22 Nm).

32. When installing the exhaust system, use new gaskets and torque the flange bolts to 27 ft. lbs. (36 Nm).

33. Install the remaining components in order of removal and connect the wiring and hoses.

VAN

The engine and transmission are removed together from under the vehicle. The crossmember under the engine and the suspension leading link attached to it must also be removed.

1. Locate and remove the fuel pump fuse. Run the engine until it stalls, then disconnect the battery cables.

2. Wrap a rag around the fuel filter outlet and remove the hose.

3. Drain the engine oil and the cooling system, including the block drains. Dispose of old fluids properly.

4. Remove the air cleaner duct and place a clean rag in the throttle body to prevent dirt from entering the engine. Remove the distributor cap and spark plug wires as an assembly. Remove the rotor.

5. Disconnect the cooling system hoses from the engine. If equipped with an automatic transmission, disconnect and plug the transmission oil cooler lines from the radiator.

6. If equipped with air conditioning, loosen the belt tension and remove the belt. Disconnect the wiring, remove the compressor and secure it out of the way. Do not disconnect the pressure hoses.

7. If equipped with power steering, remove the drive belt and the power steering pump and secure it out of the way. Do not disconnect the pressure hoses.

8. Label and disconnect all wiring and vacuum hoses that can be reached from above. Disconnect the accelerator cable.

9. Raise and safely support the vehicle.

10. Disconnect the speedometer cable and all wiring from the transmission. To disconnect the transmission shift linkage without disturbing the adjustments, remove the pin clips and slide the levers off the shafts. Remove the cables and the mounting bracket from the transmission.

11. Matchmark the driveshaft to the differential flange and remove the driveshaft. Plug the transmission opening to prevent oil leakage.

12. Without disconnecting the hydraulic line, remove the clutch release cylinder from the transmission and secure it out of the way.

13. Disconnect the exhaust pipe from the manifold and remove the pipe from the catalytic converter.

14. Remove the leading links that connect the front suspension to the crossmember. The rubber bushings are mounted on the link are not interchangable, identify them for re-assembly.

15. Check to make sure all wiring, cables and hoses are disconnected. Support the engine and transmission with a jack and remove the rear transmission mount.

16. Remove the crossmember bolts and lower the engine and transmission from the vehicle.

17. If equipped with an automatic transmission, matchmark the torque converter to the driveplate and remove the torque converter–to–driveplate bolts. Push the torque converter back so it does not fall out.

18. Separate the engine and transmission and install the engine on a work stand to remove the crossmember and mounts.

To install:

19. If equipped with a manual transmission, lightly grease the input shaft spline before joining the engine and transmission. Torque the long bolts to 36 ft. lbs. (49 Nm) and the short bolts to 29 ft. lbs. (39 Nm).

20. If equipped with an automatic transmission:

a. Use a dial indicator to check the driveplate runout while turning the crankshaft. Maximum allowable runout is 0.020 in. (0.5mm); if beyond specifications, replace the driveplate.

b. Measure and adjust how far the torque converter is recessed into the transmission housing. The distance between the front mounting surface of the transmission and the torque converter–to–driveplate bolt boss should be at least 1.380 in. (35mm).

c. Join the engine and transmission and torque the long bolts to 36 ft. lbs. (49 Nm), the short bolts to 24 ft. lbs. (32 Nm).

d. Align the matchmarks on the torque converter and driveplate and install the bolts. Torque the bolts to 36 ft. lbs. (49 Nm). Turn the crankshaft to make sure there is no binding at the driveplate.

21. Raise the engine and transmission into place and start all the mounting bolts. If the front mount fasteners are already tight, loosen them and torque the rear mount bolts, then the crossmember bolts, then the front mount bolts.

22. Install the front suspension links and torque the bolts and the nut to 30 ft. lbs. (40 Nm).

23. Install the driveshaft with the matchmarks aligned and torque the bolts to 33 ft. lbs. (44 Nm).

24. Use new gaskets to install the exhaust pipe and torque the bolts to 25 ft. lbs. (34 Nm).

25. Connect the shifter cables and wiring to the transmission. On automatic transmissions, install the dipstick tube and connect the cooling system lines. On manual transmissions, install the clutch release cylinder.

26. Install the remaining components and connect the wiring, hoses and control cables.

AXXESS

The engine and transaxle are lowered as a unit from the vehicle but the unit must be supported from above to remove the mount member. On 4WD models, the front crossmember bar must be removed. On all models, the halfshafts must be removed. The torque on the front axle nut is very high and an assistant is required to hold the brake pedal when tightening or loosening it.

1. Locate and remove the fuel pump fuse. Run the engine until it stalls, then disconnect the battery cables.

68–87 FT. LBS. (92–118 NM)

REAR SUPPORT BRACKET

57–72 FT. LBS. (77–98 NM)

REAR INSULATOR

COLLAR

15–20 FT. LBS. (21–26 NM)

REAR BRACKET A/T MODEL

57–72 FT. LBS. (77–98 NM)

REAR BRACKET M/T MODEL

23–30 FT. LBS. (31–41 NM)

30–38 FT. LBS. (41–52 NM)

32–41 FT. LBS. (43–55 NM)

23–30 FT. LBS. (31–41 NM)

23–30 FT. LBS. (31–41 NM)

FRONT BRACKET R.H.

FRONT BRACKET L.H.

HEAT SHIELD PLATE

FRONT INSULATOR R.H.

FRONT INSULATOR L.H.

FRONT SUPPORT BRACKET R.H.

FRONT SUPPORT BRACKET L.H.

23–31 FT. LBS. (31–42 NM)

23–30 FT. LBS. (31–41 NM)

23–31 FT. LBS. (31–42 NM)

15–20 FT. LBS. (21–26 NM)

CENTER MEMBER

15–20 FT. LBS. (21–26 NM)

23–31 FT. LBS. (31–42 NM)

Engine and transmission mount torque values on Van

2. Wrap a rag around the fuel filter outlet and remove the hose.

3. Drain the engine oil and the cooling system, including the block drains. Dispose of old fluids properly.

4. Remove the air duct, the battery and the air cleaner and air flow meter assembly.

5. Disconnect the cooling system hoses from the engine. If equipped with an automatic transaxle, disconnect and plug the transaxle oil cooler lines from the radiator.

6. If equipped with air conditioning, loosen the belt tension and remove the belt. Disconnect the wiring, remove the compressor and secure it out of the way. Do not disconnect the pressure hoses.

7. If equipped with automatic transaxle, disconnect the transaxle–throttle control cable from the throttle. The nut towards the cable end is the locknut; mark the position of the adjusting nut and loosen the locknut to disconnect the cable. Disconnect the shifter cable from the transaxle.

8. Label and disconnect all wiring and vacuum hoses. Disconnect the accelerator cable.

9. Disconnect the speedometer cable and all wiring from the transaxle. If equipped with a manual transaxle, remove the clutch release cylinder without disconnecting the hydraulic line and secure it out of the way.

10. Raise and safely support the vehicle. Disconnect the manual transaxle shift linkage and the support rod.

11. If equipped with power steering, remove the drive belt and the power steering pump and secure it out of the way. Do not disconnect the pressure hoses.

12. Disconnect the exhaust pipe from the manifold and remove the pipe from the catalytic converter.

13. On 4WD models, matchmark the drive flanges and disconnect the driveshaft from the transfer case. If it is decided that the driveshaft is in the way of engine removal, matchmark the rear flange and remove the entire driveshaft. Do not disassemble the driveshaft and protect the CV-joint boot when moving the driveshaft.

14. Make sure the vehicle is securely supported and have an assistant hold the brake pedal. Remove the front axle cotter pin, adjusting cap and washer and loosen the axle nut. The torque is very high; if possible, loosen and tighten this nut with the wheels installed and the vehicle on the ground.

15. Without disconnecting the hydraulic hose, remove the brake calipers and hang them from the body. Do not let the caliper hang by the hose. Be sure to remove the caliper, pads and carrier as an assembly. Do not remove the sliding pin bolts.

16. Disconnect the tie rod end from the steering knuckle. Turn the knuckle all the way out at the front and use a soft hammer to tap the axle out of the hub.

17. Carefully pry the right inner CV-joint from the transaxle or transfer case.

18. On 2WD with automatic transaxle, insert a thin drift pin through the right side of differential and tap the left inner CV-joint out. Be careful not to damage the mate pinion shaft or side gear inside the differential.

19. On all other models, pry the left CV-joint out the same way as the right.

20. Carefully support the engine and transaxle from above and remove the mount member from 2WD or crossmember from 4WD.

21. Support the engine and transaxle with floor jacks, remove the remaining mounts and lower the unit out of the vehicle. Remove the starter.

22. Before removing the automatic transaxle from the engine, matchmark the torque converter to the driveplate for re-assembly and remove the torque converter–to–driveplate bolts. When separating the engine and transaxle, be careful that the torque converter does not fall out.

To install:

23. If equipped with a manual transaxle, lightly grease the input shaft spline before joining the engine and transaxle. Torque

the long bolts (1¾ in. or longer) to 36 ft. lbs. (49 Nm) and the short bolts (1½ or shorter) to 30 ft. lbs. (40 Nm).

24. If equipped with an automatic transaxle:

a. Use a dial indicator to check the driveplate runout while turning the crankshaft. Maximum allowable runout is 0.020 in. (0.5mm); if beyond specifications, replace the driveplate.

b. Measure and adjust how far the torque converter is recessed into the transaxle housing. The distance between the front mounting surface of the transaxle and the torque converter–to–driveplate bolt boss should be at least ¾ in. (19mm).

c. Join the engine and transaxle and torque the bolts to 33 ft. lbs. (44 Nm).

d. Align the matchmarks on the torque converter and driveplate and install the bolts. Torque the bolts to 43 ft. lbs. (59 Nm). Turn the crankshaft to make sure there is no binding at the driveplate.

25. Install the engine and transaxle and start all the mount bolts. When all the mounts and support members are in place, torque the bolts as shown.

26. Install the halfshafts:

a. Carefully insert the inner CV-joint into the differential gear to make sure the splines engage properly.

b. Push the shaft in to click the circlip into place. Pull out on the halfshaft to make sure the clip is seated.

c. When installing the right side extension shaft on 2WD models, torque the support bearing bracket bolts to 26 ft. lbs. (35 Nm).

d. When installing the left side halfshaft on 4WD models, torque the inner CV-joint bolts to 36 ft. lbs. (45 Nm).

e. Make sure the outer axle splines are clean and insert the axle into the hub. Connect the tie rod end to the steering knuckle and torque the nut to 29 ft. lbs. (39 Nm) and tighten as required to install a new cotter pin.

f. Install the washer and nut onto the axle but do not torque the nut yet.

27. Install the brake calipers and torque the carrier bolts to 72 ft. lbs. (97 Nm).

When inserting a tool to push the left inner CV-joint out of the differential, be careful not to damage the pinion mate shaft or side gear—Axxess with 2WD and automatic transaxle

2WD model
A/T

M/T

41 FT. LBS. (55 NM)

41 FT. LBS. (55 NM)

55 FT. LBS. (75 NM)

41 FT. LBS. (55 NM)

41 FT. LBS. (55 NM)

55 FT. LBS. (75 NM)

41 FT. LBS. (55 NM)

41 FT. LBS. (55 NM)

55 FT. LBS. (75 NM)

41 FT. LBS. (55 NM)

65 FT. LBS. (88 NM)

TO ENGINE BLOCK

41 FT. LBS. (55 NM)

55 FT. LBS. (75 NM)

55 FT. LBS. (75 NM)

55 FT. LBS. (75 NM)

55 FT. LBS. (75 NM)

55 FT. LBS. (75 NM)

41 FT. LBS. (55 NM)

72 FT. LSB. (98 NM)

M/T

41 FT. LBS. (55 NM)

41 FT. LBS. (55 NM)

55 FT. LBS. (75 NM)

72 FT. LSB. (98 NM)

Engine and transaxle mounts on 2WD Axxess

4WD model

A/T

41 FT. LBS. (55 NM)

41 FT. LBS. (55 NM)

65 FT. LBS. (88 NM)

M/T

55 FT. LBS. (75 NM)

41 FT. LBS. (55 NM)

41 FT. LBS. (55 NM)

55 FT. LBS. (75 NM)

41 FT. LBS. (55 NM)

41 FT. LBS. (55 NM)

55 FT. LBS. (75 NM)

41 FT. LBS. (55 NM)

30 FT. LBS. (40 NM)

55 FT. LBS. (75 NM)

41 FT. LBS. (55 NM)

30 FT. LBS. (40 NM)

41 FT. LBS. (55 NM)

41 FT. LBS. (55 NM)

TO ENGINE BLOCK

41 FT. LBS. (55 NM)

TO TRANSFER CASE

41 FT. LBS. (55 NM)

41 FT. LBS. (55 NM)

72 FT. LBS. (98 NM)

Engine and transaxle mounts on 4WD Axxess

28. On 4WD models, connect the driveshaft and torque the bolts to 33 ft. lbs. (44 Nm). If the driveshaft was removed, torque the center bearing support bolts to 30 ft. lbs. (41 Nm).

29. When installing the exhaust pipe, use new gaskets and torque the manifold flange nuts to 37 ft. lbs. (50 Nm), the catalytic converter flange bolts to 31 ft. lbs. (42 Nm).

30. Complete the installation of the remaining components. When the vehicle is resting on at least 3 wheels, have an assistant hold the brake pedal and torque the front axle nuts to 231 ft. lbs. (314 Nm). Install the adjusting cap and an new cotter pin.

Cylinder Head

Removal and Installation

2.4L Engine

1. Relieve the fuel system pressure. Disconnect the negative battery cable.

2. Remove the air cleaner. Disconnect the accelerator cable from the throttle body.

3. Drain the engine coolant, including the block drain.

4. Label and disconnect all wiring and hoses as required.

5. Remove the intake and exhaust manifolds.

6. Remove the steering pump, alternator and/or air conditioner compressor as required and remove the brackets as required. When removing the steering pump or air conditioner compressor, disconnect the drive belt, remove the unit pump and move it aside; do not disconnect the pressure hoses.

7. Remove the distributor cap and rotor and disconnect the wires from the spark plugs.

8. Remove the valve cover.

9. Rotate the crankshaft until the No. 1 cylinder is on the TDC of its compression stroke. Make sure the TDC mark on the crankshaft pulley is aligned with the pointer. The silver link on the timing chain should be aligned with the mark on the camshaft sprocket and the knock pin on the camshaft will be at the top.

10. To remove the camshaft sprocket:

  a. Fabricate a wooden wedge tool to hold the timing chain in place.

  b. Remove the camshaft sprocket bolt and the camshaft sprocket. Hold the sprocket up to keep tension on the chain.

  c. Install the wedge tool and rest the chain on the tool with the driver's side of the chain pulled snug against the crankshaft sprocket. If the chain falls off the crankshaft sprocket or if the crankshaft is turned, the front cover must be removed to properly set the valve timing.

11. Remove the cylinder head–to–timing chain cover bolts.

12. Carefully loosen the cylinder head bolts one turn at a time in the reverse order of the tightening sequence. When all bolts are loose, remove the bolts and remove the cylinder head.

To install:

13. Throughly clean all gasket surfaces and inspect the head and block for damage to the surfaces. Before installing, check the cylinder head for warping. The limit is 0.006 in. (0.15mm). Make sure the threads on the bolts and in the block are clean and that the bolts turn easily in the threads. Do not oil the threads.

14. Make sure the camshaft knock pin is at the top; both valves for No. 1 cylinder will be closed.

15. Install the new gasket and carefully install the cylinder head. Torque the cylinder head bolts in the sequence shown in 5 steps:

  Step 1 – 22 ft. lbs. (29 Nm)
  Step 2 – 58 ft. lbs. (78 Nm)
  Step 3 – loosen all bolts
  Step 4 – 22 ft. lbs. (29 Nm)
  Step 5 – 54–61 ft. lbs. (74–83 Nm)

16. Correctly position the camshaft sprocket into the timing chain with the silver link aligned with the mark on the sprocket. Install the sprocket onto the camshaft, install the sprocket bolt but do not fully torque it yet.

Make a wooded wedge to support the timing chain when removing 2.4L engine cylinder head

Remove the camshaft sprocket with chain attached— 2.4L engine

Support the chain with the wedge to keep it engaged with the crankshaft sprocket

Cylinder head bolt torque sequence—1988–89 2.4L engine

Cylinder head bolt torque sequence—1990–92 2.4L engine

KNOCK PIN

SILVER LINK

To install the camshaft sprocket, the knock pin will be at the top and the silver link will align with the mark

17. Carefully turn the crankshaft 2 full turns and make sure the timing marks still line up. If not, remove the camshaft sprocket and try again. Torque the sprocket bolt to 87–116 ft. lbs. (118–157 Nm).

18. Adjust the valves.

19. Use a silicone sealer when installing the rubber covers at each end of the camshaft. Install the valve cover with a new gasket and torque the bolts in a circular pattern to 7 ft. lbs. (10 Nm). Loosen all the bolts and torque them again in the same pattern.

20. Complete the installation of the remaining components. Change the oil before running the engine.

3.0L Engine

1. Relieve the fuel system pressure. Disconnect the negative battery cable.

2. Remove the air cleaner. Disconnect the accelerator cable from the throttle body.

3. Drain the engine coolant, including the block drain.

4. Label and disconnect all wiring and hoses as required.

5. Disconnect the exhaust pipes and on 1988–89 models, remove the exhaust manifolds.

6. Remove the distributor and spark plug wires as an assembly.

7. Remove the timing belt covers and the timing belt.

8. On 1988–89 models with throttle body fuel injection:

   a. Disconnect the wiring and the hoses from the throttle body.

   b. Carefully loosen the intake manifold bolts 1 turn at a time in the reverse order of the torque sequence. This is important to prevent warping the manifold.

   c. Remove the bolts and lift the manifold off.

9. On 1990–92 models with multi-point fuel injection:

   a. Remove the upper intake manifold section (5 bolts).

   b. Label and disconnect the wiring to the fuel injectors and disconnect the fuel supply and return hoses.

   c. Remove the injectors and rail as an assembly. Place the assembly where it will stay clean.

   d. Loosen the intake manifold bolts 1 turn at a time in the reverse order of the torque sequence. This is important to prevent warping the manifold.

   e. Remove the bolts and lift the manifold off.

10. Mark the camshaft sprockets left and right for proper installation and remove them.

11. Remove the rear timing belt cover.

12. Without disconnecting the hydraulic or coolant hoses, remove the power steering pump and the air conditioner compressor and secure them out of the way. Remove the brackets from the cylinder heads.

13. Remove the rocker arm covers.

NOTE: It may be necessary to remove the rocker shafts and valve lifter guide to provide access to the cylinder head bolts. Before removing the valve lifter guide, secure the valve lifters with a safety wire to keep them in their original positions.

14. To prevent warping the heads, loosen the cylinder head bolts 1 turn at a time in the reverse order of the torque sequence. When they are all loose, remove the bolts and lift the heads off the engine.

Wire

Secure the lifters with wire before removing the guide assembly—3.0L engine

R.H. SIDE

NO. 1   NO. 3   NO. 5

L.H. SIDE

NO. 2   NO. 4   NO. 6

Cylinder head bolt torque sequence—3.0L engine

View of the camshaft sprocket timing marks—3.0L engine

To install:

15. Throughly clean all gasket surfaces and inspect the head and block for damage to the surfaces. Before installing, check the cylinder head for warping. The limit is 0.004 in. (0.10mm). Make sure the threads on the bolts and in the block are clean and that the bolts turn easily in the threads. Do not oil the threads.

16. Set the crankshaft to TDC on No. 1 cylinder and make sure the mark on the sprocket aligns with the mark on the oil pump body. Make sure the knock pin on the camshaft is at the top.

17. On 1990–92 models, use new gaskets and install the exhaust manifolds. Torque the nuts or bolts in the proper sequence to 16 ft. lbs. (22 Nm).

18. Apply sealant to the block cooling system drain plugs and install the plugs.

19. Make sure the new head gaskets are properly fitted and install the cylinder heads. When installing the bolts, the long bolts go into positions 4, 5, 12 and 13; the flat side of the washer goes towards the head.

20. Torque the cylinder head bolts in the proper sequence in five steps:

    Step 1 — 22 ft. lbs. (30 Nm)
    Step 2 — 43 ft. lbs. (58 Nm)
    Step 3 — loosen all bolts
    Step 4 — 22 ft. lbs. (30 Nm)
    Step 5 — 40–47 ft. lbs. (54–64 Nm) or;
    Step 5 alternate — 22 ft. lbs. (30 Nm) plus 65 degrees

21. If the lifter guide and rocker arms were removed, install them now and tighten the bolts 1 turn at a time to draw the shafts down evenly against the valve springs without bending the shafts. Torque the bolts to 16 ft. lbs. (22 Nm).

22. Install the rocker arm covers and torque the bolts to 25 inch lbs. (3 Nm).

23. Install the rear timing belt cover and the camshaft sprockets. Make sure the sprockets are on the correct side and torque the sprocket bolts to 65 ft. lbs. (88 Nm).

24. Make sure the crankshaft and camshafts are properly positioned to install the timing belt. Be careful if it is necessary to turn either shaft; this is not a free wheeling engine and the valves will contact the pistons if the crankshaft is turned without the timing belt in place.

25. Install the timing belt, set the tension and turn the crankshaft 2 full turns to make sure the timing marks still align properly.

26. Use a new gasket to install the intake manifold and torque the nuts bolts in the proper sequence in 3 steps. Torque the nuts to 20 ft. lbs. (27 Nm) and the bolts to 14 ft. lbs. (20 Nm).

27. On 1988–89 models, use new gaskets and install the exhaust manifolds; torque the manifold nuts to 16 ft. lbs. (22 Nm).

28. Connect the exhaust pipes to the manifolds and torque the bolts to 20 ft. lbs. (27 Nm).

29. Install the remaining components using new gaskets, O-rings or seals as required. Adjust belt tensions and change the oil before starting the engine.

30. When the engine is first started, the hydraulic valve lifters may be noisy. Run the engine for 10–20 minutes at about 1000 rpm. If the noise has not subsided, the lifter will probably never pump up and must be replaced.

Valve Lash

Arrangement

2.4L ENGINE

I–E–E–I–I–E–E–I (front-to-rear)

3.0L ENGINE

Right Side

E–I–E–I–E–I (front-to-rear)

Left Side

I–E–I–E–I–E (front-to-rear)

Adjustment

1988 2.4L ENGINE

NOTE: Adjustment can be made with the engine hot or cold.

1. Disconnect the negative battery cable. Remove the valve cover.

2. Using a socket wrench on the crankshaft pulley bolt, rotate the crankshaft until the No. 1 cylinder is on the TDC of the compression stroke. Both camshaft lobes on No. 1 will be down.

Valve numbers for adjustment—1988 2.4L engine

Check the clearance between the valve stem and the adjuster screw—1988 2.4L engine

3. Check and/or adjust valves 1, 2, 4 and 6. Loosen the locknut, adjust the valve and tighten the locknut to 16 ft. lbs. (22 Nm). Check the clearance again after tightening the locknut.

4. Rotate the crankshaft 180 degrees to position the No. 4 cylinder on the TDC of its compression stroke. Both camshaft lobes will be pointed down.

5. Adjust valves 3, 5, 7 and 8 and check again with the locknut tightened.

6. Clean the gasket mounting surfaces and install the rocker arm cover with a new gasket.

   Intake valve clearance: 0.008 in. (0.21mm) cold or 0.012 in. (0.30mm) hot.

   Exhaust valve clearance: 0.009 in. (0.23mm) cold or 0.012 in. (0.30mm) hot.

Rocker Arms and Valve Lifters

Removal and Installation

2.4L ENGINE

On 1989–92 models, the hydraulic lifters are built into the rocker arms. Do not allow the arms to lay on their side or they will become air bound. Keep the rocker arms upright or lay them in a pan of new engine oil. On all models, the same bolts that hold the rocker arm assembly also hold the camshaft bearing caps. To avoid damage to the bearing surfaces, the camshaft sprocket must be removed.

1. Relieve the fuel system pressure and disconnect the negative battery cable.

2. Remove the rocker arm cover and turn the crankshaft to align the timing marks at TDC on No. 1 cylinder.

3. Use a wire tie or wire to secure the timing chain to the camshaft sprocket.

4. Hold the camshaft sprocket to loosen the bolt and remove the sprocket. Secure the sprocket so the chain does not fall off the crankshaft sprocket.

5. Loosen each rocker shaft bolt 1 turn at a time to prevent bending the shafts.

6. When all the bolts are loose, remove the rocker arm shafts with the bolts still in the shafts. This will hold the assembly together.

7. If the rocker arms are to be removed from the shafts, mark them so they can be returned into their original position. Remove the bolts from the shaft assembly and remove the parts. Keep the rocker arms upright or lay them in a pan of new engine oil. Note the punch marks on the front of each shaft that tell

Rocker arm assembly on 2.4L engine with manual lash adjusters

Make sure the rocker arm shafts are returned to their correct position—2.4L engine with hydraulic adjusters shown

Rocker arm shaft tightening sequence—2.4L engine

which shaft is for the intake side and which is for the exhaust side. This is important for correct rocker arm oiling.

To install:

8. Lubricate the shafts with engine oil and assemble them

Rocker arm assembly on 2.4L engine with hydraulic lash adjusters

with the punch marks facing up. Use the bolts to hold the assembly together. Make sure the camshaft and the bearing surfaces are in good condition and lubricate with engine oil. Make sure the pin on the camshaft sprocket end is up.

9. Install the rocker arm shafts and tighten the bolts in the proper sequence 1 turn at a time to draw the shafts down evenly against the valve springs without bending the shafts. Torque the bolts to 16 ft. lbs. (22 Nm).

10. Install the camshaft sprocket and remove the tie securing the chain. Install the sprocket bolt but don't torque it yet. Rotate the crankshaft 2 full turns to make sure the timing marks line up. When the valve timing is correct, torque the sprocket bolt to 116 ft. lbs. (157 Nm).

11. If required, adjust the valves.

12. Use a silicone sealer on the rubber end plugs and install the rocker arm cover with a new gasket. Torque the bolts to 7 ft. lbs. (10 Nm) in a crisscross pattern starting at the middle. Install the remaining components.

13. When the engine is first started, the hydraulic valve lifters may be noisy. Run the engine for 10–20 minutes at about 1000 rpm. If the noise has not subsided, the lifter will probably never pump up and must be replaced.

3.0L ENGINE

1. Relieve the fuel system pressure and disconnect the negative battery cable.

2. Remove the rocker arm covers.

3. Turn the crankshaft to align the timing marks at TDC on No. 1 cylinder. Remove the distributor cap and matchmark the position of the rotor to the distributor body and to the engine. Remove the distributor.

4. Loosen each rocker shaft bolt 1 turn at a time to prevent bending the shafts.

5. When all the bolts are loose, remove the rocker arm shafts with the bolts still in the shafts. This will hold the assembly together.

6. If the lifters are to be removed:

   a. Secure the valve lifters in the guide assembly with safety wire to keep them in their original positions, then remove the entire assembly.

   b. Before removing a lifter from the guide assembly, tag the lifters to make sure they are returned to their original position. Do not disassemble a lifter.

   c. Keep the lifters upright to prevent air from getting in or lay them down in a pan of new engine oil.

   d. Check the lifter for signs of wear or damage. Measure the outside diameter of the lifter and the inside diameter of the bore it came from. The clearance should be 0.0017–0.0026 in. (0.043–0.066mm).

7. If the rocker arms are to be removed from the shafts, mark them so they can be returned into their original position. Remove the bolts from the shaft assembly and remove the rockers. Tag each shaft to tell which shaft is for the intake side and which is for the exhaust side. This is important for correct rocker arm oiling.

To install:

8. Lubricate the shafts with new engine oil and install the rockers in their original positions. Lubricate the lifters and install them into their original positions. Wire the lifters into the guide assembly.

9. Make sure the engine is at TDC on No. 1 cylinder. Install the left bank lifter guide assembly, remove the safety wire and install the rocker arm shafts. Tighten the bolts 1 turn at a time to draw the shafts down evenly. Torque the bolts to 16 ft. lbs. (22 Nm).

10. Rotate the crankshaft to bring cylinder No. 4 to TDC. Set the right bank lifter guide assembly into place, remove the safety wire and install the rocker arm shafts. Tighten the bolts 1 turn at a time to 16 ft. lbs. (22 Nm).

11. Use new gaskets to install the rocker arm covers and torque the bolts to 24 inch lbs. (3 Nm). Install the remaining components.

Hold the lifters in place with wire before removing the guide assembly—3.0L engine

Make sure rocker arm shafts are installed in their original position—3.0L engine

12. When the engine is first started, the hydraulic valve lifters may be noisy. Run the engine for 10–20 minutes at about 1000 rpm. If the noise has not subsided, the lifter will probably never pump up and must be replaced.

Intake Manifold

Removal and Installation

2.4L ENGINE

Except 1990 Axxess

1. Release the fuel pressure. Disconnect the negative battery cable.

2. Remove the air cleaner assembly together with all of the attending hoses. Remove the EGR tube.

3. Label and disconnect all wiring and hoses as required.

4. Drain the engine coolant to a level below the thermostat housing, then, disconnect the upper coolant hose from the thermostat housing.

5. Disconnect the throttle linkage from the throttle body. The throttle body and/or fuel injectors can be removed from the manifold at this point or the entire assembly can be removed.

6. Remove the manifold bracket, if equipped, and remove the bolts and the intake manifold.

To install:

7. Clean the gasket mounting surfaces and use new gaskets. Install the manifold and tighten the bolts in 2 steps working from the center out. Torque the bolts to 15 ft. lbs. (21 Nm).

8. If it was removed, install the throttle body with a new gasket and torque the nuts to 13 ft. lbs. (18 Nm). Use new O-rings to install the injectors.

9. Install the remaining components and connect the wiring

Intake manifold assembly on 1990–92 2.4L engine except Axxess

Intake manifold assembly on 2.4L engine with throttle body injection

Intake manifold assembly on 1988–89 3.0L engine

Intake manifold bolt torque sequence—1988–89 3.0L engine

and hoses. Fill the cooling system and run the engine to check ignition timing and idle speed.

1990 Axxess

1. Release the fuel pressure. Disconnect the negative battery cable.
2. Remove the air duct from the throttle body. Remove the EGR tube.
3. Label and disconnect the electrical wiring and hoses as required.
4. Drain the engine coolant to a level below the thermostat housing, then, disconnect the upper coolant hose from the thermostat housing.
5. Disconnect the throttle linkage and vacuum lines from the throttle body.

6. Remove the throttle body-to-intake manifold collector bolts and the throttle body.
7. Remove the intake manifold stays.
8. Remove the intake manifold collector-to-intake manifold, the collector and the gasket.
9. Remove the intake manifold-to-engine bolts and the intake manifold.
10. Clean the gasket mounting surfaces and install new gaskets.
11. Install the manifold and torque the bolts in 2 steps, working from the center out, to 15 ft. lbs. (21 Nm).
12. Install the collector with a new gasket and torque the bolts in 2 steps to 15 ft. lbs. (21 Nm).
13. If the fuel injectors were removed, use new O-rings and gaskets to install them.
14. Install the remaining components and connect the wiring and hoses. Fill the cooling system and run the engine to check ignition timing and idle speed.

3.0L ENGINE

1988–89

1. Relieve the fuel system pressure and disconnect the negative battery cable.
2. Drain the cooling system to a level below the intake manifold.
3. Remove the air cleaner. Disconnect the accelerator linkage from the throttle body.
4. Remove the upper radiator hose from the water outlet housing and the exhaust tube from the EGR valve. If necessary, remove the EGR valve-to-intake manifold nuts and the EGR valve.

INTAKE MANIFOLD
COLLECTOR — THROTTLE BODY

INTAKE MANIFOLD STAY

BPT VALVE

EGR CONTROL
VALVE

AIR CUT VALVE

EGR PASSAGE

IAA UNIT

ENGINE
TEMPERATURE
SENSOR

BPT VALVE BRACKET

INJECTOR

FUEL PRESSURE
REGULATOR

INTAKE MANIFOLD

Intake manifold assembly on Axxess

5. Using a shop rag, wrap it around the fuel line and disconnect it from the throttle body. Remove the throttle body-to-intake manifold nuts, the throttle body and the heater mixture assembly.

6. To prevent warping, loosen the intake manifold nuts and bolts 1 or 2 turns at a time in the reverse of the torque sequence. Remove the manifold.

To install:

7. Clean the gasket surfaces and install new gaskets.

8. Install the intake manifold and torque the nuts and bolts in 2 steps in the proper sequence. Torque the nuts to 20 ft. lbs. (27 Nm) and the bolts to 14 ft. lbs. (19 Nm).

9. Use new gaskets to install the remaining components. Torque the EGR valve nuts to 17 ft. lbs. (23 Nm) and the throttle body nuts to 13 ft. lbs. (18 Nm).

10. Refill the cooling system and run the engine to check ignition timing and idle speed.

1990–92

1. Release the fuel system pressure and disconnect the negative battery cable. 2. Drain the cooling system to a level below the intake manifold.

3. Remove the air duct from the throttle body. Disconnect the accelerator linkage from the throttle body.

4. Remove the upper radiator hose from the water outlet housing and the exhaust tube from the EGR valve. If necessary, remove the EGR valve-to-intake manifold nuts and the EGR valve.

5. Label and disconnect the wiring and hoses as required.

Intake manifold bolt torque sequence—1990–92 3.0L engine

6. Remove the 5 intake manifold collector-to-intake manifold bolts and the lift the collector off the engine.

7. Remove the fuel rail and the injectors as an assembly from the intake manifold.

8. To prevent warping, loosen the intake manifold nuts and bolts 1 or 2 turns at a time in the reverse of the torque sequence. Remove the manifold.

To install:

9. Clean the gasket surfaces and install new gaskets.

10. Install the intake manifold and torque the nuts and bolts in the proper sequence in the following steps:
Step 1: all to 43 inch lbs. (5 Nm).

Step 2: bolts to 14 ft. lbs. (20 Nm), nuts to 20 ft. lbs. (27 Nm).

Step 3: repeat Step 2.

11. Use new O-rings and install the fuel injectors and rail assembly. Connect the wiring.

12. Use a new gasket and install the intake manifold collector. Torque the bolts to 12 ft. lbs. (16 Nm).

13. Install the remaining components and connect the wiring and hoses. Refill the cooling system and run the engine to check ignition timing and idle speed.

Exhaust Manifold

Removal and Installation

2.4L ENGINE

1. Disconnect the negative battery cable.

2. If equipped, remove the hot air duct from the exhaust manifold cover.

3. Disconnect the spark plug wires from the exhaust side of the engine; if necessary, remove the spark plugs from the exhaust side of the engine.

4. If necessary, raise and safely support the vehicle.

5. If equipped, remove the air induction tubes from the exhaust manifold. Remove the EGR tube from the exhaust manifold.

6. Remove the hot air cover and the exhaust pipe from the exhaust manifold.

7. Remove the exhaust manifold-to-engine nuts and the manifold from the engine.

To install:

8. Clean the gasket mounting surfaces and install new gaskets.

9. Install the manifold and torque the nuts/bolts to 15 ft. lbs. (20 Nm), working from the center to the ends, in 2 steps.

10. Use new gaskets and connect the exhaust pipe to the manifold. Torque the nuts to 27 ft. lbs. (36 Nm).

11. Install the remaining components and run the engine to check for leaks.

3.0L ENGINE

Left Side

1. Disconnect the negative battery cable.

2. Remove the hot air tube from the exhaust manifold cover.

12–15 ft. lbs. (16–21 NM)

3–3.5 ft. lbs. (4–5 NM)

COVER

EXHAUST GAS SENSOR
30–37 ft. lbs. (40–50 NM)

EXHAUST MANIFOLD
12–15 ft. lbs. (16–21 NM)

Exhaust manifold—2.4L engine

R.H. EXHAUST MANIFOLD

FRONT

L.H. EXHAUST MANIFOLD

FRONT

Exhaust manifolds—3.0L engine

Remove the exhaust manifold cover-to-exhaust manifold bolts and cover.

3. Remove the EGR and the AIR tubes from the exhaust manifold, if equipped.

NOTE: If the alternator is in the way, remove the drive belt and the alternator.

4. Raise and safely support the vehicle.

5. Remove the exhaust pipe-to-exhaust manifold nuts and separate the exhaust pipe from the manifold.

6. Remove the exhaust manifold-to-cylinder head bolts and the manifold from the engine.

7. Clean the gasket mounting surfaces.

8. To install, use new gaskets and reverse the removal procedures. Torque the exhaust manifold-to-cylinder head nuts to 16 ft. lbs. (22 Nm) and the exhaust pipe-to-exhaust manifold bolts to 20 ft. lbs. (27 Nm).

Right side

1. Disconnect the negative battery cable.

2. Remove the upper/lower exhaust manifold cover-to-exhaust manifold bolts and covers.

3. Remove the AIR tube from the exhaust manifold, if equipped.

4. Raise and safely support the vehicle.

5. Remove the exhaust pipe-to-exhaust manifold bolts and separate the exhaust pipe from the manifold.

6. Remove the exhaust manifold-to-cylinder head bolts and the manifold from the engine.

7. Clean the gasket mounting surfaces.

8. To install, use new gaskets and reverse the removal procedures. Torque the exhaust manifold-to-cylinder head nuts to 16 ft. lbs. (22 Nm) and the exhaust pipe-to-exhaust manifold bolts to 20 ft. lbs. (27 Nm).

Timing Chain Front Cover

Removal and Installation

2.4L ENGINE

Except Axxess

1. Disconnect the negative battery cable. Drain the cooling system. Remove the upper and lower coolant hoses from the engine and the radiator.

2. Loosen the alternator adjusting bolt and remove the drive belt. Remove the alternator bracket-to-engine bolts and move the alternator aside.

3. If equipped with air conditioning, remove the drive belt. If necessary, remove the air conditioner compressor and move it aside without disconnecting the coolant hoses.

4. If equipped with power steering, remove the drive belt.

Timing chain assembly—1988–89 2.4L engine

Labels in figure:
- TIMING CHAIN
- CAMSHAFT SPROCKET
- 87–116 FT. LBS. (118–157 NM)
- CHAIN GUIDE
- CHAIN TENSIONER
- FRONT COVER
- FRONT OIL SEAL
- CRANKSHAFT PULLEY
- 87–116 FT. LBS. (118–157 NM)
- FRONT COVER GASKET
- OIL THROWER
- CRANKSHAFT SPROCKET
- CAMSHAFT
- CYLINDER HEAD
- CYLINDER HEAD GASKET
- CYLINDER BLOCK
- CRANKSHAFT

5. Rotate the crankshaft to position the No. 1 cylinder on TDC of it's compression stroke.

6. Drain the oil and remove the oil pan.

7. Remove the distributor cap. Matchmark the rotor to the distributor housing and the distributor housing to the timing chain cover. Remove the distributor hold-down bolt and the distributor.

8. Remove the oil pump-to-timing cover bolts, the oil pump and its drive spindle.

9. On RWD vehicles, remove the cooling fan-to-water pump bolts, the fan, the fan coupling if equipped and the water pump pulley.

10. Remove the crankshaft pulley-to-crankshaft bolt and the crankshaft pulley.

11. Remove the timing chain cover-to-cylinder head bolts, the timing chain cover-to-engine bolts, and remove the cover. Clean the gasket mounting surfaces.

To install:

NOTE: Whenever the timing cover is removed, replace the oil seal.

12. Install a new oil seal and use new gaskets and silicone sealant as necessary to install the front cover.

13. Install the oil pan.

14. When installing the oil pump. place the new gasket over the shaft and make sure the drive spindle mark aligns with the hole in the pump body. This will align the shaft properly for the distributor.

15. Install the distributor and make sure the rotor aligns with the matchmark.

TIMING CHAIN

CAMSHAFT SPROCKET

87–116 FT. LBS. (118–157 NM)

CHAIN TENSIONER

5–6 FT. LBS. (7–8 NM)

CHAIN GUIDE

9–14 FT. LBS. (13–19 NM)

FRONT COVER

FRONT OIL SEAL

CRANKSHAFT PULLEY

87–116 FT. LBS. (118–157 NM)

OIL THROWER

CRANKSHAFT SPROCKET

9–14 FT. LBS. (13–19 NM)

CRANKSHAFT

Timing chain assembly—1990–92 2.4L engine except Axxess

16. Install the crankshaft pulley and torque the bolt to 116 ft. lbs. (157 Nm).

17. Install the remaining components and refill the cooling system. Run the engine to check ignition timing and idle speed.

Axxess

The right side engine mount must be removed, an engine hoist is required.

1. Disconnect the negative battery cable. Drain the cooling system. Remove the upper and lower coolant hoses from the engine and the radiator.

2. Loosen the alternator adjusting bolt and remove the drive belt. Remove the alternator and the adjusting bracket.

3. If equipped with air conditioning, remove the drive belt. If necessary, remove the air conditioner compressor and move it aside without disconnecting the coolant hoses.

4. If equipped with power steering, remove the drive belt.

5. Rotate the crankshaft to position the No. 1 cylinder on TDC of it's compression stroke.

6. Raise and safely support the vehicle and remove the underpan.

7. Remove the crankshaft pulley and the oil pump drive boss.

8. Drain the oil and remove the oil pan and the oil pick-up tube and strainer.

9. Remove the rocker arm cover.

10. Attach a chain hoist to the engine, remove the right side mount and lower the engine slightly.

11. Remove the bolts and remove the front cover.

TIMING CHAIN

CAMSHAFT SPROCKET

87–116 FT. LBS. (118–157 NM)

CHAIN TENSIONER

CHAIN GUIDE

FRONT COVER

FRONT OIL SEAL

CRANKSHAFT PULLEY

5–6 FT. LBS. (7–8 NM)
12–15 FT. LBS. (16–21 NM)

87–116 FT. LBS. (118–157 NM)

12–15 FT. LBS. (16–21 NM)

CRANKSHAFT SPROCKET

OIL PUMP DRIVE BOSS

CRANKSHAFT

5–6 FT. LBS. (7–8 NM)

TO MAIN BEARING BEAM

Timing chain assembly on Axxess

To install:

12. Install a new front cover oil seal and lubricate the seal with lithium grease. Use new gaskets, O-rings or silicone sealant as necessary to install the front cover, the oil pick-up tube and the oil pan.

13. Raise the engine, install the engine mount and torque the nuts and bolts to 41 ft. lbs. (55 Nm).

14. Install the oil pump drive boss and the crankshaft pulley. Torque the pulley bolt to 116 ft. lbs. (157 Nm).

15. Install the remaining components, adjust the drive belt tensions and refill the cooling system. Run the engine to check ignition timing and idle speed.

Front Cover Oil Seal

Replacement

2.4L ENGINE

1. Disconnect the negative battery cable.

2. Remove the radiator shroud as required and remove crankshaft pulley.

3. Carefully pry the front oil seal out of the timing cover without damaging the crankshaft.

4. Lubricate the new seal with light grease. Using an oil seal installation tool, drive the new oil seal into the timing cover un-

CAMSHAFT SPROCKET

CRANKSHAFT SPROCKET

● : PUNCHMARK

Timing chain and sprocket marks on 2.4L engine; later models may have only 1 timing mark on the camshaft sprocket

til it seats. Clean all oil and grease away from the seal and crankshaft area.

5. To complete the installation, reverse the removal procedures. Torque the crankshaft pulley-to-crankshaft bolt to 116 ft. lbs. (157 Nm). Start the engine, allow it reach normal operating temperatures and check for leaks.

Timing Chain and Sprockets

Removal and Installation

2.4L ENGINE

1. Disconnect the negative battery cable.
2. Rotate the crankshaft to align the timing marks on the crankshaft pulley at TDC of No. 1 cylinder. Remove the timing chain cover and the rocker arm cover.
3. Make sure the No. 1 piston is at TDC of its compression stroke; the No. 1 camshaft lobes will both be down. The timing marks on the camshaft sprocket and crankshaft sprocket should align with the silver links on the timing chain. If the chain has no silver links, paint alignment marks on the chain.
4. Remove the chain tensioner.

NOTE: When the chain tensioner bolts are removed, the tensioner will come apart. Hold on to the piston and don't drop any of the parts into the oil pan. There is no need to remove the chain guide unless it is being replaced.

5. Hold the camshaft sprocket from turning, remove the bolt and remove the sprocket along with the chain.
To install:
6. Inspect the timing chain for cracked links, wear and/or

damage; if necessary, replace the chain. Inspect the guides and sprockets for wear or damage and replace as necessary. If replacing a sprocket, always replace the chain.

7. Install the timing chain and camshaft sprocket, making sure to align all the timing marks. Install the camshaft sprocket bolt but do not torque it yet.
8. Install the chain tensioner and torque the bolts to 72 inch lbs. (8 Nm).
9. Rotate the crankshaft 2 full turns and make sure the timing marks still align. When the chain is correctly installed, torque the camshaft sprocket bolt to 116 ft. lbs. (157 Nm).
10. Install the front cover, crankshaft pulley and all remaining components. Run the engine to check ignition timing and idle speed.

Timing Belt Front Cover

Removal and Installation

3.0L ENGINE

1. Disconnect the negative battery cable and remove the engine under cover.
2. Drain the coolant and remove the hoses and the lower fan shroud. Remove the radiator and main shroud as an assembly.
3. Remove the accessory drive belts and remove the fan and water pump pulley.
4. Remove the spark plugs and the fresh air intake tube to the rocker arm cover.
5. Remove the idler pulley bracket and the water inlet hose.
6. Remove the crankshaft pulley bolt and use a puller to remove the crankshaft pulley. Put a spacer (a stack of washers or a large nut) on the pulley bolt and install the bolt so the crankshaft can be turned with the socket or wrench.
7. Remove the front timing belt covers. To remove the rear covers, the timing belt and camshaft sprockets must be removed.
8. Installation is the reverse of removal. Torque the crankshaft pulley bolt to 98 ft. lbs. (132 Nm).

Oil Seal Replacement

3.0L ENGINE

The front oil seal is a part of the oil pump.
1. Remove the oil pump.
2. Carefully pry the oil seal from the oil pump.
3. Lubricate the new seal with light grease. Using an oil seal installation tool, drive the new oil seal into the oil pump housing until it seats. Clean all oil and grease away from the seal.
4. To complete the installation, use new gaskets and reverse the removal procedures.

Timing Belt and Tensioner

Adjustment

3.0L ENGINE

1. This procedure is for adjusting the belt tension only if the belt has not been removed. If the belt was removed, see the Removal and Installation procedure. Disconnect the negative battery cable and remove the front timing belt covers.
2. Loosen the tensioner pulley locknut and allow the spring to hold the pulley against the belt.
3. Set a 0.014 in. (0.35mm) feeler gauge between the belt and pulley on the crankshaft side of the pulley. The feeler gauge should be at least ½ in. (12.7mm) wide.
4. Rotate the crankshaft clockwise to make the feeler gauge roll up between the tensioner pulley and the belt. Make sure the gauge is centered on the tensioner pulley.
5. Push in on the belt halfway between the tensioner pulley and the camshaft sprocket with a force of 22 lbs. (98 N) and torque the locknut to 43 ft. lbs. (58 Nm).

REAR BELT COVER

CYLINDER BLOCK

RIGHT CAMSHAFT SPROCKET

CONICAL WASHER

BELT TENSIONER NUT

FRONT UPPER COVER

COARSE THREAD STUD

LEFT CAMSHAFT SPROCKET

TENSIONER SPRING

BELT TENSIONER

FRONT LOWER COVER

TIMING BELT PLATE

CRANKSHAFT SPROCKET

PULLEY PLATE

CRANKSHAFT PULLEY

Timing belt and cover assembly on 3.0L engine

6. Rotate the crankshaft to remove the feeler gauge. Install the covers.

Removal and Installation

3.0L ENGINE

1. Disconnect the negative battery cable and remove the timing belt cover.

2. Put a spacer (a stack of washers or a large nut) on the crankshaft pulley bolt and install the bolt so the crankshaft can be turned with a socket wrench.

3. Rotate the crankshaft to position the No. 1 piston on the TDC of its compression stroke. The marks on the camshaft and crankshaft sprockets will align with marks on the rear timing belt cover and the oil pump housing.

4. If the belt is to be re-used, paint an arrow on the belt pointing towards the front of the vehicle.

5. Loosen the belt tensioner pulley nut, move the pulley with an Allen wrench and remove the belt.

To install:

6. Spin the tensioner pulley and make sure it turns smoothly. If there is any doubt, replace it. Examine the belt for wear or damage, replace as necessary.

7. Make sure all the sprockets are correctly aligned with the timing marks. Be careful when turning the crankshaft or camshafts, this is not a free wheeling engine.

8. Turn the tensioner pulley clockwise to move it out of the way, install the timing belt and allow the tensioner to slowly return on its spring. Make sure all the timing marks are still aligned. When the belt is correctly installed, there will be 40 teeth between the camshaft sprocket timing marks and 43 teeth between the crankshaft and left camshaft sprocket timing marks.

FEELER GAUGE

TENSIONER PULLEY

TIMING BELT

CRANKSHAFT SPROCKET

Make sure the feeler gauge is centered between the tensioner pulley and the belt—3.0L engine

CRANKSHAFT SPROCKET

TENSIONER PULLEY

FEELER GAUGE

FEELER GAUGE

TIMING BELT

THICKNESS: 0.0138 IN. (0.3500MM)

Place the feeler gauge under the tensioner pulley— 3.0L engine

Timing belt and sprockets on 3.0L engine

Move the tensioner pulley with an Allen wrench

9. Turn the tensioner approximately 70–80 degrees clockwise with the wrench and tighten the locknut.

10. To adjust the belt tension, turn the crankshaft clockwise several times and slowly set the No. 1 piston to TDC of the compression stroke.

11. Set a 0.014 in. (0.35mm) feeler gauge between the belt and pulley on the crankshaft side of the pulley. The feeler gauge should be at least ½ in. (12.7mm) wide.

12. Rotate the crankshaft clockwise to make the feeler gauge roll up between the tensioner pulley and the belt. Make sure the gauge is centered on the tensioner pulley.

13. Loosen the tensioner pulley locknut, push in on the belt halfway between the tensioner pulley and the camshaft sprocket with a force of 22 lbs. (98 N) and torque the locknut to 43 ft. lbs. (58 Nm).

14. Rotate the crankshaft to remove the feeler gauge. Install the covers.

Timing Sprockets

Removal and Installation

3.0L ENGINE

1. Disconnect the negative battery cable.

2. Remove the timing belt cover and the timing belt.

3. Use an appropriate tool to prevent the camshafts from turning and remove the sprocket bolts. Pull the sprockets straight off.

4. Installation is the reverse of removal. Torque the camshaft sprocket bolts to 65 ft. lbs. (88 Nm). Install the timing belt.

Camshaft

Removal and Installation

2.4L ENGINE

The same bolts that hold the rocker arm assembly also hold the camshaft bearing caps and on 1988 models, the rocker arm shaft holder is the bearing cap. On 1989–92 models, the hydraulic lifters are built into the rocker arms. If the rocker arm shafts are disassembled, do not allow the arms to lay on their side or they will become air bound. Keep the rocker arms upright or lay them in a pan of new engine oil.

1. Relieve the fuel system pressure and disconnect the negative battery cable.

2. Remove the rocker arm cover and turn the crankshaft to align the timing marks at TDC on No. 1 cylinder.

3. If the timing chain is not being removed, use a wire tie or wire to secure the timing chain to the camshaft sprocket.

4. Hold the camshaft sprocket to loosen the bolt and remove the sprocket. Secure the sprocket so the chain does not fall off the crankshaft sprocket.

5. Loosen each rocker shaft bolt 1 turn at a time to prevent bending the shafts.

6. When all the bolts are loose, remove the rocker arm shafts with the bolts still in the shafts. This will hold the assembly together.

7. If they are not already identified, mark the bearing caps so they can be installed in their original position facing the same direction. Lift the caps off and lift the camshaft out.

To install:

8. Inspect the camshaft and the bearings:

   a. Make sure the camshaft and the bearing surfaces are in good condition.

   b. Install the bearing caps without the camshaft, torque the rocker arm shaft bolts to specification and measure the inside diameter of the bearing circle.

   c. Measure the diameter of the camshaft bearings.

   d. The difference between the measurements is the cam-

Camshaft removal on 1988 2.4L engine; the rocker arm shaft holders are also the bearing caps

Camshaft removal on 1989–92 2.4L engine

shaft journal clearance; it should be no more than 0.0047 in. (0.12mm)

e. Install the camshaft without the rocker arms and torque the bolts to specification. The camshaft end-play should be no more than 0.008 in. (0.2mm).

9. Lubricate the camshaft with engine oil and set it in place. Make sure the pin on the sprocket end is up.

10. Install the rocker arm shafts and tighten the bolts in the proper sequence 1 turn at a time to draw the shafts down evenly against the valve springs without bending the shafts. Torque the bolts to 16 ft. lbs. (22 Nm).

11. Install the camshaft sprocket and remove the tie securing the chain. Install the sprocket bolt but don't torque it yet. Rotate the crankshaft 2 full turns to make sure the timing marks line up. When the valve timing is correct, torque the sprocket bolt to 116 ft. lbs. (157 Nm).

12. On 1988 models, adjust the valves.

13. Use a silicone sealer on the rubber end plugs and install the rocker arm cover with a new gasket. Torque the bolts to 7 ft. lbs. (10 Nm) in a crisscross pattern starting at the middle. Install the remaining components.

14. When the engine is first started, the hydraulic valve lifters may be noisy. Run the engine for 10–20 minutes at about 1000 rpm. If the noise has not subsided, the lifter will probably never pump up and must be replaced.

3.0L ENGINE

The camshafts can be removed without removing the cylinder heads. When removing the timing belt covers, the radiator must be removed. This should provide the clearance for removing the camshafts.

1. Relieve the fuel system pressure and disconnect the negative battery cable.

2. Remove the rocker arm covers.

3. Turn the crankshaft to align the timing marks at TDC on No. 1 cylinder. Remove the timing belt cover and the timing belt.

4. Hold the camshafts from turning and remove the camshaft sprockets. Remove the rear timing belt cover.

5. Loosen each rocker shaft bolt 1 turn at a time to prevent bending the shafts. When all the bolts are loose, remove the rocker arm shafts with the bolts still in the shafts. This will hold the assembly together.

6. Secure the valve lifters in the guide assembly with safety wire to keep them in their original positions, then remove the entire assembly.

NOTE: Before removing a lifter from the guide assembly, tag the lifters to make sure they are returned to their original position. Keep the lifters upright to keep them from becoming air bound or lay them down in a pan of new engine oil. Do not disassemble a lifter.

Camshaft removal on 3.0L engine can be done without removing the cylinder head

7. Remove the plates from the front and rear of the cylinder heads and pry the oil seals out. Remove the bolt at the rear of the camshafts and remove the locating plates. Carefully withdraw the camshafts out towards the front.

To install:

8. Inspect the camshaft and the bearing surfaces:
   a. Make sure the camshaft and the bearing surfaces are in good condition.
   b. Measure the inside diameter of the bearing circle.
   c. Measure the diameter of the camshaft bearings.
   d. The difference between the measurements is the camshaft journal clearance; it should be no more than 0.0059 in. (0.15mm).
   e. To check endplay, install the camshaft and the locating plates and torque the bolts to 65 ft. lbs. (88 Nm). The camshaft endplay should be no more than 0.0024 in. (0.06mm).

9. Lubricate the camshaft with engine oil and carefully set it in place. Install the locating plate at the rear and torque the bolt to 65 ft. lbs. (88 Nm). Turn the camshaft so the pin on the sprocket end is up.

10. Install the rear camshaft cover plate with a new gasket.

11. Lubricate a new camshaft front oil seal with grease and use an appropriate seal installation tool to carefully drive the new seal into place. Make sure the seal seats in the cylinder head.

12. With the rocker arm assemblies removed, all the valves will be closed. The rear timing belt cover, sprockets and timing belt can be installed without risk of damage to valves or pistons. Adjust timing belt tension according to correct procedure.

13. Make sure the engine is at TDC on No. 1 cylinder. Install the left bank lifter guide assembly, remove the safety wire and install the rocker arm shafts. Tighten the bolts 1 turn at a time to draw the shafts down evenly. Torque the bolts to 16 ft. lbs. (22 Nm).

14. Rotate the crankshaft to bring cylinder No. 4 to TDC. Set the right bank lifter guide assembly into place, remove the safety wire and install the rocker arm shafts. Tighten the bolts 1 turn at a time to 16 ft. lbs. (22 Nm).

15. Use new gaskets to install the rocker arm covers and torque the bolts to 24 inch lbs. (3 Nm). Install the remaining components.

16. When the engine is first started, the hydraulic valve lifters may be noisy. Run the engine for 10–20 minutes at about 1000 rpm. If the noise has not subsided, the lifter will probably never pump up and must be replaced.

Piston and Connecting Rod

Positioning

Piston and rod orientation on 2.4L engine

Piston and rod orientation on 3.0L engine

ENGINE LUBRICATION

Oil Pan

Removal and Installation

2.4L ENGINE

Except Axxess

1. Raise and safely support the vehicle.
2. Remove the engine undercover and drain the engine oil.
3. On 4WD models, perform the following procedures:
   a. Remove the bolt from the front differential carrier member.
   b. Position a floor jack under the front differential carrier and remove the mounting bolts.
   c. Remove the transmission-to-rear engine mount bracket nuts.
   d. Remove the engine mount nuts and bolts.
   e. Attach an engine hoist and raise the engine slightly.
4. On 2WD models, remove the front crossmember.
5. Remove the oil pan-to-engine bolts. Insert a seal cutter tool between the cylinder block and the oil pan and tap it around the circumference of the pan with a hammer. Remove the oil pan.

NOTE: Be careful not to drive the seal cutter into the oil pump or rear oil seal retainer as damage may occur.

To install:

6. Clean the gasket mounting surfaces.
7. Apply a continuous ⅛ in. bead of silicone sealant to the oil pan mounting surface; be sure to trace sealant bead to the inside of the bolt holes where there is no groove.
8. Install the oil pan and torque the bolts in sequence to 60 inch lbs. (7 Nm).
9. To complete the installation, reverse the removal procedures.
10. Wait at least 30 minutes and refill the crankcase. Start the engine and allow it to reach normal operating temperatures and check for leaks.

Axxess

1. Raise and safely support the vehicle.
2. Drain the engine oil.
3. Remove the front exhaust tube and the front side gusset.
4. On 2WD models, remove the crossmember.
5. Remove the oil pan-to-engine bolts. Insert a seal cutter tool between the cylinder block and the oil pan and tap it around the circumference of the pan with a hammer. Remove the oil pan.

NOTE: Be careful not to drive the seal cutter into the oil pump or rear oil seal retainer as damage may occur.

To install:

6. Clean the gasket mounting surfaces.
7. Apply a continuous ⅛ in. bead of silicone sealant to the oil pan mounting surface; be sure to trace sealant bead to the inside of the bolt holes where there is no groove.
8. Install the oil pan and torque the bolts in sequence to 7 ft. lbs. (10 Nm).
9. To complete the installation, reverse the removal procedures.
10. Wait at least 30 minutes and refill the crankcase. Start the engine and allow it to reach normal operating temperatures and check for leaks.

3.0L ENGINE

1. Raise and safely support the vehicle.
2. Remove the undercover and drain the engine oil.
3. On 2WD models, remove the stabilizer bar bracket bolts.
4. On 4WD models, remove the front driveshaft and disconnect the halfshafts at the transfer case. Position a floor jack un-

Oil pan bolt tightening sequence on 2.4L engine

Oil pan bolt loosening sequence on 3.0L engine—tighten the bolts in the reverse of this sequence

der the front differential carrier and remove the mounting bolts.
5. On 2WD models, remove the front crossmember.
6. Remove the idler arm and the starter motor.
7. On 4WD models, remove the transmission-to-rear engine mount bracket nuts and the engine mount nuts/bolts.
8. Remove the engine gussets.
9. On 4WD models, attach a hoist to the engine and raise the engine slightly.
10. Remove the oil pan-to-engine bolts in the correct sequence to avoid warping the pan. Insert a seal cutter tool between the cylinder block and the oil pan and tap the tool around the circumference with a hammer to remove the oil pan.

NOTE: Be careful not to drive the seal cutter into the oil pump or rear oil seal retainer for damage may occur.

11. Clean the gasket mounting surfaces.
To install:
12. Apply silicone sealant to the oil pump and oil seal retainer gasket.
13. Apply a continuous ⅛ in. bead of sealant to the oil pan mounting surface; be sure to trace sealant bead to the inside of the bolt holes where there is no groove.
14. Install the oil pan and torque the bolts in sequence to 60 inch lbs. (7 Nm).
15. To complete the installation, reverse the removal procedures.
16. Wait at least 30 minutes and refill the crankcase. Start the engine and allow it to reach normal operating temperatures and check for leaks.

Oil Pump

Removal and Installation

2.4L ENGINE

Except Axxess

The oil pump is an external type, mounted to the right side of the crankshaft pulley.

1. Disconnect the negative battery cable.
2. Rotate the crankshaft to position the No. 1 cylinder on the TDC of the compression stroke.
3. If equipped with a splash pan, remove it. If necessary, remove the stabilizer bar.
4. Remove the oil pump-to-housing bolts and the oil pump from the engine.
5. Clean the gasket mounting surfaces.

To install:

6. Install a new gasket onto the pump and fill the pump with oil.
7. Align the distributor drive spindle punch mark with the oil hole on the oil pump. This will properly align the drive spindle with the distributor.
8. Insert the oil pump into the housing until the drive spindle tang fits into the distributor shaft notch. Torque the oil pump-to-engine housing bolts to 11 ft. lbs. (15 Nm).
9. Start the engine to check the ignition timing and to check for leaks.

Axxess

The oil pump rides on the crankshaft and is attached to the front cover.

1. Disconnect the negative battery cable.
2. Raise and safely support the vehicle. Drain the cooling system.
3. Drain the engine oil.
4. Remove the oil pan and the front cover.
5. Remove the oil pump cover-to-front cover bolts, the cover and the oil pump gears.

NOTE: Whenever the oil pump is removed, replace the oil seal.

6. Inspect and/or replace the oil pump gears.
7. Using petroleum jelly, pack the oil pump cavity and reverse the removal procedures.

3.0L ENGINE

The oil pump is mounted at the front of the engine behind the crankshaft pulley.

1. Disconnect the negative battery cable.
2. Raise and safely support the vehicle. Drain the cooling system and the crankcase.
3. Remove the oil pan and the timing belt.

When installing the oil pump on 2.4L engine, align the mark on the shaft with the oil hole

Oil pump on Axxess engine is part of the front cover

4. Remove the crankshaft timing sprocket using a wheel puller and the timing belt plate.
5. Remove the oil pump strainer and the pickup tube from the oil pump.
6. Remove the oil pump-to-engine bolts and the oil pump from the engine.
7. Clean the gasket mounting surfaces.

NOTE: Whenever the oil pump is removed, replace the oil seal.

8. To install, use new gaskets or silicone sealant. Pack the oil pump cavity with petroleum jelly and reverse the removal procedures. Torque as follows:
   Oil pump-to-engine:
   6mm bolts—60 inch lbs. (7 Nm)
   8mm bolts—12 ft. lbs. (16 Nm)
   Pickup tube-to-oil pump bolts—15 ft. lbs. (21 Nm)

Checking

To check the oil pump clearances, the oil pump must be removed from the engine and disassembled. If the parts do not meet specifications, replace the oil pump as an assembly.

2.4L ENGINE

Except Axxess

Using a feeler gauge, check the following clearances:
   Inner rotor tip-to-outer rotor—0.0047 in. (0.12mm) max.
   Outer rotor-to-housing—0.0059–0.0083 in. (0.15–0.21mm)
   Side clearance (with gasket)—0.0016–0.0031 in. (0.04–0.07mm)

Oil pump on 3.0L engine is on the front of the engne block

Inspecting oil pump rotor clearance—2.4L engine except Axxess

Inspecting oil pump side clearance—2.4L engine except Axxess

Inspecting oil pump rotor clearance on 3.0L and 2.4L Axxess engines

Axxess

Using a feeler gauge, check the following clearances:
    Pump body-to-outer gear—0.0043–0.0079 in. (0.11–0.20mm)
    Inner gear-to-cressent—0.0087–0.0130 in. (0.22–0.33mm)
    Outer gear-to-cressent—0.0083–0.0126 in. (0.21–0.32mm)
    Housing-to-inner gear—0.0020–0.0035 in. (0.05–0.09mm)
    Housing-to-outer gear—0.0020–0.0043 in. (0.05–0.11mm)

3.0L ENGINE

Using a feeler gauge, check the following clearances:
    Pump body-to-outer gear—0.0043–0.0079 in. (0.11–0.20mm)
    Inner gear-to-cressent—0.0047–0.0091 in. (0.12–0.23mm)
    Outer gear-to-cressent—0.0083–0.0126 in. (0.22–0.33mm)
    Housing-to-inner gear—0.0020–0.0035 in. (0.05–0.09mm)
    Housing-to-outer gear—0.0020–0.0043 in. (0.05–0.11mm)

Inspecting oil pump side clearance on 3.0L and 2.4L Axxess engines

Rear Main Bearing Oil Seal

Removal and Installation

EXCEPT AXXESS

1. Disconnect the negative battery cable.
2. Raise and safely support the vehicle. Remove the starter.
3. Remove the transmission from the vehicle.
4. If equipped with a manual transmission, remove the clutch-to-flywheel bolts and the clutch assembly from the vehicle.
5. Remove the flywheel-to-crankshaft bolts and the flywheel from the engine.
6. Remove the rear oil seal retainer-to-engine bolts, the rear oil seal retainer-to-oil pan bolts and the retainer.
7. Carefully pry the rear oil seal from the retainer; be careful not to damage the mounting surfaces. Clean the oil seal mounting surfaces.
8. Using an appropriate oil seal installation tool, lubricate the new oil seal lips with engine oil and drive the the seal into the retainer until it seats.
9. To complete the installation, reverse the removal procedures. Start the engine and check for leaks.

AXXESS

1. Disconnect the negative battery cable.
2. Raise and safely support the vehicle. Remove the starter.
3. On 2WD models, remove the halfshafts from the transaxle.
4. On 4WD models, remove the driveshafts and halfshaft from the transaxle/transfer case assembly.
5. Remove the transaxle-to-engine bolts, the transaxle-to-transfer case bolts for 4WD, and lower the transaxle from the vehicle.

Removing the rear oil seal from the retainer; the transmission and flywheel must be removed

6. If equipped with a manual transaxle, remove the clutch-to-flywheel bolts and the clutch assembly from the vehicle.

7. Remove the flywheel-to-crankshaft bolts and the flywheel from the engine.

8. Remove the rear oil seal retainer-to-engine bolts, the rear oil seal retainer-to-oil pan bolts and the retainer.

9. Carefully pry the rear oil seal from the retainer; be careful not to damage the mounting surfaces. Clean the oil seal mounting surfaces.

10. Using an appropriate oil seal installation tool, lubricate the new oil seal lips with engine oil and drive the the seal into the retainer until it seats.

11. To complete the installation, reverse the removal procedures. Start the engine and check for leaks.

TORQUE SPECIFICATIONS

Component	English	Metric
Camshaft sprocket bolt		
2.4L engine	87–116 ft. lbs.	118–157 Nm
3.0L engine	65 ft. lbs	88 Nm
Connecting rod bearing cap bolts		
Step 1	12 ft. lbs.	16 Nm
Step 2	33 ft. lbs.	44 Nm
Crankshaft pulley bolt		
2.4L engine	116 ft. lbs.	157 Nm
3.0L engine	98 ft. lbs.	132 Nm
Crossmember-to-chassis bolts		
2WD	38 ft. lbs.	32 Nm
4WD	31 ft. lbs.	42 Nm
Cylinder Head bolt		
2.4L engine		
Step 1	22 ft. lbs.	29 Nm
Step 2	58 ft. lbs.	78 Nm
Step 3	loosen all bolts	
Step 4	22 ft. lbs.	29 Nm
Step 5	54–61 ft. lbs.	74–83 Nm
3.0L engine		
Step 1	22 ft. lbs.	30 Nm
Step 2	43 ft. lbs.	58 Nm
Step 3	loosen all bolts	
Step 4	22 ft. lbs.	30 Nm
Step 5	40–47 ft. lbs.	54–64 Nm
Step 5 alternate	22 ft. lbs. + 65 degrees	30 Nm + 65 degrees
Engine mount bolts	31 ft. lbs.	42 Nm
Engine-to-transmission		
2.4L engine		
60 and 65mm bolts	36 ft. lbs.	49 Nm
All others	18 ft. lbs.	25 Nm
3.0L engine		
60 and 65mm bolts	36 ft. lbs.	49 Nm
All others	36 ft. lbs.	49 Nm
Exhaust manifold		
2.4L engine	15 ft. lbs.	21 Nm
3.0L engine	16 ft. lbs.	22 Nm
Exhaust pipe-to-exhaust manifold nuts	27 ft. lbs.	36 Nm
Flywheel/flex plate-to-crankshaft bolts		
2.4L engine		
Manual transmission	112 ft. lbs.	152 Nm
Automatic transmission	76 ft. lbs.	103 Nm
3.0L engine	80 ft. lbs.	108 Nm
Intake Manifold		
2.4L engine		
Intake manifold	15 ft. lbs. in 2 steps	21 Nm in 2 steps
Collector	15 ft. lbs. in 2 steps	21 Nm in 2 steps
3.0L engine		
Upper chamber	16 ft. lbs.	22 Nm
Intake manifold		
nuts	20 ft. lbs. in 3 steps	27 Nm in 3 steps
bolts	14 ft. lbs. in 3 steps	20 Nm in 3 steps

TORQUE SPECIFICATIONS

Component	English	Metric
Main bearing cap bolts		
2.4L engine	38 ft. lbs. in 3 steps	52 Nm in 3 steps
3.0L engine	74 ft. lbs. in 3 steps	100 Nm in 3 steps
Oil Pan	60 inch lbs.	7 Nm
Oil pan drain plug	29 ft. lbs.	39 Nm
Oil pump attaching bolts		
2.4L engine	11 ft. lbs.	15 Nm
3.0L engine		
6mm bolts	60 inch lbs.	7 Nm
8mm bolts	12 ft. lbs.	16 Nm
Oil pump cover screws		
2.4L engine	7 ft. lbs.	10 Nm
Rocker arm shafts		
2.4L engine	16 ft. lbs.	22 Nm
3.0L engine	16 ft. lbs.	22 Nm
Lifter guide assembly		
3.0L engine	16 ft. lbs.	22 Nm
Rocker (Valve) Cover	24 inch lbs.	3 Nm
Spark plug	18 ft. lbs.	25 Nm
Starter-to-block bolts	36 ft. lbs.	49 Nm
Thermostat housing		
2.4L engine	72 inch lbs.	8 Nm
3.0L engine	15 ft. lbs.	21 Nm
Throttle body-to-manifold bolts	13 ft. lbs.	18 Nm
Torque converter–to–flywheel bolts	36 ft. lbs.	49 Nm
Transfer case–to–transmission bolts	30 ft. lbs.	41 Nm
Water Pump		
2.4L engine		
6mm bolts	7 ft. lbs.	10 Nm
8mm bolts	12 ft. lbs.	16 Nm
3.0L engine	15 ft. lbs.	21 Nm
Water pump pulley		
2.4L engine	6 ft. lbs.	8 Nm
3.0L engine	15 ft. lbs.	21 Nm

MANUAL TRANSMISSION

For further information, please refer to Chilton's Transmission Service Manual.

Transmission Assembly

Removal and Installation

PICK-UP AND PATHFINDER

1. Disconnect the negative battery cable.
2. Remove the shifter knob and boot and remove the snapring to lift the shift lever out of the transmission. Stuff a rag in the opening to keep dirt out of the transmission.
3. Raise and safely support the vehicle. If equipped, remove the splash pan or skid plate.
4. Remove the starter and drain the oil from the transmission.
5. Matchmark the driveshaft flange at the rear pinion flange and remove the driveshaft. Plug the extension housing opening to prevent dirt from getting in.
6. If equipped with 4WD, matchmark both front driveshaft flanges so the shaft can be installed in the same position. Remove the driveshaft.
7. Disconnect the exhaust pipe from the manifolds and from the catalytic converter and remove the pipe.
8. Disconnect the speedometer cable and the wiring from the transmission.
9. Without disconnecting the hydraulic hose, remove the clutch slave cylinder from the transmission and secure it aside.
10. If equipped with 4WD, the torsion bars must be removed.

   a. Working under the vehicle, measure and record the length of the threads on the torsion bar adjustment. At the front of the bar, pull the boot back and matchmark the bar to the mounting plate. The spline on the bar must be re-installed in the same position on the plate.

   b. Remove the locknut and adjustment nut from both torsion bars. Remove the 3 nuts at the mounting plate and remove the bars. Mark the bars left and right side for proper installation.

   c. Remove the transfer case shift lever assembly from the transfer case.

d. If necessary, the transfer case can be removed at this point so the jack will be available to remove the transmission.

e. If equipped with a 3.0L engine, remove the gusset securing the engine to the transmission.

11. Using a chain hoist, attach it to the engine and lift the engine slightly to take the weight off the mounts. Using an appropriate transmission jack, properly support the transmission and remove the transmission mount and crossmember.

12. Remove the transmission–to–engine bolts and move the transmission back away from the engine. Lower the transmission carefully from the vehicle.

To install:

13. Lightly grease the input shaft splines. On 4WD, apply a silicone sealant to the engine block or rear plate to seal the engine to the transmission.

14. Fit the transmission into place and start all the engine–to–transmission bolts. Make sure the input shaft fits properly into the clutch disc and pilot bearing.

15. Torque the 2.36 in. (60mm) and 2.56 in. (65mm) engine-to-transmission bolts to 36 ft. lbs. (49 Nm).

16. Torque the remaining bolts to 18 ft. lbs. (25 Nm) on the 2.4L engine or 29 ft. lbs. (39 Nm) on the 3.0L engine.

17. Install the crossmember and torque the crossmember-to-chassis bolts to 38 ft. lbs. (52 Nm) on 2WD or 31 ft. lbs. (42 Nm) on 4WD.

18. Install the rear transmission mount bolts, loosen the engine mount bolts, then torque all the mount bolts to 31 ft. lbs. (42 Nm), starting at the rear.

19. If the torsion bars were removed, install them in their original location. Make sure the splines are in their original position and set the adjustment to its original position.

20. If the transfer case was removed, apply silicone sealant to seal the case to the transmission. Install the transfer case and torque the bolts to 30 ft. lbs. (41 Nm). Install the shift lever.

21. When installing the driveshafts, be sure to align the matchmarks. Torque the bolts on the front driveshaft (4WD) to 33 ft. lbs. (44 Nm). On single piece rear driveshafts, torque the bolts to 65 ft. lbs. (88 Nm). On 2 piece driveshafts, torque the bolts to 33 ft. lbs. (44 Nm). Torque the center bearing bracket bolts to 16 ft. lbs. (22 Nm).

22. When installing the exhaust system, use new gaskets and torque the flange bolts to 27 ft. lbs. (36 Nm).

23. Install the remaining components in order of removal and connect the wiring and speedometer cable. Refill the transmission with oil.

VAN

1. Disconnect the negative battery cable.
2. Raise and safely support the vehicle and remove the starter.

Manual transmission shifter system on Van

3. Disconnect the speedometer cable and all wiring from the transmission.

4. Without disconnecting the hydraulic line, remove the clutch release cylinder from the transmission and secure it out of the way.

5. To disconnect the transmission shift linkage without disturbing the adjustments, remove the pin clips and slide the levers off the shafts. Remove the cables and the mounting bracket from the transmission.

6. Matchmark the driveshaft to the differential flange and remove the driveshaft. Plug the transmission opening to prevent oil leakage.

7. Disconnect the exhaust pipe from the manifold and remove the pipe from the catalytic converter.

8. Support the transmission with a jack and support the engine with a second jack and wood under the oil pan.

9. Remove the long rear transmission mount bolt or, if they are easier to reach, remove the bolts that hold the rear transmission mount to the body.

10. Remove the transmission-to-engine bolts, pull the transmission rearward until the pilot shaft is free of the engine and lower the transmission from the vehicle.

To install:

11. Lightly grease the input shaft spline and fit the transmission into place. Make sure the shaft engages the clutch disc properly and that the transmission fits up against the engine evenly.

12. Start all the bolts, then torque the long bolts to 36 ft. lbs. (49 Nm) and the short bolts to 29 ft. lbs. (39 Nm).

13. Install the rear mount. Torque the long bolt to 72 ft. lbs. (98 Nm) and the mount–to–body bolts to 20 ft. lbs. (26 Nm).

14. Install the driveshaft with the matchmarks aligned and torque the bolts to 33 ft. lbs. (44 Nm).

15. Attach the shift cable brackets to the transmission and connect the cables.

16. Use new gaskets to install the exhaust pipe.

17. Install the remaining components and check for proper operation of the shift linkage. Refill the transmission with oil.

Linkage Adjustment

VAN

1. To adjust the selector cable:
   a. Remove the console cover and loosen the adjuster locknut.
   b. Raise and support the vehicle safely.
   c. Working under the vehicle, put the transmission into **3rd** or **4th** gear by moving the shift change lever on the transmission.
   d. From inside the vehicle, adjust the selector cable length using the adjuster.
   e. After adjustment, tighten the locknut and make sure the shifter lever moves smoothly between the 1st–2nd and 3rd–4th gates (side to side).
2. To adjust the shifter cable:
   a. From under the vehicle, loosen the trunnion-to-shift cable locknut.
   b. Remove the shift cable trunnion from the cross shaft.
   c. Make sure the transmission is out of gear.
   d. At the shift lever, insert a 0.160 in. (4mm) pin into the adjustment index hole. This will align the shift lever vertically.
   e. Adjust the shifter cable to align the trunnion with the cross shaft and connect the trunnion. Tighten the locknut.

MANUAL TRANSAXLE

For further information, please refer to Chilton's Transmission Service Manual.

Transaxle Assembly

Removal and Installation

AXXESS

On 4WD models, the left suspension arm and gusset plate must be removed. On all models, the halfshafts must be removed. The torque on the front axle nut is very high and an assistant is required to hold the brake pedal when tightening or loosening it.

1. Disconnect the negative battery cable. Remove the battery and bracket.
2. Remove the air cleaner with the air flow meter.
3. Remove the air duct.
4. Remove the air injection vent (AIR) unit.
5. Remove the slave cylinder-to-transaxle bolts and move the cylinder aside.
6. Remove the clutch hose clamp.
7. Disconnect the speedometer pinion and the position switch connectors.
8. Remove the breather hose clamp.
9. Disconnect the electrical connectors from the starter. Remove the starter-to-transaxle bolts and the starter.
10. Remove the shift control rod and support rod from the transaxle.
11. Raise and safely support the vehicle and drain the transaxle.
12. On 4WD models, matchmark the drive flanges and disconnect the driveshaft from the transfer case. If it is decided that the driveshaft is in the way of engine removal, matchmark the

rear flange and remove the entire driveshaft. Do not disassemble the driveshaft and protect the CV-joint boot when moving the driveshaft.

13. On 4WD models, remove the front exhaust pipe and disconnect the transfer case shift linkage.

14. Make sure the vehicle is securely supported and have an assistant hold the brake pedal. Remove the front axle cotter pin, adjusting cap and washer and loosen the axle nut. The torque is very high: if possible, loosen and tighten this nut with the wheels installed and the vehicle on the ground.

15. Without disconnecting the hydraulic hose, remove the brake calipers and hang them from the body. Do not let the cali-

● M/T TO ENGINE (GUSSET)
⊗ ENGINE (GUSSET)
○ M/T TO STARTER MOTOR

Transaxle–to–engine bolt torque sequence on Axxess with 2WD

- • M/T TO ENGINE (GUSSET)
- ⊗ ENGINE (GUSSET) TO M/T
- ○ TRANSFER TO M/T
- ◐ M/T TO TRANSFER
- ● M/T TO STARTER MOTOR
- ⊕ END PLATE TO ENGINE

Transaxle–to–engine bolt torque sequence on Axxess with 4WD

Remove the suspension arm and the gusset to remove transaxle—Axxess with 4WD

per hang by the hose. Be sure to remove the caliper, pads and carrier as an assembly. Do not remove the sliding pin bolts.

16. Disconnect the tie rod end from the steering knuckle. Turn the knuckle all the way out at the front and use a soft hammer to tap the axle out of the hub.

17. Carefully pry the inner CV-joints from the transaxle and remove the halfshafts. On the right side of 2WD models, remove the intermediate shaft bearing and the shaft.

18. On 4WD models, remove the left side lower suspension arm and the gusset.

19. Position a jack under the engine oil pan and another jack under the transaxle. Do not position the jack under the oil pan drain plug.

20. Remove the transaxle mount–to–body bolt or the transfer case mount and lower the transaxle jack enough to clear the mount. Remove the transaxle-to-engine bolts and move the transaxle away from the engine. Carefully lower it from the vehicle.

To install:

21. Lightly grease the input shaft spline before joining the engine and transaxle. Carefully fit the transaxle into place and start all the bolts.

22. With the transaxle flush against the engine, torque the bolts in the sequence shown.

On 2WD, torque bolts 1, 5 and 6 to 36 ft. lbs. (49 Nm) and bolts 2, 3 and 4 to 30 ft. lbs. (40 Nm).

On 4WD, torque bolts 1, 3, 7 and 8 to 36 ft. lbs. (49 Nm) and bolts 2, 4, 5, 6 and 9 to 30 ft. lbs. (40 Nm).

23. If the mount was removed from the transaxle, install it and torque the bolts to 41 ft. lbs. (55 Nm). Install the transaxle mount bolt and torque it to 58 ft. lbs. (78 Nm).

24. On 4WD, install the suspension arm and gusset plate. Torque the bolts to 108 ft. lbs. (147 Nm).

25. To install the halfshafts:

   a. Carefully insert the inner CV-joint into the differential gear to make sure the splines engage properly.

   b. Push the shaft in to click the circlip into place. Pull out on the halfshaft to make sure the clip is seated.

   c. On 2WD, when installing the right side extension shaft, torque the support bearing bracket bolts to 26 ft. lbs. (35 Nm).

   d. Make sure the outer axle splines are clean and insert the axle into the hub. Connect the tie rod end to the steering knuckle, torque the nut to 29 ft. lbs. (39 Nm) and tighten as required to install a new cotter pin.

   e. Install the washer and nut onto the axle but do not torque the nut yet.

26. Install the brake calipers and torque the carrier bolts to 72 ft. lbs. (97 Nm).

27. Complete the installation of the remaining components. When the vehicle is resting on at least 3 wheels, have an assistant hold the brake pedal and torque the front axle nuts to 231 ft. lbs. (314 Nm). Install the adjusting cap and a new cotter pin. Don't forget to refill the transaxle.

28. Check and/or adjust the front wheel alignment.

CLUTCH

Clutch Assembly

Removal and Installation

1. Disconnect the negative battery cable. Raise and safely support the vehicle.

2. Remove the transmission or the transaxle.

3. Using a piece of chalk, paint or a center punch, mark the clutch assembly-to-flywheel relationship so it can be reassembled in the same position from which it is removed.

4. Using a clutch aligning tool, insert it into the clutch disc hub.

5. Loosen the clutch cover-to-flywheel bolts, a turn at a time in an alternating sequence, until the spring tension is relieved to avoid distorting or bending the clutch cover. Remove the clutch assembly.

6. Inspect the flywheel for scoring, roughness or signs of overheating. Light scoring may be cleaned up with emery cloth,

but any deep grooves or overheating (blue marks) warrant replacement or refacing of the flywheel. If the clutch facings or flywheel are oily, inspect the transmission/transaxle front cover oil seal, the pilot bushing and engine rear seals, etc. for leakage; replace any leaking seals before replacing the clutch.

7. If the crankshaft pilot bushing is worn, replace it. Install it using a soft hammer. The factory supplied part does not have to be oiled, but check the procedure if using an aftermarket part. Inspect the clutch cover for wear or scoring and replace it, if necessary.

NOTE: The pressure plate and spring cannot be disassembled; replace the clutch cover as an assembly.

To install:

8. Inspect the clutch release bearing. If it is rough or noisy, it should be replaced. The bearing can be removed from the sleeve with a puller; this requires a press to install the new bearing. After installation, coat the sleeve groove, the release lever contact

surfaces, the pivot pin/sleeve and the release bearing-to-transmission/transaxle contact surfaces with a light coat of grease. Be careful not to use too much grease, which will run at high temperatures and get onto the clutch facings. Reinstall the release bearing on the lever.

9. Apply a thin coat of grease to the pressure plate wire ring, diaphragm spring, clutch cover grooves and the pressure plate drive bosses.

10. Apply a thin coat of Lubriplate® to the splines in the driven plate. Slide the clutch disc onto the splines and move it back and forth several times. Remove the disc and wipe off the excess lubricant. Be very careful not to get any grease on the clutch facings.

11. Assemble the clutch cover and the clutch plate on the clutch alignment arbor.

12. To complete the installation, align the clutch assembly-to-flywheel alignment marks and install the bolts. Tighten the bolts 1 or 2 turns at a time in a crisscross pattern to avoid distorting the cover. Torque the bolts to 22 ft. lbs. (30 Nm).

13. Install the transmission/transaxle and adjust the pedal height as necessary.

Pedal Height/Free-Play Adjustment

The pedal height is the distance from the top of the clutch pedal to the floor board without the carpet.

The pedal free-play is the distance the clutch pedal pad moves from the released position to the point where resistance is felt.

1. To adjust the pedal height on Pick-Up and Pathfinder:
   a. From under the dash, loosen the pedal stopper locknut.
   b. Turn the pedal stopper until the specified pedal height is obtained: 9.29–9.69 in. (236–246mm) with the 2.4L engine or 8.94–9.33 in. (227–236mm) with the 3.0L engine.
   c. After adjustment, torque the pedal stopper locknut to 16 ft. lbs. (22 Nm).
2. To adjust the pedal height on Axxess:
   a. From under the dash, loosen the pedal stopper locknut.
   b. Turn the pedal stopper until the specified pedal height is obtained: 6.97–7.36 in. (177–187mm).
   c. After adjustment, torque the pedal stopper locknut to 16 ft. lbs. (22 Nm).
3. To adjust the pedal height on the Van, perform the following procedure:
   a. From under the dash, loosen the clutch switch locknut.
   b. Turn the clutch switch until the specified pedal height is obtained: 6.97–7.36 in. (117–187mm).

Clutch pedal on all except Van

c. After adjustment, torque the clutch switch locknut to 11 ft. lbs. (15 Nm).

4. To adjust the pedal free-play, perform the following procedures:
   a. Loosen the clutch pedal, pushrod locknut.
   b. Using a ruler, measure the clutch pedal free-play.
   c. Turn the clutch pedal pushrod to set the free-play at 0.040–0.120 in. (1–3mm).
   d. After adjustment, torque the locknut to 9 ft. lbs. (12 Nm).

Clutch Master Cylinder

Removal and Installation

The master cylinder is attached to a bracket located under the dash.

1. Disconnect the negative battery cable.

Clutch pedal assembly on Van

Clutch master cylinder assembly

2. From under the dash, remove the clevis pin snap pin and pull the clevis pin from the clutch pedal.

3. Disconnect the clutch pedal arm from the pushrod clevis. Remove the dust cover (boot) from the master cylinder body and pushrod. It will not go through the cowl without tearing.

4. Disconnect and plug the hydraulic line from the clutch master cylinder.

NOTE: Take precautions to keep brake fluid from coming in contact with any painted surfaces.

5. Remove the clutch master cylinder.

To install:

6. Installation is the reverse of removal. Torque the clutch master cylinder-to-cowl bolts/nuts to 14 ft. lbs. (19 Nm) on Van or to 9 ft. lbs. 12 Nm) on all others.

7. Bleed the clutch hydraulic system.

Clutch Slave Cylinder

Removal and Installation

1. If necessary, raise and safely support the vehicle.

2. Remove the slave cylinder-to-clutch housing bolts and the pushrod from the shift fork.

3. Disconnect and plug the hydraulic hose from the slave cylinder, then, remove the cylinder from the vehicle.

To install:

4. To install, reverse the removal procedures. Torque the slave cylinder-to-clutch housing bolts to 30 ft. lbs. (40 Nm).

5. Bleed the clutch hydraulic system.

Hydraulic Clutch System Bleeding

1. Check and refill the clutch fluid reservoir to the full mark.

1. Pushrod
2. Dust cover
3. Piston spring
4. Piston
5. Operating cylinder
6. Bleeder screw

Clutch slave cylinder

During the bleeding process, continue to check and replenish the reservoir to prevent the fluid level from getting lower than ½ full.

2. Connect a clear vinyl hose to the bleeder screw on the slave cylinder. Immerse the other end of the hose in a clear jar ½ filled with brake fluid.

3. Have an assistant pump the clutch pedal several times and hold it down. Loosen the bleeder screw slowly.

4. Tighten the bleeder screw and release the clutch pedal gradually. Repeat this operation until the air bubbles disappear from the brake fluid being expelled out through the bleeder screw.

5. When the air is completely removed, securely tighten the bleeder screw and replace the dust cap.

6. Check and refill the master cylinder reservoir as necessary.

7. Depress the clutch pedal several times to check the operation of the clutch and check for leaks.

AUTOMATIC TRANSMISSION

For further information, please refer to Chilton's Transmission Service Manual.

Transmission Assembly

Removal and Installation

PICK-UP AND PATHFINDER

1. Disconnect the negative battery cable.

2. Raise and safely support the vehicle. If equipped, remove the splash pan or skid plate.

3. Remove the starter.

4. Matchmark the driveshaft flange at the rear pinion flange and remove the driveshaft. Plug the extension housing opening to prevent fluid from leaking out.

5. If equipped with 4WD, matchmark both front driveshaft flanges so the shaft can be installed in the same position. Remove the driveshaft.

6. Disconnect the exhaust pipe from the manifolds and from the catalytic converter and remove the pipe.

7. Disconnect the speedometer cable and the wiring from the transmission.

8. Disconnect the selector lever and throttle cables from the transmission.

9. Remove the dipstick tube and disconnect the cooling lines from the transmission.

10. Remove the torque converter housing dust cover. Matchmark the torque converter with the driveplate for reassembly; these are balanced together at the factory. Remove the torque converter-to-driveplate (flywheel) bolts. Use a wrench on

the crankshaft pulley bolt to rotate the crankshaft to expose the hidden torque converter bolts.

11. If equipped with 4WD, the torsion bars must be removed.

a. Working under the vehicle, measure and record the length of the threads on the torsion bar adjustment. At the front of the bar, pull the boot back and matchmark the bar to the mounting plate. The spline on the bar must be re-installed in the same position on the plate.

b. Remove the locknut and adjustment nut from both torsion bars. Remove the 3 nuts at the mounting plate and remove the bars. Mark the bars left and right side for proper installation.

c. Remove the transfer case shift lever assembly from the transfer case.

d. If necessary, the transfer case can be removed at this point.

e. If equipped with a 3.0L engine, remove the gusset securing the engine to the transmission.

12. Using a chain hoist, attach it to the engine and lift the engine slightly to take the weight off the mounts. Using an appropriate transmission jack, properly support the transmission and remove the transmission mount and crossmember.

13. Remove the transmission–to–engine bolts and move the transmission back away from the engine. Lower the transmission carefully from the vehicle.

To install:

14. Use a dial indicator to check the driveplate runout while turning the crankshaft. Maximum allowable runout is 0.020 in. (0.5mm); if beyond specification, replace the driveplate.

15. Measure and adjust how far the torque converter is recessed into the transmission housing. The distance between the

front mounting surface of the transmission and the torque converter-to-driveplate bolt boss should be at least 1.024 in. (26mm).

16. Install the transmission and torque the 4 upper transmission-to-engine bolts to 36 ft. lbs. (49 Nm). Torque to transmission-to-engine gusset bolts to 29 ft. lbs. (39 Nm). Torque the remaining bolts to 18 ft. lbs. (25 Nm) on the 2.4L engine or 29 ft. lbs. (39 Nm) on the 3.0L engine.

17. Install the crossmember and torque the crossmember-to-chassis bolts to 38 ft. lbs. (52 Nm) on 2WD or 31 ft. lbs. (42 Nm) on 4WD.

18. Install the rear transmission mount bolts, loosen the engine mount bolts, then torque all the mount bolts to 31 ft. lbs. (42 Nm), starting at the rear.

19. Align the matchmarks on the driveplate and torque converter, install the bolts and torque to 36 ft. lbs. (49 Nm). Turn the crankshaft after tightening the bolts to make sure there is no binding at the driveplate.

20. If the torsion bars were removed, install them in their original location. Make sure the splines are in their original position and set the adjustment to its original position.

21. If the transfer case was removed, apply silicone sealant to seal the case to the transmission. Install the transfer case and torque the bolts to 30 ft. lbs. (41 Nm). Install the shift lever.

22. When installing the driveshafts, be sure to align the matchmarks. Torque the bolts on the front driveshaft (4WD) to 33 ft. lbs. (44 Nm). On single piece rear driveshafts, torque the bolts to 65 ft. lbs. (88 Nm). On 2 piece driveshafts, torque the bolts to 33 ft. lbs. (44 Nm). Torque the center bearing bracket bolts to 16 ft. lbs. (22 Nm).

23. When installing the exhaust system, use new gaskets and torque the flange bolts to 27 ft. lbs. (36 Nm).

24. Install the remaining components in order of removal and connect the wiring, cooling lines and speedometer cable. Refill the transmission with fluid and adjust as required.

VAN

1. Disconnect the negative battery cable and raise and safely support the vehicle.

2. Disconnect the speedometer cable and all wiring from the transmission. Disconnect the cooling lines. Disconnect the transmission shift linkage without disturbing the adjustments.

3. Matchmark the driveshaft to the differential flange and remove the driveshaft. Plug the transmission opening to prevent oil leakage.

4. Disconnect the exhaust pipe from the manifold and remove the pipe from the catalytic converter.

5. Matchmark the torque converter to the driveplate and remove the torque converter-to-driveplate bolts. Push the torque converter back so it does not fall out.

6. Support the transmission with a jack and support the engine with a second jack and wood under the oil pan.

7. Remove the long rear transmission mount bolt or, if they are easier to reach, remove the bolts that hold the rear transmission mount to the body.

8. Remove the transmission-to-engine bolts, pull the transmission rearward until the pilot shaft is free of the engine and lower the transmission from the vehicle.

To install:

9. Before installing an automatic transmission:

   a. Use a dial indicator to check the driveplate runout while turning the crankshaft. Maximum allowable runout is 0.020 in. (0.5mm); if beyond specifications, replace the driveplate.

   b. Measure and adjust how far the torque converter is recessed into the transmission housing. The distance between the front mounting surface of the transmission and the torque converter-to-driveplate bolt boss should be at least 1.380 in. (35mm).

10. Fit the transmission into place and start all the transmission-to-engine bolts. Torque the long bolts to 36 ft. lbs. (49 Nm), the short bolts to 24 ft. lbs. (32 Nm).

11. Align the matchmarks on the torque converter and driveplate and install the bolts. Torque the bolts to 36 ft. lbs. (49 Nm). Turn the crankshaft to make sure there is no binding at the driveplate.

12. Install the rear mount. Torque the long bolt to 72 ft. lbs. (98 Nm) and the mount-to-body bolts to 20 ft. lbs. (26 Nm).

13. Install the driveshaft with the matchmarks aligned and torque the bolts to 33 ft. lbs. (44 Nm).

14. Attach the shift linkage and the dipstick tube. Connect the wiring and cooling lines.

15. Use new gaskets to install the exhaust pipe.

16. Install the remaining components and check for proper operation of the shift linkage. Refill the transmission with oil.

Shift Linkage Adjustment
PICK-UP AND PATHFINDER
2WD Floor Shift Models

1. Place the shift selector in the **P** position.
2. Raise and safely support the vehicle.
3. From under the vehicle, loosen the shift lever locknuts.
4. Tighten the rear locknut **X** until it touches the trunnion.
5. Pull the selector lever toward the **R** position without pushing the button. Back off the rear locknut **X** a complete revolution, adjust the front locknut **Y** and torque the locknuts to 8.0 ft. lbs. (11 Nm).
6. After adjustment, move the selector lever through the gears to make sure it moves smoothly.

2WD Column Shift Models

1. Place the shift selector in the **P** position.
2. Raise and safely support the vehicle.
3. From under the vehicle, loosen the shift lever locknuts.
4. Tighten the front locknut **A** until it touches the trunnion.

Automatic Pick-Up and Pathfinder with 2WD and floor shift

Automatic Pick-Up and Pathfinder with 2WD and column shift adjustment

5. Pull the selector lever toward the **R** position without pushing the button. Back off the front locknut **A** 2 complete revolutions, adjust the rear locknut **B** and torque the locknuts to 8.0 ft. lbs. (11 Nm).

6. After adjustment, move the selector lever through the gears to make sure it moves smoothly.

4WD Floor Shift Models

1. Place the shift selector in the **P** position.
2. Raise and safely support the vehicle.
3. Remove the console cover.
4. Loosen the turn buckle locknuts.
5. Tighten the turn buckle until it aligns with the inner cable.
6. Pull the selector lever toward the **R** position without pushing the button. Back off the turn buckle a complete revolution, torque the locknuts to 48 inch lbs. (5 Nm).
7. After adjustment, move the selector lever through the gears to make sure it moves smoothly.

VAN

1. Place the shift selector in the **P** position.
2. Raise and safely support the vehicle.
3. From under the vehicle, loosen the shift lever locknuts.
4. Tighten the front locknut **X** until it touches the trunnion.
5. Pull the selector lever toward the **R** position without pushing the button. Back off the front locknut **X** a ¼ revolution, adjust the rear locknut **Y** and torque the locknuts to 9 ft. lbs. (12 Nm).
6. After adjustment, move the selector lever through the ranges to make sure it moves smoothly.

Kickdown Switch Adjustment

PICK-UP AND PATHFINDER WITH 71B TRANSMISSION

A kickdown switch is located inside the vehicle at the upper post of the accelerator pedal. Its purpose is to provide transmission

Automatic Pick-Up and Pathfinder with 4WD

Automatic floor shifter adjustment on Van

Downshift solenoid on Pick-Up and Pathfinder with 71B transmission

downshifting when the accelerator pedal is fully depressed; a click can be heard just before the pedal bottoms out.

With the ignition switch in the **ON** position and the engine **OFF**, when the accelerator pedal is depressed fully, the kickdown switch contacts should be closed and the downshift solenoid activated, emitting a clicking sound. If the components fail to operate in this manner, check for continuity at the switch and then at the solenoid. Replace either of the components as necessary.

Vacuum Modulator Adjustment

PICK-UP AND PATHFINDER

With 71B Transmission

1. Raise and safely support the vehicle.
2. Remove the vacuum modulator from the transmission.
3. Using a depth gauge, measure the **L** depth; be sure the vacuum throttle valve is pushed into the valve body as far as possible.
4. Select the correct length rod and install it into the vacuum modulator.
5. Using a new O-ring, install the modulator into the transmission.

Vacuum diaphragm on Pick-Up and Pathfinder with 71B transmission

Measured depth "L" mm (in)	Rod length mm (in)	Part number
Under 25.55 (1.0059)	29.0 (1.142)	31932-X0103
25.65 - 26.05 (1.0098 - 1.0256)	29.5 (1.161)	31932-X0104
26.15 - 26.55 (1.0295 - 1.0453)	30.0 (1.181)	31932-X0100
26.65 - 27.05 (1.0492 - 1.0650)	30.5 (1.201)	31932-X0102
Over 27.15 (1.0689)	31.0 (1.220)	31932-X0101

Vacuum diaphragm rod selection chart—71B transmission

Throttle Linkage Adjustment
PICK-UP AND PATHFINDER
With RL4R01A Transmission

1. Press the lock plate and move the adjusting tube in the direction **T**.
2. Release the lock plate.
3. Quickly move the throttle drum from P_2-to-P_1.
4. Ensure the throttle wire stroke **L** is within specified range between full throttle and idle; the throttle wire stroke **L** should be 1.50–1.65 in. (38–42mm).

NOTE: Adjust the throttle wire stroke when the throttle wire/accelerator wire is installed. Place marks on the throttle wire to facilitate measuring the wire stroke.

5. If the throttle wire stroke is not adjusted, the following problems may arise:
   a. When full-open position P_1 of the throttle drum is closer to the direction **T**, the kickdown range will greatly increase.
   b. When the full-open position P_1 of the throttle drum is closer to the direction **U**, the kickdown range will not occur.

P_1 (FULL THROTTLE POSITION)
THROTTLE DRUM
DIRECTION U
P_2 (IDLING POSITION)
DIRECTION T
(AT P_1)
L
(AT P_2)
ADJUSTING TUBE
ENGINE SIDE BRACKET
LOCK PLATE
RETURN SPRING
THROTTLE WIRE CASE

Throttle wire adjustment on 1990 Pick-Up and Pathfinder with RL4R10A transmission

"P" RANGE
LOCKNUT Y
LOCKNUT X

View of the throttle wire adjustment—RL2R01A

Neutral Safety Switch Adjustment

The neutral safety switch is located on the transmission shift selector lever. The switch operates the back-up lights and controls the operation of the starter. The starter should only operate when the transmission is in **P** or **N**.

PICK-UP AND PATHFINDER
With 71B Transmission

1. Unscrew the securing nut of the shift selector lever and the switch-to-transmission screws.
2. Position the shift selector to the **N** position (in vertical detent position). Move the switch slightly aside so the screw hole will be aligned with the pin hole of the shift selector lever.
3. Using a 0.080 in. (2mm) diameter alignment pin, place it in the alignment holes of the neutral start switch and the shift selector lever.

NOTE: A No. 47 drill bit will substitute for the pin gauge.

4. Secure the switch body with the screws and pull out the pin.

NOTE: If the neutral safety switch does not perform satisfactorily after adjustment, replace it with a new one.

With "R" Series Transmission

1. Unscrew the securing nut of the shift selector lever and the switch-to-transmission screws.

Neutral safety switch alignment—Pick-Up and Pathfinder with 71B transmission

PIN. DIA.
0.16 IN. (4MM)

Neutral safety switch alignment—Pick-Up and Pathfinder with "R" series transmission

2. Position the shift selector to the **N** position (in vertical detent).

3. Using a 0.16 in. (4mm) diameter alignment pin, place it in the alignment holes of the neutral start switch and the shift selector lever.

4. Secure the switch body with the screws and pull out the pin.

NOTE: If the neutral safety switch does not perform satisfactorily after adjustment, replace it with a new one.

AUTOMATIC TRANSAXLE

For further information, please refer to Chilton's Transmission Service Manual.

Transaxle Assembly

Removal and Installation

AXXESS

On all models, the halfshafts must be removed. The torque on the front axle nut is very high and an assistant is required to hold the brake pedal when tightening or loosening it.

1. Disconnect the negative battery cable. Remove the battery and bracket.
2. Remove the air cleaner with the air flow meter.
3. Remove the air duct.
4. Disconnect the heater hose from the dash panel.
5. Remove the starter.
6. Disconnect the transaxle–throttle control cable from the throttle. The nut towards the cable end is the locknut; mark the position of the adjusting nut and loosen the locknut to disconnect the cable. Disconnect the shifter cable from the transaxle.
7. Disconnect the speedometer cable and all wiring from the transaxle.
8. Raise and safely support the vehicle.
9. Disconnect the exhaust pipe from the manifold and remove the pipe from the catalytic converter.
10. On 4WD models, matchmark the drive flanges and disconnect the driveshaft from the transfer case. If it is decided that the driveshaft is in the way of engine removal, matchmark the rear flange and remove the entire driveshaft. Do not disassemble the driveshaft and protect the CV-joint boot when moving the driveshaft.
11. On 4WD models, remove the transfer case gusset under the intake manifold. Use a long socket extension and work from above the manifold.
12. Make sure the vehicle is securely supported and have an assistant hold the brake pedal. Remove the front axle cotter pin, adjusting cap and washer and loosen the axle nut. The torque is very high, if possible; tighten this nut with the wheels installed and the vehicle on the ground.
13. Without disconnecting the hydraulic hose, remove the brake calipers and hang them from the body. Do not let the caliper hang by the hose. Be sure to remove the caliper, pads and carrier as an assembly. Do not remove the sliding pin bolts.
14. Disconnect the tie rod end from the steering knuckle. Turn the knuckle all the way out at the front and use a soft hammer to tap the axle out of the hub.
15. Carefully pry the right inner CV-joint from the transaxle or transfer case. On the right side of 2WD models, remove the intermediate shaft bearing and the shaft.
16. On 2WD, insert a thin drift pin through the right side of differential and tap the left inner CV-joint out. Be careful not to damage the mate pinion shaft or side gear inside the differential.
17. On 4WD, pry the left CV-joint out the same way as the right.
18. On 4WD models, remove the left side lower suspension arm and the gusset.

19. On 2WD, remove the center frame member and remove the transaxle mount. Reinstall the center member and support the engine with a wood block under the oil pan.
20. Matchmark the torque converter to the driveplate for reassembly and remove the torque converter–to–driveplate bolts. When separating the engine and transaxle, be careful that the torque converter does not fall out.
21. Position a jack under the transaxle, remove the transaxle mount–to–body mount bolts or the transfer case mounts and lower the transaxle jack enough to clear the mount. Remove the transaxle-to-engine bolts and move the transaxle away from the engine. Carefully lower it from the vehicle.

To install:

22. Check the driveplate and mount the torque converter:

   a. Use a dial indicator to check the driveplate runout while turning the crankshaft. Maximum allowable runout is 0.020 in. (0.5mm); if beyond specifications, replace the driveplate.

   b. Measure and adjust how far the torque converter is recessed into the transaxle housing. The distance between the front mounting surface of the transaxle and the torque converter–to–driveplate bolt boss should be at least ¾ in. (19mm).

23. Fit the transaxle into place and start all the engine bolts, then torque them to 33 ft. lbs. (44 Nm).
24. Raise the transaxle to engage the mounts. On 2WD models, remove the center member and install the mounts. When all the mounts and support members are in place, tighten the bolts starting at the rear and working forward. Torque all mount–to–transaxle bolts to 41 ft. lbs. (55 Nm), the mount–to–body bolts to 58 ft. lbs. (78 Nm) and the long mounting bolts to 58 ft. lbs. (78 Nm).
25. Align the matchmarks on the torque converter and driveplate and install the bolts. Torque the bolts to 43 ft. lbs. (59 Nm). Turn the crankshaft to make sure there is no binding at the driveplate.
26. Install the halfshafts:

   a. Carefully insert the inner CV-joint into the differential gear to make sure the splines engage properly.

   b. Push the shaft in to click the circlip into place. Pull out on the halfshaft to make sure the clip is seated.

   c. When installing the right side extension shaft on 2WD models, torque the support bearing bracket bolts to 26 ft. lbs. (35 Nm).

   d. When installing the left side halfshaft on 4WD models, torque the inner CV-joint bolts to 36 ft. lbs. (45 Nm).

   e. Make sure the outer axle splines are clean and insert the axle into the hub. Connect the tie rod end to the steering knuckle and torque the nut to 29 ft. lbs. (39 Nm) and tighten as required to install a new cotter pin.

   f. Install the washer and nut onto the axle but do not torque the nut yet.

27. Install the brake calipers and torque the carrier bolts to 72 ft. lbs (97 Nm).
28. On 4WD models, connect the driveshaft and torque the bolts to 33 ft. lbs. (44 Nm). If the driveshaft was removed, torque the center bearing support bolts to 30 ft. lbs. (41 Nm).
29. When installing the exhaust pipe, use new gaskets and torque the manifold flange nuts to 37 ft. lbs. (50 Nm), the catalytic converter flange bolts to 31 ft. lbs. (42 Nm).

30. Complete the installation of the remaining components. When the vehicle is resting on at least 3 wheels, have an assistant hold the brake pedal and torque the front axle nuts to 231 ft. lbs. (314 Nm). Install the adjusting cap and an new cotter pin.

Shift Linkage Adjustment

1. Remove the center console.
2. Move the selector lever from **P-to-1** range and return to **P**; make sure the lever can move smoothly and without sliding noise. Leave the lever in **P**.
3. At the bottom of the shift lever, loosen both locknuts.
4. Make sure the manual lever on the transaxle is locked into the **P** position.
5. Adjust the rear locknut until it touches the trunnion and tighten both locknuts to 16 ft. lbs. (22 Nm).
6. Move the selector lever from **P** to **1** range; make sure the lever can move smoothly and without sliding noise.
7. Using grease, apply to the contact areas of the selector lever and the select rod.
8. Install the center console.

Throttle Linkage Adjustment

1. Loosen the throttle wire locknuts **A** and **B**.
2. With the throttle drum set at **P₁** (fully open), move the fitting **Q** fully in the **T** direction and tighten the nut **B** in the **U** direction.
3. Loosen the **B** 2¾–3¼ turns in the **T** direction and tighten the **A** nut, securely.
4. Make sure the throttle wire stroke **L** is 1.54–1.69 in. (39–43mm) between full throttle and idle.

NOTE: Adjust the throttle wire stroke when the throttle wire/accelerator wire is installed. Place marks on the throttle wire to facilitate measuring the wire stroke.

5. If the throttle wire stroke is not adjusted, the following problems may arise:
   a. When full-open position **P₁** of the throttle drum is closer to the direction **T**, the kickdown range will greatly increase.
   b. When the full-open position **P₁** of the throttle drum is closer to the direction **U**, the kickdown range will not occur.

Neutral Safety Switch Adjustment

The neutral safety switch is attached to the right, rear side of the cylinder head. The switch operates the back-up lights and controls the operation of the starter. The starter should only operate when the transaxle is in **P** or **N**.
1. Loosen the neutral safely switch-to-engine bolts.
2. Position the shift selector to the **N** position, in the vertical detent.
3. Using a 0.16 in. (4mm) diameter alignment pin, place it in the alignment holes of the neutral start switch and the shift selector lever.
4. Secure the switch body with the screws and pull out the pin.

Throttle linkage adjustment on Axxess with automatic transaxle

Neutral safety switch on Axxess is on the cylinder head

NOTE: If the neutral safety switch does not perform satisfactorily after adjustment, replace it with a new one.

TRANSFER CASE

Transfer Case Assembly

Removal and Installation
EXCEPT AXXESS

1. Disconnect the negative battery cable.
2. Raise and safely support the vehicle. If equipped, remove the splash pan or skid plate.

3. Remove the starter. Drain the oil from both the transmission and the transfer case.
4. Matchmark the driveshaft flange at the rear differential pinion flange and at both front driveshaft flanges. Remove both driveshafts.
5. Disconnect the selector lever assembly from the transfer case.
6. The torsion bars must be removed:

a. Working under the vehicle, measure and record the length of the threads on the torsion bar adjustment.

b. At the front of the bar, pull the boot back and matchmark the bar to the mounting plate. The spline on the bar must be re-installed in the same position on the plate.

c. Remove the locknut and adjustment nut and remove the 3 nuts at the mounting plate to remove each bar. Mark the bars left and right side for proper installation.

7. Using an appropriate transmission jack, properly support the transmission and remove the transmission mount and crossmember.

8. Remove the transfer case–to–transmission bolts and move the unit back away from the transmission.

To install:

9. Clean the mating surfaces and apply a bead of silicone sealant to the transfer case mounting flange.

10. Carfully fit the case into place and start all the mounting bolts. Torque the bolts to 30 ft. lbs. (41 Nm).

11. Install the crossmember and torque the bolts to 58 ft. lbs. (78 Nm). Install the mount bolts and torque to 38 ft. lbs. (52 Nm).

12. Install the driveshafts and make sure to align the matchmarks:

a. On the front driveshaft, torque the bolts to 33 ft. lbs. (44 Nm).

b. On 2 piece rear driveshafts, torque the flange bolts to 33 ft. lbs. (44 Nm) and the center bearing bracket bolts to 16 ft. lbs. (22 Nm).

c. On single piece rear driveshafts, torque the flange bolts to 65 ft. lbs. (88 Nm).

13. Install the selector lever assembly.

14. Install the torsion bars in their original location. Make sure the splines are in their original position and set the adjustment to its original position.

15. Install the remaining components and fill the transfer case and transmission with oil. Check and adjust front suspension height.

AXXESS

The transaxle must be removed to remove the transfer case.

1. Disconnect the negative battery cable.

2. If equipped with a manual transaxle, remove the breather clamp from the transfer case.

⊙ TRANSFER CASE TO TRANSAXLE
⊗ TRANSAXLE TO TRANSFER CASE

Bolt torque sequence for installing transfer case on Axxess

3. Remove the transaxle/transfer case assembly from the vehicle.

4. Remove the transfer case-to-transaxle bolts and the transfer case.

To install:

5. Using multi-purpose grease, lubricate the transaxle's oil seal on the transfer case side.

6. Using sealant, apply it around the ring gear oil seal on the transfer case.

NOTE: Be careful not to damage the transaxle oil seal when inserting the spline portion of the transfer ring gear and placing the shaft into the transaxle.

7. Torque the transfer case-to-transaxle bolts in the correct sequence to 30 ft. lbs. (40 Nm).

8. Install the transaxle and fill the transfer case with oil.

9. Test the vehicle by performing the following procedures:

a. Position the vehicle so all 4 wheels are not touching the ground and are free to turn.

b. Position the transfer case into the 4WD position.

c. Make sure the rear wheels are turning.

NOTE: Never test drive the vehicle with the transfer case in the 2WD position.

DRIVE AXLE

Halfshaft

Removal and Installation

PICK-UP AND PATHFINDER WITH 4WD

The front steering knuckle must be removed to remove the halfshaft.

1. Raise and safely support the vehicle.

2. Have an assistant depress the brake pedal and remove the halfshaft-to-differential flange bolts.

3. Remove the locking hub and front drive clutch assemblies.

4. Remove the steering knuckle with the halfshaft and clamp the knuckle in a vise.

5. Using a hammer and a block of wood, tap the halfshaft from the steering knuckle.

6. Installation is the reverse of removal. Torque the inner halfshaft drive flange bolts to 33 ft. lbs. (44 Nm).

7. Measure halfshaft end-play with a dial indicator against the end of the shaft; it should be 0.004–0.012 in. (0.1–0.3mm).

Endplay can be adjusted with different thickness snaprings avaliable at the dealer.

AXXESS

Front Halfshafts

1. With the hub cap and grease cap removed, have an assistant hold the brake pedal. Remove the front axle cotter pin, adjusting cap and washer and loosen the axle nut. The torque is very high, if possible this nut should be tightened and loosened with the wheels installed and the vehicle on the ground.

2. Raise and safely support the vehicle.

3. Without disconnecting the hydraulic hose, remove the brake calipers and hang them from the body. Do not let the caliper hang by the hose.

4. Disconnect the tie rod end from the steering knuckle. Turn the knuckle all the way out at the front and use a soft hammer to tap the axle out of the hub.

Front halfshaft on 4WD Pick-Up and Pathfinder with 3.0L engine

Front halfshaft on 4WD Pick-Up and Pathfinder with 2.4L engine

5. Carefully pry the right inner CV-joint from the transaxle or transfer case.

6. On 2WD with automatic transaxle, insert a thin drift pin through the right side of differential and tap the left inner CV-joint out. Be carefull not to damage the mate pinion shaft or side gear inside the differential.

7. On all other models, pry the left CV-joint out the same way as the right.

To install:

8. Carefully insert the inner CV-joint into the differential gear to make sure the splines engage properly.

9. Push the shaft in to click the circlip into place. Pull out on the halfshaft to make sure the clip is seated.

10. When installing the right side extension shaft on 2WD models, torque the support bearing bracket bolts to 26 ft. lbs. (35 Nm).

Front halfshaft on 2WD Axxess

11. When installing the left side halfshaft on 4WD models, torque the inner CV-joint bolts to 36 ft. lbs. (45 Nm).

12. Make sure the outer axle splines are clean and insert the axle into the hub. Connect the tie rod end to the steering knuckle and torque the nut to 29 ft. lbs. (39 Nm) and tighten as required to install a new cotter pin.

13. Install the washer and nut onto the axle but do not torque the nut yet.

14. Install the brake calipers and torque the carrier bolts to 72 ft. lbs. (97 Nm).

15. With all 4 wheels on the ground, torque the axle nuts to 231 ft. lbs. (314 Nm). Install the cap and cotter pin and install the grease cap.

Rear Halfshaft

1. Remove the grease cap, the cotter pin and loosen the wheel bearing locknut.

2. Raise and safely support the vehicle.

3. Using a drift and a hammer, lightly separate the halfshaft from the knuckle; be sure to drive it inward.

4. Using shop cloths, cover the halfshaft boots to prevent damaging them.

5. Remove the parallel link-to-knuckle bolt and the radius rods-to-knuckle bolts.

6. Pull the knuckle outward and remove the halfshaft from it.

7. While supporting the halfshaft, use a prybar to separate the halfshaft from the differential.

To install:

8. To install, insert the halfshaft into the differential until the circlip snaps into position.

9. Position the halfshaft into the hub and assemble the rear suspension. Torque the radius rods-to-knuckle bolts to 72 ft. lbs. (98 Nm), the parallel link-to-knuckle bolt to 72 ft. lbs. (98 Nm) and the hub nut to 231 ft. lbs. (314 Nm).

Driveshaft and U-Joints

Removal and Installation

PICK-UP AND PATHFINDER

One Piece Rear Driveshaft

1. Raise and safely support the vehicle.

2. Matchmark the driveshaft flange to the pinion flange on the differential.

3. Remove the flange bolts, lower the driveshaft and pull it from the transmission.

4. Using a clean rag, plug the rear of the transmission to keep the oil from leaking out.

5. To install, insert the sleeve yoke into the transmission, align the matchmarks and fit the driveshaft into place. Torque the driveshaft flange nuts/bolts to 65 ft. lbs. (88 Nm).

Front halfshaft on 4WD Axxess

Two Piece Rear Driveshaft

1. Raise and safely support the vehicle.
2. Matchmark the driveshaft flange to the pinion flange on the differential and to the transmission drive flange.
3. Remove the bolts from both flanges, then remove the bolts from the center bearing flange-to-chassis bracket and lower the driveshaft out of the vehicle.
4. Using a clean rag, plug the rear of the transmission to keep the oil from leaking out.
5. If necessary, separate the front section of the driveshaft from the rear section.
6. To install, align the matchmarks and reverse the removal procedures. Torque as follows:

    Center bearing-to-chassis bolts to 16 ft. lbs. (22 Nm)
    Driveshaft-to-differential flange nuts/bolts
        Model 3S63 — 33 ft. lbs. (44 Nm)
        Model 3S80 — 65 ft. lbs. (88 Nm)
7. If the center bearing was separated from the front driveshaft, torque as follows:

    Companion flange-to-front driveshaft nut — 174–203 ft. lbs. (235–275 Nm)
    Rear driveshaft-to-center bearing flange nuts/bolts
        Model 3S63 — 17–24 ft. lbs. (24–32 Nm)
        Model 3S71H — 29–33 ft. lbs. (39–44 Nm)
        Model 3S80 — 58–65 ft. lbs. (78–88 Nm)

4WD Front Driveshaft

1. Raise and safely support the vehicle.
2. Matchmark the driveshaft flange to the pinion flange on the differential and to the transfer case drive flange.
3. Remove the nuts and bolts and remove the front driveshaft.
4. To install, align the matchmarks and reverse the removal procedures. Torque the all the flange nuts and bolts to 33 ft. lbs. (44 Nm).

VAN

1. Raise and safely support the vehicle.
2. Matchmark the driveshaft flange to the pinion flange on the differential.
3. Remove the flange bolts, lower the driveshaft and pull it from the transmission.
4. Using a clean rag, plug the rear of the transmission to keep the oil from leaking out.
5. To install, insert the sleeve yoke into the transmission, align the matchmarks and fit the driveshaft into place. Torque the driveshaft flange nuts/bolts to 33 ft. lbs. (44 Nm).

AXXESS

With 4WD

1. Raise and safely support the vehicle.

STRUT MOUNTING
INSULATOR
ASSEMBLY

BOUND BUMPER

DUST COVER

COIL SPRING

SUSPENSION MEMBER

REAR STABILIZER

23–31 FT. LBS. (31–42 NM)

87–101 FT. LBS. (118–137 NM)

DIFFERENTIAL MOUNTING
MEMBER

33–40 FT. LBS. (44–54 NM)

23–31 FT. LBS.
(31–42 NM)

72–87 FT. LBS.
(98–118 NM)

DIFFERENTIAL MOUNTING INSULATOR

43–58 FT. LBS. (59–78 NM)

65–80 FT. LBS. (88–108 NM)

DRIVESHAFT

PARALLEL LINK

RADIUS ROD

58–72 FT. LBS. (78–98 NM)

Rear differential and halfshafts on 4WD Axxess

SNAPRING

JOURNAL BEARING

DRIVE SHAFT TUBE

58–65 FT. LBS. (78–88 NM)

SLEEVE YOKE

JOURNAL

Single piece driveshaft used on Pick-Up and Pathfinder, Van similar

WASHER
APPLY A COAT OF MULTI-
PURPOSE LITHIUM GREASE
TO THE END FACE
OF THE CENTER BEARING
AND BOTH SIDES OF THE
WASHER

CENTER BEARING UPPER
MOUNTING BRACKET

LOCKNUT
181–217 FT. LBS. (245–294 NM) – 4WD
174–203 FT. LBS. (235–275 NM) – 2WD

DRIVE SHAFT 2ND TUBE

12–16 FT. LBS.
(16–22 NM)

JOURNAL BEARING

JOURNAL

29–33 FT. LBS. (39–44 NM) – 71H
58–65 FT. LBS. (78–88 NM) – 80B

WASHER

COMPANION FLANGE

29–33 FT. LBS. (39–44 NM) – 71H
58–65 FT. LBS. (78–88 NM) – 80B

CENTER BEARING ASSEMBLY

DRIVE SHAFT
1ST TUBE

CENTER BEARING LOWER
MOUNTING BRACKET

SNAPRING

Two piece driveshaft used on Pick-Up and Pathfinder

GREASING POINT

29–33 FT. LBS. (39–44 NM)

DRIVE SHAFT TUBE

FLANGE YOKE

JOURNAL

JOURNAL BEARING

SNAPRING

29–33 FT. LBS. (39–44 NM)

Front driveshaft used on 4WD Pick-Up and Pathfinder

Three piece driveshaft used on Axxess with 4WD

2. Matchmark the driveshaft flange to the pinion flange on the differential and to the transmission drive flange.

3. Remove the bolts from both flanges, then remove the bolts from the center bearing flange-to-chassis brackets and lower the driveshaft out of the vehicle. Take care to not damage the center CV-joints by bending them too far.

4. Using a clean rag, plug the rear of the transmission to keep the oil from leaking out.

5. If necessary, separate the driveshaft sections for repair or replacement.

6. To install, align the matchmarks and reverse the removal procedures. Torque the flange nuts and bolts to 33 ft. lbs. (44 Nm) and the center bearing bracket bolts to 30 ft. lbs. (41 Nm).

Rear Axle Shaft, Bearing and Seal

Removal and Installation

PICK-UP AND PATHFINDER

Single Rear Wheels

1. Raise and safely support the vehicle and remove the rear wheels.

2. Using a floor jack, support the differential.

3. If equipped with rear drum brakes:
   a. Remove the brake drum.
   b. Disconnect the parking brake cable from the brake shoes.
   c. Disconnect and plug the hydraulic line from wheel cylinder.
   d. Remove the brake shoe assembly.

4. If equipped with rear disc brakes:
   a. Disconnect the parking brake cable from the caliper.
   b. Remove the caliper-to-knuckle bolts and hang the cali-

per from the body on a piece of wire. Do not disconnect the hydraulic line.
   c. Remove the rotor disc.

5. Remove the backing plate nuts.

6. Attach a slide hammer to the wheel lugs and pull the axle shaft/backing plate assembly from the axle housing. Whenever the axle shaft is removed, the oil seal should be replaced.

To install:

7. To replace the wheel bearing, leave the slide hammer attached to the lugs and secure it in a vise with the axle pointing up.
   a. At the rear of the backing plate, unbend and discard the lockwasher.
   b. Using a brass drift and a hammer, loosen and remove the locknut.
   c. Using a shop press, press the axle shaft out of the bearing.
   d. Press the bearing out of the bearing housing.

8. To install the wheel bearing:
   a. Press the new bearing into the housing. Be sure to press only on the outer race of the bearing.
   b. Grease the inside of the bearing housing.
   c. To install a new oil seal, lubricate the seal lips and carefully press it into the bearing housing.
   d. Position the back plate on the bearing housing, support the inner bearing race and press the axle into the bearing.
   e. Grease the flat washer and lockwasher, lay them into place and install the locknut. Torque the locknut to 217 ft. lbs. (294 Nm).
   f. Bend the lockwasher tabs into place.

9. Lubricate the bearing housing and recess in the axle housing with wheel bearing grease. Coat the axle splines with gear oil. Coat the seal surface of the shaft with grease.

10. Install a new axle housing seal behind the shim pack and

WHEEL BEARING LOCKNUT   108–145 FT. LBS. (147–196 NM)

WHEEL BEARING LOCK WASHER

PLAIN WASHER

WHEEL BEARING

WHEEL BEARING OUTER RACE

BEARING SPACER

WHEEL BEARING CAGE

BEARING GREASE SEAL

BAFFLE PLATE

REAR AXLE CASE

FILLER PLUG
43–72 FT. LBS
(59–98 NM)

AXLE SHAFT

DRAIN PLUG
43–72 FT. LBS.
(59–98 NM)

AIR BREATHER

39–46 FT. LBS. (53–63 NM)

25–33 FT. LBS. (34–44 NM)

CASE SEAL

AXLE CASE END SHIM

OIL SEAL TO SEAL LIP

Rear axle assembly on Pick-Up and Pathfinder with single rear wheels

Unbend the lockwasher and remove the locknut, then press the bearing off—Pick-Up and Pathfinder with single rear wheels

install the axle into the housing. Torque the nuts to 46 ft. lbs. (63 Nm) and check the endplay of the axle with a dial indicator.

11. The axle endplay should be 0.0008–0.0059 in. (0.02–0.15mm) when servicing only one axle. When servicing both sides, endplay should be 0.0118–0.0354 in. (0.30–0.90mm) for the first axle, 0.0008–0.0059 in. (0.02–0.15mm) for the second axle. Add or remove shims as required to adjust endplay.

12. Install the remaining components and adjust the brakes as required.

Dual Rear Wheels

1. Raise and safely support the vehicle and remove the rear wheels.

2. Remove the bolts and slide the axle shaft out of the housing. Be prepared to catch the oil that leaks out.

3. Remove the screw to remove the lockwasher and use a pin wrench to remove the locknut. The torque on the locknut is very high, do not use a hammer and drift pin to remove it.

REAR AXLE CASE

FILLER PLUG
43–72 FT. LBS. (59–98 NM)

AIR BREATHER

WHEEL BEARING LOCKNUT
123–145 FT. LBS. (167–196 NM)

OUTER WHEEL BEARING

LOCK WASHER

2.9–3.6 FT. LBS. (4–5 NM)

AXLE SHAFT

62–80 FT. LBS.
(84–108 NM)

25–33 FT. LBS. (34–44 NM)

DRAIN PLUG
43–72 FT. LBS. (59–98 NM)

OIL SEAL TO SEAL LIP

42–55 FT. LBS. (57–75 NM)

INNER WHEEL BEARING

181–217 FT. LBS. (245–294 NM)

GREASE CATCHER

BRAKE DRUM

WHEEL HUB

Rear axle assembly on Pick-Up with dual rear wheels

4. With the locknut off, the brake drum/wheel hub assembly will pull off easily with both bearings inside. Be careful not to drop the outer bearing.

5. Pry the grease seal out of the hub to remove the inner bearing for inspection. The bearing races can be removed from the hub with a hammer and a soft drift pin.

To install:

6. To replace the oil seal, pry the old seal out of the axle housing. Lubricate and carefully install the new seal with an appropriate seal installation tool. Make sure it goes in evenly and bottoms against the seat.

7. Carefully install new bearing races into the hub. Make sure they go in evenly and bottom against the seat.

8. Pack both bearings with grease and install the inner bearing into the hub. Pack some grease into the hub.

9. Lubricate and press the new wheel bearing seal into the hub. Wipe away the excess grease.

10. Slip the hub/brake drum assembly onto the axle and install the outer bearing. Grease the locknut and install it onto the axle housing.

11. To adjust the bearing preload:

a. Use a pin wrench to torque the locknut to 125–145 ft. lbs. (167–196 Nm). Turn the hub in both directions several times while torquing the nut.

b. The new grease may make it stiff but make sure the hub turns smoothly without catching or roughness. Attach a pull scale to one of the wheel studs and measure the pull required to turn the hub.

c. If it is not smooth or if more than 4.7 lbs. of pull is re-

quired to turn the hub, remove the hub and look for improperly installed bearing races or dirt in the bearings.

12. Install the axle shaft and torque the bolts to 55 ft. lbs. (75 Nm).

13. Install the wheels, check the oil level in the axle housing and adjust the brakes as required.

VAN

1. Raise and safely support the vehicle and remove the rear wheels.

2. Using a floor jack, support the differential.

3. Remove the rear brakes:

a. Remove the brake drum.

b. Disconnect the parking brake cable from the brake shoes.

c. Disconnect and plug the hydraulic line from wheel cylinder.

d. Remove the brake shoe assembly.

4. Remove the backing plate nuts.

5. Attach a slide hammer to the wheel lugs and pull the axle shaft/backing plate assembly from the axle housing. Whenever the axle shaft is removed, the oil seal should be replaced.

6. To remove the rear bearing, the bearing collar must be cut off the axle shaft with a cold chisel. Be careful not to damage the axle shaft.

7. Use a press or a bearing puller to pull the bearing housing and bearing off the axle shaft.

To install:

8. Install the bearing spacer with the chamfer facing the axle

OIL SEAL SPACER

OIL SEAL

BEARING COLLAR

BEARING

BEARING SPACER

REAR AXLE BEARING CAGE

AXLE SHAFT

BRAKE DRUM

33–40 FT. LBS.
(44–54 NM)

REAR AXLE CASE

AXLE CASE END SHIM

Rear axle assembly on Van

flange (facing out). Make sure there is no oil or grease on the axle shaft or the other parts.

9. Install the bearing, collar and housing in the correct order and press them onto the axle shaft. Be sure to support the proper bearing race when pressing or the bearing will be damaged.

10. To set the correct bearing clearance:

    a. Use a depth caliper to measure the depth of the outer bearing race in the bearing housing, Dimension **A**.

    b. Remove the shim pack and clean the axle housing flange. Measure the distance between the flange and the end of the axle housing, Dimension **B**.

    c. Subtract **A** from **B**. The difference must be 0–0.004 in. (0–0.1mm). If **A** is larger than **B**, the bearing outer race will be squeezed between the axle housing and the bearing housing and the bearing will wear quickly. Measure the shims and adjust the shim pack as required.

11. Pry the old oil seal out of the axle housing. Lubricate the new oil seal and use an appropriate seal installation tool to make sure it is evenly seated in the housing.

12. Install the axle shaft and torque the bearing housing bolts to 40 ft. lbs. (54 Nm).

13. Install the brakes and bleed and adjust as required.

To remove the rear axle bearing on Van, the bearing collar must be cut

Measure the bearing clearance when installing Van rear axle shaft

Front Wheel Hub, Knuckle and Bearings

Removal and Installation

PICK-UP AND 1988 PATHFINDER WITH 2WD

1. Raise and safely support the vehicle and remove the front wheels.

2. Disconnect the brake hose from the bracket on the knuckle.
3. Without disconnecting the hydraulic line, remove the brake caliper and hang it from the body on a wire. Do not let it hang by the hose.
4. Remove the wheel hub cup, the cotter pin, the adjusting cap and hub nut.
5. Remove the wheel hub and brake disc assembly. Be careful not to drop the outer wheel bearing.

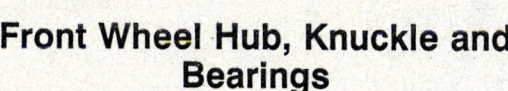

KNUCKLE SPINDLE

58–108 FT. LBS. (78–147 NM) TO UPPER BALL JOINT

87–141 FT. LBS. (118–191 NM) TO LOWER BALL JOINT

53–72 FT. LBS. (72–97 NM) TO KNUCKLE ARM

2.4–3.2 FT. LBS. (3.2–4.3 NM)

GREASE SEAL

INNER WHEEL BEARING

WHEEL HUB (INNER SIDE)

OUTER WHEEL BEARING

WASHER

BEARING SPACER

BAFFLE PLATE

36–51 FT. LBS. (49–69 NM)

ROTOR DISC

WHEEL BEARING LOCKNUT

WHEEL BEARING LOCKNUT CAP

COTTER PIN

WHEEL HUB CAP

Front wheel bearing on Pick-Up and 1988 Pathfinder with 2WD

ROTOR DISC

WHEEL HUB

36–51 FT. LBS. (49–69 NM)

0.9–1.2 FT. LBS. (1.2–1.6 NM)

Auto-lock free-running hub

AUTO-LOCK FREE-RUNNING
HUB ASSEMBLY

18–25 FT. LBS. (25–34 NM)

GREASE SEAL "A"

INNER BEARING

OUTER BEARING

WHEEL BEARING LOCKNUT

SNAPRING

LOCK WASHER

DRIVE CLUTCH

SNAPRING

Manual-lock free-running hub

MANUAL-LOCK FREE-RUNNING
HUB SUB-ASSEMBLY

HALFSHAFT ASSEMBLY

GREASE SEAL "C"

SPACER

NEEDLE BEARING

KNUCKLE

GREASE SEAL "B"

BAFFLE PLATE

2.5–3.6 FT. LBS. (3.4–4.9 NM)

Front wheel bearing and hub assembly on 1989–92 Pathfinder and all Pick-Up and Pathfinder with 4WD

6. To remove the inner bearing, pry out the grease seal. Discard the seal.

7. To remove the knuckle, remove the cotter pins from the upper and lower ball joint nuts and the tie rod nut. Remove the tie rod nut and loosen the ball joint nuts but do not remove them yet.

8. Place a jack under the lower suspension arm. The arm is connected to the torsion bar and will spring down if not supported.

9. Use a ball joint press and disconnect the tie rod end and upper and lower ball joints. Remove the front spindle.

To install:

10. Install the spindle and start all the nuts. Torque the lower ball joint nuts to 141 ft. lbs. (191 Nm) and the upper ball joint nuts to 108 ft. lbs. (147 Nm). Install new cotter pins.

11. Make sure the bearings are clean and in good condition. Pack the bearings and the hub with new grease and install the bearings into the hub. Install a new grease seal.

12. Make sure the spindle is clean. Install the spacer with the chamfer facing in on the spindle.

13. Lightly grease the lips on the seal and slide the hub and bearings onto the spindle. Install the washer and nut and adjust the pre-load on the bearing. Check and adjust front wheel alignment.

1989–92 PATHFINDER AND ALL 4WD

With the exception of the front locking hubs, the front wheel bearings are the same on 1989–92 Pathfinder as on all 4WD models.

1. Raise and safely support the vehicle and remove the front wheels.

2. Have an assistant hold the brake pedal and loosen the locking front hub housing bolts. Remove the hub assembly housing, the snapring and the hub assembly.

3. Without disconnecting the hydraulic line, remove the brake caliper and hang it from the body with wire. Do not allow the caliper to hang by the hose.

4. Remove the locking screw and remove the lock washer. Use a pin wrench to loosen the wheel bearing locknut. The torque may be fairly high, do not use a hammer and drift pin.

5. Remove the locknut and pull the hub off with the bearings. Pry the inner grease seal out to remove the inner bearing. Discard the seal.

6. Use a block of wood and hammer to tap on the end of the halfshaft to break it loose from the hub spline.

7. To remove the knuckle, remove the cotter pins from the upper and lower ball joint nuts and the tie rod nut. Remove the tie rod nut and loosen the ball joint nuts but do not remove them yet.

8. Place a jack under the lower suspension arm. The arm is connected to the torsion bar and will spring down if not supported.

9. Use a ball joint press and disconnect the tie rod end and upper and lower ball joints. Remove the front spindle.

To install:

10. Clean all parts of grease and check the condition of the bearings. If bearings are to be replaced, the inner races can be removed from the hub with a hammer and soft drift pin. Be careful not to damage the hub.

11. Install the spindle and start all the nuts. Torque the lower ball joint nuts to 141 ft. lbs. (191 Nm) and the upper ball joint nuts to 108 ft. lbs. (147 Nm). Install new cotter pins.

12. Connect the tie rods and torque the nuts to 72 ft. lbs. (98 Nm). Install new cotter pins.

13. Carefully install the new inner races with the drift pin, making sure they seat in the hub.

14. Pack the bearings with new grease and pack grease into the hub. Install the inner bearing and press a new inner seal into the hub.

15. Slip the hub assembly onto the spindle and install the out-

er bearing. Grease the locknut, thread it into place and set the bearing pre-load. Check and adjust front wheel alignment.

Bearing Pre-load Adjustment

PICK-UP AND 1988 PATHFINDER WITH 2WD

1. With the bearings and hub properly cleaned and lubricated, install the nut and torque it to 25 ft. lbs. (34 Nm).

2. Spin the hub several times in both directions, then torque the nut to 29 ft. lbs. (39 Nm).

3. Loosen the nut 45 degrees. Install the locknut cap and a new cotter pin.

1989–92 PATHFINDER AND ALL 4WD

1. Use a pin wrench to torque the locknut to 58–72 ft. lbs. (78–98 Nm). Turn the hub in both directions several times while torquing the nut.

2. Loosen the locknut, then torque again to 13 inch lbs. (1.5 Nm).

3. Turn the hub several times and check the nut torque again.

4. Install the lock washer. When installing the screw, make sure the locknut turns no more than 30 degrees in either direction.

5. When bearing pre-load is properly set, there will be no endplay in the hub and it will require no more than 4.7 lbs. of pull at the wheel stud to turn the hub.

6. Install the locking hub and the brake caliper. Torque the caliper carrier bolts to 72 ft. lbs. (98 Nm) and the hub bolts to 25 ft. lbs. (34 Nm).

VAN

1. With the vehicle on the ground, remove the hub cap and loosen the wheel bearing locknut. The torque on this nut is high enough to cause the vehicle to fall off the supports.

2. Raise and safely support the vehicle and remove the wheels.

3. Without disconnecting the hydraulic line, remove the brake caliper and hang it from the body with wire. Do not allow the caliper to hang by the hose.

4. Remove the locknut and lock washer and pull the hub and disc assembly off.

5. To remove the bearing, remove the circlip and press the bearing out of the hub. Discard the bearing.

6. To remove the knuckle, remove the cotter pins and disconnect the tie rod ends.

7. Place a jack under the lower suspension arm, remove the cotter pins and loosen the ball joint nuts.

8. Press the upper ball joint out of the knuckle first, reinstall the nut finger tight to hold the knuckle in place, then press out the lower ball joint. Remove the nut and remove the knuckle.

To install:

9. Make sure the ball joint tapered studs are clean and dry. Use a floor jack to hold the lower suspension arm up and fit the knuckle to the ball joints. Install both nuts.

10. Torque the upper ball joint nut to 72 ft. lbs. (98 Nm), then torque the lower ball joint nut to 141 ft. lbs. (191 Nm). Install new cotter pins.

11. Connect the tie rod end and torque the nut to 72 ft. lbs. (98 Nm). Install new cotter pins.

12. When pressing the new bearing into the hub, be sure to press only on the outer race or the bearing will be damaged. Make sure the lips of the grease seal on the bearing face the circlip.

13. Install a new circlip and lightly grease the lips of the seal.

14. Install the hub, lock washer and locknut onto the spindle. Do not fully tighten the locknut yet.

15. Install the brake caliper and wheel and lower the vehicle to the ground.

Front wheel bearing assembly on Van

16. With the vehicle on all 4 wheels, torque the locknut to 260 ft. lbs. (353 Nm). Install the hub cap. Check and adjust front wheel alignment.

AXXESS

1. With the vehicle on the ground, remove the hub cap, cotter pin, adjusting cap and insulator and loosen the wheel bearing locknut. The torque on this nut is high enough to cause the vehicle to fall off the supports.

2. Raise and safely support the vehicle and remove the wheels.

3. Without disconnecting the hydraulic line, remove the brake caliper and hang it from the body with wire. Do not allow the caliper to hang by the hose.

4. Remove the wheel bearing locknut and washer and hold a piece of wood against the axle. Tap the wood with a hammer to loosen the axle spline in the hub.

5. To remove the knuckle, remove the cotter pin and disconnect the tie rod end. Matchmark the adjusting pin to the strut and remove the knuckle-to-strut bolt and the lower ball joint nut. Use a ball joint press to separate the joint.

6. To remove the bearing from the knuckle:
   a. Pry out the seal and press the hub out of the bearing with a hydraulic press. The inner bearing race will probably stay on the hub.
   b. Remove the snaprings and press the bearing out towards the halfshaft side of the knuckle. Be careful not to bend the brake backing plate. Discard the bearing.

To install:

7. Carefully inspect the hub for signs of wear or cracks. If the bearing has been replaced before and seems to have failed early, the hub is distorted and should be replaced.

8. With all parts clean and dry, install the inner snapring and press the new bearing into the knuckle. Be sure to press only on the outer race or the bearing will be damaged.

9. Install the outer snapring. Pack the new grease seals with clean grease and install them.

10. Press the hub into the inner race. Be sure the inner race is properly supported or the bearing will be damaged. While the hub and bearing are still clamped in the press, turn the knuckle to make sure it turns smoothly on the bearing.

11. Make sure the halfshaft splines are clean and install the knuckle. With the adjusting pin matchmarks aligned, torque the knuckle-to-strut bolt to 91 ft. lbs. (124 Nm) and the lower ball joint nut to 64 ft. lbs. (86 Nm). Tighten as required to install a new cotter pin.

FRONT

KNUCKLE

BAFFLE PLATE

82–91 FT. LBS. (112–124 NM)

HALFSHAFT

INNER GREASE SEAL

SNAPRING

WHEEL BEARING ASSEMBLY

SNAPRING

WHEEL BOLT

OUTER GREASE SEAL

WHEEL HUB

PLAIN WASHER

WHEEL BEARING LOCKNUT
174–231 FT. LBS. (235–314 NM)

INSULATOR

DISC ROTOR

ADJUSTING CAP

COTTER PIN

WHEEL NUT
72–87 FT. LBS. (98–118 NM)

Front wheel bearing and knuckle on Axxess

12. Connect the tie rod end, torque the nut to 29 ft. lbs. (39 Nm) and tighten as required to install a new cotter pin.

13. Install the brake caliper and torque the carrier bolts to 72 ft. lbs. (97 Nm). Install the wheel and lower the vehicle. Do not roll the vehicle before tightening the wheel bearing locknut.

14. With the vehicle on all 4 wheels, install the washer and wheel bearing locknut and torque the nut to 231 ft. lbs. (314 Nm). Install the adjusting cap and a new cotter pin. Check and adjust front wheel alignment.

Rear Wheel Hub, Knuckle and Bearings

Removal and Installation
AXXESS
2WD Models
The rear knuckle and wheel spindle are a part of the rear strut

KNUCKLE SPINDLE

BAFFLE PLATE

WHEEL HUB BEARING

WASHER

FRONT

28–38 FT. LBS. (38–52 NM)

WHEEL BEARING LOCKNUT
137–188 FT. LBS. (186–255 NM)

COTTER PIN

HUB CAP

Rear wheel bearing on 2WD Axxess is part of the hub

HALFSHAFT

INNER GREASE SEAL

SNAPRING

KNUCKLE

BAFFLE PLATE

WHEEL BEARING ASSEMBLY

SNAPRING

OUTER GREASE SEAL

WHEEL HUB

WASHER

28–38 FT. LBS. (38–52 NM)

WHEEL BEARING LOCKNUT
174–231 FT. LBS. (235–314 NM)

INSULATOR

ADJUSTING CAP

COTTER PIN

Rear wheel bearing on 4WD Axxess is similar to front

and must be replaced as an assembly. The wheel bearing lock-nut torque is very high; loosen and tighten this nut with the vehicle on the ground.

1. Remove the hub cap and cotter pin.
2. Apply the brakes and loosen the wheel bearing locknut.
3. Raise and safely support the vehicle, remove the wheel.
4. Remove the wheel bearing nut, washer and wheel hub. The bearing is part of the hub and cannot be replaced separately.

To install:

5. Install the hub, washer and locknut. Do not fully tighten the locknut yet.
6. With the vehicle on all 4 wheels, torque the bearing locknut to 188 ft. lbs. (255 Nm). Install a new cotter pin.

4WD Models

1. The wheel bearing locknut torque is very high; loosen and tighten this nut with the vehicle on the ground. Remove the hub cap, cotter pin, the adjusting cap and insulator.
2. Apply the brakes and loosen the wheel bearing locknut.
3. Raise and safely support the vehicle and remove the wheel.
4. Remove the wheel bearing nut and washer.
5. Disconnect the hydraulic line from the wheel cylinder and parking brake cable from the brake shoes.
6. Using shop cloths, cover the halfshaft boots.
7. Using a mallet, tap in on the halfshaft to loosen it from the wheel hub.
8. Remove the radius rods-to-knuckle bolts and the parallel link-to-knuckle bolt.
9. Support the knuckle and remove the strut-to-knuckle nuts and bolts. Remove the knuckle assembly from the vehicle and position the assembly in a vise.
10. Using a piece of pipe and a hammer, drive the wheel hub from the knuckle. The inner bearing race will probably stay on the hub. Use a press and a bearing puller to remove it.
11. Remove the inner and outer snaprings and use the press to remove the bearing.

To install:

12. Carefully inspect the hub for signs of wear or cracks. If the bearing has been replaced before and seems to have failed early, the hub is distorted and should be replaced.
13. With all parts clean and dry, install the inner snapring and press the new bearing into the knuckle. Be sure to press only on the outer race or the bearing will be damaged.
14. Install the outer snapring. Pack the new grease seals with clean grease and install them. Install the brake backing plate.
15. Press the hub into the inner race, do not exceed 3 tons pressure. Be sure the inner race is properly supported or the bearing will be damaged. While the hub and bearing are still clamped in the press, turn the knuckle to make sure it turns smoothly on the bearing.
16. When installing the knuckle, be sure the halfshaft spline is clean and insert it into the wheel hub. Torque the knuckle-to-strut bolts to 91 ft. lbs. (124 Nm) and the remaining knuckle mounting bolts to 72 ft. lbs. (98 Nm).
17. Install the parking brake cable and the pressure line to the wheel cylinder. Install the wheel bearing locknut but do not fully tighten it yet.
18. With all 4 wheels on the ground, torque the wheel hub locknut to 231 ft. lbs. (314 Nm).
19. Check and adjust rear wheel alignment and bleed and adjust the rear brakes.

Manual Locking Hubs

Removal and Installation

1. Raise and safely support the vehicle and remove the wheels.
2. Set the knob of the manual lock to the **FREE** position.
3. Have an assistant hold the brake pedal and use a Torx® wrench to remove the locking hub housing bolts.

Manual locking hubs used on 4WD Pick-Up and Pathfinder

4. Remove the snapring to disassemble the drive clutch.
5. Installation is the reverse of removal. Make sure the parts are clean and lubricated with new grease. With the hub in the **FREE** position, torque the bolts to 25 ft. lbs. (34 Nm).

Automatic Locking Hubs

Removal and Installation

1. Raise and safely support the vehicle and remove the wheels.
2. Set the knob of the manual lock to the **FREE** position.
3. Have an assistant hold the brake pedal and use a Torx® wrench to remove the locking hub housing bolts.
4. Remove the snapring to disassemble the drive clutch.
5. Installation is the reverse of removal. Make sure the parts are clean and lubricated with new grease. With the hub in the **FREE** position, torque the bolts to 25 ft. lbs. (34 Nm).

Pinion Seal

Removal and Installation
PICK-UP AND PATHFINDER

The pinion oil seal on Models H190A, H233B and C200 differentials can not be replaced without disassembling the differential. A collapsible spacer is used to set pinion bearing pre-load.

1. Raise and safely support the vehicle.
2. Remove the driveshaft.
3. Using a socket wrench and the differential flange holding tool, hold the differential flange and the remove the differential pinion nut.
4. Using a wheel puller tool, pull the pinion flange from the differential.
5. Using a small prybar, pry the oil seal from the differential.
6. Using the oil seal driver tool (Model R180A and H190A differentials), lubricate the new oil seal lips with multi-purpose grease and drive the new seal into the differential housing until it is flush with the end of the housing.
7. Using a soft hammer, tap the pinion flange onto the pinion shaft.
8. Using a socket wrench and the differential flange holding tool (Model H233B), hold the differential flange and torque the pinion flange nut as follows:

Model R180 – 123–145 ft. lbs. (166–196 Nm)
Model R190A – 94–217 ft. lbs. (127–294 Nm)
Model H233B – 145–181 ft. lbs. (196–245 Nm)

9. Check the oil level in the differential and install the driveshaft and wheels.

VAN

1. Raise and safely support the vehicle. Remove the driveshaft.
2. Using a socket wrench and the differential flange holding tool, hold the differential flange and the remove the differential pinion nut.

Automatic locking hubs used on 4WD Pick-Up and Pathfinder

Labels in figure: SCREW 0.9–1.2 FT. LBS. (1.2–1.6 NM); HALFSHAFT; WHEEL BEARING LOCKNUT; LOCKWASHER; BRAKE "B"; WASHER "A"; WASHER "B"; SNAPRING; BRAKE "A"; SPRING; O-RING; 18–25 FT. LBS. (25–34 NM); HOUSING (WITH SUB-ASSEMBLY); AUTO-LOCK FREE-RUNNING HUB ASSEMBLY

3. Using a wheel puller tool, pull the pinion flange from the differential.

4. Using a small prybar, pry the oil seal from the differential.

5. Using the oil seal driver tool, lubricate the new oil seal lips with multi-purpose grease and drive the new seal into the differential housing until it is flush with the end of the housing.

6. Using a soft hammer, tap the pinion flange onto the pinion shaft.

7. Using a socket wrench and the differential flange holding tool, hold the differential flange and torque the pinion flange nut to 94 ft. lbs.

8. Turn the pinion flange, in both directions, several times to set the bearings. Using a small torque wrench, measure the pinion preload; it should be 9.5–14.8 inch lbs. (1–1.7 Nm). If the preload value is not obtained, repeat the pinion torquing procedure.

9. Check the oil level in the differential and install the driveshaft and wheels.

AXXESS

4WD Models

1. Raise and safely support the vehicle.
2. Remove the driveshaft.
3. Using a spanner wrench and a socket wrench, remove the drive pinion nut.
4. Using a wheel puller tool, press the companion flange from the differential.
5. Using an oil seal remover tool, press the oil seal from the differential.

To install:

6. Using a new oil seal, lubricate it with multi-purpose grease.
7. Using an oil seal installation tool, drive the new oil seal into the differential.
8. Install the companion flange and torque the drive pinion nut to 123–145 ft. lbs. (167–196 Nm).
9. Install the driveshaft and lower the vehicle.

Differential Carrier

Removal and Installation

PICK-UP AND PATHFINDER (4WD)

Front

1. Raise and safely support the vehicle. Drain the differential.

When removing the front differential from 4WD Pick-Up and Pathfinder, remove the crossmember

Label in figure: DIFFERENTIAL MOUNTING MEMBER

2. Matchmark and disconnect the front halfshafts from the front differential.

3. Matchmark the front driveshaft to the flanges and remove the driveshaft.

4. Attach a chain hoist to the engine, remove the front engine mount bolts and raise the engine slightly.

5. Remove the differential crossmember-to-chassis bolts and lower the differential with the crossmember as an assembly.

To install:

6. Fit the differential without the crossmember into place and start all the bolts. Torque all nuts and bolts to 64 ft. lbs. (87 Nm) in the following sequence to avoid excess vibration:

    a. First tighten the differential mounts to the frame.

    b. Tighten the 2 long differential mount bolts.

    c. Install the crossmember and tighten the differential mount bolts.

    d. Tighten the crossmember mount bolts.

7. Install the front driveshaft and halfshafts, making sure to align the matchmarks.

Rear

EXCEPT MODELS C200 DIFFERENTIAL

1. Raise and safely support the vehicle.

43–58 FT. LBS. (59–78 NM)

DIFFERENTIAL CROSSMEMBER

AIR BREATHER

43–58 FT. LBS. (59–78 NM)

FILLER PLUG

43–72 FT. LBS. (59–98 NM)

DRAIN PLUG

43–72 FT. LBS. (59–98 NM)

HALFSHAFT

REAR DIFFERENTIAL GEAR ASSEMBLY

43–58 FT. LBS. (59–78 NM)

DIFFERENTIAL MOUNTING INSULATOR

Rear differential assembly on Axxess with 4WD

2. Matchmark the driveshaft to the differential flange and remove the driveshaft.

3. Drain all fluid from the differential carrier and remove the axle shafts.

4. Remove the differential carrier-to-axle housing bolts and remove the carrier.

5. Installation is the reverse of removal. Be sure the gasket is correctly installed and torque the bolts to 18 ft. lbs. (25 Nm).

6. Install the remaining components and fill the differential with oil.

AXXESS

A differential carrier is used only with 4WD models.

1. Raise and safely support the vehicle.

2. Matchmark and disconnect the driveshaft. Remove the halfshafts.

3. Disconnect the breather hose from the differential carrier.

4. Using a floor jack, support the differential carrier.

5. Remove the all differential mounting bolts, move it forward to clear the rear mount, then lower it and move it back to clear the crossmember.

To install:

6. Installation is the reverse of removal. Torque the mounting bolts to 58 ft. lbs. (78 Nm).

7. Install the halfshafts, connect the driveshaft and fill the differential with oil.

Axle Housing

Removal and Installation

PICK-UP

1. Block the front wheels.

2. Raise and safely support the vehicle. Using a floor jack, position it under the differential and support its weight.

3. Remove the rear wheel/tire assemblies.

4. Matchmark the driveshaft to the differential flange and remove the driveshaft.

5. If equipped with drum brakes, remove the brake drum and disconnect the parking brake cable from the brake assembly. If equipped with disc brakes, disconnect the parking brake cable from the caliper.

6. Disconnect and plug the brake hydraulic lines from the wheel cylinders or calipers. Disconnect the brake line from the retaining clips.

7. Disconnect the shock absorber from the lower mount.

8. On vehicles with 2WD, remove all 4 leaf spring mount bolts and remove the axle housing and leaf springs together. Remove the U-bolts to remove the springs from the axle housing.

9. On vehicles with 4WD, remove the nuts from the U-bolts and lower the axle housing away from the leaf springs.

To install:

10. Raise the axle housing into position and start all the mounting bolts and nuts.

11. On 2WD vehicles, torque the rear leaf spring mount nuts to 50 ft. lbs. (68 Nm), then the front mount nuts to 72 ft. lbs. (98 Nm).

12. On 4WD vehicles, torque the U-bolt nuts to 72 ft. lbs. (98 Nm).

13. Connect the shock absorbers to the lower mounts and torque the nut to 30 ft. lbs. (40 Nm).

14. Connect the brake parking cable and hydraulic line and bleed and adjust the brakes.

15. Install the driveshaft with the matchmarks aligned.

PATHFINDER AND VAN

1. Raise and safely support the vehicle and remove the rear wheels.

2. Using a floor jack, position it under the differential and support its weight.

3. Matchmark the driveshaft to the differential flange and remove the driveshaft.

4. Remove the brake drum and disconnect the parking brake cable from the brake assembly.

5. Disconnect and plug the main brake line from the differential junction block.

6. Disconnect the stabilizer bar from the axle housing and from the body and remove the stabilizer bar.

7. Disconnect the shock absorber from its upper mount. On Van, the mounting nuts are inside the vehicle.

8. Remove the panhard rod-to-chassis nut/bolt and lower the rod.

9. Remove the upper and lower links-to-chassis nuts/bolts, then separate the links from the chassis supports.

37–50 FT. LBS. (50–68 NM)

22–30 FT. LBS. (30–40 NM)

12–16 FT. LBS. (16–22 NM)

37–50 FT. LBS. (50–68 NM)

FRONT

Rear axle housing on Pick-Up with 4WD; with 2WD, the leaf springs must be removed to remove the axle housing

UPPER SPRING SEAT

COIL SPRING

SHOCK ABSORBER

BOUND BUMPER

12–16 FT. LBS. (16–22 NM)

80–108 FT. LBS. (108–147 NM)

PANHARD ROD

22–30 FT. LBS. (30–40 NM)

36–51 FT. LBS. (49–69 NM)

LOWER SPRING SEAT

22–30 FT. LBS. (30–40 NM)

STABILIZER BAR

19–24 FT. LBS. (25–32 NM)

STABILIZER BAR CONNECTING ROD

32–41 FT. LBS. (43–55 NM)

80–108 FT. LBS. (108–147 NM)

UPPER LINK

LOWER LINK

80–108 FT. LBS. (108–147 NM)

80–108 FT. LBS. (108–147 NM)

80–108 FT. LBS. (108–147 NM)

19–24 FT. LBS. (25–32 NM)

Rear axle housing removal on Van, Pathfinder similar

10. Lower the axle housing and remove the coil springs.

To install:

11. Raise the axle housing into position and start all the mounting nuts and bolts.

12. Lower the vehicle to the ground, bounce the vehicle several times and torque all nuts and bolts as shown.

13. Connect the brake cable and hydraulic line and bleed and adjust the brakes.

14. Install the driveshaft.

STEERING

Steering Wheel

Removal and Installation

1. Position the steering wheel in the straight-ahead position.
2. Disconnect the negative battery cable.
3. Remove the horn pad by removing the screws from the rear of the steering wheel crossbar.
4. Matchmark the top of the steering column shaft and the steering wheel flange.
5. Remove the attaching nut and remove the steering wheel with a puller.

NOTE: Do not strike the shaft with a hammer, the steering column may collapse.

To install:

6. Install the steering wheel so the punchmarks are aligned. Torque the steering wheel nut to 22–29 ft. lbs. (29–39 Nm).
7. Install the horn pad and connect the negative battery cable.

Manual Steering Gear

Removal and Installation

EXCEPT AXXESS

1. Raise and safely support the vehicle.
2. Remove the steering gear-to-rubber coupling bolt.
3. Matchmark the pitman arm and sector shaft and with the wheels in a straight-ahead position, remove the idler arm-to-sector shaft nut.
4. Using the steering gear arm puller tool, press the arm from the steering gear.
5. Remove the steering gear-to-chassis bolts and the steering gear from the vehicle.
6. To install, reverse the removal procedures. Torque as follows:

    Steering gear-to-coupling bolt—17–22 ft. lbs. (24–29 Nm)
    Steering gear-to-pitman arm nut—94–108 ft. lbs. (127–147 Nm)
    Steering gear-to-frame bolts—62–71 ft. lbs. (84–96 Nm)

Adjustment

WORM GEAR PRELOAD

For this procedure, the steering gear must be removed from the vehicle and placed in a vise.

1. Using the locknut wrench tool, loosen the locknut.
2. Rotate the worm shaft a few times, in both directions, to settle the worm bearing and check the preload.
3. Using the adjusting plug wrench, the torque wrench and an adapter socket, check the worm bearing preload; it should be 1.7–5.2 inch lbs. (0.20–0.59 Nm).
4. To adjust the worm gear preload, turn the adjusting plug with the special pin wrench and recheck the preload.
5. With the worm gear preload set, hold the adjusting plug and tighten the locknut. Check preload again.

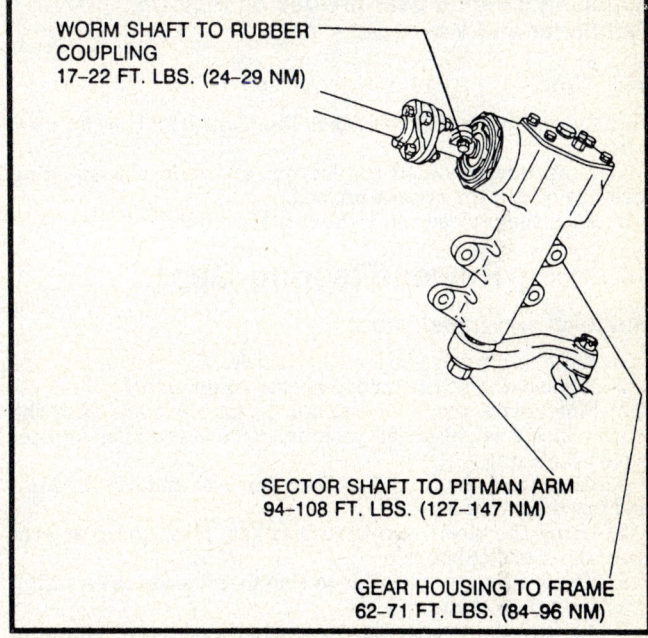

WORM SHAFT TO RUBBER COUPLING
17–22 FT. LBS. (24–29 NM)

SECTOR SHAFT TO PITMAN ARM
94–108 FT. LBS. (127–147 NM)

GEAR HOUSING TO FRAME
62–71 FT. LBS. (84–96 NM)

Steering gear box used on all except Axxess

KV48101400

KV48100700

ST3127S000

Use the special wrench to adjust worm gear preload—Pick-Up, Pathfinder and Van

STEERING GEAR PRELOAD

1. Loosen the adjusting screw locknut.
2. Rotate the worm shaft a few times in both directions to settle the worm bearing and check the preload.
3. Set the worm gear in the straight ahead position.
4. Using the torque wrench tool and an adapter socket, check the worm gear preload; it should be 7.4–10.9 inch lbs. (0.83–1.23

Adjusting steering gear preload on Pick-Up, Pathfinder and Van

Minor steering rack adjustment on Axxess can be made on the vehicle

Nm) for new parts or 5.2–8.7 inch lbs. (0.59–0.98 Nm) for used parts.

5. If necessary, loosen the locknut and turn the adjusting screw to obtain the correct preload.

6. With the preload set, tighten the locknut.

Power Steering Gear

Removal and Installation

1. Raise and safely support the vehicle.
2. Remove the wormshaft-to-rubber coupling bolt.
3. Matchmark the idler arm and sector shaft and with the wheels in a straight-ahead position, remove the idler arm-to-sector shaft nut.
4. Disconnect the fluid lines from the gear and cap the lines and openings in the gear.
5. Using the steering gear arm puller, press the gear arm from the steering knuckle.
6. Remove the steering gear-to-chassis bolts and the steering gear from the vehicle.
7. To install, reverse the removal procedures. Torque as follows:

Steering gear coupling bolt—17–22 ft. lbs. (49–51 Nm)

Steering gear-to-pitman arm nut—101–130 ft. lbs. (137–177 Nm)

Steering gear-to-frame bolts—62–71 ft. lbs. (84–96 Nm).

8. Refill the power steering pump reservoir and bleed the system.

Adjustment

1. Remove the power steering gear and position it in a vise.
2. Loosen the adjusting screw locknut.
3. Set the worm gear in the straight-ahead position.
4. Using the torque wrench and an adapter socket, check the turning torque; it should be 0.9–3.5 inch lbs. (0.1–0.4 Nm).
5. If necessary, use a screwdriver, then, turn the adjusting screw to obtain the correct preload.
6. With the preload set, tighten the adjusting screw nut.

Power Steering Rack

Removal and Installation

1. Raise and safely support the vehicle and remove the front wheels.
2. Remove the cotter pins and nuts and use a ball joint press to separate the tie rod ends from the steering knuckles.
3. Remove the rubber coupling pinch bolt.
4. Disconnect and plug the hydraulic lines coming from the pump.

5. Remove the bracket bolts and remove the rack from the chassis.

6. Installation is the reverse of removal. Torque the bracket bolts to 72 ft. lbs. (98 Nm). Torque the coupling pinch bolt to 22 ft. lbs. (29 Nm).

7. Connect the tie rod ends and torque the nuts to 29 ft. lbs. (39 Nm). Tighten as required to install new cotter pins.

8. Use new O-rings to connect the hydraulic lines. Fill and bleed the system.

Adjustment
ON VEHICLE

1. Drive the vehicle on a flat road and turn the steering wheel about 20 degrees. If the wheel returns to center when released, no adjustment is required.

2. If the wheel does not self-center from a slight turn, loosen the locknut and loosen the adjusting screw.

3. If there is excessive play in the steering that is definitely in the rack, loosen the locknut and tighten the adjusting screw.

4. Road test the vehicle again. All adjustments should be made in very small increments. Under normal use, the steering rack should not require any adjustment. If adjustment does not cure the symptom, look for other problems in the steering system such as contaminated fluid, pump or suspension failure or incorrect wheel alignment.

OFF VEHICLE

For a complete adjustment, the power steering rack must be removed from the vehicle and positioned in a vise.

1. Without fluid in the rack, set the gears in the neutral position (wheels straight-ahead).

2. Lubricate the adjusting screw with locking sealant and screw it in.

3. Lightly, tighten the locknut.

4. Torque the adjusting screw to 43–52 inch lbs. (4.9–5.9 Nm).

5. Loosen the adjusting screw and retorque it to 0.43–1.74 inch lbs. (0.05–0.20 Nm).

6. Move the rack over its entire stroke several times.

7. Using an inch lb. torque wrench, measure the pinion rotating torque within the range of 180 degrees from the neutral position.

8. Loosen the adjusting screw and retorque it to 43–52 inch lbs. (4.9–5.9 Nm).

9. Loosen the adjusting screw 40–60 degrees.

10. While securing the adjusting screw in position, torque the locknut to 29–43 ft. lbs. (39–59 Nm).

11. Using a spring gauge, connect it to the tie rod end, pull the tie rod to check the frictional sliding force; it should be 27.6–37.5 lbs. (122.6–166.7 N) at neutral point or 27.6–41.9 lbs. (122.6–186.3 N) other than neutral point.

Power Steering Pump

Removal and Installation

1. Disconnect the negative battery cable.
2. Remove the drive belt from the power steering pump.
3. Place a container under the power steering pump, disconnect and plug the pressure lines and drain the fluid into the container. Remove the bolts to remove the pump from the vehicle.
4. Remove the bolts to remove the pump from the vehicle.
5. To install, reverse the removal procedures. Adjust the drive belt tension. Bleed the power steering system.

Belt Adjustment

1. To check belt deflection, press on the belt at a point midway between the pulleys with a force of 22 lbs. (98 N) and measure how far the belt moves.
2. Loosen the adjuster locking bolt and turn the adjuster bolt as required. Be careful not to make the belts too tight or bearings will fail. Check belt deflection specifications.
3. Torque the adjuster locking bolt to 12 ft. lbs. (17 Nm).

Axxess
    Used belt – 0.24–28 in. (6–7mm)
    New belt – 0.20–0.24 in. (5–6mm)

Pick-Up and Pathfinder
  2.4L Engine
    Used belt – 0.35–0.43 in. (9–11mm)
    New belt – 0.28–0.35 in. (7–9mm)
  3.0L Engine
    Used belt – 0.43–0.51 in. (11–13mm)
    New belt – 0.35–0.43 in. (9–11mm)

Van
    Used belt – 0.35–0.39 in. (9–10mm)
    New belt – 0.28–0.35 in. (7–9mm)

System Bleeding

1. Raise and support the vehicle safely.
2. Check and add fluid to the reservoir, if necessary.
3. Start the engine. Turn the steering wheel quickly (all the way), right and left, just touching the stops; turn the steering wheel at least 10 times.

NOTE: When bleeding the system, make sure the temperature of the fluid reaches 140–176°F (60–80°C).

4. Stop the engine, check the fluid level, add as required.
5. Start and run the engine for 3–5 seconds.
6. Stop the engine, check the fluid level, add as required.
7. Start the engine. Turn the steering wheel (all the way) right and left, just touching the stops; turn the steering wheel at least 10 times.
8. Stop the engine, check the fluid level, add as required.
9. Repeat the steps until all of the air is bled from the system.
10. If the air cannot be bleed from the system, turn and hold the steering wheel at each stop for at least 5 seconds but never more than 15 seconds.

Tie Rod Ends

Removal and Installation

EXCEPT AXXESS

1. Raise and safely support the vehicle. Remove the wheel/tire assembly.
2. If removing the tie rod as an assembly:
    a. Remove the tie rod-to-cross rod cotter pin and nut.
    b. Remove the tie rods-to-steering knuckle cotter pin and nut.

40–72 FT. LBS. (54–98 NM)

TIE ROD (L.H.) ASSEMBLY

TIE ROD CLAMP NUT
10–14 FT. LBS. (14–20 NM)

TIE ROD (R.H.) ASSEMBLY

PITMAN ARM

58–72 FT. LBS. (78–98 NM)

BOOT BAND

CROSS ROD

40–72 FT. LBS. (54–98 NM)

MANUAL STEERING
94–108 FT. LBS. (127–147 NM)

POWER STEERING
101–130 FT. LBS. (137–177 NM)

IDLER ARM

40–72 FT. LBS. (54–98 NM)

40–51 FT. LBS. (54–69 NM)

Steering linkage on 2WD Pick-Up and Pathfinder

SWIVEL JOINT

CROSS ROD

19–25 FT. LBS. (25–33 NM)

STEERING DAMPER PIN

40–72 FT. LBS. (54–98 NM)

TIE ROD ASSEMBLY (R.H.)

40–72 FT. LBS. (54–98 NM)

58–72 FT. LBS. (78–98 NM)

27–36 FT. LBS. (37–49 NM)

STEERING DAMPER

BOOT BAND

TIE ROD ASSEMBLY (L.H.)

IDLER ARM

13–17 FT. LBS. (18–24 NM)

PITMAN ARM

40–72 FT. LBS. (54–98 NM)

MANUAL STEERING 94–108 FT. LBS. (127–147 NM)

POWER STEERING 101–130 FT. LBS. (137–177 NM)

LOCKNUT 58–72 FT. LBS. (78–98 NM)

DUST COVER

40–51 FT. LBS. (54–69 NM)

40–72 FT. LBS. (54–98 NM)

Steering linkage on 4WD Pick-Up and Pathfinder

DUST COVER

40–51 FT. LBS. (54–69 NM)

62–80 FT. LBS. (84–108 NM)

WASHER

GREASE SEAL

BUSHING

IDLER BODY

40–72 FT. LBS. (54–98 NM)

58–72 FT. LBS. (78–98 NM)

TIE ROD

RELAY ROD ASSEMBLY

BUSHING

DUST SEAL

GREASE SEAL

COTTER PIN

40–72 FT. LBS. (54–98 NM)

IDLER ARM

40–72 FT. LBS. (54–98 NM)

40–72 FT. LBS. (54–98 NM)

40–72 FT. LBS. (54–98 NM)

FRONT

58–72 FT. LBS. (78–98 NM)

62–80 FT. LBS. (84–108 NM)

DRAG LINK ASSEMBLY

40–72 FT. LBS. (54–98 NM)

40–72 FT. LBS. (54–98 NM)

RELAY LEVER ASSEMBLY

Steering linkage on Van

12–15 FT. LBS. (16–21 NM)

REAR HOUSING COVER

REAR HOUSING ASSEMBLY

LOCKNUT
29–43 FT. LBS.
(39–59 NM)

ADJUSTING SCREW

SPRING

SPRING DISC

WASHER

PINION
SEAL RING

PINION ASSEMBLY

O-RING

SHIM

PINION OIL SEAL

GEAR HOUSING TUBE
14–20 FT. LBS. (20–26 NM)

SPRING SEAT

RETAINER

CENTER BUSHING

RACK OIL SEAL

RACK SEAL RING

GEAR HOUSING

RACK OIL SEAL

RACK ASSEMBLY

O-RING

END COVER ASSEMBLY
43–54 FT. LBS. (59–74 NM)

DUST BOOT

BOOT CLAMP

TIE ROD

BOOT BAND

LOCK PLATE

TIE ROD INNER SOCKET   58–72 FT. LBS. (78–98 NM)

2WD: 27–34 FT. LBS. (37–46 NM)
4WD: 58–72 FT. LBS. (78–98 NM)

TIE ROD OUTER
DO NOT DISASSEMBLE
22–29 FT. LBS. (29–39 NM)

COTTER PIN

Steering linkage on Axxess

14-83

c. Using the ball joint remover tool, press the tie rod from the steering knuckle and the tie rod from the cross rod.

3. If removing a defective tie rod end:

a. Remove the cotter pin and nut from the end being removed.

b. Loosen the tie rod clamp or locknut.

c. Using the ball joint remover tool, press the tie rod from the cross rod or steering knuckle and unscrew the tie rod end from the tie rod.

d. Measure the tie rod end-to-tie rod clamp distance.

e. Unscrew the tie rod end from the tie rod.

f. Using a new tie rod end, screw the new tie rod end into the tie rod clamp until the measured distance is the same, then, torque the tie rod clamp bolt to 10–14 ft. lbs. (14–20 Nm) or nut to 58–72 ft. lbs. (78–98 Nm).

4. Inspect the tie rod ball joint for wear; if necessary, replace it.

5. To install, use new cotter pins and reverse the removal procedures. Torque the tie rod-to-steering knuckle nut to 40–72 ft. lbs. (54–98 Nm) and the tie rod-to-cross rod nut to 40–72 ft. lbs. (54–98 Nm). Check and/or adjust the front-end alignment.

AXXESS

1. Raise and safely support the vehicle.

2. Remove the wheel assembly.

3. Remove the tie rod end-to-steering knuckle cotter pin and nut. Using a tie rod removal tool, separate the tie rod end from the steering knuckle.

4. Loosen the tie rod end locknut.

5. While counting the number of turns, remove the tie rod end from the tie rod.

6. To install, screw the tie rod end onto the tie rod the same number of turns necessary to remove it.

7. Install the tie rod end into the steering knuckle. Torque as follows:

Tie rod end-to-steering knuckle nut—22–29 ft. lbs. (29–39 Nm)

Tie rod locknut
2WD—27–34 ft. lbs. (37–46 Nm)
4WD—58–72 ft. lbs. (78–98 Nm)

8. To complete the installation, reverse the removal procedures. Check and or adjust the front wheel alignment.

BRAKES

For all brake system repair and service procedures not detailed below, please refer to "Brakes" in the Unit Repair section.

Master Cylinder

NOTE: Be careful not to spill brake fluid on the painted surfaces of the vehicle; it will damage the paint.

Removal and Installation

1. Using a syringe, remove the brake fluid from the master cylinder.

2. Disconnect and plug the hydraulic lines at the master cylinder.

3. If equipped, disconnect the fluid level warning switch connector from the master cylinder.

4. Remove the clevis pin connecting the master cylinder to the pedal.

5. Remove the nuts or bolts securing the master cylinder to the firewall or power brake booster unit and pull the master cylinder out.

6. To install, reverse the removal procedures. Torque the

Master cylinder assembly on Van, Axxess similar

Master cylinder assembly on Pick-Up and Pathfinder

master cylinder nuts to 8 ft. lbs. (11 Nm) and the brake lines-to-master cylinder to 13 ft. lbs. (18 Nm). Refill the master cylinder with new brake fluid and bleed the brake system.

NOTE: Before tightening the master cylinder mounting nuts or bolts, screw the hydraulic line fitting into the cylinder body a few turns.

Load Sensing Proportioning Valve

The purpose of this valve is to control the fluid pressure applied to the brakes to prevent rear wheel lock-up during weight transfer at high speed stops.

Removal and Installation

1. Raise and safely support the vehicle.
2. Disconnect and plug the lines going to the valve.
3. Remove the valve-to-chassis bolts and the valve.
4. To install, reverse the removal procedures.
5. Bleed the brake system.

Adjustment

PICK-UP AND PATHFINDER

1989

1. Position approximately 220 lbs. (100 kg) of weight over the rear axle.
2. Install pressure gauges at the front and rear brakes.
3. Depress the brake pedal until the front brake is approximately 711 psi (4900 KPa) Check that the rear brake pressure is 327–469 lbs. (2255–3234 KPa).
4. Depress the brake pedal until the front brake pressure is approximately 1422 lbs. (1928 KPa). Check that the rear brake pressure is 455–654 lbs. (3137–4509 KPa).
5. If the rear brake pressure is not within specifications, move the spring bracket to the left if the pressure is high or to the right if the pressure is low. Repeat this process until the rear brake pressure is correct.

1990–92

1. Ensure the fuel tank, the cooling system and the engine crankcase are filled. Make sure the spare tire, the jack, the hand tools and the mats are installed.
2. Position a person in the driver's seat and one on the rear end;, then have the person on the rear end slowly get off.
3. Attach a lever to the stopper bolt and adjust the length **L** to approx. 7.44 in. (189mm).
4. Install pressure gauges at the front and rear brakes.
5. Depress the brake pedal until the front brake pressure is approximately 1422 psi (9805 KPa). Check that the rear brake pressure is 327–441 psi (2255–3041 KPa).
6. Slowly, set a 220 lbs. (100 kg) weight on the rear axle.
7. Depress the brake pedal until the front brake pressure is approximately 1422 psi. Check that the rear brake pressure is 711–995 psi (4902–6861 KPa) for all except heavy duty or 640–924 psi (4413–6371 KPa) for heavy duty.
8. If the rear brake pressure is above specification, adjust the bracket away from the valve.
9. If the rear brake pressure is below specification, adjust the bracket towards the valve.

AXXESS

1. Position a person in the driver's seat and position 1544 lbs. (702 kg) over the rear axle.
2. Install pressure gauges at the front and rear brakes.
3. Bleed the air from the front and rear brake lines.
4. Depress the brake pedal until the front brake is approximately 711 psi (4902 KPa). Check the rear brake pressure:
    455–597 psi (3137–4116 KPa)—2WD, 5-passenger model
    412–555 psi (4909–3827 KPa)—2WD, 7-passenger model
    370–512 psi (2551–3530 KPa)—4WD, 5-passenger model
    341–483 psi (2351–3330 KPa)—4WD, 7-passenger model

BLEEDER
4.3–6.5 FT. LBS. (6–9 NM)

LOAD SENSING VALVE
DO NOT DISASSEMBLE

12–15 FT. LBS. (17–21 NM)

SENSOR SPRING

BRACKET

12–15 FT. LBS. (17–21 NM)

2.2–3.3 FT. LBS. (2.9–4.4 NM)

Load sensing brake valve—Pick-Up and Pathfinder

L

STOPPER BOLT

LEVER

LOOSEN THESE BOLTS

Adjust load sensing valve spring length—Pick-Up and Pathfinder

5. Depress the brake pedal until the front brake pressure is approximately 1422 psi. (9805 KPa). Check the rear brake pressure:
    455–597 psi (3137–4116 KPa)—2WD, 5-passenger model
    412–555 psi (4909–3827 KPa)—2WD, 7-passenger model
    370–512 psi (2551–3530 KPa)—4WD, 5-passenger model
    341–483 psi (2351–3330 KPa)—4WD, 7-passenger model
6. If the rear brake pressure is above specification, adjust the bracket in the **A** direction.
7. If the rear brake pressure is below specification, adjust the bracket in the **B** direction.
8. If necessary, repeat the pressure procedure.
9. If the pressure is outside the specified range after the spring length is adjusted, replace the load sensing valve assembly.

14–18 FT. LBS. (20–25 NM)

LOAD SENSING VALVE ASSEMBLY

9–11 FT. LBS. (12–15 NM)

SENSOR SPRING

ADJUSTING BOLT 11–14 FT. LBS. (15–20 NM)

23–31 FT. LBS. (31–42 NM)

Load sensing valve on Axxess

SENSOR SPRING

BRACKET

LOAD SENSING VALVE ASSEMBLY

A

B

ADJUSTING BOLT

Load sensing valve adjustment on 2WD Axxess

SENSOR SPRING

A

B

LOAD SENSING VALVE ASSEMBLY

BRACKET

ADJUSTING BOLT

Load sensing valve adjustment on 4WD Axxess

Power Brake Booster

Removal and Installation

1. Remove the master cylinder from the power brake booster.
2. Remove the vacuum hose form the power brake booster.
3. Working under the instrument panel, remove the brake pedal-to-brake booster rod clevis pin. Remove the power brake booster mounting bolts and the booster from the vehicle.
4. To install, reverse the removal procedures. Torque the power brake booster-to-cowl nuts to 5.8–8 ft. lbs. (8–11 Nm). Check and/or adjust the brake pedal height.

NOTE: When installing the power brake booster, make sure there is 0.40–0.41 in. (10–10.5mm) clearance between the pushrod end and the master cylinder piston.

Brake Caliper

Removal and Installation

1. Raise and safely support the vehicle. Remove the wheel assembly.
2. Remove the lower sliding pin bolt and swing the caliper up to remove disc brake pads from the caliper.
3. Disconnect and plug the brake hose from the brake caliper.
4. Remove the caliper torque member bolts and the caliper from the vehicle.
5. Make sure the caliper moves freely on the sliding pins. Clean, repair or replace as necessary. Use a small amount of light grease to lubricate the pins.
6. To install, reverse the removal procedures. Torque the sliding pin bolts to 31 ft. lbs. (42 Nm). If the torque member was removed, torque the bolts to 72 ft. lbs. (97 Nm) on front calipers, 38 ft. lbs. (52 Nm) on rear calipers.
7. Bleed the brake system.

Single piston front caliper used on Pick-Up and Pathfinder

Single piston front caliper, Axxess shown

Dual piston front caliper used on Pick-Up, Pathfinder and Van

Disc Brake Pads

Removal and Installation

1. Raise and safely support the vehicle. Remove the wheels and the brake fluid reservoir cap.

2. Remove the bottom sliding pin bolt and swing the caliper upward.

3. Remove the pad retainers, the inner/outer retainers and the brake pads.

4. Using a medium C-clamp and a block of wood, place the wood against the caliper piston(s) and use the C-clamp press the piston into the caliper. Some brake fluid may be expelled from the reservoir.

5. Inspect the caliper for signs of fluid leakage; if necessary, replace or rebuild the caliper.

6. Make sure the caliper moves freely on the sliding pins. Clean, repair or replace as necessary. Use a small amount of light grease to lubricate the pins.

7. To install, use new brake pads and reverse the removal procedures. Torque the sliding pin bolts to 31 ft. lbs. (42 Nm).

Front Brake Rotor

Removal and Installation

PICK-UP AND PATHFINDER

2WD

1. Raise and safely support the vehicle. Remove the wheel assembly.

2. Without disconnecting the hydraulic hose, remove the and

torque member bolts and hang the caliper from the body with wire. Do not let the caliper hang by the hose.

3. Remove the wheel bearing grease cup, cotter pin, adjusting nut cap, hub nut, thrust washer and wheel bearing.

4. Pull the wheel hub/brake rotor assembly from the wheel spindle.

5. From the rear of the brake rotor, remove the rotor-to-wheel hub bolts and the rotor.

6. Inspect the rotor for cracks, wear and/or other damage; if necessary, replace it.

To install:

7. Install the rotor to the hub and torque the bolts to 51 ft. lbs. (69 Nm).

8. Install the hub and wheel bearings and adjust the bearing pre-load according to the proper procedure.

9. Install the caliper and pump the brake pedal to adjust the brakes.

4WD

1. Raise and support the vehicle safely under the axle case. Remove the wheels and brake calipers.

2. Block the wheels or hold the brake pedal and remove the Torx® screws to remove the locking hubs.

3. Remove the snapring from the end of the halfshaft and remove the locking hub parts.

4. From the halfshaft, remove the thrust washer, the snapring, the lockwasher screw and the lockwasher.

5. Use the proper pin wrench to loosen and remove the wheel bearing locknut.

6. Pull the wheel hub/rotor assembly from the spindle.

7. Remove the bolts to remove the rotor from the hub.

PIN BOOT

MAIN PIN BOLT

TORQUE MEMBER

28-38 FT. LBS. (38-52 NM)

TO PAD CONTACT AREA

PIN BOOT

PAD RETAINER

BRAKE HOSE

SHIM COVER

INNER SHIM B

INNER SHIM A

EYE BOLT
12-14 FT. LBS. (17-20 NM)

23-30 FT. LBS.
(31-41 NM)

COPPER WASHER

5.1-6.5 FT. LBS. (7-9 NM)

CYLINDER BODY

PAD

OUTER SHIM

PISTON SEAL

PISTON

DUST SEAL

RETAINER

Single piston rear caliper used on Pick-Up and Pathfinder

To install:

8. Install the rotor to the hub and torque the bolts to 51 ft. lbs. (69 Nm).

9. Install the hub and bearings and adjust the wheel bearing pre-load according to the proper procedure.

10. Install the brake caliper.

11. Install the locking hub assembly and torque the Torx® bolts to 25 ft. lbs. (34 Nm).

VAN

1. With the vehicle on the ground, remove the hub cap and loosen the wheel bearing locknut. The torque on this nut is high enough to cause the vehicle to fall off the supports.

2. Raise and safely support the vehicle and remove the wheels.

3. Without disconnecting the hydraulic line, remove the brake caliper and hang it from the body with wire. Do not allow the caliper to hang by the hose.

4. Remove the locknut and lock washer and pull the hub and rotor assembly off. The brake rotor and the hub are all one piece and the bearing is pressed into the hub.

To install:

5. Install the hub, lock washer and locknut onto the spindle. Do not fully tighten the locknut yet.

6. Install the brake caliper and wheel and lower the vehicle to the ground.

7. With the vehicle on all 4 wheels, torque the locknut to 260 ft. lbs. (353 Nm). Install the hub cap. Check and adjust front wheel alignment.

AXXESS

1. Raise and safely support the vehicle and remove the front wheels.

2. Without disconnecting the hydraulic hose, remove the and torque member bolts and hang the caliper from the body with wire. Do not let the caliper hang by the hose.

3. The rotor can be pulled off the hub. If it sticks, use a penetrating lubricant and a soft mallet to break it free.

4. Installation is the reverse of removal.

Rear Brake Rotor

Removal and Installation

PICK-UP AND PATHFINDER

1. Raise and safely support the vehicle.

2. Remove the wheel assembly.

3. Without disconnecting the hydraulic hose, remove the and torque member bolts and hang the caliper from the body with wire. Do not let the caliper hang by the hose.

4. Remove the rotor from the hub.

5. To install, reverse the removal procedures.

Brake Drums

Removal and Installation

1. Raise and safely support the vehicle.
2. Remove the wheel assembly.
3. Pull the brake drum from the wheel hub. It may be necessary to back off the brake adjustment.
4. Inspect and/or replace the brake drum.
5. To install, reverse the removal procedures.

Brake Shoes

Removal and Installation

1. Fully release the parking brake.
2. Raise and safely support the vehicle. Remove the wheel assembly.
3. If equipped with rear disc brakes and drum type parking brakes, remove the brake caliper. Without disconnecting the hydraulic hose, remove the torque member bolts and hang the caliper from the body with wire. Do not let the caliper hang by the hose.
4. Remove the brake drum. If the drum is difficult to remove, insert 2—8mm × 1.25 screws in the disc/drum holes, tighten the screws to press the drum from the hub.
5. When removing the brake shoes and springs, be sure to remove only one side at a time so the other side is available as a reference. Remove the brake shoe retainers and the springs.
6. Separate the parking brake cable from the from the parking brake lever.

To install:

7. Using brake grease, lubricate the shoe adjuster and the backing plate contact points.
8. Turn the shoe adjuster all the way inward.
9. To install, reverse the removal procedures. Adjust the parking brakes by turning the adjuster wheel.

Adjustment

1. Raise and safely support the vehicle. Make sure the parking brake lever is fully released.
2. From the rear of the backing plate, remove the adjuster hole plug.
3. Using a small prybar, rotate the adjuster wheel until the wheel will not turn.
4. Back off the adjuster wheel 7–8 notches. Make sure the wheel turns freely.
5. Install the adjuster hole plug.

Rear brake shoe assembly on vehicles with rear disc brakes and drum parking brakes; lightly lubricate the backing plate in the areas indicated with arrows – Pick-Up and Pathfinder

Wheel Cylinder

Removal and Installation

1. Raise and safely support the vehicle.
2. Remove the wheel, brake drum and brake shoes.
3. Disconnect the hydraulic line from the rear of the wheel cylinder.
4. Remove the wheel cylinder-to-backing plate bolts and the wheel cylinder from the backing plate.
5. To install, reverse the removal procedures. Torque the wheel cylinder-to-backing plate nuts to bolt to 65 inch lbs. (7 Nm). Bleed the brake hydraulic system.

Parking Brake Cable

Removal and Installation

REAR CABLE

1. Fully release the parking brake handle.
2. Raise and safely support the vehicle.
3. Loosen the adjusting nut at the adjuster cable lever.
4. Disconnect the cable from the balance lever or adjuster.
5. Disconnect the rear parking brake cable(s) from the parking brake toggle levers of the rear service brake assemblies.
6. Remove the rear parking brake cable brackets-to-chassis bracket screws.
7. Remove parking brake cable(s) from the vehicle.
8. To install, reverse the removal procedures. Apply a light coat of grease to the cables to make sure they slide properly. Adjust the parking brake cables.

FRONT CABLE

1. Fully release the parking brake control lever.
2. Raise and safely support the vehicle.
3. Loosen the adjusting nut at the adjuster cable lever.
4. Disconnect the cable from the balance lever or adjuster.
5. Remove the front cable bracket-to-chassis bolt(s) and the cable from the vehicle.
6. To install, reverse the removal procedures. Apply a light coat of grease to the cable to make sure it slides properly. Adjust the parking brake cables.

Adjustment

1. Raise and safely support the vehicle.
2. Adjust the rear brakes.
3. From under the vehicle, adjust the parking brake cable locknut(s). Turn the adjusting nut until the parking brake control lever operating stroke is (using 44 lbs. force):

    10–12 clicks—console lever—Pick-Up and Pathfinder
    10–12 clicks—stick lever—2WD Pick-Up and 2WD Pathfinder
    9–11 clicks—stick lever—4WD Pick-Up and 4WD Pathfinder
    7–9 clicks—Van
    8–9 clicks—2WD Axxess
    10–11 clicks—4WD Axxess

4. Release the parking brake and make sure the rear wheels turn freely with no drag.

Brake System Bleeding

1. Raise and safely support the vehicle.
2. Make sure the brake fluid reservoir is full. Keep checking the level during the procedure, do not allow the level to fall too low.
3. Have an assistant pump the brake pedal, then hold pressure on the pedal.
4. Connect a tube to the bleeder at the right rear wheel and put the other end in a container. Open the bleeder until the pressure is released, then close it before releasing pressure on the pedal.
5. Repeat the procedure until fluid flows from the bleeder with no air bubbles. If the bubbles do not stop, a problem is indicated in the master cylinder.
6. Repeat the procedure on the left rear, right front, then left front brakes in order.
7. Fill the fluid reservoir.

FRONT SUSPENSION

Shock Absorbers

Removal and Installation

EXCEPT AXXESS

1. Raise and safely support the vehicle. Remove the wheel assembly.
2. While holding the upper stem of the shock absorber, remove the shock absorber-to-chassis nut and/or bolt, washer and rubber bushing.
3. Remove the lower shock absorber-to-lower control arm nut and/or bolt and remove the shock absorber from the vehicle.
4. To install, use new rubber bushings and reverse the removal procedures. Torque the shock absorber-to-lower control arm nut/bolt to 58 ft. lbs. (78 Nm) and the shock absorber-to-chassis nut to 16 ft. lbs. (22 Nm) on Pick-Up and Pathfinder or nut/bolt to 30 ft. lbs. (41 Nm) on Van.

MacPherson Strut

Removal and Installation

AXXESS

1. Raise and safely support the vehicle; position support under the front of the frame.
2. Remove the wheel assembly.
3. Matchmark the strut-to-steering knuckle position.
4. Remove the strut-to-steering knuckle nut/bolts.
5. Remove the strut-to-chassis nuts and the strut from the vehicle.
6. To install, reverse the removal procedures. Align the strut-to-steering knuckle matchmarks. Torque the strut-to-chassis nuts to 40 ft. lbs. (54 Nm) and the strut-to-steering knuckle nuts/bolts to 91 ft. lbs. (124 Nm).
7. Check and/or adjust the front end alignment.

Leaf Springs

Removal and Installation

VAN

1. Raise and safely support the vehicle; position supports under the frame.
2. Remove the wheel assembly.
3. Remove the lower control arm from one side.
4. From the opposite side, loosen the leaf spring-to-lower control arm bolt.
5. Remove the leaf spring by sliding it from the opposite lower control arm.
6. Inspect the spring for wear and/or cracks; if necessary, replace the spring.
7. To install, reverse the removal procedures.

Torsion Bars

Removal and Installation

PICK-UP AND PATHFINDER

1. Raise and safely support the vehicle with supports placed under the frame. Remove the wheel assemblies.
2. Remove the torsion bar spring adjusting nut.
3. Remove the dust cover and the snapring from the anchor arm.
4. Pull the anchor arm off rearward and remove the torsion bar spring. Keep them separated left and right, they are not interchangable.
5. Remove the torque arm.

To install:

6. Check the torsion bars for wear, cracks or other damage; replace them if necessary.

Front suspension on Van

Adjusting torsion bar anchor arm bolt length L on 2WD Pick-Up and Pathfinder

Adjusting torsion bar on 4WD Pick-Up and Pathfinder

Adjust dimension H with vehicle on the ground; 2WD Pick-Up and Pathfinder

Anchor arm length G on 4WD Pick-Up and Pathfinder

7. Install the torque arm on the lower link (control arm) and torque the bolts to 50 ft. lbs. (68 Nm).

8. Install the snapring and dust cove on the torsion bar.

9. Coat the splines on the inner end of the torsion bar with chassis lube and install it into the torque arm. The torsion bars are marked **L** and **R** and are not interchangeable. Adjust the torsion bars.

Adjustment

2WD MODELS

1. Position a floor jack under the lower suspension arm and raise it so the clearance between the arm and the rebound bumper is 0.

2. Install the anchor arm so the dimension **L** is 0.24–0.71 in. (6–18mm).

3. Install the snapring to the anchor arm and dust cover. Make sure the snapring is properly installed in the groove of the anchor arm.

4. Tighten the anchor arm adjusting nut until dimension **L** is 1.38 in. (35mm) for heavy duty, cab/chassis and std models or 1.93 in. (49mm) for all other models.

5. Lower the vehicle so it is resting on the wheels and bounce it several times to set the suspension. Turn the anchor bolt adjusting nut so dimension **H** is 4.25–4.65 in. (108–118mm).

4WD MODELS

1. Position a floor jack under the lower suspension arm and raise it so the clearance between the arm and the rebound bumper is 0.

2. Install the anchor arm so the dimension **G** is 01.97–2.36 in. (50–60mm).

3. Install the snapring to the anchor arm and dust cover.

Torsion bar adjusting bolt length L on 4WD Pick-Up and Pathfinder

Adjust dimension H with vehicle on the ground; 4WD Pick-Up and Pathfinder

Make sure the snapring is properly installed in the groove of the anchor arm.

4. Tighten the anchor arm adjusting nut until dimension **L** is 3.03 in. (77mm).

5. Lower the vehicle so it is resting on the wheels and bounce it several times to set the suspension. Turn the anchor bolt adjusting nut so dimension **H** is 1.61–2.01 in. (41–51mm).

Upper Ball Joints

Inspection
EXCEPT AXXESS

The ball joint(s) should be replaced when play becomes excessive. The manufacturer does not publish specifications on just what constitutes excessive play, relying instead on a method of determining the force (in inch lbs.) required to keep the ball joint turning. An effective way to determine ball joint play is to raise the vehicle until the wheel is just a few inches off the ground and the ball joint is unloaded, which means not to jack directly under the ball joint. Place a long bar under the tire and move the wheel and tire assembly up and down; place one hand on top of the tire while you are doing this. If there is over ¼ in. of play at the top of the tire, the ball joint is probably bad. This assuming that the wheel bearings are in good shape and properly adjusted. As a double check, have someone watch the ball joint while you move the tire up and down with the bar. If considerable play is seen, besides feeling play at the top of the wheel, the ball joints need to be replaced.

Removal and Installation
EXCEPT AXXESS

1. Raise and safely support the vehicle.
2. Remove the wheel/tire assembly.

NOTE: On the Pick-Up and Pathfinder, it may be necessary to loosen the torsion bar anchor lock and adjusting nuts to relieve spring tension.

3. Place a floor jack under the steering knuckle and support it.

4. Remove and discard the cotter pin from the ball joint stud, then loosen the nut. Using the ball joint removal tool, press the upper ball joint from the lower control arm. Remove the upper ball joint nut.

5. Remove the upper ball joint-to-upper control arm bolts and the ball joint from the vehicle.

6. To install, use a new ball joint, a new cotter pin and reverse the removal procedures. Torque as follows:

Upper ball joint-to-upper control arm bolts—16 ft. lbs. (22 Nm)

Upper ball-to-steering knuckle nut
Pick-Up and Pathfinder—108 ft. lbs. (146 Nm)
Van—72 ft. lbs. (98 Nm)

Use a ball joint press to disconnect the ball joints and tie rod ends—Pick-Up and Pathfinder

7. Check and/or adjust the ride height and the front end alignment.

Lower Ball Joints

Removal and Installation

The lower control arm ball joint on the 2WD Pick-Up and 2WD Pathfinder models are not removable; if the ball joint is defective, replace the lower control arm.

1. Raise and safely support the vehicle.
2. Remove the wheel/tire assembly.

NOTE: On the Pick-Up and Pathfinder, loosen the torsion bar spring anchor lock and adjusting nuts and remove the anchor arm bolt from the anchor arm. Remove the snapring, then move the anchor arm and torsion bar fully rearward. This procedure is to relieve the spring pressure on the lower control arm.

3. If equipped, it may be necessary to disconnect the sway bar from the lower arm.

4. Disconnect the tension rod from the lower arm.

5. Remove the cotter pin from the ball joint stud and loosen the nut.

6. Using the ball joint separator tool, press the ball joint from the steering knuckle.

7. Remove the lower ball joint-to-lower control arm bolts and the ball joint.

8. To install, use a new cotter pin and reverse the removal procedures. Torque as follows:

Ball joint-to-control arm bolts
4WD Pick-Up and 4WD Pathfinder—45 ft. lbs. (61 Nm)
Axxess—80 ft. lbs. (108 Nm)
Ball joint-to-steering knuckle nut
Pick-Up and Pathfinder—141 ft. lbs. (190 Nm)
Axxess—64 ft. lbs. (87 Nm)
Van—141 ft. lbs. (190 Nm)

9. Check and/or adjust the torsion bar ride height assembly and the front end alignment.

Upper Control Arms

Removal and Installation
PICK-UP AND PATHFINDER

1. Raise and safely support the vehicle.
2. Remove the wheels.
3. Remove the upper shock absorber-to-chassis nut and compress the shock absorber.

NOTE: If may be necessary to loosen the torsion bar anchor lock and adjusting nuts to relieve the torsion bar tension.

4. Remove the upper ball joint-to-upper control arm bolts.
5. Using a floor jack, raise the lower control arm.
6. Remove the upper control arm-to-chassis bolts and the upper control arm from the vehicle.

NOTE: If shims are used, be sure to keep them in order for reinstallation purposes.

7. Inspect the ball joint, replace as required.
8. To install, replace the shims, if used, in their original locations and reverse the removal procedures. Torque the upper control arm-to-chassis bolts to 108 ft. lbs. (146 Nm), the ball joint-to-upper control arm bolts to 15 ft. lbs. (20 Nm) and the upper shock absorber-to-chassis nut to 16 ft. lbs. (21 Nm).

9. Lower the vehicle and adjust the ride height. Check and/or adjust the front end alignment.

VAN

1. Raise and safely support the vehicle. Remove the wheel assembly.
2. Using a floor jack, support the lower control arm.
3. Remove the upper ball joint-to-upper control arm bolts and separate the ball joint from the upper control arm.
4. Remove the upper control arm-to-chassis bolts and the control arm from the vehicle.

NOTE: If shims are used, be sure to keep them in order for reinstallation purposes.

5. To install, replace the shims, if used, in their original locations and reverse the removal procedures. Torque the upper control arm-to-chassis bolts to 50 ft. lbs. (68 Nm) and the upper ball joint-to-upper control arm bolts to 22 ft. lbs. (30 Nm).
6. Check and/or adjust the front end alignment.

Lower Control Arms

Removal and Installation

2WD PICK-UP

1. Raise and safely support the vehicle and remove the front wheels.
2. Remove the shock absorber.
3. Remove the torsion bar.
4. Disconnect the stabilizer bar linkage from the lower control arm.
5. Disconnect the tension rod-to-lower control arm bolts.
6. Remove the cotter pin from the ball joint and use a ball joint press to separate the ball joints from the control arm.
7. Remove the lower control arm-to-chassis nut/bolt, tap the pivot shaft from the bushing. Push down on the tension rod and remove the lower control arm.

Bolt tightening sequence for installing lower control arm on Axxess with 2WD and 4WD

To install:

8. Install the control arm and the pivot bolt and torque the bolt to 108 ft. lbs. (147 Nm).
9. Connect the lower ball joint and sway bar. Torque the ball joint nut to 141 ft. lbs. (191 Nm) and tighten as required to install a new cotter pin.
10. Connect the tension rod and torque the bolts to 47 ft. lbs. (64 Nm). Install the stabilizer bar linkage and torque to 16 ft. lbs. (22 Nm).
11. Install the torsion bar and shock absorber. Adjust the torsion bar height and front wheel alignment.

4WD AND PATHFINDER

1. Raise and safely support the vehicle and remove the front wheels.
2. Remove the torsion bar.
3. Remove the shock absorber.
4. Disconnect the stabilizer bar linkage.
5. Remove the cotter pin and lower ball joint nut and use a ball joint press to separate the ball joint from the lower control arm.
6. Remove the lower arm spindle bolt and the bushing nut and remove the lower control arm.

To install:

7. Fit the arm into place and start the bushing nut. Torque this nut when the vehicle is on the wheels. Torque the spindle bolt to 108 ft. lbs. (147 Nm).
8. Connect the lower ball joint and torque the nut to 141 ft. lbs. (191 Nm) and tighten as required to install a new cotter pin.
9. Connect the stabilizer bar linkage and install the shock absorber. Torque the stabilizer bar linkage when the vehicle is on the wheels to 16 ft. lbs. (22 Nm).
10. Install the torsion bar and adjust the bar and front wheel alignment.

VAN

1. Raise and safely support the vehicle and remove the wheels.
2. Remove the brackets to remove the stabilizer bar.
3. Support the lower control arm with a floor jack. Disconnect the shock absorber from the control arm.
4. Disconnect the compression rod from the lower control arm.
5. Use wire or rope to support the upper control arm and steering knuckle assembly to the body so it does not fall when the lower arm is removed.
6. Remove the nut from the lower ball joint and use a ball joint press to separate the lower ball joint from the control arm.
7. Carefully lower the floor jack to release the leaf spring tension. Remove the nuts securing the spring to the bump stop.
8. Remove the lower control arm pivot bolt and remove the arm.

To install:

9. Install the lower control arm and temporarily tighten the pivot bolt.
10. Raise the arm into position to engage the leaf spring with the bump stop bolt. Make sure the washer is fully on the spring and torque the nut to 27 ft. lbs. (37 Nm).
11. Connect the ball joint and torque the nut to 141 ft. lbs. (191 Nm). Install a new cotter pin.
12. Connect the compression rod and torque the bolts to 30 ft. lbs. (41 Nm).
13. Connect the shock absorber and stabilizer bar. Torque the nuts and bolts to 31 ft. lbs. (42 Nm).
14. With all of the suspension pieces connected, set the vehicle on the wheels and torque the control arm pivot bolt to 101 ft. lbs. (137 Nm). Check and adjust the front wheel alignment.

AXXESS

1. Raise and safely support the vehicle and remove the front wheels.
2. Remove the stabilizer bar.

3. Remove the bolts securing the control arm to the lower ball joint. Remove the bolts securing the control arm to the frame and remove the arm.

To install:

4. Install the control arm and temporarily tighten the bolts.
5. Torque the ball joint nuts to 80 ft. lbs. (109 Nm).
6. Install the stabilizer bar.
7. With the vehicle resting on all 4 wheels, torque the numbered bolts in the sequence shown to 108 ft. lbs. (147 Nm). Torque the front bushing nut to 87 ft. lbs. (118 Nm).
8. Check and adjust front wheel alignment.

Stabilizer Bar

Removal and Installation

PICK-UP AND PATHFINDER

1. Raise and safely support the vehicle.
2. From both sides of the vehicle, remove the stabilizer bar-to-lower control arm connecting rod nut, bushings and tube.
3. Remove the bracket bolts and brackets and remove the stabilizer bar.
4. Installation is the reverse of removal. Make sure the brackets are to the outside of the white painted marks on the stabilizer bar. Torque the bracket bolts to 16 ft. lbs. (22 Nm) and the connecting rod nut to 22 ft. lbs. (30 Nm).

VAN

1. Raise and safely support the front of the vehicle.
2. From both sides of the vehicle, remove the stabilizer bar-to-lower control arm bracket bolts and brackets. Note the orientation of the bushings so they can be installed the same way.
3. Remove the stabilizer bar-to-chassis bracket bolts and remove the bar. Note the orientation of the bushings so they can be installed the same way.
4. When installing the stabilizer bar, make sure the bushings are installed correctly. With the vehicle on all 4 wheels, torque the bolts to 31 ft. lbs. (42 Nm).

AXXESS

A stabilizer bar is used on the 2WD models only.
1. Raise and safely support the front of the vehicle.
2. Remove the stabilizer bar-to-connecting rod nut.
3. Remove the stabilizer bar clamp-to-chassis bolts and the stabilizer bar from the vehicle.
4. To install, reverse the removal procedures. Torque the stabilizer bar clamp-to-chassis bolts to 31 ft. lbs. (42 Nm). and the stabilizer bar-to-connecting rod nuts to 38 ft. lbs. (51 Nm).

Front Wheel Bearings

For the FWD Axxess, the 4WD Pick-Up and 4WD Pathfinder models, please refer to the Drive Axle section.

Removal and Installation

2WD PICK-UP

1. Raise and safely support the vehicle and remove the front wheels.
2. Disconnect the brake hose from the bracket on the knuckle.
3. Without disconnecting the hydraulic line, remove the brake caliper and hang it from the body on a wire. Do not let it hang by the hose.
4. Remove the wheel hub cup, the cotter pin, the adjusting cap and hub nut.
5. Remove the wheel hub and brake disc assembly. Be careful not to drop the outer wheel bearing.
6. To remove the inner bearing, pry out the grease seal. Discard the seal.

To install:

7. Make sure the bearings are clean and in good condition. Replace as required. Pack the bearings and the hub with new grease and install the bearings into the hub. Install a new grease seal.
8. Make sure the spindle is clean. Install the spacer with the chamfer facing in on the spindle.
9. Lightly grease the lips on the seal and slide the hub and bearings onto the spindle. Install the washer and nut.
10. To adjust the pre-load on the bearing:
    a. Torque the wheel bearing nut to 25 ft. lbs. (34 Nm).
    b. Spin the hub several times in both directions, then torque the nut to 29 ft. lbs. (39 Nm).
    c. Loosen the nut 45 degrees. Install the locknut cap and a new cotter pin.
11. Install the brake caliper and torque the caliper carrier bolts to 72 ft. lbs. (98 Nm).

2WD PATHFINDER

1. Raise and safely support the vehicle and remove the front wheels.
2. Without disconnecting the hydraulic line, remove the brake caliper and hang it from the body with wire. Do not allow the caliper to hang by the hose.
3. Remove the hub cap and locking screw and remove the lock washer. Use a pin wrench to loosen the wheel bearing locknut. The torque may be fairly high, do not use a hammer and drift pin.
4. Remove the locknut and pull the hub off with the bearings. Pry the inner grease seal out to remove the inner bearing. Discard the seal.

To install:

5. Clean all parts of grease and check the condition of the bearings. If bearings are to be replaced, the inner races can be removed from the hub with a hammer and soft drift pin. Be careful not to damage the hub.
6. Carefully install the new inner races with the drift pin, making sure they seat in the hub.
7. Pack the bearings with new grease and pack grease into the hub. Install the inner bearing and press a new inner seal into the hub.
8. Slip the hub assembly onto the spindle and install the outer bearing. Grease the locknut and thread it into place.
9. To adjust bearing pre-load:
    a. Use a pin wrench to torque the locknut to 58–72 ft. lbs. (78–98 Nm). Turn the hub in both directions several times while torquing the nut.
    b. Loosen the locknut, then torque again to 13 inch lbs. (1.5 Nm).
    c. Turn the hub several times and check the nut torque again.
    d. Install the lock washer. When installing the screw, make sure the locknut turns no more than 30 degrees in either direction.
    e. When bearing pre-load is properly set, there will be no endplay in the hub and it will require no more than 4.7 lbs. of pull at the wheel stud to turn the hub.
10. Install the brake caliper and torque the caliper carrier bolts to 72 ft. lbs. (98 Nm).

VAN

1. Loosen the wheel lug nuts. Raise and safely support the vehicle. Remove the wheel/tire assembly.
2. Remove the caliper-to-steering knuckle bolts and the caliper. Using a wire, suspend the caliper from the vehicle; do not disconnect the brake hose from the caliper.
3. Remove the grease cap from the wheel hub.

4. Remove the wheel bearing nut and the lockwasher. Pull the rotor/wheel hub from the spindle.

5. Remove the lock ring from the rotor/wheel hub.

6. Using a hydraulic press, press the wheel bearing and grease seal from the rotor/wheel hub assembly.

7. Using a new bearing, press it into the rotor/wheel hub assembly until it seats; use no more than 3 tons pressure. Install a new lock ring into the rotor/wheel hub.

8. To complete the installation, reverse the removal procedures. Torque the wheel bearing nut to 195–260 ft. lbs.

REAR SUSPENSION

Shock Absorbers

Removal and Installation

1. Raise and safely support the vehicle.
2. Remove the upper shock-to-vehicle nut, the lower shock-to-vehicle nut and the shock from the vehicle.

NOTE: The weight of the vehicle must be on the rear wheels before tightening the shock absorber attaching nuts.

3. To install, reverse the removal procedures. Torque as follows:
   Upper shock-to-vehicle nut
   Pick-Up and Pathfinder—22–30 ft. lbs.
   Van—12–18 ft. lbs.
   Lower shock absorber-to-axle nut
   2WD Pick-Up and 2WD Pathfinder—12–16 ft. lbs.
   4WD Pick-Up and 4WD Pathfinder—22–30 ft. lbs.
   Van—53–72 ft. lbs.

MacPherson Strut

Removal and Installation

AXXESS

2WD Model

On the 2WD models, the wheel spindle and knuckle are a part of the strut.

1. Remove the hub cap and cotter pin.
2. Apply the brakes and loosen the wheel bearing locknut.
3. Raise and safely support the vehicle. Remove the wheel assembly.
4. Remove the wheel bearing nut, washer and wheel hub bearing.

NOTE: The wheel hub bearing must be replaced as an assembly if the bearing is defective.

5. Disconnect and plug the brake line from the wheel cylinder.
6. Remove radius rod-to-knuckle nut/bolt, the stabilizer rod-to-knuckle nut/bolt and the parallel rods-to-knuckle nut/bolt.
7. From inside the vehicle, remove the strut cover.
8. Remove the strut-to-chassis nuts and the strut.

To install:

9. Install strut and the strut-to-chassis nuts and torque to 58 ft. lbs. (78 Nm).
10. Install the parallel rods-to-knuckle nut/bolt and torque to 87 ft. lbs. (118 Nm).
11. Install the stabilizer rod-to-knuckle nut/bolt and torque to 58 ft. lbs. (78 Nm).
12. Install the radius rod-to-knuckle nut/bolt and torque to 87 ft. lbs. (118 Nm).
13. Complete the installation of the remaining components. Torque the wheel hub bearing assembly to 137–188 ft. lbs. (186–255 Nm). Bleed the rear brakes and inspect the rear wheel alignment.

14. Using a dial indicator, measure the bearing axial endplay; it should be 0.0020 in. (0.05mm) or less.

4WD Models

1. Raise and safely support the vehicle. Remove the wheel assembly.
2. Matchmark the strut-to-knuckle location.
3. Support the knuckle and remove the strut-to-knuckle nuts and bolts.
4. From inside the vehicle, remove the strut-to-chassis nuts.
5. Remove the strut from the vehicle.
6. To install, reverse the removal procedures. Torque the strut-to-chassis nuts to 51 ft. lbs. (69 Nm) and the strut-to-knuckle nuts/bolts to 91 ft. lbs. (124 Nm).
7. To complete the installation, reverse the removal procedures. Inspect the rear wheel alignment.

Coil Springs

Removal and Installation

VAN

1. Raise and safely support the vehicle.
2. Lower the axle housing and remove the coil spring(s).
3. To install, reverse the removal procedures.

Leaf Springs

Removal and Installation

PICK-UP AND PATHFINDER

——————————— **CAUTION** ———————————

The leaf springs are under a considerable amount of tension. Be very careful when removing or installing them; they can exert enough force to cause serious injuries.

1. Raise and safely support the vehicle. Using a floor jack, support the axle housing.
2. Disconnect the shock absorbers at their lower end.
3. Remove the axle housing-to-spring pad U-bolt nuts and the spring pad.
4. Raise the axle housing to remove the weight off the springs.
5. Remove the spring shackle nuts, drive out the shackle pins and remove the spring from the vehicle.

NOTE: The weight of the vehicle must be on the rear wheels before torquing the front pin, shackle and shock absorber nuts.

6. To install, reverse the removal procedures. Torque as follows:
   Front pin and shackle nuts—94 ft. lbs. (127 Nm)
   U-bolt nuts—72 ft. lbs. (98 Nm)
   Shock absorber lower end nut
   2WD—16 ft. lbs. (22 Nm)
   4WD—30 ft. lbs. (41 Nm)

Rear Control Arms

Removal and Installation

VAN

Lower Link

1. Raise and safely support the vehicle.
2. Remove the lower link-to-axle housing nut/bolt and the lower link-to-chassis nut/bolt.
3. Remove the lower link from the vehicle.
4. To install, reverse the removal procedures. Torque the lower link-to-chassis nut/bolt and the lower link-to-axle housing nut/bolt to 94 ft. lbs. (127 Nm).

Upper Link

1. Raise and safely support the vehicle.
2. Remove the upper link-to-axle housing nut/bolt and the upper link-to-chassis nut/bolt.
3. Remove the upper link from the vehicle.
4. To install, reverse the removal procedures. Torque the upper link-to-chassis nut/bolt and the upper link-to-axle housing nut/bolt to 94 ft. lbs. (127 Nm).

Panhard Rod

1. Raise and safely support the vehicle.
2. Remove the panhard rod-to-axle housing nut and the panhard rod-to-chassis nut/bolt.
3. Remove the panhard rod from the vehicle.
4. To install, reverse the removal procedures. Torque the panhard rod-to-chassis nut/bolt to 94 ft. lbs. (127 Nm) and the panhard rod-to-axle housing nut to 50 ft. lbs. (68 Nm).

AXXESS

2WD Models With Radius Rod

1. Raise and safely support the vehicle.
2. Remove the wheel assembly.
3. Remove the radius rod-to-knuckle nut and bolt.
4. Remove the radius rod-to-chassis nut/bolt and the rod.
5. To install, reverse the removal procedures. Torque the radius rod-to-chassis nut/bolt to 80 ft. lbs. (108 Nm) and the radius rod-to-knuckle nut/bolt to 80 ft. lbs. (108 Nm).

2WD Models With Parallel Rods

Dual rods are connected from the chassis to the knuckle.
1. Raise and safely support the vehicle.
2. Remove the wheel assembly.
3. Remove the parallel rods-to-knuckle nut and bolt.
4. Remove the parallel rods-to-chassis nut/bolt and the rods.
5. To install, reverse the removal procedures. Torque the parallel rods-to-chassis nut/bolt and the parallel rods-to-knuckle nut/bolt to 87 ft. lbs. (118 Nm).

4WD Models With Radius Rod

1. Raise and safely support the vehicle.
2. Remove the wheel assembly.
3. Remove the radius rod-to-knuckle nut and bolt.
4. Remove the radius rod-to-chassis nut/bolt and the rod.
5. To install, reverse the removal procedures. Torque the radius rod-to-chassis nut/bolt to 80 ft. lbs. (108 Nm) and the radius rod-to-knuckle nut/bolt to 72 ft. lbs. (98 Nm).

4WD With Parallel Rods

Dual rods are connected from the chassis to the knuckle.
1. Raise and safely support the vehicle.
2. Remove the wheel assembly.
3. Remove the parallel rods-to-knuckle nut and bolt.
4. Remove the parallel rods-to-chassis nut/bolt and the rods.
5. To install, reverse the removal procedures. Torque the parallel rods-to-chassis nut/bolt and the parallel rods-to-knuckle nut/bolt to 72 ft. lbs. (98 Nm).

Rear Wheel Bearings

For RWD models, refer to the drive axle section.

Removal and Installation

AXXESS

1. Remove the hub cap, the grease cap and the cotter pin.
2. Loosen the wheel hub nut; do not remove it.
3. Raise and safely support the vehicle.
4. Remove the wheel assembly and the brake drum.
5. Remove the hub nut, the washer and the wheel hub assembly.

NOTE: If the wheel bearings are defective, replace the entire wheel hub bearing assembly.

6. To install, reverse the removal procedures. With the vehicle on all 4 wheels, torque the wheel hub nut to 137–188 ft. lbs. (186–255 Nm).

SPECIFICATIONS

ENGINE IDENTIFICATION

Year	Model	Engine Displacement cu. in. (cc/liter)	Engine Series Identification	No. of Cylinders	Engine Type
1988	Samurai	80.8 (1324/1.3)	5	4	SOHC
1989	Samurai	80.8 (1324/1.3)	5	4	SOHC
	Sidekick	79.2 (1298/1.3)	5	4	SOHC
	Sidekick	97.0 (1590/1.6)	0	4	SOHC
1990	Samurai	79.2 (1298/1.3)	5	4	SOHC
	Sidekick	97.0 (1590/1.6)	0	4	SOHC
1991	Samurai	79.2 (1298/1.3)	5	4	SOHC
	Sidekick	97.0 (1590/1.6)	0	4	SOHC
1992	Samurai	79.2 (1298/1.3)	5	4	SOHC
	Sidekick	97.0 (1590/1.6)	0	4	SOHC

SOHC—Single Overhead Cam

GENERAL ENGINE SPECIFICATIONS

Year	Model	Engine Displacement cu. in. (cc)	Fuel System Type	Net Horsepower @ rpm	Net Torque @ rpm (ft. lbs.)	Bore × Stroke (in.)	Compression Ratio	Oil Pressure @ rpm
1988	Samurai	80.8 (1324)	2 bbl	NA	NA	2.91 × 3.03	8.9:1	42.7–59.7 ①
1989	Samurai	80.8 (1324)	2 bbl	64 @ 5500	74 @ 3500	2.91 × 3.03	8.9:1	42.7–59.7
	Sidekick	79.2 (1298)	2 bbl	64 @ 5500	73 @ 3500	2.91 × 2.97	8.7:1	NA
	Sidekick	97.0 (1590)	EFI	80 @ 5400	94 @ 3000	2.95 × 3.54	8.9:1	51.2–62.6 ①
1990	Samurai	79.2 (1298)	EFI	66 @ 6000	76 @ 3500	2.91 × 2.97	9.5:1	42.7–59.7
	Sidekick	97.0 (1590)	EFI	80 @ 5400	94 @ 3000	2.95 × 3.54	8.9:1	51.2–62.6 ①
1991	Samurai	79.2 (1298)	EFI	66 @ 6000	76 @ 3500	2.91 × 2.97	9.5:1	42.7–59.7
	Sidekick	97.0 (1590)	EFI	80 @ 5400	94 @ 3000	2.95 × 3.54	8.9:1	51.2–62.6 ①
1992	Samurai	79.2 (1298)	EFI	66 @ 6000	76 @ 3500	2.91 × 2.97	9.5:1	42.7–59.7
	Sidekick	97.0 (1590)	EFI	80 @ 5400	94 @ 3000	2.95 × 3.54	8.9:1	51.2–62.6 ①

NA—Not available
EFI—Electronic Fuel Injection
① @ 3000 rpm.

GASOLINE ENGINE TUNE-UP SPECIFICATIONS

Year	Model	Engine Displacement cu. in. (cc)	Spark Plugs Type	Spark Plugs Gap (in.)	Ignition Timing (deg.) MT	Ignition Timing (deg.) AT	Compression Pressure (psi)	Fuel Pump (psi)	Idle Speed (rpm) MT	Idle Speed (rpm) AT	Valve Clearance In. Ex.
1988	Samurai	80.8 (1324)	BPR5ES	0.027–0.031	10B	NA	170–199	3–4	800	NA	①
1989	Samurai	80.8 (1324)	BPR5ES	0.027–0.031	NA	NA	NA	NA	NA	NA	NA
	Sidekick	79.2 (1298)	BPR5ES	0.027–0.031	10B	NA	170–199	34.1–39.8	800	NA	①
	Sidekick	97.0 (1590)	BPR5ES	0.027–0.031	8B	8B	170–199	34.1–39.8	800	800	①
1990	Samurai	79.2 (1298)	BPR5ES	0.027–0.031	8B	NA	170–199	34.1–39.8	800	NA	①
	Sidekick	97.0 (1590)	BPR5ES	0.027–0.031	8B	8B	170–199	34.1–39.8	800	800	①
1991	Samurai	79.2 (1298)	BPR5ES	0.027–0.031	8B	NA	170–199	34.1–39.8	800	NA	①
	Sidekick	97.0 (1590)	BPR5ES	0.028–0.031	8B	8B	170–199	34.1–39.8	800	800	①
1992	Samurai	79.2 (1298)	BPR5ES	0.027–0.031	8B	NA	170–199	34.1–39.8	800	NA	①
	Sidekick	97.0 (1590)	BPR5ES	0.028–0.031	8B	8B	170–199	34.1–39.8	800	800	①

NA—Not available
① Intake

Cold—0.0051–0.0067 in.
Hot—0.009–0.011 in.

Exhaust
Cold—0.0063–0.0079 in.
Hot—0.0102–0.0118 in.

FIRING ORDERS

NOTE: To avoid confusion, always install spark plug wires one at a time.

1.3L and 1.6L Engines
Engine Firing Order: 1–3–4–2
Distributor Rotation: Clockwise

CAPACITIES

Year	Model	Engine Displacement cu. in. (cc)	Engine Crankcase with Filter	Engine Crankcase without Filter	Transmission (pts.) 4-Spd	Transmission (pts.) 5-Spd	Transmission (pts.) Auto.	Drive Axle (pts.)	Fuel Tank (gal.)	Cooling System (qts.)
1988	Samurai	80.8 (1324)	3.7	3.5	NA	2.7	NA	②	10.6	5.1
1989	Samurai	80.8 (1324)	3.7	3.5	NA	2.7	NA	②	10.6	5.1
	Sidekick	79.2 (1298)	3.7	3.5	NA	3.2	NA	③	11.1	①
	Sidekick	97.0 (1590)	4.5	4.3	NA	3.2	10.8	③	11.1	①
1990	Samurai	79.2 (1298)	3.7	3.5	NA	2.7	NA	②	10.6	5.1
	Sidekick	97.0 (1590)	4.5	4.3	NA	3.2	10.8	③	11.1	①
1991	Samurai	79.2 (1298)	3.7	3.5	NA	2.7	NA	②	10.6	5.1
	Sidekick	97.0 (1590)	4.5	4.2	NA	3.2	6.0	③	11.1	①
1992	Samurai	79.2 (1298)	3.7	3.5	NA	2.7	NA	②	10.6	5.1
	Sidekick	97.0 (1590)	4.5	4.2	NA	3.2	6.0	③	11.1	①

NA—Not available
① Manual transmission—5.6 qts.
　Automatic transmission—5.5 qts.
② Front—4.2 pts.
　Rear—3.2 pts.
③ Front—2.1 pts.
　Rear—4.6 pts.

CAMSHAFT SPECIFICATIONS
All measurements are given in inches.

Year	Engine Displacement cu. in. (cc)	Journal Diameter 1	2	3	4	5	Lobe Lift In.	Lobe Lift Ex.	Bearing Clearance	Camshaft End Play
1988	80.8 (1324)	1.7372–1.7381	1.7451–1.7460	1.7530–1.7539	1.7609–1.7618	1.7687–1.7697	1.4763–1.4724	1.4763–1.4724	0.0020–0.0036①	0.0039
1989	79.2 (1298)	1.7372–1.7381	1.7451–1.7460	1.7530–1.7539	1.7609–1.7618	1.7687–1.7697	1.4763–1.4724	1.4763–1.4724	0.0020–0.0036①	0.0039
	80.8 (1324)	1.7372–1.7381	1.7451–1.7460	1.7530–1.7539	1.7609–1.7618	1.7687–1.7697	1.4763–1.4724	1.4763–1.4724	0.0020–0.0036①	0.0039
	97.0 (1590)	1.7372–1.7381	1.7451–1.7460	1.7530–1.7539	1.7609–1.7618	1.7687–1.7697	1.4763–1.4724	1.4763–1.4724	0.0020–0.0036①	0.0039
1990	79.2 (1298)	1.7372–1.7381	1.7451–1.7460	1.7530–1.7539	1.7609–1.7618	1.7687–1.7697	1.4763–1.4724	1.4763–1.4724	0.0020–0.0036①	0.0039
	80.8 (1324)	1.7372–1.7381	1.7451–1.7460	1.7530–1.7539	1.7609–1.7618	1.7687–1.7697	1.4763–1.4724	1.4763–1.4724	0.0020–0.0036①	0.0039
	97.0 (1590)	1.7372–1.7381	1.7451–1.7460	1.7530–1.7539	1.7609–1.7618	1.7687–1.7697	1.4763–1.4724	1.4763–1.4724	0.0020–0.0036①	0.0039

CAMSHAFT SPECIFICATIONS

All measurements are given in inches.

Year	Engine Displacement cu. in. (cc)	Journal Diameter					Lobe Lift		Bearing Clearance	Camshaft End Play
		1	2	3	4	5	In.	Ex.		
1991	79.2 (1298)	1.7372–1.7381	1.7451–1.7460	1.7530–1.7539	1.7609–1.7618	1.7687–1.7697	1.4763–1.4724	1.4763–1.4724	0.0020–0.0036 ①	0.0039
	97.0 (1590)	1.7372–1.7381	1.7451–1.7460	1.7530–1.7539	1.7609–1.7618	1.7687–1.7697	1.4763–1.4724	1.4763–1.4724	0.0020–0.0036 ①	0.0039
1992	79.2 (1298)	1.7372–1.7381	1.7451–1.7460	1.7530–1.7539	1.7609–1.7618	1.7687–1.7697	1.4763–1.4724	1.4763–1.4724	0.0020–0.0036 ①	0.0039
	97.0 (1590)	1.7372–1.7381	1.7451–1.7460	1.7530–1.7539	1.7609–1.7618	1.7687–1.7697	1.4763–1.4724	1.4763–1.4724	0.0020–0.0036 ①	0.0039

① .0059 Limit.

CRANKSHAFT AND CONNECTING ROD SPECIFICATIONS

All measurements are given in inches.

Year	Engine Displacement cu. in. (cc)	Crankshaft				Connecting Rod		
		Main Brg. Journal Dia.	Main Brg. Oil Clearance	Shaft End-play	Thrust on No.	Journal Diameter	Oil Clearance	Side Clearance
1988	80.8 (1324)	①	0.0008–0.0016 ②	0.0044–0.0122 ③	3	1.6529–1.6535	0.0012–0.0019 ④	0.0039–0.0078 ⑤
1989	79.2 (1298)	①	0.0008–0.0016 ②	0.0044–0.0122 ③	3	1.6529–1.6535	0.0012–0.0019 ④	0.0039–0.0078 ⑤
	80.8 (1324)	①	0.0008–0.0016 ②	0.0044–0.0122 ③	3	1.6529–1.6535	0.0012–0.0019 ④	0.0039–0.0078 ⑤
	97.0 (1590)	⑥	0.0012–0.0023	0.0100–0.0149	3	1.7316–1.7323	0.0008–0.0031	0.0039–0.0137
1990	79.2 (1298)	①	0.0008–0.0016 ②	0.0044–0.0122 ③	3	1.6529–1.6535	0.0012–0.0019 ④	0.0039–0.0078 ⑤
	97.0 (1590)	⑥	0.0012–0.0023	0.0100–0.0149	3	1.7316–1.7323	0.0008–0.0031	0.0039–0.0137
1991	79.2 (1298)	①	0.0008–0.0016 ②	0.0044–0.0122 ③	3	1.7710–1.7716	0.0012–0.0019 ④	0.0039–0.0078 ⑤
	97.0 (1590)	⑥	0.0012–0.0023	0.0100–0.0149	3	1.7316–1.7323	0.0008–0.0031	0.0039–0.0137
1992	79.2 (1298)	①	0.0008–0.0016 ②	0.0044–0.0122 ③	3	1.7710–1.7716	0.0012–0.0019 ④	0.0039–0.0078 ⑤
	97.0 (1590)	⑥	0.0012–0.0023	0.0100–0.0149	3	1.7316–1.7323	0.0008–0.0031	0.0039–0.0137

① Bearing cap stamped
  No. 1—1.7714–1.7716 in.
  No. 2—1.7712–1.7714 in.
  No. 3—1.7710–1.7712 in.

② Maximum clearance—0.0023
③ Maximum clearance—0.0149
④ Maximum clearance—0.0031
⑤ Maximum clearance—0.0137

⑥ Bearing cap stamped
  No. 1—2.0470–2.0472
  No. 2—2.0468–2.0470
  No. 3—2.0465–2.0468

VALVE SPECIFICATIONS

Year	Engine Displacement cu. in. (cc)	Seat Angle (deg.)	Face Angle (deg.)	Spring Test Pressure (lbs.)	Spring Installed Height (in.)	Stem-to-Guide Clearance (in.)		Stem Diameter (in.)	
						Intake	Exhaust	Intake	Exhaust
1988	80.8 (1324)	45	45	54.7–64.3 @ 1.63 in.	1.9409	0.0008–0.0019 ①	0.0014–0.0025 ②	0.2742–0.2748	0.2737–0.2742

VALVE SPECIFICATIONS

Year	Engine Displacement cu. in. (cc)	Seat Angle (deg.)	Face Angle (deg.)	Spring Test Pressure (lbs.)	Spring Installed Height (in.)	Stem-to-Guide Clearance (in.)		Stem Diameter (in.)	
						Intake	Exhaust	Intake	Exhaust
1989	79.2 (1298)	45	45	54.7–64.3 @ 1.63 in.	1.9409	0.0008–0.0019 ①	0.0014–0.0025 ②	0.2742–0.2748	0.2737–0.2742
	80.8 (1324)	45	45	54.7–64.3 @ 1.63 in.	1.9409	0.0008–0.0019 ①	0.0014–0.0025 ②	0.2742–0.2748	0.2737–0.2742
	97.0 (1590)	45	45	54.7–64.3 @ 1.63 in.	1.9074	0.0008–0.0019 ①	0.0014–0.0025 ②	0.2742–0.2748	0.2737–0.2742
1990	79.2 (1298)	45	45	54.7–64.3 @ 1.63 in.	1.9409	0.0008–0.0019 ①	0.0014–0.0025 ②	0.2742–0.2748	0.2737–0.2742
	97.0 (1590)	45	45	54.7–64.3 @ 1.63 in.	1.9074	0.0008–0.0019 ①	0.0014–0.0025 ②	0.2742–0.2748	0.2737–0.2742
1991	79.2 (1298)	45	45	54.7–64.3 @ 1.63 in.	1.9409	0.0008–0.0019 ①	0.0014–0.0025 ②	0.2742–0.2748	0.2737–0.2742
	97.0 (1590)	45	45	54.7–64.3 @ 1.63 in.	1.9074	0.0008–0.0019 ①	0.0014–0.0025 ②	0.2742–0.2748	0.2737–0.2742
1992	79.2 (1298)	45	45	54.7–64.3 @ 1.63 in.	1.9409	0.0008–0.0019 ①	0.0014–0.0025 ②	0.2742–0.2748	0.2737–0.2742
	97.0 (1590)	45	45	54.7–64.3 @ 1.63 in.	1.9074	0.0008–0.0019 ①	0.0014–0.0025 ②	0.2742–0.2748	0.2737–0.2742

① Maximum clearance—.0027 in.
② Maximum clearance—.0035 in.

PISTON AND RING SPECIFICATIONS

All measurements are given in inches.

Year	Engine Displacement cu. in. (cc)	Piston Clearance	Ring Gap			Ring Side Clearance		
			Top Compression	Bottom Compression	Oil Control	Top Compression	Bottom Compression	Oil Control
1988	80.8 (1324)	0.0008–0.0015	0.0079–0.0129 ①	0.0079–0.0137 ①	0.0079–0.0275 ②	0.0012–0.0027	0.0008–0.0023	NA
1989	79.2 (1298)	0.0008–0.0015	0.0079–0.0129 ①	0.0079–0.0137 ①	0.0079–0.0275 ②	0.0012–0.0027	0.0008–0.0023	NA
	80.8 (1324)	0.0008–0.0015	0.0079–0.0129 ①	0.0079–0.0137 ①	0.0079–0.0275 ②	0.0012–0.0027	0.0008–0.0023	NA
	97.0 (1590)	0.0008–0.0015	0.0079–0.0129 ①	0.0079–0.0137 ①	0.0079–0.0275 ②	0.0012–0.0027	0.0008–0.0023	NA
1990	79.2 (1298)	0.0008–0.0015	0.0079–0.0129 ①	0.0079–0.0137 ①	0.0079–0.0275 ②	0.0012–0.0027	0.0008–0.0023	NA
	97.0 (1590)	0.0008–0.0015	0.0079–0.0129 ①	0.0079–0.0137 ①	0.0079–0.0275 ②	0.0012–0.0027	0.0008–0.0023	NA
1991	79.2 (1298)	0.0008–0.0015	0.0079–0.0129 ①	0.0079–0.0137 ①	0.0079–0.0275 ②	0.0012–0.0027	0.0008–0.0023	NA
	97.0 (1590)	0.0008–0.0015	0.0079–0.0137 ①	0.0079–0.0137 ①	0.0079–0.0275 ②	0.0012–0.0027	0.0008–0.0023	NA
1992	79.2 (1298)	0.0008–0.0015	0.0079–0.0129 ①	0.0079–0.0137 ①	0.0079–0.0275 ②	0.0012–0.0027	0.0008–0.0023	NA
	97.0 (1590)	0.0008–0.0015	0.0079–0.0137 ①	0.0079–0.0137 ①	0.0079–0.0275 ②	0.0012–0.0027	0.0008–0.0023	NA

NA—Not available
① Limit—.0275 in.
② Limit—.0708 in.

TORQUE SPECIFICATIONS
All readings in ft. lbs.

Year	Engine Displacement cu. in. (cc)	Cylinder Head Bolts	Main Bearing Bolts	Rod Bearing Bolts	Crankshaft Pulley Bolts	Flywheel Bolts	Manifold Intake	Manifold Exhaust	Spark Plugs
1988	80.8 (1324)	46–50	36–41	24–26	7–9	41–47	13–20	13–20	14–21
1989	79.2 (1298)	46–50	36–41	24–26	7–9	41–47	13–20	13–20	14–21
	80.8 (1324)	46–50	36–41	24–26	7–9	41–47	13–20	13–20	14–21
	97.0 (1590)	54	36–41	24–26	7–9	57–58	13–20	13–20	14–21
1990	79.2 (1298)	46–50	36–41	24–26	7–9	41–47	13–20	13–20	14–21
	97.0 (1590)	54	36–41	24–26	7–9	57–58	13–20	13–20	14–21
1991	79.2 (1298)	46–50	36–41	24–26	7–9	41–47	13–20	13–20	14–21
	97.0 (1590)	51–54	36–41	24–26	7–9	54–57	13–20	13–20	14–21
1992	79.2 (1298)	46–50	36–41	24–26	7–9	41–47	13–20	13–20	14–21
	97.0 (1590)	51–54	36–41	24–26	7–9	54–57	13–20	13–20	14–21

BRAKE SPECIFICATIONS
All measurements in inches unless noted

Year	Model	Lug Nut Torque (ft. lbs.)	Master Cylinder Bore	Brake Disc Minimum Thickness	Brake Disc Maximum Runout	Standard Brake Drum Diameter	Minimum Lining Thickness Front	Minimum Lining Thickness Rear
1988	Samurai	36–57	NA	0.394	0.334	8.66	0.236 ①	0.120 ②
1989	Samurai	36–57	NA	0.394	0.334	8.66	0.236 ①	0.120 ②
	Sidekick	36–57	NA	0.394	0.334	8.66	0.236 ①	0.120 ②
1990	Samurai	36–57	NA	0.394	0.334	8.66	0.236 ①	0.120 ②
	Sidekick	36–57	NA	0.394	0.334	8.66	0.236 ①	0.120 ②
1991	Samurai	36–57	NA	0.394	0.334	8.66	0.236 ①	0.120 ②
	Sidekick	58–78	NA	0.394	0.315	8.66	0.315 ①	0.120 ②
1992	Samurai	36–57	NA	0.394	0.334	8.66	0.236 ①	0.120 ②
	Sidekick	58–78	NA	0.394	0.315	8.66	0.315 ①	0.120 ②

NA—Not available
① Lining plus pad rim
② Lining plus shoe rim

WHEEL ALIGNMENT

Year	Model	Caster Range (deg.)	Caster Preferred Setting (deg.)	Camber Range (deg.)	Camber Preferred Setting (deg.)	Toe-in (in.)	Steering Axis Inclination (deg.)
1988	Samurai	2½P–4½P	3½P	¼P–1¾P	1P	5/32–15/32	9
1989	Samurai	2½P–4½P	3½P	¼P–1¾P	1P	5/32–15/32	9
	Sidekick	½P–2½P	1½P	½N–1½P	½P	5/16–¼	NA
1990	Samurai	2½P–4½P	3½P	¼P–1¾P	1P	5/32–15/32	9
	Sidekick	½P–2½P	1½P	½N–1½P	½P	5/16–¼	NA
1991	Samurai	2½P–4½P	3½P	½P–1¾P	1P	5/32–15/32	9
	Sidekick	½P–2½P	1½P	½N–1½P	½P	5/16–¼	NA
1992	Samurai	2½P–4½P	3½P	½P–1¾P	1P	5/32–15/32	9
	Sidekick	½P–2½P	1½P	½N–1½P	½P	5/16–¼	NA

NA—Not available
N—Negative
P—Positive

ENGINE ELECTRICAL

NOTE: Disconnecting the battery cable on some vehicles may interfere with the functions of the on board computer systems and may require the computer to undergo a relearning process, once the negative battery cable is disconnected.

Distributor

Removal

1. Disconnect the negative battery terminal at the battery.
2. Disconnect the electrical connections and the vacuum hoses.

NOTE: Do not bend or twist the spark plug wires to avoid internal damage. Grip the the wire boot when removing or installing the wires.

3. Remove the distributor cap.
4. Mark the rotor position on the distributor housing and the distributor housing position on the engine.
5. Remove the distributor flange bolt and remove the distributor.

NOTE: Do not crank the engine with the distributor removed.

Installation

TIMING NOT DISTURBED

1. Install the distributor and align the marks on the distributor housing and on the engine.
2. Tighten the flange bolt and install the distributor cap.
3. Connect the electrical connections and the vacuum hoses.
4. Connect the negative battery cable and set the timing to specification.

TIMING DISTURBED

1. Rotate the crankshaft in a clockwise position until the specified timing mark on the flywheel aligns with the timing matchmark on the engine.

NOTE: After aligning the 2 marks, remove the cylinder head cover to visually check that the rocker arms are not riding on the camshaft cams at No. 1 cylinder. If the arms are found to be riding on the cams, turn the crankshaft 360 degrees to realign the 2 marks.

Timing mark alignment—Samurai
The timing marks are visible by removing the rubber plug in the bell housing

Timing marks—Sidekick

Installed jumper wire at monitor coupler

2. Position the rotor to the No. 1 cylinder position and install the distributor.
3. Connect the vacuum and electrical connections.
4. Connect the negative battery cable and set the timing to specification.

Ignition Timing

Adjustment

1. Start the engine and warm up to normal operating temperature. Prior to any adjustment, be sure all the electrical accessories are OFF .
2. After warming up, make sure the idle speed is within the proper specification.
3. Remove cap from monitor coupler next to battery and connect terminals C and D with a jumper wire. Connect the timing light to the No. 1 cylinder spark plug wire.
4. With the engine running at the specified idle speed, direct the timing light to the crankshaft pulley. If the specified timing mark on the timing tab is aligned with the timing notch on the crankshaft pulley the ignition is properly timed.
5. If the timing is out of adjustment, loosen the distributor flange bolt and turn the distributor housing to advance or retard the timing. Turn the distributor counterclockwise to advance the timing and clockwise to retard the timing.
6. After the adjustment, tighten the flange bolt and recheck the timing.

Alternator

For further information, please refer to "Alternators" in the Unit Repair section.

Belt Tension Adjustment

1. Disconnect the negative battery cable.

2. Loosen the alternator bolt and pivot bolts.

3. Adjust the belt tension to 0.24 – 0.32 in. of deflection using a belt tension gauge and measuring at the midpoint between the 2 pulleys.

Removal and Installation

1. Disconnect the negative battery cable.

2. Disconnect the wire coupler and white lead wire from the alternator.

3. Remove the radiator shroud from under the radiator.

4. Remove the alternator mounting bolt and alternator drive belt adjusting bolt.

5. Remove the alternator from the vehicle.

To install:

6. Install the alternator and tighten the mounting bolt and drive belt adjusting bolt. Adjust the drive belt tension.

7. Install the shroud under the radiator and connect the wire coupler to the alternator.

8. Connect the negative battery cable.

Starter

For further information, please refer to "Starters" in the Unit Repair section.

Removal and Installation

1. Disconnect the negative battery cable.

2. Raise and support the vehicle safely.

3. Disconnect the lead wire and battery cable from the starter motor.

4. Support the starter and remove the 2 mounting bolts.

5. Remove the starter.

To install:

6. Install the starter and tighten the 2 mounting bolts to 22 ft. lbs..

7. Connect the lead wire and battery cable to the starter.

8. Lower the vehicle and connect the negative battery cable.

CHASSIS ELECTRICAL

Heater Blower Motor

Removal and Installation

SAMURAI

1. Disconnect the negative battery cable. Drain the cooling system.

2. Disconnect the inlet and outlet heater hoses from the heater core.

3. Remove the horn pad and the steering wheel retaining nut and remove the steering wheel by using the proper puller.

4. Disconnect and tag the radio and cigar lighter wires. Remove the radio from the vehicle.

5. Remove the ash tray and mounting plate.

6. Disconnect the hood release cable from the release lever.

7. Disconnect and tag the heater control cables and wires at the controls.

8. Remove the heater control lever knobs and facing plate. Loosen the lever case screws.

9. Remove the defroster and side ventilator hoses.

10. Disconnect the lead wires and speedometer cable from the speedometer and remove the lead wires from the heater controls.

11. Disconnect the wiring harness clamps from the instrument panel.

12. Loosen the instrument panel mounting screws and remove the instrument panel.

NOTE: When removing the heater lever case which is fitted in the steering column holder, be very careful not to damage it.

13. Loosen the front door opening stop screws and remove the steering column bracket.

14. Disconnect and tag the blower motor and resistor connections at the coupler.

15. Loosen the heater case securing nut on the engine side.

16. Remove the heater assembly from the vehicle.

17. Remove the blower motor from the case.

To install:

18. Install the blower motor in the heater case and install the assembly in the vehicle.

19. Tighten the heater case securing nut on the engine side.

20. Install the blower motor and resistor connections at the coupler.

21. Tighten the front door opening stop screws and install the steering column holder.

22. Tighten the instrument panel mounting screws and replace the instrument panel.

23. Reconnect the wiring harness clamps to the instrument panel.

24. Reconnect the lead wires and speedometer cable to the speedometer.

25. Install the defroster and side ventilator hoses.

26. Install the heater control knobs and plate, and tighten the lever case screws.

27. Reconnect the heater control cables at the controls.

28. Reconnect the hood release cable to the release lever.

29. Install the ash tray and mounting plate.

30. Reconnect the radio and cigar lighter wires. Install the radio in the vehicle.

31. Install the horn pad and steering wheel retaining nut and install the steering wheel.

32. Reconnect the inlet and outlet heater hoses to heater core.

33. Refill the cooling system with the proper coolant. Install the negative battery cable.

SIDEKICK

1. Disconnect the negative battery cable.

2. Remove the glove box assembly.

3. Disconnect the blower motor and resistor wire connectors.

4. Disconnect the fresh air control cable from the blower motor case.

5. Loosen but do not remove the blower housing fastener bolts.

6. Remove the 3 blower motor mounting screws.

7. Remove the blower motor.

To install:

8. Install the blower motor and install the 3 mounting screws.

9. Tighten the blower housing fastener bolts.

10. Connect the fresh air control cable to the blower motor case.

11. Connect the blower motor and resistor wire connectors.

12. Install the glove box assembly and connect the negative battery cable.

Windshield Wiper Motor

Removal and Installation

SAMURAI

Soft Top

1. Disconnect the negative battery cable.
2. Remove the wiper linkage to wiper mounting nut.
3. Disconnect the wire connector from the wiper motor.
4. Remove the 3 wiper mounting bolts and remove the wiper motor.

To install:

5. Install the wiper motor and install the 3 mounting bolts.
6. Connect the wire connector and linkage to the wiper motor and tighten the linkage mounting nut.
7. Connect the negative battery cable.

Hard Top

NOTE: On some models, the windshield frame may have to be removed.

1. Disconnect the negative battery cable.
2. Remove the wiper linkage to wiper mounting nut.
3. Disconnect the wire connector from the wiper motor.
4. Remove the 3 wiper mounting bolts and remove the wiper motor.

To install:

5. Install the 3 wiper motor mounting bolts and install the motor.
6. Install the linkage and mounting nut and connect the negative battery cable.

SIDEKICK

1. Disconnect the negative battery cable.
2. Remove the right and left cowl grilles.
3. Remove the wiper linkage to wiper mounting nut.
4. Disconnect the wire connector from the wiper motor.
5. Remove the 4 wiper mounting bolts and remove the wiper motor.

To install:

6. Install the 4 wiper mounting bolts and the wiper motor.
7. Connect the wiper motor wire connector and wiper linkage.
8. Install the right and left cowl grilles and connect the negative battery cable.

Instrument Cluster

Removal and Installation

1. Disconnect the negative battery cable.
2. Remove the lower instrument panel cover.
3. Loosen, but do not remove the 2 upper and 4 lower steering column mounting bolts. Lower and support the steering column, if neccessary.
4. Remove the outer instrument cluster cover.
5. Remove the 4 cluster mounting screws and slide the cluster outwards.
6. Disconnect the lead wires and speedometer cable from the speedometer.
7. Remove the speedometer.
8. Disconnect and tag the wire connector from the rear of the instrument cluster.
9. Remove the instrument cluster.

To install:

10. Install the instrument cluster and connect the wire connector to the rear.
11. Install the speedometer and connect the speedometer cable and lead wires.
12. Install the 4 cluster mounting screws.
13. Install the outer instrument cluster cover.

14. Secure the steering column and the column mounting bolts.
15. Install the lower instrument cover panel and connect the negative battery cable.

Combination Switch

The combination switch incorporates the turn signal, windshield wiper, dimmer and headlight switches into 1 switch.

Removal and Installation

1. Disconnect the negative battery cable.
2. Remove the horn button and remove the steering wheel retaining nut and remove the steering wheel.
3. Remove the upper and lower column cover screws and remove the covers.
4. Disconnect the lead wires from the combination switch at the connector.
5. Remove the combination switch assembly screws.
6. Remove the combination switch from the steering column.

To install:

7. Install the combination switch to the steering column and install the assembly screws.
8. Connect the lead wires at the connector to the combination switch.
9. Install the lower and upper column covers and reinstall the steering wheel.
10. Install the horn button and connect the negative battery cable.

Ignition Switch

Removal and Installation

1. Disconnect the negative battery cable.
2. Remove the steering wheel from the vehicle.
3. Disconnect the wire connector at the ignition switch.
4. With the ignition switch in the **OFF** position, remove the mounting bolts and remove the switch.

To install:

5. With the ignition switch in the **OFF** position, install the switch and the mounting bolts.
6. Connect the wire connector at the ignition switch.
7. Install the steering wheel and horn pad and connect the negative battery cable.

Ignition Lock

Removal and Installation

1. Disconnect the negative battery cable.
2. Remove the steering wheel.
3. Disconnect the lead wires to the ignition and combination switches.
4. Disconnect the steering joint by removing the joint bolt.
5. Remove the steering column fastening bolts.
6. Remove the steering column assembly.
7. Using a center punch, loosen and remove the steering lock mounting bolts.
8. Turn the key to **ACC** or **ON** position and remove the steering lock assembly from the steering column.

To install:

9. To install the switch position the oblong hole of the steering shaft in the center of the hole in the steering column.
10. Turn the ignition key to the **ACC** or **ON** position and install the steering lock assembly onto the column.

11. Turn the ignition key to the **LOCK** position and remove it.
12. Align the hub on the lock with oblong hole of the steering shaft.
13. Rotate the shaft to assure that the steering shaft is locked.
14. Tighten the 2 new steering lock mounting bolts.
15. Turn the ignition key to the **ACC** or **ON** position and check to be sure the steering shaft rotates smoothly and check the lock mechanism operation.
16. Install the steering column assembly by attaching the joint and joint bolt.
17. Install the steering column attaching bolts.
18. Connect the wires to the ignition and combination switches.
19. Install the steering wheel and connect the negative battery cable.

Stoplight Switch

Removal and Installation

1. Disconnect the negative battery cable. Remove the under dash trim panel, if equipped.
2. Push the brake pedal down and remove the stoplight locknut.
3. Disconnect the wire connector at the switch.
4. Remove the switch from the bracket.

To install:

5. Install the new switch on the bracket.
6. Adjust the switch so there is 0.02–0.04 in. clearance between the switch and the brake pedal.
7. Install the locknut and tighten to 7.5–10.5 ft. lbs.
8. Install the negative battery cable.

Clutch Switch

Removal and Installation

SIDEKICK

1. Disconnect the negative battery cable. Remove the under dash trim panel, if equipped.
2. Disconnect the start switch connector beside the clutch pedal bracket.
3. Remove the locknut and start switch.

To install:

4. Installation is the reverse of the removal procedure.

Fuses and Relays

Location

The fuse box and turn signal relay are located under the driver side of the dashboard.

View of the cruise control adjustment

Computers

Location

SIDEKICK

The Electronic Control Module computer is located under the dash on the driver side of the vehicle.

Cruise Control

For further information, please refer to Chilton's Chassis Electronics Service Manual.

Adjustment

SIDEKICK

1. Remove the top cover from the actuator assembly.
2. Loosen the lock nuts on the cable.
3. Adjust the cable so the play range is between 0.04–0.08 in. when the actuator lever is fully closed.
4. Tighten the locknut to 4 ft. lbs. and replace the top cover.

ENGINE COOLING

Radiator

Removal and Installation

1. Disconnect the negative battery cable.
2. Drain the cooling system.
3. Disconnect and plug the transmission cooler lines, if equipped.
4. Loosen the water pump drive belt tension.
5. Remove the cooling fan and radiator shroud.

6. Disconnect the water hoses to the radiator.
7. Remove the radiator retaining bolts and remove the radiator.

To install:

8. Install the radiator mounting bolts and install the radiator.
9. Reconnect the water hoses to the radiator.
10. Install the cooling fan and radiator shroud.
11. Tighten the water pump drive belt to the proper tension.

12. Reconnect the transmission cooler lines, if necessary, to the radiator.
13. Refill the cooling system.
14. Reconnect the negative battery cable.

Heater Core

For further information, please refer to Chilton's Air Conditioning and Heating Manual.

Removal and Installation
SAMURAI

1. Disconnect the negative battery cable. Drain the cooling system.
2. Disconnect the heater hoses from the heater core.
3. Disconnect the radio and cigar lighter lead wires, and remove the radio from the vehicle.
4. Remove the ash tray and mounting plate.
5. Disconnect the hood release cable from the release lever.
6. Disconnect and tag the heater control cables and wires at the controls.
7. Remove the heater control lever knobs and facing plate, and loosen the lever case screws.
8. Remove the defroster and side ventilator hoses.
9. Disconnect the lead wires and speedometer cables from the speedometer.
10. Disconnect the wiring harness from the instrument panel.
11. Loosen the instrument panel mounting screws and remove the instrument panel.
12. Loosen the front door opening stop screws and remove the steering column holder.
13. Disconnect and tag the blower motor and resistor connections at the coupler.
14. Loosen the heater securing nut on the engine side.
15. Remove the heater assembly from the vehicle.
16. Remove the clips holding the heater case together, separate the case and remove the heater core.
To install:
17. Install the heater core into the heater case and install the clips holding the case together.
18. Install the heater assembly in the vehicle and tighten the securing nut on the engine side.
19. Reconnect the blower motor and resistor connections at the coupler.
20. Install the steering column holder and tighten the front door opening stop screws.
21. Install the instrument panel and tighten panel mounting screws.
22. Reconnect the wiring harness to the instrument panel.
23. Install the defroster and side ventilator hoses.
24. Tighten the heater control case screws and install the control knobs and facing plate.
25. Reconnect the heater control cable and wires to the heater control.
26. Reconnect the hood release cable the release lever.
27. Install the ash tray and mounting plate.
28. Install radio and connect the cigar lighter and radio wires.
29. Reconnect the heater hoses to the heater core.
30. Refill the cooling system to the proper with the proper coolant. Install the negative cable.

SIDEKICK

1. Disconnect the negative battery cable. Drain the cooling system.
2. Disconnect the 2 water hoses from the heater assembly.
3. Remove the steering wheel. Disconnect the lead wires from the ignition and combination switches.
4. Disconnect the wiring harness and remove the instrument panel and related parts.

5. Disconnect all the wiring connections and cables from the heater controls.
6. Disconnect the defroster duct and speedometer cable retaining bracket from the heater case.
7. Remove the heater assembly and remove the heater core.
To install:
8. Install the heater core and install the heater assembly.
9. Reconnect the defroster duct and speedometer cable retaining bracket to the heater case.
10. Reconnect the wiring connections and cables to the heater controls.
11. Reconnect the wiring harness and install the instrument panel.
12. Connect the lead wires to the ignition and combination switches and install the steering wheel.
13. Connect the water hoses to the heater assembly.
14. Refill the cooling system with the proper coolant and replace the negative battery cable.

Water Pump

Removal and Installation

1. Disconnect the negative battery cable.
2. Drain the cooling system.
3. Loosen the drive belt tension and remove the drive belt. If equipped, loosen the air conditioning belt tension and remove the air conditioning belt.
4. Remove the radiator fan shroud mounting bolts and radiator fan mounting bolts. Remove the radiator shroud, fan and water pump pulley from the vehicle.
5. Remove the crankshaft pulley bolts and remove the crankshaft pulley.

NOTE: The crankshaft pulley bolt can be removed without removing the center crankshaft bolt.

6. Remove the timing belt cover mounting bolts and remove the cover.
7. Loosen the timing belt tensioner adjusting bolt and pivot nut. Hold the tensioner to loosen the timing belt and remove the belt from the camshaft pulley.
8. Remove the timing belt tensioner mounting bolts and remove the tensioner plate and spring.
9. Remove the water pump mounting bolts and remove the water pump assembly.
10. On Sidekick, it is necessary to remove the dipstick tube and the alternator bracket from the vehicle.
To install:
11. Clean and inspect the surface of the engine before installation.
12. Using a new gasket, install the new water pump on the engine. Torque the mounting bolts to 8 ft. lbs.
13. On Sidekick, install the dipstick tube and the alternator bracket to the vehicle.
14. Install the rubber seals between the water pump to cylinder head and water pump to oil pump.
15. Install the timing belt tensioner plate, tensioner and spring.
16. Align the marks on the timing belt and the camshaft sprocket. Install the timing belt in the same position on the camshaft sprocket as when removed.
17. Adjust the timing belt to be free of any slack. Torque the tensioner bolts to 7.5–9.0 ft. lbs.
18. Install the crankshaft and water pump pulleys. Torque the crankshaft and water pulley bolts to 7.5–9.0 ft. lbs.
19. Install the timing belt cover, cooling fan/clutch, shroud and drive belt. Adjust the belt tension.
20. As required, adjust the intake and exhaust valve lash.
21. Refill the cooling system with the proper coolant and replace the negative battery cable.

Thermostat

Removal and Installation

1. Disconnect the negative battery cable.
2. Drain the cooling system.
3. Disconnect the thermostat cap from the intake manifold and remove the thermostat.

To install:
4. Clean and inspect the surfaces of the housing and the engine.
5. Install the new thermostat with the spring facing towards the engine.
6. Install a new gasket and the thermostat cap to the intake manifold.
7. Refill the cooling system with the proper coolant and replace the negative battery cable.

FUEL SYSTEM

Fuel System Service Precaution

When working with the fuel system, certain precautions should be taken; always work in a well ventilated area, keep a dry chemical (Class B) fire extinguisher near the work area. Always disconnect the negative battery cable and do not make any repairs to the fuel system until all the necessary steps for repair have been reviewed.

Relieving Fuel System Pressure

The fuel pressure must be relieved before performing any service on the fuel system.
1. Disconnect the negative battery cable.
2. Remove the fuel filler cap from the fuel filler neck to release the fuel vapor pressure in the fuel tank. Reinstall the fuel cap.
3. Raise and support the vehicle safely.
4. Place an appropriate container under the fuel filter.
5. Cover the plug bolt on the fuel filter inlet union bolt with a rag and loosen the plug bolt slowly to release the fuel pressure gradually.
6. When the pressure has been released, tighten the plug bolt to 7.5 ft. lbs. so the fuel does not leak.
7. Lower the vehicle.
8. Reconnect the negative battery cable.

Fuel Filter

Removal and Installation

1. Disconnect the negative battery cable.
2. Remove the fuel filler cap to release the fuel vapor pressure in the fuel tank. After releasing pressure, reinstall filler cap.
3. Raise and support the vehicle safely.
4. Release the fuel pressure.
5. Disconnect the inlet and outlet hoses from the fuel filter.
6. Remove the fuel filter from the chassis frame.
To install:
7. Install the new fuel filter to the frame and connect the inlet and outlet hoses.
8. Lower the vehicle and connect the negative battery cable.

Mechanical Fuel Pump

Removal and Installation

1.3L ENGINE

1. Disconnect the negative battery cable.
2. Remove the fuel filler cap to release the fuel vapor pressure in the fuel tank.
3. Disconnect and tag the fuel inlet, outlet and return hoses from the fuel pump.
4. Remove the fuel pump mounting bolts and remove the fuel pump.
5. Remove the fuel pump mounting rod from the engine and lubricate it with engine oil before installation.

To install:
6. Clean the engine mounting surface and install the fuel pump using a new gasket and tighten to 10 ft. lbs.
7. Connect the inlet, outlet and return hoses to the fuel pump.
8. Reconnect the negative battery cable. Run the engine and check for leaks when finished.

Electric Fuel Pump

Pressure Testing

1.6L ENGINE

1. Remove the fuel filler cap to release the fuel vapor pressure in the fuel tank. Reinstall the cap.
2. Raise and support the vehicle safely.
3. Release the fuel pressure in the fuel feed line.
4. Remove the plug bolt on the fuel filter union bolt and connect the proper fuel pressure gauge to the fuel filter inlet union bolt.

NOTE: If the pressure in the fuel tank is not released prior to system service, the fuel in the fuel tank may be forced out through the fuel hoses during disconnection.

5. Start the engine and warm up to the proper operating temperature.
6. Measure the fuel pressure under each of the following conditions.
    a. At a sp ecified idle speed or with the fuel pump operating and the engine stopped the fuel pressure should read: 34.1–39.8 psi.
    b. Within 1 minute after the fuel pump has stopped the fuel pressure should read: 21.3 psi.
7. Release the fuel pressure and remove the fuel pressure gauge.
8. Install the plug bolt to the fuel filter inlet bolt. Use a new gasket.
9. Start the engine and check for leaks.
10. Lower the vehicle.

FUEL FILTER

Checking fuel pump pressure

Removal and Installation

1.6L ENGINE

The fuel pump is located in the fuel tank. The fuel pump and the fuel gauge sending unit are located on the upper part of the fuel tank.

1. Disconnect the negative battery cable.
2. Remove the rear bumper assembly.
3. Disconnect the fuel gauge sending unit and fuel pump electrical connectors from the fuel tank.
4. Relieve the fuel system pressure.
5. Disconnect the fuel tank filler hose cover, filler hose, and fuel tank inlet valve (breather hose).
6. Disconnect the inlet pipe from the fuel filter and remove the fuel vapor and return hoses.
7. If necessary, drain the fuel from the tank using a hand operated pump.
8. Disconnect the fuel tank protector and remove the fuel tank and cover from the vehicle.
9. Remove the fuel pump from the fuel tank.

To install:

10. Install the fuel pump to the fuel tank using a new gasket.
11. Install the fuel tank and cover to the vehicle and connect the fuel tank protector.
12. Install the fuel vapor and return hoses and connect the inlet pipe to the fuel filter.
13. Reconnect the fuel tank inlet valve (breather hose), filler hose, and fuel tank filler hose cover.
14. Connect the fuel pump and fuel gauge sending sending unit electrical connectors to the fuel tank.
15. Install the bumper assembly and reconnect the negative battery cable.
16. If necessary, refill the fuel tank with any fuel that had been drained.
17. Start the engine and check for leaks when finished.

Carburetor

Removal and Installation

1.3L ENGINE

1. Disconnect the negative battery cable. Drain the cooling system.
2. Remove the air intake case from the carburetor.
3. Disconnect and tag the micro switches, switch vent solenoid valve, fuel cut off valve, vacuum switch valve and Mixture Control Valve (MCSV) lead wires at their couplers.
4. Disconnect the EGR valve bracket from the carburetor.
5. Disconnect the water inlet and outlet hoses from the carburetor.
6. Disconnect the accelerator cable from the carburetor.
7. Relieve the fuel pressure by removing the fuel filler cap and reinstalling it. Remove the fuel inlet hose from the carburetor.
8. Remove the carburetor mounting nuts and remove the carburetor from the intake manifold.

To install:

9. Install the carburetor to the intake manifold and install the mounting nuts. Torque the carburetor mounting nuts to 20 ft. lbs.
10. Install the fuel inlet hose and connect the accelerator cable to the carburetor.
11. Reconnect the water inlet and outlet hoses to the carburetor.
12. Connect the EGR valve bracket to the carburetor.
13. Reconnect the micro switches, switch vent solenoid valve, fuel cut off valve, vacuum switch valve and (MCSV) lead wires to their couplers.
14. Install the air intake hose to the carburetor.
15. Refill the cooling system with the proper coolant and connect the negative battery cable.

Idle Speed Adjustment

NOTE: Before starting the engine, place the gear shift lever in neutral for manual transmission or P for automatic transmission. Set the parking brake and block the drive wheels.

1. Warm up the engine to the normal operating temperature.
2. Check the idle speed to see if within specifications; 750–850 rpm.
3. If idle speed is not within specifications, adjust by turning the idle speed adjusting screw.
4. After idle speed adjustment, check idle-up for operation with the electrical accessories **ON** one at a time.

Idle Mixture Adjustment

1. Remove the carburetor from the intake manifold to obtain access to the cap covering the mixture adjusting screw.
2. Drive out the mixture adjusting screw pin using about 0.18 in. thick iron rod.
3. Reinstall the carburetor.
4. Before starting the engine, place the gear shift lever in neutral for manual transmission or **P** for automatic transmission. Set the parking brake and block the drive wheels.
5. Start the engine and warm up to normal temperature.
6. Check and adjust the idle speed if necessary.
7. Remove the rubber seal of the dwell check coupler and connect the positive terminal of a dwell meter to the blue and red wire and negative terminal to the black and green wire.
8. Run the engine at 1500–2000 rpm for 30 seconds and adjust the idle speed.
9. Adjust the idle mixture adjusting screw slowly, allowing for the dwell to stabilize after turning screw to obtain a dwell of 10–50 degrees at 750–850 rpm.
10. Recheck the engine idle speed.

Idle adjustment—1.3L engine

Idle mixture adjustment—1.3L engine

Idle adjustment—1.6L engine

11. Install the rubber seal to the dwell check coupler and drive in idle mixture adjusting pin.

Service Adjustment

For all carburetor service adjustment procedures and Specifications, please refer to "Carburetor Service" in the Unit Repair section.

Fuel Injection

For further information, please refer to Chilton's Electronic Engine Controls Manual.

Idle Speed Adjustment

NOTE: Before starting the engine, place the gear shift lever in neutral for manual transmission or P for automatic transmission. Set the parking brake and block the drive wheels.

1. Warm the engine to the normal operating temperature.
2. Race the engine until the engine speed exceeds 1500 rpm and then let it slow down to idle speed.
3. Check and see if the idle speed is within 750–850 rpm.

Fuel Injector

Removal and Installation

1.6L ENGINE

1. Disconnect the negative battery cable.
2. Release the fuel pressure.
3. Remove the the air intake case from the throttle body.
4. Remove the fuel feed pipe clamp from the intake manifold and disconnect the fuel feed pipe from the throttle body.
5. Remove the injector cover.
6. Disconnect the injector coupler, release its wire harness from the clamp and remove its grommet from the throttle body.
7. Place a cloth over the injector and a hand on top of it. Using an air gun, blow low pressure compressed air into the fuel inlet port of the throttle body and the injector can be removed.

NOTE: Be precise about the pressure of the compressed air. Using excessively high pressure may force the injector to jump out and may cause damage, not only to the injector itself but also to other parts.
To install:
8. Apply thin coating of gasoline to O-rings and then install the fuel injector to the throttle body.
9. Connect fuel injector wire connector and install injector cover.
10. Connect fuel feed pipe to throttle body.
11. Connect the negative battery cable and turn the ignition ON for 3 seconds and then OFF until fuel pressure is felt at the return hose.
12. Install air intake case assembly.
13. Secure all wires and check for any leaks in the system.

EMISSION CONTROLS

Emission Warning Lamps

For further information, please refer to Chilton's Emission Controls Manual.

The CHECK ENGINE light automatically comes on at 50,000, 80,000 and 100,000 miles.

Resetting

The lamp reset switch is located on the left side of the dashboard, mounted on the steering column support. The lamp can be reset by moving the switch upwards and then downwards. If the switch remains on after being reset, check the system.

1. Cancel switch (USA) —Check switch (CANADA)
2. Instrument panel
3. Steering column bracket
4. Steering wheel

Resetting the check engine light

ENGINE MECHANICAL

NOTE: Disconnecting the battery cable on some vehicles may interfere with the functions of the on board computer systems and may require the computer to undergo a relearning process, once the negative battery cable is disconnected.

Engine

Removal and Installation

1. Disconnect both cables at the battery.
2. Remove the hood from the vehicle and drain the cooling system.
3. Remove the radiator reservoir tank, fan shroud, cooling fan and radiator.
4. Properly discharge the air conditioning system and remove the air conditioning condenser, if equipped.
5. Remove the air cleaner outlet hose.
6. Disconnect the accelerator and the automatic transmission kickdown cable from the throttle body, if equipped.
7. Disconnect and tag the throttle opener VSV and EGR VSV wires at the coupler.
8. Disconnect and tag the water temperature, oil pressure, air temperature and ground cable wires at the intake manifold.
9. Disconnect and tag the injector, throttle position sensor and idle speed control solenoid valve wires at their couplers, if equipped.
10. Disconnect the PTC heater wires at the coupler for automatic transmission vehicles, if equipped.
11. Disconnect and tag the wires at the starter and alternator.
12. Disconnect and tag the oxygen sensor and distributor wires at their couplers. Remove the coil wire.
13. Remove the starter motor and disconnect the ground wires from the distributor.
14. Remove the fuel tank filler cap to relieve the pressure. Reinstall the cap.
15. Relieve the fuel pressure in the fuel feed line. Disconnect and tag the fuel feed and return hoses.
16. Remove the gear shift lever mounting bolts and remove the shifter.
17. Disconnect the canister purge hose and remove the pressure sensor hose from the fuel filter, if equipped.
18. Disconnect the brake booster hose from the intake manifold.
19. Remove the vacuum hose from the intake manifold, if equipped with automatic transmission.
20. Disconnect the heater hoses from the intake manifold and from the heater core outlet.
21. Raise and safely support the vehicle.
22. Drain the engine oil and disconnect the exhaust pipe from the exhaust manifold and muffler.
23. Disconnect the clutch cable, if equipped with manual transmission.
24. Drain the automatic transmission fluid, if equipped.
25. Disconnect the clutch (torque converter) housing lower plate.
26. Remove the lock driveplate, using the special tool, if equipped with automatic transmission.
27. Lower the vehicle.
28. Remove the nuts and bolts between the cylinder block and transmission.
29. Support the transmission, using an appropriate stand or jack.
30. Support the engine from the top using a chain type hoist.
31. Remove the engine mount assemblies.

NOTE: Before lifting the engine, check to ensure all the hoses, wires and cables are disconnected from the engine.

32. Remove the engine assembly from the chassis and transmission by sliding towards the front and carefully hoist the engine.

To install:

33. Install the engine into the engine compartment and connect to the transmission.
34. Install the engine mounts with the chassis side mounting brackets. Tighten to 41 ft. lbs.
35. Remove the lifting device.
36. Install the nuts and bolts fastening the cylinder block and transmission.
37. Raise and safely support the vehicle.
38. Install the lock driveplate, if equipped.
39. Connect the clutch (torque converter) housing lower plate.
40. Connect the automatic transmission lines, if equipped.
41. Reconnect the clutch cable to the bracket, if equipped with manual transmission.
42. Connect the exhaust pipe to the exhaust manifold and muffler.
43. Lower the vehicle.
44. Reconnect the heater hoses to the outlet pipe and the intake manifold.
45. Install the vacuum hose for the automatic transmission to the intake manifold, if equipped.
46. Reconnect the brake booster hose to the intake manifold.
47. Install the pressure sensor hose to the fuel filter and connect the canister purge hose, if equipped.
48. Install the fuel return and feed hoses.
49. Install the starter motor and connect the ground wire to the distributor.
50. Install the coil wire and connect the oxygen sensor and distributor wires to their couplers.
51. Reconnect the wires at the alternator and starter motor.
52. Install the PTC heater wires at the coupler, if equipped with automatic transmission.
53. Install the idle speed control solenoid valve, throttle position sensor and injector wires at their couplers, if equipped.
54. Connect the ground cable, air temperature, oil pressure and water temperature wires to the intake manifold.
55. Reconnect the throttle opener VSR and EGR VSR wires to their couplers, if equipped.
56. Connect the accelerator cable and the automatic transmission kickdown cable, if equipped, to the throttle body.
57. Install the air cleaner outlet hose. Refill the engine oil and the transmission oil to the proper level.
58. Install the air conditioning condenser and properly recharge the air conditioning system, if equipped.
59. Install the radiator, cooling fan, fan shroud and radiator reservoir tank.
60. Install the hood and refill the cooling system with the proper coolant.
61. Reconnect the positive and negative battery cables.
62. Adjust the accelerator, clutch and the automatic transmission kickdown cable, if equipped.
63. Before starting the engine, check to see if all the parts disassembled are back in place securely.
64. Start the engine and check the timing. Check for any oil leaks.

Cylinder Head

Removal and Installation

NOTE: When removing the cylinder head, remove the pools from the top of the cylinder head before loosening the head bolts to avoid possible contamination.

1. Disconnect the negative battery cable. Drain the cooling system.

Cylinder head bolt tightening sequence

2. Disconnect the air intake case.

3. Disconnect the brake booster hose from the intake manifold and the air valve water hose from the throttle body.

4. Disconnect the accelerator and the automatic transmission kickdown cable, if equipped, from the throttle body.

5. Disconnect and tag the throttle opener VSV and EGR VSV wires at the coupler.

6. Disconnect and tag the water temperature, oil pressure, air temperature sensor and ground cable wires at the intake manifold.

7. Disconnect and tag the injector, throttle position sensor and idle speed control solenoid valve wires at their couplers, if equipped.

8. Disconnect the PTC heater wires at the coupler, if equipped with automatic transmission.

9. Disconnect and tag the oxygen sensor and distributor wires at their couplers. Remove the coil wire.

10. Disconnect the ground wires from the distributor assembly.

11. Remove the fuel tank filler cap to relieve the pressure. Reinstall the cap.

12. Release the fuel pressure in the fuel feed line.

13. Disconnect the fuel feed and return hoses.

14. Disconnect the canister purge hose and remove the pressure sensor hose from the fuel filter, if equipped.

15. Remove the vacuum hose for the automatic transmission from the intake manifold, if equipped.

16. Disconnect the radiator cooling fan, fan shroud, water pump drive belt and water pump pulley.

17. Disconnect the crankshaft pulley, timing belt cover and the timing belt.

18. Raise and safely support the vehicle.

19. Disconnect the exhaust pipe from the exhaust manifold and lower the vehicle.

20. Disconnect the air conditioner compressor adjusting arm, if equipped.

21. Remove the cylinder head cover mounting bolts and remove the cylinder head cover.

22. Loosen all the valve adjusting screw locknuts, turn the adjusting screws back all the way to allow all the valves to close.

23. Remove the intake manifold with the carburetor attached, from the cylinder head.

24. Remove the distributor and distributor housing from the cylinder head.

25. Remove the cylinder head mounting bolts and remove the cylinder head from the engine.

26. Remove any oil and water in the cylinder bores and on top of the pistons.

27. Clean and inspect the sealing surfaces of the cylinder head and the engine block.

To install:

28. Install the cylinder head using a new gasket.

29. Install the cylinder head mounting bolts and tighten to 46–54 ft. lbs.

30. Install the distributor and distributor housing to the cylinder head.

31. Install the intake manifold with the carburetor attached, to the cylinder head.

32. Tighten all the valve adjusting screw nuts.

33. Adjust the valve lash.

34. Install the cylinder head cover and connect the air conditioning compressor adjusting arm, if equipped.

35. Raise and safely support the vehicle.

36. Connect the exhaust pipe to the exhaust manifold and safely lower the vehicle.

37. Reconnect the timing belt, timing belt cover and crankshaft pulley.

38. Install the water pump pulley, water pump drive belt, fan shroud and the radiator cooling fan.

39. Install the vacuum hose for the automatic transmission to the intake manifold, if equipped.

40. Install the pressure sensor hose to the fuel filter and connect the canister purge hose, if equipped.

41. Install the fuel return and feed hoses.

42. Connect the ground wires to the distributor assembly.

43. Install the coil wire. Connect the oxygen sensor and distributor wires to their couplers.

44. Connect the PTC wires to the coupler.

45. Connect the idle speed control valve, throttle position sensor and injector wires to their couplers, if equipped.

46. Reconnect the ground cable, air temperature, oil pressure and water temperature sensor wires to the intake manifold.

47. Install the throttle opener VSV and EGR VSV wires to their couplers.

48. Connect the accelerator and the automatic transmission kickdown cables, if equipped, to the throttle body.

49. Install the air valve water hose to the throttle body and connect the brake booster hose to intake manifold.

50. Reconnect the air intake case.

51. Refill the cooling system with the proper coolant and connect the negative battery.

52. Check for any water and oil leaks when finished.

Valve Lash

Adjustment

Valve lash can be adjusted with the engine hot or cold. Specifications are provided for both adjustments.

1. Remove the air intake case and cylinder head cover.

2. On the 1.3L engine, remove the rubber plug from the transmission case to gain access to the timing marks.

3. Turn the crankshaft clockwise so:

   a. The **T** mark punched on the flywheel is aligned with the matchmark on the transmission on the 1.3L engine.

   b. The **V** mark on the crankshaft pulley is aligned with the **0** mark on the timing belt cover on the 1.6L engine.

4. Remove the distributor cap and confirm that the rotor is

Valve lash adjustment screw and locknut

Valve adjustment sequence

Locking the camshaft in position

facing the No. 1 firing position. If the rotor is out of place, turn the crankshaft 360 degrees.

5. With the engine in this position, check the valve lash at valves 1, 2, 5 and 7.

NOTE: The valves are adjusted by loosening the locknut on the valve adjuster and turning the adjusting screw to obtain the proper clearance. Once the proper clearance is obtained, the locknut must be torqued to 11–13 ft. lbs. while holding the adjusting screw. Check the clearance after the locknut is torqued.

Clearance should be: Intake: 0.0051–0.0067 in. (0.13–0.17mm.) cold or 0.009–0.011 in. (0.23–0.27mm.) hot. Exhaust: 0.0063–0.0079 in. (0.16–0.20mm.) cold or 0.0102–0.0118 in. (0.26–0.30mm.) hot.

6. Rotate the crankshaft 360 degrees, and check the valve lash at valves 3, 4, 6 and 8.

7. After adjusting and checking all the valves, install the cylinder head cover, distributor cover and intake hose.

Rocker Arms/Shafts

Removal and Installation

NOTE: The rocker arm shafts are not identical and must be kept in the proper order for installation. If the shafts get mixed up before installation, the intake rocker shaft has a 14mm stepped end and the exhaust rocker shaft has a 13mm stepped end. The stepped end of the intake rocker shaft faces the front of the engine and the stepped end of the exhaust rocker shaft faces the rear of the engine.

1. Disconnect the negative battery cable. Drain the cooling system.

2. Remove the front grille for Sidekick.

3. Remove the radiator cooling fan and fan shroud. Properly discharge the air conditioning system and remove the air conditioning flexible suction hose, if equipped.

4. Remove the radiator for Sidekick.

5. Remove the water pump drive belt and the water pump pulley.

6. Remove the timing belt outside cover, timing belt and the tensioner.

7. Disconnect the air intake case and remove the cylinder head cover.

8. Remove the camshaft timing belt pulley and timing belt inside cover. Insert the proper size rod into the hole in the camshaft to lock the camshaft and loosen the pulley nut.

9. Loosen all the valve lash adjusting screw locknuts and turn the adjusting screws out all the way.

10. Remove the rocker arm shaft screws.

11. Remove the intake and exhaust rocker arm shafts, rocker arms and springs.

12. Keep all the valve train parts in the order that they were removed.

To install:

13. Apply engine oil to the rocker arms, springs and shafts. Install the shafts in the correct direction, into the cylinder head by placing the rocker arms and springs on the shafts as they are installed. With the rocker arms, springs and shafts installed, torque the rocker shaft mounting screws to 7.0–8.5 ft. lbs.

14. Install the timing belt pulley and inside cover by locking the camshaft with the proper size rod.

15. With the camshaft locked, tighten the camshaft pulley bolt to 41–46 ft. lbs.

16. The remainder of the installation is the reverse of the removal procedure.

Intake Manifold

Removal and installation

1. Disconnect the negative battery cable. Drain the cooling system.

2. Remove the air intake case from the manifold.

3. Disconnect the accelerator cable and the automatic transmission kickdown cable, if equipped.

4. Disconnect the injector, throttle position sensor and idle speed control solenoid valve wires at their couplers, if equipped.

5. Disconnect the vacuum hoses from the throttle body and throttle opener. Remove the water hose from the air valve, if equipped.

6. Remove the fuel filler cap to release the fuel pressure in the fuel tank. Reinstall the cap.

7. Release the fuel pressure in the fuel line.

8. Disconnect the fuel line from the throttle body or carburetor and intake manifold.

9. Remove the fuel return hose.

10. Disconnect the throttle body or carburetor from the intake manifold and remove the PCV hose from the cylinder head cover.

11. Disconnect the pressure sensor hose from the fuel filter, if equipped, and remove the brake booster hose from the intake manifold.

12. Disconnect the vacuum hose for the automatic transmission from the intake manifold, if equipped.

13. Remove the VSV (for throttle opener) hose from the intake manifold.

14. Disconnect the water hose from the thermostat cap. Remove the heater inlet and water bypass hose from the intake manifold.

15. Disconnect the hoses at the EGR valve and remove the ground wire from the intake manifold.

16. Disconnect the wire couplers from the air temperature

sensor, water temperature sensor, water temperature gauge and PTC heater, if equipped with automatic transmission.

17. Disconnect the wire harnesses from their clamps.

18. Remove the intake manifold mounting bolts and remove the intake manifold from the cylinder head.

19. Remove the PCV valve, EGR valve, fuel filter, thermostat from the intake manifold.

20. Clean and inspect the sealing surfaces of the intake manifold and the cylinder head.

To install:

21. Install the thermostat, fuel filter, EGR valve and PCV valve to the intake manifold.

22. Using a new gasket, install the intake manifold and tighten the mounting bolts to 13–20 ft. lbs.

23. Reconnect the wiring harnesses to their clamps and fasten the wire couplers to the air temperature sensor, water temperature sensor, water temperature gauge and PTC heater, if equipped with automatic transmission.

24. Reconnect the ground wire to the intake manifold and replace the hoses at the EGR valve.

25. Install the water heater inlet and bypass hose to the intake manifold. Install the water hose to the thermostat cap.

26. Install the VSV (for throttle opener) hose to the intake manifold.

27. Connect the automatic transmission vacuum hose to the intake manifold, if equipped.

28. Install the brake booster hose to the intake manifold and connect the pressure sensor to the fuel filter, if equipped.

29. Reconnect the fuel line to the throttle body or carburetor to the intake manifold.

30. Install the water hose to the air valve. Connect the vacuum hoses to the throttle body and throttle opener, if equipped.

31. Reconnect the injector, throttle position sensor and idle speed control wires to their couplers, if equipped.

32. Connect the accelerator cable and the automatic transmission kickdown cable, if equipped, to the throttle body.

33. Install the air intake case to the manifold.

34. Refill the cooling system with the proper coolant. Connect the negative battery cable.

35. Check for vacuum, water and oil leaks when finished.

Exhaust Manifold

Removal and Installation

1. Disconnect the negative cable.

2. Raise and safely support the vehicle.

3. Disconnect the exhaust pipe from the exhaust manifold and lower the vehicle.

4. Disconnect the oxygen sensor lead wire at the coupler and remove the air intake case bracket for 1.6L engine.

5. Disconnect the exhaust manifold upper and lower covers or heat shields from the exhaust manifold.

6. Remove the exhaust manifold mounting bolts and remove the exhaust manifold from the cylinder head.

To install:

7. Clean and inspect the sealing surfaces of the exhaust manifold and the cylinder head.

8. Using new gaskets, install the exhaust manifold to the cylinder head and tighten the mounting bolts to 13–20 ft. lbs.

9. The remainder of the installation is the reverse of the removal procedure.

10. Check for exhaust leaks when finished.

Timing Belt Front Cover

Removal and Installation

1. Disconnect the negative battery cable.

2. Remove the radiator cooling fan and fan shroud.

3. If equipped, disconnect the air conditioning compressor

drive belt, properly discharge the air conditioning system and remove the air conditioning compressor flexible suction hose.

4. Loosen the alternator mounting bolts and remove the water pump drive belt and pulley.

5. Remove the crankshaft mounting bolts and remove the crankshaft pulley.

NOTE: The crankshaft drive belt pulley can be removed without loosening the center crankshaft bolt.

6. Disconnect the timing belt cover mounting bolts and remove the timing belt cover.

To install:

7. Clean and inspect all mounting surfaces.

8. Install the timing belt cover and tighten the bolts to 7.0–9.0 ft. lbs.

9. Install the crankshaft pulley. Install the 5 mounting bolts and tighten to 7.0–9.0 ft. lbs.

10. Install the water pump drive belt pulley and install the drive belt.

11. Adjust the belt tension and tighten the alternator mounting bolts.

12. Install the air conditioning flexible suction hose and replace the air conditioning compressor drive belt. Adjust the belt tension and properly recharge the air conditioning system, if equipped.

13. Install the radiator cooling fan and fan shroud.

14. Connect the negative battery cable.

Oil Seal Replacement

1. Disconnect the negative battery cable.

2. Remove the the timing belt and the crankshaft sprocket.

3. Insert a suitable tool between the crankshaft and the oil seal and pull the seal outwards to remove it.

NOTE: Use care when removing or installing the oil seal, not to damage the crankshaft or the oil pump sealing surfaces.

TIMING BELT
DRIVE SIDE

TENSIONER
WASHER

TENSIONER
STUD AND NUT

TENSIONER
PLATE

TENSIONER
SPRING SCREW

SPRING TENSIONER

Exploded view of the timing belt and the tensioner assembly

Timing marks on the crankshaft pulley

Timing marks on the camshaft pulley

4. Clean and inspect the surfaces of the crankshaft and the oil pump assembly.

5. Install the crankshaft sleeve, using the proper tool, onto the crankshaft.

6. Install the new seal over the crankshaft and into the oil pump, making sure the oil seal lip is not upturned.

7. Install the crankshaft sprocket and the timing belt. Check the timing.

8. Connect the negative battery cable.

Timing Belt and Tensioner

Adjustment

1. Disconnect the negative battery cable.

2. Remove the radiator cooling fan and fan shroud.

3. If equipped, disconnect the air conditioning compressor drive belt, properly discharge the air conditioning system and remove the air conditioning compressor flexible suction hose.

4. Loosen the alternator mounting bolts and remove the water pump drive belt and pulley.

5. Remove the crankshaft mounting bolts and disconnect the crankshaft pulley.

NOTE: The crankshaft drive belt pulley can be removed without loosening the center crankshaft bolt.

6. Disconnect the timing belt cover mounting bolts and remove the timing belt cover. Loosen but do not remove the tensioner bolt.

7. Disconnect the air intake case from the intake manifold.

8. Remove the cylinder head cover and loosen all the valve adjusting screws to permit free rotation of the camshaft.

9. Turn the camshaft pulley clockwise and align the timing marks.

10. Turn the crankshaft clockwise, using a 17mm wrench to crank the timing belt pulley bolt.

11. Align the punch mark on the timing belt pulley with the arrow mark on the oil pump.

12. With the 4 marks aligned, remove any slack from the drive side of the belt. Tighten the tensioner bolt to 17.5–21.5 ft. lbs.

13. To allow the belt to be free of any slack, turn the crankshaft clockwise 2 full rotations. Confirm that the 4 marks are aligned.

14. Install the timing cover and tighten the bolts to 7.0–8.5 ft. lbs.

15. Adjust the valve lash and install the cylinder head cover, using a new gasket.

16. Connect the air intake case to the throttle body.

17. Install the crankshaft pulley and install the 5 mounting bolts. Tighten to 7.0–8.5 ft. lbs.

18. Install the water pump pulley, water pump drive belt and tighten the alternator mounting bolts.

19. Install the air conditioning compressor flexible suction hose and the air compressor belt. Properly recharge the air conditioning system, if equipped.

20. Install the radiator cooling fan and fan shroud.

21. Connect the negative battery cable.

22. Properly recharge the air conditioning system, if equipped. Run the engine and check for any leaks.

Removal and Installation

1. Disconnect the negative battery cable.

2. Remove the radiator cooling fan and fan shroud.

3. If equipped, disconnect the air conditioning compressor drive belt, properly discharge the air conditioning system and remove the air conditioning compressor flexible suction hose.

4. Loosen the alternator mounting bolts and remove the water pump drive belt and pulley.

5. Remove the crankshaft mounting bolts and disconnect the crankshaft pulley.

NOTE: The crankshaft drive belt pulley can be removed without loosening the center crankshaft bolt.

6. Disconnect the timing belt cover mounting bolts and remove the timing belt cover. Loosen but do not remove the tensioner bolt.

7. Disconnect the air intake case from the intake manifold.

8. Loosen the timing belt tensioner adjusting bolt and pivot nut. Hold pressure on the tensioner to loosen the timing belt and remove the timing belt from the camshaft and crankshaft pulleys.

9. Remove the timing belt tensioner, tensioner plate and tensioner spring.

To install:

10. Install the timing belt tensioner, plate and spring. Hand tighten the tensioner bolt and stud only at this time.

11. Remove the cylinder head cover and loosen all the valve adjusting screws to permit free rotation of the camshaft.

12. Turn the camshaft pulley clockwise and align the timing marks.

13. Turn the crankshaft clockwise, using a 17mm wrench to crank the timing belt pulley bolt.

14. Align the punch mark on the timing belt pulley with the arrow mark on the oil pump

15. With the 4 marks aligned, remove any slack from the drive side of the belt. Tighten the tensioner bolt to 17.5–21.5 ft. lbs.

16. To allow the belt to be free of any slack, turn the crankshaft clockwise 2 full rotations. Confirm that the 4 marks are aligned.

17. Install the timing cover and tighten the bolts to 7.0–8.5 ft. lbs.

18. Adjust the valve lash and install the cylinder head cover, using a new gasket.

19. Connect the air intake case to the intake manifold.

20. Install the crankshaft pulley and install the mounting bolts. Tighten to 7.0–8.5 ft. lbs.

21. Install the water pump pulley, water pump drive belt and tighten the alternator mounting bolts.

22. If equipped, install the air conditioning compressor flexible suction hose and install the air conditioning compressor belt.

23. Install the radiator cooling fan and fan shroud.

24. Connect the negative battery cable.

25. If equipped, properly recharge the air conditioning system. Run the engine and check for any leaks.

Timing Sprockets

Removal and Installation

1. Disconnect the negative battery cable.

2. Remove the radiator cooling fan/clutch and fan shroud.

3. If equipped, disconnect the air conditioning compressor drive belt, properly discharge the air conditioning system and remove the air conditioning compressor flexible suction hose.

4. Loosen the alternator mounting bolts and remove the water pump drive belt and pulley.

5. Remove the crankshaft mounting bolts and disconnect the crankshaft pulley.

NOTE: The crankshaft drive belt pulley can be removed without loosening the center crankshaft bolt.

6. Disconnect the timing belt cover mounting bolts and remove the timing belt cover. Loosen, but do not remove the tensioner bolt.

7. Disconnect the air intake case from the throttle body.

8. Remove the cylinder head cover and loosen all the valve adjusting screws to permit rotation of the camshaft.

9. Remove the camshaft timing belt pulley by inserting a proper size rod into the hole in the camshaft to lock the camshaft.

10. Remove the camshaft sprocket mounting bolt, sprocket and sprocket pin.

To install:

11. Install the camshaft sprocket pin in the sprocket and replace the sprocket and the bolt on the camshaft.

12. With the camshaft locked, tighten the sprocket bolt to 41–46 ft. lbs.

13. Remove the crankshaft sprocket by using a gear stopper to hold the flywheel (driveplate for automatic transmission vehicles). Remove the crankshaft timing belt pulley bolt, sprocket and key.

14. With the crankshaft locked, install the crankshaft timing belt sprocket and key. Install the crankshaft pulley bolt and tighten to 47–54 ft. lbs.

15. Align the camshaft and crankshaft timing marks, install the timing belt and tighten the timing belt tensioner.

16. Adjust the valve lash and install the cylinder head cover.

17. Reconnect the air intake hose to the throttle body.

18. If equipped, install the air conditioning compressor flexible suction hose and install the air conditioning compressor belt.

19. Install the water pump pulley and install the water pump drive belt.

20. Install the radiator cooling fan and fan shroud.

21. Install the water pump pulley and install the water pump drive belt.

22. Connect the negative battery cable.

23. If equipped, properly recharge the air conditioning system. Run the engine and check for any leaks.

Camshaft

Removal and Installation

1. Disconnect the negative battery cable. Drain the cooling system.

2. Disconnect the air intake case.

3. Disconnect the brake booster hose from the intake manifold and the air valve water hose from the throttle body.

Camshaft removal

4. Disconnect the accelerator and the automatic transmission kickdown cable, if equipped, from the throttle body.

5. Disconnect and tag the throttle opener VSV and EGR VSV wires at the coupler.

6. Disconnect and tag the water temperature, oil pressure, air temperature sensor and ground cable wires at the intake manifold.

7. Disconnect and tag the injector, throttle position sensor and idle speed control solenoid valve wires at their couplers, if equipped.

8. Disconnect the PTC heater wires at the coupler, if equipped with automatic transmission.

9. Disconnect and tag the oxygen sensor and distributor wires at their couplers. Remove the coil wire.

10. Disconnect the ground wires from the distributor assembly.

11. Remove the fuel tank filler cap to relieve the pressure. Reinstall the cap.

12. Release the fuel pressure in the fuel feed line.

13. Disconnect the fuel feed and return hoses.

14. Disconnect the canister purge hose and remove the pressure sensor hose from the fuel filter, if equipped.

15. Remove the vacuum hose for the automatic transmission from the intake manifold, if equipped.

16. Disconnect the radiator cooling fan, fan shroud, water pump drive belt and water pump pulley.

17. Disconnect the crankshaft pulley, timing belt cover and the timing belt.

18. Raise and safely support the vehicle.

19. Disconnect the exhaust pipe from the exhaust manifold and lower the vehicle.

20. Disconnect the air conditioner compressor adjusting arm, if equipped.

21. Remove the cylinder head cover mounting bolts and remove the cylinder head cover.

22. Loosen all the valve adjusting screw locknuts, turn the adjusting screws back all the way to allow all the valves to close.

23. Remove the intake manifold with the carburetor attached, from the cylinder head.

24. Remove the distributor and distributor housing from the cylinder head.

25. Remove the cylinder head mounting bolts and remove the cylinder head from the engine.

26. Remove any oil and water in the cylinder bores and on top of the pistons.

27. Clean and inspect the sealing surfaces of the cylinder head and the engine block.

28. Disconnect the timing belt gear from the camshaft and remove the rocker arms, springs and rocker arm shafts.

29. Keep all the valve train parts in the order that they were removed.

30. Remove the camshaft from the rear of the cylinder head.

To install:

31. To install, lubricate the lobes and journals of the camshaft and the oil seal on the cylinder head with engine oil.

32. Install the camshaft to the cylinder head from the transmission side.

33. Install the cylinder head using a new gasket.

34. Install the cylinder head mounting bolts and tighten to 46–54 ft. lbs.

35. Install the distributor and distributor housing to the cylinder head.

36. Install the intake manifold with the carburetor attached, to the cylinder head.

37. Tighten all the valve adjusting screw nuts.

38. Adjust the valve lash.

39. Install the cylinder head cover and connect the air conditioning compressor adjusting arm, if equipped.

40. Raise and safely support the vehicle.

41. Connect the exhaust pipe to the exhaust manifold and safely lower the vehicle.

42. Reconnect the timing belt, timing belt cover and crankshaft pulley.

43. Install the water pump pulley, water pump drive belt, fan shroud and the radiator cooling fan.

44. Install the vacuum hose for the automatic transmission to the intake manifold, if equipped.

45. Install the pressure sensor hose to the fuel filter and connect the canister purge hose, if equipped.

46. Install the fuel return and feed hoses.

47. Connect the ground wires to the distributor assembly.

48. Install the coil wire. Connect the oxygen sensor and distributor wires to their couplers.

49. Connect the PTC wires to the coupler.

50. Connect the idle speed control valve, throttle position sensor and injector wires to their couplers, if equipped.

51. Reconnect the ground cable, air temperature, oil pressure and water temperature sensor wires to the intake manifold.

52. Install the throttle opener VSV and EGR VSV wires to their couplers.

53. Connect the accelerator and the automatic transmission kickdown cables, if equipped, to the throttle body.

54. Install the air valve water hose to the throttle body and connect the brake booster hose to intake manifold.

55. Reconnect the air intake case.

56. Refill the cooling system with the proper coolant and connect the negative battery.

57. Check for any water and oil leaks when finished.

Piston and Connecting Rod

Positioning

1. Top ring
2. Second ring
3. Oil ring
4. Piston
5. Connecting rod
6. Connecting rod bearing cap
7. Connecting rod bearing
8. Piston pin

Exploded view of the piston and rod assembly

CRANKSHAFT PULLEY SIDE FLYWHEEL SIDE

Piston arrow marks to the cylinder head

ENGINE LUBRICATION

Oil Pan

Removal and Installation

1. Raise and safely support the vehicle.

2. On Sidekick, drain and remove the front differential assembly from the chassis.

3. Drain the engine oil.

4. Remove the clutch housing lower plate or the torque converter housing lower plate on the Sidekick.

5. Remove the oil pan mounting bolts and remove the pan.

To install:

6. Clean and inspect the sealing surfaces on the oil pan and the engine block.

7. Using new gaskets, install the oil pan and tighten the oil pan bolts to 7.0–8.5 ft. lbs.

NOTE: Tightening should begin at the center moving outward on both sides.

8. Install the oil drain plug and tighten to 22.0–28.5 ft. lbs.

9. Install the clutch housing lower plate or the torque converter on the Sidekick.

10. Install the front differential assembly to the chassis and fill with differential oil on the Sidekick.

11. Lower the vehicle.

12. Refill the engine with engine oil. Run the engine and check for leaks.

Oil Pump

Removal and Installation

1. Disconnect the negative battery cable.

2. Remove the radiator cooling fan, fan shroud, water pump pulley and water pump drive belt.

3. Remove the timing belt outside cover, timing belt and timing belt tensioner.

4. Disconnect the alternator and remove the bracket, if necessary.

5. If equipped, properly discharge the air conditioning system and remove the air compressor and bracket.

6. Disconnect the crankshaft timing belt pulley and the timing belt guide.

NOTE: To lock the crankshaft, engage a special tool (gear stopper) with the flywheel ring gear (driveplate

Oil pump installation—bolt location

Oil pump installation

ring gear for automatic transmission vehicles). With the crankshaft locked, remove the crankshaft timing belt pulley bolt.

7. Raise and safely support the vehicle. Drain the engine oil.
8. Remove the clutch (torque converter) housing lower plate.
9. Remove the oil pan mounting bolts and remove the oil pan. Disconnect the oil pump strainer.
10. Remove the oil pump mounting bolts and remove the oil pump.

To install:

11. Clean and inspect the sealing surfaces of the oil pump and the engine block.
12. Using a new gasket, install the oil pump to the engine.
13. Install the No. 1 and No. 2 mounting bolts and tighten to 7.0–8.5 ft. lbs.

NOTE: To prevent the oil seal lip from being damaged when installing the oil pump to the crankshaft, use a proper seal guide tool when installing. After installing

the oil pump, check to be sure the oil lip is not upturned, then remove the special tool. The edge of the oil pump gasket might bulge out. If it does, cut off bulge with knife.

14. With the crankshaft locked, install the crankshaft timing belt guide and the timing belt pulley.
15. Install the clutch (torque converter) housing lower plate.
16. If equipped, install the air conditioning bracket, the air conditioning compressor and properly rechargew the air conditioning system.
17. Install the alternator and the alternator bracket, if necessary.
18. Reinstall the timing belt tensioner, timing belt and timing belt outside cover.
19. Install the water pump drive belt, water pump pulley, radiator cooling fan and fan shroud.
20. Refill the engine with engine oil and connect the negative battery cable.
21. Run the engine and check for any leaks.

Checking

With the oil pump removed from the engine, certain clearances must be checked on the oil pump, if it is being reused.

1. The radial clearance is the clearance between the oil pump outer rotor and the oil pump case. The maximum clearance is 0.0122 in.
2. The side clearance is measured with a straightedge across the mounting surface of the oil pump. The measurement is taken between the oil pump gears and the straightedge. The maximum clearance is 0.0059 in.

Rear Main Bearing Oil Seal

Removal and Installation

1. Raise and safely support the vehicle.
2. Support the engine and remove the transmission from the vehicle.
3. Disconnect the clutch and flywheel, for manual transmission vehicles or the driveplate, for automatic transmission vehicles.
4. Using a suitable tool, remove the seal by pulling it outwards. Use care not to damage the sealing surface of the crankshaft.

To install:

5. Clean and inspect the sealing surfaces of the crankshaft and seal housing.
6. Using a seal driver, install the new seal into the seal housing with the lip of the seal facing the engine.
7. Install the flywheel and clutch, for manual transmission vehicles or the driveplate, for automatic transmission vehicles.
8. Install the transmission in the vehicle.
9. Lower the vehicle and check all the fluids. Run the engine and check for any leaks.

TORQUE SPECIFICATIONS

Component	English	Metric
Camshaft sprocket bolt	45 ft. lbs.	62 Nm
Carburetor-to-manifold bolts	17 ft. lbs.	25 Nm
Connecting rod bearing cap bolts	25 ft. lbs.	35 Nm
Crankshaft pulley bolt	9 ft. lbs.	13 Nm

TORQUE SPECIFICATIONS

Cylinder Head bolt		
1.3L Engine		
Step 1:	21 ft. lbs.	30 Nm
Step 2:	33 ft. lbs.	45 Nm
Step 3:	48 ft. lbs.	65 Nm
1.6L Engine		
Step 1:	25 ft. lbs.	35 Nm
Step 2:	40 ft. lbs.	54 Nm
Step 3:	54 ft. lbs.	75 Nm
Engine-to-transmission	18 ft. lbs.	25 Nm
Exhaust manifold	19 ft. lbs.	26 Nm
Exhaust pipe-to-exhaust manifold nuts	43 ft. lbs.	60 Nm
Flywheel/flexplate-to-crankshaft bolts	55 ft. lbs.	78 Nm
Flywheel-to-converter bolts	38 ft. lbs.	53 Nm
Front engine mount through bolt	36 ft. lbs.	50 Nm
Intake manifold	20 ft. lbs.	28 Nm
Main bearing cap bolts	25 ft. lbs.	34 Nm
Oil pan	8.5 ft. lbs.	12 Nm
Oil pan drain plug	28.5 ft. lbs.	40 Nm
Oil pump attaching bolts	8.5 ft. lbs.	12 Nm
Oil pump cover screws	8.5 ft. lbs.	12 Nm
Rocker arm pivot bolt	8.5 ft. lbs.	12 Nm
Rocker (valve) cover	8.5 ft. lbs.	12 Nm
Spark plug	21.5 ft. lbs.	30 Nm
Starter-to-block bolts	20 ft. lbs.	28 Nm
Thermostat housing	20 ft. lbs.	27 Nm
Timing belt cover	8.5 ft. lbs.	12 Nm
Water Pump	9 ft. lbs.	13 Nm
Water pump pulley	36 ft. lbs.	50 Nm

MANUAL TRANSMISSION

For further information, please refer to Chilton's Transmission Service Manual.

Transmission Assembly

Removal and Installation

1. Disconnect the negative battery cable.
2. Remove the console cover, remove the 4 gear shift boot mounting bolts and slide the boot upwards on the gear shifter.
3. On Samurai, loosen the 3 gear shift lever mounting bolts and remove the gear shift lever.
4. On the Sidekick remove the boot clamp and remove the second boot from the shift lever case.
5. Push the gear shift lever control case down with fingers, turn it counterclockwise and remove the shift control lever.
6. Remove the transfer case shift control lever the same way.
7. Disconnect the breather hose and clamp at the rear of the cylinder head.
8. Remove the clamp at the rear of the intake manifold to free up the wiring harness. Disconnect the harness coupler.
9. Raise and safely support the vehicle. Drain the oil from the transmission and the transfer case.
10. Disconnect the starter lead wires and mounting bolts and remove the starter.

11. Remove the fuel line clamp on the transmission. Disconnect the bolts fastening the engine to the transmission.
12. Disconnect the flange bolts from the front driveshaft and remove and mark the shaft.
13. Disconnect the flange bolts from the rear driveshaft and remove and mark the shaft.
14. Disconnect the clutch cable and remove the clutch housing lower plate.
15. Disconnect the center exhaust pipe and remove the nuts from the joint with the engine.
16. Disconnect the speedometer cable from the transfer case.
17. Position a transmission jack and remove the engine rear mounting member from the vehicle. Move the transmission and transfer case rearwards and lower.
18. Disconnect the wiring harness and breather hose at the transmission.
19. Separate the gear shift lever case and transfer case from the transmission. Remove the transmission from the vehicle.

To install:
20. Install the gear shift lever case and transfer case to the transmission.
21. Install the transmission wiring harness and breather hose.
22. Raise the transmission and transfer case on the transmission jack and place under the vehicle.
23. Install the engine rear mounting member and tighten the

bolts. Tighten the Samurai mounting bolts to 19 ft. lbs. or the Sidekick mounting bolts to 37 ft. lbs.

24. Connect the speedometer cable to the transfer case and joint with the engine.

25. Remove the transmission jack and install the center exhaust pipe.

26. Install the clutch housing lower plate and connect the clutch cable.

27. Install the front and rear driveshaft and install the flange bolts. Tighten the Samurai flange bolts to 20 ft. lbs. or the Sidekick flange bolts to 37 ft. lbs.

28. Connect the bolts attaching the engine to the transmission and install the fuel line clamp on the transmission.

29. Install the starter and install the mounting bolts and the lead wires to the starter.

30. Lower the vehicle. Refill the transmission and transfer case with the recommended gear oil.

31. Connect the wiring coupler and install the clamp holding the wiring harness at the rear of the intake manifold.

32. Install the breather hose and clamp at the rear of the cylinder head.

33. Install the transfer case and the gear shift control levers. Install the gear shift lever boots and the console cover.

34. Connect the negative battery cable. Run the engine and check for any leaks.

CLUTCH

Clutch Assembly

Removal and Installation

1. Disconnect the negative battery cable.
2. Raise and safely support the vehicle.
3. Support the engine and remove the transmission from the vehicle.
4. Support the pressure plate and remove the 6 pressure plate to flywheel mounting bolts.
5. Remove the pressure plate and the clutch disc from the flywheel.
6. Inspect the condition of the flywheel, pressure plate and clutch disc and install as necessary.
7. Remove the flywheel mounting bolts and remove the flywheel.

To install:

8. Install the new flywheel and install the mounting bolts, tighten to 41–47 ft. lbs.
9. Inspect the condition of the clutch release bearing and the input shaft bearing and install if necessary.
10. Align the clutch disc to the flywheel using a clutch disc alignment tool.
11. Install the pressure plate and evenly tighten the pressure plate bolts to 13–20 ft. lbs.

NOTE: Before assembling, make sure the clutch disc and the pressure plate are clean and dry.

12. With the engine supported, install the transmission in the vehicle.
13. Lower the vehicle. Connect the negative battery cable.
14. Check and adjust the clutch pedal height. Check the clutch operation when finished.

Pedal Height/Free-play Adjustment

The only adjustment possible is the clutch pedal free-play. The free-play is adjusted by moving the joint nut on the release bearing arm. Clutch linkage free-play should be between 0.8–1.1 in. for the Samurai or 0.6–1.1 in. for the Sidekick.

Clutch Cable

Removal and Installation

1. Disconnect the negative battery cable.
2. Raise and safely support the vehicle.
3. Disconnect the cable adjusting nuts on the clutch release and remove the adjusting nuts on the cable support bracket.
4. Disconnect the clutch cable from the 3 cable clamps.
5. Remove the clutch cable support bolts. Lower the vehicle.

1. Flywheel
2. Cover bolt
3. Release shaft seal
4. Release shaft bushing
5. Clutch release shaft
6. Release return spring
7. Clutch release bearing
8. Clutch cover
9. Clutch disc
10. Input shaft bearing

Exploded view of the clutch assembly

A Free travel of release arm 0.02–0.06 in. (0.5–1.5mm)
1. Inner cable
2. Joint nut
3. Joint pin
4. Clutch release arm
5. Cable outer nut
6. Clutch cable bracket

Clutch cable free travel adjustment

6. Disconnect the cable hook at the clutch pedal shaft arm and remove the clutch cable.

To install:

7. Install the cable after first applying grease to the cable end hook and the joint pin.

8. Install the clutch cable support bolts and connect the cable to the 3 clamps.

BRAKE PEDAL
CLUTCH PEDAL
CLUTCH CABLE ASSEMBLY
ADJUSTING BOLT

HEIGHT DIFFERENCE 0.2 IN. (5MM.)

Clutch pedal height adjustment

9. Connect the clutch cable adjusting nuts and adjust to proper setting.

10. Lower the vehicle and connect the negative battery terminal.

Adjustment

Adjust the clutch pedal height by adjusting the bolt located on the pedal bracket so the clutch pedal exceeds the height of the brake pedal by 0.2 in. (5mm.) Tighten the locknut.

AUTOMATIC TRANSMISSION

For further information, please refer to Chilton's Transmission Service Manual.

Transmission Assembly

Removal and Installation

1. Disconnect the negative battery cable.
2. Disconnect the transmission shift control lever and remove the transfer case shift control lever knob.
3. Disconnect the breather hose from the clamp at the rear of the cylinder head.
4. Disconnect the wiring harness clamp at the rear end of the intake manifold to free up the harness.
5. Disconnect the wiring harness coupler and remove the detent cable at the throttle body, if equipped.
6. Remove the vacuum modulator hose at the intake manifold.
7. Raise and safely support the vehicle.
8. Disconnect the starter lead wires and mounting bolts, remove the starter motor.
9. Drain the oil from the transmission and transfer case.
10. Disconnect the flange bolts from the front driveshaft, remove and mark the shaft.
11. Disconnect the flange bolts from the rear driveshaft, remove and mark the shaft.
12. Disconnect the select cable from the transmission and the speedometer cable from the transfer cases.
13. Remove the torque converter housing lower plate and disconnect and plug the oil cooler lines.
14. Disconnect the transfer case skid plate and remove the kickdown cable from the transmission.
15. Remove the exhaust bracket at the catalytic converter and at the transmission. Disconnect the center exhaust pipe, if necessary.
16. Remove the transmission to engine retaining bolts and nuts.
17. Support the transmission using a transmission jack or equivalent. Disconnect the transmission crossmember mounting bolts and remove the crossmember.
18. Disconnect the lead wires and breather hose at the transmission and lower the transmission with the transfer case from the vehicle. Remove the torque converter-to-flywheel bolts.
19. Disconnect the transmission-to-transfer case bolts and separate the transmission from the transfer case.

To install:

20. Connect the transfer case to the transmission and tighten the bolts to 20 ft. lbs. Install the torque converter to flywheel bolts.
21. Raise the transmission, connect the lead wires and breather to the transmission.
22. Install the transmission to engine retaining bolts and tighten to 62 ft. lbs.
23. Install the transmission cross member and tighten the bolts to 62 ft. lbs.
24. Connect the exhaust bracket to the catalytic converter and the transmission.
25. Reconnect the center exhaust pipe, if necessary.
26. Connect the transfer case skid plate and install the kickdown cable to the transmission.
27. Install the torque converter housing lower plate and connect the transmission cooler lines.
28. Reconnect the select cable to the transmission and the speedometer cable to the transfer case.
29. Install the front and rear driveshafts and tighten the flange bolts to 37 ft. lbs.
30. Install the starter and connect the lead wires to the starter.
31. Lower the vehicle and connect the vacuum modulator hose to the intake manifold.
32. Connect the wiring coupler at the rear of the intake manifold and install the wiring harness clamp in the proper position.
33. Connect the breather hose to the clamp at the rear of the cylinder head.
34. Install the transmission shift control lever and install the transfer case shift control lever knob.
35. Connect the negative battery cable and refill the transmission. Run the engine and check for leaks.

ACCELERATOR CABLE
ADJUSTING NUT
LOCKNUT
CABLE PLAY

Accelerator cable adjustment

Shift Linkage Adjustment

1. Adjust the shift cable assembly by moving the shift selector to the **N** position and placing a pin in the selector to hold that position.
2. Put the manual select lever in **L** position and set the cable to the cable bracket with the E-clip.

3. Adjust the manual select lever back to the **N** position and tighten the cable end locknut to 5ft. lbs.

NOTE: When the manual selector is moved to the N position, there should be a little clearance between the lever and the adjusting nut.

Throttle linkage Adjustment

Adjust the cable by loosening the cable locknut and adjust the cable to specifications. The cable endplay should be 0.12–0.20 in. when the throttle valve is in the idle position.

Detent Cable Adjustment

1. Make sure accelerator play is within specifications.
2. Loosen the kickdown cable nut and adjusting nut.
3. With the accelerator pedal fully depressed and the cable pulled towards the firewall, adjust the locknut-to-bracket clearance to 0.039 in. by turning the locknut

NOTE: When adjusting the clearance make sure the adjusting nut does not rub against the bracket.

4. Release the accelerator pedal and adjust the locknut-to-bracket clearance by tightening the adjusting nut. Tighten the locknut securely.

TRANSFER CASE

Transfer Case Assembly

Removal and Installation

1. Disconnect the negative battery cable.
2. Raise and safely support the vehicle.
3. Support the transmission and transfer case using a suitable transmission jack.
4. Disconnect the speedometer cable from the transfer case.
5. Remove the transmission and transfer case from the vehicle.

6. Remove the 10 transmission-to-transfer case mounting bolts and separate the transfer case from the transmission.

To install:
7. Install the 10 transmission-to-transfer case mounting bolts and tighten the bolts to 20 ft. lbs.
8. Install the transmission and transfer case into the vehicle and tighten the mounting bolts to 20 ft. lbs. on the Samurai or 37 ft. lbs. on the Sidekick.
9. Connect the speedometer cable to the transfer case.
10. Lower the vehicle and connect the negative battery cable.

DRIVE AXLE

Halfshaft

Removal and Installation

SIDEKICK

1. Raise and safely support the vehicle. Drain the transmission.
2. Remove the front wheels and disconnect the locking hubs.
3. Disconnect the halfshaft snaprings and remove the stabilizer bar links.
4. Disconnect the tie rod ends and remove the brake caliper and brake disc. Support the brake caliper.
5. Disconnect the wheel hub and remove the steering knuckle.
6. Disconnect the differential side joint snapring and remove the right side halfshaft by prying the joint away from the differential assembly.
7. Disconnect the left side halfshaft bolts and remove the halfshaft from the left inner axle flange.

To install:
8. Install the left side halfshaft and the halfshaft bolts and tighten to 37 ft. lbs.
9. Install the right side halfshaft and install the snapring.
10. Install the steering knuckle and wheel hub assembly.
11. Install the brake caliper and connect the tie rod ends.
12. Install the left side driveshaft snapring and connect the stabilizer bar links.
13. Install the front wheels and lower the vehicle.
14. Refill the transmission with the proper fluid.

Driveshaft and U-Joints

Removal and Installation

1. Raise and safely support the vehicle.
2. Matchmark the driveshafts to the yokes on the transfer case and the differential.
3. Drain the transfer case oil, when servicing the front driveshaft shaft.

Exploded view of the halfshaft assembly

4. Support the driveshaft and remove the attaching bolts.
5. Remove the driveshaft from the vehicle.
To install:
6. Install the driveshaft, by aligning the matchmarks to the vehicle.
7. Tighten the mounting bolts to 17–21 ft. lbs. on Samurai or 37 ft. lbs. on the Sidekick.
8. Refill the transfer case and lower the vehicle.

Front Axle Shaft

Removal and Installation

SAMURAI

1. Raise and safely support the vehicle.
2. Drain the oil in the front differential.
3. Remove the front wheels and disconnect the brake caliper. Support the brake caliper.
4. Disconnect the tie rod end from the steering knuckle. The tie rod end removal may require the use of a puller.
5. Remove the 8 oil seal cover mounting bolts and disconnect the felt pad, oil seal and the retainer from the steering knuckle.
6. Mark the upper and lower kingpins. Remove the 4 mounting bolts and disconnect the kingpins from the steering knuckle.
7. Remove the axle shaft from the housing with the steering knuckle attached.
To install:
8. Transfer the steering knuckle to the new axle.
9. Align the marks on the upper and lower kingpins and install the kingpins and tighten to 14–21 ft. lbs..
10. Install the steering knuckle oil seal and install the 8 mounting bolts and tighten to 6–8 ft. lbs.
11. Connect the tie rod end to the steering knuckle and tighten the bolts to 22–39 ft. lbs. Install the front brake caliper assembly.
12. Install the front wheels and refill the differential with the proper fluid.
13. Lower the vehicle.

Front Axle Shaft, Bearing and Seal

Removal and Installation

SAMURAI

1. Raise and safely support the vehicle. Drain the front differential assembly.
2. Disconnect the front wheel hub and remove the bearing.
3. Support the hub and drive out the seal in the hub.
4. Using a seal driver, install the new seal in the hub until it is flush with the hub face. Apply a thin film of oil to the lip of the seal before installation to the vehicle.
5. Install the hub and the bearing to the vehicle.
6. Refill the front differential assembly and safely lower the vehicle.

Rear Axle Shaft, Bearing and Seal

Removal and Installation

SAMURAI

1. Raise and safely support the vehicle. Drain the rear differential assembly.
2. Make sure the rear brake is released.
3. Remove the rear wheels and remove the rear brake drums from the vehicle.
4. Disconnect the parking brake cables from the levers. Remove the parking brake lever stop plates.
5. Disconnect and plug the brake lines to the wheel cylinders.
6. Remove the backing plate mounting bolts.
7. Remove the rear axles with the backing plates attached using a slide hammer type puller.
8. Using a suitable tool, remove the axle seal from the housing.
9. If the axle, axle bearing or backing plate is being replaced, support the axle in a vise with additional support under the shaft next to the bearing.

─── **CAUTION** ───

Eye protection must be worn during the 3 steps. Failure to do so could cause injury.

10. With the axle shaft supported properly, grind the top and bottom of the axle bearing retainer to remove it without damaging the axle shaft.

11. Using a chisel, finish removing the retainer from the axle shaft.

12. Using a press or suitable bearing puller, remove the axle shaft bearing from the axle shaft.

13. Remove the backing plate from the axle shaft.

To install:

14. Using a seal driver, install the new seal with the lip facing the housing to the same depth as the old seal.

15. Install the backing plate on the axle shaft and using a press, install the bearing and the retainer on the axle shaft.

16. Install the axle shaft in the housing.

17. Install the backing plate mounting bolts and connect the brake lines to the wheel cylinders.

18. Install the parking brake lever plates and connect the brake cables to the parking brake lever.

19. Install the rear brake drums and install the rear wheels.

20. Adjust the brakes and bleed the brake system.

21. Refill the rear differential and safely lower the vehicle.

SIDEKICK

1. Raise and safely support the vehicle.

2. Remove the rear wheels and remove the rear brake drums from the vehicle.

3. Drain the gear oil from the rear axle housing.

4. Remove the rear wheel bearing retainer nuts from the rear axle housing.

5. Using a suitable tool, remove the axle shaft from the housing.

NOTE: Do not remove the backing plate with the axle. This may cause damage to the inner seal.

6. If the axle, axle bearing or backing plate is being replaced, support the axle in a vise with additional support under the shaft next to the bearing.

─── **CAUTION** ───

Eye protection must be worn during the 3 steps. Failure to do so could cause injury.

7. With the axle shaft supported properly, grind the top and bottom of the axle bearing retainer to remove it without damaging the axle shaft.

8. Using a chisel, finish removing the retainer from the axle shaft.

9. Using a press or suitable bearing puller, remove the axle shaft bearing from the axle shaft.

10. Using a suitable tool, remove the seal from the axle housing.

11. Using a seal driver, install the new seal with the lip facing the housing to the same depth as the old seal.

12. Install the new bearing and the retainer on the axle shaft using a suitable press.

13. Install the axle shaft in to the rear axle housing and install the rear wheel bearing retaining nuts, tighten to 17 ft. lbs.

14. Install the rear brake drums and install the rear tires on the vehicle.

15. Refill the rear axle housing with the proper gear oil and safely lower the vehicle.

Front Wheel Hub, Knuckle and Bearings

Removal and Installation

SAMURAI

1. Raise and safely support the vehicle. Remove the front wheels.

2. Disconnect the locking hub. Remove the caliper mounting bolts and move the caliper out of position with the brake line attached.

NOTE: Do not allow the caliper to hang on the brake hose. Support it by the mounting bracket.

3. Install 2 (8mm) bolts into the threaded holes and tighten evenly. This will remove the rotor from the hub assembly.

4. Remove the front axle shaft cap and the circlip. Remove the drive flange from the steering knuckle.

5. Straighten the bent lock washer and remove the hub nut and washer.

6. Remove the front wheel hub and bearing from the spindle.

7. Remove the oil seal and race from the wheel hub.

8. Clean and inspect the hub and bearing seats. Install the new bearing, race and grease seal in the same position.

9. Loosen the upper and lower kingpin bolts but do not remove the kingpins.

10. Disconnect the disc dust cover and remove the spindle.

11. Disconnect the tie rod end from the steering knuckle.

12. Remove the 8 joint seal cover bolts and remove the cover, pad, oil seal and retainer from the knuckle.

13. Mark the upper and lower kingpins. Remove the 4 mounting bolts and disconnect the kingpins from the steering knuckle.

14. Remove the steering knuckle while noting the upper from the lower kingpin positions during the removal of the knuckle.

To install:

15. Install the kingpin bearings in the new knuckle and install the knuckle to the vehicle.

16. Install the kingpins and tighten the mounting bolts to 14–21 ft. lbs.

17. Install the joint seal cover, pad oil seal and retainer. Tighten the joint seal cover bolts to 6.0–8.5 ft. lbs.

18. Connect the tie rod end to the steering knuckle.

19. Install the spindle and connect disc dust cover.

20. Install the front wheel hub and bearing to the spindle.

21. Install the front hub nut and lock washer and install the drive flange to the steering knuckle.

22. Install the front axle cap and circlip. Connect the rotor to the hub assembly.

23. Place the brake caliper into position and install the caliper mounting bolts.

24. Reconnect the locking hub assembly and install the front wheels.

25. Lower the vehicle.

SIDEKICK

1. Disconnect the negative battery cable. Raise and safely support the vehicle.

2. Remove the wheels and disconnect the locking hub assembly.

3. Remove the caliper mounting bracket and position the caliper out of the way. Support the caliper.

4. Disconnect the front wheel bearing lock plate and washer and remove the wheel hub complete with bearings and seals.

5. Remove the oil seal and race from the wheel hub.

6. Clean and inspect the hub and bearing seats. Install the new bearing, race and grease seal in the same position.

7. Support the suspension with a jack and remove the dust cover.

8. Disconnect the spindle by tapping with a hammer.

Wheel hub "LOCK" and "FREE" positions

9. Remove the strut bracket bolts from the steering knuckle.
10. Disconnect the tie rod end from the knuckle and the knuckle from the control arm.
11. Remove the dust seal and the spindle from the knuckle.
To install:
12. Install the new seal and the spindle to the knuckle.
13. Connect the knuckle to the ball joint and tighten the nut to 40 ft. lbs.
14. Connect the knuckle to the strut damper and tighten the bolts to 66 ft. lbs.
15. Install the tie rod end to the knuckle and tighten the nut 30 ft. lbs.
16. Install the spindle and install the dust cover and remove the jack from under the suspension.
17. Install the wheel hub assembly and connect the locking hub.
18. Install the wheels and lower the vehicle.
19. Connect the negative battery cable.

Manual Locking Hubs

Removal and Installation

1. Disconnect the negative battery cable and remove the locking hub cover.
2. Raise and support the vehicle safely.
3. Remove the locking hub body assembly.

NOTE: The manual locking hubs must not be packed with grease.
To install:
4. Install a new O-ring to the locking hub assembly.
5. Install the locking hub body assembly to the wheel hub flange and tighten the hub body bolts to 18 ft. lbs.
6. Install a new gasket in the manual locking hub cover.
7. Install the locking hub cover and tighten the bolts to 106 inch lbs.
8. Connect the negative battery cable and lower the vehicle.

NOTE: The O mark on the hub knob must be in the FREE position.

Automatic Locking Hubs

Removal and Installation

1. Disconnect the negative battery cable and remove the automatic locking hub cover.
2. Disconnect the automatic hub body assembly.

To install:
3. Install a new O-ring to the automatic locking hub body assembly.
4. Connect the automatic locking hub body assembly to the wheel hub flange. Tighten the hub body assembly bolts to 18 ft. lbs.
5. Install a new gasket in the automatic locking hub cover and install the hub cover.
6. Connect the negative battery cable.

Pinion Seal

Removal and Installation

1. Raise and safely support the vehicle.
2. Matchmark and remove the driveshaft.
3. Check the turning torque of the pinion before proceeding.
4. Using a pinion flange holding tool, remove the pinion nut and the washer.
5. Remove the pinion flange from the differential carrier and pry out the pinion seal.
To install:
6. Clean and inspect the sealing surface of the carrier.
7. Using a seal driver, install the new seal into the carrier until the flange of the seal is flush with the carrier.

NOTE: Tightening the flange nut will preload the pinion bearings. Exceeding the preload specifications will compress the collapsible spacer to far and require the spacer to be replaced.

8. Install the pinion flange and using the pinion flange holding tool, install the pinion nut and washer. Tighten the pinion nut to the same torque as before.
9. Align the matchmarks and install the driveshaft.
10. Check the level of the differential fluid when finished.

Differential Carrier

Removal and Installation

1. Raise and safely support the vehicle. Drain the oil from the rear differential.
2. Remove the left and right axle shafts.
3. Disconnect the driveshaft.
4. Remove the 4 mounting bolts to the upper rear suspension arm.
5. Support the differential carrier with a proper jack.
6. Remove the differential case nuts and lower the differential assembly from the rear housing.

7. Clean and inspect the sealing surfaces of the carrier and the housing.

To install:

8. Using a liquid sealant on the carrier, install the carrier in the housing and tighten the nuts to 16 ft. lbs.

9. Install the 4 mounting bolts to the upper rear suspension arm and tighten to 41 ft. lbs.

10. Connect the rear driveshaft and install the left and rear axles.

11. Refill the rear differential to the proper level with SAE 75W–90W API GL5 Hypoid Gear Oil.

12. Lower the vehicle.

Front Axle Housing

Removal and Installation

SAMURAI AND SIDEKICK

1. Raise and safely support the vehicle. Remove the front wheels.

2. Drain the oil from the front differential.

3. Remove caliper assembly from brake disc and support caliper assembly.

4. Remove the tie rod end from the steering knuckle using a tie rod end remover.

5. Remove the 8 oil seal cover bolts and separate the felt pad, seal and retainer.

6. Remove the 4 kingpin bolts from the top and bottom and remove the kingpins from the knuckle.

7. Remove axle shafts from housing by pulling outward gradually.

8. Remove the bolts between the flange yoke and companion flange and disconnect the front drive shaft.

9. Remove the 8 U-joint nuts and remove the housing assembly.

To install:

10. Install the housing and torque the housing U-bolt nuts to 43 ft. lbs.

11. Connect the front drive shaft and install the bolts.

12. Install the front axle shafts and install the kingpins. Apply Loctite® to the kingpin bolts.

13. Install oil seal, felt pad and retainer and tighten the 8 cover bolts.

14. Install the tie rod end to the steering knuckle.

15. Install the front caliper to the disc and install the front wheels.

16. Refill the differential with the proper lubricant and bleed the brake system when finished.

Rear Axle Housing

Removal and Installation

SAMURAI

1. Raise and safely support the vehicle. Drain the rear differential assembly.

2. Make sure the parking brake is in the released position.

3. Remove the rear wheels and remove the rear brake drums from the vehicle.

4. Disconnect the parking brake cables from the levers. Remove the parking brake lever stop plates.

5. Disconnect and plug the brake lines to the wheel cylinders.

6. Remove the backing plate mounting bolts and remove the axle shafts with the backing plates attached.

7. Disconnect the driveshaft and remove from the transmission.

8. Remove the brake line from the flexible hose and remove the E-clip.

9. Disconnect the brake clamps and remove the brake lines from the rear housing.

10. Disconnect the mounting bolts to the rear suspension arm and remove the housing to leaf spring U-bolts and nuts.

11. Remove shock absorber lower mount bolt.

12. Slide the housing to one side while tilting the opposite side under the leaf spring and remove the housing from the vehicle.

To install:

13. Install the housing and connect the shock absorber lower bolt.

14. Connect the U-bolts to the leaf spring and tighten the bolts to 50 ft. lbs.

15. Connect brake lines to the rear housing and install the driveshaft.

16. Install the axle shafts with backing plates attached and tighten the backing plate bolts to 19 ft. lbs.

17. Connect the brake lines to the rear wheel cylinders.

18. Install the parking brake lever stop plates and connect the parking brake cables.

19. Install the rear brake drums and install the rear wheels.

20. Lower the vehicle and refill the rear differential with the proper fluid.

SIDEKICK

1. Raise and safely support the vehicle. Drain the rear differential assembly.

2. Make sure the parking brake is in the released position.

3. Remove the rear wheels and remove the rear brake drums from the vehicle.

4. Disconnect the parking brake cables from the levers. Remove the parking brake lever stop plates.

5. Disconnect and plug the brake lines to the wheel cylinders.

6. Remove the rear wheel bearing retainer nuts and remove the axle shafts from the vehicle. Do not remove the axle shafts with the backing plates attached.

7. Remove the rear axle carrier assembly.

8. Disconnect the brake line from the flexible hose and remove the E-clip. Remove the brake lines from the rear housing.

9. Remove the breather hose from the axle housing and disconnect the rear driveshaft.

10. Support the rear axle housing with a jack.

11. Remove the ball joint bracket from the differential carrier and remove the carrier assembly.

12. Loosen the rear mount nut of the trailing rod. Do not remove it.

13. Disconnect the shock absorber lower mount bolt.

14. Lower the jack to relieve the tension of the coil springs and remove the rear mount bolt of the trailing rod.

15. Remove the rear axle housing.

To install:

16. Place the rear axle housing on a jack and install the trailing rod rear mounting bolts. Mount the nuts but do not tighten.

17. Install the coil spring on the spring seat and raise the axle housing.

18. Install the shock absorber lower mounting bolts. Do not tighten.

19. Install the differential carrier assembly and install the rear upper ball joint bracket onto the carrier assembly and tighten to 37 ft. lbs.

20. Install the rear driveshaft and remove the jack from under the axle housing.

21. Install the breather hose and brake lines to axle housing. Tighten them securely.

22. Connect the flexible brake hose to the bracket on the axle housing and secure with the E-clip.

23. Tighten the trailing rod nuts and the shock absorber nuts to 66 ft. lbs.

24. Install the brake line to the flexible hose and install the axle shafts.

25. Install the brake line to the wheel cylinders and install the brake drums.

26. Install the wheels and refill the rear differential assembly.

27. Bleed the brake system and lower the vehicle.

STEERING

Steering Wheel

Removal and Installation

1. Disconnect the negative battery cable.
2. Disconnect the horn button and remove the steering wheel shaft nut.
3. Make matchmarks on the steering wheel and the shaft to use as a guide during reinstallation.
4. Remove the steering wheel, using a suitable steering wheel puller.

To install:

5. Install the steering wheel onto the shaft, aligning the matchmarks.
6. Install and tighten the shaft nut to 24 ft. lbs.
7. Install the horn button and connect the negative battery cable.

Manual Steering Gear

Removal and Installation

SAMURAI

1. Remove the steering shaft coupler bolt and disconnect the coupler from the steering box. As required, raise and support the vehicle safely.
2. Remove the radiator under cover and disconnect the ball stud of the drag rod. Remove the steering damper from the pitman arm.
3. Support the steering gear and remove the mounting bolts.
4. Remove the steering gear from the vehicle.

To install:

5. Install the steering gear in the vehicle and tighten the nuts to 55 ft. lbs.
6. Install the steering damper to the pitman arm tighten the nut to 30 ft. lbs.
7. Install the radiator under cover and connect the drag rod.
8. Connect the steering coupler to the steering box and tighten the bolt to 18 ft. lbs. Lower the vehicle.

SIDEKICK

1. As required, raise and support the vehicle safely. Disconnect the steering lower shaft mounting bolts.
2. Disconnect the center link end from the pitman arm.
3. Remove the 3 steering gear box mounting bolts.
4. Disconnect the steering lower shaft joint and remove the steering gear.

To install:

5. Install the steering gear box by connecting to the lower shaft joint.

NOTE: Align the flat part of the steering gear worm shaft with the bolt hole of the lower shaft joint.

6. Install the steering gear box mounting bolts and tighten to 60 ft. lbs.
7. Attach the center link to the pitman arm and tighten the nut to 35 ft. lbs.
8. Connect the lower shaft mounting bolts and tighten to 18 ft. lbs.

Adjustment

1. Check the worm shaft to make sure it is free from thrust play.
2. Place the pitman arm in a position that is nearly parallel with the worm shaft.
3. With the pitman arm in this position, the front wheels should be in a straight forward position.

Adjusting the steering gear assembly

4. Measure the worm shaft starting torque from it's straight foward position. The torque should be 0.4–0.7 ft. lbs.
5. Adjust the worm shaft adjusting bolt to specifications.

Power Steering Gear

Removal and Installation

1. Disconnect the negative battery cable.
2. Remove the coolant reservoir tank from the radiator.
3. Disconnect the steering column lower shaft from the gear box.
4. Raise and safely support the vehicle.
5. Remove the center link nut and lock washer and disconnect the center link from the pitman arm, using a piman arm puller.
6. Lower the vehicle. Remove the pressure hose from the power steering gear assembly and plug.
7. Disconnect the return hose and plug. Remove the 3 power steering gear mounting bolts.
8. Remove the power steering gear. Disconnect the pitman arm from the gear assembly, note the alignment marks.

To install:

9. Align the matchmarks on the pitman arm and the power steering gear secter shaft. Install the pitman arm to the gear assembly and tighten the nut to 95 ft. lbs.
10. Install the power steering gear assembly on the vehicle and tighten the mounting bolts to 72 ft. lbs.
11. Connect the power steering pressure and return hoses.
12. Raise and safely support the vehicle.
13. Install the center link to the pitman arm and tighten the nut to 40 ft. lbs. Lower the vehicle.
14. Connect the steering column lower shaft to the gear assembly and tighten the bolts to 29 ft. lbs.
15. Install the coolant reservoir tank to the radiator. Refill the power steering pump.
16. Connect the negative battery cable. Run the engine and operate the power steering. Recheck the fluid level and for any leaks.

Adjustment

1. Check the worm shaft to make sure it is free from thrust play.
2. Place the pitman arm in a position that is nearly parallel with the worm shaft.
3. With the pitman arm in this position, the front wheels are in a straight-forward state.
4. Measure the worm shaft starting torque from it's straight-forward state. The torque should be 0.5 ft. lbs.
5. Adjust the worm shaft adjusting bolt tospecifications.

Power steering Pump

Removal and Installation

NOTE: Before disconnecting the power steering pressure and return line at the pump assembly, make sure any dirt or grease is removed.

1. Disconnect the negative battery cable. Remove the coolant reservoir tank from the radiator.
2. Loosen the air conditioning compressor adjusting and pivot bolts, if equipped.
3. Loosen the power steering pump adjusting and mounting bolts, if not equipped with air conditioning.
4. Remove the power steering belt.
5. Disconnect the power steering pressure and return hose and plug.
6. Disconnect the power steering pressure switch lead wire at the switch terminal.
7. Remove the engine oil filter.
8. Remove the power steering pump mounting and adjusting bolts.
9. Remove the power steering pump.

To install:
10. Install the power steering pump and install the pump mounting bolts. Do not tighten.
11. Install the power steering pump pressure switch lead wire to the switch terminal.
12. Install the power steering pressure and return hoses.
13. Install the power steering belt and tighten the power steering pump mounting bolts to 21 ft. lbs.
14. Tighten the air conditioning mounting bolts to 21 ft. lbs., if equipped.
15. Install the coolant reservoir tank to the radiator and connect the negative battery cable. Refill the power steering pump.
16. Install the oil filter and fill the crankcase to the proper level.
17. Run the engine and operate the power steering. Recheck the fluid level and for any leaks.

Belt Adjustment

1. To adjust the power steering belt tension, loosen the adjusting bolt of the air conditioning compressor, if equipped, or that of the power steering pump for vehicles without air conditioning.
2. Adjust the belt tension to 0.30 in. deflection, using the proper belt tension gauge and measuring at the midpoint between the 2 pulleys.
3. Tighten the proper adjusting and mounting bolts to the specified torque.

System Bleeding

1. Raise and support the vehicle safely.
2. Fill the power steering reservoir to the specified level.
3. Run the engine for 3–5 minutes, stop the engine and add fluid if necessary to reach specified level.
4. With the engine stopped, turn the steering wheel to the left and to the right as far as it turns. Repeat a few times and refill the reservoir.
5. With the engine running at idle speed, bleed air from the system by loosening the bleeder valve at the gear assembly.
6. Repeat the stop to stop turn of the steering wheel until all the foam is gone.
7. Tighten the bleed valve securely. Recheck the fluid level in the reservoir.

NOTE: When air bleeding is not complete, it is indicated by a foaming fluid on the level indicator or a humming noise from the power steering pump.

Tie Rod Ends

Removal and Installation

1. Raise and safely support the vehicle and remove the wheels.
2. Remove the tie rod end from the steering knuckle, using a suitable tie rod end remover tool.
3. Mark the tie rod end locknut position on the tie rod thread.
4. Loosen the locknut and remove the tie rod end from the tie rod.

To install:
5. Install the tie rod end locknut and the tie rod end to the tie rod. Align the locknut with the mark on the tie rod thread and tighten the locknut to 48 ft. lbs.
6. Connect the tie rod end to the steering knuckle. Tighten the castle nut until the holes of the split pin are aligned but only within the specified torque 33 ft. lbs.

BRAKES

Master Cylinder

Removal and Installation

1. Disconnect the negative battery cable. Remove the air cleaner case.
2. Disconnect the reservoir lead wire.
3. Clean the outside of the reservoir and drain the fluid from the reservoir.
4. Disconnect and plug the brake fluid lines at the master cylinder.
5. Remove the master cylinder to booster mounting bolts and remove the master cylinder.

To install:
6. Install the new master cylinder and tighten the mounting bolts to 12 ft. lbs.
7. Install the hydraulic brake lines to the master cylinder and tighten and tighten the flare nuts to 13 ft. lbs.
8. Install the reservoir lead wire, if equipped.
9. Fill the reservoir with the specified brake fluid. Install the air cleaner case.
10. Bleed the air from the brake hydraulic system and check the brake pedal play.

Proportioning Valve

Removal and Installation

1. Raise and safely support the vehicle.
2. Disconnect and plug the hydraulic brake lines from the proportioning valve assembly.
3. Remove the proportioning valve from the vehicle body.

NOTE: The proportioning valve should be removed with the spring attached.

To install:
4. Install the proportioning valve to the vehicle body and tighten the mounting bolts to 20 ft. lbs.

5. Connect the hydraulic brake lines to the proportioning valve and tighten the flare nuts to 13 ft. lbs.

6. Fill the brake reservoir to the proper level and bleed the brake hydraulic system. Lower the vehicle.

NOTE: Bleed the air from the proportioning valve bleeder valve.

Power Brake Booster

Removal and Installation

1. Disconnect the negative battery cable. Remove the air cleaner case.

2. Drain the fluid from the brake reservoir and remove the master cylinder.

3. Disconnect the vacuum hose from the booster. Remove the pushrod clevis pin and cotter pin from the brake pedal arm.

4. Disconnect the brake booster mounting nuts and remove the brake booster from the vehicle.

5. Disconnect the pedal attachment from the booster.

To install:

6. Connect the pedal attachment to the booster and install the booster to the vehicle. Tighten the mounting nuts to 7.5–11.5 ft. lbs.

7. Install the pushrod clevis pin and cotter pin to the brake pedal arm.

8. Connect the vacuum hose to the booster and install the master cylinder to the booster.

9. Install the air cleaner case and connect the negative battery cable.

10. Fill the brake reservoir and bleed the brake hydraulic system.

Brake Caliper

Removal and Installation

1. Disconnect the negative battery cable. Raise and safely support the vehicle.

2. Remove the wheels. Disconnect and plug the brake line.

3. Remove the caliper mounting bolts and remove the caliper from the vehicle.

To install:

4. Install the caliper on the vehicle. Tighten the mounting bolts to 65 ft. lbs.

5. Connect the hydraulic brake line, using 2 new washers. Replace the front wheels.

6. Lower the vehicle. Connect the negative battery cable.

7. Fill the brake reservoir and bleed the hydraulic brake system.

Disc Brake Pads

Removal and Installation

1. Disconnect the negative battery cable. Raise and safely support the vehicle.

2. Remove the wheels.

3. Disconnect the brake caliper.

NOTE: Do not allow the caliper hang from the brake hose. Support it by the mounting bracket.

4. Remove the disc pads from the caliper. Disconnect the anti-rattle springs.

1. Anti-rattle outer spring
2. Brake caliper carrier
3. Disc brake outer pad
4. Disc brake inner pad
5. Cylinder boot
6. Disc brake piston
7. Piston seal
8. Disc brake caliper
9. Caliper pin bolt
10. Caliper pin
11. Caliper mounting bolt
12. Bleeder plug cap
13. Bleeder plug
14. Anti-noise shim

Exploded view of the front disc brake assembly

To install:

5. Connect the anti-rattle springs and install the brake pads on to caliper assembly.

6. Connect the brake caliper and install the front wheels.

7. Lower the vehicle. Connect the negative battery cable.

Brake Rotor

Removal and Installation

1. Disconnect the negative battery cable.

2. Raise and safely support the vehicle. Remove the front wheels.

3. Remove the brake caliper mounting bracket, with the caliper and the brake line attached, move it out of the way and support it.

NOTE: Do not allow the caliper hang from the brake hose. Support it by the mounting bracket.

4. Install 2 bolts into the threaded holes in the brake rotor and tighten them evenly. This will remove the rotor from the hub assembly.

To install:

5. Install the new brake rotor on the hub and install the caliper assembly.

6. Install the front wheels and tighten to 65 ft. lbs.

7. Lower the vehicle and connect the negative battery terminal.

Brake Drums

Removal and Installation

1. Disconnect the negative battery cable. Raise and safely support the vehicle.

2. Make sure the parking brake is released.

3. Remove the wheels and the rear drum nuts from the vehicle.

4. Remove the brake drum, using a slide hammer.

To install:

5. Install the brake drum, tighten the brake drum nuts to 58 ft. lbs.

6. Install the rear wheels and lower the vehicle. Connect the negative battery cable.

Brake Shoes

Removal and Installation

1. Disconnect the negative battery cable. Raise and safely support the vehicle.

2. Remove the rear wheels from the vehicle. Remove the rear brake drums.

3. Remove the brake shoe hold-down springs.

4. Disconnect the parking brake cable from the parking brake shoe lever and remove the brake shoes.

To install:

5. Install the brake shoes and install the parking brake lever and cable to the assembly.

6. Install the brake shoe hold-down springs and install the rear brake drums.

7. Install the rear wheels, lower the vehicle and connect the negative battery terminal.

Wheel Cylinder

Removal and Installation

1. Disconnect the negative battery cable. Raise and safely support the vehicle.

1. Shoe hold-down pin
2. Brake backing plate
3. Wheel cylinder assembly
4. Rod spring
5. Parking brake rod
6. Shoe hold-down spring
7. Brake shoe
8. Shoe return spring
9. Shoe return upper spring

Exploded view of the rear brake drum assembly

2. Remove the rear wheels and brake drums from the vehicle.

3. Remove the rear brake shoes and disconnect the brake line from the rear of the wheel cylinder. Plug the brake lines.

4. Remove the 2 rear wheel cylinder mounting bolts. Remove the rear wheel cylinder.

To install:

5. Install the wheel cylinder and tighten the mounting bolts to 7 ft. lbs.

6. Connect the brake line to the wheel cylinder and install the rear brake shoes.

7. Install the rear brake drums and the rear wheels.

8. Lower the vehicle. Connect the negative battery cable.

9. Bleed the brake system and check for any leaks when finished.

Parking Brake Cable

Removal and Installation

1. Disconnect the parking brake cable from the parking lever.

2. Raise and safely support the vehicle. Remove the rear wheels and brake drums from the vehicle.

3. Remove the rear brake shoes and disconnect the park brake cable from the park brake shoe lever.

4. Remove the cable from the brake backing plate by squeezing the park brake cable stop ring.

To install:

5. Install the cable to the backing plate and to the brake shoe lever.

6. Install the brake shoes and install the rear brake drums.

7. Install the rear wheels and lower the vehicle. Connect the cable to the parking brake lever.

Adjustment

1. Adjust the parking brake lever by loosening or tightening the self locking nut at the park brake lever.

2. The proper adjustment is when the park brake lever is within 7–9 notches, when the lever is pulled up at 44 lbs.

3. Check the rear drum for dragging after adjustment.

FRONT SUSPENSION

Shock Absorbers

Removal and Installation

1. Raise and safely support the vehicle.

2. Support the axle assembly and remove the upper shock absorber mounting nut.

3. Remove the lower shock absorber mounting nut and remove the shock absorber.

To install:

4. Install the shock absorber and install the lower mounting nut to the bolt.

5. Torque the upper mounting nut to 20 ft. lbs. and the lower nut to 33 ft. lbs. and lower the vehicle.

MacPherson Strut

Removal and Installation

1. Disconnect the negative battery cable.

2. Raise and safely support the vehicle. Allow the front suspension to hang free.

3. Remove the front wheel. Disconnect the E-clip mounting the brake hose and remove the brake hose from the strut bracket.

4. Remove the strut bracket to steering knuckle bolts.

5. Lower the vehicle. Remove the strut support nuts, while holding the strut by hand. Remove the strut assembly.

To install:

6. Install the strut assembly and tighten the strut support nuts to 18 ft. lbs.

7. Raise and safely support the vehicle.

8. Install the strut bracket to steering knuckle bolts and tighten to 66 ft. lbs.

9. Connect the brake hose to the strut bracket using the E-clip.

10. Install the front wheels and lower the vehicle.

11. Connect the negative battery cable.

Coil Springs

Removal and Installation
SIDEKICK

1. Disconnect the negative battery cable.

2. Raise and safely support the vehicle. Allow the front suspension to hang free.

3. Remove the front wheel and the locking hub assembly.

4. Remove the front axle circlip and washer.

5. Remove the brake caliper mounting bracket, with the caliper and the brake line attached, move it out of the way and support it.

6. Remove the brake disc and disconnect the stabilizer link from the control arm.

7. Disconnect the tie rod end and support the lower control arm using a jack.

8. Disconnect the strut bracket and remove the ball joint castle nut.

9. Remove the steering knuckle and the wheel hub assembly while lowering the jack.

10. Remove the coil spring from the vehicle.

To install:

11. Install the coil spring in the vehicle and install the wheel hub and steering knuckle while raising the jack.

12. Connect the strut bracket and install the ball joint castle nut.

13. Connect the tie rod end and connect the stabilizer link to the control arm.

14. Install the brake disc and connect the caliper assembly.

15. Install the front axle circlip and washer and install the locking hub assembly.

16. Install the front wheels, lower the vehicle and connect the negative battery cable.

Leaf Springs

Removal and Installation
SAMURAI

1. Disconnect the negative battery cable.

2. Raise and safely support the vehicle. Allow the front suspension to hang free.

3. Remove the stabilizer bar pivot bolt.

4. Support the front axle assembly with an adjustable stand.

5. Remove the leaf spring to spring plate mounting U-bolts.

6. Remove the shackle pin and the nut from the front of the leaf spring.

7. Disconnect the leaf spring bolt and remove the leaf spring.

SMOOTH ROTATION

Checking ball joint play

NOTE: Removal of the leaf spring causes the axle housing to hang. Support it with a safety stand to prevent it from damaging the U-joint of the driveshaft.

To install:

8. Install the leaf spring and leaf spring bolts and tighten to 57 ft. lbs.

9. Install the shackle pin and nut to the front of the leaf spring and install the spring plate and U-bolts.

10. Install the stabilizer bar pivot bolt.

11. Lower the vehicle and connect the negative battery terminal.

Lower Ball Joints

Inspection

SIDEKICK

1. Inspect for the smoothness of the rotation.
2. Check the ball stud for damage.
3. Inspect the dust shield for damage.

Removal and Installation

SIDEKICK

1. Disconnect the negative battery cable. Remove the coil spring from the vehicle.
2. Remove the control arm mounting bolts.
3. Remove the control arm.
4. Disconnect the ball joint from the control arm and remove the ball joint.

To install:

5. Install the ball joint to the control arm and tighten the bolts to 63 ft. lbs.

6. Install the control arm to the chassis and tighten the bolts to 74 ft. lbs.

7. Install the coil spring and connect the negative battery cable.

Lower Control Arms

Removal and Installation

SIDEKICK

1. Disconnect the negative battery cable. Remove the coil spring from the vehicle.
2. Remove the control arm mounting bolts.
3. Remove the control arm.

To install:

4. Install the control arm to the chassis and tighten the bolts to 74 ft. lbs.

5. Install the coil spring and connect the negative battery cable.

Stabilizer Bar

Removal and Installation

1. Disconnect the negative battery cable. Raise and safely support the vehicle.
2. Disconnect the left and the right stabilizer ball joints from the front control arms on the Sidekick.
3. Disconnect the stabilizer bar pivot bolts on the Samurai.
4. Remove the stabilizer bar mount bushing bracket bolts and nuts.
5. Remove the stabilizer bar.
6. Remove the stabilizer links on the Sidekick.

To install:

7. Install the new stabilizer bar, using new bushings.

8. Torque the stabilizer bar pivot bolts to 51–65 ft. lbs. and the mounting bracket nuts to 13–20 ft. lbs. for the Samurai. Torque the stabilizer link nuts to 21 ft. lbs. and the stabilizer bar bracket bolts and nuts to 37 ft. lbs. for the Sidekick.

9. Lower the vehicle and connect the negative battery cable.

Kingpin and Bushings

Removal and Installation

SAMURAI

1. Raise and safely support the vehicle.
2. Remove the steering knuckle from the vehicle.

NOTE: When the steering knuckle is pulled, the lower kingpin bearing sometimes falls off.

3. Remove the upper and the lower kingpins, mark them. Check the number of shims on each side.

To install:

4. Install the new kingpin bearings in the steering knuckle holding them in with grease.

5. Install the steering knuckle on the axle assembly.

6. Install the new kingpins in the steering knuckle, shim them correctly and torque the bolts to 17 ft. lbs.

NOTE: The correct procedure for installing the kingpins is to check the turning torque of the spindle while pulling it outwards from the tie rod end hole. A spring type gauge is required for this procedure. The correct force should be 2.20–3.96 lbs. of force require to turn the spindle without the oil seal being installed. Use additional shims, if necessary, to correct the turning torque.

7. With the turning torque of the spindle correct and the oil seal installed, install the front wheels and lower the vehicle.

REAR SUSPENSION

Shock Absorbers

Removal and Installation

1. Raise and safely support the vehicle. Support the rear axle housing.
2. Remove the upper and lower shock absorber mounting bolts.
3. Remove the rear shock absorber.

To install:

4. Install the the rear shock absorber.
5. On the Sidekick, install the upper mounting bolts and tighten to 21 ft. lbs. Install the lower mounting bolts and tighten to 63 ft. lbs.
6. On Samurai, tighten the upper and the lower mounting bolts to 25 ft. lbs.

Coil Springs

Removal and Installation

SIDEKICK

1. Raise and safely support the vehicle. Remove the rear wheels.
2. Support the rear axle housing, using a floor jack.
3. Remove the shock absorber lower mounting bolt and disconnect the parking brake cable hangers.
4. Lower the rear axle housing so the coil spring can be removed.
5. Remove the coil spring from the vehicle.

To install:

6. Install the coil spring to the spring seat and raise the axle housing.

7. Install the lower shock absorber mounting bolt but do not tighten.
8. Connect the parking brake cable hangers and install the rear wheels.
9. Lower the vehicle and tighten the lower shock absorber nut to 64 ft. lbs.

Leaf Springs

Removal and Installation

SAMURAI

1. Raise and safely support the vehicle. Remove the rear wheels.
2. Safely support the axle housing separately and disconnect the shocks.
3. Disconnect the stabilizer bar from the shackle plate under the leaf spring.

NOTE: Do not let the axle housing hang on the brake hoses or lines.

4. Remove the rear axle housing U-bolt nuts and remove the bolts.
5. Raise the rear axle housing to release spring tension and remove the shackle plate.
6. Support the leaf spring and disconnect the rear leaf spring mounting bolts.
7. Remove the leaf spring assembly.

To install:

8. Install the leaf spring and shackle assembly and tighten the mounting bolts to 56 ft. lbs.
9. Install the U-bolt nuts and tighten to 50 ft. lbs.
10. Connect the stabilizer bar under the shackle plate. Install the shocks and tighten to 30 ft. lbs.
11. Install the rear wheels and lower the vehicle.

SPECIFICATIONS

ENGINE IDENTIFICATION

Year	Model	Engine Displacement cu. in. (cc/liter)	Engine Series Identification	No. of Cylinders	Engine Type
1988	Pick-Up	144.4 (2366/2.4)	22R	4	OHC
	Pick-Up	144.4 (2366/2.4)	22R-E	4	OHC
	Pick-Up	144.4 (2366/2.4)	22R-TE	4	OHC-Turbo
	Pick-Up	180.5 (2959/3.0)	3VZ-E	6	OHC
	4Runner	144.4 (2366/2.4)	22R	4	OHC
	4Runner	144.4 (2366/2.4)	22R-E	4	OHC
	4Runner	144.4 (2366/2.4)	22R-TE	4	OHC-Turbo
	4Runner	180.5 (2959/3.0)	3VZ-E	6	OHC
	Van	136.5 (2237/2.2)	4Y-EC	4	OHC
	Land Cruiser	241.3 (3956/4.0)	3F-E	6	OHV
1989	Pick-Up	144.4 (2366/2.4)	22R	4	OHC
	Pick-Up	144.4 (2366/2.4)	22R-E	4	OHC
	Pick-Up	180.5 (2959/3.0)	3VZ-E	6	OHC
	4Runner	144.4 (2366/2.4)	22R-E	4	OHC
	4Runner	180.5 (2959/3.0)	3VZ-E	6	OHC
	Land Cruiser	241.3 (3956/4.0)	3F-E	6	OHV
	Van	136.5 (2237/2.2)	4Y-EC	4	OHC
1990	Pick-Up	144.4 (2366/2.4)	22R	4	OHC
	Pick-Up	144.4 (2366/2.4)	22R-E	4	OHC
	Pick-Up	180.5 (2959/3.0)	3VZ-E	6	OHC
	4Runner	144.4 (2366/2.4)	22R-E	4	OHC
	4Runner	180.5 (2959/3.0)	3VZ-E	6	OHC
	Land Cruiser	241.3 (3956/4.0)	3F-E	6	OHV
1991–92	Pick-Up	144.4 (2366/2.4)	22R-E	4	OHC
	Pick-Up	180.5 (2959/3.0)	3VZ-E	6	OHC
	4Runner	144.4 (2366/2.4)	22R-E	4	OHC
	4Runner	180.5 (2959/3.0)	3VZ-E	6	OHC
	Land Cruiser	241.3 (3956/4.0)	3F-E	6	OHV
	Previa	146.4 (2399/2.4)	2TZ-FE	4	DOHC

OHC—Overhead cam
OHV—Overhead valves
DOHC—Dual overhead cam

GENERAL ENGINE SPECIFICATIONS

Year	Model	Engine Displacement cu. in. (cc)	Fuel System Type	Net Horsepower @ rpm	Net Torque @ rpm (ft. lbs.)	Bore × Stroke (in.)	Compression Ratio	Oil Pressure @ rpm
1988	Pick-Up	144.4 (2366)	2 bbl	96 @ 4800	129 @ 2800	3.62 × 3.50	9.3:1	36–71 @ 3000
	Pick-Up	144.4 (2366)	EFI	116 @ 4800	140 @ 2800	3.62 × 3.50	9.3:1	36–71 @ 3000
	Pick-Up	144.4 (2366)	EFI①	135 @ 4800	173 @ 2800	3.62 × 3.50	7.5:1	36–71 @ 3000
	Pick-Up	180.5 (2959)	EFI	150 @ 4800	180 @ 3400	3.44 × 3.23	9.0:1	36–71 @ 4000
	4Runner	144.4 (2366)	2 bbl	96 @ 4800	129 @ 2800	3.62 × 3.50	9.3:1	36–71 @ 3000
	4Runner	144.4 (2366)	EFI	116 @ 4800	140 @ 2800	3.62 × 3.50	9.3:1	36–71 @ 3000

GENERAL ENGINE SPECIFICATIONS

Year	Model	Engine Displacement cu. in. (cc)	Fuel System Type	Net Horsepower @ rpm	Net Torque @ rpm (ft. lbs.)	Bore × Stroke (in.)	Compression Ratio	Oil Pressure @ rpm
1988	4Runner	144.4 (2366)	EFI①	135 @ 4800	173 @ 2800	3.62 × 3.50	7.5:1	36–71 @ 3000
	Van	136.5 (2237)	EFI	101 @ 4000	132 @ 3000	3.58 × 3.40	8.8:1	50–70 @ 3000
	Land Cruiser	241.3 (3956)	EFI	154 @ 4000	220 @ 3000	3.70 × 3.74	8.1:1	36–71 @ 4000
1989	Pick-Up	144.4 (2366)	2 bbl	103 @ 4800	133 @ 2800	3.62 × 3.50	9.3:1	36–71 @ 3000
	Pick-Up	144.4 (2366)	EFI	116 @ 4800	140 @ 2800	3.62 × 3.50	9.3:1	36–71 @ 3000
	Pick-Up	180.5 (2959)	EFI	150 @ 4800	180 @ 3400	3.44 × 3.23	9.0:1	36–71 @ 4000
	4Runner	144.4 (2366)	EFI	116 @ 4800	140 @ 2800	3.62 × 3.50	9.3:1	36–71 @ 3000
	4Runner	180.5 (2959)	EFI	150 @ 4800	180 @ 3400	3.44 × 3.23	9.0:1	36–71 @ 4000
	Land Cruiser	241.3 (3956)	EFI	154 @ 4000	220 @ 3000	3.70 × 3.74	8.1:1	36–71 @ 4000
	Van	136.5 (2237)	EFI	101 @ 4000	132 @ 3000	3.58 × 3.40	8.8:1	50–70 @ 3000
1990	Pick-Up	144.4 (2366)	2 bbl	103 @ 4800	133 @ 2800	3.62 × 3.50	9.3:1	36–71 @ 3000
	Pick-Up	144.4 (2366)	EFI	116 @ 4800	140 @ 2800	3.62 × 3.50	9.3:1	36–71 @ 3000
	Pick-Up	180.5 (2959)	EFI	150 @ 4800	180 @ 3400	3.44 × 3.23	9.0:1	36–75 @ 3000
	4Runner	144.4 (2366)	EFI	116 @ 4800	140 @ 2800	3.62 × 3.50	9.3:1	36–75 @ 3000
	4Runner	180.5 (2959)	EFI	150 @ 4800	180 @ 3400	3.44 × 3.23	9.0:1	36–75 @ 3000
	Land Cruiser	241.3 (3956)	EFI	155 @ 4000	220 @ 3000	3.70 × 3.74	8.1:1	36–71 @ 4000
1991–92	Pick-Up	144.4 (2366)	EFI	116 @ 4800	140 @ 2800	3.62 × 3.50	9.3:1	36–71 @ 3000
	Pick-Up	180.5 (2959)	EFI	150 @ 4800	180 @ 3400	3.44 × 3.23	9.0:1	36–75 @ 3000
	4Runner	144.4 (2366)	EFI	116 @ 4800	140 @ 2800	3.62 × 3.50	9.3:1	36–71 @ 3000
	4Runner	180.5 (2959)	EFI	150 @ 4800	180 @ 3400	3.44 × 3.23	9.0:1	36–75 @ 3000
	Land Cruiser	241.3 (3956)	EFI	155 @ 4000	220 @ 3000	3.70 × 3.74	8.1:1	36–71 @ 4000
	Previa	146.4 (2399)	EFI①	138 @ 5000	154 @ 4000	3.74 × 3.39	9.1:1	36–71 @ 3000

EFI—Electronic Fuel Injection
① Turbocharged

GASOLINE ENGINE TUNE-UP SPECIFICATIONS

Year	Model	Engine Displacement cu. in. (cc)	Spark Plugs Type	Gap (in.)	Ignition Timing (deg.) MT	Ignition Timing (deg.) AT	Compression Pressure (psi)	Fuel Pump (psi)	Idle Speed (rpm) MT	Idle Speed (rpm) AT	Valve Clearance In.	Valve Clearance Ex.
1988	Pick-Up①	144.4 (2366)	W16-EXRU	0.031	0④	0④	142–171	2.1–4.3	700	750	0.008	0.012
	Pick-Up②	144.4 (2366)	W16-EXRU	0.031	5B⑤	—	142–171	36–38	750	—	0.008	0.012
	Pick-Up③	144.4 (2366)	W16-EXRU	0.031	5B⑤	—	142–171	36–38	800	—	0.008	0.012
	Pick-Up	180.5 (2959)	Q16-RU	0.031	10B	10B	142–171	38–44	800	800	⑨	⑨
	4Runner①	144.4 (2366)	W16-EXRU	0.031	0④	0④	142–171	2.1–4.3	700	750	0.008	0.012
	4Runner②	144.4 (2366)	W16-EXRU	0.031	5B⑤	—	142–171	36–38	750	—	0.008	0.012
	4Runner③	144.4 (2366)	W16-EXRU	0.031	5B⑤	—	142–171	36–38	800	—	0.008	0.012
	4Runner	180.5 (2959)	Q16-RU	0.031	10B	10B	142–171	38–44	800	800	⑨	⑨
	Van	136.5 (2237)	P-16R	0.043	12B⑤	—	128–178	27–31	700	750	Hyd.	Hyd.
	Land Cruiser	241.3 (3956)	W16-EXRU	0.031	7B④	7B	114–149	37–46	650	650	0.008	0.014
1989	Pick-Up①	144.4 (2366)	W16-EXRU	0.031	0④	0④	142–171	2.1–4.3	700	750	0.008	0.012
	Pick-Up②	144.4 (2366)	W16-EXRU	0.031	5B⑤	—	142–171	36–38	750	—	0.008	0.012
	Pick-Up	180.5 (2959)	Q16-RU	0.031	10B	10B	142–171	38–44	800	800	⑨	⑨
	4Runner②	144.4 (2366)	W16-EXRU	0.031	5B⑤	—	142–171	36–38	750	—	0.008	0.012
	4Runner	180.5 (2959)	Q16-RU	0.031	10B	10B	142–171	38–44	800	800	⑨	⑨

GASOLINE ENGINE TUNE-UP SPECIFICATIONS

Year	Model	Engine Displacement cu. in. (cc)	Spark Plugs Type	Gap (in.)	Ignition Timing (deg.) MT	AT	Compression Pressure (psi)	Fuel Pump (psi)	Idle Speed (rpm) MT	AT	Valve Clearance In.	Ex.
1989	Land Cruiser	241.3 (3956)	W16-EXRU	0.031	7B④	7B	114–149	37–46	650	650	0.008	0.014
	Van	136.5 (2237)	P-16R	0.043	12B⑤	—	128–178	27–31	700	750	Hyd.	Hyd.
1990	Pick-Up①	144.4 (2366)	W16-EXRU	0.031	0④	0	142–171	2.1–4.3	750	850	0.008	0.012
	Pick-Up②	144.4 (2366)	W16-EXRU	0.031	5B	5B	142–171	38–44	750	850	0.008	0.012
	Pick-Up	180.5 (2959)	K16-RU	0.031	10B	10B	142–171	38–44	800	800	⑨	⑨
	4Runner	144.4 (2366)	W16-EXRU	0.031	5B	5B	142–171	38–44	750	750	0.008	0.012
	4Runner	180.5 (2959)	K16-RU	0.031	10B	10B	142–171	38–44	800	800	⑨	⑨
	Land Cruiser	241.3 (3956)	W16-EXRU	0.031	—	7B	114–149	37–46	650	650	0.008	0.014⑪
1991	Pick-Up②	144.4 (2366)	W16-EXRU	0.031	5B	5B	142–171	38–44	750	850	0.008	0.012
	Pick-Up	180.5 (2959)	K16-RU	0.031	10B	10B	142–171	38–44	800	800	⑨	⑨
	4Runner②	144.4 (2366)	W16-EXRU	0.031	5B	5B	142–171	38–44	750	750	0.008	0.012
	4Runner	180.5 (2959)	K16-RU	0.031	10B	10B	142–171	38–44	800	800	⑨	⑨
	Land Cruiser	241.3 (3956)	W16-EXR-U11	0.043	—	7B	114–149	37–46	650	650	0.008	0.014⑪
	Previa⑥	146.4 (2399)	PK16R11	0.043	5B	5B	128–178	38–44	700	750	⑦	⑧
1992	SEE UNDERHOOD STICKER											

Hyd.—Hydraulic
① 2 bbl
② EFI
③ Turbocharged
④ 950 rpm

⑤ "T" terminal shorted
⑥ DOHC
⑦ Intake: 0.006–0.010 (cold)
⑧ Exhaust: 0.010–0.014 (cold)

⑨ Intake: 0.007–0.011 (cold)
   Exhaust: 0.009–0.013 (cold)
⑩ Intake: 0.010–0.014 (cold)
   Exhaust: 0.011–0.015 (cold)
⑪ Engine hot

FIRING ORDERS

NOTE: To avoid confusion, always replace spark plug wires one at a time.

22R, 22R–E, 22R–TE, 2TZ–FE and 4Y–EC Engines
Engine Firing Order: 1–3–4–2
Distributor Rotation: Clockwise

3F–E Engines
Engine Firing Order: 1–5–3–6–2–4
Distributor Rotation: Clockwise

3VZ–E Engine
Engine Firing Order: 1–2–3–4–5–6
Distributor Rotation: Counterclockwise

CAPACITIES

Year	Model	Engine Displacement cu. in. (cc)	Engine Crankcase with Filter	Engine Crankcase without Filter	Transmission (qts.) 4-Spd	Transmission (qts.) 5-Spd	Transmission (qts.) Auto.	Drive Axle (qts.)	Fuel Tank (gal.)	Cooling System (qts.)
1988	Pick-Up[1]	144.4 (2366)	4.5	4.0	2.5	2.5	[7]	[8]	[9]	8.9
	Pick-Up[2]	144.4 (2366)	4.5	4.0	—	4.1	[7]	[8]	[9]	8.9
	Pick-Up[3]	144.4 (2366)	4.5	4.0	—	4.1	[7]	[8]	[9]	8.9
	Pick-Up	180.5 (2959)	4.8	4.4	—	3.2	—	2.5	17.2	[11]
	4Runner[1]	144.4 (2366)	4.5	4.0	2.5	2.5	[7]	[8]	[9]	8.9
	4Runner[2]	144.4 (2366)	4.5	4.0	—	4.1	[7]	[8]	[9]	8.9
	4Runner[3]	144.4 (2366)	4.5	4.0	—	4.1	[7]	[8]	[9]	8.9
	4Runner	180.5 (2959)	4.8	4.4	—	3.2	[7]	2.5	17.2	[11]
	Van	136.5 (2237)	3.7	3.2	—	2.5	6.9	1.5[10]	15.9	7.5
	Land Cruiser	258.1 (4200)	8.2	7.4	—	—	15.9	2.2[6]	22.2[4]	17.5[5]
1989	Pick-Up[1]	144.4 (2366)	4.5	4.0	2.5	2.5	[7]	[8]	[9]	8.9
	Pick-Up[2]	144.4 (2366)	4.5	4.0	—	4.1	[7]	[8]	[9]	8.9
	Pick-Up	180.5 (2959)	4.8	4.4	—	3.2	—	2.5	17.2	[11]
	4Runner	144.4 (2366)	4.5	4.0	—	4.1		[8]	17.2	[11]
	4Runner	180.5 (2959)	4.8	4.4	—	3.2	[7]	2.5	17.2	[11]
	Van	136.5 (2237)	3.7	3.2	—	2.5	6.9	1.5[10]	15.9	7.5
	Land Cruiser	241.3 (3956)	8.2	7.4	—	—	15.9	2.2[6]	22.2[4]	17.5[5]
1990	Pick-Up[1]	144.4 (2366)	4.5	4.0	2.5	[16]	8.7	[17]	[9]	[15]
	Pick-Up[2]	144.4 (2366)	4.5	4.0	2.5	[16]	8.7	[17]	[9]	[15]
	Pick-Up	180.5 (2959)	4.8	4.4	—	[16]	8.7	[17]	[9]	[11]
	4Runner	144.4 (2366)	4.5	4.0	—	[16]	8.7	[17]	17.2[14]	[15]
	4Runner	180.5 (2959)	4.8	4.4	—	[16]	8.7	[17]	17.2[14]	[11]
	Land Cruiser	241.3 (3956)	8.2	7.4	—	—	5.3	2.6[13]	25.1	18.5[12]
1991–92	Pick-Up[1]	144.4 (2366)	4.5	4.0	—	[16]	[18]	[17]	[9]	[15]
	Pick-Up	180.5 (2959)	4.8	4.4	—	[16]	[18]	[17]	[9]	[11]
	4Runner	144.4 (2366)	4.5	4.0	—	[16]	[18]	[17]	17.2[14]	[15]
	4Runner	180.5 (2959)	4.8	4.4	—	[16]	[18]	[17]	17.2[14]	[11]
	Land Cruiser	241.3 (3956)	8.2	7.4	—	—	6.3	3.0	25.1	18.5[12]
	Previa	146.4 (2399)	6.1	5.8	—	[19]	2.5	[20]	19.8	12.3

[1] 2 bbl
[2] EFI
[3] Turbocharged
[4] 23.8 gallon optional
[5] Wagon—18.3 qts.
[6] Front Axle—1.7 pts. for Pick-Up and 4Runner
    3.2 pts. for Land Cruiser
[7] A43D Automatic Transmission—6.9 qts.
    A340E Automatic Transmission—7.3 qts.
    A340H Automatic Transmission—10.9 qts.
[8] 2WD
    7.5 in: 1.42 qts.
    8 in: 1.9 qts.
    4WD
    22R and 22R Engines: 2.3 qts.
    22R-TE Engine: 2.5 qts.
[9] Short bed—13.7 gallons
    Long bed—17.2 gallons
    Long bed 4WD—19.3 gallons

[10] 4WD—2.0 qts.
[11] Manual Transmission—11.0 qts.
    Automatic Transmission—10.8 qts.
[12] With rear heater—20.6 qts.
[13] Front axle—3.2 qts.
[14] 19.3 gallons optional
[15] 4WD automatic transmission—9.6 qts.
    Except 4WD automatic transmission—8.9
[16] 2WD—2.5 qts.
    4WD:
    G58—4.1 qts.
    W56 and R150F—3.2 qts.
[17] 2WD:
    7.5 in.—1.4 qts.
    8.0 in.—1.9 qts.

    4WD Front
    Standard—1.7 qts.
    A.D.D.—2.0 qts.
    4WD Rear—2.3 qts.
[18] 2WD:
    A340E—1.7 qts.
    A44D—2.5 qts.
    4WD:
    A340F—1.7 qts.
    A340H—4.8 qts.
[19] 2WD—2.3 qts.
    4WD—2.7 qts.
[20] 2WD—1.6 qts.
    4WD:
    Front—1.1 qts.
    Rear—1.6 qts.

CAMSHAFT SPECIFICATIONS

All measurements given in inches.

| Year | Engine Displacement cu. in. (cc) | Journal Diameter | | | | | Lobe Lift | | Bearing Clearance | Camshaft End Play |
		1	2	3	4	5	In.	Ex.		
1988	144.4 (2366)	1.2984–1.2992	1.2984–1.2992	1.2984–1.2992	1.2984–1.2992	—	1.6783–1.6891	1.6807–1.6842	0.0004–0.0020	0.0031–0.0071
	136.5 (2237)	1.8291–1.8297	1.8192–1.8199	1.8094–1.8100	1.7996–1.8002	1.7913–1.7929	1.5205–1.5244	1.5208–1.5248	0.0010–0.0032	0.0028–0.0087
	180.5 (2959)	1.3370–1.3376	1.3370–1.3376	1.3370–1.3376	1.3370–1.3376	—	1.6783–1.6891	1.6807–1.6842	0.0010–0.0030	0.0031–0.0075
	241.3 (3956)	1.8880–1.8888	1.8289–1.8297	1.7699–1.7707	1.7108–1.7116	—	1.5102–1.5142	1.5059–1.5098	0.0010–0.0030	0.0079–0.0103
1989	144.4 (2366)	1.2984–1.2992	1.2984–1.2992	1.2984–1.2992	1.2984–1.2992	—	1.6783–1.6891	1.6807–1.6842	0.0004–0.0020	0.0031–0.0071
	136.5 (2237)	1.8291–1.8297	1.8192–1.8199	1.8094–1.8100	1.7996–1.8002	1.7913–1.7929	1.5205–1.5244	1.5208–1.5248	0.0010–0.0032	0.0028–0.0087
	180.5 (2959)	1.3370–1.3376	1.3370–1.3376	1.3370–1.3376	1.3370–1.3376	—	1.6783–1.6891	1.6807–1.6842	0.0010–0.0030	0.0031–0.0075
	241.3 (3956)	1.8880–1.8888	1.8289–1.8297	1.7699–1.7707	1.7108–1.7116	—	1.5102–1.5142	1.5059–1.5098	0.0010–0.0030	0.0079–0.0103
1990	144.4 (2366)	1.2984–1.2992	1.2984–1.2992	1.2984–1.2992	1.2984–1.2992	—	1.6783–1.6891	1.6807–1.6842	0.0004–0.0020	0.0031–0.0071
	180.5 (2959)	1.3370–1.3376	1.3370–1.3376	1.3370–1.3376	1.3370–1.3376	—	1.8701–1.8870	1.8701–1.8870	0.0010–0.0039	0.0031–0.0098
	241.3 (3956)	1.8880–1.8888	1.8289–1.8297	1.7699–1.7707	1.7108–1.7116	—	1.5102–1.5142	1.5059–1.5098	0.0010–0.0030	0.0079–0.0130
1991–92	144.4 (2366)	1.2984–1.2992	1.2984–1.2992	1.2984–1.2992	1.2984–1.2992	—	1.6783–1.6891	1.6807–1.6842	0.0004–0.0020	0.0031–0.0071
	146.4 (2399)	1.0614–1.0620	1.0614–1.0620	1.0614–1.0620	1.0614–1.0620	—	1.7839–1.7878	1.7740–1.7779	0.0010–0.0031	0.0016–0.0047
	180.5 (2959)	1.3370–1.3376	1.3370–1.3376	1.3370–1.3376	1.3370–1.3376	—	1.8701–1.8870	1.8701–1.8870	0.0010–0.0039	0.0031–0.0098
	241.3 (3956)	1.8880–1.8888	1.8289–1.8297	1.7699–1.7707	1.7108–1.7116	—	1.5102–1.5142	1.5059–1.5098	0.0010–0.0030	0.0079–0.0130

CRANKSHAFT AND CONNECTING ROD SPECIFICATIONS

All measurements are given in inches.

| Year | Engine Displacement cu. in. (cc) | Crankshaft | | | | Connecting Rod | | |
		Main Brg. Journal Dia.	Main Brg. Oil Clearance	Shaft End-play	Thrust on No.	Journal Diameter	Oil Clearance	Side Clearance
1988	144.4 (2366)	2.3616–2.3622	0.0010–0.0022	0.0008–0.0087	3	2.0861–2.0866	0.0010–0.0022	0.0008–0.0087
	136.5 (2237)	2.2829–2.2835	0.0008–0.0020	0.0008–0.0087	3	1.8892–1.8898	0.0008–0.0020	0.0063–0.0123
	180.5 (2959)	2.5195–2.5197	0.0009–0.0017	0.0008–0.0098	3	2.1648–2.1654	0.0009–0.0021	0.0059–0.0130
	241.3 (3956)	①	0.0008–0.0017	0.0024–0.0063	3	2.1252–2.1260	0.0008–0.0024	0.0043–0.0091

CRANKSHAFT AND CONNECTING ROD SPECIFICATIONS

All measurements are given in inches.

Year	Engine Displacement cu. in. (cc)	Crankshaft				Connecting Rod		
		Main Brg. Journal Dia.	Main Brg. Oil Clearance	Shaft End-play	Thrust on No.	Journal Diameter	Oil Clearance	Side Clearance
1989	144.4 (2366)	2.3616–2.3622	0.0010–0.0022	0.0008–0.0087	3	2.0861–2.0866	0.0010–0.0022	0.0008–0.0087
	136.5 (2237)	2.2829–2.2835	0.0008–0.0020	0.0008–0.0087	3	1.8892–1.8898	0.0008–0.0020	0.0063–0.0123
	180.5 (2959)	2.5195–2.5197	0.0009–0.0017	0.0008–0.0098	3	2.1648–2.1654	0.0009–0.0021	0.0059–0.0130
	241.3 (3956)	①	0.0008–0.0017	0.0006–0.0080	3	2.0861–2.0866	0.0008–0.0020	0.0063–0.0118
1990	144.4 (2366)	2.3616–2.3622	0.0010–0.0022	0.0008–0.0087	3	2.0861–2.0866	0.0010–0.0022	0.0008–0.0087
	180.5 (2959)	2.5195–2.5197	0.0009–0.0017	0.0008–0.0098	3	2.1648–2.1654	0.0009–0.0021	0.0059–0.0130
	241.3 (3956)	①	0.0008–0.0017	0.0006–0.0080	3	2.0861–2.0866	0.0008–0.0020	0.0063–0.0118
1991–92	144.4 (2366)	2.3616–2.3622	0.0010–0.0022	0.0008–0.0087	3	2.0861–2.0866	0.0010–0.0022	0.0008–0.0087
	146.4 (2399)	2.3617–2.3622	0.0008–0.0019	0.0008–0.0087	3	2.0861–2.0866	0.0012–0.0023	0.0063–0.0123
	180.5 (2959)	2.5195–2.5197	0.0009–0.0017	0.0008–0.0098	3	2.1648–2.1654	0.0009–0.0021	0.0059–0.0130
	241.3 (3956)	①	0.0008–0.0017	0.0006–0.0080	3	2.0861–2.0866	0.0008–0.0020	0.0063–0.0118

① No. 1—2.6367–2.6376
No. 2—2.6957–2.6967
No. 3—2.7548–2.7557
No. 4—2.8139–2.8148

VALVE SPECIFICATIONS

Year	Engine Displacement cu. in. (cc)	Seat Angle (deg.)	Face Angle (deg.)	Spring Test Pressure (lbs.)	Spring Installed Height (in.)	Stem-to-Guide Clearance (in.)		Stem Diameter (in.)	
						Intake	Exhaust	Intake	Exhaust
1988	144.4 (2366)	45①	44.5	66	1.909②	0.0010–0.0024	0.0012–0.0026	0.3138–0.3144	0.3136–0.3142
	136.5 (2237)	45①	44.5	64–77	1.850②	0.0010–0.0024	0.0012–0.0026	0.3138–0.3144	0.3136–0.3142
	180.5 (2959)	45①	44.5	57	1.594	0.0010–0.0024	0.0012–0.0026	0.3138–0.3144	0.3136–0.3142
	241.3 (3956)	45	44.5	71.6	1.693	0.0012–0.0024	0.0016–0.0028	0.3140	0.3137
1989	144.4 (2366)	45①	44.5	66	1.909②	0.0010–0.0024	0.0012–0.0026	0.3138–0.3144	0.3136–0.3142
	136.5 (2237)	45①	44.5	64–77	1.850②	0.0010–0.0024	0.0012–0.0026	0.3138–0.3144	0.3136–0.3142
	180.5 (2959)	45①	44.5	57	1.594	0.0010–0.0024	0.0012–0.0026	0.3138–0.3144	0.3136–0.3142
	241.3 (3956)	45	44.5	71.6	1.693	0.0012–0.0024	0.0016–0.0028	0.3140	0.3137

VALVE SPECIFICATIONS

Year	Engine Displacement cu. in. (cc)	Seat Angle (deg.)	Face Angle (deg.)	Spring Test Pressure (lbs.)	Spring Installed Height (in.)	Stem-to-Guide Clearance (in.)		Stem Diameter (in.)	
						Intake	Exhaust	Intake	Exhaust
1990	144.4 (2366)	45①	44.5	63–66	1.909②	0.0010–0.0024	0.0012–0.0026	0.3138–0.3144	0.3136–0.3142
	180.5 (2959)	45①	44.5	54–57	1.850②	0.0010–0.0024	0.0012–0.0026	0.3138–0.3144	0.3136–0.3142
	241.3 (3956)	45③	45③	60–72	2.028②	0.0010–0.0024	0.0014–0.0028	0.3138–0.3144	0.3134–0.3140
1991–92	144.4 (2366)	45①	44.5	63–66	1.909②	0.0010–0.0024	0.0012–0.0026	0.3138–0.3144	0.3136–0.3142
	146.4 (2399)	45①	44.5	57–63	1.406②	0.0010–0.0024	0.0012–0.0026	0.2350–0.2356	0.2348–0.2354
	180.5 (2959)	45①	44.5	54–57	1.850②	0.0010–0.0024	0.0012–0.0026	0.3138–0.3144	0.3136–0.3142
	241.3 (3956)	45③	45③	60–72	2.028②	0.0010–0.0024	0.0014–0.0028	0.3138–0.3144	0.3134–0.3140

① Blend the seat with 30° and 60° cutters to center the 45° portion on the valve face.
② Free length
③ Intake:
Blend the seat with 25° and 70° cutters to center the 45° portion of the valve face.
Exhaust:
Blend the seat with 60° cutters to center the 45° portion of the valve face.

PISTON AND RING SPECIFICATIONS

All measurements are given in inches.

Year	Engine Displacement cu. in. (cc)	Piston Clearance	Ring Gap			Ring Side Clearance		
			Top Compression	Bottom Compression	Oil Control	Top Compression	Bottom Compression	Oil Control
1988	144.4 (2366)	0.0008–0.0016①	0.0098–0.0421	0.0236–0.0559	0.0079–0.0461	0.0012–0.0080	0.0012–0.0080	0.0012–0.0080
	136.5 (2237)	0.0026–0.0033	0.0091–0.0189	0.0063–0.0173	0.0051–0.0185	0.0012–0.0028	0.0012–0.0028	0.0012–0.0028
	180.5 (2959)	0.0031–0.0039	0.0091–0.0327	0.0150–0.0366	0.0059–0.0354	0.0012–0.0028	0.0012–0.0028	0.0012–0.0028
	241.3 (3956)	0.0011–0.0019	0.0079–0.0165	0.0197–0.0283	0.0079–0.0323	0.0012–0.0028	0.0020–0.0035	snug
1989	144.4 (2366)	0.0008–0.0016①	0.0098–0.0421	0.0236–0.0559	0.0079–0.0461	0.0012–0.0080	0.0012–0.0080	0.0012–0.0080
	136.5 (2237)	0.0026–0.0033	0.0091–0.0189	0.0063–0.0173	0.0051–0.0185	0.0012–0.0028	0.0012–0.0028	0.0012–0.0028
	180.5 (2959)	0.0031–0.0039	0.0090–0.0327	0.0150–0.0366	0.0060–0.0354	0.0012–0.0028	0.0012–0.0028	0.0012–0.0028
	241.3 (3956)	0.0011–0.0019	0.0079–0.0165	0.0197–0.0283	0.0079–0.0323	0.0012–0.0028	0.0020–0.0035	snug
1990	144.4 (2366)	0.0006–0.0014	0.0098–0.0421	0.0236–0.0559	0.0079–0.0461	0.0012–0.0080	0.0012–0.0080	0.0012–0.0080
	180.5 (2959)	0.0031–0.0039	0.0091–0.0327	0.0150–0.0366	0.0059–0.0354	0.0012–0.0028	0.0012–0.0028	0.0012–0.0028
	241.3 (3956)	0.0011–0.0019	0.0079–0.0165	0.0197–0.0283	0.0079–0.0323	0.0012–0.0028	0.0020–0.0035	snug
1991–92	144.4 (2366)	0.0006–0.0014	0.0098–0.0421	0.0236–0.0559	0.0079–0.0461	0.0012–0.0080	0.0012–0.0080	0.0012–0.0080
	146.4 (2399)	0.0012–0.0020	0.0118–0.0406	0.0177–0.0472	0.0051–0.0386	0.0008–0.0028	0.0012–0.0028	snug

PISTON AND RING SPECIFICATIONS

All measurements are given in inches.

Year	Engine Displacement cu. in. (cc)	Piston Clearance	Ring Gap			Ring Side Clearance		
			Top Compression	Bottom Compression	Oil Control	Top Compression	Bottom Compression	Oil Control
1991–92	180.5 (2959)	0.0031–0.0039	0.0091–0.0327	0.0150–0.0366	0.0059–0.0354	0.0012–0.0028	0.0012–0.0028	0.0012–0.0028
	241.3 (3956)	0.0011–0.0019	0.0079–0.0402	0.0197–0.0520	0.0079–0.0559	0.0012–0.0028	0.0020–0.0035	snug

① 22R-TE Engine—0.0022–0.0030
② Maximum

TORQUE SPECIFICATIONS

All readings in ft. lbs.

Year	Engine Displacement cu. in. (cc)	Cylinder Head Bolts	Main Bearing Bolts	Rod Bearing Bolts	Crankshaft Pulley Bolts	Flywheel Bolts	Manifold	
							Intake	Exhaust
1988	144.4 (2366)	53–63	69–83	40–47	102–130	73–86	13–19	29–36
	136.5 (2237)	②	58	36	116	61①	36	36
	180.5 (2959)	③	⑪	⑩	181	65①	13	29
	241.3 (3956)	87–93	④	40–46	247–259	60–68	⑤	⑤
1989	144.4 (2366)	53–63	69–83	40–47	102–130	73–86	13–19	29–36
	136.5 (2237)	②	58	36	116	61①	36	36
	180.5 (2959)	③	43–47	16–20	176–186	63–67	11–15	25–33
	241.3 (3956)	87–93	④	40–46	247–259	60–68	⑤	⑤
1990	144.4 (2366)	58⑨	76	51	116	80①	14	33
	180.5 (2959)	③	⑪	⑩	181	65①	13	29
	241.3 (3956)	90⑫	④	43	253	64	⑤	⑤
1991–92	144.4 (2366)	58⑨	76	51	116	80①	14	33
	146.4 (2399)	⑥	⑨	⑦	192	65①	15	36
	180.5 (2959)	③	⑪	⑩	181	65①	13	29
	241.3 (3956)	90⑫	④	43	253	64	⑤	⑤

① Drive plate—54 ft. lbs.
② 12 mm bolt—14 ft. lbs.
  14 mm bolt—65 ft. lbs.
③ Step 1—27
  Step 2—33
  Step 3—90 degree turn
  Step 4—90 degree turn
④ 19 mm bolt—99 ft. lbs.
  17 mm bolt—85 ft. lbs.

⑤ 14 mm bolt—37 ft. lbs.
  17 mm bolt—51 ft. lbs.
  Nut—41 ft. lbs.
⑥ Step 1—29 ft. lbs.
  Step 2—90 degree turn
  Step 3—90 degree turn
⑦ Step 1—22 ft. lbs.
  Step 2—90 degree turn
⑧ Step 1—29 ft. lbs.

  Step 2—90 degree turn
⑨ Step 1—20 ft. lbs.
  Step 2—35 ft. lbs.
  Step 3—58 ft. lbs.
⑩ Step 1—18 ft. lbs.
  Step 2—90 degree turn
⑪ Step 1—45 ft. lbs.
  Step 2—90 degree turn
⑫ Torque in 3 steps

BRAKE SPECIFICATIONS

All measurements in inches unless noted.

Year	Model	Lug Nut Torque (ft. lbs.)	Master Cylinder Bore	Brake Disc		Standard Brake Drum Diameter	Minimum Lining Thickness	
				Minimum Thickness	Maximum Runout		Front	Rear
1988	Pick-Up	65–86	NA	①	0.0059	②	0.039	0.039
	4Runner	65–86	NA	①	0.0059	②	0.039	0.039
	Van	65–86	NA	0.748	0.0059	10.00	0.039	0.039
	Land Cruiser	65–86	NA	0.748	0.0059	11.61	0.040	0.059

BRAKE SPECIFICATIONS
All measurements in inches unless noted.

Year	Model	Lug Nut Torque (ft. lbs.)	Master Cylinder Bore	Brake Disc Minimum Thickness	Brake Disc Maximum Runout	Standard Brake Drum Diameter	Minimum Lining Thickness Front	Minimum Lining Thickness Rear
1989	Pick-Up	65–86	NA	①	0.0059	②	0.039	0.039
	4Runner	65–86	NA	①	0.0059	②	0.039	0.039
	Van	65–86	NA	0.748	0.0059	10.00	0.039	0.039
	Land Cruiser	65–86	NA	0.748	0.0059	11.61	0.040	0.059
1990	Pick-Up	65–86	NA	⑤	⑥	⑦	0.039	0.039
	4Runner	65–86	NA	0.709	0.0035	11.61	0.039	0.039
	Land Cruiser	65–86	NA	0.748	0.0059	11.61	0.039	0.059
1991–92	Pick-Up	65–86	NA	⑤	⑥	⑦	0.039	0.039
	4Runner	65–86	NA	0.709	0.0035	11.61	0.039	0.039
	Land Cruiser	65–86	NA	0.906	0.0059	11.61	0.039	0.059
	Previa	65–86	NA	0.827③	0.0028④	10.00	0.039	0.039

NA—Not available
① 2WD with PD60 Brake Disc—0.945
   2WD with FS17 Brake Disc—0.827
   4WD—0.748
② 2WD—10.00
   4WD—11.64

③ Rear disc—0.669
④ Rear disc—0.0039
⑤ PD60—0.907
   PD66—1.102
   FS17, 18—0.787
   S12 & 12—0.709

⑥ PD60—0.0035
   PD66—0.0047
   FS17, 18—0.0035
   S12 & 12—0.0035
⑦ 2WD—10.00
   4WD—11.70

WHEEL ALIGNMENT

Year	Model	Caster Range (deg.)	Caster Preferred Setting (deg.)	Camber Range (deg.)	Camber Preferred Setting (deg.)	Toe-in (in.)	Steering Axis Inclination (deg.)
1988	Pick-Up 2WD① :						
	Extra long bed	1/2P–1 1/2P	1P	0–1P	1/2P	1/8–3/16	10
	Cab & Chassis	1/16P–1 1/16P	9/16P	0–1P	1/2P	1/8–3/16	10
	Dual rear wheels	1/16P–1 1/16P	9/16P	0–1P	1/2P	1/8–3/16	10
	Extra long cab	5/16P–1 5/16P	13/16P	0–1P	1/2P	1/8–3/16	10
	1 ton	1/16P–1 1/16P	9/16P	0–1P	1/2P	1/8–3/16	10
	Pick-Up 4WD	13/16P–1 13/16P	1 5/16P	1/8P–1 1/8P	5/8P	5/64–5/32	11 5/16
	4Runner	1 5/8P–2 5/8P	2 1/8P	1/8P–1 1/8P	5/8P	5/64–5/32	11 15/16
	Van 2WD	2P–3P	2 1/2P	9/16N–7/16P	1/16N	3/64–3/64	10 9/16
	Van 4WD	1 11/16P–2 9/16P	2 13/16P	5/16N–11/16P	3/16P	3/64–3/64	12 7/16
	Land Cruiser	3/16N–1 13/16P	13/16P	1/4P–1 3/4P	1P	0–5/64	9 1/2
1989	Pick-Up 2WD① :						
	RN80LTRKR, TRTR	3/16P–1 3/16P	11/16P	1/16N–15/16P	7/16P	3/64–7/64	10
	RN80LTRLD, TRMR	1/4P–1 1/4P	3/4P	0–1P	1/2P	1/32–3/32	10
	RN85LTRLD, TRMD	1/2P–1 1/2P	1P	1/16N–15/16P	7/16P	1/64–1/8	10 1/32
	RN90LCRLD, CRMD	5/8P–1 5/8P	1 1/8P	1/8N–7/8P	3/8P	1/8–3/16	10 1/8
	RN80LTRMD, TRSD	1/4P–1 1/4P	3/4P	0–1P	1/2P	1/32–3/32	10
	RN85LTRMD, TRSD	1/2P–1 1/2P	1P	1/16N–15/16P	7/16P	1/16–1/8	10 1/32
	RN85LTRMS, TRSS	11/16P–1 11/16P	1 3/16P	1/8N–7/8P	3/8P	1/8–3/16	10 1/8
	RN90LCRMD, CRDS	10/16P–1 11/16P	1 3/16P	1/8N–7/8P	3/8P	1/8–3/16	10 1/8
	RN90LCRMS, CRSS	7/8P–1 7/8P	1 3/8P	5/16N–11/16P	3/16P	7/32–9/32	10 5/16
	VZ85LTRMD, TRSD	5/8P–1 5/8P	1 1/8P	1/16N–15/16P	7/16P	1/16–1/8	10
	VZ85LTHMD, THSD	1/16P–1 1/16P	9/16P	1/16P–1 1/16P	9/16P	3/16–1/4	9 29/32

WHEEL ALIGNMENT

Year	Model	Caster Range (deg.)	Caster Preferred Setting (deg.)	Camber Range (deg.)	Camber Preferred Setting (deg.)	Toe-in (in.)	Steering Axis Inclination (deg.)
1989	VZ85LTRMR, TRSR	7/16N–9/16P	1/16P	1/16P–1 1/16P	9/16P	11/64–15/64	9 15/16
	VZN90LCRMD, CRSD	13/16P–1 13/16P	1 5/16P	1/8N–7/8P	3/8P	3/32–5/32	10 3/32
	VZN90LCRMG, CRPG	15/16P–1 15/16P	1 7/16P	3/16N–13/16P	5/16P	5/32–7/32	10 3/16
	VZN95LTWMR, TWSR	3/8N–5/8P	1/8P	1/16P–1 1/16P	9/16P	5/32–7/32	9 15/16
	Pick-Up 4WD	2P–3P	2 1/2P	1/4P–1 1/4P	3/4P	0–1/16	11 13/16
	4Runner	1 5/8P–2 5/8P	2 1/8P	1/8P–1 1/8P	5/8P	5/64–5/32	11 15/16
	Van 2WD	2P–3P	2 1/2P	9/16N–7/16P	1/16N	3/64–3/64	10 9/16
	Van 4WD	1 11/16P–2 9/16P	2 13/16P	5/16N–11/16P	3/16P	3/64–3/64	12 7/16
	Land Cruiser	1/16P–1 9/16P	13/16P	1/4P–1 3/4P	1P	3/64–9/64	9 1/2
1990	Pick-Up 2WD① :						
	RN80LTRTR	1/16N–15/16P	7/16P	0–1P	1/2P	1/32–3/32	10
	RN80LTRMR	1/8P–1 1/8P	5/8P	0–1P	1/2P	1/32–3/32	10
	RN85LTRLD	3/16P–1 3/16P	11/16P	0–1P	1/2P	1/64–5/64	10
	RN85LTRMD, TRLD	7/16P–1 7/16P	15/16P	1/16N–15/16P	7/16P	1/16–1/8	10
	RN90LCRLDL	3/4P–1 3/4P	1 1/4P	1/8N–7/8P	3/8P	3/32–5/32	10 3/32
	RN80LTRKR	3/16P–1 3/16P	11/16P	0–1P	1/2P	1/32–3/32	10
	RN80LTRSD, TRMD	3/16P–1 3/16P	11/16P	0–1P	1/2P	1/64–5/64	10
	RN85LTRMD, TRSD	7/16P–1 7/16P	15/16P	1/16N–15/16P	7/16P	1/16–1/8	10
	RN85LTRMS, TRSS	5/8P–1 5/8P	1 1/8P	1/8N–7/8P	3/8P	1/4–3/8	10 1/8
	RN90LCRMD, CRSD	3/4P–1 3/4P	1 1/4P	1/8N–7/8P	3/8P	3/32–5/32	10 3/32
	RN90LCRMJ, CRSS	7/8P–1 7/8P	1 3/8P	5/16N–11/16P	3/16P	3/16–1/4	10 1/4
	VZN85LTRMD, TRSD	3/8P–1 3/8P	7/8P	1/16N–15/16P	7/16P	1/16–1/8	10
	VZN85LTHMD, THSD	1/16P–1 1/16P	9/16P	0–1P	1/2P	5/32–7/32	10
	VZN85LTRMR, TRSR	7/16N–9/16P	1/16P	0–1P	1/2P	5/32–7/32	10
	VZN85LTWMR, TWSR	3/4P–1 3/4P	1 1/4P	0–1P	1/2P	3/16–1/4	10
	VZN90LCRMD, CRSD	11/16P–1 11/16P	1 3/16P	1/16N–15/16P	7/16P	3/32–5/32	10 1/16
	VZN90LCRMG, CRPG	11/16P–1 11/16P	1 3/16P	1/16N–15/16P	7/16P	1/16–1/8	10 1/16
	VZN95LTWMR, TWSR	1/2N–1/2P	0	0–1P	1/2P	3/16–1/4	10
	Pick-Up 4WD	2P–3P	2 1/2P	1/4P–1 1/4P	3/4P	0–1/16	11 13/16
	4Runner	2P–3P	2 1/2P	1/4P–1 1/4P	3/4P	1/32–3/32	11 13/16
	Land Cruiser	1/16P–1 9/16P	13/16P	1/4P–1 3/4P	1P	3/64–9/64	9 1/2
1991-92	Pick-Up 2WD① :						
	RN80LTRSD, TRMD	0–1 1/2P	3/4P	1/4N–1 1/4P	1/2P	1/32–5/32	10
	RN80LTRMR	1/16N–1 7/16P	11/16P	5/16N–1 3/16P	7/16P	1/32–5/32	10
	RN85LTRMD, TRSD	7/32P–1 23/32P	31/32P	5/16N–1 3/16P	7/16P	0–3/16	10 1/32
	RN90LCRSD, CRMD	1/2P–2P	1 1/4P	3/8N–1 1/8P	3/8P	1/32–7/32	10 3/32
	VZN85LTHMD	3/16N–1 15/16P	9/16P	1/4N–1 1/4P	1/2P	1/8–5/16	10
	VZN85LTHSD	3/16N–1 15/16P	9/16P	1/4N–1 1/4P	1/2P	3/32–9/32	10
	VZN85LTWMR, TWSR	1P–2 1/2P	1 3/4P	1/4N–1 1/4P	1/2P	3/32–9/32	10
	VZN90LCRMD, CRSD	7/16P–1 15/16P	1 3/16P	3/8N–1 1/8P	3/8P	1/32–7/32	10 3/32
	VZN90LCRMG, CRPG	7/16P–1 15/16P	1 3/16P	5/16N–1 3/16P	7/16P	1/32–7/32	10 1/16
	VZN95LTWMR, TWSR	1P–2 1/2P	1 3/4P	1/4N–1 1/4P	1/2P	1/8–5/16	10
	Pick-Up 4WD	2P–3P	2 1/2P	1/4P–1 1/4P	3/4P	0–1/16	11 13/16

WHEEL ALIGNMENT

Year	Model	Caster		Camber		Toe-in (in.)	Steering Axis Inclination (deg.)
		Range (deg.)	Preferred Setting (deg.)	Range (deg.)	Preferred Setting (deg.)		
1991–92	4Runner	2P–3P	2½P	¼P–1¼P	¾P	1/32–3/32	11¹³/₁₆
	Land Cruiser with 10.5R tire	1¹¹/₁₆P–2¹¹/₁₆P	1¹¹/₁₆P	¼P–1³/₄P	1P	0–3/16	13
	W/O 10.5R tire	2P–4P	3P	¼P–1³/₄P	1P	0–3/16	13
	Previa 2WD	4³/₄P–6¹/₄P	5½P	21/32N–27/32P	3/32P	0–3/16	10¹⁹/₃₂
	Previa 4WD	4¹⁹/₃₂P–6³/₃₂P	5¹¹/₃₂P	½N–1P	¼P	1/32–7/32	10¹¹/₃₂

N—Negative
P—Positive

① **NOTE:** Front end alignment specifications are given according to Vehicle Identification Number. Before using this information, verify that the Vehicle Identification Number is correct for the alignment data that is used.

ENGINE ELECTRICAL

NOTE: **Disconnecting the battery cable on some vehicles may interfere with the functions of the on board computer systems and may require the computer to undergo a relearning process, once the negative battery cable is disconnected.**

Distributor

Removal

3F–E, 22R, 22R–E, 22R–TE AND 3VZ–E ENGINES

1. Disconnect the negative battery cable. Label and disconnect the high tension cables from the spark plugs. Remove the high tension cable from the coil.
2. Remove the primary wire or the electrical connector and the vacuum line, if equipped, from the distributor. Remove the distributor cap spring clips or screws, then the cap.
3. Using a piece of chalk, matchmark the rotor-to-distributor housing and the distributor-to-engine block. This will aid in correct positioning of the distributor during installation.
4. Remove the distributor hold-down clamp bolt and the distributor from the engine.

NOTE: **It is easier to install the distributor if the engine timing is not disturbed while it is removed.**

4Y–EC ENGINE

1. Disconnect the negative battery terminal from the battery.
2. Remove the front-right seat from the vehicle.
3. Remove the engine service hole cover.
4. Disconnect the distributor vacuum advance hoses.
5. Disconnect the high tension cables from the spark plugs.

DISTRIBUTOR HOUSING O-RING PACKING ROTOR DISTRIBUTOR CAP HEAT INSULATOR

Distributor assembly—2TZ–FE engine

6. Using a piece of chalk, matchmark the rotor-to-distributor housing and the distributor housing-to-engine.

7. Remove the distributor-to-engine bolt and the distributor from the engine.

2TZ–FE ENGINE

1. Disconnect the negative battery cable.
2. Label and disconnect the spark plug wires.
3. Disconnect the distributor connector and ventilation hoses.
4. Remove the cap and packing.
5. Set the No. 1 cylinder to TDC of the compression stroke. Install the service bolt and nut into the equipment driveshaft to turn the crankshaft pulley. Turn the crankshaft 1 turn if the rotor is not facing No. 1 spark plug wire.
6. Remove the distributor hold-down and pull the distributor out of the engine.

Installation

TIMING NOT DISTURBED

All Engines

1. Insert the distributor into the engine block by aligning the matchmarks made during removal.
2. Engage the distributor drive with the oil pump drive shaft.
3. Install the distributor hold-down clamp, the cap, the high tension wire, the primary wire or the electrical connector and the vacuum line(s).
4. Install the spark plugs cables.
5. Connect the negative battery cable.

TIMING DISTURBED

3F–E, 22R, 22R–E, 22R–TE and 3VZ–E Engines

If the engine has been cranked, dismantled or the timing otherwise lost, proceed as follows:

1. Determine the Top Dead Center (TDC) of the No. 1 cylinder's compression stroke by removing the spark plug from the No. 1 cylinder and placing a finger or a compression gauge over the spark plug hole.

NOTE: Using a wrench, turn the crankshaft until the compression pressure starts to build up. Continue cranking the engine until the timing marks indicate TDC (0 degrees).

2. Turn the crankshaft to align the timing marks on the 22R–E and 22R–TE engines to 5 degrees BTDC or on the 22R and 3VZ–E engines to 0 degree TDC.
3. Temporarily install the rotor on the distributor shaft so the rotor is pointing toward the No. 1 terminal of the distributor cap.
4. Using a small prybar, align the slot on the distributor drive (oil pump driveshaft) with the key on the bottom of the distributor shaft.
5. Install the distributor in the block by rotating it slightly (no more than a gear tooth in either direction) until the driven gear meshes with the drive.

NOTE: Oil the distributor drive gear and the oil pump driveshaft end before installation.

6. Temporarily tighten the lock bolt.
7. Remove the rotor, then install the dust cover, the rotor and the distributor cap.
8. Install the primary wire or the electrical connector and the vacuum line(s).
9. Install the No. 1 cylinder spark plug. Connect the cables to the spark plugs in the proper order. Install the high tension wire on the coil.
10. Start the engine and adjust the ignition timing.

Exhaust camshaft positioning—2TZ–FE engine

4Y–EC Engine

1. Remove the No. 1 spark plug, place a finger over the opening and rotate the crankshaft, using a turning tool, in the clockwise direction, until pressure is felt, then replace the spark plug.

NOTE: Make sure the notch on the crankshaft pulley is aligned with the 0 degree mark on the timing plate.

2. Position the oil pump drive rotor slot 30 degrees from the centerline.
3. On the distributor, align the groove on the housing with the pin of the driven gear (the drill mark side).
4. Insert the distributor by aligning the flange center with the bolt hole in the engine block.
5. Lightly tighten the hold-down bolt.
6. To complete the installation, reverse the removal procedures. Adjust the ignition timing.

2TZ–FE Engine

1. Remove the No. 1 spark plug, place a finger over the opening and rotate the equipment driveshaft, using a turning tool, in the clockwise direction, until pressure is felt, then replace the spark plug.

NOTE: Make sure the slit in the exhaust camshaft is in the proper position.

2. Remove the service bolt and nut.
3. Align the cut out portion of the coupling with the groove on the housing.
4. Install the distributor and align the center of the flange with the bolt hole on the cylinder head.
5. Install the hold-down bolt loosely.
6. Install the seal packing, distributor cap and connect the wiring.
7. Adjust the timing to specifications and torque the hold-down bolt to 14 ft. lbs. (19 Nm).

Ignition Timing

Adjustment

EXCEPT 2TZ–FE ENGINE

NOTE: The timing mark locations differ between the

engines used in the Pick-Up and 4Runner for 22R, 22R–E, 22R–TE and 3VZ–E engines; Van for 4Y–EC engine and Land Cruiser for 3F–E engine. On the 22R, 22R–E, 22R–TE, 4Y–EC and 3VZ–E engines, the timing marks are located on the crankshaft pulley (painted notch) and the timing cover (plate). On the 3F–E engine the timing marks are located on the flywheel (ball) and the bell housing (pointer).

1. Set the parking brake and block the wheels.

2. Clean off the timing marks and mark them with chalk or paint. The crankshaft may have to rotated to find the marks.

3. Warm the engine to operating temperatures. Connect a tachometer to the engine, then, check and/or adjust the engine idle speed.

NOTE: On the 22R, 22R–E, 22R–TE and 3VZ–E engines, connect the positive (+) tachometer terminal either to the negative (−) ignition coil terminal or to the yellow service connector. On the 4Y–EC engine, connect the positive (+) tachometer to the service connector on the ignition coil/igniter assembly. Do not connect it to the distributor side. Improper connections will damage the transistorized igniter. On the 4Y–EC and 3VZ–E engines, use a service wire to short the engine check connector

4. Turn off the engine and connect a timing light according to the manufacturer's directions.

5. On the 22R–E and 22R–TE engines, disconnect and short the **T** and the **E₁** connector of the engine check harness (near the front of the vehicle). On all other engines, disconnect and plug the vacuum hose(s) from the distributor vacuum unit.

NOTE: If equipped with a High Altitude Compensation (HAC) system there are 2 vacuum hoses which connect to the distributor. Both must be disconnected and plugged. These systems require an extra step in the timing procedure.

6. Be sure the timing light wires are clear of the fan and pulleys, then start the engine.

7. Allow the engine to run at the specified idle speed with the shift selector in neutral for manual transmission or **D** for automatic transmission.

8. Point the timing light at the marks. With the engine at the specified idle, the marks should align.

9. If the timing is incorrect, loosen the bolt at the base of the distributor just enough so the distributor can be turned. Hold the distributor by its base and turn it slightly to advance or retard the timing as required. Once the marks are seen to align properly, tighten the bolt.

10. After tightening the distributor bolt or adjusting the octane selector, recheck the timing. Turn off the engine, then, disconnect the timing light and connect the vacuum line(s) at the distributor or the electrical **T** and **E₁** connector, except on engines with HAC.

11. On engines with HAC after setting the initial timing, reconnect the vacuum hoses at the distributor. Recheck the timing.

12. If the advance is still low, pinch the hose between the HAC valve and the 3 way connector; it should now be to specifications. If not, the HAC valve should be checked for proper operation.

2TZ–FE ENGINE

NOTE: On the 2TZ–FE engine the timing mark is on the equipment driveshaft U-joint and front cover.

1. Ground terminals **TE1** and **E1** of the check connector using tool 0984318020 or equivalent. The check connector is next to the emergency brake lever.

Timing mark location – 4Y–EC engine

Timing mark location – 22R, 22R–E and 22R–TE engines

Timing mark location – 3VZ–E engine

Grouding the ckeck connector and timing location – 2TZ–FE engine

2. Connect a timing light terminal to terminal **30** of the starter and test probe to the No. 1 spark plug wire (light blue).

3. Start the engine and warm up. Slowly turn the distributor unitl the timing mark on the crankshaft pulley is aligned with the **5** mark. Tighten the distributor bolt and recheck timing.

4. Remove the grounding tool from the check connector and timing light.

Alternator

For further information, please refer to "Alternators" in the Unit Repair section.

Precautions

Several precautions must be observed with alternator equipped vehicles to avoid damage to the unit.

- If the battery is removed for any reason, make sure it is reconnected with the correct polarity. Reversing the battery connections may result in damage to the one-way rectifiers.
- When utilizing a booster battery as a starting aid, always connect the positive to positive terminals and the negative terminal from the booster battery to a good engine ground on the vehicle being started.
- Never use a fast charger as a booster to start vehicles.
- Disconnect the battery cables when charging the battery with a fast charger.
- Never attempt to polarize the alternator.
- Do not use test lights of more than 12 volts when checking diode continuity.
- Do not short across or ground any of the alternator terminals.
- The polarity of the battery, alternator and regulator must be matched and considered before making any electrical connections within the system.
- Never separate the alternator on an open circuit. Make sure all connections within the circuit are clean and tight.
- Disconnect the battery ground terminal when performing any service on electrical components.
- Disconnect the battery if arc welding is to be done on the vehicle.

Belt Tension Adjustment

Inspection and adjustment to the alternator drive belt should be performed every 30,000 miles or if the alternator has been removed.

1. Inspect the drive belt to see that it is not cracked or worn. Be sure its surfaces are free of grease or oil.

2. If not using a belt tension gauge, push down on the belt halfway between the fan and the alternator pulleys, (or crankshaft pulley) with thumb pressure; belt deflection should be $\frac{3}{8}$–$\frac{1}{2}$ in.

3. If using the an appropriate belt tension gauge, position it in the middle of the drive belt and check the belt tension; a new belt should be 170–180 lbs. (230–244 N) for Van or 100–150 lbs. (135–202 N) for Pick-Up and 4Runner, a used belt should be 95–135 lbs. (130–182 N) for Van or 60–100 lbs. (81–136 N) for Pick-Up and 4Runner.

4. If the belt tension requires adjustment, loosen the adjusting link bolt and move the alternator until the proper belt tension is obtained.

5. Tighten the adjusting link bolt.

Removal and Installation

NOTE: On some engines the alternator is mounted very low. On these engines it may be necessary to remove the gravel shield and work from under the vehicle in order to gain access to the alternator.

EXCEPT 2TZ–FE ENGINE

1. Disconnect the negative battery cable.

2. Remove the air cleaner, if necessary, to gain access to the alternator.

3. On the 22R remove the vane pump pulley.

4. On the 22R–E and 22R–TE engines, drain the engine coolant. If necessary, remove the under engine cover.

5. If equipped with power steering, remove the water inlet pipe bolts and the water inlet hose from the engine.

NOTE: If equipped with air conditioning, it may be necessary to remove the No. 2 fan shroud.

6. Remove the nut or the wiring connector and the wire(s) from the alternator.

7. Remove the adjusting lock, the pivot and the adjusting bolt(s), then the drive belt from the alternator.

8. Remove the alternator attaching bolt and then withdraw the alternator from its bracket.

9. To install, reverse the removal procedures. Rotate the drive belt 8 revolutions for new belt or 5 revolutions for used belt. Adjust the drive belt tension.

10. Refill the cooling system, if it was drained.

11. Connect the negative battery cable.

2TZ–FE ENGINE

NOTE: To service many engine components, the engine service hole covers may have to be removed. Remove the front seats, scuff plate and seat legs to access the service hole covers.

1. Disconnect the negative battery cable.

2. Raise the vehicle and safely support it.

3. Disconnect the alternator connectors.

4. Loosen the lock bolt, adjusting bolt and pivot bolt. Remove the drive belt.

5. Remove the pivot and lock bolts. Remove the alternator.

To install:

6. Install the alternator and bolts.

7. Install the belt and adjust. Do not pry against the housing.

8. Connect the alternator wiring and battery cable.

9. Lower the vehicle and check operation.

Starter

For further information, please refer to "Starters" in the Unit Repair section.

Removal and Installation

EXCEPT 2TZ–FE ENGINE

1. If necessary, raise and support the vehicle safely.

2. Disconnect the negative battery terminal from the battery.

NOTE: On some 22R, 22R–E and 22R–TE engines, equipped with an automatic transmission, it may be necessary to remove the transmission oil filler tube.

3. Disconnect the wiring connectors and the wiring from the starter.

4. Remove the starter-to-engine bolts and the starter from the engine.

5. To install, reverse the removal procedures.

2TZ–FE ENGINE

1. Disconnect the negative battery cable.

2. Raise the vehicle and safely support it.

3. Disconnect the starter connectors.

4. Remove the front driveshaft for 4WD only.

5. Remove the clutch release cylinder (manual transmission only).

6. Remove the 3 bolts and starter for 2WD. Remove the 4 bolts, 2 nuts, center support bracket and starter for 4WD.

To install:

7. Install the starter and torque the long bolts to 41 ft. lbs. (54 Nm) and short bolts to 30 ft. lbs. (41 Nm).

8. Connect the starter connectors.

9. Install the front driveshaft and clutch release cylinder, if removed.

10. Connect the battery cable and lower the vehicle.

CHASSIS ELECTRICAL

Heater Blower Motor

Removal and Installation

PICK-UP, VAN AND 4RUNNER

1. Disconnect the negative battery cable.
2. Disconnect the electrical connector from motor.
3. Remove the blower motor-to-case screws and lift the motor from the case.
4. To install, reverse the removal procedures. Make sure the seal around the motor flange is in good condition.

LAND CRUISER

1. Disconnect the negative battery cable. Disconnect the electrical connector from the blower motor.
2. Disconnect the flexible tube from the side of the blower motor.
3. Remove the blower motor fasteners and lower the blower motor out of the air inlet duct.
4. To install, reverse the removal procedures. During installation, be sure to position the motor so the flexible tube can be attached to the motor.

PREVIA

1. Disconnect the negative battery cable and open the hood.
2. Remove the air duct and disconnect the motor connectors.
3. Remove the blower motor from the housing.
4. Installation is the reverse of removal.

Windshield Wiper Motor

Removal and Installation

PICK-UP, VAN AND 4RUNNER

Front

1. Disconnect the negative battery cable. Disconnect the wiring from the wiper motor. Remove the motor from the fire wall.
2. Remove the nut, then, pry the wiper link from the crank arm.
3. Remove the motor.
4. To install, reverse the removal procedures and inspect he operation.

Rear

1. Disconnect the negative battery cable. At the rear of the vehicle, remove the wiper motor cover panel.
2. Remove the wiper arm from the wiper motor.
3. Disconnect the electrical connector from the wiper motor.
4. Remove the wiper motor-to-door bolts and the motor from the vehicle.
5. To install, reverse the removal procedures and inspect the operation.

LAND CRUISER AND PREVIA

NOTE: On these vehicles, the wiper motor is removed with the linkage assembly.

1. Disconnect the negative battery cable. Remove the wiper arm retaining nuts, then, the wiper arm/blade assemblies.

Blower motor location—Previa

2. Remove both wiper arm pivot covers and the pivot-to-cowl attaching screws.
3. Remove the service hole covers from the cowl area of the engine compartment.
4. Disconnect the wiring from the wiper motor.
5. From the engine compartment, remove the wiper motor plate-to-cowl screws. Withdraw the wiper motor and the linkage from the cowl panel as an assembly.
6. Pry the linkage from of the wiper motor.
7. To install, reverse the removal procedures.

Windshield Wiper Linkage

Removal and Installation

PICK-UP, VAN, 4RUNNER AND PREVIA

1. Disconnect the negative battery cable. Remove the wiper motor.
2. Remove the wiper arms by removing their retaining nuts and working them off their shafts.
3. Remove the wiper shafts nuts/spacers and push the shafts down into the body cavity. Pull the linkage out of the cavity through the wiper motor hole.
4. To install, reverse the removal procedures.

LAND CRUISER

1. Disconnect the negative battery cable. Remove the wiper arm assemblies.
2. Remove the end plate from the pivot housing.
3. Remove the wiper motor with the linkage cable.
4. Separate the wiper motor and the transmission.
5. Remove the linkage cable.
6. To install, reverse the removal procedures.

Windshield Wiper Switch

Removal and Installation

FRONT

1. Disconnect negative battery terminal from the battery.
2. Remove the upper and the lower steering column shrouds.
3. Disconnect the combination switch electrical connector.
4. Remove the terminal from the horn contact.

Typical combination switch assembly

5. To remove the windshield/wiper switch wires from the electrical connector, place a small prybar into the end of the connector, pry up on the retaining tab and pull the wire(s) from the connector.

6. Remove the windshield/wiper switch-to-combination switch screw and the switch.

7. Installation is the reverse of the removal procedure. To install, place the wire(s) into the electrical connector's slots, place a suitable tool behind the wire terminal and push the wire into the connector until the retaining tab locks it into place.

REAR

If equipped with a rear wiper switch, it will be located in the center of the dash.

1. Disconnect the negative battery cable. Using a small prybar, pry the rear wiper switch from the center of the dash.

2. Disconnect the electrical connector from the rear of the switch.

3. To install, reverse the removal procedures.

Instrument Cluster

Removal and Installation

PICK-UP, VAN AND 4RUNNER

1. Disconnect the negative battery terminal from the battery.

2. Remove the upper and lower steering column covers.

3. Remove the instrument trim panel screws and the panel.

4. Disconnect the speedometer cable from the speedometer.

5. Remove the instrument panel screws and pull the panel forward. Disconnect the electrical connectors from the back of the panel and remove the panel.

6. To install, reverse the removal procedures.

LAND CRUISER

1. Disconnect the negative battery terminal from the battery.

2. Disconnect the speedometer cable. Remove the instrument panel screws.

3. Loosen the steering column clamp by removing the attaching bolts.

4. Pull out the instrument panel and the speedometer, disconnect the electrical connectors and remove the panel.

5. To install, reverse the removal procedures.

PREVIA

1. Disconnect the negative battery cable.

2. Remove the cluster finish panel by removing the 2 screws and prying on the left side with a prybar. Be careful not to damage the plastic components.

3. Remove the 4 screws and disconnect the cable from the automatic transmission indicator. Remove the cable from the roller and cluster.

INSTRUMENT PANEL

LOWER FINISH PANEL NO. 2

LOWER FINISH PANEL NO. 1

GLOVE COMPARTMENT DOOR

COMBINATION METER

INSTRUMENT PANEL NO. 1 RESISTER

LOWER CENTER FINISH PANEL

HEATER RESISTER DUCT NO. 1

METER HOOD

CLUSTER FINISH PANEL

KEY CYLINDER COVER

HEATER CONTROL

COWL SIDE TRIM

RADIO

ASHTRAY

Typical instrument cluster and panel assembly—Pick-Up and 4Runner

4. Disconnect the electrical connectors and remove from the vehicle.

5. To install, reverse the removal procedures.

Speedometer Cable

Removal and Installation

1. Disconnect the negative battery cable. Remove the instru-ment cluster and disconnect the cable from the speedometer.

2. Disconnect the other end of the speedometer cable from the transmission extension housing and pull the cable from its jacket at the transmission end.

NOTE: If the cable is being replace because it is bro-ken, be sure to remove both pieces of the broken cable.

3. Using graphite, lubricate the new speedometer cable and insert it into the cable jacket at the lower end.

Instrument cluster finish panel removal—Previa

4. Connect the speedometer cable to the transmission, then, to the instrument cluster.

5. To complete the installation, reverse the removal procedures.

Headlight/Dimmer Switch

Removal and Installation

1. Disconnect the negative battery terminal from the battery.

2. Remove the upper and lower steering column covers.

3. Disconnect the electrical connector from the combination switch.

4. Remove the headlight switch-to-combination switch screws and the headlight switch from the combination switch.

5. To install, reverse the removal procedures.

Turn Signal Switch

Removal and Installation

1. Disconnect negative battery terminal.

2. Remove the upper and the lower steering column shrouds.

3. Disconnect the combination switch electrical connector.

4. At the left-rear of the combination switch, remove the mounting screws and the turn signal switch.

5. If necessary to the remove the turn signal switch wires from the electrical connector, place a small prybar into the end of the connector, pry up on the retaining tab and pull the wire(s) from the connector.

6. To install, place the wire(s) into the electrical connector's slots, place a prybar behind the wire terminal and push the wire into the connector until the retaining tab locks it into place.

7. To complete the installation, reverse the removal procedures.

Combination Switch

Removal and Installation

The combination switch is composed of the turn signal, the headlight control, the dimmer, the hazard, the wiper and the washer switches.

1. Disconnect the negative battery cable. Remove the steering wheel.

2. Remove the upper and lower steering column shroud screws and the shrouds.

3. Remove the combination switch screws and the switch from the column.

4. Disconnect the electrical connector from the combination switch. To remove the wires from the electrical connector, perform the following procedures.

a. Using a small prybar, insert it into the open end between the locking lugs and the terminal.

Ignition lock assembly

b. Pry the locking lugs upward and pull the terminal out from the rear.

c. To install the terminals, simply push them into the connector until they lock securely in place.

5. To complete the installation, reverse the removal procedures.

Ignition Lock/Switch

Removal and Installation

The ignition lock/switch is located behind the combination switch on the steering column.

1. Disconnect the negative battery terminal.

2. Remove the upper and lower steering column covers.

3. Disconnect the ignition switch from the electrical connector.

4. Using the key in the ignition switch, turn it to the **ACC** position.

5. Using a thin rod, place it into the hole of the cylinder lock housing. Pushing down on the thin rod, pull out the cylinder lock.

6. Remove the unlock warning switch-to-combination switch screws and the unlock warning switch.

7. Remove the ignition switch-to-combination switch screw and the ignition switch.

8. To install, push the ignition switch into the housing and install the screw. Using the key, install cylinder lock into the housing until the retaining tab locks it in place.

9. To complete the installation, reverse the removal procedures.

Stoplight Switch

Removal and Installation

1. Disconnect the negative battery cable.

2. Remove the electrical connector from the switch at the brake pedal.

3. Remove the mounting nut and remove the switch from the bracket.

4. Installation is the reverse of the removal procedure.

Clutch Switch

Removal and Installation

1. Disconnect the negative battery cable.

2. Remove the electrical connector from the switch at the clutch pedal.

3. Remove the mounting nut and remove the switch from the bracket.

4. Installation is the reverse of the removal procedure.

Fuses, Circuit Breakers and Relays

Location

There are 3 fuse boxes on the Pick-Up, 4Runner and Land Cruiser. One is located in the engine compartment, 1 at the drivers side kick panel and 1 behind the glove box. The Van has a combination fuse box and relay panel, located behind a panel on the passengers side of the instrument panel. The junction/relay and fuse block is located behind the heater controls, under the center instrument panel hood.

Each fuse box has the fuse numbers and circuits protected on the lid of the box.

Computer

Location

The ECU is located at the right kick panel for the Pick-Up and 4Runner, behind the glove compartment for the Land Cruiser, at the left door pillar for the Van, behind the trim panel or under the driver's seat for the Previa.

Flashers

The turn signal/hazard flasher is located under the instrument panel near the steering column for the Pick-Up, 4Runner and Previa. The flasher unit is located behind the heater controls for the Van and in the relay block at the left kick panel for the Land Cruiser.

Cruise control actuator adjustment—Van

Cruise Control

For further information, please refer to Chilton's Chassis Electronics Service Manual.

Adjustment

PICK-UP, 4RUNNER AND LAND CRUISER

1. Inspect that the control cable freeplay is less than 0.39 in. (10mm).

2. Connect the positive lead from the battery to terminals **1** and **2** and negative lead to terminal **3** of the actuator.

3. Slowly apply vacuum from 0–11.81 in. Hg. (0–300mm Hg), check that the control cable can be pulled smoothly and the cable stroke is at least 1.42 in. (36mm).

VAN

Inspect that the control cable freeplay is less than 0.08 in. (2mm).

ENGINE COOLING

Radiator

Removal and Installation

1. Disconnect the negative battery cable. Drain the cooling system.

2. Unfasten the hose clamps and disconnect the hoses from the radiator. On Land Cruiser equipped with air conditioning, properly discharge the system.

3. Disconnect the transmission cooling lines, if equipped with an automatic transmission. Disconnect the air conditioning air intake duct on Previa vehicles.

4. On the 22R–TE engine, disconnect the No. 1 turbocharger cooling line.

5. Raise the vehicle, support safely and remove the engine under cover on Van.

6. Remove the fan shrouds, if equipped.

7. Remove the grille assembly and remove the hood lock from the radiator support. On Land Cruiser with air conditioning, remove the condensor to radiator bolts.

8. Remove the coolant recovery tank. Unbolt the radiator and remove it from the vehicle.

To install:

9. Install the radiator into position.

10. On Land Cruiser with air conditioning, install the condensor-to-radiator bolts.

11. Install the hood lock assembly and install the grille.

12. Connect the radiator hoses and the transmission cooler lines.

13. On the 22R–TE engine, connect the turbocharger water line. Connect the air conditioning intake duct on Previa vehicles.

14. Install the coolant recovery bottle. Refill the cooling system to the correct level.

15. Run the engine and check for leaks.

Heater Core

Removal and Installation

NOTE: If equipped with air conditioning, the heater and the air conditioner are completely separate units. Be certain when working under the dashboard that only the heater hoses are disconnected.

—————— **CAUTION** ——————

The air conditioning hoses are under pressure; if disconnected, the escaping refrigerant will freeze any surface with which it comes in contact, including skin and eyes.

PICK-UP, VAN, 4RUNNER AND PREVIA

1. Disconnect the negative battery terminal from the battery.

2. Drain the cooling system.

3. Remove the glove box, the defroster hoses, the air damper, the air duct and the 2 side defroster ducts.

4. Remove the control unit from the instrument panel.

5. Disconnect the heater hoses from the core tubes.

6. Remove the retaining bolts and lift out the heater unit. At this point, the core may be pulled from the case.

7. To install, reverse the removal procedures. Refill the cooling system.

LAND CRUISER

Front Heater

NOTE: The entire heater unit must be removed to gain access to the heater core. This procedure requires almost complete disassembly of the instrument panel and lowering of the steering column.

1. Disconnect the negative battery terminal. Remove the glove box and the glove box door.

2. Remove the lower heater ducts. Remove the large heater duct from the passenger side of the heater unit.

3. Remove the ductwork from behind the instrument panel. Remove the radio.

4. Disconnect the wiring connector from the right-side inner portion of the glove opening.

5. Remove the instrument panel pad. Remove the hood release lever. Disconnect the hand throttle control cable.

6. Remove the retaining screw from the left-side of the fuse block.

7. Remove the steering column-to-instrument panel attaching nuts and carefully lower the steering column. Tag and disconnect the wiring as necessary in order to lower the column assembly.

8. Disconnect the electrical connector from the rheostat located to the left of the steering column opening.

9. Remove the center dual outlet duct which is attached to the upper portion of the heater unit.

10. Remove the lower instrument panel.

11. Tag and disconnect the hoses from the heater unit. Remove the heater unit-to-firewall fasteners and the heater unit.

12. Remove the heater core-to-heater unit pipe clamps and the heater core retaining clamp, then, withdraw the heater core from the heater unit.

13. To install, reverse the removal procedures. Torque the steering column-to-instrument panel fasteners to 14–15 ft. lbs. (18–20 Nm). Refill the cooling system.

Rear Heater

1. Turn off the water valve and disconnect both hoses from the rear heater core.

2. Disconnect the wiring from the rear heater.

3. Remove the mounting bolts and lift out the core.

4. To install, reverse the removal procedures. Refill the cooling system.

Typical heater unit and ducts – Land Cruiser

Water Pump

Removal and Installation

22R, 22R–E AND 22R–TE ENGINES

1. Disconnect the negative battery cable. Drain the cooling system.

2. If equipped, remove the fan shroud bolts and the shroud.

3. Loosen the alternator adjusting link bolt and remove the drive belt, then, swing the alternator toward the engine.

4. If equipped with an air pump, air conditioning compressor or power steering pump drive belts, it may be necessary to loosen the adjusting bolt, remove the drive belt(s) and move the component(s) aside.

5. Remove the fan from the fluid coupling, the fluid coupling and pulley from the water pump, then, the water pump-to-engine bolts and the pump.

6. Clean the gasket mounting surfaces.

7. To install, use a new gasket, sealant and reverse the removal procedures. Adjust the drive belt(s) tension. Refill the cooling system.

4Y–EC ENGINE

1. Disconnect the negative battery cable. Drain the cooling system. Disconnect the drive belt from the water pump.

2. Remove the fan from the fluid coupling and the fluid coupling/pulley from the water pump.

3. Remove the drive belt adjusting bar from the water pump, the water pump-to-engine bolts and the water pump.

4. Clean the gasket mounting surfaces.

5. To install, use a new gasket, sealant and reverse the removal procedures.

6. Torque the water pump nuts/bolts to 13 ft. lbs. (17 Nm), the drive belt adjusting bar to 29 ft. lbs. (40 Nm), the pulley/fluid coupling-to-water pump nuts to 10 ft. lbs. (14 Nm) and the fan-to-fluid coupling nuts to 10 ft. lbs. (14 Nm). Adjust the drive belt tension. Refill the cooling system.

3F–E ENGINE

1. Disconnect the negative battery cable.

2. Drain the engine coolant.

3. Remove the accessory drive belt. Loosen the power steering pump mount, idler pulley and adjusting bolts.

4. Disconnect the overflow tank hose.

5. Disconnect the radiator inlet hose and remove the fan shroud.

6. Remove the fan, fluid coupling and the water pump pulley.

7. Remove the alternator. Disconnect the hoses from the water pump.

8. Remove the water pump, power steering idler pulley and bracket as an assembly.

9. Installation is the reverse of the removal procedure. Torque the water pump mounting bolts to 27 ft. lbs. (37 Nm).

3VZ–E ENGINE

1. Disconnect the negative battery cable.

Water pump mounting bolt locations – 3VZ–E engine

WATER BYPASS HOSE

HEATER WATER HOSE

WATER PUMP PLATE

WATER INLET HOSE

WATER PUMP PULLEY

GASKET

GASKET

OIL COOLER WATER HOSE

PULLEY SEAT

WATER PUMP

FAN

FLUID COUPLING

DRIVE BELT

Water pump assembly—3F–E engine

TENSION SPRING BRACKET

WATER OUTLET

WATER PUMP

GASKET

THERMOSTAT

Water pump assembly—3VZ–E engine

Water pump assembly—2TZ-FE engine

2. Remove the timing belt assembly.
3. Remove the thermostat.
4. Remove the idler pulley.
5. Remove the water pump mounting bolts and remove the water pump.

To install:

6. Clean the mounting surface.
7. Use new seal packing on the water pump and install it in position on the engine.
8. Torque the bolts marked **A** to 13 ft. lbs. (18 Nm) and the bolts marked **B** to 14 ft. lbs. (20 Nm).
9. Install the thermostat and the idler pulley.
10. Install the timing belt assembly.
11. Connect the negative battery cable and refill the cooling system.

2TZ-FE ENGINE

1. Disconnect the negative battery cable and drain the engine coolant.
2. Raise the vehicle and support safely.
3. Disconnect the heater hose and radiator outlet hoses.
4. Remove the oil filter bracket.
5. Remove the pump retaining bolts and pump from the timing cover.

To install:

6. Install the water pump with new O-rings.
7. Torque the bolts to 21 ft. lbs. (28 Nm).
8. Reconnect the coolant hoses and oil filter bracket.
9. Refill the engine coolant and check for leaks.

Thermostat

Removal and Installation

22R, 22R-E AND 22R-TE ENGINES

1. Disconnect the negative battery cable. Partially drain the cooling system to a level below the thermostat.

NOTE: Unless the upper radiator hose is positioned over one of the thermostat housing (water outlet) bolts, it is not necessary to detach the hose.

2. Remove the mounting bolts, the water outlet and the thermostat from the intake manifold.
3. Clean the gasket mounting surfaces.
4. To install, use a new gasket, sealant and reverse the removal procedures. Refill the cooling system.

NOTE: When installing a new thermostat, be sure the thermostat is positioned with the spring down.

5. Bleed the cooling system.

4Y-EC ENGINE

1. Disconnect the negative battery cable. Drain the cooling system to a level below the thermostat.
2. Disconnect the radiator outlet hose from the thermostat housing.
3. Remove the mounting bolts, the thermostat housing and the thermostat.
4. Clean the gasket mounting surfaces.
5. To install, use a new gasket, sealant and reverse the removal procedures, making sure the jiggle valve is placed at the upper-left position. Torque the thermostat housing to 9 ft. lbs. (12 Nm). Refill the cooling system.

NOTE: When installing a new thermostat, be sure the thermostat is positioned with the spring facing the engine block.

6. Bleed the cooling system.

3F-E ENGINE

1. Disconnect the negative battery cable.
2. Drain the cooling system.
3. Disconnect the cold start injector wire and the BVSV vacuum lines.

4. Remove the thermostat housing bolts and remove the housing.

5. Remove the thermostat housing.

6. Installation is the reverse of removal. Torque the housing bolts to 13 ft. lbs. (18 Nm).

7. Refill the cooling system. Bleed the cooling system.

3VZ–E ENGINE

1. Disconnect the negative battery cable.

2. Drain the coolant.

3. Remove the radiator outlet hose from the housing.

4. Remove the thermostat housing and thermostat from the engine.

5. Installation is the reverse of the removal procedure. Use a new gasket for installation.

6. Torque the housing bolts to 14 ft. lbs. (20 Nm). Refill and bleed the cooling system.

2TZ–FE ENGINE

1. Raise the vehicle and support safely. Drain the engine coolant.

2. Disconnect the radiator outlet hose.

3. Remove the retaining bolts, water inlet and thermostat.

4. Installation is the reverse of removal. Torque the retaining bolts to 14 ft. lbs. (20 Nm). Refill the engine with coolant.

Cooling System bleeding

After working on the cooling system, even to replace the thermostat, it must be bled. Air trapped in the system will prevent proper filling and leave the radiator coolant level low, causing a risk of overheating.

1. To bleed the system, start with the system cool, the radiator cap off and the radiator filled to about an inch below the filler neck.

2. Start the engine and run it at slightly above normal idle speed. This will insure adequate circulation. If air bubbles appear and the coolant level drops, fill the system with an anti-freeze/water mixture to bring the level back to the proper level.

3. Run the engine this way until the thermostat opens. When this happens, coolant will move abruptly across the top of the radiator and the temperature of the radiator will suddenly rise.

4. At this point, air is often expelled and the level may drop quite a bit. Keep refilling the system until the level is near the top of the radiator and remains constant.

5. If the vehicle has an overflow tank, fill the radiator right up to the filler neck. Replace the radiator filler cap.

FUEL SYSTEM

Fuel System Service Precaution

When working with the fuel system certain precautions should be taken; always work in a well ventilated area, keep a dry chemical (Class B) fire extinguisher near the work area. Always disconnect the negative battery cable and do not make any repairs to the fuel system until all the necessary steps for repair have been reviewed.

Relieving Fuel System Pressure

1. Disconnect the negative battery terminal from the battery.

2. Allow the system enough time to bleed off the fuel pressure through the fuel return line.

3. Before disconnecting any fuel line component, place a rag under the item to catch any excess fuel.

4. After installation, install the negative battery terminal, turn **ON** the ignition switch and check for fuel leaks.

Fuel Tank

Removal and Installation

1. Disconnect the negative battery cable. Relieve the fuel pressure.

2. This procedure should be done with the tank less than ¼ full. Place a suitable drain pan under fuel tank and remove the drain plug. If the tank is more than ¼ full, use an approved syphon to remove the fuel from the tank.

3. Disconnect all hoses, wiring and tubes that can be accessed at this point.

4. Place a jack under the tank and remove the tank protector.

5. Remove the tank straps or retaining bolts.

6. Lower the tank far enough to disconnect the remaining hoses, wiring and tubes. Be careful not to damage the nylon fuel lines when removing the tank.

7. Drain the remaining fuel from the tank.

To install:

8. Raise the tank and connect the hoses, wiring and tubes.

9. Install the retaining bolts or straps and torque to 29 ft. lbs. (39 Nm).

10. Connect the remaining hoses or wiring.

11. Refill the fuel tank and check for leaks.

12. Check the battery cable and check operation.

Fuel Filter

Removal and Installation

EXCEPT 22R ENGINE

The fuel filter is located in the engine compartment, at the inlet line to the fuel rail.

1. Disconnect the negative battery cable.

2. Relieve the fuel system pressure.

3. Disconnect and plug the inlet and outlet lines from the filter.

4. Remove the filter retaining bolts and remove the filter.

5. Installation is the reverse of the removal procedure.

6. Use new O-rings and tighten the lines to 22 ft. lbs. (29 Nm).

7. Connect the negative battery cable. Run the engine and check for leaks.

22R ENGINE

The fuel filter is located under the rear of the vehicle, next to the fuel tank.

1. Disconnect the negative battery cable.

2. Raise and safely support the vehicle.

3. Remove the protective cover from the filter.

4. Disconnect and plug the inlet and outlet lines from the filter.

5. Remove the filter retaining bolts and remove the filter.

6. Installation is the reverse of the removal procedure.

7. Use new O-rings and tighten the lines to 22 ft. lbs. (29 Nm).

8. Connect the negative battery cable. Run the engine and check for leaks.

Mechanical Fuel Pump

Pressure Testing

1. Attach a pressure gauge to the pressure side of the fuel line. If equipped with a vapor return system, squeeze off the return hose.
2. Run the engine at idle and note the reading on the gauge. Stop the engine and compare the reading with the specification. If the pump is operating properly, the pressure will be as specified and will be constant at idle speed. If the pressure varies or is too high or low, the pump should be repaired or replaced.
3. Remove the pressure gauge.

Flow Test

1. Disconnect the fuel line from the carburetor. Run the fuel line into a suitable measuring container.
2. Run the engine at idle until there is one pint of fuel in the container. One pint should be pumped in 30 seconds or less.
3. If the flow is below minimum, check for a restriction in the line.

Removal and Installation

22R ENGINE

1. Disconnect the negative battery terminal from the battery.
2. Drain the cooling system to a level below the upper radiator hose and remove the upper radiator hose.
3. Remove all 3 lines from the fuel pump, the mounting bolts, the fuel pump and the gasket.

NOTE: The fuel pump is not repairable. It must be replaced as a complete unit.

4. Clean the gasket mounting surfaces.
5. To install, use a new gaskets and reverse the removal procedures. Refill the cooling system. Start the engine and check for leaks.

Electric Fuel Pump

An electric fuel pump is used on all fuel injected engines. The fuel pump is wired into the ignition switch and oil pressure switch circuits. In the event of an oil pressure loss, the fuel pump is turned **OFF** so the engine will stall, thus preventing engine damage due to the oil pressure loss. The fuel pump will operate only when the ignition switch is turned to the **START** position and when the oil pressure is normal.

Operation Testing

1. Disconnect the electrical clip from the oil pressure switch.
2. Turn the ignition switch to the **ON** position; do not start the engine.
3. Short the **Fp** and the **+B** terminals of the check connector. Check the cold start injector hose for pressure.
4. Check for a smooth flow of gasoline from the fuel filter outlet. If the pump is noisy, it is probably defective. If the pump does not run, check the pump resistor and relay.
5. Disconnect the jumper wire and reconnect the check connector. Turn the ignition switch **OFF**.

Pressure Testing

1. Disconnect the negative battery terminal from the battery and the wiring connector from the cold start injector.
2. Place a container or a shop towel near the end of the delivery tube.
3. Slowly loosen the cold start injector union bolt, then, remove the bolt and the gaskets. Drain the fuel line.
4. Using pressure gauge tool 09268–45011 or equivalent, connect it in line with the cold start injector. Reconnect the battery cable.

Typical mechanical fuel pump

Typical electric fuel pump

Testing the fuel pump pressure

5. Short the **Fp** and **+B** terminals of the check connector wire. Turn the ignition switch to the **ON** position and measure the fuel pump pressure. It should be as follows:

22R–E, 2TZ–FE, 3VZ–E, 4Y–E engines—38–44 psi (265–304 kPa)

22R–TE engine—33–38 psi (226–265 kPa)

3F–E engine—37–46 psi (255–314 kPa)

6. Turn the ignition switch **OFF**.

NOTE: If the pressure is high, replace the pressure regulator; if the pressure is low, check the hoses, the connections, the fuel pump, the fuel filter or the pressure regulator.

6. Remove the jumper wire from the check connector. Start the engine. Disconnect and plug the vacuum sensing hose at the pressure regulator, then, measure the fuel pressure at idle. It should be as follows:

22R–E, 2TZ–FE, 3VZ–E, 4Y–E engines—38–44 psi (265–304 kPa)

22R–TE engine—33–38 psi (226–265 kPa)

3F–E engine—37–46 psi (255–314 kPa)

7. Reconnect the vacuum sensing hose to the pressure regulator. The pressure should now be as follows; if not, check the vacuum hose and/or the pressure regulator.

22R–E, 2TZ–FE, 3VZ–E, 4Y–E engines—33–38 psi (226–265 kPa)

22R–TE engine—27–31 psi (186–216 kPa)

3F–E engine—33–37 psi (226–265 kPa)

8. Stop the engine and check that the fuel pressure remains at 21 psi. for 5 minutes. If not, check the fuel pump, the pressure regulator and/or the injectors.

Removal and Installation

1. Disconnect the negative battery cable. Drain the fuel tank.

2. Disconnect the electrical connector and the fuel lines from the fuel tank.

3. Remove the inlet tube and mounting bolts/straps, then, the fuel tank from the vehicle.

4. Remove the access plate-to-fuel tank bolts, then, pull out the plate/fuel pump assembly.

5. Disconnect the electrical connectors from the fuel pump. Pull the bracket from the lower-side of the fuel pump, then, remove the fuel pump from the fuel hose.

6. Remove the rubber cushion, the clip and the fuel filter from the bottom of the fuel pump.

To install:

7. Install the fuel pump and use new gaskets.

8. Install the fuel tank and connect all electrical and fuel connections.

9. Torque the fuel pump bracket-to-fuel tank to 43 inch lbs. (5.3 Nm). Refill the fuel tank and check for leaks.

Carburetor

Removal and Installation

1. Disconnect the negative battery terminal from the battery.

2. Label and disconnect the emission control hoses. Disconnect the air intake hose. Remove the mounting and butterfly nuts, then, lift the air cleaner from the carburetor.

3. If equipped with an automatic transmission, disconnect the throttle cable or rod. Disconnect the fuel hose, the emission control hose, the PCV hose and the wiring connector(s) from the carburetor.

4. Disconnect the accelerator linkage and the choke pipe, if equipped.

5. Remove the carburetor-to-manifold nuts/bolts and lift it from the manifold.

6. Cover the open manifold with a clean cloth to prevent dirt

FUEL PUMP CHECK CONNECTOR

SERVICE WIRE

Fuel pump check connector—Van

and small objects from entering into the engine. Clean the gasket mounting surfaces.

To install:

7. Install a new gasket and carburetor. Torque the retaining nuts to 56 inch lbs. (6.4 Nm).

8. Reconnect all electrical, vacuum and fuel connectors.

9. Install the remaining components. Adjust the idle speed.

Idle Speed and Mixture Adjustment

22R ENGINE

NOTE: The idle mixture screw is preset at the factory and adjustment should not be necessary.

The idle speed should be adjusted under the following conditions: the air cleaner must be installed, the choke fully opened, the transmission should be in **N**, all accessories should be turned **OFF**, all vacuum lines should be connected and the ignition timing should be set to specification.

1. Start the engine and allow it to reach normal operating temperatures.

2. Check the float setting; the fuel level should be just about even with the spot on the sight glass. If the fuel level is too high or low, adjust the float level.

NOTE: Do not connect the tachometer to the distributor side; damage to the transistorized ignition could result. Never allow the tachometer terminal to touch ground for damage to the igniter or the ignition coil could result.

3. Connect a tachometer in accordance with its manufacturer's instructions. However, connect the tachometer positive (+) lead to the coil's (−) negative terminal or to the igniter's service connector, if provided.

NOTE: If the idle mixture caps have been removed, turn the idle mixture screws to the fully closed position, then, open them 3½ turns.

4. Using a pair of pliers, remove the caps from the idle speed adjusting screw. Turn the idle speed adjusting screw to obtain the correct idle speed: 700 rpm for a manual transmission or 750 rpm for an automatic transmission.

5. Disconnect the tachometer and install new idle speed adjusting screw cap.

Float Level Adjustment

22R ENGINE

For this procedure, the air horn must be removed from the carburetor and the gasket removed from the air horn.

1. Position the air horn with the floats facing upward; allow the float to rest by itself.

2. Using tool 09240–00014 or equivalent, position it between the floats and the air horn; the measurement should be 0.386 in.

METERING NEEDLE

FUEL UNION

METERING NEEDLE GUIDE

OUTER VENT CONTROL VALVE

SECONDARY MAIN JET

CHOKE BREAKER

AAP

POWER PISTON AND VALVE

NEEDLE VALVE

CHOKE OPENER

SLOW JET

FLOAT

PRIMARY MAIN JET

CARBURETOR BODY

ACCLERATOR PUMP

SOLENOID VALVE

FAST IDLE CAM

CARBURETOR FLANGE

IDLE UP DIAPHRAGM

IDLE SPEED ADJUSTING SCREW

PLUG

IDLE MIXTURE ADJUSTING SCREW

FAST IDLE ADJUSTING SCREW

Carburetor components — 22R, 22R-E and 22R-TE engines

If adjustment is necessary, bend the tang at the float pivot point.

3. Using a vernier caliper, raise the float and measure the distance between the bottom of the float and the air horn; the distance should be 1.89 in. If adjustment is necessary, bend the tang at the pivot point.

4. After adjustment, replace the air horn onto the carburetor.

Service Adjustments

For all carburetor service adjustment procedures and specifications, please refer to "Carburetor Service" in the Unit Repair section.

Fuel Injection

Idle Speed Adjustment

22R-E, 22R-TE, 4Y-EC AND 3VZ-E ENGINES

The engines are equipped with a computer activated, electronic fuel injection system. Prior to adjusting the idle speed, make sure the air cleaner is installed. All vacuum hoses are connected. All pipes and hoses in the air intake system are connected and in good condition. All fuel injection system wiring is connected and in good condition. The engine is at normal operating temperature. All accessories are **OFF**. Transmission selector lever in **N**.

1. Connect the tachometer positive (+) lead to the coil's (−)

Idle speed adjusting screw—22R-E, 22R-TE and 3VZ-E engines shown, 4Y-EC engine similar

Checking Idle Speed Control (ISC) valve—3F-E engine

Checking ISC valve—2TZ-FE engine

negative terminal or to the igniter's service connector, if provided.

2. Run the engine at 2500 rpm for 2 minutes.

3. Run the engine at idle and turn the idle speed adjusting screw to obtain the correct idle speed.

4. Disconnect and remove the tachometer.

Checking ISC valve—3F-E engine

3F-E AND 2TZ-FE ENGINES

These engines are equipped with electronic fuel injection. The idle speed is controlled by a Idle Speed Control (ISC) valve. The idle speed is preset at the factory and requires no adjustment. There is no idle speed adjusting screws.

1. 3F-E engine: check that there is a clicking sound immediately after stopping the engine. Check the valve using an ohmmeter. Measure the resistance between the terminals.

Terminals **B1–S1** or **S3**—10–30 ohms
Terminals **B2–S2** or **S4**—10–30 ohms

2. If not within specifications, replace the ISC valve.

3. 2TZ-FE engine: using an ohmmeter, measure the resistance between terminals **B+** and the other 2. The resistance should be 18.8–22.8 ohms.

4. If the valve check OK, remove the valve and clean the mounting area with carburetor cleaner. Install new gaskets and valve

Idle Mixture Adjustment

The idle mixture adjustment is preset at the factory and controlled by the electronic control unit. There is no adjustment necessary or possible.

Cold Start Injector

The EFI engines have a cold start injector located in the intake air chamber which aids in cold weather starting.

Removal and Installation

1. Disconnect the negative battery cable and the cold start injector wire.

2. Place a shop towel or a container under the fuel delivery pipe and drain the fuel from the pipe.

3. Disconnect the fuel pipe from the cold start injector.

4. Remove the mounting bolts and the cold start injector from the intake air chamber.

5. To install, use new gaskets and reverse the removal procedures. Torque the injector bolts to 44–60 inch lbs. (5.4–6.8 Nm).

Fuel Pressure Regulator

The fuel pressure regulator is located on the fuel delivery pipe of the fuel system, it maintains a constant fuel pressure in the injection system.

Removal and Installation

1. Relieve the fuel pressure. Disconnect the vacuum sensing hose from the pressure regulator.

NOTE: On the 22R–E and 22R–TE engines, remove the No. 1 EGR pipe.

2. Place a shop towel or a container under the fuel hose connection and disconnect the fuel return hose from the regulator.

3. Remove the locknut for 22R–E, 22R–TE and 3F–E engines, the mounting bolts for 4Y–EC and 3VZ–E engines and the pressure regulator from the fuel delivery pipe.

4. To install, reverse of removal. Torque the locknut to 22 ft. lbs. (30 Nm) for 22R–E, 22R–TE and 3F–E engines or bolts to 44–60 inch lbs. (5.4–6.8 Nm) for 4Y–EC and 3VZ–E engines. Start the engine and check for fuel leaks.

Fuel Injector

Testing

EXCEPT 2TZ–FE ENGINE

Each injector may be tested for operation while on the engine, in 2 ways.

1. Listen for a clicking at the injector.

2. Using an ohmmeter, check the continuity at each injector's terminal; the resistance should be 1.5–3.0 ohms.

Removal and Installation

EXCEPT 2TZ–FE ENGINE

1. Disconnect the negative battery terminal from the battery and the ground strap from the rear side of the engine.

2. Disconnect the accelerator wire. If equipped with an automatic transmission, disconnect the throttle cable from the bracket and the clamp.

3. Disconnect the No. 1 and No. 2 PCV hoses.

4. If equipped with a 22R–TE engine, disconnect the No. 2 PCV hose and the Vacuum Control Valve (VCV).

5. Disconnect the following items:
   a. Brake power booster hose
   b. Air control valve hoses
   c. Vacuum Switching Valve (VSV)
   d. Evaporative emission control hose
   e. EGR vacuum hose and modulator
   f. Pressure regulator hose for 2WD
   g. Fuel pressure-up (VSV) and hose
   h. No. 1 and No. 2 air valve hose from the throttle body
   i. No. 2 and No. 3 water bypass hoses from the throttle body
   j. Cold start injector wire
   k. Throttle position wire

6. Remove the following items:
   a. Cold start injector-to-plenum chamber bolt.
   b. No. 1 EGR pipe-to-plenum chamber bolts.
   c. Manifold stay-to-plenum chamber bolts.
   d. Fuel hose clamp, 4 bolts, 2 nuts and the bond strap.
   e. The plenum chamber with the throttle body and gaskets.

7. Disconnect the fuel return hose.

Removing the fuel delivery pipe

Injector installation into delivery pipe

8. Disconnect the following wires:
   a. Auxiliary air valve wire
   b. Knock sensor wire
   c. Oil pressure sender gauge/switch
   d. Starter wire (terminal 50)
   e. Transmission wires
   f. Air conditioning compressor wires
   g. Injector wires
   h. Water temperature sender gauge wire
   i. Overdrive temperature switch wire (air conditioning)
   j. Oxygen sensor and igniter wire
   k. Vacuum Switching Valve (VSV) wire (air conditioning)
   l. Cold start injector time switch wire
   m. Water temperature sensor wire

9. Disconnect the fuel hose from the delivery pipe with the pulsation damper and gaskets.

10. Remove the injectors from the engine. Take care in handling the injectors.

NOTE: Injector performance tests are possible but special tools are required. If these tools are unavailable, use the test procedures above.

11. To install, use new O-rings and reverse the removal procedures. Torque the hold-down bolts to 14 ft. lbs. (20 Nm). Check for fuel leakage.

NOTE: Each injector should have 4 insulators. Prior to installation, coat the O-rings with clean gasoline. Prior to tightening the hold-down bolts, make sure the injector rotates smoothly in its bore. If not, the O-rings are twisted.

2TZ–FE ENGINE

1. Relieve the fuel pressure and disconnect the negative battery cable.

2. Remove the right engine service hole.

3. Disconnect the PCV hose, engine wiring harness-to-injectors, vacuum hoses and fuel rail pipes.

4. Remove the fuel rail and spacers.

5. Remove the 4 bolts from the injector covers.

6. Using an injector remover tool 0926874010 and remove the injector from the fuel rail.

To install:

7. Lubricate the O-rings with spindle oil or gasoline. Install new O-rings.

8. Push the injector into the fuel rail. Check the connectors are along the center line of the fuel rail.

9. Install the insulator onto each injector.

10. Install the injector covers and fuel rail onto the engine.

11. Torque the fuel rail retaining bolts to 14 ft. lbs. (20 Nm).

12. Install the remaining components, connect the battery cable and check for leaks.

Injector removal—2TZ–FE engine

EMISSION CONTROLS

For further information, please refer to Chilton's Emission Controls Manual.

ENGINE MECHANICAL

NOTE: **Disconnecting the negative battery cable on some vehicles may interfere with the functions of the on board computer systems and may require the computer to undergo a relearning process, one the negative battery cable is reconnected.**

Engine Assembly

Removal and Installation

22R, 22R–E AND 22R–TE ENGINES

1. Disconnect the negative battery cable.

2. Remove the engine undercover.

3. Disconnect the windshield washer hose and then remove the hood. Scribe matchmarks around the hinges for easy installation.

4. Drain the engine oil. Drain the engine coolant from the radiator and the cylinder block.

5. Drain the automatic transmission fluid on models so equipped.

6. Disconnect the air cleaner hose and then remove the air cleaner.

7. Remove the radiator and shroud. Disconnect the No. 1 turbocharger water line on the 22R–TE engine.

8. Remove the coupling fan.

9. Disconnect the heater hoses at the engine.

10. If equipped with automatic transmissions, disconnect the accelerator and throttle cables at their bracket.

11. Disconnect the following:
   a. No. 1 and No. 2 PCV hoses
   b. Brake booster hose
   c. Air control valve hoses
   d. EVAP hose at the canister
   e. Actuator hose on vehicles with cruise control
   f. Vacuum modulator hose at the EGR valve
   g. Air valve hoses at the throttle body and chamber
   h. Two water bypass hoses at the throttle body
   i. Air control valve hose at the actuator
   j. Pressure regulator hose at the chamber
   k. Cold start injector pipe

l. BVSV hose.

12. Tag and disconnect the cold start injector wire and the throttle position sensor wire.

13. Remove the EGR valve from the throttle chamber.

14. Disconnect the throttle chamber at the stay. Remove the chamber-to-intake manifold mounting bolts and lift off the throttle chamber.

15. Tag and disconnect the following wires:
   a. Cold start injector time switch wire
   b. Water temperature sensor wire
   c. If equipped with air conditioning: VSV and air conditioning compressor wires
   d. Oxygen sensor wire for 22R–TE engine only
   e. OD temperature switch wire (with automatic transmission)
   f. Injector wires
   g. Knock sensor connector
   h. Air valve wire
   i. Oil pressure switch wire
   j. Starter wire.

16. Remove the power steering pump from its bracket, if equipped. Disconnect the ground strap from the bracket.

17. If equipped with air conditioning, loosen the drive belt and remove the air conditioning compressor. Position it aside with the refrigerant lines attached.

18. Disconnect the engine ground straps at the rear and right side of the engine.

19. If equipped with a manual transmission, remove the shift lever from inside the vehicles.

20. Raise and safely support the vehicle. Drain the engine oil. Remove the rear driveshaft.

21. If equipped with automatic transmission, disconnect the manual shift linkage at the neutral start switch. On 4WD vehicles with automatic transmission, disconnect the transfer shift linkage.

22. Disconnect the speedometer cable. Be sure not to lose the felt dust protector and washers.

23. Remove the transfer case undercover on 4WD vehicles.

24. Remove the stabilizer bar on 4WD vehicles.

25. Remove the front driveshaft on 4WD vehicles.

26. Remove the No. 1 frame crossmember.

27. Disconnect the front exhaust pipe at the manifold and tail pipe and remove the exhaust pipe.

28. If equipped with manual transmission, remove the clutch release cylinder and its bracket from the transmission.

29. Remove the No. 1 front floor heat insulator and the brake tube heat insulator on 4WD vehicles.

30. On 2WD vehicles, remove the rear engine mount bolts, raise the transmission slightly with a floor jack and then remove the support member mounting bolts.

31. On 4WD vehicles, remove the 4 rear engine mount bolts, raise the transmission slightly with a floor jack and then remove the bolts from the side member and remove the No. 2 frame crossmember.

32. Lower the vehicle. Attach an engine hoist chain to the lifting brackets on the engine. Remove the engine mount nuts and bolts and slowly lift the engine/transmission out of the truck.

To install:

33. Slowly lower the engine assembly into the engine compartment.

34. Raise the transmission onto the crossmember with a floor jack.

35. Align the holes in the engine mounts and the frame, install the bolts and then remove the engine hoist chain.

36. On 2WD vehicles, raise the transmission slightly and align the rear engine mount with the support member and tighten the bolts to 9 ft. lbs. (13 Nm). Lower the transmission until it rests on the extension housing and then tighten the bracket mounting bolts to 19 ft. lbs. (25 Nm).

37. On 4WD vehicles, raise the transmission slightly and tighten the No. 2 frame crossmember-to-side frame bolts to 70 ft. lbs. (95 Nm). Lower the transmission and tighten the rear engine mount bolts to 9 ft. lbs. (13 Nm).

38. On 4WD vehicles, install the brake tube and front floor heat insulators.

39. Install the clutch release cylinder and its bracket to the manual transmission. Tighten the bracket bolts to 29 ft. lbs. (39 Nm) and the cylinder bolts to 9 ft. lbs. (13 Nm).

40. Reconnect the exhaust pipe. Install the No. 1 frame crossmember.

41. On 4WD vehicles, install the front driveshaft, stabilizer bar and the transfer case undercover.

42. Connect the speedometer cable. Connect the transfer shift linkage on 4WD vehicles with automatic transmission.

43. Connect the manual shift linkage to the neutral start switch (automatic transmission only).

44. Install the rear driveshaft. Install the shift lever for manual transmission only.

45. Connect the engine ground straps. Install the air conditioning compressor.

47. Install the power steering pump and connect the ground strap.

48. Connect all of the following wires:
  a. Cold start injector time switch wire
  b. Water temperature sensor wire
  c. If equipped with air conditioning: VSV and air conditioning compressor wires
  d. Oxygen sensor wire for 22R–TE engine only
  e. OD temperature switch wire for automatic transmission
  f. Injector wires
  g. Knock sensor connector
  h. Air valve wire
  i. Oil pressure switch wire
  j. Starter wire

49. Connect all of the following parts:
  a. No. 1 and No. 2 PCV hoses
  b. Brake booster hose
  c. Air control valve hoses
  d. EVAP hose at the canister
  e. Actuator hose on vehicles with cruise control
  f. Vacuum modulator hose at the EGR valve

  g. Air valve hoses at the throttle body and chamber
  h. Two water bypass hoses at the throttle body
  i. Air control valve hose at the actuator
  j. Pressure regulator hose at the chamber
  k. Cold start injector pipe
  l. BVSV hose.

50. Connect the accelerator and throttle cables to the bracket for automatic transmission only.

51. Connect the heater hoses and install the coupling fan. Install the radiator and shroud.

52. Install the air cleaner. Refill the engine with oil and the radiator with coolant. Install the engine undercover.

53. Install and adjust the hood.

54. Connect the battery cable, start the engine and road test the vehicle.

4Y–EC ENGINE

1. Disconnect the negative battery terminal.

2. Remove the right seat and the engine service hole cover.

3. Drain the coolant from the radiator. Remove the reservoir tank, the heater hoses and the radiator.

4. Remove the air cleaner, the breather tube, the brake booster, the charcoal canister and the fuel hoses from the engine.

5. If equipped with power steering, remove the drive belt, the pulley, the Woodruff key and the pump from the engine, then, move the pump aside.

NOTE: When removing the power steering pump, do not disconnect the pressure lines unless it is absolutely necessary.

6. Disconnect the accelerator cable with the bracket from the throttle body.

7. Disconnect the following wiring connectors from the: water temperature sender, oil pressure switch, IIA unit, air conditioning compressor, idle-up solenoid, VSV, water temperature switch (automatic transmission), alternator connector and wire, air flow meter and solenoid resistor.

8. Remove the fan shroud, the fan, the fluid coupling and the water pump pulley.

9. From inside the vehicle, remove the center pillar cover, the seat belt retractor and cover, then, disconnect the electrical connectors from the ECU.

10. If equipped with air conditioning, remove the drive belt and the compressor mounting bolts, then, move the compressor aside.

11. Raise and safely support the vehicle.

12. Drain the engine oil. Remove the driveshaft and the front exhaust pipe.

13. Remove the transmission selector and shift cables, then, the clutch release cylinder for manual transmission.

14. Disconnect the starter wires, the mounting bolts and the starter from the engine.

15. Remove the speedometer cable, the bond cable and the back-up light switch connector.

16. If equipped with a rear heater, disconnect the mode selector and the air mix damper cable from the damper. Disconnect the heater hoses to the rear heater unit.

17. Disconnect the bond cable(s) from the engine mount(s). Remove the engine under cover.

18. Disconnect the oil level sensor and the oil cooler hoses, if equipped with automatic transmission.

19. Place matchmarks on the front strut bar and the rear mounting nut. Remove the rear nut, the strut bar-to-lower control arm bolts and the strut.

20. Using an engine saddle, place it under the engine and support it. Place a floor jack under the transmission and support it.

NOTE: If equipped with a manual transmission, remove the engine rear mounting bracket from the body. If equipped with automatic transmission, remove the engine mounting member-to-transmission through bolt.

21. Remove the engine mounts-to-body nuts/bolts and lower the engine/transmission assembly, then, remove the engine mounting member from the engine.

22. Remove the transmission from the engine.

To install:

23. Install the engine to the transmission.

24. Install the engine mounts-to-body nuts/bolts and lower the engine/transmission assembly.

25. Remove the engine support and floor jack.

26. Install the front strut bar and the rear mounting nut. Install the rear nut, the strut bar-to-lower control arm bolts and the strut.

27. Connect the oil level sensor and the oil cooler hoses, if equipped with automatic transmission.

28. Connect the bond cable(s) to the engine mount(s). Install the engine under cover.

29. If equipped with a rear heater, connect the mode selector and the air mix damper cable to the damper. Connect the heater hoses to the rear heater unit.

30. Install the speedometer cable, the bond cable and the back-up light switch connector.

31. Connect the starter wires, the mounting bolts and the starter to the engine.

32. Install the transmission selector and shift cables, then, the clutch release cylinder for manual transmission.

33. Refill the engine oil. Install the driveshaft and the front exhaust pipe.

34. Lower the vehicle.

35. If equipped with air conditioning, install the drive belt and the compressor mounting bolts.

36. From inside the vehicle, install the center pillar cover, the seat belt retractor and cover.

37. Install the fan shroud, the fan, the fluid coupling and the water pump pulley.

38. Connect the following wiring connectors to the: water temperature sender, oil pressure switch, IIA unit, air conditioning compressor, idle-up solenoid, VSV, water temperature switch for automatic transmission, alternator connector and wire, air flow meter and solenoid resistor.

39. Connect the accelerator cable with the bracket to the throttle body.

40. If equipped with power steering, install the drive belt, the pulley, the woodruff key and the pump to the engine.

41. Install the air cleaner, the breather tube, the brake booster, the charcoal canister and the fuel hoses to the engine.

42. Refill the coolant and install the reservoir tank, the heater hoses and the radiator.

43. Install the right seat and the engine service hole cover.

44. Connect the negative battery terminal to the battery and check for leaks.

3F–E ENGINE

1. Disconnect the negative battery cable. Drain the engine coolant.

2. Scribe matchmarks around the hood hinges and then remove the hood.

3. Remove the battery and its tray.

4. Disconnect the accelerator and throttle cables.

5. Remove the air intake hose, air flow meter and air cleaner assembly.

6. Remove the coolant reservoir tank.

7. Remove the radiator.

8. Tag and disconnect the following wires and connectors:
   a. Oil pressure connector
   b. High tension cord at the coil
   c. Neutral start switch and transfer connectors near the starter
   d. Front differential lock connector
   e. Starter wire and connector
   f. Starter ground strap

g. O_2 sensor connectors
   h. Alternator wire and connector
   i. Cooling fan connector
   j. Check connector.

9. Disconnect the following hoses:
   a. Heater hoses
   b. Fuel hoses
   c. Transfer case hose
   d. Brake booster hose
   e. Air injection hoses
   f. Distributor hose
   g. Emission control hoses

10. Remove the glove box, pull out the 4 connectors and then pull the EFI wiring harness from the cowl.

11. Unbolt the power steering pump and position it aside with the hoses still connected.

12. Do the same with the air conditioning compressor.

13. Raise the vehicle and remove the transfer case undercover. Drain the engine oil.

14. Remove the front and rear driveshafts.

15. Disconnect the speedometer cable.

16. Disconnect the engine ground strap.

17. Disconnect the 2 vacuum hoses at the diaphragm cylinder under the transfer case.

18. Remove the clip and pin and then disconnect the shift rod at the transfer case. Remove the nut, disconnect the washers and the shift lever at the shift rod.

19. Disconnect the transmission control rod.

20. Disconnect the exhaust pipe at the manifold.

21. With a floor jack under the transmission, remove the bolts and nuts that attach the frame crossmember and then remove the crossmember. Lower the vehicle.

22. Attach an engine hoist to the lifting brackets on the engine. Remove the engine mount nuts and bolts and slowly lift the engine/transmission out of the vehicle.

To install:

23. Slowly lower the engine assembly into the engine compartment.

24. Raise the transmission onto the crossmember with a floor jack.

25. Align the holes in the engine mounts and the frame, install the bolts and then remove the engine hoist chain.

26. Raise the transmission slightly and tighten the frame crossmember-to-chassis bolts to 29 ft. lbs. (39 Nm). Tighten the 2 nuts to 43 ft. lbs. (59 Nm).

27. Install the exhaust pipe with a new gasket and tighten the nuts to 46 ft. lbs. (62 Nm).

28. Connect the transmission control rod. Connect the transfer case shift lever.

29. Connect the engine ground strap. Connect the speedometer cable.

30. Install the front and rear driveshafts. Tighten the nuts to 65 ft. lbs. (88 Nm).

31. Install the transfer case undercover. Install the air conditioning compressor. Install the power steering pump and tighten the pulley nut to 35 ft. lbs. (47 Nm).

32. Connect the EFI wiring harness at the ECU. Connect all of the following hoses:
   a. Heater hoses
   b. Fuel hoses
   c. Transfer case hose
   d. Brake booster hose
   e. Air injection hoses
   f. Distributor hose
   g. Emission control hoses

33. Connect all of the following the wires and connectors:
   a. Oil pressure connector
   b. High tension cord at the coil
   c. Neutral start switch and transfer connectors near the starter

d. Front differential lock connector
e. Starter wire and connector
f. Starter ground strap
g. Oxygen sensor connectors
h. Alternator wire and connector
i. Cooling fan connector
j. Check connector
34. Install the radiator and the coolant reservoir tank.
35. Install the air intake hose, air flow meter and air cleaner. Connect the accelerator and throttle cables.
36. Refill the engine with oil and the radiator with coolant. Install the engine undercover. Install the battery.
37. Install and adjust the hood.
38. Install the battery, start the engine and road test the vehicle.

3VZ–E ENGINE

1. Disconnect the battery cables and remove the battery.
2. Remove the engine undercover.
3. Disconnect the windshield washer hose and then remove the hood. Scribe matchmarks around the hinges for easy installation.
4. Drain the engine coolant from the radiator and the cylinder block.
5. Raise and safely support the vehicle. Drain the engine oil. Drain the automatic transmission fluid, if equipped.
6. Lower the vehicle. Disconnect the air cleaner hose and then remove the air cleaner.
7. Remove the radiator.
8. Remove all drive belts and then remove the fluid coupling and fan pulley.
9. Tag and disconnect the following wires and connectors:
a. Left side and rear ground straps
b. Alternator connector and wire
c. Igniter connector
d. Oil pressure switch connector
e. ECU connectors
f. VSV connectors
g. Starter relay connector for manual transmission only
h. Solenoid resistor connector
i. Check connector
j. Air conditioning compressor connector
10. Tag and disconnect the following hoses:
a. Power steering hoses at the gas filter and air pipe
b. Brake booster hose
c. Cruise control vacuum hose, if equipped
d. Charcoal canister hose at the canister
e. VSV vacuum hoses.
11. Disconnect the accelerator, throttle and cruise control cables where applicable.
12. Unbolt the power steering pump and position it aside with the hydraulic lines still connected.
13. Properly discharge the air conditioning system. Remove the air conditioning compressor if equipped.
14. Disconnect the clutch release cylinder hose for manual transmission only.
15. Disconnect the 2 heater hoses.
16. Disconnect and plug the fuel inlet and outlet lines.
17. Remove the shift levers for manual transmission only.
18. Raise and safely support the vehicle. Remove the rear driveshaft.
19. Disconnect the manual shift linkage for automatic transmission only.
20. Disconnect the speedometer cable, don't lose the felt dust protector and washers.
21. Remove the transfer case undercover. Remove the stabilizer bar.
22. Remove the front driveshaft. Remove the front exhaust pipe.
23. Remove the No. 1 front floor heat insulator and the brake tube heat insulator.

24. Remove the rear engine mount bolts, raise the transmission slightly with a floor jack and then remove the 4 bolts from the side member and remove the No. 2 frame crossmember. Lower the vehicle.
25. Attach an engine hoist chain to the lifting brackets on the engine. Remove the engine mount nuts and bolts and slowly lift the engine/transmission out of the vehicle.

To install:
26. Slowly lower the engine assembly into the engine compartment.
27. Raise the transmission onto the crossmember with a floor jack.
28. Align the holes in the engine mounts and the frame, install the bolts and then remove the engine hoist chain.
29. Raise the transmission slightly and tighten the No. 2 frame crossmember-to-side frame bolts to 70 ft. lbs. (95 Nm). Lower the transmission and tighten the 4 rear engine mount bolts to 9 ft. lbs. (13 Nm).
30. Install the brake tube and front floor heat insulators. Reconnect the exhaust pipe.
31. Install the No. 1 frame crossmember. Install the front driveshaft, stabilizer bar and the transfer case undercover.
32. Connect the speedometer cable. Connect the manual shift linkage for automatic transmission only.
33. Install the rear driveshaft. Install the shift levers for manual transmission only.
34. Install the fuel inlet and outlet lines. Connect the heater hoses.
35. Connect the clutch release cylinder hose. Install the air conditioning compressor.
36. Install the power steering pump and connect the ground strap.
37. Connect the throttle, cruise control and accelerator cables.
38. Connect the following hoses:
a. Power steering hoses at the gas filter and air pipe
b. Brake booster hose
c. Cruise control vacuum hose, if equipped
d. Charcoal canister hose at the canister
e. VSV vacuum hoses.
39. Install the fan pulley, belt guide, fluid coupling and drive belt. Connect the following wires:
a. Left side and rear ground straps
b. Alternator connector and wire
c. Igniter connector
d. Oil pressure switch connector
e. ECU connectors
f. VSV connectors
g. Starter relay connector for manual transmission only
h. Solenoid resistor connector
i. Check connector
j. Air conditioning compressor connector
40. Install the air conditioning belt. Install the power steering pump and connect the ground strap.
41. Install the radiator and shroud. Install the air cleaner. Refill the engine with oil and the radiator with coolant.
42. Install the engine undercover. Install the battery. Install and adjust the hood.
43. Install the battery, start the truck and road test it.

2TZ–FE ENGINE

1. Disconnect the negative battery cable and drain the engine coolant and oil.
2. Raise the vehicle and support safely. Remove the engine under covers.
3. Remove the accessory drive belt and service bolts and nut at the front end of the driveshaft. Matchmark and disconnect the equipment driveshaft from the crankshaft pulley.
4. Label and disconnect all hoses, electrical connectors, vacuum lines and cables from the engine and position aside.
5. Disconnect the front driveshaft for 4WD only.

6. Remove the air intake connector and disconnect the engine wiring from the floor pan.

7. Remove the exhaust pipe from the manifold and disconnect the oxygen sensor connector.

8. Remove the rear driveshaft.

9. Place a engine/transmission jack under the engine and remove the engine and transmission mount bolts.

9. With the vehicle on a hoist, lower the engine with the transmission from the bottom of the vehicle.

To install:

10. Raise the engine/transmission into the vehicle and torque the mount bolts and nuts to 27 ft. lbs. (34 Nm).

11. Connect all electrical connectors, vacuum hoses, coolant hoses and cables to the engine.

12. Install the exhaust pipe and torque to 32 ft. lbs. (43 Nm).

13. Install the front (4WD) and rear driveshafts and torque to 14 ft. lbs. (21 Nm).

14. Install the equipment drive shaft to the pulley and torque the bolts to 38 ft. lbs. (54 Nm). Install the belt and adjust.

15. Refill the engine with oil and coolant.

16. Connect the battery cable, start the engine and check for leaks.

Engine Mounts

Removal and Installation

1. Raise the vehicle and support safely.
2. Remove the engine-to-mount bolt or nut.
3. Position a suitable jack under the engine block.
4. Raise the engine far enough to take the weight off of the mount. Wedge a piece of wood between the engine and chassis in case the engine jack slips.
5. Remove the mount-to-body bolts and remove the mount.

To install:

6. Install the mount and torque the bolts to 34 ft. lbs. (46 Nm).
7. Remove the wood and lower the jack to engage the mount.
8. Torque the mount nut to 25 ft. lbs. (34 Nm).
9. Lower the vehicle and check for proper operation.

Cylinder Head

Removal and Installation

22R ENGINE

1. Disconnect the negative battery cable.
2. Drain the cooling system.
3. Mark all vacuum hoses and disconnect them.
4. Remove the air cleaner assembly, complete with hoses, from the carburetor.

NOTE: Cover the carburetor with a clean shop cloth so nothing can fall into it.

5. Remove all linkages, fuel lines, etc., from the carburetor, cylinder head, and manifolds. Remove the wire supports.

6. Mark the spark plug leads and disconnect them from the plugs.

7. Matchmark the distributor housing and block. Disconnect the primary lead and remove the distributor.

8. Unfasten the 14mm nuts which secure the cam cover. Remove the cam cover.

9. Remove the rubber camshaft seals. Turn the crankshaft until the No. 1 piston is at TDC on its compression stroke. Matchmark the timing sprocket to the cam chain, and remove the semi-circular lug. Using a 19mm wrench, remove the cam sprocket bolt. Slide the distributor drive gear and spacer off the cam and wire the cam sprocket in place.

10. Remove the timing chain cover 14mm bolt at the front of the head. This must be done before the head bolts are removed. Remove the exhaust pipe flange nuts and disconnect the pipe.

Cylinder head bolt removal sequence—22R, 22R-E and 22R-TE engines

Cylinder head bolt installation sequence—22R, 22R-E and 22R-TE engines

11. Remove the cylinder head bolts in the correct order. Improper removal could cause head damage.

12. Using prybars applied evenly at the front and the rear of the valve rocker assembly, pry the assembly off its mounting dowels.

13. Lift the head off its dowels. Do not pry it off.

14. Drain the engine oil from the crankcase after the head has been removed, because the oil will become contaminated with coolant while the head is being removed.

To install:

15. Apply liquid sealer to the front corners of the block and install the head gasket.

16. Lower the head over the locating dowels; do not attempt to slide it into place.

17. Rotate the camshaft so the sprocket aligning pin is at the top. Remove the wire and hold the cam sprocket. Manually rotate the engine so the sprocket hole is also at the top. Wire the sprocket in place.

18. Install the rocker arm assembly over its positioning dowels.

19. Tighten the cylinder head bolts evenly, in 3 stages and in the correct order.

20. Install the timing chain cover bolt and tighten it to 7–11 ft. lbs. (9.5–14 Nm).

21. Remove the wire and fit the sprocket over the camshaft dowel. If the chain won't allow the sprocket to reach, rotate the crankshaft back and forth, while lifting up on the chain and sprocket.

22. Install the distributor drive gear and tighten the crankshaft bolt to 51–65 ft. lbs. (68–88 Nm).

23. Set the No. 1 piston at TDC of its compression stroke and adjust the valves.

24. After completing valve adjustment, rotate the crankshaft 352 degrees, so the 8 BTDC mark on the pulley aligns with the pointer.

Exploded view of the cylinder head assembly — 22R, 22R-E and 22R-TE engines

25. Install the distributor.

26. Install the spark plugs and leads.

27. Make sure the oil drain plug is installed. Fill the engine with oil after installing the rubber cam seals. Pour the oil over the distributor drive gear and the valve rockers.

28. Install the rocker cover and tighten the bolts to 8–11 ft. lbs. (11–15 Nm).

29. Connect all the vacuum hoses and electrical leads which were removed during disassembly. Install the spark plug lead supports. Fill the cooling system. Install the air cleaner.

30. Tighten the exhaust pipe-to-manifold flange bolts to 25–33 ft. lbs. (34–45 Nm).

31. Reconnect the battery. Start the engine and allow it to reach normal operating temperature. Check and adjust the timing and valve clearance. Adjust the idle speed and mixture. Road test the vehicle.

22R-E AND 22R-TE ENGINES

1. Relieve the fuel system pressure. Disconnect the negative battery cable.

2. Drain the coolant from the radiator and the cylinder block. Raise and safely support the vehicle. Drain the engine oil.

3. Remove the turbocharger on the 22R-TE engine.

4. Disconnect and remove the air cleaner hose on the 22R-E engine.

5. Disconnect the oxygen sensor wire. Remove the nuts attaching the manifold to the exhaust pipe and then separate them.

6. Remove the oil dipstick. Remove the distributor with the spark plug leads attached.

7. Disconnect the upper radiator hose and the heater hoses where they attach to the engine and then position them aside.

8. Disconnect the actuator cable, the accelerator cable and

Service Tips

CYLINDER HEAD GASKET MATERIAL REVISION

To improve the corrosion resistance on the cylinder head gasket that is used on the 22R engine, the manufacturer has changed the sealing surfaces from steel to stainless steel.

When replacing the cylinder head gasket, make sure the sealing surfaces of the new head gasket are stainless steel. Consult the dealer for part number information.

the throttle cable for the automatic transmission at their bracket.

9. Tag and disconnect the following:
  a. Both PCV vacuum hoses
  b. Brake booster hose
  c. Actuator hose, if equipped with cruise control
  d. Air control valve hoses
  e. Air control valve.

10. Tag and disconnect the EGR vacuum modulator hoses and then remove the modulator itself along with the bracket.

11. Tag and disconnect the following:
  a. Green and brown BVSV hoses
  b. Vacuum advance hoses
  c. The 2 air valve hoses; one at the throttle body, the other at the air chamber
  d. Air control valve hose, if equipped with air conditioning
  e. Pressure regulator hose at the air chamber
  f. Cold start injector pipe and wire
  g. Throttle position sensor wire.

12. Remove the bolt holding the EGR valve to the air chamber. Disconnect the chamber from the stay. Remove the air chamber-to-intake manifold bolts and then lift off the chamber with the throttle body.

13. Disconnect the fuel return hose.

14. Tag and disconnect the following:
  a. Water temperature sender gauge wire
  b. Temperature sensor wire
  c. Start injection time switch wire
  d. Fuel injector wires.

15. Remove the pulsation damper. Remove the bolt holding the fuel hose to the delivery pipe and then disconnect and remove the fuel hose.

16. Disconnect the wire and hose and then remove the air valve from the intake manifold.

17. Disconnect the bypass hose at the intake manifold on the 22R–E engine. On the 22R–TE engine, disconnect the oil cooler hose at the manifold.

18. If equipped with power steering, remove the pump and position it aside without disconnecting the hydraulic lines.

19. Remove the 4 nuts and then remove the cylinder head cover.

20. Remove the rubber camshaft seals. Turn the crankshaft until the No. 1 piston is at TDC of its compression stroke. Matchmark the timing sprocket to the timing chain and then remove the semi-circular plug. Using a 19mm wrench, remove the camshaft sprocket bolt. Slide the distributor drive gear and spacer off the camshaft and wire the cam sprocket in place.

21. Remove the timing chain cover bolt in front of the cylinder head.

NOTE: This must be done before the cylinder head bolts are removed.

22. Remove the cylinder head bolts gradually, in 2–3 stages, in the correct order.

23. Using prybars applied evenly at the front and rear of the rocker arm assembly, pry the assembly off of its mounting dowels.

24. Lift the cylinder head off of its mounting dowels.

To install:

25. Apply liquid sealer to the front corners of the block and install the head gasket.

26. Lower the head over the locating dowels. Do not attempt to slide it into place.

27. Rotate the camshaft so the sprocket aligning pin is at the top. Remove the wire and hold the cam sprocket. Manually rotate the engine so the sprocket hole is also at the top. Wire the sprocket in place.

28. Install the rocker arm assembly over its positioning dowels.

29. Tighten the cylinder head bolts evenly, in 3 stages and in the correct order.

30. Install the timing chain cover bolt and tighten it to 7–11 ft. lbs. (11–15 Nm).

31. Remove the wire and fit the sprocket over the camshaft dowel. If the chain won't allow the sprocket to reach, rotate the crankshaft back and forth, while lifting up on the chain and sprocket.

32. Install the distributor drive gear and tighten the crankshaft bolt to 51–65 ft. lbs. (68–88 Nm).

33. Set the No. 1 piston at TDC of its compression stroke and adjust the valves.

34. After completing valve adjustment, rotate the crankshaft 352 degrees, so the 8 BTDC mark on the pulley aligns with the pointer.

35. Install the distributor.

36. Install the spark plugs and leads.

37. Make sure the oil drain plug is installed. Fill the engine with oil after installing the rubber cam seals. Pour the oil over the distributor drive gear and the valve rockers.

38. Install the rocker cover and tighten the bolts to 8–11 ft. lbs. (11–15 Nm).

39. Connect all the vacuum hoses and electrical leads which were removed during disassembly. Install the spark plug lead supports. Fill the cooling system. Install the air cleaner.

40. Tighten the exhaust pipe-to-manifold flange bolts to 25–33 ft. lbs. (34–45 Nm).

41. Reconnect the battery. Start the engine and allow it to reach normal operating temperature. Check and adjust the timing and valve clearance. Adjust the idle speed and mixture. Road test the vehicle.

4Y–EC ENGINE

1. Disconnect the negative battery terminal from the battery.

2. Remove the right-front seat and the engine service hole cover.

3. Raise and safely support the vehicle. Drain the engine coolant at the radiator. Drain the engine oil. Lower the vehicle.

4. If equipped with power steering, perform the following:
  a. Remove the air hoses from the air control valve
  b. Drain the fluid from the reservoir tank
  c. Disconnect the return hose from the pump
  d. Disconnect the pressure hose from the pump
  e. Remove the drive belt, the pulley nut, the pulley, the Woodruff key, the mounting bolts and the pump

5. Remove the exhaust pipe and the bracket. Remove the air cleaner pipe and the hoses.

6. Disconnect the accelerator cable with the bracket from the throttle body.

7. Disconnect the water temperature sender gauge connector from the cylinder head.

8. Disconnect the following EFI connectors from the:
   a. The water thermo sensor
   b. The cold start injector time switch
   c. The cold start injector
   d. The air valve
   e. The throttle position sensor
   f. The oxygen sensor
   g. The water temperature switch
9. Disconnect the following hoses from the:
   a. The radiator inlet
   b. The radiator breather
   c. The reserve tank
   d. The heater outlet
   e. The PCV valve
   f. The water bypass
   g. The brake booster vacuum
   h. The charcoal canister
   i. Label and disconnect the emission control
10. Remove the throttle body from the air intake chamber.
11. Remove the EGR valve nuts from the intake chamber and the exhaust manifold-to-EGR valve union.
12. Disconnect the cold start injector pipe, the water bypass hoses and the pressure regulator hose.
13. Using a 12mm offset box wrench, remove the air intake chamber brackets, then, the chamber with the air valve.
14. Remove the wire clamp bolts and the injector connectors from the injectors.
15. Remove the exhaust manifold bracket, the heater pipe bracket, the fuel inlet pipe union bolt from the fuel filter and the fuel outlet hose.
16. Remove the spark plugs and the tubes.
17. Remove the cap nuts, the seal washers, the cylinder head cover and the gasket.
18. Remove the rocker arm shaft assembly nuts/bolts a little at a time, in 3–4 steps. Remove the pushrods, keeping them in order.
19. Remove the cylinder head bolts, a little at a time, in 3 passes. Lift the cylinder head off of the engine.
20. Remove the valve lifters from the cylinder block.

To install:
21. Clean the gasket mounting surfaces.
22. To install, use new gaskets and reverse the removal procedures. Torque the cylinder head bolts, in 3 passes, to 65 ft. lbs. (88 Nm) for 14mm bolt or 14 ft. lbs. (19 Nm) for 12mm bolt, the rocker arm shaft-to-cylinder head bolts, in 3 passes, to 17 ft. lbs. (24 Nm), the spark plugs to 13 ft. lbs. (18 Nm), the air intake chamber bolts to 9 ft. lbs. (12 Nm), the throttle body-to-intake chamber to 9 ft. lbs. (12 Nm) and the exhaust pipe-to-exhaust manifold to 29 ft. lbs. (41 Nm).
23. Adjust the drive belts.
24. Refill the cooling system and the engine with oil.
25. Check and/or adjust the timing.

NOTE: Use special tool 09270–71010 or equivalent, to hold the pushrods in position when installing the pushrods.

3F–E ENGINE

1. Drain the coolant.
2. Disconnect the negative battery cable.
3. Scribe matchmarks around the hood hinges and then remove the hood.
4. Disconnect the accelerator and throttle cables.
5. Remove the air intake hose, air flow meter and air cleaner cap.
6. Unbolt the power steering pump and position it aside without disconnecting the hydraulic lines.
7. Unbolt the air conditioning compressor and position it aside without disconnecting the refrigerant lines.
8. Remove the power steering pump and air conditioning compressor brackets.

9. Disconnect the high tension leads from the spark plugs and the coil.
10. Disconnect and remove the heater water (oil cooler) pipe.
11. Disconnect the upper radiator hose.
12. Disconnect and plug the fuel lines.
13. Disconnect the exhaust pipe at the manifold.
14. Remove the air pump.
15. Remove the fuel delivery pipe along with the fuel injectors.
16. Remove the air injection manifold.
17. Remove the intake and exhaust manifolds.
18. Disconnect the water bypass hose at the water outlet and then remove the outlet.
19. Remove the spark plugs.
20. Remove the cylinder head cover and its gasket.
21. Loosen the bolts and nuts that attach the rocker shaft assembly in several stages and then remove the rocker shaft.
22. Remove the pushrods.
23. Remove the cylinder head bolts in the reverse of the tightening sequence. Remove the air pump bracket and engine hanger.
24. Lift the cylinder head off of its mounting dowels.

To install:
25. Install the cylinder head on the cylinder block using a new gasket.
26. Lightly coat the threads of the cylinder head bolts with engine oil and then install them into the head. Tighten in several stages, to the correct torque.
27. Install the pushrods in the order that they were removed.
28. Position the rocker shaft assembly on the cylinder head and align the rocker arm adjusting screws with the heads of the pushrods. Tighten the mounting bolts with a 12mm head to 17 ft. lbs. (24 Nm); tighten the bolts with a 14mm head to 25 ft. lbs. (33 Nm).
29. Adjust the valve clearance and install the spark plugs. Install the cylinder head cover and tighten the cap nuts to 78 inch lbs. (8.8 Nm).
30. Install the water outlet and connect the bypass hose. Tighten the bolts to 18 ft. lbs. (25 Nm).
31. Install the intake and exhaust manifolds using a new gasket. Make sure the front mark on the gasket is towards the front of the engine.
32. Install the heat insulators and the manifold stay.
33. Install the air injection manifold and tighten the union nuts and clamp bolts to 15 ft. lbs. (21 Nm).
34. Install the fuel injector/delivery pipe assembly.
35. Install the air pump and connect the air hose.
36. Connect the exhaust pipe to the manifold. Use a new gasket and tighten the bolts to 46 ft. lbs. (62 Nm).
37. Connect the fuel lines and the upper radiator hose.
38. Install the heater water pipe.
39. Connect the high tension cords.
40. Install the air conditioning compressor and the power steering pump. Remember to adjust the belt tension later.
41. Install the air intake hose, the air flow meter and the air cleaner cap.
42. Connect and adjust the accelerator and throttle cables.
43. Connect the battery cable, fill the engine with coolant, start the engine and check for any leaks. Road test the vehicle.

3VZ–E ENGINE

1. Disconnect the negative battery cable.
2. Remove the air cleaner hose and case.
3. Drain the engine coolant.
4. Remove the radiator.
5. Unbolt the power steering pump and position it aside with the hoses still attached.
6. Remove all drive belts and then remove the fluid coupling and fan pulley.
7. Tag and disconnect all wires and connectors that will interfere with cylinder head removal.

Cylinder head bolt installation sequence – 3F–E engine

Cylinder head bolt removal sequence – 3VZ–E engine

CAMSHAFT HOUSING REAR COVER

CAMSHAFT HOUSING PLUG

CAMSHAFT

SHIM

VALVE LIFTER

KEEPER

VALVE SPRING RETAINER

OIL SEAL

SNAPRING

VALVE GUIDE BUSHING

BEARING CAP

VALVE SPRING

VALVE SPRING SEAT

VALVE

OIL SEAL

NO. 1 ENGINE HANGER

NO. 4 CAMSHAFT BEARING CAP

NO. 1 EXHAUST MANIFOLD HEAT INSULATOR

OIL SEAL

PS PUMP BRACKET

LH CYLINDER HEAD

NO. 2 ENGINE HANGER

RH EXHAUST MANIFOLD

GASKET

RH CYLINDER HEAD

GASKET

GASKET

LH EXHAST MANIFOLD

NO. 4 TIMING BELT COVER

GASKET

NO. 3 TIMING BELT COVER

ALTERNATOR BRACKET

NO. 2 EXHAUST MANIFOLD

Exploded view of the cylinder head assembly – 3VZ–E engine

Camshaft bearing cap loosening sequence—3VZ–E engine

Camshaft bearing cap bolt tightening sequence—3VZ–E engine

Cylinder head gasket installation—3VZ–E engine

Cylinder head torque sequence—2TZ–FE engine

Cylinder head bolt tightening sequence—3VZ–E engine

Cylinder head loosengine sequence—2TZ–FE engine

8. Disconnect the following hoses:
a. Power steering air hoses
b. Brake booster hose
c. Cruise control vacuum hose
d. Charcoal canister has at the canister
e. VSV vacuum hose.

9. Disconnect the accelerator, throttle and cruise control cables.

10. Disconnect the clutch release cylinder hose for manual transmission only.

11. Disconnect the heater hoses and the fuel lines.

12. Remove the left side scuff plate and disconnect the O_2 sensor and then remove the front exhaust pipe.

13. Remove the timing belt as detailed later in this chapter.

14. Remove the distributor with the spark plug leads attached; position it aside.

15. Remove the air intake chamber.

16. Disconnect the connectors and then remove the engine wire.

17. Remove the Nos. 2 and 3 fuel pipes.

18. Remove the No. 4 timing belt cover.

19. Remove the No. 2 idler pulley and the No. 3 timing belt cover.

20. Disconnect the hose and remove the water bypass outlet.

21. Remove the intake manifold.

22. Remove the exhaust crossover pipe.

23. For the right side, remove the following:
a. Remove the reed valve with the No. 1 air injection manifold.
b. Remove the water bypass pipe mounting bolt.
c. Remove the cylinder head cover.
d. Remove the camshaft.
e. Loosen the cylinder head bolts in several stages, in the opposite order of the tightening sequence. Remove the air pump bracket and engine hanger.
f. Lift the cylinder head off of its mounting dowels, do not pry it off.

24. For the left side, remove the following:
a. Remove the alternator.
b. Remove the oil dipstick guide tube:

c. Remove the cylinder head cover.

e. Remove the camshaft.

f. Loosen the cylinder head bolts in several stages, in the opposite order of the tightening sequence. Remove the air pump bracket and engine hanger.

g. Lift the cylinder head off of its mounting dowels, do not pry it off.

To install:

25. Install the cylinder head on the cylinder block using a new gasket.

26. Lightly coat the threads of the cylinder head bolts with engine oil and then install them into the head. Tighten them in several stages, in the correct order. After the initial tightening, mark the front side the the top of the bolt with paint. Tighten the bolts an additional 90 degrees (¼ turn) and check that the mark is now facing the side of the head. Tighten the bolts an additional 90 degrees and check that the mark is now facing the rear of the head. Install the bolt (A) and tighten it to 27 ft. lbs. (37 Nm).

27. Install the camshaft.

28. Install the alternator and the water bypass pipe mounting bolt.

29. Install the reed valve with the No. 1 injection manifold.

30. Install the oil dipstick tube.

31. Install the crossover pipe and tighten it to 29 ft. lbs. (39 Nm).

32. Connect the oxygen sensor wire.

33. Install the intake manifold with new gaskets and tighten the mounting bolts to 29 ft. lbs. (39 Nm).

34. Install the water bypass outlet and tighten the bolts to 13 ft. lbs. (18 Nm).

35. Install the fuel delivery pipes and injectors.

36. Install the No. 2 idler pulley. Install the Nos. 3 and 4 timing belt covers and tighten the bolts to 74 inch lbs. (8.3 Nm).

37. Install the fuel pipes and tighten the union bolts to 22 ft. lbs. (29 Nm).

38. Install the timing belt. Install the cylinder head covers.

39. Install the air intake chamber and tighten the nuts and bolts to 13 ft. lbs. (18 Nm).

40. Install the EGR valve and connect all hoses and lines. Install the distributor and the front exhaust pipe.

41. Connect the fuel lines and heater hoses. Connect the clutch release cylinder hose.

42. Connect the power steering pump. Connect all cables and adjust, hoses and wires previously removed.

43. Install the fan pulley, fluid coupling and drive belts. Install the radiator.

44. Install the air cleaner hose, refill the engine with coolant and connect the battery cable.

2TZ–FE ENGINE

1. Disconnect the negative battery cable.

2. Remove the engine/transmission assembly from the vehicle.

3. Remove the engine wiring from the engine and move aside.

4. Remove the No. 2 valve cover.

5. Mark the spark plug wires and disconnect. Matchmark the distributor, rotor and cylinder head. Remove the distributor and disconnect the wiring.

6. Remove the EGR valve.

7. Remove the fuel rail and water outlet.

8. Remove the intake and exhaust manifold assembly.

9. Remove the exhaust manifold heat insulator and oil return pipe.

10. Remove the No. 1 valve cover.

11. Place matchmarks on the timing sprocket and chain. Hold the camshaft with a wrench and remove the sprocket bolt.

12. Remove the chain tensioner and gasket.

13. Remove the No. 6 camshaft bearing cap.

14. Set the knock pin hole of the exhaust camshaft at the 5–30

degree BTDC. Uniformly loosen the camshaft bearing caps and remove the exhaust camshaft from the head.

15. Set the knock pin hole of the intake camshaft at the 75–100 degree BTDC. Uniformly loosen the camshaft bearing caps and remove the exhaust camshaft from the head.

16. Remove the 2 bolts in front of the head before removing the cylinder haed retaining bolts.

17. Using a 12 sided socket wrench, remove the 10 cylinder head retaining bolts in sequence and remove the head from the engine.

To install:

18. Clean the gasket mating surfaces and check for warpage.

19. Install the head gasket and install the cylinder head.

20. Oil the bolts and torque in 3 steps, in sequence. If any of the bolts break, deform or do not meet the torque specification replace them.

21. Install and torque the 2 front bolts to 15 ft. lbs. (21 Nm).

22. Grease to all camshaft journals and caps.

23. Place the intake camshaft at 75–100 degrees BTDC. Install the bearing caps with the marking arrows facing forward. Uniformly torque the bearing cap bolts to 12 ft. lbs. (16 Nm).

Intake camshaft bearing cap torque sequence–2TZ–FE engine

Exhaust camshaft bearing cap torque sequence–2TZ–FE engine

Service **T**ips

CYLINDER HEAD COOLANT CORE PLUG REVISION

On 1991–92 vehicle with a 2TZ–FE engine, a design change has been made to the cylinder head coolant plug and gasket.

Always replace the plugs and gaskets as a set with the revised style (9034127006). Torque the new plug to 62 ft. lbs. (83 Nm) and do not apply anaerobic sealant to the threads.

24. Apply sealant to the bearing cap next to the timing chain sprocket. Place the intake camshaft at 5–30 degrees BTDC. Install the bearing caps with the marking arrows facing forward. Uniformly torque the bearing cap bolts to 12 ft. lbs. (16 Nm). Make sure the exhaust and intake camshaft gear alignment marks are facing each other. The one gear has 2 dots and the other has 1 dot.

25. Install the timing chain sprocket and torque the bolt to 54 ft. lbs. (74 Nm).

26. Release the ratchet pawl and fully push the plunger and apply the hook on the tensioner so it can not spring out.

27. Install the tensioner and torque the bolts to 15 ft. lbs. (21 Nm). Turn the crankshaft to the left so the hook of the tensioner is released from the pin. If it does not spring out, pull the slipper into the tensioner to release the hook.

28. Install the cylinder head covers and torque to 69 inch lbs. (7.8 Nm).

29. Install the intake and exhaust manifolds.

30. Install the remaining components onto the engine.

31. Install the engine/transmission assembly into the vehicle.

32. Refill the engine coolant and oil. Connect the battery cable and check for leaks.

Valve Lifters

Removal and Installation

Always replace the camshaft and lifters as a set. If not replacing, label all components for exact reinstallation.

4Y–EC AND 3F–E ENGINES

1. Disconnect the negative battery cable.
2. Remove the spark plugs and tubes.
3. Remove the valve cover.
4. Uniformly loosen and remove the rocker arm shaft bolts and nuts. Remove the rocker shaft and pushrods. Label all components for installation.
5. Using a piece of wire or magnetic finger, remove the 8 valve lifters for 4Y–EC engine.

NOTE: Always keep the lifters upright and in correct order.

6. Remove the pushrod cover. Remove the 12 lifters for 3F–E engine.

To install:

7. Lubricate the lifters with prelube and install into their original location.
8. Install the pushrod cover and torque to 35 inch lbs. (3.9 Nm) for 3F–E engines.
9. Install the rocker arms and torque to 17 ft. lbs. (24 Nm) and 25 ft. lbs. (33 Nm) for the bolt/nut combination.
10. Install the rocker arm cover and torque to 69 inch lbs. (7.8 Nm).
11. Install the remaining components and check for leaks.

Valve Lash

Adjustment

22R, 22R–E AND 22R–TE ENGINES

1. Start the engine and allow it to reach normal operating temperatures above 175° F.
2. Stop the engine. Remove the air cleaner assembly, the hoses and the bracket, then any cables, hoses, wires and etc., which are attached to the valve cover. Remove the valve cover.
3. Set the No. 1 cylinder to TDC of the compression stroke. Place a wrench on the crankshaft pulley bolt and turn the engine until the notch on the crankshaft pulley is aligned with the 0 degree mark on the timing plate; the engine is at TDC.

NOTE: The rocker arms on cylinder No. 1 should be loose and the rocker arms on cylinder No. 4 should be tight.

4. With the engine hot, the valve clearances are 0.008 in. for intake or 0.012 in. for exhaust.

NOTE: The clearance is measured with a feeler gauge between the valve stem and the adjusting screw.

5. To adjust the valve clearance, loosen the locknut and turn the adjusting screw until the specified clearance is obtained. Tighten the locknut and check the clearance again. Adjust the intake valves of No. 1 and 2 cylinders; the exhaust valves of No. 1 and 3 cylinders.

6. Turn the crankshaft one full revolution, 360 degrees. Adjust the intake valves of No. 3 and 4 cylinders; the exhaust valves of No. 2 and 4 cylinders.

7. To install the components, reverse the removal procedures.

4Y–EC ENGINE

The valve tappets of this engine are hydraulic; no adjustment is necessary.

Valve adjustment sequence—22R, 22R–E and 22R–TE engines

First step of the valve adjustment procedure—22R, 22R–E and 22R–TE engines

Second step of the valve adjustment procedure—22R, 22R–E and 22R–TE engines

Valve clearance check—2TZ–FE engine

Adjusting valve clearance—3F–E engine

2TZ–FE ENGINE

Check the valve clearance with the engine cold.
1. Remove the front seat and engine service hole cover.
2. Remove the valve cover.
3. Install a service bolt and nut into the equipment driveshaft.
4. Set the No. 1 cylinder to TDC/compression stoke.
5. Measure the clearance of the first set of valves and record the measurements. The clearance should be 0.006–0.010 in. (0.15–0.25mm) for intake and 0.010–0.014 in. (0.25–0.35mm) for exhaust.
6. Turn the equipment driveshaft 1 full revolution and measure the second set of valves.
7. Using a shim removing tool 0924855010 or equivalent, press down the lifter and remove the shim with a small pick.
8. Determine the replacement shim size by measuring the old shim using a micrometer and calculate the thickness of the new shim using the following formula:

T = thickness of the used shim
A = valve clearance measured
N = thickness of new shim
Intake: $N = T + (A - 0.008 \text{ in. } (0.20\text{mm})$
Exhaust: $N = T + (A - 0.012 \text{ in. } (0.30\text{mm})$

9. Select a shim with the thickness as close as possible to the calculated values. Shims are available in 17 sizes, in increments of 0.002 in. (0.050mm). The thickness is stamped on the shim.
10. Install the shims and recheck the clearance.
11. Install the valve cover and torque the bolts to 69 inch lbs. (7.8 Nm).
12. Install the remaining components and check for leaks.

3F–E ENGINE

Check the valve clearance with the engine at normal operating temperature.
1. Remove the air cleaner and valve cover.
2. Set the No. 1 cylinder to TDC. Make sure the No. 1 rocker arms are loose and the No. 6 are tight. If not turn the crankshaft 1 turn and align the timing marks to 0.
3. Adjust the first set of valves to 0.008 in. (0.20mm) for intake and 0.014 in. (0.35mm) for exhaust valves.
4. After tightening the lock nut, recheck the valve clearance.
5. Install the valve cover and air cleaner.

3VZ–E ENGINE

Check the valve clearance with the engine cold.
1. Remove the valve cover.
2. Set the No. 1 cylinder to TDC/compression.
3. Measure the clearance of the lifters with the camshaft lobe at the base circle and record the measurements. The clearance should be as follows:

    1988—0.010–0.014 in. (0.25–0.35mm) intake
    1988—0.011–0.015 in. (0.27–0.37mm) exhaust
    1989–92—0.007–0.011 in. (0.18–0.28mm) intake
    1989–92—0.009–0.013 in. (0.22–0.32mm) exhaust

4. Using a shim removing tool 0924855010 or equivalent, press down the lifter and remove the shim with a small pick.
5. Determine the replacement shim size by measuring the old shim using a micrometer and calculate the thickness of the new shim using the following formula:

T = thickness of the used shim
A = valve clearance measured
N = thickness of new shim
1988 Intake: $N = T + (A - 0.0118 \text{ in. } (0.30\text{mm})$
1988 Exhaust: $N = T + (A - 0.0126 \text{ in. } (0.32\text{mm})$
1989–92 Intake: $N = T + (A - 0.0091 \text{ in. } (0.23\text{mm})$
1989–92 Exhaust: $N = T + (A - 0.0126 \text{ in. } (0.32\text{mm})$

6. Select a shim with the thickness as close as possible to the calculated values. Shims are available in 25 sizes, in increments of 0.002 in. (0.050mm). The thickness is stamped on the shim.
7. Install the shims and recheck the clearance.
8. Install the valve cover and torque the bolts to 69 inch lbs. (7.8 Nm).
9. Install the remaining components and check for leaks.

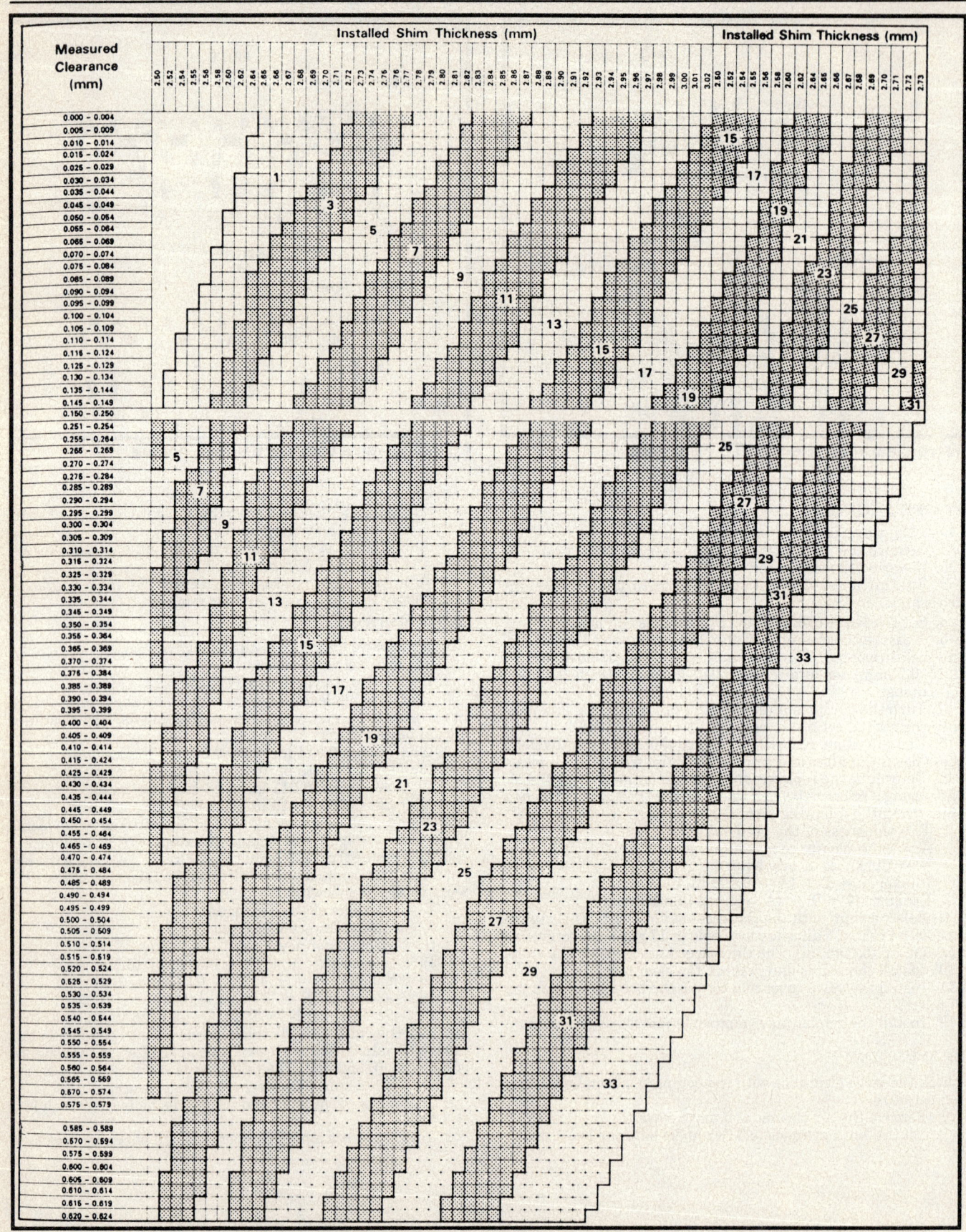

Intake shim selection chart (cont) — 2TZ–FE engine

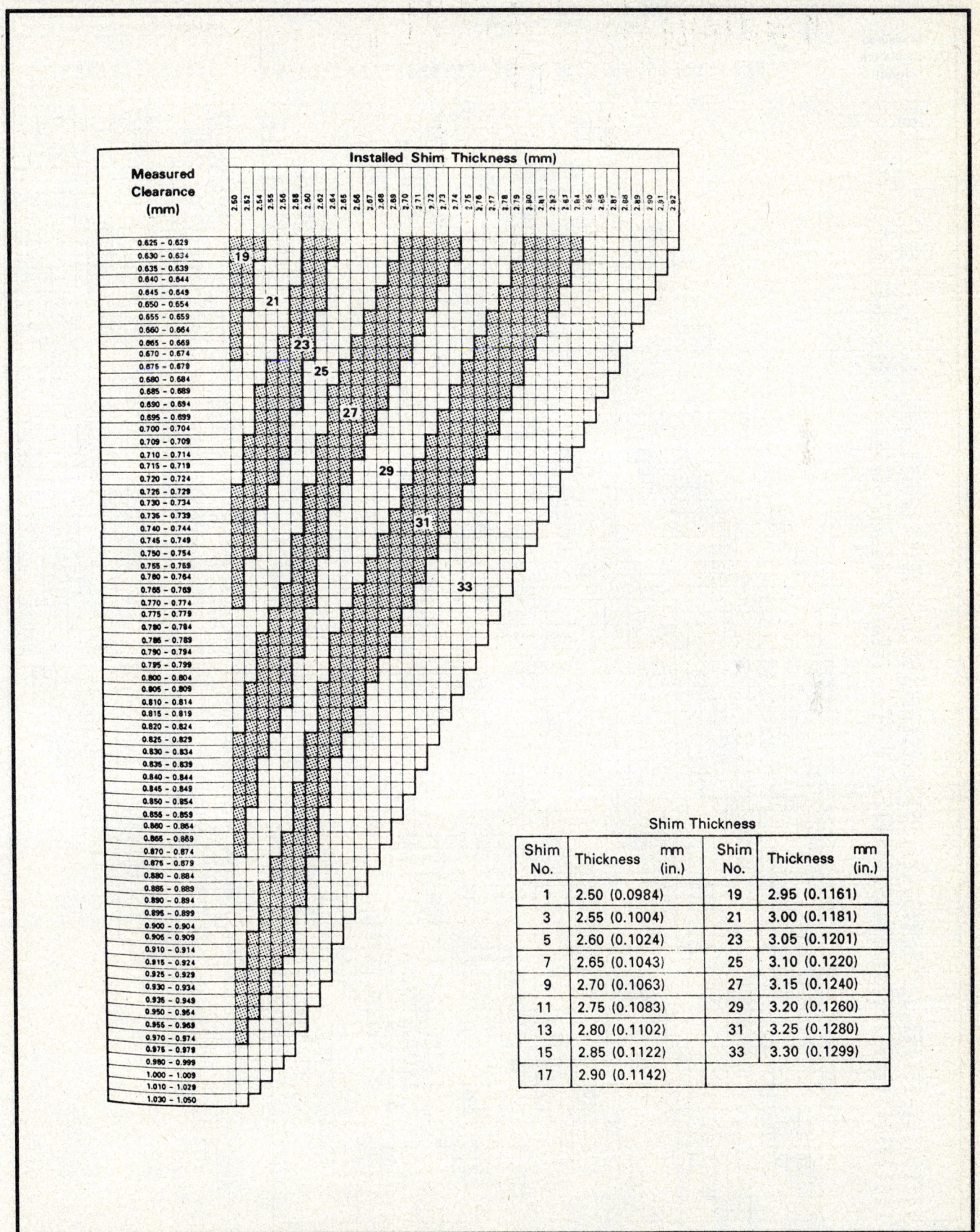

Intake shim selection chart (cont) – 2TZ–FE engine

Shim No.	Thickness mm (in.)	Shim No.	Thickness mm (in.)
1	2.50 (0.0984)	19	2.95 (0.1161)
3	2.55 (0.1004)	21	3.00 (0.1181)
5	2.60 (0.1024)	23	3.05 (0.1201)
7	2.65 (0.1043)	25	3.10 (0.1220)
9	2.70 (0.1063)	27	3.15 (0.1240)
11	2.75 (0.1083)	29	3.20 (0.1260)
13	2.80 (0.1102)	31	3.25 (0.1280)
15	2.85 (0.1122)	33	3.30 (0.1299)
17	2.90 (0.1142)		

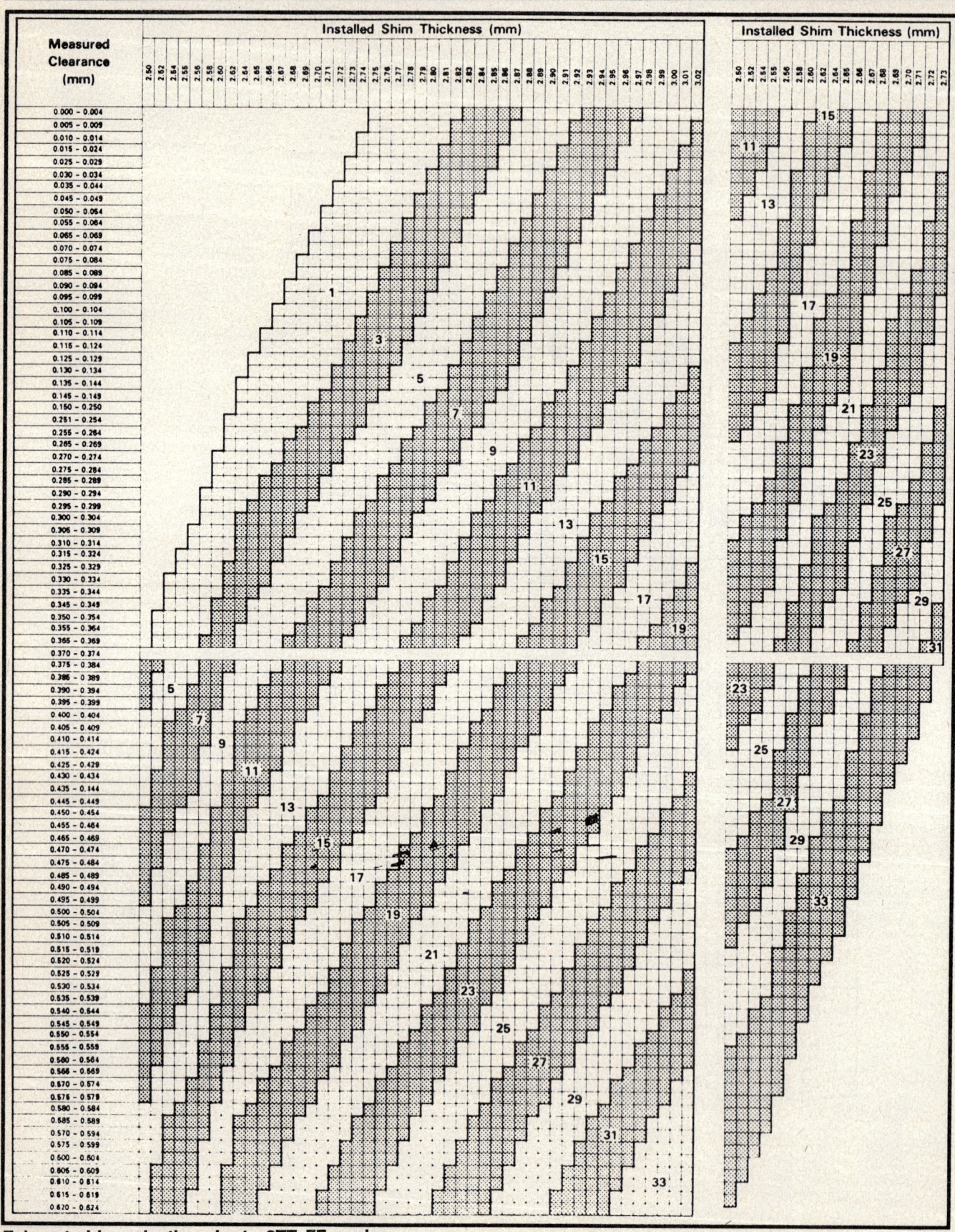

Exhaust shim selection chart—2TZ-FE engine

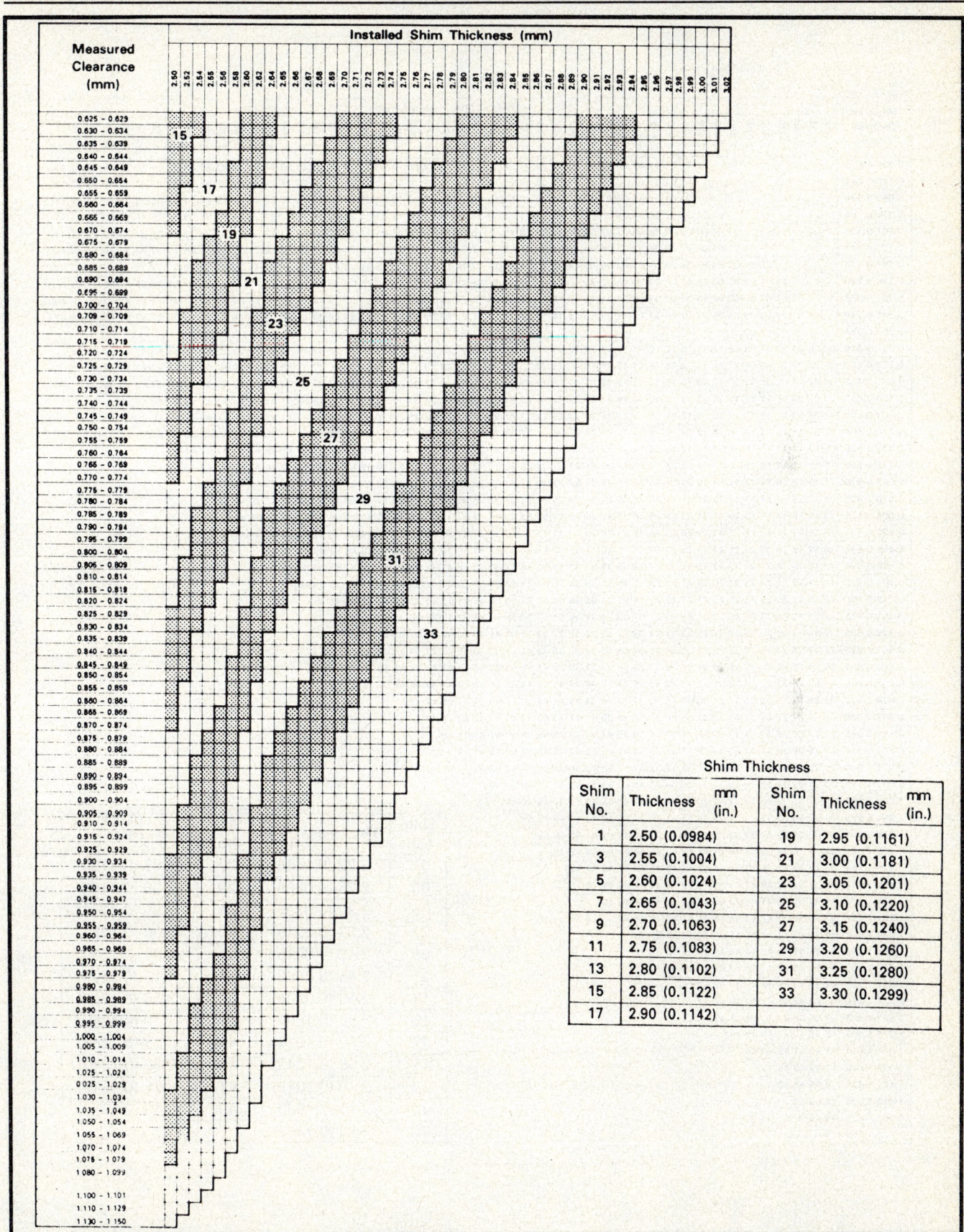

Exhaust shim selection chart (cont) – 2TZ–FE engine

Shim Thickness

Shim No.	Thickness mm (in.)	Shim No.	Thickness mm (in.)
1	2.50 (0.0984)	19	2.95 (0.1161)
3	2.55 (0.1004)	21	3.00 (0.1181)
5	2.60 (0.1024)	23	3.05 (0.1201)
7	2.65 (0.1043)	25	3.10 (0.1220)
9	2.70 (0.1063)	27	3.15 (0.1240)
11	2.75 (0.1083)	29	3.20 (0.1260)
13	2.80 (0.1102)	31	3.25 (0.1280)
15	2.85 (0.1122)	33	3.30 (0.1299)
17	2.90 (0.1142)		

Intake shim selection chart — 1988 3VZ–E engine

Measured Clearance (mm)	2.200	2.225	2.250	2.275	2.300	2.325	2.350	2.375	2.400	2.425	2.450	2.475	2.500	2.525	2.550	2.575	2.600	2.625	2.650	2.675	2.700	2.725	2.750	2.775	2.800	2.825	2.850	2.875	2.900	2.925	2.950	2.975	3.000	3.025	3.050	3.075	3.100	3.125	3.150	3.175	3.200	3.225	3.250	3.275	3.300	3.325	3.350	3.375	3.400
0.000-0.025											01	01	01	03	03	05	05	07	07	09	09	11	11	13	13	15	15	17	17	19	19	21	21	23	23	25	25	27	27	29	29	31	31	33	33	35	35	37	37
0.026-0.050										01	01	01	03	03	05	05	07	07	09	09	11	11	13	13	15	15	17	17	19	19	21	21	23	23	25	25	27	27	29	29	31	31	33	33	35	35	37	37	39
0.051-0.075									01	01	01	03	03	05	05	07	07	09	09	11	11	13	13	15	15	17	17	19	19	21	21	23	23	25	25	27	27	29	29	31	31	33	33	35	35	37	37	39	39
0.076-0.100								01	01	01	03	03	05	05	07	07	09	09	11	11	13	13	15	15	17	17	19	19	21	21	23	23	25	25	27	27	29	29	31	31	33	33	35	35	37	37	39	39	41
0.101-0.125							01	01	01	03	03	05	05	07	07	09	09	11	11	13	13	15	15	17	17	19	19	21	21	23	23	25	25	27	27	29	29	31	31	33	33	35	35	37	37	39	39	41	41
0.126-0.150						01	01	01	03	03	05	05	07	07	09	09	11	11	13	13	15	15	17	17	19	19	21	21	23	23	25	25	27	27	29	29	31	31	33	33	35	35	37	37	39	39	41	41	43
0.151-0.175					01	01	01	03	03	05	05	07	07	09	09	11	11	13	13	15	15	17	17	19	19	21	21	23	23	25	25	27	27	29	29	31	31	33	33	35	35	37	37	39	39	41	41	43	43
0.176-0.200				01	01	01	03	03	05	05	07	07	09	09	11	11	13	13	15	15	17	17	19	19	21	21	23	23	25	25	27	27	29	29	31	31	33	33	35	35	37	37	39	39	41	41	43	43	45
0.201-0.225			01	01	01	03	03	05	05	07	07	09	09	11	11	13	13	15	15	17	17	19	19	21	21	23	23	25	25	27	27	29	29	31	31	33	33	35	35	37	37	39	39	41	41	43	43	45	45
0.226-0.249		01	01	01	03	03	05	05	07	07	09	09	11	11	13	13	15	15	17	17	19	19	21	21	23	23	25	25	27	27	29	29	31	31	33	33	35	35	37	37	39	39	41	41	43	43	45	45	47
0.250-0.360																																																	
0.351-0.375	03	05	05	07	07	09	09	11	11	13	13	15	15	17	17	19	19	21	21	23	23	25	25	27	27	29	29	31	31	33	33	35	35	37	37	39	39	41	41	43	43	45	45	47	47	49	49	49	
0.376-0.400	05	07	07	09	09	11	11	13	13	15	15	17	17	19	19	21	21	23	23	25	25	27	27	29	29	31	31	33	33	35	35	37	37	39	39	41	41	43	43	45	45	47	47	49	49	49			
0.401-0.425	05	07	07	09	09	11	11	13	13	15	15	17	17	19	19	21	21	23	23	25	25	27	27	29	29	31	31	33	33	35	35	37	37	39	39	41	41	43	43	45	45	47	47	49	49	49			
0.426-0.450	07	09	09	11	11	13	13	15	15	17	17	19	19	21	21	23	23	25	25	27	27	29	29	31	31	33	33	35	35	37	37	39	39	41	41	43	43	45	45	47	47	49	49	49					
0.451-0.475	07	09	09	11	11	13	13	15	15	17	17	19	19	21	21	23	23	25	25	27	27	29	29	31	31	33	33	35	35	37	37	39	39	41	41	43	43	45	45	47	47	49	49	49					
0.476-0.500	09	11	11	13	13	15	15	17	17	19	19	21	21	23	23	25	25	27	27	29	29	31	31	33	33	35	35	37	37	39	39	41	41	43	43	45	45	47	47	49	49	49							
0.501-0.525	09	11	11	13	13	15	15	17	17	19	19	21	21	23	23	25	25	27	27	29	29	31	31	33	33	35	35	37	37	39	39	41	41	43	43	45	45	47	47	49	49	49							
0.526-0.550	11	13	13	15	15	17	17	19	19	21	21	23	23	25	25	27	27	29	29	31	31	33	33	35	35	37	37	39	39	41	41	43	43	45	45	47	47	49	49	49									
0.551-0.575	11	13	13	15	15	17	17	19	19	21	21	23	23	25	25	27	27	29	29	31	31	33	33	35	35	37	37	39	39	41	41	43	43	45	45	47	47	49	49	49									
0.576-0.600	13	15	15	17	17	19	19	21	21	23	23	25	25	27	27	29	29	31	31	33	33	35	35	37	37	39	39	41	41	43	43	45	45	47	47	49	49	49											
0.601-0.625	13	15	15	17	17	19	19	21	21	23	23	25	25	27	27	29	29	31	31	33	33	35	35	37	37	39	39	41	41	43	43	45	45	47	47	49	49	49											
0.626-0.650	15	17	17	19	19	21	21	23	23	25	25	27	27	29	29	31	31	33	33	35	35	37	37	39	39	41	41	43	43	45	45	47	47	49	49	49													
0.651-0.675	15	17	17	19	19	21	21	23	23	25	25	27	27	29	29	31	31	33	33	35	35	37	37	39	39	41	41	43	43	45	45	47	47	49	49	49													
0.676-0.700	17	19	19	21	21	23	23	25	25	27	27	29	29	31	31	33	33	35	35	37	37	39	39	41	41	43	43	45	45	47	47	49	49	49															
0.701-0.725	17	19	19	21	21	23	23	25	25	27	27	29	29	31	31	33	33	35	35	37	37	39	39	41	41	43	43	45	45	47	47	49	49	49															
0.726-0.750	19	21	21	23	23	25	25	27	27	29	29	31	31	33	33	35	35	37	37	39	39	41	41	43	43	45	45	47	47	49	49	49																	
0.751-0.775	19	21	21	23	23	25	25	27	27	29	29	31	31	33	33	35	35	37	37	39	39	41	41	43	43	45	45	47	47	49	49	49																	
0.776-0.800	21	23	23	25	25	27	27	29	29	31	31	33	33	35	35	37	37	39	39	41	41	43	43	45	45	47	47	49	49	49																			
0.801-0.825	21	23	23	25	25	27	27	29	29	31	31	33	33	35	35	37	37	39	39	41	41	43	43	45	45	47	47	49	49	49																			
0.826-0.850	23	25	25	27	27	29	29	31	31	33	33	35	35	37	37	39	39	41	41	43	43	45	45	47	47	49	49	49																					
0.851-0.875	23	25	25	27	27	29	29	31	31	33	33	35	35	37	37	39	39	41	41	43	43	45	45	47	47	49	49	49																					
0.876-0.900	25	27	27	29	29	31	31	33	33	35	35	37	37	39	39	41	41	43	43	45	45	47	47	49	49	49																								
0.901-0.925	25	27	27	29	29	31	31	33	33	35	35	37	37	39	39	41	41	43	43	45	45	47	47	49	49	49																								
0.926-0.950	27	29	29	31	31	33	33	35	35	37	37	39	39	41	41	43	43	45	45	47	47	49	49	49																										
0.951-0.975	27	29	29	31	31	33	33	35	35	37	37	39	39	41	41	43	43	45	45	47	47	49	49	49																										
0.976-1.000	29	31	31	33	33	35	35	37	37	39	39	41	41	43	43	45	45	47	47	49	49	49																												
1.001-1.025	29	31	31	33	33	35	35	37	37	39	39	41	41	43	43	45	45	47	47	49	49	49																												
1.026-1.050	31	33	33	35	35	37	37	39	39	41	41	43	43	45	45	47	47	49	49	49																														
1.051-1.075	31	33	33	35	35	37	37	39	39	41	41	43	43	45	45	47	47	49	49	49																														
1.076-1.100	33	35	35	37	37	39	39	41	41	43	43	45	45	47	47	49	49	49																															
1.101-1.125	33	35	35	37	37	39	39	41	41	43	43	45	45	47	47	49	49	49																															
1.126-1.150	35	37	37	39	39	41	41	43	43	45	45	47	47	49	49	49																																	
1.151-1.175	35	37	37	39	39	41	41	43	43	45	45	47	47	49	49	49																																	
1.176-1.200	37	39	39	41	41	43	43	45	45	47	47	49	49	49																																			
1.201-1.225	37	39	39	41	41	43	43	45	45	47	47	49	49	49																																			
1.226-1.250	39	41	41	43	43	45	45	47	47	49	49	49																																					
1.251-1.275	39	41	41	43	43	45	45	47	47	49	49	49																																					
1.276-1.300	41	43	43	45	45	47	47	49	49	49																																							
1.301-1.325	41	43	43	45	45	47	47	49	49	49																																							
1.326-1.350	43	45	45	47	47	49	49	49																																									
1.351-1.375	43	45	45	47	47	49	49	49																																									
1.376-1.400	45	47	47	49	49	49																																											
1.401-1.425	45	47	47	49	49	49																																											
1.426-1.450	47	49	49	49																																													
1.451-1.475	47	49	49	49																																													
1.476-1.500	49	49	49																																														
1.501-1.525	49	49																																															
1.526-1.550	49																																																

Shim Thickness

Shim No.	Thickness mm (in.)	Shim No.	Thickness mm (in.)
01	2.20 (0.0866)	27	2.85 (0.1122)
03	2.25 (0.0886)	29	2.90 (0.1142)
05	2.30 (0.0906)	31	2.95 (0.1161)
07	2.35 (0.0925)	33	3.00 (0.1181)
09	2.40 (0.0945)	35	3.05 (0.1201)
11	2.45 (0.0965)	37	3.10 (0.1220)
13	2.50 (0.0984)	39	3.15 (0.1240)
15	2.55 (0.1004)	41	3.20 (0.1260)
17	2.60 (0.1024)	43	3.25 (0.1280)
19	2.65 (0.1043)	45	3.30 (0.1299)
21	2.70 (0.1063)	47	3.35 (0.1319)
23	2.75 (0.1083)	49	3.40 (0.1339)
25	2.80 (0.1102)		

Measured Clearance (mm)	Installed Shim Thickness (mm)																																																	
	2.200	2.225	2.250	2.275	2.300	2.325	2.350	2.375	2.400	2.425	2.450	2.475	2.500	2.525	2.550	2.575	2.600	2.625	2.650	2.675	2.700	2.725	2.750	2.775	2.800	2.825	2.850	2.875	2.900	2.925	2.950	2.975	3.000	3.025	3.050	3.075	3.100	3.125	3.150	3.175	3.200	3.225	3.250	3.275	3.300	3.325	3.350	3.375	3.400
0.000-0.020													01	01	03	03	05	05	07	07	09	09	11	11	13	13	15	15	17	17	19	19	21	21	23	23	25	25	27	27	29	29	31	31	33	33	35	35	37
0.021-0.045												01	01	03	03	05	05	07	07	09	09	11	11	13	13	15	15	17	17	19	19	21	21	23	23	25	25	27	27	29	29	31	31	33	33	35	35	37	37
0.046-0.070											01	01	03	03	05	05	07	07	09	09	11	11	13	13	15	15	17	17	19	19	21	21	23	23	25	25	27	27	29	29	31	31	33	33	35	35	37	37	39
0.071-0.095										01	01	03	03	05	05	07	07	09	09	11	11	13	13	15	15	17	17	19	19	21	21	23	23	25	25	27	27	29	29	31	31	33	33	35	35	37	37	39	39
0.096-0.120									01	01	03	03	05	05	07	07	09	09	11	11	13	13	15	15	17	17	19	19	21	21	23	23	25	25	27	27	29	29	31	31	33	33	35	35	37	37	39	39	41
0.121-0.145								01	01	03	03	05	05	07	07	09	09	11	11	13	13	15	15	17	17	19	19	21	21	23	23	25	25	27	27	29	29	31	31	33	33	35	35	37	37	39	39	41	41
0.146-0.170							01	01	03	03	05	05	07	07	09	09	11	11	13	13	15	15	17	17	19	19	21	21	23	23	25	25	27	27	29	29	31	31	33	33	35	35	37	37	39	39	41	41	43
0.171-0.195						01	01	03	03	05	05	07	07	09	09	11	11	13	13	15	15	17	17	19	19	21	21	23	23	25	25	27	27	29	29	31	31	33	33	35	35	37	37	39	39	41	41	43	43
0.196-0.220					01	01	03	03	05	05	07	07	09	09	11	11	13	13	15	15	17	17	19	19	21	21	23	23	25	25	27	27	29	29	31	31	33	33	35	35	37	37	39	39	41	41	43	43	45
0.221-0.245				01	01	03	03	05	05	07	07	09	09	11	11	13	13	15	15	17	17	19	19	21	21	23	23	25	25	27	27	29	29	31	31	33	33	35	35	37	37	39	39	41	41	43	43	45	45
0.246-0.269			01	01	03	03	05	05	07	07	09	09	11	11	13	13	15	15	17	17	19	19	21	21	23	23	25	25	27	27	29	29	31	31	33	33	35	35	37	37	39	39	41	41	43	43	45	45	47
0.270-0.370																																																	
0.371-0.395	03	05	05	07	07	09	09	11	11	13	13	15	15	17	17	19	19	21	21	23	23	25	25	27	27	29	29	31	31	33	33	35	35	37	37	39	39	41	41	43	43	45	45	47	47	49	49		
0.396-0.420	05	05	07	07	09	09	11	11	13	13	15	15	17	17	19	19	21	21	23	23	25	25	27	27	29	29	31	31	33	33	35	35	37	37	39	39	41	41	43	43	45	45	47	47	49	49			
0.421-0.445	05	07	07	09	09	11	11	13	13	15	15	17	17	19	19	21	21	23	23	25	25	27	27	29	29	31	31	33	33	35	35	37	37	39	39	41	41	43	43	45	45	47	47	49	49				
0.446-0.470	07	07	09	09	11	11	13	13	15	15	17	17	19	19	21	21	23	23	25	25	27	27	29	29	31	31	33	33	35	35	37	37	39	39	41	41	43	43	45	45	47	47	49	49					
0.471-0.495	07	09	09	11	11	13	13	15	15	17	17	19	19	21	21	23	23	25	25	27	27	29	29	31	31	33	33	35	35	37	37	39	39	41	41	43	43	45	45	47	47	49	49						
0.496-0.520	09	09	11	11	13	13	15	15	17	17	19	19	21	21	23	23	25	25	27	27	29	29	31	31	33	33	35	35	37	37	39	39	41	41	43	43	45	45	47	47	49	49							
0.521-0.545	09	11	11	13	13	15	15	17	17	19	19	21	21	23	23	25	25	27	27	29	29	31	31	33	33	35	35	37	37	39	39	41	41	43	43	45	45	47	47	49	49								
0.546-0.570	11	11	13	13	15	15	17	17	19	19	21	21	23	23	25	25	27	27	29	29	31	31	33	33	35	35	37	37	39	39	41	41	43	43	45	45	47	47	49	49									
0.571-0.595	11	13	13	15	15	17	17	19	19	21	21	23	23	25	25	27	27	29	29	31	31	33	33	35	35	37	37	39	39	41	41	43	43	45	45	47	47	49	49										
0.596-0.620	13	13	15	15	17	17	19	19	21	21	23	23	25	25	27	27	29	29	31	31	33	33	35	35	37	37	39	39	41	41	43	43	45	45	47	47	49	49											
0.621-0.645	13	15	15	17	17	19	19	21	21	23	23	25	25	27	27	29	29	31	31	33	33	35	35	37	37	39	39	41	41	43	43	45	45	47	47	49	49												
0.646-0.670	15	15	17	17	19	19	21	21	23	23	25	25	27	27	29	29	31	31	33	33	35	35	37	37	39	39	41	41	43	43	45	45	47	47	49	49													
0.671-0.695	15	17	17	19	19	21	21	23	23	25	25	27	27	29	29	31	31	33	33	35	35	37	37	39	39	41	41	43	43	45	45	47	47	49	49														
0.696-0.720	17	17	19	19	21	21	23	23	25	25	27	27	29	29	31	31	33	33	35	35	37	37	39	39	41	41	43	43	45	45	47	47	49	49															
0.721-0.745	17	19	19	21	21	23	23	25	25	27	27	29	29	31	31	33	33	35	35	37	37	39	39	41	41	43	43	45	45	47	47	49	49																
0.746-0.770	19	19	21	21	23	23	25	25	27	27	29	29	31	31	33	33	35	35	37	37	39	39	41	41	43	43	45	45	47	47	49	49																	
0.771-0.795	19	21	21	23	23	25	25	27	27	29	29	31	31	33	33	35	35	37	37	39	39	41	41	43	43	45	45	47	47	49	49																		
0.796-0.820	21	21	23	23	25	25	27	27	29	29	31	31	33	33	35	35	37	37	39	39	41	41	43	43	45	45	47	47	49	49																			
0.821-0.845	21	23	23	25	25	27	27	29	29	31	31	33	33	35	35	37	37	39	39	41	41	43	43	45	45	47	47	49	49																				
0.846-0.870	23	23	25	25	27	27	29	29	31	31	33	33	35	35	37	37	39	39	41	41	43	43	45	45	47	47	49	49																					
0.871-0.895	23	25	25	27	27	29	29	31	31	33	33	35	35	37	37	39	39	41	41	43	43	45	45	47	47	49	49																						
0.896-0.920	25	25	27	27	29	29	31	31	33	33	35	35	37	37	39	39	41	41	43	43	45	45	47	47	49	49																							
0.921-0.945	25	27	27	29	29	31	31	33	33	35	35	37	37	39	39	41	41	43	43	45	45	47	47	49	49																								
0.946-0.970	27	27	29	29	31	31	33	33	35	35	37	37	39	39	41	41	43	43	45	45	47	47	49	49																									
0.971-0.995	27	29	29	31	31	33	33	35	35	37	37	39	39	41	41	43	43	45	45	47	47	49	49																										
0.996-1.020	29	29	31	31	33	33	35	35	37	37	39	39	41	41	43	43	45	45	47	47	49	49																											
1.021-1.045	29	31	31	33	33	35	35	37	37	39	39	41	41	43	43	45	45	47	47	49	49																												
1.046-1.070	31	31	33	33	35	35	37	37	39	39	41	41	43	43	45	45	47	47	49	49																													
1.071-1.095	31	33	33	35	35	37	37	39	39	41	41	43	43	45	45	47	47	49	49																														
1.096-1.120	33	33	35	35	37	37	39	39	41	41	43	43	45	45	47	47	49	49																															
1.121-1.145	33	35	35	37	37	39	39	41	41	43	43	45	45	47	47	49	49																																
1.146-1.170	35	35	37	37	39	39	41	41	43	43	45	45	47	47	49	49																																	
1.171-1.195	35	37	37	39	39	41	41	43	43	45	45	47	47	49	49																																		
1.196-1.220	37	37	39	39	41	41	43	43	45	45	47	47	49	49																																			
1.221-1.245	37	39	39	41	41	43	43	45	45	47	47	49	49																																				
1.246-1.270	39	39	41	41	43	43	45	45	47	47	49	49																																					
1.271-1.295	39	41	41	43	43	45	45	47	47	49	49																																						
1.296-1.320	41	41	43	43	45	45	47	47	49	49																																							
1.321-1.345	41	43	43	45	45	47	47	49	49																																								
1.346-1.370	43	43	45	45	47	47	49	49																																									
1.371-1.395	43	45	45	47	47	49	49																																										
1.396-1.420	45	45	47	47	49	49																																											
1.421-1.445	45	47	47	49	49																																												
1.446-1.470	47	47	49	49																																													
1.471-1.495	47	49	49																																														
1.496-1.520	49	49																																															
1.521-1.545	49																																																

Exhaust shim selection chart — 1988 3VZ–E engine

Intake shim selection chart—1989–92 3VZ–E engine

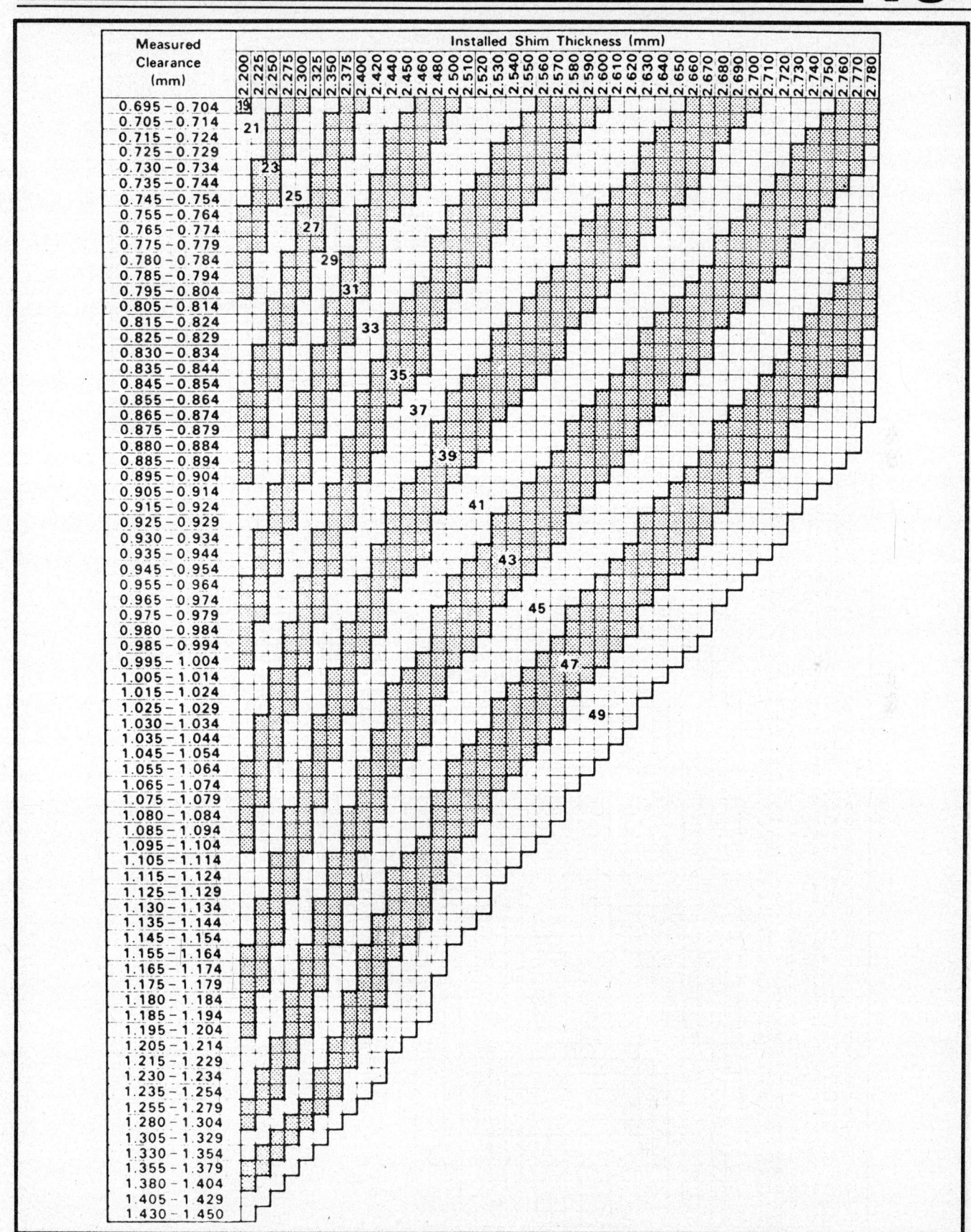

Intake shim selection chart (cont) — 1989-92 3VZ-E engine

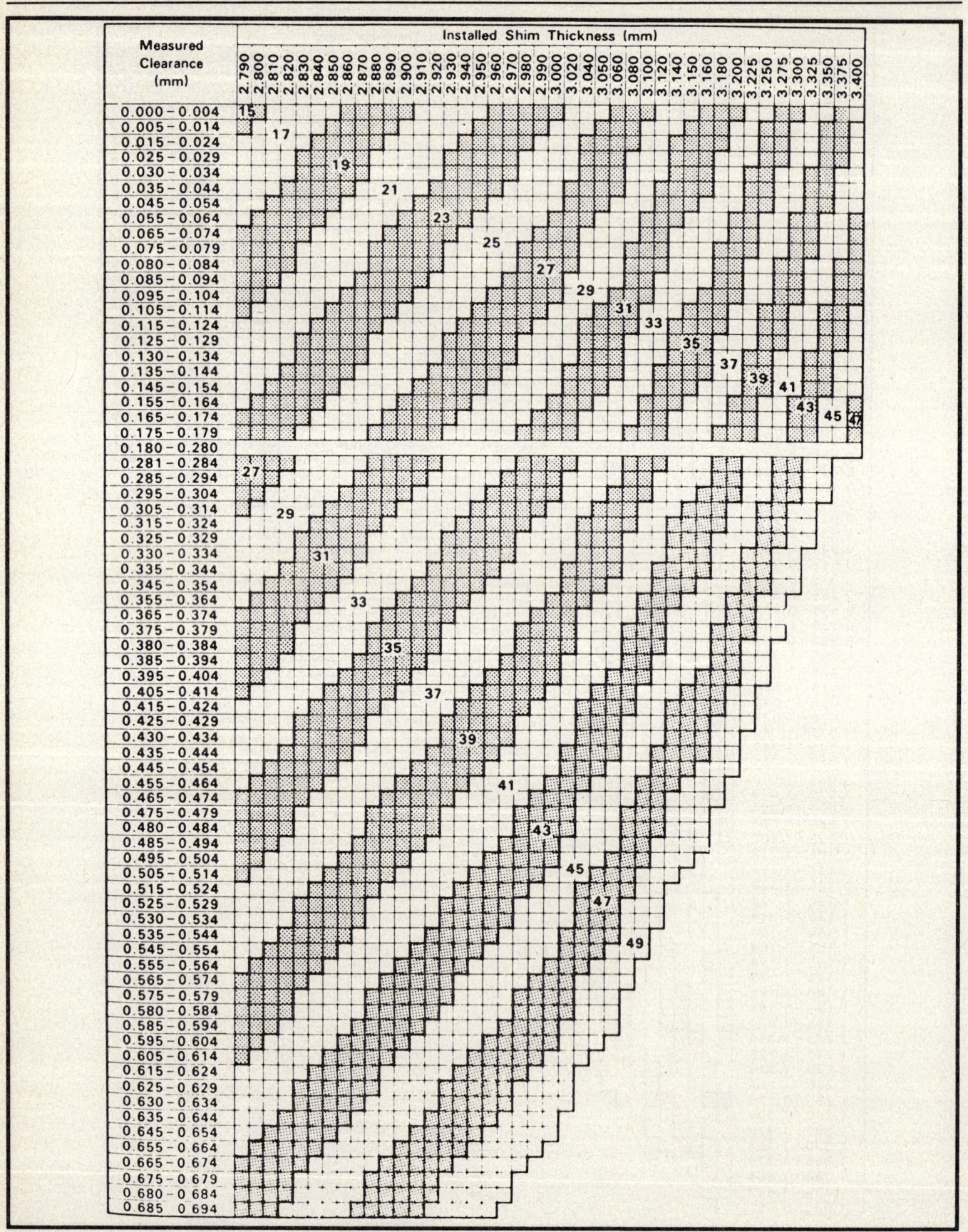

Intake shim selection chart (cont) – 1989–92 3VZ–E engine

Shim Thickness

Shim No.	Thickness mm (in.)	Shim No.	Thickness mm (in.)
01	2.20 (0.0866)	27	2.85 (0.1122)
03	2.25 (0.0886)	29	2.90 (0.1142)
05	2.30 (0.0906)	31	2.95 (0.1161)
07	2.35 (0.0925)	33	3.00 (0.1181)
09	2.40 (0.0945)	35	3.05 (0.1201)
11	2.45 (0.0965)	37	3.10 (0.1220)
13	2.50 (0.0984)	39	3.15 (0.1240)
15	2.55 (0.1004)	41	3.20 (0.1260)
17	2.60 (0.1024)	43	3.25 (0.1280)
19	2.65 (0.1043)	45	3.30 (0.1299)
21	2.70 (0.1063)	47	3.35 (0.1319)
23	2.75 (0.1083)	49	3.40 (0.1339)
25	2.80 (0.1102)		

Intake shim selection chart (cont) — 1989–92 3VZ–E engine

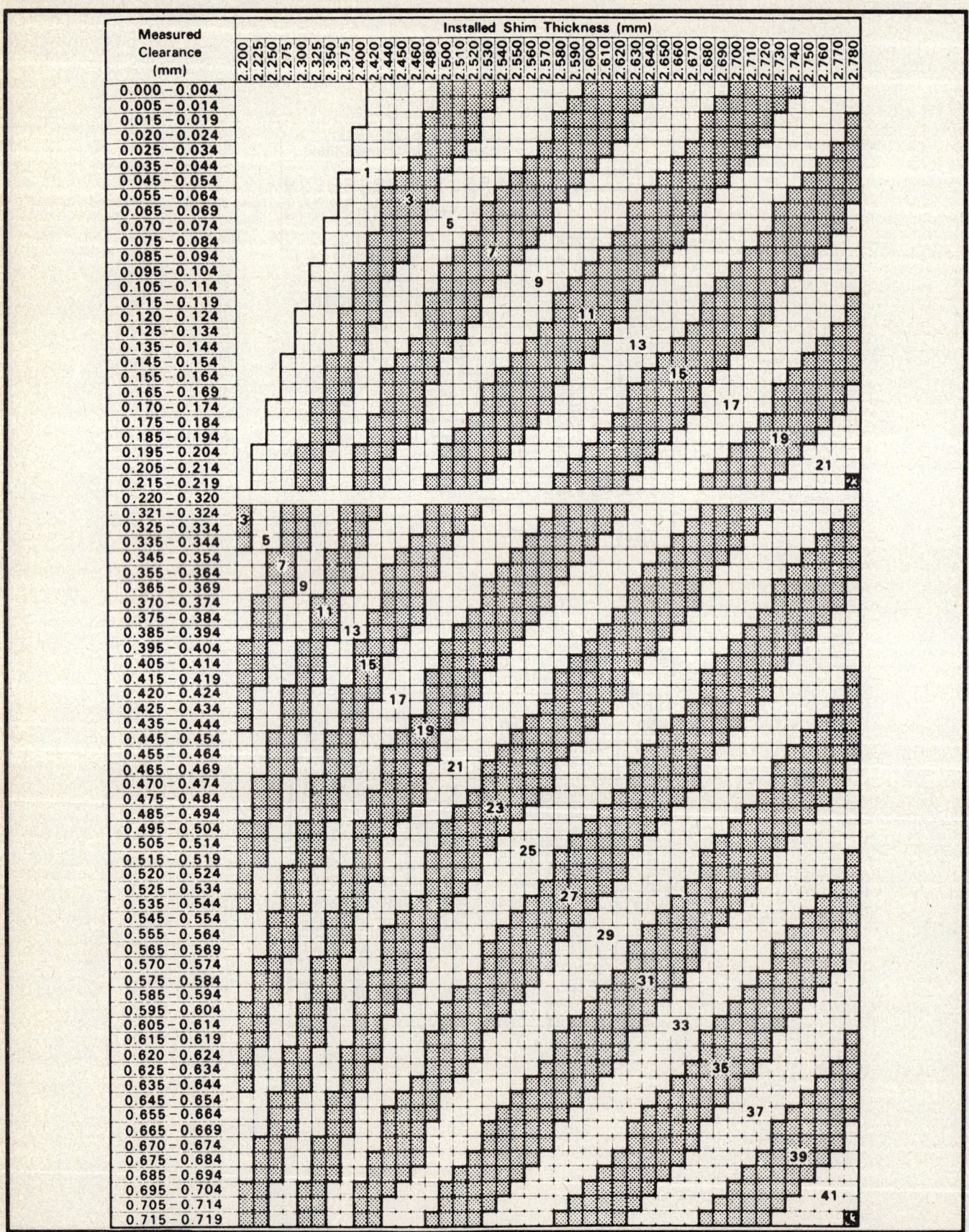

Exhaust shim selection chart—1989–92 3VZ–E engine

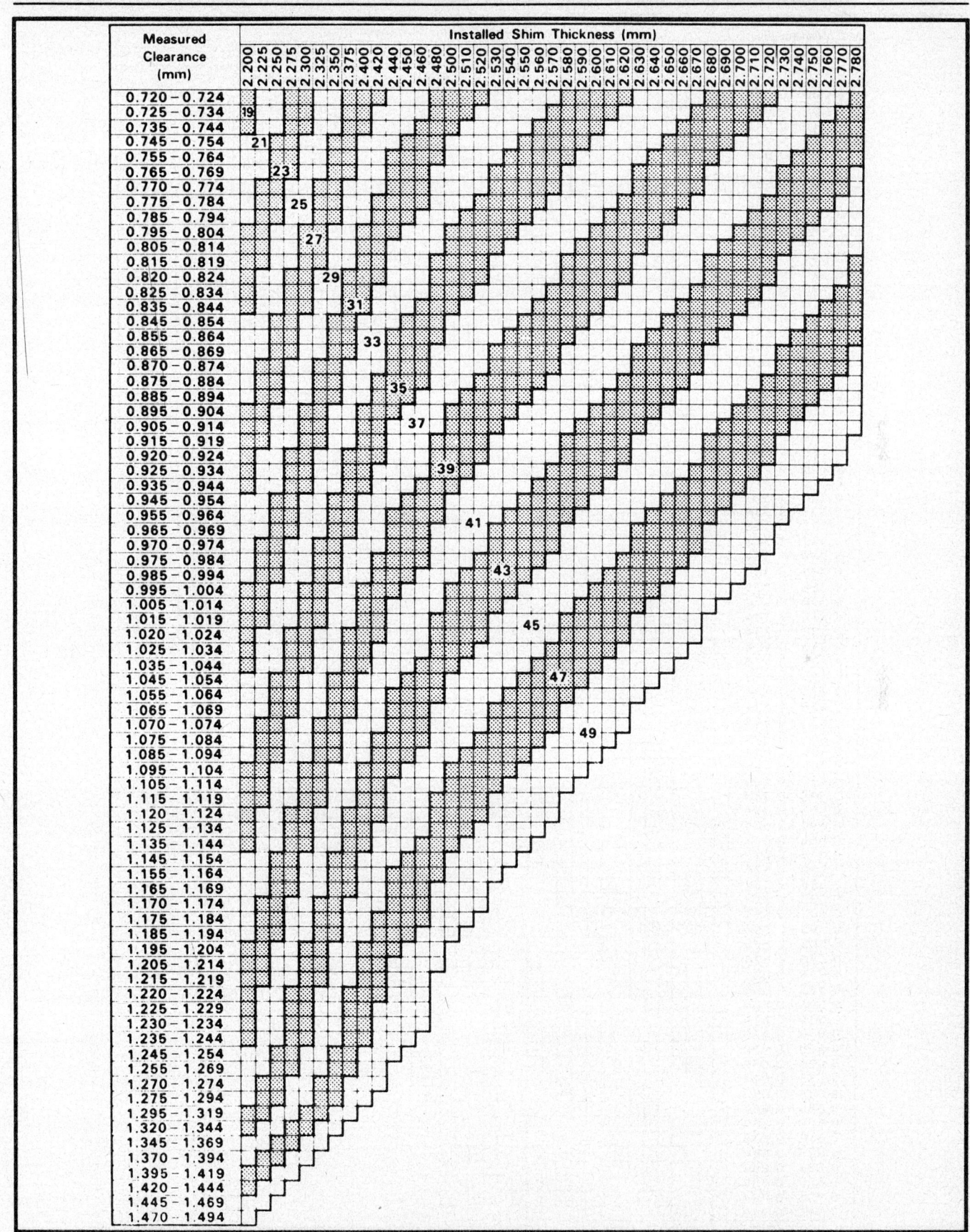

Exhaust shim selection chart (cont) – 1989–92 3VZ–E engine

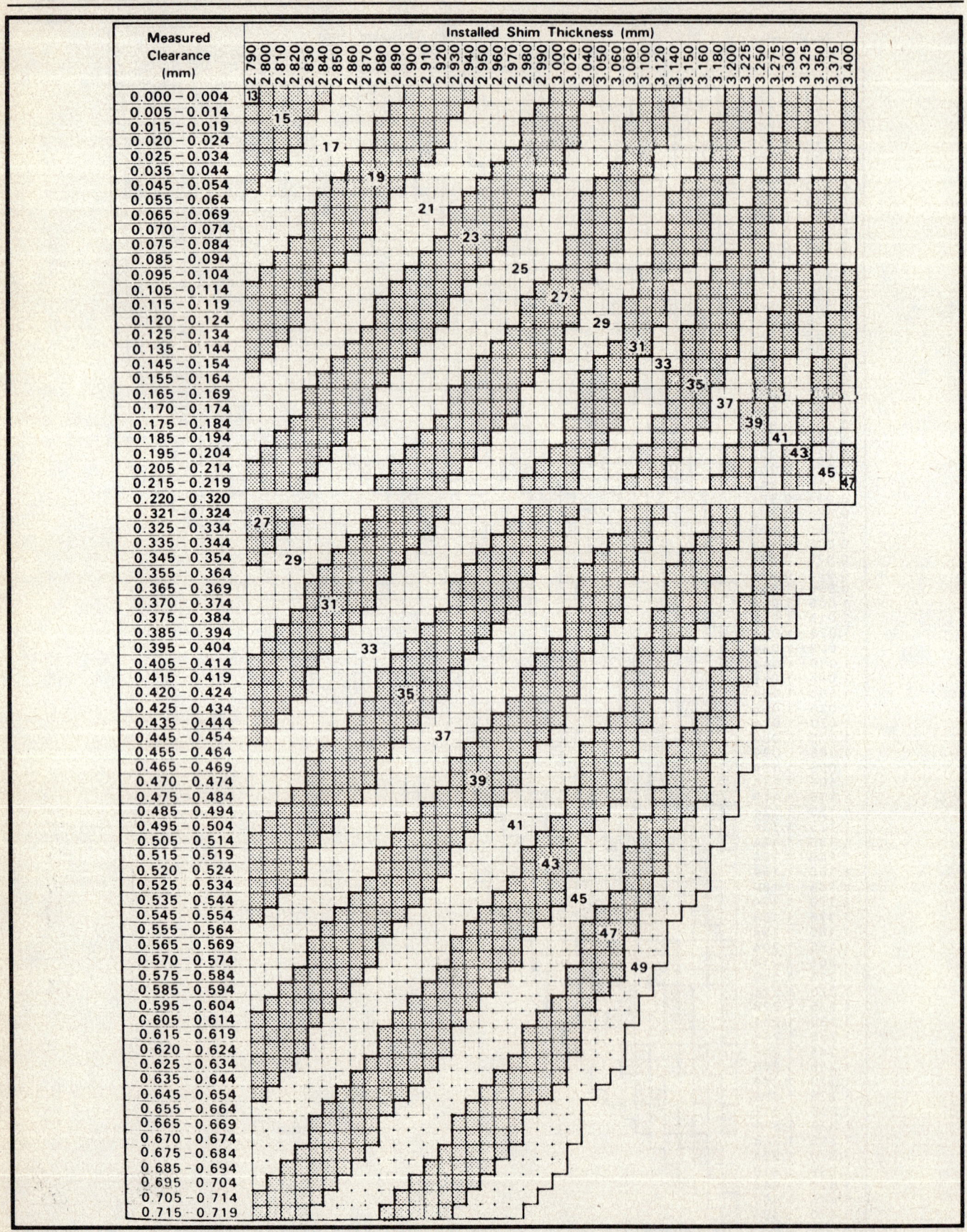

Exhaust shim selection chart (cont) — 1989–92 3VZ–E engine

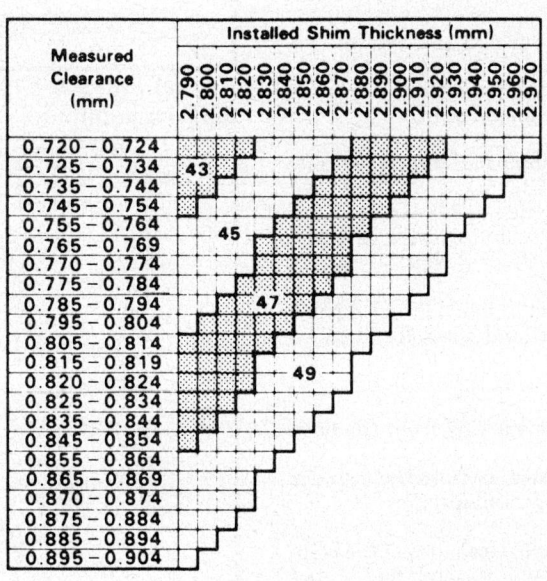

Shim Thickness

Shim No.	Thickness mm (in.)	Shim No.	Thickness mm (in.)
01	2.20 (0.0866)	27	2.85 (0.1122)
03	2.25 (0.0886)	29	2.90 (0.1142)
05	2.30 (0.0906)	31	2.95 (0.1161)
07	2.35 (0.0925)	33	3.00 (0.1181)
09	2.40 (0.0945)	35	3.05 (0.1201)
11	2.45 (0.0965)	37	3.10 (0.1220)
13	2.50 (0.0984)	39	3.15 (0.1240)
15	2.55 (0.1004)	41	3.20 (0.1260)
17	2.60 (0.1024)	43	3.25 (0.1280)
19	2.65 (0.1043)	45	3.30 (0.1299)
21	2.70 (0.1063)	47	3.35 (0.1319)
23	2.75 (0.1083)	49	3.40 (0.1339)
25	2.80 (0.1102)		

Rocker Arm Shafts

Removal and Installation

22R, 22R-E AND 22R-TE ENGINES

1. Remove the valve cover.
2. Remove the timing chain sprocket and secure the sprocket and chain to the engine with wire to ensure correct valve timing.
3. Remove the distributor drive gear and fuel pump for 22R engine.
4. Uniformly loosen the 10 shaft bolts in the opposite sequence of tightening.
5. Remove the rocker arm shaft assembly from the cylinder head. Keep the assembly together for installation.

To install:

6. Install the rocker arm shaft assembly and torque the bolts in 3 steps, in sequence to 58 ft. lbs. (78 Nm).
7. Install the chain cover bolt and torque to 9 ft. lbs. (13 Nm).
8. Install timing chain sprocket, distributor drive gear and thrust plate. Torque the bolt to 58 ft. lbs. (78 Nm).
9. Adjust the valve clearance.
10. Install the valve cover and torque to 69 ft. lbs. (7.8 Nm).
11. Install the remaining components and check for leaks.

3F-E AND 4Y-EC ENGINES

1. Remove the valve cover.
2. Uniformly loosen the shaft bolts starting from the ends and working inward.
3. Remove the rocker arm shaft assembly from the cylinder head. Keep the assembly together for installation.

To install:

4. Install the rocker arm shaft assembly and torque the bolts in 3 steps, start in the middle and move to the ends and torque in sequence to 17 ft. lbs. (24 Nm) and 25 ft. lbs. (33 Nm) for the bolt and nut combination.
5. Adjust the valve clearance.
6. Install the valve cover and torque to 69 ft. lbs. (7.8 Nm).
7. Install the remaining components and check for leaks.

Intake Manifold

Removal and Installation

22R ENGINE

1. Disconnect the negative battery cable.
2. Drain the cooling system.
3. Remove the air cleaner assembly, complete with hoses, from the carburetor.
4. Disconnect the vacuum lines from the EGR valve and carburetor. Mark them first to aid in the installation.
5. Remove the fuel lines, electrical leads, accelerator linkage, and water hose from the carburetor.
6. Remove the water bypass hose from the manifold.
7. Unbolt and remove the intake manifold, complete with carburetor and EGR valve.
8. Cover the cylinder head ports with clean shop cloths to keep anything from falling into the cylinder head or block.

To install:

9. When installing the manifold, replace the gasket with a new one. Torque the mounting bolts to 14 ft. lbs. (19 Nm). Tighten the bolts in several stages working from the inside bolts outward.
10. Connect the bypass line and all other lines and hoses.
11. Install the air cleaner and refill the cooling system.

22R-E AND 22R-TE ENGINES

1. Relieve the fuel system pressure. Disconnect the negative battery cable.
2. Drain the cooling system.
3. Disconnect the air intake hose from both the air cleaner assembly on one end and the air intake chamber on the other.

Rocker arm shaft torque sequence—22R, 22R-E, 22R-TE engines

Intake manifold assembly—22R-E and 22R-TE engines

4. Tag and disconnect all vacuum lines attached to the intake chamber and manifold.
5. Tag and disconnect the wires to the cold start injector, throttle position sensor and the water hoses from the throttle body.
6. Remove the EGR valve from the intake chamber.
7. Tag and disconnect the actuator cable, accelerator cable and throttle valve cable, if equipped, from the cable bracket on the intake chamber.
8. Unbolt the air intake chamber from the intake manifold and remove the chamber with the throttle body attached.
9. Disconnect the fuel hose from the fuel delivery pipe.
10. Tag and disconnect the air valve hose from the intake manifold.
11. Make sure all hoses, lines and wires are tagged for later installation and disconnected from the intake manifold. Unbolt the manifold from the cylinder head, removing the delivery pipe and injection nozzle with the manifold.

To install:

12. Clean the gasket mating surfaces and check for warpage.
13. Install the gasket and manifold. Torque the bolts to 13 ft. lbs. (18 Nm) starting from the middle and move outward.
14. Install the remaining components and check for leaks.

3VZ-E ENGINE

1. Relieve the fuel system pressure. Disconnect the negative battery cable.
2. Drain the cooling system.
3. Disconnect the air intake hose from both the air cleaner assembly on one end and the air intake chamber on the other.
4. Tag and disconnect all vacuum lines attached to the intake chamber and manifold.
5. Disconnect the throttle position sensor connector at the air chamber. Disconnect the PCV hose at the union.

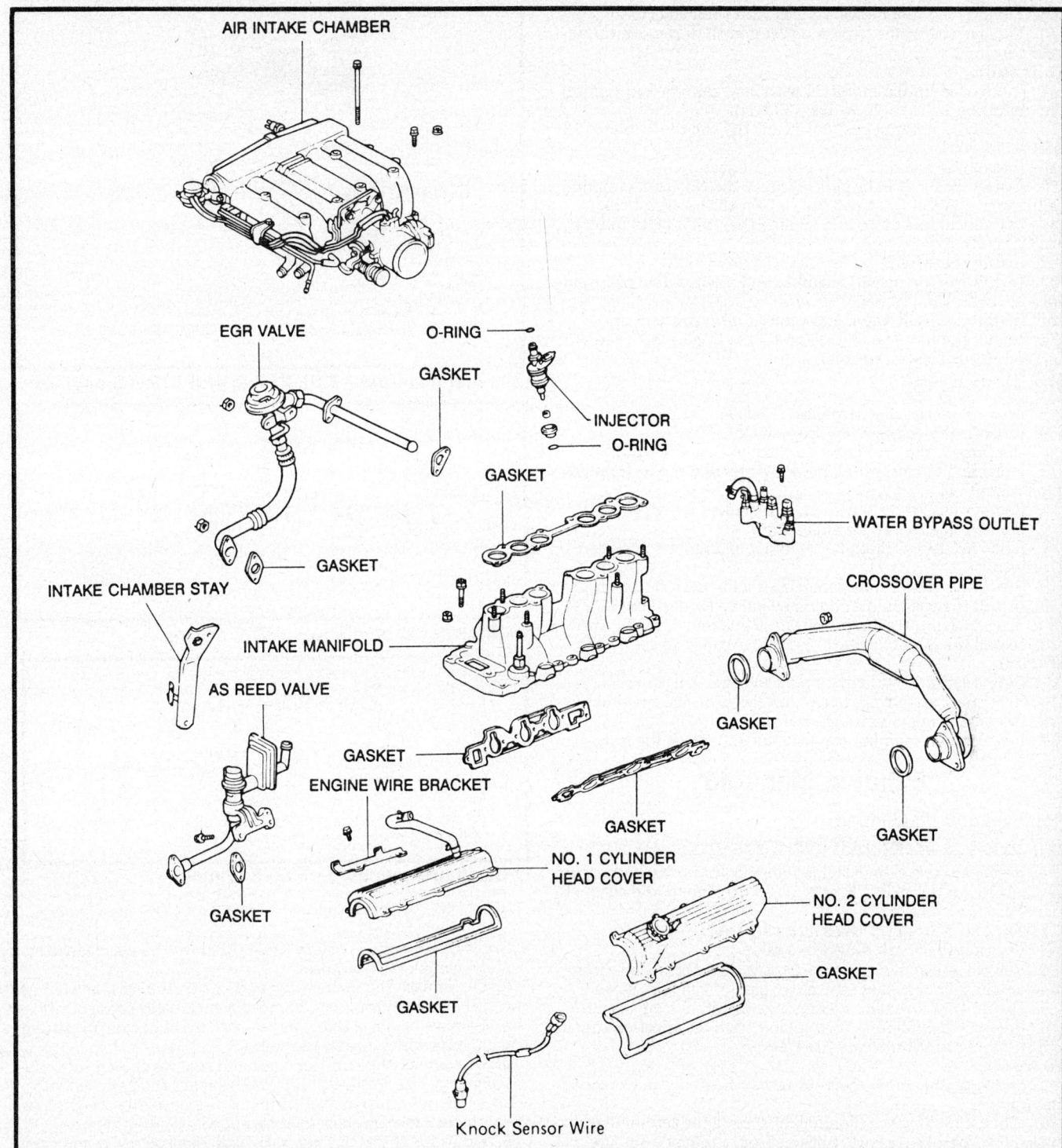

AIR INTAKE CHAMBER

EGR VALVE

O-RING

GASKET

INJECTOR

O-RING

GASKET

WATER BYPASS OUTLET

GASKET

CROSSOVER PIPE

INTAKE CHAMBER STAY

INTAKE MANIFOLD

GASKET

GASKET

AS REED VALVE

GASKET

ENGINE WIRE BRACKET

GASKET

NO. 1 CYLINDER HEAD COVER

GASKET

GASKET

NO. 2 CYLINDER HEAD COVER

GASKET

GASKET

Knock Sensor Wire

Intake manifold assembly – 3VZ–E engine

6. Disconnect the No. 4 water bypass hose at the manifold. Remove the No. 5 bypass hose at the water bypass pipe.

7. Disconnect the cold start injector and the vacuum hose at the fuel filter.

8. Remove the union bolt and gaskets, then remove the cold start injector tube.

9. Disconnect the EGR gas temperature sensor and the EGR vacuum hoses from the air pipe and the vacuum modulator.

10. Remove the EGR valve.

11. Disconnect the No. 1 air hose at the reed valve.

12. Remove the air intake chamber and then remove the engine wire.

13. Remove the union bolts and then remove the No. 2 and 3 fuel pipes.

14. Remove the No. 4 timing belt cover. Remove the the No. 2 idler pulley and the No. 3 timing belt cover.

15. Remove the fuel delivery pipes with their injectors.

16. Remove the water bypass outlet and then remove the intake manifold.

To install:

17. Install the intake manifold with new gaskets and tighten the mounting bolts to 29 ft. lbs. (39 Nm).

18. Install the water bypass outlet and tighten the 2 bolts to 13 ft. lbs. (18 Nm).

19. Install the fuel delivery pipes and injectors.

20. Install the No. 2 idler pulley. Install the No. 3 and 4 timing belt covers and tighten the bolts to 74 inch lbs. (8.3 Nm).

21. Install the fuel pipes and tighten the union bolts to 22 ft. lbs. (29 Nm).

22. Install the engine wire.

23. Install the air intake chamber and tighten the nuts and bolts to 13 ft. lbs. (18 Nm).

24. Install the EGR valve and connect all hoses and lines.

25. Install the air cleaner hose, refill the engine with coolant and connect the battery cable.

2TZ–FE ENGINE

1. Disconnect the negative battery cable.

2. Remove the engine from the vehicle.

3. Disconnect the fuel pipes and remove the fuel rail.

4. Label and disconnect all hoses, wiring and cables from the intake manifold.

5. Remove the water outlet and disconnect the PCV hose.

6. Remove the intake manifold stays.

7. Remove the retaining bolts, intake manifold and gasket.

To install:

8. Clean the gasket mating surfaces and check for warpage.

9. Install the gasket, manifold and bolts. Torque the bolts to 15 ft. lbs. (21 Nm), starting from the inside and work outward.

10. Install the manifold stays and torque the bolts to 27 ft. lbs. (37 Nm).

11. Connect the water bypass pipe and fuel rail.

12. Reconnect all wiring, hoses and cables to the manifold.

13. Install the engine into the vehicle.

14. Install the remaining components and check for leaks.

Exhaust Manifold

Removal and Installation

22R, 22R–E, 22R–TE AND 3VZ–E ENGINES

1. Remove the 3 exhaust pipe flange bolts for turbocharger flange bolts on the 22R–TE engine and disconnect the exhaust pipe from the manifold.

2. Tag and disconnect the spark plug leads.

3. Position the spark plug wires aside.

4. Remove the air cleaner tube from the heat stove, on carbureted engines, and remove the outer part of the heat stove.

5. Use a 14mm wrench to remove the manifold securing nuts.

6. Remove the manifold(s), complete with air injection tubes and the inner portion of the heat stove.

To install:

7. Separate the inner portion of the heat stove from the manifold.

8. When installing the manifold(s), torque the retaining nuts to 29–36 ft. lbs. (41–49 Nm), working from the inside out, and in several stages. Install the distributor and set the timing. Tighten the exhaust pipe flange nuts to 25–32 ft. lbs. (34–45 Nm).

9. Install the remaining components and check for leaks.

Combinaton Manifold

Removal and Installation

3F–E ENGINE

1. Relieve the fuel system pressure on the 3F–E engine. Dis-

1. Inner heat stove
2. Exhaust manifold
3. Gasket
4. Gasket
5. Outer heat stove

Exhaust manifold—22R, 22R–E and 22R–TE engines

Right exhaust manifold—3VZ–E engine

Left exhaust manifold—3VZ–E engine

connect the negative battery cable. Remove the air cleaner assembly, complete with hoses.

2. Disconnect the accelerator and choke linkages, as well as the fuel and vacuum lines. Remove the throttle linkage.

3. Remove or move aside, any of the emission control system components which are in the way.

4. Disconnect the oil filter lines and remove the oil filter assembly from the intake manifold. Unfasten the solenoid valve wire from the ignition coil terminal. Remove the EGR pipes from the exhaust gas cooler, if equipped.

5. Unfasten the retaining bolts and remove the carburetor from the manifold. On the fuel injected engine, disconnect the throttle chamber from the manifold.

6. Loosen the manifold retaining nuts, working from the inside out, in 2–3 stages.

7. Remove the intake/exhaust manifold assembly from the cylinder head as a complete unit.

To install:

8. Clean the gasket mating surfaces and check for warpage.

9. When installing the manifolds, always use new gaskets. Torque the bolts to 36 ft. lbs. (49 Nm) working from the inside out.

SEAL WASHER

CYLINDER HEAD COVER

GASKET

ROCKER ARM AND SPRING

ROCKER ARM SHAFT

PUSH ROD

SPARK PLUG

SPARK PLUG TUBE

VALVE KEEPER

GASKET

SPRING RETAINER

VALVE SPRING

EGR GAST TEMP. SENSOR

OIL SEAL

CYLINDER HEAD

GASKET

EGR VALVE

SPRING SEAT

ENGINE REAR PLATE

SNAP RING

VALVE GUIDE BUSHING

AIR INTAKE
CHAMBER

WATER OUTLET

GASKET

GASKET

GASKET

GASKET

HEATER OUTLET
VALVE

GASKET

CYLINDER HEAD GASKET

GASKET

VALVE

THROTTLE BODY

MANIFOLD STAY

INTAKE AND EXHAUST MANIFOLD

Intake manifold assembly – 4YE–C engine

4Y–EC ENGINE

1. Relieve the fuel system pressure. Disconnect the negative battery terminal from the battery. Remove the right seat and the engine service hole cover.
2. Drain the engine coolant to a level below the throttle body.
3. Remove the air cleaner-to-throttle body hose.
4. Remove the accelerator cable with the bracket from the throttle body.
5. Disconnect the air valve connector, the throttle position sensor connector and the O_2 sensor connector.
6. Disconnect the PCV hose from the air intake chamber, the water bypass hoses from the throttle body, the booster vacuum hose and the charcoal canister hose, then label and disconnect the emission control hoses.
7. Remove the throttle body from the air intake chamber, the EGR tube union nut from the exhaust manifold, the EGR valve from the air intake chamber.
8. Disconnect the cold start injector tube, the water bypass hoses and the pressure regulator hose from the intake manifold.
9. Remove the air intake chamber brackets and the air intake chamber with the air valve from the intake manifold.
10. Remove the wire clamp bolt from the fuel injector rail, then, the fuel injector rail from the fuel injectors.
11. Remove the exhaust manifold-to-intake manifold bracket, the exhaust manifold-to-engine bracket, the exhaust pipe from the exhaust manifold, the fuel inlet and outlet tubes union nut from the fuel rail.
12. Remove the spark plug wires, the spark plugs and the tubes.
13. Remove the retaining bolts, then, the intake/exhaust manifolds as an assembly.

To install:
14. Clean the gasket mounting surfaces and check for leakage.
15. Use new gaskets and reverse the removal procedures. Torque the manifold-to-cylinder head bolts to 36 ft. lbs. (48 Nm), the air intake chamber-to-intake manifold bolts to 9 ft. lbs. (14 Nm) and the throttle body bolts to 9 ft. lbs. (14 Nm).
16. Refill the cooling system. Start the engine, allow it to reach operating temperatures and check for leaks.

Turbocharger

Removal and Installation

22R–TE ENGINE

1. Disconnect the negative battery cable.
2. Drain the coolant.
3. Disconnect the oxygen sensor wire clamp and connector.
4. Disconnect the No. 1 and 3 PCV hoses.
5. Disconnect the No. 1 and 2 turbocharger water hoses.
6. Loosen the clamp on the throttle body, remove the nuts and lift off the air tube assembly.
7. Remove the No. 1 air cleaner hose assembly and the No. 2 air cleaner hose.
8. Remove the exhaust manifold and turbocharger heat insulators.
9. Disconnect the No. 3 turbocharger water hose.
10. Raise and safely support the vehicle. Disconnect the exhaust pipe from the turbine outlet.
11. Remove the turbocharger bracket stay.
12. Disconnect the turbocharger oil pipe.
13. Remove the turbocharger and exhaust manifold as an assembly.
14. Remove the No. 2 turbocharger water pipe.
15. Remove the oil pipe.
16. Remove the No. 1 water pipe.
17. Remove the turbine outlet elbow with the O_2 sensor attached.
18. Disconnect the turbocharger from the manifold.

To install:
19. Pour approximately 20cc of new oil into the oil inlet and then turn the turbocharger impeller wheel so as to wet the bearing.
20. Using a new gasket, attach the turbocharger to the manifold and tighten the nuts to 29 ft. lbs. (39 Nm).
21. Install the turbine outlet elbow and tighten the nuts to 19 ft. lbs. (25 Nm).
22. Install the No. 1 water pipe. Install the turbo oil pipe and tighten the nuts to 14 ft. lbs. (19 Nm).
23. Install the No. 2 water pipe and then mount the assembly to the cylinder head.
24. Install the oil pipe and tighten the union bolt to 20 ft. lbs. (27 Nm). Tighten the nuts to 14 ft. lbs. (19 Nm).
7. Install the turbocharger bracket stay.
25. Connect the exhaust pipe to the turbine outlet elbow and tighten the nuts to 32 ft. lbs. (43 Nm). Lower the truck.
26. Connect the No. 3 water hose and install the heat insulators.
27. Install the No. 2 air cleaner hose with the arrow facing the turbocharger and fasten the clip as shown.
28. Install the air tube assembly. Connect the O_2 sensor and clamp.
29. Refill the engine with coolant, start it and check for leaks.

Timing Chain Front Cover

Removal and Installation

22R, 22R–E AND 22R–TE ENGINES

1. Disconnect the negative battery cable. Remove the cylinder head.
2. Remove the radiator.
3. Remove the alternator. Remove the oil pan.
4. On engines equipped with air pumps, unfasten the adjusting link bolts and the drive belt. Remove the hoses from the pump; remove the pump and bracket from the engine.
5. Remove the fan and water pump as a complete assembly.

NOTE: To prevent the fluid from running out of the fan coupling, do not tip the assembly over on its side.

6. Unfasten the crankshaft pulley securing bolt and remove the pulley with a suitable puller.
7. Remove the water bypass pipe.
8. Remove the fan belt adjusting bar.
9. Disconnect and remove the heater water outlet pipe. On the 22R–TE engine, remove the No. 3 turbocharger water pipe.
10. Remove the bolts securing the timing chain cover. Remove the cover.

To install:
11. Install the cover and tighten the 8mm bolts to 9 ft. lbs. (13 Nm). Tighten the 10mm bolts to 29 ft. lbs. (39 Nm). Apply sealer to the gaskets for both the timing chain cover and the oil pan.
12. Install the fan belt adjusting bar and tighten it to 9 ft. lbs. (13 Nm).

Timing chain cover removal—3F–E engine

Exhaust manifold and turbocharger assembly—22R– TE engine

13. Install the heater water outlet pipe and the No. 3 turbo water hose. Install the water bypass pipe.

14. Install the crankshaft pulley and tighten the bolt to the proper torque.

15. Install the water pump and fluid coupling. Install the air conditioning compressor and then adjust the tension on all drive belts.

16. Install the oil pan. Install the radiator and then install the cylinder head.

17. Refill the engine with oil and coolant. Road test the vehicle and check for leaks.

3F–E ENGINE

1. Disconnect the negative battery cable and drain the coolant.

2. Disconnect the accelerator and throttle cables.

3. Remove the air intake hose, air flow meter and air cleaner as an assembly.

Timing chain and sprockets—22R, 22R–E and 22R–TE engines

4. Loosen the power steering pump drive pulley nut.

5. Remove the fluid coupling with the fan and water pump pulley.

6. Remove the power steering pump and the air conditioning compressor. Remove their brackets. Remove the power steering pump idler pulley and its bracket.

7. Remove the cylinder head cover. Remove the rocker shaft assembly.

8. Remove the distributor.

9. Remove the pushrod cover and then remove the valve lifters. Be certain that they are kept in order.

10. Loosen the 6 bolts and then slide the power steering pump pulley off the crankshaft.

11. Using special tool 09213–58011 or equivalent, and a 46mm socket wrench, remove the crankshaft pulley bolt. Remove the pulley.

12. Remove the oil cooler pipe and its hose.

13. Remove the timing gear cover and gasket.

To install:

14. There are 3 sizes of timing gear cover bolts. Apply adhesive to the two **A** bolts. Install a new gasket and then position the cover. Finger tighten all bolts. Align the crankshaft pulley set key with the groove of the pulley; gently tap the pulley onto the crankshaft. Tighten the cover bolts marked **A** to 18 ft. lbs. (25 Nm). Tighten those marked **B** or **C** to 43 inch lbs. (5 Nm). Tighten the pulley bolt to 253 ft. lbs. (343 Nm).

15. Position the power steering pulley on the crankshaft and tighten the bolts to 13 ft. lbs. (18 Nm).

16. Insert the valve lifters into their bores and install the pushrod cover. Tighten the bolts to 35 inch lbs. (4 Nm). Make sure the valve lifters are installed in the same bore that they were removed from.

17. Install the rocker shaft assembly, the cylinder head cover and the distributor.

18. Install the water pump pulley, fluid coupling and fan.

19. Install the power steering pump idler pulley and bracket. Install the power steering pump and air conditioning compressor. Adjust the drive belts.

20. Install the air cleaner assembly and then connect and adjust the accelerator and throttle cables.

21. Fill the engine with coolant and connect the battery cable. Start the engine and check for leaks. Check the ignition timing.

4Y–EC ENGINE

1. Disconnect the negative battery terminal from the battery. Drain the cooling system.

2. If equipped with an automatic transmission, remove and plug the oil cooler lines at the radiator.

3. Remove the fan shroud, the radiator hoses, the coolant reservoir hose and the upper radiator bolt. Raise and safely support the vehicle. Remove the engine under cover, the mounting bolts and the radiator. Lower the vehicle.

4. Remove the drive belts, the fan, the fluid coupling and the water pump pulley from the water pump.

5. Using the appropriate tools, remove the crankshaft pulley center bolt. Using an appropriate puller, pull the crankshaft pulley from the crankshaft.

6. Remove the front cover mounting bolts. Using a small prybar, lift the front cover from the engine.

To install:

7. Using a putty knife, clean the gasket mounting surfaces.

8. Use a new gasket, sealant and reverse the removal procedures.

9. Using a soft faced hammer, drive the crankshaft pulley onto the crankshaft. Torque the crankshaft pulley bolt to 80 ft. lbs. (108 Nm).

10. Adjust the drive belts and refill the cooling system.

11. Start the engine, allow it to reach normal operating temperatures and check for leaks.

2TZ–FE ENGINE

1. Disconnect the negative battery cable.
2. Remove the engine from the vehicle.
3. Remove the cylinder head from the engine.
4. Remove the crankshaft pulley bolt by using a holding tool 0921358012 and 0933000021 or equivalent. Using a pulley pulling tool 0995020017 or equivalent, remove the crankshaft pulley.
5. Remove the left engine mounting.
6. Remove the oil pressure switch and engine ventilation case.
7. Remove the oil pan using a pan removing tool 0903200100 or equivalent. Remove the oil baffle.
8. Remove the 3 bolts and oil filter bracket from the timing cover.
9. Remove the 12 bolts, 2 nuts and timing cover. 3 bolts are in the back of the cover. Be careful not to damage the mating surfaces during removal.

To install:

10. Clean the gasket surfaces and check for warpage.
11. Install new gaskets and torque the (A) bolts to 14 ft. lbs. (21 Nm), (B) bolts to 21 ft. lbs. (28 Nm) and the (C) bolts to 32 ft. lbs. (43 Nm).
12. Install the oil filter bracket and torque to 14 ft. lbs. (21 Nm).
13. Install the crankcase baffle plate, oil pan and ventilation case.
14. Install the oil pressure switch and left engine mount.
15. Install the crankshaft pulley and torque the bolt to 192 ft. lbs. (260 Nm).
16. Install the cylinder head and engine assembly into the vehicle.
17. Install the remaining components and check for leaks.

Front Cover Oil Seal

Replacement

22R, 22R–E AND 22R–TE ENGINES

1. Disconnect the negative battery cable. Remove the crankshaft pulley.
2. Using a small prybar, pry the oil seal from the oil pump housing.
3. Using the appropriate seal installer, drive the new seal into the oil pump housing. Apply multi-purpose grease to the lip of the new seal.
4. To complete the installation, reverse the removal procedures.

3F–E ENGINE

1. Disconnect the negative battery cable. Remove the crankshaft pulley.
2. Using a small prybar, pry the oil seal from the front cover.
3. Using the appropriate seal installer, drive the new seal into the front cover. Apply multi-purpose grease to the lip of the new seal.
4. To complete the installation, reverse the removal procedures.

4Y–EC ENGINE

Front Cover Removed

1. Using a drift punch and a hammer, drive the oil seal from the front cover.
2. Using an appropriate seal installer and a hammer, drive the new oil seal into the front cover.
3. Apply grease to the lip of the new seal.

Timing chain cover torque sequence—2TZ–FE engine

Front Cover Installed

1. Disconnect the negative battery cable. Remove the crankshaft pulley.
2. Using the appropriate seal remover, pull the oil seal from the front cover.
3. Apply multi-purpose grease to the lip of the new seal.
4. Using the appropriate seal installer and a hammer, drive the new oil seal into the front cover.
5. To complete the installation, reverse the removal procedures.

Timing Chain and Tensioner

Removal and Installation

22R, 22R–E AND 22R–TE ENGINES

1. Disconnect the negative battery cable. Remove the cylinder head and timing chain cover.
2. Separate the chain from the damper and remove the chain, complete with the camshaft sprocket.
3. Remove the crankshaft sprocket and the oil pump drive with a puller.
4. Inspect the chain for wear or damage. Replace it if necessary.
5. Inspect the chain tensioner for wear. If it measures less than 11mm, replace it.
6. Check the dampers for wear. If their measurements are below the following specifications, replace them. The specification for the upper damper is 5.0mm and the lower damper is 4.5mm.

To install:

7. Rotate the crankshaft until its key is at TDC. Slide the sprocket in place over the key.
8. Place the chain over the sprocket so its single bright link aligns with the mark on the camshaft sprocket.
9. Install the cam sprocket so the timing mark falls between

Aligning the crankshaft gear with the single bright link of the timing chain—22R, 22R–E and 22R–TE engines

Aligning the camshaft sprocket mark between the 2 bright links of the timing chain—22R, 22R–E and 22R–TE engines

Aligning the timing chain and sprockets—4Y–EC engine

Installing the timing chain on the sprockets—4Y–EC engine

Timing chain alignment marks—2TZ–FE engine

the two bright links on the chain.

10. Fit the oil pump drive spline over the crankshaft key.

11. Install the timing cover gasket on the front of the block.

12. Rotate the camshaft sprocket counterclockwise to remove the slack from the chain.

13. Install the timing chain cover and cylinder head.

4Y–EC ENGINE

1. Disconnect the negative battery cable. Remove the front cover.

NOTE: Using a tension gauge, measure the slack of the timing chain, it should be 0.531 in. at 22 lbs. (29 N) pressure.

2. Remove the mounting bolts and the timing chain tensioner.

3. Install the crankshaft pulley on the crankshaft. Using the proper tools, secure the crankshaft pulley, remove the camshaft mounting bolt with a socket wrench and remove the crankshaft pulley.

4. Using an appropriate puller tool, uniformly remove the camshaft sprocket with the crankshaft sprocket and chain.

5. Clean the gasket mounting surfaces.

6. Upon installation, align the timing chain with the timing marks on the sprockets, then install the sprockets on their respective shafts.

7. To complete the installation, use new gaskets, sealant and reverse the removal procedures. Torque the camshaft mounting bolt to 67 ft. lbs. (90 Nm), the timing chain tensioner bolts to 13 ft. lbs. (18 Nm), the crankshaft pulley bolt to 80 ft. lbs. (108 Nm). Adjust the drive belt tension and refill the cooling system. Check and/or adjust the engine timing.

2TZ–FE ENGINE

1. Remove the timing chain cover. There are 3 bolts in back of the cover.

2. Remove the cylinder head assembly.

3. Remove the chain slipper, damper and oil nozzle.

4. Remove the oil pump drive chain and idle gear.

5. Remove the crankshaft sprocket using a puller 0921336020 or equivalent.

To install:

6. Install the crankshaft sprocket using an installer tool 0960806040 or equivalent.

7. Install the idle sprocket, chain and tensioner. Torque the bolts to 14 ft. lbs. (21 Nm).

8. Check the spring is operating normally against the chain guide by pressing on the chain with a finger and then release. With the guide against the chain, torque the tensioner bolt to 14 ft. lbs. (20 Nm).

9. Install the oil nozzle and torque to 13 ft. lbs. (18 Nm).

10. Install the timing chain damper and slipper. Torque the bolts to 20 ft. lbs. (26 Nm).

11. Place the timing chain on the camshaft sprocket so the timing mark is between the bright chain links and at 12 o'clock.

12. Place the timing chain on the crankshaft sprocket with the single bright link indicated aligned with the timing mark on the crankshaft sprocket at 6 o'clock.

13. Turn the camshaft sprocket counterclockwise to take the slack out of the chain.

14. Tie the timing chain with a cord.

15. Install the timing chain cover and cylinder head.

16. Install the remaining components and check for leaks.

Timing Gears

Removal and Installation

3F–E ENGINE

1. Disconnect the negative battery cable. Remove the cylinder head and the front cover from the engine.

2. Remove the oil slinger from the crankshaft. Remove the camshaft thrust plate retaining bolts, by working through the holes provided in the camshaft timing gear.

3. Remove the camshaft through the front of the cylinder block. Support the camshaft while removing it, so the bearings or the lobes do not become damaged.

NOTE: The timing gear is a press-fit and cannot be removed without removing the camshaft.

4. Inspect the crankshaft timing gear. Replace it if it has worn or damaged teeth.

5. Remove the sliding key, then, pull the crankshaft timing gear from the crankshaft with a gear puller.

6. Use a large piece of pipe to drive the timing gear onto the crankshaft. Lightly and evenly tap the end of the pipe until the gear is in its original position.

To install:

7. Apply a coat of engine oil to the camshaft journals and bearings, then, insert the camshaft into the block.

8. Align the mating marks on the timing gears. Slip the camshaft into position. Torque the camshaft thrust plate bolts to 14.5 ft. lbs. (20 Nm).

9. Using a feeler gauge, check the gear backlash, inserted between the crankshaft and the camshaft timing gears. The maximum backlash should be 0.002–0.005 in.; if it exceeds this, replace one or both of the gears, as required.

10. Using a dial indicator, check the gear run-out. Maximum run-out, for both gears, is 0.008 in.; if not, replace the gear.

11. Install the oil nozzle, if removed, by screwing it in place with a screwdriver and punching it in 2 places, to secure it.

NOTE: Be sure the oil hole in the nozzle is pointed toward the timing gear before securing it.

12. To complete the installation, use new gaskets, sealant and reverse the removal procedures.

Timing Belt Front Cover

Removal and Installation

3VZ–E ENGINE

1. Disconnect the negative battery cable and drain the coolant.

2. Remove the radiator and shroud.

3. Remove the power steering belt and pump.

4. Remove the spark plugs.

5. Disconnect the No. 2 and 3 air hoses at the air pipe.

6. Disconnect the No. 1 water bypass hose at the air pipe and then remove the water outlet.

7. Remove the air conditioning belt. Remove the alternator drive belt, fluid coupling, guide and fan pulley.

8. Disconnect the high tension cords and their clamps at the No. 2 (upper) timing belt cover and then remove the cover and its gaskets.

9. Rotate the crankshaft pulley until the groove on its lip is aligned with the **0** on the No. 1 (lower) timing belt cover, this should set the No. 1 cylinder at TDC of its compression stroke. The matchmarks on the camshaft timing pulleys must be in alignment with those on the No. 3 (upper rear) timing cover. If not, rotate the engine 360 degrees (1 complete revolution).

10. Remove the crankshaft pulley using a puller.

11. Remove the fan pulley bracket and then remove the No. 1 timing belt cover.

To install:

12. Install the No. 1 cover with the 2 gaskets and tighten the bolts to 48 inch lbs. (5.4 Nm).

13. Install the fan pulley bracket and tighten it to 30 ft. lbs. (41 Nm).

14. Install the No. 2 cover and tighten the bolts 48 inch lbs. (5.4 Nm).

15. Position the crankshaft pulley so the groove in the pulley is aligned with the Woodruff key in the crankshaft. Tighten the bolt to 181 ft. lbs. (245 Nm).

16. Install the fan pulley, guide, fluid coupling and alternator drive belt. Adjust the belt tension.

17. Install the power steering pump and belt. Install the air conditioning belt. Adjust the belt tension.

18. Install the water outlet and connect the bypass hose. Connect the No. 2 and 3 air hoses.

19. Install the spark plugs. Install the radiator, fill with coolant and road test the vehicle. Check for leaks and check the ignition timing.

Timing Belt and Tensioner

Removal and Installation

3VZ–E ENGINE

1. Disconnect the negative battery cable. Remove the timing belt covers.

2. Draw a directional arrow on the timing belt and matchmark the belt to each of the pulleys. Remove the timing belt guide and then remove the tension spring.

3. Loosen the idler pulley bolt and shift it left as far as it will go. Tighten the set bolt and relieve the tension on the timing belt. Remove the belt.

4. Remove the crankshaft and camshaft sprocket timing pulleys. Remove the No. 1 idler pulley.

To install:

5. Align the groove in the crankshaft pulley with the key on the crankshaft and press the pulley onto the shaft.

6. Install the idler pulley. Align the groove on the pulley with the cavity of the oil pump and then force it to the left as far as it will go. Temporarily tighten it to 27 ft. lbs. (37 Nm).

7. Position the camshaft pulleys on the camshafts so the match holes in each pulley are in alignment with those on the No. 3 (upper rear) timing cover. Align the pulley matchmark with the one on the cover.

NOTE: Do not install the match pin. Check that the bolt head is not touching the pulley.

8. Install the timing belt around the timing pulleys. If reusing the old belt, make sure the arrow and matchmarks all line up with those made earlier on the pulleys.

9. Move the idler pulley to the right as far as it will go. Install the tension spring and then loosen the pulley bolt until the pulley moves lightly with the tension spring force.

10. Check the valve timing and belt tension by turning the crankshaft 2 complete revolutions clockwise. Check that each

NO. 2 TIMING BELT COVER — NO. 2 IDLER PULLEY — CAMSHAFT TIMING PULLEY (RH)

HIGH TENSION CORD CLAMP — CAMSHAFT TIMING PULLEY (LH)

TENSION SPRING — NO. 1 IDLER PULLEY — GASKET

WATER OUTLET

FAN — BELT GUIDE — FAN PULLEY — DRIVE BELT

MATCH PIN

CRANKSHAFT TIMING PULLEY

TIMING BELT GUIDE

TIMING BELT

NO. 1 TIMING BELT COVER

CRANKSHAFT PULLEY

PS BELT PULLEY

Timing belt components—3VZ-E engine

Aligning the timing marks with the rear cover—3VZ-E engine

Rechecking the sproket alignment—3VZ-E engine

Installing the timing belt—3VZ-E engine

pulley aligns with its timing marks. Retighten the idler pulley bolt to 27 ft. lbs. (37 Nm).

11. Remove the camshaft timing pulley bolts and align the match pin hole with the match pin hole in the camshaft. Install the pin and bolt and tighten to 80 ft. lbs. (108 Nm).

12. Remove the crankshaft timing pulley bolt and position the belt guide over the crankshaft pulley so the cupped side is out.

13. Install the timing covers. Connect the negative battery cable.

Oil Seal Replacement

Remove the crankshaft pulley, timing belt cover and pry the seal from the retainer. Be careful not to damage the crankshaft. Install the seal with a seal installer 0930937010 or equivalent.

Camshaft

Removal and Installation

22R, 22R–E AND 22R–TE ENGINES

1. Disconnect the negative battery cable. Remove the cylinder head cover.

2. Remove the rocker arm assembly from the cylinder head.

NOTE: It may be necessary to use a small prybar to lift the rocker arm assembly from the cylinder head.

3. Using a feeler gauge, measure the thrust bearing clearance at the front of the camshaft; the standard clearance is 0.003–0.007 in., it should not exceed 0.0098 in.

4. Remove the camshaft bearing caps and lift out the camshaft. Keep the bearings in order so they may be installed in their original position.

5. Check the camshaft journal caps for damage. Clean all of the bearing surfaces, including the caps, cam journal and the cylinder head.

To install:

6. With the camshaft in place on the cylinder head, lay small strips of plastigage® on each of the camshaft journals (at the tops of the journals, facing front-to-rear).

7. Reinstall the journal caps in their original locations, arrows facing forward, and torque the caps to 13–16 ft. lbs. (18–22 Nm).

8. Remove the journal caps and gauge the width of the plastigage® against the chart on the plastigage® package. Maximum journal clearance is 0.004 in. If the journal clearance is greater than specified, measure the cam journal diameters with a micrometer. If the diameter of any cam journal is less than specified, obtain a new camshaft and recheck the journal clearance. If the clearance is still excessive, the cylinder head must be replaced.

9. To complete the installation, use new gaskets, sealant and reverse the removal procedures. Refill the cooling system. Torque the camshaft bearing cap bolts to 14 ft. lbs. (19 Nm), the cylinder head-to-engine block to 58 ft. lbs. (79 Nm), the timing chain cover-to-cylinder head bolt to 9 ft. lbs. (12 Nm), the camshaft sprocket-to-camshaft bolt to 58 ft. lbs. (79 Nm), the intake manifold bolts to 14 ft. lbs. (19 Nm), the exhaust manifold bolts to 33 ft. lbs. (45 Nm) and the rocker arm cover to 7–12 ft. lbs. (10–15 Nm). Replace the cooling system fluid and the engine oil. Adjust the valves, the drive belts, then, check and/or adjust the timing.

NOTE: If a new cam is installed, use an assembly lube on the cam lobes and engine oil on the journals. Change the engine oil and filter.

3F–E ENGINE

1. Disconnect the negative battery cable. Remove the cylinder head and the front cover from the engine.

2. Remove the oil slinger from the crankshaft. Remove the camshaft thrust plate retaining bolts, by working through the holes provided in the camshaft timing gear.

3. Remove the camshaft through the front of the cylinder block. Support the camshaft while removing it, so the bearings or the lobes do not become damaged.

4. Inspect the crankshaft timing gear. Replace it if it has worn or damaged teeth.

5. Remove the sliding key, then, pull the crankshaft timing gear from the crankshaft with a gear puller.

6. Use a large piece of pipe to drive the timing gear onto the crankshaft. Lightly and evenly tap the end of the pipe until the gear is in its original position.

To install:

7. Apply a coat of engine oil to the camshaft journals and bearings, then, insert the camshaft into the block.

8. Align the mating marks on the timing gears. Slip the camshaft into position. Torque the camshaft thrust plate bolts to 14.5 ft. lbs. (20 Nm).

9. Using a feeler gauge, check the gear backlash, inserted between the crankshaft and the camshaft timing gears. The maximum backlash should be 0.002–0.005 in.; if it exceeds this, replace one or both of the gears, as required.

10. Using a dial indicator, check the gear run-out. Maximum run-out, for both gears, is 0.008 in.; if not, replace the gear.

11. Install the oil nozzle, if removed, by screwing it in place and punching it in 2 places, to secure it.

NOTE: Be sure the oil hole in the nozzle is pointed toward the timing gear before securing it.

12. To complete the installation, use new gaskets, sealant and reverse the removal procedures.

4Y–EC ENGINE

1. Disconnect the negative battery cable. Remove the timing chain from the engine.

2. Remove the right-front seat, the service hole cover and the distributor.

3. Disconnect the cold start injector connector, place a shop towel under the injector tube, then, remove the cold start injector union bolts, the injector and the gaskets. Remove the valve cover, the mounting bolts and the rocker arm assembly.

4. Remove the pushrods, keeping them in order. Using a wire hook or a magnetic finger, remove the valve lifters, keeping them in order.

5. Remove the thrust plate mounting bolts and the plate.

6. While turning the camshaft, slowly pull it out through the front of the engine, making sure not to damage the bearings, the camshaft lobes or the camshaft bearing surfaces.

To install:

7. Install the thrust plate, the camshaft sprocket and bolt onto the camshaft. Using a feeler gauge, measure the thrust bearing clearance, it should be 0.0028–0.0087 in.; if the clearance exceeds 0.012 in., replace the thrust plate.

8. Using a micrometer, check the bearing diameters of the camshaft. Using an internal micrometer, check the camshaft bearing diameters on the engine block.

9. Clean the gasket surfaces.

NOTE: Before installing the valve lifters, coat them with oil.

10. Use new gaskets, sealant and reverse the removal procedures. Torque the camshaft thrust bearing plate bolts to 13 ft. lbs. (17 Nm), the camshaft sprocket bolt to 67 ft. lbs. (93 Nm), the timing chain tensioner bolts to 13 ft. lbs. (17 Nm) and the crankshaft pulley bolt to 80 ft. lbs. (108 Nm). Adjust the drive belts and refill the cooling system. Check and/or adjust the timing.

3VZ–E ENGINE

1. Disconnect the negative battery cable.

Removing the camshaft bearing bolts

2. Remove the timing belt covers and remove the timing belt.

3. Disconnect all wires and hoses to the air intake chamber.

4. Remove the bolts retraining the air intake chamber and remove the air intake chamber from the intake manifold.

5. Remove the rear timing belt cover.

6. Remove the idler pulley and timing cover.

7. Remove the fuel rail and injectors from the intake manifold.

8. Remove the cylinder head cover.

9. Remove the camshaft housing rear cover. Loosen the camshaft retaining bolts a little at a time in the correct sequence.

10. Remove the camshaft from the cylinder head.

11. Installation is the reverse of the removal procedure. When installing the bearing caps, make sure the arrow faces the front of the engine. Torque the caps to 12 ft. lbs. (16 Nm) in the correct sequence.

2TZ-FE ENGINE

1. Disconnect the negative battery cable.

2. Remove the engine from the vehicle.

3. Remove the valve cover.

4. Place the matchmarks on the camshaft sprocket and chain facing 12 o'clock with the engine upright.

5. Hold the camshaft with a wrench and remove the sprocket bolt.

6. Remove the chain tensioner, timing chain and sprocket. Hold to the side with a wire to maintain camshaft timing.

7. Remove the No. 6 camshaft bearing cap.

8. To remove the exhaust camshaft:

   a. Set the knock pin hole of the camshaft at 5–30 degrees BTDC.

   b. Secure the camshaft sub-gear to the main gear with a service bolt.

   c. Uniformly loosen and remove the bearing caps No. 1, No. 2, No. 3 and No. 5., in that order. Leave No. 4 tight.

   d. Loosen and remove the No. 4 bearing cap.

9. To remove the intake camshaft:

   a. Set the knock pin hole of the camshaft at 75–100 degrees BTDC.

   b. Uniformly loosen and remove the bearing caps No. 1, No. 2, No. 4 and No. 5., in that order. Leave No. 3 tight.

   c. Loosen and remove the No. 3 bearing cap.

To install:

10. To install the intake camshaft:

    a. Set the knock pin hole of the camshaft at 75–100 degrees BTDC.

    b. Apply prelube to the camshaft journals and lobes.

    c. Tighten caps No. 1 and No. 3 to draw the camshaft to the cylinder head.

    d. Uniformly torque the bearing caps in several steps to ensure the camshaft does not bend.

    e. Torque the bolts to 12 ft. lbs. (16 Nm).

11. To install the exhaust camshaft:

    a. Set the knock pin hole of the camshaft at 5–30 degrees BTDC.

    b. Apply prelube to the camshaft journals and lobes.

    c. Tighten caps No. 2 and No. 4 to draw the camshaft to the cylinder head.

    d. Uniformly torque the bearing caps in several steps to ensure the camshaft does not bend.

    e. Torque the bolts to 12 ft. lbs. (16 Nm).

12. Apply sealer to the bottom of No. 6 bearing cap and install. Torque the cap to 12 ft. lbs. (16 Nm).

13. Install the camshaft sprocket and chain. Torque the bolt to 54 ft. lbs. (74 Nm).

14. Release the chain tensioner ratchet pawl. Fully push in the plunger and apply the hook to the pin so the plunger can not spring out and install the tensioner. Torque the bolts to 15 ft. lbs. (21 Nm).

15. Set the tensioner by pulling back on the slipper to release the hook.

16. Check the valve clearances.

17. Install the remaining components and check for leaks.

Piston and Connecting Rod

Positioning

Piston and connecting rod positioning—22R, 22R-E and 22R-TE, 3F-E and 4Y-EC engines

Piston and connecting rod positioning—3VZ-E engine, 2TZ-FE similar

Service Tips

PISTON SLAP NOISE

On 1988 vehicles equipped with the 22R, 22R-E and 4Y-EC engines may produce a muffled, hollow, bell-like sound during cold engine operation. This sound may be caused by a piston slap. Run the engine and carefully disconnect each spark plug wire for a short period of time. If the noise goes away after shorting, piston slap may be the cause.

Different size pistons are available if the cylinder bore is okay. After confirming that the source of the engine noise is caused by engine piston slap, select and install new style pistons with the same bore size mark as that is on the cylinder block, below each bore at the gasket surface. If the piston size cannot be found, measure the bore and install the appropriate size pistons.

Consult the dealer for part number information and availability.

ENGINE LUBRICATION

Oil Pan

Removal and Installation

PICK-UP, VAN AND 4RUNNER

1. Raise the hood and disconnect the negative battery cable.
2. Raise and safely support the vehicle.
3. Drain the engine oil.
4. Remove the steering relay rod and the tie rods from the idler arm, pitman arm, and steering knuckles.
5. Remove the engine stiffening plates.
6. Remove the splash pans from under the engine.
7. Position a floor jack under the transmission and raise the engine/transmission assembly slightly.
8. Remove the front motor mount attaching bolts.
9. Remove the oil pan bolts and remove the oil pan.
10. Scrape the cylinder block and oil pan mating surfaces clean of any old sealing material. Apply gasket sealer to the oil pan when installing a new gasket. If equipped with the 22R, 22R-E, 22R-TE or 4Y-EC engine, apply 5mm bead of gasket sealer; if equipped with the 3F-E or 3VZ-E engine, use 3mm bead. The parts should be installed within 5 minutes of applying the sealer.
11. The oil pan bolts should be tightened to 9 ft. lbs. (12 Nm) on the 22R, 22R-E, 22R-TE or 4Y-EC engines; 6 ft. lbs. (10 Nm) (bolt), 52 inch lbs. (70 Nm) for the 3F-E or 3V-ZE engines. Tighten the bolts in a circular pattern, starting in the middle of the pan and working out towards the ends.
12. Lower the engine and tighten the motor mount bolts. Install the splash shields and stiffening plates.
13. Install any steering arms removed in Step 4 and then lower the vehicle; tighten all suspension components and the motor mounts to their final torque with the vehicle resting on the ground.
14. Fill the engine with oil, road test the vehicle and check for leaks.

LAND CRUISER

1. Raise and safely support the vehicle. Remove the engine skid plates.
2. Remove the flywheel side cover and skid plate.
3. Disconnect the front driveshaft from the engine.
4. Drain the engine oil.
5. Remove the bolts which secure the oil pan. Remove the pan and its gasket.
6. Scrape away any old gasket material and then apply gasket sealer to the cylinder block mating surface and the No. 1 and No. 4 main bearing caps.
7. Install the oil pan and tighten the bolts to 69 inch lbs. (7.8 Nm). Always use a new pan gasket.
8. Connect the driveshaft, skid plate and flywheel side cover.
9. Lower the vehicle, fill the engine with oil and check for any leaks.

PREVIA

This engine has 2 oil pans. If the crankshaft is going to be serviced, the side crankcase pan has to be removed. If the oil pump sump is going to be serviced, the bottom oil pan has to be removed.

1. Drain the engine oil and disconnect the battery cable.
2. Remove the oil level sensor and gasket. Be careful not to drop the sensor when removing.
3. Remove the 14 bolts and 2 nuts.
4. Using a pan removing tool 0903200100 or equivalent, pry the pan from the engine, being careful not to damage the flange.

To install:
5. Clean the gasket mating surfaces and apply gasket sealer No. 0882600080 or equivalent, to the pan and assembly within 5 minutes.
6. Install the pan and torque the bolts and nuts to 48 inch lbs. (5.4 Nm).
7. Install the gasket, oil sensor and torque to 9 ft. lbs. (13 Nm).
8. Install the remaining components.
9. Refill the engine with oil and check for leaks.

Oil Pump

Removal and Installation

22R, 22R-E AND 22R-TE ENGINES

1. Raise and safely support the vehicle. Drain the oil, and remove the oil pan and the oil strainer and pick-up tube.
2. Remove the drive belts from the crankshaft pulley.
3. Remove the crankshaft bolt, and remove the pulley with a gear puller.
4. Remove the 5 bolts from the oil pump and remove the oil pump assembly.
5. Inspect the drive spline, driven gear, pump body, and timing chain cover for excessive wear or damage. If necessary, replace the gears or pump body or cover. Unbolt the relief valve (the vertical bolt on the pump body) when attached to the engine) and check the pistons, oil passages, and sliding surfaces for burrs or scoring. Inspect the crankshaft front oil seal and replace if worn or damaged.
6. When installing, use a new O-ring if necessary.
7. Apply a sealer to the upper bolt and install the 5 bolts.
8. Install the crankshaft pulley and use a new gasket on the oil strainer and oil pan. Be sure to apply sealer to the corners of the oil pan gasket before installing the pan.

3F-E ENGINE

1. Disconnect the negative battery cable. Raise and safely support the vehicle. Remove the oil pan.
2. Remove the oil strainer and unfasten the union nuts on the oil pump pipe.
3. Remove the lock wire and the oil pump retaining bolt and pipe from the engine.
4. Remove the oil pump cover and inspect the following parts for nicks, scoring, grooving, etc.:
   a. pump cover
   b. drive and driven gears
   c. pump body
5. Replace either the damaged parts or the complete pump if damage is excessive.
To install:
6. Install the oil pump so the slot in the oil pump shaft is in alignment with the protrusion on the governor shaft of the distributor. Tighten the mounting bolts to 13 ft. lbs. (18 Nm).
7. Install the outlet pipe and tighten the union bolt to 33 ft. lbs. (44 Nm); use new gaskets.
8. Install the oil pan, fill the engine with oil and check for leaks.

NOTE: Be sure to check all of the gaskets and replace if necessary.

4Y-EC ENGINE

1. Disconnect the negative battery cable. Raise and safely support the vehicle. Remove the oil pan.
2. Remove the oil pump mounting bolts, then pull out the pump assembly.
3. Using a gasket scraper, clean the gasket mounting surfaces.

Oil pan and pump assembly—3VZ–E engine

4. To install, use new gaskets, sealant and reverse the removal procedures. Torque the oil pump bolts to 13 ft. lbs. (17 Nm).

3VZ–E ENGINE

1. Disconnect the negative battery cable.
2. Remove the timing belt.
3. Raise and safely support the vehicle. Remove the engine under cover.
4. Remove the front differential.
5. Drain the oil.
6. Remove the crankshaft timing pulley.
7. Raise the engine slightly and remove the oil pan.
8. Remove the oil strainer. Insert a drift between the cylinder block and the oil pan baffle plate, cut off the sealer and remove the baffle plate.

NOTE: When removing the baffle plate with the drift, do not damage the baffle plate flange.

9. Remove the oil pump and O-ring.

To install:

10. Apply sealer to the oil pump mating surface running the bead on the inside of the bolts holes. Position a new O-ring in the groove in the cylinder block and install the pump so the spline teeth of the drive gear engage the large teeth on the crankshaft. Tighten the mounting bolts to 14 ft. lbs. (20 Nm).
11. Remove any old sealer and install the baffle plate with new sealer.
12. Install the oil strainer and tighten the bolts to 61 inch lbs. (7 Nm).
13. Install the oil pan, crankshaft pulley and the timing belt.
14. Install the front differential and the undercovers.
15. Fill the engine with oil and check for leaks.

2TZ–FE ENGINE

1. Remove the oil level sensor. Be careful not to drop the sensor when removing.
2. Remove the pan retaining bolts and pry the pan from the engine using a prying tool 0903200100 or equivalent. Be careful not to damage the flange.

Oil pump assembly—22R, 22R–E and 22R–TE engines

To install:

3. Clean the gasket mating surfaces with a scraper and solvent.
4. Apply a bead of sealer 0882600080 or equivalent to the pan surface and install within 5 minutes.
5. Torque the pan bolts and nuts to 48 inch lbs. (5.4 Nm).
6. Install the oil sensor and torque the bolts to 9 ft. lbs. (13 Nm).
7. Install the remaining components and refill the with engine oil.

Rear Main Bearing Oil Seal

Removal and Installation

22R, 22R–E AND 22R–TE ENGINES

1. Raise and safely support the vehicle. Remove the transmis-

sion and the clutch assembly, if equipped. Remove the transfer case, if equipped.

2. Remove the flywheel or the flexplate from the crankshaft. Remove the cover plate from the rear of the engine.

3. Remove oil pan-to-oil seal retaining plate bolts, the oil seal retaining plate-to-engine bolts and oil seal retaining plate.

4. Carefully pry or drive the old seal from the retaining plate. Be careful not to damage the retaining plate.

5. Using an oil seal driver tool, drive the new seal into the oil seal retaining plate, until the surface is flush.

6. Lubricate the lips of the seal with multi-purpose grease.

7. Clean the gasket mounting surfaces.

8. To install, use new gaskets and reverse the removal procedures. Adjust the clutch.

3F–E ENGINE

1. Raise and safely support the vehicle. Remove the transfer case, the transmission and the clutch assembly.

2. Remove the flywheel from the crankshaft.

3. Using a small prybar, carefully pry the oil seal from the rear of the crankshaft.

4. Lubricate the lips of the seal with multipurpose grease.

5. Using an oil seal driver tool, drive the new seal into the rear of the crankshaft.

6. Clean the gasket mounting surfaces.

7. To install, reverse the removal procedures. Adjust the clutch.

4Y–EC AND 3VZ–E ENGINES

1. Raise and safely support the vehicle. Remove the transmission and the clutch assembly, if equipped. Remove the transfer case, if equipped.

2. Remove the flywheel or the flexplate from the crankshaft. Remove the cover plate from the rear of the engine.

3. To replace the oil seal with the retaining plate removed:

a. Remove oil pan-to-oil seal retaining plate bolts, the oil seal retaining plate-to-engine bolts and oil seal retaining plate.

b. Carefully pry or drive the old seal from the retaining plate. Be careful not to damage the retaining plate.

c. Using an oil seal driver tool, drive the new seal into the oil seal retaining plate, until the surface is flush.

d. Lubricate the lips of the seal with multipurpose grease.

4. To replace the oil seal with the retaining plate installed:

a. Cut off the oil seal lip.

b. Using a small prybar, pry the oil seal from the retaining plate.

c. Apply multi-purpose grease to the new oil seal.

d. Using an oil seal driver tool, drive the new seal into the oil seal retaining plate until the surface is flush.

5. Clean the gasket mounting surfaces.

6. To complete the installation, reverse the removal procedures. Adjust the clutch.

2TZ–FE ENGINE

1. Remove the transmission from the vehicle.

2. Separate the transmission from the engine.

3. Remove the flywheel or flexplate.

4. Using a knife, cut off the lip of the oil seal.

5. Using a suitable prybar, pry the seal out of the seal carrier. Be careful not to damage the crankshaft.

To install:

6. Clean the seal mating surfaces with solvent.

7. Apply grease to the seal lip.

8. Using an installer tool 0922356010 or equivalent, install the seal. Make sure the seal is seated properly. If not, the seal will leak and the engine will have to be removed again.

9. Install the engine/transmission assembly.

10. Install the remaining components and check for leaks.

TORQUE SPECIFICATIONS

Component	English	Metric
Camshaft cap bolts		
2.4L (22R, 22R-E, 22R-TE) engine	14 ft. lbs.	20 Nm
2.4L (2TZ-FE) engine	12 ft. lbs.	16 Nm
3.0L (3VZ-E) engine	12 ft. lbs.	16 Nm
Camshaft sprocket bolt		
2.2L (4Y-EC) engine	67 ft. lbs.	90 Nm
2.4L (22R, 22R-E, 22R-TE) engine	58 ft. lbs.	78 Nm
2.4L (2TZ-FE) engine	54 ft. lbs.	74 Nm
3.0L (3VZ-E) engine	80 ft. lbs.	108 Nm
Camshaft thrust plate		
2.2L (4Y-EC) engine	13 ft. lbs.	18 Nm
4.0L (3F-E) engine	9 ft. lbs.	12 Nm
Connecting rod bearing cap nuts		
2.2L (4Y-EC) engine	36 ft. lbs.	49 Nm
2.4L (22R, 22R-E, 22R-TE) engine	51 ft. lbs.	69 Nm
2.4L (2TZ-FE) engine		
Step 1:	22 ft. lbs.	29 Nm
Step 2:	+ 90°	+ 90°
3.0L (3VZ-E) engine		
Step 1:	18 ft. lbs.	25 Nm
Step 2:	+ 90°	+ 90°
4.0L (3F-E) engine	43 ft. lbs.	59 Nm
Crankshaft pulley bolt		
2.2L (4Y-EC) engine	116 ft. lbs.	157 Nm
2.4L (22R, 22R-E, 22R-TE) engine	116 ft. lbs.	157 Nm
2.4L (2TZ-FE) engine	192 ft. lbs.	260 Nm
3.0L (3VZ-E) engine	181 ft. lbs.	245 Nm
4.0L (3F-E) engine	253 ft. lbs.	343 Nm

TORQUE SPECIFICATIONS

Component	English	Metric
Crankshaft seal retainer bolts		
2.2L (4Y-EC) engine	9 ft. lbs.	12 Nm
2.4L (22R, 22R-E, 22R-TE) engine	13 ft. lbs.	18 Nm
2.4L (2TZ-FE) engine	10 ft. lbs.	13 Nm
3.0L (3VZ-E) engine	69 inch lbs.	7.8 Nm
Cylinder head bolt		
2.2L (4Y-EC) engine		
12mm bolt	27 ft. lbs.	37 Nm
14mm bolt		
Step 1:	33 ft. lbs.	44 Nm
Step 2:	65 ft. lbs.	88 Nm
1988 2.4L (22R, 22R-E) engine *		
Step 1:	27 ft. lbs.	37 Nm
Step 2:	33 ft. lbs.	44 Nm
Step 3:	+ 90°	+ 90°
Step 4:	+ 90°	+ 90°
1989–92 2.4L (22R-E) engine		
Step 1:	26–32 ft. lbs.	36–43 Nm
Step 2:	53–65 ft. lbs.	72–88 Nm
2.4L (2TZ-FE) engine *		
Step 1:	29 ft. lbs.	39 Nm
Step 2:	+ 90°	+ 90°
Step 3:	+ 90°	+ 90°
3.0L (3VZ-E) engine *		
Step 1:	27 ft. lbs.	37 Nm
Step 2:	33 ft. lbs.	44 Nm
Step 3:	+ 90°	+ 90°
Step 4:	+ 90°	+ 90°
4.0L (3F-E) engine		
Step 1:	40 ft. lbs.	54 Nm
Step 2:	90 ft. lbs.	123 Nm
EGR valve		
2.2L (4Y-EC) engine	13 ft. lbs.	18 Nm
2.4L (22R, 22R-E, 22R-TE) engine	9 ft. lbs.	13 Nm
2.4L (2TZ-FE) engine	13 ft. lbs.	18 Nm
3.0L (3VZ-E) engine	22 ft. lbs.	29 Nm
4.0L (3F-E) engine	13 ft. lbs.	18 Nm
EGR valve-to-spacer plate		
3.0L (3VZ-E) engine	13 ft. lbs.	18 Nm
4.0L (3F-E) engine	13 ft. lbs.	18 Nm
EGR supply tube		
2.2L (4Y-EC) engine	25 ft. lbs.	34 Nm
2.4L (22R, 22R-E, 22R-TE) engine	9 ft. lbs.	13 Nm
2.4L (2TZ-FE) engine	58 ft. lbs.	78 Nm
3.0L (3VZ-E) engine	9 ft. lbs.	12 Nm
4.0L (3F-E) engine	47 ft. lbs.	64 Nm
Engine-to-transaxle		
2.2L (4Y-EC) engine	47 ft. lbs.	64 Nm
2.4L (22R, 22R-E, 22R-TE) engine	29 ft. lbs.	39 Nm
2.4L (2TZ-FE) engine	53 ft. lbs.	72 Nm
3.0L (3VZ-E) engine	30 ft. lbs.	41 Nm
4.0L (3F-E) engine		
Engine/transaxle mounts		
2.2L (4Y-EC) engine	29 ft. lbs.	39 Nm
2.4L (22R, 22R-E, 22R-TE) engine	33 ft. lbs.	44 Nm
2.4L (2TZ-FE) engine	33 ft. lbs.	45 Nm
3.0L (3VZ-E) engine	30 ft. lbs.	40 Nm
4.0L (3F-E) engine	47 ft. lbs.	64 Nm
Exhaust manifold		
2.2L (4Y-EC) engine	36 ft. lbs.	49 Nm
2.4L (22R, 22R-E, 22R-TE) engine	33 ft. lbs.	44 Nm

TORQUE SPECIFICATIONS

Component	English	Metric
2.4L (2TZ-FE) engine	36 ft. lbs.	49 Nm
3.0L (3VZ-E) engine	29 ft. lbs.	39 Nm
4.0L (3F-E) engine		
14mm bolt:	37 ft. lbs.	50 Nm
17mm bolt:	51 ft. lbs.	69 Nm
Nut:	41 ft. lbs.	56 Nm
Exhaust manifold-to-heat shield nuts	15–22 ft. lbs.	20–30 Nm
Exhaust flange-to-manifold nuts		
2.2L (4Y-EC) engine	46 ft. lbs.	62 Nm
2.4L (22R, 22R-E, 22R-TE) engine	35 ft. lbs.	47 Nm
2.4L (2TZ-FE) engine	46 ft. lbs.	62 Nm
3.0L (3VZ-E) engine	29 ft. lbs.	39 Nm
4.0L (3F-E) engine	46 ft. lbs.	62 Nm
Flywheel/flex plate-to-crankshaft bolts		
2.2L (4Y-EC) engine		
Manual transmission	65 ft. lbs.	88 Nm
Automatic transmission	54 ft. lbs.	74 Nm
2.4L (22R, 22R-E, 22R-TE) engine		
Manual transmission	80 ft. lbs.	108 Nm
Automatic transmission	61 ft. lbs.	88 Nm
2.4L (2TZ-FE) engine		
Manual transmission	65 ft. lbs.	88 Nm
Automatic transmission	54 ft. lbs.	74 Nm
3.0L (3VZ-E) engine		
Manual transmission	65 ft. lbs.	88 Nm
Automatic transmission	61 ft. lbs.	83 Nm
4.0L (3F-E) engine	64 ft. lbs.	87 Nm
Flywheel-to-converter bolts	30 ft. lbs.	41 Nm
Fuel rail-to-intake manifold bolts		
2.2L (4Y-EC) engine	13 ft. lbs.	18 Nm
2.4L (22R, 22R-E, 22R-TE) engine	13 ft. lbs.	18 Nm
2.4L (2TZ-FE) engine	48 inch lbs.	5.4 Nm
3.0L (3VZ-E) engine	9 ft. lbs.	13 Nm
4.0L (3F-E) engine	9 ft. lbs.	13 Nm
Intake manifold		
2.2L (4Y-EC) engine	36 ft. lbs.	49 Nm
2.4L (22R, 22R-E, 22R-TE) engine	13 ft. lbs.	18 Nm
2.4L (2TZ-FE) engine	15 ft. lbs.	21 Nm
3.0L (3VZ-E) engine	13 ft. lbs.	18 Nm
4.0L (3F-E) engine		
14mm bolt:	37 ft. lbs.	50 Nm
17mm bolt:	51 ft. lbs.	69 Nm
Nut:	41 ft. lbs.	56 Nm
Intake plenum-to-lower manifold		
2.2L (4Y-EC) engine	9 ft. lbs.	12 Nm
2.4L (22R, 22R-E, 22R-TE) engine	13 ft. lbs.	18 Nm
3.0L (3VZ-E) engine	13 ft. lbs.	18 Nm
4.0L (3F-E) engine	18 ft. lbs.	25 Nm
Main bearing cap bolts		
2.2L (4Y-EC) engine	58 ft. lbs.	78 Nm
2.4L (22R, 22R-E, 22R-TE) engine	76 ft. lbs.	103 Nm
2.4L (2TZ-FE) engine		
Step 1:	29 inch lbs.	39 Nm
Step 2:	+ 90°	+ 90°
3.0L (3VZ-E) engine		
Step 1:	45 inch lbs.	61 Nm
Step 2:	+ 90°	+ 90°
4.0L (3F-E) engine		
17mm bolt:	85 ft. lbs.	115 Nm
19mm bolt:	99 ft. lbs.	135 Nm

TORQUE SPECIFICATIONS

Component	English	Metric
Oil filter adapter	13 ft. lbs.	18 Nm
Oil pan–to–block		
2.2L (4Y-EC) engine	9 ft. lbs.	13 Nm
2.4L (22R, 22R-E, 22R-TE) engine	9 ft. lbs.	13 Nm
2.4L (2TZ-FE) engine	48 inch lbs.	5.4 Nm
3.0L (3VZ-E) engine	48 inch lbs.	5.4 Nm
4.0L (3F-E) engine	69 inch lbs.	7.8 Nm
Oil pan drain plug	18 ft. lbs.	25 Nm
Oil low level sensor	20–30 ft. lbs.	27–41 Nm
Oil pressure sending unit	12–16 ft. lbs.	16–22 Nm
Oil pump attaching bolts		
2.2L (4Y-EC) engine	13 ft. lbs.	18 Nm
2.4L (22R, 22R-E, 22R-TE) engine		
8mm bolt:	9 ft. lbs.	13 Nm
10mm bolt:	29 ft. lbs.	39 Nm
2.4L (2TZ-FE) engine	13 ft. lbs.	18 Nm
3.0L (3VZ-E) engine	14 ft. lbs.	20 Nm
4.0L (3F-E) engine	13 ft. lbs.	18 Nm
Oil pump cover		
2.2L (4Y-EC) engine	69 inch	7.8 Nm
2.4L (22R, 22R-E, 22R-TE) engine	13 ft. lbs.	18 Nm
2.4L (2TZ-FE) engine	43 inch lbs.	4.9 Nm
3.0L (3VZ-E) engine	61 inch lbs.	6.9 Nm
4.0L (3F-E) engine	7 ft. lbs.	10 Nm
Rocker arm bolt		
2.2L (4Y-EC) engine	17 ft. lbs.	24 Nm
2.4L (22R, 22R-E) engine	58 ft. lbs.	78 Nm
4.0L (3F-E) engine		
12mm bolt:	17 ft. lbs.	24 Nm
14mm bolt:	25 ft. lbs.	33 Nm
Rocker (valve) cover		
2.2L (4Y-EC) engine	48 inch lbs.	5.4 Nm
2.4L (22R, 22R-E, 22R-TE) engine	52 inch lbs.	5.9 Nm
2.4L (2TZ-FE) engine	48 inch lbs.	5.4 Nm
3.0L (3VZ-E) engine	48 ft. lbs.	5.4 Nm
4.0L (3F-E) engine	78 inch lbs.	8.8 Nm
Spark plug	5–12 ft. lbs.	7–16 Nm
Starter-to-block bolts	15–20 ft. lbs.	20–27 Nm
Thermostat housing		
2.2L (4Y-EC) engine	13 ft. lbs.	18 Nm
2.4L (22R, 22R-E, 22R-TE) engine	14 ft. lbs.	19 Nm
2.4L (2TZ-FE) engine	13 ft. lbs.	18 Nm
3.0L (3VZ-E) engine	13 ft. lbs.	18 Nm
4.0L (3F-E) engine	13 ft. lbs.	18 Nm
Throttle body nuts	15–22 ft. lbs.	20–30 Nm
Timing chain tensioner bolt		
2.2L (4Y-EC) engine	13 ft. lbs.	18 Nm
2.4L (22R, 22R-E, 22R-TE) engine	13 ft. lbs.	18 Nm
2.4L (2TZ-FE) engine	15 ft. lbs.	21 Nm
3.0L (3VZ-E) engine	13 ft. lbs.	18 Nm
4.0L (3F-E) engine	13 ft. lbs.	18 Nm
Timing cover		
2.2L (4Y-EC) engine	13 ft. lbs.	18 Nm
2.4L (22R, 22R-E, 22R-TE) engine		
8mm bolt:	9 ft. lbs.	13 Nm
10mm bolt:	29 ft. lbs.	39 Nm
2.4L (2TZ-FE) engine	21 ft. lbs.	28 Nm
3.0L (3VZ-E) engine	48 inch lbs.	5.4 Nm

TORQUE SPECIFICATIONS

Component	English	Metric
4.0L (3F-E) engine		
10mm bolt:	43 inch lbs.	4.9 Nm
14mm bolt:	18 ft. lbs.	25 Nm
Water pump		
2.2L (4Y-EC) engine	13 ft. lbs.	18 Nm
2.4L (22R, 22R-E, 22R-TE) engine	13 ft. lbs.	18 Nm
2.4L (2TZ-FE) engine	14 ft. lbs.	20 Nm
3.0L (3VZ-E) engine		
Short bolt:	14 ft. lbs.	20 Nm
Long bolt:	13 ft. lbs.	18 Nm
4.0L (3F-E) engine	27 ft. lbs.	37 Nm
Water pump pulley hub bolts		
2.2L (4Y-EC) engine	13 ft. lbs.	18 Nm
2.4L (22R, 22R-E, 22R-TE) engine	15 ft. lbs.	21 Nm
3.0L (3VZ-E) engine	48 inch lbs.	5.4 Nm
4.0L (3F-E) engine	13 ft. lbs.	18 Nm

* NOTE: Use new bolts and oil the threads

MANUAL TRANSMISSION

Transmission Assembly

For further information, please refer to Chilton's Transmission Service Manual.

Removal and Installation

2WD PICK-UP AND VAN

1. Disconnect the negative battery terminal.
2. Perform the following:
   a. Remove the center floor console, if equipped.
   b. Remove the shift lever handle, then the floor mat or carpet along with the shift lever boot in order to gain access to the shift lever.
   c. Using an shift lever removal tool, remove the shift lever.

NOTE: On the Pick-Up, remove the boot and the shift lever from inside the vehicle.

3. Raise and safely support the vehicle. Drain the transmission fluid.
4. Make matchmarks on the driveshaft flange and the differential pinion flange to indicate their relationships; these marks must be aligned during installation.
5. Remove the driveshaft flange bolts and the center support bearing-to-frame bolts, if equipped with a 2-piece driveshaft. Lower the driveshaft out of the vehicle. Using an appropriate tool, insert it into the end of the transmission to prevent oil leakage.
6. On the Van, disconnect the shift and the select cables from the select outer levers, the clips and the cables.
7. Disconnect the back-up lamp switch electrical connector and the speedometer cable from the transmission, then tie the cable aside.
8. Disconnect the wiring at the starter. Remove the starter mounting bolts and lower the starter out of the vehicle.
9. Remove the exhaust pipe clamp and the exhaust pipe.
10. If the hydraulic line from the clutch release cylinder is clamped to the frame, remove the clamp retaining bolt. Remove the release cylinder mounting bolts and the fork spring, if equipped. Tie the release cylinder aside.

NOTE: It is not necessary to disconnect the hydraulic line from the release cylinder.

11. On column shift vehicles, disconnect the shift selector linkage at the transmission and remove the transmission cross shafts.
12. Support the rear of the transmission with a jack and remove the transmission-to-crossmember bolts, the crossmember-to-frame bolts and the crossmember from the vehicle.

NOTE: When removing the crossmember, raise the rear of the transmission, just enough to take the weight off of the crossmember.

13. Place a support under the engine with a wooden block (¾ in. thick) between the support and the engine oil pan.

NOTE: The wooden block and support should be no more than about ¼ in. away from the engine so when the engine is lowered, damage will not occur to any underhood components. If possible, shim the support so the wooden block touches the engine.

14. Remove the transmission-to-engine bolts, draw the transmission rearward and down, away from the engine.
To install:
15. Raise the transmission into position under the vehicle.
16. Install the transmission-to-engine bolts.
17. Torque transmission-to-engine bolts to 53 ft. lbs. (70 Nm), the stiffener plate bolts to 27 ft. lbs. (38 Nm), the transmission mount/bracket bolts to 19 ft. lbs. (28 Nm), the rear engine mount bracket-to-crossmember bolts to 9 ft. lbs. (12 Nm).
18. Connect the exhaust pipes and brackets. Install the starter and the clutch release cylinder.
19. Tighten the exhaust pipe-to-manifold bolts to 29 ft. lbs. (40 Nm), the upper exhaust pipe bracket-to-clutch housing bolts to 27 ft. lbs. (38 Nm), the lower exhaust pipe bracket-to-clutch housing bolts to 51 ft. lbs. (68 Nm), the lower starter bolt/release cylinder tube bracket bolt to 29 ft. lbs. (41 Nm), the clutch release cylinder bolts to 9 ft. lbs. (12 Nm).
20. Connect the remaining linkages and connect the driveshaft, aligning the matchmarks made during removal.

21. Refill the transmission to the correct level.
22. Install the shift lever and the center console.
23. Connect the negative battery cable.

4WD PICK-UP, 4RUNNER AND VAN

1. Disconnect the negative battery terminal. Remove the starter upper mounting bolt.
2. Working inside the vehicle, pull up the shift lever boot and pull out the shift lever. If equipped with a 22R–E engine, pull up the shift lever boot, then, remove the mounting bolts and pull out the shift lever.
3. Using needle nose pliers, remove the transfer case shift lever snapring and the shift lever.
4. Raise and safely support the vehicle.
5. Drain the lubricant from both the transmission and the transfer case.
6. Make matchmarks on the driveshaft flanges and the differential pinion flanges to indicate their relationships. These marks must be aligned during installation.
7. Remove the driveshaft mounting bolts and remove the front driveshaft assembly.

NOTE: Do not disassemble the front driveshaft to remove it.

8. Using a piece of chalk, place matchmarks on the rear driveshaft and the slip yoke to indicate their relationships; these marks must be aligned during installation.
9. Remove the mounting bolts from the rearward flange of the rear driveshaft. Lower the driveshaft out of the vehicle. Remove the mounting bolts from the slip yoke flange, then, remove the flange and yoke assembly.
10. Unbolt the clutch release cylinder and tie it aside.

NOTE: It is not necessary to disconnect the hydraulic line from the clutch release cylinder.

11. Disconnect the starter motor electrical connectors. Remove the starter bolts and lower the starter from the vehicle.
12. At the transfer case, disconnect the speedometer cable (tie it aside), the back-up light switch connector and the 4WD indicator switch connector.
13. Disconnect the exhaust pipe clamp and the exhaust pipe from the transmission housing.
14. Remove the clutch release cylinder and the tube bracket, then, move the cylinder aside.

NOTE: When removing the clutch release cylinder, do not disassemble the hydraulic line from the cylinder.

15. Remove the crossmember-to-transfer case mounting bolts. Using a jack, raise the transmission and transfer case assembly off of the crossmember. Remove the crossmember-to-frame attaching bolts and remove the crossmember.
16. Place a support under the engine oil pan, with a wooden block (¾ in. thick) between the support and the engine oil pan.

NOTE: The wooden block and support should be no more than about ¼ in. away from the engine so when the engine is lowered, damage will not occur to any underhood components. If possible, shim the support so the wooden block touches the engine.

17. Lower the jack until the engine rests on the support.

18. Remove the exhaust pipe bracket and the stiffener plate bolts.
19. Remove the transmission-to-engine bolts, draw the transmission/transfer case assembly rearward and down away from the engine.
20. Remove the transmission-to-transfer case adapter bolts and pull the transfer case from the transmission.

To install:

21. Raise the transmission into position under the vehicle.
22. Install the transmission-to-engine bolts.
23. Torque transmission-to-engine bolts to 53 ft. lbs. (73 Nm), the stiffener plate bolts to 27 ft. lbs. (38 Nm), the transmission mount/bracket bolts to 19 ft. lbs. (27 Nm), the rear engine mount bracket-to-crossmember bolts to 9 ft. lbs. (12 Nm).
24. Connect the exhaust pipes and brackets. Install the starter and the clutch release cylinder.
25. Tighten the exhaust pipe-to-manifold bolts to 29 ft. lbs. (40 Nm), the upper exhaust pipe bracket-to-clutch housing bolts to 27 ft. lbs. (38 Nm), the lower exhaust pipe bracket-to-clutch housing bolts to 51 ft. lbs. (69 Nm), the lower starter bolt/release cylinder tube bracket bolt to 29 ft. lbs. (40 Nm), the clutch release cylinder bolts to 9 ft. lbs. (12 Nm).
26. Connect the remaining linkages and connect the driveshaft, aligning the matchmarks made during removal.
27. Refill the transmission to the correct level.
28. Install the shift lever and the center console.
29. Connect the negative battery cable.

PREVIA

1. Disconnect the negative battery cable and drain the transmission fluid.
2. Raise the vehicle and support safely.
3. Remove the starter motor. Matchmark the driveshafts-to-flange and remove the front (4WD) and rear driveshafts.
4. Remove the clutch release cylinder, hose and bracket.
5. Remove the exhaust pipe and bracket.
6. Disconnect the control cables/bracket and speed sensor connector.
7. Remove the engine-to-transmission stiffener plate.
8. Place a suitable transmission jack under the transmission.
9. Remove the engine rear mounting bolts and raise the rear side of the engine.
10. Remove the engine-to-transmission bolts, pull the transmission toward the rear and remove.

To install:

11. Align the input shaft with the clutch disc and push the transmission fully into position.
12. Install the transmission bolts and torque to 53 ft. lbs. (72 Nm).
13. Install the rear engine mounts and stiffener plate. Torque the bolt to 27 ft. lbs. (37 Nm).
14. Connect the speed sensor and control cables.
15. Install the exhaust pipe and torque the bracket to 37 ft. lbs. (51 Nm).
16. Install the clutch release cylinder, starter and driveshafts. Torque the starter to 41 ft. lbs. (56 Nm) and driveshaft bolts to 20 ft. lbs. (25 Nm).
17. Lower the vehicle.
18. Connect the battery cable and refill with transmission fluid.

CLUTCH

Clutch Assembly

Removal and Installation

1. Raise and safely support the vehicle. Remove the transmission from the vehicle.

2. Make matchmarks on the clutch cover and flywheel, indicating their relationship.
3. Loosen the clutch cover-to-flywheel retaining bolts a turn at a time. The pressure on the clutch disc must be released gradually.

4. Remove the clutch cover-to-flywheel bolts. Remove the clutch cover and the clutch disc.

5. If the clutch release bearing is to be replaced, perform the following:

    a. Remove the bearing retaining clip(s), the bearing and hub.

    b. Remove the release fork and the boot.

    c. The bearing is press fitted to the hub.

    d. Clean all parts and lightly grease the input shaft splines and all of the contact points.

    e. Install the bearing/hub assembly, the fork, the boot and the retaining clip(s) in their original locations.

To install:

6. Inspect the flywheel surface for cracks, heat scoring (blue marks) and warpage. Replace or resurface the flywheel, if any damage is present.

NOTE: Before installing any new parts, make sure they are clean. During installation, do not get grease or oil on any of the components, as this will shorten clutch life considerably.

7. Using an clutch alignment tool, position the clutch disc against the flywheel. The raised center section of the disc faces the transmission.

8. Install the clutch cover over the disc and install the bolts loosely. Align the pressure plate-to-flywheel matchmarks. If a new or rebuilt clutch cover assembly is installed, use the matchmark on the old cover assembly as a reference. Torque the pressure plate-to-flywheel bolts to 14 ft. lbs. (19 Nm), using a criss-cross pattern.

9. Install the transmission into the vehicle.

Pedal Height/Free-Play Adjustment

The pedal height measurement is gauged from the angled section of the floorboard to the center of the clutch pedal pad. The correct pedal height is 6.7–7.3 in. for Van, 6.12 for Pick-Up and 4Runner or 6.46 in. for Previa.

If necessary, adjust the pedal height by loosening the locknut and turning the pedal stop bolt which is located above the pedal towards the drivers seat. Tighten the locknut after the adjustment.

Clutch Master Cylinder

Removal and Installation

PICK-UP AND 4RUNNER

1. Disconnect the negative battery cable. Disconnect the master cylinder pushrod pin from the top of the clutch pedal.

2. Remove the hydraulic line from the master cylinder, being careful not to damage the compression fitting.

3. Remove the master cylinder-to-cowl nuts/ bolts.

4. To install, reverse the removal procedures. Partially tighten the hydraulic line before tightening the master cylinder mounting nut(s). Torque the nuts/bolts to 9 ft. lbs. (12 Nm). Bleed the clutch system. Adjust the push rod play clearance.

VAN

1. Disconnect the negative battery terminal from the battery.

2. Remove the reservoir cap from the cluster finish panel, the mounting screws, then, pull the cluster finish panel forward and remove it.

3. Remove the mounting screws and pull the instrument panel forward, then, disconnect the speedometer and the electrical connectors from it.

4. Remove the No. 3, the No. 1 and the No. 2 air ducts.

5. Disconnect and plug the reservoir hose at the master cylinder. Disconnect the clutch line union.

6. Remove the mounting bolts and the master cylinder.

Clutch disc installation

Clutch pedal adjustment points

7. To install, reverse the removal procedures. Bleed the clutch system. Adjust the clutch pedal.

PREVIA

1. Disconnect the negative battery cable.

2. Remove the instrument panel lower finish panel and steering column cover.

3. Remove the clip and clevis pin.

4. Disconnect the reservoir hose and clutch union line.

5. Remove the mounting bolts and pull out the master cylinder.

6. Installation is the reverse of removal. Torque the mounting bolts to 9 ft. lbs. (12 Nm).

7. Bleed the clutch hydraulic system.

8. Connect the battery cable and check operation.

Adjustment

PUSHROD

The pedal pushrod play is the distance between the clutch master cylinder piston and the pedal pushrod located above the pedal towards the firewall. Since it is nearly impossible to measure this distance at the source, it must be measured at the pedal pad, preferably with a dial indicator gauge. The pushrod play specification is: 0.040–0.200 for Land Cruiser and Previa or 0.039–0.197 for Vans, Pick-Ups and 4Runner.

If necessary, adjust the pedal play by loosening the pedal pushrod locknut and turning the pushrod. Tighten the locknut after the adjustment.

FREE-PLAY

The free-play measurement is the total travel of the clutch pedal from the fully released position to where resistance is felt as the pedal is pushed downward. The free-play specification is: 0.20–0.59 for all vehicles.

Clutch Slave Cylinder

Removal and Installation

1. Raise and safely support the vehicle.
2. If equipped, remove the tension spring on the clutch fork.
3. Remove the hydraulic line from the release cylinder. Be careful not to damage the fitting.
4. Turn the release cylinder pushrod in sufficiently to gain clearance from the fork.
5. Remove the mounting bolts and withdraw the cylinder.
6. To install, reverse the removal procedures. Bleed the clutch system. Adjust the fork tip clearance.

Hydraulic Clutch System Bleeding

1. Fill the master cylinder reservoir with brake fluid.
2. Remove the cap and loosen the bleeder screw on the clutch release cylinder. Cover the hole with a finger.
3. Pump the clutch pedal several times. Take the finger off the hole while the pedal is being depressed so the air in the system can be released. Put a finger back on the hole and release the pedal.
4. When fluid pressure can be felt tighten the bleeder screw.
5. Place a short length of hose over the bleeder screw and the other end in a jar half full of clean brake fluid.
6. Depress the clutch pedal and loosen the bleeder screw. Allow the fluid to flow into the jar.
7. Tighten the plug, then release the clutch pedal.
8. Repeat this procedure until no air bubbles are visible in the bleeder tube.
9. When there are no more air bubbles in the system, tighten the plug fully with the pedal depressed. Replace the plastic cap.
10. Refill the master cylinder to the correct level with brake fluid. Check the system for leaks.

AUTOMATIC TRANSMISSION

For further information, please refer to Chilton's Transmission Service Manual.

Transmission Assembly

Removal and Installation

1. Disconnect the negative battery terminal from the battery. On the Pick-Up and 4Runner, remove the air cleaner assembly.
2. Disconnect the transmission throttle cable from the carburetor linkage or the throttle body.
3. Raise and safely support the vehicle. Drain the transmission fluid.
4. Disconnect the wiring connectors (near the starter) for the neutral start switch and the back-up light switch. If equipped, disconnect the solenoid (overdrive) switch wiring at the same location. Disconnect the oil level gauge for Previa.
5. Disconnect the starter wiring at the starter. Remove the mounting bolts and the starter from the engine.
6. Make matchmarks on the rear driveshaft flange and the differential pinion flange. These marks must be aligned during installation.
7. Unbolt the rear driveshaft flange. If the vehicle has a 2 piece driveshaft, remove the center bearing bracket-to-frame bolts. Remove the driveshaft from the vehicle.
8. Disconnect the speedometer cable (tie it aside) and the shift linkage from the transmission.
9. Disconnect the transmission oil cooler lines at the transmission.
10. Disconnect the exhaust pipe clamp and remove the oil filler tube.
11. Support the transmission, using a jack with a wooden block placed between the jack and the transmission pan. Raise the transmission, just enough to take the weight off of the rear mount.
12. On the Pick-Up and 4Runner, remove the rear engine mount with the bracket and the engine under cover, to gain access to the engine crankshaft pulley. On the Van, remove the fuel tank mounting bolts and support the fuel tank; remove the transmission mount through bolt. Remove the stiffener plates on 2WD Previa.

13. Place a wooden block (or blocks) between the engine oil pan and the front frame crossmember.
14. Slowly, lower the transmission until the engine rests on the wooden block.
15. Remove the rubber plug(s) from the service holes located at the rear of the engine in order to gain access to the torque convertor bolts.
16. Rotate the crankshaft (to remove the torque convertor bolts) to access the bolts through the service holes.
17. Obtain a bolt of the same dimensions as the torque convertor bolts. Cut the head off of the bolt and hacksaw a slot in the bolt opposite the threaded end.

NOTE: **This modified bolt is used as a guide pin. Two guides pins are needed to properly install the transmission.**

18. Thread the guide pin into one of the torque convertor bolt holes. The guide pin will help keep the convertor with the transmission.
19. Remove the stiffener plates from the transmission.
20. Remove the transmission-to-engine bolts, then carefully move the transmission rearward by prying on the guide pin through the service hole.
21. Pull the transmission rearward and lower it (front end down) out of the vehicle.

To install:

22. Apply a coat of multi-purpose grease to the torque convertor stub shaft and the corresponding pilot hole in the flywheel.
23. Install the torque convertor into the front of the transmission. Push inward on the torque convertor while rotating it to completely couple the torque convertor to the transmission.
24. To make sure the convertor is properly installed, measure the distance between the torque convertor mounting lugs and the front mounting face of the transmission. The proper distance is 0.080 in.
25. Install guide pins into 2 opposite mounting lugs of the torque convertor.
26. Raise the transmission to the engine, align the transmission with the engine alignment dowels and position the convertor guide pins into the mounting holes of the flywheel.
27. Install and tighten the transmission-to-engine mounting bolts. Torque the bolts to 47 ft. lbs. (63 Nm).
28. Remove the convertor guide pins and install the convertor

mounting bolts. Rotate the crankshaft as necessary to gain access to the guide pins and bolts through the service holes. Evenly, tighten the convertor mounting bolts to 13 ft. lbs. (17 Nm). Install the rubber plugs into the access holes.

29. Install the engine undercover. Raise the transmission slightly and remove the wood block(s) from under the engine oil pan.

30. Install the transmission crossmember. Torque the crossmember-to-frame bolts to 26–36 ft. lbs. (34–48 Nm).

31. Lower the transmission onto the crossmember and install the transmission mounting bolts. Torque the bolts to 19 ft. lbs. (26 Nm).

32. Install the oil filler tube and connect the exhaust pipe clamp.

33. Connect the oil cooler lines to the transmission and torque the fittings to 25 ft. lbs. (34 Nm).

34. To complete the installation, reverse the removal procedures. Adjust the transmission throttle cable. Refill the transmission with Dexron®II fluid. Road test the vehicle and check for leaks.

Shift Linkage Adjustment

1. Loosen the adjustment nut on the transmission shift cable.
2. Push the manual lever of the transmission fully rearward except for Previaor downward for Previa.
3. Move the manual lever back 2 notches, which is the **N** position except for Previa or 3 notches for Previa.
4. Set the gearshift selector lever in the **N** position.
5. Apply a slight amount of forward pressure on the selector lever and tighten the shift cable adjustment nut.

Throttle Linkage Adjustment

1. Remove the air cleaner assembly.
2. Push the accelerator to the floor and check that the throttle valve opens fully; if not, adjust the accelerator link, so it does.
3. Push back the rubber boot from the throttle cable which runs down to the transmission. Loosen the throttle cable adjustment nuts so the cable housing can be adjusted.
4. Fully open the carburetor throttle by pressing the accelerator all the way to the floor.
5. Adjust the cable housing so, with the throttle wide open,

Throttle linkage adjustment

the distance between the outer cable end rubber cap to the inner cable stopper is 0–0.04 in. (0–1mm).

6. Tighten the nuts and double check the adjustment. Install the rubber boot and the air cleaner.

Neutral Start Switch Adjustment

The neutral safety switch prevents the vehicle from starting unless the gearshift selector is in either the **P** or **N** positions. If the vehicle will start in these positions, adjustment of the switch is required.

1. Loosen the neutral start switch bolt.
2. Place the selector lever in the **N** position.
3. Disconnect the wires from the neutral start switch.
4. Connect an ohmmeter between the terminals of the switch.
5. Adjust the switch until there is continuity between the N and B terminals.
6. Reconnect the wires. Torque the bolt to 48 inch lbs. (65 Nm).

TRANSFER CASE

Transfer Case Assembly

Removal and Installation

The transfer case and transmission are connected together. It is recommended by the manufacturer that they be removed from the vehicle as an assembly and then separated for repairs.

DRIVE AXLE

Front Halfshaft

Removal and Installation

4WD PICK-UP, 4RUNNER AND VAN

1. Remove the 4WD hub (with the flange) from the axle hub.
2. Raise and safely support the vehicle. Remove the wheel and tire assembly.
3. Disconnect and plug the brake line from the caliper. Remove the caliper from the axle hub.

4. Using a drift punch and a hammer, drive the lock washer tabs away from the locknut.

5. Remove the locknut from the halfshaft. Remove the lock washer, the adjusting nut, the thrust washer, the outer bearing and the axle hub/disc assembly from the vehicle.

6. Remove the knuckle spindle bolts, the dust seal and the dust cover. Using a brass bar and a hammer, tap the steering spindle from the steering knuckle.

7. Turn the halfshaft until a flat spot on the outer shaft is in the upper position, then pull the halfshaft from the steering knuckle.

8. Using a slide hammer, pull the oil seal from the axle housing.

9. Using a clean shop towel, wipe the grease from inside the steering knuckle housing and the halfshaft.

To install:

10. Using an oil seal installation tool, drive a new oil seal into the axle housing until it seats.

11. Install the halfshaft into the axle housing.

12. Using multi-purpose grease, fill the steering knuckle cavity to about ¾ full.

13. To complete the installation, use new seals/gaskets and reverse the removal procedures.

14. Torque the steering spindle-to-steering knuckle bolts to 38 ft. lbs. (52 Nm), the axle hub adjusting nut to 18 ft. lbs. (25 Nm), the axle hub locknut to 33 ft. lbs. (44 Nm), the free wheel/locking hub nuts to 23 ft. lbs. (33 Nm) and the brake caliper to 65 ft. lbs. (88 Nm).

NOTE: To install the wheel bearings with the axle hub, torque the adjusting nut to 43 ft. lbs. (58 Nm), turn the axle hub (back and forth, several times), loosen the nut and retorque the adjusting nut to 18 ft. lbs. (24 Nm).

15. Install the wheel and tire assembly. Lower the vehicle.

4WD PREVIA

1. Raise and safely support the vehicle. Remove the wheel and tire assembly.

2. Using a drift punch and a hammer, drive the lock washer tabs away from the locknut.

3. Remove the locknut from the halfsahft. Remove the lock washer, the adjusting nut and the thrust washer.

4. Using a tie rod remover 0962810011 or equivalent, remove the tie rod end from the knuckle.

5. Remove the 6 bolts from the inner shaft joint.

6. Disconnect the knuckle from the lower ball joint by removing the 2 bolts.

7. Remove the halfshaft by pulling the knuckle outward and remove the halfshaft from the wheel hub. If the outer shaft will not come out of the hub, soak the splines with penetrating lube, install the nut and tap on the halfshaft with a soft hammer. Be careful not to damage the shaft threads.

To install:

NOTE: Coat the halfshaft splines with anti-seize compound to prevent spline secure. This will help for future halfshaft removal.

8. Connect the lower ball joint and torque the bolts to 94 ft. lbs. (127 Nm).

9. Install the inner halfshaft joint-to-drive axle and torque the bolts to 51 ft. lbs. (61 Nm).

10. Install the tie rod end, torque the nut to 36 ft. lbs. (49 Nm) and install a new cotter pin.

11. Install the halfshaft nut and torque to 76 ft. lbs. (103 Nm).

12. Install the remaining components and check operation.

CV-Boot

Removal and Installation

INNER BOOT

1. Remove the halfshaft from the vehicle.

2. Clean the halfshaft with soap and water. Remove the 2 inner boot clamps and slide the inner boot off the the joint.

3. Place matchmarks on the inner joint outer race and shaft. Remove the outer race from the shaft. Some joints have a large snapring on the inner side of the race that has to be removed.

4. Remove the snapring from the end of the inner joint. Pull the inner joint and boot from the shaft splines.

To install:

5. Install the boot, inner joint and snapring.

6. Fill the boot and joint with special CV-boot grease. The grease ussually comes with replacement boot kits.

7. Slide the boot into position and install the clamps.

OUTER BOOT

1. Remove the inner joint and boot from the shaft.

2. Tape the inner splines to protect the boots.

3. Remove the 2 outer boot clamps and slide the outer boot off the the joint.

4. Installation is the reverse of removal. Clean the outer joint from all old grease and repack with special CV-boot grease.

Driveshaft and U-Joints

Removal and Installation

4WD VEHICLES EXCEPT LONG BED PICK-UP

Rear

1. Raise and safely support the vehicle and place a drain pan under the transmission.

2. Paint a mating mark on the halves of the rear universal joint flange.

3. Remove the bolts which hold the rear flange together.

4. Remove the splined end of the driveshaft from the transmission. The Previa rear shaft is bolted at both ends.

NOTE: Plug the end of the transmission with a rag or dummy flange to avoid losing transmission oil.

5. Remove the driveshaft from under the vehicle.

6. To install, reverse the removal procedures. Grease the splined end of the shaft before installing. Torque bolts to 31 ft. lbs. (42 Nm) for Van and Previa or 54 ft. lbs. (75 Nm) for Pickup and 4Runner.

ALL 4WD VEHICLES

Front

1. Raise and safely support the vehicle.

2. Matchmark the driveshaft flange at the front axle housing and the transfer case.

3. On Vans, remove the differential support bracket. On Previa, remove the center support bracket.

4. On Pick-Up and 4Runner, remove the flange dust cover.

5. Remove the bolts retaining the driveshaft and remove the driveshaft from the vehicle.

6. Install the driveshaft by aligning the matchmarks made during removal.

7. Torque the retaining bolts to 54–58 ft. lbs. (74–78 Nm). Torque the center support bracket bolts to 35 ft. lbs. (48 Nm). Make sure the drain hole is facing downward.

2WD LONG BED PICK-UP

Rear

1. Raise and safely support the vehicle.

2. Paint mating marks on all 6 flange halves.

3. Remove the bolts attaching the rear universal joint flange to the drive pinion flange.

4. Drop the rear section of the shaft slightly and pull the unit out of the center bearing sleeve yoke.

5. Remove the center bearing support from the crossmember.

6. Unbolt the driveshaft flange from the rear of the transmission and remove driveshaft along with center bearing support.

7. To install, align the matchmarks and reverse the removal procedures. Torque the flange bolts to 54 ft. lbs. (75 Nm).

FRONT DRIVESHAFT ASSEMBLY

SPIDER BEARING

CENTER BEARING   FLANGE

SPIDER   INTERMEDIATE SHAFT

FLANGE YOKE

SPIDER BEARING

SPIDER

FLANGE YOKE

FLANGE YOKE   SLEEVE YOKE

DRIVESHAFT

Driveshaft assemblies—Pick-Up and 4Runner

Front Axle Shaft

Removal and Installation

LAND CRUISER

1. Raise and safely support the vehicle. Remove the wheel and tire assembly.
2. Plug the brake master cylinder reservoir to prevent brake fluid leakage from the disconnected brake flexible hose.
3. Remove the outer axle shaft flange cap for automatic locking hub, the hub cover bolts and the cover for free wheel locking hub and the shaft snapring from the axle hub.
4. Remove the outer axle shaft flange for automatic locking hub or the hub ring-to-axle hub bolts, then alternately, screw 2 service bolts into the shaft flange or hub ring and remove the shaft flange or the hub ring with it's gasket.
5. Remove the caliper and disc.
6. Straighten the lock washer and remove the front wheel bearing adjusting nuts with front wheel adjusting nut wrench or similar tool.
7. Remove the front axle hub together with its claw washer, bearings and oil seal.
8. Remove the clip and disconnect the brake flexible hose from the brake tube.
9. Cut and remove the lock wire.
10. Using a soft mallet, lightly, tap the steering knuckle spindle and remove the spindle with it's gasket.

NOTE: When removing the steering knuckle spindle, if equipped with the ball joint type axle shaft joint, be prepared for the disconnection of the outer axle shaft from the joint. Prevent the shaft joint ball from falling from the joint.

11. If equipped with the ball type axle shaft joint, slide the inner front axle shaft out of the axle housing. If equipped with the Birfield constant velocity joint type of axle shaft joint, remove the entire axle shaft assembly from the axle housing.
12. Using a bearing puller, remove the bushing from inside of knuckle spindle and the axle housing oil seal. Using a metal tube as a seating tool, drive oil seal into the axle housing and the new bushing into the knuckle spindle.

NOTE: If equipped with the ball joint type axle joint, install the inner axle with its proper spacer in position until the splines are fully meshed with the differential. If equipped with the Birfield constant velocity joint axle joint, install the axle into the housing and rotate the axle shaft until its splines mesh with the differential. Fill the steering knuckle about ¾ full with grease and place the joint ball on the inner shaft end.

13. To complete the installation, reverse the removal procedures. Adjust the wheel bearing preload.

Front Axle Bearing

Removal and Installation

EXCEPT 4WD PREVIA

1. Raise and safely support the vehicle. Remove the 4WD hubs.
2. Using a small prybar, pry the grease seal from the rear of the disc/hub assembly, then remove the inner bearing from the assembly.
3. Using a shop cloth, wipe the grease from inside the disc/hub assembly.
4. Using a brass drift, drive the outer bearing races from each side of the disc/hub assembly.
5. Using solvent, clean all of the parts and blow dry with compressed air.

Front drive axle assembly—Pick-Up and 4Runner

Labels on diagram: INBOARD JOINT TULIP, SNAPRING, CLAMP, FREE WHEELING HUB COVER, GASKET, TRIPOD JOINT, DRIVESHAFT, SPACER, GASKET, BOOT, CLAMP, SNAPRING, CLAMP, BOOT, FREE WHEELING HUB BODY, CLAMP, DUST DEFLECTOR

To install:

6. Using a bearing installation tool, drive the outer races into the disc/hub assembly until they seat against the shoulder.

7. Using multi-purpose grease, coat the area between the races and pack the bearings.

8. Place the inner bearing into the rear of the disc/hub assembly. Using a bearing installation tool, drive a new grease seal into the rear of the disc/hub assembly until it is flush with the housing.

9. Install the disc/hub assembly onto the axle shaft, the outer bearing, the thrust washer and the adjusting nut.

10. To adjust the bearing preload, perform the following:
   a. Torque the adjusting nut to 43 ft. lbs. (58 Nm).
   b. Turn the disc/hub assembly 2–3 times, from the left to the right.
   c. Loosen the adjusting nut until it can be turned by hand.
   d. Retorque the adjusting nut to 18 ft. lbs. (25 Nm).
   e. Install the lock washer and the locknut. Torque the locknut to 33 ft. lbs. (44 Nm).
   f. Check that the bearing has no play.
   g. Using a spring gauge, connect it to a wheel stud, the gauge should be held horizontal, then measure the rotating force, it should be 6–12 lbs. (8–15 Nm).

11. Lower the vehicle.

4WD PREVIA

1. Remove the steering knuckle from the vehicle. Place the assembly in a vise.

2. Using a hub remover tool (slide hammer) 0952000031 or equivalent, remove the wheel hub from the knuckle.

3. Remove the bearing from the hub using a press and arbor tool 0955010012 or equivalent.

4. Remove the dust protector and oil seal.

5. Remove the bearing snapring from the knuckle and press the inner bearing from the knuckle.

To install:

6. Using a press and arbor tool 0960810010 or equivalent, press the bearing into the knuckle.

7. Install the outer oil seal and dust cover.

8. Press the axle hub onto the knuckle.

9. Install the knuckle assembly onto the vehicle.

Rear Axle Shaft and Bearings

Removal and Installation

PICK-UP AND 4RUNNER

1. Loosen the rear wheel lug nuts, then raise and safely support the vehicle. Remove the wheel and tire assembly.

2. Place a pan under the axle, remove the plug and drain the axle housing.

3. For 2WD vehicles, remove the clip/clamp-to-frame bolts and disconnect the parking brake cable from the equalizer. For 4WD vehicles, remove the pin and disconnect the rear parking brake cable from the bell crank.

4. Remove the brake drum securing screw and the drum.

5. Disconnect the brake line from the wheel cylinder and plug it, being careful not to damage the fitting.

6. Remove the brake backing plate-to-axle housing nuts and pull the backing plate with the axle from the axle housing.

NOTE: When removing the axle shaft, be careful not to damage the oil seal.

7. Using a pair of snapring pliers, remove the snapring from the axle shaft.

8. Slip tool 09521–25011 or equivalent, over the axle shaft

and fasten it to the backing plate. Using 2 metal blocks and a press, press the axle from the backing plate assembly.

9. If necessary to remove the bearing from backing plate, perform the following:

a. Remove the brake spring, the retracting spring clamp bolt, the lower springs, the shoe strut, the brake shoes and the parking brake lever.

b. Using a slide hammer puller, pull the outer oil seal from the backing plate.

c. Press the bearing from the backing plate.

d. Using the proper installation tools, press the new bearing into the backing plate.

e. Using the proper seal installation tool, press the new oil seal into the backing plate.

f. Reassemble the brake components to the backing plate.

10. Using a slide hammer, pull the oil seal from the axle housing.

To install:

11. Using the installation tool and a hammer, drive a new oil seal into the axle housing.

12. Using a press, press the axle shaft into the backing plate and the bearing retainer. Using snapring pliers, install the snapring onto the axle shaft.

13. Clean the gasket mounting surfaces.

14. To complete the installation, reverse the removal procedures. Torque the backing plate-to-axle housing nuts to 51 ft. lbs. (69 Nm). Adjust the brake shoe clearance and bleed the brake system. Refill the axle housing with SAE 90W GL5 gear oil.

VAN AND PREVIA

1. Loosen the rear wheel nuts. Raise and safely support the vehicle. Remove the wheel and tire assembly.

2. Remove the brake drum or caliper and rotor.

3. Working through the hole in the axle flange, remove the backing plate-to-axle housing bolts.

4. Using a slide hammer puller, pull the axle shaft from the housing.

5. Using a grinder, grind down the inner bearing retainer on the axle shaft. Using a chisel and a hammer, cut off the retainer and remove it from the shaft.

6. Using a arbor press, press the bearing from the axle shaft.

7. Using a slide hammer puller, pull the oil seal from the axle housing.

To install:

8. Lubricate the new oil seal with multi-purpose grease. Using the proper seal installation tool and a hammer, drive the new oil seal into the axle housing to a depth of 0.236 in.

9. To install, use new gaskets and reverse the removal procedures. Torque the axle retainer-to-housing bolts to 48 ft. lbs. (65 Nm).

LAND CRUISER

Semi-Floating Type

1. Loosen the rear wheel nuts. Raise and safely support the vehicle. Remove the wheel and tire assembly.

2. Place a pan under the axle, remove the plug and drain the oil from the differential.

3. Remove the brake drum and related parts, as follows:

a. Remove the cover from the back of the differential housing.

b. Remove the pin from the differential pinion shaft.

c. Withdraw the pinion shaft and it's spacer from the case.

d. Use a mallet to tap the rear axle shaft toward the differential, then remove the C-lock from the axle shaft.

e. Withdraw the axle shaft from the housing.

4. Using a bearing puller, remove axle bearing and oil seal together from the axle housing. Using a metal tube and a hammer, drive the bearing and the seal into the housing until they seat.

NOTE: Do not mix the parts of the left and right axle shaft assemblies.

5. To complete the installation, reverse the removal procedures. Refill the axle housing with SAE 90W GL5 gear oil.

NOTE: After installing the axle shaft, C-lock, spacer and pinion shaft, measure the clearance between the axle shaft and the pinion shaft spacer with a feeler gauge. The clearance should fall between 0.0024–0.0181 in. If the clearance is not within specifications, use one of the following spacers to adjust it:

a. 1.172–1.173 in.

b. 1.188–1.189 in.

c. 1.204–1.205 in.

Full Floating Type

1. Loosen the rear wheel nuts. Raise and safely support the vehicle. Remove the wheel and tire assembly.

2. Place a pan under the axle, remove the plug and drain the oil from the differential.

3. Remove the rear axle shaft plate nuts.

4. Remove the cone washers from the mounting studs by tapping the slits of the washers with a tapered punch.

5. Install bolts into the 2 unused holes of the axle shaft plate.

6. Tighten the bolts to draw the axle shaft assembly out of the housing.

7. To install, use a new gasket, sealant and reverse the removal procedures. Torque the axle shaft nuts to 21–25 ft. lbs. (27–34 Nm).

Front Wheel Hub, Knuckle and Bearing

Removal and Installation

2WD PICK-UP AND VAN

1. Raise and safely support the vehicle. Remove the wheel and tire assembly.

2. Remove the brake caliper. Do not disconnect the brake hose from the caliper. Suspend it on a wire.

3. Remove axle hub dust cap, the cotter pin, the nut lock, the adjusting nut, the thrust washer and the outer bearing, then pull the hub/disc assembly from the axle spindle.

4. Remove the backing plate cotter pins and the mounting nuts or bolts, then the backing plate.

5. Remove steering knuckle arm from the back of the steering knuckle.

6. Remove the nuts, the retainers and the bushings, then the shock absorber from the lower control arm.

7. Support the lower arm with a jack and raise to put pressure on spring.

NOTE: Be careful not to unbalance vehicle support stands when jacking up lower arm.

8. Remove cotter pins, then the upper and lower ball joint nuts. Using a ball joint removal tool, separate the ball joints from the steering knuckle.

9. Remove the steering knuckle from the vehicle.

NOTE: Whenever the hub/disc assembly is removed from the vehicle, it is good practice to replace the grease seal.

10. To install, reverse the removal procedures. Torque the upper ball joint nut to 80 ft. lbs. (109 Nm) for Pick-Up or 58 ft. lbs. (78 Nm) for Van, the lower ball joint nut to 105 ft. lbs. (142 Nm) for Pick-Up or 76 ft. lbs. (109 Nm), the steering knuckle arm-to-steering knuckle bolts to 80 ft. lbs. (109 Nm) for Pick-Up or 61 ft. lbs. (90 Nm) for Van, the shock absorber-to-lower control arm nuts to 19 ft. lbs. (27 Nm) and the backing plate-to-steering

knuckle bolts to 80 ft. lbs. (109 Nm) for Pick-Up or 61 ft. lbs. (90 Nm) for Van. Adjust the wheel bearing.

4WD VEHICLES

1. Remove the front axle shaft assembly from the vehicle.
2. Remove the oil seal retainer and the oil seal set from the rear of the steering knuckle.
3. At the drag link end of the steering knuckle arm, remove the cotter pin. Using the proper tool, remove the plug from the drag link, then disconnect the drag link from the steering knuckle arm.
4. Remove the tie rod-to-steering knuckle, cotter pin and nut. Using the proper ball joint removal tool, separate the tie rod from the steering knuckle arm.
5. Remove the steering knuckle arm-to-steering knuckle (top) nuts and the steering knuckle-to-bearing cap (bottom) nuts. Using a tapered punch, tap the cone washers slits and remove the washers.

NOTE: Do not mix or lose the upper and lower bearing cap shims.

6. Using a bearing removal tool (without a collar), press the steering knuckle arm with the shims from the steering knuckle.
7. Using a bearing removal tool (without a collar), press the bearing cap with the shims from the steering knuckle.
8. Remove the steering knuckle from the vehicle.

To install:

9. To install the steering knuckle, use a suitable tool to support the upper inner bearing. Using a hammer, tap the steering knuckle arm into the bearing inner race.
10. Using the proper tool, support the lower bearing inner race. Using a hammer, tap the bearing cap into the bearing inner race.

NOTE: When installing the drag link-to-steering knuckle arm, torque the plug all the way, then loosen it 1⅓ turns and secure it with the cotter pin.

11. To install, use gaskets, seals, pack the steering knuckle with multi-purpose grease and reverse the removal procedures for the Land Cruiser.
    a. Torque the steering knuckle arm-to-steering knuckle nuts to 71 ft. lbs. (95 Nm).
    b. Torque the bearing cap-to-steering knuckle nuts to 71 ft. lbs. (95 Nm).
    c. Torque the tie rod-to-steering knuckle arm nut to 67 ft. lbs. (91 Nm).
    d. Torque the axle spindle-to-steering knuckle bolts to 38 ft. lbs. (51 Nm).
12. To install, reverse the removal procedures for the Pick-Up, 4Runner and Van.
    a. Torque the upper ball joint nut to 80 ft. lbs. (109 Nm) for Pick-Up and 4Runner or 58 ft. lbs. (78 Nm) for Van.
    b. Torque the lower ball joint nut to 105 ft. lbs. (142 Nm) for Pick-Up and 4Runner or 76 ft. lbs. (109 Nm) for Van.
    c. Torque the steering knuckle arm-to-steering knuckle bolts to 80 ft. lbs. (109 Nm) for Pick-Up and 4Runner or 61 ft. lbs. (90 Nm) for Van.
    d. Torque the shock absorber-to-lower control arm nuts to 19 ft. lbs. (27 Nm).
    e. Torque the backing plate-to-steering knuckle bolts to 80 ft. lbs. (109 Nm) for Pick-Up and 4Runner or 61 ft. lbs. (90 Nm) for Van.
13. Adjust the wheel bearing preload.

NOTE: To test the knuckle bearing preload, attach a spring scale to the tie rod end hole (at a right angle) in the steering knuckle arm. The force required to move the knuckle from side to side should be 6.6–13 lbs. (10–17 N) except for Land Cruiser or 4–5 lbs. (5–7 N) for Land Cruiser. If the preload is not correct, adjust by replacing shims.

Front hub and steering knuckle—typical 2WD vehicle

PREVIA

1. Loosen the halfshaft nut. Raise the vehicle and support safely.
2. Remove the front wheels and disconnect the ABS sensor, if equipped.
3. Remove the front caliper and rotor. Secure the caliper to the vehicle with wire.
4. Remove the the halfshaft nut for 4WD.
5. Remove the MacPherson strut-to-knuckle bolts and lower ball joint bolts.
6. Separate the tie rod end using a remover tool 0962810011 or equivalent.
7. Make sure the halfshaft splines are loose and remove the halfshaft from the knuckle.
8. Remove the steering knuckle/hub assembly.
9. 2WD only, remove the grease cap. Using a chisel, release the nut stake and nut.
10. Using a hub remover tool (slide hammer) 0952000031 or equivalent, remove the wheel hub from the knuckle.
11. Remove the bearing from the hub using a press and arbor tool 0955010012 or equivalent.
12. Remove the dust protector and oil seal.
13. Remove the bearing snapring from the knuckle and press the inner bearing from the knuckle.

To install:

14. Using a press and arbor tool 0960810010 or equivalent, press the bearing into the knuckle.

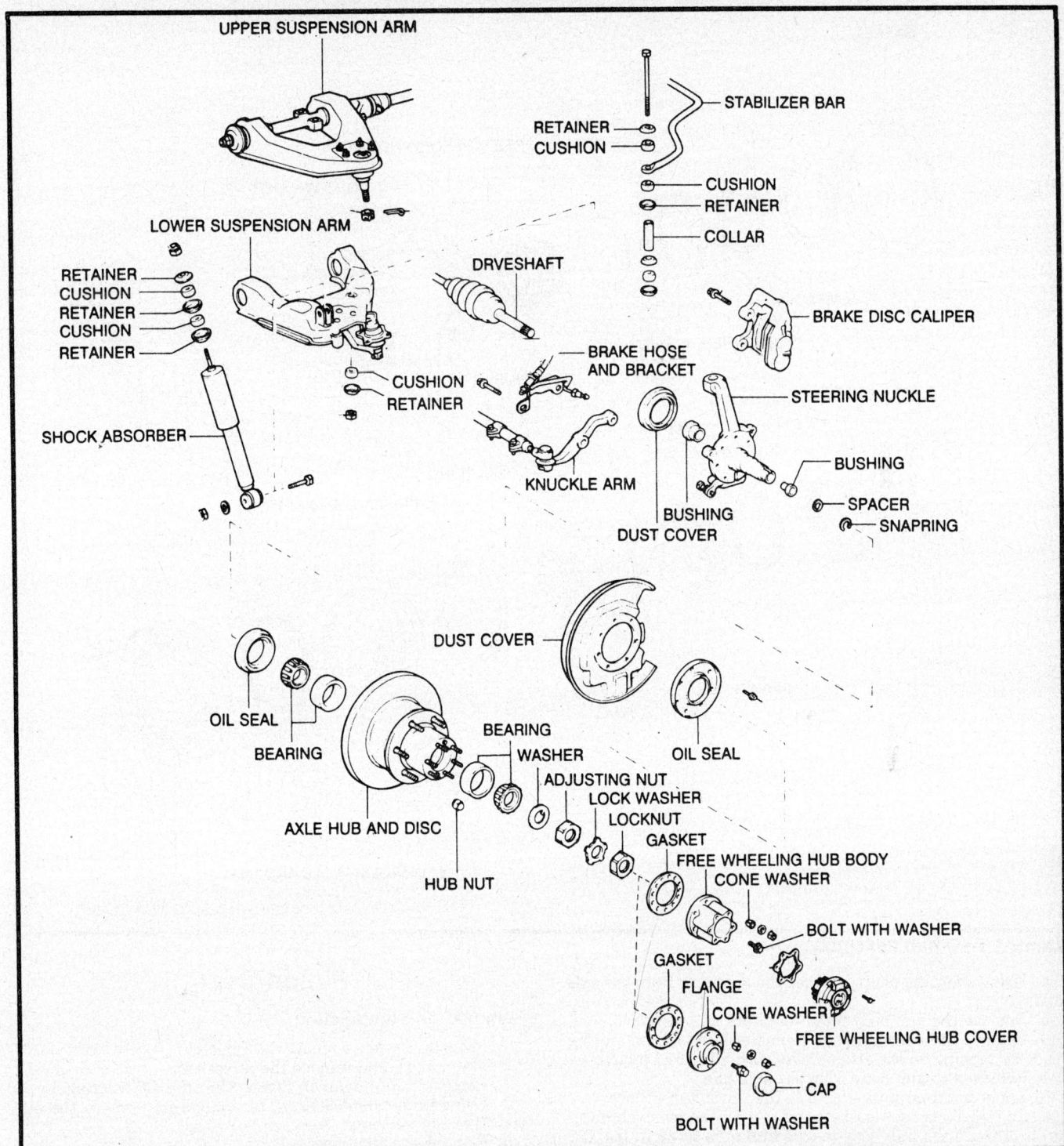

UPPER SUSPENSION ARM

STABILIZER BAR

RETAINER
CUSHION

CUSHION
RETAINER
COLLAR

LOWER SUSPENSION ARM

DRVESHAFT

BRAKE DISC CALIPER

RETAINER
CUSHION
RETAINER
CUSHION
RETAINER

BRAKE HOSE
AND BRACKET

STEERING NUCKLE

CUSHION
RETAINER

BUSHING

SHOCK ABSORBER

KNUCKLE ARM

BUSHING
DUST COVER

BUSHING
SPACER
SNAPRING

DUST COVER

OIL SEAL

BEARING

BEARING
WASHER
ADJUSTING NUT
LOCK WASHER
LOCKNUT
GASKET
FREE WHEELING HUB BODY
CONE WASHER

OIL SEAL

AXLE HUB AND DISC

HUB NUT

BOLT WITH WASHER

GASKET
FLANGE
CONE WASHER

FREE WHEELING HUB COVER

CAP

BOLT WITH WASHER

Front hub and steering knuckle—typical 4WD vehicle

15. Install the outer oil seal and dust cover.
16. Press the axle hub onto the knuckle.
17. 2WD only, install the lock nut and torque to 147 ft. lbs. (199 Nm). Stake the nut and install the dust cover.
18. Install the knuckle assembly onto the vehicle. Torque the tie rod ends to 36 ft. lbs. (49 Nm), strut bolts to 231 ft. lbs. (314 Nm), lower ball joint bolts to 94 ft. lbs. (147 Nm) and 4WD halfshaft nut to 137 ft. lbs. (186 Nm).

Locking Hubs

Removal and Installation

1. If equipped with free-wheeling hubs, turn the hub control handle to the **FREE** position.
2. Remove the hub cover bolts and pull off the cover.
3. If equipped with automatic locking hubs, remove the axle bolt with the washer.

GASKET

SNAPRING

SPACER

FREE WHEELING HUB BODY

CONE WASHER

SNAPRING

FREE WHEELING HUB RING

INNER HUB

BOLT WITH WASHER

CLUTCH

PAWL

SNAPRING

STEEL BALL AND SPRING

GASKET

SPRING

SPRING

CONTROL HANDLE AND SEAL

FREE WHEELING HUB COVER

Manual 4WD hub assembly

4. Using snapring pliers, remove the snapring from the axle shaft.

5. Remove the hub body mounting nuts.

6. Remove the cone washers from the hub body mounting studs by tapping on the washer slits with a tapered punch.

7. Remove the hub body from the axle hub.

8. Apply multi-purpose grease to the inner hub splines.

9. To install, use new gaskets and reverse the removal procedures. Torque the hub body-to-axle hub nuts to 23 ft. lbs. (31 Nm), the plate washer/bolt to 13 ft. lbs. (17 Nm) for auto. locking hub and the hub cover-to-hub body bolts to 7 ft. lbs. (10 Nm).

NOTE: To install the snapring onto the axle shaft, install a bolt into the axle shaft, pull it out and install the snapring.

Pinion Seal

Removal and Installation

1. Raise and safely support the vehicle.

2. Matchmark and remove the driveshaft.

3. Remove the companion flange from the differential.

4. Using puller 09308–10010 or equivalent, remove the oil seal from the housing.

5. Remove the oil slinger.

6. Remove the bearing and spacer.

To install:

7. Install the bearing spacer and bearing.

NOTE: Lubricate the seal lips with multi-purpose grease before installing it.

8. Install the oil slinger and using seal installer 09554–30011 or equivalent, install the oil seal.

9. Drive the seal into place, to a depth of 0.59 in below the housing lip for 7.5 in. axles and 0.39 in. below the lip for 8 in. axles.

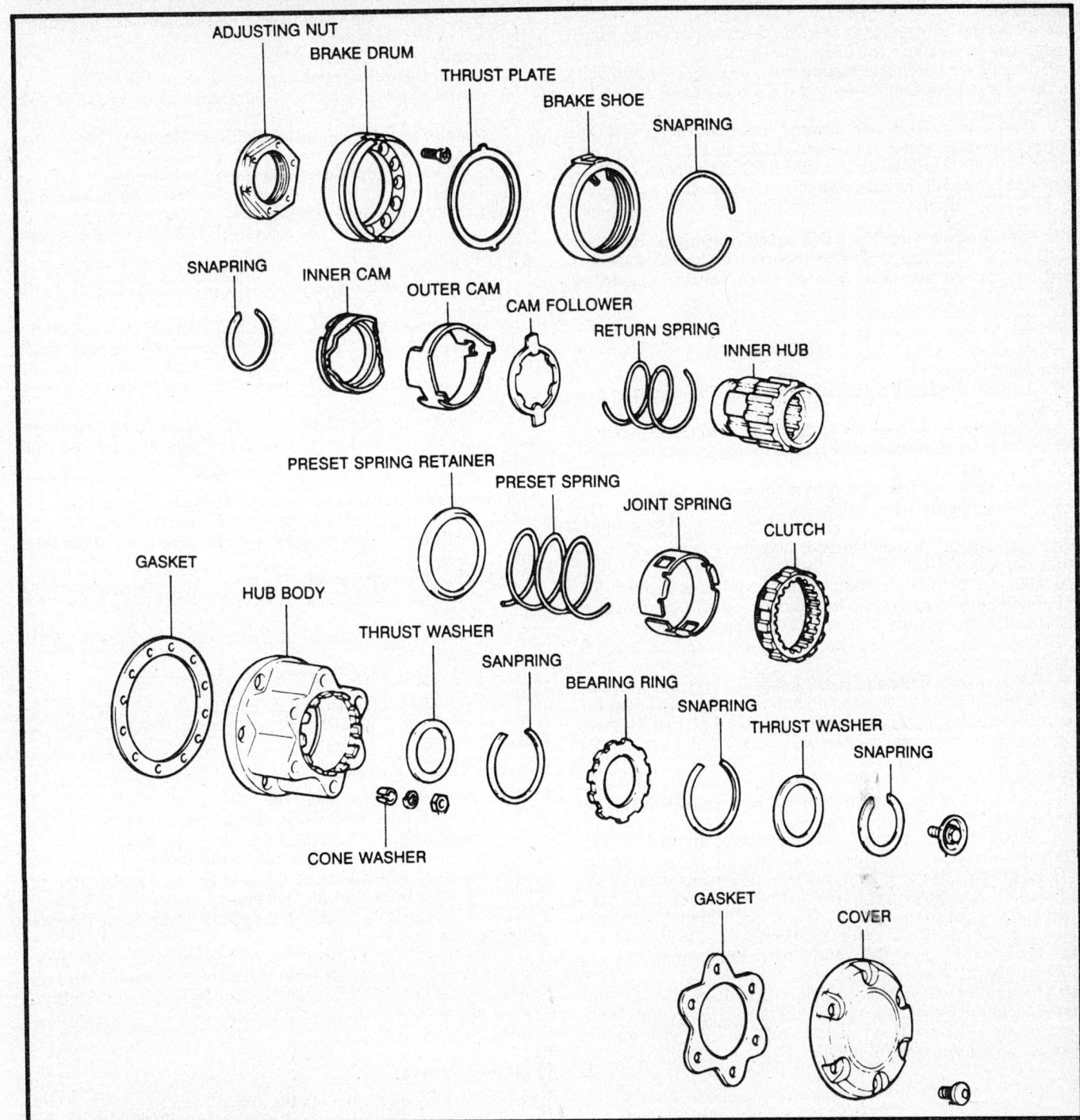

Automatic 4WD hub assembly

10. Install the companion flange and install the driveshaft.
11. Lower the vehicle.

Differential Carrier

Removal and Installation

REAR AND LAND CRUISER FRONT

1. Raise and safely support the vehicle. Drain the lubricant from the differential.

2. Remove the axle shafts from the axle housing.
3. Matchmark the driveshaft flange to the differential flange. Remove the mounting bolts and separate the driveshaft from the differential.
4. Remove the differential retaining nuts and pull the assembly out of the differential housing.
5. Place matchmarks on the bearing caps, carrier housing and adjusting nuts.
6. Remove the 4 bolts and bearing caps. Lift the carrier assembly with the side bearings out of the housing. Tag the parts to show the location for reassembly.

To install:

7. Place the bearing outer races on their respective bearings. Install the carrier into the differential housing.

8. Install the bearing adjusting nuts, bearing caps and bolts to the original position. Torque the cap bolts to 58 ft. lbs. (78 Nm).

9. Use new gaskets and reverse the removal procedures. Torque the differential-to-axle nuts to 23 ft. lbs. (31 Nm) and the driveshaft flange-to-differential flange nuts/bolts to 31 ft. lbs. (43 Nm). Refill the axle with 80W–90 gear oil to a level of ¼ in. below the fill hole.

NOTE: Before installing the carrier, apply a thin coat of liquid or silicone sealer to the carrier housing gasket and to the carrier side face of each carrier retaining nut.

FRONT

1. Raise and safely support the vehicle. Drain the lubricant from the differential.

2. Remove the front axle shafts or halfshafts from the axle housing.

3. Matchmark the front driveshaft flange to the differential flange. Remove the mounting bolts and separate the driveshaft from the differential.

4. Remove the differential carrier cover.

5. Using needle nose pliers or equivalent, remove the snapring from the side gear shafts. Pull the side gear shafts from the housing. A slide hammer may have to be used to remove the side shafts.

6. Remove the A.D.D actuator from the left side of the differential assembly. Remove the intermediate shaft using a puller 0935020015 or equivalent, for A.D.D equipped vehicles.

7. Place matchmarks on the bearing caps, carrier housing and adjusting nuts.

8. Remove the 4 bolts and bearing caps. Using carrier removing tool 0950422011 or equivalent, and a hammer. Dislodge the carrier assembly and lift the carrier assembly with the side bearings out of the housing. Tag the parts to show the location for reassembly.

To install:

9. Install the carrier, bearing races and adjusting shims into the housing.

10. Install the bearing caps and torque the bolts to 58 ft. lbs. (78 Nm).

11. Install the side gear shaft oil seals and side shafts.

12. Install new snaprings to the end of the shafts.

13. Apply sealer to the A.D.D actuator and install. Torque the bolts to 15 ft. lbs. (21 Nm) for A.D.D only.

14. Apply sealer to the differential cover and torque the bolts to 34 ft. lbs. (47 Nm).

15. Torque the differential-to-axle nuts to 19 ft. lbs. (27 Nm) and the front driveshaft flange-to-differential flange nuts/bolts to 54 ft. lbs. (74 Nm). Refill the axle with 80W–90 gear oil to a level of ¼ in. below the fill hole.

Axle Housing

Removal and Installation

FRONT

4WD Vehicles, Except Previa

1. Raise and safely support the vehicle.
2. Matchmark and remove the front driveshaft.
3. Disconnect the axle shafts from the axle assembly.
4. Disconnect vacuum hoses, if equipped with automatic locking hubs.
5. Disconnect the 4WD indicator. Remove the front differential mounting bolt.

6. Support the axle housing with an suitable jack and remove the rear mounting bolts.

To install:

7. Install the differential in position under the vehicle.

8. Install the rear mounting bolts and torque to 123 ft. lbs. (167 Nm).

9. Install the front mounting bolt and torque to 108 ft. lbs. (147 Nm).

10. Connect vacuum hoses and the 4WD indicator.

11. Install the axle shafts and the driveshaft, aligning matchmarks made during removal.

12. Refill the axle with the correct oil and lower the vehicle.

4WD Previa

1. Raise the vehicle and safely support it and drain the axle housing.

2. Disconnect the driveshaft and halfshafts. Hange the shafts aside with wire. Be careful not to damage the rubber shaft boots.

3. Remove the left engine undercover and differential support protectors.

4. Place a jack under the axle housing and remove the 3 support bolts and 6 cushions. Lower the jack and remove the assembly.

To install:

5. Raise the assembly and install the collars, cushions and support bolts. Torque the bolts to 54 ft. lbs. (73 Nm).

6. Install the support protectors and torque the bolts to 9 ft. lbs. (12 Nm).

7. Install the under cover.

8. Install the halfshafts and torque the bolts to 51 ft. lbs. (69 Nm).

9. Install the front driveshaft and torque the bolts to 27 ft. lbs. (37 Nm).

10. Refill the axle housing with hypoid gear oil.

REAR

Except Van and Previa

1. Raise and safely support the vehicle.
2. Remove the tire and wheel assemblies.
3. Support the axle housing with a suitable jack.
4. Disconnect the shock absorber lower bolts.
5. Disconnect the stabilizer bar and lateral rod. Disconnect the brake lines from the axle housing.
6. Remove the leaf spring U-bolts and carefully lower the axle housing from the vehicle.
7. Installation is the reverse of the removal procedure. Torque the shock absorber lower bolts to 19 ft. lbs (25 Nm) on 2WD vehicles or to 47 ft. lbs (64 Nm) on 4WD vehicles. Tighten the U-bolt nuts to 90 ft. lbs (123 Nm).

Van and Previa

1. Raise and safely support the vehicle.
2. Remove the tire and wheel assemblies.
3. Support the axle housing with a suitable jack.
4. Disconnect the shock absorber lower bolts.
5. Disconnect the stabilizer bar and lateral rod. Also, disconnect the upper and lower control arms.
6. Remove the brake lines from the axle housing.
7. Slowly lower the axle housing from the vehicle.
8. Installation is the reverse of the removal procedure. Observe the following torques:
   a. Shock absorber bottom bolts – 27 ft. lbs (37 Nm) for 2WD, 94 ft. lbs. (127 Nm) for 4WD vehicles.
   b. Upper control arm bolts – 105 ft. lbs. (142 Nm).
   c. Lower control arm bolts – 105 ft. lbs. (142 Nm).
   d. Stabilizer bar bolts – 19 ft. lbs. (25 Nm).

STEERING

Steering Wheel

Removal and Installation

1. Disconnect the negative battery cable.
2. Position the wheels in a straight ahead position.
3. Remove the steering wheel center cover, some vehicles use a screw to retain the cover.
4. Disconnect the horn wire. Matchmark the wheel and the shaft.
5. Using an appropriate wheel puller tool 0960920011 or equivalent, remove the steering wheel.
6. Installation is the reverse of the removal procedure. Tighten the steering wheel nut to 25 ft. lbs. (34 Nm).

Steering Column

Removal and Installation

1. Disconnect the negative battery cable.
2. Remove the instrument panel and steering column finish panels.
3. Disconnect all electrical connectors from the column.
4. Remove the lower joint protectors, if equipped.
5. Remove the pinch bolt and nut from the intermediate shaft or flex joint. Disconnect the intermediate shaft from the column shaft or disconnect the flex joint from the steering gear.
6. Remove the column bracket-to-instrument panel nuts.
7. Remove the floor boot retainers and pull the boot away from the floor.
8. Remove the column from the vehicle. Do not hammer on the shaft.

To install:

9. Install the column into the vehicle. Make sure the plastic retainers are properly aligned. Torque the column-to-instrument panel nuts to 18 ft. lbs. (25 Nm).
10. Install the floor boot and retainers. Make sure the boot is sealed from water. Use sealer between the floor and boot.
11. Connect the intermediate shaft to the column shaft or connect the flex joint to the steering gear. Install the pinch bolt and nut to the intermediate shaft or flex joint. Torque the bolt to 26 ft. lbs. (35 Nm).
12. Install the lower joint protectors, if equipped.
13. Connect all electrical connectors to the column.
14. Install the instrument panel and steering column finish panels.
15. Connect the negative battery cable and check operation.

Manual Steering Gear

Adjustment

PICK-UP AND 4RUNNER

1. Install a special socket 0961600010 or equivalent, and inch lbs. torque wrench on the worm shaft.
2. Turn the adjusting screw while measuring the preload. It should be 6.9–9.5 inch lbs. (0.8–1.1 Nm).
3. Install the lock nut and torque to 34 ft. lbs. (46 Nm).

VAN

1. Loosen the lock nut and torque the rack guide spring cap to 18 ft. lbs. (25 Nm).
2. Return the cap 30 degrees.
3. Turn the control valve shaft right and left 1 or 2 times. Loosen the spring cap until the rack guide compression spring is not functioning.
4. Using an inch lbs. torque wrench on the worm shaft, tight-en the rack guide cap until the preload is within 4.3–11.3 inch lbs. (0.7–1.3 Nm).
5. Apply sealer to the lock nut threads and torque the locknut to 41 ft. lbs. (56 Nm).

Removal and Installation

2WD PICK-UP

1. Raise and safely support the vehicle. Remove the pitman arm-to-relay rod cotter pin and nut. Separate the relay rod from the pitman arm.
2. Matchmark the flexible steering coupling-to-steering gear, then remove the lock bolt and separate the steering coupling from the steering gear.
3. Remove the steering gear housing mounting bolts and the gear housing.
4. To install, reverse the removal procedures. Torque the housing-to-frame bolts to 48 ft. lbs. (62 Nm), the pitman arm-to-relay rod nut 67 ft. lbs. (93 Nm) and the steering gear-to-coupling yoke to 15–20 ft. lbs. (20–27 Nm).

4WD PICK-UP AND 4RUNNER

1. Raise and safely support the vehicle. Remove the stone shield from the gear housing, if equipped.
2. Matchmark the intermediate shaft-to-steering gear and disconnect them.
3. Remove the cotter pin and plug from the drag link.
4. Disconnect the drag link from the pitman arm.
5. Remove the pitman arm nut. Using a puller tool, separate the pitman arm from the steering gear.
6. Remove the steering gear housing-to-frame bolts and the gear housing.
7. To install, reverse the removal procedures. Torque the steering gear-to-frame bolts to 42 ft. lbs. (56 Nm), the steering gear-to-intermediate bolts to 29 ft. lbs. (40 Nm), the pitman arm-to-steering gear nut to 127 ft. lbs. (170 Nm).

NOTE: When installing the drag link to the pitman arm, tighten the plug completely and loosen it $1\frac{1}{3}$ turns.

VAN

1. Raise and safely support the vehicle.
2. Remove the wheel and tire assemblies.
3. Disconnect the tie rod ends from the steering knuckle.
4. Matchmark and disconnect the intermediate shaft from the gear.
5. Remove the retaining bolts from the 2 brackets and slide the rack out from under the vehicle.
6. Installation is the reverse of the removal procedure. Torque the bracket bolts to 56 ft. lbs (76 Nm), the coupling bolts to 26 ft. lbs. (35 Nm) and the tie rod bolts to 43 ft. lbs. (59 Nm).

LAND CRUISER

1. Raise and safely support the vehicle. Remove the worm yokes from the worm and the main shaft.
2. Remove the intermediate shaft assembly.
3. Remove the pitman arm from the sector shaft.
4. Remove the steering gear-to-frame bolts and the steering gear from the vehicle.
5. To install, reverse the removal procedures. Torque the pitman arm to 119–141 ft. lbs. (163–190 Nm).

NOTE: The intermediate shaft must be installed with the wheels in a straight-ahead position and the steering wheel straight-ahead.

Power Steering Gear

Adjustment

PICK-UP AND 4RUNNER

1. Install a special socket 0961600010 or equivalent, and inch lbs. torque wrench on the worm shaft.
2. Turn the adjusting screw while measuring the preload. It should be 2.6–4.8 inch lbs. (0.3–0.5 Nm).
3. Install the lock nut and torque to 34 ft. lbs. (46 Nm).

VAN AND PREVIA

1. Loosen the lock nut and torque the rack guide spring cap to 18 ft. lbs. (25 Nm).
2. Return the cap 30 degrees.
3. Turn the control valve shaft right and left 1 or 2 times. Loosen the spring cap until the rack guide compression spring is not functioning.
4. Using an inch lbs. torque wrench on the worm shaft, tighten the rack guide cap until the preload is within 7.8–11.3 inch lbs. (0.9–1.3 Nm) for the Van or 6.1–11.3 inch lbs. (0.7–1.3 Nm) for the Previa.
5. Torque the lock nut to 41 ft. lbs. (56 Nm).

LAND CRUISER

1. Turn the worm shaft in both directions to determine the exact center.
2. Install special socket 0961600010 or equivalent, and an inch lbs. torque wrench to the worm shaft.
3. Turn the adjusting screw while measuring the preload. It should be 6.5–9.5 inch lbs. (0.7–1.1 Nm).
4. Install a new seal and torque the locknut to 34 ft. lbs. (46 Nm).

Removal and Installation

2WD PICK-UP

1. Raise and safely support the vehicle. Disconnect and plug the pressure line clamp bolts at the steering gear.
2. Matchmark the intermediate shaft-to-steering gear, then, remove the coupling bolt and separate the intermediate shaft from the steering gear.

Power steering gear assembly—all except Van

Steering gear removal—Van

3. Remove the pitman arm-to-steering gear and the pitman arm-to-relay rod nuts.

4. Using a puller tool, separate the pitman arm from the relay rod and the pitman arm from the steering gear.

5. Remove the steering gear-to-frame bolts and the steering gear from the vehicle.

6. To install, reverse the removal procedures. Torque the steering gear-to-frame bolts to 48 ft. lbs. (66 Nm), the pitman arm-to-steering gear nut to 90 ft. lbs. (122 Nm), the pitman arm-to-relay rod nut to 67 ft. lbs. (92 Nm), the intermediate shaft-to-steering gear bolt to 19 ft. lbs. and the pressure line nuts to 33 ft. lbs. (45 Nm). Bleed the power steering system.

4WD PICK-UP AND 4RUNNER

1. Remove the battery and the engine lower gravel shield.

2. Raise and safely support the vehicle. Disconnect and plug the pressure lines at the steering gear.

3. Remove the steering gear stone shield.

4. Matchmark the intermediate shaft-to-steering gear, then remove coupling bolt and the intermediate shaft from the steering gear.

5. Remove the pitman arm-to-steering gear nut. Using a puller tool, separate the pitman arm from the steering gear.

6. Remove the gear housing-to-frame bolts and the steering gear from the vehicle.

7. To install, reverse the removal procedures. Torque the steering gear-to-frame bolts to 42 ft. lbs. (57 Nm), the pitman arm-to-steering gear nut to 127 ft. lbs. (172 Nm), the intermediate shaft-to-steering gear bolt to 29 ft. lbs. (41 Nm) and the pressure line union nuts to 33 ft. lbs. (44 Nm). Bleed the power steering system.

VAN

1. Raise and safely support the vehicle.

2. Remove the wheel and tire assemblies.

3. Disconnect and plug the power steering fluid lines from the gear.

4. Disconnect the tie rod ends from the steering knuckle.

5. Matchmark and disconnect the intermediate shaft from the gear.

6. Remove the retaining bolts from the 2 brackets and slide the rack out from under the vehicle.

7. Installation is the reverse of the removal procedure. Torque the bracket bolts to 56 ft. lbs. (76 Nm), the coupling bolts to 26 ft. lbs. (35 Nm) and the tie rod bolts to 43 ft. lbs. (59 Nm).

LAND CRUISER

1. Raise and safely support the vehicle. Disconnect the pressure lines from the steering gear.

2. Remove the intermediate shaft-to-steering gear bolt and the steering column-to-firewall bolts.

3. Loosen the steering column-to-dash bolts. Remove the pitman arm-to-steering gear nut.

4. Using a puller, separate the relay rod from the pitman shaft and the pitman arm from the steering gear.

5. Pull the steering column towards the passenger compartment to uncouple the steering shaft from the steering gear.

6. Remove the steering gear-to-frame bolts and the steering gear from the vehicle.

7. To install, reverse the removal procedures. Torque the steering gear-to-frame bolts to 40–63 ft. lbs. (54–86 Nm), the pitman arm-to-steering gear nut to 120–141 ft. lbs. (163–190 Nm), the intermediate shaft-to-steering gear bolt to 22–32 ft. lbs. (29–43 Nm), the pressure hose fitting to 29–36 ft. lbs. (40–48 Nm) and the return hose fitting to 24–30 ft. lbs. (35–41 Nm). Bleed the power steering system.

NOTE: During installation of the hydraulic lines, position each line clear of any surrounding components, then tighten the fittings.

PREVIA

1. Raise the vehicle and support safely.

2. Disconnect the tie rod ends using a separator tool 0961112010 or equivalent.

3. Place matchmarks on the universal joint and shaft. Remove the lower and upper joint bolts and slide the joint upward to disconnect.

4. Disconnect the pressure and return pipes using flarenut wrenches.

5. 4WD only: remove the front differential assembly, equipment driveshaft housing insulator and drive housing stay.

6. Remove the bracket bolts and grommets. Turn the housing toward the back side and slide the housing to the right side. Put the left tie rod end in the body panel. Pull the housing out through the opening in the left lower side of the body.

To install:

7. Install the gear housing and torque the mounting bolts to 56 ft. lbs. (76 Nm).

8. 4WD only: install the front differential assembly, equipment driveshaft housing insulator and drive housing stay.

9. Connect the pressure and return pipes using flarenut wrenches. Torque the fittings to 33 ft. lbs. (44 Nm).

10. Install the lower and upper joint bolts. Torque the bolts to 26 ft. lbs. (35 Nm).

11. Connect the tie rod ends, torque to 36 ft. lbs. (49 Nm) and install a new cotter pin.

12. Align the front end and lower the vehicle.

Power Steering Pump

Removal and Installation

PICK-UP, LAND CRUISER AND 4RUNNER

NOTE: Disconnect the air hoses from the air control valve and the high tension wires from the distributor.

1. Disconnect the negative battery cable. Loosen the power steering pump pulley nut.

NOTE: Use the drive belt as a brake to keep the pulley from rotating.

2. Place a container under the pump. Disconnect the return line and the pressure tube, then drain the fluid into the container.

3. Loosen the idler pulley nut and the adjusting bolt, then remove the drive belt.

4. Remove the drive pulley and the Woodruff key from the pump shaft.

5. Remove the mounting bolts and the power steering pump from the vehicle.

6. To install, reverse the removal procedures. Torque the pump pulley mounting bolt to 29 ft. lbs. (40 Nm), the pump pulley nut to 32 ft. lbs. (42 Nm) and the pressure hoses to 33 ft. lbs. (45 Nm). Adjust the drive belt tension. Bleed the power steering system.

VAN

1. Disconnect the negative battery cable. Disconnect the air hoses from the air control valve of the power steering pump.

2. Drain the fluid from the power steering reservoir tank.

3. At the power steering pump, disconnect the return hose and the pressure tube.

4. Loosen the power steering pump adjusting bolt, then, remove the drive belt, the pulley and the Woodruff key.

5. Remove the mounting bolts, the power steering pump and the bracket from the vehicle.

6. To install, reverse the removal procedures. Torque the power steering pump-to-engine bolts to 29 ft. lbs. (40 Nm), the pulley set nut to 32 ft. lbs. (42 Nm) and the pressure tube to 33 ft. lbs. (45 Nm).

Belt Adjustment

Use a belt tension gauge and make sure the tension is 105 lbs. (140 N) for new or 85 lbs. (115 N) for and old belt. Loosen the air pump mounting and adjust the pump until the proper tension is obtained. tighten the mounting brackets and check operation.

System Bleeding

1. Raise and safely support the vehicle.
2. Fill the pump reservoir with power steering fluid.
3. With the engine running, rotate the steering wheel from lock to lock several times. Add fluid as necessary.

NOTE: Perform the bleeding procedure until all of the air is bled from the system.

4. The fluid level should not have risen more than $^2/_{10}$ in.; if it does, check the pump.

Tie Rod Ends

Removal and Installation

1. Raise and safely support the vehicle.
2. Remove the wheel and tire assembly. Remove the cotter pin and nut.

Drive belt adjustment

3. Using a tie rod end puller, disconnect the tie rod from the relay rod.
4. Using a tie rod end puller remove the tie rod from the steering knuckle.
5. Remove the tie rod end from the vehicle.
6. Installation is the reverse of the removal procedure. Tighten the clamp nuts to 19 ft. lbs. (25 Nm) and the knuckle-to-arm nuts to 67 ft. lbs. (90 Nm). Always install a new cotter pin.

BRAKES

For all brake system repair and service procedures not detailed below, please refer to "Brakes" in the Unit Repair section.

Master Cylinder

Removal and Installation

PICK-UP, 4RUNNER, LAND CRUISER AND PREVIA

1. Disconnect the negative battery cable. Using a syringe, remove the brake fluid from the master cylinder.
2. Disconnect and plug the hydraulic lines at the master cylinder.
3. If equipped, disconnect the level warning switch connector from the master cylinder.
4. Remove the master cylinder-to-power booster nuts and the master cylinder assembly from the power brake unit.
5. To install, reverse the removal procedures. Torque the master cylinder mounting bolts to 9 ft. lbs. (12 Nm) and the brake lines-to-master cylinder to 11 ft. lbs. (15 Nm). Refill the master cylinder with new brake fluid and bleed the brake system.

VAN

1. Disconnect the negative battery terminal.
2. To expose the master cylinder, perform the following:
   a. Remove the master cylinder reservoir cap, located at the left-side of the instrument panel.
   b. Remove the instrument cluster finish panel and the lower cluster finish panel. Disconnect the electrical connectors and the speedometer cable from the instrument panel, then remove the instrument panel.
   c. Remove the No. 1, 2 and 3 air ducts.
3. Using a syringe, remove the brake fluid from the master cylinder reservoir.
4. Remove the reservoir hoses from the master cylinder. Disconnect and plug the brake lines at the master cylinder.
5. Remove the master cylinder mounting nuts, the vacuum check valve bracket and the master cylinder from the vehicle.

6. To install, reverse the removal procedures. Torque the master cylinder mounting nuts to 9 ft. lbs. (12 Nm) and the brake lines-to-master cylinder to 11 ft. lbs. (15 Nm). Refill the master cylinder with new brake fluid and bleed the brake system.

Load Sensing Proportioning Valve

Removal and Installation

1. Raise and safely support the vehicle, so it is level.
2. Disconnect the No. 2 shackle from the bracket.
3. Disconnect and plug the brake lines from the load sensing valve.
4. Remove the load sensing valve bracket from the frame.
5. To install, reverse the removal procedures. Torque the load sensing valve-to-frame bolts to 14 ft. lbs. (18 Nm) and the brake tubes to 11 ft. lbs. (15 Nm). Bleed the brake system.

Adjustment

EXCEPT PREVIA

1. Adjust the load sensing valve and the rear axle load.
2. Check and/or adjust the length of the No. 2 shackle for distance from the center of the No. 2 shackle-to-shackle bracket bolt to the center of the No. 1 shackle-to-spring bolt, 3.07 in. for 2WD Pick-Up, Van and 1989–92 Land Cruiser, 4.72 in. for 4WD Pick-Up, 4Runner and 1988 Land Cruiser or 1.18 in. for Previa.
3. Shortening the **A** length raises the pressure to the rear brakes and lengthening lowers the pressure. 1 turn will adjust the pressure to the rear brakes 28–51 psi (196–353 kPa).

Power Brake Booster

Removal and Installation

EXCEPT VAN

1. Disconnect the negative battery cable. Separate the master cylinder from the power brake booster.

Removing the brake booster and master cylinder— Van

CLUSTER FINISH PANEL

COMBINATION METER

VACUUM HOSE

MASTER CYLINDER

BRAKE BOOSTER AND PEDAL BRACKET

CLUSTER FINISH LOWER PANEL

STEERING COLUMN ASSEMBLY

RESERVOIR HOSE

AIR DUCT

AIR DUCT

AIR DUCT

Load sensing proportioning valve adjustment— Except Previa

Load sensing proportioning valve adjustment— Previa

2. Remove the vacuum hose form the power brake booster.

3. Working under the instrument panel, remove the brake pedal-to-brake booster rod clevis pin. Remove the power brake booster mounting bolts and the booster from the vehicle.

4. To install, reverse the removal procedures. Torque the power brake booster nuts to 9 ft. lbs. (12 Nm).

5. Adjust the length of the booster pushrod. Install the master cylinder gasket on the booster. Set the measurement tool 0973700010 or equivalent, so the pin slightly touches the piston.

6. Turn the tool upside down and measure the clearance between the booster pushrod and pin head. The clearance should be **0**.

NOTE: When installing a new booster, make sure there is a little clearance between the pushrod end and the master cylinder piston.

VAN

1. Disconnect the negative battery terminal.

2. To expose the master cylinder, perform the following:

a. Remove the master cylinder reservoir cap, located at the left-side of the instrument panel.

b. Remove the instrument cluster finish panel and the lower cluster finish panel. Disconnect the electrical connectors and the speedometer cable from the instrument panel, then remove the instrument panel.

c. Remove the No. 1, 2 and 3 air ducts.

3. Using a syringe, remove the brake fluid from the master cylinder reservoir.

4. Remove the reservoir hoses from the master cylinder. Disconnect and plug the brake lines at the master cylinder.

5. Remove the master cylinder mounting nuts, the vacuum check valve bracket and the master cylinder from the vehicle.

6. Remove the bolts retaining the brake pedal and booster bracket. Remove the bracket from the vehicle.

7. To install, reverse the removal procedures. Torque the master cylinder mounting nuts to 9 ft. lbs. (12 Nm) and the brake lines-to-master cylinder to 11 ft. lbs. (15 Nm). Refill the master cylinder with new brake fluid and bleed the brake system.

Brake Caliper

Removal and Installation

1. Raise ands safely support the vehicle.
2. Remove the wheel and tire assembly.
3. Remove the 2 wire clips at the ends of the brake pad pins.
4. Pull out the pads and anti-rattle springs.
5. Lift out the anti squeal shims.
6. Plug the vent hole on the master cylinder cap, to prevent fluid leakage. Disconnect and plug the brake line from the caliper.
7. Remove the 2 caliper mounting bolts and remove the caliper.

To install:

8. Position the caliper and install the mounting bolts. Tighten the caliper mounting bolts to 18 ft. lbs. (25 Nm) on Previa, 29

ft. lbs. (41 Nm) on 2WD vehicles or to 90 ft. lbs. (122 Nm) on 4WD vehicles.

9. Install the brake pads. Install the wheel and tire assembly and lower the vehicle.

10. Road test the vehicle.

Disc Brake Pads

Removal and Installation

2WD VEHICLE

1. Raise and safely support the vehicle.
2. Remove the wheel and tire assembly.
3. Remove the bottom caliper retaining bolt and loosen the top bolt.
4. Pivot the caliper upward and suspend it with wire, do not disconnect the brake line.
5. Remove the anti-squeal springs, brake pads, anti-squeal shims, wear indicator plates and the 4 pad support plates.
6. Installation is the reverse of the removal procedure. Compress the caliper piston into the bore using a C-clamp. Torque the caliper bolts to 29 ft. lbs. (39 Nm).

4WD VEHICLE

1. Raise and safely support the vehicle.
2. Remove the wheel and tire assembly.
3. Remove the brake pad retaining clips, 2 locating pins, anti-rattle spring, brake pads and anti-squeal shims.
4. Installation is the reverse of the removal procedure. Compress the caliper piston into the bore using a C-clamp. Torque the caliper bolt to 27 ft. lbs. (36 Nm).

Front brake assembly—typical 2WD vehicle

Front brake assembly—typcal 4WD vehicle

Brake Rotor

Removal and Installation

1. Raise and safely support the vehicle.
2. Remove the wheels and tires.
3. Remove the caliper and brake pads. Hange from the suspension with a wire.
4. Remove the brake torque plate.
5. On 2WD vehicles, remove the grease cap, cotter pin and nut from the hub, except Previa.
6. On 4WD vehicles, remove the bolt retaining the locking hub assembly and lift it off the hub. Remove the nuts and washer from the inside of the hub.
7. Remove the rotor from the vehicle. Be careful not to drop the bearings from the hub.

To install:

8. Install the rotor. Be careful not to drop the bearings from the hub.
9. On 4WD vehicles, install the hub bolts.
10. On 2WD vehicles, install the grease cap, cotter pin and nut to the hub. Adjust the bearing preload.
11. Install the brake torque plate and torque the bolts to 77 ft. lbs. (104 Nm).
12. Install the caliper and brake pads.
13. Install the wheels and tires.
14. Bleed the brake system.

Brake Drums

Removal and Installation

1. Raise and safely support the vehicle.
2. Remove the wheel and tire assemblies.

3. Remove the brake drum retaining screws.
4. Remove the drum from the vehicle. If the drum is difficult to remove, release the brake adjusters from behind the drum.
5. Install the drum on the vehicle and install the retaining screws.
6. Install the wheel and tire assemblies.
7. Lower the vehicle. Check the operation of the brakes and adjust as needed.

Brake Shoes

Removal and Installation

1. Raise and safely support the vehicle.
2. Remove the wheel and tire assemblies.
3. Remove the brake drum retaining screws and remove the brake drum.
4. Disconnect the return spring from the rear shoe.
5. Remove the rear shoe hold-down spring, cups and pin. Disconnect the anchor spring from the shoe and remove the shoe.
6. Remove the front shoe hold-down spring, cups and pin. Disconnect the parking brake cable from the lever and remove the front shoe with the adjuster.
7. Remove the adjuster from the front shoe.
8. Installation is the reverse of the removal procedure.
9. Adjust the brake shoes after the drum is installed. Once the vehicle is lowered, pump the brakes several times to seat the shoes.

Wheel Cylinder

Removal and Installation

1. Raise and safely support the vehicle.
2. Remove the wheel and tire assemblies.

3. Remove the brake drum and the brake shoes.

4. Disconnect and plug the brake line from the wheel cylinder.

5. Remove the wheel cylinder mounting bolts and remove the wheel cylinder from the vehicle.

6. Installation is the reverse of the removal procedure. Torque the mounting bolts to 7 ft. lbs. (10 Nm).

7. Bleed the brake system after installation.

Parking Brake Cable

Adjustment

2WD PICK-UP

1. Working under the vehicle, tighten the adjusting nut at the equalizer until the travel is within limits and there is no drag at the rear shoes.

2. Apply the parking brake several times and again check that there is no drag with the brake released.

4WD PICK-UP AND 4RUNNER

1. Working under the vehicle, tighten the bellcrank stopper screw until the play at the rear brake links is gone, then loosen the nut one full turn. Tighten the locknut.

2. Tighten one of the adjusting nuts on the intermediate lever while loosening the other, until the travel is correct. Tighten the locknuts.

3. Confirm that the bellcrank is in contact with the backing plate.

VAN AND PREVIA WITH REAR DRUMS

1. Raise and safely support the rear of the vehicle.

2. Remove the shift knob and the console box.

3. At the parking brake handle, loosen the cable locknut. Pull the hand brake upward about 7–9 clicks for Van or 4–5 clicks for Previa.

4. Turn the adjust nut until the rear wheels can no longer be turned, then, tighten the locknut.

5. Install the console and the shift knob.

PREVIA WITH REAR DISCS

1. Raise the vehicle and support safely. Remove the rear wheel.

2. Temporarily install lug nuts and remove the plug hole in the rotor.

3. Turn the adjuster and expand the shoes until the rotor disc locks.

4. Back off the adjuster 8 notches and install the hole plug.

5. Make sure there is no excessive drag on the parking brake.

6. Install the wheel and lower the vehicle.

7. Loosen the 2 adjusting nuts under the vehicle and adjust the parking brake No. 1 cable until the parking brake lever clicks 4–5 times.

Parking Brake Shoes

Removal and Installation

Previa With Rear Discs

1. Raise the vehicle and support safely. Remove the rear wheels.

2. Remove the shoe return spring using a remover tool 0971720010 or equivalent.

3. Remove the shoe strut and spring. Remove the shoe hold-down cups.

4. Remove the front shoe, adjuster and tension spring.

5. Remove the rear shoe and disconnect the parking brake cable.

6. Remove the parking brake shoe lever by spreading the clip with a prybar.

To install:

7. Lubricate all moving parts with high temperature lithium

Parking brake shoes—Previa with rear disc brakes

grease. Install the parking brake lever and new clip. Bend the clip around the shaft with a pliers.

8. Connect the cable to the parking brake lever.
9. Install the rear shoe and hold-down.
10. Install the front shoe, tension spring and adjuster.
11. Install the strut with spring and shoe return springs.
12. Install the rotor and remaining components.
13. Adjust the parking brake and lower the vehicle.

Bleeding the Brake System

1. Fill reservoir to the maximum fill mark.
2. Bleed the brakes in the following sequence: right rear, left rear, right front, left front and load sensing proportioning valve.
3. Attach a bleed hose to the caliper or wheel cylinder being bled, immerse the end of the bleed hose in a glass container partially filled with brake fluid.
4. Have a helper apply brake pedal to pressurize the system. Open the bleed screw ½ turn. Close the bleed screw when the fluid entering the glass container is free of bubbles.
5. Check the reservoir fluid level and add fluid to the **MAX** fill mark.
6. Repeat bleeding operations at remaining wheels.

NOTE: Do not allow the master cylinder reservoir to run dry while bleeding the brakes. Running dry will allow air to re-enter the system making a second bleeding operation necessary.

Anti-lock Brake System Service

Precautions

● When welding with an electric welding unit, unplug the electric control unit.
● During paint jobs, the electronic control unit may be exposed to a maximum of 203°F (95°C) for up to 2 hours or 185°F (85°C) if more time is needed.
● When removing the rear axle centerpiece, make sure the correct toothed wheel with the correct ratio for the wheel speed sensor is installed. If a wheel with the wrong number of teeth is installed, this fault will not show up when checking the system with the ABS tester. The stopping distance, however, will be increased during controlled braking.
● If work was done to non-ABS brake components, a simple operational test will be sufficient. This means that after driving about 5 mph, the warning light on the instrument panel should go out if the ABS system is intact.
● If ABS components have been replaced, the entire system should be checked using the appropriate tester in combination with brake test bench or an adaptor in combination with a multimeter.

Relieving Anti-lock Brake System Pressure

Pump the brake pedal at least 20 times with the ignition key in the OFF position. Place a shop rag around the hydraulic line fitting and wear safety glasses when disconnecting the hydraulic lines.

Anti-Lock Brake Actuator

Removal and Installation

PREVIA

1. Disconnect the negative battery cable.
2. Remove the brake fluid from the master cylinder with a syringe.
3. Remove the plastic cover from the actuator.
4. Disconnect the hydraulic lines from the actuator. Plug the lines to prevent loss of fluid.

5. Disconnect the electrical connectors from the actuator.
6. Remove the actuator from the bracket.
7. Installation is the reverse of the removal procedure. Fill and bleed the system.
8. Connect the battery cable, start the engine and check brake system operation before driving the vehicle.

PICK-UP AND 4RUNNER

1. Disconnect the negative battery cable.
2. Remove the brake fluid from the master cylinder with a syringe.
3. Remove the battery and tray.
4. Disconnect the electrical connectors from the actuator.
5. Using a flarenut wrench, disconnect the hydraulic lines from the actuator.
6. Turn the steering wheel clockwise until it locks before disconnecting the power steering lines at the actuator. Using a flarenut wrench, disconnect the power steering lines from the actuator.
7. Remove the actuator and bracket.

To install:

8. Install the actuator and torque the bolts to 21 ft. lbs. (28 Nm).
9. Connect the hydraulic lines and torque to 11 ft. lbs. (15 Nm) and the power steering lines to 34 ft. lbs. (47 Nm).
10. Connect the electrical connectors and install the remaining components.
11. Bleed the brake system.

ABS Electronic Control Unit (ECU)

Removal and Installation

1. Disconnect the negative battery cable.
2. On Pick-up and 4Runner, remove the glove compartment assembly, disconnect the ECU and remove. The unit is located above the engine ECU.
3. On Previa, remove the audio power amplifier, if equipped.
4. Remove the ABS ECU and disconnect the wiring.
5. Installation is the reverse of removal.

Brake system bleeding when the power steering system at the actuator is disconnected—Pick-Up and 4Runner with ABS

Anti-lock Brake System Bleeding

PREVIA

Use the conventional brake system bleeding procedure.

PICK-UP AND 4RUNNER

Use the conventional brake system bleeding procedure unless the power steering hoses are disconnected from the brake actuator.

1. Bleed the power steering system using the conventional method.
2. Bleed the brake system with the engine running.
3. Bleed the brake system with the engine not running.
4. Disconnect the connector from the actuator and solenoid relay.

5. Connect an actuator tester tool 0999000150 and 0999099205 or equivalent, to the actuator solenoid relay and body side of the wiring harness through a sub-wire.
6. Connect the red cable of the tester to the battery positive terminal and the black wire to the negative terminal.
7. Start the engine and run at idle.
8. Turn the selector switch on the tester to **AIR BLEED**.
9. Strongly depress the brake pedal and hold.
10. Push **ON** and release the ON/OFF switch, 3 seconds each for 5 times.
11. Release the switch and brake pedal.
12. Check the power steering fluid level and add Dexron®II fluid.
13. Remove the tester and reconnect the actuator and solenoid.

FRONT SUSPENSION

Shock Absorber

Removal and Installation

2WD PICK-UP AND VAN

1. Raise and safely support the vehicle. Remove the wheel and tire assembly.
2. Unfasten the double nuts at the top end of the shock absorber. Remove the cushions and the cushion retainers.
3. Remove the shock absorber-to-lower control arm bolts.
4. Compress the shock absorber and remove it from the vehicle.
5. To install, reverse the removal procedures. Torque the shock absorber-to-lower control arm bolts to 13 ft. lbs. (18 Nm) and the shock absorber-to-body nuts to 19 ft. lbs. (26 Nm).

4WD PICK-UP, 4RUNNER AND VAN

1. Raise and safely support the vehicle. Remove the wheel and tire assembly.
2. Unfasten the double nuts at the top end of the shock absorber. Remove the cushions and the cushion retainers.
3. Remove the shock absorber-to-axle housing bolt.
4. Compress the shock absorber and remove it from the vehicle.
5. To install, reverse the removal procedures. Torque the shock absorber-to-suspension arm nut/bolt to 101 ft. lbs. (137 Nm) for Pick-Up and 4Runner or 70 ft. lbs. (95 Nm) for Van and the shock absorber-to-body nuts to 19 ft. lbs. (27 Nm).

LAND CRUISER

1. Raise and safely support the vehicle. Remove the wheel and tire assembly.
2. Remove mounting bolts from the top and the bottom of the shock and remove shock.
3. To install, reverse the removal procedures.

MacPherson Strut

Removal and Installation

PREVIA

1. Raise the vehicle and support safely.
2. Remove the halfshaft cotter pin and nut for 4WD only.
3. Disconnect the brake hose from the strut by removing the clips.
4. Loosen the 2 strut-to-knuckle bolts, do not remove.
5. Removethe stabilizer bar from the strut.
6. Remove the 3 upper strut mount nuts and remove the strut from the vehicle.

To install:

7. Install the strut and torque the upper nuts to 47 ft. lbs. (64 Nm).
8. Install the strut-to-knuckle bolts and torque to 231 ft. lbs. (314 Nm).
9. Install the stabilizer bar and torque the bolt to 76 ft. lbs. (103 Nm).
10. Install the halfshaft nut and torque to 136 ft. lbs. (187 Nm). Install a new cotter pin.
11. Install the remaining components and align the front end.

Coil Springs

Removal and Installation

1991–92 LAND CRUISER

1. Raise the vehicle and support the body and frame.
2. Raise the front axle assembly.
3. Hold the shock piston rod with a wrench and remove the upper mounting nut.
4. Disconnect the stabilizer bar with the cushion and bracket.
5. Lower the jack and install a spring compressor tool 0972730020 or equivalent. Compress the spring to take the load off the the upper mount.
6. Remove the upper spring retaining nuts and remove the spring.

To install:

7. Compress the coil spring and position into the vehicle. Align the spring end with the lower seat. Torque the upper mount nuts to 30 ft. lbs. (40 Nm).
8. Remove the spring compressor and raise the jack.
9. Connect the stabilizer bar and shock absorber. Torque the stabilizer and shock nut to 51 ft. lbs. (69 Nm).

Leaf Springs

Removal and Installation

1988–90 LAND CRUISER

1. Raise and safely support the vehicle. Support the axle housing with a floor jack. Remove the wheel and tire assembly.
2. Lower the floor jack to take the tension off of the spring. Remove the shock absorber mounting nuts/bolts and the shock absorber.
3. Remove the cotter pins and the nuts from the lower end of the stabilizer link. Detach the link from the axle housing.
4. Remove the spring-to-axle housing U-bolt nuts, the spring bumper and the U-bolt.

Front suspension components—Previa

UPPER ARM

UPPER BALL JOINT

UPPER ARM BUSHING

STEERING KNUCKLE

STABILIZER BAR

ANCHOR ARM

LOWER ARM BUSHING

LOWER ARM SHAFT

TORQUE ARM

SHOCK ABSORBER

TORSION BAR SPRING

LOWER ARM

LOWER BALL JOINT

STRUT BAR

Front suspension components—2WD vehicle

5. At the front of the spring, remove the hanger pin bolt. Disconnect the spring from the bracket.

6. Remove the spring shackle retaining nuts and the spring shackle inner plate, then carefully pry out the spring shackle with a pry bar.

7. Remove the spring from the vehicle.

To install:

8. To install, perform the following procedure:

a. Install the rubber bushings in the eye of the spring.

b. Align the eye of the spring with the spring hanger bracket and drive the pin through the bracket holes and rubber bushings.

NOTE: Use soapy water as lubricant, if necessary, to aid in pin installation. Never use oil or grease.

c. Finger-tighten the spring hanger nuts/bolts.

d. Install the rubber bushings in the spring eye at the opposite end of the spring.

e. Raise the free end of the spring. Install the spring shackle through the bushings and the bracket.

f. Install the shackle inner plate and finger-tighten the retaining nuts.

g. Center the bolt head in the hole which is provided in the spring seat on the axle housing.

h. Fit the U-bolts over the axle housing. Install the spring bumper and the nuts.

9. To complete the installation, reverse the removal procedures. Torque the U-bolt nuts to 90 ft. lbs. (122 Nm), the hanger pin-to-frame nut to 67 ft. lbs. (93 Nm), the shackle pin nuts to 67 ft. lbs. (93 Nm), the shock absorber bolts to 47 ft. lbs. (65 Nm).

NOTE: When installing the U-bolts, tighten the nuts so the length of the bolts are equal.

Torsion Bars

Removal and Installation

2WD PICK-UP AND VAN

The vehicles are equipped with torsion bar front springs.

NOTE: Great care must be taken to make sure springs are not mixed after removal. It is strongly suggested that before removal, each spring be marked with paint, showing front and rear of spring and from which side of the vehicle it was taken. If the springs are installed backwards or on the wrong sides of the vehicle, they could fracture. If replacing the springs, it is not necessary to mark them.

1. Raise and safely support the front of the vehicle.
2. Slide the boot from the rear of torsion bar spring, then paint an alignment mark from the torsion bar spring onto the anchor arm and the torque arm. There are right and left identification marks on the rear end of the torsion bar springs.
3. On the rear torsion bar spring holder, there is a long bolt that passes through the arm of the holder and up through the frame crossmember. Remove the locking nut only from this bolt.
4. Using a small ruler, measure the length from the bottom of the remaining nut to the threaded tip of the bolt and record this measurement.
5. Place a jack under the rear torsion bar spring holder arm and raise the arm to remove the spring pressure from the long bolt. Remove the adjusting nut from the long bolt.
6. Slowly lower jack.
7. Remove the long bolt, the spacers, the anchor arm and the torsion bar spring. The torsion bar should be easily pulled out of the anchor and the torque arms.

NOTE: Inspect all parts for wear damage or cracks. Check the boots for rips and wear. Inspect the splined ends of the torsion bar spring and the splined holes in the rear holder and the front torque arm for damage. Replace as necessary.

To install:

8. Coat the splined ends of the torsion bar with multi-purpose grease.
9. If installing the old torsion bars, perform the following:
   a. Slide the front of the torsion bar spring into the torque arm, making sure the alignment marks are matched.
   b. Slide the anchor arm onto the rear of the torsion bar spring, making sure the alignment marks are matched. Install the long bolt and it's spacers.
   c. Tighten the adjusting nut so it is the same length as it was before removal.

NOTE: Do not install the locknut.

10. When installing a new torsion bar spring, perform the following:
   a. Raise the front of the vehicle, replace the wheel and tire assembly, place a wooden block (7½ in. high) under the front tire. Lower the jack until the clearance between the spring bumper (on the lower control arm) and the frame is ½ in.
   b. Slide the front of the torsion bar spring into the torque arm.
   c. Install the anchor arm into the rear of the torsion bar spring, then the long bolt and the spacers. the distance from the top of the upper spacer to the tip of the threaded end of bolt is 0.310–1.100 in. for ½ ton vehicles or 0.430–1.220 in. for ¾ ton vehicles.

NOTE: Make sure the bolt and bottom spacer are snuggly in the holder arm while measuring.

   d. Remove the wooden block and lower the vehicle until it rests on the jackstands.
   e. Install and tighten the adjusting nut until the distance from the bottom of the nut to the tip of the threaded end of the bolt is 2.7–3.5 in.

NOTE: Do not install the locknut.

11. Apply multi-purpose grease to the boot lips, then refit the boots to the torque and the anchor arms.
12. Lower the vehicle to the floor and bounce it several times to settle the suspension. With the wheels on the ground, measure the distance from the ground to the center of the lower control arm-to-frame shaft. Adjust the vehicle height using the adjusting nut on the anchor arm. The height should be approximately 10.31 in.

NOTE: If, after achieving the correct vehicle height, the distance from the bottom of the adjusting nut to the top of the threaded end of the long bolt is not within 2.7–3.5 in., change the position of the anchor arm-to-tension bar spring spline and reassemble.

13. Install and torque the locknut on the long bolt to 61 ft. lbs. (83 Nm).

NOTE: Make sure the adjusting nut does not move when tightening locknut.

4WD VAN

NOTE: Great care must be taken to make sure springs are not mixed after removal. It is strongly suggested that before removal, each spring be marked with paint, showing front and rear of spring and from which side of the vehicle it was taken. If the springs are installed backwards or on the wrong sides of the vehicle, they could fracture. If replacing the springs, it is not necessary to mark them.

1. Raise and safely support the vehicle.
2. Using a piece of chalk, remove the boots, then, matchmark the torsion bar spring, the anchor arm and the torque arm.
3. Remove the locknut.
4. Measure the protruding length of the adjusting arm bolt, from the nut to the end of the bolt.

NOTE: The adjusting arm bolt measurement is used as a reference to establish the chassis ground clearance.

5. Remove the adjusting nut, the anchor arm and the torsion bar spring.

NOTE: When installing the torsion bar springs, be sure to check the left/right indicating marks on the rear end of the springs; be careful not to interchange the springs.

To install:

6. Using molybdenum disulphide lithium base grease, apply a coat to the torsion bar spring splines.
7. If installing a used torsion bar spring, perform the following procedures:
   a. Align the matchmarks and install the torsion bar spring to the torque arm.
   b. Align the matchmarks and install the anchor arm to the torsion bar spring.
   c. Tighten the adjusting nut until the bolt protrusion is the same as it was before.
8. If installing a new torsion bar spring, perform the following procedures:
   a. Make sure the upper and lower arms rebound.
   b. Install the boots onto the torsion bar spring.
   c. Install one end of the torsion bar spring to the torque arm.
   d. Install the torsion bar spring onto the opposite end of the anchor arm.
   e. Finger tighten the adjusting nut until the adjusting bolt protrudes about 1.570 in.
   f. Tighten the adjusting nut until the adjusting bolt protrudes about 2.480 in. for 4WD Van/Wagon or 2.400 in., for 4WD Van or 2.76 in. for 2WD Van.

g. Install the wheel(s) and lower the vehicle. Bounce the front of the vehicle to stabilize the suspension.

9. To adjust the ground clearance, turn the adjusting nut until the center of the cam plate nut, located of the front end of the lower suspension arm, is 11.17 in. for 4WD Van/Wagon, 11.99 in. for 4WD Van or 10.00 for 2WD Van above the ground.

10. After adjusting the ground clearance, torque the locknut to 58 ft. lbs. (78 Nm), then, install the boots.

4WD PICK-UP AND 4RUNNER

These vehicles are equipped with torsion bar front springs.

NOTE: Great care must be taken to make sure springs are not mixed after removal. It is strongly suggested that before removal, each spring be marked with paint, showing front and rear of spring and from which side of the vehicle it was taken. If the springs are installed backwards or on the wrong sides of the vehicle, they could fracture. If replacing the springs, it is not necessary to mark them.

1. Raise and safely support the vehicle.

2. Using a piece of chalk, remove the boots. Matchmark the torsion bar spring, the anchor arm and the torque arm.

3. Remove the locknut.

4. Measure the protruding length of the adjusting arm bolt, from the nut to the end of the bolt.

NOTE: The adjusting arm bolt measurement is used as a reference to establish the chassis ground clearance.

5. Remove the adjusting nut, the anchor arm and the torsion bar spring.

NOTE: When installing the torsion bar springs, be sure to check the left/right indicating marks on the rear end of the springs; be careful not to interchange the springs.

To install:

6. Using molybdenum disulphide lithium base grease, apply a coat to the torsion bar spring splines.

7. If installing a used torsion bar spring, perform the following procedures:

a. Align the matchmarks, install the torsion bar spring to the torque arm.

b. Align the matchmarks and install the anchor arm to the torsion bar spring.

c. Tighten the adjusting nut until the bolt protrusion is the same as it was before.

8. If installing a new torsion bar spring, perform the following procedures:

a. Make sure the upper and lower arms rebound.

b. Install the boots onto the torsion bar spring.

c. Install one end of the torsion bar spring to the torque arm.

d. Install the torsion bar spring onto the opposite end of the anchor arm.

e. Finger tighten the adjusting nut until the adjusting bolt protrudes about 1.570 in.

f. Tighten the adjusting nut until the adjusting bolt protrudes about 3.430 in.

g. Install the wheel(s) and remove the jackstands. Bounce the front of the vehicle to stablize the suspension.

9. To adjust the ground clearance, turn the adjusting nut until the center of the cam plate nut, located of the front end of the lower suspension arm, about 11.220 in. above the ground.

10. After adjusting the ground clearance, torque the locknut to 61 ft. lbs. (83 Nm), then, install the boots.

Upper Ball Joints

Inspection

1. Raise the vehicle and place jackstands under the lower control arms and check for excess play.

2. Move the suspension arm up and down. Maximum vertical play should be 0.

3. If the ball joints are within specifications and a looseness problem still exists, check the other suspension parts for wheel bearings, tie rods and etc.

4. The bottom of the tire should not move more than 0.200 in. when the tire is pushed and pulled inward and outward. The tire should not move more than 0.090 in. up and down.

5. If the play is greater than these figures, replace the ball joint.

Removal and Installation

1. Raise and safely support the vehicle. Remove the wheel and tire assembly.

2. Support the lower control arm with a floor jack.

3. Remove the brake caliper and support it aside, with a wire.

4. Using a ball joint removal tool, separate the tie rod end from the knuckle arm.

5. Remove the ball joint-to-control arm mounting bolts and separate the joint from the arm.

6. To install, reverse the removal procedures. Torque the ball joint-to-upper control arm bolts 20 ft. lbs. (27 Nm) for 2WD Pick-Up, 25 ft. lbs. (34 Nm) for 4WD Pick-Up or 22 ft. lbs. (30 Nm) for 2WD Van, the ball joint-to-lower control arm bolts to 51 ft. lbs. (69 Nm) for Pick-Up or 49 ft. lbs. (68 Nm) for Van, and the lower ball joint-to steering knuckle nut to 25 ft. lbs. (34 Nm) for 4WD Pick-Up, 76 ft. lbs. (103 Nm) for 2WD Van or 83 ft. lbs. (115 Nm) for 4WD Van.

NOTE: Be sure to grease the ball joints before moving the vehicle.

Lower Ball Joint

Inspection

1. Raise the vehicle and place jackstands under the lower control arms and check for excess play.

2. Move the suspension arm up and down. Maximum vertical play should be 0.

3. If the ball joints are within specifications and a looseness problem still exists, check the other suspension parts for wheel bearings, tie rods and etc.

4. The bottom of the tire should not move more than 0.200 in. when the tire is pushed and pulled inward and outward. The tire should not move more than 0.090 in. up and down.

5. If the play is greater than these figures, replace the ball joint.

Removal and Installation

1. Raise and safely support the vehicle. Remove the wheel and tire assembly.

2. Support the lower control arm with a floor jack.

3. Remove the brake caliper and support it aside, with a wire.

4. Using a ball joint removal tool, separate the tie rod end from the knuckle arm.

5. Using a ball joint removal tool, separate the upper ball joint from the steering knuckle.

6. Remove the ball joint-to-control arm mounting bolts and separate the joint from the arm.

7. To install, reverse the removal procedures. Torque the ball joint-to-upper control arm bolts 20 ft. lbs. (27 Nm) for 2WD Pick-Up, 25 ft. lbs. (34 Nm) for 4WD Pick-Up or 22 ft. lbs. (30 Nm) for 2WD Van, the upper ball joint-to-steering knuckle nut to 80 ft. lbs. (122 Nm) for 2WD Pick-Up, 105 ft. lbs. (140 Nm)

for 4WD Pick-Up, 58 ft. lbs. (79 Nm) for 2WD Van or 83 ft. lbs. (115 Nm) for 4WD Van.

NOTE: Be sure to grease the ball joints before moving the vehicle.

Knuckle Joint Bearings

Removal and Installation

LAND CRUISER

1. Raise the vehicle and support safely. Remove the front wheels.
2. Remove the caliper, axle hub and rotor.
3. Remove the spindle mounting bolts, dust seal and cover.
4. Using a brass drift, tap the spindle off of the steering knuckle. Tap around the side to dislodge.
5. Position 1 flat part of the outer shaft upward and pull out the axle shaft.
6. Using a tie rod remover 0961122012 or equivalent, remove the tie rod end.
7. Remove the oil seal and retainer from the rear of the knuckle.
8. Remove the upper and lower knuckle arm and bearing caps. Tap with a brass drift on the cone washers and remove them from the arm or bearing cap.
9. Using a bearing remover tool 0960660020 or equivalent, push the bearing cap and shims from the steering knuckle. Label each bearing set upper and lower for installation.
10. Remove the outer race using a brass drift.

To install:

11. Using a race installer tool 0960560010 or equivalent, drive in the new bearing outer races.
12. Coat the knuckle bearings with molybdenum lithium grease.
13. Mount the bearings on tool 0963460013 or equivalent.
14. Add preload to the bearing by tightening the upper nut on the bearings installation tool. Preload should be 6.6–13.2 lbs. (29–59 N).
15. Measure distance **A** and **B**. The difference between the 2 measurements is required to maintain the correct bearing preload (shim thickness).
16. Install the oil seal into the axle housing using tool 0951860010 or equivalent.
17. Install the felt dust seal, rubber seal and steel ring to the knuckle.
18. Pack the bearings with molybdenum lithium grease.
19. Install the bearings into position on the knuckle and axle housing. Insert the knuckle on the axle housing.
20. Using a support tool 0960660020 or equivalent, to support the bearings. Install the knuckle over the shims that were originally used or selected in the adjustment operation.
21. Using a hammer, tap the knuckle arm into the bearing inner races.
22. Install the bearing cap over the shims and tap with a hammer.
23. Install the cone washers and torque the nuts to 71 ft. lbs. (96 Nm).
24. Install the tie rod end and torque to 67 ft. lbs. (91 Nm). Install a new cotter pin.
25. Install the seal set to the knuckle.
26. Install the axle shaft and pack with grease.
27. Install the spindle dust cover and axle hub.
28. Install the remaining components and check operation.

Upper Control Arm

Removal and installation

PICK-UP AND 4RUNNER

1. Raise and safely support the vehicle. Remove the wheel and tire assembly.

Knuckle joint bearings—Land Cruiser

Knuckle bearing preload—Land Cruiser

2. Using a floor jack, support the lower control arm.
3. Remove the upper ball joint-to-upper control arm nuts/bolts, then, disconnect the upper control arm.
4. Remove the upper control arm-to-chassis bolts and camber adjusting shims and the upper control arm.

NOTE: When removing the camber adjusting shims, be sure to record their location and thickness of shims, so they may be reinstalled in their original positions.

5. To install, reverse the removal procedures. Torque the upper control arm-to-chassis bolts to 72 ft. lbs. (96 Nm) and the upper control arm-to-upper ball joint nuts/bolts to 20 ft. lbs. (27 Nm). Check and/or adjust the front wheel alignment.

2WD VAN

1. Raise and safely support the vehicle. Remove the torsion bar spring.

2. Remove the cool air intake duct.

3. Remove the upper control arm-to-upper ball joint nuts/bolts and separate the upper control arm from the ball joint.

4. Remove the upper control arm-to-chassis bolts and the control arm from the vehicle.

5. To install, reverse the removal procedures. Torque the upper control arm-to-chassis bolts to 65 ft. lbs. (88 Nm) for front and 112 ft. lbs. (150 Nm) for rear, then, the upper control arm-to-ball joint nuts/bolts to 22 ft. lbs. (29 Nm). Check and/or adjust the front end alignment.

4WD VAN

1. Raise and safely support the vehicle. Remove the torsion bar spring. Lower the vehicle.

2. Remove the front-right seat and the console box. Disconnect the control and shift cables from the shift levers, then, remove the transmission/transfer shifting levers with retainer.

3. Disconnect the parking brake cable from the brake lever, then, remove the parking brake lever assembly from the vehicle.

4. Disconnect the parking brake cable from the intermediate lever and remove it. Disconnect the shift cable from the transmission and remove it.

5. Remove the seat floor panel.

6. Remove the fan shroud, the radiator mounting bolts/nuts and move it aside; do not drain the coolant. Raise and safely support the vehicle.

7. Remove the shock absorber-to-frame nuts and disconnect the shock absorber from the frame.

8. From the upper ball joint, remove the cotter pin and the nut. Using a ball joint removal tool, press the ball joint from the steering knuckle.

9. Remove the upper control arm-to-chassis bolts and the arm from the vehicle.

10. To install, reverse the removal procedures. Torque the upper control arm-to-chassis bolts to 112 ft. lbs. (152 Nm), the upper ball joint-to-steering knuckle nut to 83 ft. lbs. (122 Nm).

Lower Control Arm

Removal and Installation

2WD PICK-UP

1. Raise and safely support the vehicle. Remove the torsion bar spring.

2. Remove the shock absorber, the stabilizer bar and the strut bar from the lower arm.

3. Remove the shock absorber from the lower arm.

4. From the lower ball joint, remove the cotter pin and the nut. Using a ball joint removal tool, press the ball joint from the lower control arm.

NOTE: If the lower ball joint is not to be replaced, simply unbolt it from the lower control arm. It is not necessary to separate the ball joint from the steering knuckle.

5. Remove the lower control arm shaft nut. Remove the spring torque arm from the other side of the lower control arm, then, remove the lower arm shaft bolt and the lower arm.

6. To install, reverse the removal procedures.

7. Tighten the bolt(s) holding the lower control arm to the frame but do not torque them until the vehicle is on the ground.

8. Torque the ball joint-to-lower control arm nuts/bolts to 51 ft. lbs. (69 Nm), the strut bar-to-lower control arm bolts to 70 ft. lbs. (95 Nm), the stabilizer bar-to-lower control arm bolts to 9 ft.

lbs. (12 Nm), the lower shock absorber bolt to 13 ft. lbs. (18 Nm), upper shock absorber bolt to 18 ft. lbs. (25 Nm) and the lower arm mounting nuts to 166 ft. lbs. (220 Nm).

9. Check and/or adjust the front end alignment.

NOTE: Do not torque the control arm bolts fully until the vehicle is lowered and bounced several times; if the bolts are tightened with the control arm(s) hanging, excessive bushing wear will result.

4WD PICK-UP AND 4RUNNER

1. Raise and safely support the vehicle. Remove the shock absorber.

2. Disconnect the stabilizer bar from the lower suspension arm.

3. Remove the lower ball joint-to-lower control arm bolts, then, separate the control arm from the ball joint.

4. Using a piece of chalk, place matchmarks on the front/rear adjusting cams.

5. Remove the nuts and adjusting cams and the lower control arms.

6. To install, reverse the removal procedures. Torque the lower ball joint-to-lower control arm bolts to 20 ft. lbs. (27 Nm), the stabilizer bar-to-lower control arm bolts to 19 ft. lbs. (26 Nm), the shock absorber-to-lower control arm nut/bolt to 101 ft. lbs. (137 Nm).

7. Lower the vehicle to the ground, bounce it a few times, align the matchmarks and torque the adjusting cam nuts to 203 ft. lbs. (270 Nm). Check and/or adjust the front wheel alignment.

2WD VAN

1. Raise and safely support the vehicle.

2. Remove the stabilizer bar and the strut bar from the lower arm.

3. Remove the shock absorber from the lower arm. If necessary, disconnect the tie rod end from the steering knuckle.

4. From the lower ball joint, remove the cotter pin and the nut. Using a ball joint removal tool, press the ball joint from the lower control arm.

NOTE: If the lower ball joint is not to be replaced, simply unbolt it from the lower control arm. It is not necessary to separate the ball joint from the steering knuckle.

5. Using a piece of chalk, matchmark the adjusting cam of the lower control arm.

6. Remove the adjusting cam, the nut and the lower control arm.

7. To install, reverse the removal procedures. Align the cam matchmarks and finger-tighten the nut:

Torque the ball joint-to-lower control arm nuts/bolts to 49 ft. lbs. (68 Nm), the lower ball joint-to-steering knuckle nut to 76 ft. lbs. (103 Nm).

Torque the strut bar-to-lower control arm bolts to 49 ft. lbs. (68 Nm).

Torque the stabilizer bar-to-lower control arm bolts to 9 ft. lbs. (12 Nm).

Torque the tie rod end-to-steering knuckle nut to 43 ft. lbs. (58 Nm).

Torque the lower shock absorber bolt to 13 ft. lbs. (17 Nm).

Torque the upper shock absorber bolt to 19 ft. lbs. (25 Nm).

Torque the adjusting cam unit to 152 ft. lbs. (205 Nm).

8. Check and/or adjust the front end alignment.

NOTE: Do not torque the control arm bolts fully until the vehicle is lowered and bounced several times.

4WD VAN

1. Raise and safely support the vehicle.

2. Remove the stabilizer bar from the lower control arm.

3. Remove the shock absorber from the lower control arm.

4. From the lower ball joint, remove the cotter pin and the nut. Using a ball joint removal tool, press the ball joint from the lower control arm.

NOTE: If the lower ball joint is not to be replaced, simply unbolt it from the lower control arm. It is not necessary to separate the ball joint from the steering knuckle.

5. Using a piece of chalk, matchmark the adjusting cam of the lower control arm.

6. Remove the adjusting cam, the nut and the lower control arm.

7. To install, reverse the removal procedures. Align the cam matchmarks and finger-tighten the nut:

Torque the ball joint-to-lower control arm nuts/bolts to 83 ft. lbs. (110 Nm).

Torque the stabilizer bar-to-lower control arm bolts to 14 ft. lbs. (17 Nm).

Torque the tie rod end-to-steering knuckle nut to 43 ft. lbs. (57 Nm).

Torque the lower shock absorber bolt to 70 ft. lbs. (95 Nm).

Torque the adjusting cam nut to 152 ft. lbs. (205 Nm).

8. Check and/or adjust the front end alignment.

NOTE: Do not torque the control arm bolts fully until the vehicle is lowered and bounced several times.

1991-92 LAND CRUISER

1. Raise the vehicle and support safely.

2. Support the frame and body. Support the axle assembly with a floor jack.

3. Remove the lower control arm-to-frame bolt.

4. Remove the 2 bolts and nuts from the axle housing and remove the control arm.

To install:

5. Install the control and bolts loosely. Do not tighten at this time.

6. Install the front wheels and lower the vehicle. Bounce the front end to stabilize the front suspension.

7. Torque the retaining bolts to 127 ft. lbs. (171 Nm).

PREVIA

1. Raise the vehicle and support safely. Remove the front wheel.

2. Remove the under cover and disconnect the lower ball joint from the knuckle.

3. Remove the 2 bolts and lower arm bracket, nut and arm shaft and lower control arm with ball joint.

To install:

4. Install the lower arm and retainers. Do not tighten at this time.

5. Connect the lower ball joint and torque to 94 ft. lbs. (127 Nm).

6. Install the front wheels and lower the vehicle.

7. Bounce the suspension up and down several times.

8. Raise the vehicle and support under the control arms with jackstands.

9. Torque the lower arm retainers to 121 ft. lbs. (164 Nm).

10. Install the remaining components and lower the vehicle.

Sway Bar

Removal and Installation

1. Raise the vehicle and support safely.

2. Remove the under covers.

3. Disconnect the sway bar links-to-control arms.

4. Disconnect the sway bar-to-frame bolts and remove the sway bar.

5. Installation is the reverse of removal. torque the frame bracket bolts to 14 ft. lbs. (19 Nm) and the link nuts to 76 ft. lbs. (103 Nm).

Front Wheel Bearings

Removal and Installation

RWD vehicles only, refer to drive axle for 4WD vehicles.

PICK-UP AND VAN

1. Raise the vehicle and support safely. Remove the front wheel.

2. Remove the brake caliper and suspend with a wire.

3. Remove the bearing cap, cotter pin, nut and outer bearing. Do not drop the bearing.

4. Remove the rotor/hub assembly.

5. Pry the inner grease seal from the hub and remove the inner bearing.

6. Clean the grease out of the hub using shop rags and compressed air. Do not use solvent to remove grease.

7. Using a brass drift and hammer, drive out the bearing outer races. Do not use old races with new bearings.

NOTE: Grind the outer circumference of the old bearing race with a grinder. Use this race to press in the new race.

8. Install the outer race into the hub using a press. If the new race gets damaged, replace with a new one.

9. Pack the bearings with high temperature bearing grease and install inner bearing.

10. Install the grease seal with tool 0960804100 or equivalent.

11. Install the rotor, outer bearing, washer, nut and nut lock.

12. Torque the nut to 25 ft. lbs. (34 Nm). Loosen the nut until it can be turned by hand.

13. Using a spring tension gauge attached to a lug bolt.

14. Tighten the nut until the bearing preload is 0.9-2.2 lbs. (3.9-9.8 N) for dual wheel vehicles or 1.3-4.0 lbs. (5.9-17.7 N) for single wheel vehicles.

15. Install nut lock, new cotter pin and grease cap.

16. Install the remaining components and check operation.

2WD PREVIA

1. Remove the steering knuckle from the vehicle. Place the assembly in a vise.

2. Remove the grease cap and lock nut. Remove the spacer or speed sensor rotor.

3. Using a hub remover tool (slide hammer) 0952000031 or equivalent, remove the wheel hub from the knuckle.

4. Remove the bearing from the hub using a press and arbor tool 0955010012 or equivalent.

5. Remove the dust protector and oil seal.

6. Remove the bearing snapring from the knuckle and press the inner bearing from the knuckle.

To install:

7. Using a press and arbor tool 0960810010 or equivalent, press the bearing into the knuckle.

8. Install the outer oil seal and dust cover.

9. Press the axle hub onto the knuckle.

10. Install the new nut and torque to 147 ft. lbs. (199 Nm). Stack the nut using a chisel. Install the grease cap.

11. Install the knuckle assembly onto the vehicle.

REAR SUSPENSION

Shock Absorbers

Removal and Installation

PICK-UP, 4RUNNER AND LAND CRUISER

1. Raise and safely support the vehicle.
3. Remove the upper shock absorber retaining bolts from the upper frame member.
4. Remove the lower end bolt of the shock absorber from the spring seat.
5. Remove the shock absorber from the vehicle.

NOTE: Inspect the shock for wear, leaks or other signs of damage.

6. To install, reverse the removal procedures. Torque the upper bolt to 19 ft. lbs. (25 Nm) for 2WD vehicle or 47 ft. lbs. (63 Nm) for 4WD vehicle and the lower bolt to 19 ft. lbs. (25 Nm) for 2WD vehicle or 47 ft. lbs. (63 Nm) for 4WD vehicle.

VAN

1. Raise and safely support the vehicle.
2. Remove the shock absorber-to-axle housing bolt.
3. Working inside the vehicle, remove the locknut, the retaining nut, the retainers and the rubber bushings from the top of the shock absorber.

NOTE: When removing the retaining nut, from the top of the shock absorber, it may be necessary to hold the top of the shock to keep it from turning.

4. Remove the shock absorber from the vehicle.
5. To install, reverse the removal procedures. Torque the shock absorber-to-body nut to 16–24 ft. lbs. (22–33 Nm) and the shock absorber-to-axle housing bolt to 27 ft. lbs. (38 Nm).

PREVIA

1. Raise the vehicle and support safely.
2. Support the axle housing with a jack.
3. Disconnect the shock from the lower control arm. Hold the shaft with a suitable tool and remove the nut.
4. Remove the upper mount bolt and shock absorber.
To install:
5. Install the shock and torque the upper mount to 27 ft. lbs. (37 Nm) and tighten the lower mount nut until the shaft protrudes 0.0059 in. (1.5mm).
6. Lower the vehicle and check operation.

Coil Spring

Removal and Installation

VAN AND PREVIA

1. Raise and safely support the vehicle. Support the axle housing with a floor jack. Remove the wheel and tire assembly.
2. Remove the shock absorber-to-axle housing bolt.
3. Remove the stabilizer-to-axle housing bar bushing bracket bolts.
4. Remove the lateral control arm-to-axle housing nut and disconnect the lateral control arm.
5. Lower the floor jack, then remove the coil spring(s) and the insulators.

NOTE: While lowering the axle housing, be careful not to snag the brake line of the parking brake cable.

6. To install, reverse the removal procedures. Torque the shock absorber bolt to 27 ft. lbs. (34 Nm), the lateral control

Rear suspension—except Van

arm-to-axle housing nut to 43 ft. lbs. (60 Nm) and the stabilizer-to-axle housing bolts to 27 ft. lbs. (34 Nm).

NOTE: Before tightening the lateral control arm and the stabilizer nuts/bolts, bounce the vehicle to stabilize the suspension.

Leaf Springs

Removal and Installation

1. Raise and safely support the vehicle. Support the axle housing with a floor jack. Remove the wheel and tire assembly.
2. Lower the floor jack to take the tension off of the spring. Remove the shock absorber mounting nuts/bolts and the shock absorber.
3. Remove the cotter pins and the nuts from the lower end of the stabilizer link. Detach the link from the axle housing.
4. Remove the spring-to-axle housing U-bolt nuts, the spring bumper and the U-bolt.
5. At the front of the spring, remove the hanger pin bolt. Disconnect the spring from the bracket.
6. Remove the spring shackle retaining nuts and the spring shackle inner plate, then carefully pry out the spring shackle with a pry bar.
7. Remove the spring from the vehicle.
To install:
8. To install, perform the following procedure:
   a. Install the rubber bushings in the eye of the spring.
   b. Align the eye of the spring with the spring hanger bracket and drive the pin through the bracket holes and rubber bushings.

NOTE: Use soapy water as lubricant, if necessary, to aid in pin installation. Never use oil or grease.

Rear suspension – Van

c. Finger-tighten the spring hanger nuts/bolts.

d. Install the rubber bushings in the spring eye at the opposite end of the spring.

e. Raise the free end of the spring. Install the spring shackle through the bushings and the bracket.

f. Install the shackle inner plate and finger-tighten the retaining nuts.

g. Center the bolt head in the hole which is provided in the spring seat on the axle housing.

h. Fit the U-bolts over the axle housing. Install the lower spring seat for 2WD vehicle or spring bumper for 4WD vehicle and the nuts.

9. To complete the installation, reverse the removal procedures. Torque the U-bolt nuts to 90 ft. lbs. (122 Nm), the hanger pin-to-frame nut to 67 ft. lbs. (90 Nm), the shackle pin nuts to 67 ft. lbs. (90 Nm), the shock absorber bolts to 47 ft. lbs. (65 Nm) for 4WD vehicle.

NOTE: When installing the U-bolts, tighten the nuts so the length of the bolts are equal.

Rear Control Arms

Removal and Installation

VAN AND PREVIA

1. Raise and safely support the vehicle. Place a floor jack under the axle housing to support it.

2. Remove the upper control arm-to-body bolt, the upper control arm-to-axle housing bolt and the upper control arm from the vehicle.

3. Disconnect the brake line from the lower control arm.

4. Remove the lower control arm-to-body bolt, the lower control arm-to-axle housing bolt and the lower control arm from the vehicle.

To install:

5. Install the upper control arm to the body and to the axle housing with the nuts. Do not tighten the nuts.

6. Install the lower control arm to the body and to the axle housing with the nuts. Do not tighten the nuts.

7. Remove the jack and the supports from under the vehicle. Bounce the vehicle to stabilize the suspension.

8. Using the floor jack under the axle housing, raise the vehicle. Place jackstands under the frame but do not let them touch the frame.

9. To complete the installation, torque the upper control arm-to-body bolt to 105 ft. lbs. (140 Nm), the upper control arm-to-axle housing bolt to 105 ft. lbs. (140 Nm), the lower control arm-to-body bolt to 130 ft. lbs. (176 Nm) and the lower control arm-to-axle housing bolt to 105 ft. lbs. (140 Nm).

Lateral Control Rod

Removal and Installation

VAN AND PREVIA

1. Raise and safely support the vehicle. Place a floor jack under the axle housing and support it.

2. Remove the lateral control rod-to-axle housing nut.

3. Remove the lateral control rod-to-body nut and the control rod from the vehicle.

To install:

4. Raise the axle housing until the frame is just free of the jack.

5. Install the lateral control rod-to-body with the nut. Do not tighten the nut.

6. Install the lateral control rod-to-axle housing in the following order: washer, bushing, spacer, lateral control rod, bushing, washer and nut. Do not tighten the nut.

7. Remove the jack, lower the vehicle to the floor and bounce it to stabilize the suspension.

8. Using the floor jack under the axle housing, raise the vehicle. Torque the lateral control rod-to-body nut to 81 ft. lbs. (110 Nm) and the lateral control rod-to-axle housing nut to 43 ft. lbs. (58 Nm).

SPECIFICATIONS

ENGINE IDENTIFICATION

Year	Model	Engine Displacement cu. in. (cc/liter)	Engine Series Identification	No. of Cylinders	Engine Type
1988	Vanagon	129 (2109/2.1)	MV	4	OHV
	Vanagon Syncro	129 (2109/2.1)	MV	4	OHV
1989	Vanagon	129 (2109/2.1)	MV	4	OHV
	Vanagon Syncro	129 (2109/2.1)	MV	4	OHV
1990	Vanagon	129 (2109/2.1)	MV	4	OHV
	Vanagon Syncro	129 (2109/2.1)	MV	4	OHV
1991–92	Vanagon	129 (2109/2.1)	MV	4	OHV
	Vanagon Syncro	129 (2109/2.1)	MV	4	OHV

OHV—Overhead valves

GENERAL ENGINE SPECIFICATIONS

Year	Model	Engine Displacement cu. in. (cc)	Fuel System Type	Net Horsepower @ rpm	Net Torque @ rpm (ft. lbs.)	Bore × Stroke (in.)	Compression Ratio	Oil Pressure @ rpm
1988	Vanagon	129 (2109)	EFI	90 @ 4800	117 @ 3200	3.70 × 2.99	9.0:1	29 @ 2000
1989	Vanagon	129 (2109)	EFI	90 @ 4800	117 @ 3200	3.70 × 2.99	9.0:1	29 @ 2000
1990	Vanagon	129 (2109)	EFI	90 @ 4800	117 @ 3200	3.70 × 2.99	9.0:1	29 @ 2000
1991–92	Vanagon	129 (2109)	EFI	90 @ 4800	117 @ 3200	3.70 × 2.99	9.0:1	29 @ 2000

EFI—Electronic Fuel Injection

GASOLINE ENGINE TUNE-UP SPECIFICATIONS

Year	Model	Engine Displacement cu. in. (cc)	Spark Plugs Type	Spark Plugs Gap (in.)	Ignition Timing (deg.) MT	Ignition Timing (deg.) AT	Compression Pressure (psi)	Fuel Pump (psi)	Idle Speed (rpm) MT	Idle Speed (rpm) AT	Valve Clearance In.	Valve Clearance Ex.
1988	Vanagon	129 (2109)	W7CC0	0.028	5BTDC	5BTDC	145–190	29	830–930	830–930	Hyd. ①	Hyd. ①
1989	Vanagon	129 (2109)	W7CC0	0.028	5BTDC	5BTDC	145–190	29	830–930	830–930	Hyd. ①	Hyd. ①
1990	Vanagon	129 (2109)	W7CC0	0.028	5BTDC	5BTDC	145–190	29	830–930	830–930	Hyd. ①	Hyd. ①
1991	Vanagon	129 (2109)	W7CC0	0.028	5BTDC	5BTDC	145–190	29	830–930	830–930	Hyd. ①	Hyd. ①
1992	REFER TO UNDERHOOD STICKER											

Hyd.—Hydraulic
① Must be adjusted when overhauling cylinder head

FIRING ORDERS

NOTE: To avoid confusion, always replace spark plug wires one at a time.

2.1L Engine
Engine Firing Order: 1–4–3–2
Distributor Rotation: Clockwise

CAPACITIES

Year	Model	Engine Displacement cu. in. (cc)	Engine Crankcase with Filter	Engine Crankcase without Filter	Transmission (pts.) 4-Spd	Transmission (pts.) 5-Spd	Transmission (pts.) Auto.	Drive Axle (pts.)	Fuel Tank (gal.)	Cooling System (qts.)
1988	Vanagon	129 (2109)	4.7	4.7	3.2③	—	12.8	②	15.9①	16.9
1989	Vanagon	129 (2109)	4.8	4.8	3.2③	—	12.8	②	15.9①	16.9
1990	Vanagon	129 (2109)	4.8	4.8	3.2③	—	12.8	②	15.9①	16.9
1991–92	Vanagon	129 (2109)	4.8	4.8	3.2③	—	12.8	②	15.9①	16.9

① Syncro—18.4 gal.
② Front drive axle on Syncro—1.6 pts.
③ Syncro equipped with extra low gear—3.7 pts.

CRANKSHAFT AND CONNECTING ROD SPECIFICATIONS

All measurements are given in inches.

Year	Engine Displacement cu. in. (cc)	Crankshaft Main Brg. Journal Dia.	Crankshaft Main Brg. Oil Clearance	Crankshaft Shaft End-play	Crankshaft Thrust on No.	Connecting Rod Journal Diameter	Connecting Rod Oil Clearance	Connecting Rod Side Clearance
1988	129 (2109)	2.126	0.001–0.003	0.003–0.007	1	1.811	0.001–0.003	0.015
1989	129 (2109)	2.126	0.001–0.003	0.003–0.007	1	1.811	0.001–0.003	0.015
1990	129 (2109)	2.126	0.001–0.003	0.003–0.007	1	1.811	0.001–0.003	0.015
1991–92	129 (2109)	2.126	0.001–0.003	0.003–0.007	1	1.811	0.001–0.003	0.015

VALVE SPECIFICATIONS

Year	Engine Displacement cu. in. (cc)	Seat Angle (deg.)	Face Angle (deg.)	Spring Test Pressure (lbs.)	Spring Installed Height (in.)	Stem-to-Guide Clearance (in.) Intake	Stem-to-Guide Clearance (in.) Exhaust	Stem Diameter (in.) Intake	Stem Diameter (in.) Exhaust
1988	129 (2109)	45	45	NA	NA	0.047	0.047	0.313–0.314	0.3508–0.3512
1989	129 (2109)	45	45	NA	NA	0.047	0.047	0.313–0.314	0.3508–0.3512
1990	129 (2109)	45	45	NA	NA	0.047	0.047	0.313–0.314	0.3508–0.3512
1991–92	129 (2109)	45	45	NA	NA	0.047	0.047	0.313–0.314	0.3508–0.3512

NA—Not available

PISTON AND RING SPECIFICATIONS

All measurements are given in inches

Year	Engine Displacement cu. in. (cc)	Piston Clearance	Ring Gap Top Compression	Ring Gap Bottom Compression	Ring Gap Oil Control	Ring Side Clearance Top Compression	Ring Side Clearance Bottom Compression	Ring Side Clearance Oil Control
1988	129 (2109)	0.001–0.008	0.0120–0.0180	0.0120–0.0200	0.0100–0.0160	0.0020–0.0030	0.0020–0.0030	0.0010–0.0020
1989	129 (2109)	0.001–0.008	0.0120–0.0180	0.0120–0.0200	0.0100–0.0160	0.0020–0.0030	0.0020–0.0030	0.0010–0.0020
1990	129 (2109)	0.001–0.008	0.0120–0.0180	0.0120–0.0200	0.0100–0.0160	0.0020–0.0030	0.0020–0.0030	0.0010–0.0020
1991–92	129 (2109)	0.001–0.008	0.0120–0.0180	0.0120–0.0200	0.0100–0.0160	0.0020–0.0030	0.0020–0.0030	0.0010–0.0020

TORQUE SPECIFICATIONS

All readings are given in ft. lbs.

Year	Engine Displacement cu. in. (cc)	Cylinder Head Bolts	Main Bearing Bolts	Rod Bearing Bolts	Crankshaft Pulley Bolts	Flywheel Bolts	Manifold Intake	Manifold Exhaust	Spark Plugs
1988	129 (2109)	①	37②	22	257③	80	15	18	14
1989	129 (2109)	①	37②	22	257③	80	15	18	14
1990	129 (2109)	①	37②	22	257③	80	15	18	14
1991–92	129 (2109)	①	37②	22	257③	80	15	18	14

① Coat the bolts with sealing compound. Torque in sequence to 7 ft. lbs., then retorque in sequence to 37 ft. lbs.
② Coat with sealing compound before assembling case
③ Triple V-belt pulley only. If equipped with single belt pulley, 44 ft. lbs.

BRAKE SPECIFICATIONS

All measurements are given in inches

Year	Model	Lug Nut Torque (ft. lbs.)	Master Cylinder Bore	Brake Disc Minimum Thickness	Brake Disc Maximum Runout	Standard Brake Drum Diameter	Minimum Lining Thickness Front	Minimum Lining Thickness Rear
1988	Vanagon	132	NA	0.512	NA	9.921	0.276	0.098
1989	Vanagon	132	NA	0.512	NA	9.921	0.276	0.098
1990	Vanagon	132	NA	0.512	NA	9.921	0.276	0.098
1991–92	Vanagon	132	NA	0.512	NA	9.921	0.276	0.098

NA—Not available

WHEEL ALIGNMENT

Year	Model	Caster Range (deg.)	Caster Preferred Setting (deg.)	Camber Range (deg.)	Camber Preferred Setting (deg.)	Toe-in (in.)	Steering Axis Inclination (deg.)
1988	Vanagon	7P–7½P	7¼P	½N–½P	0	11/64	NA
	Vanagon Syncro	4⁷/₁₆P–4¹⁵/₁₆P	4¹¹/₁₆P	0–¹¹/₁₆P	¹¹/₃₂P	5/64	NA
1989	Vanagon	7P–7½P	7¼P	½N–½P	0	11/64	NA
	Vanagon Syncro	4⁷/₁₆P–4¹⁵/₁₆P	4¹¹/₁₆P	0–¹¹/₁₆P	¹¹/₃₂P	5/64	NA
1990	Vanagon	7P–7½P	7¼P	½N–½P	0	11/64	NA
	Vanagon Syncro	4⁷/₁₆P–4¹⁵/₁₆P	4¹¹/₁₆P	0–¹¹/₁₆P	¹¹/₃₂P	5/64	NA
1991–92	Vanagon	7P–7½P	7¼P	½N–½P	0	11/64	NA
	Vanagon Syncro	4⁷/₁₆P–4¹⁵/₁₆P	4¹¹/₁₆P	0–¹¹/₁₆P	¹¹/₃₂P	5/64	NA

NA—Not available
N—Negative
P—Positive

ENGINE ELECTRICAL

NOTE: If equipped with a theft protected radio, obtain the security reset code before disconnecting the negative battery cable. Vehicles with a single battery have the battery under the front passenger seat. Campers with an electric refrigerator have a battery under both front seats.

Removing the distributor shaft with a puller

ROTOR
DUST COVER
DISTRIBUTOR SHAFT
SHIMS
PLASTIC WASHER
SCREW
HALL SENDER
DISTRIBUTOR
SPRING
DISTRIBUTOR DRIVESHAFT
BRACKET
GASKET
SHIMS
PLASTIC WASHER
THRUST WASHER
CLUTCH
PIN
RETAINING SPRING

Distributor and driveshaft assembly

Distributor

Removal

1. Make sure the ignition switch is **OFF**.
2. Remove the distributor cap and shield and disconnect the wiring at the distributor.
3. Rotate the engine so the rotor points to the No. 1 spark plug wire notch on the distributor body. Check to see that the engine timing marks are aligned and matchmark the distributor body to the engine case.
4. Remove the distributor bracket bolt and lift the distributor straight out of the engine with the bracket. The driveshaft should remain in the crankcase.

Installation

1. The distributor drive is an off-set key that fits into an off-set slot. The distributor cannot be installed incorrectly if the driveshaft has not been removed. Sometimes the driveshaft lifts with the distributor but falls back in without coming all the way out. Make sure the shaft is installed correctly.
2. If the bracket was removed from the distributor body, loosen the clamp bolt and slide the bracket onto the distributor.
3. Lubricate the O-ring and insert the distributor into the engine. If the clutch does not engage the driveshaft, turn the distributor shaft until it drops into the slot. The driveshaft slot is off-set and the distributor cannot be installed "180 degrees out".
4. Align the matchmarks on the body and the engine case and tighten the bracket and clamp bolt.
5. Install the cap, connect the wiring and check ignition timing.

Distributor Driveshaft

Removal and Installation

1. With the distributor removed, the shaft can be pulled straight out with a magnet or expanding finger tool.
2. To install, make sure the crankshaft pulley timing mark is aligned at TDC on No. 1 cylinder. If necessary, remove the passenger side valve cover and make sure both valves on the front cylinder (No. 1) are closed and the rocker arms move slightly.

The small side of the distributor driveshaft off-set is towards the water pump when the engine is at TDC No. 1 cylinder

The mark on the inner pulley is the timing mark, the outer pulley had the TDC mark

3. With the small side of the driveshaft off-set towards the water pump, insert the driveshaft with the slot parallel to the crankcase center line.

4. As the driveshaft falls into place, the gears will engage and the slot will turn clockwise and end up being almost aligned with the distributor hold-down stud.

5. Lubricate the O-ring and insert the distributor into the engine. If the clutch does not engage the driveshaft, turn the distributor shaft until it drops into the slot.

6. Align the matchmarks on the body and the engine case and tighten the bracket and clamp bolt.

7. Install the cap, connect the wiring and check ignition timing.

Ignition Timing

Adjustment

1. Run the engine until it reaches normal operating temperature, then stop the engine.

2. Connect a timing light and tachometer. Start the engine and raise the speed to 2000–2500 rpm for about 10 seconds.

3. Allow the engine to idle, check and adjust idle speed as necessary to 830–930 rpm.

4. Aim the timing light at the crankshaft pulley. The timing mark on the inner pulley should be aligned with the split in the crankcase. If using a timing light with adjustable advance, using the TDC mark will show 5 degrees BTDC.

5. Loosen and rotate the distributor to adjust the ignition timing. When the timing is correct, tighten the distributor clamp and recheck the timing.

6. If using a timing light with adjustable advance, timing should be 30–40 degrees BTDC at 3000 rpm.

Alternator

For further information, please refer to "Alternators" in the Unit Repair section.

Precautions

Several precautions must be observed with alternator equipped vehicles to avoid damage to the unit.

• If the battery is removed for any reason, make sure it is reconnected with the correct polarity. Reversing the battery connections may result in damage to the one-way rectifiers.

• When utilizing a booster battery as a starting aid, always connect the positive to positive terminals and the negative terminal from the booster battery to a good engine ground on the vehicle being started.

• Never use a fast charger as a booster to start vehicles.

• Disconnect the battery cables when charging the battery with a fast charger.

• Never attempt to polarize the alternator.

• Do not use test lights of more than 12 volts when checking diode continuity.

• Do not short across or ground any of the alternator terminals.

• The polarity of the battery, alternator and regulator must be matched and considered before making any electrical connections within the system.

• Never separate the alternator on an open circuit. Make sure all connections within the circuit are clean and tight.

• Disconnect the battery ground terminal when performing any service on electrical components.

• Disconnect the battery if arc welding is to be done on the vehicle.

Belt Tension Adjustment

1. Loosen the alternator pivot and mounting bolts.

2. Pivot the alternator to adjust the belt tension.

3. The correct tension is measured by pressing the belt with the thumb. Deflection should be 0.079 in. (2.0mm) on a new belt or 0.197 in. (5.0mm) on a used belt.

4. After the tension is adjusted, tighten the mounting and pivot bolts to 14 ft. lbs. (19 Nm).

Removal and Installation

1. Disconnect the negative battery cable.

2. Label and disconnect the alternator wiring.

3. Remove the dipstick and oil filler neck.

4. Loosen the alternator adjusting bolt and remove the drive belt.

5. Remove the right rear engine cover plate and alternator cover plate.

6. Remove the mounting bolt and remove the alternator from above.

7. Installation is the reverse of the removal procedure. Use care to ensure that the rubber grommet on the intake cover for the wiring harness is installed correctly.

8. After installation, adjust the drive belt tension.

Starter

For further information, please refer to "Starters" in the Unit Repair section.

Removal and Installation

1. Disconnect the negative battery cable.

2. Disconnect and tag the wiring at the starter.

3. Remove the upper starter mounting bolt through the engine compartment.

4. Raise and support the vehicle safely.

5. On Vanagon Syncro, it may make the job easier to disconnect the halfshaft at the inner drive flange and to remove the differential lock servo.

6. Remove the lower starter mounting bolt and remove the starter.

To install:

7. Before installing the starter, lubricate the outboard bushing in the nose with grease. Apply sealing compound to the mating surfaces between the starter and transaxle.

8. Locate the starter on the transaxle housing and install the lower mounting bolt. If removed, install the differential lock servo and halfshaft bolts.

9. Lower the vehicle and install the upper mounting bolt.

10. Connect the starter wiring and battery cable.

CHASSIS ELECTRICAL

Heater Blower Motor

Removal and Installation

FRONT

1. Disconnect the negative battery cable.
2. Drain the cooling system, using the following procedures:
   a. Set the heater temperature control to full hot.
   b. Open the expansion tank cap.
   c. Position a catch pan under the water pump.
   d. Disconnect the lower and the center coolant hoses from the water pump.
3. Disconnect the wiring and vacuum hoses from the center heater unit under the instrument panel. Disconnect the air ducts from the housing.
4. Remove the heater housing mounting bolts and remove the housing from under the instrument panel.
5. Remove the top cover and remove the blower from the housing.

To install:

6. Install the blower motor in position in the housing and install the cover.
7. Install the heater assembly in position under the instrument panel.
8. Connect the wiring, the vacuum hoses and air ducts to the housing.
9. Connect the negative battery cable and fill the cooling system. Run the engine at 2500 rpm and check that water flows at the breather valve with no bubbles.
10. Check the operation of the blower motor.

REAR

1. Make sure the ignition switch is **OFF**.
2. Remove the kick panel from under the rear seat.
3. Remove the 4 bolts retaining the auxiliary heater unit to the floor.
4. Pivot the heater unit outward, do not disconnect the heater hoses or the cables from the housing.
5. Disconnect the blower wiring and remove the blower from the housing.
6. Installation is the reverse of the removal procedure.
7. Check the operation of the blower.

Windshield Wiper Motor

Removal and Installation

1. Place the wiper arms in the park position.
2. Make sure the ignition switch is **OFF**.
3. Remove both wiper arms.
4. Remove the glove compartment.
5. Remove the bearing cover and nut from the motor.
6. Remove the heater branch connections under the instrument panel.
7. Disconnect the wiper motor wiring.
8. Remove the wiper motor mounting screws and remove the motor.

To install:

9. Install the wiper motor in position under the instrument panel.
10. Install the bearing cover and nut to the motor.
11. Before attaching the linkage, turn the ignition switch and the wiper switch **ON** to run the motor. Turn the wiper switch **OFF**. When the motor stops in the park position, attach the crank to the motor shaft.
12. Install the fresh air ducts and reconnect the wiring.
13. Install the glove compartment.
14. Install the wiper arms. The blades should be 2¾ in. (70mm) from the bottom of the windshield.

Rear Wiper Motor

Removal and Installation

1. Make sure the ignition switch is **OFF**.
2. Remove the rear wiper arm.
3. Raise the rear hatch and remove the interior panel.
4. Disconnect the wiring and remove the screws to remove the motor.
5. Installation is the reverse of removal. Before attaching the linkage, turn the ignition switch and the wiper switch **ON** to run the motor. Turn the wiper switch **OFF**. When the motor stops in the park position, attach the crank to the motor shaft.
6. Install the wiper arm. The blade should be 2¾ in. (70mm) from the bottom of the windshield.

HEATER/VENTILATION WITH FRESH AIR FAN

CONTROL VALVE

FRESH AIR/HEATING CONTROL

AIR DISTRIBUTOR

Front heater and fresh air distribution system

Instrument cluster assembly

Windshield Wiper Switch

Removal and Installation

1. Disconnect the negative battery cable.
2. Matchmark and remove the steering wheel.
3. Disconnect the combination switch wiring and remove the combination switch.
4. Disconnect the wiper switch wiring and remove the wiper switch.
5. Installation is the reverse of the removal procedure.
6. Align the steering wheel matchmarks during installation and torque the nut to 36 ft. lbs. (50 Nm).

Instrument Cluster

Removal and Installation

1. Disconnect the negative battery cable.
2. Grasp the rear of the instrument cluster cover by the 2 recesses and pull the cover off.
3. Remove the 2 screws retaining the instrument cluster and pull it forward.
4. Disconnect the speedometer cable and remove the cluster from the vehicle.
5. All instruments can be removed from the rear of the cluster.
6. Installation is the reverse of the removal procedure.

Combination Switch

Removal and Installation

The combination switch incorporates the headlight, turn signal, dimmer and cruise control switches.
1. Disconnect the negative battery cable.
2. Matchmark and remove the steering wheel.
3. Pry off the switch cover on the end of the steering column.
4. Disconnect and tag the switch wiring.
5. Remove the switch mounting screws and remove the switch from the steering column.
6. Installation is the reverse of the removal procedure.
7. Align the steering wheel matchmarks during installation. Tighten the steering wheel retaining nut to 36 ft. lbs. (50 Nm).

Remove 3 screws to remove the wiper and combination switch assembly

Ignition Lock/Switch

Removal and Installation

1. Disconnect the negative battery cable.
2. Remove the steering wheel, steering column covers and the windshield wiper/combination switch assembly.
3. Use a ⅛ in. (3mm) drill to carefully drill a hole into the cylinder housing at the intersection of lines **A** and **B**. Dimension **A** is 0.472 in. (12mm); dimension **B** is 0.394 in. (10mm).
4. Carefully insert a punch into the hole and push in on the spring loaded detent.
5. With the key in the cylinder and turned to the **ON** position, pull the lock cylinder out.
6. To install a cylinder, insert the key into the cylinder and push it into place. Make sure the pin engages correctly and that the retainer fits easily in place. Do not force any parts together. When they are correctly aligned, they will fit easily into place.

Stoplight Switch

Removal and Installation

The stoplight switch is located in the side of the master cylinder.
1. Disconnect the negative battery cable.
2. Remove the instrument cluster cover.
3. Remove the instrument cluster from the vehicle.
4. Disconnect the electrical lead from the stoplight switch.
5. Place a rag under the stoplight switch. Unscrew the switch and quickly plug the opening in the master cylinder.

NOTE: It is important that the switch opening be plugged immediately to prevent the brake fluid from leaking out and to protect the interior trim components from damage.

Dimensions for drilling the ignition lock cylinder

To install:

6. Install the switch into the master cylinder and reconnect the electrical lead.
7. Fill the master cylinder to the correct level.
8. Install the instrument cluster and cover.
9. Connect the negative battery cable.
10. Check the operation of the switch and the operation of the brake system.

Neutral Safety Switch

Adjustment

1. The combination neutral start and back-up light switch is mounted inside the shifter housing.
2. The engine should start in **P** or **N** only and the back-up lights should only come on only in **R**.
3. Adjust the switch by loosening the screws and moving it on it's mounts.
4. After any adjustment or replacement, check that the engine starts only with the switch in **P** or **N** and the back-up lights come on only in **R**.

Fuses and Relays

Location

The fuse and relay panel is located behind a panel, under the left side of the instrument panel. The panel can be removed by lifting it from the bottom and pulling it upward. The fuse ratings and circuits protected are listed on the fuse box cover.

Engine Control Unit

Location

The main engine ECU is mounted on the floor behind the rear seat of passenger models. On cargo models, the ECU is under a panel at the rear of the load bed.

Flashers

Location

The turnsignal flashers and all other relays are on the main fuse panel under the left side of the dashboard.

ENGINE COOLING

Radiator

Removal and Installation

1. Disconnect the negative battery cable. Drain the cooling system.
2. Remove the grille retaining screws and remove the grille.
3. Raise and safely support the vehicle.
4. Remove the spare tire from the spare tire tray and remove the spare tire tray bracket.
5. Remove the lower radiator cover.
6. Disconnect the hoses from the radiator and remove the radiator lower bolts.

NOTE: If equipped with air conditioning, the system does not have to be discharged. The condenser can be lowered with the radiator and supported aside.

7. Lower the radiator partially and disconnect the electrical lead from the thermo-time switch.
8. Carefully remove the radiator from the vehicle. If equipped with air conditioning, use care not to kink the refrigerant lines. Remove the condenser-to-radiator bolts and support the condenser aside.

To install:

9. If equipped with air conditioning, attach the condenser to the radiator.
10. Raise the radiator assembly into position and install the lower retaining bolts. Tighten to 11 ft. lbs. (15 Nm).
11. Connect the electrical lead to the thermo-time sensor.
12. Connect the hoses to the radiator. Install the lower radiator cover.
13. Install the spare tire tray bracket and tire. Lower the vehicle.
14. Install the grille assembly. Connect the negative battery cable.
15. Fill and bleed the cooling system.

Electric Cooling Fan

Removal and Installation

1. Disconnect the negative battery cable.

2. Remove the grille assembly.
3. Raise and safely support the vehicle.
4. Remove the spare tire and spare tire bracket.
5. Lower the radiator from the vehicle, it is not necessary to disconnect the hoses from the radiator or to drain the coolant. Support the radiator assembly aside.
6. Disconnect the fan electrical lead and remove the fan retaining bolts.
7. Remove the fan from the vehicle.
8. Installation is the reverse of the removal procedure. Check the operation of the fan.

Heater Core

For further information, please refer to Chilton's Air Conditioning and Heating Manual.

Removal and Installation

1. Disconnect the negative battery cable.
2. Drain the cooling system.
3. Locate and remove the heater core cover in the side of the heater box.
4. Disconnect the heater hoses from the heater core.

NOTE: It may be necessary to remove the heater box from the vehicle. If so, disconnect and tag the wiring and cables at the heater box.

5. If the unit has a core cover on the side, remove the screws or unclip the cover and remove the core. The core should pull straight out.
6. If the heater box is separated in halves, separate the halves and remove the heater core. It may be held together with clips or glue joints. To separate a glue joint:
   a. Place a knife along the length of the joint.
   b. Strike the back of the knife with a hammer. The joint should pop open cleanly.

To install:

7. Installation is the reverse of the removal procedure.
8. Fill the cooling system and check the operation of the heater when finished.

Water pump assembly on waterboxer engine

9. If the heater box was removed, check the heater controls to insure that there is full travel with the controls.

Water Pump

Removal and Installation

1. Drain the cooling system. Loosen the water pump pulley bolts.
2. Remove the drive belt and pulley from the water pump.
3. Disconnect the coolant hoses and remove the left side coolant elbow from the water pump.
4. Remove the right side coolant elbow from the pump.
5. Remove the water pump.

To install:

6. Clean and inspect the mounting surfaces of the water pump and engine.
7. Lightly grease the O-ring and install the water pump on the engine.
8. Torque the bolts to 15 ft. lbs. (20 Nm).

9. Install the left side coolant elbow with a new O-ring and torque the bolts to 15 ft. lbs. (20 Nm).
10. Install the right side coolant elbow with a new O-ring and torque the bolts to 15 ft. lbs. (20 Nm).
11. Install the drive belt pulley and torque the retaining bolts to 15 ft. lbs. (20 Nm). Install the drive belt. Adjust the belt tension.
12. Fill the cooling system, run the engine and check for leaks.

Thermostat

Removal and Installation

The thermostat is mounted in the top of the coolant distribution housing, above the water pump.

1. Drain the coolant from the engine.
2. Remove the hoses from the top of the housing.
3. Remove the housing top retaining bolts and remove the top from the housing.
4. Remove the thermostat from the housing.

To install:

5. Replace the O-ring in the top of the thermostat housing.

6. Install the thermostat in position and install the top of the housing.

7. Tighten the retaining bolts to 15 ft. lbs. (20 Nm). Connect the hoses and refill the cooling system.

8. Connect the battery cable and bleed the cooling system.

Bleeding Cooling System

NOTE: The manufacturer specifies the use of a specially-formulated coolant, part ZVW 237 102 in this engine. Anti-freeze other than this may cause corrosion of the cooling system, leading to engine damage.

1. Set the heater control to **MAX** heat.

2. If equipped, open the control valve for the auxiliary heater under the rear seat.

3. Remove the radiator grille.

4. Raise and safely support the vehicle approximately 15¾ in. (400mm) at the front, under the crossmember.

5. Open the bleeder screw on the radiator.

6. Open the bleeder valve in the engine compartment.

7. Fill the coolant expansion tank until the tank is full.

8. Start the engine. Increase the engine speed to 2000 rpm and continue to fill the tank until coolant flows from the bleeder screw on the radiator. Wait until the coolant is flowing free of bubbles.

9. Add more coolant until the tank is full. Close the tank cap.

10. Turn the engine **OFF**. Restart the engine after 20 seconds.

11. At 2000 rpm, open the expansion cap.

12. Close the bleeder screw on the radiator when coolant flows out. Add coolant if necessary and close the tank cap.

13. Close the bleeder screw in the engine compartment and turn **OFF** the engine. If necessary, check and fill the expansion tank.

FUEL SYSTEM

Fuel System Service Precautions

When working with the fuel system certain precautions should be taken; always work in a well ventilated area, keep a dry chemical (Class B) fire extinguisher near the work area. Always disconnect the negative battery cable and do not make any repairs to the fuel system until all the necessary steps for repair have been reviewed.

Relieving Fuel System Pressure

The Digifant fuel injection system used in this vehicle will maintain a residual pressure up to 36 psi (2.5 BAR) for 10–30 minutes after the ignition is switched OFF. If the system is working properly, the pressure is generated any time the ignition is switched ON, with or without the engine running. The fuel pump stops running after about 2 seconds if the engine is not turning over, but this is enough time to build pressure. To relieve the system pressure, locate the Tee fitting near the distributor and loosen the bolt to open the fitting. Cover the fitting with a shop rag to catch the fuel spray and dispose of the rag properly.

Fuel Tank

Removal and Installation

1. Disconnect the negative battery cable. On Vanagon Syncro, remove the transaxle.

2. Raise and safely support the vehicle. Empty the fuel tank.

3. Disconnect the filler pipe. Label and disconnect the vent hoses and supply and return hoses.

RELAYS AND FUSES

CONTROL UNIT

FUEL PUMPS

COMBUSTION AIR VALVE

Fuel pump location

4. Remove the splash shield from under the body.

5. Remove the fuel tank.

6. Installation is the reverse of removal. Use new gaskets and seals and make sure the vent hoses are properly connected.

Fuel Filter

Removal and Installation

The fuel filter is located under the right side of the vehicle, just behind the fuel tank. Some vehicles also have a small in-line filter before the fuel pump.

1. Relieve the fuel system pressure.

2. Raise and safely support the vehicle.

3. Disconnect the fuel lines from the filter.

4. Remove the filter bracket retaining bolt and remove the filter.

5. Install the new filter in position, note the direction of the arrows for fuel flow.

6. Reconnect the fuel lines and lower the vehicle.

7. Run the engine and check for leaks.

Electric Fuel Pump

Pressure Testing

1. Connect tool VW-1318 or equivalent, 0–60 psi (4 BAR) gauge to the Tee fitting next to the distributor. Locate the fuel pressure regulator near the center of the intake manifold.

2. Run the engine at idle and check the pressure reading. The pressure should be 29 psi. (2 BAR) with the vacuum line connected to the regulator or 36 psi. (2.5 BAR) with the vacuum line disconnected.

3. Stop the engine and wait 10 minutes, the pressure should not drop below 29 psi (2 BAR). If the pressure is not maintained;

   a. Run the engine again to build pressure, then stop the engine.

   b. Check the fuel pump check valve by clamping off the line from the fuel pump to the regulator and observing the gauge.

   c. Check the pressure regulator by clamping off the return line to the fuel tank and observing the gauge.

   d. Check the injectors by clamping the lines between the injectors and the regulator.

4. If the pressure drop stops or slows down, the problem is in the unit tested by clamping the line.

Flow Rate Testing

1. Disconnect the fuel return hose from the pressure regulator and plug the hose.
2. Attach a hose to the pressure regulator and place the other end into a measuring container.
3. Locate and remove the fuel pump relay in the separate box near the main ECU. When the sockets for terminals **30** and **87** are jumpered, the fuel pump will run.
4. Run the pump for 30 seconds and measure the fuel flow. The minimum specification is 17 oz. (500 cc) in 30 seconds. If the flow is less and no other leak is found, replace the pump.

Removal and Installation

1. Disconnect the negative battery cable. Relieve the fuel system pressure.
2. Raise and safely support the vehicle. Disconnect the fuel pump wiring. Pull the plug from the pump but do not pull on the wiring.
3. Disconnect and plug the fuel hoses.
4. Remove the fuel pump mounting nuts and remove the pump.
5. Reconnect the fuel pump hoses and wiring.
6. Install the pump on the vehicle.

Sample point for exhaust analyser probe

Oxygen sensor (1) and idle stabilizer valve (2) connectors

Idle speed adjustment screw (1) and air/fuel mixture (CO) adjustment screw (2)

Fuel Injection

For further information, please refer to Chilton's Electronic Engine Controls Manual.

Idle Speed and Mixture Adjustment

1. Run the engine until it reaches normal operating temperature.
   a. Turn **OFF** all electrical accessories and take readings when the radiator fan is not running.
   b. Check that the throttle valve switch on the throttle body is in the closed position at idle.
   c. The crankcase breather hose should be removed from the oil vent and plugged.
   d. Check to see that the idle stabilizer is operating properly. With the ignition turned **ON**, the valve should hum or vibrate.
2. With the ignition switch **OFF**, connect a tachometer and timing light to the engine. Power is available at the alternator output terminal. Connect the tachometer to terminal **1** of the ignition coil for the rpm signal.
3. Connect the CO meter to the sample tap on the left side exhaust pipe.
4. With the ignition switch **OFF**, disconnect the oxygen sensor connector and the idle stabilizer control valve connector.
5. Start the engine and run it at idle speed. After 2 minutes, adjust as necessary by turning the adjusting screw on the throttle valve housing. The idle speed should be 880 ± 50 rpm.
6. Check the CO reading on the exhaust analyzer; the CO should be 0.3–1.1%. If the vehicle has an emissions information sticker in the engine compartment, use the CO specification on the sticker. The CO is set at the factory and controlled by the ECU, which is able to adapt to various altitudes and engine conditions to maintain correct air/fuel mixture. If the CO value is not correct, look for other problems with the engine, such as a vacuum leak or poor electrical connection, before adjusting the air/fuel mixture.
7. If the air/fuel mixture must be adjusted, the seal must be removed from the CO adjustment screw.
   a. Center punch the sheet metal plug in the CO adjusting hole. Drill a $\frac{3}{32}$ in. (2.5mm) hole in the center of the plug. Keep the area clean of metal shavings.
   b. Screw a sheet metal screw into the plug.
   c. Remove the plug by pulling straight out on the screw with pliers.
8. Start the engine and alternately turn the adjusting screws to obtain the correct CO and idle speed specifications.
9. Reconnect the oxygen sensor connector and idle stabilizer connector. Let the engine idle for approximately 2 minutes. Check the CO, idle speed and ignition timing and correct, if necessary, by repeating the above procedure.
10. Stop the engine. Install a new plug over the air/fuel mixture screw until it is flush with the housing.

Fuel Injector

Removal and Installation

1. Injectors are removed in pairs from each intake manifold. Relieve the fuel system pressure.
2. Remove the electrical connectors from both injectors.
3. Disconnect the fuel supply and return lines from the fuel rail.
4. Pull both injectors straight out of the manifold. Loosen the clamps to remove each injector from the rail.
5. Installation is the reverse of removal. Use new O-rings and check for fuel and vacuum leaks after assembly.

EMISSION CONTROLS

For further information, please refer to Chilton's Emission Controls Manual.

Emission Warning Lamps

Resetting

The emission systems incorporates a mileage counter which activates the oxygen sensor warning light on the instrument panel. The counter will illuminate the light at 60,000 mile intervals. The oxygen sensor must be replaced when the light comes ON. The light can reset by pushing the button on the milage counter with a pencil. Locate the counter under the left front of the instrument panel, in line with the speedometer cable.

Push the button on the milage counter to reset the OXS light

ENGINE MECHANICAL

NOTE: If equipped with a theft protected radio, obtain the reset security code before disconnecting the negative battery cable.

Engine

Removal and Installation

1. The engine is removed from below without removing the transaxle. Disconnect the negative battery cable. Some models have 2 batteries, one under each front seat.
2. Remove the air cleaner, the air flow sensor and air intake duct.
3. Disconnect and tag the alterntor wires at the alternator.
4. Disconnect and tag the connectors at the fuel injectors, the plug at the throttle valve switch and the plug at the auxiliary air regulator.
5. Disconnect and tag the hoses at the charcoal filter valve.
6. Disconnect and plug the fuel hoses near the distributor. Remove the accelerator cable from the throttle valve lever. On automatic transaxle equipped vehicles, remove the circlip and spring from the accelerator rod.
7. Disconnect and tag the connector at the oxygen sensor, the distributor, oil pressure switch, temperature sensor, temperature sender and coolant level warning switch (located at the coolant expsansion tank).
8. Clamp the coolant hoses and open the coolant expansion tank cap. Remove the drain plugs from the cylinder heads and drain the coolant. The drain plugs are above the pushrod tubes.

Engine carrier bolts at the top of their slots

NOTE: Always replace the sealing rings under the drain plugs during installation.

9. Disconnect the brake booster hose and all coolant hoses. Remove the coolant expansion tank.
10. If equipped with power steering and/or air conditioning, remove the pump or compressor without disconnecting the hoses. Secure the pump or compressor out of the way, do not let it hang by the hoses.
11. Raise and support the vehicle safely. Remove the engine-to-transaxle bolts and nuts on both sides.
12. If equipped with automatic transaxle, remove the bolts which attach the torque converter to the driveplate through the hole on the top of the transaxle housing.

Check the position of the engine carrier

Transaxle shift linkage coupling, remove the square head bolt

13. Disconnect and tag the starter motor wiring.

14. If equipped with automatic transaxle, disconnect the accelerator rod.

15. On Vanagon Syncro, loosen the large mounting bolts on the front differential about 3 turns.

16. Support the engine and transaxle separately with jacks that can be lowered.

17. Loosen the transaxle mount bolt at the front of the transaxle.

18. Remove the engine carrier bolts. Carefully lower the engine and transaxle assembly slightly. Keep the wiring harness aside so it can pass the oil filler tube. Lower the assembly more, to have access to the lower engine mounting bolts. Remove the engine from the transaxle and lower it out of the vehicle.

To install:

19. Check the clutch release bearing for wear and replace, if necessary.

20. Lubricate the clutch release bearing and main shaft splines lightly with grease. Do not lubricate the guide sleeve for the release bearing.

21. On Vanagon Syncro, clean the engine–to–transaxle mounting face and apply a bead of silicone sealer to the transaxle.

22. Carefully raise the engine into place and start all the engine–to–transaxle bolts. When they are all started, torque the bolts to 22 ft. lbs. (30 Nm).

23. Raise the engine and transaxle assembly into position and start all the engine and transaxle mounting bolts. Torque the transaxle mount bolts to 22 ft. lbs. (30 Nm) and the engine carrier–to–body bolts to 18 ft. lbs. (25 Nm). Make sure the carrier bolts are correctly positioned at the top of their holes.

24. If equipped with an automatic transaxle, install all the torque converter bolts, then torque them to 15 ft. lbs. (20 Nm).

25. Connect the accelerator rod and the wiring to the starter. Install the coolant expansion tank and reconnect all coolant lines.

26. Reconnect all electrical leads on the engine. Reconnect all of the fuel lines to the injectors and the fuel pressure regulator.

27. Connect the wiring to the alternator and install the air cleaner assembly.

28. Connect the negative battery cable. Refill the cooling system, using the correct procedure.

29. Run the engine to normal operating temperature and check for leaks. Check the idle speed and transmission operation.

Cylinder head bolt torque sequence

Cylinder heads can be removed with the engine installed

Cylinder Head

Removal and Installation

NOTE: It is not necessary to remove or lower the en-

Replace the metal gasket and the O-ring

gine to remove the cylinder heads. **Either head can be removed and installed while the engine is in place in the vehicle. The manufacturer specifies use of a beam or dial type torque wrench for installing the cylinder head nuts, and specifically recommends against using a click type torque wrench.**

1. Relieve the fuel system pressure. Disconnect the negative battery cable. Some models have 2 batteries.

2. Drain the cooling system by disconnecting the radiator hoses at the front of the vehicle. Remove the coolant drain plugs on the bottom of each cylinder head just above the pushrod tubes.

3. Remove the coolant pump and the coolant crossover pipes from the front and rear of the engine.

4. Remove the exhaust system, including the crossover pipes, muffler and catalytic converter and heat shields.

5. Remove the crankshaft pulley and the power steering pump. Set the pump aside without disconnecting the hydraulic hoses.

6. Disconnect the fuel injector wiring and hoses. Remove the intake manifolds from the cylinder heads.

7. Remove the valve covers, rocker arms and pushrods. Mark the pushrods to they can be installed into their original position.

8. Remove the 8 nuts and remove the cylinder head. The cylinder head is held in place on 8 studs and the cylinder head also holds the cylinders in place. It may be necessary to hold the cylinders in place when removing the head.

To install:

9. Make sure all sealing surfaces are clean and free of damage. To prepare the pushrod tubes for installation, stretch them so they are at least 7.6 in. (194mm) long. The small end goes towards the cylinder head, make sure the seam is up and use new sealing rubbers.

NOTE: If the pushrod tube rests on the edge of the valve lifter, the basic valve setting will be incorrect and the lifter(s) will be damaged when the engine is started.

10. Make sure the sealing surfaces are clean and apply a small bead of silicone sealer to the cylinder water jacket. Install a new gasket onto the water jacket and install new O-rings and metal gaskets onto the cylinder liners. Apply the sealer to the face of the cylinder head cap nuts. Be careful not to use too much sealer.

11. Slide the cylinder head partially onto the studs. Hold a pushrod tube up to the crankcase and insert the correct pushrod through the cylinder head to hold the tube in place. Install all the pushrod tubes the same way.

12. Carefully push the cylinder head onto the studs, making sure the pushrod tubes fit properly into their holes. Tighten the No. 1 cap nut just enough so the remaining 7 cap nuts can be installed.

13. Torque all nuts in sequence in 3 steps to 37 ft. lbs. (50 Nm). Use a beam type or dial type torque wrench, avoid using a click type torque wrench, if possible.

14. Make sure the pushrods are properly seated in the lifters and install the rocker arm assembly. Tighten the nuts 2 turns at a time to draw the shaft down evenly, then torque the nuts to 18 ft. lbs. (25 Nm). Adjust the valve lash.

15. Complete the installation in the reverse order of the removal procedures. Be sure to use new gaskets, seals and O-rings as needed, especially at the cylinder head coolant drain plugs.

Valve Lifters

Removal and Installation

1. Valve lifters can be removed without removing the cylinder head. Remove the valve cover, rocker arm assembly and pushrods.

2. Push the pushrod tube towards the crankcase to compress the tube and pull it out of the cylinder head. Remove the tubes.

LOCKRING — PUSHROD SOCKET — PLUNGER — BALL CHECK VALVE — CHECK VALVE SPRING — CHECK VALVE RETAINER — PLUNGER SPRING — VALVE BODY — BORE HOLE

Valve lifter must be filled with oil before assembly

3. Use a magnet to remove the lifters from the crankcase.

4. Installation is the reverse of removal. Replace any lifter that appears badly worn or damaged. Bleed the lifters and use new pushrod tube seals. Adjust the valve lash.

Lifter Bleeding

1. Before installing a lifter, use a finger to push in where the pushrod contacts the lifter. If the lifter moves (collapses), it must be bled.

2. Remove the lockring that holds the lifter together and remove all the internal parts.

3. Fill the body with clean oil up to the bore hole and install all the internal parts, except the lockring.

4. Insert an old valve guide or a sawed-off pushrod into the lifter socket. With the bore hole facing up, slowly press the lifter and tool in a vise to collapse the lifter enough to install the lockring. If the lifter still moves after being filled with oil, replace the lifter.

Valve Lash

Adjustment

NOTE: No routine valve adjustment is necessary or recommended. However the valves must be adjusted whenever the cylinder heads or rocker arms have been removed. The rocker arms are equipped with conventional locknut-type adjusters.

1. Make sure the ignition switch is **OFF**. If the lifters were removed, make sure they are properly bled. Unscrew the adjusting screws on the rocker arms so the ball shaped end is flush with the surface of the rocker arm.

2. Rotate the crankshaft until No. 1 cylinder is at TDC on compression. Both valves should be closed and the mark on the distributor rotor should be in line with the mark on the distributor housing.

3. Turn the adjusting screws in so they just touch the valve stems.

4. Turn the adjusting screws 2 turns clockwise and tighten the locknuts.

5. Rotate the crankshaft 180 degrees and adjust cylinder No. 2. Repeat the procedure on cylinder No. 3 and 4 until all valves are adjusted.

6. Intermittent valve train noise is normal during starting, sudden acceleration, high temperature or high engine speed.

Rocker Arms/Shafts

Removal and Installation

1. Make sure the ignition switch is **OFF**. Pull the clip that retains the rocker cover over the cover and remove the cover.

2. Loosen the rocker arm retaining nuts 1 or 2 turns at a time to avoid bending the shafts. Remove the rocker arm assembly and the stud seals.

3. Inspect the assembly for signs of excess wear or lack of lubrication. Before installing the rocker arm assembly, be sure the parts are as clean as possible.

To install:

4. Install new stud seals. When installing the rocker arm assembly, the slot on the rocker shaft support faces upward.

5. Tighten the nuts 1 or 2 turns at a time to avoid bending the shaft. Make sure the pushrods stay engaged in the rocker arms. Torque the nuts to 18 ft. lbs. (24 Nm).

6. Adjust the valve lash and install the rocker cover using a new gasket.

Intake Manifold

Removal and Installation

1. Relieve the fuel system pressure. Disconnect the negative battery cable. Remove the air cleaner.

2. Remove the pressure switch which is mounted under the right pair of intake manifold pipes. Disconnect the injector wiring.

3. Disconnect the fuel lines to the injectors and remove the fuel injectors.

4. Disconnect the hoses from the intake air distributor to the manifold pipes.

5. Remove the manifold retaining nuts. Remove the manifold from its mounting.

To install:

6. Using new gaskets, install the manifold in position on the cylinder head.

7. Tighten the intake manifold bolts to 15 ft. lbs. (20 Nm).

8. Connect the hoses from the intake air distributor to the manifold pipes.

9. Install the injectors, using new O-rings. Reconnect the fuel and electrical leads to the injectors.

10. Install the pressure switch to the right manifold.

11. Connect the negative battery cable.

12. Run the engine and check for leaks.

Intake Air Distributor

Removal and Installation

The intake air distributor is located at the center of the engine at the junction of the intake manifold pipes. The throttle valve housing and the air inlet pipes are connected to it.

NOTE: It is not necessary to remove the distributor if only the manifold pipes are to be removed.

1. Disconnect the negative battery cable. Relieve the fuel system pressure. Remove the air cleaner and pressure switch which are located under the right pair of manifold pipes.

2. Push the 4 rubber hoses onto the intake manifold pipes and away from the intake air distributor.

3. Remove the accelerator cable and the throttle valve switch.

4. Disconnect the accelerator cable.

5. Disconnect and tag the leads to the ignition distributor and the pressure sensor.

6. Disconnect the vacuum hose at the auxiliary air regulator.

7. Remove the retaining bolts and remove the throttle valve housing from the crankcase.

To install:

8. Install the air intake distributor in position on the crankcase.

9. Connect the vacuum hoses and auxiliary air regulator. Connect the distributor electrical leads.

10. Connect the accelerator cable and the throttle valve switch.

11. Reposition the rubber hoses from the intake pipes to the air distributor.

12. Install the pressure switch and the air cleaner.

13. Connect the negative battery cable. Check the operation of the accelerator cable and adjust the idle as needed.

Exhaust Manifold

Removal and Installation

1. Disconnect the negative battery cable. Raise and support the vehicle safely and remove the rear wheels.

2. Remove the pipe connecting the manifold assembly to the catalytic converter.

3. Remove the nuts and bolts holding the exhaust manifold to the front and rear exhaust pipes.

4. Remove the front and rear exhaust pipes as required for the job.

5. Installation is the reverse of removal. Use new gaskets and torque all fasteners to 18 ft. lbs. (25 Nm).

Crankcase

Disassembly

1. Relieve the fuel system pressure and disconnect the negative battery cable. Drain the engine oil and the cooling system.

2. The crankshaft pulley bolt should be loosened and tightened with the engine in the vehicle.

   a. The torque on the bolt is extremely high and a special tool is available to hold the pulley. Remove the right side rubber mount-to-engine carrier bolt.

   b. To loosen the pulley bolt, turn the crankshaft so the small hole in the pulley is up. Install tool 3102 or equivalent, into the pulley and the carrier bolt hole and loosen the bolt with a socket wrench.

   c. To tighten the bolt, turn the crankshaft so the small hole is down, install the holding tool and torque the bolt.

3. Remove the engine and position it in a suitable holding fixture.

4. Remove the flywheel. To remove the torque converter driveplate from automatic transaxle models, install an M18 x 1.5 x 60mm bolt in the center of the driveplate. Tighten the bolt to press the driveplate off the crankshaft.

5. Remove the distributor and the intake and exhaust manifolds.

6. Remove the cylinder heads, valve lifters, cylinders and pistons. Mark all parts so they can be returned to the same crankcase bore.

7. Remove the oil filter, oil cooler, oil pressure switch and oil pump.

8. Remove the nuts holding the crankcase halves together.

9. Use a rubber hammer to break the seal between the crankcase halves.

NOTE: Never insert sharp metal tools, wedges, or any prying device between the crankcase halves.

10. After the seal between the crankcase halves is broken, remove the right-hand crankcase half. The crankshaft assembly, camshaft and oil seals can now be lifted out of the crankcase half.

11. Remove the bearing shells and oil pressure relief valve. Throughly clean all parts for inspection.

FRONT EXHAUST PIPE

GASKET (METAL SIDE TOWARDS CYLINDER HEAD)

FRONT BRACKET

REAR EXHAUST PIPE

EXHAUST MANIFOLD

REAR BRACKET

EXHAUST MANIFOLD

GASKET

5 DIAPHRAGM SPRINGS

WASHER

EXHAUST PIPE

Exhaust system components

Inspection

Whenever the crankcase is split, the crankshaft, camshaft and the crankcase should be carefully inspected for wear or damage. The crankshaft should be examined using magnetic or fluoroscopic crack detection equipment. Mount the crankshaft and camshaft on V-blocks or in a lathe and use a dial indicator to make sure run-out is not more than 0.0015 in. (0.04mm). See the specifications charts for journal diameters. If either shaft shows wear or damage, it should be reconditioned or replaced.

The crankcase halves should be inspected for deep cracks or warping. Check carefully around the cylinder head studs for signs of the stud inserts pulling out. Check the lifter bores for signs of scoring or deformation. Use solvent and compressed air to clean out all the oil passages. Clean the mating surfaces and assemble the empty case halves to check the alignment of the crankshaft and camshaft bores.

Before grinding the crankshaft or line-boring the case, check to see what oversize bearings are available. The crankshaft is painted with color code dots according to main journal size and crankshaft application. A green color code indicates the crankshaft for the 2.1L Digifant engine. The color dots between the journals must be the same on the new bearings. If in doubt, clean and temporarily assemble the crankcase with the crankshaft and the old or new bearings, and use Plastigage® to measure bearing clearances. This can be done before or after line-boring the case.

1. Camshaft
2. Crankshaft and connecting rod assembly
3. Main bearing No. 1
4. Main bearing No. 2
5. End cap for camshaft bore
6. No. 1 camshaft bearing shell
7. No. 2 camshaft bearing shell
8. No. 3 camshaft bearing shell
9. Crankshaft bearing dowel pin
10. No. 2 crankshaft bearing half
11. Left crankcase half

Crankcase assembly

TRIPLE V-BELT PULLEY

SEALING RING

WOODRUFF KEY

RUBBER ENGINE MOUNT

BOLT WITHOUT WASHER

ENGINE CARRIER

TOOL NO. 3102

A special tool is required to hold the crankshaft pulley when loosening or tightening the bolt

Thrust washer tab (1) and bearing shell tabs (2) at the case split line

The camshaft gear timing mark must be between the 2 crankshaft gear timing marks

Assembly

1. Install the No. 3 crankshaft bearing dowel into the left crankcase half. Lubricate the case and install the bearing shells. The left case half has the oil holes, make sure the bearings are correctly installed.

2. The crankshaft thrust washer fits onto the flywheel end of the crankshaft. The tab points towards the main bearing and the split line of the case.

3. Lubricate and install the camshaft bearings, making sure the tabs fit properly into the notches in the case.

4. Temporarily lay the crankshaft and camshaft into the left crankcase half. Make sure the dowel fits into the rear bearing. Use a dial indicator to check camshaft endplay; it should be no more than 0.006 in. (0.16mm). The rear camshaft bearing determines endplay.

5. Use a dial indicator to check timing gear backlash; it should be 0.002 in. (0.05mm).

   a. Set the dial indicator against a camshaft gear tooth and measure how far it moves without moving the crankshaft. Backlash should be hardly noticeable.

   b. If no backlash is measured, turn the crankshaft counter-clockwise, viewed from the pulley end. If the camshaft tries to lift out of the case, the gears are too tight.

   c. Different size camshaft gears are available to adjust timing gear backlash. The gears are marked on the back side with a number indicating hundredths of a millimeter larger or smaller than standard. The marks appear as + 0.1, + 0.2, – 0.1, etc. or 0, which indicates a standard gear. Do not confuse this "0" with the timing mark on the front face of the gear.

   d. A camshaft gear is removed by drilling out the rivets. When a camshaft gear is changed, make sure the rivets are tight before installing the camshaft.

6. Install the oil pressure relief valve.

7. Install the oil pick-up tube and screen.

8. With the connecting rods and gears assembled onto the

A. Thrust washer
B. 81mm shim
C. 75mm adjustment shims
D. 94mm shim
E. Oil seal
F. O-ring

Install crankshaft thrust washer with tab A towards crankshaft bearing, install only shims B and D to check/adjust crankshaft endplay

crankshaft, lay the crankshaft into place. Make sure the dowel fits into the rear main bearing. Install the camshaft with the timing marks aligned. Use plenty of oil on the shaft bearing journals during assembly.

9. Install the camshaft end plug using sealing compound.

10. If necessary, use grease or petroleum jelly to hold the bearings into the right case half.

11. Spread a thin film of VW AMV 188–001–02 or equivalent, sealing compound on the crankcase joining faces, place the halves together and start all the nuts.

12. First tighten the 8mm nut located at the upper right of the lifter bore on the flywheel end, then tighten all the 10mm nuts, then the remaining 8mm nuts. Torque all nuts in 3 steps to 37 ft. lbs. (50 Nm). Between steps, carefully turn the crankshaft to make sure it turns smoothly. If the crankshaft gets stiff or binds, there is a problem with the crankcase bore alignment or maybe a bearing has moved.

13. Set the crankshaft endplay to 0.003–0.005 in. (0.07–0.13mm) with 3 shims mounted behind the flywheel.

NOTE: Always use a total of 3 shims when setting crankshaft endplay or the crankcase may be damaged.

   a. Temporarily install the flywheel or torque converter driveplate with shims **B** and **D** and without the third shim **C**, O-ring and oil seal. Torque at least 2 opposing bolts to 80 ft. lbs. (110 Nm).

   b. Attach a dial indicator base to the crankcase and set the gauge on the flywheel. Move the crankshaft in and out to measure the endplay.

   c. To determine the required thickness of the third shim, subtract 0.004 in. (0.10mm) from the dial indicator reading. That number is the required thickness of shim **C**.

   d. Remove the flywheel, install the correct shims, O-ring and oil seal and install the flywheel. Use a thread locking compound on the flywheel bolts and torque to 80 ft. lbs. (110 Nm).

14. Install the crankshaft pulley with a new oil seal and sealing ring and snug the bolt. Torque the bolt only with the engine installed.

15. Install the cylinders and pistons. Install the cylinder heads.

16. Install the intake and exhaust manifolds.

17. Install the engine in the vehicle and torque the crankshaft pulley bolt. Use the pulley holding tool with the small hole in the pulley on the bottom and torque the bolt to 258 ft. lbs. (350 Nm).

Pistons and Cylinders

Removal and Installation

1. With the engine removed from the vehicle and mounted in a work stand, remove the intake and exhaust manifolds and the cooling system components.

2. Remove the rocker arm assemblies, pushrods, cylinder heads and pushrod tubes. When removing the cylinder heads, do not let the cylinder come off with the head.

Piston and cylinder assembly

Use the puller to draw the cylinder part way out, then work through the coolant passage to remove circlips and wrist pins

3. Matchmark the pistons and the liners to each other and to the crankcase. Pistons and liners must be installed in the same locations. Note the boss on the inner side of each liner.

4. Set one of the rear pistons at TDC. Using the clamping tool 3092 or equivalent sleeve puller, pull out that cylinder until the piston pin circlip is visible through the coolant passage on the rear (drive belt side) of the engine. Remove the circlip.

5. Remove the wrist pin through the same coolant passage using wrist pin puller 3091 or equivalent. If the wrist pin is difficult to remove, there is a burr in the piston just outside of the circlip groove. Remove the wrist pin tool and use tool 3159 or equivalent, to remove the burr from the piston.

6. With the pin removed, remove the piston and cylinder together. To remove the front piston on that side, work through the same coolant passage to remove the circlip and wrist pin.

To install:

7. The maximum allowable weight difference between the pistons with wrist pins is 0.35 oz. (10 grams). Make sure the cylinder–to–crankcase mating surfaces are clean. The sealing rings on the top and bottom of the cylinders must always be replaced. The upper ring is a thin green rubber O-ring and the ring at the crankcase end is thick and black in color.

8. To install the piston into the cylinder:

   a. The small arrow stamped into the piston faces the flywheel side of the engine.

   b. The gap on the oil scraper ring must be at the top of the piston. The compression ring gaps must be offset by 180 degrees.

   c. Install the flywheel-side wrist pin circlip into the piston.

   d. Lubricate the piston and cylinder bore with clean engine oil.

   e. Install a ring compressor onto the piston and install the piston into the crankcase end of the cylinder up to the wrist pin bore.

9. Set the flywheel end connecting rod to TDC. Install a connecting rod support tool 3090 or equivalent, onto the stud. Position the finger to hold the connecting rod up so the wrist pin can be installed through the coolant passage. Secure the tool in place with a rubber band around the other finger and another stud.

10. Check to make sure the flywheel side wrist pin circlip is installed. Install the piston/cylinder assembly.

Connecting rod support tool used to align the rod for installing the wrist pin

11. The piston should be protruding from the bottom of the sleeve just enough so the entire wrist pin area is exposed. Using tool 3091 or equivalent, install the wrist pin through the coolant passage. Install the other wrist pin clip and slide the cylinder down into the crankcase.

12. Repeat this procedure for all cylinders and install the cylinder heads.

Crankshaft and Connecting Rods

Disassembly and Assembly

1. Before removing the connecting rods, note their position on the crankshaft;

   a. A raised forge mark is on the side of each rod. When the connecting rod is installed, this mark faces up.

   b. A number is stamped on the rod with a matching number on the cap at the split.

   c. Check the clearance between the side of the connecting rod and the crankshaft journal with a feeler gauge. If clearance is more than 0.028 in. (0.7mm) on any single rod, replace the connecting rods as a set.

   d. Mark the connecting rod so it can be installed on the same journal.

2. Remove the nuts to remove the bearing caps and connecting rods. Discard the nuts.

3. If the threads on the bearing cap studs are damaged, the studs can be replaced by pressing out both studs at once in a vise.

4. With the outer oil thrust ring and No. 4 main bearing removed, remove the circlip from the end of the crankshaft.

5. Use a press to remove the timing gear and distributor gear together. There is a spacer between the gears.

6. Note the position of the No. 3 main bearing before removing it. If there is a projection on the bearing, it should be off-set towards the flywheel.

7. Weigh the connecting rods with the caps; the weight difference between them must be no more than 0.35 oz. (10 grams).

8. Inspect the crankshaft and connecting rods, recondition or replace as required.

To assemble:

9. Oil the crankshaft and install the No. 3 main bearing in the proper position.

Crankshaft and connecting rod assembly

10. Heat the timing and distributor drive gears to about 175°F (80°C) in an oven or on a hot plate.

11. Install the Woodruff keys and press the gears onto the crankshaft. On the small distributor gear key, the flat side faces the circlip. Don't forget the spacer between the gears. Install the circlip.

12. Lubricate the connecting rods, caps and new bearings and install the bearings.

13. When fitting the connecting rods, make sure they are fitted to their original journal with the forge mark facing up. When installing the cap, make sure the numbers are next to the numbers on the rod.

14. Lubricate and install new connecting rod nuts and torque to 22 ft. lbs. (30 Nm) in 2 steps. Between steps, tap lightly with a hammer on the rod/cap split to relieve the tendency to pinch the bearing.

15. If the connecting rods move smoothly on the crankshaft, the assembly is ready for installation.

Piston Positioning

A = stamped arrow, must point to flywheel when piston is installed;
B = paint dot, blue indicates standard size, pink indicates oversize;
C = weight group (+ or −);
D = piston size in mm

Piston identification and positioning marks

ENGINE LUBRICATION

Oil Pump

Removal and Installation

With the muffler and catalytic converter removed, it should be possible to remove the oil pump without removing the engine. On some models, it may be necessary to remove the rear engine carrier.

1. Remove the muffler and catalytic converter.
2. If required, support the engine and remove the carrier.
3. Drain the engine oil.
4. Remove the 4 oil pump sealing nuts and discard them. Remove the cover and the oil pump gears.
5. To remove the oil pump housing, install the special puller tool VW201 and tighten the nut to pull the pump housing out of the engine.

To install:

6. Prior to assembly, check the oil pump body for wear, especially the gear seating surface. If the pump body is worn, the result will be loss of oil pressure. Check the driven gear shaft for

CRANKCASE BREATHER
HEATING PIPE
OIL FILLER TUBE
OIL FILLER CAP
OIL DIPSTICK
OIL PUMP HOUSING
OIL PUMP GEARS
SEALING NUT
OIL PUMP COVER
OIL PRESSURE SWITCH
PRESSURE SWITCH
OIL DRAIN PLUG
OIL PRESSURE RELIEF VALVE

Oil pump assembly and lubrication system

tightness and if necessary, peen it tightly into place or replace the pump housing. The gears should be checked for excessive wear, backlash and endplay. Maximum endplay without a gasket is 0.004 in. (1mm).

7. The endplay can be checked using a T-square and a feeler gauge. Check the mating surface of the pump body and the crankcase for damage and cleanliness.

8. Install the pump housing into the crankcase with a new gasket. Do not use any sealing compound. Install the driven gear while turning it to engage the camshaft. When it falls into place, install the other gear.

9. Install the cover with a new gasket. Install new sealing nuts with the seal facing the cover and torque the nuts to 18 ft. lbs. (25 Nm).

10. After installing the exhaust components and engine mount, refill the crankcase and run the engine to check for leaks.

Crankshaft Oil Seals

Removal and Installation

FLYWHEEL OIL SEAL

1. Remove the engine from the vehicle and support it in a suitable holding fixture. Remove the clutch, if equipped.

2. Remove the flywheel or torque converter driveplate.

3. Once the flywheel is removed, inspect the surface on the flywheel joining flange where the seal makes contact. If there is a deep groove or any other damage, the flywheel must be replaced.

4. Remove the oil seal by prying it out of it's bore. Note the

position of the shims so they can be installed in the porper order.

5. Before installing a new seal, clean the crankcase oil seal recess and lubricate the new seal. Install the crankshaft endplay shims in the correct order.

6. Use an appropriate installation tool to press the seal in evenly. Be sure the seal rests squarely on the bottom of its recess. Make sure the correct side of the lip of the seal is facing inward, towards the crankcase.

7. Reinstall the flywheel after coating the oil seal contact surface with oil. Be careful not to damage the seal when sliding the flywheel into place. Use a thread locking compound and torque the flywheel bolts to 80 ft. lbs. (108 Nm).

CRANKSHAFT PULLEY OIL SEAL

1. Remove the accessory drive belts.

2. To loosen the crankshaft pulley bolt:

  a. The torque on the bolt is extremely high and a special tool is available to hold the pulley. Remove the right side rubber mount–to–engine carrier bolt.

  b. To loosen the pulley bolt, turn the crankshaft so the small hole in the pulley is up. Install tool 3102 or equivalent, into the pulley and the carrier bolt hole and loosen the bolt with a socket wrench.

3. Carefully pry out the oil seal.

4. Lubricate the new seal and use an appropriate installation tool to press the seal evenly into place.

5. To tighten the pulley bolt, turn the crankshaft so the small hole is down, install the holding tool and torque the bolt to 258 ft. lbs. (350 Nm).

TORQUE SPECIFICATIONS

Component	English	Metric
Connecting rod bearing cap bolts	22 ft. lbs.	30 Nm
Crankcase half nuts	37 ft. lbs.	50 Nm
Crankshaft pulley bolt	258 ft. lbs.	350 Nm
Cylinder head nuts	37 ft. lbs.	50 Nm
Engine mount bolts	18 ft. lbs.	25 Nm
Engine-to-transaxle	22 ft. lbs.	30 Nm
Exhaust manifold	18 ft. lbs.	25 Nm
Flywheel/flexplate-to-crankshaft bolts	80 ft. lbs.	110 Nm
Intake manifold	15 ft. lbs.	20 Nm
Oil pump cover	18 ft. lbs.	25 Nm
Rocker arm shaft nuts	18 ft. lbs.	25 Nm
Spark plug	14 ft. lbs.	19 Nm
Starter bolts	22 ft. lbs.	30 Nm
Thermostat housing	15 ft. lbs.	20 Nm
Transaxle mount bolts	22 ft. lbs.	30 Nm
Torque converter–to–flywheel bolts	15 ft. lbs.	20 Nm
Water pump	15 ft. lbs.	20 Nm
Water pump pulley	15 ft. lbs.	20 Nm

MANUAL TRANSAXLE

For further information, please refer to Chilton's Transmission Service Manual.

Transaxle Assembly

Removal and Installation

1. Disconnect the negative battery cable.
2. Raise and safely support the vehicle.
3. Remove the top engine-to-transaxle bolts.
4. Remove the rear skid plate on Vanagon Syncro.
5. On Vanagon Syncro, loosen the side bolts of the front differential mounting bracket so the differential can move. Do not remove the bolts.

Front differential side mount bolts on Vanagon Syncro

Front differential housing mount bolt on Vanagon Syncro

Front transaxle mount bolt on Vanagon Syncro

6. On Vanagon Syncro, remove the driveshaft-to-flange bolts and support the driveshaft aside.

7. Remove the left side halfshaft bolts and support the axle shaft aside.

8. Disconnect the clutch line bracket from the side of the transaxle. Do not disconnect the hydraulic line.

9. Remove the clutch slave cylinder from its bracket and support it aside.

10. Disconnect the back-up light switch wiring.

11. Remove the right side halfshaft bolts and support the halfshaft aside.

12. Disconnect the shift linkage from the transaxle. If equipped with a locking rear differential, disconnect the vacuum hose and wiring from the lock servo.

13. Place a suitable support under the engine and place a floor jack under the transaxle. Remove the front transaxle mounting bracket and lower the front of the transaxle approximately 6 in.

14. Disconnect the starter wiring and the vent hose from the transaxle.

15. Remove the bottom transaxle mounting bolts and pull the transaxle off the engine guides.

16. Lower the transaxle from the vehicle.

To install:

17. Lightly lubricate the input shaft with molybdenum grease. Raise the transaxle into position.

18. Install the lower transaxle mounting bolts, tighten to 22 ft. lbs. (30 Nm).

19. Reconnect the starter cables and install the vent hose. Raise the transaxle and install the front mounting bracket.

20. Connect the shift linkage to the transaxle and connect both halfshafts. Tighten the halfshaft bolts to 26 ft. lbs. (35 Nm).

21. Connect the back-up light switch and vacuum hose to the servo, if equipped. Install the slave cylinder in its bracket.

22. Connect the clutch line bracket to the transaxle.

23. On Vanagon Syncro, connect the driveshaft to the drive flange and tighten the bolts to 26 ft. lbs. (35 Nm). Tighten the front differential housing bolts.

24. Install the transaxle bracket side mounting bolts.

25. Install the skid plate, if equipped.

26. Install the top transaxle mounting bolts. Tighten to 22 ft. lbs. (30 Nm).

27. Lower the vehicle and connect the battery cable.

28. Check the operation of the transaxle and check the clutch operation.

CLUTCH

Clutch Assembly

Removal and Installation

1. Disconnect the negative battery cable.
2. Raise and safely support the vehicle.
3. Remove the transaxle from the vehicle.
4. Remove the pressure plate securing bolts a turn at a time until all spring pressure is released.
5. Remove the bolts and remove the clutch assembly.

NOTE: Note which side of the clutch disc faces the flywheel and install the new disc in the same direction.

6. Before installing the new clutch, check the condition of the flywheel. It should not have excessive heat cracks and the friction surface should not be scored or warped. Check the condition of the throw out bearing. If the bearing is worn, replace it.

To install:

7. Lubricate the pilot bearing in the end of the crankshaft with grease.

8. Insert a pilot shaft, used for centering the clutch disc, through the clutch disc and place the disc against the flywheel. The pilot shaft will hold the disc in place.

NOTE: Make sure the correct side of the clutch disc is facing outward. The disc will rub the flywheel if it is incorrectly positioned.

9. After making sure the pressure plate aligning dowels will fit into the pressure plate, tighten the bolts a turn at a time until the plate is pulled into place. Torque the bolts to 18 ft. lbs. (25 Nm).

10. Remove the pilot shaft and install the transaxle.

11. Lower the vehicle. Bleed the clutch system.

12. Connect the negative battery cable. Check the operation of the clutch.

Clutch Pedal Free-Play Adjustment

1. The clutch pedal should have a free-play of 0.20–0.28 in. (5–7mm) and a 7 in. (178mm) total travel. If either of the above are not to specifications, adjust the master cylinder as follows.

2. Loosen the master cylinder pushrod locknut and shorten the pushrod length slightly.

Adjusting clutch pedal free-play

Clutch pedal stop screw adjustment

3. Loosen the master cylinder bolts and push the cylinder as far forward as it will go. Retighten the bolts.

4. Remove the rubber cap from the clutch pedal stop screw and adjust distance to 0.89 in. (22mm). Install the rubber cap.

5. Lengthen the pushrod as necessary to obtain a pedal free-play of 0.20–0.28 in. (5–7mm). Tighten the pushrod locknut.

6. Road test the vehicle to insure proper clutch operation.

Hydraulic clutch system components

Clutch Master Cylinder

Removal and Installation

1. Disconnect the negative battery cable.
2. Siphon the hydraulic fluid from the clutch master cylinder reservoir.
3. Pull back the carpeting from the pedal area and place some absorbent rags under the reservoir.
4. Pull the elbow connection from the top of the clutch master cylinder.

5. Disconnect and plug the pressure line from the rear of the master cylinder.
6. Remove the master cylinder mounting bolts and remove the cylinder from the rear.
7. Installation is the reverse of the removal procedure. Bleed the clutch system when finished.

Clutch Slave Cylinder

Removal and Installation

1. Raise and support the vehicle safely.
2. Locate the slave cylinder on the bellhousing.
3. Disconnect and plug the pressure line from the slave cylinder.
4. Disconnect the return spring from the pushrod.
5. Remove the retaining circlip from the boot and remove the boot.
6. Remove the circlip and slide the slave cylinder rearwards from its mount.
7. Remove the spring clip from the mount.
8. Installation is the reverse of the removal procedure. Bleed the system and check the operation of the clutch.

Bleeding Hydraulic Clutch System

NOTE: Use brake fluid that meets DOT 3 or DOT 4 specifications.

1. Fill the clutch fluid reservoir and make sure the cap vent is open.
2. Locate the slave cylinder bleed nipple and remove all dirt and grease from the valve. Attach a hose to the nipple and submerge the other end of the hose in a glass jar containing clean brake fluid.
3. Have an assitant operate the clutch pedal. Depresses the clutch pedal slowly to the floor, open the bleeder valve 1 turn. Hold the pedal on the floor until the bleeder valve is closed. Repeat this operation several times until no air bubbles are emitted from the tube.

NOTE: During the procedure, check the fluid level in the fluid reservoir. Never let the level fall below the ½ full mark.

4. After bleeding, discard the old fluid and top up the reservoir.

AUTOMATIC TRANSAXLE

For further information, please refer to Chilton's Transmission Service Manual.

Transaxle Assembly

Removal and Installation

1. Disconnect the negative battery cable.
2. Remove the 3 torque converter-to-flywheel bolts through the hole in the top of the transaxle housing. Rotate the crankshaft to bring each bolt into position. Remove the top transaxle-to-engine bolts.
3. Raise and safely support the vehicle.
4. Disconnect both halfshafts from the transaxle, support them aside.
5. Disconnect the starter wiring and remove the starter.
6. Loosen the transaxle fluid dipstick tube.
7. Disconnect the accelerator linkage and accelerator cable.

8. Remove the circlip from the selector lever.
9. Support the engine with a suitable support bar.
10. Remove the ground strap and selector lever cable. Remove the side mounting bracket.
11. Support the transaxle with a suitable lifting device. Remove the rear transaxle support.
12. Remove the lower transaxle-to-engine bolts. Slowly lower the transaxle out of the vehicle. Use care not to drop the torque converter from the input shaft.

To install:

13. Make sure the torque converter is properly mounted on the one-way clutch and firmly seated into place. If the torque converter slips out of place when installing the transaxle, the oil pump driveshaft could be pulled out of the pump. This will cause serious damage when bolting the transaxle to the engine.
14. Raise the transaxle into position and start the bolts. Keep checking that the torque converter turns freely when tightening the bolts. If there is any binding, the torque converter has slipped off the clutch support and must be re-installed.

15. When the transaxle is fully in place against the engine, torque the lower bolts to 22 ft. lbs. (30 Nm).

16. Install the rear transaxle support.

17. Install the ground strap and selector lever cable. Install the side mounting bracket.

18. Remove the engine support bar and connector the selector lever.

19. Connect the accelerator cable and linkage. Attach the dipstick tube.

20. Install the starter and connect the wiring.

21. Connect the halfshafts and tighten the bolts to 33 ft. lbs. (45 Nm).

22. Install the upper transaxle bolts, tighten to 22 ft. lbs. (35 Nm).

23. Lower the vehicle and install the torque converter bolts. Tighten to 22 ft. lbs. (35 Nm).

24. Adjust the linkage as required. Connect the negative battery cable and check the operation of the transaxle.

Shift Linkage Adjusment

1. Make sure the shift cable is not kinked or bent and that the linkage and cable are properly lubricated.

2. Move the gear shift lever to the **P** position.

3. Loosen the shift rod bolt at the bottom of the selector, under the vehicle.

4. Operate the transaxle control by hand to make sure it is in park.

5. Push the shift rod towards the rear and tighten the bolt.

DRIVE AXLE

Halfshaft

Removal and Installation

VANAGON SYNCRO

Front

— CAUTION —

Torque on the axle nut is very high and loosening it with a breaker bar may cause the vehicle to fall off the supports. Do not loosen or tighten this nut unless the vehicle is on all 4 wheels.

1. With the vehicle on the ground, remove the front halfshaft end-nut and washer.

2. Raise and support the vehicle safely. Remove the wheel and tire assembly.

3. Remove the socket head bolts retaining the halfshaft to the differential.

4. Remove the bolts holding the ball joint to the lower control arm.

5. Removing the ball joint from the control arm will give enough clearance to remove the axle shaft. It pulls right out of the wheel bearing hub.

6. Installation is the reverse of the removal procedure. Front wheel alignment should not be effected.

7. Always use a new halfshaft end-nut when installing. Tighten the halfshaft to differential bolts to 26 ft. lbs. (35 Nm), the

Front suspension and differential on Vanagon Syncro

ball joint bolts to 22 ft. lbs. (30 Nm) and the halfshaft end-nut to 258 ft. lbs. (350 Nm).

Rear

1. Raise and support the vehicle safely.

2. Matchmark the halfshaft to the transaxle and to the stub axle.

3. Remove the bolts which secure the halfshaft at each end.

4. Tilt the halfshaft downwards and remove the halfshaft from the vehicle.

5. Install the halfshaft in position, aligning the matchmarks made during removal.

6. Torque the axleshaft bolts to 33 ft. lbs. (45 Nm).

Driveshaft and U-Joints

Removal and Installation

VANAGON SYNCRO

1. Raise and safely support the vehicle. Loosen the front differential mounting bolts but do not remove them.

2. Matchmark the driveshaft ends to the flanges.

3. Remove the driveshaft retaining bolts and remove the driveshaft from the vehicle.

4. Install the driveshaft in position, aligning the matchmarks.

5. Torque the bolts to 26 ft. lbs. (35 Nm). Tighten the differential mounting bolts.

Front halfshaft assembly on Vanagon Syncro

Front Wheel Bearing and Seal

Removal and Installation

VANAGON

1. Raise and support the vehicle safely. Remove the wheel and tire assembly.
2. Remove the brake pads and pins.
3. Without disconnecting the hydraulic hose, remove the brake caliper from the wheel bearing housing and support it out of the way. Do not let it hang by the hose.
4. Remove the cotter pin and bearing retaning nut. Remove the rotor/hub assembly.
5. To remove the bearing races, pry the seal out of the hub and use a drift pin to tap the race out.

To install:

6. Carefully install new inner bearing races and make sure they are fully seated in the hub. Pack the new bearings with new grease and install the inner wheel bearing into the hub. Press the new seal into place on the hub.
7. Installation of the hub is the reverse of the removal procedure. Torque the caliper bolts to 116 ft. lbs. (160 Nm).
8. To adjust the wheel bearing;
   a. Tighten the nut firmly while turning the hub.
   b. Back off the nut just enough so the thrust washer can be moved without prying.
   c. Install the retaining nut and a new cotter pin.

VANAGON SYNCRO

CAUTION

The torque on the axle nut is very high and loosening it with a breaker bar may cause the vehicle to fall off the supports. Do not loosen or tighten this nut unless the vehicle is on all 4 wheels.

1. Remove the front axle nut and washer with the vehicle on the ground.
2. Raise and support the vehicle safely. Remove the wheel and tire assembly.
3. Without disconnecting the hydraulic hose, remove the brake caliper from the wheel bearing housing and support it out of the way. Do not let it hang by the hose.
4. Remove the disc brake rotor and the splash shield.
5. Remove the lower ball joint bracket bolts and separate the ball joint from the lower control arm.
6. Remove the lower shock absorber mounting bolt.
7. Remove the tie rod end nut and separate the tie rod from the wheel bearing housing.
8. Support the halfshaft in place with wire and pull the wheel

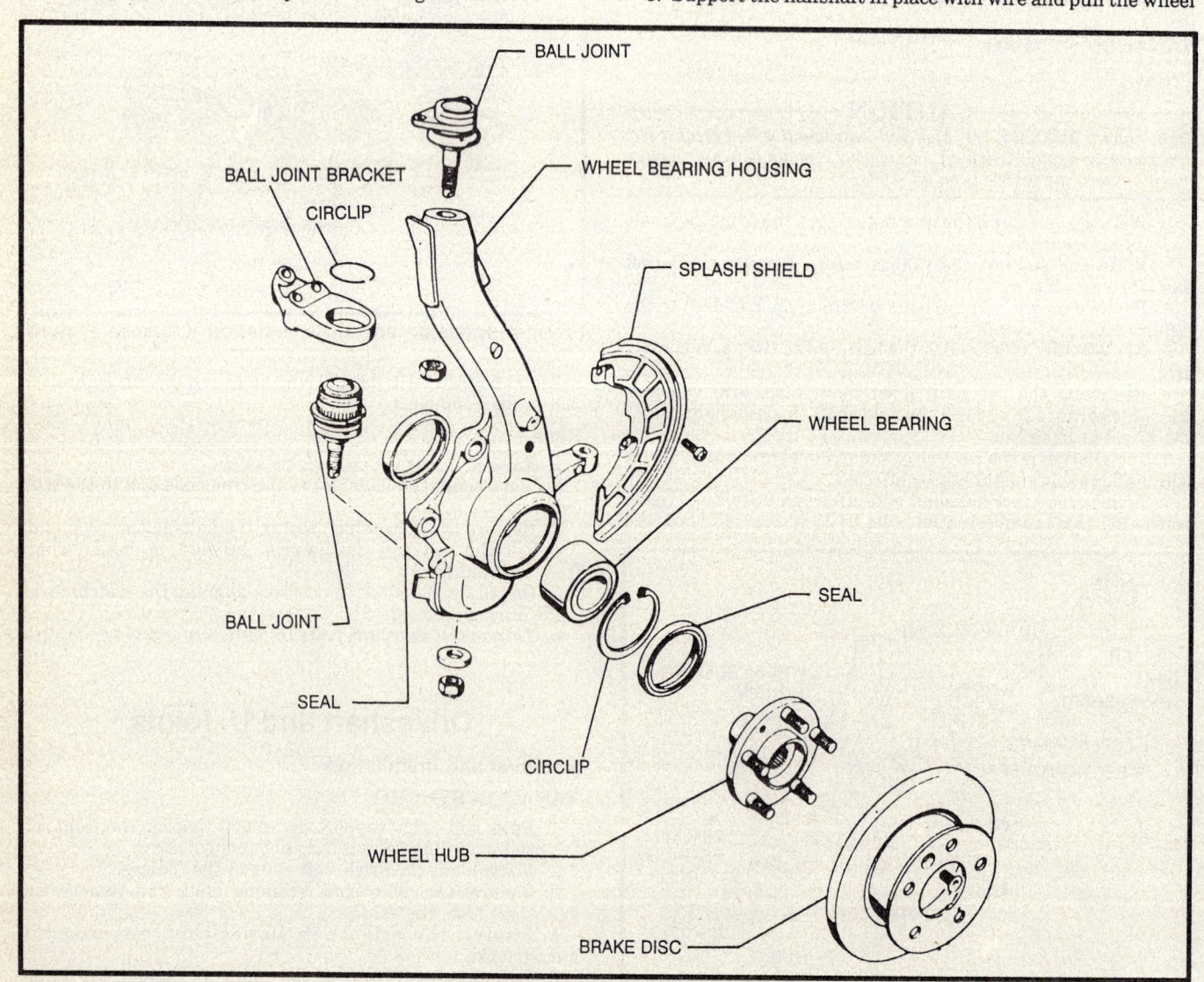

BALL JOINT

BALL JOINT BRACKET

CIRCLIP

WHEEL BEARING HOUSING

SPLASH SHIELD

WHEEL BEARING

BALL JOINT

SEAL

SEAL

CIRCLIP

WHEEL HUB

BRAKE DISC

Front wheel bearing and seal assemly on Vanagon Syncro

bearing housing off the halfshaft. Do not let the halfshaft hang by the inner CV-joint.

9. Remove the upper ball joint bolts and remove the wheel bearing housing assembly from the vehicle.

10. Support the wheel bearing housing in a press and press the wheel hub out of the bearing. If the inner bearing race comes off with the hub, secure the hub in a vise and use a puller to remove the inner race from the hub shaft.

11. Remove the circlip and press the bearing out of the wheel bearing housing. Be sure to press on the outer bearing race.

12. Thoroughly clean and inspect all parts. The bearing and seals must be replaced any time they are removed. If there are signs of wear on the hub or if the bearing has already been replaced and has failed, replace the hub.

To install:

13. Carefully press the new bearing into the housing. Be sure to press only on the outer race or the bearing will be damaged. Install the circlip.

14. Lubricate and install the new seals. Make sure they are installed evenly and fully seated in place.

15. When pressing the hub into the bearing, be sure to properly support the inner bearing race or the bearing will be damaged.

16. Make sure the halfshaft splines are clean and install the wheel bearing housing onto the control arms. Torque the ball joint–to–control arm nuts or bolts to 44 ft. lbs. (60 Nm). If the ball joint was removed from the wheel bearing housing, torque the nut to 74 ft. lbs. (100 Nm).

17. Connect the tie rod and torque the nut to 22 ft. lbs. (30 Nm). Tighten the nut as required to install a new cotter pin.

18. Install the splash shield and brake caliper. Torque the caliper carrier bolts to 185 ft. lbs. (250 Nm).

19. With the vehicle resting on all 4 wheels, torque the axle nut to 258 ft. lbs. (350 Nm).

Rear Stub Axle, Bearing and Seal

Removal and Installation

CAUTION

Torque on the axle nut is very high and loosening it with a breaker bar may cause the vehicle to fall off the supports. Do not loosen or tighten this nut unless the vehicle is on all 4 wheels.

1. Remove the cotter pin and loosen the axle nut.
2. Raise and support the vehicle safely.
3. Remove the wheel and tire.

4. Remove the axle nut and use a puller to remove the brake drum and hub as an assembly. The bearing and spacer should stay on the axle.

5. Disconnect the parking brake cable and the brake hydraulic hose. Remove the bolts to remove the brake backing plate and brake assembly.

6. Remove the halfshaft–to–stub axle bolts.

7. Remove the 4 wheel bearing housing retaining bolts and remove the housing.

8. Use a press to remove the stub axle from the wheel bearing housing.

9. Pry out the grease seal and remove the spacer sleeve and outer bearing race. Drive the outer bearing out with a brass drift pin.

10. Use a press to remove the inner bearing.

To install:

11. Pack the new inner wheel bearing with grease and press it into the housing. Make sure to press only on the outer race and seat the bearing in the housing.

12. Fill the space between the bearings with grease and install the spacer sleeve. Pack the new outer bearing with grease and press the outer bearing into the housing.

13. Install the outer bearing race, the circlip and new grease seals.

14. Carefully press the stub axle into the new bearings. Make sure it moves smoothly.

15. Install the bearing housing assembly and torque the bolts to 101 ft. lbs. (140 Nm).

16. Install the halfshaft bolts and torque to 33 ft. lbs. (45 Nm). Install the brake assembly and torque the backing plate bolts to 14 ft. lbs. (20 Nm).

17. Connect the parking brake cable and hydraulic hose, install the brake drum and tighten the axle nut by hand.

18. With the vehicle resting on all 4 wheels, torque the axle nut to 369 ft. lbs. (500 Nm), then turn the nut farther as required to install a new cotter pin. Bleed and adjust the brakes.

Front Differential

Removal and Installation

VANAGON SYNCRO

1. Raise and support the vehicle safely. Remove the skid plate.

2. Loosen but do not remove the front differential mounting bolt and the side differential mounting bracket bolts.

Rear wheel bearing housing removal

3. Matchmark and remove the driveshaft bolts from the front differential flange. Support the driveshaft.

4. Disconnect the halfshafts, speedometer cable and vent hose from the differential. Support the halfshafts.

5. Remove the differential rear mounting bolt. Remove the bracket from the frame.

6. Support the differential and remove the front mounting bolts.

7. Carefully lower the differential from the vehicle.

To install:

8. Raise the differential into position.

9. Install the rear mounting bolts, do not tighten. Install the bracket to the frame.

10. Connect the halfshafts, speedometer cable and vent hose.

11. Install the front mounting bolts but do not tighten yet.

12. Align the matchmarks and connect the driveshaft and halfshafts. Torque the bolts to 26 ft. lbs. (35 Nm).

13. Tighten the differential mounts and bolts last.

Pinion Seals

Removal and Installation

VANAGON SYNCRO

1. This procedure applies to both front and rear driveshaft flange seals. Matchmark and remove the driveshaft.

2. Bolt tool 3145 or equivalent, to the driveshaft flange to hold it from turning and remove the flange nut.

3. Use a puller to remove the flange. Pry the old seal out.

4. Carefully drive a new seal into the housing, making sure it seats evenly.

5. Lubricate the seal lips and install the driveshaft flange. Hold the flange with the tool and torque the nut to 118 ft. lbs. (160 Nm).

6. Install the driveshaft with the matchmarks aligned and torque the bolts to 26 ft. lbs. (35 Nm).

STEERING

Steering Wheel

Removal and Installation

1. Disconnect the negative battery cable.

2. Remove the horn pad from the steering wheel. Pull the horn pad up by hand to remove it.

3. Disconnect the electrical lead from the horn pad.

4. Matchmark the steering wheel and the steering shaft.

5. Remove the steering wheel nut and pull the steering wheel straight off.

6. To install the steering wheel, align the matchmarks made during removal and install the wheel.

7. Tighten the retaining nut to 36 ft. lbs. (50 Nm).

8. Install the horn pad. Connect the negative battery cable.

Manual Rack and Pinion

Removal and Installation

1. Raise and safely support the vehicle.

2. Detach the connecting shaft from the coupling disc.

3. Remove both tie rod end nuts and separate the tie rod ends from the wheel bearing housings.

Steering assembly

4. At the coupling, remove the bolts connecting the steering gear flange to the connecting shaft flange.

5. Remove the clamps from the subframe and remove the steering gear assembly.

6. Installation is the reverse of removal. Use new self-locking nuts on the subframe clamps and the connecting shaft flange. Torque the clamp bolts to 18 ft. lbs. (25 Nm), the flange bolts to 14 ft. lbs. (20 Nm) and the tie rod end nuts to 22 ft. lbs. (30 Nm). Turn the tie rod end nuts tighter as required to install a new cotter pin.

7. Check and adjust front wheel alignment.

Power Rack and Pinion

Removal and Installation

1. Raise and safely support the vehicle.

2. Detach the connecting shaft from the coupling disc.

3. Remove both tie rod end nuts and separate the tie rod ends from the wheel bearing housings.

4. At the steering gear pinion, remove the universal joint clamp bolt.

5. Disconnect and plug the power steering lines from the steering gear housing. Place a drain pan under the power steering pump suction hose to catch the fluid when removing the power steering lines, then discard the fluid.

6. Remove the clamps from the subframe and remove the steering gear assembly.

7. Installation is the reverse of removal. Use new self-locking nuts on the subframe clamps and torque the clamp bolts to 18 ft. lbs. (25 Nm). Torque the tie rod end nuts to 22 ft. lbs. (30 Nm), then turn them tighter as necessary to install a new cotter pin.

8. Use new O-rings when connecting the hydraulic lines and refill with new fluid. Bleed the system and check and adjust front wheel alignment.

Power Steering Pump

Removal and Installation

1. Disconnect the negative battery cable. Place a pan under the power steering pump when draining the fluid.

2. Remove the suction hose and pressure line from the pump, then drain the fluid into the pan.

3. Loosen the belt tensioning bolt at the front of the bracket and remove the drive belt from the pulley.

4. Remove the pump mounting bolts and remove the pump from the vehicle.

5. Installation is the reverse of removal. Set the belt tension and torque the mounting bolts to 15 ft. lbs. (20 Nm).

6. Fill the reservoir with approved power steering fluid and bleed the system.

System Bleeding

1. Fill the power steering reservoir to **MAX** with Dexron® II automatic transmission fluid.

2. Raise and safely support the vehicle.

3. With the engine off, rotate the steering wheel from lock to lock.

4. Fill the reservoir to the **MAX** mark.

5. Start the engine several times, turning it off immediately after the engine starts. Add fluid as necessary, maintaining the level at the **MAX** mark.

NOTE: Never let the reservoir run out of fluid. Damage to the pump and/or steering gear may result.

6. When the fluid level no longer drops, start and run the engine. Rotate the steering wheel lock to lock several times. Check that no bubbles appear in the reservoir and that the level remains steady.

7. If air bubbles appear, repeat the procedure until the fluid is clear.

Tie Rod Ends

Removal and Installation

1. Raise and safely support the vehicle.

2. Remove the cotter pins and nuts and separate the tie rod ends from the wheel bearing housing.

3. Loosen the locknut at the inner end and count the number of turns required to remove the tie rod end.

4. Installation is the reverse of removal. Be sure to install the tie rod end the same number of turns into the tie rod, then tighten the nut.

5. Install the tie rod end into the wheel bearing housing. Torque the tie rod end nut to 22 ft. lbs. (30 Nm), then turn it tighter as necessary to install a new cotter pin.

6. Check and adjust the toe in when finished.

BRAKES

For all brake system repair and service procedures not detailed below, please refer to "Brakes" in the Unit Repair section.

Master Cylinder

Removal and Installation

NOTE: In order to remove the master cylinder reservoir, the intrument cluster must first be removed.

1. Disconnect the negative battery cable. Grasp the recesses provided on the back of the instrument cluster frame and pull it forward.

Master cylinder and booster assembly

2. Disconnect and tag the wiring leading to the back of the instrument cluster and then remove the cluster.

3. Disconnect and plug the brake lines at the master cylinder.

4. Disconnect the electrical plug from the sending unit for the brake failure switch.

5. Remove the master cylinder mounting nuts.

6. Lift the master cylinder and reservoir out of the vehicle.

NOTE: Do not depress the brake pedal while the master cylinder is removed.

To install:

7. Position the master cylinder and reservoir assembly onto the mounting studs and install the washers and nuts. Tighten the nuts to 14 ft. lbs. (20 Nm).

8. Remove the plugs and connect the brake lines to the master cylinder.

9. Connect the wiring to the sending unit for the brake failure switch.

10. Install the instrument cluster. Connect the negative battery cable.

11. Fill the master cylinder and bleed the brake system.

12. Install the instrument cluster cover.

Power Brake Booster

Removal and Installation

1. Disconnect the negative battery cable.

2. Remove the instrument cluster. Remove the steering column covers and remove the steering column bolts (there are 2 shear bolts that retain the column, these must be drilled out and replaced).

3. Remove the glove box and remove the center dash panel. Pull off the heater controls levers.

4. Remove the screws inside the center cover and to the side of the instrument cluster opening.

5. Disconnect the air ducts under the instrument panel. Remove the instrument panel retaining screws at the top of the panel and at the sides. Remove the instrument panel from the firewall.

6. Disconnect the electrical leads from the stoplight switch.

7. Remove the bolts that retain the pedal bracket to the firewall and remove the booster/pedal bracket assembly from the vehicle. Disconnect the pushrod from the pedal assembly.

8. Remove the booster retaining bolts and remove the booster from the bracket.

To install:

9. Install the booster to the bracket assembly. Tighten the nuts to 11 ft. lbs. (15 Nm).

10. Install the booster/pedal bracket assembly to the firewall. Connect the pedal to the pushrod and connect the stoplight switch lead.

11. Install the instrument panel to the firewall. Use new shear bolts at the steering column.

12. Install the master cylinder.

13. Install the instrument cluster.

14. Bleed the brake system.

15. Connect the negative battery cable and install the instrument cluster hood.

Brake Caliper

Removal and Installation

1. Raise and support the vehicle safely. Remove the wheel and tire assembly.

2. Remove the brake pads from the caliper.

3. Disconnect and plug the brake fluid line at the caliper.

4. Remove the brake caliper mounting bolts and remove the caliper.

To install:

5. Position the caliper on the mount and install the mounting bolts.

NOTE: The upper caliper mounting bolt has a shoulder on the top of the bolt. This bolt must be installed on the top.

6. Torque the mounting bolts to 116 ft. lbs. (160 Nm).

7. Connect the brake fluid line to the caliper. Install the brake pads, pins and clips.

8. Fill and bleed the entire brake system.

Disc Brake Pads

Removal and Installation

1. Raise and support the vehicle safely. Remove the wheel and tire assembly.

2. Using a $^3/_{32}$ in. (2.4mm) drift pin, carefully drive the brake pad retaining pins inward.

3. Remove the brake pads.

4. Push the caliper piston into the caliper until it bottoms out.

Front brake caliper and rotor assembly on 2WD

To install:

5. Install the new brake pads and retaining pins. Check that the pins are fully seated in the caliper.

6. Install the wheel and tire assembly.

7. Repeat the procedure for the opposite side. Check the brake fluid level in the reservoir when finished.

8. Depress the brake pedal several times until pressure is felt before moving the vehicle.

Brake Rotor

Removal and Installation

VANAGON

1. Raise and support the vehicle safely. Remove the wheel and tire assembly.

2. Remove the brake pads and pins.

3. Without disconnecting the hydraulic hose, remove the brake caliper from the wheel bearing housing and support it out of the way. Do not let it hang by the hose.

4. Remove the cotter pin and bearing retaning nut. Remove the rotor/hub assembly.

5. Installation is the reverse of the removal procedure. Torque the caliper bolts to 116 ft. lbs. (160 Nm).

6. To adjust the wheel bearing;

   a. Tighten the nut firmly while turning the hub.

   b. Back off the nut just enough so the thrust washer can be moved without prying.

VANAGON SYNCRO

1. Raise and support the vehicle safely. Remove the wheel and tire assembly.

2. Remove the brake pads and pins.

3. Without disconnecting the hydraulic hose, remove the brake caliper from the wheel bearing housing and support it out of the way. Do not let it hang by the hose.

4. Remove the screws and pull the rotor off the hub.

5. Installation is the reverse of the removal procedure. Torque the caliper bolts to 116 ft. lbs. (160 Nm).

Brake Drums

Removal and Installation

1. Raise and safely support the vehicle.

2. Remove the wheel and tire assembly.

3. Remove the drum retaining screws.

4. Remove the brake drum. If the drum will come off on easily, turn the adjuster through the hole near the top of the backing plate.

5. Installation is the reverse of removal. Adjust the brakes as required.

Brake Shoes

Removal and Installation

1. Raise and safely support the vehicle.

2. Remove the wheel and tire assembly.

3. Remove the brake drum.

4. Remove the brake shoe hold-down springs and pins.

5. Unhook the parking brake lever at the leading brake shoe.

6. Remove the lower return spring and the adjuster spring.

7. Move the brake shoes out of the lower support and unhook the return springs.

8. Remove the brake shoes and the push/adjusting rod.

To install:

9. Make sure the adjuster turns easily. Install the return springs and adjuster/push rod on the brake shoes.

10. Install the shoes on the backing plate and into the lower support.

11. Pull the top of the brake shoes around the wheel cylinder.

12. Install the hold-down spring and the pins.

13. Install the adjuster spring.

14. Attach the parking brake lever. Install the lower return spring.

15. Turn the brake adjuster to pre-adjust the shoes so they are about 0.060 in. (1.5mm) smaller diameter than the inside diameter of the drum.

16. Install the brake drum. Install the wheel and tire assembly.

17. Check the adjustment of the brakes.

Wheel Cylinder

Removal and Installation

1. Raise and support the vehicle safely. Remove the wheel and tire assembly. Remove the brake drum and brake shoes.

2. Disconnect and plug the brake line on the rear of the wheel cylinder.

3. Remove the bolts and lockwashers that attach the wheel cylinder to the backing plate and remove the wheel cylinder.

4. Position the new wheel cylinder on the backing plate and install the attaching bolts and lockwashers.

5. Connect the brake line.

6. Install the brake drum, brake shoes, wheel and tire assembly. Bleed the wheel cylinder.

Parking Brake Cable

Removal and Installation

1. Disconnect the cables at the hand brake lever by removing the nuts which secure the cables to the lever. Pull the cables rearward to remove that end from the lever bracket.

2. Raise and support the vehicle safely. Remove the wheel and tire assemblies.

3. Remove the brake drum and detach the cable end from the lever attached to the rear brake shoe.

4. Remove the brake cable bracket from the backing plate and remove the cable from the vehicle.

5. Installation is the reverse of the removal procedure.

6. Adjust the parking brake.

Adjustment

1. Brake cable adjustment is performed at the hand brake le-

Parking brake lever and cable assembly

ver in the passenger compartment. There is a cable for each rear wheel with an adjusting nut and a locknut on each cable. Loosen the locknuts.

2. Raise and safely support the rear wheels so they can be turned by hand.

3. Turn one adjusting nut until a very slight drag is felt as the wheel on that side is turned. Do the same for the other side.

4. Back off on the adjusting nuts until the lever can be pulled up 3 notches. Tighten the locknuts.

FRONT SUSPENSION

Shock Absorber

Removal and Installation

1. Raise and support the vehicle safely so the front suspension is hanging freely. Remove the wheel and tire assembly.

2. Support the lower control arm and remove the upper and lower shock absorber mounting bolts, nuts and washers.

3. Remove the shock absorber from the vehicle.

4. Install the shock absorber, rubber boot and stopper.

5. Tighten the upper shock absorber mounting nut until the rubber washer is compressed to the same width as the metal washer.

6. Raise the lower control arm and tighten the lower shock absorber mounting bolt to 29 ft. lbs. (39 Nm).

7. Install the wheel and tire assembly. Lower the vehicle.

Coil Spring

Removal and Installation

1. Raise and safely support the vehicle.

2. Remove the wheel and tire assembly.

3. Remove the shock absorber.

4. With the shock absorber removed, the coil spring can be removed.

5. Remove the coil spring, noting the position of the rubber stopper.

To install:

6. Install the new coil spring and seat the spring in the lower control arm seat.

7. Install the shock absorber.

8. Install the wheel and tire assembly.

SPACER RING

OUTER CV JOINT

HALFSHAFT

PROTECTIVE BAND

SPLASH RING

STABILIZER BAR

V SECTIONED SEAL

RADIUS ROD

SHOCK ABSORBER WITH SPRING

LOWER BALL JOINT

UPPER CONTROL ARM WITH ECCENTRIC ADJUSTER

UPPER CONTROL ARM

LOWER CONTROL ARM

INNER SEAL

UPPER BALL JOINT

WHEEL BEARING HOUSING

WHEEL BEARING

OUTER SEAL

HUB

Front suspension components on Vanagon Syncro

Upper Ball Joint

Inspection

1. Raise and support the vehicle safely so the front wheels are hanging freely.
2. Insert a prybar between the ball joint pinch bolt and upper control arm.
3. Measure the distance of ball joint play.
4. If the play exceeds 0.1 in. (2.5mm), replace the ball joint.

Removal and Installation

1. Raise and support the vehicle safely. Remove the wheel and tire assembly.
2. Place a floor jack under the lower control arm as close to the wheel bearing housing as possible. Raise the control arm enough to put a slight load on the coil spring.
3. Loosen the ball joint nut but do not remove it yet. Free the ball joint from the wheel bearing housing, using a ball joint press.

Upper ball joint mounting bolts on Vanagon Syncro and Vanagon

4. Remove the upper ball joint to upper control arm bolts and remove the ball joint.
5. Installation is the reverse of the removal procedure. Install

Lower ball joint bracket bolts on

a new ball joint nut and torque to 80 ft. lbs. (110 Nm). Torque the bolts to 44 ft. lbs. (60 Nm). Check the front wheel alignment.

Lower Ball Joint

Inspection

1. Raise and support the vehicle safely so the front wheels are hanging freely.
2. Insert a prybar between the ball joint pinch bolt and lower control arm.
3. Measure the distance of ball joint play.
4. If the play exceeds 0.1 in. (2.5mm), replace the ball joint.

Removal and Installation

VANAGON

1. The wheel bearing spindle must be removed and the lower ball joint pressed out. Raise and support the vehicle safely. Remove the wheel and tire assembly.
2. Place a floor jack under the lower control arm as close to the wheel bearing housing as possible and place a slight load on the coil spring.
3. Without disconnecting the hydraulic hose, remove the brake caliper from the wheel bearing housing and support it out of the way. Do not let it hang by the hose. Remove the hub and brake rotor and the splash shield.
4. Loosen but do not remove the upper ball joint nut and the tie rod end nut. Use a ball joint press to separate the ball joint and tie rod end from the wheel bearing spindle, then remove the nuts.
5. Remove the lower ball joint to lower control arm nut and remove the ball joint from the control arm. Remove the spindle.
6. Remove the circlip and press the ball joint out of the spindle.
To install:
7. Press a new ball joint in place, with the flat side facing the spindle. Install the circlip.
8. Install the wheel bearing spindle onto the control arms. Use new self-locking ball joint nuts and torque them to 80 ft. lbs. (110 Nm).
9. Torque the tie rod end nut to 22 ft. lbs. (30 Nm).
10. Install the splash shield, hub and rotor and adjust the wheel bearing. When installing the brake caliper, torque the bolts to 115 ft. lbs. (160 Nm). Make sure the bolt with the shoulder is in the upper caliper mounting hole.
11. Check and adjust front wheel alignment.

VANAGON SYNCRO

1. On 4WD models, the lower ball joint can be changed without removing the wheel bearing housing. Raise and safely support the vehicle and remove the wheel.
2. Support the upper control arm so the wheel bearing housing will not be hanging on the halfshaft. Place a floor jack under the lower control arm and lift slightly to keep the spring in place.

3. Loosen the ball joint nut and use a ball joint press to separate the ball joint from the wheel bearing housing.
4. Remove the bolts to remove the ball joint bracket from the lower control arm.
5. Remove the circlip and press the ball joint out of the bracket.
To install:
6. Press the new ball joint into the bracket and install the circlip.
7. Install the ball joint bracket into the control arm and torque the bolts to 44 ft. lbs. (60 Nm).
8. Fit the ball joint into the wheel bearing housing and install a new self-locking nut. Torque the nut to 74 ft. lbs. (100 Nm).
9. Check and adjust front wheel alignment.

Upper Control Arms

Removal and Installation

1. Raise and support the vehicle safely. Remove the wheel and tire assembly.
2. Raise the lower control arm to place a slight load on the coil spring.
3. Disconnect the upper ball joint from the bearing housing.
4. Remove the upper control arm camber adjustment bolt and remove the control arm.
To install:
5. Fit the control arm in place and install the long bolt with the eccentric washers.
6. Connect the upper ball joint and torque the bolts to 44 ft. lbs. (60 Nm).
7. Check and adjust front wheel alignment.

Lower Control Arms

Removal and Installation

1. Raise and support the vehicle safely. Remove the wheel and tire assembly.
2. Remove the shock absorber and coil spring.
3. On the radius rod, measure the length of the threads so it can be installed with the same caster adjustment. Remove the radius rod and disconnect the stabilizer bar linkage from the control arm.
4. Remove the lower control arm bushing bolt and remove the control arm.
To install:
5. Install the lower control arm in position, install the mounting bolt and torque to 65 ft. lbs. (90 Nm).
6. Install the radius rod in the original position. Torque the locknut at the control arm to 133 ft. lbs. (180 Nm), torque the bushing nuts to 74 ft. lbs. (100 Nm).
7. Connect the stabilizer bar linkage and torque the nut to 22 ft. lbs. (30 Nm).
8. Install the shock and coil spring.
9. Install the wheel and tire and check and adjust the front wheel alignment.

Stabilizer Bar

Removal and Installation

1. Raise and safely support the vehicle.
2. Remove the wheel and tire assemblies.
3. Remove the stabilizer bar linkage nuts on each side.
4. Remove the upper stabilizer bar brackets and bushings.
5. Remove the stabilizer bar from the vehicle.
To install:
6. Install the stabilizer in position. Install the brackets and bushings and torque the nuts or bolts to 18 ft. lbs. (25 Nm).
7. Install the stabilizer bar linkage and torque the nuts to 22 ft. lbs. (30 Nm).

Radius Rod

Removal and Installation

VANAGON

1. Raise and safely support the vehicle.
2. Remove the wheel and tire assemblies.
3. Disconnect the stabilizer bar from the radius rod.
4. On the radius rod, measure the length of the threads so it can be installed with the same caster adjustment. Remove the front retaining nut from the radius rod.
5. Remove the rear radius rod mounting nuts from the lower control arm.
6. Remove the radius rod from the vehicle.

To install:

7. Install the radius rod in position. Install the rear retaining nuts in the same position marked during removal and torque to 133 ft. lbs. (180 Nm).
8. Install the front rod nut and torque the nut to 111 ft. lbs. (150 Nm).
9. Connect the stabilizer bar to the radius rod, torque the nut to 22 ft. lbs. (30 Nm). Check and adjust front wheel alignment.

VANAGON SYNCRO

1. Raise and safely support the vehicle.
2. Remove the wheel and tire assemblies.
3. Disconnect the stabilizer bar from the radius rod.
4. Support the lower control arm with a floor jack and remove the ball joint bracker bolts.

Front radius rod on Vanagon Syncro

5. On the radius rod, measure the length of the threads so it can be installed with the same caster adjustment. Remove the front retaining nut and remove the radius rod.

To install:

6. Install the radius rod in position. Install the rear retaining nuts in the same position marked during removal and torque to 133 ft. lbs. (180 Nm).
7. Install the ball joint bracket bolts and torque to 74 ft. lbs. (100 Nm).
8. Connect the stabilizer bar linkage and torque the nut to 22 ft. lbs. (30 Nm). Check and adjust front wheel alignment.

REAR SUSPENSION

Shock Absorber

Removal and Installation

1. Raise and safely support the vehicle.
2. Remove the wheel and tire assemblies.
3. Support the trailing arm assembly and remove the upper and lower shock mounting bolts. Remove the shock absorber from the vehicle.
4. Installation is the reverse of the removal procedure. Torque the shock mounting bolts to 65 ft. lbs. (88 Nm).

Coil Springs

Removal and Installation

1. Raise and safely support the vehicle.
2. Remove the wheel and tire assembly.
3. Support the trailing arm and remove the shock absorber.
4. Lower the trailing arm slightly and remove the coil spring.
5. Installation is the reverse of the removal procedure.

Trailing Arms

Removal and Installation

—— **CAUTION** ——

Torque on the axle nut is very high and loosening it with a breaker bar may cause the vehicle to fall off the supports. Do not loosen or tighten this nut unless the vehicle is on all 4 wheels.

1. With the vehicle on all 4 wheels, remove the cotter pin and loosen the rear axle nut.

Rear suspension components on all models

FRONT FINAL DRIVE WITH
VISCOUS COUPLING

DRIVESHAFT

PROTECTIVE RAILS FOR
DRIVESHAFT

TRANSAXLE

Vanagon Syncro drive line lay-out

2. Raise and safely support the vehicle. Remove the wheel and tire.

3. Remove the axle nut and use a wheel puller to remove the hub.

4. Disconnect and plug the brake hydraulic line and disconnect the parking brake cable.

5. Remove the the backing plate assembly from the trailing arm. The brake shoes do not need to be removed.

6. Remove the halfshaft. Remove the wheel bearing and stub axle assembly.

7. Disconnect and remove the shock absorber and the coil spring.

8. Remove the trailing arm pivot bolt and lower the trailing arm from the vehicle.

To install:

9. Install the trailing arm in position and torque the pivot bolts to 74 ft. lbs. (100 Nm).

10. Install the shock absorber and coil spring.

11. Connect the halfshaft to the transaxle and torque the bolts to 33 ft. lbs. (45 Nm).

12. Install the wheel bearing and stub axle assembly to the trailing arm and torque the bolts to 101 ft. lbs. (140 Nm).

13. Install the brake backing plate and torque the bolts to 14 ft. lbs. (20 Nm). Connect the parking brake cable and hydraulic line.

14. Install the hub and hand tighten the axle nut. Install the brake drum and bleed and adjust the brakes as required.

15. With the vehicle resting on all 4 wheels, torque the rear axle nut to 360 ft. lbs. (500 Nm). Install a new cotter pin.

ELECTRICAL DIAGNOSIS

To satisfy the growing trend toward organized engine diagnosis and tune-up, the following gauge and meter hook-ups, as well as diagnosis procedures are covered. The most sophisticated tune-up and diagnostic facilities are no more than a complex of the basic gauges and meters in common, everyday use. Therefore, to understand gauge and meter hook-ups, their applications and procedures, is to be equipped with the know how to perform the most exacting diagnosis.

KNOW YOUR INSTRUMENTS

OHMMETER

An ohmmeter is used to measure electrical resistance in a unit or circuit. The ohmmeter has a self contained power supply. In use, it is connected across (or in parallel with) the terminals of the unit being tested.

AMMETER

An ammeter is used to measure the amount of electricity flowing through a unit, or circuit. Ammeters are always connected in series with the unit or circuit being tested.

VOLTMETER

A voltmeter is used to measure voltage pushing the current through a unit, or circuit. The meter is connected across the terminals of the unit being tested.

ALTERNATORS AND REGULATORS

Diagnosis

The first step in diagnosing troubles of the charging system, is to identify the source of failure. Does the fault lie in the alternator or the regulator? The next move depends upon preference or necessity, either repair or replace the defective unit.

If the system is equipped with an external voltage regulator, it is easy to separate an alternator, electrically, from the regulator. Alternator output is controlled by the amount of current supplied to the field circuit of the system.

An alternator is capable of producing substantial current at idle speed. Higher maximum output is also a possibility. This presents a potential danger when testing. As a precaution, a field rheostat should be used in the field circuit when making the following isolation test. The field rheostat permits positive control of the amount of current allowed to pass through the field circuit during the isolation test. Unregulated alternator capacity could ruin the unit.

Most manufacturers of precision gauges offer special test connectors, in sets, that will adapt to the leads and connections of any charging system.

ALTERNATOR TEST PLANS

The following is a procedure pattern for testing the various alternators and their control systems.

There are certain precautionary measures that apply to alternator tests in general. These items are listed in detail to avoid repetition when testing each make of alternator and to encourage a habit of good test procedure.

1. Check alternator drive belt for condition and tension.
2. Disconnect the battery cables. Check physical, chemical and electrical condition of battery.
3. Be absolutely sure of polarity before connecting any battery in the circuit. Reversed polarity will ruin the diodes.
4. Never use a battery charger to start the engine.
5. Disconnect both battery cables when making a battery recharge hook-up.

Checking field circuit current draw—as a precaution, a field rheostat should be used to control the amount of current allowed to pass through the circuit during isolation test

Checking current output of the charging system—if an overcharge of 10–15 amps is indicated, check for a faulty regulator

Checking charging system resistance to determine the amount of voltage drop between the alternator output terminal wire and the battery

6. Be sure of polarity hook-up when using a booster battery for starting.
7. Never ground the alternator output or battery terminal.
8. Never ground the field circuit between alternator and regulator.
9. Never run any alternator on an open circuit with the field energized.
10. Never try to polarize an alternator, unless directed by the manufacturer.
11. Do not attempt to motor an alternator.
12. When making engine idle speed adjustments, always consider potential load factors that influence engine rpm. To compensate for electrical load, switch **ON** the lights, radio, heater, air conditioner, etc.

Diagnosis

LOW OR NO CHARGING

1. Blown fuse

2. Broken or loose fan belt
3. Voltage regulator not working
4. Brushes sticking
5. Slipring dirty
6. Open circuit
7. Faulty wiring connections
8. Faulty diode rectifier
9. High resistance in charging circuit
10. Grounded stator

11. May be open rectifiers (check all 3 phases)
12. If rectifiers are found or open, check capacitor

NOISY UNIT

1. Damaged rotor bearings
2. Poor alignment of unit
3. Broken or loose belt
4. Open diode rectifiers.

CHRYSLER CORPORATION

GENERAL INFORMATION

There is a great deal of interchangeability among Chrysler alternators. Four types were widely used among domestic Chrysler products. Alternators were made by Bosch, Nippondenso, Mitsubishi and Chrysler. Often the same replacement part number applies to alternators with different nominal amperages, even different makes. The major difference between alternators is in the pulley grooves. From 2–8 pulley grooves were used, some for conventional Vee-belts, others for Serpentine belts. Use care when ordering parts.

The alternators used on 1990 and later Chrysler vehicles may be considered not serviceable and a defective unit may have to be replaced with a new one. Always check parts availability before attempting to overhaul an alternator.

With very few exceptions, the alternators covered in this section all have their output regulated by the electronic engine controller. In most cases, with the proper equipment, the computer can be accessed for diagnostic codes.

Chrysler 90 and 120 Amp Alternator

GENERAL DESCRIPTION

The charging system consists of a battery, alternator, voltmeter

and connecting wires. The 90 amp unit has 6 built-in silicon rectifiers, while the 120 amp has 12 built-in silicon rectifiers. The voltage regulator is built into the power and logic modules. The rectifiers convert AC current into DC current. Current at the alternator battery terminal is DC. The alternator's main components are rotor, stator, capacitor, rectifiers, end shields, brushes, bearings, drive pulley and fan.

The electronic voltage regulator is contained within the engine electronics power module and logic module. It is a device that regulates vehicle electrical system voltage by limiting output voltage that is generated by the alternator. This is accomplished by controlling the amount of current that is allowed to pass through the alternator field winding. The alternator field is turned **ON** by a driver in the power module which is controlled by a predriver in the logic module.

The logic module looks at battery temperature to determine control voltage. The field is then driven at a duty cycle proportional to the difference between battery voltage and desired control voltage. One important feature of the electronic regulator is the ability of its control circuit to vary regulated system voltage up or down as temperature changes. This provides varying charging conditions for battery throughout seasons of the year.

TESTING

Resistance Test

Alternator output wire resistance test will show amount of volt-

Alternator electrical schematic—Chrysler 120 amp

Alternator electrical schematic—Chrysler 90 amp

age drop across alternator output wire between alternator BAT terminal and positive battery post.

1. Before starting test, make sure vehicle has a fully charged battery.
2. Turn **OFF** ignition switch.
3. Disconnect negative battery cable.
4. Disconnect alternator output wire from alternator output battery terminal.
5. Connect a 0–150 ampere scale DC ammeter in series between alternator BAT terminal and disconnected alternator

output wire. Connect positive lead to alternator BAT terminal and negative lead to disconnected alternator output wire.

6. Connect positive lead of a test voltmeter (range 0–18 volts minimum) to disconnected alternator output wire. Connect negative lead of test voltmeter to positive battery cable at positive post.

7. Remove air hose between power and module and air cleaner.

8. Connect an end of a jumper wire to ground and with other

Chrysler 90 amp alternator with engine electronics — output wire resistance test

Chrysler 90 amp alternator with engine electronics — current output test

end probe green R-3 lead wire on dash side of black 8-way connector.

NOTE: Do not connect the blue J-2 lead of the 8-way connector to ground. Both R-3 and J-2 leads are green on the alternator side of the 8-way connector. At the dash end of the connector, R-3 is green and J-2 is blue.

9. Connect an engine tachometer and reconnect negative battery cable.

10. Connect a variable carbon pile rheostat between battery terminals. Be sure carbon pile is in **OPEN** or **OFF** position before connecting leads.

11. Start engine. Immediately after staring, reduce engine speed to idle. Adjust engine speed and carbon pile to maintain 20 amperes flowing in circuit. Observe voltmeter reading. Voltmeter reading should not exceed 0.5 volts.

12. If a higher voltage drop is indicated, inspect, clean and tighten all connections between alternator BAT terminal and positive battery post.

13. A voltage drop test may be performed at each connection to locate connection with excessive resistance. If resistance tested satisfactorily, reduce engine speed, turn **OFF** carbon pile and turn **OFF** ignition switch.

14. Disconnect negative battery cable. Remove test ammeter, voltmeter, carbon pile and tachometer. Remove jumper wire between 8-way black connector and ground.

15. Connect alternator output wire to alternator BAT terminal post. Tighten 45–75 inch lbs. Reconnect negative battery cable. Reconnect hose between power module and air cleaner.

Current Output Test

Current output test determines whether or not alternator is capable of delivering its rated current output.

1. Before starting any tests, make sure vehicle has a fully charged battery.

2. Disconnect negative battery cable.

3. Disconnect alternator output wire at the alternator battery terminal.

4. Connect a 0–150 ampere scale DC ammeter in series be-

tween alternator BAT terminal and disconnected alternator output wire. Connect positive lead to alternator BAT terminal and negative lead to disconnected alternator output wire.

5. Connect positive lead of a test voltmeter (range 0–18 volts minimum) to alternator BAT terminal.

6. Connect negative lead of test voltmeter to a good ground.

7. Connect an engine tachometer and reconnect negative battery cable.

8. Connect a variable carbon pile rheostat between battery terminals. Be sure carbon pile is in **OPEN** or **OFF** position before connecting leads.

9. Remove air hose between power module and air cleaner.

10. Connect 1 end of a jumper wire to ground and with other end probe green R-3 lead wire on dash side of Black 8-way connector.

NOTE: Do not connect the blue J-2 lead of the 8-way connector to ground. Both R-3 and J-2 leads are green on the alternator side of the 8-way connector. At the dash end of the connector, R-3 is green and J-2 is blue.

11. Start engine. Adjust carbon pile and engine speed in increments until a speed of 1250 rpm and voltmeter reading of 15 volts is obtained. Do not allow the voltmeter to read above 16 volts.

12. The ammeter reading must be within the proper limits.

13. If reading is less than specified and alternator output wire resistance is not excessive alternator should be removed from vehicle and bench tested.

14. After current output test is completed, reduce engine speed, turn **OFF** carbon pile and ignition switch. Disconnect negative battery cable.

15. Remove test ammeter, voltmeter, tachometer and carbon pile. Remove jumper wire between 8-way black connector and ground. Disconnect alternator output wire to alternator BAT terminal post.

16. Reconnect negative battery cable. Reconnect air hose between power module and air cleaner.

CHRYSLER ALTERNATOR DIAGNOSTIC CHART

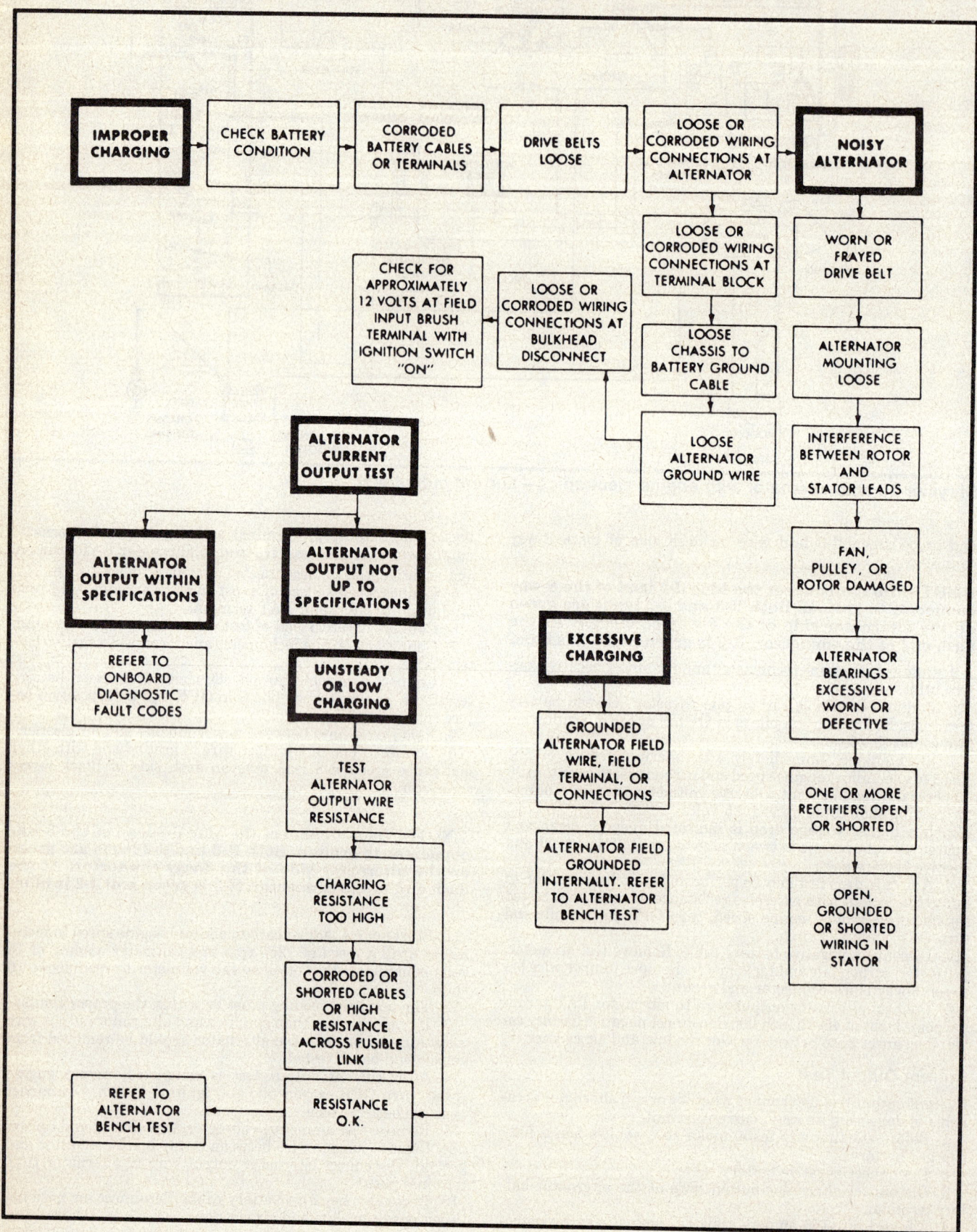

Voltage Regulator Test

On board diagnostic fault codes play a major role in case of a charging system failure.

Fault codes are 2 digit numbers that identify which circuit is at fault. In most cases, they do not identify which component in a circuit is at fault. Therefore, a fault code is only a result, not necessarily a reason for the problem. It is important that the test procedure be followed in order to understand the fault codes of the on-board diagnostic system.

DIAGNOSTIC READOUT BOX OPERATION

The diagnostic readout box is used to put the on-board diagnostic system in 3 different modes of testing as called for in the driveability test procedure, only one of which is used in charging system diagnosis.

DIAGNOSTIC MODE

1. Connect diagnostic readout box C–4805 to the mating connector located in the wiring harness by right front shock tower.
2. Place read/hold switch on readout box in **READ** position.
3. Turn ignition switch **ON/OFF**, **ON/OFF**, on within 5 seconds.
4. Record all codes, displaying of codes may be stopped by moving read/hold button to **HOLD** position. Returning to **READ** position will continue displaying of codes.
5. If for some reason diagnostic readout box is not available, logic module can show fault codes by means of flashing power loss light on instrument cluster.

HOW TO USE POWER LOSS OR POWER LIMIT LIGHT FOR CODES

To activate this function, turn ignition key **ON/OFF/ON/OFF/ON** within 5 seconds. The power loss light will turn **ON** for 2 seconds as a bulb check. Immediately following this it will display a fault code by flashing on and off. There is a short pause between flashes and a longer pause between digits. All codes displayed are 2 digit numbers with a 4 second pause between codes. An example of a code is as follows.
1. Light on for 2 seconds then turns off.
2. Light flashes 4 times, pauses and flashes once.
3. Light pauses for 4 seconds, flashes 4 times, pauses and flashes 7 times.
4. The 2 codes are 41 and 47. Any number of codes can be displayed as long as they are in memory. The light will flash until all of them are displayed.

CHARGING SYSTEM FAULT CODES

Perform test procedure categories using the following guide lines.
1. Each category is made up of many tests. Always start at the first test of a category. Starting at any other test will only give incorrect results.
2. Each test may have many steps. Only perform steps indicated under action required. It is not necessary to perform all steps in a test.
3. At the end of each test (not step) reconnect all wires and turn the engine **OFF** and reinstall any components that were removed for testing.
4. The vehicle being tested must have a fully charged battery.

Diagnostic Testing With Readout Box

TEST 1

Checking Battery Sensing Circuit Code 16

This test will check for direct battery feed to logic module. Circuit is also memory feed to logic module. Code 16 with lower battery voltage will turn **ON** power loss light.
1. Turn the ignition switch **OFF**.

2. Disconnect the (black on EFI, blue on turbocharged engines) connector from the logic module.
3. Connect a voltmeter to cavity No. 22 of logic module connector and ground.
4. Voltmeter should read within 1 volt of battery voltage. Voltage okay, replace logic module. Before replacing logic module, make sure the terminal in cavity No. 22 is not crushed so it cannot touch logic module pin.
5. Zero volts, repair wire of cavity No. 22 for an open circuit to the wiring harness splice.

TEST 2

Checking Charging System Codes 41 and 46
STEP A
1. Disconnect the power module 10-way connector.
2. Connect a voltmeter between cavity No. 8 of 10-way connector and ground.
3. Turn ignition switch to **RUN** position.
4. Voltmeter should read within 1 volt of battery voltage. Not within 0–1 volts, repair alternator field circuit for short to ground. Voltage okay, perform Step B.

STEP B
1. Turn the ignition switch **OFF**.
2. Reconnect the power module 10-way connector.
3. Disconnect the power module 12-way connector.
4. Connect a voltmeter between **F2** terminal on alternator and ground.
5. Turn the ignition switch to the **RUN** position.
6. Voltage should read within 1 volt of battery voltage. Not within 0–1 volt, replace power module. Voltage okay, perform Step C.

STEP C
1. Turn the ignition switch **OFF**.
2. With power module 12-way connector disconnected.
3. Disconnect the logic module (white on EFI, red on turbocharged engines) connector.
4. Connect an ohmmeter between cavity No. 11 of power module 12-way connector and ground.
5. Ohmmeter should not show continuity. No continuity, replace logic module. Continuity repair wire of cavity No. 11 for short circuit to ground.

TEST 3

Checking Codes 41 and 47
STEP A
1. Connect a voltmeter between battery positive and ground.
2. Connect an end of jumper wire to a good engine ground.
3. Start the engine and note reading of voltmeter.
4. Very quickly touch other end of jumper wire to **F2** terminal on alternator and watch voltmeter.
5. Voltmeter should show an increase in voltage. Voltage increases, this indicates alternator is operating correctly. Move on to Step B, for field circuit check. Voltage does not increase, this indicates alternator is not operating. If this is the case, perform Step E which checks for voltage to alternator field.

STEP B
1. Connect a voltmeter between cavity No. 2 of logic module (black on EFI, blue on turbocharged engines) connector and ground.
2. Connect an end of a jumper wire to cavity No. 5 of the logic module white connector.
3. Very quickly touch other end of jumper wire to logic module mounting stud and watch voltmeter.
4. Voltmeter should show an increase in voltage. If voltage in-

creases, this indicates all components of system, except logic module, are operating correctly.

5. Before replacing the logic module, be sure the terminal in cavity No. 5 is not crushed so it cannot touch the logic module pin. If terminal in cavity 5 is not damaged, replace logic module. If no increase is indicated, move on to Step C.

STEP C

1. Turn the engine **OFF**.

2. Disconnect logic module (white on EFI, red on turbocharged engines) connector.

3. Connect a voltmeter between cavity No. 5 of logic module connector and ground.

4. Turn the ignition switch to **RUN** position. Voltmeter should read within 1 volt of battery voltage. Zero volts, disconnect power module 12-way and connect an ohmmeter between cavity 5 of logic module (white on EFI, red on turbocharged engines) connector and cavity 11 of power module. If open, repair wire or connector. If meter shows continuity replace power module. If voltage shown is within 1 volt of battery voltage, go on to Step D.

STEP D

1. Turn ignition switch **OFF**.

2. Disconnect 10-way connector from power module.

3. Connect a voltmeter between cavity No. 8 of 10-way connector and ground.

4. Turn ignition switch to **RUN** position. Voltmeter should read within 1 volt of battery voltage. If voltage shown is within 1 volt of battery voltage, replace power module.

5. Zero volts, turn ignition switch **OFF** and place an ohmmeter between cavity 8 of power module 10-way connector and **F2** terminal of alternator. If open, repair wire or connector. If meter shows continuity, proceed to Step E.

STEP E

1. Turn ignition switch to **OFF** position.

2. Connect a voltmeter between **F1** terminal of alternator and ground.

3. Turn ignition switch to **RUN** position.

4. Voltmeter should read within 1 volt of battery voltage. If voltage shown is within 1 volt of battery voltage, alternator is not functioning properly and must be removed form vehicle and repaired.

5. If no voltage is shown, this indicates an open circuit and the wire from the **F1** terminal to ignition switch must be repaired.

TEST 4

Checking Code 44

STEP A

1. Turn the ignition switch **OFF**.

2. Disconnect the logic module (black connector on EFI, blue connector on turbocharged engines).

3. Connect an ohmmeter between cavity No. 20 of logic module (black on EFI, blue on turbocharged engines) connector and ground.

4. Ohmmeter should show resistance, amount of resistance should be 8–29 kilo-ohms. Correct resistance, replace logic module. If 0 resistance, perform Step B. Open circuit, perform Step C.

STEP B

1. Ohmmeter connected between cavity No. 20 of logic module (black on EFI, blue on turbocharged engines) connector and ground.

2. Disconnect power module 12-way connector.

3. Ohmmeter should show an open circuit. Open circuit, replace power module. If 0 resistance, repair wire of cavity No. 20 and cavity No. 3 of power module 12-way connector.

STEP C

1. Disconnect power module 12-way connector.

2. Connect an ohmmeter between pin 3 of power module 12-way and ground.

3. Ohmmeter should show resistance, amount of resistance should be between 8–29 kilo-ohms.

4. Correct resistance, repair wire in cavity No. 20 of logic module (black on EFI, blue on turbocharged engines) and cavity No. 3 of power module 12-way connector. Open circuit, replace power module.

OVERHAUL

Disassembly

1. Remove the dust cover mounting nut. Remove the dust cover.

2. Remove the brush holder assembly mounting screws. Remove the brush holder assembly.

3. Remove the stator to rectifier mounting screws. Remove the stator-to-rectifier assembly mounting screws. Remove the rectifier insulator. Remove the capacitor mounting screw. Remove the rectifier assembly.

4. Remove the through bolts. Carefully pry between the stator and the drive end shield, using a suitable tool and separate the end shields. The stator is laminated, do not burr the stator or the end shield.

5. Position the drive end of the alternator over the bosses of the holding fixture. Do not position the rotor plastic termination plate over the fixture boss or damage to the assembly will result.

6. Bolt the drive end of the assembly to shield fixture. Loosen the pulley mounting nut. Remove the pulley mounting nut. Remove the pulley washer.

7. Remove the poly-vee pulley. Remove the fan. Remove the front bearing spacer. Press the rotor assembly out of the drive end shield.

8. Remove the inner bearing spacer. Position the alternator bearing puller tool under the rear rotor bearing. Tighten the right puller bolt a ½ turn. Tighten the left puller bolt a ½ turn. Continue tightening the tool a ½ turn on each bolt until the rear rotor bearing is free. Remove the rear rotor bearing assembly from the rotor.

9. Position the rotor assembly in the holding fixture. Position the rear rotor bearing onto the rotor shaft.

10. Drive the rear rotor bearing onto the rotor until it bottoms. The rear rotor position is critical and must be installed using special tools C-4885 and C-4894.

11. Remove the front bearing retaining screws. Press the front bearing out of the drive end shield.

12. Carefully remove the stator from the rectifier end shield.

Inspection

ROTOR ASSEMBLY TEST

Check the outside circumference of slipring for dirtiness and roughness. Clean or polish with fine sandpaper, if required. A badly roughened slipring or a worn down slipring should be replaced.

Sliprings are not serviced as a separate item; they are serviced with the rotor assembly.

ROTOR FIELD COILS FOR
OPENS AND SHORTS TEST

To check for an open rotor field coil connect an ohmmeter between sliprings. Ohmmeter readings should be between 1.5–2 ohms on rotor field coils at room temperature. Resistance between 2.5–3.0 ohms would result from alternator rotor field coils that have been operated on vehicle at higher engine compartment temperatures. Readings about 3.5 ohms would indicate high resistance rotor field coils and further testing or replacement may be required.

To check for a shorted rotor field coil, connect an ohmmeter between both sliprings. If the reading is below 1.5 ohms, the rotor field coil is shorted.

ROTOR FIELD COIL FOR GROUND TEST

To check for a grounded rotor field coil, connect an ohmmeter from each slipring to rotor shaft. Ohmmeter should be set for infinite reading when probes are apart and 0 when probes are shorted. The ohmmeter should read infinite. If the reading is 0 or low in value, rotor is grounded.

STATOR ASSEMBLY TEST

Stator Coil for Ground Test

1. Remove varnish from a spot on the stator frame.
2. Press an ohmmeter test probe firmly onto cleaned spot on frame. Be sure varnish has been removed from stator so spot is bare.
3. Press the other ohmmeter test probe firmly to each of the 3 phase (stator) lead terminals 1 at a time. If ohmmeter reads 0 or low in value stator lead is grounded.
4. Replace stator if stator tested grounded.

Stator for Open or Short Circuit Test

The stator windings are delta wound. Therefore, they cannot be tested for opens or shorts with an ohmmeter. They can only be tested for these items with test equipment not common to automotive service test equipment. If stator is not grounded and all other electrical circuits and components of alternator test okay, it can be suspected that stator could possibly be open or shorted and must be replaced.

Rectifier Assemblies Test

When testing rectifiers with an ohmmeter, disconnect the 3 phase stator lead terminals from rectifier assembly. Pry stator lead terminals away from rectifier assembly.

Positive Rectifier Test

With an ohmmeter check for continuity between each positive (+) rectifier strap and positive (+) heat sink. Reverse test probes and retest. There should be continuity in one direction only. If there is continuity in both directions, rectifier is short circuited. If there is no continuity in either direction, rectifier is open. If rectifier is shorted or open, replace rectifier assembly.

Negative Rectifier Test

With an ohmmeter, check for continuity between each negative (−) rectifier strap and negative (−) heat sink. Reverse test probes and retest. There should be continuity in one direction only. If there is continuity in both directions, rectifier is short circuited. If there is no continuity in either direction, rectifier is open. If rectifier is shorted or open, replace rectifier assembly. When installing a new rectifier assembly, apply 3 dabs (0.1 grams each) of heat sink compound to bottom of negative rectifier prior to mounting rectifier assembly to rectifier end shield.

Brushes and Brush Springs Continuity Test

When testing brushes and brush springs make sure brushes move smoothly in brush holder. Sticking brushes require replacement of brush holder assembly.

Inner Brush Circuit Test

With an ohmmeter, touch a test probe to inner brush and another probe to field terminal. If there is no continuity, replace the brush assembly.

Outer Brush Circuit Test

With an ohmmeter, touch a test probe to outer brush and other

probe to field terminal. If there is no continuity, replace brush assembly.

Cleaning Alternator Parts

Do not immerse stator field coil assembly, rotor assembly or rectifier assembly in cleaning solvent, as solvent will damage these parts.

Assembly

1. Be sure to repair or replace defective components as required.
2. To the front of the rotor, install the inner bearing spacer and press the drive end shield onto the rotor.

NOTE: The front drive end shield bearing must be replaced anytime the rotor or drive end shield is removed, for the front bearing is a press fit and may be damaged upon removal.

3. Position the drive end shield into a holding fixture so the fixture bosses do not contact the rotor plastic termination plate and tighten the holding bolt.
4. At the front of the drive end shield, install the pulley spacer (flat side up), the fan, the pulley, the washer and the pulley nut. Torque the pulley nut to 80–105 ft. lbs. (108–125 Nm).
5. Remove the drive end shield and rotor assembly from the holding fixture.
6. To assemble the rear end housing on the 90 amp unit, perform the following procedures:
   a. Apply joint compound to the rectifier end shield surface, under the rectifier mounting position.
   b. Position the rectifier assembly to the rectifier drive end housing.
   c. Install the rectifier insulator, the insulator mounting screws and torque the screws to 36–46 inch lbs. (4–6 Nm).
   d. Install the capacitor terminal over the rectifier assembly battery terminal stud and torque the mounting screw to 36–48 inch lbs. (4–6 Nm).
   e. Install the alternator battery terminal nut and torque to 30–50 inch lbs. (3–6 Nm).
   f. Install the stator-to-rectifier screws and torque to 12–18 inch lbs. (1–2 Nm).
   g. Slide the brushes into their cavity, Install the brush holder assembly and torque the screws to 12–18 inch lbs. (1–2 Nm).
   h. Install the dust cover and torque the nut to 12–18 inch lbs. (1–2 Nm).
7. To assemble the rear housing on the 120 amp unit, perform the following procedures:
   a. Apply joint compound to the rectifier end shield surface, under the rectifier mounting position.
   b. Position the rectifier assemblies No. 1 and No. 2 to the rectifier drive end housing.
   c. Install the rectifier insulators, the insulator mounting screws and torque to 36–46 inch lbs. (4–6 Nm).
   d. Install the capacitor terminal over the rectifier assembly No. 2 battery terminal stud and torque the mounting screw to 36–48 inch lbs. (4–6 Nm).
   e. Install the alternator battery terminal nut and torque to 30–50 inch lbs. (3–6 Nm).
   f. Position a jumper strap between the rectifier assemblies No. 1 and No. 2.; torque the nut to 36–48 inch lbs. (4–6 Nm) and the screw to 15–35 inch lbs. (2–4 Nm).
   g. Position the 3 buss bars to the rectifier assemblies and torque the screws to 12–18 inch lbs. (1–2 Nm).
   h. Slide the brushes into their cavity, Install the brush holder assembly and torque the screws to 12–18 inch lbs. (1–2 Nm).
   i. Install the dust cover and torque the nut to 12–18 inch lbs. (1–2 Nm).

8. Assemble the rear end housing to the drive end shield and rotor assembly. Install the through bolts and torque to 48–72 inch lbs. (5–8 Nm).

9. Install the rear bearing oil seal.

Bosch 90 Amp Alternator

GENERAL INFORMATION

The voltage regulator is built into the Single Module Engine Controller (SMEC). Vehicle application is 1990–92 Chrysler Corporation full size RWD pickups and vans, Dakota pickups and Caravan/Voyager mini-vans.

TESTING

Alternator Output Wire Resistance Test

Alternator output wire resistance test will show the amount of voltage drop across the alternator output wire between the alternator BAT terminal and the battery positive post.

1. Be sure the battery is fully charged.
2. Turn ignition switch **OFF**.
3. Disconnect the negative battery cable.
4. Disconnect the alternator output wire from the alternator output BAT terminal.
5. Connect a 0–150 ampere scale DC ammeter in series between alternator output BAT terminal and disconnected BAT terminal wire. Connect positive lead to alternator output BAT terminal and negative lead to disconnected alternator output BAT lead.
6. Connect positive lead of a test voltmeter (range 0–18 volts

minimum) disconnected alternator output wire. Connect negative lead of test voltmeter to battery positive cable at the positive post.

7. Remove the air hose between the engine controller and the air cleaner.
8. Connect an end of a jumper wire to ground and with other end, probe the green R-3 lead wire at the back of the alternator. This will generate a fault code. Do not connect blue J-2 lead of wiring to ground.
9. Connect an engine tachometer and reconnect negative battery cable.
10. Connect a variable carbon pile rheostat to the battery terminals. Be sure carbon pile is in **OPEN** or **OFF** position before connecting leads.
11. Start engine. Immediately after starting, reduce engine speed to idle.
12. Adjust engine speed and carbon pile to maintain 20 amperes flowing in circuit. Observe voltmeter reading. Voltmeter reading should not exceed 0.5 volts.

NOTE: If a higher voltage drop is indicated, inspect, clean and tighten all connections between the alternator BAT terminal and the battery positive post. A voltage drop test may be performed at each connection to locate connection with excessive resistance. If charging circuit resistance tested satisfactorily, reduce engine speed, turn OFF carbon pile and turn OFF ignition switch.

13. Disconnect negative battery cable.
14. Remove test ammeter, voltmeter, carbon pile and tachometer.
15. Remove jumper wire from the back of the alternator and ground.

Bosch 90 RS amp alternator—charging system resistance test—adjust engine speed and carbon pile to maintain 20 amps, voltmeter reading should not exceed 0.5 volts

Bosch 90 RS amp alternator—current output test— adjust engine speed and carbon pile increments until an engine speed of 1250 rpm is reached, voltmeter reading should not exceed 15 volts

16. Connect BAT lead to alternator output BAT terminal post.
17. Reconnect negative battery cable.
18. Reconnect single module engine controller and air cleaner.
19. Use the factory DRB II scan tool or its equivalent to erase fault codes.

Current Output Test

The current output test determines whether or not the alternator is capable of delivering its rated current output.
1. Be sure the battery is fully charged.
2. Disconnect negative battery cable.
3. Disconnect the BAT lead wire at the alternator output terminal.
4. Connect a 0–150 ampere scale DC ammeter in series between alternator output BAT terminal and negative lead to disconnected BAT terminal.
5. Connect positive lead of a test voltmeter (range 0–18 volts minimum) to alternator output BAT terminal.
6. Connect negative lead of test voltmeter to a good ground.
7. Connect an engine tachometer and reconnect negative battery cable.
8. Connect a variable carbon pile rheostat tool between battery terminals. Be sure carbon pile is in **OPEN** or **OFF** position before connecting leads.
9. Remove air hose between the single module engine controller and air cleaner.
10. Connect 1 end of a jumper wire to ground and with other end, probe the green wire R-3 terminal at the back of the alternator. This will generate a fault code. Do not the blue J-2 lead of the wiring to ground.

11. Start engine. Immediately after starting reduce engine speed to idle.
12. Adjust carbon pile and engine speed in increments until a speed of 1250 rpm and voltmeter reading of 15 volts is obtained. Do not allow voltage meter to read above 16 volts.
13. The ammeter reading must be within the proper limits (40–90 amps).
14. If reading is less than specified and alternator output wire resistance is not excessive, the alternator should be replaced.
15. After current output is completed reduce engine speed, turn **OFF** carbon pile and turn **OFF** ignition switch.
16. Disconnect negative battery cable.
17. Remove test ammeter, voltmeter, tachometer and carbon pile.
18. Remove jumper wire.
19. Connect BAT lead to alternator output BAT terminal post.
20. Reconnect negative battery cable.
21. Reconnect hose between the single module engine controller and air cleaner.
22. Use the factory DRB II scan tool or equivalent to erase the codes.

Operation of the On-Board Diagnostic System

The Engine Controller monitors critical input and output circuits of the charging system making sure they are okay. Some are checked continuously, and some are only checked under certain conditions.

If the on-board diagnostic system senses that one of the critical circuits is bad during a predetermined amount of time during the monitoring cycle, it will consider this a real problem and puts a fault code into memory. Each input and output circuit

CHRYSLER CHARGING SYSTEM DIAGNOSTIC CHART

IMPROPER CHARGING

- CHECK BATTERY CONDITION SEE BATTERY SECTION FOR DETAILS
- CORRODED BATTERY CABLES OR TERMINALS
- DRIVE BELTS LOOSE
- LOOSE OR CORRODED WIRING CONNECTIONS AT ALTERNATOR
- LOOSE OR CORRODED WIRING CONNECTIONS AT TERMINAL BLOCK
- LOOSE CHASSIS TO BATTERY GROUND CABLE
- LOOSE ALTERNATOR GROUND WIRE
- LOOSE OR CORRODED WIRING CONNECTIONS AT BULKHEAD DISCONNECT
- CHECK FOR APPROXIMATELY 12 VOLTS AT FIELD INPUT BRUSH TERMINAL WITH IGNITION SWITCH "ON"

UNSTEADY OR LOW CHARGING

- TEST ALTERNATOR OUTPUT WIRE RESISTANCE
- CHARGING RESISTANCE TOO HIGH
- CORRODED OR SHORTED CABLES OR HIGH RESISTANCE ACROSS FUSIBLE LINK
- RESISTANCE O.K.
- TEST ALTERNATOR CURRENT OUTPUT
- CURRENT OUTPUT O.K.
- REFER TO USING ON-BOARD DIAGNOSTIC SYSTEM
- FAULTY ALTERNATOR

OVER CHARGING

- GROUNDED ALTERNATOR FIELD WIRE, FIELD TERMINAL, OR CONNECTIONS
- REFER TO USING ON-BOARD DIAGNOSTIC SYSTEM
- FAULTY ALTERNATOR

NOISY ALTERNATOR

- WORN OR FRAYED DRIVE BELT
- ALTERNATOR MOUNTING LOOSE
- FAULTY ALTERNATOR

CHRYSLER ALTERNATOR FAULT CODE CHART

Fault Code	Type	Check Engine Lamp	Circuit	When Monitored By the Logic Module	When Put into Memory	Actuator Test	Sensor Read Test
41	Fault	Yes	Alternator Field Control (Charging System)	All the time when the ignition switch is on.	If the field control fails to switch properly or excessive alt. field current detected.	Yes	None
46	Fault	Yes	Charging System Voltage	All the time when the engine is running.	If the battery sense voltage is more than 1 volt above the desired control voltage for more than 20 seconds.	None	Yes
47	Fault	Yes	Charging System Voltage	Engine rpm above 1,500 rpm	Battery voltage sense input below desired charging voltage during engine operation and no change in voltage during internal SBEC test performed on alternator field.	None	Yes

monitored by the on-board diagnostic system has its own fault code. The fault code will stay in memory as long as the circuit continues to be bad. However, if the problem does not happen again after the fault code is put into memory, the engine controller is programmed to clear the memory after 50–100 engine starts.

Fault Codes

Fault codes are 2-digit numbers flashed by the Check Engine light that identify which circuit is bad. In most cases they do not identify which component in a circuit is bad. A fault description can be read using the factory DRB II tester or equivalent. A fault code is only a result, not necessarily the reason for the problem. However, in some cases, as a result of the design of the driveability test procedure, a fault code can be the reason for the problem. It is important that the test procedures be followed in order to understand what the fault codes of the on-board diagnostic system are trying to tell.

How To Use CHECK ENGINE Light for Fault Codes

To activate this function, cycle the ignition switch **ON–OFF–ON–OFF–ON** within 5 seconds and any fault stored in the engine controller will be displayed. The CHECK ENGINE light will display a fault code by flashing on and off. There is a short pause between flashes and a longer pause between digits. All codes displayed are 2-digit numbers with a 4 second pause between codes.

An example of a code is as follows:
1. Light ON for 2 seconds, then turns off.
2. Light flashes 4 times, pauses and then flashes 1 time.
3. Light pauses for 4 seconds, flashes 4 times, pauses, then flashes 7 times.

The 2 codes are 41 and 47. Any number of codes can be displayed up to a maximum of 8 faults, as long as they are in memory. The light will flash until all of the codes are displayed, including code 55 which means End Of Test.

Nippondenso Alternators

GENERAL INFORMATION

The voltage regulator is built into the Single Module Engine

Controller (SMEC) on all vehicles except some 1988 vehicles with the 90 amp alternator which use an external electronic voltage regulator. Vehicle application for these alternators in their various forms is Chrysler Corporation full size RWD pickups and vans, Dakota pickups and Caravan/Voyager mini-vans.

Before starting an alternator overhaul, check parts availability. In most cases, from 1990 and later, the factory considers alternators not serviceable and does not recommend overhaul, only replacement if defective.

OVERHAUL

Disassembly

1. Remove the B+ insulator nut and insulator. Remove the rear cover nuts and cover.
2. Remove the brush holder screws and the brush holder.
3. Remove the field block screws and the block.
4. Remove the rectifier and stator terminal screws and the rectifier.
5. Remove the stator terminal rubber insulators and the end shield through stud nuts.

Separating the end shields—Nippondenso 75, 90 and 120 amp alternators

Testing the inner brush continuity—Nippondenso 75, 90 and 120 amp alternators

Testing the outer brush continuity—Nippondenso 75, 90 and 120 amp alternators

Testing the field block R–3 terminal—Nippondenso 75, 90 and 120 amp alternators

Testing the field block J–2 terminal—Nippondenso 75, 90 and 120 amp alternators

Testing the field block R–3 to J–2 terminals—Nippondenso 75, 90 and 120 amp alternators

6. With the drive pulley facing downward, tap rectifier end shield upward and separate the 2 end shields.

7. Remove the drive pulley nut and the drive pulley.

NOTE: Do not handle the sliprings of the rotor with the bare hands for oil or grease may restrict contact.

8. Pull the rotor assembly from the drive end shield.

9. Using a wheel puller, press the rectifier end shield bearing from the rotor shaft.

NOTE: When removing the bearing, be careful not to damage the sliprings.

10. From the drive end shield, remove the bearing retainer screws and the retainer.

11. Using a socket and a light hammer, place the drive end shield on a work surface and tap the bearing from the shield.

Inspection

BRUSH HOLDER TESTS

1. Make sure the brushes move smoothly and return fully to the stops when released; if not, replace the brush holder assembly.

2. Using an ohmmeter, test inner brush-to-field terminals continuity; 1 field terminal should be open and the other closed. If not, replace the brush holder.

3. Using an ohmmeter, test outer brush-to-field terminals continuity; a field terminal should be open and the other closed. If not, replace the brush holder.

FIELD BLOCK TESTS

1. Using an ohmmeter, test the outer brush terminal to **R–3**

field terminal for continuity; the circuit should be closed. If not, replace the field block.

2. Using an ohmmeter, test the inner brush terminal to **J–2** field terminal for continuity; the circuit should be closed. If not, replace the field block.

3. Using an ohmmeter, test the **R–3** field terminal to the **J–2** terminal for continuity; the circuit should be open. If not, replace the field block.

4. Turn the field block over. Using an ohmmeter, test the radio suppression capacitor terminals for continuity; the circuit should be open. If not, replace the field block.

ROTOR TESTS

1. Check the field sliprings for excessive wear or roughness; fine emery cloth may be used to repair minor damage. If the rings are excessively damaged, replace the rotor.

2. Using an ohmmeter, test for continuity between the sliprings; the circuit should be closed. If not, replace the rotor.

3. Using an ohmmeter, test for continuity between the

Testing the field block radio capacitor—Nippondenso 75, 90 and 120 amp alternators

Testing the diodes—Nippondenso 75, 90 and 120 amp alternators

sliprings and the rotor shaft or core; the circuit should be open. If not, replace the rotor.

STATOR TESTS

1. Check the stator for signs damage—weak or broken leads, distorted frame or burned windings; if necessary, replace the stator.

NOTE: Scrape clean a portion of the stator frame to assure good electrical contact.

2. Using an ohmmeter, test for continuity between the stator leads and frame; the circuit should be open. If not, replace the stator.

3. Using an ohmmeter, test for continuity between the stator leads; the circuit should be closed. If not, replace the stator.

RECTIFIER TESTS

1. Inspect the rectifier assembly for poor solder joints, cracks, loose terminals or signs of overheating.

2. At each diode location, scrape a small area of the coating to assure good electrical contact while testing.

NOTE: Using an analog ohmmeter or a digital volt ohmmeter, perform the following tests.

3. Position the negative test probe on the stator terminal and the positive test probe on a negative diode; the resistance should be 7–11 ohms or 0.4–0.6 volts. Position the positive test probe on a positive diode; there should be no continuity. Perform this procedure on each terminal to diode set. If failure is detected, replace the rectifier.

4. Position the positive test probe on the stator terminal and

the negative test probe on a positive diode; the resistance should be 7–11 ohms or 0.4–0.6 volts. Position the negative test probe on a negative diode; there should be no continuity. Perform this procedure on each terminal to diode set. If failure is detected, replace the rectifier.

Assembly

1. Using a socket, slightly smaller than the bearing, tap the bearing into the drive end shield.

2. Install the bearing retainer in the drive end shield.

3. Using a shop press, press the rectifier end shield bearing onto the rotor shaft.

NOTE: When installing the bearing, be careful not to damage the sliprings.

4. Install the rotor assembly into the drive end shield.

5. Install the drive pulley and nut.

6. Using solvent, clean the sliprings on the rotor shaft.

7. Align the rectifier end shield and assemble it to the drive end shield.

8. Install the through stud nuts and the stator terminal insulators.

9. Position the rectifier and install the screws.

10. Position the field block and install the screws.

11. Retract the brushes into the brush holder, slide the assembly over the commutator rings and install the screws.

12. Install the rear cover and nuts.

13. Align the B+ insulator guide boss into the rear cover hole and install the nut.

Mitsubishi Alternator With Internal Regulator

GENERAL INFORMATION

This is a conventional alternator with a built-in electronic voltage regulator. It has been manufactured in a number of different amp ratings depending on the vehicle and options into which is installed.

The main components of the alternator are the rotor, stator, rectifiers, end shields, pulley, fan and capacitor. The electronic voltage regulator is very compact and is built into the rectifier end shield of the alternator. Chrysler application is Mitsubishi built import pickups such as Ram 50 and Ram Raider.

Before starting an alternator overhaul, check parts availability. In most cases, from 1990 and later, the factory considers alternators not serviceable and does not recommend overhaul, only replacement if defective.

Testing

CHARGING CIRCUIT RESISTANCE TEST

1. With the ignition switch in the **OFF** position, disconnect the negative battery cable and the output wire from the alternator battery cable.

2. Using a 0–100 amp DC ammeter, connect it in series between the alternator **BAT** terminal and the disconnected alternator output wire; connect the positive (+) wire to the alternator **BAT** terminal and the negative (−) wire to the disconnected alternator output wire.

3. Using a 0–18 volt voltmeter, connect its positive (+) lead to the disconnected alternator output wire and its negative (−) lead to the positive (+) battery post.

4. Install the tachometer to the engine.

5. Using a variable carbon pile rheostat, connect it between the battery posts; be sure the pile is in the **OPEN** or **OFF** position before connecting the leads.

6. Start the engine and allow it to idle.

Mitsubishi 75 and 90 amp alternators with internal voltage regulator—charging system resistance test—adjust engine speed and carbon pile to maintain 20 amps, voltmeter reading should not exceed 0.5 volts

7. Adjust the engine speed and the carbon pile to maintain 20 amps flowing in the circuit; the voltmeter should not exceed 0.5 volts.

8. If a higher voltage drop is indicated, clean and tighten the alternator output wire circuit connections.

9. If the resistance is satisfactory, reduce the engine speed, turn OFF the carbon pile and the ignition switch.

10. Remove the test equipment. Reconnect the alternator output wire and the negative battery cable.

VOLTAGE REGULATOR TEST

1. With the ignition switch in the OFF position, disconnect the positive cable from the battery and place a knife switch on the battery post and connect the cable to the knife switch.

2. Install the leads from an ammeter to the knife switch connectors and open the switch-to-battery current.

3. Connect the leads of a voltmeter between the L terminal of the alternator and a good ground.

4. The voltage reading should be 0 volts. Should voltage be present, a defective alternator or wiring is indicated.

5. If no voltage is present, turn the ignition switch ON position. The voltage present should be lower than battery voltage, by about 1 volt or less. If the voltage reading is higher or at battery voltage, a defective alternator is indicated.

6. Connect a tachometer to the engine and close the knife switch, mounted on the battery post. Start the engine. Do not apply any starting current through the ammeter when starting the engine. The ammeter can be ruined.

7. After the engine is operating, open the knife switch and increase the engine speed to approximately 2500 rpm and observe the ammeter reading.

8. If the ammeter reading is 10 amps or less, observe the voltage reading. This reading is the charging voltage.

NOTE: The charging voltage varies with the ambient temperature. It is necessary to measure the temperature of the air around the rear of the alternator and correct the charging voltage reading as required.

9. If the ammeter reading is more than 10 amps, continue to charge the battery until the reading falls under 10 amps or replace the battery with a fully charged one. An alternate method is to limit the charging circuit by connecting a ¼ ohm (25 watt) resistor in series with the battery.

10. Disconnect all test equipment, remove knife switch and reinstall the battery positive cable.

CURRENT OUTPUT TEST

The purpose of this test is to determine the capability of the alternator to deliver its rated current output.

1. With the ignition switch in the OFF position, disconnect the battery ground cable.

2. Disconnect the BAT lead wire from the terminal of the alternator.

3. Connect a 0–100 scaled ammeter in series, between the BAT terminal and the BAT lead wire.

4. Connect the positive lead of a voltmeter to the BAT terminal of the alternator and ground the negative lead.

5. Disconnect the green field wire (to voltage regulator) at the alternator.

6. Connect a tachometer to the engine and reconnect the negative battery cable.

7. Connect a carbon pile rheostat between the battery terminals. Be sure the carbon pile is in the OPEN or OFF position before connecting the leads.

8. Start the engine and operate at idle.

9. Adjust the carbon pile and accelerate the engine to the

specified speed and measure the output current. The current should be within specifications. Do not allow the voltage to increase over 16 volts.

10. The ammeter reading must be within the specified limits. If not the alternator should be removed and bench tested.

11. After the tests, disconnect the test equipment from the components.

OVERHAUL

Disassembly

1. Place the alternator in a vise or similar holding fixture, mark the body components and remove the through body bolts.

2. Pry between the stator and the drive end shield and carefully separate the drive end plate, the pulley and the rotor assembly from the stator and rectifier end shield assembly.

3. Carefully clamp the rotor and remove the pulley nut from the end of the shaft. Remove the pulley, the pulley fan, the pulley fan spacer and the alternator drive end shield from the rotor shaft.

4. The front bearing can be removed from the front drive housing by the removal of the dust seals, front and rear, the bearing retainer screws, the retainer, exposing the bearing so it can be tapped from the drive housing.

5. To remove the stator assembly. The 6 stator leads must be unsoldered from the rectifiers, as per the manufacturer's recommendation.

6. Remove the rectifiers from the stator end shield housing.

7. Remove the brush holder and regulator retaining screw.

8. Remove the BAT terminal retaining nut and remove the capacitor from the terminal.

9. Remove the regulator and rectifier assembly. Unsolder 1 rectifier-to-regulator assembly and remove the other rectifier assembly by sliding the battery stud out of the regulator.

View of the alternator terminals—Mitsubishi 75 and 90 amp alternators

10. Inspect the rotor bearing surface for scores and make the necessary off vehicle test on the electrical components.

Inspection

ROTOR ASSEMBLY

1. Check the outside circumference of the slipring for dirtiness and roughness. Clean or polish with fine sandpaper, if required. A badly roughened slipring or a slipring worn down beyond the service limit should be replaced.

Exploded view of the alternator assembly—Mitsubishi 75 and 90 amp alternators

Testing the rotor field coils—Mitsubishi 75 and 90 amp alternators

Testing the rotor for ground—Mitsubishi 75 and 90 amp alternators

Stator coil continuity test—Mitsubishi 75 and 90 amp alternators

Stator coil ground test—Mitsubishi 75 and 90 amp alternators

Testing the positive rectifiers—Mitsubishi 75 and 90 amp alternators

Testing the negative rectifiers—Mitsubishi 75 and 90 amp alternators

2. Check for continuity between the field coil and slipring. If there is no continuity, the field coil is defective. Replace the rotor assembly.

3. Check for continuity between the slipring and shaft (or core). If there is continuity, the coil or slipring is grounded. Replace the rotor assembly.

STATOR ASSEMBLY

Check for continuity between the leads of the stator coil. If there is no continuity the stator coil is defective. Replace the stator assembly.

Testing the rectifier trio—Mitsubishi 75 and 90 amp alternators

RECTIFIER ASSEMBLY

Positive (+) Heat Sink Assembly

Check for continuity between the positive (+) heat sink and stator coil lead connection terminal with a continuity tester. If there is continuity in both directions the diode is short circuited. Replace the rectifier assembly.

Negative (−) Heat Sink Assembly

Check for continuity between the negative (−) heat sink and stator coil lead connection terminal. If there is continuity in both directions the diode is short circuited. Replace the rectifier assembly.

RECTIFIER TRIO TEST

Using a circuit tester check the 3 diodes for continuity in both directions. If there is either continuity or an open circuit in both directions the diode is defective. Replace the rectifier assembly.

Assembly

1. The assembly of the alternator is the reverse of the removal procedure. Certain steps must be performed as the alternator is assembled.
2. Install the seals in the front and in the rear of the front bearing with the angled lip away from the bearing.
3. Push the brushes into the brush holder and insert a wire to hold them in the raised position. Install the rotor and remove the holding wire.

GENERAL MOTORS CORPORATION

SI Alternators

GENERAL INFORMATION

Delcotron alternators are available with different idle outputs and rated amp outputs.

All alternators incorporate a solid state voltage regulator which is mounted inside the alternator. The construction and operation of each alternator is basically the same. The Delcotron alternator consists of a forward and rear end frame assembly, a rotor, a stator, brushes, sliprings and diodes. The rotor is supported in the drive end frame by ball bearings and in the slipring end frame by roller bearings. The bearings do not require periodic lubrication.

There are 2 brushes which carry current through the sliprings to the field coil. The field coil is mounted on the rotor. The stator windings are assembled on the inside of a laminated core that is part of the alternator frame. The rectifier bridge which is connected to the stator windings contains 6 diodes, 3 of which are negative and 3 of which are positive. The positive and negative diodes are molded into the assembly. The rectifier bridge changes stator AC voltage into DC voltage which appears at the output BAT terminal.

The blocking action of the diodes prevents the battery from discharging, back through the alternator. The need for a cutout relay is eliminated because of this blocking action. The alternator field current is supplied through a diode trio, which is connected to the stator windings. A capacitor is mounted in the end frame to protect the rectifier bridge and the 6 diodes from high voltage and radio interference. Periodic alternator adjustment or maintenance is not required. The voltage regulator is preset and needs no adjustment.

TESTING

On Vehicle Service

INDICATOR LIGHT OPERATION TEST

1. Check the indicator light for normal operation. If the indi-

Typical Delcotron charging system wiring schematic

TROUBLESHOOTING GM INTERNAL REGULATOR ALTERNATORS

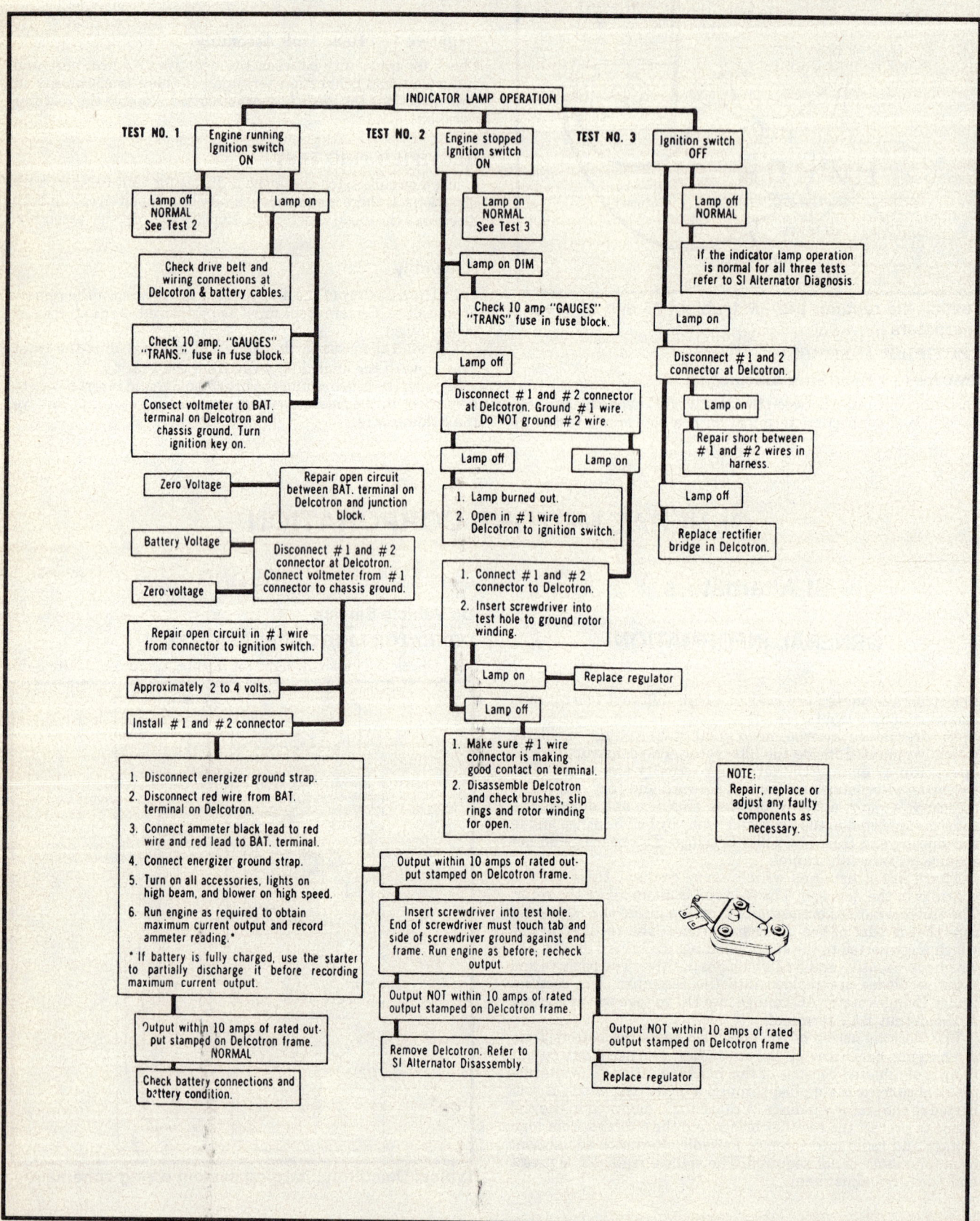

INDICATOR LAMP OPERATION

TEST NO. 1 — Engine running Ignition switch ON

Lamp off NORMAL See Test 2

Lamp on

Check drive belt and wiring connections at Delcotron & battery cables.

Check 10 amp. "GAUGES" "TRANS." fuse in fuse block.

Consect voltmeter to BAT. terminal on Delcotron and chassis ground. Turn ignition key on.

Zero Voltage → Repair open circuit between BAT. terminal on Delcotron and junction block.

Battery Voltage

Zero-voltage → Disconnect #1 and #2 connector at Delcotron. Connect voltmeter from #1 connector to chassis ground.

Repair open circuit in #1 wire from connector to ignition switch.

Approximately 2 to 4 volts.

Install #1 and #2 connector

1. Disconnect energizer ground strap.
2. Disconnect red wire from BAT. terminal on Delcotron.
3. Connect ammeter black lead to red wire and red lead to BAT. terminal.
4. Connect energizer ground strap.
5. Turn on all accessories, lights on high beam, and blower on high speed.
6. Run engine as required to obtain maximum current output and record ammeter reading.*

* If battery is fully charged, use the starter to partially discharge it before recording maximum current output.

Output within 10 amps of rated output stamped on Delcotron frame. NORMAL

Check battery connections and battery condition.

TEST NO. 2 — Engine stopped Ignition switch ON

Lamp on NORMAL See Test 3

Lamp on DIM

Check 10 amp "GAUGES" "TRANS" fuse in fuse block.

Lamp off

Disconnect #1 and #2 connector at Delcotron. Ground #1 wire. Do NOT ground #2 wire.

Lamp off

1. Lamp burned out.
2. Open in #1 wire from Delcotron to ignition switch.

Lamp on

1. Connect #1 and #2 connector to Delcotron.
2. Insert screwdriver into test hole to ground rotor winding.

Lamp on → Replace regulator

Lamp off

1. Make sure #1 wire connector is making good contact on terminal.
2. Disassemble Delcotron and check brushes, slip rings and rotor winding for open.

Output within 10 amps of rated output stamped on Delcotron frame.

Insert screwdriver into test hole. End of screwdriver must touch tab and side of screwdriver ground against end frame. Run engine as before; recheck output.

Output NOT within 10 amps of rated output stamped on Delcotron frame.

Remove Delcotron. Refer to SI Alternator Disassembly.

TEST NO. 3 — Ignition switch OFF

Lamp off NORMAL

If the indicator lamp operation is normal for all three tests refer to SI Alternator Diagnosis.

Lamp on

Disconnect #1 and 2 connector at Delcotron.

Lamp on

Repair short between #1 and #2 wires in harness.

Lamp off

Replace rectifier bridge in Delcotron.

NOTE:
Repair, replace or adjust any faulty components as necessary.

Output NOT within 10 amps of rated output stamped on Delcotron frame

Replace regulator

cator light operates properly, refer to the undercharged battery test. If the indicator light does not operate properly, proceed accordingly.

2. Switch **OFF**, light **ON**. Unplug the connector from the alternator No. 1 and No. 2 terminals. If the light stays **ON**, there is a short between these 2 leads. If the light goes out, replace the rectifier bridge.

3. Switch **ON**, light **OFF**, engine stopped. This condition can be caused by the defects listed above or by an open in the circuit. To determine where an open exists proceed as follows. Check for a blown fuse, or fusible link, a burned out bulb, defective bulb socket or an open in No. 1 lead circuit between alternator and ignition switch. If no defects have been found, proceed to undercharged battery test.

4. Switch **ON**, light **ON**, engine running. Check for a blown fuse, (where used), between indicator light and switch and also in air conditioning circuit.

UNDERCHARGED BATTERY TEST

1. Be sure the undercharged battery condition has not been caused by accessories that have been left **ON** for an extended period of time.

2. Check the alternator belt for proper belt tension. Inspect the battery for physical defects replace as required.

3. Inspect the wiring for defects. Check all connections for proper contact and cleanliness, including the slip connectors at the alternator and bulkhead connections.

4. With ignition switch **ON** and all wiring harness leads connected, connect a voltmeter from the alternator BAT terminal to ground, from the alternator No. 1 terminal to ground and from the alternator No. 2 terminal to ground. A zero reading indicates an open circuit between voltmeter connection and battery.

5. Delcotron alternators have a built in feature, which prevents overcharge and accessory damage by preventing the alternator from turning on if there is an open circuit in the wiring harness connected to the No. 2 alternator terminal.

6. If Steps 1–5 check out okay, check the alternator as follows. Disconnect negative battery cable. Connect an ammeter or alternator tester in the circuit at the BAT terminal of the alternator. Reconnect negative battery cable.

7. Turn **ON** radio, windshield wipers, lights high beam and blower motor on high speed. Connect a carbon pile across the battery (or use alternator tester). Operate engine about 2000 rpm and adjust carbon pile as required, to obtain maximum current output. If ampere output is within 10 amperes of rated output as stamped on alternator frame, alternator is not defective. Recheck Steps 1–5.

8. If ampere output is not within 10 percent of rated output, determine if test hole is accessible. Ground the field winding by inserting a suitable tool into the test hole. Tab is within ¾ in. of casting surface. Do not force suitable tool deeper than 1 in. into end frame to avoid damaging alternator.

9. Operate engine at moderate speed as required and adjust carbon pile as required to obtain maximum current output.

Delcotron Alternator Availability Chart

Alternator Type	Rated Amp Output
10SI	37, 42, 63
12SI	56, 66, 78, 94
15SI	70, 85
17SI	—
27SI	65, 80, 100

Delcotron alternator sizes

Delcotron alternator—showing location of components—typical

Delcotron alternator—voltage test

Testing Delcotron alternator stator—use an ohmmeter to check for opens or grounds

Bench test hook-up for testing the Delcotron alternator

10. If output is within 10 amperes of rated output, check field winding, diode trio and rectifier bridge. Test regulator with an approved regulator tester.

11. If output is not within 10 amperes of rated output, check the field winding, diode trio, rectifier bridge and stator. If test hole is not accessible, disassemble alternator and repair as required.

OVERCHARGED BATTERY TEST

1. Check the condition of the battery before any testing is done.

2. If an obvious overcharging condition exists, remove the alternator from the vehicle and check the field windings for grounds or shorts. If defective, replace the rotor. Test the regulator.

Alternator Diagnostic Tester (J–26290)

This special diagnostic tester is designed to determine if the alternator should be removed from the vehicle.

1. Install tester J–26290 according to manufacturers instructions.

2. With the engine **OFF** and all lights and accessories **OFF**, test the alternator as follows. Light flashes, go to Step 3. Light **ON**, indicates fault in tester which should be replaced. Light **OFF**, pull plug from alternator. One flashing light, indicates

Delcotron alternator—if test hole is accessible, ground the field winding by inserting a suitable tool into the test hole (max. of 1 in.)

Delcotron alternator—voltage regulator test (on vehicle) voltage regulator setting should be 13.5–16.0 volts

Delcotron alternator drive end bearing and related components

that the alternator should be removed and the rectifier bridge replaced. Light **OFF**, indicates faulty tester or no voltage to tester. Check for 12 volts at No. 2 terminal of harness connector. Repair wiring or terminals if 12 volts is not available. Replace tester if 12 volts is available.

3. With the engine at fast idle and all accessories and lights **OFF**, test the alternator as follows. Light **OFF** indicates that the charging system good, do not remove alternator. Light **ON** indicates a component failure within the alternator. Remove alternator and check diode trio, rectifier bridge and stator. Light flashing indicates a problem within the alternator. Remove alternator and check regulator, rotor field coil, brushes and sliprings.

Voltage Regulator Test

ALTERNATOR ON VEHICLE

1. Connect a battery charger and a voltmeter to the battery.

2. Turn the ignition **ON** and slowly increase the charge rate. The alternator light in the vehicle will dim at the voltage regula-

tor setting. Voltage regulator setting should be 13.5–16.0 volts. This test works if the rotor setting is good, even if the stator rectifier bridge or diode trio is bad.

ALTERNATOR OFF VEHICLE

1. Remove the alternator from the vehicle.
2. Disassemble the alternator and remove the voltage regulator.
3. Connect a voltmeter and a fast charger to a 12 volt battery. Connect a test light to the regulator and observe the battery polarity.
4. The test light should light.
5. Turn **ON** the fast charger and slowly increase the charge rate. Observe the voltmeter, the light should go out at the voltage regulator setting. The voltage regulator setting specification is 13.5–16.0 volts.

OVERHAUL

Disassembly

1. Remove the alternator from the vehicle. Position the assembly in a suitable holding fixture.
2. Make scribe marks on the alternator case end frames to aid in reassembly.
3. Remove the through bolts that retain the assembly together. Separate the drive end frame assembly from the rectifier end frame assembly.
4. Remove the rectifier attaching nuts and the regulator attaching screws from the end frame assembly.
5. Separate the stator, diode trio and voltage regulator from the end frame assembly.

1. Nut	16. Diode	25. Capacitor
2. Washer	17. Screw	26. Screw
3. Pulley	18. Washer	27. Screw
4. Fan	19. Terminal	28. Washer
5. Collar	20. Bridge	29. Brush
6. Frame	21. Spring	30. Regulator
7. Slinger	22. Frame	31. Seal
8. Bearing	23. Bolt	32. Bearing
9. Plate	24. Screw	33. Resistor
10. Collar		
11. Rotor		
12. Stator		
13. Screw		
14. Nut		
15. Washer		

Delcotron alternator—exploded view showing assembly sequence of components

Delcotron alternator end frame—showing location of related components

Delcotron alternator brush installation

Delcotron alternator—rotor test use an ohmmeter to check for opens or grounds

6. On the 10SI alternator, check the stator for opens using an ohmmeter. If high readings are obtained, replace the stator.
7. Check the stator for grounds using an ohmmeter. If readings are low, replace the stator.
8. Using an ohmmeter check the rotor for grounds. The ohmmeter reading should be very high. If not, replace the rotor.
9. Using an ohmmeter, check the rotor for opens. If the ohmmeter reading is not 2.4–3.5 ohms replace the rotor.
10. To check the diode trio connect the ohmmeter to the diode trio and then reverse the lead connections. The ohmmeter should read high and low if not replace the diode trio. Repeat the same test between the single connector and each of the other connectors.
11. Check rectifier bridge with ohmmeter connected from grounded heat sink to flat metal on terminal. Reverse leads. If both readings are the same replace rectifier bridge.
12. Repeat test between grounded heat sink and other 2 flat metal clips.

13. Repeat test between insulated heat sink and 3 flat metal clips.

14. Clean or replace the alternator brushes as required. Position the brushes in the brush holder and retain them in place using the brush retainer wire or equivalent.

15. To remove the rotor and drive end bearing, remove the shaft nut, washer and pulley, fan and collar. Push the rotor from the housing.

16. Remove the retainer plate from inside the drive end frame. Push the bearing out. Clean or replace parts as required.

Inspection

ALTERNATOR BENCH TEST

1. Remove the alternator from the vehicle. Position the unit in a suitable test stand.

2. Connect the alternator in series, but leave the carbon pile disconnected.

NOTE: Ground polarity of the battery must be the same as the alternator. Be sure to use a fully charged battery and a 10 ohm resistor rated at 6 watts or more between the alternator No. 1 terminal and the battery.

3. Increase the alternator speed slowly and observe the voltage.

4. If the voltage is uncontrolled with speed and increases above 15.5 volts, test regulator with an approved regulator tester and check field winding. If voltage is below 15.5 volts, connect the carbon pile.

5. Operate the alternator at moderate speed as required and adjust the carbon pile as required to obtain maximum current output.

6. If output is within 10 amperes of rated output as stamped on alternator frame, alternator is good. If output is not within 10 amperes of rated output, keep battery loaded with carbon pile and ground alternator field.

7. Operate alternator at moderate speed and adjust carbon pile as required to obtain maximum output. If output is within 10 amperes of rated output, test regulator with an approved regulator tester and check field winding.

8. If output is not within 10 amperes of rated output, check the field winding, diode trio, rectifier bridge and stator.

Assembly

1. Press against the outer bearing race to push the bearing in. On some alternators it will be necessary to fill the bearing cavity with lubricant. Other alternators use a sealed bearing and lubricant is not required for assembly.

2. Press rotor into end frame. Assemble collar, fan, pulley, washer and nut. Torque shaft nut 40–60 ft. lbs.

3. Push slipring end bearing out from outside toward inside of end frame.

4. On 10SI and 15SI, place flat plate over new bearing and press from outside toward inside until bearing is flush with end frame.

USE THINWALL TUBE TO PUSH BEARING FLUSH WITH HOUSING

Delcotron alternator rectifier end bearing installation

BRUSH HOLDER · REGULATOR · INSULATED HEAT SINK · GROUNDED HEAT SINK · INSULATING WASHER · OHMMETER

Testing Delcotron alternator rectifier bridge using an ohmmeter

OHMMETER · SINGLE CONNECTOR · 3 CONNECTORS

Testing Delcotron alternator diode trio using an ohmmeter

5. On 15SI alternators use the thin wall tube in the space between the grease cup and the housing to push the bearing in flush with the housing.

6. Assemble brush holder, regulator, resistor, diode trio, rectifier bridge and stator to slipring end frame.

7. Assemble end frames together with through bolts. Remove brush retainer wire.

CS Alternators

GENERAL INFORMATION

The alternator with internal regulator is designed for high amperage output per pound of weight. It does not use a diode trio. The delta stator, rectifier bridge and rotor with sliprings and brushes are electrically similar to other alternators. The CS stands for Charging System and the number of the alternator (130 or 144) indicates the outside diameter of the stator laminations in millimeters. The bearings are sealed with lifetime lubrication in both end frames. No periodic maintenance is required.

The voltage regulator setting varies with temperature and limits system voltage by controlling rotor field current. It switches rotor field current **ON** or **OFF** at a fixed frequency of about 400 cycles per second. By varying the **ON/OFF** time, correct average field current for proper system voltage control is obtained. At high speeds, the **ON** time may be 10 percent and the **OFF** time 90 percent. At low speeds, with high electrical loads, **ON/OFF** time may be 90 percent and 10 percent respectively.

Unlike 3 wire alternators, the 130 and 144 may be used with only 2 connections, the battery positive and an L terminal to the

Schematic of the Delcotron CS series charging system

Location of the components—CS-130 alternator

Cross-sectional view of the alternator drive end bearing assembly—Delcotron CS-130 alternator

Top: CS-130 alternator; Bottom: CS-144 alternator

charge indicator bulb. Use of P, F and S terminals is optional. The P terminal is connected to the stator and may be connected externally to a tachometer or other device. The F terminal is connected internally to field positive and may be used as a fault indicator. The S terminal may be connected externally to a voltage, such as battery voltage, to sense voltage to be controlled.

As on other charging systems, the charge indicator lights when the switch is closed and goes out when the engine is run-

A: CONNECT RESISTOR TO L TERMINAL

CARBON PILE
VOLTMETER
BATTERY
RESISTOR
A
PLIS BAT
ALTERNATOR
AMMETER

Test hookups for CS alternators

ning. If the charge indicator is **ON** with the engine running, a charging system defect is indicated. For all kinds of defects, the indicator will glow at full brilliance, not half lit. Also, the charge indicator will be **ON** with the engine running if system voltage

is too high or too low. The regulator voltage setting varies with temperature and limits system voltage by controlling rotor field current.

TESTING

On Vehicle Service

When operating normally, the indicator light will illuminate when the ignition switch is turned **ON** and go out when the engine starts. If the light operates abnormally or if an undercharged or overcharged battery condition occurs, the following procedure may be used to diagnose the charging system.

To diagnose the CS–130 and CS–144 charging systems, use the following procedure.

1. Visually check the belt and wiring.
2. For vehicles without charge indicator light, go to Step 5.
3. With switch **ON**, engine stopped, light should illuminate. If not, detach harness at alternator and ground **L** terminal. If the light turns ON, repair or replace the alternator. If the light does not turn ON, locate open circuit between grounding lead and ignition switch. Light may be open.
4. With switch **ON**, engine running at moderate speed, light should illuminate. If not, detach wiring harness at alternator. If the light goes off, replace or repair alternator. If the light stays on, check for grounded **L** terminal wire in harness.
5. Battery undercharged or overcharged. Detach wiring harness connector from alternator. With switch **ON**, engine not running, connect voltmeter from ground to **L** terminal. Zero reading indicates open circuit between terminal and battery. Correct as required. Reconnect harness connector to alternator, run engine at moderate speed. Measure voltage across battery. If above 16 volts, replace or repair alternator.
6. Turn **ON** accessories, load battery with carbon pile to obtain maximum amperage. Maintain voltage at 13 volts or above.

1. Nut	7. Drive end frame	13. Rotor	19. Brush spring
2. Washer	8. Drive end bearing	14. Regulator connector	20. Regulator
3. Pulley	9. Inside collar	15. Insulated screw	21. Rectifier bridge
4. Fan collar	10. Retainer	16. Capacitor	22. Sliping end bearing
5. Fan	11. Screw	17. Grounded screw	23. Sliping end frame
6. Outside collar	12. Stator	18. Brush holder	24. BAT terminal
			25. Through bolt

CS–144 alternator internal components

If within 15 amperes of rated output, alternator is okay. If not within 15 amperes of rated output, repair or replace the alternator.

Alternator Ouput—Bench Test

1. Place alternator in suitable test stand and hook up voltmeter and ammeter. Leave the carbon pile disconnected. The ground polarity of the alternator and battery must be the same. The battery must be fully charged. Use a 30–500 ohms resistor between the battery and the **L** terminal.
2. Slowly increase the alternator speed and observe the voltage.
3. If the voltage is uncontrolled and increases above 16 volts, the rotor field is shorted or grounded or the regulator is bad or both. A shorted or grounded rotor field coil can cause problems in the regulator.
4. If the voltage is below 16 volts, increase the speed and adjust the carbon pile to obtain maximum amperage output. Maintain voltage above 13 volts.
5. If the output is within 15 amps of the rated output, the alternator is okay. If the output is not within 15 amps of the rated output, repair or replace the alternator.

OVERHAUL

Disassembly and Assembly

Before starting alternator overhaul, check parts availability.

The CS–130 alternator is not considered serviceable and should be replaced as an assembly only. It should not be disassembled for any reason.

CS–144

1. Remove the alternator from the vehicle. Scribe marks on the end frames to facilitate assembly.
2. Remove the through bolts and separate the end frames.
3. Check the rotor for grounds using an ohmmeter. The reading should be infinite, if not, replace the rotor.
4. Check the rotor for shorts and opens. Replace the rotor as required.
5. Remove the attaching nuts and the stator from the end frame.
6. Check the stator for grounds using an ohmmeter. If the reading is low replace the stator.
7. Unsolder the connections, remove the retaining screws and connector from the end frame. Separate the regulator and the brush holder from the end frame.
8. Check the rectifier bridge using an ohmmeter. Replace as required. Check the heat sink, using an ohmmeter. Replace as required. Clean the brushes. Replace them as required.
9. To remove the rotor and drive end bearing, Hold the rotor using a hex wrench in the shaft end while removing the nut. Push the rotor from the housing. Remove the plate and push the bearing out.
10. Assembly is the reverse of the disassembly procedure. Repair or replace defective components as required.

FORD MOTOR COMPANY

GENERAL INFORMATION

Ford pickups and motorhome vehicles can be equipped with 1 of 2 types of alternator charging systems, internal regulator type alternator (IAR) or external voltage regulator type alternator (EVR).

The alternator charging system is a negative ground system consisting of an alternator, regulator, charge indicator (ammeter or voltmeter), storage battery, fuse link and associated wiring.

Motorhome vehicles use 1 or 2 maintenance free batteries depending on engine application. Vehicles equipped with the 7.5L and 5.8L engines use 1 battery, while vehicles equipped with 7.3L diesel engine require 2 batteries for additional cranking power.

When an auxiliary battery is used, it is connected in parallel with the main battery. When the ignition switch is in OFF, the auxiliary battery relay is de-energized, and the camper/trailer circuits are powered only from the auxiliary battery. The prevents discharging the main battery when camper or trailer is being used.

External Voltage Regulator Alternator (EVR)

GENERAL INFORMATION

The Ford charging system is a negative ground system. It includes an alternator, electronic regulator, a charge indicator or an ammeter and a storage battery.

TESTING

NOTE: If the current indicator is to give an accurate reading, the battery cables must be of the same gauge and length as the original equipment.

1. With the engine running and all electrical systems turned OFF, position a current indicator over the positive battery cable.
2. If a charge of about 5 amps is recorded, the charging system is working. If a draw of about 5 amps is recorded, the system is not working. The needle moves toward the battery when a charge condition is indicated and away from the battery when a draw condition is indicated. If a draw is indicated continue to the next testing procedure. If an overcharge of 10–15 amps is indicated check for a faulty regulator or a bad ground at the regulator or the alternator.

Ignition Switch to Regulator Circuit Test

1. Disconnect the regulator wiring harness from the regulator.
2. Turn ON the key. Using a test light or voltmeter check for voltage between the **I** wire and ground. Check for voltage between the **A** wire and ground. If voltage is present at this part of the system the circuit is OK. If there is no voltage at the **I** wire check for a burned out charge indicator bulb, a burned-out resistor, or a break or short in the wiring. If there is no voltage present at the **A** wire check for a faulty connection at the starter relay or a break or short in the wire.

Isolation Test

This test determines whether the regulator or the alternator is faulty after the rest of the circuit is found to be in good working order.

1. Disconnect the regulator wiring harness from the regulator.
2. Connect a jumper wire from the **A** wire to the **F** wire in the wiring harness plug.
3. Connect a voltmeter to the battery. The positive voltmeter lead goes to the positive terminal and the negative lead to the negative terminal. Record the reading on the voltmeter.
4. Turn OFF all of the electrical systems and start the engine. Do not race the engine.

Ford alternator with external regulator—rear terminal alternator charging system schematic with indicator light

Ford alternator with external regulator—rear terminal alternator charging system schematic with ammeter

TROUBLESHOOTING FORD ALTERNATORS

USE JUMPER WIRE TO CONNECT A AND
F TERMINALS AT REGULATOR PLUG

USE OF JUMPER WIRE AT REGULATOR
PLUG TO TEST ALTERNATOR FOR
NORMAL OUTPUT AMPS AND FOR FIELD
CIRCUIT WIRING CONTINUITY

**Using a jumper wire at the regulator plug to test the
alternator for normal output amps and for field circuit
wiring continuity—Ford alternator with external
regulator**

CONTACT STATOR SCREW

CONTACT EACH SCREW

STATOR WIRES
DISCONNECTED

**Testing diodes with stator wires connected—Ford
alternator with external regulator**

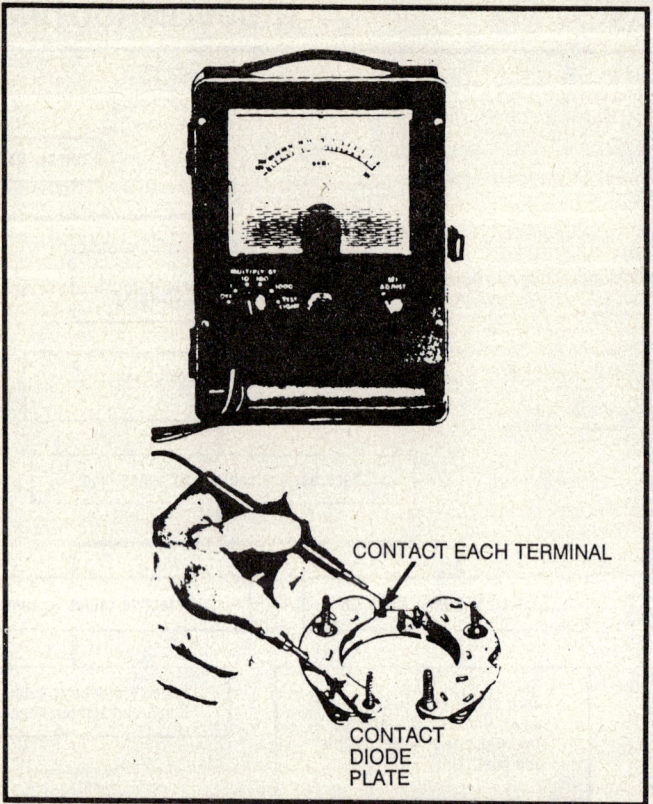

CONTACT EACH TERMINAL

CONTACT
DIODE
PLATE

**Testing diodes—Ford alternator with external
regulator**

5. Gradually increase engine speed 1500–2000 rpm. The voltmeter reading should increase above the previously recorded
battery voltage reading by at least 1–2 volts. If there is no increase the alternator is not working correctly. If there is an increase the voltage regulator needs to be replaced.

OVERHAUL

Disassembly

1. Matchmark both end housings for assembly.

REAR
BEARING

REAR
HOUSING

BRUSH TERMINAL
AND INSULATOR

BRUSHES

RECTIFIER ASSEMBLY

STATOR

ROTOR

STOPRING

BEARING
RETAINER

FRONT HOUSING

FAN

PULLEY

INSULATORS

BRUSH
SPRINGS

BRUSH HOLDER

BEARING
SPACER

FRONT BEARING

FAN SPACER

Exploded view of the rear terminal alternator used with an external voltage regulator

View of stator and rectifier assemblies and terminals—Ford alternator with external regulator

Rectifier assemblies and related components—Ford alternator with external regulator

2. Remove the housing through bolts.

3. Separate the front housing and rotor from the stator and rear housing.

4. Remove the nuts from the rectifier to rear housing mounting studs and remove rear housing.

5. Remove the brush holder mounting screws and the holder, brushes, springs, insulator and terminal.

6. If replacement is necessary press the bearing from the rear end housing while supporting the housing on the inner boss.

7. If rectifiers are to be replaced carefully unsolder the leads from the terminals. Use only a 100 watt soldering iron. Leave the soldering iron in contact with the diode terminals only long enough to remove the wires. Use pliers as temporary heat sinks in order to protect the diodes.

8. There are various types of rectifier assembly circuit boards installed in production. One type has the circuit board spaced away from the diode plates and the diodes are exposed. Another type consists of a single circuit board with integral diodes; and still another has integral diodes with an additional booster diode plate containing 2 diodes.

9. This last type is used only on the 8 diode (61 amp) alternator. To disassemble use the following procedures. Exposed diodes: Remove the screws from the rectifier by rotating bolt heads ¼ turn clockwise to unlock and unscrewing. Integral diodes: Press out the stator terminal screw, making sure not to twist it while doing this. Do not remove grounded screw. Booster diodes: Press out the stator terminal screw about ¼ in., remove the nut from the end of the screw and lift screw from circuit board. Be sure not to twist it as it comes out.

10. Remove the drive pulley and fan. On alternator pulleys with threaded holes in the outer end of the pulley use a standard puller for removal.

11. Remove the front bearing retainer screws and the front housing. If the bearing is to be replaced press it from the housing.

Brush Replacement

1. Remove the brush holder and cover assembly from the rear housing.

2. Remove the terminal bolts from the brush holder and cover assembly. Remove the brush assemblies.

3. Position the new brush terminals on the terminal bolts and assemble the terminals, bolts, brush holder washers and nuts. The insulating washer mounts under the **FLD** terminal nut. The entire brush and cover assembly also is available for service.

4. Depress the brush springs in the brush holder cavities and insert the brushes on top of the springs. Hold the brushes in position by inserting a stiff wire in the brush holder. Position the brush leads properly.

5. Install the brush holder and cover assembly into the rear housing. Remove the brush retracting wire and put a dab of silicone cement over the hole.

Inspection

1. The rotor, stator, diode rectifier assemblies and bearings are not to be cleaned with solvent. These parts are to be wiped off with a clean cloth. Cleaning solvent may cause damage to the electrical parts or contaminate the bearing internal lubricant. Wash all other parts in solvent and dry them.

2. Rotate the front bearing on the driveshaft. Check for any scraping noise, looseness or roughness that indicates that the bearing is excessively worn. As the bearing is being rotated look for excessive lubricant leakage. If any of these conditions exist replace the bearing. Check rear bearing and rotor shaft.

3. Place the rear end housing on the slipring end of the shaft and rotate the bearing on the shaft. Make a similar check for noise, looseness or roughness. Inspect the rollers and cage for damage. Replace the bearing if these conditions exist or if the lubricant is missing or contaminated.

4. Check both the front and rear housings for cracks.

5. Check all wire leads on both the stator and rotor assemblies for loose soldered connections and for burned insulation. Solder all poor connections. Replace parts that show burned insulation.

6. Check the sliprings for damaged insulation and runout. If the sliprings are more than 0.005 in. out of round, take a light cut (minimum diameter limit 1.220 in.) from the face of the rings to true them. If the sliprings are badly damaged the entire rotor will have to be replaced as an assembly.

7. Replace any parts that are burned or cracked. Replace brushes that are worn to less than $\frac{5}{16}$ in. in length. Replace the brush spring if it has less than 7–12 oz. tension.

FIELD CURRENT DRAW TEST

1. Remove the alternator from the vehicle. Connect a test ammeter between the alternator frame and the positive post of a 12 volt test battery.

2. Connect a jumper wire between the negative test battery post and the alternator field terminal.

3. Observe the ammeter. Little or no current flow indicates high brush resistance, open field windings, or high winding resistance. Current in excess of specifications (approximately 2.9 amps for most models) indicates shorted or grounded field windings, or brush leads touching.

NOTE: The alternator, may produce current output at low engine speeds, but cease to produce current at higher speeds. This can be caused by centrifugal force expanding the rotor windings to the point where they short to ground. Place in a test stand and check field current draw while spinning alternator.

DIODE TESTS

Disassemble the alternator. Disconnect diode assembly from stator and make tests. To test one set of diodes contact 1 ohmmeter probe to the diode plate and contact each of the 3 stator lead terminals with the other probe. Reverse the probes and repeat the test. All 6 tests (8 for 61 amp 8-diode models) should show a reading of about 60 ohms in one direction and infinite ohms in the other. If 2 high readings or 2 low readings are obtained after reversing probes, the diode is faulty and must be replaced.

STATOR TESTS

Disassemble the stator from the alternator assembly and rectifiers. Connect test ohmmeter probes between each pair of stator leads. If the ohmmeter does not indicate equally between each pair of leads the stator coil is open and must be replaced.

Connect test ohmmeter probes between one of the stator leads and the stator core. The ohmmeter should not show any reading. If it does show continuity the stator winding is grounded and must be replaced.

Assembly

1. Press the front bearing into the front housing boss by putting pressure on outer race only. Install bearing retainer.

2. If the stop ring on the driveshaft was damaged install a new stop ring. Push the new ring onto the shaft and into the groove.

3. Position the front bearing spacer on the driveshaft against the stop ring.

4. Place the front housing over the shaft with the bearing positioned in the front housing cavity.

5. Install fan spacer, fan, pulley, lockwasher and retaining nut and tighten nut 60–100 ft. lbs. while holding the shaft with an Allen key.

6. If rear bearing was removed, press a new one into rear housing.

7. Assemble brushes, springs, terminal and insulator in the brush holder, retract the brushes and insert a short length of ⅛ in. rod or stiff wire through the hole in the holder to hold the brushes in the retracted position.

8. Position the brush holder assembly in the rear housing and install mounting screws. Position brush leads to prevent shorting.

9. Wrap the 3 stator winding leads around the circuit board terminals and solder them using only rosin core solder and a solder iron. Position the stator neutral lead eyelet on the stator terminal screw and install the screw in the rectifier assembly.

10. Exposed diodes, insert the special screws through the wire lug, dished washers and circuit board. Turn ¼ turn counterclockwise to lock in place. Integral diodes, insert the screws straight through the holes.

NOTE: The dished washers are to be used on the molded circuit boards only. Using these washers on a fiber board will result in a serious short circuit, as only a flat insulating washer between the stator terminal and the board is used on fiber circuit boards.

11. Booster diodes, position the stator wire terminal on the stator terminal screw, then position screw on rectifier. Position square insulator over the screw and into the square hole in the rectifier, rotate terminal screw until it locks, then press it in fingertight. Position the stator wire, then press the terminal screw into the rectifier and insulator with a vise.

12. Place the radio noise suppression condenser on the rectifier terminals. With molded circuit board and install the STA and BAT terminal insulators. With fiber circuit board place the square stator terminal insulator in the square hole in the rectifier assembly, then position BAT terminal insulator.

13. Position the stator and rectifier assembly in the rear housing, making sure all terminal insulators are seated properly in the recesses. Position STA, BAT and FLD insulators on terminal bolts and install the nuts.

14. Clean the rear bearing surface of the rotor shaft with a rag and then position rear housing and stator assembly over rotor. Align matchmarks made during disassembly and install the through bolts. Remove brush retracting wire and place a dab of silicone sealer over the hole.

Internal Alternator/Regulator (IAR)

GENERAL INFORMATION

The Ford alternator with internal regulator is manufactured by Motorcraft division of the Ford Motor Company. The field current is supplied from the alternator regulator which is mounted on the rear of the alternator, to the rotating field of the alternator through 2 brushes and 2 sliprings.

The alternator produces power in the form of alternating current. The alternating current is rectified to direct current by 6 diodes. The alternator regulator automatically adjusts the alternator field current to maintain the alternator output voltage within prescribed limits to correctly charge the battery. The alternator is self current limiting.

The regulator voltage control circuit is turned on when the ignition switch is **ON** and voltage is applied to the regulator **I** terminal through a resistor in the **I** circuit. When the ignition switch is **OFF** the control circuit is turned off and no field current flows to the alternator.

On warning light equipped vehicles, the warning light is connected across the terminals of a 500 ohm resistor at the instrument cluster. Current passes through the warning light when the ignition switch is in the **RUN** position and there is no voltage at terminal **S**. When voltage at **S** rises to a preset value the regulator switching circuits stop the flow of current into terminal **I** and the light turns off.

System voltage is sensed and alternator field current is drawn through terminal **A**. The regulator switching circuits will turn the warning light on, indicating a system fault, if terminal **A** voltage is excessively high or low or if the terminal **S** voltage signal is abnormal. A fusible link is included in the charging system wiring on all models. The fusible link is used to prevent damage to the wiring harness and alternator if the wiring harness should become grounded, or if a booster battery is connected to the charging system with the wrong polarity.

TESTING

ON VEHICLE TESTING

NOTE: The following diagnostic tests are made with the alternator installed in the vehicle. Be sure the battery is fully charged before any testing is done.

Battery Voltage Test

1. Connect a voltmeter to the positive and negative battery terminals.
2. Record the battery voltage. If battery voltage is not within specification, correct as required.

Load Test

1. Be sure the battery is fully charged before performing this test.
2. Connect the tachometer to the engine.
3. Start the engine. Turn the heater/air condition switch to the **HIGH** blower position. Turn **ON** the headlights with the high beams. Increase engine speed to 2000 rpm.
4. Voltmeter should indicate a minimum of a 0.5 volt increase over battery voltage.
5. If the system is working the above readings will be obtained. Be sure not to ground the A terminal of the voltage regulator.

No Load Test

1. Be sure the battery is fully charged before performing this test.
2. Connect a tachometer to the engine. Start the engine and increase the engine speed to 1500 rpm with no electrical load.
3. The voltmeter reading should be taken when the voltmeter

Schematic of the charging system—Ford alternator with internal regulator

needle stops moving. The voltmeter reading should be 1–2 volts above the voltage of the battery.

4. If the voltage increased properly proceed with another test.

High Voltage Test

1. Be sure the battery is fully charged before performing this test.

2. Turn the ignition switch to the **ON** position. Connect the voltmeter negative lead to the rear of the alternator housing.

3. Connect voltmeter positive lead to alternator output terminal and record voltage. Connect voltmeter positive lead to the A terminal of regulator. Compare voltage difference recorded at alternator output terminal.

4. If voltage difference is greater than 0.5 volt, repair or replace wiring circuit to A terminal.

5. If high voltage condition still exists check ground connections at regulator to alternator, alternator to engine, firewall to engine and engine to battery.

6. If high voltage condition still exists connect voltmeter negative lead to rear of alternator housing. With ignition to **OFF** position connect voltmeter positive lead to **A** terminal of regulator and record reading. Connect voltmeter positive lead to **F** terminal of regulator.

7. Check if different voltage is present at **A** and **F** terminals. Different voltage readings indicate a defective regulator, grounded brush leads or grounded rotor coil.

8. If same voltage is present at both terminals and circuits tested in previous steps are good replace the regulator.

Low Voltage Test

1. Be sure the battery is fully charged before performing this test.

2. Disconnect the wiring plug from the voltage regulator and install the ohmmeter between terminals **A** and **F**.

3. The ohmmeter reading should indicate more than 2.2 ohms. If the reading is less than 2.2 ohms, replace the voltage regulator and check the alternator for a shorted rotor or open field circuit. Repeat the load test. Do not replace the voltage regulator before a shorted rotor coil or field circuit has been determined not to be the problem. If not, damage to the new regulator could occur.

4. If the field circuit is okay, more than 2.2 ohms, reconnect the voltage regulator wiring plug and connect the voltmeter negative lead to the rear of the alternator. Connect the positive lead of the voltmeter to terminal **A** of the voltage regulator. Battery voltage should be present, if so go on. If not, repair wiring in circuit **A**.

5. With the ignition switch in the **OFF** position connect the positive lead of the voltmeter to the **F** terminal of the voltage regulator.

6. If battery voltage is present, go on. If not, replace the voltage regulator. Repeat the load test.

7. Turn the ignition switch to the **ON** position. The voltmeter should indicate 1.5 volts or less. If the reading is more than 1.5 volts, perform the regulator **I** circuit test. Replace the voltage regulator if required. Repeat the load test.

8. If the voltmeter reading is 1.5 volts or less, disconnect the alternator wiring plug and connect a 12 gauge jumper wire between the alternator plug terminal and the wiring harness connector.

9. Connect the positive lead of the voltmeter to 1 of the **B** terminals. Repeat the load test.

10. If the reading is 0.5 volt above battery voltage, repair the wiring harness from the alternator to the starter relay.

11. If the voltmeter reading is less than 0.5 volt above battery voltage, connect a jumper wire from the rear of the alternator housing to terminal **F** of the voltage regulator.

12. Repeat the load test. If the voltmeter reading is more than 0.5 volt, replace the voltage regulator. If the reading is less than 0.5 volt, repair the alternator.

Voltage Regulator Circuit I Test

1. Disconnect the voltage regulator wiring plug harness.

2. Connect the voltmeter negative lead to the battery ground. Connect the voltmeter positive lead to the harness side of terminal **I**.

3. With the ignition switch in the **OFF** position, voltage should not be present. If voltage is present repair the circuit as necessary.

4. With the ignition switch in the **ON** position, battery voltage should be present. If voltage is not present, check the wiring for an open or grounded circuit. Repair as required.

5. If the voltage readings are within specification, check the resistance of the **I** circuit resistor. If equipped with an indicator light the resistance is 500 ohms. If equipped with a gauge, the resistance is 300 ohms. If the specification obtained is not within ± 50 ohms, replace the resistor. Repeat the load test.

6. Disconnect the voltage regulator wiring plug and remove the indicator light bulb, if equipped, before performing this test.

Field Circuit Drain Test

1. Connect the negative lead of the voltmeter to the rear of the alternator housing. Turn the ignition switch to the **OFF** position. Connect the positive lead of the voltmeter to the **F** terminal of the voltage regulator.

2. Battery voltage should be present. If no voltage is present, proceed.

3. If voltage is less than battery voltage, check **I** circuit. Dis-

Ford alternator with internal regulator rear housing and related components.

View of the voltage regulator and brush holder—Ford alternator with internal regulator

Exploded view of the Ford alternator with internal regulator

connect regulator wiring harness. Connect voltmeter positive lead to **S** terminal of wiring plug. If voltage is present, proceed to Step 4. If no voltage is present replace regulator.

4. Disconnect wiring plug from alternator. Check **S** terminal for voltage. If no voltage is present, replace alternator rectifier assembly. If voltage is still present, replace or repair wiring between alternator and regulator plugs.

OVERHAUL

Disassembly and Assembly

1. Remove the alternator from the vehicle. Position the unit in a suitable holding fixture.

2. Remove the voltage regulator and the brush holder from the rear of the alternator assembly.

3. Remove the brush holder-to-voltage regulator screws and separate the components.

4. Matchmark the alternator end housings and stator frame to aid in installation.

5. Remove the alternator through bolts. Separate the front housing and the rotor assembly from the stator and the rear housing.

6. Unsolder the 3 stator leads from the rectifier assembly. Be careful that the rectifiers are not in contact with the solder iron, overheating them will cause damage.

7. Remove the rectifier assembly from the rear of the alternator housing. Press the rear alternator housing bearing from the rear housing.

8. From the front housing of the alternator remove the drive pulley nut from the rotor shaft.

9. Remove the lockwasher, drive pulley, fan and fan spacer from the rotor shaft.

10. Remove the rotor from the front housing. Remove the front bearing spacer from the rotor shaft. Do not remove the rotor stop ring unless it must be replaced.

11. Remove the front housing bearing retainer and bearing.

12. Assembly of the alternator is the reverse of the disassembly procedure. Be sure to clean and check all parts for wear and defects. Repair or replace defective components as required.

Inspection

NOTE: In performing the following tests, digital meters cannot be used.

STATOR GROUND TEST

1. Using an ohmmeter connect 1 test lead to the **B** terminal and the other test lead to the **S** terminal.

2. Reverse the test leads and repeat the test. The ohmmeter should read about 6.5 ohms in 1 direction and infinity when the test probes are reversed.

3. A reading in both directions indicates a faulty positive diode or a shorted radio suppression capacitor.

4. Perform the same test using the **S** terminal and the alternator rear housing.

5. Readings in both directions indicate a faulty negative di-

Stator coil open test, using an ohmmeter. If meter does not respond, an open is present and the stator should be replaced—Ford alternator with internal regulator

ode, grounded stator winding, grounded stator terminal or a shorted radio suppression capacitor.

6. If the ohmmeter needle does not move in 1 direction or high resistance in the other direction exists, there is an open circuit in the rectifier assembly. Correct the problem as required.

FIELD OPEN OR SHORT CIRCUIT TEST

1. Using an ohmmeter connect 1 test lead to terminal **A** on the voltage regulator. Connect the other test lead to terminal **F** of the voltage regulator. Spin the alternator pulley. Reverse the ohmmeter connections and repeat the test.

2. In one test the ohmmeter should read between 2.2–100 ohms. The reading may fluctuate while the pulley is spinning.

3. In the other test the ohmmeter should read between 2.2–9 ohms.

4. An infinite reading in one test and a 9 ohm reading in the other test indicates an open brush lead, worn or stuck brushes, faulty rotor assembly or loose voltage regulator to brush holder retaining screws.

5. A reading of less than 2.2 ohms in both tests indicates a shorted rotor or a faulty voltage regulator.

6. A reading greater than 9 ohms in both tests indicates a defective voltage regulator or a loose **F** terminal screw.

7. Connect 1 ohmmeter test lead to the rear of the alternator. Connect the other test lead to terminal **A** of the voltage regulator and then to terminal **F** of the voltage regulator. The ohmmeter should read infinity at both points.

8. A test reading of less than infinity at both points indicates a grounded brush lead, grounded rotor or a faulty voltage regulator.

RECTIFIER ASSEMBLY TEST

1. Remove rectifier assembly from alternator. To test the

positive set of diodes contact 1 ohmmeter test lead to **B** terminal and contact each of 3 stator lead terminals with other test lead.

2. Reverse the test leads and repeat test. All diodes should show readings of approximately 6.5 ohms in 1 direction and infinite readings with probes reversed.

3. Repeat test for negative set of diodes by connecting a test lead to rectifier assembly base plate and to other 3 terminals. If meter readings are not as specified replace rectifier assembly.

RADIO SUPPRESSION CAPACITOR TEST

NOTE: This is an open or shorted circuit test only and does not measure capacitance value.

1. Contact the ohmmeter test leads to the **B** terminal and the rectifier base plate assembly. Reverse the test leads while observing the indicator needle.

2. If the needle jumps momentarily and then returns to previous position, capacitor is okay. If needle does not jump replace rectifier assembly. Radio suppression capacitor must be replaced as a complete rectifier assembly.

STATOR COIL GROUND TEST

1. Remove the stator from the alternator.

2. Using an ohmmeter connect a test lead to a stator lead and the other test lead to the stator laminated core. The reading should be infinity.

3. If the meter needle moves then the stator winding is shorted to the core. Replace the stator. Repeat this test for each stator lead.

NOTE: Do not touch the metal test leads or the stator leads, an incorrect test reading will result.

STATOR COIL OPEN TEST

1. Disconnect the stator from the rectifier assembly.

2. Using an ohmmeter, connect a test lead to a stator lead and the other test lead to another stator lead.

3. If the meter does not respond, an open circuit is present and the stator should be replaced. Repeat the test with the other wire combinations. A single open phase cannot be detected on alternators using a delta connected stator.

ROTOR OPEN OR SHORT CIRCUIT TEST

1. Remove the rotor assembly from the alternator.

2. Using an ohmmeter contact each test lead to a rotor slipring. The ohmmeter should read 2.0–3.9 ohms.

3. If the readings are higher than specification it would indicate a damaged slipring solder connection or a broken wire.

4. If the readings are lower than specification it would indicate a shorted wire or slipring.

5. Replace the rotor if it is damaged. Connect an test lead of the ohmmeter to a rotor slipring and the other test lead to the rotor shaft.

6. The ohmmeter reading should be infinity. If this is not the case, the rotor is shorted to the shaft. Replace the rotor if the unit is shorted.

JEEP

Delco SI–Series

GENERAL INFORMATION

The charging system is an integrated AC generating system containing a built in voltage regulator. The regulator is mounted in-

side the slipring end frame. All regulator components are enclosed in an epoxy molding and the regulator cannot be adjusted.

TESTING

INDICATOR LIGHT OPERATION TEST

1. Check the indicator light for normal operation. If the indi-

Schematic of the Delcotron charging system—Jeep

Cross-sectional view of the Delcotron alternator—Jeep

cator light operates properly, refer to the undercharged battery test. If the indicator light does not operate properly, proceed with the following tests.

2. Switch **OFF**, light **ON**. Unplug the connector from the alternator No. 1 and No. 2 terminals. If the light stays **ON**, there is a short between these 2 leads. If the light goes out, replace the rectifier bridge.

3. Switch **ON**, light **OFF**, engine stopped. This condition can be caused by the defects listed above or by an open in the circuit. To determine where an open exists, proceed as follows. Check for a blown fuse or fusible link, a burned out bulb, defective bulb socket or an open in No. 1 lead circuit between alternator and ignition switch. If no defects have been found, proceed to undercharged battery test.

4. Switch **ON**, light **ON**, engine running. Check for a blown fuse, (where used), between indicator light, ignition switch and also in air conditioning circuit.

UNDERCHARGED BATTERY TEST

1. Be sure the undercharged battery condition has not been

caused by accessories that have been left **ON** for an extended period of time.

2. Check the alternator belt for proper belt tension. Inspect the battery for physical defects. Replace as required.

3. Inspect the wiring for defects. Check all connections for proper contact and cleanliness, including the slip connectors at the alternator and bulkhead connections.

4. With ignition switch **ON** and all wiring harness leads connected, connect a voltmeter from the alternator BAT terminal-to-ground, from the alternator No. 1 terminal-to-ground and from the alternator No. 2 terminal-to-ground. A zero reading indicates an open between voltmeter connection and battery.

5. Delcotron alternators have a built in feature which prevents overcharge and accessory damage by preventing the alternator from turning **ON** if there is an open in the wiring harness connected to the No. 2 alternator terminal.

6. If Steps 1 through 5 check out, inspect the alternator as follows. Disconnect negative battery cable. Connect an ammeter or alternator tester in the circuit at the **BAT** terminal of the alternator. Reconnect negative battery cable.

7. Turn **ON** radio, windshield wipers, lights (high beam) and blower motor on **HIGH** speed. Connect a carbon pile across the battery (or use alternator tester). Operate engine about 2000 rpm and adjust carbon pile as required, to obtain maximum current output. If ampere output is within 10 amperes of rated output as stamped on alternator frame, alternator is not defective. Recheck Steps 1 through 5.

8. If ampere output is not within 10 percent of rated output, determine if test hole is accessible. Ground the field winding by inserting a suitable tool into the test hole. Tab is within ¾ inch of casting surface. Do not force suitable tool deeper than an 1 inch into end frame to avoid damaging alternator.

9. Operate engine at moderate speed as required and adjust carbon pile as required to obtain maximum current output.

10. If output is within 10 amperes of rated output, check field winding, diode trio and rectifier bridge. Test regulator with an approved regulator tested.

11. If output is not within 10 amperes of rated output, check the field winding, diode trio, rectifier bridge and stator. If test hole is not accessible, disassemble alternator and repair as required.

OVERCHARGED BATTERY TEST

1. Check the condition of the battery before any testing is done.

2. If an obvious overcharging condition exists, remove the alternator from the vehicle and check the field windings for grounds or shorts. If defective, replace the rotor. Test the regulator.

Delcotron alternator diagnostic tester (J–26290). Use tester according to manufacturers instructions

Testing the voltage regulator—Delcotron alternator—Jeep

Voltage regulator test (on vehicle) voltage regulator setting should be 13.5–16.0 volts—Delcotron alternator—Jeep

ALTERNATOR DIAGNOSTIC TESTER (J-26290)

This special diagnostic tester is designed to determine if the alternator should be removed from the vehicle.

1. Install tester J-26290 according to manufacturer's instructions.
2. With the engine **OFF** and all lights and accessories **OFF**, test the alternator as follows. Light flashes, go to Step 3. Light **ON**, indicates fault in tester which should be replaced. Light **OFF**, pull plug from alternator. A flashing light, indicates the alternator should be removed and the rectifier bridge replaced. Light **OFF**, indicates faulty tester or no voltage to tester. Check for 12 volts at No. 2 terminal of harness connector. Repair wiring or terminals if 12 volts is not available. Replace tester if 12 volts is available.
3. With the engine at fast idle and all accessories and lights **OFF**, test the alternator as follows. Light **OFF** indicates the charging system good, do not remove alternator. Light **ON** indicates a component failure within the alternator. Remove alternator and check diode trio, rectifier bridge and stator. Light flashing indicates a problem within the alternator. Remove alternator and check regulator, rotor field coil, brushes and sliprings.

VOLTAGE REGULATOR TEST (ALTERNATOR ON VEHICLE)

1. Connect a battery charger and a voltmeter to the battery.
2. Turn the ignition switch **ON** and slowly increase the charge rate. The alternator light in the vehicle will dim at the voltage regulator setting. Voltage regulator setting should be 13.5–16.0 volts. This test is performed to determine if the voltage regulator setting is within specifications. This test is accurate even if the stator rectifier bridge or diode trio is faulty.

VOLTAGE REGULATOR TEST (ALTERNATOR OFF VEHICLE)

1. Remove the alternator from the vehicle.
2. Disassemble the alternator and remove the voltage regualtor.
3. Connect a voltmeter and a fast charger to a 12 volt battery. Connect a test light to the regulator and observe the battery polarity.
4. The test light should light.
5. Turn **ON** the fast charger and slowly increase the charge rate. Observe the voltmeter, the light should go out at the voltage regulator setting. The voltage regulator setting specification is 13.5–16.0 volts.

ALTERNATOR BENCH TEST

1. Remove the alternator from the vehicle. Position the unit in a suitable test stand.
2. Connect the alternator in series but leave the carbon pile disconnected.

NOTE: Ground polarity of the battery must be the same as the alternator. Be sure to use a fully charged battery and a 10 ohm resistor rated at 6 watts or more between the alternator No. 1 terminal and the battery.

3. Increase the alternator speed slowly and observe the voltage.
4. If the voltage is uncontrolled with speed and increases above 15.5 volts on a 12 volt system or 31 volts on a 24 volt system, test regulator with an approved regulator tester and check field winding. If voltage is below 15.5 volts on a 12 volt system or 31 volts on a 24 volt system, connect the carbon pile.
5. Operate the alternator at moderate speed as required and adjust the carbon pile as required to obtain maximum current output.
6. If output is within 10 amperes of rated output as stamped on alternator frame, alternator is good. If output is not within 10 amperes of rated output, keep battery loaded with carbon pile and ground alternator field.
7. Operate alternator at moderate speed and adjust carbon

Bench test hook-up for testing—Delcotron alternator—Jeep

1. Rotor
2. Front bearing retainer plate
3. Inner collar
4. Bearing
5. Front housing
6. Inner collar
7. Fan
8. Pulley
9. Lockwasher
10. Pulley nut
11. Terminal assembly
12. Bridge rectifier
13. Regulator
14. Brush assembly
15. Screw
16. Stator
17. Insulating washer
18. Capacitor
19. Diode trio
20. Rear housing
21. Through bolt
22. Bearing and seal assembly

Exploded view of Delcotron alternator—Jeep

pile as required to obtain maximum output. If output is within 10 amperes of rated output, test regulator with an approved regulator tester and check field winding.

8. If output is not within 10 amperes of rated output, check the field winding, diode trio, rectifier bridge and stator.

OVERHAUL

Disassembly and Assembly

1. Remove the alternator from the vehicle. Position the assembly in a suitable holding fixture.

2. Make scribe marks on the alternator case end frames to aid in reassembly.

3. Remove the assembly through bolts and separate the drive end frame assembly from the rectifier end frame assembly.

4. Remove the rectifier nuts and the regulator screws from the end frame assembly.

5. Separate the stator, diode trio and voltage regulator from the end frame assembly.

6. Check the stator for opens using an ohmmeter. If high readings are obtained, replace the stator.

7. Check the stator for grounds, using an ohmmeter. If readings are low, replace the stator.

8. Using an ohmmeter, check the rotor for grounds. The ohmmeter reading should be very high. If not, replace the rotor.

9. Using an ohmmeter, check the rotor for opens. If the ohmmeter reading is not 2.4–3.5 ohms, replace the rotor.

10. To check the diode trio connect the ohmmeter to the diode trio and then reverse the lead connections. The ohmmeter should read high and low. If not, replace the diode trio. Repeat the same test between the single connector and each of the other connectors.

11. Check rectifier bridge with ohmmeter connected from grounded heat sink to flat metal on terminal. Reverse leads. If both readings are equal then replace rectifier bridge.

12. Repeat test between grounded heat sink and other 2 flat metal clips.

13. Repeat test between insulated heat sink and 3 flat metal clips.

Exploded view of Delcotron alternator—Jeep

Installing the brushes into the holder—Delcotron alternator—Jeep

Location of the related end frame components—Delcotron alternator—Jeep

14. Clean or replace the alternator brushes as required. Position the brushes in the brush holder and retain them in place using the brush retainer wire or equivalent.

Using an ohmmeter to check the rotor for opens or grounds—Delcotron alternator—Jeep

Using an ohmmeter to check the stator for opens or grounds—Delcotron alternator—Jeep

Grounding the field winding by inserting a tool into the test hole to no more than a depth of 1 in.—Delcotron alternator—Jeep

15. To remove the rotor and drive end bearing, remove the shaft nut, washer and pulley, fan and collar. Push the rotor from the housing.

16. Remove the retainer plate from inside the drive end frame. Push the bearing out. Clean or replace parts as required.

To assemble:

17. Assembly is the reverse of the removal procedure. Press against the outer bearing race to push the bearing in.

18. Press rotor into end frame. Assemble collar, fan, pulley, washer and nut. Torque shaft nut 40–60 ft. lbs.

19. Push slipring end bearing out from outside toward inside of end frame.

20. Place flat plate over new bearing and press from outside toward inside until bearing is flush with end frame.

21. Use the thin wall tube in the space between the grease cup and the housing to push the bearing in flush with the housing.

22. Assemble brush holder, regulator, resistor, diode trio, rectifier bridge and stator-to-slipring end frame.

23. Assemble end frames together with through bolts. Remove brush retainer wire.

CHRYSLER IMPORTS

Mitsubishi Alternator

GENERAL INFORMATION

The alternator used on imported Chrysler pickups such as the Ram Raider and Ram 50 is a conventional design with an internal voltage regulator. Different rated outputs of the same basic unit are installed depending on engine size and vehicle options. Note that some vehicles such as the Ram Raider if equipped with air conditioning and the 2.6L engine, may require that the air conditioning system be discharged and the compressor removed before accessing the alternator.

OVERHAUL

Disassembly

NOTE: Before starting alternator overhaul, check parts availability to make sure required parts can be obtained.

1. Clamp the alternator in a soft jaw vise, remove the retaining nut, alternator drive pulley and the seal ring under it. Remove the case bolts and carefully separate the alternator end frames from the stator core.

2. Remove the alternator rotor assembly.

3. Remove the rotor rear bearing by using a small puller.

4. Remove the front frame bearing cover and remove the front bearing. In some cases, a small amount of heat may be required to allow the bearing to be pulled out.

5. Remove the stator and rectifier assembly as well as the nut of the **B** terminal and the insulation bushing. Remove the rectifier retaining screws and the brush holder retaining screw. Separate the rear bracket and stator.

6. Remove the internal voltage regulator.

7. Remove the solder from the rectifier and stator leads.

NOTE: Do not use the soldering iron for more than 5 seconds as the rectifier may be damaged if overheated.

8. The brush may be removed by removing the solder from the pigtail.

Testing

ROTOR

1. Using an ohmmeter, check for continuity at the slip end rings. If there is no continuity, replace the rotor.

2. Using an ohmmeter, make an insulation test. Check for continuity between the slipring and the rotor core. If continuity exists, replace the rotor.

3. Measure the slipring outer diameter for wear. Minimum diameter is 1.18 in. (30mm).

1. Pulley
2. Seal
3. Rotor assembly
4. Rear bearing
5. Bearing retainer
6. Front bearing
7. Front bracket
8. Stator
9. Terminal
10. Plate
11. Regulator and brush holder
12. Brush
13. Brush spring
14. Slinger
15. Rectifier assembly
16. Rear bracket

Exploded view of Chrysler alternator—2.6L engine

1. Pulley
2. Seal
3. Rotor assembly
4. Rear bearing
5. Bearing retainer
6. Front bearing
7. Front bracket
8. Stator
9. Terminal
10. Plate
11. Regulator and brush holder

12. Brush
13. Brush spring
14. Slinger
15. Rectifier assembly
16. Rear bracket

Exploded view of Chrysler alternator—3.0L engine

STATOR

1. Using an ohmmeter, make a continuity test between the stator lead wires. If there is no continuity, replace the stator.
2. Using an ohmmeter, make an insulation test between the stator core and the lead wire. If the continuity exists, replace the stator.

DIODE

1. Using and ohmmeter, perform a continuity test on diodes in both directions.
2. Replace as necessary.

BRUSHES

1. Check for smooth movement of the brush and clean the brush holder if necessary.
2. Check for brush wear by looking at the wear limit line (box around 3–Diamond emblem) on the brush and replace if necessary. Melt out old solder and resolder new brush pigtails.

Assembly

1. Assembly of the alternator is the reverse of disassembly with the following instructions:
2. When installing the front bearing, use a socket which exactly fits the outer race of the bearing, then use a hand press or vise and press the bearing in evenly. When pressing the rear bearing on, first heat the rear bracket, then press it so the groove at the bearing circumference is at the slipring side. When soldering a new brush, solder the pigtail so the wear limit line of the brush projects 0.079–0.118 in. out from the end of the brush holder. Fit the stopper spring into the eccentric groove of the rear bearing circumference. The protruding part of the spring should be fit into the deepest part of the groove. This makes assembly much easier.
3. Before assembly, use a finger to push the brush into the brush holder, then pass a wire through the hole and secure the brush into position. After reassembly, manually turn the pulley to make sure the rotor turns easily.

DAIHATSU

Internal Regulator Alternator

GENERAL INFORMATION

Daihatsu vehicles use a conventional, Japanese-produced alternator with an internal voltage regulator.

TESTING

1. Check the fusible links.
2. Check the EFI No. 1 fuse (top, right fuse in fuse box).
3. Check engine fuse and gauge fuses.
4. Check the alternator wiring, listen for abnormal noises.

Exploded view of alternator assembly—Daihatsu Rocky

OVERHAUL

Disassembly and Assembly

1. Remove the alternator pulley locknut with an impact wrench and remove the front pulley.
2. Remove the nut and terminal insulator from the **BAT** terminal and remove the 3 nuts from the back cover. Remove the rear cover.
3. Remove the brush holder.
4. Remove the rectifier holder and regulator assembly. In order to remove the rectifier holder, the stator wire must be straightened.
5. Remove the rectifier end frame assembly.
6. Remove the rotor from the drive end frame assembly.

Inspection

1. Check the rotor for open circuit with an ohmmeter. Measure between the sliprings. Specification is 2.9 ± 0.2 ohms. If out of specification, replace the rotor.

2. Check the rotor for ground with an ohmmeter. Measure between sliprings and rotor core. If continuity exists, replace rotor.
3. Check sliprings for wear, roughness or burns. Minimum slipring diameter is 0.550 inch (14mm). If necessary, replace the rotor.
4. Inspect the stator with an ohmmeter to see if an open circuit exists between any of the coil leads. If no continuity exists, replace the stator/end frame assembly.
5. Inspect the stator with an ohmmeter to see if a short circuit exists between the stator coil and the end frame. Check between the leads and the frame. If continuity exists, the stator is shorted and the assembly must be replaced.
6. Check the brushes for wear. Standard exposed brush length is 0.410 inch (10.5mm). Minimum exposed length is 0.060 inch (1.5mm). If brushes must be replaced, unsolder and install replacements. New brush pigtails must be resoldered. Check that the brushes move freely in their holder.
7. Check the positive side of the rectifier with an ohmmeter. Continuity should exist between the positive stud bolt of the

rectifier holder and the rectifier terminal. Place the ohmmeter negative probe on the terminal, and the positive probe on 1 of the 3 stud bolts. Check each stud bolt in turn. There should be continuity. If not, replace the rectifier holder. Reverse the ohmmeter leads and check again. There should be no continuity. If there is, replace the rectifier holder.

8. Check the negative side of the rectifier with an ohmmeter. Place the ohmmeter positive lead on the terminal stud and the negative lead on 1 of the 3 negative terminals. Continuity should exist between each of the negative terminals of the rectifier holder and each rectifier terminal. Resistance should be about 900 ohms. If no continuity exists, replace the rectifier holder. Reverse the ohmmeter leads and check again. There should be no continuity. If there is, replace the rectifier holder.

9. Check the bearings for wear. Bearings should turn smoothly. Replace if necessary.

Assembly

1. Assembly is the reverse of the removal procedure. Use a suitable size socket or driver to press a replacement bearing into the front frame.

2. If the rear bearing is be replace, use a suitable puller to remove from the rotor. Use care not to damage the fan during removal. Use a suitable drive and press to install a replacement rear bearing.

3. Install the rotor into the drive end frame assembly.

4. Install the rectifier end frame on the drive end frame, install the nuts and bolts. Use care not to damage coil wire at installation.

5. Install rectifier holder, regulator and brush assembly. Attach rectifier holder to the end frame with the coil wires passed through the opening of the rectifier holder.

6. Wind the coil wire around the rectifier attaching bolt.

7. Install the regulator assembly and screws. Install the brush holder in such a way that as gap of at least 1mm (0.040 inch) is provided between the brush holder and the regulator assembly. Secure with the screws.

8. Install the rear cover and tighten the nuts. Install the terminal insulator and nut.

9. Install the front pulley and locknut. Make sure the rotor turns smoothly.

GEO

Internal Regulator Alternator

GENERAL INFORMATION

The Geo Tracker uses a conventional internal voltage regulator alternator. It is built by Mitsubishi and is similar to those used on other Japanese vehicles.

OVERHAUL

Disassembly

1. Place alignment matchmarks on the cases.

2. Remove the through bolts from the alternator.

3. The rear alternator bearing uses a small spring clip that fits into a shallow groove that goes around the outside of the bearing. This clip retains the rear housing. To remove the housing, the rear bearing housing must be heated to expand it away from the spring clip. Using a 200W soldering iron, position it against the bearing box at the rear of the alternator housing and heat the bearing box to a temperature of 122–140°F (50–60°C).

4. Using a small prybar, position it between the stator core and the front housing, then, separate the front housing from the rear housing.

5. Position the rotor/front housing into a soft jawed vise.

6. Remove the pulley nut and the pulley.

1. Rear housing
2. Solid state voltage regulator
3. Stator coil
4. Pulley
5. Front housing
6. Bearing
7. Retainer
8. Rotor coil
9. Rectifier
10. Brush

Exploded view of alternator assembly—1991–92 GEO Tracker

7. Remove the front housing from the rotor.

8. Remove the front bearing by performing the following procedures:

    a. Remove the front bearing retainer screws and the retainer.

    b. Using a shop press, press the bearing from the front housing.

9. Remove the stator-to-rear housing screws, the battery terminal nut and the stator.

10. If necessary to remove the brushes from the brush holder, use a soldering iron to unsolder the brush wire(s).

11. Remove the rectifier and condenser assembly from the rear housing.

12. Assembly is the reverse of the removal procedure.

Inspection

1. Using an ohmmeter, check the resistance between the rotor sliprings; if there is no continuity, replace the rotor.

2. Using an ohmmeter, check the resistance between the rotor slipring and the rotor; if there is continuity, replace the rotor.

3. Inspect the rotor sliprings for scoring or roughness; if rough or scored, replace the rotor.

4. Using an ohmmeter, check for continuity between the leads; if there is no continuity, replace the stator.

5. Using an ohmmeter, check for continuity between the leads and the stator core; if there is continuity, replace the stator.

6. Inspect the brushes for wear; the brush wear limit is 0.55 in. (14mm), if worn past the limit, replace the brushes.

7. Using an ohmmeter, check for continuity, in both directions, between the upper and lower rectifier bodies and each diode lead; if continuity exists in both directions, replace the rectifier.

Assembly

1. Installation is the reverse of the removal procedure. Install the rectifier and condenser assembly into the rear housing.

2. If the brushes were removed, be sure to solder them to the regulator terminal.

3. Using a stiff wire, depress the brushes into the holder and insert the wire, through the hole in the rear housing, to hold the brushes in place.

4. Install the stator to the rear housing.

5. Using a shop press, press the bearing into the front housing.

6. Install the bearing retainer to the front housing.

7. Using a 200W soldering iron, heat the bearing box of the rear housing to 122–140°F (50–60°C).

8. Install the rotor into the front housing, the pulley and the pulley nut; torque the nut to 48 ft. lbs. (65 Nm).

9. Align the matchmarks and assemble the front housing/rotor assembly to the rear housing.

10. Install the through bolts and remove the brush support wire.

11. Make sure the rotor turn freely within the assembly.

ISUZU

Internal Regulator Alternator

GENERAL INFORMATION

The alternators used in Isuzu vehicles are a conventional design. The electronic voltage regulator is mounted internally.

Isuzu Rodeo, Amigo, Trooper/Trooper II and Pick-Up models 1990 and later equipped with 3.1L V6 engines may be equipped with Delco CS–130 type alternators. These alternators are not considered serviceable, no internal repair parts are available from the factory and must be replaced as a unit if defective. Complete troubleshooting information on CS type alternators can be found in the General Motors section of this chapter.

OVERHAUL

Disassembly

EXCEPT CS TYPE ALTERNATOR

1. Remove the through bolts and disconnect the lead wires at the connector.

2. Separate the alternator assembly into front and rear sections. The stator should be on the rear side.

3. Carefully clamp the rotor in a vise and remove the pulley nut, then remove the pulley fan and rotor.

4. Remove the bearing retainer screws, then remove the ball bearing.

5. Remove the rear side nuts, then remove the stator from the rear cover together with the diodes, brush and capacitor.

6. Unsolder the diode-to-stator coil connections, then separate the diodes from the stator together with the brush and capacitor.

7. Remove the screws retaining the brush holder, then remove the diodes, brush and capacitor.

8. Assembly of the alternator is the reverse of disassembly with the following instructions.

9. Before assembling the front and rear sections. insert a wire into the hole in the rear face of the rear cover from the outboard side to support the brush in the raised position, then insert the front section to which the rotor is assembled

Inspection

EXCEPT CS TYPE ALTERNATOR

1. Measure the resistance between **F** and **E** terminals (rotor coil resistance): The rotor coil circuit is normal if resistance measured across the terminals is 5 ohms. If resistance is higher than 5 ohms, the trouble is poor contact between the brushes and commutator. If no continuity exists between terminals **F** and **E**, the trouble is either an open coil rotor circuit, brush sticking or a broken lead wire. If resistance is lower than 5 ohms, it may be an indication of rotor coil layer short or the circuit being grounded.

2. Test the rectifying diodes in the following manner: Connect the positive (+) lead of a tester to the alternator **N** terminal and the tester negative (−) lead to the alternator **A** terminal. If there exists a continuity between terminals, it indicates that 1 or more of the 3 diodes in the positive side are shorted. Connect the positive (+) lead of a tester to the alternator **E** terminal and the tester negative (−) lead to the alternator **N** terminal. If there exists a continuity, it indicates that 1 or more of the 3 diodes in the negative side are shorted.

ROTOR

1. Using an ohmmeter, check for continuity at the slip end rings. If there is no continuity, replace the rotor.

2. Using an ohmmeter, make an insulation test. Check for continuity between the slipring and the rotor core. If continuity exists, replace the rotor.

1. Bolts
2. Nut
3. Pulley
4. Rotor assembly
5. Screw
6. Bearing assembly
7. Front bearing
8. Front cover
9. Nuts
10. Rear cover
11. Stator assembly
12. Nuts
13. Fan terminal
14. Battery terminal
15. Condenser
16. Diode assembly
17. Brush and IC regulator assembly

Exploded view of Isuzu alternator—2.0L engine

STATOR

1. Using an ohmmeter, make a continuity test between the stator lead wires. If there is no continuity, replace the stator.

2. Using an ohmmeter, make an insulation test between the stator core and the lead wire. If the continuity exists, replace the stator.

DIODE

1. Using and ohmmeter, perform a continuity test on diodes in both directions.

2. Replace as necessary.

BRUSH

1. Check for smooth movement of the brush and clean the brush holder if necessary.

2. Check for brush wear by looking at the wear limit line on the brush and replace if necessary.

Assembly

1. Assembly of the alternator is the reverse of disassembly with the following instructions: Resolder the IC regulator lead wires. To prevent heat from being transferred to the diodes, use long nose pliers to hold the stator coil leads and diode leads and solder as quickly as possible.

U.V.W. INDIATE STATOR COIL LEAD TERMINALS

POSITIVE SIDE (+) DIODES

AUXILIARY DIODES

L

BAT

NEGATIVE SIDE (–) DIODES

E

DIRECTION OF FLOW OF CURRENT

Testing the diodes—Isuzu

2. Carefully clamp the rotor in a vise and torque the pulley nut to 33–43 ft. lbs.

3. Align the holes in the front cover and rear cover flange then install the through bolts. Make sure the brush is installed in the brush holder correctly.

4. Turn pulley and check that the alternator spins freely.

Exploded view of Isuzu alternator—Trooper with 2.0L engine

1. Bolts
2. Front cover assembly (with rotor assembly)
3. Nut
4. Pulley
5. Fan
6. Cover assembly
7. Front bearing
8. Rear cover and stator assembly
9. Stator assembly
10. Brush assembly and diode assembly
11. Brush and condenser assembly

MAZDA

Internal Regulator Alternator

GENERAL INFORMATION

The alternators used in Mazda vehicles are a conventional design. The electronic voltage regulator is mounted internally.

The Mazda Navajo is built by Ford Motor Company domestically. Like other Ford products in its size class, it is equipped with a Ford Integral Alternator/voltage Regulator (IAR) system rated at 95 amps. The alternator is not considered serviceable, no internal repair parts are available from the factory and it must be replaced as a unit if defective. Complete troubleshooting information can be found in the Ford Motor Company section of this chapter.

TESTING

Checking Regulated Voltage With No Load

1. Disconnect the wiring connected to alternator terminal **B**.
2. Connect an ammeter (more than 40 amps) between the alternator terminal **B** and the battery positive terminal.
3. Connect a voltmeter between alternator terminal **L** and ground.
4. Start the engine and increase the engine speed to approximately 2000 rpm. Turn off all unnecessary electrical loads and read the value shown on the ammeter.
5. When the amperage in Step 4 is less than 5 amp., read the voltage (regulated voltage) of terminal **L**. The regulated voltage should be 14.1–14.7 volts.

Checking the charging system—Mazda

Alternator terminal identification—Mazda

Checking the regulated voltage with no load—Mazda

Checking the current output—Mazda

Checking Output Current

1. Disconnect the wiring connected to the alternator terminal **B**.

2. Connect an ammeter (more than 40 amp) between the alternator terminal **B** and the battery positive terminal.

3. Start the engine and increase the engine speed to more than 2500 rpm and read the maximum value shown on the ammeter. Apply all electrical loads. If the value shown on the ammeter is more than 90 percent of the rated output, the alternator is normal.

OVERHAUL

1988

1. Place a soldering iron on the rear bearing box for approximately 3–4 minutes to heat it, then pull out the bolts and insert

Exploded view of alternator—1988 Mazda

1. Bolt
2. Front bracket
3. Rotor and fan
4. Locknut
5. Rear bracket
6. Stator
7. Brush holder assembly
8. Rectifier

1. Pulley
2. Front cover
3. Rotor
4. Stator
5. Brush holder
6. Rectifier
7. Rear bracket

Exploded view of alternator—1989–92 Mazda

a flat tip tool between the stator and front bracket and separate them.

> **NOTE: The bearing box must be heated or the bearing cannot be pulled out.**

2. Separate the front and rear sections, being careful not to lose the stopper spring that fits around the circumference of the rear bearing.

3. Remove the pulley nut, then disassemble the pulley, rotor and front bracket.

4. The rear bearing can be removed by using a bearing puller.

5. Remove the nut of the **B** terminal and the insulation bushing. Remove the rectifier retaining screws and the brush holder retaining screw and then separate the rear bracket and stator.

6. Remove the IC regulator.

7. Remove the solder from the rectifier and stator leads.

> **NOTE: Do not use the soldering iron for more than 5 seconds as the rectifier may be damaged if overheated.**

8. The brush may be removed by removing the solder from the pigtail.

1989–92

1. Remove the alternator through bolts and separate the rear case/stator assembly from the front case/rotor assembly.

2. Secure the rotor and remove the pulley nut, the washer and the pulley.

3. Pull the rotor from the front case.

4. Remove the front bearing retainer-to-front case bolts, the retainer and the bearing.

5. From the rear case, remove the stator, the brush holder/rectifier assembly-to-rear case nuts/washers, the brush holder assembly and the rectifier.

Testing

ROTOR

1. Using an ohmmeter, check for continuity at the slip end rings. If there is no continuity, replace the rotor.

2. Using an ohmmeter, make a ground test. Check for continuity between the slipring and the rotor core. If continuity exists, replace the rotor.

3. Measure the slipring outer diameter for wear. Minimum diameter is 1.18 in. (30mm).

STATOR

1. Using an ohmmeter, make a continuity test between the stator lead wires. If there is no continuity, replace the stator.

2. Using an ohmmeter, make a ground test between the stator core and the lead wire. If the continuity exists, replace the stator.

DIODE

1. Using and ohmmeter, perform a continuity test on diodes in both directions.

2. Replace as necessary.

BRUSHES

1. Check for smooth movement of the brush and clean the brush holder, if necessary.

2. Check for brush wear by looking at the wear limit line on the brush and replace, if necessary.

Assembly

1988

1. Assemble the alternator by reversing the order of disassembly, while observing the following instructions:

2. When installing the front bearing, use a socket which exactly fits the outer race of the bearing, then use a hand press or vise to press the bearing in evenly.

3. When pressing the rear bearing on, first heat the rear bracket, then press it so the groove at the bearing circumference is at the slipring side.

4. When soldering a new brush, solder the pigtail so the wear limit line of the brush projects 0.079–0.118 in. out from the end of the brush holder.

5. Install the stopper spring into the eccentric groove of the rear bearing circumference. The protruding part of the spring should be fit into the deepest part of the groove; this makes assembly much easier.

6. Before assembly, use a finger to push the brush into the brush holder, then, pass a wire through the hole in the brush holder and secure the brush into position.

7. After assembly, manually turn the pulley to make sure the rotor turns easily.

1989–92

1. Install the front bearing into the front cover.

2. Install the front bearing retainer and torque the bolts to 26–39 inch lbs. (2.9–4.4 Nm).

3. Install the rotor into the front case. Install the pulley and torque the nut to 43–58 ft. lbs. (58–78 Nm).

4. Install the rectifier, the brush holder assembly and stator to the rear housing. Torque the bolts to 26–39 inch lbs. (2.9–4.4 Nm).

5. Using a wire, depress the brushes into the brush holder and secure them in place.

6. Assemble the alternator halves.

7. Install the through bolts and torque to 35–48 ft. lbs. (3.9–5.4 Nm).

8. Remove the wire securing the brushes.

9. Turn the pulley to make sure the rotor turns easily.

MITSUBISHI

Internal Regulator Alternator

GENERAL INFORMATION

The alternator used on Mitsubishi pickups and vans is a conventional design with an internal voltage regulator. Different rated outputs of the same basic unit are installed depending on engine size and vehicle options. Note that some vehicles such as the Montero if equipped with air conditioning and the 2.6L engine, may require that the air conditioning system be discharged and the compressor removed before accessing the alternator.

TESTING

Troubleshooting (On Vehicle)

1. Place the ignition switch in the **OFF** position.

2. Disconnect the battery ground cable.

3. Disconnect the cable from terminal **B** of the alternator and connect an ammeter between the terminal **B** and the cable.

4. Connect a voltmeter between terminal **B** (+) and ground (−).

5. Set the engine tachometer.

6. Connect the battery ground cable to the battery. The voltmeter should indicate the battery voltage.

7. Start the engine.

8. Turn **ON** the lights, accelerate the engine to the speed specified and measure the current. At room temperature, the regulated voltage should be approximately 13.9–14.9 volts.

OVERHAUL

Disassembly

NOTE: Before starting alternator overhaul, check parts availability to make sure required parts can be obtained.

1. Remove alternator from vehicle.

2. Remove the through bolts from the alternator body.

3. Insert an appropriate pry tool between the front bracket and stator. Pry the front bracket away from the stator. Remove the front bracket along with the rotor.

NOTE: If the tool is inserted too deeply, the stator coil might be damaged.

4. Hold the rotor in a vise and remove the pulley nut. Then remove the pulley, fan, spacer and seal. Remove the rotor from the front bracket and remove the seal.

5. Unsolder the rectifier from the stator coil lead wires and remove the stator assembly.

NOTE: Make sure the solder is removed quickly (in less than 5 seconds). If a diode is heated to more than 150°C, it might be damaged.

6. Remove the condenser from terminal **B**.

7. Unsolder the plates **B** and **L** from the rectifier assembly.

8. Remove the mounting screw and terminal **B** bolt and remove the electronic voltage regulator and brush holder. The regulator and brush holder cannot be separated.

1. Pulley
2. Seal
3. Rotor assembly
4. Rear bearing
5. Bearing retainer
6. Front bearing
7. Front bracket
8. Stator
9. Terminal
10. Plate
11. Regulator and brush holder
12. Brush
13. Brush spring
14. Slinger
15. Rectifier assembly
16. Rear bracket

Exploded view of alternator—Mitsubishi—2.6L engine

1. Pulley
2. Seal
3. Rotor assembly
4. Rear bearing
5. Bearing retainer
6. Front bearing
7. Front bracket
8. Stator
9. Terminal
10. Plate

11. Regulator and brush holder
12. Brush
13. Brush spring
14. Slinger
15. Rectifier assembly
16. Rear bracket

Exploded view of alternator—Mitsubishi—3.0L engine

9. Remove the rectifier assembly.

10. When only a brush or brush spring is to be replaced, it is not necessary to remove the stator, etc. Raise the brush holder assembly and unsolder the wire pigtail of the brush and remove the brush.

NOTE: Be very careful when bending the plates B and L so as not to disturb the rectifier moulding.

Inspection

1. Check the outside circumference of the slipring for dirtiness and roughness. Clean or polish with armature paper, if required. A badly damaged slipring or a slipring worn down beyond the service limit should also be replaced. The service limit for the slipring outside diameter is 1.268 in.

2. Check for continuity between the field coil and slipring. If

there is not continuity, the field coil is defective and the rotor must be replaced.

3. Check for continuity between the slipring and the shaft. If there is continuity, the rotor assembly must be replaced.

4. Check for continuity between the leads of the stator coil. If there is no continuity, the stator coil is defective.

5. Check for an open circuit between the stator coil leads and the stator core. If there is continuity between the stator core and the coil leads, the stator assembly must be replaced.

6. Check for continuity between the positive (+) heat sink and the stator coil lead connection terminal with a circuit tester. If there is continuity in both directions, the diode is short circuited and the rectifier assembly must be replaced.

7. Perform Step 6 between the negative (−) heat sink and the stator coil lead connection.

8. Using a circuit tester, check the 3 diodes for continuity in both directions. If there is either continuity or an open circuit in both directions, the diode is defective and must be replaced.

9. Measure the length of the brush. If it is worn below 0.315 in., it must be replaced.

Assembly

1. Assembly is the reverse of disassembly. Install new seals when replacing bearings.

2. To install the rotor assembly in the rear bracket, push the brushes into the brush holder, insert a wire to hold them in the raised position and install the rotor. Remove the wire.

3. After assembly, turn the alternator to make sure it spins freely.

NISSAN

Internal Voltage Regulator Alternator
GENERAL INFORMATION

Nissan pickups and vans use conventional alternators with internal voltage regulators.

One area of caution when serving these alternators is that the rear cover may be difficult to separate from the rotor. This is due to a small lockring that fits into a groove that goes around the rear bearing's outer circumference. This holds the bearing to the rear cover. To remove, use a large soldering iron (200 watts) on the outside of the rear bearing housing to expand the

bearing bore so the lockring releases its grip. Do not use a heat gun because the heat will not be concentrated on the bearing housing and the diodes could be overheated and damaged.

OVERHAUL

Disassembly

1. Remove the through bolts and separate the front cover from the rear cover.

2. Place the rear cover side of the rotor in a vise and remove the pulley nut and pulley.

Exploded view of alternator—1988–89 Nissan

Exploded view of alternator—1990–92 Nissan PickUp and Pathfinder with 2.4L engine

Exploded view of alternator—1990–92 Nissan PickUp and Pathfinder with 3.0L engine

Exploded view of alternator—1990–92 Nissan Axxess with 2.4L engine

3. Remove the screws from the bearing retainer.
4. Remove the attaching nuts and take out the stator assembly.
5. Use a bearing puller or a press and pull the rear bearing from the rotor assembly.

NOTE: The bearing cannot be reused and must be replaced with a new one.

6. To remove the stator, disconnect the stator coil lead wires from the diode terminals, using a soldering iron.

Inspection

ROTOR

1. Using an ohmmeter, check for continuity at the slip end rings. If there is no continuity, replace the rotor.

Performing rotor continuity test—Nissan

Performing stator continuity test—Nissan

Performing rotor ground test—Nissan

Performing stator ground test—Nissan

Using an ohmmeter to test the positive side diodes

Using an ohmmeter to test the negative side diodes

2. Using an ohmmeter, make an insulation test. Check for continuity between the slipring and the rotor core. If continuity exists, replace the rotor.

3. Measure the slipring outer diameter for wear. Minimum diameter is 1.18 in. (30mm).

View of the brush limit lines

STATOR

1. Using an ohmmeter, make a continuity test between the stator lead wires. If there is no lead wires, replace the stator.

2. Using an ohmmeter. make an insulation test between the stator core and the lead wire. If the continuity exists, replace the stator.

DIODE

1. Using an ohmmeter, perform a continuity test on diodes in both directions.

2. Replace diodes as necessary.

BRUSH

1. Check for smooth movement of the brush and clean the brush holder if necessary.

2. Check for brush wear at the wear limit line on the brush and replace if necessary.

Assembly

1. Assembly of the alternator is the reverse of disassembly with the following instructions: Solder each stator coil lead wire to the diode assembly terminal as quickly as possible. When soldering the brush lead wire, position the brush so it extends 0.43 in. from the brush holder and wrap the coil lead wire at least 1.5 times around the terminal groove. Solder the outside of the terminal.

2. Tighten the pulley nut to 29–43 ft. lbs.

3. Before installing the front and rear sides of the alternator, push the brush up and retain the brush by inserting a wire from the outside into a lift hole. After installing the front and rear sides of the alternator, move the brush by pushing towards the center.

NOTE: Do not pull brush. Lift by pushing towards the outside of the cover as it will damage the slipring as it slides.

SUZUKI

Internal Voltage Regulator Alternator

GENERAL INFORMATION

Suzuki pickups use conventional alternators with internal voltage regulators.

One area of caution when serving these alternators is that the rear cover may be difficult to separate from the rotor. This is due to a small lockring that fits into a groove that goes around the rear bearing's outer circumference. This holds the bearing to the rear cover. To remove, use a large soldering iron (200 watts) on the outside of the rear bearing housing to expand the bearing bore so the lockring releases its grip. Do not use a heat gun because the heat will not be concentrated on the bearing housing and the diodes could be overheated and damaged.

1. Pulley nut
2. Pulley
3. Drive end frame
4. Stator
5. Stud bolt
6. Drive end bearing
7. Bearing retainer
8. Rotor
9. End housing bearing
10. Bearing cover
11. Wave washer
12. Rear end frame
13. Frame bolt
14. Rectifier
15. Insulator
16. Regulator
17. Brush
18. Brush holder
19. Rear end cover

Exploded view of alternator—Suzuki

OVERHAUL

Disassembly

SAMURAI

1. Remove the nut and terminal insulator, the nuts and end cover.
2. Remove the screws, the brush holder and the brush holder cover.
3. Remove the screws and the IC regulator.
4. Remove the rectifier holder screws and the holder.
5. Remove the terminal insulator.
6. Loosen the alternator pulley nut and the pulley.
7. Remove the nuts from the rear end frame. Using a puller, remove the rear end frame.
8. Remove the rotor from the drive end frame.
9. If necessary, remove the front bearing by removing the screws from the bearing retainer.
10. If necessary, remove the rear bearing by using a puller. Remove the rear bearing with the cover from the rotor shaft.

SIDEKICK

1. Matchmark front and rear housing.
2. Remove the housing bolts.

3. Apply heat with soldering iron to rear bearing housing. Pry apart between stator and front housing/rotor assembly.
4. Pad bench vise with clean cloth, hold rotor in vise and remove pulley nut. Take off pulley and separate front housing from rotor.
5. Remove front bearing retainer screws and remove front bearing.
6. Remove rear bearing with a suitable puller or press.
7. Remove the screws and terminal nut from the rear housing to take out stator assembly.
8. To remove the brush, remove the wire cover from the brush holder and then disconnect the brush wire from the regulator terminal by unsoldering.

Inspection

1. Using an ohmmeter, check for continuity between the sliprings. Standard resistance is 2.8–3.0 ohms for Samurai or 3.1–3.5 ohms for Sidekick. If there is no continuity, replace the rotor.
2. Using an ohmmeter, check that there is no continuity between the slipring and rotor; if there is continuity, replace the rotor.
3. Using an ohmmeter, check all leads for continuity. If there is no continuity, replace the drive end frame assembly.

4. Using an ohmmeter, check for continuity between the coil leads and the drive end frame; if there is continuity, replace the drive end frame assembly.

5. Measure the exposed brush length and replace, if necessary. Minimum length is 0.200 in. for Samurai or 0.080 in. for Sidekick. Also check that the brush moves smoothly in the brush holder.

6. Inspect the front and rear bearings for roughness and replace, if necessary.

Assembly

1. If it is necessary to replace the rear bearing, use a shop press and press the rear bearing and cover onto the rotor shaft.

2. Install the rotor to the drive end frame.

3. Using a plastic hammer, lightly tap the rear end frame on the drive end frame and install the nuts.

4. Install the alternator pulley and torque to approximately 37–47 ft. lbs.

5. Install the terminal insulators on the lead wires.

6. Install the rectifier holder with the screws.

7. If it is necessary to install a new brush, unsolder and remove the brush and spring. Put the new brush wire through the spring and insert it into the brush holder. Solder the wire to the brush holder and cut off any excess.

8. Install the brush holder with the IC regulator and the screws to the IC regulator. Install the retaining screws and the brush holder cover to the rear end frame.

9. Install the end cover with the retaining nuts and install the terminal insulator and nut.

10. Make sure the rotor rotates smoothly.

TOYOTA

Internal Voltage Regulator Alternators

GENERAL INFORMATION

Toyota pickups and vans including Previa use a conventional alternator with an internal solid state voltage regulator.

OVERHAUL

Disassembly
EXCEPT LAND CRUISER

1. Remove the nut and terminal insulator. Remove the nuts and end cover.

2. Remove the screws, the brush holder and brush holder cover.

3. Remove the screws and the IC regulator.

4. Remove the rectifier holder screws and the holder.

5. Remove the terminal insulator(s).

6. To remove the pulley and nut, use tool 09820–63010 to perform the following procedure:

   a. Hold the tool at point **A** with a torque wrench and tighten at point **B** clockwise to 29 ft. lbs. (39 Nm).

   b. Confirm that the tool **A** is secured to the pulley shaft.

   c. Grip tool **C** in a vise and install the alternator into special tool **C**.

   d. Loosen the pulley nut by turning tool **A** counterclockwise.

Exploded view of alternator—Toyota PickUp and 4Runner—22R and 22R–E engines

Exploded view of alternator—Toyota PickUp and 4Runner—3VZ–E engine

Exploded view of alternator—Toyota Van

Exploded view of alternator—Toyota Land Cruiser

PULLEY — FAN — SPACE COLLAR — DRIVE END FRAME — FRONT BEARING — SNAPRING — ROTOR — REAR BEARING — STATOR — SPACER RING — BEARING RETAINER — CONDENSER — TERMINAL INSULATOR — REAR END FRAME — INSULATOR WASHER — VOLTAGE REGULATOR ASSEMBLY — RECTIFIER HOLDER

Installing the removal tool to the rotor shaft—Toyota alternator—PickUp, Van and 4Runner

Removing the pulley nut and pulley from the shaft—Toyota alternator—PickUp, Van and 4Runner

NOTE: To prevent damage to the rotor shaft, do not loosen the pulley nut more than ½ turn.

e. Turn the tool at point **B** and remove all the tool components.

f. Remove the pulley nut and the pulley.

7. Remove the nuts from the rear end frame. Using a puller, tool 09286–46011, remove the rear end frame.

8. Remove the rotor from the drive end frame.

9. If necessary, remove the front bearing by removing the screws from the bearing retainer.

10. If necessary, remove the rear bearing by using a puller, tool 09820–00020. Remove the rear bearing with the cover from the rotor shaft.

Removing the rear frame—Toyota alternator—PickUp, Van and 4Runner

LAND CRUISER

1. Remove the through bolts.
2. Using a prybar, pry the drive end frame/rotor assembly from the stator.
3. Mount the rotor assembly into a soft jawed vise.
4. Remove the pulley nut, the spring washer, the pulley and fan from the rotor.
5. Remove the spacer collar, drive end frame, the spacer ring and snapring.
6. From the rectifier end frame, remove the nuts, the condenser and the terminal insulators.
7. Remove the rectifier end frame and the insulator washer from the rectifier holder stud.
8. Using needle-nose pliers to hold the IC regulator terminal, unsolder the terminals.

NOTE: Protect the rectifiers from heat.

9. Using needle-nose pliers to hold the stator coil lead, unsolder the leads.

Inspection
EXCEPT LAND CRUISER

1. Using an ohmmeter, check for continuity between the sliprings; standard resistance is 2.8–3.0 ohms. If there is no continuity, replace the rotor.
2. Using an ohmmeter, check that there is no continuity between the slipring and rotor. If there is continuity, replace the rotor.
3. Using an ohmmeter, check all leads for continuity. If there is no continuity, replace the drive end frame assembly.
4. Using an ohmmeter, check that there is no continuity between the coil leads and the drive end frame. If there is continuity, replace the drive end frame assembly.
5. Measure the exposed brush length and replace, if necessary; minimum length is 0.059 in. (1.5mm). Also check that the brush moves smoothly in the brush holder.
6. Inspect the front and rear bearings for roughness and replace if necessary.

LAND CRUISER

1. Using an ohmmeter, check for continuity between the sliprings; standard resistance is 2.8–3.0 ohms. If there is no continuity, replace the rotor.
2. Using an ohmmeter, check that there is no continuity between the slipring and rotor. If there is continuity, replace the rotor.
3. Using an ohmmeter, check all leads for continuity; if there is no continuity, replace the stator.
4. Using an ohmmeter, check that there is no continuity between the coil leads and the stator core; if there is continuity, replace the stator.
5. Measure the exposed brush length and replace, if necessary; minimum length is 0.217 in. (5.5mm). Also check that the brush moves smoothly in the brush holder.
6. Inspect the front and rear bearings for roughness and replace if necessary.
7. Using an ohmmeter, inspect the diodes of the rectifier assembly; good diodes will show continuity in one direction and no continuity in the other direction.

Assembly
EXCEPT LAND CRUISER

1. If it is necessary to replace the rear bearing, use bearing installation and press the rear bearing and cover onto the rotor shaft.

2. Install the rotor to the drive end frame.
3. Using a plastic hammer, lightly tap the rear end frame on the drive end frame and install the nuts.
4. Install the pulley in the following manner:
   a. Using the pulley onto the rotor shaft and tighten the pulley nut by hand.
   b. Using tool 09820–63010, hold it at point **A** with a torque wrench and tighten tool **B** clockwise to 29 ft. lbs. (39 Nm).
   c. Confirm tool **A** is secured to the pulley shaft.
   d. Grip special tool **C** in a vise and then install the alternator to tool **C**.
   e. To torque the pulley nut, turn tool **A** and tighten to 81 ft. lbs. (110 Nm).
   f. Turn tool **B** and remove all the tool components.
5. Install the terminal insulators on the lead wires.
6. Install the rectifier holder with the screws.
7. If it is necessary to install a new brush, unsolder and remove the brush and spring. Put the new brush wire through the spring and insert it into the brush holder. Solder the wire to the brush holder and cut off any excess.
8. Install the brush holder with the IC regulator and install the screws to the IC regulator. Install the retaining screws and the brush holder cover to the rear end frame.
9. Install the end cover with the retaining nuts and install the terminal insulator and nut. Make sure the rotor rotates smoothly.

LAND CRUISER

1. Using needle-nose pliers to hold the stator coil lead, solder the leads.

NOTE: Protect the rectifiers from heat.

2. Using needle-nose pliers to hold the IC regulator terminal, solder the terminals.
3. Install the rectifier end frame-to-rectifier holder by performing the following procedures:
   a. Position the insulator washer onto the positive (+) stud of the rectifier holder.
   b. Position both cushions onto the brush holder and alternator terminal.
   c. Position the rectifier end frame onto the rectifier holder.
   d. Position both terminal insulators onto the positive (+) studs of the rectifier holder.
   e. Install the condenser and nuts.
4. Install the drive end frame, the fan and pulley to the rotor by performing the following procedures:
   a. Install the snapring and spacer ring onto the rotor shaft.
   b. Position the rotor into the soft jawed vise.
   c. Install the drive end frame and spacer collar.
   d. Install the fan, the pulley and spring washer onto the rotor shaft.
   e. Torque the pulley nut to 65 ft. lbs. (88 Nm).
5. Assemble the drive end frame and the rectifier end frame by performing the following procedures:
   a. Bend the rectifier lead wires back to clear the rotor.
   b. Push the brushes into the holder, as far as they will go, and insert a stiff wire through the access hole, in the rectifier frame, to hold the brushes in place.
   c. Assemble the drive end frame and the rectifier end frame.
   d. Install the through bolts.
   e. Remove the stiff wire from the access hole.
   f. Turn the rotor to make sure it turns freely.
   g. Seal the access hole.

VOLKSWAGEN

Bosch Alternators

OVERHAUL

Disassembly

45 AMP AND 65 AMP

1. Remove the alternator from the vehicle. Mount the unit in a suitable holding fixture.
2. Hold the alternator pulley and remove the pulley retaining nut.
3. Remove the pulley lockwasher, pulley fan spacer and pulley from the alternator assembly.
4. Remove the Woodruff® key from the rotor shaft.

5. From the rear of the alternator remove the brush holder retaining screws. Remove the brush holder.
6. To test the inner and outer brush circuits, use an ohmmeter and touch 1 test probe to the inner brush and the other test probe to the brush terminal. If continuity does not exist replace the brush assembly. Repeat the same test for the outer brush circuit.
7. Disconnect the capacitor electrical connection and remove the capacitor retaining screw. Remove the capacitor from its mounting on the alternator.
8. Remove the ground stud nut and stud washer.
9. Remove the alternator through bolts that retain the unit together.
10. Using the proper tool, separate the stator and the drive end shield.

Exploded view of Bosh 45 amp and 65 amp alternators—Volkswagen

O-RING

BEARING
SLIPRING SIDE

ROTOR

Note
Always use new bearings, avoid damaging slip rings

SUPPRESSION CONDENSER

VOLTAGE REGULATOR/BRUSHES

SPACER DISC

BEARING
DRIVE SIDE

ALTERNATOR HOUSING

ENDPLATE

DIODE PLATE

V-BELT PULLEY

STATOR

Exploded view of Bosh 90 amp alternators— Volkswagen

11. To test the positive and negative rectifiers use tool C–3929–A or equivalent.

NOTE: Do not break the plastic cases of the rectifiers. These cases are for protection against corrosion. Be sure to always touch the test probe to the metal pin of the nearest rectifier.

12. Position the rear end shield and the stator assembly on an insulated surface. Connect the test lead clip to the alternator battery output terminal.

13. Plug in tool C–3829–A or equivalent. Touch the metal pin of each of the positive rectifiers with the test probe.

14. Reading for satisfactory rectifiers will be 1¾ amperes or more. Reading should be approximately the same and meter needle must move in the same direction for all 3 rectifiers.

15. When some rectifiers are good and 1 is shorted, the reading taken at good rectifiers will be low and the reading at shorted rectifiers will be 0. Disconnect stator lead to rectifiers reading 0 and retest. Reading of good rectifiers will now be within satisfactory range.

16. When a rectifier is open, it will read approximately 1 ampere and good rectifiers will read within satisfactory range.

17. To test the negative rectifiers, connect the test clip of tool C–3829–A to the rectifier end housing.

18. Touch the metal pin of each of the negative rectifiers with the test probe.

19. Test specifications are the same and test results will be approximately same as for positive case rectifiers except that the meter will read on opposite side of scale.

NOTE: If a negative rectifier shows a shorted condition, remove stator from rectifier assembly and retest. It is possible that a stator winding could be grounded to stator laminations or to an rectifier end shield which would indicate a shorted negative rectifier.

20. Remove the battery (B+) stud nut, stud lockwasher, stud flatwasher and stud insulator.

21. Remove the rectifier assembly retaining screws. Remove the stator assembly along with the rectifier unit. Unsolder the stator to rectifier leads.

22. Check for continuity between stator coil leads. Press test probe firmly to each of 3 phase (stator) lead terminals separately. If there is no continuity, stator coil is defective. Replace stator assembly.

23. To test stator for ground, check for continuity between stator coil leads and stator coil frame. If there is continuity stator is grounded. Replace stator assembly.

24. Remove the rear bearing oil and dust seal. Check the rotor bearing surface for wear and scoring. Replace as required.

25. Remove the inner battery (B+) stud insulator.

26. Press the rotor out of the drive end shield and remove the spacer.

27. Check outside circumference of slipring for dirtiness and roughness. Clean or polish with fine sandpaper, if required. A badly roughened slipring or a worn down slipring should be replaced.

28. Check for continuity between field coil and sliprings. If there is no continuity, field coil is defective. Replace rotor assembly.

29. Check for continuity between sliprings and shaft (or core). If there is continuity, it means that coil or slipring is grounded. Replace rotor assembly.

30. Using a puller remove the rotor bearing.

31. Remove the front bearing from the drive end shield by removing the front bearing retaining screws.

32. Press out the drive end shield bearing. Remove the front drive bearing from the front drive end shield.

90 AMP

1. Remove the alternator from the vehicle. Position the unit in a suitable holding fixture.

2. Remove the pulley nut and lockwasher. Remove the alternator pulley.

3. Remove the pulley to fan spacer and pulley fan.

4. Remove the Woodruff key from the rotor shaft.

5. From the rear of the alternator disconnect the electrical terminal from the capacitor. Remove the capacitor retaining screw and the capacitor.

6. Remove the brush holder retaining screw and remove the brush holder from its mounting on the rear of the alternator.

7. Remove the alternator through bolts. Using a suitable tool pry between the stator and the drive end shield and carefully separate the assembly.

8. Press the rotor out of the drive end shield and remove the spacer. Remove the pulley fan spacer.

9. Remove the front alternator drive end bearing screws.

10. Remove the drive end shield bearing retainer and press out the drive end shield bearing.

11. Remove the front drive bearing from the front of the drive end shield.

12. To test the positive and negative rectifiers use tool C-3929–A or equivalent.

NOTE: Do not break the plastic cases of the rectifiers. These cases are for protection against corrosion. Be sure to always touch the test probe to the metal pin of the nearest rectifier.

13. Position the rear end shield and the stator assembly on an insulated surface. Connect the test lead clip to the alternator battery output terminal.

14. Plug in tool C–3829–A or equivalent. Touch the metal pin of each of the positive rectifiers with the test probe.

15. Reading for satisfactory rectifiers will be 1¾ amperes or more. Reading should be approximately the same and meter needle must move in same direction for all 3 rectifiers.

16. When some rectifiers are good and 1 is shorted, the reading taken at good rectifiers will be low and the reading at shorted rectifiers will be 0. Disconnect stator lead to rectifiers reading 0 and retest. Reading of good rectifiers will now be within satisfactory range.

17. When a rectifier is open it will read approximately 1 ampere and the good rectifiers will read within satisfactory range.

18. Touch the metal pin of each of the negative rectifiers with the test probe.

19. Test specifications are the same and the test results will be approximately same as for positive case rectifiers except that the meter will read on opposite side of scale.

NOTE: If a negative rectifier shows a shorted condition remove stator from rectifier assembly and retest. It is possible that a stator winding could be grounded to stator laminations or to an rectifier end shield, which would indicate a shorted negative rectifier.

20. Unsolder the stator to rectifier leads. Mark the stator coil frame, to aid in reinstallation of the stator. Remove the stator from the rectifier end shield assembly.

21. Remove the 3 rectifier assembly mounting screws. Remove the rectifier assembly.

22. Remove the inner battery (B+) stud insulator.

23. Remove the B+ stud insulator, stud nut, stud flatwasher and stud insulating washer.

24. Remove the rear bearing oil and dust seal. Check the rotor bearing surface for scoring.

25. Using puller C–4068 or equivalent, remove the rear rotor bearing.

26. Check outside circumference of slipring for dirtiness and roughness. Clean or polish with fine sandpaper, as required. A badly roughened slipring or a worn down slipring should be replaced.

27. To check for an open rotor field coil, connect an ohmmeter to sliprings. Ohmmeter reading should be between 1.5–2.0 ohms on rotor coils at room ambient conditions. Resistance between 2.5–3.0 ohms would result from alternator rotors that have been operated on vehicle at higher engine compartment temperatures. Readings above 3.5 ohms would indicate high resistance rotor coils and further testing or replacement may be required.

28. To check for a shorted field coil connect an ohmmeter to sliprings. If reading is below 1.5 ohms field coil is shorted.

29. To check for a grounded rotor field coil connect an ohmmeter from each slipring to rotor shaft.

NOTE: Ohmmeter should be set for infinite reading when probes are apart and 0 when probes are touching. The ohmmeter should read infinite. If reading is 0 or higher, rotor is grounded.

30. Check for continuity between leads of stator coil. Press test probe firmly to each of 3 phase (stator) lead terminals separately. If there is no continuity, stator coil is defective. Replace stator assembly.

31. To test the stator for ground check for continuity between the stator coil leads and the stator coil frame. If there is no continuity the stator is grounded and must be replaced.

32. To test the inner and outer brush circuit, use an ohmmeter and touch 1 test probe to the inner brush and the other test probe to the brush terminal. If continuity does not exist replace the brush assembly. Repeat the same procedure for the outer brush.

Assembly

45 AMP AND 65 AMP

1. Be sure to check all parts for wear and replace the defective components as required.

2. Install the rear rotor bearing oil and dust seal.

3. Install the inner alternator battery terminal insulator.

4. Solder the stator leads to the rectifier assembly; be sure to use needle nose pliers as a heat sink.

5. Position the stator and rectifier assembly. Install the recti-

fier mounting screws, both terminal insulators, the insulator washer, the insulator lockwasher and the insulator nut.

6. Position and press the front bearing into the drive end shield. Install the bearing retainer.

7. Position the drive end shield and spacer over the rotor. Press the drive end shield onto the rotor.

8. Install the rectifier end shield over the drive end shield. Install the through bolts and tighten.

9. Install the capacitor and terminal plug onto the alternator assembly.

10. Push the brushes into the brush holder and install the brush holder onto the alternator assembly.

11. Install the Woodruff key into the shaft and the fan over the shaft.

12. Install the drive pulley-to-fan spacer, the pulley, the lockwasher and the nut over the shaft. Secure the pulley and tighten the nut.

90 AMP

1. Be sure to check all parts for wear and replace the defective components as required.

2. Install the rear rotor bearing oil and dust seal.

3. Install the inner alternator battery B + terminal insulator.

4. Position the rectifier assembly. Install the rectifier mount-ing screws, the insulator, the insulator washer, the insulator lockwasher and the insulator nut.

5. Position the stator assembly into the rectifier end shield. Align the scribe marks on the stator and the rectifier end shield.

6. Solder the stator leads to the rectifier assembly; be sure to use needle nose pliers as a heat sink.

7. Position and press the front bearing into the drive end shield. Install the bearing retainer and the pulley fan spacer onto the drive end shield.

8. Position the drive end shield and spacer over the rotor. Using a socket wrench, press the drive end shield onto the rotor.

9. Install the rectifier end shield and stator assembly into the drive end shield and rotor assembly. Install the through bolts and tighten.

10. Push the brushes into the brush holder and install the brush holder onto the alternator assembly.

11. Install the capacitor and terminal plug onto the alternator assembly.

12. Install the Woodruff key into the shaft and the fan over the shaft.

13. Install the drive pulley-to-fan spacer, the pulley, the lockwasher and the nut over the shaft. Secure the pulley and tighten the nut.

HYDRAULIC BRAKE SYSTEM SERVICE

HYDRAULIC BRAKE SYSTEM TROUBLE DIAGNOSIS

Condition	Cause	Correction
Insufficient brakes	1. Improper brake adjustment. 2. Worn lining. 3. Sticking brakes. 4. Brake valve pressure low. 5. Master cylinder low on brake fluid.	1. Adjust brakes. 2. Replace brake lining and adjust brakes. 3. Lubricate brake pivots and support platforms. 4. Inspect for leaks and obstructed brake lines. 5. Fill master cylinder and inspect for leaks.
Brakes apply slowly	1. Improper brake adjustment or lack of lubrication. 2. Excessive leakage with brakes applied. 3. Restriction in brake line or hose.	1. Adjust brakes and lubricate linkage. 2. Inspect all fittings and lines for leaks and repair as necessary. 3. Clean or replace brake line or hose.
Spongy pedal	1. Air in hydraulic system. 2. Swollen rubber parts due to contaminated brake fluid. 3. Improper brake shoe adjustment. 4. Brake fluid with low boiling point. 5. Brake drums ground excessively.	1. Fill and bleed hydraulic system. 2. Clean hydraulic system and recondition wheel cylinders and master cylinder. 3. Adjust brakes. 4. Flush hydraulic system and refill with proper brake fluid. 5. Replace brake drums.
Erratic brakes	1. Linings soaked with grease or brake fluid. 2. Primary and secondary shoes mounted in wrong position.	1. Correct the leak and replace brake lining. 2. Match the primary and secondary shoes and mount in proper position.
Chattering brakes	1. Improper adjustment of brake shoes. 2. Loose front wheel bearings. 3. Hard spots in brake drums. 4. Out-of-round brake drums. 5. Grease or brake fluid on lining.	1. Adjust brakes. 2. Clean, pack and adjust wheel bearings. 3. Grind or replace brake drums. 4. Grind or replace brake drums. 5. Correct leak and replace brake lining.
Squealing brakes	1. Incorrect lining. 2. Distorted brakedrum. 3. Bent brake support plate. 4. Bent brake shoes. 5. Foreign material embedded in brake lining. 6. Dust or dirt in brake drum. 7. Shoes dragging on support plate. 8. Loose support plate. 9. Loose anchor bolts. 10. Loose lining on brake shoes or improperly ground lining.	1. Install correct lining. 2. Grind or replace brake drum. 3. Replace brake support plate. 4. Replace brake shoes. 5. Replace brake shoes. 6. Use compressed air and blow out drums and support plate and shoes. 7. Sand support plate platforms and lubricate. 8. Tighten support plate attaching nuts. 9. Tighten anchor bolts. 10. Replace brake shoes and cam-grind lining.

HYDRAULIC BRAKE SYSTEM TROUBLE DIAGNOSIS — CONT'D

Condition	Cause	Correction
Brakes fading	1. Improper brake adjustment. 2. Improper brake lining. 3. Improper type of brake fluid. 4. Brake drums ground excessively.	1. Adjust brakes correctly. 2. Replace brake lining. 3. Drain, flush and refill hydraulic system. 4. Replace brake drums.
Dragging brakes	1. Improper brake adjustment. 2. Distorted cylinder cups. 3. Brake shoe seized on anchor bolt. 4. Broken brake shoe return spring. 5. Loose anchor bolt. 6. Distorted brake shoe. 7. Loose wheel bearings. 8. Obstruction in brake line. 9. Swollen cups in wheel cylinder or master cylinder. 10. Master cylinder linkage improperly adjusted.	1. Correct adjust brakes. 2. Recondition or replace cylinder. 3. Clean and lubricate anchor bolt. 4. Replace brake shoe return spring. 5. Adjust and tighten anchor bolt. 6. Replace defective brake shoes. 7. Lubricate and adjust wheel bearings. 8. Clean or replace brake line. 9. Recondition wheel or master cylinder. 10. Correctly adjust master cylinder linkage.
Wheel locks	1. Loose or torn brake lining. 2. Incorrect wheel bearing adjustment. 3. Wheel cylinder cups sticking. 4. Saturated brake lining.	1. Replace brake lining. 2. Clean, pack and adjust wheel bearings. 3. Recondition or replace the wheel cylinder. 4. Reline front, rear or all four brakes.
Brakes fade (high speed)	1. Improper brake adjustment. 2. Distorted or out of round brake drums. 3. Overheated brake drums. 4. Incorrect brake fluid (low boiling temperature). 5. Saturated brake lining.	1. Adjust brakes and check fluid. 2. Grind or replace the drums. 3. Inspect for dragging brakes. 4. Drain, flush and refill and bleed the hydraulic brake system. 5. Reline brakes as necessary.
Uneven brake action (brakes pull)	1. Incorrect tire pressure. 2. Front end out of alignment. 3. Loose suspension parts. 4. Worn out brake linings. 5. Incorrect lining material. 6. Malfunctioning caliper assembly. 7. Loose calipers. 8. Contaminated brake linings. 9. Malfunctioning rear brakes.	1. Inflate evenly on both sides to specifications. 2. Check and align to specifications. 3. Check all the suspension mountings. 4. Replace with lining of the correct material. 5. Replace with linings of the correct material. 6. Check for frozen or sluggish pistons and the lubrication of the retainer bolts. Caliper should slide. 7. Check and torque. 8. Repair as necessary. Replace the linings in complete axle sets. 9. Check for inoperative self adjusters. Weak return springs. Leaking wheel cylinders.

HYDRAULIC BRAKE SYSTEM TROUBLE DIAGNOSIS — CONT'D

Problem	Cause	Correction
Uneven brake action (brakes pull)	10. Leaking wheel or piston cylinder seal.	10. Repair as necessary.
	11. Restricted brake tubes or hoses.	11. Check for collapsed rubber hoses or damaged lines. Repair as necessary.
	12. Unmatched tires on the same axle.	12. Same style tires with about the same tread should be used on the same axle.
Slow pedal return	Compensating (peripheral) holes in the quick take-up valve are clogged.	Replace the master cylinder.
Brake pedal pulsates	1. Excessive rotor lateral runout.	1. Check per instructions. If within specifications, machine the rotor.
	2. Rear drums out of round.	2. Check per instructions. If within specifications, machine the drum.
	3. Heat spotted rotors or drums.	3. Check per instructions. If within specifications, machine the drum.
	4. Incorrect wheel bearing adjustments.	4. Repair as necessary.
	5. Out of balance wheel assembly.	5. Repair as necessary.
	6. Brake assembly attachments missing or loose.	6. Repair as necessary.
Excessive pedal effort	1. Leaking vacuum system.	1. Repair as necessary.
	2. Malfunctioning power brake unit.	2. Repair as necessary.
	3. Worn out linings.	3. Replace the linings.
	4. Malfunctioning proportioning valve.	4. Replace the combination valve.
	5. Incorrect lining material.	5. Replace with linings of the correct materials.
	6. Incorrect wheel cylinder.	6. Replace with the correct size wheel cylinder.
	7. Center orifice in quick take-up valve clogged.	7. Replace the master cylinder.
Brake warning light comes on	1. Air in the brake system.	1. Check the fluid level. Check for leaks in the lines, wheel cylinders, or master cylinder. Bleed the system.
	2. Malfunctioning master cylinder.	2. Check for malfunctioning or leaking metering valve. Repair as necessary.
	3. Contaminated or improper brake fluid.	3. Repair as necessary.
	4. Parking brake on or not fully released.	4. Check the parking brake. Repair as necessary.
	5. Worn out brake lining.	5. Replace the linings.
	6. Incorrect wheel bearing adjustment.	6. Repair as necessary.
	7. Malfunctioning self adjusters.	7. Repair as necessary.
	8. Brake assembly attachments missing or loose.	8. Replace or repair as necessary.
	9. Improperly adjusted master cylinder pushrod.	9. Adjust the pushrod length.
	10. RWAL system malfunction.	**10. Refer to REAR WHEEL ANTILOCK BRAKE SYSTEM**

HYDRAULIC BRAKE SYSTEM TROUBLE DIAGNOSIS—CONT'D

Problem	Cause	Correction
Excessive pedal travel	1. Fluid level low in the master cylinder reservoir.	1. Fill the reservoir with approved brake fluid. Check for leaks and air in the system. Check the warning light.
	2. Air in the brake system.	2. Check for leaks in the lines, wheel cylinders, or master cylinder. Bleed the system.
	3. Malfunctioning self adjusters.	3. Repair as necessary.
	4. Master cylinder.	4. Replace or repair as necessary.
	5. Incorrect wheel bearing adjustment.	5. Repair as necessary.
	6. Improperly adjusted master cylinder pushrod.	6. Adjust the master cylinder pushrod.
	7. Fluid bypassing quick take-up valve to the reservoir.	7. Replace the master cylinder.
	8. Leaking brake line or connection.	8. Repair as necessary.
	9. Leaking wheel cylinder or caliper.	9. Repair as necessary.

Hydraulic System Basics

CAUTION

When servicing brake parts, do not create dust by grinding the linings or by blowing them clean with compressed air. Many brake parts contains asbestos fibers which can become airborne if dust is generated during brake servicing. Continuously breathing this dust can cause serious bodily harm. A dampened cloth or a spray bottle with water should be used to remove brake dust prior to work. Equipment is also commercially available for safe brake servicing.

The hydraulic system controls the braking operation and consists of a master cylinder, hydraulic lines and hoses, control valves and calipers and/or wheel cylinders. When the brake pedal is depressed, the master cylinder forces brake fluid regulated by the proportioning valve to the calipers and/or cylinders, via lines and hoses. Rubber seals throughout the system contain the fluid and prevent leakage.

Servicing the hydraulic brake system is chiefly a matter of adjustments, replacement of worn or damaged parts and correcting the damage caused by grit, dirt or contaminated brake fluid. Always make sure the brake system is clean and tightly sealed when a brake job is completed and that only approved heavy duty brake fluid is used.

Return springs in the master cylinder help the brake pedal return to the original unapplied position. Check valves (in most

Typical brake system schematic

cases) regulate the return flow of the fluid to the master cylinder. Other valves, such as the metering valve, proportioning valve or combination valve, regulate the flow of fluid to the caliper/wheel cylinder, to achieve even and efficient braking.

Dual Braking Systems

Dual braking systems were introduced on many light Pick-Ups and Vans during the late 1960's. The main difference is the use of a tandem master cylinder which is essentially 2 master cylinders in one. Two separate pistons share 1 bore and 2 fluid reservoirs are built into 1 housing. Dual brake lines split the calipers and/or wheel cylinders into 2 groups, each actuated by its own, separate master cylinder piston. In the event of failure of 1 of the dual systems, the other should provide enough braking to safely stop the vehicle. The development of dual braking systems is an improvement over the older single systems where a leak anywhere would allow the fluid to escape resulting in loss of braking.

The dual system usually includes a red warning light on the instrument panel which is activated by a pressure differential valve. The valve is sensitive to any loss of hydraulic pressure that might result from a braking failure on either side of the system.

Light Pick-Ups are equipped with either a front/rear wheel split or a diagonally split system. On front/rear systems, the front wheels are connected to one circuit while the rear wheels are connected to the other circuit. Diagonally split systems have diagonally opposite wheels connected to each circuit.

These systems are the most popular ever since front disc brakes were introduced. Since a greater amount of brake fluid is moved in a disc brake system, one chamber of the the master cylinder feeds the front discs, while the other chamber feeds the rear wheel cylinders.

Brake Fluid

Approved DOT 3 heavy duty type brake fluid retains the correct consistency throughout the widest range of temperature variation, will not affect rubber cups or seals, helps protect the metal parts of the brake system against failure and has a high boiling point to assure long trouble free brake operation when properly maintained.

Never use brake fluid from a container that has been used for any other liquid. Mineral oil, alcohol, antifreeze or cleaning solvents, even in very small quantities, will contaminate brake fluid. Contaminated brake fluid will cause rubber parts within the hydraulic system to swell or deteriorate. Always return the cap to the fluid container after using the brake fluid. This will prevent the fluid from absorbing moisture from the surrounding air, which will lower its boiling point. Do not use brake fluid that has been sitting in an unopened container for an extending amount of time.

Brake fluid will also absorb moisture from the air. Over time, brake fluid stored for long periods and fluid inside the brake system will be affected by this moisture. Rust, corrosion and pitting of system components result. Some fleet managers change the brake fluid in their vehicles every year or 2 to avoid brake system problems caused by moisture.

Use extreme care when using brake fluid. It will damage painted surfaces.

Hydraulic Line Repair

Steel tubing is used for the hydraulic lines and special flexible hoses connect moving parts such as front calipers which turn with the steering and the connection between the body and rear axle.

When replacing steel lines or flexible brake hose, use only exact replacements, in both size and quality.

NOTE: Never use copper tubing for hydraulic brake lines. Copper is subject to fatigue cracking and corrosion which could result in brake failure. Use specially made steel brake lines only. Tighten all connections securely.

After replacement, bleed the brake system at each wheel and at the booster, if equipped with a bleeder screw.

If a length of steel brake line tubing must be replaced and the end flared, a special double flaring tool must be used. Always inspect newly formed flares for defects. Double lap flaring tools must be used. Single flares cannot hold the high pressures in the brake system and tend to crack. When bending brake tubing to fit the frame or rear axle contours, be careful not to crack or kink the tube. Always clean the inside of even new brake tube with clean isopropyl alcohol.

Steel tubing is used for the hydraulic lines between any 2 parts that do not move independent of one another, like the master cylinder and the front brake tube connector or along the axle tubes between the brake tee and the rear brake cylinders. Brake hoses provide a flexible connection between the tube and a part that moves independently, like the hose that connects the brake tube to the front brake calipers or the tube that runs along the body of the vehicle connected by hose down to the axle.

BRAKE TUBING

If a section of the brake tube becomes damaged, the entire section should be replaced with tubing of the same type, size, shape and length. Copper tubing should not be used in the hydraulic system. When bending brake tubing to fit the frame or axle contours, be careful not to kink or crack the tube.

All brake tubing should be double flared to provide good leak proof connections. Always clean the inside of a new brake tube with clean isopropyl alcohol before installing.

BRAKE HOSE

All flexible brake hoses should be carefully inspected often. They should be replaced if they show any signs of softening, cracking, swelling or other damage. Flexible hoses should be inspected for any signs of road damage, cracks or chafing any of which requires immediate hose replacement.

When installing a new brake hose, make sure it is not twisted and is positioned to avoid contact with other vehicle components under any suspension condition. Hoses feeding front brake calipers are often equipped with a copper washer for a seal. This should also be replaced when hoses are renewed. After hose installation, make sure the hose is not twisted. Many hoses have a painted stripe on them to help the technician determine if the hose is twisted.

Hydraulic Control Valves

PRESSURE DIFFERENTIAL VALVE

The valve activates a panel warning light in event of pressure loss failure. As pressure fails in one split system, the other system's normal pressure causes a piston in the switch to compress a spring and move until an electrical circuit is completed lighting the dash light. Normally, the spring balanced piston automatically recenters when the brake pedal is released, thus flashing the warning light only during brake application and will recenter automatically after repairs are successfully completed and the system is properly bled.

METERING VALVE

Often used on vehicles equipped with front disc and rear drum brakes, the metering valve improves braking balance during

A. METERING VALVE
B. WARNING VALVE
C. PROPORTIONER

Brake proportioning valve—typical

Height sensing valve—General Motors, typical

COMBINATION VALVE

A valve combining 2 or 3 functions (metering, proportioning and/or brake warning) may be used. The combination valve is usually mounted under the hood close to the master cylinder, where the brake lines can be easily routed to the front and rear wheels. The combination valve is a non-serviceable unit and if found to be malfunctioning, must be replaced as a unit.

HEIGHT SENSING VALVE

Most light Pick-Ups have some sort of height sensing valve. The vehicle braking force is distributed to the front and rear wheels as determined be either a light or heavy payload. The valve is usually mounted on the frame and a linkage connects the valve to a bracket mounted on the axle.

Adding suspension accessories or other equipment, such as load leveling kits, lift kits, extra springs, etc., or making modifications that will change the distance between the axle and frame without changing the load will provide a false reading to the sensing valve. This could result in unsatisfactory brake performance which could result in an accident and possibly personal injury.

Disc Brakes

CALIPERS

Caliper disc brakes can be divided into 3 types: dual piston floating caliper, single piston floating caliper and single piston sliding caliper.

On the floating caliper types, the inner pad is hydraulically pushed into contact with the disc, while the reaction force generated is used to pull the outer pad into contact with the other side of the disc, made possible by allowing the caliper to move slightly along the axle's center line. Two pistons may be may be used to accomodate more severe braking requirements on heavier vehicles. All disc brake systems are self-adjusting and have no provision for manual adjustment.

With the sliding caliper type, the caliper assembly slides along the smooth and lubricated surface of a key or stopper, nomenclature varies between manufacturers, which is held stationary by cotter pins or retaining bolts. The caliper is held against the key or stopper with 1 or 2 support springs.

One of the recent developments in brake equipment materials includes the use of aluminum calipers for the purpose of saving weight. A vast array of anti-rattle springs, clips and anti-squeal pads and shims are used by manufacturers to prevent the pads from making any undesirable noises. In addition, most brake pads are comprised of semi-metallic materials for improved stopping power. Unfortunately, these pads often produce an annoying brake squeal as they are used, but the squeal itself should not reduce the stopping ability of the pads. If the pad kit includes plates or shims, use them when servicing the disc brakes. Aftermarket spreads and sprays are also available to quiet noisy pads. It is always a good idea to replace calipers in pairs.

ROTORS

Rotors provide the surface upon which the brake pads stop the vehicle. It is important to inspect the rotor carefully. Manufacturers differ some on permissable runout (warpage) of the rotor but excessive runout can usually be felt as a pulsation at the brake pedal regardless of the specification.

A wobble pump effect is created when the rotor is not perfectly flat and the pad hits a high spot forcing fluid back into the master cylinder. This alternating pressure causes a pulsation. It can often be felt at the pedal when the brakes are applied. But

light brake applications by preventing application of the front disc brakes unitl the pressure to the rear brakes overcomes the tension of the rear brake shoe return springs. Thus, when the front brake pads contact the rotor the rear brakes shoes move outward to contact the brake drum at approximately the same time.

The metering valve should be inspected whenever the brakes are serviced. A slight amount of moisture inside the boot does not indicate a defective valve, however a great deal of fluid indicates a faulty valve and replacement is recommended. Make sure to install the brake lines in the correct ports when installing a new valve, crossed lines will cause the hydraulic system to malfunction.

PROPORTIONING VALVE

The proportioning valve is used to transmit full input pressure to the rear brakes up to a certain point (the split point). Beyond the split point, it reduces the amount of pressure to the rear brakes according to a certain ratio, which is built into the valve. On light pedal applications, equal braking pressure is transmitted to to the front and rear brakes. During heavier brake applications, however, the pessure delivered to the rear brakes is lower than that at the front brakes to prevent rear wheel lockup and skidding.

Whenever the brakes are serviced, the valve should be inspected. To check valve operation, install hydraulic gauges ahead of and behind the valve and determine that it has an operative transition point above which rear brake pressure is proportioned. If the valve is leaking replacement is required.

Excessive runout of parallelism

Wobble pump action resulting from a warped rotor

more importantly, as the piston wobbles in and out, it acts like a small pump and air can be drawn into the system past the dust boot and caliper piston seal. This is especially a problem on multi-piston calipers.

An excessive amount of runout can cause the pads to be out of adjustment because they cannot hold themselves against the rotor at all times. It is always a good idea to replace rotors in pairs.

To check the actual runout of the rotor, fist tighten the spindle nut to remove all endplay. Fasten a dial indicator on the suspension on a convenient location so the pin contacts the rotor surface about 1 in. from its outer edge. Set the dial at 0 and check the runout while turning the rotor 1 full revolution. If the rotor is warped beyond limits, the rotor should be replace. Rotors the are not warped beyond the specification can be resurfaced, as long as the final thickness is not below the minumum thickness requirement of the rotor.

Lateral Runout: The wobbly movement of the rotor from side-to-side as it rotates. Excessive lateral runout causes the rotor faces to knock bask the pads and can cause brake chatter, shudder or vibration.

Parallelism (lack of): This refers to the amount of variation in the thickness of the rotor. Excessive variation of parallelism can cause a pulsating pedal, front end vibrations or grabbing condiions; a condition comparable to an out-of-round brake drum. Check parallelism with a micrometer. Measure the thickness of the rotor a 8 or more equally spaced locations on the rotor, equally distant from the outer edge, preferably at the midpoint of the braking surface. A lack of parallelism results if the difference between the highest and lowest measurement is beyond the parallelism specification.

Surface or Micro-inch finish, flatness and smoothness: These terms all refer to the degree of perfection of the flat surfaces on each side fo the rotor. Visually inspecting the rotor, the machined surface should have a fine ground polish with a swirling pattern to reduce brake squeal.

DISC BRAKE PADS

The brake pads are the tools that the vehicle uses to stop, so they should be inspected very carefully. Pads should be replaced only in sets, both sides of the same axle, if any of the pads is damaged, cracked, burnt or separated from the plate that it is glued or riveted to. Replace the pads if any of their lining is worn down to $\frac{1}{16}$ in. thickness. If the lining is allowed to wear beyond this point, severe and costly damage to the rotor may result. Note that individual state inspection guidelines take precedence over these general recommendation.

Floating caliper type disc brake pads may wear at an angle; the measurement should always be taken at the narrowest end of the taper. Tapered lining should be replaced if the amount of tapering exceeds $\frac{1}{8}$ in. from end to end and the cause of the taper should be investigated and repaired, if possible.

To prevent potentially costly paint damage, remove some brake fluid from the master fluid reservoir and install the reservoir cover before servicing the pads. When installing new pads, the caliper piston is forced back into its bore and fluid is pushed back into the master cylinder. The fluid could spill and remove paint from any painted surface that it comes in contact with.

When the caliper is removed from its mouning adaptor, do not allow it to dangle by the brake hose. This can damage the hose and create a dangerous situation. Always rest the caliper on a suspensiion member of suspent it from the frame with a wire or rope.

Drum Brakes

WHEEL CYLINDERS

The wheel cylinder performs in response to the master cylinder. It receives fluid from the hydraulic tube through its inlet port. As the pressure increases, the wheel cylinder cups and pistons are forced apart. As a result, the hydraulic pressure is converted into mechanical force acting on the brake shoes. The variation in wheel cylinder size (diameter) is one of the factors controlling the distribution of braking force in a vehicle. Bleeder screws are provided to remove air or vapor trapped in the system.

Wheel cylinders may need reconditioning or replacement whenever the brake shoes are replaced or when required to correct a leak condition. On many designs, the wheel cylinders can be diassembled without removing them from the backing plate. On some designs, however, the cylinder is mounted in an indention in the backing plate or a cylinder piston stop is welded to the backing plate. When servicing brakes of this type, the cylinder must be removed from the backing plate before being disassembled.

Leaks which coat the boot and the cylinder with fluid or result in a dropped reservoir fluid level or dampen and stain the brake linings are dangerous. Such leaks can cause the brakes to grab or fail and should be immediately corrected. A leakage, not immediately apparent, can be detected by pulling back the cylinder boot. A small amount of fluid seepage dampening the interior of the boot is normal, however a dripping boot is not. Unless other conditions causing a brake to pull, grab or drag becomes obvious, the wheel cylinder is a suspect and should be included in general reconditioning. It is always a good idea to service wheel cylinders in pairs.

Cylinder binding may be caused by rust, deposits, grime or swollen cups due to fluid contamination or by a cup wedged into an excessive piston clearance. If the clearance between the pistons and the bore wall exceeds allowable values, a condition called heel drag may exist. It can result in rapid cup wear and can cause the pistons to retract very slowly when the brakes are released. A ring of a hard, crystal like substance is sometimes noticed in the cylinder bore where the piston stops after the brakes are released.

BRAKE DRUMS

The condition of the brake drum surface is equally as important as the surface of the lining. All drum braking surfaces should be clean, smooth, free of hark spots, heat damage, scoring and forign material embedded in the braking surface. The drum should not be out-of-round, bell mouthed or barrel shaped. Drums should be checked with a drum micrometer before resurfacing to see if it within over-size limits. If the drum is within safe limints, it should be machined to true the drum surface and to remove any contamination in the surface from previous linings and road matter. Too much metal removed from the drum is unsafe and may result in brake fade due to the thin drum not being able to absorb the heat generated, vibration from ensuing drum distortion and generally unsafe conditions.

Brake drum runout should not exceed 0.005 in. Drums machined to more than 0.060 in. oversize are unsafe and should be replaced. It is always good practice to replace drums on both whels at the same time to ensure even braking.

If the drums are in good condition, smooth up any slight scoring by sanding with coarse sand paper, then polishing with emery cloth. If deep scores or grooves are present, machine the drums to restore them to good operating condition.

DRUM BRAKE SHOES

The brake shoes should also be inspected very carefully. Shoes should be replaced only in sets, both sides of the same axle, if any of the shoes are bent, damaged, cracked, burnt or separated from the plate that it is glued or riveted to. Replace the shoes if any of their lining is worn down to $\frac{1}{16}$ in. thickness. If the lining is allowed to wear beyond this point, severe and costly damage to the drum may result. Note that individual state inspection guidelines take precedence over these general recommendation.

Rear brakes with weak return springs may create a bell-mouthed condition which causes the shoes to wear at an angle; if so, the measurement should always be taken at the narrowest end of the taper. Tapered linings should be replaced, if the amount of tapering is excessive and the cause of the taper should be investigated and repaired, if possible.

Disassemble and assemble one side at a time to prevent improper assembly. This will also provide a model that can be checked if the installation doen not look right. Always complete the brake shoe adjustment with the wheels installed and adjust the parking brake cable last.

STAR AND SCREW ADJUSTER

Star and screw self-adjusters are used on most model vehicles. This system requires manual adjustment only when the shoes have been replaced, when the star wheel has been disturbed or when the star wheel is not operating properly.

As the star wheel is turned, it expands or contracts the shoes accordingly.

In most cases, the brakes can be initially adjusted by removing the drum, measuring the internal diameter of the drum and setting the shoes to slightly less than that measurement. Normally, the brakes will self-adjust when the vehicle is backed up and the brakes are firmly applied.

General Diagnosis

LOW PEDAL

Normal brake lining wear reduces pedal reserve. Low pedal reserve may also be caused by the lack of brake fluid in the master cylinder. This means a brake adjustment is required. Check fluid level in the master cylinder and add as required.

FLUID LOSS

If the master cylinder requires constant addition of brake fluid, fluid may be leaking past the piston cups in the master cylinder, calipers or wheel cylinders, the brake lines or hoses or through loose connections. Brake hoses often have copper sealing washers which may need to be replaced. Replace worn or damaged components, refill and bleed the system.

FLUID CONTAMINATION

To determine if contamination exists in the brake fluid as indicated by swollen, deteriorated rubber parts like wheel cylinder cups, the following tests can be made.

Place a small amount of the drained brake fluid into a clear glass bottle. Separation of the fluid into distinct layers will indicate mineral oil content. Be safe and discard the old brake fluid that has been bled from the system since it may contain dirt and other contamination and should not be reused.

BRAKE ADJUSTMENT

Self adjusting brakes usually do not require manual adjustment. When installing new brake shoes, it may be advisable to make the initial adjustment manually to speed up adjusting time.

AUTOMATIC ADJUSTER CHECK

On most vehicles, drum brakes appear only on the rear axle. Brake adjustments are automatic and are made during reverse brake applications.

Raise and safely support the vehicle, have a helper in the driver's seat to apply brakes. If equipped, remove the plug from the adjustment slot in the backing plate to observe the star wheel. Some models are adjusted through the face of the brake drum; others through the backing plate. Tighten the adjusting star wheel screw until the wheel can just be turned by hand. The brake drag should be equal at both wheels. Back off the adjusting star wheel about 30-35 notches. The brakes should have no drag after the adjuster has been backed off about 15 notches. If heavy drag is present, the parking brake likely needs service and/or adjustment.

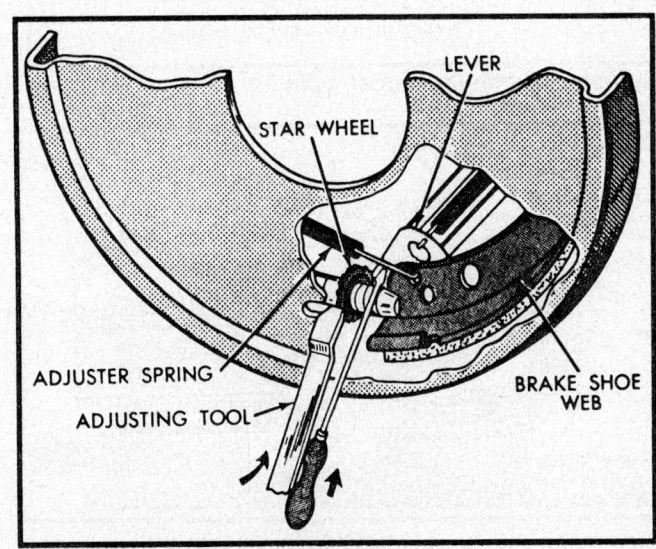

Drum brake adjustment – typical

CHRYSLER CORPORATION

Master Cylinder Service

Chrysler Corporation uses a dual master cylinder which contains a double hydraulic cylinder with 2 fluid reservoirs and primary and secondary hydraulic pistons. On most models, the master cylinder is assisted by a vacuum booster. The unit is mounted on a 90 degree bracket on some models, directly to the dashboard on others. Hydraulic rear drum brakes with automatic adjusters and self-adjusting front disc brakes are standard on all models.

The front outlet tube of the master cylinder is connected to the hydraulic system control valve and then to the rear brakes. This is referred the secondary system. The rear outlet tube is connected to the control valve and to the front brakes. This system is referred to as the primary system. No residual pressure valves are used in the master cylinder outlets.

During normal operation, the fluid level in the master cylinder will rise during brake operation and fall during release. It is also expected that the fluid level will decrease with brake pad wear. In addition, a trace of brake fluid on the booster shell below the master cylinder mounting flange will often be found as a result of the normal lubricating action of the master cylinder bore and seal. All of these conditions are considered normal and are not indications the master cylinder needs service.

Two types of master cylinders were used by Chrysler Corporation; 1) a cast iron master cylinder with built-in reservoir and separate proportioning valve and 2) a master cylinder with a pressed on plastic reservoir. The body of the two-piece master cylinder is made of anodized aluminum and the reservoir is made of nylon. Both compartments of the reservoir are interconnected to permit equalization of the fluid level. However, a sufficient quantity of fluid is retained in the reservoir of the unaffected system to permit operation of that half of the master cylinder even if the other half of the reservoir is drained due to a hydraulic leak.

Use extra care when servicing aluminum master cylinders not to cross thread brake line fittings and do not overtighten any threaded connection.

In the event of a front brake system malfunction the proportioning valve with a bypass feature allows full hydraulic pressure to the rear brake system.

Disassembly and Assembly

The manufacturer does not recommend that either the cast iron or the aluminum master cylinder be overhauled but replaced only. Do not attempt to hone the bore of the aluminum master cylinder or the hard anodized surface will be removed.

On the aluminum master cylinders, the plastic reservoir may be replaced using the following procedure:

1. Clean the outside of the master cylinder and remove the caps. Drain and discard remaining brake fluid.
2. Hold the master cylinder in a soft-jaw vise and grasp the plastic reservoir. Firmly rock reservoir from side-to-side to and remove it from the master cylinder housing. Don't pry the reservoir off with a tool that could damage the plastic body.
3. Remove and discard the reservoir grommets from the master cylinder body.
4. To assemble, lubricate the new grommets with brake fluid and install in the master cylinder body.
5. Place the reservoir in position. Make sure it is positioned properly and that the lettering can be read from the left side of the master cylinder. Install by rocking the reservoir while pressing down. Seat the reservoir until the bottom of the reservoir touches the top of the grommets.

Brake Booster Service

Chrysler Corporation models covered here are equipped with vacuum boosters.

Under normal operating conditions, with brakes released, a vacuum suspended booster operates with vacuum on both sides of its diaphragm, or both diaphragms in a tandem diaphragm unit. When the brakes are applied, air at atmospheric pressure is admitted to one side of the diaphragm, or both diaphragms in a tandem diaphragm unit, to provide the power assist.

Brake boosters used by Chrysler Corporation are not repairable and if defective, the booster must be replaced as a unit, including the check valve. Do not remove the check valve.

Brake Booster Vacuum Pump

On gasoline engines, engine vacuum is used to power the vacuum booster brake. On diesel engines, there is not enough vacuum available for vacuum booster brake operation.

On diesel engines, vacuum is supplied from a pump. If equipped with Cummins Turbo Diesel, the vacuum pump and power steering pump is one assembly which is driven from a common shaft from the front gear train. To service either pump, the complete assembly must be removed from the front gear housing.

In addition, these vehicles will have an engine warning light panel on the dash which contains 5 warning indicator lights: brake, water in fuel, wait to start, anti-lock and low fuel. The Brake light is connected to a sensor that monitors vacuum in the brake booster system. The brake light when lit indicates low

Chrysler aluminum master cylinder

Removing plastic reservoir from master cylinder body

Power steering and vacuum pump on Cummins diesel engine

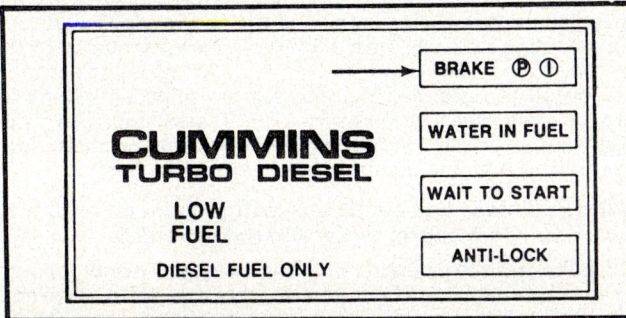

Message center includes low vacuum and anti-lock system warning lights

Vacuum sensor under the left hood hinge is supplied by line from booster check valve

vacuum. If this light comes ON, the brake system must be serviced.

NOTE: The brake light will also be activated when the parking brake is on or there is a hydraulic brake failure.

The vacuum pump provides vacuum for the brake booster and dash controllers. The vacuum sensor is mounted under the left hood hinge in the engine compartment. Vacuum is supplied by a hose teed off the check valve in the brake booster. The sensor will activate the brake light on the warning light panel in 10 seconds or less when the vacuum drops to 8.5 in. Hg or less in the brake system.

Removal and Installation

1. Remove the vacuum pump and power steering pump as-

Removing power steering and vacuum pump assembly from engine's gear drive

Fabricate pin for pressing off drive gear

sembly by removing the 2 bolts which should need an 18mm wrench.

2. Clean the gasket from the engine rear cover.

3. Install the pump assembly with a new gasket. Torque the bolts to 57 ft. lbs.

Disassembly and Assembly

1. Before starting pump disassembly, make a pin 2 in. long and 0.312 in. diameter. Use an 8mm bolt or a piece of drill rod. This pin must be hard so make it from a 10.9 grade metric bolt or at least an SAE Grade 8 capscrew.

2. Insert the pin into the pump shaft and screw a M14-2mm threaded capscrew in against the pin.

3. Tighten the capscrew against the pin to draw off the gear/eccentric/bearing assembly off of the power steering pump shaft.

4. Inspect the gear for excessive wear or damage. If the gear/eccentric is not damaged, do not separate them. If the gear is damaged, use a press to press the eccentric out of the gear. Use a

Insert pin, tighten capscrew against the pin to draw gear assembly from pump shaft

Remove the pushrods from the housing

Remove vacuum diaphragm assemblies, then O-rings

Use ⅜–18 Grade 8 capscrew to draw assembly onto pump shaft

Lube pushrods and O-rings with engine oil at assembly

flat plate over the new gear and press it onto the eccentric until it bottoms.

5. Inspect the bearing, turning it by hand. If the bearing looks good and feels smooth to turn, do not separate them. If the bearing/eccentric is bad, press the eccentric out of the bearing, using the appropriate size socket or tool that will press only on the inner race of the bearing. Press it on until it bottoms.

6. With a 15mm wrench, remove the 4 nuts and separate the power steering pump from the vacuum pump housing. Remove the 2 short pushrods from the housing. Inspect the pushrods. They should move smoothly but should not move side-to-side.

7. With a 10mm wrench, remove the diaphragm assemblies from the housing. If the diaphragms are bad, they must be replaced as a unit. Remove and discard the O-rings from the center bore and pushrod bores.

8. Clean all parts and dry with compressed air.

9. Install the 2 spacers on the studs on the back of the power steering pump.

10. Install the vacuum pump housing onto the power steering pump using a new O-ring lubricated with engine oil. Install the four retaining nuts and with a 15mm wrench, torque to 18 ft. lbs.

11. Install the gear/eccentric/bearing assembly by pulling it onto the power steering shaft with a ⅜–18 thread capscrew with a flat washer threaded into the power steering pump shaft. Pull it on until it bottoms. Remove capscrew and washer.

NOTE: This is a press fit and will require a minimum of SAE Grade 8 capscrew for thread strength.

12. Lubricate the pushrods with engine oil and install then in the housing. Install new O-rings, also lubricated with engine oil.

13. With a 10mm wrench, install the diaphragm assemblies. Torque to 7 ft. lbs.

14. Install the assembly to the engine with new gaskets. Torque bolts to 57 ft. lbs.

Combination Valve

All models have a hydraulic system control valve in the brake system. The valve is usually mounted on the frame rail below the master cylinder. The control valve assembly in B-150 and B-250 models combines a brake warning switch with a hold-off and proportioning valve assembly. A brake warning switch and hold-off valve assembly are combined and used on B-350 models. Hold-off and Proportioning valves are used because of different braking characteristics between disc and drum brakes.

A height sensing proportioning valve regulates the front to rear braking balance based upon vehicle load conditions. The valve senses vehicle loads through variations in rear suspension height. With a light load on the rear axle, the valve reduces hydraulic pressure to the rear brakes. As the load increases, more hydraulic pressure is released to the rear brakes.

HOLD-OFF VALVE

The hold-off valve section of the combination valve holds off pressure to the front disc brakes to allow the rear drum brake shoes to overcome the return springs and begin to contact the drums. This valve keeps the output pressure to the front brakes in the 3–30 psi range until the hold-off pressure is reached (117 psi) and then blends back to give full output pressure to the front brakes under heavy brake applications. This feature helps keep the front brakes from locking under light pedal applications when driving on icy surfaces. The hold-off valve has no effect on front brake pressure during hard stops.

Checking the Hold-Off Valve

A visual check will show that the valve stem extends slightly when the brakes are applied and retracts when the brakes are released.

Combination warning switch/hold-off/proportioning valve assembly—typical

Brake warning switch/hold-off valve

In case of a hold-off valve malfunction, remove the valve and install a new combination valve assembly.

BRAKE WARNING SWITCH

The hydraulic brake system is split. The front brakes are part of one system and the rear brakes are part of the other. Both systems are routed through, but hydraulically separated by the pressure differential switch. The function of this switch is to alert the driver to a malfunction in one of the hydraulic systems. Since the brake system is split, a failure in one part of the brake system does not result in failure of the entire hydraulic brake system.

The brake warning light on the instrument panel will come ON if one of the brake systems should fail after the brake pedal is depressed. The warning light switch is the latching type. It will automatically recenter itself after the repair is made and the pedal is depressed.

The instrument panel bulb can be checked each time the ignition switch is turned to **ON, START** or the parking brake is set.

Checking the Brake Warning Switch Unit

The brake warning light is lit only when the parking brake is applied with the ignition key turned **ON**. The same light will also illuminate should 1 of the 2 service brake systems fail.

To test the service brake warning system, raise the vehicle on a hoist and open a wheel cylinder bleeder while a helper depresses the brake pedal and watches the warning light. If the light fails to light, check for a burned out bulb, disconnected socket or a broken or disconnected wire at the switch. If the bulb is not burned out and the wire continuity is uninterupted check the service brake warning switch operation with a test light between the switch terminal and a voltage source.

If the light still fails to light, disconnect the brake tubes from the valve assembly and install a new valve assembly. If a new is installed, bleed the system. The warning switch is not serviced separately. Do not remove the swicth or attempt to repair.

After repairing and bleeding the brake system applying the brakes with moderate force will hydraulically recenter the valve's piston and automatically turn off the warning light. Do not disassemble to reset the piston.

Caliper Service

Chrysler Corporation calipers are one-piece castings with the in-

Caliper assembly—typical

Remove piston seal without scratching bore

Clean up bore with light honing

Lubricate piston seal with brake fluid and install

board side containing the piston bore. A square cut rubber seal is located in a groove in the piston bore which provides the hydraulic seal between the piston and the cylinder wall.

As the brake pedal is pressed, hydraulic pressure is applied against the piston. This pressure pushes the inboard brake lining against the inboard braking surface of the rotor. As the force increases against the rotor, the caliper assembly moves inboard and provides a clamping action on the rotor.

When brake pressure is released, the piston seal returns to its normal position, pulling the piston back into the caliper bore. This creates a running clearance between the inner brake lining and rotor.

Disassembly and Assembly

1. Chrysler Corporation does not recommend using air pressure to remove the piston from the caliper due to the possibility of personal injury. Their suggested procedure is to remove the caliper from its vehicle mount, remove the outboard shoe and support the caliper on top of the control arm on shop towels to absorb brake fluid. Carefully depress the brake pedal and allow hydraulic pressure to push the piston out of the bore.

NOTE: The brake pedal will fall away when the piston has passed the bore opening. Prop the brake pedal to any position below the first inch of pedal travel to prevent loss of brake fluid. If both front caliper pistons are to be removed, disconnect the flexible brake line at the frame bracket after removing the first piston. Plug the brake line to remove the piston from the opposite caliper.

2. Remove the flexible brake line from the caliper.
3. Mount the caliper in a soft-jaw vise. Do not use too much pressure or the bore will be distorted and the piston will bind.
4. Remove the dust boot and, using a small, pointed wooden stick, work the piston seal out of its groove in the caliper bore. Do not use any metal tool which might nick or scratch the bore. Discard the seal.

To assemble:

5. Assembly is the reverse of the disassembly procedure. Clean all parts well using alcohol and blow dry. Inspect the piston bore for scoring or pitting. Install a new piston if it is pitted, scored or the plating is worn. Some pistons are plastic. Bores that show light scratches can be cleaned with fine crocus cloth. Deeper scratches may need to be honed.

NOTE: The bore must not be honed more than 0.002 in. oversize, only 0.001 in. oversize on Caravan, Voyager and Town & Country models. Measure the bore accurately before honing. If the bore does not clean up within this specification, a new housing must be installed. Black stains on the piston are caused by the piston seal and will do no harm.

6. Clean all parts well, dip the new piston seal in brake fluid and install in the bore. Position the seal at one area at a time and, using fingers, gently work the seal into the groove.
7. Coat the new piston boot with brake fluid leaving a generous amount inside the boot. Position the boot on the piston and install the piston into the bore, pushing it past the piston seal until it bottoms in the bore.
8. Position the dust boot and with a circular driver, seal into the caliper.
9. Install the flexible brake hose with new seals.

Wheel Cylinder Service

The rear brakes are drum type with internal expanding shoes. The rear brakes are of the single anchor type, mounted to the same anchor and actuated by 1 wheel cylinder. The wheel cylinder has 2 pistons. Brake adjustments are automatic and are made during reverse brake applications.

Wheel cylinders may need reconditioning or replacement whenever the brake shoes are replaced or when required to correct a leak condition. Leaks which coat the boot and the cylinder with fluid or result in a dropped reservoir fluid level or dampen and stain the brake linings are dangerous. Such leaks can cause the brakes to grab or fail and should be immediately corrected. A leakage, not immediately apparent, can be detected by pulling back the cylinder boot. A small amount of fluid seepage dampening the interior of the boot is normal. However, a dripping boot is not. Unless other conditions causing a brake to pull, grab or drag become obvious, the wheel cylinder is suspect and should be included in general reconditioning.

Cylinder binding may be caused by rust, deposits, grime or swollen cups due to fluid contamination or by a cup wedged into an excessive piston clearance.

Hydraulic system parts should not be allowed to come into contact with oil or grease, neither should those be handled with greasy hands. Even a trace of any petroleum based product is sufficient to cause damage to the rubber parts.

Disassembly and Assembly

1. Remove the brake bleeder screw.
2. Remove the dust boots, allow any brake fluid to drain out.
3. Remove the pistons, seals and inner spring.

Rear wheel cylinder for Chrysler 11 and 12 inch brake—typical

4. Inspect the bore for scoring and corrosion. The inside of the bore may be cleaned with fine crocus cloth. If bore is scored, replace cylinder. Black stains on the cylinder walls are caused by the piston cups and will not impair operation of the cylinder. Clean the cylinder with alcohol or brake fluid.

5. Lubricate the seals with brake fluid and install. Cup lips should always face inward. Install the spring assembly and seals.

6. Carefully install the pistons and dust boots.

7. Install the bleeder screw.

Anti-Lock Braking Systems

Despite advances in brake design over the years, even the best systems in use can still lock up during certain road conditions, such as wet road surfaces. When the brakes lock up, the driver can lose control of the vehicle, because a locked wheel cannot absorb any cornering or lateral forces and steering is lost. It is impossible to brake to a maximum and at the same time steer the vehicle when the front wheels are locked. If the back wheels are locked the vehicle will become unstable and start to slide.

While many different ways have been tried over the years to solve this problem, mechanical sensors could not provide sufficient information about wheel rotation speed and mechanical control units could not operate the brakes fast enough to prevent brake lockup.

The growth of the electronics industry has allowed small computers (microprocessors) to be reduced in both size and cost. Coupled with fast reacting electronic sensors, anti-lock braking has become more reliable with widespread application.

REAR WHEEL ANTI-LOCK BRAKE SYSTEM

Chrysler Corporation's Rear Wheel Anti-lock brake system (RWAL) is designed to prevent rear wheel lockup under heavy braking conditions. Anti-lock braking allows a vehicle to stop without locking the wheels and therefore maintains directional stability.

The RWAL system uses a standard master cylinder and booster arrangement with a vertical split hydraulic circuit. An electronic control module, rear wheel speed sensor and a dual sole-noid control valve (hydraulic valve) are the major components added to this system. No hydraulic pumps are used. Braking pressure comes directly from pushing on the brake pedal.

The system will provide vehicle stability by allowing at least 1 rear wheel to remain unlocked. Since the system works on the rear wheels only it is possible to lock the front wheels. In addition, the system benefit is somewhat limited when a 4WD vehicle is in the 4WD mode.

The system utilizes an amber antilock warning light in the instrument panel along with the standard red brake warning light. These 2 lights work together to notify the driver the driver

RWAL connection locations—typical

RWAL electronic brake control module—typical

RWAL electronic brake control module pin locations

that the system is working correctly. These lights are also used to blink fault codes for system diagnosis.

Major Components

The system continually monitors rear wheel speed with a sensor mounted on the rear axle. A toothed exciter ring is press fit onto the differential case next to the differential ring gear and provides a signal for the sensor. When the teeth on the exciter ring pass the sensor pole piece, an AC voltage is induced in the sensor circuit with a frequency proportional to the average rear wheel speed. In the event of an impending lockup condition during braking, the RWAL modulates hydraulic pressure to the rear brakes. This inhibits rear wheel lockup.

The electronic brake control module is located behind the glove box on most models. The control module monitors the rear wheel speed and controls the dual solenoid valve.

The control module determines if the rear wheels are decelerating too quickly and sends a signal to the dual solenoid hydraulic valve to prevent rear wheel lockup. The control module also performs a system self check every time the ignition key is turned **ON**.

The dual solenoid hydraulic valve is located between the rear brakes and the proportioning valve and is attached on the left frame rail near the rear axle.

Under normal conditions, the valve will allow brake fluid to flow freely between the master cylinder and the rear brakes. Once anti-lock braking begins the control module will trigger the valve to either isolate or reduce pressure to the rear wheels.

The electronic control module has the capability of generating and storing fault codes. Only one code can be stored and shown at any one time. Also, if a fault code is generated the electronic control module will retain the code even after a key **OFF** condition.

If a problem is detected the electronic control module will illuminate the amber anti-lock brake warning light and set a fault code. When a fault code is set the red brake warning light will also be lit. To determine what the fault code is, momentarily ground the RWAL diagnostic connector and count the flashes of the amber anti-lock warning light. The initial flash will be a long flash followed by a number of short flashes. The long flash indicates the beginning of the fault number sequence and the short flashes are a continuation of that sequence. Count the long flash with the short flashes to have an accurate fault code count.

To clear a fault code disconnect the control module connector from the module or disconnect the battery for at least 5 seconds. During system retest, wait 30 seconds to make sure the fault code does not reappear.

Removal and Installation
RWAL SPEED SENSOR

1. Raise and safely support vehicle.
2. Remove sensor hold down-bolt.
3. Remove sensor shield and sensor from differential by pulling sensor out of differential.
4. Disconnect wiring from sensor.
5. To install, connect wiring to sensor. Be sure the seal is in place between the sensor and wiring connector.
6. Install the sensor into the differential housing with a new O-ring.
7. Install sensor shield.
8. Install sensor hold down bolt. Torque to 170–230 inch lbs.
9. Lower vehicle.

ELECTRONIC BRAKE CONTROL MODULE

1. Remove the right side sill plate.
2. Remove the right side cowl cover.
3. Remove the three screws that attach electronic brake control module to side cowl.
4. Disconnect the wiring from the module.
5. When installing, connect the wiring first, then install the three mounting screws.
6. Install the right side cowl cover and sill plate.

DUAL SOLENOID HYDRAULIC VALVE

1. Raise and safely support vehicle.
2. Remove the brake lines from the valve.
3. Remove the 2 nuts that hold the valve to the frame.
4. Remove the valve from the frame and disconnect the wiring.
5. When installing, connect the wiring first, then install the valve. Torque the hold-down nuts to 16–25 ft. lbs.
6. Bleed the solenoid valve and the rear brakes.
7. Lower hoist.

CHRYSLER CORPORATION BRAKE SYSTEM TROUBLE DIAGNOSIS

Test Step	What to do	Condition	Yes	No
TEST 1 VISUAL INSPECTION				
1.1	Inspect RWAL connectors and ground for defects and good connections	Are connectors free of defects and connected properly?	Go to Test 2	Repair or connect terminals as required
TEST 2 SYSTEM SELF CHECK				
2.1	Turn ignition switch to run position	Both lamps illuminate for 2 seconds then go out as system performs self check	Go to Test 3	Choose another condition
		Antilock and brake lamp stay on	Go to Test 6	Choose another condition
		Antilock lamp off and will not self check, brake lamp checked OK	Go to Test 7	Choose another condition
		Brake lamp on, antilock lamp off and does self check	Go to Test 8	Choose another condition
		Antilock and brake lamps flashing	Go to Test 9	Choose another condition
		Brake lamp off, antilock lamp on, antilock lamp does self check	Go to Test 10	Choose another condition
TEST 3 CHECKING SENSOR OUTPUT AND PHYSICAL CONDITION				
3.1	Apply service brakes and check stop lights	Stop lamps illuminate	Go to Test 3.2	Repair stop lamp circuit
3.2	Remove sensor from differential and inspect exciter ring for damage	Exciter ring in good condition	Reinstall sensor. Go to Test 3.3	Replace exciter ring and retest system
3.3	Lift rear wheels, start engine, run wheels at 5 mph. Make sure vehicle is properly positioned on hoist or jack stands. **WARNING: STAY CLEAR OF ROTATING WHEELS.** Using a voltmeter set on 2 volt AC scale and connect between B01 PK and B02 LG/OR wires of the sensor connector	Is voltage 650 MV (RMS) or greater?	Go to Test 5	Go to Test 3.4
3.4		Has sensor been replaced?	Go to Test 3.5	Replace sensor and go to Test 3.3
3.5	Disconnect 14 way module connector. Disconnect sensor connector and connect an ohmmeter between B01 RD/VT wire in module connector and B01 PK wire in sensor connector	Is there continuity?	Go to Test 3.6	Repair open circuit
3.6	Connect an ohmmeter between B01 RD/VT wire in module connector and ground	Is there continuity?	Repair circuit for a short to ground	Go to Test 3.7
3.7	Connect an ohmmeter between B02 WT/VT wire in module connector and B02 LG/OR wire in sensor connector	Is there continuity?	Repair circuit for an open circuit	Go to Test 3.8
3.8	Connect an ohmmeter between B02 WT/VT wire in module connector and ground	Is there a short to ground?	Repair circuit for short to ground	Go to Test 4

CHRYSLER CORPORATION BRAKE SYSTEM TROUBLE DIAGNOSIS—CONT'D

Step	What to do	Condition	Yes	No
TEST 4 CHECKING SENSOR GAP				
4.1	Remove sensor from differential. Measure height of sensor pole piece from mounting face of sensor (should be 1.07"–1.08"). Measure top of exciter ring teeth from sensor mounting face on differential (should be 1.085"–1.12"). Subtract measurements as shown to obtain sensor gap. Gap must be a minimum of 0.005" and a maximum of 0.05"	Was gap within specifications?	Go to Test 5	Go to Test 4.2
4.2	Look at sensor measurement from Test 4.1 (should be 1.07"–1.08")	Was sensor measurement within specifications?	Repair differential and retest system	Replace sensor and retest system
TEST 5 CHECKING FOR BRAKE MECHANICAL PROBLEMS				
5.1	Check rear brakes for mechanical problems such as grabbing, locking or pulling	Are the rear brakes functioning properly?	Replace module and retest system	Repair mechanical problem and retest system
TEST 6 CHECKING THE DIAGNOSTIC CONNECTOR GROUND				
6.1	Locate the black 2-way diagnostic connector below RWAL module. Connect a jumper wire between the diagnostic connector and ground	Is there a flashout code?	Go to Test 11	Go to 6.2
6.2	Turn ignition off. Disconnect 14-way connector from module and connect an ohmmeter between the BK in the 14-way connector and the BK in the 2-way diagnostic connector	Is there continuity?	Go to Test 6.3	Repair open circuit and retest system
6.3	Check brake fluid level in master cylinder reservoir	Is brake fluid level correct?	Go to Test 6.4	Find and repair leak and retest system
6.4	Reconnect 14-way module connector. Disconnect connector from the pressure differential switch. Turn ignition to run position	Do both antilock lamp and brake lamp stay on?	Go to Test 6.5	Check brake system for air in lines or mechanical damage
6.5		Does the vehicle have a diesel engine?	Go to Test 6.6	Go to Test 6.7
6.6	Disconnect harness connector from vacuum warning switch. Turn the ignition switch to the run position	Do both lamps stay on?	Go to Test 6.7	Check complete vehicle vacuum system, repair as required and retest system
6.7	Disconnect 14-way module connector. Turn ignition switch to the run position	Are both antilock lamp and brake lamp off?	Go to Test 6.8	Choose another condition
		Antilock lamp on, brake lamp off	Repair AT1 orange wire for short to ground between module and antilock lamp	Repair short to ground in differential switch sensor wiring, B01 PK and B02 LG/OR
6.8	Remove and inspect antilock fuse	Is fuse open?	Check and repair all circuits fuse is protecting. Replace fuse	Go to Test 6.9

CHRYSLER CORPORATION BRAKE SYSTEM TROUBLE DIAGNOSIS—CONT'D

Step	What to do	Condition	Yes	No
6.9	Connect a voltmeter between pin 3 RD/YL wire of 14-way module connector and ground	Is voltage greater than 9 volts?	Go to Test 6.10	Repair the D1 RD/YL wire for an open
6.10	Remove and inspect the stop lamp fuse.	Is the fuse open?	Check and repair all circuits fuse is protecting for shorts and replace fuse	Go to Test 6.11
6.11	Connect a voltmeter between pin 9 of the 14-way module connector and ground	Is voltage greater than 9 volts?	Replace module and retest system	Repair the D3B PK/DB wire for open circuit.

TEST 7 CHECKING MODULE GROUND AND POWER

Step	What to do	Condition	Yes	No
7.1	Make sure module connector is fully-plugged into module	Is connector plugged in?	Go to Test 7.2	Plug connector in and retest system
7.2	Disconnect battery and 14-way module connector. With an ohmmeter set on 200 ohm scale, check resistance between pin 10 BK/LG wire on the 14-way harness connector and ground	Is resistance less than 1 ohm?	Go to Test 7.3	Repair H40 BK/LG for an open or damaged circuit
7.3	Remove and inspect antilock lamp fuse	Is fuse open?	Check and repair all circuits fuse is protecting for shorts and replace fuse	Go to Test 7.4
7.4	Connect battery and turn ignition to run position. With a voltmeter set on 20 volt DC scale, check voltage between Pin 2 Orange wire of the 14-way module connector and ground	Is voltage less than 9 volts?	Go to Test 7.5	Replace the module and retest system
7.5	Check antilock bulb	Is bulb open?	Replace bulb and retest system	Repair AT1 orange wire for open circuit between pin 2 and fuse

TEST 8 CHECKING PARKING SYSTEM AND MODULE

Step	What to do	Condition	Yes	No
8.1	Turn ignition to run position. Pull lever to release parking brake	Does the brake lamp go off?	Disregard failure, retest antilock and brake lamp for 2 second self check	Go to Test 8.2
8.2	Pull park brake release lever with one hand and pull pedal up with other hand	Did brake lamp go off	Repair park brake mechanism or switch	Go to Test 8.3
8.3	Disconnect black 1-way park brake switch connector	Did brake lamp go off	Adjust or replace park brake switch and retest system	Go to Test 8.4
8.4	Disconnect 14-way module connector	Did brake lamp go off?	Replace module and retest system	Repair P5 BK/GY wire for a short to ground

CHRYSLER CORPORATION BRAKE SYSTEM TROUBLE DIAGNOSIS — CONT'D

Step	What to do	Condition	Yes	No
TEST 9 CHECKING FOR INTERMITTENT PROBLEMS				
9.1	Disconnect 14-way module connector. With a voltmeter set on 20 volt DC scale, check voltage between pin 3 RD/YL wire on the 14-way module connector and ground. Turn ignition to run position and shake the instrument panel harness	Is voltage steady at 9 volts?	Go to Test 9.2	Repair D1 RD/YL for open circuit
9.2	Disconnect battery, set ohmmeter on 200 scale and connect between pin 12 BK wire of the 14-way module connector and ground, then shake the instrument panel harness	Is resistance 100K or greater and steady?	Go to Test 9.3	Repair DK/BK/ wire for a short to ground
9.3	With ohmmeter set on 200 ohm scale, connect between Pin 10 BK/LG wire of the 14-way module connector and ground, then shake instrument panel harness.	Is resistance steady at 1 ohm?	Replace module and retest system	Repair open circuit in H40 BK/LG
TEST 10 CHECKING FOR OPEN OR DISCONNECTED PARK BRAKE SWITCH CONNECTOR				
10.1	Make sure the P5 BK/GY wire at the park brake switch is connected	Is P5 wire connected to park brake switch?	Go to Test 10.2	Connect and retest system
10.2	Disconnect park brake switch connector. Disconnect message center black 6-way connector. Connect an ohmmeter between P5 BK/BY wire in both connectors	Is there continuity?	Go to Test 10.3	Repair P5 BK/GY wire for open circuit
10.3	Inspect instrument cluster printed circuit board for damage	Is printed circuit board damaged?	Replace printed circuit board	Replace brake warning lamp bulb
TEST 11 FLASHCODES				
11.1	Connect a jumper wire between the diagnostic connector and ground. Count the flashes including the long flash that starts the flash code count. Choose the proper condition	Antilock lamp and brake lamp flash 1 time	Go to Test 12	
		Antilock lamp and brake lamp flash 2 times.	G to Test 13	
		Antilock lamp and brake lamp flash 3 times.	G to Test 14	
		Antilock lamp and brake lamp flash 4 times.	G to Test 15	
		Antilock lamp and brake lamp flash 5 times.	G to Test 16	
		Antilock lamp and brake lamp flash 6 times.	G to Test 17	
		Antilock lamp and brake lamp flash 7 times.	G to Test 18	
		Antilock lamp and brake lamp flash 8 times.	G to Test 19	
		Antilock lamp and brake lamp flash 9 times.	G to Test 20	
		Antilock lamp and brake lamp flash 10 times.	G to Test 21	
		Antilock lamp and brake lamp flash 11 times.	G to Test 22	
		Antilock lamp and brake lamp flash	G to Test 23	

CHRYSLER CORPORATION BRAKE SYSTEM TROUBLE DIAGNOSIS — CONT'D

Step	What to do	Condition	Yes	No
11.1		12 times.		
		Antilock lamp and brake lamp flash 13 times.	G to Test 24	
		Antilock lamp and brake lamp flash 14 times.	G to Test 25	
		Antilock lamp and brake lamp flash 15 times.	G to Test 26	
		Antilock lamp and brake lamp flash 16 times.	G to Test 27	

TEST 12 ONE FLASH

12.1	One flash code should not occur. Perform flashcode procedure several times	Are you still getting code 1?	Go to Test 5	Go to Test 11

TEST 13 TWO FLASHES

13.1	Disconnect battery and 14-way module connector. Set an ohmmeter on 200 ohm scale and connect between pin 1 LG wire of the 14-way module connector and ground	Does the circuit have over 6 ohms?	Go to test 13.2	Replace the module and retest system
13.2	Disconnect valve harness connector from valve connector. Connect an ohmmeter between B09 GY/WT of harness connector and ground	Is resistance greater than 1 ohm?	Repair B09 GY/WT wire for an open circuit or high resistance. Check for contaminated or loose connector pins and retest system	Go to Test 13.3
13.3	Connect an ohmmeter between IS1 LG/ and B09 GY/WT wires in the 4-way black valve connector	Does circuit have over 6 ohms?	Replace antilock valve and retest system	Repair the IS1 LG/ for open circuit from valve to computer module and retest system

TEST 14 THREE FLASHES

14.4	Disconnect battery. Remove 14-way module harness connector from module. Set ohmmeter on 200 ohm scale and connect to pin 8 DS1 WT/BR and ground	Does circuit have over 3 ohms?	Go to Test 14.2	Replace module and retest system
14.2	Disconnect the 4-way valve harness connector. Connect an ohmmeter between DS1 WT and B09 GY/NT wires in valve connector	Does circuit have over 3 ohms?	Replace antilock valve and retest system	Repair DS1 WT wire for open between module connector and valve connector

TEST 15 FOUR FLASHES

15.1	Disconnect the 4-way valve harness connector from valve connector. Set ohmmeter on 20K scale and connect between VS1 LB wire in valve body and ground	Is resistance greater than 10K ohms?	Go to Test 15.2	Replace the antilock valve and retest system
15.2	Connect an ohmmeter between VS1 LB and B09 GY/WY wires in the valve connector	Is resistance greater than 10K ohms?	Go to Test 15.3	Replace the antilock valve and retest system

CHRYSLER CORPORATION BRAKE SYSTEM TROUBLE DIAGNOSIS—CONT'D

Step	What to do	Condition	Yes	No
15.3	Disconnect battery. Disconnect the 14-way module harness connector from module. Set ohmmeter on 200K scale and connect to pin 11, VS1 LB of 14-way connector and ground	Is resistance greater than 100K ohms?	Replace module and retest system	Repair VS1 LB wire for a short to ground between valve and module. Retest system
TEST 16 FIVE FLASHES				
16.1	Did the failure occur in 2 wheel drive mode?		Go to Test 16.2	Go to Test 16.3
16.2	Disconnect 14-way module connector from module to deactivate antilock system. Drive the vehicle in 2 wheel drive mode and make normal and safe stops to determine the condition of the rear brakes	Are the brakes functioning normally?	Replace the antilock valve and retest system	Repair rear brakes and retest system
16.3	Disconnect 14-way module connector from module. Turn ignition key to run position. Shift into 4 wheel drive. Set a voltmeter to 20 vdc and connect between pin 4, X4 LG/BR wire and ground	Is voltage greater than 1 volt?	Repair X4 wire for an open or 4 wheel drive indicator switch. Retest system	Replace antilock valve and retest system
TEST 17 SIX FLASHES				
17.1	Recheck flashcode after driving vehicle	Antilock light and brake light flash 6 times	Go to Test 17.2	Go to Test 11
17.2	Disconnect battery. Disconnect 14-way module connector. Set ohmmeter on 200 ohm scale and connect between pin 13, B02 WT/VT and pin 14, B01 RD/VT of harness connector. Shake antilock wiring harness from differential to module	Is resistance constant at 1000–2000 ohms?	Go to Test 17.3	Repair circuit. Retest system
17.3	Remove sensor from the differential and inspect for build up of metal chips on sensor pole piece	Are metal chips present?	Drain and clean differential. Check exciter ring for broken or chipped teeth. Retest system	Go to Test 17.4
17.4	Look into sensor hole in differential and rotate exciter ring and check for damage (missing or bent teeth)	Is exciter ring intact?	Go to 17.5	Replace exciter ring. Retest system
17.5	Reinstall sensor. Disconnect 2-way RWAL sensor connector. With a voltmeter on 2 volt scale, connect between B01 PK and B2 LG/OR wires of sensor connector. Raise rear wheels off floor and run at 5 mph. **WARNING: STAY CLEAR OF ROTATING WHEELS**	Is voltage greater than 650 MV and steady?	Replace module. Retest system	Replace sensor. Recheck sensor output. Retest system
TEST 18 SEVEN FLASHES				
18.1	Disconnect 4-way valve harness connector from valve connector. Connect an ohmmeter between IS1 LG/ and B09 GY/WT wire in valve connector	Is resistance less than 3 ohms?	Replace antilock valve. Retest system	Go to Test 18.2

CHRYSLER CORPORATION BRAKE SYSTEM TROUBLE DIAGNOSIS — CONT'D

Step	What to do	Condition	Yes	No
18.2	Disconnect battery. Disconnect 4-way valve harness connector from valve connector. Disconnect 14-way module harness connector from module. Set ohmmeter on 20K ohms scale and connect between Pin 1, IS1 LG/ wire in harness connector and ground	Is resistance greater than 20K ohms?	Replace module. Retest system	Repair IS1 LG/* for a short between antilock valve and module. Retest system

TEST 19 EIGHT FLASHES

Step	What to do	Condition	Yes	No
19.1	Disconnect 4-way valve harness from valve connector. Set ohmmeter on 200 ohm scale and connect between DS1 WT and B09 GY/WT wires in valve connector	Is resistance less than 1 ohm?	Replace antilock valve. Retest system	Go to Test 19.2
19.2	Disconnect battery. Disconnect 4-way valve connector. Disconnect 14-way module connector. Set ohmmeter on 20K ohm scale and connect between pin 8, DS1 WT/BR and ground	Is resistance greater than 20K ohms?	Replace module	Repair DS1 WT/BR for a short to ground between antilock valve and module. Retest system

TEST 20 NINE FLASHES

Step	What to do	Condition	Yes	No
20.1	Disconnect 2-way sensor harness connector from sensor on differential housing. Set ohmmeter on 20K scale and connect to B01 PK and B02 LG/OR wire on sensor	Is resistance greater than 2500 ohms?	Replace sensor. Recheck resistance. **Make sure seal is in place between sensor and connector.** Retest system	Go to Test 20.2
20.2	Reconnect sensor harness **making sure seal is in place.** Disconnect battery. Disconnect 14-way module connector. Connect an ohmmeter between pin 13, B02 WT/VT and pin 14, B01 RD/VT wires in module harness connector	Is resistance greater than 2500 ohms?	Repair B02 WT/VT and B01 RD/VT for open circuits between the module and sensor. Retest system	Replace computer module. When reconnecting sensor, **make sure seal is in place.** Retest system

TEST 21 TEN FLASHES

Step	What to do	Condition	Yes	No
21.1	Set ohmmeter on 20K ohm scale. Disconnect 2-way sensor connector from sensor on differential. Connect an ohmmeter between B01 PK and B02 LG/OR wires on sensor	Is resistance less then 1000 ohms?	Replace sensor. Recheck resistance. **Make sure seal is in place between sensor and connector.** Retest system	Go to Test 21.2
21.2	Disconnect battery. Disconnect 14-way module. Connect an ohmmeter between pin 14, B01 RD/VT and ground	Is resistance greater than 20K ohms?	Go to Test 21.3	Repair B01 RD/VT circuit between the module and sensor. When reconnecting sensor, **make sure seal is in place.** Retest system

CHRYSLER CORPORATION BRAKE SYSTEM TROUBLE DIAGNOSIS — CONT'D

Step	What to do	Condition	Yes	No
21.3	Connect an ohmmeter between pin 13, B02 WT/VT and pin 14 B01 RD/VT wire in module harness connector	Is resistance greater than 20K ohms?	Replace module. Retest system	Repair B01 RD/ VT and B02 WT/ VT circuit. When reconnecting sensor, **make sure seal is in place.** Retest system

TEST 22 ELEVEN FLASHES

Step	What to do	Condition	Yes	No
22.1	Recheck flash code after driving vehicle at 35 mph or greater.	Antilock light and brake light flash 11 times	Go to Test 22.1	Go to Test 11
22.2	Apply vehicle service brakes and check vehicle stop lights	Are stop lights operating correctly?	Go to Test 22.3	Repair the stop lamp circuit. Retest system
22.3	Turn ignition switch off. Disconnect 14-way module connector from module. Connect a voltmeter between pin 7, D4 WT of harness connector and ground while stepping on brake pedal	Is voltage less than 9 volts?	Repair D4 WT for open circuit between stop light switch and module. Retest system	Check 4-way flasher, directional wiring, and feedback through stop light circuit. Also check for proper operation of cruise control. Recheck antilock and brake lights for proper 2 second bulb check

TEST 23 TWELVE FLASHES

Step	What to do	Condition	Yes	No
23.1	This code should not occur. Read flashcodes several times	Are 12 flashes still present?	Replace module. Retest system	Go to Test 11

TEST 24 THIRTEEN FLASHES

Step	What to do	Condition	Yes	No
24.1	Read flashcode	Are 13 flashes present?	Replace module. Retest system	Go to Test 11

TEST 25 FOURTEEN FLASHES

Step	What to do	Condition	Yes	No
25.1	Read flashcode	Are 14 flashes present?	Replace module. Retest system	Go to Test 11

TEST 26 FIFTEEN FLASHES

Step	What to do	Condition	Yes	No
26.1	Read flashcode	Are 15 flashes present?	Replace module. Retest system	Go to Test 11

TEST 27 SIXTEEN OR MORE FLASHES

Step	What to do	Condition	Yes	No
27.1	Read flashcode	Are 16 or more flashes present?	Replace module. Retest system	Go to Test 11

FORD MOTOR COMPANY

Master Cylinder Service

Ford Motor Company uses a dual master cylinder which contains a double hydraulic cylinder with 2 fluid reservoirs and primary and secondary hydraulic pistons. The rear wheel brakes are connected to the secondary outlet port and are actuated by the secondary piston assembly. The front wheel brakes are connected to the primary outlet port (nearest the dash panel) and are actuated by the primary piston assembly. Both primary and secondary pistons function together. On most models, the master cylinder is assisted by a vacuum booster. Both single and double diaphragm Bendix models are used. Hydraulic rear drum

Ford master cylinder with see-through reservoir and integral proportioning valve.

Plastic reservoir with fluid level indicator

brakes with automatic adjusters and self-adjusting front disc brakes are standard on all models.

The Ford Motor Company master cylinder uses a pressed on plastic see-through reservoir with the proportioning valve built into or integral with the master cylinder. In the event of a front brake system malfunction the proportioning valve with a bypass feature allows full hydraulic pressure to the rear brake system.

The Aerostar uses a Recessed Cartridge Master Cylinder (RCMC) which contains the primary and secondary hydraulic springs and pistons, reservoir with fluid level indicator and integral bypass proportioning valve and differential pressure activation system. The integral proportioning valve eliminates addition tubing and connections.

A Fluid Level Indicator (FLI) is built into the reservoir. It is serviced as part of the reservoir assembly.

During normal operation, the fluid level in the master cylinder will rise during brake operation and fall during release. It is also expected that the fluid level will decrease with brake pad wear. In addition, a trace of brake fluid on the booster shell below the master cylinder mounting flange will often be found as a result of the normal lubricating action of the master cylinder bore and seal. All of these conditions are considered normal and are not indications the master cylinder needs service.

Disassembly and Assembly

1. Clean the outside of the master cylinder and remove the cap and gasket. Drain and discard remaining brake fluid.
2. Remove the proportioning valve from the master cylinder.
3. Remove the stop-bolt from the bottom of the master cylinder assembly.
4. Depress the secondary piston, remove the snapring from the bore and remove the secondary piston assembly.
5. Remove the primary piston assembly by directing a little compressed air into the outlet at the blind end of the bore while plugging the other outlet port.
6. Inspect the pistons, seals and cylinder bore for etching, pitting, scoring or other damage. If bore is damaged, discard and replace with a new master cylinder. Do not attempt to hone the bore. If the bore is not damaged, use the proper repair kit to rebuild.

To assemble:

7. If plastic reservoir is to be removed, carefully pry the reservoir from the master cylinder body. The plastic reservoir is a push-fit with rubber grommets making the seal. Whenever the plastic reservoir is replaced, the grommets must also be replaced.
8. Dip the repair kit piston assemblies in clean heavy duty brake fluid to lubricate the seals. Carefully insert the complete primary piston assembly into the master cylinder bore, followed by the secondary piston assembly.
9. Depress the secondary piston and install snapring. Install the stop bolt in the bottom of the master cylinder bore.
10. Install the proportioning valve assembly in the master cylinder.
11. If the reservoir was removed, lubricate new retainer grommets with brake fluid and insert the grommets into the master cylinder body. Press the plastic reservoir into the grommets. The reservoir should snap into place indicating that it is secure. Make sure the fluid level indicator socket is facing the correct direction for the vehicle on which it is to be installed.
12. Install plastic cap on the master cylinder.

Brake Booster Service

Three types of brake boosters are used, a single diaphragm, a tandem diaphragm and a hydraulic booster (Hydro-Boost).

Under normal operating conditions, with brakes released, a vacuum suspended booster operates with vacuum on both sides of its diaphragm, or both diaphragms in a tandem diaphragm unit. When the brakes are applied, air at atmospheric pressure is admitted to one side of the diaphragm, or both diaphragms in a tandem diaphragm unit, to provide the power assist.

The hydraulic brake booster (Hydro-Boost) uses the power steering pump to power the system and a pneumatic accumulator as a reserve system. In this system no special fluids are used. However, care must be taken to use the correct fluids. The master cylinder and brake system operate on standard brake fluid. The hydraulic pump uses power steering fluid.

Vacuum pump installation—typical

BRACKET

ALTERNATOR

ALTERNATOR ADJUSTMENT ARM

ALTERNATOR SUPPORT BRACKET

J-NUT

ADJUSTMENT BOLT

PIVOT BOLT

ALTERNATOR MOUNTING BRACKET

VACUUM PUMP MOUNTING BOLTS

VACUUM PUMP ADJUSTMENT PLATE

VACUUM PUMP

VACUUM PUMP PULLEY

BOLT

VACUUM OUTLET MANIFOLD

3/8" PORT TO VACUUM PUMP
5/16" PORT TO SPEED CONTROL
1/4" PORT TO LOW VAC. IND. SW.
1/4" PORT TO AIR CONDITIONING
1/4" PORT TO REGULATOR VALVE
3/8" PORT TO BRAKE BOOSTER

COWL INNER PANEL (REF.)

HOSE CLAMP

HOSE

HOSE

TRANSMISSION VACUUM LINE

VIEW Z

VACUUM OUTLET MANIFOLD

HOSE CLAMP

HOSE

HOSE
ROUTE TUBE BETWEEN BRAKE BOOSTER AND MASTER CYLINDER AS SHOWN

TRANSMISSION VACUUM TUBE (REF.)

CLIP PART OF AIR CLEANER

STRAP

VIEW Z

TRANSMISSION REG. VALVE (REF.)

VACUUM HOSE TO BE OUTSIDE OF HEATER HOSE AS SHOWN

LOW VACUUM INDICATOR SWITCH

SCREW

FENDER APRON (REF.)

5" TO 8" ABOVE CONNECTION

HOSE CLAMP

VACUUM PUMP

HOSE

E-250 - E-350 INSTALLATION

Vacuum pump layout—Econoline shown—typical

FORD PICK-UP BRAKE BOOSTER VACUUM PUMP TESTING—DIESEL ENGINES

TEST	PROCEDURE
Test 1	Isolating Problem A. Disconnect Low Vacuum Switch. Run engine at idle, apply brakes. 　　If brake warning light comes on, the problem is in the hydraulic brake system. 　　If brake warning light does not come on, the problem is in the vacuum pump (perform Test 2).
Test 2	Vacuum Pump Output Check A. Hook up vacuum gauge to hose at brake booster. At normal idle, vacuum should reach 21 inches Hg within 30 seconds (approximately 16 inches Hg at high altitudes—5,000 ft.). 　　If vacuum is okay, reconnect booster base and "TEE" vacuum gauge near pump inlet. Check vacuum at idle. There should be no more than 3 inches Hg vacuum drop. If drop is greater, look for vacuum leaks at hoses or vacuum accessories. 　　If vacuum is okay, repeat test with brake pedal held down. If vacuum drops, replace brake booster. If vacuum is within specs, check brake hydraulic system. 　　If vacuum is not okay, check gauge and connector for leaks. Make sure pulley is not slipping on shaft, and belt tension is okay. Make sure engine idle speed is correct. If vacuum output is still low, replace vacuum pump.

NOTE: When making tests, block all wheels, place transmission in Park or Neutral before starting engine.

VACUUM DIAPHRAGM BRAKE BOOSTER

Both the Bendix single diaphragm and Bendix tandem diaphragm booster are not repairable and the booster must be replaced as a unit. The booster check valve is the only component which can be serviced on the booster assembly.

The Bendix Hydro-Boost uses the hydraulic pressure supplied by the power steering pump to provide a power assist to brake application. It has identifying information stamped into the housing near the inlet.

The Hydro-Boost power brake booster is not to be disassembled and is to be serviced as a unit.

Brake Booster Vacuum Pump

On gasoline engines, engine vacuum is used to power the vacuum booster brake. On diesel engines, there is not enough engine vacuum available for vacuum booster brake operation.

On diesel engines, vacuum is supplied from a pump usually located on the top right side of the engine. It is usually driven by a single belt off the alternator or from the back of the alternator rotor shaft.

Diesel engine equipped vehicles will also usually have a low-vacuum indicator switch which activates the BRAKE warning light when vacuum gets below a certain level. The switch senses vacuum through a fitting in the vacuum manifold (sometimes called a vacuum tree). Note that the BRAKE light will glow until vacuum builds up to normal level.

The low-vacuum switch for Ford E-Series vehicles is located to the left side fender panel. On F-250—F-350 Series vehicles the switch is located on the right side of the engine compartment adjacent to the vacuum pump.

The vacuum pump is not to be disassembled. It is only serviced as a unit. The pulley is serviced as a separate item.

Caliper Service

Ford Motor Company uses several types of brake calipers, a Heavy Duty (HD) Pin Rail caliper, a Light Duty (LD) sliding brake caliper and a Light Duty (LD) Pin Rail caliper.

The HD caliper has 2 pistons on the same side of the rotor. Pin Rail type calipers slide on 2 pins that also attach the caliper to the spindle, or anchor plate on some F-Super Duty rear disc brakes. The caliper is a one-piece casting with the inboard side containing the piston bore(s). A square cut rubber seal is located in a groove in the piston bore which provides the hydraulic seal between the piston and the cylinder wall.

Front caliper—Ford HD rail slider type

Disc caliper—Front and rear F-Super duty

Disc caliper—Ford LD sliding caliper

As the brake pedal is pressed, hydraulic pressure is applied against the piston(s). This pressure pushes the inboard brake lining against the inboard braking surface of the rotor. As the force increases against the rotor, the caliper assembly moves inboard and provides a clamping action on the rotor.

When brake pressure is released, the piston seal returns to its normal position, pulling the piston back into the caliper bore. This creates a running clearance between the inner brake lining and rotor.

NOTE: Some Ford Pick-Ups were available with 4 wheel disc brakes.

Disassembly and Assembly

1. Remove pads from caliper. Different types of anti-rattle springs have been used. Note their positions for reassembly. Drain all fluid from the caliper.
2. Pad interior of caliper with clean shop towels or soft wood block and slowly and carefully use just enough compressed air to ease the piston out of the bore.

CAUTION

Do not place fingers in front of piston to try to catch piston or protect it when applying compressed air. This could result in serious injury. Use just enough air to ease the piston out. If piston is blown out, even with padding, it may be damaged. If the piston is jammed or cocked and will not come out readily, release the air pressure and tap sharply on the end of the piston with a soft (brass) hammer or plastic mallet to straighten the piston. Do not use a sharp tool to pry the piston out of the bore.

3. Remove and discard seal boot, being careful not to scratch bore.
4. Remove and discard square cut seal from caliper bore groove.
5. Remove bleeder valve.
6. Clean all parts with denatured alcohol, blow dry with compressed air. Inspect all parts for scoring, corrosion or damage. If the caliper assembly is leaking, replace the piston assemblies. If the cylinder bores are scored, corroded or excessively worn, replace the caliper. Do not hone the cylinder bores. Piston assemblies are not available for oversize bores.

NOTE: Some versions of Ford calipers came with phenolic (plastic) pistons. These do not have to be replaced for small cosmetic surface irregularities or small chips between the piston boot grooves and the shoe face.

To assemble:

7. Lubricate the new piston seals, caliper bore and piston with clean brake fluid and install the seal in the caliper bore groove. Make sure seal is not twisted.

8. Lubricate the retaining lips of the dust boots with clean brake fluid and install them in the boot retaining grooves in the cylinder bores. Insert the pistons into the dust boots and start them into the cylinder by hand until they are beyond the piston seals. Be careful not to damage or dislodge the piston seal. Place a wood block over 1 piston and press the piston into the cylinder being careful not to cock the piston in the cylinder. Install the second (of dual piston calipers) in the same manner. Make sure boots are correctly seated.
9. Install bleeder screw.
10. Install shoe and lining assemblies, using care to get the anti-rattle clips correctly positioned. New copper washers should be used when the caliper is installed and the brake hose reconnected. The machined surfaces of the caliper mount should be wire brushed smooth and clean so the caliper will be able to more freely.

NOTE: After the caliper has been installed and the system bled, before moving the vehicle, pump the brake pedal several times until the pedal is firm. Do not move the vehicle until a firm pedal is obtained. Check the fluid level in the master cylinder after pumping the brakes.

Wheel Cylinder Service

The rear brakes are drum type with internal expanding shoes. The rear brakes are of the single anchor type, mounted to the same anchor and actuated by one wheel cylinder. The wheel cylinder has 2 pistons. Brake adjustments are automatic and are made during reverse brake applications.

Wheel cylinders may need reconditioning or replacement whenever the brake shoes are replaced or when required to correct a leak condition. Leaks which coat the boot and the cylinder with fluid or result in a dropped reservoir fluid level or dampen and stain the brake linings are dangerous. Such leaks can cause the brakes to grab or fail and should be immediately corrected. A leakage, not immediately apparent, can be detected by pulling back the cylinder boot. A small amount of fluid seepage dampening the interior of the boot is normal. However, a dripping boot is not. Unless other conditions causing a brake to pull, grab or drag become obvious, the wheel cylinder is suspect and should be included in general reconditioning.

Cylinder binding may be caused by rust, deposits, grime or swollen cups due to fluid contamination or by a cup wedged into an excessive piston clearance.

Hydraulic system parts should not be allowed to come into contact with oil or grease, neither should those be handled with greasy hands. Even a trace of any petroleum based product is sufficient to cause damage to the rubber parts.

Disassembly and Assembly

1. Remove the brake bleeder screw.
2. Remove the dust boots, allow any brake fluid to drain out.
3. Remove the pistons, seals and inner spring.
4. Inspect the bore for scoring and corrosion. The inside of the bore may be cleaned with fine crocus cloth. If bore is scored, replace cylinder. Clean the cylinder with brake fluid.
5. Lubricate the seals with brake fluid and install. Cup lips should always face inward. Install the spring assembly and seals.
6. Carefully install the pistons and dust boots.
7. Install the bleeder screw.

Anti-Lock Braking Systems

Despite advances in brake design over the years, even the best systems in use can still lock up during certain road conditions, such as wet road surfaces. When the brakes lockup, the driver can lose control of the vehicle, because a locked wheel cannot absorb any cornering or lateral forces and steering is lost. It is impossible to brake to a maximum and at the same time steer the vehicle when the front wheels are locked. If the back wheels are locked the vehicle will become unstable and start to slide.

While many different ways have been tried over the years to solve this problem, mechanical sensors could not provide sufficient information about wheel rotation speed and mechanical control units could not operate the brakes fast enough to prevent brake lockup.

The growth of the electronics industry has allowed small computers (microprocessors) to be reduced in both size and cost. Coupled with fast reacting electronic sensors, anti-lock braking has become more reliable with widespread application.

REAR WHEEL ANTI-LOCK BRAKE SYSTEM

Description

Ford Motor Company's Rear Anti-lock Brake System (RABS) continually monitors rear wheel speed with a sensor mounted on the rear axle. When the teeth on an exciter ring, mounted inside the rear axle on the differential gear case, pass the sensor pole piece, an AC voltage is induced in the sensor circuit with a frequency proportional to the average rear wheel speed. In the event of an impending lockup condition during braking, the RABS modulates hydraulic pressure to the rear brakes. This inhibits rear wheel lockup.

When the brake pedal is applied, the RABS module senses the drop in rear wheel speed. If the rate of deceleration is too great, indicating the wheel lockup is going to occur, the RABS module activates the electro-hydraulic valve causing isolation valve to close. With the isolation valve closed, the rear wheel cylinders are isolated from the master cylinder and the rear brake pressure cannot increase. If the rate of deceleration is still too great, the RABS module will energize the dump solenoid with a series of rapid pulses to bleed off rear wheel cylinder fluid into an accumulator built into the RABS valve. This will reduce the rear wheel cylinder pressure and allow the rear wheels to spin back up to vehicle speed. Continuing under RABS module control, the dump and isolation solenoids will be pulsed in a manner that will keep the rear wheels rotating while still maintaining high levels of deceleration during braking.

At the end of the stop, when the operator releases the brake pedal, the isolation valve de-energizes and any fluid in the accumulator is returned to the master cylinder. Normal brake operation is resumed.

System Self Test

The RABS module performs system tests and self-tests during startup and normal operation. The valve, sensor and fluid level circuits are monitored for proper operation. If a fault is found the RABS will be deactivated and the REAR ANTI-LOCK light will be illuminated. Most faults will cause the light to stay illuminated until the ignition is turned **OFF**. While the light is illuminated a diagnostic flashout code may be obtained. However, there are certain faults (those associated with the fluid level switch or loss of power to the module) that will cause the light to be deactivated and the REAR ANTI-LOCK light to be illuminated but will not provide a diagnostic flashout code will be available.

Warning Lights

The RABS uses both the BRAKE and REAR ANTI-LOCK instrument panel warning lights to alert the driver to a system malfunction. Both lights must be working properly to assist in problem diagnosis. The red BRAKE warning light is used to indicate a low fluid level condition, parking brake applied condition or if equipped with diesel engine a low vacuum condition. To check this light, turn the key to **START**. The light should glow in this position. If it fails to glow, service of the electrical system is required.

NOTE: If the red light continues to glow after the key is in the RUN position, repair the brake system as required. If the brake system checks out OK, troubleshooting will be required to diagnose the RABS problem.

The yellow REAR ANTI-LOCK warning light is used to indicate an RABS malfunction and a deactivation of the RABS. To check this light, turn the key to **ON**. The light should perform a self-check, glowing for about 2 seconds. If the light fails to glow or continues to glow after 2 seconds, troubleshooting of the warning lights is required.

A diode/resistor is located on the main trunk of the instrument panel wiring harness where the RABS module connector pigtail intersects the main trunk. The diode/resistor isolates the RABS module from the parking brake switch and the low vacuum switch for diesel engine. If the diode/resistor did not prevent voltage from reaching the RABS module, the yellow REAR ANTI-LOCK light would turn ON and the system would be shut down whenever the parking brake was applied or the low vacuum switch was closed.

Flashout Codes

Whenever the yellow REAR ANTI-LOCK light comes ON during normal operation, a flashout code may be obtained to aid in problem diagnosis. If the vehicle is shut off before the code is read, the code will be lost. In some cases the code may reappear when the vehicle is restarted. In other cases, the vehicle may have to be driven to reproduce the problem and, if the problem was associated with an intermittent condition, it may be difficult to reproduce. Therefore, whenever possible, it is recommended that the code be read before the vehicle is shut off.

NOTE: Place blocks behind the rear wheels and in front of the front wheels to prevent the vehicle from moving while the flashout code is being taken. If the BRAKE light is also ON due to a grounding of the fluid level circuit (perhaps low brake fluid), no flashout code will be flashed and the REAR ANTI-LOCK light will remain on steadily. If there is more than one system fault only the first recognized flashout code may be obtained.

Obtaining the Flashout Code

A flashout code may be obtained only when the yellow REAR ANTI-LOCK light is ON. No code will be flashed, if the system is operating properly.

Before obtaining the flashout code, drive the vehicle to a level area and place the shift lever in **P** for automatic transmissions or neutral for manual transmissions.

Notice whether the red BRAKE light is ON or not for future reference and then apply the parking brake. Keep the ignition switch **ON** so the code will not be lost.

NOTE: Place blocks behind the rear wheels and in front of the front wheels to prevent the vehicle from moving while the flashout code is being taken.

To obtain the flashout code, locate the RABS diagnostic connector (with the black/orange wire) and attach a jumper wire to it. Momentarily ground it to the chassis. When the ground is made and then broken the REAR ANTI-LOCK light should begin to flash.

NOTE: If the red BRAKE light was on (as noticed before the parking brake was applied) the problem may be with the low fluid level circuit and in this case no flashout code will be flashed and the light will remain ON steadily.

The code consists of a number of short flashes and ends with a long flash. Count the short flashes and include the following long flash in the count to obtain the proper code number. For example, 3 short flashes followed by 1 long flash indicates Flashout Code 4. The code will continue to repeat itself until the

FORD REAR WHEEL ANTI-LOCK BRAKE SYSTEM DIAGNOSTIC CODES

Codes Are Yellow REAR ANTILOCK Light Flashing—Count Flashes

CODE	SYSTEM PROBLEM
CODE 1	This code is not used and should not occur
CODE 2	Open isolate circuit
CODE 3	Open dump circuit
CODE 4	Check RABS valve
CODE 5	Check RABS valve/4 × 4 indicator switch (4WD)
CODE 6	Check sensor for loose connections, chips, bad exciter ring
CODE 7	No isolate valve self test
CODE 8	No dump valve self test
CODE 9	Check sensor wiring for high resistance
CODE 10	Check sensor wiring for low resistance (shorted)
CODE 11	Check stop lamp switch
CODE 12	Check for low fluid level, bad brake light wiring
CODE 13	RABS module failure—replace
CODE 14	RABS module failure—replace
CODE 15	RABS module failure—replace
CODE 16	This code is not used and should not occur

NOTE: CODES 1 and 16 are not used. When checking resistance in the antilock brake system, always disconnect the battery. Improper resistance readings will occur with the vehicle battery connected.

key is turned OFF. It is recommended that the code be verified by reading it several times. In addition, the first code flashed may be too short because it may have been started in the middle. It should be ignored.

COMPONENT LOCATION

F SERIES AND BRONCO

The RABS consists of the following components:

RABS module—located in the cab to the right of the brake pedal under the upper dash panel.

RABS valve (dual solenoid electro-hydraulic)—located on the left frame rail just behind the No. 1 crossmember.

RABS speed sensor—located on the rear axle housing and the exciter ring is located inside on the gear carrier.

Yellow REAR ANTI-LOCK warning light—in the instrument cluster.

RABS diagnostic connector—located in the cab and clipped on the main instrument panel wiring harness about 6 inches from the firewall near the parling brake pedal.

Diode/resistor element—located on the main trunk of the instrument panel wiring harness where the RABS module connector pigtail intersects the main harness trunk.

Speed Sensor test connector (with weatherproof cap)—located under the hood on the left wheel well.

E SERIES

The RABS consists of the following components:

RABS module—located in the cab on the driver's inside cowl panel just outboard of the parking brake mechanism.

RABS valve (dual solenoid electro-hydraulic)—located on the left inside frame rail just behind the engine mount crossmember.

RABS speed sensor—located on the rear axle housing and the exciter ring is located inside on the gear carrier.

Yellow REAR ANTI-LOCK warning light—in the instrument cluster.

RABS diagnostic connector—located just off the module connector harness.

Diode/resistor element—located on the main trunk of the instrument panel wiring harness where the RABS module connector pigtail intersects the main harness trunk.

Speed sensor test connector (with weatherproof cap)—located under the hood between the battery and the right side engine compartment wall.

RANGER/BRONCO II

The RABS consists of the following components:

RABS module—located in the dash under the instrument panel. Mounted to a brace, center of panel area.

RABS valve (dual solenoid electro-hydraulic)—located approximately 5 inches rearward of the No. 1 crossmember on the inboard side of the left side frame rail.

RABS speed sensor and exciter ring—the sensor is located on the rear axle housing and the exciter ring is located inside on the gear carrier.

Yellow REAR ANT-ILOCK warning light—in the instrument cluster.

RABS diagnostic connector—located on the main wire bundle inside of cab under dash, slightly rearward of the No. 53 pin connector, driver's side.

Diode/resistor element—located in the master cylinder fluid level sensor wiring harness on the left splash apron.

Speed sensor test connector (with weatherproof cap)—located under the hood slightly rearward of the washer bottle.

AEROSTAR

The RABS consists of the following components:

RABS module—mounted to the driver's side of the engine cover under the instrument panel.

RABS valve (dual solenoid electro-hydraulic)—located on the fender apron below the master cylinder.

RABS speed sensor and exciter ring—the sensor is located on the rear axle housing and the exciter ring is located inside on the gear carrier.

Yellow REAR ANTI-LOCK warning light—in the instrument cluster.

RABS diagnostic connector—located on the main wire bundle inside of cab under dash, slightly rearward of the No. 53 pin connector, driver's side.

Diode/resistor element—located approximately 3 inches left of the cluster connector takeouts in the instrument panel wiring harness.

Speed sensor test connector (with weatherproof cap)—located forward of the No. 53 pin connector on the left side fender apron.

Component Location F-150—F-350, Bronco

YELLOW REAR ANTILOCK WARNING LAMP

RED BRAKE WARNING LAMP

SECTION A

VIEW Z

VIEW Y

VIEW W

SENSOR TEST CONNECTOR

REAR ANTILOCK BRAKE SYSTEM COMPONENT LOCATION

FRONT OF VEHICLE

SENSOR TEST CONNECTOR LOCATED ON LH FENDER APRON

SPEED SENSOR

EXCITOR RING

SPEED SENSOR AND EXICTOR RING SECTION A

DUAL SOLENOID ELECTRO-HYDRAULIC VALVE VIEW W

DIAGNOSTIC CONNECTOR

DIAGNOSTIC CONNECTOR VIEW Y

DIODE/RESISTOR

RABS MODULE

VIEW Z

RABS component location—F-Series, Bronco shown—typical

Removal and Installation
RABS MODULE

The RABS module, valve and sensor are serviced as assemblies and are not to be disassembled. The exciter ring is pressed on the differential case and, if removed for any reason, must be discarded.

Except E Series Vans

1. Disconnect the wire harness from the RABS module by depressing the plastic tab on the connector and pulling the connector off.

2. Remove the 2 screws that retain the module to the dash panel or engine cover for Aerostar. Remove the module.

3. Place the module in position on the dash panel or engine cover for Aerostar. Install and tighten the 2 retaining screws.

4. Connect the wiring harness to the module. Check the system for proper operation.

E Series

1. Remove the parking brake actuator assembly. Start by loosening the adjusting nut at the equalizer. On Super Duty series vehicles remove the clevis pin at the parking brake. Working from the engine compartment, remove the nuts attaching the parking brake control assembly to the dash panel.

2. Working under the instrument panel, remove the bolt attaching the control assembly to the lower flange of the instrument panel. Remove the parking brake cable from the control assembly clevis by compressing the conduit end fitting prongs (using ½ inch box wrench) holding the cable assembly to the control, remove the cable from the control. Remove the parking brake control.

3. Remove the 2 screws that hold the module to the cowl panel. Remove the module.

4. Disconnect the wiring harness from the RABS module by depressing the plastic tab on the connector and pulling the connector off.

To install:

5. Connect the wiring harness to the RABS module.

6. Place module in position on the cowl panel. Install and tighten the two retaining screws.

7. Install the parking brake actuator by connecting the forward ball end of the parking brake cable to the clevis of the control assembly and insert the cable assembly into the control assembly. Install hair pin retainer.

8. Position the control assembly on the lower flange of the instrument panel and install the attaching bolt.

9. Working from the engine compartment, install and tighten the nuts that attach the parking brake control assembly to the dash panel. Torque to 15 ft. lbs.

10. Adjust the parking brake equalizer lever to its original position. On Super Duty serie vehicles, install the parking brake clevis pin. Check cable tension and adjust if necessary.

11. Check the RABS and parking brake systems for proper operation.

RABS DUAL SOLENOID ELECTRO-HYDRAULIC VALVE

The purpose of this valve assembly is to control hydraulic fluid pressure to the rear wheels based on RABS module signals.

Except E Series Vans

1. Disconnect the inlet and outlet brake lines from the RABS valve. Cap the lines.

2. Disconnect the wiring harness to the valve.

3. Remove the nuts retaining the valve to the frame rail or fender apron on Aerostar and remove the valve.

To install:

4. Position the RABS valve on the frame rail or fender apron on Aerostar. Install the 3 nuts and torque to 12–17 ft. lbs.

5. Connect the brake lines and tighten the larger fitting to

RABS Module—F-Series, Bronco

RABS Module—E-Series

10–17 ft. lbs. and the smaller to 10–15 ft. lbs. Do not overtighten the fittings.

6. Bleed the brake system. It is not necessary to energize the valve electrically to bleed the rear brakes.

RABS VALVE

E Series Vans

1. Disconnect the inlet and outlet brake lines from the RABS valve. Cap the lines.

2. Disconnect the wiring harness from the valve harness.

3. Remove the 3 screws holding the valve to the frame rail liner and remove the valve.

4. Position the RABS valve on the frame rail liner, install the three screws and torque to 19–24 ft. lbs.

5. Connect the brake valve wiring harness to the main harness connector.

6. Connect the brake lines and tighten the larger fitting to 10–17 ft. lbs. and the smaller to 10–15 ft. lbs. Do not overtighten the fittings.

7. Bleed the brake system. It is not necessary to energize the valve electrically to bleed the rear brakes.

Speed sensor mounts to rear axle housing

Exciter ring for speed sensor is pressed on gear carrier

RABS SENSOR

1. The RABS sensor is located on the rear axle housing. Remove the wiring connector.
2. Remove the sensor hold-down bolt and remove the sensor from the axle housing.
3. When installing, clean the axle mounting surface. Use care to keep dirt from entering the axle housing.
4. Inspect and clean the magnetized sensor pole piece to ensure that it is free from loose metal particles which could cause erratic system operation. Inspect the sensor O-ring for damage and replace if necessary.
5. Lightly lubricate the sensor O-ring with motor oil, align the sensor bolt hole and install. Do not apply force to the plastic sensor connector. The sensor flange should slide to the mounting surface. This will insure the air gap setting is between 0.005–0.045 in.
6. Inspect the blue sensor connector seal and replace it, if missing or damaged. Push the connector on the sensor.

NOTE: The clearance between the sensor and the excitor ring should be no greater than 0.050 inches. To measure, remove the sensor from the axle carrier and measure the height of the pole piece from the mounting face of the flange. Sensor pole should be 1.07–1.08 in. Measure the depth from axle housing mounting surface to the top of the exciter teeth. Subtract the 2 measurements to get the sensor gap.

EXCITER RING

The exciter ring is pressed onto the differential case. To inspect it, remove the sensor from the axle housing.

View the exciter ring teeth through the sensor hole. Rotate the rear axle and check the exciter ring teeth for damage or breakage. Dented or broken teeth could cause the RABS system to function when not required. To replace the exciter ring, the differential case must be removed from the axle housing and the exciter ring pressed off the case. Upon removal, the exciter ring must be discarded. It is not to be reused.

FUSES

Three replaceable fuses are involved with RABS. The fuses are located in the fuse box. A 20 amp fuse protects the total RABS. A 15 amp fuse protects the red BRAKE and yellow REAR ANTI-LOCK warning lights. Another 15 amp fuse protects the four-way stoplight cluster.

GENERAL MOTORS CORPORATION

Master Cylinder Service

In addition to standard master cylinder functions, a quick take-up feature in included on most models. This provides a large volume of fluid to the wheels at low pressure with the initial brake application. This large volume of fluid is needed to overcome the clearance created by the seals retracting the pistons into the front calipers and the spring retraction of the rear brake shoes.

NOTE: General Motors Corporation does not recommend honing the bores of either cast iron or composite master cylinders. When the brake master cylinder is overhauled, it is recommended that the cylinder body be replaced rather than attempting to clean up a scuffed cylinder by honing the bore. The master cylinder has a hard, highly polished surface which is produced by diamond boring followed by ball or roller burnishing under heavy pressure. Honing will destroy this surface which will cause rapid wear of rubber cups. Do not use kerosene, gasoline or other solvents for cleaning or flushing master cylinder and components. The use of these solvents or any other with a trace of mineral oil, will damage rubber parts.

DELCO CAST IRON MASTER CYLINDER

Disassembly and Assembly

1. Remove cover, rubber diaphragm and drain reservoir.
2. Remove snapring and primary piston assembly.

3. Plug rear port and apply low pressure air to front port. Secondary piston will pop out. Use shop cloth to catch piston. Use caution. The piston may come out with considerable force. Remove seals from secondary piston.

4. If tube seats must be replaced, thread in self-tapping screw into seat, remove with locking pliers.

To assemble:

5. Clean all metal parts in denatured alcohol, the rubber parts in brake fluid.

6. A stained or discolored bore may be cleaned with fine crocus cloth. Do not attempt to hone the bore.

7. Lube all seals and the bore with clean brake fluid. Install seals on pistons and assemble.

8. Push primary piston with smooth rounded end tool and install snapring.

9. If tube seats are replaced, seat with spare brake tube nut.

10. Install diaphragm into cover and install cover.

BENDIX MASTER CYLINDER

Disassembly and Assembly

1. Remove cover, rubber diaphragm and drain reservoir.

2. Locate and remove the reservoir to body bolts and remove reservoir.

3. Remove the seals, poppet valves and springs from cylinder body.

4. Remove snapring and primary piston.

5. Plug rear port and apply low pressure air to front port. Secondary piston will pop out. Use shop cloth to catch piston. Use caution. The piston may come out with considerable force. Remove seals from secondary piston.

To assemble:

6. Clean all metal parts in denatured alcohol, the rubber parts in brake fluid.

Bendix master cylinder—GM Pick-Up

Composite master cylinder—GM Pick-Up

7. A stained or discolored bore may be cleaned with fine crocus cloth. Do not attempt to hone the bore.

8. Lube all seals and the bore with clean brake fluid. Install seals on pistons and assemble.

9. Push primary piston with smooth rounded end tool and install snapring.

10. Install O-ring, springs, valve poppets and compensating valve seals.

11. Bolt on reservoir, replace diaphragm and cover.

Cast iron master cylinder—GM Pick-Up

PROPORTIONER
VALVE CAP

PROPORTIONER
VALVE
PISTON

FLUID
LEVEL
SENSOR

RESERVOIR
O-RINGS

SECONDARY SEAL

SECONDARY
PISTON

PRIMARY SEAL

PRIMARY PISTON
ASSEMBLY

Master cylinder assembly—Lumina APV

DELCO COMPOSITE MASTER CYLINDER

Disassembly and Assembly

EXCEPT LUMINA APV, SILHOUETTE AND TRANS SPORT

1. Remove cover, rubber diaphragm and drain reservoir.
2. Clamp mounting flange of cylinder in vise and pry reservoir off. Remove reservoir grommet.
3. Remove snapring and primary piston.
4. Plug rear port and apply low pressure air to front port. Secondary piston will pop out. Use shop cloth to catch piston. Use caution. The piston may come out with considerable force. Remove seals from secondary piston.

To assemble:

5. Clean all metal parts in denatured alcohol, the rubber parts in brake fluid.
6. A stained or discolored bore may be cleaned with fine crocus cloth. Do not attempt to hone the bore.
7. Lube all seals and the bore with clean brake fluid. Install seals on pistons and assemble.
8. Push primary piston with smooth rounded end tool and install snapring.
9. Install grommets and press reservoir on with rocking motion. Install diaphragm and cover.

LUMINA APV, SILHOUETTE AND TRANS SPORT

1. Remove cover, rubber diaphragm and drain reservoir.
2. Remove fluid level sensor switch using needle-nose pliers to compress switch locking tabs at the inboard side of master cylinder.
3. Remove proportioner valve assemblies by unscrewing cap assemblies, removing the O-rings and springs. Remove pistons with needle-nose pliers. Use care. Do not scratch piston stems.
4. Remove snapring and primary piston.

5. Apply low pressure air into upper outlet port at blind end of bore. Plug all other ports. Secondary piston will pop out. Use shop cloth to catch piston. Use caution. The piston may come out with considerable force. Remove seals from secondary piston.
6. To remove reservoir, clamp flange (never the body) of master cylinder in vise. Drive out spring pins with ⅛ in. punch. Pull reservoir straight up and remove O-rings from grooves in reservoir.

To assemble:

7. Clean all metal parts in denatured alcohol, the rubber parts in brake fluid.
8. Inspect the bore for scoring or corrosion. If noted, replace master cylinder. No abrasives should be used in bore. Do not attempt to hone the bore.
9. Install new seals on reservoir, press into cylinder body and install spring pins.
10. Lube all seals and the bore with clean brake fluid. Install seals on pistons and assemble.
11. Push primary piston with smooth rounded end tool and install snapring.
12. Install proportioner valve assemblies and fluid level sensor, making sure locking tabs snap into place.
13. Install diaphragm and cover.

Brake Booster Service

Three types of brake boosters are used: a single diaphragm, a tandem diaphragm and a hydraulic booster (Hydro-Boost).

The vacuum boosters may have a vacuum switch to activate a brake warning light in case of low booster vacuum or vacuum pump malfunction. Under normal operating conditions, with brakes released, a vacuum suspended booster operates with vacuum on both sides of its diaphragm or both diaphragms in a tandem diaphragm unit. When the brakes are applied, air at atmospheric pressure is admitted to one side of the diaphragm or both diaphragms in a tandem diaphragm unit to provide the power assist.

The hydraulic brake booster (Hydro-Boost) uses a hydraulic pump to power the system and a pneumatic accumulator as a reserve system. In this system no special fluids are used. However, care must be taken to use the correct fluids. The master cylinder and brake system operate on standard brake fluid. The hydraulic pump, which is driven by pressure from the power steering pump, uses power steering fluid.

VACUUM DIAPHRAGM BRAKE BOOSTERS

Disassembly and Assembly

SINGLE DIAPHRAGM BOOSTER

NOTE: A special brake booster disassembly tool is recommended for this procedure.

1. With the booster unit off the vehicle and the master cylinder removed from the booster, take off the boot and silencer disc from the booster's mounting (rear) side. Remove the vacuum check valve, grommet and the front housing seal from the face side.
2. Scribe a mark across the front and rear housings to aid assembly.
3. Clamp the base in a vise with the power section facing up. Separate the front and rear housings by pressing down, using the special disassembly tool, if available, and rotating the housing counterclockwise to the unlocked position. Loosen carefully as it is spring loaded.
4. Remove the large return spring and the power piston which will likely still have the pedal pushrod attached.
5. Remove the power piston bearing from the rear housing.
6. Remove the reaction body retainer, the master cylinder piston rod and reaction retainer.

1. Check valve and grommet
2. Front housing seal
3. Front housing
4. Piston rod
5. Reaction retainer
6. Return springs
7. Reaction body retainer
8. Power piston and pushrod assembly
9. Diaphragm support
10. filter
11. Diaphragm
12. Diaphragm retainer
13. Rear housing
14. Power piston bearing
15. Silencer disc
16. Boot

Single diaphragm booster—GM Pick-Up

Special tool presses down while housing is turned

Installing diaphragm retainer with pipe driver

Using special GO NO-GO gauge to check pushrod

A Stake
B Unstaked Tab
C Staking Tab Socket

Staking the booster tabs

7. Remove the filter with an awl or similar tool.

8. Separate the power piston and pedal pushrod. To do this, grasp the outside edge of the diaphragm support and diaphragm. Hold the pushrod down against a hard surface and use slight force to dislodge the diaphragm retainer.

9. Remove the diaphragm from the diaphragm support.

To assemble:

10. Inspect all parts for corrosion, nicks, cracks, cuts, scoring, distortion or excessive wear. Replace as required. Clean all parts in denatured alcohol, but do not immerse the power piston and pushrod assembly in alcohol. Dry with compressed air.

11. Lubricate the inside diameter of the diaphragm lip with a thin layer of silicone grease and install the diaphragm into its support.

12. Install the diaphragm and support onto the power piston and pushrod assembly. Use a new retainer and install with a pipe-like driver.

13. Install filter, reaction retainer, piston rod and reaction body retainer.

14. Install the reaction body retainer disc. Lubricate the inside and outside of the power piston bearing with silicone grease and install in rear housing.

15. Install power piston group into rear housing, put in the return spring and assemble front housing to rear housing. Align mating marks made before disassembly.

1. Boot
2. Silencer
3. Vacuum check valve
4. Grommet
5. Front housing seal
6. Primary piston bearing
7. Rear housing
8. Front housing
9. Return spring
10. Piston rod
11. Reaction retainer
12. Power head silencer
13. Diaphragm retainer
14. Primary diaphragm
15. Primary support plate
16. Secondary piston bearing
17. Housing divider
18. Secondary diaphragm
19. Secondary support plate
20. Reaction disc
21. Reaction piston
22. Reaction body retainer
23. Reaction body
24. Air valve spring
25. Reaction bumper
26. Retaining ring
27. Filter
28. Retainer
29. O-ring
30. Air valve pushrod assembly
31. Power piston

Tandem diaphragm vacuum booster components

16. Apply pressure in clockwise direction to lock housings together. Stake the housing at two tabs 180 degrees apart. Do not stake a tab that has been previously staked.

17. Lubricate the check valve grommet with silicone grease and install it and the check valve in the front cover.

18. Install the front housing seal, silencer disc and boot.

19. The piston rod should be checked with a special GO, NO-GO gauge. If not within limits, replace the rod.

TANDEM DIAPHRAGM BOOSTER

NOTE: A special brake booster disassembly tool is recommended for this procedure.

1. With the booster unit off the vehicle and the master cylinder removed from the booster, take off the boot and silencer disc from the booster's mounting (rear) side. Remove the vacuum check valve, grommet and the front housing seal from the face side.

2. Scribe a mark across the front and rear housings to aid assembly.

3. Clamp the base in a vise with the power section facing up. Separate the front and rear housings by pressing down, using the special disassembly tool, if available, and rotating the housing counterclockwise to the unlocked position. Loosen carefully as it is spring loaded.

4. Remove the large return spring and the power piston which will likely still have the pedal pushrod attached.

5. Remove the power piston bearing from the rear housing.

6. Remove the piston rod, reaction retainer and power head silencer ring.

7. Remove the power piston assembly and pushrod. Grasp the assembly at the outside edge of the housing divider and both diaphragms. Hold the pushrod down against a hard surface. Tap to dislodge diaphragm retainer.

8. Remove the primary diaphragm (rear) and primary support plate from the housing divider and separate the primary diaphragm from its support plate.

9. Remove the secondary diaphragm (front) and secondary support plate from the housing divider. Remove the secondary piston bearing from the center of the housing divider and separate the secondary diaphragm from its support plate.

10. Remove the reaction plate retainer, reaction body, reaction disc and reaction piston from the reaction body.

11. Remove the air valve spring and reaction bumper from the end of the pushrod. Carefully remove the retaining ring from the pushrod and remove the pushrod by inserting a suitable tool through the eyelet end and pulling straight out. Considerable force will be required.

12. Remove the filter, retainer and O-ring from the pushrod assembly.

To assemble:

13. Inpect all parts for corrosion, nicks, cracks, cuts, scoring, distortion or excessive wear. Replace as required. Clean all parts in denatured alcohol, but do not immerse the power piston and pushrod assembly in alcohol. Dry with compressed air.

14. Using silicone grease, lubricate the O-ring for the pushrod and install the pushrod into the power piston, then install the retainer and seat.

15. Install the filter over the pushrod eyelet and into the power piston and install the retaining ring.

16. Assemble the reaction bumber, air valve spring, reaction piston and reaction disc into the reaction body. Install the reaction body retainer.

17. Using silicone grease, lubricate the inside diameter of both the primary and secondary diaphragm as well as the secondary piston bearing.

18. Assemble the secondary diaphragm to its support plate and slide the assembly over the power piston/pushrod assembly.

19. Install the secondary piston bearing into the housing divider. The flat surface of the bearing goes on the same side as the 6 raised lugs on the divider. Install this assembly over the power piston/pushrod assembly.

20. Assemble the primary diaphragm to its support plate, by folding the diaphragm up, away from the support plate and slide the assembly over the power piston/pushrod assembly. Fold the primary diaphragm back into position and pull the outside edge of the diaphragm over the formed flange of the housing divider.

NOTE: Check that the beads on the secondary diaphragm are seated evenly around the complete circumference.

21. Install a new diaphragm retainer and install with a pipe-like driver.

22. Install the silencer ring, reaction retainer and piston rod.

23. Lubricate the inside and outside diameters of the primary piston bearing with silicone grease and install into the rear housing.

1. Nut
2. C-clamp
3. Adapter

Removing the accumulator—Hydro-Boost

24. Install the power piston assembly into the rear housing.

25. Install the return spring and assemble front housing to rear housing. Align mating marks made before disassembly.

26. Apply pressure in clockwise direction to lock housings together. Stake the housing at 2 tabs 180 degrees apart. Do not stake a tab that has been previously staked.

27. Lubricate the check valve grommet with silicone grease and install it and the check valve in the front cover.

28. Install the front housing seal, silencer disc and boot.

29. The piston rod should be checked with a special GO, NO-GO gauge. If not within limits, replace the rod.

HYDRO-BOOST

The Bendix Hydro-Boost uses the hydraulic pressure supplied

1. Retainer	16. Cover
2. Accumulator	17. Bracket
3. O-Ring	18. Nut
4. Retainer	19. Boot
5. Plug	20. Pedal Rod
6. O-Ring	21. Pin
7. Spring	22. Piston Assembly
8. Housing	23. Seal
9. Bolt	24. Retainer
10. Seal	25. Piston Return Spring
11. Accumulator Valve	26. Retainer
12. Return Line Fitting	27. Baffle
13. Spool Valve	28. Output Pushrod
14. Seal	
15. Seal	

Hydro-Boost components

1. Input rod seal
2. Power piston seal
3. Housing seal
4. Spool valve plug seal
5. Accumulator seal
6. Return plug port

Possible Hydro-Boost seal leak areas

by the power steering pump to provide a power assist to brake application. It has identifying information stamped into the housing near the inlet line. When servicing this unit, there are some special tools that are recommended for these procedures.

Disassembly and Assembly

CAUTION

This system uses an accumulator that contains compressed gas. Do not apply heat to the accumulator. Use caution or personal injury may result. Do not attempt to repair a defective accumulator. Always replace with a new unit. Dispose of an inoperative accumulator by drilling a $^1/_{16}$ in. diameter hole through the end of the accumulator can opposite the O-ring.

1. Remove the accumulator. Note that an adapter (a piece of strap metal with a hole drilled to accommodate a mounting stud) is used along with a C-clamp. Depress the accumulator with the C-clamp, insert a punch into the hole on the housing and remove the snapring retainer. Release the C-clamp, remove the accumulator and O-ring.
2. Remove the retainer from the small port above the mounting flange and remove the plug, O-ring and spring.
3. Remove the star-shaped retainer from the mounting flange bore and remove the output pushrod, baffle, piston return spring and inner retainer.
4. Remove the pedal rod boot and mounting bracket, if installed. On some installations it may be necessary to saw off the eyelet of the pedal rod. Make sure exact replacements or the replacement parts kit is available before cutting the original part.
5. Remove the cover bolts and separate the cover from the housing. Remove the seals (a large figure 8 shaped seal and a smaller seal on the end of the piston assembly).
6. Remove the piston assembly and the O-ring seal on the housing side of the piston.
7. Remove the spool valve.
8. Remove the accumulator valve. It may be necessary to fish this small valve out with a thin wire hook.
9. Remove the return line fitting and seal.

To assemble:
10. Clean all parts in power steering fluid. Inspect the spool valve for corrosion, nicks and scoring. If found, replace the complete booster. Discoloration of the spool or bore is not harmful and is no cause for replacement. Check all components for damage or wear, especially the tube seat in the housing. This seat can be removed with an Easy-Out type remover and its replacement installed by tapping gently into place.

11. Lubricate all seals and friction metal parts with power steering fluid.
12. Install the return line fitting and seal.
13. Install the accumulator valve and spool valve.
14. Install the seal and piston assembly, place the small seal on the piston assembly end and the figure 8 shaped seal into the housing. Install the cover and torque the bolts to 22 ft. lbs.
15. Install the mounting bracket and pushrod boot.
16. On the master cylinder side of the unit, install the output pushrod, baffle, piston return spring and retainer.
17. Install the accumulator and O-ring using a large C-clamp as in disassembly procedure.
18. Install the jam nut from the repair kit onto the pedal rod and install the eyelet onto the pedal rod.

Combination Valve

The combination valve (also called a proportioning valve) is made up of 3 sections, each serving a different function.

The metering or hold-off section of the valve limits the pressure to the front disc brakes until a predetermined front input pressure is reached, enough to overcome the rear shoe retractor springs. There is no restriction to the inlet pressures below 3 psi to allow for pressure equalization during no-apply periods.

The proportioning section of the combination valve proportions outlet pressure to the rear brakes after a predetermined rear input pressure has been reached. This is done to prevent rear wheel lockup on vehicles with light rear wheel loads.

The valve is designed to have a bypass feature which ensures full system pressure to the rear brakes in the event of a front brake system malfunction. Full front pressure is retained in the event of rear malfunction.

The pressure-differential warning switch is designed to constantly compare front and rear brake pressure from the master cylinder and energize the warning light on the instrument panel in the event of a front or rear system malfunction. The valve and switch are designed so the switch will latch in the warning postion once a malfunction has occurred. The only way the light can be turned off is to repair the malfunction and apply a pedal force required to develop about 450 psi line pressure (a firm brake application).

Valve Overhaul

The combination valve is not repairable and must be replaced as a complete assembly.

Caliper Service

The disc brake assembly consists of a caliper and piston assem-

Caliper components—typical

Bleeder Valve
Seal
Piston
Boot
Spring Assembly
Seal
Piston
Boot

Wheel cylinder components—typical

bly, rotor, linings and an anchor plate. The caliper is mounted to the anchor plate, which allows the caliper to move laterally against the rotor. The caliper is a one-piece casting with the inboard side containing the piston bore. A square cut rubber seal is located in a groove in the piston bore which provides the hydraulic seal between the piston and the cylinder wall.

As the brake pedal is pressed, hydraulic pressure is applied against the piston. This pressure pushes the inboard brake lining against the inboard braking surface of the rotor. As the force increases against the rotor, the caliper assembly moves inboard and provides a clamping action on the rotor.

When brake pressure is released, the piston seal returns to its normal position, pulling the piston back into the caliper bore. This creates a running clearance between the inner brake lining and rotor.

Disassembly and Assembly

1. Drain all fluid from caliper.

2. Pad interior of caliper with clean shop towels and use just enough compressed air to ease the piston out of the bore.

CAUTION

Do not place fingers in front of piston to try to catch piston or protect it when applying compressed air. This could result in serious injury. Use just enough air to ease the piston out. If piston is blown out, even with padding, it may be damaged.

3. Remove boot, being careful not to scratch bore.
4. Remove square cut seal from caliper bore groove.
5. Remove bleeder valve.

To assemble:

6. Clean all parts with denatured alcohol, blow dry with compressed air. Inspect all parts for scoring, corrosion or damage to chrome plating on piston. Replace if damaged. Fine crocus cloth can be used to polish out any light corrosion.

7. Lubricate the new piston seal, caliper bore and piston with clean brake fluid and install the seal in the caliper bore groove. Make sure seal is not twisted.

8. Install the boot on the piston, slide the piston into the bore and gently tap the boot into the counterbore of the caliper housing using a suitable driver.

9. Install bleeder screw.

CAUTION

After the caliper has been installed and the system bled, before moving the vehicle, pump the brake pedal several times until the pedal is firm. Do not move the vehicle until a firm pedal is obtained. Check the fluid level in the master cylinder after pumping the brakes.

Wheel Cylinder Service

The drum brake assembly is a duo-servo design. Force which is applied by the wheel cylinder to the primary shoe is multiplied by the primary shoe friction to provide a large applied force to the secondary shoe. The torque from the brake shoes is transferred to the anchor pin and through the backing plate, the the axle flange. Brake adjustments are automatic and are made during reverse brake applications.

Wheel cylinders may need reconditioning or replacement whenever the brake shoes are replaced or when required to correct a leak condition. In some cases, the wheel cylinders can be disassembled without removing them from the backing plate.

- - - - ELECTRIC
——— HYDRAULIC

A. To Front Brakes
1. Master cylinder
2. Brake light switch
3. Instrument cluster
4. Digital ratio adapter
5. Speed sensor
6. Transmission
7. Isolation/dump valve
8. RWAL control module
9. Brake warning light
10. Combination valve

Rear Wheel Anti-lock (RWAL) brake system—General Motors Corporation

Rear Wheel Anti-lock (RWAL) brake system wiring diagram

On others, the cylinder must be removed before being disassembled.

Leaks which coat the boot and the cylinder with fluid or result in a dropped reservoir fluid level or dampen and stain the brake linings are dangerous. Such leaks can cause the brakes to grab or fail and should be immediately corrected. A leakage, not immediately apparent, can be detected by pulling back the cylinder boot. A small amount of fluid seepage dampening the interior of the boot is normal. However, a dripping boot is not. Unless other conditions causing a brake to pull, grab or drag become obvious, the wheel cylinder is suspect and should be included in general reconditioning.

Cylinder binding may be caused by rust, deposits, grime or swollen cups due to fluid contamination or by a cup wedged into an excessive piston clearance.

Hydraulic system parts should not be allowed to come into contact with oil or grease, neither should those be handled with greasy hands. Even a trace of any petroleum based product is sufficient to cause damage to the rubber parts.

Disassembly and Assembly

1. Remove the brake bleeder screw.
2. Remove the dust boots, allow any brake fluid to drain out.
3. Remove the pistons, seals and inner spring.
4. Inspect the bore for scoring and corrosion. The inside of the bore may be cleaned with fine crocus cloth. If bore is scored, replace cylinder. Clean the cylinder with brake fluid.
5. Lubricate the seals with brake fluid and install. Cup lips should always face inward. Install the spring assembly and seals.

6. Carefully install the pistons and dust boots.
7. Install the bleeder screw.

Anti-Lock Braking Systems

Despite advances in brake design over the years, even the best systems in use can still lockup during certain road conditions, such as wet road surfaces. When the brakes lockup, the driver can lose control of the vehicle, because a locked wheel cannot absorb any cornering or lateral forces and steering is lost. It is impossible to brake to a maximum and at the same time steer the vehicle when the front wheels are locked. If the back wheels are locked the vehicle will become unstable and start to slide.

While many different ways have been tried over the years to solve this problem, mechanical sensors could not provide sufficient information about wheel rotation speed and mechanical control units could not operate the brakes fast enough to prevent brake lockup.

The growth of the electronics industry has allowed small computers (microprocessors) to be reduced in both size and cost. Coupled with fast reacting electronic sensors, anti-lock braking has become more reliable with widespread application.

REAR WHEEL ANTI-LOCK BRAKE SYSTEM

General Motors Corporation's system is called the Rear Wheel Anti-Lock (RWAL) System and its application is on selected 2WD models. It is designed to reduce the occurrence of the rear wheel lockup during a severe brake application.

Rear Wheel Anti-lock (RWAL) brake system connectors

RWAL ECU and isolation/dump valve

Transmission speed sensor installation

Digital ratio adapter controller mounting

The system functions by regulating the rear hydraulic brake line pressure. The pressure regulation is accomplished by a control valve which is located under the master cylinder. The control valve is made up of 2 valves, a dump valve which releases pressure into an accumulator and an isolation valve which maintains rear brake pressure. The valve is controlled by a microcomputer which is part of the Electronic Control Unit (ECU). The ECU is mounted next to the master cylinder. In a severe brake application as pressure is applied to the brake pedal, the ECU is designed to permit the valve to do 1 of 3 functions or a combination of all 3. The ECU will allow the valve to either maintain the same amount of hydraulic pressure. release hy-

draulic pressure through the dump valve into the accumulator or increase the pressure by pulsing the isolation valve.

The ECU operates by receiving signals from the speed sensor which is located in the transmission and the brake light switch. The speed sensor sends its signal to the digital ratio adapter which is part of the instrument cluster. If the axle ratio or tire size is changed, it will be necessary to recalibrate the digital ratio adapter.

The RWAL system is connected to the existing brake warning light located on the dash. An indication of the RWAL operation

REAR WHEEL ANTI-LOCK BRAKE SYSTEM DIAGNOSTIC CODES

CODE	SYSTEM PROBLEM
CODE 1	Electronic control unit malfunction
CODE 2	Open isolation valve or faulty ECU
CODE 3	Open dump valve or faulty ECU
CODE 4	Grounded antilock valve switch
CODE 5	Excessive actuations of dump valve during an anti-lock stop
CODE 6	Erratic speed signal
CODE 7	Shorted isolation valve or faulty ECU
CODE 8	Shorted dump valve or faulty ECU
CODE 9	Open circuit to the speed signal
CODE 10	Brake lamp switch circuit
CODE 11	Electronic control unit malfunction
CODE 12	Electronic control unit malfunction
CODE 13	Electronic control unit malfunction
CODE 14	Electronic control unit malfunction
CODE 15	Electronic control unit malfunction

Trouble codes are available at the ALDL (Assembly Line Diagnostic Link), the twelve terminal connector wired to the Electronic Control Module and located under the instrument panel in the passenger compartment. These codes are ready by jumping terminal A (which is ground) of the ALDL to terminal H of the ALDL and observing the flashing of the brake warning light.

is a bulb check performed each time the ignition is turned ON. The warning light will remain on for about 2 seconds. A RWAL system malfunction is indicated by a brake warning light.

To aid in diagnosing problems, trouble codes are produced by the system. Trouble codes are available at the Assembly Line Diagnostic Link (ALDL), the 12-terminal connector wired to the Electronic Control Module and located under the instrument panel in the passenger compartment. These codes are read by jumping terminal **A** (which is ground) of the ALDL to terminal **H** of the ALDL and observing the flashing of the brake warning light. The terminals must be jumped for about 20 seconds before the code will begin to flash. In counting code pulses, count the number of short flashes starting from the long flash. Include the long flash as a count.

NOTE: Sometimes the first count sequence will be short. However, subsequent counts will be accurate. If there is more than 1 failure, only the first recognized failure code will be retained and flashed.

To clear trouble codes, with the ignition **OFF**, remove the brake fuse, wait 5 seconds and then reinstall fuse.

Circuit Maintenance and Repair

All electrical connections must be kept clean and tight. Make sure connectors are properly seated and all of the sealing rings on weather-proof connections are in place. With the low current and voltage levels found in some circuits, it is important that all connections be the best possible. Special tools are required for servicing GM's Weather-Pack connectors. This special tool is required to remove the pin and sleeve terminals. If removal is attempted with an ordinary pick, there is a good chance that the terminal will be bent or deformed. These terminals cannot be straightened once they are bent.

Use care when probing the connections or replacing terminals in them. It is possible to short between opposite terminals. If this happens to the wrong terminal part, it is possible to damage certain components. Always use jumper wires between connectors for circuit checking. Never probe through Weather-Pack seals.

When diagnosing for possible open circuits, it is often difficult to locate them by sight because oxidation or terminal misalignment are hidden by the connectors. Merely wiggling a connector on a sensor or in the wiring harness may correct the open circuit condition. This should always be considered when an open cir-

cuit is indicated while troubleshooting. Intermittent problems may also be caused by oxidized or loose connections.

Removal and Installation

RWAL ELECTRONIC CONTROL UNIT

The RWAL Electronic Control Unit (ECU) is not serviceable. It should be replaced when diagnosis shows it to be malfunctioning.

NOTE: Do not touch the electrical connections and pins or allow them to come into contact with brake fluid as this will damage the RWAL ECU.

1. Disconnect the electrical connectors.
2. Remove the RWAL ECU by prying the tab at the rear of the ECU and pulling it forward toward the front of the vehicle.
3. To install, simply slide the RWAL ECU into its bracket on the master cylinder until the tab locks into the hole.
4. Install the electrical connectors. If brake fluid has gotten on the connectors, clean then with water followed by isopropyl alcohol.

ISOLATION/DUMP VALVE

The Isolation/Dump valve is not serviceable. It should be replaced when diagnosis shows it to be malfunctioning.

NOTE: Do not touch the electrical connections and pins or allow them to come into contact with brake fluid as this will damage the RWAL ECU.

1. Disconnect the brake line fittings and remove the bolts holding the valve to the bracket.
2. Disconnect the electrical connector from the RWAL ECU. Do not allow the valve to hang by the pigtail.
3. Remove the valve from the vehicle.
4. When installing replacement valve, torque bolts to 21 ft. lbs., brake line fittings to 18 ft. lbs.
5. Install the electrical connectors. If brake fluid has gotten on the connectors, clean them with water followed by isopropyl alcohol.
6. Bleed brake system.

SPEED SENSOR

The vehicle speed sensor is a permanent magnet signal generator located on the transmission output shaft housing. The vehi-

VEHICLE SPEED SENSOR AND DIGITAL RATIO ADAPTER CONTROLLER DIAGNOSIS

Condition	Cause	Correction
Speedometer and odometer are inaccurate	Incorrect digital ratio adapter.	Check for the correct digital ratio adapter.
Speedometer and odometer do not operate properly	1. Inoperative digital ratio adapter.	1. Disconnect the digital ratio adapter, and place the ignition in run. Check for voltage between the pink/black wire in the harness and a good chassis ground. If the voltage is less than the battery voltage, check for an open or short in the pink/black wire.
	2. Poor ground path from the digital ratio adapter.	2. Check for voltage between the pink/black wire in the harness and the black/white wire. If the voltage is less than battery voltage, check for an open or short in the black/white wire.
	3. No signal from the vehicle speed sensor.	3. Raise and support the vehicle, start the engine, and place the transmission in drive. Check for AC voltage that changes with the engine rpm between the purple/white wire, and the light green/black wire at the digital ratio adapter. If there is not AC voltage at these wires, check for opens in the purple/white wire and the light green wire. If there are not shorts or opens, replace the vehicle speed sensor.
	4. Inoperative digital ratio adapter (speedometer output).	4. Raise and support the vehicle, start the engine, and place the transmission in drive. Check for AC voltage that changes with the engine rpm between the light blue/black and the black/white wires at the digital ratio adapter connector (connector attached) if AC voltage varies with RPM, replace the digital ratio adapter.
	5. Inoperative digital ratio adapter (cruise output).	5. Raise and support the vehicle, start the engine, and place the transmission in drive. Check for AC voltage that changes with the engine rpm between the yellow and the black/white wires at the digital ratio adapter connector (connector attached) if AC voltage varies with rpm, replace the digital ratio adapter.
	6. Inoperative instrument cluster.	6. Refer to DIAGNOSIS OF THE ELECTRONIC INSTRUMENT CLUSTER.

TERMINAL IDENTIFICATION

A GROUND	**F** T.C.C. (IF USED)
B DIAGNOSTIC TERMINAL	**G** FUEL PUMP (CK)
C A.I.R. (IF USED)	**H** BRAKE SENSE SPEED INPUT (CK)
E SERIAL DATA (V6/V8)	**M** SERIAL DATA (L4)

ALDL Connector

cle speed sensor sends an analog signal proportional to the propeller shaft speed. This signal goes to the Digital Ratio Adapter Controller (DRAC) which is used to change the speed sensor signal to a digital signal for the electronic instrument cluster.

The speed sensor is not serviceable. It should be replaced when necessary. The sensor is located in the left rear of the transmission on 2WD models or on the transfer case of 4WD models.

The resistance of the speed sensor should be 900–2000 ohms.

1. Remove the electrical connector.
2. Most applications will use a bolt retainer which is removed. Pull the speed sensor out of transmission housing. Have container ready to catch transmission fluid.
3. Always use new O-ring seal when installing speed sensor. Coat the seal with a thin film of transmission fluid.
4. Install retainer bolt if used and connect electrical harness.

Four wheel drive anti-lock wiring diagram

NOTE: The speedometer must recalibrated when rear axle ratio or tire size is changed.

FOUR WHEEL ANTI-LOCK BRAKE SYSTEM

In 1990, selected G.M. models with All Wheel Drive (AWD) could be equipped with a Four Wheel Anti-Lock System (4WAL). It too is designed to to reduce wheel lockup during severe braking. Like the Rear Wheel Anti-Lock system, it works by regulating hyrdaulic brake line pressure. An Electro-Hydraulic Control Unit (EHCU) valve located under the master cylinder, is made up of 2 types of valves. Isolation valves main-

A. To Ignition Switch (B+)
B. To Battery (B+)
C. ALDL
1. 4WAL EHCU Valve
2. Combination Valve
3. Master Cylinder
4. Brake Pedal Switch
5. Park Brake Switch
6. Wheel Speed Sensors
7. Warning Lamps

Four wheel drive anti-lock brake system schematic

G.M. FOUR WHEEL ANTI-LOCK BRAKE SYSTEM DIAGNOSTIC CODES

CODE	SYSTEM PROBLEM
CODE 21	Right front speed sensor or circuit open
CODE 22	Missing right front speed signal (set with vehicle in motion)
CODE 23	Erratic right front speed sensor
CODE 25	Left front speed sensor or circuit open
CODE 26	Missing left front speed signal (set with vehicle in motion)
CODE 27	Erratic left front speed sensor
CODE 28	Erratic speed sensor signal (two drop-outs above 20 mph)
CODE 29	Simultaneous drop-out of all four sensors (at speeds above 8 mph)
CODE 31	Right rear speed sensor or circuit open
CODE 32	Missing right rear speed signal (set with vehicle in motion)
CODE 33	Erratic right rear speed sensor
CODE 35	Left rear speed sensor or circuit open
CODE 36	Missing left rear speed signal (set with vehicle in motion)
CODE 37	Erratic left rear speed sensor
CODE 38	Wheel speed error (set with vehicle in motion)
CODES 41 thru 66 and 71 thru 74	4WAL control unit
CODE 67	Open motor circuit or shorted ECU output
CODE 68	Locked motor or shorted motor circuit
CODES 68, 43, 44, 47, 48, 53 and 54	Loss of power ground
CODE 81	Brake switch circuit shorted or open
CODE 85	Open antilock warning lamp
CODE 86	Shorted antilock warning lamp
CODE 88	Shorted brake warning lamp

tain pressure to each front wheel separately and to the rear wheels combined. Dump valves dump pressure to each front wheel separately and to the rear wheels combined. The valves are controlled by a microcomputer which is part of the EHCU valve. Under severe braking, the EHCU valve will allow the valves to either maintain the same hydraulic pressure, release hydraulic pressure through the dump valves into the accumulator or increase pressure.

The EHCU valve operates by receiving signals from the speed sensors, located at each wheel and the brake light switch. The speed sensors are connected directly to the EHCU valve through the 8 pin connector.

The 4WAL system is connected to the ANTI-LOCK warning light in the instrument panel. An indication of 4WAL operation and a bulb check is performed each time the ignition is turned ON. The warning light will remain on for about 2 seconds. A 4WAL system malfunction is indicated by the ANTI-LOCK warning light.

To aid in diagnosing problems, trouble codes are produced by the system. Trouble codes are available at the Assembly Line Diagnostic Link (ALDL) the 12-terminal connector wired to the Electronic Control Module and located under the instrument panel in the passenger compartment. These codes are read by jumping terminal **A** of the ALDL to terminal **H** of the ALDL and observing the flashing of the ANTI-LOCK light. The terminals must be jumped for a few seconds before the code will begin to flash. The ANTI-LOCK light will flash in a manner similar to

the SERVICE ENGINE SOON light for the fuel and emissions system.

In counting code pulses, count the number of short flashes starting from the long flash. Include the long flash as a count.

NOTE: Sometimes the first count sequence will be short. However, subsequent counts will be accurate. If there is more than one failure, only the first recognized failure code will be retained and flashed.

To clear trouble codes, turn the ignition switch to **RUN**. Use a jumper wire to ground the ALDL terminal **H** to **A** for 2 seconds. Remove the jumper wire for two seconds. Repeat the grounding and ungrounding 2 more times. Check that the memory is cleared by making a diagnostic request. Turn ignition **OFF**.

Removal and Installation

ELECTRO-HYDRAULIC CONTROL UNIT (EHCU) VALVE

The EHCU valve is not serviceable. It should be replaced when diagnosis shows it to be malfunctioning.

1. Mark relationship between the intermediate steering shaft upper universal joint yoke to steering shaft and the lower yoke to steering gear wormshaft. Remove the upper and lower universal yoke pinch bolt.

2. Remove the steering gear frame bolts. Lower the steering

36–38° ANGLE
MUST NOT EXCEED
39° MAXIMUM OR
34° MINIMUM

INTERMEDIATE SHAFT

STEERING GEAR

Remove steering intermediate shaft to remove EHCU

EHCU VALVE

BRACKET

EHCU valve mounting

TO REAR WHEELS

TO LEFT FRONT WHEEL

TO RIGHT FRONT WHEEL

EHCU valve brake line connections

gear. It is not necessary to disconnect the pitman arm from the steering gear pitman shaft.

3. Remove the intermediate steering shaft and universal joint assembly.

4. Remove the brake lines from the bottom of the combination valve. Remove the electrical connector.

5. Remove the master cylinder and combination valve assembly.

6. Remove the brake lines from the EHCU valve. Remove the electrical connectors from the EHCU valve.

7. Remove mounting bolt and nuts and remove EHCU from vehicle. Remove EHCU from its mounting bracket.

To install:

8. Install the EHCU valve to its mounting bracket. Tighten the 6 mounting bolts to only 60 inch lbs. Overtightening the bolts could result in excessive noise transfer from the EHCU valve.

9. Install the EHCU valve and bracket assembly into the vehicle and install the fasteners. Torque the bolt to 33 ft. lbs., the nuts to 20 ft. lbs.

10. Install the electrical connectors and the brake lines to the EHCU valve.

11. Install the master cylinder and combination valve assem-

bly. Connect the electrical connector and the brake lines to the combination valve.

12. Install the steering intermediate shaft. Start by placing the lower yoke onto the steering gear wormshaft. Align the match marks made at removal. Install the pinch bolt which must pass through the shaft undercut. Torque to 30 ft. lbs.

13. Raise the steering gear into position while guiding the upper yoke onto the steering shaft. Align the matchmarks made at removal. Tighten the steering gear to frame bolts to 55 ft. lbs. Install the pinch bolt which must pass through the shaft undercut. Torque to 30 ft. lbs.

14. Bleed the brake system including the EHCU valve.

NOTE: The EHCU valve should be bled after replacement only. It should not be necessary to bleed the valve during normal brake system bleeding. The valve should be bled after the wheel cylinders and calipers have been bled. Use the 2 bleed screws on the EHCU valve for bleeding. There are also 2 bleeders on the front of the unit that look like normal brake bleeders. These are not the correct bleeders for bleeding the EHCU valve and they should not be turned. A special tool is used to depress the high pressure accumulator bleed stem of the EHCU valve. This is similar to tools used to hold the stem of proportioning valves during bleeding.

15. Bleed the wheel cylinders and calipers as usual (right rear, left rear, right front, left front).

16. Install the special hold-down tool on the left high pressure accumulator bleed stem of the EHCU valve.

17. Slowly depress brake pedal one time and hold. Loosen the left bleeder screw ¼–½ turn to purge air from the EHCU valve. Tighten the bleeder screw and slowly release the pedal.

Front wheel speed sensor—2WD vehicles

Front wheel speed sensor—4WD vehicles

INTERNAL
BLEED
SCREW

EHCU VALVE TO
BRACKET BOLTS

EHCU VALVE TO
BRACKET BOLTS

EHCU VALVE TO
BRACKET BOLTS

DEPRESS DURING BLEEDING

EHCU valve bleeders

BOLTS

Rear wheel speed sensor

18. Wait 15 seconds then repeat this sequence including the 15 second wait until all air is purged from the EHCU valve.

19. Repeat these steps on the right side of the EHCU valve.

20. Remove valve depressor tool.

FRONT WHEEL SPEED SENSOR

2WD Vehicles

1. Raise and safely support vehicle. Remove wheel and tire assembly.

2. Remove brake caliper.

3. Remove hub and bearing assembly.

4. Remove rotor assembly.

5. Disconnect the sensor wire connector and unclip from upper control arm.

6. Remove bolts holding speed sensor/splash shield assembly and remove unit from vehicle.

To install:

7. Install speed sensor/splash shield assembly and torque bolts to 11 ft. lbs.

8. Clip wire to upper control arm and reconnect electrical connection.

9. Apply recommended lubricant to the spindle and inside of hub. Install hub and outer wheel bearing and washer with a generous amount of lubricant. Tighten nut to 12 ft. lbs. while turning the hub forward to seat the bearing. Back off the nut to the just loose position. Hand tighten nut, then back off until the hole in the spindle lines up with a slot on the nut. The nut should not be backed off more than ½ a flat. Install new cotter pin.

10. Install brake rotor.

11. Install caliper. Bushings should be lubricated with silicone grease. Make sure the brake line is not twisted.

12. Install wheel and tire assembly. Lower vehicle.

4WD Vehicles

1. Raise and safely support vehicle. Remove wheel and tire assembly.

2. Remove brake caliper.

3. Remove brake rotor.

4. Remove hub and bearing assembly. On all-wheel drive models, remove the drive axle nut and washer. Use a puller to ease the hub from the drive axle.

5. Disconnect the sensor wire connector and unclip from upper control arm.

6. Remove bolts holding speed sensor/splash shield assembly and remove unit from vehicle.

To install:

7. Install speed sensor/splash shield assembly to the steering knuckle and torque the bolts to 11 ft. lbs.

8. Clip wire to upper control arm and reconnect electrical connection.

9. Install hub and bearing assembly, align threaded holes and tighten bolts to 66 ft. lbs.

10. Install outer axle washer and nut. Torque to 175 ft. lbs.

11. Install brake rotor and caliper.

12. Install wheel and tire. Lower vehicle.

REAR WHEEL SPEED SENSOR

4WD Vehicles

1. Raise and safely support vehicle. Remove wheel and tire assembly.

2. Remove brake drum.

3. Remove the primary brake shoe.

4. Disconnect the sensor electric wire connector and wire from its axle clips.

5. Remove the retainer bolts and take out speed sensor by pulling the wire through the hole in the backing plate.

To install:

6. Install the speed sensor and bolts. Torque to 26 ft. lbs.

7. Install sensor wire to axle clips and hook up connector.

8. Install primary brake shoe, brake drum and wheel and tire assembly. Lower vehicle.

JEEP

Master Cylinder Service

Jeep uses a dual master cylinder which contains a double hydraulic cylinder with 2 fluid reservoirs and primary and secondary hydraulic pistons. The master cylinder is assisted by a vacuum booster. Hydraulic rear drum brakes with automatic adjusters and self-adjusting front disc brakes are standard on all models.

The front outlet tube of the master cylinder is connected to the hydraulic system control valve and then to the rear brakes. This is referred the secondary system. The rear outlet tube is connected to the control valve and to the front brakes. This system is referred to as the primary system. No residual pressure valves are used in the master cylinder outlets.

During normal operation, the fluid level in the master cylinder will rise during brake operation and fall during release. It is also expected that the fluid level will decrease with brake pad wear. In addition, a trace of brake fluid on the booster shell below the master cylinder mounting flange will often be found as a result of the normal lubricating action of the master cylinder bore and seal. All of these conditions are considered normal and are not indications the master cylinder needs service.

Two types of master cylinders were used; 1) a cast iron master cylinder with built-in reservoir and separate proportioning valve and, 2) a master cylinder with a pressed on plastic reservoir. The body of the 2-piece master cylinder is made of anodized aluminum and the reservoir is made of nylon. The 2 compartments of the reservoir are interconnected to permit equalization of the fluid level. However, a sufficient quantity of fluid is retained in the reservoir of the unaffected system to permit operation of that half of the master cylinder even if the other half of the reservoir is drained due to a hydraulic leak. There is another type of master cylinder used on vehicles equipped with anti-lock brakes. See anti-lock section.

Use extra care when servicing aluminum master cylinders not to cross thread brake line fittings and do not overtighten any threaded connection.

In the event of a front brake system malfunction the proportioning valve with a bypass feature allows full hydraulic pressure to the rear brake system.

Disassembly and Assembly

While the manufacturer does give overhaul procedures for the master cylinder, the manufacturer does not permit that either the cast iron or aluminum master cylinder be honed in an at-

Use air pressure to remove secondary piston

tempt to restore the surface. Replace the cylinder if the bore is corroded or if doubt exists about cylinder bore condition.

CAST IRON MASTER CYLINDER

Except Anti-Lock

1. Remove the cover and drain fluid. Examine cover seal for damage.

2. Mount cylinder in vise and press in primary piston. Remove snapring.

3. Remove the primary piston and discard. It is serviced only as an assembly.

4. Apply a small amount of compressed air to secondary outlet while covering small ports at bottom of rear reservoir to ease secondary piston from bore.

5. Disassemble secondary piston. Discard seals, spring and retainer.

To assemble:

6. Inspect bore carefully, clean and dry with compressed air. Do not hone bore if scored. Replace the assembly.

Secondary piston components

Bleeding master cylinder—typical

7. Coat the cylinder bore and new piston assemblies with clean brake fluid. Assemble the secondary piston, making sure the seals are facing the proper direction. Assemble the retainer and return spring and insert assembly into the cylinder bore.

8. Install the primary piston into the bore, push in and install the snapring.

9. Bench-bleed the master cylinder before installation.

ALUMINUM MASTER CYLINDER

Except Anti-Lock

1. Remove the reservoir cover, seal and drain fluid.

2. Mount the cylinder in a vise. Clamp vise jaws on one of the mounting ears so cylinder bore not be distorted.

3. Remove reservoir with a rocking motion. Remove the seal grommets.

4. Remove the cylinder snapring.

5. Remove the primary piston and discard. It is serviced only as an assembly.

6. Apply a small amount of compressed air to secondary outlet to ease secondary piston from bore.

7. Disassemble secondary piston. Discard seals, spring and retainer.

8. Inspect the cylinder check valve. Remove the valve snapring and replace the valve, if necessary. The tube seats can also be replaced. Remove by forcing in a hardened self-tapping screw, then pry upwards to remove the seat.

9. Inspect bore carefully, clean and dry with compressed air. Do not hone bore if scored. Replace the assembly.

To assemble:

10. Coat the cylinder bore and new piston assemblies with clean brake fluid. Assemble the secondary piston, making sure the seals are facing the proper direction. Assemble the retainer and return spring and insert assembly into the cylinder bore.

11. Install the primary piston into the bore, push in and install the snapring.

12. Install new reservoir grommets into the cylinder body.

13. Turn reservoir upside down and place on flat surface. Press the master cylinder onto the reservoir with a rocking motion. Be sure it is fully seated.

14. Bench bleed the master cylinder before installation.

Brake Booster Service

Jeep models covered are equipped with vacuum boosters, except those equipped with the anti-lock brake system. Anti-lock master cylinder/power brake booster units are not repairable and must be replaced as a complete assembly.

Aluminum master cylinder

Aluminum master cylinder components

Installing the reservoir to the master cylinder body

Caliper components—typical

Under normal operating conditions, with brakes released, a vacuum suspended booster operates with vacuum on both sides of its diaphragm or both diaphragms in a tandem diaphragm unit. When the brakes are applied, air at atmospheric pressure is admitted to one side of the diaphragm or both diaphragms in a tandem diaphragm unit to provide the power assist.

Brake boosters used by Jeep are not repairable and if defective, the booster must be replaced as a unit. The brake boosters used on different models of Jeeps are different sizes and are not interchangeable.

Combination Valve

All models have a hydraulic system control valve in the brake system. A combination proportioning valve/pressure differential switch is used on all models. Comanche series Pick-Ups are equipped with a rear brake height sensing proportioning valve.

The valve adjusts front-rear brake proportioning to maintain brake balance when the vehicle is loaded.

A dual purpose warning light is located in the instrument cluster. The primary function of this light is to alert the driver, if a pressure differential exists between the front and rear brake hydraulic systems. The light also functions as an indicator to alert the driver when the parking brake is applied.

Caliper Service

Jeep calipers are 1-piece castings with the inboard side containing the piston bore. A square cut rubber seal is located in a groove in the piston bore which provides the hydraulic seal between the piston and the cylinder wall.

As the brake pedal is pressed, hydraulic pressure is applied against the piston. This pressure pushes the inboard brake lining against the inboard braking surface of the rotor. As the force increases against the rotor, the caliper assembly moves inboard and provides a clamping action on the rotor.

When brake pressure is released, the piston seal returns to its normal position, pulling the piston back into the caliper bore. This creates a running clearance between the inner brake lining and rotor.

Disassembly and Assembly

1. Place shop towels under the caliper piston to protect it during removal. Apply a little compressed air to slowly ease the piston out of the bore.

2. Remove the dust boot and using a small, pointed wooden

Install dust boot on piston, then fold back

stick, work the piston seal out of its groove in the caliper bore. Do not use a screwdriver or metal tool which might nick or scratch the bore. Discard the seal.

To assemble:

3. Clean all parts well using alcohol and blow dry. Inspect the piston bore for scoring or pitting. Install a new piston if it is pitted, scored or the plating is worn. Jeep does not recommend honing calipers or using any type of abrasives on the basis that abrasives will ruin the piston plating and cause it to corrode and bind. Replace the piston if damaged in any way.

4. Clean all parts well, dip the new piston seal in brake fluid and install in the bore. Position the seal at one area at a time and, using fingers, gently work the seal into the groove.

5. Slide the metal retainer part of the new dust boot over the open end of the piston. Pull the retainer rearward until the boot lip seats in the groove at the end of the piston. Push the metal

Rear drum brakes—Comanchee, Cherokee, Wrangler shown—typical

retainer part of the boot forward until flush with the rim at the open end of the piston. Then snap boot folds in place. Finally, install the piston in the caliper bore with a twisting motion being careful not to unseal the piston seal.

6. Seal the metal retainer part of the dust boot in the caliper with a circular driver.

7. Install new mounting bushings in the caliper as required. Install bleeder screw if removed.

8. Install the flexible brake hose with new seals.

Wheel Cylinder Service

The rear brakes are drum type with internal expanding shoes. The rear brakes are of the single anchor type, mounted to the same anchor and actuated by one wheel cylinder. The wheel cylinder has 2 pistons. Brake adjustments are automatic and are made during reverse brake applications.

Wheel cylinders may need reconditioning or replacement whenever the brake shoes are replaced or when required to correct a leak condition. Leaks which coat the boot and the cylinder with fluid or result in a dropped reservoir fluid level or dampen and stain the brake linings are dangerous. Such leaks can cause the brakes to grab or fail and should be immediately corrected. A leakage, not immediately apparent, can be detected by pulling back the cylinder boot. A small amount of fluid seepage dampening the interior of the boot is normal. However, a dripping boot is not. Unless other conditions causing a brake to pull, grab or drag become obvious, the wheel cylinder is suspect and should and should be included in general reconditioning.

Cylinder binding may be caused by rust, deposits, grime or swollen cups due to fluid contamination or by a cup wedged into an excessive piston clearance.

Hydraulic system parts should not be allowed to come into contact with oil or grease, neither should those be handled with greasy hands. Even a trace of any petroleum based product is sufficient to cause damage to the rubber parts.

Disassembly and Assembly

1. Remove the brake bleeder screw.
2. Remove the dust boots, allow any brake fluid to drain out.
3. Remove the pistons, seals and inner spring.
4. Inspect the bore for scoring and corrosion. If bore is scored, replace cylinder. Do not hone the cylinder bores or polish the pistons. Replace the cylinder as an assembly if the bore is damaged. Black stains on the cylinder walls are caused by the piston cups and will not impair operation of the cylinder. Clean the cylinder with alcohol or brake fluid.
5. Lubricate the seals with brake fluid and install. Cup lips should always face inward. Install the spring assembly and seals.
6. Carefully install the pistons and dust boots.
7. Install the bleeder screw.

Anti-Lock Braking Systems

Despite advances in brake design over the years, even the best systems in use can still lockup during certain road conditions, such as wet road surfaces. When the brakes lockup, the driver can lose control of the vehicle, because a locked wheel cannot absorb any cornering or lateral forces and steering is lost. It is impossible to brake to a maximum and at the same time steer the vehicle when the front wheels are locked. If the back wheels are locked the vehicle will become unstable and start to slide.

While many different ways have been tried over the years to solve this problem, mechanical sensors could not provide sufficient information about wheel rotation speed and mechanical control units could not operate the brakes fast enough to prevent brake lockup.

The growth of the electronics industry has allowed small computers (microprocessors) to be reduced in both size and cost. Coupled with fast reacting electronic sensors, anti-lock braking has become more reliable with widespread application.

Jeep's anti-lock brake system is available on 70 Series (Cherokee/Wagoneer Sport Pick-Ups) models with Select-Track 4-wheel drive. It is an electronically operated, power assisted, all wheel brake control system. The system is designed to retard wheel lockup during periods of high wheel slip when braking. Retarding wheel lockup is accomplished by modulating fluid pressures to the wheel brake units.

The 70 Series anti-lock system is a 3 channel design. The front wheel brakes are controlled individually and the rear wheel brakes in tandem.

System pressure is modulated according to wheel speed, degree of wheel slip and rate of deceleration. A sensor at each wheel converts wheel speed into electronic signals. The signals are transmitted to the brake system control unit for processing and determination of deceleration rate and wheel slip.

Basic system components include wheel sensors, fluid level and pressure switches, a pressure modulator, an accumulator, an electric booster pump, a master cylinder/power boost unit and an electronic control unit. Two instrument cluster indicator lights (1 red, 1 yellow) are used to signal system condition and operating status.

The anti-lock electronic control system is separate from other electrical circuits in the vehicle. A specially programmed ECU is used for operational control.

The accumulator tank and the small accumulator on the booster pump both contain high pressure gas charges which assist in maintaining boost pressure. Do not puncture or attempt to disassemble either of these components at any time.

When servicing the anti-lock system, keep system components clean. Do not allow any dirt or foreign material to enter the system. Clean the reservoir cap and exterior thoroughly before removing the cap to add fluid. Dirt or foreign material in the system could result in poor brake system performance and possible component failure.

The manufacturer recommends Mopar brake fluid or equivalent, meeting DOT 3 standards only. Never use reclaimed fluid or fluid from an open container that has been allowed to stand for any length of time.

CAUTION

The normal working pressure of the anti-lock boost system is 1650–2050 psi. System pressure must be pumped down before any pressure lines are loosened or disconnected. Failure to do so could result in personal injury. To reduce system pressure, turn the ignition key OFF. Then apply the brakes 45–50 times (until pedal is firm) to reduce fluid pressure in the accumulator, booster, pump and lines. Wear safety goggles when disconnecting fluid lines.

MAJOR COMPONENTS

Master Cylinder/Power Booster Unit

The master cylinder and power booster pistons are located in a single, cast aluminum cylinder body. A fluid reservoir is attached to the body with rubber seals.

The fluid reservoir is internally separated into 3 sections by bulkheads. A common fluid fill is used for the 3 sections.

The power booster is a demand type component. Power assist occurs only when the brakes are applied. Power assist is from high pressure brake fluid supplied by the electric motor driven booster pump. The pump is connected to the system accumulator. The accumulator is connected to the booster unit in the master cylinder.

Pump and Motor Assembly

The booster pump is powered by an electric motor. The motor and pump are combined in a common housing. The pump piston

Anti-lock master cylinder/power booster unit

Anti-lock booster pump and motor assembly

Pressure modulator channels—typical

Accumulator and low pressure switch

Rear wheel sensor and tone wheel

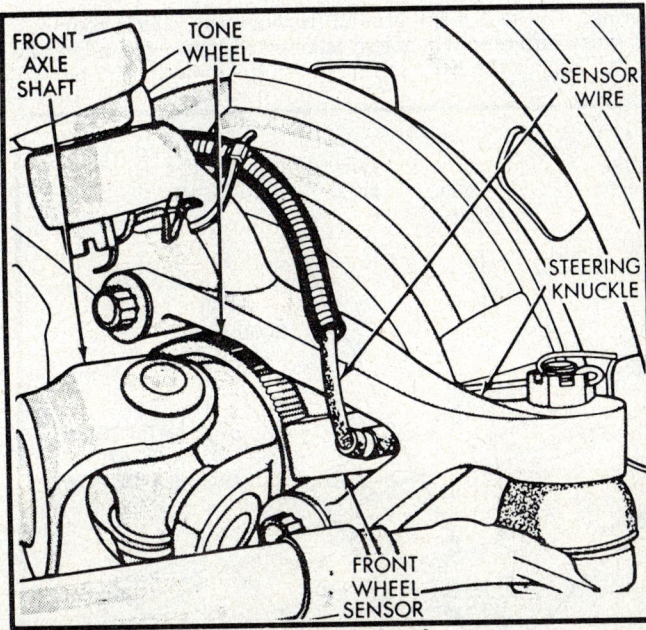

Front wheel sensor and tone wheel

Boost pressure differential and low fluid switch locations

operates off an eccentric drive. An internal relief valve and a pressure switch control pump output. The housing contains a small accumulator which operates in tandem with the main accumulator.

The pump supplies fluid boost pressure for both standard and anti-lock brake operation. Pump operating pressure range is 1650–2050 psi. The pump motor is equipped with a thermal fuse which stops the pump if operating temperatures approach overheat range. The fuse does not reset once it is tripped.

Pressure Modulator

The pressure modulator is a hydro-electric component. It provides 3 channels of pressure control to the front/rear brakes. One channel controls the rear wheel brakes in tandem. The 2 remaining channels control the front wheel brakes individually. Modulator inputs are both hydraulic and electronic.

The modulator contains a total of nine solenoid valves. Three valves are assigned to each control channel. The illustration shows 1 channel section of the modulator.

The 3 solenoid valves in each control channel have separate functions. The isolation solenoid valves isolate the master cylinder line to a caliper or wheel cylinder. The decay solenoid valves provide a controlled decrease (drop) in pressure to the wheel brakes in the anti-lock mode. The build solenoid valves provide controlled pressure build (increase) to the wheel brakes in the anti-lock mode.

Accumulator and Low Pressure Switch

The accumulator stores fluid under pressure for power brake and anti-lock operation. The low pressure switch monitors fluid pressure and is connected to the ECU.

If pressure falls below a minimum value of approximately 1050 psi, the switch triggers the ECU which stops cycling the modulator solenoids. The yellow indicator light illuminates when the solenoids cease operation in the anti-lock mode.

The pressure switch is grounded through the vehicle body during normal operation but reverts to an open circuit, if pressure drop occurs. An open circuit will trigger the instrument cluster indicator lights.

The accumulator is connected to the pump and power booster unit respectively.

Wheel Sensors

A sensor is used at each wheel. The sensors convert wheel speed into an electronic signal which is transmitted to the anti-lock ECU. A toothed-type tone wheel serves as the trigger mechanism for each sensor. The tone wheels are mounted at the outboard ends of the front and rear axle shafts.

Boost Pressure Differential Switch

The boost pressure differential switch is mounted in the pressure modulator. The switch checks the pressure differential between modulated boost pressure and the master cylinder primary system pressure.

The switch is in circuit with the ECU and instrument panel indicator lights. The switch is open when pressure differential is

Anti-lock electronic control unit

normal. The switch will ground (through the vehicle body) if a pressure differential problem is detected. Once grounded, the switch signals the ECU to illuminate the indicator lights.

Anti-lock modulator/indicator light relays and harness location

PUMP MOTOR RELAY AND HARNESS

PUMP AND COOLANT BRACKET

HARNESS CONNECTOR

PUMP/MOTOR ASSEMBLY

Pump motor relay and harness

Fluid Level Switch

A fluid level switch is located in the master cylinder reservoir. The switch activates the red indicator light if the fluid level falls below the required level. The yellow light also comes on if the vehicle speed is above approximately 2.5 mph.

Electronic Control Unit

A separate Electronic Control Unit (ECU) is used to monitor and control the entire anti-lock system. The ECU is attached to a bracket located under the rear seat. The power up voltage source for the ECU is through the ignition switch in the ON or RUN position.

The anti-lock ECU is separate from the other vehicle electronic systems. It contains a self-diagnostic program which triggers the indicator lights when a system fault is detected. Faults are stored in a diagnostic program memory. Faults remain in memory until cleared. However, if the battery is disconnected, stored faults are erased.

The ECU is also equipped with a mercury switch. The switch monitors the degree of vehicle deceleration to determine what type of surface the vehicle is on. The switch provides input to the ECU for improved operation in the 4WD mode on low traction (slippery) road surfaces.

NOTE: Proper mounting angle of the ECU is critical to correct and accurate operation of the mercury switch.

System Relays

There are 3 system relays. The yellow indicator light and modulator power relays are located on the driver side inner fender

BOOSTER PUMP AND MOTOR

MASTER CYLINDER/POWER BOOSTER

BOOST PRESSURE SWITCH (IN MODULATOR)

PRESSURE MODULATOR

PROPORTIONING VALVE/DIFFERENTIAL SWITCH

ECU

SENSOR CONNECTORS/WIRE

ACCUMULATOR AND PRESSURE SWITCH

LEFT FRONT SENSOR

REAR WHEEL SENSORS

RIGHT FRONT SENSOR

Anti-lock component layout and connectors

panel. The relay wires are in the engine compartment wire harness.

The pump/motor relay is part of the pump motor harness and is located at the passenger side of the engine compartment.

The modulator power relay is connected to the pressure modulator solenoids and the ECU. When the system is powered up, the ECU supplies the operating voltage (12 volts) to the solenoids through the relay.

The indicator light relay is connected to the modulator solenoid relay and the indicator light. The relay turns the yellow light on when the modulator power relay is off. The yellow light is turned off when the modulator power relay is energized.

The pump motor relay starts/stops the pump motor when signaled by the pump switch.

Ignition Switch

The anti-lock ECU and indicator lights are in the standby mode with the ignition switch in the **OFF** or **ACCESSORY** position. No operating voltage is supplied.

In the **ON** and **RUN** positions, the switch supplies the ECU, pump motor and indicator lights with a 12 volt power supply.

In the **START** position, only the indicator lights are supplied with operating voltage. The remaining system components are in the standby mode.

System Indicator Lights

Two indicator lights are used with the anti-lock system. One light is red and the other yellow. Both are in the instrument cluster. The lights are in circuit with the self diagnostic program in the ECU and signal both normal operation and system faults.

The yellow light indicates anti-lock system condition. It is in circuit with the modulator solenoids and relay. The light illuminates at start-up and goes out when the self-diagnostic program determines system operation is normal.

If a fault occurs, the yellow light remains on until the fault is either corrected, the battery is disconnected or the ignition switch is cycled (turned **OFF** and then **ON**). Cycling the ignition switch may not turn the light off after some faults.

The yellow light illuminates in tandem with the red warning light to indicate certain types of faults. The pressure modulator solenoids are in circuit with the yellow indicator light. When the yellow light is on (system fault occurred), the solenoids are disabled.

The red light serves as the system warning light (low fluid, parking brake on, system pressure differential, etc.). The light illuminates in tandem with the yellow anti-lock light when certain system faults occur.

There are time delays built into indicator light illumination. These delays are provided as a means of identifying some system faults.

Proportioning Valve

The combination front/rear brake pressure switch and proportioning valve is connected between the master cylinder and modulator. The switch and valve operate normally in the standard braking mode. In the anti-lock mode, the proportioning valve is isolated to enable brake pressure modulation during anti-lock system operation. The pressure differential switch is only activated by a difference in pressure between the front and rear (primary and secondary) brake circuits.

Parking Brake Switch

The switch is connected to the ECU low fluid circuit. When the switch is activated, the red indicator light illuminates. If vehicle speed is above approximately 2.5 mph, the yellow light will also illuminate.

SYSTEM OPERATION

Component Connections

The booster pump and accumulator provide the fluid pressure needed for power assist. The accumulator is connected to the pump by a high pressure feed line. A second high pressure line connects the accumulator to the booster section of the master cylinder. A low pressure supply line connects the reservoir to the booster pump.

Fluid from the master cylinder is channeled to the calipers and wheel cylinders through the pressure modulator. The 3 solenoid valves (isolation – decay – build) in each modulator control channel are contained within the modulator body.

The wheel sensors are connected directly to the ECU. The sensor triggering devices (tone wheels), are mounted on the axle shafts.

System Power Up

The anti-lock system is in standby mode with the ignition switch in **OFF** or **ACCESSORY** position. When the switch is moved to the **START** position, voltage through the switch activates the indicator lights only. The ECU and other system components are still the standby mode.

The indicator lights illuminate as part of the self test feature and remain on until the switch is in the **RUN** position.

In the **ON** and **RUN** position, 12 volts are supplied through the ignition switch to power up the ECU and system components.

When the vehicle is motionless (no wheel speed inputs) and the ignition switch is in the **ON** or **RUN** position, the modulator solenoids are activated and briefly exercised. This serves two purposes: It checks solenoid function as part of the self diagnostic feature and ensures proper solenoid operation after periods of inactivity.

Boost Pressure and Fluid Supply

The system main fluid supply is contained in the master cylinder reservoir and the accumulator. Additional fluid is also contained in the booster pump accumulator. The pump and main accumulator provide the reserve fluid pressure needed for power brake assist.

Fluid stored in the accumulator is at normal working pressure of 1650–2050 psi. The accumulator contains enough pressurized fluid for 25–30 power assisted brake applications if a pump fault should occur.

Pump motor operation is controlled by the pump relay and by a pressure switch within the pump/motor assembly. The pump operates only when the ignition switch is in the **ON** or **RUN** position.

The pump does not run continuously. It cycles on/off with the pump pressure switch. The pump is capable of running with or without connection to the ECU. Pressurized fluid from the pump is transmitted to the accumulator and power booster unit.

The booster pump motor is equipped with thermal protection. If the motor approaches an overheat condition, a thermal fuse inside the pump will blow and shut off the motor. The fuse is not a reset-type and is not serviceable.

Sensor Inputs and Pressure Modulation

The wheel sensors and tone wheels supply wheel speed inputs to the ECU whenever the vehicle is in motion.

The ECU determines the degree of deceleration and wheel slip and provides optimum brake pressures for each control channel based on this data. The 70 Series (Cherokee/Wagoneer) anti-lock system provides 3 channel control. The front wheels are controlled individually. The rear wheels are controlled in tandem.

The ECU activates the pressure modulator solenoids which either build (increase), decay (decrease) or hold (maintain) fluid pressure as dictated by the ECU. The isolation solenoids isolate normal fluid pressure from the master cylinder to the rear wheels or to the left or right front wheel as needed. Wheel brake isolation occurs prior to build/decay solenoid operation.

Solenoid operation is not entirely constant in the anti-lock mode. Operation occurs in brief, rapid cycles front-to-rear and side-to-side. Rapid changes in input data will produce equally rapid changes in pressure modulation. The isolation, decay and build functions are capable of function changes and cycle times measured in milliseconds.

SERVICE DIAGNOSIS

Wheel/Tire Size and Input Signals

Anti-lock system operation is dependent on signals from the wheel sensors. The vehicle wheels and tires must all be the same size and type in order to generate accurate signals. Variations in wheel/tire size will produce inaccurate input signals resulting in incorrect pressure modulation.

Operational Sound Levels

The booster pump and/or relay may produce a clicking sound as they cycle on and off. In addition, the booster pump and motor and the pressure modulator solenoids may generate a buzzing-type sound when operating. The sound is due to normal pump motor and system operation and is not indicative of a system fault. Under most conditions, the sound should not be audible.

Vehicle Response in Anti-lock Mode

During anti-lock braking, the pressure modulator solenoids cycle rapidly in response to ECU inputs.

As the solenoids in each channel isolate, build and decay pressure as needed, the driver may experience a slight pulsing sensation within the vehicle. A firmer brake pedal and some brake pedal pulsation may also be noted during anti-lock mode braking.

The pulsing sensation occurs as the individual brake units apply/release during anti-lock mode braking. Pulsing is a result of normal front-to-rear and side-to-side pressure modulation.

Indicator Light Operation

The red warning light and the yellow anti-lock indicator light both go on at start-up and go off when the engine is running. The 1 or 2 second illumination is part of a system self-test feature and indicates normal operation. System faults are indicated when 1 or both of the lights illuminate after initial start-up system check.

Driver Induced System Faults

Some driving or operational situations can induce faults in an anti-lock system that is actually operating correctly.

Induced faults are not true faults; a component malfunction as not actually occurred. Instead, they are a result of driver actions recognized by the diagnostic program as improper operation.

Anti-lock three channel schematic

JEEP ANTI-LOCK BRAKE SYSTEM DIAGNOSTIC CHART
SERVICE DIAGNOSIS

CONDITION	CAUSE	INDICATOR LIGHT DISPLAY
LOW FLUID	SYSTEM LEAK. ACCUMULATOR CHARGE LOW OR LOST.	RED LIGHT ON. YELLOW LIGHT ON WITHIN ½ SECOND WHEN VEHICLE SPEED EXCEEDS 2.5 MPH.
PARKING BRAKES APPLIED	PARKING BRAKES NOT RELEASED BEFORE DRIVING VEHICLE.	RED LIGHT ON. YELLOW LIGHT ON IF VEHICLE SPEED EXCEEDS 2.5 MPH.
PRESSURE DROP AT ACCUMULATOR	ACCUMULATOR GAS CHARGE LOST. SYSTEM LEAK. PUMP/MOTOR MALFUNCTION. PROLONGED STOP ON ICY SURFACE WITH TRANSMISSION IN GEAR.	YELLOW LIGHT ON. RED LIGHT WILL ALSO COME ON WITHIN 20 SECONDS.
DIFFERENTIAL PRESSURE SWITCH (IN PROPORTIONING VALVE) ACTUATED	SYSTEM LEAK. MASTER CYLINDER MALFUNCTION (SECONDARY PISTON). AIR IN SYSTEM.	RED LIGHT ON. YELLOW LIGHT COMES ON AT VEHICLE SPEED OF 3 MPH.
PRESSURE DROP AT BOOST PRESSURE SWITCH AND PRESSURE DIFFERENTIAL SWITCH	MASTER CYLINDER MALFUNCTION (PRIMARY PISTON). SYSTEM LEAK. AIR IN SYSTEM.	RED LIGHT ON. YELLOW LIGHT COMES ON AT VEHICLE SPEED OF 3 MPH.
WHEEL SENSOR FAULT (FRONT ONLY)	SENSOR-TO-TONE WHEEL SPACING INCORRECT (SPACE TOO LARGE). DAMAGED SENSOR WIRE, SENSOR, OR TONE WHEEL. SENSOR AND TONE WHEEL MISALIGNED. SENSOR DISCONNECTED.	YELLOW LIGHT ON (AFTER 15 MPH).
WHEEL SENSOR FAULT (FRONT OR REAR, ONE OR TWO MISSING SIGNALS)	DAMAGED SENSOR, WIRE, OR CONNECTOR. SENSOR DISCONNECTED. EXCESSIVE WHEEL SPIN. MISALIGNED OR DAMAGED TONE WHEEL. OPEN SENSOR OR WIRE.	YELLOW LIGHT ON AT 15 MPH IF FAULT OCCURRED <u>BEFORE</u> VEHICLE DRIVE-OFF. OR, ORANGE LIGHT ON AT 8 MPH IF FAULT OCCURRED <u>AFTER</u> VEHICLE DRIVE-OFF.
EXCESSIVE DECAY SOLENOID OPERATION	MODULATOR/SOLENOID FAULT. WHEEL SENSOR FAULT. EXTREMELY LOW AMBIENT TEMPERATURES. VEHICLE ON ICE-COVERED SURFACE. TIRES HYDROPLANING ON WATER-COVERED ROAD SURFACE.	YELLOW LIGHT ON WITHIN 1–2 SECONDS.
PRESSURE MODULATOR SOLENOID FAULT	SOLENOID SHORTED OR OPEN. DECAY AND BUILD SOLENOID ON AT SAME TIME. OPEN/SHORT IN MODULATOR HARNESS.	YELLOW LIGHT ON.
PUMP/MOTOR RUN-ON	EXCESSIVE RUN TIME. RELAY SHORTED, MOTOR SWITCH SHORTED.	RED LIGHT ON IF PUMP RUNS MORE THAN 4 MINUTES WITH NO BRAKE.
PUMP/MOTOR INOPERATIVE	PUMP RELAY FAULT. NO VOLTAGE TO MOTOR. DAMAGED PUMP OR MOTOR. PUMP GAS CHARGE LOST.	YELLOW LIGHT ON. RED LIGHT ON AFTER 20 SECONDS.
LOW VOLTAGE	SYSTEM VOLTAGE BELOW 9V. SHORT, OPEN IN FEED WIRES OR RELAY. FUSE BAD. POOR GROUND. LOOSE, DISCONNECTED WIRE IN SYSTEM. BATTERY LOW OR DISCHARGED.	YELLOW LIGHT ON.
NO BRAKE SIGNAL	SYSTEM LEAK. MASTER CYLINDER MALFUNCTION. PUMP/MOTOR MALFUNCTION. ACCUMULATOR OR MODULATOR FAULT.	RED LIGHT ON DURING BRAKING.
RELAY FAULT	RELAY SHORTED OR OPEN.	YELLOW LIGHT ON.
ECU SELF DIAGNOSTIC FEATURE INOPERATIVE (SOLENOIDS NOT TEST-EXERCISED AT START-UP)	IGNITION SWITCH IN OFF POSITION. PARKING BRAKES ON (NOT RELEASED AT DRIVE-OFF). SYSTEM COMPONENT HAS MALFUNCTIONED. LOW FLUID LEVEL/LEAK IN SYSTEM.	YELLOW LIGHT ON.

Improper parking brake use can induce faults in the self-diagnostic program. If a driver attempts to move the vehicle with the parking brakes applied, a system fault will register. Or, if the parking brake is applied while the vehicle is in motion, a system fault will also register. One or both indicator lights will illuminate in either situation. The red light illuminates for parking brake faults. The yellow light illuminates if a fault is sensed.

Faults can be induced in the system through excessive wheel spin. Wheel spin due to low traction surfaces or high speed acceleration can induce a fault in a system that is operating normally. In addition, if system pressure is not restored after a repair, a fault will register when the vehicle is driven.

Pumping or riding the brake pedal may also induce a fault causing the indicator light to go on.

Steering Response

A modest amount of steering input is required during extremely high deceleration braking or when braking on differing traction surfaces. An example of differing traction surfaces would be when the left side wheels are on ice and the right side wheels are on dry pavement.

Loss of Sensor Input

Sensor malfunctions will most likely be due to loose connections, damaged sensor wires or incorrect sensor-to-tone wheel air gap adjustment. Additional causes of sensor faults would be sensor and tone wheel misalignment or a damaged tone wheel.

System Diagnosis Procedures

Anti-lock system diagnosis involves three basic procedures. The first requires observation of indicator light display sequence. The second is a visual examination of system components for low fluid levels, leak points or visible damage. The third involves using the manufacturer's diagnostic tester to check operation and locate a malfunctioning circuit.

The 2 indicator lights will illuminate separately, simultaneously or with varying delays depending on the fault. The lights signal low fluid levels, pressure drops and other hydro-electrical faults. The service diagnosis charts for indicator light display can be used when a fault is detected.

COMPONENT SERVICEABILITY

The master cylinder/power booster unit, pressure modulator, accumulator, pump/motor and proportioning valve are not repairable components. If diagnosis indicates a malfunction has occurred, these components are to be replaced as a complete assembly.

The fluid level switch in the master cylinder and the boost pressure switch in the modulator are also not serviceable. The switches cannot be removed from their respective components.

The electrical harnesses, pump bracket, pump high pressure and supply hose, system relays and wheel sensors can be serviced individually.

The tone wheels are permanently attached to the axle shafts and are not replaceable. If a tone wheel becomes damaged, it will be necessary to replace the tone wheel and axle shaft as an assembly.

The wheel brake components such as calipers, brake shoes, wheel cylinders, rotors and drums are all serviced the same as standard brake system components.

Wheel Sensors

The wheel sensors have a polyethylene spacer strip attached to the sensor contact face. When installing a sensor, be very sure this spacer strip actually touches the tone wheel. The strips are made in the exact thickness needed for correct sensor-to-tone wheel spacing (air gap). If the spacing (air gap) is too great, the sensors will not transmit accurate speed signals to the ECU.

If the spacer strip is missing from an original or not provided on a replacement sensor, the correct sensor-to-tone wheel air gap will have to be established with a brass feeler gauge. A brass feeler gauge must be used to avoid disrupting sensor polarity

System components and location

Front sensor wire routing

Sensor contacts (spacer strip removed)

Sensor spacer strip

If the sensor strip is missing from a reuseable sensor, set the sensor-to-tone wheel air gap as follows:
Set front sensor air gap to 0.013–0.019 in.
Set rear sensor air gap to 0.030–0.036 in.

Removal and Installation

FRONT WHEEL SENSOR

1. Raise and safely support vehicle and turn wheel outward for easier access to sensor.

2. Note the sensor wire routing for installation reference. Cut the tie straps holding wire to steering knuckle and brake line.

3. If sensor is covered with heavy accumulations of dirt or mud, clean the sensor and surrounding area before proceeding. This is necessary to avoid possible damage when removing the sensor.

4. Remove the sensor attaching screw and remove the sensor from the steering knuckle.

5. Unseat the grommet holding the sensor wire in the wheel house panel.

Adjusting sensor-to-wheel air gap

6. In the engine compartment, disconnect the sensor wire connector at the anti-lock harness plug. Remove sensor and wire.

7. Before installing a new or reinstalling an original front wheel sensor, note the condition of the spacer strip. If the strip is securely attached and in good condition, a spacing (air gap) adjustment will not be needed. However, if the strip is loose or damaged, the correct air gap will have to be established with a brass feeler gauge.

To install:

8. Route the wire through the wheelhouse grommet hole and connect the sensor to the harness plug. Seat the grommet.

9. Position the sensor on the steering knuckle and install the bolt finger-tight.

10. If the sensor strip was in good condition and securely attached, lightly press the sensor against the tone wheel and tighten the bolt to 11 ft. lbs.

11. If the sensor spacer strip is missing, loose or damaged and the sensor contacts are exposed, perform the following steps:

   a. Remove the spacer strip if completely loose or torn. Wipe sensor contacts clean with a shop towel.

   b. Set sensor-to-tone wheel air gap to 0.013 – 0.019 in. with a brass feeler gauge.

   c. Tighten the sensor bolt to 11 ft. lbs. and recheck spacing.

12. Secure the sensor wire to the brake line and steering knuckle with new tie straps.

REAR WHEEL SENSOR

1. Raise and fold the rear seat forward for access to the rear sensor connectors. They are located near the ECU. Separate both sensor connections.

Rear sensor grommets

Rear sensor wire routing and attachment

Rear sensor installation

2. Push the sensor grommets and sensor wires through the floorpan.

3. Raise and safely support the vehicle and remove the wheel and brake drum.

4. Cut and remove the tie straps securing the sensor wires to the axle and rear brake hose.

5. Unseat the sensor backing plate grommet, remove the sensor attach bolt and remove the sensor by pulling the wire through the grommet hole in the backing plate.

To install:

6. Before installing a new or reinstalling an original rear wheel sensor, note the condition of the spacer strip. If the strip is securely attached and in good condition, a spacing (air gap) adjustment will not be needed. However, if the strip is loose or damaged, the correct air gap will have to be established with a brass feeler gauge.

7. If the sensor spacer strip is missing, loose or damaged and the sensor contacts are exposed, perform the following steps:

   a. Remove the spacer strip if completely loose or torn. Wipe sensor contacts clean with a shop towel.

   b. Set sensor-to-tone wheel air gap to 0.030 – 0.036 in. with a brass feeler gauge.

   c. Tighten the sensor bolt to 11 ft. lbs. and recheck spacing.

8. Route the sensor wires to the rear seat area, feed the wires through the access holes and seat the grommets in the floorpan.

9. Secure the sensor wire with wire ties to the rear brake hose and axle. Make sure the wire is clear or rotating components.

10. Install the brake drum and wheel then lower vehicle.

11. Connect the sensors to the harness connects, reposition carpet and fold down rear seat.

BOOSTER PUMP AND MOTOR

————— **CAUTION** —————

The normal working pressure of the anti-lock boost system is 1650–2050 psi. System pressure must be pumped down before any pressure lines are loosened or disconnected. Failure to do so could result in personal injury. To reduce system pressure, turn the ignition key OFF. Then apply the brakes 45–50 times (until pedal is firm) to reduce fluid pressure in the accumulator, booster, pump and lines. Wear safety goggles when disconnecting fluid lines.

1. Turn the ignition switch to the **OFF** position and apply the brakes (pump pedal) 45–50 times (until pedal is firm on initial apply) to reduce system fluid pressure.

NOTE: When the reserve pressure is depleted, the reservoir fluid level will rise above the MAX fill mark but will not overflow unless the reservoir was overfilled to begin with.

2. Disconnect the battery negative cable.

3. Remove the coolant pressure bottle retaining strap and move the reservoir aside. It is not necessary to disconnect the bottle hoses, just move the bottle aside for working clearance.

4. Remove the bolts holding the two-piece mounting bracket to the dash and inner fender panels. Rotate the bracket and pump/motor assembly to one side for access to the wires and hoses. Disconnect the pump motor harness from the engine harness.

5. Slowly loosen the pump pressure line at the pump and allow any residual fluid pressure to bleed off, then disconnect the line from the pump.

6. Put a drain container under the pump return line, loosen the return line hose clamp and remove the line from the pump. Discard any drained fluid.

7. Remove the pump/motor and bracket as an assembly. Remove the relay from the bracket and separate the components.

To install:

8. Position the pump/motor assembly on the bracket and install the assembly attaching screws along with the relay.

9. Connect the pressure and return lines to the pump as well as the motor harness.

10. Position the mounting bracket on the dash panel and install the attaching bolts and screws. Check the line routing, making sure the lines are not kinked or touching the engine.

11. Clean the master cylinder exterior and cap. Fill the reservoir to the top of the V-shaped MAX indicator mark with DOT 3 rated brake fluid.

NOTE: Do not overfill the reservoir. Overfilling will cause overflow and could damage the reservoir. Add fluid to the V-shaped MAX indicator only.

12. Connect the battery and turn the ignition to **ON** to start the pump running. While the pump is running, listen for an rpm drop which indicates the pump is pressurizing. If the pump rpm does not drop after 20 seconds, immediately turn the ignition **OFF** and check the pump hydraulic connections.

NOTE: Do not allow the pump to run if it does not pressurize. If the pump rpm does not drop after 20 seconds run time, turn the ignition OFF immediately to avoid pump damage.

13. Add fluid to master cylinder reservoir if necessary.

MASTER CYLINDER

The master cylinder, modulator and accumulator are serviced as an assembly only. Do not attempt to disassemble or repair these components.

───── **CAUTION** ─────

The normal working pressure of the anti-lock boost system is 1650–2050 psi. System pressure must be pumped down before any pressure lines are loosened or disconnected. Failure to do so could result in personal injury. To reduce system pressure, turn the ignition key OFF. Then apply the brakes 45–50 times (until pedal is firm) to reduce fluid pressure in the accumulator, booster, pump and lines. Wear safety goggles when disconnecting fluid lines.

1. Pump system pressure down by turning the ignition **OFF** and applying the brake pedal 45–50 times until the pedal becomes firm.

2. Disconnect the battery. Remove the windshield washer fluid reservoir attaching screrws, disconnect the hoses and wires and remove the reservoir.

3. Remove the air cleaner assembly, disconnect the ECU harness wire connectors at the pressure modulator and disconnect the wires at the proportioning valve differential switch.

Pump motor harness and relay

Pump pressure and supply line connections

4. Disconnect the high pressure line at the accumulator block. Cap the line to keep out dirt.

5. Disconnect the supply line at the reservoir. Cap the line to keep out dirt. Discard any fluid that drains from the line.

6. Disconnect the low pressure switch wires and the wires at the modulator boost pressure and fluid level switches.

7. Disconnect the front brakelines at the outboard side of the pressure modulator.

8. In the passenger compartment, remove the instrument panel lower trim cover for access to the brake pedal. Disconnect the brakelight switch wires, remove the master cylinder pushrod bolt and disconnect the pushrod from the pedal. Discard the pushrod bolt nuts as they are not reuseable.

9. Remove the master cylinder mounting bracket stud nuts.

10. In the engine compartment, pull the brake hydraulic components and mounting bracket forward until the bracket studs are clear of the dash. Lift the assembly up and out of the engine compartment.

To install:

11. Place pad on the mounting bracket and position assembled bracket and brake components on dash panel. Be sure bracket studs are seated in dash panel holes.

12. Position master cylinder/modulator/accumulator assembly on dash panel. Tighten stud nuts to 27 ft. lbs.

13. Connect the harness wires to the modulator, low pressure switch, differential switch and the low fluid and boost pressure switches.

14. In the passenger compartment, install the nuts of the mounting studs and torque to 31 ft. lbs.

15. Align the brake pedal, brakelight switch, master cylinder push rod and install the pushrod bolt.

NOTE: The pushrod bolt must be installed correctly to avoid interference with the dash bracket. The bolt must be installed with the bolt head at the left side of the pedal.

16. Install new nuts on the pushrod bolt. Tighten the inner lock nut to 25 ft. lbs. and the outer jam nut to only 75 inch lbs. Connect the brake light switch wires and install the lower trim panel.

17. In the engine compartment, connect the brake lines to the proportioning valve and connect the pressure and return lines to the accumulator.

18. Install the air cleaner assembly, connect the hoses and wires to the washer reservoir and install the reservoir to the fender panel.

19. Clean the master cylinder exterior and cap. Fill the reservoir to the top of the V-shaped MAX indicator mark with DOT 3 rated brake fluid.

20. Connect the battery and turn the ignition to ON to start the pump running. While the pump is running, listen for an rpm drop which indicates the pump is pressurizing. If the pump rpm does not drop after 20 seconds, immediately turn the ignition OFF and check the pump hydraulic connections.

NOTE: Do not allow the pump to run if it does not pressurize. If the pump does not drop after 20 seconds run time, turn the ignition OFF immediately to avoid pump damage.

21. Add fluid to master cylinder reservoir if necessary.
22. Bleed the brake system.

ELECTRONIC CONTROL UNIT (ECU)

1. Make sure the ignition is OFF, then fold the rear seat cushion forward for access to the ECU.

ECU harness and fluid connections

Fluid line connections

Removing/installing master cylinder, modulator and accumulator assembly

2. Remove the screws attaching the ECU mounting bracket to the floorpan, remove the screws attaching the ECU to the mounting bracket, unplug the ECU and remove.

3. At installation, connect the harness of the replacement ECU.

4. Install the replacement ECU on the bracket and install the bracket to the floorpan.

5. Fold down rear seat.

SYSTEM BLEEDING

1. Fill reservoir to V-shaped maximum fill mark.
2. Bleed the brakes in the following sequence: right rear, left rear, right front, left front.
3. Attach a bleed hose to the caliper or wheel cylinder being

Anti-lock ECU wiring diagram

bled, immerse the end of the bleed hose in a glass container partially filled with brake fluid.

4. Turn the ignition **ON** to cycle the pump.

5. Have a helper apply brake pedal to pressurize the system. Open the bleed screw ½ turn. Close the bleed screw when the fluid entering the glass container is free of bubbles.

6. Check the reservoir fluid level and add fluid to the **MAX** fill mark.

7. Repeat bleeding operations at remaining wheels.

NOTE: Do not allow the master cylinder reservoir to run dry while bleeding the brakes. Running dry will allow air to re-enter the system making a second bleeding operation necessary. More importantly, if air re-enters the system, it could damage the pump seriously enough to require replacement.

ECU mounting bracket

Jeep anti-lock brake system

CHRYSLER IMPORTS

NOTE: When cleaning brake system components, use only brake fluid or denatured isopropyl alcohol. Never use a mineral-based solvent such as gasoline or paint thinner; these fluids will leave a residue that may swell and deteriorate rubber parts within the system. All alcohol must be removed from the system when the work is done because alcohol mixed with brake fluid lowers its boiling point.

Do not hone any aluminum bores. There is a hard anodized coating on the aluminum which will be removed if honed. This will allow the aluminum to wear quickly and will damage the component.

Master Cylinder Service

Disassembly and Assembly

1. Remove the brake fluid reservoir retainer screw, if equipped, and remove the reservoir and seals or remove the reservoir unions and seals.

2. Push the primary piston in and remove the stopper bolt and gasket.

3. Hold the pistons in and remove the snapring.

NOTE: Do not disassemble either piston assembly as the individual parts are not serviceable.

1. Brake fluid lever sensor connector
2. Brake tube
3. Brake line connector block
4. Master cylinder
5. Reservoir cap
6. Diaphragm
7. Float
8. Reservoir retainer screw
9. Reservoir
10. Reservoir seals
11. Piston stopper bolt
12. Gasket
13. Snapring
14. Primary piston assembly
15. Secondary assembly

Chrysler Import master cylinder

1. Lock pin bolt
2. Guide pin bolt
3. Caliper adaptor
4. Guide pin sleeve
5. Lock pin sleeve
6. Lock pin boot
7. Guide pin boot
8. Boot retaining ring
9. Piston boot
10. Piston
11. Piston seal

Chrysler Import caliper

4. Let the primary piston spring out and remove the primary piston assembly.

5. Remove the secondary piston assembly. This may be accomplished by carefully blowing low pressure compressed air through the secondary side outlet port, if it does not come out easily.

6. Remove the brake line connector block and washers.

To assemble:

7. Coat the master cylinder bore and secondary and primary piston seals liberally with brake fluid.

8. Install both assemblies to the master cylinder.

9. Push the pistons in and install a new snapring.

10. Hold the pistons in and install the stopper bolt with a new gasket.

1. Wheel cylinder boot
2. Piston assembly
3. Piston
4. Piston cup
5. Wheel cylinder body

Chrysler Import wheel cylinder

11. Install the brake fluid reservoir or unions with new seals. Install the reservoir retaining screw, if equipped.

12. Install the connector block with new washers.

Brake Booster Service

The brake boosters installed on these vehicles are not serviceable. If the unit is defective, replace the entire assembly.

Caliper Service

Disassembly and Assembly

1. Remove the bleeder screw.
2. Drain the brake fluid from the caliper.
3. Remove the dust boot ring and the dust boot.
4. Position a shop rag opposite the top of the piston. Apply low pressure compressed air to the fluid inlet and carefully blow the piston out of the bore.

——— CAUTION ———

Do not put fingers where the piston will land when it is blown out of the caliper. The force of the piston can crush fingers and cause personal injury.

5. Remove the piston seal from inside the bore.

To assemble:

6. Blow out all fluid passages with low pressure compressed air.

7. Slight corrosion or rust can be removed with commutator paper or crocus cloth. Replace pistons that are pitted, scored, peeling or otherwise damaged.

8. Lubricate the caliper bore with brake fluid. Lubricate the seal and install it in the groove.

9. Lubricate the piston and install it to the bore until it bottoms. If the piston will not go in by hand, it is probably cocked. Remove it and reinstall.

10. Apply lubricant to the dust boot mounting groove and install the boot. Install the retaining ring.

11. Apply rust penetrant to the bleeder screw threads and install to the caliper. Tighten it until it is just snug against its seat.

Wheel Cylinder Service

Disassembly and Assembly

1. Remove the bleeder screw, if equipped.
2. Remove both rubber boots.
3. Remove the piston assemblies, each consisting of the piston and cup.
4. Remove the piston cups from the pistons, being careful not to scratch the piston.
5. Remove the return spring.
6. Hone the cylinder bore if it is not damaged, to provide a smooth sealing surface. Wash and dry the bore after honing.

To assemble:

7. Lubricate the cylinder bore with brake fluid.

8. Lubricate the new piston cups and install them to the pistons, with their lips facing upward. Install the assemblies to the cylinder.

9. Apply lubricant to the boot mounting groove and install the boot.

10. Apply rust penetrant to the bleeder screw threads and install to the wheel cylinder. Tighten it until it is just snug against its seat.

DAIHATSU

NOTE: When cleaning brake system components, use only brake fluid or denatured isopropyl alcohol. Never use a mineral-based solvent such as gasoline or paint thinner; these fluids will leave a residue that may swell and deteriorate rubber parts within the system. All alcohol must be removed from the system when the work is done because alcohol mixed with brake fluid lowers its boiling point.

Do not hone any aluminum bores. There is a hard anodized coating on the aluminum which will be removed if honed. This will allow the aluminum to wear quickly and will damage the component.

Master Cylinder Service

Disassembly and Assembly

1. Remove the stopper bolt that is between the the brake line openings.

2. Push the primary piston in and remove the snapring.

3. Remove the primary piston assembly.

4. Remove the secondary piston assembly.

5. Remove the reservoir clamp and take off the reservoir.

To assemble:

6. Coat the master cylinder bore and secondary and primary piston seals liberally with brake fluid. Install both assemblies to the master cylinder.

7. Push the pistons in and install a new snapring.

8. Install the stopper bolt with a new gasket.

9. Install the brake fluid reservoir. Install the reservoir retaining clamp.

Brake Booster Service

Disassembly and Assembly

1. Remove the lockring and gasket from the attaching side of the vacuum brake booster.

2. With a suitable prying tool, pry the upper half of the booster from its base.

3. Remove the oil seals and snaprings from the booster mounting studs and remove the bracket and diaphragm spring assembly.

4. Remove the boots from the mounting studs and the reaction ring from the center.

5. Lift off the booster piston assembly.

6. Remove the snaprings from the base of the mounting studs and remove the booster body from the studs. Remove the O-rings that were under the studs.

7. Remove the center bushing and piston seal.

8. Remove the expander ring and diaphragm.

9. Loosen the locknut and remove the pushrod clevis.

10. Remove the spring seat, the sponge seal, the snapring and poppet valve from the center of the booster base.

11. Remove the pushrod and the output rod.

To assemble:

12. Inspect all parts for wear or damage, especially the springs.

13. Apply silicone grease to the valve stopper and install the pushrod, valve stopper and poppet spring.

14. Install the valve spring and its snapring, the poppet valve and its snapring.

15. Install the diaphragm and secure with the expander ring.

16. Apply silicone grease to the piston seal and install along with the bushing.

17. Assemble the O-rings and mounting studs.

18. Install the booster piston, the reaction ring in the center and the boots on the mounting studs.

19. Install the diaphragm spring and bracket over the mounting studs. Secure with proper clips and seals.

20. Install the booster cover, gasket and snaprings.

Caliper Service

Disassembly and Assembly

1. Remove the bleeder screw.

2. Drain the brake fluid from the caliper.

3. Remove the dust boot ring and the dust boot.

4. Position a shop rag opposite the top of the piston. Apply low pressure compressed air to the fluid inlet and carefully blow the piston out of the bore.

— CAUTION —

Do not put fingers where the piston will land when it is blown out of the caliper. The force of the piston can crush fingers and cause personal injury.

5. Remove the piston seal from inside the bore.

To assemble:

6. Blow out all fluid passages with low pressure compressed air.

7. Slight corrosion or rust can be removed with commutator paper or crocus cloth. Replace pistons that are pitted, scored, peeling or otherwise damaged.

8. Lubricate the caliper bore with brake fluid. Lubricate the seal and install it in the groove.

9. Lubricate the piston and install it to the bore until it bottoms. If the piston will not go in by hand, it is probably cocked. Remove it and reinstall.

10. Apply lubricant to the dust boot mounting groove and install the boot. Install the retaining ring.

11. Apply rust penetrant to the bleeder screw threads and install to the caliper. Tighten it until it is just snug against its seat.

Wheel Cylinder Service

Disassembly and Assembly

1. Remove the bleeder screw.

2. Remove both rubber boots.

3. Remove the pistons from the cylinder.

4. Remove the piston cups.

5. Remove the return spring.

6. Hone the cylinder bore if it is not damaged, to provide a smooth sealing surface. Wash and dry the bore after honing.

To assemble:

7. Lubricate the cylinder bore with brake fluid. Install the return spring.

8. Lubricate the new piston cups and install them to the cylinder. Lubricate and install the pistons.

9. Apply lubricant to the boot mounting groove and install the boot.

10. Apply rust penetrant to the bleeder screw threads and install to the wheel cylinder. Tighten it until it is just snug against its seat.

1. Reservoir cap
2. Cap spacer
3. Reservoir diaphragm
4. Reservoir float
5. Reservoir assembly
6. Reservoir clamp
7. Master cylinder body
8. Stop bolt seal
9. Stop bolt
10. Primary and secondary piston assemblies
11. Booster gasket
12. Shim
13. Seal
14. Circlip
15. Tie rod stud seal
16. Snapring
17. Booster piston rod
18. Piston boot
19. Reaction disc
20. Booster piston
21. Booster diaphragm band
22. Piston stop ring
23. Rod adjusting nut
24. Rod adjusting locknut
25. Lockring
26. Retainer
27. Tie rod stud
28. O-ring
29. Locknut
30. Clevis
31. Cotter pin
32. Clevis pin

Brake booster and master cylinder—Daihatsu

GEO

NOTE: When cleaning brake system components, use only brake fluid or denatured isopropyl alcohol. Never use a mineral-based solvent such as gasoline or paint thinner; these fluids will leave a residue that may swell and deteriorate rubber parts within the system. All alcohol must be removed from the system when the work is done because alcohol mixed with brake fluid lowers its boiling point.

Do not hone any aluminum bores. There is a hard anodized coating on the aluminum which will be removed if honed. This will allow the aluminum to wear quickly and will damage the component.

Master Cylinder Service

Disassembly and Assembly

1. Remove the brake fluid reservoir retainer which will be either a screw or roll pin and remove the reservoir. Remove the reservoir to master cylinder seals.
2. Push the primary piston in and remove the snapring.
3. Let the primary piston spring slowly out and remove piston stopper, cups and the primary piston assembly.
4. Remove the secondary piston stopper bolt.
5. Remove the secondary piston assembly. This may be accomplished by carefully blowing low pressure compressed air through the secondary side outlet port if it does not come out easily. Disassemble the secondary piston.

To assemble:

6. Assemble the secondary piston assembly. Coat the master cylinder bore and secondary and primary piston seals liberally with brake fluid. Install both assemblies to the master cylinder.
7. Install the cups and stoppers. Install the snapring.
8. Push the pistons in and install the stopper bolt.
9. Install the fluid reservoir and seals.

1. Master cylinder reservoir
2. Reservoir connector grommet
3. Retainer pin
4. Master cylinder seal boot
5. Master cylinder body
6. Secondary stopper bolt
7. Secondary piston return spring
8. Secondary return spring seat
9. Secondary piston cup
10. Secondary piston
11. Secondary piston pressure cup
12. Primary piston cup
13. Primary piston
14. Cylinder cup and plate
15. Piston stopper
16. C-clip

A—PRIMARY PISTON
B—SECONDARY PISTON

Master cylinder assembly and components—Geo Tracker

Brake Booster Service

Disassembly and Assembly

1. Remove the pushrod clevis.
2. Remove the locknut.

3. Mount the booster on the holding tool set 09950–88210. Do not tighten the 2 outer nuts to more than 30 inch lbs. or the booster may become deformed.

4. Turn the special tool bolt clockwise until the projection and depression in the bodies match. Matchmark the bodies at that location.

1. Attaching nut
2. Fluid reservoir
3. Brake vacuum hose
4. Brake booster assembly
5. Operating rod locknut
6. Safety lock pin
7. Operating rod clevis
8. Bracket gasket
9. Booster retaining nuts
10. Dash panel
11. Clevis pin
12. Master cylinder assembly
13. Booster front shell
14. Diaphragm spring
15. Rod retainer
16. Piston rod assembly
17. Reaction disc
18. Booster piston
19. Operating rod assembly
20. Valve stopper key
21. Key cushion
22. Diaphragm
23. Diaphragm retainer
24. Diaphragm stopper ring
25. Booster rear body
26. Rear body oil seal
27. Filter separator
28. Filter element
29. Body boot

Brake booster components—Geo Tracker

1. Locking hub
2. Disc brake rotor
3. Disc brake caliper
4. Brake line union bolt
5. Seal washers
6. Brake caliper carrier
7. Outer brake pad
8. Inner brake pad
9. Anti-rattle spring
10. Piston dust boot
11. Piston
12. Piston seal
13. Caliper pin boot
14. Caliper pin
15. Caliper body
16. Bleeder screw
17. Bleeder screw cover
18. Caliper mounting
    bolt

Brake caliper components—Geo Tracker

5. Remove the booster from the tool and separate the bodies.

—————— **CAUTION** ——————

The rear body is spring loaded. Loosen it slowly and carefully or personal injury may result.

6. Remove the piston rod, boot, air cleaner elements and air cleaner separator from the rear body.
7. Remove the valve stopper key cushion.
8. Push the air valve down and remove the stopper key. Remove the air valve assembly from the booster piston.
9. Remove the diaphragm circular ring from the booster piston. Remove the diaphragm from the pressure plate.
10. Remove the reaction disc from the booster piston.
11. Remove the seal from the rear body.
To assemble:
12. Lubricate and install a new seal to the rear body.

13. Install the retainer to the diaphragm. Install the diaphragm to the booster piston and install the new diaphragm circular ring.
14. Lubricate and install the booster air valve to the booster piston. Compress the valve and install the stopper key. Install the cushion to the notch in the stopper.
15. Install the booster piston to the rear body.
16. Install the new air cleaner separator and elements to the air valve rod.
17. Install the boot to the rear body.
18. Lubricate the face and install the reaction disc to the booster piston.
19. Place the front body on the special tool and place the return spring, rod retainer and piston rod on it.
20. Place the assembled rear body on the return spring and compress. Turn the special bolt counterclockwise until the projection and depression line up.
21. Install the piston rod into the booster piston.
22. Install the locknut and clevis.

Caliper Service

Disassembly and Assembly

1. Remove the bleeder screw.
2. Drain the brake fluid from the caliper.
3. Remove the cylinder boot.
4. Position a shop rag opposite the top of the piston. Apply low pressure compressed air to the fluid inlet and carefully blow the piston out of the bore.

------ CAUTION ------

Do not put fingers where the piston will land when it is blown out of the caliper. The force of the piston can crush fingers and cause personal injury.

5. Remove the piston seal from inside the bore.

To assemble:

6. Blow out all fluid passages with low pressure compressed air.
7. Slight corrosion or rust can be removed with commutator paper or crocus cloth. Replace pistons that are pitted, scored, peeling or otherwise damaged.
8. Lubricate the caliper bore with brake fluid. Lubricate the seal and install it in the groove.
9. Lubricate the piston and install it to the bore until it bottoms. If the piston will not go in by hand, it is probably cocked. Remove it and reinstall.
10. Apply lubricant to the cylinder boot mounting groove and install.

1. Rear wheel cylinder assembly
2. Outer boot
3. Piston
4. Cup seal
5. Wheel cylinder body
6. Wheel cylinder spring
7. Brake shoe hold-down pin
8. Wheel bearing retainer nut
9. Brake backing plate
10. Parking brake strut rod
11. Brake hold-down spring clip
12. Upper return spring
13. Return springs
14. Brake shoes

Brake wheel cylinder components—Geo Tracker

11. Apply rust penetrant to the bleeder screw threads and install to the caliper. Tighten it until it is just snug against its seat.

Wheel Cylinder Service

Disassembly and Assembly

1. Remove the bleeder screw, if equipped.
2. Remove both rubber boots.
3. Remove the piston assemblies, each consisting of the piston and cup.
4. Remove the piston cups from the pistons, being careful not to scratch the piston.
5. Remove the return spring.
6. Hone the cylinder bore if it is not damaged, to provide a smooth sealing surface. Wash and dry the bore after honing.

To assemble:

7. Lubricate the cylinder bore with brake fluid.
8. Lubricate the new piston cups and install them to the pistons, with their lips facing upward. Install the assemblies to the cylinder.
9. Apply lubricant to the boot mounting groove and install the boot.
10. Apply rust penetrant to the bleeder screw threads and install to the wheel cylinder. Tighten until it is just snug against its seat.

Anti-Lock Braking Systems

GENERAL DESCRIPTION

The purpose of the Rear Wheel Anti-lock (RWAL) brake system is to minimize rear wheel lockup during heavy braking on most road surfaces and conditions. The RWAL brake system performs this function by monitoring the speed of the rear axle and controlling the brake fluid pressure to both rear wheels during a braking maneuver. This allows the driver to retain directional stability and better steering capability.

NOTE: Do not use lubricated compressed air on brake parts. Lubricated compressed air can damage rubber brake system components.

When working on brake systems, the following cautions should be observed:

1. Replace all components provided in repair kits used to service this system.
2. Lubricate rubber parts with clean brake fluid to make assembly easier.
3. If any hydraulic component is removed or disconnected, it may be necessary to bleed all or part of the brake system. Any torque values specified are for dry, unlubricated fasteners.
4. Perform service operations on a clean work area, free from all mineral oil materials.
5. Use of tire sizes other than those recommended may result in a reduction in the optimal performance of the RWAL brake system.

Normal and Anti-lock Braking

Under normal conditions, the RWAL brake system functions much like a conventional brake system.

If rear wheel locking tendency is noted during a brake application, the RWAL Brake System will enter the anti-lock mode. During anti-lock braking, hydraulic pressure in the rear wheel circuit is modulated by a pressure limiting valve to prevent the rear wheels from locking. The pressure limiting valve is located under the master cylinder and actually consists of 2 separate valves. One is a dump valve which releases pressure into an accumulator. The other is an isolation valve which maintains rear wheel brake pressure.

During anti-lock braking, a series of rapid pulsations will be felt in the pedal caused by the rapid changes in position of the pressure limiting valve. This pedal pulsation is present during anti-lock braking and will stop when normal braking is resumed or when the vehicle comes to a stop. During anti-lock braking on dry pavement, the rear tires may make "chirping" noises as they approach lockup. These noises and pedal pulsations should be considered normal during anti-lock operation.

Vehicles equipped with RWAL brake systems may be stopped by applying normal force to the brake pedal. Pedal operation during normal braking should be no different than previous vacuum-boost systems. When the anti-lock mode is in effect, the brake pedal may rise slightly while the brakes are being applied. This condition should also be considered normal. Maintaining a constant force on the pedal will provide the shortest stopping distance.

Warning System Operation

The brake system continuously monitors all of its components and uses several methods of determining if a fault exists. Should a fault be detected, the RWAL brake system notifies the driver of a malfunction

When the vehicle is started, a functional check of the RWAL brake system is performed. Self-check functional tests are also performed during normal driving conditions once the vehicle is moving.

When any fault is detected, anti-lock functions are stopped and the BRAKE light is lit to notify the driver of a problem in the braking system.

BRAKE Warning Light

The BRAKE warning light in the instrument panel cluster will illuminate to warn the driver of conditions in the brake system which may result in reduced braking capability. It will also illuminate when the parking brake is applied or not fully released. Conditions which turn on the BRAKE warning light include the following:

1. Parking brake not fully released. If the parking brake is applied or not fully released, the switch on the parking brake lever assembly will ground the BRAKE warning light circuit and cause the light to turn on.
2. Low brake fluid level. If the brake fluid level drops in the reservoir, the brake fluid level switch will ground the BRAKE warning light and cause the light to turn on.
3. Instrument panel bulb check. When the ignition switch is turned to **BULB TEST**, the BRAKE warning light circuit is grounded and the light turns on. The light should go out when the ignition switch is released to **ON**.

Electronic Brake Control Module (EBCM)

The Electronic Brake Control Module (EBCM) is a small control computer, mounted behind the left side of the instrument panel near the fuse block. The EBCM monitors the speed of the rear axle and the electrical status of the pressure limiting valve. The primary functions of the EBCM are to detect wheel locking tendencies, control the brake system while in anti-lock mode and monitor the system for normal electrical operation. The EBCM also emits diagnostic codes while in the diagnostic mode.

The EBCM continuously checks the speed of the rear axle to determine if the rear wheels are beginning to lock. If a wheel locking tendency is detected, the EBCM commands the pressure limiting valve to modulate the rear hydraulic circuit to prevent wheel lockup and provide optimum braking performance. The EBCM continues to control pressure until a locking tendency is no longer detected.

The RWAL Brake System is electronically monitored by the EBCM for proper operation. If an error is detected anywhere in

- - - - - ELECTRICAL CIRCUIT
————— HYDRAULIC CIRCUIT

6. 4WD switch
7. Transmission
8. EBCM
9. BRAKE warning light
10. Parking brake switch
11. Reset switch
12. Pressure limiting valve
13. Proportioning/differential valve
14. Differential switch

A. To front brakes
B. To 12V (+) ignition
1. Master cylinder
2. Stoplight switch
3. Rear brake circuit
4. Rear differential
5. Rear wheel speed sensor

Rear Wheel Anti-lock brake system layout—Geo Tracker

the system, the EBCM will light the BRAKE warning light in the instrument cluster and diagnosis of the system is required.

Rear Wheel Speed Sensor

The rear wheel speed sensor is mounted to the rear differential carrier. The sensor transmits rear wheel speed information to the EBCM by means of a low-voltage AC voltage signal. This voltage signal is generated through magnetic induction and is caused by passing a toothed exciter ring past the stationary magnetic coil of the rear wheel speed sensor. The AC voltage signal is then transmitted to the EBCM through 2 wires from the rear wheel speed sensor. Voltage signals to the EBCM increase in both frequency and amplitude as the rear wheel speed increases.

1. Master cylinder
2. Pressure limiting valve
3. Inlet
4. Outlet
5. Bleeder plug
6. Rear wheel speed sensor
7. Air gap
8. Exciter ring

Master cylinder, pressure limiting valve and rear wheel speed sensor—Geo Tracker

Pressure Limiting Valve

The pressure limiting valve is mounted under the brake master cylinder and is connected in the brake hydraulic circuit between the proportioning/differential valve and the rear brake circuit.

The main components of the pressure limiting valve are an isolation valve, a dump valve, an accumulator and a reset switch. During normal (nonanti-lock) braking operation, the isolation valve is open to allow hydraulic pressure to be applied to the rear wheels. Under heavy (anti-lock) braking applications, the isolation valve functions in unison with the dump valve and accumulator to maintain, decrease or increase the hydraulic pressure applied to the rear wheels in response to signals from the EBCM

During anti-lock brake application, when wheel and vehicle speed conditions dictate that hydraulic pressure to the rear wheels remains constant, the EBCM applies voltage to the isolation valve. The isolation valve is normally open and only closes when the EBCM applies voltage. During conditions under which constant hydraulic pressure is desired, the EBCM only applies voltage to the isolation valve, which closes both the isolation and dump valves. With both valves closed, brake fluid volume (and therefore pressure) in the rear brake circuit remain constant.

If wheel and vehicle speed conditions dictate that a decrease in pressure is required, the EBCM applies a voltage pulse to the dump valve. The dump valve, upon receiving voltage, opens and allows brake fluid to be released into the accumulator. When brake fluid is released, the brake fluid volume (and therefore pressure) in the rear brake circuit is reduced.

If wheel and vehicle speed conditions dictate that an increase in pressure is required, the EBCM stops applying voltage to the isolation valve and the dump valve. Under these conditions, the isolation valve is open, allowing brake fluid to flow from the master cylinder to the rear wheels and the dump valve is closed, not allowing any fluid to be released into the accumulator. This action causes more fluid to enter the rear brake circuit and increase pressure proportionally.

REAR WHEEL SPEED CONTROL

The ECBM, by monitoring the frequency of the AC voltage sig-nal from the rear wheel speed sensor, determines the speed and deceleration rate of the rear wheels during all braking conditions. For any given wheel speed, an optimum deceleration rate has been programmed into the EBCM which will stop the vehicle quickly and safely.

When the difference between the optimum rear wheel speed (programmed) and the true rear wheel speed (from the rear wheel speed sensor) reaches the first programmed set value, the EBCM applies voltage to the isolation valve in the pressure limiting valve. This action closes the isolation valve and maintains a constant hydraulic pressure in the rear brake circuit. Under these conditions, this pressure will remain constant regardless of pressure applied to the brake pedal.

If rear wheel speed should continue to decelerate faster than desired and the difference between optimum rear wheel speed and true rear wheel speed increases to the second programmed set value, the EBCM determines that the rear wheels are going to lock and applies a voltage pulse to the dump valve in the pressure limiting valve. Upon receiving the voltage pulse, the dump valve opens, brake fluid is released into the accumulator and pressure in the rear wheel circuit drops. If one pulse is not enough to recover rear wheel speed to the optimum value, the pulse signal will be applied repeatedly.

As the pressure is reduced, the rear wheels regain speed and the difference between optimum rear wheel speed and true rear wheel speed reaches the third set value, the EBCM determines that rear wheel lockup has been prevented and stops pulsing voltage to the dump valve. The EBCM may also temporarily stop applying voltage to the isolation valve. Under these conditions, the dump valve remains closed, the isolation valve temporarily opens and pressure in the rear brake circuit increases. With increased pressure in the rear brake circuit, rear wheel speed will again begin to decrease rapidly. If one pulse of opening the isolation valve is not enough to slow the rear wheels sufficiently, the pulse will be applied repeatedly until a satisfactory rear wheel speed has been achieved. If rear wheel speed decreases too rapidly and a possible lockup condition is again detected by the EBCM, the entire cycle is repeated.

IZUSU

NOTE: When cleaning brake system components, use only brake fluid or denatured isopropyl alcohol. Never use a mineral-based solvent such as gasoline or paint thinner; these fluids will leave a residue that may swell and deteriorate rubber parts within the system. All alcohol must be removed from the system when the work is done because alcohol mixed with brake fluid lowers its boiling point.

Do not hone any aluminum bores. There is a hard anodized coating on the aluminum which will be removed if honed. This will allow the aluminum to wear quickly and will damage the component.

Master Cylinder Service

Disassembly and Assembly

1. Remove the brake fluid reservoir retainer screw.
2. Remove the reservoir and seals.
3. Remove the dust seal from the end of the master cylinder.
4. Push the primary piston in and remove the stopper bolt and gasket.
5. Hold the pistons in and remove the snapring.

NOTE: Do not disassemble either piston assembly as the individual parts are not serviceable.

6. Let the primary piston spring out and remove the primary piston assembly and end washer, if equipped.
7. Remove the secondary piston assembly. This may be accomplished by carefully blowing low pressure compressed air through the secondary side outlet port, if it does not come out easily.

To assemble:

8. Coat the master cylinder bore and secondary and primary piston seals liberally with brake fluid. Install both assemblies to the master cylinder.
9. Push the pistons in and install a new snapring.
10. Hold the pistons in and install the stopper bolt with a new gasket.
11. Install the brake fluid reservoir with new seals. Install the reservoir retaining screw.

Brake Booster Service

SINGLE VACUUM SERVO

Disassembly and Assembly

1. Remove the clevis yoke and locknut from the actuator rod.

1. Dust seal
2. Screw
3. Brake fluid reservoir
4. Grommet
5. Snapring
6. Stopper bolt
7. Gasket
8. Primary piston assembly
9. Secondary assembly
10. Secondary piston spring
11. Reservoir cover
12. Seal
13. Float magnet
14. Cylinder body

Isuzu master cylinder

1. Clevis yoke
2. Locknut
3. Rubber boot
4. Rear shell
5. Retainer
6. Bearing
7. Valve body seal
8. Retainer
9. Filter and silencer
10. Retainer
11. Rear diaphragm
12. Rear diaphragm plate
13. C-ring
14. Stopper key
15. Actuating rod assembly
16. Center plate
17. Retainer
18. Seal
19. Bearing
20. Retainer
21. Front diaphragm
22. Front diaphragm plate
23. Valve body and O-ring
24. Pushrod
25. Reaction disc
26. Retainer
27. Spring
28. Front shell
29. Retainer
30. Plate and seal

Isuzu tandem vacuum servo—Pick-Up and Amigo with 2.6L engine.

1. Clevis yoke
2. Locknut
3. Servo retainer
4. Seal
5. Rubber boot
6. Rear shell assembly
7. Front shell assembly
8. Servo spring
9. Diaphragm plate assembly
10. Servo retainer
11. Servo bearing
12. Valve body seal
13. Vacuum servo diaphragm
14. Servo retainer
15. Vacuum filter
16. Vacuum silencer
17. Actuating rod stopper key
18. Actuating rod
19. Reaction disc
20. Valve body
21. Diaphragm plate
22. Pushrod assembly

Isuzu single vacuum servo booster

2. Pry out the servo retainer and seal from the front of the shell.
3. Remove the rubber boot.

— **CAUTION** —

The rear shell is spring loaded. Loosen it slowly and carefully or personal injury may result.

4. Matchmark the front and rear shells. Using wrench J-9504–01 and holder J–34250, separate the 2 shells slowly. Remove the servo spring.
5. Remove the entire diaphragm plate assembly.
6. Pry out the servo retainer, bearing and valve body seal from the rear shell.
7. Using a knife, cut the vacuum servo diaphragm and remove. Make sure not to damage the valve body when cutting.
8. Remove the servo retainer from the valve body.
9. Remove the vacuum filter and silencers from the valve body.
10. Push in the actuating rod and remove the rod stopper key. Remove the actuating rod assembly.
11. Remove the reaction disc, valve body, diaphragm plate and pushrod assembly.

Isuzu tandem vacuum servo—Trooper/Trooper II

5. Rear shell and diaphragm assembly
6. Spring
7. Front shell
8. Rubber boot
9. Retainer
10. Bearing
11. Body seal
12. Nut
13. Front diaphragm plate
14. Front diaphragm
15. Center plate
16. Retainer
17. Center plate seal
18. Bearing
19. Pushrod
20. Key
21. Key retainer
22. Reaction disc hub
23. Reaction disc
24. O-ring
25. Center body
26. Rear diaphragm plate
27. Rear diaphragm
28. Valve body and rod
29. Retainer
30. Actuating rod
31. Retainer
32. Filter
33. Silencer
34. Filter

1. Clevis yoke
2. Locknut
3. Retainer
4. Seal

To assemble:

12. Install the new actuating rod assembly to the valve body. Push the rod in and install the rod stopper key.

13. Install the new vacuum silencers and filter.

14. Install the new retainer to the rear shell.

15. Install the diaphragm plate and carefully attach the new vacuum servo diaphragm to the valve body.

16. Apply silicone grease to the new reaction disc and install to the valve body. Install the pushrod and spring.

17. Apply silicone grease to the rear shell seal and install.

18. Mount the holding tool J–34350 in a vise and mount the front shell on the tool. Assemble the entire diaphragm plate assembly to the rear shell. Install the bearing and new retainer.

19. To assemble the unit, connect a vacuum source to the vacuum intake pipe on the front shell. Using the matchmarks as guides, apply vacuum and assemble the unit using tool J–9504–01. Make sure the bent area of the of the diaphragm does not drop against the front and rear shell engaging areas.

20. Rotate the rear shell clockwise until the notch on the rear shell is fully against the stopper. Tighten until the matchmarks are perfectly aligned.

21. Install the new rubber boot, locknut and clevis yoke.

22. Apply silicone grease to the last seal and install to the front shell. Install the remaining retainer over the seal.

TANDEM VACUUM SERVO

Disassembly and Assembly

EXCEPT 1988–90 TROOPER/TROOPER II

1. Remove the clevis yoke and locknut from the actuator rod.

2. Remove the rubber boot.

3. Install holding tool J–34350 to the mounting studs and clamp in a vise. Matchmark the front and rear shells. Install wrench J–9504–01 to the rear shell studs.

CAUTION

The rear shell is spring loaded. Loosen it slowly and carefully or personal injury may result.

---

4. Connect a vacuum source to the vacuum intake pipe on the front shell. Rotate the lever counterclockwise slightly (about $\frac{1}{20}$ turn). The front shell caulking tab must be aligned with the V-groove on the outside of the rear shell. Exhaust the vacuum and pry the rear shell from the front shell.

5. Remove the retainer, bearing and seal from the rear shell.

6. Remove the retainer and remove the filter and silencers from the actuating rod.

7. Remove the retainer and remove the rear diaphragm from the valve body. Remove the rear diaphragm plate.

8. Remove the C-ring from the valve body. Push the actuating rod down, remove the stopper key and remove the actuating rod from the valve body.

9. Remove the center plate and remove the retainer, seal and bearing from the plate.

10. Remove the retainer and remove the front diaphragm from the valve body.

11. Raise the catch that holds the valve body and front diaphragm plate together. Turn the plate and remove it from the valve body.

12. Remove the pushrod, reaction disc, retainer and spring from the front shell.

13. Remove the retainer and seal from the front shell.

To assemble:

14. Apply silicone grease to the seal and install to the front shell and install the retainer over the seal. Lubricate the diaphragm sliding surfaces on the inside of the shell with the same grease.

15. Lubricate the pushrod stem and install to the hub reaction disc.

16. Lubricate and install a new O-ring to the valve body. Set the diaphragm plate on the valve body and rotate it to install. Install the new front diaphragm and retainer.

17. Lubricate and install the bearing, seal and retainer to the center plate.

18. Use installer J-38595 to install the center plate assembly to the valve body.

19. Align the arrow mark on the rear diaphragm plate with the mark on the valve body and install the plate with a tilting motion. Install a new retainer to the front diaphragm.

20. Lubricate and install the actuating rod to the valve body and install the C-ring. Push the actuating rod and install the stopper key.

21. Install the first filter, the silencer then the second filter to the valve body and install the new retainer.

22. Lubricate and install the seal, bearing and retainer to the rear shell.

23. Mount the holding tool J-34350 in a vise and mount the front shell on the tool. Assemble the entire center plate assembly to the rear shell.

24. To assemble the unit, connect a vacuum source to the vacuum intake pipe on the front shell. Using the matchmarks as guides, apply vacuum and assemble the unit using tool J-9504-01. Make sure the bent area of the of the diaphragm does not drop against the front and rear shell engaging areas.

25. Rotate the rear shell clockwise until the notch on the rear shell is fully against the stopper. Tighten until the matchmarks are perfectly aligned.

26. Install the new rubber boot, locknut and clevis yoke.

27. Adjust the pushrod length to 0.7 in. (18.2mm) from the base of the front shell.

1988-90 TROOPER/TROOPER II

1. Remove the clevis yoke and locknut from the actuator rod.

2. Pry out the servo retainer and seal from the front of the shell.

──────── **CAUTION** ────────

The rear shell is spring loaded. Loosen it slowly and carefully or personal injury may result.

───────────────────

3. Matchmark the front and rear shells. Using wrench J-9504-01 and holder J-34250 (holes elongated to fit), separate the 2 shells slowly. Remove the servo spring.

4. Remove the rubber boot.

5. Remove the retainer, bearing and seal from the rear shell.

6. To disassemble the diaphragm assembly, remove the large nut with a 1½ in. wrench.

7. Remove the front diaphragm plate, front diaphragm and center plate.

8. Remove the retainer, center plate seal and bearing from the center plate.

9. Remove the pushrod and carefully pry the key out of the valve body. Remove the key retainer.

10. Rotate the reaction disc hub 90 degrees and release it from the center body. Remove the reaction disc and O-ring.

11. Remove the center body and diaphragm from the rear diaphragm plate.

12. Remove the valve body assembly. Remove the retainer and remove the actuating rod.

13. Remove the retainer and remove the filters and silencer from the rod.

To assemble:

14. Install the valve body to the rear diaphragm plate. Install the retainer with the cutouts to the valve body lugs and install the actuating rod.

15. Install the new rear diaphragm.

16. Install the center body and new lubricated O-ring. Set the retainer against the outer pawl of the reaction and rotate the reaction disc 90 degrees to install.

17. Install the key retainer, push in the actuating rod and install the stopper key.

18. Install the new filter, silencer, second filter and retainer.

19. Install the reaction disc (with the stepped side inward) and pushrod.

20. Lubricate and install the bearing, center plate seal and retainer to the center plate.

21. Install the front diaphragm to its plate and install 1½ in. nut.

22. Lubricate and install the seal, bearing and retainer to the rear shell. Install the new rubber boot.

23. Mount the holding tool J-34350 in a vise and mount the front shell on the tool. Assemble the entire diaphragm assembly, spring and the rear shell.

24. To assemble the unit, connect a vacuum source to the vacuum intake pipe on the front shell. Using the matchmarks as guides, apply vacuum and assemble the unit using tool J-9504-01. Make sure the bent area of the of the diaphragm does not drop against the front and rear shell engaging areas.

25. Rotate the rear shell clockwise until the notch on the rear shell is fully against the stopper. Tighten until the matchmarks are perfectly aligned.

26. Install locknut and clevis yoke.

27. Apply silicone grease to the last seal and install to the front shell. Install the remaining retainer over the seal.

Caliper Service

Disassembly and Assembly

FRONT CALIPER

1. Remove the bleeder screw.
2. Drain the brake fluid from the caliper.
3. Remove the dust boot ring and the dust boot.
4. Position a shop rag opposite the top of the piston. Apply low pressure compressed air to the fluid inlet and carefully blow the piston out of the bore.

──────── **CAUTION** ────────

Do not put fingers where the piston will land when it is blown out of the caliper. The force of the piston can crush fingers and cause personal injury.

───────────────────

5. Remove the piston seal from inside the bore.

To assemble:

6. Blow out all fluid passages with low pressure compressed air.

7. Slight corrosion or rust can be removed with commutator paper or crocus cloth. Replace pistons that are pitted, scored, peeling or otherwise damaged.

1. Sleeve
2. Sleeve dust boot
3. Guide pin dust boot
4. Bleeder and cap
5. Dust seal ring
6. Dust seal
7. Piston
8. Piston seal
9. Caliper body

Isuzu front caliper

1. Sleeve
2. Sleeve dust boot
3. Guide pin dust boot
4. Bleeder and cap
5. Dust seal ring
6. Dust seal
7. Piston
8. Piston seal
9. O-ring
10. Caliper body
11. Parking brake lever
12. Parking brake lever dust boot

Isuzu rear caliper

8. Lubricate the caliper bore with brake fluid. Lubricate the seal and install it in the groove.

9. Lubricate the piston and install it to the bore until it bottoms. If the piston will not go in by hand, it is probably cocked. Remove it and reinstall.

10. Apply lubricant to the dust boot mounting groove and install the boot. Install the retaining ring.

11. Apply rust penetrant to the bleeder screw threads and install to the caliper. Tighten it until it is just snug against its seat.

REAR CALIPER

1. Remove the sleeve and its dust boot. Remove the mounting pin dust boot.

2. Remove the bleeder screw.

3. Drain the brake fluid from the caliper. Remove the dust boot ring and the dust boot.

4. To remove the piston, unscrew it using tool J–37617. Remove the piston seal.

5. Remove the snapring at the bottom of the caliper bore. Pull out the pad adjusting spindle along with the retainer, spring, spring plate and stopper. Remove the O-ring from the spindle.

6. Remove the parking brake link from the bottom of the caliper bore.

7. Remove the parking brake lever, spring and dust boot.

8. Remove the return spring and dust boot.

To assemble:

9. Apply brake system compatible grease to the parking brake link and install.

10. Lubricate and install the new O-ring to the pad adjusting spindle. Attach the stopper, spring plate, spring and retainer to the spindle. Turn the embossed side of the stopper to the outer side and align the cutaways of the stopper and retainer.

11. Insert the spindle assembly into the caliper bore fitting the stopper to the groove at the bottom of the bore. Install the snapring and position it so the open area between ends aligns with the bleeder.

12. Lubricate the piston seal and install to the groove in the caliper. Install the piston and using tool J–37617, turn the piston clockwise until it bottoms. Align the piston cutouts with the inspection window in the caliper body. If this is not done, the brake pads will wear unevenly.

13. Apply lubricant to the dust boot mounting groove and install the boot. Install the retaining ring.

14. Apply rust penetrant to the bleeder screw threads and install to the caliper. Tighten it until it is just snug against its seat.

15. Install the new parking brake lever dust boot, spring and lever. Torque the retaining bolt to 35 ft. lbs. (47 Nm).

Wheel Cylinder Service

Disassembly and Assembly

1. Remove the bleeder screw.

2. Remove both rubber boots.

3. Remove the pistons from the cylinder.

4. Remove the piston cups.

5. Remove the return spring.

6. Hone the cylinder bore if it is not damaged, to provide a smooth sealing surface. Wash and dry the bore after honing.

To assemble:

7. Lubricate the cylinder bore with brake fluid. Install the return spring.

8. Lubricate the new piston cups and install them to the cylinder. Lubricate and install the pistons.

9. Apply lubricant to the boot mounting groove and install the boot.

10. Apply rust penetrant to the bleeder screw threads and install to the wheel cylinder. Tighten it until it is just snug against its seat.

MAZDA

NOTE: When cleaning brake system components, use only brake fluid or denatured isopropyl alcohol. Never use a mineral-based solvent such as gasoline or paint thinner; these fluids will leave a residue that may swell and deteriorate rubber parts within the system. All alcohol must be removed from the system when the work is done because alcohol mixed with brake fluid lowers its boiling point.

Do not hone any aluminum bores. There is a hard anodized coating on the aluminum which will be removed if honed. This will allow the aluminum to wear quickly and will damage the component.

Master Cylinder Service

Disassembly and Assembly

1. Remove the brake fluid reservoir retainer screw.
2. Remove the reservoir and seals.
3. Remove the dust seal from the end of the master cylinder.
4. Push the primary piston in and remove the stopper bolt and gasket.
5. Hold the pistons in and remove the snapring.
6. Let the primary piston spring out and remove the primary piston assembly and end washer, if equipped.
7. Remove the secondary piston assembly. This may be accomplished by carefully blowing low pressure compressed air through the secondary side outlet port, if it does not come out easily.

To assemble:

8. Assemble the secondary piston assembly, if it was disassembled. Coat the master cylinder bore and secondary and primary piston seals liberally with brake fluid. Install both assemblies to the master cylinder.
9. Push the pistons in and install a new snapring.
10. Hold the pistons in and install the stopper bolt with a new gasket.
11. Install the brake fluid reservoir with new seals. Install the reservoir retaining screw.

Brake Booster Service

The brake booster on the MPV is not serviceable. If the unit is defective, replace the entire assembly.

SINGLE DIAPHRAGM

Disassembly and Assembly

2WD PICK-UP

1. Remove the clevis yoke and locknut from the actuator rod.
2. Pry out the servo retainer and seal from the front of the shell.
3. Remove the rubber boot.

— CAUTION —

The rear shell is spring loaded. Loosen it slowly and carefully or personal injury may result.

4. Matchmark the front and rear shells. Using the special tools, separate the 2 shells slowly. Remove the servo spring.
5. Remove the entire diaphragm and plate assembly.
6. Pry out the retainer, bearing and seal from the rear shell.
7. Using a knife, cut the vacuum diaphragm and remove. Make sure not to damage the power piston assembly when cutting.
8. Remove the retainer from the power piston.
9. Remove the vacuum filter and silencers from the power piston.
10. Push in the valve rod and remove the retainer key. Remove the valve rod assembly.

1. Fluid level sensor	5. Stopper screw and O-ring
2. Screw	6. Snapring
3. Reservoir tank	7. Primary piston assembly
4. Seal	8. Secondary assembly

Mazda master cylinder

1. Rubber boot	10. Power piston assembly
2. Rear shell assembly	11. Retainer key
3. Retainer	12. Valve rod and plunger assembly
4. Bearing	13. Reaction disc
5. Dust seal	14. Spring
6. Retainer	15. Pushrod
7. Air filter	16. Front shell assembly
8. Air silencer	17. Retainer
9. Diaphragm and plate	18. Seal

Mazda single diaphragm booster

1. Clevis
2. Nut
3. Rear shell assembly
4. Front shell assembly
5. Boot
6. Rear shell
7. Retainer
8. Bearing
9. Seal
10. Locknut
11. Front diaphragm
12. Front diaphragm plate
13. Center plate
14. Retainer
15. Seal
16. Bearing
17. Stopper and key
18. Retainer
19. Retainer
20. Air filter
21. Air silencer
22. Valve rod and plunger assembly
23. Valve body
24. O-ring
25. Reaction disc hub
26. O-ring
27. Reaction disc
28. Rear diaphragm
29. Rear diaphragm plate
30. Spring
31. Pushrod
32. Front shell
33. Retainer
34. Seal

Mazda double diaphragm booster

11. Remove the reaction disc, power piston, diaphragm plate and pushrod assembly.

To assemble:

12. Install the new valve rod assembly to the power piston. Push the rod in and install the retainer key.

13. Install the new vacuum silencers and filter.

14. Install the new retainer to the rear shell.

15. Install the diaphragm plate and carefully attach the new vacuum diaphragm to the power piston.

16. Apply silicone grease to the new reaction disc and install to the power piston. Install the pushrod and spring.

17. Apply silicone grease to the rear shell seal and install.

18. Mount the front shell in a vise. Assemble the entire diaphragm plate assembly to the rear shell. Install the bearing and new retainer.

19. To assemble the unit, connect a vacuum source to the vacuum intake pipe on the front shell. Using the matchmarks as guides, apply vacuum and assemble the unit using the special tool. Make sure the bent area of the of the diaphragm does not drop against the front and rear shell engaging areas.

20. Rotate the rear shell clockwise until the notch on the rear shell is fully against the stopper. Tighten until the matchmarks are perfectly aligned.

21. Install the new rubber boot, locknut and clevis yoke.

22. Apply silicone grease to the last seal and install to the front shell. Install the remaining retainer over the seal.

DOUBLE DIAPHRAGM

Disassembly and Assembly

4WD PICK-UP

1. Remove the clevis yoke and locknut from the actuator rod.

2. Pry out the servo retainer and seal from the front of the shell.

—————— **CAUTION** ——————

The rear shell is spring loaded. Loosen it slowly and carefully or personal injury may result.

————————————————————

3. Matchmark the front and rear shells. Using the special tools, separate the shells. Remove the rubber boot.

4. Clamp holding tool 49–U043–002 in a vise and mount the rear shell assembly to the tool. Uncrimp the reaction disc hub. Remove the locknut using wrench 49–U043–001.

5. Remove the retainer, bearing and seal from the rear shell.

6. Remove the front diaphragm plate, front diaphragm and center plate.

7. Remove the retainer, center plate seal and bearing from the center plate.

8. Remove the pushrod and carefully pry the key out of the valve body.

9. Remove the key retainer.

10. Rotate the reaction disc hub 90 degrees and release it from the center body. Remove the reaction disc and O-ring.

11. Remove the center body and diaphragm from the rear diaphragm plate.

12. Remove the valve body assembly. Remove the retainer and remove the actuating rod.

13. Remove the retainer and remove the filters and silencer from the rod.

To assemble:

14. Install the valve body to the rear diaphragm plate. Install the retainer with the cutouts to the valve body lugs and install the actuating rod.

15. Install the new rear diaphragm.

16. Install the center body and new lubricated O-ring. Set the retainer against the outer pawl of the reaction and rotate the reaction disc 90 degrees to install.

17. Install the key retainer, push in the actuating rod and install the stopper key.

18. Install the new filter, silencer, second filter and retainer.

19. Install the reaction disc (with the stepped side inward) and pushrod.

20. Lubricate and install the bearing, center plate seal and retainer to the center plate.

21. Install the front diaphragm to its plate and install locknut using the special wrench. Crimp the reaction disc hub in the 2 notched grooves of the locknut.

22. Lubricate and install the seal, bearing and retainer to the rear shell. Install the new rubber boot.

23. Align the notches of the rear shell and center plate. Make sure the bent area of the of the diaphragm does not drop against the front and rear shell engaging areas.

24. Push down and rotate the rear shell clockwise until the notch on the rear shell is fully against the stopper. Tighten until the matchmarks are perfectly aligned.

25. Install locknut and clevis yoke.

26. Apply silicone grease to the last seal and install to the front shell. Install the remaining retainer over the seal.

Caliper Service

Disassembly and Assembly

1. Remove the bleeder screw.
2. Drain the brake fluid from the caliper.
3. Remove the dust boot.
4. Position a shop rag opposite the top of the piston. Apply low pressure compressed air to the fluid inlet and carefully blow the piston out of the bore.

CAUTION

Do not put fingers where the piston will land when it is blown out of the caliper. The force of the piston can crush fingers and cause personal injury.

---

5. Remove the piston seal from inside the bore.

To assemble:

6. Blow out all fluid passages with low pressure compressed air.

7. Slight corrosion or rust can be removed with commutator paper or crocus cloth. Replace pistons that are pitted, scored, peeling or otherwise damaged.

8. Lubricate the caliper bore with brake fluid. Lubricate the seal and install it in the groove.

9. Lubricate the piston and install it to the bore until it bottoms. If the piston will not go in by hand, it is probably cocked. Remove it and reinstall.

10. Apply lubricant to the dust boot mounting groove and install the boot.

1. Piston
2. Dust seal
3. Piston seal
4. Bleeder and cap
5. Pin boot
6. Pin
7. Bushing

Mazda caliper

LEFT SIDE ONLY

REPLACE

1. Dust boots
2. Pistons
3. Piston rubber cups
4. Piston cups
5. Spring
6. Rubber cap
7. Bleeder
8. Steel ball

Mazda wheel cylinder

11. Apply rust penetrant to the bleeder screw threads and install to the caliper. Tighten it until it is just snug against its seat.

Wheel Cylinder Service

Disassembly and Assembly

1. On the left side, remove the bleeder screw and check ball.
2. Remove both dust boots.
3. Remove the pistons.
4. Remove the piston cups.
5. Remove the return spring.
6. Hone the cylinder bore if it is not damaged, to provide a smooth sealing surface. Wash and dry the bore after honing.

To assemble:

7. Lubricate the cylinder bore with brake fluid. Install the return spring.

8. Lubricate the new piston cups and install them to the cylinder. Lubricate and install the pistons.

9. Apply lubricant to the boot mounting groove and install the boot.

10. Apply rust penetrant to the bleeder screw threads and install it with the check ball to the wheel cylinder. Tighten until just snug.

MITSUBISHI

NOTE: When cleaning brake system components, use only brake fluid or denatured isopropyl alcohol. Never use a mineral-based solvent such as gasoline or paint thinner; these fluids will leave a residue that may swell and deteriorate rubber parts within the system. All alcohol must be removed from the system when the work is done because alcohol mixed with brake fluid lowers its boiling point.

Do not hone any aluminum bores. There is a hard anodized coating on the aluminum which will be removed if honed. This will allow the aluminum to wear quickly and will damage the component.

Master Cylinder Service

Disassembly and Assembly

1. Remove the brake fluid reservoir retainer screw, if equipped, and remove the reservoir and seals or remove the reservoir unions and seals.
2. Push the primary piston in and remove the stopper bolt and gasket.
3. Hold the pistons in and remove the snapring.

NOTE: Do not disassemble either piston assembly as the individual parts are not serviceable.

4. Let the primary piston spring out and remove the primary piston assembly.
5. Remove the secondary piston assembly. This may be accomplished by carefully blowing low pressure compressed air through the secondary side outlet port, if it does not come out easily.

6. Remove the brake line connector block and washers.

To assemble:

7. Coat the master cylinder bore and secondary and primary piston seals liberally with brake fluid.
8. Install both assemblies to the master cylinder.
9. Push the pistons in and install a new snapring.
10. Hold the pistons in and install the stopper bolt with a new gasket.
11. Install the brake fluid reservoir or unions with new seals. Install the reservoir retaining screw, if equipped.
12. Install the connector block with new washers.

Brake Booster Service

The brake boosters are not serviceable. If the unit is defective, replace the entire assembly.

Caliper Service

Disassembly and Assembly

1. Remove the bleeder screw.
2. Drain the brake fluid from the caliper.
3. Remove the dust boot ring and the dust boot.
4. Position a shop rag opposite the top of the piston. Apply low pressure compressed air to the fluid inlet and carefully blow the piston out of the bore.

— CAUTION —

Do not put fingers where the piston will land when it is blown out of the caliper. The force of the piston can crush fingers and cause personal injury.

1. Vacuum fitting
2. Booster vacuum line
3. Reservoir cap
4. Cap diaphragm
5. Fluid level float
6. Fluid level sensor connector
7. Reservoir seals
8. Reservoir bolt
9. Connector seals— not reuseable
10. Brake tube connection
11. Brake tubes
12. Master cylinder body
13. Stopper bolt
14. Stopper bolt seal
15. Secondary piston assembly
16. Primary piston assembly
17. Piston stopper lockring
18. Pushrod clevis pin

Master cylinder and booster assembly—Mitsubishi Pick-Ups, typical

1. Lock pin bolt
2. Guide pin bolt
3. Guide pin sleeve
4. Lock pin boot
5. Lock pin sleeve
6. Guide pin boot
7. Bleeder screw and cap

8. Caliper body
9. Piston seal
10. Piston assembly
11. Piston dust boot
12. Dust boot ring

13. Caliper support
14. Brake pad clip
15. Inner shoe shim
16. Disc brake pads
17. Outer shim

Front caliper and brake assembly—Mitsubishi Pick-Ups, typical

Install longer side to shoe and lever assembly

Identification groove to be directed outward

1. Brake line connection
2. Shoe hold-down pins
3. Adjusting hole cover
4. Backing plate
5. Shoe and lining assembly
6. Return spring and adjuster
7. Shoe retainer spring
8. Parking brake connection
9. Shoe and lever assembly

10. Bleeder screw
11. Wheel cylinder boot
12. Piston assembly
13. Piston cup
14. Wheel cylinder body
15. Brake drum

Rear brake assembly—Mitsubishi Pick-Ups, typical

5. Remove the piston seal from inside the bore.

To assemble:

6. Blow out all fluid passages with low pressure compressed air.

7. Slight corrosion or rust can be removed with commutator paper or crocus cloth. Replace pistons that are pitted, scored, peeling or otherwise damaged.

8. Lubricate the caliper bore with brake fluid. Lubricate the seal and install it in the groove.

9. Lubricate the piston and install it to the bore until it bottoms. If the piston will not go in by hand, it is probably cocked. Remove it and reinstall.

10. Apply lubricant to the dust boot mounting groove and install the boot. Install the retaining ring.

11. Apply rust penetrant to the bleeder screw threads and install to the caliper. Tighten it until it is just snug against its seat.

Wheel Cylinder Service

Disassembly and Assembly

1. Remove the bleeder screw, if equipped.

2. Remove both rubber boots.

3. Remove the piston assemblies, each consisting of the piston and cup.

4. Remove the piston cups from the pistons, being careful not to scratch the piston.

5. Remove the return spring.

6. Hone the cylinder bore if it is not damaged, to provide a smooth sealing surface. Wash and dry the bore after honing.

To assemble:

7. Lubricate the cylinder bore with brake fluid.

8. Lubricate the new piston cups and install them to the pistons, with their lips facing upward. Install the assemblies to the cylinder.

9. Apply lubricant to the boot mounting groove and install the boot.

10. Apply rust penetrant to the bleeder screw threads and install to the wheel cylinder. Tighten it until it is just snug against its seat.

NISSAN

NOTE: When cleaning brake system components, use only brake fluid or denatured isopropyl alcohol. Never use a mineral-based solvent such as gasoline or paint thinner; these fluids will leave a residue that may swell and deteriorate rubber parts within the system. All alcohol must be removed from the system when the work is done because alcohol mixed with brake fluid lowers its boiling point.

Do not hone any aluminum bores. There is a hard anodized coating on the aluminum which will be removed if honed. This will allow the aluminum to wear quickly and will damage the component.

Master Cylinder Service

Disassembly and Assembly

1. Remove the brake fluid reservoir and seals or hoses.

2. Push the primary piston in and remove the stopper cap.

3. Let the primary piston spring slowly out and remove the primary piston assembly.

4. Inspect the stopper cap carefully. If either claw is damaged in any way, replace it.

5. Remove the secondary piston assembly. This may be accomplished by carefully blowing low pressure compressed air through the secondary side outlet port if it does not come out

Nissan master cylinder—Pick-Up and Pathfinder

Nissan master cylinder—Van and Axxess

Nissan single piston front caliper

Nissan double piston caliper

Nissan rear caliper

easily. Disassemble the secondary piston on Pick-Up and Pathfinder only. The secondary pistons on Axxess and Van are not serviceable.

To assemble:

6. Assemble the secondary piston assembly, if disassembled. Coat the master cylinder bore and secondary and primary piston seals liberally with brake fluid. Install both assemblies to the master cylinder.

7. Push the pistons in and install the stopper cap.

8. Install the fluid reservoir and seals, if equipped.

Brake Booster Service

The brake boosters are not serviceable. If the unit is defective, replace the entire assembly.

Caliper Service

SINGLE PISTON TYPE

Disassembly and Assembly

1. Remove the bleeder screw.

2. Drain the brake fluid from the caliper.

3. Remove the dust seal ring (rear caliper only) and the dust seal.

4. Position a shop rag opposite the top of the piston. Apply low pressure compressed air to the fluid inlet and carefully blow the piston out of the bore.

— **CAUTION** —

Do not put fingers where the piston will land when it is blown out of the caliper. The force of the piston can crush fingers and cause personal injury.

5. Remove the piston seal from inside the bore.

To assemble:

6. Blow out all fluid passages with low pressure compressed air.

7. Slight corrosion or rust can be removed with commutator paper or crocus cloth. Replace pistons that are pitted, scored, peeling or otherwise damaged.

8. Lubricate the caliper bore with brake fluid. Lubricate the seal and install it in the groove.

9. Lubricate the piston and install it to the bore until it bottoms. If the piston will not go in by hand, it is probably cocked. Remove it and reinstall.

10. Apply lubricant to the dust seal mounting groove and install the seal. Install the retaining ring, if equipped.

11. Apply rust penetrant to the bleeder screw threads and install to the caliper. Tighten it until it is just snug against its seat.

Nissan wheel cylinder

DOUBLE PISTON TYPE

Disassembly and Assembly

1. Remove the bleeder screw.
2. Drain the brake fluid from the caliper.
3. Remove the dust covers.
4. Position a shop rag opposite the top of the piston. Apply low pressure compressed air to the fluid inlet and carefully blow the pistons out of their bores. If both pistons do not come out, install the extracted piston back into its bore just enough to seal; then hold it place with a suitable spacer. Blow out the remaining piston.

— **CAUTION** —

Do not put fingers where the piston will land when it is blown out of the caliper. The force of the piston can crush fingers and cause personal injury.

5. Remove the piston seals from inside the bore.

To assemble:

6. Blow out all fluid passages with low pressure compressed air.
7. Slight corrosion or rust can be removed with commutator paper or crocus cloth. Replace pistons that are pitted, scored, peeling or otherwise damaged.
8. Lubricate the caliper bore with brake fluid. Lubricate the seals and install in the grooves.
9. Lubricate the pistons and install them to the bores until they bottom. If either piston will not go in by hand, it is probably cocked. Remove it and reinstall.
10. Apply lubricant to the dust seal mounting grooves and install the seals.
11. Apply rust penetrant to the bleeder screw threads and install to the caliper. Tighten it until it is just snug against its seat.

Wheel Cylinder Service

Disassembly and Assembly

1. Remove the bleeder screw.
2. Remove both dust covers.
3. Remove the pistons.
4. Remove the piston cups.
5. Remover the return spring.
6. Hone the cylinder bore if it is not damaged, to provide a smooth sealing surface. Wash and dry the bore after honing.

To assemble:

7. Lubricate the cylinder bore with brake fluid. Install the return spring.
8. Lubricate the new piston cups and install them to the cylinder. Lubricate and install the pistons.
9. Apply lubricant to the dust cover mounting groove and install the cover.
10. Apply rust penetrant to the bleeder screw threads and install to the wheel cylinder. Tighten it until it is just snug against its seat.

SUZUKI

NOTE: When cleaning brake system components, use only brake fluid or denatured isopropyl alcohol. Never use a mineral-based solvent such as gasoline or paint thinner; these fluids will leave a residue that may swell and deteriorate rubber parts within the system. All alcohol must be removed from the system when the work is done because alcohol mixed with brake fluid lowers its boiling point.

Do not hone any aluminum bores. There is a hard anodized coating on the aluminum which will be removed if honed. This will allow the aluminum to wear quickly and will damage the component.

Master Cylinder Service

Disassembly and Assembly

1. Remove the brake fluid reservoir screw of roll pin and remove the reservoir. Remove the seals.
2. Push the primary piston in and remove the snapring.
3. Let the primary piston spring slowly out and remove piston stopper, cups and the primary piston assembly.
4. Remove the secondary piston stopper bolt.
5. Remove the secondary piston assembly. This may be accomplished by carefully blowing low pressure compressed air through the secondary side outlet port, if it does not come out easily. Disassemble the secondary piston.

To assemble:

6. Assemble the secondary piston assembly. Coat the master cylinder bore and secondary and primary piston seals liberally with brake fluid. Install both assemblies to the master cylinder.
7. Install the cups and stoppers. Install the snapring.
8. Push the pistons in and install the stopper bolt.
9. Install the fluid reservoir and seals.

1. Master cylinder assembly
2. Piston set
3. Snapring
4. Stopper bolt
5. Stopper seal ring
6. Seal rings
7. Cylinder cup
8. Master cylinder seal ring
9. Reservoir retainer screw
10. Reservoir seals
11. Fluid reservoir
12. Strainer
13. Reservoir cap
14. Breather capp
15. Gasket
16. Booster

Suzuki master cylinder—Samarai

1. Snapring
2. Piston stopper
3. Cylinder cup and plate
4. Primary piston
5. Piston cup
6. Secondary piston pressure cap
7. Piston cup
8. Secondary piston
9. Return spring secondary seat
10. Secondary piston return spring
11. Stopper bolt
12. Cylinder body
13. Seal

Suzuki master cylinder—Sidekick

Brake Booster Service

SINGLE DIAPHRAGM TYPE

SAMURAI

1. Remove the piston rod from the booster.
2. Remove the pushrod clevis and locknut.
3. Mount the booster on the holding tool set 09950–88210. Do not tighten the 2 outer nuts to more than 30 inch lbs. or the booster may become deformed.
4. Turn the special tool bolt clockwise until the projection and depression in the bodies match. Matchmark the bodies at that location.
5. Remove the booster from the tool and separate the bodies.

—————————— **CAUTION** ——————————

The rear body is spring loaded. Loosen it slowly and carefully or personal injury may result.

————————————————————————————————

6. Remove the boot, air cleaner elements and air cleaner separator from the rear body.
7. Turn the booster piston counterclockwise and remove from the rear body.
8. Push the air valve down and remove the stopper key. Remove the air valve assembly from the booster piston.
9. Remove the diaphragm from the pressure plate.
10. Remove the reaction disc from the booster piston.
11. Remove the seal from the from the rear body.

To assemble:

12. Lubricate and install a new seal to the rear body.
13. Lubricate and install the booster air valve to the booster piston.
14. Compress the valve and install the stopper key.
15. Install the new diaphragm to the pressure plate. Make sure the diaphragm is seated securely in its groove in the pressure plate.
16. Lubricate the face and install the reaction disc to the booster piston.
17. Install the booster piston to the rear body by turning it clockwise into place.

1. Vacuum check valve
2. Grommet
3. Front body
4. Piston rod
5. Reaction disc
6. Booster piston return spring
7. Valve stopper key
8. Booster piston
9. Booster air valve assembly
10. Pressure plate
11. Diaphragm
12. Rear body
13. Seal
14. Air cleaner separator
15. Air cleaner element
16. Rubber boot
17. Nut
18. Bracket
19. Pushrod clevis

Suzuki single diaphragm booster—Samarai

1. Front body
2. Booster piston return spring
3. Piston rod retainer
4. Piston rod
5. Reaction disc
6. Booster piston
7. Key cushion
8. Valve stopper key
9. Booster air valve assembly
10. Diaphragm
11. Diaphragm retainer
12. Retainer
13. Rear body
14. Seal
15. Air cleaner separator
16. Air cleaner element
17. Rubber boot
18. Nut
19. Bracket
20. Clevis pin
21. Pushrod clevis
22. Cotter pin

Suzuki single diaphragm booster—Sidekick

1. Guide pin
2. Guide pin sleeve
3. Guide pin boot
4. Guide pin cap
5. Bleeder cap
6. Bleeder
7. Caliper body
8. Piston seal
9. Piston
10. Boot
11. Brake pad
12. Adaptor
13. Anti-rattle clip

Suzuki caliper—typical

Suzuki wheel cylinder—typical

18. Install the new air cleaner separator and elements to the air valve rod.
19. Install the boot to the rear body.
20. Place the front body on the special tool and place the return spring on it large end up.
21. Place the assembled rear body on the return spring and compress. Turn the special bolt counterclockwise until the projection and depression line up.
22. Install the piston rod into the booster piston.
23. Install the locknut and clevis.

SIDEKICK

1. Remove the pushrod clevis.
2. Remove the locknut.
3. Mount the booster on the holding tool set 09950–88210. Do not tighten the 2 outer nuts to more than 30 inch lbs. or the booster may become deformed.
4. Turn the special tool bolt clockwise until the projection and depression in the bodies match. Matchmark the bodies at that location.
5. Remove the booster from the tool and separate the bodies.

— CAUTION —
The rear body is spring loaded. Loosen it slowly and carefully or personal injury may result.

6. Remove the piston rod, boot, air cleaner elements and air cleaner separator from the rear body.
7. Remove the valve stopper key cushion.

8. Push the air valve down and remove the stopper key. Remove the air valve assembly from the booster piston.
9. Remove the diaphragm circular ring from the booster piston. Remove the diaphragm from the pressure plate.
10. Remove the reaction disc from the booster piston.
11. Remove the seal from the from the rear body.
To assemble:
12. Lubricate and install a new seal to the rear body.
13. Install the retainer to the diaphragm. Install the diaphragm to the booster piston and install the new diaphragm circular ring.
14. Lubricate and install the booster air valve to the booster piston. Compress the valve and install the stopper key. Install the cushion to the notch in the stopper.
15. Install the booster piston to the rear body.
16. Install the new air cleaner separator and elements to the air valve rod.
17. Install the boot to the rear body.
18. Lubricate the face and install the reaction disc to the booster piston.
19. Place the front body on the special tool and place the return spring, rod retainer and piston rod on it.
20. Place the assembled rear body on the return spring and compress. Turn the special bolt counterclockwise until the projection and depression line up.
21. Install the piston rod into the booster piston.
22. Install the locknut and clevis.

Caliper Service

Disassembly and Assembly

1. Remove the bleeder screw.
2. Drain the brake fluid from the caliper.
3. Remove the cylinder boot.
4. Position a shop rag opposite the top of the piston. Apply low pressure compressed air to the fluid inlet and carefully blow the piston out of the bore.

— CAUTION —
Do not put fingers where the piston will land when it is blown out of the caliper. The force of the piston can crush fingers and cause personal injury.

5. Remove the piston seal from inside the bore.
To assemble:
6. Blow out all fluid passages with low pressure compressed air.
7. Slight corrosion or rust can be removed with commutator paper or crocus cloth. Replace pistons that are pitted, scored, peeling or otherwise damaged.
8. Lubricate the caliper bore with brake fluid. Lubricate the seal and install it in the groove.
9. Lubricate the piston and install it to the bore until it bottoms. If the piston will not go in by hand, it is probably cocked. Remove it and reinstall.
10. Apply lubricant to the cylinder boot mounting groove and install.
11. Apply rust penetrant to the bleeder screw threads and install to the caliper. Tighten it until it is just snug against its seat.

Wheel Cylinder Service

Disassembly and Assembly

1. Remove the bleeder screw, if equipped.
2. Remove both rubber boots.
3. Remove the piston assemblies, each consisting of the piston and cup.
4. Remove the piston cups from the pistons, being careful not to scratch the piston.

5. Remove the return spring.

6. Hone the cylinder bore if it is not damaged, to provide a smooth sealing surface. Wash and dry the bore after honing.

To assemble:

7. Lubricate the cylinder bore with brake fluid.

8. Lubricate the new piston cups and install them to the pis-

tons, with their lips facing upward. Install the assemblies to the cylinder.

9. Apply lubricant to the boot mounting groove and install the boot.

10. Apply rust penetrant to the bleeder screw threads and install to the wheel cylinder. Tighten until it is just snug against its seat.

TOYOTA

NOTE: When cleaning brake system components, use only brake fluid or denatured isopropyl alcohol. Never use a mineral-based solvent such as gasoline or paint thinner; these fluids will leave a residue that may swell and deteriorate rubber parts within the system. All alcohol must be removed from the system when the work is done because alcohol mixed with brake fluid lowers its boiling point.

Do not hone any aluminum bores. There is a hard anodized coating on the aluminum which will be removed if honed. This will allow the aluminum to wear quickly and will damage the component.

Master Cylinder Service

Disassembly and Assembly

1. Remove the brake fluid reservoir retainer screw, if

equipped, and remove the reservoir and seals or remove the reservoir unions and seals.

2. Remove the boot. Push the primary piston in and remove the stopper bolt and gasket.

3. Hold the pistons in and remove the snapring.

NOTE: Do not disassemble either piston assembly on the Pick-Up and 4Runner. The individual parts are not serviceable.

4. Let the primary piston spring out and remove the primary piston assembly.

5. Remove the secondary piston assembly. This may be accomplished by carefully blowing low pressure compressed air through the secondary side outlet port if it does not come out easily.

To assemble:

6. Assemble the pistons, if they were disassembled.

7. Coat the master cylinder bore and secondary and primary piston seals liberally with brake fluid.

8. Install both assemblies to the master cylinder.

9. Push the pistons in and install a new snapring.

10. Hold the pistons in and install the stopper bolt with a new gasket. Install a new boot.

11. Install the brake fluid reservoir or unions with new seals. Install the reservoir retaining screw, if equipped.

Brake Booster Service

The brake boosters are not serviceable. If the unit is defective, replace the entire assembly.

Toyota master cylinder

Toyota single piston caliper

Toyota four-piston caliper

Caliper Service

SINGLE PISTON TYPE

Disassembly and Assembly

1. Remove the bleeder screw.
2. Drain the brake fluid from the caliper.
3. Remove the boot.
4. Position a shop rag opposite the top of the piston. Apply low pressure compressed air to the fluid inlet and carefully blow the piston out of the bore.

─── CAUTION ───

Do not put fingers where the piston will land when it is blown out of the caliper. The force of the piston can crush fingers and cause personal injury.

5. Remove the piston seal from inside the bore.

To assemble:

6. Blow out all fluid passages with low pressure compressed air.
7. Slight corrosion or rust can be removed with commutator paper or crocus cloth. Replace pistons that are pitted, scored, peeling or otherwise damaged.
8. Lubricate the caliper bore with brake fluid. Lubricate the seal and install it in the groove.
9. Lubricate the piston and install it to the bore until it bottoms. If the piston will not go in by hand, it is probably cocked. Remove it and reinstall.
10. Apply lubricant to the boot mounting groove and install the boot.
11. Apply rust penetrant to the bleeder screw threads and install to the caliper. Tighten it until it is just snug against its seat.

FOUR PISTON TYPE

Disassembly and Assembly

1. Remove the bleeder screw.
2. Drain the brake fluid from the caliper.
3. Remove the boot set rings and boots.
4. Position a block of wood across the caliper and use an old brake pad to keep 1 pair of pistons in their bores. Apply low pressure compressed air to the fluid inlet and carefully blow the pistons out of their bores. Reinsert the piston just enough to seal and reverse the old brake pad in order to blow out the remaining pistons.

─── CAUTION ───

Do not put fingers where the piston will land when it is blown out of the caliper. The force of the piston can crush fingers and cause personal injury.

WHEEL CYLINDER ASSEMBLY

Toyota wheel cylinder

5. Remove the piston seals from inside the bore.

To assemble:

6. Blow out all fluid passages with low pressure compressed air.
7. Slight corrosion or rust can be removed with commutator paper or crocus cloth. Replace pistons that are pitted, scored, peeling or otherwise damaged.
8. Lubricate the caliper bore with brake fluid. Lubricate the seals and install in the grooves.
9. Lubricate the pistons and install them to the bores until they bottom. If any of the pistons will not go in easily, it is probably cocked. Remove it and reinstall.
10. Apply lubricant to the boot mounting grooves and install the boots and rings.
11. Apply rust penetrant to the bleeder screw threads and install to the caliper. Tighten it until it is just snug against its seat.

Wheel Cylinder Service

Disassembly and Assembly

1. Remove the bleeder screw.
2. Remove both boots.
3. Remove the pistons.
4. Remove the piston cups.
5. Remover the return spring.
6. Hone the cylinder bore if it is not damaged, to provide a smooth sealing surface. Wash and dry the bore after honing.

To assemble:

7. Lubricate the cylinder bore with brake fluid. Install the return spring.
8. Lubricate the new piston cups and install them to the cylinder. Lubricate and install the pistons.
9. Apply lubricant to the dust cover mounting groove and install the cover.
10. Apply rust penetrant to the bleeder screw threads and install to the wheel cylinder. Tighten it until it is just snug against its seat.

VOLKSWAGEN

NOTE: When cleaning brake system components, use only brake fluid or denatured isopropyl alcohol. Never use a mineral-based solvent such as gasoline or paint thinner; these fluids will leave a residue that may swell and deteriorate rubber parts within the system. All alcohol must be removed from the system when the work is done because alcohol mixed with brake fluid lowers its boiling point.

Master Cylinder Service

Disassembly and Assembly

1. Remove the brake fluid reservoir and seals. Remove the brake light switches, if equipped.
2. Push the primary piston in and remove the stopper bolt and gasket.

Volkswagen master cylinder and brake booster

1. Master cylinder assembly
2. Gasket
3. Nut
4. Brake light switch
5. Seal

3. Hold the pistons in and remove the snapring.

4. Let the primary piston spring out and remove the primary piston assembly.

5. Remove the secondary piston assembly. This may be accomplished by carefully blowing low pressure compressed air through the secondary side outlet port, if it does not come out easily.

6. Disassemble the pistons.

To assemble:

7. Assemble the pistons using all parts provided with the kit. Coat the master cylinder bore and secondary and primary piston seals liberally with brake fluid.

8. Install both assemblies to the master cylinder.

9. Push the pistons in and install a new snapring.

10. Hold the pistons in and install the stopper bolt with a new gasket.

11. Install the brake fluid reservoir and new seals.

12. Install the switches.

Brake Booster Service

The brake boosters are not serviceable. If the unit is defective, replace the entire assembly.

Caliper Service

Disassembly and Assembly

1. Remove the bleeder screw.
2. Drain the brake fluid from the caliper.
3. Remove the dust boot.
4. Position a shop rag opposite the top of the piston. Apply low pressure compressed air to the fluid inlet and carefully blow the piston out of the bore.

—————— **CAUTION** ——————
Do not put fingers where the piston will land when it is blown out of the caliper. The force of the piston can crush fingers and cause personal injury.

5. Remove the piston seal from inside the bore.

To assemble:

6. Blow out all fluid passages with low pressure compressed air.

7. Slight corrosion or rust can be removed with commutator paper or crocus cloth. Replace pistons that are pitted, scored, peeling or otherwise damaged.

8. Lubricate the caliper bore with brake fluid. Lubricate the seal and install it in the groove.

9. Lubricate the piston and install it to the bore until it bottoms. If the piston will not go in by hand, it is probably cocked. Remove it and reinstall.

10. Apply lubricant to the dust boot mounting groove and install the boot.

11. Apply rust penetrant to the bleeder screw threads and install to the caliper. Tighten it until it is just snug against its seat.

Wheel Cylinder Service

Disassembly and Assembly

1. Remove the bleeder screw.
2. Remove both dust covers.
3. Remove the pistons.
4. Remove the piston cups.
5. Remover the return spring.
6. Hone the cylinder bore if it is not damaged, to provide a smooth sealing surface. Wash and dry the bore after honing.

To assemble:

7. Lubricate the cylinder bore with brake fluid. Install the return spring.

8. Lubricate the new piston cups and install them to the cylinder. Lubricate and install the pistons.

9. Apply lubricant to the dust cover mounting groove and install the cover.

10. Apply rust penetrant to the bleeder screw threads and install to the wheel cylinder. Tighten it until it is just snug against its seat.

CARBURETOR IDENTIFICATION

All carburetors are identified by code numbers, either stamped on the attaching flange side, the main body or on a metal tag retained by a bowl cover screw. This identification number is important in order to obtain the correct carburetor replacement or parts and to properly adjust the carburetor when matched to a specific engine.

Motorcraft carburetors for Ford usage—typical

Rochester 2-bbl models—typical

Carter carburetors for Jeep usage—typical

Rochester 1-bbl models—typical

Motorcraft carburetors for Jeep usage—typical

Rochester 2-bbl models—typical

SPECIAL TOOLS

An angle degree tool is recommended by Rochester Products Division for use to confirm adjustments to the choke valve and related linkages on late model 2 and 4 barrel carburetors in place of the plug type gauges. Decimal and degree conversion charts are provided for use with the angle degree tool. To use the angle gauge, rotate the degree scale until 0 is opposite the pointer. With the choke valve completely closed, place the gauge magnet squarely on top of the choke valve and rotate the bubble until it is centered. Make the necessary adjustments to have the choke valve at the specified degree angle opening as read from the degree angle tool. The carburetor may be off the engine for adjustments but make sure the carburetor is held firmly during the use of the angle gauge.

A variety of other special adjustment tools may be necessary during the overhaul of different carburetors covered in this section. Most carburetor overhaul kits contain the float level gauges and specifications necessary for complete rebuilding and if specifications differ from those given in the following charts, use the values listed in the overhaul instructions with a specific kit. Before beginning any overhaul procedures, read through each section to make sure all required special tools are on hand in order to complete the repair.

Typical degree angle tool

Carburetor Overhaul Tips

When the carburetor is disassembled, wash all parts (except diaphragms, electric choke units, pump plunger, and any other plastic, leather, fiber, or rubber parts) in clean carburetor solvent. Do not leave parts in the solvent any longer than is necessary to sufficiently loosen the deposits. Excessive cleaning may remove the special finish from the float bowl and choke valve bodies, leaving these parts unfit for service. Rinse all parts in clean solvent and blow them dry with compressed air or allow them to air dry. Wipe clean all cork, plastic, leather and fiber parts with a clean, lint-free cloth.

Blow out all passages and jets with compressed air and be sure there are no restrictions or blockages. Never use wire or similar tools to clean jets, fuel passages or air bleeds. Clean all jets and valves separately to avoid accidental interchange. Check all parts for wear or damage. If wear or damage is found, replace the defective parts. Especially check the following:

1. Check the float needle and seat for wear. If wear is found, replace the complete assembly.
2. Check the float hinge pin for wear and the float(s) for dents or distortion. Replace the float if fuel has leaked into it.
3. Check the throttle and choke shaft bores for wear or an out-of-round condition. Damage or wear to the throttle arm, shaft or shaft bore will often require replacement of the throttle body. These parts require a close tolerance of fit. Wear may allow air leakage, which could affect starting and idling.

NOTE: Throttle shafts and bushings are not included in overhaul kits. They can be purchased separately.

4. Inspect the idle mixture adjusting needles for burrs or grooves. Any such condition requires replacement of the needle, since you will not be able to obtain a satisfactory idle.
5. Test the accelerator pump check valves. They should pass air one way but not the other. Test for proper seating by blowing and sucking on the valve. Replace the valve if necessary. If the valve is satisfactory, wash the valve again to remove breath moisture.
6. Check the bowl cover for warped surfaces with a straightedge.
7. Closely inspect the valves and seats for wear and damage, replacing as necessary.
8. After the carburetor is assembled, check the choke valve for freedom of operation.

Carburetor overhaul kits are recommended for each overhaul. These kits contain all gaskets and new parts to replace those that deteriorate most rapidly. Failure to replace all parts supplied with the kit (especially gaskets) can result in poor performance later.

After cleaning and checking all components, reassemble the carburetor, using new parts and referring to the exploded view. When reassembling, make sure all screws and jets are tight in their seats but do not overtighten as the tips will be distorted. Tighten all screws gradually, in rotation. Do not tighten needle valves into their seats; uneven jetting will result. Always use new gaskets. Be sure to adjust the float level, following the instructions contained in the rebuilding kit, when reassembling.

GENERAL MOTORS CORPORATION

Rochester Carburetors

Refer to the individual sections for idle speed and idle mixture adjustments, using the propane enrichment procedure on non-electronic controlled engine carburetors and with the use of a dwellmeter on the electronic controlled carburetor equipped engines.

MODEL 1MEF

ROCHESTER MODEL 1MEF
(All measurements in inches)

Year	Carburetor Number	Float Level	Choke Unloader Setting	Choke Coil Lever Setting	Fast Idle Speed (rpm)	Metering Rod Setting	Fast Idle Cam 2nd Step	Choke Vacuum Break
1988	17086096	¹¹/₃₂	0.520	0.120	①	0.090	0.275	0.200
	17086101	¹¹/₃₂	0.520	0.120	①	0.090	0.275	0.200

① See emission label under hood

6. Choke shaft, lever and link assembly
7. Choke link
8. Choke housing and bearing assembly
9. Choke housing attaching screw
10. Choke housing attaching screw
11. Choke shaft and lever assembly
12. Choke stat lever
13. Stat lever attaching screw
14. Electric choke cover and stat assembly
15. Connector and bracket assembly
16. Choke cover retainer
17. Choke cover attaching rivet
18. Bowl side vacuum breat assembly
19. Vacuum Break Hose
20. Vacuum break lever and link assembly
21. Vacuum break link
22. Lever attaching screw
23. Air horn assembly
24. Air horn to float bowl gasket
25. Air horn to float bowl (long) screw assembly
26. Air horn to float bowl screw assembly
27. Air horn to float bowl (countersunk) screw
28. Air cleaner bracket
29. Air cleaner bracket attaching screw assembly
30. Float bowl assembly
31. Fuel inlet nut
32. Fuel inlet nut gasket
33. Fuel inlet filter
34. Fuel filter spring
35. Float
36. Float hinge pin
37. Float needle
38. Float needle seat
39. Float needle gasket
40. Pump rod
41. Pump rod seal
42. Pump assembly
43. Pump plunger B cup
44. Pump plunger spring
45. Pump return spring
46. Pump discharge spring guide
47. Pump discharge ball
48. Power piston rod
49. Power piston rod seal
50. Power piston rod seal retainer
51. Power valve piston assembly
52. Power piston spring
53. Metering rod and spring assembly
54. Main metering jet
55. Idle tube assembly
56. Throttle body assembly
57. Float bowl to throttle body gasket
58. Float bowl to throttle body screw assembly
59. Pump and power rod lever
60. Pump lever attaching screw
61. Power rod link
62. Pump link
63. Idle mixture needle
64. Idle mixture needle spring
65. Idle mixture needle limiter
66. Idle mixture needle plug
67. Idle stop solenoid
68. Idle stop solenoid spring
69. Throttle return spring anchor bracket
70. Bracket attaching (countersunk) screw
71. Bracket attaching screw
1. Air cleaner gasket
2. Flange gasket
3. Fast idle cam
4. Fast idle cam attaching screw
5. Fast idle cam link

Rochester 1MEF carburetor—exploded view

Rochester 1MEF float level adjustment

② GAUGE FROM TOP OF CASTING TO TOP OF INDEX POINT AT TOE OF FLOAT

③ BEND HERE TO ADJUST FLOAT UP OR DOWN

① HOLD FLOAT RETAINING PIN FIRMLY IN PLACE — PUSH DOWN ON END OF FLOAT ARM, AGAINST TOP OF FLOAT NEEDLE

Rochester 1MEF metering rod adjustment

③ HOLD POWER PISTON DOWN AND SWING METERING ROD HOLDER OVER FLAT SURFACE (GASKET REMOVED) OF BOWL CASTING NEXT TO CARBURETOR BORE

① REMOVE METERING ROD BY HOLDING THROTTLE VALVE WIDE OPEN. PUSH DOWNWARD ON METERING ROD AGAINST SPRING TENSION, THEN SLIDE METERING ROD OUT OF SLOT IN HOLDER AND REMOVE FROM MAIN METERING JET.

⑤ BEND HERE TO ADJUST

BENDING TOOL

④ SPECIFIED PLUG GAUGE — SLIDE FIT

② BACK OUT IDLE STOP SOLENOID — HOLD THROTTLE VALVE COMPLETELY CLOSED

Rochester 1MEF choke coil lever adjustment

② HOLD CHOKE VALVE COMPLETELY CLOSED

④ BEND LINK TO ADJUST

③ .120" PLUG GAUGE MUST PASS THROUGH HOLE IN LEVER AND ENTER HOLE IN CASTING

① PLACE FAST IDLE CAM FOLLOWER ON HIGHEST STEP OF FAST IDLE CAM

Rochester 1MEF fast idle cam adjustment

② HOLD DOWN ON CHOKE VALVE – ROD IN END OF SLOT.

③ GAUGE BETWEEN LOWER EDGE OF CHOKE VALVE (AT CENTER) AND INSIDE AIR HORN WALL.

④ BEND ROD AT POINT SHOWN TO ADJUST.

① WITH FAST IDLE ADJUSTMENT MADE, FAST IDLE CAM FOLLOWER MUST BE HELD FIRMLY ON SECOND STEP OF FAST IDLE CAM AGAINST HIGHTEST STEP.

Rochester 1MEF vacuum break adjustment

④ PLACE GAUGE BETWEEN LOWER EDGE OF CHOKE VALVE AND INSIDE AIR HORN WALL.

ON DELAY FEATURE MODELS, COVER PLUG AND PURGE BLEED HOLE WITH 1" SQUARE PIECE OF MASKING TAPE. REMOVE AFTER ADJUSTMENT.

HOLD GAUGE VERTICAL.

③ PUSH DOWN ON CHOKE VALVE (COMPRESS PLUNGER BUCKING SPRING AND SEAT PLUNGER STEM ON MODELS SO EQUIPPED).

② USE OUTSIDE VACUUM SOURCE TO SEAT DIAPHRAGM.

⑤ BEND LINK TO ADJUST.

① PLACE FAST IDLE CAM FOLLOWER ON HIGHEST STEP OF CAM.

Rochester 1MEF unloader adjustment

① INSTALL CHOKE COIL IN CHOKE HOUSING AND INDEX PROPERLY (SEE NOTE).

NOTE: IF CHOKE COIL IS WARM, COOL DOWN TO POINT WHERE CHOKE VALVE WILL CLOSE FULLY.

② HOLD THROTTLE VALVE WIDE OPEN.

③ GAUGE BETWEEN LOWER EDGE OF CHOKE VALVE AND INSIDE AIR HORN WALL (SEE NOTE).

④ BEND TANG TO ADJUST (SEE INSET).

MODELS M4MED AND M4MEF

ROCHESTER MODEL M4MEF QUADRAJET
General Motors Corporation
(All measurements in inches or degrees)

Year	Carburetor Number	Float Level	Pump Rod Hole	Pump Rod Setting	Choke Rod ① Setting	Air Valve Rod	Vacuum Break Front	Vacuum Break Rear	Air Valve Turns	Choke Unloader	Propane Enrichment (rpm)
1988	17085004	13/32	inner	9/32	46°	0.025	23°	—	7/8	35°	—
	17085212	13/32	inner	9/32	46°	0.025	23°	—	7/8	35°	—
	17088040	13/32	inner	9/32	46°	0.025	27°	—	7/8	35°	—
	17088041	13/32	inner	9/32	46°	0.025	27°	—	7/8	35°	—
1989	17085004	13/32	inner	9/32	46°	0.025	23°	—	7/8	35°	—
	17085212	13/32	inner	9/32	46°	0.025	23°	—	7/8	35°	—

NOTE: Specified angle for use with angle degree tool. Choke coil lever setting is 0.120 in. for all carburetors.

1. REMOVE AIR HORN, GASKET, POWER PISTON AND METERING ROD ASSEMBLY, AND FLOAT BOWL INSERT.

2. ATTACH J-34817-1 OR BT-8227A-1 TO FLOAT BOWL.

3. PLACE J-34817-3 OR BT-8227A IN BASE WITH CONTACT PIN RESTING ON OUTER EDGE OF FLOAT LEVER.

4. MEASURE DISTANCE FROM TOP OF CASTING TO TOP OF FLOAT, AT POINT 3/16" FROM LARGE END OF FLOAT. USE J-9789-90 OR BT-8037.

5. IF MORE THAN ±2/32" FROM SPECIFICATION, USE J-34817-25 OR BT-8427 TO BEND LEVER UP OR DOWN. REMOVE BENDING TOOL AND MEASURE, REPEATING UNTIL WITHIN SPECIFICATION.

6. CHECK FLOAT ALIGNMENT.

7. REASSEMBLE CARBURETOR.

Rochester M4MEF float adjustment

1. Air cleaner gasket
2. Flange gasket
3. Air horn assembly
4. Secondary metering rod holder attaching screw
5. Secondary metering rod holder
6. Secondary metering rod
7. Choke lever
8. Choke lever attaching screw
9. Pump lever
10. Pump lever hinge pin

11. Air horn to throttle body screw assembly
12. Air horn to float bowl screw assembly
13. Air horn to float bowl (countersunk) screw
14. Air horn baffle
15. Primary side (front) vacuum break assembly
16. Primary side (front) vacuum break assembly attaching screw
17. Primary side (front) vacuum break hose

18. Primary side vacuum break — air valve lever link
19. Pump stem seal retainer
20. Pump stem seal
21. Float bowl assembly
22. Air horn to float bowl gasket
23. Pump plunger spring
24. Pump plunger cup
25. Pump assembly
26. Pump return spring
27. Power valve piston assembly
28. Primary metering rod
29. Primary metering rod spring
30. Power piston spring
31. Float bowl insert
32. Float hinge pin
33. Float
34. Float needle pull clip
35. Float needle
36. Float needle seat
37. Float needle seat gasket
38. Primary metering jet
39. Pump discharge (retainer) plug
40. Pump discharge ball
41. Pump well baffle
42. Choke cover attaching rivet
43. Choke cover retainer
44. Electric choke cover and stat assembly
45. Choke housing assembly
46. Choke housing to float bowl screw and washer assembly
47. Choke stat lever attaching screw
48. Choke stat lever
49. Intermediate choke shaft — lever and link assembly
50. Fast idle cam assembly
51. Intermediate choke lever
52. Choke lever
53. Secondary throttle lockout lever
54. Intermediate choke shaft seal
55. Fuel inlet nut
56. Fuel inlet nut gasket
57. Fuel inlet filter
58. Fuel filter spring
59. Throttle stop screw
60. Throttle stop srew spring
61. Throttle body assembly
62. Float bowl to throttle body gasket
63. Float bowl to throttle body screw assembly
64. Pump link
65. Idle mixture needle
66. Idle mixture needle spring
67. Idle mixture needle plug
68. Fast idle adjusting screw
69. Fast idle adjusting screw spring
70. Solenoid and bracket assembly
71. Bracket attaching screw

Rochester M4MEF carburetor exploded view—1988–89

③ GAGE FROM TOP OF CHOKE VALVE WALL, NEXT TO VENT STACK, TO TOP OF PUMP STEM AS SPECIFIED

SCALE

⑤ BEND PUMP LEVER AT NOTCH TO ADJUST

④ SUPPORT LEVER WITH SCREWDRIVER WHILE BENDING LEVER

① ROD IN SPECIFIED HOLE

② BE SURE FAST IDLE CAM FOLLOWER LEVER IS OFF STEPS OF FAST IDLE CAM. BACK OFF THROTTLE STOP SCREW FROM CONTACT WITH THROTTLE LEVER

Rochester M4MEF pump adjustment

① ATTACH RUBBER BAND TO GREEN TANG OF INTERMEDIATE CHOKE SHAFT

② OPEN THROTTLE TO ALLOW CHOKE VALVE TO CLOSE

③ SET UP ANGLE GAGE AND SET ANGLE TO SPECIFICATION

④ ON QUADRAJET, HOLD SECONDARY LOCKOUT LEVER AWAY FROM PIN

⑤ HOLD THROTTLE LEVER IN WIDE OPEN POSITION

⑥ ADJUST BY BENDING TANG OF FAST IDLE LEVER UNTIL BUBBLE IS CENTERED

PIN

CHOKE COVER

FAST IDLE CAM

④ LOCKOUT LEVER

Rochester M4MEF unloader adjustment

③ CENTER LEVELING BUBBLE

① CHOKE VALVE CLOSED

② ROTATE DEGREE SCALE UNTIL ZERO IS OPPOSITE POINTER

MAGNET

④ ROTATE SCALE TO SPECIFIED ANGLE (SEE SPECIFICATIONS)

⑤ ADJUST LINKAGE TO CENTER THE BUBBLE

Rochester M4MEF choke valve angle gauge usage

① ATTACH RUBBER BAND TO GREEN TANG OF INTERMEDIATE CHOKE SHAFT.

② OPEN THROTTLE TO ALLOW CHOKE VALVE TO CLOSE.

③ SET UP ANGLE GAGE AND SET ANGLE TO SPECIFICATION.

④ RETRACT VACUUM BREAK PLUNGER, USING VACUUM SOURCE, AT LEAST 18" HG. PLUG AIR BLEED HOLES WHERE APPLICABLE.

④A ON QUADRAJETS, AIR VALVE ROD MUST NOT RESTRICT PLUNGER FROM RETRACTING FULLY. IF NECESSARY, BEND ROD HERE TO PERMIT FULL PLUNGER TRAVEL. WHERE APPLICABLE, PLUNGER STEM MUST BE EXTENDED FULLY TO COMPRESS PLUNGER BUCKING SPRING.

⑤ TO CENTER BUBBLE, EITHER:
  A. ADJUST WITH 1/8" HEX WRENCH (VACUUM STILL APPLIED)

  -OR-

  B. SUPPORT AT "S" AND BEND VACUUM BREAK ROD (VACUUM STILL APPLIED)

Rochester M4MEF rear (secondary) vacuum break adjustment

③ TURN TENSION-ADJUSTING SCREW CLOCKWISE UNTIL AIR VALVE JUST CLOSES. THEN TURN ADJUSTING SCREW CLOCKWISE SPECIFIED NUMBER OF TURNS.

④ TIGHTEN LOCK SCREW

⑤ APPLY LITHIUM BASE GREASE TO LUBRICATE CONTACT AREA.

① LOOSEN LOCK SCREW USING 3/32" HEX WRENCH.

② TURN TENSION-ADJUSTING SCREW COUNTERCLOCKWISE UNTIL AIR VALVE OPENS PART WAY.

Rochester M4MEF air valve spring adjustment

⑥ BEND CHOKE ROD HERE TO ADJUST

CHOKE VALVE CLOSED

③ PUSH UP ON CHOKE COIL LEVER TO CLOSE CHOKE VALVE.

⑤ LOWER EDGE OF LEVER SHOULD JUST CONTACT GAGE.

④ INSERT .120" PLUG GAGE.

① IF RIVETED, DRILL OUT AND REMOVE RIVETS. REMOVE CHOKE COVER AND COIL ASSEMBLY.

② PLACE FAST IDLE CAM FOLLOWER ON HIGH STEP OF FAST IDLE CAM.

Rochester M4MEF coil lever adjustment

PLUGGING AIR BLEED HOLES

PUMP CUP OR VALVE STEM SEAL

TAPE HOLE IN TUBE

TAPE END OF COVER

BUCKING SPRINGS

Plunger Stem Extended (Spring Compressed)

PLUNGER BUCKING SPRING

Spring Seated

LEAF TYPE BUCKING SPRING

Rochester M4MEF vacuum break inspection

CHOKE VALVE

PUSH DOWN FAST IDLE CAM (STEP 2)

LOCKOUT LEVER

CHOKE VALVE CLOSED

THROTTLE VALVES CLOSED

BEND PIN TO ADJUST

015 MAX CLEARANCE

SECONDARY LOCKOUT LEVER ① SIDE CLEARANCE

HOLD CHOKE VALVE WIDE OPEN BY PUSHING DOWN ON TAIL OF FAST IDLE CAM

CHECK LOCKOUT PIN FOR CLEARANCE

FILE END OF PIN FOR CLEARANCE (CHECK FOR NO BURRS AFTER FILING)

015 GAGE

SECONDARY LOCKOUT ② OPENING CLEARANCE

Rochester M4MEF secondary lockout adjustment

1. Plug vacuum break bleed holes, if applicable. Air valves (A) close. Apply 15 in. Hg vacuum to seat vacuum break plunger
2. Gauge the clearance between air valve link and end of slot in lever
3. Adjust, if necessary, by bending link

Rochester M4MEF air valve rod adjustment—1988–89

1. Attach rubber band to vacuum break lever of intermediate choke shaft
2. Open throttle to allow choke valve to close
3. Set up angle gauge and set to specification
4. Plug vacuum break bleed holes, if applicable. Apply 15 in. Hg vacuum to seat vacuum break plunger. Seat bucking spring (A), if applicable. On quadrajets, if necessary, bend air valve link (B) to permit full plunger travel and reapply vacuum
5. Adjust, if bubble is not recentered, by turning screw

J-26701-A or BT-7704

Rochester M4MEF front (primary) vacuum break adjustment—1988–89

1. Attach rubber band to green tang of intermediate choke shaft
2. Open throttle to allow choke valve to close
3. Set up angle gauge and set angle to specifications
4. Place cam follower on 2nd step of cam, against the rise of the highest step. If the cam follower does not contact cam, turn in fast idle speed screw additional turn(s)
5. Adjust a bending tang of fast idle cam until bubble is centered

PLIERS ON TANG

FAST IDLE CAM

FAST IDLE SPEED SCREW

Rochester M4MEF choke rod fast idle cam adjustment

CHRYSLER CORPORATION

Holley Carburetors

MODEL 6520

HOLLEY MODEL 6520
Chrysler Corporation
(All measurements in inches)

Year	Carburetor Number	Float Level	Choke Vacuum Kick	Accelerator Pump Hole	Fast Idle Speed	Propane Idle Speed
1988	R40308-1	0.500	0.082	—	①	①
	R40309-1	0.500	0.082	—	①	①

① Refer to underhood specification sticker

Holley 6520 float drop measurement

Holley 6520 choke vacuum kick adjustment

Holley 6520 dry float setting

Holley 6520 carburetor side view

CURB IDLE ADJUSTING SCREW

SOLE KICKER

VACUUM OPERATED SECONDARY DIAPHRAGM

VENDOR PART NUMBER

CHRYSLER PART NUMBER

FUEL INLET

VACUUM OPERATED SECONDARY CONTROL SOLENOID

AIR FILTER

VACUUM HOSE

IDLE ADJUSTING SCREW

SOLE KICKER

CHOKE BLADE

HEATED AIR DOOR AND CHOKE VACUUM TUBE

PRIMARY MAIN AIR ALTITUDE TUBE

CHOKE VACUUM TUBE

CHOKE VACUUM KICK ADJUSTMENT SCREW

ANTI-DIESEL ADJUSTING SCREW

PRIMARY MAIN AIR ALTITUDE TUBE

CHOKE VACUUM TUBE

EGR TUBE

CONCEALMENT PLUG

PRIMARY IDLE ALTITUDE TUBE

MANIFOLD VACUUM NIPPLE

ACCLERATOR PUMP

VACUUM OPERATED SECONDARY CONTROL SOLENOID

BOWL VENT TUBE

FUEL INLET

1. Needle and seat
2. Power valve
3. Main metering jet
4. Float
5. Air horn gasket
6. Switch vent solenoid
7. Choke diaphragm
8. Pump cup
9. Duty-cycle solenoid

10. Idle-stop solenoid
11. Idle needle plug
12. Throttle modulator

Holley 6520 carburetor exploded view

Rochester Carburetors

QUADRAJET

ROCHESTER QUADRAJET MODELS
Chrysler Corporation
(All measurements in inches or degrees)

Year	Carburetor Number	Float Level	Air Valve Spring Turns	Fast Idle Cam	Choke Rod	Vacuum Kick	Air Valve Rod	Choke Unloader	Propane rpm
1988	17085431	13/32	1/2	20°	0.125	23°	0.025	32°	①
	17086425	15/32	1/2	20°	0.125	23°	0.025	32°	①
	17087175	13/32	3/4	20°	0.125	26°	0.025	38°	①
	17087176	13/32	3/4	20°	0.125	26°	0.025	30°	①
	17087177	13/32	1	20°	0.125	27°	0.025	33°	①
	17087245	15/32	5/8	20°	0.125	23°	0.025	32°	①

NOTE: Specified angle for use with angle gauge tool Choke coil lever adjustment is 0.120 in. on all models
① Refer to underhood specification sticker

1. Air cleaner gasket
2. Flange gasket
3. Air horn assembly
4. Secondary metering rod holder attaching screw
5. Secondary metering rod holder
6. Secondary metering rod
7. Choke lever
8. Choke lever attaching screw
9. Pump lever
10. Pump lever hinge pin
11. Air horn to throttle body screw assembly
12. Air horn to float bowl screw assembly

13. Air horn to float bowl (countersunk) screw
14. Air horn baffle
15. Pump stem seal retainer
16. Pump stem seal
17. Air horn to float bowl gasket
18. Pump assembly
19. Pump return spring
20. Power valve piston assembly
21. Primary metering rod
22. Primary metering rod (M2M, M4M only) spring
23. Power piston spring

24. Float bowl insert
25. Float hinge pin
26. Float
27. Float needle pull clip
28. Float needle
29. Float needle seat
30. Float needle seat gasket
31. Primary metering jet
32. Pump discharge (retainer) plug

33. Pump discharge ball
34. Pump well baffle
35. Throttle body to "T" hose
36. Secondary side vacuum break (choke diaphragm) "T" vacuum hose
37. "T" to secondary side vacuum break (choke diaphragm) hose
38. Secondary side (rear) vacuum break assembly (choke diaphragm)
39. Secondary side (rear) vacuum break assembly (choke diaphragm) attaching screw
40. Secondary side (rear) vacuum break (choke diaphragm) to choke link
41. Secondary side vacuum break (choke diaphragm) air valve lever link
42. Choke cover attaching rivet
43. Choke cover retainer
44. Electric choke cover and stat assembly
45. Choke housing assembly
46. Choke housing to float bowl screw and washer assembly
47. Choke stat lever attaching screw
48. Choke stat lever
49. Intermediate choke shaft lever and link assembly
50. Fast idle cam assembly
51. Intermediate choke lever
52. Choke link
53. Secondary throttle lockout lever
54. Intermediate choke shaft seal
55. Fuel inlet nut
56. Fuel inlet nut gasket
57. Fule inlet filter
58. Fuel filter spring
59. Throttle stop screw
60. Throttle stop srew spring
61. Throttle body assembly
62. Float bowl to throttle body gasket
63. Float bowl to throttle body screw assembly
64. Pump link
65. Idle mixture needle
66. Idle mixture needle spring
67. Idle mixture needle plug
68. Fast idle adjusting screw
69. Fast idle adjusting screw spring
70. Hose
71. Solenoid and bracket assembly
72. Bracket attach screw

Rochester Quadrajet carburetor exploded view

Rochester Quadrajet secondary metering adjustment

Rochester Quadrajet air valve spring adjustment

Rochester Quadrajet secondary lockout adjustment

Rochester Quadrajet secondary opening adjustment

Rochester Quadrajet air valve dashpot adjustment

Rochester Quadrajet vacuum break adjustment

Rochester Quadrajet idle vent adjustment

Rochester Quadrajet fast idle adjustment

Rochester Quadrajet float level adjustment

Rochester Quadrajet secondary closing adjustment

Rochester Quadrajet pump rod adjustment

Rochester Quadrajet choke coil lever adjustment

Rochester Quadrajet choke rod adjustment

FORD MOTOR COMPANY

Emission Calibration Numbers

Emission calibration numbers are used by Ford Motor Company to provide the technician with the necessary specifications to adjust a specific engine to the proper emission control levels.

The calibration numbers are listed on the lower right of the Vehicle Emission Control Information label, which is attached to the engine valve cover.

The information on the decal must be used when differences exist between the decal and other specification tables, unless otherwise noted by Ford Motor Company.

Asian Carburetor

MODEL Y

ASIAN MODEL Y
Ford Motor Company

(All measurements in millimeters and degrees)

Year	Carburetor Number	Choke Pulldown Setting	Fast Idle Cam Setting	Dechoke Setting	Float Setting (Dry)	Choke Cap Setting	Fast Idle
1988	E87E-9510-AA	18°	14.5° ①	195 sec.	47.1 mm	20°C	3200 ②

① On step #1   ② 3100 rpm for vehicles with less than 100 miles.

Aisan model Y carburetor—exploded view

JEEP

Carter Carburetors

MODEL BBD

CARTER MODEL BBD-2
Jeep
(All measurements in inches)

Year	Carburetor Number	Float Level	Step-up Piston Gap	Initial Choke Clearance	Fast Idle Cam Setting	Choke Cover Setting	Choke Unloader (Min.)	Fast Idle Speed (rpm) [1]
1988	8383	0.250	0.035	0.140	0.095	1 Rich	0.280	1850
	8384	0.250	0.035	0.140	0.095	1 Rich	0.280	1700
1989	8383	0.250	0.035	0.140	0.095	1 Rich	0.280	1850
	8384	0.250	0.035	0.140	0.095	1 Rich	0.280	1700
1990	8383	0.250	0.035	0.140	0.095	1 Rich	0.280	1850
	8384	0.250	0.035	0.140	0.095	1 Rich	0.280	1700

[1] On second step of fast idle cam with TCS solenoid and EGR disconnected.

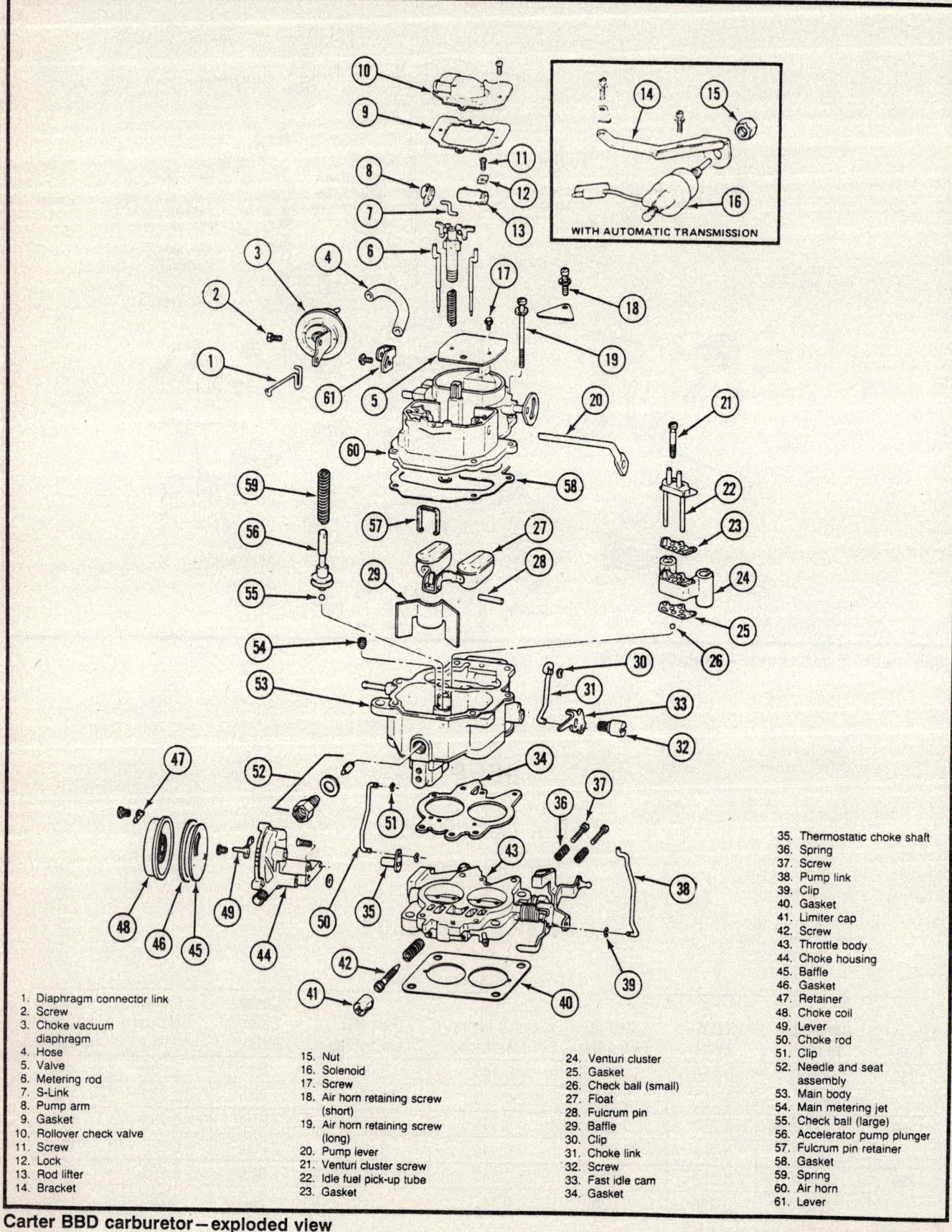

WITH AUTOMATIC TRANSMISSION

1. Diaphragm connector link
2. Screw
3. Choke vacuum diaphragm
4. Hose
5. Valve
6. Metering rod
7. S-Link
8. Pump arm
9. Gasket
10. Rollover check valve
11. Screw
12. Lock
13. Rod lifter
14. Bracket

15. Nut
16. Solenoid
17. Screw
18. Air horn retaining screw (short)
19. Air horn retaining screw (long)
20. Pump lever
21. Venturi cluster screw
22. Idle fuel pick-up tube
23. Gasket

24. Venturi cluster
25. Gasket
26. Check ball (small)
27. Float
28. Fulcrum pin
29. Baffle
30. Clip
31. Choke link
32. Screw
33. Fast idle cam
34. Gasket

35. Thermostatic choke shaft
36. Spring
37. Screw
38. Pump link
39. Clip
40. Gasket
41. Limiter cap
42. Screw
43. Throttle body
44. Choke housing
45. Baffle
46. Gasket
47. Retainer
48. Choke coil
49. Lever
50. Choke rod
51. Clip
52. Needle and seat assembly
53. Main body
54. Main metering jet
55. Check ball (large)
56. Accelerator pump plunger
57. Fulcrum pin retainer
58. Gasket
59. Spring
60. Air horn
61. Lever

Carter BBD carburetor—exploded view

Float Adjustment

1. Remove the air horn.
2. Apply light finger pressure to the vertical float tab to exert gentle pressure against the inlet needle.
3. Lay a straight-edge across the float bowl and measure the gap between the straight-edge and the top of the float at its highest point. The gap should be 0.250 in.
4. To adjust, remove the float and bend the lower tab. Replace the float and check the gap.

Fast Idle Cam Adjustment

1. Loosen the choke housing cover and turn it ¼ turn right. Tighten one screw.
2. Slightly open the throttle and place the fast idle screw on the second cam step.
3. Measure the distance between the choke plate and the air horn wall. The distance should be 0.095 in.
4. If adjustment is necessary, bend the fast idle cam link down to increase and up to decrease the gap.
5. Return the choke cover cap to the original setting.

Initial Choke Valve Clearance

1. Position the fast idle screw on the top step of the fast idle cam.
2. Using a vacuum pump, seat the choke vacuum break.

3. Apply light closing pressure in the choke plate to position the plate as far closed as possible without forcing it.
4. Measure the distance between the air horn wall and the choke plate, it should be 0.140 in. If it is not, bend the choke vacuum break link until it is.

Unloader Adjustment

1. With the throttle held fully open, apply pressure on the choke valve toward the closed position and measure the clearance between the lower edge of the choke valve and the air horn wall.

Carter BBD float level adjustment

Carter BBD initial choke valve adjustment

Carter BBD fast idle cam adjustment

Carter BBD choke unloader adjustment

2. The measurement should be 0.280 in. Adjust by bending the tang on the throttle lever which contacts the fast idle cam. Bend toward the cam to increase the clearance.

NOTE: Do not bend the unloader down so it binds or interferes with any other component.

Vacuum (Step Up) Piston Gap

1. Turn the adjusting screw, mounted on top of the unit, so the gap between the metering rod lifter lower edge and the top of the vacuum piston, is 0.035 in.
2. Counting the number of turns involved, turn the curb idle adjustment screw counterclockwise, until the throttle valves are completely closed.
3. Fully depress the vacuum piston, while exerting moderate pressure on the metering rod lifter tab. In this position, tighten the rod lifter lock screw.
4. Release the piston and rod lifter.

NOTE: The accelerator pump should now be adjusted.

5. Return the curb idle adjustment screw to its original position.

Accelerator Pump

1. Counting the number of turns involved, turn the curb idle adjustment screw counterclockwise, until the throttle valves are completely closed.
2. Open the choke valve so the fast idle cam will allow the throttle valves to seat in their bores.
3. Turn the curb idle adjustment screw clockwise, so it just barely touches the stop, then, turn it 2 full turns further.
4. Measure the distance between the surface of the air horn and the top of the accelerator pump shaft with a T-scale. The distance should be 0.520 in.
5. If the dimension is not correct, loosen the pump arm adjusting screw and rotate the sleeve to adjust the pump travel. Tighten the lock screw.
6. Return the curb idle screw to its original position.

Carter BBD piston gap adjustment

Carter BBD accelerator pump adjustment

Motorcraft Carburetors

MODEL 2150

MOTORCRAFT MODEL 2150
Jeep
(All measurements in inches)

Year	Carburetor Number	Float Level (Dry)	Fuel Level (Wet)	Initial Choke Valve Clearance	Fast Idle Cam Setting ②	Choke Cover Setting	Choke Unloader Valve Clearance	Fast Idle Speed ①	Bowl Vent Clearance	Rod Pump Location Hole
1988	4RHA2	0.575	0.930	0.136	0.086	2 Rich	0.350	1600	0.120	—
	5RHA2	0.328	0.930	0.118	0.076	Y	0.420	1600	NA	—
1989	5RHA2	0.328	0.930	0.118	0.076	Y	0.420	1600	NA	—
1990	5RHA2	0.328	0.930	0.118	0.076	V	0.420	1600	NA	—
1991-92	0RHA2	0.328	0.930	0.118	0.076	V	0.420	1600	NA	—

NA—Not available

① TCS solenoid and EGR disconnected, fast idle screw on 2nd cam step

② Measured between choke valve and air horn fast idle screw on 2nd cam step

Motorcraft 2150 carburetor—exploded view

Dry Float Adjustment

1. With the air horn assembly and the gasket removed raise the float by pressing down on the float tab until the fuel inlet needle is lightly seated.

2. Using a T-scale, measure the distance from the fuel bowl machined surface to either corner of the float ⅛ in. (3mm) from the free end.

3. To adjust bend the float tab and hold the fuel inlet needle

off its eat in order to prevent damage to the seat and the tip of the needle.

Wet Float Adjustment

— CAUTION —

Exercise extreme care when performing this adjustment as fuel vapors and liquid fuel are present and could cause personal injury if ignited.

1. Place the vehicle on a flat, level surface and run the engine to normal operating temperature. Turn off the engine and remove the air cleaner.
2. Remove the air horn attaching screws but leave the air horn in place.
3. Start the engine and let it idle for 1 minute. Shut off the engine and remove the air horn and gasket.
4. Use a T-scale to measure the vertical distance between the machined surface of the carburetor body and the fuel level in the bowl. Make this measurement as near the center of the bowl as possible. The proper distance is ¼ in. To adjust, bend the float tab.

NOTE: Every time an adjustment is made, the air horn must be replaced and the engine started and idled for 1 minute to stabilize the fuel level.

5. Install the air horn and gasket when adjustment is completed.

Fast Idle Cam Adjustment

1. Push down on the fast idle cam lever until the fast idle speed adjusting screw is contacting the second step (index) and against the shoulder of the high step.
2. Measure the clearance between the lower edge of the choke valve and air horn wall.
3. Adjust by turning the fast idle cam lever screw to obtain the proper specification.

Initial Choke Valve Clearance

1. Remove the choke cover shield.
2. Loosen the choke cover coil retaining screws. If rivets are used grind away and replace with screws.
3. Open the throttle and rotate the choke cover until the choke valve is held close.
4. Tighten 1 cover retaining screw.
5. Close the throttle with the fast idle screw adjustment screw on the top step of the cam.
6. Use a hand held vacuum pump and apply vacuum to hold the choke diaphragm aganst the setscrew.
7. Measure the clearance between the lower edge of the choke valve and the top of the air horn.
8. Adjust the clearance by turning the screw at the rear of the choke vacuum diaphragm.
9. Make a fast idle cam adjustment.

Choke Setting

The automatic choke setting is made by loosening the choke cover in the desired direction as indicated by an arrow on the face of the cover. the original setting will be satisfactory for most driving conditions. However, if the engine stumbles or stalls on acceleration during warmup, the choke may be set richer or leaner no more than 2 graduations from the original setting.

Unloader Adjustment

1. With the throttle held fully open, apply pressure on the choke valve toward the closed position and measure the clear-ance between the lower edge of the choke valve and the air horn wall.
2. Adjust by bending the tang on the throttle lever which contacts the fast idle cam. Bend toward the cam to increase the clearance.

NOTE: Do not bend the unloader down so it binds or interferes with any other component.

3. A clearance of 0.070 in. (1.8mm) must be between the unloader tang and the edge of the fast idle cam. Final unloader adjustment must always be done on the vehicle. The throttle should be fully opened by depressing the accelerator pedal to the floor. This is to assure that full throttle is obtained.

Motorcraft 2150 dry float level adjustment

Motorcraft 2150 wet float level adjustment

Motorcraft 2150 fast idle cam adjustment

Motorcraft 2150 initial choke valve clearance adjustment

Motorcraft 2150 choke unloader adjustment

Motorcraft 2150 unloader to fast idle cam clearance

CHRYSLER IMPORTS

Float Level Adjustment

1. Invert the float chamber cover assembly without a gasket.
2. Position a float gauge and measure the distance from the bottom of the float to the surface of the float chamber cover.
3. If not within specification the shim under the needle seat must be changed.
4. Adding or removing a shim will change the float level by 3 times the thickness of the shim.

Choke Breaker Opening

1. Disconnect the vacuum hose (yellow stripe) from the choke breaker.

2. With the engine idling, close the choke valve lightly until the choke valve stops.

3. Measure the choke valve to choke bore clearance to see if it is within the 1st stage specification. If necessary, remove the bi-

metal assembly and adjust the rod end opening to be within the 1st stage specification.

NOTE: When removing the bimetal assembly, put a mark on the electric choke body.

4. Reconnect the vacuum hose (yellow stripe) from the choke breaker and remeasure the choke valve to choke bore clearance.
5. If the clearance is not within the 2nd stage specification, adjust by the adjusting screw.

Throttle Position Sensor Adjustment

RAM 50 AND RAM RAIDER

1. Loosen the accelerator cable.
2. Turn the No. 1 and 2 idle speed adjusting screws counterclockwise enough to close the throttle valve completely. Record the number of turns. At this time, the fast idle control should have been released (the lever not resting on the fast idle cam).
3. Turn the ignition switch to **LOCK**.
4. Disconnect the large and small harness connector from the engine control unit.
5. Set the check switch of the ECI switch **OFF**.
6. Set the select switch of the ECI checker tool MD998451 to **A**.
7. Connect a carburetor test harness MD998456 to the engine control unit and the harness connectors.
8. Connect a voltmeter to the extension terminals of the ECI checker, then change the extension switch from **CHECK METER** down to the extension position.
9. Set the select switch and the check switch on the ECI checker to **A** and **3** respectively.
10. Turn the ignition switch to **ON** but do not start the engine.
11. Measure the output voltage of the TPS. The standard value is 0.25 volts.
12. If adjustment is necessary, loosen the TPS attaching screw and adjust by turning the TPS to the standard value.

NOTE: Turning the TPS clockwise increases the output voltage.

13. Set the check switch of the ECI checker to **OFF**.
14. Set the ignition switch to **LOCK**.
15. Disconnect the connectors of the ECI checker and the carburetor test harness from the engine control unit and body side harness connectors.
16. Connect the body side harness connectors to the engine control unit.
17. Tighten the No. 1 and No. 2 idle speed adjusting screws recorded earlier.
18. Adjust the play of the accelerator cable.
19. Check that the idle speed is as specified on the emission control label.

Dashpot Adjustment

1. Make sure the curb idle speed is correct, the engine temperature is at normal operating temperature, lights and accessories OFF, manual transmission in neutral or automatic transmission in **P**.
2. Start the engine and run at idle.
3. Close the throttle valve until the No. 2 idle speed adjusting screw contacts the free lever. Check the engine speed at that moment. If the engine speed is not as specified, adjust the dashpot by turning the No. 3 idle speed adjustment screw.
4. Release the free lever and verify that the engine returns to the idle speed slowly.

Chrysler No. 2 and No. 3 idle speed adjustment screws – 1988–89

ISUZU

Stromberg Carburetor

ISUZU CARBURETORS
Stromberg Models
(All measurements in inches)

Year	Carburetor Number	Float Level	Primary Throttle Valve	Choke Valve Opening	Unloader	Primary and Secondary Throttle Valve
1988	DFP384-205	0.059	—	0.031–0.050	0.105–0.050	0.272–0.331
1989	DFP384-205	0.059	—	0.031–0.050	0.105–0.050	0.272–0.331
1990	DFP384-205	0.059	—	0.031–0.050	0.105–0.129	0.272–0.331
1991–92	DFP384-205	0.059	—	0.031–0.050	0.105–0.129	0.272–0.331

1. Pump lever spring
2. Throttle return spring
3. Pump lever
4. Fuel nipple and strainer
5. Vent valve switch
6. Pump rod
7. Vacuum hose
8. Choke chamber assembly

9. Clip
10. Diaphragm assembly
11. Float chamber assembly
12. Throttle chamber assembly
13. Accelerator pump plunger assembly
14. Float needle assembly
15. Level gauge cover
16. Float
17. Diaphragm chamber
18. Jets
19. Injector weight plug, injector weight and check ball
20. Power jet
21. Main jet plugs and primary
22. Primary show air bleed

Isuzu (Stromberg) carburetor disassembled view— DFP384 models

44. Accelerator lever
45. Cruise lever
46. Kick lever
47. Spring hanger
48. Spring hanger
49. Main spring
50. Assist spring
51. Pump rod
52. Sleeve
53. Shaft collar
54. Shaft collar
55. Pump lever spring
56. Lock lever
57. Return spring
58. Throttle spring
59. Adjusting lever
60. Fast idle screw

61. Cam spring
62. Piston return spring
63. Level gauge cover
64. Level gauge
65. Injector weight
66. pump set screw
67. Injector spring
68. Collar
69. Rubber seal
70. Cylinder plate
71. Dust cover
72. Piston
73. Nipple set screw
74. Fule drain plug
75. Taper plug
76. Filter
77. Slow jet spring
78. Lead wire connector
79. O-ring
80. Needle valve
81. Wire clip
82. Main jet
83. Main jet
84. Main air bleed
85. Main air bleed
86. Slow jet
87. Slow jet
88. Slow air Bleed
89. Slow air Bleed
90. Power valve

1. Choke chamber
2. Counter choke lever
3. Not used
4. Solenoid switch vent valve
5. Float chamber
6. Solenoid slow cut valve
7. Throttle chamber
8. Throttle adjusting screw
9. Throttle adjusting spring
10. Idle adjusting screw
11. Idle adjusting spring
12. Idle adjusting washer
13. Rubber seal
14. Diaphragm chamber
15. Diaphragm
16. Diaphragm spring
17. Carburetor gasket kit
18. Screw and washer kit (A)
19. Screw and washer kit (B)
20. Fuel nipple
21. Stopping plate
22. Fast idle cam
23. Lead wire holder
24. Connector hanger
25. Fast idle adjusting lever
26. Fuel float
27. Drain plug lock plate
28. Connector hanger
29. Actuator bracket
30. Pipe connector holder
31. Connector pipe
32. Rubber hose
33. Rubber hose
34. Rubber hose
35. 2P connector
36. 1P connector
37. 3P connector
38. Rubber mounting
39. Rubber mounting plate
40. rubber mounting collar
41. Main actuator
42. Slow actuator
43. Pump lever

Isuzu (Stromberg) carburetor disassembled view — DCH340 models

1. Assist spring
2. Pump rod split pin with washer
3. Pump lever and split pin with washer
4. Return spring
5. Main spring
6. Slow cut solenoid valve
7. Fast idler cam and spring
8. Choke chamber screw and washer
9. Choke chamber assembly
10. Choke and float chamber gasket
11. Throttle chamber screw and washer
12. Float chamber assembly
13. Float and throttle chamber assembly
14. Throttle chamber assembly

Isuzu (Stromberg) carburetor disassembled view of the major components

10. Secondary main jet No. 170
11. Primary main jet No. 88
12. Piston
13. Pump cover
14. Piston return spring
15. Pump set screw
16. Injector spring
17. Injector weight
18. Taper plug

To slow cut solenoid valve

1. Vent cover
2. Duty solenoid valve
3. Choke chamber
4. Fuel nipple
5. Fuel filter
6. Level gauge cover
7. Level gauge and rubber seal
8. Float and collar
9. Needle valve

19. Slow jet spring
20. Primary slow jet No. 52
21. Secondary slow jet No. 100
22. Primary main air bleed No. 100
23. Secondary main air bleed No. 60
24. Primary slow air bleed
25. Float chamber

Isuzu (Stromberg) carburetor disassembled view of the choke chamber and float chamber

1. Diaphragm chamber assembly
2. Diaphragm chamber cover
3. Diaphragm spring
4. Diaphragm
5. Idler adjusting screw
6. Throttle adjusting screw
7. Throttle shaft nut and washer
8. Throttle lever
9. Spring hanger
10. Shaft collar
11. Fast idle adjusting lever and screw
12. Kick lever
13. Return spring
14. Return plate and sleeve
15. Adjusting lever
16. Throttle chamber

Isuzu (Stromberg) carburetor disassembled view of the throttle chamber

Float Level Adjustment

The fuel level is normal if it is within the mark on the window. If the level is outside the line, adjust by bending the float seat. The needle valve should have an effective stroke of about 0.059 in. The float stroke may be measured as follows:

1. Hold the carburetor with the bottom side up and fully raise the float.
2. Measure the distance between the valve stem (resting at its bottom position) and the float seat.
3. Normal clearance is 0.059 in. Bend the float stopper as necessary to adjust.

Choke Valve Opening Adjustment

1. Move the fast idle screw tip against the 2nd step of the fast idle cam.
2. Measure the clearance between the choke valve and the choke valve chamber wall.

3. If the clearance measured is not between 0.031–0.050 in., bend the counter lever tang to adjust.

Unloader Adjustment

1. Open the primary valve fully.
2. Measure the clearance between the choke valve and the choke valve chamber wall.
3. If the clearance measured is not between 0.105–0.129 in., bend the adjusting lever tang to adjust.

Primary and Secondary Throttle Valve Adjustment

1. Slowly open the primary throttle valve until the kick lever tang contacts the return plate.
2. Measure the clearance between the choke valve and the choke valve chamber wall.
3. If the clearance measured is not between 0.272–0.331 in., bend the kick lever tang to adjust.

Isuzu (Stromberg) float level adjustment

Isuzu (Stromberg) unloader adjustment

Isuzu (Stromberg) choke valve opening

Isuzu (Stromberg) primary and secondary throttle valve adjustment

MAZDA

MAZDA CARBURETORS
(All measurements in inches)

Year	Model	Fast Idle Cam	Fast Idle Opening	Float Level	Choke Valve Opening	Choke Diaphragm	Choke Unloader	Dashpot (rpm)	Secondary Throttle Valve
1988	B-2200	0.033–0.041	—	①	0.024–0.045	0.067–0.085	0.110–0.143	—	0.289–0.325
	B-2600	—	0.026–0.030	0.748–0.827	—	—	—	②	—
1989	B-2200	0.033–0.041	—	①	0.024–0.045	0.067–0.085	0.110–0.143	—	0.289–0.325
1990	B-2200	0.033–0.041	—	①	0.024–0.045	0.067–0.085	0.110–0.143	—	0.289–0.325
1991	B-2200	0.033–0.041	—	①	0.024–0.045	0.067–0.085	0.110–0.143	—	0.289–0.325
1992	B-2200	0.033–0.041	—	①	0.024–0.045	0.067–0.085	0.110–0.143	—	0.289–0.325

① Manual transmission: 0.457–0.496
Automatic transmission: 0.421–0.461

② Manual transmission: 1400–1600 rpm
Automatic transmission: 1900–2100 rpm

1. Accelerator pump connecting rod
2. Connecting spring
3. Air vent solenoid valve
4. Choke rod
5. Air horn
6. Automatic choke assembly
7. Float
8. Needle valve assembly
9. Accelerator pump plunger
10. Fuel bowl sight glass
11. Idle switch
12. Slow fuel cut solenoid valve
13. Coasting richer solenoid valve
14. Dashpot
15. Accelerator pump outlet check ball and spring
16. Accelerator pump inlet check ball
17. Primary slow jet
18. Secondary slow jet
19. Primary main jet
20. Secondary main jet
21. Plug
22. Primary venturi and nozzle
23. Secondary venturi and nozzle
24. Primary main air bleed
25. Secondary main air bleed
26. Main body
27. Vacuum diaphragm
28. Throttle link
29. Throttle body
30. Mixture adjusting screw

Mazda carburetor disassembled view—B2200

Float Level Adjustments

B2200

1. Without the gasket turn the air horn upside down and allow the float to lower by its own weight.
2. Measure the clearance between the float and the air horn.
3. Bend the float seat lip until the proper clearance is obtained.
4. Turn the air horn to its normal position and allow the float to lower by its own weight.
5. Measure the clearance between the bottom of the float and the air horn. If the clearance is not between 1.811–1.850 in., bend the float stopper to adjust.

B2600

1. Invert the float chamber cover assembly.
2. Measure the clearance between the bottom of the float to the surface of the float chamber cover without the gasket in place.
3. Add or remove needle valve seat shims to adjust the fuel level to specifications as follows:
   a. Pull out the float lever pin and remove the float.
   b. Remove the needle valve and retainer.
   c. Use pliers and remove the needle valve seat.
   d. Insert the necessary shims for adjustment and reinstall the needle valve, float and float chamber cover.

Choke Diaphragm Adjustment

B2200

1. Using a vacuum pump, apply a vacuum of about 15.7 in. Hg to the choke diaphragm vacuum tube.
2. Push the choke valve lightly to close it and measure the clearance.

Mazda float level adjustment with the air horn upside down—B2200

Mazda float level adjustment with the air horn at its normal position—B2200

Mazda float needle valve seat and retainer—B2600

Mazda float level measurement—B2600

Mazda choke diaphragm adjustment—B2200

Mazda valve seat shim location—B2600

3. If the clearance is not within specification, adjust by bending the choke lever.

Fast Idle Cam Adjustment

B2200

1. Set the fast idle cam to the second position.
2. Adjust the throttle valve clearance by turning the adjusting screw.

NOTE: The clearance will become larger as the screw is turned clockwise.

Fast Idle Opening Adjustment

B2600

1. With the carburetor at normal room temperature, insert the specified drill between the choke valve and the choke valve chamber wall.
2. Adjust the fast idle opening by using the fast idle adjusting screw.

Choke Valve Clearance Adjustment

B2200

1. Set the fast idle cam select to the second position.
2. Make sure the choke valve clearance is within specification.
3. Adjust the choke valve clearance by bending the starting arm. If a large adjustment is required, bend the choke rod.

Mazda float and pin—B2600

Mazda fast idle cam adjustment—B2200

Mazda fast idle opening adjustment—B2600

Mazda choke valve clearance adjustment—B2200

Choke Valve Setting Adjustment

B2600

1. Remove the choke cover. It may be necessary to grind off the rivet heads and replace with locking screws.
2. Remove the 2 lock screws and remove the choke valve pinion assembly.
3. Install the strangler spring to the choke lever.
4. Assemble, aligning the inscribed line or black painted line on the teeth of the choke pinion with the inscribed line on the cam lever.
5. Loosely tighten the new lock screws.
6. Set the choke valve by moving the pinion arm up or down, align the punch mark on the float chamber cover with the center of the 3 inscribed lines and secure the pinion arm with the lock screws.

Dashpot Adjustment

B2600

1. Warm the engine to normal operating temperature.
2. Connect a tachometer to the engine.
3. Push the dashpot rod up and loosen the dashpot adjusting screw.
4. Turn the adjusting screw clockwise and and set the engine speed to specification.

Unloader Adjustment

B2200

1. Open the primary throttle valve all the way.
2. Measure the choke valve clearance and if not within specification adjust by bending the tab.

Secondary Throttle Valve Adjustment

B2200

1. The secondary throttle valve should start to open when the primary throttle valve opens (50–52 degrees), and should be completely open at the same time that the primary throttle valve is fully open.
2. Check the clearance between the primary throttle valve and the wall of the throttle bore when the secondary throttle valve starts to open.
3. If the clearance is not within specification, bend the tab to adjust.

Fit the strangler spring to the choke lever—Mazda B2600

Aligning the cam lever and choke pinion—Mazda B2600

Mazda dashpot adjustment—B2200

Pinion arm lock screws—Mazda B2600

Mazda unloader adjustment—B2200

Align the center line with the punch mark—Mazda B2600

Mazda secondary throttle valve adjustment—B2200

MITSUBISHI

CHRYSLER IMPORTS/MITSUBISHI CARBURETORS
(All measurements in inches)

Year	Carburetor Number	Fast Idle Opening	Float Level	Choke Breaker Opening	Throttle Position Sensor (volts)	Dashpot (rpm)
1988	DIDEF-400	—	—	①	0.25	2000
	DIDEF-401	—	—	①	0.25	1500
	DIDEF-402	—	—	①	0.25	2000
	DIDEF-403	—	—	①	0.25	1500
	DIDEF-420	—	—	②	0.25	2000
	DIDEF-421	—	—	②	0.25	1500
	DIDEF-429	—	—	②	0.25	2000
	DIDEF-430	—	—	②	0.25	1500
	DIDEF-431	—	—	③	0.25	2000
	DIDEF-432	—	—	③	0.25	1500
	DIDEF-435	—	—	②	0.25	2000
	DIDEF-436	—	—	②	0.25	1500
	DIDEF-437	—	—	②	0.25	2000
	DIDEF-438	—	—	②	0.25	1500
	DIDEF-441	—	—	③	0.25	2000
	DIDEF-442	—	—	③	0.25	1500
	DIDEF-443	—	—	③	0.25	2000
	DIDEF-444	—	—	③	0.25	1500
1989	DIDEF-400	—	—	①	0.25	2000
	DIDEF-401	—	—	④	0.25	1500
	DIDEF-402	—	—	①	0.25	2000
	DIDEF-403	—	—	①	0.25	1500
	DIDEF-420	—	—	①	0.25	2000
	DIDEF-428	—	—	①	0.25	1500
	DIDEF-429	—	—	②	0.25	2000
	DIDEF-430	—	—	②	0.25	1500
	DIDEF-431	—	—	③	0.25	2000
	DIDEF-435	—	—	②	0.25	2000
	DIDEF-436	—	—	②	0.25	1500
	DIDEF-437	—	—	②	0.25	2000
	DIDEF-438	—	—	②	0.25	1500
	DIDEF-441	—	—	③	0.25	2000
	DIDEF-443	—	—	③	0.25	2000

① 1st stage: 0.087–0.094
   2nd stage: 0.114–0.122
② 1st stage: 0.098–0.106
   2nd stage: 0.126–0.133
③ 1st stage: 0.091–0.098
   2nd stage: 0.118–0.126
④ 1st stage: 0.079–0.087
   2nd stage: 0.114–0.122

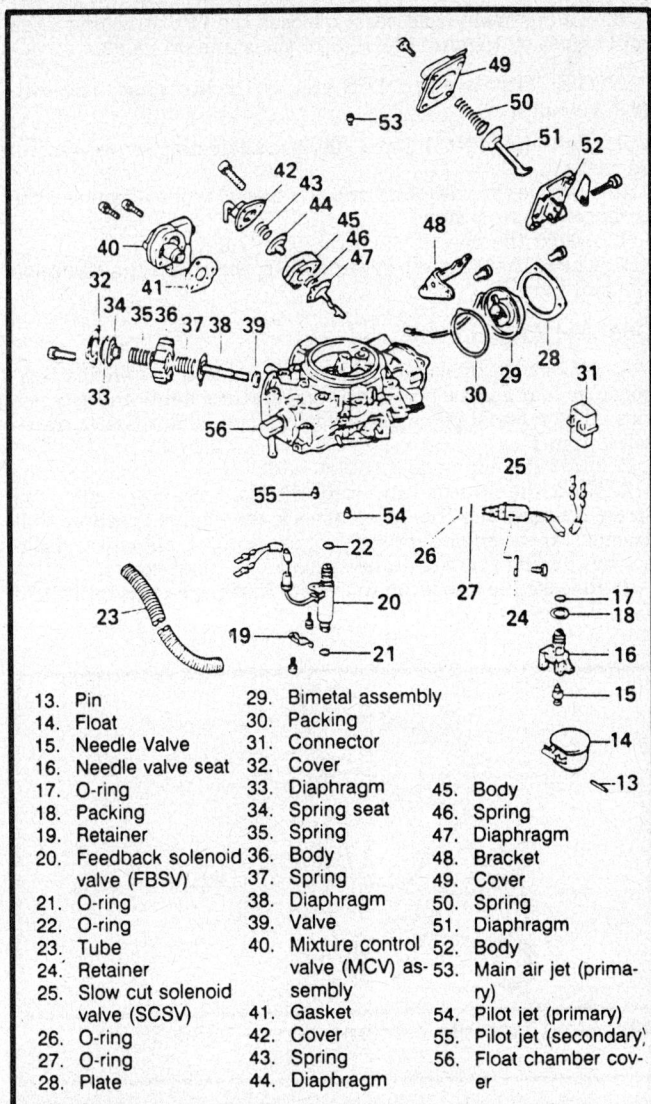

Mitsubishi carburetor upper half exploded view

Mitsubishi carburetor lower half exploded view

13. Pin	29. Bimetal assembly	
14. Float	30. Packing	
15. Needle Valve	31. Connector	
16. Needle valve seat	32. Cover	
17. O-ring	33. Diaphragm	45. Body
18. Packing	34. Spring seat	46. Spring
19. Retainer	35. Spring	47. Diaphragm
20. Feedback solenoid valve (FBSV)	36. Body	48. Bracket
21. O-ring	37. Spring	49. Cover
22. O-ring	38. Diaphragm	50. Spring
23. Tube	39. Valve	51. Diaphragm
24. Retainer	40. Mixture control valve (MCV) assembly	52. Body
25. Slow cut solenoid valve (SCSV)	41. Gasket	53. Main air jet (primary)
26. O-ring	42. Cover	54. Pilot jet (primary)
27. O-ring	43. Spring	55. Pilot jet (secondary)
28. Plate	44. Diaphragm	56. Float chamber cover

57. Steel ball	71. Enrichment jet	85. Vacuum hose
58. Weight	72. Spring	86. Depression chamber
59. Ball	73. Ball	87. Throttle position sensor
60. Plug	74. Pump cover assembly	88. Throttle lever
61. O-ring	75. Diaphragm	89. Cam follower
62. Ball	76. Spring	90. Fast idle adjusting screw
63. Screw	77. Pump body	91. Free lever
64. Gasket	78. Gasket	92. Apartment plate
65. Main jet (primary)	79. Hose	93. Idle speed adjusting screw
66. Main jet (secondary)	80. Auxiliary accelerator pump cover	94. Spring
67. Cover	81. Spring	95. Secondary lever
68. Spring	82. Diaphragm	96. Idle speed adjusting screw
69. Diaphragm	83. Check valve	97. Plug
70. Enrichment jet valve	84. Mixing body	98. Mixture adjusting screw
		99. Throttle body

Float Level Adjustment

1. Invert the float chamber cover assembly without a gasket.
2. Position a float gauge and measure the distance from the bottom of the float to the surface of the float chamber cover.
3. If not within specification the shim under the needle seat must be changed.
4. Adding or removing a shim will change the float level by 3 times the thickness of the shim.

Choke Breaker Opening

1. Disconnect the vacuum hose (yellow stripe) from the choke breaker.
2. With the engine idling, close the choke valve lightly until the choke valve stops.
3. Measure the choke valve to choke bore clearance to see if it is within the 1st stage specification. If necessary, remove the bimetal assembly and adjust the rod end opening to be within the 1st stage specification.

Mitsubishi float level adjustment

NOTE: When removing the bimetal assembly, put a mark on the electric choke body.

4. Reconnect the vacuum hose (yellow stripe) from the choke breaker and remeasure the choke valve to choke bore clearance.

5. If the clearance is not within the 2nd stage specification, adjust by the adjusting screw.

Throttle Position Sensor Adjustment

MONTERO AND PICK-UP

1. Loosen the accelerator cable.
2. Turn the No. 1 and 2 idle speed adjusting screws counterclockwise enough to close the throttle valve completely. Record the number of turns. At this time, the fast idle control should have been released (the lever not resting on the fast idle cam).
3. Disconnect the carburetor connectors.
4. Connect the special test harness tool MD998474 between the disconnected connectors.
5. Connect a digital voltmeter between the No. 2 red sensor output terminal and the No. 8 blue sensor (ground) of the carburetors connectors.
6. Turn the ignition switch to **ON** but do not start the engine.
7. Measure the output voltage of the TPS. The standard velue is 0.25 volts.

8. If adjustment is necessary, loosen the TPS attaching screw and adjust by turning the TPS to the standard value.

NOTE: Turning the TPS clockwise increases the output voltage.

9. Tighten the No. 1 and 2 idle speed adjusting screws recorded earlier.
10. Remove the voltmeter and the special tool and connect the carburetor's connector.
11. Adjust the play of the accelerator cable.
12. Check that the idle speed is as specified on the Emission Control Label.

Dashpot Adjustment

1. Make sure the curb idle speed is correct, the engine temperature is at normal operating temperature, lights and accessories OFF, manual transmission in neutral or automatic transmission in **P**.
2. Start the engine and run at idle.
3. Close the throttle valve until the No. 2 idle speed adjusting screw contacts the free lever. Check the engine speed at that moment. If the engine speed is not as specified, adjust the dashpot by turning the No. 3 idle speed adjustment screw.
4. Release the free lever and verify that the engine returns to the idle speed slowly.

Mitsubishi choke breaker opening measurement

Mitsubishi No. 1 and No. 2 idle speed adjusting screws—1988–89

Mitsubishi fast idle cam and lever—1988–89

Mitsubishi TPS adjustment—1988–89

SUZUKI

SUZUKI CARBURETORS
(All measurements in inches)

Year	Model	Float Level	Choke Unloader	Fast Idle Clearance	Choke Piston	Choke Valve Clearance
1988	Samurai	0.31	0.10–0.12	0.10–0.12	①	0.004–0.023②
1989	Samurai	0.31	0.10–0.12	0.10–0.12	①	0.004–0.023②
	Sidekick	0.31	0.10–0.12	0.118–0.137	①	0.004–0.023②

① See procedure in text
② At 75°F (25°C)

Float Adjustment

The fuel level in the float chamber should be within the round mark at the center of the level gauge. If the level is not found within the round mark adjust as follows:

1. Remove the air horn and invert it.
2. To find the float level, measure the distance between the float and the mating surface of the air horn without the gasket.
3. If the float level is not to specification, bend the tongue up or down to adjust.
4. Check the float height with the float weight applied to the needle valve. Use a gauge such as a drill or bolt that is the correct thickness and bend the tongue to adjust.

1. Level gauge
2. Round mark
3. Fuel level

Suzuki fuel level adjustment

1. Air horn
2. Float
3. Float level
4. Tongue

Suzuki float level adjustment

Choke Valve Clearance Adjustment

1. Check the choke valve for smooth movement.
2. Make sure the choke valve is closed almost completely when ambient temperature is below 77°F and the engine is cold.
3. Measure the clearance between the choke valve and the carburetor bore.
4. If the clearance is found excessively large or small, check the strangler spring, choke piston and each link in the choke system for smooth operation. Lubricate as necessary.
5. If clearance is still out of specification, remove the carbure-

FEELER GAUGE

CHOKE VALVE

Suzuki choke valve to carburetor bore measurement

1. Choke piston
2. Choke valve shaft
3. Strangler spring

Suzuki choke linkage

1. Air Horn
2. Float chamber
3. Throttle chamber
4. Pump boot
5. Pump lever
6. Pump rod
7. Bracket
8. Screw
9. Thermo element holder
10. Seal
11. Thermo element
12. Choke piston
13. Delay valve
14. Switch vent solenoid
15. Vacuum switching valve
16. 3-way joint
17. Vacuum transmitting valve
18. Primary slow air No. 1 bleeder
19. Secondary slow air bleeder
20. Mixture control solenoid
21. Solenoid valve seal
22. Needle valve filter
23. Needle valve gasket
24. Needle valve
25. Float
26. Air horn gasket
27. Connector (5 terminal)
28. Connector (4 terminal)
29. Connector (1 terminal)
30. Injector weight
31. Injector spring
32. Injector weight
33. Ball
34. Primary slow air No. 2 bleeder
35. Primary slow jet
36. Primary main air bleeder
37. Secondary main air bleeder
38. Spring
39. Secondary slow jet
40. Idle micro jet
41. Wide open micro switch
42. Idle up actuator
43. Solenoid valve
44. Washer
45. Level gauge seal
46. Level gauge
47. Level gauge gasket
48. Micro switch bracket
49. Primary main jet
50. Secondary main jet
51. Drain plug gasket
52. Drain plug
53. Float pin
54. Insulator
55. Secondary actuator (diaphragm)

Suzuki (Samurai) carburetor exploded view

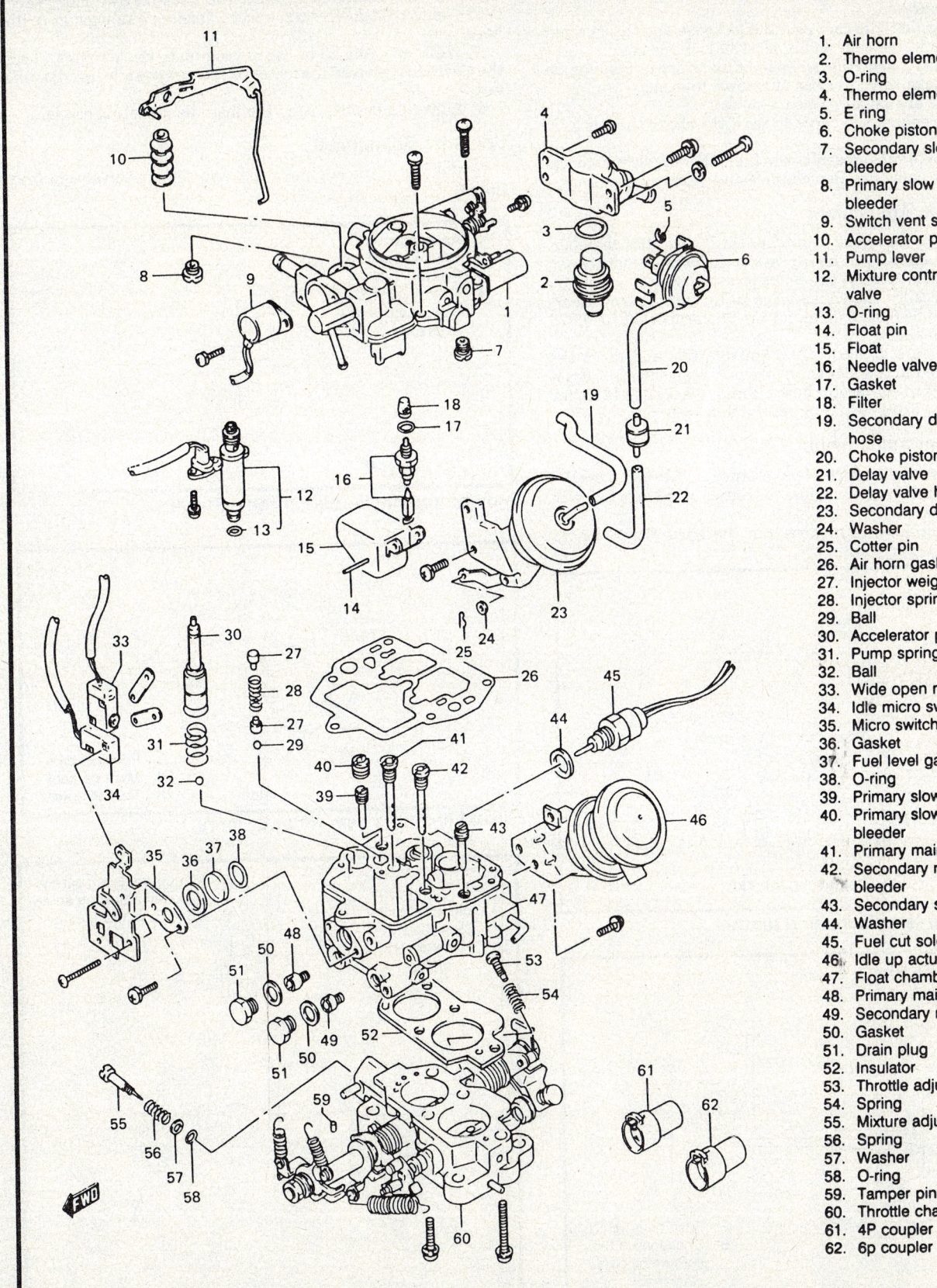

1. Air horn
2. Thermo element
3. O-ring
4. Thermo element holder
5. E ring
6. Choke piston
7. Secondary slow air bleeder
8. Primary slow air Noi. 1 bleeder
9. Switch vent solenoid
10. Accelerator pump boot
11. Pump lever
12. Mixture control solenoid valve
13. O-ring
14. Float pin
15. Float
16. Needle valve
17. Gasket
18. Filter
19. Secondary diaphragm hose
20. Choke piston hose
21. Delay valve
22. Delay valve hose
23. Secondary diaphragm
24. Washer
25. Cotter pin
26. Air horn gasket
27. Injector weight
28. Injector spring
29. Ball
30. Accelerator pump piston
31. Pump spring
32. Ball
33. Wide open micro switch
34. Idle micro switch
35. Micro switch bracket
36. Gasket
37. Fuel level gauge
38. O-ring
39. Primary slow jet
40. Primary slow air No. 2 bleeder
41. Primary main air bleeder
42. Secondary main air bleeder
43. Secondary slow jet
44. Washer
45. Fuel cut solenoid valve
46. Idle up actuator
47. Float chamber
48. Primary main jet
49. Secondary main jet
50. Gasket
51. Drain plug
52. Insulator
53. Throttle adjusting screw
54. Spring
55. Mixture adjusting screw
56. Spring
57. Washer
58. O-ring
59. Tamper pin
60. Throttle chamber
61. 4P coupler
62. 6p coupler

Suzuki (Sidekick) carburetor exploded view

tor from the intake manifold and remove the idle up actuator from the carburetor.

6. Turn the fast idle cam counterclockwise and insert a pin into the holes in the cam and bracket to lock the cam.

7. Using pliers, bend the choke lever up or down. Bending up causes the choke valve to close and down to open.

8. Start the engine and warm it up fully.

9. Stop the engine and check to see if the choke valve is fully open.

10. If the choke valve doesn't open fully, the wax element or its link system is defective. Replace defective parts as necessary.

Choke Piston Adjustment

1. Disconnect the choke piston hose at the throttle chamber.

2. While pushing down lightly on the choke valve to its closed position, apply vacuum to the choke piston hose with a vacuum gauge and measure the choke valve to carburetor bore clearance. It should be 0.04–0.05 in. for the Samarai or 0.070–0.078 in. for the Sidekick.

3. With vacuum applied, use a suitable tool and move the choke piston rod in towards the choke piston and check to see if the choke valve to carburetor bore clearance is 0.13–0.14 in. for the Samarai or 0.142–0.163 in. on the Sidekick.

Fast Idle Cam Adjustment

1. Make sure the ambient temperature is between 71–81°F and that the mark on the cam and the center of the cam follower are in alignment.

2. Disconnect the vacuum hose from the Three Way Solenoid

Valve (TWSV) on the Samurai or the Vacuum Switching Valve (VSV) on the Sidekick and connect a vacuum pump gauge to it's hose.

3. While applying 15 in. Hg of vacuum to the actuator, check the clearance between the actuator rod and the idle up adjusting screw.

4. Adjust as needed using the fast idle adjusting screw.

Unloader Adjustment

1. Make sure the engine is cool and the choke valve is fully closed.

1. Apply vacuum
2. Choke piston rod
3. Suitable tool
4. Choke valve to carburetor bore clearance

Moving the choke piston rod—Suzuki

1. Fast idle cam
2. Mark on cam
3. Cam follower

Suzuki cam and cam follower mark

CHOKE LEVER TAB

Suzuki choke lever adjusting tab

1. Choke piston hose
2. Choke piston
3. Apply vacuum
4. Choke valve

5. Push here lightly
6. Choke valve to carburetor bore clearance

Suzuki choke piston measurement

1. TWSV
2. Vacuum hose
3. Idle up actuator
4. Clearance
5. Actuator rod
6. Idle up adjusting screw
7. Fast idle adjusting screw
8. Vaccum pump gauge

Applying vacuum to the TWSV—Samurai

2. Fully open the throttle valve and measure the choke valve to carburetor bore clearance.

3. If necessary, bend the unloader arm to adjust.

1. Unloader arm
2. Fast idle cam
3. Accelerator cable

Suzuki unloader lever arm

1. VSV
2. Vacuum hose
3. Idle up actuator
4. Actuator rod
5. Idle up adjusting screw
6. Fast idle adjusting screw
7. Vaccum pump gauge
8. Clearance

Applying vacuum to the VSV—Sidekick

TOYOTA

TOYOTA CARBURETORS
(All measurements in inches or degrees)

Year	Carburetor Number	Float Level	Throttle Valve Angle	Secondary Touch Angle	Fast Idle Angle	Choke Unloader Angle	Idle-Up Angle
1988	All	②	90°	59°	23°	45°	16.5°
1989	All	②	90°	59°	①	45°	16.5°
1990	All	②	90°	59°	①	45°	16.5°

NOTE: Use angle degree tool for angle specifications
① Federal and Canada: 24.5 degrees
    California: 23.0 degrees
② Raised position: 0.386 in.
    Lowered position: 1.89 in.

Fuel Level

The fuel level is about even with the center of the sight glass.

Float Level Adjustment

1. Allow the float to hang down by its own weight.
2. Measure the clearance between the float top and the air horn without the gasket.
3. The float level (raised position), should be 0.386 in. If necessary, bend the upper portion of the float tab to adjust to specification.
4. Lift up the float and measure the distance between the air horn and the float bottom.
5. The float level (lowered position), should be 0.189 in. If necessary, bend the lower portion of the float tab to adjust to specification.

Throttle Valve Opening (Angle) Adjustment

1. Measure the full opening angle of the of the primary and secondary throttle valves.

2. Both the primary and secondary throttle valve openings should be 90 degrees from the horizontal plane.

3. Adjust by bending the respective throttle arm levers of either valve.

Fuel Level

Toyota float level sight glass

Secondary Touch Angle Measurement

1. Measure the primary throttle valve opening at the same time the second throttle valve just starts to open.
2. The standard angle is 59 degrees from the horizontal plane.
3. Adjustment is not necessary, this is a rebuilding reference only.

Fast Idle Angle Adjustment

1. Set the throttle shaft lever to the first step of the fast idle cam.
2. Measure the primary throttle valve angle with the choke valve fully closed.
3. Adjust by turning the fast idle adjusting screw.

Choke Unloader Adjustment

1. Measure the choke valve angle with the primary throttle valve fully opened.
2. Adjust by bending the primary throttle arm.

Idle-Up Angle Adjustment

1. Apply vacuum to the idle-up diaphragm.
2. Measure the throttle valve opening angle.
3. Adjust the angle by turning the idle adjusting screw.

Dashpot Adjustment

1. Open the throttle valve until the throttle lever separates from the dashpot end.
2. Release the throttle valve gradually, and check the dashpot touch angle when the throttle lever touches the dashpot end.
3. If the dashpot touch angle is not 24½ degrees from the horizontal plane, unlock the locknut and adjust the angle by turning the dashpot diaphragm.

Toyota fast idle angle adjustment

Toyota throttle valve opening adjustment

Toyota choke unloader adjustment

Toyota secondary touch angle adjustment

Toyota idle-up adjustment

DRIVE AXLES

Differential Operation

GENERAL INFORMATION

The differential is an arrangement of gears that permits the wheels to turn at different speeds when cornering and divides the torque between the axle shafts. The differential gears are mounted on a pinion shaft and the gears are free to rotate on this shaft. The pinion shaft is fitted in a bore in the differential case and is at right angles to the axle shafts.

The front drive axle on four wheel drive vehicles is similar to the rear drive axle. In additional, most Pick-Ups are available with an optional limited slip or "locking differential" providing extra traction for heavy-duty conditions such as snow plowing. Limited slip differentials are usually limited to the rear drive axle of 4WD vehicles.

Power flow through the differential is as follows. The drive pinion, which is turned by the driveshaft, turns the ring gear. The ring gear, which is bolted to the differential case, rotates the case. The differential pinion forces the pinion gears against the side gears. In cases where both wheels have equal traction, the pinion gears do not rotate on the pinion shaft, because the input force of the pinion gear is divided equally between the 2 side gears. Consequently the pinion gears revolve with the pinion shaft, although they do not revolve on the pinion shaft itself. The side gears, which are splined to the axle shafts and meshed with the pinion gears, rotate the axle shafts.

Gear Ratios and Axle Identification

The drive axle of a vehicle is said to have a certain axle ratio. This number (usually a whole number and a decimal fraction) is actually a comparison of the number of gear teeth on the ring gear and the pinion gear. For example, a 4:11 rear means that theoretically, there are 4:11 teeth on the ring gear to every tooth on the pinion. Actually, on a typical 4:11 rear gear, there are 37 teeth on the ring gear and nine teeth on the pinion gear. By dividing the number of teeth on the pinion gear into the number of teeth on the ring gear, the numerical axle ratio (4:11) is obtained.

Many axles will have a small metal tag either pinned to the axle housing or attached to one of the cover or gear carrier bolts. This tag may contain axle identification information and often will have the gear ratio numbers on it. Use care not to loose this tag when servicing the axle. Always reinstall at axle assembly.

General Motors corporate axles should be identified by the alphabetic code on the right axle tube near the carrier.

Dana axles are identified by the part number on the right axle tube next to the carrier. The model number is cast on the carrier. The carrier cover does not have a drain plug. There is a fill plug on the cover.

Drive Axle Types

FULL FLOATING AXLES

Support of the vehicle and the payload weight is by the axle housing. The wheels are driven by splined shafts which float on bearings within the axle housing. These axles usually contain an inboard and outboard bearing which helps contain the axle if it should break. It can usually be identified by the large outboard drive hub. This type of axle is often found on heavy-duty trucks.

SEMI-FLOATING AXLE

This axle design provides for the support of the payload and vehicle weight to be carried by the axle shaft through the wheel bearings to the axle housing. Usually, only an outboard bearing is used. This is most common type of drive axle in use.

SINGLE REDUCTION AXLE

Final drive ratio is obtained by the use of a single ring gear and pinion set.

LOCK-UP TYPE DIFFERENTIALS

Unlike the standard differential, the limited slip or locking differential equally divides the torque load between the driving wheels. Usually a clutch-pack arrangement is used in this type axle.

A vehicle equipped with a locking differential can be operated on any surface (sand, snow, etc.) with a minimum of slippage through one wheel and provides the greatest power to the wheel getting traction. A vehicle with a standard differential provides power to the wheel that's easiest to turn; that is, the one experi-

Drive axle identification tags. Note gear ratio markings. Ford application shown—typical

Integral carrier rear axle with full-floating axles. Note heavy duty outboard hub to help identify this axle type. 1990 Ford setup for rear anti-lock brakes shown—typical

Integral carrier rear axle with semi-floating axles. Note the flange for the brake backing plate instead of an outboard hub to help identify this axle. 1990 Ford setup for rear anti-lock brakes shown—typical

encing the poorest traction while the other wheel may be gripping well.

When negotiating a turn, the locking differential allows the outer wheel to turn faster than the inner. When traveling in a straight direction, and the vehicle loses traction over a rough or slippery road, the clutches will lock-up and neither wheel will spin. A specified lubricant must be used for locking differentials.

Identification of locking axles can often be made by lifting both rear wheels off the ground and turning them. If both rear wheels turn in the same direction at the same time, the vehicle is equipped with a locking or limited-slip differential. Another means of identification is by removing the filler plug if on the rear cover and using a flashlight to look through the filler hole to identify the type of differential case.

Note that some axles which provide better traction than a conventional differential are more of a "limited slip" axle and really are not a true locking differential. Extreme differences in traction conditions at the driving wheels may permit one wheel to spin.

The overhaul procedures are basically the same as for the conventional rear axle assemblies. The differences are within the differential carrier case where the lock-up mechanism is located.

In some instances where wear is noted within the lock-up mechanism, the lock-up assembly should be replaced as a unit.

Lubrication

Proper axle lubrication is a key to drive axle life. In some cases, a multi-purpose gear lubricant rated GL-5 will be used. Hypoid gear type axles in which the center line of the drive pinion is mounted below the center line of the ring gear, require a lubricant designed to protect this type of axle. Generally, hypoid axle lube has extra Extreme Pressure (EP) additives. Most Pick-Ups use a type of hypoid axle. Vehicles equipped with locking type differentials may also require a special lubricant and/or additive or the differential will chatter and wear.

Some axles such as Dana do not have a drain plug. The cover should be loosened and removed from the housing to allow drainage. Reseal cover with Room Temperature Vulcanizing (RTV) silicone rubber sealer.

Should a drive axle become submerged in water as in launching a boat or in off-road use, the lubricant must be changed immediately to avoid the possibility of early axle failure resulting from the contamination of the lubricant by water.

PINION GEARS

PINION SHAFT

SIDE GEAR CLUTCH

SIDE GEAR CLUTCH

PINION SHAFT LOCK BOLTS   SIDE GEARS

PINION SHAFT

CASE

PINION SHAFT LOCK BOLT

SIDE GEAR

PLATE

DISC

DISHED SPACER

PINION

WASHER

RETAINER CLIP

Exploded view of locking rear differential showing clutch plates, differential carrier and side gears— typical

Differential Diagnosis

The most essential part of axle service is proper diagnosis of the problem. Any gear driven unit will produce a certain amount of noise. Acceptable or normal noise can be classified as a slight noise heard only at certain speeds or under unusual conditions. This noise tends to reach a peak at 40–60 mph depending on the road condition, load, gear ratio and tire size. Frequently, other noises are mistakenly diagnosed as coming from the axle assembly. Vehicle noises from tires, transmission, driveshaft, U-joints and front and rear wheel bearings will often be mistaken as coming from the front or rear axle assemblies.

EXTERNAL NOISE ELIMINATION

It is advisable to make a thorough road test to determine whether the noise originates in the axle assembly or whether it originates from the tires, engine transmission, wheel bearings or road surface. Noise originating from other places cannot be corrected by overhauling the axle assemblies.

ROAD NOISE

Brick roads or rough surfaced concrete, may cause a noise which can be mistaken as coming from the axle assembly. Driving on a different type of road (smooth asphalt or dirt) will determine whether the road is the cause of the noise. Road noise is usually the same on drive or coast conditions.

TIRE NOISE

Tire noise can be mistaken as axle assembly noises. Snow tread and mud tread tires or tires worn unevenly will frequently cause vibrations which seem to originate elsewhere. To check, temporarily and for test purposes only, inflate the tires to 40–50 lbs. This will significantly alter the noise produced by the tires, but will not alter noise from the axle assembly. Noises from the axle assembly will normally cease at speeds below 30 mph on coast, while tire noise will continue at lower tone as vehicle speed is decreased. The axle noise will usually change from drive conditions to coast conditions, while tire noise will not. Do not forget to lower the tire pressure to normal after the test is complete.

ENGINE AND TRANSMISSION NOISE

Engine and transmission noises can also be mistaken for axle noise. Road test the vehicle and determine at which speeds the noise is most pronounced. Stop the vehicle in a quiet place to avoid interfering noises. With the transmission in **N** position, run the engine slowly through the engine speeds corresponding to the vehicle speed at which the noise was most noticeable. If a similar noise was produced with the vehicle standing still, the noise is not in the axle assemblies but somewhere in the engine or transmission.

FRONT WHEEL BEARING NOISE

Front wheel bearing noises, sometimes confused with axle noises, will not change when comparing drive and coast conditions. While holding the vehicle speed steady, lightly apply the footbrake. This will often cause wheel bearing noise to lessen, as some of the weight is taken off the bearing. Front wheel bearings are easily checked by raising the wheels and spinning the wheels. Shaking the wheels will also determine if the wheel bearings are excessively loose.

AXLE ASSEMBLY NOISE

If a logical test of the vehicle shows that the noise is not caused by external items, it can be assumed that the noise originates from the axle assembly. The axle assembly should be tested on a smooth level road to avoid road noise. It is not advisable to test the axle by raising the wheels and running the vehicle.

True axle noises generally fall into 2 classes; gear noise and bearing noises and can be caused by a faulty driveshaft, faulty wheel bearings, worn differential or pinion shaft bearings, U-joint misalignment, worn differential side gears and pinions, or mismatched, improperly adjusted, or scored ring and pinion gears.

REAR WHEEL BEARING NOISE

A rough rear wheel bearing causes a vibration or growl which will continue with the vehicle coasting or in neutral. A brinelled rear wheel bearing will also cause a knock or click noise. Raise the rear wheels and spin the wheel slowly, listening for signs of a rough or brinelled wheel bearing.

DIFFERENTIAL SIDE GEAR AND PINION NOISE

Differential side gears and pinions seldom cause noise since their movement is relatively slight on straight ahead driving. Noise produced by these gears will be more noticeable on turns.

PINION BEARING NOISE

Pinion bearing failures can be distinguished by their speed of rotation, which is higher than side bearings or axle bearings. Rough or brinelled pinion bearings cause a continuous low pitch whirring or scraping noise beginning at low speeds.

SIDE BEARING NOISE

Side bearings produce a constant rough noise, which is slower than the pinion bearing noise.

Bearing Diagnosis

This section will help in the diagnosis of bearing failure and the causes. Bearing diagnosis can be very helpful in determining the cause of axle assembly failure.

When disassembling an axle assembly, the general condition of all bearings should be noted and classified where possible. Proper recognition of the cause will help in correcting the problem and avoiding a repeat failure. Some of the common causes of bearing failure are:

1. Abuse during assembly or disassembly.
2. Improper assembly methods.
3. Improper or inadequate lubrication.
4. Bearing contact with dirt or water.
5. Wear caused by dirt or metal chips.
6. Corrosion or rust.
7. Seizing due to overloading.
8. Overheating.
9. Fretting of the bearing seats.
10. Brinelling from impact or shock loading.
11. Manufacturing defects.
12. Pitting due to fatigue.

To avoid damage to the bearing from improper handling, it is best to treat a used bearing the same as a new bearing. Always work in a clean area with clean tools. Remove all outside dirt from the housing before exposing a bearing and clean all bearing seats before installing a bearing. Never spin a bearing either by hand or with compressed air.

Drive Axle Service

COMPONENT INSPECTION AND REPLACEMENT

Cleaning Bearings

Proper bearing cleaning is important. Bearings should always be cleaned separately from other rear axle parts.

1. Soak all bearings in clean kerosene or diesel fuel oil.

NOTE: Gasoline should not be used nor should bearings be cleaned in hot caustic solution tank.

2. Soak bearings in cleaning solution until all old lubricant is loosened. Brush bearings with soft bristled brush until all dirt has been removed. Remove loose particles of dirt by striking flat against a wood block.

3. Rinse bearings in clean fluid. While holding races to prevent rotation, blow dry with compressed air.

NOTE: Do not spin bearings while drying.

4. After bearings have been inspected, lubricate thoroughly with regular axle lubricant. Wrap each bearing in clean cloth or paper until ready to use.

Cleaning Parts

Immerse all parts in cleaning fluid and clean thoroughly. Use a stiff bristle brush as required to remove foreign deposits. Clean all lubricant passages or channels in pinion cage, carrier, caps and retainers. Make certain the interior of housing is thoroughly cleaned. Clean vent plugs and breathers.

Small parts such as cap screws, bolts, studs, nuts and etc., should be cleaned thoroughly.

Inspection

Magna Flux or equivalent test all steel parts, except ball and roller bearings, to detect presence of wear and cracks.

Bearings

Rotate each bearing and check to see if the rollers are worn, chipped, rough or in any other way damaged. Check the cage to see if it is in any way damaged. If either the bearing rollers or the cage are damaged the bearing must be replaced.

Gears

Examine drive gear and drive pinion, differential pinions and differential side gears carefully, for damaged teeth, worn spots in surface hardening, distortion and where drive gear is attached to differential case with rivets, inspect rivets for looseness, replace loose rivets. Check radial clearances between differential side gears and differential case. Check fit of differential pinions on spider.

Differential Case

Inspect case for cracks, distortion or damage. If in good condition, thoroughly clean case and cover. Assemble case with bolts and mount in lathe centers or V-block stand. If a lathe is not available, install differential side bearings and mount case in differential carrier. Install dial indicator and check differential case run out.

Differential case with drive gear installed is checked in the same manner, except that dial indicator reading must be taken at gear instead of at case flange.

Axle Shafts

Examine splined end of axle shaft for twisted or cracked splines, twisted shaft and worn dowel holes in flange. Install new shafts if necessary.

If available, install axle shaft assembly in lathe centers and check shaft run out with dial indicator. Set up so dial indicator shaft end contacts inner surface of flange near outer edge of flange. Check flange run out.

Shims

Carefully inspect shims for uniform thickness. Where various thickness of shims are used in a pack, it is recommended that the thickest shims be used between the thin shims.

Thrust Washers

Replace all thrust washers upon installation.

Spider Assembly

Carefully inspect spider components for wear or defects. "Spin-Out" damage is common on differential spiders. This results when one wheel is on dry pavement and the other on a slippery surface. A non-locking drive axle will spin the wheel with no traction. An inattentive driver can exceed the vehicle's axle speed design limits and damage the spider gear assembly from lack of lubrication and overheating. These components should always be carefully inspected at overhaul.

Pinion Bushings

Examine bushings (when used) for excessive wear, looseness or damage. Check fit or gears on spider for excessive clearance.

Axle Housing Sleeves

Sleeves showing damaged threads, wear or other damage should be replaced as necessary.

Housing Check

BEFORE REMOVAL

A check for bent axle housing can be made with unit in vehicle; however, conventional alignment instruments can be used, if available.

1. Raise and safely support rear axle. Block the axle under each spring seat.

2. Check wheel bearing adjustment and adjust, if necessary. Check wheels for looseness and tighten wheel nuts, if necessary.

3. Place a chalk mark on outer side wall of tires at bottom. Measure across tires at chalk marks with a toe-in gauge.

4. Turn wheels half-way around so the chalk marks are posi-

tioned opposite of original location. Measure across tires again. If second measurement is 1/8 in. or more smaller than second measurement, axle housing has sagged and is bent. If second measurement exceeds first dimension by 1/8 in. or more, axle housing is bent at ends.

5. Turn chalk marks on both wheels so the marks are level with axle and at rear of vehicle. Take measurement with toe-in gauge at chalk marks; then, turn both chalk marks to front and level with axle and take another measurement. If measurement at front exceeds rear dimension by 1/8 in. or more, axle is bent to the rear. If the measurement condition is the reverse, the axle is bent forward.

AFTER REMOVAL

Place 2 straight-edges across the housing flanges and measure the distance between the ends of the straight-edges at a point about 12 inches from the tube center. Relocate the straight-edge 180 degrees and remeasure. If the straight-edges are parallel in both measurements within 3/32 in., the housing is serviceable.

Oil Seals

The surface of metal parts contacted by oil seals must be free of corrosion, pits and grooves. If abrasive cleaning fails to clean up the seal contact surface and restore smooth finish, a new part must be installed. Many oil seals now come with a thin stainless steel sleeve that is permanently installed on the shaft providing a smooth surface for the new seal at very little cost. This often saves an expensive and/or hard to get part.

Oil seals can be removed with a drift pin, preferably a soft brass drift. When removing a seal, be careful it does not become cocked and result in damage to the retainer. Clean surface of retainer carefully, so the seal will seat properly in retainer. Coat outer surface of seal retainer with a light coat of sealer to prevent lubricant leaks. Carefully start seal in retainer. Cutting, scratching or curling of lip of seal seriously impairs its efficiency and usually results in premature replacement. Lip of seal should be coated with a high temperature grease containing zinc oxide to help prevent scoring and damage to parts during installation. Seals must always be installed so the seal lip is toward the lubricant.

Measuring the pinion bearing preload torque with the pinion in a shop press. Rockwell 12 inch axle pinion shown, Chevrolet application — typical

Pinion Bearing Adjustments (Preload)

Pinion bearing must be adjusted for preload before assembly is installed in carrier. Do not install oil seal until after adjustment is made. Installation of seal would produce false rotating torque.

1. With pinion bearings and adjusting spacers (or shims) installed in cage, check bearing contact by rotating cage.

2. Using a press, apply pressure (approx. 20,000 lbs.) to outer bearing.

3. Wrap a length of soft wire around cage and pull on horizon-

tal line with spring scale. Rotating (not starting) torque should be within limits recommended by manufacturer.

NOTE: Another method of determining inch-pounds torque with a scale is to determine radius of cage. Multiply radius in inches by pounds pull required to rotate cage to determine inch-pounds torque. Example: An 8 in. diameter divided by 2 equals 4 in. radius. Multiply 4 in. (radius) by 5 pounds (pull) equals 20 in. pounds torque.

4. If press is not available, check preload torque by installing propeller shaft yoke, washer, and nut and torque to specifications; then check as previously explained. Remove yoke after correct adjustment is obtained.

Bevel Gear Shaft Bearing Adjustment

Bevel gear shaft bearings must be adjusted for preload before pinion and cage assembly and differential assembly are installed in carrier.

1. Wrap several turns of soft wire around gear teeth on cross shaft and pull on a horizontal line with spring scale. Rotating (not starting) torque should be used.

NOTE: Method of determining inch lbs. torque with scale is to determine radius. Multiply radius in inches by pounds pull required to rotate shaft to determine inch-pounds torque. Example: An 8 in. diameter divided by 2 equals 4 in. radius times 5 pounds (pull) equals 20 inch lbs. torque.

2. Remove or add shims from under cage or cap opposite bevel gear to obtain specified bearing preload.
3. When making bevel gear and pinion tooth contact or backlash adjustments it is sometimes necessary to remove or add shims from one side.

NOTE: Always remove or add an equal thickness to the opposite side so to maintain correct preload.

Gear Tooth Contact and Backlash
PINION DEPTH MEASUREMENT METHOD

Methods of adjusting pinions to obtain the proper depths will vary with the axle type and the manufacturer's recommendations. Pinion depth settings and gear teeth contact may be determined by the use of pinion setting gauges or by the use of marking dye on the gear teeth.

Drive axle major parts layout showing gear relationship and how shim placement affects that relationship including backlash and bearing preload—Dana axle shown—typical

Installation of pinion depth tools used to determine pinion position shim—Dana axle shown—typical

Checking pinion depth with special arbor tool and selective fit shims placed between crossbore arbor tool and gauge block.

Checking pinion depth with pinion blocks, arbor and discs which temporarily replace the bearings. A dial indicator is moved across the arbor to read deflection. Adjustment is by shims.

When using the gauge method, backlash is established after the pinion has been properly set. With the dye method, backlash is obtained first then the proper pinion tooth contact is established.

The pinion gauge method usually involves a direct reading micrometer, mounted on or through an arbor bar, set in adapter discs and located in the side carrier bearing cup locations on the differential housing and held in place by the bearing cup caps. The arbor bar coincides with and represents the center line of the axle shafts. A reading is taken by the mounted micrometer, from the arbor bar to the head of the pinion to determine the need to add to or remove shims from the shim pack total, to adjust the pinion to the proper nominal assembly dimension or standard pinion depth.

Another method using the arbor bar and discs, is the use of a gauge block with a spring loaded plunger and a thumb screw to lock the plunger upon expansion. A micrometer is used to measure the gauge block after the plunger has been allowed to ex-

Final drive gear tooth contact patterns: A—Desired contact pattern with light load; B—Incorrect pattern, increase depth shim thickness; C—Tooth pattern after depth shim thickness is increased; D—Incorrect pattern, decrease depth shim thickness; E—Tooth pattern after depth shim thickness is decreased

pand between the arbor bar and the pinion head. As in the mounted micrometer procedure, the shim pack thickness is determined by the reading obtained.

A third method is the use of a gauge block tool, installed in the housing in place of the pinion gear, and a large arbor bar placed in the axle housing differential bearing seats and tightened securely. A measurement is taken between the arbor bar and the pinion tool by either a feeler gauge or the use of individual shims from the shim pack. This measurement represents the shim pack needed for a zero marked pinion.

GEAR TOOTH CONTACT (DYE)

Gear tooth contact cannot be successfully accomplished until pinion and bevel gear bearings are in proper adjustment and gear backlash is within specified limits.

Check for proper tooth contact by painting a few teeth of bevel gear with marking dye or white grease. Turn pinion in direction of normal rotation, then check tooth impression on bevel gear.

GEAR BACKLASH

Gears used in extended service form running contacts due to

Avoid overlap of worn section of gear teeth during backlash adjustments when using original gears

Pinion identification markings and an example of how pinion standard depth/distance is determined—Dana model 60 and 70 shown—typical

AXLE MODEL	PINION SETTING
60	3.125 (79.37mm)
70	3.500 (88.9mm)

Checking ring gear backlash with a dial indicator

wear of teeth. Therefore, the original shim pack (between pinion cage and carrier) should be maintained when checking backlash. If backlash exceeds maximum tolerance, reduce backlash only in the amount that will avoid overlap of worn tooth section. Smoothness and roughness can be noted by rotating bevel gear.

If a slight overlap is present at worn tooth section, rotation will be rough.

If new gears are installed, check backlash with dial indicator.

Backlash is increased by moving bevel gear away from pinion and may be decreased by moving bevel gear toward pinion.

When the drive gear is attached to the differential, backlash is accomplished by the bearing adjusting rings. It should be remembered, when one ring is tightened, the opposite ring must be loosened an equal amount to maintain previously established bearing adjustment.

On axles where the bevel gear is supported by cross shaft, backlash is accomplished by adding or removing shims under bearing cages.

TERMS USED

Certain dimensions must be determined when using the pinion setting gauge:

1. **Nominal Assembly Dimension:** (standard pinion depth) This dimension (varying with axle model) is the distance between the center line of the drive gear (or differential carrier bore) and the end of the drive pinion. This dimension may be marked on the pinion or listed on the Nominal Assembly Dimension and Adapter Disc chart.

2. **Individual Variation Distance:** (pinion depth variance) This dimension is a plus or minus variation of the **Nominal Assembly Dimension** on each individual pinion which may be caused by manufacturing variations.

3. **Corrected Nominal Dimension:** (desired pinion depth) This dimension is the **Nominal Assembly Dimension** plus or minus the **Individual Variation Distance**.

4. **Corrected Micrometer Distance** is the **Corrected Nominal Dimension** less the thickness of the gauge set step plate (for example, 0.400 in.) mounted on end of pinion.

5. **Initial Micrometer Reading** is the dimension taken by micrometer to the gauge step plate.

6. **Shim Pack Correction** is determined by the difference between the **Corrected Micrometer Distance** and the **Initial Micrometer Reading** and represents the amount of shim pack to be added or removed as later explained.

7. **Measured Pinion Depth.** This measurement is the distance between the axle center line and the top of the pinion gear. If a step plate or other type gauge tool is used, this measurement is included in the total.

Pinion and Drive Gear Identification

Drive gears and pinions are tested at the time of manufacture to detect machining variances and to obtain desirable tooth contact and quietness. When the correct setting is achieved, the gears are considered matched and a set of numbers, along with other identifying marks are etched on the gear set.

A plus (+) or minus (−) sign is used, followed by a digit to represent the factory setting where the tooth contact and quietness were the best. This is called the pinion depth variance or individual variation distance.

If the pinion is marked +5 for example, this means the distance from the pinion gear rear face to the axle shaft center line is 0.005 in. more than the standard setting and if the pinion gear is marked −5, this means the distance is 0.005 in. less than the standard setting. To move the pinion to the standard setting, compensating for the variation, shims must be either added to subtracted from the total shim pack, located under the rear pinion bearing cup, between the pinion cage and the differential carrier or under the rear pinion bearing, depending upon the differential model being serviced.

The procedures to follow in the adjustment of the pinion and drive gears are outlined in the respective differential model disassembly and assembly sections.

As a rule of thumb on the addition or removal of shims for the pinion depth adjustment, draw a diagram as shown and determine which way the pinion must be moved to obtain the desired pinion depth.

Standard Torque Specifications and Capscrew Markings

Because of the varied bolt sizes used in the many models of differentials, the torque specifications are not always available for a specific bolt. By determining the grade of bolt, size and thread, the proper torque limit can be determined.

STANDARD TORQUE SPECIFICATIONS

BOLT TORQUE

BOLT SIZE	GRADE 5		GRADE 8	
	N·m	ft-lbs (In-lbs)	N·m	ft-lbs (In-lbs)
1/4-20	11	(95)	14	(125)
1/4-28	11	(95)	17	(150)
5/16-18	23	(200)	31	(270)
5/16-24	27	20	34	25
3/8-16	41	30	54	40
3/8-24	48	35	61	45
7/16-14	68	50	88	65
7/16-20	75	55	95	70
1/2-13	102	75	136	100
1/2-20	115	85	149	110
9/16-12	142	105	183	135
9/16-18	156	115	203	150
5/8-11	203	150	264	195
5/8-18	217	160	285	210
3/4-16	237	175	305	225

SAE CLASSIFICATION		
GRADE 5		GRADE 8

MARKINGS FOUND ON TOP OF BOLT HEAD INDICATE GRADE

120°   60°

GRADE 2   GRADE 5   GRADE 8

(SAE) BOLTS—IDENTIFICATION MARKS CORRESPOND TO BOLT STRENGTH—INCREASING NUMBERS REPRESENT INCREASING STRENGTH.

METRIC BOLTS—IDENTIFICATION CLASS NUMBERS CORRESPOND TO BOLT STRENGTH— INCREASING NUMBERS REPRESENT INCREASING STRENGTH.

If torque specifications are not available, determine bolt size and type and tighten to the appropriate standard torque specifications

CHRYSLER CORPORATION

Front Axle Assembly—4WD

7¼ INCH RING GEAR AXLE

This axle is designed for use with independent front suspension. The 4WD front hub and bearings are serviced as a complete unit. The hub is attached to the steering knuckle with 4 bolts. The hub and CV-joint driveshaft stub are engaged via splines located within the hub bearing. They are retained by the hub washer and nut. Multi-purpose hypoid gear lubricant should be used in front differentials on 4WD Dakota Pick-Ups. If the front axle is submerged in water, the differential lubricant must be replaced immediately. Lubricant level should be ¼–½ inch below the fill hole. Overfilling can result in lubricant foaming and overheating.

The 7¼ ring gear front axle is used on Dodge Dakota 4WD Pick-Ups.

Removal and Installation

LEFT AXLE SHAFT, SEAL AND BEARING

1. Raise and safely support vehicle.
2. Disconnect the left CV-joint driveshaft from the axle shaft flange.
3. Clean all dirt and foreign material from the housing cover area.
4. Loosen the housing cover bolts, drain the lubricant, then remove the cover.
5. Turn the differential case so the differential shaft lock screw is accessible. Remove the lock screw and pinion shaft.
6. Force the left axle shaft toward the center of the vehicle, remove the axle shaft C-clip from the axle shaft and remove the axle shaft from the differential housing. Use care not to damage the bearing.
7. Inspect the axle shaft for brinelling, spalling and pitting. If any of these condition exist, the axle and bearing should be replaced. Normal bearing contact on the shaft will be dull gray and it could appear to be lightly dented.
8. Pry the axle shaft seal from the housing.
9. Do not remove the bearing unless it appears to be damaged. If necessary, remove the axle shaft bearing from the housing with a suitable slide hammer puller.

To install:

10. Do not reuse the original seal and bearing, if removed. Wipe the housing bearing bore clean. Inspect the bore for burrs and remove, if necessary. Insert the replacement bearing into the bore and seat firmly against the shoulder with a suitable driver.
11. Install a replacement seal with a suitable driver.
12. Lubricate the axle shaft, bearing bore and seal lip. Insert the axle shaft and engage the splines with the side gear. Use care to prevent the shaft splines from damaging the axle shaft seal lip.
13. Insert the C-clip into the axle groove. Force the axle shaft outward to seat the C-clip lock.
14. Insert the pinion gear shaft into the case, install the thrust washers and pinion gears, if removed. Align the shaft with the lock screw hole, install the lock screw and tighten to 8 ft. lbs.
15. Clean the cover, apply a bead of silicone sealer and install.
16. Install the CV-joint driveshaft. Tighten the flange bolts to 65 ft. lbs.
17. Test drive vehicle to check axle for proper operation.

RIGHT AXLE SHIFT MOTOR

1. Disconnect shift motor vacuum hoses and electrical connections.
2. Remove the shift motor cover and gasket from the housing.

3. Remove the E-clips from the shift motor. Remove the shift motor and shift fork from the cover.
4. Remove the O-ring and shift fork pads.

To install:

5. Clean and inspect all components. If any component is worn or damaged, it should be replaced. Install a replacement O-ring and replacement pads on the shift fork.
6. Insert the shift motor into the housing cover and through shift fork.
7. Install the E-clips on the shift motor.
8. Install the shift motor cover and a replacement gasket. Make sure the shift fork is correctly engaged in the shift collar groove.
9. Install the cover, tighten the bolts to 10 ft. lbs. Connect the vacuum lines and electrical connector to the shift motor.

RIGHT (DISCONNECT) AXLE AND INTERMEDIATE AXLE SHAFT

1. Remove the shift motor, housing cover and gasket.
2. Remove the bearing seal/retainer attaching screws. They are accessible through the holes in the axle shaft flange.
3. Remove the outer axle shaft from the differential housing.
4. Remove the snapring and splined gear from the outer axle shaft.
5. Remove the bearing and seal from the outer axle shaft using a suitable puller.
6. Remove the shift collar from the shift motor housing.
7. Loosen the housing cover bolts, drain the lubricant, then remove the cover.
8. Turn the differential case so the differential shaft lock screw is accessible. Remove the lock screw and pinion shaft.
9. Force the intermediate, or inner axle shaft toward the center of the vehicle, remove the axle shaft C-clip from the axle shaft and remove the intermediate axle shaft from the differential housing.
10. Remove the bearings, if necessary, from the inner axle shaft with a suitable bearing puller.

To install:

11. Install replacement bearings on the intermediate shaft, if necessary. Lubricate the bearings and install the axle shaft into

Exploded view of the disconnected housing cover assembly—front axle assembly—Chrysler

Exploded view of the right axle shaft—front axle assembly—Chrysler

View of the inner axle shaft, bearing and shift collar—front axle assembly—Chrysler

Removing the needle bearing from the inner axle shaft—front axle assembly—Chrysler

the axle tube, push inward, install the C-clip, then force outward to seat the clip.

12. Insert the pinion gear shaft into the case, install the thrust washers and pinion gears, if removed. Align the shaft with the lock screw hole, install the lock screw and tighten to 8 ft. lbs.

13. Install the shift collar on the splined end of the intermediate axle shaft. Install the seal/retainer on the outer axle shaft.

Press on the replacement bearing. Install the splined gear and retaining snapring.

14. Insert the outer axle shaft into the shift motor housing. Use care when guiding the end of the shaft into the intermediate axle shaft needle bearing. Tighten the attaching screws to 200 inch lbs.

15. Install the shift motor housing cover.

16. Clean the cover, apply a bead of silicone sealer and install. Refill with lubricant.

17. Test drive vehicle to check axle for proper operation.

PINION SEAL

NOTE: The following procedure should be used so the correct pinion bearing preload torque is retained. If this procedure is not completely followed, the results can be premature failure of the front axle.

1. Raise and safely support vehicle.

2. Mark the U-joint, pinion yoke and pinion shaft for reference.

3. Disconnect the front drive shaft from the pinion yoke. Secure the driveshaft in an upright position to prevent damage to the rear U-joint.

4. Shift the axle to 2WD operation. This will prevent any drag from causing a possible false bearing preload torque measurement.

5. Use an inch-pound torque wrench to measure the pinion bearing preload. Rotate the pinion shaft several times with the torque wrench. Note the indicated torque as the wrench is moved through several revolutions. Record this torque number. This measurement is very important because the bearing preload torque must be carefully readjusted after the replacement seal is installed.

6. Use a suitable yoke holding tool and remove the pinion shaft nut and washer.

7. Remove the yoke using a suitable puller.

8. Lower the front of the vehicle, if possible, to prevent lubricant leakage.

9. Remove the pinion shaft seal from the differential housing.
To install:

10. Clean the seal contact surface of the housing. Examine the splines on the pinion shaft for burrs or wear and clean the shaft. Check for cracks, worn splines or worn seal contact surface. Repair or replace the yoke as necessary.

11. The outer perimeter of original equipment seals are pre-coated with a special sealant. An additional application of sealant is not required. Install the replacement pinion shaft seal with a suitable installer. The seal is correctly installed when the seal flange contacts the face of the differential housing flange.

12. Position the pinion yoke on the end of the shaft with the reference marks aligned. Seat the yoke. Install a suitable yoke holding tool. Install the washer. The convex side of the washer must face outward. Install the pinion nut.

13. Tighten the pinion shaft nut to 210 ft. lbs. Rotate the pinion shaft several complete revolutions to ensure the bearing rollers are seated. Use an inch-pound torque wrench to measure the pinion gear bearing preload.

NOTE: Never loosen the pinion gear nut to decrease the pinion gear bearing preload torque. If the specified torque is exceeded, a replacement collapsible spacer must be installed. The torque sequence will have to be repeated.

14. Continue tightening and measuring the bearing preload torque until it is the same as the original. The bearing preload torque should never be greater than 10 inch-lbs. more than the recorded value. The bearing preload torque should be constant during a complete revolution of the pinion gear. If the preload torque varies, this indicates a binding condition which must be corrected before the installation of the driveshaft.

15. If the specified torque is not obtained with 210 ft. lbs. of

torque, continue tightening the nut in small increments until the recorded bearing preload torque is obtained.

16. The differential will be unacceptable for use if the final nut torque is less than 210 ft. lbs. If the preload torque is not within the specified range, this is also unacceptable.

17. Install the front drive shaft with the marks aligned. Tighten the U-joint yoke clamp screws to 14 ft. lbs.

18. Level the vehicle and check the differential fluid level. Add lubricant, if necessary.

DIFFERENTIAL

1. Remove the axle housing cover.

2. Clean the inside of the differential case with solvent and blow dry with compressed air.

3. Turn the differential case to make the differential pinion shaft lock screw accessible and remove the lock screw and pinion shaft.

4. Remove the left axle shaft by performing the following procedures:

    a. Remove the C-lock from the recessed groove of the axle shaft.

    b. Remove the axle shaft from the housing.

5. Remove the right axle shaft and inner axle shaft by performing the following procedures:

    a. Remove the disconnect housing cover assembly-to-axle housing screws and the assembly and the gasket.

    b. Remove the axle bearing seal retainer-to-axle housing screws and the axle/bearing retainer assembly from the axle housing.

    c. Remove the shift collar from the disconnect housing.

    d. Remove the C-lock from the recessed groove of the axle shaft.

    e. Remove the needle bearing from the inner axle shaft.

    f. Using an axle puller tool, pull the inner axle shaft from the axle housing.

6. Check for differential side-play by inserting a prybar between the left side of the axle housing and the differential case flange. Using a prying motion, determine whether side-play exists; there should be no side-play.

7. Paint the ring gear teeth and make a gear tooth contact pattern. Determine if proper depth of mesh can be obtained.

8. If side-play was found in Step 6, proceed to Step 9. If no side-play was found in Step 6, check the drive gear run-out by performing the following procedures:

    a. Mount a dial indicator and index the indicator stem at right angles in the rear face of the ring gear.

    b. Rotate the ring gear and mark the ring gear and case at the point of greatest run-out.

    c. Total indicator reading should not exceed 0.005 in.; if it does, the possibility exists that the case must be replaced.

9. Using an inch lb. torque wrench, measure and record the pinion bearing preload.

10. Matchmark the axle housing and the differential bearing caps.

11. Remove the threaded adjusters and the differential bearing caps; there is a special wrench to do this through the axle tube.

12. Remove the differential case from the housing.

NOTE: The differential bearing cups and threaded adjuster must be kept together so they can be installed in their original position.

13. Clamp the differential case and ring gear in a vise with soft jaws.

14. Remove the ring gear bolts (left-hand thread). Tap the ring gear loose with a soft-faced mallet.

15. If the ring gear run-out exceeded 0.005 in., recheck the case as follows:

    a. Install the differential case, cups, caps and adjusters into the housing.

    b. Turn the adjusters to eliminate all side-play and tighten the differential cap bolts snugly.

    c. Measure the run-out at the ring gear flange face; total indicator reading should not exceed 0.003 in.

NOTE: It is often possible to reduce run-out by removing the ring gear and reinstalling it 180 degrees from its original position.

    d. Remove the differential case from the housing.

16. Remove the pinion shaft lock-screw and remove the pinion shaft.

17. Rotate the differential side gears until the differential pinion shafts can be removed through the opening in the case.

18. Remove the differential side gears and thrust washers.

19. Using a bearing puller, press side bearing from the differential.

To install:

20. Lubricate all parts, before assembly, with rear axle lubricant.

21. Install the thrust washers on the differential side gears and install the side gears into the case.

22. Place thrust washers on both differential pinions and, working through the opening in the case, mesh the pinion gears with the side gears. The pinions should be exactly 180 degrees apart.

23. Rotate the side gears 90 degrees to align the pinions and thrust washers with the pinion shaft holes.

24. From the pinion shaft lockpin hole side of the case, insert the slotted end of the pinion shaft through the case and conical thrust washer; install the pinion shaft through one of the pinion gears.

25. Install a thrust block through the side gear hub, so the slot is centered between the side gears.

26. Hold all of the parts in alignment and align the lockpin holes in the pinion shaft and case. Install the lockpin from the pinion shaft side of the ring gear flange, temporarily.

27. With a stone, relieve the edge of the chamfer on the inside diameter of the ring gear.

28. Heat the ring gear (fluid bath or heat lamp) to a temperature not exceeding 300°F; do not heat ring gear with a torch.

29. Align the ring gear with the case. Insert the ring gear screws through the case flange and into the ring gear.

30. Alternately, tighten each cap screw to 80 ft. lbs. (108 Nm).

31. Position each differential bearing cone on the hub of the differential case (taper away from ring gear) and install the bearing cones; a shop press may be helpful.

32. Install the differential into the axle housing.

33. Install the right and inner axle shaft by performing the following procedures:

    a. Using the axle shaft removal/installation tool, install the inner axle shaft into the housing.

    b. Install the C-clip on the other end of the shaft to retain it.

    c. Install the needle bearing into the end of the inner axle shaft.

    d. Install the shift collar onto the splined end of the inner axle shaft.

    e. Install the axle shaft/bearing retainer assembly into the disconnect housing and torque the bearing retainer-to-disconnect housing screws to 200 inch lbs. (23 Nm).

    f. Using a new gasket, install the disconnect housing cover assembly onto the disconnect housing and torque the bolts to 10 ft. lbs. (14 Nm).

34. Install the left axle shaft into the axle housing and secure it with the C-clip.

35. To complete the installation, reverse the removal procedures.

PINION GEAR

1. Remove the pinion nut, washer and pinion flange.

2. Remove and discard the pinion oil seal.

3. Using a brass hammer, drive the pinion rearward out of the bearing. This will result in damage to the bearing and cup. The bearing cone and cup must be replaced with new parts. Discard the collapsible spacer.

4. Using a brass drift and a hammer, drive the front and rear bearing cups from the housing.

5. Remove the shim from behind the rear bearing cup and record the thickness.

6. Using a bearing puller, press the rear bearing cone from the pinion stem.

7. Perform the following inspections:

   a. Clean the differential components in solvent and use compressed air to dry them; do not use compressed air on the bearings, only shop towels.

   b. Check the components for wear or damage; replace them, if necessary.

   c. Inspect the bearings and bearing cups for wear, cracks or scoring; replace them, if necessary.

   d. Inspect the differential side and pinion gears for wear, cracks or chips; replace them, if necessary.

   e. Inspect the ring and pinion gears for wear and/or damage; replace them, if necessary.

   f. Inspect the differential case for cracks or damage; replace it, if necessary.

To install:

8. The proper pinion setting (relative to the ring gear) is determined by a shim which has been selected before the pinion is to be installed in the carrier. Pinion bearing shims are available in 0.001 in. increments.

9. The head of the pinion is marked with a plus (+) or a minus (−) mark that is followed by a number ranging from 0–4. If the old and new pinions have the same marking and the old bearing is being installed, use a shim of the original thickness. If the old pinion is marked zero (0), however and the new pinion is marked +2, try a shim that is 0.002 in. thinner. If the new pinion is marked axle housing cup bore and install −2, try a shim that is 0.002 in. thicker.

10. Position the selected shim in the bore of the rear bearing cup. Install the cup.

NOTE: Special pinion depth measuring tools are available. When using the special tools, follow the manufacturer's recommended procedures. Without the special tools, complete the following procedure and check the pinion depth by examining the pinion to ring gear tooth contact pattern. Correct as required by adding or subtracting shims controlling the pinion depth.

11. Place the rear pinion bearing cone on the pinion stem (small side away from pinion head).

12. Lubricate the front and rear bearing cones and install the rear pinion bearing cone onto the pinion stem with an arbor press.

13. Insert the pinion bearing and collapsible spacer assembly through the carrier and install the front bearing cone. Install the companion flange.

NOTE: During installation of the pinion bearing do not collapse the spacer.

14. Install the drive pinion oil seal into the carrier; be sure to properly seat the seal.

15. Support the pinion in the carrier.

16. Install the dished washer (convex side up) and pinion nut.

17. Hold the companion flange and tighten the pinion nut to remove all end play, while rotating the pinion to ensure proper bearing seating. Remove the tools and rotate the pinion several revolutions.

18. Torque the pinion nut to 210 ft. lbs. (285 Nm). Using an inch lbs. torque wrench, measure the pinion bearing preload;

the torque is 20–35 inch lbs. for new bearings or 10 inch lbs. over the original figure for the old pinion bearing.

NOTE: The correct preload reading can only be obtained with the carrier nose upright. The final assembly is incorrect if the final pinion nut torque is below 210 ft. lbs. (285 Nm) or if the pinion bearing preload is not within specifications. Under no circumstances should the pinion nut be backed off to reduce the pinion bearing preload; if this is done, a new collapsible spacer will have to be installed and the unit adjusted again until proper preload is obtained.

Adjustment

DIFFERENTIAL BEARING PRELOAD AND RING GEAR-TO-PINION BACKLASH

The threaded adjuster uses a hex drive hole and requires a special tool C–4164 to adjust the side bearing preload through the axle tube. An adjuster lock with 2 pointed teeth which engage in the exposed adjuster thread when the lock is tightened is provided. The shims will range from 0.020–0.038 in. and will be equipped with internal centering tabs. The shims, marked with a number which represents its thickness in thousandths of an in., can be installed with either side against the pinion head.

1. Index the gears so the same gear teeth are in contact throughout the adjustment.

2. The differential bearing cups will not always move with the adjusters. It is important to seat the bearings by rotating them 5–10 times in each direction, each time the adjusters are moved.

3. With the pinion bearings installed and the preload set, install the differential with adjusters, caps and bearings. Lubricate the bearings and adjuster threads. Tighten the top cap screws on the right and left to 10 ft. lbs. Tighten the bottom cap screws finger-tight until the head is just seated on the bearing cap.

4. Using the tool, make sure the adjuster rotates freely. Turn both adjusters in until bearing play is eliminated with some drive gear backlash (0.010 in.). Seat the bearing rollers.

5. Install and register a dial indicator against the drive side of a gear tooth. Check the backlash at 4 positions to find the point of minimum backlash. Rotate the gear to the position of least backlash and mark the tooth so the readings will be taken at the same point.

6. Loosen the right adjuster and turn it until the backlash is 0.003–0.004 in. with each adjuster tightened to 10 ft. lbs. Seat the bearings rollers.

7. Tighten the differential bearing cap screws to 45 ft. lbs. (61 Nm).

8. Tighten the right adjuster to 70 ft. lbs. and seat the rollers, until the torque remains constant at 70 ft. lbs. Measure the backlash, if the backlash is not 0.006–0.008 in. increase the torque on the right adjusters and seat the rollers until the correct backlash is obtained.

9. Tighten the left adjuster to 70 ft. lbs. and seat the bearings until the torque remains constant.

10. If the assembly is properly done, the initial reading on the left adjuster will be approximately 70 ft. lbs. If it is substantially less, the entire procedure should be repeated.

11. After the adjustments are complete, install the adjuster locks; be sure the teeth are engaged in the adjuster threads. Torque the lockscrews to 90 inch lbs.

SPICER 8½ INCH MODEL 44 AXLE

Disassembly

DIFFERENTIAL

1. Remove the housing cover and drain the lubricant.

Sectional view of the left disconnect axle assembly— model 44 front axle assembly—Chrysler

Removing the inner axle shaft—model 44 front axle assembly—Chrysler

2. Remove the left axle shaft and the inner axle shaft by performing the following procedures:

a. Using an axle puller, press the left axle shaft from the axle housing.

b. Remove the disconnect housing assembly-to-axle housing screws, the housing and the gasket.

c. Remove the shift collar from the inner axle shaft.

d. Using an inner axle shaft removal/installation tool, attach it to the inner axle shaft and carefully, slide the inner axle shaft from the axle housing.

3. Using an axle spreader tool, mount it onto the axle housing and spread the housing enough to remove the differential.

4. Using a dial indicator, measure the amount the opening is being spread; do not spread the housing more than 0.015 in. (0.38mm), for damage to the housing may occur.

5. Mark the differential bearing caps for reassembly purposes.

6. Loosen the bearing caps until 2–3 threads are engaged.

7. Using a prybar, pry the differential loose.

8. Remove the bearing caps and the differential.

9. Mount the differential into a vise.

10. Remove and discard the ring gear bolts; they are not reusable.

11. Using a brass drift and a hammer, tap the ring gear from the differential.

12. Using a differential bearing puller, press the differential bearings from the differential.

13. Remove the differential bearing shims.

14. Remove the pinion shaft lockpin and pinion shaft.

15. Rotate the pinions to remove them through the case opening.

16. Remove the side gears and thrust washers.

PINION GEAR

1. Remove the differential case from the axle housing.

2. Using a pinion yoke holding tool, remove the pinion gear nut.

3. Remove the pinion washer. Using a pinion yoke holder tool and a pinion puller tool, press the yoke from the pinion gear.

4. Using an oil seal remover tool, remove the pinion gear oil seal and discard it. Remove the slinger, the gasket, the upper pinion bearing cone and preload shim pack; measure and record the shim thickness.

5. Press drive the pinion gear and inner bearing cone assembly from the axle housing.

6. Using a shop press, press the inner bearing cone from the pinion gear.

7. Remove and record the shim thicknesses from behind the inner pinion bearing cup.

Inspection

1. Clean the differential components in solvent and use compressed air to dry them; do not use compressed air on the bearings, only shop towels.

2. Check the components for wear or damage; replace them, if necessary.

3. Inspect the bearings and bearing cups for wear, cracks or scoring; replace them, if necessary.

4. Inspect the differential side and pinion gears for wear, cracks or chips; replace them, if necessary.

5. Inspect the ring and pinion gears for wear and/or damage; replace them, if necessary.

6. Inspect the differential case for cracks or damage; replace it, if necessary.

PINION GEAR VARIATION CHART

Original Pinion Gear Depth Variance	Replacement Pinion Gear Depth Variance								
	−4	−3	−2	−1	0	+1	+2	+3	+4
+4	+0.008	+0.007	+0.006	+0.005	+0.004	+0.003	+0.002	+0.001	0
+3	+0.007	+0.006	+0.005	+0.004	+0.003	+0.002	+0.001	0	−0.001
+2	+0.006	+0.005	+0.004	+0.003	+0.002	+0.001	0	−0.001	−0.002
+1	+0.005	+0.004	+0.003	+0.002	+0.001	0	−0.001	−0.002	−0.003
0	+0.004	+0.003	+0.002	+0.001	0	−0.001	−0.002	−0.003	−0.004
−1	+0.003	+0.002	+0.001	0	−0.001	−0.002	−0.003	−0.004	−0.005
−2	+0.002	+0.001	0	−0.001	−0.002	−0.003	−0.004	−0.005	−0.006
−3	+0.001	0	−0.001	−0.002	−0.003	−0.004	−0.005	−0.006	−0.007
−4	0	−0.001	−0.002	−0.003	−0.004	−0.005	−0.006	−0.007	−0.008

Assembly

PINION GEAR

1. Make sure the ring and pinion are a matched set.
2. Measure the thickness of the original pinion shim and note the variance on the pinion gear.
3. Perform the following procedure to determine the pinion starter shim thickness:

    a. If the original ring and pinion are being installed, use the original shim.

    b. If a replacement gear set is being installed, determine the best starter shim thickness.

    c. Refer to the pinion variance chart and observe where the old and new pinion marking column intersect.

    d. If the old pinion is +2 and the new pinion is −2, the intersecting figure is +0.004 in. (0.10mm); add this amount to the original shim. Or, if the old pinion is −3 and the new pinion is −2, the intersecting figure is −0.001 in. (−0.025mm); subtract this amount from the original shim.

4. Install the starter shim in the pinion rear bearing cup bore; if the shim is chamfered on one side, position the chamfered side so it faces the bottom of the bore.
5. Using a driver tool, install the pinion rear bearing cup into the axle housing.
6. Install the front bearing cup.
7. Using a shop press, press the rear bearing onto the pinion gear.
8. Install the pinion gear into the axle housing and the front bearing onto the pinion; do not install the slinger or the seal.
9. Install the yoke, the pinion nut washer and the old pinion nut; tighten the nut enough to remove the end play.
10. Adjust the backlash and gear tooth contact.

DIFFERENTIAL

1. Install the side gears, the thrust washers and the pinion gears into the differential case.

NOTE: If new gears and washers are used, it will not be necessary to check the gear backlash. Correct fit is provided due to the close manufacturing tolerances.

2. Install the pinion shaft and lockpin into the case.
3. Assemble the original differential bearing shim packs, then, remove approximately 0.20 in. (0.50mm) shim thickness from each pack; the remaining shims will serve as a starter shim pack.
4. Install the starter shim packs and bearing onto the case.
5. Align and install the ring gear. Using new bolts, torque the ring gear-to-differential case bolts to 45–60 ft. lbs. (61–81 Nm).
6. Install the spreader tool onto the axle housing. Using a dial indicator, spread the axle housing no more than 0.015 in. (0.38mm).

NOTE: Do not spread the housing more than 0.015 in. (0.038mm), for damage may occur to the case.

7. Install the differential; it may be necessary to tap the differential bearing cups, with a soft hammer, to seat them.
8. Install the differential bearing caps and torque the bolts to 70–90 ft. lbs. (95–122 Nm).
9. Remove the spreader tool and dial indicator.
10. Adjust the ring and pinion gear.

Installing the inner axle shaft bearing — model 44 front axle assembly — Chrysler

Exploded view of the 7¼ inch rear axle assembly

11. Using silicone sealant, apply a bead of it to the axle housing. Install the cover and torque the bolts to 35 ft. lbs. (47 Nm).

Adjustment

PINION BEARING PRELOAD

1. Using a yoke holding tool, torque the pinion nut to 200–220 ft. lbs. (271–298 Nm). Rotate the drive pinion several complete revolutions to seat the bearing rollers.

2. Using an inch lb. torque wrench, measure the torque necessary to rotate the pinion; the torque should be 20–40 inch lbs. (2–5 Nm).

NOTE: If the torque is not correct, add a shim to decrease the preload or subtract a shim to increase the preload.

3. Remove the pinion nut, the washer and the yoke after setting the preload; be sure to discard the old nut.

4. Lubricate the new pinion oil seal lip and install the seal into the axle housing.

5. Install the yoke, the washer and a new pinion nut; torque the nut to 200–220 ft. lbs. (271–298 Nm).

DIFFERENTIAL BEARING PRELOAD AND DRIVE GEAR AND PINION BACKLASH

1. Install the differential and tighten the bearing caps.

2. Using a dial indicator, mount it onto the housing, position the stylus against the drive side of one ring gear tooth; be sure the stylus is at a right angle to the tooth.

3. Move the ring gear toward the dial indicator and zero it.

4. Move the ring gear away from the pinion until the backlash and note the reading on the dial indicator.

NOTE: The reading represents the thickness of the shim pack necessary to take up the clearance between the bearing cup and the case on the ring gear side of the differential assembly.

Exploded view of the 8¼ inch rear axle assembly

5. Subtract this reading from the previously recorded total reading to obtain the amount of shims necessary to take up the clearance between the bearing cup and the case at the pinion side of the differential.

6. Remove the differential and ring gear assembly from the carrier.

7. Remove the differential bearing covers. Install the correct thickness shim pack between the bearing cone and differential case hub shoulder. Add an additional 0.015 in. (0.38mm) shim to the drive gear side of the differential and install the differential bearing cones.

8. Install the spreader tool to the axle housing. Using a dial indicator, spread the housing to 0.015–0.020 in. (0.38–0.51mm). Install the differential assembly into the axle housing.

9. Install the bearing caps, remove the spreader tool and torque the bearing caps snugly.

10. Using a soft hammer, tap the drive gear to seat the differential bearing and cups.

NOTE: When seating the bearing and cups, be careful not to nick the ring gear or drive pinion teeth.

11. Torque the bearing cap bolts to 70–90 ft. lbs. (95–122 Nm).

12. Attach a dial indicator to the carrier, with the stylus contacting a ring gear tooth, and measure the backlash between the ring gear and the drive pinion.

13. Check the backlash at 4 equally spaced points around the circumference of the ring gear; the backlash must be between 0.04–0.009 in. (0.102–0.229mm) and cannot vary more than 0.002 in. (0.508mm) between the 4 check positions.

NOTE: If the backlash does not fall within these specifications, change the shim pack thickness on both the differential bearing hubs to maintain the proper bearing preload and backlash.

Exploded view of the 8³/₈ inch rear axle assembly

SPICER—MODEL 60 AXLE

For overhaul information, refer to the Spicer 60 axle, in the rear axle assembly section.

Rear Axle Assembly—4WD

Some Dodge/Plymouth Pick-Ups use a 7¼, 8¼, 8⅜ or 9¼ in. semi-floating axle. Others use a Spicer 60, 60 HD (heavy duty) or 70 full-floating axle.

7¼, 8¼, 8⅜ AND 9¼ INCH RING GEAR AXLE

Disassembly
DIFFERENTIAL

1. Remove the axle housing cover.

2. Clean the inside of the differential case with solvent and blow dry with compressed air.

3. Check for differential side-play by inserting a prybar between the left side of the axle housing and the differential case flange. Using a prying motion, determine whether side-play exists; there should be no side-play.

4. Paint the ring gear teeth and make a gear tooth contact pattern. Determine if proper depth of mesh can be obtained.

5. If side-play was found in step 3, proceed to step 6. If no side-play was found in step 3, check the drive gear run-out by performing the following procedures:

    a. Mount a dial indicator and index the indicator stem at right angles in the rear face of the ring gear.

    b. Rotate the ring gear and mark the ring gear and case at the point of greatest run-out.

    c. Total indicator reading should not exceed 0.005 in.; if it does, the possibility exists that the case must be replaced.

6. Using an inch lb. torque wrench, measure and record the pinion bearing preload.

Exploded view of the 9¼ inch rear axle assembly

7. Matchmark the axle housing and the differential bearing caps.

8. Remove the threaded adjusters and the differential bearing caps; there is a special wrench to do this through the axle tube.

9. Remove the differential case from the housing.

NOTE: The differential bearing cups and threaded adjuster must be kept together so they can be installed in their original position.

10. Clamp the differential case and ring gear in a vise with soft jaws.

11. Remove the ring gear bolts (left-hand thread). Tap the ring gear loose with a soft-faced mallet.

12. If the ring gear run-out exceeded 0.005 in., recheck the case as follows:

   a. Install the differential case, cups, caps and adjusters into the housing.

   b. Turn the adjusters to eliminate all side-play and tighten the differential cap bolts snugly.

   c. Measure the run-out at the ring gear flange face; total indicator reading should not exceed 0.003 in.

NOTE: It is often possible to reduce run-out by removing the ring gear and reinstalling it 180 degrees from its original position.

   d. Remove the differential case from the housing.

13. Remove the pinion shaft lock-screw and remove the pinion shaft.

14. Rotate the differential side gears until the differential pinion shafts can be removed through the opening in the case.

15. Remove the differential side gears and thrust washers.

16. Using a bearing puller, press side bearing from the differential.

PINION GEAR

1. Remove the pinion nut, washer and pinion flange.

2. Remove and discard the pinion oil seal.

3. Using a brass hammer, drive the pinion rearward out of the bearing. This will result in damage to the bearing and cup. The bearing cone and cup must be replaced with new parts. Discard the collapsible spacer.

4. Using a brass drift and a hammer, drive the front and rear bearing cups from the housing.

5. Remove the shim from behind the rear bearing cup and record the thickness.

6. Using a bearing puller, press the rear bearing cone from the pinion stem.

Inspection

1. Clean the differential components in solvent and use compressed air to dry them; do not use compressed air on the bearings, only shop towels.

2. Check the components for wear or damage; replace them, if necessary.

3. Inspect the bearings and bearing cups for wear, cracks or scoring; replace them, if necessary.

4. Inspect the differential side and pinion gears for wear, cracks or chips; replace them, if necessary.

5. Inspect the ring and pinion gears for wear and/or damage; replace them, if necessary.

6. Inspect the differential case for cracks or damage; replace it, if necessary.

Assembly

PINION GEAR

1. The proper pinion setting (relative to the ring gear) is determined by a shim which has been selected before the pinion is to be installed in the carrier. Pinion bearing shims are available in 0.001 in. increments.

2. The head of the pinion is marked with a plus (+) or a minus (−) mark that is followed by a number ranging from 0–4. If the old and new pinions have the same marking and the old bearing is being installed, use a shim of the original thickness. If the old pinion is marked zero (0), however and the new pinion is marked +2, try a shim that is 0.002 in. thinner. If the new pinion is marked axle housing cup bore and install −2, try a shim that is 0.002 in. thicker.

3. Position the selected shim in the bore of the rear bearing cup. Install the cup.

NOTE: Special pinion depth measuring tools are available. When using the special tools, follow the manufacturer's recommended procedures. Without the special tools, complete the following procedure and check the pinion depth by examining the pinion to ring gear tooth contact pattern. Correct as required by adding or subtracting shims controlling the pinion depth.

4. Place the rear pinion bearing cone on the pinion stem (small side away from pinion head).

5. Lubricate the front and rear bearing cones and install the rear pinion bearing cone onto the pinion stem with an arbor press.

6. Insert the pinion bearing and collapsible spacer assembly through the carrier and install the front bearing cone. Install the companion flange.

NOTE: During installation of the pinion bearing do not collapse the spacer.

7. Install the drive pinion oil seal into the carrier; be sure to properly seat the seal.

8. Support the pinion in the carrier.

9. Install the dished washer (convex side up) and pinion nut.

10. Hold the companion flange and tighten the pinion nut to remove all end play, while rotating the pinion to ensure proper

bearing seating. Remove the tools and rotate the pinion several revolutions.

11. Torque the pinion nut to 210 ft. lbs. (285 Nm). Using an inch lbs. torque wrench, measure the pinion bearing preload; the torque is 20–35 inch lbs. for new bearings or 10 inch lbs. over the original figure for the old pinion bearing.

NOTE: The correct preload reading can only be obtained with the carrier nose upright. The final assembly is incorrect if the final pinion nut torque is below 210 ft. lbs. (285 Nm) or if the pinion bearing preload is not within specifications. Under no circumstances should the pinion nut be backed off to reduce the pinion bearing preload; if this is done, a new collapsible spacer will have to be installed and the unit adjusted again until proper preload is obtained.

DIFFERENTIAL

1. Lubricate all parts, before assembly, with rear axle lubricant.

2. Install the thrust washers on the differential side gears and install the side gears into the case.

3. Place thrust washers on both differential pinions and, working through the opening in the case, mesh the pinion gears with the side gears. The pinions should be exactly 180 degrees apart.

4. Rotate the side gears 90 degrees to align the pinions and thrust washers with the pinion shaft holes.

5. From the pinion shaft lockpin hole side of the case, insert the slotted end of the pinion shaft through the case and conical thrust washer; install the pinion shaft through one of the pinion gears.

6. Install a thrust block through the side gear hub, so the slot is centered between the side gears.

7. Hold all of the parts in alignment and align the lockpin holes in the pinion shaft and case. Install the lockpin from the pinion shaft side of the ring gear flange, temporarily.

8. With a stone, relieve the edge of the chamfer on the inside diameter of the ring gear.

9. Heat the ring gear (fluid bath or heat lamp) to a temperature not exceeding 300°F; do not heat ring gear with a torch.

10. Align the ring gear with the case. Insert the ring gear screws through the case flange and into the ring gear.

11. Alternately tighten each cap screw to:

    80 ft. lbs. (108 Nm) − 7¼ in axle
    70 ft. lbs. (95 Nm) − 8¼ in., 8⅜ in. and 9¼ in. axles

12. Position each differential bearing cone on the hub of the differential case (taper away from ring gear) and install the bearing cones; a shop press may be helpful.

Adjustment

DIFFERENTIAL BEARING PRELOAD AND RING GEAR-TO-PINION BACKLASH

The threaded adjuster uses a hex drive hole and requires a special tool C-4164 to adjust the side bearing preload through the axle tube. An adjuster lock with 2 pointed teeth which engage in the exposed adjuster thread when the lock is tightened is provided. The shims will range from 0.020–0.038 in. and will be equipped with internal centering tabs. The shims, marked with a number which represents its thickness in thousandths of an inch, can be installed with either side against the pinion head.

1. Index the gears so the same gear teeth are in contact throughout the adjustment.

2. The differential bearing cups will not always move with the adjusters. It is important to seat the bearings by rotating them 5–10 times in each direction, each time the adjusters are moved.

3. With the pinion bearings installed and the preload set, install the differential with adjusters, caps and bearings. Lubricate the bearings and adjuster threads. Tighten the top cap

screws on the right and left to 10 ft. lbs. Tighten the bottom cap screws finger-tight until the head is just seated on the bearing cap.

4. Using the tool, make sure the adjuster rotates freely. Turn both adjusters in until bearing play is eliminated with some drive gear backlash (0.010 in.). Seat the bearing rollers.

5. Install and register a dial indicator against the drive side of a gear tooth. Check the backlash at 4 positions to find the point of minimum backlash. Rotate the gear to the position of least backlash and mark the tooth so the readings will be taken at the same point.

6. Loosen the right adjuster and turn it until the backlash is

Using a long bar tool with hex end to adjust the differential bearing preload and gear backlash

0.003–0.004 in. with each adjuster tightened to 10 ft. lbs. Seat the bearings rollers.

7. Tighten the differential bearing cap screws to:
   100 ft. lbs. (136 Nm) — 8¼ in. and 9¼ in axles
   45 ft. lbs. (61 Nm) — 7¼ in. axle
   70 ft. lbs. (95 Nm) — 8⅜ in axle

8. Tighten the right adjuster to 70 ft. lbs. and seat the rollers, until the torque remains constant at 70 ft. lbs. Measure the backlash, if the backlash is not 0.006–0.008 in. increase the torque on the right adjusters and seat the rollers until the correct backlash is obtained.

9. Tighten the left adjuster to 70 ft. lbs. and seat the bearings until the torque remains constant.

10. If the assembly is properly done, the initial reading on the left adjuster will be approximately 70 ft. lbs. If it is substantially less, the entire procedure should be repeated.

11. After the adjustments are complete, install the adjuster locks; be sure the teeth are engaged in the adjuster threads. Torque the lockscrews to 90 inch lbs.

SPICER — MODELS 60, 60 HD AND 70 AXLES

Disassembly

DIFFERENTIAL

1. Remove the housing cover and drain the lubricant.

2. Using an axle spreader tool, mount it onto the axle housing and spread the housing enough to remove the differential.

3. Using a dial indicator, measure the amount the opening is being spread; do not spread the housing more than 0.015 in. (0.38mm), for damage to the housing may occur.

4. Mark the differential bearing caps for reassembly purposes.

5. Loosen the bearing caps until 2–3 threads are engaged.

Exploded view of the Spicer 60 and 60 HD rear axle assembly

Exploded view of the Spicer model 70 rear axle assembly

Exploded view of the Spicer model 70 differential

6. Using a prybar, pry the differential loose.
7. Remove the bearing caps and the differential.
8. Mount the differential into a vise.
9. Remove and discard the ring gear bolts; they are not reusable.
10. Using a brass drift and a hammer, tap the ring gear from the differential.

11. Using a differential bearing puller, press the differential bearings from the differential.
12. Remove the differential bearing shims.
13. Remove the pinion shaft lockpin and pinion shaft.
14. Rotate the pinions to remove them through the case opening.
15. Remove the side gears and thrust washers.

PINION GEAR

1. Remove the differential case from the axle housing.
2. Using a pinion yoke holding tool, remove the pinion gear nut.
3. Remove the pinion washer. Using a pinion yoke holder tool and a pinion puller tool, press the yoke from the pinion gear.
4. Using an oil seal remover tool, remove the pinion gear oil seal and discard it. Remove the slinger, the gasket, the upper pinion bearing cone and preload shim pack; measure and record the shim thicknesses.
5. Press drive the pinion gear and inner bearing cone assembly from the axle housing.
6. Using a shop press, press the inner bearing cone from the pinion gear.
7. Remove and record the shim thicknesses from behind the inner pinion bearing cup.

Inspection

1. Clean the differential components in solvent and use compressed air to dry them; do not use compressed air on the bearings, only shop towels.
2. Check the components for wear or damage; replace them, if necessary.
3. Inspect the bearings and bearing cups for wear, cracks or scoring; replace them, if necessary.
4. Inspect the differential side and pinion gears for wear, cracks or chips; replace them, if necessary.
5. Inspect the ring and pinion gears for wear and/or damage; replace them, if necessary.
6. Inspect the differential case for cracks or damage; replace it, if necessary.

Assembly
PINION GEAR

1. Make sure the ring and pinion are a matched set.
2. Measure the thickness of the original pinion shim and note the variance on the pinion gear.
3. Perform the following procedure to determine the pinion starter shim thickness:
    a. If the original ring and pinion are being installed, use the original shim.
    b. If a replacement gear set is being installed, determine the best starter shim thickness.
    c. Refer to the pinion variance chart and observe where the old and new pinion marking column intersect.
    d. If the old pinion is +2 and the new pinion is −2, the intersecting figure is +0.004 in. (0.10mm); add this amount to the original shim. Or, if the old pinion is −3 and the new pin-

ion is −2, the intersecting figure is −0.001 in. (−0.025mm); subtract this amount from the original shim.
4. Install the starter shim in the pinion rear bearing cup bore; if the shim is chamfered on one side, position the chamfered side so it faces the bottom of the bore.
5. Using a driver tool, install the pinion rear bearing cup into the axle housing.
6. Install the front bearing cup.
7. Using a shop press, press the rear bearing onto the pinion gear.
8. Install the pinion gear into the axle housing and the front bearing onto the pinion; do not install the slinger or the seal.
9. Install the yoke, the pinion nut washer and the old pinion nut; tighten the nut enough to remove the end play.
10. Adjust the backlash and gear tooth contact.

DIFFERENTIAL

1. Install the side gears, the thrust washers and the pinion gears into the differential case.

NOTE: If new gears and washers are used, it will not be necessary to check the gear backlash. Correct fit is provided due to the close manufacturing tolerances.

2. Install the pinion shaft and lockpin into the case.
3. Assemble the original differential bearing shim packs, then, remove approximately 0.20 in. (0.50mm) shim thickness from each pack; the remaining shims will serve as a starter shim pack.
4. Install the starter shim packs and bearing onto the case.
5. Align and install the ring gear. Using new bolts, torque the ring gear-to-differential case bolts to 100–120 ft. lbs. (136–163 Nm).
6. Install the spreader tool onto the axle housing. Using a dial indicator, spread the axle housing no more than 0.015 in. (0.38mm).

NOTE: Do not spread the housing more than 0.015 in. (0.038mm), for damage may occur to the case.

7. Install the differential; it may be necessary to tap the differential bearing cups, with a soft hammer, to seat them.
8. Install the differential bearing caps and torque the bolts to 70–90 ft. lbs. (95–122 Nm).
9. Remove the spreader tool and dial indicator.
10. Adjust the ring and pinion gears.
11. Using silicone sealant, apply a bead of it to the axle housing. Install the cover and torque the bolts to 35 ft. lbs. (47 Nm).

PINION GEAR VARIATION CHART

Old Pinion Marking	New Pinion Marking (U.S. Standards)								
	−4	−3	−2	−1	0	+1	+2	+3	+4
+4	+0.008	+0.007	+0.006	+0.005	+0.004	+0.003	+0.002	+0.001	0
+3	+0.007	+0.006	+0.005	+0.004	+0.003	+0.002	+0.001	0	−0.001
+2	+0.006	+0.005	+0.004	+0.003	+0.002	+0.001	0	−0.001	−0.002
+1	+0.005	+0.004	+0.003	+0.002	+0.001	0	−0.001	−0.002	−0.003
0	+0.004	+0.003	+0.002	+0.001	0	−0.001	−0.002	−0.003	−0.004
−1	+0.003	+0.002	+0.001	0	−0.001	−0.002	−0.003	−0.004	−0.005
−2	+0.002	+0.001	0	−0.001	−0.002	−0.003	−0.004	−0.005	−0.006
−3	+0.001	0	−0.001	−0.002	−0.003	−0.004	−0.005	−0.006	−0.007
−4	0	−0.001	−0.002	−0.003	−0.004	−0.005	−0.006	−0.007	−0.008

Adjustment

PINION BEARING PRELOAD

1. Using a yoke holding tool, torque the pinion nut to 250–270 ft. lbs. (339–366 Nm). Rotate the drive pinion several complete revolutions to seat the bearing rollers.
2. Using an inch lb. torque wrench, measure the torque necessary to rotate the pinion; the torque should be 10–20 inch lbs. (1–3 Nm).

NOTE: If the torque is not correct, add a shim to decrease the preload or subtract a shim to increase the preload.

3. Remove the pinion nut, the washer and the yoke after setting the preload; be sure to discard the old nut.
4. Lubricate the new pinion oil seal lip and install the seal into the axle housing.
5. Install the yoke, the washer and a new pinion nut; torque the nut to 250–270 ft. lbs. (339–366 Nm).

DIFFERENTIAL BEARING PRELOAD AND DRIVE GEAR AND PINION BACKLASH

1. Install the differential and tighten the bearing caps.
2. Using a dial indicator, mount it onto the housing, position the stylus against the drive side of one ring gear tooth; be sure the stylus is at a right angle to the tooth.
3. Move the ring gear toward the dial indicator and zero it.
4. Move the ring gear away from the pinion until the backlash and note the reading on the dial indicator.

NOTE: The reading represents the thickness of the shim pack necessary to take up the clearance between the bearing cup and the case on the ring gear side of the differential assembly.

5. Subtract this reading from the previously recorded total reading to obtain the amount of shims necessary to take up the clearance between the bearing cup and the case at the pinion side of the differential.
6. Remove the differential and ring gear assembly from the carrier.
7. Remove the differential bearing covers. Install the correct thickness shim pack between the bearing cone and differential case hub shoulder. Add an additional 0.015 in. (0.38mm) shim to the drive gear side of the differential and install the differential bearing cones.
8. Install the spreader tool to the axle housing. Using a dial indicator, spread the housing to 0.015–0.020 in. (0.38–0.51mm). Install the differential assembly into the axle housing.
9. Install the bearing caps, remove the spreader tool and torque the bearing caps snugly.
10. Using a soft hammer, tap the drive gear to seat the differential bearing and cups.

NOTE: When seating the bearing and cups, be careful not to nick the ring gear or drive pinion teeth.

11. Torque the bearing cap bolts to 70–90 ft. lbs. (95–122 Nm).
12. Attach a dial indicator to the carrier, with the stylus contacting a ring gear tooth, and measure the backlash between the ring gear and the drive pinion.
13. Check the backlash at 4 equally spaced points around the circumference of the ring gear; the backlash must be between 0.04–0.009 in. (0.102–0.229mm) and cannot vary more than 0.002 in. (0.508mm) between the 4 check positions.

NOTE: If the backlash does not fall within these specifications, change the shim pack thickness on both the differential bearing hubs to maintain the proper bearing preload and backlash.

TRAC-LOK DIFFERENTIAL

Operational Test

If a noisy or rough operation such as a chatter occurs when turning corners, the most probable cause of this chatter or noise is incorrect or contaminated lubricant. Before removing the Trac-Lok unit for repair, drain, flush and refill the axle with the specified lubricant. A complete lubricant drain and refill with the specified fluid will usually correct the chatter problem. A quick operational test of the Trac-Lok differential can be done easily by performing the following steps.

1. Position one wheel on solid dry pavement and the opposite wheel on ice, mud grease or a similar low traction surface.
2. Gradually, increase the engine rpm to obtain the maximum traction prior to a breakaway. The ability to move the vehicle effectively will demonstrate the proper performance.

NOTE: If the test is performed on extremely slick surfaces such as ice or grease coated surfaces, some question may exist as to proper performance. In these extreme cases, a properly performing Trac-Lok will provide greater pulling power by lightly applying the parking brake.

Disassembly

DIFFERENTIAL

1. Remove the housing cover and drain the lubricant.
2. Using an axle spreader tool, mount it onto the axle housing and spread the housing enough to remove the differential.
3. Using a dial indicator, measure the amount the opening is being spread; do not spread the housing more than 0.015 in. (0.38mm), for damage to the housing may occur.
4. Mark the differential bearing caps for reassembly purposes.
5. Loosen the bearing caps until 2–3 threads are engaged.
6. Using a prybar, pry the differential loose.
7. Remove the bearing caps and the differential.
8. Mount the differential into a vise.
9. Remove and discard the ring gear bolts; they are not reusable.
10. Using a brass drift and a hammer, tap the ring gear from the differential.

Section view of the Spicer model 70 Trak-Lok differential

11. Using a differential bearing puller, press the differential bearings from the differential.

12. Remove the differential bearing shims.

13. Remove the pinion shaft lockpin and pinion shaft.

14. Rotate the pinions to remove them through the case opening.

15. Remove the side gears and thrust washers.

Inspection

If any member of either clutch pack shows evidence of excessive wear or scoring, the complete clutch pack must be replaced on both sides.

1. Clean each part in solvent.

2. Towel dry bearings or allow them to air dry, do not use compressed air to dry bearings as damage might result. Dry all other parts with compressed air or shop towels. If the parts are not to be assembled immediately, cover them to prevent dust or dirt contamination.

3. Inspect the housing for cracks and sand holes. Replace the housing if it is cracked or porous. Check for burrs and deep scratches or nicks on the gasket and oil seal surfaces. An oil stone or fine tooth file may be used to remove nicks or burrs.

4. Inspect the bearing cup bores for nicks or burrs that may have been created during bearing cup removal.

5. Inspect and clean the axle tubes. Inspect the vent to be sure it is not obstructed.

6. Check housing for bent or loose tubes or other physical damage.

7. Inspect the side gears for worn, cracked or chipped teeth. The gears should fit snugly on the axle shaft splines. Also, inspect the fit of the gears in the differential case bore.

Assembly

DIFFERENTIAL

1. Install the side gears, the thrust washers and the pinion gears into the differential case.

NOTE: If new gears and washers are used, it will not be necessary to check the gear backlash. Correct fit is provided due to the close manufacturing tolerances.

2. Install the pinion shaft and lockpin into the case.

3. Assemble the original differential bearing shim packs, then, remove approximately 0.20 in. (0.50mm) shim thickness from each pack; the remaining shims will serve as a starter shim pack.

4. Install the starter shim packs and bearing onto the case.

5. Align and install the ring gear. Using new bolts, torque the ring gear-to-differential case bolts to 100–120 ft. lbs. (136–163 Nm).

6. Install the spreader tool onto the axle housing. Using a dial indicator, spread the axle housing no more than 0.015 in. (0.38mm).

NOTE: Do not spread the housing more than 0.015 in. (0.038mm), for damage may occur to the case.

7. Install the differential; it may be necessary to tap the differential bearing cups, with a soft hammer, to seat them.

8. Install the differential bearing caps and torque the bolts to 70–90 ft. lbs. (95–122 Nm).

9. Remove the spreader tool and dial indicator.

10. Adjust the ring and pinion gear.

11. Using silicone sealant, apply a bead of it to the axle housing. Install the cover and torque the bolts to 35 ft. lbs. (47 Nm).

Front Drive Assembly All Wheel Drive

FRONT DRIVE AXLE

The All Wheel Drive (AWD) system is available on all Caravan/Voyager models equipped with 3.3L V6 engine and Ultradrive transaxle. Under normal driving 90 percent of the torque is allocated to the front wheels. A viscous coupling allows more torque to the rear wheels in accordance with the amount of the slippage at the front wheels. The rear drive line module assembly consists of 5 main parts: the rear carrier, torque tube, overrunning clutch assembly, a vacuum operated dog clutch and a viscous coupling. The rear carrier contains a conventional open differential with hypoid ring gear and pinion gear set. The hypoid gears are lubricated by SAE 85W–90 gear lubricant.

The Power Transfer Unit (PTU) is attached to a modified automatic transaxle case where the right half shaft extension housing would normally be located. The PTU is sealed from the transaxle and has its own oil sump, holding 1.22 quarts. The PTU fill plug is located on the end cover. Do not mistake the black plastic inspection plug located on the PTU case for the fill plug.

Power Transfer Unit (PTU) fill plug, major component and weep hole locations—Caravan/Voyager with All Wheel Drive (AWD)

Power Transfer Unit (PTU) seal and major component identification—Caravan/Voyager with All Wheel Drive (AWD)

PTU Overhaul

Service of the PTU is limited to the seals, gaskets and 1 ball bearing. If the ring gear and pinion, any tapered roller bearings, case, covers or pinion carrier fail, the entire unit must be replaced.

PTU Reseal

For accurate seal diagnosis and repair, correct seal names and locations are critical. When diagnosing fluid leaks on the PTU assembly, note that 2 weep holes are provided to diagnose certain seal leaks. These holes are located on the bottom side of the assembly. If fluid leak is detected from either weep hole, seal replacement is necessary. Do not attempt to repair the leak by sealing the weep holes. They must be kept open for proper seal operation.

If fluid is leaking from weep hole **A** the type of fluid leaking will determine which seal needs to be replaced. If the fluid leaking is red in color, it is transmission fluid which indicates that the transmission carrier seal should be replaced. If the fluid leaking is light brown, it is gear lube which indicates that the PTU input seal should be replaced.

If fluid is leaking from weep hole **B**, the one closest to the driveshaft boot, the type of fluid leaking will determine which seal needs to be replaced. If the fluid leaking is red in color, it is transmission fluid which indicates that the input shaft end seal should be replaced. If the fluid leaking is light brown, it is gear lube which indicates that the halfshaft inner seal and PTU input shaft cover seal should be replaced.

Before condemning any seal or gasket be sure the rear rocker arm cover on the engine is not the cause of the oil leak. Oil leaking from the rocker arm cover is easily mistaken for a leaking power transfer unit.

The power transfer unit must be removed from the vehicle for reseal.

PTU END COVER RESEAL

1. With the PTU removed from the vehicle, remove the PTU end cover bolts.

2. Locate the small rectangular ears on the case cover. Gently tap on the end cover ears with a soft mallet to separate the end cover from the case.

To assemble:

3. Clean and inspect the sealer surfaces.

PTU end cover removal and bolt tightening pattern—Caravan/Voyager with All Wheel Drive (AWD)

Remove input shaft and ring gear. Use seal puller to remove input shaft seal

4. Apply Mopar Gasket Maker 4318083, Loctite Gasket Eliminator No. 518 or equivalent to sealing surfaces.

5. Reinstall the cover. Use care not to damage the PTU input shaft cover seal. Tighten the bolts to 250 inch lbs. in a crisscross pattern. Retighten the first bolt after all others are tight.

6. Reinstall PTU into vehicle. Fill and check fluid levels.

PTU INPUT SHAFT SEAL

1. With the PTU removed from the vehicle, remove the PTU end cover bolts.

2. Locate the small rectangular ears on the case cover. Gently tap on the end cover ears with a soft mallet to separate the end cover from the case.

3. Remove the ring gear oil slinger trough.

4. Remove the input shaft and ring gear from the case.

5. A special factory seal puller is recommended to remove the seal from the PTU case.

To assemble:

6. Clean and inspect seal area. Lay the housing on bench and install a new seal with a suitable seal driver. The seal must be installed with the spring side facing towards the the ring gear. Drive the seal in until it bottoms against the case shoulder.

7. Install the input shaft and oil trough.

8. Apply Mopar Gasket Maker 4318083, Loctite Gasket Eliminator No. 518 or equivalent to sealing surfaces.

9. Reinstall the cover. Use care not to damage the PTU input shaft cover seal. Tighten the bolts to 250 inch lbs. in a crisscross pattern. Retighten the first bolt after all others are tight.

10. Reinstall PTU into vehicle. Fill and check fluid levels.

TRANSAXLE DIFFERENTIAL CARRIER SEAL

1. Remove the PTU from the vehicle.

2. Use a suitable prying tool to remove the seal from the retainer plate. Be careful not to damage the seal journal when removing the seal.

To assemble:

3. Using a large socket, install new seal. The spring side of the seal must face the transaxle differential.

4. Reinstall PTU into vehicle. Fill and check fluid levels.

PTU REAR COVER O-RING

1. With the vehicle safely supported, remove the rear cover retaining bolts.

2. Matchmark the rear cover to the case for later reassembly.

3. Pull the rear cover out of the PTU case.

4. Locate the rear cover O-ring which is in a groove in the cover near the pinion gear.

To assemble:

5. Assembly is the reverse of the disassembly procedure. Use care not to damage or twist the O-ring.

6. Be sure to align the matchmarks made at disassembly.

Removing and installing PTU differential carrier seal

7. Reinstall PTU into vehicle. Fill and check fluid levels.

PTU OUTPUT SEAL AND/OR FLANGE

1. With the PTU removed from the vehicle, remove the rear cover retaining bolts.

2. Matchmark the rear cover to the case for later reassembly.

3. Pull the rear cover/pinion assembly from the PTU case.

4. Clamp the rear cover/output shaft assembly in a soft-jaw vise and remove the output flange nut. Before removing the flange use paint to make a matchmark on both the output flange and the end of the pinion shaft.

5. Using a hydraulic press, press off the output flange from the pinion.

6. Using a suitable prying tool, remove the output seal.

7. If the output flange is damaged and is being replaced, a new shim may be required. Replacement of the output flange requires installation of the correct size shim to maintain bearing preload. The shim must protrude from the new output flange the same distance that the original shim protruded from the original flange. It can checked using the following proceedure.

  a. Stand the original output flange on end with the shim side pointing up.

  b. Place the original shim into the groove in top of the flange.

  c. Place a straight-edge across the shim.

  d. Using a feeler gauge, measure the distance between the straight-edge and the top of the flange. Record this measurement.

  e. Repeat Steps a through d using the new replacement flange and the original shim. Record the measurement.

  f. If the measurements are not equal, use a new shim that will protrude from the new output flange the same amount that the original shim protruded from the original output flange. Example: The original shim protrudes 0.075 inch from the original output flange. Place the original shim into the the new output flange. The protrusion of the shim in the new flange is 0.085 inch. This indicates that a 0.010 inch thinner shim is required to maintain the original protrusion.

To assemble:

8. Clean all parts well. Install the new seal with a suitable driver.

9. If the original flange is used, align the matchmarks made

Matchmark PTU rear cover, remove cover and output shaft, remove and replace O-ring

at disassembly and press the flange onto the pinion. If a new flange is used, disregard the matchmarks and press the flange onto the pinion.

10. Install the flange nut and torque to 120 ft. lbs.

11. Install the rear cover. Use care not to damage the rear cover O-ring.

12. Reinstall the cover. Use care not to damage the PTU input shaft cover seal. Tighten the bolts to 250 inch lbs. in a crisscross

Input shaft cover seal replacement first requires removal of the bearing race, then the seal.

Remove output flange nut and matchmark as shown. Flange replacement requires shim checking using straight-edge.

pattern. Retighten the first bolt after all others are tight.

13. Reinstall PTU into vehicle. Fill and check fluid levels.

PTU INPUT SHAFT COVER SEAL

The PTU input shaft cover seal is the longer of the 2 seals located on the inside of the end cover. The differential bearing cup must be removed to service this seal. The PTU must be removed from the vehicle to perform this operation.

1. With the PTU removed from the vehicle, remove the PTU end cover bolts.

2. Locate the small rectangular ears on the case cover. Gently tap on the end cover ears with a soft mallet to separate the end cover from the case.

3. Use a suitable puller to remove the differential bearing race located in the end cover. The race must be removed to gain access to the seal.

4. Place the end cover is a soft-jaw vise and with a suitable tool, remove the input shaft cover seal.

To assemble:

5. Clean and inspect the seal are. With a suitable driver, install the replacement seal. The spring side of the seal must face toward the installation driver.

6. Reinstall the original bearing race and shim with a suitable driver. The original shim must be installed behind the bearing cup to maintain proper bearing preload.

7. Clean and inspect the sealer surfaces.

8. Apply Mopar Gasket Maker 4318083, Loctite Gasket Eliminator No. 518 or equivalent to sealing surfaces.

9. Reinstall the cover. Use care not to damage the PTU input shaft cover seal. Tighten the bolts to 250 inch lbs. in a crisscross pattern. Retighten the first bolt after all others are tight.

10. Reinstall PTU into vehicle. Fill and check fluid levels.

Input shaft cover seal is driven in place, the original shim is placed under the bearing cup which is then installed with a driver.

PTU half shaft inner seal removal and installation

PTU HALF SHAFT INNER SEAL

The PTU half shaft inner seal is the smaller of the 2 seals located on the inside of the end cover. The PTU must be removed from the vehicle to perform this operation.

1. With the PTU removed from the vehicle, remove the PTU end cover bolts.

2. Locate the small rectangular ears on the case cover. Gently tap on the end cover ears with a soft mallet to separate the end cover from the case.

3. Drive the seal out with a suitable small tool.

PTU input shaft end seal removal

PTU outer half shaft seal may be removed and installed with the PTU assembly still in the vehicle

PTU end cover ball bearing may be removed and installed with the PTU assembly still in the vehicle after first removing the seal for access to the snapring. Use a bearing puller to remove the bearing

To assemble:

4. Clean and inspect the seal area. Install the replacement seal with a $1^1/_{16}$ inch socket as a driver. The seal must be installed with the spring side of the seal facing the end cover ball bearing. The seal should bottom against a machined shoulder in the cover.

5. Apply Mopar Gasket Maker 4318083, Loctite Gasket Eliminator No. 518 or equivalent to sealing surfaces.

6. Reinstall the cover. Use care not to damage the PTU input shaft cover seal. Tighten the bolts to 250 inch lbs. in a crisscross pattern. Retighten the first bolt after all others are tight.

7. Reinstall PTU into vehicle. Fill and check fluid levels.

PTU INPUT SHAFT END SEAL

The input shaft end seal is located on the end of the input shaft and the cover must be removed to access the seal.

1. With the PTU removed from the vehicle, remove the PTU end cover bolts.

2. Locate the small rectangular ears on the case cover. Gently tap on the end cover ears with a soft mallet to separate the end cover from the case.

3. Pry out the seal with a suitable small tool.

To assemble:

4. Clean and inspect the seal area. Remove the input shaft

from the housing and stand on soft block of wood. Install the input shaft end seal with a suitable driver. Lubricate the seal lip after installing the seal into the input shaft.

5. Apply Mopar Gasket Maker 4318083, Loctite Gasket Eliminator No. 518 or equivalent to sealing surfaces.

6. Reinstall the cover. Use care not to damage the PTU input shaft cover seal. Tighten the bolts to 250 inch lbs. in a crisscross pattern. Retighten the first bolt after all others are tight.

7. Reinstall PTU into vehicle. Fill and check fluid levels.

PTU OUTER HALFSHAFT SEAL

The outer halfshaft seal is located on the outside of the end cover. The PTU does not have to be removed to replace this seal.

1. Raise and safely support vehicle.
2. Remove the right front halfshaft from vehicle.
3. Remove the seal with a suitable prybar.

To assemble:

4. Clean and inspect seal area.
5. Install new seal with suitable driver.
6. Reinstall the right front halfshaft.
7. Fill and check fluid levels.

PTU END COVER BALL BEARING

The end cover ball bearing can be removed and installed without removing the PTU from the vehicle. When replacing the bearing the output shaft seal must be removed to gain access to the bearing.

1. Raise and safely support vehicle.
2. Remove the right front halfshaft from vehicle.
3. Remove the output seal with a suitable prybar.
4. Remove the bearing retaining snapring.

5. Use a suitable bearing puller to draw the bearing out of the end cover.

To assemble:

6. Use a suitable bearing driver to install the bearing. Install the snapring.
7. Install new seal with suitable driver. Do not reuse the old seal.
8. Reinstall the right front halfshaft.
9. Fill and check fluid levels.

REAR DRIVE LINE MODULE ASSEMBLY (ALL WHEEL DRIVE)

The All Wheel Drive (AWD) system is available on all Caravan/Voyager models equipped with 3.3L V6 engine and Ultradrive transaxle. Under normal driving 90 percent of the torque is allocated to the front wheels. A viscous coupling allows more torque to the rear wheels in accordance with the amount of the slippage at the front wheels.

The rear drive line module assembly consists of 5 main parts: the rear carrier, torque tube, overrunning clutch assembly, a vacuum operated dog clutch and a viscous coupling. The rear carrier contains a conventional open differential with hypoid ring gear and pinion gear set. The hypoid gears are lubricated by SAE 85W–90 gear lubricant.

A torque tube assembly attaches to the overrunning clutch case. The front torque shaft bearing is located in the torque tube, is permanently sealed and does not require maintenance. The torque shaft is located within the torque tube assembly. The vacuum reservoir and solenoid assembly are attached to the top of the torque tube.

All Wheel Drive rear drive line module oil seal locations

All Wheel Drive rear carrier output shaft and seal removal

Remove inner race snapring, overrunning clutch inner race and dog clutch snapring

The overrunning clutch allows the rear wheels to overrun the front wheels during a rapid front wheel lock braking maneuver. The overrunning action prevents any feedback of front wheel braking torque to the rear wheels and allows the braking system to control the braking behavior as a 2 Wheel Drive (2WD) vehicle.

The overrunning clutch has a separate oil sump and is filled independently from the differential. The fill plug is located on the side of the overrunning clutch case. When filling the overrunning clutch with lubricant, use Mopar type 7176 Automatic Transmission fluid or equivalent.

The dog clutch provides all wheel drive in reverse by bridging and locking out the overrunning clutch. The dog clutch is operated by a double-acting servo using intake manifold vacuum as its power source. Two vacuum solenoids, controlled by the back-up light switch, engage and disengage the dog clutch. A spring in the vacuum servo disengages the dog clutch, if vacuum is lost.

Located in front of the torque tube is the viscous coupling. The viscous coupling controls and distributes torque/power to the rear wheels. The coupling is similar to a multi-plate clutch and consists of a series of closely spaced discs, alternately connected to the front and rear drive units, which operate in silicone fluid. The unit is totally sealed and partially filled with silicone fluid. There is no adjustment, maintenance or fluid checks required during the life of the unit.

Fluid Leak Diagnosis

When diagnosing fluid leaks on the rear drive line module assembly, 2 weep holes are provided to diagnose seal leaks. These

TORQUE TUBE

BEARING SHIELD

SNAP RING

OVERRUNNING CLUTCH CASE

OUTER TORQUE SHAFT BEARING SNAP RING

TORQUE SHAFT REAR BEARING

Remove torque shaft snapring and rear bearing snap ring to access overrunning clutch seal

holes are located on the bottom side of the assembly. If fluid leak is detected from either weep hole, seal replacement is necessary. Do not attempt to repair the leak by sealing the weep holes. They must be kept open for proper seal operation.

If fluid is leaking from weep hole **A** and it is identified to be automatic transmission fluid by its red color, this indicates that the front overrunning clutch seal is leaking. If fluid is leaking from weep hole **B** the type of fluid leaking will determine which seal needs to be replaced. If the fluid leaking is red in color, it is transmission fluid which indicates that the rear overrunning clutch seal should be replaced. If the fluid leaking is light brown, it is hypoid gear lube which indicates that the input pinion seal should be replaced.

Removal and Installation
REAR CARRIER OUTPUT SHAFT SEALS

The rear drive line module assembly does not have to be removed from the vehicle to service the carrier output shaft seals. The output shaft seals are located on the rear carrier unit.

1. Remove the inner halfshaft retaining bolts to separate the

half shafts from the output shaft drive flange. Use care not to allow the halfshafts to hang freely. Tie up with wire to keep the shaft level and the joint straight.

2. Use suitable prybars and wood blocks to pop out the output shafts.

3. Using a suitable prybar, pry out the oil seal being careful not to damage the race.

To install:

4. Installation is the reverse of the removal procedure. Clean and inspect the shaft and seal area.

5. Install the oil seal with a suitable driver.

6. Install the output shaft. Lightly tap the shaft in order to seat the retainer ring into the differential side gear.

7. Install the halfshaft.

8. Check fluid level, fill as required.

FRONT OVERRUNNING CLUTCH SEAL

The rear drive line module must be removed to service this seal. A number of snaprings must be removed. The front overrunning clutch seal is located in the overrunning clutch case.

1. Remove the rear drive line module assembly from the vehicle.

2. Remove the viscous coupling unit.

3. Remove the overrunning clutch cover assembly.

4. Drain fluid from overrunning clutch case.

5. Remove the overrunning clutch case to rear carrier bolts and separate the clutch case from the rear carrier case.

6. Locate and remove the overrunning clutch inner race snapring and slide the clutch inner race off the shaft.

7. Locate and remove the shaft snapring and slide the dog clutch off the shaft.

8. Locate and remove the torque shaft snapring and torque tube bearing shield.

9. Remove the torque tube retaining bolts.

10. Locate and remove the inner torque shaft bearing snapring.

11. Separate the overrunning clutch case from the torque tube.

12. Remove the rear torque shaft bearing retaining outer snapring in the overrunning clutch case and remove the bearing.

13. Using a suitable driver, remove the seal.

To install:

14. Installation is the reverse of the removal procedure. Clean and inspect the shaft sealing surface and case for nicks or grooves. Replace as required.

15. Using a suitable driver, install the new seal. The seal should seat flush with the outside edge of the case.

16. Install the rear torque shaft bearing and outer snapring.

17. Install the overrunning clutch case onto the torque tube and tighten the bolts to 250 inch lbs.

18. Install the torque shaft inner snapring. Slide the dog clutch onto the shaft and install the snapring. Slide the overrunning clutch inner race onto the shaft and install the retaining snapring with the tapered end of the inner race facing outward.

19. Clean sealing surfaces and apply a bead of Mopar Gasket Maker 4318083, Loctite Gasket Eliminator No. 518 or equivalent and reinstall the overrunning clutch housing to the rear carrier case. Install the bolts and tighten to 250 inch lbs.

20. Apply a bead of Mopar Gasket Maker 4318083, Loctite Gasket Eliminator No. 518 or equivalent and reinstall the overrunning clutch cover. When installing the cover be sure the overrunning clutch fork engages into the overrunning clutch dog.

21. Install the rear drive line module assembly into the vehicle. Check and fill fluid levels as required.

DRIVE PINION SEAL AND/OR
REAR OVERRUNNING CLUTCH SEAL

The rear drive line module must be removed to service these seals. The drive pinion seal is located in the front carrier cover

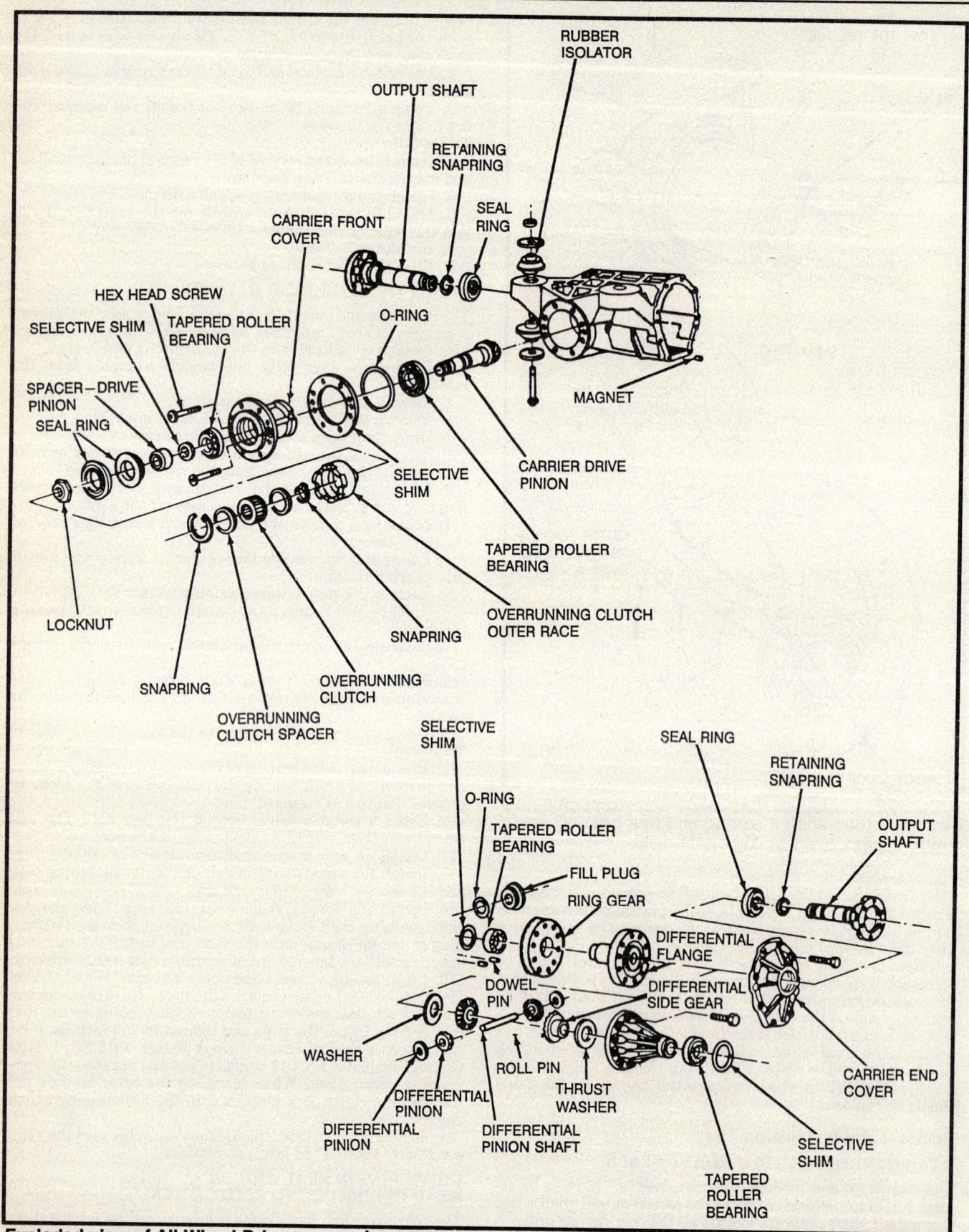

Exploded view of All Wheel Drive rear carrier components

FRONT CARRIER COVER

DRIVE PINION BEARING SHIM

PINION SPACER

PINION SHAFT

WOOD BLOCK

MICROMETER

DRIVE PINION SPACER

FRONT CARRIER COVER

DRIVE PINION SPACER

OVERRUNNING CLUTCH OUTER RACE

SNAP RING

CARRIER CASE

PINION

OVERRUNNING CLUTCH OUTER RACE

PINION NUT

WRENCH

SPECIAL TOOL

Remove overrunning clutch snapring, the outer race and pinion nut

Remove the drive pinion spacer, measure the spacer and replace the spacer

behind the overrunning clutch rear seal. The overrunning clutch seal must be removed to gain access to the input pinion seal. Do not reuse the overrunning clutch seal.

1. Remove the rear drive line module from the vehicle.

2. Remove the overrunning clutch care to rear carrier bolts and separate the overrunning clutch case from the differential carrier case.

3. Remove the overrunning clutch outer race snapring and slide the overrunning clutch outer race off of the shaft.

4. Remove the pinion nut. A special spline socket tool is required to hold the shaft while the pinion nut is loosened.

5. Remove the front carrier cover retaining screw and remove the cover from the case. The pinion will come off with the cover. Note that there should be shim under the pinion spacer. Handle carefully as this shim must be reused. It is installed with the front carrier cover to avoid the potential of cutting the O-ring with the shim.

6. Place a block of wood under the end of the pinion shaft. Hold the shaft vertically with the spline end downwards. Tap the end of the pinion shaft against the wood to drive the pinion spacer off of the pinion shaft.

7. Reinstall the front carrier cover into the carrier case. Tighten the retaining bolts to 105 inch lbs. Use a suitable seal puller to remove the overrunning clutch seal and drive pinion seal. Note that to gain access to the drive pinion seal, the overrunning clutch seal must first be removed. The overrunning clutch seal must be replaced after the drive pinion seal is installed. Do not reuse an old seal.

To install:

8. Installation is the reverse of the removal procedure. Clean and inspect the seal area. Apply a light coat of oil onto the drive pinion seal and install with a suitable driver. The seal must be installed with the spring side in towards the rear carrier case.

NOTE: If the drive pinion spacer is grooved or damaged, it must be replaced. A new drive pinion bearing shim may be required. Refer to Drive Pinion Bearing Shim Selection procedure before continuing.

9. Apply a light coat of oil onto the drive pinion spacer and slide onto the pinion shaft with the tapered side facing outward. Apply a light coat of oil onto the overrunning clutch seal and install with a suitable driver. The seal must be installed with the spring side away from the rear carrier case.

10. Install the pinion nut and tighten to 150 ft. lbs.

11. Install the overrunning clutch outer race and snapring. Clean sealing surfaces and apply a bead of Mopar Gasket Maker 4318083, Loctite Gasket Eliminator No. 518 or equivalent and reinstall the overrunning clutch case to rear carrier case.

12. Install the rear drive line module assembly into the vehicle. Check and fill fluid levels as required.

DRIVE PINION BEARING SHIM SELECTION

This procedure must be performed whenever the drive pinion spacer has been replaced.

1. Using a 1 inch micrometer, measure the thickness of the original spacer.

2. Measure the thickness of the new spacer the same way that the original spacer was measured.

3. The difference in the measurements will determine which shim to use. If the new drive pinion spacer is the same thickness as the original drive pinion spacer, use the original shim.

4. If the new drive pinion spacer is thinner than the original drive pinion spacer, a thicker shim will have to be used to compensate for the difference in size. Use the following procedure:

    a. Determine the difference in size between the new spacer and the original spacer. Record this dimension.

    b. Measure the thickness of the original shim. Record this dimension.

    c. Add together to 2 dimensions and use a shim that is equal to this size. For example: If the new spacer is 0.010 in.

thinner than the original spacer. If the original shim measures 0.205 in., adding 0.205 and 0.010 equals a new shim thickness of 0.215 in.

5. If the new spacer is 0.010 in thinner than the original drive pinion spacer, a thinner shim will have to be used to compensate for the difference in size. Use the following procedure:

    a. Determine the difference in size between the new spacer and the original spacer. Record this dimension.

    b. Measure the thickness of the original shim. Record this dimension.

    c. Subtract the 2 dimensions and use a shim that is equal to this size. For example: If the new spacer is 0.010 in. thicker than the original spacer. If the original shim measures 0.205 in., subtracting 0.010 from 0.205 equals a new shim thickness of 0.195 in.

REAR DRIVE LINE MODULE DIFFERENTIAL SIDE GEARS

1. Disconnect both halfshafts from the rear drive line module.

2. Using 2 suitable prybars, pop out and remove the output shaft.

3. Remove the end cover retaining bolts and take off the cover.

4. Remove the differential assembly from the rear drive line case.

5. Remove the ring gear bolts and separate the differential case from the differential body.

6. Using a suitable punch and hammer, remove the differential pinion shaft pin and slide the differential pinion shaft out of the differential case.

To install:

7. Installation is the reverse of the removal procedure. Inspect and replace pinion gears, pinion shaft or pinion washers as required.

8. Torque ring gear bolts to 70 ft. lbs.

9. Clean sealing surfaces and apply a bead of Mopar Gasket Maker 4318083, Loctite Gasket Eliminator No. 518 or equivalent and install end cover. Tighten bolts to 250 inch lbs. in a criss-cross pattern. Retighten first bolt after all others are tightened.

10. Install output shafts, reconnect halfshafts and fill differential with lubricant.

DIFFERENTIAL CARRIER END COVER RESEAL

1. Disconnect left half shaft.

2. Using 2 suitable prybars, pop out and remove the output shaft.

3. Remove the differential end cover retaining bolts and take off the cover.

To install:

4. Installation is the reverse of the removal procedure. Clean sealing surfaces and apply a bead of Mopar Gasket Maker 4318083, Loctite Gasket Eliminator No. 518 or equivalent and install end cover. Tighten bolts to 250 inch lbs. in a criss-cross pattern. Retighten first bolt after all others are tightened.

5. Install output shafts, reconnect halfshaft and fill differential with lubricant.

OVERRUNNING CLUTCH COVER RESEAL

1. Remove the rear drive line module assembly from the vehicle.

2. Matchmark the hoses for reassembly. Cut the clamps and disconnect the hoses to the vacuum motor.

3. Remove the overrunning clutch cover assembly mounting bolts and lift the clutch cover off the clutch housing.

To install:

4. Installation is the reverse of the removal procedure. Clean sealing surfaces and apply a bead of Mopar Gasket Maker 4318083, Loctite Gasket Eliminator No. 518 or equivalent and

All Wheel Drive torque tube and overrunning clutch components

Removing overruning clutch vacuum motor and shift fork

reinstall cover and vacuum line clip. When installing the cover be sure the overrunning clutch fork engages into the overrunning clutch dog. Tighten bolts to 250 inch lbs.

5. Reinstall the rear drive line module assembly into the vehicle.

6. Check and fill the fluid levels as required. Use only Mopar type 7176 automatic transmission fluid or equivalent in the overrunning clutch case.

OVERRUNNING CLUTCH CASE TO REAR CARRIER CASE RESEAL

1. Remove rear drive line module assembly from vehicle.
2. Drain fluid from overrunning clutch case.
3. Remove overrunning clutch case to rear carrier bolts and separate overrunning clutch case from rear carrier unit.

To install:

4. Installation is the reverse of the removal procedure. Clean sealing surfaces and apply a bead of Mopar Gasket Maker 4318083, Loctite Gasket Eliminator No. 518 or equivalent to sealing surfaces and reassemble.

5. Reinstall the rear drive line module assembly into the vehicle.

6. Check and fill the fluid levels as required. Use only Mopar type 7176 automatic transmission fluid or equivalent in the overrunning clutch housing.

OVERRUNNING CLUTCH VACUUM MOTOR

1. Remove rear drive line module assembly from vehicle.
2. Cut clamps and disconnect vacuum hoses to the vacuum motor.
3. Remove overrunning clutch cover assembly mounting bolts. Lift clutch cover with vacuum motor assembly off of the clutch case.
4. Clamp overrunning clutch cover assembly in soft jawed vise. Remove the 2 E-clips from the vacuum motor shaft.
5. Holding the overrunning clutch shift fork, slide the shift motor out of the housing.

NOTE: Shift fork can be installed backwards by mistake. Note the position of the shift fork before removing. Paint matchmarks if required.

6. Clean and inspect all parts and sealing surfaces. Replace worn or damaged parts.

To install:

7. Installation is the reverse of the removal procedure. Slide the vacuum shift motor into the housing through the shift fork. The shift fork offset angle must be angled away from the vacuum motor.

8. Install the 2 E-clips. One goes on the vacuum shift motor shaft and 1 on the vacuum motor bushing.

9. Clean sealing surfaces and apply a bead of Mopar Gasket Maker 4318083, Loctite Gasket Eliminator No. 518 or equivalent and reinstall cover. When installing cover be sure the overrunning clutch fork engages into the overrunning clutch dog. Tighten the cover bolts to 250 inch lbs.

10. Reinstall the rear drive line module assembly into the vehicle.

11. Check and fill the fluid levels as required.

FORD MOTOR COMPANY

Front Axle Assembly

DANA—MODEL 28, 35, 44 AND 50 AXLES

Several models of Dana front-drive axles are available for Ford vehicle applications.

The Dana Model 28 and 35 front drive axle is used on the Ranger and Bronco II 4WD applications. Before performing any service procedures check the axle identification tag. A code

F07A will appear on the identification tag if the vehicle is equipped with a Dana 35 IFS axle. If a code of E87A appears on the identification tag, the vehicle is equipped with a Dana 28 IFS axle. The axle is equipped with automatic or optional manual locking hubs. The front axle is of the integral carrier housing hypoid-gear type. The differential carrier is made of aluminum and mounts directly to the left axle arm assembly. The right hand axle stub shaft is retained in the carrier by a C-clip in the differential case. To remove the axle shaft the carrier must

Exploded view of the Dana model 44 front axle assembly – model 50 is similar

RIGHT SHAFT
CAMBER ADJUSTER
RIGHT AXLE ARM
KEYSTONE CLAMP
RUBBER BOOT
KEYSTONE CLAMP
SLIP YOKE
YOKE
SEAL
CUP
WASHER
OIL SLINGER
BEARING
COLLAPSIBLE SPACER
SLIP YOKE AND STUB SHAFT
C-CLIP
BEARING
OIL SEAL
DIFFERENTIAL BEARING
CARRIER HOUSING
BEARING CUP
BEARING CAP
RTV GASKET SEALANT
SHIMS
DIFFERENTIAL CASE
OIL BAFFLE
INNER BEARING CUP
INNER BEARING
OIL SLINGER
LEFT AXLE ARM
LOCK PIN
DRIVE PINION
PIVOT BUSHING
RING GEAR
UPPER BALL JOINT
CAMBER ADJUSTER
LOWER BALL JOINT
LEFT SHAFT AND JOINT ASSEMBLY
STEERING KNUCKLE
INNER WHEEL BEARING
SEAL
SPLASH SHIELD
BEARING CUP
NEEDLE BEARING SEAL
SPINDLE NEEDLE BEARING
BEARING CUP
SPINDLE SEAT
OUTER WHEEL BEARING
SPINDLE
MANUAL LOCKING HUB
GREASE SEAL
ROTOR
AUTOMATIC LOCKING HUB

Exploded view of the Dana model 28 front axle assembly

21–44

be removed from the support arm. Bearing and pinion adjustment is by shims. The cover for the axle carrier is integral with the left hand axle assembly. A manufacturing date code and a complete part number is stamped on the left carrier arm between the fill plug and axle end. The Model 28 should not be confused with the Dana Model 28-2 used in Aerostar Electronic Four Wheel Drive (E-4WD) vehicles which can be easily identified by its use of halfshafts and CV-joints.

The Dana model 44 front drive axle is used on Bronco and F-150 4WD applications. The Dana 44 Independent Front Suspension–Heavy Duty (IFS-HD) is available on F-250 4WD applications. The Dana 50 IFS is available on F-250 4WD equipped with heavy duty front end option or F-250 Super Cab models.

All axles are basically alike with some minor differences such as hub type. The cover for the axle carrier is integral with the left hand axle assembly. A metal tag, stamped with the gear ratio and part number is secured to the housing by one of the carrier mounting bolts.

Disassembly

DIFFERENTIAL

1. Remove the left axle arm-to-carrier case bolts, the left arm and drain the lubricant.
2. Remove the right axle stub shaft by performing the following procedures:
   a. Rotate the stub shaft so the open end of the snapring is exposed.
   b. Using 2 prybars, force the snapring from the stub shaft.
   c. Remove the stub shaft from the carrier.
3. Using an axle spreader tool, mount it onto the axle housing and spread the housing enough to remove the differential.
4. Using a dial indicator, measure the amount the opening is being spread; do not spread the housing more than 0.010 in. (0.25mm), for damage to the housing may occur.
5. Mark the differential bearing caps for reassembly purposes.

6. Loosen the bearing caps until 2–3 threads are engaged.
7. Using a prybar, pry the differential loose.
8. Remove the bearing caps and the differential.
9. Mount the differential into a vise.
10. Remove and discard the ring gear bolts; they are not reusable.
11. Using a brass drift and a hammer, tap the ring gear from the differential.
12. Using a differential bearing puller, press the differential bearings from the differential.
13. Remove the differential bearing shims.
14. Remove the pinion shaft lockpin and pinion shaft.
15. Rotate the pinions to remove them through the case opening.
16. Remove the side gears and thrust washers.

PINION GEAR

1. Remove the differential case from the axle carrier housing.
2. Using a pinion yoke holding tool, remove the pinion gear nut.
3. Remove the pinion washer. Using a pinion yoke holder tool and a pinion puller tool, press the yoke from the pinion gear.
4. Using a soft hammer, drive the pinion gear assembly from the axle carrier housing.
5. Using a bearing cup puller tool and a slide hammer, remove the pinion gear oil seal and discard it. Remove the outer

Installing the inner and outer bearing cups—Dana model 44 and 50 front axle assemblies

View of the depth gauge tool set

Old Pinion Marking	New Pinion Marking								
	−4	−3	−2	−1	0	+1	+2	+3	+4
+4	+0.008	+0.007	+0.006	+0.005	+0.004	+0.003	+0.002	+0.001	0
+3	+0.007	+0.006	+0.005	+0.004	+0.003	+0.002	+0.001	0	−0.001
+2	+0.006	+0.005	+0.004	+0.003	+0.002	+0.001	0	−0.001	−0.002
+1	+0.005	+0.004	+0.003	+0.002	+0.001	0	−0.001	−0.002	−0.003
0	+0.004	+0.003	+0.002	+0.001	0	−0.001	−0.002	−0.003	−0.004
−1	+0.003	+0.002	+0.001	0	−0.001	−0.002	−0.003	−0.004	−0.005
−2	+0.002	+0.001	0	−0.001	−0.002	−0.003	−0.004	−0.005	−0.006
−3	+0.001	0	−0.001	−0.002	−0.003	−0.004	−0.005	−0.006	−0.007
−4	0	−0.001	−0.002	−0.003	−0.004	−0.005	−0.006	−0.007	−0.008

Pinion shim selection sizes

pinion bearing and the oil slinger from the carrier input bore.

6. Remove the pinion bearing preload shims.

7. Using a shop press, press the inner pinion bearing cup and baffle from the bore.

8. Rotate the carrier housing. Using a shop press, press the outer pinion bearing cup from the bore.

9. Using a universal bearing remover tool, press the bearing and the oil slinger from the pinion gear.

Inspection

1. Clean the differential components in solvent and use compressed air to dry them. Do not use compressed air on the bearings, only shop towels.

2. Check the components for wear or damage; replace them, if necessary.

3. Inspect the bearings and bearing cups for wear, cracks or scoring; replace them, if necessary.

4. Inspect the differential side and pinion gears for wear, cracks or chips. Replace them, if necessary.

5. Inspect the ring and pinion gears for wear and/or damage. Replace them, if necessary.

6. Inspect the differential case for cracks or damage. Replace it, if necessary.

Assembly

PINION GEAR

1. Make sure the ring and pinion are a matched set.

2. Perform the depth gauge check, performing the following procedures:

   a. Using pinion bearing cup replacer tools and the forcing screw from the depth gauge tool set, install the inner and outer pinion cups.

   b. Place a new rear pinion bearing over the aligning adapter and insert it into the pinion bearing retainer assembly. Place the front pinion bearing into the bearing cup in the carrier and assemble the handle onto the screw and hand tighten.

NOTE: The 3/8 in. drive in the handle is to be used for obtaining the proper pinion bearing preload.

   c. Center the gauge tube into the differential bearing bore. Install the bearing caps and tighten the handle until the bearing preload is 20–40 inch lbs. (2.3–4.5 Nm).

   d. Using a feeler gauge or shims, select the thickest feeler shim that will fit between the gauge tube and the gauge block. Insert the feeler gauge or shims directly along the gauge block to insure a correct reading. The feeler gauge, installed between the gauge tube and the gauge block, should have a slight drag feeling.

   e. After the correct shims or feeler gauge thickness is obtained, check the reading, this is the thickness of shim(s) required, provided that upon inspection of the service pinion gear, the button is etched 0.

NOTE: If the service pinion gear is marked with a (+) plus reading, this amount must be subtracted from the thickness dimension obtained in Step d; example: +2 (−0.002 in.). If the service pinion gear is marked with a (−) minus reading, this amount must be added to the thickness dimension obtained in Step d; example: −2 (+0.002 in.). Be sure to use the exact same new rear pinion bearing that was used in the previous steps.

   f. Using a micrometer, measure the shims to verify the sizes.

3. Place the oil slinger (if used) onto the pinion. Using a pinion bearing cone installer tool, press the bearing onto the pinion gear.

4. Remove the bearing cup and install the oil baffle (1st) and

the required amount of shims into the inner pinion bearing bore.

5. Using the inner pinion bearing cup replacer tool and the forcing screw tool, press the inner pinion bearing cup; be careful not to cock the cup.

6. Lubricate the ends of the outer pinion bearings rollers with long life lubricant and install the outer bearing cone.

7. Measure the original preload shims and replace with new shims of equal size.

8. Install the pinion into the carrier. Install the shims over the pinion, the outer pinion and oil slinger.

9. Assemble the yoke end, the washer, the deflector and slinger onto the pinion shaft and align.

10. Using a companion flange holder tool, seat the yoke, install a new pinion nut and torque to 175 ft. lbs. (237 Nm) for model 28 or 200–220 ft. lbs. (271–298 Nm) except for model 28.

11. Using an inch lb. torque wrench, rotate the pinion gear and check the preload; it should be 20–40 inch lbs. (2.25–4.52 Nm).

NOTE: To increase the preload, remove shims; to decrease the preload, install shims.

12. After the preload is adjusted, remove the yoke and washer.

13. Lubricate the pinion oil seal lip. Using an oil seal installation tool, drive a new oil seal into the carrier housing.

14. Using a companion flange holder tool, seat the yoke, install a new pinion nut and torque to 175 ft. lbs. (237 Nm) or 200–220 ft. lbs. (271–298 Nm) except for model 28.

DIFFERENTIAL

1. Install the side gears, the thrust washers and the pinion gears into the differential case.

2. Install the pinion shaft and lockpin into the case; peen some differential case metal over the pin to lock it in 2 places 180 degrees apart.

3. Assemble the ring gear to the differential case and torque the bolts, alternately, to 45–60 ft. lbs. (61–81 Nm).

4. Place the differential assembly into the carrier housing with the master bearings installed.

5. Adjust the pinion and ring gear backlash.

6. Install the right stub shaft by performing the following procedures:

   a. Insert the stub shaft into the differential carrier.

   b. Position the carrier so the snapring may be installed onto the stub shaft.

   c. Using 2 prybars, press the snapring onto the stub shaft.

7. Using silicone sealant, apply a bead of it to the axle housing. Install the cover and torque the bolts to 35 ft. lbs. (47 Nm) except for model 28 or 40–50 ft. lbs. (54–68 Nm) for model 28.

Adjustment

PINION AND RING GEAR BACKLASH

1. Install the differential and tighten the bearing caps.

2. Force the differential case away from the drive pinion gear, until it is completely seated against the cross bore face of the carrier. Using a dial indicator, position it so the stylus rests on the differential case bolt and zero the indicator.

3. Force the ring gear against the pinion gear. Rock the ring gear, slightly, to make sure the gear teeth are in contact. Then, force the ring gear away from the pinion gear, making sure the dial indicator returns to zero; repeat this procedure until the dial indicator reading is the same.

NOTE: The reading reveals the amount of shims necessary between the differential case and the differential bearing on the ring gear side.

4. Remove the differential case from the carrier and the master bearings from the case.

5. As determined in Step 3, place the required amount of shims onto the ring gear hub of the differential case. Example: if

the reading was 0.045 in. (1.14mm), place 0.045 in. (1.14mm) shims onto the hub of the ring gear side of the differential case.

6. Install the bearing cone onto the hub of the ring gear side of the differential case. Using a differential side bearing replacer tool and a shop press, press the bearing onto the hub.

7. To determine the correct amount of shims to be installed on the hub of the drive pinion side, subtract the reading obtained in step 3 from the differential total case end play. When this amount is determined, add 0.010 in. (0.26mm) to the amount; this is the required amount of shims to be placed on the hub of the drive pinion side of the differential.

Example: Total case end play was 0.091 in. (2.30mm) and the reading in Step 3 was 0.045 in. (1.14mm). Subtract the reading from the end play; the result is 0.046 in. (1.16mm). Then, add 0.010 in. (0.26mm) to the result; 0.056 in. (1.42mm) is the amount of shims to be added on the hub of the drive pinion side of the differential case.

8. Place the required amount of shims onto the hub of the drive pinion side of the differential case.

9. Install the bearing cone onto the hub of the drive pinion side of the differential case. Using a step plate tool, placed on the ring gear side bearing, and a differential side bearing replacer tool, drive the bearing onto the hub of the drive pinion side of the differential case.

10. Using a differential bearing replacer tool, install the bearing cone onto the pinion side of the differential case; be sure to position a pinion bearing cone replacer tool on the ring gear bearing to prevent damage to it.

11. Install the differential bearing cups onto the bearing cones.

12. Using a case spreader tool and a dial indicator, spread the carrier housing to 0.015 in. (0.25mm) max.

13. Install the differential case into the carrier; it may be necessary to use a soft hammer to seat the differential case into the carrier case cross bore.

14. Install the bearing caps; make sure the letters or numbers stamped on the caps correspond in both direction and position with the numbers stamped in the carrier. Torque the bolts to 35–40 ft. lbs. (48–54 Nm) for model 28 or 80–90 ft. lbs. (108–122 Nm) except for model 28.

15. Install a dial indicator to the case and check the ring gear backlash at 3 equally spaced points; the backlash should be 0.005–0.009 in. (0.13–0.23mm) and should not vary more than 0.003 in. (0.08mm) between the points.

NOTE: If the backlash is high, the ring gear must be moved closer to the pinion, by moving the shims to the ring gear side from the opposite side. If the backlash is low, the ring gear must be moved away from the pinion by moving the shims from the ring gear side to the opposite side.

16. Check and/or adjust the gear tooth pattern.

17. Install the right stub shaft by performing the following procedures:

    a. Insert the stub shaft into the differential carrier.

    b. Position the carrier so the snapring may be installed onto the stub shaft.

    c. Using 2 prybars, press the snapring onto the stub shaft.

18. Using silicone sealant, apply it to the mating surface of the carrier support arm.

19. Using 2 guide pins, assemble the carrier housing to the carrier support arm and torque the new bolts to 30–40 ft. lbs. (41–54 Nm) except for model 28 or 40–50 ft. lbs. (54–68 Nm) for model 28.

20. Except for model 28, install the support arm tab bolt to the side of the carrier and torque the bolts to 85 ft. lbs. (115–136 Nm).

21. For model 28, assemble the carrier shear bolt and nut, then, torque to 75–95 ft. lbs. (102–129 Nm).

DANA 60 MONOBEAM AXLE

The differential side bearing shims are located between the side bearing cup assembly and the differential case. The axle use inner and outer shims on the pinion gear. The inner shims are used to control the pinion depth in the housing, while the outer shims are used to preload the pinion bearings. The axle uses a solid differential carrier with a removable side and pinion gear shaft.

Disassembly

DIFFERENTIAL CARRIER

1. The axle assembly can be overhauled either in or out of the vehicle. Either way, the free-floating axles must be removed.

2. Drain the lubricant and remove the rear cover and gasket.

3. Matchmark the bearing caps and the housing for reassembly in the same position. Remove the bearing caps and bolts.

4. Using a spreader tool mounted to the carrier housing, spread the housing a maximum of 0.015 in.

NOTE: Do not exceed this measurement. The housing could be permanently damaged. The use of a dial indicator is recommended to prevent over-stretching the housing.

5. Using a prybar, remove the differential case from the housing. Remove the spreader tool from the housing.

6. Remove the differential side bearing cups and tag to identify the side, if they are to be used again.

7. Remove the differential gear pinion shaft lock pin and remove the shaft. Rotate the side and pinion gears to remove them from the carrier. Remove the thrust bearings.

8. Remove the bearing cones and rollers from the carrier, marking and noting the shim locations.

9. Remove the ring gear bolts and tap the ring gear from the carrier housing.

10. Inspect the components.

DRIVE PINION

1. Remove the pinion nut and flange from the pinion gear.

2. Remove the pinion gear assembly from the housing. It may be necessary to tap the pinion from the housing with a soft faced hammer. Catch the pinion so as not to allow it to drop on the floor.

3. With a long drift, remove the inner bearing cup, pinion seal, slinger, gasket, outer pinion bearing and the shim pack. Label the shim pack for reassembly.

4. Remove the rear pinion bearing cup and shim pack from the housing. Label the shims for reassembly.

5. Remove the rear pinion bearing from the pinion gear with an arbor press and special plates.

Inspection

1. Clean the gears, bearings and component parts with solvent and inspect for scoring, chipping or excessive wear.

2. Inspect the flanges and splines for excessive wear.

3. Replace the necessary parts as required.

PINION SHIM SELECTION

Ring gears and pinions are supplied in matched sets only. The matched numbers are etched on both gears for verification. On the rear face of the pinion, a plus (+) or a minus (−) number will be etched, indicating the best running position for each particular gear set. This dimension is controlled by the shimming behind the inner bearing cup. Whenever baffles or oil slingers are used, they become part of the adjusting shim pack. An example: If a pinion is etched +3, this pinion would require 0.003 in. less shims than a pinion etched 0. This means by removing shims, the mounting distance of the pinion is increased by 0.003 in., which is just what a plus (+) etching indicates. If a pinion is

Exploded view of the Dana 60 Monobeam front axle differential assembly

Assembled view of the Dana 60 Monobeam front axle assembly

Old Pinion Marking	New Pinion Marking								
	−10	−8	−5	−3	0	+3	+5	+8	+10
+10	+.20	+.18	+.15	+.13	+.10	+.08	+.05	+.03	0
+ 8	+.18	+.15	+.13	+.10	+.08	+.05	+.03	0	−.03
+ 5	+.15	+.13	+.10	+.08	+.05	+.03	0	−.03	−.05
+ 3	+.13	+.10	+.08	+.05	+.03	0	−.03	−.05	−.08
0	+.10	+.08	+.05	+.03	0	−.03	−.05	−.08	−.10
− 3	+.08	+.05	+.03	0	−.03	−.05	−.08	−.10	−.13
− 5	+.05	+.03	0	−.03	−.05	−.08	−.10	−.13	−.15
− 8	+.03	0	−.03	−.05	−.08	−.10	−.13	−.15	−.18
−10	0	−.03	−.05	−.08	−.10	−.13	−.15	−.18	−.20

Pinion shim selection sizes

etched −3, it would be necessary to add 0.003 in. more shims than would be required if the pinion was etched 0. By adding the 0.003 in. shims, the mounting distance of the pinion is decreased 0.003 in., which is just what the minus (−) etching indicates. Pinion adjusting shims are available in thicknesses of 0.003 in. (0.08mm), 0.005 in. (0.13mm), 0.010 in. (0.25mm) and 0.030 in. (0.76mm). An example: If a new gear set is used and the old pinion reads +2 and the new pinion reads −2, add 0.004 in. shims to the original shim pack.

Assembly

DRIVE PINION

1. Select the correct pinion depth shims and install in the rear pinion bearing cup bore.
2. Install the rear bearing cup in the axle housing.
3. Add or subtract an equal amount of shim thickness to or from the preload or outer shim pack, as was added or subtracted from the inner shim pack.
4. Install the front pinion bearing cup into its bore in the axle housing.
5. Press the rear pinion bearing onto the pinion gear shaft and install the pinion gear with bearing into the axle housing.
6. Install the preload shims and the front pinion bearing; do not install the oil seal at this time.
7. Install the flange with the holding bar tool attached, the washer and the nut on the pinion shaft end. Torque the nut to 240–300 ft. lbs. (326–406 Nm).
8. Remove the holding bar from the flange and with an inch lb. torque wrench, measure the rotating torque of the pinion gear. The rotating torque should be 10–20 inch lbs. with the original bearings or 20–40 inch lbs. with new bearings. Disregard the torque reading necessary to start the shaft to turn.
9. If the preload torque is not in specifications, adjust the shim pack as required.
   a. To increase preload, decrease the thickness of the preload shim pack.
   b. To decrease preload, increase the thickness of the preload shim pack.
10. When the proper preload is obtained, remove the nut, washer and flange from the pinion shaft.
11. Install a new pinion seal into the housing and reinstall the flange, washer and nut. Using the holder tool, torque the nut to 240–300 ft. lbs. (326–406 Nm).

DIFFERENTIAL CARRIER

1. Install the differential side gears, the differential pinion gears and new thrust washers into the differential carrier.
2. Align the pinion gear shaft holes and install the pinion shaft into the carrier. Align the lock pin hole in the shaft and carrier. Install the lock pin and peen the hole to avoid having the pin drop from the carrier.
3. Install the differential case side bearings with the proper installation tools. Do not install the shims at this time.
4. Place the carrier assembly into the axle housing with the bearing cups on the bearing cones. Install the bearing caps in their original position and tighten the bearing cap bolts enough to keep the bearing caps in place.
5. Install a dial indicator on the housing so the indicator button contacts the carrier flange. Press the differential carrier to prevent side-play and center the dial indicator. Rotate the carrier and check the flange for run-out. If the run-out is greater than 0.002 in., the defect is probably due to the bearings or to the carrier and should be corrected.
6. Remove the assembly and install the ring gear. Torque the retaining bolts and reinstall the assembly into the housing. Install the bearing caps in their original position and tighten the cap bolts to keep the bearings caps in place.
7. Install the dial indicator and position the indicator button to contact the ring gear back surface. Rotate the assembly and

the run-out should be less than 0.002 in. If over 0.002 in., remove the assembly and relocate the ring gear 180 degrees. Reinstall the assembly and recheck. If the run-out remains over the 0.002 in. tolerance, the ring gear is defective. If the measurement is within tolerances, continue on with the assembly.

8. Position 2 prybars between the bearing cap and the housing on the side opposite the ring gear. Pull on the prybars and force the differential carrier as far as possible towards the dial indicator. Rock the assembly to seat the bearings and reset the dial indicator to zero.
9. Reposition the prybars to the opposite side of the carrier and force the carrier assembly as far towards the center of the housing. Read the dial indicator scale. This will be the total amount of shims required for setting the backlash during the reassembly, less the bearing preload. Record the measurement.
10. With the pinion gear installed and properly set, position the differential carrier assembly into the axle housing and install the bearing caps in their proper positions. Tighten the cap bolts just to hold the bearing cups in place.
11. Install a dial indicator on the axle housing with the indicator button contacting the back of the ring gear.
12. Position 2 prybars between the bearing cup and the axle housing on the ring gear side of the case and pry the ring gear into mesh with the pinion gear teeth, as far as possible. Rock the ring gear to allow the teeth to mesh and the bearings to seat. With the pressure still applied by the prybars, set the dial indicator to zero.
13. Reposition the prybars on the opposite side of ring gear and pry the gear as far as it will go. Take the dial indicator reading. Repeat this procedure until the same reading is obtained each time. This reading represents the necessary amount of shims between the differential carrier and the bearing on the ring gear side.
14. Remove the bearing from the differential carrier on the ring gear side and install the proper amount of shims. Reinstall the bearing.
15. Remove the differential carrier bearing from the opposite side of the ring gear. To determine the amount of shims needed, use the following method.
   a. Subtract the size of the shim pack just installed on the ring gear side of the carrier from the reading obtained and recorded when measurement was taken without the pinion gear in place.
   b. To this figure, add an additional 0.015 in. to compensate for preload and backlash. An example: If the first reading was 0.085 in. and the shims installed on the ring gear side of the carrier were 0.055 in., the correct amount of shims would be 0.085 − 0.055 + 0.015 = 0.045 in.
16. Install the required shims as determined under step 15 and install the differential side bearing. The installation of the shims should give the proper preload to the bearings and the proper backlash to the ring and pinion gears.
17. Spread the axle housing with the spreader tool no more than 0.015 in. Install the differential bearing outer cups in their correct locations and install the cups in their respective locations.
18. Install the bolts and tighten finger-tight. Rotate the differential carrier and ring gear and tap with a soft-faced hammer to insure proper seating of the assembly in the axle housing.
19. Remove the spreader tool and torque the cap bolts to 80–90 ft. lbs. (108–122 Nm).
20. Install a dial indicator and check the ring gear backlash at 4 equally spaced points of the ring gear circle. The backlash must be within a range of 0.004–0.009 in. and must not vary more than 0.003 in. between the points checked.
21. If the backlash is not within specifications, the shim packs must be corrected to bring the backlash within limits.
22. Check the tooth contact pattern and verify.
23. Install the cover and torque the bolts to 30–40 ft. lbs. (41–54 Nm). Refill to proper level with lubricant and operate to verify proper assembly.

PRELOAD
BACKLASH
SHIMS

DIFF. BEARING
CUP

SELECTIVE SHIM

INNER PINION
BEARING CUP

INNER PINION BEARING
CONE

BAFFLE

COLLAPSIBLE SPACER

OUTER PINION BEARING CUP

OUTER PINION BEARING
CONE

PINION SEAL

COMPANION FLANGE
ASSEMBLY

C-CLIPS

FILL
PLUG

DIFF.
BEARING CONE

BREATHER

1. NUT (PINION)
2. WASHER (PINION)
3. COMPANION FLANGE
4. PINION SEAL
5. THRUST WASHER (OUTER PINION BEARINGS)
6. OUTER PINION BEARING CONE
7. OUTER PINION BEARING CUP
8. COLLAPSIBLE SPACER
(PINION BEARING PRELOAD)
9. BAFFLE
10. INNER PINION BEARING CUP
11. INNER PINION BEARING CONE
12. PINION POSITION SHIM
13. DIFFERENTIAL BEARING CAP SCREW
14. DIFFERENTIAL BEARING CUP
15. DIFFERENTIAL BEARING CONE
16. DIFFERENTIAL BEARING PRELOAD
AND BACKLASH SHIMS
17. ROLL PIN (PINION MATE SHAFT)
18. DIFFERENTIAL CASE
19. RING GEAR SCREW

20. COVER PLATE
21. COVER SCREW
22. RTV SEALANT
23. AXLE SHAFT (RIGHT HAND)
24. SEAL (AXLE SHAFT)
25. BEARING (AXLE SHAFT)
26. AXLE SHAFT (LEFT HAND)
27. FILL PLUG
28. VENT
29. RING GEAR AND DRIVE PINION ASSEMBLY
30. MOUNTING BRACKET
31. SCREW (MOUNTING BRACKET)
32A*. HOUSING
32B*. DIFFERENTIAL BEARING CAP
33. SIDE GEAR THRUST WASHER
34. SIDE GEAR
35. PINION MATE GEAR THRUST WASHER
36. DIFFERENTIAL PINION MATE GEAR
37. SNAP RING (AXLE SHAFT RETENTION)
38. DIFFERENTIAL PINION MATE SHAFT

*DIFFERENTIAL BEARING CAPS ARE
PART OF THE HOUSING AND CANNOT
BE SERVICED SEPARATELY

Carrier assembly—Ford Aerostar with E-4WD all wheel drive

Top: removing axle snaprings. Bottom: Installing axle snaprings. Note position of tool to push snapring. Push as shown. Do not push on center of snapring or it will spread and be damaged.

DANA MODEL 28-2

The Dana Model 28-2 is used on Aerostar vans equipped with Electronic Four-Wheel Drive (E-4WD). The drive axle assembly has an integral carrier housing containing a spiral bevel gear. The pinion is in line with the centerline of the ring gear. Specified lubrication is approximately 35 ounces of Motorcraft Mercon Multi-Purpose Automatic Transmission Fluid or equivalent.

The differential carrier is made of aluminum and is mounted to a sub-frame assembly. The axle shafts are retained in the carrier by C-clips in the differential case. To remove the axle shafts, the axle assembly must be removed from the sub-frame.

Adjustment of the differential bearings is by shims. The bearings are preloaded by the squeezing action of the carrier housing and bearing caps. A spreader must be used on the axle housing to relieve tension on the bearings and permit removal and installation of the differential.

The drive pinion gear shaft is supported by 2 opposed tapered roller bearings which are assembled in the carrier housing. Pinion depth is controlled by a selective oil slinger installed in front of the drive pinion inner bearing cone. Pinion bearing preload is controlled by a collapsible spacer on the drive pinion.

Pulling oil seal and caged needle bearing using slide hammer and adapters

The differential case assembly is supported by 2 opposed tapered roller bearings and cups, which are retained in the housing by removeable caps. Shims, installed between each differential bearing and the shoulder of the case, perform 3 functions: they take up the differential case side clearance, they adjust the backlash between ring gear and drive pinion, and they establish differential bearing preload.

Disassembly and Assembly

AXLE SHAFTS, CARRIER OIL SEAL AND BEARING

1. Remove the axle assembly from the sub-frame and the vehicle.
2. Remove the cover plate and drain lubricant.
3. Mount the axle assembly in a suitable fixture.
4. Rotate the shafts so the open side of the snapring is exposed. Remove the snaprings from the shafts.
5. Remove the shafts from the assembly.
6. Use a suitable puller to remove the axle shaft oil seals and caged needle bearings from the axle carrier. Take note of the bearing installation. It should have been installed with the manufacturer name and part number facing outwards. Replacement bearings must be installed in the same manner. Discard both the seals and bearings.

To assemble:

7. Assembly is the reverse of the disassembly procedure. Make sure the bearing bore is free from nicks and burrs. Install a new caged needle bearing using a suitable installation driver. Drive the needle bearing unit in until it is seated in the bore.
8. Coat the axle oil seal with multi-purpose lubricant. Drive the seal into the carrier using a suitable driver.
9. Install the axle shafts into the carrier so the groove in the shaft is visible in the differential case.
10. Install the snapring in the groove in the shaft. Force the snapring into position. Do not tap on the center of the snapring. This may damage the snapring. Push against the groove in the snapring ears.
11. Clean all traces of sealer from carrier and cover. Apply a

1/8–1/4 in. bead of RTV sealer and install the cover plate.

12. Allow 1 hour for the sealant to cure. Fill the carrier with lubricant and install the axle assembly into the vehicle.

CARRIER ASSEMBLY

1. Remove the axle assembly from the sub-frame and the vehicle.

2. Remove the cover plate and drain lubricant.

3. Mount the axle assembly in a suitable fixture.

4. Rotate the shafts so the open side of the snapring is exposed. Remove the snaprings from the shafts.

5. Remove the shafts from the assembly.

6. Remove the bearing caps. Note the matched numbers or letters stamped on the cap and carrier. If these marks are missing or unreadable, punch new matchmarks. These marks must be matched at assembly.

7. Remove the differential case from the carrier. A case spreading tool should be used. It may be necessary to pry the case from the carrier. Use care not to damage any machined surfaces. Remove and tag bearing cups to indicate from which side of the carrier they were removed. Remove spreader tool.

8. Turn the nose of the carrier upwards. Hold the companion flange with a suitable holding tool. Remove the pinion shaft nut and washer. Use a suitable puller to remove the companion flange. Inspect the companion flange for signs of wear at the point of seal contact. If worn, replace the flange.

9. Remove the drive pinion by tapping on the end with a rawhide or plastic mallet. Catch the pinion to prevent damage. Use care. The pinion teeth have sharp edges.

10. Remove the pinion shaft oil seal.

11. Remove the outer pinion bearing cone, oil slinger, and collapsible spacer.

12. Using a suitable puller, remove the inner pinion bearing cup. Remove the oil baffle from the inner bearing cup bore. An oil baffle is located between the inner bearing cup and carrier bore. If the baffle is damaged during cup removal, measure the thickness of the baffle and replace with one of equal thickness.

13. Turn the nose of the carrier down and remove the outer pinion bearing cup with a suitable driver.

14. Using a suitable puller, remove the differential case bearings and shims from the case. Wire the shims, bearing cup and cone together and identify from which side of the differential case they were removed. If any shims were damaged, replace with new ones at assembly.

15. Pad the jaws of a bench vise with several layers of shop towels to protect the gear teeth and place the differential case in the vise. Remove the ring gear screws and discard them. They should not be reused. Tap the ring gear with a rawhide mallet to free it from the case. Remove the case and ring gear from the vise.

16. With a suitable puller, remove the inner pinion bearing cone and oil splinger/position shim from the drive pinion. Note that for controlling drive pinion depth, an oil slinger with a selected thickness is located between the inner pinion bearing cone and drive pinion head. Be careful not to damage the oil slinger when removing the bearing. If the oil slinger is damaged, measure the thickness and replace with an oil slinger of equal thickness.

To assemble:

17. Assembly is the reverse of the removal procedure. Inspect all parts for damage. Clean all parts to be reused. A number of checks will be made during the assembly process.

18. To check total differential case end play use the following procedure:

   a. Attach the ring gear to the differential case using new screws. Tighten alternately to 45–65 ft. lbs.

   b. The factory recommends so-called master bearings be placed on the differential. Remove all burrs and nicks from the hubs so the master bearings rotate freely.

   c. Place the differential case into the carrier without the pinion. The differential case should move freely in the carrier.

   d. Mount a dial indicator with minimum travel of 0.200 in. so its pintle locates on the flat surface of the top of one ring gear screws. Force the differential case toward the dial indicator as far as possible and zero the dial indicator still applying force to the differential case.

   e. Force the differential case away from the dial indicator as far as it will go. Repeat this procedure until the same reading is obtained. Call this reading **Measurement A** and record this dial indicator reading. It will be used later during axle buildup. This reading indicates the amount of shims needed behind the differential side bearings to take up the total clearance between the differential bearing and case.

   f. Remove the differential case from the carrier but do not remove the master bearings at this time.

19. Two separate adjustments affect contact between the ring gear and drive pinion: Pinion Depth and Pinion/Ring Gear Backlash. Pinion depth is controlled by an oil slinger with a selective thickness located between the drive pinion head and inner pinion bearing cone and an oil baffle located between the inner bearing cup and carrier bore. Pinion/ring gear backlash is controlled by preload shims located between the differential bearings and differential case. In the pinion depth adjustment, the size of the selected thickness oil slinger and the oil baffle controls pinion position. Increasing the oil slinger thickness moves the pinion toward the ring gear. Decreasing the oil slinger thickness moves the pinion away from the ring gear.

20. To perform a depth gauge check, use the following procedure:

   a. Assemble the recommended gauge tube tool set and adapters. The same depth gauge tool set used to service other Dana axles may be used.

   b. Install the oil baffle in the inner bearing cup bore in the carrier.

   c. Install the inner and outer pinion bearing cups with an appropriate driver.

   d. Place a new rear pinion bearing over the proper aligning adapter and insert into the pinion bearing retainer assembly. Install into the carrier.

   e. Center the proper gauge tube into the differential bearing bore. Install the bearing caps, torque to 30–45 ft. lbs. Preload the bearing by turning the gauge tube tool handle to about 20–40 inch lbs.

   f. Using a feeler gauge tool, select the thickest feeler gauge that will enter between the gauge tube and gauge block. There should be a slight drag on the feeler gauge. Record the size of the feeler gauge. This is the thickness of the oil slinger required providing that upon inspection of the service pinion gear, there are no markings. If the service pinion gear is marked with a plus (+) reading, this amount must be subtracted from the thickness of the feeler gauge. Make all checks using the exact same bearing.

21. Measure the oil slinger with a micrometer to verify the slinger size. Place the oil slinger on the pinion and press on the bearing using a hydraulic press and appropriate adapters. Continue to build the remaining components with proper pinion and differential bearing preload torques and ring gear backlash.

22. To check the drive pinion preload, use the following procedure:

   a. Install a new collapsible spacer, outer bearing cone and thrust washer. Never reuse a collapsible spacer. Always discard the spacer and install a new one.

   b. Coat the pinion seal with hypoid gear lubricant and install the seal with a appropriate driver. After installation, check to make sure the garter spring didn't pop out. If the spring came out, remove and replace the seal.

   c. Install the companion flange, washer and pinion nut. Torque nut to 140 ft. lbs.

   d. Place an inch-pound torque wrench on the pinion nut and turn the pinion. Rotational torque should be 15–35 inch lbs. except for 3.73 ration axle or 2–4 inch lbs. for 3.73 ratio axle. If the reading is less than 15 inch lbs., tighten the pinion nut in small amounts until the proper specification is reached. Do not tighten the pinion nut more than 275 ft. lbs.

e. If the reading is more than 15–35 inch lbs., the collapsible spacer has been compressed too far. The spacer must be removed and a new collapsible spacer installed.

23. If the differential case is to be disassembled, place the case in a vise and drive out the lock pin that retains the pinion shaft. With a hammer and soft drift pin, drive out the pinion shaft. Rotate the pinion gears and side gears until they can be removed through the openings in the differential case. Take out the gears and thrust washers.

24. Inspect the pinion gears and parts for wear. If wear exists on all parts, replace the entire differential case assembly. If 1 gear shows signs of wear, replace both pinion mate and side gears as a set.

25. Clean parts well and lubricate. Hold side gears in place in the case with 1 hand and install the pinion mate gears and washers with the other hand. Rotate the side gears and pinion gears until the holes in the washers and pinion gears align exactly with the holes in the case. Insert the pinion shaft and align the lock pin hole. Insert lock pin and peen some metal of the case over the pin to lock it in place.

26. Assemble the ring gear to the differential case. Use new screws and tighten alternately to 45–65 ft. lbs. Place differential case into the carrier. Note that the master bearings used in checking differential case end play previously in Step 18 should still be installed. Mount dial indicator to housing for pinion and ring gear backlash check using the following procedure:

a. Force the differential case away from the drive pinion gear until it is completely seated against the cross bore face of the carrier. Position the dial indicator tip so it rests on a differential case screw. Zero the indicator.

b. Force the ring gear against the pinion gear. Rock the ring gear slightly to make sure the gear teeth are in contact. Then force the ring gear away from the drive pinion gear making sure the dial indicator returns to zero. Repeat this procedure until the dial indicator reading is the same. Call this reading **Measurement B**. Record this reading and compare it the the reading obtained in Step 18, **Measurement A**.

c. Remove the differential case from the carrier and remove the master bearings.

d. Make the calculations for the proper shim selection: **A** minus **B** equal **C**. For example, if the total amount of space measured in Step 18 without the gearset assembled in the carrier was 0.090 in. (**A**), and total amount of space measured in Step 26 with the gear set assembled into the housing was 0.045 in. (**B**), then **A**, 0.090 minus **B**, 0.045 equals **C** 0.045.

e. Assemble the shim packs onto the differential case hubs with new bearing cones. Continue to build the axle.

27. Spread the case no more than 0.010 inch and install the differential carrier. Use care not to nick gears. Align marks on ring and pinion, if any.

28. Install bearing caps and bolts. Check that matchmarks are properly aligned. Tighten bolts to 30–45 ft. lbs.

29. Paint ring gear teeth with marking compound and rotate ring gear 1 complete revolution while load is being applied with a prybar between the carrier casting and differential case flange. Check mesh pattern. Adjust shims accordingly.

a. A dial indicator may be mounted to check backlash. Check at 3 equally spaced locations. Backlash specification on this axle is 0.005–0.008 inch and may not vary more than 0.003 inch between checkpoints.

b. If backlash is high, the ring gear should be moved closer to the pinion by moving differential bearing shims to the ring gear side from the pinion side. If backlash is low, move the ring gear away from the pinion.

c. When a change in backlash is required, backlash shims should be changed in the range of 1½ times the amount of backlash required. For example, if the backlash needed to be changed 0.004 inch, the shim pack should be changed by 0.006 inch as a starting point.

30. Assemble axle shafts into carrier, apply RTV to cover and install. Allow 1 hour for RTV to cure. Install axle, fill axle with 35 ounces Motorcraft Mercon ATF.

Rear Axle Assembly

FORD—10¼ AND 8.8 INCH RING GEAR AXLES

Disassembly

DIFFERENTIAL CARRIER

1. Remove the cover and clean the lubricant from the internal parts.

2. Using a dial indicator, measure and record the ring gear backlash and the runout; the backlash should be 0.008–0.015 in. and the runout should be less than 0.004 in.

3. Mark 1 differential bearing cap to ensure it is installed its original position.

4. Loosen the differential bearing cap bolts.

5. Using a prybar, pry the differential carrier until the bearing cups and shims are loose in the bearing caps.

6. Remove the bearing caps and the differential assembly.

7. If necessary, remove ring gear-to-differential case bolts. Using a hammer and a punch, strike the alternate bolt holes around the ring gear to dislodge it from the differential.

8. If necessary, remove the ABS excitor ring by striking it with a soft hammer.

9. Remove the pinion shaft lock bolt from the differential case. Remove the differential pinion shaft, the pinion gears and the thrust washers.

10. Remove the side gears and thrust washers.

11. Using a bearing puller tool, press the bearings from the differential carrier.

PINION GEAR

1. Remove the differential carrier assembly.

2. Using a companion flange holding tool, remove the companion flange nut.

3. Using a puller tool, press the companion flange from the pinion gear.

4. Using a soft hammer, drive the pinion gear from the housing.

5. Using a prybar, remove the pinion gear oil seal from the housing.

6. Remove the oil slinger and the front pinion bearing.

7. Using a shop press, press the bearing cone from from the pinion gear.

8. Remove and record the shim from the pinion gear.

Inspection

1. Clean the differential components in solvent and use compressed air to dry them; do not use compressed air on the bearings, only shop towels.

2. Check the components for wear or damage; replace them, if necessary.

3. Inspect the bearings and bearing cups for wear, cracks or scoring; replace them, if necessary.

4. Inspect the differential side and pinion gears for wear, cracks or chips; replace them, if necessary.

5. Inspect the ring and pinion gears for wear and/or damage; replace them, if necessary.

6. Inspect the differential case for cracks or damage. Replace it, if necessary.

Assembly
PINION GEAR

NOTE: When replacing the ring and pinion gear, the correct shim thickness for the new gear set to be installed is determined by following procedure using a pinion depth gauge tool set.

1. Assemble the appropriate aligning adapter, the gauge disc and gauge block to the screw.
2. Place the rear pinion bearing over the aligning tool and insert it into the rear portion of the bearing cup of the carrier. Place the front bearing into the front bearing cup and assemble the tool handle into the screw. Roll the assembly back and forth a few times to seat the bearings while tightening the tool handle, by hand, to 20 ft. lbs. (27 Nm).

NOTE: The gauge block must be offset 45 degrees to obtain an accurate reading.

3. Center the gauge tube into the differential bearing bore. Install the bearing caps and tighten the bolts to 70–85 ft. lbs. (96–115 Nm); be sure to install the caps with the triangles pointing outward.
4. Place the selected shim(s) on the pinion and press the pinion bearing cone and roller assembly until it is firmly seated on the shaft, using the pinion bearing cone replacer and the axle bearing/seal plate.
5. Place the collapsible spacer on the pinion stem against the pinion stem shoulder.
6. Install the front pinion bearing and oil slinger in the housing bore and install the pinion seal on the pinion seal replacer. Using a hammer, install the seal until it seats.
7. From the rear of the axle housing, install the drive pinion assembly into the housing pinion shaft bore.
8. Lubricate the pinion shaft splines and install the companion flange.
9. Using a companion flange holder tool, torque the pinion nut to 160 ft. lbs. (217 Nm); rotate the pinion gear, occasionally, to ensure proper bearing seating.
10. Using an inch pound torque wrench, frequently, measure the pinion bearing preload. It should be 9–14 inch lbs. for used bearings or 16–29 inch lbs. for new bearings.

NOTE: If the preload is higher than the specification, tighten to the original reading as recorded. Never back off the pinion nut.

DIFFERENTIAL CARRIER

1. If the bearings were removed, use a shop press to press them onto the differential case.
2. Install the side gears and thrust washers. Install the pinion gears, the thrust washer, the pinion shaft and the pinion shaft lock bolt.
3. Using a shop press, align the excitor ring tab with the differential case slot and press the ring gear and excitor ring onto the differential case. Install the ring gear-to-differential case bolts and torque them to 100–120 ft. lbs. (135–162 Nm).
4. Place the differential case with the bearing cups into the housing.
5. On the left side, install a 0.265 in. shim. Install the bearing cap and tighten the bolts finger-tight.
6. On the right side, install progressively larger shims until the largest can be installed by hand. Install the bearing cap.
7. Torque the bearing cap-to-housing bolts to 70–85 ft. lbs. (95–115 Nm).
8. Rotate the assembly to ensure free rotation.
9. Adjust the ring gear backlash.

Backlash Change Required	Thickness Change Required	Backlash Change Required	Thickness Change Required
.001	.002	.009	.012
.002	.002	.010	.014
.003	.004	.011	.014
.004	.006	.012	.016
.005	.006	.013	.018
.006	.008	.014	.018
.007	.010	.015	.020
.008	.010		

Pinion shim selection sizes

Backlash adjustement by changing shims

Adjustment
RING GEAR AND PINION BACKLASH

1. Using a dial indicator, measure the ring gear and pinion backlash; it should be 0.008–0.015 in. If the backlash is 0.001–0.007 in. or greater than 0.015 in. proceed to Step 3. If the backlash is zero, proceed to Step 2.
2. If the backlash is zero, add 0.020 in. shim(s) to the right side and subtract a 0.020 in. shim(s) from the left side.
3. If the backlash is within specification, go to Step 7. If the backlash is 0.001–0.007 in. or greater than 0.015 in., increase the thickness of a shim on 1 side and decrease the same thickness of another shim on the other side, until the backlash comes within range.
4. Install and torque the bearing cap bolts to 80–95 ft. lbs. (109–128 Nm).
5. Rotate the assembly several times to ensure proper seating.
6. Recheck the backlash, if it is not within specification, go to Step 7.
7. Remove the bearing caps. Increase the shim sizes, on both sides by 0.006 in.; make sure the shims are fully seated and the assembly turns freely. Use a shim driver to install the shims.
8. Install the bearing caps and torque the bearing caps to 80–95 ft. lbs. (109–128 Nm). Recheck the backlash. If not to specification, repeat this entire procedure.

COVER ASSEMBLY · U-WASHER · SIDE GEAR AND THRUST WASHER · DIFFERENTIAL CASE · DIFFERENTIAL BEARING CUP · ADJUSTABLE SHIM · LIQUID GASKET · DIFFERENTIAL BEARING · RING AND PINION GEAR · BEARING ASSEMBLY · AXLE HOUSING · PINION SHIM · BEARING CUP · FILLER PLUG · WHEEL BEARING SEAL · BEARING CUP · AXLE SHAFT · PINION NUT · SPACER · SLINGER · FLANGE · BEARING ASSEMBLY · BEARING ASSEMBLY · SEAL

Exploded view of the 7½ inch ring gear axle assembly—Ford Motor Company

FORD—7½ INCH RING GEAR AXLE

Disassembly

DIFFERENTIAL CASE

1. Check and record the ring gear runout and backlash.
2. Mark on differential bearing cap to help position the caps properly during assembly.
3. Loosen the differential bearing cap bolts and bearing caps.

NOTE: The direction of arrows on bearing caps must be noted. When reassembled, the arrows must be pointing in the same direction as before removal.

4. Pry the differential case, bearing cups and shims out until they are loose in the bearing caps. Remove the bearing caps and the differential assembly from the carrier.

NOTE: If the ring gear is removed, discard the bolts. Install new bolts, coated with thread locking compound. Tighten to 70–85 ft. lbs. (95–115 Nm).

DRIVE PINION

1. Hold the rear axle companion flange with the proper tool and remove the pinion nut.
2. Remove the companion flange. With a soft-faced hammer, drive the pinion out of the front bearing cone and remove it through the rear of the carrier casting.
3. Remove the drive pinion oil seal with tool 1125–AC and

T50T–100–A or their equivalent. Remove the front pinion bearing cone, the roller and slinger from the housing.
4. To remove the pinion rear bearing cone, use tool T71P–4621–B or equivalent. Measure the shim found under the bearing cone with a micrometer. Record the thickness of the shim.

NOTE: Before assembling the rear bearing cone to the pinion, it will be necessary to adjust pinion depth.

Inspection

1. Clean the differential components in solvent and use compressed air to dry them. Do not use compressed air on the bearings, only shop towels.
2. Check the components for wear or damage; replace them, if necessary.
3. Inspect the bearings and bearing cups for wear, cracks or scoring. Replace them, if necessary.
4. Inspect the differential side and pinion gears for wear, cracks or chips. Replace them, if necessary.
5. Inspect the ring and pinion gears for wear and/or damage. Replace them, if necessary.
6. Inspect the differential case for cracks or damage. Replace it, if necessary.

Assembly

DRIVE PINION

1. Place the selected shim(s) on the pinion shaft and press the pinion bearing until firmly seated on the shaft.

2. Place the rear pinion bearing (new or used if in good condition) over the aligning disc and insert it into the pinion bearing cup of the carrier. Place the front bearing into the front bearing cup and assemble the tool handle into the screw and tighten to 20 ft. lbs. (27 Nm).

NOTE: The gauge block must be offset to obtain an accurate reading.

3. Center the gauge tube into the differential bearing bore. Install the bearing caps and torque the bolts to specification; the caps must be installed with the arrows point outboard.

4. Make sure the gauge handle adapter screw, aligning adapter, gauge disc and gauge block assembly are securely mounted between front and rear bearing. Recheck tool handle torque prior to gauging to ensure the bearings are properly seated. This can affect final shim selection when improperly assembled. Clean bearing cups and differential pedestal surfaces thoroughly. Apply only light oil film on bearing assemblies prior to gauging.

5. Gauge block should then be rotated several ½ turns to ensure rollers are properly seated in bearing cups. Rotational torque on the gauge assembly should be 20 inch lbs. with new bearings. Final position should be approximately 45 degrees across the gauge tube to ensure the gauge block is aligned with gauge tube high point. This area should be utilized for pinion shim selection. Selection of pinion shim with gauge block not aligned with tube high point will cause improper shim selection and may result in axle noise.

6. Utilize pinion shims as the gauge for shim selection. This will minimize errors in attempting to stack feeler gauge stock together or simple addition errors in calculating correct shim thickness.

NOTE: Shims must be flat. Do not use dirty, bent, nicked or mutilated shims as a gauge.

7. It is important to utilize a light drag on the shim for the correct selection. Do not attempt to force the shim between the gauge block and gauge tube. This will minimize selection of a shim thicker than required which results in a deep tooth contact in final assembly for integral axles.

8. If the pinion has a plug (+) marking, subtract his amount from the feeler gauge measurement. If the pinion has a minimum (−) marking, add this amount to the feeler gauge measurement.

DIFFERENTIAL CASE

For shim selection after a complete replacement of the rear axle housing, the differential assembly or differential side bearings use the following instructions. For a ring and pinion replacement only or a backlash adjustment, follow Steps 9 through 13 and Step 15, using the side bearing shims that were originally in the axle.

1. With pinion depth set and pinion installed, place differential case gear assembly with bearings and cups into the carrier.

2. Install a 0.265 in. (6.73mm) shim on left side.

3. Install left bearing cap and tighten bolts finger-tight.

4. Install progressively larger shims on the right side until the largest shim selected can be assembled with a slight drag feel.

NOTE: Apply pressure towards the left side to ensure bearing cup is seated.

5. Install right side bearing cap and tighten bearing cup bolts to 70–85 ft. lbs. (95–115 Nm).

6. Rotate assembly to ensure free rotation.

7. Check the ring gear and pinion backlash. If the backlash is 0.008–0.015 in. (0.20–0.38mm) with 0.012–0.015 in. (0.304–0.381mm) preferred, proceed to Step 14. If backlash is not within specifications, go to Step 10, unless zero backlash is measured, then, go to Step 8.

SHIM CODE CHART

NUMBER OF STRIPES AND COLOR CODE	DIM.
2 — C-COAL	.3070- .3075
1 — C-COAL	.3050- .3055
5 — BLU	.3030- .3035
4 — BLU	.3010- .3015
3 — BLU	.2990- .2995
2 — BLU	.2970- .2975
5 — PINK	.2930- .2935
4 — PINK	.2910- .2915
3 — PINK	.2890- .2895
2 — PINK	.2870- .2875
1 — PINK	.2850- .2855
5 — GRN	.2830- .2835
4 — GRN	.2810- .2815
3 — GRN	.2790- .2795
2 — GRN	.2770- .2775
1 — GRN	.2750- .2755
5 — WH	.2730- .2735
4 — WH	.2710- .2715
3 — WH	.2690- .2695
2 — WH	.2670- .2675
1 — WH	.2650- .2655
5 — YEL	.2630- .2635
4 — YEL	.2610- .2615
3 — YEL	.2590- .2595
2 — YEL	.2570- .2575
1 — YEL	.2550- .2555
5 — ORNG	.2530- .2535
4 — ORNG	.2510- .2515
3 — ORNG	.2490- .2495
2 — ORNG	.2470- .2475
1 — ORNG	.2450- .2455
2 — RED	.2430- .2435
1 — RED	.2410- .2415

BACKLASH ADJUSTMENTS

MORE BACKLASH
LESS BACKLASH

DECREASE — FOR MORE BACKLASH LEFT SIDE

INCREASE + FOR LESS BACKLASH

DECREASE — FOR LESS BACKLASH

INCREASE + FOR MORE BACKLASH RIGHT SIDE

BACKLASH SPECIFICATIONS

BACKLASH CHANGE REQUIRED (INCH)	THICKNESS CHANGE REQUIRED (INCH)	BACKLASH CHANGE REQUIRED (INCH)	THICKNESS CHANGE REQUIRED (INCH)
.001	.002	.009	.012
.002	.002	.010	.014
.003	.004	.011	.014
.004	.006	.012	.016
.005	.006	.013	.018
.006	.008	.014	.018
.007	.010	.015	.020
.008	.010		

Shim changes for ring gear and pinion backlash

8. If a zero backlash conditions occurs, add 0.020 in. to the right side and subtract 0.020 in. from the left side to allow backlash indication.

9. Recheck backlash.

10. If backlash is not to specification, correct backlash by increasing thickness of one shim and decreasing thickness on the other shim the same amount.

11. Install shim and bearing caps. Tighten cap bolts to 70–85 ft. lbs. (95–115 Nm).

12. Rotate assembly several times.

13. Recheck backlash. If backlash is within specification, go to Step 14. If backlash is not within specification, repeat Step 10. Backlash specification is 0.008–0.015 in. (0.20–0.38mm). Preferred range is 0.012–0.015 in. (0.304–0.381mm).

14. Increase both left and right shim sizes by 0.006 in. and install for correct differential bearing preload. Make sure shims are fully seated and assembly turns freely.

15. Utilize white marking compound to obtain a tooth mesh contact pattern in the assembly.

NOTE: Pattern inspection is intended to detect gross errors in set up prior to complete reassembly. Pattern contact should be within the primary area of the ring gear tooth surface avoiding any narrow or hard contact with outer perimeter of tooth (top to root, toe to heel). Pattern inspection should be on the drive (pull) side. Correct assembly of drive pattern will result in satisfactory coast performance. If gross pattern error is detected, the preferred backlash of 0.012–0.015 in. (0.30–0.38mm), recheck pinion shim selection.

16. Install bearing caps and tighten cap bolts to 70–85 ft. lbs. (95–115 Nm).

17. Install the axle shafts.

18. Remove the oil seal replacer from the transmission extension housing. Install the driveshaft in the extension housing. align the scribe marks on the flange and driveshaft and connect the driveshaft at the drive pinion flange. Apply thread locking compound to the threads of the attaching bolts and torque to 70–95 ft. lbs. (90–128 Nm).

19. Install the brake drum and attaching shakeproof retainers. Install the wheel and tire on the brake drum. Install the wheel covers.

20. Clean the gasket mating surface of the rear axle housing and cover. Apply a new continuous bead of silicone rubber sealant to the carrier casting face.

NOTE: Make sure the machined surfaces on both cover and carrier are clean before installing the new silicone sealant. Inside of axle must be covered when cleaning the machined surface to prevent axle contamination.

21. Install the cover and torque the bolts to 25–35 ft. lbs. (34–47 Nm), except the ratio tag bolt, which is tightened to 15–25 ft. lbs. (20–34 Nm).

NOTE: Cover assembly must be installed within 15 minutes of application of the silicone or new sealant must be reapplied.

22. Add EOAZ–19580–A (ESP-MC2154–A) or equivalent lubricant through the filler hole until the lubricant level is ⅜ in. (9.5mm) below the filler hole with the axle in the running position.

23. Lower vehicle and road test.

Adjustment
DRIVE PINION AND DRIVE PINION BEARING PRELOAD

1. Install the pinion front bearing and slinger.

2. Apply grease, C1AZ–19590–B or equivalent, between the lips of the pinion seal and install the pinion seal.

3. Insert the companion flange into the seal and hold it firmly against the pinion front bearing cone. From the rear of the carrier casting, insert the pinion shaft, with a new spacer, into the flange.

4. Start new pinion nut. Hold the flange with special tool T78P–4851–A or equivalent, and tighten the pinion nut. As the nut is tightened, the pinion shaft is pulled into the front bearing cone and into the flange.

5. As the pinion shaft is pulled into the front bearing cone, pinion shaft end play is reduced. While there is still end play in the pinion shaft, the flange and bearing cone will be felt to bottom on the collapsible spacer.

6. From this point, a much greater torque must be applied to turn the pinion nut, since the spacer must be collapsed. Very slowly, tighten the nut but check the pinion shaft end play often to see the pinion bearing preload does not exceed the limits.

7. If the pinion nut is tightened to the point that pinion bearing preload exceeds the limits, the pinion shaft must be removed and a new collapsible spacer installed.

NOTE: Do not decrease the preload by loosening the pinion nut. This will remove the compression between the pinion front and rear bearing cones and the collapsible spacer and may permit the front bearing cone to turn on the pinion shaft.

8. As soon as there is a preload on the bearings, turn the pinion shaft in both directions several times to seat the bearing rollers.

9. Adjust the bearing preload to specification. Measure the preload.

DANA–MODEL 30 AXLE

Disassembly
DIFFERENTIAL CARRIER

1. The axle assembly can be overhauled either in or out of the vehicle. Either way, the free-floating axles must be removed.

2. Drain the lubricant and remove the rear cover and gasket.

3. Matchmark the bearing caps and the housing for reassembly in the same position. Remove the bearing caps and bolts.

4. Using a spreader tool mounted to the carrier housing, spread the housing a maximum of 0.015 in.

NOTE: Do not exceed this measurement. The housing could be permanently damaged. The use of a dial indicator is recommended to prevent over-stretching the housing.

5. Using a prybar, remove the differential case from the housing. Separate the shims and record the dimensions. Remove the spreader tool from the housing.

6. Remove the differential side bearing cups and tag to identify the side, if they are to be used again.

7. Remove the differential gear pinion shaft lock pin and remove the shaft. Rotate the side and pinion gears to remove them from the carrier. Remove the thrust bearings.

8. Remove the bearing cones and rollers from the carrier, marking and noting the shim locations.

9. Remove the ring gear bolts and tap the ring gear from the carrier housing.

10. Inspect the components.

DRIVE PINION

1. Remove the pinion nut and flange from the pinion gear.

2. Remove the pinion gear assembly from the housing. It may be necessary to tap the pinion from the housing with a soft faced hammer. Catch the pinion so as not to allow it to drop on the floor.

3. With a long drift, remove the inner bearing cup, pinion

Exploded view of the Dana model 30 rear axle assembly

seal, slinger, gasket, outer pinion bearing and the shim pack. Label the shim pack for reassembly.

4. Remove the rear pinion bearing cup and shim pack from the housing. Label the shims for reassembly.

5. Remove the rear pinion bearing from the pinion gear with an arbor press and special plates.

Inspection

1. Clean the gears, bearings and component parts with solvent and inspect for scoring, chipping or excessive wear.

2. Inspect the flanges and splines for excessive wear.

3. Replace the necessary parts as required.

PINION SHIM SELECTION

Ring gears and pinions are supplied in matched sets only. The matched numbers are etched on both gears for verification. On the rear face of the pinion, a plus (+) or a minus (−) number will be etched, indicating the best running position for each particular gear set. This dimension is controlled by the shimming behind the inner bearing cup. Whenever baffles or oil slingers are used, they become part of the adjusting shim pack. An example: If a pinion is etched +3, this pinion would require 0.003 in. less shims than a pinion etched 0. This means by removing shims, the mounting distance of the pinion is increased by 0.003 in., which is just what a plus (+) etching indicates. If a pinion is etched −3, it would be necessary to add 0.003 in. more shims than would be required if the pinion was etched 0. By adding the 0.003 in. shims, the mounting distance of the pinion is decreased 0.003 in., which is just what the minus (−) etching indicates. Pinion adjusting shims are available in thicknesses of 0.003, 0.005 and 0.010 in. An example: If a new gear set is used and the old pinion reads +2 and the new pinion reads −2, add 0.004 in. shims to the original shim pack.

Assembly
DRIVE PINION

1. Select the correct pinion depth shims and install in the rear pinion bearing cup bore.

2. Install the rear bearing cup in the axle housing.

3. Add or subtract an equal amount of shim thickness to or from the preload or outer shim pack, as was added or subtracted from the inner shim pack.

4. Install the front pinion bearing cup into its bore in the axle housing.

5. Press the rear pinion bearing onto the pinion gear shaft and install the pinion gear with bearing into the axle housing.

6. Install the preload shims and the front pinion bearing; do not install the oil seal at this time.

7. Install the flange with the holding bar tool attached, the washer and the nut on the pinion shaft end. Torque the nut to 200–220 ft. lbs. (271–298 Nm).

8. Remove the holding bar from the flange and with an inch lb. torque wrench, measure the rotating torque of the pinion gear. The rotating torque should be 10–20 inch lbs. with the original bearings or 20–40 inch lbs. with new bearings. Disregard the torque reading necessary to start the shaft to turn.

9. If the preload torque is not in specifications, adjust the shim pack as required.

   a. To increase preload, decrease the thickness of the preload shim pack.

   b. To decrease preload, increase the thickness of the preload shim pack.

10. When the proper preload is obtained, remove the nut, washer and flange from the pinion shaft.

11. Install a new pinion seal into the housing and reinstall the flange, washer and nut. Using the holder tool, torque the nut to 200–220 ft. lbs. (271–298 Nm).

DIFFERENTIAL CARRIER

1. Install the differential side gears, the differential pinion gears and new thrust washers into the differential carrier.

2. Align the pinion gear shaft holes and install the pinion shaft into the carrier. Align the lock pin hole in the shaft and carrier. Install the lock pin and peen the hole to avoid having the pin drop from the carrier.

3. Install the differential case side bearings with the proper installation tools. Do not install the shims at this time.

4. Place the carrier assembly into the axle housing with the bearing cups on the bearing cones. Install the bearing caps in their original position and tighten the bearing cap bolts enough to keep the bearing caps in place.

5. Install a dial indicator on the housing so the indicator button contacts the carrier flange. Press the differential carrier to prevent side-play and center the dial indicator. Rotate the carrier and check the flange for run-out. If the run-out is greater than 0.002 in., the defect is probably due to the bearings or to the carrier and should be corrected.

6. Remove the assembly and install the ring gear. Torque the retaining bolts and reinstall the assembly into the housing. Install the bearing caps in their original position and tighten the cap bolts to keep the bearings caps in place.

7. Install the dial indicator and position the indicator button to contact the ring gear back surface. Rotate the assembly and the run-out should be less than 0.002 in. If over 0.002 in., remove the assembly and relocate the ring gear 180 degrees. Reinstall the assembly and recheck. If the run-out remains over the 0.002 in. tolerance, the ring gear is defective. If the measurement is within tolerances, continue on with the assembly.

8. Position 2 prybars between the bearing cap and the housing on the side opposite the ring gear. Pull on the prybars and force the differential carrier as far as possible towards the dial indicator. Rock the assembly to seat the bearings and reset the dial indicator to zero.

9. Reposition the prybars to the opposite side of the carrier and force the carrier assembly as far towards the center of the housing. Read the dial indicator scale. This will be the total amount of shims required for setting the backlash during the reassembly, less the bearing preload. Record the measurement.

10. With the pinion gear installed and properly set, position the differential carrier assembly into the axle housing and install the bearing caps in their proper positions. Tighten the cap bolts just to hold the bearing cups in place.

11. Install a dial indicator on the axle housing with the indicator button contacting the back of the ring gear.

12. Position 2 prybars between the bearing cup and the axle housing on the ring gear side of the case and pry the ring gear into mesh with the pinion gear teeth, as far as possible. Rock the ring gear to allow the teeth to mesh and the bearings to seat. With the pressure still applied by the prybars, set the dial indicator to zero.

13. Reposition the prybars on the opposite side of ring gear and pry the gear as far as it will go. Take the dial indicator reading. Repeat this procedure until the same reading is obtained each time. This reading represents the necessary amount of shims between the differential carrier and the bearing on the ring gear side.

14. Remove the bearing from the differential carrier on the ring gear side and install the proper amount of shims. Reinstall the bearing.

15. Remove the differential carrier bearing from the opposite side of the ring gear. To determine the amount of shims needed, use the following method.

   a. Subtract the size of the shim pack just installed on the ring gear side of the carrier from the reading obtained and recorded when measurement was taken without the pinion gear in place.

   b. To this figure, add an additional 0.015 in. to compensate for preload and backlash. An example: If the first reading was 0.085 in. and the shims installed on the ring gear side of the carrier were 0.055 in., the correct amount of shims would be 0.085 − 0.055 + 0.015 = 0.045 in.

16. Install the required shims as determined under step 15 and install the differential side bearing. The installation of the shims should give the proper preload to the bearings and proper backlash to the ring and pinion gears.

17. Spread the axle housing with the spreader tool no more than 0.015 in. Install the differential bearing outer cups in their correct locations and install the cups in their respective locations.

18. Install the bolts and tighten finger-tight. Rotate the differential carrier and ring gear and tap with a soft-faced hammer to insure proper seating of the assembly in the axle housing.

19. Remove the spreader tool and torque the cap bolts to specifications.

20. Install a dial indicator and check the ring gear backlash at 4 equally spaced points of the ring gear circle. The backlash must be within a range of 0.004–0.009 in. and must not vary more than 0.002 in. between the points checked.

21. If the backlash is not within specifications, the shim packs must be corrected to bring the backlash within limits.

22. Check the tooth contact pattern and verify.

23. Complete the assembly, refill to proper level with lubricant and operate to verify proper assembly.

Limited Slip Differentials

TRACTION-LOCK—FORD 7.5 AND 8.8 INCH RING GEAR AXLES

Limited Slip axle assemblies, except for the differential case and internal components, are identical to a conventional axle. The 7.5 and 8.8 Ford Traction-Lock differentials and service procedures are similar. The Limited Slip differential employs 2 sets of multiple-disc clutches to control differential action. The side gear mounting distance is controlled by 7 plates on each side. The clutch pack for 7.5 inch axles have 3 steel plates, 4 friction plates and 1 or 2 steel shims. The 8.8 inch axle clutch pack has 4 steel plates, 3 friction plates and 1 steel shim. These steel shims are of the selective type to control side gear position.

The plates are stacked on the side gear hub and are housed in the differential case. Between the side gears is a 1-piece S-shaped preload spring which applies an initial force to the clutch packs. Additional clutch capacity is delivered from the side gears thrust loads. Splined plates are splined to the side gear hubs which, in turn, are splined to the left and right axle shaft. The eared friction plates are dogged to the case so the clutch packs are always engaged.

Noise Acceptability

A gear-driven unit, especially a drive axle, will produce a certain amount of noise. Some noise is acceptable and may be audible at certain speeds or under various driving conditions, as on a newly paved blacktop road. The slight noise is in no way detrimental to operation of the rear axle and must be considered normal. Vehicles equipped with a Limited Slip differential may exhibit a slight stick-slip noise on tight turns after extended highway driving. This is considered acceptable and has no detrimental effect.

Diagnosis and Testing

A Limited Slip differential can be checked for proper operation without removing the differential from the axle housing

NOTE: A vehicle equipped with a Limited Slip differential will always have both wheels driving. If, while the vehicle is being serviced, only 1 wheel is raised off the floor and the rear axle is driven by the engine, the wheel on the floor could drive the vehicle off the stand or jack.

1. Raise 1 rear wheel and remove the wheel cover. Adapters are available that bolt to the axle shaft wheel studs and connect to a torque wrench.

2. Using a torque wrench, preferably of the dial type with a capacity of at least 200 ft. lbs., rotate the axle shaft. Be sure the transmission is in Neutral, 1 rear wheel is on the floor and the other rear wheel is raised off the floor. The break-away torque

DIFFERENTIAL CASE

DIFFERENTIAL CLUTCH PACK SHIM

DIFFERENTIAL SHAFT LOCK BOLT

DIFFERENTIAL PINION GEAR THRUST WASHER

DIFFERENTIAL PINION SHAFT

DIFFERENTIAL CLUTCH PACK

S-SHAPED PRELOAD SPRING

DIFFERENTIAL PINION GEAR THRUST WASHER

DIFFERENTIAL SIDE GEAR

Ford Traction-Lok limited slip rear axle differential assembly components—8.8 inch ring gear axle shown

required to start rotation should be at least 20 ft. lbs. The initial break-away torque may be higher than the continuous turning torque, but this is normal. The axle shaft should turn with even pressure throughout the check without slipping or binding. If the torque reading is less than specified, check the differential for proper assembly.

Clutch Pack Preload Adjustment

In-vehicle adjustments are possible on this unit without removing the differential case from the axle housing. If the operational check was not to specification, the following procedures can be used.

Before the clutch pack preload can be adjusted, both axle shafts must be removed. The shafts must be removed all the way from the housing so the oil seals will not be damaged.

Disassembly and Assembly

FORD 7.5 INCH RING GEAR AXLE

1. Clean all dirt from the axle carrier cover with a wire brush and/or cloth. Loosen the axle cover to drain the lubricant, then remove the cover. Remove the differential assembly. The procedure is the same as a conventional axle. It is not necessary to remove the differential cone and roller assemblies from the case journals unless they are damaged. If the bearings remain on the case during service, keep them clean.

2. Remove the bolts that attach the ring gear to the differen-

tial case. Remove the ring gear from the case by striking at alternate holes around the gear with a soft drift pin. If equipped with ABS, do not damage the excitor ring when removing the ring gear. If the excitor ring is removed, it must be replaced with a new one.

3. Remove the differential pinion shaft lock bolt and remove the pinion shaft. With a suitable drift, drive out the S-shaped preload spring. Use care. The spring is under tension.

4. Rotate the pinion gears until the gears and thrust washers can be removed. Remove the side gears, thrust washers. Remove the right and left side gear and clutch pack with the shim and tag the parts R.H. and L.H. Clean and inspect the remaining parts of the differential case assembly for wear or damage. Replace parts as required.

5. Clean and inspect the clutch packs for wear and replace parts as necessary. Do not use acids or solvents when cleaning clutch components. Wipe parts with a clean lint-free cloth only.

6. Assemble the clutch packs without shims on the respective side gears. Prelubricate all friction plates with Ford Friction Modifier C8AZ-19B546-A or equivalent. Do not mix clutch plates or shims from one side with the other.

7. A special tool is available from Ford under part number T84P-4946-A Traction-Lok Clutch Gauge. It is a combination holding fixture/checking gauge and is recommended in the following procedure. Assemble the clutch gauge. Stack the right side clutch pack and side gear without the differential clutch pack shim over the base of the tool. Install the top portion of the

Traction-Lock special tools. Top: torque tool for checking breakaway torque. Bottom: clutch plate gauge allows checking for proper shim size—8.8 inch ring gear axle shown

tool and the nut onto the base stud. Tighten the nut to 60 inch lbs.

8. Using a feeler gauge, select the thickest blade that will enter between the tool and the clutch pack. This reading will be the thickness of the new shim. Repeat for other side clutch pack shim. Be sure to lubricate the friction plates with the proper Ford Friction Modifier C8AZ-19B546-A or equivalent prior to reassembly.

To assemble:

9. Assembly is the reverse of the removal procedure. Mount the differential case in a soft jaw vise and place the clutch packs and side gears in their proper cavities in the differential case.

10. Place the pinion gears and thrust washers on the side gears and rotate the pinion gears until the bores in the gear are aligned with the pinion shaft holes in the differential case.

11. Hold the S-shaped preload spring up to the differential case window and with a soft-faced mallet or drift, tap the spring into position.

12. Install the pinion shaft. Apply thread locking compound on the lock bolt and install. Clean the tapped holes in the ring gear with solvent. Check that new replacement ring gear bolts have thread locking compound on them. If not apply compound prior to installation. Torque to 70–85 ft. lbs.

Removing and installing S-shaped preload spring— 8.8 inch ring gear axle shown

13. Install differential case and ring gear assembly into axle housing. Apply RTV sealant to the case and install the cover.

14. Allow the RTV to cure. Fill 7.5 inch ring gear axles as follows:

a. Aerostar—3½ pints hypoid gear lubricant and 4 ounces of friction modifier additive Ford number C8AZ-19B546-A or equivalent.

b. Ranger—5 pints hypoid gear lubricant and 4 ounces of friction modifier additive Ford number C8AZ-19B546-A or equivalent.

c. Bronco II—5½ pints hypoid gear lubricant and 4 ounces of friction modifier additive Ford number C8AZ-19B546-A or equivalent.

FORD 8.8 INCH RING GEAR AXLE

1. The differential assembly need not be removed from the axle housing. Clean all dirt from the axle carrier cover with a wire brush and/or cloth. Loosen the axle cover to drain the lubricant, then remove the cover. Locate and remove the differential pinion shaft lock bolt and take out the pinion shaft.

2. Push the flanged end of the axle shafts inboard and remove the C-lock from the button end of each axle shaft. Use care not to damage the rubber O-ring which is in the axle shaft groove under the C-lock. The O-ring is used to hold the C-lock in position until the axle shafts are pulled back in place at reassembly.

3. Remove the axle shaft from the housing, being careful not to damage the oil seal.

4. With a suitable drift, drive the S-shaped preload spring half-way out of the differential case. Rotate the differential case

180 degrees. Hold the S-shaped preload spring with a pair of pliers and pull/tap outward until it is removed. Use care. The preload spring is under tension.

5. Rotate the pinion gears until the gears can be removed from the differential.

6. Remove the right and left side gear and clutch pack with the shim and tag the parts R.H. and L.H. Clean and inspect the remaining parts of the differential case assembly for wear or damage. Replace parts as required.

7. Clean and inspect the clutch packs for wear and replace parts as necessary. Do not use acids or solvents when cleaning clutch components. Wipe parts with a clean lint-free cloth only.

8. Assemble the clutch packs without shims on the respective side gears. Prelubricate all friction plates with Ford Friction Modifier C8AZ-19B546-A or equivalent. Do not mix clutch plates or shims from one side with the other.

9. A special tool is available from Ford under part number T87T-4946-A Traction-Lok Clutch Gauge. It is a combination holding fixture/checking gauge and is recommended in the following procedure. Assemble the clutch gauge using a bench vise and stack the right side clutch pack and side gear without the differential clutch pack shim over the base of the tool. Install the top portion of the tool and the nut onto the base stud. Tighten the nut to 60 inch lbs.

10. Using a feeler gauge, select the thickest blade that will enter between the tool and the clutch pack. This reading will be the thickness of the new shim. Be sure to lubricate the friction plates with the proper Ford Friction Modifier C8AZ-19B546-A or equivalent prior to reassembly.

11. Install the right side gear, clutch pack and new shim into the cavity in the differential case. Repeat for the left side.

12. Place the pinion gears and thrust washers 180 degrees apart on the side gears. Align the pinion gears and install.

13. Hold the S-shaped preload spring up to the differential case window and with a soft-faced mallet, hammer the spring into position. Apply RTV sealant to the case and install the cover.

14. Allow the RTV to cure. Fill Ford 8.8 inch ring gear axles with 5½ pints hypoid gear lubricant and 4 ounces of friction modifier additive Ford number C8AZ-19B546-A or equivalent.

LIMITED SLIP—FORD 10.25 INCH RING GEAR AXLE

This limited slip differential is available on Ford F-250–F-350 vehicles equipped with 10.25 inch ring gear rear axles.

The limited slip assembly, except for the differential case and its internal components, is identical to the conventional axle. The limited slip differential employs 2 sets of multiple-disc clutches to control differential action. The side gear mounting distance is controlled by 10 plates and 1 dished spring plate. The clutch pack consists of 2 plate designs: a splined plate that engages the splines of the side gear hub an an alternate-tabbed or stationary plates.

Diagnosis and Testing

If roughness or noises such as chatter are present while turning corners, the probable cause is incorrect or contaminated lubricant. Before a differential is removed and disassembled for chatter concerns, the lubricant level should be determined.

Drain and refill the axle with the correct amount (6½ pints) of hypoid gear lubricant and 8 ounces of friction modifier additive Ford number C8AZ-19B546-A or equivalent. Warm the axle up and recheck for chatter by making a minimum of 10 figure-8 type turns.

Noise Acceptability

A gear-driven unit, especially on a drive axle, will produce a certain amount of noise. Some noise will be acceptable and may be audible at certain speeds or under various diving conditions. The slight noise is in no way detrimental to the operation of the rear axle and must be considered normal.

If noise level is unacceptable, a complete lubricant drain, flush and refill will usually correct chatter. Use the following procedure:

1. Warm the lubricant by vehicle road operation or 5 minutes of operation in gear with both rear wheels off the ground on a hoist.

Ford limited slip rear axle differential assembly components—10.25 inch ring gear axle

NOTE: A vehicle equipped with a limited slip differential will always have both wheels driving. If one wheel is raised off the floor and the rear axle is driven by the engine, the wheel on the floor could drive the vehicle off the stand or jack. Always be sure both wheels are off the ground.

2. Drain lubricant while warm. Remove the axle cover to drain completely.

3. Clean the gasket surface of both the housing and cover.

4. Apply a bead of RTV silicone rubber on the carrier casting face inside the cover holes.

5. Install the cover, tighten bolts to 25–35 ft. lbs. in a crosswise pattern.

6. Add 8 ounces of friction modifier additive Ford number C8AZ-19B546-A or equivalent. Add lubricant through the fill hole until the level reaches the bottom of the fill hole. This should be approximately 6½ pints. Note that approximately 7½ pints are required after an out-of-axle repair.

7. Operate the vehicle for approximately 10 miles making a minimum of 10 figure-8 type turns to flush the old lubricant out of the clutch pack.

SPECIAL TOOLS

DIFFERENTIAL ROTATING HANDLE
T86T-4205-A

NUT

SPLINED HOLDING TOOL
D83T-4205-A

DOWEL BAR

STEP PLATE
D83T-4205-C2

HEX HEAD SCREW

NOTE: HEX HEAD SCREW, DOWEL BAR AND NUT ARE INCLUDED IN KIT D83T-4205-C

MOUNT DIFFERENTIAL HOLDING TOOL D83T-4205-A IN VISE AS SHOWN

Ford limited slip rear axle special tools—10.25 inch ring gear axle

HEX HEAD SCREW
PART OF KIT D83T-4205-C

NUT
PART OF KIT D83T-4205-C

DOWEL BAR
PART OF KIT D83T-4205-C

NUT
PART OF KIT D83T-4205-C

PINION GEAR

USE FEELER GAUGE TO PUSH THRUST WASHER FROM BETWEEN PINION GEAR AND DIFFERENTIAL CASE

Ford limited slip rear axle differential pinion and thrust washer removal using special forcing screw—10.25 inch ring gear axle

8. Repeat the draining procedure in Steps 2 through 6.

9. It is possible that a slight chatter may remain requiring addition vehicle operation. If chatter persists, after 100 miles of operation or chatter is severe after the flushing operation, disassembly and repair will be necessary.

Disassembly and Assembly

1. Note that some special tools are required especially to remove the side gears and clutch packs. Clean all dirt from the axle carrier cover with a wire brush and/or cloth. Loosen the axle cover to drain the lubricant, then remove the cover. Remove the differential assembly. The procedure is the same as a conventional axle. It is not necessary to remove the differential cone and roller assemblies from the case journals unless they are damaged. If the bearings remain on the case during service, keep them clean.

2. With the differential case assembly out of the vehicle, locate and remove the differential pinion shaft lockbolt.

3. Install a differential splined holding tool (or cut-off axle stub) in a vise and install the differential assembly on it with the ring gear side facing upwards.

4. With a hammer and soft drift pin, drive the pinion shaft from the differential case.

5. Assemble Ford kit D83T-4205-C or equivalent into the differential case. Tighten the forcing screw to force the side gears away from the pinion mating gears. With an appropriate size feeler gauge, push the pinion gear thrust washers out from between the pinion gears and the differential case. Remove the thrust washers, then back off the forcing screw until it is just loose.

6. Turn the case to "walk" the pinion gears out to the differential case windows and remove the pinions. Use caution and make sure the vise is tightened securely for this step.

7. Remove the special tool forcing screw and stop plate from the case. Remove the side gears, retainer clips and clutch pack assemblies.

8. Remove the retainer clips from both clutch packs to allow separation of the discs and plates for cleaning and inspection.

NOTE: When separating the clutch plates and discs, note the sequence in which they are assembled. They must be reassembled in the same sequence.

To install:

9. Assembly is the reverse of the removal procedure. Prelubricate each disc and plate by soaking in a container of friction modifier additive Ford number C8AZ-19B546-A or equivalent. Prelubricate the thrust face of the side gear. Assemble the plates and discs to the side gear splines in exactly the same sequence in which they were removed. Assemble the retainer clips to the ears of the plates. Make sure both clips are completely assembled and seated onto the ears of the plates.

10. Install a differential splined holding tool (or cut-off axle stub) in a vise and install the differential assembly on it with the ring gear side facing upwards.

11. Insert the clutch pack and side gear assemblies into the differential case. Make sure the clutch packs stay assembled to the side gear splines and that the retainer clips are completely seated in the pockets of the differential case. Hold the upper clutch pack and side gear assembly in place to prevent it from falling out of the differential case.

12. Assemble Ford forcing screw kit D83T-4205-C or equivalent into the differential case. Tighten the forcing screw to hold the side gears. Position the pinion gears in the case opening so they mesh with the side gear teeth. Hold the pinion gears in place. Make sure the pinion gears are 180 degrees apart so they will correctly align with the pinion shaft bore.

13. Rotate the case so the pinion gears engage the side gears and "walk" into the differential case. Rotate the case until the pinion mating shaft holes are lineup exactly with the holes in

the pinion gears. It may be necessary to adjust the forcing screw kit as the pinions turn into place.

14. Prelube both sides of the pinion thrust washers with hypoid gear lubricant. Tighten the forcing screw kit to allow clearance to insert the thrust washers. Insert the pinion gear thrust washers between the pinion gears and the differential case with the concave side facing in. Be sure to align the thrust washers with the bore in the differential case prior to installing the differential pinion shaft.

15. Remove the forcing screw kit. Install the pinion shaft and tighten the lockbolt to 15–30 ft. lbs. If removed, reinstall the ring gear with new bolts.

16. After the differential has been reinstalled, and the cover is back in place, add 8 ounces of friction modifier Ford number C8AZ-19B546-A or equivalent and 6.5 pints of hypoid gear lubricant, or until the level reaches the bottom of the fill hole.

DANA LIMITED SLIP AXLES

The limited slip Dana Trac-Lok Model 44 IFS, Model 44 IFS-HD and Model 60-1U 2 pinion axle and the 4 pinion Dana Power-Loc Model 70 have a power flow identical to the conventional rear axle, plus a more direct power flow which automatically takes effect as driving conditions demand. This more direct power flow is from the differential case to each axle shaft through clutches.

Although there are many similarities among these axles, the clutch plates and some other parts vary. Each clutch plate and disc pack consists of steel plates set between the case and side gear ring. Each clutch pack is premeasured for proper stack height. Do not separate packs and intermix the plates and discs from the packs. The side gears are splined to the axle shafts and act as a pressure plate for the clutch pack. Since the side gear ring fits against the pinions on the cross shaft (mate shaft), any outward force exerted by the mate shaft and its pinions will press the ring against the the clutch pack and thus connect the differential case directly to the axle shaft.

Unlike the cross shafts of the conventional unit, the 4 pinion limited slip differential mate shafts in Dana Model 70 axles are not rigidly attached to the differential case, nor are they attached to each other. At both ends of the mate shafts there are 2 flat surfaces so arranged that they form a V which mates with corresponding V-shaped surfaces (ramps) cut in the shaft openings of the differential case. The mate shafts are assembled in the case with enough clearance so when the case tries to rotate, they resist rotation. They are then forced to bear against 1 side of the V ramps. Since the 2 V ramps of 1 mate shaft point in a direction opposite to those of the other pin, the 2 shafts with their pinions will be forced apart as they resist rotation. This mate shaft movement compresses the clutch pack through the pinion gears and side gear rings.

Diagnosis and Testing

If roughness or noises such as chatter are present while turning corners, the probable cause is incorrect or contaminated lubricant. Before a differential is removed and disassembled for chatter concerns, the lubricant level should be determined.

Drain and refill the axle with the correct amount of hypoid gear lubricant and 8 ounces (rear axles, 2 ounces for front axles) of friction modifier additive Ford number C8AZ-19B546-A or equivalent. Warm the axle up and recheck for chatter by making a minimum of 10 figure-8 type turns.

Noise Acceptability

A gear-driven unit, especially on a drive axle, will produce a certain amount of noise. Some noise will be acceptable and may be audible at certain speeds or under various diving conditions. The slight noise is in no way detrimental to the operation of the rear axle and must be considered normal.

If noise level is unacceptable, a complete lubricant drain,

flush and refill will usually correct chatter. Use the following procedure:

1. Warm the lubricant by vehicle road operation or 5 minutes of operation in gear with both rear wheels off the ground on a hoist.

NOTE: A vehicle equipped with a limited slip differential will always have both wheels driving. If one wheel is raised off the floor and the rear axle is driven by the engine, the wheel on the floor could drive the vehicle off the stand or jack. Always be sure both wheels are off the ground.

2. Drain lubricant while warm. Remove the axle cover to drain completely.

3. Clean the gasket surface of both the housing and cover.

4. Apply a bead of RTV silicone rubber on the carrier casting face inside the cover holes.

5. Install the cover. It may help to install the bolts at the 8 o'clock and 2 o'clock position first to guide the cover into position. Tighten bolts to 30–40 ft. lbs. in a cross-wise pattern. Allow 1 hour for the sealer to cure before adding lubricant.

6. Add 8 ounces (for rear axle, 2 ounces for front axle) of friction modifier additive Ford number C8AZ-19B546-A or equivalent. Add lubricant through the fill hole until the level reaches the bottom of the fill hole. This should be approximately 6½ pints. Note that approximately 7½ pints are required after an out-of-axle repair.

7. Operate the vehicle for approximately 10 miles making a minimum of 10 figure-8 type turns to flush the old lubricant out of the clutch pack.

8. Repeat the draining procedure in Steps 2 through 6.

9. It is possible that a slight chatter may remain requiring addition vehicle operation. If chatter persists, after 100 miles of operation or chatter is severe after the flushing operation, disassembly and repair will be necessary.

Disassembly and Assembly

The differential bearings need not be removed to overhaul the limited slip differential. However, the ring gear will have to be removed first.

To remove and install the side gears, washers and clutch packs during diasassembly and assembly requires special procedures and tools. An axle placed in a vise with the splines extending above the jaws of the vise not more than 3 inches, makes an excellent holding fixture after the case has been removed from the housing.

EXCEPT MODEL 70 4-PINION POWER-LOK

1. Mount the differential case assembly onto the holding fixture or axle shaft held in a vise. The flange or ring gear side should be down. For Model 44IFS and 60-1U full float axles, use a small drift to remove the roll pin retaining the cross shaft. For model 60-1U semi-float axles, a lock screw is used to secure the slip fit cross shaft. Remove the cross shaft for the full float axles with a soft drift pin. The semi-float axle cross shaft is a slip fit and may be lifted out without tools.

2. Assemble Ford kit D83T-4205-A or equivalent into the differential case. Tighten the forcing screw to force the side gears away from the pinion mating gears and relieve the normal loaded condition. Using a piece of 0.030 inch thick shim stock, push out the differential spherical washers. Back off the forcing screw momentarily. This is important top relieve the pressure of

Special tools recommended to remove the clutch packs—Dana Model 44 and 60 Trac-Lok limited slip differentials

the clutch pack. Retighten the forcing screw until a very slight movement of the differential pinion gears can be seen.

3. Insert an appropriate round tool into the pinion mate shaft bore and rotate the case. Continue this until the differential pinion gears can be removed through the large openings in the case. Some loosening and tightening of the forcing screw will probably be required to permit gear movement.

4. Holding the top gear and clutch pack, remove the forcing screw and tooling. Carefully remove the top gear and clutch pack. Keep the stack of plates and discs in exact order.

5. Turn the case over so the flange, or ring gear side is up. As this is being done, ease the side gear and clutch pack out of the case. Keep the stack of plates and discs in exact order.

6. Remove the retainer clips from both clutch packs to allow separation of the discs and plates for cleaning and inspection. Again, keep the stack of plates and discs in exact order.

To assemble:

7. Assembly is the reverse of the removal procedure. Whether the original plates and discs or new ones are used, assemble them in exactly the same order as the originals. Always replace the entire kit of plates and discs even if only 1 component requires it.

8. Prelubricate the thrust faces of the side gear and assemble the plates and discs to the side gear splines, prelubricating each part with hypoid gear lubricant and/or friction modifier additive Ford number C8AZ-19B546-A or equivalent.

NOTE: The Model 60 discs may have the newer design, coated but without grooves. These plates must be soaked in friction modifier additive Ford number C8AZ-19B546-A or equivalent for at least 20 minutes before assembly.

9. Assemble the retainer clips to the ears of the plates. Make sure both clips are completely assembled or seated onto the ears of the plates. Place the differential case on the workbench.

10. Assemble 1 clutch pack and side gear into the case. Make sure the clutch pack stays assembled to the side gear splines and that the retainer clips are completely seated into the pockets of the case. To prevent the pack from falling out of the case, hold them in place by hand while re-positioning the case on the bench.

11. Assemble the other clutch pack and side gear into the case. Make sure the clutch pack stays assembled to the side gear splines and that the retainer clips are completely seated into the pockets of the case. Assemble Ford kit D83T-4205-A or equivalent into the differential case. Tighten the forcing screw to hold the side gears and clutch packs in the differential case as the differential case is moved.

12. Place the differential case onto the holding fixture or axle shaft held in a vise by aligning the splines of the side gear with those of the axle shaft.

13. Position both differential pinion gears opposite one another through the openings in the case. Be sure the holes of the gears are aligned with each other. Hold the gears in place by hand. Tighten the forcing screw so the side gears will move away from the differential pinion gears and relieve the loaded condition.

14. Rotate the differential case and allow the differential pinion gears to rotate and enter the case. It will probably be necessary to adjust the forcing screw by loosening or tightening to allow the side gear and differential pinion gears to rotate.

15. Turn the case until the holes of both differential pinion gears are aligned exactly with those of the case. Prelube both sides of the spherical washers with hypoid gear lube. Apply pressure to the forcing screw to allow clearance to assemble the washers. Do not over-tighten the forcing screw or the clutch plates may be damaged. Align the holes in the washers, pinion gear and case very carefully. Remove the forcing screw tool kit.

16. Install the pinion shaft into the differential case. Install the cross shaft locking pin.

NOTE: PLATE WITH HOLE IN LUG IS
ASSEMBLED AGAINST CLUTCH RING

Differential internal parts—Dana Model 70 4-Pinion Power-Lok

CLUTCH PLATES

PINION FLANGE USED TO SUPPORT SIDE GEAR RING

CLUTCH DISC

SIDE GEAR RING

SIDE GEAR RING

SIDE GEAR

PINION MATE SHAFT

PINION GEAR THRUSTWASHERS

AXLE SHAFTS MUST BE INSERTED ALL THE WAY ON EACH SIDE TO ALIGN BOTH SPLINES.

Assembling the differential and aligning the side gears using the axle shafts—Dana Model 70 4-Pinion Power-Lok

17. Install the ring gear on the differential case. Use new bolts and thread locking compound. Torque to 60–100-120 ft. lbs. Install differential assembly into axle.

18. Apply a bead of RTV silicone rubber on the carrier casting face inside the cover holes. Install the cover. It may help to install the bolts at the 8 o'clock and 2 o'clock position first to guide the cover into position. Tighten bolts to 30–40 ft. lbs. in a crosswise pattern. Allow 1 hour for the sealer to cure before adding lubricant.

19. Add 8 ounces (for rear axle, 2 ounces for front axle) of friction modifier additive Ford number C8AZ-19B546-A or equivalent. Add lubricant through the fill hole until the level reaches the bottom of the fill hole. About 7½ pints are required after an out-of-axle repair.

MODEL 70 4-PINION POWER-LOK

1. Remove the differential assembly from the axle. Note that the bearings need not be removed to overhaul the limited slip differential.

2. Mark (paint is suggested) the ring gear half and cover half of the differential case so they can be reassembled in the same relative positions. Mark the pinion mate shafts and their corresponding ramps so they too can be reassembled in the same positions.

3. Clamp the differential assembly in a soft-jawed vise and loosen but do not remove the bolts that hold the case halves together.

4. Place the differential assembly on the bench with the ring half of the case down. Remove the case attaching bolts and then remove the cover half of the case.

5. Remove the pinion mate gear, side gear ring and clutch pack. Keep these parts with the cover half of the case so they can be reinstalled in their original positions. Tag the parts if necessary to identify.

6. Remove the corresponding parts from the drive gear half of the case.

7. Clean all parts well and dry carefully with low pressure compressed air. Inspect the clutch plates and discs for cracks, excessive wear and distortion. If 1 or more of the plates or discs need replacing, the entire stack of clutch plates on each side should be replaced. Inspect all other parts for wear and replace any that appears to be worn or damaged. Inspect the pinion mate shaft surfaces and the ramp surfaces on the case for excessive wear or pitting. Inspect the side gear and pinion gear teeth and the side gear rings. Inspect the pinion gear races that bear on the side gear rings.

To install:

8. Assembly is the reverse of the removal procedure. Place the side gear ring from the drive gear half of the case on a pinion flange or something similar so it is blocked up about 4 inches above the bench. Coat and install the clutch plates with hypoid gear lubricant and/or friction modifier additive Ford number C8AZ-19B546-A.

NOTE: The plates of the new design (without grooves) must be soaked in friction modifier additive Ford number C8AZ-19B546-A or equivalent for at least 20 minutes before assembly.

9. Place the ring gear half of the case over the clutch pack and side gear ring. Make sure the clutch plate lugs enter the slots in the case and that the case bottoms on the clutch pack.

10. Grasp the flange and the case to hold the assembly together and then turn the case half upside down.

11. Place the proper side gear in the side gear ring. Place the mate shaft and pinions on the side gear ring, aligning the matchmarks made at disassembly.

12. Install the cover half mate shaft and pinions, aligning the matchmarks made at disassembly.

13. Place the side gear on the pinions and then place the side gear ring on the side gear and pinions.

14. Assemble the clutch pack, align the plate lugs and install all parts into the case.

NOTE: There may be circumstances of continuing chatter/bumping in turns despite replacement of parts and lubricant, particularly in vehicles operating at close to GVW rating. Typical situations are emergency vehicles and 5th wheel trailers. In these cases, it is permissible to reassemble the clutch pack with the disc next to the side gear ring, resulting in 2 plates together. This results in 3 friction surfaces instead of the normal 5 and will result in lowering the torque to rotate the wheel by 40 percent.

15. Place the cover half over the assembly, align the matchmarks made at disassembly and install the case bolts, turning just a few threads. Case bolts must be clean and dry. Using both axle shafts, align the splines of the side gear and the side gear ring on both sides of the case. With the axle shafts in position, tighten the case bolts evenly and alternately to 65–70 ft. lbs.

NOTE: If bolt heads have "180" or 7 radial lines stamped on the head, tighten the case bolts to 90–100 ft. lbs.

16. Remove the axle shafts. If the differential has been properly assembled, each pinion mate cross shaft should be tight on its ramp; or, if there is clearance between the cross shaft and the ramp, it should be not more than 0.010 inch and equal at all 4 cross shaft ends.

GENERAL MOTORS CORPORATION

Front Axle Assembly

GMC—8½ INCH RING GEAR AXLE

For overhaul information, refer to the General Motors Corporation 8½ in. ring gear axle, in the rear axle assembly section.

DANA—9¾ INCH RING GEAR AXLE

For overhaul information, refer to the Dana 9¾ in. ring gear axle, in the rear axle assembly section.

GMC—7¼ INCH RING GEAR AXLE

This axle is available on small cab General Motors Pick-Ups and vans. It is available either with or without a center disconnect feature which allows shifting into and out of 4WD when the vehicle is in motion under most conditions. Vehicles with All Wheel Drive do not have the disconnect feature but are otherwise similar.

This front axle could be called a "split case" design since the gear carrier is unlike an integrated carrier axle or an axle with a removeable cast gear carrier. For that reason, use care when disassembling. Fasteners must always be reinstalled in the same location from which they were removed. Replacement fasteners, if required, must be the correct part number for the application.

The axle uses a convention ring and pinion gear. The pinion is supported by 2 tapered roller bearings. The pinion depth is set by a shim pack located between the gear end of the pinion and the roller bearing that is pressed onto the pinion. The pinion bearing preload is set by crushing a collapsible spacer between the pinion bearings in the axle housing. Note that the ring gear is bolted to the differential case with left-hand thread bolts.

The differential case is supported in the axle housing by 2 tapered roller bearings. The differential and ring gear are located in relationship to the pinion by threaded adjusters.

The axle identification code is located on a tag attached to the right side axle tube.

Inspection

Before disassembly, a few checks should be made to help diagnose problems.

1. Drain the axle lubricant. Check for metal bits or chips.
2. Check the ring gear backlash. This information can be used to determine the cause of the axle problem. It will also help when setting up the shim packs for locating and preloading the differential case. It is possible to read backlash at the pinion flange without disassembling the axle. Use the following procedure:

    a. Install a dial indicator so the button contacts the outer edge of the pinion flange. The plunger must be at right angle to the pinion flange.

    b. Move the pinion flange through its free-play while holding the differential carrier from moving. Record the dial indicator reading.

    c. Divide the dial indicator reading by 2 to obtain the actual backlash when using this method. Example: A dial indicator reading of 0.006 inch (0.16mm) means there is actually 0.003 in. (0.08mm backlash). Backlash specification for this axle is:

    d. 0.003–0.010 inch (0.08–0.25mm)

    e. 0.005–0.007 inch (0.13–0.18mm) preferred

Disassembly and Assembly

1. With the unit removed from the vehicle, remove the right

Dial indicator set up on pinion flange for measuring backlash before the axle is disassembled—General Motors 7¼ inch ring gear split case front axle

1. Axle shaft
2. Deflector
3. Oil seal
4. Axle shaft bearing
5. Axle tube
6. Flange bolts
7. Thrust washer
8. Retaining ring
9. Carrier connector
10. Shift cable
11. Shift cable housing
12. Gasket
13. Indicator switch
14. Spring
15. Seal
16. Spring
17. Shift shaft and fork
18. Bolt
19. Lock tab
20. Thrust washer
21. Differential pilot bearing
22. Sleeve
23. Output shaft
24. Washer
25. Plug
26. Washer
27. Pin
28. Bolt
29. Carrier case

30. Bearing
31. Insert
32. Sleeve
33. Side bearing
34. Bolt
35. Differential case
36. Bolt
37. Ring and pinion gears
38. Shim
39. Bearing
40. Spacer
41. Bearing
42. Seal
43. Deflector
44. Flange
45. Washer
46. Nut

47. Plug
48. Bushing
49. Vent hose
50. Vent
51. Fitting
52. Shaft
53. Thrust washer
54. Side gear
55. Thrust washer
56. Differential pinion gear
57. Cover
58. Bolt
59. Output shaft

Exploded view—General Motors 7¼ inch ring gear split case front axle

Separating the carrier case halves. Pry at location A—General Motors 7¼ inch ring gear split case front axle

CARRIER CASE   SLEEVE   LOCK TAB   BOLT

Removing the side bearing adjuster lock tabs—General Motors 7¼ inch ring gear split case front axle

side axle tube flange bolts, shift cable housing and the small spring inside. Take off the axle tube and remove the thrust washer. Remove the large spring, shift shaft and fork.

2. Clamp the right side axle tube in a vise being careful to clamp only on the mounting flange. Strike the inside of the shaft flange with a brass hammer to dislodge the axle shaft. Remove the axle shaft and oil deflector.

3. Remove the right side gear-like carrier connector and retaining ring. Take off the thrust washer, sleeve and pull out the right side output shaft along with the washer under it from the differential housing. The output shaft differential pilot bearing may be removed, if necessary, with a suitable small puller.

4. Using a suitable slide hammer puller and adapter, remove the left side output shaft from the case. Remove the retaining bolts and the left side axle cover and seal.

5. Remove the differential case through bolts. Separate the case halves by first locating the slots provided in the case. With suitable small prying tools, separate the case halves.

6. Remove the differential case and set aside.

7. Locate and remove the bolts and lock tabs from the side bearing adjuster sleeves. A special tool is recommended to turn the adjuster sleeves until the sleeves and the bearing cups are pushed from the case. The bearings can be removed from the sleeves using a bench press.

8. Use a suitable holding fixture to secure the pinion flange.

Remove the flange nut. A special holding fixture is available to hold the left carrier case. Mount the left carrier case in this fixture. With a suitable puller, remove the universal joint flange and the deflector under it.

9. Remove the pinion with spacer, pinion bearing and shim. Take the spacer off the pinion and remove the bearing from the pinion. A bench press and suitable adapters will be required. remove the shim after the bearing is off.

10. Remove the bearing and cup from the differential case using a suitable puller and adapters.

11. Remove the pinion shaft lock bolt and remove the pinion shaft from the differential case.

12. Remove the differential pinions and thrust washers.

13. Remove the side gears and thrust washers. Matchmark the side gears and case so they can be installed in their original location.

14. Remove the ring gear bolts and remove the ring gear. Do not pry between the ring gear and the case. Drive the ring gear off with a soft brass drift pin.

15. Remove the differential side bearings with a suitable puller.

To assemble:

16. Assembly is the reverse of the disassembly procedure. Parts should be clean and dried with clean air, not rags. Inspect all parts before assembly. Check the carrier bore for nicks or burrs or any damage that would prevent the pinion seal from sealing. Check the large end of roller bearings for wear. This is where tapered roller bearing wear is most evident. Lubricate parts with axle lubricant prior to assembly.

17. Assemble the thrust washers and side gears into the differential case. If the same gears and washers are being used, install them in the same locations as they were removed, using the matchmarks made at teardown.

18. Position 1 pinion gear between the side gears and rotate the gears until the pinion gear is directly opposite the opening in the case. Place the other pinion gear between the side gears, making sure the hole in the pinion gears lines up. Install the thrust washers by rotating the pinion gears toward the opening just enough to permit the sliding in of the thrust washers. Install the pinion shaft and lock bolt.

19. Install the ring gear onto the differential case. Make sure the ring gear and the differential case flange are perfectly clean. Foreign mattter between the ring gear and flange will result in uneven backlash at assembly. Do not reuse the old bolts. Always use new bolts. Torque to 60 ft. lbs.

20. Install the side bearings onto the differential using a suitable press/driver.

21. Using suitable pullers and adapters, install the outer and inner pinion bearing cups into the carrier case.

22. Set the pinion depth. Special tools are required. Use the following procedure:

    a. Pinion depth is adjusted by selecting a shim of the proper thickness.

    b. Lubricate the inner and outer pinion bearings liberally with axle lubricant.

    c. Hold the pinion bearings in position and install the special tools.

    d. The special tooling using a dial indicator to first read off the bearing bore, then the dial indicator is turned to read out of the bearing bore.

    e. The dial indicator reading is equal to the required shim size. Example: If the dial indicator reads 0.84mm, a 0.84mm shim is required. Shim kits are available in a number of sizes ranging from 0.53–0.94mm.

    f. After determining pinion depth shim size, remove the special tools and bearing cones.

23. Install the proper size pinion depth shim on the pinion. Install the pinion inner bearing using a suitable driver. Install a new spacer on the pinion, and the outer bearing and seal into the case. Slide the pinion gear into the case.

24. Install the deflector, universal joint flange and pinion nut.

A. BUTTON LOCATED IN BEARING BORE
B. BUTTON MOVED OUT OF BEARING
BORE

Measuring pinion depth with special tools and dial indicator—General Motors 7¼ inch ring gear split case front axle

DIAL INDICATOR READS DIRECTLY AGAINST RING GEAR

Measuring backlash at the ring gear—General Motors 7¼ inch ring gear split case front axle

Use thread locking compound on the pinion threads and on both sides of the washer. Using a suitable holding tool, tighten the pinion nut until no end play is detectable. No further tightening should be attempted until the bearing preload has been checked.

25. Measure the bearing preload using the following procedure:

a. Use a inch-pound torque wrench and suitable socket/adapters to turn the pinion nut.

b. Rotate the pinion with the torque wrench and observe the reading.

c. The correct preload is 15–25 inch lbs.

d. If the preload is below specifications, tighten the pinion nuts in small amounts. Check the preload after each tightening. Use care. If the preload is exceeded, the pinion will have to be removed and new collapsible spacer installed.

e. Once the preload has been obtained, rotate the pinion several times to make sure the bearings have been seated. Recheck the preload and readjust, if neceesary.

26. Install the output shaft bearings into the sleeves with a suitable driver. Install the sleeves into the carrier case. Thread in all the way. Install the bearing cups into the carrier case with a suitable tool.

27. Install the differential assembly into the carrier case half which contains the pinion gear. Turn the left sleeve in toward the differential case. A special tool fits the lugs on the sleeve. This tool is important and will be used in several adjustment steps. Turn until backlash is felt between the ring and pinion gear.

28. Join the carrier halves together. Do not use any sealer at this time. If the carrier halves do not make complete contact, back out the right side adjusting sleeve. Install 4 case through bolt and tighten to 37 ft. lbs.

29. Adjust the backlash using the following procedure:

a. Using the special tool, tighten the right side adjusting sleeve to 100 ft. lbs.

b. Using the special tool, tighten the left side adjusting sleeve to 100 ft. lbs.

c. Mark the location of the adjusting sleeves in relation to the carrier halves so the notches in the adjusting sleeves can be counted when turned.

d. Turn the right adjusting sleeve out 2 notches.

e. Turn the left adjusting sleeve in 1 notch.

f. Rotate the pinion several times to seat the bearings.

g. Jig up a dial indicator to read off the ring gear through the opening next to the adjuster sleeve. Place the indicator

stem at the heel end (the end of the tooth away from the pinion or to the outside of the ring gear) of a tooth.

h. Check and record the backlash at 3 or 4 points around the ring gear. The pinion must be held stationary when checking backlash. The backlash should be the same at each point within 0.002 inch (0.05mm). If the backlash varies more than this, check for burrs, a distorted case flange, uneven bolting or dirt between the case and ring gear.

i. Gear backlash should be between 0.003–0.010 inch (0.08–0.25mm) with a preferred specification of 0.005–0.007 inch (0.13–0.18mm).

j. If the backlash is incorrect, adjust the sleeves as necessary. Always maintain "1 notch" preload on the side bearings. Example: If it was necessary to turn the right sleeve in 1 notch, the left sleeve must be turned out 1 notch.

k. To increase backlash, turn the left sleeve in and turn the right sleeve out an identical amount. To decrease backlash, turn the right sleeve in and turn the left sleeve out an identical amount.

l. When the backlash is correct, mark the position of the sleeves so they can be kept in the same location.

30. It is possible to read backlash at the pinion flange without disassembling the axle. Use the following procedure:

a. Install a dial indicator so the button contacts the outer edge of the pinion flange. The plunger must be at right angle to the pinion flange.

b. Move the pinion flange through its free-play while holding the differential carrier from moving. Record the dial indicator reading.

c. Divide the dial indicator reading by 2 to obtain the actual backlash when using this method. Example: A dial indicator reading of 0.006 inch (0.16mm) means there is actually 0.003 inch (0.08mm) backlash. Backlash specification for this axle is:

d. 0.003–0.010 inch (0.08–0.25mm)

e. 0.005–0.007 inch (0.13–0.18mm) preferred

31. Before final assembly, a gear tooth contact pattern check should be performed. This check is not a substitute for adjusting pinion depth and backlash. It is to verify the correct running position of the gear set. Use the following procedure:

a. Wipe oil out of the carrier and carefully clean each tooth of the ring gear.

b. Use gear marking compound and apply this mixture sparingly with a stiff brush.

c. Apply a load until a torque to 40–50 ft. lbs. is required to turn the pinion. A test made without loading the gears will not give a satisfactory pattern. Turn the pinion flange with a wrench so the ring gear rotates 1 full revolution then reverse the rotation so the ring gear rotates 1 revolution in the opposite direction. Excessive turning of the ring gear is not recommended.

d. Observe the ring gear pattern to determine if changes are needed.

e. Both backlash and drive pinion depth affect tooth contact. It may be necessary to change both setting to obtain correct pattern. The position of the drive pinion is changed through shims. Backlash is adjusted by means of the side bearing adjusting sleeves which move the entire case and ring gear assembly closer to, or farther from the drive pinion.

f. To increase backlash, turn the left sleeve in and turn the right sleeve out. The decrease backlash, turn the right sleeve in and turn the left sleeve out an identical amount. It is important that the contact pattern be centrally located up and down on the face of the ring gear teeth.

32. After all adjustments have been determined to be correct, remove the 4 through bolts for the case and lift off the right carrier case half. Clean the sealing surfaces well with carburetor cleaner. Apply a bead of sealer such as Loctite 514 or equivalent to one carrier case surface. Set the right case half in place, install the bolts and torque to 35 ft. lbs.

1. Shaft
2. Deflector
3. Seal
4. Bearing
5. Tube
6. Bolt
7. Thrust washer
8. Retaining ring
9. Carrier connector
10. Shift cable
11. Shift cable housing
12. Gasket
13. Indicator switch
14. Spring
15. Seal
16. Spring
17. Shift shaft and fork
18. Bolt
19. Tab washer
20. Thrust washer
21. Differential pilot bearing
22. Sleeve
23. Output shaft
24. Washer
25. Plug
26. Washer
27. Pin
28. Bolt
29. Carrier case
30. Bearing
31. Insert
32. Sleeve
33. Side Bearing
34. Ring gear bolt
35. Differential case
36. Screw
37. Ring and pinion set
38. Shim
39. Bearing
40. Spacer
41. Bearing
42. Seal
43. Deflector
44. Yoke
45. Washer
46. Pinion nut
47. Plug
48. Bushing
49. Vent hose
50. Vent
51. Hose fitting
52. Pinion shaft
53. Thrust washer
54. Side gear
55. Thrust washer
56. Differential pinion gear
57. Cover
58. Bolt
59. Output shaft

Exploded view of the 8¼ and 9¼ inch front differential assembly—General Motors

33. Make sure all the adjusting sleeves are in the right place as marked. Install locks and tighten the bolts to 70 inch lbs.

34. Install the left seal to the left side cover plate. Install the cover plate with Loctite 514 or equivalent. Torque the bolts to 18 ft. lbs.

35. Install the left side axle shaft with deflector.

36. Assemble the right side axle shaft and seals including the shift housing seal.

37. Install the differential pilot bearing, the washer to the output shaft and the output shaft to the carrier assembly.

38. Assemble and install the shift fork and housing assembly.

39. Assemble the axle tube assembly to the carrier case. Torque the bolts to 35 ft. lbs.

GMC—8¼ AND 9¼ INCH RING GEAR AXLE

Disassembly

1. Remove the drain plug and drain the fluid from the axle.

2. Measure and record the backlash for it may help to determine the cause of an axle problem.

3. Using a holding tool, remove the pinion flange nut and washer.

4. Using a pinion flange removal tool, press the pinion flange from the differential.

5. Using an oil seal puller, pull the pinion oil seal from the differential.

6. Remove the solenoid and the indicator switch.

7. Remove the right axle tube-to-carrier case bolts and the tube with the shaft.

8. Remove the sleeve, shift fork, shaft, spring and shim.

9. Clamp the axle shaft tube in a vise, using the mounting flange. Strike the inside of the shaft flange to dislodge the carrier connector. Remove the carrier connector and the retaining ring.

10. Remove the snapring, the washer and the thrust washer.

11. Remove the axle shaft with the deflector.

12. Remove the sleeve, the bearing and the output shaft.

13. Using a removal tool, press the differential pilot bearing.

14. Using a prybar and a soft faced hammer, remove the shaft and the deflector.

15. Using a prybar, remove the seal from the axle tube.

16. Remove the bearing from the carrier case.

17. Remove the carrier case bolts, tap on the carrier case lugs to separate the right side carrier case half.

18. Pry up the locks and remove the differential assembly.

19. Remove the bolt, the lock, the sleeves and the side bearing cups; turn the sleeves to push the cups from the bores.

20. Remove the adjuster plug with the side bearing cup and the O-ring, if equipped.

21. Remove the pinion with the shim, the bearing cone and the spacer.

22. Using a bearing removal tool, press the bearing from the pinion.

23. Remove the shim, the seal, the bearing cup and the cone.

24. Using the puller tool, press the bearing cup from the pinion.

25. Remove the side bearings.

NOTE: The ring gear bolts are left handed threads.

26. Remove the ring gear bolts. Using a brass drift, drive the ring gear from the differential case.

27. Using a drift and a hammer, drive the roll pin from the differential case.

Inspection

1. Clean the gears, bearings and component parts with solvent and inspect for scoring, chipping or excessive wear.

2. Inspect the flanges and splines for excessive wear.

3. Replace the parts, if necessary.

Assembly

1. Install the roll pin into the differential case.

2. Install the ring gear to the differential case and torque the bolts to 52–66 ft. lbs. (70–90 Nm).

3. Install the side bearings.

4. Using a shop press, press the bearing cup onto the pinion.

5. Install the cone, the bearing cup, the seal and the shim onto the pinion.

6. Using a shop press, press the bearing onto the pinion.

7. Install the spacer, the bearing cone and the shim onto the pinion.

8. Install the O-ring, if equipped, and the adjuster plug with the side bearing cup.

9. While turning the sleeves to install the cups, install the side bearing cups, the sleeves, the lock and the bolt.

10. Install the differential assembly and secure with the locks.

11. Using a new gasket, assemble the carrier case halves and install the bolts; torque the carrier bolts to 30–40 ft. lbs. (40–55 Nm).

12. Press the bearing into the carrier case.

13. Install the new seal into the axle tube.

14. Install the deflector and the shaft.

15. Press the differential pilot bearing into the carrier case.

16. Install the output shaft, the bearing and the sleeve.

17. Install the deflector with the axle shaft, the thrust washer, the washer and the snapring.

18. Install the retaining ring and the carrier connector.

19. Install the shim, the spring, the shaft, the shift fork and the sleeve.

20. Using a new gasket, install the axle shaft tube to the carrier case and torque the bolts to 15–20 ft. lbs. (20–27 Nm).

21. Install the indicator switch and the solenoid.

22. Using an oil seal installer tool, install a new pinion oil seal.

23. Install the pinion flange onto the pinion. Install the washer and the flange nut. Tighten the nut a little at a time until the preload is 3–5 inch lbs. (0.3–0.6 Nm). The maximum pinion nut torque is 15 ft. lbs. (20 Nm).

24. Refill the axle with lubricant.

Rear Axle Assembly

The rear axles are categorized by the ring gear diameter and are identified as follows: 7½, 7⅝, 8½, 9½ in. (GMC) semi-floating axles; 9¾, 10½ in. (Dana) full floating axles; 10½ in. (GMC) full floating axles and 12 in. (Rockwell) full floating axles.

GMC—7½ AND 7⅝ INCH RING GEAR AXLE

Disassembly

REAR AXLE CASE

1. Before removing the rear axle case from the housing, check the ring gear-to-drive pinion backlash. This will indicate gear or bearing wear or an error in backlash or preload setting which will help in determining cause of axle noise.

2. Mark the bearing caps **R** and **L** to make sure they will be reassembled in their original location. Remove rear axle bearing cap bolts.

3. Remove rear axle case. Exercise caution in prying on carrier so the gasket sealing surface is not damaged. Place right and left bearing outer races and shims in sets with marked bearing caps so they can be reinstalled in their original positions.

4. If rear axle side bearings are to be replaced, use a puller to remove them.

5. Remove rear axle pinions, side gears and thrust washers from case. Mark the side gear and case after removing bolts. Using a brass drift and hammer, drive it off; do not pry between ring gear and case.

Checking the pinion preload

DRIVE PINION, BEARING AND RACES

1. Check drive pinion bearing preload. If there is no preload reading, check for looseness of pinion assembly by shaking. Looseness could be caused by defective bearings or worn pinion flange. If rear axle was operated for an extended period with very loose bearings, the ring gear and drive pinion will also require replacement.
2. Remove pinion flange nut and washer.
3. Remove pinion flange.
4. Install a drive pinion remover tool and drive out pinion. Apply heavy hand pressure on the pinion remover toward rear axle housing to keep front bearing seated to avoid damage to outer race.

NOTE: The rear pinion bearing must be removed when it becomes necessary to change the pinion depth adjustment.

5. With drive pinion removed from carrier, press bearing from the pinion gear.
6. Drive pinion oil seal from carrier and remove front pinion bearing. If this bearing is to be replaced, remove outer race from carrier.
7. If rear pinion bearing is to be replaced, remove outer race from carrier using a punch in slots provided for this purpose.

Cleaning and Inspection

1. Clean all rear axle bearings thoroughly in clean solvent (do not use a brush). Examine bearings visually and by feel. All bearings should feel smooth when oiled and rotated while applying as much hand pressure as possible. Minute scratches and pits appear on rollers and races at low mileage are due to the initial preload and bearings having these marks should not be rejected.
2. Examine sealing surface of pinion flange for nicks, burrs or rough tool marks which would cause damage to the seal and result in an oil leak. Replace if damaged.
3. Examine carrier bore and remove any burrs that might cause leaks around the outside diameter of the pinion seal.
4. Examine the ring gear and drive pinion teeth for excessive wear and scoring. If any of these conditions exist, replacement of the gear set will be required.
5. Inspect the pinion gear shaft for unusual wear; also check the pinion and side gears and thrust washers.
6. Check the press fit of the side bearing inner race on the rear axle case hub by prying against the shoulder at the puller recess in the case. Side bearings must be a tight press fit on the hub.
7. Diagnosis of a rear axle failure such as: chipped bearings, loose (lapped-in) bearings, chipped gears, etc., is a warning that some foreign material is present; therefore, the axle housing must be cleaned.

Checking the pinion depth

Assembly

DRIVE PINION

1. If a new rear pinion bearing is to be installed, install new outer races.
2. If a new front pinion bearing is to be installed, install new outer race.

NOTE: Pinion depth is set with pinion setting gauge. The pinion setting gauge provides in effect, a normal or zero pinion as a gauging reference. Instructions are included in gauge set.

3. Make certain all of the gauge parts are clean.
4. Lubricate front and rear pinion bearings liberally with rear axle lubricant.
5. While holding bearings in position, install depth setting gauge assembly.
6. Hold stud stationary with a wrench positioned over the flats on the ends of stud and tighten nut to 20 inch lbs. (2.2 Nm) torque. Rotate gauge plate assembly several complete revolutions to seat the bearings. Tighten nut until a torque between 15–25 inch lbs. (1.6–2.2 Nm) is obtained to keep the gauge plate in rotation.
7. Rotate the gauge plate tool until the gauging areas are parallel with the discs.
8. Make certain rear axle side bearing support bores are clean and free of burrs.
9. Install the correct discs on the gauge shaft.
10. Position the gauge shaft assembly in the carrier so the dial indicator rod is centered on the gauging area of the gauge block and the discs seated fully in the side bearing bores. Install side bearing caps and torque bolts to 55 ft. lbs. (75 Nm). Use a dial indicator reading from 0.00–100.0 inch (0.0–2.5mm).
11. Set dial indictor at zero. Then position on mounting post of the gauge shaft with the contact button touching the indicator pad. Push dial indicator downward until the needle rotates approximately ¾ turn clockwise. Tighten the dial indicator in this position and recheck.
12. Rotate gauge shaft slowly back and forth until the dial indicator reads the greatest deflection. At the point of greatest deflection, set the dial indicator to zero. Repeat rocking action of gauge shaft to verify the zero setting.
13. After the zero setting is obtained, rotate gauge shaft until the dial indicator rod does not touch the gauge block.
14. Record dial reading at pointer position. Example: If pointer moved counterclockwise 0.067 in. (1.70mm) to a dial reading of

0.033 in. (0.84mm) record the reading of 0.033 inch, not 0.067 inch. The dial indicator should be within the range of 0.020–0.050 inch (0.50–1.27mm).

15. Loosen the stud tool and remove gauge plate, washer and both bearings from carrier.

16. Position correct shim on drive pinion and install the drive pinion rear bearings.

REAR AXLE CASE

Before assembling the rear axle case, lubricate all parts with rear axle lubricant.

1. Place side gear thrust washer over side gear hubs and install side gears in case. If same parts are reused, install in original sides.

2. Position one pinion, without washer, between the side gears and rotate gears until pinion is directly opposite from loading opening in case. Place other pinion between side gears so the pinion shaft holes are in line; then, rotate gears to make sure holes in pinions align with the holes in case.

3. If the holes align, rotate pinions back toward loading opening just enough to permit sliding in pinion thrust washers.

4. After making certain the mating surfaces of case and ring gear are clean and free of burrs, thread 2 bolts into opposite sides of ring gear; then, install ring gear on case. Install new ring gear attaching bolts snug; never reuse old bolts. Torque bolts alternately in progressive stages to 90 ft. lbs. (120 Nm).

5. If case side bearings were removed, reinstall bearings.

NOTE: The side bearing preload adjustment is to be made before installing the pinion.

6. If the pinion is installed, remove ring gear. Case side bearing preload is adjusted by changing the thickness of both the right and left shims by an equal amount. By changing the thickness of both shims equally, the original backlash will be maintained. Production shims are cast iron and vary in thickness from 0.210–0.272 in. (5.33–6.91mm) in increments of 0.002 in. (0.05mm). Standard service spacers are 0.170 in. (4.32mm) thick and steel service shims are available from 0.040–0.082 in. (1.02–2.08mm) in increments of 0.002 in. (0.05mm).

NOTE: Do not attempt to reinstall the production shims as they may break when tapped into place. If service shims were previously installed, they can be reused but, whether using new or old bearings, adhere to the following procedure in all cases.

7. Before installing of the case assembly, make sure the side bearing surfaces in the carrier are clean and free of burrs. If the same bearings are being reused, they must have the original outer races in place.

8. Determine the approximate thickness of shims needed by measuring each production shim or each service spacer and shim pack.

9. In addition to the service spacer, a service shim will be needed. To select a starting point in service shim thickness, use the following chart.

10. Place case with bearing outer races in position in carrier. Slip the service spacer between each bearing race and carrier housing with chamfered edge against housing.

NOTE: Install the left bearing cap loose so the case may be moved while checking adjustments. Another bearing cap bolt can be added in the lower right bearing cap hole. This will prevent case from dropping while making shim adjustments.

11. Select 1 or 2 shims totaling the amount shown in the right-hand column and position between the right bearing race and the service spacer. Be sure left bearing race and spacer are against left side of housing.

12. Insert progressively larger feeler gauge sizes 0.010 in.

4.32mm (.170″) SERVICE SPACER	
Total Thickness of Both Prod. Shims Removed	Total Thickness of Service Shims to be Used as a Starting Point
10.57mm .420″	1.52mm .060″
10.92mm .430″	1.78mm .070″
11.18mm .440″	2.03mm .080″
11.43mm .450″	2.29mm .090″
11.68mm .460″	2.54mm .100″
11.94mm .470″	2.79mm .110″
12.19mm .480″	3.05mm .120″
12.45mm .490″	3.30mm .130″
12.70mm .500″	3.56mm .140″
12.95mm .510″	3.81mm .150″
13.21mm .520″	4.06mm .160″
13.46mm .530″	4.32mm .170″
13.97mm .550″	4.83mm .190″

General Motors shim spacer sizes

Installing the case side bearings

(0.25mm), 0.012 in. (0.30mm), 0.014 in. (0.36mm) or etc. between the right shim and service spacer until there is noticeable increased drag. Push the feeler gauge downward until the end of the gauge makes contact with the carrier bore so as to obtain a correct reading. The point just before additional drag begins is correct feeler gauge thickness. Rotate case while using feeler gauge to assure an even reading.

NOTE: The original light drag is caused by weight of the case against the carrier while additional drag is caused by side bearing preload. By starting with a thin feeler gauge, a sense of feel is obtained so the beginning of preload can be recognized to obtain zero clearance. It will be necessary to work case in and out and to the left in order to insert the feeler gauge.

13. Remove left bearing cap and shim from carrier. The total shim pack needed (with no preload on side bearings) is the feeler gauge reading in Step 12 plus thickness of shims installed in Step 10.

14. Select 2 shims of approximately equal size whose total thickness is equal to the value obtained in Step 12. These shims will be installed between each side bearing race and service spacer when the case is installed in the carrier.

NOTE: **The objective is to obtain the equivalent of a slip fit of the case in the carrier. For convenience in setting backlash, the preload will not be added until the final step.**

15. If the pinion is in position, install the ring gear and adjust the rear axle backlash.

DRIVE PINION, BEARING AND RACES

1. Install a new collapsible spacer on pinion and position assembly in carrier. Lubricate the pinion bearings with rear axle lubricant before installing pinion.
2. Hold the pinion forward in the case assembly.
3. Install the front bearing onto pinion and the drive bearing onto pinion shaft until sealed in the race.
4. Position and install the pinion oil seal in the carrier.
5. Lubricate the pinion oil seal lips and seal surface of pinion flange. Install pinion flange on pinion by tapping with a soft hammer until a few pinion threads project through the flange.
6. Install the pinion washer and nut. While holding the pinion flange, intermittently, rotate the pinion to seat pinion bearings. Tighten the pinion flange nut until the end play begins to disappear. When no further end play is detectable and the holder will no longer pivot freely as the pinion is rotated, the preload specifications are being approached. No further tightening should be attempted until the preload has been checked.
7. Check the preload by using an inch lb. torque wrench. After the preload has been checked, final tightening should be done very carefully.

NOTE: **If when checking, preload was found to be 5 inch lbs. (0.6 Nm), any additional tightening of the pinion nut can add many additional inch lbs. of torque. Therefore, the pinion nut should be further tightened only a little at a time, for the preload specifications will compress the collapsible spacer too far and require the installation of a new collapsible spacer.**

8. While observing the preceding note, carefully set preload at 24–32 inch lbs. (2.7–3.6 Nm) on new bearings or 8–12 inch lbs. (1.0–1.4 Nm) for used bearings.
9. Rotate pinion several times to assure the bearings have been seated. Check the preload again, if preload has been reduced by rotating pinion, reset preload to specifications.

Adjustment

REAR AXLE BACKLASH

1. Install rear axle case into carrier, using shims as determined by the side bearing preload adjustment.
2. Rotate the rear axle case several times to seat bearings, then, mount a dial indicator. Use a small button on the indicator stem so contact can be made near heel end of tooth. Set the dial indicator so the stem is aligned as nearly as possible with gear rotation and perpendicular to tooth angle for accurate backlash reading.
3. Check the backlash at 3 or 4 points around ring gear. Lash must not vary more than 0.002 in. (0.05mm) around ring gear. The pinion must be held stationary when checking backlash; if variation is greater than 0.002 in. (0.05mm) check for burrs, uneven bolting conditions or distorted case flange and make corrections, as necessary.
4. Backlash at the point of minimum lash should be between 0.005–0.009 in. (0.13–0.23mm) for all new gears.
5. If backlash is not within specifications, correct by increasing thickness of one shim and decreasing thickness of other shim the same amount. This will maintain correct rear axle side bearing preload.
   a. For each 0.001 in. (0.03mm) change in backlash desired, transfer 0.002 in. (0.05mm) in shim thickness.
   b. To decrease backlash 0.001 in. (0.03mm), decrease thickness of right shim 0.002 in. (0.05mm) and increase thickness of left shim 0.002 in. (0.05mm).

   c. To increase backlash 0.002 in. (0.05mm), increase thickness of right shim 0.004 in. (0.10mm) and decrease thickness of left shim 0.004 in. (0.10mm).
6. When the backlash is correctly adjusted, remove both bearing caps and both shim packs. Keep the packs in their respective position, right or left side. Select a shim 0.004 in. (0.10mm) thicker than the one removed from left side, then, insert left side shim pack between the spacer and the left bearing race. Loosely install bearing cap.
7. Select a shim 0.004 in. (0.10mm) thicker than the one removed from right side and insert between the spacer and the right bearing race; it will be necessary to drive the right shim into position.
8. Torque to 55 ft. lbs. (75 Nm).
9. Recheck backlash and correct if necessary.
10. Install the axles.
11. Install a new cover gasket, the cover and torque the bolts to 20 ft. lbs. (27 Nm).
12. Refill the rear axle to the proper level.

GMC – 8½ AND 9½ INCH RING GEAR AXLE

This axle assembly is the semi-floating type with a hypoid type drive pinion and ring gears. The drive pinion gear is supported by 2 bearings. The differential case contains 2 pinion gears. The carrier assembly is not removable since it is part of the axle assembly but the design allows for the differential assembly to be serviced while the axle is still in the vehicle. The ring gear is bolted to a 1 piece differential case is supported by 2 preloaded roller bearings.

1. Companion Flange	15. Ring gear	
2. Deflector	16. Side gear	
3. Pinion oil seal	17. Bearing cap	
4. Pinion front bearing	18. Axle shaft	
5. Pinion bearing spacer	19. Thrust washer	
6. Differential carrier	20. Differential pinion	
7. Differential case	21. Shim	
8. Shim (A) with service shim	22. Pinion rear bearing	
9. Gasket	23. Drive pinion	
10. Differential bearing		
11. C-lock		
12. Pinion shaft lock bolt		
13. Cover		
14. Pinion shaft		

Cross-sectional view of the General Motors 8½ and 9½ inch rear axle assembly

Disassembly

DIFFERENTIAL CASE

1. Remove the inspection cover from the axle housing and drain the gear lubricant into a pan.

2. Remove the screw or pin that holds the pinion shaft in place and remove the shaft.

3. Push the axle shaft(s) in a little and remove the C-locks from the ends of the shafts. Remove the axle shafts from the housing.

4. Measure and record the backlash. This will allow the old gears to be reassembled at the same amount of lash to avoid changing the gear tooth pattern. It also helps to indicate if there is gear or bearing wear and if there is any error in the original backlash setting.

5. Remove the differential pinions, the side gears and thrust washers from the case; be sure to mark the pinions and side gears so they may be reassembled in their original position.

6. Mark the bearing caps and housing and loosen the retaining bolts. Tap the caps lightly to loosen them. When the caps are loose, remove the bolts and reinstall them, just a few turns; this will keep the case from falling out of the housing when it is pried loose.

7. Using a prybar, carefully pry the case assembly loose. Be careful not to damage the gasket surface on the housing when prying. The case assembly may suddenly come free if the bearings were preloaded, so pry very slowly.

8. When the case assembly is loose, remove the bearing cap bolts and the caps. Place the caps so they may be reinstalled in the same position. Place any shims that were removed with the cap.

9. Using a bearing puller, pull the differential bearing from the case.

10. To remove the drive pinion bearing, perform the following procedures:

   a. Depending on the bearing that is being replaced, remove the front or rear bearing cup from the carrier assembly.

   b. With the pinion gear mounted in a press, press the rear bearing from the pinion shaft. Be sure to record the thicknesses of the shims that were removed from between the bearing and the gear.

DRIVE PINION

1. With the differential removed, check the pinion preload. Do this by checking the amount of torque needed to turn the pinion gear. For a new bearing, it should be 20–25 inch lbs. and for a used bearing it should be 10–15 inch lbs. If there is no preload reading check the pinion for looseness. If there is any looseness, replace the bearing.

2. Using a holder assembly to secure the flange, remove the flange nut and washer.

3. Using a puller, press the flange from the pinion splines.

4. Thread the pinion nut, a few turns, onto the pinion shaft. Using a brass drift and hammer, lightly tap the end of the pinion shaft to remove the pinion from the carrier. Be careful not to allow the pinion to fall out of the carrier.

5. With the pinion removed from the carrier, discard the old seal pinion nut and collapsible spacer; install new ones when reassembling.

RING GEAR

1. Remove the ring gear-to-differential case bolts and tap the ring gear from the case with a soft hammer.

NOTE: Do not try to pry the ring gear off the case. This will damage the machined surfaces.

2. Clean all dirt from the case assembly and lubricate the case with gear lube.

Cleaning and Inspection

1. Clean all parts in solvent and blow dry.

2. Check all of the parts for any signs of wear, chips, cracks or distortion. Replace any parts that are defective.

3. Check the fit of the differential side gears in the case and the fit of the side gear and axle shaft splines.

Assembly

DRIVE PINION BEARING

1. Using a bearing driver, install a new bearing cup for each one that was removed. Make sure the cups are seated fully against the shoulder in the housing.

2. The pinion depth must be checked to determine the nominal setting. This allows for machining variations in the housing and enables selection of the proper shim so the pinion depth can be set for the best bear tooth contact.

3. Clean the housing and carrier assemblies to insure accurate measurement of the pinion depth.

4. Lubricate the front and rear pinion bearings with gear lubricant and install them in their races in the carrier assembly.

5. Using a pinion setting gauge, select the proper clover leaf plate and install it on the preload stud.

6. Using the proper pilot, insert the stud through the rear bearing, with the proper size pilot on the stud and through the front bearing. Install the hex nut and tighten it until it is snug.

7. Using a wrench to hold the preload stud, torque the hex nut until 20 inch lbs. of torque are required to rotate the bearings.

8. Install the side bearing discs on the ends of the arbor assembly, using the step of the disc that fits the bore of the carrier.

9. Install the arbor and plunger assembly into the carrier. Make sure the side bearing discs fit properly.

10. Install the bearing caps in the carrier assembly finger-tight. Make sure the discs do not move.

11. Mount a dial indicator on the mounting post of the arbor with the contact button resting on the top surface of the plunger.

13. Preload the dial indicator by turning it ½ revolution and tightening it in this position.

14. Use the button on the gauge plate that corresponds to the ring gear size and turn the plate so the plunger rests on top of it.

15. Rock the plunger rod back and forth across the top of the button until the dial indicator reads the greatest amount of variation. Set the dial indicator to zero at the point of most variation. Repeat the rocking of the plunger several times to check the setting.

16. Turn the plunger until it is removed from the gauge plate button. The dial indicator will now read the pinion shim thickness required to set the nominal pinion depth; record the reading.

17. Check for the pinion code number, located on the rear face of the pinion gear. The number will indicate the necessary change to the pinion shim thickness.

NOTE: If the pinion is marked with a plus (+) and a number, add that much to the reading of the dial indicator. If the pinion has no mark, use the reading from the dial indicator as the correct shim thickness. If the pinion is marked with a minus (−) and a number, subtract that amount from the reading on the dial indicator.

18. Remove the depth gauge tools from the carrier assembly and install the proper size shim on the pinion gear.

19. Lubricate the bearing with gear lubricant and use a shop press to press the bearing onto the pinion shaft.

DRIVE PINION

1. Lubricate the front bearing and install it into the front cup.

2. Using a seal driver and a gauge plate, drive the pinion seal into the bore until the gauge plate is flush with the shoulder of the carrier.

RING GEAR SIDE		OPPOSITE SIDE		
.250"	Thickness of Tool J-22779 required to force ring gear into contact with pinion	Combined total of: Service Spacer (A) Service Shim (B) Feeler Gauge (C)		.265"
– .010" .240"	TO MAINTAIN PROPER BACKLASH (.005" – .008"), ring gear is moved away from pinion by subtracting .010" shims from ring gear side and adding .010" shims to other side			+ .010" .275"
+ .004"	TO OBTAIN PROPER PRELOAD on side bearings, add .004" shims to each side.			+ .004"
.244"	Shim dimension required for ring gear side	Shim dimension required for opposite side		.279"

Shim pack selection—General Motors

Gauge tools installed in the carrier

3. Lubricate the seal lips and install a new bearing spacer on the pinion gear.

4. Install the pinion gear into the carrier assembly. Using a large washer and nut, draw the pinion gear through the front bearing, far enough to install the companion flange.

5. With the companion flange installed on the pinion shaft, use a holder assembly and tighten the pinion nut until all of the end play is removed from the drive pinion.

6. When no more end play exists, check the preload; the preload should be 20–25 inch lbs. on new bearings or 10–15 inch lbs. on used bearings. Tighten the pinion nut until these figures are reached; do not over tighten the pinion, for this will collapse the spacer too much and make it necessary to replace it.

7. Turn the pinion gear several times to make sure the bearings are seated and recheck the preload.

RING GEAR

1. Align the ring gear bolt holes with the carrier holes and lightly press the ring gear onto the case assembly.

2. Install the bolts and tighten them all evenly, using a crisscross pattern to avoid cocking the ring gear.

3. When the ring gear is firmly seated against the case, torque the bolts to 60 ft. lbs.

DIFFERENTIAL CASE ASSEMBLY

1. Place the new differential bearing onto the case hub with the thick side of the inner race toward the case. Using a bearing driver, drive the bearing onto the case until it seats against the shoulder on the case.

2. Install the thrust washers and side gears into the case assembly. If the original parts are being used, be sure to place them in their original position.

3. Place the pinions in the case so they are 180 degrees apart as they engage the side gears.

4. Turn the pinion gears so the case holes align with the gear holes. When the holes are aligned, install the pinion shaft and lock screw; do not tighten the lock screw too tightly at this time.

5. Check the bearings, bearing cups, cup seat and carrier caps to make sure they are in good condition.

6. Lubricate the bearings with gear lube. Install the cups on the bearings and the differential assembly into the carrier. Support the carrier assembly to keep it from falling.

7. Install a support strap on the left side bearing and tighten the bearing bolts to an even, snug fit.

8. With the ring gear tight against the pinion gear, insert a gauge tool between the left side bearing cup and the carrier housing.

9. While lightly shaking the tool back and forth, turn the adjusting wheel until a slight drag is felt and tighten the locknut.

10. Between the right side bearing and carrier, install a 0.170 in. thick service spacer, a service shim and a feeler gauge. The feeler gauge must be thick enough so a light drag is felt when it is moved between the carrier and the shim.

11. Add the total of the service spacer, service shim and the feeler gauge. Remove the gauge tool from the left side of the carrier, then, using a micrometer, measure the thickness in at least 3 places. Average the readings and record the result.

12. Refer to the chart to determine the proper thickness of the shim packs.

13. Install the left side shim first, then, the right side shim between the bearing cup and spacer. Position the shim so the chamfered side is facing outward or next to the spacer.

NOTE: If there is not enough chamfer around the outside of the shim, file or grind the chamfer a little to allow for easy installation.

14. If there is difficulty in installing the shim, partially remove the case from the carrier and slide both the shim and case back into place.

15. Install the bearing caps and torque them to 60 ft. lbs. Tighten the pinion shaft lock screw.

NOTE: The differential side bearings are now preloaded. If any adjustments are made in later procedures, make sure not to change the preload. Do not change the total thickness of the shim packs.

16. Mount a dial indicator on the carrier assembly with the indicator button perpendicular to the tooth angle and aligned with the gear rotation.

17. Measure the amount of backlash between the ring and pinion gears; it should be between 0.005–0.008 in. Take readings at 4 different spots on the gear; there should not be variations greater than 0.002 in.

18. If there are variations greater than 0.002 in. between the readings, check the runout between the case and ring gear; the gear runout should not be greater than 0.003 in. If the runout

Checking the gear tooth contact

1. Companion flange
2. Oil deflector
3. Oil seal
4. Bearing retainer
5. Shim
6. Pinion front bearing
7. Collapsible spacer
8. Pinion rear bearing
9. Drive pinion
10. Straddle bearing
11. Ring gear
12. Differential spider
13. Differential case
14. Differential pinion
15. Differential side gear
16. Side bearing
17. Side bearing adjusting nut
18. Adjusting nut retainer
19. Retainer screw
20. Bearing cap
21. Case-to-ring gear bolt
22. Differential cover
23. Bearing cap bolt
24. Cover screw
25. Axle shaft

Cross-sectional view of the General Motors 10½ inch rear axle.

exceeds 0.003 in., check the case and ring gear for the deformation or dirt between the case and gear.

19. If the gear backlash exceeds 0.008 in., increase the thickness of the shims on the ring gear side and decrease the thickness of the shims on the opposite side, an equal amount.

20. If the backlash is less than 0.005 in., decrease the shim thickness on the ring gear side and increase the shim thickness on the opposite side an equal amount.

GEAR PATTERN CHECK

Before final assembly of the differential, a pattern check of the gear teeth must be made. This determines if the teeth of the ring and pinion gears are meshing properly, for low noise level and long life of the gear teeth. The most important thing to note is if the pattern is located centrally up and down on the face of the ring gear.

1. Wipe any oil from the carrier and all dirt and oil from the teeth of the ring gear.

2. Coat the teeth of the ring gear with a gear marking compound.

3. With the bearing caps torqued to 55 ft. lbs., expand the brake shoes until it takes 20–30 ft. lbs. of torque to turn the pinion gear.

4. Turn the companion flange so the ring gear makes a full rotation in 1 direction, then, turn it a full rotation in the opposite direction.

5. Check the pattern on the teeth and refer to the chart for any adjustments necessary.

6. With the gear tooth pattern checked and properly adjusted, install the axle housing cover gasket and cover and tighten securely. Refill the axle with gear lube to the correct level.

7. Road test the vehicle to check for any noise and proper operation of the rear.

GMC—10½ INCH RING GEAR AXLE

This axle is a full floating type that uses special hypoid type drive and pinion gears. The pinion gear is supported by 3 bearings, 2 in front of the pinion gear and 1 behind. The differential assembly has either 2 or 4 pinions depending on the application of the axle. This axle assembly must be removed from the vehicle to remove and service the differential.

Disassembly

DIFFERENTIAL

1. Place the axle assembly in a vise or holding fixture.

2. Remove the cover bolts, the cover and allow the gear lubricant to drain into a pan.

3. Remove the axle shafts from the axle assembly.

NOTE: Measure and record the pinion backlash so if the same gears are reused they may be installed at the same backlash to avoid changing the gear tooth pattern.

4. From the bearing caps, remove the adjusting nut lock retainers.

5. Mark the bearing caps so they may be reinstalled in the same position and remove the bearing caps.

6. Loosen the side bearing adjusting nut and remove the differential carrier from the axle housing.

PINION

1. Remove the differential assembly from the axle.

2. Check the pinion bearing for the proper preload. The force required to turn the pinion should be 25–35 inch lbs. for used bearings. If there is no reading, shake the companion flange to check for any looseness in the bearing. If there is any looseness present, replace the bearing.

3. Remove the pinion bearing retainer-to-axle housing bolts.

4. Remove the bearing retainer and pinion assembly from the axle housing. It may be necessary to tap the pilot end of the pinion shaft to help remove the pinion assembly from the carrier.

5. Record the thickness of the shims that are removed from between the carrier assembly and the bearing retainer assembly.

DRIVE PINION

1. With the pinion assembly clamped in a vise, install a holder assembly on the flange.

2. Using the proper size socket, remove the pinion nut and washer from the pinion.

NOTE: When reassembling the pinion use a new nut and washer assembly.

3. With the holder assembly still in place, use a puller to remove the flange from the pinion.

4. With the bearing retainer supported in a shop press, press the pinion out of the retainer assembly. Be careful not to allow the pinion gear to fall onto the floor because this can damage the gear.

5. Separate the pinion flange, the oil seal, the front bearing and the bearing retainer. If the oil seal needs to be replaced it may have to be driven from the retainer.

6. Using a drift, drive the front and rear bearing cups from the bearing retainer.

7. Support the pinion assembly in a press, with the bearing supported. Press the bearing from the pinion gear.

8. Using a drift, drive the straddle bearing from the carrier assembly.

DIFFERENTIAL CASE

1. Scribe a line across both halves of the differential case so they may be reassembled in the same position and with the ring gear removed, separate the halves.

2. Remove the ring gear bolts and washers. Using a soft hammer tap the ring gear from the case.

3. Remove the internal parts from the case and set them aside in order so they may be reassembled in the same position.

4. If removing the side bearing, perform the following procedures:

    a. Install a bearing puller on the bearing and press the bearing assembly from the differential case.

    b. Check the bearings for any signs of wear on distortion.

Cleaning and Inspection

1. Clean all of the parts in solvent and blow dry.

2. Check the differential gears, pinions, thrust washers and spider for any signs of unusual wear, chips, cracks or pitting.

3. Check the pinion gear for signs of wear, chips, cracks or any other imperfections. Check the splines for signs of wear or distortion.

4. Check all mating surfaces for signs of wear.

5. Check the bearings for signs of wear or pitting on the rollers and races and check the bearing cage for dents and bends. Check the bearing retainer for any cracks, pits, grooves or corrosion.

6. Check the pinion flange splines for any signs of wear or distortion.

7. Replace parts that show any of the signs mentioned above.

Assembly

DIFFERENTIAL CASE

1. If the side bearing was removed, perform the following procedures:

    a. Install a new bearing on the differential case.

    b. Using a bearing driver, drive the bearing onto the case assembly until it seats against the shoulder on the case.

2. Using a good quality gear lubricant coat all of the parts.

3. Assemble the differential pinions and thrust washers onto the spider and install the assembly into the differential case.

4. Align the scribe marks on both halves of the differential case and install the ring gear.

5. Install the ring gear washers and bolts and torque the bolts to approx. 10 ft. lbs.

DRIVE PINION

1. Coat all of the parts with a good quality gear lubricant.

2. Position the pinion gear into a shop press and press the rear bearings onto the pinion assembly.

3. Using a bearing driver, install the front and rear bearing cups into the bearing retainer.

4. Using a bearing driver, install the straddle bearing assembly in the axle housing.

5. Install the bearing retainer, with the bearing cups, onto the pinion gear and install a new collapsible spacer.

6. Using a shop press, press the front bearing onto the pinion gear.

7. Lubricate the oil seal with a good quality high pressure grease and install the seal into the retainer bore; be sure to press the seal until it rests against the internal shoulder.

8. Install the pinion flange and oil deflector onto the pinion gear splines, then, install a new lock washer and pinion nut.

9. With the pinion flange clamped in a vise and a holder assembly installed on the flange, tighten the nut to obtain the proper preload; 25–35 inch lbs. for a new bearing or 5–15 inch lbs. for a used bearing. To preload the bearing, tighten the pinion nut to approx. 350 ft. lbs. and take a reading of the torque required to turn the pinion. Continue tightening the nut until the proper preload is obtained.

NOTE: Do not tighten the nut too tightly because it will collapse the spacer too much. This will make replacement necessary.

DRIVE PINION

1. If installing a new pinion gear, check the top of the new gear for the depth code number.

2. Compare the new number with the old number on top of the old pinion and check the pinion depth chart for preliminary setting of the pinion depth.

3. Check the thickness of the original shims removed from the pinion and either add or subtract from the shims according to the chart.

4. Place the shim on the carrier assembly and align the holes with those in the axle housing. Make sure the surfaces are clean of all dirt and grease.

5. Install the retainer and pinion assembly in the housing making sure the holes align. Install the retaining bolts and torque to approx. 45 ft. lbs.

DIFFERENTIAL CASE

1. Place the bearing cups over the side bearings on the differential assembly and place the unit into the carrier in the axle housing.

2. Align the marks and install the bearing caps and the bolts. Tighten the bearing retaining bolts.

3. Loosen the right side nut and tighten the left side nut until the ring gear comes in contact with the pinion gear. Do not force the gears together. This brings the gears to zero lash.

4. Back off the left side adjusting nut about 2 slots and install the lock fingers into the nut.

5. In this order, tighten the right side adjusting nut firmly to force the case assembly into tight contact with the left side adjusting nut, then loosen the right side nut until it is free from the bearing.

6. Again, retighten the right side adjusting nut until it comes

		CODE NUMBER ON ORIGINAL PINION				
		+2	+1	0	-1	-2
	+2	—	ADD .001	ADD .002	ADD .003	ADD .004
CODE NUMBER ON SERVICE PINION	+1	SUBT. .001	—	ADD .001	ADD .002	ADD .003
	0	SUBT. .002	SUBT. .001	—	ADD .001	ADD .002
	-1	SUBT. .003	SUBT. .002	SUBT. .001	—	ADD .001
	-2	SUBT. .004	SUBT. .003	SUBT. .002	SUBT. .001	—

Pinion depth codes and corresponding shim thicknesses

in contact with the bearing. Tighten the right adjusting nut about 2 slots for an old bearing or 3 slots for a new bearing.

7. Install the lock retainers into the slots and torque the bearing cap bolts to 100 ft. lbs. This insures the bearings are preloaded properly. If more adjustments are made, make sure the preload stays the same. To do this, 1 adjusting nut must be loosened the same amount the other nut is tightened.

8. Install a dial indicator on the housing and measure the amount of backlash between the ring and pinion gear. The backlash should measure between 0.003–0.012 in. with the best figure being between 0.005–0.008 in.

9. If the backlash is more than 0.012 in., loosen the right side adjusting nut 1 slot and tighten the left side 1 slot. If the backlash is less than 0.003 in., loosen the left side nut 1 slot and tighten the right side 1 slot. These adjustments should bring the backlash measurement into an acceptable range.

PATTERN CHECK

1. Clean all the oil from the ring gear. Using a gear marking compound, coat the teeth of the ring gear.

2. Make sure the bearing caps are torqued to 110 ft. lbs. and apply load to the gears while rotating the pinion. Rotate the ring gear a full turn in both directions.

NOTE: Load must be applied to the assembly while rotating or the pattern will not show completely.

3. Check the pattern on the ring gear, adjust the assembly to get the contact pattern located centrally on the face of the ring gear teeth.

DANA — 9¾ AND 10½ INCH RING GEAR AXLES

The Dana Corporation's 9¾ and 10½ in. ring gear axle assem-

blies are basically the same but with certain exceptions. The differential side bearing shims are located between the side bearing cup assembly and the differential case on the 9¾ in. ring gear axle assembly, while on the 10½ in. ring gear axle assembly, the side bearing shims are located between the side bearing cup and the axle housing. Both axles use inner and outer shims on the pinion gear. The inner shims are used to control the pinion depth in the housing, while the outer shims are used to preload the pinion bearings. The 9¾ in. ring gear axle uses a solid differential carrier with a removable side and pinion gear shaft. The 10½ in. ring gear axle uses a split differential carrier with the side and pinion gears mounted on a cross shaft.

Disassembly

DIFFERENTIAL CARRIER

9¾ Inch

1. The axle assembly can be overhauled either in or out of the vehicle. Either way, the free-floating axles must be removed.

2. Drain the lubricant and remove the rear cover and gasket.

3. Matchmark the bearing caps and the housing for reassembly in the same position. Remove the bearing caps and bolts.

4. Using a spreader tool mounted to the carrier housing, spread the housing a maximum of 0.015 in.

NOTE: Do not exceed this measurement. The housing could be permanently damaged. The use of a dial indicator is recommended to prevent over-stretching the housing.

5. Using a prybar, remove the differential case from the housing. Separate the shims and record the dimensions and location. Remove the spreader tool from the housing.

6. Remove the differential side bearing cups and tag to identify the side, if they are to be used again.

6. Outer pinion oil slinger
7. Outer pinion bearing cone and roller
8. Outer pinion bearing cup
9. Outer pinion bearing shims
10. Inner pinion oil slinger
11. Inner pinion bearing shims
12. Inner pinion bearing cup
13. Inner pinion bearing cone and roller
14. Ring and pinion
15. Housing cover gasket
16. Housing retaining screw and washer
17. Cover and plug
18. Pinion shaft lock pin
19. Differential case
1. Nut
2. Washer
3. Companion flange
4. Pinion oil seal
5. Gasket
20. Differential bearing shims
21. Differential bearing cone and roller
22. Differential bearing cup
23. Differential bearing cap
24. Differential bearing bolt
25. Ring gear bolt
26. pinion shaft
27. Pinion thrust washer
28. Pinion
29. Side gear
30. Side gear thrust washer

Exploded view of the Dana 9¾ inch differential assembly

8. Preload shim pack
9. Pinion depth shim pack
10. Rear bearing cup
11. Pinion rear bearing
12. Drive pinion
13. Ring gear
14. Differential case
15. Ring gear bolt
16. Differential side bearing
17. Side bearing cup
18. Side bearing adjusting shims
19. Bearing cap
20. Bearing cap bolt
21. Differential spider
22. Differential side gear
23. Washer
24. Pinion gear
25. Washer
26. Gasket
27. Cover
28. Cover screw
29. Drain plug

1. Nut
2. Washer
3. Companion flange
4. Oil seal
5. Oil slinger
6. Pinion front bearing
7. Front bearing cup

Exploded view of the Dana 10½ inch differential assembly

7. Remove the differential gear pinion shaft lock pin and remove the shaft. Rotate the side and pinion gears to remove them from the carrier. Remove the thrust bearings.

8. Remove the bearing cones and rollers from the carrier, marking and noting the shim locations.

9. Remove the ring gear bolts and tap the ring gear from the carrier housing.

10. Inspect the components.

10½ Inch

1. The axle assembly can be overhauled either in or out of the vehicle. Either way, the free-floating axles must be removed.

2. Drain the lubricant and remove the rear cover and gasket.

3. Matchmark the bearing caps and the housing for reassembly in the same position. Remove the bearing caps and bolts.

4. Using a spreader tool mounted to the carrier housing, spread the housing a maximum of 0.015 in.

NOTE: Do not exceed this measurement. The housing could be permanently damaged. The use of a dial indicator is recommended to prevent over-stretching the housing.

5. Using a prybar, remove the differential case from the housing. Separate the shims and record the dimensions and location. Remove the spreader tool from the housing.

6. Using puller tools, press the differential side bearings from the case.

7. Remove the ring gear bolts and tap the ring gear from the case with a soft-faced hammer.

8. Matchmark the case halves for reassembly and remove the retaining bolts.

9. Tap the upper part of the case to separate it from the bottom part. Remove the internal gears, washers and cross.

DRIVE PINION

1. Remove the pinion nut and flange from the pinion gear.

2. Remove the pinion gear assembly from the housing. It may be necessary to tap the pinion from the housing with a soft faced hammer. Catch the pinion so as not to allow it to drop on the floor.

3. With a long drift, remove the inner bearing cup, pinion seal, slinger, gasket, outer pinion bearing and the shim pack. Label the shim pack for reassembly.

4. Remove the rear pinion bearing cup and shim pack from the housing. Label the shims for reassembly.

5. Remove the rear pinion bearing from the pinion gear with an arbor press and special plates.

Inspection

1. Clean the gears, bearings and component parts with solvent and inspect for scoring, chipping or excessive wear.

2. Inspect the flanges and splines for excessive wear.

3. Replace the necessary parts as required.

SIDE BEARING SHIM SELECTION

10½ Inch

1. With the pinion gear not in the axle housing, place the bearing cups over the side bearings and install the differential carrier into the axle housing.

2. Place the shim that was originally installed on the ring gear side into its original position.

3. Install the bearing caps in their proper positions and tighten the bolts to keep the bearings in place.

Old Pinion Marking	New Pinion Marking								
	- 4	- 3	- 2	- 1	0	+ 1	+ 2	+ 3	+ 4
+ 4	+ 0.008	+ 0.007	+ 0.006	+ 0.005	+ 0.004	+ 0.003	+ 0.002	+ 0.001	0
+ 3	+ 0.007	+ 0.006	+ 0.005	+ 0.004	+ 0.003	+ 0.002	+ 0.001	0	- 0.001
+ 2	+ 0.006	+ 0.005	+ 0.004	+ 0.003	+ 0.002	+ 0.001	0	- 0.001	- 0.002
+ 1	+ 0.005	+ 0.004	+ 0.003	+ 0.002	+ 0.001	0	- 0.001	- 0.002	- 0.003
0	+ 0.004	+ 0.003	+ 0.002	+ 0.001	0	- 0.001	- 0.002	- 0.003	- 0.004
- 1	+ 0.003	+ 0.002	+ 0.001	0	- 0.001	- 0.002	- 0.003	- 0.004	- 0.005
- 2	+ 0.002	+ 0.001	0	- 0.001	- 0.002	- 0.003	- 0.004	- 0.005	- 0.006
- 3	+ 0.001	0	- 0.001	- 0.002	- 0.003	- 0.004	- 0.005	- 0.006	- 0.007
- 4	0	- 0.001	- 0.002	0.003	- 0.004	- 0.005	- 0.006	- 0.007	- 0.008

Removing the differential hub bearings

4. Mount a dial indicator on the axle housing with the indicator button contacting the back of the ring gear.

5. Position 2 prybars between the bearing shim and the housing on the ring gear side of the differential carrier. Force the differential carrier away from the dial indicator and set the indicator to zero.

6. Reposition the prybars to the opposite side of the differential carrier and force the carrier back towards the dial indicator. Repeat several times until the same reading is obtained each time.

7. To the dial indicator reading, add the thickness of the shim and record the results to be used later in the assembly.

PINION SHIM SELECTION

Ring gears and pinions are supplied in matched sets only. The matched numbers are etched on both gears for verification. On the rear face of the pinion, a plus (+) or a minus (−) number will be etched, indicating the best running position for each particular gear set. This dimension is controlled by the shimming behind the inner bearing cup. Whenever baffles or oil slingers are used, they become part of the adjusting shim pack. An example: If a pinion is etched + 3, this pinion would require 0.003 in. less shims than a pinion etched 0. This means by removing shims, the mounting distance of the pinion is increased by 0.003 in., which is just what a plus (+) etching indicates. If a pinion is etched − 3, it would be necessary to add 0.003 in. more shims than would be required if the pinion was etched 0. By adding the 0.003 in. shims, the mounting distance of the pinion is decreased 0.003 in., which is just what the minus (−) etching indicates. Pinion adjusting shims are available in thicknesses of 0.003, 0.005 and 0.010 in. An example: If a new gear set is used and the old pinion reads + 2 and the new pinion reads − 2, add 0.004 in. shims to the original shim pack.

Assembly

DRIVE PINION

1. Select the correct pinion depth shims and install in the rear pinion bearing cup bore.

2. Install the rear bearing cup in the axle housing.

3. Add or subtract an equal amount of shim thickness to or from the preload or outer shim pack, as was added or subtracted from the inner shim pack.

4. Install the front pinion bearing cup into its bore in the axle housing.

5. Press the rear pinion bearing onto the pinion gear shaft and install the pinion gear with bearing into the axle housing.

6. Install the preload shims and the front pinion bearing; do not install the oil seal at this time.

7. Install the flange with the holding bar tool attached, the washer and the nut on the pinion shaft end. Torque the nut to 250 ft. lbs. for the 10½ in. or 255 ft. lbs. for the 9¾ in.

8. Remove the holding bar from the flange and with an inch lb. torque wrench, measure the rotating torque of the pinion gear. The rotating torque should be 10–20 inch lbs. with the original bearings or 20–40 inch lbs. with new bearings. Disregard the torque reading necessary to start the shaft to turn.

9. If the preload torque is not in specifications, adjust the shim pack as required.

 a. To increase preload, decrease the thickness of the preload shim pack.

 b. To decrease preload, increase the thickness of the preload shim pack.

10. When the proper preload is obtained, remove the nut, washer and flange from the pinion shaft.

11. Install a new pinion seal into the housing and reinstall the flange, washer and nut. Using the holder tool, torque the nut to 250 ft. lbs. for the 10½ in. or 255 ft. lbs. for the 9¾ in.

DIFFERENTIAL CARRIER

9¾ Inch

1. Install the differential side gears, the differential pinion gears and new thrust washers into the differential carrier.

2. Align the pinion gear shaft holes and install the pinion shaft into the carrier. Align the lock pin hole in the shaft and carrier. Install the lock pin and peen the hole to avoid having the pin drop from the carrier.

3. Install the differential case side bearings with the proper installation tools. Do not install the shims at this time.

4. Place the carrier assembly into the axle housing with the bearing cups on the bearing cones. Install the bearing caps in their original position and tighten the bearing cap bolts enough to keep the bearing caps in place.

5. Install a dial indicator on the housing so the indicator button contacts the carrier flange. Press the differential carrier to

prevent side-play and center the dial indicator. Rotate the carrier and check the flange for run-out. If the run-out is greater than 0.002 in., the defect is probably due to the bearings or to the carrier and should be corrected.

6. Remove the assembly and install the ring gear. Torque the retaining bolts and reinstall the assembly into the housing. Install the bearing caps in their original position and tighten the cap bolts to keep the bearings caps in place.

7. Install the dial indicator and position the indicator button to contact the ring gear back surface. Rotate the assembly and the run-out should be less than 0.002 in. If over 0.002 in., remove the assembly and relocate the ring gear 180 degrees. Reinstall the assembly and recheck. If the run-out remains over the 0.002 in. tolerance, the ring gear is defective. If the measurement is within tolerances, continue on with the assembly.

8. Position 2 prybars between the bearing cap and the housing on the side opposite the ring gear. Pull on the prybars and force the differential carrier as far as possible towards the dial indicator. Rock the assembly to seat the bearings and reset the dial indicator to zero.

9. Reposition the prybars to the opposite side of the carrier and force the carrier assembly as far towards the center of the housing. Read the dial indicator scale. This will be the total amount of shims required for setting the backlash during the reassembly, less the bearing preload. Record the measurement.

10. With the pinion gear installed and properly set, position the differential carrier assembly into the axle housing and install the bearing caps in their proper positions. Tighten the cap bolts just to hold the bearing cups in place.

11. Install a dial indicator on the axle housing with the indicator button contacting the back of the ring gear.

12. Position 2 prybars between the bearing cup and the axle housing on the ring gear side of the case and pry the ring gear into mesh with the pinion gear teeth, as far as possible. Rock the ring gear to allow the teeth to mesh and the bearings to seat. With the pressure still applied by the prybars, set the dial indicator to zero.

13. Reposition the prybars on the opposite side of ring gear and pry the gear as far as it will go. Take the dial indicator reading. Repeat this procedure until the same reading is obtained each time. This reading represents the necessary amount of shims between the differential carrier and the bearing on the ring gear side.

14. Remove the bearing from the differential carrier on the ring gear side and install the proper amount of shims. Reinstall the bearing.

15. Remove the differential carrier bearing from the opposite side of the ring gear. To determine the amount of shims needed, use the following method.

   a. Subtract the size of the shim pack just installed on the ring gear side of the carrier from the reading obtained and recorded when measurement was taken without the pinion gear in place.

   b. To this figure, add an additional 0.015 in. to compensate for preload and backlash. An example: If the first reading was 0.085 in. and the shims installed on the ring gear side of the carrier were 0.055 in., the correct amount of shims would be 0.085 − 0.055 + 0.015 = 0.045 in.

16. Install the required shims as determined under step 15 and install the differential side bearing. The installation of the shims should give the proper preload to the bearings and the proper backlash to the ring and pinion gears.

17. Spread the axle housing with the spreader tool no more than 0.015 in. Install the differential bearing outer cups in their correct locations and install the cups in their respective locations.

18. Install the bolts and tighten finger-tight. Rotate the differential carrier and ring gear and tap with a soft-faced hammer to insure proper seating of the assembly in the axle housing.

19. Remove the spreader tool and torque the cap bolts to specifications.

20. Install a dial indicator and check the ring gear backlash at 4 equally spaced points of the ring gear circle. The backlash must be within a range of 0.004–0.009 in. and must not vary more than 0.002 in. between the points checked.

21. If the backlash is not within specifications, the shim packs must be corrected to bring the backlash within limits.

22. Check the tooth contact pattern and verify.

23. Complete the assembly, refill to proper level with lubricant and operate to verify proper assembly.

10½ Inch Ring Gear

1. Install new thrust washers to the side gears and lubricate the contact surfaces.

2. Assemble the side gears, pinion bears, washers and cross shaft into the flanged part of the case.

3. Install the upper case to the bottom making sure the scribe marks are aligned.

4. Install the retaining bolts finger-tight, then, torque the bolts alternately.

5. If a new ring gear is to be installed or the old one used, install it to the differential case and align the bolt holes and torque the bolts alternately.

6. Install the side carrier bearings.

7. Install the differential carrier, with the side bearings and cups installed, in place in the axle housing.

8. Select the smallest of the original shims as a gauge shim and place it between the bearing cup and the housing on the ring gear side.

9. Install the bearing caps and tighten the bolts to hold the cups in place.

10. Mount a dial indicator on the ring gear side of the axle housing and position the indicator button on the rear side of the ring gear.

11. Position 2 prybars between the bearing cup and the housing on the side opposite the ring gear. With the prybars, force the differential carrier towards the dial indicator and set the indicator dial to zero.

12. Reposition the prybars on the ring gear side of the carrier and force the ring gear into mesh with the pinion gear while observing the dial indicator reading. Repeat this operation until the same reading is obtained each time.

13. Add this indicator reading to the gauging shim thickness to determine the correct shim dimension for installation on the ring gear side of the differential carrier.

14. An example: If the gauging shim was 0.115 in. and the indicator reading was 0.017 in., the correct shim would be 0.115 + 0.017 = 0.172 in.

15. Remove the gauge shim and install the correct shim into position between the bearing cup and the axle housing on the ring gear side of the housing.

16. To determine the correct dimension for the remaining shim, refer to the side bearing shim selection for the 10½ in. and obtain the recorded shim size. From that figure, subtract the size of the shim installed in Step 14 and add 0.006 in. for the bearing preload and backlash.

17. An example: If the reading of the shim just installed on the ring gear side of the carrier was 0.172 in. and the reading obtained during the checking of clearance without the pinion installed was 0.329, the correct shim dimension would be as follows: 0.329 − 0.172 = 0.157 + 0.006 = 0.163 in.

18. Spread the axle housing with a spreader tool, no more than 0.015 in. The carrier assembly is in place in the housing.

19. Assemble the shim, as determined previously, into place between the bearing cup and the housing. Remove the spreader tool.

20. Install the bearing caps in their marked positions and torque the bolts to specifications.

21. Install a dial indicator and check the ring gear backlash at 4 equally spaced points around the ring gear.

22. The backlash must be within 0.004–0.009 in. and must not vary more than 0.002 in. between the positions checked.

23. Whenever the backlash is not within the allowable limits, it must be corrected. Changing of the shim packs is required.

    a. Low backlash is corrected by decreasing the shim on the ring gear side and increasing the opposite side shim an equal amount.

    b. High backlash is corrected by increasing the shim on the ring gear side and decreasing the opposite side shim an equal amount.

24. Check the tooth contact pattern and correct as required.

25. Complete the assembly, refill to the correct level and operate to verify correct repairs.

ROCKWELL—12 INCH RING GEAR AXLE

Disassembly

DIFFERENTIAL

1. Remove locknut, adjusting screw and thrust block.
2. Remove 2 adjuster lock cap screws and locks.
3. Punch-mark bearing caps and carrier to help in locating caps for assembly. Remove bearing adjusters and bearing caps.

NOTE: Do not pry caps free with a prybar or distort locating dowels.

4. Carefully remove differential assembly from carrier.
5. Use a differential side bearing remover to pull bearing cones off each side of case.
6. Make sure the differential case halves are punch-marked so they can be reassembled in same position.
7. Remove drive gear and separate case halves.
8. Remove 2 side gears, the differential spider and the 4 differential pinions.
9. Remove pinion and side gear thrust washers.

DRIVE PINION

1. Remove seal retainer and gasket from carrier.
2. Using brass drift against inner end of pinion, drive out the pinion and bearing assembly.
3. Remove shim pack from carrier from those models having tapered roller outer bearings.
4. It may be necessary to use a drift to remove the pinion rear bearing.
5. Clamp yoke in soft-jawed vise. Remove yoke nut and washer and separate drive pinion from yoke.
6. Separate yoke from oil seal retainer.
7. Place retainer in a soft-jawed vise and, using a hammer and chisel, remove oil seal and then the felt oil seal.
8. If equipped with a tapered roller outer bearing, remove bearing cup, outer tapered bearing cone and bearing spacer from drive pinion.
9. Using a bearing remover press plate with shop press, press the bearing cone or roller bearing from the drive pinion.
10. If equipped, remove the bearing lock ring and use press plates with shop press to press the roller bearing from inner end of drive pinion.

Inspection

1. Clean the gears, bearings and component parts with solvent and inspect for scoring, chipping or excessive wear.
2. Inspect the flanges and splines for excessive wear.
3. Replace the necessary parts as required.

Assembly

NOTE: Thoroughly clean and lubricate all components with axle lubricant before reassembling.

DRIVE PINION

1. Clean counterbore of oil seal retainer. Saturate the felt seal in oil and install evenly in retainer. Soak oil seal in light engine oil for about 1 hour before installing. Coat outer surface of seal lightly with sealing compound to prevent oil leaks between seal and retainer.

2. Install oil seal into retainer with lip of seal toward inner side of retainer. Using a seal installer, press oil seal into retainer with face of seal flush with retainer face.

3. Retainer surface must be clean and smooth to prevent oil leaks between retainer and carrier.

4. Using a shop press, press bearing into place into carrier bore or the roller bearing into position on drive pinion with chamfered side of inner race facing toward pinion shoulder. Position bearing lock ring to secure bearing on drive pinion.

NOTE: Opposed tapered roller bearing cones, 2 bearing cups and spacer are serviced and replaced as a unit. The spacer is a preselected one to provide proper bearing adjustment.

5. Models with tapered roller bearings:

    a. Press inner bearing cone into place with largest side of cone facing the pinion gear end.

    b. Install original shim pack in carrier. If original ring gear and pinion are reinstalled, use shims that were removed. Shims are available in 5 thicknesses: 0.012, 0.015, 0.018, 0.021 and 0.024 in. When using new gears, start with a 0.021 in. shim and check the pinion depth.

    c. Insert the pinion assembly into carrier, align roller bearing with carrier boss. Install bearing spacer, bearing cup and bearing cone with the wide side facing pinion splines.

6. If equipped with double-row ball bearing: Using a 2 in. pipe or tubing, drive bearing unit into proper seating position.

7. With pinion assembly properly positioned in carrier, install new gasket. Install seal retainer onto yoke and assemble yoke and retainer assembly onto splined end of drive pinion.

8. Secure the retainer to carrier with lock washers and cap screws and torque.

9. Secure the pinion assembly with yoke washer and nut and torque to 220 ft. lbs.

DIFFERENTIAL

1. To facilitate installation of drive gear, install 2 guide pins (½ × 20 × 2 in. bolts) in gear. Start the guide pins through the case flange holes and tap drive gear onto case. If a differential gear is bad, the complete set should be replaced.

2. Lubricate the differential case inner walls and all component parts with axle lubricant. Place the differential pinions and thrust washers onto the spider.

3. Assemble the side gears, pinions, side gear and pinion thrust washers onto the left half of differential.

4. Assemble the drive gear half, right half of differential, being sure to align marks on both halves.

5. Install differential-to-drive gear cap screw and lock washers and tighten evenly until drive gear is flush with case flange. Remove guide pins and install cap screws and torque.

6. Using an installer tool, install the differential side bearing cones.

7. Install the bearing cap locating dowels into the caps. Lubricate the side bearings and place the bearing cups on bearings.

8. Install the differential assembly into the carrier. Carefully install the bearing adjusters into the carrier.

9. Install the bearing caps by aligning the punch marks previously made. Be sure the bearing adjuster threads are engaged with carrier and caps. Tighten the adjusters alternately and evenly. Tighten the bearing cap screws until the lock washers are flat.

Adjustment

DRIVE GEAR AND PINION

1. Loosen the bearing cap screws, enough, to loosen the right-hand bearing adjuster (pinion side) and tighten the left-hand bearing adjuster (opposite pinion side.) Using the adjuster, remove all backlash between the drive gear and pinion.

2. Back off the left-hand bearing adjuster about 2 notches to point where notch in adjuster is aligned with lock. Tighten the right-hand bearing adjuster solidly to seat the bearing. Loosen right-hand adjuster, enough, to free the bearing; then, retighten against the bearing. Draw up right-hand adjuster 1–2 more notches until adjuster notch aligns with the lock.

3. Using a dial indicator on carrier adjuster, slowly oscillate the drive gear and measure the backlash; it should be 0.005–0.008 in.

4. If backlash exceeds 0.008 in., loosen the right-hand adjuster 1 notch; then, tighten the left-hand adjuster 1 notch. If less than 0.005 in., loosen the left-hand adjuster 1 notch and tighten the right-hand adjuster 1 notch.

5. After the backlash has been adjusted, tighten the bearing cap screws until their respective lock washers flatten out.

6. Check the drive gear run-out.

7. Install the side bearing adjusting locknut and secure with cap screws and lock washers.

CHECKING PINION DEPTH

NOTE: This procedure is performed if the pinion is equipped with tapered roller bearings.

1. Coat the drive gear with red lead.

2. Turn the pinion shaft several revolutions in both directions while applying considerable drag on drive gear.

3. Pinion depth is determined by shim pack selection. Shim packs are available in thicknesses of: 0.012, 0.015, 0.018, 0.021 and 0.024 in.

4. Changing the pinion depth will again require adjusting backlash. After pinion depth and backlash have been adjusted, torque bearing caps.

THRUST BLOCK

1. Install the thrust block and locknut to the adjusting screw.

2. Thread the screw and block into the carrier until the block contacts the drive gear.

3. Rotate the gear and note the drag change.

4. Adjust these parts until point of greatest drag is reached. Back off the screw about 30 degrees to provide 0.005–0.007 in. clearance between the block and gear. Make certain screw does not turn at all when torquing the locknut to 135 ft. lbs.

Locking Differentials

7½, 7⅝, 8½, 9½ INCH RING GEAR

Disassembly and Assembly

1. With the differential assembly out of the vehicle, start by removing the governor bushing from the differential. A special C-clamp type tool is suggested to press out the bushing.

2. Remove the E-clips that hold the latching bracket in place on the bracket shaft. Move the bracket down the shaft.

3. Remove the latching bracket busing. A special C-clamp type tool is suggested to press out the bushing.

4. Remove the latching bracket, shaft and spring from the case.

5. Remove the governor assembly from the case.

6. On 9½ inch differentials only, remove the stop pin.

7. Remove the lockscrew and pinion shaft.

8. Roll the gears out of the case by rotating 1 of the side gears. Take out both the pinion gears and thrust washers. Remove the thrust block.

A. 7½ in. ring gear
B. 8½ in. ring gear
C. 9½ in. ring gear
1. Differential case
2. Stop pin (9½ only)
3. Lock screw
4. Governor bushing
5. Latching bracket bushing
6. Pinion thrust washer
7. Pinion gear
8. Side gear thrust washer
9. Clutch plates
10. Side gear
11. Latching bracket
12. Clutch plates
13. Side gear thrust washer
14. Side thrust sleeve (9½ only)
15. Wave washer
16. Cam plate
17. Thrust block
18. Pinion shaft
19. Guide clip
20. Guide clip
21. Side cam gear
22. Retaining ring
23. Governor

Differential components—General Motors 7½, 7⅝, 8½ and 9½ ring gear locking differential

Top: removing the governor bushing: Bottom: view of governor and latching bracket—General Motors 7½, 7⅝, 8½ and 9½ ring gear locking differential

9. Remove the right side gear, right side clutch pack and side thrust washer.

10. Remove the left side gear, cam plate and clutch pack as an assembly.

11. Remove the side gear thrust washer.

12. Disassemble the cam unit on 7½, 7⅝ and 8½ inch differentials using the following procedure:
   a. Remove the snapring.
   b. Take off the clutch plates.
   c. Remove the guide clips.
   d. Remove the wave spring.
   e. Remove the cam plate.
   f. Remove the cam side gear.

13. Disassemble the cam unit on 9½ inch differentials using the following procedure:
   a. Measure and record the overall length of the gear pack assembly from the front of the gear to the back of the thrust sleeve including the side gear washer. Remove the guide clips.
   b. Remove the thrust sleeve using a press to remove the sleeve from the side gear.
   c. Remove the lock plates.
   d. Remove the wave spring.
   e. Remove the cam plate.
   f. Remove the cam side gear.

Measurements required when overhauling locking differential. Top: checking cam gear backlash. Center: measuring side gear spread. Note drift pin wedges. Bottom: measuring the thrust block— General Motors 7½, 7⅝, 8½ and 9½ ring gear locking differential

To assemble:

14. Installation is the reverse of the removal procedure. Clean all parts well with solvent and blow dry with low pressure air. Check all parts for excessive wear, cracks or damage. Check the fit of the axles and side gears. Check the thrust sleeve for wear. Do not replace unless necessary.

15. Assemble the cam unit on 7½, 7⅝ and 8½ inch differentials using the following procedure:

a. Install the cam plate to the side gear. Install the wave spring.

b. Assemble the clutch pack, alternating the plates. 7½ and 7⅝ differentials use 8 plates. 8½ differentials use 10 plates.

c. Install the snapring and guide clips to the plates. Use grease in the clips to hold them in place on the plates.

16. Assemble the cam unit on 9½ inch differentials using the following procedure:

a. Install the cam plate to the cam side gear. Install the wave spring.

b. Assemble the clutch pack, alternating the plates.

c. Install the thrust sleeve. Press the sleeve flush with the side gear disc splines.

d. Install the guide clips to the plates. Use grease in the clips to hold them in place on the plates.

e. If the side gear or thrust sleeve has been replaced, measure and record the overall length of the gear assembly from the front of the gear to the back of the thrust sleeve including the side gear washer. Compare this reading with the reading obtained earlier. If the new reading is more than 0.003 inch higher or lower than the original, select a thrust washer that will return the reading closest to the original reading.

Adjustment

If it is necessary to replace the cam gear, the right side gear or the thrust block, the entire differential must be adjusted. The differential is adjusted by using selective thickness washers behind each side gear and selective thickness thrust washers behind the reaction blocks.

It is important to build up the differential properly as the proper clearance between parts is necessary for the proper operation of the units. There are 3 adjustments to be made: Left side gear backlash, right side gear backlash and thrust block clearance.

LEFT SIDE GEAR BACKLASH ADJUSTMENT

1. Install the cam unit and thrust washer to the flange end of the case.

2. Place the differential gears and thrust washers into the differential, aligning with the pinion shaft hole.

3. Press down the side gear and install the pinion shaft and lock screw. If the side gear cannot be pressed down far enough to install the pinion shaft replace the thrust washer with a thinner washer.

4. Rotate the pinion gear closest to the lock screw so one of the teeth is pointing downward, perpendicular to the ring gear flange.

5. Insert a large tapered tool or drift pin firmly between the side gear and the pinion shaft.

6. Mount a dial indicator to the ring gear flange and place the stem of the indicator on 1 of the teeth on the pinion gear closest to the lock screw. Pull the pinion gear firmly into its seat and rotate the gear back and forth while reading the dial indicator. Record the reading.

7. Repeat these steps on the opposite pinion gear.

8. The backlash should be between 0.254–0.457mm (0.010–0.018 inch). If the backlash is too high, use a thicker thrust washer. If too low, a thinner washer.

RIGHT SIDE GEAR BACKLASH ADJUSTMENT

1. Assemble the clutch pack, alternating the plates. Use grease to hold the guide clips in place.

2. Install the thrust washer, clutch plate assembly and right side gear to the differential.

3. Place the pinion gears and thrust washers into the differential aligning them with the pinion shaft hole. Press down on the side gear and install the pinion shaft and lock screw. If the side gear cannot be pressed down far enough to install the pinion shaft, replace the thrust washer with a thinner washer.

4. Rotate the pinion gear closest to the lock screw so one of

teeth is pointing downward, perpendicular to the ring gear flange.

5. Insert a large tapered tool or drift pin firmly between the side gear and the pinion shaft.

6. Mount a dial indicator to the ring gear flange and place the stem of the indicator on 1 of the teeth on the pinion gear closest to the lock screw. Pull the pinion gear firmly into its seat and rotate the gear back and forth while reading the dial indicator. Record the reading.

7. Repeat these steps on the opposite pinion gear.

8. The backlash should be between 0.002–0.010 inch (0.051–0.243mm). If the backlash is too high, use a thicker thrust washer. If too low, a thinner washer.

THRUST BLOCK CLEARANCE ADJUSTMENT

1. Install the left thrust washer, cam unit and right thrust washer to the differential.

2. Install the clutch packs and right side gear to the differential.

3. Install the pinion shaft and lock screw. Insert a large tapered tool or drift pin firmly between each side gear and the pinion shaft.

4. Insert a 1–2 inch telescoping measuring gauge ("snap gauge") between the side gear faces, not the gear teeth. Measure the side gear spread. Remove the telescoping gauge and measure with a micrometer. Record this number.

5. Measure the original thrust block at the outer corner with a micrometer. If the thrust block thickness is not 0.000–0.006 inch less than the side gear spread, adjust the clearance by:

a. Selecting a new thrust block the correct size to obtain 0.000–0.006 inch clearance.

b. Reshimming the right and/or left clutch pack. The backlash must remain 0.002–0.010 inch.

Final Assembly

1. Install the left thrust washer.

2. Install the assembled cam unit.

3. Install the right thrust washer, clutch pack and side gear.

4. Install the thrust block, thrust washer and pinion gear by placing the pinion gears into the differential 180 degrees apart. Rotate the gears ad thrust block into position. The open side window of the thrust block must face toward the small window opening.

5. Install the pinion shaft. Install a new lockscrew, turning finger-tight. Tighten to 27 ft. lbs. (37 ft. lbs. for 9½ axle) after the differential is installed in the vehicle.

6. Install the governor assembly and latching bracket. The straight end of the latching bracket spring must be over and outside the governor assembly shaft.

7. On 9½ inch axles, install the stop pin. Press the pin flush with the case.

8. Install the governor bushing. Use the bushing with a straight hole, not a tapered hole. Press the bushing in far enough to give 0.004–0.020 inch shaft end play.

9. Install the latching bracket bushing. Press the bushing in far enough to eliminate all end play.

10½ INCH RING GEAR

Disassembly and Assembly

1. With the differential assembly out of the vehicle, start by removing the ring gear and the differential bearings.

2. Set the differential unit on the right side case half. Remove the differential case screws and separate the case halves by prying apart at the yoke hole location. Hold the side gear in the left side case half as the halves come apart.

3. Remove the governor assembly.

4. Remove the latching bracket assembly.

5. Remove the left side gear, clutch pack, guide clips and left thrust washer.

1. Differential case halves
2. Screw
3. Cam plate
4. Guide clip
5. Thrust sleeve
6. Side gear thrust washer
7. Plates
8. Pinion thrust washer
9. Pinion gear
10. Side cam gear
11. Reaction block
12. Pinion yoke
13. Governor and latching bracket
14. Plates
15. Side gear thrust washer
16. Side gear
17. Guide clip
18. Governor

Differential components—General Motors 10½ ring gear locking differential

6. Remove the reaction blocks, pinion yoke, pinion gears and pinion thrust washers.

7. Remove the right cam unit from the differential. Measure and record the overall length of the gear assembly from the front of the gear to the back of the thrust sleeve including the side gear washer. Remove the right thrust washer.

8. Remove the thrust sleeve from the side gear with a suitable press.

9. Remove the remaining clutch plates, guide clips, wave spring cam plate and cam side gear.

To assemble:

10. Installation is the reverse of the removal procedure. Installation is the reverse of the removal procedure. Clean all parts well with solvent and blow dry with low pressure air. Check all parts for excessive wear, cracks or damage. Check the fit of the axles and side gears. Check the thrust sleeve for wear. Do not replace unless necessary.

11. Assemble the cam plate to the side gear. Install the wave washer and clutch pack alternating the plates. Make sure the wave washer is properly positioned.

12. Press the thrust sleeve flush with the side gear disc spline.

13. Install the guide clips to the plates. Use grease in the clips to hold them in place on the plates.

   a. If the side gear or thrust sleeve has been replaced, measure and record the overall length of the gear assembly from the front of the gear to the back of the thrust sleeve including the side gear washer.

   b. Compare this reading with the reading obtained earlier.

   c. If the new reading is more than 0.003 inch higher or lower than the original, select a thrust washer that will return the reading closest to the original reading.

Adjustment

If it is necessary to replace the cam gear, the right side gear or the reaction blocks, the entire differential must be adjusted. The differential is adjusted by using selective thickness thrust washers behind each side gear and selective thickness thrust washers between the reaction blocks.

It is important to build up the differential properly as the proper clearance between parts is necessary for the proper operation of the unit. There are 3 adjustments to be made: Left side gear backlash, right side gear backlash and thrust block clearance.

RIGHT SIDE GEAR BACKLASH ADJUSTMENT

  1. Install the cam unit and thrust washer to the right case half.

  2. Clamp the cam unit in place using a set of washers, nut and a bolt long enough to hold the cam unit in place.

Clamp the cam unit in place with a nut and bolt, then install the pinion yoke—General Motors 10½ ring gear locking differential

Measurements required when overhauling locking differential. Top: checking pinion gear backlash. Center: chceking reaction block clearance by first measuring side gear spread with a depth micrometer. Bottom: measuring the reaction block—General Motors 10½ ring gear locking differential

3. Place the pinion gears and thrust washers on the pinion yoke and install the yoke firmly to the differential case half. A soft mallet may be needed to tap into place.

4. Loosen the holding nut and index 1 pinion gear tooth to point downward, perpendicular to the case face. Retighten the holding nut.

5. Mount a dial indicator on the case half face using a magnetic base. Place the stem of the dial indicator on the pinion gear tooth. Pull the pinion gear firmly into its seat and rotate the gear back and forth while reading the dial indicator. Use care not to unseat the pinion yoke. This will make the backlash reading inaccurate. Record the reading.

6. Repeat these steps on the remaining 2 pinions.

7. The backlash should be 0.010–0.018 inch (0.254–0.457mm). If the backlash is too high, use a thicker thrust washer. If the backlash is too low, use a thinner thrust washer.

LEFT SIDE GEAR BACKLASH ADJUSTMENT

1. Assemble the clutch pack, alternating the plates. Use grease to hold the guide clips in place.

2. Install the thrust washer, clutch plate assembly and left side gear to the differential.

3. Clamp the side gear in place using a set of washers, nut and a bolt long enough to hold the side gear in place.

4. Place the pinion gears and thrust washers on the pinion yoke and install the yoke firmly to the differential case half. A soft mallet may be needed to tap into place.

5. Loosen the holding nut and index 1 pinion gear tooth to point downward, perpendicular to the case face. Retighten the holding nut.

6. Mount a dial indicator on the case half face using a magnetic base. Place the stem of the dial indicator on the pinion gear tooth. Pull the pinion gear firmly into its seat and rotate the gear back and forth while reading the dial indicator. Use care not to unseat the pinion yoke. This will make the backlash reading inaccurate. Record the reading.

7. Repeat these steps on the remaining 2 pinions.

8. The backlash should be 0.002–0.010 inch (0.051–0.254mm). If the backlash is too high, use a thicker thrust washer. If the backlash is too low, use a thinner thrust washer.

REACTION BLOCK CLEARANCE ADJUSTMENT

1. Install the left thrust washer, clutch plates and side gear to the differential. Use a long bolt washers and nut to hold them in place as before.

2. Install the right thrust washer and cam assembly. Use a long bolt washers and nut to hold them in place as before.

3. Measure the distance from the side gear face to the case half face using suitable straight-edges and a depth micrometer. Do this to both sides of the gear case. Remember to subtract the thickness of the straight-edges. Add the measurement of both sides together. This is the side gear spread.

4. With a micrometer, measure the thickness of the original reaction blocks and the reaction block thrust washers together. If the combined reaction block and thrust washer thickness is not 0.000–0.006 in. (0.000–0.152mm) less than the side gear spread, adjust the clearance by:

   a. Selecting a new thrust block of the correct thickness to obtain 0.000–0.006 in. clearance.

   b. Reshimming the right and/or left clutch pack. The side gear backlash must be maintained.

   c. Note that some older models of this differential had select fit reaction blocks without the thrust washer between them. These models require replacing the reaction blocks with the correct thickness block.

Final Assembly

1. Install the right thrust washer.

2. Install the right cam unit.

3. Install the reaction blocks, reaction block thrust washer, pinion yoke, pinion gears and pinion thrust washers.

4. Install the left thrust washer. Make sure the clutch plates are assembled properly.

5. Install the left side gear.

6. Install the latching bracket assembly.

7. Install the governor assembly. The straight end of the latching bracket spring must be over and outside the governor assembly shaft.

8. Join the 2 case halves together, holding the side gear in the left side case half.

9. Install the case screws.

10. Install the ring gear with new bolts. Note that these bolts are left-hand thread. Tighten alternately to 120 ft. lbs. Install the differential bearings with a suitable drive.

11. Install differential into axle assembly. Refill with 80W90 GL-5 gear lubricant. Do not use limited slip additive.

JEEP

Jeep models are currently using Dana Model 30 and Model 44 front drive axles. Model 30 axles are used on Wrangler, Comanche and Cherokee. It is a semi-floating axle shaft type with a 7.125 (7⅛) inch ring gear. Selec-Trac models are the non-disconnect type. Command-Trac axles have a disconnect feature.

Model 44 front drive axles are used on the Grand Wagoneer. It is a full-floating type with an 8.50 (8½) inch ring gear. All use 75W-90 GL5 hypoid gear lubricant. The Model 30 uses approximately 2.5 pints, the Model 44 uses approximately 3.75 pints. Note that the Model 30 with Command-Trac disconnect axle, uses an intermediate axle and seal inside the axle tube. This means that an additional 5 ounces of lubricant must be added to the front axle shift motor housing opening.

Current Jeep models use the Dana Model 35 and Model 44 rear drive axles. The Model 35 uses a $7^9/_{16}$ ring gear. It is used on the Wrangler, Comanche (except Heavy Duty Metric Ton option) and Cherokee. The Model 44 uses an 8.50 (8½) inch ring gear and is standard on the Grand Wagoneer. Note that front axles are very similar to rear axles and most of the procedures are the same.

The differential assembly consists of a cast iron case containing 2 differential side gears, 2 differential pinion gears and a pinion shaft on which the pinion gears are mounted. The differential side and pinion gears are in constant mesh.

The axle ratio and the ring and pinion gear tooth combinations are stamped on a tag attached to the differential housing cover. On the Jeep rear axles, the axle code letters are stamped on the right side axle housing tube boss.

NOTE: The Trac-Lok limited slip differentials are available as an option. The Trac-Lok is used only in rear axles and there are 2 Trac-Lok units used.

Front Axle Assembly
MODEL 30 AND 44 FRONT AXLE

Disassembly and Assembly

1. Raise and safely support vehicle.

2. Remove the differential cover and drain the lubricant.

3. Make matchmarks for reference on the yokes and disconnect the front driveshaft from the pinion yoke.

Exploded view Model 44 front drive axle—Jeep

1. Fill plug
2. Differential housing cover
3. RTV sealant
4. Bearing cap bolt
5. Bearing cap
6. Bearing cup
7. Pinion mate shaft
8. Thrust washer
9. Side gear
10. Pinion gear
11. Thrust washer
12. Ring gear mounting bolts
13. Bearings
14. Bearing preload shims
15. Differential case
16. Pinion mate shaft pin
17. Ring gear
18. Pinion drive gear
19. Slinger
20. Pinion bearing
21. Drive pinion bearing cup
22. Drive pinion depth shims
23. Baffle
24. Differential housing
25. Drive pinion preload shims
26. Oil seal
27. Dust cap
28. Yoke
29. Washer
30. Drive pinion nut
31. Upper ball stud split ring seat
32. Upper ball stud nut
33. Cotter pin
34. Lower ball stud jamnut
35. Upper ball stud
36. Spindle
37. Seal
38. Bearing
39. Bearing cup
40. Hub
41. Inner locknut
42. Washer
43. Outer locknut
44. Spring cup
45. Pressure spring
46. Drive gear
47. Snapring
48. Hub cap
49. Spindle bearing
50. Washer
51. Seal
52. Seal seat
53. Axle shaft
54. Steering knuckle
55. Steering stop bolt
56. Lower ball stud
57. Snapring
58. Tie rod
59. Tie rod end nut
60. Inner oil seal

Command-Trac disconnect axle on Model 30 front drive axle—Jeep

4. Remove the front wheels, disc brake rotors and hubs and bearings.
5. Remove the shift motor and housing if equipped with Command-Trac disconnect axle.
6. Remove the axle shafts.
7. If equipped with Command-Trac disconnect axle, remove the intermediate axle shaft retaining C-clip. Disengage the shaft from the right side differential side gear.
8. Make matchmarks for reference on the differential bearing caps and loosen but do not remove the bolts.
9. Disconnect the steering tie rod from the left steering knuckle. Disconnect the track bar from the frame rail bracket.
10. Install a differential spreader tool on the housing. Use a dial indicator to make sure the housing is not overspread which could damage the axle. Spread the axle only enough to remove the differential case. For Wrangler, Comanche and Cherokee, separate a maximum of 0.020 inch. For Grand Wagoneers, separate a maximum of 0.015 inch.
11. After spreading the differential, remove the differential bearing caps. Position a prybar under a ring gear bolt head and another prybar under the differential case. Pry the differential case upward to remove it.

12. Remove the spreader tool after removing the differential case to avoid the possibility of the housing taking a "set."

13. Clamp the differential housing in a vise. Remove and discard the ring gear bolts. Use a soft drift pin to drive off the ring gear. Do not try to pry off the gear or the case could be damaged.

14. Use a small pin punch to drive out the differential pinion gear mate shaft lockpin then remove the shaft.

15. Rotate the differential pinion gears until the gears are aligned with the case opening. Remove the differential pinion gears and thrust washers.

16. Measure the side gear clearance with 2 feeler gauges. Insert a gauge blade between each thrust washer and the differential case. Vary the blade thickness until the blade fits tight. Do not exceed 0.007 inch between washers and case. Replace both thrust washers if the clearance exceeds the clearance specification. After checking, remove the differential side gears and the thrust washers.

17. Mark the differential bearing cups for installation reference and remove them. Remove the differential bearing with a suitable puller.

18. With a suitable holding tool secure the pinion yoke. Remove the pinion nut and washer. Use a puller to remove the yoke from the pinion. On Model 44 axles, remove the dust cap from the pinion.

19. Remove the pinion gear. Strike the end of the shaft with a rawhide hammer to force it out of the pinion gear bearing and housing.

20. Remove the pinion gear front bearing, the bearing preload spacer, shims, oil slinger and seal. Use a 2x2 inch piece of wood or suitable size pipe to drive the bearing, spacer, oil slinger and seal out of the housing. Discard the seal and spacer (Model 30 axles). If reuseable, save the shims for installation. Pinion bearing cups may be removed from the housing with a brass drift punch. Save any shims.

To assemble:

21. Assembly is the reverse of the removal procedure. Clean all parts well. Inspect parts for wear or damage, especially the side

Special tools used for removing and installing intermediate axle shaft seal and bearing on Command-Trac disconnect axle on Model 30 front drive axle. Top: removing seal, Middle: Installing the seal, Bottom: Using special hook tool to remove intermediate shaft bushing—Jeep

Replacing inner axle seals on Comanche, Cherokee and Grand Wagoneer with Select-Trac non-disconnect axles—Jeep

JEEP PINION GEAR DEPTH VARIATION CHART—DANA 30 FRONT AXLE

PINION GEAR DEPTH VARIANCE

Original Pinion Gear Depth Variance	Replacement Pinion Gear Depth Variance								
	−4	−3	−2	−1	0	+1	+2	+3	+4
+4	+0.008	+0.007	+0.006	+0.005	+0.004	+0.003	+0.002	+0.001	0
+3	+0.007	+0.006	+0.005	+0.004	+0.003	+0.002	+0.001	0	−0.001
+2	+0.006	+0.005	+0.004	+0.003	+0.002	+0.001	0	−0.001	−0.002
+1	+0.005	+0.004	+0.003	+0.002	+0.001	0	−0.001	−0.002	−0.003
0	+0.004	+0.003	+0.002	+0.001	0	−0.001	−0.002	−0.003	−0.004
−1	+0.003	+0.002	+0.001	0	−0.001	−0.002	−0.003	−0.004	−0.005
−2	+0.002	+0.001	0	−0.001	−0.002	−0.003	−0.004	−0.005	−0.006
−3	+0.001	0	−0.001	−0.002	−0.003	−0.004	−0.005	−0.006	−0.007
−4	0	−0.001	−0.002	−0.003	−0.004	−0.005	−0.006	−0.007	−0.008

gears and pinion gears. If only one gear is damaged, replace all gears.

22. Wrangler, Comanche and Cherokee with Command-Trac disconnect axles, will have a right side axle shaft inner seal and bushing. Both the seal and bushing require special tools to replace. The factory tool is a long threaded shaft with a series of adapters to alternately drive out, then pull into place the replacement parts.

23. Wrangler, Comanche and Cherokee with Command-Trac disconnect axles, will have a left side axle shaft inner seal. The seal requires special tools to replace. After prying the inner seal out of the axle shaft tube bore in the differential housing, the factory tool, a long threaded shaft with a series of adapters, to force the replacement seal into place.

24. Comanche, Cherokee and Grand Wagoneer with Selec-Trac non-disconnect axles also have left and right inner axle seals. After prying the inner seals out of the axle shaft tube bore in the differential housing, the factory tool, a turnbuckle-like spreader tool is used to press the replacement seals into place.

25. Ring and pinion gears must be replaced as matched sets and set up properly to get the correct tooth contact pattern. Note that front differentials require an oil slinger to be located between the pinion gear rear bearing and the gear head. The slinger must be installed on the shaft to correctly adjust the pinion gear depth for the best possible gear teeth contact pattern. Install the drive pinion gear using the following procedure:

a. If applicable, verify that the replacement ring and pinion gear are a matched set. If the original ring and pinion is being installed, use the original shim(s).

b. Determine the depth when using a replacement ring and pinion. Add or subtract the original depth shim to establish pinion depth. Note the depth variance etched in the original and replacement drive pinion gear. Refer to the pinion gear variance chart. Move to where the original and replacement columns intersect. Note the value. It will be either plus (+), zero (0), or minus (−). This is the amount of change from the original thickness.

c. Clean the bearing cup bores and install the "initial" depth shim(s) in the housing rear bearing cup bore. If the depth shim is chamfered on 1 side, position the chamfered side so it faces the bottom of the bearing cup bore. Install the pinion gear bearing cups and the oil slinger on the pinion.

d. Install the rear pinion bearing on the pinion gear with a suitable driver.

e. Install pinion gear in the housing but do not install the bearing preload spacer at this time. Install and seat the front bearing. Do not install the seal.

f. Install the pinion yoke and the original nut on the pinion gear. Tighten the nut enough to remove the shaft "end play."

g. Install the bearings on the differential case hubs with a suitable driver. Do not install the bearing shims at this time.

h. Install the bearing cups, observing the matchmarks made at teardown.

i. Install an axle spreading tool to the carrier housing. Use a dial indicator to make sure the spread does not exceed 0.020 inch (0.015 inch on Model 44). Install the differential into the housing. Insert enough spare shims between 1 of the differential bearings and the housing to eliminate all differential case "side play."

j. Install the bearing caps using the matchmarks made at teardown.

k. Install a dial indicator so the tip rests against the ring gear flange. Turn the flange to check runout. Total case flange runout should not exceed 0.002 inch.

l. Loosen the bearing cap bolts on both sides. Remove the spare shims used to eliminate case side-play in Step i. Install a 0.142 inch thick shim between each differential bearing and the housing. These shims will provide an "end play" coarse adjustment.

m. Pry the differential case to 1 side of the housing. Zero the dial indicator. Pry the differential case to the opposite side of the housing. Record the dial indicator end play. This measurement is the additional thickness required for zero end play. For example: if the end play is 0.008 inch, an additional

Differential case runout check and bearing shim installation—Jeep

Checking differential side gear/thrust washer clearance—Jeep

0.004 inch shim will be added at each side for zero end play. Obtain the necessary differential bearing shims and set them aside for for later installation.

　n. Install the spreader tool and remove the differential.
26. Install the side gears with their thrust washers and the pinion gears with their thrust washers in the differential case. Measure the side gear clearance. if the clearance exceeds 0.007 inch per side with the original thrust washers, replace them. If the clearance exceeds 0.007 inch per side with the replacement thrust washers, replace the side gears. Install the pinion shaft and lockpin.
27. Remove the differential hub bearings with a suitable puller and install the saved zero end play shims (Step 25—m) on each side of the differential case. Install the differential bearings and cups, observing matchmarks made at teardown.
28. Install the ring gear on the differential case. Use new bolts, torqued to 55 ft. lbs. Check ring gear backlash and drive pinion gear depth adjustment using the following procedure:

　a. The pinion gear is adjusted by changing the thickness of the shims. The shims are located under the rear bearing cup. The ring gear position backlash is adjusted by changing the side-to-side shims. The 2 adjustments interact.
　b. Install the differential case in the housing using the spreader tool. Tap the outer edges of the bearing cups with a rawhide mallet to seat them. Observe the matchmarks made at teardown. Tighten the bolts securely.
　c. Attach a dial indicator to the housing. Position the indicator plunger against the "drive" side of 1 ring gear tooth at right angles to the tooth. Pry the ring gear toward the dial indicator and zero the indicator while at this position.
　d. Pry the ring gear away from the drive pinion gear until the gear "backlash" indicated is 0.005–0.009 inch. Temporarily insert shims between one differential bearing nearest the ring gear and the housing to maintain the established gear "backlash" during the remainder of the adjustment.
　e. Apply gear marking compound to the ring gear and turn 1 complete revolution in both directions, to imprint the gear teeth contact patterns. Analyze the patterns for corrective action.
　f. To increase backlash, use a thinner shim pack on the ring gear side of the case. Subtract the amount needed from the ring gear pack. Add the same amount to the opposite shim pack.
　g. To decrease backlash, use a thinner shim pack on the ring gear side of the case. Add the amount needed to the ring gear shim pack. Subtract the same amount from the opposite shim pack.
29. Remove the differential case assembly and remove the pinion gear. Replace the shims as necessary to adjust the gear positions for the best possible gear teeth contact and backlash.
30. Install the pinion gear and differential case. As before, use care not to spread the case more than 0.020 inch (0.015 inch on Model 44). Apply gear marking compound and rotate the ring gear 1 complete revolution in both directions. Analyze the gear teeth contact patterns. Change pinion gear depth shims as required.
31. Check the drive pinion gear bearing preload torque adjustment using the following procedure:

　a. The pinion gear yoke nut is used to adjust the preload torque.
　b. Use the spreader tool to spread the axle housing and remove the differential. Clean the gear marking compound from the ring gear teeth.

c. Remove the pinion gear and install a replacement pre-load spacer and install the pinion gear back in the housing along with a lubricated new seal.

d. Install the driveshaft yoke and a new replacement nut. Tighten the nut only enough to remove the end play. Do not over-tighten or the spacer will be collapsed too much and will need to be replaced.

e. With a suitable socket and torque wrench, rotate the shaft and measure the turning torque. Use a suitable holding tool on the yoke and slowly tighten the nut in small increments until the torque required to rotate the pinion gear is in the range of 20–40 inch lbs. for new replacement bearings or 15–25 inch lbs. with original bearings. Measure the preload frequently to avoid over-tightening the nut.

32. Before installing the differential case, the differential bearings must be preloaded. Use additional shims to compensate for heat and the engine torque during vehicle operation. Note the installation matchmarks made earlier and install the originally selected differential bearing shims on each case hub. Add an additional 0.004 inch shim to each case hub. Install the differential bearings on the case hubs with a suitable driver.

33. Lubricate the bearings, gears and thrust washers with axle lubricant. Spread the axle housing no more than 0.020 inch (0.015 inch on Model 44). Install the bearing cups and then the differential case in the housing. Tap the outer edges of the bearing cups with a rawhide mallet to seat them.

34. Remove the differential spreader. Install the bearing caps and bolts. Torque to 57 ft. lbs.

35. Check the ring gear backlash. If it has changed, it must be readjusted.

Rear Axle Assembly

MODEL 35 AND 44 REAR AXLE

The ring gear and pinion gear in Model 35 axles are supplied in matched sets. Do not interchange with other sets. Verify that the ID numbers are the same before installation. The ring gear and differential case in current Model 35 rear axles are also a matched set. They are not interchangeable with 1987 and earlier Model 35 axles.

Model 35 rear axles use 2½ pints 75W–90 GL5 hypoid gear lubricant. Synthetic 80W–140 hypoid gear lubricant is recommended for trailer towing. If equipped with Trac-Lok, add a container of limited slip additive.

Disassembly and Assembly

MODEL 35 DIFFERENTIAL

1. Using a puller tool and adapters, remove the differential bearings.

NOTE: When using this tool, be sure the differential case is secure. When the bearing is removed the differential case can drop if not supported.

2. Remove the ring gear-to-differential case bolts.

NOTE: Do not chisel or wedge the gear from the case.

3. Remove the ring gear from the case. Using a brass drift and hammer, tap the ring gear from the case; do not nick the ring gear face of the differential case or drop the gear.

4. Using a drift, remove the pinion mate shaft lockpin. Remove the pinion mate shaft and the thrust block.

5. Rotate the pinion gears on the side gears until the pinion gears are aligned with the case opening. Remove the pinion gears with the thrust washers and the side gears with the thrust washers.

6. Using a pinion yoke holding tool, remove the pinion nut. Using a pinion yoke removal tool, remove the axle yoke.

7. Install the axle housing cover to prevent the pinion gear

Removing the pinion lock pin

Removing the pinion shaft and thrust block

Removing the axle yoke

from falling out when the gear is driven out of the bearings and housing. Loosely attach the cover using 2 bolts.

8. Using a seal removal tool, remove the pinion seal. Tap the end of the pinion gear with a soft face mallet to drive the pinion gear out of the front bearing. Remove the front bearing and collapsible spacer. Discard the spacer.

NOTE: The collapsible spacer is used to control the pinion bearing preload. Discard this spacer after removal, it is not reusable.

9. Remove the axle housing cover, the pinion gear and the rear bearing. Using bearing removal tools, remove the rear bearing cup.

NOTE: The pinion gear depth adjustment shims are located under the rear bearing cup; label these shims for assembly reference.

10. Using bearing removal tool, remove the front bearing cup.

NOTE: Keep the bearing cup remover tool seated squarely on the cup to prevent damaging the cup bores during removal.

Inspection

AXLE HOUSING

1. Place 2 straight-edges across the tube flanges and measure the distance between the flange ends. If the straight-edges are parallel within $^{3}/_{32}$ in. at a distance of 11 inches from the tube centerline, the axle housing is serviceable.
2. Perform this inspection with the straight-edges placed in horizontal and vertical positions.

DIFFERENTIAL

1. Clean each part thoroughly in solvent.
2. Towel dry the bearings or allow them to air dry, do not use compressed air to dry bearings as damage might result. Dry all other parts with compressed air or shop towels. If the parts are not to be assembled immediately, cover them to prevent dust or dirt contamination.
3. Inspect the housing for cracks and sand holes. Replace the housing if it is cracked or porous. Check for burrs and deep scratches or nicks on the gasket and oil seal surfaces. An oil stone or fine tooth file may be used to remove nicks or burrs.
4. The bearing cup bores should be carefully inspected for

nicks or burrs that may have been created during bearing cup removal.
5. Inspect and clean the axle tubes. Inspect the vent to be sure it is not obstructed.
6. Check housing for bent or loose tubes or other physical damage.
7. Inspect the shaft for scoring and wear. The shaft should be a press fit of 0.000–0.010 in. in the case. Replace the shaft if worn or scored.
8. Inspect the side gears for worn, cracked or chipped teeth. The gears should fit snugly on the axle shaft splines. Also inspect the fit of the gears in the differential case bore.
9. With the gears installed, side clearance must not exceed 0.007 in. Excessive side clearance must be corrected to avoid driveline backlash resulting in a clunk noise when the transmission is initially engaged in **D** or **R** with automatic transmission.

Assembly

PINION GEAR

Ring and pinion gear sets are factory tested to detect machining variances. Tests are started at a standard setting which is then varied to obtain the most desirable tooth contact pattern and quiet operation. When this setting is determined, the ring and pinion gear are etched with identifying numbers.

The ring gear receives one number. The pinion gear receives 2 numbers which are separated by a plus (+) or a minus (−) sign. The 2nd number on the pinion gear indicates pinion position, in relation to the centerline of the axle shafts, where tooth contact was best and gear operation was most quiet. This number represents pinion depth variance and indicates the amount in thousands of an inch the gear set varied from the standard setting.

The number on the ring gear and 1st number on the pinion gear identify the gears as a matched set; do not attempt to use a ring and pinion set having different numbers. The standard setting for Jeep axles is 2.547 in. If the pinion is marked + 2, the gear set varied from standard by + 0.002 in. and will require 0.002 in. less shims than a gear set marked zero (0).

When a gear set is marked plus (+), the distance from the pinion end face to the axle shaft centerline must be more than the standard setting. If the pinion gear is marked − 3, the gear set varied from standard by 0.003 in. more shims than a set marked zero (0). When a set is marked minus (−), the distance from the pinion end face to the axle shaft centerline must be less than the standard setting.

NOTE: On some factory installed gear sets, an additional 0.010 or 0.020 in. may have been machined off the pinion gear bottom face. This does not affect the gear operation but does affect the pinion gear marking and depth measurement.

Pinion gears machined in this fashion have different identifying numbers. For example, if the pinion is marked + 23, the number 2 indicates 0.020 in. was removed from the pinion bottom face and the number 3 indicates variance from the standard setting is + 0.003 in. If the pinion is marked + 16, the number 1 indicates 0.010 in. was removed from the pinion bottom face and the number 6 indicates variance from the standard setting is + 0.006 in.

Gear sets with additional amounts machined off the pinion bottom face are factory installed items exclusively. All service replacement gear sets will be machined to standard settings only. In addition, replacement gear sets marked ± 0.009 in. or more or sets with mismatched identifying numbers must be returned to the parts distributor center; do not attempt to install these gear sets.

The chart provided in this section will help to determine the approximate starter shim thickness needed for the initial pinion depth measurement. However, the chart will not provide the exact shim thickness required for final adjustment and must not

(11 in)

(11 in)

Checking the axle housing alignment

be used as a substitute for an actual pinion depth measurement. The chart should be used as follows.

1. Measure the thickness of the original pinion depth shim. Note the pinion depth variance numbers marked on the old and new pinion gears.

2. Now use the chart to determine the starter shim thickness. An example of this is as follows:

If the old pinion is marked −3 and the new pinion is marked +2, the chart procedure would be as follows. Go to the old pinion column and locate the −3, then go across the chart until the +2 figure is reached in the new pinion column. The box where the 2 columns intersect will indicate the amount of starter shim thickness required.

DIFFERENTIAL

1. Install the differential bearings on the case using tools J–21784 and J–8092 or equivalent.

2. Install the thrust washers on the differential side gears and install the gears in the differential case. Install the differen-

tial pinion gears in the case. Install the thrust washers behind the pinion gears and align the pinion gear bores.

3. Rotate the differential side and pinion gears until the pinion mate shaft bores in the pinion gears are aligned with the shaft bores in the case.

4. Install the thrust block in the case. Insert the block through the side gear bore. Align the bore in the block with the pinion mate shaft bores in the pinion gears and case.

5. Install the pinion mate shaft. Align the lockpin bore in the shaft with the bore in the case and install the shaft lockpin.

RING GEAR

1. Position the ring gear on the differential case. Install the 2 ring gear bolts in the opposite holes and tighten the bolts to pull the gear into position.

2. Install the remaining ring gear bolts and tighten to within 105 ft. lbs. torque.

3. Position the shims previously selected to remove the differential bearing side-play on the bearing cups and install the differential assembly in the axle housing. Install the bearing cap bolts and tighten the bolts with 85 ft. lbs. torque.

4. Attach the dial indicator to the housing. Position the indicator so the indicator stylus contacts the drive side of a ring gear tooth and at a right angle to the tooth. Move the ring gear back and forth and note the movement registered on the dial indicator. The ring gear backlash should be 0.005–0.009 in., with 0.008 in. desired.

5. Adjust the backlash as follows: to increase the backlash, install the thinner shim on the ring gear side and the thicker shim on the opposite side. To decrease the backlash, reverse the procedure; however, do not change the total thickness of the shims.

Pinion and ring gear identifying numbers

NOTE: The following is an example on how to decrease backlash. The side-play was removed using 0.090 in. shims on each side totaling 0.180 in. Backlash is checked and found to be 0.011 in. To correct the backlash, add 0.004 in. the the shim on the ring gear side and subtract 0.004 in. from the shim on the opposite side. This will result in 0.094 in. shim on the ring gear side and 0.086 in. shim on the other side. The backlash will be approximately 0.007–0.008 in. The total shim thickness remains 0.180 in.

JEEP PINION GEAR DEPTH VARIATION CHART — DANA 35 REAR AXLE

Old Pinion Marking	New Pinion Marking								
	− 4	− 3	− 2	− 1	0	+ 1	+ 2	+ 3	+ 4
+ 4	+ 0.008	+ 0.007	+ 0.006	+ 0.005	+ 0.004	+ 0.003	+ 0.002	+ 0.001	0
+ 3	+ 0.007	+ 0.006	+ 0.005	+ 0.004	+ 0.003	+ 0.002	+ 0.001	0	− 0.001
+ 2	+ 0.006	+ 0.005	+ 0.004	+ 0.003	+ 0.002	+ 0.001	0	− 0.001	− 0.002
+ 1	+ 0.005	+ 0.004	+ 0.003	+ 0.002	+ 0.001	0	− 0.001	− 0.002	− 0.003
0	+ 0.004	+ 0.003	+ 0.002	+ 0.001	0	− 0.001	− 0.002	− 0.003	− 0.004
− 1	+ 0.003	+ 0.002	+ 0.001	0	− 0.001	− 0.002	− 0.003	− 0.004	− 0.005
− 2	+ 0.002	+ 0.001	0	− 0.001	− 0.002	− 0.003	− 0.004	− 0.005	− 0.006
− 3	+ 0.001	0	− 0.001	− 0.002	− 0.003	− 0.004	− 0.005	− 0.006	− 0.007
− 4	0	− 0.001	− 0.002	0.003	− 0.004	− 0.005	− 0.006	− 0.007	− 0.008

Measuring the ring gear backlash

Installing the gauge arbor tool, discs and gauge block tool

Adjustment

PINION DEPTH MEASUREMENT

1. Measure the thickness of the original pinion depth shim. Note the pinion depth variance numbers marked on the old and new pinion gears.

2. Determine the starter shim thickness. Using the chart, determine the amount to be added or subtracted from the original shim thickness for starter shim thickness.

NOTE: The starter shim thickness must not be used as a final shim setting. An actual pinion depth measurement must be performed and the final shim thickness adjusted, as necessary.

3. Install the ring bearing on the pinion gear with the large diameter of the bearing cage facing the gear end of the pinion. Press the bearing against the rear face of the gear.

4. Clean the pinion bearing bores in the axle housing thoroughly. This is important in obtaining the correct pinion gear depth adjustment. Install the starter pinion depth shim in the housing rear bearing cup bore. Be sure the shim is centered in the bearing cup bore.

NOTE: If the shim is chamfered, be sure the chamfered side faces the bottom of the bearing cup bore.

5. Install the ring bearing cup using tools J–8092 and J–8608 or equivalent. Install the front bearing cup using tools J–8092 and J–8611–01 or equivalent. Install the pinion gear in the rear bearing cup.

6. Install the front bearing, rear universal joint yoke and original pinion nut on the pinion gear. Tighten the pinion nut only enough to remove the bearing end play.

NOTE: Do not install a replacement pinion nut and collapsible spacer at this time as the pinion gear will be removed after depth measurement.

7. Note the pinion depth variance marked on the pinion gear. If the number is preceded by a plus (+) sign, add that amount (in thousandths) to the standard setting for the axle model being overhauled. If the number is preceded by a minus (−) sign, subtract that amount (in thousandths) from the standard setting. The result of this addition or subtraction is the desired pinion depth. Record this figure for future reference.

Measuring the anvil with a micrometer

Installing the shim(s) on the side of the differential bearing cup

Installation of the dial indicator

8. Assemble an arbor tool J–5223–4 and discs J–5223–23 or equivalent, install the assembled tools in the differential bearing cup bores; be sure the discs are completely seated in bearing cup bores.

9. Install the bearing caps over the discs and install the bearing cap bolts. Tighten the bearing cap bolts securely but not with the specified torque.

10. Position a gauge block tool J–5223–20 or equivalent, on the end face of the pinion gear with the anvil end of the gauge block seated on the gear and the gauge plunger under the arbor tool J–5223–4 or equivalent.

11. Assemble and mount the clamp tool J–5223–24 and bolt J–5223–29 or equivalent, on the axle housing. Use the axle housing cover bolt to attach the clamp to the housing.

12. Extend the clamp bolt until it presses against the gauge block with enough force to prevent the gauge block from moving. Loosen the gauge block thumb screw to release the gauge block plunger. When the plunger contacts the arbor tool, tighten the thumbscrew to lock the plunger in position; do not disturb the plunger position.

13. Remove the clamp and bolt assembly from the axle housing. Remove the gauge block and measure the distance from the end of the anvil to the end of the plunger using a 2–3 in. micrometer. This dimension represents the measured pinion depth. Record this dimension for assembly reference.

14. Remove the bearing caps, the arbor tool and discs from the axle housing. Remove the pinion gear, the rear bearing cup and pinion depth shim from the axle housing.

15. Measure the thickness or the depth shim. Add this dimension to the measured pinion depth. From this total, subtract the desired pinion depth. The result represents the correct shim thickness required.

NOTE: The desired pinion depth is the standard setting plus or minus the pinion depth variance.

PINION GEAR BEARING PRELOAD

1. Install the correct thickness pinion depth shim(s) in the axle housing bearing cup bore. Install the rear bearing cup and pinion gear.

NOTE: The collapsible spacer controls the pinion bearing preload; do not reuse the old spacer, use a replacement spacer only.

2. Install the replacement collapsible spacer and front bearing on the pinion gear. Install the pinion oil seal using tool J–22661 or equivalent.

3. Install the pinion yoke, replace the pinion nut and tighten the pinion nut finger-tight. Tighten the pinion nut enough to remove end play and seat the pinion bearings. Using tool J–22575 or equivalent, tighten the nut and use tool J–86141–01 or equivalent, to hold the yoke while tightening the nut.

4. Rotate the pinion, while tightening the nut, to seat the bearings evenly. Remove the tools.

NOTE: Do not exceed the specified preload torque or loosen the nut to reduce the preload torque, if the specified torque is exceeded.

5. Using an inch lb. torque wrench and adapter tool J–22575 or equivalent, measure the torque required to turn the pinion gear; the correct pinion bearing preload torque is 17–25 inch lbs. Continue tightening the pinion nut until the required preload torque is obtained.

6. If the pinion bearing preload torque is exceeded, remove the pinion gear, replace the collapsible spacer and pinion nut and adjust the preload again.

DIFFERENTIAL BEARING

1. Place the bearing cup over each differential bearing and install the differential case assembly in the axle housing.

2. Install the shim on each side between the bearing cup and the housing; use 0.080 in. shims as the starting point.

3. Install the bearing caps and tighten the bolts finger-tight. Mount the dial indicator on the housing. Using a prybar, pry between the shims and housing. Pry the assembly to one side and zero the indicator, then, pry the assembly to the opposite side and read the indicator.

NOTE: Do not zero or read the indicator while prying.

4. The amount read on the indicator is the shim thickness that should be added to arrive at the zero preload and zero end play. Repeat the procedure to ensure accuracy and adjust if necessary; shims are available in thicknesses from 0.080–0.110 in. in increments of 0.002 in.

5. When the side-play is eliminated, a slight bearing drag will be noticed. Install the bearing caps and tighten the bearing cap bolts to with 85 ft. lbs. torque.

6. Attach the dial indicator to the axle housing and check the ring gear mounting face of the differential case for runout; runout should not exceed 0.002 in.

7. Remove the case from the housing. Retain the shims used to adjust the side-play.

DIFFERENTIAL AND BEARING PRELOAD

NOTE: The differential bearings must be preloaded to compensate for heat and loads during operation. The differential bearings are preloaded by increasing the shim pack thickness at each side of the differential by 0.004 in. for a total of 0.008 in.

1. Remove the differential assembly from the housing. Be sure to keep the differential bearing shim packs together for the proper assembly. Do not distort the shims in the axle housing bearing bores.

2. Install the differential bearing cups on the differential bearings. The cups should cover the differential bearing rollers completely. Position the differential assembly in the housing so the bearings just start into the housing bearing bores.

NOTE: Slightly tipping the bearing cups will ease starting them into the bores. Also keep the differential assembly square in the housing during installation and push it in as far as possible.

3. Tap the outer edge of the bearing cups until the differential is seated in the housing.

4. Install the differential bearing caps. Position the caps accordingly to the alignment punch marks made at disassembly. Tighten the bearing cap bolts with 85 ft. lbs. torque. Preloading the differential bearings may change the backlash setting. Check and correct the backlash, if necessary.

5. Install the propeller shaft, aligning the index marks made at disassembly. Install the axle shafts, bearings, seals and brake support plates. Fill the rear axle with the specified axle lubricant.

6. Check and adjust the axle shaft end play, if necessary. Adjust the end play at the left side of the axle shaft only. Install the hubs, drums and wheels.

7. Lower the vehicle and road test the vehicle to check the rear axle assembly for proper operation.

MODEL 44 AXLE

Disassembly
MODEL 44 DIFFERENTIAL

1. Remove the housing cover and drain the lubricant.
2. Using an axle spreader tool, mount it onto the axle housing and spread the housing enough to remove the differential.
3. Using a dial indicator, measure the amount the opening is being spread; do not spread the housing more than 0.015 in. (0.38mm), for damage to the housing may occur.
4. Mark the differential bearing caps for reassembly purposes.
5. Loosen the bearing caps until 2–3 threads are engaged.
6. Using a prybar, pry the differential loose.
7. Remove the bearing caps and the differential.
8. Mount the differential into a vise.
9. Remove and discard the ring gear bolts; they are not reusable.
10. Using a brass drift and a hammer, tap the ring gear from the differential.
11. Using a differential bearing puller, press the differential bearings from the differential.
12. Remove the differential bearing shims.
13. Using 2 sets of feeler gauges, insert them between each side of the side gear thrust washer and differential case and

measure the side gear clearance; the clearance should not exceed 0.007 in. (0.18mm). Replace both thrust washers, if the clearance exceeds the tolerance.
14. Remove the pinion shaft lockpin and pinion shaft.
15. Rotate the pinions to remove them through the case opening.
16. Remove the side gears and thrust washers.

PINION GEAR

1. Remove the differential case from the axle housing.
2. Using a pinion yoke holding tool, remove the pinion gear nut.
3. Using a pinion yoke holder tool and a pinion puller tool, press the yoke from the pinion gear. Remove the pinion washer.
4. Using a soft mallet, drive the pinion gear from the axle housing.
5. Remove the pinion gear, the bearings and the preload spacers.
6. Remove and discard the pinion seal.
7. Using a shop press and the bearing removal tool, press the bearing from the pinion gear.

Inspection

1. Clean the differential components in solvent and use compressed air to dry them; do not use compressed air on the bearings, only shop towels.
2. Check the components for wear or damage; replace them, if necessary.
3. Inspect the bearings and bearing cups for wear, cracks or scoring; replace them, if necessary.
4. Inspect the differential side and pinion gears for wear, cracks or chips; replace them, if necessary.
5. Inspect the ring and pinion gears for wear and/or damage; replace them, if necessary.
6. Inspect the differential case for cracks or damage; replace it, if necessary.

Assembly
PINION GEAR

1. Make sure the ring and pinion are a matched set.

Spreading the axle housing

Measuring the side gear clearance

Exploded view of the Dana Model 44-8½ inch rear differential assembly

2. Measure the thickness of the original pinion shim and note the variance on the pinion gear.

3. Perform the following procedure to determine the pinion starter shim thickness:

a. If the original ring and pinion are being installed, use the original shim.

b. If a replacement gear set is being installed, determine the best starter shim thickness.

c. Refer to the pinion variance chart and observe where the old and new pinion marking column intersect.

d. If the old pinion is +1 and the new pinion is −3, the intersecting figure is +0.004 in. (0.10mm); add this amount to the original shim. Or, if the old pinion is −3 and the new pinion is −2, the intersecting figure is −0.001 in. (−0.025mm); subtract this amount from the original shim.

4. Install the starter shim in the pinion rear bearing cup bore; if the shim is chamfer on one side, position the chamfered side so it faces the bottom of the bore.

5. Using a driver tool, install the pinion rear bearing cup into the axle housing.

6. Install the front bearing cup.

7. Using a shop press, press the rear bearing onto the pinion gear.

8. Install the pinion gear into the axle housing and the front bearing onto the pinion; do not install the slinger or the seal.

9. Install the yoke, the pinion nut washer and the old pinion nut; tighten the nut enough to remove the end play.

10. Adjust the backlash and gear tooth contact.

DIFFERENTIAL

1. Install the side gears, the thrust washers and the pinion gears into the differential case.

NOTE: Be sure to install new side gear thrust washers, if the clearance measured at disassembly exceeded 0.007 in. (0.18mm).

2. Using 2 sets of feeler gauges, insert them between each side of the side gear thrust washer and differential case and measure the side gear clearance; the clearance should not exceed 0.007 in. (0.18mm). Replace both thrust washers, if the clearance exceeds the tolerance.

3. Install the pinion shaft and lockpin into the case.

4. Assemble the original differential bearing shim packs, then, remove approximately 0.20 in. (0.50mm) shim thickness from each pack; the remaining shims will serve as a starter shim pack.

5. Install the starter shim packs and bearing onto the case.

6. Align and install the ring gear. Using new bolts, torque the ring gear-to-differential case bolts to 55 ft. lbs. (75 Nm).

7. Install the spreader tool onto the axle housing. Using a dial indicator, spread the axle housing no more than 0.015 in. (0.38mm).

NOTE: Do not spread the housing more than 0.015 in. (0.038mm), for damage may occur to the case.

8. Install the differential; it may be necessary to tap the differential bearing cups, with a soft hammer, to seat them.

9. Install the differential bearing caps and torque the bolts to 57 ft. lbs. (77 Nm).

10. Remove the spreader tool and dial indicator.

11. Adjust the ring and pinion gear.

12. Using silicone sealant, apply a bead of it to the axle housing. Install the cover and torque the bolts to 35 ft. lbs. (47 Nm).

Adjustment

RING AND PINION

1. Using gear marking compound, coat the drive and coast sides of the ring gear teeth.

2. Install the differential and tighten the bearing caps.

3. Using a dial indicator, mount it onto the housing, position the stylus against the drive side of one ring gear tooth; be sure the stylus is at a right angle to the tooth.

4. Move the ring gear toward the dial indicator and zero it.

5. Move the ring gear away from the pinion until the backlash

Ring gear tooth part names

is 0.005–0.009 in. (0.13–0.23mm). Insert shims or feeler gauges between the differential bearings and housing to maintain the backlash during the remainder of the adjustment.

NOTE: To increase the backlash, subtract shims from the ring gear side of the case. To decrease the backlash, add shims to the ring gear side of the case.

6. Move the dial indicator aside and recoat any necessary ring gear teeth with the ferrous oxide compound.

7. Rotate the ring gear a complete revolution in both directions and note the tooth contact pattern imprinted in the compound.

8. Adjustments can be made as follows:

   a. Decreasing the backlash moves the drive and coast side pattern slightly lower and toward the toe.

   b. Increasing the backlash move the drive and coast side pattern slightly higher and toward the heel.

   c. A thicker pinion shim moves the pinion closer to the ring gear. The drive pattern moves deeper on the tooth and slightly towards the heel.

   d. A thinner pinion shim moves the pinion away from the ring gear. Drive pattern moves toward the top of the tooth and toward the heel. Coast pattern moves toward the top of the tooth and slightly toward the toe.

9. Remove the differential and pinion gear.

10. Change the pinion and differential shims, as necessary.

11. Install the pinion and differential.

12. Recheck the tooth contact pattern and backlash; adjust, as necessary.

PINION BEARING PRELOAD

1. Using a yoke holding tool, torque the pinion nut to a minimum of 210 ft. lbs. (285 Nm).

2. Using an inch lb. torque wrench, measure the torque necessary to rotate the pinion; the torque should be 20–40 inch lbs. (2–5 Nm).

NOTE: If the torque is not correct, add shims to increase the preload or subtract shims to decrease the preload.

3. Remove the pinion nut, the washer and the yoke after setting the preload; be sure to discard the old nut.

4. Lubricate the new pinion oil seal lip and install the seal into the axle housing.

5. Install the yoke, the washer and a new pinion nut; torque the nut to a minimum of 210 ft. lbs. (285 Nm).

DIFFERENTIAL BEARING PRELOAD

1. Remove the differential bearing from the side of the case opposite the ring gear.

2. Add a 0.015 in. (0.38mm) shim the shim pack on the side of the case.

3. Reinstall the bearing onto the case.

4. Clean the marking compound from the ring and pinion gears, then, lubricate the differential gears and bearings with axle lubricant.

5. Install the spreader tool onto the axle housing. Using a dial indicator, spread the axle housing no more than 0.015 in. (0.38mm).

NOTE: Do not spread the housing more than 0.15 in. (0.38mm), for damage may occur to the case.

6. Install the differential; it may be necessary to tap the differential bearing cups, with a soft hammer, to seat them.

7. Install the differential bearing caps and torque the bolts to 57 ft. lbs. (77 Nm).

8. Recheck the backlash; it should be 0.005–0.009 in. (0.13–0.23mm). If necessary, reset the backlash.

TRAC-LOK DIFFERENTIAL

Operational Test

If a noisy or rough operation such as a chatter occurs when turning corners, the most probable cause of this chatter or noise is incorrect or contaminated lubricant. Before removing the Trac-Lok unit for repair, drain, flush and refill the axle with the specified lubricant. A complete lubricant drain and refill with the specified fluid will usually correct the chatter problem. A quick operational test of the Trac-Lok differential can be done easily by performing the following steps.

1. Position one wheel on solid dry pavement and the opposite wheel on ice, mud grease or a similar low traction surface.

2. Gradually, increase the engine rpm to obtain the maximum traction prior to a breakaway. The ability to move the vehicle effectively will demonstrate the proper performance.

NOTE: If the test is performed on extremely slick surfaces such as ice or grease coated surfaces, some question may exist as to proper performance. In these extreme cases, a properly performing Trac-Lok will provide greater pulling power by lightly applying the parking brake.

Disassembly

DIFFERENTIAL

1. Remove the differential from the axle housing as previously outlined in this section. Install one axle shaft in the vise with the spline end facing upward and tighten the vise.

2. Do not allow more than 2¾ in. of the shaft to extend above the top of the vise. This prevents the shaft from fully entering the side gear, causing interference with the step plate tool used to remove the differential gears.

3. Mount the differential case on the axle shaft with the ring gear bolt heads facing upward. Place some shop towels under the ring gear to protect the gear when it is removed from the case.

4. Remove and discard the ring gear bolts. Remove the ring gear from the case, using a rawhide hammer. Remove the differential case from the axle shaft and remove the ring gear and remount the differential case on the axle shaft.

5. Use suitable tools to disengage the snaprings from the pinion mate shaft. Place a shop towel on the opposite opening of the case to prevent the snaprings from flying out of the case. Remove the pinion mate shaft using a hammer and brass drift.

1. Thrust block
2. Snapring
3. Pinion gear
4. Thrust washer
5. Pinion shaft
6. Retainer clip
7. Clutch pack
8. Belleville spring
9. Side gear
10. Case
11. Ring gear

Exploded view of the Trac-Loc differential

Removing the snapring from the pinion mate shaft

Install the step plate tool

NOTE: A special gear rotating tool J–23781–3 or equivalent, is required to perform the following steps. The tool consists of 3 parts; the gear rotating tool, forcing screw and step plate.

6. Install step plate tool into the lower differential side gear. Position the pawl end of the gear rotating tool onto the step plate.

7. Insert the forcing screw tool through the top of the case and thread it into the gear rotating tool. Before using the forcing screw tool, apply a small amount of grease to the centering hole in the step plate and oil the threads of the forcing screw.

8. Center the forcing screw in the step plate and tighten the screw to move the differential side gears away from the differential pinion gears. Remove the differential pinion gear thrust washers using a feeler gauge or a shim stock of 0.030 in. thickness. Insert the feeler gauge or shim stock between the washer and the case and withdraw the shim stock with the thrust washer.

9. Tighten the forcing screw until a slight movement of the differential pinion gear is observed. Insert the pawl end of the gear rotating tool between the teeth of one differential side gear.

10. Pull the handle of the tool to rotate the side gears and pinion gears. Remove the pinion gears as they appear in the case opening. It could be necessary to adjust the tension applied on the dished washers by the forcing screw before the gears can be rotated in the case.

11. Retain the upper side gear and clutch pack in the case by placing a hand on the bottom of the rotating tool while removing the forcing screw. Remove the rotating tool, upper side gear and clutch pack.

12. Remove the differential case from the axle shaft. Invert the case with the flange or ring gear side up and remove the step plate tool, lower the side gear and clutch pack from the case. Remove the retainer clips from both the clutch packs to allow separation of the plates and discs.

Inspection

If any member of either clutch pack shows evidence of excessive wear or scoring, the complete clutch pack must be replaced on both sides.

Install the gear rotating tool

Removing the pinion gear thrust washers

Installing the clutch packs

Keeping the side gear in place

Installing the forcing screw into the rotating tool

1. Thoroughly clean each part in solvent.
2. Towel dry bearings or allow them to air dry, do not use compressed air to dry bearings as damage might result. Dry all other parts with compressed air or shop towels. If the parts are not to be assembled immediately, cover them to prevent dust or dirt contamination.
3. Inspect the housing for cracks and sand holes. Replace the housing if it is cracked or porous. Check for burrs and deep scratches or nicks on the gasket and oil seal surfaces. An oil stone or fine tooth file may be used to remove nicks or burrs.
4. Inspect the bearing cup bores for nicks or burrs that may have been created during bearing cup removal.
5. Inspect and clean the axle tubes. Inspect the vent to be sure it is not obstructed.
6. Check housing for bent or loose tubes or other physical damage.
7. Inspect the side gears for worn, cracked or chipped teeth. The gears should fit snugly on the axle shaft splines. Also, inspect the fit of the gears in the differential case bore.

Assembly

DIFFERENTIAL

1. Lubricate all the differential components with the specified gear lubricant. Assemble the clutch packs. Install the plates and discs in the same position as when removed regardless of whether they are replacement or original parts.
2. Install the clutch retainer clips on the ears of the clutch plates. Be sure the clutch packs are completely assembled and seated on the ears of the plates. Install the clutch packs on the differential side gears and install the assembly in the case.
3. Make sure the clutch pack stays assembled on the side gear splines and the retainer clips are completely seated in the case

pockets. To prevent the pack from falling out of the case, it will be necessary to hold it in place by hand while mounting the case on the axle shaft.

NOTE: When installing the differential case on the axle shaft, make sure the splines of the side gears are aligned with those of the axle shaft. Make sure the clutch pack is still properly assembled in the case after installing the case on the axle shaft.

4. Mount the case assembly on the axle shaft. Install the step plate tool in the side gear and apply a small amount of grease in the centering hole of the step plate.

5. Install the remaining clutch pack and side gear. Make sure the clutch pack stays assembled on the side gear splines and the retainer clips are completely seated in the pockets of the case.

6. Position the gear rotating tool in the upper side of the gear. Keep the side gear and rotating tool in position by holding them with your hand. Insert the forcing screw through the top of the case and thread it into the rotating tool.

7. Install both of the differential pinion gears in the case; be sure the bores of the gears are aligned. Hold the gears in place by hand. Tighten the forcing screw to compress the springs and provide clearance between the teeth of the pinion gears and the side gears.

8. Position the pinion gears in the case and insert the rotating tool pawl between the side gear teeth. Rotate the side gears by pulling on the tool handle and install the pinion gears.

NOTE: If the side gears will not rotate, the spring load will have to be adjusted. If adjustment is necessary, loosen or tighten the forcing screw slightly until the gears will rotate.

9. Rotate the side gears, using the rotating tool handle, until the shaft bores in both the pinion gears are aligned with the case bore. Lubricate both sides of the pinion gear thrust washers.

10. Tighten or loosen the forcing screw to permit the thrust washer installation. Install the thrust washers and using a suitable tool, guide the washers into position. Make sure the shaft bores in the washers and gears are aligned with the case bores.

11. Remove the forcing screw, rotating tool and step plate. Lubricate the pinion mate shaft and seat the shaft in the case. Be sure the snapring grooves in the shaft are exposed to allow the snapring installation.

12. Install the pinion mate shaft snaprings, remove the case from the axle shaft and install the ring gear on the case. Be sure to use replacement ring bolts only; do not reuse the original bolts.

13. Align the ring gear and case bolt holes and install the ring gear bolts finger-tight only. Remove the case on the axle shaft and tighten the bolts evenly to the proper torque specifications.

14. Install the differential assembly into the axle housing.

Installing the thrust washers

Component	Service Set-To Torque	Service Recheck Torque
Wheel Lug Nuts	102 N·m (75 ft-lbs)	81-122 N·m (60-90 ft-lbs)
Brake Support Plate Nuts	43 N·m (32 ft-lbs)	34-54 N·m (25-40 ft-lbs)
U-Joint Strap Bolts	19 N·m (170 in-lbs)	15-23 N·m (140-200 in-lbs)
Differential Bearing Cap Bolts	77 N·m (57 ft-lbs)	64-91 N·m (47-67 ft-lbs)
Ring Gear-to-Case Bolts	70 N·m (52 ft-lbs)	57-88 N·m (42-65 ft-lbs)
Rear Axle Cover Screws	19 N·m (170 in-lbs)	17-21 N·m (150-190 in-lbs)
Rear Axle Filler Plug	34 N·m (25 ft-lbs)	27-41 N·m (20-30 ft-lbs)

Component	Service Set-To Torque	Service Recheck Torque
Axle Housing Cover Bolts	19 N·m (170 in-lbs)	17-21 N·m (150-190 in-lbs)
Brake Tube-to-Rear Wheel Cylinder	11 N·m (97 in-lbs)	10-12 N·m (90-105 in-lbs)
Differential Bearing Cap Bolts	115 N·m (85 ft-lbs)	102-129 N·m (75-95 ft-lbs)
Ring Gear-to-Case Bolt	142 N·m (105 ft-lbs)	135-149 N·m (95-115 ft-lbs)
Rear Brake Support Plate Bolts	43 N·m (32 ft-lbs)	34-54 N·m (25-40 ft-lbs)
Universal Joint Strap Bolts	19 N·m (170 in-lbs)	16-22 N·m (140-200 in-lbs)

Torque specifications for the Trac-Loc differential

CHRYSLER IMPORT

Front Drive Axle

Inspection Before Dissassembly

1. Position the removed differential carrier assembly in a suitable holding fixture. Remove the differential cover.

2. With the drive pinion locked in place, measure the final drive gear (ring gear) backlash with a dial indicator on the drive gear. Measure at 4 points or more on the drive gear. If the backlash is not within specification, adjust it by using the correct side bearing spacer.

3. The final drive gear backlash specification is 0.0043–0.0063 in. on all engines.

4. Measure the drive gear runout at the shoulder on the reverse side of the drive gear the limit is 0.0020 in. on all engines.

5. While locking the side gear with a wedge or equivalent, measure the differential gear backlash with a dial indicator on the pinion gear. The standard valve is 0–0.0030 in. The service limit is 0.008 in. on all engines.

6. Check the final drive gear tooth contact by the following steps:

   a. Apply a thin uniform coat of gear markinmg compound to both surfaces of the drive gear teeth.

   b. Insert a tool between the differential carrier and the differential case and then rotate the companion flange by hand (once in normal direction and once reverse direction) while applying a load to the drive gear so the revolution torque (about 2.5 ft. lbs.) is applied to the drive pinion.

   c. If the drive gear is rotated too much, contact pattern will become unclear and difficult to read. If a correct pattern cannot be obtained (drive gear and pinion worn beyond allowable limits), replace the drive gear and the drive pinion as a set.

1.	Vent plug	
2.	Carrier	
3.	Oil seals	
4.	Drive pinion front bearing outer race	
5.	Drive pinion rear bearing outer race	
6.	Drive pinion	
7.	Front shim	
8.	Drive pinion front bearing inner race	
9.	Drive pinion rear bearing inner race	
10.	Oil seal	
11.	Rear shim	
12.	Drive pinion spacer	
13.	Drive pinion assembly	
14.	Companion flange	
15.	Washer	
16.	Flange nut	
17.	Differential Case	
18.	Side gear thrust spacers	
19.	Side gear	
20.	Pinion washers	
21.	Pinion gears	
22.	Pinion shaft	
23.	Lock pin	
24.	Drive gear	
25.	Bolts	
26.	Side bearing inner races	
27.	Side bearing outer races	
28.	Side bearing adjusting spacers	
29.	Differential case assembly	
30.	Bearing caps	
31.	Cover	

Differential gear set

Final drive gear set

Exploded view of front differential assembly— Chrysler Import 4WD Pick-Up

STEP 1

C-3281

STEP 2

Adjustment of drive pinion preload on front differential carrier—Chrysler Import 4WD Pick-Up

Disassembly and Assembly

1. Position the removed differential carrier assembly in a suitable holding fixture. Remove the differential cover.

2. Matchmark and remove the bearing (carrier) caps and pry out the differential assembly.

3. Remove the differential side bearings. Be sure to keep the right and left bearings and shims separated. Remove side bearings inner and outer races.

4. Matchmark ring gear assembly and loosen the ring gear mounting bolts in diagonal sequence. Remove the ring gear.

5. Drive the pinion shaft lock pin out from the rear of the ring gear using a punch and remove the pinion shaft assembly.

6. Remove the pinion gears and washers. Remove the side gears with their spacers. Keep left and right side gears and spacers separate. Remove the differential case.

7. Hold the end yoke (companion flange) and remove the self-locking nut and washer. Matchmark for correct installation then remove the companion flange.

8. Tap the end of the drive pinion shaft (matchmark shaft assembly for correct installation) with a plastic hammer and force out the drive pinion along with its adjusting shim, the rear inner race, the drive pinion spacer and the preload adjusting shim. The rear bearing inner race can be pressed off the pinion shaft.

9. Remove the front and rear pinion bearing outer races. Remove the oil seals. Remove the vent plug if necessary and gear carrier case.

To assemble:

10. Assembly is the reverse of the removal procedure. Install the vent plug to the gear carrier case if necessary. Install oil seals.

11. Press the drive pinion front and rear bearing outer races into the differential carrier case. Make sure the races do not tilt and that they sit fully in the case.

12. At this point of the reassembly, adjust the drive pinion height by following this procedure:

    a. Install special service tool C–4626 and drive pinion front and rear bearing inner races to the gear carrier in the correct sequence.

    b. Gradually tighten the nut of the special tool until the standard valve of the drive pinion turning torque is reached.

STEP 1

C-4626

STEP 2

C-4626

STEP 3

C-4626

STEP 4

MB990552

C-4626

Drive pinion front shim

Adjustment of drive pinion height on front differential carrier—Chrysler Import 4WD Pick-Up

    c. Measure the drive pinion turning torque without the oil seal installed. The standard specification is 1–2 inch lbs. of turning torque for all engines except 3.0L engine. The specification is 3–4 inch lbs. of turning torque for 3.0L engine.

    d. Because 1 rotation cannot be made when the special tool is in contact with the gear carrier, move it a few times and after seating the bearing measure the rotation torque.

    e. Mount the special service tool MB990552 in the side bearing seat of the gear carrier and then select a drive pinion

Adjustment of differential gear backlash on front differential carrier — Chrysler Import 4WD Pick-Up

$$+ \frac{\text{Clearance}}{2} + \frac{0.05 \text{ mm}}{(.002 \text{ in.})}$$

= Thickness of the spacer on one side

STEP 5 — If backlash is too small —

Thinner spacer   Thicker spacer

Thicker spacer   Thinner spacer

— If backlash is too large —

Adjustment of final drive backlash on front differential carrier — Chrysler Import 4WD Pick-Up

front height adjusting shim (keep front shims to a minimum) of a thickness which corresponds to the gap between the special tools. Be sure to clean the side bearing seat thoroughly. When mounting the special tool be sure the cut-out sections are in the correct position and also confirm that the tool is in close contact with the side bearing seat.

f. Install the selected drive pinion front shim(s) to the drive pinion. Using special tool MB990802, press fit the drive pinion front bearing inner race.

13. At this point of the reassembly, adjust the drive pinion preload (turning torque) by following this procedure:

a. Without the oil seal installed insert the drive pinion into the gear carrier and then install from the front side of the carrier, the driver pinion spacer, drive pinion rear shim, drive pinion rear bearing inner race and the companion flange in that order.

b. Tighten the companion flange to 115–160 ft. lbs. on all engines except the 3.0L engine. On the 3.0L engine torque the companion flange to 140–180 ft. lbs. Measure the drive pinion turning torque without the oil seal installed. The standard specification is 1–2 inch lbs. turning torque for all engines except the 3.0L engine. This should be 3–4 inch lbs. turning torque for the 3.0L engine.

c. Adjust the turning torque by replacing the drive pinion rear shim(s) or the drive pinion spacer. Reduce number of drive pinion rear shims by replacing drive pinion spacer(s) as necessary.

d. Remove the companion flange and drive pinion once again.

14. Install drive pinion rear bearing inner race. Install oil seal into the gear carrier using suitable tools.

15. Install the drive pinion assembly and companion flange in the correct position. Tighten the companion flange to 116–159 ft. lbs. on all engines except the 3.0L engine. On the 3.0L engine torque the companion flange to 140–180 ft. lbs.

16. Measure the drive pinion turning torque with oil seal installed. The standard specification is 3–4 inch lbs. of turning torque for all engines except the 3.0L engine. The specification for the 3.0L engine is 5–6 inch lbs. of turning torque.

17. If not within the standard specification, check for faulty installation of the oil seal or wrong torque on the companion flange locking nut.

18. At this point of the reassembly, adjust the differential gear backlash by following this procedure:

a. Install the side gears, side gear thrust spacers, pinion gear and pinion washers into the differential case. Temporarily install the pinion shaft. Do not drive the lock pin in place yet.

b. While locking the side gear with a wedge or equivalent, measure the differential gear backlash with a dial indicator on the pinion gear. The standard specification is 0–0.0030 in. and the service limit is 0.008 in. for all axles.

c. If the differential gear backlash exceeds the limit adjust the backlash by installing thicker side gear thrust spacers. If adjustment is not possible replace the side gears and pinion gears as a set.

19. Align the pinion shaft lock pin hole with the differential case lock pin hole.

20. Drive the lock pin in and stake the pin with a suitable tool in 2 different locations.

21. Install the drive gear onto the differential case with matchmarks in the correct position. Torque (with locking adhesive or equivalent on threads) drive gear attaching bolts to 58–65 ft. lbs. in a diagonal sequence for all engines.

22. Press fit the side bearing inner races to the differential case using suitable tools.

23. At this point of the reassembly, adjust the final drive gear backlash as follows:

a. Install the side bearing adjusting spacers (both sides same size-thin spacers as possible) to the side bearing outer races, then mount ther differential case assembly into the gear carrier.

b. Push the differential case assembly to one side. Measure the clearance between the gear carrier and the side bearing adjusting spacer with a feeler gauge.

c. Measure the thickness of the side bearing adjusting spacers on a side. Select 2 pairs of spacers which correspond to that thickness plus ½ of the clearance plus 0.002 in. and then install one pair each to the drive pinion side and the drive gear side.

24. Install the side bearing adjusting spacers and differential case assembly in the gear carrier.

25. Tap the side bearing adjusting spacers with a brass tool to position them to the side bearing outer races.

26. Align the mating marks on the gear carrier and the bearing caps and tighten the bearing caps to 40–50 ft. lbs. on all axles.

27. Attach a dial indicator to the ring gear teeth and measure the final drive gear backlash at 4 different locations. Final drive gear backlash standard specification is 0.0043–0.0063 in. for all axles. Change the side bearing spacers as necessary for correct adjustment. When increasing the number of side bearing adjust-

ing spacers, use the same number for each side and as few as possible.

28. Measure the ring gear runout in 2 or more locations. Runout should be 0.002 in. or less on all axles.

29. If necessary make a ring gear tooth pattern check. Apply gear oil to all moving parts and use sealant and or gasket when assembling to the axle housing.

Rear Drive Axle

Inspection Before Disassembly

1. Position the removed differential carrier assembly in a suitable holding fixture.

2. With the drive pinion locked in place, measure the final drive gear (ring gear) backlash with a dial indicator on the drive gear. Measure at 4 points or more on the drive gear.

3. The final drive gear backlash specification for 2.0L, 2.4L and 2.6L engines is 0.0043–0.0063 in. The specification for 3.0L engine is 0.0051–0.0071 in.

4. Measure the drive gear runout at the shoulder on the reverse side of the drive gear the limit is 0.0020 in. on all engines.

5. On a conventional differential asssembly the differential gear backlash must be checked. While locking the side gear with a wedge or equivalent, measure the differential gear backlash with a dial indicator on the pinion gear. The differential gear backlash (conventional) for the 2.0L, 2.4L and 2.6L engines specification is 0.0004–0.0030 in. The specification for the 3.0L engine is 0–0.0030 in. The service limit is 0.008 in. on all engines.

6. Check the final drive gear tooth contact by the following steps:

a. Apply a thin uniform coat of machine blue or equivalent to both surfaces of the drive gear teeth.

b. Insert a tool between the differential carrier and the differential case and then rotate the companion flange by hand (once in normal direction and once reverse direction) while applying a load to the drive gear so the revolution torque (about 2.5 ft. lbs.) is applied to the drive pinion.

c. If the drive gear is rotated too much, contact pattern will become unclear and difficult to read. If a correct pattern cannot be obtained (drive gear and pinion worn beyond allowable limits), replace the drive gear and the drive pinion as a set.

Disassembly and Assembly

1. Position the differential assembly in a suitable holding fixture. Remove the lock bolts and plates holding the side bearing nut in place.

2. Remove the side bearing nuts with the special adjusting tool spanner wrench MB990201 or equivalent.

3. Matchmark and remove the carrier caps and pry out the differential.

4. Pull off the differential side bearings. Be sure to keep the right and left bearings and shims separated. Remove side bearings inner and outer races.

5. Matchmark ring gear assembly and loosen the ring gear mounting bolts in diagonal sequence. Remove the ring gear.

6. Drive the pinion shaft lock pin out from the rear of the ring gear using a punch and remove the pinion shaft assembly.

7. Remove the thrust block, pinion gears and washers. Remove the side gears with their spacers. Keep left and right side gears and spacers separate. Remove the differential case.

8. On limited slip differential vehicles, remove limited slip differential case assembly.

9. Hold the end yoke (companion flange) and remove the self-locking nut and washer. Matchmark for correct installation then remove the companion flange.

10. Tap the end of the drive pinion shaft (matchmark shaft assembly for correct installation) with a plastic hammer and force out the drive pinion along with its adjusting shim, the rear inner race, the drive pinion spacer and the preload adjusting shim.

Inspection of rear differential carrier before disassembly—Chrysler Import 4WD Pick-Up

The rear bearing inner race can be pressed off the pinion shaft.

11. Remove the front and rear pinion bearing outer races. The front inner race should be removed with its oil seal. Remove the differential carrier case.

NOTE: Do not reuse the old oil seal. If the unit is to be assembled using no replacement parts except oil seals, the same spacers and shims can generally be used. If either pinion bearing or ring gear and drive pinion are being replaced, new shims should be used. Only replace the drive pinion and ring gear in matched sets.

Adjustment of final drive gear backlash on rear differential carrier—Chrysler Import 4WD Pick-Up

Standard tooth contact pattern

1 Toe
2 Drive-side
3 Heel
4 Coast-side

Problem	Solution

Tooth contact pattern resulting from excessive pinion height

The drive pinion is positioned too far from the center of the drive gear.

Increase the thickness of the pinion height adjusting shim, and position the drive pinion closer to the center of the drive gear.
Also, for backlash adjustment, position the drive gear farther from the drive pinion.

Tooth contact pattern resulting from insufficient pinion height

The drive pinion is positioned too close to the center of the drive gear.

Decrease the thickness of the pinion height adjusting shim, and position the drive pinion farther from the center of the drive gear.
Also, for backlash adjustment, position the drive gear closer to the drive pinion.

Differential tooth contact pattern—Chrysler Import 4WD Pick-Up

To assemble:
12. Assembly is the reverse of the removal procedure. Press the drive pinion front and rear bearing outer races into the differential carrier case. Make sure the races do not tilt and that they sit fully in the case.

13. At this point of the reassembly, adjust the drive pinion height by following this procedure:

   a. Install special service tool MB991169 (use special adapter head tool C–4626 for 3.0L engine only) and drive pinion front and rear bearing inner races to the gear carrier in the correct sequence.

   b. Gradually tighten the nut of the special tool until the standard valve of the drive pinion turning torque is reached.

   c. Measure the drive pinion turning torque without the oil seal installed. The standard specification for all engines is 3–4 inch lbs. of turning torque.

   d. Mount the special service tool MB990552 in the side bearing seat of the gear carrier and then select a drive pinion height adjusting shim (keep rear shims to a minimum) of a thickness which corresponds to the gap between the special tools. Be sure to clean the side bearing seat thoroughly. When mounting the special tool be sure the cut-out sections are in the correct position and also confirm that the tool is in close contact with the side bearing seat.

Exploded view of rear differential assembly— Chrysler Import 4WD Pick-Up

1. Carrier
2. Drive pinion rear bearing outer race
3. Drive pinion front bearing outer race
4. Drive pinion
5. Rear shim
6. Drive pinion rear bearing inner race
7. Drive pinion front bearing inner race
8. Oil seal
9. Front shim
10. Drive pinion spacer
11. Drive pinion assembly
12. Companion flange
13. Washer
14. Flange nut
15. Differential Case

16. Limited slip differential case assembly
17. Side gear thrust spacers
18. Side gear
19. Pinion washers
20. Pinion gears
21. Thrust block
22. Pinion shaft
23. Lock pin
24. Drive gear
25. Bolts
26. Side bearing inner races
27. Side bearing outer races
28. Differential case assembly
29. Bearing caps
30. Side bearing nuts
31. Lock plates

STEP 1

For 3.0L
Engine only
MB991169
Attachment

C-4626

STEP 2

MB990552

Drive pinion
rear shim

C-4626

Adjustment of pinion height — rear differential carrier

e. Install the selected drive pinion rear shim(s) to the drive pinion. Using special tool MB990802, press fit the drive pinion rear bearing inner race.

14. At this point of the reassembly, adjust the drive pinion preload (turning torque) by following this procedure:

a. Without the oil seal installed fit the drive pinion front shims between the drive pinion spacer and the drive pinion front bearing inner race.

b. Tighten the companion flange to 135–180 ft. lbs. on all engines. Measure the drive pinion turning torque without the oil seal installed. The standard specification is 3–4 inch lbs. turning torque for all engines.

c. Adjust the turning torque by replacing the drive pinion front shim(s) or the drive pinion spacer. Reduce number of drive pinion front shims by replacing drive pinion spacer as necessary.

d. Remove the companion flange and drive pinion once again.

15. Install drive pinion front bearing inner race. Install oil seal into the gear carrier using suitable tools.

16. Install the drive pinion assembly and companion flange in the correct position. Torque the companion flange locking nut to 135–180 ft. lbs. on all engines.

17. Measure the drive pinion turning torque with oil seal installed. The standard specification is 5–6 inch lbs. of turning torque on all engines.

18. On limited slip differential vehicles, install limited slip differential case assembly.

19. At this point of the reassembly (conventional differential), adjust the differential gear backlash by following this procedure:

a. Install the side gears, side gear thrust spacers, pinion gear and pinion washers into the differential case. Temporarily install the pinion shaft. Do not drive the lock pin in place yet.

1. Screw
2. Differential case
3. Thrust washer
4. Spring plate
5. Spring disc
6. Friction plate
7. Friction disc
8. Friction plate
9. Friction disc
10. Pressure ring
11. Side gear
12. Thrust block
13. Differential pinion gear
14. Differential pinion shaft
15. Thrust block
16. Side gear
17. Pressure ring
18. Friction disc
19. Friction plate
20. Friction disc
21. Friction plate
22. Spring disc
23. Spring plate
24. Thrust washer
25. Differential case

Differential gear set

Exploded view of limited slip differential carrier — Chrysler Import 4WD Pick-Up

b. While locking the side gear with a wedge or equivalent, measure the differential gear backlash with a dial indicator on the pinion gear. The differential gear backlash for the 2.0L, 2.4L and 2.6L engines standard specification is 0.0004–0.0030 in. The standard specification for the 3.0L engine is 0–0.0030 in. The service limit is 0.008 in. on all engines.

c. If the differential gear backlash exceeds the limit adjust the backlash by installing thicker side gear thrust spacers. If adjustment is not possible replace the side gears and pinion gears as a set.

20. Install the thrust block. Align the pinion shaft lock pin hole with the differential case lock pin hole.

21. Drive the lock pin in and stake the pin with a suitable tool in 2 different locations.

22. Install the drive gear onto the differential case with matchmarks in the correct position. Torque (with locking adhesive or equivalent on threads) drive gear attaching bolts to 58–65 ft. lbs. on conventional and limited slip differentials in a diagonal sequence.

23. Press fit the side bearing inner races to the differential case using suitable tools.

24. Install the differential case assembly.

25. Install the carrier (bearing) caps with their mating marks in line with the marks on the carriers and finger-tighten the 4 set bolts.

26. Install the side bearing nuts and tighten the carrier cap bolts to 40–50 ft. lbs. on all engines.

27. Screw in the side bearing nuts to adjust the final drive gear backlash. Each nut should be tightened to the state just before preloading of the side bearing.

28. Attach a dial indicator to the ring gear teeth and measure the final drive gear backlash in 4 different locations. The final drive gear backlash standard specification for 2.0L, 2.4L and 2.6L engines is 0.0043–0.0063 inch. The standard specification for 3.0L engine is 0.0051–0.0071 inch.

NOTE: If the backlash has to be adjusted, loosen the bearing nut on the back side of the ring gear and tighten the bearing nut on the teeth side by the same amount.

29. After adjusting backlash, tighten the bearing nuts ½ pitch. One pitch is the space between 2 adjacent holes on the side of the bearing nut.

30. Again measure the backlash and install a 1 or 2 pronged lock plate whichever lines up with the bearing nut holes. Tighten the lock plate bolts to 11–16 ft. lbs.

31. Measure the ring gear runout in 2 or more locations. Runout should be 0.002 in. or less on all engines.

32. If necessary make a ring gear tooth pattern check. Apply gear oil to all moving parts and use sealant and/or gasket when assembling to the axle housing.

GEO

Front And Rear Drive Axles

Disassembly and Assembly

1. Position the removed differential carrier assembly in a suitable holding fixture.

2. Matchmark side differential side bearing caps for correct installation.

3. Remove the bearing side lock plates and bearing caps. Remove bearing adjusters and outer races. Remove ring gear complete assembly.

4. Remove the flange nut using suitable tools to hold flange.

5. Remove the pinion shaft assembly from the carrier. Remove the pinion shaft oil seal using suitable tools.

6. Remove the outer pinion bearing from the differential carrier.

7. Remove the outer and inner pinion bearing races from the differential carrier.

8. Remove the ring gear bolts and remove the ring gear from the differential assembly.

9. Drive out spring pin (3 spring pins are used on 4 pinion type rear assembly) and remove the differential side gears, selective shims, pinion gears, thrust washers and cross shafts.

10. Remove the collapsible spacer and inner pinion bearing using tool and suitable press. Discard the collapsible spacer.

11. Clean disassembled parts completely. Repair or replace any damaged or faulty parts. If replacing drive pinion or ring gear, replace as a set. All taper roller bearings and races must be replaced as a set.

To assemble:

12. Assembly is the reverse of the removal procedure. Install the differential side gears, thrust washers, cross shaft and side gears with the correct selective shim in the differential case.

13. Measure the differential side gear end play. The specification is 0.005–0.14 in. select the correct shim to obtain the spec.

14. Drive the spring pin (3 spring pins are used on 4 pinion type rear assembly) for the differential side pinion shaft until it is flush with the case surface.

15. When correct end play is obtained install the ring gear to differential case. Torque the ring gear (special) retaining bolts to 70 ft. lbs.

16. Install the right and left side differential bearings using suitable tools. Hold one side bearing when installing the other side bearing to prevent damage to any component.

17. Install pinion gear inner bearing race into the differential case using suitable tool and a press.

18. Install pinion gear outer bearing race into the differential case using suitable tool and a press.

19. At this point of the reassembly, set pinion depth. The pinion setting gauge provides in effect a nominal or zero pinion as reference.

20. Lubricate inner and outer pinion bearings with axle lubricant. While holding pinion bearings in the correct position install the pinion depth gauge.

21. Tighten depth gauge stud nut to 18 inch lbs. Rotate the gauge plate several times to seat the bearings. Retighten the locknut on stud of tool to 18 inch lbs.

22. Install special tool side bearing discs and arbor in the correct position in the side bearing bores of the housing.

23. Rotate the gauge plate until the correct area are parallel with the 2 side bearing discs.

24. Position a dial indicator rod over the lower step (94mm) of the gauging plate for front drive axle. Position a dial indicator rod over the higher step (97mm) of the gauging plate for rear drive axle.

25. Connect the dial indicator to the arbor and position gauge shaft over the dial indicator rod.

26. Install the side bearing caps and torque the bolts to 65 ft. lbs.

27. Position the dial indicator to the zero setting. Slowly rotate the arbor on the lower step (94mm) front drive axle or higher step (97mm) rear driver axle of the gauge plate to determine the point of the greatest deflection. At this point reset the dial indicator to zero setting.

28. Slowly rotate the arbor until the dial indicator is no longer on the gauge plate.

29. Record the dial indicator reading. This reading indicates

the selective shim required for the correct pinion depth. The selective shims range from 0.012–0.050 in.

30. Install the correct pinion shim on the pinion gear shaft.

31. Assembly the inner pinion bearing on the pinion gear shaft using suitable press plate and press.

32. Install new collapsible spacer on the pinion gear shaft.

33. Install the outer pinion bearing in the differential carrier using suitable tools.

34. Apply lubricant to the oil seal lip. Install the new pinion oil seal using a suitable seal installer or equivalent.

35. Install pinion flange, pinion washer and nut. Hold the pinion flange with a suitable flange holding tool while frequently rotating pinion to seal pinion bearings. Tighten pinion flange nut a little at a time until end play is taken up. Measure preload with torque wrench the standard specification for all applications is 11 inch lbs. of starting torque, not rotating torque. Exceeding preload specification will compress the collapsible spacer.

36. After final preload has be reached rotate the pinion several times to make sure the bearings have been seated. Recheck the preload specification.

37. Install the ring gear and differential carrier assembly, side bearing outer races, bearing adjusters and bearing caps to housing. Align all identification marks.

38. Rotate pinion gear to ensure the side bearings seat. Tighten bearing caps 15 ft. lbs. on the front and rear drive axle assembly.

39. Using suitable tool turn the bearing adjusters to push side bearings lightly from outside so outer races are in contact with inner races. Apply a small amount of lubricant to bearings. With dial indicator installed to differential carrier and carrier at 0.0 backlash (ring gear fully engaged into pinion gear) set or check preload. The differential side bearing preload is 0.002–0.006 in.

40. Rotate pinion gear to ensure the side bearings seat. Tighten bearing caps to 44 ft. lbs. on the front drive axle assembly or 65 ft. lbs. on the rear drive axle assembly.

41. Check backlash using a dial indicator installed to the differential ring gear. The standard specification for all applications is 0.008–0.015 in. If adjustment is necessary loosen one adjuster nut and tighten the opposite nut an equal amount. This will move the ring gear away from or toward the pinion gear and maintain side bearing preload.

42. When turning the side bearing adjusters the final movement must be made in the tightening direction to ensure correct side bearing preload.

43. Install the side bearing lock plates. Torque the side bearing lock plate bolts to 25 ft. lbs.

44. Paint the ring gear with gear marking compound and rotate the pinion flange to obtain a tooth mesh contact pattern.

45. Inspect pattern contact and adjust or service the assembly as required. After all adjustments and correct pattern contact is obtained stake the pinion flange locknut.

46. Apply gear oil to all moving parts and use sealant and or gasket when assembling to the axle housing.

ISUZU

Front Drive Axle

Disassembly and Assembly

1. Position the removed differential carrier assembly in a suitable holding fixture.

2. Matchmark and remove the side bearing caps.

3. Remove the differential cage assembly. Keep the right and left side bearing races and shims in separate groups for reinstallation in same positions.

4. Remove the differential side bearings from the case by using puller J–22888 and plug J–8107–2 or equivalent. Carefully record the thickness of each side bearing and each shim(s) removed for later use in reassembly and keep separated. Puller arms must not pull against roller cage. Use care to position legs against inner race. As bearing is being removed, check for free rotation of bearing. If bearing does not rotate freely, check position of puller legs.

5. Remove the companion flange nut while holding flange with suitable tools. Remove the flange assembly with puller if necessary.

6. Drive the pinion assembly from the carrier using suitable tools and brass punch. The outer (front) bearing will fall loose in the carrier, while the inner (rear) bearing will remain pressed on the drive pinion. Both races will remain in the carrier bores.

7. Remove rear bearing from the drive pinion by use of a press and tool J–22912–01 or equivalent.

8. Remove the oil seal and then drive the 2 outer races from the carrier by use of a brass drift and suitable tools.

9. Remove the ring gear bolts and separate the ring gear from the differential case. Use care when removing ring gear to prevent damage to differential case or ring gear. Do not force a chisel or other tools between the joining faces.

10. Drive out the pinion shaft lock pin with a long drift. It may be necessary to first break the stake on lock pin using a 0.020 diameter drill or equivalent.

11. Remove the pinion shaft with a drift pin and take out the pinion gears, side gears and thrust washers from the differential case.

NOTE: It is important to clean and assemble parts with care and to follow adjustment procedures. Axles which are contaminated with dirt or other foreign material, or which are incorrectly adjusted may be noisy and have short life. Be sure to use new seals, gaskets and flange nut when reassembling axle.

12. Wash the bearings in a suitable solvent. Examine bearings carefully for wear, separation, cracks, seizure and other abnormal conditions. Replace bearings as necessary.

13. Check the ring gear and drive pinion teeth for wear, chipping, cracks, pitting and abnormal contact. Check the drive pinion splines for cracks, distortion and step wear. Replace parts if needed. Ring gear and drive pinion come only in matched sets. If either item is defective, both parts must be replaced. Torque ring gear replacement bolts to 75–90 ft. lbs. in diagonal sequence.

14. Check the pinion gears and side gears for wear, chipped teeth and separation and replace if needed.

15. Check and replace the thrust blocks if so equipped and thrust washers, if worn or damaged.

16. Check the lock pin for bending, dents and other abnormal conditions. Replace if necessary.

17. Check the side gear-to-axle shaft fit. Also check the fit of the pinion shaft to pinion gears. Examine the contact surfaces between side gears and differential case and between ring gear and case.

18. The standard specification for the clearance between the differential pinion and the cross pin is 0.002–0.005 in. and the service limit is 0.008 in.

19. The standard specification for the clearance between the

1. Differential carrier
2. Outer bearing outer race
3. Inner bearing outer race
4. Shim
5. Inner bearing
6. Collapsible spacer
7. Pinion gear
8. Outer bearing
9. Oil seal
10. Dust cover
11. Flange
12. Flange nut
13. Shim
14. Side bearing
15. Bearing outer race
16. Differential cage assembly
17. Bearing cap
18. Bolt
19. Case
20. Differential assembly
21. Bolt

Exploded view of front differential assembly—Isuzu

STEP 1

STEP 2

STEP 3

Dial indicator
Gaging arbor
Plunger
Gage plate

STEP 4

STEP 5

Example = Dial indicator reading of 0.075

STEP 6

+2

Adjustment of drive pinion mounting distance

Pinion marking / Dial indicator reading (Inches)	+10	+8	+6	+4	+2	0	−2	−4	−6	−8	−10
0.081											2.18(0.0858)
0.082										2.18(0.0858)	2.20(0.0866)
0.083									2.18(0.0858)	2.20(0.0866)	2.24(0.0882)
0.084								2.18(0.0858)	2.20(0.0866)	2.24(0.0882)	2.26(0.0890)
0.085							2.18(0.0858)	2.20(0.0866)	2.24(0.0882)	2.26(0.0890)	2.28(0.0898)
0.086						2.18(0.0858)	2.20(0.0866)	2.24(0.0882)	2.26(0.0890)	2.28(0.0898)	2.32(0.0914)
0.087					2.18(0.0858)	2.20(0.0866)	2.24(0.0882)	2.26(0.0890)	2.28(0.0898)	2.32(0.0914)	2.34(0.0921)
0.088				2.18(0.0858)	2.20(0.0866)	2.24(0.0882)	2.26(0.0890)	2.28(0.0898)	2.32(0.0914)	2.34(0.0921)	2.36(0.0929)
0.089			2.18(0.0858)	2.20(0.0866)	2.24(0.0882)	2.26(0.0890)	2.28(0.0898)	2.32(0.0914)	2.34(0.0921)	2.36(0.0929)	2.38(0.0937)
0.090		2.18(0.0858)	2.20(0.0866)	2.24(0.0882)	2.26(0.0890)	2.28(0.0898)	2.32(0.0914)	2.34(0.0921)	2.36(0.0929)	2.38(0.0937)	2.42(0.0953)
0.091	2.18(0.0858)	2.20(0.0866)	2.24(0.0882)	2.26(0.0890)	2.28(0.0898)	2.32(0.0914)	2.34(0.0921)	2.36(0.0929)	2.38(0.0937)	2.42(0.0953)	2.44(0.0961)
0.092	2.20(0.0866)	2.24(0.0882)	2.26(0.0890)	2.28(0.0898)	2.32(0.0914)	2.34(0.0921)	2.36(0.0929)	2.38(0.0937)	2.42(0.0953)	2.44(0.0961)	2.46(0.0969)
0.093	2.24(0.0882)	2.26(0.0890)	2.28(0.0898)	2.32(0.0914)	2.34(0.0921)	2.36(0.0929)	2.38(0.0937)	2.42(0.0953)	2.44(0.0961)	2.46(0.0969)	2.48(0.0977)
0.094	2.26(0.0890)	2.28(0.0898)	2.32(0.0914)	2.34(0.0921)	2.36(0.0929)	2.38(0.0937)	2.42(0.0953)	2.44(0.0961)	2.46(0.0969)	2.48(0.0977)	2.52(0.0992)
0.095	2.28(0.0898)	2.32(0.0914)	2.34(0.0921)	2.36(0.0929)	2.38(0.0937)	2.42(0.0953)	2.44(0.0961)	2.46(0.0969)	2.48(0.0977)	2.52(0.0992)	2.54(0.1000)
0.096	2.32(0.0914)	2.34(0.0921)	2.36(0.0929)	2.38(0.0937)	2.42(0.0953)	2.44(0.0961)	2.46(0.0969)	2.48(0.0977)	2.52(0.0992)	2.54(0.1000)	2.56(0.1008)
0.097	2.34(0.0921)	2.36(0.0929)	2.38(0.0937)	2.42(0.0953)	2.44(0.0961)	2.46(0.0969)	2.48(0.0977)	2.52(0.0992)	2.54(0.1000)	2.56(0.1008)	
0.098	2.36(0.0929)	2.38(0.0937)	2.42(0.0953)	2.44(0.0961)	2.46(0.0969)	2.48(0.0977)	2.52(0.0992)	2.54(0.1000)	2.56(0.1008)		
0.099	2.38(0.0937)	2.42(0.0953)	2.44(0.0961)	2.46(0.0969)	2.48(0.0977)	2.52(0.0992)	2.54(0.1000)	2.56(0.1008)			
0.000	2.42(0.0953)	2.44(0.0961)	2.46(0.0969)	2.48(0.0977)	2.52(0.0992)	2.54(0.1000)	2.56(0.1008)				
0.001	2.44(0.0961)	2.46(0.0969)	2.48(0.0977)	2.52(0.0992)	2.54(0.1000)	2.56(0.1008)					
0.002	2.46(0.0969)	2.48(0.0977)	2.52(0.0992)	2.54(0.1000)	2.56(0.1008)						
0.003	2.48(0.0977)	2.52(0.0992)	2.54(0.1000)	2.56(0.1008)							
0.004	2.52(0.0992)	2.54(0.1000)	2.56(0.1008)								
0.005	2.54(0.1000)	2.56(0.1008)									
0.006	2.56(0.1008)										

Shim selection chart—Isuzu front and rear conventional drive axles

LOW FLANK CONTACT
DECREASE PINION SHIM

TOE CONTACT
INCREASE BACKLASH

HEEL CONTACT
DECREASE BACKLASH

HIGH FACE CONTACT
INCREASE PINION SHIM

Differential tooth contact pattern—Isuzu

side gear and the differential assembly is 0.001–0.004 in. and the service limit is 0.006 in.

20. The standard specification for play (backlash) in splines between the side gear and the axle shaft is 0.001–0.006 in. and the service limit is 0.010 in.

To assemble:

21. Assembly is the reverse of the removal procedure. Install the side gears and thrust washers in the differential case.

22. Position the pinion gears 180 degrees apart. Roll gears into position, making sure they are in alignment, to allow installation of the pinion shaft.

23. Place the thrust block if equipped between the pinion gears and drive the pinion shaft into position. Make sure the lock pin hole in cross shaft aligns with the hole in the case.

24. Measure the amount of backlash between the differential gears and the pinion gears. If the backlash is greater than 0.001–0.003 in., make the necessary adjustment with the thrust washers.

25. Install lock pin into cross shaft and stake the cage to prevent loosening of the pin.

26. Apply Loctite or equivalent, to the threaded portion of the bolts. Install the ring gear in position on the differential case. Tighten the bolts (always use new retaining bolts) in diagonal sequence to 75–90 ft. lbs.

27. To set pinion depth install the drive pinion front and rear bearing outer races into carrier bores. Use drive handle J–8092 with J–24256 for front bearing race and J–24252 or equivalent for rear bearing race.

28. Lubricate and position the front and rear bearings to be used for final assembly into their respective races.

29. Install gauging plate J–23597–7 and preload stud and pilot J–23597–9 or their equivalent through front and rear bearings and tighten nut snugly.

30. Rotate the bearings to insure proper seating and tighten locknut until 20 inch lbs. of torque are required to rotate new bearings; 8–10 inch lbs. for used bearings.

31. Place discs J–23597–8 onto arbor J–23597–1 or equivalent and place tool into position in side bearing bores.

32. Install bearing caps and torque to 65–72 ft. lbs.

33. Mount dial indicator J–8001 or equivalent on arbor post and preload dial ½ revolution. Tighten indicator in this position.

34. Position the indicator plunger on the gauge plate and slowly swing across until the highest reading is obtained. Zero the indicator on the highest reading of the gauge plate.

35. Carefully swing the plunger off the gauge plate. Note the indicator reading. Recheck to verify the reading. Record the number the dial indicator needle points to. The reading on the dial is the correct dimension for the rear pinion depth shim. Convert the dial indicator reading (inches) to pinion marking (depth code) specification.

36. Record pinion depth code on the head of the drive pinion. The number indicates a necessary change in the pinion mounting distance. A plus number indicates the need for a greater mounting distance (which can be achieved by decreasing the shim thickness). A minus number indicates the need for a smaller mounting distance (which can be achieved by increasing the shim thickness). If examination reveals no pinion depth code, the pinion is nominal. Determine the proper shim variation to compensate for plus or minus markings.

37. Place the shim on the drive pinion, then install the rear bearing, using J–6133–01 or equivalent. Do not press on roller cage press only on inner race.

38. To set pinion bearing preload place the drive pinion and spacer (always use new spacer) into the carrier.

39. Lubricate, then position the front bearing to be used in final assembly into the carrier. Install new oil seal.

40. Install companion flange to drive pinion. Apply hypoid lubricant to pinion threads. Install new pinion nut and torque to 130–200 ft. lbs. using J–8614–01 or equivalent to hold companion flange.

41. Rotate drive pinion to insure that bearings are seated. Measure the bearing preload by using a torque wrench. Note the scale reading required to rotate the flange.

42. Continue tightening until the correct starting torque is obtained. The standard specification for starting torque is 5–10 inch lbs. The pinion nut should be tightened only in small increments and the scale should be checked after each small amount of tightening. Exceeding preload specifications may compress the collapsible spacer too far and require its replacement.

43. Install the side bearings to be used in final assembly onto the differential case. Do not install shims at this time. Use J–24244 or equivalent for the first bearing installation.

44. Support case on plug J–8107–2 or equivalent for opposite bearing installation.

45. Install the differential cage assembly into carrier bores.

46. Using 2 sets of feeler gauges, insert a feeler gauge of sufficient thickness between each bearing outer race and the carrier to remover all end play. Make certain the feeler gauge is pushed to the bottom of the bearing bores.

47. Install a dial indicator on the carrier so the stem of the tool is at a right angle to a tooth on the ring gear.

48. Adjust feeler gauge thickness from side to side until the gear backlash is 0.005–0.007 in.

49. With zero end play and correct backlash established, remove the feeler gauge. Determine the thickness of the shims (always use new shims) required and add 0.002 in. to each shim pack to provide side bearing preload.

50. Remove the case from the carrier. Carefully remove both side bearings. Install shims as determined behind each bearing, install bearings onto case.

51. Install case onto carrier, tapping carefully into place. Install side bearing caps in original position. Tighten to 65–80 ft. lbs.

52. Measure the runout of the ring gear. If the runout exceeds 0.002 in., correct by replacement.

53. Apply a thin coat of gear marking compound to the faces of 7–9 teeth of the ring gear. Check the impression of the contact on the ring gear teeth and make the necessary adjustments.

54. Apply gear oil to all moving parts and use sealant and or gasket when assembling to the axle housing.

Rear Drive Axle

Disassembly and Assembly

1. Position the removed differential carrier assembly in a suitable holding fixture. Perform tooth pattern check to help determine what service should be performed on the differential components.

2. Matchmark and remove the side bearing caps.

3. Remove the differential cage assembly. Keep the right and left side bearing races and shims in separate groups for reinstallation in same positions.

4. Remove the differential side bearings from the case by using puller J–22888 and plug J–8107–2 or equivalent (some special tools may be different on the limited slip differential carrier). Carefully record the thickness of each side bearing and each shim(s) removed for later use in reassembly and keep separated. Puller arms must not pull against roller cage. Use care to position legs against inner race. As bearing is being removed, check for free rotation of bearing. If bearing does not rotate freely, check position of puller legs.

5. Remove the companion flange nut while holding flange with suitable tools. Remove the flange assembly with puller if necessary.

6. Drive the pinion shaft assembly from the carrier using suitable tools and brass punch. The outer (front) bearing will fall loose in the carrier, while the inner (rear) bearing will remain pressed on the drive pinion. Both races will remain in the carrier bores.

7. Remove rear bearing from the drive pinion by use of a

1. Outer bearing outer race
2. Inner bearing outer race
3. Shim
4. Inner bearing
5. Collapsible spacer
6. Drive pinion assembly
7. Outer bearing
8. Oil seal
9. Flange assembly
10. Flange nut
11. Shim
12. Side bearing
13. Side bearing outer race
14. Differential cage
    assembly and ring gear
15. Bearing cap
16. Bolt
17. Differential assembly

Exploded view rear differential assembly—Isuzu

press and tool J–22912–01 or equivalent on conventional differential carrier. On limited slip differential carrier use special tool J–37452 and a press.

8. Remove the oil seal and then drive the 2 outer races from the carrier by use of a brass drift and suitable tools.

9. Remove the ring gear bolts (diagonal pattern) and separate the ring gear from the differential case. Use care when removing ring gear to prevent damage to differential case or ring gear. Do not force a chisel or other tools between the joining faces.

10. At this point of the reassembly, check the amount of backlash before removal. The standard specification for backlash is 0.001–0.003 in. for conventional differential. The standard specification for backlash is 0.005–0.007 in. for limited slip differential.

11. On conventional differential carrier drive out the pinion shaft lock pin with a long drift. It may be necessary to first break the stake on lock pin using a 0.020 in. diameter drill or equivalent.

12. On conventional differential carrier remove the pinion

shaft with a drift pin and take out the pinion gears, side gears, thrust block and thrust washers from the differential case.

13. On limited slip differential remove the limited slip differential carrier assembly.

14. Wash the bearings in a suitable solvent. Then examine bearings carefully for wear, separation, cracks, seizure and other abnormal conditions. Replace bearings as necessary.

15. Check the ring gear and drive pinion teeth for wear, chipping, cracks, pitting and abnormal contact. Check the drive pinion splines for cracks, distortion and step wear. Replace parts if needed. Ring gear and drive pinion come only in matched sets. If either item is defective, both parts must be replaced.

16. Check the pinion gears and side gears for wear, chipped teeth and separation and replace if needed.

17. Check and replace the thrust blocks on conventional differential and thrust washers, if worn or damaged.

18. On conventional differential check the lock pin for bending, dents and other abnormal conditions. Replace if necessary.

19. Check the clearance between pinion gear and cross pin.

1. Box
2. Thrust washer
3. Spring
4. Disc plate
5. Friction plate
6. Friction disc
7. Friction plate
8. Friction disc
9. Pressure ring
10. Side gear
11. Pinion gear and shaft
12. Side gear
13. Pressure ring
14. Friction disc
15. Friction plate
16. Friction disc
17. Friction plate
18. Disc plate
19. Spring
20. Thrust washer
21. Box cover
22. Bolt

Exploded view limited slip differentail carrier — Isuzu

Dial indicator reading (inches) / Pinion marking	+10	+8	+6	+4	+2	0	-2	-4	-6	-8	-10
0.073											
0.074										1.94(0.0764)	1.96(0.0772)
0.075									1.94(0.0764)	1.96(0.0772)	1.98(0.0779)
0.076								1.94(0.0764)	1.96(0.0772)	1.98(0.0779)	2.00(0.0787)
0.077							1.94(0.0764)	1.96(0.0772)	1.98(0.0779)	2.00(0.0787)	2.02(0.0795)
0.078						1.94(0.0764)	1.96(0.0772)	1.98(0.0779)	2.00(0.0787)	2.02(0.0795)	2.04(0.0803)
0.079					1.94(0.0764)	1.96(0.0772)	1.98(0.0779)	2.00(0.0787)	2.02(0.0795)	2.04(0.0803)	2.06(0.0811)
0.080	1.94(0.0764)	1.96(0.0772)	1.98(0.0779)	2.00(0.0787)	2.02(0.0795)	2.04(0.0803)	2.06(0.0811)	2.08(0.0819)	2.10(0.0827)	2.12(0.0835)	2.14(0.0842)
0.081	1.96(0.0772)	1.98(0.0779)	2.00(0.0787)	2.02(0.0795)	2.04(0.0803)	2.06(0.0811)	2.08(0.0819)	2.10(0.0827)	2.12(0.0835)	2.14(0.0842)	2.16(0.0850)
0.082	1.98(0.0779)	2.00(0.0787)	2.02(0.0795)	2.04(0.0803)	2.06(0.0811)	2.08(0.0819)	2.10(0.0827)	2.12(0.0835)	2.14(0.0842)	2.16(0.0850)	2.18(0.0858)
0.083	2.00(0.0787)	2.02(0.0795)	2.04(0.0803)	2.06(0.0811)	2.08(0.0819)	2.10(0.0827)	2.12(0.0835)	2.14(0.0842)	2.16(0.0850)	2.18(0.0858)	2.20(0.0866)
0.084	2.04(0.0803)	2.06(0.0811)	2.08(0.0819)	2.10(0.0827)	2.12(0.0835)	2.14(0.0842)	2.16(0.0850)	2.18(0.0858)	2.20(0.0866)	2.22(0.0874)	2.24(0.0882)
0.085	2.06(0.0811)	2.08(0.0819)	2.10(0.0827)	2.12(0.0835)	2.14(0.0842)	2.16(0.0850)	2.18(0.0858)	2.20(0.0866)	2.22(0.0874)	2.24(0.0882)	2.26(0.0890)
0.086	2.08(0.0819)	2.10(0.0827)	2.12(0.0835)	2.14(0.0842)	2.16(0.0850)	2.18(0.0858)	2.20(0.0866)	2.22(0.0874)	2.24(0.0882)	2.26(0.0890)	2.28(0.0898)
0.087	2.12(0.0835)	2.14(0.0842)	2.16(0.0850)	2.18(0.0858)	2.20(0.0866)	2.22(0.0874)	2.24(0.0882)	2.26(0.0890)	2.28(0.0898)	2.30(0.0906)	2.32(0.0913)
0.088	2.14(0.0842)	2.16(0.0850)	2.18(0.0858)	2.20(0.0866)	2.22(0.0874)	2.24(0.0882)	2.26(0.0890)	2.28(0.0898)	2.30(0.0906)	2.32(0.0913)	2.34(0.0921)
0.089	2.16(0.0850)	2.18(0.0858)	2.20(0.0866)	2.22(0.0874)	2.24(0.0882)	2.26(0.0890)	2.28(0.0898)	2.30(0.0906)	2.32(0.0913)	2.34(0.0921)	2.36(0.0929)
0.090	2.18(0.0858)	2.20(0.0866)	2.22(0.0874)	2.24(0.0882)	2.26(0.0890)	2.28(0.0898)	2.30(0.0906)	2.32(0.0913)	2.34(0.0921)	2.36(0.0929)	
0.091	2.22(0.0874)	2.24(0.0882)	2.26(0.0890)	2.28(0.0898)	2.30(0.0906)	2.32(0.0913)	2.34(0.0921)	2.36(0.0929)			
0.092	2.24(0.0882)	2.26(0.0890)	2.28(0.0898)	2.30(0.0906)	2.32(0.0913)	2.34(0.0921)	2.36(0.0929)				
0.093	2.26(0.0890)	2.28(0.0898)	2.30(0.0906)	2.32(0.0913)	2.34(0.0921)	2.36(0.0929)					
0.094	2.28(0.0898)	2.30(0.0906)	2.32(0.0913)	2.34(0.0921)	2.36(0.0929)						
0.095	2.32(0.0913)	2.34(0.0921)	2.36(0.0929)								
0.096	2.34(0.0921)	2.36(0.0929)									
0.097	2.36(0.0929)										

Shim selection chart — Isuzu rear limited slip differential drive axle

The standard specification for the clearance between the differential pinion and the cross pin is 0.002–0.005 in. and the service limit is 0.008 in. on both differential carriers.

20. Check the clearance between the side gear and differential box. The standard specification for the clearance between the side gear and the differential assembly is 0.001–0.004 in. and the service limit is 0.006 in. on conventional carrier. The standard specification for the clearance between the side gear and the differential assembly is 0.002–0.004 in. and the service limit is 0.006 in. on limited slip differential carrier.

21. Check the play in splines between the side gear and axle shafts. The standard specification for play (backlash) in splines between the side gear and the axle shaft is 0.001–0.006 in. and the service limit is 0.010 in. on the conventional differential. The standard specification for play in splines between the side gear and the axle shaft is 0.03–0.15 in. and the service limit is 0.010 in. on the limited slip differential.

To assemble:

22. Assembly is the reverse of the removal procedure. Install the side gears and thrust washers in the differential case. Position the pinion gears 180 degrees apart. Roll gears into position, making sure they are in alignment, to allow installation of the pinion shaft.

23. Place the thrust block on conventional differential between the pinion gears and drive the pinion shaft into position. Make sure the lock pin hole in cross shaft aligns with the hole in the case.

24. Measure the amount of backlash between the differential gears and the pinion gears. The standard specification is 0.001–0.003 in. on conventional differential or 0.005–0.007 in. on limited slip differential. Make the necessary adjustment with the thrust washers.

25. Install lock pin into cross shaft and stake the cage to prevent loosening of the pin.

26. Apply Loctite or equivalent to the threaded portion of the bolts. Install the ring gear in position on the differential case. Tighten the bolts (always use new retaining bolts) in diagonal sequence to 75–90 ft. lbs. on conventional and limited slip differentials.

27. To set pinion depth install the drive pinion front and rear bearing outer races into carrier bores. Use drive handle J–8092 with J–24256 (conventional carrier) or J–37262 for limited slip differential carrier for front bearing race and J–24252 (conventional carrier) and J–24252 for limited slip differential carrier for rear bearing race.

28. Lubricate and position the front and rear bearings to be used for final assembly into their respective races.

29. Install gauging plate J–23597–7 and preload stud and pilot J–23597–9 or their equivalent through front and rear bearings and tighten nut snugly. On limited slip differential carriers special tool numbers may change.

30. Rotate the bearings to insure proper seating and tighten locknut until 20 inch lbs. of torque are required to rotate new bearings or 8–10 inch lbs. for used bearings.

31. Place discs J–23597–8 onto arbor J–23597–1 or equivalent (special tool numbers may change on limited slip differential carrier) and place tool into position in side bearing bores. Install bearing caps and torque to 65–75 ft. lbs. on conventional carrier or 75–90 ft. lbs. on limited slip differential carrier.

32. Mount dial indicator J–8001 or equivalent on arbor post and preload dial ½ revolution. Tighten indicator in this position.

33. Position the indicator plunger on the gauge plate and slowly swing across until the highest reading is obtained. Zero the indicator on the highest reading of the gauge plate. Repeat procedure if necessary for correct readings.

34. After zero setting is obtained carefully swing the plunger off the gauge plate. Note the indicator reading. Recheck to verify the reading. Record the number the dial indicator needle points

to. The reading on the dial is the correct dimension for the rear pinion depth shim. Convert the dial indicator reading (inches) to the correct pinion marking (depth code) specification.

35. Record pinion depth code on the head of the drive pinion. The number indicates a necessary change in the pinion mounting distance. A plus number indicates the need for a greater mounting distance (which can be achieved by decreasing the shim thickness). A minus number indicates the need for a smaller mounting distance (which can be achieved by increasing the shim thickness). If examination reveals no pinion depth code, the pinion is nominal. Determine the proper shim variation to compensate for plus or minus markings.

36. Place the shim on the drive pinion with chamfered side toward the pinion head then install the rear bearing, using J–6133–01 or equivalent. Do not press on roller cage press only on inner race.

37. To set pinion bearing preload place the drive pinion and spacer (always use new spacer) into the carrier.

38. Lubricate, then position the front bearing to be used in final assembly into the carrier. Install new oil seal.

39. Install companion flange to drive pinion. Apply hypoid lubricant to pinion threads. Install new pinion nut and torque to 130–200 ft. lbs. using J–8614–01 or equivalent to hold companion flange. On limited slip differential carrier torque new pinion nut to 180–220 ft. lbs. using suitable tools to hold flange.

40. Rotate drive pinion to insure that bearings are seated. Measure the bearing preload by using a torque wrench. Note the scale reading required to rotate the flange.

41. Continue tightening until the correct starting toque is obtained. The standard specification for starting torque is 5–10 inch lbs. on conventional differential or 6–12 inch lbs. on limited slip differential carrier. The pinion nut should be tightened only in small increments and the scale should be checked after each small amount of tightening. Exceeding preload specifications may compress the collapsible spacer too far and require its replacement.

42. Install the side bearings to be used in final assembly onto the differential case. Do not install shims at this time. Use J–24244 or equivalent for the first bearing installation (on limited slip differential carrier special tools numbers may be different).

43. Support case on plug J–8107–2 or equivalent for opposite bearing installation.

44. Install the differential cage assembly into carrier bores.

45. Using 2 sets of feeler gauges, insert a feeler gauge of sufficient thickness between each bearing outer race and the carrier to remover all end play. Make certain the feeler gauge is pushed to the bottom of the bearing bores.

46. Install a dial indicator on the carrier so the stem of the tool is at a right angle to a tooth on the ring gear.

47. Adjust feeler gauge thickness from side to side until the gear backlash is 0.005–0.007 in. on conventional differential or 0.006–0.008 in. on limited slip differential.

48. With zero end play and correct backlash established, remove the feeler gauge. Determine the thickness of the shims (always use new shims) required and add 0.002 in. to each shim pack to provide side bearing preload.

49. Remove the case from the carrier. Carefully remove both side bearings. Install shims as determined behind each bearing, install bearings onto case.

50. Install case onto carrier, tapping carefully into place. Install side bearing caps in original position. Tighten bearing caps to 65–80 ft. lbs. on conventional differential carrier or 75–90 ft. lbs. on limited slip differential carrier.

51. Measure the runout of the ring gear. If the runout exceeds 0.002 in., correct by replacement. Apply a thin coat of gear marking compound to the faces of 7–9 teeth of the ring gear. Check the impression of the contact on the ring gear teeth and make the necessary adjustments.

52. Apply gear oil to all moving parts and use sealant and or gasket when assembling to the axle housing.

MAZDA

Front And Rear Drive Axles

Disassembly and Assembly

1. Position the removed differential carrier assembly in a suitable holding fixture.

2. Matchmark the carrier, differential bearing caps and adjusters for correct reassembly.

3. Remove the adjuster lock plates.

4. Loosen the bolts securing the bearing cap and slowly back off the adjuster slightly to relieve the preload.

5. Remove the nuts, bearing caps and adjusters. Keep each bearing cap with its own adjuster.

6. Lift out the differential assembly and keep each bearing outer race with its own bearing.

7. If the differential bearings are to be replaced, mark for correct installation and remove using a suitable puller.

8. Remove the bolts (in diagonal pattern) and washers retaining the ring gear to the case.

9. Remove the ring gear. On conventional differential position the assembly in a vise or equivalent and remove the lock pin (tap out toward the ring gear side) with a suitable punch (0.16 in. diameter size).

10. On conventional differential remove the pinion shaft and the thrust block. Rotate the differential pinion gears 90 degrees and remove. Remove the differential side gears and thrust washers.

11. On limited slip differential remove the limited slip differential carrier assembly.

12. Using a holding tool, steady the companion flange and remove the nut.

13. Remove the companion flange using suitable puller.

14. Remove the front bearing, drive pinion and rear bearing from the carrier, which may require tapping with a plastic mallet or equivalent. Guide the pinion assembly to avoid damage to any component.

15. Remove the oil seal and the front bearing.

16. The pinion bearing outer races (cups) can be removed (mark for correct installation) from the carrier by tapping out using a drift in the slots provided.

17. Remove the rear bearing from the pinion (support the pinion during bearing removal) using suitable press and separator plate.

18. Check the drive pinion for damaged or worn teeth, damaged bearing journals or splines. Inspect the ring gear again for worn or chipped teeth. If any of the above conditions are found, replace both drive pinion and ring gear as a set.

19. Inspect bearing cones and cups and replace any showing wear, flaking or damage. Replace only in sets. Do not use an old cup with a new bearing or an old bearing with a new cup.

20. Check the companion flange carefully for cracks or worn splines. If either exist, the part should be replaced. Check for rough or scratched oil seal contact surface. If only slight scratches appear, it may be possible to repair with crocus cloth. Otherwise, replace it. Be sure to use a new oil seal when reassembling the carrier.

21. On conventional differential assemble the side gears, thrust washers, thrust block, pinion gears, pinion shaft and lock pin. After installing lock pin stake pin so pin cannot come out of gear case.

22. On conventional differential assemble press the side bearings (correct location) onto the gear case using suitable tools. Adjust the backlash of the side gears and pinion gear as follows:

   a. Position a dial indicator against the pinion gear. Secure one of the side gears.

   b. Move the pinion gear and measure the backlash at the end of the pinion gear.

   c. The standard specification for backlash is 0–0.004 in. on all vehicles. If backlash exceeds the standard specification use suitable thrust washer to adjust.

23. On conventional and limited slip differential carriers apply thread locking compound install ring gear to differential assembly. Torque the retaining bolts to 50–60 ft. lbs. all vehicles in a diagonal pattern.

24. Press fit the companion flange side bearing outer races using bearing installer set.

25. Press fit the ring gear side bearing outer races using bearing installer set.

NOTE: Special tools are required to check and adjust the pinion height, these include a drive pinion model tool 498531565, a pinion height adjustment gauge body tool 490727570 and a gauge block tool 400305555.

1. Locknut
2. Washer
3. Flange
4. Oil seal
5. Front bearing
6. Collapsible spacer
7. Drive pinion
8. Rear bearing
9. Spacer
10. Bearing outer races

Exploded view of drive pinion assembly—Mazda

1. Bolts
2. Lock plates
3. Bearing caps
4. Adjustment screws
5. Bearing outer races
6. Differential gear assembly

Exploded view of differential carrier—Mazda

1. Bolt
2. Ring gear
3. Pin
4. Pinion shaft
5. Pinion gears
6. Thrust block
7. Side gears
8. Thrust washer
9. Bearings
10. Gear case

Exploded view standard differential assembly—Mazda

1. Ring gear
2. Screw
3. Differential cover
4. Thrust washer
5. Spring
6. Friction plate
7. Friction disc
8. Friction plate
9. Friction disc
10. Pressure ring
11. Side gear
12. Spider
13. Pinion gear
14. Thrust block
15. Side gear
16. Pressure ring
17. Friction disc
18. Friction plate
19. Friction disc
20. Friction plate
21. Spring
22. Thrust washer
23. Differential case

Exploded view limited slip differential assembly — Mazda

26. At this point of the reassembly, adjust the pinion height as follows:

a. Fit the spacer, rear bearing and collar onto the drive pinion model. Secure the collar with an O-ring and install in the assembly in the carrier.

b. Attach the front bearing, collar, companion flange, washer and nut to the drive pinion model. Use the same spacer and nut which were removed at disassembly. Be careful to install collars in their correct position facing in the correct direction.

c. Tighten the nut until the drive pinion model can be turned by hand without any apparent play.

d. Install a dial indicator on the pinion height adjustment gauge body. Place the gauge block on top of the drive pinion model and then set the pinion height adjustment gauge body on top of the gauge block.

e. Place the measuring probe of the dial indicator so it contacts the location where the side bearing is installed in the carrier. Zero and set up the indicator to measure the lowest point. Measure both the left and right sides. Add the 2 values (right and left side readings) and divide the total by 2. The standard specification is 0 in. on all vehicles. Install correct spacer as necessary to adjust pinion height.

27. Install the correct spacer(s) on the pinion shaft (facing in the proper direction) and press the bearing on the pinion shaft.

28. Install the drive pinion, spacer, front bearing, collapsible spacer and companion flange in the carrier and temporarily tighten the locknut. Do not install the pinion oil seal at this time.

29. At this point of the reassembly, adjust preload of the drive pinion as follows:

a. Rotate the companion flange by hand to seat the bearing.

b. Use a torque wrench to tighten the locknut. Tighten slowly until the required preload drag of 8–12 inch lbs. is

reached with a locknut torque of 95–130 ft. lbs. for all applications except MPV vehicle.

c. On MPV vehicle, slowly tighten until the preload drag of 11–16 inch lbs. is reached with a locknut torque of 95–210 ft. lbs.

d. If the specified preload cannot be maintained within the locknut tightening range, install a new collapsible spacer and repeat the process if necessary.

e. On all applications except MPV vehicle remove the locknut and flange. Install the pinion seal, flange and new locknut. Tighten the locknut to the ft. lbs. specification torque giving the correct preload.

f. On MPV vehicle, remove the locknut and flange. Install the pinion seal, flange and new locknut. Retighten the locknut to the preload drag of 14–18 inch lbs. is reached with a locknut torque of 95–210 ft. lbs.

30. Install the differential gear assembly in the carrier. Note the identification marks on the adjusters and install each to its respective side. Install the bearing caps making sure the identification marks on the caps correspond with those on the carrier and install the bolts.

31. Loosely tighten the bearing cap mounting bolts and completely tighten the adjustment screws by hand. Then, while turning the ring gear, alternately tighten the left and right adjustment screws using a suitable tool.

32. At this point of the reassembly, adjust the drive pinion and ring gear backlash and side bearing preload as follows:

a. Mark the ring gear at 4 points at approximately 90 degree intervals and mount a dial indicator to the carrier flange so the feeler comes in contact at right angles with one of the ring gear teeth.

b. Turn both bearing adjusters equally until backlash becomes (standard specification for all vehicles) 0.0035–0.0043 in.

Adjustment of drive pinion and ring gear backlash

Differential tooth contact pattern—Mazda

STEP 1

Gauge block   Drive-pinion model

`49 8531 565`

Spacer

Rear bearing

`49 H027 001`

Front bearing

`49 U027 001`

STEP 2

Adjustment of drive pinion height

c. Check the backlash at the other 3 marked points and make sure minimum backlash is more than 0.002 in. and the difference in the specification of the maximum and minimum backlash is less than 0.0028 in.

d. After adjusting the backlash, tighten the adjustment screws equally until the distance between both pilot sections on the bearing caps becomes the standard distance. The standard distance is 7.3004–7.3031 in. for B2000 (2WD) and B2200 (2WD) rear axle assemblies and B2600 (4WD) front axle assembly. The standard distance is 8.0484 in. plus or minus 0.028 in. for B2600 (2WD and 4WD) rear axle assemblies and the MPV rear axle assembly. When adjusting the differential bearing preload, care must be taken not to affect the backlash of the drive pinion gear and ring gear.

33. Tighten the bearing caps to specification: B2000 (2WD) and B2200 (2WD) rear axles and B2600 (4WD) front axle assembly is 27–38 ft. lbs. The specification for B2600 (2WD and 4WD) rear axle assemblies is 41–59 ft. lbs. The specification for the MPV vehicle is 51–61 ft. lbs.

34. Install the adjuster lock plates.

35. Coat both surfaces of 6–8 teeth of the ring gear uniformly with a thin coat of gear marking compound.

36. While moving the ring gear back and forth by hand, rotate the drive pinion several times and check the tooth contact.

37. If pattern is not correct readjust the pinion height then the backlash.

38. Apply gear oil to all moving parts and use sealant and/or gasket when assembling to the axle housing.

MITSUBISHI

Front Drive Axle

Inspection Before Disassembly

1. Position the removed differential carrier assembly in a suitable holding fixture. Remove the differential cover.

2. With the drive pinion locked in place, measure the final drive gear (ring gear) backlash with a dial indicator on the drive gear. Measure at 4 points or more on the drive gear. If the backlash is not within specification, adjust it by using the correct side bearing spacer.

3. The final drive gear backlash specification is 0.0043–0.0063 in. on all engines.

4. Measure the drive gear runout at the shoulder on the reverse side of the drive gear the limit is 0.0020 in. on all engines.

5. While locking the side gear with a wedge or equivalent, measure the differential gear backlash with a dial indicator on the pinion gear. The standard valve is 0–0.0030 in. The service limit is 0.008 in. on all engines.

6. Check the final drive gear tooth contact by the following steps:

   a. Apply a thin uniform coat of gear markinmg compound to both surfaces of the drive gear teeth.

   b. Insert a tool between the differential carrier and the differential case and then rotate the companion flange by hand (once in normal direction and once reverse direction) while applying a load to the drive gear so the revolution torque (about 2.5 ft. lbs.) is applied to the drive pinion.

   c. If the drive gear is rotated too much, contact pattern will become unclear and difficult to read. If a correct pattern cannot be obtained (drive gear and pinion worn beyond allowable limits), replace the drive gear and the drive pinion as a set.

Disassembly and Assembly

1. Position the removed differential carrier assembly in a suitable holding fixture. Remove the differential cover.

2. Matchmark and remove the bearing (carrier) caps and pry out the differential assembly.

3. Remove the differential side bearings. Be sure to keep the right and left bearings and shims separated. Remove side bearings inner and outer races.

4. Matchmark ring gear assembly and loosen the ring gear mounting bolts in diagonal sequence. Remove the ring gear.

5. Drive the pinion shaft lock pin out from the rear of the ring gear using a punch and remove the pinion shaft assembly.

6. Remove the pinion gears and washers. Remove the side gears with their spacers. Keep left and right side gears and spacers separate. Remove the differential case.

7. Hold the end yoke (companion flange) and remove the self-locking nut and washer. Matchmark for correct installation then remove the companion flange.

8. Tap the end of the drive pinion shaft (matchmark shaft assembly for correct installation) with a plastic hammer and force out the drive pinion along with its adjusting shim, the rear inner race, the drive pinion spacer and the preload adjusting shim. The rear bearing inner race can be pressed off the pinion shaft.

9. Remove the front and rear pinion bearing outer races. Remove the oil seals. Remove the vent plug if necessary and gear carrier case.

To assemble:

10. Assembly is the reverse of the removal procedure. Install the vent plug to the gear carrier case if necessary. Install oil seals.

11. Press the drive pinion front and rear bearing outer races into the differential carrier case. Make sure the races do not tilt and that they sit fully in the case.

12. At this point of the reassembly, adjust the drive pinion height by following this procedure:

   a. Install special service tool C–4626 and drive pinion front and rear bearing inner races to the gear carrier in the correct sequence.

   b. Gradually tighten the nut of the special tool until the standard valve of the drive pinion turning torque is reached.

   c. Measure the drive pinion turning torque without the oil seal installed. The standard specification is 1–2 inch lbs. of turning torque for all engines except 3.0L engine. The specification is 3–4 inch lbs. of turning torque for 3.0L engine.

   d. Because 1 rotation cannot be made when the special tool is in contact with the gear carrier, move it a few times and after seating the bearing measure the rotation torque.

   e. Mount the special service tool MB990552 in the side bearing seat of the gear carrier and then select a drive pinion front height adjusting shim (keep front shims to a minimum) of a thickness which corresponds to the gap between the special tools. Be sure to clean the side bearing seat thoroughly. When mounting the special tool be sure the cut-out sections are in the correct position and also confirm that the tool is in close contact with the side bearing seat.

   f. Install the selected drive pinion front shim(s) to the drive pinion. Using special tool MB990802, press fit the drive pinion front bearing inner race.

13. At this point of the reassembly, adjust the drive pinion preload (turning torque) by following this procedure:

   a. Without the oil seal installed insert the drive pinion into the gear carrier and then install from the front side of the carrier, the driver pinion spacer, drive pinion rear shim, drive pinion rear bearing inner race and the companion flange in that order.

   b. Tighten the companion flange to 115–160 ft. lbs. on all engines except the 3.0L engine. On the 3.0L engine torque the companion flange to 140–180 ft. lbs. Measure the drive pinion turning torque without the oil seal installed. The standard specification is 1–2 inch lbs. turning torque for all engines except the 3.0L engine. This should be 3–4 inch lbs. turning torque for the 3.0L engine.

   c. Adjust the turning torque by replacing the drive pinion rear shim(s) or the drive pinion spacer. Reduce number of drive pinion rear shims by replacing drive pinion spacer(s) as necessary.

   d. Remove the companion flange and drive pinion once again.

14. Install drive pinion rear bearing inner race. Install oil seal into the gear carrier using suitable tools.

15. Install the drive pinion assembly and companion flange in the correct position. Tighten the companion flange to 116–159 ft. lbs. on all engines except the 3.0L engine. On the 3.0L engine torque the companion flange to 140–180 ft. lbs.

16. Measure the drive pinion turning torque with oil seal installed. The standard specification is 3–4 inch lbs. of turning torque for all engines except the 3.0L engine. The specification for the 3.0L engine is 5–6 inch lbs. of turning torque.

17. If not within the standard specification, check for faulty installation of the oil seal or wrong torque on the companion flange locking nut.

18. At this point of the reassembly, adjust the differential gear backlash by following this procedure:

   a. Install the side gears, side gear thrust spacers, pinion gear and pinion washers into the differential case. Temporarily install the pinion shaft. Do not drive the lock pin in place yet.

   b. While locking the side gear with a wedge or equivalent, measure the differential gear backlash with a dial indicator on the pinion gear. The standard specification is 0–0.0030 in. and the service limit is 0.008 in. for all axles.

   c. If the differential gear backlash exceeds the limit adjust the backlash by installing thicker side gear thrust spacers. If adjustment is not possible replace the side gears and pinion gears as a set.

19. Align the pinion shaft lock pin hole with the differential case lock pin hole.

20. Drive the lock pin in and stake the pin with a suitable tool in 2 different locations.

21. Install the drive gear onto the differential case with matchmarks in the correct position. Torque (with locking adhesive or equivalent on threads) drive gear attaching bolts to 58–65 ft. lbs. in a diagonal sequence for all engines.

22. Press fit the side bearing inner races to the differential case using suitable tools.

23. At this point of the reassembly, adjust the final drive gear backlash as follows:

a. Install the side bearing adjusting spacers (both sides same size-thin spacers as possible) to the side bearing outer races, then mount ther differential case assembly into the gear carrier.

b. Push the differential case assembly to one side. Measure the clearance between the gear carrier and the side bearing adjusting spacer with a feeler gauge.

c. Measure the thickness of the side bearing adjusting spacers on a side. Select 2 pairs of spacers which correspond to that thickness plus ½ of the clearance plus 0.002 in. and then install one pair each to the drive pinion side and the drive gear side.

24. Install the side bearing adjusting spacers and differential case assembly in the gear carrier.

25. Tap the side bearing adjusting spacers with a brass tool to position them to the side bearing outer races.

26. Align the mating marks on the gear carrier and the bearing caps and tighten the bearing caps to 40–50 ft. lbs. on all axles.

27. Attach a dial indicator to the ring gear teeth and measure the final drive gear backlash at 4 different locations. Final drive gear backlash standard specification is 0.0043–0.0063 in. for all axles. Change the side bearing spacers as necessary for correct adjustment. When increasing the number of side bearing adjusting spacers, use the same number for each side and as few as possible.

28. Measure the ring gear runout in 2 or more locations. Runout should be 0.002 in. or less on all axles.

29. If necessary make a ring gear tooth pattern check. Apply gear oil to all moving parts and use sealant and or gasket when assembling to the axle housing.

Rear Drive Axle

Inspection Before Disassembly

1. Position the removed differential carrier assembly in a suitable holding fixture.

2. With the drive pinion locked in place, measure the final drive gear (ring gear) backlash with a dial indicator on the drive gear. Measure at 4 points or more on the drive gear.

3. The final drive gear backlash specification for 2.0L, 2.4L and 2.6L engines is 0.0043–0.0063 in. The specification for 3.0L engine is 0.0051–0.0071 in.

4. Measure the drive gear runout at the shoulder on the reverse side of the drive gear the limit is 0.0020 in. on all engines.

5. On a conventional differential asssembly the differential gear backlash must be checked. While locking the side gear with a wedge or equivalent, measure the differential gear backlash with a dial indicator on the pinion gear. The differential gear backlash (conventional) for the 2.0L, 2.4L and 2.6L engines specification is 0.0004–0.0030 in. The specification for the 3.0L engine is 0–0.0030 in. The service limit is 0.008 in. on all engines.

6. Check the final drive gear tooth contact by the following steps:

a. Apply a thin uniform coat of machine blue or equivalent to both surfaces of the drive gear teeth.

b. Insert a tool between the differential carrier and the differential case and then rotate the companion flange by hand (once in normal direction and once reverse direction) while applying a load to the drive gear so the revolution torque (about 2.5 ft. lbs.) is applied to the drive pinion.

c. If the drive gear is rotated too much, contact pattern will become unclear and difficult to read. If a correct pattern cannot be obtained (drive gear and pinion worn beyond allowable limits), replace the drive gear and the drive pinion as a set.

Disassembly and Assembly

1. Position the differential assembly in a suitable holding fixture. Remove the lock bolts and plates holding the side bearing nut in place.

2. Remove the side bearing nuts with the special adjusting tool spanner wrench MB990201 or equivalent.

3. Matchmark and remove the carrier caps and pry out the differential.

4. Pull off the differential side bearings. Be sure to keep the right and left bearings and shims separated. Remove side bearings inner and outer races.

5. Matchmark ring gear assembly and loosen the ring gear mounting bolts in diagonal sequence. Remove the ring gear.

6. Drive the pinion shaft lock pin out from the rear of the ring gear using a punch and remove the pinion shaft assembly.

7. Remove the thrust block, pinion gears and washers. Remove the side gears with their spacers. Keep left and right side gears and spacers separate. Remove the differential case.

8. On limited slip differential vehicles, remove limited slip differential case assembly.

9. Hold the end yoke (companion flange) and remove the self-locking nut and washer. Matchmark for correct installation then remove the companion flange.

10. Tap the end of the drive pinion shaft (matchmark shaft assembly for correct installation) with a plastic hammer and force out the drive pinion along with its adjusting shim, the rear inner race, the drive pinion spacer and the preload adjusting shim. The rear bearing inner race can be pressed off the pinion shaft.

11. Remove the front and rear pinion bearing outer races. The front inner race should be removed with its oil seal. Remove the differential carrier case.

NOTE: Do not reuse the old oil seal. If the unit is to be assembled using no replacement parts except oil seals, the same spacers and shims can generally be used. If either pinion bearing or ring gear and drive pinion are being replaced, new shims should be used. Only replace the drive pinion and ring gear in matched sets.

To assemble:

12. Assembly is the reverse of the removal procedure.

Press the drive pinion front and rear bearing outer races into the differential carrier case. Make sure the races do not tilt and that they sit fully in the case.

13.

At this point of the reassembly, adjust the drive pinion height by following this procedure:

a. Install special service tool MB991169 (use special adapter head tool C-4626 for 3.0L engine only) and drive pinion front and rear bearing inner races to the gear carrier in the correct sequence.

b. Gradually tighten the nut of the special tool until the standard valve of the drive pinion turning torque is reached.

c. Measure the drive pinion turning torque without the oil seal installed. The standard specification for all engines is 3–4 inch lbs. of turning torque.

d. Mount the special service tool MB990552 in the side bearing seat of the gear carrier and then select a drive pinion height adjusting shim (keep rear shims to a minimum) of a thickness which corresponds to the gap between the special tools. Be sure to clean the side bearing seat thoroughly. When mounting the special tool be sure the cut-out sections are in the correct position and also confirm that the tool is in close contact with the side bearing seat.

e. Install the selected drive pinion rear shim(s) to the drive pinion. Using special tool MB990802, press fit the drive pinion rear bearing inner race.

14. At this point of the reassembly, adjust the drive pinion preload (turning torque) by following this procedure:

a. Without the oil seal installed fit the drive pinion front shims between the drive pinion spacer and the drive pinion front bearing inner race.

b. Tighten the companion flange to 135–180 ft. lbs. on all engines. Measure the drive pinion turning torque without the oil seal installed. The standard specification is 3–4 inch lbs. turning torque for all engines.

c. Adjust the turning torque by replacing the drive pinion front shim(s) or the drive pinion spacer. Reduce number of drive pinion front shims by replacing drive pinion spacer as necessary.

d. Remove the companion flange and drive pinion once again.

15. Install drive pinion front bearing inner race. Install oil seal into the gear carrier using suitable tools.

16. Install the drive pinion assembly and companion flange in the correct position. Torque the companion flange locking nut to 135–180 ft. lbs. on all engines.

17. Measure the drive pinion turning torque with oil seal installed. The standard specification is 5–6 inch lbs. of turning torque on all engines.

18. On limited slip differential vehicles, install limited slip differential case assembly.

19. At this point of the reassembly (conventional differential), adjust the differential gear backlash by following this procedure:

a. Install the side gears, side gear thrust spacers, pinion gear and pinion washers into the differential case. Temporarily install the pinion shaft. Do not drive the lock pin in place yet.

b. While locking the side gear with a wedge or equivalent, measure the differential gear backlash with a dial indicator on the pinion gear. The differential gear backlash for the 2.0L, 2.4L and 2.6L engines standard specification is 0.0004–0.0030 in. The standard specification for the 3.0L engine is 0–0.0030 in. The service limit is 0.008 in. on all engines.

c. If the differential gear backlash exceeds the limit adjust the backlash by installing thicker side gear thrust spacers. If adjustment is not possible replace the side gears and pinion gears as a set.

20. Install the thrust block. Align the pinion shaft lock pin hole with the differential case lock pin hole.

21. Drive the lock pin in and stake the pin with a suitable tool in 2 different locations.

22. Install the drive gear onto the differential case with matchmarks in the correct position. Torque (with locking adhesive or equivalent on threads) drive gear attaching bolts to 58–65 ft. lbs. on conventional and limited slip differentials in a diagonal sequence.

23. Press fit the side bearing inner races to the differential case using suitable tools.

24. Install the differential case assembly.

25. Install the carrier (bearing) caps with their mating marks in line with the marks on the carriers and finger-tighten the 4 set bolts.

26. Install the side bearing nuts and tighten the carrier cap bolts to 40–50 ft. lbs. on all engines.

27. Screw in the side bearing nuts to adjust the final drive gear backlash. Each nut should be tightened to the state just before preloading of the side bearing.

28. Attach a dial indicator to the ring gear teeth and measure the final drive gear backlash in 4 different locations. The final drive gear backlash standard specification for 2.0L, 2.4L and 2.6L engines is 0.0043–0.0063 inch. The standard specification for 3.0L engine is 0.0051–0.0071 inch.

NOTE: If the backlash has to be adjusted, loosen the bearing nut on the back side of the ring gear and tighten the bearing nut on the teeth side by the same amount.

29. After adjusting backlash, tighten the bearing nuts ½ pitch. One pitch is the space between 2 adjacent holes on the side of the bearing nut.

30. Again measure the backlash and install a 1 or 2 pronged lock plate whichever lines up with the bearing nut holes. Tighten the lock plate bolts to 11–16 ft. lbs.

31. Measure the ring gear runout in 2 or more locations. Runout should be 0.002 in. or less on all engines.

32. If necessary make a ring gear tooth pattern check. Apply gear oil to all moving parts and use sealant and/or gasket when assembling to the axle housing.

NISSAN

Front Drive Axle

Inspection Before Disassembly

1. Position the removed differential carrier assembly in a suitable holding fixture.

2. Check total preload by turning drive pinion in booth directions several times to set bearings. Using accurate dial-type torque wrench. The standard specification for model R180 and R180A differential carriers is 8.7–20 inch lbs. of turning torque. The standard specification for model R200A is 11–20 inch lbs. of turning torque.

3. Check the backlash of ring gear with a dial indicator at several points. The standard specification for ring gear to drive pinion backlash is 0.0051–0.0071 in., on all vehicles.

4. Check runout of ring gear with a dial indicator at several points. The standard specification is 0.0020 in. of runout for R180A and R200A models. The standard specification is 0.0030 in. of runout for R180 model.

5. Using suitable equipment check differential tooth contact for correct pattern as follows:

a. Thoroughly clean ring gear and drive pinion teeth.

b. Apply gear marking compound to several teeth on the ring gear drive side.

c. Hold companion flange steady by hand and rotate the ring gear in both directions.

d. Check contact marks left on the ring gear assembly. Gear tooth contact pattern check is necessary to verify correct relationship between ring gear and drive pinion.

6. On R180 model, check backlash of side gear. Using a thickness gauge, measure clearance between side gear and differential case. The standard specification is 0.006 in. of side gear clearance.

Disassembly and Assembly

1. Position the removed differential carrier assembly in a suitable holding fixture.

2. On R180A and R200A models remove the extension tube

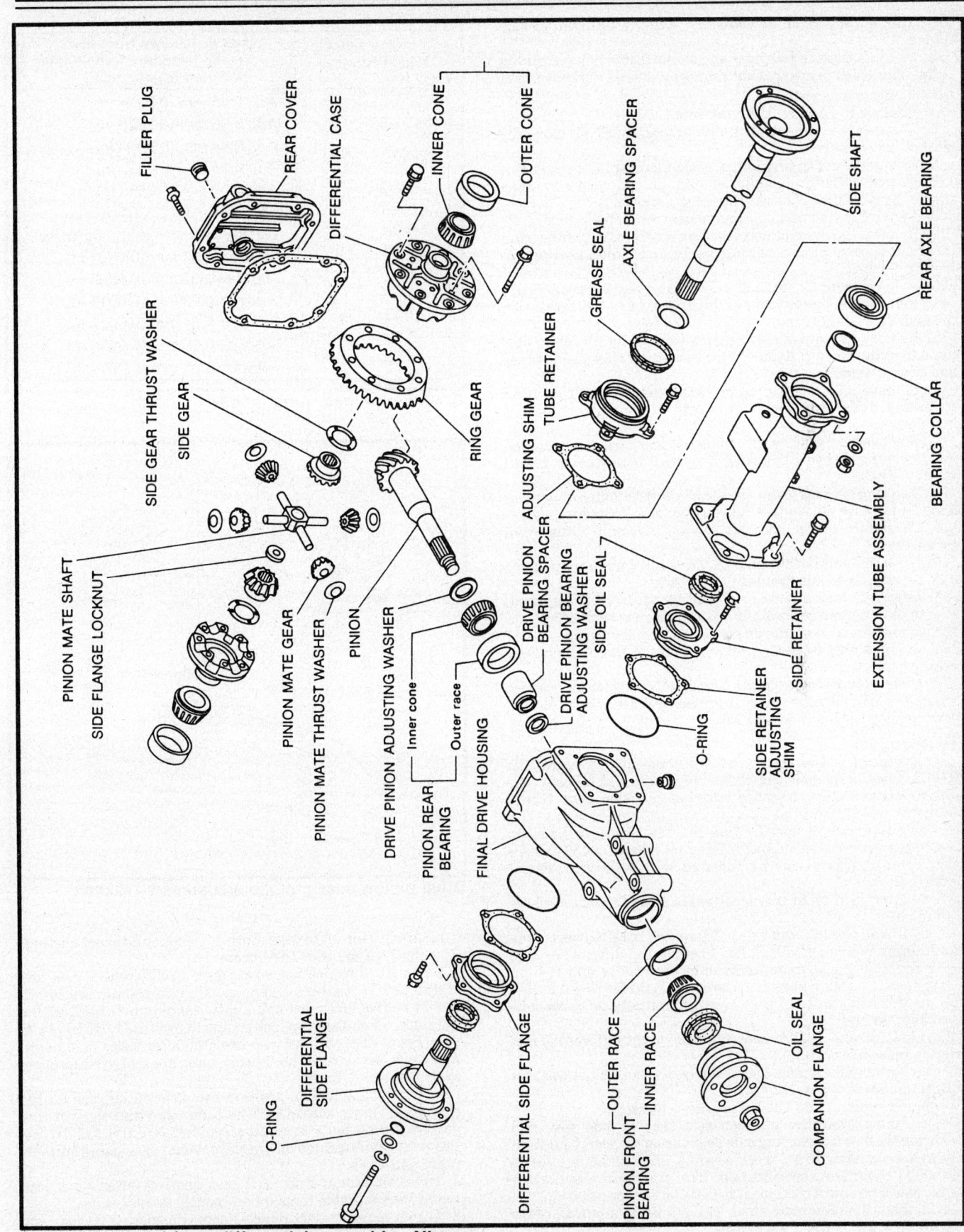

Exploded view of front differential assembly — Nissan

and differential side shaft assembly. Remove differential side flanges.

3. Matchmark side retainers and shims (some have retaining bolts) with paint to ensure that they are replaced in proper position during reassembly.

4. Remove the differential case from the final drive housing.

5. Remove the side bearing outer races. Mark all parts for correct installation.

6. Remove the side bearing oil seals using suitable puller.

7. Attach a flange holding wrench or equivalent to keep flange from turning. Loosen the drive pinion nut.

8. Remove the companion flange using suitable puller.

9. Remove the drive pinion together with pinion rear bearing inner cone, drive pinion bearing spacer and pinion bearing adjusting washer.

10. Remove front oil seal and pinion front bearing inner cone.

11. Remove the pinion front and rear bearing outer races with brass drift from housing.

12. Remove the pinion rear bearing inner cone and drive pinion adjusting washer. Remove rear bearing with suitable press and separator plate.

13. Remove side bearing inner race assembly with a puller from the differential carrier. Mark all parts for correct installation.

14. Remove ring gear by spreading out lock straps if equipped and loosening ring gear bolts in a criss-cross pattern. Remove all retaining bolts.

15. Tap ring gear off gear case using a soft hammer or equivalent. Tap evenly all around to keep ring gear from binding.

16. On R180A model, separate the left and right differential case halves.

17. On R180 and R200A models, drive out pinion mate shaft lock pin with drift pin from ring gear side.

18. Draw out pinion mate shaft and thrust block if equipped. Rotate pinion mate gears out of case and remove side gears and thrust washers. Put marks on gears and thrust washers so they can be reinstalled in their original positions from which they were removed.

19. Clean disassembled parts completely. Repair or replace any damaged or faulty parts. If replacing drive pinion or ring gear, replace with a new gear set.

To assemble:

20. Assembly is the reverse of the removal procedure. On R180A model, assemble the differential carrier as follows:

   a. Measure the clearance between the side gear thrust washer and differential case.

   b. The standard specification for the clearance between side gear thrust washer and differential case is 0.0039–0.0079 in. The clearance can be adjusted with side gear thrust washer.

   c. Apply gear oil to gear tooth surfaces and thrust surfaces and check to see they turn properly.

   d. Install the left and right differential case halves torque retaining bolts to 45–55 ft. lbs. Position the differential case on the ring gear. Apply Locktite or equivalent and tighten ring gear retaining bolts to (criss-cross fashion) 75–90 ft. lbs.

   e. Press fit side bearings on the differential case using suitable press and tools.

21. On R180 and R220A models, assemble the differential carrier as follows:

   a. Install pinion mate gears, side gears and thrust washers into differential case.

   b. Fit pinion mate shaft and thrust block.

   c. Adjust clearance between rear face of side gear and thrust washer by selecting side gear thrust washer. The standard specification for clearance on R200A model is 0.0039–0.0079 in. specification. The standard specification for clearance on R180 model is 0–0.006 in. specification.

   d. Install pinion mate shaft lock pin using a punch. Make sure lock pin is flush with case.

Pinion Head Height Number	Add or Remove from the Standard Pinion Height Washer Thickness Measurement
−6	Add 0.06 mm (0.0024 in)
−5	Add 0.05 mm (0.0020 in)
−4	Add 0.04 mm (0.0016 in)
−3	Add 0.03 mm (0.0012 in)
−2	Add 0.02 mm (0.0008 in)
−1	Add 0.01 mm (0.0004 in)
0	Use the selected washer thickness
+1	Subtract 0.01 mm (0.0004 in)
+2	Subtract 0.02 mm (0.0008 in)
+3	Subtract 0.03 mm (0.0012 in)
+4	Subtract 0.04 mm (0.0016 in)
+5	Subtract 0.05 mm (0.0020 in)
+6	Subtract 0.06 mm (0.0024 in)

Drive pinion gear height chart—Nissan

Drive pinion gear preload adjustment—Nissan

   e. Apply gear oil to gear tooth surfaces and thrust surfaces and check to see they turn properly.

   f. On R180 model, place ring gear on differential case and install new lock straps and bolts. Tighten bolts to 90–100 ft. lbs. in a criss-cross fashion, lightly tapping bolt head with a hammer. Then bend up lock straps to lock the bolts in place.

   g. Press fit front and rear bearing outer races using suitable tools. Make sure the bearing races are seated squarely in their respective bores.

   h. On R200A model, position the differential case on the ring gear. Apply thread locking compound and tighten ring gear retaining bolts to (criss-cross fashion) 100–115 ft. lbs. Press fit side bearings on the differential case using suitable press and tools.

22. Press fit pinion front and rear bearing outer races into housing with suitable tools on all models as necessary.

23. On all models select pinion bearing adjusting washer and drive pinion bearing spacer as follows:

a. Make sure all parts are clean and that bearings are well lubricate. Assemble the pinion gear bearings into the pinion preload shim selector tool J–34309 or equivalent. Make sure the front and rear bearings are in the correct position on the special tool (rear bearing first).

b. Install the pinion preload shim selector tool or equivalent into the final drive axle housing. Make sure the pinion height gauge will make a full turn and tighten the 2 sections by hand. Turn the special tool with bearings installed on it several times to seat the bearings.

c. Measure the turning torque at the end of the tool with a torque wrench. The standard specification for the R180A model is 5–9 inch lbs. The standard specification for the R200A model is 9–11 inch lbs. The standard specification for the R180 model is 8–15 inch lbs.

d. Place correct pinion height adapter (each model has different pinion height adapter) onto the gauge plate and tighten it by hand.

e. Insert the pinion bearing adjusting spacer squarely into the recessed portion of the correct special tool. Select the correct thickness of the pinion bearing preload adjusting washer using a standard specification plus the distance between spacer and gauge anvil tool. The exact measurement you get with the standard specification and distance between spacer and special tool is the thickness of the adjusting washer required. The standard specification for the R180A model is 0.24 in. or 0.138 in. for the R200A model. The standard specification is 0.118 in. for R180 model.

f. On R180A model position the side bearing discs tool J–25269–4 and arbor firmly in the side bearing bores. On R200A model install tool as previous described and torque the side bearing cap bolts to 65–75 ft. lbs.

g. Select the correct standard pinion height adjusting washer thickness using a standard specification plus the distance between pinion height adapter tool and the arbor. The standard specification for the R180A and R200A models is 0.12 in. On R180 model use the appropriate service tool for this operation and measure the thickness of the lead washer.

h. Correct the pinion height washer size by referring to the pinion head number. There are 2 numbers on the pinion gear. The first one refers to the pinion and ring gear as a matched set and the number should be the same on the ring gear. The second number is the pinion head height number and it refers to the ideal pinion height for proper operation. Use this number to determine the correct pinion height washer. Select the correct pinion height washer and remove the special tools with pinion bearings from housing.

24. Install pinion height adjusting washer in drive pinion, bevel side toward gear and press fit rear bearing inner race in it, using press and special tools.

25. Lubricate front bearing with gear oil and place it in gear housing.

26. Carefully fit a new oil seal into carrier. Make sure oil seal is flush with end of carrier and apply multi-purpose grease into cavity between lips.

27. Install the drive pinion bearing spacer, pinion bearing adjusting washer and drive pinion in housing.

28. Install companion flange into drive pinion by tapping with a soft hammer or equivalent.

29. Hold companion flange and temporarily tighten pinion nut, until there is no axial play. Check that threaded portion of drive pinion and pinion nut are free from oil or grease. Tighten pinion nut by degrees to the specified preload while checking the preload with torque wrench. Preload with oil seal is 8–15 inch lbs. for R180 and R180A models or 10–15 inch lbs. for the R200A model.

30. When checking preload, turn drive pinion in both directions several times set bearing rollers. After preload is reached torque pinion nut to 125–145 ft. lbs. on R180 and R180A models or 140–220 ft. lbs. on R200A model. Preload and final pinion nut torque must both be attained for correct operation of axle unit.

31. On the R180 and R180A models select the side retaining washer as follows:

a. Make sure all parts are cleaned and well lubricated.

b. Install the differential carrier and side bearing assembly into the housing.

c. Install all old bearing preload shims onto side bearing retainer. Install both bearing retainers onto housing and torque retaining bolts to 6–7 ft. lbs.

d. Turn carrier several times to seat bearings. Measure the carrier turning torque with a tool at the ring gear retaining bolt. The standard specification of pulling force at the ring gear bolt is 8–9 ft. lbs. Add or subtract shims as necessary. Increase shim thickness to decrease turning torque and decrease shim thickness to increase turning torque. Record correct shim(s) thickness and remove carrier and bearings.

32. On the R220A model select the side retaining washer as follows:

a. Make sure all parts are cleaned and well lubricated.

b. Install the differential carrier with side bearings and bearing races installed into gear housing.

c. Install side bearing spacer on the ring gear end of the carrier.

d. Install old preload shims using suitable tools on the carrier end opposite the ring gear.

e. Install side bearing caps and torque retaining bolts to 65–75 ft. lbs.

f. Turn carrier several times to seat bearings. Measure the carrier turning torque with a tool at the ring gear retaining bolt. The standard specification of pulling force at the ring gear bolt is 8–9 ft. lbs. Add or subtract shims as necessary. Increase shim thickness to decrease turning torque and decrease shim thickness to increase turning torque. Record correct shim(s) thickness and remove carrier and bearings.

33. On R180 and R180A model, press fit side bearing outer race into side retainer using suitable tools.

34. Install oil seals. Install differential case assembly. Place side retainer (correct marked position) adjusting shims and O-ring on side retainer and install on housing.

35. On R200A model install differential case assembly with side bearings outer races into housing. Insert the correct bearing adjusting washers between side bearings and housing. Drive in side bearing spacer with suitable tools.

36. Align mark on bearing caps and install caps torque to 65–75 ft. lbs.

37. Measure the ring gear to drive pinion backlash with a dial indicator. The standard specification is 0.0051–0.0071 in. If backlash is too small, decrease thickness of right shim and increase thickness of left shim by the same amount. If backlash is to great reverse the above procedure. Never change the total amount of shims as it will change the bearing preload.

38. Check total preload with torque wrench, turn drive pinion several times in both directions to set bearings. The standard specification for total preload is 9–20 inch lbs. for R180 and R180A models. The standard specification for total preload is 10–20 inch lbs. for R200A model.

39. On R180 and R180A models, if preload is too great, add the same amount of shims to each side. If preload is too small, remove the same amount of shims from each side. Never add or remove a different number of shims for each side as it will change ring gear to drive pinion backlash.

40. On R200A model, if preload is too great, remove the same amount of shims from each side. If preload is too small, add the same amount of shims to each side. Never add or remove a different number of shims for each side as it will change ring gear to drive pinion backlash.

41. Recheck ring gear to drive pinion backlash. Check runout of ring gear the standard specification for R180 and R180A models is 0.0031 in. or 0.0020 in. for the R200A model.

42. Check tooth contact pattern as necessary.

43. Install rear cover and gasket on all models. Install extension tube and differential side shaft assembly on R180A and

R200A models. Install the side flange in correct position on R180 model.

Rear Drive Axle

Inspection Before Disassembly

1. Position the removed differential carrier assembly in a suitable holding fixture.

2. Check total preload by turning drive pinion in booth directions several times to set bearings. Use an accurate dial-type torque wrench. The standard specification for model H190A and C220 models is 10–19 inch lbs. of turning torque. The standard specification for H233B model is 9–18 inch lbs. of turning torque.

3. Check backlash of ring gear with a dial indicator at several points. The standard specification for models H190A and C220 ring gear to drive pinion backlash is 0.0051–0.0071 in. or 0.0059–0.0079 in. for H233B model.

4. Check runout of ring gear with a dial indicator. The standard specification is 0.0031 in. of runout for all models.

5. Using suitable equipment check differential tooth contact for correct pattern as follows:

   a. Thoroughly clean ring gear and drive pinion teeth.

   b. Sparingly apply gear marking compound to 3 or 4 teeth of ring gear drive side.

   c. Hold companion flange steady by hand and rotate the ring gear in both directions.

   d. Inspect contact marks left on the ring gear assembly. Gear tooth contact pattern check is necessary to verify correct relationship between ring gear and drive pinion.

6. On all models, check backlash of side gear. Using a thickness gauge, measure clearance between side gear thrust washer and differential case. The standard specification is 0.039–0.0079 in. of side gear clearance.

Disassembly and Assembly

1. Position the removed differential carrier assembly in a suitable holding fixture.

2. Matchmark side bearing caps and shims if equipped to ensure that they are replaced in proper position during reassembly.

3. On H233B model, remove the side lock fingers and side bearing caps. Remove side bearings with suitable tools.

4. Remove the differential case from the final drive housing. Mark all parts for correct installation.

5. Attach a flange holding wrench or equivalent to hold flange from turning. Remove the drive pinion nut.

6. Remove the companion flange using suitable puller.

7. Remove the drive pinion together with pinion rear bearing inner cone, drive pinion bearing spacer and pinion bearing adjusting washer.

8. Remove front oil seal and pinion front bearing inner cone.

9. Remove the side oil seals as required.

10. Remove the pinion front and rear bearing outer races with brass drift from housing.

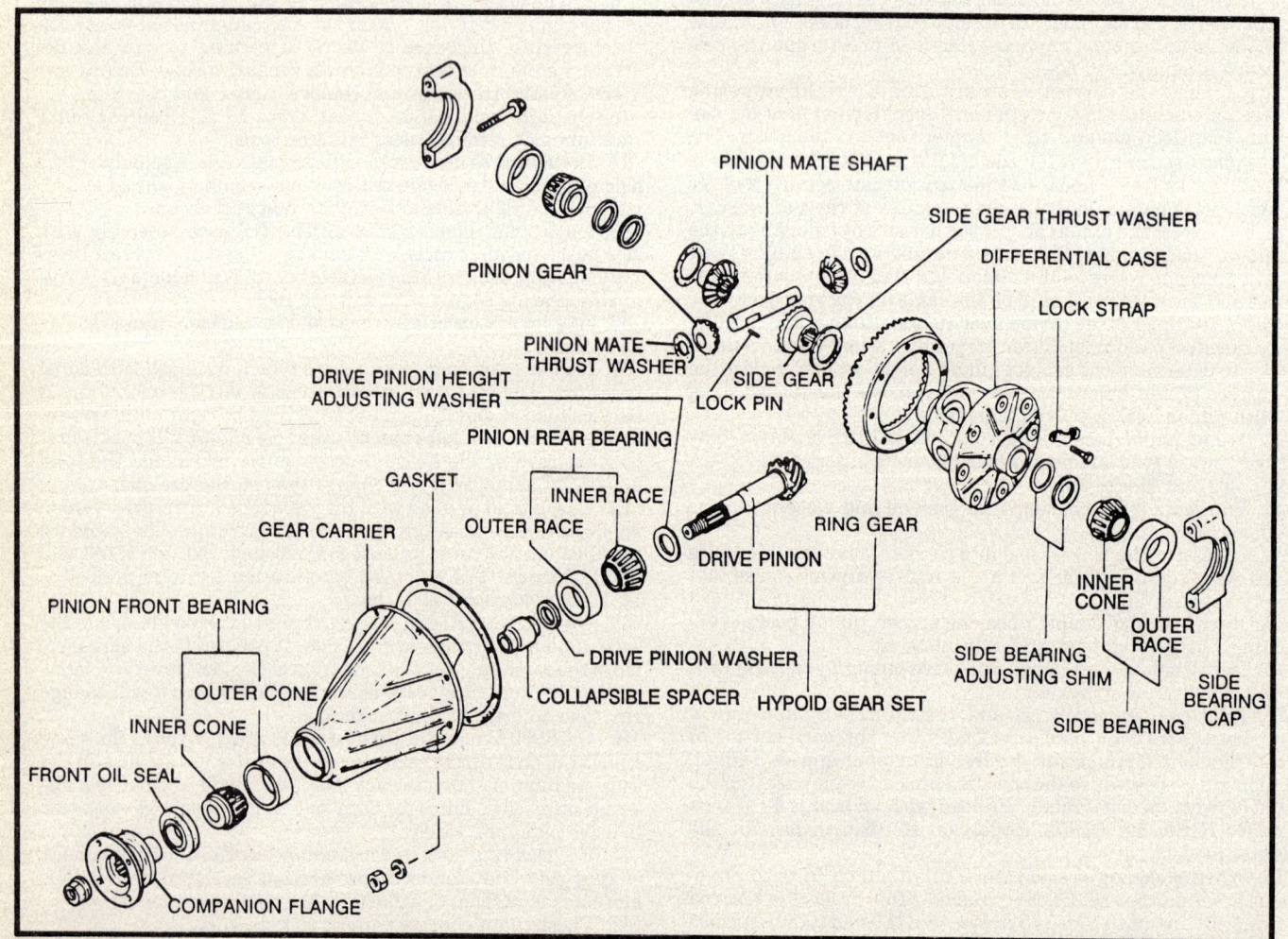

Exploded view of standard rear differential assembly—Nissan

Exploded view of limited slip rear differential assembly—Nissan

11. Remove the pinion rear bearing inner cone and drive pinion adjusting washer. Remove rear bearing with suitable press and separator plate.

12. Remove side bearing inner race assembly with a puller from the differential carrier. Mark all parts for correct installation.

13. Remove ring gear by spreading out lock straps if equipped and loosening ring gear bolts in a criss-cross pattern. Remove all retaining bolts.

14. Tap ring gear off gear case using a soft hammer or equivalent. Tap evenly all around to keep ring gear from binding.

15. On C200 and H233B models, separate the left and right differential case halves.

16. On R190A model, drive out pinion mate shaft lock pin with drift pin from ring gear side.

17. Draw out pinion mate shaft and thrust block if equipped. Rotate pinion mate gears out of case and remove side gears and thrust washers. Put marks on gears and thrust washers so they can be reinstalled in their original positions from which they were removed.

18. Clean disassembled parts completely. Repair or replace any damaged or faulty parts. If replacing drive pinion or ring gear, replace gears as a set.

To assemble:

19. Assembly is the reverse of the removal procedure. On C200 and H233B models, assemble the differential carrier as follows:

    a. Measure the clearance between the side gear thrust washer and differential case.

    b. The standard specification for the clearance between side gear thrust washer and differential case is 0.0039–0.0079 in. The clearance can be adjusted with side gear thrust washer.

    c. Apply gear oil to gear tooth surfaces and thrust surfaces and check to see they turn properly.

    d. Install the left and right differential case halves torque retaining bolts to 40–50 ft. lbs. Position the differential case on the ring gear. Apply thread locking compound and tighten ring gear retaining bolts to (criss-cross pattern) 100–112 ft. lbs. bend up lock straps if equipped.

    e. Press fit side bearings on the differential case using suitable press and tools.

20. On R190A model, assemble the differential carrier as follows:

    a. Install pinion mate gears, side gears and thrust washers into differential case.

    b. Fit pinion mate shaft and thrust block.

    c. Adjust clearance between rear face of side gear and thrust washer by selecting side gear thrust washer. The standard specification for clearance on R190A model is 0.0039–0.0079 in. specification.

    d. Install pinion mate shaft lock pin using a punch. Make sure lock pin is flush with case.

    e. Apply gear oil to gear tooth surfaces and thrust surfaces and check to see they turn properly.

    f. Place ring gear on differential case and install new lock straps and bolts. Tighten bolts to 100–112 ft. lbs. in a criss-cross pattern, lightly tapping bolt head with a hammer. Then bend up lock straps to lock the bolts in place.

    g. Press fit front and rear bearing outer races using suitable tools. Make sure the bearing races are seated squarely in their respective bores.

21. Press fit pinion front and rear bearing outer races into housing with suitable tools on all models as necessary.

22. On all models select pinion bearing adjusting washer and drive pinion bearing spacer as follows:

    a. Make sure all parts are clean and that bearings are well lubricated. Assemble the pinion gear bearings into the pinion preload shim selector tool J–34309 or equivalent. Make sure the front and rear bearings are in the correct position on the special tool (rear bearing first).

    b. Install the pinion preload shim selector tool or equivalent into the final drive axle housing. Make sure the pinion height gauge will make a full turn and tighten the 2 sections by hand. Turn the special tool with bearings installed on it several times to seat the bearings.

    c. Measure the turning torque at the end of the tool with a torque wrench. The standard specification for the H190A and C200 models is 9–12 inch lbs. The standard specification for the R233B model is 4–8 inch lbs. The standard specification for the R180 model is 8–15 inch lbs.

    d. Place correct pinion height adapter (each model has different pinion height adapter) onto the gauge plate and tighten it by hand.

    e. Insert the pinion bearing adjusting spacer squarely into the recessed portion of the correct special tool. Select the correct thickness of the pinion bearing preload adjusting washer using the distance between spacer and gauge anvil tool. The exact measurement you get with the distance between spacer and special tool is the thickness of the adjusting washer required.

f. Position the side bearing discs tool J–25269–4 and arbor firmly in the side bearing bores and torque the side bearing cap bolts to 36–44 ft. lbs. on the H190A model, 65–72 ft. lbs. on the C200 model or 70–76 ft. lbs. on the H233B model.

g. Select the correct standard pinion height adjusting washer thickness using a standard specification plus the distance between pinion height adapter tool and the arbor. The standard specification for the C200 is 0.138 in. The standard specification for the H190A is 0. The standard specification for the H233B is either 0.098, 0.118 or 0.138 in.

h. Correct the pinion height washer size by referring to the pinion head number. There are 2 numbers on the pinion gear. The first one refers to the pinion and ring gear as a matched set and the number should be the same on the ring gear. The second number is the pinion head height number and it refers to the ideal pinion height for proper operation. Use this number to determine the correct pinion height washer. Select the correct pinion height washer and remove the special tools with pinion bearings from housing.

23. Install pinion height adjusting washer in drive pinion, bevel side toward gear and press fit rear bearing inner race in it, using press and special tools.

24. Lubricate front bearing with gear oil and place it in gear housing.

25. Carefully fit a new oil seal into carrier. Make sure oil seal is flush with end of carrier and apply multi-purpose grease into cavity between lips.

26. Install the drive pinion bearing spacer, pinion bearing adjusting washer and drive pinion in housing.

27. Install companion flange into drive pinion by tapping with a soft hammer or equivalent.

28. Hold companion flange and temporarily tighten pinion nut, until there is no axial play. Ascertain that threaded portion of drive pinion and pinion nut are free from oil or grease. Tighten pinion nut by degrees to the specified preload while checking the preload with torque wrench. Preload with oil seal is 10–14 inch lbs. for H190A model or 10–15 inch lbs. for the C200 model. The preload with oil seal is 4–9 inch lbs. for H233B model.

29. When checking preload, turn drive pinion in both directions several times to seat bearing rollers. After preload is reached torque pinion nut to 95–220 ft. lbs. for H190A and C200 models. Torque the pinion nut to 145–180 ft. lbs. on H233B model. Preload and final pinion nut torque must both be attained for correct operation of axle unit.

30. On the H190A model select the side retaining washer as follows:

a. Make sure all parts are cleaned and well lubricated.

b. Remove the side bearings with suitable tools. Install side bearing old shims on the carrier side away from the ring gear.

c. Reinstall carrier side bearings using suitable press.

d. Install the assembly into the housing. Install side bearing caps and torque retaining bolts to 36–44 ft. lbs.

e. Turn carrier several times to seat bearings. Measure the carrier turning torque with a tool at the ring gear retaining bolt. The standard specification of pulling force at the ring gear bolt is 8–9 ft. lbs. Add or subtract shims as necessary. Increase shim thickness to increase turning torque and decrease

shim thickness to decrease turning torque. Record correct shim(s) thickness and remove carrier and bearings.

31. On the C200 model select the side retaining washer as follows:

a. Make sure all parts are cleaned and well lubricated with automatic transmission fluid.

b. Install the differential carrier with side bearings and bearing races installed into gear housing.

c. Install side bearing spacer on the ring gear end of the carrier.

d. Install old preload shims using suitable tools on the carrier end opposite the ring gear.

e. Install side bearing caps and torque retaining bolts to 65–72 ft. lbs.

f. Turn carrier several times to seat bearings. Measure the carrier turning torque with a tool at the ring gear retaining bolt. The standard specification of pulling force at the ring gear bolt is 8–9 ft. lbs. Add or subtract shims as necessary. Record correct shim(s) thickness and remove carrier and bearings.

32. On all models press fit side bearing outer race into side case retainer using suitable tools.

33. On H190A model install differential case assembly with side bearings outer races into housing. On C200 model insert left and right side bearing adjusting washers between side bearing and carrier. Install differential assembly and side bearing spacer using suitable tools.

34. On H233B model install the side bearing adjusters on gear carrier, screw adjusters lightly at this stage.

35. Align mark on bearing caps and install bearing caps torque to 36–44 ft. lbs. on H190A model or 65–72 ft. lbs. on C200 model. On the H223 model do not fully tighten at this point to allow further tightening of side bearing adjusters.

36. On the H190A and C200 models measure the ring gear to drive pinion backlash with a dial indicator. The standard specification is 0.0051–0.0071 in. If backlash is too small, decrease thickness of right shim and increase thickness of left shim by the same amount. If backlash is to great reverse the above procedure. Never change the total amount of shims as it will change the bearing preload.

37. On the H233B model tighten both right and left bearing adjusters alternately and measure the backlash and total preload at the same time. The standard specification is 0.0059–0.0079 in. Tighten side bearing caps to 69–76 ft. lbs. and install side lock clip in correct position.

38. On the H190A and C200 models check total preload with torque wrench, turn drive pinion several times in both directions to set bearings. The standard specification for total preload is 10–19 inch lbs. for H190A model or 10–20 inch lbs. for the C200 model.

39. On H190 and C200 models if preload is too great, remove the same amount of shims from each side. If preload is too small, add the same amount of shims to each side. Never add or remove a different number of shims for each side as it will change ring gear to drive pinion backlash.

40. Recheck ring gear to drive pinion backlash. Check runout of ring gear the standard specification for runout is 0.0031 in. on all models.

41. Check tooth contact pattern as necessary. Apply gear oil to all moving parts and use sealant and or gasket when assembling to the axle housing. On the C200 model install rear cover and gasket.

SUZUKI

Front And Rear Drive Axles

Disassembly and Assembly

1. Position the removed differential carrier assembly in a suitable holding fixture.

2. Matchmark side differential side bearing caps for correct installation.

3. Remove the bearing side lock plates and bearing caps. Remove bearing adjusters and outer races. Remove ring gear complete assembly.

4. Remove the flange nut using suitable tools to hold flange.

5. Remove the pinion shaft assembly from the carrier. Remove the pinion shaft oil seal using suitable tools.

6. Remove the outer pinion bearing from the differential carrier.

7. Remove the outer and inner pinion bearing races from the differential carrier.

8. Remove the ring gear bolts and remove the ring gear from the differential assembly.

9. Drive out spring pin (3 spring pins are used on 4 pinion type rear assembly) and remove the differential side gears, selective shims, pinion gears, thrust washers and cross shafts.

10. Remove the collapsible spacer and inner pinion bearing using tool and suitable press. Discard the collapsible spacer.

11. Clean disassembled parts completely. Repair or replace any damaged or faulty parts. If replacing drive pinion or ring gear, replace as a set. All taper roller bearings and races must be replaced as a set.

To assemble:

12. Assembly is the reverse of the removal procedure. Install the differential side gears, thrust washers, cross shaft and side gears with the correct selective shim in the differential case.

13. Measure the differential side gear end play. The specification is 0.005–0.14 in. select the correct shim to obtain the spec.

14. Drive the spring pin (3 spring pins are used on 4 pinion type rear assembly) for the differential side pinion shaft until it is flush with the case surface.

15. When correct end play is obtained install the ring gear to differential case. Torque the ring gear (special) retaining bolts to 70 ft. lbs.

16. Install the right and left side differential bearings using

J-21777-101
J-23597-1
J-8001-3
J-8001-2
J-21777-101
J-21777-102
J-23597-12
J-21777-43
J-21777-42
97MM
94MM
A

1. Bearing cap
2. Bevel ring gear
3. Bevel pinion
4. Collapsible spacer
5. Pinion outer bearing
6. Differential carrier
7. Pinion inner bearing

Pinion depth measurement—Suzuki

1. Shim
2. Side gear
3. Cross shaft joint
4. Pinion gear thrust washer
5. Cross shaft
6. Pinion gear
7. Pinion gear
8. Pinion gear thrust washer
9. Side gear
10. Shim
11. Pinion gear
12. Cross shaft
13. Pinion gear thrust washer
14. Differential case
15. Case bolt
16. Lock plate
17. Lock plate bolt
18. Adjuster nut
19. Side bearing
20. Gear set
21. Pinion selective shim
22. Side bearing cap bolt
23. Side bearing cap washer
24. Flange nut
25. Flange lock washer
26. Flange
27. Oil seal
28. Outer pinion bearing
29. Differential carrier
30. Carrier nut
31. Collapsible spacer
32. Inner pinion bearing
33. Differential case
34. Pinion gear thrust washer
35. Side bearing
36. Adjuster nut
37. Lock plate
38. Lock plate bolt
39. Cross shaft
40. Spring pin

Exploded view of standard rear differential assembly—Suzuki

Contact patterns	Diagnosis and remedy
Outer end / Drive side / Coast side / Inner end	**NORMAL**
	HIGH CONTACT Pinion is too far back, therefore, increase bevel pinion adjusting shim.
	LOW CONTACT Pinion is too far out from differential carrier. Decrease bevel pinion adjusting shim.

Contact patterns	Diagnosis and remedy
	Replace differential carrier.
	1. Check seating of bevel gear or differential case. 2. Replace pinion and gear set. 3. Replace differential carrier.
	1. Replace pinion and gear set. 2. Replace differential case.

Differential tooth contact pattern—Suzuki

suitable tools. Hold one side bearing when installing the other side bearing to prevent damage to any component.

17. Install pinion gear inner bearing race into the differential case using suitable tool and a press.

18. Install pinion gear outer bearing race into the differential case using suitable tool and a press.

19. At this point of the reassembly, set pinion depth. The pinion setting gauge provides in effect a nominal or zero pinion as reference.

20. Lubricate inner and outer pinion bearings with axle lubricant. While holding pinion bearings in the correct position install the pinion depth gauge.

21. Tighten depth gauge stud nut to 18 inch lbs. Rotate the gauge plate several times to seat the bearings. Retighten the locknut on stud of tool to 18 inch lbs.

22. Install special tool side bearing discs and arbor in the correct position in the side bearing bores of the housing.

23. Rotate the gauge plate until the correct area are parallel with the 2 side bearing discs.

24. Position a dial indicator rod over the lower step (94mm) of the gauging plate for front drive axle. Position a dial indicator rod over the higher step (97mm) of the gauging plate for rear drive axle.

25. Connect the dial indicator to the arbor and position gauge shaft over the dial indicator rod.

26. Install the side bearing caps and torque the bolts to 65 ft. lbs.

27. Position the dial indicator to the zero setting. Slowly rotate the arbor on the lower step (94mm) front drive axle or higher step (97mm) rear driver axle of the gauge plate to determine the point of the greatest deflection. At this point reset the dial indicator to zero setting.

28. Slowly rotate the arbor until the dial indicator is no longer on the gauge plate.

29. Record the dial indicator reading. This reading indicates the selective shim required for the correct pinion depth. The selective shims range from 0.012–0.050 in.

30. Install the correct pinion shim on the pinion gear shaft.

31. Assembly the inner pinion bearing on the pinion gear shaft using suitable press plate and press.

32. Install new collapsible spacer on the pinion gear shaft.

33. Install the outer pinion bearing in the differential carrier using suitable tools.

34. Apply lubricant to the oil seal lip. Install the new pinion oil seal using a suitable seal installer or equivalent.

35. Install pinion flange, pinion washer and nut. Hold the pinion flange with a suitable flange holding tool while frequently rotating pinion to seal pinion bearings. Tighten pinion flange nut a little at a time until end play is taken up. Measure preload with torque wrench the standard specification for all applications is 11 inch lbs. of starting torque, not rotating torque. Exceeding preload specification will compress the collapsible spacer.

36. After final preload has be reached rotate the pinion several times to make sure the bearings have been seated. Recheck the preload specification.

37. Install the ring gear and differential carrier assembly, side bearing outer races, bearing adjusters and bearing caps to housing. Align all identification marks.

38. Rotate pinion gear to ensure the side bearings seat. Tighten bearing caps 15 ft. lbs. on the front and rear drive axle assembly.

39. Using suitable tool turn the bearing adjusters to push side bearings lightly from outside so outer races are in contact with inner races. Apply a small amount of lubricant to bearings. With dial indicator installed to differential carrier and carrier at 0.0 backlash (ring gear fully engaged into pinion gear) set or check preload. The differential side bearing preload is 0.002–0.006 in.

40. Rotate pinion gear to ensure the side bearings seat. Tighten bearing caps to 44 ft. lbs. on the front drive axle assembly or 65 ft. lbs. on the rear drive axle assembly.

41. Check backlash using a dial indicator installed to the differential ring gear. The standard specification for all applications is 0.008–0.015 in. If adjustment is necessary loosen one adjuster nut and tighten the opposite nut an equal amount. This will move the ring gear away from or toward the pinion gear and maintain side bearing preload.

42. When turning the side bearing adjusters the final movement must be made in the tightening direction to ensure correct side bearing preload.

43. Install the side bearing lock plates. Torque the side bearing lock plate bolts to 25 ft. lbs.

44. Paint the ring gear with gear marking compound and rotate the pinion flange to obtain a tooth mesh contact pattern.

45. Inspect pattern contact and adjust or service the assembly as required. After all adjustments and correct pattern contact is obtained stake the pinion flange locknut.

46. Apply gear oil to all moving parts and use sealant and or gasket when assembling to the axle housing.

TOYOTA

Front and Rear Drive Axles

Disassembly and Assembly

1. Position the removed differential carrier assembly in a suitable holding fixture.

2. Measure the side gear backlash while holding one pinion gear toward the case. The standard specification is 0.0020–0.0079 in. on all except Land Cruiser. The standard specification for Land Cruiser is 0.0008–0.0079 in.

3. Check ring gear runout. Maximum runout is 0.0028 in. on all except Land Cruiser. The standard specification for Land Cruiser is 0.0039 in.

NOTE: On rear axle assembly with 7½ in. ring gear the runout is 0.0028. On rear axle assembly with 8 in. ring gear the runout is 0.0039 in.

4. Hold drive pinion flange check ring gear backlash (several different locations). The standard specification is 0.0051–0.0071 in. on all except Land Cruiser. The standard specification for Land Cruiser is 0.0059–0.0079 in.

5. Inspect tooth contact between ring gear and drive pinion using suitable marking compound.

6. Using a torque wrench measure the (starting) preload of the backlash between the drive pinion and ring gear. The standard specification is 5–9 inch lbs. for all vehicles except Land Cruiser and Vans. The standard specification specification for Land Cruiser is 6–9 inch lbs. or 4–7 inch lbs. for Vans.

NOTE: On rear axle assembly with 7½ in. ring gear the drive pinion preload is 5–9 inch lbs. On rear axle assembly with 8 in. ring gear 2 pinion type the drive pinion preload is 8–12 inch lbs. or 4–7 inch lbs. on 4 pinion type.

7. The total preload standard specification is 1–3 inch lbs. for all vehicles except Land Cruiser and Vans. The specification for Land Cruiser is 3–5 inch lbs. or 2–4 inch lbs. for Vans. This measurement is total preload (starting) also adding drive pinion preload to the specification.

8. Loosen the the staked part of the flange retaining nut. Remove the nut using a suitable tool to hold flange. Remove flange using a puller or equivalent.

9. Remove the companion flange oil seal and slinger from the housing.

10. Remove the rear bearing spacer and rear bearing from the drive pinion.

11. Put alignment marks on the bearing cap and differential carrier.

12. Remove both bearing caps. Remove both side bearing preload adjusting washers.

13. Remove the differential case with bearing outer races (mark for correct installation) from the carrier.

14. Remove the drive pinion from the differential carrier.

15. Remove the front bearing from the drive pinion using a suitable tool and press.

16. Remove the drive pinion front and rear bearing outer races from the housing.

17. Remove the side bearing from the differential case using suitable puller. Puller jaws must align with notches in the differential case.

18. Remove the ring gear retaining bolts and lock plates.

19. Place matchmarks on the ring gear then using a plastic tool or equivalent separate it from the differential case.

20. Drive out the straight pin and remove the pinion shaft, pinion gears, side gears and thrust washers.

To assemble:

21. Assembly is the reverse of the removal procedure. Assemble the differential case by installing the correct (check backlash with dial indicator) thrust washer to side gears. Try to select washers of the same thickness for both sides. Install the thrust washer and side gears in the differential case.

NOTE: On some rear axle assemblies the differential case splits. The retaining torque for left and right case halves is 35 ft. lbs.

22. Temporarily install the side gear shaft. Measure the side gear backlash. The specification is 0.0020–0.0079 in. on all vehicles except Land Cruiser. The specification for Land Cruiser is 0.0008–0.0079 in.

23. Drive the straight pin through the case and pinion shaft. Stake the pin and differential case.

24. Clean the contact surface of the differential case before installing the ring gear to the assembly.

25. Heat the ring gear in oil bath to about 212°F. then quickly install the ring gear on the differential case. Caution should be used when performing this service operation.

26. Align the matchmarks on the ring gear differential case. Coat the ring gear bolts with gear oil, install the lock plates and retaining bolts.

27. After the ring gear cools down enough, torque the retaining bolts uniformly and little at a time. The standard specification torque for ring gear installation is 70 ft. lbs. on all vehicles except Land Cruiser. The standard specification for Land Cruiser is 80 ft. lbs. Stake the lock plates on all applplications.

28. Using a suitable press plate and press install the side bearings into the differential case.

29. Install the differential case onto the carrier assembly. Install the plate washers where there is no play in the bearings.

30. Install the bearing caps using a dial indicator measure the runout of the ring gear. The specification for runout is 0.0028 in. on all except Land Cruiser. The specification for Land Cruiser is 0.0039 in. After runout inspection is performed remove the assembly from the carrier.

SIDE GEAR SHAFT

OIL SEAL

SNAPRING

DIFFERENTIAL CARRIER

DRIVE PINION

SPACER

FRONT BEARING

CARRIER COVER

SPACER

OIL SLINGER

COMPANION FLANGE

WASHER

REAR BEARING

OIL SEAL

DIFFERENTIAL TUBE

SNAPRING

PLATE WASHER

SIDE BEARING

SIDE GEAR SHAFT

LOCK PLATE

DIFFERENTIAL CASE

STRAIGHT PIN

RING GEAR

SIDE BEARING

THRUST WASHER

SIDE GEAR

PINION GEAR

THRUST WASHER

PINION SHAFT

Side Bearing Cap

PLATE WASHER

Exploded view of front differential assembly—Toyota

NOTE: On rear axle assembly with 7½ in. ring gear the runout is 0.0028. On rear axle assembly with 8 in. ring gear the runout is 0.0039 in.

31. Install the front and rear pinion bearing outer races to the carrier.

32. Install the drive pinion assembly (rear bearing) and front bearing in housing. Install the companion flange with a suitable tool to hold flange in place.

33. Rotate the flange several times to seat the bearing. Adjust the drive pinion preload by tightening the flange nut. Use a torque wrench to measure the preload. The specification for preload (starting torque) is 10–17 inch lbs. on Pick-Ups. The specification for preload (starting torque) is 9–14 inch lbs. on Vans. The standard specification for preload (starting torque) specification is 11–18 inch lbs. on Land Cruiser. In order to measure the total preload, record this preload specification.

NOTE: On rear axle assembly with 7½ in. ring gear the preload (starting torque) is 10–17 inch lbs. On rear axle assembly with 8 in. ring gear 2 pinion type the preload (starting torque) specification is 16–23 inch lbs. or 9–14 inch lbs. on 4 pinion type.

34. Install the bearing outer races in the correct location. Install the differential case in the carrier.

35. At this point of reassembly, on all front drive axle vehicles except Land Cruiser use the following procedure:

   a. Insure the ring gear has backlash. Install only the plate washer on the ring gear back side.

   b. Snug down on the washer and bearing by pushing the ring gear into the housing.

   c. Hold the side bearing boss on the teeth surface of the ring gear and measure the backlash. The standard specification for backlash is 0.0051 in. Select a ring gear plate washers as required.

   d. Install both (as required) the adjusting washers and differential case into the carrier.

   e. Using a dial indicator, measure the ring gear backlash again to obtain the standard specification. Adjust by either increasing or decreasing the number of washers on both sides by a equal amount. Insure that ring gear has standard specification of backlash.

36. Adjust the side bearing preload by removing the ring gear adjusting washer and measure the thickness. Using the backlash as a reference specification select a correct washer to obtain the standard specification of backlash (0.0051–0.0071 in.) by increasing or decreasing the washer thickness on both sides by an equal amount.

37. Install the side bearing caps in the correct position. Torque the side bearing cap bolts to 58 ft. lbs.

38. Measure the total preload using a torque wrench. The total preload specification is 2–3 inch lbs. for all trucks except for trucks with automatic disconnecting differential assembly which is 4–5 inch lbs. The specification for vans 3–4 inch lbs. This measurement is total preload (starting) also add drive pinion preload to the specification.

39. At this point of reassembly, on rear drive axle vehicles and Land Cruiser use the following procedure:

   a. Install the adjusting nuts in the correct location in the carrier.

   b. Align the marks on the cap and carrier. Insure that bearing caps and adjusting nuts are installed properly.

   c. Torque the bearing caps bolts until the spring washers are slightly compressed.

   d. Tighten the adjusting nuts (equal amount on both sides) on the ring gear side until the ring gear backlash is 0.0051–0.0071 in. for all Pick-Ups and Vans rear axle assemblies and 0.0059–0.0079 in. on Land Cruiser.

40. Install the side bearing caps in the correct position. Torque the side bearing cap bolts to 58 ft. lbs.

41. Recheck the ring gear backlash.

42. Measure the total preload using a torque wrench. The total preload specification standard specification is 4–5 inch lbs. This measurement is total preload (starting) also add drive pinion preload to the specification.

43. On all applications inspect tooth pattern contact between ring gear and drive pinion. Adjust as required.

44. Remove the companion flange and drive pinion bearing. Install new bearing spacer on the drive pinion. Install the bearing.

45. Install oil slinger and new oil seal. The oil seal drive in depth is 0.059 in. for Pick-Ups, 0.0079 in. for Vans or 0.0039 in. for Land Cruiser.

NOTE: On rear axle assembly with 7½ in. ring gear the oil seal drive depth is 0.059 in. On rear axle assembly with 8 in. ring gear the oil seal drive depth is 0.039 in.

46. Using suitable tools, install the companion flange. Coat the threads of the new nut with lubricant or equivalent.

47. The torque specification for the companion flange is 90 ft. lbs. on Pick-Ups, 80 ft. lbs. on Vans or 180 ft. lbs. on Land Cruiser.

PROPER CONTACT

HEEL CONTACT   FACE CONTACT

Select an adjusting shim that will bring the drive pinion closer to the ring gear.

TOE CONTACT   FLANK CONTACT

Select an adjusting shim that will shift the drive pinion away from the ring gear.

Exploded view of rear differential assembly—Toyota

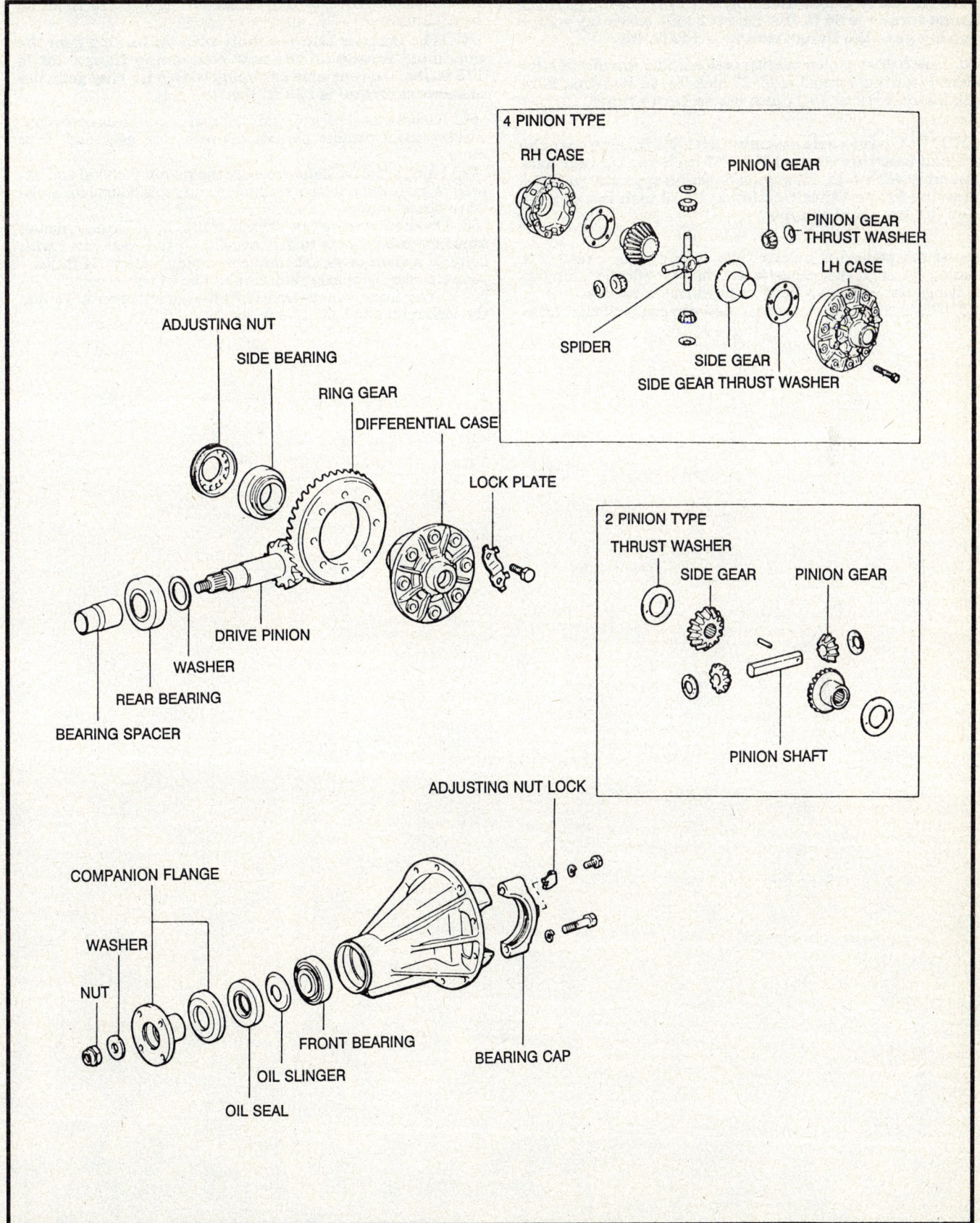

Exploded view of rear differential assembly—Toyota

4 PINION TYPE

RH CASE · PINION GEAR · PINION GEAR THRUST WASHER · LH CASE · SPIDER · SIDE GEAR · SIDE GEAR THRUST WASHER

2 PINION TYPE

THRUST WASHER · SIDE GEAR · PINION GEAR · PINION SHAFT

ADJUSTING NUT · SIDE BEARING · RING GEAR · DIFFERENTIAL CASE · LOCK PLATE

DRIVE PINION · WASHER · REAR BEARING · BEARING SPACER

ADJUSTING NUT LOCK

COMPANION FLANGE · WASHER · NUT · OIL SEAL · OIL SLINGER · FRONT BEARING · BEARING CAP

NOTE: On rear axle assembly with 7½ in. ring gear the flange torque is 80 ft. lbs. On rear axle assembly with 8 in. ring gear the flange torque is 145 ft. lbs.

48. Check drive pinion bearing preload. The specification for preload (starting torque) is 10–17 inch lbs. on Pick-Ups, 9–14 inch lbs. on Vans or 11–17 inch lbs. on Land Cruiser.

NOTE: On rear axle assembly with 7½ in. ring gear the preload (starting torque) is 10–17 inch lbs. On rear axle assembly with 8 in. ring gear 2 pinion type the preload (starting torque) specification is 17–23 inch lbs. or 9–14 inch lbs. on 4 pinion type.

49. If the preload is greater than specification, replace the bearing spacer. If the preload is less than specification, retighten flange nut (little at a time) until preload is reached.

50. The maximum torque on the new companion flange nut is 165 ft. lbs. on Pick-Ups, 175 ft. lbs. on Vans or 325 ft. lbs on Land Cruiser.

NOTE: On rear axle assembly with 7½ in. ring gear the maximum torque on the new companion flange nut is 175 ft. lbs. On rear axle assembly with 8 in. ring gear the maximum torque is 250 ft. lbs.

51. Recheck total preload and ring gear backlash as necessary. Inspect tooth contact pattern between ring gear and drive pinion.

52. Using a dial indicator measure the runout (vertical and lateral) of companion flange, maximum runout is 0.0039 in. Stake drive pinion nut.

53. On all front drive axle vehicles except Land Cruiser, install attaching components to axle housing. Install rear cover with suitable sealant or gasket torque retaining bolts to 34 ft. lbs.

54. On rear drive axle vehicles and Land Cruiser vehicles select correct locks, whichever wiil fit the adjusting nuts. Torque the lock retaining bolts to 9 ft. lbs.

FRONT END TROUBLE DIAGNOSIS

Condition	Cause	Correction
Hard steering	1) Steering linkage needs lubrication 2) Low or uneven front tire pressure 3) Incorrect front wheel alignment (manual steering)	1) Lubricate the linkage 2) Inflate tires to the recommended pressure 3) Check and align the front suspension
Poor directional stability	1) Steering linkage need lubrication 2) Low or uneven tire pressure 3) Loose wheel bearings 4) Incorrect front wheel alignment (caster) 5) Broken springs 6) Malfunctioning shock absorber 7) Broken stabilizer bar or a missing link	1) Lubricate the linkage 2) Inflate tires to the recommended pressure 3) Adjust or replace the wheel bearings 4) Check and align the front suspension 5) Replace the springs 6) Check and replace the shock absorber 7) Replace the stabilizer bar or link
Front wheel shimmy (smooth road shake)	1) Tire and wheel are out of balance or out of round 2) Worn or loose wheel bearings 3) Worn ball joints 4) Malfunctioning shock absorber	1) Balance the tires, check run-out 2) Adjust the wheel bearings 3) Replace the ball joints 4) Check and replace the shock absorber
Vehicle pulls to one side (no braking action)	1) Low or uneven tire pressure 2) Front or rear brakes dragging 3) Broken or sagging front spring 4) Incorrect front wheel alignment (camber)	1) Inflate the tires to the recommended pressure 2) Adjust the brakes 3) Replace the spring 4) Check and align the front suspension
Noise in the front end	1) Steering linkage needs lubrication 2) Loose shock absorber or worn bushings 3) Worn control arm bushings 4) Worn or loose wheel bearings 5) Loose stabilizer bar 6) Loose wheel nuts 7) Spring is improperly positioned 8) Loose suspension bolts	1) Lubricate at the recommended intervals 2) Tighten the bolts or replace the shock absorber 3) Replace the bushings or control arm 4) Adjust or replace the wheel bearings 5) Tighten all the stabilizer bar attachments 6) Tighten the wheel nuts 7) Reposition the spring 8) Tighten to specifications or replace
Wheel tramp	1) Tire and the wheel are out of balance 2) Tire and the wheel are out of round 3) Blister or bumb on the tire 4) Improper shock absorber action	1) Balance the wheels 2) Replace the tire 3) Replace the tire 4) Replace the shock absorber
Excessive or uneven tire wear	1) Underinflated or overinflated tires 2) Improper toe-in 3) Wheels are out of balance 4) Hard driving 5) Overloading the vehicle	1) Inflate the tire to the recommended pressure 2) Adjust toe-in setting 3) Balance the wheels 4) Follow proper driving techniques 5) Do not exceed the maximum recommended payload rating
Scuffed tires	1) Toe-in is incorrect 2) Excessive speed on turns 3) Tires are improperly inflated 4) Suspension arm is bent or twisted	1) Adjust toe-in setting 2) Follow proper driving techniques 3) Inflate the tires to the recommended pressure 4) Replace the suspension arm
Noisy shocks	1) Loose mounting	1) Check all mounting torques (bolt and/or nut)
Excessive road shock	1) Tire air pressure is too high 2) Loose wheel bearings	1) Deflate to correct pressure 2) Adjust bearings

FRONT END TROUBLE DIAGNOSIS

Condition	Cause	Correction
Excessive road shock	3) Camber adjustment is incorrect (negative camber contributes to road shock)	3) Adjust camber
	4) Weak or broken front spring	4) Replace the spring
	5) Loose suspension components	5) Inspect, repair, and adjust as necessary
Leaky shocks	1) Seals are worn out	1) Replace shocks
Weak shocks	1) Shocks are worn out	1) Replace shocks
	2) Loss of shock fluid	2) Replace shocks
Vibration and shimmy	1) Seal damage resulting in loss of lubricant, corrosion, excessive wear	1) Replace damaged parts as necessary
	2) Tires and wheels, or brake drums, are out of balance	2) Balance the tires and wheels, turn the brake drums
	3) Bent wheel or tire is out of round	3) Replace the wheel and remount, or replace the tire
	4) Wheel stud nuts torqued unevenly	4) Retorque the wheel stud nuts
	5) Loose steering linkage	5) Adjust, torque or repair as necessary
	6) Wheel is loose on the hub	6) Inspect the wheel bolt for damage Replace the wheel if needed. Replace all wheel studs
	7) Driveline universal joints are rough or defective (may be confused with steering vibration)	7) Repair driveline
	8) Malfunctioning shock absorbers	8) Replace the shock absorbers
Cupped tires	1) Front shock absorbers are defective	1) Replace the shock absorbers
	2) Worn ball joints	2) Replace the ball joints
	3) Wheel bearings are incorrectly adjusted or worn	3) Adjust or replace the wheel bearings (also replace the races)
	4) Wheel and tire is out of balance	4) Balance the wheel and tire
	5) Excessive tire or wheel runout	5) Check and compensate for runout

GENERAL INFORMATION

Wheel Alignment

For a vehicle to have safe steering control with a minimum of tire wear, certain established rules must be followed. These rules fix the values of planes, angles and radii relative to each other and to vehicle and tire dimensions. Some factors are built in, with no provision for adjustment; others are adjustable within limits. The entire system depends upon all value factors, separately and combined. It is therefore difficult to change some of the established settings without influencing others.

This system is called steering geometry or wheel alignment and requires a complete check of all the factors involved. Definitions of these factors and the effect each has on the vehicle are as follows.

STEERING WHEEL POSITION

Always check steering wheel alignment in conjunction with and at the same time as toe-in. In fact, the steering wheel spoke position, with the vehicle on a straight section of highway, may be the first indication of front end misalignment.

If the vehicle has been wrecked or indicates evidence of steering gear or linkage disturbance, the pitman arm should be disconnected from the sector shaft. The steering wheel (or gear)

CENTERING BAR

Steering wheel positioning

should be turned from extreme right to extreme left to determine the halfway point in its turning scope. This will be the spot on the gear that is in action during straight ahead driving and in

A = CAMBER (DEGREES POSITIVE)
B = KINGPIN INCLINATION (DEGREES)

C MINUS D = TOE-IN (INCHES)
E = CASTER (DEGREES POSITIVE)

Typical steering geometry

Caster/camber adjustment suspension using upper control arms

Caster angle showing both positive and negative caster

Typical steering geometry on turns

Camber adjustment suspension using struts

which position the steering gear should be adjusted. With the steering wheel in the straight ahead position and the steering gear adjusted to 0 lash status, reconnect the pitman arm.

CAMBER ANGLE

Camber is the amount that the front wheels are inclined outward or inward at the top. Camber is spoken of, and measured, in degrees from the perpendicular. The purpose of the camber angle is to take some of the load off the spindle outboard bearing.

CASTER ANGLE

Caster is the amount that the kingpin (or in the case of vehicles without kingpins, the knuckle support pivots) is tilted towards the back or front of the vehicle. Caster is usually spoken of, and measured, in degrees. Positive caster means that the top of the kingpin is tilted toward the back of the vehicle. Positive caster is indicated by the sign +.

Negative caster is exactly the opposite; the top of the kingpin is tilted toward the front of the vehicle. This is generally indicat-

ed by the sign —. Negative caster is sometimes referred to as reverse caster.

The effect of positive caster is to cause the vehicle to steer in the direction in which it tends to go. Positive caster in the front wheels may cause the vehicle to steer down off a crowned road or steer in the direction of a cross wind. For this reason, a number of our modern vehicles are arranged with negative caster so the opposite is true, which is that the vehicle tends to steer up a crowned road and into a cross wind.

Caster angle specifications are based on the vehicle load limits, which will usually result in a level frame. Since load requirements may vary, the frame does not always remain level and must be considered when determining the correct caster angle.

Because of their naturally straight running characteristics, front wheel drive vehicles are not overly sensitive to caster, therefore caster is not adjustable.

To measure the caster angle, the vehicle should be on a smooth and level surface. Place a bubble protractor on the frame rail and measure the degree of frame tilt and in what direction, either front or rear.

Two methods of determining caster angles are used. The first method is to determine the caster angle from the wheel with

Alignment measurement—example one

Alignment measurement—example two

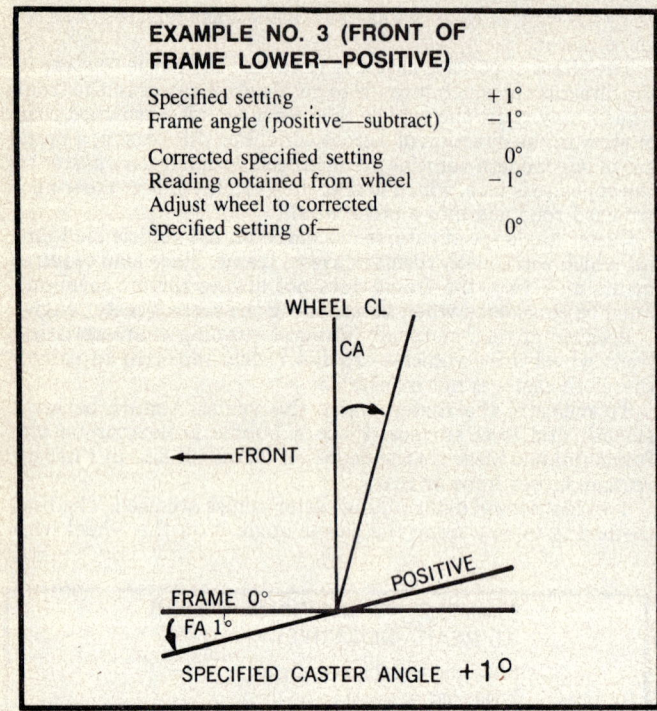

EXAMPLE NO. 3 (FRONT OF FRAME LOWER—POSITIVE)

Specified setting	+1°
Frame angle (positive—subtract)	−1°
Corrected specified setting	0°
Reading obtained from wheel	−1°
Adjust wheel to corrected specified setting of—	0°

Alignment measurement—example three

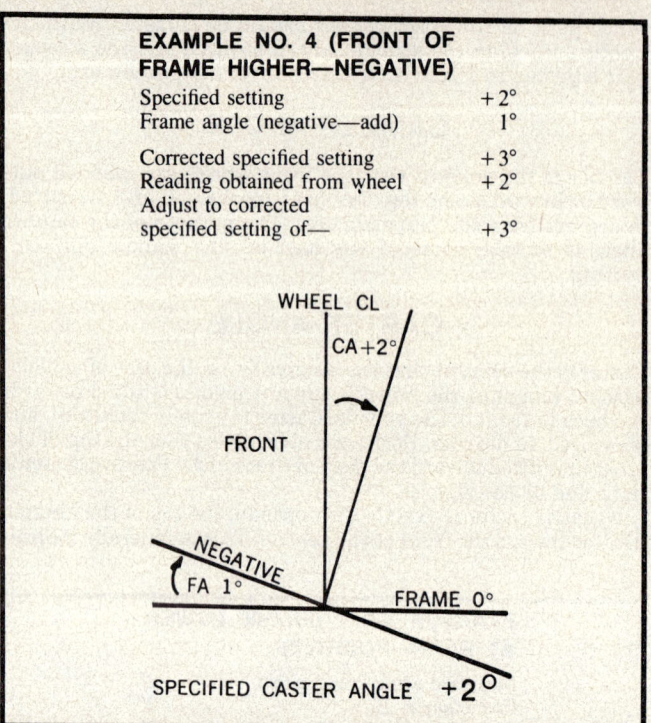

EXAMPLE NO. 4 (FRONT OF FRAME HIGHER—NEGATIVE)

Specified setting	+2°
Frame angle (negative—add)	1°
Corrected specified setting	+3°
Reading obtained from wheel	+2°
Adjust to corrected specified setting of—	+3°

Alignment measurement—example four

A. A "DOWN IN REAR" frame angle must be SUBTRACTED from a POSITIVE caster reading.

FRAME ANGLE = 1·1/4" DOWN
CASTER ANGLE READING = + (2·1/4°)
ACTUAL (CORRECTED) CASTER ANGLE = + (1°)

B. A "UP IN REAR" frame angle must be ADDED to a POSITIVE caster reading.

FRAME ANGLE = 1° UP
CASTER ANGLE READING = + (2°)
ACTUAL (CORRECTED) CASTER ANGLE = + (3°)

C. A "DOWN IN REAR" frame angle must be ADDED to a NEGATIVE caster reading.

FRAME ANGLE = 1/2° DOWN
CASTER ANGLE READING = - (·1/4°)
ACTUAL (CORRECTED) CASTER ANGLE = - (1·3/4°)

D. An "UP IN REAR" frame angle must be SUBTRACTED from a NEGATIVE caster reading.

FRAME ANGLE = 1 1/4° UP
CASTER ANGLE READING = - (1/4°)
ACTUAL (CORRECTED) CASTER ANGLE = + (1°)

Typical caster measurements

alignment equipment; the second method is to obtain the desired caster angle from the specification charts. The frame angle is then added to or subtracted from the caster angles as necessary.

METHOD ONE

1. Determine the frame angle.
   a. If the frame is high at rear; the frame angle is negative.
   b. If the frame is low at rear; the frame angle is positive.

Frame angle determination—method one

Frame angle determination—method two

2. Determine the caster angle at the wheel with the alignment checking equipment.

3. Add or subtract frame angle to determine caster angle.

a. Negative frame angle is added to positive caster angle.

b. Positive frame angle is subtracted from positive caster angle.

c. Negative frame angle is subtracted from negative caster angle.

d. Positive frame angle is added to negative caster angle.

4. Determine the correct caster angle and the specified caster angle. Correct the vehicle caster, as required.

METHOD TWO

1. Measure the frame angle.

a. If the front of the frame is down; the frame angle is positive.

b. If the front of the frame is up; the frame angle is negative.

2. From the specifications, determine the specified or desired caster setting.

3. Add or subtract the frame angle from the specified caster setting.

a. Positive frame angle is subtracted from the specified setting.

b. Negative frame angle is added to the specified caster setting.

4. Using wheel alignment equipment, obtain the measured caster angle from the wheel and determine the corrected specified setting.

KINGPIN INCLINATION ANGLE

In addition to the caster angle, the kingpins, if equipped, (or knuckle support pivots) are also inclined toward each other at the top. This angle is known as kingpin inclination and is usually spoken of and measured, in degrees.

The effect of kingpin inclination is to cause the wheels to steer in a straight line, regardless of outside forces such as crowned roads, cross winds, etc., which may tend to make the vehicle steer at a tangent. As the spindle is moved from extreme right to extreme left it apparently rises and falls. The spindle reaches its highest position when the wheels are in the straight ahead position. In actual operation, the spindle cannot rise and fall because the wheel is in constant contact with the ground.

Therefore, the vehicle itself will rise at the extreme right turn and come to its lowest point at the straight-ahead position and

Included angle, kingpin and camber measurement locations

again rise for an extreme left turn. The weight of the vehicle will tend to cause the wheels to come to the straight-ahead position, which is the lowest position of the vehicle.

KINGPIN INCLUDED ANGLE

Included angle is the name given to that angle which includes kingpin inclination and camber. It is the relationship between the centerline of the wheel and the centerline of the kingpin or the knuckle support pivots. This angle is built into the knuckle (spindle) forging and will remain constant throughout the life of the vehicle, unless the spindle itself is damaged.

When checking a vehicle on the front end alignment machine, always measure kingpin inclination as well as camber unless some provision is made on the stand for checking condition of the spindle. Where no such provision is made, add the kingpin inclination to the camber for each side of the vehicle. The totals should be exactly the same, regardless of how far from the norm the readings may be.

For example, the left side of the vehicle checks 5½ degrees kingpin inclination and 1 degree positive camber the total is 6½ degrees. Since both sides check exactly the same for the included angle, it is unlikely that both spindles, in this instance, are bent. Adjusting to correct for camber will automatically set correct kingpin inclination.

A bent spindle would show up as follows. The left side of the vehicle has ¾ degree positive camber with 5¼ degree kingpin inclination, the total being 6 degrees included angle. The right side of vehicle has 1¼ degree positive camber with 6 degree kingpin inclination, the total being 7¼ degrees included angle. One of the spindles is bent and if adjustments are made to correct camber, the kingpin inclination will be incorrect due to the bent spindle.

Since the most common cause of a bent spindle is striking the curb when parking, which causes the spindle to bend upward, the side having the greater included angle usually has the bent spindle. It will be impossible to achieve good alignment and minimum tire wear unless the bent spindle is replaced.

TOE-IN

Toe-in is the amount that the front wheels are closer together at the front than they are at the back. This dimension is usually measured, in inches or fractions of an inch.

Generally speaking, the wheels are toed-in because they are cambered. When a vehicle operates with 0 degrees camber it will be found to operate with 0 toe-in. As the required camber increases, so does the toe-in. The reason is the cambered wheel tends to steer in the direction in which it is cambered. Therefore it is necessary to overcome this tendency by compensating very slightly in the direction opposite to that in which it tends to roll. Caster and camber both have an effect on toe-in. Therefore toe-in is the last component on the front end which should be corrected.

TOE-OUT

When a vehicle is steered into a turn, the outside wheel of the vehicle scribes a much larger circle than the inside wheel. Therefore, the outside wheel must be steered to a somewhat less angle than the inside wheel. This difference in the angle is often called toe-out.

The change in angle from toe-in in the straight-ahead position to toe-out in the turn is caused by the relative position of the steering arms to the kingpin and to each other.

If a line were drawn from the center of the kingpin through the center of the steering arm tie rod attaching hole at each wheel the lines would be found to cross almost exactly in the center of the rear axle.

If the front end angles, including toe-in, are set correctly, and the toe-out is found to be incorrect, one or both of the steering arms are bent.

TOE-OUT   TOE-IN

CAMBER

SPRUNG OR SAGGING AXLE

Exaggerated examples of alignment problems

WHEEL BASE

Frame measurement point locations

Parallel wheel track measurement

Bent frame measurement point locations

TRACKING

While tracking is more a function of the rear axle and frame, it is difficult to align the front suspension when the vehicle does not track straight. Tracking means that the centerline of the rear axle follows exactly the path of the centerline of the front axle when the vehicle is moving in a straight line.

On vehicles that have equal tread, front and rear, the rear tires will follow in exactly the thread of the front tires, when moving in a straight line. However, there are many vehicles whose rear tread is wider than the front tread. On such vehicles, the rear axle tread will straddle the front axle tread an equal amount on both sides, when moving in a straight line.

Perhaps the easiest way to check a vehicle for tracking is to stand directly in back of it and watch it more in a straight line down the street. If the observer will stand as near to the center of the vehicle as possible, he can readily observe, even with the difference in perspective between the front and rear wheels, whether or not they are tracking properly. If the vehicle is found to track incorrectly, the difficulty will be found in either the frame or in the rear axle alignment.

Another more accurate method to check tracking is to park the vehicle on a level floor and drop a plumb line from the extreme outer edge of the front suspension lower A-frame. Use the same drop point on each side of the vehicle. Make a chalk line where the plumb line strikes the floor. Do the same with the rear axle, selecting a point on the rear axle housing for the plumb line.

Measure diagonally from the left rear mark to the right front mark and from the right rear mark to the left front mark. These diagonal measurements should be the same but a ¼ in. variation is acceptable.

If the diagonal measurements taken are different, measure from the right rear mark to the right front mark and from the left rear to the left front. These measurements should also be the same within ¼ in.

If the diagonal measurements are different but the longitudinal measurements are the same, the frame is swayed (diamond shaped).

However, in the event that the diagonal measurements are unequal and the longitudinal measurements are also unequal, and the vehicle is tracking incorrectly, the rear axle is misaligned.

If the diagonal and longitudinal measurements are both unequal but the vehicle appears to track correctly on the street, a kneeback is indicated.

NOTE: A kneeback means that a complete side of the front suspension is bent back. This is often caused by crimping the front wheels against the curb when parking the vehicle, then starting up without straightening the wheels out.

TIRE AND WHEEL DIAGNOSIS

Condition	Cause	Correction
Tires show excess wear on edge of tread	1) Under inflated tires 2) Vehicle overloaded 3) High-speed cornering 4) Incorrect toe setting	1) Adjust air pressure in tires 2) Correct as required 3) Correct as required 4) Set to to specification
Tires show excess wear in center of tread	1) Tires over inflated	1) Adjust air pressure in tires
Other excessive tire wear problems	1) Improper tire pressure 2) Incorrect tire/wheel usage 3) Loose or leaking shock absorbers 4) Front end out of alignment 5) Front wheel bearings out of adjustment 6) Loose, worn or damaged suspension components, bushings and ball joints 7) Wheels and tires out of balance 8) Excessive lateral and/or radial runout of wheel or tire 9) Tires need rotating	1) Adjust air pressure in tires 2) Install correct tire and wheel combination 3) Tighten or replace as necessary 4) Align front end 5) Adjust front wheel bearings 6) Inspect, repair or replace as required 7) Balance wheels and tires 8) Check, repair or replace as required. Use dial indicator to accurately determine runout 9) Rotate tires
Excessive vehicle vibration, rough steering, or severe tire wear	1) Loose or improper attaching parts 2) Overloading or unbalanced loads	1) Tighten or replace 2) Check wheel and tire specs against work load requirements. Recommend correct tire and rim. Check on loading procedure
Vehicle vibrations	1) Loose or worn driveline or suspension parts 2) Improper front end alignment 3) Excessive lateral runout (wheel or tire). Use a dial indicator to accurately verify runout reading 4) Bent or distorted wheel disc from overloading, road impact hazards or improper handling 5) Loose mountings—damaged studs, cap nuts, enlarged stud holes, worn or broken hub face or foreign material on mounting surfaces 6) Out-of-balance wheel and/or tire or hub and drum assembly 7) Out-of-round wheel or tire (excessive radial runout). Use a dial indicator to accurately verify runout reading 8) Wheel stud runout 9) Water in tires	1) Identify location of vibration carefully as it may be transmitted through frame making a rear end vibration appear to come from the front. Repair or replace loose and worn parts 2) Align front end 3) Replace wheel or tire 4) Replace wheel. Attempts to straighten wheel can result in fractures in the steel and weakening of the disc or the weld between disc and rim. Check loading and operating conditions and shop practices 5) Tighten and/or replace worn or damaged parts. Clean mounting surfaces 6) Determine the out-of-balance component and balance or replace 7) Replace the wheel or tire and check for overloading and unbalanced loads, rugged operating conditions, proper wheel and tire specifications 8) Replace hub or axle shaft 9) Remove water

TIRE AND WHEEL DIAGNOSIS

Condition	Cause	Correction
Wheel mounting is difficult	1) Improper application or mismatched parts, including studs and nuts 2) Corroded or worn parts	1) Follow manufacturers' specifications 2) Clean or replace
Wheel-rust or corrosion	1) Poor maintenance	1) Keep clean and protect with paint
Cracked or broken wheel discs. Cracks develop in the wheel disc from hand hole to hand hole, from hand hole to rim, or from hand hole to stud. Stud holes become worn, elongated or deformed. Metal builds up around stud hole edges, cracks develop from stud hole to stud hole. Related driver complaints: unusual operating noise or vibration and on the road failures	1) Metal fatigue resulting from abusive handling 2) Vehicle operated with loose wheel mounting	1) Replace wheel. Check position of wheel on vehicle for working load specifications 2) Replace wheel and check for: —Installation or correct studs and nuts, and recommend exact specifications —Cracked or broken studs, and replace —Worn hub face. Machine if not excessive, or replace if severe —Broken or cracked hub barrel, replace —Worn stud grooves, replace or install recommended serrated bolts —Clean mounting surfaces and re-torque cap nut periodically NOTE: Rust streaks fanning out from stud holes are a sure indication that the cap nuts are or have been loose
Cracks develop in rim base back flange (rim bead seat) or the gutter area (drop well radii)	1) Overloading or abuse 2) Improper use of tools	1) Replace rim or wheel. Check loading and operating conditions. Avoid over inflation of tires. Check specs for rim load capacity, working loads, tire size, ply rating and tire construction 2) Check mounting, demounting, and maintenance procedures
Damaged stud threads	1) Sliding wheel across studs during assembly	1) Replace studs. Follow proper wheel installation procedure
Loose drum	1) Stud too long	1) Replace stud with proper length stud
Broken studs	1) Loose lug nuts 2) Overloading	1) Replace studs. Follow proper torque procedure 2) Replace studs. Compare actual load against vehicle load ratings
Stripping threads	1) Excessive torque	1) Replace studs. Follow proper torque procedure
Rust streaks from stud holes	1) Loose lug nuts	1) Check complete assembly. Replace damaged parts. Follow proper torque procedure
Damaged lug nuts	1) Loose wheel assembly	1) Replace lug nuts. Check for proper stud standout. Follow proper torque procedure
Frozen lug nuts	1) Corrosion or galling	1) If corrosion is slight, wire brush away corrosion If corrosion is excessive, replace studs and nuts If condition persists, lubricate first three threads of each stud with a graphite-based lubricant NOTE: Do not permit lubricant to get on cone seats of stud holes or on cone face of lug nuts

Tire and Wheel Service

TIRE AND WHEEL BALANCE

There are 2 types of tire and wheel balancing procedures. They are the dynamic balance and the static balance.

The dynamic balance is the equal distribution of weight on each side of the centerline, so when the tire and wheel assembly spins there is no tendency for the assembly to move from side-to-side. Tire and wheel assemblies that are dynamically unbalanced may cause wheel shimmy.

The static balance is the equal distribution of weight around the wheel. Tire and wheel assemblies that are statically unbalanced cause a bouncing action called wheel tramp. This condition will eventually cause uneven tire wear.

Before the tire and wheel assembly can be properly balanced all deposits of mud, etc must be removed from the inside of the rim area. Stones and other foreign matter should be removed from the tire tread area. The tire and wheel assembly should be

Tire data explanation

inspected for any signs of external damage. Once these conditions have been met the tire and wheel assembly is ready to be balanced according to manufacturer's instructions.

TIRE ROTATION

To ensure that all tires wear evenly tire rotation should be done every 8000 miles. If a tire shows excessive wear the wear problem should be corrected before rotating the tires. If equipped with a temporary spare tire, do not include it in the tire rotation procedure.

LUG NUT TORQUE

When reinstalling tire and wheel lug nuts, be sure they are torqued properly and to the correct specification. Tighten the lug nuts in a criss-cross manner until all the lug nuts are snug against the wheel assembly. Torque the lug nuts to specification and in the proper sequence.

TIRE REPLACEMENT

Specialized tools and equipment have been designed for use in the replacement of a tire on multipiece rims. The manufacturer's instructions should be followed in the use of the machines in the mounting and dismounting of tires to avoid personal injury.

For the safety of the repairman, the word **DIP** should be remembered when working with tires and wheels.

1. **D**—deflate the tire before working on it.
2. **I**—inspect the rim, rings, lug holes and tires for damage and proper sealing.
3. **P**—protect yourself by placing the tire and wheel assembly in a cage before inflating it.

Tire and wheel balancing points

Tire servicing procedure

CHRYSLER CORPORATION

Wheel Alignment

Prior to any wheel adjustments, perform a preliminary inspection of the following:

1. Check that tires of the correct designated size are mounted on the rims.

2. Check the tires for wear, proper inflation and balance.

3. Check the brake disc and the wheel runout.

4. Check the front wheel bearings for looseness.

5. Check the steering linkage and the front suspension for looseness. Check the tie rod ends and ball joints for wear.

6. Check the operation of the front shocks. Jounce the front and rear of the vehicle several times and allow to settle to normal ride height.

7. Park the vehicle on a level surface. With the front wheels place in a straight-ahead position, center the steering wheel.

NOTE: To center the steering wheel, adjust the tie rods to shorten 1 side and lenghten the other side.

8. Make sure the steering box does not have excessive play and the wheel lug nuts are tightened to specifications.

9. Make sure the vehicle ride height is correct, the fuel tank is full and the spare tire is in the vehicle; all other excessive weight should be removed.

10. Use approved wheel alignment equipment for checking the wheel alignment.

Toe Adjustment

2WD DAKOTA AND ALL FWD VEHICLES

1. Center the steering wheel and clamp it into position; the wheel should be in the straight-ahead position.

NOTE: Adjust each front wheel to ½ of the total toe position; this will ensure that the steering wheel will remain in the straight-ahead position.

2. Loosen the tie rod adjustment locknuts and rotate the tie rod to obtain the specific wheel toe position.

NOTE: Be careful not to twist the tie rod-to-steering rod rubber boots.

3. After adjustment, torque the tie rod end locknuts to 55 ft. lbs. (75 Nm). Reposition the rubber boot and remove the steering wheel clamp.

Adjusting the toe position—Except 2WD Dakota and All FWD Vehicles

EXCEPT 2WD DAKOTA AND ALL FWD VEHICLES

1. Center the steering wheel and clamp it into position; the wheel should be in the straight-ahead position.

NOTE: If equipped with power steering, start the engine before centering the steering wheel. Also, the engine should be in operation while adjusting the toe.

2. Loosen the tie rod adjusting sleeve clamp bolts.

NOTE: Adjust each front wheel to ½ of the total toe position; this will ensure that the steering wheel will remain in the straight-ahead position.

3. Turn the tie rod adjustment sleeves to adjust the wheel toe position.

4. Avoid a binding condition at the tie rods. Rotate both adjusting sleeves equally, in the direction of sleeve travel; this will ensure that both ends will be centered, in their travel, when the sleeve clamp bolts are tightened.

5. Position the sleeve clamps so their ends are not located at the adjustment sleeve slot. Torque the clamp bolts to 17 ft. lbs. (23 Nm) for Dakota, 160 inch lbs. (18 Nm) for D350 and all 4WD models with heavy duty tie rods.

NOTE: Ensure that the clamp nut/bolt are positioned so they do not extend above the to the sleeve.

Adjusting the toe position—2WD Dakota and All FWD Vehicles

View of the caster and camber adjustment location—Dakota

Camber and Caster Adjustment
DAKOTA

1. Loosen the pivot bar mounting nuts. Move the upper suspension arm ends either in or out to obtain the proper camber and caster angles.

2. To change the caster angle significantly, move the rear position of the pivot bar in or out.

3. To change the camber angle significantly, move the front position of the pivot bar in or out.

NOTE: To increase the positive caster angle, move the rear position of the pivot bar inward—toward the engine. Move the front of the pivot bar outward, away from the engine, slightly until the original camber angle is obtained.

View of the caster and caster adjustment location—D Series and 2WD Ramcharger

CARVAN, TOWN & COUNTRY AND VOYAGER

The caster is not adjustable on FWD vehicles.

1. On each side of the vehicle, loosen the cam and through bolts.

2. To move the top of the wheel in or out, rotate the cam bolt.

3. To keep the cam bolt from rotating, hold it with a wrench; then, tighen the cam bolt nuts to 75 ft. lbs. (100 Nm) plus ¼ turn beyond the specified torque.

D SERIES AND 2WD RAMCHARGER

1. Clean the adjusting bolt threads.

2. Record the camber and caster measurements; then, loosen the adjusting bolt retaining nuts.

3. Adjust the camber angle as near as possible to the preferred angle.

NOTE: The caster should be the same on both sides of the vehicle.

4. Torque the adjusting bolts to 70 ft. lbs. (95 Nm).

W SERIES AND 4WD RAMCHARGER

NOTE: The wheel camber angle is preset at the factory and connect be adjusted. If the camber angle is not correct, the component(s) causing the incorrect angle must be replaced.

1. The caster angle can be adjusted by installing tapered shims between the front axle pads and the spring brackets.

2. Adjust the caster angle as near as possible to the perferred angle and should be the same at both sides of the vehicle.

Wheel Service

Tire Rotation

Rotate the tires periodically to ensure uniform wear of the tires. If the spare wheel is of a different type from the other 4 wheels, the 4 wheel rotation method should be used.

FORD MOTOR COMPANY

Wheel Alignment

The wheel alignment refers to the angular relationship between the front wheels and the steering axis. Caster, camber and toe are the 3 main, measurable, alignment parameters that most affect tire wear and directional stability.

Toe-In Adjustment

1. Loosen the adjusting sleeve clamp bolts at each end of the tie rod and link assemblies where they connect to the spindles.
2. Turn the sleeve until the proper toe alignment is achieved.
3. Center the clamps between the adjustment sleeve lock ring nibs on 2WD models or ³⁄₁₆ inch from the sleeve end on the 4WD models.
4. On the E150, E250 and E350 the adjusting sleeve must be positioned so the threaded end of the clamp bolts face downward. On the F150, F250, F350, F super duty and the Bronco, the left adjusting sleeve must be positioned so the threaded end of the bolts point towards the front of the vehicle. The right adjusting sleeve must be positioned so the threaded end of the bolts faces the rear of the vehicle.

WHEN SETTING TOE, THE ADJUSTING SLEEVE CLAMP BOLTS MUST BE POSITIONED WITHIN THE LIMIT OF ± 45 DEGREES OF THE CORRECT SETTING. THE LEFT SIDE BOLT SHOULD POINT THE THREADED END TOWARD THE FRONT OF THE VEHICLE. THE RIGHT SIDE BOLT SHOULD POINT THE THREADED END TOWARD THE REAR OF THE VEHICLE.

Clamp bolt settings—F150, F250, F350, F-Super duty and Bronco

CAMBER/CASTER SERVICE ADJUSTMENT CHART—F-SERIES 2WD

F-SERIES 4x2 ADJUSTABLE CAMBER/CASTER

Service Adjuster Type (Degrees)	Position Slot in Axle (Degrees)	LH Axle		RH Axle	
		Camber Change (Degrees)	Caster Change (Degrees)	Camber Change (Degrees)	Caster Change (Degrees)
1/2	0	− 0.5	0	+ 0.5	0
1	0	− 1.0	0	+ 1.0	0
1-1/2	0	− 1.5	0	+ 1.5	0
1/2	45	− 0.25	+ 0.25	+ 0.25	+ 0.25
1	45	− 0.75	+ 0.75	+ 0.75	+ 0.75
1-1/2	45	− 1.00	+ 1.00	+ 1.00	+ 1.00
1/2	90	0	+ 0.5	0	+ 0.5
1	90	0	+ 1.0	0	+ 1.0
1-1/2	90	0	+ 1.5	0	+ 1.5
1/2	135	+ 0.25	+ 0.25	− 0.25	+ 0.25
1	135	+ 0.75	+ 0.75	− 0.75	+ 0.75
1-1/2	135	+ 1.00	+ 1.00	− 1.00	+ 1.00
1/2	180	+ 0.5	0	− 0.5	0
1	180	+ 1.0	0	− 1.0	0
1-1/2	180	+ 1.5	0	− 1.5	0
1/2	225	+ 0.25	− 0.25	− 0.25	− 0.25
1	225	+ 0.75	− 0.75	− 0.75	− 0.75
1-1/2	225	+ 1.00	− 1.00	− 1.00	− 1.00
1/2	270	0	− 0.5	0	− 0.5
1	270	0	− 1.0	0	− 1.0
1-1/2	270	0	− 1.5	0	− 1.5
1/2	315	− 0.25	− 0.25	+ 0.25	− 0.25
1	315	− 0.75	− 0.75	+ 0.75	− 0.75
1-1/2	315	− 1.00	− 1.00	+ 1.00	− 1.00

Camber and Caster Adjustment

E150, E250, E350

Camber is not adjustable on the Econoline series. Caster can be adjusted by use of service kit E5TZ-3K064-A. This kit includes an adjustment cam that is to be added to the bottom of the front radius arm.

BRONCO, F150 AND F250 (4WD)

1. Measure camber with proper gauge, if out of specification continue to next step.
2. Raise and safely support the vehicle. Remove the front wheels.
3. Remove the upper ball joint cotter pin and nut. Loosen the lower ball joint nut to the end of the stud.
4. Strike the inside of the spindle near the upper and lower ball joints to break the spindle assembly loose.
5. Remove the camber adjuster sleeve.
6. Install the replacement service camber adjuster sleeve.
7. To increase camber, point the arrow on the adjuster outward. To decrease camber, point the arrow on the adjuster inward.
8. Partially tighten the lower nut to 40 ft. lbs. Install the new upper nut and tighten to 100 ft. lbs.
9. Replace the cotter pin and tighten the lower nut to 110 ft. lbs.
10. Install the front wheels and lower the vehicle.
11. Check camber and set toe as needed.

F250 4WD WITH LEAF SPRING SUSPENSION

The Caster adjustment on the F250-F350 4x4 with the leaf spring type suspension can be adjusted by inserting a shim between the axle and the spring.

F150, F250, F350 2WD WITH BALL JOINT SYSTEM

1. Measure the vehicle caster and camber. If not within specifications continue with the next step.
2. Raise and safely support the vehicle. Remove the front wheels.

WHEN SETTING TOE, THE ADJUSTING SLEEVE CLAMP BOLTS MUST BE POSITIONED WITHIN A LIMIT OF ± 45 DEGREES WITH THE THREADED END OF THE BOLT POINTING DOWN.

Clamp bolt settings—E150, E250 and E350

3. Loosen the pinch bolt at the upper ball joint and remove the adjuster from the axle.
4. Install the new adjuster and set as per the Camber/Caster Service Adjustment chart.
5. Tighten the pinchbolt to 65 ft. lbs. and install the front wheels.
6. Lower the vehicle and check alignment and toe specifications.

Wheel Service

Tire Rotation

To equalize tire wear, rotate the tires every 7500 miles. Proper tire rotation will ensure uniform wear.

GENERAL MOTORS CORPORATION

Wheel Alignment

Prior to making any wheel adjustments, perform a preliminary inspection of the following:
1. Check tires for proper inflation pressures.
2. Check front wheel bearings for proper adjustment.
3. Check ball joints, tie rod ends and relay rods for looseness.
4. Check wheels and tires for proper run-out.
5. Check steering gear for looseness at the frame.
6. Check shock absorbers for leaks or abnormal noise.
7. Check control arm or stabilizer shaft for looseness.
8. Check suspension and linkage components for excessive stiffness.
9. Use approved wheel alignment equipment for checking the alignment.

Toe-In Adjustment

1. Place the front wheels in a straight-ahead position.
2. Measure the toe-in with a proper gauge.

NOTE: When the tie rod ends are mounted ahead of the steering knuckle they must be decreased in length to increase toe-in. When the tie-rod ends are mounted behind the steering knuckle they must be lengthened in order to increase toe-in.

3. Adjust the toe-in by changing the length of the tie rod ends.

Camber and Caster Adjustment

C/K SERIES

NOTE: The control arm cannot be adjusted for caster and camber, without first removing the frame bracket knockout. The frame bracket knockout can only be removed by using knockout removal tool J-38794 or equivalent. To prevent any possible incorrect reading of the caster or camber, move the vehicle up and down a few times prior to inspection.

1. Raise and safely support the vehicle.
2. Support the lower control arms.
3. Remove the front wheels mark the adjustment bolt setting.
4. Using tool J-36202 or equivalent, increase the tension on the adjustment arm.
5. Remove the adjuster bolt and release the tension on the torsion bar.
6. Remove the nut, both cams, and the bolt from the upper control arm bracket.
7. Lift the upper control arm up and to the side to gain access to the inner portion of the bracket.

A. Caster
B. Camber
C. Remove shims from here to increase positive caster
D. Frame
E. Add shims here to ncrease positive caster
F. Subtract shims equally to increase positive camber

FWD

Caster and camber adjustment—S-Series and G- Series

C MODELS

K MODELS

1. Frame bracket
2. Upper control arm
3. Frame
4. Knockout with hole
5. Bolt
6. Cam
7. Nut

Knockout removal—C/K Series

1. Frame
2. Cam nut
3. Cam
4. Upper control arm

Caster and camber adjustment—T-Series

8. Using tool J–38794 or equivalent, tighten the T-bolt against the knockout until the knock out breaks free. Do not exceed 75 ft. lbs.
9. Repeat the procedure on the other frame bracket.
10. Install the control arms and partially tighten the bolts.
11. Measure the caster and frame angle and make adjustments as needed.

12. Tighten the upper control arm nuts to 82 ft. lbs. and the tie rod adjuster nuts to 14 ft. lbs.

13. Install the front wheels and lower the vehicle.

ASTRO, SAFARI, G VAN, S SERIES

Caster and camber adjustments are made by inserting shims between the upper control arm shaft and the frame bracket. Caster is adjusted by transferring shims from front to rear or from rear to front. Camber adjustments are made by adding or removing an equal number of shims from the front and rear of the cross shaft.

T SERIES

Caster and camber adjustments are made by moving the cams on the upper control arm frame attaching bolts. Loosen the upper control arm attaching nuts at the frame. Turn cam by turning bolt. Adjust camber and caster to specification. Tighten the nuts to 65 ft. lbs.

LUMINA APV

Caster is not adjustable. Camber can be adjusted by loosening both strut-to-knuckle bolts. Loosen the bolts enough to make adjustment and move the top of the wheel in or out to specification. Tighten the nuts to 140 ft. lbs.

R/V SERIES

Caster can be adjusted by adding and subtracting shims from the upper control arm-to-frame mounting bolts. By adding a shim to the front bolt and by removing a shim from the rear bolt, caster will be increased. Camber can be adjusted by adding or subtracting shims from both the front and rear upper control arm-to-frame mounting bolts equally. To increase camber add shims equally. Tighten bolts to 70 ft. lbs. on R1 models and to 105 ft. lbs. on all other models.

Wheel Service

Tire Rotation

Rotating the tires evens out tire wear and prolongs the tire life. Tire rotation should be performed every 7500 miles for maximum performance.

A. Caster
B. Camber
C. To increase caster add shims here
D. Frame
E. To increase caster subtract shims here
F. To increase camber add shims here equally

Caster and camber adjustment—R/V Series

JEEP

Wheel Alignment

Prior to making any adjustments perform a preliminary check of the following:

1. Check tire pressures and make sure the vehicle is parked on a level surface.
2. Inspect the steering gear to column shaft alignment.
3. Check the steering knuckle pivots, spindle and wheel bearings for looseness.
4. Check the brakes, shock absorbers and springs for sagging.
5. Check the steering gear to assure that it is centered.
6. Check the spring center bolts to assure that none are broken.
7. Check that all front suspension and steering bolts and nuts are tight.

Toe-In Adjustment

GRAND WAGONEER, PICK-UP AND WRANGLER

1. Measure the toe-in with an appropriate toe-in gauge.
2. Loosen the tie rod clamp bolts and adjust the tie rod in or out.
3. When done adjusting the toe-in, position the tie rod adjust-

Tie rod/drag link clamp bolts—Jeep SJ/YJ vehicles

Tie rod/drag link clamp bolts—Jeep MJ/XJ vehicles

ment sleeve clamp bolts so that they face upward and rearward.

4. Tighten the adjustment sleeve clamp bolts to 30 ft. lbs.

COMANCHE, CHEROKEE AND WAGONEER

1. Measure the toe-in with an appropriate toe-in gauge.

2. Adjust the toe-in for the right wheel by turning the drag link adjustment sleeve.

3. Adjust the toe-in for the left wheel by turning the tie rod adjustment sleeve.

4. When right wheel adjustments are completed, tighten the bolts on the drag link adjustment sleeve so the bolt thread ends face the rear of the vehicle. Tighten to 14 ft. lbs.

5. When left wheel adjustments are completed, tighten the tie rod adjustment sleeve bolts so the bolt heads face the rear of the vehicle. Tighten the bolts to 36 ft. lbs.

Camber and Caster Adjustment

GRAND WAGONEER, PICK-UP AND WRANGLER

The camber cannot be adjusted. The caster can be adjusted by installing the correct size, tapered shims between the front axle pads and the spring brackets.

COMANCHE, CHEROKEE AND WAGONEER

The camber cannot be adjusted. The caster can be adjusted by adding or removing shims at the rear of the lower suspension arms.

Wheel Service

Tire Rotation

To equalize tire wear, rotate the tires and wheels every 7500 miles.

CHRYSLER IMPORT

Wheel Alignment

Measure the wheel alignment with the vehicle parked on a level ground and with the front wheels place in a straight-ahead position. The front suspension, steering system tires and wheels should be serviced to the should be serviced to the proper condition prior to the measurement of the wheel alignment. Use approved wheel alignment equipment for checking the wheel alignment.

Toe-In Adjustment

1. Measure the toe-in with an appropriate toe-in gauge.

2. Adjust the toe-in by turning the left and the right tie rod turnbuckles the same amount in opposite directions. The toe-in value will decrease if the left turnbuckle is turned toward the front of the vehicle and the right one is turned to the rear.

3. Adjust to specifications and tighten the tie rod turnbuckles.

Camber and Caster Adjustment

RAIDER

1. Adjust the tire inflation pressure to the proper specifications.

2. Remove the front wheeling hub assembly.

3. Loosen the upper arm mounting bolts and adjust by increasing or decreasing the amount of the adjusting shims between the upper arm shaft and the crossmember.

4. Remove the upper arm from the crossmember and turn the upper arm shaft to adjust the caster.

EXCEPT RAIDER

1. Adjust the tire inflation pressure to the proper specifications.

2. Place the vehicle on a turning radius gauge and level the vehicle.

3. Adjust the camber by rotating the lower arm's shaft assembly on the Van.

4. Loosen the upper mounting bolts and increase or decrease the amount of shims between the upper arm shaft and the crossmember to adjust the camber and caster except on the Van.

Wheel Service

Tire Rotation

Rotate the tires periodically to ensure uniform wear of the tires. If the spare wheel is of a different type from the other 4 wheels, the 4 wheel rotation method should be used.

Tire rotation sequence—Chrysler Import

DAIHATSU

Wheel Alignment

Prior to any adjustments to the front wheel alignment, perform a preliminary inspection of the following:

    a. Check that tires of the correct designated size are mounted on the rims.

    b. Check the tires for wear and proper inflation.

    c. Check the brake disc and the wheel runout.

    d. Check the front wheel bearings for looseness.

    e. Check the steering linkage and the front suspension for looseness.

    f. Check the operation of the front shocks.

Toe-in Adjustment

1. Place the front wheels in straight-ahead position.
2. Align a suitable toe-in gauge with the center height at the rear side of each front wheel.
3. Apply center marks to each wheel, then take the measurement of distance A between the center marks on each wheel.
4. Slowly, move the vehicle forward until the center marks turn 180 degrees.
5. Take the measurement of distance A between the center marks at the front end.
6. The toe-in equals B minus A.
7. To adjust the toe-in, loosen the locknuts on the tie rod adjusting tubes at both sides of the vehicle and turn the tie rod adjusting tubes the same distance falls into specification.

Camber and Caster Adjustment

1. Position the wheel on a turning radius gauge.
2. Remove the wheel cover.
3. Align the forward end of the center rod of the camber, caster and kingpin gauge with the center of the halfshaft section. Bring the forward end of the center rod into contact with the hub body.

Marking the wheels for checking the toe-in—Daihatsu

4. The camber and caster may be adjusted by adding or removing adjusting shims located at the frame surface of the upper arm shaft.

Wheel Service

Tire Rotation

It is recommended that the tires and wheels be rotated every 7500 miles to ensure uniform wear.

View of the tie rod adjusting tube—Daihatsu

View of the camber and caster adjusting location—Daihatsu

GEO

Wheel Alignment

The wheel alignment refers to the angular relationship between the front wheels, the front suspension mounting parts and the ground. Generally the only adjustment required is toe-in.

Toe-In Adjustment

The toe is adjusted by changing the tie rod length. Adjust by loosening the locknuts first the rotate the left and the right tie rod by the same amount. In this adjustment the left and the right tie rod should become equal in length.

Camber and Caster Adjustment

The camber and caster cannot be adjusted for this vehicle. To prevent any possible incorrect reading of the camber or caster, move the front of the vehicle up and down a few times before inspection.

Tire rotation sequence—GEO

Wheel Service

Tire Rotation

To equalize tire wear, rotate the tire and wheels at 7500 miles

Toe-in adjustment—GEO

and every 15,000 miles thereafter. The tire and wheel assemblies should be rotated whenever uneven tire wear is noticed.

ISUZU

Wheel Alignment

The wheel alignment should be checked periodically to ensure proper wear of the tires and excessive wear of the suspension components.

Toe-In Adjustment

1. Place the front wheels in straight-ahead position.
2. Align a suitable toe-in gauge with the center height of each wheel at the front end.
3. Apply center marks to each wheel, then take the measurement of distance A between the center marks on each wheel.
4. Slowly, move the vehicle rearward until the center marks reach the rear end position.
5. Take the measurement of distance B between the center marks at the rear end.
6. The toe-in equals B minus A.
7. To adjust the toe-in, loosen the locknut on the outer tie rod end and turn the outer track rod the same distance right and left.

Camber and Caster Adjustment

1. The camber angle can be adjusted by the means of camber pins installed in position between the chassis frame and the fulcrum pins. Adding shims decreases the camber angle and removing shims increases the camber angle.
2. The caster angle on the 2WD vehicles can be adjusted by varying the length of the strut bar. Adjust with the locknut. Shims should not be used for this adjustment.
3. The caster angle on the 4WD and Amigo can be adjusted by means of the caster shims installed in position between the frame and fulcrum pins. Adding shims to the front side decreases the caster angle while removing shims increases the angle. Adding shims to the rear side increases the caster angle while removing shims increases the angle.

Steering Angle Adjustment

1. The maximum steering angle on the front wheels can be adjusted with the stopper bolts under the frame side members.

Measuring distance for toe-in adjustment—Isuzu

Caster angle adjustment—Isuzu 4WD and Amigo

2. Position each front wheel on a suitable turning radius gauge in a straight-ahead position.

3. Adjust the inside angle of each side with the stopper bolts.

NOTE: The maximum steering angles should be set after adjusting the front wheel alignment.

Tire rotation sequence—Isuzu

Wheel Service

Tire Rotation

Rotating the tires evens out tire wear and prolongs the tire life. Tire rotation should be performed every 7500 miles for maximum performance.

MAZDA

Wheel Alignment

Measure the wheel alignment with the vehicle parked on a level ground and with the front wheels place in a straight-ahead position. The front suspension, steering system tires and wheels should be serviced to the should be serviced to the proper condition prior to the measurement of the wheel alignment. Use approved wheel alignment equipment for checking the wheel alignment.

Toe-In Adjustment

1. Raise and safely support the front of the vehicle.
2. Turn the wheels by hand, mark a line in the center of each tire tread using a proper scribing tool.
3. Place the front wheels in a straight-ahead position and lower the vehicle.
4. Measure the distance between the marked lines at the front and the rear of the wheels.
5. To adjust, loosen the left and the right tie rod locknuts and turn the tie rods by the same degree.
6. Adjust the toe-in after adjusting the steering angle except on the MPV.

Toe-in adjustment on the vehicle—Mazda B2200 and B2600

Camber and Caster Adjustment

EXCEPT MPV

1. Position the front wheels on a turning radius guage.
2. Remove the front wheel hub on 4WD vehicles.
3. Remove the wheel cap and the wheel hub nut on 2WD vehicles. Attach a suitable gauge adapter to the hub.
4. Attach a suitable camber and caster guage to the hub or the adapter and measure the camber and the caster.
5. The camber and the caster are adjusted by adding or subtracting the amount of the shims.

MPV

1. Raise and safely support the front of the vehicle.
2. Remove the blocks that hold the mounting block to the fender.
3. Push the mounting block down and turn it to the desired position.
4. Adjust the camber and the caster by changing the position of the mounting block. Retighten the nuts to the specified torque.

Checking toe-in with a suitable gauge—Mazda

Location of the adjusting shims for the camber and caster—Mazda

Tire rotation sequence—Mazda

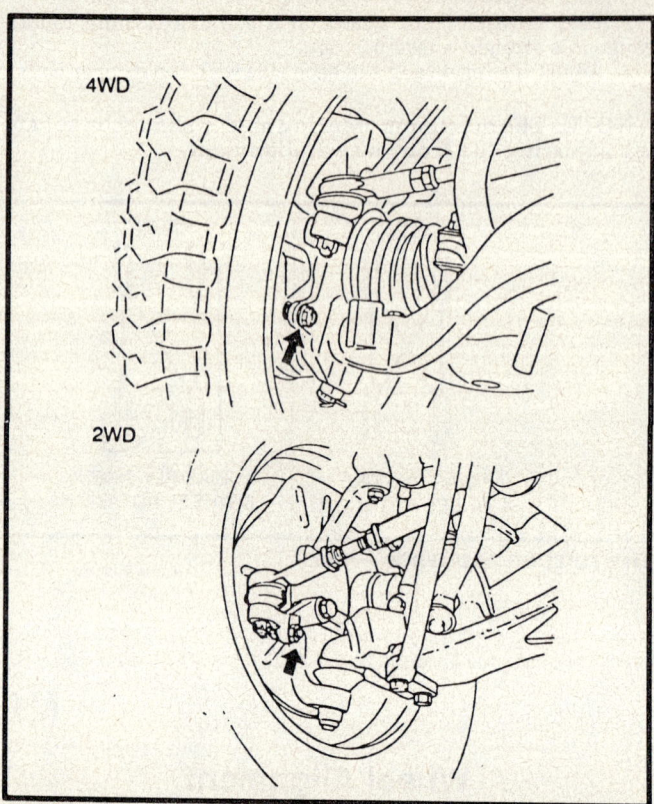

Checking the steering angle—Mazda 2WD and 4WD vehicles

Steering Angle

The steering angle is measured by placing the front wheels on a turning radius gauge. Adjust the steering angle by adjusting the bolt fitted on the steering knuckle arm except on the MPV.

Wheel Service

Tire Rotation

In order to prolong tire life and assure uniform wear, the tires should be rotated every 3750 miles. Do not include the temporary spare in the rotation.

MITSUBISHI

Wheel Alignment

Measure the wheel alignment with the vehicle parked on a level ground and with the front wheels place in a straight-ahead position. The front suspension, steering system tires and wheels should be serviced to the should be serviced to the proper condition prior to the measurement of the wheel alignment. Use approved wheel alignment equipment for checking the wheel alignment.

Toe-In Adjustment

1. Measure the toe-in with an appropriate toe-in gauge.
2. Adjust the toe-in by turning the left and the right tie rod turnbuckles the same amount in opposite directions. The toe-in value will decrease if the left turnbuckle is turned toward the front of the vehicle and the right one is turned to the rear.

3. Adjust to specifications and tighten the tie rod turnbuckles.

Camber and Caster Adjustment

MONTERO

1. Adjust the tire inflation pressure to the proper specifications.
2. Remove the front wheeling hub assembly.
3. Loosen the upper arm mounting bolts and adjust by increasing or decreasing the amount of the adjusting shims between the upper arm shaft and the crossmember.
4. Remove the upper arm from the crossmember and turn the upper arm shaft to adjust the caster.

EXCEPT MONTERO

1. Adjust the tire inflation pressure to the proper specifications.

2. Place the vehicle on a turning radius gauge and level the vehicle.

3. Loosen the upper mounting bolts and increase or decrease the amount of shims between the upper arm shaft and the cross-member to adjust the camber and caster.

Wheel Service

Tire Rotation

Rotate the tires periodically to ensure uniform wear of the tires. If the spare wheel is of a different type from the other 4 wheels, the 4 wheel rotation method should be used.

Tire rotation sequence—Mitsubishi

NISSAN

Wheel Alignment

Prior to any adjustments to the front wheel alignment, perform a preliminary inspection of the following:

a. Check the tires for wear and proper inflation.
b. Check the wheel runout.
c. Check the front wheel bearings for looseness.
d. Check the steering linkage and the front suspension for looseness.
e. Check the operation of the front shocks.

Toe-In Adjustment

1. Draw a line across the tread of the tire and set the steering wheel in a straight-ahead position.
2. Measure distance A and B at the same height as the hub center, this is the toe-in.
3. Adjust the toe-in by varying the length of the steering rods and turning the tie rod tubes clockwise and counterclockwise an equal amount.

Camber and Caster Adjustment

1. To adjust the camber and caster, increase or decrease the number of adjusting shims inserted between the upper link spindle and the frame.

NOTE: The camber, caster and the king pin inclination are preset at the factory and cannot be adjusted on the Axxess.

2. Do not install 3 or more shims at one place.
3. To adjust the camber, equalize the thickness of the front and rear shims by adding or subtracting shim(s).
4. To adjust the caster, make a difference between the front and rear shims.
5. When the caster is adjusted the camber angle changes and must be readjusted.

Steering Angle Adjustment

1. Set the wheels in a straight-ahead position.
2. Move the vehicle forward until the front wheels rest on the turning radius gauge properly.
3. Rotate the steering wheel all the way to the right and the left and check the turning angle.

Wheel Service

Tire Rotation

Do not include the T type spare and small type spares in the rotation. Make sure the wheel nuts are tightened to specifications when completed.

BASE LINE

LINE PARALLEL TO CENTER LINE OF BODY

A

B

θ

FRONT

TOE-IN = A - B

Toe-in adjustment—Nissan

FRONT

FRONT

FRONT

4 WHEELS

5 WHEELS

DUAL WHEELS TYPE

Tire rotation sequence—Nissan

SUZUKI

Wheel Alignment

The wheel alignment refers to the angular relationship between the front wheels, the front suspension mounting parts and the ground. Generally the only adjustment required is toe-in.

Toe-In Adjustment

The toe is adjusted by changing the tie rod length. Adjust by loosening the locknuts first the rotate the left and the right tie rod by the same amount. In this adjustment the left and the right tie rod should become equal in length.

Toe-in adjustment—Suzuki

Camber and Caster Adjustment

The camber and caster cannot be adjusted for this vehicle. To prevent any possible incorrect reading of the camber or caster, move the front of the vehicle up and down a few times before inspection.

Wheel Service

Tire Rotation

To equalize tire wear, rotate the tire and wheels at 7500 miles and every 15,000 miles thereafter. The tire and wheel assemblies should be rotated whenever uneven tire wear is noticed.

Tire rotation sequence—Suzuki

TOYOTA

Wheel Alignment

Follow the specific instructions of the equipment manufacturer the wheel alignment.

Toe-In Adjustment

1. Rock the vehicle up and down to stabilize the suspension.
2. Mark the center of each rear tread at spindle height and measure the distance between the marks on the right and left tires.
3. Advance the vehicle until the marks on the rear side of the tires come to the front.

NOTE: The toe-in should be measured at the same point on the tire and at the same level.

4. Measure the distance between the marks on the front side of the tires.
5. Adjust the toe-in by turning the left and the right tie rod tubes an equal amount. Make sure the tie rods are the same length.

Camber and Caster Adjustment

1. For 2WD Pick-Ups, adjust the camber and the caster by adding or removing shims on the upper arm. If the steering axis

Toe-in adjustment—Toyota

inclination is not as specified after the camber and caster have been properly adjusted, recheck the steering knuckle for bending or looseness.

NOTE: For the Previa, the camber and caster are not adjustable. If the measurements are not within specification, inspect and replace the suspension parts.

Camber and caster adjustment—Toyota 4WD vehicles

Camber and caster adjustment—Toyota 2WD Vans

2. For 2WD vans, adjust the camber and caster by turning the adjusting cam or the strut bar nut. The adjusting cam should not be turned more than 4.5 graduations from the neutral position. Do not turn the strut bar more than 3 threads from the original position.

3. For 4WD vehicles, adjust the camber and the caster by adjusting the front and rear adjusting cams. Refer to the service specifications for the adjustment standards.

Steering wheel angle—Toyota

Tire rotation sequence—Toyota

Steering Angle Adjustment

1. Remove the caps of the steering knuckle stopper bolts.
2. Loosen the knuckle stopper bolt locknuts and tighten the stopper bolts by hand.

NOTE: For the Previa, the steering angle is not adjustable. If the measurement is not within specification, inspect and replace the suspension parts.

3. Remove the boot clips and loosen the tie rod end locknuts.
4. Adjust the maximum wheel angle by turning the left and the right tie rod ends an equal amount.
5. Check that the lengths of the left and right tie rods are the same distance.

Wheel Service

Tire Rotation

It is recommended that the tires and wheels be rotated every 7500 miles to ensure uniform wear.

VOLKSWAGEN

Wheel Alignment

The vehicle should have been run from 625–1250 miles to let the coil springs settle before performing an alignment. The vehicle should be empty.

Toe-In Adjustment
FRONT WHEELS

1. Place the steering gear in the center position by turning the steering wheel from lock-to-lock and count the number of turns. Turn the wheel back ½ the number of turns.

2. Align the lug on the rubber washer on the pinion shaft with the notch in the steering housing.

3. Loosen the locknuts and turn both tie rods until the desired setting is reached. Retighten the locknuts.

4. Check that the bellows are not twisted after turning the tie rods.

5. The specification of the total toe at the front axle is determined by the ride height of the vehicle.

Caster adjustment—Vanagon

REAR WHEELS

1. Loosen the outer bolt on the trailing arm.
2. Adjust the camber by moving the trailing arm up or down with the proper tool.
3. Tighten the bolt.

Tire rotation sequence—Vanagon

Camber and Caster Adjustment

FRONT WHEELS

1. Adjust the caster by adjusting the length of the radius bar A at location B.
2. To adjust the camber, loosen the nut on the upper control arm shaft. Turn the upper control arm shaft to obtain the desired setting. Tighten the nut.

REAR WHEELS

1. Loosen the inner bolt on the trailing arm.
2. Adjust the toe by moving the trailing arm to the front or rear, using the proper tool.
3. Tighten the bolt.

Wheel Service

Tire Rotation

It is recommended that the tires and wheels be rotated every 7500 miles to ensure uniform wear. After the rotation torque the wheel nuts diagonally.

CHRYSLER CORPORATION

Single and Dual Point Fuel Injection Systems

GENERAL INFORMATION

The electronic fuel injection system is a computer regulated single point fuel injection system that provides precise air/fuel ratio for all driving conditions. At the center of this system is a digital pre-programmed computer known as the Single Module Engine Controller (SMEC) on 1988–89 vehicles or the Single Board Engine Controller (SBEC) on 1990–92 vehicles, that regulates ignition timing, air/fuel ratio, emission control devices, idle speed and cooling fan and charging system. This component has the ability to update and revise its programming to meet changing operating conditions.

Various sensors provide the input necessary for the SMEC/SBEC to correctly regulate the fuel flow at the fuel injector. These include the manifold absolute pressure, throttle position, oxygen sensor, coolant temperature, vehicle speed (distance) sensors and throttle body temperature. In addition to the sensors, various switches also provide important information. These include the neutral-safety switch, air conditioning clutch relay and auto shut-down relay.

All inputs to the SMEC/SBEC are converted into signals which are used by the computer. Based on these inputs, air-fuel ratio, ignition timing or other controlled outputs are adjusted accordingly.

The SMEC/SBEC tests many of its own input and output circuits. If a fault is found in a major system this information is stored in the memory. Information on this fault can be displayed to a technician by means of the instrument panel check engine light or by connecting a diagnostic read out and reading a numbered display code which directly relates to a specific fault.

COMPONENTS AND OPERATION

Single Module Engine Controller (SMEC) and Single Board Engine Controller (SBEC)

The SMEC/SBEC contain the circuits necessary to drive the ignition coil, fuel injector and the alternator field. The SMEC/SBEC is digital computer containing a microprocessor. The module receives input signals from various switches and sensors. These are high current devices and have been isolated to minimize any electrical noise in the passenger compartment.

The Automatic Shut Down (ASD) relay is mounted externally but is turned on and off by the SMEC/SBEC. Distributor pick-

Fuel injection system components—Chrysler Single Point Injection

Fuel injection system components—Chrysler Dual Point Injection

up signal goes to the SMEC/SBEC. In the event of no distributor signal, the ASD relay is not activated and power is shut off from the fuel injector and ignition coil. The SMEC/SBEC contains a voltage convertor which converts battery voltage to a regulated 9.0 volt output. This 9.0 volt output powers the distributor pickup. The internal 5 volt supply which, in turn, powers the MAP sensor and TPS.

The SMEC/SBEC is a digital computer containing a microprocessor. The module receives input signals from various switches and sensors. It then computes the fuel injector pulse width, spark advance, ignition coil dwell, idle speed, purge and cooling fan turn on and alternator charge rate.

The SMEC/SBEC tests many of its own input and output circuits. If a fault is found in a major system, this information is stored in the SMEC/SBEC. Information on this fault can be displayed to a technician by means of the instrument panel check engine light or by connecting the diagnostic read out tool and reading a numbered display code which directly relates to a general fault.

Manifold Absolute Pressure (MAP) Sensor

The Manifold Absolute Pressure (MAP) sensor is a device which monitors manifold vacuum. It is connected to a vacuum nipple on the throttle body and electrically to the SMEC/SBEC. The sensor transmits information on manifold vacuum conditions and barometric pressure to the SMEC/SBEC. The MAP sensor data on engine load is used with data from other sensors to determine the correct air/fuel mixture. It is located as follows:

All 1988 Models—Mounted underhood on the dash panel

All 1989–92 Models (except Dakota)—Mounted underhood on the shock tower

1989–92 Dakota Single Point Injection—Mounted underhood on the dash panel

1989–92 Dakota Dual Point Injection—Mounted underhood on the throttle body

Heated Oxygen Sensor (O_2 Sensor)

The oxygen sensor (O_2 sensor) is a device which produces an electrical voltage when exposed to the oxygen present in the exhaust gases. The sensor is mounted in the exhaust manifold and is electrically heated internally for faster switching when the engine is running. When there is a large amount of oxygen present (lean mixture), the sensor produces a low voltage. When there is a lesser amount present (rich mixture) it produces a higher voltage. By monitoring the oxygen content and converting it to electrical voltage, the sensor acts as a rich-lean switch. The voltage is transmitted to the SMEC/SBEC which changes the fuel injector's pulse width. The injector changes the mixture.

Coolant Temperature Sensor

The coolant temperature sensor is a device that monitors coolant temperature, which is the same as engine operating temperature,. It is mounted in the thermostat housing. This sensor provides data on engine operating temperature to the SMEC/SBEC. This allows the SMEC/SBEC to demand slightly richer air/fuel mixtures and higher idle speeds until normal operating temperatures are reached. This sensor is also used for cooling fan control.

Switch Input

Various switches provide information to the SMEC/SBEC. These include the neutral safety, air conditioning clutch, speed control and brake light switches. If one or more of these switches is is sensed as being in the **ON** position, the SMEC/SBEC signals the automatic idle speed motor to increase idle speed to a scheduled rpm.

Check Engine Light

The light comes on each time the ignition key is turned **ON** and stays on for a few seconds as a bulb test. If the SMEC/SBEC receives an incorrect signal or no signal from certain sensors or emission related systems (California vehicles only) the light on the instrument panel is illuminated. This is a warning that the SMEC has gone into limp-in mode in an attempt to keep the system operating. It signals an immediate need for service.

The light can also be used to display fault codes. Cycle the ignition switch **ON, OFF, ON, OFF, ON,** within 5 seconds and any fault code stored in the memory will be displayed.

Canister Purge Solenoid

The purge solenoid is controlled by the SMEC/SBEC. During warm-up and for a specified time period after hot starts, the SMEC/SBEC grounds the purge solenoid causing it to energized. This prevents vacuum from reaching the charcoal canister valve. When the engine reaches a specified operating temperature and the time delay interval has occurred, the solenoid is deenergized by turning off the ground. Once this occurs vacuum will flow to the canister purge valve and purge fuel vapors through the throttle body. The purge solenoid will also be energized during certain idle conditions. This is to update the fuel delivery calibration.

Air Conditioning Cutout Relay

The air conditioning cutout relay is connected, in series, electrically with the air conditioning damped pressure switch, the air conditioning switch and, on some models, the air conditioning fan relay. This relay is in the energized, closed (on), position during engine operation. When the module senses low idle speeds and wide open throttle through the throttle position sensor, it will deenergize the relay, open its contacts and prevent air conditioning clutch engagement.

Throttle Body

The throttle body assembly replaces a conventional carburetor and is mounted on top of the intake manifold. The throttle body houses the fuel injector(s), pressure regulator, throttle position sensor, automatic idle speed motor and throttle body temperature sensor. Air flow through the throttle body is controlled by a cable operated throttle blade located in the base of the throttle body. The throttle body itself provides the chamber for metering atomizing and distributing fuel throughout the air entering the engine.

Fuel Injector(s)

The fuel injector(s) is an electric solenoid driven by the SMEC/SBEC. The SMEC/SBEC, based on sensor inputs, determines when and how long the fuel injector(s) should operate. When an electric current is supplied to the injector, a spring loaded ball is lifted from it's seat. This allows fuel to flow through 6 spray orifices and deflects off the sharp edge of the injector nozzle. This action causes the fuel to form a 45 degree cone shaped spray pattern before entering the air stream in the throttle body.

Fuel is supplied to the injector constantly at regulated 14.5 psi; the unused fuel is returned to the fuel tank.

Fuel Pressure Regulator

The pressure regulator is a mechanical device located downstream of the fuel injector on the throttle body. Its function is to maintain a constant 14.5 psi (100 kPa) across the fuel injector tip. The regulator uses a spring loaded rubber diaphragm to uncover a fuel return port. When the fuel pump becomes operational, fuel flows past the injector into the regulator and is restricted from flowing any further by the blocked return port. When fuel pressure reaches the predetermined setting, it pushes on the diaphragm, compressing the spring and uncovers the fuel return port. The diaphragm and spring will constantly move from an open to closed position to keep the fuel pressure constant.

Throttle Position Sensor (TPS)

The Throttle Position Sensor (TPS) is an electric resistor which is activated by the movement of the throttle shaft. It is mounted on the throttle body and senses the angle of the throttle blade opening. The voltage that the sensor produces increases or decreases according to the throttle blade opening. This voltage is transmitted to the SMEC/SBEC, where it is used along with data from other sensors to adjust the air/fuel ratio to varying conditions and during acceleration, deceleration, idle and wide open throttle operations.

Automatic Idle Speed (AIS) Motor
SINGLE POINT FUEL INJECTION

The Automatic Idle Speed (AIS) motor is operated by the SMEC/SBEC. Data from the throttle position sensor, speed sensor, coolant temperature sensor and various switch operations, (safety/neutral, brake) are used by the module to adjust engine idle to an optimum during all idle conditions. The AIS adjusts the air portion of the air/fuel mixture through an air bypass on the back of the throttle body. Basic (no load) idle is determined by the minimum air flow through the throttle body. The AIS opens or closes off the air bypass as an increase or decrease is needed due to engine loads or ambient conditions. The module senses an air/fuel change and increases or decreases fuel proportionally to change engine idle. Deceleration die out is also prevented by increasing engine idle when the throttle is closed quickly after a driving (speed) condition.

Idle Speed Control (ISC) Actuator
DUAL POINT FUEL INJECTION

The Idle Speed Control (ISC) actuator adjusts the idle speed by physically moving the throttle lever. The moving of the throttle lever will change the air flow which results in the SMEC/SBEC changing the amount of fuel supplied. The ISC compensates for varying engine loads and ambient temperature.

Throttle Body Temperature Sensor

The throttle body temperature sensor is a device that monitors throttle body temperature which is the same as fuel temperature. It is mounted in the throttle body. This sensor provides information on fuel temperature which allows the SMEC/SBEC, to provide the correct air/fuel mixture for a hot restart condition.

Fuel Pump

The fuel pump used in this system is a positive displacement, roller vane immersible pump with a permanent magnet electric motor. The fuel is drawn in through a filter sock and pushed through the electric motor to the outlet. The pump contains 2 check valves. One valve is used to relieve internal fuel pump pressure and regulate maximum pump output. The other check valve, located near the pump outlet, restricts fuel movement in either direction when the pump is not operational. Voltage to operate the pump is supplied through the Auto Shutdown relay (ASD).

FORD MOTOR COMPANY

GENERAL INFORMATION

The Ford Electronic Fuel Injection systems use the Electronic Engine Control (EEC) IV system on vehicles. EEC–IV is similar to previous Ford engine control systems in that the heart of the system is a microcomputer called an Electronic Control Assembly (ECA). The ECA receives data (system inputs) from sensors, switches, relays and other electronic components and issues command signals (system outputs) to various devices in order to control engine operation under a variety of loads and ambient conditions. The ECA is calibrated according to the powertrain, axle ratio and Gross Vehicle Weight (GVW) to optimize fuel economy and driveability while minimizing harmful emissions.

The EEC–IV engine control system is used in conjunction with a multi-point (EFI and SEFI) injection fuel delivery system depending on the year, model and powertrain. Although the individual system components vary, the electronic control system operation is basically the same. The major difference is the number and type of output devices being controlled by the ECA.

The EEC–IV system electronically controls the fuel injectors to maintain a 14.7:1 air/fuel ratio under all driving conditions. This 14.7:1 air/fuel mixture allows the 3-way catalytic converter to operate at peak efficiency while getting the most performance and economy from the engine. Ignition spark timing, deceleration fuel cut-off, EGR function (on or off), curb and fast idle speed, evaporative emissions purge, air conditioning cut-off during wide open throttle, cold engine start and enrichment, electric fuel pump and self-test engine diagnostics are also controlled by the ECA to maintain consistent driveability across a wide range of operating conditions, temperatures and altitudes. The EEC–IV system is self-adjusting for operation at high altitude elevations (over 4000 ft. above sea level) and can actually compensate for engine component wear (a worn timing chain, for example).

The ECA in the EEC–IV system is similar in appearance to earlier control units, except that the calibration module is located within the ECA assembly instead of being attached to the outside as on earlier systems. The harness connectors are edge-card type contacts which provide a more positive connection. The ECA is usually mounted in the passenger compartment, under the front section of the center console, but the location will vary on different models. The ECA could also be located under the right (passenger) seat or behind the right front (passenger) kick panel, for example.

Typical Ford EEC–IV Engine Control System

The EEC–IV engine control system is divided into 3 major subsystems:

Fuel Delivery Subsystem

Which includes the fuel tank and lines, fuel pump and fuel injection components. On fuel injected models, this includes the fuel supply manifold, fuel pressure regulator, injectors and fuel filter.

Air Induction Subsystem

Which includes the air cleaner and ducts, intake manifold, fuel injection throttle body, throttle air bypass valve, vane airflow meter and related vacuum hoses and air ducts.

Electronic Control Subsystem

Which consists of the ECA and its various engine sensors (such as the oxygen sensor and coolant temperature sensor, etc.), along with the wiring harness, relays, fuses, battery and self-diagnostic system. On fuel injected models, it would include the throttle position switch and the wire harness to the fuel injectors but not the fuel injectors themselves.

Multi-Point (EFI) and Sequential (SEFI) Fuel Injection Systems

The EFI and SEFI fuel subsystems include a high pressure in-line electric fuel pump, a low-pressure tank-mounted fuel pump, fuel charging manifold, pressure regulator, fuel filter and both solid and flexible fuel lines. The fuel charging manifold includes 4, 6 or 8 electronically controlled fuel injectors, each mounted directly above an intake port in the lower intake manifold. On the 4 cylinder EFI system, all injectors are energized simultaneously and spray once every crankshaft revolution, delivering a predetermined quantity of fuel into the intake air stream. On 6 cylinder engines, the injectors are energized in 2 banks of 3, once each crankshaft revolution. On the V8 EFI engines, the injectors are energized in 2 banks of 4, once each crankshaft revolution. On the SEFI system, each injector fires once every crankshaft revolution, in sequence with the engine firing order.

The fuel pressure regulator maintains a constant pressure drop across the injector nozzles. The regulator is referenced to intake manifold vacuum and is connected parallel to the fuel injectors and positioned on the far end of the fuel rail. Any excess fuel supplied by the pump passes through the regulator and is returned to the fuel tank via a return line.

NOTE: The pressure regulator reduces fuel pressure to 39–40 psi under normal operating conditions. At idle or high manifold vacuum condition, fuel pressure is reduced to approximately 30 psi.

The fuel pressure regulator is a diaphragm operated relief valve in which the inside of the diaphragm senses fuel pressure and the other side senses manifold vacuum. Normal fuel pressure is established by a spring preload applied to the diaphragm. Control of the fuel system is maintained through the EEC power relay and the EEC–IV control unit, although electrical power is routed through the fuel pump relay and an inertia switch. The fuel pump relay is normally located on a bracket somewhere above the Electronic Control Assembly (ECA) and the inertia switch is located in the trunk. The in-line fuel pump is usually mounted on a bracket at the fuel tank, or on a frame rail. Tank-mounted pumps can be either high or low-pressure, depending on the model.

The inertia switch opens the power circuit to the fuel pump in the event of a collision. Once tripped, the switch must be reset manually by pushing the reset button on the assembly. Check that the inertia switch is reset before diagnosing power supply problems to the fuel pump circuit.

Fuel Injectors

The fuel injectors used with the EFI and SEFI system are electromechanical (solenoid) type designed to meter and atomize fuel delivered to the intake ports of the engine. The injectors are mounted in the lower intake manifold and positioned so their spray nozzles direct the fuel charge in front of the intake valves. The injector body consists of a solenoid actuated pintle and needle valve assembly. The control unit sends an electrical impulse that activates the solenoid, causing the pintle to move inward off the seat and allow the fuel to flow. The amount of fuel delivered is controlled by the length of time the injector is energized (pulse width), since the fuel flow orifice is fixed and the fuel pressure drop across the injector tip is constant. Correct atomization is achieved by contouring the pintle at the point where the fuel enters the pintle chamber.

NOTE: Exercise care when handling fuel injectors during service. Be careful not to lose the pintle cap and replace O-rings to assure a tight seal. Never apply direct battery voltage to test a fuel injector.

The injectors receive high pressure fuel from the fuel manifold (fuel rail) assembly. The complete assembly includes a single, preformed tube with 4, 6 or 8 injector connectors, mounting flange for the pressure regulator, mounting attachments to locate the manifold and provide the fuel injector retainers and a Schrader® quick-disconnect fitting used to perform fuel pressure tests.

The fuel manifold is normally removed with fuel injectors and pressure regulator attached. Fuel injector electrical connectors are plastic and have locking tabs that must be released when disconnecting the wiring harness.

Throttle Air Bypass Valve

The throttle air bypass valve is an electro-mechanical (solenoid) device whose operation is controlled by the EEC–IV control unit. A variable air metering valve controls both cold and warm idle air flow in response to commands from the control unit. The valve operates by bypassing a regulated amount of air around the throttle plate; the higher the voltage signal from the control unit, the more air is bypassed through the valve. In this manner, additional air can be added to the fuel mixture without moving the throttle plate. At curb idle, the valve provides smooth idle for various engine coolant temperatures, compensates for air conditioning load and compensates for transaxle load and no-load conditions. The valve also provides fast idle for start-up, replacing the fast idle cam, throttle kicker and anti-dieseling solenoid common to previous models.

There are no curb idle or fast idle adjustments. As in curb idle operation, the fast idle speed is proportional to engine coolant temperature. Fast idle kick-down will occur when the throttle is kicked. A time-out feature in the ECA will also automatically kick-down fast idle to curb idle after a time period of approximately 15–25 seconds; after coolant has reached approximately 160°F (71°C). The signal duty cycle from the ECA to the valve will be at 100 percent (maximum current) during the crank to provide maximum air flow to allow no touch starting at any time (engine cold or hot).

Electronic Engine Control

The electronic engine control subsystem consists of the ECA and various sensors and actuators. The ECA reads inputs from engine sensors, then outputs a voltage signal to various components (actuators) to control engine functions. The period of time that the injectors are energized ("ON" time or "pulse width") determines the amount of fuel delivered to each cylinder. The longer the pulse width, the richer the fuel mixture.

NOTE: The operating reference voltage (Vref) between the ECA and its sensors and actuators is 5 volts. This allows these components to work during the crank operation even though the battery voltage drops.

In order for the ECA to properly control engine operation, it must first receive current status reports on various operating conditions. The control unit constantly monitors crankshaft position, throttle plate position, engine coolant temperature, exhaust gas oxygen level, air intake volume and temperature, air conditioning (On/Off), spark knock and barometric pressure.

Universal Distributor

The primary function of the TFI–IV ignition system universal distributor is to direct the high secondary voltage to the spark plugs. In addition, the universal distributor supplies crankshaft position and frequency information to the ECA using a Profile Ignition Pick-up (PIP) sensor in place of the magnetic pick-up or the crankshaft position sensor used on other models. This distributor does not have any mechanical or vacuum advance. The universal distributor assembly is adjustable for resetting base timing, if required, by disconnecting the spout connector.

NOTE: The PIP replaces the crankshaft position sensor found on other EEC–IV models.

The PIP sensor has an armature with 4 windows and 4 metal tabs that rotates past the stator assembly (Hall effect switch). When a metal tab enters the stator assembly, a positive signal (approximately 10 volts) is sent to the ECA, indicating the 10 degrees BTDC crankshaft position. The ECA calculates the precise time to energize the spark output signal to the TFI module. When the TFI module receives the spark output signal, it shuts off the coil primary current and the collapsing field energizes the secondary output.

NOTE: Misadjustment of the base timing affects the spark advance in the same manner as a conventional solid-state ignition system.

Thick Film Ignition (TFI–IV) Module

The TFI–IV ignition module has 6 connector pins at the engine wiring harness that supply the following signals:
- Ignition switch in **RUN** position
- Engine cranking
- Tachometer
- PIP (crankshaft position to ECA)
- Spark advance (from ECA)
- Internal ground from the ECA to the distributor

The TFI–IV module supplies the spark to the distributor through the ignition coil and calculates the duration. It receives its control signal from the ECA (spark output).

Distributorless Ignition System (DIS)

The DIS ignition systems eliminates the need for a distributor by using multiple coils, which fire 2 spark plugs at the same time. This system uses either a dual function crank sensor or a crank sensor and cam sensor. The cam sensor provides the Cylinder Identification (CID) signal, used to choose which coil to fire. The crank sensor provides a Profile Ignition Pick-up (PIP) signal for spark timing. The dual function crank sensor provides both CID and PIP signals to the DIS module.

Distributorless Ignition System (DIS) Module

The DIS module controls coil firing from the ECA commands similar to the way the TFI–IV module does. The DIS module functions include:
- Selection of Coil(s)
- Drives the coils
- Drives the tachometer

- PIP (crankshaft position to ECA)
- CID (cylinder identification)
- LOS (limited operation strategy — base timing)

Throttle Position (TP) Sensor

The TP sensor is mounted on the throttle body. This sensor provides the ECA with a signal that indicates the opening angle of the throttle plate. The sensor output signal uses the 5 volt reference voltage (Vref) previously described. From this input, the ECA controls:
1. Operating modes, which are Wide Open Throttle (WOT), Part Throttle (PT) and Closed Throttle (CT).
2. Fuel enrichment at WOT.
3. Additional spark advance at WOT.
4. EGR cut off during WOT, deceleration and idle.
5. Air conditioning cut off during WOT (30 seconds maximum).
6. Cold start kick-down.
7. Fuel cut off during deceleration.
8. WOT dechoke during crank mode (starting).

On the EEC–IV system, the TP sensor signal to the ECA only changes the spark timing during the WOT mode. As the throttle plate rotates, the TP sensor varies its voltage output. As the throttle plate moves from a closed throttle position to a WOT Position, the voltage output of the TP sensor will change from a low voltage (approximately 1.0 volt) to a high voltage (approximately 4.75 volts). The TP sensor used is not adjustable and must be replaced if it is out of specification. The EEC–IV programming compensates for differences between sensors.

Engine Coolant Temperature (ECT) Sensor

The ECT sensor is located either in the heater supply tube at the rear of the engine, or in the lower intake manifold. The ECT is a thermistor (changes resistance as temperature changes). The sensor detects the temperature of engine coolant and provides a corresponding signal to the ECA. From this signal, the ECA will modify the air/fuel ratio (mixture), idle speed, spark advance, EGR and Canister purge control. When the engine coolant is cold, the ECT signal causes the ECA to provide enrichment to the air/fuel ratio for good cold drive away as engine coolant warms up, the voltage will drop.

Exhaust Gas Oxygen (EGO) Sensor

The EGO or HEGO sensor on the EEC–IV system is a little different from others used and is mounted in its own mounting boss, located between the 2 downstream tubes in the header near the exhaust system. On supercharged or turbocharged models, the EGO sensor is mounted in the exhaust elbow. The EGO sensor works between 0–1 volt output, depending on the presence (lean) or absence (rich) of oxygen in the exhaust gas. A voltage reading greater than 0.6 volts indicates a rich air/fuel ratio, while a reading of less than 0.4 volts indicates a lean ratio.

NOTE: Never apply voltage to the EGO sensor because it could destroy the sensor's calibration. This includes the use of an ohmmeter. Before connecting and using a voltmeter, make sure it has a high-input impedance (at least 10 megohms) and is set on the proper resistance range. Any attempt to use a powered voltmeter to measure the EGO voltage output directly will damage or destroy the sensor.

Operation of the sensor is the same as previous models. A difference that should be noted is that the rubber protective cap used on top of the sensor on the earlier models has been replaced with a metal cap. In addition, later model sensors incorporate a heating element to bring the sensor up to operating temperature more quickly and keep it there during extended idle periods to prevent the sensor from cooling off and placing the system into open loop operation.

Vane Meter

The vane meter is actually 2 sensors in 1 assembly—a Vane Air Flow (VAF) sensor and Vane Air Temperature (VAT) sensor. This meter measures air flow to the engine and the temperature of the air stream. The vane meter is located either behind or under the air cleaner.

Air flow through the body moves a vane mounted on a pivot pin. The more air flowing through the meter, the further the vane rotates about the pivot pin. The air vane pivot pin is connected to a variable resistor (potentiometer) on top of the assembly. The vane meter uses the 5 volt reference voltage. The output of the potentiometer to the ECA varies between 0 and Vref (5 volts), depending on the volume of air flowing through the sensor. A higher volume of air will produce a higher voltage output.

The volume of air measured through the meter has to be converted into an air mass value. The mass (weight) of a specific volume of air varies with pressure and temperature. To compensate for these variables, a temperature sensor in front of the vane measures incoming air temperature. The ECA uses the air temperature and a programmed pressure value to convert the VAF signal into a mass air flow value. This value is used to calculate the fuel flow necessary for the optimum air/fuel ratio. The VAT also affects spark timing as a function of air temperature.

Air Conditioning Clutch Compressor (ACC) Signal

Anytime battery voltage is applied to the air conditioning clutch, the same signal is also applied to the ECA. The ECA then maintains the engine idle speed with the throttle air bypass valve control solenoid (fuel injection), or throttle kicker (carburetor), to compensate for the added load created by the air conditioning clutch operation. Shutting down the air conditioning clutch will have a reverse effect. The ECA will maintain the engine idle speed at 850–950 rpm.

Knock Sensor (KS)

The knock sensor is used to detect detonation. In situations of excessive knock the ECA receives a signal from this sensor and retards the spark accordingly. The operation of the knock sensor during boost on turbocharged models improves the engine's durability. It is mounted in the lower intake manifold at the rear of the engine.

Barometric (BAP) Sensor

The barometric sensor is used to compensate for altitude variations. From this signal, the ECA modifies the air/fuel ratio, spark timing, idle speed and EGR flow. The barometric sensor is a design that produces a frequency based on atmospheric pressure (altitude). The barometric sensor is mounted on the right-hand fender apron.

Manifold Absolute Pressure (MAP) Sensor

The MAP sensor is used to measure manifold vacuum using a frequency. This gives the ECA information on engine load. It replaces the BAP sensor by providing the ECA updated barometric pressure readings during key **ON** engine **OFF** and every wide open throttle. The MAP sensor output is used by the ECA to control spark advance, EGR flow and air/fuel ratio.

EGR Shut-Off Solenoid

The electrical signal to the EGR shut-off solenoid is controlled by the ECA. The signal is either **ON** or **OFF**. It is **OFF** during cold start, closed throttle or WOT. It is **ON** at all other times.

NOTE: The canister purge valve is controlled by vacuum from the EGR solenoid. The purge valve is a standard-type valve and operates the same as in previous systems.

The solenoid is the same as the EGR control solenoid used on previous EEC systems. It is usually mounted on the LH side of the dash panel in the engine compartment, or on the RH shock tower in the engine compartment. The solenoid is normally closed and the control vacuum from the solenoid is applied to the EGR valve.

GENERAL MOTORS CORPORATION

GENERAL INFORMATION

The electronic throttle body fuel injection system is a fuel metering system with the amount of fuel delivered by the Throttle Body Injector(s) (TBI) determined by an electronic signal supplied by the Electronic Control Module (ECM) or Powertrain Control Module (PCM). The ECM monitors various engine and vehicle conditions to calculate the fuel delivery time (pulse width) of the injector(s). The fuel pulse may be modified by the ECM to account for special operating conditions, such as cranking, cold starting, altitude, acceleration and deceleration.

The Throttle Body Injection (TBI) system provides a means of fuel distribution for controlling exhaust emissions within legislated limits. The TBI system, by precisely controlling the air/fuel mixture under all operating conditions, provides as near as possible complete combustion.

This is accomplished by using an Electronic Control Module (ECM) (a small on-board microcomputer) that receives electrical inputs from various sensors about engine operating conditions. An oxygen sensor in the main exhaust stream functions to provide feedback information to the ECM as to the oxygen content, lean or rich, in the exhaust. The ECM uses this information from the oxygen sensor and other sensors, to modify fuel delivery to achieve, as near as possible, an ideal air/fuel ratio of 14.7:1. This air/fuel ratio allows the 3-way catalytic converter to be more efficient in the conversion process of reducing exhaust emissions while at the same time providing acceptable levels of driveability and fuel economy.

ELECTRONIC CONTROL MODULE

The ECM program electronically signals the fuel injector in the TBI assembly to provide the correct quantity of fuel for a wide range of operating conditions. Several sensors are used to determine existing operating conditions and the ECM then signals the injector to provide the precise amount of fuel required.

The ECM used on EFI vehicles has a learning capability. If the battery is disconnected to clear diagnostic codes or for repair, the learning process has to begin all over again. A change may be noted in vehicle performance. To teach the vehicle, make sure the vehicle is at operating temperature and drive at part throttle, under moderate acceleration and idle conditions, until performance returns.

With the EFI system, the TBI assembly is centrally located on the intake manifold where air and fuel are distributed through a single bore in the throttle body, similar to a carbureted engine. Air for combustion is controlled by a single throttle valve which is connected to the accelerator pedal linkage by a throttle shaft and lever assembly. A special plate is located directly under the throttle valve to aid in mixture distribution.

General Motors TBI fuel injection system components

Fuel for combustion is supplied by 1 or 2 fuel injector(s), mounted on the TBI assembly, whose metering tip is located directly above the throttle valve. The injector is pulsed or timed open or closed by an electronic output signal received from the ECM. The ECM receives inputs concerning engine operating conditions from the various sensors (coolant temperature sensor, oxygen sensor, etc.). The ECM, using this information, performs high speed calculations of engine fuel requirements and pulses or times the injector, open or closed, thereby controlling fuel and air mixtures to achieve, as near as possible, ideal air/fuel mixture ratios.

When the ignition key is turned **ON**, the ECM will initialize (start program running) and energize the fuel pump relay. The fuel pump pressurizes the system to approximately 10 psi. If the ECM does not receive a distributor reference pulse (telling the ECM the engine is turning) within 2 seconds, the ECM will then de-energize the fuel pump relay, turning off the fuel pump. If a distributor reference pulse is later received, the ECM will turn the fuel pump back on.

The ECM controls the exhaust emissions by modifying fuel delivery to achieve, as near as possible and air/fuel ratio of 14.7:1. The injector on-time is determined by various inputs to the ECM. By increasing the injector pulse, more fuel is delivered, enriching the air/fuel ratio. Decreasing the injector pulse, leans the air/fuel ratio. Pulses are sent to the injector in 2 different modes: synchronized and nonsynchronized.

Synchronized Mode

In synchronized mode operation, the injector is pulsed once for each distributor reference pulse. In dual injector throttle body systems, the injectors are pulse alternately.

Nonsynchronized Mode

In nonsynchronized mode operation, the injector is pulsed once every 12.5 milliseconds or 6.25 milliseconds depending on calibration. This pulse time is totally independent of distributor reference pulses. Nonsynchronized mode results only under the following conditions:

1. The fuel pulse width is too small to be delivered accurately by the injector (approximately 1.5 milliseconds).
2. During the delivery of prime pulses (prime pulses charge the intake manifold with fuel during or just prior to engine starting).
3. During acceleration enrichment.
4. During deceleration leanout.

The basic TBI unit is made up of 2 major casting assemblies: (1) a throttle body with a valve to control airflow and (2) a fuel body assembly with an integral pressure regulator and fuel injector to supply the required fuel. An electronically operated device to control the idle speed and a device to provide information regarding throttle valve position are included as part of the TBI unit.

The fuel injector(s) is a solenoid-operated device controlled by the ECM. The incoming fuel is directed to the lower end of the injector assembly which has a fine screen filter surrounding the injector inlet. The ECM actuates the solenoid, which lifts a normally closed ball valve off a seat. The fuel under pressure is injected in a conical spray pattern at the walls of the throttle body bore above the throttle valve. The excess fuel passes through a pressure regulator before being returned to the vehicle's fuel tank.

The pressure regulator is a diaphragm-operated relief valve with injector pressure on one side and air cleaner pressure on the other. The function of the regulator is to maintain a constant pressure drop across the injector throughout the operating load and speed range of the engine.

The throttle body portion of the TBI may contain ports located at, above, or below the throttle valve. These ports generate the vacuum signals for the EGR valve, MAP sensor and the canister purge system.

The Throttle Position Sensor (TPS) is a variable resistor used to convert the degree of throttle plate opening to an electrical signal to the ECM. The ECM uses this signal as a reference point of throttle valve position. In addition, an Idle Air Control (IAC) assembly, mounted in the throttle body s used to control idle speeds. A cone-shaped valve in the IAC assembly is located in an air passage in the throttle body that leads from the point beneath the air cleaner to below the throttle valve. The ECM monitors idle speeds and, depending on engine load, moves the IAC cone in the air passage to increase or decrease air bypassing the throttle valve to the intake manifold for control of idle speeds.

Cranking Mode

During engine crank, for each distributor reference pulse the ECM will deliver an injector pulse (synchronized). The crank air/fuel ratio will be used if the throttle position is less than 80 percent open. Crank air fuel is determined by the ECM and ranges from 1.5:1 at $-33°F$ ($-36°C$) to 14.7:1 at 201°F (94°C).

The lower the coolant temperature, the longer the pulse width (injector on-time) or richer the air/fuel ratio. The higher the coolant temperature, the less pulse width (injector on-time) or the leaner the air/fuel ratio.

Clear Flood Mode

If for some reason the engine should become flooded, provisions have been made to clear this condition. To clear the flood, the driver must depress the accelerator pedal enough to open to wide-open throttle position. The ECM then issues injector pulses at a rate that would be equal to an air/fuel ratio of 20:1. The ECM maintains this injector rate as long as the throttle remains wide open and the engine rpm is below 600. If the throttle position becomes less than 80 percent, the ECM then would immediately start issuing crank pulses to the injector calculated by the ECM based on the coolant temperature.

Run Mode

There are 2 different run modes. When the engine rpm is above 400, the system goes into open loop operation. In open loop operation, the ECM will ignore the signal from the oxygen (O_2) sensor and calculate the injector on-time based upon inputs from the coolant and manifold absolute pressure sensors.

During open loop operation, the ECM analyzes the following items to determine when the system is ready to go to the closed loop mode:

1. The oxygen sensor varying voltage output; this is dependent on temperature.
2. The coolant sensor must be above specified temperature.
3. A specific amount of time must elapse after starting the engine. These values are stored in the PROM.

When these conditions have been met, the system goes into closed loop operation In closed loop operation, the ECM will modify the pulse width (injector on-time) based upon the signal from the oxygen sensor. The ECM will decrease the on-time if the air/fuel ratio is too rich and will increase the on-time if the air/fuel ratio is too lean.

The pulse width, thus the amount of enrichment, is determined by manifold pressure change, throttle angle change and coolant temperature. The higher the manifold pressure and the wider the throttle opening, the wider the pulse width. The acceleration enrichment pulses are delivered nonsynchronized. Any reduction in throttle angle will cancel the enrichment pulses. This way, quick movements of the accelerator will not over-enrich the mixture.

Acceleration Enrichment Mode

When the engine is required to accelerate, the opening of the throttle valve(s) causes a rapid increase in Manifold Absolute Pressure (MAP). This rapid increase in the manifold pressure causes fuel to condense on the manifold walls. The ECM senses this increase in throttle angle and MAP and supplies additional fuel for a short period of time. This prevents the engine from stumbling due to too lean a mixture.

Deceleration Leanout Mode

Upon deceleration, a leaner fuel mixture is required to reduce

emission of Hydrocarbons (HC) and Carbon Monoxide (CO). To adjust the injection on-time, the ECM uses the decrease in manifold pressure and the decrease in throttle position to calculate a decrease in pulse width. To maintain an idle fuel ratio of 14.7:1, fuel output is momentarily reduced. This is done because of the fuel remaining in the intake manifold during deceleration.

Deceleration Fuel Cut-Off Mode

The purpose of deceleration fuel cut-off is to remove fuel from the engine during extreme deceleration conditions. Deceleration fuel cut-off is based on values of manifold pressure, throttle position and engine rpm stored in the calibration PROM. Deceleration fuel cut-off overrides the deceleration enleanment mode.

Battery Voltage Correction Mode

The purpose of battery voltage correction is to compensate for variations in battery voltage to fuel pump and injector response. The ECM modifies the pulse width by a correction factor in the PROM. When battery voltage decreases, pulse width increases.

Battery voltage correction takes place in all operating modes. When battery voltage is low, the spark delivered by the distributor may be low. To correct this low battery voltage problem, the ECM can do any or all of the following:

1. Increase injector pulse width (increase fuel)
2. Increase idle rpm
3. Increase ignition dwell time

Fuel Cut-Off Mode

When the ignition is **OFF**, the ECM will not energize the injector. Fuel will also be cut off if the ECM does not receive a reference pulse from the distributor. To prevent dieseling, fuel delivery is completely stopped as soon as the engine is stopped. The ECM will not allow any fuel supply until it receives distributor reference pulses which prevents flooding.

Backup Mode

When in this mode, the ECM is operating on the fuel backup logic calibrated by the CalPak. The CalPak is used to control the fuel delivery if the ECM fails. This mode verifies that the backup feature is working properly. The parameters that can be read on a scan tool in this mode are not much use for service.

Highway Mode

When driven at highway speeds the system may enter highway or semi-closed loop mode. This improves fuel economy by leaning out fuel mixture slightly. The ECM must see correct engine temperature, ignition timing, canister activity and a constant vehicle speed before if will enter this mode. The system will switch back to closed loop periodically to check all system functions.

A scan tool scan determine highway mode by looking at the integrator/block learn values and oxygen sensor voltage. Integrator and block learn will show very little change and the oxygen sensor voltage is be less than 100 millivolts.

ALCL/ALDL Connector

The Assembly Line Communication Link (ALCL) or Assembly Line Diagnostic Link (ALDL) is a diagnostic connector located in the passenger compartment. It has terminals which are used in the assembly plant to check that the engine is operating properly before it leaves the plant. This connector is a very useful tool in diagnosing EFI engines. Important information from the ECM is available at this terminal and can be read with one of the many popular scanner tools.

NOTE: Some models refer to the ALCL as the Assembly Line Diagnostic Link (ALDL). Either way it is referred to, they both still perform the same function.

FUEL INJECTION SUBSYSTEMS

Electronic Fuel Injection (EFI) is the name given to the entire fuel injection system. Various subsystems are combined to form the overall system. These subsystems are:

1. Fuel supply system
2. Throttle Body Injector (TBI) assembly
3. Idle Air Control (IAC)
4. Electronic Control Module (ECM)
5. Data sensors
6. Electronic Spark Timing (EST)
7. Emission controls

Fuel Supply System

Fuel, supplied by an electric fuel pump mounted in the fuel tank, passes through an in-line fuel filter to the TBI assembly. To control fuel pump operation, a fuel pump relay is used.

When the ignition switch is turned to the **ON** position, the fuel pump relay activates the electric fuel pump for 1.5–2.0 seconds to prime the injector. If the ECM does not receive reference pulses from the distributor after this time, the ECM signals the relay to turn the fuel pump off. The relay will once again activate the fuel pump when the ECM receives distributor reference pulses.

The oil pressure sender is the backup for the fuel pump relay. The sender has 2 circuits, 1 for the instrument cluster light or gauge, the other to activate the fuel pump if the relay fails. If the fuse relay has failed, the sender activates the fuel pump when oil pressure reaches 4 psi. Thus a failed fuel pump relay would cause a longer crank, especially in cold weather. If the fuel pump fails, a no start condition exists.

NOTE: On the 7.4L engine or a G-Series van with the 5.7L engine and all other 5.7L engines over 8500 GVW, a fuel module will override the ECM 2 second timer and the fuel pump will run for 20 seconds and then shut off, if the vehicle is not started. This circuit corrects a hot restart (vapor lock) during a high ambient condition.

Throttle Body Injector (TBI) Assembly

The basic TBI model 700 is used on 4 cylinder engines, it is made up of 2 major casting assemblies: (1) a throttle body with a valve to control airflow and (2) a fuel body assembly with an integral pressure regulator and fuel injector to supply the required fuel. A device to control idle speed (IAC) and a device to provide information about throttle valve position (TPS) are included as part of the TBI unit.

The model 220 is used on V6 and V8 engines, consists of 3 major castings. (1) fuel meter cover with pressure regulator, (2) Fuel meter body with injectors and (3) throttle body with IAC valve and TPS sensor.

The throttle body portion of the TBI unit may contain ports located at, above, or below the throttle valve. These ports generate the vacuum signals for the EGR valve, MAP sensor and the canister purge system.

The fuel injector is a solenoid-operated device controlled by the ECM. The incoming fuel is directed to the lower end of the injector assembly which has a fine screen filter surrounding the injector inlet. The ECM turns on the solenoid, which lifts a normally closed ball valve off a seat. The fuel, under pressure, is injected in a conical spray pattern at the walls of the throttle body bore above the throttle valve. The excess fuel passes through a pressure regulator before being returned to the vehicle fuel tank.

The pressure regulator is a diaphragm-operated relief valve with the injector pressure on one side and the air cleaner pressure on the other. The function of the regulator is to maintain constant pressure (approximately 11 psi) to the injector throughout the operating loads and speed ranges of the engine. If the regulator pressure is too low, below 9 psi, it can cause poor performance. Too high a pressure could cause detonation and a strong fuel odor.

Idle Air Control (IAC)

The purpose of the Idle Air Control (IAC) system is to control engine idle speeds while preventing stalls due to changes in engine load. The IAC assembly, mounted on the throttle body, controls bypass air around the throttle plate. By extending or retracting a conical valve, a controlled amount of air can move around the throttle plate. If rpm is too low, more air is diverted around the throttle plate to increase rpm.

During idle, the proper position of the IAC valve is calculated by the ECM based on battery voltage, coolant temperature, engine load and engine rpm. If the rpm drops below a specified rate, the throttle plate is closed. The ECM will then calculate a new valve position.

Three designs are used for the IAC conical valve. The first design used is single 35 taper while the second design used is a dual taper. The third design is a blunt valve. Care should be taken to insure use of the correct design when service replacement is required.

The IAC motor has 255 different positions or steps. The zero or reference position, is the fully extended position at which the pintle is seated in the air bypass seat and no air is allowed to bypass the throttle plate. When the motor is fully retracted, maximum air is allowed to bypass the throttle plate. When the motor is fully retracted, maximum air is allowed to bypass the throttle plate.

The ECM always monitors how many steps it has extended or retracted the pintle from the zero or reference position; thus, it always calculates the exact position of the motor. Once the engine has started and the vehicle has reached approximately 40 mph, the ECM will extend the motor 255 steps from whatever position it is in. This will bottom out the pintle against the seat. The ECM will call this position 0 and thus keep its zero reference updated.

The IAC only affects the engine's idle characteristics. If it is stuck fully open, idle speed is too high (too much air enters the throttle bore) If it is stuck closed, idle speed is too low (not enough air entering). If it is stuck somewhere in the middle, idle may be rough and the engine won't respond to load changes.

Idle Speed Control (ISC)

Incorrect diagnosis and/or misunderstanding of the idle speed control systems used on EFI engines may lead to unnecessary replacement of the IAC valve. Engine idle speed is controlled by the ECM which changes the idle speed by moving the IAC valve. The ECM adjusts idle speed in response to fluctuations in engine load (air conditioning, power steering, electrical loads, etc.) to maintain acceptable idle quality and proper exhaust emission performance.

The following is provided to assist the technician to better understand the system and correctly respond to the following customer concerns:

1. Rough idle/low idle speed
2. High idle speed/warm-up idle speed; no kickdown

Rough Idle/Low Idle Speed

The ECM will respond to increases in engine load, which would cause a drop in idle speed, by moving the IAC valve to maintain proper idle speed. After the induced load is removed the ECM will return the idle speed to the proper level.

During air conditioning compressor operation (MAX, BI-LEVEL, NORM or DEFROST mode) the ECM will increase idle speed in response to an air conditioning-ON signal, thereby compensating for any drop in idle speed due to compressor load. On some vehicles, the ECM will also increase the idle speed in response to high power steering loads.

During periods of especially heavy loads (air conditioning-ON plus parking maneuvers) significant effects on idle quality may be experienced. These effects are more pronounced on 4-cylinder engines. Abnormally low idle, rough idle and idle shake may occur if the ECM does not receive the proper signals from the monitored systems.

High Idle Speed/Warm-Up Idle Speed (No Kickdown)

Engine idle speeds as high as 2100 rpm may be experienced during cold starts to quickly raise the catalytic converter to operating temperature for proper exhaust emissions performance. The idle speed attained after a cold start is ECM controlled and will not drop for 45 seconds regardless of driver attempts to kickdown.

It is important to recognize the EFI engines have no accelerator pump or choke. Idle speed during warm-up is entirely ECM controlled and cannot be changed by accelerator kickdown or pumping.

Abnormally low idle speeds are usually caused by an ECM system-controlled or monitored irregularity, while the most common cause for abnormally high idle speed is an induction (intake air) leak. The idle air control valve may occasionally lose its memory function and it has an ECM programmed method of relearning the correct idle position. This reset, when required, will occur the next time the vehicle exceeds 35 mph. At this time the ECM seats the pintle of the IAC valve in the throttle body to determine a reference point. Then it backs out a fixed distance to maintain proper idle speed.

DATA SENSORS

A variety of sensors provide information to the ECM regarding engine operating characteristics. These sensors and their functions are described below. Be sure to take note that not every sensor described is used with every engine application.

Engine Coolant Temperature

The Coolant Temperature Sensor (CTS) is a thermister (a resistor which changes value based on temperature) mounted on the engine coolant stream. As the temperature of the engine coolant changes, the resistance of the coolant sensor changes. Low coolant temperature produces a high resistance (100,000 ohms at −40°F/−40°C), while high temperature causes low resistance (70 ohms at 266°F/130°C).

The ECM supplies a 5 volt signal to the coolant sensor and measures the voltage that returns. By measuring the voltage change, the ECM determines the engine coolant temperature. The voltage will be high when the engine is cold and low when the engine is hot. This information is used to control fuel management, IAC, spark timing, EGR, canister purge and other engine operating conditions.

A failure in the coolant sensor circuit should either set a Code 14 or 15. These codes indicate a failure in the coolant temperature sensor circuit.

Oxygen Sensor

The exhaust oxygen sensor is mounted in the exhaust system where it can monitor the oxygen content of the exhaust gas stream. The oxygen content in the exhaust reacts with the oxygen sensor to produce a voltage output. This voltage ranges from approximately 100 milli-volts (high oxygen—lean mixture) to 900 milli-volts (low oxygen—rich mixture).

By monitoring the voltage output of the oxygen sensor, the ECM will determine what fuel mixture command to give to the injector (lean mixture—low voltage—rich command, rich mixture—high voltage—lean command).

Remember that oxygen sensor indicates to the ECM what is happening in the exhaust. It does not cause things to happen. It is a type of gauge: high oxygen content = lean mixture; low oxygen content = rich mixture. The ECM adjusts fuel to keep the system working.

The oxygen sensor, if open should set a Code 13. A constant low voltage in the sensor circuit should set a Code 44 while a constant high voltage in the circuit should set a Code 45. Codes 44 and 45 could also be set as a result of fuel system problems.

Manifold Absolute Pressure Sensor

The Manifold Absolute Pressure (MAP) sensor measures the changes in the intake manifold pressure which result from engine load and speed changes. The pressure measured by the MAP sensor is the difference between barometric pressure (outside air) and manifold pressure (vacuum). A closed throttle engine coastdown would produce a relatively low MAP value (approximately 20–35 kPa), while wide-open throttle would produce a high value (100 kPa). This high value is produced when the pressure inside the manifold is the same as outside the manifold and 100 percent of outside air (or 100 kPa) is being measured. This MAP output is the opposite of what you would measure on a vacuum gauge. The use of this sensor also allows the ECM to adjust automatically for different altitude.

The ECM sends a 5 volt reference signal to the MAP sensor. As the MAP changes, the electrical resistance of the sensor also changes. By monitoring the sensor output voltage the ECM can determine the manifold pressure. A higher pressure, lower vacuum (high voltage) requires more fuel, while a lower pressure, higher vacuum (low voltage) requires less fuel. The ECM uses the MAP sensor to control fuel delivery and ignition timing. A failure in the MAP sensor circuit should set a Code 33 or Code 34.

Intake Air Temperature Sensor

The Intake Air Temperature (IAT) and Manifold Air Temperature (MAT) are the same sensor. This sensor is a thermistor mounted in the intake manifold or air intake. A thermistor is a resistor which changes resistance based on temperature. Low manifold air temperature produces a high resistance (100,000 ohms at −40°F/−40°C), while high temperature cause low resistance (70 ohms at 266°F/130°C).

The ECM supplies a 5 volt signal to the MAT/IAT sensor through a resistor in the ECM and monitors the voltage. The voltage will be high when the manifold air is cold and low when the air is hot. By monitoring the voltage, the ECM calculates the air temperature and uses this data to help determine the fuel delivery and spark advance. A failure in the MAT/IAT circuit should set either a Code 23 or Code 25.

Vehicle Speed Sensor

NOTE: A vehicle equipped with a speed sensor, should not be driven without a the speed sensor connected, as idle quality may be affected.

The Vehicle Speed Sensor (VSS) is mounted behind the speedometer in the instrument cluster or on the transmission/speedometer drive gear. It provides electrical pulses to the ECM from the speedometer head. The pulses indicate the road speed. The ECM uses this information to operate the IAC, canister purge and TCC.

Some vehicles equipped with digital instrument clusters use a Permanent Magnet (PM) generator to provide the VSS signal. The PM generator is located in the transmission replaces the speedometer cable. The signal from the PM generator drives a stepper motor which drives the odometer. A failure in the VSS circuit should set a Code 24.

Throttle Position Sensor

The Throttle Position Sensor (TPS) is connected to the throttle shaft and is controlled by the throttle mechanism. A 5 volt reference signal is sent to the TPS from the ECM. As the throttle valve angle is changed (accelerator pedal moved), the resistance of the TPS also changes. At a closed throttle position, the resistance of the TPS is high, so the output voltage to the ECM will be low (approximately 0.5 volts). As the throttle plate opens, the resistance decreases so, at wide open throttle, the output voltage should be approximately 5 volts. At closed throttle position, the voltage at the TPS should be less than 1.25 volts.

By monitoring the output voltage from the TPS, the ECM can determine fuel delivery based on throttle valve angle (driver demand). The TPS can either be misadjusted, shorted, open or loose. Misadjustment might result in poor idle or poor wide-open throttle performance. An open TPS signals the ECM that the throttle is always closed, resulting in poor performance. This usually sets a Code 22. A shorted TPS gives the ECM a constant wide-open throttle signal and should set a Code 21. A loose TPS indicates to the ECM that the throttle is moving. This causes intermittent bursts of fuel from the injector and an unstable idle. On some vehicles, the TPS is adjustable and therefore can be adjusted to correct any complications caused by to high or to low of a voltage signal.

Crankshaft and Camshaft Sensor

These sensors are mounted on the engine block, near the engine crankshaft and also near the camshaft on some engines. The sensors are used to send a signal through the Direct Ignition System (DIS) module to the ECM. The ECM uses this reference signal to calculate engine speed and crankshaft position.

In a typical 4 cylinder engine application, a sensor is mounted with the ignition module and 2 ignition coils to comprise the direct ignition assembly. When mounted on the engine block, the sensor tip is very close to a metal disk wheel with slots which is mounted on the crankshaft.

The sensor tip contains a small magnet and a small coil of wire. As the metal disk wheel with the slots rotates past the sensor tip, the magnetic field of the permanent magnet is changed and a voltage is induced into the coil. This voltage signal is sent to the ignition module. The ignition module is able to determine engine speed from the frequency of the voltage curve, which changes with engine speed.

A 6 cylinder engine may use a different type of sensor called a hall effect switch. With the direct ignition connected to the vehicle electrical system, the system voltage is applied to the hall effect switch located near the tip of the sensor. A small permanent magnet creates a magnetic field in the hall effect switch circuit. As the disc wheel with the slots rotates past the sensor tip, the magnetic field in the hall effect switch changes and a change in the voltage occurs at the hall effect switch output terminal.

Since this terminal is connect to the ignition module, the module senses this change in voltage and correlates the frequency of the voltage curve to determine the engine speed. The ignition module then uses this voltage input to help determine when to close and open the ignition coil primary circuit and fire the spark plug.

Park/Neutral Switch

NOTE: Vehicle should not be driven with the park/neutral switch disconnected as idle quality may be affected in PARK or NEUTRAL and a Code 24 (VSS) may be set.

This switch indicates to the ECM when the transmission is in **P** or **N**. The information is used by the ECM for control on the torque converter clutch, EGR and the idle air control valve operation.

Air Conditioner Request Signal

This signal indicates to the ECM that an air conditioning mode is selected at the switch and that the air conditioning low pressure switch is closed. The ECM controls the air conditioning and adjusts the idle speed in response to this signal.

Torque Converter Clutch Solenoid

The purpose of the Torque Converter Clutch (TCC) system is designed to eliminate power loss by the converter (slippage) to increase fuel economy. By locking the converter clutch, a more effective coupling to the flywheel is achieved. The converter clutch is operated by the ECM controlled torque converter clutch solenoid.

Power Steering Pressure Switch

The Power Steering Pressure Switch (PSPS) is used so the power steering oil pressure pump load will not effect the engine idle. Turning the steering wheel increase the power steering oil pressure and pump load on the engine. The power steering pressure switch will close before the load can cause an idle problem.

Oil Pressure Switch

The oil pressure switch is usually mounted on the back of the engine, just below the intake manifold. Some vehicles use the oil pressure switch as a parallel power supply, with the fuel pump relay and will provide voltage to the fuel pump, after approximately 4 psi (28 kPa) of oil pressure is reached. This switch will also help prevent engine seizure by shutting off the power to the fuel pump and causing the engine to stop when the oil pressure is lower than 4 psi.

Electronic Spark Timing

Electronic Spark Timing (EST) is used on all engines. The EST distributor contains no vacuum or centrifugal advance and uses a 7-terminal distributor module. It also has 4 wires going to a 4-terminal connector in addition to the connectors normally found on HEI distributors. A reference pulse, indicating both engine rpm and crankshaft position, is sent to the ECM. The ECM determines the proper spark advance for the engine operating conditions and sends an EST pulse to the distributor.

The EST system is designed to optimize spark timing for better control of exhaust emissions and for fuel economy improvements. The ECM monitors information from various engine sensors, computes the desired spark timing and changes the timing accordingly. A backup spark advance system is incorporated in the module in case of EST failure.

Electronic Spark Control

When engines are equipped with Electronic Spark Control (ESC) in conjunction with EST, ESC is used to reduce spark advance under conditions of detonation. A knock sensor signals a separate ESC controller to retard the timing when it senses engine knock. The ESC controller signals the ECM which reduces spark advance until no more signals are received from the knock sensor.

Direct Ignition System

Components of the Direct Ignition System (DIS) are a coil pack, ignition module, crankshaft reluctor ring, magnetic sensor and the ECM. The coil pack consists of 2 separate, interchangeable, ignition coils. These coils operate in the same manner as previous coils. Two coils are needed because each coil fires for 2 cylinders. The ignition module is located under the coil pack and is connected to the ECM by a 6 pin connector. The ignition module controls the primary circuits to the coils, turning them on and off and controls spark timing below 400 rpm and if the ECM bypass circuit becomes open or grounded.

The magnetic pickup sensor inserts through the engine block, just above the pan rail in proximity to the crankshaft reluctor ring. Notches in the crankshaft reluctor ring trigger the magnetic pickup sensor to provide timing information to the ECM. The magnetic pickup sensor provides a cam signal to identify correct firing sequence and crank signals to trigger each coil at the proper time.

This system uses EST and control wires from the ECM, as with the distributor systems. The ECM controls the timing using crankshaft position, engine rpm, engine temperature and manifold absolute pressure sensing.

JEEP

Throttle Body Fuel Injection (TBI) System

GENERAL INFORMATION

The Renix Throttle Body Fuel Injection (TBI), used on 1988–1990 2.5L Jeep engines is an electronically controlled single-point system. The engine is found in the Cherokee and Wagoneer (XJ Models), the Comanche (MJ) and the Wrangler (YJ) models.

The Electronic Control Unit (ECU) is a microprocessor or small computer that receives signals from many sensors. These signals are combined and interpreted within the ECU. The control unit sends actuating signals to the outputs based on the input signals. The single fuel injector meters fuel to the engine based on an output signal from the ECU. The operating time of the injector (pulse width) determines the amount of fuel admitted to the engine and is solely controlled by the ECU.

Additionally, the ECU controls the ignition timing. Based on pre-programmed values within the computer, the ECU will vary the ignition timing to meet changing load and engine conditions. The timing is not manually adjustable. The combination of precise fuel delivery and exact ignition timing allow the engine to operate efficiently under all operating conditions. The ECU is capable of adapting its programming to compensate for changing operating conditions.

Correct input signals are vital to the proper operation of the system. The ECU makes all decisions based on information received. If the input signal is faulty or absent, the output signal—and the resulting engine operation—will not be correct for the operating condition. When diagnosing a driveability or emission-related problem, remember that the output signal to the fuel and ignition systems can only be as accurate as the signals input to the control unit.

Fuel Pump Relay

The ECU grounds terminal 85 of the fuel pump relay when the ignition switch is in the **START** or **RUN** position. When a ground is provided and the relay coil energized, battery power is supplied to the electric fuel pump. The fuel pump relay is located on the relay board at the right inner fender.

NOTE: The relay has an internal resistor to protect it from voltage spikes. If necessary to replace the relay, make certain a resistor-type, not a diode type, relay is used.

Electric Fuel Pump

Located in the fuel tank, the 12 volt fuel pump is combined with the fuel gauge sending unit. The pump contains a ball-and-spring check valve to prevent fuel backflow. Operation of the pump is controlled by the ECU through the fuel pump relay. When the pump is operating, fuel line pressure is maintained at 14–15 psi (97–103 kPa). The pump also contains a pressure relief valve which will divert fuel internally if line pressure exceeds 90 psi.

Fuel Filter

The fuel filter is located on the under the vehicle on the left frame rail, ahead of the fuel tank.

Fuel Pressure Regulator

The fuel pump delivers more fuel than is required by the engine. The fuel pressure regulator, mounted on the throttle body, maintains a constant pressure at the injector and allows excess fuel to be routed back to the fuel tank. The regulator contains a spring and diaphragm calibrated at approximately 14.5 psi.

As fuel pressure builds within the regulator, the diaphragm is forced back, opening the relief valve. The spring tension is controlled by the adjusting screw at the bottom of the regulator.

Both the regulator spring chamber and the tip of the fuel injector are vented to outside air. Since both chambers are vented to the same atmospheric pressure, the volume of fuel injected is dependent only on the length of time the injector is energized.

Fuel Injector

Mounted on the throttle body above the throttle blade, the fuel injector is a solenoid type with a plunger and ball valve. When energized by the ECU, the solenoid armature pulls the plunger and ball valve upward or off the valve seat. Fuel is allowed to pass through the spray nozzle until the injector is de-energized; an internal spring forces the plunger and ball valve onto the seat, cutting off the flow of fuel.

Electronic Control Unit (ECU)

On XJ and MJ models, the ECU is located above the accelerator pedal between the steering column and the heater housing. On YJ vehicles, the ECU is mounted on a bracket above the glove box.

The Electronic Control Unit controls fuel injector operation and ignition timing based on signals from many sensors. These sensors transmit data regarding air-fuel temperature, exhaust oxygen content, engine speed (position), throttle position, coolant temperature, battery voltage and manifold absolute pressure. Certain models also provide switched inputs based on power steering pump pressure, wide open throttle and automatic transmission gear selection.

ECU INPUTS

Manifold Absolute Pressure (MAP) Sensor

The Manifold Absolute Pressure (MAP) sensor converts a vacuum signal from the intake manifold to a variable electrical signal usable by the ECU. It receives a constant 5 volts from the ECU and sends back a changing voltage directly proportional to the vacuum in the throttle body. As the engine load changes, manifold pressure varies, causing the MAP sensor's resistance to change. The input voltage level supplies the ECU with information relating to ambient barometric pressure during engine start-up (cranking) and to engine load while the engine is running.

In general, the MAP signal voltage will be low when the engine load is low (high manifold vacuum), such as idle or part-throttle cruise. Voltages will be approximately 0.5–1.8 volts at warm idle or part-throttle cruise. Conversely, signal voltages will increase with engine load. With allowance for atmospheric conditions, MAP voltage will range between 3.9–4.84 volts at wide open throttle. The ECU uses this information to adjust the fuel delivery and ignition timing as well as positioning the idle speed actuator motor and activating the instrument panel shift light.

The MAP sensor is mounted under the hood on the firewall and is connected to the throttle body with a vacuum line.

Throttle Position Sensor (TPS)

The TPS is mounted on the left side of the throttle body and is connected to the throttle valve shaft. The sensor is a variable resistor that provides the ECU with an input voltage representing throttle position. The input voltage to the ECU from the TPS varies from low at idle to high at open throttle. The increase or decrease in voltage is directly proportional to the change in throttle position. The ECU uses TPS input voltages to determine current engine operating conditions.

There a 2 types of sensors, 1 for manual transmissions and 1 with automatic transmissions. The manual transmission TPS has a 3-terminal connector. The automatic version has both the 3-terminal connector and a 4-terminal connector. In all cases, the 3-terminal connector connects the sensor to the ECU; the additional connector on the automatic sensor conveys throttle information to the transmission controller.

Of the 3 wires in the TPS connector, 1 is used to supply the controller with a constant 5 volts from the controller. One wire grounds the sensor and the third wire carries the voltage signal from the TPS to the ECU.

The throttle position sensor is adjustable but adjustment should only be done using the DRB-II scan tool with the Jeep/Eagle adapter (preferred) or by using the Idle Speed Actuator Motor Exerciser tool 7088 or equivalent, and a digital volt-ohm-meter. Random adjustments must never be made; an incorrect voltage from the TPS can cause severe driveability problems.

NOTE: When using the DRB-II to adjust the TPS on a vehicle with automatic transmission, the jumper connections must be made at the 4-pin transmission connector. The adjustment for the transmission takes precedence over the fuel injection system.

Engine Speed Sensor

This sensor is attached to the transmission bell housing. The magnetic sensor detects the flywheel/driveplate teeth as they pass during engine operation and provides engine speed and crankshaft angle (position) information to the ECU by means of a low voltage signal.

The flywheel/driveplate has a larger trigger tooth and a notch located 90 degrees before Top Dead Center (TDC) for piston No. 1. There are 12 small teeth between the notch and TDC.

When a small tooth and notch pass under the magnet core in the sensor, the concentration and then collapse of the magnetic flow induces a small voltage into the sensor coil winding. These small voltage spikes enable the ECU to count the teeth as they pass the sensor.

When the larger tooth and notch pass under the magnet core in the sensor, the signal to the ECU stops momentarily. This indicates to the ECU that the piston will be at TDC 12 teeth later. The ignition timing for the cylinder is either advanced or retarded as necessary by the ECU according to the sensor inputs.

Coolant Temperature Sensor

The coolant temperature sensor is installed in the intake manifold coolant jacket and provides a variable input voltage to the ECU. The voltage signal from the sensor to the ECU is inversely proportional to coolant temperature; that is, when the coolant is cold the signal voltage is high. As the coolant temperature increases, the voltage signal decreases.

The ECU uses this voltage signal to provide extra fuel for cold engine operation as well as determining idle speed actuator motor position, ignition advance, open or closed loop emission control and EGR operation.

The coolant temperature sensor is not adjustable but its signals and behavior may be monitored with the DRB-II scan tool.

Manifold Air Temperature (MAT) Sensor

This sensor is installed in the intake manifold with the sensor element extending into the air/fuel stream. Like the coolant temperature sensor, the MAT sensor output voltage is inversely proportional to the temperature. The ECU uses this signal to determine when cold air is entering the engine. Engine coolant temperature alone does not allow a complete picture of engine operation.

The manifold air temperature sensor is not adjustable but its signals and behavior may be monitored with the DRB-II scan tool.

Oxygen Sensor

The oxygen sensor is mounted in the exhaust pipe. It sends an electrical signal to the ECU representing the amount of oxygen present in the exhaust stream. The sensor receives ignition voltage which is used to power an internal heating element. The heating element keeps the sensor at proper operating temperature during all operating modes.

When at operating temperature—approximately 1475°F—the oxygen sensor accurately translates the oxygen content to a very low voltage signal. The signal voltage centers on 500 milli-volts. When the engine is running rich (and the exhaust is proportionately low in oxygen), the voltage rises above 500 milli-volts. As the air/fuel ratio becomes lean (exhaust gas oxygen is high), the signal drops below 500 milli-volts.

The signal from the oxygen sensor is always sent to the ECU when the engine is operating; programming within the control unit determines when the system enters closed loop operation. The system will enter closed loop operation during warm idle, part-throttle cruise and deceleration; the system will function in open loop during wide-open throttle, engine start or cold engine operation.

Shift Selector or PARK/NEUTRAL Switch

Located on the automatic transmission case, this switch signals the ECU that a driving range has been selected. The controller, in turn, uses this information to adjust the idle speed actuator motor.

Power Steering High Pressure Switch

A pressure sensing switch is placed in the power steering fluid pressure line running from the pump. Engine rpm drops when the pump is under load. The switch provides an input to the ECU during periods of high pump load; the ECU adjusts the idle speed actuator motor to provide a stable idle when necessary.

When the power steering pump pressure exceeds 275 ± 25 psi (1896 kPa) with the air conditioning clutch not engaged, the ECU will increase the engine idle speed to prevent the engine from stalling. If the air conditioning compressor clutch is engaged when the power steering pump pressure exceeds the specified amount, the ECU will disengage the air conditioning clutch to compensate for the increased engine load.

One wire running to the pressure switch brings 5 volts from the ECU. The second wire provides ground through the ECU. When pressure exceeds the trip point, the circuits are connected and the voltage signal drops below 3 volts. The ECU recognizes this voltage drop and takes appropriate action(s) to maintain idle speed and quality.

Battery Voltage Signal

The ECU monitors the operating voltage from the alternator and battery to insure precise fuel injector operation. The injector contains an electromagnet, used to raise the plunger and valve from the valve seat. Since voltage within the electrical system varies constantly, the response time of the electromagnet will also vary. These minor variations in injector function can cause noticeable driveability and emission problems.

The ECU notes the present system voltage, then adjusts the injector duration (pulse width) so the precise amount of fuel is delivered. The ECU will compensate for a wide range of system voltage but will not attempt to operate if the voltage is extremely low or extremely high.

Engine Start Signal

The ECU receives a signal that the engine is being cranked. The signal originates at the ignition switch on Comanche, Cherokee and Wagoneer vehicles. The Wrangler start signal is taken from the starter relay.

When engine speed is detected during cranking, the ECU provides ground for the fuel pump relay. Additionally, the ECU uses signals from the coolant temperature sensor, MAP sensor, manifold air mixture temperature sensor and throttle position sensor to control fuel delivery during cranking and start-up. Fuel delivery is cut off if the wide open throttle is noted during cranking; this allows clearing a flooded engine. The wide open throttle signal will be ignored if engine speed exceeds 400 rpm.

During cranking, the EGR/Canister purge solenoid is grounded by the ECU, preventing operation of the EGR valve and purging of the vapor canister.

Air Conditioning Select Switch

This input is used only on Cherokee and Wagoneer vehicles. When the manually operated air conditioning select switch on the dashboard is in the air conditioning position, voltage is supplied to the ECU through the low pressure switch. Voltage is also provided to the thermostat in the evaporator housing. Reception of this signal places the ECU in readiness to operate the air conditioning clutch relay.

The thermostat switch closes when the evaporator temperature is higher than desired. The closing of the thermostat is called the air conditioning request signal. The request signal will get no response from the ECU if the air conditioning select signal is not present. When the dashboard select switch, the low pressure switch and the thermostatic switch are all closed, the ECU will ground the air conditioning clutch relay, allowing the compressor to function. The air conditioning relay will be disabled during periods of wide open throttle or high power steering pump pressure. When the compressor is operating, the ECU will adjust the position of the idle speed actuator motor.

Closed Throttle Switch

The closed throttle switch in integral with the Idle Speed Actuator (ISA) motor and provides an input voltage to the ECU. This input enables the ECU to increase or decrease the throttle stop angle (by extending or retracting the ISA) in response to the operating conditions.

When not at idle, the throttle lever does not contact the ISA plunger; a 5 volt reference signal is sent to the ECU. At idle, the contact between the plunger and the throttle lever grounds the voltage signal, dropping it below 1 volt. By this voltage change, the ECU is signaled that the throttle is closed.

ECU CONTROLLED OUTPUTS

Air Conditioning Clutch Relay

Used only on XJ models—Cherokee and Wagoneer—the relay is located on the right inner fender panel. Once the ECU has received the air conditioning Select and Request signals, the ground circuit to the relay is closed by the ECU. The ground will not be provided, if the ECU receives a wide open throttle or power steering high pressure signal.

Once the ground is present, the air conditioning relay provides power to the compressor clutch and the compressor engages.

Power Latch Relay

After the engine is switched **OFF**, the ECU adjusts the idle speed actuator motor position in preparation for the next start. The power latch relay provides voltage to the ISA motor for approximately 5 seconds after the engine is stopped.

During engine start up, the power latch relay is provided with a ground by the ECU. When energized by the ECU, system voltage is supplied to the idle speed actuator motor through the relay.

The power latch relay is located on the right inner fender panel.

Fuel Pump Relay

The fuel pump control relay provides voltage to the electric fuel pump. When the ignition switch is turned **ON**, the ECU provides voltage to the relay coil and contact points. At initial Key On, the ECU also supplies ground to the relay coil for 3 seconds. This brief period allows the pump to run, building up fuel pressure in the lines and pressure regulator. If the ECU does not re-

ceive an engine start (cranking) or engine speed signal, the ground to the relay is switched off. This prevents the pump from running.

Once the engine is started, the ECU maintains the relay ground and permits continuous operation of the fuel pump.

Shift Indicator Light

Some manual transmission vehicles are equipped with a shift indicator or upshift light on the dashboard. The purpose of the light is to remind the operator of optimum shift points to achieve best fuel economy.

The light is controlled by the ECU and is triggered at pre-programmed intervals based on engine speed and MAP sensor values. If the operator chooses not to shift when the light is lit, the light will extinguish after approximately 5 seconds. A high gear switch within the transmission prevents the light from lighting when the vehicle is in the highest gear.

The light should illuminate when the key is turned **ON**, then go off when the engine is started.

EGR/Canister Purge Solenoid

On the Wrangler model, this solenoid controls both the EGR function and the canister purge function. On all except Wrangler models, the solenoid controls only the EGR function; the canister is purged through the air cleaner whenever the engine is running.

When energized by the ECU, the solenoid restricts vacuum flow and thereby prevents operation of the EGR and canister purge valves. Under proper operating conditions, the ECU de-energizes the solenoid and allows vacuum to flow to the controlled components.

The purge solenoid is located near the relay board in the engine compartment.

Fuel Injector

Located in the top of the throttle body, the fuel injector receives a constant supply of battery voltage from the fuel pump relay. The engine control unit provides ground to the injector; when the circuit is complete, the injector opens and fuel is admitted to the intake manifold. The amount of time the injector is open is termed pulse width and is measured in thousandths of a second or milli-seconds. The injector is energized once per intake stroke per cylinder.

NOTE: The ECU monitors the electrical signals to the injector and will react to faulty or missing signals. The ECU receives no signal regarding the condition or function of the injector; a plugged or mechanically malfunctioning injector will not set a code or trigger the dash warning light.

The ECU uses the input signals to to determine the correct pulse width for all operating conditions. Pulse width is longer for cold engine operation and shorter for warm operation. The pulse width is also varied according to conditions of wide open throttle, part-throttle cruise, deceleration and warm or cold idle.

Idle Speed Actuator (ISA) Motor

The Idle Speed Actuator (ISA) is mounted on the throttle body and is controlled by the ECU. The throttle lever rests against the adjustment screw of the actuator (plunger).

NOTE: The idle speed is not adjustable. The initial adjustment screw is only used to establish the initial positioning of the actuator when the ISA motor has been replaced. When a new ISA motor is installed, tool 7088, ISA motor exerciser or equivalent, should be used.

The actuator (plunger) extends or retracts to control the engine idle speed and to set the throttle stop angle during deceleration. Based on the inputs from the various engine sensors and switches, the ECU supplies current to the ISA motor to adjust the actuator (plunger) position for the particular operating conditions.

Once the engine has been shut off, current is momentarily supplied to ISA motor through the Power Latch relay causing the actuator to extend to a set position for the next start up. When the engine is next started it operates at a fast idle until sensor inputs tell the ECU that the engine has reached normal operating temperature. The ECU then retracts the actuator until the idle is set to a programmed rpm for current operating conditions. Programming in the ECU can provide a fast idle of 1300 rpm for a cold engine; warm idle is maintained at 700–900 rpm with 750 rpm preferred.

Multi-Point Fuel Injection System

GENERAL INFORMATION

1988–1990 Vehicles

The Renix multi-point fuel injection system, used in 1988–1990 Jeep vehicles equipped with the 4.0L engine, is controlled by a digital microprocessor called the Electronic Control Unit or ECU. The ECU receives information from various input sensors. Based on this information, the ECU is programmed to provide a precise amount of fuel and the correct ignition timing to meet existing engine speed and load conditions.

The ECU also calculates ignition timing and operates the ignition power module. The ignition timing is modified by the ECU to meet any engine operating condition. Information such as air temperature, engine coolant temperature, engine speed, absolute pressure in the intake manifold or the presence of spark knock is used by the ECU when calculating the correct ignition timing.

The ECU controls the engine by receiving input signals from the Manifold Absolute Pressure (MAP) sensor, the engine speed sensor, knock sensor, exhaust oxygen sensor, throttle position switch, coolant temperature sensor, air temperature sensor and battery voltage. Based on the information received from the input sensors, the ECU then sends control (output) signals to the fuel pump relay, fuel injectors, idle speed regulator, ignition power module and the EGR valve.

1991-92 Vehicles

All 1991–92 fuel injected Jeep vehicles employ a sequential multi-point fuel injection system. The system, found on both 2.5L and 4.0L engines, is controlled by the second generation Single Board Electronic Controller or SBEC-II. The engine controller is a pre-programmed dual microprocessor digital computer. It regulates ignition timing, air/fuel ratio, emission control devices, charging system, speed control (if equipped) and idle speed.

Typical Jeep MPI fuel system components

The SBEC-II system is capable of receiving more inputs and controlling more outputs than the previous Renix or ECU system. It can perform computation and comparisons on a higher level than the previous system. While there are many similarities between the systems in function and diagnosis, the newer SBEC-II system allows extended test functions with the DRB-II as well as providing improved engine and emission control in all operating conditions.

The engine controller receives inputs from several sensors on the engine. Based on the information received regarding present conditions, the controller provides a precise amount of fuel and the correct ignition timing to meet existing engine speed and load requirements. The engine controller limits the amount of time each injector delivers fuel to the cylinder. The fuel pressure remains constant; this method of injector control is referred to a pulse-width control. The SBEC-II system is capable of adapting the internal programming to compensate for changing operating conditions.

Although the engine controller receives inputs regarding the exhaust gas oxygen content, coolant temperature, manifold absolute pressure, engine speed, throttle position, battery voltage, air conditioning selection, automatic tranmission gear position and speed control operation, the engine speed and manifold absolute pressure signals are the primary signals that determine fuel injector pulse width.

SYSTEM OPERATION

As input signals to the controller change, the computer adjusts its signals to the output devices. For example, a different injector pulse width and ignition timing must be calculated for idle than for Wide Open Throttle (WOT). There are 8 different modes of operation for the ECU system and 9 for the SBEC-II system. These modes determine how and why the computer responds to various input signals. The modes are:

1. Key **ON**
2. Engine start-up or cranking
3. Engine warmup
4. Warm idle
5. Part-throttle cruise
6. Deceleration
7. Acceleration (SBEC-II only)
8. Wide Open Throttle (WOT)
9. Key **OFF**

The operating modes are further divided into Open Loop or Closed Loop operation. When in any of the Open Loop modes, the controller receives the input signals but uses pre-programmed values in the computer to control the fuel delivery and ignition timing. The signal from the oxygen sensor is not used as a control factor during Open Loop operation.

In Closed Loop operating modes, the computer uses the signal from the oxygen sensor to control the injector pulse width. The calculated pulse width should result in the ideal 14.7:1 air/fuel ratio.

Key ON

The key ON operating mode is an Open Loop function. When the ignition switch is turned to the **ON** position (engine off), the controller responds to inputs from the MAP sensor, air temperature sensor, coolant temperature sensor, throttle position switch and the battery voltage signal. The fuel pump is energized through the fuel pump relay and either the ASD relay or B+ Latch relay will be energized for about 3 seconds.

Although the signal from the oxygen sensor is not used by the computer in this mode, the heating element within the sensor is energized. This allows the sensor to be at the correct operating temperature sooner in the driving cycle. Additionally, at key **ON**, the manual transmission upshift light is illuminated and, on SBEC-II systems, the automatic idle speed motor is positioned by the engine controller.

Engine Start-up

The controller operates in Open Loop during engine starting. When the engine is cranking, the computer responds to inputs from the MAP sensor, engine speed sensor, MAT sensor, coolant temperature sensor, throttle position switch, starter relay, sync signal and the battery voltage signal. The ballast resistor is bypassed during engine cranking. Injector pulse width is based primarily on the signals from the coolant and MAT sensors.

On Renix systems, the ECU restricts EGR and canister purge operation by energizing the EGR/canister purge solenoid. Voltage is supplied to the injectors and the ECU controls the injector pulse width by controlling the length of time that the injector circuit ground path remains completed.

When the ignition switch is turned to the **START** position, a crank signal is sent to the control unit. The computer monitors either the engine speed (Renix) or crankshaft position (SBEC-II) signal. If a signal is not seen within 3 seconds of cranking the engine, the fuel injection system is disabled by the engine controller. If, during cranking, the computer detects a wide open throttle, the computer responds by shutting off the fuel injection to allow clearing a flooded engine. This flood-recovery function is found on both Renix and SBEC-II systems.

Warm-up

This is an Open Loop operating mode. During engine warm-up, the ECU responds to input signals from the MAP sensor, engine speed sensor or crankshaft position sensor, MAT sensor, coolant temperature sensor, throttle position sensor, gear indicator for automatic transmission, air conditioning select and request signal (if equipped), sync signal, battery voltage signal and on the Renix system, the knock sensor.

On Renix sysems, the ECU restricts EGR and canister purge operation by energizing the EGR/canister purge solenoid. For both systems, voltage is supplied to the injectors and the computer controls the injector pulse width by controlling the length of time that the injector circuit ground path remains closed. The computer also controls the air conditioning operation if the system has been selected by the operator and requested by the evaporator thermostat. If equipped with a manual transmission, the upshift light is operated by the ECU.

On both systems, the idle speed will be controlled by positioning either the idle speed stepper motor (Renix) or the AIS motor (SBEC-II). When the engine hsa reached normal operating temperature, the computer will begin monitoring the oxygen sensor input. The system will leave the warm-up mode and enter Closed Loop operation, generally in either the Idle or Cruise mode.

Idle

With the engine at normal operating temperature, this is a Closed Loop function. During engine idle, the ECU responds to input signals from the MAP sensor, engine speed sensor or crankshaft position sensor, MAT sensor, coolant temperature sensor, throttle position sensor, battery voltage signal, sync signal, oxygen sensor, air conditioning select and request signals (if equipped) and the gear indicator or neutral safety switch signal on automatic transmissions. The ECU on the Renix system receives input from the knock sensor; the SBEC-II engine controller receives an additional input from the power steering high pressure switch.

Voltage is supplied to the injectors and the computer controls the injector pulse width by controlling the length of time that the injector circuit ground path remains closed. Idle speed is controlled as necessary in response to air conditioning function and/or high pressure in the power steering system.

The computer monitors the signal from the exhaust oxygen sensor and fine tunes the injector pulse width to maintain high efficiency and low emissions. On both systems, the computer also controls air conditioning operation if the system has been selected by the operator and requested by the evaporator thermostat.

Cruise

To enter this Closed Loop operating mode, the engine must be at normal operating temperature. Addtionally, the computer must receive signals indicating throttle position above idle but below wide-open, engine speed above idle.

When the vehicle is moving at road speed, the controller responds to input signals from the MAP sensor, engine speed sensor or crankshaft position sensor, MAT sensor, coolant temperature sensor, throttle position sensor, battery voltage signal and sync signal, oxygen sensor and air conditioner select and request signals (if equipped) and the automatic transmission gear position or neutral safety switch. The ECU for the Renix system also receives signals from the knock sensor.

The computer monitors the signal from the exhaust oxygen sensor and fine tunes the injector pulse width to maintain high efficiency and low emissions. On both systems, the computer also controls air conditioning operation if the system has been selected by the operator and requested by the evaporator thermostat. The Renix ECU breaks the ground path for the EGR valve solenoid. This allows vacuum to reach the EGR valve transducer in anticipation of EGR operation.

Acceleration—SBEC-II Only

When the engine controller notes an abrupt increase in throttle position or manifold absolute pressure, it enters the acceleration mode. The system enters Open Loop operation. Injector pulse width is increased or extended in response to the increased throttle position.

Wide Open Throttle (WOT)

During WOT operation, the computer responds to input signals from the MAP sensor, MAT sensor, speed sensor or crankshaft positon sensor,coolant temperature sensor, battery voltage signal and sync signal and the throttle position sensor. The ECU for the Renix system also receives input from the knock sensor.

When the system enters wide open throttle operation, the ballast resistor is bypassed; battery voltage is applied to the fuel pump through either the oxygen sensor heater relay (Renix), the ballast bypass relay (SBEC-II, XJ and MJ) or the fuel pump relay (YJ). The system enters Open Loop and the signal from the oxygen sensor is ignored by the computer; a pre-determined amount of fuel is admitted to the engine by adjusting the injector pulse width.

If the air conditioning is operating at the time WOT is engaged, the computer will disengage the air conditioning compressor clutch for approximately 15 seconds. In addition, the upshift light will be illuminated on manual transmission vehicles.

Deceleration Mode

This Open Loop mode can only be entered with the engine at normal operating temperature. The system will enter this mode during periods of closed throttle with engine RPM above 1200 for SBEC-II or 1500 for Renix. When in this mode, the computer responds to input signals from the MAP sensor, MAT sensor, Coolant temperature sensor, speed sensor or crankshaft position sensor, throttle position sensor, automatic transmission gear selection or neutral safety switch signal, battery signal, sync signal and air conditioning select and request signals.

Once the computer senses hard deceleration with the proper rpm and throttle position, the signal from the oxygen sensor is ignored. The computer shuts off the fuel injectors, completely eliminating engine fuel delivery during this period. Based on the inputs to the computer, idle speed and ignition timing are also controlled. If the air conditioning is engaged, the SBEC-II system will disengage the compressor clutch during hard deceleration. When the input signals show that hard deceleration has ceased, the system re-enters the appropriate operating mode such as cruise or idle.

Key OFF Mode

When the ignition switch is moved to the **OFF** position, the computer stops the operation of the fuel injectors and ignition. The ASD or Latch relay is de-energized as is the fuel pump relay. On the Renix system, the ECU positions the idle speed stepper motor in anticipation of the next engine start.

SYSTEM COMPONENTS

Electric Fuel Pump

All 1990–92 fuel injected Jeep vehicles employ an electric fuel pump immersed in the fuel tank. The pump is a gear and rotor type, driven by a 12 volt electric motor. The pump is integrated with the fuel level sender.

The pump is equipped with an internal check-valve. When operating, pump pressure overcomes the spring tension within the valve and fuel is admitted to the lines. When the pump is off, the check-valve closes and fuel is prevented from flowing back into the tank.

When the pump is operating and vacuum is applied to the fuel pressure regulator, line pressure is maintained at approximately 31 psi (214 kPa). If the vacuum supply is interrupted or not present, system line pressure will increase by 8–10 psi. When the fuel pump is not operating, the fuel pressure regulator and the pump check valve combine to maintain line pressure at 19–39 psi. (131–269 kPa). This pressure can be maintained within the system for an extended period of time.

------------------------------ CAUTION ------------------------------

The fuel system is under constant pressure, even when the engine has not been run for a period of time. To avoid injury and/or property damage, always safely relieve the fuel system pressure before servicing any fuel or return line component.

Fuel Pump Control

CHEROKEE, WAGONEER AND COMANCHE

The engine control computer energizes the fuel pump by grounding the fuel pump relay. The relay is located in the relay board or power distribution center at the right inner fender.

Once energized, the relay supplies power to the fuel pump through the ballast resistor. On SBEC-II systems, the ballast resistor is bypassed during periods of wide-open throttle, with power being routed through the ballast bypass resistor. The Renix ECU bypasses the fuel pump ballast during periods of engine start-up or wide-open throttle. During starting, the power to the fuel pump is routed through the starter relay; during WOT, the power is routed through the oxygen sensor heater relay.

WRANGLER

The engine controller energizes the fuel pump through the fuel pump relay. Battery voltage is applied to the relay by the ignition switch; when the computer closes the relay ground circuit, power is provided to the fuel pump. The engine controller operates the fuel pump through the fuel pump relay under all operating conditions. The fuel pump relay is located in the power distribution center next to the battery.

Fuel Pressure Regulator

The fuel pressure regulator used with MPI systems is non-adjustable. It is a mechanical unit not controlled by the engine computer and employs manifold vacuum as an internal control or balance circuit. The regulator is mounted at the output end of the fuel injection rail and is connected to intake manifold vacuum by a hose. The fuel return hose also connects to the regulator.

The regulator contains a diaphragm, calibrated spring and a fuel return valve. Fuel pressure acts on one side of the diaphragm while vacuum and spring pressure operate on the other. Without vacuum applied, the spring is calibrated to open the fuel return outlet when the pressure differential between the injectors and the intake manifold reaches approximately 39 psi. (269 kPa). Since manifold vacuum varies as a function of engine operating conditions, the amount of vacuum applied within the regulator varies. Fuel pressure will rise and fall according to engine load. For example, with low vacuum such as during wide-open throttle, minimal vacuum is available. The regulator spring firmly seals the return outlet and fuel pressure is allowed to build within the system. Conversely, at idle, vacuum is high within the regulator; the return outlet opens sooner and line pressures are reduced.

Fuel Filter

The fuel filter is located under the vehicle on the left frame rail, ahead of the fuel tank.

Fuel Rail

Mounted on the intake manifold, the fuel rail provides fuel to the individual injectors. The fuel pressure test port is located on the fuel rail. The fuel rail assembly is not repairable under any condition.

Fuel Injectors

The fuel injectors are attached to the fuel rail; the nozzle ends are placed in the intake manifold just above the intake ports of the cylinder head. The injectors are energized sequentially and individually by the engine control computer.

On Renix systems, the injectors are provided a permanent ground. The ECU supplies battery voltage to the injector and controls the pulse width. SBEC-II systems supply voltage to the injectors through the ASD relay at start-up or through the charging system when the engine is running. The SBEC-II engine controller controls injector operation by switching the injector ground on and off.

Engine Control Units

RENIX

The Renix ECU is located under the instrument panel, between the steering column and the heater housing, roughly above the accelerator pedal. During the initial power-up period in the Key On mode, the ECU checks certain critical circuits for faults. Once a fault is identified, a code is assigned and retained in memory until the key is switched **OFF**.

When the engine is running, the ECU maintains a continuous check on certain input circuits as well as the transitions between Open and Closed Loop operation. If a fault or lack of transition is detected, the fault and its identifying code are stored in Keep Alive Memory (KAM). A fault must be present for at least 2 seconds to be stored in memory. These faults are retained in memory even after the ignition is switched **OFF**.

NOTE: Faults stored during the power-up cycle are generally hard or permanent occurrences. Faults noted during engine operation and stored in the Keep Alive Memory have a higher likelihood of being intermittent. Once a fault is stored, it will not be cleared from memory even if the problem self-corrects.

SBEC-II

The SBEC-II engine control unit is located on the left inner fender panel of Wagoneer, Cherokee and Comanche. On Wrangler, the control unit is located behind the washer fluid reservoir, near the brake master cylinder.

The SBEC-II control unit is a sophisticated computing unit containing 2 microprocessors. In addition to overseeing fuel and ignition functions, the engine control unit also controls alternator current regulation, radiator fan function (XJ and MJ with 4.0L engine only), the emission maintenance reminder light, air

conditioning clutch function, tachometer operation, the shift indicator light (manal trans), speed control system and the vehicle security/alarm system.

As with the older ECU system, SBEC-II constantly tests and monitors circuits in the system and will set a fault code when an abnormality is detected. If a fault self-corrects or does not recur, the engine controller will cancel the stored code after 51 engine starts. Besides the ability to identify a missing signal, the SBEC-II evaluates the quality of the signal. The engine controller is programmed to expect an electrical input signal within a certain voltage range. Should the circuit become damaged, the controller is capable of setting faults indicating that the signal voltage is out of range, either too high or too low. This additional refinement can be of great value when troubleshooting the system.

The SBEC-II engine controller contains certain stored values which may be substituted in case of signal loss from a critical circuit. Should a signal be interrupted, the controller will use the pre-programmed value in its place. The controller can provide back-up values for the MAP, MAT, coolant temperature, oxygen and throttle position sensors. This value may not be exactly correct for the driving condition but the engine will remain in operation. This is referred to as the limp-in or default mode of operation. In most cases, the operator will note reduced performance when this mode is entered.

The engine controller contains a voltage convertor providing a regulated 8.0 volts to the crankshaft position sensor and the sync sensor. Additionally, the the controller provides the 5.0 volt signal to the MAP and TPS sensors.

Input Components

AIR CONDITIONING SELECT SIGNAL

When the factory installed air conditioning is switched to the **ON** position, an input signal is sent to the control unit informing it that the air conditioning has been selected. The ECU or engine controller uses this signal to determine correct idle speed.

AIR CONDITIONING REQUEST SIGNAL

Once air conditioning has been selected, the air conditioning request signal provides information to the from the evaporator switch indicating that the evaporator temperature is in the proper range for air conditioning application. The computer uses this input to cycle the air conditioning compressor clutch and to determine correct idle speed stepper motor position.

ALTERNATOR OUTPUT – SBEC-II ONLY

This signal advises the engine controller of alternator output voltage to the ignition coil and fuel injectors. The computer adjusts fuel injector pulse width and alternator field based on this input.

BATTERY VOLTAGE

The battery voltage input to the controller is monitored so the injector is energized for the proper amount of time. As the battery voltage input varies, such as during engine cranking, the controller varies the injector pulse width to compensate. Additionally, the SBEC-II system uses this signal to control the alternator field.

BRAKE SWITCH – SBEC-II ONLY

The engine controller receives this input when the brake pedal is pressed. The signal is used to adjust both the idle speed and the speed control function.

COOLANT TEMPERATURE SENSOR (CTS)

The coolant temperature sensor is located on the left side of the cylinder block below the exhaust manifold on 1990 vehicles. 1991–92 vehicles position the sensor next to the thermostat housing. The CTS provides an engine coolant temperature input to the controller, which will then enrich the fuel mixture delivered by the injectors when the engine coolant is cold. Based on the CTS signal, the computer will also control engine warmup idle speed, increase ignition advance and, on Renix systems, inhibit EGR operation when the coolant is cold.

SPEED SENSOR OR CRANKSHAFT POSITION SENSOR – RENIX SYSTEM

The speed sensor is mounted to flywheel/driveplate housing and is non-adjustable. The speed sensor senses TDC and engine speed by detecting the flywheel teeth as they pass during engine operation.

The ECU converts the rate of change of crankshaft angle to engine rpm and the crankshaft angle to piston position. The flywheel has 3 trigger notches, 120 degrees apart. Each trigger notch represensts pairs of pistons, 1 and 6, 2 and 5 or 3 and 4. The trigger notch for each pair is located before a series of evenly spaced teeth on the flywheel or driveplate.

As the teeth spin past the sensor, a voltage spike is induced in the sensor and is noted by the ECU. These spikes allow the ECU to count the teeth as they pass the sensor. When the trigger notch passes, a pause occurs in the electrical input; the ECU is programmed to recognize the pause as an indication that the pair of pistons will be at TDC 12 voltage spikes later. By knowing both engine position and speed, the ECU can accurately control both fuel delivery and ignition timing.

CRANKSHAFT POSITION SENSOR – SBEC-II SYSTEM

The Hall effect sensor is attached to the flywheel or driveplate housing. The flywheel or driveplate have groups of 4 notches. As the notches spin past the sensor, electrical pulses are generated and sent to the engine controller. For each engine revolution, the 4 cylinder flywheel sends out 2 groups of 4 pulses and the 6 cylinder flyweel emits 3 groups of 4 pulses.

The trailing edge of the 4th notch in each group is 4 degrees before TDC for the corresponding piston. After computing both engine speed and position, the engine controller adjusts fuel delivery and ignition timing according to the exisiting conditions.

The engine will not operate if no signal is received from the crankshaft position sensor.

IGNITION CIRCUIT ON – SBEC-II ONLY

When the ignition switch is switched **ON**, a signal is sent to the engine controller. The controller, in turn, activates certain outputs in preparation for an engine start.

MANIFOLD ABSOLUTE PRESSURE (MAP) SENSOR

The manifold absolute pressure sensor is mounted on the firewall behind the engine. The MAP sensor reads the absolute pressure in the intake manifold and converts the vacuum signal to an electrical signal. This voltage signal is sent to the computer.

The MAP sensor is connected to the manifold or throttle body by a vacuum hose and to the ECU by a wiring harness.

MANIFOLD AIR TEMPERATURE (MAT) SENSOR

The manifold air temperature sensor is located in the intake manifold. The MAT sensor reacts to the temperature of the air in the intake manifold and provides an input to the computer, allowing it to compensate for air density changes during high temperature operation.

As the temperature of the air/fuel stream in the manifold varies, sensor resistance also changes, resulting in a different voltage input to the controller.

HEATED OXYGEN (O₂) SENSOR

The oxygen sensor is located in the exhaust manifold or in the down pipe below the manifold. The voltage output from this sensor, which varies with the oxygen content in the exhaust gas, is supplied to the computer. The O_2 sensor is equipped with a ceramic, resistance heating element that keeps the sensor at the proper operating temperature – approx. 1000°F. – during all engine operating modes. Maintaining correct sensor tempera-

ture at all times allows the system to enter closed loop operation sooner.

KNOCK SENSOR – RENIX ONLY

The knock sensor is located on the lower left side of the cylinder block, just above the oil pan. The knock sensor provides and input to the ECU that indicates detonation (knock) during engine operation. When detonation occurs, the ECU retards the ignition timing advance to eliminate the detonation at the applicable cylinder(s).

NEUTRAL SAFFETY SWITCH

If equipped with an automatic transmission, a gear selection indicator signal is sent to the controller from the neutral safety switch. When the transmission is in gear, the controller will adjust the engine idle speed to compensate for increased engine load as well as adjusting the injector pulse width and the ignition timing.

POWER STEERING PRESSURE SWITCH – 2.5L ENGINE WITH SBEC-II ONLY

A pressure sensing switch in the high pressure fluid line is used to control a signal to the engine controller. When power steering pump pressure exceeds 275 psi and engine rpm is low, a voltage signal is sent to the controller. The controller increases the engine idle speed to prevent stalling.

SERIAL COMMUNICATIONS INTERFACE (SCI) – SBEC-II ONLY

This circuit is used by the engine controller to receive information from the DRB-II during diagnosis. The scan tool cannot communicate with the controller if this circuit is not intact.

SPEED CONTROL SWITCHES – SBEC-II ONLY

The engine controller receives signals from 3 speed control switches. The ON/OFF switch signals that speed control has been enabled or disengaged. SET informs the controller of a request for a constant speed and RESUME indicates a request to return to the previously set speed.

These signals, along with the vehicle speed sensor signal, allow the engine controller to maintain both the requested speed and engine effieciency.

START SIGNAL

The computer receives a signal from the ignition switch or starter relay indicating that the switch is in the **START** position. This causes the computer to enter the Start Mode, activating the fuel pump and injectors.

SYNC SIGNAL

The sync signal works in conjunction with the engine speed sensor to provide the computer with inputs to establish and maintain correct injector firing order.

The sync signal generator is located in the distributor and provides a signal relative to the positions of pistons No. 1 and 6. A pulse ring is mounted on the distributor shaft and rotates through a Hall effect signal generator. When the leading edge of the ring enters the generator, the resulting magnetic field induces a voltage rise in the sensor. This causes a 5 volt signal to be sent to the engine control computer.

On the Renix system, this indicates to the ECU that piston No. 1 is due at TDC. As the trailing edge of the pulse ring leaves the signal generator field, the line voltage drops to 0. This advises the ECU that piston No. 6 is approaching TDC.

On SBEC-II 4-cylinder engines, the voltage rise indicates that piston No. 4 is coming to TDC. Six cylinder engines with SBEC-II use the voltage rise to indicate the approach of cylinder No. 3 to TDC. When the signal voltage falls to 0 volts, a 4 cylinder engine has piston No. 1 approaching TDC and a 6 cylinder engine has piston No. 4 approaching TDC.

The sync signal input combined with other data allow the engine controller to establish the necessary reference point for proper injector operation.

THROTTLE POSITION SENSOR

The TPS is a variable resistor; as the position of the throttle changes so does the resistance of the sensor. The throttle position sensor is mounted on the throttle plate assembly and provides the computer with an input voltage proportional to throttle position. At minimum throttle opening, a signal input of approximately 1 volt is transmitted. As the throttle opening increases, voltage increases to a maximum of approximately 5 volts for Renix or 4 volts for SBEC-II, at the wide open throttle position.

A dual TPS is used on 1988–1990 models equipped with the Renix system and automatic transmission. This dual TPS not only provides the ECU with input voltages, but also supplies the automatic transmission TCU with an input of throttle position.

VEHICLE DISTANCE/SPEED SENSOR – SBEC-II ONLY

The sensor input is used by the engine controller to determine vehicle speed and distance traveled. On 2WD vehicles, the sensor is located on the transmission extension housing. On 4WD vehicles, the sensor is located on the transfer case extension housing.

The sensor generates 8 pulses per sensor revolution. The engine controller uses this signal in conjunction with the TPS signal to determine idle, deceleration and speed control system functions. The signal is also used as a reference for the emission maintenance light.

CHRYSLER IMPORT

Multi-Point Injection (MPI) System

GENERAL INFORMATION

The Multi-Point Injection (MPI) system controls the fuel flow, idle speed and ignition timing. The basic function of the MPI system is to control the air/fuel ratio according to operational conditions through the Electronic Control Unit (ECU), based on data from various sensors. The MPI System is roughly divided into 3 areas — the fuel system, intake system and control system.

Fuel System

The fuel is supplied by the electronic in tank fuel pump and is distributed to the respective injectors via the main pipe and fuel filter. The fuel pressure applied to the injector is constant and is higher than the pressure in the intake manifold. The pressure is controlled by the pressure regulator. The excess fuel, after its regulation, is returned to the fuel tank through the return pipe.

When an electric current flows in the injector, the injector valve is fully opened to inject the fuel. Since the fuel pressure is constant, the amount of the fuel injected from the injector into the manifold is increased or decreased in proportion to the time the electric current flows. Based on ECU signals, the injectors inject fuel to the cylinder manifold ports in firing order.

Intake System

The flow rate of the air drawn through the air cleaner is measured by the air flow sensor. The air enters the air intake plenum through the throttle body.

The air is distributed to each cylinder manifold from the air intake plenum. In the manifold, the air is mixed with the fuel from the injectors and is drawn into the cylinder. The air flow rate is controlled according to the degree of the throttle valve and the servo motor openings.

The amount of air drawn during idling is adjusted by the idle speed control (ISC) servo controlled by the ECU. Further, the amount of air drawn during warm-up and deceleration is also controlled by the ISC servo.

Control System

The control system is composed of a sensor section, which monitors engine conditions and an Electronic Control Unit (ECU), which calculates the injection timing and rate according to the signals from the sensors. The sensors convert such conditions as the amount of intake air, amount of oxygen in the exhaust gas, coolant temperature, intake air temperature, engine revolution speed and driving speed into electric signals, which are sent to the ECU.

Analyzing these signals, the ECU determines the amount of fuel to inject according to driving conditions and drives the injectors. The fuel injection is by sequential injection type, in which 4 or 6 injectors are sequentially driven.

During idling, the ISC Servo is driven according to the load to assure stable idling.

SYSTEM OPERATION

The air fuel ratio control is achieved by controlling the driving time of each injector installed at each intake air port. After passing through the in-line filter, fuel is force-fed by the in-tank pump so as to be sent to the delivery pipe through the main pipe and fuel filter and is distributed to each injector by the delivery pipe. The fuel pressure applied to the injector is maintained at a fixed level by the fuel pressure regulator so it may be higher than the internal pressure of the intake manifold where fuel injection takes place. After pressure regulation, excess fuel is returned to the fuel tank through the return hose. When the injector is energized, the valve inside the injector opens fully to inject the fuel. Since the fuel pressure is kept at a fixed level, supply of fuel injected from the injectors into the intake manifold varies with the energizing time. The injectors inject fuel to each manifold port, in the sequential firing order of each cylinder, according to ECU signals.

SYSTEM COMPONENTS

Injectors

Injectors are electromagnetic type injection nozzles which inject fuel according to signals calculated and provided by the ECU. When there is continuity at the solenoid coil, the plunger and the needle valve unified with it are pulled and, as a result, fuel is sprayed from the nozzle. Because the stroke of the needle valve is always constant, the amount of fuel spray (injection) is determined by the continuity time of the solenoid coil.

Using a stethoscope or similar tool, check for operating sound as engine idles. Each injector gives a distinct ticking as it opens and closes. Check that the sound occurs at shorter intervals as the engine speed increases. Listen carefully; other injectors may produce similar sound even if the injector being checked is not working.

Pressure Regulator

The pressure regulator maintains the fuel volume at a fixed amount relative to fuel injection time. As a means to improve precision, the pressure regulator controls the fuel pressure applied to the injectors at a constant pressure relative to the surge tank negative pressure.

Surge tank negative pressure is applied to the diaphragm chamber of the pressure regulator. When the fuel pressure within the pressure regulator reaches a pressure of approximately 36 psi (250 kPa) or higher, extra fuel is bypassed to the return hose and is returned to the fuel tank.

Fuel Pulsation Damper

The fuel pulsation damper absorbs the slight fluctuations of fuel pressure which occur when the injectors inject the fuel.

The fuel pressure is constantly maintained by the pressure regulator at a pressure of approximately 36 psi (250 kPa) but slight fluctuations of the fuel pressure do occur when the injector sprays the fuel. The fuel pulsation damper, through the action of the diaphragm, absorbs these minor fluctuations of the fuel pressure to create smoother engine operation.

Resistor

The resistor is used to lower the source voltage to a level suitable for the injector. The resistor is connected in series with the injector. It reduces the voltage to approximately ¼ of the source voltage. These resistors protect the injectors from alternator voltage surges and the effects of other components in the vehicle's electrical system.

Spark-Advance Switching Solenoid Drive

The spark-advance switching solenoid is activated in order to advance the ignition timing at high altitudes where the atmospheric pressure is low or during cold weather.

At a barometric pressure of less than 660mm Hg or a water temperature of less than 95°F (35°C), the spark-advance control solenoid is driven and, by leading the surge tank negative pressure to the boost control, the ignition timing is advanced 5 degrees.

Air Conditioning Relay Control

The air conditioning relay is switched off, even when the air conditioner switch is switched **ON**, according to the engine rpm and the throttle opening. The air conditioner relay is also switched off at an engine rpm of 400 rpm or less. Additionally, this relay is switched off for 5 seconds if the ECU detects full throttle acceleration.

Air Flow Sensor

This measures the intake airflow; utilizing the Karman vortex phenomenon, it counts the number of vortices and converts this data to electric pulses which are then sent to the ECU. The ECU uses these signals to determine the basic injection time.

If the air flow sensor fails, the intake air volume cannot be measured and as a result, normal fuel injection control is no longer available. The engine will run using the default value built into the ECU.

Intake Air Temperature Sensor

Part of the air flow sensor assembly, this sensor detects the temperature of the intake air and converts this data to voltage which is sent to the ECU. Based on these signals, the ECU performs air/fuel ratio feedback control and configures usable information.

Barometric Pressure Sensor

This sensor, also integral with the air flow sensor, detects the barometric pressure and converts this data to voltage which is

sent to the ECU. The ECU uses these signals for correct the fuel injection amount and the ignition timing.

Throttle Position Sensor (TPS)

The TPS detects the degree of throttle opening; this data is converted to voltage and is sent to the ECU. The ECU uses these signals to calculate the changes in the degree of throttle opening and to sense the variable speed condition.

Idle Switch

This switch detects the fact that the throttle valve is in the idle position and sends this data as signals to the ECU. The ECU senses that the engine is idling and then controls the fuel injection amount, the ignition timing, the ISC servo, etc.

Coolant Temperature Sensor

This sensor detects the temperature of the engine's coolant and converts this data to voltage which is sent to the ECU. The ECU uses these signals for correction of the fuel injection amount and the ignition spark advance.

Oxygen Sensor

This sensor measures the amount of oxygen in the exhaust gas and sends these signals to the ECU. The ECU, based on these signals, performs air/fuel ratio feedback control.

Top Dead Center (TDC) Sensor

Built into the distributor, this sensor identifies the reference signal applicable to each cylinder. The disc slit is read by the light-emitting diode and the photo diode; this data is sent from the unit assembly to the ECU as electrical pulses. The ECU uses these signals and the signals from the crankshaft angle sensor to determine the injection timing.

Crankshaft Angle Sensor

Also built into the distributor, this sensor detects the position of the crankshaft (and therefore, the piston). The 360 slits in the disc are read by the light-emitting diode and the photo diode and this data is sent from the unit assembly to the ECU as electrical pulses.

Power Steering Oil Pressure Switch

This switch detects a load on the power steering system and increases the idle to compensate.

Idle Speed Control (ISC) Servo

The ISC system provides the following 4 modes of control:

Start Control: The throttle valve opening is controlled to optimum position for start according to the engine coolant temperature and the altitude (atmospheric pressure).

Fast Idle Control: When the idle switch is on, the engine speed is controlled to a target rpm according to the engine coolant temperature (rpm feedback control). When the idle switch is off, the ISC servo is actuated to move the throttle valve to a target opening position (throttle valve opening position) according to the engine coolant temperature (target opening control).

Idle Control: When the air conditioner switch is turned on or when the transmission is shifted from **N** to **D**, the system causes the idle speed to increase to the target rpm according to the load (rpm feedback control).

Dash Pot Control: The system provides dash pot control according to deceleration conditions to alleviate shock at deceleration.

DAIHATSU

Electronic Fuel Injection
GENERAL INFORMATION

The EFI system consists of the following 3 systems; fuel system, intake system and control system. The Electronic Control Unit (ECU) incorporating a microcomputer, controls the EFI system based on signals inputted from various sensors. Besides this function the ECU controls various functions such as the fuel pump control, Idle Speed VSV Control (ISC), Exhaust Gas Recirculating (EGR) VSV control, Barometric VSV (PVSV) control, self diagnostic and fail safe functions.

Fuel System

The fuel system is the system which supplies the injectors with the fuel necessary for combustion. This system is composed of the fuel pump, fuel pipes, fuel filter, pressure regulator, fuel delivery pipe and injectors. Fuel sucked up from the fuel tank by means of the fuel pump is sent under a pressurized condition to the fuel delivery pipe through the fuel filter. The pressure regulator mounted at the delivery pipe keeps the fuel pressure at a value about 36.3 psi. higher than the intake manifold inner pressure. Such difference between the intake manifold inner pressure and and the fuel line inner pressure prevents any variation in the fuel injection rate. Any excess fuel returns to the fuel tank through the pressure regulator. This makes it possible for the fuel at comparatively low temperature in the fuel tank to to be supplied into the fuel line, thus preventing percolation. The fuel pump is driven by the ECU.

Intake System

The intake system is a system which supplies the air needed for combustion. Air at a low temperature is sucked into the surge tank through the air cleaner and air chamber, depending on the opening degree of the the throttle valve. The air then goes through the intake manifold into the cylinders.

Control System

The control system is a system which controls the fuel amount, using the ECU, by detecting the engine operating conditions and the vehicle running conditions, based on the input signals of the various engine sensors.

Self Diagnosis Function

This system has a self diagnostic function that is invoked when any of the sensor inputs do not conform to the memorized values in the ECU. This malfunction sets a code in the ECU that records the malfunction, which is retained in the ECU by battery back-up. The code remains stored until cleared by disconnecting the battery. When the malfunction code is set, the CHECK ENGINE lamp is illuminated on the instrument panel. The code can be read from memory by shorting the test terminal, located at the right fender panel in the engine compartment.

Fail Safe Function

In the case of a major sensor failure or the ECU's inability to operate correctly the fail safe mode is evoked. This mode uses stored values from the ECU to operate the vehicle in a serviceable mode. Normal vehicle performance can not be expected in this mode of operation.

GEO

Throttle Body Injection (TBI) System
GENERAL INFORMATION

Used in the Tracker the Electronic Fuel Injection (EFI) system supplies the combustion chambers with an air/fuel mixture of optimized ratio under varying driving conditions.

The TBI system consists of a single injector which injects fuel into a throttle body bore. This system consists of 2 major subsystems: An air/fuel delivery system and the electronic control system.

The main components of the air/fuel delivery system consists of the fuel tank, fuel pump, fuel filter, throttle body assembly, fuel feed and return lines, air cleaner and the Idle Speed Control (ISC) solenoid valve.

The electronic control system consists of the Electronic Control Module (ECM), which controls various devices according to signals received from sensors. Functionally, the air/fuel control system is divided into 5 sub-systems. These sub-systems are as follows:

Fuel injection control system
ISC solenoid valve control system
Fuel pump control system
EGR control system (California)
Shift-up indicator light control system, if equipped with manual transmission

Also, if equipped with automatic transmission, the ECM sends a throttle valve opening signal to an automatic transmission control module to control the transmission.

The TBI system includes a self-diagnosis function which is controlled by the ECM. If a fault is detected when the ignition switch is **ON** and the engine is running, the ECM will response by turning on or flashing the check engine light. The self-diagnosis system includes the following components; however, not all vehicles used every components listed below:

Oxygen Sensor
Water Temperature Sensor (WTS)
Throttle Position Sensor (TPS)
Air Temperature Sensor (ATS)
Pressure Sensor
Ignition signal
EGR system
Idle switch circuit
Lock-up circuit – automatic transmission
5th Switch circuit – manual transmission only
Central Processing Unit (CPU) of the ECM

When the ignition switch is turned **ON** and the engine is stopped, the check engine light will light. This is only to check the check engine light bulb and circuit. However, if the self-diagnosis system detects trouble in the EFI system, the ECM will turn **ON** the check engine light with the engine running to warn the driver of such trouble and at the same time it stores the trouble area in the ECM backup memory. The check engine light will remain **ON** as long as the trouble exists but will turn **OFF** when the normal condition is restored.

The EFI system also includes a fail-safe function. Should a malfunction occur in the EFI system, the ECM will control such functions as the injector, ISC solenoid valve and others on the basic of a standard program pre-stored in the ECM. During a fail-safe condition, the ECM will ignore the failure signal and/or the CPU and thus provide the vehicle with a deminished level of engine performance.

SYSTEM OPERATION

When the ignition switch is turn **ON**, power is supplied to the fuel pump via the fuel pump relay. The fuel pump is activated and the fuel system is pressurized. Simultaneously, an ignition signal is sent from the ignition coil primary circuit. An engine start signal is also sent to the ECM via the engine starter circuit. The ECM uses the engine start signal to determine whether the engine is cranking or not and thus control the fuel injector and fuel pump relay accordingly.

While the engine is cranking, the ECM keeps the Idle Speed Control (ISC) solenoid valve **ON**. This provides the engine with a better start. After the engine has started, the ECM gradually reduces the ISC solenoid valve **ON** time to maintain the specified idle speed.

When the injector (solenoid coil) is energized by the ECM, the needle valve, which is incorporated with the plunger, opens and the injector, which is under pressure, injects fuel in a conical dispersion into the throttle body bore. The injected fuel is mixed with the air which has been filtered through the air cleaner in the throttle body. The air/fuel mixture is drawn through the clearance between the throttle valve, throttle bore and an idle bypass passage into the intake manifold. The intake manifold then distributes the air/fuel mixture to each combustion chamber. Should the fuel system pressure exceed a preset level, a valve in the fuel pressure regulator opens and excess fuel returns to the fuel tank via the return line.

An air valve, located in the throttle body supplies bypass air into the intake manifold without letting the air pass through the throttle valve when the engine is cold. This condition causes the engine speed to increase (fast idle state) and thus provides engine warm-up. As the engine is warmed up, a piston inside the air valve gradually blocks the amount of air passing through the air valve and simultaneously the engine speed is reduced. As the engine coolant temperature reaches approximately 176°F (80°C), the valve is fully open and the engine speed returns to normal idle speed.

The ECM also uses the following signals to compensate for engine speeds and/or fuel injection **ON** time:

Air Conditioning Signal — The ECM uses this signal to determine whether the air conditioner is operating or not and uses it as 1 of the signals for controlling the ISC valve operation.

Battery Voltage — The fuel injector is driven by its solenoid coil based upon the ECM output. However, there is some delay, called "ineffective injection time," which doesn't provide fuel, between the ECM signal and the valve action. The ineffective injection time depends on the battery voltage signal. The ECM takes this information to compensate for fuel injection time.

R, D, 2 or **L Range Signal** — When in these ranges, the automatic transmission module sends a battery voltage signal to the ECM. The ECM uses this signal as 1 of the signals to control the fuel injector and the ISC solenoid valve.

SYSTEM COMPONENTS

Electronic Control Module (ECM)

The ECM consists of a microcomputer, analog/digital converter and an Input/Output unit. The ECM controls the fuel injectors, ISC solenoid valve, fuel pump relay, self-diagnosis and the fail-safe functions.

Fuel Pump

The fuel pump, located in the fuel tank, consists of an armature, magnet, impeller, brush and a check valve. Fuel is drawn into the inlet port of the fuel pump and while under pressure, it is discharged through the outlet port. The fuel pump is also equipped with a check valve to keep the fuel system pressurized when the fuel pump is not operating. The ECM controls fuel pump operation.

Throttle Body

The throttle body consists of the main bore, air and fuel passage, vacuum passage, air induction passage, fuel injector, fuel pressure regulator, throttle valve, air valve and a throttle position sensor.

Fuel Pressure Regulator

The fuel pressure regulator is a diaphragm operated relief valve consisting of a diaphragm, spring and valve. The fuel pressure regulator maintains the fuel pressure to the injector at 25.6 psi (180 kpa) higher than that in the intake manifold at all times. If the pressure increase more than 25.6·psi (180 kpa) higher than the intake manifold pressure, a valve in the regulator opens and excess fuel returns to the fuel tank via the return line.

Fuel Injector

The fuel injector is an electromagnetic type solenoid valve, which injects fuel in the throttle body bore according to a signal from the ECM. The amount of fuel injected at any given time is determined by the length of time (duration) the solenoid coil is energized.

Pressure Sensor

The pressure sensor, consisting of a semi-conductor element, senses pressure changes in the intake manifold and converts it into a signal voltage. As the manifold pressure changes, the electrical resistance of the pressure sensor also changes. The ECM uses the voltage signal from the pressure sensor as one of the signals to control the fuel injectors.

Throttle Position Sensor (TPS)

The TPS, connected to the throttle valve shaft, consists of a contact point (idle switch) and a potentiometer which detects throttle valve angle. The throttle position in the idle state is detected by the idle switch but beyond idle position, it is detected by the output voltage across the the potentiometer. The ECM not only uses the TPS signal to control the injector but also sends it to the automatic transmission control module, where it is used as 1 of the signals to control the automatic transmission.

Air Temperature Sensor (ATS)

The ATS, located on the side of the air cleaner assembly, measures the temperature of the incoming air and converts the air temperature into resistance values. When the air temperature is low, the resistance increases and when the air temperature is high, the resistance decreases. The ECM monitors the resistance of the air temperature sensor and adjusts the amount of fuel injection accordingly.

Idle Speed Control (ISC) Valve

The ISC solenoid regulates the amount of air entering the intake manifold. The valve opens and closes an air bypass passage according to the signal from the ECM. The ECM controls the ISC solenoid valve **ON** and **OFF** time at a rate of 12 times per second.

Water Temperature Sensor (WTS)

The WTS, located at the side of the throttle body, measures the temperature of the engine coolant and signal the ECM with resistance changes. When the coolant temperature is low, the resistance value increases and when the coolant temperature is high, the resistance decreases.

Oxygen Sensor

The oxygen sensor, located on the exhaust manifold, detects the concentration of oxygen in the exhaust gases. The sensor zirconia element, generates an electromotive force when a difference in oxygen concentration exists between its faces.

ISUZU

Multi-Port Injection (MPI) I-TEC System

GENERAL INFORMATION

2.6L ENGINE

The I-TEC fuel injection control system constantly monitors and controls engine operation, which in turn helps lower emissions while maintaining the fuel economy and driveabiltiy. The Electronic Control Unit (ECU) controls the fuel injection and ignition systems.

The fuel injection system basically consists of the following components: the crank angle sensor, the throttle valve switch, the vehicle speed sensor, the coolant temperature sensor, air flow sensor, oxygen sensor, fuel injectors and the ECU.

Throttle Body Injection (TBI) System

2.8L AND 3.1L ENGINES

The electronic throttle body fuel injection system used on the 2.8L and 3.1L engines is a fuel metering system with the amount of fuel delivered by the throttle body dual injectors, determined by an electronic signal supplied by the Electronic Control Module (ECM). The ECM monitors various engine and vehicle parameters to calculate the fuel delivery time (pulse width) of the injectors. The fuel pulse may be modified by the ECM to account for special operating conditions such as cranking, cold starting, altitude, acceleration and deceleration.

The ECM controls the exhaust emissions by modifying fuel delivery to achieve, as near as possible, an air/fuel ratio of 14.7:1. The injector on-time is determined by various inputs to the ECM. By increasing the injector pulse, more fuel is delivered, enriching the air/fuel ratio. Decreasing the injector pulse leans the air/fuel ratio. Pulses are sent to each injector in synchronized and nonsynchronized modes.

Synchronized Mode

In synchronized mode operation, the injector is pulsed once for each distributor reference pulse. In the dual injector throttle body systems, the injectors are pulsed alternately.

Non-Synchronized Mode

In non-synchronized mode operation, the injector is pulsed once every 12.5 milliseconds or 6.25 milli-seconds depending on its particular calibration. This pulse time is totally independent of distributor reference pulses.

Non-synchronized mode results only under the following conditions:

1. The fuel pulse width is too small to be delivered accurately by the injector (approximately 1.5 milli-seconds).
2. During the delivery of prime pulses (prime pulses charge the intake manifold with fuel during or just prior to engine starting).
3. During acceleration enrichment.
4. During deceleration leanout.

The basic TBI unit is made up of 2 major casting assemblies: a throttle body with a valve to control airflow and a fuel body assembly with an integral pressure regulator and fuel injector to supply the fuel. An electronically operated device to control the idle speed and a device to provide information regarding throttle valve position are included as part of the TBI unit.

The Throttle Position Sensor (TPS) is a variable resistor used to convert the degree of throttle plate opening to an electrical signal to the ECM. The ECM uses this signal as a reference point of throttle valve position. In addition, an Idle Air Control (IAC) assembly, mounted in the throttle body is used to control idle speeds. A cone-shaped valve in the IAC assembly is located in an air passage in the throttle body that leads from the point beneath the air cleaner to below the throttle valve. The ECM monitors idle speeds and, depending on engine load, moves the IAC cone in the air passage to increase or decrease air bypassing the throttle valve to the intake manifold for control of idle speeds.

The pressure regulator is a diaphragm-operated relief valve with injector pressure on one side and air cleaner pressure on the other. The function of the regulator is to maintain a constant pressure drop across the injector throughout the operating load and speed range of the engine.

The throttle body portion of the TBI may contain ports located at, above or below the throttle valve. These ports generate the vacuum signals for the EGR valve, MAP sensor and the canister purge system.

SELF-DIAGNOSIS SYSTEM

The self-diagnosis system is so designed that the circuits handling the input signals from the sensors and output signals for the driving actuator are continuously monitored by the control unit. In the event of a failure, the control unit stores it in memory and operates the **CHECK ENGINE** light on the instrument panel when the nature of trouble is important, to warn the operator of failure.

The self-diagnosis system is capable of trouble-shooting the electrical circuits in the Closed Loop Emission Control system only and does not cover the trouble in the sensors, actuators or the engine itself.

When a failure has developed in the following systems while driving, the **CHECK ENGINE** light within the instrument panel is operated to warn the driver of a system failure.

1. Air flow sensor system
2. Coolant temperature sensor
3. Fuel injector system
4. Micro computer
5. Oxygen sensor
6. Vehicle speed sensor

When the diagnosis lead in the vicinity of the control unit is connected with the ignition switch in the **ON** position (engine not running), the trouble code stored in the memory is displayed by the **CHECK ENGINE** light.

After completion of the service operation, clear the trouble codes stored in memory by disconnecting the 60A main fuse in the fuse junction block, then check that only Code 12 is displayed.

All the codes stored in memory will be cleared automatically when the 13-pole connector in the control unit is disconnected. Since all the memory will be cleared when number 4 fuse is disconnected, it will be necessary to reset the clock and other electrical equipment.

SYSTEM COMPONENTS

Air Conditioning Request Signal

This signal indicates to the ECM that an air conditioning mode is selected at the switch and that the air conditioning low pressure switch is closed. The ECM controls the air conditioning and adjusts the idle speed in response to this signal. This signal is only included with the 2.8L and 3.1L engine TBI systems.

Isuzu I-TEC fuel injection system—component diagram

Air Flow Sensor

The air flow sensor is located in the air cleaner housing assembly. The purpose of the air flow sensor is to measure the volume (rate) of air that is coming into the engine. This sensor generates voltage corresponding to the mass flow of the air drawn through the air cleaner assembly and into the engine. The changing voltage is transformed into a usable electrical signal and sent oto the ECM. The air flow sensor is only included with the 2.6L engine MPI system.

Back-up Control System

Programmed into the ECU in vehicles equipped with the 2.8L and 3.1L engines only, this useful system is used in case there is a malfunction with the microcomputer within the ECU, the back-up control system works to maintain the necessary functions of the control unit to permit continuous operation of the vehicle.

Coolant Temperature Sensor

2.6L ENGINE

This sensor is located on the engine block, under the intake manifold. It sends the coolant temperature information back to the ECU. The ECU then uses this information to determine the engine temperature for calculating the required air/fuel mixture.

2.8L AND 3.1L ENGINES

The coolant sensor is a thermistor, a resistor which changes value based on temperature, mounted in the engine coolant stream. As the temperature of the engine coolant changes, the resistance of the coolant sensor changes. Low coolant temperature produces a high resistance (100,000 ohms at $-40°F/-40°C$), while high temperature causes low resistance (70 ohms at 266°F/130°C).

The ECM supplies a 5 volt signal to the coolant sensor and measures the voltage that returns. By measuring the voltage change, the ECM determines the engine coolant temperature. The voltage will be high when the engine is cold and low when the engine is hot. This information is used to control fuel management, spark timing, EGR use, canister purge and other engine operating conditions.

Crank Angle Sensor

The crank angle sensor is usually located inside the distributor housing on the 2.6L engine. It is used to detect the engine speed and relative position of each piston in its cylinder. Using these parameters, the ECU calculates the proper ignition timing and dwell angle. The ECU then sends a signal to the transistorized ignition coil to create a spark.

Crankshaft and Camshaft Sensors

These sensors are mounted on the engine block, near the crankshaft and also near the camshaft on the 2.8L and 3.1L engines. They are used to send a signal through the Direct Ignition System (DIS) module to the ECM. The ECM uses this reference signal to calculate engine speed and crankshaft position.

The engine uses a sensor called a Hall effect switch. With the direct ignition connected to the vehicle electrical system, the system voltage is applied to the Hall effect switch located near the tip of the sensor. A small permanent magnet creates a magnetic field in the Hall effect switch circuit. As the disc with the slots rotates past the sensor tip, the magnetic field in the Hall effect switch changes and a change in the voltage occurs at the Hall effect switch output terminal.

Since this terminal is connected to the ignition module, the module senses this change in voltage and correlates the frequency of the voltage curve to determine the engine speed. The ignition module uses this voltage input to help determine when to close and open the ignition coil primary circuit and fire the spark plug.

Electronic Control Unit (ECU)

The ECU is usually located under the instrument panel. The ECU analyzes all electrical data signals from the sensors. It controls the fuel injection system and the ignition system. The ECU has a built in back-up, diagnostic and fail safe control systems.

Electronic Spark Control (ESC)

When engines are equipped with ESC in conjunction with electronic spark timing, ESC is used to reduce spark advance under conditions of detonation. A knock sensor signals a separate ESC controller to retard the timing when it senses engine knock. The ESC controller signals the ECM which reduces spark advance until no more signals are received from the knock sensor. Included with the 2.8L and 3.1L engines TBI electronics.

Fuel Injector

Each fuel injector is a solenoid operated device controlled by the vehicles's controlling unit. The incoming fuel is directed to the lower end of the injector assembly which has a fine screen filter surrounding the injector inlet. The control unit actuates the solenoid, which lifts a normally closed ball valve off a seat. The fuel, under pressure, is injected in a conical spray pattern. The excess fuel passes through a pressure regulator before returning to the vehicle's fuel tank.

Manifold Absolute Pressure (MAP) Sensor

Included in the 2.8L engine TBI system, the Manifold Absolute Pressure (MAP) sensor measures the changes in the intake manifold pressure which result from engine load and speed changes. The pressure measured by the MAP sensor is the difference between barometric pressure (outside air) and manifold pressure (vacuum). A closed throttle engine coastdown would produce a relatively low MAP value (approximately 20–35 kPa), while wide-open throttle would produce a high value (100 kPa). This high value is produced when the pressure inside the manifold is the same as outside the manifold and 100 percent of outside air (or 100 kPa) is being measured. This MAP output is the opposite of what would be measured on a vacuum gauge. The use of this sensor also allows the ECM to adjust automatically for different altitudes.

The ECM sends a 5 volt reference signal to the MAP sensor. As the pressure changes, the electrical resistance of the sensor also changes. By monitoring the sensor output voltage the ECM can determine the manifold pressure. A higher pressure, lower vacuum (high voltage) requires more fuel, while a lower pressure, higher vacuum (low voltage) requires less fuel. The ECM uses the MAP sensor to control fuel delivery and ignition timing.

Manifold Air Temperature (MAT) Sensor

The Manifold Air Temperature (MAT) sensor is a thermistor mounted in the intake manifold. A thermistor is a resistor which changes resistance based on temperature. Low manifold air temperature produces a high resistance (100,000 ohms at $-40°F/-40°C$), while high temperature cause low resistance (70 ohms at 266°F/130°C).

The ECM supplies a 5 volt signal to the MAT sensor through a resistor in the ECM and monitors the voltage. The voltage will be high when the manifold air is cold and low when the air is hot. By monitoring the voltage, the ECM calculates the air temperature and uses this data to help determine the fuel delivery and spark advance. The MAT sensor is also on the 2.8L and 3.1L engines TBI system only.

Oil Pressure Switch

The oil pressure switch is mounted on the back of the 2.8L and 3.1L engines, just below the intake manifold. Some vehicles use the oil pressure switch as a parallel power supply (with the fuel pump relay) and will provide voltage to the fuel pump after approximately 4 psi (28 kPa) of oil pressure is reached. This switch will also help prevent engine seizure by shutting off the power to the fuel pump and causing the engine to stop when the oil pressure is lower than 4 psi.

Oxygen Sensor

2.6L ENGINE

This sensor is usually threaded into the exhaust manifold. The oxygen sensor measures and produces an electrical signal proportional to the amount of the oxygen present in the exhaust gases.

2.8L AND 3.1L ENGINES

The exhaust oxygen sensor is mounted in the exhaust system where it can monitor the oxygen content of the exhaust gas stream. The oxygen content in the exhaust reacts with the oxygen sensor to produce a voltage output. This voltage ranges from approximately 100 milli-volts (high oxygen — lean mixture) to 900 milli-volts (low oxygen — rich mixture).

By monitoring the voltage output of the oxygen sensor, the ECM will determine what fuel mixture command to give to the injector (lean mixture — low voltage — rich command, rich mixture — high voltage — lean command). The oxygen sensor only indicates to the ECM what is happening within the exhaust system; it does not cause things to happen. It is simply a type of gauge: high oxygen content = lean mixture; low oxygen content = rich mixture. The ECM adjusts fuel to keep the system working.

Power Steering Pressure Switch

The power steering pressure switch is used so the power steering pump load will not effect the engine idle. Turning the steering wheel increases the power steering oil pressure and pump load on the engine. The power steering pressure switch will close before the load can cause an idle problem. This switch is mounted in-line with the power steering fluid on the 2.8L and 3.1L engines only.

Throttle Position Sensor (TPS)

The Throttle Position Sensor (TPS) is connected to the throttle shaft and is controlled by the throttle mechanism. A 5 volt reference signal is sent to the TPS from the ECM. As the throttle valve angle is changed (accelerator pedal moved), the resistance of the TPS also changes. At a closed throttle position, the resistance of the TPS is high, so the output voltage to the ECM will be low (approximately 0.5 volts). As the throttle plate opens, the resistance decreases so, at wide open throttle, the output voltage should be approximately 5 volts. At closed throttle position, the voltage at the TPS should be less than 1.25 volts.

By monitoring the output voltage from the TPS, the ECM can determine fuel delivery based on throttle valve angle (driver demand). The TPS can either be misadjusted, shorted, open or loose. Misadjustment might result in poor idle or poor wide-open throttle performance. An open TPS signals the ECM that the throttle is always closed, resulting in poor performance. A loose TPS indicates to the ECM that the throttle is moving. This causes intermittent bursts of fuel from the injector and an unstable idle. On some vehicles, the TPS is adjustable and therefore can be adjusted to correct any complications caused by a voltage signal that is too high or low.

Vacuum Switching Valve

The vacuum switching valve is controlled by a signal from the ECU. This valve controls the fuel pressure according to the vacuum developed in the intake manifold. Included in the 2.6L engine I-TEC system only.

Vehicle Speed Sensor

The speed sensor is mounted behind the speedometer in the instrument cluster or on the transmission/speedometer drive gear. It provides electrical pulses to the ECM from the speedometer head. The pulses indicate the road speed. The ECM uses this information to operate several of its parameters.

Some vehicles equipped with digital instrument clusters use a Permanent Magnet (PM) generator to provide the VSS signal. The PM generator is located in the transmission and replaces the speedometer cable. The signal from the PM generator drives a stepper motor which drives the odometer.

A vehicle equipped with a speed sensor, should not be driven without the speed sensor connected or idle quality may be affected.

MAZDA

Multi-Point Fuel Injection (MPI) System

GENERAL INFORMATION

NOTE: The Mazda Navajo uses the Ford MPI fuel Injection System, which can be found earlier in this section.

Intake Air System

The air intake system controls the air that is induced into the engine for efficient operation. The system consists of the air duct work, air cleaner assembly, air flow sensor, throttle body, dynamic chamber, extension manifolds or plenums and intake manifolds. The intake air system may contain the Variable Resonance Induction System (VRIS) and Idle Speed Control (ISC) system for improved engine power and idle smoothness.

Some air flow sensor are equipped with a self-cleaning feature (burn off control system) that momentarily super-heats the hot wire to burn off contaminants that may have collected over time. This operation will only occur after the vehicle has been shut off after after being operated.

Idle Speed Control (ISC) System

The ISC system controls the intake air amount (detected by the air flow meter), by regulating the amount of bypass air that passes through the throttle body, which is instrumental in maintaining a steady idle speed. The ISC system consists of the Bypass Air Control (BAC) valve and its control system.

Variable Resonance Induction System (VRIS)

This system is only included in the MPV with the 3.0L engine to enhance low speed torque capabilities. This system consists of the dynamic chamber, shutter valve actuator, extension manifolds, intake manifold and its control system.

The shutter valve is installed on the dynamic chamber and its operation is controlled by engine control unit. The resonance

Mazda EGI fuel injection system

charge uses pressure waves from the intake air caused by the closing and opening of the intake valve. As each cylinder's intake valve operates, it forces air to fill the other cylinders. The engine speed at which this actually takes place is determined by the dynamic chamber capacity and the length of the passage between cylinders.

Fuel System

The fuel system supplies the necessary fuel to the injectors to achieve combustion at a constant pressure. Fuel is metered and injected into the intake manifold according to the signals from the engine control unit coming from the various sensors.

The fuel system consists of the fuel pump, fuel filter, distribution pipe, pressure regulator, injectors, transfer pump (4WD vehicles) and a circuit opening relay.

Engine Control Unit (ECU)

The ECU, through various input signals, monitors battery voltage, engine rpm, amount of air intake, cranking signal, intake temperature, coolant temperature, oxygen concentration in the exhaust gases, throttle opening, atmospheric pressure gearshift position, clutch engagement, braking, power steering operation and air conditioning compressor operation.

The ECU controls the operation of the fuel injection system, idle-up system, fuel evaporation system and ignition timing. The ECU has a built in fail-safe mechanism. If a fault is generated while driving, The ECU will substitute pre-programmed values for the faulty one(s). Driving performance will be affected, but the vehicle will still be driveable.

Pressure Regulator Control (PRC) System

By cutting the vacuum to the pressure regulator, this system prevents fuel percolation and eventual loss during idle after the engine is started while it is still hot. The PRC system causes an increase in fuel pressure to overcome the percolating effect.

Evaporative Emission Control (EEC) System

This system is controlled by signals sent from the water thermo sensor, intake air thermo sensor, air flow sensor and the engine speed sensor (ignition coil). The ECU calculates the engine operating conditions from the signals and controls the EEC system by the operation of the solenoid valves for the No. 1 purge control valve and the vacuum switching valve.

Deceleration Control System

This system, only available on the MPV with the 3.0L engine, consists of the fuel cut operation and dashpot unit. The fuel cut feature is used to improve fuel economy and prevent bucking during deceleration. The dashpot prevents the throttle valve from closing suddenly and causing an undesirable braking action.

Air Conditioning Cut-Off System

To improve idle smoothness just after engine start up and acceleration performance, this cut-off system is used. The air conditioning compressor will be turned off when all of the following condition are met:
1. The air conditioning is **ON**.
2. The transmission is in gear and the clutch pedal is released, if equipped with a manual transmission.
3. The automatic transmission is not in **P** or **N**, if equipped.
4. The throttle valve is at least half opened.
5. The air conditioning is cut off for about 10 seconds after the engine is started.

MITSUBISHI

Multi-Point Injection (MPI) System

GENERAL INFORMATION

The Multi-Point Injection (MPI) system controls the fuel flow, idle speed and ignition timing. The basic function of the MPI system is to control the air/fuel ratio according to operational conditions through the Electronic Control Unit (ECU), based on data from various sensors. The MPI System is roughly divided into 3 areas — the fuel system, intake system and control system.

Fuel System

The fuel is supplied by the electronic in tank fuel pump and is distributed to the respective injectors via the main pipe and fuel filter. The fuel pressure applied to the injector is constant and is higher than the pressure in the intake manifold. The pressure is controlled by the pressure regulator. The excess fuel, after its regulation, is returned to the fuel tank through the return pipe.

When an electric current flows in the injector, the injector valve is fully opened to inject the fuel. Since the fuel pressure is constant, the amount of the fuel injected from the injector into the manifold is increased or decreased in proportion to the time the electric current flows. Based on ECU signals, the injectors inject fuel to the cylinder manifold ports in firing order.

Intake System

The flow rate of the air drawn through the air cleaner is measured by the air flow sensor. The air enters the air intake plenum through the throttle body.

The air is distributed to each cylinder manifold from the air intake plenum. In the manifold, the air is mixed with the fuel from the injectors and is drawn into the cylinder. The air flow rate is controlled according to the degree of the throttle valve and the servo motor openings.

The amount of air drawn during idling is adjusted by the idle speed control (ISC) servo controlled by the ECU. Further, the amount of air drawn during warm-up and deceleration is also controlled by the ISC servo.

Control System

The control system is composed of a sensor section, which monitors engine conditions and an Electronic Control Unit (ECU), which calculates the injection timing and rate according to the signals from the sensors. The sensors convert such conditions as the amount of intake air, amount of oxygen in the exhaust gas, coolant temperature, intake air temperature, engine revolution speed and driving speed into electric signals, which are sent to the ECU.

Analyzing these signals, the ECU determines the amount of fuel to inject according to driving conditions and drives the injectors. The fuel injection is by sequential injection type, in which 4 or 6 injectors are sequentially driven.

During idling, the ISC Servo is driven according to the load to assure stable idling.

SYSTEM OPERATION

The air fuel ratio control is achieved by controlling the driving time of each injector installed at each intake air port. After passing through the in-tank filter, fuel is force-fed by the in-tank pump so as to be sent to the delivery pipe through the main pipe

Mitsubishi—MPI fuel system components

and fuel filter and is distributed to each injector by the delivery pipe. The fuel pressure applied to the injector is maintained at a fixed level by the fuel pressure regulator so it may be higher than the internal pressure of the intake manifold where fuel injection takes place. After pressure regulation, excess fuel is returned to the fuel tank through the return hose. When the injector is energized, the valve inside the injector opens fully to inject the fuel. Since the fuel pressure is kept at a fixed level, supply of fuel injected from the injectors into the intake manifold varies with the energizing time. The injectors inject fuel to each manifold port, in the sequential firing order of each cylinder, according to ECU signals.

SYSTEM COMPONENTS

Injectors

Injectors are electromagnetic type injection nozzles which inject fuel according to signals calculated and provided by the ECU. When there is continuity at the solenoid coil, the plunger and the needle valve unified with it are pulled and, as a result, fuel is sprayed from the nozzle. Because the stroke of the needle valve is always constant, the amount of fuel spray (injection) is determined by the continuity time of the solenoid coil.

Using a stethoscope or similar tool, check for operating sound as engine idles. Each injector gives a distinct ticking as it opens and closes. Check that the sound occurs at shorter intervals as the engine speed increases. Listen carefully; other injectors may produce similar sound even if the injector being checked is not working.

Pressure Regulator

The pressure regulator maintains the fuel volume at a fixed amount relative to fuel injection time. As a means to improve precision, the pressure regulator controls the fuel pressure applied to the injectors at a constant pressure relative to the surge tank negative pressure.

Surge tank negative pressure is applied to the diaphragm chamber of the pressure regulator. When the fuel pressure within the pressure regulator reaches a pressure of approximately 36 psi (250 kPa) or higher, extra fuel is bypassed to the return hose and is returned to the fuel tank.

Fuel Pulsation Damper

The fuel pulsation damper absorbs the slight fluctuations of fuel pressure which occur when the injectors inject the fuel.

The fuel pressure is constantly maintained by the pressure regulator at a pressure of approximately 36 psi (250 kPa) but slight fluctuations of the fuel pressure do occur when the injector sprays the fuel. The fuel pulsation damper, through the action of the diaphragm, absorbs these minor fluctuations of the fuel pressure to create smoother engine operation.

Resistor

The resistor is used to lower the source voltage to a level suitable for the injector. The resistor is connected in series with the injector. It reduces the voltage to approximately ¼ of the source voltage. These resistors protect the injectors from alternator voltage surges and the effects of other components in the vehicle's electrical system.

Spark-Advance Switching Solenoid Drive

The spark-advance switching solenoid is activated in order to advance the ignition timing at high altitudes where the atmospheric pressure is low or during cold weather.

At a barometric pressure of less than 660mm Hg or a water temperature of less than 95°F (35°C), the spark-advance control solenoid is driven and, by leading the surge tank negative pressure to the boost control, the ignition timing is advanced 5 degrees.

Air Conditioning Relay Control

The air conditioning relay is switched off, even when the air conditioner switch is switched **ON**, according to the engine rpm and the throttle opening. The air conditioner relay is also switched off at an engine rpm of 400 rpm or less. Additionally, this relay is switched off for 5 seconds if the ECU detects full throttle acceleration.

Air Flow Sensor

This measures the intake airflow; utilizing the Karman vortex phenomenon, it counts the number of vortices and converts this data to electric pulses which are then sent to the ECU. The ECU uses these signals to determine the basic injection time.

If the air flow sensor fails, the intake air volume cannot be measured and as a result, normal fuel injection control is no longer available. The engine will run using the default value built into the ECU.

Intake Air Temperature Sensor

Part of the air flow sensor assembly, this sensor detects the temperature of the intake air and converts this data to voltage which is sent to the ECU. Based on these signals, the ECU performs air/fuel ratio feedback control and configures usable information.

Barometric Pressure Sensor

This sensor, also integral with the air flow sensor, detects the barometric pressure and converts this data to voltage which is sent to the ECU. The ECU uses these signals for correct the fuel injection amount and the ignition timing.

Throttle Position Sensor (TPS)

The TPS detects the degree of throttle opening; this data is converted to voltage and is sent to the ECU. The ECU uses these signals to calculate the changes in the degree of throttle opening and to sense the variable speed condition.

Idle Switch

This switch detects the fact that the throttle valve is in the idle position and sends this data as signals to the ECU. The ECU senses that the engine is idling and then controls the fuel injection amount, the ignition timing, the ISC servo, etc.

Coolant Temperature Sensor

This sensor detects the temperature of the engine's coolant and converts this data to voltage which is sent to the ECU. The ECU uses these signals for correction of the fuel injection amount and the ignition spark advance.

Oxygen Sensor

This sensor measures the amount of oxygen in the exhaust gas and sends these signals to the ECU. The ECU, based on these signals, performs air/fuel ratio feedback control.

Top Dead Center (TDC) Sensor

Built into the distributor, this sensor identifies the reference signal applicable to each cylinder. The disc slit is read by the light-emitting diode and the photo diode; this data is sent from the unit assembly to the ECU as electrical pulses. The ECU uses these signals and the signals from the crankshaft angle sensor to determine the injection timing.

Crankshaft Angle Sensor

Also built into the distributor, this sensor detects the position of the crankshaft (and therefore, the piston). The 360 slits in the disc are read by the light-emitting diode and the photo diode and this data is sent from the unit assembly to the ECU as electrical pulses.

Power Steering Oil Pressure Switch

This switch detects a load on the power steering system and increases the idle to compensate.

Idle Speed Control (ISC) Servo

The ISC system provides the following 4 modes of control:

Start Control: The throttle valve opening is controlled to optimum position for start according to the engine coolant temperature and the altitude (atmospheric pressure).

Fast Idle Control: When the idle switch is on, the engine speed is controlled to a target rpm according to the engine coolant temperature (rpm feedback control). When the idle switch is off, the ISC servo is actuated to move the throttle valve to a target opening position (throttle valve opening position) according to the engine coolant temperature (target opening control).

Idle Control: When the air conditioner switch is turned on or when the transmission is shifted from **N** to **D**, the system causes the idle speed to increase to the target rpm according to the load (rpm feedback control).

Dash Pot Control: The system provides dash pot control according to deceleration conditions to alleviate shock at deceleration.

NISSAN

Electronic Concentrated Control System (ECCS)

GENERAL INFORMATION

The Nissan ECCS is a throttle body or multi-port fuel injection system used on all fuel injected vehicles. The electronic control unit consists of a microcomputer, inspection lights, a diagnostic mode selector and connectors for signal input and output and for power supply. The Electronic Concentrated Control System (ECCS) computer controls the amount of fuel injected, ignition timing, mixture ratio feedback, idle speed, fuel pump operation, mixture heating, Air Injection Valve (AIV) operation, Exhaust Gas Recirculation (EGR) and vapor canister purge operation.

SYSTEM OPERATION

In operation, the on-board computer (control unit) calculates the basic injection pulse width by processing signals from the crank angle sensor and air flow meter. Receiving signals from each sensor which detects various engine operating conditions, the computer adds various enrichments (which are preprogrammed) to the basic injection amount. In this manner, the optimum amount of fuel is delivered through the injectors. The fuel is enriched when starting, during warm-up, when accelerat-

EGR CONTROL VALVE

BPT VALVE

EXHAUST GAS TEMPERATURE SENSOR (FOR CALIFORNIA MODEL)

EXHAUST GAS SENSOR

EGR CONTROL SOLENOID VALVE

IGNITION COIL AND POWER TRANSISTOR

FUEL FILTER

AIV CASE

AIR FLOW METER

DISTRIBUTOR

THROTTLE SENSOR

THROTTLE CHAMBER

AIV CONTROL SOLENOID VALVE

ENGINE TEMPERATURE SENSOR

INJECTOR

CRANK ANGLE SENSOR

Nissan fuel injection system components—4 cylinder engines

ing, when cylinder head temperature is high and when operating under a heavy load. The fuel is leaned during deceleration according to the closing rate of the throttle valve. Fuel shut-off is accomplished during deceleration, when vehicle speed exceeds 137 mph or when engine speed exceeds 6400 rpm for about 500 revolutions.

The mixture ratio feedback system (closed loop control) is designed to control the air/fuel mixture precisely to the stoichiometric or optimum point so the 3-way catalytic converter can minimize CO, HC and NOx emissions simultaneously. The optimum air/fuel fuel mixture is 14.7:1. Some systems use an exhaust gas (oxygen) sensor located in the exhaust manifold to give an indication of whether the fuel mixture is richer or leaner than the stoichiometric point. The control unit adjusts the injection pulse width according to the sensor voltage so the mixture ratio will be within the narrow window around the stoichiometric fuel ratio. The system goes into closed loop as soon as the oxygen sensor heats up enough to register. The system will operate under open loop when starting the engine, when the engine temperature is cold, when exhaust gas sensor temperature is cold, when driving at high speeds or under heavy load, at idle (after mixture ratio learning is completed), during deceleration, if the exhaust gas sensor malfunctions, or when the exhaust gas

sensor monitors a rich condition for more than 10 seconds and during deceleration.

Ignition timing is controlled in response to engine operating conditions. The optimum ignition timing in each driving condition is preprogrammed in the computer. The signal from the control unit is transmitted to the power transistor and controls ignition timing. The idle speed is also controlled according to engine operating conditions, temperature and gear position. On manual transmission models, if battery voltage is less than 12 volts for a few seconds, a higher idle speed will be maintained by the control unit to improve charging function.

There is a fail-safe system built into the ECCS control unit. If the output voltage of the air flow meter is extremely low, the ECU will substitute a preprogrammed value for the air flow meter signal and allow the vehicle to be driven as long as the engine speed is kept below 2000 rpm. If the cylinder head temperature sensor circuit is open, the control unit locks the warmup enrichment at a certain amount. This amount is almost the same as that when the cylinder head temperature is between 68–176°F (20–80°C). If the fuel pump circuit malfunctions, the fuel pump relay comes on until the engine stops. This allows the fuel pump to receive power from the relay.

Nissan fuel injection system components – 6 cylinder engines

SYSTEM COMPONENTS

Crank Angle Sensor

The crank angle sensor is a basic component of the entire system. It monitors engine speed and piston position and sends other signals which the control unit uses to calculate ignition timing and other functions. The crank angle sensor has a rotor plate and a wave forming circuit. The rotor plate has 360 slits for 1 degree signals (engine speed) and 4 slits for 180 degree signals (crank angle). Light emitting diodes (LED's) and photo diodes are built in the wave forming circuit. When the rotor plate passes the space between the LED and the photo diode, the slits of the rotor plate continually cut the light which is sent to the photo diode from the LED, causing rough shaped pulses. These pulses are converted into on-off signals by the wave forming circuit and sent to the control unit as input signals.

Air Flow Meter

The air flow meter measures the intake air flow rate by taking a part of the entire flow. Measurements are made in such a manner that the control unit receives electrical output signals varied by the amount of heat emitted from a hot wire placed in the stream of intake air. When intake air flows into the intake manifold through a route around the hot wire, the heat generated by the wire is taken away by the passing air. The amount of heat removed depends on the air flow but the maximum temperature of the hot wire is automatically controlled, requiring more electrical current to maintain the controlled temperature in the wire as the amount of intake air increases. By measuring the amount of current necessary to maintain the hot wire temperature, the control unit measures the amount of intake air passing the wire and therefore knows the volume of air entering the engine.

Before removing the air flow meter, remove the throttle valve switch. When removing the air flow meter, pull it out vertically, taking care not to bend or damage the plug portion. Never touch the sensor portion with your finger and apply silicone grease to the mating surface between the air flow meter and throttle body when installing to allow heat to escape. Failure to use silicone grease for heat dissipation will result in air flow meter failure.

Water Temperature Sensor

The water temperature sensor, located on the front side of the intake manifold, detects engine coolant temperature and sends signals to the control unit. The air temperature sensor is installed in the air cleaner and senses the temperature of the intake air. The water and air temperature sensors employs a thermistor which is sensitive to changes in temperature. The electrical resistance of this type of thermistor decreases as temperature rises.

Exhaust Gas Sensor

The exhaust gas sensor, which is placed in the exhaust pipe, monitors the amount of oxygen in the exhaust gas. The sensor is made of ceramic titania which changes electrical resistance at the ideal air/fuel ratio (14.7:1). The control unit supplies the sensor with approximately 1 volt and takes the output voltage of the sensor depending on its resistance. The oxygen sensor is equipped with a heater to bring it to operating temperature quickly.

Throttle Sensor/Hard Idle Switch

The throttle sensor/hard idle switch is attached to the throttle body and operates in response to accelerator pedal movement. This sensor has 2 functions; it contains an idle switch and throttle position sensor. The idle switch closes when the throttle valve is positioned at idle and opens when it is in any other position. The throttle sensor is a potentiometer which transforms the throttle valve position into output voltage and feeds the voltage signal to the control unit. In addition, the throttle sensor detects the opening or closing speed of the throttle valve and feeds the rate of voltage change to the control unit.

Power Steering Oil Pressure Switch

A power steering oil pressure switch is attached to the power steering high pressure line and detects the power steering load, sending a load signal to the control unit which then sends the idle-up signal to the Idle Speed Control (ISC) valve.

Fuel Pressure Regulator

A fuel pressure regulator is built into the side of the throttle body. It maintains fuel pressure at a constant 14 psi. Since the injected fuel amount depends on injection pulse duration, it is necessary to keep the fuel pressure constant. The fuel pump with a fuel damper is located in the fuel tank. The pump is an electric, vane roller type.

Fuel Injector

The fuel injector is basically a small solenoid valve. As the control unit sends injection signals to the injector, high pressure fuel, which is supplied to the coil built into the injector, pulls the ball valve back and the fuel is injected onto the throttle valve through the nozzle. The amount of injected fuel is controlled by the computer by means of longer or shorter signals (pulse duration) to the injector. A mixture heater is located between the throttle valve and the intake manifold. This is designed and operated for atomizing fuel in the cold engine start condition. The heater is also controlled by the computer. Injectors make a clicking noise when functioning properly.

Mixture Heater

If equipped, the mixture heater is located between the throttle valve and the intake manifold. This is designed and operated for atomizing fuel in the cold engine start condition. The ECU controls the heater.

Idle Speed Control (ISC) Valve

The Idle Speed Control (ISC) valve is a rotary solenoid valve that receives a pulse signal from the control unit. This pulse signal determines the position of the slider, thereby varying bypass air quantity which raises or lowers the idle speed. The ISC valve has additional functions which include idle-up after cold start (fast idle), idle speed feedback control, idle-up for air conditioner and power steering (fast idle control device) and deceleration vacuum control.

Electronic Control Unit (ECU)

The ECU consists of a microcomputer, inspection lights, a diagnostic mode selector and connectors for signal input and for power supply. The unit has control of the injected fuel amount, ignition timing, mixture ratio feedback, idle speed, fuel pump operation, mixture heating, AIV operation and EGR and canister purge operation.

SUZUKI

Throttle Body Injection (TBI) System

GENERAL INFORMATION

Used in the Suzuki Sidekick the Electronic Fuel Injection (EFI) system supplies the combustion chambers with an air/fuel mixture of optimized ratio under varying driving conditions.

The TBI system consists of a single injector which injects fuel into a throttle body bore. This system consists of 2 major subsystems: An air/fuel delivery system and the electronic control system.

The main components of the air/fuel delivery system consists of the fuel tank, fuel pump, fuel filter, throttle body assembly, fuel feed and return lines, air cleaner and the Idle Speed Control (ISC) solenoid valve.

The electronic control system consists of the Electronic Control Module (ECM), which controls various devices according to signals received from sensors. Functionally, the air/fuel control system is divided into 5 sub-systems. These sub-systems are as follows:

Fuel injection control system
ISC solenoid valve control system
Fuel pump control system
EGR control system (California)
Shift-up indicator light control system, if equipped with manual transmission

Also, if equipped with automatic transmission, the ECM sends a throttle valve opening signal to an automatic transmission control module to control the transmission.

The TBI system includes a self-diagnosis function which is controlled by the ECM. If a fault is detected when the ignition switch is **ON** and the engine is running, the ECM will response by turning on or flashing the check engine light. The self-diagnosis system includes the following components; however, not all vehicles used every components listed below:

Oxygen Sensor
Water Temperature Sensor (WTS)
Throttle Position Sensor (TPS)
Air Temperature Sensor (ATS)
Pressure Sensor
Ignition signal
EGR system
Idle switch circuit
Lock-up circuit—automatic transmission
5th Switch circuit—manual transmission only
Central Processing Unit (CPU) of the ECM

When the ignition switch is turned **ON** and the engine is stopped, the check engine light will light. This is only to check the check engine light bulb and circuit. However, if the self-diagnosis system detects trouble in the EFI system, the ECM will turn **ON** the check engine light with the engine running to warn the driver of such trouble and at the same time it stores the trouble area in the ECM backup memory. The check engine light will remain **ON** as long as the trouble exists but will turn **OFF** when the normal condition is restored.

The EFI system also includes a fail-safe function. Should a malfunction occur in the EFI system, the ECM will control such functions as the injector, ISC solenoid valve and others on the basic of a standard program pre-stored in the ECM. During a fail-safe condition, the ECM will ignore the failure signal and/or the CPU and thus provide the vehicle with a deminished level of engine performance.

SYSTEM OPERATION

When the ignition switch is turn **ON**, power is supplied to the fuel pump via the fuel pump relay. The fuel pump is activated and the fuel system is pressurized. Simultaneously, an ignition signal is sent from the ignition coil primary circuit. An engine start signal is also sent to the ECM via the engine starter circuit. The ECM uses the engine start signal to determine whether the engine is cranking or not and thus control the fuel injector and fuel pump relay accordingly.

While the engine is cranking, the ECM keeps the Idle Speed Control (ISC) solenoid valve **ON**. This provides the engine with a better start. After the engine has started, the ECM gradually reduces the ISC solenoid valve **ON** time to maintain the specified idle speed.

When the injector (solenoid coil) is energized by the ECM, the needle valve, which is incorporated with the plunger, opens and the injector, which is under pressure, injects fuel in a conical dispersion into the throttle body bore. The injected fuel is mixed with the air which has been filtered through the air cleaner in the throttle body. The air/fuel mixture is drawn through the clearance between the throttle valve, throttle bore and an idle bypass passage into the intake manifold. The intake manifold then distributes the air/fuel mixture to each combustion chamber. Should the fuel system pressure exceed a preset level, a valve in the fuel pressure regulator opens and excess fuel returns to the fuel tank via the return line.

An air valve, located in the throttle body supplies bypass air into the intake manifold without letting the air pass through the throttle valve when the engine is cold. This condition causes the engine speed to increase (fast idle state) and thus provides engine warm-up. As the engine is warmed up, a piston inside the air valve gradually blocks the amount of air passing through the air valve and simultaneously the engine speed is reduced. As the engine coolant temperature reaches approximately 176°F (80°C), the valve is fully open and the engine speed returns to normal idle speed.

The ECM also uses the following signals to compensate for engine speeds and/or fuel injection **ON** time:

Air Conditioning Signal—The ECM uses this signal to determine whether the air conditioner is operating or not and uses it as 1 of the signals for controlling the ISC valve operation.

Battery Voltage—The fuel injector is driven by its solenoid coil based upon the ECM output. However, there is some delay, called "ineffective injection time," which doesn't provide fuel, between the ECM signal and the valve action. The ineffective injection time depends on the battery voltage signal. The ECM takes this information to compensate for fuel injection time.

R, D, 2 or L Range Signal—When in these ranges, the automatic transmission module sends a battery voltage signal to the ECM. The ECM uses this signal as 1 of the signals to control the fuel injector and the ISC solenoid valve.

SYSTEM COMPONENTS

Electronic Control Module (ECM)

The ECM consists of a microcomputer, analog/digital converter and an Input/Output unit. The ECM controls the fuel injectors, ISC solenoid valve, fuel pump relay, self-diagnosis and the fail-safe functions.

Fuel Pump

The fuel pump, located in the fuel tank, consists of an armature, magnet, impeller, brush and a check valve. Fuel is drawn into the inlet port of the fuel pump and while under pressure, it is discharged through the outlet port. The fuel pump is also equipped with a check valve to keep the fuel system pressurized when the fuel pump is not operating. The ECM controls fuel pump operation.

Throttle Body

The throttle body consists of the main bore, air and fuel passage, vacuum passage, air induction passage, fuel injector, fuel pressure regulator, throttle valve, air valve and a throttle position sensor.

Fuel Pressure Regulator

The fuel pressure regulator is a diaphragm operated relief valve consisting of a diaphragm, spring and valve. The fuel pressure regulator maintains the fuel pressure to the injector at 25.6 psi (180 kpa) higher than that in the intake manifold at all times. If the pressure increase more than 25.6 psi (180 kpa) higher than the intake manifold pressure, a valve in the regulator opens and excess fuel returns to the fuel tank via the return line.

Fuel Injector

The fuel injector is an electromagnetic type solenoid valve, which injects fuel in the throttle body bore according to a signal from the ECM. The amount of fuel injected at any given time is determined by the length of time (duration) the solenoid coil is energized.

Pressure Sensor

The pressure sensor, consisting of a semi-conductor element, senses pressure changes in the intake manifold and converts it into a signal voltage. As the manifold pressure changes, the electrical resistance of the pressure sensor also changes. The ECM uses the voltage signal from the pressure sensor as one of the signals to control the fuel injectors.

Throttle Position Sensor (TPS)

The TPS, connected to the throttle valve shaft, consists of a contact point (idle switch) and a potentiometer which detects throttle valve angle. The throttle position in the idle state is detected by the idle switch but beyond idle position, it is detected by the output voltage across the the potentiometer. The ECM not only uses the TPS signal to control the injector but also sends it to the automatic transmission control module, where it is used as 1 of the signals to control the automatic transmission.

Air Temperature Sensor (ATS)

The ATS, located on the side of the air cleaner assembly, measures the temperature of the incoming air and converts the air temperature into resistance values. When the air temperature is low, the resistance increases and when the air temperature is high, the resistance decreases. The ECM monitors the resistance of the air temperature sensor and adjusts the amount of fuel injection accordingly.

Idle Speed Control (ISC) Valve

The ISC solenoid regulates the amount of air entering the intake manifold. The valve opens and closes an air bypass passage according to the signal from the ECM. The ECM controls the ISC solenoid valve **ON** and **OFF** time at a rate of 12 times per second.

Water Temperature Sensor (WTS)

The WTS, located at the side of the throttle body, measures the temperature of the engine coolant and signal the ECM with resistance changes. When the coolant temperature is low, the resistance value increases and when the coolant temperature is high, the resistance decreases.

Oxygen Sensor

The oxygen sensor, located on the exhaust manifold, detects the concentration of oxygen in the exhaust gases. The sensor zirconia element, generates an electromotive force when a difference in oxygen concentration exists between its faces. A large concentration (lean mixture) difference results in approximately 1 volt and a small difference (rich mixture) results in slightly higher than 0 volt.

TOYOTA

Toyota Computer Control System (TCCS)

GENERAL INFORMATION

Fuel System

An electric fuel pump supplies sufficient fuel, under a constant pressure, to the fuel injectors. These injectors inject a metered quantity of fuel into the intake manifold in accordance with signals from the Electronic Control Computer (ECU). Each injector simultaneously injects ½ the fuel required for ideal combustion with each engine revolution.

Air Induction System

The air induction system provides sufficient air for the engine operation. This includes the primary and auxiliary air valves, throttle body, air intake device and idle control components.
    Separation of the oil dipstick, oil filler cap, PCV hose, etc. may cause the engine to run out of tune. Disconnection, loosenes or cracks between the air flow meter components and the cylinder head will throw the air induction system off and also cause the engine to run out of tune.

Auxiliary Air Valve

Some models are equipped with an auxiliary air valve. This air valve operates in the same manner as the main air valve. To remove the auxiliary air valve, the throttle body must first be removed and then the auxiliary air valve can be removed. This valve can be tested in the same manner as the main air valve.

ELECTRONIC CONTROL SYSTEM

All vehicles are equipped with a Toyota Computer Control System (TCCS) which centrally controls the electronic fuel injection, electronic spark advance, Idle Speed Control (ISC), electronic transmission, if equipped and diagnostics system. The ECU and the TCCS control the following functions:

Electronic Fuel Injection (EFI)

The ECU receives signals from the various sensors indicating changing engine operations conditions such as:
1. Intake air volume
2. Intake air temperature
3. Coolant temperature sensor
4. Engine rpm
5. Acceleration/deceleration
6. Exhaust oxygen content
    These signals are utilized by the ECU to determine the injection duration necessary for an optimum air-fuel ratio.

EQUIPMENT MOUNTING LOCATION

The ECU has been designed so it will not be affected by outside interference. However, if equipped with a mobile radio system, it may have an effect on the ECU's performance. The following precautions should be observed to prevent adverse effects:

1. Make sure the antenna mast is located as far from the ECU as possible.

2. Keep the antenna feeder wire at least 8 in. away from the ECU. More precisely, do not wind the antenna feeder cable with any of the wires going to or coming from the ECU.

3. Make sure the radio equipment trimmers are properly adjusted.

4. Ground the equipment directly to the vehicle body only.

5. Do not use powerful mobile radio systems.

6. Do not open the ECU case; if the IC terminals are touched, the IC may be destroyed by static electricity.

Electronic Spark Advance (ESA)

The ECU is programmed with data for optimum ignition timing during all operating conditions. Using the data provided by sensors which monitor various engine functions (rpm, intake air volume, coolant temperature, etc.), the microcomputer (ECU) triggers the spark at precisely the right moment.

EGR Temperature Sensor

The ECU detects the coolant temperature and controls the EGR operations accordingly. The EGR sensor is available on California vehicles.

Fail-Safe and Back-Up Functions

When an abnormality occurs in any of the ECU input signals, the ECU substitutes nominal values stored in the microcomputer's memory to provide enough driveability to keep the vehicle moving. In the event of serious problems, the ECU may stop the engine.

Self-Diagnosis

The ECU contains a built-in self diagnosis system by which troubles with the engine signal the engine signal network are detected. The check engine light on the instrument panel informs the driver that a malfunction has been detected. The light goes out automatically when the malfunction has been cleared.

The check engine warning light will come on when the ignition switch is placed **ON** and the engine is not running. When the engine is started, the check engine warning light should go out. If the light remains on, the diagnosis system has detected a malfunction in the system.

Idle Speed Control (ISC)

The ECU is programmed with specific engine speed values to respond to different engine conditions (coolant temperature, air conditioner on/off, etc.). Sensors transmit signals to the ECU which controls the flow of air through the bypass of the throttle valve and adjusts the idle speed to the specified value. Some vehicles use a ISC valve while others use an air valve to control throttle body bypass air flow.

VOLKSWAGEN

Digifant System

GENERAL INFORMATION

Using a single control unit, all of the functions of the fuel system, ignition system and oxygen sensor system are controlled to provide optimum mixture and ignition control for improved acceleration, deceleration and driveability.

The Digifant system features a 50mm throttle bore and an idle stabilization system to eliminate the need for a digital idle stabilizer or auxiliary air regulation. Electronic fuel injection control is based on the measurement of air entering the air intake and engine speed measured by the Hall sender. The coolant temperature sensor provides for correction during cold engine running.

The oxygen sensor, intake air temperature sensor and throttle switch provide the control unit with the required additional measurements to ensure smooth performance under all driving conditions. A separate control unit is used for the idle stabilization valve. Ignition timing control is determined by engine speed signal from the Hall sender and a load signal from the air sensor.

SYSTEM COMPONENTS

Electronic Control Unit (ECU)

The ECU used with the Digifant system incorporates all the functions of the fuel system and ignition system and provides both the actuation signals for the injectors and optimum ignition timing point for all engine operating conditions. Injection duration opening signals are provided based on the following inputs:

Engine speed
Intake air volume
Coolant temperature
Oxygen content in the exhaust gas
Battery voltage
Throttle position
Intake air temperature

Coolant Temperature Sensor

This sensor is a negative coefficient resistor. The resistance signal it produces is utilized by the ECU to determine the amount of cold start and warm-up enrichment, ignition advance and idle stabilization when the different sensor's functions are activated. The resistance of the sensor should decrease as the temperature of its thermistor increases.

Fuel Pump

The electronic fuel pump is a roller cell design. Centrifugal force seals the rollers against the walls of the pressure chamber as the rotor spins. Fuel that is trapped between the rollers is pressurized and forces out the delivery port. The pump is designed to be cooled and lubricated by the fuel flowing through it. The pump constantly delivers more fuel than is needed by the engine. Excess fuel is returned to the fuel tank by the fuel regulator.

The regulator also maintains a constant pressure to the injectors. It responds to intake manifold fluctuations and compensates different engine load requirement. When the engine is shut off, the regulator seals the system and maintains a residual pressure to provide for good start up.

Fuel Injectors

Digifant fuel injectors are electronically controlled on/off valves. A solenoid activates a needle valve allowing fuel to be forces out the nozzle. All 4 injectors open at the same time and inject fuel directly into the intake manifold near the intake valve. Injection quantity is controlled by the amount of time the injectors stay open. The resistance between the injector's terminals should be 14–18 ohms.

Digifant injectors with a yellow body are not interchangeable with injectors from other non-compatible Volkswagen injection systems.

Air Flow Sensor

The air flow sensor measures the amount of air entering the intake manifold and sends a voltage signal to the ECU accordingly. Intake air opens the air flow sensor flap which actuates a potentiometer to determine the voltage signal. This signal and the engine speed signal are used as principal parameters to determine the injector opening duration and ignition timing. compensation flap connected to the air sensor dampens sudden movement of the air sensor flap due to changes in intake air.

Intake Air Sensor

This sensor is mounted in the air flow sensor housing. Like the coolant temperature sensor, this sensor is a negative coefficient resistor. The resistance signal it produces is utilized by the ECU to modify the fuel injection rate depending on intake air temperature. The resistance of the sensor should decrease as the temperature of its thermistor increases.

Throttle Switch

Digifant uses a single throttle switch to signal the ECU when the throttle plate fully closed at idle or fully open. The signal enables the ECU to determine that 1 of 3 auxiliary functions (idle stabilization, deceleration fuel shut-off or full load enrichment) is required and activates the appropriate circuit.

The throttle switch is normally open unless actuated. The contact arm is actuated by a cam with 2 eccentrics which attach to the throttle plate shaft. One eccentric closes the the contacts when the plate is closed and the other fulfills the duty at wide open throttle.

Oxygen Sensor

The oxygen sensor is comprised of a ceramic material called Zir-conium dioxide. The inner and outer surfaces of the ceramic is coated with platinum. The outer platinum surface is exposed to the exhaust gases, while the inside surface is exposed to outside air.

The difference in the amount of oxygen contacting the inner and outer surfaces of the sensor create a pressure differential which results in a small voltage signal ranging from 175–1100 milli-volts supplied to the ECU. The amount of voltage supplied is determined by the fuel mixture.

The oxygen sensor is electrically heated to keep it at a constant operating temperature. This ensures continuously accurate sensor reaction regardless of the surrounding conditions. The heated oxygen sensor has 3 leads: 2 for heating it and a signal wire to the ECU. Power is supplied to the heating element all the time when the ignition is on.

Idle Stabilization

This system ensures that the idle speed will remain constant at the predetermined level. The system controls the amount of air bypassing the throttle plate. If engine idle speed varies from the value stored in the control unit, the idle stabilizer valve will adjust the volume of air induced into the engine at idle. This action maintains idle speed within certain limits.

The idle stabilizer valve is operated by a control unit located in the engine compartment near the air cleaner intake duct. The control unit receives input values from the following components:

Throttle switch
Coolant temperature sensor
Air condition compressor clutch
Ignition coil terminal No. 1
Automatic transmission selector switch
Power steering pressure switch
Since the idle speed is now automatically adjusted, other regulatory systems are not needed and periodic adjustment is accomplished electronically.

24 Electronic Ignition Systems 24

CHRYSLER CORPORATION

Electronic Control Unit (ECU) Ignition System/Electronic Ignition System (EIS)

GENERAL INFORMATION

The system consists of battery, ignition switch, ignition resistor, control unit, coil, single or dual pickup distributor, dual pickup start/run relay, spark plugs and necessary components for routing of primary and secondary current.

The ECU/EIS system allows use of a dual pickup distributor without electronic spark advance. Advance is applied mechanically through a vacuum advance unit on the side of the distributor.

The system is made up of 3 circuits. The primary, secondary and pickup circuits. The primary circuit consists of battery, ignition switch, 1.2 ohm ignition resistor, primary windings of the ignition coil, power switching transistor of control unit, vehicle frame and dual pickup start/run relay.

The secondary circuit consists of the coil secondary windings, distributor cap and rotor, spark plug cables, spark plugs and vehicle frame. On 5.9L engine, the ignition resistor is bypassed during starting, applying full battery voltage to the ignition coil.

The pickup circuit is used to sense the proper timing for the control unit switching transistor. The reluctor, rotating with the distributor shaft, produces a voltage pulse in the magnetic pickup each time a spark plug should be fired. This pulse is transmitted through the pickup coil to the power switching transistor in the control unit. The transistor interrupts the current flow through the primary circuit. This break in the primary circuit induces a high voltage in the secondary coil circuit and fires the spark plug. The length of time that the switching transistor allows the flow of current in the primary circuit is determined by the circuitry within the ECU. Ignition maintenance is reduced to inspection of distributor cap, rotor, wiring and cleaning or replacing spark plugs as necessary.

The main relay in the EIS system is the dual pickup/start run relay. The dual pickup/start run relay allows the use of a dual pickup distributor without the use of electronic spark advance. This has benefits of increased timing and improved fuel economy. During engine cranking, the dual pickup start-run relay is energized through the starter solenoid circuit, which allows the start pickup to adjust the timing for starting purposes only. As soon as the starter solenoid is de-energized, the start-run relay switches the sensing function back to the run pickup.

Electronic Spark Control (ESC) System

GENERAL INFORMATION

The electronic spark control system consists of a Spark Control Computer (SCC), various sensors, a specially calibrated carburetor and a single or dual pickup distributor. The system accurately controls the air/fuel mixture delivered to the engine.

The spark control computer controls the entire ignition system. It gives the capability of igniting the fuel mixture according to different engine conditions during the run drive cycle. It can deliver infinite electronic spark advance curves. The SCC has a built-in microprocessor which receives continuous input from

Chrysler Electronic Ignition System (EIS) components

the engine sensors. The computer electronically advances or retards the timing to provide even driveability.

During the crank-start period, the computer will provide a set amount of advanced timing to assure a quick, efficient start. The amount of electronic spark advance provided by the computer is determined by changes in coolant temperature, engine rpm and available manifold vacuum. The SCC also receives information from the oxygen sensor and the idle stop carburetor switch.

There are 2 functional modes of the computer, start and run. The start mode will only function during engine cranking and starting. The run mode only functions after the engine start and during engine operation. Both modes will never operate together.

For cranking and starting, the pickup coil in the distributor feeds its signal to the computer. During this time the start mode is functioning and the run mode is bypassed. A fixed quantity of advance will be established in the ignition system because of the permanent position of the pickup coil. The amount of advance in this mode will be determined by the position of the distributor.

After the engine starts and during engine operation, the pickup coil (run pickup on dual pickup distributors) signal continues to feed into the computer. Now the run mode is functioning and the start mode is bypassed. The amount of advance will now be determined by the computer based on information received from all the sensors. If the run mode should fail during operation, the system will switch back to the start mode. The engine will keep running, but since timing in the start mode is fixed, performance and driveability will be below standard. This is also known as the "limp-in" or default mode. Should a failure of the pickup coil(s) or the start mode of the computer occur, the engine will not start or run.

The pickup coil signal is a reference signal. When the signal is received by the computer the maximum amount of timing advance is made available. Based on the data from all the sensors, the computer determines how much of this maximum advance is needed at that instant.

The amount of spark advance is determined by 2 factors, engine speed and engine vacuum. However, when it happens depends on the following conditions: Advance based on vacuum will be given by the computer when the carburetor switch is open. The amount is programmed into the computer and is proportioned to the amount of vacuum and engine rpm. Advance based on speed is given by the computer when the carburetor switch is open and is programmed to engine rpm.

Hall Effect Electronic Ignition System

GENERAL INFORMATION

The Hall Effect Pickup ignition system is used in conjunction with a Single Board Engine Controller (SBEC), with the exception of the 2.2L turbocharged engine. The ignition system on the 2.2L turbocharged engine operates in conjunction with a Single Module Engine Controller (SMEC). Both the SBEC and the SMEC controls the entire ignition. The engine controller gives the capability of igniting the fuel mixture over all operating conditions, by delivering an infinite amount of variable electronic spark advance curves.

The Hall Effect Pickup ignition system consists of an engine controller (SBEC or SMEC), a conventional but pointless distributor, a hall effect pickup, an ignition coil, an Auto Shutdown (ASD) relay and primary and secondary ignition wiring.

SYSTEM OPERATION

A shutter, sometimes referred to as an interrupter, is attached

Chrysler fuel injection system diagram showing ignition system components—Hall Effect ignition system

to the distributor shaft. The shutter contains a set of blades, 1 for each cylinder. A switch plate is mounted to the distributor housing above the shutter. The switch plate contains the distributor pickup (hall effect device) through which the shutter blades rotate. As the shutter blades pass through the pickup, they interrupt the magnetic field. The hall effect device in the pickup senses the change in the magnetic field and switches ON and OFF, generating input signal (pulses) to the engine controller.

The engine controller energizes the ignition coil through the ASD relay. When the relay is energized by the controller, battery voltage is supplied to the ignition coil positive terminal. The engine controller will not energize the ASD relay until it receives input from the distributor pickup. The engine controller calculates engine speed through the number of pulses generated.

On the 2.5L turbo I engine, 1 of the shutter blades has a window cut into it. The controller determines injector synchronization from that window.

During the crank-start period, the engine controller will provide a set amount of advanced timing to assure a quick efficient start. The amount of electronic spark advance provided by the engine controller is determined by 3 input factors:
- Coolant temperature
- Engine rpm
- Manifold Absolute Pressure (MAP)

The engine controller also receives information from the oxygen sensor and electronically adjusts the air fuel mixture to assure the most efficient fuel burn possible.

SYSTEM COMPONENTS

Engine Controller

The engine controller has a built in microprocessor which continuously monitor various engine sensors. The computer will then electronically advance or retard the ignition timing to provide even driveability during operation.

Hall Effect Pickup

The hall effect pickup, located in the distributor, supplies the engine controller with engine rpm, fuel injection synchronization (turbo engines) and ignition timing information.

Manifold Absolute Pressure (MAP) Sensor

The MAP sensor, mounted under the hood, is a device which transmits information on manifold vacuum conditions and barometric pressure to the SBEC. The MAP sensor data, along with data from other sensors, is used to determine proper air/fuel mixture.

Coolant Temperature Sensor

The coolant temperature sensor is located on the thermostat housing and provides the SBEC with engine temperature data. The SBEC uses this data to control various engine functions such as spark advance, fuel mixture, emission controls operation and radiator fan.

Auto Shutdown (ASD) Relay

The ASD relay is used basically as a fuel delivery safety factor. The ASD relay interrupts the power to the electrical fuel pump, fuel injectors and ignition coil if the ignition key is in **RUN** and there is no need for fuel delivery.

Detonation (Knock) Sensor

The detonation (knock) sensor, used on 2.5L turbo I engine, is a device that generates a signal when spark knock occurs in the combustion chamber. The engine controller use this information to modify spark advance in order to eliminate detonation.

Cutaway view of the optical distributor—Chrysler

Optical Distributor Ignition System

GENERAL INFORMATION

The Optical Distributor ignition system, is used in conjunction with the Chrysler Single Board Engine Controller (SBEC). The SBEC controls the entire ignition. It gives the capability of igniting the fuel mixture over all operating conditions, by delivering an infinite amount of variable electronic spark advance curves.

The Optical Distributor ignition system consists of an engine controller (SBEC), an optical distributor, an ignition coil, an Auto Shutdown (ASD) relay and primary and secondary ignition wiring.

SYSTEM OPERATION

During the crank-start period, the SBEC receives engine speed and crankshaft position signals from the optical distributor. These signals are used to control fuel injection, ignition timing and idle speed. The timing member in the distributor is a thin disk, driven at ½ the engine speed from the forward left bank camshaft. The disk is equipped with 2 slots. The outer set of slots (high rate data) occurs at intervals of 2 degrees of crankshaft rotation. This information is used for ignition timing at engine speeds up to 1200 rpm to increase timing accuracy. During cranking and idle, engine speed changes with the firing pulses of each cylinder. The high data rate signal is used to trigger the ignition at the correct crankshaft position, regardless of these speed changes. The inner set of slots (low rate data) contains 6 slots. Each slot coordinate with TDC for each cylinder. This information is used to trigger the fuel injection system. It also used for ignition timing at engine speeds above 1200 rpm where speed changes due to individual firing pulses is small.

Light Emitting Diodes (LED's) and photo diodes are mounted in facing positions on opposite sides of the photo disk in line with the slots. Marks over the LED's and the photo diodes focus the light beams onto the photo diodes. As each slot passes between the diodes, the light beam is turned ON and OFF. This creates an alternating voltage in each photo diode which is converted into ON-OFF pulses by an integrated circuit within the distributor. These pulses are transmitted to the engine controller.

A cover located between the rotor and case, in the distributor, protects against high voltage damage to the electronic circuitry and optical system contamination.

SYSTEM COMPONENTS

Single Board Engine Controller (SBEC)

The SBEC (engine controller) has a built in microprocessor which continuously monitor various engine sensors. The computer will then electronically advance or retard the ignition timing to provide even driveability during operation.

Optical Distributor

The optical distributor provides the SBEC with information on crankshaft position and engine speed. It also delivers the firing pulses from the coil to each individual cylinder through a cap and rotor.

Coolant Temperature Sensor

The coolant temperature sensor is located on the thermostat housing and provides the SBEC with engine temperature data. The SBEC uses this data to control various engine functions such as spark advance, fuel mixture, emission controls operation and radiator fan.

Manifold Absolute Pressure (MAP) Sensor

The MAP sensor, mounted under the hood, is a device which transmits information on manifold vacuum conditions and barometric pressure to the SBEC. The MAP sensor data, along with data from other sensors, is used to determine proper air/fuel mixture.

Auto Shutdown (ASD) Relay

The ASD relay is used basically as a fuel delivery safety factor. The ASD relay interrupts the power to the electrical fuel pump, fuel injectors and ignition coil if the ignition key is in **RUN** and there is no need for fuel delivery.

Direct Ignition System (DIS)

GENERAL INFORMATION

The Direct Ignition System (DIS) eliminates the conventional distributor and all its components, by using multiple ignition coils. Two coils for 4-cylinder or 3 coils for 6-cylinder, are mounted together in a coil pack. Basic timing and all ignition advance is controlled by the Single Board Engine Controller (SBEC). This eliminate the need for timing adjustment.

The significant advantages of the DIS system over conventional ignition system include the follow:

- Peak output voltage is 20 percent higher than previously used ignition systems.
- No distributor cap or rotor to replace.
- No timing adjustment required.

In the DIS ignition system, each coil fires 2 spark plugs at the same time. The plugs are paired so the plug on the compression stroke fires, while the other plug is on its exhaust stroke. The next time the coil is fired, the plug that was on the exhaust will be on the compression and the one that was on the compression will be on the exhaust. The spark in the exhaust cylinder is wasted but little of the coil energy is lost.

The DIS ignition system consists of the following components:

- Crankshaft timing sensor
- Camshaft reference sensor
- Single Board Engine Controller (SBEC)
- Ignition coil pack
- Detonation sensor

To control spark and fuel operation, the SBEC also use information from the coolant sensor, Manifold Absolute Pressure (MAP) sensor and the Auto Shutdown (ASD) Relay.

SYSTEM OPERATION

The engine controller receives its engine speed and crankshaft position signal from a sensor located on the transaxle housing.

When the ignition is turned to the **START** position and the engine is being cranked, the transaxle driveplate rotates. Solid areas and open slots, located around an extension on the torque converter driveplate, passes the end of the crankshaft timing sensor. When a solid area is in line with the crankshaft timing sensor, a low voltage (less than 0.3 volts) is sent to the SBEC. When an open slot passes the sensor, the output voltage goes to approximately 5 volts.

The crankshaft timing sensor, used on the Monaco and Premier 3.0L engine, also senses slots (4 per cylinder) located around the torque converter driveplate. These slots are located at 65, 45, 25 and 5 degrees BTDC. One set of slots have a wide slot at the 45 degree position to be used to indicate cylinder No. 6 or cylinder No. 2.

The camshaft reference sensor operates similar to the operation of the crankshaft sensor. The camshaft timing gear has 5 areas with notched slots. There are 2 areas with a single slot, 2 areas with 2 slots and 1 area with 3 slots. The camshaft timing gear also has 1 long and 4 short solid unnotched surfaces. The cam sensor will supply cylinder identification information; thereby, allowing fuel and spark operation for start and run conditions. The cam pickup will sense slots located on the cam timing gear.

Camshaft Reference Sensor locations:

3.0L engine—left rear cylinder head
3.3L and 3.8L engines—timing chain case cover
2.2L turbo III engine—front of the head

Each ignition coil primary is joined to the power wire from the automatic shutdown relay. Base on information from the crankshaft timing sensor, the SBEC will provide a ground for each coil primary which causes the spark plugs to fire.

The DIS ignition system also uses a detonation sensor to control ignition timing. The detonation sensor provides signal to the SBEC in response to internal engine noises. When detonation occurs, the SBEC reduces ignition advance for all cylinders.

During the crank-start period the engine controller will provide a set amount of advanced timing to assure a quick efficient start. The amount of electronic spark advance is determined by the coolant sensor, available manifold vacuum and engine rpm.

SYSTEM COMPONENTS

Crankshaft Timing Sensor

The crankshaft timing sensor is a hall-effect switch, which sends engine speed and crankshaft position signals to the SBEC. This signal is in response to the slots in the transaxle driveplate.

Single Board Engine Controller (SBEC)

The SBEC receives information about engine speed, load and crankshaft position from various sensors. The SBEC has complete control of ignition timing during all modes of engine operation.

Ignition Coil Assembly

The ignition coil assembly is a single unit containing 3 individual ignition coils.

Camshaft Reference Sensor

The camshaft reference sensor, mounted through an access hole at the top of the timing chain case cover, is a hall-effect switch used by the SBEC to determine camshaft position relative to crankshaft position.

Detonation Sensor

The detonation sensor, mounted on the lower portion of the engine block, provides signal to the SBEC in response to internal engine noises.

FORD MOTOR COMPANY

Dura Spark Ignition System

GENERAL INFORMATION

The Dura Spark II ignition system consists of the typical electronic primary and conventional secondary circuits, designed to carry higher voltages. The primary and secondary circuits consists of the following components:

Primary Circuit

- Battery
- Ignition switch
- Ballast resistor start bypass (wire)
- Ignition coil primary winding
- Ignition module
- Distributor stator assembly

Secondary Circuit

- Battery
- Ignition switch
- Ignition coil secondary winding
- Distributor rotor
- Distributor cap
- Ignition wires
- Ballast resistor start bypass (wire)
- Spark plugs

The Dura Spark II system uses both a Dura Spark II and the universal ignition module, with continual updating from year to year, as required.

The Dura Spark II ignition control module is equipped with an altitude sensor, an economy modulator or pressure switches. This module, when combined with the additional switches and sensor, varies the base engine timing according to altitude and engine load conditions. The Dura Spark II ignition control modules use 3 wiring harness connectors.

Both ignition modules perform the function of turning off current flow through the ignition coil in response to a control signal. In the Dura Spark II ignition system, this signal comes from the distributor stator assembly. Additionally, the Univer-

sal Ignition Module (UIM), can respond to another control signal from either an ignition barometric pressure switch or the Microprocessor Control Unit (MCU), depending upon the engine's calibration. In responding to this second control signal, the UIM provides additional spark timing control for certain operating conditions by turning off the ignition coil current flow at a different time than what would happen from just the distributor signal.

The universal ignition module has a programmable run/retard feature in a smaller, more compact module. This programmable run/retard function can be programmed as a step change by an external programming switch/resistor combination for altitude and some economy calibrations or as a variable controlled element in the closed loop system, such as with the spark control mode system. The switch/resistor combinations change resistance inside the module to determine the amount of compensation the module will make.

SYSTEM OPERATION

With the ignition switch in the **RUN** position, the primary circuit current is directed from the battery, through the ignition switch, the ballast resistor, the ignition coil (in the positive side, out the negative side), the ignition module and back to the battery through the ignition system ground in the distributor. This current flow causes a magnetic field to be built up in the ignition coil. When the poles on the armature and the stator assembly align, the ignition module turns the primary current flow off, collapsing the magnetic field in the ignition coil. The collapsing field induces a high voltage in the ignition coil secondary windings. The ignition coil wire then conducts the high voltage to the distributor where the cap and rotor distributes it to the appropriate spark plug.

A timing device in the ignition module turns the primary current back on after a very short period of time. High voltage is produced each time the magnetic field is built up and collapsed.

The red ignition module wire provides operating voltage for the ignition module for the ignition module electronic components in the run mode. The white ignition module wire and start

Ford Dura Spark II ignition system schematic

bypass provide increased voltage for the ignition module and ignition coil, respectively, during start mode.

The distributor provides a signal to the ignition module, which controls the timing of the spark at the spark plugs. This signal is generated as the armature, attached to the distributor shaft, rotates past the stator assembly. The rotating armature causes fluctuations in a magnetic field produced by the stator assembly magnet. These fluctuations induce a voltage in the stator assembly pickup coil. The signal is connected to the ignition module by the vehicle wiring harness.

The occurrence of the signal to the ignition module, in relation to the initial spark timing, is controlled by centrifugal and vacuum advance mechanisms. The centrifugal advance mechanism controls spark timing in response to engine rpm. The vacuum advance mechanism controls spark timing in response to engine load.

The centrifugal advance mechanism varies the relationship of the armature to the stator assembly. The sleeve and plate assembly, on which the armature is mounted rotates in relation to the distributor shaft. This rotation is caused by centrifugal weights moving in response to the engine rpm. The movement of the centrifugal weights change the initial relationship of the armature to stator assembly ahead of its static position on the distributor shaft. This results in spark advance. The rate of movement of the centrifugal weights is controlled by calibrated springs.

The vacuum spark control mechanism can provide spark advance if a single diaphragm assembly is used or spark advance and retard if a dual diaphragm assembly is used. The diaphragm assembly used depends on the engine calibration.

The single vacuum diaphragm assembly also varies the armature to stator assembly relationship. In this case the stator assembly positioned is changed by means of vacuum applied to the diaphragm assembly. The diaphragm assembly is attached to the stator assembly by the diaphragm rod. The stator assembly

is mounted on the upper plate assembly. The vacuum applied to the diaphragm and attached diaphragm rod to move, compressing the advance spring, which controls the rate of spark advance. The rate of spark advance is controlled by a calibrated spring.

Spark advance is obtained with a dual diaphragm assembly in the same manner as with a single diaphragm assembly. In this case, vacuum applied to the vacuum advance port cause the advance diaphragm rod to move, other wise the action is the same. Spark retard is obtained by applying vacuum to the vacuum retard port. This causes the retard diaphragm to move, compressing the retard spring, which controls the rate of spark retard. Compressing the retard spring allows the diaphragm rod stop to move due to force applied by an advance spring pushing against the it by means of a diaphragm rod. The result is the diaphragm rod moves, causing the attached stator assembly to change position with respect to the armature. In this instance, the direction of the stator assembly movement is opposite that occurring during vacuum advance, resulting spark retard. It should be noted that vacuum applied to the advance port overrides any spark retard caused by vacuum applied to the retard port.

SYSTEM COMPONENTS

Dura Spark II and Universal Ignition Modules

Both ignition modules perform the function of turning off current flow through the ignition coil in response to a control signal.

Distributor Assembly

The distributor distributes the secondary voltage from the ignition coil to each spark plug. It also provides a signal to the ignition module, which controls the timing of the spark at the spark plugs.

Ford TFI-IV ignition system components

Ford TFI-IV ignition system schematic

The centrifugal advance mechanism varies the relationship of the armature to the stator assembly. The vacuum spark control mechanism provides part throttle spark advance.

Thick Film Integrated (TFI-IV) System

GENERAL INFORMATION

The Thick Film Integrated (TFI-IV) ignition system is used for all EEC-IV electronic fuel injected vehicles. The TFI-IV system module has 6 pins and uses an E-Core ignition coil, named after the shape of the laminations making up the core.

There are 2 type of TFI-IV system, and are as follow:

• PUSH START—this first TFI-IV system featured a "push start" mode which allow manual transmission vehicles to be push started. Automatic transmission vehicles must not be push started.

• COMPUTER CONTROLLED DWELL—this second TFI-IV system features an EEC-IV controlled ignition coil charge time.

The TFI-IV ignition system can be equipped with either a "Universal" or "Close Bowl" type distributor.

The TFI-IV ignition system with "Close Bowl" distributor, can be easily identified by its externally mounted TFI-IV ignition module. This module is generally mounted at the radiator support bracket or behind the engine at cowl area.

NOTE: The TFI-IV module, on 1992 Ford vehicles, have been moved from the engine to the fender. This new location is to help avoid heat and vibration problems.

The TFI-IV ignition system with "Universal" distributor has a distributor base mounted TFI ignition module and a hall effect stator assembly. The distributor also contains a provision to change the basic distributor calibration with the use of a replaceable octane rod, from the standard of 0 degrees to either 3 or 6 degree retard rods. No other calibration changes are possible.

NOTE: Initial timing adjustments are not required unless the distributor has been removed from the engine or moved from its initial factory setting.

Both the Push Start and Computer Controlled Dwell TFI-IV systems operates in the same manner. The TFI-IV module supplies voltage to the Profile Ignition Pickup (PIP) sensor, which sends the crankshaft position information to the TFI-IV module. The TFI-IV module then sends this information to the EEC-IV module, which determines the spark timing and sends an electronic signal to the TFI-IV ignition module to turn off the coil and produce a spark to fire the spark plug.

SYSTEM OPERATION

The operation of the universal distributor is accomplished through the Hall Effect stator assembly, causing the ignition coil to be switched off and on by the ECC-IV computer and TFI-IV modules. The vane switch is encapsulated package consisting of a Hall sensor on one side and a permanent magnet on the other side.

A rotary armature, made of ferrous metal, is used to trigger the Hall Effect switch. When the window of the armature is between the magnet and the Hall Effect device, a magnetic flux field is completed from the magnet through the Hall Effect device back to the magnet. As the vane passes through the opening, the flux lines are shunted through the vane and back to the magnet. A voltage is produced while the vane passes through the opening. When the vane clears the opening, the window causes the signal to go to 0 volts. The signal is then used by the EEC-IV system for crankshaft position sensing and the computation of the desired spark advance based on the engine demand and calibration. The voltage distribution is accomplished through a conventional rotor, cap and ignition wires.

Distributorless Ignition System (DIS)

GENERAL INFORMATION

In the Distributorless Ignition System (DIS), all engine timing and spark distribution is handled electronically with no moving parts. This system has fewer parts that require replacement and provides a more accurately timed spark. During basic operation, the EEC-IV determines the ignition timing required by the engine and a DIS module determines which ignition coil to fire.

The purpose of the DIS module is to deliver a full energy spark at a crank angle targeted by the EEC-IV and to provide the EEC-IV module with speed and position information. An Ignition Diagnostic Monitor (IDM) Clean Tach Out (CTO) line is also provided. The DIS inputs and outputs are listed below;

a. Inputs—Variable Reluctance Sensor (VRS) input and Spark Advance Word (SAW).

b. Outputs—Coil drivers, one for every 2 cylinders. Profile Ignition Pickup (PIP) and Ignition Diagnostic Monitor (IDM) Clean Tach Out (CTO) line.

The Variable Reluctance Sensor (VRS) input is derived by sensing the passage of the teeth from a 36 minus one tooth crankshaft mounted wheel. The signal is processed by the DIS in order to identify the missing tooth. Once the missing tooth is found, the module is said to be synchronized. Synchronization is essential to the DIS in order to ascertain and track the angular position of the crankshaft relative to a fixed reference. Since the missing tooth is indexed from Top Dead Center (TDC) of the No. 1 cylinder, the cylinder pair of No. 1 and No. 4 is identified for 4 cylinder DIS. Cylinder pair indentification is a requirement for the Distributorless Ignition Systems (DIS) which fires a pair of simultaneous sparks (one on compression and one on exhaust).

A Profile Ignition Pickup (PIP) output is synthesized from the High Data Rate (HDR) VRTS signal and sent to the EEC-IV control module. This signal is a 50 percent duty cycle square wave with its rising edge at 10 degrees before TDC of each cylinder event. The PIP signal is required by the EEC-IV control module to determine engine speed and position. Once the EEC-IV control module recognizes the the PIP signal, fuel and spark functions are enable. The calculated spark target is sent to the DIS module as a pulse width modulated digital signal (SAW). This signal is sent once per cylinder event. It is then up to the DIS module to decode the SAW signal and to fire the next spark at the command spark target.

Coil firing is initiated by energizing the DIS coil in sequence referenced to the missing tooth (example 4 cylinder A-B) and firing at the command spark target; default spark advance is 10 de-

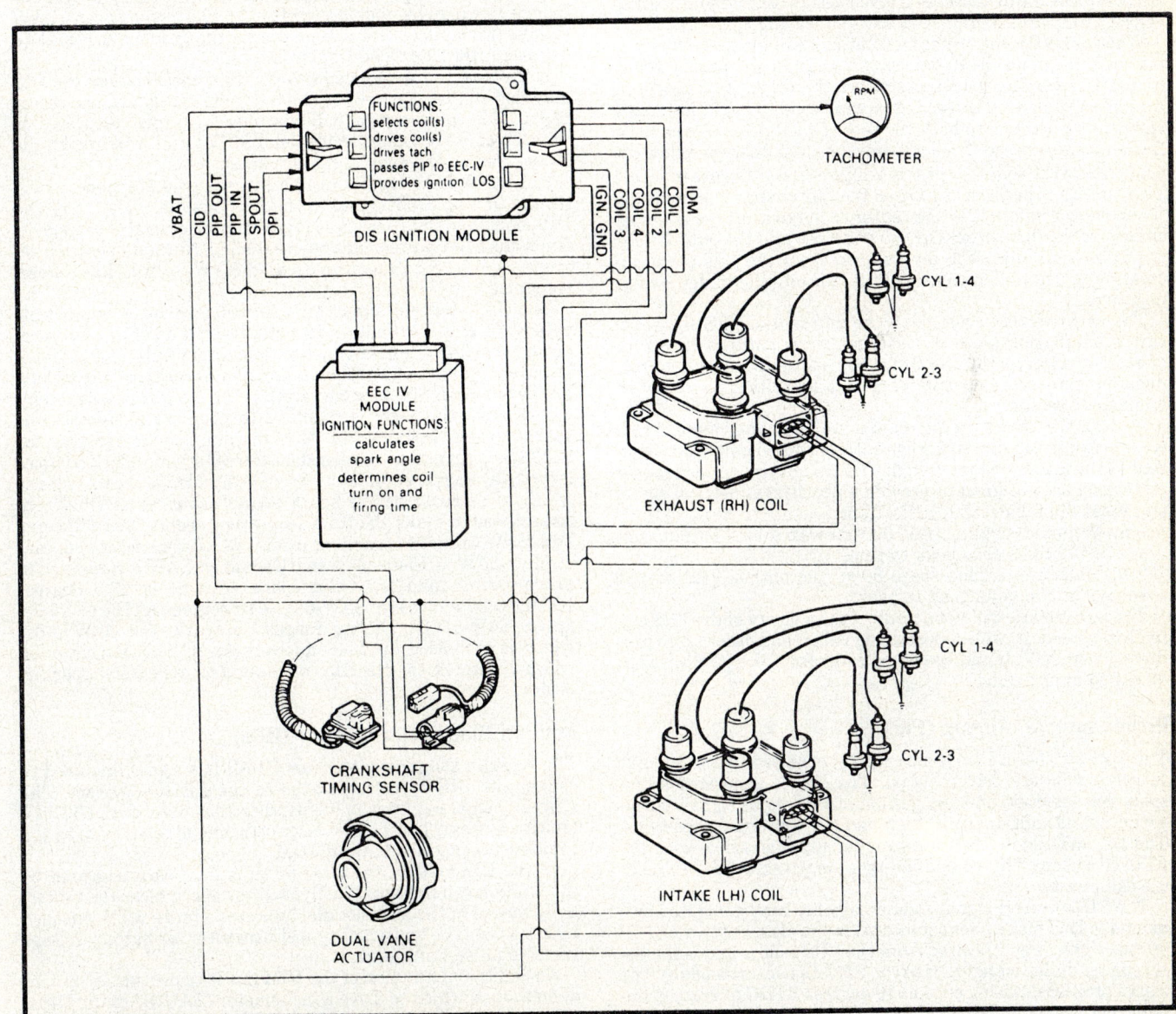

Ford Distributorless Ignition System (DIS) schematic—Ranger with 2.3L engine

grees BTDC. By energizing the primary side of the coils in proper sequence and by connecting the secondary wires in accordance with the engine firing order, a power stroke is achieved on each cylinder event with a wasted spark fired in the exhausting cylinder. In addition, an IDM/CTO signal is transmitted on each spark firing. This signal is intended to communicate diagnostic information by pulse width modulation and provide a clean buffered signal, proportional to engine speed, for tachometer operation. A brief description of the system components and their operation follows:

SYSTEM COMPONENTS

Variable Reluctance Sensor (VRS)

The Variable Reluctance Sensor (VRS) is a magnetic transducer with a pole piece wrapped with fine wire which , when exposed to a change in flux linkage will induce a differential voltage across the terminals of the wire windings. The output differential voltage of the transducer is a function of the sensor to tooth air gap (voltage increase with decreasing air gap), tooth and sensor pole piece width (fixed for a given design) and engine angular velocity (the voltage increases with increasing rpm).

When the VRS encounters a rotating timing wheel, the passing ferro-magnetic teeth causes a change in the sensor reluctance. The varying reluctance alters the amount of magnetic flux linkage passing through the wire windings and induces a voltage proportional to both the rate of change in the magnetic flux and the number of coil windings. As a tooth approaches the pole piece of the sensor, a positive differential voltage is induced. This voltage is positive as long as the flux change is increasing. When the pole piece is in the center of the tooth there is no net change in the flux across the coil windings and the output voltage is zero. As the tooth moves away from the pole piece (increasing reluctance, decreasing flux), the output voltage swings negative.

The negative zero crossing of the differential VRS signal occurs when the pole piece of the sensor corresponds to the center of each physical tooth. The DIS module is sensitive only to this negative zero crossing and uses this transition to establish crankshaft position.

At normal engine running speeds, the VRS signal waveform is an approximation of a sine wave with increased amplitude adjacent to the missing tooth region. The variable reluctance sensor and wheel are designed to provide a nearly symmetrical signal and meet the following specifications:

a. Minimum engine speed 30 rpm with a VRS output voltage of 150 milli-volts peak to peak.
b. Maximum engine speed 8000 rpm with a VRS output voltage of 300 volts peak to peak.

The DIS module will not operate if the polarity of the VRS signal is reversed. In addition, starting cables and other noise producing elements should be routed away from the VRS wires so as not to induce noise.

Profile Ignition Pickup (PIP)

The DIS synthetic PIP is not a hardware sensor output but rather a software driven signal. The PIP is generated in response to detection and recognition of VRS input signals corresponding to traditional PIP high and PIP low engine positions. The DIS module is hardware functionally compatible with the EEC-IV system. This compatibility minimizes the EEC-IV module complexity.

The PIP interface signal , historically has been generated by a magnetic Hall pick up sensor located in the distributor. The PIP output signal is synthesized from the VRS sensor and is the basic engine timing signal sent to the EEC-IV control module. The signal profile is a rising edge at 10 degrees BTDC of every cylinder event with a 50 percent duty cycle, i.e. (the falling edge is 90 degrees later on a 4 cylinder; 60 degrees later on a 6 cylinder and

45 degrees later on an 8 cylinder). This signal characteristic is a battery voltage square wave.

Spark Angle Word (SAW)

The Spark Angle Word (SAW) is a pulse width encoded spark advance word generated by the EEC-IV control module. In conventional TFI-IV systems, this signal line is called the Spout for spark out. The EEC-IV system hardware is identical for both of these systems.

In the conventional systems, a rising edge Spout corresponds to a spark firing event; the falling edge is used for dwell control. The EEC-IV control module is tasked with real time control for both spark placement and dwell. Additionally in the event of an EEC-IV control module failure, the EEC-IV system will enter a Limited Operation Strategy (LOS) mode which, among other things will put the Spout in a tri-state (i.e. high impedance state). This loss of Spout will by default force the TFI-IV to a 10 degrees BTDC fixed spark timing.

The DIS system utilizes a SAW signal. SAW is a pulse width modulated signal typically produced once per cylinder event. A SAW signal is required a minimum of once every 5 cylinder firings, but may be updated as often as every spark event. SAW may be transmitted at any time during the cylinder except at 10 degrees After Top Dead Center (ATDC).

If the SAW value received is not within specification, the DIS module will target sparks to the last valid spark advance recognized. This spark timing will continue for 5 misinterpreted or unreceived SAW values. Additional SAW faults will invoke the 10 degrees BTDC default spark timing.

In EEC-IV LOS, the Spout line enters a tri-state mode, which results in a no SAW signal to the DIS module. This forces the DIS module to the 10 degrees BTDC timing after the criteria for 5 missing SAW pulses have been satisfied. Normal operation resumes when 3 consecutive valid SAW values have been recognized.

The SAW transfer function was designed to be compatible with 4, 6, and 8 cylinder DIS modules. To do this, it was required that the transfer function maximum pulse width be allowed enough time for transmission at a worse case DIS module for 8 cylinder at 800 rpm operating point. To insure a sufficient guard band, the SAW is specified to decrease in duration as spark advance is increased. At high rpm, the alotted time for SAW transmission is decreased; at the same time spark advance is typically increased. It is therefore desirable for the SAW pulse width to decrease as the spark target advances. A final constraint was to make the SAW easily decodeable. The following DIS SAW transfer function meets all of the described constraints SAW = 1540 – 25.6 spark advance. SAW is measured in micro-seconds and the valid spark advance is 57.5 degrees BTDC (+57.5 degrees: SAW-68) to 10 degrees ATDC (– 10 degrees: SAW-1792). During respective spark, the SAW pulse width is increased by 2048 micro-seconds. This longer pulse width indicates to the DIS module that repetitive spark is desired.

Ignition Diagnostic Monitor (IDM)

The Ignition Diagnostic Monitor (IDM) is a signal line used to convey the DIS operating status to the EEC-IV system. The EEC-IV signal circuitry is identical to that used in the TFI-IV ignition system. The TFI-IV diagnostic line is referred to as the Ignition Diganostic Monitor (IDM).

In the DIS system, the IDM pulse is hardware triggered by the ignition coil flyback. The flyback voltage, which when internally sensed in the DIS module, indicates a pulse width encoded IDM output. The ignition diagnostic monitor is a battery voltage variable pulse width signal.

An additional function of the IDM line is to provide an optional method in which to drive a tachometer (TACH). In the DIS 4 cylinder system this signal is brought out on 2 pins, IDM and Clean Tach Out (CTO). The IDM and CTO driven tach lines may be used to provide a buffered TACH signal. This buffered tach signal eliminates radiated noise emissions associated with the high voltage IDM line signal harness.

Crankshaft Timing Sensor

Besides the PIP signal there is another signal generated called the Cylinder Identification (CID). The CID signal is used to synchronize the ignition coils, due to the fact that the Ranger uses a 2 ignition coil pack DIS system.

The Dual Hall Effect crankshaft sensor contains 2 hall digital output devices (PIP and CID) in one package. The sensor is located on a bracket mounted near the crankshaft damper. Two rotary vane cups (or wheels) are mounted on the damper and used to trigger the Hall sensors.

When the window of the vane cup is between the magnet and the Hall Effect device, a magnetic flux field is completed from the magnet through the Hall Effect device back to the magnet the output signal will be low (0 volts). However, as the vane passes through the gap between the Hall Effect device and the magnet, the flux lines are shunted through the vane and back to the magnet and the output will change from a low voltage to a high voltage.

The PIP cup has 2 teeth resulting in a 2 positive going edges each revolution of the crankshaft, where as the CID cup has 1 tooth and generates a signal that is high half of the crankshaft revolution and low the other half. The CID is used by the DIS module to enable it to select the proper coils to fire. When the CID is high, coils 2 and 3 are enabled and when the CID is low 1 and 4 are enabled. The EEC-IV control module tells the DIS module when to fire but the DIS module has to select one of the 2 coils based on the CID (which 2 of 4 if in the DPI mode).

Ignition Coil Pack

There are 2 ignition coil packs used on the 2.3L dual plug engine. The 2 ignition coil packs are triggered by the DIS module and are timed by the EEC-IV control module. Each coil pack contains 2 separate ignition coils for a total of 4 ignition coils. Each ignition coil fires 2 spark plugs simultaneously, 1 spark plug on the compression stroke and 1 on the exhaust stroke. The spark plug fired on the exhaust stroke uses very little of the ignition coils stored energy and the majority of the ignition coils energy is used by the spark plug on the compression stroke. Since these 2 spark plugs are are connected in series, the firing voltage of one of the spark plugs will be negative with respect to ground, while the other one will be positive with respect to ground.

DIS Module

The main function of the DIS module is to switch between the ignition coils and trigger the coils to spark. The DIS ignition module receives the PIP and the CID signals from the crankshaft timing sensor and the Spout (spark out) signal from the EEC-IV control module. During normal operation, the PIP signal is passed onto the EEC-IV control module and provides base timing and rpm information. The CID signal provides the DIS module with information required to switch between the coils for cylinders No. 1 and No. 4 and the coils for cylinders No. 2 and No. 3. The Spout signal (from the EEC-IV control module) contains the optimum spark timing and dwell time information. The spark angle is determined by the rising edge of the Spout while the falling edge of the Spout controls the coil current on or dwell time. The dwell time is controlled or varied by varying the duty cycle of the Spout signal.

This feature is called Computer Controlled Dwell (CCD). With the proper inputs of the PIP, CID and Spout the DIS module turns the ignition coils on and off in the proper sequence for spark control.

Electronic Distributorless Ignition System (EDIS)
GENERAL INFORMATION

The new high data rate EDIS system is controlled by an EDIS module and the EEC-IV module operating in union. The system is designed to deliver a full energy spark at a crank angle selected by the EEC-IV. This system is a modified version of the Distributorless Ignition System (DIS). The EDIS consists of a Variable Reluctance Sensor (VRS), an EDIS module, an EEC-IV processor and a coil pack.

Technically speaking, the EDIS functions similarly to the DIS. The most obvious difference has to do with the Profile Ignition Pickup (PIP) signal. In the DIS, the PIP is a signal generated by a hall-effect device and passed through the DIS module to the EEC-IV. PIP provided the EEC-IV with base timing information. In the EDIS, the crankshaft position sensing and rpm is accomplished by the use of a trigger wheel and a Variable Reluctance Sensor (VRS). The position is determined by a missing tooth on the sensor wheel.

SYSTEM OPERATION

The EDIS operates by sending crankshaft position information from the VRS to the EDIS module. The VRS senses the passage of teeth from the 36 minus 1 tooth trigger wheel, creating an input signal for the EDIS module. The module process the signal indicated by the missing tooth, generates a PIP signal and sends it to the EEC-IV processor. The processor responds with a Spark Angle Word (SAW) signal containing advance or retard timing information back to the EDIS module. The ignition coil pack, turned ON and then OFF by the EDIS module. This condition fires 2 spark plugs at once, one for the cylinder on its compression stroke and the other for the mating cylinder which is on its exhaust stroke. The next time the coil is fired, the situation is reversed.

The module generates an Ignition Diagnostic Monitor (IDM) signal to the processor which is used to indicate a failure mode and also provide a tach output signal. In addition, the IDM line indicates Key ON/Engine OFF (KOEO) status. By providing a pulse, the KOEO signal communicates module power on status.

SYSTEM COMPONENTS
Coil Pack

The coil pack is controlled by the EDIS module, firing 2 spark plugs at once. One is for the cylinder being fired, which is on its compression stroke and the other is for the cylinder on its exhaust stroke.

EDIS Module

The EDIS module is a microprocessor based device with coil drivers which make decisions about spark timing and coil firing. The module controls the coil, based on information from the VRS signal and a pulse width modulated signal (SAW) generated from the EEC-IV processor.

Variable Reluctance Sensor (VRS)

The VRS is a passive electromagnetic device which senses movement of a 36 minus 1 tooth wheel located behind the crankshaft pulley. The sensor generates an AC voltage signal, which increases with engine rpm and provides engine speed and crankshaft position information to the EDIS module.

EEC-IV Processor

The EEC-IV processor is an electronic unit which receives Ignition, Ground and PIP signals from the EDIS module then generates a SAW output signal based upon engine speed, load, temperature and other sensor information.

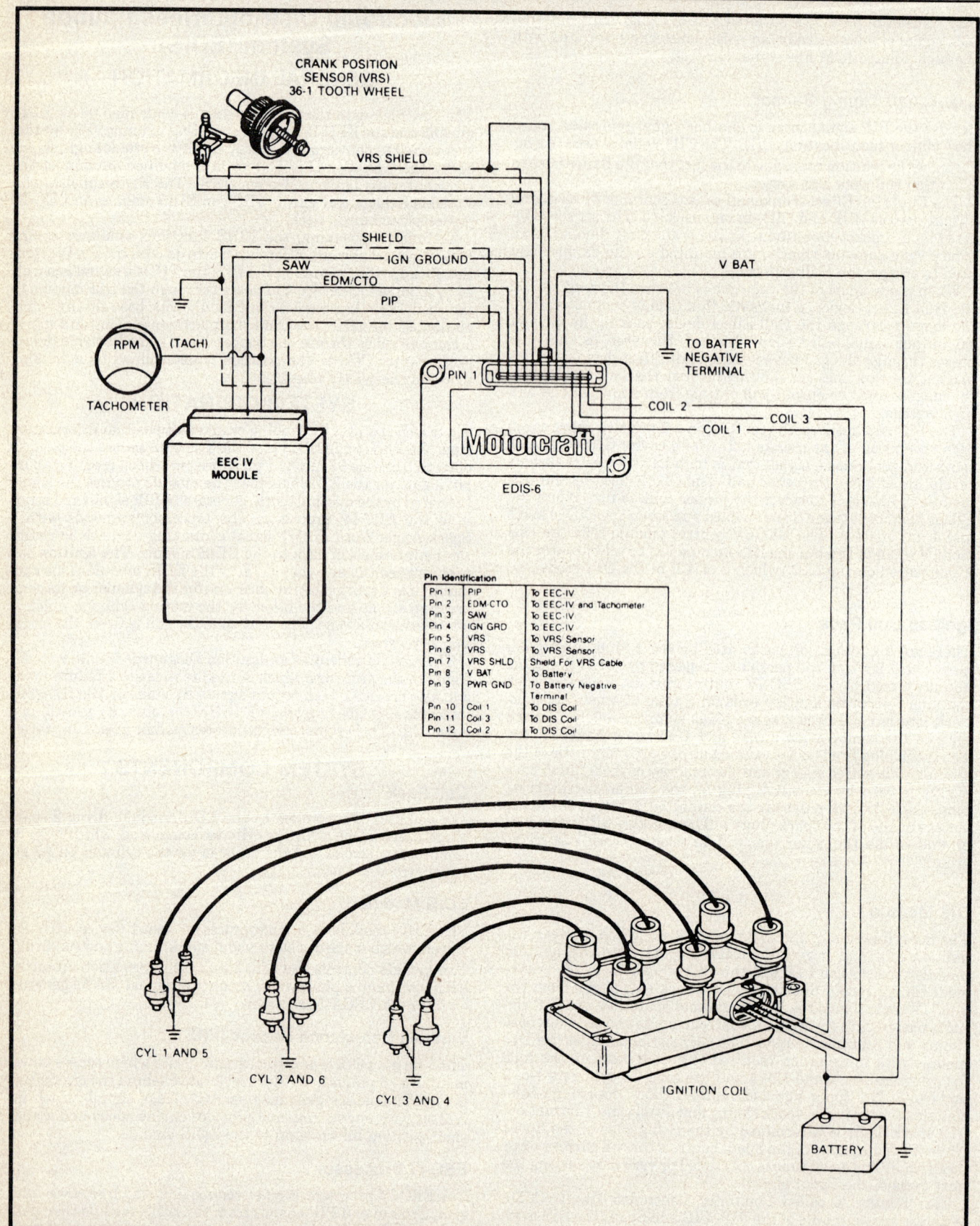

CRANK POSITION SENSOR (VRS) 36-1 TOOTH WHEEL

VRS SHIELD

SHIELD

IGN GROUND

SAW

EDM/CTO

PIP

V BAT

TO BATTERY NEGATIVE TERMINAL

RPM (TACH)

TACHOMETER

EEC IV MODULE

PIN 1

Motorcraft

EDIS-6

COIL 2

COIL 3

COIL 1

Pin Identification

Pin 1	PIP	To EEC-IV
Pin 2	EDM·CTO	To EEC-IV and Tachometer
Pin 3	SAW	To EEC-IV
Pin 4	IGN GRD	To EEC-IV
Pin 5	VRS	To VRS Sensor
Pin 6	VRS	To VRS Sensor
Pin 7	VRS SHLD	Shield For VRS Cable
Pin 8	V BAT	To Battery
Pin 9	PWR GND	To Battery Negative Terminal
Pin 10	Coil 1	To DIS Coil
Pin 11	Coil 3	To DIS Coil
Pin 12	Coil 2	To DIS Coil

CYL 1 AND 5

CYL 2 AND 6

CYL 3 AND 4

IGNITION COIL

BATTERY

Ford Electronic Distributorless Ignition System (EDIS) schematic

GENERAL MOTORS CORPORATION

High Energy Ignition (HEI) Systems

GENERAL INFORMATION

The Delco Remy High Energy Ignition (HEI) system is a breakerless, pulse triggered, transistor controlled, inductive discharge ignition system. There are only nine external electrical connections; the ignition switch feed wire and the eight spark plug leads. The ignition coil is located within the distributor cap, connecting directly to the rotor. All others have a separate coil. There are 2 basic systems that are used in conjunction with the basic high energy distributor, Electronic Spark Control (ESC) and Electronic Spark Timing (EST). Each uses an HEI system distributor with an increased number of sensors over the base HEI system.

The magnetic pick up assembly located inside the distributor contains a permanent magnet, a pole piece with internal teeth, and a pickup coil. When the teeth of the rotating timer core and pole piece align, an induced voltage in the pickup coil signals the electronic module to open the coil primary circuit. As the primary current decreases, a high voltage is induced in the secondary windings of the ignition coil, directing a spark through the rotor and high voltage leads to fire the spark plugs. The dwell period is automatically controlled by the electronic module and is increased with increasing engine rpm. The HEI System features a longer spark duration which is instrumental in firing lean and EGR diluted fuel/air mixtures. The condenser (capacitor) located within the HEI distributor is provided for noise (static) suppression purposes only and is not a regularly replaced ignition system component.

Some engines use an Electronic Spark Timing (EST) distributor. This unit replaces vacuum and centrifugal advance units with an electronic actuator (Hall Effect stator). A vacuum sensor provides manifold vacuum information and a reference pulse is generated by a pulse generator located near the engine vibration damper. These signals are fed to an Electronic Control Module (ECM) which, in turn, sends a signal to the EST distributor for ignition timing determination.

Some engines also use an Electronic Spark Control (ESC) which responds to engine detonation with retardation of ignition timing. An engine block mounted sensor detects the presence of vibration generated by detonation and signals the ESC controller to process the signal and adjust the timing via the actuator on the distributor. The system gradually retards the spark until detonation has disappeared. A failed sensor would produce occasional detonation.

These ESC equipped engines also have a "tip in" vacuum switch. When the throttle is suddenly opened and manifold vacuum is suddenly decreased, the switch contacts close to send a signal to the ESC controller to arbitrarily retard the spark to prevent knock. Thus, if the engine knocks for a very short time after a rapid opening of the throttle, this switch may be at fault.

Vehicles equipped with the 2.5L engine have distributors that contain a Hall Effect Switch which provides a voltage signal to the ECM when the rotating iron vane blocks the magnetic flux between the permanent magnet and the switch circuit. On these distributors, the **R** terminal on the module inside the distributor is not used.

The majority of system diagnosis is performed in conjunction with the computer command control system diagnosis and requires the reading of engine failure codes from the ECM.

General Motors High Energy Ignition (HEI) system schematic

HEI (EST) DISTRIBUTOR

1. Capacitor
2. 7-Terminal module
3. Mainshaft assembly
4. To ECM connector
5. Cover
6. Coil
7. Cap
8. Rotor
9. Housing

HEI distributor assembly—General Motors

JEEP

Solid-State ECU Ignition (SSI) System

GENERAL INFORAMTION

The Solid-State Ignition (SSI) system consists of a conventional pointless distributor. The main components of this system are as follow:

- A Solid-State Ignition Control Module (ICM)
- Ignition distributor
- An Electronic Control Unit (ECU)
- A speed sensor, with flywheel trigger
- A sync pulse (Stator) signal for the 4.0L engine

The ICM consists of a solid-state ignition circuit, an integrated ignition circuit and an integrated ignition coil. These components can be removed and service separately, if necessary. The ICM has only 2 outputs:

- Tachometer signal and diagnostic connector
- High voltage from the to the distributor

The ECU provides inputs to the ICM. Electronic signals from the ECU to the ICM determine the amount of ignition timing advance or retard is needed to meet the engine load requirements.

The Crankshaft Position Sensor (CPS)/speed sensor, attached to the torque converter/flywheel driveplate housing, provides an input signal to the ECU relating to crankshaft angle. The ECU converts the rate of change of crankshaft angle into engine rpm and the crankshaft angle to piston position. The speed sensor senses TDC, BDC and engine speed by detecting the flywheel teeth as they pass during engine operation. The speed sensor is non-adjustable.

The flywheel driveplate, on the 2.5L engine, has a large trigger tooth and notch located 90 degrees before each TDC position. There are 12 small teeth between the notch and TDC.

When a tooth and notch pass the magnet core of the speed sensor, a voltage spike is induced in the sensor pickup coil winding. The voltage spikes allows the ECU to count the teeth as

Jeep Solid State Ignition (SSI) system schematic

they pass the sensor. When a trigger notch passes the speed sensor there is a longer than usual delay between voltage spikes. This longer delay tells the ECU that a piston will be at TDC position 12 voltage spike later. The ECU uses information from the speed sensor to control spark timing and fuel injection timing for each cylinder.

The 4.0L MPFI engine uses a sync signal generator (stator), located in the distributor. The stator operates in conjunction with the engine speed sensor to provide the ECU with inputs necessary to establish and maintain correct injector firing order.

The 5.9L engine, is a carbureted engine equipped with a micro-computer controlled Fuel Feedback system. The Solid-State Ignition (SSI) system is ultimately controlled by a Micro-Computer Unit (MCU). The MCU monitors various engine sensors, which indicate engine operating conditions. The system consists of a Micro Computer Unit (MCU), electronic ignition control unit, ignition coil, resistance wire, distributor assembly, knock sensor, spark plugs and wires.

The flywheel/driveplate, on the 2.5L and 4.0L engines for 1991–92, has groups of 4 notches at its edge. On the 2.5L engine there are 2 sets of slots; 4.0L engine is equipped with 3 sets of slots. As with earlier 2.5L and 4.0L engine, the notches cause pulse signals to be generated when they pass within the sensor path. The pulses are input into the SBEC (engine controller). The trailing edge of the forth notch is 4 degrees BTDC of the corresponding piston.

The engine will not operate if the engine controller does not receive a CPS input.

SYSTEM OPERATION

Based on control system inputs, the Electronic Control Unit (ECU) triggers the ignition coil, via the Ignition Control Module (ICM).

Ignition signals from the ECU is received by the ICM in the form of a 5 volt square wave. As the leading edge of the wave contacts the ignition circuitry in the ICM, the ICM charges the coil primary windings. When coil saturation occurs, the module circuitry opens the primary windings to collapse the magnetic field in the windings. This induces the high voltage in the coil secondary windings, which is then transmitted to the spark plugs via the coil wire, distributor cap and rotor.

The ECU is able to advance or retard ignition timing by controlling the ignition coil through the ICM.

SYSTEM COMPONENTS

Ignition Control Module (ICM)

The ICM, used with 2.5L and 4.0L engines for 1990, is mounted to the ignition coil. The ICM is used to generate the voltage for spark plug firing.

Single Board Engine Controller (SBEC)

The SBEC (engine controller), used with 2.5L and 4.0L engines for 1991–92, controls the ignition coil to adjust ignition timing for changing engine operating conditions.

Micro-Computer Unit (MCU)

The MCU, used on the 5.9L engine, monitors various engine sensors, processes the ignition signals and then sends them to the ignition module.

Speed Sensor With Flywheel Trigger

The speed sensor, attached to the torque converter driveplate housing, along with flywheel trigger is used to input crankshaft angle position for the ECU.

Sync Pulse Signal (Stator)

The sync signal generator, located in the distributor, operates in conjunction with the engine speed sensor. This component provides the ECU with inputs to establish and maintain correct injector firing order.

CHRYSLER IMPORT

Electronic Ignition System

GENERAL INFORMATION

The ignition system consists of a battery, distributor (built-in ignitor), ignition coil, spark plugs, high tension cable, ignition switch and connection wires.

The distributor contains a signal generator (signal rotor and pickup, the latter being built into the ignitor), primary current controller (ignitor), timing controller (governor and vacuum controller) and distributor (rotor and distributor cap).

IGNITOR OPERATION

As the signal rotor rotates, the protrusion of the signal rotor either moves away from or comes face to face with the detector core.

When the protrusion moves away from the core, the oscillator circuit starts oscillation and when it comes face to face with the core, alternating magnetic flux from the core goes through the signal rotor. This increase in the loss causes oscillation to stop.

This oscillation is sent to the detection circuit, the output from which is amplified and used to drive the power transistor. When oscillating, current is allowed to flow to the ignition coil

Electronic Ignition System (EIS) schematic—Chrysler Imports

and when oscillation stops, current is shut off. The transistor is protected from over current by the current detection circuit.

Electronic Control Ignition Timing (ECIT) System

GENERAL INFORMATION

Ignition timing is controlled by the Electronic Control Ignition Timing (ECIT) system. The standard ignition timing data for engine operating conditions are programmed into the fuel injection computer (ECU) at the time of manufacture. The computer uses these pre-planned values to maintain the best engine timing under all operating conditions. This results in improved economy and lowered emissions.

The engine conditions (rpm, load, coolant temperature, barometric pressure and others) are detected by the various sensors. Signals from these sensors are compared to the standard ignition timing data within the computer. Optimum timing is computed and signals to interrupt the primary current are sent to the power transistor. The ignition coil is activated, and the ignition timing is in this way controlled.

DAIHATSU

Electronic Ignition System

GENERAL INFORMATION

The ignition system consists of a battery, distributor (built-in ignitor), ignition coil, spark plugs, high tension cable, ignition switch and connection wires.

The distributor contains a signal generator (signal rotor and pickup, the latter being built into the ignitor), primary current controller (ignitor), timing controller (governor and vacuum controller) and distributor (rotor and distributor cap).

IGNITOR OPERATION

As the signal rotor rotates, the protrusion of the signal rotor either moves away from or comes face to face with the detector core.

When the protrusion moves away from the core, the oscillator circuit starts oscillation and when it comes face to face with the core, alternating magnetic flux from the core goes through the signal rotor. This increase in the loss causes oscillation to stop.

This oscillation is sent to the detection circuit, the output from which is amplified and used to drive the power transistor. When oscillating, current is allowed to flow to the ignition coil and when oscillation stops, current is shut off. The transistor is protected from over current by the current detection circuit.

Daihatsu electronic ignition system schematic

1. Battery
2. Main fuse
3. Main switch
4. Main relay
5. Ignition coil
6. Power unit
7. Noise suppressor
8. Distributor
9. Rotor
10. Signal rotor
11. Crank angle sensor
12. Spark plug
13. AFS
14. TPS
15. WTS
16. Speed sensor
17. Test switch terminal

Geo electronic ignition system schematic

GEO

Electronic Ignition System
GENERAL INFORMATION

The Geo Tracker uses a solid state ignition system with conventional distributor. The principal components of the ignition system are the spark plugs, ignition coil and distributor. The distributor has a rotor, a module, a pole piece, a vacuum advance, a centrifugal advance and ignition coil.

The signal generator (pickup coil) is used to generate the ignition signal and consists of a signal rotor (pole piece), a magnet and a signal generator (pickup coil). The pole piece is attached to the distributor shaft, and the magnet and the pickup coil are attached to the pickup coil base plate.

When the distributor shaft rotates, the magnetic flux passing through the pickup coil varies due to the change in the air gap between the pickup coil and the pole piece. As a result, the alternating current voltage is induced in the pickup coil. The induced voltage turns the module on and off which switches the ignition coil primary current off. Thus, the high voltage is induced in the secondary winding of the ignition coil and ignition sparks are generated at the spark plugs.

ISUZU

Electronic Ignition System
GENERAL INFORMATION

EXCEPT 2.8L ENGINE

There are 2 types of ignition systems used on Isuzu vehicles: one uses a conventional centrifugal advance type distributor and the other uses a fully transistorized type distributor.

Conventional type distributors are made up of the distributor shaft, rotor shaft, rotor head, breaker assembly, reluctor, governor flyweight, pinion gear and vacuum control unit.

Transistorized distributors consist of dust bushing, rotor, pinion and a crank angle sensor built into the distributor housing. The crank angle sensor uses a photo-electric pickup to measure piston position and engine speed.

2.8L ENGINE

The computer controlled Electronic Spark Timing (EST) ignition system used on the 2.8L engine consists of the battery, distributor, engine control switch, spark plugs, primary and secondary wiring.

The computer, or Electronic Control Module (ECM), monitors the information from the engine sensor network. The ECM uses this information to calculate the proper spark timing and tell the distributor when to make timing modifications.

The distributor does not have centrifugal advance weights, springs or a vacuum advance unit.

The 2.8L engine is equipped with Electronic Spark Control (ESC). At the heart of the ESC system is the knock sensor which is mounted to the engine block. The knock sensor is connected to the electronic spark control module which is located on the right fender panel in the engine compartment or on a bracket mounted to the block. In response to engine knock, the sensor transmits a signal to the electronic spark module ("half function box"). The spark control module sends the signal to the ECM which in turn tells the distributor to retard the spark timing up to 20 degrees to reduce spark knock in the engine.

Isuzu electronic ignition system schematic

MAZDA

Electronic Ignition System

GENERAL DESCRIPTION

The Mazda electronic ignition system, uses a solid state ignition system with conventional distributor. This system is used on the B series Pick-Ups. The principal components of the ignition system are the spark plugs, ignition coil and distributor. The distributor has a rotor, a module, a signal rotor, a vacuum advance, a centrifugal advance, ignitor and ignition coil.

The pickup coil is used to generate the ignition signal and consists of a signal rotor, a magnet and a signal generator. The pole piece is attached to the distributor shaft, and the magnet and the pickup coil are attached to the pickup coil base plate.

When the distributor shaft rotates, the magnetic flux passing through the pickup coil varies due to the change in the air gap between the pickup coil and the pole piece. As a result, the alternating current voltage is induced in the pickup coil. The induced voltage turns the module on and off which switches the ignition coil primary current off. Thus, the high voltage is induced in the secondary winding of the ignition coil and ignition sparks are generated at the spark plugs.

Electronic Distributorless Ignition System (EDIS)

GENERAL INFORMATION

NOTE: The Mazda Navajo uses the Ford Electronic Distributorless Ignition System (EDIS).

The high data rate EDIS system is controlled by an EDIS module and the EEC-IV module operating in union. The system is designed to deliver a full energy spark at a crank angle selected by the EEC-IV. This system is a modified version of the Distributorless Ignition System (DIS). The EDIS consists of a Variable Reluctance Sensor (VRS), an EDIS module, an EEC-IV processor and a coil pack.

Technically speaking, the EDIS functions similarly to the DIS. The most obvious difference has to do with the Profile Ignition Pickup (PIP) signal. In the DIS, the PIP is a signal generated by a hall-effect device and passed through the DIS module to the EEC-IV. PIP provided the EEC-IV with base timing information. In the EDIS, the crankshaft position sensing and rpm is accomplished by the use of a trigger wheel and a Variable Reluctance Sensor (VRS). The position is determined by a missing tooth on the sensor wheel.

SYSTEM OPERATION

The EDIS operates by sending crankshaft position information from the VRS to the EDIS module. The VRS senses the passage of teeth from the 36 minus 1 tooth trigger wheel, creating an input signal for the EDIS module. The module process the signal indicated by the missing tooth, generates a PIP signal and sends it to the EEC-IV processor. The processor responds with a Spark Angle Word (SAW) signal containing advance or retard timing information back to the EDIS module. The ignition coil pack, turned ON and then OFF by the EDIS module. This condition fires 2 spark plugs at once, one for the cylinder on its compression stroke and the other for the mating cylinder which is on its exhaust stroke. The next time the coil is fired, the situation is reversed.

The module generates an Ignition Diagnostic Monitor (IDM) signal to the processor which is used to indicate a failure mode and also provide a tach output signal. In addition, the IDM line indicates Key ON/Engine OFF (KOEO) status. By providing a pulse, the KOEO signal communicates module power on status.

SYSTEM COMPONENTS

Coil Pack

The coil pack is controlled by the EDIS module, firing 2 spark plugs at once. One is for the cylinder being fired, which is on its compression stroke and the other is for the cylinder on its exhaust stroke.

EDIS Module

The EDIS module is a microprocessor based device with coil drivers which make decisions about spark timing and coil firing. The module controls the coil, based on information from the VRS signal and a pulse width modulated signal (SAW) generated from the EEC-IV processor.

Variable Reluctance Sensor (VRS)

The VRS is a passive electromagnetic device which senses movement of a 36 minus 1 tooth wheel located behind the crankshaft pulley. The sensor generates an A.C. voltage signal, which increases with engine rpm and provides engine speed and crankshaft position information to the EDIS module.

EEC-IV Processor

The EEC-IV processor is an electronic unit which receives Ignition, Ground and PIP signals from the EDIS module then generates a SAW output signal based upon engine speed, load, temperature and other sensor information.

MITSUBISHI

Electronic Ignition System

GENERAL INFORMATION

The ignition system consists of a battery, distributor (built-in ignitor), ignition coil, spark plugs, high tension cable, ignition switch and connection wires.

The distributor contains a signal generator (signal rotor and pickup, the latter being built into the ignitor), primary current controller (ignitor), timing controller (governor and vacuum controller) and distributor (rotor and distributor cap).

Electronic Ignition System (EIS) schematic – Mitsubishi

IGNITOR OPERATION

As the signal rotor rotates, the protrusion of the signal rotor either moves away from or comes face to face with the detector core.

When the protrusion moves away from the core, the oscillator circuit starts oscillation and when it comes face to face with the core, alternating magnetic flux from the core goes through the signal rotor. This increase in the loss causes oscillation to stop.

This oscillation is sent to the detection circuit, the output from which is amplified and used to drive the power transistor. When oscillating, current is allowed to flow to the ignition coil and when oscillation stops, current is shut off. The transistor is protected from over current by the current detection circuit.

NISSAN

Electronic Concentrated Control (Ignition) System (ECCS)

GENERAL INFORMATION

The ignition timing is controlled by the central electronic control unit adjusting to engine operating conditions. The signals used for the determination of the ignition timing are water temperature, engine rpm, engine load, etc. Then, the signal from the central electronic control unit is transmitted to the power transistor of the ignition coil and controls the ignition timing.

The ignition system is an integral part of the fuel control (ECCS) system.

SYSTEM COMPONENTS

Crank Angle Sensor

The crank angle sensor detects engine rpms and the crank angle (piston position). It also sends a signal to the control unit to control various operations. This sensor is built into the distributor.

Signal Rotor Plate

The signal rotor plate is located in the distributor, it has 360 slits for 1 degree signals (crank angle). The signal rotor also has 4 larger slits for 180 degree signals (engine speed). These signals are sent to the ECCS control unit.

Ignition Coil

The ignition coil has a built power transistor. The signal from the control unit is amplified by the power transistor. This signal is then used to connect and disconnect the ignition coils primary current to generate high voltage across the secondary coil and thereby creating a spark at the spark plug.

SUZUKI

Transistorized Ignition System

GENERAL INFORMATION

The ignition system is fully transistorized. The basic components of the system includes the battery, ignition switch, ignition coil, distributor and spark plugs. The distributor has a rotor, an ignitor, a signal generator, a vacuum advancer and a centrifugal advancer. The signal generator consists of a signal rotor, a magnet and a pickup coil. The signal rotor is attached to the distributor shaft and the magnet and pickup coil are attached to the generator

When the distributor shaft rotates, the air gap between the pickup coil and the signal rotor changes. As a result, the magnetic flux passing through the pickup coil varies and creates an alternating current voltage to be induced in the pickup coil. The voltage signal turns on and off the ignitor which switches off the ignition coil primary circuit. When the ignition coil primary circuit is interrupted, a high voltage is induced in the secondary winding of the ignition coil and an ignition spark is generated at the spark plugs via the rotor and high tension wires. A brief description of the system components follows:

SYSTEM COMPONENTS

Distributor

The distributor acts basically as a rotary switch. It connects the high voltage from the ignition coil secondary winding to the spark plugs via the rotor, distributor cap and high tension wires. The distributor shaft, from its driven gear end to the rotor carrying end, is a 2 piece shaft connected together through the timing advancer.

Vacuum Advancer

The vacuum advance mechanism, attached to the distributor, is a vacuum controlled device which assist in ignition timing advancement. When vacuum in the carburetor gets high, the pressure acting on the diaphragm overcomes the spring force in the vacuum advancer and a controller rod attached to the diaphragm is pulled. The controller rod in turns pulls the generator base plate counter to the direction of distributor shaft rotation to advance the ignition timing.

Centrifugal Advancer

The centrifugal advancer, located inside the distributor, is essentially a flyweight mechanism which assist in ignition timing advancement. Timing advancement is accomplished by twisting the top shaft piece (slightly ahead) relative to the bottom shaft piece in the same direction of distributor shaft rotation. The twisting movement is produced by the speed dependent radial movements of the 2 flyweights.

Ignition Coil

The ignition coil is basically a step-up transformer. The primary and secondary windings are so close to each other that any fluctuation in the primary current induces a very large voltage in the secondary winding. The ignition coil has 3 terminals, 1 high tension terminal and 2 low tension terminals.

1. Battery
2. Main fuse
3. Main switch
4. Main relay
5. Ignition coil
6. Power unit
7. Noise suppressor
8. Distributor
9. Rotor
10. Signal rotor
11. Crank angle sensor
12. Spark plug
13. AFS
14. TPS
15. WTS
16. Speed sensor
17. Test switch terminal

Suzuki Transistorized Igniton System schematic

TOYOTA

Electronic Spark Advance (ESA) System

GENERAL INFORMATION

The electronic control unit is programmed with data for optimum ignition timing under any and all operating conditions. Using data provided by the sensors which monitor various engine functions (rpm, intake air volume, engine temperature, etc.) the electronic control unit (microcomputer triggers the spark at precisely the right instant.

Integrated Ignition Assembly (IIA)

GENERAL INFORMATION

The Integrated Ignition Assembly (IIA) is a typical electronic ignition system. The major components consist of an integral ignition coil, signal generator (pickup), ignitor, vacuum and governor weight advance system and a rotor and distributor cap distribution system.

VOLKSWAGEN

Map Controlled Hall Effect System

GENERAL INFORMATION

The map controlled ignition system operates on the principle of a timing map programmed into the Electronic Control Unit (ECU). Information on engine load, speed and coolant temperature are provided to the ECU in the form of voltage signals. In the ECU these signals are processed so the ignition coil is controlled at its No. 1 terminal using the information from the ignition timing map.

The distributor contains a Hall Effect switch, which is activated by a trigger wheel with 4 openings in it, one for each cylinder. The distributor has no vacuum or centrifugal advance. From the signal generated by the Hall Effect switch, the ECU can determine engine speed and crankshaft position.

STARTING SYSTEMS

Starter Motor Testing

TESTING THE STARTER CIRCUIT

The starter circuit should be divided and tested in 4 separate phases:
1. Cranking voltage check
2. Amperage draw
3. Voltage drop on grounded side
4. Voltage drop on battery side

NOTE: **The battery must be in good condition. To accurately check battery condition, use equipment designed to measure its capacity under a load. Instructions accompanying the equipment should be followed.**

Cranking Voltage

Connect voltmeter leads to battery posts; observe polarity and reverse meter leads, if necessary. Remove the high tension wire from the distributor cap, if equipped, and ground it to prevent starting. With electronic ignition, disconnect the control box harness from the distributor. Turn the key to **START**. Observe both voltmeter reading and cranking speed. Cranking speed should be even and at a satisfactory rate of speed, with a voltmeter reading of at least 9.6 volts.

Amperage Draw

The amount of amperage current the starter motor draws is usually (but not always) associated with the mechanical problems involved in cranking the engine. Mechanical trouble in the engine, frozen or worn starter parts, misaligned starter or starter components, thick engine oil, etc. can all cause high starter draw. Because starter motor amperage draw is directly influenced by anything restricting the free turning of the engine or starter, it is important the engine and all components be at operating temperatures when testing.

To measure starter current draw, remove the high tension wire from the center of the distributor cap, if equipped, and ground it to prevent starting. With electronic ignition, disconnect the control box harness from the distributor. A very simple and inexpensive starter current indicator is available at auto stores. This indicator is an induction type gauge and shows, without disconnecting any wires, starter current draw.

Place the yoke of the meter directly over the insulated starter supply cable (cable must be straight for a minimum of 2 in.). Turn the ignition switch to the **START** position for about 20 seconds, watch the meter dial and record the average reading. If the indicator swings in the wrong direction, reverse the position of the meter.

The cranking amperage draw can vary from 150–400 amperes, depending on the engine size, engine compression and starter type.

NOTE: **When starter specifications are not available, average starter draw amperage can be derived from testing a like starter unit, known to be operating satisfactorily.**

More accurate but complex equipment is available from many manufacturers. This equipment consists of a combination voltmeter, ammeter and carbon pile rheostat. When using this equipment, follow the equipment manufacturer's procedures and recommendations.

High amperage and lazy performance would suggest an excessively tight engine, friction in the starter or starter drive, grounded starter field or armature.

Normal amperage and lazy performance suggest high resistance or possibly poor connections somewhere in the starter circuit.

Low amperage and lazy or no performance suggest battery condition poor, bad cables or connections along the line.

Voltage Drop On Grounded Side

With a voltmeter on the 3 volt scale, without disconnecting any wires, connect negative test lead of the voltmeter to the grounded battery post. The positive test lead is connected to a cleaned, bare metal portion of the starter motor housing. Turn the ignition switch to the **START** position and note the voltmeter reading. If the reading is the same as battery reading, the ground circuit is open somewhere between the battery and the starter. In many cases the reading will be very small. The reading shown will indicate voltage drop (loss) between battery ground post and starter housing. The drop should not exceed 0.2 volts. If the voltage drop is above the specified amount, the next step is to isolate and correct the cause. It can be a bad cable or connection anywhere in the battery-to-starter ground circuit. A check of this type should progress along the various points of possible trouble, between the battery ground post and the starter motor housing, until the trouble spot has been located.

Voltage Drop On Battery Side

Bad starter cranking may result from poor connections or faulty components of the battery or hot phase of the starter motor circuit. To check this phase of the circuit, without disconnecting any wires, connect a lead of a voltmeter to the hot post of the battery and the other voltmeter lead to the field terminal of the starting motor. The meter should be set to the 16–20 volt scale. Before closing the starter switch, the voltmeter reading will be that of the battery. After closing the starter switch, change the selector on the voltmeter to the 3 volt scale. With a jumper wire between the relay battery terminal and the relay starter switch terminal, crank the engine. If the starting motor cranks the engine, the relay (solenoid) is operating.

While the engine is being cranked, watch the voltmeter. It should not register more than 0.5 volts. If more than this, check each part of the circuit for voltage drop to isolate the trouble, (high resistance).

Without disturbing the voltmeter-to-battery hook-up, move the free voltmeter lead to the battery terminal of the relay (solenoid) and crank the engine. The voltmeter should show no more than 0.1 volts.

If this reading is correct, move the same voltmeter lead to the starting motor terminal of the relay (solenoid). While the engine is being cranked, the voltmeter should show no more than 0.3 volts. If it does, the trouble lies in the relay.

If the reading is correct, the trouble is in the cable or connections between the relay and the starting motor.

DIAGNOSIS

Starter Won't Turn Over Engine

1. Dead battery
2. Open starter circuit, such as:
   a. Broken, corroded or loose battery cables/connectors
   b. Inoperative starter motor solenoid
   c. Broken or loose wire from starter switch-to-solenoid
   d. Poor solenoid or starter ground
   e. Faulty starter switch
3. Defective starter internal circuit, such as:
   a. Dirty or burned commutator
   b. Stuck, worn or broken brushes
   c. Open or shorted armature
   d. Open or grounded fields

4. Starter motor mechanical faults, such as:
   a. Jammed armature end bearings
   b. Faulty bearings, allowing armature to rub fields
   c. Bent shaft
   d. Broken starter housing
   e. Faulty starter worm or drive mechanism
   f. Faulty starter drive or flywheel driven gear

5. Engine hard or impossible to crank such as:
   a. Hydrostatic lock, water in combustion chamber
   b. Crankshaft seizing in bearings
   c. Piston or ring seizing
   d. Bent or broken connecting rod
   e. Seizing of connecting rod bearing
   f. Flywheel jammed or broken

6. Starter spins free, won't engage such as a sticking or broken drive mechanism

CHRYSLER CORPORATION

Overhaul

REDUCTION GEAR STARTER

Before beginning overhaul on any Chrysler starter motor, check parts availability. Many late model starters are not designed for repair but replacement only.

Disassembly and Assembly

CHRYSLER

1. Support assembly in a soft jawed vise. Be careful not to distort or damage the die cast aluminum.
2. Matchmark the starter housings for reassemlby. Remove the through bolts and the end housing.
3. To disassemble the starter motor, perform the following procedures:
   a. Carefully pull the armature up and out of the gear housing and the starter frame and field assembly.
   b. Remove the steel and fiber thrust washer.
   c. Carefully pull the frame and field assembly up enough to expose the terminal screw and the solder connection of the shunt field at the brush terminal.

d. Place 2 wood blocks between the starter frame and starter gear housing to facilitate removal of the terminal screw.
   e. Unsolder the shunt field wire at the brush terminal.

NOTE: **The starting motors have the wire of the shunt field coil soldered to the brush terminal. A pair of brushes are connected to this terminal. Another pair of brushes are attached to the series field coils by means of a terminal screw.**

4. Support the brush terminal with a finger behind terminal and remove the screw. Unsolder the shunt field coil lead from the brush terminal and housing.
5. The brush holder plate (with terminal contact) and brushes are serviced as an assembly. Clean all old sealer from around plate and housing.
6. Remove the brush holder screw. On the shunt type, unsolder the solenoid winding from the brush terminal.
7. Remove the $^{11}/_{32}$ in. nut, washer and insulator from solenoid terminal. Remove the brush holder plate with brushes as an assembly and the gear housing ground screw.
8. The solenoid assembly can be removed from the well. Remove the nut, washer and seal from starter battery terminal and the terminal from the plate.

Exploded view of the reduction gear starter motor — Chrysler Corporation

9. Remove the solenoid contact and plunger from solenoid and the coil sleeve. Remove the solenoid return spring, coil retaining washer, retainer and the dust cover from the gear housing.

10. Release the snapring that locates the driven gear on pinion shaft. Release the front retaining ring.

11. Push the pinion shaft rearward and remove the snapring, thrust washers, clutch/pinion and the 2 nylon shift fork actuators.

12. Remove the driven gear and friction washer. Pull the shifting fork forward and remove the moving core.

13. Remove the fork retaining pin and shifting fork assembly. The gear housing with bushings is serviced as an assembly.

14. Brushes that are worn to ½ the length of new brushes or oil soaked, should be replaced.

15. When resoldering the shunt field and solenoid lead, make a strong low resistance connection using a high temperature solder and resin flux; do not use acid or acid core solder. Be careful not to break the shunt field wire units when removing and installing the brushes.

16. Do not immerse the starter clutch unit in a cleaning solvent. The outside of the clutch and pinion must be cleaned with a cloth so the lubricant is not washed from inside the clutch.

17. Rotate the pinion. The pinion gear should rotate smoothly, in 1 direction only. If the starter clutch unit does not function properly or the pinion is worn, chipped or burred, replace the starter clutch unit.

18. Inspect the commutator and the surface contacted by the brushes when the starter is assembled, for flat spots, out of roundness or excessive wear.

19. Reface the commutator, if necessary, removing only a sufficient amount of metal to provide a smooth even surface.

20. Using light pressure scrape the commutator grooves with a broken hacksaw blade; do not remove any metal or expand the grooves.

Cross-sectional view of the reduction gear starter motor—Chrysler Corporation

Removing the starter drive gear snapring—reduction gear starter motor—Chrysler Corporation

Shift fork and clutch arrangement—reduction gear starter motor—Chrysler Corporation

Removing the starter drive gear retaining ring—reduction gear starter motor—Chrysler Corporation

Removing the clutch assembly—reduction gear starter motor—Chrysler Corporation

21. To assemble, lubricate the bushings and reverse the disassembly procedures. The shifter fork consists of 2 spring steel plates held together by 2 rivets. Before assembling the starter check the plates for side movement. After lubricating between the plates with a small amount of SAE 10 engine oil they should have about ¹⁄₁₆ in. side movement to insure proper pinion gear engagement.

NIPPONDENSO

1. Position the assembly in a soft jawed vise. Remove the rubber boot from the field coil terminal, the nut from the field coil terminal stud and the field coil terminal from the stud.

Exploded view of the Nippondenso reduction gear starter motor—Chrysler Corporation

Exploded view of the Bosch reduction gear starter motor—Chrysler Corporation

2. Remove the through bolts and the splash shield. Remove the end shield screws from the brush plate and the end shield.

3. Slide the brushes from the holders. Pry the retaining springs back for access and remove the brush plate.

4. Slide the armature from the starter housing. Remove the starter housing from the gear housing and the solenoid terminal cover.

5. Remove the solenoid terminal nut/washer, the battery terminal nut/washer and the solenoid terminal assembly from the terminal posts.

6. Remove the solenoid terminal and the battery terminal from the insulator.

7. Remove the solenoid cover screws, the solenoid cover, the seal, the solenoid plunger from the housing and the plunger spring.

8. Remove the gear housing-to-solenoid screws and separate the gear housing from the solenoid housing.

9. Remove the reduction gear and clutch assembly from the gear housing.

10. Remove the reduction gear, pinion gear, retainer and roller assembly from the gear housing.

11. Inspect and clean all parts, as required. Repair or replace defective parts as required. Brushes that are worn less than ½ the length of new brushes or oil soaked should be replaced.

12. To assemble, reverse the disassembly procedures.

BOSCH

1. Position the assembly in a soft jawed vise. Remove the field terminal nut, the terminal and the washer.

2. Remove the solenoid-to-starter screws. Work the solenoid from the shift fork and remove the solenoid from the starter.

3. Remove the starter end shield bushing cap screws, the starter end shield bushing cap, the end shield bushing and C-washer.

4. Remove the starter end shield bushing washer and seal.

5. Remove the starter through bolts, the starter end shield and the brush plate.

6. Slide the field frame from the starter and over the armature. Remove the armature assembly from the drive end housing.

7. Remove the rubber seal from the drive end housing. Remove the starter drive gear train.

8. Remove the dust plate. Press the stop collar from the snapring. Using snapring pliers, loosen the snapring.

9. Remove the output shaft snapring, the clutch stopring collar and the clutch assembly from the starter.

10. Remove the clutch shift lever bushing, the clutch shift lever and the C-clip retainer.

11. Remove the retaining washer, the sun and the planetary gears from the annulus gear.

12. To assemble, lubricate the necessary parts and reverse the disassembly procedures. Replace all defective components as required.

FORD MOTOR COMPANY

Overhaul

DIRECT DRIVE STARTERS

Disassembly and Assembly

FORD POSITIVE ENGAGEMENT STARTER

1. Remove the starter from the vehicle. Position the unit in a soft jawed vise.

2. Remove the cover screw, the cover, through bolts, starter drive end housing and the starter drive plunger lever return spring.

3. Remove the pivot pin from the starter gear plunger lever, the lever and the armature. Remove the stopring retainer and the thrust washer from the armature shaft.

4. Remove the stopring from the groove in the armature shaft and discard it. Remove the starter drive gear assembly, the brush end plate and insulator assembly.

5. Remove the brushes from the plastic brush holder and lift out the brush holder. Note the location of the holder in relation to the end terminal.

6. Remove the ground brush screws. Remove the sleeve and the retainer by bending up the edge of the sleeve which is inserted in the rectangular hole of the frame.

7. Using the tool 10044-A or equivalent, remove the pole retaining screws. An arbor press may have to be used in conjunction with the special tool.

8. Cut the positive brush leads from the coil fields as close to the field connection as possible.

To assemble:

9. Check the commutator for runout. If the commutator is rough, has flat spots or is more than 0.005 in. out of round, reface it.

10. Inspect the armature shaft and the bearings for scoring and excessive wear; replace it, if necessary. Inspect the starter

Exploded view of the 4 inch plunger pole positive engagement starter motor—Ford Motor Company

Cross-sectional view of the Delco 42 MT starter. Ford diesel application shown—typical—Ford Motor Company

drive; if the gear teeth are pitted, broken or excessively worn, replace the starter drive.

11. Lubricate the necessary parts and reverse the disassembly procedures.

12. Solder the field coil-to-starter switch terminal posts. Check for continuity and grounds in the assembled coils.

13. Position the ground brushes-to-starter frame and rivet securely.

14. Install the starter motor drive gear assembly onto the armature shaft. Install a new stopring, a new stopring retainer and thrust washer.

15. Install the armature.

16. Position the drive gear plunger lever to the frame and starter drive assembly. Fill the end housing bearing bore a ¼ full or grease. Position the drive end housing onto the frame and make sure the return spring engages the lever tang. Install the pivot pin.

17. Install the brush holder, the brushes and the brush springs; make sure the brushes are positioned properly to avoid grounding.

18. Install the brush end plate; be sure the end plate insulator is positioned correctly on the end plate.

19. Install the through bolts and torque to 55–80 inch lbs. (6–9 Nm).

20. Install the starter drive plunger ever cover and tighten the screw.

21. Check the starter no-load current draw. It should be 80 amps.

DELCO 42MT STARTER

1. Remove the starter from the vehicle. Position the unit in a soft jawed vise.

2. Remove the field coil connector screw and the solenoid-to-starter screws. Rotate the solenoid 90 degrees and remove it along with the plunger return spring.

3. Remove the starter through bolts, the commutator end frame and washer.

4. Remove the field frame assembly from the drive gear housing.

5. If equipped, remove the center bearing screws. Remove the drive gear housing from the armature shaft.

6. To remove the overrunning clutch from the armature shaft, perform the following procedures:

    a. Remove the washer or collar from the armature shaft.

    b. Using a ⅝ in. deep socket, slide it over the shaft and against the retainer. Using the socket as a driving tool, tap it with a hammer to move the retainer of the snapring.

    c. Remove the snapring from the groove in the shaft; if the snapring is distorted, replace it.

    d. Remove the retainer and the clutch assembly from the armature shaft.

7. If required, the shaft lever and the plunger can be disassembled by removing the roll pin.

8. To replace the starter brushes, remove the brush holder pivot pin which positions the insulated and the ground brushes. Remove the brush spring.

To inspect:

9. Inspect armature commutator, shaft and bushings, overrunning clutch pinion, brushes and springs for discoloration, damage or wear; replace the damaged parts.

10. Check fit of armature shaft in bushing in drive housing. The shaft should fit snugly in the bushing. If worn, replace it.

11. Inspect armature commutator. If commutator is rough, it should be refinished on a lathe. Do not undercut or turn to less than 1.650 in. O.D. Inspect the points where the armature conductors join the commutator bars to make sure they have a good connection. A burned commutator bar is usually evidence of a poor connection.

12. Using a growler and holding hacksaw blade over armature core while armature is rotated, inspect the armature for short circuits. If saw blade vibrates, armature is shorted.

13. Using a test lamp place a lead on the shunt coil terminal and connect the other lead to a ground brush. The test should be made using both ground brushes to insure continuity through the brushes and leads. If the lamp fails to light, the field coil is open and will require replacement.

14. Using a test lamp place a lead on the series coil terminal and the other on the insulated brush. If the lamp fails to light the series coil is open and will require repair or replacement. The test should be made from each insulated brush to check brush and lead continuity.

15. If equipped with a shunt coil separate the series and shunt coil strap terminals during the test. Do not allow the strap terminals to touch case or other ground. Using a test lamp place a lead on the grounded brush holder and the other lead on either insulated brush. If the lamp lights a grounded series coil is indicated and must be repaired or replaced.

NOTE: If the solenoid has not been removed from the starter, the connector strap terminals must be removed before making the following tests. Complete the tests as fast as possible in order to prevent overheating the solenoid.

16. To check the starter winding, connect an ammeter in series with 12 volt battery and the switch terminal on the solenoid. Connect a voltmeter to the switch terminal and to ground. Connect a carbon pile across battery. Adjust the voltage to 10 volts and note the ammeter reading. It should be 14.5–16.5 amperes.

17. To check both windings, connect as for previous test and ground the solenoid motor terminal. Adjust the voltage to 10 volts and note the ammeter reading. It should be 41–47 amperes.

18. Current draw readings over specifications indicate shorted turns on a ground in the windings of the solenoid; the solenoid should be replaced. Current draw readings under specifications indicate excessive resistance. No reading indicates an open circuit. Check the connections and replace the solenoid, if necessary. Current readings will decrease as the windings heat up.

To assemble:

19. Reverse the disassembly procedures. Be sure to replace or repair all defective components as required.

NOTE: When the starter has been disassembled or the solenoid replaced, it is necessary to check the pinion clearance. Pinion clearance must be checked in order to prevent the buttons on the shift lever yoke from rubbing on the clutch collar during engine cranking.

20. To check the pinion clearance, perform the following procedures:

   a. Disconnect the motor field coil connector from the solenoid motor terminal and insulate the terminal.

   b. Connect the positive 12 volt battery lead to the solenoid switch terminal and the negative lead to the starter frame.

   c. Touch a jumper lead momentarily from the solenoid motor terminal to the starter frame; this will shift the pinion into cranking position and remain there until the battery is disconnected.

   d. Using a feeler gauge, push the pinion back as far as possible and check the clearance; the clearance should be 0.010–0.140 in.

   e. Pinion clearance adjustment is not provided on the starter motor. If the clearance does not fall within limits check for improper installation and replace all worn parts.

GENERAL MOTORS CORPORATION

Overhaul

DIRECT DRIVE STARTERS

Disassembly and Assembly

DELCO 5MT, 10MT, 27MT AND 28MT STARTER MOTORS

NOTE: In 1989, the identification for the 5MT starter was converted to the SD200/SD250 starters and the 10MT was converted to the SD300 starter. The 28MT is used with the diesel engine.

1. Remove the starter from the vehicle. Position the unit in a soft jawed vise.

2. Remove the field coil connector screw and the solenoid-to-starter screws. Rotate the solenoid 90 degrees and remove it along with the plunger return spring.

3. Remove the starter through bolts, the commutator end frame and washer.

4. Remove the field frame assembly from the drive gear housing.

5. If equipped, remove the center bearing screws. Remove the drive gear housing from the armature shaft.

6. To remove the overrunning clutch from the armature shaft, perform the following procedures:

   a. Remove the washer or collar from the armature shaft.

   b. Using a ⅝ in. deep socket, slide it over the shaft and against the retainer. Using the socket as a driving tool, tap it with a hammer to move the retainer of the snapring.

   c. Remove the snapring from the groove in the shaft; if the snapring is distorted, replace it.

   d. Remove the retainer and the clutch assembly from the armature shaft.

7. If required, the shaft lever and the plunger can be disassembled by removing the roll pin.

8. To replace the starter brushes, remove the brush holder pivot pin which positions the insulated and the ground brushes. Remove the brush spring.

9. On 5MT starters, to replace the brushes remove the screw from the brush holder and separate the brushes from the holder.

To inspect:

10. Inspect armature commutator, shaft and bushings, overrunning clutch pinion, brushes and springs for discoloration, damage or wear; replace the damaged parts.

11. Check fit of armature shaft in bushing in drive housing. The shaft should fit snugly in the bushing; if it is worn, replace it.

12. Inspect armature commutator. If commutator is rough, it should be refinished on a lathe. Do not undercut or turn to less than 1.650 in. O.D. Inspect the points where the armature conductors join the commutator bars to make sure they have a good connection. A burned commutator bar is usually evidence of a poor connection.

13. Using a growler and holding hacksaw blade over armature core while armature is rotated, inspect the armature for short circuits. If saw blade vibrates, armature is shorted.

14. Using a test lamp place a lead on the shunt coil terminal and connect the other lead to a ground brush. The test should be made using both ground brushes to insure continuity through the brushes and leads. If the lamp fails to light, the field coil is open and will require replacement.

15. Using a test lamp place a lead on the series coil terminal and the other on the insulated brush. If the lamp fails to light the series coil is open and will require repair or replacement. The test should be made from each insulated brush to check brush and lead continuity.

16. If equipped with a shunt coil separate the series and shunt coil strap terminals during the test. Do not allow the strap terminals to touch case or other ground. Using a test lamp place a lead on the grounded brush holder and the other lead on either insulated brush. If the lamp lights a grounded series coil is indicated and must be repaired or replaced.

NOTE: If the solenoid has not been removed from the starter, the connector strap terminals must be removed before making the following tests. Complete the tests as fast as possible in order to prevent overheating the solenoid.

17. To check the starter winding, connect an ammeter in series with 12 volts battery and the switch terminal on the solenoid. Connect a voltmeter to the switch terminal and to ground. Connect a carbon pile across battery. Adjust the voltage to 10

1. Shift lever
2. Plunger
3. Solenoid
4. Spring
5. Armature assembly
6. Grommet
7. Commutator end bearing
8. Brake washer
9. Plug
10. Shift lever retainer
11. Thrust collar
12. Drive shield
13. Drive end bearing

14. Shield attachment nut
15. Solenoid shield
16. Drive end frame
17. Drive assembly
18. Pinion stop retaining ring
19. Pinion stop collar
20. End frame
21. Field lead attachment nut
22. Solenoid attachment clamp

23. Solenoid attachment screws
24. Drain tube
25. Frame and field assembly including brushes
26. Through bolts

Delco SD-200 and SD-260 starter motors—General Motors Corporation

volts and note the ammeter reading. It should be 14.5–16.5 amperes.

18. To check both windings, connect as for previous test and ground the solenoid motor terminal. Adjust the voltage to 10 volts and note the ammeter reading. It should be 41–47 amperes.

19. Current draw readings over specifications indicate shorted turns on a ground in the windings of the solenoid; the solenoid should be replaced. Current draw readings under specifications indicate excessive resistance. No reading indicates an open circuit. Check the connections and replace the solenoid, if necessary. Current readings will decrease as the windings heat up.

To assemble:

20. To assemble, reverse the disassembly procedures. Be sure to replace or repair all defective components as required.

NOTE: When the starter has been disassembled or the solenoid replaced, it is necessary to check the pinion clearance. Pinion clearance must be checked in order to prevent the buttons on the shift lever yoke from rubbing on the clutch collar during engine cranking.

21. To check the pinion clearance, perform the following procedures:

a. Disconnect the motor field coil connector from the solenoid motor terminal and insulate the terminal.

b. Connect the positive 12 volt battery lead to the solenoid switch terminal and the negative lead to the starter frame.

c. Touch a jumper lead momentarily from the solenoid motor terminal to the starter frame. This will shift the pinion into cranking position and remain there until the battery is disconnected.

d. Using a feeler gauge, push the pinion back as far as possible and check the clearance. The clearance should be 0.010–0.140 in.

e. Pinion clearance adjustment is not provided on the starter motor. If the clearance does not fall within limits check for improper installation and replace all worn parts.

1. Clutch
2. Shift lever
3. Plunger
4. Solenoid
5. Bearing
6. Armature
7. TIG welds
8. Return spring
9. Planetary gear reduction assembly
10. Permanent magnet field
11. Brushes
12. Welded connections
13. Pinion stop

Cross-sectional view of the Permanent Magnet Gear Reduction (PMGR) starter—Delco starter—General Motors Corporation

REDUCTION GEAR STARTER

Disassembly and Assembly

DELCO PERMANENT MAGNET GEAR REDUCTION (PMGR) STARTER

1. Remove the starter from the vehicle. Position the unit in a soft jawed vise.
2. Remove the field coil screw, the field frame through bolts and separate the field frame assembly from the drive gear assembly. Separate the armature and the commutator end frame from the field frame.
3. Remove the solenoid screws and the solenoid from the drive housing.
4. Remove the retaining ring, shift lever shaft and housing through bolts. Separate the drive assembly, drive housing and gear assembly.
5. To remove the overrunning clutch from the armature shaft, perform the following procedures:
   a. Remove the washer or collar from the armature shaft.
   b. Using a ⅝ in. deep socket, slide it over the shaft and against the retainer. Use the socket as a driving tool, tap the socket with a hammer to move the retainer off of the snapring.
   c. Remove the snapring from the groove in the shaft. If the snapring is distorted, replace it.
   d. Remove the retainer and the clutch assembly from the armature shaft.
6. To replace the starter brushes, remove the brush holder pivot pin which positions the insulated and the ground brushes. Remove the brush spring.

To inspect:

7. Inspect armature commutator, shaft and bushings, overrunning clutch pinion, brushes and springs for discoloration, damage or wear; replace the damaged parts, if necessry. Check the armature shaft fit in drive housing bushing; the shaft should fit snugly in the bushing. If the bushing is worn, it should be replaced.
8. Inspect armature commutator. If commutator is rough, it should be refinished on a lathe. Do not undercut or turn to less than 1.650 in. O.D. Inspect the points where the armature conductors join the commutator bars to make sure they have a good

connection. A burned commutator is usually evidence of a poor connection.

9. Using a growler and holding hacksaw blade over armature core while armature is rotated, check the armature for short circuits; if the saw blade vibrates, the armature is shorted.
10. Using a test lamp, place a lead on the shunt coil terminal and the other lead to a ground brush. The test should be made from both ground brushes to insure continuity through both brushes and leads. If the lamp fails to light, the field coil is open and will require replacement.
11. Using a test lamp, place a lead on the series coil terminal and the other lead on the insulated brush. If the lamp fails to light, the series coil is open and will require repair or replacement. The test should be made from each insulated brush to check brush and lead continuity.
12. If equipped with a shunt coil, separate the series and shunt coil strap terminals during this test; do not allow the strap terminals to touch the case or other ground. Using a test lamp, place a lead on the grounded brush holder and the other lead on either insulated brush. If the lamp lights, a grounded series coil is indicated and must be repaired or replaced.

NOTE: If the solenoid has not been removed from the starter, the connector strap terminals must be removed before making the following tests. Complete the tests as fast as possible in order to prevent overheating the solenoid.

13. To check the starter winding, connect an ammeter in series with a 12 volt battery, the switch terminal and to ground. Connect a carbon pile across the battery. Adjust the voltage to 10 volts and note the ammeter reading; it should be 14.5–16.5 amperes.
14. To check both windings, connect as for previous test. Ground the solenoid motor terminal, adjust the voltage to 10 volts and note the ammeter reading. It should be 41–47 amperes.
15. Current draw readings above specifications indicate shorted turns or a ground in the windings of the solenoid; the solenoid should be replaced. Current draw readings under specifications indicate excessive resistance. No reading indicates an open circuit. Check the connections and replace solenoid, if necessary. Current readings will decrease as windings heat up.

16. The roller bearing in the drive housing and the roller bearings in the gear housing must be replaced if they are dry. Do not lubricate or reuse the bearings.

17. To replace the gear housing bearing, use a tube or solid cylinder that just fits inside the housing to push bearing toward the armature side. In the opposite direction, use the tube or cylinder to press bearing flush with housing.

18. To replace the gear housing driveshaft bearing, use a tube or collar that just fits inside the housing and press bearing out; press against the open end of bearing. To install a new bearing, press against the closed end, using a thin wall tube or collar that fits in space between bearing and housing. Do not press against the flat end of the bearing; this will bend the thin metal of the bearing. As required, replace the drive housing bearing.

To assemble:

19. Assembly is the reverse of the removal procedure. Be sure to replace or repair all defective components as required.

NOTE: When the starter has been disassembled or the solenoid replaced, it is necessary to check the pinion clearance. The pinion clearance must be checked in order to prevent the buttons on the shift lever yoke from rubbing on the clutch collar during engine cranking.

20. To check the pinion clearance, perform the following procedures:

a. Disconnect the motor field coil connector from the solenoid motor terminal and insulate the terminal.

b. Connect the positive (+) 12 volt battery lead to the solenoid switch terminal and the other to the starter frame.

c. Touch a jumper lead momentarily from the solenoid motor terminal to the starter frame; this will shift the pinion into cranking position and retain it until the battery is disconnected.

d. Using a feeler gauge, push the pinion back as far as possible, to take up any movement, and check the clearance. The clearance should be 0.010–0.140 in.

e. Means for adjusting pinion clearance is not provided on the starter motor. If the clearance does not fall within limits, check for improper installation and replace worn parts.

JEEP

Overhaul

BOSCH REDUCTION GEAR STARTERS

Disassembly and Assembly

NOTE: When performing disassembly procedures, do not strike the thin wall stator frame with a hammer or any other instrument. Do not clamp the thin wall stator frame in the jaws of a vise. This may result in damage to the permanent magnets and the stator housing. The starter may be clamped by the mounting flange only.

1. Position the starter motor assembly in a suitable holding fixture, ensuring that it is secured by the mounting flange only. Remove the field terminal nut. Remove the field coil wire (Terminal 45) from the solenoid switch terminal post. Remove the field washer.

2. Remove the solenoid switch mounting screws. Disengage the solenoid switch from the fork lever and withdraw the solenoid switch with the armature and return spring from the housing.

3. Loosen the closure cap screws, but do not remove them.

4. Remove the stator frame-to-shield housing hexagon screws, the stator frame with the cover plate, armature and commutator end shield.

5. Remove the cover plate from the surface of the drive end bearing ring gear. Carefully press the armature with the commutator end shield out of the stator frame. At the same time, push out terminal 45 with the sealing rubber.

6. Remove the closure cap screws and remove the closure cap from the commutator end shield. Remove the retaining washer

1. Starter
2. Solenoid
3. Relay
4. Ignition switch
5. Battery
A. Solenoid terminal
B. Battery terminal
C. Ignition terminal
D. Ground terminal

Schematic of the Bosch starter motor circuit—Jeep

1. Bushing
2. Screw
3. Shield
4. Solenoid switch
5. Retainer
6. Stop ring
7. Bushing
8. Overrunning clutch drive
9. Fork
10. Bearing pedestal
11. Sealing rubber
12. Planetary gear system
13. Armature
14. Stator frame
15. Brush frame
16. Gasket
17. Commutator end shield
18. Bushing
19. Seal ring
20. Shim
21. Shim
22. Retaining washer
23. Closure
24. Through bolt
25. Screw
26. Coverplate

Exploded view of the Bosch starter—Jeep

Removing the overrunning clutch and planetary gear system—Bosch starter—Jeep

Removing the armature—Bosch starter—Jeep

and shims from the armature shaft and remove the commutator end shield.

7. Using the proper tool, remove the brush plate from the armature shaft.

8. Remove the sealing rubber from the bearing pedestal. Remove the planetary gear system with the overrunning clutch and fork assembly from the drive end shield. Mount both assemblies onto a suitable mounting base in the verticle position.

9. Using the proper tool, drive the stop ring down the input shaft.

10. With snapring pliers, separate the ends of the retainer far

enough to allow removal from the driveshaft without damage. If necessary, carefully remove any burrs or nicks from the driveshaft, otherwise damage to the drive bushing may occur.

Inspection

1. The armature windings, overrunning clutch and relay must be cleaned with compressed air and a clean dry rag. Other parts, such as screws and the armature shaft may be cleaned with cleaning solvent. Inspect all parts, seals, bushings and gaskets for wear and damage. Replace all worn parts as required.

2. Inspect the stator frame and permanent magnets for damage. Do not remove the magnets from the stator frame. If the stator frame or magnets are damaged, then replace the stator frame.

3. Loosen and remove the retainer from the planetary gear drive. Remove the ring gear from the driveshaft. Inspect the ring gear for cracks and wear. Check the bushings in the ring gear for excessive play, out of roundness and wear by moving the driveshaft from side-to-side. Check the driveshaft bushing in the drive end shield and commutator end shield with the proper tool. Inspect the driveshaft in the ring gear for wear or damage. Replace the shaft and ring gear, if worn.

4. Inspect the fork lever and bearing pedestal for damage, replace if necessary. Inspect the bearing bushing in the overrunning clutch for wear. Replace the overrunning clutch, if the bearing bushing is worn.

5. Remove and inspect the carbon brushes for excessive wear. The length of a new brush is $^{11}/_{16}$ in. If the existing brushes are worn more than ½ the length of a new brush or they are oil soaked, replace the existing brushes.

6. Place the drive unit on the armature shaft and support the armature by hand. Grasp the armature and rotate the drive pinion. The drive pinion should rotate smoothly in 1 direction only. Some resistance may be encountered when rotating the drive pinion; however, as long as the rotation is smooth then the drive unit is in good operating condition. If the clutch unit does not function properly or if the pinion is worn, chipped or burred, then replace the unit.

ARMATURE GROUND TEST

1. Position the armature in the growler jaws and turn the power switch to **TEST** position.

2. Touch a test probe-to-armature core (1). Touch the other test probe-to-commutator bar (2), 1 at a time and observe the test lamp. The test lamp should not light. If the test lamp lights on any bar, the armature has a short circuit-to-ground and must be replaced.

ARMATURE SHORT TEST

NOTE: Never operate the growler with the power switch in the TEST position without the armature in the growler jaws.

1. Place the armature in the growler jaws and turn the power switch to the **GROWLER** position.

2. Hold the steel blade parallel to and touching, the armature core (3). Slowly, rotate the armature 1 or more revolutions in the growler jaws. If the steel blade vibrates at any 1 area of the core, the windings have a short circuit and the armature must be replaced.

ARMATURE BALANCE TEST

1. Place the armature in the growler jaws and turn the power switch to the **GROWLER** position.

2. Place the contact fingers of the meter test probe (4) across adjacent commutator bars at the side of the commutator.

3. Adjust the voltage control until the pointer indicates the highest voltage on the scale.

4. Test each commutator bar until all bars have been tested; 0 volts across any pair indicates a short circuit and requires the armature be replaced.

ARMATURE RUNOUT TEST

Check that the armature runout is within the range shown on the specifications chart. If the runout is not within tolerance, then replace the armature.

Assembly

1. Assembly is the reverse of the removal procedure. Place a light film of 20W SAE oil onto the surface of the overrunning clutch pinion bearing surface.

Performing the armature ground test—Jeep

Performing the armature short test—Jeep

Performing the armature balance test—Jeep

2. Lightly grease the planetary gear spiral spline with Lubriplate® grease.

3. Slide the overrunning clutch with the fork lever and bearing pedestal onto the driveshaft.

4. Slide the stop ring onto the armature shaft.

NOTE: When installing the retainer, be careful not to scratch the armature shaft.

5. With snapring pliers, separate the ends of the retainer and carefully install onto the groove in the armature shaft.

6. Using the proper tool, seat the stop ring.

7. The planetary gear bearing is located forward of the planetary gears. Lubricate this bearing thoroughly, but lightly, with 20W SAE oil.

8. Insert the planetary gear train with the the pinion, overrunning clutch, fork lever and bearing pedestal into the drive housing.

9. Install the rubber seal onto the pedestal bearing.

10. Position and install the cover plate on the surface of the ring gear, ensuring the recess in the cover plate mates with the lug machined in the surface of the ring gear.

11. Using the proper tool, position the brush plate onto the end of the commutator shaft. Slide the brush plate over the commutator, ensuring the brush holders are properly seated in the anchor point. After the brush holders are properly seated, remove the tool.

12. Place a light coat of 20W SAE oil onto the felt ring gasket and install the gasket on the commutator end of the armature shaft.

13. Place a light coat of Lithium-based lubricant onto the commutator end shield bushing and install the bushing onto the armature shaft.

14. Slide the commutator end shield onto the armature shaft.

15. Set the armature end play by installing a shim and the retaining washer. After installing the shim, check the end play with the appropriate feeler gauges. The end play should be within the range of 0.002–0.016 in. Should additional shims be required, 3 sizes are available: 0.004 in., 0.047 in. and 0.055 in.

16. After setting the armature end play, place a light coat of lubricant onto the retaining washer.

17. Position the seal ring against the commutator end shield and place the closure cap into installation position.

18. Install the closure cap screws far enough to hold the closure cap into place but do not tighten at this time.

19. Support the stator frame by hand and slide the armature with the brush plate and commutator end shield carefully into the stator frame, ensuring that a sufficient gap is left to allow installation of the rubber seal.

20. Install the rubber seal onto terminal 45 and slide the rubber seal into the groove of the stator frame.

21. With moderate force, rotate the pinion gear until the armature spline meshes evenly with the planetary gears.

NOTE: When positioning the stator frame ensure the groove in the stator frame is aligned with and fits into the sealing rubber of the bearing pedestal.

22. Rotate the commutator end shield until the groove on the commutator end shield is aligned with the sealing rubber on the bearing pedestal.

23. When the proper alignment is achieved, install the stator frame-to-drive shield screws and torque to 2.0–2.6 ft. lbs.

24. Torque the closure cap screws to 1.0–1.5 ft. lbs.

25. Engage the solenoid switch armature with the fork lever and insert the armature return spring.

26. Install and tighten the solenoid switch housing screws.

27. Install the field washer and terminal wire (Terminal 45) onto the field terminal post. Install the field terminal nut.

Assembling the overrunning clutch and planetary gear system—Jeep

Seating the stop ring—Jeep

MITSUBISHI REDUCTION GEAR STARTERS

Disassembly

This starter is a light-weight unit with planetary gear drive and permanent magnets. It is highly sensitive to hammering, shocks and external pressure. Never clamp the starter motor armature frame in a vise. It will damage the magnets. Clamp by the mounting flange only. Work on a clean bench. Metal chips will be attracted by the permanent magnets and could lead to starter failure. Clean the parts with compressed air. Do not use liquid solvent.

1. Remove the solenoid terminal nut and disconnect the brush holder connecting wire.

2. Remove the 2 solenoid screws and remove the solenoid and plunger.

3. Loosen but do not remove the 2 screws that attach the commutator shield to the brush holder plate

4. Remove the 2 armature frame through bolts.

5. Slide the armature frame away from the overrunning clutch housing and remove the retainer and washer.

6. Remove the overrunning clutch housing from the armature frame. Use care not to loose the armature shaft ball when removing the frame.

7. Remove the clutch fork from the clutch and take the clutch off the armature.

8. Remove the 2 screws holding the end cover to the armature. Remove the cover but do not remove the brush holder plate.

9. Install a 22mm socket on the armature shaft against the brush holder. Slide the brush holder up and onto the socket.

Leave the socket in the brush holder for inspection and assembly.

10. Remove the seal ring from the planetary gear assembly, then remove the gears.

11. Remove the gear carrier and pinion shaft from the planetary annulus gear.

12. Place a 17mm socket on the bench as a holder and place the planetary gear/overrunning clutch assembly in a vertical position on end so the entire assembly rests upright on the socket.

13. Unseat the stop ring using a 12 point 14mm socket. Install the socket on the pinion shaft and against the stop ring. Then strike the socket with a hammer to unseat the stop ring and expose the snap ring. Remove the 14mm socket. Remove the snapring and stop ring from the drive shaft and slide the overrunning clutch from the pinion shaft.

Inspection

1. Clean the armature, frame, clutch, solenoid and brush holder assembly with clean dry cloths or compressed air. Do not use any liquid solvents on these components. All other starter components may be cleaned with mineral spirits.

2. Inspect all parts for wear or damage. Inspect the armature shaft bushings for wear. If they have worn to the point where the armature-to-frame contact has occurred, replace the starter motor assembly. Do not remove the 22mm socket from the brush holder unless the assembly is be replaced. The minimum length for the brushes is 0.035 inch (9mm).

3. Standard armature tests with a growler may be performed on the armature.

Assembly

1. Assembly is the reverse of the removal procedure. Install the planetary annulus gear on the gear carrier and pinion shaft. Lubricate the drive shaft and bushing in the overrunning clutch with 20W motor oil. Lubricate the spiral splines in the clutch bore with white lithium grease and install the clutch on the pinion shaft.

2. Install the stop ring and snapring on the pinion shaft. Use care not to scratch the shaft. A battery terminal puller is suggested to draw the stop ring against the snapring. Make sure the stop ring is seated on and over the snapring.

3. Install the clutch fork on the clutch. Install the clutch assembly in the housing, making sure the locating lugs on the planetary annulus are properly aligned and seated in the housing.

4. Lubricate the planetary gears with chassis grease and install the 3 gears on the planetary carrier shafts. Install the seal ring on the clutch housing with the largest lug on the seal ring at the top.

5. If replacement bushes were installed in the holder, reinsert the 22mm socket through the brush holder to keep the brushes in position. Hold the socket against the armature commutator and slide the brush holder and brushes onto the commutator and remove the socket. Make sure the brushes and brush retainers are seated in the holder.

6. Install the bearing and washer on the armature shaft and position the end cover on the brush holder. Align the brush connector wire and grommet in the end cover and push the cover in place. Install but do not tighten the screws.

7. Install the armature frame on the assembled armature, brush holder and shield. Be sure to align and seat the brush connector wire grommet in the frame.

8. Install the ball in the splined end of the armature shaft. Use chassis grease to hold in place. Install the armature and frame on the clutch housing. Rotate the armature frame until the alignment tabs on the frame seat in the clutch housing slots. Be sure the armature shaft splines are seated in the planetary gears and the armature shaft is seated in the planetary bushing bore.

RUBBER SEAL

22 MILLIMETER SOCKET

BRUSH HOLDER

22 MILLIMETER SOCKET

STOP RING

17MM SOCKET

12 POINT 14MM SOCKET

PLANETARY GEAR/ OVERRUNNING CLUTCH

Using sockets as disassembly/assembly tools on Mitsubishi gear drive starter motor—Top and Middle: using 22mm socket to remove and install brushes; Bottom: using 14mm and 17mm sockets to disassembly planetary gear case—1991 Jeep 4.0L and 5.9L engine

Exploded view of Mitsubishi gear drive starter motor—1991 Jeep 4.0L and 5.9L engine shown

1. Bushing
2. Overrunning clutch housing
3. Snapring
4. Stop ring
5. Overrunning clutch
6. Clutch yoke
7. Yoke washer
8. Retainer
9. Solenoid
10. Planetary annulus gear
11. Planetary carrier and pinion shaft
12. Planetary gears
13. Armature shaft ball
14. Seal ring
15. Armature frame and magnet assembly
16. Armature
17. Bearing
18. Washer
19. Carbon brushes
20. Brush holder
21. Armature grame bolts
22. End cover

9. Install the bolts that attach the armature frame to the clutch housing. Tighten the brush holder screws.

10. Install the solenoid by engaging the plunger in the fork, installing the return spring, spacer washer and solenoid housing.

Install and tighten the solenoid attaching screws.

11. Attach the brush connecting wire to the motor terminal of the solenoid.

CHRYSLER IMPORT

Overhaul

DIRECT DRIVE TYPE

Disassembly and Assembly

MITSUBISHI TYPE

1. Position the assembly in the soft jawed vise. Disconnect the field coil wire from the solenoid terminal.

2. Remove the solenoid-to-starter screws and the solenoid.

3. Remove the through bolts and the commutator end frame cover. Remove both brushes and the brush plate. Slide the field frame from the armature.

4. Remove the shift lever pivot bolt, the rubber gasket and plate.

5. Press the stop collar from the snapring and remove the snapring, stop collar and clutch.

6. Brushes that are worn less than ½ the length of new brushes or oil soaked should be replaced; new brushes are $^{11}/_{16}$ in. long.

To assemble:

7. Do not immerse the starter clutch unit in cleaning solvent; lubricant will be washed from inside the clutch.

8. Place the drive unit on the armature shaft and while holding the armature, rotate the pinion. The drive pinion should rotate smoothly in 1 direction only. The pinion may not rotate easily but as long as it rotates smoothly it is in good condition. If the clutch unit does not function properly or if the pinion is worn, chipped or burred replace the unit.

9. Lubricate the bushings/splines and reverse the disassembly procedures.

10. Install the clutch, stop collar, lock ring and shaft fork on the armature.

11. Install the armature assembly and shift fork in the drive end housing.

12. To complete the installation, reverse the removal procedures.

FORD TYPE

1. Position the starter in a soft jawed vise.

2. Remove the field strap-to-solenoid nut and the field strap.

3. Remove the solenoid-to-drive end housing screws. Remove the solenoid from the housing by guiding it away from the drive end housing and the plunger.

4. Disconnect the plunger from the drive yoke. If shims are present between the solenoid and the starter, save them for

1. Magnetic switch retaining screw
2. Front bracket
3. Washer
4. Snapring
5. Stopring
6. Overrunning clutch and pinion

7. Armature
8. Magnetic switch
9. Washer set
10. Spring retainer
11. Lever spring
12. Spring seat
13. Lever
14. Washer

15. Yoke
16. Brush holder assembly
17. Brush spring
18. Rear bracket
19. Brush holder retaining screw
20. Through bolt

Exploded view of the Mitsubishi type direct drive starter—Chrysler Import

reinstallation. The shims determine the starter pinion depth clearance.

5. Remove the starter housing through bolts. Separate the starter housing from the drive end housing.

6. Remove the rear cover-to-field frame screws, separate the strap grommet from the rear cover and remove the rear cover.

7. Using a small prybar, lift the retaining springs and remove the brushes from their channels.

NOTE: Before removing the brush plate, remove the brushes from the plate; this will prevent possible damage to the brushes.

8. Note the position of the yoke and separate it from the drive pinion. Remove the armature and the drive pinion from the drive housing.

9. From the drive housing, remove the yoke, seal and washer.

NOTE: When removing the drive pinion, do not clamp it in a vise, for damage to the internal parts may occur.

10. Using a deep socket or equivalent, drive the armature collar towards the armature to expose the snapring. Remove the snapring from the armature's groove and slide the drive pinion from the armature.

11. Using an ohmmeter, check the each commutator-to-armature core for grounds; there should be no movement of the ohmmeter indicator. If the ohmmeter indicates a ground, replace the armature.

12. Inspect the commutator burn spots, scored surface and/or dirt. Using a set of V-blocks and a dial indicator, check the commutator runout. If the runout is greater than 0.002 in., refinish the commutator or replace the armature.

13. Using a micrometer, check the commutator's outer diameter; if it is less than 1.220 in., replace the armature.

1. Magnetic switch retaining screw
2. Magnetic switch
3. Packing
4. Plate
5. Screw
6. Through bolt
7. Rear bracket
8. Rear bearing

9. Brush holder assembly
10. Yoke assembly
11. Armature
12. Lever
13. Washer
14. Snapring
15. Stopring
16. Overrunning clutch
17. Front bracket

Exploded view of the Ford type direct drive starter— Chrysler Import

NOTE: Never use emery cloth to clean the commutator face.

14. Inspect the depth of the insulating material between the commutator segments; it should be greater than 0.008 in. If necessary to undercut the insulating material, use a broken hacksaw blade and scrap the material to a depth of 0.020–0.031 in.

15. If the armature core shows signs of scuffing, the bushings are probably worn and need replacement.

16. Inspect the field coil for corrosion, insulation burnt/bare spots and/or deterioration. If necessary, replace the field coil housing assembly.

17. Using an ohmmeter, check the field strap connector-to-brushes for continuity. If there is no continuity, replace the field coil housing assembly.

18. Using an ohmmeter, check for continuity between the field strap connector and the field coil housing; if there is continuity, replace the field coil housing assembly. When performing this test, be certain the brushes and wires are not touching the housing.

19. Measure the brush lengths for wear, if they are near or beyond 0.453 in., replace the brushes.

20. To inspect the drive pinion, perform the following procedures:

  a. Inspect the drive pinion teeth for excessive wear or milling. If either condition exists, the drive pinion and flywheel (manual) or flexplate (automatic) must be replaced.

  b. To check the one-way clutch, try to turn the drive pinion in both directions; it should turn freely one-way and lock up the other way.

To assemble:

21. Lubricate the armature splines with Lubriplate® 777 or equivalent. Install the drive pinion and the locking collar on the armature. Install the snapring and pull the collar over the snapring to secure it.

22. Using Lubriplate® 777 or equivalent, lubricate the shift fork and install it into the drive end housing. Engage the armature assembly into the drive end housing and couple the shift fork with the drive pinion.

23. Position the drive end housing into a soft jawed vise (nose down) and install the plug and seal into the housing recess.

24. Lower the field coil housing over the armature and seat it onto the drive end housing; position the housing so the field strap is on the solenoid side.

25. Install the washers onto the armature. Load the brushes into the brush plate holders. With the brushes pull all the way back in the holders, position the brush springs on the brush sides.

26. Install the brush plate over the commutator. Push the brushes toward the commutator until the springs snap onto the brush ends. Make sure the brush wires do not contact any metal parts.

27. Seat the field strap grommet and the rear cover. Install the through bolts and torque them to 55–75 ft. lbs. Install the solenoid and shims, if equipped.

28. To check the pinion depth, perform the following procedures:

  a. If the field strap was connected to the solenoid terminal, disconnect it.

  b. Using a 12 volt battery, attach the negative (–) terminal to the solenoid's M-terminal and the positive (+) terminal to the solenoid's S-terminal; this will energize the solenoid.

NOTE: When energizing the solenoid, do not engage it for more than 20 seconds. Between each engagement, allow it to cool for at least 3 minutes.

  c. Using a feeler gauge and the solenoid energized, check the drive pinion-to-collar gap; it should be 0.020–0.080 in. If necessary, add or subtract shims between the solenoid and drive end housing until the desired depth is achieved.

REDUCTION DRIVE TYPE

Disassembly and Assembly

MITSUBISHI TYPE

NOTE: Do not place the stator frame in a vise or strike it with a hammer for damage to the permanent magnets could occur.

1. Disconnect the coil wire from the solenoid.

2. Remove the solenoid-to-front end frame screws and the solenoid.

3. Loosen, do not remove the commutator shield-to-brush holder screws.

4. Remove the through bolts, the rubber retainer (under solenoid) and the coin washer.

NOTE: When removing the output shaft assembly, do not loose the armature shaft ball.

1. Magnetic switch retaining screw	12. Packing A
2. Magnetic switch	13. Packing B
3. Screw	14. Plate
4. Through bolt	15. Planetary gear
5. Rear bracket	16. Lever
6. Brush holder	17. Snapring
7. Brush	18. Stopring
8. Rear bearing	19. Overrunning clutch
9. Armature	20. Internal gear
10. Yoke assembly	21. Planetary gear holder
11. Ball	22. Front bracket

Exploded view of the Mitsubishi type reduction drive starter—Chrysler Import

5. Remove the stator frame, the commutator shield and output shaft assembly as a unit. Separate the clutch fork from the output shaft assembly.

6. From the stator frame, pull the output shaft assembly forward, then, push the armature and commutator shield to the rearward.

7. Remove the commutator shield-to-brush holder plate screws and the shield; do not remove the brush holder assembly.

8. Using a 22mm socket, slide it up against the commutator, slide the brush holder assembly onto the socket and position the socket/brush holder assembly aside.

9. To disassemble the output shaft assembly, perform the following procedures:

  a. Remove the rubber packing ring and the gears.

  b. Using a 17mm socket, position it into the armature end of the driveshaft and position the assembly in the vertical position, resting on the socket.

  c. Using a 12 point 14mm socket, position it against the stopring (on the clutch end). Using a hammer, strike the socket to unseat the stopring and expose the snapring.

  d. Remove the socket, the snapring and the stopring from the driveshaft.

e. Using fine sandpaper, remove any burrs from the drive-shaft. Remove the overrunning clutch.

10. Using compressed air or dry cloths, clean the armature, the stator frame, the overrunning clutch, the solenoid and the brush holder. Using mineral spirits, clean all other components.

11. Inspect the following parts for damage and replace, if necessary:
    a. The stator frame and permanent magnets
    b. The driveshaft bushing (armature side)
    c. The planetary gear set and driveshaft
    d. The starter motor bushing and bearing
    e. The carbon brushes for cracks, distortion and wear below 0.354 in.

NOTE: When inspecting the brushes, do not remove the socket from the brush holder.

12. Using a growler and a hacksaw blade (placed on top of the armature), rotate the armature and check it for a shorted condition. If the hacksaw blade vibrates, a short exists; replace the armature.

13. Using a test light, place a lead on the armature's core and the other on each commutator segment, inspect the armature for a grounded condition. If a ground exists, the test light will turn **ON**; replace the armature.

14. Using a test light, place the leads on the adjacent commutator segments. If the test light turns **ON** between any 2 segments, the armature is shorted and must be replaced.

15. Inspect the commutator out-of-round, if it is more than 0.001 in., reface it on a lathe.

To assemble:

16. Using motor oil, lubricate the driveshaft and the overrunning clutch bushing. Using Lubriplate®, lubricate the overrunning clutch spiral cut splines.

17. Install the overrunning clutch on the driveshaft/planetary gear assembly, followed by the stopring and the snapring. Be sure to seat the snapring in the shaft groove and crimp the it with a pair of pliers.

18. Using a battery terminal puller, attach it to the driveshaft tip and press the stopring over the snapring.

NOTE: When installing the stopring, be careful not to scratch the driveshaft.

19. Install the clutch fork, with the assembled planetary gear set, lubricated with lithium grease, into the front end housing; make sure the locating lugs are properly seated in the front end housing.

20. Install the coin washer and the rubber fork retainer.

21. Install the rubber backing ring by placing the largest rubber lug at the top.

22. Install the brush holder onto the armature's commutator; make sure the brushes and brush holders are seated in the holder. Inspect the flex washer and install the commutator shield onto the armature. Install the brush holder screws but do not tighten them.

23. Install the armature assembly into the stator frame and seat the wire grommet into the frame.

24. Be sure the armature spline gear is seated in the planetary gear seat with the armature shaft ball in place. Seat the armature shaft in the shaft bushing bore; rotate the stator frame to align the tabs on the drive housing frame.

25. Install the through bolts and torque to 28 inch lbs. Torque the brush holder screws to 18 inch lbs.

26. To complete the assembly, reverse the disassembly procedures.

GEO

Overhaul

REDUCTION GEAR TYPE

Dissassembly and Assembly

1. Position the starter in a soft jawed. Disconnect the field coil wire from the solenoid terminal.

2. Remove the solenoid mounting screws and work the solenoid from the shift fork. Remove the bearing cover, the armature shaft lock, the washer, the spring and the seal.

3. Remove the commutator end frame cover through bolts, the cover, the brushes and the brush plate.

4. Slide the field frame from over the armature. Remove the shift lever pivot bolt, the rubber gasket and the metal plate.

5. Remove the armature assembly and the shift lever from the drive end housing. Press the stop collar from the snapring, then remove the snapring, the stop collar and the clutch assembly.

6. If the brushes are worn more than ½ the length of new brushes or are oil-soaked, should be replaced; the new brushes are 0.630 in. long.

7. Do not immerse the starter clutch unit in cleaning solvent as the solvent will wash the lubricant from the clutch. Place the drive unit on the armature shaft, then, while holding the armature, rotate the pinion.

NOTE: The drive pinion should rotate smoothly in one direction only. The pinion may not rotate easily but as long as it rotates smoothly it is in good condition. If the clutch unit does not function properly or if the pinion is worn, chipped or burred, replace the unit.

To assemble:

8. Lubricate the armature shaft and splines with lubricant.

9. Install the clutch, the stop collar, the lock ring and the shift fork onto the armature.

10. Install the armature assembly into the drive end housing.

11. Install the field frame housing over the armature and onto the drive end housing.

12. Position the brushes into the brush holder and position the brush holder over the armature's commutator.

13. Install the commutator end housing and the through bolts.

14. Install the cap end gasket, the armature brake spring, the armature plate and the commutator end cap.

ISUZU

Overhaul

DIRECT DRIVE TYPE

Disassembly and Assembly

1. Position the starter in a soft jawed vise. Disconnect the field coil wire from the solenoid terminal.

2. Remove the solenoid mounting screws and work the solenoid from the shift fork. Remove the bearing cover, the armature shaft lock, the washer, the spring and the seal.

3. Remove the commutator end frame cover through bolts, the cover, the brushes and the brush plate.

4. Slide the field frame from over the armature. Remove the shift lever pivot bolt, the rubber gasket and the metal plate.

5. Remove the armature assembly and the shift lever from the drive end housing. Press the stop collar from the snapring, then remove the snapring, the stop collar and the clutch assembly.

6. If the brushes are worn more than ½ the length of new brushes or are oil-soaked, should be replaced; the new brushes are 0.630 in. long.

7. Do not immerse the starter clutch unit in cleaning solvent as the solvent will wash the lubricant from the clutch. Place the drive unit on the armature shaft, then, while holding the armature, rotate the pinion.

NOTE: The drive pinion should rotate smoothly in one direction only. The pinion may not rotate easily but as long as it rotates smoothly it is in good condition. If the clutch unit does not function properly or if the pinion is worn, chipped or burred, replace the unit.

To assemble:

8. Lubricate the armature shaft and splines with lubricant.

9. Install the clutch, the stop collar, the lock ring and the shift fork onto the armature.

10. Install the armature assembly into the drive end housing.

11. Install the field frame housing over the armature and onto the drive end housing.

12. Position the brushes into the brush holder and position the brush holder over the armature's commutator.

13. Install the commutator end housing and the through bolts.

14. Install the cap end gasket, the armature brake spring, the armature plate and the commutator end cap.

REDUCTION DRIVE TYPE

Disassembly and Assembly

1. Position the starter in a soft jawed vise. Remove the nut and disconnect the motor wire from the magnetic switch terminal.

2. Remove the through bolts and pull the field frame (with the armature) from the magnetic switch assembly.

3. Remove the starter housing to magnetic switch assembly bolts and separate the housing from the assembly. Remove the pinion gear, the pinion retainer/bearings and the clutch assembly.

4. Using a magnetic finger, remove the spring and the steel ball from the hole in the clutch assembly shaft. Remove the field frame end cover.

5. Using a small prybar, separate the brush springs, then remove the brushes from the brush holder and pull the brush holder from the field frame.

6. Remove the armature from the field frame. Using an ohmmeter, make sure there is no continuity between the commutator and the armature coil core. If there is continuity, replace the armature.

1. Magnetic switch lead	5. Brush holder assembly
2. Solenoid switch assembly	6. Field coil assembly
3. Dust cover and snapring	7. Armature assembly with shift lever
4. Rear cover assembly	8. Pinion stop clip
	9. Pinion assembly

Exploded view of the Isuzu direct drive starter—Isuzu

1. Lead wire	5. Brush and brush holder
2. Through bolt	6. Armature
3. Yoke assembly	7. Drive side housing
4. Cover yoke	8. Overrunning clutch
	9. Return spring
	10. Steel ball
	11. Idler gear
	12. Retainer
	13. Roller

Exploded view of the Isuzu reduction drive starter— Isuzu

7. Using an ohmmeter, check for continuity between the commutator segments. If there is no continuity between any of the segments, replace the armature.

8. If the commutator is dirty, burnt or the runout exceeds 0.002 in., use a lathe to reface the surface. Do not machine the diameter to less than 1.140 in. diameter.

9. Using an ohmmeter, make sure there is continuity between the lead wire and the brush lead of the field coil. If there is no continuity, replace the field frame.

10. Using an ohmmeter, make sure there is no continuity between the field coil and the field frame. If there is continuity, replace the field frame.

11. If the brush length is less than 0.394 in., replace the brush and dress with emery cloth.

12. Check the gear teeth for wear or damage, if damaged, replace them. Turn the clutch assembly pinion clockwise and make sure it rotates freely, try to turn the pinion counterclockwise and make sure it locks. If the pinion does not respond correctly, replace it.

13. While applying inward force on the bearings, turn each by hand; if resistance or sticking is noticed, replace the bearings. To replace the bearings, use the tool 09286–46011 or equiva- lent, to pull the bearing(s) from the armature shaft. Using the tool 09285–76010 or equivalent, and an arbor press, press the new bearing(s) onto the armature shaft.

14. Using an ohmmeter, check for continuity between the grounded terminal and the insulated terminal, then between the grounded terminal and the housing. If there is no continuity in either case, replace the magnetic switch assembly.

To assemble:

15. Lubricate the gears, the shafts and bearings with high temperature grease.

16. Install the over-running clutch, the pinion and the retainers with the rollers into the housing.

17. Install the spring to the magnetic switch and assembly the housing and the magnetic switch.

18. Install the brushes into the brush holder; make sure the positive brush leads are not grounded.

19. Install the rear end frame to the yoke, engage the tab with the wire grommet and install the cover.

20. Install the yoke to the magnetic switch, engage the tab on the yoke with the magnetic switch notch.

21. To complete the installation, reverse the removal procedures.

MAZDA

Overhaul

DIRECT DRIVE TYPE

Disassembly and Assembly

1. Remove the starter from the engine.

2. Disconnect the field strap from the solenoid.

3. Remove the screws attaching the solenoid to the drive end housing. Disengage the solenoid plunger hook from the shift fork and remove the solenoid.

4. Remove the shift fork pivot bolt, nut and lockwasher.

5. Remove the through bolts and separate the drive end housing from the starter frame. At the same time, disengage the shift fork from the drive assembly.

6. Remove the brush end bearing cover-to-brush end cover screws.

7. Remove the C-washer, washer and spring from the brush end of the armature shaft.

8. Pull the brush end cover from the starter frame.

9. Slide the armature from the starter frame and brushes.

10. Slide the drive stop-ring retainer toward the armature and remove the stop-ring. Slide the retainer and drive assembly off the armature shaft.

11. Remove the field brushes from the brush holder and separate the brush holder from the starter frame.

To assemble:

12. Position the drive assembly on the armature shaft.

13. Position the drive stop-ring retainer on the armature shaft and install the drive stop-ring. Slide the stop-ring retainer over the stop-ring to secure the stop-ring on the shaft.

14. Position the armature in the starter frame. Install the brush holder on the armature and starter frame. Install the brushes in the brush holder.

15. Install the drive end housing on the armature shaft and starter housing. Engage the shift fork with the starter drive assembly as the drive end housing is moved toward the starter frame.

16. Install the brush end cover on the starter frame making sure that the rear tabs of the brush holder are aligned with the through-bolt holes.

1. Magnetic switch
2. Rear housing
3. Brush holder assembly
4. Field coil
5. Lever
6. Front cover
7. Drive pinion
8. Armature

Exploded view of the Mazda direct drive starter — Mazda

17. Install the through-bolts.

18. Install the rubber washer, spring, washer and C-washer on the armature shaft at the brush end. Install the brush end bearing cover on the brush end cover and install the attaching screws. If the brush end cover is not properly positioned, the bearing cover screws cannot be installed.

19. Align the shift fork with the pivot bolt hole and install the pivot bolt, lockwasher and nut. Tighten the nut securely.

20. Position the solenoid on the drive end housing. Be sure that the solenoid plunger hook is engaged with the shift fork.

21. Install both solenoid retaining screws and washers.

22. Apply 12 volts to the solenoid **S** terminal (ground the **M** terminal) and check the clearance between the starter drive and the stop-ring retainer. The clearance should be 0.080–0.200 in.

1. Magnetic switch
2. Rear housing
3. Front cover
4. Drive pinion
5. Internal gear
6. Gear shaft
7. Planetary gear
8. Magnet coil
9. Armature
10. Brush holder assembly

Exploded view of the Mazda coaxial reduction drive starter—Mazda

1. Magnetic switch
2. Rear housing
3. Drive pinion
4. Front cover
5. Reduction gear
6. Center bracket
7. Armature
8. Field coil
9. Brush holder assembly

Exploded view of the Mazda non-coaxial reduction drive starter—Mazda

If not, the solenoid plunger is not properly adjusted. The clearance can be adjusted by inserting an adjusting shim between the solenoid body and drive end housing.

23. Install the field strap and tighten the nut.

24. Install the starter. Check the operation of the starter.

REDUCTION DRIVE COAXIAL TYPE

Disassembly and Assembly

1. Position the starter in a soft jawed vise. Disconnect the field coil wire from the solenoid terminal.

2. Remove the solenoid mounting screws and work the solenoid from the shift fork. Remove the bearing cover, the armature shaft lock, the washer, the spring and the seal.

3. Remove the commutator end frame cover through bolts, the cover, the brushes and the brush plate.

4. Slide the field frame from over the armature. Remove the shift lever pivot bolt, the rubber gasket and the metal plate.

5. Remove the armature assembly and the shift lever from the drive end housing. Press the stop collar from the snapring, then remove the snapring, the stop collar and the clutch assembly.

6. If the brushes are worn more than ½ the length of new brushes or are oil-soaked, should be replaced. The new brushes are 0.630 in. long.

7. Do not immerse the starter clutch unit in cleaning solvent as the solvent will wash the lubricant from the clutch. Place the drive unit on the armature shaft, then, while holding the armature, rotate the pinion.

NOTE: The drive pinion should rotate smoothly in one direction only. The pinion may not rotate easily but as long as it rotates smoothly it is in good condition. If the clutch unit does not function properly or if the pinion is worn, chipped or burred, replace the unit.

To assemble:

8. Lubricate the armature shaft and splines with lubricant.

9. Install the clutch, the stop collar, the lock ring and the shift fork onto the armature.

10. Install the armature assembly into the drive end housing.

11. Install the field frame housing over the armature and onto the drive end housing.

12. Position the brushes into the brush holder and position the brush holder over the armature's commutator.

13. Install the commutator end housing and the through bolts.

14. Install the cap end gasket, the armature brake spring, the armature plate and the commutator end cap.

REDUCTION DRIVE NON-COAXIAL TYPE

Disassembly and Assembly

1. Remove the starter from the vehicle. Position the unit in a soft jawed vise.

2. Remove the field connector nut, the solenoid switch screws and the solenoid.

3. If equipped with shims between the solenoid and the drive end housing, retain these for installation purposes.

4. Remove the starter through bolts and the brush holder bolts. Remove the commutator end frame from the armature and bearing assembly. Remove the field frame assembly and the armature from the center housing.

5. Pry back each brush spring so each brush can be backed away from the armature about ¼ in. Release the spring to hold the brushes in the backed out position, then remove the armature from the field frame and brush holder.

6. Remove the shaft cover-to-center housing screws and the shaft cover. Remove the C-shaped washer and plate. Remove the center housing bolts, the center housing shim and thrust washers.

7. Remove the reduction gear, the spring holder and the lever springs.

8. To remove the drive pinion, perform the following procedures:

a. Using a ⅝ in. socket, slide it over the shaft against the stopper.

b. Using the socket as a driving tool, tap it with a hammer to move the stopper off the ring.

c. Remove the stopper and the drive pinion.

9. Remove the pinion shaft and the lever assembly. Note the direction of the lever and the lever holders.

10. Clean all parts in the proper cleaning solution. Inspect all parts for wear and damage; replace or repair defective components as required. Inspect all bearings for wear, roughness or dryness; replace damaged bearings with new ones.

11. Inspect the armature commutator. If the commutator is rough, it should be refinished on a lathe. Do not turn the commutator to less than 1.480 in. outside diameter.

12. With the brush holder assembly still attached to the field frame, test the field coils for open. Using a test lamp, place a test lead on the field coil connector and the other test lead on the positive (+) brush.

13. The test light should turn **ON**. If the test light fails to light, the field coil is open; the field coil must be replaced. Repeat the test on the other positive brush.

14. To test the field coil for ground, place a test light lead on the field coil connector and the other lead on the field frame; the test light should stay **OFF**. If the test light turns **ON**, the field coils are grounded to the field frame assembly, the field frame must be replaced.

To assemble:

15. To replace the brushes, remove the positive brushes from the brush holder, the brush holder and the negative brush assembly from the field frame.

16. Cut the old brush leads off of their mountings as close to brush connection point as possible. Solder the new brushes as required. Careful installation of the positive side is necessary to prevent grounding of the brush connection point having no insulation.

17. Reinstall the positive and negative brushes in the brush holder assembly and position the assembly in the starter housing.

18. In order to replace the drive end bearing, it will be necessary to press the bearing out of the drive end housing using a press. Replace the armature commutator end bearing and the armature drive end bearing.

19. To assemble, reverse the disassembly procedures. Be sure to check all parts for wear and damage; repair or replace defective parts.

20. If either the drive end housing, pinion shaft, reduction gear, shim washers or center housing were replaced, it will be necessary to check the end play for the pinion shaft. Install the plate and C-shaped washer onto the end of the pinion shaft.

21. With the drive end housing mounted in a soft jawed vise, measure the end play. Insert feeler gauge between C-washer and cover plate, pry the pinion shaft in the axial direction to check the end play. It should be 0.004–0.020 in.

22. If the end play is not correct, remove the plate, C-shaped washer, center bracket and add or remove the shim thrust washers to adjust the end play and recheck.

NOTE: Shim thrust washers are available in 2 thicknesses 0.010 in. and 0.020 in.

23. When the starter has been disassembled or the solenoid switch has been replaced, it is necessary to check the pinion position. Pinion position must be correct to prevent the top of the lever from rubbing on the clutch collar during cranking.

24. Connect the positive lead of a 12 volt battery to the "S" terminal on the switch and momentarily connect the other to the starter frame. This will shift the pinion into cranking posi-

tion and will retain it until the battery is disconnected. Do not leave engaged more than 30 seconds at a time.

25. Using a dial indicator (with pinion engaged), push the pinion shaft back by hand and measure the amount of pinion shaft movement; the clearance should be 0.020–0.080 in.

26. If the amount does not fall within limits, adjust it by adding or removing the shims which are located between the switch and the front bracket; adding shims decreases the amount of the movement. Solenoid switch shims are available in 2 thicknesses 0.020 in. and 0.010 in.

MITSUBISHI

Overhaul

DIRECT DRIVE TYPE

Disassembly and Assembly

1. Remove the wire connecting the starter solenoid to the starter.
2. Remove the starter solenoid-to-starter drive housing screws and the solenoid.
3. Remove both long through bolts from the rear of the starter and separate the armature yoke from the armature.
4. Carefully remove the armature and the starter drive engagement lever from the front bracket, noting the way they are positioned along with the spring and spring retainer.
5. Loosen both screws and remove the rear bracket.
6. Tap the stopper ring at the end of the drive gear engagement shaft in towards the drive gear to expose the snapring. Remove the snapring.
7. Pull the stopper, drive gear and overrunning clutch from the end of the shaft.
8. Inspect the pinion and spline teeth for wear or damage. If the engagement teeth are damaged, visually check the flywheel ring gear through the starter hole to insure that it is not damaged. It will be necessary to turn the engine over by hand to completely inspect the ring gear.
9. Check the brushes for wear. Their service limit length is 0.453 in. Replace if necessary.

To assemble:

10. Install the spring retainer and spring on the armature shaft.
11. Install the overrunning clutch assembly on the armature shaft.
12. Fit the stopper ring with its open side facing out on the shaft.
13. Install a new snapring and, using a gear puller, pull the stopper ring into place over the snapring.
14. Fit the small washer on the front end of the armature shaft.
15. Fit the engagement lever into the overrunning clutch and refit the armature into the front housing.
16. Fit the engagement lever spring and spring retainer into place and slide the armature yoke over the armature. Position the yoke with the spring retainer cut-out space in line with the spring retainer.

NOTE: Make sure the brushes are seated on the commutator.

17. Replace the rear bracket and retainer screws.
18. Install the through bolts in the end of the yoke.
19. Refit the starter solenoid, fitting the plunger over the engagement lever. Install the screws and connect the wire running from the starter yoke to the starter solenoid.

REDUCTION DRIVE TYPE

Disassembly and Assembly

1. Remove the wire connecting the starter solenoid to the starter.

1. Screw	10. Yoke assembly
2. Magnetic switch	11. Armature
3. Packing	12. Lever
4. Plate	13. Washer
5. Screw	14. Snapring
5. Through bolt	15. Stopring
7. Rear bracket	16. Overrunning clutch
8. Rear bearing	17. Front bracket
9. Brush holder assembly	

Exploded view of the Mitsubishi direct drive starter—Mitsubishi

2. Remove the solenoid screws, pull it out, unhook and disengage it from the engagement lever.
3. Remove the through bolts in the end of the starter and the bracket screws. Pull off the rear bracket.

NOTE: Since the conical spring washer is contained in the rear bracket, be sure to take it out.

4. Remove the yoke and brush holder assembly while pulling the brush upward.
5. Pull the armature assembly out of the mounting bracket.

6. In the side of the mounting bracket that the armature fits into, there is a small dust cap held by screws. Remove it and remove the snapring and washer under it.

7. Remove the remaining bolts in the mounting bracket and split the reduction case.

NOTE: Several washers will come out when the case is split. These adjust the end play for the pinion shaft. Do not lose them.

8. Remove the reduction gear, lever and lever spring from the front bracket.

9. Using a brass drift or deep socket, knock the stopper ring on the end of the shaft in toward the pinion. Remove the snapring. Remove the stopper, pinion and pinion shaft assembly.

10. Remove the ball bearings at both ends of the armature.

NOTE: The ball bearings are pressed in the front bracket and are not replaceable. Replace them together with the bracket.

11. Inspect the pinion and spline teeth for wear or damage. If the engagement teeth are damaged, visually check the flywheel ring gear through the starter hole to insure that it is not damaged also. It will be necessary to turn the engine over by hand to completely inspect the ring gear.

12. Check the brushes for wear. Their service limit length is 0.453 in. Replace if necessary.

13. Assembly is the reverse of disassembly. Be sure to replace all adjusting and thrust washers. When replacing the rear bracket, fit the conical spring pinion washer with its convex side facing out. Make sure the brushes seat on the commutator.

NISSAN

Overhaul

DIRECT DRIVE TYPE

Disassembly and Assembly

MITSUBISHI TYPE

1. Position the assembly in the soft jawed vise. Disconnect the field coil wire from the solenoid terminal.

2. Remove the solenoid-to-starter screws and the solenoid from the shifting fork.

3. Remove the through bolts and the commutator end frame cover. Remove the 2 brushes and the brush plate. Slide the field frame from the armature.

4. Remove the shift lever pivot bolt, the rubber gasket and plate.

5. Remove the snapring, the clutch assembly and the drive end housing from the armature.

6. Press the stop collar from the snapring and remove the snapring, stop collar and clutch.

7. Brushes that are worn less than ½ the length of new brushes or oil soaked should be replaced; new brushes are $^{11}/_{16}$ in. long.

To assemble:

8. Do not immerse the starter clutch unit in cleaning solvent; lubricant will be washed from inside the clutch.

9. Place the drive unit on the armature shaft and while holding the armature, rotate the pinion. The drive pinion should rotate smoothly in one direction only. The pinion may not rotate easily but as long as it rotates smoothly it is in good condition. If the clutch unit does not function properly or if the pinion is worn, chipped or burred replace the unit.

10. To assemble, lubricate the bushings/splines and reverse the disassembly procedures.

11. Install the clutch, stop collar, lock ring and shaft fork on the armature.

12. Install the armature assembly and shift fork in the drive end housing. Check the end play, it should be 0.002–0.021 in.

HITACHI TYPE

1. Support the starter in a soft jawed vise.

2. Remove the rear mounting bracket-to-starter nuts, the bracket and the plastic cap.

3. Disconnect the field wire from the solenoid.

4. Remove the solenoid-to-starter nuts and the solenoid.

5. From the end cover, remove the nuts, the through bolts and the end cover.

6. Using a pin punch at the drive end housing, drive the yoke axle pin from the housing.

7. At the positive brushes, move the brush spring clips to the side of the brushes and pull the brushes away from the armature. Carefully pull the field housing from the drive end housing.

8. Remove the pinion yoke and armature from the drive end housing.

9. Using a deep socket which fits over the armature shaft, tap the stop collar (driving it toward the armature) to expose the snapring. Remove the snapring from the groove and slide it from the shaft.

NOTE: When removing the snapring, be careful not to bend or distort it.

10. Remove the stop collar, the drive pinion and the support plate.

11. Using compressed air or a brush, clean the drive pinion, the drive end frame, the armature, the field coils and the starter frame. All other parts can be cleaned in solvent.

12. Inspect the condition of the starter parts, perform the following procedures:

    a. Check for broken wires or badly soldered connections.

    b. Replace any bushings which are scored or badly worn.

    c. If the armature's commutator is more than 0.005 in. out of round, reface it on a lathe.

NOTE: Never use emery cloth to clean a commutator.

    d. The drive pinion should be free of excessive wear or damage.

    e. If the brushes are cracked, broken, distorted or worn to less than 0.314 in., replace them.

    f. Using a growler and a hacksaw blade (placed on top of the armature), rotate the armature and check it for a shorted condition. If the hacksaw blade vibrates, a short exists; replace the armature.

    g. Using a test light, place a lead on the armature's core and the other on each commutator segment, inspect the armature for a grounded condition. If a ground exists, the test light will turn **ON**; replace the armature.

    h. Using a test light, check for continuity between the positive brushes; if no continuity exists, replace the winding. Repeat this test for the negative windings.

PINION ASSEMBLY — TORSION SPRING — ADJUSTING PLATE
PLATE THICKNESS:
0.020 IN. (0.50MM)
0.031 IN. (0.80MM)

SHIFT LEVER

MAGNETIC SWITCH ASSEMBLY

DUST COVER

HOUSING

ARMATURE

FRONT BUSHING

PINION STOPPER

STOPPER CLIP

BRUSH SPRING

FIELD COIL

YOKE

BRUSH (+)

BRUSH (−)

DUST COVER

E-RING

THRUST WASHER

REAR COVER

REAR BUSHING

BUSH HOLDER

Exploded view of the Hitachi direct drive starter without center bracket—Nissan

i. Using a test light, place a lead on the coil housing and the other on each coil lead, make sure there is NO continuity; if continuity exists, replace the winding(s).

To assemble:

13. Lubricate the necessary parts and place the support plate onto the armature, followed by the drive pinion and the stop collar. Carefully slide the snapring into the armature groove. Slide the stop collar over the snapring until it locks.
14. Position the armature and pinion yoke into the drive end housing. Install the pinion yoke axle pin.
15. Install the coil housing over the armature and onto the drive end housing. Position the brush holder onto the coil housing. Install the brushes and secure the brush springs.
16. Install the solenoid to the drive end housing. Position the field wire grommet to the coil housing and connect field wire to the solenoid.
17. Install the end cover to the coil housing and the install the through bolts/nuts. Install the armature brake assembly, the plastic cover and the mounting bracket.

REDUCTION GEAR TYPE

Disassembly and Assembly

MITSUBISHI TYPE

NOTE: Do not place the stator frame in a vise or strike it with a hammer for damage to the permanent magnets could occur.

1. Disconnect the coil wire from the solenoid.
2. Remove the solenoid-to-front end frame screws and the solenoid.
3. Loosen, do not remove the commutator shield-to-brush holder screws.

4. Remove the through bolts, the rubber retainer (under solenoid) and the coin washer.

NOTE: When removing the output shaft assembly, do not loose the armature shaft ball.

5. Remove the stator frame, the commutator shield and output shaft assembly as a unit. Separate the clutch fork from the output shaft assembly.
6. From the stator frame, pull the output shaft assembly forward, then, push the armature and commutator shield to the rearward.
7. Remove the commutator shield-to-brush holder plate screws and the shield; do not remove the brush holder assembly.
8. Using a 22mm socket, slide it up against the commutator, slide the brush holder assembly onto the socket and position the socket/brush holder assembly aside.
9. To disassemble the output shaft assembly, perform the following procedures:
    a. Remove the rubber packing ring and the gears.
    b. Using a 17mm socket, position it into the armature end of the driveshaft and position the assembly in the vertical position, resting on the socket.
    c. Using a 12 point 14mm socket, position it against the stopring (on the clutch end). Using a hammer, strike the socket to unseat the stopring and expose the snapring.
    d. Remove the socket, the snapring and the stopring from the driveshaft.
    e. Using fine sandpaper, remove any burrs from the driveshaft. Remove the overruning clutch.
10. Using compressed air or dry cloths, clean the armature, the stator frame, the overrunning clutch, the solenoid and the brush holder. Using mineral spirits, clean all other components.

11. Inspect the following parts for damage and replace, if necessary:
   a. The stator frame and permanent magnets
   b. The driveshaft bushing (armature side)
   c. The planetary gear set and driveshaft
   d. The starter motor bushing and bearing
   e. The carbon brushes for cracks, distortion and wear below 0.354 in.

NOTE: When inspecting the brushes, do not remove the socket from the brush holder.

12. Using a growler and a hacksaw blade (placed on top of the armature), rotate the armature and check it for a shorted condition. If the hacksaw blade vibrates, a short exists; replace the armature.

13. Using a test light, place a lead on the armature's core and the other on each commutator segment, inspect the armature for a grounded condition. If a ground exists, the test light will turn **ON**; replace the armature.

14. Using a test light, place the leads on the adjacent commutator segments. If the test light turns **ON** between any 2 segments, the armature is shorted and must be replaced.

15. Inspect the commutator out-of-round, if it is more than 0.001 in., reface it on a lathe.

To assemble:

16. Using motor oil, lubricate the driveshaft and the overrunning clutch bushing. Using Lubriplate®, lubricate the overrunning clutch spiral cut splines.

17. Install the overrunning clutch on the driveshaft/planetary gear assembly, followed by the stopring and the snapring; sure to seat the snapring in the shaft groove and crimp the it with a pair of pliers.

18. Using a battery terminal puller, attach it to the driveshaft tip and press the stopring over the snapring.

NOTE: When installing the stopring, be careful not to scratch the driveshaft.

19. Install the clutch fork, with the assembled planetary gear set, lubricated with lithium grease, into the front end housing; make sure the locating lugs are properly seated in the front end housing.

20. Install the coin washer and the rubber fork retainer.

21. Install the rubber backing ring by placing the largest rubber lug at the top.

22. Install the brush holder onto the armature's commutator; make sure the brushes and brush holders are seated in the holder. Inspect the flex washer and install the commutator shield onto the armature. Install the brush holder screws but do not tighten them.

23. Install the armature assembly into the stator frame and seat the wire grommet into the frame.

24. Be sure the armature spline gear is seated in the planetary gear seat with the armature shaft ball in place. Seat the armature shaft in the shaft bushing bore. Rotate the stator frame to align the tabs on the drive housing frame.

25. Install the through bolts and torque to 28 inch lbs. Torque the brush holder screws to 18 inch lbs.

26. To complete the assembly, reverse the disassembly procedures.

HITACHI TYPE

With Planetary Gears

1. Position the assembly in a soft jawed vise. Remove the field terminal nut, the terminal and the washer.

2. Remove the solenoid-to-starter screws. Work the solenoid from the shift fork and remove the solenoid from the starter.

3. Remove the starter end shield bushing cap screws, the starter end shield bushing cap, the end shield bushing and C-washer.

Exploded view of the Hitachi reduction drive starter with planetary gears—Nissan Pick-Up and Pathfinder

4. Remove the starter end shield bushing washer and seal.

5. Remove the starter through bolts, the starter end shield and the brush plate.

6. Slide the field frame from the starter and over the armature. Remove the armature assembly from the drive end housing.

7. Remove the rubber seal from the drive end housing. Remove the starter drive gear train.

8. Remove the dust plate. Press the stop collar from the snapring. Using snapring pliers, loosen the snapring.

9. Remove the output shaft snapring, the clutch stopring collar and the clutch assembly from the starter.

10. Remove the clutch shift lever bushing, the clutch shift lever and the C-clip retainer.

11. Remove the retaining washer, the sun and the planetary gears from the annulus gear.

12. To assemble, lubricate the necessary parts and reverse the disassembly procedures. Replace all defective components as required.

Without Planetary Gears

1. Remove the starter from the vehicle. Position the unit in a soft jawed vise.

2. Remove the field coil screw, the field frame through bolts and separate the field frame assembly from the drive gear assembly. Separate the armature and the commutator end frame from the field frame.

3. Remove the solenoid screws and the solenoid from the drive housing.

4. Remove the retaining ring, shift lever shaft and housing through bolts. Separate the drive assembly, drive housing and gear assembly.

5. To remove the overrunning clutch from the armature shaft, perform the following procedures:

    a. Remove the washer or collar from the armature shaft.

    b. Using a 5/8 in. deep socket, slide it over the shaft and against the retainer. Use the socket as a driving tool, tap the socket with a hammer to move the retainer off of the snapring.

    c. Remove the snapring from the groove in the shaft. If the snapring is distorted, replace it.

    d. Remove the retainer and the clutch assembly from the armature shaft.

6. To replace the starter brushes, remove the brush holder pivot pin which positions the insulated and the ground brushes. Remove the brush spring.

7. Inspect armature commutator, shaft and bushings, overrunning clutch pinion, brushes and springs for discoloration, damage or wear; replace the damaged parts, if necessary. Check the armature shaft fit in drive housing bushing; the shaft should fit snugly in the bushing. If the bushing is worn, it should be replaced.

8. Inspect armature commutator. If commutator is rough, it should be refinished on a lathe. Do not undercut or turn to less than 1.650 in. O.D. Inspect the points where the armature conductors join the commutator bars to make sure they have a good connection. A burned commutator is usually evidence of a poor connection.

9. Using a growler and holding hacksaw blade over armature core while armature is rotated, check the armature for short circuits; if the saw blade vibrates, the armature is shorted.

10. Using a test lamp, place a lead on the shunt coil terminal and the other lead to a ground brush. The test should be made from both ground brushes to insure continuity through both brushes and leads. If the lamp fails to light, the field coil is open and will require replacement.

11. Using a test lamp, place a lead on the series coil terminal and the other lead on the insulated brush. If the lamp fails to light, the series coil is open and will require repair or replace-

ment. The test should be made from each insulated brush to check brush and lead continuity.

12. If equipped with a shunt coil, separate the series and shunt coil strap terminals during this test; do not allow the strap terminals to touch the case or other ground. Using a test lamp, place a lead on the grounded brush holder and the other lead on either insulated brush. If the lamp lights, a grounded series coil is indicated and must be repaired or replaced.

NOTE: If the solenoid has not been removed from the starter, the connector strap terminals must be removed before making the following tests. Complete the tests as fast as possible in order to prevent overheating the solenoid.

13. To check the starter winding, connect an ammeter in series with a 12 volt battery, the switch terminal and to ground. Connect a carbon pile across the battery. Adjust the voltage to 10 volts and note the ammeter reading; it should be 14.5–16.5 amperes.

14. To check both windings, connect as for previous test. Ground the solenoid motor terminal, adjust the voltage to 10 volts and note the ammeter reading; it should be 41–47 amperes.

15. Current draw readings above specifications indicate shorted turns or a ground in the windings of the solenoid; the solenoid should be replaced. Current draw readings under specifications indicate excessive resistance. No reading indicates an open circuit. Check the connections and replace solenoid, if necessary. Current readings will decrease as windings heat up.

To assemble:

16. The roller bearing in the drive housing and the roller bearings in the gear housing must be replaced, if they are dry; do not lubricate or reuse the bearings.

17. To replace the gear housing bearing, use a tube or solid cylinder that just fits inside the housing to push bearing toward the armature side. In the opposite direction, use the tube or cylinder to press bearing flush with housing.

18. To replace the gear housing driveshaft bearing, use a tube or collar that just fits inside the housing and press bearing out; press against the open end of bearing. To install a new bearing, press against the closed end, using a thin wall tube or collar that fits in space between bearing and housing. Do not press against the flat end of the bearing; this will bend the thin metal of the bearing. As required, replace the drive housing bearing.

19. To assemble, reverse the disassembly procedures. Be sure to replace or repair all defective components as required.

NOTE: When the starter has been disassembled or the solenoid replaced, it is necessary to check the pinion clearance. The pinion clearance must be checked in order to prevent the buttons on the shift lever yoke from rubbing on the clutch collar during engine cranking.

20. To check the pinion clearance, perform the following procedures:

    a. Disconnect the motor field coil connector from the solenoid motor terminal and insulate the terminal.

    b. Connect the positive (+) 12 volt battery lead to the solenoid switch terminal and the other to the starter frame.

    c. Touch a jumper lead momentarily from the solenoid motor terminal to the starter frame; this will shift the pinion into cranking position and retain it until the battery is disconnected.

    d. Using a feeler gauge, push the pinion back as far as possible, to take up any movement, and check the clearance; the clearance should be 0.010–0.140 in.

    e. Means for adjusting pinion clearance is not provided on the starter motor. If the clearance does not fall within limits, check for improper installation and replace worn parts.

SUZUKI

Overhaul

DIRECT DRIVE TYPE

Dissassembly and Assembly

1. Remove the nut securing the end of the field coil lead to the terminal on the head of the magnetic switch.
2. Remove the magnetic switch mounting screws and the switch from the motor body.
3. Loosen the bolts and screws and remove the commutator end cover.
4. Separate the drive housing and armature from the yoke.
5. Draw the brushes out of the holder.
6. Draw the stopring toward the clutch side and remove the armature ring and slide off the overrunning clutch.
7. To assemble, reverse the disassembly procedures. Replace brushes that are worn more than 0.450 in. New brushes are 0.670 in.

REDUCTION GEAR TYPE

Disassembly and Assembly

1. Position the starter in a soft jawed. Disconnect the field coil wire from the solenoid terminal.
2. Remove the solenoid mounting screws and work the solenoid from the shift fork. Remove the bearing cover, the armature shaft lock, the washer, the spring and the seal.
3. Remove the commutator end frame cover through bolts, the cover, the brushes and the brush plate.

4. Slide the field frame from over the armature. Remove the shift lever pivot bolt, the rubber gasket and the metal plate.
5. Remove the armature assembly and the shift lever from the drive end housing. Press the stop collar from the snapring, then remove the snapring, the stop collar and the clutch assembly.
6. If the brushes are worn more than ½ the length of new brushes or are oil-soaked, should be replaced. New brushes are 0.630 in. long.
7. Do not immerse the starter clutch unit in cleaning solvent as the solvent will wash the lubricant from the clutch. Place the drive unit on the armature shaft, then, while holding the armature, rotate the pinion.

NOTE: The drive pinion should rotate smoothly in one direction only. The pinion may not rotate easily but as long as it rotates smoothly it is in good condition. If the clutch unit does not function properly or if the pinion is worn, chipped or burred, replace the unit.

To assemble:

8. Lubricate the armature shaft and splines with lubricant.
9. Install the clutch, the stop collar, the lock ring and the shift fork onto the armature.
10. Install the armature assembly into the drive end housing.
11. Install the field frame housing over the armature and onto the drive end housing.
12. Position the brushes into the brush holder and position the brush holder over the armature's commutator.
13. Install the commutator end housing and the through bolts.
14. Install the cap end gasket, the armature brake spring, the armature plate and the commutator end cap.

TOYOTA

Overhaul

REDUCTION DRIVE TYPE

Disassembly and Assembly

1. Position the assembly in a soft jawed vise. Remove the nut and disconnect the motor wire from the magnetic switch terminal.
2. Remove the through bolts and pull the field frame (with the armature) from the magnetic switch assembly.
3. On the 1.0 KW type, remove the felt seal from the armature shaft; on the 1.4 KW type, remove the field frame to magnetic switch assembly O-ring.
4. Remove the starter housing to magnetic switch assembly bolts and separate the housing from the assembly.
5. On the 1.0 KW type, remove the idler gear and the clutch assembly. On the 1.4 KW type, remove the pinion gear, the idler gear and the clutch assembly.
6. Using a magnetic finger, remove the spring and the steel ball from the hole in the clutch assembly shaft.
7. Remove the field frame end cover. On the 1.4 KW type, remove the large O-ring.
8. Using a small prybar, separate the brush springs, remove the brushes from the brush holder and pull the brush holder from the field frame. Remove the armature from the field frame.
9. Using an ohmmeter, make sure there is no continuity between the commutator and the armature coil core; if there is continuity, replace the armature.

10. Using an ohmmeter, check for continuity between the commutator segments. If there is no continuity between any of the segments, replace the armature.
11. If the commutator is dirty, burnt or the runout exceeds 0.0020 in., use a lathe to clean the surface; do not machine the diameter to less than 1.14 in. diameter.
12. Using an ohmmeter, make sure there is continuity between the lead wire and the brush lead of the field coil; if there is no continuity, replace the field frame.
13. Using an ohmmeter, make sure there is no continuity between the field coil and the field frame; if there is continuity, replace the field frame.
14. If the brush length is less than 0.335 in. (1.0 KW) or 0.394 in. (1.4 KW), replace the brush and dress with emery cloth.
15. Check the gear teeth for wear or damage, if damaged, replace them. Turn the clutch assembly pinion clockwise and make sure that it rotates freely, try to turn the pinion counterclockwise and make sure that it locks. If the pinion does not respond correctly, replace it.
16. While applying inward force on the bearings, turn each by hand; if resistance or sticking is noticed, replace the bearings. To replace the bearings, use the tool 09286–46011 or equivalent, to pull the bearing(s) from the armature shaft. Using the tool 09285–76010 or equivalent, and an arbor press, press the new bearing(s) onto the armature shaft.
17. Using an ohmmeter, check for continuity between the grounded terminal and the insulated terminal, then between the grounded terminal and the housing. If there is no continuity in either case, replace the magnetic switch assembly.
18. To inspect the armature, perform the following procedures:

a. Using digital volt-ohmmeter, check for continuity between the commutator's segments and core; if there is continuity, replace the armature. Check for continuity between the commutator's segments and the shaft. It there is continuity, replace the armature.

b. Using a set of V-blocks and a dial micrometer, measure the commutator's runout. If the runout is more than 0.002 in. (0.05mm), lightly turn the commutator on a lathe. If the commutator's runout is excessive, replace the armature.

c. Using a micrometer, check the commutator's outer diameter. If it is less than 1.14 in. (29mm), replace the armature.

d. Using commutator sand paper, clean the commutator's face of burnt spots and/or scoring; do not use emery cloth.

e. If the depth between the commutator segments is less than 0.008 in. (0.2mm), use a broken hacksaw blade to undercut the insulating material to 0.008–0.024 in. (0.2–0.6mm).

19. Inspect the armature bearing for looseness, binding or abnormal noise; if necessary, replace it.

20. Inspect the clutch/drive assembly gear teeth for wear, milling and/or chipping; if necessary, replace the assembly.

21. Inspect the pinion and idler gears for wear and/or damage; replace the gears if, necessary.

22. Inspect the brushes for wear by measuring the amount of useable brush remaining; the wear limit is 0.39 in. (10.0mm). Check the brushes for free movement in the brush holder; if necessary, clean the brush channels.

To assemble:

23. Lubricate the gears, shafts and bearings with high temperature grease. Install the armature into the frame and field assembly.

24. Position the brushes into the brush holder.

25. Install a new O-ring onto the frame and field assembly.

26. Install the commutator end housing and screws.

27. Install the pinion gear, the idler gear bearing, the idler gear and the clutch/drive assembly; be sure to mesh the idler gear with the clutch and drive assembly during installation.

28. Install the spring into the solenoid assembly.

29. Install the drive housing to the solenoid screws.

30. Using a new O-ring, install it onto the drive housing side of the field frame assembly.

31. Align the matchmarks and install the field frame assembly onto the drive housing. Install and torque the through bolts to 33 ft. lbs. (45 Nm).

32. Install the lead wire to the starter solenoid terminal and torque the nut to 26 ft. lbs. (35 Nm).

VOLKSWAGEN

Overhaul

Disassembly and Assembly

1. Position the assembly in the soft jawed vise. Disconnect the field coil wire from the solenoid terminal.

2. Remove the solenoid-to-starter screws and the solenoid, for automatic transmissions, and work the solenoid plunger, for automatic transmissions, from the shifting fork.

3. Remove the end shield bearing cap screws, the cap and washers.

4. Remove the through bolts and the commutator end frame cover. Remove the 2 brushes and the brush plate. Slide the field frame from the armature.

5. Remove the shift lever pivot bolt, the rubber gasket and plate.

6. For the automatic transmission models, remove the armature assembly and shift lever from the drive end housing. For the manual transmission models, press the stop collar from the snapring. Remove the snapring, the clutch assembly and the drive end housing from the armature.

7. For the automatic transmission model, press the stop collar from the snapring and remove the snapring, stop collar and clutch.

8. Brushes that are worn less than ½ the length of new brushes or oil soaked should be replaced. New brushes are $^{11}/_{16}$ in. long.

9. Do not immerse the starter clutch unit in cleaning solvent; lubricant will be washed from inside the clutch.

10. Place the drive unit on the armature shaft and while holding the armature, rotate the pinion. The drive pinion should rotate smoothly in 1 direction only. The pinion may not rotate easily but as long as it rotates smoothly it is in good condition. If the clutch unit does not function properly or if the pinion is worn, chipped or burred replace the unit.

To assemble:

11. To assemble, lubricate the bushings/splines and reverse the disassembly procedures.

12. On the automatic transmission models, install the clutch, stop collar, lock ring and shaft fork on the armature. On the manual transmission models, install the drive end housing on the armature, the clutch, stop collar and snapring on the armature.

13. On the automatic transmission models, install the armature assembly and shift fork in the drive end housing. Install the shim and armature shaft lock. Check the end play, it should be 0.002–0.021 in.

MANUAL STEERING GEARS
STEERING TROUBLE DIAGNOSIS
Manual Steering

Condition	Possible Cause	Correction
Excessive play or looseness in the steering	1. Steering gear shaft adjusted too loose or shaft and/or bushing badly worn.	1. Replace worn parts and adjust according to instructions.
	2. Excessive steering gear worm end play due to bearing adjustment.	2. Adjust according to instructions.
	3. Steering linkage loose or worn.	3. Replace worn parts.
	4. Front wheel bearings improperly adjusted.	4. Adjust wheel bearings.
	5. Steering arm loose on steering gear shaft.	5. Inspect for damage to the gear shaft and steering arm, replace parts as necessary.
	6. Steering gear housing attaching bolts loose.	6. Tighten the attaching bolts to specifications.
	7. Steering arms loose at steering knuckles.	7. Tighten according to specifications.
	8. Working pins or bushings.	8. Replace king pins and bushings.
	9. Loose spring shackles.	9. Adjust or replace parts as necessary.
Hard steering	1. Low or uneven tire pressure.	1. Inflate the tires to recommended pressures.
	2. Insufficient lubricant in the steering gear housing or in steering linkage.	2. Lubricate as necessary.
	3. Steering gear shaft adjusted too tight.	3. Adjust according to instructions.
	4. Improper caster or toe-in.	4. Align the wheels.
Wheel tramp (excessive vertical motion of wheels)	1. Incorrect tire pressure.	1. Inflate the tires to recommended pressures.
	2. Improper balance of wheels, tires and brake drums.	2. Balance as necessary.
	3. Loose tie rod ends or steering connections.	3. Inspect and repair as necessary.
	4. Worn or inoperative shock absorbers.	4. Replace the shock absorbers.
Shimmy	1. Badly worn and/or unevenly worn tires.	1. Rotate tires or replace if necessary.
	2. Wheels and tires out of balance.	2. Balance wheel and tire assemblies.
	3. Worn or loose steering linkage parts.	3. Replace parts as required.
	4. Worn king pins and bushings.	4. Replace king pins and bushings.
	5. Loose steering gear adjustments.	5. Adjust steering gear as necessary.
	6. Loose wheel bearings.	6. Adjust wheel bearings.
	7. Improper caster setting.	7. Adjust caster to specifications.
	8. Weak or broken springs.	8. Replace as required.
	9. Incorrect tire pressure or tire sizes not uniform.	9. Check tire sizes and inflate tires to recommended pressure.
	10. Faulty shock absorbers.	10. Replace as necessary.
Pull to one side (tendency of the vehicle to veer in one direction only)	1. Incorrect tire pressure or tires not uniform.	1. Check tire sizes and inflate the tires to recommended pressures.
	2. Wheel bearings improperly adjusted.	2. Adjust wheel bearings.
	3. Dragging brakes.	3. Inspect for weak, or broken brake shoe spring, binding pedal.
	4. Improper caster, camber or toe-in.	4. Adjust to specifications.
	5. Grease, dirt, oil or brake fluid on brake linings.	5. Inspect, replace and adjust as necessary.
	6. Broken or sagging rear springs.	6. Replace the rear springs.
	7. Bent front axle, linkage or steering knuckle.	7. Replace the parts as necessary.
	8. Worn or tight king pin bushings.	8. Lubricate or replace as necessary.

STEERING TROUBLE DIAGNOSIS
Manual Steering

Condition	Possible Cause	Correction
Wander or weave	1. Improper caster, camber or toe-in.	1. Adjust to specifications.
	2. Worn king pin and bushings.	2. Replace parts as required.
	3. Worn or improperly adjusted front wheel bearings.	3. Adjust or replace parts as necessary.
	4. Loose spring shackles.	4. Adjust or replace parts as necessary.
	5. Incorrect tire pressure or tire sizes not uniform.	5. Check tire sizes and inflate tires to recommended pressure.
	6. Loose steering gear mounting bolts.	6. Tighten to specifications.

CHRYSLER CORPORATION

Recirculating Ball and Nut

Disassembly and Assembly

1. Position the steering gear assembly in a suitable holding fixture and thoroughly clean the outside surface before disassembly.

2. Loosen the sector shaft adjusting screw locknut and back out the adjusting screw about 2 turns to relieve the mesh load between the ball nut rack and the sector gear teeth.

3. Position the steering gear worm shaft in a straight-ahead position.

4. Remove the attaching bolts from the sector shaft cover and slowly remove the sector shaft while sliding an arbor tool into the housing. Remove the locknut from the adjusting screw and remove the screw from the cover by turning it clockwise. Slide the adjustment screw and its shim out of the slot in the end of the sector shaft.

5. Loosen the worm shaft bearing adjuster locknut and remove the locknut. Slide the worm adjuster off the shaft.

6. Remove the wormshaft and the ball nut assembly from the housing.

NOTE: Make sure the ball nut does not run down to either end of the wormshaft, as the ball guide ends can be damaged if the ball nut is allowed to rotate until stopped at the end of the worm.

7. Remove the remaining wormshaft bearing from the gear housing.

8. Remove the lower bearing by using a suitable tool to pry off the bearing retainer from the adjuster plug.

9. Remove the locknut from the sector shaft adjusting screw and remove the screw from the cover by turning the screw clockwise. Slide the adjuster screw and shims from the slot in the end of the sector shaft.

10. Remove the wormshaft and the sector shaft seals.

11. Support the steering gear housing in an arbor press. Press the sector shaft bearing and seal from the housing using a special tool inserted in the lower end of the housing.

12. Remove the worm shaft oil seal from the worm shaft bearing adjuster by inserting a blunt punch behind the seal and tapping alternately on each side of the seal until it is driven out of the adjuster. Remove the worm shaft in the same manner.

13. Remove the lower cup, if necessary. Pull the bearing cup out.

14. Wash all parts in clean solvent and dry thoroughly. Inspect all parts for wear, scoring, pitting, etc. Test the operation of the worm shaft and ball nut assembly. If ball nut does not travel smoothly and freely on the worm shaft or if there is binding, replace the assembly.

NOTE: The ball nut teeth are wider and deeper on one side than the other. When assembling the wormshaft and the ball nut, position the ball nut so the wider/deeper side of the teeth are closer to the housing cover opening after the installation.

15. Inspect the sector shaft for wear and check the fit of the shaft in the housing bearings. Inspect the fit of the shaft pilot bearing in the housing. Be sure the worm shaft is not bent or damaged.

To assemble:

16. Assembly is the reverse of the removal procedure. Install the sector shaft lower bearing. Press the bearing into the housing far enough to leave enough space to install the new oil seal.

17. Install the upper bearing in the same manner and press it into the inside end of the housing bore flush with the inside end of the bore surface.

18. Install the worm shaft bearing cups (upper and lower) by placing them and their spacers in the adjuster nut and press them into place.

19. Install the worm shaft oil seal by placing the seal in the worm shaft adjuster with the metal seal retainer up. Drive the seal into place with a suitable sleeve until it is just below the end of the bore in the adjuster.

NOTE: Apply a coating of steering gear lubricant to all moving parts during assembly. Also, put lubricant on and around oil seal lips.

20. Clamp the holding fixture and housing in a bench vise with the bearing adjuster opening upward.

21. With the upper bearing on the wormshaft, insert the wormshaft and ball nut assembly into the housing, positioning the wormshaft through the upper ball bearing race and seal.

22. Assemble the ball bearing and the seal into the wormshaft adjuster plug. Press the retainer into position.

23. Place the adjuster and the locknut into position guiding the wormshaft into the bearing. Tighten the adjuster until very little wormshaft end play remains.

24. Install the sector shaft adjusting screw, with shim, in the slotted end of the sector shaft. With the adjuster screw positioned in the slot end of the sector shaft, check the end clearance of the screw.

25. Keep the clearance to 0.002 in. or less. A selection of 4 shims with various degrees is available.

26. Lubricate the the steering gear with steering gear grease. If not available, use NLGI Grade 2 E.P. or equivalent.

27. Turn the wormshaft until the ball nut is at the end of its travel. Pack as much lubricant into the housing as possible.

28. Turn the wormshaft until the ball is at the other end of its travel. Pack as much lubricant into the housing as possible.

Exploded view of manual recirculating ball steering gear—Chrysler

29. Rotate the wormshaft to bring the ball nut to the center of it's travel.

30. Install the sector shaft assembly, including the adjuster screw and the shim, into the housing.

31. Engage the center tooth of the sector with the tooth space of the ball nut.

32. Pack more lubricant into the housing and install the side cover gasket.

33. Install the side cover.

34. Turn the the adjuster screw counterclockwise until the screw bottoms, then turn ½ turn in the opposite direction. Replace the locknut but do not tighten.

35. Install the side cover bolts and tighten to 25 ft. lbs.

36. Tighten the wormshaft adjusting locknut to 5–8 inch lbs. and the sector shaft adjusting locknut to 35 ft. lbs.

Adjustments

WORM BEARING PRELOAD

1. Remove the steering gear arm and lockwasher from the sector shaft, using a suitable gear puller.

2. Remove the horn button or horn ring.

3. Loosen the sector shaft adjusting screw locknut and back out the adjusting screw about 2 turns.

4. Turn the steering wheel 2 complete turns from the

straight-ahead position and place an inch lb. torque wrench on the steering shaft nut.

5. Rotate the steering shaft at least 1 turn toward the straight-ahead position while measuring the torque on the torque wrench. The torque should be between 4–6 inch lbs. to move the steering wheel. If torque is not within these limits, loosen the worm shaft bearing adjuster locknut and turn the adjuster clockwise to increase the preload or counterclockwise to decrease the preload. When the preload is correct, hold the adjuster screw steady and tighten the locknut. Recheck the preload.

BALL NUT RACK AND SECTOR MESH

NOTE: This adjustment can be accurately made only after proper preloading of worm bearing.

1. Turn the steering wheel gently stop to stop and count the number of turns. Turn the steering wheel back exactly half way, to the center position.

2. Turn the sector shaft adjusting screw clockwise to remove all lash between ball nut rack and the sector gear teeth, then tighten adjusting screw locknut to 35 ft. lbs.

3. Turn the steering wheel about ¼ turn away from the center or high spot position. With the torque wrench on the steering wheel nut measure the torque required to turn the steering wheel through the high spot at the center position. The reading should be between 8–11 inch lbs. This is the total of the worm shaft bearing preload and the ball nut rack and sector gear mesh load. Readjust the sector shaft adjustment screw, if necessary, to obtain a correct torque reading.

4. After completing the adjustments, place the front wheels in a straight-ahead position, and with the steering wheel and steering gear centered, install the steering arm on sector shaft. Tighten the steering arm retaining nut to 175 ft. lbs.

Manual Rack and Pinion

The manual rack and pinion gear is permanently lubricated at the factory and cannot be adjusted or serviced. If a malfunction occurs, the complete rack and pinion must be replaced.

FORD MOTOR COMPANY

Recirculating Ball and Nut (Koyo)

Disassembly and Assembly

1. Rotate the steering shaft from stop to stop, counting the total number of turns. Then turn exactly ½ way back, placing the gear on center.

2. Remove the sector adjusting cover bolts, then remove the sector shaft with the cover. Remove the cover from the shaft by turning the screw clockwise. Keep the shim with the screw.

3. Using a special locknut wrench, loosen the worm bearing adjuster locknut and remove the adjuster plug and wormshaft thrust bearing.

Exploded view of Koyo manual recirculating ball steering gear—Ford

4. Carefully pull the wormshaft and ball nut assembly from the housing and remove the upper thrust bearing.

NOTE: To avoid damage to the return guides, keep the ball nut from running down to either end of the worm.

5. Pry out the sector shaft and wormshaft seals and discard them.

NOTE: Do not disassemble the wormshaft assembly. If the worm cannot rotate freely in the ball nut, replace the entire assembly.

6. The adjuster/plug bearing cup can be removed using a puller tool and slide hammer.

7. The housing bearing cup can be removed from the housing using a hammer and a suitable size bearing driver or socket.

8. The sector cover bushing is not serviceable. If found to be defective the entire sector cover including the bushing must be replaced.

9. The sector shaft needle bearing is serviced only as part of the housing unit and is not serviced separately. If one or more needles fall out, they may be cleaned and put back using steering gear lube to hold them in place.

10. Clean all the parts with the proper cleaning solvent and check for any cracks, chips or any excessive wear.

11. Check the clearance between the sector adjusting screw head and the bottom of the sector shaft T-slot. If the clearance is more than 0.004 in. install a new shim as required to reduce the clearance to 0.004 in. or less. A steering gear lash adjuster kit is available containing 5 different size shims. While holding the sector adjusting screw, turn the sector shaft back and forth. The sector shaft must turn freely. If the sector shaft does not turn freely, increase the T-slot clearance using an appropriate shim from the lash adjuster kit. Make sure the resulting clearance is not more than 0.004 in.

To assemble:

12. Installation is the reverse of the removal procedure. If the wormshaft bearing cup was removed from the housing, install a new cup using the proper tool for installing.

13. If the adjuster plug bearing cup was removed, install a new cup using the proper tool.

14. Install the sector shaft seal in the housing using the proper tool. Press the seal until it bottoms out.

15. Tap the wormshaft seal in the housing, using a suitable size socket and a hammer. Assemble the seal flush with the housing surface.

16. Clamp the steering gear housing in a vise with the wormshaft bore horizontal and the sector cover opening up.

17. Inspect the ball nut and wormshaft assembly for any binding. If any tightness is felt, discard and replace with a new assembly.

18. Apply steering gear grease to the wormshaft bearings, sector shaft needle bearing in the housing and the sector cover bushing.

19. Slip one of the wormshaft bearings over the wormshaft splined end. Insert the wormshaft and ball nut assembly into the housing. Feed the splined end of the wormshaft through the bearing cup and seal. Place the remaining wormshaft thrust bearing in the adjuster plug bearing cup.

20. Install the adjuster plug and locknut into the housing opening being careful to guide the wormshaft end into the bearing until nearly all end play has been removed from the wormshaft.

21. Position the sector adjusting screw and shim into the sector shaft slot. Check the clearance between the screw head and the sector shaft T-slot. If the clearance is more than 0.004 in. install a new shim as required to reduce the clearance to 0.004 in. or less. A steering gear lash adjuster kit is available containing five different size shims. While holding the sector adjusting

Exploded view of manual rack and pinion steering gear—Ford

screw, turn the sector shaft back and forth. The sector shaft must turn freely. If the sector shaft does not turn freely, increase the T-slot clearance using an appropriate shim from the lash adjuster kit. Make sure the resulting clearance is not more than 0.004 in.

22. Lubricate the steering gear with 10–15 ounces of steering gear grease. Rotate the wormshaft until the ball nut is near the end of its travel. Pack as much grease into the housing as possible without loosing it out at the sector shaft opening. Rotate the wormshaft to move the ball nut near the other end of its travel and pack more grease into the housing.

23. Rotate the wormshaft until the ball nut is in the center of its travel.

24. Insert the sector shaft assembly containing the adjuster screw and shim into the housing so the center tooth of the sector gear enters the center rack tooth space in the ball nut. Rotate the ball nut teeth slightly up to aid in alignment of the gear teeth and installation of the sector shaft.

25. Pack the remaining grease into the housing.

26. Apply an ⅛ in. wide by an ⅛ in. high bead of silicone rubber sealant to the mating surfaces of the sector cover and the housing. After waiting about 5 minutes, engage the sector adjuster screw with the tapped hole in the center of the center cover by turning the screw counterclockwise until the sector cover is flush with the housing.

27. Install the sector cover to housing attaching washer and bolts. Do not torque the bolts unless there is a lash between the sector shaft and wormshaft. The lash can be obtained by turning the screw counterclockwise.

28. Tighten the sector cover attaching bolts to 40 ft. lbs.

29. Adjust the steering gear preload and meshload.

Adjustments

PRELOAD AND MESHLOAD

1. Tighten the sector cover bolts to 40 ft. lbs.

2. Loosen the preload adjuster locknut and tighten the worm bearing adjuster nut until all end play has been removed. Lubricate the wormshaft seal with a drop of Type F automatic transmission fluid.

3. Using an $^{11}/_{16}$ in., 12 point socket and an inch lbs. torque wrench, turn the wormshaft all the way to the right. Measure the left turn torque required to rotate the wormshaft at a constant speed for approximately 1½ turns. This torque reading is preload.

4. Tighten or loosen the adjuster nut as required until the correct preload of 5–7 inch lbs. is obtained. Tighten the adjuster locknut to 188 ft. lbs.

5. Rotate the wormshaft from stop to stop, counting the total number of turns, then turn back halfway, placing the gear at the center.

6. Observe the highest reading while the wormshaft is turned approximately 90 degree(s) either way across center. If the highest reading (meshload) is not within 9–11 inch lbs. and at least 4 inch lbs. over the preload, turn the sector shaft adjusting screw as required.

7. Hold the sector shaft adjusting screw and tighten the locknut to 25 ft. lbs.

Manual Rack and Pinion

Disassembly and Assembly

1. Clean the exterior of the steering gear and place in a suitable holding device.

2. Place the gear in the on-center position as follows:

a. Rotate the pinion shaft from one lock position to the other (entire gear travel). Record the number of pinion shaft rotations.

b. Divide the number of pinion shaft rotations by two. This provides the required number of turns to place the gear in the on-center position.

c. From one lock position, rotate the pinion the exact number of turns determined to place the gear in the on-center position. The white marks on the pinion shaft and lower bearing should be in alignment.

3. Using the proper tool, hold the yoke plug in place and remove the yoke locking nut with the proper tool.

4. Remove the yoke plug.

5. Remove the spring from the yoke and remove the yoke from the housing.

NOTE: It may be necessary to use snapring pliers to remove the yoke.

6. Remove the dust cover from the pinion shaft.

7. Using the correct tool, hold the pinion plug lock plug in place and remove the pinion plug locknut.

8. Using the correct tool, remove the pinion plug.

9. Remove the pinion and bearing assembly from the housing.

To assemble:

10. Coat the pinion teeth and the upper bearing with steering grease.

11. Install the pinion and bearing assembly into the housing. Make sure the pinion is seated in the lower bearing.

12. Carefully, slide the pinion plug and seal assembly over the pinion shaft. Hand start the plug and seal into the housing. Using the proper tool, tighten the plug to 20–35 inch lbs. to set the pinion bearing preload.

13. Apply threadlocking compound/sealer to the pinion plug threads.

14. Hand start the pinion plug locknut onto the pinion plug. Hold the pinion plug in place using the proper tool, then tighten the locknut using tool, to 50–65 ft. lbs.

15. Pack the dust cover with steering gear grease and install it over the pinion shaft on the housing.

16. Inspect the yoke to make sure the plastic insert is firmly seated flush with the shallow rim provided on the metal portion of the yoke assembly.

NOTE: There should be no visible gap between the plastic insert and the metal.

17. Coat the plastic yoke insert and the rack bar surface that slides against the yoke with grease.

18. Install the yoke in the housing bore against the Y-section of the rack.

19. Coat both ends of the spring with grease. Install the spring in the recess in the back of the yoke.

20. If necessary, install a new service yoke plug onto the spring. Hand tighten the plug, then tighten to 65 inch lbs.

21. Mark the housing directly across from the triangle marking on the yoke plug. Back off the yoke plug about 30 degree(s), until the bar (−) marking on the yoke plug aligns with the scribed mark on the housing. This adjusts the clearance between the yoke plug and the yoke.

22. Apply threadlocking compound/sealer to the yoke plug threads.

23. Hand start the locknut on the yoke plug. Hold the plug in place, then tighten the locknut using the correct tool, to 44–58 ft. lbs.

24. Verify that the bar (−) marking on the yoke plug aligns with the scribed mark on the housing.

GENERAL MOTORS CORPORATION

Saginaw 525 and 535

Disassembly and Assembly

1. Place the steering gear in a suitable holding device, clamping onto 1 of the mounting tabs. The wormshaft should be in a horizontal position.

2. Rotate the wormshaft from stop to stop and count the total number of turns. Turn back exactly halfway, placing the gear on center.

3. Remove the self-locking bolts which attach the sector cover to the housing.

4. Using a plastic hammer, tap lightly on the end of the sector shaft and remove the sector cover and sector shaft assembly from the gear housing.

NOTE: It may be necessary to turn the wormshaft by hand until the sector will pass through the opening in the housing.

1. Worm bearing adjuster locknut
2. Worm bearing adjuster
3. Lower wormbearing cup
4. Lower worm bearing
5. Lower bearing retainer
6. Ball nut
7. Wormshaft
8. Upper worm bearing
9. Upper wormbearing cup
10. Sector shaft seal
11. Housing
12. Wormshaft seal
13. Side cover gasket
14. Sector shaftneedle bearings
15. Sector shaft
16. Preload adjuster
17. Preload adjuster shim
18. Side cover
19. Preload adjuster nut
20. Side cover bolts
21. Ball guide clamp screw
22. Ball guide clamp
23. Ball guide
24. Balls
25. Lockwasher
26. Sector arm nut
27. Top studded side cover bolt (usedon some models)

Exploded view of Saginaw 535 steering gear — General Motors Corporation

Exploded view of Saginaw 525 steering gear— General Motors Corporation

5. Remove the locknut from the adjuster plug and remove the adjuster plug assembly.

6. Pull the wormshaft and ball nut assembly from the housing.

NOTE: Damage may result to the ends of the ball guides if the ball nut is allowed to rotate to the end of the worm.

7. Remove the worm shaft upper bearing from inside the gear housing.

8. Pry the wormshaft lower bearing retainer from the adjuster plug housing and remove the bearing.

9. Remove the locknut from the lash adjuster screw in the sector cover. Turn the lash adjuster screw clockwise and remove it from the sector cover. Slide the adjuster screw and shim out of the slot in the end of the sector shaft.

10. Pry out and discard both the sector shaft and wormshaft seals.

11. Clean all the parts and inspect for any damage.

12. If there is any indication of binding or tightness when the ball nut is rotated on the worm, the unit should be disassembled, cleaned and inspected as follows:

a. Remove the screws and clamp retaining the ball guides in the ball nut. Pull the guides out of the ball nut.

b. Turn the ball nut upside down and rotate the wormshaft back and forth until all the balls have dropped out of the ball nut, count the number. The ball nut can now be pulled endwise off the worm.

c. Clean all the parts in solvent. Inspect the worm and nut grooves and the surface of all balls for signs of indentation. Check all ball guides for damage at the ends. Replace any damaged parts.

d. Slip the ball nut over the worm with the ball guide holes up and the narrow end of the ball nut teeth to the left from the steering wheel position. Sight through the ball guide to align the grooves in the worm.

e. Place the 2 ball guide halves together and insert them in the upper circuit in the ball nut. Place the 2 remaining guides together and insert them in the lower circuit.

f. Count out the correct number of balls and place them in a suitable container. This is the proper amount for one circuit.

g. Load the correct number of balls into one of the guide holes while turning the wormshaft gradually away from that hole.

h. Fill the remaining ball circuit in the same manner.

i. Assemble the ball guide clamp to the ball nut and tighten the screws to 4 ft. lbs.

j. Check the assembly by rotating the ball nut on the worm to see that it moves freely.

NOTE: Do not rotate the ball nut to the end of the worm threads as this may damage the ball guides.

To assemble:

13. Coat the threads of the adjuster plug, sector cover bolts and lash adjuster with a non-drying oil resistant sealing compound.

NOTE: Do not apply compound to the female threads. Use extreme care when applying compound to the bearing adjuster so it does not come in contact with the wormshaft bearing.

14. Place the steering gear housing in a suitable holding device with the wormshaft bore horizontal and the sector cover opening up.

15. Make sure all seals, bushings and bearing cups are installed in the gear housing and that the ball nut is installed on the wormshaft.

16. Slip the wormshaft upper bearing assembly over the wormshaft and insert the wormshaft and ball nut assembly into the housing, feeding the end of the shaft through the upper ball bearing cup and seal.

17. Place the wormshaft lower bearing assembly in the adjuster plug bearing cup and press the stamped retainer into place with a suitable size socket.

18. Install the adjuster plug and locknut into the lower end of the housing while carefully guiding the end of the wormshaft into the bearing until nearly all end play has been removed from the wormshaft.

19. Position the lash adjuster including the shim in the slotted end of the sector shaft.

NOTE: End clearance should not be greater than 0.002 in. If the end clearance is greater than 0.002 in., a shim package is available.

20. Lubricate the steering gear with steering gear grease. Rotate the wormshaft until the ball nut is at the other end of its travel and then pack as much new lubricant into the housing as possible without losing out the sector shaft opening. Rotate the wormshaft until the ball nut is at the other end of its travel and pack as much lubricant into the opposite end as possible.

21. Rotate the wormshaft until the ball nut is in the center of travel. This is to make sure the sector shaft and ball nut will engage properly with the center tooth of the sector entering the center tooth space in the ball nut.

22. Insert the sector shaft assembly including lash adjuster screw and shim into the housing so the center tooth of the sector enters the center tooth space in the ball nut.

23. Pack the remaining portion of the lubricant into the housing and also place some in the sector cover bushing hole.

24. Place the sector cover gasket on the housing.

25. Install the sector cover onto the sector shaft, using the proper tool, and turning the lash adjuster screw counterclockwise until the screw bottoms, then back the screw off ½ turn. Loosely install a new locknut onto the adjuster screw.

26. Install and tighten the sector cover bolts. On 525 models, tighten to 30 ft. lbs; on 535 models tighten to 13 ft. lbs.

Adjustments

WORM BEARING PRELOAD

1. Tighten the worm bearing adjuster until it bottoms then loosen ¼ turn.

2. Carefully turn the wormshaft all the way to the end of travel, then turn back ½ turn.

3. Tighten the adjuster plug to 5–8 inch lbs.

4. Tighten the locknut, using a punch against the edge of the slot.

OVER CENTER PRELOAD

1. Back off the preload adjuster until it stops, then turn it 1 full turn.

2. With the gear at the center of travel, check the torque to turn the stub shaft and record the reading.

3. Turn the adjuster in until the torque reads 4–10 inch lbs. greater than the above reading.

4. Tighten the adjuster locknut to 25 ft. lbs. on 525 or 22 ft. lbs. on 535 gears. Prevent the adjusting screw from turning while tightening the locknut.

JEEP

Recirculating Ball and Nut

Disassembly and Assembly

1. Secure the gear assembly in a proper holding device.

2. Rotate the wormshaft from one stop to the other and count the total number of turns.

3. Turn the wormshaft back ½ the total numbers of turns to center the shaft and the nut.

4. Remove the sector shaft adjusting screw locknut and remove the side cover mounting bolts and the side cover.

5. Slide the adjustment screw head out of the sector shaft and remove the shim(s). Retain the shims for end play adjustment during assembly.

6. Remove the sector shaft, wormshaft bearing adjuster locknut and the adjustment cap.

7. Remove the wormshaft and the ball nut.

NOTE: Do not allow the ball nut to rotate freely and bottom at the end of the wormshaft. This can damage the tangs at the end of the ball guides.

8. Remove the sector shaft and the wormshaft seals from the housing.

9. If there is any indication of binding or tightness when the ball nut is rotated on the worm the unit should be disassembled, cleaned and inspected as follows:

a. Remove the upper bearing from the wormshaft.

b. Remove the ball guide clamp mounting screws and remove the clamp and the ball guides.

c. Separate the guide halves and save the ball bearings that remained in the guides.

d. Remove the remaining balls from the ball nut circuits by rotating the wormshaft back and forth, until the bearings fall out. Use a cloth to catch the balls. There are a total of 50 ball bearings in the ball nut, with 25 in each circuit.

e. Remove the wormshaft from the ball nut. Clean all the parts with the proper solvent and inspect for any damage.

f. Position the ball nut with the ball guide holes facing up and the deep side of the ball nut teeth facing down.

g. Install the wormshaft in the ball nut and thread the shaft into the nut until an equal number of shaft threads are visible at each end of the nut.

NOTE: The ball nut teeth are machined to a greater width and depth on one side. When assembling the wormshaft and the ball nut, position the ball nut so the wider-deeper side of the teeth will face the housing side cover opening.

h. Install 1 bearing in each ball guide hole. Move the wormshaft up and down until the bearings roll into the ball nut threads under the wormshaft and support the wormshaft.

i. Assemble and install the ball guides in the ball nut.

COVER
RETAINING
BOLT

ADJUSTMENT
SCREW
LOCKNUT

COVER

ADJUSTMENT
SCREW AND
SHIMS

GASKET

PITMAN
SHAFT

SEAL

UPPER
BEARING

BEARING
CAP

RECIRCULATING
BALLS

GUIDE
CLAMP
AND RETAINING
SCREWS

WORMSHAFT

HALF-GUIDES

SEAL

WASHER

RETAINING
NUT

LOWER
BEARING

ADJUSTMENT
CAP

LOCKNUT

BALL
NUT

RETAINER

BEARING
CAP

Exploded view of manual recirculating ball steering gear—Jeep

j. Install 24 bearings in each ball nut circuit through the holes in the ball guides. Rotate the wormshaft back and forth to ease in the installation.

k. Position the ball guide clamp on the ball nut and install the clamp mounting screws.

l. Lubricate the wormshaft threads and upper bearing with chassis lubricant. Install the bearing on the wormshaft.

10. Clean the housing with a proper cleaning solvent and inspect the parts for any damage or excessive wear.

To assemble:

11. Assembly is the reverse of the removal procedure. Install the wormshaft and the ball nut in the steering gear housing.

12. Install the wormshaft bearing adjustment cap in the housing and tighten it only enough to remove the wormshaft end play.

13. Install the locknut on the wormshaft bearing adjuster cap. Do not tighten.

14. Pack the gear housing with as much chassis grease as possible. Place the ball nut in the centered position.

15. Lubricate the sector shaft with chassis grease and insert into the gear housing. Engage the center tooth on the shaft with the center groove on the ball nut.

16. Install the shim(s) on the adjustment screw and thread the screw into the cover 2–3 threads.

17. Slide the head of the adjustment screw into the sector shaft and rotate the screw counterclockwise to thread it into the cover. Rotate the screw until the cover almost comes into contact with the gasket.

18. Install the cover mounting bolts. Do not tighten.

19. Tighten the adjustment screw until the cover is tight against the gasket and then loosen the screw ½ turn.

20. Tighten the cover mounting bolts to 45 ft. lbs.

21. Install the sector shaft and wormshaft seals.

Adjustments

WORMSHAFT BEARING PRELOAD

1. Tighten the worm bearing adjuster until it bottoms then loosen ¼ turn.

2. Carefully turn the wormshaft all the way to the end of travel, then turn back ½ turn.

3. Tighten the adjuster plug to 5–8 inch lbs.

4. Tighten the adjustment cap locknut to 50 ft. lbs. Measure the preload torque.

SECTOR SHAFT OVER CENTER DRAG TORQUE

1. Rotate the wormshaft from stop-to-stop, count the number of rotations and rotate the wormshaft in the opposite direction ½ number of rotations to center the ball nut with the sector shaft.

2. While rotating the wormshaft back and forth over center, tighten the sector shaft adjustment screw until the torque required to rotate the wormshaft over center is the same as the wormshaft bearing preload torque.

3. The overcenter drag torque should be equal to the wormshaft bearing preload torque plus 4–10 inch lbs.

4. While rotating the wormshaft overcenter, tighten the sector shaft adjustment screw until the drag torque is increased by 4–10 inch lbs.

5. Hold the sector shaft adjustment screw and tighten the locknut to 25 ft. lbs.

CHRYSLER IMPORT

Recirculating Ball and Nut

Disassembly and Assembly

1. Place the gear assembly in a holding fixture and record the total mainshaft starting torque.

2. Remove the breather plug and drain the gear oil.

3. Remove the upper cover mounting bolts.

4. Loosen the locknut of the adjusting bolt and screw in the the adjusting bolt a couple of turns.

5. Place the mainshaft and the cross-shaft in a center position. Tap the bottom of the cross-shaft with the proper tool to remove the cross-shaft and the upper cover.

NOTE: Do not damage the cross-shaft oil seal.

6. Turn the adjusting bolt and separate the upper cover and the cross-shaft. Keep the spacer.

7. Remove the end cover and the mainshaft adjusting shims. Keep the adjusting shims.

8. Remove the mainshaft assembly and the bearings from the gear housing.

NOTE: Do not disassemble the mainshaft and the ball nut assembly.

9. Remove the cross-shaft and mainshaft oil seal using a suitable pry tool.

10. Inspect all the parts for damage and excessive wear. Check the operation of the ball nut and the mainshaft for a smooth rotation.

NOTE: Do not attempt to move the ball nut to either end of the mainshaft fully.

To assemble:

11. Check the pitman arm for damage or deformation and check the ball stud for looseness.

12. If the ball joint starting torque is below the lower limit, the pitman arm can be reused as long there is no play and it turns smoothly.

13. Lubricate the cross-shaft and mainshaft oil seals and install using the proper tool.

14. Secure the gear housing in a holding device and insert the mainshaft assembly into the gear housing. Hold the mainshaft horizontally.

15. Install the gasket, shim(s) and the end cover to the housing. Tighten the locknut to 11–14 ft. lbs.

16. Measure the mainshaft starting torque with the proper tool. The measured value should be approximately 3–5 inch lbs.

17. Adjust the value by increasing or decreasing the assembled thickness of the adjusting shim(s).

18. Remove the end cover and apply a proper sealer to the mating surfaces of the gear housing and the end cover.

19. Reassemble the adjusting shim and the end cover.

20. Mount the adjusting spacer onto the adjusting bolt and insert the adjusting bolt into the "T" groove in the cross-shaft.

21. Measure the gap between the "T" groove in the cross-shaft and the adjusting bolt. The measurement should be 0.002 in. or less.

22. Adjust by using the proper thickness of spacer.

23. Apply a suitable sealer to the adjusting bolt threads in the cross-shaft and install the upper cover onto the cross-shaft.

24. Install the cross-shaft and the packing to the gear housing and tighten the upper cover to 18–25 ft. lbs.

NOTE: Do not apply any sealer to the breather plug mounting hole.

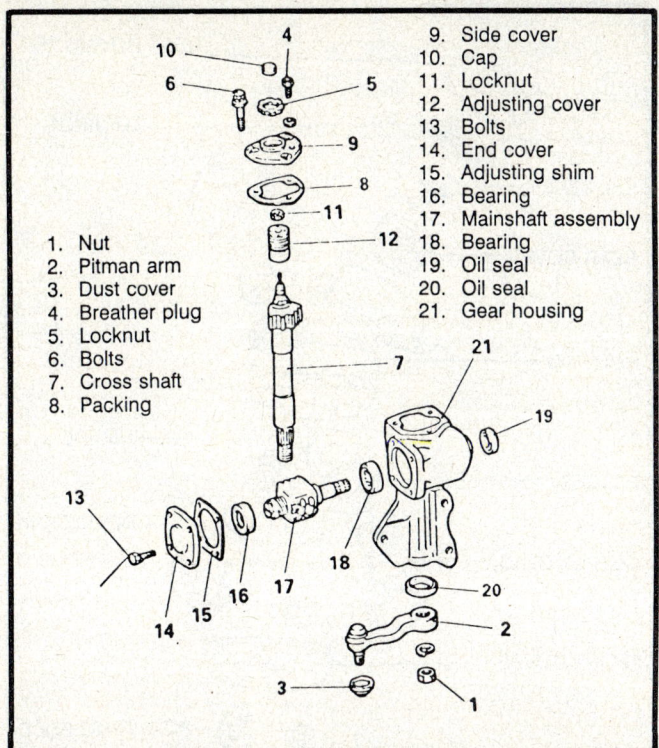

1. Nut
2. Pitman arm
3. Dust cover
4. Breather plug
5. Locknut
6. Bolts
7. Cross shaft
8. Packing
9. Side cover
10. Cap
11. Locknut
12. Adjusting cover
13. Bolts
14. End cover
15. Adjusting shim
16. Bearing
17. Mainshaft assembly
18. Bearing
19. Oil seal
20. Oil seal
21. Gear housing

Exploded view of manual steering gear—Chrysler Import

25. Refill the gear assembly with the proper gear oil.

Adjustments

STEERING GEAR BACKLASH

1. Inject a small amount of gear oil into the breather plug and lubricate the bearing parts and the gear teeth of each shaft.
2. Tighten the adjusting bolt until it engages the gear teeth. Rotate the pitman arm back and forth to make sure it is engaged with the gear teeth.
3. Position an indicator at the end of the pitman arm and move the pitman arm to measure the backlash. The steering gear backlash limit is 0.020 in.
4. Turn the adjusting bolt in or out to adjust the backlash.

NOTE: Measure the steering gear backlash when the mainshaft, cross-shaft and the pitman arm in the straight-ahead position.

5. Measure the mainshaft starting torque at the neutral position using the proper tool. The mainshaft starting torque should be approximately 8–9 inch lbs.

Manual Rack and Pinion

Disassembly and Assembly

1. Place the rack assembly in a holding fixture.
2. Loosen the locknut and remove the tie rod end.
3. Lift the tab washer using a suitable tool and remove the tie rod from the rack assembly.
4. Remove the locknut, adjusting cover and remove the rack support from the housing.

Exploded view of manual rack and pinion steering— Chrysler Import

5. Remove the dust cover, oil seal, snapring and remove the pinion with the bearing attached, from the housing.

6. Remove the rack from the gear housing in the proper direction.

NOTE: If the rack is pulled out in the wrong direction, the bushing in the gear assembly may be damaged by the rack threads.

7. Remove the stopper ring and using the proper tool, press out the rack bushing from the gear housing.

8. Inspect the rack support, pinion teeth, bearings and the rack bushing for any excessive wear or damage.

To assemble:

9. Assembly is the reverse of the removal procedure. Pack the rack bushing with multi-purpose grease.

10. Align the rack bushing retainer with the hole in the gear housing. Match the stopper ring peak with the hole in the housing. Install the rack bushing with the proper tool.

11. Install the rack in the gear housing from the proper direction.

12. Apply multi-purpose grease to the rack serrations an the surfaces contacting the rack bushing.

13. Install the pinion with the bearing attached in the housing and replace the snapring oil seal and the dust cover.

14. Install the rack support and tighten the locknut to 29–43 ft. lbs.

15. Tighten the adjuster cover to 7 ft. lbs. Rotate the pinion at a rate of 1 turn in 4–6 seconds using the proper tool and measure the pinion torque.

16. The torque should be 5–10 inch lbs. Turn the adjuster cover to reach the specifications. Install the locknut.

17. Measure the total pinion torque rotating 180 degrees in both directions from the neutral position.

18. Adjust the total pinion torque to the highest setting within specifications.

19. Install the tie rod to the rack using the proper tool. Replace the wire clamp to lock the boot in position.

20. Install the tie rod end so the left and right lengths are 7.0 in. from the edge of the boot to the edge of the locknut. Tighten the locknut to 47–58 ft. lbs.

Adjustments

TOTAL PINION TORQUE

1. Using the proper tool, rotate the pinion at a speed of one rotation in 4–6 seconds. Measure the total pinion torque.

2. Remove the boots from the gear housing and turn the pinion 180 degrees in either direction from the neutral position to measure.

3. Adjust to 5–10 inch lbs.

Bevel Gear

Disassembly and Assembly

1. Secure the gear assembly in a proper holding fixture.

2. Remove the locknut using the proper tool.

3. Remove the front cover mounting bolts, adjusting bolt and remove the front cover.

4. Remove the locknut and loosen the rear cover with the proper tool, until the input gear separates from the output gear.

5. Remove both the input gear and the output gear from the housing.

6. Inspect the gear teeth, bearings and the dust cover for any cracks or excessive damage.

7. Install the input and the output gear into the gear housing so the teeth mesh properly.

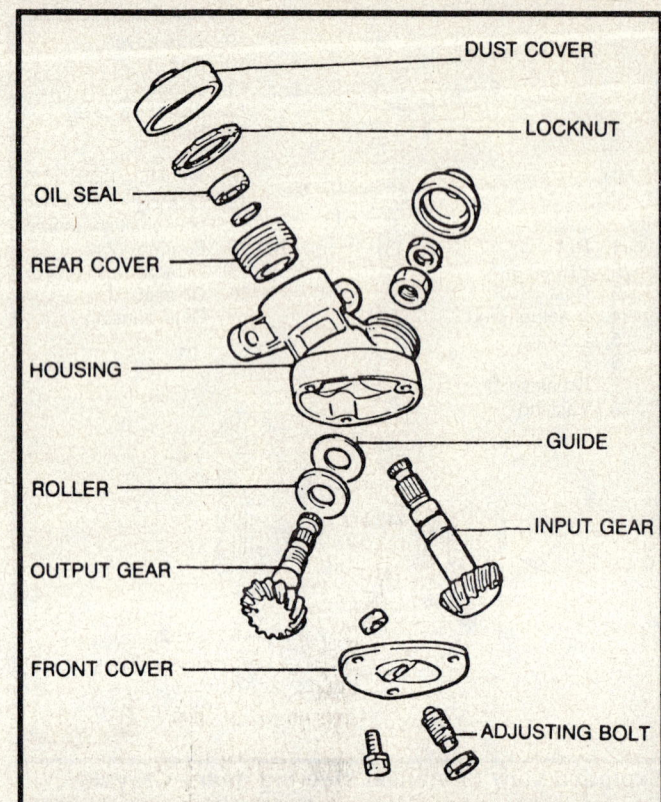

Exploded view of bevel gear assembly—Chrysler Import

8. Tighten the rear cover, using the proper tool. Replace the locknut and tighten to 47–87 ft. lbs. depending on which tool was used.

9. Install the front cover and replace the mounting bolts. Tighten to 12–19 ft. lbs.

10. Install the adjusting bolt and replace the locknut and tighten to 12–19 ft. lbs.

Adjustments

OUTPUT GEAR ROTATIONAL TORQUE

1. Turn the output gear, using the proper tool, at a speed of one rotation every 4–6 seconds. Measure the rotational torque.

2. Adjust the nut so the output side gear rotational torque is 0.4–0.9 inch lbs.

3. Tighten the locknut to 47–87 ft. lbs., depending on which tool was used.

TOTAL BEVEL GEAR ROTATIONAL TORQUE

1. Turn the input gear, using the proper tool, at a speed of one rotation every 4–6 seconds. Measure the rotational torque.

NOTE: Return the adjustment bolt to a position where there is no contact with the input side gear.

2. Using the proper tool, tighten the rear cover assembly so the input side gear rotational torque is 2.2–3.9 inch lbs.

3. Tighten the adjustment bolt so the total bevel gear rotational torque is 2.6–4.8 inch lbs.

4. Install the locknut and tighten to 47–87 ft. lbs., depending on which tool was used.

DAIHATSU

Recirculating Ball and Nut

The steering gear assembly is not serviceable. If a malfunction occurs, replace with a new unit. Lubricate with 90W gear oil.

GEO

Recirculating Ball and Nut

The steering gear assembly is not serviceable. If a malfunction occurs, replace with a new unit.

ISUZU

Recirculating Ball

Disassembly and Assembly

1. Secure the gear in a holding fixture. Remove the locknut on the side cover.

2. Turn the adjusting screw counterclockwise and remove the side cover mounting bolt.
3. Turn the adjusting screw clockwise with the side cover kept from turning and remove the side cover.
4. Remove the gasket, adjusting screw and adjusting shim.

1. Gear assembly
2. Oil seal
3. Bearing
4. Beraing
5. Ball nut and wormshaft
6. Oil seal
7. O-ring
8. End cover
9. Locknut
10. Sector shaft
11. Needle bearing
12. Adjusting shim
13. Adjusting screw
14. Gasket
15. Side cover
16. Locknut

Exploded view of typical manual steering gear assembly—Isuzu

5. Hold the sector shaft in the straight-ahead position and remove it from the gear assembly. Do not remove the sector shaft from the gear assembly with a hammer or any impact tools.

6. Remove the locknut using the proper tool.

7. Remove the end cover using the proper tool and remove the oil seal and O-ring.

8. Remove the ball nut and wormshaft assembly. Hold it in the horizontal position so the ball nut will not slide out.

9. Remove the bearings, oil seal and the bushing

10. Inspect the parts for any wear or excessive damage.

To assemble:

11. Assembly is the reverse of the removal procedure. Install the bushing, oil seal and the bearings into the gear housing, using the proper tool.

12. Install the ball nut and the wormshaft assembly, while holding in the horizontal position.

13. Replace the oil seal and the O-ring. Install the end cover.

NOTE: Tape the splines to prevent damage to the oil seal.

14. Adjust the bearing preload with the proper tool to approximately ¼–½ ft. lbs.

15. Replace the locknut and tighten to 116–145 ft. lbs. Recheck the bearing preload.

16. Install the sector shaft by aligning the center tooth of the ball nut with that of the sector shaft.

17. Adjust the clearance to 0.004 in. and check that the adjusting screw turns freely. There are 5 different thickness adjusting shims available.

18. Install the side cover using the proper sealer applied to the mounting surfaces and replace the locknut. Tighten to 14–22 ft. lbs.

Adjustments

BACKLASH PRELOAD

1. Position the sector shaft in a straight-ahead position.

2. Turn the adjusting screw to approximately ¼–¾ ft. lbs.

3. Lock the adjusting screw with the locknut and tighten to 14–22 ft. lbs.

MAZDA

Recirculating Ball and Nut

Disassembly and Assembly

1. Secure the gear assembly in a holding fixture. Remove the pitman arm nut and washer and remove the pitman arm using a puller, then remove the seal.

2. Remove the locknut and bolt, then remove the side cover and gasket.

3. Remove the adjusting shim and adjusting screw, then pull out the sector shaft while keeping it in the middle position.

4. Remove the locknut with the proper tool.

5. Remove the oil seal and the adjusting nut with the proper tool.

1. Nut and washer
2. Pitman arm
3. Oil seal
4. Locknut
5. Bolt
6. Side cover
7. Gasket
8. Adjusting shim
9. Adjusting screw
10. Sector shaft
11. Locknut
12. Oil seal
13. Adjusting nut
14. Bearing
15. Worm and ball nut
16. Bearing

Exploded view of typical manual steering gear assembly—Mazda

6. Remove the bearing then the worm ball nut and the bearing at the end of the ball nut.

To assemble:

7. Assembly is the reverse of the removal procedure. Clean all the parts and check for any damage or excessive wear. Check the rotation of the ball nut assembly to be free of any binding.

8. Apply grease or oil to the lips of all oil seals.

9. Installation is the reverse of the removal procedure.

Adjustments

WORMSHAFT PRELOAD

Preload of the worm ball nut is 0.7–1.3 lbs., using a pull scale (without sector). If an adjustment is to be made loosen the locknut and adjust with the adjusting screw. Tighten the locknut to 116–144 ft. lbs.

NOTE: The wormshaft preload will be 1.3–2.4 lbs. after installing the sector shaft.

SECTOR SHAFT

1. Set the adjusting screw and shim, in the "T" groove on the top of the sector shaft and measure the clearance in the axial direction. If the clearance is more than 0.004 in., adjust by selecting the proper size shim.

2. When installing the sector shaft, make sure the teeth of the sector shaft mesh with the center part of the teeth of the worm ball nut. The side cover tightening torque is 12–17 ft. lbs.

STEERING GEAR BACKLASH

1. Adjust the backlash by turning the adjusting screw.

2. Adjust the backlash while keeping the steering gear in the straight forward position. Backlash should be 0mm.

Rack and Pinion Assembly

The rack and pinion assembly is not serviceable. If a malfunction occurs, replace with a new unit.

MITSUBISHI

Recirculating Ball and Nut

Disassembly and Assembly

1. Place the gear assembly in a holding fixture and record the total mainshaft starting torque.

2. Remove the breather plug and drain the gear oil.

3. Remove the upper cover mounting bolts.

4. Loosen the locknut of the adjusting bolt and screw in the the adjusting bolt a couple of turns.

5. Place the mainshaft and the cross-shaft in a center position. Tap the bottom of the cross-shaft with the proper tool to remove the cross-shaft and the upper cover.

NOTE: Do not damage the cross-shaft oil seal.

6. Turn the adjusting bolt and separate the upper cover and the cross-shaft. Keep the spacer.

7. Remove the end cover and the mainshaft adjusting shims. Keep the adjusting shims.

8. Remove the mainshaft assembly and the bearings from the gear housing.

NOTE: Do not disassemble the mainshaft and the ball nut assembly.

9. Remove the cross-shaft and mainshaft oil seal using a suitable pry tool.

10. Inspect all the parts for damage and excessive wear. Check the operation of the ball nut and the mainshaft for a smooth rotation.

NOTE: Do not attempt to move the ball nut to either end of the mainshaft fully.

To assemble:

11. Check the pitman arm for damage or deformation and check the ball stud for looseness.

12. If the ball joint starting torque is below the lower limit, the pitman arm can be reused as long there is no play and it turns smoothly.

13. Lubricate the cross-shaft and mainshaft oil seals and install using the proper tool.

14. Secure the gear housing in a holding device and insert the mainshaft assembly into the gear housing. Hold the mainshaft horizontally.

15. Install the gasket, shim(s) and the end cover to the housing. Tighten the locknut to 11–14 ft. lbs.

16. Measure the mainshaft starting torque with the proper tool. The measured value should be approximately 3–5 inch lbs.

17. Adjust the value by increasing or decreasing the assembled thickness of the adjusting shim(s).

18. Remove the end cover and apply a proper sealer to the mating surfaces of the gear housing and the end cover.

19. Reassemble the adjusting shim and the end cover.

20. Mount the adjusting spacer onto the adjusting bolt and insert the adjusting bolt into the "T" groove in the cross-shaft.

21. Measure the gap between the "T" groove in the cross-shaft and the adjusting bolt. The measurement should be 0.002 in. or less.

22. Adjust by using the proper thickness of spacer.

23. Apply a suitable sealer to the adjusting bolt threads in the cross-shaft and install the upper cover onto the cross-shaft.

24. Install the cross-shaft and the packing to the gear housing and tighten the upper cover to 18–25 ft. lbs.

NOTE: Do not apply any sealer to the breather plug mounting hole.

25. Refill the gear assembly with the proper gear oil.

Adjustments

STEERING GEAR BACKLASH

1. Inject a small amount of gear oil into the breather plug and lubricate the bearing parts and the gear teeth of each shaft.

2. Tighten the adjusting bolt until it engages the gear teeth. Rotate the pitman arm back and forth to make sure it is engaged with the gear teeth.

3. Position an indicator at the end of the pitman arm and move the pitman arm to measure the backlash. The steering gear backlash limit is 0.02 in.

4. Turn the adjusting bolt in or out to adjust the backlash.

NOTE: Measure the steering gear backlash when the mainshaft, cross-shaft and the pitman arm in the straight-ahead position.

5. Measure the mainshaft starting torque at the neutral position using the proper tool. The mainshaft starting torque should be approximately 8–9 inch lbs.

Manual Rack and Pinion

Disassembly and Assembly

1. Place the rack assembly in a holding fixture.
2. Loosen the locknut and remove the tie rod end.
3. Lift the tab washer using a suitable tool and remove the tie rod from the rack assembly.
4. Remove the locknut, adjusting cover and remove the rack support from the housing.
5. Remove the dust cover, oil seal, snapring and remove the pinion with the bearing attached, from the housing.
6. Remove the rack from the gear housing in the proper direction.

NOTE: If the rack is pulled out in the wrong direction, the bushing in the gear assembly may be damaged by the rack threads.

7. Remove the stopper ring and using the proper tool, press out the rack bushing from the gear housing.
8. Inspect the rack support, pinion teeth, bearings and the rack bushing for any excessive wear or damage.

To assemble:

9. Assembly is the reverse of the removal procedure. Pack the rack bushing with multi-purpose grease.
10. Align the rack bushing retainer with the hole in the gear housing. Match the stopper ring peak with the hole in the housing. Install the rack bushing with the proper tool.
11. Install the rack in the gear housing from the proper direction.
12. Apply multi-purpose grease to the rack serrations an the surfaces contacting the rack bushing.
13. Install the pinion with the bearing attached in the housing and replace the snapring oil seal and the dust cover.
14. Install the rack support and tighten the locknut to 29–43 ft. lbs.
15. Tighten the adjuster cover to 7 ft. lbs. Rotate the pinion at a rate of 1 turn in 4–6 seconds using the proper tool and measure the pinion torque.
16. The torque should be 5–10 inch lbs. Turn the adjuster cover to reach the specifications. Install the locknut.
17. Measure the total pinion torque rotating 180 degrees in both directions from the neutral position.
18. Adjust the total pinion torque to the highest setting within specifications.
19. Install the tie rod to the rack using the proper tool. Replace the wire clamp to lock the boot in position.
20. Install the tie rod end so the left and right lengths are 7.0 in. from the edge of the boot to the edge of the locknut. Tighten the locknut to 47–58 ft. lbs.

Adjustments

TOTAL PINION TORQUE

1. Using the proper tool, rotate the pinion at a speed of one rotation in 4–6 seconds. Measure the total pinion torque.

2. Remove the boots from the gear housing and turn the pinion 180 degrees in either direction from the neutral position to measure.
3. Adjust to 5–10 inch lbs.

Bevel Gear

Disassembly and Assembly

1. Secure the gear assembly in a proper holding fixture.
2. Remove the locknut using the proper tool.
3. Remove the front cover mounting bolts, adjusting bolt and remove the front cover.
4. Remove the locknut and loosen the rear cover with the proper tool, until the input gear separates from the output gear.
5. Remove both the input gear and the output gear from the housing.
6. Inspect the gear teeth, bearings and the dust cover for any cracks or excessive damage.
7. Install the input and the output gear into the gear housing so the teeth mesh properly.
8. Tighten the rear cover, using the proper tool. Replace the locknut and tighten to 47–87 ft. lbs. depending on which tool was used.
9. Install the front cover and replace the mounting bolts. Tighten to 12–19 ft. lbs.
10. Install the adjusting bolt and replace the locknut and tighten to 12–19 ft. lbs.

Adjustments

OUTPUT GEAR ROTATIONAL TORQUE

1. Turn the output gear, using the proper tool, at a speed of one rotation every 4–6 seconds. Measure the rotational torque.
2. Adjust the nut so the output side gear rotational torque is 0.4–0.9 inch lbs.
3. Tighten the locknut to 47–87 ft. lbs., depending on which tool was used.

TOTAL BEVEL GEAR ROTATIONAL TORQUE

1. Turn the input gear, using the proper tool, at a speed of one rotation every 4–6 seconds. Measure the rotational torque.

NOTE: Return the adjustment bolt to a position where there is no contact with the input side gear.

2. Using the proper tool, tighten the rear cover assembly so the input side gear rotational torque is approximately 2–4 inch lbs.
3. Tighten the adjustment bolt so the total bevel gear rotational torque is approximately 3–5 inch lbs.
4. Install the locknut and tighten to 47–87 ft. lbs., depending on which tool was used.

NISSAN

Recirculating Ball

Disassembly and Assembly

1. Secure the gear assembly in a holding fixture.
2. Place the worm gear in a straight-ahead position.
3. Remove the sector shaft with the sector cover.

NOTE: Do not remove the sector shaft needle bearings. If necessary, replace the gear housing.

4. Loosen the adjusting plug locknut with the proper tool.
5. Remove the worm gear with the worm bearing.

NOTE: Do not allow the ball nut to run down to either

Exploded view of typical manual steering gear assembly — Nissan

end of the worm. Do not detach the ball nut from the wormshaft assembly.

To assemble:

6. Assembly is the reverse of the removal procedure. Fill the space between the sealing lips of the sector shaft and the adjusting plug oil seals with multi-purpose grease.

7. Inspect the parts for any damage or excessive wear. The ball nut must rotate smoothly on the worm gear.

8. Install the worm gear assembly with the worm gear into the gear housing.

9. Adjust the worm bearing preload with the proper tool.

10. Apply a suitable sealant around the locknut inner surface and tighten the locknut to 181–231 ft. lbs.

11. Turn the worm gear several times to break in the worm bearing. Check the steering gear preload.

12. Install the oil seal with the proper tool.

13. Measure the total preload and check the backlash.

Adjustments

WORM BEARING PRELOAD

1. Turn the adjusting plug in the tighten direction.

2. Rotate the wormshaft a few turns in both directions and measure the preload.

3. The preload should be approximately 2–6 inch lbs., without seals. The steering gear total preload with seals should be approximately 7–11 inch lbs. for a new gear and 5–9 inch lbs. for a used gear.

STEERING GEAR BACKLASH

Measure the backlash at the pitman arm top end in a straight-ahead position. The backlash should read 0.004 in. or less for a new gear or 0.012 in. or less for a used gear.

SUZUKI

Recirculating Ball and Nut

The steering gear assembly is not serviceable. If a malfunction occurs, replace with a new unit.

TOYOTA

Recirculating Ball and Nut

Disassembly and Assembly

2WD VEHICLES

1. Secure the gear assembly in a holding fixture. Remove the oil filler plug and drain the gear oil.

2. Using a puller, remove the pitman arm from the sector shaft.

3. Remove the adjusting screw locknut and the 3 retaining bolts from the end cover.

4. Remove the end cover by turning the adjusting screw clockwise.

5. Pull the sector shaft and the adjusting screw from the housing.

NOTE: Remove the needle bearings from the housing at this time, if equipped.

6. Remove the locknut and the bearing adjusting screw with the proper tool.

7. Remove the wormshaft from the gear housing.

NOTE: Do not disassemble the ball nut from the steering wormshaft.

8. Clean and inspect all the components for any damage or excessive wear.

To assemble:

9. If necessary to replace the oil seal, remove it with an appropriate prying tool, then install a new seal with the proper tool.

10. If necessary to replace the outer race in the gear housing use the proper tool to remove it then install a new one.

11. If necessary to replace the outer race from the adjusting nut, perform the following: Remove the oil seal with an appropriate prying tool. Using the proper tool remove the outer race from the nut. Using the proper tool, install a new race and then a new seal into the nut.

12. If necessary, remove the inner races from the shaft with a press, then using the proper tool, press the new ones into the shaft.

13. Measure the shaft thrust clearance with the proper tool.

The maximum clearance should be less than 0.0020 in. If necessary, install a new thrust washer between the sector shaft and the adjusting screw to provide the minimum clearance.

14. Apply MP grease to the bushing needle, roller bearings and oil seals. If necessary, remove and replace the oil seal with the proper tool.

15. Place the worm bearings on the shaft and insert the shaft into the housing.

16. Install the bearing adjusting screw and using the proper tool, gradually tighten the adjusting screw until it is snug.

17. Using a torque wrench and the same special tool, measure the bearing preload in both directions. Turn the adjusting screw until the preload is correct. The preload starting is approximately 2–4 ft. lbs. Hold the adjusting screw in position then tighten the locknut to 80 ft. lbs. vehicles. Recheck the preload. Apply MP grease to the needle rollers and install them into the housing.

18. Install the adjusting screw and thrust washer onto the sector shaft, then set the ball nut at the center of the wormshaft. Insert the sector shaft into the gear housing so the center teeth mesh together.

19. Apply liquid sealer to the gasket and end cover and install the end cover. Loosen the adjusting screw as far as possible, then install the 4 cover bolts.

20. Place the wormshaft in the neutral position by counting the total shaft rotations, then turning the shaft half of that number. Place matchmarks on the wormshaft and the housing to show the neutral position.

21. Using a torque wrench and special tool, turn the adjusting screw while measuring the preload until it is correct. Make sure the wormshaft is in the neutral position. The preload is approximately 7–9 inch lbs.

22. Apply liquid sealer to the locknut, then hold the screw with a suitable tool and tighten the locknut to 20 ft. lbs. Recheck the preload.

23. Measure the sector shaft backlash. There should be no backlash within 100 degrees of the right and left sides from the neutral position.

24. Install the pitman arm and replenish with gear oil. Install the filler plug.

Exploded view of typical manual steering gear assembly—Toyota

4WD VEHICLES

1. Secure the gear assembly in a holding fixture and drain the oil.
2. Using a puller, remove the pitman arm from the sector shaft, if necessary.
3. Remove the adjusting screw locknut and 4 retaining bolts from the end cover.
4. Remove the end cover by turning the adjusting screw clockwise.
5. Remove the sector shaft by tapping on it with a suitable tool to remove it.
6. Remove the locknut and the bearing adjusting screw with the proper tool.
7. Remove the wormshaft from the gear housing.

NOTE: Do not disassemble the ball nut from the steering wormshaft.

8. Clean and inspect all the components for any damage or excessive wear.

To assemble:

9. If it is necessary to replace the oil seal, remove it with an appropriate prying tool, then install a new seal with the proper tool.
10. If it is necessary to replace the outer race in the gear housing use the proper tool to remove it then install a new one.
11. If it is necessary to replace the outer race from the adjusting nut, remove the oil seal with an appropriate prying tool. Using the proper tool remove the outer race from the nut. Using the proper tool, install a new race and then a new seal into the nut.
12. If necessary remove the inner races from the shaft with a press, then using the proper tool, press the new ones into the shaft.
13. Measure the shaft thrust clearance with the proper tool. The maximum clearance should be less than 0.002 in. If necessary, install a new thrust washer between the sector shaft and the adjusting screw to provide the minimum clearance.
14. Apply MP grease to the bushing needle, roller bearings and oil seals. If necessary, remove and replace the oil seal with the proper tool.

15. Place the worm bearings on the shaft and insert the shaft into the housing.
16. Install the bearing adjusting screw and using the proper tool, gradually tighten the adjusting screw until it is snug.
17. Using a torque wrench and the same special tool, measure the bearing preload in both directions. Turn the adjusting screw until the preload is correct. The preload starting torque is approximately 3–4 inch lbs. Hold the adjusting screw in position then tighten the locknut to 80 ft. lbs. Recheck preload. Apply MP grease to the needle rollers and install them into the housing.
18. Install the adjusting screw and thrust washer onto the sector shaft, then set the ball nut at the center of the wormshaft. Insert the sector shaft into the gear housing so the center teeth mesh together.
19. Apply liquid sealer to the gasket and end cover and install the end cover. Loosen the adjusting screw as far as possible, then torque the four cover bolts to 72 ft. lbs.
20. Place the wormshaft in the neutral position by counting the total shaft rotations, then turning the shaft half of that number. Place matchmarks on the wormshaft and housing to show the neutral position.
21. Using a torque wrench and special tool, turn the adjusting screw while measuring the preload until it is correct. Make sure the wormshaft is in the neutral position. The preload is approximately 7–10 inch lbs.
22. Apply liquid sealer to the locknut, then hold the screw with a suitable tool and tighten the locknut to 33 ft. lbs. Recheck the preload.
23. Measure the sector shaft backlash. There should be no backlash within 100 degrees of the right and left sides from the neutral position.

Manual Rack and Pinion

Disassembly and Assembly

1. Secure the gear assembly in a holding fixture.
2. Loosen the locknut and place matchmarks on the tie rod ends and the rack ends.

Exploded view of typical manual rack and pinion assembly—Toyota

3. Remove the clips, clamps and the rack boots.

4. Unstake the claw washers. Remove the rack ends and the claw washers.

5. Remove the rack ends with the proper tool. Mark the left and right ends.

6. Remove the rack guide spring clamp with the proper tool and remove the rack guide spring.

7. Remove the rack guide and the rack seat.

8. Remove the pinion bearing adjusting screw locknut and remove the pinion bearing adjusting screw.

9. Fully pull the rack from the rack side and remove the pinion together with the upper bearing.

NOTE: Be careful not to damage the serrations.

10. Remove the rack from the pinion side without revolving it.

NOTE: If the rack is pulled from the tube, there is a possibility of damaging the bushing with the rack teeth surface.

11. Inspect the rack for runout and tooth damage. The maximum runout is 0.012 in. Do not use a wire brush when cleaning.

12. If necessary, replace the rack bushing with the proper tool.

13. If necessary, replace the pinion seal with the proper tool.

To assemble:

14. Pack rack components with molybdenum disulphide lithium base grease.

15. Install the rack into the housing from the pinion side. Set the notched portion so pinion can be positioned inside.

16. Install the pinion into the housing. Make sure the pinion end is securely in the lower bearing.

17. Apply a liguid sealer to the screw threads and install the pinion bearing adjusting screw, using the proper tool. Tighten to 15–18 ft. lbs.

18. Apply a liquid sealer to the locknut threads and install the locknut, tighten to 67–83 ft. lbs.

19. Install the rack guide and spring.

20. Apply a liquid sealer to the spring cap threads. Temporarily install the spring cap and mesh the rack with the pinion.

21. Using the proper tool, torque the rack guide spring cap to 18 ft. lbs. Return the rack guide spring cap 30 degrees.

22. Adjust the total preload, using a torque wrench, to approximately 4–12 inch lbs.

23. Apply a liquid sealer to the locknut threads and the housing surface. Tighten the locknut to 41–51 ft. lbs.

24. Install the dust cover.

25. Install the claw washers and align the claw of the claw washer with the rack groove.

26. Install the rack ends, using the proper tool and tighten to 61 ft. lbs. Stake the claw washers.

27. Install the rack boots. The left and right boots are different. Be careful not to interchange them.

28. Install the clamps and the clips. Stake the clamps to bend upward.

29. Screw the locknuts and the tie rod ends onto the rack ends until the matchmarks are aligned.

Bevel Gear

Disassembly and Assembly

1. Secure the gear in a holding fixture.

2. Remove both dust covers and the adjusting screw locknut.

3. Remove the adjusting screw with the proper tool and pull out the spring.

4. Remove the housing cover bolts and remove the housing cover.

5. Loosen the locknut and adjusting bolt. Remove the plate set bolts and plate.

6. Take out the adjusting bolt seat, spring and spring holder. Wipe the grease off the gear teeth.

7. Inspect the tooth contact between the No. 1 and No. 2 bevel gear.

8. Push in the No. 2 bevel gear and pull out the No. 1 bevel gear and thrust washer.

9. Tap out the No. 2 bevel gear and remove the bearing and spring retainer.

10. Inspect all the components for any damage or excessive wear.

To assemble:

11. If necessary, replace the No. 1 bevel gear oil seal. Remove and replace, using the proper tool.

12. If necessary, replace the No. 2 bevel gear oil seal. Remove and replace, using the proper tool.

13. Pack components with molybdenum disulphide lithium base grease.

14. Insert the No. 2 gear into the housing. Use a suitable tool to press in the bearing.

15. Install the thrust washer to the No. 1 bevel gear.

16. Install the No. 1 bevel gear into the housing.

NOTE: Line up the cutout portion of the No. 1 and No. 2 bevel gear.

17. Install the spring with the spring holder to the No. 2 bevel gear.

18. Install the plate with the 2 bolts and tighten to 69 inch lbs.

19. Install the adjusting bolt seat. Screw in the adjusting bolt until it touches the seat.

20. Using the proper tool adjust the No. 1 bevel gear preload. Adjust to 0.7–1.3 inch lbs.

21. Hold the adjusting bolt and install the locknut, tighten to 7 ft. lbs.

22. Install the spring retainer into the housing

23. Install the spring to the adjusting screw and apply a sealant to the threads of the adjusting screw.

24. Install the adjusting screw to the housing.

25. Using the proper tool, tighten the adjusting screw until the No. 1 and No. 2 bevel gears backlash is 0. Turn the No. 1 bevel gear left and right 5 times and snug it.

26. Loosen the adjusting screw to set the total preload; total preload should be approximately 1–4 inch lbs.

27. Install the adjusting screw locknut and tighten to 64 ft. lbs. Pack molybdenum disulphide lithium base grease into the gear housing.

28. Apply the proper sealant to the contact surface of the housing cover and install the cover. Tighten the bolts to 69 inch lbs.

29. Install both dust covers.

VOLKSWAGEN

The rack and pinion steering gear is not adjustable or serviceable, it must be replaced as a complete unit.

POWER STEERING GEARS

STEERING TROUBLE DIAGNOSIS
Power Steering

Condition	Possible Cause	Correction
Hard steering	1. Low or uneven tire pressure.	1. Inflate the tires to recommended pressure.
	2. Insufficient lubricant in the steering gear housing or in steering linkage.	2. Lubricate as necessary.
	3. Steering gear shaft adjusted too tight.	3. Adjust according to instructions.
	4. Improper caster or toe-in.	4. Align the wheels.
	5. Steering column misaligned.	5. See ''Steering Gear Alignment.''
	6. Loose, worn or broken pump belt.	6. Adjust or replace belt.
	7. Air in system.	7. Bleed air from system.
	8. Low fluid level in the pump reservoir.	8. Fill to correct level.
	9. Pump output pressure low.	9. See ''Pressure Test.''
	10. Leakage at power cylinder piston rings. (Linkage type).	10. Replace piston rings and repair as required.
	11. Binding or bent cylinder linkage. (Linkage type).	11. Replace or repair as required.
	12. Valve spool and/or sleeve sticking. (Linkage type).	12. Free-up or replace as required.
Intermittent or no power assist	1. Belt slipping and/or low fluid level.	1. Adjust or replace belt. Add fluid as necessary.
	2. Piston or rod binding in power cylinder. (Linkage type).	2. Repair or replace piston and rod.
	3. Sliding sleeve stuck in control valve. (Linkage type).	3. Free-up or replace sleeve.
Poor or no recovery from turns	1. Improper caster setting.	1. Adjust to specifications.
	2. Steering gear adjustments too tight.	2. Adjust according to instructions.
	3. Improper spool nut adjustment. (Linkage type).	3. Adjust according to instructions.
	4. Valve spool installed backwards. (Linkage type).	4. Install valve spool correctly.
	5. Low tire pressure.	5. Inflate tires to recommended pressure.
	6. Tight steering linkage.	6. Lubricate as necessary.
	7. King pins frozen.	7. Lubricate as necessary.
Lack of effort (both turns)	1. Improper sector shaft adjustment.	1. Adjust Sector Shaft.
	2. Pressure plates on wrong side of reactions rings.	2. Gear Recondition.
Lack of effort (left turn only)	1. Left turn reaction seal ''O'' ring worn, damaged or missing.	1. Gear Recondition.
	2. Left turn reaction oil passageway not drilled in housing or cylinder head.	2. Replace parts as required.
	3. Left turn reaction ring sticking in cylinder head.	3. Replace parts as required.
Lack of effort (right turn only)	1. Right turn U-shaped reaction seal worn, damaged, or missing.	1. Gear Recondition.
	2. Right turn reaction oil passageway not drilled in housing head, or ferrule pin.	2. Replace parts as required.
	3. Right turn reaction ring sticking in housing head.	3. Replace parts as required.
Lack of assist (left turn only)	1. Left turn reaction seal ''O'' ring worn, damaged, or missing.	1. Gear Recondition.

STEERING TROUBLE DIAGNOSIS
Power Steering

Condition	Possible Cause	Correction
Lack of assist (right turn only)	1. Right turn U-shaped reaction seal worn, damaged, or missing.	1. Gear Recondition.
	2. Worn sealing ring (teflon) worn sleeve seal, ferrule pin "O" ring damaged or worn.	2. Gear Recondition.
	3. Excessive internal leakage thru piston end plug and/or side plugs.	3. Replace worn-piston assembly.
Lack of assist (both turns)	1. Low oil level in pump reservoir (usually accompanied by pump noise).	1. Fill to proper level.
	2. Loose pump belt.	2. Adjust belts.
	3. Pump output low.	3. Pressure test pump.
	4. Engine idle too low.	4. Adjust engine idle.
	5. Excessive internal leakage thru piston end plug and/or side plugs.	5. Replace worn-piston assembly.

CHRYSLER CORPORATION

Recirculating Ball Type

Disassembly and Assembly

1. Drain the gear assembly. Remove the cover retainer ring from the housing.

2. Rotate the ring until one end is near the hole in the side of the housing, then pry it out.

3. Remove the end cover from the housing by turning the stub shaft counterclockwise.

NOTE: Do not turn the stub shaft further than neces-

1. Locknut	14. Spool valve
2. Retaining ring	15. Teflon O-rings
3. Dust seal	16. O-rings
4. Oil seal	17. Valve body
5. Bearing	18. Stub shaft
6. Adjuster plug	19. O-ring
7. O-ring	20. Wormshaft
8. Thrust washer (large)	21. Thrust washer
9. Thrust bearing	22. Thrust bearing
10. Thrust washer (small)	23. Thrust washer
11. Spacer	24. Housing
12. Retainer	25. Locknut
13. O-ring	26. Cover bolts andwashers
	27. Side cover
	28. O-ring
	29. Sector shaft
	30. Retaining screws and lockwashers
	31. Guide retainer
	32. Ball return guide
	33. Recirculating balls
	34. Rack piston
	35. Oil seal
	36. O-ring
	37. Plug
	38. O-ring
	39. Housing end cover
	40. Retaining ring
	41. Needle bearing
	42. Oil seal
	43. Backup washer
	44. Oil seal
	45. Backup washer
	46. Retaining ring

Exploded view of power recirculating ball steering gear—Chrysler sary to remove the end plug. The balls from the rack piston will fall and lay loose inside the rack piston chamber.

4. Remove the rack piston end plug.

5. Loosen the sector screw adjusting locknut. Remove the 4 side cover mounting bolts.

6. Turn the side cover until the rack piston and the sector teeth are visible, then turn the stub shaft until the sector is centered in the housing opening.

7. Remove the side cover and the sector shaft from the housing. Tap the end of the sector shaft with a soft hammer to remove.

NOTE: Do not disassemble the sector shaft, it is serviced and replaced as a unit only.

8. Insert a special tool into the rack of the piston bore with the pilot of the tool seated in the end of the worm.

9. Turn the stub shaft counterclockwise forcing the rack piston onto the tool.

10. Remove the rack piston from the housing, keeping the ball retainer tool in place to hold the balls in position.

11. Remove the adjuster plug locknut. Remove the adjuster plug assembly, using a spanner wrench.

12. Remove the complete valve assembly from the housing by pulling outward on the splined end of the stub shaft.

13. Remove the wormshaft lower thrust bearing and the conical bearing races from the wormshaft. Note the position of each race for reinstallation.

14. Remove the dust seal from the rear of the housing and discard the seal.

15. Remove the snapring from the valve housing.

16. Turn the fixture to place the valve housing in an inverted position.

17. Insert the special tool in the valve body assembly opposite the seal end and gently tap the bearing and the seal out of the housing.

NOTE: Do not damage the housing when installing or removing the tools.

18. Remove the fluid inlet and outlet seats with the proper tool, if damaged.

19. Coat the inlet and the outlet seats with petroleum jelly or the equivalent.

20. Install the bearing with the metal side covering the rollers, facing outward.

21. Seat the bearing in the valve housing using the proper tool. Be sure the bearing rotates freely.

22. Dip the new seal in gear lubricant (SAE 80W), then place it in the housing with the metal side of the seal facing outward.

23. Drive the seal into the housing until the outer edge of the seal does not quite clear the snapring groove.

24. Place the snapring in the housing and drive on the ring using the proper tool until the snapring seats in the groove.

25. Place the dust seal in the housing with the dished side (rubber side) facing out. Drive the dust seal into place.

26. The seal must be located behind the undercut in the input shaft when it is installed.

27. Pack the area between the 2 seals with multi-purpose grease.

28. Install the wormshaft conical bearing races and the lower thrust bearing in the same sequence that they were removed.

29. Both of the conical races must be installed so the top of each cone faces the bottom of the gear housing.

30. Install the stub shaft seal so it is seated against the inner edge of the stub shaft cap.

NOTE: Do not press against the stub shaft to seat the valve body. This could cause the stub shaft and the cap to separate from the valve body and allow the spool valve dampener O-ring to slip into the valve body fluid

grooves. Seat the valve body only by pushing on the outer diameter of the valve body with your fingertips. Make sure the Teflon® rings do not bind inside the housing. the valve body is properly seated when all or most of the fluid return hole in the steering gear housing is visible.

31. Align the narrow slot in the valve body with the locating pin in the wormshaft and insert the valve body into the steering gear housing.

32. Install a seal protector tool over the end of the stub shaft and place the adjustment cap over the end of the stub shaft.

33. Tighten the adjustment cap, using a spanner wrench, until it seats against the valve body. Tighten to 20 ft. lbs.

34. Remove the seal protector after installing the adjustment cap.

35. Install the rack piston into the steering gear housing until the wormshaft engages with the valve body and the stub shaft.

36. Rotate the stub shaft clockwise to force the rack piston into the steering housing. Do not remove the arbor tool until the valve body piston ring has entered the housing bore.

37. Rotate the stub shaft until the rack piston center groove is aligned with the center of the sector shaft bearing bore.

38. Lubricate the sector shaft adjustment screw cover gasket and place it on the cover. Make sure the rubber seal in the gasket is properly seated in the cover groove.

39. Place the cover over the sector shaft and thread the cover onto the adjustment screw until it makes contact with the sector shaft.

40. Install the sector shaft and with the adjustment screw cover gasket properly in place, install the cover to the steering gear housing.

41. Tighten the bolts to 45 ft. lbs.

42. Thread the adjustment screw locknut halfway on the adjustment screw and install the end plug in the rack piston. Tighten the plug to 50 ft. lbs.

43. Lubricate the steering gear housing end plug O-ring seal with power steering fluid and place it on the end plug.

44. Install and seat the end plug in the steering housing.

45. Install the end plug retaining ring with the ring end gap not aligned with the hole inside the steering gear housing. Tap the plug lightly to make sure the ring is seated properly.

46. Adjust the wormshaft bearing preload torque and the sector shaft over center drag torque to specifications.

Sector shaft over center adjustment on power recirculating ball steering gear—Chrysler

Adjustments

WORM THRUST BEARING

1. Remove the adjuster plug locknut and turn the adjuster plug clockwise until the thrust bearing is firmly seated, approximately 20 ft. lbs. torque.

2. Mark the housing even with one of the adjuster plugs. Measure back counterclockwise $3/16$–$1/4$ in. and mark the housing.

3. Rotate the adjuster counterclockwise until the hole in the adjuster is in line with the second mark.

4. Tighten the locknut securely and hold the adjuster plug to maintain the alignment of the hole with the mark.

5. Using a torque wrench, rotate the stub shaft clockwise to the stop then conterclockwise $1/4$ of a turn.

6. Measure the torque, the reading should be with the the torque wrench at/or near the vertical position. The reading should be within 4–6 inch lbs.

7. If reading is not within specifications, loose the sector shaft preload adjustment screw locknut and turn the preload adjustment screw counterclockwise $1 1/2$ turns.

8. Retighten the locknut, loosen (do not remove) the adjuster plug locknut.

9. Loosen the adjuster plug 1 turn counterclockwise and turn the stub shaft to the right stop and then back $1/4$ turn.

10. Bottom the adjuster plug firmly (20 ft. lbs.) by turning it clockwise.

11. Then back it off until the total torque reading is 3–4 inch lbs. in excess of the drag torgue.

12. Tighten the adjuster plug locknut securely.

NOTE: The preload torque tends to drop off when the locknut is tightened. The torque reading must be rechecked with the locknut tight. It is not possible to adjust the thrust bearing preload properly unless the adjuster plug is firmly bottomed out and the torque set while the adjuster plug is being loosened. Never attempt to adjust the thrust preload while tightening or advancing the adjuster plug into the gear assembly.

SECTOR SHAFT OVER CENTER

1. With the gear on center, loosen the locknut and tighten the sector shaft lash adjusting screw. Retighten the locknut.

2. Measure the gear over center torque, rotating the torque

Thrust bearing preload adjustment on power recirculating ball steering gear—Chrysler

SPANNER WRENCH

12 POINT SOCKET

TORQUE WRENCH

wrench in a 90 degree arc on each side of the center. Note the highest reading.

3. The locknut must be tight when taking this reading.

4. The over center torque of a new gear should show an increase of 4–8 inch lbs. over the thrust bearing adjustment but not exceed 18 inch lbs.

5. The over center torque of a used gear should be a 4–5 inch lbs. increase but not exceed 14 inch lbs. total.

6. The total over center torque includes the thrust bearing, over center and drag torque.

Power Rack and Pinion

NOTE: The power rack and pinion steering gear is permanently lubricated at the factory and cannot be adjusted or serviced. If a malfunction or fluid leak occurs, the complete rack and pinion must be replaced as a unit.

FORD MOTOR COMPANY

Integral Power Steering Gear

Steering gears are identified by a service identification tag fastened to the assembly under 1 of the cover-to-housing bolts. Tags contain information needed to order replacement parts. F-Super Duty commercial stripped chassis and motor home chassis vehicles use Bendix steering gears.

Disassembly and Assembly

FORD ROTARY VALVE INTEGRAL GEAR

1. Position the steering gear over a drain pan in an inverted position and cycle the input shaft several times to drain the remaining fluid from the gear assembly.

2. Secure the gear in a proper holding fixture.

3. Remove the nut from the sector shaft adjusting screw.

4. Rotate the input shaft to either stop, then turn the shaft back 2 turns to the center of the gear.

NOTE: The indexing flat portion on the input shaft spline should be facing downward.

5. Remove the sector shaft cover mounting bolts.

6. Tap the lower end of the sector shaft with a soft hammer to loosen it. Remove the cover and the shaft from the housing as an assembly.

7. Remove the valve housing mounting bolts and lift the valve housing off the steering gear housing.

8. Remove the valve housing and control valve gasket. Discard the gasket.

9. Hold the piston so the ball guide faces up and remove the ball guide clamp screws and clamp.

10. Place a finger over the opening in the ball guide, turn the piston so the ball guide faces down. Let the guide tubes fall, using a suitable container.

11. Rotate the input shaft from stop to stop until all the balls fall from the piston.

12. Remove the valve assembly from the piston.

13. Inspect the piston bore to insure that all the balls have been removed.

14. Position the valve body in a proper holding fixture and loosen the Allen head race nut screw from the valve housing.

Exploded view of the rotary valve type integral power steering gear—Ford

Rotary valve type integral power steering gear—Ford

15. Remove the worm bearing race nut.
16. Carefully slide the input shaft, worm and valve assembly out of the valve housing.
17. Remove the dust seal from the rear of the housing and discard the seal.
18. Remove the snapring from the valve housing.
19. Turn the fixture to place the valve housing in an inverted position.
20. Insert the special tool in the valve body assembly opposite the seal end and gently tap the bearing and the seal out of the housing.

NOTE: Do not damage the housing when installing or removing the tools.

Exploded view of valve housing on integral power steering gear—Ford

21. Remove the fluid inlet and outlet seats with the proper tool, if damaged.
22. Coat the inlet and the outlet seats with petroleum jelly or the equivalent.
23. Install the bearing with the metal side covering the rollers, facing outward.
24. Seat the bearing in the valve housing using the proper tool. Be sure the bearing rotates freely.
25. Dip the new seal in gear lubricant (SAE 80W), then place it in the housing with the metal side of the seal facing outward.
To assemble:
26. Place the valve housing in a proper holding fixture, with the flanged end up.
27. Apply a light coat of gear lubricant (SAE 80W) or equivalent to the Teflon® rings on the valve sleeve.
28. Carefully install the worm shaft and valve into the housing.

29. Install the worm bearing race nut in the housing and tighten to 55–90 ft. lbs.

30. Install the Allen head race nut set screw through the valve housing and tighten to 15–25 inch lbs.

31. Place the power cylinder piston in a proper holding fixture with the ball guide holes facing up.

32. Insert the worm shaft into position so the first groove is in line with the hole nearest the center of the piston.

33. Install the ball guides in the piston.

34. Turn the worm shaft counterclockwise and place the same amount of balls that were removed into the ball guide. A minimum of 27 balls are required.

35. Rotate the input shaft from one stop to the other to ensure the proper input of balls into the guide.

36. Secure the guides in the ball nut with the clamp and tighten the screws to 42–70 inch lbs.

37. Apply petroleum jelly or the equivalent to the Teflon® seal on the piston.

38. Place a new control valve O-ring on the valve housing and slide the piston and the valve into the gear housing, being careful not to damage the piston ring.

39. Align the oil passage in the valve housing with the passage in the gear housing. Place a new O-ring onto the oil passage hole of the gear housing.

40. Install the mounting bolts, do not tighten.

41. Rotate the ball nut so the teeth are in the same plane as the sector teeth. Tighten the valve housing mounting bolts to 30–45 ft. lbs.

42. Place the sector shaft cover O-ring into the steering gear housing and turn the input shaft to center the piston.

43. Apply petroleum jelly or the equivalent to the sector shaft journal and place the sector shaft and the cover assembly in the gear housing.

44. Install the sector shaft cover mounting bolts and tighten to 55–70 ft. lbs.

45. Place a torque wrench on the input shaft and adjust the mesh load to the proper specifications.

Bendix C-300N Power Steering Gear

Disassembly and Assembly

1. Clean gear assembly and secure to workbench. A large vise with jaw protectors may be used. Clamp across mounting bolt holes. Do not overtighten.

2. Remove the external dust boot from the spindle assembly's input shaft spline. Scribe a line or otherwise matchmark the relationship of the valve body to the housing. Using a 19mm wrench, remove the 4 bolts that secure the valve body to the housing.

3. Separate the valve body from the housing by rotating the output shaft using the pitman arm. It may be necessary to hold or rotate the input shaft during this operation. Continue to separate the valve body from the housing until both O-rings on the valve body can be seen.

4. Scribe a line or otherwise matchmark the relationship of the pitman arm to the output shaft, then remove the pitman arm and the dust boot under it. Clean away any dirt and corrosion from the exposed portion of the output shaft.

5. Using a 19mm wrench, loosen and remove the locknut from the adjusting screw on the side cover. Scribe a line or otherwise matchmark the relationship of the side cover to the housing. Using a 19mm wrench, remove the 4 bolts that secure the side cover to the housing. Separate the side cover from the housing by turning the adjusting screw clockwise with a 7mm socket. Continue turning the adjusting screw until the side cover can be removed from the housing.

NOTE: When the side cover is removed from the housing the 17 rollers in the side cover bearing will fall out. The rollers must not be interchanged with the rollers in the housing bearing. Do not attempt to remove the outer race of the roller bearing from the side cover.

6. Loosely install the pitman arm and use it to center the piston and output shaft gear teeth inside the side cover opening of the housing. Remove the pitman arm and then remove the output shaft by tapping gently on the splined end with a soft mallet.

NOTE: When the output shaft is removed from the housing the 17 rollers in the housing bearing will fall out. The rollers must not be interchanged with the rollers in the side cover bearing. Do not attempt to remove the outer race of the roller bearing from the housing.

7. While preventing rotation of the input shaft end of the spindle assembly, pull the valve body and piston out of the housing.

8. Remove the retaining ring, ball tube cover, the ball tube and 7 of the 26 balls from the piston. Remove the sealing ring from the piston.

9. In order to remove the remaining 19 balls from the piston, rotate the input shaft in the direction, clockwise or counterclockwise, that threads the spindle assembly out of the piston. Separate the valve body and the spindle from the piston. Check the inside of the piston for any stray balls that may have been removed in the operation. A total of 26 balls, 7 from the ball tube and 19 from the piston should be accounted for.

10. Remove the sealing ring and the O-ring below it from the groove in the piston.

11. Remove the steering limiting valve seats and sealing washers from the piston. Remove the 2 balls and spring from the piston.

12. Remove the small plug covering the steering limiting valve stem from the bottom of the housing. Retrieve the limiting valve stem from its bore and remove the O-ring from the valve stem.

13. Remove the O-ring, seal and split nylon backup ring from the side cover bore. Do not remove the outer race of the roller bearing from the side cover.

14. Locate and remove by prying the dust seal from the housing output shaft bore.

15. Reach through the side cover opening of the housing and remove the output shaft seal and its nylon backup ring. Do not remove the outer race of the roller bearing from the housing.

16. On the valve body, remove the input shaft dust seal. With a drift punch, unlock the safety point between the valve nut and the valve body. Use a spanner wrench or equivalent to loosen and remove the valve nut from the valve body.

17. Grasp the input shaft end of the spindle assembly and lift the spindle assembly out of the valve body. It will come out with the ball cage, 17 balls and half of the outer race. Separate the outer race, ball cage and the 17 balls from the spindle assembly. Do not remove the other half of the ball bearing outer race in the valve body.

18. Remove the retaining ring and then the seal from the valve nut. Remove the 2 outside O-rings from the valve body then the 3 Teflon® rings and the corresponding 3 O-rings from the spindle bore.

19. If the steering gear is equipped with a steering limiting feature, check the condition and length of the limiting stem in the valve body. The length of the stem measured from the surface of the valve body to the tip of the stem should be 0.736 inch (18.7mm). If the limiting stem is of the correct length and in good condition, do not remove it. The limiting stem can be removed if necessary by heating the poppet stem to loosen the thread locking compound, then turning counterclockwise.

20. Remove the retaining ring, adjusting screw and its spacer from the output shaft.

21. Begin disassembly of the pressure relief valve by removing the plug and its sealing washer from the valve body. Remove the spring, spring seat adjusting shims and the valve piston. Use a wide bladed suitable tool to remove the valve seat and its sealing washer.

Bendix C-300N power steering gear—Ford medium Pick-Ups

Legend for exploded view:

1. Valve nut
2. External dust seal
3. Spindle assembly
4. Internal dust seal
5. Seal
6. Ball cage
7. Valve body
8. Ball race
9. Ball
10. Teflon® ring
11. O-ring
12. O-ring
13. Steering limiting stem
14. Seal ring
15. O-ring
16. Spring
17. Valve seat
18. Sealing washer
19. Steering limiting stem
20. O-ring
21. Plug
22. Housing
23. Piston
24. Tube cover
25. Output shaft
26. Rollers
27. O-ring
28. Backup ring
29. Seal
30. Retaining ring
31. Side cover
32. Nut
33. Adjusting screw
34. Adjusting screw spacer
35. Ball tube
36. Retaining ring
37. O-ring
38. Dust seal
39. Dust boot
40. Bolt
41. Adjusting shims
42. Pressure relief valve plug
43. Spring
44. Sealing washer
45. Spring seat
46. Valve piston
47. Seal washer
48. Valve seat
49. Bolt
50. Retaining ring
51. Seal washer
52. Drain plug

22. Do not attempt to disassemble the spindle assembly which contains the rotary valve. Individual replacement parts are not available. It must be treated as a single component. In addition, the piston must be purchased (piston and spindle kit) due to the match of the grinding of the components.

To assemble:

23. Wash all parts individually in clean solvent and dry thoroughly. All non-metallic parts should be discarded and replaced with new. Inspect all parts well. If the outer races of the roller bearings contained in the side cover or the housing are not serviceable, the entire housing or side cover must be replaced. If the outer ball bearing race in the valve body must be replaced, the entire valve body must be replaced. Minor scuffing of the piston exterior and housing bore is normal. If deep scoring is detected, the affected parts should be replaced. Do not attempt honing or boring of these parts as leakage rates will increase.

24. From the appropriate maintenance kits, install the sealing washer around the pressure relief valve seat. Use a large blade suitable tool to install both in the valve body. Tighten to 15–18 ft. lbs. Install the pressure relief valve piston spring seat and spring in the valve body. Make sure the small end of the seat goes into the spring or the assembly will malfunction and the valve will be damaged.

25. Install the pressure adjusting shims, the seal washer on the plug. Use the shims that were removed during disassembly, although it may be necessary to add or subtract shims in order to properly set the pressure relief valve. Use a 26mm socket to torque plug to 66–73 ft. lbs.

26. Install the 3 O-rings and 3 Teflon® rings in the appropriate grooves in the valve body. A special tool is recommended to form (expand) the rings in their grooves.

27. If the steering limiting valve was removed from the valve body, install the stem now. Apply Locktite® 222 to the threads and screw the limiting stem into the valve body until a stem height of 0.736 inch (18.7mm) above the valve body surface is obtained. Use care in applying the thread locking compound to prevent this material from coming into contact with other surfaces of the valve body. Allow sufficient time to cure. Install the large O-rings in the valve body.

28. Install the ball cage on the input end of the spindle assembly. Using grease to hold the balls in place, install the 17 balls in the cage.

29. Install the outer ball bearing race half over the input end of the spindle assembly and insert the spindle assembly into the valve body. A special tool is available from Bendix to seat the O-rings as the spindle is installed. Make sure the 17 balls of the bearing assembly are resting against the outer race in the valve body.

30. Position the pressure side of the seal in the bore of the non-pressure side of the valve nut. Install the seal with a suitable driver. A piece of round stock such as brass bar 1.550 inch diameter is suggested. Carefully drive the seal into the bore until the snap ring groove within the bore is visible. Install the retaining ring making certain it is completely seated in the groove. After installing the retaining ring, gently tap the seal from the opposite side until it rests squarely against the snap ring.

31. Apply Locktite® 932 or 567 to the thread of the valve nut. Due to the close proximity of the spindle ball bearing, use extreme care in applying the thread locking compound. Making certain not to damage the seal, install the valve nut over the input shaft end of the spindle assembly and into the valve body. Use a suitable spanner wrench to tighten the valve nut to 220–260 ft. lbs. Reset the safety point between the valve nut and valve body using a drift punch. Install the dust seal in the valve nut.

32. Begin to assemble the piston by installing 1 of the 2 steering limiting valve seals and its sealing washer into the piston. Insert 1 of the 2 balls then the valve spring into the piston from the opposite end and install the remaining ball, sealing washer and seat into the piston. Take care not to damage the valve seals while torquing each to 88–132 inch lbs.

33. Install the O-ring into its groove in the piston. Thoroughly heat the glide ring to approximately 285°–320°F in preparation for installation on the piston. Do not use an open flame to heat the glide ring. A heat lamp or similar device should be used. Install the heated glide ring over the O-ring in the piston's groove.

NOTE: The glide ring should be distorted as little as possible during installation. Using an automotive piston ring compressor or a smooth piece of sheetmetal and an appropriately large screw type hose clamp, reshape the glide ring in the piston groove. Allow about 10 minutes cooling time before removing the compression tool from the piston.

34. Install the O-ring in its groove in the ball return opening of the piston.

35. Insert the valve body and spindle assembly all the way into the piston making certain the stroke limiting stem is not damaged and that it mates with the valve seat in the piston. Insert 19 balls, 1 at a time, into 1 of the recirculating tube holes in the ball return opening in the piston. Rotate the input shaft end of the spindle slightly in 1 direction only and do not alternate from clockwise to counterclockwise.

NOTE: When this operation is performed correctly, the spindle and valve body should screw out of the piston and the balls inserted in 1 recirculating tube hole should appear at the opposite hole. Before proceeding, make certain the balls are at an equal depth in both holes of the piston. This will assure correct installation of the return tube. Incorrect assembly of this group may result in 1 or more balls falling inside the piston or coming out at the top and lodging in the housing.

36. Install the remaining 7 balls in the recirculating tube halves and use lithium base grease to retain them in the tube. Seat the assembled tube halves containing the 7 balls in the recirculating tube holes in the piston. Lightly grease the sealing surfaces of the tube cover and install it in the piston making certain the slot in the underside of the cover mates with recirculating tube in the piston. Install the retaining ring in the piston to secure the tube cover making certain it is completely seated in its groove. After assembly, check for smooth rotation of the spindle assembly in both directions.

37. Begin assembly of the housing by reaching through the side cover opening of the housing and installing the seal with its pressure side toward the interior of the housing. Do not distort this "flexible" seal any more than is necessary for this installation. Install the split nylon backup ring, which is a separate part of the seal, in the groove formed by the backside (non-pressure side) of the seal and the housing. Make certain the split surfaces of the ring mate properly. Use care when installing. This seal prevents pressurized fluid from leaking out of the housing around the output shaft.

38. Install the dust seal in the housing with its sealing lip toward the outside of the housing. This seal is intended to prevent water and dirt from entering the housing.

39. Install the O-ring in the groove around the steering limiting stem and screw the stem into the housing about 5–6 full turns.

40. Install the 17 rollers of the bearing in the outer race contained in the housing. Use lithium grease to hold the rollers in place. Note that these 17 rollers must be the same rollers that were removed from this bearing during disassembly.

41. Align the steering limiting valve seat in the valve body with the steering limiting valve seat in the piston. Insert the piston into the housing so the rack teeth of the piston are visible in the side cover opening in the housing. Make certain the valve body is oriented in the housing so the marks made during disassembly align. Slide the piston and valve body assembly completely into the housing taking special care not to damage the piston glide ring and valve body O-rings. Secure the valve body to the housing using 4 bolts. Torque the bolts to 80–88 ft. lbs. using a

19mm socket. Rotate the input shaft of the spindle until the rack teeth of the piston are centered in the side cover opening in the housing.

42. Install the shim washer over the adjusting screw and secure both in the output shaft using the retaining screw. The maximum end play permitted for these parts is 0.002 inch. If end play is excessive, it may be necessary to install a different shim washer. The shim washer is available in 8 different thickness to provide the proper end play.

43. Install the seal in the side cover with the pressure side toward the outer race of the side cover roller bearing. This seal prevent fluid leakage around the output shaft. Do not distort this "flexible" seal more than is necessary for installation.

44. Install the split nylon backup ring which is a separate part of the seal, by "winding" it into the groove formed by the side cover and the backside of the seal. Make certain the split ring is completely seated and that the diagonal split surfaces of the ring mate properly. Install the O-ring in its groove in the side cover.

45. Install the 17 rollers of the bearing in the outer race contained in the side, retaining the rollers with lithium grease. Note that these 17 rollers must be the same rollers that were removed from this bearing during disassembly.

46. Lightly lubricate the seals contained in both the housing and side cover with lithium grease. Lubricate the sealing surface of the output shaft on the adjusting screw end only. Using a 7mm socket, install the assembled side cover on the output shaft adjuster screw and screw it on as far as it will go, then back it off ⅛ of a turn.

47. Prior to inserting the output shaft into the housing, wrap a single layer of masking tape around the splines to protect the housing seal. Lubricate the exterior of the tape with lithium grease and insert the shaft and side cover assembly into the housing with a twisting motion. Remove the masking tape from the output shaft splines.

48. Secure the side cover to the housing using 4 bolts. Make certain the side cover is positioned so the marks made during disassembly are aligned. Tighten the bolts to 80–88 ft. lbs. using a 19mm socket. Pack the cavities with lithium grease then install the exterior dust boot on the output shaft and the exterior dust seal on the input shaft.

Adjustment

ADJUSTING THE PISTON TO OUTPUT SHAFT GEAR BACKLASH

The piston and output shaft gear backlash is correct when a 4–18 inch lb. increase in torque is noted at the input shaft as it is rotated and the piston passes through the midpoint of its total travel in the housing. The torque increase at the input shaft will occur only as the piston travels through the midpoint of its travel and should disappear as the piston moves past the midpoint.

1. To obtain the adjustment stated above, make certain the adjusting screw is turned counterclockwise as far as it will go. Rotate the input shaft as far as possible in both directions. Count the total revolutions in either direction and at the same time measure the average torque to rotate the shaft.

2. To obtain the proper backlash adjustment, rotate the input shaft 180 degrees in both directions past the midpoint of piston travel. The midpoint of piston travel is approximately ½ the number of input shaft revolutions possible is a single direction.

3. Each time the direction of input shaft rotation is changed, turn the output shaft adjustment screw clockwise ⅛–¼ turn. Continue this procedure until a 4–18 inch lb. increase is noted in the torque required to rotate the input shaft.

4. When the adjustment is correct, install the locknut and tighten to 74–88 ft. lbs. with a 19mm crowfoot on a torque wrench while holding the adjustment screw in position with a 7mm socket and torque wrench.

5. Check that the power steering gear runs smoothly throughout its entire motion and that the backlash at the center position is as described above.

Integral Power Rack and Pinion

The Ford Integral Power Rack and Pinion Steering Gear as used on Aerostar incorporates a constant diameter rack. The gear is mounted to the front of the crossmember under the vehicle. The gear housing and valve housing are combined into a 1-piece aluminum die casting. The gear design incorporates quick connect fittings for the pressure and return lines that allow the lines to swivel. This is normal and does not indicate loose fittings. If the fittings leak, check the fittings to assure that they are tightened to 10–15 ft. lbs. Do not overtighten. If the leak is not corrected, replace the fitting seals or hydraulic O-rings.

Disassembly and Assembly

1. Remove the rack from the vehicle and mount in a suitable holding fixture.

2. Mark the position of the tie rod ends on the tie rods. Loosen the jam nuts and remove the tie rod ends. Count and record the number the turns required to remove the ends from the tie rod. Remove the jam nuts.

3. Remove the 4 clamps retaining the rubber bellows to the gear housing. Remove the bellows along with the breather tube from the housing.

4. To remove the ball socket at the inboard end of the tie rods, a special locknut pin removal tool is recommended. Thread the point of the tool or equivalent, into the coiled pin in the ball socket. Tighten the tool, then remove and discard the coiled pin.

5. Some racks will have ball sockets equipped with rivets instead of the coiled pins. On these racks, use a sharp chisel to gently tap around the rivet head so it lifts away from the ball joint. Use caution so the center pin of the rivet is not sheared off. When the rivet head is lifted enough, use side cutter pliers to pry out (not cut off) the rivet.

6. Remove the housing from the fixture. This prevents damaging the gear teeth due to rack twisting during tie rod removal. Rotate the input shaft to move the rack so several teeth are exposed. Hold the rack with an adjustable wrench on the teeth end only, while loosening the ball socket nuts. Remove the ball socket and wrench assembly. With the adjustable wrench still on the end teeth, remove the opposite ball socket and tie rod assembly.

7. Remove the input shaft and valve assembly from the gear housing. Thoroughly clean the input shaft valve housing, yoke locknut and plug and the pinion bearing plug.

8. Do not remove the external pressure lines (right and left turn lines) unless they are leaking or damaged. If the lines are removed new Teflon® seals must be installed.

9. Using the proper tool, loosen the yoke plug locknut and the yoke plug to relieve pressure on the rack.

10. Remove the pinion bearing plug.

11. Install the proper tool on the input shaft. Hold the input shaft and remove the pinion bearing locknut.

NOTE: Do not allow the rack to reach full travel when loosening or tightening the locknut.

12. Using a suitable tool, pry the input shaft dust seal from the housing.

13. Remove the snapring, located beneath the dust seal, from the valve housing.

14. Install a valve body puller on the input shaft. Tighten the nut on the tool to remove the input shaft and valve assembly.

15. To remove the lower pinion shaft seal, insert the proper seal remover tool and the spacer tool until it bottoms. Hold the large nut and tighten the small nut on the tool until the expander fully tightens.

16. Install slide hammer in the rear of the seal remover tool and pull the lower pinion shaft seal from the housing.

17. If the pinion bearing needs replacement use a proper slide hammer and puller attachment to remove the bearing.

18. The only serviceable components on the input shaft and valve assembly are the 4 plastic O-rings. For removal, push the

Exploded view of major components of power rack and pinion—Ford Aerostar

Exploded view of the rack and pinion input shaft and valve assembly—Ford Aerostar

rings to one side, insert a small knife under each ring and cut it off. Use care not to scratch the valve sleeve. It is not necessary to replace these seals each time the valve is removed unless they are damaged.

19. Coat the lower pinion oil seal with the proper steering gear grease. Place the seal on a suitable seal replacer tool, with the seal facing towards the tool. Support the housing on a clean flat surface and drive the seal until it is seated against the shoulder.

20. If the valve O-rings were removed install as follows:

    a. Mount the pinion end of the valve assembly in a suitable holding device.

    b. Lubricate the proper tool with Type F automatic transmission fluid. Install the proper tool over the valve assembly. Slide one valve sleeve O-ring over the tool.

    c. Push down on the ring pusher and force the O-ring down into the fourth groove of the valve sleeve. Repeat this step 3 more times and each time add one more spacer. By adding a spacer each time, the special tool will line up with the next groove on the valve sleeve.

21. After installing the 4 valve seal O-rings, apply a light coat of the proper steering gear grease to the sleeve and O-rings.

22. Install the correct spacer over the input shaft to act as a pilot. Slowly, install the proper sizing tube over the sleeve valve end of the input shaft onto the valve sleeve O-rings.

NOTE: Make sure the O-rings are not being bent over as the sizing tube is slid over them.

23. Remove the sizing tube and check the condition of the O-rings and make sure the O-rings turn freely in the grooves.

24. Position the rack in the housing so the right end of the rack protrudes $9/16$ in. (14mm) from the socket to the housing.

25. Insert the proper tool into the top of the valve housing. Line up the D-flat on the input shaft 180 degree(s) from the yoke plug hole center and insert the valve assembly into the bore. The D-flat must point straight to the rear when the gear is installed in the vehicle with the gear in the "on center" (straight-ahead) position. If necessary rotate the input shaft slightly from side to side to mesh the pinion to the rack teeth. Push the valve assembly in by hand until seated properly.

26. Insert the proper tool on the input shaft. Check if the pinion is centered by rotating the input shaft and counting the number of turns from center to each stop. If the number of turns is unequal, pull the valve assembly out far enough to free

the pinion teeth. Rotate the input shaft 60 degree(s) (1 tooth) in the direction that requires the least turns. Reinsert the valve assembly and check if the pinion is centered. Repeat if necessary.

27. Install the nut on the pinion end of the valve assembly. Hold the input shaft with the correct tool and tighten the nut to 30–40 ft. lbs. The rack must be away from the stops during this operation.

28. Position the input shaft bearing over the shaft in the bore. Drive the bearing into the bore with correct tool until firmly seated.

29. Coat the input shaft seal with a thin coat of the proper steering gear grease.

30. Install the input shaft seal with the lip towards the gear housing.

31. Install the input shaft seal over the seal protector tool, so the seal lip faces the valve.

32. Drive the seal into the bore with the proper seal installer until seated.

33. Install the snapring into the valve bore.

34. Coat the input shaft in the dust seal area with a suitable grease.

35. Install the input shaft seal tool over the input shaft.

36. Install the input shaft dust seal and drive into position using a suitable seal installer. Remove the tool from the seal and the input shaft. This allows trapped air to be released.

37. Install the bearing cap and tighten to 50 ft. lbs.

38. Remove the yoke plug locknut using the suitable tool.

39. Remove the yoke plug from the housing using a suitable socket.

40. Remove the yoke spring and yoke from the gear housing. The yoke may be removed by gripping on the guide post with a pair of pliers.

41. From the right end of the gear (opposite the pinion), push the rack into the housing far enough to gain access to the snapring.

42. Remove the snapring from the right end of the gear housing.

43. Using a hammer and a brass drift, slowly drive the rack out of the right side of the housing along with the bushing. Remove the rack from the housing.

44. To remove the high pressure rack oil seal, insert the correct tool into the housing until it bottoms.

45. Activate the expander with a wrench until the expander fully tightens against the oil seal.

45. Pull the seal from the housing, using the proper tool. Discard the seal.

NOTE: On the first attempt, the plastic insert may pull out of the seal, leaving the seal in the housing. Repeat the procedure until the seal is removed.

46. Remove the plastic O-ring and the rubber O-ring from the rack piston with a suitable tool.
47. To remove the rack bushing seal, grip the seal in a suitable holding fixture and squeeze the seal to distort it. Repeat this procedure if the bushing slips out of the holding device. With the seal distorted, it can easily removed using a suitable prying tool.
48. Mark the center tooth (the eleventh tooth) on the rack so the mark will be visible in the valve bore.
49. Slide the proper tool onto the rack until it seats on the piston. Install the rubber O-ring in the rack piston groove.
50. Slide the plastic O-ring over the tool into the piston groove over the rubber O-ring.
51. Remove the plastic insert from the rack seal. Save the insert for reinstallation.
52. Install the proper rack seal protector tool over the rack teeth.
53. Lubricate the rack and the protector tool with type F transmission fluid.
54. Install the seal so the lip faces the piston. Push the seal all the way against the piston. Remove the rack seal protector tool.
55. Install the plastic insert in the rack seal.
56. Pack the rack teeth with steering gear grease and apply a light coat to the yoke contact area in back of the rack teeth.
57. Lubricate the piston seal and and rack seal outside diameter with type F transmission fluid.
58. Install the proper ring sizing tool into the end of the gear housing.
59. Carefully install the rack without scratching the housing piston bore.
60. Carefully push the piston through the sizing tool. Continue pushing on the rack until it bottoms. Remove the sizing tool.
61. Seat the rack seal with the rack by driving the end of the rack with a drift and plastic mallet.

NOTE: Do not remove the rack.

62. Install the left tie rod and ball socket on the rack and hand tighten.
63. Thread the proper sleeve protector over the threads on the right side of the rack. Coat the protective sleeve with type F transmission fluid.

NOTE: The rack must not move too far from the center since excessive travel can cause the rack teeth to cut the left (inner) oil seal.

64. Apply steering grease to the outer rack oil seal, then install the high pressure oil seal in the rack bushing using the correct tool.
65. Lubricate the short protective sleeve on the rack end and the seal outside diameter on the rack bushing with steering grease.
66. Start the bushing on the rack with the seal facing forward.

Pass the bushing and the seal over the protective sleeve and into the housing bore. Using the proper ring sizing tool, apply hand pressure to the rack bushing until the bushing seats in the gear housing. If hand pressure will not seat the bushing, use an 1⅛ in., 12 point socket or larger and a plastic mallet and tap the bushing in place.
67. Install the snapring in the right end of the gear housing.
68. Install the right tie rod assembly. Tighten both tie rod sockets at the same time to 55–65 ft. lbs. by holding one and turning the other.
69. Tap new coiled pins in the sockets until fully seated.
70. Fill the yoke plug hole with 2 ounces of steering gear grease or the equivalent.
71. Install the yoke plug in the gear housing.
72. Install the yoke in the gear housing.
73. Install the yoke spring in the yoke.
74. Start the yoke plug and locknut in the gear housing.
75. Install the input shaft and valve assembly.
76. Adjust the rack plug preload.
77. Apply lubricant to the undercut in the tie rods where the bellows clamp to the tie rods. This is required to keep the bellows from twisting during toe-in adjustment.
78. Install the bellows and breather tube. Install new clamps retaining the bellows to the gear housing.
79. Install the clamps retaining the bellows to the tie rods.
80. Install the jam nuts to the tie rod ends on the rods.

Adjustment
RACK YOKE PLUG PRELOAD

1. Attach the gear to a proper holding device.
2. Do not remove the external pressure lines unless necessary.
3. Drain the power steering fluid by rotating the input shaft lock-to-lock twice using the proper tool. Cover the ports with a shop towel while draining.
4. Insert an inch lb. torque wrench with a maximum capacity of 30–60 ft. lbs. into the tool, then position the adapter tool and torque wrench on the input shaft splines.
5. Loosen the yoke plug locknut using the proper tool
6. Loosen the yoke plug with an appropriate socket.
7. Rotate the input shaft so the rack is in the center of travel by counting the number of complete revolutions of the input shaft and dividing by two.
8. Tighten the yoke plug to 45–50 inch lbs.

NOTE: Clean the threads of the yoke plug prior to tightening to prevent a false reading.

9. Back off the yoke plug approximately ⅛ turn (44 degrees minimum to 54 degrees maximum) until the torque required to initiate and sustain rotation of the input shaft is 7–18 inch lbs.
10. Install the proper tool to hold the yoke plug locknut. While holding the yoke plug, tighten the locknut 44–66 ft. lbs.

NOTE: Do not allow the yoke plug to move while tightening or the preload will be affected.

11. Recheck the input shaft torque after tightening the locknut.

GENERAL MOTORS CORPORATION

Saginaw Integral
Power Steering Gear

Disassembly and Assembly

1. Place the gear assembly in a proper holding fixture.

2. Pry out the retaining ring from the groove in the gear housing.
3. Turn the stub shaft counterclockwise to force the housing end plug out of the cylinder.
4. Remove the seal and the rack piston end plug.
5. Remove the adjusting nut, bolt and the side cover bolts.

1. Nut
2. Spring washer
3. Retaining ring
4. Washer
5. Seal
6. Bearing
7. Screw
8. Clamp
9. Ball guide
10. Balls
11. Rack piston
12. Plug
13. Seal
14. Ring
15. Seal
16. Plug
17. Retaining ring
18. Sector shaft
19. Adjuster screw
20. Seal
21. Side cover
22. Bolt
23. Nut
24. Housing
25. Connectors
26. Seal
27. Seal
28. Rings
29. Spacer
30. Bearing retainer
31. Spacer
32. Race
33. Bearing
34. Race
35. Seal
36. Adjuster plug
37. Bearing
38. Seal
39. Washer
40. Retaining ring
41. Nut
42. Races
43. Bearing
44. Wormshaft
45. Seal
46. Valve body
47. Stub shaft
48. Valve spool

Exploded view of the Saginaw integral power steering gear assembly—except CK (GMT400)—General Motors Corporation

Exploded view of the Saginaw integral power steering gear assembly—CK (GMT400)—General Motors

USED ON SOME MODELS

USED ON SOME MODELS

1. Housing
2. Race
3. Worm bearing
4. Race
5. Worm assembly
6. Seal
7. Stub shaft
8. Valve spool
9. Seal
10. Valve body
11. Rings
12. Seal
13. Retainer
14. Spacer
15. Race
16. Bearing
17. Race
18. Seal
19. Adjuster plug
20. Bearing
21. Seal
22. Seal
23. Retaining ring
24. Locknut
25. Bearing
26. Seal
27. Washer
30. Retaining ring
31. Washer
32. Nut
33. Nut
34. Ball
35. Guide
36. Clamp
37. Screw assembly
38. Plug
39. Seal
40. Ring
41. Seal
42. Plug
43. Retaining ring
44. Gear assembly
45. Seal assembly
46. Housing cover
47. Hex head bolt
48. Lash adjuster nut
49. Dust seal
50. Boot
51. Bolt
52. Coupling
53. Check valve

6. Turn the adjuster screw clockwise to separate the side cover from the sector shaft. Remove the side cover and gasket.

7. Turn the stub shaft counterclockwise to disengage the sector shaft teeth from the rack piston. Remove the sector shaft.

8. Remove the retaining ring and the sector shaft bearing using the proper tool.

9. Remove the rack piston and balls from the bore in the gear housing.

10. Remove the adjuster plug locknut using the proper tool and remove the adjuster plug.

11. Remove the adjusting plug retaining ring and remove the seal and the bearing using the proper tool.

12. Remove the valve and the wormshaft as an assembly with both races and the bearings and separate the worm from the valve assembly.

13. Hold the valve assembly and lightly, tap the stub shaft until the shaft cap is free from the valve body.

14. Remove the shaft assembly from the spool by disengaging the shaft pin and remove the spool from the valve body by rotating it.

15. Remove the screws, clamp and ball guide from the rack piston. Remove the balls.

16. Clean and thoroughly inspect all the parts for any burrs, cracks or any other excessive wear.

To assemble:

17. Lubricate the 24 balls with power steering fluid. Install the balls, alternating by color into the ball guide.

18. Use petroleum jelly to hold the balls in the ball guide.

19. Install the ball guide to the rack piston.

20. Lubricate the stub shaft with power steering fluid and insert the stub shaft into the valve body.

21. Lubricate the valve spool and seals with power steering fluid and install into the valve body.

22. Install the O-ring in the valve body so it is seated against the lower shaft cap and lubricate the valve body, rings and seals with power steering fluid.

Loading the recirculating balls into the power steering gear—General Motors Corporation

RACK PISTON

BALLS

BALL GIUDES

CLAMP

SCREW

23. Align the narrow notch in the valve body with the pin in the worm and install the unit into the gear housing, by exerting pressure on the valve body and not the stub shaft.

24. Install the wormshaft bearing races and bearing and insert the valve body

25. Install the seal on the adjuster plug and using the proper tool insert the needle bearing in the adjuster plug.

26. Install the seal, washer and the retaining ring in the adjuster plug.

NOTE: The retainer should not extend beyond the washer when the retainer ring is seated. The washer must be free to rotate.

27. Install the wormshaft and the valve assembly into the gear housing.

28. Install the adjuster plug into the gear housing, using the proper tool.

29. Adjust the thrust bearing preload by tightening the adjuster plug to 20 ft. lbs. to seat the thrust bearings.

30. With the ball retaining tool in position, lubricate and install the primary rack piston into the gear housing until the retaining tool bottoms against the center of the worm.

31. Turn the stub shaft clockwise to thread the rack piston onto the worm. Keep the retaining tool tight against the worm while turning the stub shaft.

32. Remove the ball retainer tool when the rack piston is completely threaded onto the worm. Center the rack teeth in the sector shaft opening.

33. Install the secondary rack piston in the gear housing and line up the center tooth space with the teeth of the primary rack piston.

34. Install the sector shaft bearing and seal, using the proper tool.

35. Install the retaining ring and slide the sector shaft into the gear housing with the tapered teeth engaging the primary rack piston.

36. Install a new O-ring on the side cover and push the cover into the housing until contact is made with the preload adjuster screw. With the aid of an Allen wrench inserted through the cover, turn the adjusting screw counterclockwise until the cover bottoms on the housing.

37. Install the side cover bolts and tighten to 40 ft. lbs. Install the rack piston plug and torque to 75 ft. lbs.

38. Install the primary and secondary end covers, O-rings and the retainer rings.

39. With the steering gear on center, tighten the sector adjusting screw. Install and tighten the locknut and check the over center torque.

Adjustments

THRUST BEARING PRELOAD

1 Turn the adjuster plug counterclockwise, using the proper tool, until the plug and the bearing are firmly seated—about 20 ft. lbs.

2. Mark the adjuster in line with a hole in the adjuster plug.

3. Measure back counterclockwise ½ in. and re-mark the housing.

4. Rotate the adjuster counterclockwise until the hole in the adjuster is in line with the second mark.

5. Install the adjuster nut and tighten to 80 ft. lbs. Hold the adjuster nut to maintain the alignment of the hole with the mark.

6. Check the turning torque of the stub shaft, using a suitable torque wrench. The reading should be taken with the beam of the wrench near vertical while turning the wrench counterclockwise.

7. The reading should be 4–10 inch lbs. Lubricate the stub shaft area outside the dust seal with a suitable chassis lubricant.

SECTOR SHAFT OVER-CENTER PRELOAD

1. Center the steering gear by turning the stub shaft to the left then to the right counting the number of turns, using the proper tool.

2. Turn the shaft back ½ way to the center position.

Marking the housing for the thrust bearing preload—General Motors Corporation

Remarking the housing for the thrust bearing preload—General Motors Corporation

3. Check the ball and bearing preload by turning the torque wrench through the center of travel. Note the highest reading.

4. Tighten the adjusting screw until the reading is 6–10 inch lbs. higher than the previous reading.

5. The total reading should not exceed 20 inch lbs. Tighten the adjusting nut to 20 ft. lbs.

Power Rack and Pinion

Disassembly and Assembly

1. Place the rack and pinion assembly in a suitable holding device.

2. Remove the adjuster plug locknut from the adjuster plug.

3. Remove the adjuster plug, spring and the rack bearing from the housing.

4. Remove the retaining ring from the valve bore of the housing.

5. Remove the dust cover from the bottom of the housing.

1. Housing
2. Upper pinion bushing
3. Pinion shaft seal
4. Pinion valve assembly
5. Valve body ring
6. Stub shaft seal retaining ring
7. Stub shaft needle bearing
8. Stub shaft bearing annulus
9. Stub shaft seal
10. Stub shaft dust seal
11. Stub shaft seal retaining ring
12. Stub shaft seal adapter
13. Rack bearing
14. Adjuster spring
15. Adjuster plug
16. Adjuster plug locknut
17. Steering gear shock dampener ring
18. Inner tie rod, left
19. Boot clamp–56mm
20. Left side boot
21. Hex nut–14mm x 1.5mm
22. Outer tie rod, left
23. Lube fitting
24. Tie rod seal
25. Slotted hex nut–12mm x 1.25mm
26. Cotter pin
27. Pinion bearing
28. Bearing retaining ring
29. Locknut
30. Dust cover
31. Tie rod end boot clamp
32. Boot clamp–56mm
33. Right side boot
34. Breather tube
35. Pressure line O-ring seal
36. Pressure line O-ring seal
37. Right side pressure line
38. Left side pressure line
39. O-ring seal
40. Inner rack seal
41. Piston and steering rack
42. Piston ring
43. Cylinder inner bulkhead
44. Bulkhead seal
45. O-ring bulkhead seal
46. Cylinder outer bulkhead
47. Bulkhead retaining ring
48. Inner tie rod
49. Outer tie rod

VIEW A-A

Exploded view of power rack and pinion assembly—General Motors U-Body vehicles—1990–92 Chevrolet Lumina APV, Pontiac TranSport and Oldsmobile Silhouette

NOTE: The stub shaft must be held to prevent damage to the pinion teeth.

6. While holding the stub shaft, remove the hex locknut from the pinion and valve assembly.

7. With the rack centered, mark the location of the stub shaft notch on the housing and measure the distance to the end of the boot.

NOTE: Do not hammer or pound on the pinion and

Housing reference mark and rack centering measurement—General Motors Corporation

valve assembly. This will cause damage or loosen the drive pin.

8. Using a suitable press, press on the threaded end of the pinion to remove the pinion and the valve assembly from the housing. Just before the removal of the pinion and valve assembly, mark the second location of the stub shaft notch on the housing.

9. Remove the stub shaft dust seal, stub shaft seal, stub shaft bearing assembly and the pinion and valve assembly, with the retaining ring and the valve body rings attached.

10. Remove the valve body rings from the pinion and valve assembly.

11. Clean the valve assembly ring grooves. Inspect the pinion and valve assembly for a broken drive pin. If a broken pin is found, replace the gear assembly.

To assemble:

12. Assembly is the reverse of the removal procedure. Apply grease to each ring groove and to the new valve body rings when installed to hold the rings in position.

13. Connect the new valve body rings to the pinion and the valve assembly.

14. Place the pinion and valve assembly into a clear protective device. This allows the valve rings to be properly sized.

15. Place the valve assembly in the protector so the valve body is flush with the bottom of the protector.

16. Center the rack in the housing according to the marks that were taken.

17. Lubricate the valve housing bore with a liberal amount of grease.

18. Align the mark on the valve stub shaft with the second mark on the housing.

19. Place the pinion and valve assembly, with the spool shaft retaining rings and the valve body rings installed, into the housing. Use the proper tool to prevent damage to the valve ring.

20. Set the pinion and valve assembly onto the rack and pinion housing assembly using the proper tool. Do not hammer or use excessive force.

21. When the pinion and valve assembly is fully seated, the

DUST SEAL
STUB SHAFT SEAL
BEARING
VALVE BODY RINGS
RETAINING RING
VALVE ASSEMBLY
HOUSING

Rack and pinion valve assembly and seals—General Motors Corporation

notch in the stub shaft and the first mark on the housing must line up while the rack is centered in the housing.

22. Install the hex locknut onto the pinion, while holding the stub shaft and tighten to 26 ft. lbs.

23. Install the dust cover to the housing and place the stub shaft bearing assembly onto the valve stub shaft.

24. Place the special protector tool onto the valve stub shaft apply a small amount of grease between the seals and the tool.

25. Place the stub shaft seal and the stub shaft dust seal over the protector and into the housing.

26. Install the retaining ring into the groove in the housing.

27. Coat the rack bearing, adjuster spring and the adjuster plug with a lithium base grease and install in the housing.

28. With the rack centered in the housing, turn the adjuster plug clockwise until it bottoms in the housing. Then back off 50–70 degrees and check the pinion. Maximum pinion preload is 18 inch lbs.

29. Install the plug locknut to the adjuster. Tighten firmly against the housing while holding the adjuster plug stationary.

JEEP

Recirculating Ball Power Steering Gear

Disassembly and Assembly

1. Place the gear assembly in a proper holding fixture and drain the fluid from the gear.

2. Pry out the retaining ring from the groove in the gear housing.

3. Turn the stub shaft counterclockwise to force the housing end plug out of the cylinder.

4. Remove the seal and the rack piston end plug.

5. Remove the adjusting nut, bolt and the side cover bolts.

6. Turn the adjuster screw clockwise to separate the side cover from the sector shaft. Remove the side cover and gasket.

1. Piston end plug
2. Teflon® ring
3. O-ring seal
4. Piston assembly
5. Black and silver balls
6. Ball half-guide
7. Ball half-guide
8. Clamp
9. Clamp bolt
10. Gear housing
11. Pitman shaft
12. Cover gasket
13. Cover
14. Locknut
15. Bolt
16. Hose connector seat
17. Check valve
18. Check valve spring
19. Hose cpnnector seat
20. Stub shaft
21. Valve body
22. O-ring seal
23. Teflon ring
24. O-ring seal
25. Teflon ring
26. O-ring seal
27. Teflon ring
28. Spool valve
29. O-ring seal
30. O-ring seal
31. Wormshaft
32. Bearing race
33. Thrust bearing
34. Bearing race
35. Needle bearing
36. Dust seal
37. Retaining snapring
38. Seal
39. Adjustment cap
40. O-ring seal
41. Large thrust washer
42. Thrust bearing
43. Small thrust washer
44. Spacer
45. Retaining ring
46. Needle bearing
47. Single lip seal
48. Backup washer
49. Double lip seal
50. Backup washer
51. Retaining snapring
52. Spring washer
53. Retaining nut
54. O-ring seal
55. Housing end plug
56. Retaining ring

Exploded view of power steering gear—Jeep

7. Turn the stub shaft counterclockwise to disengage the sector shaft teeth from the rack piston. Remove the sector shaft.

8. Remove the retaining ring and the sector shaft bearing using the proper tool.

9. Remove the rack piston and balls from the bore in the gear housing.

10. Remove the adjuster plug locknut using the proper tool and remove the adjuster plug.

11. Remove the adjusting plug retaining ring and remove the seal and the bearing using the proper tool.

12. Remove the valve and the wormshaft as an assembly with both races and the bearings attached and separate the worm from the valve assembly.

13. Hold the valve assembly and lightly, tap the stub shaft until the shaft cap is free from the valve body.

14. Remove the shaft assembly from the spool by disengaging the shaft pin and remove the spool from the valve body by rotating it.

15. Remove the screws, clamp and ball guide from the rack piston. Remove the balls.

16. Clean and thoroughly inspect all the parts for any burrs, cracks or any other excessive wear.

To assemble:

17. Assembly is the reverse of the removal procedure. Lubricate the 24 balls with power steering fluid. Install the balls, alternating by color into the ball guide.

18. Use petroleum jelly to hold the balls in the ball guide.

19. Install the ball guide to the rack piston.

20. Lubricate the stub shaft with power steering fluid and insert the stub shaft into the valve body.

21. Lubricate the valve spool and seals with power steering fluid and install into the valve body.

22. Install the O-ring in the valve body so it is seated against the lower shaft cap and lubricate the valve body, rings and seals with power steering fluid.

23. Align the narrow notch in the valve body with the pin in the worm and install the unit into the gear housing, by exerting pressure on the valve body and not the stub shaft.

24. Install the wormshaft bearing races and bearing and insert the valve body.

25. Install the seal on the adjuster plug and using the proper tool insert the needle bearing in the adjuster plug.

26. Install the seal, washer and the retaining ring in the adjuster plug.

NOTE: The retainer should not extend beyond the washer when the retainer ring is seated. The washer must be free to rotate.

27. Install the wormshaft and the valve assembly into the gear housing.

28. Install the adjuster plug into the gear housing, using the proper tool.

29. Adjust the thrust bearing preload by torquing the adjuster plug to 20 ft. lbs. to seat the thrust bearings.

30. With the ball retaining tool in position, lubricate and install the primary rack piston into the gear housing until the retaining tool bottoms against the center of the worm.

31. Turn the stub shaft clockwise to thread the rack piston onto the worm. Keep the retaining tool tight against the worm while turning the stub shaft.

32. Remove the ball retainer tool when the rack piston is completely threaded onto the worm. Center the rack teeth in the sector shaft opening.

33. Install the secondary rack piston in the gear housing and line up the center tooth space with the teeth of the primary rack piston.

34. Install the sector shaft bearing and seal, using the proper tool.

35. Install the retaining ring and slide the sector shaft into the gear housing with the tapered teeth engaging the primary rack piston.

36. Install a new O-ring on the side cover and push the cover into the housing until contact is made with the preload adjuster screw. With the aid of an Allen wrench inserted through the cover, turn the adjusting screw counterclockwise until the cover bottoms on the housing.

37. Install the side cover bolts and tighten to 45 ft. lbs. Install the rack piston plug and torque to 50 ft. lbs.

38. Install the primary and secondary end covers, O-rings and install the retainer rings.

39. With the steering gear on center, tighten the sector adjusting screw. Install and tighten the locknut and check the over center torque.

Adjustments

WORMSHAFT BEARING PRELOAD

1. Tighten the wormshaft bearing adjustment cap until it is seated in the gear housing.

2. Place an index mark on the gear housing opposite one of the holes in the adjuster plug. Measure back counterclockwise from the index mark and remark the housing.

3. Turn the adjuster plug counterclockwise until hole in the adjuster plug is aligned with the second mark on the housing.

4. Install the adjuster plug locknut and tighten to 85 ft. lbs.

5. Turn the stub shaft clockwise to the stop, then turn it back ¼ turn. Record the torque reading.

6. The torque required to turn the stub shaft should be 4–10 inch lbs.

SECTOR SHAFT OVER CENTER DRAG TORQUE

1. Turn the sector shaft adjuster screw counterclockwise until fully extended, then turn back clockwise ½ turn.

2. Rotate the stub shaft from stop-to-stop and count the number of turns. Turn the stub shaft back ½ turn from either stop. This is the gear center.

NOTE: When the gear is centered, the flat potion of the stub shaft should face up and be parallel to the side cover.

3. Rotate the torque wrench 45 degree(s) on each side of center and measure the highest drag torque on or near the center.

4. Adjust the over center drag torque by turning the sector shaft adjusting screw clockwise until the desired reading is obtained.

   a. On new steering gears, add 4–8 lbs. to the previously measured worm bearing preload torque.

   b. On used gears, add 4–5 lbs. to the previously measured worm bearing preload torque.

5. Tighten the sector shaft adjusting screw locknut to 20 ft. lbs.

CHRYSLER IMPORT

Recirculating Ball and Nut

Disassembly and Assembly

1. Secure the gear assembly in a suitable holding device and loosen the adjusting bolt locknut and remove it.
2. With the gear in neutral position, tap the bottom of the cross-shaft with a plastic hammer to remove the cross-shaft.
3. Remove the side cover bolts and screw in the adjusting bolt a couple turns.
4. Remove the valve housing nut with the proper tool.
5. Remove the valve housing bolts and take out the valve housing and rack piston, holding the rack piston to avoid turning it.
6. Be careful not to let the rack piston fall off of the shaft.
7. To remove the rack piston, turn it counterclockwise.

NOTE: There are 26 steel balls in the rack piston which will probably fall out when removed from the shaft. Do not lose them.

8. To disassemble the rack piston, remove the circular holder, the circulator, the steel balls, the seal ring and the O-ring. Do not disassemble the rack piston end cap.
9. Loosen the top cover and remove it and the input wormshaft from the valve housing.
10. Remove wormshaft thrust plate, thrust needle roller bearing, the seal rings and the O-rings.
11. Screw in the adjusting bolt at the tip of the cross-shaft and remove the side cover.

NOTE: There are 33 needle bearing rollers which may fall out when the cross-shaft is removed. Do not lose them.

12. Remove the O-ring, needle bearings, adjusting bolt and adjusting plate from the side cover.

NOTE: If no oil leaks through the threads of the adjusting bolt, do not remove the sealing at the rear of the needle bearing seat.

13. Remove the seal ring and O-ring from the valve housing.
14. Remove the ball bearing and oil seal from the top cover, using a suitable tool.
15. Remove the oil seal and seal ring from the gear housing using a suitable tool.

To assemble:

16. Assembly is the reverse of the removal procedure. Clean and inspect all parts for wear or damage. Always use new gaskets and oil seals and coat indicated parts with Dexron®II before installing.
17. Apply a thin coat of multi-purpose grease to the bearing race in the side cover and insert the 33 roller bearings. Apply a dab of grease to bottom of the side cover. Be careful not to disturb the needle bearings.
18. Install the side cover O-ring.
19. With the adjusting bolt and adjusting plate inserted in the top of the cross-shaft, measure the clearance between the bolt head and the cross-shaft. It should be 0.002 in. or less. Adjust clearance by replacing with an appropriate adjusting spacer.

Exploded view of power recirculating ball steering gear—Chrysler Import

Exploded view of input wormshaft assembly for power recirculating ball steering gear—Chrysler Import

NOTE: Install the adjusting plate with its chamfered side in contact with the surface of the cross-shaft.

20. Align the cross-shaft with the side cover and install. Attach them by tightening the adjusting bolt. Take care not to disturb the needle bearings while installing the cross-shaft. Make sure not to damage the oil seal. Tighten the adjusting bolt locknut temporarily.

21. To assemble the top cover, apply a thin coat of multipurpose grease to the lip of the oil seal.

22. Press the oil seal and the bearing into position, using the proper tool.

23. Apply a thin coat of multi-purpose grease to the packing and the lip of the oil seal. Press them in, using the proper tool.

24. Lubricate the O-ring, seal ring, needle roller bearing and the thrust plate with the specified transmission fluid.

25. Install the O-ring and the seal ring (in that order) to the input wormshaft.

26. Install the thrust plate, thrust needle bearing and the thrust plate in that order to the input wormshaft.

27. Install the O-rings and the seal ring into their seats in the valve housing without using undue force. The seal ring should be compressed into a heart shape when fit.

28. Install the input wormshaft in the valve housing.

29. Install the thrust plate, needle roller bearing and the thrust plate in that order to the top cover.

NOTE: Install the thinner thrust plate on the top cover side.

30. Temporarily tighten the top cover to the valve housing. Take care not to disturb the thrust plate and needle roller bearing in the top cover.

31. Tighten the top cover bolts to 12–16 inch lbs. Turn the input wormshaft and check for smooth rotation and noise.

32. Tighten the valve housing nut to 130–166 ft. lbs. Do not allow the top cover to rotate while tightening the nut.

33. Measure the starting preload of the input wormshaft. It should be from 2–6 inch lbs. If not, adjust by loosening the valve housing nut. Install the O-ring and seal ring to the rack piston in that order.

34. Insert the rack piston into the input wormshaft until the piston reaches the end of its travel. Rotate the input shaft and align the ball running surface with the ball insertion hole. Insert 19 balls into the hole, pushing them lightly with a suitable tool.

NOTE: Do not rotate the wormshaft on rack piston at this point or the balls might enter other grooves.

35. After installing all 19 of the balls, make sure the last ball is

about ½ in. below the end of the rack piston. If there is more clearance than that, it probably means 1 or more of the balls has fallen into a different worm groove. Remove the piston and reinstall the balls.

36. Insert 7 of the balls in the circulator, holding them in place with grease. Install the circulator.

37. Secure the gear assembly in a suitable holding fixture and install the ball screw unit.

38. Tighten the valve housing to 33–39 ft. lbs. After installation, rotate the input wormshaft to move the piston to the neutral (center) position. Be careful not to damage the seal ring when installing the piston.

39. Install the cross-shaft assembly (with side cover) in to the gear housing and tighten the side cover to 33–39 ft. lbs. When installing the cross-shaft, apply a thin coat of ATF to the teeth and shaft of the rack piston and multi-purpose grease to the oil seal lip. Do not rotate the side cover during installation to prevent damage to the O-ring. Wrap tape around the splined end of the cross-shaft to prevent damage to the seals.

40. Measure the total starting torque of the input wormshaft to neutral position (center), using the proper tool. Make sure the ball screw operates smoothly throughout its entire travel. Starting torque should be between 4–8 inch lbs.

41. Install the pitman arm on the cross-shaft and tighten the pitman arm nut to 94–108 ft. lbs.

Adjustments
STEERING GEAR BACKLASH

1. Inject a small amount of gear oil into the breather plug and lubricate the bearing parts and the gear teeth of each shaft.

2. Tighten the adjusting bolt until it engages the gear teeth. Rotate the pitman arm back and forth to make sure it is engaged with the gear teeth.

3. Position a suitable indicator at the end of the pitman arm and move the pitman arm to measure the backlash. The steering gear backlash limit is 0.020 in.

4. Turn the adjusting bolt in or out to adjust the backlash.

NOTE: Measure the steering gear backlash when the mainshaft, cross-shaft and the pitman arm in the straight-ahead position.

5. The steering gear backlash should be 0.020 in.

Power Rack and Pinion

Disassembly and Assembly

1. Secure the rack housing in a suitable holding fixture.

2. Loosen the locknut and remove the tie rod end.

3. Disconnect the bellows band and remove the bellows.

4. Lift up the tab washer caulking and remove the tie rod from the rack housing

5. Disconnect the tab washer and dust cover and remove the feed tubes from the rack.

6. Disconnect the end plug caulking and remove the end plug.

7. Disconnect the locking nut and remove the rack support cover, using the proper tool.

8. Take out the rack support spring and remove the rack support.

9. Remove the snapring, using the proper tool, and pull out the pinion and valve assembly with the oil seals

10. Rotate the rack clockwise until the end of the circlip comes out of the slot in the rack housing.

11. Turn the rack stopper counterclockwise to remove the circlip.

12. Pull the rack out slowly and remove the rack stopper and the rack bushing at the same time.

13. Using the proper tool, remove the oil seals and the bearings from the rack housing.

14. Clean all the parts and check for any damage or excessive wear.

To assemble:

15. Assembly is the reverse of the removal procedure. Press the backup washer and the oil seal into the rack housing, using the proper tool.

16. Lubricate the bearing and the seal with the proper transmission fluid and install into the rack housing, using a suitable tool.

NOTE: Press the bearing in straight, as the valve housing is aluminum. Be sure the oil seal faces in the correct direction.

17. Lubricate the oil seal for the rack bushing and install the oil seal until it touches the rack bushing end.

18. Apply a coating of multi-purpose grease to the rack teeth. Align the oil seal center with the rack and slowly, insert the rack from the power cylinder side.

19. Wrap the end of the rack with a vinyl tape, lubricate with transmission fluid and install the rack bushing and the rack stopper.

NOTE: Do not allow the oil seal retainer to slip out.

20. Align the rack stopper mark with the cylinder hole and install the circlip while turning the rack stopper clockwise.

21. Press fit the oil seal, using the proper tool.

22. Apply the proper sealant to the threaded part of the end plug and install the end plug.

23. Secure the threaded part of the end plug at 2 places, using a suitable punch.

24. Adjust the total pinion torque and install the tie rods to the rack and fold the tab washer into position.

Adjustments
TOTAL PINION TORQUE

1. Position the rack at it's center.

2. Tighten the rack support cover to 11 ft. lbs., using the proper tool.

3. In the neutral position, rotate the pinion shaft clockwise, one turn in 4–6 seconds. Return the rack support cover 30–60 degrees and adjust the torque to 6–12 inch lbs.

4. Lock the rack cover support with the locknut.

Bevel Gear Assembly

Disassembly and Assembly

1. Secure the gear assembly in a proper holding fixture.

2. Remove the locknut using the proper tool.

3. Remove the front cover mounting bolts, adjusting bolt and remove the front cover.

4. Remove the locknut and loosen the rear cover with the proper tool, until the input gear separates from the output gear.

5. Remove both the input gear and the output gear from the housing.

6. Inspect the gear teeth, bearings and the dust cover for any cracks or excessive damage.

To assemble:

7. Assembly is the reverse of the removal procedure. Install the input and the output gear into the gear housing so the teeth mesh properly.

8. Tighten the rear cover, using the proper tool. Replace the locknut and tighten to 47–87 ft. lbs. depending on which tool was used.

9. Install the front cover and replace the mounting bolts. Tighten to 12–19 ft. lbs.

10. Install the adjusting bolt and replace the locknut and tighten to 12–19 ft. lbs.

Adjustments
OUTPUT GEAR ROTATIONAL TORQUE

1. Turn the output gear, using the proper tool, at a speed of one rotation every 4–6 seconds. Measure the rotational torque.

2. Adjust the nut so the output side gear rotational torque is 0.4–0.9 inch lbs.

3. Tighten the locknut to 47–87 ft. lbs., depending on which tool was used.

TOTAL BEVEL GEAR ROTATIONAL TORQUE

1. Turn the input gear, using the proper tool, at a speed of one rotation every 4–6 seconds. Measure the rotational torque.

NOTE: Return the adjustment bolt to a position where there is no contact with the input side gear.

2. Using the proper tool, tighten the rear cover assembly so the input side gear rotational torque is 2.2–3.9 inch lbs.

3. Tighten the adjustment bolt so the total bevel gear rotational torque is 2.6–4.8 inch lbs.

4. Install the locknut and tighten to 47–87 ft. lbs., depending on which tool was used.

DAIHATSU

Recirculating Ball

The power steering gear assembly is not serviceable. If a malfunction occurs, replace with a new unit. Specified fluid is Dexron®II.

GEO

Recirculating Ball

The power steering gear assembly is not serviceable. If a mal-function occurs, replace with a new unit.

ISUZU

Integral Gear

Disassembly and Assembly

1. Secure the gear in a suitable holding fixture. Remove the dust cover, retaining ring and back up ring.
2. Clean the faces of the stub shaft extended outward and plug the hose fitting on the inlet side. Remove the oil seal by applying compressed air through the hole in the outlet side.
3. Remove the adjusting screw locknut and turn the adjusting screw counterclockwise to remove the preload between the sector gear and the rack piston. Remove the top cover bolts.
4. Hold the top cover stationary, turn the adjusting screw clockwise to raise and free the cover, then remove the cover.
5. Remove the O-ring and needle bearing.
6. Position the stub shaft in a straight-ahead position and remove the sector shaft.

NOTE: Do not use a hammer or any impact tools to remove the sector shaft.

7. Remove the ball nut and valve housing assembly.

NOTE: Always keep the ball nut and valve housing assembly in the horizontal position, or the rack piston will fall off onto the end of the worm, causing the rack piston to slip out of the wormshaft and the balls to fall out.

8. Remove the dust seal and ring from the gear housing.
9. Apply a thin coat of grease to the lips of all seals and O-rings.

To assemble:

10. Install the seal ring and dust seal into the the gear housing.
11. Install the needle bearing into the housing, using the proper tool.
12. Install the both O-rings and the seal ring onto the ball nut and valve assembly.
13. Install the ball nut and valve assembly and tighten the valve housing retaining bolts to 27–30 ft. lbs.

NOTE: Be careful not to drop the O-ring fitted to the oil passage in the valve housing. Keep the ball screw and valve housing assembly in a horizontal position.

1. Gear assembly
2. Seal ring
3. Dust seal
4. Needle bearing
5. O-ring
6. Seal ring
7. O-ring
8. Ball nut and valve housing assembly
9. Oil seal
10. Back-up ring
11. Retaining ring
12. Dust cover
13. Sector shaft
14. Needle bearing
15. O-ring
16. Top cover assembly
17. Locknut

Exploded view of typical power steering gear assembly—Isuzu

14. Install the oil seal using the proper tool, then install the back up ring and retaining ring. Turn the face with the rounded edge (outer circumference) to the oil seal.

15. Install the dust cover.

16. Tape the sector shaft serration to protect the seal ring from damage, then align the center tooth of the ball nut with that of the sector shaft and install the sector shaft.

17. Install the needle bearing, O-ring and top cover. Tighten the top cover bolts to 29–39 ft. lbs.

18. Install the locknut and adjust the backlash between the sector gear and ball nut.

Adjustments

WORM GEAR AND BALL NUT BACKLASH

1. Rotate the worm gear to a straight-ahead position.

2. Set the wormshaft backlash to below 4 inch lbs. with the sector shaft adjusting screw.

3. Measure the wormshaft backlash with the worm gear turned all the way around in both directions.

4. The worm gear backlash in these positions should be only 0.8–1.6 inch lbs. lower than in the straight-ahead position.

5. Lock the sector shaft adjusting screw with the locknut. Tighten the locknut to 25–35 ft. lbs.

MAZDA

Recirculating Ball and Nut

Disassembly and Assembly

1. Secure the gear assembly in a suitable holding fixture.

2. Plug the openings of all pipe installation fittings and clean the exterior of the gear assembly.

3. Remove the locknut and the pitman arm, using the proper puller.

4. Loosen the locknut and side cover mounting bolts. Remove the side cover.

5. Place the sector shaft in the middle position and tap the lower end of the shaft, using the proper tool.

6. Remove the sector shaft from the gear housing.

7. Remove the dust cover and pry out the oil seal with the proper tool.

8. Remove the dust cover, snapring, washer and pry out the oil seal with the proper tool.

9. Loosen the mounting bolts and remove the valve and piston assembly.

10. Remove the O-ring and the piston seal ring.

11. Clean all the parts and check for any damage or excessive wear.

To assemble:

12. Apply the proper fluid to the lips of the oil seals and all the sliding surfaces.

13. Insert the valve and piston assembly into the gear housing. Tighten the mounting bolts to 28–36 ft. lbs.

NOTE: Do not scratch the O-ring and the seal ring on the piston against the side of the housing.

14. Install the dust cover and the oil seal into the proper groove using a suitable seal installer tool.

15. Insert the sector shaft and replace the side cover. Tighten the mounting bolts to 29–36 ft. lbs.

16. Install the pitman arm and tighten the locknut to 108–130 ft. lbs.

Adjustments

WORMSHAFT PRELOAD

1. Place the wormshaft in the center position.

1. Nut and washer
2. Pitman arm
3. Locknut
4. Bolt
5. Side cover
6. O-ring
7. Sector shaft
8. Dust cover
9. Oil seal
10. Dust cover
11. Snapring
12. Washer
13. Oil seal
14. Bolt
15. Valve and pinion assembly
16. O-ring
17. Piston seal ring

Exploded view of typical power steering gear assembly—Mazda

2. Set the sector shaft adjusting screw so the preload is 1.3–2.0 lbs.

3. The preload at the center position must be 0.4–0.9 lbs. higher than the preload when the wormshaft is turned 360 degrees to the left and the right.

4. Tighten the sector screw locknut to 25–35 ft. lbs.

Power Rack and Pinion

The power rack and pinion assembly is not adjustable or serviceable, must be replaced as an entire unit.

MITSUBISHI

Recirculating Ball

Disassembly and Assembly

1. Secure the gear assembly in a suitable holding device and loosen the adjusting bolt locknut and remove it.

2. With the gear in neutral position, tap the bottom of the cross-shaft with a plastic hammer to remove the cross-shaft.

3. Remove the side cover bolts and screw in the adjusting bolt a couple turns.

4. Remove the valve housing nut with the proper tool.

5. Remove the valve housing bolts and take out the valve

housing and rack piston, holding the rack piston to avoid turning it.

6. Be careful not to let the rack piston fall off of the shaft.
7. To remove the rack piston, turn it counterclockwise.

NOTE: There are 26 steel balls in the rack piston which will probably fall out when removed from the shaft. Do not lose them.

8. To disassemble the rack piston, remove the circular holder, the circulator, the steel balls, the seal ring and the O-ring. Do not disassemble the rack piston end cap.
9. Loosen the top cover and remove it and the input wormshaft from the valve housing.
10. Remove wormshaft thrust plate, thrust needle roller bearing, the seal rings and the O-rings.
11. Screw in the adjusting bolt at the tip of the cross-shaft and remove the side cover.

NOTE: There are 33 needle bearing rollers which may fall out when the cross-shaft is removed. Do not lose them.

12. Remove the O-ring, needle bearings, adjusting bolt and adjusting plate from the side cover.

NOTE: If no oil leaks through the threads of the adjusting bolt, do not remove the sealing at the rear of the needle bearing seat.

13. Remove the seal ring and O-ring from the valve housing.
14. Remove the ball bearing and oil seal from the top cover, using a suitable tool.
15. Remove the oil seal and seal ring from the gear housing using a suitable tool.

To assemble:
16. Assembly is the reverse of the removal procedure. Clean and inspect all parts for wear or damage. Always use new gaskets and oil seals and coat indicated parts with Dexron®II before installing.
17. Apply a thin coat of multi-purpose grease to the bearing race in the side cover and insert the 33 roller bearings. Apply a dab of grease to bottom of the side cover. Be careful not to disturb the needle bearings.
18. Install the side cover O-ring.
19. With the adjusting bolt and adjusting plate inserted in the top of the cross-shaft, measure the clearance between the bolt head and the cross-shaft. It should be 0.002 in. or less. Adjust clearance by replacing with an appropriate adjusting spacer.

NOTE: Install the adjusting plate with its chamfered side in contact with the surface of the cross-shaft.

20. Align the cross-shaft with the side cover and install. Attach them by tightening the adjusting bolt. Take care not to disturb the needle bearings while installing the cross-shaft. Make sure not to damage the oil seal. Tighten the adjusting bolt locknut temporarily.
21. To assemble the top cover, apply a thin coat of multi-purpose grease to the lip of the oil seal.
22. Press the oil seal and the bearing into position, using the proper tool.
23. Apply a thin coat of multi-purpose grease to the packing and the lip of the oil seal. Press them in, using the proper tool.
24. Lubricate the O-ring, seal ring, needle roller bearing and the thrust plate with the specified transmission fluid.
25. Install the O-ring and the seal ring (in that order) to the input wormshaft.
26. Install the thrust plate, thrust needle bearing and the thrust plate in that order to the input wormshaft.
27. Install the O-rings and the seal ring into their seats in the valve housing without using undue force. The seal ring should be compressed into a heart shape when fit.
28. Install the input wormshaft in the valve housing.

29. Install the thrust plate, needle roller bearing and the thrust plate in that order to the top cover.

NOTE: Install the thinner thrust plate on the top cover side.

30. Temporarily tighten the top cover to the valve housing. Take care not to disturb the thrust plate and needle roller bearing in the top cover.
31. Tighten the top cover bolts to 12–16 inch lbs. Turn the input wormshaft and check for smooth rotation and noise.
32. Tighten the valve housing nut to 130–166 ft. lbs. Do not allow the top cover to rotate while tightening the nut.
33. Measure the starting preload of the input wormshaft. It should be from 2.2–5.6 inch lbs. If not, adjust by loosening the valve housing nut. Install the O-ring and seal ring to the rack piston in that order.
34. Insert the rack piston into the input wormshaft until the piston reaches the end of its travel. Rotate the input shaft and align the ball running surface with the ball insertion hole. Insert 19 balls into the hole, pushing them lightly with a suitable tool.

NOTE: Do not rotate the wormshaft on rack piston at this point or the balls might enter other grooves.

35. After installing all 19 of the balls, make sure the last ball is about ½ in. below the end of the rack piston. If there is more clearance than that, it probably means one or more of the balls has fallen into a different worm groove. Remove the rack piston and reinstall the balls.
36. Insert 7 of the balls in the circulator, holding them in place with grease. Install the circulator and tighten to 2.6–3.2 ft. lbs.
37. Secure the gear assembly in a suitable holding fixture and install the ball screw unit.
38. Tighten the valve housing to 33–39 ft. lbs. After installation, rotate the input wormshaft to move the rack piston to the neutral (center) position. Be careful not to damage the seal ring when installing the rack piston.
39. Install the cross-shaft assembly (with side cover) in to the gear housing and tighten the side cover to 33–39 ft. lbs. When installing the cross-shaft, apply a thin coat of ATF to the teeth and shaft of the rack piston and multi-purpose grease to the oil seal lip. Do not rotate the side cover during installation to prevent damage to the O-ring. Wrap tape around the splined end of the cross-shaft to prevent damage to the seals.
40. Measure the total starting torque of the input wormshaft to neutral position (center), using the proper tool. Make sure the ball screw operates smoothly throughout its entire travel. Starting torque should be between 4.4–7.8 inch lbs.
41. Install the pitman arm on the cross-shaft and tighten the pitman arm nut to 94–108 ft. lbs.

Adjustments

STEERING GEAR BACKLASH

1. Inject a small amount of gear oil into the breather plug and lubricate the bearing parts and the gear teeth of each shaft.
2. Tighten the adjusting bolt until it engages the gear teeth. Rotate the pitman arm back and forth to make sure it is engaged with the gear teeth.
3. Position a suitable indicator at the end of the pitman arm and move the pitman arm to measure the backlash. The steering gear backlash limit is 0.02 in.
4. Turn the adjusting bolt in or out to adjust the backlash.

NOTE: Measure the steering gear backlash when the mainshaft, cross-shaft and the pitman arm in the straight-ahead position.

5. The steering gear backlash should be 0.020 in.

Power Rack and Pinion

Disassembly and Assembly

1. Secure the rack housing in a suitable holding fixture.
2. Loosen the locknut and remove the tie rod end.
3. Disconnect the bellows band and remove the bellows.
4. Lift up the tab washer caulking and remove the tie rod from the rack housing
5. Disconnect the tab washer and dust cover and remove the feed tubes from the rack.
6. Disconnect the end plug caulking and remove the end plug.
7. Disconnect the locking nut and remove the rack support cover, using the proper tool.
8. Take out the rack support spring and remove the rack support.
9. Remove the snapring, using the proper tool, and pull out the pinion and valve assembly with the oil seals
10. Rotate the rack clockwise until the end of the circlip comes out of the slot in the rack housing.
11. Turn the rack stopper counterclockwise to remove the circlip.
12. Pull the rack out slowly and remove the rack stopper and the rack bushing at the same time.
13. Using the proper tool, remove the oil seals and the bearings from the rack housing.

To assemble:

14. Assembly is the reverse of the removal procedure. Clean all the parts and check for any damage or excessive wear.
15. Press the backup washer and the oil seal into the rack housing, using the proper tool.
16. Lubricate the bearing and the seal with the proper transmission fluid and install into the rack housing, using a suitable tool.

NOTE: Press the bearing in straight, as the valve housing is aluminum. Be sure the oil seal faces in the correct direction.

17. Lubricate the oil seal for the rack bushing and install the oil seal until it touches the rack bushing end.
18. Apply a coating of multi-purpose grease to the rack teeth. Align the oil seal center with the rack and slowly, insert the rack from the power cylinder side.
19. Wrap the end of the rack with a vinyl tape, lubricate with transmission fluid and install the rack bushing and the rack stopper.

NOTE: Do not allow the oil seal retainer to slip out.

20. Align the rack stopper mark with the cylinder hole and install the circlip while turning the rack stopper clockwise.
21. Press fit the oil seal, using the proper tool.
22. Apply the proper sealant to the threaded part of the end plug and install the end plug.
23. Secure the threaded part of the end plug at 2 places, using a suitable punch.
24. Adjust the total pinion torque and install the tie rods to the rack and fold the tab washer into position.

Adjustments

TOTAL PINION TORQUE

1. Position the rack at it is centered.
2. Tighten the rack support cover to 11 ft. lbs., using the proper tool.
3. In the neutral position, rotate the pinion shaft clockwise, one turn in 4–6 seconds. Return the rack support cover 30–60 degrees and adjust the torque to 6–12 inch lbs.
4. Lock the rack cover support with the locknut.

Bevel Gear Assembly

Disassembly and Assembly

1. Secure the gear assembly in a proper holding fixture.
2. Remove the locknut using the proper tool.
3. Remove the front cover mounting bolts, adjusting bolt and remove the front cover.
4. Remove the locknut and loosen the rear cover with the proper tool, until the input gear separates from the output gear.
5. Remove both the input gear and the output gear from the housing.
6. Inspect the gear teeth, bearings and the dust cover for any cracks or excessive damage.

To assemble:

7. Assembly is the reverse of the removal procedure. Install the input and the output gear into the gear housing so the teeth mesh properly.
8. Tighten the rear cover, using the proper tool. Replace the locknut and tighten to 47–87 ft. lbs. depending on which tool was used.
9. Install the front cover and replace the mounting bolts. Tighten to 12–19 ft. lbs.
10. Install the adjusting bolt and replace the locknut and tighten to 12–19 ft. lbs.

Adjustments

OUTPUT GEAR ROTATIONAL TORQUE

1. Turn the output gear, using the proper tool, at a speed of one rotation every 4–6 seconds. Measure the rotational torque.
2. Adjust the nut so the output side gear rotational torque is 0.4–0.9 inch lbs.
3. Tighten the locknut to 47–87 ft. lbs., depending on which tool was used.

TOTAL BEVEL GEAR ROTATIONAL TORQUE

1. Turn the input gear, using the proper tool, at a speed of one rotation every 4–6 seconds. Measure the rotational torque.

NOTE: Return the adjustment bolt to a position where there is no contact with the input side gear.

2. Using the proper tool, tighten the rear cover assembly so the input side gear rotational torque is 2–4 inch lbs.
3. Tighten the adjustment bolt so the total bevel gear rotational torque is 3–5 inch lbs.
4. Install the locknut and tighten to 47–87 ft. lbs., depending on which tool was used.

NISSAN

Recirculating Ball

Disassembly and Assembly

MODEL PB56S

1. Secure the gear assembly in suitable holding fixture.

2. Remove the adjusting screw locknut and replace the O-ring.
3. Set the stub shaft in a straight-ahead position. The straight-ahead position is where the stub shaft is turned 2.14 turns from the lock position.
4. Disconnect the sector shaft cover bolt.

Exploded view of Model PR26C power rack and pinion steering gear assembly—Nissan

Adjustments

TURNING TORQUE

1. Measure the turning torque at a 360 degrees position.
2. Turn the stub shaft all the way to the right and left several times.
3. Measure the turning torque at 360 degrees position from the straight ahead position (6–11 inch lbs.). If it is beyond specification, the gear must be replaced as an assembly.
4. Measure the torque at a straight ahead position.
5. Set the worm gear in the straight ahead position. This is 2.13 turns from the lock position.
6. Measure the turning torque at this position. It should be 1–3½ inch lbs. higher than at 360 degrees.
7. After the adjustment is completed, tighten the locknut to 25–30 ft. lbs. If the turning torques are not within specification, replace the gear assembly.

Power Rack and Pinion

Disassembly and Assembly

MODEL PR26SC

1. Secure the gear assembly in a suitable holding fixture and drain the fluid.
2. Prior to disassembling, measure the pinion rotating torque. Record the pinion rotating torque as a reference.
3. Remove the pinion gear being careful not to damage the pinion gear when removing the pinion seal ring.
4. Remove the tie rod outer sockets and boots.
5. Loosen the tie rod inner socket by prying up on the staked portion. Remove the inner socket.
6. Remove the adjusting screw, spring, spring seat and lift out the retainer.

7. Remove the rear housing cover and assembly. Remove the pinion assembly.

8. Drill the staked portion of the gear housing with a drill of 0.079–0.098 in. diameter, until the staking is eliminated.

9. Remove the end cover, using the proper tool. Draw out the rack assembly.

10. Remove the rack seal ring. Heat the ring with approximately 104°F of heat to remove.

NOTE: Be careful not to damage the rack.

11. Remove the center bushing and the rack oil seal using the proper tool. Do not scratch the inner surfaces of the pinion housing.

To assemble:

12. Heat the rack seal ring and install it onto the rack.

13. Compress the rack seal ring into position and secure it on the rack with the proper tool. Always insert the tool from the rack side.

14. Place a plastic film into the rack oil seal to prevent damage to the rack teeth.

15. Insert the rack oil seal into position and remove the plastic film. Make sure the lips of the oil seal face each other.

16. Install the center bushing and the rack oil seal with the rack assembly.

17. Replace the end cover assembly and tighten to 43–54 ft. lbs., using the proper tool.

18. Set the rack in a neutral position.

19. Lubricate the lip of the oil seal with a multi-purpose grease and install the new oil seal to the housing, using the proper tool.

20. Install the pinion bearing adjusting shims, using the same number of shims that were removed.

21. Heat the pinion seal and install it on the pinion gear assembly. Make sure the pinion seal ring is properly settled in the valve groove.

22. Lubricate the oil seal lip and the needle bearing roller. Install the pinion assembly to the pinion housing of the gear housing.

NOTE: Be careful not to damage the pinion oil seal.

23. Lubricate the rear oil seal with a multi-purpose grease and install the seal into the rear housing, using the proper tool.

24. Install the rear cover cap being careful not to damage the worm ring and the oil seal.

25. Install the retainer spring and the adjusting screw temporarily.

26. Install the new lock plate and screw the inner socket into the rack and tighten to 58–72 ft. lbs. Cinch the 2 places of the lock plate at the racks groove.

27. Install the outer tie rod and tighten the locknut to 27–34 ft. lbs. on 2WD vehicles or 58–72 ft. lbs. on 4WD vehicles.

28. Coat the surfaces between the tie rod and the boot with grease and install the boot.

29. Install the boot clamps, making sure the clamps do not contact the boot.

Adjustments
PINION ROTATING TORQUE

1. Set the gears to neutral without fluid in the gear. Lightly tighten the adjusting screw.

2. Tighten the adjusting screw to 43–52 inch lbs.

3. Loosen the adjusting screw, then retighten the screw to ½–1¾ inch lbs.

4. Move the rack over it's entire stroke several times.

5. Measure the rotating pinion torque within a range of 180 degrees from the neutral position. Stop the gear at the point of maximum torque.

6. Loosen the adjusting screw, then retighten to 43–52 inch lbs.

7. Loosen the adjusting screw by 40–60 degrees and tighten the locknut to 30–44 ft. lbs.

8. Check the steering gear for the rack sliding frictional force. Around the neutral point of the rack stroke the frictional force should be 28–38 lbs., except for the neutral point which should be 28–42 lbs.

9. Measure the pinion rotating torque within a range of plus or minus 100 degrees from the neutral point. The average rotating torque is 7–11 inch lbs. The maximum rotating torque is 16 inch lbs. and the minimum is 5 inch lbs.

SUZUKI

Recirculating Ball

The power steering gear assembly is not serviceable. If a malfunction occurs, replace with a new unit.

TOYOTA

Recirculating Ball

Disassembly and Assembly

1. Secure the gear housing in a suitable holding fixture.

2. Remove the bolts, solenoid valve and the O-rings on 2WD vehicles.

3. Remove the adjusting screw locknut and the 4 bolts. Screw in the adjusting screw and remove the end cover.

4. Tap on the cross-shaft with the proper tool and remove the cross-shaft.

5. Remove the plunger guide nut, using the proper tool.

6. Remove the spring, plunger, plunger guide and pry out the O-ring.

7. Remove the cap bolts from the housing.

8. Turn the wormshaft clockwise while holding the power piston nut so it cannot move. Pull out the valve body and the power piston assembly.

NOTE: Make sure the power piston nut does not come off the wormshaft.

9. Remove the O-ring, using the proper tool.

10. Secure the valve body in a suitable holding fixture. Move the worm gear up and down to check the ball clearance. The maximum clearance is 0.0059 in.

11. Secure the cross-shaft in a suitable holding fixture and check the adjusting screw thrust clearance. The thrust clearance is 0.0012–0.0020 in.

12. Pry out the oil seal and remove the snapring with the proper tools.

WASHER
BLEEDER PLUG
END COVER
O-RING
LOCKNUT
CROSS-SHAFT ADJUSTING SCREW
CROSS-SHAFT
SOLENOID VALVE
O-RING
NEEDLE ROLLER BEARING
UNION SEAT
PLUNGER GUIDE NUT
O-RING
SPRING
O-RING
PLUNGER GUIDE
PLUNGER
WORM GEAR VALVE ASSEMBLY
GEAR HOUSING
TEFLON RING   O-RING
O-RING
TEFLON RING
SPACER
SNAPRING
OIL SEAL

Exploded view of typical power steering gear assembly—Toyota

13. Remove the metal spacer, Teflon® ring and the O-ring. Press out the bearing.

To assemble:

14. Install a new lower bearing with the proper tool so it is positioned 0.909 in. away from the housing inner end surface.

15. Install a new upper bearing with the proper tool so it aligns with the housing end surface.

16. Install a new O-ring, metal spacer and replace the snapring.

17. Insert a new Teflon® ring into the housing.

NOTE: The Teflon® ring must be squeezed before installing the sector shaft or damage may result.

18. Drive a new seal into the housing, using the proper tool.

19. If necessary, replace the control valve Teflon® ring. Be careful not to damage or over expand the Teflon® ring.

20. If necessary, replace the union seat.

21. Install the O-rings to the gear housing and the valve body. Install the 4 bolts and tighten 34 ft. lbs.

22. Check the worm gear preload. The preload should be; 3–5 inch lbs.

23. Install the plunger, plunger guide and the spring.

24. Install a new O-ring to the plunger guide nut. Replace the nut and tighten to 15 ft. lbs.

25. Install a new O-ring on the end cover and assemble the cross-shaft to the end cover.

26. Loosen the adjusting screw and set the worm gear at the center of the housing.

27. Insert and push the cross-shaft into the gear housing so the center teeth mesh together.

28. Install the mounting bolts and tighten to 34 ft. lbs.

29. Turn the wormshaft fully in both directions to determine the exact center position. Place matchmarks on the wormshaft and the housing to show the neutral position.

30. Install new O-rings to the solenoid valve and insert the solenoid valve. Tighten the bolts to 7 ft. lbs. on 2WD vehicles.

Adjustments

THRUST CLEARANCE

1. Secure the cross-shaft in a suitable holding fixture.

2. Remove the locknut stake, using the proper tool. Loosen the locknut.

3. Turn the adjusting screw for correct clearance; 0.0012–0.0020 in.

4. Tighten and stake the locknut.

WORM BEARING PRELOAD

1. Remove the locknut, using the proper tool.

2. Tighten the adjusting screw and turn the wormshaft to the right and the left to snug the bearing.

3. Slightly loosen the adjusting screw.

4. Tighten the adjusting screw with the proper tool until the preload is correct. The preload should be 2½–5 inch lbs.

TOTAL PRELOAD

1. Install a suitable torque wrench on the center wormshaft.

2. Turn the adjusting screw until the preload is correct.

3. The total preload should be 4–8 inch lbs.

Bevel Gear

Disassembly and Assembly

1. Secure the gear in a suitable holding fixture.

2. Remove both dust covers and the adjusting screw locknut.

3. Remove the adjusting screw with the proper tool and pull out the spring.

4. Remove the housing cover bolts and remove the housing cover.

5. Loosen the locknut and adjusting bolt. Remove the plate set bolts and plate.

6. Take out the adjusting bolt seat, spring and spring holder. Wipe the grease off the gear teeth.

7. Inspect the tooth contact between the No. 1 and No. 2 bevel gear.

8. Push in the No. 2 bevel gear and pull out the No. 1 bevel gear and thrust washer.

9. Tap out the No. 2 bevel gear and remove the bearing and spring retainer.

10. Inspect all the components for any damage or excessive wear.

To assemble:

11. If necessary, replace the No. 1 bevel gear oil seal. Remove and replace, using the proper tool.

12. If necessary, replace the No. 2 bevel gear oil seal. Remove and replace, using the proper tool.

13. Pack these components with molybdenum disulphide lithium base grease.

14. Insert the No. 2 gear into the housing. Use a suitable tool to press in the bearing.

15. Install the thrust washer to the No. 1 bevel gear.

16. Install the No. 1 bevel gear into the housing.

NOTE: Line up the cutout portion of the No. 1 and No. 2 bevel gear.

17. Install the spring with the spring holder to the No. 2 bevel gear.

18. Install the plate with the 2 bolts and tighten to 69 inch lbs.

19. Install the adjusting bolt seat. Screw in the adjusting bolt until it touches the seat.

20. Using the proper tool adjust the No. 1 bevel gear preload. Adjust to 0.7–1.3 inch lbs.

21. Hold the adjusting bolt and install the locknut, tighten to 7 ft. lbs.

22. Install the spring retainer into the housing

23. Install the spring to the adjusting screw and apply a sealant to the threads of the adjusting screw.

24. Install the adjusting screw to the housing.

25. Using the proper tool, tighten the adjusting screw until the No. 1 and No. 2 bevel gears backlash is zero. Turn the No. 1 bevel gear left and right a couple times and snug it.

26. Loosen the adjusting screw to set the total preload; total preload should be 1.3–3.5 inch lbs.

NOTE: When loosening the adjusting screw make sure the backlash is not more than 0.0142 in.

27. Install the adjusting screw locknut and tighten to 64 ft. lbs. Pack molybdenum disulphide lithium base grease into the gear housing.

28. Apply the proper sealant to the contact surface of the housing cover and install the cover. Tighten the bolts to 69 inch lbs.

29. Install the 2 dust covers.

Power Rack and Pinion

Disassembly and Assembly

1. Secure the gear housing in a suitable holding fixture.

2. Remove the left and the right turn pressure tubes with the proper tool.

3. Loosen the locknuts and make matchmarks on the tie rod ends and the rack ends. Remove the tie rod ends and the locknuts.

4. Remove the clips, clamps and the rack boots.

5. Unstake the claw washers to remove the rack ends and the claw washers.

Exploded view of typical bevel gear power steering gear assembly—Toyota

TIE ROD END

TEFLON RING

O-RING

CLIP

CLAW WASHER

RACK

RACK BOOT

RACK END

O-RING

PRESSURE TUBE

CLAMP

CYLINDER END STOPPER

OIL SEAL

SPACER

O-RING

RACK HOUSING

CONTROL VALVE

OIL SEAL

SEAT

CONTROL VALVE HOUSING

RACK GUIDE

DUST COVER

SPRING

RACK GUIDE SPRING CLAMP

LOCKNUT

TEFLON RING

BEARING GUIDE NUT

BEARING

OIL SEAL

Exploded view of typical power rack and pinion steering gear assembly—Toyota

6. Remove the rack guide spring cap locknut, using the proper tool.

7. Remove the rack guide, spring and the seat.

8. Place matchmarks on the valve housing and the rack housing. Remove the mounting bolts.

9. Pull out the valve with the valve housing and remove the O-ring.

10. Remove the stopper nut with the proper tool. Pry out the O-ring.

11. Using a press, remove the oil seal and the rack.

NOTE: Be careful not to damage the inside of the cylinder tube.

12. Remove the oil seal with the spacer.

13. Remove the dust cover and loosen the bearing guide nut.

14. Tap out the control valve with the bearing guide nut and remove the O-ring, using the proper tool.

15. Inspect the rack for teeth wear and damage. Check for runout; maximum runout is 0.012 in.

16. If necessary, replace the control valve bearing and the oil seal. Press out the oil seal and the bearing, using the proper tool.

To assemble:

17. Coat the lip of the oil seal with power steering fluid and install into the control valve housing.

18. Press the new bearing into the control valve housing with the proper tool.

19. If necessary, replace the bearing nut guide oil seal. Use the proper tool to tap out and press in the new seal.

20. If necessary, replace the Teflon® ring and the O-ring. Pry out the Teflon® ring and the O-ring.

NOTE: Be careful not to damage the steering rack.

21. Install a new O-ring and Teflon® ring. Coat the Teflon® ring with power steering fluid and snug it down with your fingers.

22. If necessary, replace the control valve Teflon® rings. Use the proper tool to remove and install the rings.

23. If necessary, replace the union seat. Use the proper tool to remove and install the seat.

24. Lubricate moving parts on the rack assembly with molybdenum disulphide lithium base grease.

25. Coat the oil seal lip with power steering fluid. Install the oil seal and the spacer into the rack housing, using the proper tool.

26. Place the protective sleeve onto the rack, coat the sleeve with power steering fluid.

27. Insert the rack into the cylinder and remove the protective sleeve.

28. Coat the oil seal with power steering fluid and wrap vinyl tape in the steering rack end.

29. Install the oil seal by pushing it into the cylinder, without tilting.

30. Install a new O-ring to the end stopper, tighten to 58 ft. lbs. Stake the housing and the stopper.

31. Coat the Teflon® ring and the O-ring with power steering fluid. Install the O-ring to the control valve housing. Push the control valve into the housing.

32. Install the bearing guide nut with the proper tool and tighten to 18 ft. lbs.

33. Stake the nut and install the dust cover.

34. Install a new O-ring to the valve housing. Align the marks on the valve housing and the rack housing.

35. Install the control valve and tighten the bolts to 13 ft. lbs.

36. Install the rack guide, seat and rack guide spring.

37. Apply a sealant to the threads of the spring cap and install the rack guide spring cap.

38. Using the proper tool, torque the rack guide spring cap to 18 ft. lbs. Return the rack guide spring cap 30 degrees.

39. Turn the control valve shaft right and left a couple of times. Loosen the spring cap until the rack guide compression spring is not functioning.

40. Tighten the rack guide spring cap until the preload is 8–12 inch lbs.

41. Apply a sealant to the screws of the spring cap locknut. Install the locknut and tighten to 41 ft. lbs.

42. Stake the locknut and the cap. Install new claw washers.

NOTE: Align the claw of the claw washer with the rack groove.

43. Install the rack ends and tighten them to 65 ft. lbs. Stake the claw washer.

44. Install the rack boots, clamps and clips. Make sure the tube hole is not clogged with grease.

45. Screw the locknuts and the tie rod ends onto the rack ends until the matchmarks are aligned. Tighten the locknuts to 50 ft. lbs.

46. Install new union seats and replace the right and left turn pressure tubes, tighten to 14 ft. lbs.

VOLKSWAGEN

The rack and pinion steering gear is not adjustable or serviceable, it must be replaced as a complete unit.

POWER STEERING PUMPS

STEERING TROUBLE DIAGNOSIS
Power Steering Pump

Condition	Possible Cause	Correction
No assist	1. Pump seizure.	1. Replace pump.
	2. Broker slipper spring(s).	2. Recondition pump or replace as necessary.
	3. Flow control bore plug ring not in place.	3. Replace snapring. Inspect groove for depth.
	4. Flow control valve sticking.	4. Pressure test pump and service as necessary.
No assist when parking only	1. Wrong pressure relief valve.	1. Install proper relief valve.
	2. Broken "O" ring on flow control bore plug.	2. Replace "O" ring.
	3. Loose pressure relief valve.	3. Tighten valve.
	4. Low pump efficiency.	4. Pressure test pump and service as necessary.
Noisy pump	1. Low fluid level.	1. Inspect and correct fluid level.
	2. Belt noise.	2. Inspect for pulley alignment, paint or grease on pulley and correct. Adjust belt.
	3. Foreign material blocking pump housing oil inlet hole.	3. Remove reservoir, visually check inlet oil hole and service as necessary.

STEERING TROUBLE DIAGNOSIS
Power Steering Pump

Condition	Possible Cause	Correction
Intermittent assist	1. Flow control valve sticking.	1. Pressure test pump and service as necessary.
	2. Slipping belt.	2. Adjust belt.
	3. Low fluid level.	3. Inspect and correct fluid level.
	4. Low pump efficiency.	4. Pressure test pump and service as necessary.
Pump vibration	1. Pump hose interference with sheet metal or brake lines.	1. Reroute hoses.
	2. Belt loose.	2. Adjust belt.
	3. Pulley loose or out of round.	3. Replace pulley.
	4. Crankshaft pulley loose or damaged.	4. Replace crankshaft pulley.
	5. Bracket pivot bolts loose.	5. If unable to tighten, replace bracket.
Pump leaks	1. Cap or filler neck leaks.	1. Correct fluid level.
	2. Reservoir solder joints leak.	2. Resolder or replace reservoir as necessary.
	3. Reservoir "O" ring leaking.	3. Inspect sealing area of reservoir. Replace "O" ring or reservoir as necessary.
	4. Shaft seal leaking.	4. Replace seal.
	5. Loose rear bracket bolts.	5. Tighten bolts.
	6. Loose or faulty high pressure ferrule.	6. Tighten fitting.
	7. Rear bolt holes stripped or casting cracked.	7. Repair, if possible, or replace pump.
Objectionable hiss	1. Noisy valve	1. Do not replace valve unless "hiss" is extremely objectionable. A replacement valve will also exhibit slight noise and is not always a cure for the objection.
Rattle or chuckle noise in steering gear	1. Gear loose on frame.	1. Check gear mounting bolts. Torque bolts to specifications.
	2. Steering linkages looseness.	2. Check linkage pivot points for wear. Replace if necessary.
	3. Pressure hose touching other parts of truck.	3. Adjust hose position. Do not bend tubing by hand.
	4. Loose Pitman shaft over center adjustment. **NOTE:** A slight rattle may occur on turns because of increased clearance off the "high point". This is normal and clearance must not be reduced below specified limits to eliminate this slight rattle.	4. Adjust.
	5. Loose Pitman arm.	5. Torque Pitman arm pinch bolt.

CHRYSLER CORPORATION

Vane Type Pump

Disassembly and Assembly

1. Secure pump securely in a suitable holding device.
2. Remove the pump pulley, using a proper puller.
3. Remove the mounting brackets from the pump.
4. Remove the 2 mounting studs and the pressure hose fittings. Gently tap the reservoir tube back and forth and remove the reservoir from the pump body.

5. Using a punch, tap the end cover retaining ring until one end of the ring is near the hole in the pump body. Insert the punch in the hole far enough to disengage the ring from the groove in the pump bore and remove the ring.

6. Tap the end cover with a plastic hammer to jar it loose and remove the cover.

7. Remove the pump body and place in a inverted position on a flat surface and tap the end of the driveshaft with a plastic hammer to loosen the pressure plate, rotor and thrust plate assembly from the pump body.

Exploded view of typical vane type power steering pump assembly—Chrysler

8. Lift the pump body from the rotor assembly. The flow control valve and spring should slide out of the bore.

a. Remove the valve from the holding fixture and remove the pressure relief ball, guide and spring.

b. Install the spring, guide and pressure relief ball in the end of the flow control valve.

c. Install the flow valve spring and the valve in the bore.

9. Pry out the driveshaft oil seal. Clean and inspect the seal bore in the housing.

10. Disconnect the pressure plate and the cam ring from the rotor and remove the 10 vanes from the slots in the rotor.

11. Secure the driveshaft in a suitable holding fixture.

12. Remove the rotor lock ring and pry off the driveshaft.

13. Remove the rotor and the thrust plate from the shaft. Discard the lock ring, the reservoir O-rings, the 2 mounting stud and the pressure fitting O-rings.

14. Clean and inspect all the parts.

To assemble:

15. Assembly is the reverse of the removal procedure. Install the new driveshaft seal into the bore until the seal bottoms on the shoulder, using the proper tool.

16. Lubricate the seal with power steering fluid and secure the pump body in a suitable fixture.

17. Install the end cover and pressure plate O-rings in the grooves of the pump cavity. Lubricate with power steering fluid.

18. Lubricate the large pump body to reservoir O-ring and install on the pump body.

19. With the driveshaft secure, install the thrust plate on the driveshaft with the ported side up.

20. Slide the rotor over the splines with the counterbore of the rotor facing down. Install the rotor lock ring making sure the ring is seated in the groove.

NOTE: Regardless of which locking ring was originally used, always replace with a new ring.

21. Install 2 dowel pins in the holes in the pump cavity. Insert the driveshaft, rotor and thrust plate assembly into the pump cavity.

22. Slide the cam ring over the rotor on the dowel pins with the arrow on the ring facing UP.

23. Install the 10 vanes in the rotor slots and lubricate with power steering fluid.

24. Place the pressure plate on the dowel pins. Install the pressure plate assembly on the O-ring in the pump cavity with the proper tool.

25. Place the spring in the groove in the pressure plate and position the end cover lip edge up over the spring.

26. Press the end cover down below the retaining ring groove and install the retaining ring. Make sure it is seated in the groove.

27. Tap the retainer ring ends around in the groove until the gap is in line with the flow control valve bore.

28. Install the reservoir, the 2 mounting stud and the flow control valve O-ring on the pump body.

29. Lubricate with power steering fluid and position the reservoir on the pump body.

30 Tap the reservoir down on the pump and insert the flow control valve spring and the valve with the slotted end up.

31. Replace the O-ring on the pressure hose fitting and install the pressure hose fitting and tighten to 35 ft. lbs. Tighten the mounting studs to 35 ft. lbs.

NOTE: Be sure the O-ring is installed on the upper groove of the pressure hose fitting.

32. Install the pulley on the shaft using the proper tool.

FORD MOTOR COMPANY

Saginaw Pump

Disassembly and Assembly

1. Drain as much fluid as possible and clean the outside of the pump.
2. Remove the bracket and the pulley from the pump using a suitable pulley remover tool.
3. Clamp the front hub of the pump in a suitable holding device so the extending portion of the shaft points down.

NOTE: Do not clamp the pump too tightly or bearing damage might occur.

4. Remove the pressure union, O-ring assembly and both mounting bolts from the back of the reservoir. Discard the seals and the O-rings.
5. Rock the reservoir slightly back and forth to unseat the O-ring seal. Remove the O-ring and discard.
6. Remove the reservoir.
7. Remove the mounting bolt and the pressure union seals from the counterbored spaces in the pump housing. Discard the seals.
8. Rotate the end plate retaining ring so one end of the ring is over the hole in the housing. Insert a small punch in the ⅛ in. diameter hole in the housing opposite the flow control valve hole.
9. Compress the retaining ring with the punch and pry out the retaining ring.
10. Remove the end plate. The end plate is spring loaded and will generally sit above the housing level for easy removal. If the plate sticks, rock it back and forth to free remove it.
11. Remove the pressure plate spring.
12. Remove the pump from the holding device and turn it over to allow the flow control valve and spring to fall out.

NOTE: Do not disassemble the flow control valve. Service it as a unit.

13. Tap the end of the shaft lightly until the pressure plate falls free.
14. Remove the cam ring and the vanes from the rotor.
15. Remove the retaining ring by clamping the shaft in a proper holding device and pry the ring off the shaft. Do not damage the shaft. Discard the retaining ring.
16. Remove the thrust plate from the shaft and both dowel pins from the housing.
17. Remove the pressure plate and end plate O-ring seals from the housing bore and discard them.
18. Remove the shaft seal only if it is worn and damaged. Removal will destroy the seal.
   a. To remove the rotor shaft seal insert a sharp tool between the rotor shaft seal and the housing. Pry out the seal. Do not pry against the shaft or the housing bore.
   b. Place the new seal on the shaft with the metal backing facing the pulley end of the shaft.
   c. Install the seal using a suitable seal installer tool.

To assemble:
19. Clean all the metal parts with the proper solvent.
20. Lubricate a new pressure plate O-ring seal with a premium power steering fluid or equivalent and install it in the third groove from the rear of the housing.
21. Clamp the end hub of the housing in a suitable holding device with the extending portion of the shaft pointing down. Do not clamp too tightly.
22. Insert both dowel pins and install the thrust plate on the shaft with the ports facing the splined end of the shaft.
23. Install the rotor on the shaft with the counterbored end toward the thrust plate.
24. Clamp the shaft in a proper holding device.
25. Install a new retaining ring on the splined end of the shaft by prying the ring open and sliding it down over the shaft until it seats in the ring groove. Do not damage the shaft.
26. Insert the shaft in the housing and lubricate with a suitable power steering fluid. Make sure the thrust plate slides properly on the dowel pins.

Exploded view of typical Saginaw vane type power steering pump assembly—Ford

SEAL

DISC SPRING

PUMP HOUSING PLATE

CAM AND ROTOR ASSEMBLY

RETAINER

C-CLIP

SHAFT

SHAFT SEAL

LOWER PLATE

HIGH DISPLACEMENT CAM

SEAL

SEAL

CAP

DOWEL PINS

RESERVOIR

VALVE COVER

VALVE ASSEMBLY

SEAL

RETAINING RING

SPRING

SEAL

OUTLET FITTING

UPPER PLATE

Exploded view of typical C-11 type power steering pump assembly—Ford

27. Install the cam ring on the dowel pins with the rotation arrow toward the rear of the housing.

28. Install the vanes in the rotor slots with the rounded edge of the vanes facing out. Make sure the vanes slide freely.

29. Lubricate the pressure plate with premium power steering fluid.

30. Install the pressure plate on the dowel pins with the circular spring depression toward the rear of the housing. The narrow slots in the plate should engage the dowel pins.

31. Press the pressure plate over the O-ring about $\frac{1}{16}$ of an in. to seat properly.

32. Lubricate a new end plate O-ring and install it in the second groove from the rear of the housing.

33. Install the pressure plate spring in the groove in the pressure plate.

34. Lubricate the end plate with a suitable power steering fluid and press it in the housing, using a suitable arbor press. Depress the end plate just enough to install the retaining ring in its groove.

35. Install the end plate retaining ring and release the press.

36. Place the control valve spring in it's hole and insert the control valve, with the screened end facing the front of the housing.

37. Install new mounting bolt and pressure union seals in the countersunk holes.

38. Lubricate a new O-ring seal and install it on the housing.

39. Lubricate the inside edge of the reservoir with power steering fluid and install it on the housing. Align the holes in the reservoir with the housing.

40. Install the mounting bolts and tighten to 35 ft. lbs.

41. Lubricate a new O-ring and install it on the pressure union in the groove next to the head hex. Insert the pressure union in the flow control valve hole in the back of the reservoir and tighten to 25–30 ft. lbs.

C-II Pump

Disassembly and Assembly

1. Drain as much fluid as possible and clean the outside of the pump.

2. Remove the bracket and the pulley from the pump using a suitable pulley remover tool

3. Remove the outlet fitting, flow control valve and the spring from the pump.

4. Remove the pump reservoir.

5. Place a C-clamp or equivalent in a suitable holding device.

6. Place the lower support plate tool or equivalent over the pump rotor shaft and install the upper compressor plate tool or equivalent over the pump rotor shaft.

7. Holding the upper compressor tool, place the pump assembly in the C-clamp with the rotor shaft facing down.

NOTE: Position the contour of the upper compressor tool with the contour of the pump valve cover.

8. Tighten the C-clamp until a slight bottoming of the valve cover is felt.

9. Insert a suitable tool in the small hole in the side of the pump housing plate and push in on the valve cover retaining ring. Remove the ring.

10. Loosen the C-clamp. Remove the upper compressor plate and remove the pump assembly.

11. Remove the pump valve cover. Discard the O-ring seal.

12. Push on the rotor shaft. Remove the rotor shaft, upper plate, rotor and slippers, cam insert and the 2 dowel pins.

13. The lower plate and the disc spring will remain in the pump housing plate. To remove:

   a. Place the pump housing on a flat surface.

   b. Raise slightly and slam the housing plate down flatly until the lower plate and the disc spring fall out.

   c. Discard the O-rings.

Internal pump housing components of C-11 type power steering pump assembly—Ford

14. Remove the rotor shaft seal and the retainer at the same time by prying out with a proper tool.

NOTE: This method is only used when the pump is disassembled.

To assemble:

15. Place the rotor on the rotor shaft splines and install the retaining ring in the groove at the end of the rotor shaft.

16. Position the insert cam over the rotor. Be sure the recessed flat on the insert cam is facing the reservoir.

17. With the rotor extended about ½ way out of the cam, insert a spring in a rotor spring pocket.

18. Use one of the slippers to compress the spring and install the slipper with the narrow groove facing up.

19. Hold the cam stationary, turn the rotor to the left or the right, one space at a time and install another spring and slipper until all 10 rotor cavities have been filled.

NOTE: Be careful when turning the rotor, that the springs and the slippers already installed do not fall out.

20. Install a new rotor shaft seal using a suitable seal driver

tool. Using a plastic mallet, drive the seal into the bore until it bottoms out.

21. Install the seal retainer.
22. Place the pump housing plate on a flat surface, with the pulley side facing down.
23. Insert the lower pressure plate with the O-ring seals toward the front of the pump, into the pump housing plate and over the dowel pins.
24. Position the assembly on the C-clamp. Place the proper driver tool into the rotor shaft hole and press on the lower plate until it bottoms in the pump plate housing.
25. This will seat the outer O-ring.
26. Install the cam, rotor, slippers and the rotor shaft assembly into the pump housing plate over the dowel pins.

NOTE: When installing this assembly into the pump housing plate, the stepped holes must be used for dowel pins. The recessed notch in the cam insert must face toward the reservoir and be approximately 180 degrees opposite the square pump mounting boss.

27. Position the upper pressure plate over the dowel pins.
28. The square recess on the outside of the upper plate must be facing toward the reservoir and be 180 degrees opposite the pump square mounting boss.

29. Place a new O-ring seal on the valve cover and lubricate with power steering fluid.

NOTE: Be sure the plastic baffle is securely in place in the valve cover.

30. Insert the valve cover over the dowel pins. Make sure the outlet fitting hole in the valve cover is in line with the square mounting boss of the pump housing plate.
31. Place the assembly in the C-clamp tool and compress the valve cover into the pump housing plate, until the retaining ring groove is exposed in the pump housing plate.
32. Install the valve cover retaining ring with the ends near the hole in the pump housing plate.
33. Remove the pump assembly from the C-clamp tool.
34. Place a new O-ring on the pump housing plate and lubricate with power steering fluid.
35. Install the power steering reservoir.
36. Install the flow control spring and the flow control valve into the valve cover.
37. Place new O-ring seals on the outlet fitting and lubricate.
38. Install the outlet fitting into the valve cover and tighten to 24–34 ft. lbs.

GENERAL MOTORS CORPORATION

Saginaw Type P

Disassembly and Assembly

1. Drain the pump of any fluid. Clean the exterior of the pump.
2. Remove the reservoir mounting bolt and the line fitting. Remove the reservoir.
3. Pry off the retaining ring, using the proper tool. Remove the end plate and the pressure plate spring.
4. Remove the control valve, control valve spring and the O-ring.
5. Tap lightly on the driveshaft and remove the pressure plate.

6. Remove the pump ring and the vanes.
7. Remove the shaft retaining ring, pump rotor and the thrust plate.
8. Remove the driveshaft and pry the seal from the housing.
9. Remove the dowel pins, O-rings and the seal from the housing.
10. Clean all the parts with a suitable cleaning solvent. Lubricate the O-rings, pump ring, rotor and the vanes with power steering fluid.
To assemble:
11. Assembly is the reverse of the removal procedure. Install the dowel pins and the O-rings.
12. Insert the driveshaft seal using the proper tool. Install the O-ring, driveshaft and the thrust plate.

1.	Driveshaft
2.	Seal
3.	O-ring
4.	Housing
5.	O-ring
6.	Pin
7.	Thrust plate
8.	Filler cap
9.	Flow control valve
10.	Spring
11.	O-ring
12.	Pump rotor
13.	Retaining ring
14.	Vane
15.	Pump ring
16.	Pressure plate
17.	Pressure plate spring
18.	Housing end plate
19.	Retaining ring
20.	Seal
21.	Reservoir
22.	Bolt
23.	Seal
24.	Fitting

Exploded view of Saginaw type P power steering pump assembly—General Motors Corporation

A. Used on some models
1. Housing
2. Sleeve
3. Dowel pin
4. O-ring seal
5. Pressure plate spring
6. O-ring seal
7. Pressure plate
8. Dowel pin
9. Vane
10. Rotor
11. Pump ring
12. O-ring
13. Thrust plate
14. Retaining ring
15. Return tube
16. Driveshaft seal
17. Driveshaft
18. Bearing
19. Retaining ring
20. Flow control spring
21. Control valve
22. O-ring
23. Fitting
24. Reservoir
25. O-ring
26. Clips
27. Capstick

Exploded view of Saginaw type TC power steering pump assembly — General Motors Corporation

13. Install the rotor, making sure the counterbore portion of the rotor faces the driveshaft end of the housing.

14. Install the vanes with the rounded edge of the vane facing away from the rotor.

15. Install the driveshaft retaining ring, pump ring and the pressure plate in the housing.

16. Install the seal and the reservoir. Replace the mounting bolt and the fitting. Tighten the fitting to 75 ft. lbs.

Saginaw Type TC

Disassembly and Assembly

1. Clamp the pump in a suitable holding device. Remove the retaining clips, if equipped.

2. Remove the reservoir and the O-ring, or the return tube, if equipped.

3. Remove the fitting, flow control valve, flow control valve spring and the O-ring seal.

4. Remove the retaining ring, using suitable snapring pliers.

5. Remove the driveshaft and bearing. Pry out the driveshaft seal.

6. Insert a punch into the access hole and pry out the retaining ring.

7. Press out the thrust plate, using the proper tool and remove the O-ring seal.

8. Remove the pump ring, rotor, vanes and the dowel pins from the pump assembly.

9. Disconnect the pressure plate, O-ring, pressure plate ring and O-ring seal and remove the dowel pin.

10. Remove the sleeve from the pump housing. Clean all the parts with the proper cleaning solvent.

To assemble:

11. Assembly is the reverse of the removal procedure. Inspect all the parts for any burrs, chips or excessive wear. If heavy wear is present or parts are faulty, replace the entire rotating unit.

12. Install the return tube, if equipped.

13. Replace the dowel pin, O-ring seal and the pressure plate spring.

14. Install the pressure plat and mark the top of the pressure plate directly over the pin hole in the plate. Replace the dowel pin.

15. Lubricate the O-ring, pump ring, rotor and vanes with power steering fluid.

16. Install the vanes with the rounded edge of the vanes, facing away from the rotor.

17. Install the pump ring, making sure the identification marks are facing up. Replace the O-ring seal.

18. Install the thrust plate with the dimples in the thrust plate lining up with the bolt holes on the housing. Make sure the thrust plate engages the pump ring dowel pins

1. Return tube
2. Housing
3. Seal
4. Spring
5. Control valve
6. Seal
7. Fitting
8. Driveshaft
9. Thrust plate
10. Pump ring
11. Pump ring
12. Vanes
13. Pump rotor
14. Retaining ring
15. Pressure plate
16. Seal
17. Spring
18. Seal
19. End cover
20. Retaining ring

Exploded view of Saginaw type CB power steering pump assembly—General Motors Corporation

Exploded view of driveshaft subassembly—General Motors Corporation

Saginaw Type CB

Disassembly and Assembly

1. Remove the retaining ring, using a proper tool inserted into the access hole.
2. Push on the driveshaft and remove the O-ring, pressure plate spring, pump ring and the pump vanes and the driveshaft subassembly.
3. Pry out the O-ring from the pump housing. Remove the dowel pins and the driveshaft seal.
4. Remove the pressure plate, pressure plate spring and the O-ring from the end cover.
5. Remove the shaft retaining ring, pump rotor and the thrust plate from the driveshaft.
6. Clean and inspect the parts for any burrs, chips or excessive wear.

To assemble:

7. Assembly is the reverse of the removal procedure. Lubricate the new driveshaft seal with the proper power steering fluid and install in the pump housing, using the proper tool.
8. Place the dowel pins into the housing
9. Install the thrust plate, pump rotor and the retaining ring onto the driveshaft.
10. Install the driveshaft assembly into the pump housing and place the vanes into rotor.
11. Install the pump ring with the holes aligned with the dowel pins in the housing.
12. Lubricate the new O-ring with the proper power steering fluid and install into the groove in the housing.
13. Install the pressure plate and the pressure plate spring.
14. Lubricate the new O-ring with the proper power steering fluid and install in the end cover. Lubricate the outer edge of the end cover.
15. Press the end cover into the housing and replace the retaining ring into the groove in the housing

19. Compress the thrust plate and install the retaining ring. Align the opening of the ring with the bolt hole nearest the hole.
20. Install the driveshaft seal, using the proper tool, until the seal bottoms in the housing.
21. Press the bearing onto the driveshaft and slide the assembly into the housing while rotating the driveshaft so the shaft serrations engage with the rotor.
22. Replace the retaining ring with the proper snapring pliers.
23. Install the flow control spring and the flow control valve.
24. Replace the O-ring seal and the O-ring, using a suitable seal installer tool.
25. Install the pump reservoir to the housing and connect the clips, if equipped.

JEEP

Vane-Submerged Pump

Disassembly and Assembly

1. Secure the pump in a proper holding device with the pump shaft pointing down. Drain the fluid.

2. Remove the pressure hose fitting and the mounting stud. Discard the seals and the O-ring.
3. Tilt the reservoir back and forth to unseat the O-ring seal and remove the reservoir. Discard the O-ring.
4. Remove the mounting stud and the hose fitting seals from the counterbored spaces in the pump housing. Discard the seals.

1. O-ring
2. Capstick
3. Reservoir
4. End plate
5. Spring
6. Pressure plate
7. Ring
8. Snapring
9. Vanes
10. Rotor
11. Thrust plate
12. Dowel pin ring
13. Shaft
14. O-ring
15. O-ring
16. O-ring
17. Plug
18. Plug
19. Pump housing
20. Shaft seal
21. Bushing
22. Plug
23. O-ring
24. O-ring
25. Dowel pin ring
26. Flow control valve
27. Spring
28. O-ring
29. Retaining ring
30. Mounting stud
31. Fitting

Exploded view of vane-submerged type power steering pump—Jeep

5. Insert a small punch into the hole in the pump housing opposite the flow control valve orifice. Pry up the retaining ring and remove from the pump housing.

6. Remove the end plate and the spring from the pump housing. Tap it with a plastic hammer to loosen, if necessary.

7. Remove the pump housing from the holding device.

8. Invert the pump housing and remove the flow control valve and spring from the pump housing.

9. Tap the end of the pump shaft with a plastic hammer so the pressure plate, pump ring, rotor and the thrust plate can be removed as a unit.

10. Remove the retaining ring from the pump shaft. Discard the retaining ring.

11. Remove the pump ring, rotor and the thrust plate from the shaft. Use care to prevent dropping the rotor vanes.

12. Remove the end plate O-ring seal and the shaft seal.

13. Clean all the components and inspect for any damage. Lubricate with power steering fluid.

To assemble:

14. Install the pump shaft seal, using the proper tool.

15. Lubricate with petroleum jelly and install the replacement seal in the third groove in the housing.

16. Clamp the pump housing in a suitable holding device with the large bore facing down.

17. Insert both dowel pins in the thrust plate.

18. Insert the splined end of the pump shaft through the thrust plate and the rotor and install the retaining ring on the end of the shaft.

19. Open the retaining ring only wide enough to slide it over the end of the shaft. The rotor must slide freely on the splines.

20. Insert the pump shaft in the pump housing. Make sure the dowel pins are properly engaged in the thrust plate.

21. Install the pump ring on the dowel pins with the pump rotation arrow facing up.

22. Install all 10 rotor vanes in the rotor slots with the rounded edges of the vanes facing outward.

23. Install the pressure plate on the dowel pins with the plate spring groove facing upward.

24. Using the proper tool, force the pressure plate down approximately $\frac{1}{16}$ in. to seat it.

25. Lubricate the end plate seal with petroleum jelly and install it in the second groove in the housing.

26. Install the spring in the center groove in the pressure plate.

27. Lubricate the end plate outside diameter with petroleum jelly and install the plate in the pump housing.

28. Press the end plate down and install the end plate retaining ring.

29. Install the spring over the hexnut end of the flow control valve.

30. Install the flow control valve and the spring in the pump housing bore with the hexnut end of the valve facing the inside of the housing bore.

31. Install the mounting stud seals and the pump fitting seal in the counterbored holes in the pump housing.

32. Place the reservoir O-ring on the pump housing.

33. Lubricate the inner edge of the reservoir with petroleum jelly and place the reservoir on the pump housing. Press the reservoir down to seat it on the pump housing.

34. Install the mounting studs and tighten to 35 ft. lbs.

35. Install the seal on the flow control valve fitting and install the fitting in the flow control valve bore. Tighten the fitting to 35 ft. lbs.

Vane-Nonsubmerged Pump

Disassembly and Assembly

1. Secure the pump assembly in a suitable holding device. Drain the fluid from the pump.

2. Remove the flow control valve and the valve spring from the pump housing.

1. Retaining ring
2. Pump shaft bearing
3. Pump shaft
4. Pump shaft seal
5. Fitting
6. O-ring
7. Flow control valve
8. Spring
9. Pump housing
10. Return tube
11. Dowel pin
12. Sleeve
13. O-ring
14. Spring
15. O-ring
16. Pressure plate
17. Dowel pins
18. Vanes
19. Pump rotor
20. Pump ring
21. O-ring
22. Thrust plate
23. Retaining ring

Exploded view of vane-nonsubmerged type power steering pump—Jeep

3. Remove and discard the pump shaft retaining ring.

4. Support the pump shaft bearing on its inner race and force the pump shaft from the bearing.

5. Pry the pump shaft seal from the pump body, using a suitable tool. Remove the thrust plate retaining ring.

6. Force the thrust plate from the pump body and remove and discard the thrust plate O-ring seal.

7. Remove the pressure plate spring, the dowel pin and the pump shaft sleeve O-ring seal.

8. Remove the pump shaft sleeve, using the proper tool.

9. Clean all the components with the proper cleaning solvent and inspect for any damage.

NOTE: The flow control valve is serviced as a unit only and it must not be disassembled.

To assemble:

10. Install the pump shaft sleeve into the pump body bore, using the proper tool. Make sure the sleeve is completely seated in the bore.

11. Place a new O-ring seal in the sleeve seat and install the short dowel pin in the pump body.

12. Install the pressure plate spring over the pump shaft sleeve and place a new O-ring seal on the pressure plate.

13. Make a reference mark on the top of the pressure plate directly over the dowel pin hole.

14. Install the pressure plate in the pump body. Make sure the short dowel is completely seated in the pressure plate hole.

15. Insert the 2 pump ring dowel pins in the pressure plate and install the pump ring on the dowel pins.

16. Install the pump rotor with its counterbored end facing toward the pump shaft side of the pump body.

17. Install the vanes in the pump rotor with the rounded edge of the vanes facing out.

18. Place a new thrust plate O-ring seal in the pump body and position the thrust plate in the pump body.

19. Align the reference marks on the plate with the mounting bolt holes in the pump body. Make sure the thrust plate engages with the 2 pump ring dowel pins.

20. Force the thrust plate into the pump body and install the retaining ring.

21. Install a new shaft seal into the shaft bore until it contacts the end of the counterbore.

22. Press the bearing on the pump shaft, using a proper tool. Support the bearing on its inner race while pressing it on the shaft.

23. Insert the pump shaft and the bearing into the shaft bore in the pump body and rotate it until the splines mesh with the rotor. Make sure the shaft bearing is completely against the end of the bore in the pump body.

24. Install the new pump shaft retaining ring with the large lug placed to the right of the small lug.

CHRYSLER IMPORT

Vane Type Pump

Disassembly and Assembly

RAM 50

1. Secure the pump assembly in a suitable holding fixture. Drain the fluid from the pump.

2. Remove the pump cover mounting bolts and remove the pump cover.

3. Loosen and remove the suction port assembly and remove the pressure fitting.

NOTE: On vehicles with the reservoir attached, remove the mounting bolts and remove the reservoir.

1. Cover assembly
2. Seal washer
3. O-ring
4. Cam
5. Side plate
6. O-ring
7. Side plate spring
8. Pin
9. Pulley
10. Snapring
11. Protector
12. Shaft
13. Key
14. Bearing
15. Oil seal
16. Suction connector
17. O-ring
18. O-ring
19. O-ring
20. Connector assembly
21. O-ring
22. Flow control valve
23. Flow control valve spring
24. Oil pump body
25. Terminal assembly*
26. Plug*
27. O-ring*
28. Spring*
29. Piston rod*
30. Plunger*
31. Snapring*
32. Terminal*
33. Washer*
34. Insulator*
35. O-ring*
   *:3.0 Engine with A/T

Exploded view of typical power steering pump assembly for Ram 50 Pick-Up—Chrysler Import

1. Suction connector
2. O-ring
3. Plate
4. Suction plate
5. Suction tube
6. Reservoir bracket
7. Pump cover
8. Cam case
9. O-ring
10. Cam ring
11. Vane
12. Snapring
13. Rotor
14. Pulley
15. Oil seal
16. Connector
17. O-ring
18. Flow control valve
19. Flow control spring
20. Terminal assembly*
21. Plug*
22. O-ring*
23. Spring*
24. Piston rod*

25. Plunger*
26. Snapring*
27. Terminal*
28. Washer*
29. Insulator*
30. O-ring*
31. Oil pump body*
   * with A/T

Exploded view of typical power steering pump assembly for all except Ram 50 Pick-Up—Chrysler Import

4. Remove the cam ring, vanes, O-ring, side plate assembly and the dowel pins.

5. Remove the shaft assembly snapring and the protector.

6. Press out the shaft from the bearing and remove the shaft.

NOTE: Do not allow the shaft to drop.

7. Remove the oil seal with the proper tool. Remove the suction connector.

8. Remove the connector at the top of the pump body and remove the flow control valve assembly and flow control spring.

NOTE: Do not disassemble the flow control valve.

9. Clean and check all parts for any wear or excessive damage. Always use new gaskets and lubricate all the parts with Dexron® II before assembling.

To assemble:

10. Check the amount of play between the pump shaft and the pump body. The clearance should be 0.008 in.

11. Install the flow control valve spring, flow control valve and the connecter into the pump body. Tighten the connector to 51–58 ft. lbs.

12. Install the seal into the pump body, using a suitable seal installer.

13. Press the shaft into the bearing with the proper tool.

14. Lubricate the vanes with the proper fluid and install the vanes on the rotor. Position the vanes with the rounded edge facing cam ring.

15. When installing the cam ring, align the dowel pins of the pump body with the knock holes of the cam ring. Install so the cam ring's punch mark is at the pump body side.

16. Install the pump cover and tighten the mounting bolts to 24–31 ft. lbs.

17. Install the suction connector and tighten to 10-13 ft. lbs.

RAM RAIDER

1. Secure the pump assembly in a suitable holding fixture. Drain the fluid.

2. Disconnect the suction connector and remove the O-ring.

3. Disconnect the top connector and remove the O-ring.

NOTE: On vehicles with the reservoir attached, remove the mounting bolts and remove the reservoir.

4. Remove the flow control valve and the flow control spring from the pump housing. Do not disassemble the control valve.

5. Loosen the pump cover mounting bolts and remove the pump cover.

6. Remove the cam case, O-ring and the cam ring.

7. Remove the vanes and the snapring from the rotor. Remove the rotor.

8. Tap the side of the shaft and remove the pulley assembly.

9. Remove the oil seal using the proper tool.

10. Clean and inspect the parts for any wear and excessive damage.

To assemble:

11. Install the vanes to the rotor grooves. Measure the gap between the vane and the rotor groove. The distance should be 0.0024 in.

12. Install the seal into the pump body, using the proper tool.

13. Lubricate the rotor with the proper fluid and install the rotor with the punch mark side facing the pump cover.

14. Lubricate the vanes and the cam ring with the proper fluid.

15. Align the dowel pins of the pump body with the dowel holes of the cam ring.

16. Install the vanes to the rotor with the round edge facing the cam ring.

17. Install the flow control valve, spring, O-ring and the top connector. Tighten the connector to 29–43 ft. lbs.

18. Install the cam case, O-ring and the cam ring.

19. Replace the pump cover and tighten the mounting bolts to 13–16 ft. lbs.

20. Install the oil seal, using the proper tool. Replace the pulley.

21. Replace and tighten the suction connector to 4–7 ft. lbs.

DAIHATSU

Vane Type Pump

The only parts that may be serviced in the pump pressure system are the belt, hoses and the pulley. The pump itself should be replaced if defective. Specified fluid is Dexron® II.

GEO

Vane Type Pump

Disassembly and Assembly

1. Secure the pump in a suitable holding fixture and drain the fluid.

2. Remove the pulley using the proper puller.

3. Disconnect the pressure switch and remove the suction pipe connector.

4. Remove the pressure connector and take out the flow control valve.

5. Remove the pump cam ring and remove the rotor snapring, using the proper tool.

6. Remove the rotor and the vanes.

7. Remove the pump shaft and pry out the shaft oil seal with a suitable seal remover.

8. Clean and inspect all the parts for damage or excessive wear.

To assemble:

9. Lubricate all the parts with the proper power steering fluid.

10. Insert the shaft oil seal with the proper tool.

11. Install the pump shaft and the rotor and vanes, with the vanes facing the proper direction.

12. Install the O-ring seals and replace the cam ring. Tighten the cam bolts to 15 ft. lbs.

13. Install the flow control valve and replace the pressure connector. Tighten the connector bolts to 43 ft. lbs.

14. Install the suction pipe connector and tighten the bolts to 8 ft. lbs.

15. Install the pressure switch and tighten to 20 ft. lbs.

16. Install the pump pulley and replace the nut. Tighten the nut to 32 ft. lbs.

1. Bolt
2. Nut
3. Hose connector
4. Nut and washer
5. Bracket
6. Nut and washer
7. Oil tank
8. Bolt
9. Bolt
10. Rear body
11. O-ring
12. Cam ring
13. Rotor and vane
14. Pressure plate
15. O-ring
16. O-ring
17. Front body
18. Snapring
19. Bearing and driveshaft
20. Retaining ring
21. Oil seal
22. Control valve and O-ring
23. Spring
24. Bolt and washer
25. Coonector
26. O-ring
27. Level guage and O-ring

Exploded view of typical power steering pump assembly for all except B2600—Mazda

1. Switch
2. Nut and washer
3. Bracket
4. Nut and washer
5. Pulley
6. Bolt
7. Bolt
8. Rear body
9. O-ring
10. Rotor
11. Cam
12. Vane
13. Pressure plate
14. O-ring
15. Front body
16. Bolt
17. Bracket
18. Snapring
19. Ball bearing
20. Key
21. Shaft
22. Retaining ring
23. Oil seal
24. Connector
25. O-ring
26. Connector
27. Valve assembly
28. Spring
29. Bolt
30. Connector
31. Collar
32. O-ring

Exploded view of typical power steering pump assembly for B2600—Mazda

19. Install the pressure plate.
20. Attach the vanes to the rotor with the round edge making contact with the cam. Install the the rotor.
21. Replace the cam ring and install the O-ring.
22. Place the rear body into the pump housing and install the

bolts.
23. Install the pulley and replace the nut. Tighten to 29–43 ft. lbs.
24. Replace the rear bracket and install the switch into the pump housing.

MITSUBISHI

Vane Type Pump

Disassembly and Assembly
PICK-UP

1. Secure the pump assembly in a suitable holding fixture. Drain the fluid from the pump.
2. Remove the pump cover mounting bolts and remove the pump cover.
3. Loosen and remove the suction port assembly and remove the pressure fitting.

NOTE: On vehicles with the reservoir attached, remove the mounting bolts and remove the reservoir.

4. Remove the cam ring, vanes, O-ring, side plate assembly and the dowel pins.
5. Remove the shaft assembly snapring, the protector.
6. Press out the shaft from the bearing and remove the shaft.

NOTE: Do not allow the shaft to drop.

7. Remove the oil seal with the proper tool. Remove the suction connector.
8. Remove the connector at the top of the pump body and remove the flow control valve assembly and flow control spring.

NOTE: Do not disassemble the flow control valve.

9. Clean and check all parts for any wear or excessive damage. Always use new gaskets and lubricate all the parts with Dexron® II before assembling.
To assemble:
10. Check the amount of play between the pump shaft and the pump body. The clearance should be 0.008 in.
11. Install the flow control valve spring, flow control valve and the connecter into the pump body. Tighten the connector to 51–58 ft. lbs.
12. Install the seal into the pump body, using a suitable seal installer.
13. Press the shaft into the bearing with the proper tool.
14. Lubricate the vanes with the proper fluid and install the vanes on the rotor. Position the vanes with the rounded edge facing the cam ring.
15. When installing the cam ring, align the dowel pins of the

pump body with the knock holes of the cam ring. Install so the cam ring's punch mark is at the pump body side.
16. Install the pump cover and tighten the mounting bolts to 24–31 ft. lbs.
17. Install the suction connector and tighten to 10–13 ft. lbs.

EXCEPT PICK-UP

1. Secure the pump assembly in a suitable holding fixture. Drain the fluid.
2. Disconnect the suction connector and remove the O-ring.
3. Disconnect the top connector and remove the O-ring

NOTE: On vehicles with the reservoir attached, remove the mounting bolts and remove the reservoir.

4. Remove the flow control valve and the flow control spring from the pump housing. Do not disassemble the control valve.
5. Loosen the pump cover mounting bolts and remove the pump cover.
6. Remove the cam case, O-ring and the cam ring.
7. Remove the vanes and the snapring from the rotor. Remove the rotor.
8. Tap the side of the shaft and remove the pulley assembly.
9. Remove the oil seal, using the proper tool.
10. Clean and inspect the parts for any wear and excessive damage.
To assemble:
11. Install the vanes to the rotor grooves. Measure the gap between the vane and the rotor groove. The distance should be 0.0024 in.
12. Install the seal into the pump body, using the proper tool.
13. Lubricate the rotor with the proper fluid and install the rotor with the punch mark side facing the pump cover.
14. Lubricate the vanes and the cam ring with the proper fluid.
15. Align the dowel pins of the pump body with the dowel holes of the cam ring.
16. Install the vanes to the rotor with the round edge facing the cam ring.
17. Install the flow control valve, spring, O-ring and the top connector. Tighten the connector to 29–43 ft. lbs.
18. Install the cam case, O-ring and the cam ring.
19. Replace the pump cover and tighten the mounting bolts to 13–16 ft. lbs.
20. Install the oil seal, using the proper tool. Replace the pulley.
21. Replace and tighten the suction connector to 4–7 ft. lbs.

NISSAN

Vane Type Pump

Disassembly and Assembly

VG, SD AND Z ENGINES

1. Secure the pump in a suitable holding fixture.

2. Scribe matchmarks on the rear cover and the housing.
3. Loosen the rear cover mounting bolts and remove the rear cover.
4. Remove the O-ring from the cam case, using the proper tool.
5. Remove the cam case and the O-ring.

Exploded view of typical power steering pump assembly for Z engine—Nissan

Exploded view of typical power steering pump assembly for SD engine—Nissan

6. Remove the rotor, making sure the vane does not come off the rotor.

7. Remove the snapring with the proper tool and lift out the pulley shaft. Note the direction of the rotor.

8. Remove the oil seal with the proper tool, making sure not to damage casing.

9. Remove the connector, making sure not to drop the spool.

10. Remove the suction pipe, then remove the O-ring.

11. Clean all the parts and inspect for any damage or excessive wear.

To assemble:

12. Lubricate the O-rings and the oil seals with power steering.

13. Install the O-ring and replace the suction pipe.

14. Install the spool and replace the connector. Tighten to 50–58 ft. lbs.

15. Replace the oil seal with the proper tool.

16. Insert the pulley shaft and replace the snapring using the proper tool.

17. Install the rotor with the punch mark facing the front housing and the portion without the punch mark faces the cam side.

18. Insert the O-ring and replace the cam case.

19. Install the rear cover and tighten the mounting bolts to 28–38 ft. lbs.

KA24E ENGINE

1. Secure the pump in a suitable holding fixture.

2. Remove the snapring, using the proper tool, then draw the pulley shaft out.

3. Remove the oil seal, being careful not to damage the housing.

4. Remove the connector. Be careful not to drop the control valve.

Exploded view of typical power steering pump assembly for VG engine—Nissan

Exploded view of typical power steering pump assembly for AXXESS with KA24E engine—Nissan

5. Loosen the rear housing mounting bolts and remove the rear housing.

6. Remove the pins from the pin grooves and remove the cam ring, rotor and vanes as a unit.

7. Clean and inspect each component for damage or excessive wear.

To assemble:

8. Installation is the reverse of the removal procedure. Lubricate all the components with power steering fluid.

9. Assemble the vanes to the rotor with the rounded surface of the vanes facing the cam ring side.

10. Insert the pins into the grooves of the front housing and the front side plate.

11. Install the cam ring. Replace the rear cover and tighten the mounting bolts to 23–31 ft. lbs.

12. Insert the control valve and replace the connector. Tighten to 50–58 ft. lbs.

13. Insert the pulley shaft and replace the snapring with the proper tool.

Exploded view of typical power steering pump assembly except AXXESS with KA24E engine– Nissan

SUZUKI

Vane Type Pump

Disassembly and Assembly

1. Secure the pump in a suitable holding fixture and drain the fluid.
2. Remove the puller using the proper puller.

3. Disconnect the pressure switch and remove the suction pipe connector.
4. Remove the pressure connector and take out the flow control valve.
5. Remove the pump cam ring and remove the rotor snapring, using the proper tool.
6. Remove the rotor and the vanes.

1. Pulley
2. Shaft
3. Pressure switch
4. Pump body
5. Flow control valve assembly
6. Cam ring
7. Rotor
8. Vane
9. Cover

Exploded view of typical power steering pump assembly–Suzuki

7. Remove the pump shaft and pry out the shaft oil seal with a suitable seal remover.

8. Clean and inspect all the parts for damage or excessive wear.

To assemble:

9. Lubricate all the parts with the proper power steering fluid.

10. Insert the shaft oil seal with the proper tool.

11. Install the pump shaft and the rotor and vanes, with the vanes facing the proper direction.

12. Install the O-ring seals and replace the cam ring. Tighten the cam bolts to 15 ft. lbs.

13. Install the flow control valve and replace the pressure connector. Tighten the connector bolts to 43 ft. lbs.

14. Install the suction pipe connector and tighten the bolts to 7 ft. lbs.

15. Install the pressure switch and tighten to 21 ft. lbs.

16. Install the pump pulley and replace the nut. Tighten the nut to 32 ft. lbs.

TOYOTA

Vane Type Pump

Disassembly and Assembly

1. Secure the pump in a suitable holding fixture.

2. Remove the air control valve from the rear housing on the 22R–E engine.

3. Remove the suction port union from the rear housing, if equipped.

4. Remove the reservoir tank and the O-ring on the Land Cruiser.

5. Place matchmarks on the front and rear housing.

6. Remove the 4 front housing bolts, then using the proper tool, tap off the front housing. Be careful that the vane plates, rotor and cam ring do not fall out.

7. Remove the cam ring, rotor and vane plates.

NOTE: Be careful not to scratch the cam ring, rotor or vane plates.

8. Secure the front housing in a suitable holding fixture. Pry off the oil seal using the proper tool.

9. Remove the snapring, using the proper tool. Using a plastic hammer, lightly tap the rotor shaft out of the front housing.

10. Tap the bottom end of the rear housing and remove the rear plate and spring.

11. Temporarily install a bolt to the plug. Push the bolt and remove the snapring with the proper tool.

12. Pull out the bolt and remove the plug. Remove the spring and flow control valve by hand.

NOTE: Be careful not to drop, scratch or nick the valve.

13. Remove the pressure port union.

14. Check the front housing bushing for wear or damage. If wear or damage is found, the entire housing must be replaced.

15. Check the oil clearance between the bushing and rotor shaft. Maximum oil clearance is 0.0028 in. except Land Cruiser or 0.0012 in. on Land Cruiser.

16. If necessary, replace the rotor shaft bearing.
   a. Remove the snapring with the proper tool. Using a suitable press, press out the old bearing and press in the new one.
   b. Install the snapring with the proper tool.

17. Measure the cam ring thickness. Check that the difference between the rotor and cam ring is less than the maximum 0.0024 in. If the difference is excessive, replace the cam ring with one having the same letter as the rotor.

18. Check the vane plates for wear or scratches.

19. Measure the clearance between the vane plate and the rotor groove. Maximum clearance is 0.0024 in. except Land Cruiser or 0.0012 in. for Land Cruiser.

20. Check the flow control valve for wear or damage. If necessary, replace the valve with one having the same letter on the rear housing.

21. Check that the flow control valve spring is within 1.85–1.97 in. If not replace it.

To assemble:

22. Install the flow control valve, spring, plug and snapring.

NOTE: Make sure the letter inscribed on the flow control valve matches the letter stamped on the rear of the pump body.

23. Install the pressure port union and tighten to 50 ft. lbs.

24. Install the rotor shaft to the front housing by tapping it with the proper tool.

25. Install the snapring to the front housing with the proper tool.

26. Apply a light coat of MP grease to the oil seal lip, then using the proper tool, install the oil seal.

27. Install the O-ring except on Land Cruiser.

28. Align the fluid passages of the cam ring and front housing and install the cam ring.

NOTE: Make sure the letters on the cam ring face upward.

29. Install the rotor with the camfered end facing toward the front.

Exploded view of typical power steering pump assembly for Land Cruiser—Toyota

NOTE: Be sure the letters inscribed on the cam ring and rotor match.

30. Install the vane plates with the round end facing outward.

31. Align the fluid passages of the rear plate and cam ring and install the rear plate with the spring. Place the spring on the rear plate.

32. Align the matchmarks on the front and rear housing and assemble them. Temporarily, tighten the the front and rear housing mounting bolts.

33. Install the reservoir tank and the O-ring on Land Cruiser.

34. Secure the rear housing in a suitable holding fixture, then tighten the housing bolts evenly to 34 ft. lbs. Tighten the reservoir tank bolts to 9 ft. lbs. on Land Cruiser.

35. Insert the union to the rear housing and tighten to 9 ft. lbs.

36. Install the air control valve to the rear housing and tighten to 27 ft. lbs. on the 22R-E engine.

37. Check that the rotor shaft rotates smoothly. Check the rotating torque; the rotating torque should be lees than 2.4 inch lbs.

VZN Series Pump

Disassembly and Assembly

1. Secure the pump in a suitable holding fixture.

2. Remove the air control valve and take out the union seat.

3. Remove the mounting bolts and lift off the reservoir tank. Remove the O-ring from the reservoir tank.

4. Remove the pressure port union and remove the O-ring from the union.

5. Remove the flow control valve and the spring from the housing.

6. Remove the snapring with the proper tool and tap out the rear housing. Pry out the O-ring from the rear housing.

7. Tap the end of the shaft with the proper tool and remove the rear plate. Pry out the O-ring from the rear plate.

8. Remove the pump shaft with the cam ring and vane plates from the front housing.

9. Remove the cam ring and the 10 plates from the pump shaft. Remove the longer straight pin from the front housing.

10. Remove the snapring with the proper tool and remove the rotor and front plate from the pump shaft.

11. Remove both O-rings and the straight pin from the front plate.

12. Remove the bolts and the adjusting stay.

13. Check the oil clearance with the proper tool. The maximum clearance is 0.0028 in.

14. Measure the clearance between the rotor groove and the vane plate. The maximum clearance is 0.0011 in.

15. Inspect the control valve for damage or leakage. Measure the free length of the spring. The spring free length should be 1.38–1.46 in.

16. If necessary, replace the oil seal with the proper tool.

To assemble:

17. Coat all the sliding surfaces with power steering fluid.

18. Install the adjusting stay and tighten the bolts to 30 ft. lbs.

19. Install the shorter front pin to the front plate and install new O-rings to the front plate.

20. Install the front plate to the pump shaft.

21. Install the rotor to the pump shaft with the inscribed mark facing out. Install the snapring with the proper tool.

22. Coat the oil lip with MP grease and install the longer straight pin to the front housing. Align the hole of the front plate with the straight pin and tap in the pump shaft with the proper tool.

23. Align the oval hole of the cam ring with the longer straight pin and insert the cam ring with the inscribed mark facing out.

24. Install the 10 vane plates with the round end facing outward.

25. Install a new O-ring to the rear plate and align the holes of the rear plate with the pins. Install the rear plate.

26. Install the washer and the O-ring to the rear housing.

27. Tap in the rear housing with the proper tool and install the snapring.

28. Check that the shaft rotates smoothly. Temporarily, install the pulley nut and check the rotating torque. The rotating torque should be 2.4 inch lbs. or less.

29. Install the spring and the valve into the housing and install a new O-ring in the groove of the pressure port union.

30. Install the port union and tighten to 50 ft. lbs.

Exploded view of typical VZN power steering pump assembly—Toyota

31. Install a new O-ring to the reservoir tank.

32. Install the reservoir tank to the housing and replace the bolts. Tighten the 12mm bolts to 9 ft. lbs. and the 14mm bolts to 30 ft. lbs.

33. Install a new union seat to the housing.

34. Install the air control valve and tighten the bolts to 27 ft. lbs.

RN Series Pump

Disassembly and Assembly

1. Secure the pump in a suitable holding fixture.

2. Remove the air control valve and the union seat on the 22R-E engine.

3. Remove the bolts and remove the suction port union. Pry out the O-ring from the union.

4. Remove the front housing bolts.

5. Place matchmarks on the front and rear housing. Tap off the front housing with the proper tool.

NOTE: Be careful that the vane plates, rotor and the cam ring do not fall out.

6. Remove the cam ring, rotor and vane plates, do not scratch.

7. Secure the front housing in a suitable holding fixture.

8. Pry out the oil seal and remove the snapring with the proper tools.

9. Tap the rotor shaft out of the housing.

10. Tap the bottom end of the rear housing and remove the rear plate and spring.

11. Remove the pressure port union and pry out the O-rings from the union and the housing.

12. Remove the flow control valve and spring.

13. Temporarily, install a bolt to the spring seat. Push the bolt and remove the snapring with the proper tool.

14. Pull out the bolt and remove the spring seat. Pry out the O-ring from the spring seat.

15. Check the oil clearance between the bushing and the rotor shaft. The maximum oil clearance is 0.0028 in.

16. Measure the cam thickness. Check that the difference between the rotor and the cam ring is less than 0.0024 in.

17. Measure the clearance between the vane plate and the rotor groove. The maximum clearance is 0.0024 in.

18. Check the flow control valve for wear or damage. If necessary, replace the valve with one having the same letter on the rear housing.

19. Check that the flow control valve spring is within 1.85–1.97 in. If not replace it.

To assemble:

20. Install a new O-ring to the spring seat. Insert the spring seat into the housing, install the snapring.

21. Install a new O-ring to the housing. Insert the spring and control valve to the housing. Make sure the letter marked on the flow control valve matches the letter marked on the rear of the pump body.

22. Install a new O-ring to the pressure port union. Replace the union and tighten the bolts to 50 ft. lbs.

23. Install the rotor shaft into the front housing by tapping on it with the proper tool. Install the snapring to the front housing.

24. Apply a light coat of MP grease to the oil seal lip and install the oil seal with the proper tool.

25. Install a new O-ring.

26. Align the fluid passages of the rear plate with the cam ring and install the rear plate. Place the spring on the rear plate.

27. Align the matchmarks on the front and rear housing and assemble the housings. Tighten the housing bolts evenly to 34 ft. lbs.

28. Install the suction port union and tighten to 9 ft. lbs.

29. Install a new union seat and the air control valve on the 22R-E engine.

30. Check that the rotor shaft rotates smoothly and that the rotational torque is 2.4 inch lbs. or less.

VOLKSWAGEN

Vane Type Pump

Disassembly and Assembly

1. Secure the pump in a suitable holding fixture.

2. Loosen the end housing bolts and remove the end hosing.

3. Remove the spring, pressure/flow limiting valve and valve retainer, using the proper tool.

4. Remove the seal support with the proper tool and lift out the valve plate. Remove the stator.

5. Press the rotor down and remove the circlip from the groove in the housing with the proper tool.

6. Remove the rotor and the O-ring from the front housing.

NOTE: Be careful not to let the vanes fall out.

7. Loosen the front housing cover bolts and remove the pump shaft with the flange. Remove the shaft seal with the proper tool.

To assemble:

8. Clean all the components and check for damage or excessive wear. Coat all the sealing components with power steering fluid.

9. Install the shaft seal with the proper tool. Make sure the seal bottoms.

10. Install the pump shaft with the flange and tighten the bolts to 14 ft. lbs.

11. Install the O-ring and the rotor to the shaft. Replace the circlip.

NOTE: The circlip must fit properly in the groove and be secured by the rotor.

12. Install the stator with the long pins facing downward.

13. Install the valve plate, seal and the seal support, using the proper tool.

14. Insert the pressure/flow limiting valve and replace the valve retainer with the proper tool.

15. Install the valve retainer with the angled ends positioned in the housing slot. Press down the angled ends with the proper tool.

16. Install the end cover and replace the bolts, tighten to 14 ft. lbs.